THE STORY OF
CINEMA

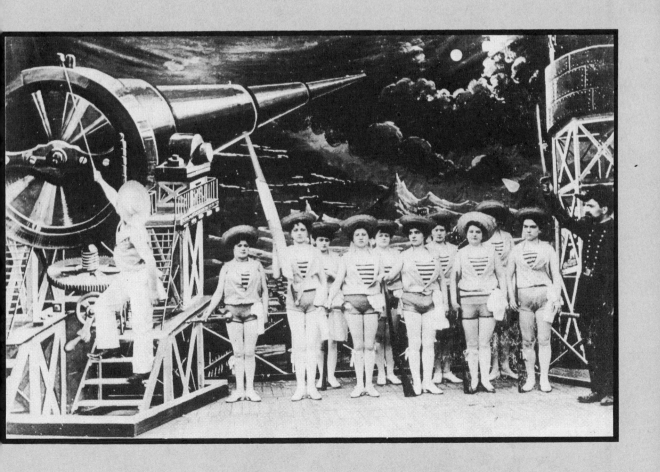

THE STORY OF CINEMA

A COMPLETE NARRATIVE HISTORY
FROM THE BEGINNINGS TO THE PRESENT

DAVID SHIPMAN

Preface by Ingmar Bergman

St. Martin's Press
New York

By the same author

THE GREAT MOVIE STARS:
Volume 1 – The Golden Years
Volume 2 – The International Years

THE STORY OF CINEMA. Copyright © 1982 by David Shipman. All rights
reserved. Printed in the United States of America. No part of this book may
be used or reproduced in any manner whatsoever without written permission
except in the case of brief quotations embodied in critical articles or reviews.
For information, address St. Martin's Press, 175 Fifth Avenue, New York,
N.Y. 10010.

Library of Congress Cataloging in Publication Data

Shipman, David.
    The story of cinema.

    1. Moving-pictures—History.   I. Title.
PN1993.5.A1S52   1984   791.43'09   84-13254
ISBN 0-312-76279-8

The Story of Cinema was originally published in Great Britain in two volumes
in 1982 by Hodder and Stoughton .

First U.S. Edition

10 9 8 7 6 5 4 3 2 1

Contents

Note to the reader: There are no pages 505-538 .

Acknowledgments

WRITING a book on the cinema is to an extent a solitary experience: one watches films without talking, one sits alone at the typewriter. When it comes to investigating or checking facts I do my own research. The job became more social watching movies on television or on the Steenbeck machine, and it became positively congenial when the following were commenting on the text and suggesting changes: Christine Medcalf, Barbara Noble, Philippa Toomey, Bruce Goldstein, Susan Lermon and Felix Brenner. My thanks to the last-named and to Frank Thomas for assistance on the index. Gratitude, too, to the late Keith Roberts, who initiated the project in the first place, and to my agent, Frances Kelly, the jewel of her profession. To my editor, Richard Cohen, and to my designer, Margaret Fraser, special thanks for our tripartite conferences, which will remain among the happiest experiences of my writing career. It has been observed that there is nothing a movie buff enjoys more than the company of other movie buffs: though Richard would come into that category Margaret would not, but I recall with great pleasure her enthusiasm as memories were evoked while we examined thousands of stills for the illustrations.

For their co-operation in supplying us with stills and/or permission to reproduce I am grateful to the following: A.J.Y.M., Avala, R. D. Bansal, Manuel Barbachano, Barrandov Studio, Ingmar Bergman, Ceskoslovensky, Ceylon Studios, Champion, The Cinema Bookshop, Cinetel, Columbia Pictures, Contemporary, Daiei, Dear Film, del Duca, Walt Disney, E.M.I., Film Polski, Filmel, Films de la Boétie, Films du Carosse, Films de la Pléiade, Les Films 13, Filmsonor, Finos, Franco London, Goldcrest, Greenwich Film, Gujarat Cooperative, Hungaro Film, Iéna, Imperia, Igor Film, I.T.C., Lira, Deana Lom, Lux, Mafilm, Merchant Ivory, M-G-M/UA, Mosfilm, John B. Murray, New South Wales Film Corporation, Nikkatsu, Nouvelles Editions de Films, Paramount, Paris Film, Pathé, Ponce, Ponti de Laurentiis, Elias Querejita, R.A.I., Rank, Satyajit Ray, Reggane, Rizzoli, R.K.O. Radio, Rome Paris Films, Safir-Film, Sandrews, Shintoho, Shochiku, Silver Film, Bernhard Sinkel, Sono, South Australia Film Corporation, Sovexport, Spéva Film, Svensk Filmindustri, Tango Film, Titanus, Transcontinental, Toei, Toho, 20th Century-Fox, Uninci, Union Générale, Universal, Vides, Warner Bros., W.D.R. and, above all, the National Film Archive of Great Britain.

Preface

IT WAS CHRISTMAS and I was nine years old. A wealthy old
lady who was a friend of the family used to give us children
rather expensive presents. Two days before Christmas Eve
her servant arrived with the gifts, which together with the
other packets were placed in a large laundry basket under the
stairs up to the attic. I saw at once that one of the packets (big
and angular, wrapped in strong brown paper) contained a
film projector. I nearly fainted with joy. For several years I
had wished for a projector; now the dream was to come true.
I went about in a trance, unable either to sleep or eat.

The great moment turned out to be a terrible disappointment. The film projector went to my brother, who was four
years older than me; I was given a bear that could growl. My
grief was agonising. My brother, who had never shown the
slightest interest in cinematic art and was moreover a clever
businessman, seized the opportunity. He sold me the
apparatus at a price of two hundred tin soldiers, that is to say,
my entire army. Two days later he declared war and invaded
my country, defeating the few gallantly fighting troops that
were left, despite our agreement that no war was to break out
until I had a chance of building up a new armed force. I fled
into the nursery's dark and spacious closet with my
'cinematograph', as the toy was called. Although simple it
was a fine little machine, but more dangerous than a bomb.

It consisted of two spools for sixty metres of 35-mm film,
a steady feeding mechanism (Maltese cross and crank), a
sector and a fairly large lens in shining brass. The lamp-house
was of black lacquered tinplate with a reflex mirror, paraffin
lamp and a backward curved chimney. In addition there was
a holder for slides. A blue box (with a pretty picture on the
lid of a young man in a sailor suit showing moving pictures
of fighting lions to an impressed family) contained a film
loop about four metres long, an everlasting film. The loop
was brown and had a pungent, rather sweet smell; like all

film at that time it was made on a nitrate base and was frightfully inflammable. Nitrate film, paraffin lamp, dusty closet, a nine-year-old projectionist – no grown-up knew just how dangerous the whole thing really was. During the next few years I spent all my pocket-money and savings on film. I must have kept thousands of metres of film in the closet, where I established my cinema in the flickering light of the paraffin lamp. The fact that the family and the old rectory survived must be put down to the constant vigilance of guardian angels.

Sometimes I have wondered at the child's wild and inexplicable excitement. It was all a mechanical process. A little machine which rattled loudly as it fed in sixteen frames a second. If I cranked frame by frame nothing, or almost nothing, happened – the frames hardly changed. If I went faster, movement was born. The shadows acted, the faces turned towards me, eyes opened, lips formed inaudible words. The darkness, the rattling, the smells, the lighted rectangle on the wall . . . I made up stories about the small, mysterious figures, they sent out magic signals, they took part in my dreams. I remember these pictures with a clarity and focus which they no doubt lacked in reality.

The rectangle of light in the dark, the shadows' unceasing movements controlled by me. Unaccountable courses of events, secret relations that extended far into the boundless twilight land of dreams. Hypnosis and magic – the nine-year-old touched the little finger of a giant's invisible hand. Today, fifty-five years later, in the murk of the cutting room I can feel the same excitement, the same tension, in the presence of the endless and the unexplored.

Fårö, 25 July 1981
© Ingmar Bergman
Translated by Alan Blair

8

Introduction

IN 1972, out of the blue, I received a letter inviting me to write a history of the cinema. It was a project which I had previously considered as too vast for one person, but I needed no persuasion once a concrete offer had been made. Even compressed, I realised it would have to be a very long book, and if at first I was unsure of my approach I wanted it to be as factually accurate as was within my power.

I had already discovered how few reliable books were available on the subject. For instance, researching *The Jazz Singer* has proved a hazardous task. As the first Talking picture and therefore of great importance in the development of the medium, it is a title to be found in the indices of all cinema histories, yet not one agreed on what was actually spoken from the screen. Some were vague, some had apparently made up the facts to suit the author's beliefs and some were inaccurate – as I discovered when I had the opportunity to see the film. The first requirement, therefore, was that I should view every film to be discussed – not at that time, however, foreseeing that that, plus further research and actual writing, would take more than ten years.

During that period the cinema's past has become available as never before, with literally hundreds of lost or forgotten films emerging from archives and dusty corners. These films in themselves called for a reinterpretation of cinema history, while the accepted classics had begun to offer meanings quite different from those accepted by their original audiences. Many valuable films, recording their times with honesty and accuracy, had been ignored or forgotten, while some much-admired films turned out to be of minimal interest. The first commentators on cinema had tended to praise any movie which raised the medium above its primary purpose – as mass entertainment – and thus a proportionately large number of experimental and avant-garde films had been welcomed beyond their intrinsic worth. From its humble beginnings, the cinema gained in respectability whenever connected to other art forms, and the earliest films publicly approved were adaptations of plays and novels, especially those with a religious or historical basis. Thus Griffith made his inflated reputation, and thus matters rested till the Soviets experimented with film form in the Twenties. In the interim the most admired movies were those of the German Expressionist movement, with their juxtaposition of an old art – the theatre – and a new science – psychiatry. Today these films provide merely a footnote to the cultural climate of the time, while those which with hindsight have become the really important films (because they show us what Germany was like then) were ignored or derided, and consequently not exported.

Very few critics or film historians were prepared to view unknown films – or so declared James Card, the curator of the Eastman House archive, in an attempt to explain why Griffith and Von Stroheim are still regarded as the best directors then working. To me, it was not only clear that Griffith had never advanced beyond a basic level of competence, but recent researches had shown his claims to innovation to be false. Similarly, *The Great Train Robbery* is still described as the most influential film in early cinema, despite the revelation, in 1959 in the Eastman House magazine, *Image*, that it was copied almost frame by frame from another film, just then rediscovered.

Such misconceptions were significantly not corrected in Paul Rotha's 'The Film Till Now', the ancestor of all serious writing on the subject. First published in 1930, this work has always been regarded as definitive, so much so that when Rotha declined to update it Richard Griffith did so, both in the Forties and the Fifties, giving it a new lease of life. Rotha's text is revealing as a guide to what constituted cinema culture at the time, but otherwise is no longer of value. He had, for instance, difficulty in concealing his contempt for all American cinema except for Griffith, Chaplin and Flaherty; and his enthusiasm for the German cinema was, as I have implied, both partial and misjudged. Yet his influence was such that his favoured films formed the basis of most of the world's film archives, thus perpetuating the myths by making those particular films alone available for study. He is sound only on Eisenstein and Pabst, though Richard Griffith's additions recognise the importance of the French directors of the Thirties and of Capra and Lubitsch. If in the post-war period we add the names of Rossellini and de Sica, together with John Ford, Minnelli and the British documentarists, we arrive at the total cinema pantheon as enshrined in the most prominent of Rotha's successors, 'The Penguin Film Review' of the late Forties and *Sight and Sound* in the early Fifties. Clearly this is an impoverished pantheon, and one may wonder what Rossellini and the British documentarists – with the outstanding exception of Humphrey Jennings – were doing there in the first place. Nowhere was there to be found any comment on the brilliant and immensely influential early Swedish cinema, virtually dismissed by Rotha. Even Arthur Knight, in his more authoritative 'The Liveliest Art', published in 1957, confines his discussion of early Swedish cinema to one of its lesser efforts, *Gosta Berling's Saga*. Meanwhile, with the possible exception of the 1939 'Rise of the American Film' by Lewis Jacobs, the most readable and informative study of early cinema continued to be Benjamin B. Hampton's 'A History of the Movies'. But that was never mentioned in 'The Penguin Film Review' or *Sight and Sound*, since it concerned the movie *industry*.

Yet the cinema is first and foremost just that – an industry – and since any motion picture is a manufactured product film cannot be profitably discussed only with reference to its highest endeavours. Were I to confine myself to the revelatory and influential films I should be limited to about one thousand, and were I to deal only with the enduringly entertaining I should probably reach the same figure: and few would duplicate the other. Some films are now of interest for the manner in which people moved, spoke, dressed or decorated their homes, and we can therefore add two further categories of films deserving attention: those which faithfully reflected their times and those which – since this is an entertainments industry not inclined towards sociology – made no attempt to do so.

Trying to say so much to so many, often in the simplest terms, film had, or had until recently, the advantage of its presentation: on a gigantic screen in a vast, darkened auditorium seating sometimes thousands; and these circumstances enabled it to become the most powerful of all means of expression. At its peak, in the Thirties and Forties, the entire populations of most civilised countries were regular cinemagoers, and it was then that films replaced literature as a principal after-dinner topic, not yet superseded in that role by television. For the purposes of this book I saw again the films of youth and childhood, and it was clear that from them as much as from any other source were derived my values – on such matters as public spirit, courage, romantic ardour, humour and the other qualities with which movie heroes were naturally endowed. Some of these films had lodged so deep in my consciousness that despite my having forgotten, I thought, everything about them, each sequence unrolled anew with vigorous familiarity. Obviously I have not restricted myself to films with a personal significance, and as far as possible I have tried to include those which were very popular. The latter have often been the industry's own favourite artefacts, and for the same reason I have usually detailed the leading awards of the American Motion Picture Academy of Arts and Sciences – though certainly not because its Oscar is any guarantee of merit.

Since the Hollywood film has been dominant in every country with which the United States has a trade agreement, often keeping local product from theatre screens, I have devoted to it the largest share of the text, certain that what has emanated from Paramount, M-G-M or Warners is as familiar in Bombay or Helsinki as in New York or New Orleans. In fact, my dissatisfaction with most previous cinema histories is that they have ignored the worldwide exposure of American films and their consequent social significance. As far as the other national industries are concerned, I began with those films which crossed frontiers and added little-known ones of such quality that they had to be included, if only to demonstrate their superiority to others which have gained attention in the international market. Except when American-financed, the odds against foreign distribution are very long indeed. 'Winchester's 1948 Screen Encyclopedia' lists approximately 250 foreign-language films publicly shown in Britain from 1920 to that time – less than the number of American films shown annually. The listing is not entirely accurate, for in the Silent days a number of European films were passed off as British or American, but it is significant that over fifty per cent of the films listed is from one source, i.e. France (a comparable listing for the United States would be difficult to compile, since many more European films were imported, but often were shown, without subtitles, only in cinemas catering to specific ethnic populations). The 'failed' German films I mentioned earlier were denigrated by the critics and shunned by the public because their subject matter was poverty – and though that could be an advantage in the eyes of foreign critics the producers concerned made little attempt to find buyers abroad. Japanese

Introduction

producers from the start never considered that there would be foreign interest in their films, despite the fact that by the mid-Thirties they were as technically advanced as those in the West and often more mature in treatment. That changed in 1951 when *Rashomon* was shown at the Venice Film Festival, and from then on 'World Cinema' was no longer confined to a handful of countries. The existence of international film festivals has become crucial to the history of the cinema, since they provide a market-place for film-makers: I have tried to see the early films of those who did not gain international prominence thereby till comparatively late in their careers – for example, Ingmar Bergman, who made at least a dozen remarkable films before achieving world renown.

Nevertheless, even he worked in an industry motivated by profit, but these films may be ascribed to him – as creator or prime mover – and the same may be said of most directors working outside America. In Hollywood more than anywhere else the story of cinema has been a prolonged battle between those who have regarded it as a means of achieving fame and wealth and those for whom it is a medium for communication and/or personal expression. Few Hollywood directors have been allowed to be creative in the sense that Bergman and, say, Antonioni are, so that for each Capra and Wilder there are dozens of honest, interpretative craftsmen, as well as many more whose work has been skilfully assembled in the cutting-room till it becomes acceptable entertainment. I regret being unable to credit all the individuals – writers, designers, photographers, editors – who make decisive contributions to any film, but as it is the text is sufficiently burdened with names. Complete cross-referencing would have made the text even longer than it is, and the use of q.v. refers only to items later in the text (including those in Volume Two): I have tended not to use this abbreviation in cases where it is obvious that there is a later discussion of the item concerned or within brackets when members of any film's cast are listed. I have assumed that the reader has some knowledge of technical terms, and have included the dates of birth and death only of leading figures – usually at that point when the individual concerned has come into prominence. Similarly I have assumed familiarity with the players and films of recent years, so that the illustrations in the early part of the book have been selected mainly as a guide to appearance, while those in the latter section represent either films which are interesting or important.

On the studios, I have the film historian's usual dilemma as to whether to refer to them in the singular or plural: the reader may take it that the plural implies the executives, 'the front office' or the production team, the singular either the corporate identity or the building itself. (In the case of 20th Century-Fox, I have in general used the more clumsy '20th' rather than the customary 'Fox' after their amalgamation, in order to avoid confusion with that operation as controlled by William Fox.) I have taken the opportunity when appropriate to discuss American cinema in terms of producer, director or star – which means that for the most part the text is divided into parallel chapters on Hollywood, that is on individuals and on the studios. I have hesitated to use the director's possessive unless convinced that it was either recognisably his work or that he was the driving force behind it.

The classic case is *Casablanca*, since it may be everyone's favourite Hollywood movie. It was produced and directed by two knowledgeable and skilled craftsmen, respectively Hal Wallis and Michael Curtiz; the former contributed to the often memorable dialogue, credited to some otherwise undistinguished veterans – but what is probably the secret of its popularity is the teaming of Humphrey Bogart and Ingrid Bergman. She has said that she barely knew Bogart, and since she has attested to the constant confusion and dissension during shooting we must conclude that the end result is the product of a team. Other popular films of that time – *Les Enfants du Paradis* and *Ladri di Biciclette* – clearly owe as much to their writers as to their directors, but they are not studio films and we credit them to their directors for convenience.

I hope that I have obtained the right balance between Hollywood and the other national industries in selecting five thousand films to tell the story of cinema; their titles are printed in the text in bold face. Among those omitted are early films which, alas, have not been preserved, and those of once-important film-makers whose later work dwindled into insignificance – and in this case I trust that I have made it clear why I stopped persevering. The dates I have given the films are not those when copyrighted, but the completion date – i.e. when they were first shown to other than studio employees and were therefore deemed to be fit for public consumption. I have assumed some knowledge of the chief European languages in keeping the original titles of French, German, Italian and Spanish films, adding the English title only when the original is likely to be unknown. In the case of all other foreign titles I have used the best-known, whether in English or not – and all of these are cross-indexed at the back of the book. Films are discussed in chronological order whenever possible, since the cinema has been particularly susceptible to influence and indeed plagiarism, and every study of it should take into account what was being done just a few months earlier. Since, however, the cinema is a volatile industry/art form I have been able to vary my approach; and since this very long text required two separate volumes I hope the reader will agree that we made the right break at the beginning of the Second World War – that as far as Hollywood was concerned *Gone with the Wind* marked the end of one era and *Citizen Kane*, released sixteen months later, the beginning of another.

Of all the films I expected to see, beyond those irretrievably lost, less than a handful were unavailable. Doubtless archivists are making further discoveries, but if I take as a starting point the two hundred 'Outstanding fiction films, 1914–48' listed as an appendix in the Rotha-Griffith book, I have seen all but twenty, of which some are officially lost and the rest – all Soviet Talkies – unheard of since that list was compiled. (An additional seventy-eight documentary and experimental films are also listed, of which I lack perhaps a dozen – and cannot be more precise since many of the titles, e.g. *Chang*, *October*, *Roma Città Aparta*, do not belong in either of the appointed categories.) This brings into question my own standards of excellence, and the plural is necessary since the cinema encompasses Eisenstein and Buster Keaton, Marilyn Monroe and Kurosawa, Bergmans Ingmar and Ingrid, Jean Arthur and Gene Kelly, Satyajit Ray and David O. Selznick, Capra and Méliès, Antonioni and W. C. Fields. Some of these contributed to entertainments which after several viewings still seem fresh, while others created films attempting to illuminate aspects of the human condition in terms which are intrinsic to themselves.

13

Introduction

Everyone in films hopes their product will reach the widest possible audience, but there are nevertheless different publics – and it is easier for me to define my ideal audience than my idea of the perfect film. The text that follows includes qualitative judgments on most of the films discussed, but those are not judgments made in isolation. If I am happiest with audiences in the cinémathèques and repertory theatres, asking to be entertained and stimulated by the cinema's past, I have also sat with other audiences: the art-house or student audience sitting reverently through one-half of a double-bill and barracking the other; and the circuit audience, sitting through *Gone with the Wind* in almost as much awe as those for whom it was originally intended, or talking noisily – vast sections of it – through *Star Wars*, which rivalled the earlier film in popularity, or so it seemed. Perhaps I seize on popularity when it supports my own taste and deplore it when it doesn't; I hope at least that I have always been able to chart the undeserved successes and the undeserved failures inevitable in a product which demands mass support.

Unfortunately many movies which were designed to wile away an idle hour are subjected to analyses undreamt of by their progenitors – which is not to say that the most commercial or mechanical artefacts cannot incidentally tell us something of the culture which gave them birth. The matter was neatly put by Robert F. Moss in the *Saturday Review* (23 June 1979): '"I'm not sure film is an art form," said Lionel Trilling one day in a seminar at Columbia University. "Certainly most film scholarship is hardly worthy of the name." Indeed, to anyone trained in an orthodox academic discipline, film studies is apt to look like a primitive outpost of intellectual activity, a mining-camp of critical anarchy and wild-eyed artistic judgments. There are marvellous exceptions of course, but even allowing for them most film criticism is a do-it-yourself undertaking in which the critic remoulds the films of his favourite director closer to his heart's desire, investing jaunty melodramas and cowboy epics with some hidden motifs and subterranean profundities that would never have occurred to the directors themselves.'

If I have found few differences of opinion on what are the cinema's highest achievements, there is equal agreement on those at the opposite end of the scale: amateur films, and I do not mean 'home movies'; cheap horror films and, indeed, all exploitation product; movies which are overlong – a proliferating species because their makers are now more in awe of their own talent than respectful of audiences; and works of no intellectual content which aspire to festival exposure by the wilful confusion of narrative – thought by their makers to provide 'enigma'. Then there are the cultists, ranging from those who find feminist messages in old Hollywood junk to self-confessed 'Marxist' theorists who only approve of films intended to bring down a bourgeois culture.

The most pernicious of the cults is the 'auteur' theory, which in the last twenty years has wrecked any rational interpretation of the cinema's past. The film historians of the early Fifties held to the same beliefs as the first writers on film, partly because they needed 'classics' and partly because there were few opportunities to see old movies without that status (thus the great films of Sjöström were unseen outside Sweden for more than a generation). Since it was accepted that such films were made by one man – Eisenstein, Griffith, Chaplin, Murnau, Lang – the auteur theorists of the late Fifties decreed that the

14

only worthwhile films were those that were clearly the work of individuals. Thus film-makers of authority within the industry, like William Wyler, who prided himself on changing his subject matter, if not his approach, were derided in favour of journeyman directors. Few of these had any individual style, and their admired consistency was due to their inability, either from lack of talent or lack of opportunity, to do other than make variations over again of the same film – except, obviously, Hitchcock, who was too commercially canny to do anything else. Thus arose a fallacy which has bewildered or bored even the most hardened movie buffs, who have in this period taken to avoiding the often second-rate directors favoured by the theorists. At the same time many excellent films have fallen into neglect because their work confuses those unable to understand creative activity of a various nature, whether of subject or quality. I have thus been particularly anxious to point up in the text both once-influential films by directors who did little else of interest and those made by talents which moved into – often spectacular – decline.

No other visual art form is so dependent on the written word. The more a film is discussed the better it is known; so that if it is new it is the more likely to earn back its investment, and if old the more likely to recover the cost of bringing it from the vault. It is therefore necessary for writers on film to be well versed in the opinions of their confreres. I have restricted myself in the text to the most influential critics working in London and New York, and when I have not quoted in admiration it is to explain why some terrible films have been accepted. It is not that cinemagoers themselves are particularly gullible, but many believe in the infallibility of critics, as if it were conferred by the distinction of having their opinions in print. The two most influential New York critics during the past thirty years have been, to say the least, erratic. The situation improved as one retired and the other, more recently, lost credence, but in the summer of 1981 Fassbinder's routine *Lili Marleen* received American notices better than those for Rosi's *Cadaveri Eccellenti*. Admittedly among European critics there is no unanimity on Fassbinder, an uneven film-maker, but throughout Europe Rosi is regarded as a master and that particular film a major work. In these cases posterity may have much to say – and it is one of my themes to show how recent reviewings have so wholeheartedly overturned past judgments. But to be just, the film historians of the past were attempting to interpret an art form in the light of their own cultural values. The reason that they have been proved wrong is because we now regard the cinema in a different light.

As a means of communication the film has been overtaken by television. In historical terms the age of cinema was minute; many of the early pioneers were still living when I began this book – and a few are still, happily, with us. The Silent cinema lasted just over thirty years. Thirty years later, movies bowed to the power of television – which is where, now, most people watch them. As a record of the twentieth century – certainly the last part of it – posterity will look to television. But that is another story.

1

Beginnings

THE CINEMA began in Paris, in 1895. The first moving pictures – and they are no more than that – are not in themselves rewarding, unless you imagine yourselves there that evening, 28 December, having paid one franc admittance to the basement of a café in the boulevard des Capucines, its one hundred serried seats occupied by only thirty-three people, watching a show lasting twenty minutes: if you can, these half-minutes of images will haunt you.

We know from artefacts that the Ancients had wanted to tell stories in pictures – which was more than the cinema did at first. The optical principles of the camera were known to the Greeks, but it was not until the early nineteenth century that efforts were made to fix images by mechanical means. Photography was invented in 1835, but the cinema film did not become possible till 1888, when George Eastman (1854–1932) devised, among other photographic products, the celluloid roll film. In the meantime, in 1873, an English-born photographer, Eadweard Muybridge (1830–1904) had been commissioned by the Governor of California to take action pictures of a favourite race-horse. He experimented to the extent that later, working with the University of Pennsylvania, he took over one hundred thousand exposures – of speeds of up to 1/2000th of a second – of people and animals in consecutive action, intended to interest art lovers and students of anatomy. Among others interested was Thomas Edison (1847–1931), who had already invented the phonograph, and when he met Muybridge in 1888 he was impressed by a machine the latter had invented, the zoopraxiscope, by which

drawings of his photographs were projected. He envisaged something similar to accompany recorded sound, and two years later his assistant, W. K. L. Dickson (1860–1935), using Eastman's new roll film, began to produce sequences of images. Edison was the first of many in the history of cinema to take credit for the work of others, and since he was the boss it was only right that the Kinetoscope be patented in his name. It was fashioned like a peepshow; the viewer peered into a box to watch mechanically operated strips of action film. In 1893 Edison constructed a work-shop near his laboratory to take pictures for the Kinetoscope; called the Black Maria, the studio could be turned, and the roof opened, to take the greatest advantage of the sun. The first film made there, reputedly, was **Fred Ott's Sneeze**, which as *Record of a Sneeze, 7 January 1894,* was the first film copyrighted. **Fun in a Chinese Laundry** (1894) was more ambitious, part of a vaudeville skit; and **Execution of Mary, Queen of Scots** (1895) offered the gruesome spectacle of that lady's headless body – effected by a dummy put in place while the camera was halted.

What was needed was to combine these strips with the principles of another toy or gadget, the magic lantern, and in February 1895 two brothers, from their father's photographic factory in Lyon, patented an 'appareil servant à l'obtention et à la vision des épreuves chronophotographiques' – in other words, a projector. August Lumière (1862–1954) and Louis (1864–1948) were only two of many scientists experimenting with film – the ability to reproduce nature on a continuous piece of celluloid – and pioneer claims have been registered most notably on behalf of William Friese-Green (1855–1931) in Britain, and Etienne-Jules Marey (1830–1904) in France, as well as Edison and Dickson. If Edison himself merely regarded the Kinetoscope as a profitable toy, Dickson, Friese-Green and Marey were among those trying to find a way of projecting moving images on to a screen. In Britain the partnership of Birt Acres (1854–1918) and Robert William Paul (1870–1943) – having counterfeited a Kinetoscope – patented a camera to take pictures for it in May 1895, and it is clear that they were giving private projections before the end of the year. On 1 November, almost two months before the public presentation in the boulevard des Capucines, a German showman, Max Skladanowsky (1863–1939), offered his Bioskop at the Berlin Wintergarten in a programme of novelties, but his machine 'was an elaborate affair using two parallel film strips and two lenses, and so hardly qualifies as a film projector in the sense we have come to understand it' (David Robinson). The Lumières did make the first film, both publicly registered and projected, if by publicly we mean to people they hoped would buy the novelty, on 22 March 1895, at 44 rue de Rennes, Paris – **Sortie des Ouvriers de l'Usine Lumière**. Among those uninterested were the Musée Grévin (whose wonders were mainly waxworks) and the Folies-Bergères, so in December they rented the 'Salon Indien' of the Grand Café, 14 boulevard des Capucines, with posters outside announcing the attraction. After the *Sortie des Ouvriers* came such tidbits as *Le Goûter de Bébé, Le Demolition d'un Mur, L'Arroseur Arrosé* (a gardener looks into the nozzle of a hose-pipe and gets a faceful) and, most sensational of all, *L'Arrivée d'un Train en Gare de la Ciotat*.

The press took little notice: only two reporters from the forty-odd Paris newspapers showed up for the first performance. 'With this new invention,' wrote one of them in *La Poste*, 'death will be no longer absolute, final. The people we have seen on the screen will be with us, moving and alive after their deaths.' Without thoughts of immortality, the public began to flock to the Salon, and one among them who asked to show

these 'animated photographs' because of their scientific interest was Quintin Hogg, founder of the Regent Street Polytechnic in London. Seen there, on 25 February 1896, they immediately attracted the attention of the Empire Music Hall, which borrowed them, and soon had to put them at the top of the bill, adding 'animated photographs' of such London landmarks as Marble Arch and Piccadilly Circus. Two months later Edison's Vitascope process was unveiled to the American public at Koster and Bial's Music Hall, on the site now covered by Macy's. Edison had purchased and patented a projection device, one of several that appeared simultaneously. The first projected film that those New Yorkers saw was of a music hall act, the Leigh Sisters in their umbrella dance, followed by a shot of waves breaking. 'Some of the people in the front rows seemed to be afraid they were going to get wet,' went the report in *The New York Dramatic Mirror*, 'and looked about to see where they could run to,' going on to note that 'the Vitascope is nothing more than an enlarged Kinetoscope.' The Lumière programme followed two months later, at Keith's: vaudeville and variety had found a new attraction.

The craze to see moving-pictures had started, and by the end of the year had spread throughout the States. Theatres projected them; carnivals and penny arcades had to make do with peepshows, but as these were cumbersome and uneconomic, with only one customer able to view at one time, their proprietors looked longingly at projectors. A fierce battle ensued between those who owned, or had patented projectors, determined to retain their exclusivity and those who wanted them; but just as rivals to the Kinetoscope came thick and fast, several companies began to market projectors. Fairgrounds began to provide both projection and peepshow, and the proliferation of tents for the former received only a temporary setback in Paris in 1897, when 140 people perished in a fire started in the cinema tent of a charity bazaar.

Despite legal injunctions, Edison's rivals multiplied. The chief competitor of the Kinetoscope had been the Mutoscope, and its owners developed the Biograph for showmen who preferred to project their pictures. Indeed, the Mutoscope, a book of pages of consecutive images which might be flicked through manually or mechanically, had been devised by Dickson with Herman Casler; Dickson had resigned from Edison and with Casler and others formed the American Mutoscope and Biograph Company, whose product was introduced in Pittsburgh in September 1896, in turn to move into Koster and Bial's two months later, and to take up what was to become a ten years' residence at Keith's the following year.

The films of both companies were still sketches – *Burning Stable, Feeding the Chickens, Easter Parade on Fifth Avenue* – but at least two were thought to be scandalous, and were much imitated: from Edison, **The Kiss** (1896), a discreet middle-aged embrace, a scene from the play 'The Widow Jones', and from Biograph, **Fatima** (1897), part of the act of a Coney Island belly-dancer. **Tearing Down the Spanish Flag** (1898) also proved sensational, appealing to the current mood, and its success caused its maker, J. Stuart Blackton (1875–1941), a former journalist and vaudeville artist – and like Dickson, British-born – to set up as a rival to Edison and Biograph; with his partner Albert E. Smith, he founded Vitagraph in 1899.

By this time, films were more likely to be projected than viewed through a peepshow. They became a popular item at smoking-concerts and church socials, and their value was proved to theatre-owners when they replaced vaudeville during a performers' strike in 1900. At the St Louis Exposition the following year one of the most popular exhibits was 'Hale's Tours and Scenes of the World', in which audiences sat in a simulated railway coach and watched the world – or some of it – flash by. Local fairgrounds were the logical venue of the novelty, along with performing seals and waxworks; eager audiences watched films in improvised auditoria behind partitions. In the U.S. the cinema, as such, did not exist till the owner of one Los Angeles amusement arcade threw out the 'amusements' and installed seats and a projector. That was in 1902, but five years earlier the Lumière brothers had opened a building in Paris for the specific showing of films. The peepshow began to die: throughout the world, stores and then theatres were converted into cinemas. In the U.S. the price of admission determined the name – the nickelodeon – and that became the generic name for the makeshift or purpose-built show places for some years.

The films remained simple. They were sold outright to exhibitors for a few cents per foot and as most of the trading was done by mail-order, more money went into the preparation of the catalogues than into filming. Alongside such early categories as 'Views' and 'Vaudeville Acts' there appeared 'News Events'. Films purporting to show action in both the Spanish-American and Boer Wars brought in wide audiences, and 'staging' became an accepted part of the game. Edison, Biograph and Vitagraph began to offer brief sketches and burlesques of stage productions, but they were no more imaginative than their 'Views'. It was a Frenchman who turned it into an art: Georges Méliès (1861–1938).

In Méliès' own opinion (as expressed in his memoir), 'in the development of the cinema I have played a more important part than Lumière', and in considering *development* this is certainly true. The Lumières photographed nature; Méliès photographed a reconstructed life. The public would have tired of watching factory-workers leave their building; Méliès offered them a realisation of their fantasies. He discovered, or invented, the fiction film.

He was thirty-four when he went into films – a designer, actor, magician, and director of the Théâtre Robert-Houdin. A visit to the Salon Indien transformed his life. When the frères Lumière would neither rent nor lend him their equipment, he purchased a camera from London; and showed his first film in April 1896. Later that year he built the first studio in Europe (at Montreuil-sous-Bois), and he made an interesting discovery: his camera jammed while filming a street scene, and when the film was projected a carriage miraculously became a hearse. Edison had been aware of this trick when recreating the decapitation of Mary Stuart, but to Méliès it offered magical opportunities: immediately he made **L'Escomptage d'un Dame**

The Magic of Méliès

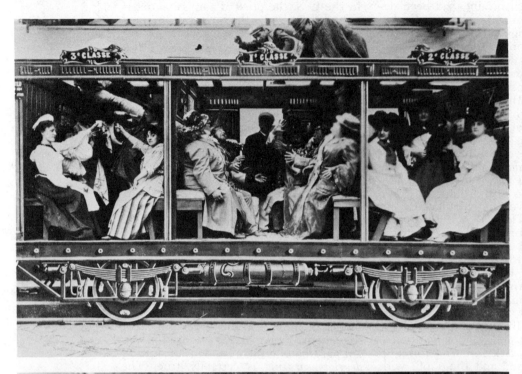

More than any
primitive films, the
brief pieces put
together by Georges
Méliès continue to
enchant. Remembered
best for his science
fiction tales, such as
*Voyage à Travers
l'Impossible,* ABOVE LEFT
and his joke fantasies,
such as *L'Homme à
la Tête de Caoutchouc,*
LEFT, he also made
reconstructions of actual
events and of stage
spectacles.

Here are two more
facets of Méliès:
allegory, as in
*Civilisation à Travers
les Ages*, ABOVE and
fairy-tale, as in *Barbe
Bleue*, RIGHT.

(1896), in which a woman temporarily becomes a skeleton. From photographing 'anything that moved' he experimented ceaselessly. In **Nouvelles Luttes Extravagantes** (1900) women wrestlers become men, and the sexes continue to rotate amidst much dismemberment; in **L'Homme Orchestre** (1900) chairs and men multiply and disappear as if by magic. Ghosts dance at the top of the screen in **Le Chaudron Infernale** (1903), and in **L'Homme à la Tête de Caoutchouc** (1902) a real head grows smaller and larger, an effect made by careful superimposition and an advancing and receding camera. Méliès hand-tinted his films, in the manner of contemporary photography, but he was reluctant to use other photographic techniques, such as the close-up. It has been claimed that the pioneers refused to use the close-up because audiences would not accept people shown chopped off at knee or waist, but indeed close-ups were common from *Fred Ott's Sneeze* onwards – at least, with those initiators who regarded the new art form as allied to photography. Méliès in fact saw it rather as a branch of the theatre, enabling him to rival the spectacles of the Théâtre du Chatelet, which he had been unable to do on the small stage of his theatre. Hence his camera in general is rooted in the stalls, and thus the meticulously painted scenery. His use of narrative, as in **Barbe Bleue** (1901), is to chop it into segments of approximately one minute each, each of which is little more than a tableau in motion; but in fantasies such as **Rêve de Noël** (1900), a sequence of pictures on Christmas themes, he is already using the dissolve.

However, if his favourite subject was not a magician on a stage, it was a scientist in a laboratory; he turned inevitably to the works of the still-living Jules Verne. His first Verne-inspired film was *Le Voyage dans la Lune* (1902), which, with his *Cendrillon* (1900), established him throughout the world – to the extent that at a time when the production cost of one reel was confined to mere salaries and a limited expenditure on costumes or sets he spent the equivalent of $7,500 on **Voyage à Travers l'Impossible** (1904). It does last for two reels, probably the first film to do so, and audiences of the day, convinced that they were at the dawn of an age of marvels, responded with enthusiasm; but today the odd, imaginative tricks and the endearing details of the short subjects tend to pall when the material is stretched out to twenty minutes. His savants, viewed satirically, tend to gesticulate like clowns, but that is also true of his characters in his reconstruction of real-life events, such as **L'Affaire Dreyfus** (1899), an elaborate, one-reel effort in nine sequences. The trial finished on 9 September 1899, with the verdict that shocked Europe, that Dreyfus was guilty 'with extenuating circumstances'; and in the light of the furore caused by *L'Affaire* it is possible to say that Méliès' final sequence, showing Dreyfus returning to prison, is inflammatory. The aspects of the case he chose to show were not so much informative as designed to play on audience emotions – and we may well wonder how many spectators thought they were seeing actuality. Some rushing across the camera by the cast indicates that Méliès did not understand the importance of action, and during the next decade his films remained inert while the medium moved on. He made fewer and longer films, but lost his pre-eminence as piracy and plagiarism ran rife in the industry; and just as the unit he set up under his brother in the U.S. collapsed under the onslaught of more important companies, so he found local conditions difficult with the industry dominated by the Pathé company (q.v.).

He was also unable to change in the light of innovations by others. By 1912 French film-makers were out in the streets of Paris shooting the chase comedies which had become so popular, but Méliès was offering *A la Conquête du Pole,* which was similar to the films he had made ten years earlier – animated tableaux set against painted sets, each of them explained in an introductory intertitle. The film is pleasing, with a suffragette determined to go on a trip of Polar exploration and its voyage among the signs of the Zodiac – represented by scantily-clad maidens holding painted stars. Once at the Pole they discover a giant, who gathers the explorers into his icicled arms, occasionally popping one into his mouth. But such matters were no longer novel to audiences and Méliès gave up making films in 1913, having made over five hundred, and some titles indicate his range: *Le Château Hanté, La Vengeance de Bouddha ou la Fontaine Sacrée, Les Sept Péchés Capitaux, Le Barbier de Séville, La Tour de Londres et les Derniers Moments d'Anne de Boleyn, Hamlet, Jeanne d'Arc, Le Tsar en France, Le Juif-Errant, New York-Paris en Automobile* and *L'Eruption du Mont-Pélé.* He was rediscovered, not long before his death, selling toys, not the first of many creative artists to find the cinema an ungrateful mistress, since virtually all the pioneers were driven out or ruined by it. His work may be primitive, but audiences of the time were enchanted; and the enchantment lingers.

Méliès was the first to make publicity films for other companies, in 1898; and he may have been the first, for the sake of publicity, to put his name on another's film. The British-based American entrepreneur, Charles Urban, engaged him to make a version of the Coronation of Edward VII, but it was in fact made by George Albert Smith (1864–1959), whose Warwick Trading Co. was financed by Urban. Smith was a follower of Méliès, but more interested in his *jeux d'esprits* than in his longer films. He had been a portrait photographer, which may be why his films are rich in close-ups; double exposure was known to photography, but Smith patented it for cinematographic use in 1898 – though others, including Méliès, were using it by 1900. Smith's films show a delight in trickery, and his **The Kiss in the Tunnel** (1899) is the earliest surviving example of action put together without intervening titles: a couple in a railway carriage embrace, framed at beginning and end by shots of a train. There is something prurient about the kiss, and Smith seems to have been a pioneer in the matter of sex. In **Let Me Dream Again** (1900) an older man is drinking and smoking with a girl, but as he leans to kiss her he finds himself in bed with his wife; the **Things Seen Through a Telescope** (1900) includes a couple embracing and a woman undressing – as are the objects seen through a keyhole by *Peeping Tom* (1901). Apart from the impish humour, there is an attempt to get audiences to accept close-ups by suggesting that they were watching objects enlarged mechanically; and

there are close-ups cut into innocent little frolics like *Grandma's Reading Glass* (1900) and *The Little Doctor and the Kitten* (1900), not to mention **Mary Jane's Mishap, or Don't Fool with the Paraffin** (1903), in which a slovenly maid blows herself up and appears as a ghost with a paraffin can.

The British were adept at trick films, and from the Hepworth company the output included *How it Feels to Be Run Over* (1900), **The Jonah Man or the Traveller Bewitched** (1904), with its disappearing coats, trolleys and trains, and **What the Curate Really Did** (1905), in which the curate's true adventures are superimposed above a number of gossiping ladies. James Williamson, also associated with Urban, offered **An Interesting Story** (1904), in which a man's absorption in his book causes many a mishap including dismemberment.

The British pioneers were indeed at one point – 1902 – the most innovative, but the French took the lead the following year, mainly due to the enterprise of the Pathé brothers. Charles Pathé (1863–1957) had become successful importing Edison's phonograph and records into France; when offered the franchise of Edison's films and the accompanying equipment he realised the importance of the new medium, observing that it was school, newspaper and theatre all combined. He was also to claim that though he did not invent the cinema it was he who industrialised it; in 1901 he left the phonograph business in the hands of his brother Emile and opened a studio in Vincennes. The following year he opened a branch in London, the beginning of a world-wide network, and it was estimated that by 1908 he controlled at least half of the movie business in the U.S., also selling in that market twice as much product as all the local companies combined.

At the time of his first expansion, in 1901, he was fortunate in appointing Ferdinand Zecca (1863–1947) to ensure a regular supply of films. Both men had worked originally in fairgrounds, and Zecca had originally been commentator for the Pathé films. He borrowed ideas and innovations from his contemporaries, and duplicates of most of Smith's films may be found in the Pathé catalogue – though it could not now be established that Smith did not plagiarise in return; but when Zecca uses a dissolve in his version of *Let Me Dream Again* instead of Smith's clumsy shift of focus, that is probably because the dissolve had not yet crossed the Channel. Zecca improved upon Méliès by disposing of the proscenium effect, and his early experience of popular taste enabled him also to widen its subject matter. He made the first French crime film, *L'Histoire d'un Crime* (1901) and the first movie religioso, *La Passion de Notre Seigneur* (1902). He also made a *Quo Vadis?* (1901), an *Ali Baba et les 40 Voleurs* (1902) and *La Conquête de l'Air* (1901), while his re-enactments of true events include another on Dreyfus and the equally popular assassination of President McKinley; some titles suggest more weighty matters – *Les Victimes de l'Alcoolisme* (1902), *La Grève* (1904), *Les Executions Capitales* – but under Zecca's leadership Pathé were most adept at fantasy. The tricks, for instance, in **Marionetten** (1904) and **Japonaiserie** (1904) are really quite extraordinary, two of a series built round acrobats in which nothing is impossible, from living people being pulled from paper cones to magic boxes forming a child's – real – face. In **L'Ingénieuse Soubrette** (1902) the lady of the title walks up walls; in **Rêve à la Lune** (1905) a drunk sees dancing champagne bottles, and there are miraculous transformations and vases with faces in **Aladin** (1906).

Zecca followed Méliès in believing that what the cinema did best was fantasy. It was by no means certain at this time that it would adopt the narrative habit, for the film-makers realised that that was something that the stage could do so much better. However, the public began to tire of magical tricks and began to favour the more narrative films, and these became possible with the invention of editing. The fantasy films prove that within a few years of the Lumières' first showings the technical vocabulary of the new medium was immense, and also that audiences were not so reluctant to accept innovation as has been pretended. The wholesale piracy of ideas and techniques is such – and the preservation of early films and cataloguing so rare – that the film historian treads a minefield in allotting credit to anyone, but we may

certainly challenge the accepted view that Edwin S. Porter (q.v.) was the inventor of editing, i.e. the creation of narrative by joining pieces of film together. With Méliès the film became an art, but it is with editing that the art of the film begins. Somewhere among the dozens of 'fire' movies listed in the catalogues is the first edited film, probably **Fire!** (1901) made in Britain by James Williamson. Warwick's **Fire Call and Fire Escape**, first shown in March 1899, suggests some sort of staged action, since a man is seen giving an alarm; but Williamson's film is longer and more sophisticated, in five scenes: 1. Policeman sees burning house; 2. Hove Fire Brigade leaves its HQ; 3. Engines rush down street; 4. Man in bedroom is rescued by fireman; 5. Fireman descends ladder with another man. Unlike, say, the narratives of Méliès, each scene depends on the one before, and Williamson had earlier made **Stop Thief**!, which in three scenes follows a thief from theft to apprehension. Among the many subsequent films on this theme is one directed by Frank Mottershaw for the Sheffield Photo Company, **A Daring Daylight Robbery** (1903), a quite elaborate affair involving a burglar, several policemen, the Sheffield Fire Brigade and, most significantly, a finale in which the burglar is apprehended as he steps off the train, as the result of a telegraph message. Clearly Williamson and Mottershaw had reasoned that if a narrative could be constructed from pieces of film, the logical progression was to decide beforehand what, beyond the props, was needed. Thus, if not the screenplay, screen-planning was born, as opposed to Méliès's meticulous preparations.

Edwin S. Porter (1869–1941) worked for the Edison Company, a projectionist-turned-cameraman who by this time was production head; the influence of Méliès (whose films Edison distributed) can be seen in **Uncle Josh at the Moving Picture Show** (1902), a little joke on the principle of what we now call 'the film within a film', and that of G. A. Smith and his imitators in **Gay Shoe Clerk** (1904), which includes a close-up of a lady's ankle. Porter was merely another plagiarist in an industry now founded on that principle, and indeed one of his jobs was to study imported film for ideas; it is generally conceded that he had *Fire!* in mind when he made **The Life of an American Fireman** (1903), but he increased audience interest by showing a woman and child in danger, heightened by cutting back to the galloping fire-engine. He does not use this discovery in an exciting way, and though in **The Great Train Robbery** (1904) he cuts from dance-hall to telegraph office to the robbers escaping, he never cuts from pursuer to pursued – so clearly this standard device of almost every Western ever since did not occur to him. The film, though based on an actual event, owed its existence to *A Daring Daylight Robbery*, which in fact the Edison Company as distributors had put into circulation some months earlier.

In the interim, Porter had directed a pet project of Edison's, and reputedly the most expensive film made in the U.S. to that time, a version of *Uncle Tom's Cabin* (1903) – and he had made it in the style current for 'classics', i.e. the moving tableau. Many American manufacturers were resisting close-ups and cutting because they thought they would bewilder and distract audiences, but audience acceptance of *The Great Train Robbery* paved the way for much livelier films. Porter himself was not carried away, and indeed, *The Seven Ages* (1905) is deliberately a series of tableaux, while *The Dream of a Rarebit Fiend* (1906) continues his copies of Méliès.

Audiences did not merely accept *The Great Train Robbery*: they went wild about it. It was copied and imitated, but its popularity was such that it was almost always the opening attraction of the nickelodeons now springing up – as a result of its success. The chase, literally, was on, and Biograph came up with **Personal** (1904) and **The Lost Child** (1905), both directed by Wallace McCutcheon Sr, respectively about a French nobleman who advertises for a wife and is pursued by the candidates, and a child kidnapper pursued by a number of passers-by, including a policeman. The latter was photographed by Billy Bitzer, later to work with Griffith, and it includes the interpolated close-up which four years later was claimed by Griffith to be his own invention.

Audiences the world over clamoured

for action, but in Britain, at least, the influence of *The Great Train Robbery* was slow to be felt – though **Raid on a Coiner's Den** (1904) is more elaborate than the little crook pieces that preceded it. Sheffield followed their *Daring Daylight Robbery* with a companion picture, **The Life of Charles Peace** (1905), which in terms of popularity far outshadowed the earlier film, and locally rivalled Porter's film – to the extent that it was also widely plagiarised. The ingredients are once more a crook, a train and the police, but in this case it was 'Taken on the Exact Spot' and the engine-driver was the same man who had driven the train taking Peace to jail. Such factors doubtless added to the thrill of being so close to crime, and the exploits of Peace, the most famous of Victorian criminals due to his daring burglaries and innumerable escapes, were still fresh in the mind of the British public. The cinema was still akin to the Chamber of Horrors, appealing to the millions who devoured the crime stories in the Sunday papers: it is not coincidental that the first hugely popular American and British 'features' were both about criminals – though neither, unlike later films, glamorises them.

Rescued by Rover (1905) is also about crime, and may well have been inspired by *The Lost Child*, since it also concerns a stolen baby – and a dog with apparently

Rescued by Rover was so popular that it was remade twice – the negatives of the first two versions wore out. Its original cost was £7.13s.6d (unnaturally low, since it was mainly a family affair); which became £10.12s.6d for positive prints sold outright.

extrasensory perception. It was made by Cecil Hepworth (1874–1953), the most successful of the British pioneers, from his 'Animated Photography', in 1897, the first book on the cinema, to his second version of *Comin' Thro' the Rye* (q.v.) in 1923. Though at this time it is unwise to attribute anything innovatory to any one person, *Rescued by Rover* may have owed its success to its cross-cutting which increased audience tension as it slipped back and forth between the baby's fate and its parents' agitation.

Certainly Porter, who had tentatively cut back and forth in *The Life of an American Fireman*, uses it to illuminate **The Kleptomaniac** (1906), telling simultaneously the stories of a rich woman caught shoplifting, and a poor woman who steals from desperation. He had done an earlier tract on social injustice, *The Ex-Convict* (1904), and **The White Caps** (1906) indicates the perils that can befall a wife-beater at the hands of a group of social do-gooders – who, since they are hooded, may be based on the Ku Klux Klan. This latter film, only attributed to Porter, is a particularly messy one, as it meanders over its fifteen locations; and the later famous **Rescued from an Eagle's Nest** (1907), a re-working of *Rescued by Rover* which is also attributed to him, was in its time greeted with particular scorn by the trade press. Another version was McCutcheon's **Her First Adventure** (1908) from Biograph, a virtual remake, even to the close-up of the dog at the end; it is more elaborate, especially in the cross-cutting at the climax – another invention which Griffith was to claim as his own. We know he saw this, because he is, in fact, its leading actor – and his first film as a director, made a few months later, **The Adventures of Dollie** (her Marvellous Experience at the Hands of the Gypsies), is another version of the same subject.

Griffith's rise as a director did nothing to improve the generally appalling quality of the American film, though the attention he attracted to himself and his supposed innovations reminded other film-makers of the diverse gifts the medium had acquired for its purpose – which was, since *The Great Train Robbery*, the telling of a story. The fact is that the industry staggered along, even retro-gressing to the tableau-form when it found itself inadequate to stuffing a long story into one reel (Vitagraph's 1909 *Oliver Twist* is a good, or rather bad, example). Between the two landmarks, Porter's film and *The Birth of a Nation* (q.v.), further requirements for narrative came into being, be it an imaginative camera set-up or the fade between scenes or the travelling camera. The latter did not become common till more than a decade later, and the fade only became extensively used *circa* 1912. These American film-makers were as enthusiastic as the more fastidious Europeans, but they lacked finesse – as, they thought, did most of their audience. There remained, too, the rivalry of the three major companies as a barrier to progress, though by the end of the decade Edison was limping behind Vitagraph and Biograph; significantly, as the public began recognising their players, for there was no 'Edison Girl' to rival 'The Biograph Girl' and 'The Vitagraph Girl'.

The subjects they chose to film ranged from the classics and Shakespeare through nineteenth-century melodramas to popular novels of the day – the latter literally stolen without acknowledgment. The historical films and literary adaptations are today very dull as stories, though the lavishness of costume, if not setting, can sometimes surprise; but it is the contemporary dramas which are exciting to watch, trite though many of them are. Here are a number of favourite themes: infidelity, which invariably means a mild flirtation on the part of the husband and the wife's discovery of it; courtship, often of a middle-aged widow by a no-good johnny; abduction, usually of children, by gypsies, Red Indians, and other untrustworthy people; seduction, or rather attempted seduction, often of a friend's wife or a pretty employee engaged to another man; deception, which may mean posing as a swell to raid a wealthy home or planting jewellery on an innocent man; revenge, perhaps on some hapless victim supposed to have wronged mother or daughter; and just about every form of crime. A vast army of young girls discovered that they didn't love the men they thought they did; a number of diabolical schemers went mad; assorted animals, but usually dogs, found themselves quicker at detection and rescue than human beings; many unfortunates accused of larceny turned out to be innocent or to have what is called extenuating circumstances; and a great many villains, invariably moustached, perished in horrible manner, often crazed with lust at the time.

These people emoted, sometimes much more naturalistically than is supposed, whether before painted scenery, on which was printed the company's insignia to prevent duping (the intertitles with the company's name or insignia had proved ineffectual, since the pirates simply incorporated new intertitles) and also in an increasing number of natural settings. Porter used fourteen scenes to tell *The Great Train Robbery:* eight years later, in 1912, D. W. Griffith used sixty-eight scenes, including intertitles, close-ups, etc., for *The Sands of Dee* – a proliferation that was not always welcome, since some cinemagoers spoke of 'confusion'. The changes in the industry from 1910 onwards are so enormous that we will trace through them carefully in a separate chapter. We move from the American industry when two of its three leaders left it – Wallace 'Old Man' McCutcheon of Biograph and Porter of Edison. The survivor was J. Stuart Blackton of Vitagraph, and as heads of production of the three companies we may regard them as the three founders of American film production. But the new maverick companies which had sprung into being were filching the assistants of these three men to turn out their own films, and even Porter left Edison in 1909 to form his own company, Rex; then in 1915 he decided that the industry needed younger blood and turned to technical experimentation till drifting away altogether from films. Adolph Zukor (q.v.) and Blackton remained with Vitagraph till 1917, but McCutcheon left Biograph in 1908 to return to the theatre – which is when Griffith took over as head of production.

Since Blackton was among those responsible for the development of the animated film, we might look at it briefly before turning to the situation in Europe. The Kinetoscope and the other machines had utilised drawings; in 1906 Blackton produced **Humorous Phases of Funny**

Faces, the first animated cartoon done in the single frame method. This series of metamorphosing faces was followed in 1908 by *The Haunted House,* which mixed drawings with live objects. It was Blackton's experience as cartoonist which prompted his interest; and it was another newspaper artist who created the most famous early film cartoon, Winsor McKay, with **Gertie the Dinosaur** (1909) – originally to accompany his vaudeville act, though a filmed prologue (showing him accept a wager that he can make drawings move) was later added for cinema showings. In France the firm of Gaumont from 1908 onwards encouraged Emil Cohl in animation, and the inventiveness of his little films still astonishes.

In France, in keeping with the attitude of the Belle Epoque, the cinema was mainly

27

devoted to frivolity, and in 1905 Pathé engaged a music hall star, André Deed, to make a series of comedy films built around a character called 'Boireau' – and Deed therefore takes credit as the first screen performer recognised by the public. It was perhaps the French who most widely appreciated the cinema as a vehicle for action, and if Britain invented the chase film, and the U.S. the chase comedy, it was France which turned the latter into high art. Something moved: it fell, or began to run, and the utmost havoc was created in the streets of Paris. Chase comedies were turned out by the thousand, and in the midst of them appeared the cinema's first great performer, Max Linder (1883–1925), who joined Pathé not long after Deed. He had had some success as an actor in the 'boulevard' theatre, but like the great American Silent comics later, it took some time for him to develop his silk-hatted screen persona, though the titles of his early films – *La Première Sortie d'un Collégien*, *Les Débuts d'un Patineur* – indicate that he soon hit upon the idea of a young man innocently causing chaos, not least to himself. He quickly discovered that the higher the young man the harder the fall, and thus became the impeccably-dressed man-about-town. Within three years of his debut, the titles of most of his films indicate his presence in them, proof that he was the first movie performer to be an attraction in his own right. From 1911 he wrote and directed most of the films in which he appeared, and here are just a few of these later titles: *Max est Distrait* (1911), *Max et son Chien Dick* (1911), *Max Professeur de Tango* (1912), *L'Anglais tel que Max Parle* (1914) and *Max Devrait Porter les Bretelles* (1915). Starting as a sketch or a situation, his films begin to tell a story, if a rudimentary one: for instance, in **Max Pédicure** (1915) – based on one of his stage sketches – the lady he has called upon passes him off as a chiropodist, and her father insists that Max treat his feet, complications which lead eventually to the real chiropodist being thrown through the window and landing on Max emerging below.

Other Linder films confirm the importance of the final gag, and he seems to have first used the comedy 'coda', as taken on later by Keaton and Lloyd. Chaplin once admitted that Linder was his master, and when he left Mutual that company invited Linder to replace him; a year later he did go to the U.S., to join Chaplin's earlier employers, Essanay, but the three two-reelers he made there did not encourage him to stay. Two successful features in Europe tempted him back to Hollywood, where he preceded the American comics into feature-length films, going further than they in that he not only wrote, produced, directed and starred, but also financed. That each had a different distributor indicates the bumpy road at the box-office – which is ironic, since both **Seven Years' Bad Luck** (1921), and **Be My Wife** (1921) are not only funnier than the first features of Lloyd, Keaton and Chaplin, but have more sustained and 'building' narratives. The misadventures of fiancé and prospective bridegroom are inventive, visually witty and endearing; his most brilliant sequence is the false mirror image – and because he is hung-over it is funnier than the version done by Groucho Marx in *Duck Soup* (q.v.). After a comic spoof of Dumas. **The Three Must-Get-Theres** (1922), he returned to Europe, and after making a film in Vienna he and his wife committed double suicide in a Paris hotel room. In 1963 his daughter collected his three American features into *En Compagnie de Max Linder*, to re-establish him among his peers; his unfortunately little seen one- and two-reelers give evidence of his astonishing superiority over the cinema's other first clowns.

It was his success which caused Itala Film of Italy to filch André Deed from Pathé, and rechristen him Cretinetti – or 'Gribouille' in France and 'Foolshead' in England: his is primitive slapstick, and it is surprising to find that he had a host of imitators within Italy, including Polidor, who is even worse. These were larcenous times: in England there was Pimple ('Flivver' in the U.S.) and Winky, the latter a round, cheery fellow whose habit of glancing at the camera for approval is remarkably successful. He played put-upon tramps and husbands for Bamforth, a Yorkshire company, and disappeared during the War because of public feeling towards his real name, Reggie Switz: with the French Onésime ('Simple Simon' in Britain) he is, after

LEFT: *La Mort* – or *L'Assassinat* – *du Duc de Guise* was much admired and influential. What actually impressed were the names of those engaged – Saint-Saëns wrote an accompanying score, the Académie Française supplied a writer for the scenario, and the Comédie Française the cast and co-directors, André Calmettes and Charles La Bargy – the latter also in the lead. The film tempted Sarah Bernhardt to put on screen her Dame aux Camélias BELOW.

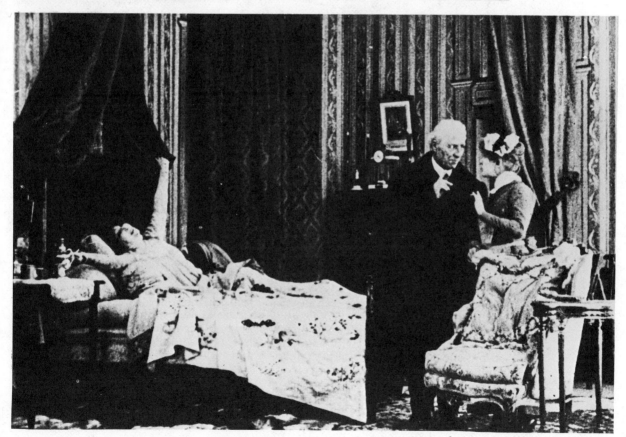

Beginnings

Gli Ultimo Giorni de Pompei was a popular subject with the early Italian film-makers, since Vesuvius had erupted four times since the beginning of the century. Caserini's second attempt at the subject was plagued by smoke which did not always come from the top of the (painted) volcano; perhaps a rival version, directed by Enrico Vidali, was more convincing.

Linder, the most accessible of the early clowns. Onésime was played by Ernest Bourbon, but he is simply a peg on which to hang the gags: one reason the Onésime comedies are so far ahead of Cretinetti is that the plot is the all-important element but another is that there is a specific point of view. Jean Durand (1882–1946) was the man who looked, for Gaumont, and he saw things in a very funny light; his editing is very tight, and his one-reelers should be much better known than they are.

It was in France that the theatre first embraced the film, when the frères Lafitte, financiers, founded the Société du Film d'Art to provide material worthy of the new medium – that is, films dealing with 'elevated' subjects. Their first film, **La Mort du Duc de Guise** (1908), overwhelmed contemporaries, as can be seen from this notice in *The New York Dramatic Mirror*: 'Its superior quality in photographic excellence, superb acting, rich settings and costumes and skilful dramatic handling of a carefully constructed picture narrative distinguishes it as one of the masterpieces of motion picture production' – none of which is today readily apparent in what is the usual series of

tableaux. Sarah Bernhardt was persuaded to immortalise her *La Tosca* (1908), and then in two reels another of her stage successes, **La Dame aux Camélias** (1912), which André Calmettes also directed. Lack of close-ups prevents comment, except to say that she is coquettish and vivacious, and that she moves awkwardly (her leg had not yet been amputated). The story, not a complicated one, has been much simplified, and yet requires lengthy intertitles despite its length.

Les Amours de la Reine Elizabeth (1912) was twice as long, and the longest film yet made: two alumni of the Film d'Art, Louis Mercanton and Henri Desfontaines, produced it – in London – with the former directing. Again adapted from one of Bernhardt's popular vehicles, it is not about her 'loves' at all (in English it was known simply as *Queen Elizabeth*), beyond her relationship with Essex. It is not, to put it mildly, historically accurate, and Bernhardt's performance, again without close-ups, is no more impressive than the earlier one: her poses are not to our taste, though I can imagine that they thrilled live audiences.

The Lafittes set up their company in

30

defiance of Pathé, who retaliated by starting a rival, the Société Cinematographique des Auteurs et Gens de Lettres, which they put in the hands of Albert Capellani, a former actor with André Antoine's 'Théâtre Libre', many of whose members joined him – and from which he took its creed of literary 'naturalism' as exemplified by Zola. Unfortunately, Capellani, like his rivals, believed that the elevated subject was the historical one, and though he tried for realism in his crowd scenes and a multiplicity of (painted) sets, his films are no more watchable than other primitive historical spectacles. Pathé, meanwhile, handled the Lafittes' films abroad, taking credit for them, and they finally succeeded in putting them out of business at the time the Bernhardt-Elizabeth was filming. Pathé not only dominated the industry in France, but their tentacles were long, and in 1908 they took the 'art' film to Italy with the foundation of the Film d'Arte Italiana. There, however, the historical spectacle was already a staple of the industry.

The first important Italian company was that founded at Turin by Arturo Ambrosio (1869–1960) and named after him. The first pioneer of the Italian industry, however, is Filoteo Alberini (1865–1937), who snatched the leadership of the industry when his Cines company made the first spectacle, *Il Sacco di Roma* (1905). Ambrosio retaliated with *Marcus Lycinus* (1907). In the same year, at Cines, Mario Caserini made an *Otello*, and among other subjects to his credit are *Catalina*, *Macbeth*, *Siegfried*, *Parsifal* and two versions of Bulwer-Lytton's novel, *Gli Ultimo Giorni de Pompei* (1908 and 1913). Apart from Shakespeare and the Romans, the most popular sources plundered were Dante and the Greek heroes. Giuseppe de Liguoro's two-reel **L'Inferno** (1909) is ambitious: a quick tour of hell, with Virgil conducting Dante, and pictorially faithful to the Doré illustrations to 'The Divine Comedy'. De Liguoro was a member of the aristocracy who ran his own company, Milano, and the superiority of his productions was recognised by contemporaries. This one indicates a tremendous amount of preparation: locations range from mountaintops to the sea, and hell is most imagina-

tively done, with a huge number of Méliès-like tricks – and hundreds of nude men, which, given the prudery of the times, suggests the poverty of the participants.

These were times of great advances: the falling pillars of Troy in Giovanni Pastrone's **La Caduta di Troia** (1910) look very much the real thing, but the Wooden Horse, awesome in long-shot, turns up in close-up to be a cardboard cut-out. The unknown director of Cines **La Sposa del Nilo** (1911) keeps the screen buzzing with people – which was one reason it was widely influential. Such spectacles found a market abroad, and with that in mind – and simultaneous with the Bernhardt-Elizabeth – Cines put into production an eight-reel version of Henryk Sienkiewicz's popular novel about Romans and Christians, **Quo Vadis?** (1912). Caserini should have directed, but defected to Ambrosio, and the job went to another pupil of Alberini, Enrico Guazzoni, whose output included an *Agrippina* (1910) and a *Brutus* (1911). 'Direction' in this case is a relative term: contemporary opinion considered that the spectacle swamped all else, but the

The 1912 *Quo Vadis?* was not the first screen adaptation of this oft-filmed tale. Like at least one later version, the spectacle was relieved by witty impersonations of Nero, right, and Petronius.

31

burning of Rome is mostly a matter of smoke(-screens), and the scenes in the arena show almost nothing crucial of the action. 'Two hours fifteen minutes to project,' said the announcements in the New York press when it opened there in May 1913; in Britain it was premiered at the Royal Albert Hall.

But as happens in films, the 'greatest' was soon superseded. The moment it was clear that *Quo Vadis?* would return its investment, Itala Film put into production **Cabiria** (1914), directed by Pastrone. It opened in New York exactly a year after *Quo Vadis?*, was two reels longer, and lasted three hours. Unlike the earlier film, it is still worth watching. The sets, designed by Camillo Innocenti, range from the magnificent – the Temple of the Moloch – to the functional and false; the venues from the Alps to the Sahara: all of them are always an integral part of the film, and there can be no doubt that the storming of Carthage was copied by Griffith for the similar scenes in *Intolerance* (q.v.). It was to convey the size of the sets that Pastrone invented the tracking-shot, which refined the occasional camera-shift by moving at an angle. His other achievement was to persuade Gabrielle d'Annunzio to write the scenario – the first major literary figure to be involved directly with films: at least, he was credited, but he merely donated the names of the characters and re-wrote Pastrone's intertitles – and very florid they are. The story, concerning the Punic Wars, includes elements from a dozen sources, and the best that can be said for it is that it never flags: this is a teeming world, but it is its carpentry and not its characters which really interested Pastrone. If I quote *The New York Dramatic Mirror* again, it is not only because that was one of the few papers to notice films, but because its rapture was tempered by caution: this was 'the summit,' it reasoned, 'but the climb upward during the last decade has been so persistent, who could venture to declare that the top has been reached?' The paper considered, however, that though it might be a nine days' wonder, 'it is going to convince many doubtful people that high art and the motion picture industry are not incompatible.'

In fact, it was a summit for the Italian industry: *Maciste*, which Pastrone made the following year was a kind of sequel; inasmuch as its eponymous hero was the popular and huge negro slave of *Cabiria* (played by a former Genovese docker), but the industry was not inclined to top it. There were modern dramas as well, surprisingly many of them managing to incorporate a troupe of lions – not then needed in arenas with Christians. We may also be surprised by the popularity of the 'divismo' dramas, so-named after the style of their leading actresses, which was based on the declamatory style of Bernhardt – and which can be seen, in aspic as it were, in the posters of Mucha. These were all dramas of high society – perhaps appropriately, because many of them were showcases for the mistresses of the aristocrats so much involved in Italian films. Among these ladies were Lyda Borelli, whose *Ma L'Amore Mio Non Muore* (1913), directed by Caserini, concerns the fatal love of an exiled primadonna and the heir to the throne, and Pina Menichelli, whose *Tigre Real* (1916), directed by Pastrone, concerns the fatal love of a Russian countess and a diplomat – though after her husband's death in a spectacular fire she recovers from consumption for a happy finish.

The acknowledged leader, however, was Francesca Bertini, who in the remnants available of *Serpe* (1919) may be found in the classic position of the vamp: exultant on a huge divan, pearls round her brow and one shoulder graced with feathers, while her victim lies below, white tie and tailed, so overcome by lust that he has drunk himself into impotency. When, earlier, the vogue for such tales had waned for a while, Bertini had made **Assunta Spina** (1915) directed by Gustavo Serena from a play by Salvatore di Giacomo (reputedly inspired by *Sperduti nel Buio* now lost, also based on a play and said to mark the beginning of realism in the Italian cinema). The plot has no new slant on the old tale of the woman who commits an indiscretion for the sake of her lover, but the details of Neapolitan life are completely integrated into it and the location photography by Alberto G. Carta is extraordinary. Its producers, Caesar, combined with Ambrosio to make **Cenere** (1916), directed by Ambrosio himself and Febo Mari; Mari wrote the scenario with Eleanora Duse, and plays her son in the picture. It is a tale of mother-love, not to our taste, but a cut above others of the genre; it is adapted from a novel by Grazia Deledda (later a Nobel prize-winner) and since hitherto Duse had refused movie offers we may assume she thought this one worthwhile; as with *Assunta Spina*, there is a delight in the minutiae of daily life, and there is Duse herself: almost alone among stage-performers of the time she doesn't disappoint. At fifty-eight, she was still beautiful; her movements are slight, but cinematically highly expressive.

If the longer film was the result of a taste for historical spectacle, it was the serial which helped to make movie-going a habit – and with both had arrived the two enduring complexes of this industry, the conjunction of size and length, and their confusion with quality, with the attendant worry of winning and keeping audiences. The serial sprang from the detective film, and that is reckoned to begin in 1908, when Victorin Jasset filmed the Nick Carter series, set in Paris. The most famous exponent of the early serial, Louis Feuillade (1873–1925), began directing in 1907, and was best known for his series with the child Bébé, for Gaumont, when he published a manifesto which claimed that film could exist on its own terms, without recourse to other media, and that above all it should be visual. He began a series of family dramas, *La Vie telle qu'elle Est*, and a series of comedies, *La Vie Drôle* – the whole point of the series being that they ensured a public for the next change of programme. The detective serial evolved from a suggestion at the end of the reel that this was not the end of the story, by leaving the hero in such a predicament that the spectator was compelled to return to find out how he gets out of it. Feuillade made his first essay in the genre in 1912, *Le Proscrit*, with René Navarre as detective Jean Dervieux – and Navarre became Fantômas, l'Empéreur du Crime, whose exploits were originally issued in thirty-two parts between 1911 and 1913. Like almost all the later master criminals, he was based on Maurice Le Blanc's then enormously popular fictional thief, Arsène Lupin. Fantômas dressed in skin-tight black, with a mask, and was adept at disguises. His enemies were Inspector Juve, of the Sûreté, and a journalist, to whom he offered a bafflling series of crimes – which meant occasionally capturing and always outwitting the two of them. I have seen only one of the *Fantômas* films, **La Mort que Tue** (1913), and it is antiquated, simple penny-plain stuff, moving so fast that you have to pay the closest attention; knowing, in fact, that you will be little rewarded by its hooded criminals, real and bogus policemen, stolen jewels, false fingerprints, hidden doors, secret chambers and mysterious spiritings-away.

Within two years the serial was established as a feature of cinema programmes throughout the world. The Nick Carter series had already had its imitators, and we may find it telling that in Britain the most popular was an intrepid naval officer, Lieutenant Rose, RN, in Germany a superman, Homunculus, and in the U.S. a young woman – as produced by the Selig Company under the title *The Adventures of Kathlyn,* although all of Kathlyn's adventures were complete in themselves and did not end with the ubiquitous 'continued next week'. The most famous of the serials proper followed Kathlyn two years later, *The Perils of Pauline* (1914) and *The Exploits of Elaine* (1915), and they starred a former trapeze artist, Pearl White, as their trouble-prone but dauntless heroine. Her producers absolutely understood the importance of the visual thrill, and we may call them French-American, inasmuch as the films were made by Pathé's American subsidiary.

Meanwhile, the Danes were making the best films, and it was due to the popularity throughout Europe of both *Afgrunden* (q.v.) and *The White Slave Trade* (q.v.) that the two-reel film was adopted there much earlier than in the U.S. Both concerned sex, but Denmark's first world-wide success had been **The Lion Hunt** (1907), which sold a total of 259 copies – and its hopeless attempt to re-stage the event of the title suggests that to that time there had been few (wild) animals in movies. The producer was the Nordisk Film Company, founded by Ole Olsen, an amusement park proprietor; his director was Viggo Larsen, who had been the barker at one of his nickelodeons, and the photographer was Axel Sørensen, who had been the fairground's engineer.

Looking for another sensational subject, Olsen had come up with a one-reel abduction story, and he remade it three years later in a two-reel version, **The White Slave Trade** (1910), reasoning that Feuillade's real-life series for Gaumont and Vitagraph's similar series (q.v.) in the U.S. had created a demand for truth. The market for the white slave traffic was enormous, since these were respectable words for marquees where the word 'whore' clearly wasn't; and if to our eyes the bordellos look equally respectable – men and women drinking, smoking and dancing to a piano – they must then have seemed the height of daring. Since, however, the ways of getting young girls into the clutches of the traffickers were dramatically limited, later films concentrated on the mechanism of escape – since no heroine, of course, could submit to what was offered. Both this film and **The White Slave Trade's Last Big Job** (1911) were directed by August Blom (1869–1942). They are fascinating examples of the early exploitation movie.

Blom was as accomplished as any film director then working, and **The Shop Girl** (1911) is another good example of the early sex drama: both the boy and girl are treated sympathetically, but whereas in American films the pregnant waifs, if any, had always been 'deceived', this boy merely turns out to be too weak to remember true love when confronted by

his parents. Consequently he suffers considerably, but the fact that her fate is much worse – she dies – indicates the harsher penalties allotted to young girls who give in to their carnal instincts.

However, the most famous example of 'the wages of sin' drama was **Afgrunden** (1910), or *The Abyss*, devised by Urban Gad as a vehicle of his wife, Asta Nielsen (q.v.), to display her abilities to the theatre managers who neglected her. One might speculate as to why, throughout movie history, so many writers/directors have cast their wives as whores or loose women, but certainly at this time the subject was a favourite of the working class who were then the most enthusiastic audiences for films. In this particular version a music-teacher prefers a circus-performer to her hard-working fiancé, which indeed starts her on the road to the abyss.

The Danish cinema had another huge success with **The Four Devils** (1911), directed by Robert Dinesen (who also played one of the leads), Alfred Lind (who also photographed) and Carl Rosenbaum, and one of the reasons, again, was sex; in one particular scene the woman guiltlessly follows the man into the bedroom. In most cases the only form of impending sex allowed to be shown was rape; in *The Shop Girl* and *Afgrunden* it is simply not shown at all – or even later in such American films as *A Fool There Was* (q.v.) – so that the suggestion here of mutual enjoyment is very rare indeed. Otherwise this version of Herman Bang's novel is crude. But there is proof that European film-makers were in advance of the Americans in realising that audiences wanted spectacle, be it circuses, wild animals, battles – or shipwrecks. The demand for the latter followed the sinking of the *Titanic*, and Nordisk's *Drama at Sea* (1912) is an early example and *Atlantis* (1913), directed by Blom, the best known. The former was directed by his colleague, Eduard Schnedler-Sørensen, whose output that year also included one of the manifold copies of *The Four Devils*, **The Great Circus Catastrophe**, whose hero, Valdemar Psilander, is chased by a pre-Hollywood attempt at a vamp. Actually, this team, with the same writer, A. Kjerulf, offered a fairly sophisticated comedy, **The**

Strongest (1912), a title that refers to putative lovers, she the pursuer and he the pursued.

At this time Nordisk was second only to Pathé in its output, and continued to be a force in Denmark long after the international demand for Danish film had ceased. Olsen's directors were trying to do too much from too few resources, and they simply did not have the visual imagination of Benjamin Christensen (1879–1959), an actor in their company who left and turned director when Olsen refused to back **The Mysterious X** (1914). Both this and **The Night of Revenge** (1916) have complicated and deftly melodramatic plots of, respectively, a wronged officer caught up in espionage and a wronged ex-convict, and in both roles Christensen himself gives performances of considerable vivacity; but his films are most remarkable for their demonstration of the care taken in camera set-up, lighting, location and editing. They are, in fact, technically adventurous, and though his later films (q.v.) demonstrate the same care they would indicate little advance in characterisation.

The Danish cinema declined with the defection of many of its leading talents to Germany, and chief among these was the actress who immediately after Max Linder became the best-known screen performer, Asta Nielsen (1890–1972). 'She is all,' wrote Guillaume Apollinaire after seeing *Afgrunden*. 'The vision of the drunkard and the dream of the hermit.' After that film she made three with Blom, and then went with her husband to Germany, where he did a variation of *Afgrunden* called **Die Arme Jenny** (1912) in which she sinks from scullery maid, betrayed by a swell, to soliciting with a cigarette in her mouth, and finally walks into a snow-drift after learning that her seducer is to marry. Less risqué, but as much in keeping with the taste of the time, is **Mädchen ohne Vaterland** (1912), about a gypsy persuaded to steal secrets – something she does without hindrance – from the barracks where her lover is stationed. A tentative statement is made about inter-racial love, and certainly the title, and the ending, make it clear that the displaced have no patriotism. *The Moving Picture World* waxed enthusiastic when the film reached the U.S. two years later: 'A more finely finished production . . . it will be hard to find. All the elements of a great and striking success are present in happy and harmonious combination.' They are not; but in Europe at least this infant art form was growing so fast that it would mesmerise even sophisticates like Apollinaire – whose view of Miss Nielsen was shared by this particular critic: her performance was, he said, 'a masterpiece'; she already knew more about screen acting than most Hollywood stars a decade later. Her skill may be compared with Mary Pickford's, since in **Engelein** (1913) she played the sort of role Miss Pickford often undertook, a sixteen-year-old – one who has to pose as a child, and suddenly grow up when the uncle who falls in love with her has qualms about being a Humbert Humbert. She is furiously inventive, whether ogling a guardsman, or smoking, or deciding that the lake is too cold for a suicide attempt – and very droll indeed.

Engelein was one of the feature films, five reels long, now common in Europe. Of the three forms open to the cinema, documentary as offered by Lumière, fantasy as promulgated by Méliès, and the narrative as (probably) developed by the British, the new medium had opted for the last named though its now multi-reel form was likely to be supported by one reel of the other two – since programmes were increasingly including the newsreel (first offered on a regular basis by Pathé in 1908) and an animated cartoon. Cinema developed faster in Europe, because most of its exponents saw it primarily as a means of expression: so far those involved in the infant American industry saw it best as a means of making money – and they had not progressed yet to the quality offered by Pathé or Nordisk. But with Europe committed to the Apocalypse, the U.S. would take the lead in film production, and from then to the present its films would predominate throughout the world.

2

The Rise of the American Industry

IT WAS not only the cutback in production entailed by the War which caused the European film industries to fall behind the American one – because, War or not, the latter was already poised to push ahead. The new medium suited the new country: it was an entertainment understandable to the new immigrant population, and it was the first complete means of communication to scattered townships in a vast country. It is doubtful whether the managers of the three pioneer companies, Edison, Biograph and Vitagraph realised what powerful potential the cinema possessed, though at Biograph D. W. Griffith did, to the extent that he was determined to ride with it to glory. There is no doubt that he realised the boundless artistic possibilities, and since he was, in his own view, an artist, it was a comparatively simple matter to make his name as synonymous with cinema as was that of Dickens with literature. Another so minded was Thomas Ince, less well-remembered, since he died in mid-career and did not have propagandists to keep his name alive as his films became forgotten. When film appreciation started, roughly at the time the Silents died, the only American authority was the poet and essayist Vachel Lindsay, and the only American director he appreciated was Griffith (significantly, he later wrote poems inspired by Griffith heroines). But if Griffith and Ince saw in the cinema a means of self-aggrandisement their achievement in drawing attention to it, in making it respectable, cannot be underestimated – and they were perhaps more honourably motivated than the new entrepreneurs, who saw in it a means to wealth. The achievement of the latter is by no means despicable, since they founded an industry which was to overshadow all other means of mass communications for the next thirty years, and which was to remain almost unchanged for another twenty.

It began in 1905, when films left the penny arcades and saloon backrooms for specially equipped premises. The practice was facilitated by the formation of film exchanges – distribution centres which bought from the manufacturers and rented to exhibitors at a quarter of the purchase price. The first was started by a cameraman, Harry J. Miles, in 1903, and within four years there were over a hundred exchanges throughout the country. Easier access to a greater number of films meant that some exhibitors could change their programmes more frequently, even daily; if they could pay bigger fees than their rivals they could get new products and advertise 'first-run' pictures; or if they owned several sites, they could pass the print from one to another – usually carried by boys on bicycles (so that 'bicycling' remains the industry term for shipping to a nearby theatre).

What is regarded as America's first cinema was opened in Pittsburgh by John P. Harris and his brother-in-law, Harry Davis – who coined for it the name nickelodeon, to suggest both the cheapness of entry and its aspirations to respectability. They had converted a disused store with trimmings from a defunct opera-house (the opening film was *The Great Train Robbery*, of course); within three years there were 10,000 nickelodeons in the U.S., their programmes usually consisting of a melodrama, a comedy and a novelty – probably a film of an actual event – each, of course, still one-reel long. The pit pianist arrived on the scene, to accompany the films, and so, sometimes, did a singer to lead the community singing in the intervals. Popcorn, candy and peanuts were hawked in the aisles – such goodies the essential accompaniment to movie-watching for years to come. In time, the price of admission might also include an orange or a toffee-apple; in lean times, admission might be obtained on presentation of a token fee and some lowly object, i.e. a jam jar. The entrances, plastered with posters, proclaimed a haven of sensational but simple entertainment; and, in the early days at least, it was not a haven found on the more elegant thoroughfares. Inevitably opposition arose to an entertainment so enthusiastically patronised by the more humble people: newspaper editorials thundered on the 'immorality' to be seen at nickelodeons, but the most strenuous agitators were those·people feeling the pinch – saloon owners, vaude-ville entrepreneurs and clergymen.

To meet criticism, the industry's trade magazine, *Views and Film Index*, began to clamour for a self-instituted censorship board, and in 1909 the National Board of Censorship of Motion Pictures – later the National Board of Review – was set up by the People's Institute of New York, in conjunction with the Motion Picture Patents Company (q.v.) but the Board was never very effective because the Patents Company did not embody all the producing companies. In Britain, the film-makers set up the British Board of Film Censors (in 1912), which always acted as an official body – though its findings could be challenged by local authorities. In the U.S. only a handful of States passed legislature controlling movies, and it wasn't till 1922 that more stringent censorship was exercised, with the formation of the Motion Picture Producers and Distributors Association – usually known as The Hays Office, after its first president, Will H. Hays, recruited from President Harding's cabinet. Again, the impetus for this came from within the industry, as a result of some scandals, and some noisy legal squabbles between theatre owners, distributors and manu-facturers – many of whom were then

one and the same – attempting either to monopolise the industry or to drive com-petitors to the wall. Many independent producers were indeed forced out, but it should be noted that the industry was never so united as when business was poor – as happened after the War.

An earlier crisis had precipitated the foundation of the Motion Picture Patents Company. As nickelodeons multiplied, so did manufacturers to fill them with product. Legally, only Edison, Biograph and Vitagraph had patents to manufacture motion pictures but in an attempt to stifle competition they combined in 1909 with the best-established of their rivals – Selig, Kalem, Essanay and Lubin, and the French-owned Pathé and Méliès. Pooling their patent claims, they were licensed to manufacture films; they arranged with Eastman Kodak, the largest supplier of raw film stock, to supply only them; and with Edison himself within their fold they charged exhibitors $2 a week to rent his equipment – a tax which was much resented. Despite it, over ten thousand exhibitors signed with them to show only their films. Those producers left outside the trust protested, and arranged under-hand deals; bootlegging of films became common – and associations were formed to fight the monopoly. In a further attempt to strengthen its hold, the Patents Company established a national film exchange, the General Film Company, in 1910, and in less than two years – by revoking licences – it had absorbed all fifty-seven of the leading exchanges. But there was one hold-out, the Greater New York Rental Company, headed by William Fox, who owned sufficient theatres to oppose the trust: he instituted a lawsuit against it, invoking restraint of trade, and though the matter was not legally resolved till 1916, the monopoly began to crumble almost immediately.

Fox (1879–1952) himself became one of the independents – a manufacturer of films – in 1912, and in 1915 he formed the Fox Film Corporation, which he headed till it amalgamated with Twenti-eth Century in 1935. The founders of the great Hollywood studios all came from similar backgrounds. In Fox's case, he was an immigrant, at the age of nine months, with his German-Jewish family; as a boy he worked in the garment industry, and entered the film business by acquiring a penny arcade in Brooklyn which expanded into a chain of fifteen cinemas.

The other leading opponent of the Patents Company was Carl Laemmle (1867–1939), who also would eventually establish one of the great, continuing, production companies, Universal. He too was a German Jew, arriving in the U.S. to work with his brother in 1884; he worked as a book-keeper and store-manager in Oshkosh, and in 1906, instead of opening his own store, as intended, he started a nickelodeon, in Chicago. He soon had a chain of cinemas and his own distribution company – the Laemmle Film Service, notably active against the trust. To compete additionally, he formed a producing company, the Independent Motion Picture Company, or I.M.P.

It was I.M.P. and Laemmle who insti-gated the movies' two abiding fantasies, Hollywood and the American film star – though to be exact the 'discovery' of Hollywood was accidental, and I.M.P. was only one of several companies which found themselves in that part of California at the height of the war with the trust. By 1912 it was imperative for these indepen-dents to get as far from the Patents Company as possible: California offered sunshine, a variety of landscape, and a welcome from workers and real-estate dealers, both of whose financial demands were lower than those in the East. Los Angeles was more attractive than San Francisco, because it was nearer the Mexican border if the Patents Company sent writs or injunctions; most of the companies settled in a suburb of L.A. known locally as Hollywood – a name which was formally adopted in 1913.

The institution of the film star also arose from the anti-trust war. In Europe theatre-players had begun to work before the cameras, but in the U.S. film per-formers were likely to be propmen or their wives or visiting relatives. As actors arrived from the stage – usually because they couldn't get work on it – the manu-facturers refused them publicity because they believed it would create a demand for higher salaries: they were slow tc seize upon the possibilities of personality cults on celluloid, but exhibitors were soon aware of them: a buzz of recognition in the audience, and then increased business as word of mouth spread. Laemmle was determined to get that lady known as 'The Biograph Girl' to I.M.P. In 1910 at Biograph she was getting $25 a week; he offered her $1,000 a week and she, not surprisingly, accepted. His war with the trust had taught him the value of publicity, and he planted a story in the St Louis press to the effect that she, Florence Lawrence, the Biograph Girl, had been killed in a streetcar accident. Then I.M.P. took an ad in *The Moving Picture World* to the effect that the story was an invention of I.M.P.'s enemies: 'We nail a lie'. And Miss Lawrence visited St Louis with I.M.P.'s leading actor, King Baggott: they were mobbed.

After I.M.P. had become Universal, in 1913, it advised exhibitors to book films with familiar faces, but by then all the companies, on both sides of the war, were advertising the names of their players. The last of the Patents group to give in to the advertising of stars was Biograph, which had twice lost the most valuable star property of them all, Mary Pickford (1893–1979), dubbed by exhibitors 'Little Mary' and 'The Girl With the Curls' dur-ing her first spell with the company. She had also been filched by I.M.P. in 1910, and did equally brief stints at Majestic, at Biograph again and in the theatre before returning to Biograph – though that com-pany was not particularly enthusiastic about her popularity, reasoning that what mattered was the product itself – and Bio-graph's films were the most favourably received by those newspapers that took note of movies. In charge of production, and making most of them, was D. W. Griffith.

David Wark Griffith (1875–1948) came to dominate the American film industry in the second decade of the century. His achievements so mesmerised his peers that for a brief while it looked as though the director – rather than the producer or financier – would have control over what actually went into movies. He is said to be the great innovator – it was certainly said by himself. When he broke with Biograph he advertised himself thus in *The New York Dramatic Mirror*: 'D. W. Griffith: producer of all the great Bio-graph successes, revolutionising the Motion Picture Drama, and founding

Of the early Griffith
two–reelers, the
1910 *An Arcadian
Maid* is among the
most pleasing –
partly because of the
rustic locations for
its story of a
washerwoman
(Mary Pickford)
persuaded to rob her
employer by a
handsome pedlar.

the modern techniques of the art. Included
in the innovations which he introduced
and which are now generally followed by
the most advanced producers are: the use
of large close-up figures, distant views,
as reproduced first in *Ramona*, the
"switchback", sustained suspense, the
"fadeout", and restraint in expression,
raising motion picture acting to recognition as a genuine art.' No one seems to
have been concerned that these claims
were false – probably because the industry
was moving so fast, probably also because
it didn't seem to matter ; the fact that
some film-writers till the present have
accepted them simply indicates that they
do not know any pre-Griffith material.
James Card, the curator of the Eastman
House archive – and the man who has
perhaps seen more antique movies than
anyone living – believes that Griffith's
reputation began with the advertisements
he placed in the trade press.

Griffith was born in Kentucky, the sor
of a doctor impoverished by the Civil
War, and he became successively theatre
critic, dramatist and actor. Unemployed
in New York, he approached the film
companies with scenarios – which were
refused by Porter of Edison, who nevertheless offered him the role of the brave
woodsman in *Rescued from the Eagle's Nest*.
Biograph, however, were prepared to use
him in both capacities, paying him $5 a day
to act, and up to $15 for any ideas contri-
buted. From the time he took over as
production head, in the summer of 1908, till
the end of the following year, he was
Biograph's sole director, turning out in that
period 131 films, a one-reeler and a half-
reeler each week, at a salary of $50 per week
plus a weekly commission of not less than
that amount. The cost of each film was
approximately $200, and since the com-
pany was clearing over $5,000 a week in
profit, against the competition of its dozen
rivals, it is clear that the industry was
growing.

Altogether, in his six years with
Biograph, Griffith made just under 450
films, working so well with his photographer, Billy Bitzer, that the latter left

Two of Vitagraph's
popular leading
men, Earle
Williams, and FAR
RIGHT, Maurice
Costello in the 1911
A Tale of Two Cities.
Williams often
sported a monocle,
but that and his
lordly manner were
suitable for the
heroes he played.
Costello was older,
and seems even less
approachable, but
audience fondness
for such favourite
players hastened the
arrival of the
feature–film: for this
version of Dickens,
released in three
parts of one reel
each, was played by
enterprising
exhibitors in one
programme. Also,
the insertion of 'It is
a far, far better
thing…' advanced
the use of dialogue
intertitles, for the
latter to this point
were invariably
descriptive.

EARLE WILLIAMS

with him in 1913 and moved with him from company to company till they quarrelled in 1924; it is recorded that they worked together so closely that it is impossible to distinguish their contributions. Given the available shooting time, it is not surprising that the quality is variable, from a family charade like **They Would Elope** (1909) to the earlier, well-achieved **The Drive for Life** (1909), respectively a comedy about an abortive elopement and a thriller about a man (Arthur Johnson) hurrying to his fiancée to prevent her eating the poisoned chocolates sent by his ex-mistress – a good example of the 'switchback' or cross-cutting which Griffith was now developing for his climactic situations; but he does not seem to have realised the value of the mobile camera (placed here on another motor car), since he seldom used it again. **Gold is Not All** (1910) is a morality tale paralleling the lives of two couples, poor and wealthy, and a shot of them divided by a wall shows a vivid sense of location; **Ramona** (1910) is an ambitious version of Helen Hunt-Jackson's popular tearjerker about a girl (Pickford) who marries an Indian (Henry B. Walthall) : the characters rush on from one side of the screen and off the other, gesticulating wildly, and the photography for which Griffith claimed credit consists only of a few shots of foreground action played against a valley and mountains beyond. **Wilful Peggy** (1910) concerns a hoyden (Pickford) who refuses a lordly suitor and runs away with his nephew who, despite or because she's in male attire, makes advances ; it does demonstrate that Miss Pickford had more vivacity than her rivals, but she was more likely to be found in roles like 'The Little Slavey' in **Simple Charity** (1910), helping a penniless couple and finding a handsome young doctor in the process.

By this time, halfway through his Biograph period, the evidence does suggest that Griffith understood the medium better than the other American directors ; his climactic cross-cutting was so much admired that he began to stage these sequences in two different settings – even when unnecessary to the plot. He had certainly realised that it was cutting which gave his films mobility – there are ninety separate shots in the fourteen-minute length of **The Voice of a Child** (1911), where most films of the time have one-third to one-half that number. The story, a favourite one of Griffith's, concerns a neglected wife (Blanche Sweet) who almost runs off with a bounder, while the unusual **Fate's Interception** (1912) tells of a rejected Mexican girl who tries to gas her American lover. 'Loneliness' is the reason given for his involvement in the first place, and the film is particularly vicious towards Mexicans : but the wooing is sympathetically done, with one long-shot, from above, with the couple framed among leaves, which is remarkable for the time. **The Musketeers of Pig Alley** (1912), like much of Griffith, has a spurious reputation – as the first gangster film. In fact it is just another cops-and-robbers' tale, and a confused one at that, apart from the central situation: the poor girl (Lillian Gish) and her musician lover (Walter Miller) caught in the crossfire. It cannot be compared to a Reliance two-reeler of the following year, *Detective Burton's Triumph*, made in the semi-documentary style which the American film industry eschewed till after the Second World War.

The industry was discovering that the transition from one- to two-reeler could be achieved only with difficulty: in Europe the longer running time was smoothly utilised, but in the U.S. the plot of the second reel tended to be convoluted and repetitive. Technically, this was a time of great change. Angleshots were becoming common, being first used in Denmark to indicate Point-of-View; the Americans would take much longer than the Danes to rid themselves of this *raison d'être*. The language of the cinema was also enriched by the discovery of the time-shift, and **Just a Shabby Doll** (1913) – a rags-to-riches production, typical of the Thanhouser Company, in which the boy finally marries his now-impoverished childhood sweetheart – dispenses with intertitles to denote past time. The future was usually a matter of dreams, as in Majestic's **The Warning** (1914), in which an indolent country girl (Dorothy Gish) thus learns of her future with 'The Drummer from the Big City', but dreams were very big anyway – in Selig's **The Devil, the Servant and the Man** (1910), a marriage grown cold is restored by some dreams and by Christ, all superimposed on the original image. The close-up came into common use, and location shooting was more rigorously exploited, as in Kalem's **A Race with Time** (1913), in which a station-agent's daughter saves a train from sabotage, and Kay-Bee Broncho's **In the Nick of Time** (1914), in which the put-upon heroine flees to a deserted rail-road station and saves it from a posse of train-robbers. The cutting speeds in both films were adjusted to their subjects, and when the latter was reissued ten years later it would not have seemed, technically, too dated : but the films of 1912 could not have been passed off as new even two years later.

In Vitagraph's **The Right Girl ?** (1914), the heroine studies a movie poster, and it lists a dozen items, including Mary Pickford (whose films could be endlessly reissued), 'Song Contest' and 'Amateurs' : the rest of the programme – now running to about two hours – consisted of comedies, melodramas, and novelty tales like

this, about a 'bach' (i.e. a bachelor) who takes his friend's advice and follows the first pretty woman he sees, who turns out to be the other's wife. The stars are Earle Williams and Anita Stewart, frequently teamed – and notably in **His Phantom Sweetheart** (1915), built around a clubman's dream. The director of both is Ralph Ince (1887–1937), brother of Thomas H. Ince ; he was also an actor, and in **His Last Flight** (1913) he saves a shipwrecked honeymoon couple from a brutal crew (for which, at the end, the bride thinks of him in flashback). The three films are so accomplished as to make one want to see more of Ince's early work. He continued into the Talkie era, though abandoning leading roles for character parts – and ended his days directing quota quickies in Britain, one of many early directors who later tried their chance across the Atlantic (others included Vitagraph's Larry Trimble and Kalem's Sidney Olcott). Earle Williams was a stalwart of Vitagraph for most of its existence, tall, dark and handsome and possibly the prototype of all movie heroes. Type-casting began early – before 1911, when the practice of identifying players became accepted – and in both **Love's Awakening** (1910) and **Coronets and Hearts** (1912) he played impoverished milords who marry American heiresses ; the former was one of Vitagraph's series 'Scenes From True Life', which Victor Sjöström acknowledged as an influence on him.

In the same vein are **The Spirit of Christmas** (1913) and **The Man That Might Have Been** (1914), directed by and starring another pillar of Vitagraph, William Humphrey, and both very sure in their mixture of melodrama and high-flown sentiment. The former concerns a poor mother tempted to steal, but forgiven and passed on to an eccentric millionaire who doesn't like the 'usual' Christmas, and the latter a man who spends his life dreaming of his dead wife and child, till re-united with them by his own death. Both were novelty items, but Vitagraph also made melodramas – such as **Conscience** (1912), about a cop's sister who elopes to marry a brute, and years later, after separation, finds herself in a wax-works where for a bet he is spending the night, and **The Fire Escape** (1915), in which a boy and girl romance is over-shadowed by some crooked politicians in the same apartment block . . . But the people who saw these films when they first came out remember Vitagraph best for their comedies with the rotund John Bunny and Mr and Mrs Sidney Drew. Bunny joined Vitagraph from the stage in 1910 and stayed till he died in 1915 – usually playing the exuberant and long-suffering husband of pinch-faced Flora Finch. The Drews also did domestic comedy, of a somewhat more urbane nature – as befits a man who was uncle to the Barrymores – but neither their films nor those of Bunny that I have seen give an indication of why they are so fondly remembered.

Among the important early directors is Sidney Olcott (1873–1949), a Canadian actor who was briefly at Biograph before joining Kalem at its inception in 1906 – a company founded on $400 cash by George Kleine, Samuel Long and Frank Marion. Writers at that time were mainly ideas men, but Olcott, invited to direct, had had experience enough to prepare a scenario, and since he liked to shoot on location this preparation proved both economical and useful for smoother continuity. His **Ben Hur** (1907) was a huge success, opening the way for more American costume films as well as clarifying the matter of screen rights: Kalem were sued by the publishers, the author's estate and the producers of the dramatised version, and though the matter wasn't settled till 1911 (for $25,000) it at once became the policy of the film companies to pay for properties of recognised value. In 1908 Olcott was working in Florida when Kalem, acknowledging his success with location-shooting, decided to send him to Europe, with a troupe including Jack Clark, the leading man, and Gene Gauntier, who also doubled as writer. Olcott made some films in Ireland, including **Rory O'Moore** (1911), a silly tale of a rebel and the redcoats which Kalem considered politically controversial (which it almost certainly was, at that time) – and moved on throughout Europe to the Middle East. I have also seen his **Captured by Bedouins** (1912), mainly notable for some shots of the garden of Shepheard's Hotel and of the Sphinx before its paws were uncovered. In Jerusalem he made *From the Manger to the Cross* (1912), which so infuriated Kalem that he was forced to resign: but instead of the public staying away, as his bosses had thought, it flocked – thus justifying its high cost (the controversy over it in Britain helped to bring about censorship), and establishing Olcott as one of the leading directors. He was active as a director till 1927, when he became production manager of British Lion, but left the industry two years later.

The first important woman director was Lois Weber (1882–1939), who with her husband, Phillips Smalley, acted in Edwin S. Porter's first independent pictures. Porter left Edison when a former carpet-dealer was placed in charge of production there; he joined the non-Patents producers, forming the Rex Picture Company. One of his first productions was *A Heroine of '76* (1911), in which a tavern wench (Weber) receives the assassination wounds intended for George Washington (Smalley). When Porter was lured from his own company by Zukor, Laemmle absorbed Rex, and his Universal distributed their films. Rex eventually disappeared, but Weber and Smalley were involved in some big Universal productions, such as *The Merchant of Venice* (1914) and *The Picture of Dorian Gray* (1914). They wrote, produced, directed and acted, sometimes in tandem; as a director, solo, she had a success with *Where Are My Children?* (1916), which touched upon abortion, and as a result Universal offered her a producer contract. She continued to direct, and made one Talkie, in 1934, at the time when Smalley's career as a character actor was beginning to falter. Among their early films, worth noting are **An Ill Wind** (1912), a familiar anecdote – used, among others, by Mrs Henry Wood in The Channings – about a young man falsely accused of stealing a cheque, and **Suspense** (1913), about a young wife alone in a lonely house, and a tramp trying to break in. Most films of this period – Westerns excepted – could as easily have been done on the stage, but the latter depends on the situation of the house, a telephone, and the husband's rush to the rescue; it also has a number of imaginative touches, including a split screen.

The first major name connected with the Western is Gilbert M. Anderson (1883–1971), born Max Aaronson and known as 'Broncho Billy'. He had been a newsboy; at seventeen, he went on the stage, and just three years later started in films – in *The Great Train Robbery*. In 1907, with George K. Spoor, he founded Essanay, which began the 'Broncho Billy' series with *Broncho Billy and the Baby* (1908), based on what would be an oft-filmed play, 'Three Godfathers'. The film Western, in fact, grew not from Edw. in S. Porter's film, but from the popular melodramas of the West – and the early Broncho Billy films are as much domestic comedy as Western. Despite a Durante-sized nose, Anderson himself is rather fetching – comely, with a thatch of hair : usually a shy man winning the girl from his more dashing rival, or unexpectedly besting the robbers, he was probably the inspiration for Will Rogers's stage personality.

The popularity of the Western was such that it was the sole product of some companies; it was also attractive because location-shooting kept the company far from the battles with Essanay and other members of the Patents Company. Important in this field was the American Manufacturing Company started in 1910 when a Chicago distributor filched most of Essanay's leading staff, including Allan Dwan (b. 1885–1982) who had been an electrician. Successively scenario editor for American and production manager with the California stock company, Dwan became a director in May 1911, and before the year was out had made sixty-eight films – at the rate of two a week, filming side-by-side on Mondays, Tuesdays and Wednesdays, and processing them on Thursdays and Fridays. Ideas were made up on the spot: thus filming by the sea at Santa Barbara meant involving smugglers with cowboys – as in **The Fear** (1912); and a handy flume suggested an odd revenge when a cowpuncher's marriage proposal has been refused – **The Poisoned Flume** (1911). Dwan was one of the talents poached by Laemmle; most of his company went with him, including the leading man, J. Warren Kerrigan, who became one of Universal's biggest stars.

Also purveyors of Westerns were the subsidiaries, under various names, of Kessel and Bauman (q.v.). **An Apache Father's Revenge** (?1911) concerns an heroic Indian so besotted with a handsome Anglo-Saxon that she dons Western clothes, and when her father attacks the fort she lights the signal – for the earliest surviving example of the Cavalry riding to the rescue. The film's attitude towards the Indians is vile, a good enough expression of prevailing opinion in the U.S. at the time. **The Wheels of Destiny** (1911), mainly the tale of a baby adopted by a drunken father, starts with an Indian massacre; and there is only one good Indian among the many treacherous ones in **Blazing the Trail** (1912), a story of attacks and counter-attacks among the covered wagons. The star and director of the latter is Francis Ford (1883–1953), elder brother of John Ford, and his vigorous handling at this time remains a pleasure. However, the best of Kessel and Bauman's directors would seem to be Reginald Barker (1886–1937) – and *The Wheels of Destiny* has been attributed to him on account of its fluidity: a lone cowboy rides across the hill and down to the camera, and the Indians pour into battle from behind the camera. Barker is credited on **Bad Buck of Santa Ynez** (1914), the tale of a man so mean and bad that he is driven out of town, but pauses to befriend a widow and her small daughter, for whom he sacrifices his life when the latter is bitten by a rattlesnake. The story is credited to Bret Harte, and it was remade as *The Toll-Gate* (q.v.), by Lambert Hillyer, who like Barker was a protégé of Thomas H. Ince. The star of both versions is William S. Hart (1870–1946); a former trailhand and stage actor, who had come into films in 1913 as a result of his friendship with Ince. Roles like this earned him the designation, 'The Good-Bad Man', and among the early stars only Asta Nielsen surpassed him in intensity – though in his case his acting is bare to the point of impassivity. *Bad Buck*, like *The Wheels of Destiny*, indicates a director's joy in the medium : it may well be that the exigencies of the Western did most to liberate movies from the techniques they took from the stage.

Another liberating factor was the feature-length movie, and in the United States that was a long time in gestation. It grew from the habit of filming the classics in multi-reel versions, of which the first may well have been a two-and-a-half reel version of *Les Misérables*, issued by Edison in 1909. There is no evidence that any enterprising exhibitor screened them together, nor Vitagraph's four-reel version of the same subject issued over a two-month period at the same time ; but Vitagraph's five-reel *The Life of Moses*, issued over a fourteen-month period, 1909–10, was shown in one New Orleans cinema in April 1910 – to what *The Moving Picture World* called 'record business'. The same company's three-reel *Uncle Tom's Cabin* (1910) was designed to be released in three weekly parts. Almost certainly that had been shown in one programme before two multi-reel Italian films were imported in 1911 – as *The Crusaders* and *Dante's Inferno*; and quite certainly there were a number of American features before July 1912, when the success of the French four-reel *Queen Elizabeth* at the Lyceum, New York, is reckoned to have reconciled exhibitors towards the longer film. In

January 1912 Atlas advertised a four-reel *Ten Nights in a Bar Room*, but the other contributions were all from the 'classics' – a five-reel *Oliver Twist* and a four-reel *Hiawatha*, while two actresses followed Bernhardt's example of immortalising herself, Blanche White in a five-reel *Resurrection*, and Helen Gardner in a six-reel *Cleopatra*, which she also produced. Adolph Zukor's Famous Players (q.v.) lured Edwin S. Porter away from his own company, Rex, to direct a five-reel *Monte Cristo*, to star James O'Neill (the father of the playwright, Eugene) – but by the time it was ready Selig had a three-reel version on the market. Zukor therefore persuaded Porter to make *The Prisoner of Zenda* in five reels, which had its premiere in February 1913. There followed a slew of European imports, including a six-reel *David Copperfield* from Britain, and the eight-reel Italian *Quo Vadis?* – which, like the Bernhardt film, was shown in a Broadway theatre, the Astor: that was in May 1913, and it cost $1.50 a seat instead of the customary fifteen cents. Thus the feature film reached America only as an adjunct of theatre and literature.

The excitement over *Quo Vadis?* reached D. W. Griffith in California, nearing the end of his winter season : Biograph refused to let him come East to see it, just as they had refused to sanction a feature after his two-reel spectaculars of 1912, *Man's Genesis* and *The Massacre* (a recreation of Custer's Last Stand), passed unnoticed. Biograph, however, were discussing a deal with Klaw and Erlanger to film their stage productions in the Famous Players manner, and Griffith, furious and without authorisation, began his own feature, **Judith of Bethulia** (1914). The company was startled by both length and cost – $36,000 – and determined to withdraw him from direction: he was offered the job of supervisor, which he countered by demanding autonomy as a director. They refused and he left. He himself in his memoir claimed of the film that 'the bosses rather liked it', but that seems unlikely, as they delayed release for eight months. 'It remains,' said Iris Barry in her Museum of Modern Art monograph (repeating Lewis Jacobs's gaffe that it was the first American feature), 'both in [Griffith's] own career and in the memories of those who saw it at the

time a real landmark.' Such, of course, has been said about such contemporaries as 'Le Sacre du Printemps', but film was an infant art and this film is a shambles – much rushing about and barnstorming, amidst which may be discerned the Bible story of Judith (Blanche Sweet) and Holofernes (Henry B. Walthall). Miss Barry's assessment of Griffith's innovations is equally absurd, and we are reminded that it was at this point that he began to advertise himself – almost certainly influenced by his association with Miss Pickford : if a mere player could achieve world-wide fame, how much worthier was a director and dramaturge!

From Biograph Griffith went to Mutual, to supervise production and direct five films – and to plan an even longer epic than *Judith*. He wanted a subject from America's past, and a member of the company, Frank Woods, recommended 'The Clansman' by the Reverend Thomas Dixon, a novel of the Reconstruction – and, as dramatised, a popular road-show attraction: Woods had done the continuity for a film version abandoned by the Kinemacolor Company. Harry Aitken was the backer of Mutual, but as the film outgrew his resources he and Griffith formed a new company, Epoch, to market it ; its eventual cost was in the region of $91,000 – which included $30,000 for publicity – and its profits around $5 million. After the West Coast opening under the original title, it opened in New York, at Dixon's suggestion, as **The Birth of a Nation** (1915), at an unprecedented $2 top – and it was immediately clear that the gamble had paid off. This was the first time in

So much legend surrounds America's first 'epic', *The Birth of a Nation* – as, for instance, that its profits were incalculable, perhaps as high as $50,000,000; but even if recent research has found them to be about one-tenth of that, that is still good money for the period. Both its plot and ethics make it difficult to sit through, but the panoramic scenes of battle remain impressive.

The Rise of the American Industry

As late as 1973 the forty most prominent American critics voted *Intolerance* the second greatest American film of all time – *Citizen Kane* was first – and *The Birth of a Nation* the third. Can any of them actually have seen it? Certainly *Intolerance* was big. As with a great many other matters, Griffith falsely claimed credit for Walter L. Hall's magnificent sets. Some survived on various backlots into the Twenties, but most were dismantled at the request of the Los Angeles Fire Department.

American cinema that a movie-maker who thought big and acted big found himself appropriately recompensed – and indeed the film was for years considered a 'great' one.

Historically important, it has today virtually no entertainment value. Its admirers point to the cross-cutting at the climax, by then a cliché in Griffith's work; they praise the famous panning shot which concludes with Sherman's army in the valley, but most sequences are as static as the view of Lumières' workers leaving their factory. Indeed, much of the film is a throwback to the days of animated tableaux – admittedly often elaborate – introduced by explanatory intertitles. The story, like most Civil War tales, is about divided families: a Northern boy (Robert Harron) falls in love with a Southern girl (Miriam Cooper), and his sister (Lillian Gish) falls in love with her brother, 'The Little Colonel' (Henry B. Walthall). Their war is a dull affair: the film is not offensive till the aftermath, with uppity Negroes shoving people off the sidewalk and putting their bare feet on the desks in the legislative chamber. Before, a white had led them raping; now they do it on their own initiative, and it's the attempted rape of his sister which causes 'The Little Colonel' to devise the Ku Klux Klan. 'In agony of soul over the degradation of his people, [he] thought of a secret army – the organisation that saved the South from agony. But not without more blood than was spilt at Gettysburg.' At the end this army rescues both the family, besieged with some Union soldiers by berserk blacks, and Miss Gish – from the lecherous clutches of the mulatto governor.

So the birth-pangs of this particular nation are reduced to 'Will Lillian be saved?' The film is, at best, an hysterical poke at a confused period, and, when it might have been balanced, as in the matter of the rapist's guilt, we're offered the shortest trial in the history of movies. Griffith's later apologists have explained away his prejudices by claiming them typical of a Southerner of the time; but if the film is not libellous to blacks (if they were uncivilised that was because education was denied them) it is manic and rabble-rousing. Movie-makers constantly made clear their contempt for

46

people of different skins, certainly a retrogression from enlightened nineteenth-century opinion; but as a study in racial intolerance, this film far outclasses those which used the dusty-shoed and the slant-eyed as their villains. Originally it was worse. There was no shooting script, so no record remains, but we do know that in response to criticism Griffith snipped and cut, and prepared new intertitles. There were riots in some towns; in New York, the Mayor and the Licence Commissioner insisted on the removal of the more inflammatory scenes. Griffith responded to the accusations of bigotry in a pamphlet, 'The Rise of Free Speech in America': 'Intolerance martyred Joan of Arc' he claimed, and what he considered his all-embracing theory of history transformed his next film. Based on a recent case, the killing of nineteen industrial workers by their employers' self-appointed militia, he added to it three stories from history to emphasise his sympathy for the oppressed: **Intolerance** (1916), 'A Drama of Comparisons' – with its subtitle changed to 'A Sun-Play of the Ages' for its New York opening, and 'Love's Struggle Through the Ages' for its 1933 revival. It was also described as 'A Drama in Two Acts and a Prologue' to explain the interval and confer respectability.

At just under three hours (and fourteen reels) it is a sight longer than *The Birth of a Nation*, having to accommodate its four stories: the modern one, originally called *The Mother and the Law*; the fall of Babylon; the famous events in Judea in AD 33; and the Massacre of the Eve of St Bartholomew in 1572. They would begin, declared Griffith, 'like four currents looked at from a hilltop. At first the four currents will flow apart, slowly and quietly. But as they flow, they grow nearer and nearer together, and faster and faster, until in the end, in the last act, they mingle in one mighty river of expressed emotion.' That is true up to a point, for one story – Judea – is merely a trickle, and another – the French one – no more than a stream; for long periods both are ignored, but the very lack of symmetry can only add surprise to a film which needs every bit of help it can get. This simultaneous unfolding of parallel stories however remains attractive, and

technically the film is a clear advance on its predecessor. It was much studied by the Russian masters, fascinated by the variety of shots – infinitely greater than in any film yet made; close-ups, medium-shots and long-shots intermingle, exactly judged and whipped away before interest is exhausted. There are some trolley-shots and an occasional shift of the camera – but not enough to suggest that Griffith really understood camera movement. The film does race along, appropriately, with the chariots which will destroy Babylon: the real triumph is in the editing.

The spectacle, also, was something to stun contemporaries. Griffith went further than any of the Europeans in construction: the walls of Babylon were 300 feet high, and the cost of Belshazzar's feast alone more than twice the total cost of *The Birth of a Nation*. Since the success of that was regarded as a fluke, the final cost of this – including, reputedly, 250 chariots on call, and 15,000 extras – was a wanton $1,900,000. (Within six years, Douglas Fairbanks would exceed that sum, but by that time movie investment was no longer considered a risk.) In a way, the money was misspent, since spectacle swamps everything: in the Babylon story Mountain Girl (Constance Talmadge) has a crush on the King, but is unable in time to warn him of the downfall of the city; but plot interest loses out entirely to effects. The two assaults are strikingly done, as based on the works of John Martin (the more colourful nineteenth-century illustrators and writers influenced all of Griffith's work); and the man whose head is struck off shocked audiences at the time. The French story is equally gory, and one might wonder – at least for the first two hours – what intolerance has to do with any of this: it is, at best, a simplification to suggest that that is what caused the Crucifixion. The modern story is explicit on the evils done by do-gooders, but it is wildly dishonest to suggest that they create the particular conditions to be overcome here – 'The Boy' wrongly convicted of murder, 'The Dear Little One' deprived of her child. In fact, the characters in all four episodes are either pure-white or jet-black, so that the audience's attitude towards intolerance is never tested – until the epilogue, which more modestly implies that intolerance caused the War in Europe (before the whole thing ends with 'us' on earth being united with 'them' in the sky). Griffith himself spoke of 'a protest against despotism and injustice in every form', but his ambitions outran his conceptions by light-years; and though few regarded this film as being of deep philosophy, he has been taken at his word by some – though even admirers concede 'absurdity' and 'sentimentality' in the telling.

The disparate stories are held together by the famous device of Lillian Gish rocking a cradle and the words 'Out of the cradle endlessly rocking' – its purpose obscure without the source, Walt Whitman's 'Endlessly rocks the cradle, Uniter of Here and Hereafter.' To the suffering audience, however, the word 'endlessly' is all too appropriate. Audiences of the time were thin, no matter how often critics confirmed its creator's genius, and it was soon clear that the film would not begin to recoup its costs. Its failure limited Griffith's independence, but did not lessen his standing, for *The Birth of a Nation* had proved something for which the powers of the industry had dared not hope – that the potential audience for films consisted not only of the more humble members of the community but of every single person in it. Less to the understanding and liking of the moguls, the two films proved that some people considered the new medium to be an art form.

With the rewards now proved so great, the in-fighting and competition were conducted with even less scruple. Laemmle and Fox were typical of the new entrepreneurs, Jewish immigrants, of little or no education, and in some cases unable to speak the language properly. This industry was an extension of familiar territory; like them, it was brash and new and not quite respectable. They wanted to make a fast buck, and as the bucks came faster than anticipated, they rose on the crest of a wave. Those who survived became the rulers of Hollywood – characterised later by S. J. Perelman as 'a dreary industrial town controlled by hoodlums of enormous wealth, the ethical sense of a pack of jackals, and taste so degraded that it befouled everything it

touched'. Their taste and cultural values touched most people in the world for at least two generations, albeit that as filtered through writers, directors and players it was in happy concurrence with what the world wanted anyway.

The war boom and the feature film helped to change the structure of the industry. The once-mighty Biograph discontinued production not long after Griffith left, and Edison called it quits in 1918, so that the only survivor of the original Patents Company was Vitagraph – and that tottered, managing to cling on by combining in 1915 with Lubin, Selig and Essanay to form a distribution company to handle their product jointly – V.S.L.E Kalem gave up the ghost around the same time, and the failure of its Max Linder films in 1917 signalled the end of Essanay. Then V.S.L.E. crumbled: Vitagraph absorbed Selig and then Lubin, to be itself swallowed by Warner Bros. in 1925 – so that the sole survivor of the companies which joined the trust in 1909 (since Méliès had folded almost immediately) was Pathé.

If the two most aggressive opponents of the trust were Laemmle and Fox, not far behind were H. E. Aitken and the team of Adam Kessel and Charles Bauman – not that any of them were allies, or if so, not for long. It was Aitken who had poached Mary Pickford from Laemmle's I.M.P. for his newly-formed Majestic, and as that increased the enmity between him and Laemmle he allied himself with John R. Freuler, a former colleague from his exchange days, to form Mutual. In retaliation, Laemmle founded Universal, comprising a number of independents, including his own I.M.P., Rex, Pat Powers and his Powers Picture Plays, and Kessel and Bauman's exchange, the New York Motion Picture Company. Kessel and Bauman had been exhibitors who, balked of getting films for their exchanges had decided to make their own: after two (in which they both appeared), they founded Bison Life Pictures, which became successful when Thomas Ince applied to them for a job.

Thomas H. Ince (1882–1924) came from theatrical stock, and began in films in 1910 acting with I.M.P. and then Biograph; he returned to I.M.P. to direct (and was briefly in Cuba filming, out of reach of the trust's agents) before going to Kessel and Bauman. They wanted him to take over the Bison Life company in California, and there he hired the Miller Brothers' 101 Ranch Wild West Show, renaming the company 101 Bison. The popularity of his Westerns enabled his bosses to start Reliance to make dramatic subjects – for which they stole Biograph's popular star, Arthur Johnson. Meanwhile, they found that they could not get on with Laemmle, and bought themselves out – leaving Universal with the name '101 Bison' to add to the other names under that umbrella. Their Western unit was renamed Broncho (later Kay-Bee Broncho), and both the Broncho and Reliance pictures were put in the hands of Aitken's Mutual, together with those of their new company, Keystone – backed for Mack Sennett, whom they had encouraged to leave Biograph. Ince moved over from Broncho to Reliance, and stayed with that company when its picture-making activities were amalgamated with those of Majestic – and it was at this point that Griffith also worked for Majestic-Reliance.

Then there was a split in Mutual – between Aitken and Freuler. Freuler was also a partner of Samuel S. Hutchinson in the American Film Company. These two made, in Europe, *The Quest* (1915), and shipped it, as was normal with American's films, to Mutual to distribute – but Mutual, in response to the presence of Griffith and Ince and the industry vogue for theatre-players, had started a policy of 'Master Pictures', and Aitken did not consider *The Quest* accorded with that policy. He shelved it, and when finally released, American's advertising stressed Hutchinson. 'The Master Producer'. More seriously, Freuler managed to oust Aitken as president of Mutual. Aitken thereupon withdrew the Majestic-Reliance product from Mutual, and persuaded his co-owners of that company, Kessel and Bauman, to withdraw Keystone; Aitken then, with the co-operation of Kessel and Bauman, formed Triangle – so named after its three directors, Griffith, Ince and Sennett, all of whom were much in the public eye. Triangle's chief aim was to solve the industry's most pressing prob-lem, the growing power of the new company formed by the amalgamation of Adolph Zukor's Famous Players with Jesse Lasky. If the chief asset of this rival was Mary Pickford, Triangle had something comparable in William S. Hart, but in emulating Zukor by contracting stage stars, Triangle had only one success – Douglas Fairbanks – which was one reason for its quick demise, especially when, at the end of his contract, Fairbanks accepted a better offer from Zukor, which included his own production company. It was because Mutual had Chaplin that that company survived the defection of Aitken's people (and Kessel and Bauman's), but it did not last long after his departure. Soon after that Triangle began to collapse, and Famous Players–Lasky, which had already added Ince to Fairbanks, hastened to grab Griffith, Sennett, Hart and Wallace Reid.

The fact that some sources claim that Triangle was founded by its three directors seems due to the exaggeration which surrounds most writing about Griffith, but also to the fact that both he and Ince were powerful enough to have real independence. From the moment when Ince had gone West to join Bison Life his energy and imagination had astounded the industry; and his films were successful enough for his employers to purchase 18,000 acres of land in Southern California for a studio christened Inceville. Unlike Griffith, he enjoyed supervising. Of the hundreds of films turned out under his aegis, it is difficult now to sort out his contribution; even when credits survive it is unwise to believe that Ince's actual work on any particular film was very great. He liked taking credit, and we may be sure that when he is said to have collaborated on direction or authorship that his contribution was minimal. I have seen two of his Triangle films, said to have been directed by him, **Civilization** (1916), which certainly was – and which deserves a paragraph of its own – and *D'Artagnan* (1916), a version of Dumas of absolutely no interest.

Civilization was meant to rival *Intolerance*, and, like that, was built on the base of an existing and completed film: it took the War in Europe not as its epilogue, but as its whole subject. There had been a number of pro-war and anti-isolationist films, of which the most notable was J. Stuart Blackton's *The Battle Cry of Peace*, based on Hudson Maxim's 'Defenseless America'. *Civilization* was Ince's rebuttal, and its success may partly have been due to timing: its $100,000 cost (*D' Artagnan* cost $15,000) made a profit seven times over. Its popularity is surprising, for there is no identifiable hero, and all is flat-out propaganda. For the box-office, there is a power-mad demagogue – the king who makes war; there is a secret league of women who desire world peace; and there is Christ coming to earth (in the body of the husband of one of them) to make the king see the error of his ways.

Directors who served under Ince at this time include Henry King, Frank Borzage and Fred Niblo; the best Ince films of this period are now attributed to Reginald Barker. We have noted his flair in his two-reel Westerns, and that is a quality to be found in **The Typhoon** (1914), a study of the Japanese community in Paris and how it protects the young doctor (Sessue Hayakawa) who has strangled a taunting showgirl. It is based on a Hungarian play by Melchior Lengyel which had been a success in New York and London – but it is far more cinematic than any of Zukor's 'Famous Plays', and it was to that company that Kessel and Bauman (presumably in a moment of truce) sold it. Even better is Barker's **The Italian** (1915), a plea for compassion in semi-documentary style on behalf of New York's immigrant community. The hero (George Beban) is a boot-black and he does suffer unusual hardship; but the incident of the politician who buys his vote, via the underworld, remains a chilling comment on public life. The writer was C. Gardner Sullivan, and the same directness of plot may be found in both **Hell's Hinges** (1916) and **The Return of Draw Egan** (1916), both of which, as it happens, have the same story. The second is directed by William S. Hart, who stars in both, and the first by Barker, with his strong visuals – the marvellous use of dust and fire in this small Western town puts it way ahead of most movies of its era. Both films were made under Ince's supervision, and Hart's film, if polished, is not as technically expert as Barker's. In both Hart is the

bad man who for love of a lady keeps the law between the rowdies and the churchgoing folk. It is equally pleasant to see him in city duds in Barker's **Between Men** (1915), a knight errant bugging the villain's office, thought in this context to be an admirable thing. House Peters is the bully-boy businessman villain, out to ruin a father and marry the daughter.

Ince left Triangle after a year to found his own company, with facilities provided by Zukor; after three years there he formed Associated Producers with some other directors, who included Allan Dwan, Mack Sennett, Marshall Neilan, King Vidor and Maurice Tourneur, but within months they had moved into the First National fold. Ince's death, incidentally, was for years one of Holly-

William S. Hart was the first movie actor with a perfected image. Audiences knew what to expect of his best–known predecessor, Broncho Billy, but Hart, having established himself as the Good–Bad Man, had to work harder at being reformed, especially when there were temptresses around like Louise Glaum. The film concerned is *The Return of Draw Egan*, and as in the very similar *Hell's Hinges* her natural habitat is the saloon.

wood's biggest scandals: he was taken ill aboard the yacht of William Randolph Hearst, the newspaper magnate, and died two days later. Because he didn't want rivals printing stories about wild drinking parties, Hearst tried to hush up the matter – which was why speculation started as to the true cause of death. Ince's legacy to Hollywood was his policy: a complete and detailed script, constructed individually but under his supervision, directed as written, and edited by himself. The studios adopted it because the re-sponsibility for expenditure did not devolve upon the director – an animal which, given its head (as Griffith with *Intolerance*) was inclined to lose it.

Triangle was founded because its owners sought position and respectability, having noticed the extent to which Famous Players-Lasky commanded respect by signing stage-players and

filming Broadway plays – and undoubt-edly, the fact that they commanded higher admission fees as well. Among the plays filmed by Triangle was **Pillars of Society** (1916), directed by Raoul Walsh, which, like Majestic-Mutual's earlier **Ghosts** (1915), directed by George Nicholls, was supervised by Griffith. Both featured Henry B. Walthall, as Karsten and Captain Alving respectively – and the presence of the Captain in *Ghosts* indicates that what interested Triangle were the melodramatic events to which Ibsen merely referred. His actual plays are confined to the final reels, but if *Ghosts* is reduced to a simple tale of retribution, complete with orgy, *Pillars* is considerably more fleshy and con-vincing than most films of the period. **Old Heidelberg** (1915) was one of several stage properties offered by a subsidiary, Fine Arts, starring Wallace Reid as the student prince and Dorothy Gish as the tavern maid: the direction is credited to John Emerson, and the film is notable for the violent anti-militarist stance injected into the material – and also as an example of Triangle's re-working of plays. Let Famous Players, they decided, bask in reflected glory: they would emphasise the fact that cinema was an independent art. The elevation of Sennett to stand with Ince and Griffith might be considered far-sighted were it not for the fact that he was acknowledged a master – though he, 'the king of the comic cut-ups', regarded his own work as trivial.

Mack Sennett (1880–1960) was born in Canada, and entered films as an actor at Biograph. He became a writer, and subsequently director, specialising in slapstick – much of it influenced by Linder and the French chase comedies. He added elements of the circus and vaudeville, using every trick device of which the camera was capable; and though today some of the chases he engineered may lack variety, it is a stony spectator who remains unamused by the car which doesn't quite go over the cliff or the bus that makes it over the level-crossing a split-second before the train. These vehicles would almost certainly contain the Keystone Cops, that band of unfailingly energetic policemen which joined his repertory when Kessel and

Bauman gave him his own company in 1912. Joining him from Biograph, from vaudeville or just by wandering in the door, were the Sennett troupe: Mabel Normand, prettiest of comediennes; Roscoe or 'Fatty' Arbuckle, melon-headed comic of immodest girth; Chester Conklin, with the forlorn moustache; Ben Turpin, of the swivelling and meeting eyes; Ford Sterling, the heavy with fuzz on his chin; and Mack Swain, most lugubriously stout of evil-doers – nor must we forget Sennett's Bathing Beauties, frowned on by some, and the nearest equivalent for the troops of World War One to the leggy pin-ups of the Second.

Sennett's films were often improvised, under various directors, utilising every prop within sight : sticks to hit with, doors to be chased through, stairs to be fallen down, water to be fallen into, walls to collapse, custard pies to be thrown, cash registers to be stolen from, sausages for dogs to steal, dogs to tear holes in pants, pants to be lost, pretty girls to be kissed, fat ladies to be sat on, soup to be spilled, dishes to be broken, and, above all, cars to chase and be chased: small cars to disgorge a score of cops; cars to proceed after being sliced in half, to pass unharmed through brick walls, to proceed without wheels, engines or sometimes drivers, always emerging triumphant and unscathed. In Sennett's world everything went to extremes – absurd, illogical and surrealistic; his films survive as entertainment, even in the form we – unfortunately – know them best, chopped-up for compilations with relentlessly jokey commentaries. Some of them, it is true, mistake energy for invention, and flounder, but parts of most of them survive the years with ease.

It was Sennett who brought Chaplin into pictures, and it was while with him at Triangle that Douglas Fairbanks emerged as the most popular male screen star after Chaplin. Both actors moved on, and in 1917 Sennett signed a contract to make two-reelers for Paramount: in 1921 he was one of the Associated Producers who moved to First National, during which time he made a number of features, with his stock company, for release by other distributors. He did not adapt to the less robust shenanigans demanded by audi-

ences towards the end of the decade, but went on to the Sound period, when he employed both Bing Crosby and W. C. Fields. The two-reel comedy remained a staple of film programmes till the Forties, but for at least a decade had lost its popularity to Mickey Mouse and his brethren.

Sennett made the first feature-length comedy, **Tillie's Punctured Romance** (1914), which sought respectability by being based on a stage play with its original star, Marie Dressler. As a coy spinster she has to be seen to be believed: her expressions provide amusement, but the slapstick is of the most rudimentary kind – much kicking, falling over, cavorting, bumping into. Chaplin, as her money-grabbing suitor, is almost totally unfunny. Theodore Huff, in his monograph on Chaplin, calls it: 'Not merely crude slapstick, however; it is brilliant satire', one of the manifold over-assessments from which Chaplin's reputation is now suffering. Sennett never went in for satire, though he liked spoofs – such as **Down on the Farm** (1920), which has a wicked landlord threatening to foreclose, and Louise Fazenda as another hopeful and heavy heroine. The enormous success of *Tillie* – confounding its backers and the reviewers, who were unsure whether the public would accept a six-reel comedy – did not encourage Sennett to move over for good to the longer film. *Down on the Farm* is a good indication of the care he took with the few he made: it has a complicated plot, a sub-plot, a chase, and a number of fights and drubbings.

Neither Sennett nor Chaplin should be judged on the shorts Chaplin made for Keystone. Charles Chaplin (1889–1977), a London-born music hall comic, became one of the best known men in the world while with that company. He moved on to Essanay, where he made fourteen films in thirteen months. Reviewing one of them, *His New Job* (1915), *The Bioscope* wrote: 'There is probably no film comedian in the world more popular with the average picture theatre audience than that famous funmaker, Charles Chaplin. . . The art of Charles Chaplin defies analysis, and disarms the critic. Just *why* he is so funny, it is impossible to say, and very probably he could not tell you himself. He possesses a naturally comic personality and his humour is accentuated by the originality of the innumerable bits of "business" with which his work is so profoundly interspersed. Scarcely a moment passes while he is on the screen, but he is up to some wild piece of mischief or committing some ludicrous folly. And perhaps the funniest thing of all is his own complete imperturbability'.

Chaplin's clowning was already spoken of as 'art': one of the problems confronting the cinema historian is the praise showered on Chaplin – certainly not justified by the silly, improvised knockabout of the Keystones and Essanays: but he *is* imperturbable. Audiences liked his pluck, his self-reliance, his cocking-a-snook at authority. He begins to be funny towards the end of the Essanay period, in **A Night in the Show** (1915), a version of one of his music hall sketches, as a drunk swell, using an expression of immense hauteur in the hope of disguising his condition. In **Police** (1916), his penchant for pathos is beginning to show, and as he adds motivation to his gags we can see him maturing. He did grow to meet the praise: almost every film he made at Mutual was an improvement on the one before. There is much less thwacking and bum-kicking, and he is able to get beautiful meaning into his expressions – the mingled admiration and horror with which he regards Eric Campbell eating spaghetti in **The Count** (1916), or the disappointment at finding the girl prefers his rival in **The Vagabond** (1916). He is learning to use props at length, and build routines round them, as in **The Pawnshop** (1916), and in which he first perfected the precision and balletic grace of his movements.

Easy Street (1917) is his first masterpiece. The earlier Mutuals had been churned out at the rate of one every three or four weeks: but this was six weeks in gestation, and there would be three to four months between the later ones. It is episodic, shifting from incident to incident in no particular order, but it hews mainly to the relationship between Chaplin and Eric Campbell. Up to this time Campbell had certainly menaced Chaplin in the Mutuals, as nemesis and rival: but the pairing of the diminutive Chaplin and the towering Campbell had never been as effective as here – Campbell had never been so fearsome a villain, so tough that a dozen police truncheons on his head go unnoticed. He is, of course, the king of Easy Street; Chaplin is a policeman. In **The Immigrant** (1917) Campbell is a waiter whose carelessness is matched only by his fierceness; Chaplin is in the title-role, delicately judging the pathos. This is a rich comedy, but **The Adventurer** (1917) – Charlie in high society – is merely a return to slapstick, with such devices as ice-creams falling into ladies' cleavages. Shortly after this Chaplin moved to First National – without Campbell, who had been killed in a car crash.

Chaplin's phenomenal popularity gave pause to those who would dismiss the movies as a visual equivalent of the penny-dreadful, as well as having a galvanising effect upon the industry. His female equivalent was Mary Pickford, and the two of them engaged in a purely private rivalry as to which could earn the most – which went at high as $10,000 a week plus bonuses (at a time when the average annual wage in the U.S. was about a thousand dollars). Undoubtedly, however, Miss Pickford was the prime factor in building the fortunes of the biggest company of the period – though the 'Divine Sarah' and the first Queen Elizabeth also had a hand. The U.S. distribution rights of the Bernhardt-Elizabeth film were owned by Adolph Zukor (1873–1976), a Hungarian who had arrived in the States just before the turn of the century, and who had moved from the fur business into nickelodeons. He merged his cinema interests with Marcus Loew, a fellow-furrier – and later, via Loews Inc., owner of M-G-M – but parted from him to handle the Bernhardt film, in which he had a financial interest. Its success led to the formation of his own production company, to feature 'Famous Players in Famous Plays' – and though he operated outside the trust, he was able to function in New York: because he also had the support of the veteran showman Daniel Frohman, who after three years of Broadway failures was looking for a way of re-establishing his once mighty prestige. He had offered to show Bernhardt's Elizabeth film in one of his theatres, an action which alone gave respectability to the film industry: he conferred respectability on Zukor by fighting the Patents Company, pointing out to its members they would do a disservice to culture by preventing showings of the film – thus helping the importation of other European films and hastening the end of the Patents monopoly. Frohman's partnership with Zukor also ensured the latter in getting the co-operation of stage players of the calibre of Minnie Maddern Fiske, Bertha Kalich, Cecilia Loftus, John Barrymore, Gaby Deslys and Pauline Frederick. The public, however, found their vehicles stuffy, and Zukor realised that his profits were from the less prestigious efforts being made in Hollywood by Mary Pickford.

It is difficult now to see why she was so much more popular than her rivals (and imitators), but undoubtedly her traditional image – gingham and golden curls – was reassuring at a time when women were asserting themselves equal to men. It is a paradox that she was not only the most famous actress who had ever lived, but also the most successful career woman: her astronomical salary demands were inevitably met by the grumbling Zukor. A further curiosity is that the public indicated a preference for those films in which she played a child. **The Poor Little Rich Girl** (1917), directed by Maurice Tourneur, finds her lonely in an ivory tower till father decides to devote himself to her and her mother after an illness – done as an extended pre-Freudian dream sequence, with Death in a long black veil carrying lilies, and Life prancing about an Arcadian meadow in white lace. In **Rebecca of Sunnybrook Farm** (1917) she is an orphan who puts a good face on adversity and wins over her mean old aunts, despite having, literally, turned their barn into a circus. She also wins the rose-gathering bachelor with the bow-tie – despite her first greeting, 'Are you the lady of the house?' – growing up miraculously in the last few minutes to achieve this happy ending. Marshall Neilan directed both this and the rather more cunning **Stella Maris** (1918), which offers two Pickfords, one to admire and one with whom to identify – thus audiences got a wilting heroine and a mischievous one, a sad one and a happy one, with endings to match. Stella is a radiant,

wealthy cripple, and Unity Blake a cockney orphan and slavey, plain if not actually deformed, and a born sufferer: both are in love with the same man (Conway Tearle) and Unity sacrifices herself to save him from his drunken and drug-addicted wife – which makes it rather unfeeling for him and Stella to be so happy at the fade-out.

It was a lady at the other end of the scale who founded the fortunes of William Fox's studio: Theda Bara (1890–1955), an obscure stage actress whose name became synonymous with all that was daring and luxuriously sinful. Copying the Italian 'divismo' films, he put her into a series of melodramas in which she flaunted herself till death, conscience or reformation caught her in the final reel. The only film to survive is the first and most famous, **A Fool There Was** (1914), which included nothing that you'd see on Main Street in a month of Sundays. It includes nothing that had much to do with life, either, but audiences were thrilled to the nth degree by this tale of a respectably married man who falls helpless prey to a designing woman. For once, his downfall does not include drugs, but as ever adultery is equated with drunkenness, and neither is found to be remotely enjoyable. She exults in his disgrace, and Fox revelled in his profits, reckoned to be a million dollars. As directed by Frank Powell, this was muck-raking, revelling in the thing it pretends to condemn, but its vague source – a poem by Kipling – is quoted extensively in the intertitles to give the thing respectability. Miss Bara, described as 'a notorious woman of the vampire species', is the only thing that links this to the twentieth century – she is more ruthless than her predecessors, and does not have to atone for her sins. She is pretty, but her acting is as incredible as her behaviour, moving from petulance to gloating triumph in a glance. From then on, American films did not have to relegate sexual misdeeds to historical subjects only.

If Zukor and Fox rode to success on the coat-tails of Pickford and Bara, Laemmle had been unlucky with Florence Lawrence, whose popularity soon faded; however, it might be said that it was another aspect of fornication which formed the basis of his success – the white

The Rise of the American Industry

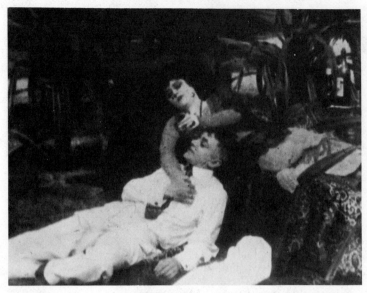

Edward Jose succumbs to Theda Bara's charms in *A Fool There Was*. He is a social reformer and diplomat, no match for this American cousin of *les Grandes Horizontales*, who even lures him in front of his child. They meet on an ocean crossing – after she has had a deckchair put over the spot where her last lover shot himself – and he will soon echo an earlier lover (now a bum), 'See what you have made of me and still you prosper, you hellcat!'

slave trade, as practised in New York. And if *A Fool There Was* owed everything to the Italian Cinema, **Traffic in Souls** (1913) was clearly inspired by the Danish films. Its instigator and director was George Loane Tucker, who shared its cost – $5,700 – with several other Laemmle people. Indeed, it was made against Laemmle's wishes, but since it was made on his time it became his property, and a pawn in his many fights with his co-directors – since it was of feature-length. Most features to that time had been the 'prestige' pieces, playing at opera-houses and legitimate theatres, but as none of these would touch this subject, the Shubert theatre chain arranged for it to be shown in a leading vaudeville house – having liked it enough to pay $33,000 for a one-third interest, thereby making a profit even before its public screening, when, advertised as 'a $200,000 spectacle', it played to 30,000 in its first week. On its profits, the following year, Laemmle built Universal City, where, mainly eschewing features for the time being, his subsidiaries turned out one- and two-reelers to be rented together to exhibitors as complete programmes.

Thus, by 1914, amidst the internecine strife, there were already in business three of the eight film companies which would dominate Hollywood in its heyday – the third being Paramount, which grew from the combination of Famous Players and

Lasky. Jesse Lasky (1880–1958) was a third-generation American and former vaudevillian, who in 1913 had launched Jesse Lasky Feature Plays, in association with his brother-in-law Sam Goldwyn (q.v.), Arthur S. Friend and Cecil B. deMille, an actor and playwright. Lasky had in fact wanted the co-operation of a young Broadway dramatist, William deMille, but had to settle for his less successful younger brother. Their aim was to photograph plays, and Cecil deMille arranged with David Belasco for the rights for his productions; he also persuaded Belasco's chief designer, Wilfred Buckland, to work with him, thus introducing art direction to the American film. Buckland's careful work, and the directorial experience of Oscar Apfel, helping deMille in his debut at that task, got the company off to a flying start on their first film, **The Squaw Man** (1914), based on a popular play, about a wrongly-disgraced English nobleman who flees to the West and falls in love with an Indian princess. 'The touches of great beauty,' said *The Moving Picture World*, 'contain a secret of success known only to screen presentation – they cause us to surrender ourselves more completely to the story . . . and to love this new art form for its own sake.

For his second film, *Brewster's Millions*, Lasky hired a legitimate theatre, and Zukor, impressed with this attempt to emulate his methods, invited Lasky into partnership. They soon joined forces with H. V. Hodkinson, who from one cinema in Utah had developed his own circuit and had subsequently become manager for the Western operations of the Patents Company. Foreseeing the demise of the Trust, he was looking for product for his own distribution company, which he called Paramount. Two years later, in 1916, the three companies merged, though the production company remained 'Famous Players-Lasky' till virtually the end of the Silent period. Hodkinson was forced out in 1917, whereupon he founded another distribution company, under his own name, which he ran till he started P.D.C. in 1924. From the merger of the three companies, Paramount dominated the industry, and just as surely Mary Pickford dominated Paramount. Her popularity enabled Zukor to institute block-booking, an iniquitous system by which exhibitors bought blind a block of films in order to get one or two they knew would do sensational business – a practice denounced and officially outlawed but still occasionally used today. Miss Pickford put a stop to it, at the time, as far as her own films were concerned, in order to get more money from 'special' bookings; and it was when she left him, in 1919, that Zukor concentrated his energies – and helped by a ten million dollar bank loan – on the acquisition and construction of theatres. He had already boasted of building the first national circuit, his growing power so alarming competitors that they formed themselves into a cooperative group which in retaliation they christened First National: and in view of his renewed aggression in the field of exhibition First National started a studio to challenge him in the field of production (q.v.).

The in-fighting of the industry at this time is exemplified by the story of Lewis J. Selznick (1870–1933), a Russian-born Jew who quit the jewelry trade for the hazards of the film business. He hitched his wagon to a star, namely Clara Kimball Young, persuading her to move from Vitagraph to World to his own organisation, set up within Universal by virtue of voting a friend's stock. Her popularity and his methods attracted other stars, enabling Selznick to use the slogan 'Features With Well-Known Players in Well-Known Plays'. As with Lasky, Zukor decided that this imitator was safer as partner, and he invited Selznick to join him as partner in a company called Select Pictures, with complete freedom but under the aegis of Famous Players-Lasky. One condition was that Selznick films could no longer be prefixed 'Lewis J. Selznick presents' but soon 'Selznick presents' preceded the titles of films ostensibly produced by another company headed by Selznick's son Myron, seventeen years old at the time. After a court battle, Lewis J. Selznick was free, and Zukor revenged himself by stealing Clara Kimball Young. The industry declined to forgive Selznick, especially when he copied another slogan, 'Mutual Movies Make Time Fly', changing it to 'Selznick Pictures Make Happy Hours'; and he was not forgiven for signing Olive Thomas against all competition when her Triangle contract finished. Miss Thomas, a former

Ziegfeld beauty, was expected to be the biggest star in pictures, and Selznick's career faced its biggest reversal when she, at the age of twenty, was found dead of drug-addiction in a Paris hotel-room. Fox and Laemmle joined Zukor and Lasky in taking Selznick's other stars, and Selznick's son David (q.v.) always believed that their vindictiveness drove him from films.

After Miss Pickford, Paramount's biggest asset was Cecil B. deMille (1881–1959), whose technical skill was equalled only by his knowledge of what the public wanted. **The Cheat** (1915) was so popular that the scenarist, Hector Turnbull, turned it into a play – the first scenario adapted for the stage. A flighty Long Island wife (Fannie Ward) misappropriates club funds to pay her debts, and turns for assistance to the Burmese playboy (Sessue Hayakawa) with whom she has been dallying, and he, later, cheated of his prize, brands her with the stamp he uses for his goods and chattels. He is clearly the villain, but deMille realised that the public would not have sympathy for the callow couple at the centre, and offered instead high society in sumptuous settings. The heroine (Cleo Ridgely) of **The Golden Chance** (1915) aspires to such settings, and is sheltered from her drunken husband by a society couple. While deMille pondered as to which sort of heroine fitted best into such sumptuousness, he was asked to guide the screen career of the prima diva Geraldine Farrar – signed at $20,000 for eight weeks' work, and the culmination of the policy of getting renowned stage performers into the studio. After a *Carmen* (1915), with Wallace Reid and Pedro de Cordoba, she did the similar **Maria Rosa** (1916) with the same players, and also based on a popular play, a tale of fatal loves and vendettas. Her true love leaves jail to find her just married to a murderer, but unsullied, and indeed earlier she had avoided being raped by that gentleman – which makes this film an early example of deMille's (and Hollywood's) devious attitude towards sex. Miss Farrar is more like a Catalonian peasant than you'd expect – plump, ageing, and not very pretty; and her simple emoting includes a good deal of throat-clutching. Her stolid presence is the major drawback to **Joan the Woman** (1917), which (since the

The Rise of the American Industry

others are all terrible) manages the interesting but not considerable feat of being still the best film about Joan of Arc. The courtroom images indicate that it influenced Dreyer's film (q.v.), and it confirms deMille as a director of force and imagination, be it in the vigorous battle scenes, the numerous superimpositions, or merely in the compositions. It makes analogies with the concurrent conflict in Europe – which gets some footage – and as it progresses towards its climax it gathers, despite the liberties of the script, a degree of complexity hinged with real tragedy. Nothing in Griffith indicates that he gave as much thought as deMille (at this time) to the business of telling a story through images, and for sheer power and beauty the immolation sequence stands alone in the Silent period.

Miss Farrar was lured away by Goldwyn, now independent, for $10,000 a week, and deMille returned to melodrama, finding the high society formula he sought in **Old Wives for New** (1918), and matching it with an ironic tone. As the middle-aged husband (Elliott Dexter) leaves his frumpish wife (Sylvia Ashton) for a pretty modiste (Florence Vidor), a contrast between the wife then and the wife now is indicated by dynamic cutting. **Don't Change Your Husband** (1918) examines the same situation from the wife's point of view, and in acquiring Gloria Swanson (b. 1898) deMille found the heroine he sought – one who found that boredom with her first husband was preferable to the philandering of her second. She suffered in luxury – the girl who had everything but wasn't happy with it, bridging the gap between Bara and Pickford and their imitators, and establishing a screen type more lasting than either, the woman who was both sophisticated and sympathetic.

She, and these films of deMille's, were exactly what a restless, post-war generation wanted to see: a more relaxed attitude towards sex and a more liberal attitude towards women; a hint of corruption among the rich, of effeteness among the older generation; and a touch of the exotic – something the returning doughboy thought he had left behind in Paris cafés. **Male and Female** (1919) offers a bizarre scene with Miss Swanson

in a marble bath, as well as a quite extraneous sequence set in luxurious ancient Babylon – neither episode can be found in the play on which it is based, Barrie's 'The Admirable Crichton'. The impression of such trappings was to complement Swanson's sophistication: of going to the opera and the best resorts, of drinking cocktails to the sound of the gramophone – and indeed when the soulful wife (Swanson) loses her husband (Thomas Meighan) in **Why Change Your Wife ?** (1920) to the girl (Bebe Daniels) who prefers the Follies, she takes up smoking to win him back, learns to shimmy, and dons the once-disputed negligée. This, presumably, was the pattern of behaviour employed by the wealthy – a pattern that included the infidelities, shown as explicitly as possible, which in fact means glimpses of ankle and silken beds featuring prominently in the decor. Happy endings were vitally important, however, so that audiences might aspire to such married bliss, and the smartness and spuriousness of the pieces are indicated by the aspiring cynicism of the intertitles, e.g. a husband pondering 'the difference between his wife and the girl he married' (*Why Change Your Wife ?*) and the vamp claiming 'I'm not the type of girl for a little boy like you to play with. The place for you is home' (*The Affairs of Anatol*).

The attitudes reflected are certainly not those of Barrie – but are hopefully those of the marital comedies of Somerset Maugham and the plays of Schnitzler. DeMille's version of **The Affairs of Anatol** (1921) indicates how little his Massachusetts soul understood the spirit of the Viennese dramatist. We may overlook the fact that staying to formula Anatol (Wallace Reid) is no longer a bachelor but a bored husband; but after three episodes of dalliance – notably in the Oriental boudoir of Satan Synne (Bebe Daniels), the wickedest woman in town – he is not (as in the original) as far from his ideal as ever, but happily reunited with his wife.

DeMille, in fact, was an opportunist, but his muddled theories do not blind us to the fact that he was also technically more adroit than any of his contemporaries, notably in the matter of continuity and lighting. More genuine sophistication is to be found in the work of his brother,

On the basis of his very few surviving films, we are, however, more likely to admire Cecil's brother, William deMille, a former Broadway dramatist who took to film directing with ease. This is Thomas Meighan in *Conrad in Search of his Youth*. The proud mother is Sylvia Ashton, once his childhood sweetheart: he had not been prepared for the change, or the squawling brats.

William C. deMille (1878–1955), and especially in **Conrad in Search of His Youth** (1920). Conrad (Meighan) is an Indian Army officer who tries to relive his past. A reunion with his cousins in their childhood holiday home is a several-pronged disaster, and further disillusion follows when he seeks out his first love and the magical older woman who once gave him a good night kiss. The final sequence, in which he does find happiness, is a betrayal of the original novel (by Leonard Merrick), but it still has the sort of 'civilised' humour which appealed to the ladies who belonged to the lending libraries. **Miss Lulu Bett** (1921) also suffered on the journey from page to screen, via a Pulitzer-prizewinning play by the original writer, Zona Gale. I say 'suffered' because where *Conrad* remains a rare delight among films of the period, *Miss Lulu Bett* relies, like too many of them, on coincidence and omission. However, like the earlier film, it offered audiences identification rather than escape, and a notable portrait of family life with its squabbles and fears of what the neighbours think; the advance of Lulu (Lois Wilson) from drab skivvy to attractive wife is well done, and I'm sure audiences cheered when she smashed those dishes and marched out. William

deMille's strength was in matters of characterisation, by which he hoped to transform rather mundane subjects like these; when he could no longer interest producers in such subjects he quit directing.

Among the other directors of the period, Maurice Tourneur (1876–1961) was one of the most admired. Born in Paris, he began in films as an actor, but turned director in 1913, and crossed the Atlantic with art director Ben Carré, when their employers, Eclair, started an American branch, at Fort Lee, New Jersey – which was the major production centre for the industry until it ceded its place to Hollywood. Indeed, New Jersey recognisably doubles for Britain in **The Wishing Ring** (1914), 'An Idyll of Old England'. It is not to be expected that the 'Cranford'-like charm it seeks is achieved, but the story – the reformation of a ne'er-do-well by the daughter of an impoverished parson – is of little interest anyway. As indicated, *The Poor Little Rich Girl* is hardly better, but **A Girl's Folly** (1917) is worth notice: concocted by the director and Frances Marion, it is one of the first movies about movie-making – and like many later ones, about a film-struck girl (Doris Kenyon). Her folly is not in leaving the New Jersey fields for New York, but in staying after flunking her chance, dazzled by movie people; like a vast number of early films before the moguls' tastes began to impinge, the satiric strain is very strong – which also tells us much about the people who made them. There is nothing of this Tourneur in **The Blue Bird** (1918), a lavish production of Maeterlinck's play for Paramount, with over fifty sets, designed by Carré, which are varied and within the limitations of the time, exciting: but the film itself is a matter of staging rather than direction. It is easier to admire Tourneur for **Foolish Matrons** (1921), three stories of marriage, told simultaneously: the actress who traps an ageing doctor into matrimony, only to find that the demands of her career have turned him into a drug-addict; the woman reporter who marries the nice, promising young poet, and watches him turn into an alcoholic because he cannot get published; and the young wife from the country who succumbs to the blandishments of her husband's boss, losing both in time but achieving a sort of tarnished wealth. Victorian melodrama hangs heavily over all three tales, but the approach is ironic and the treatment entirely fresh. It is, however, New York which gives the film its distinct flavour: the many, impressive locations, separately directed by Clarence Brown, make you suddenly aware that you never before saw a convincing restaurant or bar in a movie. For such things this film is both more convincing and more entertaining than Von Stroheim's similarly-titled *Foolish Wives* (q.v.), and not a good deal less cynical or outspoken. It was a product of Associated Producers, the group of independent directors led by Ince, and on the strength of it we must regret that the company was so short-lived.

Another Frenchman, Léonce Perret (1880–1935), was also one of the superior directors of this period. A former actor, he started the 'Léonce' series, in which he also starred, for Gaumont in 1911, and they reveal both a sprightly wit and a smooth technical skill. Pathé sent him to Hollywood in 1917, and during his four years there he made a number of melo-dramas, including **Twin Pawns** (1919), which starred Mae Marsh in a double role. Perret himself wrote it, several removes from its acknowledged source, 'The Woman in White', and apart from the villain (Warner Oland) who lives by his wits it is very silly: but beyond the always imaginative and still-fresh inter-titles it holds evidence that Perret wholly understood the shape of the screen, and how it could be filled: the composition and lighting are superb, and the strong images of the factory scenes are matched by the narrative hold.

Raoul Walsh, in **Regeneration** (1915), offers a portrait of the times to stand with *The Italian* and *Foolish Matrons*. Walsh (1892–1981), a former actor with Griffith, had hitherto co-directed shorts, and he manages with accomplished ease this por-trait of New York low life, moving from beer hall to mission picnics. It is not, as Walsh and others have claimed, the first gangster film, since it has more in com-mon with the early counterfeiter tales than, say, *Little Caesar* (q.v.); it does attempt to analyse the mentality of the layabout – not the hoodlum – and is, alas, a little too pious, as the title indicates.

Rather that, though, than **Hawthorn of the U.S.A.** (1919), directed by James Cruze for Paramount, one of a number of post-war films to reiterate faith in Ameri-can-style democracy. Being Hawthorne, says the star (Wallace Reid), 'that's got every king in Europe backed off the map'; he helps the foolish king rid the country of a number of vile revolutionaries, trans-forming the country 'with Yankee gold and ginger'.

The haughty, tall Reid and burly Thomas Meighan were Paramount's leading male stars, and in the case of Reid it is difficult to see why; both pale in comparison to William S. Hart – by the time he arrived at Paramount one of the cornerstones of the industry. That strange face, blinkered and hard, was surely like that of Marley's which Scrooge found on the knocker, haunted and hunted, and not needing intertitles like 'Realising that the road of the outlaw closes all others'. The episodic nature of **The Toll Gate** (1919) indicates that neither he nor his director and co-writer, Lambert Hillyer, was yet at home with the feature-length movie, but his knowledge of the frontier was never better expressed: the film is harsh, raw and unexpected, and because of what must surely be its authentic look and spirit, the most valuable example of the

William S. Hart was one of the actors who reached near-autonomy at Triangle - as jealously watched by Adolph Zukor at Famous Players-Lasky, who regarded himself as the leader of the industry. In fact, he helped to bring about the eventual collapse of Triangle by poaching Douglas Fairbanks Sr, with the offer of his own production company. When Thomas H. Ince quarrelled with his bosses at Triangle, Zukor offered him a haven – though what mainly interested Zukor was Ince's personal contract with Hart. When it ended Zukor broke with Ince, but kept Hart – with, of course, the offer of his own company. Its first film was *The Toll Gate*, one of the finest films Hart made.

genre extant. Its title is a reference to the soul, the difference between today and yesterday, or so an intertitle tells us, but **The Testing Block** (1920) is a wife: 'Along the ladder of life every man finds a rung that is his testing block, and writes his future as he climbs' – a phrase which accurately indicates that this film goes further than its predecessor in moralising, and it is even more overplotted. Hillyer was again Hart's collaborator, but this is less a portrait of the wild and rugged West than a weepie which could just as easily have had gangsters as its desperadoes. Since the old codes had been superseded, Hart had difficulty in finding subjects.

The lawless regions he had known as a youth were now settled, which was why he played an outlaw, the 'Good-Bad Man', only able to function outside that settled community. But now post-war audiences were more alive to social injustice: they wanted to see wrongdoing punished, and though settler and city-dweller alike could not obliterate the lawless past, they could however romanticise it, and in so doing destroy the authenticity of Hart's early films. His films were increasingly regarded as naif, and Zukor finally asked him to relinquish control and act under supervision. Earlier, Zukor had offered him $200,000 per film not to join United Artists (q.v.), and it was that company he now joined to retain his independence: but after one film, **Tumbleweeds** (1925), (in my opinion, a deserved failure) he retired.

Paramount's chief female player, after Miss Pickford, was perhaps Marguerite Clark, whose only film to survive is **Silks and Satins** (1916), directed by the then admired veteran, J. Searle Dawley. The title refers to the days of powdered wigs, but for all the references to 'the tap rooms of Paris' we may recognise the Palisades, a feature of every other film at the time. The star herself is merely another dimity heroine, dark, expressive and pretty: in 'The Movies in the Age of Innocence' Edward Wagenknect says that not to have seen her is tantamount to having 'never seen a silver birch or a daffodil', and in 1932 Sam Goldwyn listed her as one of the five greatest stars. She had retired in 1921: her husband had refused to let her kiss her leading man, and that was, in Lasky's opinion, the reason for her decline in popularity.

It was scandal which ruined another of Pickford's rivals, Mary Miles Minter, whose dimples may be examined in close-up in **The Ghost of Rosy Taylor** (1918), directed for Mutual by Edward Sloman, in which she suffers every misfortune but the wolves lapping at her heels. It is fast-paced, but dim, and the mystery promised by the title is notably missing. Miss Minter became implicated in the death of the director William Desmond Taylor, which was a mystery: and it also killed the career of the comedienne Mabel Normand, whose **Mickey** (1918) was astonishingly popular and is still fondly remembered. It was the first feature set up by her own company, as founded by Sennett (in whose one-reelers she had attained stardom) – and it was the only one, since she soon succumbed to a lucrative offer from Goldwyn. In fact, the film for that reason went unreleased for two years – a long time at that period – but its episodic plot did not deter audiences. That plot is literally 'Cinderella' rewritten for a modern tomboy, and Miss Normand's sharp reactions are occasionally funny as directed by Richard Jones.

Among the other players of this period must be mentioned John Barrymore, yet another of the over-age leading men. The line began with the genteel, kindly, Maurice Costello, but the more boisterous Barrymore was invariably cast as a reprobate who sobered up and showed his worth in the last reel. He was already the Barrymore we know from his Talkies – the quizzical stare, the jaunty self-confidence, the overall aura of a déclassé Don Juan. His films for Zukor are genial enough, but avoid **Raffles, the Amateur Cracksman** (1917), directed by George Irving, a confused account of E. W. Hornung's stories about a gentleman thief who plundered jewels at house parties. Another famous novel is just recognisable in **A Tale of Two Cities** (1917), directed by Frank Lloyd for Fox, and hardly an advance on the earlier Vitagraph version. The over-age hero in this one is William Farnum, as both Darnay and Carton (in fair to good trick work), and this portly, inexpressive actor makes one realise why audiences would soon fall or Valentino (q.v.).

Lon Chaney (q.v.), another name of the future, was at this time with Universal – not a star player, but one whose features, especially the whites of his eyes, made an indelible impression. He was one of Joseph de Grasse's stock company, along with some others left by Allan Dwan when he moved on from Universal: their scenarist was usually Ida May Park, who was the wife of director de Grasse, and the others in the company included Louise Lovely, who succeeded Gretchen Lederer as leading lady, and Hayward Mack. Their last two-reeler was **Dolly's Scoop** (1916), which offers the dilemma of a young reporter (Miss Lovely) who realises that the lady in the scandal she has uncovered is the wife of her editor (Mr Mack) – just retribution, of course, because he had threatened her with the sack if she didn't spice up her copy. The tone is light and lively, even the moralising; we forgive it its hypocrisy (the editor's wife is not really guilty), and it does indicate the level at which films might have worked had audiences not demanded sex, and producers not been determined to give it to them.

It was Universal that tried to make a film-star out of Anna Pavlova, and its solution was more sensible than making Geraldine Farrar a mute Carmen: she was put into a version of Auber's opera, **The Dumb Girl of Portici** (1916), in which by tradition the leading role – the lady of the title – was played by a ballerina. Looking haggard and intense, she does a tarantella or so, is seduced by the viceroy's son, and helps the Neapolitans to shake off the Spanish yoke. The action is as daft as most opera plots, and thus no sillier than most films of this era: but Lois Weber's direction confirms her position as one of the best directors of the time. Vigorous handling is also a feature of **The Virgin of Stamboul** (1920), and this other piece of exotic melodrama in fact made the reputation of a former vaudevillian, Tod Browning (1882–1962). The title-role is played by Priscilla Dean, one of Universal's most popular players, and part-clown in the manner of female stars of the time: as pursued by a dashing American officer and a sheik whose motives are much less honourable, the film conveys a fairly libellous account of the Levant at the time.

The preoccupation with sex was not accidental, and only the most popular players could get by with just a peck on the cheeks. A minor star like Molly King could be put in something like **The On-the-Square Girl** (1917), directed by Frederick J. Ireland for Pathé, a sexual version of *The Perils of Pauline* ; in such films titillation was provided by entirely double standards – the innocent seeming to be guilty, situations set up in which nothing actually happens, and the sinners paying for their happiness with entirely unconvincing reversals. Such was the major preoccupation of writers in the latter half of the second decade of the century : the arrival of the feature film confirmed that the cinema was not a passing fad, and sex was the simplest means at hand for hanging on to audiences.

On the other hand, films were achieving cohesion, and a number of filmmakers had demonstrated that the art of film narrative required far more than having actors emote before a camera. The most important technical development since the close-up was just a couple of years away – the moving camera: occasional cameramen had pushed it about, but its fluency had hardly been considered. As the decade turned, films seemed to have only two visual inadequacies: night-filming in exteriors remained difficult (a problem for audiences only when the stock was not tinted – dark blue for night, pink for twilight, yellow for sunlight) and parts of California stood in for the rest of the world. 'A tree is a tree is a tree' went the maxim, 'Shoot it in Griffith Park.' But it was a convention slowly losing credence ; the great era of set-building was about to begin, and technically the Americans would lead the world. Yet once again in ideas and imagination, the decade belonged to the Europeans – or so thought informed opinion of the time, including the American industry, which began to raid the studios of the Continent. The great era of purchasing talent had also begun.

63

3

The Screen's First Master

IT WAS not only the confidence and aggressiveness of the American industry which made it the most successful: chance also played a part, in the form of the War. With Europe in its apparent death throes, the leading producing companies – France, Germany, Britain and Italy – finished the War with industries diminished. Within a few years the film-makers of a defeated Germany would startle the world, and so would those of a new industry of a new country – the U.S.S.R. In Scandinavia the Danish industry declined, and Sweden continued to produce a few films of high quality.

Until quite recently the achievements of the German Silent film were thought to have been surpassed only by the Russians: to such an extent has Paul Rotha's 1929 survey of film influenced film historians that most major archives were based on his enthusiasms or those of such disciples as Iris Barry and Eileen Bowser of the Museum of Modern Art. Rotha's sole remark on the native work of Victor Sjöström is a passing reference to his 'Swedish masterpieces' and it has hardly been better documented elsewhere. It is ironic that Sjöström's most celebrated film, *The Phantom Carriage*, is also the most dated. It was the first Sjöström, says Ingmar Bergman, that he saw, and it was surely in his mind when he concocted *The Seventh Seal* (q.v.). If these two films were all that we knew of Swedish cinema, they would seem to confirm our notions of gloom and guilt, but in fact Sjöström is the only film-maker of the first three decades whose work can be considered as seriously as the major novelists and dramatists of the time. His situation has been admirably set by a contemporary French critic, Jean-Loup Passek: 'Towards Sjöström posterity has shown a singular ingratitude. It is almost indecent to see a creator of his stature relegated to the Purgatory of the Seventh Art. More perfidious than a perfectly planned assassination, for him has been reserved the lowest, most hypocritical, of contempt: oblivion.'

It has not been, of course, a blanket oblivion; due obeisance has been paid to the 'lyric' qualities of Sjöström and his contemporary, Mauritz Stiller. Iris Barry has noted their achievement more accurately: 'It was the Swedish film that first depicted individual human character with amplitude and truth, and taught the screen to suggest motive and mood. Both Sjöström and Stiller consciously and in original ways sought to make the film a vehicle for expressing by purely pictorial means subtleties hitherto unknown to it.' Sjöström succeeded triumphantly, though his films are technically barren; Stiller, the better technician, only sporadically. The gulf between them is enormous; but given Sjöström's admiration for his colleague, we may conclude that this has only become apparent with the years. Comparisons are inevitable, for they were not only contemporaries and colleagues, but collaborators – Sjöström acted in several of Stiller's films – and they filmed similar subjects, notably the novels of Selma Lagerlöf. One of these, Stiller's *Gosta Berling's Saga*, is the only one of their films to be discussed at length by Arthur Knight in 'The Liveliest Art'. It is a terrible film, described by Knight as 'the last great movie to come out of Sweden for many a year', one of those judgments, so common in discussing Silent films, n which boredom is equated with great-ness. The films of Stiller are of their time, tilted and melodramatic : he imitated he Griffith movie. Sjöström in later life was not interested in discussing the films he had directed, but he conceded that some of them may have been before their ime. The Museum of Modern Art note on *The Outlaw and his Wife* makes that point, also saying that Sjöström 'created effects not found outside the work of Griffith, yet more sophisticated and complex than anything even he had done'. It is not that Sjöström was before his time; his contemporaries in the industry were behind theirs.

The first credit for Sjöström's achieve-ment should, however, go to Charles Magnusson (1878–1948), usually re-garded as the founder of the Swedish ilm. In 1911 he built at Lidingö a studio reputed to be the most advanced in Europe. In establishing a distinctive native style – as opposed to the foreign

material flooding in – he turned to dis-tinguished men of the theatre; in 1912 he persuaded both Sjöström and Stiller to join his team. Sjöström continued to work as both actor and director, and he wrote, or collaborated, on most of his screenplays. It was, he said later, 'a youthful desire for adventure' which brought him into films; but it was soon apparent, in the words of the film historians Bardeche and Brasillac, that 'here was a man really interested in what he was doing, loving the film as though it were one of the noble arts, and realising that it is, above all, a child of light'. The contribution to Sjöström's films of his cameramen cannot be under-estimated : these were usually Henrik or Julius Jaenzen, brothers, who achieved for both him and Stiller images of breath-taking beauty. They photographed night and twilight, sky and landscape, sea and mountain, in a manner which astonishes even today.

Victor Sjöström (1879–1960) was born

Nothing else in early cinema can prepare us for the power of Victor Sjöström's *Terje Vigen*. In the title–role, Sjöström himself (with the white beard) breaks through a blockade, is captured, and returns to find wife and child dead. Years later, a lonely and terrifying old man, he is offered a strange chance for revenge.

The Screen's First Master

Sjöström's *The Girl from Stormycroft* is, for a movie of its time, honest about sexual mores. He knew that the choice was not always between a demure Gish–type maiden and a city vamp; the Other Woman is nice and sensible – as is the film's attitude to her, allowing her to confess that she still 'likes' her seducer. Here is Greta Almroth, as the wronged woman, with Lars Hanson, the man who has taken her in.

in Silbodal, a small town in south-west Sweden. He grew up partly in Brooklyn; back in Sweden, at seventeen years of age, he joined a troupe of actors touring Finland, and he mainly toured till Magnusson invited him to join his company, Svenska Biografteatern. His first film he made as an actor, with Stiller directing; and Stiller wrote the screenplay for Sjöström's first film as a director, a film which was banned by the censor and never shown in Sweden. Between 1912 and 1923 he directed forty-five features, of which only thirteen survive.

The earliest survivor is **Ingeborg Holm** (1913), much praised then for its realism or naturalism – interchangeable words in cinema theory and with a common meaning, that of depicting life in reproduction as it is. The source was a play by Nils Krook, evidently so eminent that a photograph of him precedes the story. Sjöström had directed it on the stage, and the leading role is taken by a stage actress, Hilda Borgstrom: but few films of any time, let alone then, are less theatrical. The melodrama of the story is disguised by a style of extreme

simplicity, with nothing inessential to be seen, as derived from the Scandinavian literary tradition – which itself evolved from the simplicity of the landscape, with its plains, dense woods and luminous skies. To that landscape belongs this tale of a suffering woman, her children torn from her, descending into madness. Except for the coda – an unconvincing happy ending – the film is far from others on the same theme: the subject of impoverished widowhood, the poor-house, of children parted from parents, was one then of universality – and that could be one reason why Sjöström tells it without ornament. That vexing movie question of the form for the content might here have had its earliest solution.

Twenty (lost) films intervene between it and **Terje Vigen** (1917), but these two were, at the time, the most highly regarded. The source of this one is a nationalistic epic poem by Ibsen, inspired by a local legend he heard when living in Grimstad, on the south Norwegian coast. Magnusson acquired the film rights for Svenska, and Sjöström decided to make it after a visit to Grimstad. It is set at the time of the Napoleonic Wars, when British ships were blockading that part of the Norwegian coast. It is not a strong plot, but masterly handling does make effective two passages: the pursuit and capture, and Terje's return. The desperation of starvation – the mainspring of the tale, and from his other work the thing we might have expected to most interest Sjöström – is treated in cursory fashion: nor does he, this once, make much of the spirit of the community. But the piece is imbued with the spirit of the sea – omnipresent, a source of wonder and livelihood, of danger and isolation, and a worthy opponent of Terje, played by Sjöström himself and looking the role absolutely.

This was a conscious effort to drag the film into the level of art; so was **The Girl from Stormycroft** (1917), and it was far more successful. The aspirations in this case were due to the fact it was based on a novel by Selma Lagerlöf (the first to be filmed by Svenska Bio), the most admired and acclaimed of living Swedish authors. The girl of the title is Helga (Greta Almroth), who bears a child out of wedlock. Called to court to accuse the

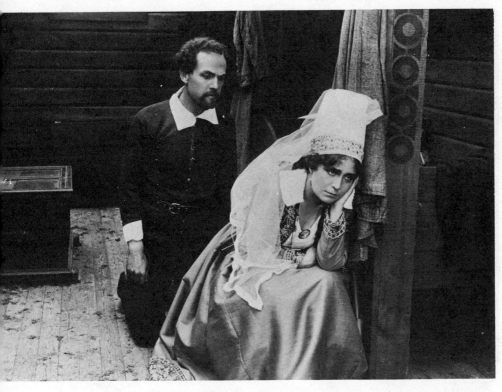

The composition of the pictures on these two pages indicates Sjöström's success in moving away from theatrical grouping and lighting. This is *The Outlaw and his Wife*, his second attempt – after *Terje Vigen* – at an epic. It fulfils all the definitions of that tough genre, while never moving towards the obvious. It is the man this time who is taken in – played by Sjöström himself; the woman is Edith Erastoff, who in life became his third (and enduring) wife.

father, she withdraws her plaint to prevent him perjuring himself, which so impresses Gudmund (Lars Hanson) that he persuades his mother to employ her as a servant, at risk to his relationship with his fiancée (Karen Molander). The plot has a gaping hole at the climax, if minimised by making Gudmund's guilt a fantasy which is his alone. There may well have been sexual attraction between him and Helga, and the point is that both girls are alike – blonde, pretty and of sunny disposition. But if the characterisation is stronger than the plot, it is the scenes from provincial life which make it the best film made up to that time: the wedding guests gossiping and drinking tea; the curious onlookers in the courtroom and the preening local bigwigs; the merry-makers in the tavern and its disapproving *patron*. Sjöström's touch is of the lightest: he merely sketches the families of the three young people, and they come alive.

The similarity with Griffith's *True-Heart Susie* (q.v.) brings that to mind, but there is nothing else like **The Outlaw and his Wife** (1917), though in power and maturity it dwarfs all other film epics to that time. The public and critical acceptance of *Terje Vigen* caused Sjöström to attempt this tale, and if its actual source is a modern Icelandic play, by Johann Sigurdonsson, its spiritual roots are in the Norse sagas. With that in mind, it is easy to accept some tall moments in the second half, but its strength is in its marvellous portrait of a primitive farming community (if filmed in Sweden rather than Iceland) – and its essential point is the integrity of its wanderer hero. Sjöström himself plays that role, and Edith Erastoff is the widow who employs him, who declares him married to her, and who when his past catches up with him flees with him to the hills. Years later, locked in mutual loathing, she asks him in vain to recall their former happiness – but that may only be found in death, since they have, as they say, worked in the ways of God. 'Love is the only law,' she declares, and 'No man can escape his fate, though he run faster than the wind': these are the film's twin themes, with both the Norse gods and Freudian psychology elbowing into its Christian

The Screen's First Master

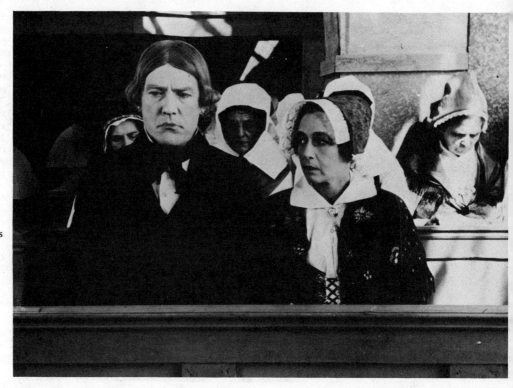

morality. The concept that deprivation can turn a happy couple into an embittered one, while not new, went wholly against the Victorian sentiment permeating all film-making in all countries ; only a great film-maker would dare offer it.

As a picture of the past **The Ingmarssons** (1919) is even more valuable: set in a far province of southern Sweden in the nineteenth century, things could hardly have changed there by the time Sjöström went on location to make it. The source is again Lagerlöf – her two-volume novel 'Jerusalem', which provided Magnusson with five films in all: this one, shown originally in two parts; Sjöström's *Karin Ingmarsdotter* (q.v.); and the later *Ingmar's Inheritance* and *To the East,* both directed by Gustav Molander, at this time writer for both Sjöström and Stiller. This description of the novel – by Professor Bergmann of Gothenburg – equally applies to Sjöström's film: 'The first part makes an impressive study of a rural community and the often subtle underplay of the individual and the collective. With its hero, Ingmar Ingmarsson, and his

struggle for moral integrity Selma Lagerlöf has created her most memorable character, at once a rational being subject to impulses he only partly understands.' This is an introspective masterpiece, and very slow – taking almost two-and-a-half hours for what is hardly more than an anecdote. In the first part he (Sjöström) marries Britta (Harriet Bosse), against her will, and finds her dislike turning to hatred, to the extent that she kills their child; in the second, with her release from prison, he tries to solve the dilemma of them both – a tale of two basically decent people who have hurt each other and are, perhaps too late, trying to make amends.

In contrast, both **His Lordship's Last Will** (1919) and **The Monastery of Sendomir** (1920) are minor. The former is a comedy about a crusty old baron and his family, adapted from a novel by Hjalmar Bergman, with whom Sjöström would collaborate further; it is mainly notable for its sketch of life on a provincial estate, and the always entrancing Miss Almroth. The other is of the 'tales told to travellers' breed – and in this case

68

he tale is of seventeenth-century adultery
and revenge, as based on a play by
Franz Grillparzer, a nineteenth-century
Viennese dramatist who wrote a number
of historical moralities. Sjöström has
clearly tried to create a visual style to
compensate for the loss of verse, but it
remains primitive melodrama, occasionally enjoyable for its guilty Countess
(Tora Teje).

Karin Ingmarsdotter (1920) takes
up the story of the Ingmarssons with
Ingmar (Sjöström) a widower and his
daughter Karin (Miss Teje) sought in
marriage by the worthy Halvor (Tor
Weiden); because of his own mistake,
Ingmar does not attempt to influence her,
but she is influenced by the fact that
Halvor's father drank and because he
himself once succumbed – so that when
she later finds herself married to an incorrigible old drunkard it is, as she says,
a judgment on her. Although endorsing
Lagerlöf's views on the evils of alcohol
(a tradition which remains in Swedish
society), Sjöström's film is not as harrowing as it sounds, and he plays his concluding scene for humour, spinning it out
dangerously, calculating rightly that the
audience is both in high good spirits and
loath to say farewell to the Ingmarssons.
Miss Teje's performance is as remarkable
as those of Miss Bosse and himself in the
earlier film. This film is less an achievement than that, and certainly less epic, a
simple and straightforward account of a
disastrous marriage. Its ending is happy,
and the Ingmarssons, for all their self-
righteousness, surely deserve that.

In **Mästerman** (1920) Sjöström is the
gentleman of the title, a Silas Marner-like
pawnbroker and the most loathed man in
the small fishing port which is its setting;
he takes as pawn the young Tora (Miss
Almroth), always refusing to believe that
her heart will ever belong to her ne'er-
do-well fiancé. This performance is a
study in depth, physically modelled on
Ibsen, with his side-whiskers, stove-hat
and voluminous cloak; despite his gruff-
ness, kindness is not unknown to him,
as when he relents to take in the budgeri-
gars, and his loneliness is clear when he
attempts to stroke the pig grazing with
her litter. Like the villagers, we never
get close – even physically. Tora has
several close-ups, but he none. Sjöström,

directing himself, has vast footage but
never hogs the camera ; his Mästerman
remains an enigma, and that is what
makes this film so rewarding. We cannot
foresee his actions; unlike other Silent
villains he has dimension. He surprises
us, and the same is true of Miss Almroth,
with her quiet strength, her merriment
and her youth, as well as the minor
characters. The set-pieces are done with
as much love and lack of self-consciousness: business in the pawnshop; the
crowds waiting at the quayside for the
sailors to dock; the open-air party to
welcome them home; the boats crossing
the water for Matins on Sunday. Hjalmar
Bergman wrote the screenplay, one of
the rare originals in Swedish films at the
time. Looking then at the Scandinavian
cinema, Carl Dreyer wrote in *Dagbladet*:
'It is not possible to mention Swedish
film without mentioning Victor
Sjöström's name in the same breath . . .
he had the courage to go against the
current. He was the first in Scandinavia
to realise that one cannot *manufacture*
films. . . Through Sjöström's work, film
was let into art's promised land . . . the
Swedish art film has acquired its distinctive character by becoming a medium for
true and genuine human representation.'

Despite the melodrama and moralising
required, some of these are great films
by any standard – *The Ingmarssons, Karin
Ingmarsdotter, The Outlaw and his Wife,
Mästerman*, and I would add to them *The
Wind* (q.v.), his best American film: yet
Sjöström was technically uninventive,
with moments of cinematic language so
few and isolated as to give doubt that
he really understood the medium. Sometimes the intertitles are so many and so
lengthy as to obscure the action, but it
is clear that his motivation was fidelity
to the text and spirit of the authors whose
work he adapted. It is perhaps by chance
that he towers over his contemporaries,
since he was allowed to work with better
material – yet we have seen what happened to Ibsen in Hollywood, and we
shall see what Stiller did with Lagerlöf.
Later, Dreyer observed that Sjöström
responded the better of the two to that
writer, because he was Swedish in
thought and mentality – 'Swedish to his
very backbone', and he added, significantly in view of Stiller's failure, 'He put

into the stylised figures of her novels the warm humanity and feelings of his own heart. Under his hands noble spirit was combined with noble form.' Ingmar Bergman, speaking of another Sjöström version of Lagerlöf, *The Phantom Carriage,* observed 'There are scenes in *Sons of Ingmar* [i.e. *The Ingmarssons*] and *Karin Ingmarsdotter* which with their precision, their genuineness and clarity, still have the same educative impression of being honest artistic products.' Sjöström was honest with his material, honest with himself, and honest with his audience: so perhaps was Griffith, but if his *Broken Blossoms* (q.v.) of this time was supposedly a film peak, we can only shake our heads. Native audiences so responded to *The Ingmarssons* that Magnusson was able to take over his rivals in the industry: he formed Svensk Filmindustri and built new studios at Rasunda. *Mästerman* was the first production made there, and the second of Sjöström's was the first Swedish film to have a large international success – after which things would never be quite the same again.

This was **The Phantom Carriage** (1921), again based on a novel by Lagerlöf, 'Korkarlen' i.e. 'The Driver', though the film has also been known by its British title, *Thy Soul Shall Bear Witness*, and it was originally shown in the U.S. as *At the Stroke of Midnight*. These titles indicate its theme, and Lagerlöf's starting point was a French legend claiming that anyone who meets with a fatal accident on New Year's Eve has to drive the carriage of death for a year. Lagerlöf's predeliction, as Dreyer observed, 'for dreams and supernatural events appealed to Sjöström's somewhat sombre artistic mind'. Contemporaries admired the film for its representation of the supernatural – in double images – and for its complexities, with flashback within flashback to depict the past life of the wastrel David Holm (Sjöström). And the moral then seemed relevant: drink is the root of all evil. In *Karin Ingmarsdotter* drunkenness was a reaction against repression, but here no reason is offered for Holm's descent into self-ruin, and the result is a moral tract, turgid and pretentious; it is a tribute to Sjöström that we take it at all seriously.

With world attention now turned towards the Swedish market, Magnusson as so many subsequent European entrepreneurs, attempted to make films for the international market. Sjöström was encouraged to film an historical novel by Hjalmar Bergman, *Vem Dömer?* – a film known to us as **Love's Crucible** (1922). The setting is said to be Florence, but the titles do not indicate this – and nor, emphatically, do the settings. After a dull exposition, events come thick and fast, having to do with the eternal triangle, a phial of poison, a sudden heart attack, a miracle – possibly echoed by Ingmar Bergman in *The Touch* (q.v.) – and a trial by fire. The climax is imaginative, but overall it is a poor film. The Swedish title means 'Who judges?', to recall to us that both the Outlaw and his wife and the Ingmarssons preferred the judgment of God to man, but it is not, otherwise, recognisably a Sjöström film.

Its public and critical failure was fast and complete, but Magnusson, not discouraged, engaged two international names (both from Britain) for *The Surrounded House* (1922) and **Hell Ship** (1923), respectively Meggie Albanesi and Matheson Lang. The former, from a French play, with Sjöström in the leading male role, has not survived, breaking the run from *Terje Vigen* to what was to be his last Swedish Silent. Hjalmar Bergman wrote the original screenplay of *Hell Ship*, like all Sjöström's major films a study in obsession – the jealousy of a ship's captain (Lang) towards the former suitor (Sjöström) of his wife (Jenny Hasselqvist). These are protagonists of weight, neither all good and bad, so carefully worked out as to remind us how seldom Sjöström put colour into his female characters (the major exception is Karin Ingmarsdotter); it is also characteristic of him that they should be reconciled at the end. The attention to detail is as vivid as ever, with one outstanding sequence – the loading of the cargo at night, in a storm – but there is here and there a dot of contrivancy, a stroke of sentimentality. An uneasy story-line was not helped by an accident to the ship (it sank), and the need to improvise a new ending. Lang's performance is almost as good as Sjöström's – and very far from the scenery-chewing stints revealed in his British films; but the film moves towards the conventional movies of the period – the movies of Hollywood, Britain or France.

There is no record of Sjöström speaking of compromise, but he had been increasingly unhappy directing films, of which the last three were failures; and Magnusson was more than content to have him go to Hollywood to study film-making. His presence in the U.S. and the success elsewhere of *The Phantom Carriage* brought Hollywood offers, and he signed with the Goldwyn Company, on the point of merging with Metro and Mayer. It has been suggested that Magnusson wanted to distribute the films of the merged companies in Sweden, and used Sjöström as a pawn: certainly he did annul Sjöström's contract and he did handle M-G-M's films.

Sjöström's departure left him with only one film-maker of repute – Mauritz Stiller; and since there is no way of discussing him without reference to Sjöström, we might note the opinion of the director Jorn Donner, 'The film histories generally state that Sjöström was more powerful, if heavy; that Stiller was more elegant, if superficial. Ingmar Bergman puts Sjöström first, partly because of Sjöström's weighty Swedishness.' Stiller (1883–1928) was of Russian-Jewish stock, born in Helsinki, at that time capital of a Russian Grand Duchy. Orphaned at the age of four, he later gravitated towards the theatre, but fled to Sweden – like most Finns, he was bi-lingual – when conscription loomed. For some years he had no more success than in his native country, till a few good notices emboldened him to apply to Magnusson for employment; his enthusiasm for films was such that he was taken on not as actor but as director. He made his first film in 1912, but the first to survive is the thirtieth, **Love and Journalism** (1916), a comedy about a journalist (Karin Molander) who inveigles herself into the home of a famous explorer (Richard Lund) to get copy. Only Stiller's comedies survive from this period, and if far from the rollicking fun of the Sennett two-reelers they are swiftly-paced and notable in their frank approach to sex. Desire runs rampant: nice young men run after nice young girls, as do older men, unless

The Scandinavian cinema's preference for tales of sex found satiric bent in the comedies of Mauritz Stiller, with the lady often taking the initiative. The provocative miss on the left is Karen Molander, in *Thomas Graal's Best Film*.

too aged except to philander with the ladies of the town – while their wives support good works; even nice young wives dream of changing partners. **Alexander the Great** (1917) is a satire on small town morals, centring on an engagement between a penniless lieutenant and a hideous spinster. Her admonition that they must have single rooms brings a look of surprise and delight to his face – a typical Stiller touch. The film, however, is hardly worth seeing: all of Stiller's films are disjointed, and this one suffered further from censorship cuts.

Both **Thomas Graal's Best Film** (1917) and **Thomas Graal's Best Child** (1918) are blessed with the presence of Sjöström, playing a writer, and the witty and pretty Miss Molander. The first is a lighthearted tale about film-making; the sequel tells us what happens when they marry – or, rather, what doesn't happen, since a hasty quarrel precludes consummation. It is often amusing, more so than the similar but better-known **Erotikon** (1920), though it was the latter, Lubitsch said, which helped him form his style, along with the sex comedies of deMille; it can be said that Stiller's characters are somewhat more believable and sophisticated than those of deMille.

The first of his serious films to survive is **Song of the Scarlet Flower** (1918),

71

the first of three film versions of a popular Finnish novel by Johannes Linnankoski – said to be a work of stature, but the film, though it plays well, is merely another melodrama about a headstrong dissolute youth (Lars Hanson) whose wayward experiences help him 'to find himself'. It is not dissimilar to *The Ingmarssons,* but whereas the supreme pleasure in Sjöström is his recreation of time past, Stiller hardly uses the brothels and taverns in which his films abound. Each of his surviving serious films does have one huge set-piece – here the log-rolling sequence, and in **Sir Arne's Treasure** (1919) the dash across the ice. That version of Lagerlöf, a tale of Scottish mercenaries and their plunder, only emphasises his inferiority, being virtually hysterical, clearly less considered than Sjöström's more naturalistic approach. Of his extant films, only **Johan** (1921) offers a valuable portrait of contemporary life – of life in a faraway place where people live off the soil and regard the opening of a canal as a momentous event. Its source is again a Finnish novel, by Juani Aho (who was much influenced

by Lagerlöf), and its plain story concerns a wife torn between day-to-day drudgery and the romance offered by a stranger. She revolts against the loveless marriage, to the extent that the advent of the stranger puts her into a mood of sexual tension: having gone away with him, she again revolts, but from guilt. As with Sjöström's people, all options are open to her and her menfolk, and they grow before our eyes, taking on facets as so few characters did in films of this time. Stiller may not say as much as Sjöström, but he uses less intertitles and his cutting is always more imaginative.

After that high point, however, he returned to stark melodrama for his last two Swedish films, both versions of Lagerlöf. **Gunnar Hedes Saga** (1922) is the wan tale of a wealthy scion who goes mad and the waif who loves him, but **Gosta Berling's Saga** (1924) is saga indeed, lasting three hours and based on Lagerlöf's first and most famous book. If the film has several English titles, it seems to have two in Swedish, one that translates as 'The Cavaliers of Ekeby' – and it concerns these cavaliers, living in

The photography of the Jaenzon brothers was as beneficial to the films of Stiller as to those of Sjöström. The highly-lipsticked men and wild-eyed over-emoting that Stiller encouraged do not, however, make for naturalism, though neither factor exactly spoils the highly melodramatic *Sir Arne's Treasure*. Certainly at the time audiences were not bothered.

a remote part of Värmland, and their effect on the community. They are privileged retainers, idle and dissipated, their vices creating chaos till they take stock and return to order. Berling himself (Mr Hanson) is a drunken, unfrocked priest, and if his behaviour is as appalling as theirs, that is the fault of direction and adaptation, ransacking the piece for ersatz excitement. Lagerlöf herself, who loathed the film, commented that Stiller had seen 'too many poor serials'. There is a good fire sequence, a famous chase across the ice, and some scenes of revelry – but since the latter lack period flavour, pleasure in them is muted. Most people know the film from the cut-down versions, but the original – as restored by the Swedish Film Archive – reveals the whole to be no more coherent. The cut copies have, naturally, retained all

the footage of Stiller's discovery, Greta Garbo (b. 1905) – originally a subsidiary character till he grew so enraptured of her that he built up her role, which may also be the reason why she is given to Gosta at the fade-out, a complete distortion of Lagerlöf's ending. Garbo evinces little actual ability, and only once towards the end does she look attractive, as the light plays on her hair. Although she regarded the homosexual Stiller as her mentor, it is uncertain to what extent he moulded the magical figure that emerged at M–G–M, and he never directed her again. When their next project failed, he loaned her to Pabst for *Die Freudlosse Gasse* (q.v.). He insisted that M–G–M take her, when that company signed him to a contract, but as she flourished, he languished; he was removed from several films, and made

Because of the presence of Greta Garbo (seated) *Gosta Berling's Saga* – also known as *The Atonement of Gosta Berling*–remains the most famous early Swedish film. A concoction of domestic drama and gloomy social injustice, mixed with roistering, it was for years a warhorse of the film societies – despite being damply received when it came out.

73

only three American films, all on loan to Paramount. Assigned to direct her in *The Divine Woman*, he was replaced by Sjöström, and these two compatriots were the only two to see him off when he left Hollywood. He died in Stockholm a year later, of a lung ailment. His films have technical virtuosity and occasional sophistication, but are mostly ordinary: the point about Sjöström's is that they are extra–ordinary.

That adjective may be the one to apply to Benjamin Christensen's **Häxan** (1922) or *Witchcraft Through the Ages*, his first film since those two we examined earlier, and in fact made in Sweden under the auspices of Magnusson. It may be the first feature-length non-fiction film, this anticlerical study of necromancy, superstition and related matters, as told in old prints and some fantastical reconstructions, with Christensen himself appearing briefly as a grinning, tempting devil. Readers of Rattray-Taylor's 'Sex in History' would find these fat priests and possessed nuns fairly treated, and if the conclusion is superficial – that doctors have replaced the devils, and mental sickness is a descendent of witchcraft – psychology as a science wasn't that advanced when this film was made. The original had interminable intertitles, but the revised version, with a Sound commentary, is very taking.

Christensen went to Hollywood via Germany, and of these Scandinavians only Carl Dreyer (1889–1968) remained working in Europe – which is maybe why he acquired the most renown. Since his later films are uniformly terrible, it is pleasant to find the early ones so good. He began in films writing intertitles for Nordisk, and progressed via the writing of scenarios to directing. His second film survives, **Leaves from Satan's Book** (1920), an examination in four episodes of the compulsion of Satan to manifest himself as a representation of the State against the individual. It moves from the Passion to sixteenth-century Seville to Revolutionary France to Helsinki just after the Russian Revolution, and if clearly influenced by *Intolerance* its great superiority is in its point of view, to be expected in a director who looked to Sjöström and Stiller for guidance: Satan's tools turn out to be good but sexually frustrated young men whose ambitions enable them to fulfil their sexual desires. Dreyer's debt to Sjöström is even clearer in **The Parson's Widow** (1920), in fact made in Sweden – for Magnusson – though set in Norway, a rather sweet but gallumphing comedy about the new parson (Einar Rød) and the elderly widow (Hildur Carlberg) he is required by tradition to marry. If Dreyer lacks Sjöström's insight into the tensions of a rural community, his picture of a drunken, lecherous priest is often funny, and there is much tenderness towards the end. **Once Upon a Time** (1922) is considerably less interesting than the German films (q.v.) he made on either side of it, though to judge from the hour-plus which survives it is not notably inferior to the Hollywood fairy-stories of the period. Dreyer's last Danish Silent (there was another in Norway) is **Master of the House** (1925), a study of a tyrannical paterfamilias, carefully and honestly done, but confirming that he was less interested in people than in strips of film – which is fatal to such slight domestic tales. It was a failure everywhere but France, which was why he was invited there to make *La Passion de Jeanne d'Arc* (q.v.).

He did not thenceforward have a lucrative career, and indeed by the beginning of Talkies the Scandinavian cinema was no longer a force in world cinema, and its achievements were already forgotten. Victor Sjöström can now be seen to tower over his contemporaries, holding at perfect balance the epic and the everyday; he had only images in which to express the thoughts, emotions, motivations and ideas of humanity, and he used them with genius. He left a tradition in Swedish cinema which, after a couple of bare decades, brought forth a worthy successor, Ingmar Bergman.

4

Germany in the Twenties: Shadows, Poverty and Prostitutes

IT IS impossible to overestimate the effect of the post-war German cinema on the intelligentsia of other countries. The Swedish cinema was immediately overshadowed: only four of Sjöström's films were shown in the U.S., and of these *The Phantom Carriage* had to wait till *The New York Times* had lamented its absence from American screens. That journal did not review *Sir Arne's Treasure*, but did, after some weeks, print a eulogy by a lady troubled at its neglect, and described as 'instructor in photoplay composition at Columbia University'. Such films were not thought accessible to the great American public – which had, said D. W. Griffith, 'the mentality of a child nine years old': and it was precisely *not* for that mentality, said *The New York Times,* that Lubitsch was making films. Its critic was reviewing his *Anna Boleyn* (q.v.), and a few months later he expressed the general view in reviewing the 1920 version of *The Golem,* 'the latest motion picture to have come from the explorative innovators of Germany'. Swedish films were too slow for American audiences; later, fear of the propaganda content of Soviet films would prevent their reaching American screens; but Germany always had a hearing – thanks in the first place, to Lubitsch and *Caligari* (q.v.). The Lubitsch spectacles were popular; *Caligari* and the other wrongly-labelled 'expressionist' films were admired out of all proportion to their worth: the Lubitsch films were historical, and the others equally respectable, with their connections to the theatre and modern art movements – and certainly the German film-makers were both exploratory and innovatory. The

German cinema thus offered in tandem biographies of historical figures and an enquiry into the nature of film and its possibilities for the fantastic, neither of relevance to a country deep in the grip of inflation – and both traditions were arriving at a dead end as the Soviet cinema exploded, and changed the concept of film. The German cinema reflected that change but slowly, though it eventually, towards the end of the decade, began to record contemporary life with vividness: Berlin of the Twenties, much written about, is also available on film.

In 1912, Berlin theatre managers had formally forbidden their artist to work in films, but the money and acclaim reaped by Asta Nielsen eventually caused the injunction to be ignored. The still-lively Danish and the equally thrusting Swedish cinema provided virtually the only foreign films available during the War, though the home industry had proved at least once able to make a film of serious appeal: *Der Student von Prag* (1913), directed by Paul Wegener, a tale of a young man who trades his soul with the devil, as borrowed from several sources. Wegener himself was a former Reinhardt actor with a strong sense of the fantastic; two years later, he made *Der Golem,* based on Czech-Jewish folklore, but this time owing something – the conception of the monster – to Mary Shelley's 'Frankenstein'. Neither film has survived, but we know them from their remakes: **Der Golem** (1920), made by Wegener and the same collaborator, Henrik Galeen, and **Der Student von Prag** (1926), directed by Galeen alone. In

75

Paul Wegener's second version of *Der Golem* was one of the first films to establish Germany as a force in the international cinema: one reason was its visual quality, and the photographer was Karl Freund, then at the start of his innovatory career – to end ignominiously in the U.S. as cameraman on 'I Love Lucy' for television.

this *Golem* the demand for magic is met at every occasion, due in part to the photography of Karl Freund: the *Student* is mainly notable for the performance of Conrad Veidt, ever-reliable as a haunted or obsessed creature – and in the title-role he is required to be both as so often in his career.

The first German film-makers came from the theatre, but unlike other early practitioners, they were successful theatre people – which is perhaps why they regarded cinema as an extension of that art form. Pre-eminent among them was Max Reinhardt (1873 – 1943), the dominant figure in German theatre, and though he directed only four films during this period his work in both mediums was the major influence for a number of years. Since he was renowned for his mounting of spectacles, the idea that the theatre was an arena for social realism was a long time catching on, at least south of the Baltic, and there was no urgency in applying it to films; but if the theatre was for drama and spectacle, well, that could best be expounded in films as fantasy – which

anyway seemed more suitable for an audience increasingly unhappy with reality. During the War the German government wanted the cinema for a third purpose: the effect of anti-German propaganda films made by the Allies had not been lost on the Kaiser's ministers, who in 1917 encouraged and part-capitalised the amalgamation of the leading companies as Universum-Film-Aktiengesellschaft, but known familiarly as Ufa. Thus this unexpected combination of official endorsement and intellectual responsibility created a cinema of competing interests, but they miraculously crossbred and coalesced – fantasy, realism and propaganda – to form a national school as strong and individual as that of Sweden.

The American cinema with its dramas of the West had created a 'national' image, but beyond a certain brash optimism, most of its product could have originated in London or Paris. For the first time in the history of the world, a popular 'literature' knew no boundaries – as the first film-makers had discovered; and for economic reasons their successors preferred to work with the international market in mind. Where there were fewer expectations of this market, as in Sweden and Germany, their films were more characteristic of their origin, and thus more highly valued – then and now. They reflected the native drama and literature, past and present; Faustian themes recur, and other echoes of the neo-Gothic, including the dichotomy of fate and chance; and a conception of the little man as a cog in the machinery of state. There was also the obsession with uniforms and/or authority, with policemen and/or cavalry officers as protectors of established order; in defeat, the government lost interest in propaganda, but the creative film-maker seized the chance to instruct and sway public opinion – and in the bewildering, changing political climate any reminder of authority was more welcome than ever. All these elements are to be found in the early films of Ernst Lubitsch, the most brilliant of the German directors, and the first to demonstrate to the world the vitality of his country's films. However, since his aim was to amuse and satirise, he cannot be said to be typical; but like his colleagues, he used at first frankly theatrical settings while exploring the plastic resources of the medium. By the time he went out into the streets and fields to shoot, he had conceived his film as an artistic entity, its visual quality balanced against the narrative. As basically theatre-people, the possibilities of decor absorbed this generation of German film-makers, and, filtered through such designs, the expressionist painters and their themes provided another influence. The themes of Dix, Schlichter, Beckmann, Grosz, Hubbuch, etc., had found their way into films before the reaction against expressionism – that movement called the *neue sachlichkeit* or the new realism; but it was the taste for theatrical excess which led to the Oriental subjects and the historical dramas. Those were the films which established the supremacy of the German 'art' film, regarded by contemporaries with far more awe and respect than the pure cinema of Sjöström or pieces like *Assunta Spina*. Art, history, literature: any film with a smattering of these – the more theatrically presented the better – could command attention, and it wasn't till the Russians worked exclusively within film that the intelligentsia 'saw' differently.

Ernst Lubitsch (1892–1947) had also worked for Reinhardt as an actor. Born in Berlin, he made a mild mark in films as a comic Jew – and if we find his beaked-nose craftiness unsympathetic, we must admit that that was the way Jewish actors edged into films and theatre at that time. His first two films to survive are both features, **Der Stolz der Firma** (1914), directed by Carl Wilhelm, and **Schuhpalast Pinkus** (1916), directed by himself, and they have virtually identical stories: in both by sheer *chutzpah* he rises from the most humble position in the store to the chief one, marrying respectively the boss's daughter and his benefactress. The former has a notable finale in which the Lubitsch of the first reel meets the Lubitsch of the last, underlining the differences in conduct and appearance and hence the advancement it is possible for a Jew to make; the second has what may be the first example of 'the Lubitsch touch', by which a narrative point is made both visually and wittily – in this case an idle

staff indicating the Lubitsch-character's (temporary) lack of success. He continued to play this character till 1919, admitting that it was its lack of success with the public which caused him to think of himself as solely a director. For the moment it was as comedy director: both **Ein Fideles Gefängnis** (1917) and **Wenn Vier Dasselbe Tun** (1917) are foreshadowings of the work for which he is remembered – witty examinations of the war between the sexes. The first of these is an adaptation of 'Réveillon', which he would film again as *So This is Paris?* (q.v.), with some of the same elaborate sight gags; *Wenn Vier Dasselbe Tun* concerns parallel romances between Ossi Oswalda – a rubber-jointed young lady who worked in many of his films – and a young poet, and between her father (Emil Jannings) and the poet's spinster boss. But Lubitsch's boss at Ufa, Paul Davidson, wanted him to try drama, and assigned him to **Die Augen der Mummie Mâ** (1918), to star Pola Negri (b. 1894), who had appeared with Lubitsch in Reinhardt's pantomime-ballet, *Sumurun*. Her forte was exotic dancing, and thus she played a temple dancer taken to Europe by a painter (Harry Liedtke), and pursued there by a vengeful priest (Jannings). According to Hans Kräly, its scenarist (and Lubitsch's chief collaborator from 1916 to the end of the Silent period), it was the first film drama taken seriously by the German press; but to us it is merely another daft melodrama, except for its glimpses of the salons and galleries of the era. It was another drama, **Carmen** (1918), which made the reputations of Lubitsch and Pola Negri throughout Europe, and though we may just see why contemporaries admired her Carmen ('wild, amoral, capricious, savage, brazenly independent, impulsive, cruel and passionate', said Theodore Huff, which is at least three adjectives too many), it is impossible to find the lightness of Lubitsch's other films of this time.

The first sustained, full-length demonstration of his skill is **Die Austernprinzessin** (1919), the tale of an American tycoon's daughter (Miss Oswalda) who determines to marry a prince and finds through a marriage agency a particularly bankrupt one (Liedtke). Lubitsch aims many a shaft at capitalists and royalty, and is particularly bright (as he would ever be) on court ritual; he is also funny but very much in favour of such matters as sexual attraction and nights on the town. **Die Puppe** (1919) is a companion burlesque, about a puppeteer's mischievous daughter (Oswalda) who impersonates one of her father's life-size dolls in order to marry a baron's nephew (Hermann Thimig). The theme is from Hoffmann, and its treatment heavy, but the humour is much less Germanic than the more acceptable **Ich Möchte Kein Mann Sein** (1919 ; released 1921), a farce about transvestism – and one which probably explores the subject more than any film hitherto. The spectacle of the tuxedoed heroine (Oswalda) being sick on a cigar or kissed by her guardian (Victor Janson) cannot amuse audiences as they once did, but the whole has an urbanity that we recognise by now as typically Lubitsch. Conversely, **Romeo und Julia im Schnee** (1920) and **Kolhiesels Töchter** (1920) are both bucolic romps, heavily dependent on their observation of (Bavarian) village mores and manners. Both themes are from Shakespeare, inasmuch as *Kolhiesels Töchter* is a part reworking of 'The Taming of the Shrew'. The success of that, however, is due almost entirely to Henny Porten in the dual role of the pretty sister and her plain, shrewish one – she was in the remake of 1930, and there was another in 1943, suggesting an abiding German amusement in ox-like farmhands, village idiots and their assorted frauleins. These still-delightful films were considered too parochial for foreign audiences, but then so was **Die Bergkatze** (1921), Lubitsch's one German masterpiece. It was also an anti-militarist satire, and the Germans were not in the mood for that, at least as it applied to them – which Lubitsch sensed, and therefore had Ernest Stern from the theatre design expressionist sets which beautifully mingled with snowy locations. But the film nevertheless was a failure. A robber's daughter (Negri) falls in love with a vain and dilettante lieutenant (Paul Heidemann), and vows to steal him from the fort and from under the eyes of the pompous commander (Victor Janson) who plans

to marry him to his daughter. The cavorting of the robbers has some funny knockabout, but is as nothing to the sharp portrait of the regimented ritual of the fort; and there is a marvellous example of the Lubitsch touch, inevitably with a door, when the daughter looks through the keyhole at the unclad lieutenant, and is pushed away by her mother, neither of them anxious to let the vision go. Alone, this film puts paid to any suggestion that Lubitsch was later bowled over by *A Woman of Paris* (q.v.) – responsibility for which rests with Herman G. Weinberg, who in his book on Lubitsch quotes Chaplin as claiming his 'was the first film to articulate irony and psychology'; Weinberg himself finds the remark only 'partly true', citing in exchange *Die Bergkatze*, *Die Austernprinzessin* and *Die Flamme* – which suggests that he hasn't seen any of them for years. Lubitsch's two extant films have far more irony and psychology than Chaplin's, and we may suppose as much of *Die Flamme* (1922), from the fifteen-minute fragment which remains. As a study of a marriage – in a Montmartre 'artistic' milieu – it would seem to be comparable to the films of Sjöström and Stiller which inspired it, and hence with irony and psychology much in advance of Chaplin's.

Certainly contemporary critics found these qualities in the historical films which were making Lubitsch very famous indeed. The European success of **Madame Dubarry** (1919) persuaded First National to buy it – for $40,000. Rechristened *Passion*, its origin hidden under the banner 'A European Spectacle', and the names of all concerned suppressed except that of Miss Negri, 'the famous continental star', it took the U.S. by storm, temporarily breaking the Hollywood dominance. 'One of the preeminent motion pictures of the present cinematograph age,' said *The New York Times*, also impressed by the way the Dubarry's 'simply sordid' affairs were 'weaved' into the setting, and by the handling of the Revolution, 'never so vividly portrayed'. The characterisations, if rudimentary, remain amusing: a Dubarry who wants to have her cake and eat it – the lot of all royal mistresses in cinema, always good-natured and guileless (which the original in this case was not); a Louis xv (Jannings) of fish-like complacency, which is as good a way as any of summarising the Bourbons; and a villain, Choiseul (Reinhold Schunzel), who happily recalls Tito Gobbi's Scarpia. It was the lighthearted treatment of these characters which so excited admiration, and we may think it civilised of the Germans in 1919 to take this view of their recent enemy: it was liked by Alfred Hugenberg not only because his huge investment in Ufa paid dividends, but because he was a fervent nationalist. So, since he considered it anti-French, he suggested an anti-English movie, also about the loves of a monarch: **Anna Boleyn** (1920), with Fraulein Porten in the title-role and Jannings as Heinrich VIII. It is at its best and worst with wholly invented matters: at its worst with Princess Maria publicly insulting Anna at her Coronation, and at its best when Heinrich disappears into the bushes with Anna to look for a tennis-ball. That's the Lubitsch touch for you, and surely the reason *The New York Times* wondered, 'Did he ever work in Paris or Vienna?' Today, there is virtually nothing to hold a modern audience, though it does have a point or two to make on the caprices of kings, and the viciousness of court life.

It has, however, more to it than has **Sumurun** (1920), Reinhardt's old (1908) Arabian Nights show, filmed by Lubitsch with visual elegance and very little else. We may wonder what audiences saw in all these Oriental junketings; this one did at least provide a vehicle for Negri, and a plum role for Lubitsch (his last acting job) as the hunchback clown in love with her. There was also for him, perhaps, the sense of competition, since Hollywood had already recently offered several similar films. With **Das Weib des Pharao** (1921) we had a scenario by Norbert Falk and Kräly that plunders from 'The Iliad' – though the setting is Egypt, with again a certain amount of borrowing (the crowd and battle scenes) from *Intolerance*. Jannings is the Pharaoh, and as with his other monarchs for Lubitsch he is a complete despot but not a complete tyrant, perhaps to be redeemed by love for the slave-girl

(Dagy Servaes). The film was in its time overwhelming; the only version now available is a reconstructed one, with some sequences curtailed or missing – yet it is much more impressive than any other primitive spectacle, including Lang's *Nibelungen* (q.v.).

Since the American press had freely referred to Lubitsch as a genius, it was only a matter of time before he went to Hollywood; meanwhile, his erstwhile colleagues laboured on in the historical literary field. Chief among them, in that respect, was the Russian-Polish Dimitri Buchowetzki, whose **Danton** (1921) and **Othello** (1922) were particularly admired: both simplify to a degree of absurdity, both use grandiose settings as if to reduce their characters to puppets, and both use a number of imaginative camera angles. They are notable for the acting partnership of Jannings, in the title-roles, and Werner Krauss, as Robespierre and Iago respectively. Jannings, inclined to give his all, is seldom effective in sympathetic or heroic roles – but since he could be seen to be acting, with 'weight' and with a number of disguises, he was the Twenties' idea of a great actor. Krauss managed make-up with genius, even suggesting changes in his flat moon-face via small twists in eye-brows, lashes and side-hair; he disappeared inside his characterisations,

The fame of Lubitsch's historical spectacles far overshadowed his other German films, a series of still-sparkling comedies. *Die Bergkatze* handled sex in that visually witty way which became known as 'The Lubitsch touch'; but its chief aim was to poke fun at the military, which it does with a mixture of wild slapstick and razor-sharp satire.

never chancing a bravura note. He was a consummate film actor, one of the wonders of the German Silent cinema – and his single-expressioned, single-minded villains are the best features of these two films.

Another Shakespeare, **Hamlet** (1920), remains one of the best known of this series, partly because Asta Nielsen plays the title-role. You didn't know Hamlet was a girl? There is more than that here to startle scholars, but to be fair the sources also include Danish legends and a German play, 'Fratricide Unpunished': for reasons of state the heiress to the throne has been brought up a boy, and she has conceived a hopeless passion for Horatio. Dying, she gets that longed-for kiss from him, as his wandering hand encounters a breast: 'Death reveals thy tragic secret,' he says. Sven Gade and Heinz Schall directed, for Miss Nielsen's own company. She is more interestingly employed in **Vanina** (1922), as the governor's daughter who plots against her father for the sake of her rebel-lover. As the governor, Paul Wegener goes beyond cruelty to sadism, and this doom-laden tale is also helped immeasurably by Walter Reimann's huge, dark craggy sets; the last, long, futile escape from the prison is one of the finest sequences from this era, as directed by Arthur von Gerlach and written – from Stendhal's novel – by Carl Mayer (1894–1944), the most imaginative of the German scenarists.

The literary and historical genres – never far apart – come together in **Carlos und Elizabeth** (1924), a version of Schiller directed by Richard Oswald with Conrad Veidt as an ambiguous but reasonably healthy Don Carlos. His quarrels with his father (Eugen Klöpfer) are set against huge flats, ornate only in detail, but Oswald otherwise worked in the *kammerspiel* tradition, usually reserved for emotional tales of the lowly.

Richard Oswald (1880–1963) was an eclectic film-maker. Born in Vienna and a former actor, his first films include a *Hoffmanns Erzählungen* (1916) and *Es Werde Licht* (1917), a study of syphilis, which achieved respectability by being sponsored by the official society organised to combat such illness. Venereal disease was a preoccupation of the War government, and Oswald was encouraged to add a second and third part to *Es Wirde Licht*; when the post-war government abolished censorship he added a fourth part. The German film industry accelerated its output on sexual matters, and Oswald made *Die Prostitution* (1919) and what was probably the first film on homosexuality, **Anders Als die Andern** (1919). The theme of the latter is spelt out in detail: unless Paragraph 175 of the Penal Code is repealed, there will be more suicides like that of the famous violinist (Conrad Veidt). It is a simple film: the acting is elementary and the set-ups obvious and few; homosexuality is denoted by a caress on the cheek, a hand on the hip, by men doing the two-step at a *thé-dansant*; and the story tells briefly of a chance-meeting at one such, the subsequent blackmail and hence ruin both of career and friendship with a student. The film was unpopular; today it strikes us as unremarkable, sympathetic, and a good deal more forthright than more recent films on this subject. The realities of life in the Weimar Republic may also be found in **Der Reigen** (1920), based on a play by Schnitzler that we know best as *La Ronde* (q.v.) – though you wouldn't recognise it from this version. Asta Nielsen has her familiar role, a girl wronged by society: up the ladder and down again, waifdom to kept woman, to mistress of the mansion, to prostitution, singularly unlucky in the men she meets (they include Herr Veidt), but when she pleads with the one man she loves to take her away, it is clear that she is a woman of her time, completely dependent on men. Without money, references or a man to support her she has only one way to support herself: that other alternatives do not immediately occur to the viewer is a measure of Oswald's persuasive handling. His Silents also include *Lady Hamilton* (1921), *Lucrezia Borgia* (1922), *Cagliostro* (1928), and a version of Wedekind's *Fruhlings Erwachen*; his Sound films, coincidentally, are mainly remakes: *Alraune* (1930), *Unheimliche Geschichten* (q.v.), a version of his 1919 horror story; *Tempête sur l'Asie* (1938), in France; and *I was a Criminal* (1942) in the U.S. as well as a version of Zuckmayer's *Der Haupt-*

mann von Köpenick (1931), which he made before fleeing the Nazis.

The Danish Carl Dreyer also attempted a film on homosexuality, **Michael** (1924) – though unlike Oswald's film, the word is never mentioned and we are left to guess the exact relationship of the painter (Benjamin Christensen) and his adopted son (Walter Slezak). The taste of the time may have dictated discretion, but the combination of subtlety and ambiguity, conscious or not, puts the film far ahead of its time, not least at the end, when the unexplained absence of protégé from the painter's deathbed is followed by an image of Woman as predator. The original novel was by Herman Bang, who was homosexual; and a knowledge of Berlin's artistic circles was clearly being utilised by the production team – Dreyer and Thea von Harbou (writers), Karl Freund (photographer) and Erich Pommer

(producer). The stimulus of his co-workers must have contributed to Dreyer's making in Berlin by far his two best films – both made with an untypical passion, and committed to tolerance of minorities. **Die Geseichneten** (1922) means approximately 'The Marked Ones' and it refers to the Jews; it is taken from a long novel by Aage Madelung, and was filmed in Germany both because resources were not available in Denmark, and there was in Berlin a large number of Russian émigrés, many of whom play leading roles. By Dreyer's own admission the novel was too long, and the compression is inadequate: but like *Leaves from Satan's Book*, it also has ideas. It offers brief portraits of ghetto life and life in St Petersburg, and we learn much of motivation: snobbery, prejudice, envy, superstition – none of them well expressed, but comprising a wider spectrum than love, hatred and

Those who know Carl Dreyer only from his later work may be surprised at the excellence of his early films, including *Michael*, the study of a homosexual artist and his protégé. The artistic milieu of Berlin is such a strong feature of many German films of the early Twenties that we may suppose it a strong influence on them – as well as being the opposite, as here, of the accepted Bohemian conception.

81

The coming to power of the Nazi party swept away most of the fine directors who were not already in Hollywood. Their fates would be various, and that of E.A. Dupont one of the saddest, to judge from the occasional poverty–row 'B' flicks he directed in the Fifties; in between-whiles he had owned a magazine and an actors' agency. He is remembered best for *Varieté*, but *Das Alte Gesetz* is altogether the more remarkable – a sensitive dual study of Jewish and theatrical life in the last century.

lust, the then-staples of movies. Both of Dreyer's films, like those of Oswald's, try for a whole range of human emotions set against a recognisable society.

As much may be said of **Das Alte Gesetz** (1923), directed by E.A. Dupont (1891–1956), a former film critic who entered films as a writer for Oswald, circa 1916. He directed his first film a year later, and though most of them are missing, this one – regardless of the later ones – establishes him as a master. It takes one Baruch (Ernst Deutsch) from the Vienna ghetto of the 1860s to supremacy as an actor, and whether dealing with Jewish life or life backstage, Dupont's evocation of the past is on a par with Sjöström's. It behoves me to say that films so bound to an ethnic cause did, eventually, prove dangerous. Did the Jews of the German film industry flaunt their Jewishness? At all events this portrait of what it was like for their parents' generation is an extremely valuable one.

Needless to say, it achieved nothing of the renown of a piece of theatrical arty-crafty called **Das Kabinett des Doktor Caligari** (1920), and, indeed, that is for many people *the* film classic. It was, says Lewis Jacobs, 'seen by comparatively few people, [but] it was nevertheless the most widely discussed

film of the time'. For a reviewer in *Exceptional Photoplays* it was 'a revelation and a challenge . . . a revelation of what the motion picture is capable of as a form of artistic expression. It challenges the public to appreciate it and the producer to learn from it.' Its producer, Eric Pommer (1889–1966), later said that he snapped up the scenario because mystery stories were popular, but its writers said they took it to him because he was a producer more adventurous than most. They were Carl Mayer, an Austrian, and Hans Janowitz, a Czech, who had based their scenario on a bizarre Hamburg murder case; to direct it Pommer brought from the theatre a man without film experience, Robert Wiene, and he gave the art direction to his own team, Walter Röhrig, Herman Warm and Walter Reimann. They used abstract sets as a matter of expediency, since there were government restrictions on power and lighting – but their distinctive style was not what the writers had had in mind.

The theatre was already tinkering with Expressionism, and thus, because of its sets, *Caligari* was linked both to culture and to the avant-garde. Within the film there is a cut-out of the somnambulist-villain which looks less like him than like Munch's painting *The Cry*: as Expressionism was a statement on emotional darkness, so was this film. It is, indeed, 'about' madness – and it arrived at a time when Freud's studies in psychology were required reading for the intelligentsia – but it is not Expressionist at all: it is Surrealist, and then only at an elementary level. Sets in the *manner* of the Expressionists cannot change the subject-matter, and perhaps only an animated cartoon could create a truly Expressionist film, i.e. one whose method of telling leads directly to its meaning, its central emotion. These sets and make-up reek disconcertingly of the theatre, and are not sufficiently imaginative to provide a lingering atmospheric charm. At its best, we are in the world of Poe – though we may feel we're watching a bad production of 'Petrushka' when Dr Caligari (Krauss) invites the crowd to watch the re-awakening of a dead man (Conrad Veidt, with black-ringed eyes and baggy black tights). The succeeding Grand Guignol events include pursuit into a madhouse, whose chief turns out to be Caligari, plus a final revelation that the whole thing is a tale told by idiots. The film is genuinely a Chinese cabinet, and it is easy to see why it was so much admired: but it was a one-of-a-kind thing, since there would only be one film which turned out to be the ravings of a madman – though there have been many films which turned out to be dreams.

That other ways than painted sets were needed to take us into private worlds was apparently proved by Wiene's *Genuine* (1920), an immediate failure. Despite their reservations about the *Caligari* sets, Mayer and Janowitz had provided the story, about a bloodthirsty vamp who drives men to ruin. Andrei Andreyev designed the sets for **Raskolnikov** (1923), and they are not inappropriate to the guilt-haunted fantasies of Dostoevsky's hero, though the film as a whole is dusty. In Vienna, still involved with horror, Wiene made **Orlacs Hande** (1924), based on a novel by Maurice Renard about a pianist (Veidt) who wakes after an accident to find that the donor of his hands-transplant was a convicted murderer, and suffers consequent twitchings whenever he holds a knife. This promising idea is indifferently handled, with a disappointed denouement as Orlac's behaviour becomes increasingly imbecilic; and as Fritz Kortner's acting is as absurd as Veidt's we may blame the director, a good example of the 'one-film' man.

The success of *Caligari* spawned a hundred imitations – that is films with weird, painted sets. Mayer wrote **Torgus** (1921), directed by Hanns Kobe, a sad tale of a weak young man who allows his aunt (Adele Sandrock) to separate him from his true love, the mother of his baby: the Icelandic setting and the Golem-like presence of the coffin-maker Torgus (Klöpfer) help the mood of gloom, but the sets neither add nor detract from the story. In fact, the public tired so quickly of expressionism that many of these films were not released, and until recently **Von Morgens bis Mitternacht** (1920) was seen only in Japan: from one point of view, it is the most important of the series – more

important than *Caligari*, since both its writer and director were established expressionists before that film was even thought of. Indeed, Georg Kaiser was considered the foremost expressionist dramatist, and as a play this had been done in 1918; the film's director and co-scenarist was Karl-Heinz Martin. Like *Caligari*, it is depressingly determined to be art: there are unreal sets, a complete absence of intertitles, and all the female roles are played by the same actress, Roma Bahn. The original was worth telling in straightforward manner – a portrait of a man (Ernst Deutsch) at the end of his tether. His symbols are those of the graphic artists – champagne-bottle, lamplight, whore, lurking death – and his odyssey from embezzlement and flight to the maelstrom of the night-city would be echoed by every other German film to the end of the Weimar Republic.

Meanwhile, the industry continued to deal with the grotesque and fantastic, and since the current mood for escapism was of pessimistic turn a number of interesting talents were attracted. Fritz Lang made **Der Müde Tod** (1921) – ennobled into *Destiny* in its English version, and in fact the struggle against destiny would be a recurring theme in his work. This primitive, operatic work concerns a woman (Lil Dagover) who consults Death when her lover (Walter Janssen) disappears, and is offered him back if she can prevent three deaths – in old Baghdad, Renaissance Venice and Ancient China. The film is enhanced by a compendium of camera tricks (Douglas Fairbanks bought the rights, in order to use them in *The Thief of Bagdad*, q.v.); and F.W. Murnau offered several in **Nosferatu, Eine Symphonie des Grauens** (1922). Some of Fritz Arno Wagner's images still startle, and the fearsome Count (Max Schreck) follows the tradition already set for movie monsters, grotesque-pathetic; but overall this tale of demonic possession – it is a pirated version by Henrik Galeen of Bram Stoker's 'Dracula' – remains powerful.

Wagner also photographed Arthur Robison's **Schatten** (1923), an attempt to tell a psychological tale entirely in terms of shadows, reflections, lights, silhouettes and what-have-you. The story concerns a jealous husband (Kortner), his wife's admirers, and the mesmerist (Alexander Granach) who makes them act out their thoughts: amidst ponderous direction and absurd acting it arrives ·at a banal ending. Its supernatural reasoning is entirely in keeping with others of its kind, and, like them, it is set in the past: this may be because the mesmerist is culled from the tales of E. T. A. Hoffman, but confirms an obsession with the neo-Gothic.

To Siegfried Kracauer, in 'From Caligari to Hitler', it was 'this extraordinary drama', but then to him one of 'the greatest achievements of film art' was the final sequence of **Das Wachsenfigurenkabinett** (1924). This film of Paul Leni (1885–1929) is in three parts, as dreamed up by a poet (Wilhelm Dieterle) in a carnival waxworks. The first is a lumbering comic anecdote about a lecherous Haroun al-Raschid (Jannings) and a baker's wife; the second is a sinister, inconclusive yarn involving Ivan the Terrible (Veidt) and a young bride; and the third a bit of brimstone about Jack the Ripper (Krauss). Money had run out by the time they reached the Ripper, and Leni, a former designer, abandoned Galeen's script to improvise – with superimpositions, multiple images, shadows and back-lighting. It is still effective, and proof of Leni's talent for the medium: but hardly worth enduring the rest of it for.

Leni's film, along with some of these other grotesqueries – *Caligari*, *Der Müde Tod*, *Nosferatu* and *Schatten* (rechristened *Warning Shadows*) – helped establish the artistic supremacy of the German cinema among foreign cineastes. *Nosferatu* is the only one amongst them to use wholly natural settings, and is indeed the least tainted by the shadow of the theatre. F. W. Murnau (1889–1931) was an alumnus of Reinhardt, but from the evidence of his few surviving early films he was immediately aware of the cinematic possibilities of his medium; among contemporary German critics, he was more widely regarded than any of his colleagues, and often called a poet. His inspiration was avowedly the cinema of Sjöström and Stiller, as we may see from his seventh film, and the first to survive, **Der Gang**

in die Nacht (1920). Carl Mayer wrote it, from a treatment by Harriet Bloch, a popular writer of the Danish cinema, and it concerns an eminent doctor (Olaf Fonss) who abandons his fiancée for a dancer, only to lose the latter to a blind painter (Conrad Veidt) after he has retired to a seaside village. The plethora of shots of the sea suggest the Scandinavian models, and Willy Haas, the critic of the *Film Kurier*, observed that the film reminded him of Ibsen; Haas also paid Murnau the great compliment of observing that he was unable to see where the director took over from the writer. Haas helped write **Der Brennende Acker** (1922) for Murnau, made after an indifferent thriller, *Schloss Vogelöd* (1921), and here again the Scandinavian influence is very strong. The protagonist is a proud, ambitious man (Wladimir Gaidarow), who becomes secretary to a Count and moves his affections from the Count's daughter (Lya de Putti) to his young, second wife (Stella Arbenina) when he realises that the latter will inherit the greater fortune, a field under which lies a huge petrol reserve. The film begins dully, but becomes involving as the young man's machinations become clearer: as in Sjöström, however, motives may remain a matter of conjecture.

Unanimous praise greeted this film, but the much superior **Phantom** (1922) was not liked: based on a novel by Gerhard Hauptmann, it was released to coincide with his sixtieth birthday celebrations and was generally considered superficial. To an extent it is just another Silent melodrama, with over-gesticulated acting and a plot founded on impossible situations. The hero (Alfred Abel) is, like so many in German films at the time, haunted and buffeted by fate: yet in the midst of clichés and conventions is a quite remarkable film. Murnau is no longer under the influence of Sjöström, and though he lacks the latter's penetration, he is far more imaginative. Lorenz is taken by a dual fancy, of becoming a famous poet and marrying a wealthy girl in the town: obsessed by her, he meets her double (Lya de Putti), daughter of an impoverished Baroness, and in paying suit to her he is financed by his aunt (Grete Berger). The interesting characters are this aunt, and her fancy-man (Anton Edthofer) – and it is he who manipulates Lorenz, leading him to his doom – and the little town itself, with its cabarets and wide squares. Murnau's use of figures in his settings is more advanced than any of his contemporaries, and his fantasies – notably when Lorenz dreams of his beloved or imagines that the town is literally falling on him – remain extraordinary.

Die Finanzen des Grossherzogs (1923) pleased contemporary German critics as being one of the few domestic films without pretensions to signficance, but Murnau himself disliked it, and we would certainly side with him. Photographed along the Dalmatian coast, it tells of a penniless Grande Duke (Harry Liedtke), the moneylender who helps to overthrow him and the Russian Grand Duchess (Mady Christians) who elects to marry him. It is clear that Murnau intended burlesque, and the piece indicates an extension of his talent: but it is no preparation for the film which made his international reputation, **Der Letzte Mann** (1924). It also made the reputation of Mayer, who wrote this story of a hotel porter (Jannings) stripped of his livery and demoted to lavatory attendant – a fact that he manages to keep from the neighbours – until rehabilitated by a wealthy American who has used the facilities: an epilogue which has been disowned by certain admirers and improbably explained away as a satire on happy endings. The critical réclame was due to the absence (again!) of intertitles, but its chief achievement is Murnau's virtuoso balancing of three rare enough elements – the authoritative (if monotonous)) performance of Jannings, and, more importantly, the probing cinematography of Karl Freund and Mayer's simple scenario. As a team, they seemed unmoved by the film's reception the world over, since **Tartüff** (1925) breaks new ground neither in subject-matter nor style – unless we include setting Molière's play (or what is left of it, since most of the characters have gone) as a film within a film. The framework – a disinherited heir shows his grandfather a film to point out the hypocrisy of his housekeeper – is dark, harsh, realistic; the 'flashback' is light and fanciful, with visual effects such as the extinguishing of the wasteful candles and the repeated image of the bulky but thin-legged Tartuffe with

Emil Jannings and Lya de Putti in Dupont's *Varieté*, which raised foreign audiences 'to a white heat of enthusiasm', in the words of Lewis Jacobs. Its 'realism' persuaded people that it offered a greater insight into the matter of adultery than Hollywood's seemingly more trivial triangle dramas.

a book to his nose. In that role Jannings comes close to genius, never venturing beyond the pious and haughty till transformed into a grinning drunken lecher, when he's very funny. As Orgon, Krauss has little to do but look fond and/or credulous. Contemporary reception centred on these two performances, but since *Der Letzte Mann* had made Murnau one of the world's most eagerly watched film-makers, he planned and came up with **Faust** (1926). The opening and the first thirty minutes are the most triumphantly visual of all Silent movies, as the forces of light and darkness argue and look down on our earth. Later it moves to, shall we say, the level of Gounod. In Germany it was unappreciated; the country at that point was not interested in 'Faustian problems' says Kracauer, dismissing it as 'another Ufa superproduction': but abroad its magic was recognised.

Dupont's **Varieté** (1925) was also photographed by Freund, and also based on a simple premise: a small-time trapeze artist (Jannings) is stung to revenge when he discovers that his wife (Lya de Putti) is unfaithful with the star (Warwick Ward) they have taken into partnership. Dupont had embraced the *neue sachlichkeit*, and the film is flawlessly done, from the razzmatazz of the music hall milieu to the details of the couple's squalid little room; and he used these with the appurtenances of the expressionists – the superimpositions, the camera-angles, the lighting. The combination was a winning one for foreign audiences; retitled *Vaudeville* its success abroad eclipsed even that of *Madame Dubarry*.

Faust was of such prestige that it was initially shown in Britain at the Royal Albert Hall, 'presented' by C. B. Cochran and 'edited and titled' by Arnold Bennett. During the same season, Pommer's first American film was shown – and the ads for *Hotel Imperial* (q.v.) featured his name in equal size to that of the star, adding, 'Germany's greatest film genius of *Vaudeville* fame'. As the fame of these films echoed round the world, their makers followed – as far as Hollywood. Lubitsch had been there for some years: Murnau went, and Dupont, Freund and Pommer, as well as Jannings, Negri and Veidt. It has been claimed that Pommer was the great force behind this burst of creativity, which may be true; but there was also much inter-stimulation and discovery between a group of people who cared for the medium; there was 'something in the air' (as George Cukor said of Hollywood at the time of *Citizen Kane*), and certainly it did not die with the defection of the leading artists. Pommer's sojourn in Hollywood was brief, and he returned to produce some more notable films for Ufa – but not again to any degree either influential and seminal; and if his were the creative juices which fed this period, they were drying up by the early Thirties. The most immediately influential was Freund, and the distinctive Ufa-style lighting was a commonplace in movies for at least ten years.

Ufa itself was in a bad way. Its films may have achieved international fame, but many – *Der Letzte Mann* and certainly *Metropolis* (q.v.) – lost a great deal of money. In 1925 the company approached Hollywood for support, and Zukor of Paramount and Marcus Loew both loaned $2 millions. Ironically, the American companies were at the root of the trouble, since with the re-establishment of the gold standard they had opened distribution offices and cinemas in Germany, swamping local com-petition: to counteract this, and to stem the flow of money from leaving the country, the quota system was introduced, similar to those to operate later – for the same reasons – in Britain and France. Fox used the situation to establish Fox-Europa, using blocked capital to make quota films, but Paramount and Loews were smarter – from their point of view: the Parufamet agreement (so named from the three companies) gave them the use of Ufa's quota certificates and an entrée into its theatres. These new obligations – plus old debts and internal mismanagement – only worsened the situation, and in 1927 the company was in a drastic state; it was solved by Hugenberg, who had expanded his communications empire since he had pressed Ufa to make *Anna Boleyn*, and he was able to acquire the whole company. His conservative, reactionary views were said to impose a threat to those major film-makers who were left – but there were probably only three of these: Lamprecht, the humanitarian, whose work did decline; Pabst, whose career owes little to Ufa; and Lang, who seems to have been unaffected.

Fritz Lang (1890–1976) studied art in his native Vienna, and entered the industry as a writer. His first scenario filmed – *Die Hochzeit in Ekzentrik Klub* (1918) – disappointed him, but he felt 'something great, a new medium, something which I usually call the art of our century'. Pommer, then head of Decla-Film, made him story-editor, and allowed him to direct *Halbblut* (1919), from his own scenario; on the next, *Das Wandernde Bild* (1920), he was joined by Thea von Harbou, who became his collaborator and wife for more than a decade. His only film to survive till *Der Müde Tod* is the two-part **Die Spinnen** (1919), conceived in fact in four parts, i.e. as a serial at a time when longer films were in vogue. 'I simply wanted to film adventurous subjects,' said Lang. 'I loved everything that was exuberant and exotic' – but adventure in this case meant a couple of locations on the Baltic Sea and a minute budget. On the evidence of this imitation-Feuillade about a secret organisation called 'The Spiders' and their involvement with an Inca priestess the cancellation of the last two parts is no deprivation.

Influenced by Sjöström, Fritz Lang did his own version of the German saga, *Die Nibelungen* – of which this is the first part, *Siegfried*. Years later Henry Fonda explained that he had disliked working with Lang because he cared too little for the performer and too much for the plastic, and it is obvious here, to the film's detriment.

The success of *Der Müde Tod* whetted Lang's ambition, and he and von Harbou came up with **Dr Mabuse der Spieler** (1922) – also a two-parter, but a long one, and much too long for the sort of thing you wouldn't give five minutes to on television with Sound and colour; though I must say for those who like this sort of thing, this is the sort of thing they like – the adventures of a mastermind (Rudolf Klein-Rogge) seeking to dominate the world. Again Feuillade-inspired, the source was a novel by Norbert Jacques, but with 'much of the social criticism eliminated' (Liam O'Laoghaire). Its narrative strength and visual boldness almost compensate for the convolutions and ramifications – the sheer amount of which finally gets through to the most restless spectator; we file out at the end of the second part, numb, but satisfied with our final view of the mastermind – sitting on the floor, mad-eyed and despairing, counting his useless money, the image of Germany in defeat. Kracauer maintains that this film, with *Caligari*, 'attempts to show how closely tyranny and chaos are interrelated', and that it portrays a society 'fallen prey to lawlessness and depravity'. But the only chaos is that projected by the tyrant; and the behaviour in the gambling parlours is exceptionally decorous. True, a doorman asks 'Cards or cocaine?', and the unremarked-upon presence within of the State Attorney does suggest a level of corruption; but one intertitle biography of a den-owner hardly qualifies as social comment among all the disguises and dropped notes and confrontations and coincidences.

That audiences sat through *Mabuse* on successive nights caused Lang to embark on another film so 'big' that it would be shown at two sittings – and though the word 'epic' is often misused in movie terms, it certainly applies to **Die Nibelungen** (1924). The cinema, he decided, was an ideal medium for the sagas, and having experimented with spectacle and fantasy he was tempted to the thing itself; the Wagner score was rearranged to accompany what was a different arrangement of the same thirteenth-century poem. In *Siegfried*, that warrior inherits the treasure of the Nibelungen, and with magic powers helps the Duke of Burgundy win the hand of Brunhild, gaining for himself the Duke's daughter, Kriemheld; but he is murdered by the aged, jealous Hagan, goaded by a Brunhild aware of the deception. In *Kriemhelds Rache* Kriemheld marries Etzel, king of the Huns (the English version calls him Attila) whom she tricks into killing Hagan and the Burgundians while ostensibly entertaining them. There is no magic here, but bleakness and horror, the very stuff of – primitive – epic; the final scenes of immolation are powerful. Yet, as with *Mabuse,* the experience is tiring. The trickery used to convey the fantastical is more developed than in *Der Müde Tod,* but the film is static. The dragon encountered is patently papier-mâché, though that instant when his eye is gouged is still not for the squeamish. Precedence was given to the costumes (those of the Huns were copies of those in the Hamburg Folk Museum) and to Otto Hunte's sets, based on the paintings of Altdorfer, Elsheimer and Böchlin – the latter not the most distinguished of painters, but like the others the most Germanic. If German audiences were encouraged to escape into fantasy, this particular film was, in the manner of the legend, a reassertion of the country's faith in itself; and though Mabuse and Siegfried are defeated, both correspond to the Nietzschean theory of a superman, always able to rise again.

Significantly the film was a great encouragement for the tyros of the Nazi party, unable to find much cheer in other German films; its huge sets and those of **Metropolis** (1927) would provide the conception of the stadium at Nuremberg, and though one film was set in the past and the other in the future, vastness – like the pyramids – was bound to last. In the city of Metropolis the gilded youth are at sport in a vast arena; and the Nazis noted with satisfaction that its mad inventor lived under the star of David.

Metropolis was made for Ufa (who had taken over Decla); for Frank Vreeland in *The New York Telegram* it was 'a sardonic Ufa dissection of our mechanical

age . . . so towering and overwhelming and unique'. Rotha noted 'a brilliant *filmic* conception' and reasoned that the abuse it invoked was due to the version shown in Britain (and the U.S.), which had five reels cut. H. G. Wells called it 'quite the silliest film' and years later Lang referred to it similarly, blaming himself as much as von Harbou. At over two million RM, it was Ufa's most expensive picture to date – in Lang's own words, 'A battle of modern science and occultism, the science of the Middle Ages.' The Krupp armaments factory in Essen, with its regimentation and 'ideal homes' and hierarchy, had undoubtedly been studied; Capek's *R.U.R.* and Wells' novels were among works poached, as were two films (q.v.) *The Four Horsemen of the Apocalypse* and *The Hunchback of Notre Dame* – and the inventor is a variation of Dr Mabuse. The result you might imagine to be a bastard, and that's a good word for it: suffice to say that it chiefly concerns the tyrannical boss (Alfred Abel), his rebellious son (Gustav Frölich), the mad inventor (Klein-Rogge), and a sort of Miss Messiah, Maria (Brigitte Helm), who has a false double, whipping the zombie-like workers into revolt and finally chaos. Lang later referred to the denouement as 'fairy-tale', and he was clearly less interested in the struggle between capital and labour than in machines and magic (much of this was cut, which is why the film is so choppy) – so that whenever things get humdrum, something comes along to stun: the huge furnace which turns into Moloch; the electronic transformation of the robot; the building of the Tower of Babel; the flood; and the city of the Future. As opposed to these – and the architectural constructions – the blunting naivety is relieved only once, when Lang intercuts the shimmy of the false Maria into the hero's dream of the Seven Deadly Sins, so that she becomes part of the dream, nudging him into a realisation of the strangeness of his beloved: *that* is a brilliant filmic conception.

With **Spione** (1928) Lang returned to the man who wanted to master the world, played again by Klein-Rogge, the tale now set in the land of political intrigue and espionage – territory later

mapped out by writers like Greene and Ambler, spurning the masterminds with dungeon palaces beneath the respectable frontage of a bank. The piece swarms with idiocies, like the vamp who casually murders as a way to meet the hero, or the spy who pretends to be a waif in order to be picked up by a diplomat (we know politicians aren't always fussy about their bed-partners, but this one carries the safety of the world in his attaché case); however, there is a sense of fatality, of ups and downs and pains and rewards: almost for the first time one recognises the later Lang. And in **Die Frau im Mond** (1929) Lang returned to the early film-makers – in this case Méliès, though a small boy's Nick Carter comics provide a clear reference. This boy has smuggled himself aboard this moon-rocket, whose daft adventures on that planet contrast with those of the international financiers who backed it. I have to report that it is liable to drive

contemporary audiences into hysteria.

Fate, as we have seen, was writ large in all these films, and a whole series of films was built round the tragedies that resulted when the bourgeoisie encountered the underworld. The prototype is *Von Morgens bis Mitternacht,* the play if not the film, and it is certainly the starting point for Karl Grune's **Die Strasse** (1923) – and Grune lifts direct from the earlier film (because it wasn't shown publicly?) the device of the women's faces which turn to skulls. Karl Grune (1890–1962) had worked with Reinhardt, and during the War had lived with foreign soldiers, whose language he didn't speak: his experiences aroused his desire to develop on the screen 'a pictorial language as communicative as the spoken one', writes Kracauer. *Die Strasse* certainly speaks; there are only a dozen intertitles, mainly to clear up the plot at the end – and the speech is in the movement. Everything

Karl Grune's *Die Strasse* was probably the most influential German film of the Twenties, standing midway between some films whose fame has been more enduring: adopting the so-called 'expressionist' motives as carried into films by *Caligari,* it started its own movement towards more realistic subjects like *Die Freudlose Gasse* and on to *Asphalt* and *Der Blaue Engel.* The gentleman in front is Eugen Klöpfer, and Aud Egede Nissen, behind, has designs on his virtue – and pocket.

The greater social inequalities of half a century ago attracted many of the best film–makers, but since the public has never cared for films about poverty few of them were popular. Gerhard Lamprecht made a number of such films – which foreign importers did not want; nor were they showy or theatrical enough to impress local reviewers to the degree that they might attract attention abroad. Lamprecht, in fact, tells more of Berlin in the Twenties, and more entertainingly, than some writers whose name we more readily associate with it. This is a scene from *Die Verrufenen* – literally 'The Discredited' – with Bernhard Götzke, Aud Egede Nissen and Arthur Berger.

moves, from the opening onwards, when the hero watches on his ceiling the shadows of a woman picking up a man; when he dreams, it is in montage with superimposition (which gave Dziga-Vertov an idea or two). The film is not particularly good, and Grune's ideas are not original: a respectable husband rejects the monotony of middle-class life for a night on the town – till the prostitute (Aud Egede Nissen) he fancies and her cohorts frame him for the murder of another of their victims. With its mostly stylised sets it belongs absolutely to its time, along with *Schatten* and *Raskilnikov*, but its success gave rise to that much healthier school – the tales of prostitution and the underbelly of society. Grune was in the forefront of those who rejected expressionism to embrace the *neue sachlichkeit*. **Die Brüder Schellenberg** (1926)

is no more entertaining than *Die Strasse*, but it sets its melodramatics against a Germany founded on fate, money and sex – a recognisable Germany, in fact. It begins with a factory holocaust (which influenced *Metropolis*, just as the scenes in the stock exchange found their way into *L'Argent*, q.v.), and that changes the life of two brothers, both played by Conrad Veidt. The suave, handsome one rises high in the world of finance and becomes a playboy and seducer; the grey-bearded bespectacled one becomes a philanthropist, and eventually 'saves' one of his brother's victims. He runs a rehabilitation centre for the poor, and it is clear that the film was intended as a comfort agathese the inflation then rampant in Germany; in the same way **Am Rande der Welt** (1927) is Grune's tract against war – but with a narrative so bizarre as to be . . . well, let us say, surrealistic. It is set in a mill near the border of two warring territories – a mill which in Robert Neppach's art direction and Fritz Arno Wagner's photography is even more fascinating than the similar setting in *Der Schatz* (q.v.) – and has one vital sequence, on the declaration of war, prefiguring *All Quiet on the Western Front* (q.v.) Grune, disillusioned, later turned to conventional historical melodramas and after the coming of the Nazis made one half-notable film in Britain, *Abdul the Damned* (q.v.).

By far the best of the *neue sachlichkeit* directors was Gerhard Lamprecht (b. 1890), another one-time actor who had come under the influence of Reinhardt, and who had entered films as a cameraman. He has left a portfolio on Berlin quite as valuable as Ozu's of Tokyo – and if he has been underrated it is because his films were overshadowed by the Berlin cartoonist who inspired them, Heinrich Zille. Zille's stories and drawings were the basis of a number of films at this time – and novels, such as Alfred Döblin's 'Berlin Alexanderplatz'. Like Döblin's book, Lamprecht's first film, **Die Verrufenen** (1925) – adapted from Zille, whose drawing of down-and-outs sets the tone at the outset – concerns the difficulty of an ex-convict (Berhard Götzke) in finding again his place in society. Since he had been both wronged and rich, we are near to Hollywood's later bromides on the subject, and indeed the story is banal, moving eventually towards contrivance and sentimentality. But it is told in modern fashion, without the 't's being crossed and the 'i's being dotted – often at the most important points; and the 'dialogue' is also ahead of its time in carrying wit, such as the prostitute-heroine's jeer to a shocked passer-by, 'What do you think I'm doing, dressed like this? Advertising a choral society?' or the hero's apology to the boss, after fixing the machine after-hours, 'I'm sorry I had to stoop to doing it in romantic fashion.' What faults of narrative there are are absent from **Menschen Untereinander** (1926), and since it adds great gusts of humour, it is an even better film. This is a collective portrait of life in an apartment-house, in the genre we know

as *Grand Hotel* (though Vicki Baum's novel of that name – in German 'Menschen in Hotel' – was written three years later, in the tradition of cross-section stories like this one), and it succeeds marvellously in juggling its half-dozen stories. The tenants are introduced to us by an inmate gossiping to the new concierge, and we mostly become involved with the desiccated lawyer (Alfred Abel) who finds it hard to forgive his wife (Aud Egede Nissen) for a fatal automobile accident, and – more than making amends for the stickiness of that – the mean, vain landlady 'caught' by an Australian adventurer met at one of her high-priced introduction parties.

Lamprecht's simple titles were indication to his audience that they were not to be offered escapism. He followed Oswald in demanding open discussion of and sympathy for those wronged by society. If it was the Americans who discovered, during the War, the cinema's ability to sway mass opinion it was the Germans who put it to social use: and **Die Unehelichen** (1926) demands thought for illegitimate children. Peter (Ralph Ludwig) is exceptionally unlucky in his foster parents, feckless and drunken – just as he is equally lucky, later, with the wealthy, generous lady who takes him under her wing; but Lamprecht neutralises his sentimental excesses at the end, when Peter has gone reluctantly to his own father (Götzke), a tough bargeman whose only relaxation from his labours is the solace of the bottle; the cross-cutting between boy on deck with dog, and father getting drunker, is as touching as it is elementary. The first and third of this trio – trilogy? – demanded not only attention from the public but the lawmakers; and **Unter der Laterne** (1928) makes great play of the fact that there is not enough work to go round, following as it does former sweethearts, he to a nice suburban home and she to the profession and death of Marguerite Gautier. In fact, her downfall began when she stayed out all night – innocently – with him, and the film is a conventional account of a whore's rise and fall. We may note some staples of the films of the period: a stunning montage when she's most successful, of lingerie, diamonds, etc.; the visit to the businessman in his apartment; and the situation *à trois* which would be copied less innocently in the Lilian Harvey musicals (q.v.). But as a whole the film is unremarkable, and we may suppose – did the same thing happen to Grune? – that Hugenberg would not permit Lamprecht to continue on his conscience-stirring path. This film does, however, have one sequence in a low-life bar to set beside the wealth of such sequences in the earlier ones, ranging from penny arcades and skittle alleys to huge boozy music halls. In Lamprecht's films there is a panorama of the times: the ballet school, the little Jewish photographer's bare apartment, the flophouse, the cellar where piece-work is paid for in schnapps, the bureaucrats' dusty office, the mansion in Lugano, the dime-a-dance cabaret or the bars where the sexes don't separate to dance . . . for in the end, there are always the bars, the dives, the cafés. At the end of *Die Verrufenen*, the hero has a tirade: 'Poverty and suffering, vice and alcohol make people what they call the Fifth Class . . . They cannot escape their fate. You can fight against it, but you cannot change it': and that was the sort of moralising that the self-righteous wanted to hear. Sjöström did it too, and next to him the Silents have no more honest observer. Lamprecht may be, in the fashion of the time, sentimental towards his hero-victims, but he never is to the poor.

His films had no great success outside Germany, or indeed within it, since audiences only liked poverty when dealt with in the manner of Pollyanna. Nor were critics immune: Pabst's **Die Freudlosse Gasse** (1925) had far more success than *Die Verrufenn*, and since Pabst is the greater film-maker, this particular film is much deeper in melodrama than Lamprecht's, though perhaps, in its mordant portrait of a divided society, it possesses more edge. It is a profoundly socialist film: the rich recklessly inflate mine shares at the expense of the middle class, disporting in cabarets while the inhabitants of the joyless street queue for bread. The irony in the cutting was influenced by *Strike* (q.v.); Pabst so admired Eisenstein that he planned a film on a German mutiny

after seeing *Potemkin*. The background is post-Hapsburg Vienna under inflation, and here is Asta Nielsen, the corrupted one, and Garbo (in her second film), about to go the same way. The latter is a silly goose, in straitened circumstances getting into the toils of Frau Greifer (Valeska Gert), and then not being nice to her 'client' – the butcher (Krauss): whereupon the hideous Greifer throws herself at him in desperation and is accepted – a touch that is absolutely Pabst, and the sort of thing that makes his work at this time so much more mature than Lang's. The butcher is presented as the immediately capitalist enemy of the people, though there are certain ladies prepared to bargain with their bodies: he is killed by the hungry mob, and Garbo is 'saved' – the moral of which is reputed to have caused the film its two year run in Paris. It played for over a year in Berlin, but censorship in other countries resulted in mutilation of the material. These included the U.S., which imported it, in 1927, on the strength of Garbo's participation. In Britain it was banned absolutely for some years.

G. W. Pabst (1885–1967) was born in Czechoslovakia and raised in Vienna; he began his career as an actor, but after one film he turned to writing scenarios for Carl Frölich's company, and Frölich gave him the chance to direct. **Der Schatz** (1924) was adapted from a novel by Rudolph Hans Bartsch, which clearly provided what was then thought paramount in the German cinema: a moral melodrama played out against bizarre settings – in this case a mill, brilliantly designed by Robert Herlth and Walter Röhrig. The plot is conventional stuff about buried treasure and greed with the miller's daughter (Lucie Mannheim) as the pawn. It is understandable that with the treasure at stake, both parents and the brutish handyman (Krauss) should forget her – but then so, momentarily, does her true love, and that is Pabst the social realist in his true voice. *Der Freudlosse Gasse* was his third film; his fifth was a psychological study, **Geheimnisse einer Seele** (1926), for its time an incredible achievement, and one of the most sober and imaginative of Silent films. With two former colleagues of Freud, Pabst

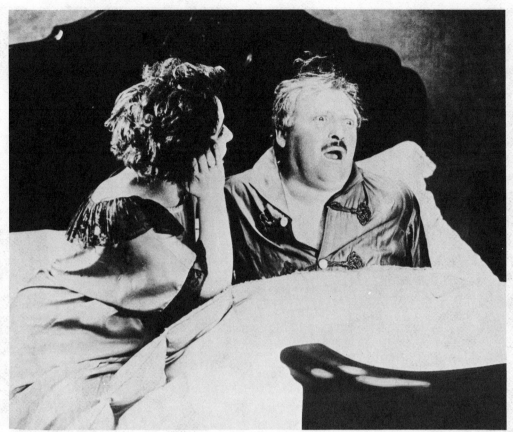

Perhaps the German directors who most consistently impressed their contemporaries were Murnau, Lang and Pabst: the Silent output of Murnau and Lang often looks dated, but the work of Pabst remains strong and vivid: *Geheimnisse einer Seele* or *Secrets of a Soul* is still a remarkable study of a mentally sick man, played by Werner Krauss. Freud disapproved of the enterprise, but gets a nod in the foreword to the effect that he, 'the university professor', had found a cure for such illnesses.

worked out a case in which a neighbourhood murder and the gift of a knife by a cousin bring out a phobia in a chemistry professor (Krauss): he cannot pick up a knife, a razor, a letter-opener, till he consults a psychiatrist, who urges from him fantasies from his past and the dreams that we have already seen. The front-door key soon becomes symbolic: the doctor finds the key – the cousin's tacit reference to the professor's *kinderlosigkeit* or impotence – and dredges from the professor's memory the moment that scarred. It is too simply resolved; but the symbolism of the dreams impresses, and the surrounding narrative envisages moments of sexual frustration.

The only other director who might – *just* – have treated the subject was Von Stroheim, and Pabst acknowledged admiration in the opening sequence of **Die Liebe der Jeanne Ney** (1927): a military orgy which surpasses any of the former's in probability and beastliness. It was easier to be more explicit in Germany; but Ufa did force upon Pabst a bowdlerised version of Ehrenburg's long novel. Briefly, it concerns the pursuit to Paris of Jeanne Ney (Edith Jehanne) and her Bolshevik lover Andreas (Udo Henning) by the scheming Khalibiev (Fritz Rasp); the latter manages to get himself affianced to her – blind – cousin (Brigitte Helm), and to pin one of his murders on Andreas – to unpin which Jeanne agrees to go away with him. In the book she becomes both his mistress and that of Andreas; gone too are the moral and political implications – replaced by a sub-plot about Bolshevik subversion in Paris, plus a hint that Andreas will see the error of his views. The film is complicated rather than complex, but Pabst constantly offers relishable details – above all, the greedy, unshaven private detective and his book-lined warren of an agency.

His interest in the darker side of man's

93

nature led him to his two masterpieces, **Die Büchse von Pandora** (1928) and **Tagebuch einer Verlorenen** (1929), so much a pair that we may stretch the word 'unique' to describe the experience they make. The former was taken from two plays by Wedekind which had shocked audiences two decades earlier, and the latter from a moralising novel by Margarete Böhme which Oswald had filmed in 1918. In *Pandora*, Lulu threads her amoral way from the conquest of a respectable doctor (Fritz Kortner) to death in London at the hands of Jack the Ripper; in *Verlorenen*, Thymian moves from seduction by her father's assistant (Rasp) to a bordello, then to marriage to a wealthy old man. Pabst subjects his players to a battery of close-ups, carrying events forward in glances and nuances; he offers a decadent wedding party and some fine, flaunting backstage scenes with the same panache that he brings to reform-school gymnastics or a family conference, cutting brilliantly to find detail. In both, Louise Brooks is not a femme fatale but a child — so delighted with everything, unable to be regretful for long, pleased to be admired. In response to the doctor's

Pabst's *Die Buchse der Pandora* and *Tagebuch einer Verlorenen* are, because of the incandescent Louise Brooks, something more than a girl's odyssey into the world of sin and luxury. LEFT, in *Pandora*, with Franz Lederer, son of her lover, and ABOVE, in *Verlorenen* with Fritz Rasp, just before embarking on that odyssey.

95

hopeless, eyes-open passion, Lulu exults without a thought in her head; when the lesbian countess hugs her on her wedding night, she gives a glimmer of a smile, aware of a new conquest. Twice Thymian knows she is going to be ravished – once by the assistant, and later by her first client in a brothel – and she closes her eyes, her head thrown back in a trance; she had already submitted, a fragile plaything and not a partner – and the ecstatic stance indicates more than willingness, since she is no longer mistress of her fate. Even without the luminous presence of this actress, we might say that there is no other *fille de joie* quite like her: in the brothel, looking at the men about her, or preparing to sip a glass of champagne (her first?), her reaction, beyond sheer delight, is unfathomable. Consequently, because of her, Pabst's two films have a deeper resonance than the other German prostitute films. They are all moral tales – finally; but Pabst comes down firmly for 'sinning' as vital to the life force. The men are all dry-throated and wet-lipped with anticipation: they are also unpersonable to a degree. Wedekind's original producer, Karl Kraus, described the plays' matter as 'the revenge of the world of men . . . for its own guilt', but Pabst feels no guilt: since sex is so much to be desired, prostitution is not to be deplored.

Prostitution in the other films of the period, including *Der Freudlosse Gasse*, is linked to poverty and inflation; it brings disease, unhappiness and death – as it does, indeed, in *Pandora*. But for Pabst it is not so easy: his clients are as likely to be in the usual image – fat, old and gross – and in the brothel it is an aged man who sweeps into the bedroom the youngest and most innocent-seeming of the girls. He is not, finally, a social realist like Lamprecht, but a satirist; the others find faults in the German haute bourgeoisie, but he concedes nothing. *His* people are not rotten because of present economic conditions: they have been rotten for generations – but they are not fixed, because humanity is capable of shifting. 'A little more love,' says Thymian's benefactor, 'and no one would be lost.'

That is a message implicit in **Das**

Gefahrliche Alter (1927), another of the prostitute or 'street' (from *Die Strasse*) films, directed by Eugen Illes. Unlike the girl who falls from grace in *Unter der Laterne*, this one – Miss Nielsen again – is a middle-aged lady, and she falls in love with one of her husband's students (Walter Rilla). For a while, this is like one of Hollywood's Florence Vidor vehicles, as much smartness as sadness, about a woman trying to retain her youth; but under the lantern she is a pathetic figure. **Dirnentragödie** (1927) was directed by Bruno Rahn, who died shortly after it was finished: alas, for on this evidence he might have been a master. The English title was *The Tragedy of the Street*, but the original means 'Whore's Tragedy'. It is the whore this time who falls – Auguste (Nielsen), first glimpsed applying a toothbrush dipped in bootblack to the roots of her hair. She has an amiable pimp (Oskar Homolka), but when she meets young Felix (Werner Pittshau) he is bribed to leave and she abandons her 'client'. To hold Felix, she uses the rest of her money for a down-payment on a grocer's shop, but the pimp returns and manoeuvres Felix into the arms of the party-girl roommate: and as tragedy sweeps away three of these people, Felix weeps in his mother's lap. I do not think experienced whores give up all at the first glimpse of a youth from a nice family, but this film suggests that this is the one act of foolishness of which such ladies are capable. Miss Nielsen, hunched now and smiling without mirth, makes us believe absolutely; and Rahn's people move furtively through the shadows, in the stylised sets still sometimes used in such films.

You might suppose, film-makers being what they are, that there would be a film combining the 'street' genre with the fantastical – and there is: **Alraune** (1927) – though to be fair, Alraune (Brigitte Helm) is femme fatale rather than street-walker. The daughter of a whore and a hanged criminal, as 'manufactured' in the lab by a scientist (Paul Wegener), her discovery of her origins leads from bad to worse, and the same can be said of the film, since its motive – her revenge on her creator – is handled in dim fashion. Or so it seems now:

at the time *The Kinematograph Weekly* spoke of 'the genius of H. H. Ewers's story and Henrik Galeen's directorial genius'. The posturing of Fraulein Helm is a distinct demerit; she played the same role in the first of the two Sound remakes.

The wholly commercial directors may be represented by Alexander Korda (1893–1956), since his films reflect the period as accurately as more famous titles. They deserve to be better known because Korda was a man of intelligence, and that quality is reflected in them; he was also an opportunist, a necessity in Weimar then and the movie industry always. He was born in Hungary of an impoverished Jewish family, and made his way into the industry via film criticism; he had directed twenty-five films there before arriving in Vienna, where he made *Seine Majestät das Bettelkind* for Sascha Film, a version of Mark Twain's 'The Prince and the Pauper', of no interest whatsoever. His second film for Sascha (it was in fact made simultaneously, on the same locations, as *Herren der Meere*, which hasn't survived) was **Eine Versunkene Welt** (1922), somewhat better, and with a subject of passionate interest at the time – indeed, it won a Gold Medal for best dramatic film at a Congress in Milan. The subject is that of a Grand Duke who embraces socialism – after, that is, embracing a dancer. In films such relationships usually lead to self-sacrifice or suicide; but the Grand Duke's suicide is due to his beliefs, he and the film having decided that socialism is a good thing in theory but unworkable in practice. There is also a political reference or so in **Samson und Delila** (1922), inasmuch as the strange young man found aboard the prince's yacht is thought to be an anarchist. He appears in the modern part of the film; the rest of it is the Biblical story, the two tied together by the notion of a *diva* about to sing Delilah. The ancient-modern device was not new in films, and this precedes the best-known one, deMille's first *Ten Commandments* (q.v.); Korda's co-writer was Ernst Vajda, who later became a writer for Lubitsch. The international success of the Mark Twain film had given Korda a taste for more, and the example of *Sumurun* had proved that spectacle films sold throughout the world – and

this particular subject offered spice from an unimpeachable source. The sets are splendid: the cost of them, despite the film's relative success (it never played the U.S.) bankrupted the backers – which was and would be the fate of most people who financed Korda.

Fleeing Austria, he gained Berlin, where he found a compatriot to back **Das Unbekannte Morgen** (1923), written with Vajda, and derived from both *Der Müde Tod* and *Schatten* – and more entertaining than either. It is an examination of the past, present and future of a potential suicide (Maria Corda, then the director's wife). Korda attacks the subject with energy, and his Teutonic London is more menacing than in other, comparable films – which would include many with bogeymen: in that role again is Herr Krauss, diabolical once more, with longish hair and monocle, developed (as an intertitle informs us) from musician to maniac, insanely plotting for carnal purposes against our poor heroine. The film's reception enabled Korda to buy his way into a distribution company, but that went into liquidation; after a film for Ufa, he obtained backing from another Hungarian for a film which Ufa released, **Tragödie in Hause Hapsburg** (1924). Lajos Biro (who would work with him in Britain) wrote it, and it is the first film on the Mayerling affair: perhaps because audiences would have been familiar with the Crown Prince, Koloman Zatony is the only one of

The incomparable Asta Nielsen continued to act up to the Sound period (she made just one Talking picture), playing, as she always did, sad ladies of unfortunate virtue. Here she is (right) with Hilde Jennings in *Dirnentragödie* – a young lady to whom she has foolishly offered a room. The looks of Miss Jennings make her a popular girl at parties of old bachelors, while Miss Nielsen's haunt is more likely to be the street – where, of course, the other will eventually end up.

several screen Rudolphs to look like him – and he also gives a tremendously affecting performance. Frau Corda is Maria Vetsera. Wrote Dorothy Gies McGuigan in her marvellous book on the Hapsburgs: 'So completely, so painstakingly, was every shred of truth, every concrete piece of factual evidence hurried out of public sight that even today, nearly eighty years later, the full truth of Mayerling continues to elude the searcher.' We must therefore admire Biro's script, keeping to the known facts – including the accepted opinion that the Prince killed himself for reasons other than love. The result is fair entertainment: Korda was never good at narrative strength, but as the film lurches on, it does so, impressively, in Schönbrunn and other locations associated with the principals.

Eine Dubarry von Heute (1927) is further reminder of Korda's abiding interest in the amours of kings – though it was designed to exploit the charms of his wife, now considerably glamorised and thus expected to be his passport to international acclaim. As written by Biro, it attempted to combine two popular film genres, royal romance and the rise of a Paris coquette. The latter, at least, is of interest – to a degree not far short of Miss Brooks's progress in Pabst's films (we may suppose Pabst saw this, since he chose an actress identical in appearance to Frau Corda here) – and we find, rare in such films, a genuine feeling between the king (Alfred Abel) and this woman of the world. It is pleasant to find that feeling in a film which borrows so much – whether it be the shots of revolving, multiple faces, or walking legs on the sidewalk: the abiding clichés of the German Silent film.

For the Germans, as for most other film-makers, Paris was the very best setting for escapist movies, since there, as everyone knows, high society and the bohemians could mingle and indulge in *l'amour* to their hearts' content: though the starting-point of films like Richard Eichberg's **Die Keusche Susanne** (1926) was surely emulation of Lubitsch's Hollywood films, even to the extent, in this case, of a huge finale – cf. *So This is Paris?* (q.v.) – in the Moulin Rouge. Adapted from a French operetta, the farcical complications are not entirely served by a cast including Ruth Weyher in the title-role, the not-so-chaste Susanne, Willy Fritsch as a gay young blade, and Lillian Harvey.

Wilhelm Thiele's **Die Dame mit der Maske** (1928) is on its own merits of little account, but it is completely of its period, absolutely representative of a Berlin crippled by inflation, and it has an opening montage on inflation (designed by Hans Richter) that is so strong that it colours all that follows. Alexander Esway and Henrik Galeen wrote the scenario, which concerns the daughter (Arlette Marchal) of a writer who goes into a scantily-clad revue rather than tell him she couldn't find a publisher for his book – and today it's very difficult to feel sympathy for a man who hopes to make a fortune from a book about his hunting days in Africa. It is all here: the Russian émigré hero and his cab-driver friend; the Jewish pawnbroker; the impresario's girlfriend who fancies herself a star; and the impresario himself (Heinrich George), who takes a shine to our heroine. Will he ravish her? Will she shoot him?

There are no such problems in **Der Geiger von Florenz** (1926) since the heroine (Elisabeth Bergner) dresses up as a boy and meets the nicest Italian artist (Walter Rilla), who has no qualms about the consequent palpitations in his breast. This version of 'As You Like It' was written and directed by Paul Czinner to perpetuate the winsome charms of his wife, Bergner – and it must be quite the daftest variation on an already impossible theme.

Italy is much better served in **Das Haus am Meer** (1924): the story is sheer melodrama – the woman whose past catches up with her – but it is attacked with new conviction by the director, Fritz Kaufman. The *haus* is on the Sorrento peninsula, an inn kept by Enrico (Gregory Chmara) and his wife (Miss Nielsen) – who is recognised in due course as a notorious camp-follower by some conscripts bound for Morocco. 'So you mean to throw me back into the depths from which you saved me?' she pleads against Vesuvius in full smoke. There is one notable sequence: the wife's dilemma and her past presented in one

The young wife (Jenny Jugo) is encouraged by her spinster neighbour (Olga Limburg) to return the attentions of a local nobleman – without, of course, arousing the suspicions of her husband (Werner Krauss). Released abroad as *A Royal Scandal*, *Die Hose* was widely regarded as one of the best films of its time, but its director, Hans Behrendt, remains a shadowy figure. From the time of this film, 1927, to the coming of the Nazis, he was prolific, specialising in satiric small town comedy. His only recorded work after being expelled from the German film industry is a Spanish film made in 1934.

montage, cutting finally to her husband, and *thus* confirming his suspicions – technique at its most imaginative. The acting (Chmara was then married to Nielsen) is Silent acting of the most vivid kind and the locations – the rough and relentless sea, the land high, hard and rugged – are heady after the hermetic world of Ufa and its clever lighting.

Another remarkable film, also set away from the contemporary scene, is **Die Hose** (1927), directed by Hans Behrendt from a scenario by Franz Schulz: its source is Carl Sternheim's 1911 play, one of his small-town satires chronicling the rise to power of the Maske family. Werner Krauss is Maske, petty official, stuffing his belly into tight trousers, blinking pale-lashed eyes over a glorious splutter of a moustache. He has a young and pretty wife (Jenny Jugo), but his moustache and his job in the Prince's household are his chief claims to fame – not that he is seen to work, but he unwraps his lunch-time sandwich methodically, with as much mental effort as he'll use all day. He is convivial with 'the boys', irritable with his wife, obsequious with the Prince, and satisfied

before a mirror: Krauss might have made him more pitiable or more overbearing, and that he doesn't is because he was, quite simply, a wonderful actor. The film is not wonderful, but it is worthy of him: I like it better than any similar film I've seen, partly because it proves that the German sense of humour was not always lumbering – and partly because it is very well made. The sets and extensive locations are appropriately charming, and as the Prince's philosopher-adviser Rudolph Forster manages a comic portrait as richly amusing as that of Krauss.

The few historical films of the decade were usually based on plays or novels, and Friedrich Zelnik, usually a specialist in Viennese operettas, made a version of Hauptmann's drama **Die Weber** (1927), about the Silesian weavers' strike in 1844. Its confrontation between the bosses and the oppressed is uneven, and without being very dynamic it is nevertheless an incitement to mob violence – in emulation of its model, Eisenstein's *Strike* (q.v.). The Soviet films were changing the German cinema, and social realism became the cry of the remaining major talents – Lang excepted – of the German film industry. The influence of Reinhardt had long gone, and expressionism along with neo-Gothic horror belonged to the nursery days before the slump. Yet years of distorted images and fancy cutting leave their mark, and Ernö Metzner put them to service in his upending of German film tradition, **Überfall** (1927). Metzner was a studio architect (i.e. constructing sets from others' designs) and a Social Democrat; in this two-reeler he suggested a new set of rules. The accident of the title was the dropping of a coin, which leads the bourgeois hero into a spot of gambling. He is skinny, pop-eyed and unappetising, and the bar is not the usual friendly haven but a bare room of evil menace; the prostitute who saves him is no Asta Nielsen, but tough-looking, sexy, beautiful – and consistently vicious; and the policeman at the end, the symbol of law and understanding, proves ineffably dense and utterly indifferent as to whether our bourgeois hero lives or dies. The film was banned, but its influence was felt within the industry.

Berlin: die Symphonie einer Gross-stadt (1927) was made at the same time and was the brainchild of that child of expressionism, Mayer, who had come to the conclusion that there was more to cinema than scripting fictions. He had thought of it – the symphony as described in the title – while standing in traffic near the Palast am Zoo, and had enlisted the help of Karl Freund, and of Walter Ruttmann, who had until then only made abstract films. Ruttmann is the credited director, as Mayer withdrew his name since he considered Ruttmann's interpretation of Berlin too superficial – and it is too much an interpretation in the manner of Dziga-Vertov (q.v.) and his Kino-Eye group, montage and image for their own sakes, rather than an attempt to get beyond the surface of a city.

The influence of the film lies heavily on Joe May's superb **Asphalt** (1929) – or is it the *Asphalt* of Erich Pommer (one of his first films on returning from Hollywood) since May did so little else of note? The long, opening sequence is one of the most evocative ever filmed – the Potsdamer Platz, with store and traffic lights blazing, workers going home and late shoppers sauntering by;

and it is followed by another long sequence, in which the prostitute-thief heroine (Betty Amann) seeks to prevent the upright young cop (Gustav Fröhlich) from sending her to jail. It's clear enough he feels lust, and it's clear enough at the end that they'll marry – so the sort of film we expect from a city of legendary decadence by no means offended the moralities of provincial German audiences.

Nor were they offended by Leo Mittler's **Jenseits der Strasse** (1929), but the whore (Lissi Arno) lives on to steal again and tread the *trottoir* while her innocent young victim floats out, face downward, in Hamburg harbour. He (Fritz Genshow) is from the country, an *arbeitsloser*, and he is befriended by a bargeman, wealthy before inflation; and when he has to choose between lust/greed and friendship/loyalty, he chooses wrongly. Such then it was: a time of desperation, when lust and booze provided a temporary respite. Still, the film is more than a metaphor: it goes further yet in the depiction of the milieu. In *Die Verrufenen* we saw a whore continue to work despite true love; here, from the low-life bar with its same-sex couples we see the customer climb the stairs behind the silk-clad legs – we see, for the first time, a whore in bed with her client. As much as in Lamprecht's film, the masses struggle for existence on the edge of the underworld while the fat cats lap up their *café mit sahne*. The lucky ones all look like the capitalists in Eisenstein – and borrowed back from the Soviets are the flashy montages, handled with such confidence by Mittler. He left nothing else of note before fleeing the Nazis, but in *Razzia in St Pauli* (q.v.) Werner Hochbaum made a Sound companion piece – more gentle and, ironically, more optimistic.

The problem of sexual frustration is frankly discussed in an extraordinary film, **Geschlect in Fesseln** (1928), directed by the actor turned director Wilhelm Dieterle (q.v.), who also plays the leading-role, that of a young salesman, hit by the Depression, who is sent to jail after killing a man who pestered his wife (Mary Johnson). After a series of sexual fantasies, imaginatively conceived, on the part of wife, husband and fellow-prisoners, he begins a relationship with a cellmate, after which he cannot or will not return to his wife. This conclusion would have been unthinkable in any other national cinema at the time, and if the inevitable result is suicide, the homosexual issue is treated with both sympathy and subtlety.

Pessimism is the sole note of Carl Junghaus's **So ist der Leben** (1929) which follows the ill-fortunes from one Saturday to the next of one family living in Prague. I much prefer what is virtually the same story with humour, **Mutter Krausens Fahrt ins Glück** (1929), and certainly it was preferred at the time by audiences. Phil Jutzi, directing, offers a portrait of everyday life as fascinating as those of Lamprecht, and we find the hero's Marxist pal quoting Zille, 'Living conditions can kill as surely as an axe' – which allows the hero to forgive his girl the loss of her virginity elsewhere and let her join him in a people's demonstration that provides a rare healthy ending, with its indication that the remedy is at hand, that there are elements within society which will fight to push out the degradation and deprivation. The late German Silents may have borrowed from the Soviets, but few bothered with their message of hope. The Nazi party must also have taken hope, if not quite the same way: for all the glorification of the workers, the film stresses the unity of the family and the joys of sport, the open-air, and the community.

These last are celebrated in a slight piece, **Menschen am Sonntag** (1930), directed by Robert Siodmak (1900–73) and Edgar G. Ulmer, with assists on script or camera by Eugen Schüfftan, Fred Zinnemann and Billy Wilder – all of them then youngsters on the fringe of the industry. Literally a lighthearted Sunday version of *Berlin: die Symphonie einer Grossstadt*, with some fictional incidents borrowed from the Soviet *House on Trubnaya Square* (q.v.), it concerns two picnicking couples, played by amateurs who were encouraged to improvise. They were accompanied by only a music track and audiences delighted in them, ensuring a last success for Silent films as Talkies

flooded German theatres. Doubtless the woods and lakes were refreshing after a decade of shadows and smoke-filled cafés, and the same was true of the mountain stretches of **Die Weisse Hölle von Piz Palü** (1929), co-directed by Pabst and Dr Arnold Fanck. During his brief spell at Ufa, Pabst had been commanded to direct in the Russian manner, and then – which he found much more difficult – in the American way. Left to himself by Nero-Film to make *Die Büchse der Pandora*, he determined to set up his own company to make *Tagebuch einer Verlorenen* – which was why, between the two, he agreed to co-operate with Fanck. Fanck, a geologist, had specialised in 'mountain' films since *Das Wunder des Schneeschuhs* (1920), their emotions and actions as awesome as their scenery. Pabst was able to cool the emotions, and for the first time one of Fanck's films was regarded as more than 'fringe' entertainment – indeed, it was a worldwide success. The visuals were then as remarkable as they still appear to be – which include the aerial shots used in the rescue attempt at the end. You must not think from that that this is just another disaster movie, but it is relatively simple: what happens when a honeymoon couple (Leni Riefenstahl, Ernst Petersen) run into a famous mountaineer (Gustav Diessl), still searching for the wife he lost in this white hell a year ago.

There is a quest, often as obsessive as this one, throughout the German films of this decade: for lost loved ones, for self-knowledge, for economic survival, for information on the forces of darkness and disillusion. They are a reflection of the prevailing gloom of a Germany in defeat, where paper money has no value and consequently little else has: it is the open-air and the mountains which offer hope that the spirit will soar, a polarisation similar to that in the American cinema and its conflict between the old, as represented by the heroes of the West and the gingham-clad heroines, and the new – the flappers, gangsters and smart-talking reporters. The two conflicts would be resolved in very different ways.

5

The U.S.S.R: Montage and Message

IN SWEDEN, the particular nature of Sjöström's genius led him to concentrate on specifically Nordic material; in Germany, the emphasis on similarly indigenous matter was dictated by the mood of the time, at first reinforced by a government aware of the advantages of a nationalistic cinema. In Russia, the new Soviet government was quick to recognise the cinema's potential as propaganda. When that country, after the Revolution, opted out of the War, the film industry was virtually non-existent. The first studio had not been built till 1907, and the cinema for years had shown the French, British and Italian burlesques, or copies thereof. In 1913 some artists had banded together to make a film considered avant-garde, but the feature films were comfortable bourgeois subjects permitted by the Czarist regime. Under the freer conditions of the Kerensky government, Yakov Protazanov did a version of a Tolstoi short story, *Father Sergius* (1918), said to be well in advance of most Russian production. With the Civil War following the Revolution, what production equipment there was was dispersed, but its re-assembly was considered a priority – to record the activities of the Red Army for exhibition to the public. Lenin declared: 'The cinema for us is the most important of the arts,' and the world's first film school was established.

There was not, however, enough raw film stock to do much more than theorise, and chief among the theorists was Vladimir Majakovski, one of the leaders of the Futurist movement; he believed passionately in film, and with a group of fellow Futurists had been responsible for that 1913 experiment, *Drama in Futurist Cabinet 13*. When the War was over he joined the Czarist film company, Neptune, but survived to co-operate with the Revolutionary authorities. He managed to make three short films: *Creation Can't Be Bought*, adapted from 'Martin Eden' by Jack London; **The Young Lady and the Hooligan** (1918), adapted from 'Cuore' by Edmondo de Amicis; and *Shackled by Film*. The last of these Majakovski somewhat respected, but the first two he dismissed as 'sentimental commissioned rubbish . . . rubbish not because they were worse than others, but because they were not better.' The only one to have survived is *The Young Lady and the Hooligan*, and it is hard to disagree. An anecdote about the new schoolteacher and the lout (Majakovski himself) who cheeks her and then falls in love with her, it never amounts to much, though presumably to Russian audiences then, hitherto kept rigidly behind class barriers, the situation of a worker soliciting a lady had a certain piquancy; the sad ending must also have suited local taste. Majakovski, at first working for the government, became one of the great, influential voices of the Revolutionary cinema, but he never directed again; from 1926 until his suicide in 1930 he wrote a number of screenplays, only two of which – both stories for children – found their way to the screen, in much altered form. Other projects were cancelled, as he himself was increasingly critical of the shackles placed by the government on freedom of expression.

Meanwhile, at the State Film School in Moscow, without film stock, there were discussions; there were classes for acting in cinematic fashion; and there were study groups – taking apart the best-known films of D. W. Griffith, and re-editing them for different effect. What stock there was was used for what the French call *actualités*, and thus, via deprivation and the inability to practise the craft, the roots of the Soviet cinema were grounded in two qualities – immediacy and, more important, editing. Chief among the teachers was Vsevolod Meyerhold (1874–1940), a former theatre man who had directed two or three films before the Revolution; after it, he surfaced with a hundred and one ideas for allying the avant-garde with the revolutionary message – and though at this point no one was quite sure how far the cinema could be separated from the theatre, there was a wide belief that it should be, to the extent that 'plays' were attempted in 'cinematic', i.e. natural, surroundings. Lev Kuleshov (1899–1970) had had practical experience before the Revolution as film designer, and he had written extensively on the new art form. His great achievement – lacking raw stock – was the discovery that the emotions of the spectator could be shaped by the selection and juxtaposition of images: he transposed the same clip of an expressionless face with different images – a child, a plate of soup, a coffin – and found that audiences read the expression not as it was but as they expected it to be. He discovered the cinema's power to deceive; he realised that the arrangement of the material, and the length to which the image could be held, could create emotions quite opposite to those created when the same images were a series of still photographs. There is a striking example in **The Man with a Movie Camera** (1928), made by another of the theorists, Dziga Vertov (1896–1954): a ball hurtles towards the camera, an athlete lets fly a javelin, a goal-keeper defends his goal – and it is a relief when he catches the ball instead of the javelin. Vertov was still a young man when assigned officially to the task of assembling the Red Army newsreels in a three-hour film, *The Anniversary of the October Revolution* (1919). In a series of manifestoes he expounded the theory we now call cinema-*vérité*, believing deeply that the only worthwhile

form of cinema was the photographing of life-as-is. He started a newsreel called Kino-Pravda (Film-Truth), because he wanted to explain the new Russia to its citizens. But truth, of course, is relative: the Soviet film-makers put their discoveries of film deceit to the service of what they saw as the truth.

Not that Vertov held entirely to the line of the greatest propaganda; his obsessive interest in the visuals led in time to this *Man with a Movie Camera* in which man and camera are interchangeable – the I, the eye of the world. It is a film of vistas, of tricks, of artificially-heightened tension, of split-screens, of montage. Its very age offers slight compensation: an authentic snatch of old Russia, looking, with its shop-fronts and an occasional Peugeot, still capitalist. Perhaps if the selection of image was less arbitrary, or if there had been a theme – or related themes – or even a building of images, it would not have been made so completely obsolete (unlike *Berlin: die Symphonie einer Grossstadt*) by the myriads of feet of film shot since.

Even less from Kuleshov's films can we see that he was one of the founders of film theory: **Extraordinary Adventures of Mr West in the Land of the Bolsheviks** (1924) was the first film made by his Experimental department at the State Film School, a direct challenge to the theatre schools and therefore a statement by his pupils as to which direction film should follow. Pudovkin and he wrote the screenplay, and Pudovkin was assistant director, art director, and one of the leading actors. It concerns a naive American in the U.S.S.R., mainly involved – as he expected – with crooks; and as the title also implies, it is a free-wheeling comedy moving in directions both fantastic and satiric, hoping to make its points visually. Since Goskino put thirty-two prints into distribution we may suppose it popular – though it was not thought suitable for export. To sit through it today with an audience requires stamina, as the left-wingers present can be relied upon to laugh at any left-wing jokes, however unfunny – and these are either galumphing or smug: the fact that I still like the picture says much for its amiable high spirits. However, there is nothing to be

103

The films of Lev Kuleshov do not, on the whole, justify his reputation as a theorist on cinema; but despite a hint of self–parody *By the Law* is superb, one of several late Silent melodramas in which a small isolated group is subjected to the elements and their own emotions.

said for **The Death Ray** (1925), the second film of the Kuleshov collective, and like its predecessor designed to display American influence – it being Kuleshov's declared aim to captivate audiences as the Hollywood film-makers did. However, like *Strike* (q.v.) – which Eisenstein was making at the same time – it set out to make the proletariat its collective hero. Pudovkin wrote the scenario, in which between the propaganda may be discerned dim affinities with Feuillade and *Mabuse*; and it is here that the collective, for all their studies, fell apart – not realising that by this time the prime virtue of the Americans was their narrative clarity. Kuleshov, explaining the film's failure, had a number of theories for that – all failing to find the point: 'the ideological slander'

it created was 'utterly undeserved', he claimed, though he did admit that the film was 'inadequate' and elsewhere quoted a critic: 'You must be completely mad futurists – you show films made out of tiny pieces that to any normal spectator seem an incredible muddle – the pieces chase each other so fast that no one can possibly find out what's going on.'

As a result of this failure the collective was abandoned, and Kuleshov was unemployed for eighteen months; he finally interested Goskino in a low-budget film, **By the Law** (1926) – one interior set, a minute cast. It was an adaptation of Jack London's story, 'The Unexpected', set in Alaska, about three goldseekers – the Swedish Hans (Sergei Komarov), his English wife (Alexandra Khokhlova), and the Irish Michael

Dennin (Vladimir Fogel). It is the Irishman who finds the gold, leading to a murder, and months-long tension as the three of them are marooned by floods. As the captive, Fogel takes all our sympathy; he was never again required to give so much of his great gift for cinema acting. But the whole film is masterly. Kuleshov in his workshop had taught the importance of movement and facial expression, and instead of tripping over himself as in the other films, he lingers: the images, powerful or seemingly banal, add to the impact. It was not seen in English-speaking countries prior to 1939, but was influential on the Continent. In its refusal to take sides – in seeing the situation in shades of grey – it bears the influence of Sjöström, who may have seen it, returning the compliment in the not-dissimilar *The Wind*. My sole reservation concerns Miss Khokhlova, overdoing things as badly as in the other two films; despite its grimness and a hint of self-parody it is one to convert anyone to Silent movies.

Such is not the case with **Aelita** (1924), a science fiction tale which was probably the best-known Russian film abroad before *Potemkin* (q.v.). Directed by the aforementioned Protazanov, it moves clumsily from a resettlement centre to a space-ship, with excursions to a Mars constructed of parallel triangles and piano strings. Two points to note: a revolution on Mars as glorious as that of October 1917, and a superb ten minutes at the end when the images destroy chronology to leave us floundering, wondrously, between dreams and reality. Other examples of this technique, in the Twenties, include *Caligari* and *Das Haus am Meer*; there is no modern example till *Blow-Up* (q.v.). **The Trial of Three Millions** (1926) shows Protazanov to have made as great an advance as Kuleshov. Adapted from a story by Umberto Notari which had as a play become popular in Russia, it attacks the standards and big business methods of a 'bourgeois kingdom' – and as such, said a contemporary review, in *Prim*, it 'should advantageously shake up the theme, mock a little less sympathetically, sting a little more . . . It is a soft film, with no spitefulness, completely inoffensive.' Certainly it is uneven; but

when in the middle the wife is entertaining in her room a handsome burglar, having speedily accepted him in lieu of her lover, and her fat old husband in his sock-suspenders is slobbering outside to be let in – well, that's in advance of Lubitsch at that point. We may laud it further: American comedy was innocuous, and wouldn't begin to bite till the following year, and in Europe only *Die Bergkatze* had had satirical thrust, eventually succeeded by *Der Liebe der Jeanne Ney*, again a year later than this film. These are not idle comparisons, since there is nothing specifically Russian about this film; the business of its three chief characters – three burglars – is far more 'American' than anything managed by Kuleshov.

Meanwhile, the teachings of Kuleshov and Meyerhold were coming to fruition in a pupil of genius. Sergei M. Eisenstein (1898–1948) had studied theatre with the latter and, once he had decided to move into films, he had looked in on the work of the Kuleshov studio. He had trained as an engineer, and had painted scenery at the Proletkult Theatre, a combination that led surely to films. He had made a short film sequence for one of his stage productions, and further experimentation led to the staging of a play – 'Gas Masks' – in a gas works, but the audience, expected to move about the premises with the actors, showed a reluctance to turn up in the first place. Eisenstein was persuaded that both the realism and freedom he needed could be realised only with film: after extended preparation and with the backing of the Proletkult collective he produced **Strike** (1924), a propagation of Soviet ideals – 'Towards the Dictatorship of the Proletariat' as the English copy is prefixed.

The argument is simple: a micrometer is stolen, and the man accused hangs himself; the workers strike, using the opportunity to demand reformed working conditions – and while management pretends to ponder, it brings in undercover men and *agents provocateurs* to create violence, and cavalry for the final massacre. However, we have not forgotten the words of Lenin quoted at the beginning, 'The strength of the working class is in its organisation.' The working

105

The three films Eisenstein made on the theme of Revolution remain among the cinema's greatest treasures. Supposedly without the trappings of fiction, they are in fact dynamic assemblies of highly emotive images. To see them, still, is to become as excited by the possibilities of the film medium as in the triumph of the 'People' which they are celebrating. ABOVE AND RIGHT, *Battleship Potemkin*, a tribute to the naval mutineers of 1905, and FAR RIGHT, both pictures, *October*, commissioned by the Soviet Government to commemorate the tenth anniversary of the Revolution itself. The young sailor is Eisenstein's representative of the proletariat, while the two pictures from *October* indicate the romanticised approach, ABOVE, and the documentary, BELOW – the invasion of the Winter Palace.

Eisenstein and the Image of Revolution

The U.S.S.R.: Montage and Message

Sergei Eisenstein

class here behaves as nobly as individual appearance suggests; the stock-holders are fat and smug, cigar-equipped. It is a strip-cartoon, racing from image to memorable image, some of them simple (a child cleaning a boot, a cat pattering along a paper-strewn corridor), some ostentatious (a bank of fire-hoses, a shanty-town of barrels), all of them chosen for maximum emotive effect. People hurry and scurry, the rushing and hiding are overdone, but the result is invigorating: film had been freed from the narrative confines imposed upon it by the novel and the theatre. The Russians had recognised that *Caligari* had advanced from a pattern of pictures, but Eisenstein went further, for *Strike* proceeds *solely* from its selection and juxtaposition of images.

There was, further, no identifiable hero; the entire crew of a ship was the hero of **Battleship Potemkin** (1925) – originally designed as a section of a longer film (to have been called *1905*), but, with the addition of the Odessa Steps sequence and the shots of the harbour at dawn, considered by its creator to be complete. The theme again was the revolt of the oppressed: the crew mutiny when ordered to eat rotten meat, and when the men ordered

to the firing squad refuse to shoot them, there is no recourse but to attack the officers – and it is a measure of the director's skill that a meek, modern audience can exult at the consequent brutality: this film makes revolutionaries of us all. When it opened abroad, it was dismissed in some quarters as propaganda: if that were so, it would not be, still, an overwhelming experience. The government, which commissioned it, got, however, exactly what it wanted; audiences were rewarded with a reconstruction of an historical incident, as immediate as if pieced together from newsreel material (that species of film we call 'documentary' had till that time only *recorded*); and Eisenstein, often improvising, advanced the innovations of *Strike*. Each shot is held for only an instant, and most of them have movement: the sea below and the surface of the deck, great factors of life at sea, are insistently with us. The film is organised like a symphony: the mutiny – the first movement – is harsh and vivid; there is the interlude, the harbour at dawn, and then the response of the populace – a movement *con brio* – gathering on the Mole; the Odessa Steps sequence – the coda; and, finally, the ship steaming out to sea, unmolested by the other units of the fleet. The Cossacks moving down the Steps, bayonets lowered, must be the most anthologised of movie sequences: it marks the high point of the discoveries in the cutting-room, joining together for total effect – what Eisenstein himself called 'shock attraction' – the varied images of the aggressor and the defenceless. It lasts longer than it could have done in life (had it happened), and one is aware of this after seeing it too often: one is aware of the artifice – and that way terror does not lie. It does, however, contribute to the cumulative effect of the most rousingly emotional of all films.

October (1928) also harks back to past dissension, and its sometime sub-title – *Ten Days that Shook the World* – indicates the throbbing, explosive nature of its happenings. It starts with the demolition of a statue of Alexander III and the proclamation of the provisional government; and ends with the storming of the Winter Palace, pausing en route to illustrate the massing of the dedicated proletariat and the death-struggles of the ruling orders – while amidst the gilded paraphernalia of despots, the doomed government waits for the voice of the people. The political elisions serve only to emphasise the nature of the tract, but Eisenstein allows one surprising – and enlivening – comment: a young sailor in the room of the Czarina, ashamed and embarrassed when confronted with something he cannot understand. In the middle reaches the mechanism falters and the rhythm slows, till the crowds move towards the lighted Palace. The action then moves inexorably towards the triumphant close – the clocks of Petrograd and Moscow, then of the world, and hands applauding. At that point, as the images blur, Sound would be superfluous. The absence of Sound cannot date any of these three films of Eisenstein; *October* is romanticised history, but in its pain and passion it reflects the spirit of the Revolution. It is the desired record, eloquently revealing the hand of a man at that time inspired.

The Soviet authorities smiled benignly on Eisenstein's achievements, but they were not shown widely within the Union; abroad, although *Strike* was a success in France and Germany – and *Potemkin* made him world famous – showings were restricted to film societies, a movement born at this time in order to see just such films, those unwanted by commercial managements. Roger Manvell later recalled: 'I well remember the emotion with which I first saw films like *Potemkin*, *October* and *Mother* some twenty years ago – a kind of artistic awe which had no conscious connection with the social system which these films were designed to advocate. It was an excitement entirely derived from the artistic form they exemplified.' Certain industry people were impressed with the 'artistic form', but except for Germany the innovations of the Russians did not influence the other film industries as the German cinema had done – because, for one thing, style and content were welded, indivisible, and instigation to revolution was not what those industries had been founded to propagate. Dr Manvell might separate the two, but others saw only a threat to democracy; cinema-owners, aware of the enthusiasm of a minority, happily decided that the style was as alienating as the content. In Britain, when the furore created by the coterie began to attract the curious, the government stepped in: *Mother* (q.v.) was banned in 1929, *Potemkin* and *Storm Over Asia* (q.v.) in 1930.

The serious film student (i.e. the member of a film society – someone convinced that the cinema, given half a chance, could be an art) was so mesmerised by the Soviet cinema that he took it for granted that it could produce two young film-makers of genius at the same time. Attempting to differentiate, Lewis Jacobs wrote, 'Where Eisenstein is all mind, Pudovkin is mostly feeling'. There are identifiable heroes in Pudovkin, some glimpses of humanity and less caricature – but despite such evidence of 'feeling' he is, finally, more dependent on the medium than was Eisenstein.

Vsevolod Pudovkin (1893–1953), after his work with Kuleshov, co-directed a still-amusing two-reel slapstick, *Chess Fever* (1925), to celebrate the International Chess Tournament then being held in Moscow. At that point the government invited him to make a commemorative film on the revolutionary events of 1905; and where Eisenstein had chosen an actual event, he selected a story by Maxim Gorki. **Mother** (1926) bears the influence of *Strike*, each shot composed for the maximum effect – and Pudovkin also works rhythmically, cross-cutting to hypnotic effect: but whereas Eisenstein worked each image against those each side of it, he preferred a judicious linking of details. To create the impression of industrial unrest he accelerates the stock shots of the factory building – they're not stock shots in the accepted sense, but they are impersonal and repeated; towards the end, the images seem to dance upon the screen; but the hastening pace reveals a dependence on the 'gathering force' techniques of Griffith. And, alas, the opening stages – the hovel, the brutal father and the cowed mother – are much more Griffith than Gorki.

Except for some vignettes at the trial (the inebriated counsel, the uninterested judge) the film is too calculated to be stirring; its shortcomings are magnified in **The End of St Petersburg** (1927), commissioned, like *October*, to mark the tenth anniversary of the Revolution and covering the same events. Its chief dissimilarity is the presence of a particular hero, a peasant involved in strike-breaking prior to the October rising; the original plan had been to cover two centuries of history. The cause is, of course, propaganda – which means that we are shown a certain truth; life as the film's perpetrators would like it to be: here, manipulations to the plot (such as it is) are matched by the care given to 'construction' – to the extent that differing interpretations can be made; each image is 'composed' to within an inch of its life. This can be effective (a soldier huddled in a trench, writing a letter; the introduction to St Petersburg – a montage of reflections in water and parts of grandiloquent statues), but it need not bear any relation to the truth. The pictorial devices are somewhat tired: the boot, eternal symbol of the oppressor (over-used in all these films, but, to be fair, also strongly suggestive of Sound); the matching of massing workers to smoke from chimneys and waves; and the close-ups of faces screaming just above camera-range, most notably (if not first) deployed on the Odessa Steps.

This is already academic film-making – perhaps the prerogative of a young man. The attack on the Winter Palace lacks the sweep and incident of Eisenstein's version: *October* is no less propaganda, but its roller-coaster exhilaration transcends its purpose.

Storm Over Asia (1928) also has its redundancies and clumping ironies, but, moving from a study of revolt to one of imperialism, it has chances to take: it seems to me one of the most mature of Silent films. It was originally known in the West as *The Heir to Jenghis Khan*, which is more faithful to the Russian title. The setting is Mongolia, and the Caucasians have arrived on their usual business – exploitation and manipulation. A fur-trapper, Bair (V. Inkishnikov), flees from them, becomes a partisan, and is captured by the White Russians and forced to become the puppet-king, heir to the great Khan. But he is eventually aroused, and his partisan army appears miraculously behind him – which is demonstrably dishonest, but the miracle would not have been lost on the masses who rose in 1917.

Pudovkin made another thirteen films – in the Sound period – mainly in collaboration; none of those shown in the West achieved any degree of recognition. It is a pity, however, that his fame and that of Eisenstein should have eclipsed some engaging minor talents. The late Russian Silent cinema is, in fact, a fine flowering, a result not only of Kuleshov and his Experimental school in Moscow, but of the Eccentrics in Leningrad – FEKS, as they called themselves – who were also great theorisers and experimenters. The most important of the FEKS are Grigori Kozintsev (1905–73) and Leonid Trauberg (b. 1902), who worked in tandem for most of their careers. They had worked together in Kiev in the theatre, and as a result of their experience with a touring studio theatre founded FEKS – the Factory of the Eccentric Actor – with Sergei Yutkevich. In 1924 they were invited by Sevzapkino to make a short comedy. Two years later they moved to Leningradkino to make **The Devil's Wheel** (1926), which was deeply indebted to the German cinema; but their commitment to the Moscow school is evident from Kozintzev's comment to the FEKS

Nikolai Batalov in Pudovkin's *Mother*, as the family is torn asunder by a strike: his father is killed and himself imprisoned, but he escapes to join the marching workers, reunited with his mother, a convert to the cause; and they die, martyrs, in mid-embrace.

group: 'All that we've been doing is childish nonsense, we must all see *Strike* again and again, until we can understand it and adopt its power for our own.' So the childish nonsense is behind them, and *The Devil's Wheel* is a story of ordinary folk. It is not, as Jay Leyda says in 'Kino' 'a drama of the gangster bands that preyed upon Petrograd during the Civil War': the town is clearly called Leningrad, and since the hero is a Soviet sailor, we may take the time to be the present; he does become involved with crooks, but they are petty hoods rather than gangsters. The sailor, a country boy, also gets involved with a girl, and booze: he goes back to his ship contrite and prepared for the worst, but the friendly smiles of his escort suggest that he'll be let off because he's only young once. Undoubtedly that is propaganda – of the sort that would eventually stifle the Soviet cinema: but at least the sailor is more human than most Russian movie heroes, and since later movies refused to allow that there was anything rotten in Russia, it is good to have a fairly comprehensive portrait of the Leningrad underworld. It is apparent throughout these early Kozintsev-Trauberg collaborations that they were fascinated by vice; they are most at home in smoke-clouded bars and bordellos – though careful not to make such places attractive to their heroes. Their cleverness here is in making their comment on the underworld in 'Eccentric' style, letting the camera go ape in the fairground or whenever there are crowds. Turning for the first time to 'everyday life' – which had never interested Russian film-makers – they have put it on the screen in a way that is honest both to the subject and to their own principles of style. Visually, the film is lively, but it seems a little trivial when set beside Pabst's more melodramatic *Die Freudlosse Gasse*. The girl's butcher father more than resembles Werner Krauss in that film: and did Pabst in return study this girl for his own portraits of women who are neither whores nor virgins but, like this one, what we'd call a good-time girl?

With **The Cloak** (1926), Kozintsev and Trauberg turned to Gogol – and it may be said to be a tale of everyday life a century earlier. Kozintsev explained later that the Leningrad cinema was dominated by historical films of stultifying stiffness: Gogol, with his grotesques and ironies, provided a counter-balance – and also a chance to be true again to the principles of FEKS. Leyda is right in seeing the central character as kin to both the somnambulist in *Caligari*, because of his appearance, and the doorkeeper in *Der Letzte Mann*, because of his pathos and isolation. The style and content have been worked out with as much thoroughness as with *The Devil's Wheel* – too much so, since the joint directors couldn't see the wood for the trees. The images may spill across the screen, but for the first half at least it is impossible to follow the narrative without a knowledge of the original novel plus some of 'The Nevsky Prospect', purloined to pad out a thin anecdote. As the clerk, Andrei Kostrichkin overplays with intelligence. In all these Russian films there is too much 'acting': the heroes and heroines are always naturalistic, but when anyone has anything half-villainous to do, they start to over-indulge – but in this case they're justified. The decor by Yevgeni Enei and the camerawork by Andrei Moskvin are in both cases superior to that on the earlier film, and they surpassed even this work in **The Club of the Big Deed** (1927). A contemporary study of the FEKS – by V. Nedborovo – calls this 'the most cinematographic' of their films, and he quotes another critic as saying that it was 'the smartest film yet produced by the Soviet Union' – by which I take it he means the most handsome. It is possible that Kozintsev and Trauberg sought historical subjects because they had these two brilliantly talented men in their team . . . but this was an historical subject in fashion with Eisenstein and Pudovkin, celebrating a revolutionary period of an earlier time – in this case the Decemberist movement of 1825. It has a collective hero, which here is an unsatisfactory device; and it has a villain who is villainous merely for the sake of it – which is hard to accept in a political film. Once again narrative clarity is not a strong point, but the sets – the gambling club of the title, the battlefield, a circus, a parade-ground – are used with great virtuosity. **New Babylon** (1929) was the only Kozintsev-

Trauberg film well received in the West; and was considered sufficiently important in the U.S.S.R. at the time for Shostakovich to write a score for it – surprisingly, not welded to the film in synchronised version after the coming of Sound. Although its title is that name given to Paris by the Prussian press of 1870, the subject is the subsequent Commune: the bourgeoisie (a theatre-owner and his actresses – the best representatives of decadence) retreat to the heights of Versailles as the Prussians advance, and the people, free of their bosses, find a new purpose in life – the Commune. The bourgeoisie can't bear to see them happy, and have the soldiers fire on them; a dying Communard shouts that they'll be back one day. For this trite tale, the French artists of the period have been ransacked, works by Doré and Daumier juxtaposed with those of Manet and Degas – for that same old purpose, irony: at the end, the film cuts back and forth between the defeated workers and corpses on the barricades and the same old effete faces swilling champagne – but with such bravura consistency that much may be forgiven. The medium is being used to its fullest extent, as putty, as a pliable toy – not as something recording the movements of actors.

The Kiss of Mary Pickford (1927) was directed by one of Kuleshov's pupils, Sergei Komarov, with due regard to his theories – the blending of fact and fiction; but since Komarov was a great admirer of the Eccentrics he gives much business to its hero, Igor Ilinskyi, one of Russia's favourite comics. The film is a satire on the local movie industry, incorporating newsreel footage of the celebrated European tour of Mary Pickford and Douglas Fairbanks; it is ironic that that tour should be best preserved via a film made in the Soviet Union – for the couple were, after all, two enormously wealthy people, major props of a capitalist industry. No one can doubt the charm and genuine pleasure of the couple, but one does notice them searching for the camera between smiles – just to make sure it's there. As with *Extraordinary Adventures of Mr West*, more might have been made of the subject, but the film is nevertheless a huge advance on that.

Another member of Kuleshov's work-shop, Boris Barnet (1902–65), made **The Girl with the Hatbox** (1927), an almost perfect comedy – richer, indeed, with visual wit than the comedies that René Clair was making at the time. The girl is Natasha (Anna Sten), who comes from the country once a week with the hats she makes: her buyer, Madame Irene, claims to the tax-inspector that the girl has a room in her house, and the girl promptly marries a destitute student (Ivan Koval-Samborsky) to give him a roof over his head. The film is inventive and enchanting, be it in the odd relationship of the girl and her 'husband', or the vile bourgeois behaviour of Madame Irene and hers. Also airy and irresistible is **House on Trubnaya Square** (1928), although it does tend to go heavy on party propaganda – though one of the funniest sequences is an amateur theatre show at the workers' club, in which lots of hackneyed jokes come up sparklingly fresh. The heroine is again a country girl (Vera Maretskaya), and the piece mainly concerns her adventures in an apartment house, clearly influenced by *Menschen Untereinander*; the most entertaining of her fellow-tenants is the jumped-up hair-dresser played in his last film role (he died in 1929) by Vladimir Fogel, the most human villain of the period.

He may also be seen in Abram Room's **Bed and Sofa** (1927), completing a *menage à trois* with Batalov and Ludmilla Semyenova, needless to say as the lodger who breaks up their marriage. In its acceptance of both adultery and abortion, the film might once have been shocking, but even allowing for the fact that Room was making a film for revolutionaries he was careful, for it's short on the necessary amorous activity. But if it is only mildly entertaining, it must be seen as another example of the Soviet film industry being ahead of any other. Like *By the Law*, the strongest influence seems to have been Sjöström, and the marriage here is not unlike that of the Ingmarssons, with no praise or blame for the trauma it undergoes. Others have seen this film as a comedy, since the situation is one of farce, and some of the devices used to indicate a marriage growing stale – husband ordering his tea

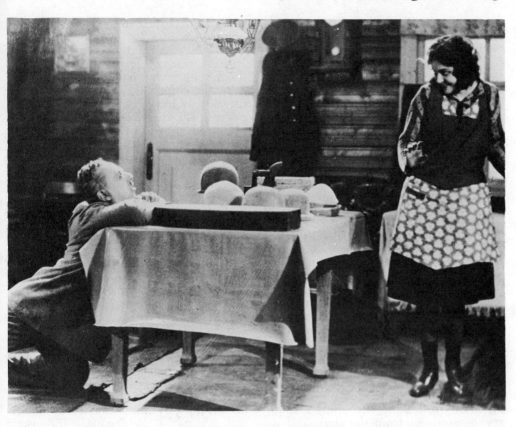

The achievements of the 'classic' Russian directors have cast too great a shadow over some lesser talents, but it is perhaps because of them that the comedies of Boris Barnet are such unexpected delights. In *The Girl with the Hatbox* the gentleman on the left is indeed proposing to Anna Sten: as her landlord he had not been particularly pleasant, but she has the winning lottery ticket – though she doesn't know it yet.

instead of asking for it – were typical of the comedy of the period. Let us say rather that it is drama treated lightly by one who finds absurdity in most human behaviour.

The same cannot be said of the Ukrainian, Alexander Dovzhenko (1894–1956), a painter who one sleepless night decided to start again in 'the one art which was fresh and new, with enormous creative potentialities and opportunities'. The first film he directed was a two-reel slapstick about a lost baby, **The Fruits of Love** (1926), a piece as inept as it is unfunny. When he turned serious, contemporary opinion placed him on a level with Eisenstein and Pudovkin, if not higher; as late as 1960 Ernest Lindgren wrote of **Earth** (1930): 'Its political moral is in its narrative framework, portraying the conflict between rich Kulaks and the collective farms which threaten to absorb their lands. But the film's more profound and more memorable content is its picture of the ever-recurring rhythm of pastoral life.

birth, love, death and sorrow following each other with the same inevitability as the ploughing, the sowing and the harvest.' Ah! there it is: peasants wresting their living from the soil – how much more worthy of attention than all those vamps, cuties, detectives and reporters!

It is the only one of Dovzhenko's pictures to enter the international repertory, but I have seen two of his preceding three features, and they are quite as dreadful. **Zvenigora** (1928) has some striking images, which is presumably why Eisenstein and Pudovkin recognised him as their equal. I find it unintelligible. Dovzhenko said, 'Do I hear the objection that some people in the audience may not understand my film? Well, I cannot help it . . . The reason you don't understand is within yourself. Maybe you are simply unable to think, whereas my purpose is to prompt your thinking while you see my film.' **Arsenal** (1929), supposedly a celebration of the Ukrainian people's struggle for liberty, plods on with pictures of armies,

113

soldiers, peasants, fields, machinery, followed by more pictures of armies, soldiers, peasants, etc. Watching it is like going to an exhibition where the pictures move – posed, artificial pictures, meant to strike us all of a heap with their artistry. Even the contemptible *Earth* does at least have a story, and I beg you to bear with me.

'Seventy-five years behind an ox-drawn plough,' says someone about an old man who promptly dies. The village goes ecstatic: a big attraction is en route. A circus? Stalin? No, a tractor – driven by the deceased's grandson, Vassil; he strays on to the land of a kulak, Khoma, who later murders him. Vassil's father wants him 'buried the new way, and we'll sing new songs about our new way of life': the whole village turns out for the burial, singing new songs about our new way of life, and ignoring the now-demented Khoma yelling out his grief. The dead man's fiancée has also gone mad, and is rushing around her hovel stark-naked; while the priest, unwanted for this important funeral, sits and stares with apprehension. The film ends with Khoma doing a wild Cossack dance in imitation of Vassil. His guilt, I might say, is apparent from the start, and the posturing intrudes upon the film's only pleasure – the plain, unfussy faces. Neither they, nor any amount of shots of rain-pelted apples, can save it; but, Lenin be praised, it only lasts just over an hour. It was John Coleman of the *New Statesman* who in 1976 prevented me from attempting Dovzhenko's next film, *Ivan* (1932): 'heavy and ludicrous' he dismissed it.

The sameness and self-consciousness of Russian cinema are reasons many avoid it: the films we have been discussing, even the comedies, are dedicated to one theme – the innate nobility of the worker/peasant. In the West, we have always preferred those concerned with revolutionary struggles, despite the over-use of irony, to those exalting the land; and when the greater of the two 'revolutionary' directors, Eisenstein, offers a study in the latter genre, we seldom programme it. **Old and New** (1929), also known as *The General Line*, co-directed with Grigori Alexandrov, was planned in 1926, but work was interrupted by *October* – and was further delayed when Stalin advised a more 'correct' ending: but all Eisenstein came up with was an epilogue – a montage, naturally – on the bond between Russian workers. The subject is the collectivisation of Soviet agriculture, via the study of one rural community. What makes the film unpalatable is that its message is simple-minded: tractors and bulls are lovely. I have to say that I am caught two ways by this film: by admiration for the images and editing – the language Eisenstein created for the cinema, so powerful that it is its own narrative; and by fatigue. All those smiling workers' faces, processions past enormous busts of Lenin, endless shots of fields and clouds . . . But then, this film wasn't made with us in mind.

6

The United Artists

IN 1919 the four most famous people working in films decided to pool their talents for their own greater financial advantage – Charles Chaplin, D. W. Griffith, Mary Pickford and her husband, Douglas Fairbanks. Despite the huge salaries they earned – particularly Chaplin and Pickford – their producers were making gigantic profits from their films, and they were in part reacting against persistent rumours that the studios would put a ceiling on star salaries. It was even said that Zukor was considering a merger with his arch-rival, First National, the more easily to achieve this; but it was an action of the latter company which triggered the foundation of the new association, when it casually refused Chaplin's request for an increase in his production budget. That talent should be its own boss was a policy the studios resisted – so strongly that all other attempts were killed until the Fifties, and then it was another long struggle before the studios bowed to the notion that talent demanded creative freedom – and as much money as it could command. The new company, United Artists, opened a distribution office, and its four principals either bought studios or hired space, relying on their reputations to have exhibitors demand their films. 'The lunatics have taken charge of the asylum,' went the industry quip, as it closed ranks against them: the cinema chains owned by the big companies refused to show United Artists' films – until they saw the profits being made by the independent theatres.

The concept, however, of United Artists was not started by one of its founder members but by a jobless executive determined to remain in the film industry. He was B. P. Schulberg (1892–1957), who in common with the other film moguls was Jewish, but unlike most of them was both American-born and literate. A former reporter, he joined Edwin S. Porter's Rex company as screenwriter and publicist, later moving with him to Famous Players. When Hiram Abrams, a New England distributor, succeeded H. V. Hodkinson within Paramount, Zukor began to realise that he no longer trusted Abrams: when he forced him out, Schulberg – by this time head of production – elected to go with him. Since the industry was controlled by Zukor, Fox, Laemmle and First National, the two men had three options open if they wished to continue in films: (1) apply to one of Zukor's rivals (2) join one of the still mushrooming minor companies, or (3) start up on their own. Schulberg believed that they could follow the last of these courses and overwhelm all competition if they gained the concurrence of the five most powerful figures in the industry. Thus Chaplin, Fairbanks, Pickford, Griffith and William S. Hart were each presented with a manifesto, '89 Reasons for United Artists'. Hart declined to join, and in the event United Artists was formed without Schulberg: for Fairbanks wanted the new company headed by William Gibbs McAdoo, a friend who was also an influential politician and son-in-law to President Wilson. McAdoo declined the offer, but proposed in his stead his press secretary, at the same time objecting to the financial arrangements to be made with Abrams and Schulberg. Abrams stayed; Schulberg left, to form his own production company (before rejoining Zukor in 1926, when Zukor coveted one of his stars,

Clara Bow. He resumed his position as head of production, till ejected from Paramount during that company's financial convulsions in 1932, along with Jesse Lasky – and like Lasky became an independent producer with only intermittent success.)

Once the experiment had proved successful, the four co-founders hired a production manager, Joseph M. Schenck (1877–1961), another immigrant and one-time theatre manager and producer; he joined them in 1924, and was virtually in control from 1926 onwards. He realised that more films were needed to feed the system of exchanges set up by Abrams as chief sales executive, and thus his own star (and brother-in-law) Buster Keaton joined the fold, as did others, including Valentino and Gloria Swanson.

Given their eminence at the time, it is not remarkable that the four founders of the company remain gigantic figures in cinema history. We still admire and enjoy the star vehicles of Pickford and Fairbanks – certainly the later ones. The same is true of the comedies of Chaplin, but not to the same extent. Up to five

or ten years ago, as throughout his lifetime, he was regarded as a genius; since then his reputation has decreased, and continues to do so. For over half a century Chaplin's position was as unassailable as that of Shakespeare: our parents and our grandparents had loved him, and then, suddenly, audiences were no longer laughing. This struck me as so astonishing that I tried to see as much Chaplin as I could with as many disparate audiences. Those that roared through most of Keaton and much of Harold Lloyd evinced only intermittent mirth with Chaplin. The most serious blow, however, to his reputation was the re-showing, in the last year of his life, of his one serious film, *A Woman of Paris* (q.v.), reputedly a masterpiece. For over fifty years he had refused requests from students to view it, and there was no copy in any Western archive; revealed, it was of appalling banality even by the standards at the time.

But though the contemporary reviews were ecstatic, what of the case of Griffith, who continued to have his admirers through the years? Aside from his false

D.W. Griffith at work: The lady to whom he is giving last minute instructions is Lillian Gish, while behind them is Robert Harron, his usual leading man. With the advent of Richard Barthelmess he was demoted to comic, or romantic lead in less important projects like *The Greatest Question.* When he shot himself it was said to be accidental, but it was after the New York premiere of *Way Down East,* which promised to be a triumph for both Griffith and Barthelmess. The film Griffith is directing in this picture is much earlier, *The Battle of the Sexes,* made in 1914.

claims to innovations, he has at least the achievement of 'bigness' with *Intolerance*; but his later films are sentimental and contrived melodramas, with virtually identical endings, as the heroine is saved from death, or a Fate Worse Than, amidst much cross-cutting. *Orphans of the Storm* (q.v.) was described by Robert E. Sherwood, in the old *Life* Magazine, as better than any previous Griffith film, and 'immeasurably better' than the two German films which had inspired it, *Danton* and *Madame Dubarry*: 'There is scarcely a moment,' Sherwood said, 'that is not charged with intense dramatic power,' and Lillian Gish in her memoir quotes another contemporary: 'A great work of art. It has the sweep of *The Birth of a Nation,* the remarkable tragic drive of *Broken Blossoms,* the terrific melodramatic appeal of *Way Down East* . . . ' It is difficult today to find these films any less dreadful than those which Griffith's admirers deplored. *Dream Street* (1921) was 'a low point' in his work, said Iris Barry, but 'too early to be considered the beginning of decline', and her colleague, Eileen Bowser, dismissed Griffith's three First National films as 'potboilers, and one suspects them to be the work of not very competent assistants'; but since she describes *The Greatest Question* (1919) as 'the usual melodramatic Griffith story' I fail to see why she could not accept that the usual Griffith was directing it.

A clue to the mystery may lie in Rotha's 1929 assessment of *Broken Blossoms* (q.v.), that its 'simple, human story [was] without the box-office attractions of silk legs and spectacle.' James Agate, writing in 1922, found 'this little picture as arresting as ever' and ten years later he bracketed it with *Way Down East* as films of which he 'personally can never tire'; another ten years on he listed it as one of the ten best films ever made. How little, you see, was expected of the cinema: would Agate as theatre critic have accepted a drama as barren and emotionally naïve?

After *Intolerance* Griffith had accepted an invitation from the British government to make a propaganda film, **Hearts of the World** (1918), which it financed together with Zukor (against Griffith's future services). Griffith, under two pseudonyms, provided the scenario – about a boy

(Robert Harron) and girl (Miss Gish) divided by war but reunited in the heat of battle, in an inn where there are Germans (literally) coming out of the woodwork. The film was eventually of little purpose, since the U.S. had entered the War by the time it was shown – but it quickly made half-a-million dollars' profit. Some of the film was shot in England, where it gathered Noël Coward as an extra, but most of it in California; the battle footage left over was incorporated into **The Girl Who Stayed at Home** (1919), which contrasts a French heiress (Carol Dempster) and her American soldier suitor (Richard Barthelmess) with two effete New Yorkers (Clarine Seymour, Mr Harron). It is a particularly shapeless film, cutting inanely between these couples and a German soldier, whose presence is finally explained when he saves the heiress from the inevitable Fate Worse Than. Griffith's work on it was supposedly perfunctory because his attention was taken up by **Broken Blossoms** (1919), a tale of miscegenation in Limehouse rendered the more excruciating by its intertitles (e.g. 'Into the dark chambers of her frightened, incredulous little heart comes warmth and light'). Agate was right to praise the performances of Barthelmess as the Yellow Man and Miss Gish as the girl who runs away from her brutal stepfather (Donald Crisp); he also liked the settings – photographed throughout, appropriately, as a stage-set, and disastrously influential: when other producers learnt that this film was shot in eighteen days at a cost of $88,000 they drew away from location shooting. It was made for Zukor, who thought it 'too poetic' and sold it to United Artists, since he knew they needed product, for $250,000: it made a profit for the new company of $700,000.

Griffith dedicated **True-Heart Susie** (1919) to all the girls who wait vainly for a husband – presumably by staying pure: the intertitles emphasise that paint and powder constitute traps of a devious nature, but the film is attractively ambivalent. We are supposed to admire the artless, plain Miss Gish, and despise the hussy Miss Seymour, but though the pure one eventually triumphs and her rival becomes slatternly and dies, we may sense the division in Griffith himself between Victorian sentimentalist and Hollywood

The photography of Billy Bitzer and the acting of Lillian Gish are virtually all that make Griffith's films watchable today. The most pleasant is *True–Heart Susie*: Miss Gish (right) sells the family cow to pay secretly for the college education of her sweetheart (Robert Harron), to lose his good opinion by taking the blame for the infidelities of his new love (Clarine Seymour).

party-man. It does, therefore, offer an accurate reflection of the changing attitude towards women, and contains also a clear and well-judged portrait of a small rural community. It was Griffith's last film for Zukor, and he reputedly signed the First National contract in order to buy his own studio – at Mamaroneck, New York. *The Greatest Question* has the hideously abused Miss Gish as an orphan skivvy, and in **Way Down East** (1920) she is seduced but abandoned. Griffith paid $175,000 for the rights to this already dated barnstormer, and it was his biggest commercial success after *The Birth of a Nation*. Readers, after all, still wept at the death of Little Nell, and the borrowings from Dickens in this film are many: that author, however, would surely have loved Miss Gish, playing a waif but with such spirit that you know she will denounce her seducer before rushing out on to the ice-floes. **Orphans of the Storm** (1921) was based on an even more venerable melodrama, reset at the time of the French Revolution because the two previous German films had such acclaim in New York; an introduction spells out the dangers of Bolshevism and

anarchy when one iniquitous government is replaced by another, while the portrayal of Danton, as an intertitle has it, makes him 'the Abraham Lincoln of France'.

When the public failed to respond in sufficient numbers, Griffith tried a mystery story, *One Exciting Night,* and another attempt to present rural America coping with the Jazz Age, *The White Rose;* but without Miss Gish to furnish her beauty and talent his films looked more old-fashioned than ever. Although he had experimented with synchronisation at the time of *Dream Street,* he advanced in no other direction. Indeed, he regressed, and in **America** (1924) attempted to do for the War of Independence what his most successful film had done for the War between the States. Also, he returned to the animated tableaux of old, and claims to historical accuracy were derided when the plot has George Washington playing Cupid to a plough-boy poet (Neil Hamilton) and a highborn lady (Carol Dempster). Stung by such criticism, Griffith tried a contemporary story, of conditions in post-war Germany, **Isn't Life Wonderful?** (1924), about childhood sweethearts (Hamilton, Dempster) who can marry if they can surmount poverty. The film does flicker to life with a sequence about queueing for meat as the Reichsmark rises by the millions, but was no better liked by press or public. Griffith was an expensive worker, and because he had given United Artists only failures since *Way Down East* his quarrels with his partners now became public. He signed a contract with Zukor – which, announced before he had severed that with United Artists, caused the latter to claim his first Paramount film, **Sally of the Sawdust** (1925) – a version of a W. C. Fields stage vehicle which foolishly shifted the emphasis from Fields to the heroine (Miss Dempster), a circus-girl finally reunited with her 'real' grandparents. Griffith's loss of independence found compensation when, after another Fields vehicle, he was assigned to an expensive project, *The Sorrows of Satan,* abandoned by deMille when he left to form his own company. But when, after costs had further mounted amidst much dispute, it too was a disaster at the box office, Griffith's lingering reputation within the industry was finally annihilated.

Nevertheless, Schenck brought him back to United Artists, inasmuch as he signed him to make five films for his Art Cinema Corporation, releasing through U.A. – for which privilege he voted Griffith's remaining stock (which Griffith hung on to till 1933) and exercised control over script and budget. Only four films were made, and **Lady of the Pavements** (1929) is at best mediocre, the story of a Parisian countess (Jetta Goudal) who revenges herself on a reluctant suitor (William Boyd) by making him fall in love with a trollop disguised as a lady. There is more to be said, however, for **Abraham Lincoln** (1930), his first Talkie. 'Shucks,' says a small boy, looking at Baby Abe, 'he'll never amount to anything'; but nothing that follows is quite as bad. The script, credited to Stephen Vincent Benét, was apparently much disregarded – which is perhaps why the Civil War consists of bitty battle scenes, punctuated by Mr Lincoln receiving news of varying import – but in the title-role Walter Huston (q.v.) has the strength and sincerity to make such badly conceived scenes seem consequential. During production, Griffith was, in his own words, in 'a nightmare of the mind and nerves', but this is a reasonably polished piece of work. It is difficult to offer more credit in view of the all-round incompetence of **The Struggle** (1931), made without studio control and as a gesture to prove that his failures had been due to 'interference'. It was made possible by a bank loan, some backing from United Artists, and a 1929 tax refund to his old company, luckily invested. There are just two good sequences: the prologue, set in 1911, in a beer garden; and an engagement party done with a more reasonable view of the proletariat than was usual in films of the era. The rest is a tract on the Evils Wrought by the Demon Drink, from the husband getting rolling drunk after being taunted for ordering a sarsaparilla, through broken marriage and vagabondage, to an attempt to murder his daughter during the last throes of D.T.s – followed by an epilogue in which he is regenerated and gets his job back, together with a raise, because the factory has adopted his invention. Griffith's own 1909 A Drunkard's Reformation could not have been less sophisticated – or less topi-

cal: despite the modern costumes, there is no reference to Prohibition. The staging is clumsy, the sound as primitive as in the very first Talkies – and audiences at its few showings, in Philadelphia, roared with laughter while Griffith cowered in his hotel room. His company went into receivership, and he lived on another sixteen years, earning enough from occasional reissues, occasional consultant's fees and the remake rights to *Broken Blossoms* – made in Britain in 1936 – to pay for a hotel room and booze. Writers on film who castigated Hollywood for not using him had presumably not seen *The Struggle* – or examined his record of failures. Hollywood, for once at least, knew better than its critics.

Mary Pickford's last film for First National was **Daddy Long Legs** (1919), in which she leaves an orphanage because of an unknown benefactor. At a time when workhouses were a prominent part of the urban scene, the orphanage must have terrified audiences, till they could relax with the pre-Raphaelite countryside of the second half; and they must have been happy that she preferred the old-world courtesy of the unknown benefactor (Marshall Neilen, who also directed) to brash young Jimmy, who almost certainly liked jazz. The difficulty with Miss Pickford today is that her interpretation of childhood varies between the kittenish and the grotesque; in the midst of tall supporting-players and sets made to scale, she pouts and grins, walking with legs wide apart and toes turned out – and it is a parody of childhood. The public's insistence that she play children was surely due to the fact that though it had taken her to its heart, it found her pallid in grown-up roles; as a child, her spirited and merry personality must have endeared her to spectators who cherished their childhoods more than we do today: there was authority to be flouted, there were crusty hearts to be melted, the poor and deprived to be cosseted. She was Cinderella in a different dress, usually in stories that adolescent girls had wept over on the printed page. She apparently loathed such tales, but chose one, **Pollyanna** (1920), for her first United Artists film because she wanted to protect her investment. 'This is really not a story,' says the foreword, but 'the rainbow born of the sunshine of a

The World's Sweetheart

ABOVE: Mary Pickford in a double-role in *Little Lord Fauntleroy*: it was her gifted photographer, Charles Rosher, who – in this film – first used double-exposure for such effects, and they are still impressive. RIGHT: After the insipidity of most of Miss Pickford's films, *My Best Girl* is a delightful surprise. In one funny sequence, the boss's son takes her home – only she thinks he's merely a store apprentice and is uncertain about this supposed dinner for two of the workers. He is played by Charles 'Buddy' Rogers, whom she married after her divorce from Fairbanks.

On the set of *Rosita*, from left to right: Charles Chaplin, Ernst Lubitsch, Mary Pickford and Douglas Fairbanks. Miss Pickford had invited Lubitsch to direct her because of his historical spectacles – and this was another. It was the critical success of Chaplin's *A Woman in Paris* which caused Lubitsch to return to the sophisticated comedies which he most enjoyed making.

little girl's smile.' The little girl learns the 'glad' philosophy from her father and imparts it to all and sundry till felled by an almost fatal accident, while trying to save a baby, of course: 'God wouldn't let those little feet be destroyed when He needs them to run His errands,' says an intertitle. **Suds** (1920), directed by Paul Powell, is more palatable both because it is short and because Miss Pickford's role is similar to the skivvy in *Stella Maris* – a cockney laundress who dreams of romance with a masher but finds love with the delivery boy. The source was a one-act play that Maude Adams used to perform, but Pickford returned to the 'classics' with **Little Lord Fauntleroy** (1921), directed by Alfred E. Green and Jack Pickford, her brother. She plays both the little lord and his mother, Dearest; he is not actually a lord, but the American heir to an earldom – melting his grandfather's heart, besting a rival claimant and introducing American democracy into an English castle. The success of the film – and of Frances Hodgson Burnett's novel – was partly due to the tingling thought that American red

blood was intermingling with British blue; what today repels is that it was thought to be the height of human ambition to be a lord.

In her other films at this time – e.g. *Tess of the Storm Country* (1922) – Miss Pickford, at that time almost thirty, plays an adolescent of uncertain age. The apparent acceptance of her Dearest encouraged her to try adult roles, but the public responded to neither **Rosita** (1923) nor *Dorothy Vernon of Haddon Hall* (1924). The former was directed by Lubitsch, after he had rejected the latter – for which Pickford had brought him to the U.S. As Rosita, a fiery street-singer whose virtue is threatened by the Spanish king, she fails to supply him with the sensuous appeal of Negri; and if it is surely the most enjoyable of her extant films, it was a regression for Lubitsch himself. In the pages of *Photoplay* Miss Pickford asked her fans what roles she should play, and the overwhelming response was Cinderella. But that would have been too easy; like her husband – and as 'king' and 'queen' of the American film industry it was befitting –

she wanted to offer her public both the best possible production and herself in a new role. The challenge, however, was never extended beyond the bounds of reasonable investment, so virtually all that is new in **Little Annie Rooney** (1925) is the milieu – she's the daughter of Officer Rooney, a New York cop. Again, she is an urchin, again she almost dies, and again she grows up miraculously at the very end for a romantic fade-out. William Beaudine directed, as with **Sparrows** (1926), where she mothers a group of orphans in the middle of an alligator-infested swamp, her resourcefulness unquestioned – to the extent that one wonders why the owners of this baby farm haven't fed her to a quicksand. They are excellent villains (Gustav von Seyffertitz and Charlotte Mineau), and the film undoubtedly has thrills of a far-fetched nature.

The Cinderella aspect of **My Best Girl** (1927) is so strong that Pickford advanced to adolescence, as stockgirl in a department store. In this last of her Silent films she proves an adept comedienne, sharing some delightful scenes with the boy (Charles 'Buddy' Rogers), the boss's son learning the business. Sam Taylor directed this almost perfect romantic comedy, a good example of the Pickford and Fairbanks films, co-operative efforts not factory-packaged. The stars were the controlling forces, assisted by the director, and, in her case, Charles Rosher (according to his own word), who photographed her films so handsomely – and probably by her mother, watching on the side of the set. The 'Elton Thomas' who wrote most of the Fairbanks films is his own pseudonym, but Allan Dwan, who directed two of them, has said that it referred to the Fairbanks crew, since every one chipped in.

The energy of Douglas Fairbanks (1883–1939) was prodigious, and it is said that his exuberance alienated his co-workers at Triangle: Anita Loos, then a scenario writer with that company, managed to harness him and present him to the public as the all-courageous, always optimistic all-American boy; her stories for him* often found him as basically

*They are credited to her and her husband, John Emerson, often also as director: but Miss Loos later insisted that Emerson's creative contribution was nil.

decent playboy or wronged black sheep of the family. He made four such films for United Artists, but only one after he started his series of swashbucklers: **The Nut** (1921), directed by Ted Reed. In this, he is a wealthy scion whose attempts to aid his fiancée's philanthropic schemes end in chaos – the same role that Keaton played in *The Saphead* (q.v.), as recommended a few months earlier by Fairbanks, who had done it on the stage in New York, borrowing in return the fantastic household gadgets from *One Week* (q.v.), to remind us how frankly dependent were these artists on each other. But he was no more a comic than he was an ardent romantic hero, and he didn't find his real screen identity till he took sword in hand. His comic sense was always apparent, however, deliciously so in his Spanish dance as Don Q, all heel-taps and bum-wriggles; his bragging and his dashing, always a mite self-mocking, took on an extra edge in his swashbucklers; and his balletic agility was entirely suited to leaping parapets, shinning walls and tackling a dozen assailants while protecting the heroine with his free arm. 'When life was life and men were men' runs an intertitle in **The Three Musketeers** (1921), and one loves this enlivening and sometimes magical performer for believing it.

He had wanted to play d'Artagnan for years, and took the chance when he decided that the troops returning from France were not in the mood for his usual optimistic subjects. First he made **The Mark of Zorro** (1920), from a magazine story about a Spanish-educated Californian don who poses as an effete buffoon by day and is by night the daring swordsman who rights the peons' wrongs. It is, alas, a throwback to the early features, since you could shuffle the incidents without harm and no character but the don has individuality; and there is little more to be said for anything other than his stunts in the Dumas film, also directed by Fred Niblo, or for **Robin Hood** (1922), directed by Allan Dwan, or for **The Thief of Bagdad** (1924), directed by Raoul Walsh. His Robin Hood finds him rather Robin Goodfellow; and not so parenthetically, his followers are not so much 'merry' as 'gay'. This has something to do with the way they were choreographed, but indeed the reverence accorded comradeship in the Fairbanks films goes beyond the buddy-buddy attitude of many American films; however innocently meant, surely only one interpretation is possible of that scene where Robin is found romping on the floor with a friend, and the king (Wallace Beery) observes, 'At a time like this 'tis befitting he shows his love for a maid.' It is the nature of such against-all-odds tales that their heroes are renegades or outlaws, a tradition that goes back at least to Hereward the Wake: Fairbanks contrived to be outside the law, either pretended or wronged, from the start, but with *Robin Hood* he found his formula. The exposition is painfully slow (to modern eyes) till the halfway mark, when the tempo will quicken, then dull till the all-out action of the final sequence. The pastiche of *The Thief of Bagdad* – inspired, incidentally, by the German spectacles – finally explodes into the marvellous final sequence with the carpet whizzing above Bagdad, its shadow over the towers to prove that it wasn't a simple matter of superimposition.

For Fairbanks believed in giving value for money. *The Three Musketeers* was by the standards of the time a 'super-production', and Edward Knoblock was engaged to handle the adaptation; also Fairbanks sensibly believed that his films had to be visually exciting, importing on occasion designers from Europe to achieve this. The famous castle set in *Robin Hood* still takes the breath away. The upper reaches of the great hall were achieved with glass-shots, i.e. backcloths painted on glass before the camera-eye or sometimes on the lens itself, an established device to enhance the spectacle at minimum cost, but the exteriors brought the budget to $2 million, the highest for any film till that time and provided by Fairbanks himself when faced with his financiers' doubts. The industry was in crisis, for it had begun to repeat itself, and the public, not then as movie-orientated as it would be during the first decade of Talkies, had begun to stay away from all but the exceptional film – and though this was, it hardly recovered its costs. *The Thief of Bagdad,* also expensive, was hugely profitable, encouraging Fairbanks to use Technicolor for **The Black Pirate** (1926)

directed by Albert Parker. Keaton the previous year had been the first to use this colour system, for the prologue of *Seven Chances* (q.v.), and until the arrival of three-tone Technicolor it was more commonly used for one-reel sequences in otherwise monochrome films – due, clearly, to its limitations. In choosing to make the first movie wholly in colour Fairbanks selected a subject and setting to suit the limited colour palette then available – for sea and sky and what was literally a desert island. The effect is other-worldly, and the fact that the film is visually satisfying owes much to the paraphernalia of sails and rigging designed by Carl Oscar Berg. It is against those sails that Fairbanks performs one of his most celebrated stunts, sliding down the sails with his knife in the canvas. Not till long after Fairbanks's death was it disclosed that he had done few of his own stunts – 'the best kept secret of the time', as Eileen Bowser puts it. (The other famous stunt – sliding down the curtain in *Robin Hood* – was done with a concealed slide.)

The Black Pirate, however, has its longueurs, but I have no reservations about the other late Fairbanks Silents. **Don Q, Son of Zorro** (1925) is a great advance on its predecessor, an adventure set in old Madrid, with the ageing Zorro crossing the Atlantic to help his son out of difficulties – Fairbanks in a double role, well supported by Donald Crisp (who also directed) as the villain, and Mary Astor as the heroine. There is a superb villain in **The Gaucho** (1927) – Gustav von Seyffertitz as Ruiz the Usurper; and instead of the usual anaemic leading lady there is a fiery senorita, Lupe Velez, a shrew to be tamed; there also lurks 'The Victim of Black Death', a figure as terrifying as any created by Lon Chaney. Fairbanks himself is head of a band of outlaws pitted against a fascist regime, and as directed by F. Richard Jones the whole film has sweep and imagination; it is ingenuous but not naïve. The duels, escapes and last-minute rescues take place in settings by Berg even more impressive than those in *The Black Pirate*, and the piece is wrapped in a religious mysticism that isn't cloying. At a time when virtually all films carried morals, the principals of United Artists were particularly strict about this, doubtless because their

The Great Swashbuckler

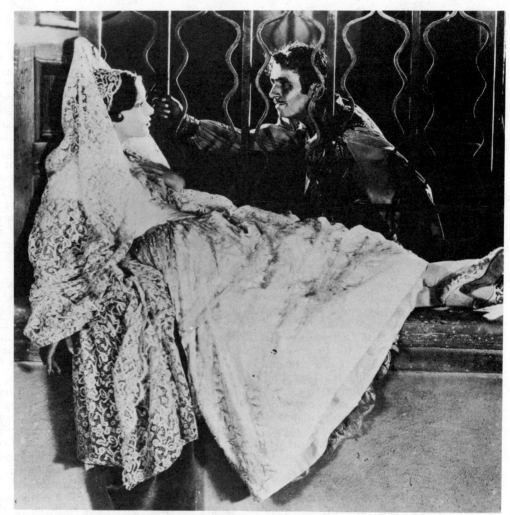

FAR LEFT: Douglas
Fairbanks about to
embark on one of his
space-defying leaps
in *The Thief of
Bagdad* and, ABOVE,
as lover with Lupe
Velez in *The Gaucho*
The latter is later and
better, since it was a
challenge to
Fairbanks to make
each vehicle more
colourful and more
exciting than the
last. His final Silent
is shown LEFT, in an
advertisement for a
reissue.

eminence decreed it; Griffith's and Pickford's moralities were fundamentally of the Sunday school, and so were those of Fairbanks. However, **The Iron Mask** (1929) is suffused – albeit in an elementary way – with a feeling of defeat, of time passing, of death and change. All the Fairbanks swashbucklers exemplify the days when movies were young and fun, but he was growing older and was conscious of it: Dwan directed this d'Artagnan to go about his derring-do with greying locks. And movies themselves were growing older: the jazz singer had sung, and now Fairbanks spoke – prologue and epilogue, and just for a moment in the middle.

The fame of Chaplin was greater even than that of 'Doug' and 'Mary' and the acclaim virtually unanimous, his 'genius' an accepted fact. Probably no film of its time was as much loved as **Shoulder Arms** (1918), in which he represented all those 'little men' who didn't want to fight the Kaiser and who endured the blitzkrieg of trench warfare. **The Kid** (1921) was an even bigger triumph, acknowledged, as Chaplin says in his autobiography, a 'classic' immediately after its New York opening, and going on to repay its $300,000 cost many times over. First National had insisted that the public did not want to see Chaplin in features, despite the success of both *A Dog's Life* (1918) and *Shoulder Arms* in three reels each and the comparative failure of the two two-reel successors, *Sunnyside* and *A Day's Pleasure*. *The Kid* was six reels long, and only released after long battles with the company, which proposed to release it as three two-reelers. Chaplin proved to be justified, for the world laughed and cried at these adventures of the tramp and the ragamuffin (Jackie Coogan), a miniature version of himself. The slapstick is particularly inventive in a sequence where the kid breaks windows and Charlie turns up as a glazier, and the pathos is well judged; however, the fantasy sequence is horrendous, and it is difficult to justify Chaplin's reputation as a social satirist by such rare, nudging touches as the shot of the hospital crucifix after the mother has been turned away from its door. Certainly he took his reputation seriously, attempting a satire on the rich in **The Idle Class** (1921). However, although that

film contains some superb comic invention (which has little to do with satire) more to be preferred is **Pay Day** (1922), which is indeed an extended music-hall sketch: in it the Little Fellow has a wife for the first time since *Getting Acquainted* in 1914, played by the same actress, Phyllis Allen. After those two-reelers he went to four for **The Pilgrim** (1922), effortlessly filling them as he is mistaken for the new preacher and thus exposed to new temptations (the collecting box; the urge to show off during his sermon), to a ghastly family and an inconvenient colleague from his convict days. The film, like *Easy Street,* is a masterpiece, throwing into relief the pretension of much of his later work.

A Woman of Paris (1923) was his first film for United Artists, written, produced and directed by him, but a vehicle for his usual leading lady, Edna Purviance – playing a demi-mondaine caught between her country sweetheart (Carl Miller) and the wealthiest bachelor (Adolphe Menjou) in Paris. As a piece of film-craft it is no better or worse than most American features of the time, though certainly inferior to the Keaton and Lloyd films released the following month; as a film about 'sin' it is in the simple-minded tradition of *A Fool There Was*, and its vaunted sophistication is not to be compared to that in the films of the brothers deMille. However, Chaplin (after commissioning Josef von Sternberg to make another film with Purviance, which he apparently destroyed in a fit of professional jealousy) was back on form with **The Gold Rush** (1925), making the Tramp a prospector in the frozen North, giving him at least three fine sequences: a hilarious one where the tramp and Big Jim (Mack Swain) are in a hut which unbeknown to them is on the edge of a precipice; and two pieces of mime, both of pathos, both at the dinner-table – the boiled old boot, its laces eaten like spaghetti, and the dancing rolls, stuck on forks, with which he entertains his girl in fantasy. But Chaplin's glances at the camera indicate his increasing self-consciousness, and the commentary he wrote and added for the 1942 reissue only confirms the mediocrity of his thought, viz. 'A city grew, and humanity warmed it, with living, loving, desiring.' **The Circus** (1928) strives to comment on humanity, as the Tramp – a clown to his employers and to the girl he vainly worships from afar – suffers the ill-will of others in the cause of goodness; and when he finally offers some slapstick on the high wire, the laughs come stumblingly. Chaplin was aware that the film was lacking, for he did not mention it in his memoirs and it was the only one of his features he did not reissue during the Fifties, when in 1970 he did allow it to be shown, the reviewers were dismissive – and indeed several of those in London recommended their readers to go instead to the Academy Cinema to see Buster Keaton.

The original reviews, however, of **City Lights** (1931) – and of its first reissue in 1950 – are unanimous in saying that it hardly falls short of perfection; Chaplin's 'genius' was confirmed by his daring to make a Silent – then regarded as the pure form – among the Talkies. Even the maudlin ending was admired, though like that of *The Kid* it dithers between his early good endings, complete rejection by society, or walking off with the Girl into the sunset, as in *Modern Times* (q.v.). Here, the Tramp has fallen in love with a blind girl and is befriended by a millionaire who recognises him only when drunk – a hugely manipulative film, bearable only for a boxing-match in which Chaplin confirms that he was a great clown. His own treacly score (poured over all his films thereafter) and the tenth-rate sets reinforce a feeling that he believed his own 'genius' was enough.

Buster Keaton (1895–1966) was liked and admired, but critically often got the crumbs from Chaplin's table. Or not even that: *The New York Times* commented – incredibly – of *Steamboat Bill Jr* that 'Buster Keaton's latest attempt to make the millions laugh is a sorry affair'. His decline and disappearance were not marked by the attention which would surely have been paid to Chaplin. When Lewis Jacobs wrote 'The Rise of the American Film' in 1939, he devoted a chapter to Chaplin and one line to Keaton. The former lived long enough to see his work decried – at least in some countries; and Keaton died not long after finding himself reinstated. The fact that the reputation of the one was inflated during the forty years in which the other was in almost total eclipse has caused all

sorts of snap-judgments as to Keaton's superiority. John Crosby was right, however, when he said, in 1975, that Chaplin 'clearly considered himself to be the clown for all ages – and that's why the stuff creaks a bit today. Buster Keaton holds up much better – and Keaton had no idea he was playing for posterity.' The truth of the matter is that Keaton is more in tune with modern taste; he was not before his time – for audiences laughed at him then – but his appeal is timeless. That Chaplin's one-man-band talent awed his admirers cannot be doubted; because Keaton worked with directors and writers, his own work with them uncredited, may be one reason he was undervalued. Our view of the cinema is different from that of their contemporaries: Chaplin never mastered the medium, Keaton did. Long after Chaplin's films had moved from a confined set, he was incapable of doing any chase or piece of action except within the equivalent of stage confines; his scenarios remained narratives with intertitles taking the place of dialogue. He never learnt to use the medium as Keaton did, using space and detail: Keaton understood the limitations of the Silent screen, and he *used* them. Not all his shorts reveal his capabilities, but the totality of his Silent films reveal him unmistakably as the screen's supreme genius of the Silent era.

He was born into a vaudeville family of acrobats, and went into movies by chance, when Roscoe 'Fatty' Arbuckle, directing and acting in **The Butcher Boy** (1917), invited him, an onlooker, to participate. Here, he is a grave young man in a flat hat wanting molasses, but he is absent-minded: before he knows it he is deep in molasses, not to be freed till a struggle reminiscent of the wrestlers in the Palazzo dell' Signoria. Keaton had fallen in love with movie-making. He continued to support Arbuckle in his two-reelers, gradually getting more of the action; when Arbuckle accepted an offer from Paramount, his producer, Joseph M. Schenck, gave Keaton the chance to replace him as his prize comic. Schenck made an agreement with Metro to release, and that company engaged Keaton independently for a feature, **The Saphead** (1920), directed by Winchell Smith, to play a foolish young man who saves the

The Little Fellow

'The Little Fellow' was the way Charles Chaplin usually referred to the character he created, seen RIGHT, at his most outrageous and engaging, in *The Pilgrim*. The slapstick *Pay Day*, BELOW RIGHT, is one of his last two-reelers and again one of the most enduring: he is a hen-pecked husband and Phyllis Allen was clearly excellent casting as the wife. He had by this time begun to inject pathos into his work, most notably in *The Kid*, BELOW FAR RIGHT, with Jackie Coogan. Chaplin's most successful blend of comedy and pathos is probably in *The Gold Rush*, ABOVE FAR RIGHT: the lady standing on the bar is Georgia Hale, to whose heart he will aspire, without, at first, much encouragement.

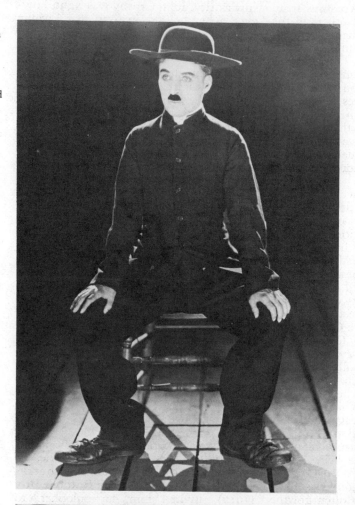

129

family fortunes by dabbling on the stock exchange. Though he returned to this figure – the solemn-faced, silk-hatted dummy whose meddling inadvertently saves the day – the film is by no means as funny as his later ones. The constant was his unsmiling face; unlike his rivals, the roles he played varied; where Chaplin's screen romances were yearnings for the unattainable, and Lloyd's directed towards nice eager girls, Buster's were exasperating and soppy. He moved through slapstick, satire, fantasy and black comedy, otherwise consistent only that he matched nimble wits and an athletic body with overwhelming odds. In his first-released starring two-reeler, **One Week** (1920), he follows tradition by wearing a clown's clothes but, free of Arbuckle, he triumphantly attacks the world of gadgetry, with a Do-It-Yourself house of which a rival has switched the numbers on the containers. **The High Sign** (1921), made first, also has a house – the home of a secret society; it is even more crazily animated, with swivelling doors and panels useful not only as escape routes but as weapons. It is less inventive, but an intertitle offers the best introduction to Keaton: 'Our hero came from *nowhere* – he wasn't going *anywhere* – he got kicked off *somewhere*.' This rootlessness is the only thing Keaton owes to Chaplin: he will attempt to earn an honest living – or at any rate a living – but misfortune and misunderstanding dog his footsteps.

In **The Goat** (1921), his eighth two-reeler, he is an innocent man thought to be a desperate criminal – he had simply been watching a prisoner being photographed, and the prisoner had ducked. **The Playhouse** (1921) also finds him at his peak, busily filling the playhouse and the screen with myriad Busters; but **The Boat** (1921) is bleak, his ingenuity so little called into play that the normal balance of adversity and eventual triumph is lost: the elements win, and with home and boat gone, the family trudge off into the darkness. In **The Paleface** (1921) the pursuer becomes the pursued: an innocent lad, blithely chasing butterflies, disturbs some Red Indians and barely escapes scalping. In **Cops** (1922), the pursuers appear to be the whole of the Los Angeles police force. It is their day for parading,

and Buster, in an odd number of manoeuvres, has acquired a horse and cart not his own, loaded with furniture not his own, and setting out for no destination. He has accepted good luck and ill, hoping for a deal and thus to marry the Mayor's daughter – the American dream, as Rudi Blesh points out in his book on Keaton. Having magnificently outwitted every single cop, Keaton is ignored by her, so he unlocks the prison door and goes inside: if you're going to be lonely and unloved, what price freedom? It was in the nature of Chaplin's tramp that society rejected him, but in Keaton's case it was actively hostile – for no good reason. Chaplin's upbringing might have brought from him a similar view, but after the amorality of his shorts he poured such affection on his character that beyond the moralising no actual philosophy is discernible. Keaton was very modern in that he never moralised; the black vision of his shorts suggests that he accepted defeat equally fatalistically in his later battles with M-G-M and alcoholism. **Daydreams** (1922) is a cry of despair, its title referring to the lies told by Buster in his letters to the girl back home of success in the city. One daydream becomes a nightmare as one cop, again, becomes an army of cops: Buster takes refuge on a ferry-boat – but it is only manoeuvring, and he finds haven in the paddle-wheel. Blesh thinks that the movie ends with him falling into the water, but in another version he is deemed to travel for ever between two shores, beyond the barriers of the law; unfortunately the most complete version concludes tamely with him returning to the girl – but it is still pessimistic, since her father throws him out.

The view of **The Three Ages** (1923) is that success, power, wealth and brutality go hand in hand, and that if the little man achieves anything against those odds, it's not going to be with elegance or panache. This is the first of the Keaton features, a look at the one thing that stays eternal – love. As he himself pointed out, it is really three two-reelers stuck together: Buster in prehistoric times, in the Roman era, and in the present day, in each outwitting his rival (Wallace Beery) to win the girl, the stories interweaving and the parallels not enforced with rigidity. **Our Hospitality** (1923) is a return to the standard of the best shorts. The title is ironic: the story was inspired by the Hatfield-McCoy feud, and Keaton is a New York boy travelling South to take up an inheritance, unaware that the girl (Natalie Talmadge, his wife at the time) on the train has brothers who have sworn to kill him on sight. How he stays alive is accomplished by a profusion of brilliant, indescribable visual gags; and it is difficult to write about **Sherlock Junior** (1924) because it is so completely magical – and since Keaton knew that magic wears off, he made the film shorter than his other features. He starts with an ordinary story, and moves into fantasy as his hero, a cinema-projectionist, walks into the screen and becomes a man-about-town detective. Keaton never threw custard pies or lost his pants; the bad men pursue and heroines doubt, but after he left Arbuckle he seldom used a conventional joke – or if he did, he built on it, ending ten steps in front. He ends thus there; and as he finishes, his look is as enigmatic as Garbo's at the end of *Queen Christina* (q.v.).

In **The Navigator** (1924) he is a rich boy, 'living proof that every family tree must have its sap'. The reason for his pedigree seems to be to emphasise his uselessness when stranded on a deserted liner – the usual Buster would have been as immediately inventive as he later becomes. By mischance the girl (Kathryn McGuire) is with him on these acres of floating iron; after learning to cook for two in a kitchen meant for hundreds, they are beset by cannibals. This climax is suspenseful rather than amusing; that in **Seven Chances** (1925) contains his most sustained brilliance. A prologue establishes his inability to propose to his girl in any of the four seasons; and then he desperately needs a bride to inherit a huge fortune – before seven o'clock on this particular evening. His first proposal is maladroit, and he is refused; he tries the ladies at his country club, and by the end of the afternoon 'had proposed to everything in skirts, including a Scotchman [sic]' – and a joke involving the female impersonator Julian Eltinge is done with equal delicacy. The dilemma has been offered to a local newspaper, armed with which brides descend upon the appointed church – by foot, horse, tram, bicycle. And when

Buster, inevitably, flees, brides converge from all directions, as many, as menacing, and about as pretty as his old enemy, the cops.

Seven Chances, with *Sherlock Junior*, are the only films on which he takes sole directorial credit – and since both are so beautifully made we need not look at his collaborators; but it is worth noting that Clyde Bruckman and Jean Havez are credited among the writers of his first five features, and neither seems to have worked on **Go West** (1925) and **Battling Butler** (1926), the weakest films of his great period. He was attracted to the former, for he wanted to see how far he could take the gag of having a cow for heroine – and one who evokes the same single-minded passion as the others; and *Battling Butler* offered the chance of a serious climax – a brutal boxing-match. It is certainly funnier than *Go West*, but not to be placed with **The General** (1926), for which Bruckman returned, also co-directing. The title refers to an engine, and the film remains the cinema's happiest exercise in playing trains; if the gags are not Keaton's most brilliant or most sustained, on no other occasion did they spring so easily from the narrative and blend with it. The girl (Marian Mack) is notably dim: she throws away a log (fuel) because there is a hole in it; she uselessly sweeps the floor of the engine's cabin; and she stokes up the fire with a twig. Buster mocks her by handing her a chip: more than Chaplin, his innate chivalry towards women dissolves when they become dangerous or *de trop*.

College (1927), possibly the greatest of the features, was inspired by Lloyd's *The Freshman* (q.v.) – but the campus is absolutely of Keaton's world. He is the school swot who, rejected by the Girl in favour of the hearties, turns up at college with every item of sporting equipment known to man: an odd man out in this athlete's world, he perseveres. He attempts the long jump, the high jump, putting the shot (it puts him), ignominiously ignored by his fellows till his antics menace their safety. As a sportsman, he gets just one thing right – and it's the one thing that doesn't matter: the stance at the starting-post. Then, strained and quivering, his unchanging face is at its most eloquent, as it is again when failing miser-

The shorts of Buster
Keaton are among
the greatest pleasures
the cinema has to
offer – even if the
woes in *The Boat*,
RIGHT, with Sybil
Sealey, are a little
too relentless. Those
in *Daydreams*, BELOW
CENTRE, are varied: In
this particular scene
the cop is too dumb
to recognise an actor
in costume, but sees
only a guy in a skirt.
The features are
miraculous –
certainly so in the
case of *Sherlock
Junior*, ABOVE FAR
RIGHT, in which
Buster is a cinema
projectionist. Unlike
Lloyd or Chaplin, he
moved about the
social scale, and in
College, BELOW FAR
RIGHT, he is a student.
His mother was
Florence Turner,
'the original Vitagraph
Girl', who had spent
more than a decade in
England, attempting
to prolong her waning
career; when it
finally halted there,
she managed to find
a few small roles in
Hollywood before
retiring.
Incidentally, as against
the possible evidence
of these stills,
Keaton's unvarying
expression was able to
convey a wide range
of emotion.

The Great Stone Face

ably as a soda-fountain clerk, his every gesture a witness to whether or not he's being watched. If, at the end, he wins both the Girl and the race (instead of the traditional football-game climax, Keaton chose a boat-race because only two mishaps can occur – the boats can collide or sink, and thus audience anticipation is keener), the consolation is temporary. Despite the film's title, no one is seen studying; it is natural to Keaton that brawn should dominate over brain.

He is again an effete young man in **Steamboat Bill Jr** (1928), the despair of his sea-dog father (Ernest Torrence). Unhappily bereft of college togs and moustache, he finds unexpected consolation in his natty naval togs; and as he saunters along, a friend suggests to his father, 'No jury would convict.' He becomes, when pressed, as stoic and enterprising as ever: and it is perhaps this that makes him so endearing, since it is always by accident that he discovers his heroic self. The adversary to be overcome this time was to have been a cyclone, and Keaton resented till he died the substitution of a flood. Starting with *The General,* Schenck had appointed a supervisor, and Keaton unhappily deferred to him; when he complained, Schenck made it clear that without supervision there would be no more Keaton films.

He lacked the courage to strike out on his own. His last three films had been made for United Artists, and he was happy to be with the company that included Chaplin; he did make one timid attempt to be independent of Schenck, but when Schenck contracted him to M-G-M, with all powers of autonomy lost, he began to sink. He produced **The Cameraman** (1928), suggested the idea, and worked out the gags with Bruckman; Edward Sedgwick directed it, but, unlike his later Metro pictures, Keaton always regarded it as his own. He is a tintype photographer determined to get a job with the M-G-M newsreel company and win the girl (Marceline Day, the prettiest of his leading ladies) who works there; his determination, and gestures, are often zombie-like, and thus half of Buster is missing – his skill, and we are surprised by his lack of ingenuity in the Tong War. It has half as many laughs as its immediate predecessor, and there are half as few

again in **Spite Marriage** (1929), in which he is a pants-presser whose dream comes true when his favourite star (Dorothy Sebastian) marries him on the rebound. The story was foisted on him, he was denied the use of Sound, his incredible athletics were forbidden as being too risky, and he had to fight to keep what he correctly thought was the funniest sequence – trying to get a tipsy bride to bed. Keaton believed that he was destroyed because M-G-M considered that they knew better how to make a Keaton film than he did, but the simultaneous deterioration of his marriage and his relationship with the once-protective Schenck – who was married to his wife's sister – may have weakened his creativity. In these two studio-controlled films, there are a number of routines clearly his own, but apart from the tipsy bride none is very good, harking back to his days in vaudeville. Is it not possible that his imagination was wearing thin? He had made twenty shorts between 1920 and 1923, and ten features in the subsequent years: the limited number of masterpieces among them suggests, on average, that he could not have gone on for ever.

The third great Silent clown, and the second best of them, is Harold Lloyd (1893–1971), though at the time both he and Keaton agreed with and accepted, at least publicly, the world's opinion that they were a rung or so below Chaplin – though Lloyd led the others at the American box office. Chaplin was unique, and copied only by blatant imitators, while all the other two-reel comics borrowed from each other. Lloyd's fascination with movies was a contributory factor to his success; he became an extra before he was twenty, and was invited by Hal Roach (b. 1892) to join him when the latter, a former Universal cowboy, founded his own company. Roach emulated Sennett: Lloyd was star and gagman, attempting to rival the other funny-clothes clowns with enthusiasm and hard work – but to little appreciation. Where others fell by the wayside or moved to supporting status, Lloyd pressed on, changing from Willie Work to Lonesome Luke to Winkle, whose spectacles and mild appearance belied his ability to flout authority and make fools of those around him. After a while the name was dropped, the silk hat gave way to the boater, and as the character evolved he became respectable, the Galahad of the college set, fighting adversity and winning the girl. Lacking the pungency of Chaplin at his best, he towered above his other rivals in the sheer inventiveness of his gags – a challenge to Keaton, starting his own two-reelers as Lloyd moved into features. Keaton eluding Red Indians in *The Paleface* was emulating Lloyd in *Take a Chance*, fleeing prison warders, while Lloyd learnt from Keaton how to deepen predicament into disaster. Both were possessed by some deep inner fantasy, though Lloyd's was probably only that of the average American male. Although he was once miscast as a doctor, the point of Lloyd's industry and invention was that it was never for the good of the community but to satisfy a girl or a dream. Silence created the movie clowns, from Max Linder onwards; if movies had talked from the beginning, their physical action might still have been confined to what was possible behind a proscenium arch. But that Lloyd deserves to stand with Keaton is made obvious when we realise that as Chaplin was putting the finishing touches to his visually stodgy *Gold Rush* they were offering the magical chases of *Girl Shy* (q.v.) and *Sherlock Junior*.

It was public response which encouraged Roach to add a third reel to the Lloyd films – something which till then only Chaplin had dared attempt; and of the many comics only they, Linder, Arbuckle, Keaton and later Harry Langdon (q.v.) made the transition to longer films. But even with his last three-reeler, **Never Weaken** (1921), Lloyd was having the usual difficulty in sustaining a theme, and it falls into three separate but prolonged gags: employing a circus contortionist to attract customers to an osteopath; trying to commit suicide because he thinks his girl is planning to marry another; and being trapped high on a building site. The first two find him often contrived and mechanical, but once trapped on that girder he becomes immortal. This extraordinary climax he tried to live up to, and though some of the gags from his shorts found their way into his features, later gags were never repeated: the sheer variety of his spectacular climaxes is one reason audiences adored

him. In **A Sailor-Made Man** (1921) he is a rich man playing at sailor who finds courage battling a sheik, and in **Grandma's Boy** (1922), a parody of *Tol'able David* (q.v.), a shy village lad who finds courage battling his uncouth rival. Discussing the latter in 'The Best Moving Pictures of 1922–3', Robert E. Sherwood noted that Lloyd 'constructed each scene as carefully as though it were the mainspring of a watch . . . There is nothing haphazard about his methods; he puzzles over every episode and situation, working it out first in his mind and then in the action itself. He had a remarkably clear vision and an acute sense of risibility; he knows instinctively what will be naturally funny, and what will be merely forced.' His collaborators included Sam Taylor and Fred Newmeyer, who singly or together directed all of his pictures till 1926; the two later Silents were directed by Ted Wilde. A small number of writers and gagmen, including Clyde Bruckman, worked for both Lloyd and Keaton. The two clowns also had in common a desire to change both comic formulae and the film itself if preview audiences did not respond, as with *The Freshman* (q.v.), when Lloyd returned to the set to lose his pants as well, because preview audiences had not laughed at what he had hoped was a new gag, a disintegrating jacket. Unlike Keaton, he was an astute businessman, and after parting amicably with Roach he left Pathé for an extremely advantageous deal with Paramount, which guaranteed complete autonomy.

The Lloyd on screen is, as James Agee observed, 'funny from the inside' – which is why his skyscraper stunt in **Safety Last** (1923) works so well. This sequence should only be seen in context (i.e. never in excerpt) for we must know his reasons for climbing, which are accidental – though he would surely have done it to please a girl. It is justly famous: and to see it today with an audience alternately roaring with laughter and gasping is one of the great experiences of cinema. Lloyd admitted, 'This sort of thrill comedy was dangerous but it wasn't as dangerous as it looked' – for once they had established the location, it proved possible to build a 'safe' portion of the 'dangerous' building with the same view beyond. He used a double in the long shots, a fact not

Master of the High and Dizzy

Harold Lloyd in *Why Worry?*, RIGHT, as a young American involved in a South American revolution – a situation reprised fifty years later by Woody Allen in *Bananas,* which has probably one–fifth of the laughs. For that matter, *Speedy,* BELOW, has a number of car chases funnier than those ubiquitous in the movies of the Sixties and Seventies; he played a cab–driver, here on his day off at Coney Island with Ann Christy, temporarily replacing Jobyna Ralston as his leading lady. The other two pictures are from *Feet First,* FAR RIGHT, discussed later, but included here to show that it wasn't only in *Safety Last* that Lloyd scaled a skyscraper – and that as long as movies are shown people will be watching Lloyd on high buildings.

HAROLD LLOYD IN "SPEEDY"
PRODUCED BY THE HAROLD LLOYD CORPORATION

137

revealed till after his death, and wore a harness; also, there were wide platforms just out of camera range. Yet we might still like to think of his task as Herculean, for he worked with a hand that had a false thumb and forefinger (because of an accident), and 'it took us sometimes over a month to make one of these sequences, because we could only work between about eleven o'clock and one o'clock, otherwise shadows would come up in the street and it wouldn't match the other scenes.'

In **Why Worry?** (1923) he is an innocent trapped amidst Latin-American revolutionaries; in **Hot Water** (1924) the possessor of both a new car and new in-laws; and in **Girl Shy** (1924) he is a country boy who from complete ignorance writes a treatise on love, and loses his girl to a bigamist. If in this case he had telephoned to stop the wedding we would have lost a climax as thrilling as that of *Safety Last*, as he employs every means of land transport to get him to the church on time – a masterpiece of precision ill-served by the copies currently in circulation, which run it at sound speed, i.e. faster, in order to accommodate a music-track. Chases also conclude both **For Heaven's Sake** (1926) and **Speedy** (1928); a football match ends **The Freshman**; and a fight of particular violence, aboard an abandoned hulk, provides a brilliant climax to **The Kid Brother** (1927). There is also a brutal free-for-all in *Speedy*, involving greybeards, and it is clear that Lloyd equated violence with the cities, changing for the worst. The screen Harold may have set out to be the all-American go-getter, but his ideals were Victorian – and it is only too typical of him that in this particular film he experiences empathy with a horse-drawn trolley. Perhaps only an old-fashioned man would indicate that the end of the world is nigh as those trousers fall apart, or be so enchanted by the crooks reformed in 'his' mission in *For Heaven's Sake* – not to mention his joy in *Speedy*, hurtling from one side of town to the other, because he has Babe Ruth in the back of his cab (thus allowing Americans to watch two current idols at the same time). Unequipped except in ingenuity to cope with the dangers of the modern world, his final emergence into triumph

might well be transitory, but it is often a great deal less precarious than Buster's.

Any of the other Silent comics, in whatever garbled form they now reach us, are worth seeing – especially Charley Chase, in his two-reelers for Roach, often a hen-pecked husband, but in his funniest film, **Limousine Love** (1928), a prospective bridegroom hampered by a naked lady on his way to the church. Then there is Roach's superb **A Pair of Tights** (1928), with its vain attempts by a girl to get her ice-creams to the car and its climax when men crash to the ground because those already lying there whack their calves. Like the trouser-tearing finish to *You're Darn Tootin'* (1929) and the pie-throwing of *The Battle of the Century* (1927) – both made by Roach with Laurel and Hardy (q.v.) – this wholesale combination of heartlessness and loss of dignity has something to say about the human condition.

Other American artists of the Twenties live on, if only in legend, and we shall look at their work in the next chapter: but there is one film-maker who should be considered at this point, because his work was so strikingly individual. Erich Von Stroheim (1885–1957) was born in Vienna of Polish Jewish parents, and had arrived in the U.S. in 1906; after collaborating on a play he drifted into films in 1914, acting and writing for Triangle, and since he claimed – falsely – to have been an officer in the Imperial army, he was much in demand to advise on the many films dealing with the European military. When the Armistice made such subjects unfashionable, he approached Carl Laemmle with a screenplay that he had written – saying that to film it would cost only $5,000, but that he must direct it himself; he also claimed that it was based on a novel by him, supposedly called 'The Pinnacle'. Laemmle agreed, and the result, actually costing $100,000 and retitled **Blind Husbands** (1919) – and now sporting a happy ending – was the biggest success that Universal had had up to that time. Its mixture of the eternal triangle and mountaineering was as opportunistic as its creator's approach to Laemmle had been fraudulent. DeMille's stories of erring wives and husbands were all the rage, and as with deMille the film has a foreword asking us to look freshly at the situation – specifically whether the husband is as guilty as the other man. But whereas de Mille had taken the characters of Schnitzler and made them into simple-minded Americans, Von Stroheim offered a mentality closer to that of his countryman. The character he himself played, an aristocrat dedicated to seduction, was clearly influenced by Schnitzler – and portrayed in such detail that he was more fascinating than most screen rakes. The fact that he was European and the couple were Americans indicated the dangers and/or delights awaiting Americans daring or wealthy enough to travel abroad. The clash of old world decadence and new world purity may have been borrowed in turn from Henry James: it became a staple in American cinema from then on, though already touched upon in the war films. The new world was full of Europeans, but none like this particular gentleman; if it was Von Stroheim's past as a penniless immigrant which attracted him to the role, he was to maintain all his life the fictions of his birth and upbringing.

The reviews immediately justified his confidence. *The New York Times* found it 'superior to most of the year's productions' because 'its outstanding pictorial quality indicates that Mr Stroheim, unlike many directors, grasps the fact that the screen is the place for moving pictures' and if 'some of the scenes are continentally frank, they are not offensive, nor more suggestive than is necessary.' This 'pictorial quality' would include the close-ups, almost wholly concerned with Von Stroheim's fetishistic interests: a woman's ankle, the details of his own uniform, the voyeurist spying of the maid, the amorous couple whose kisses emphasise the wife's neglect. Von Stroheim understood lust and eroticism, and he understood, as no other Hollywood film-maker at the time dared to, the distinctions between marriage, love and lust. His characters were as mercenary as they were sexual, with the stronger gulling the weak – a view he would have seen expressed in the theatres of his native city, if not in the seventeenth-century satirists. It was a view novel only to the cinema.

The same attitudes were propounded in *The Devil's Passkey*, which no longer exists, and in **Foolish Wives** (1922): the setting has moved from the Alps to Monte Carlo and this time Von Stroheim is supposedly a Russian count. The prey remains an American woman – though once again she is not the only one. Whether he has also had 'relations' with his cousins is not clear – if they are his cousins – and they certainly are revealed as anything but the princesses they claim to be; he has, moreover, compromised the maid (Dale Fuller), whose suicide puts an end to both her pregnancy and pleas for marriage. As retribution begins to mount, his conduct is revealed as increasingly ignoble, till at the height of his troubles he decides to ravish a half-idiot girl. He is killed by her father, who stuffs his body into a manhole. Von Stroheim had intended the Count to be even more dastardly – and by far the best thing in the mutilated copies which remain are the indications of his ruthlessness. The film originally extended to at least twenty-one ..els (though Von Stroheim claimed that there were as many as thirty-four) but had been reduced to fourteen by the time of the New York première, after which four more were removed to appease censors and critics. The re-written intertitles not only covered the gaps in continuity but softened the text, so that the American husband was demoted from Ambassador to mere business functionary. The film, despite its moral, still revels in its world of cafés and casinos. There is an odd moment when the American woman discovers that the soldier whose manners she has deplored is in fact armless – not an incident at odds with the tone of the film, but too isolated to place the film with Von Stroheim's later attempts at social realism. As it was censored the world over for its *sexual* realism, so it was praised: Harriett Underhill in *The New York Tribune* declared that Von Stroheim was a genius – a view in which he concurred – adding that she had seen 'many motion pictures and *Foolish Wives* is the best photoplay I have ever seen without any exceptions whatever.' Since *Intolerance*, it was also the most expensive, and Universal's publicists, with the short memories which mark many in the industry, advertised it as 'The First Million Dollar movie'. The company soon realised that it would have to settle for a prestige hit, for vilification kept audiences away. 'An insult to every

'The Man you Love to Hate'

Von Stroheim – the above soubriquet was coined by publicists and used extensively throughout his career – was not allowed to play the lead in *The Merry-Go-Round*, RIGHT, so he dressed Norman Kerry in the uniform he had designed for himself. He was taken off the film, and most of it is an anodyne affair; some of his ideas for it he later transferred to *The Wedding March*, BELOW. Playing his mother is Maud George, who had been his 'cousin' in *Foolish Wives*. His role was the same, wearing uniform, using perfume, smoking cigarettes six inches long breakfasting on caviar and drunk in the evening. Few men have so indulged their fantasies on the screen.

The Merry Widow hardly impresses as a version of Lehar's musical frolic, but it is unique among American films of the time in that Von Stroheim managed to set most of it in a *maison close* – and its hero, John Gilbert, was, in seeking comfort from older ladies, supposedly still a typical American male. BELOW: Gibson Gowland and Zazu Pitts in Von Stroheim's *Greed*, in one of their happier moments. She has already won the lottery prize which, with his drinking, will lead to the disintegration of their marriage – the film's true subject, rather than that indicated by the title.

American,' declared *Photoplay*, and Thomas Quinn Curtis in his book on Von Stroheim quotes a Methodist minister as denouncing 'a disgusting story of lust. Not only is gambling shown, but men and women are seen brazenly smoking cigarettes.'

For the premiere, Sigmund Romberg had composed a special score, an extra expense to add to the full-scale construction of a Monte Carlo square on the Universal lot. Elated by the notices, the studio reproduced what it called 'the Coney Island of Vienna', the Prater, for **The Merry-Go-Round** (1923). Irving Thalberg, Laemmle's new assistant, had suggested a circus picture to Von Stroheim, who decided to use a carnival background for the tale of an aristocrat in love with a pure maiden. The budget was set at $100,000, but it was soon clear that Von Stroheim had no intention of keeping to it (this was the film for which he required the military to wear silk monogrammed underwear – not, of course, to be seen on the screen); and due to his arrogance, there had been tension between him and Thalberg since Laemmle had left for a European trip. After five weeks' shooting, with only one reel completed, Von Stroheim was replaced by Rupert Julian, the sole credited director of the completed film. Since Von Stroheim shot in sequence, the first twelve minutes indicates how he spent those five weeks: an aristocratic officer (Norman Kerry) is awakened by his valet after the previous night's debauch, and the Countess, his mother, treats her servants sadistically, having them slavishly pull off her boots and massage her silk-stockinged legs as she lolls on a divan. The first sequence would be repeated in *The Wedding March* (q.v.), and the attitudes of the Countess borrowed for *The Merry Widow* (q.v.) – while the heroine (Mary Philbin) is observed with the same harsh pathos that would characterise Zazu Pitts in *Greed* (q.v.). As the film proceeds these characters lose their interest, and it is a dull thing except where some Von Stroheim touches remain, as in a party sequence with the officers and girls all with vine-leaves in their hair.

Turning from European high life to American low life, Von Stroheim made **Greed** (1924), based on Frank Norris's popular attempt at a Zolaesque novel, 'McTeague'. The Goldwyn executives backed it, having announced their hostility to the factory system and their plans to give their directors freedom; they were also on the verge of amalgamating with Metro. By the time the film was finished, the new company – M-G-M – was headed by Thalberg and Louis B. Mayer, whose idea of entertainment was not *Greed* and certainly not at this length, forty-two reels. Von Stroheim himself reduced the number to twenty-four, and the released print was of ten – or two-and-a-half hours, exactly the duration of the deleted account of McTeague's early years, reduced to a seven-minute prologue. *Greed* was not Von Stroheim's title, and the film is not, as it has been said to be, a study in miserliness: McTeague (Gibson Gowland) is a thick-witted dentist who courts and weds Trina Sieppe (Zazu Pitts), but banned from practising, he fails to hold other, demeaning jobs. He drinks because he is bored, and because they are living in increasing squalor, if held together by bouts of affection; but as he realises the extent to which her obsession with money has taken over her life, he regards her with indifference. It has been claimed that her hoarding is due to the experience of the wedding night, but the film (as it now stands) does not support that view. Her primness always indicated that she would be careful; the money becomes an obsession because they have little and will soon have less. This is the best part of the film: sober, convincing, and of concern – before the descent to melodrama.

Von Stroheim's reputation as a realist rests on *Greed*, but, said Herman G. Weinberg, 'he was essentially a romantic. The theme of loveless marriage runs through all his films' – and since we know that the most profound examination of a loveless marriage then available in film terms was *The Ingmarssons* we may assume that Von Stroheim saw it. There are numerous echoes in *Greed* of *The Phantom Carriage*, notably in its handling of the demon drink, but it has more in common with Sjöström's greatest film: both are melodramas taking on the mantle of tragedy; both are meticulous recreations of past times made chiefly on location; and apart from the common subject, both are very long or were intended to be. Norris's book provided Von Stroheim with the detail he needed for an exercise in European culture somewhat different from his earlier achievements; but once placed beside Sjöström's films the much-praised originality of *Greed* is in fact slight, and indeed Von Stroheim is revealed again as opportunistic, since he has managed 'realism' but to no discernible end. There is no point of view to be found in the film, other than that people are not very nice – the opposite of Sjöström's – and it lacks the complete cynicism of Von Stroheim's other films, with its hints of sympathy for McTeague. Realism, in Von Stroheim's terms, means a farcical wedding feast, with everyone stuffing themselves and burping, or Trina's brother wanting to pee after a theatre visit, or the courting couple on the concrete sewer by the sea. There is certainly nothing wrong in this: Robert E. Sherwood in his review spoke of 'ferocity, brutality, muscle, vulgarity, crudity naked realism, and sheer genius', and all those qualities but the last are still apparent. How many other American Silents could be described as having ferocity and muscle?

Sherwood also mentioned the film's original length, and observed wryly that Von Stroheim would have to learn 'limitations': Von Stroheim is in fact the classic example of film-makers so in awe of their own talents that nothing was too expensive and no footage too long. His vanity was legendary; when towards the end of his life Billy Wilder said that he had been ten years before his time, Von Stroheim corrected him, 'Twenty'. He has been admired because he fought the system and lost, but he lost simply because he was too arrogant to work other than in a recklessly extravagant manner. That he made good films was recognised; but he was often praised for an approach to sex and marital relations merely in advance of his backward-looking colleagues.

Certainly his changes 'improved' **The Merry Widow** (1925), which, adapted from the operetta, was handicapped as screen entertainment; but he retains at length the famous waltz, which at best would have had orchestral accompaniment and at worst silence, if the piano-player was ill. The film is more than two-thirds over when the plot of the original begins to intrude, and most of that time has been spent examining the activities of the widow's three rival suitors, as they move in a haze of lechery and drunkenness: Danilo (John Gilbert) is a seducer of inconsiderable charm, given to saucy postcards; the horrible old baron (Tully Marshall) is also a foot fetishist; and the Crown Prince (Roy d'Arcy) seems prone to every depravity going. Alas, as the object of their attentions Mae Murray is vivacious but dull, though the uniforms, it must be said, give pause.

Thalberg, having inherited Von Stroheim on *Greed*, kept him for this film because he considered his 'European' approach ideal; but M-G-M was not prepared to suffer further, for the success of *The Merry Widow* did not atone for the miserable failure of *Greed* and the loss of most of its $750,000 cost. The independent producer Pat Powers listened to Von Stroheim's advances, and allotted him a budget of $700,000 for his next project, only to find that that had been exceeded by yet another half-million. The film lasted eleven hours, which Paramount, distributing, refused to handle: Von Stroheim and subsequently others reduced the material, cutting it into two separate films, **The Wedding March** (1928) and *The Honeymoon,* which was released in Europe only and of which there are now no surviving prints. *The Wedding March* announces itself 'in its entirety an Erich Von Stroheim Production' dedicated 'to the true lovers of the world', and its combination of debauchery and innocent, romantic love is merely a repeat of what was intended in *The Merry-Go-Round*. Von Stroheim plays the usual Von Stroheim hero, introduced to us via his clothing, strewed drunkenly on the floor; his first action on waking is to paw the maid, and his subsequent conduct is no improvement. His life-style must be paid for by a wealthy marriage, so he becomes engaged to the lame daughter (Zazu Pitts) of a corn-plaster magnate, despite the fact that he has fallen in love with the daughter (Fay Wray) of an innkeeper. This becomes an everyday anecdote as handled by Von Stroheim, and perhaps only he would have handled it at such length.

The United Artists

Von Stroheim moved on to Gloria Swanson, who had been impressed by his ability to turn Mae Murray into an actress and was curious to see what he might do with her own (and acknowledged) talent. **Queen Kelly** was based on one of his own stories, and a budget was set at $800,000 with a forty-week shooting schedule, for this was to be another very long film: shooting was closed down after ten weeks, thus effectively sealing Von Stroheim's American career as a director, though as with the later *Walking Down Broadway* (q.v.) he seems to have worked quickly and as economically as he knew how to be. The chief reason for the film being abandoned was that it was clear that it would not be ready till mid–1929 and already – before the end of 1928 – it was also clear that the public wanted only Talkies. It would have been possible to start again with Sound, or add Sound sequences, but Von Stroheim was disregarding the instructions of the Hays Office in respect of the script. In the film Swanson was supposed to go to Africa to manage her aunt's brothel: Hays had insisted that the establishment become a hotel, but Von Stroheim was filming material indicating the activities that went on inside it, as girls from the bar led clients upstairs. He was concentrating on the squalor of this particular part of Africa, and had, against Hays's advice, shown a black priest administering the last rites. Swanson's chief backer, Joseph P. Kennedy (1888–1969; future ambassador to Britain and father of President Kennedy), was also a prominent Roman Catholic, and he decided that he did not want to defend a film which seemed likely to be a complete box-office failure.

The film that now exists was originally the prologue, concerning an orphan (Swanson) who attracts the attention of a Prince (Walter Byron) when she loses her knickers. He, however, is contracted to marry a Queen (Seena Owen) who is not only mad but as depraved as he, and it is with these two that Von Stroheim is at his most typical, whether showing the Prince being forcibly fed by his servants after a night of debauch or the Queen in bed, the table beside her littered with a box of veronal, a copy of the 'Decameron' and a cluttered ashtray. When the Queen discovers the Prince with the girl she horse-whips her, and the girl attempts suicide. In the ending shot for this version – probably directed by Edmund Goulding (q.v.), who directed Swanson's next film, *The Trespasser* – the Queen relents and allows him to marry the girl, but the suicide attempt has been successful. At ninety minutes, the film was exported to Europe and South America, on the assumption that in both continents were many cinemas not wired for Sound. It has been said Von Stroheim used a clause in his contract to prevent the film being released in the U.S., but it is more likely that Miss Swanson's distributors, United Artists, felt that it had no market value. Finally, it was Von Stroheim's arrogance and his penchant for length and eroticism which wrecked his career as a director. When he acted in France projects were announced by enthusiastic producers but none came to pass, apparently because producers decided that he did not well support the daily bottle of whisky stipulated in his contracts.

The ousting of Von Stroheim, though undoubtedly deserved by industry standards, was a blow to the freedom of the individual artist; and although the importance of Griffith in the Twenties has been exaggerated by historians, the same may be said of him. The ideals, other than financial, which had caused the foundation of United Artists were by the coming of the Talkies in disarray – and that was due as much to the personalities of the founders as to their eminence. Within a few years the public had deserted both Pickford and Fairbanks, and the stars who replaced them had no wish to double as executives, preferring the comfort of the studio contract. Keaton, who had had no business sense, was gone as well; Lloyd and Chaplin made only occasional films, the former regarded as a character from the past, the latter stationed on his lone pinnacle. The producers releasing through United Artists had the same mentalities and motives as those of the other major companies, and none of them wanted to employ artists with an inflated idea of their own importance, with budgets to match. Success henceforth depended not on reputation, but on profitability – though, as the idea of independence floundered, a number of people arrived, like Lubitsch and Garbo, who could with docility provide both.

7

Hollywood in the Twenties: The Studios

TECHNICALLY, the late American Silent film is often close to perfection. The luminosity of the photography and an imaginative but unshowy use of composition were welded into narrative by editors whose understanding of rhythm and dramatic tension remains extraordinary. Intertitles were reduced to the minimum, and not only had the barnstorming histrionics gone, but players were able to convey with only slight gestures a whole range of emotion – though whether, given the subject-matter, the expertise was worthwhile is debatable. It was certainly taken for granted, as critics rushed to admire the new artistic event from Europe.

One American film was much admired at the beginning of the decade, **Nanook of the North** (1922), which as the first travel-picture of feature-length eclipsed its few predecessors. This study of Eskimo life was made by Robert J. Flaherty (1884–1951), who as an amateur film-maker had taken a motion-picture camera with him when working in Hudson Bay. His first effort was destroyed by fire, and he obtained backing from Revillon Frères, the furriers, for this second attempt, taking eighteen months simply to gather the material. Both Paramount and First National passed up the chance to distribute, and it went to Pathé, which was owned by the same parent company as the fur company. Even then it stayed on the shelf till it fired the enthusiasm of S. L. 'Roxy' Rothafel, the impresario. Today its effect compares badly with modern documentaries made for television, and unlike them it offers a fictionalised climax (when, hunting far from home, the Eskimos seek refuge

in a deserted igloo); but contemporaries were enraptured, including Frances Taylor Patterson in *The New Republic*: 'We are excessively weary of adaptations from the other arts. . . Here at last begins our native screen language, as original in concept as *The Cabinet of Dr Caligari,* yet as natural as that is fantastic.'

Nanook was hardly the dead end that *Caligari* was, but by the time the industry had recognised its achievement, the hold of the German film had grown stronger: most of the admired American films were those showing the Teutonic influences – till the lessons of the Russians were assimilated. Both pushed the American film towards realism, but it was a movement as short as it was sweet; the public and the industry were seduced by Sound.

By the end of the Silent period virtually every man, woman and child in the U.S. went to the cinema at least once a week; whole populations elsewhere grew up with a detailed knowledge of American life. The tastes of audiences everywhere coincided with that of the Hollywood moguls, which was fortunate for their stock-holders. If in Europe directors often took the credit for an entire film, the fall of Griffith and Von Stroheim convinced the Hollywood moguls of the foolishness of giving power to the man who directed the action on the studio-floor. The flirtations with Flaherty proved him equally expensive and unamenable to commercial considerations; Ince was approved of, since he was able to supervise several productions simultaneously, but he died young. Replacements could be purchased from Europe, often less with enthusiasm than in the competitive spirit of ten years

145

Nita Naldi and Rudolph Valentino in *Blood and Sand*: she is 'the widow of an ambassador [sic] who has turned the heads of half the kings and diplomats of Europe' and he is a matador. This bite comes after a kiss, as she cries, 'Snake – one moment I love you – one moment I hate you – serpent from hell.'

earlier – to prevent rivals from profiting from possibly important talents; and the European director, enticed by the available money, could be bent to the moguls' will. Scenarios could be imposed on him, and decor, and players. Any freedom given to directors was the result of success with studio-imposed material, and that freedom was studio-controlled. Yet a Lubitsch survived; a film as close to its director's heart as *The Crowd* (q.v.) could emerge – but do not look for consistency among American directors of the Twenties, other than that, for most of their time, they were forced to support the star system.

Everyone loved stars: since the emergence of Mary Pickford, the necessity of stars was recognised by everyone, from the merest studio stock-holder to the most egotistical of directors. Though that lady, and her star-colleagues at United Artists, had proved capable of holding power, they were the exceptions among players: Gloria Swanson proved no more successful at business than Keaton, and Rudolph Valentino, offered a degree of

autonomy, proved a singularly inept producer. The studios kept under contract a stock of lesser names, for the factory system and the star system went hand in hand. 'Answering your letter,' wrote David O. Selznick to a contract writer in 1929, 'we are in need mostly of stories for Nancy Carroll and for Dick Arlen. Carroll's vehicles should be rather on the emotional side, with a little comedy of the precious type, if possible . . . I think that Carroll and Arlen are our most serious needs in that we have only one story ahead for Nancy, and none for Dick . . . We are in splendid shape on William Powell, and fairly well off on Clara Bow, Evelyn Brent, Ruth Chatterton, and Gary Cooper. We have two stories ahead for Buddy Rogers, but could use a couple more very nicely.' These people were, of course, commodities, as Selznick makes clear in a later memo: 'At one time, when [George] Bancroft and Bow were strong, we discussed co-starring this pair; but you felt that we would be losing a picture by it, and that subsequent pictures starring these players individually would suffer through a seeming comparative weakness after a co-starring picture. But now, with Bow on her way out, and with Bancroft certainly not as strong as he was a year ago, I think that a Bancroft-Bow picture would assume real importance; that we would be extracting the last ounce of value out of Bow before letting her go . . .'

Today we may well feel that a star's presence is a mixed blessing: certainly it is a pleasure to watch a player of accomplishment and it is painful, often, to watch a nonentity, but the presence of stars in the fictions which movies tell is almost as deleterious as if novels began with a list of characters and their functions in the plot. Consequently few films of this time hold any surprise for the modern viewer – nor did they at the time to the sophisticated filmgoer; but the mass audience, it seemed, so wanted to watch their favourite players repeat themselves that even the smallest variation came as a surprise.

'Who is the real maker of a film?' asked Jean Renoir in 1974, answering the question himself. 'In the heroic age of the American cinema it was generally the actor who put his stamp on it. As the industry prospered it became a medium for the manufacture of stars.' Earlier, Raoul Walsh had concurred: the real auteurs, he had said, were the stars. The auteur theory, started by the French in the late Fifties, and posited on the director as sole creator, has been rejected by most of its cult-figures – Walsh himself, William Wellman and Vincente Minnelli among them. Film-making, its practitioners agree, is a collaborative effort. We may notice that the films of Walsh move faster than those of James Cruze, that the comedies of LaCava are lighter than those of Clarence Badger; we may find John Ford drawn to open-air stories or Frank Borzage preferring those with sentiment; but while the star system predominated, American films, with rare exceptions, took their complexion from the looks and personality of the leading players★ – a complexion even stronger when Sound brought voice – as we may see from the various versions (q.v.) of, say, *The Prisoner*

of *Zenda* and *A Star is Born*, or the tests for *Gone with the Wind*.

'Under Zukor's management and guidance some of the most famous stars of the screen were developed,' boasted 'The Motion Picture Almanack', and Paramount for a while owned the most famous star of his time: Rudolph Valentino (1895–1926), fresh from his success in *The Four Horsemen of the Apocalypse* (q.v.). In *The Sheik* he had set a whole generation of girls dreaming of being carried off to a desert lair by a romantic Arab – though we may feel that the secret of his appeal died with him. He moved awkwardly, but in **Blood and Sand** (1922) he gives a performance of sorts – a boy-man, loving his fame, unused to his dandy's clothes, amused as he smokes his mistress's candy-striped cigarettes while she plays the harp. His chameleon-like changes from clodhopping naivety to burning intensity were utilised in relentlessly exotic situations: these particular ones were provided by Ibañez' popular novel of the bull-ring and directed by Fred Niblo. The film, like *The Sheik*, was influential in creating the taste for the more florid interior decor popular over the next decade.

Dependence on stars was sometimes waived for 'big' pictures, though **The Covered Wagon** (1923) had been bought for Mary Miles Minter (who refused it); Paramount, anxious to recoup the large sum paid to acquire Emerson Hough's novel, turned it over to James Cruze, and then poured more money into the project, hoping for an authentic American epic. The film has genuine sweep: Cruze was thought to have struck a blow for a return to the omnipotence of the director, but from his later work it is clear that he was much indebted to the cinematography of Karl Brown (working with stationary cameras and stock film insensitive to blues). In 1923 there were still alive many who had been on that particular land-rush starting out from what became Kansas City. Films in the preceding years had developed entirely different ways of treating the gunfighters and pioneers whom William S. Hart had regarded as virtually his enclave. This film, however, became the prototype for the prestige Western, and for two generations Hollywood blurb-writers linked it

---

★Perhaps the best example is *Casablanca* (q.v.), which surely would have been quickly forgotten had it starred Dennis Morgan and Hedy Lamarr, as at one time planned.

147

with a later film for effective copy: 'There was *The Covered Wagon* . . . and then *Cimarron* . . . Now, Greatest of all –' Four years later Cruze was put in charge of **Old Ironsides** (1926), a 'true' adventure of the Revolutionary War, in which Esther Ralston went to sea for love of Charles Farrell, an interpolation regretted by some critics, who otherwise did not spare their superlatives. At specified city premieres the image was enlarged at one point to reveal a huge replica of the *Constitution* itself, done by a magnifier in the projection-box; but the film's failure put an end, for the moment, to wide screens – and to Cruze's career at Paramount, despite the reviews.

Paramount's other leading director, deMille, continued his modern morality tales with **Manslaughter** (1922), about a rich girl (Leatrice Joy) who believes that 'modern girls do not sit by the fire and knit': when she is involved in an automobile accident we are told 'These overcivilised, mad young wasters must be STOPPED – or the nation will be destroyed

as Rome was destroyed,' which leads to an 'ancient' sequence as gratuitous as that in *Male and Female*. This led to the retelling of Exodus in **The Ten Commandments** (1923) in which the parting of the Red Sea was shown by photographing two bowls of water as they emptied, then playing the shots backwards and magnified. This is followed by a fable of two brothers, a good one (Richard Dix) and one (Rod La Rocque) who doesn't believe in the laws of Moses; using cheap concrete he builds a church which collapses on their mother, and La Rocque is seduced by a Eurasian vamp (Nita Naldi) before being hounded to death by the Furies, presumably representing the Almighty. As flatly made as they are opportunistic, these two films indicate deMille's decline as well as his predilection for the grandiose; he was exceptionally budget-conscious, and found that the greater outlay for spectacles was rewarded at the box office. Curiously the public considered the second film as Hollywood's atonement for the scandals which had led to the

Ronald Colman, left, in the title–role of *Beau Geste*, with Ralph Forbes as his brother John. For audiences, this was *the* Foreign Legion story, and they would also have recognised that the final sacrifice of the other Geste, Digby, was based on that of Captain Oates.

creation of the Hays Office (an event that was followed, incidentally, by another shock, the death from drug-addiction of Wallace Reid, one of Paramount's most important stars).

In **Beau Geste** (1926) divine justice is British and therefore more absolute, as adapted from P. C. Wren's story of three brothers who join the Foreign Legion when a precious stone disappears, each fleeing to protect the others. From the arresting opening – the deserted fort and the dead garrison – the film seldom falters: and if the direction by Herbert Brenon is imaginative, it owes as much to the performance of Ronald Colman, graceful and replete with aristocratic charm. That the director Brenon, like Cruze, also depended on his photographer is apparent from the two films for which he is best remembered, **Peter Pan** (1924) and **A Kiss for Cinderella** (1925) – and since these plays by J. M. Barrie had enchanted audiences for two decades Brenon seems to have taken the decision not to tamper with them. The result is a plethora of intertitles and talking-heads which is a drawback if the audience is not convinced by the story. Watching Paramount's equally poor *Alice in Wonderland* (q.v.) I felt a surge of affection for the original, but with the other two I merely wondered at Barrie's psychology – at least, as translated here, e.g. when the London bobby writes to his Cinderella, 'There are thirty-four policemen in this room but I would rather have you, my darling.' The *Peter Pan* is the more bearable, despite a Peter with a distinct shadow and the Lost Boys sporting the Stars and Stripes (though that became the Union Jack for the British version); it has a vile Captain Cook (Ernest Torrence), a jolly Nana and a crocodile, both humans in skins, and no apparent strings on the flying children. Betty Bronson's Peter, approved by Barrie himself, has sprightliness and boyishness, but her waif in the second picture is as tiresome as any of the child-women of Silent movies, with their primping and coyness and ringlets.

These two Barrie films, though they were praised by the urban critics, were aimed at less sophisticated audiences – and those who might have been tempted to stay at home with radio, which had recently become a serious competitor for after

working-hours entertainment. Such films were also offered to those who wanted traditional entertainment rather than the 'continental' tales which had started with Von Stroheim and had become entrenched with the success of Lubitsch's *The Marriage Circle* (q.v.) in 1924. Adolphe Menjou, star of that film and of *A Woman of Paris*, made some similar films for Paramount, including **Open All Night** (1924), directed by Paul Bern from stories by Paul Morand, and **A Gentleman of Paris** (1927), directed by Harry D'Abbadie D'Arrast. The former is an odd combination of sex-comedy and slapstick, wherein Thérèse (Viola Dana) gets herself taken to the Cirque d'Hiver for a bicycle race because she thinks she prefers a 'cave-man' to the courtly Menjou; the latter is an examination of a roué who frequents high-class brothels and seduces a number of ladies, including the wife of his faithful valet. In two different roles, the character remains the same, ambivalently regarded; in the second film he proves himself a man of honour when not tempted by the flesh.

The British Clive Brook played similar roles, that of the basically decent cad, and if his role of the gentleman clown in **You Never Know Women** is not quite

Viola Dana and Adolphe Menjou in *Open All Night*, one of a great number of films in which he played the eternal cad – usually, for easier acceptance, set in Paris. The films nevertheless had much to say about traditional values since the War had shifted the balance of male–female power – and they always concluded with an assurance that things hadn't really changed after all typical, the film is notable since it made the reputation of its director, William A. Wellman, and is one of the many imitations of Sjöström's *He Who Gets Slapped* (q.v.). The clown is afraid to tell the leading lady (Florence Vidor) that he loves her; the title refers to her realisation that it is reciprocal, after he has been dropped in the Hudson as a stunt and she has escaped rape by his playboy rival (Lowell Sherman). Also 'European' in feeling – specifically German – and also directed by an American, in this case Victor Schertzinger, **Forgotten Faces** (1928) mixes crime, *crime passionnel* and father-love. Brook is a silk-hatted crook, William Powell (q.v.) his accomplice, and Olga Baclanova the unfaithful wife – for whom Howard Esterbrook wrote a couple of memorable scenes: one of crazy passion at the piano with her paramour, as she bangs his head upon the keys, and another, later, when her way of life is indicated not by the usual row of bottles but the moue of disgust she makes as her hand encounters a cigar-butt by the bed.

Paramount's sophisticated lady – the female equivalent of Menjou and Brook – remained (till she left for United Artists) Gloria Swanson, the epitome of glamour to millions; and to the millions of working girls who dreamed of emulating her, she repaid the compliment by occasionally eschewing pearls and satins to impersonate one of them. Thus she is in her two best films of this period, **Manhandled** (1924) and **Stage Struck** (1925), both directed by Allan Dwan and demonstrating her superiority as a comedienne; she is particularly delightful in the former, whether enduring a rushhour subway ride to her place behind a Macy's counter, or impressing society with her bogus Russian countess – whose mannerisms were based on her new rival at the studio.

This was Pola Negri who had been transported across the Atlantic after her successes with Lubitsch: since these had included the Dubarry, she was typed as an adventuress, but when the public evinced little interest Lubitsch was borrowed from Warner Bros. to find a suitable subject. He chose an old play by Lajos Biro and Melchior Lengyal, 'The Czarina', and rechristened it **Forbidden Paradise** (1924): reviewers of the time were delighted at the concept of turning Catherine the Great into a contemporary ruler, but she is merely another movie vamp – with a passion for guardsmen. Chief object of her attention is Rod La Rocque, and Menjou is the wily chancellor who connives at the liaison. There are typical situations, and Lubitsch describes the putting-down of the Revolution in just three close-ups (the general's hand upon his sword; the proffered foreign bank account book; the general's hand loosening). Mary Pickford's dictum that Lubitsch was obsessed with doors is borne out: we see more of them than of the actual intrigues. When the public again proved indifferent, Negri was put into the hands of Mal St Clair, for a story of small towns more typical of him, **A Woman of the World** (1925). The reaction of a back-woods populace to a real-life countess in its midst was a popular theme at the time, and this one humanises the image of the star which the studio had so carefully built up. The D.A., a reform-addict, leaps about in fury at a glimpse of her cigarette-holder, and for that she horse-whips him in public – after which we find them sharing a wicked cigarettes as they leave for their honeymoon.

These two delightful comedies still did not endear Negri to American audiences, so she was entrusted to Erich Pommer during his brief spell at Paramount. He cast her in two war stories, **Hotel Imperial** (1927) and **Barbed Wire** (1927), in plebeian roles – hotel-maid and farm-girl respectively. The former is set in a hotel in Galicia in 1915, and concerns the relationship between its staff and the Russian troops in occupation; the latter concerns the effect of German P.O.W.s on a French rural community – and is as fully perceptive on the uneasy relations between the two nationalities. *Hotel Imperial,* primarily a spy story (when Billy Wilder remade it as *Five Graves to Cairo,* q.v., he sensibly kept the hotel looking very much the same), is the more enjoyable today: Mauritz Stiller directed, from a story by Biro, a Hungarian, and these European talents were almost certainly stimulated by the Americans around them, if only in the inevitable tensions. An American, Rowland V. Lee, directed the second film, and apart from Negri and Pommer a name common to both is

Pola Negri, with George Siegmann, in her best remembered American film, *Hotel Imperial*, produced by Erich Pommer. Primarily a thriller, it managed a point or two on the relationships of differing nationalities in wartime, a theme Pommer returned to in *Barbed Wire* – only to be reprimanded by the critic of the London *Sunday Express*, who called it 'an illegitimate child of the League of Nations. There is no reason why Mr Pommer and Mr Schulberg [Paramount's executive producer] should not produce German screen propaganda, but there is every reason why they should be prevented from thrusting it on the British Empire in the guise of entertainment...This American effort to instruct Britain in the attitudes she should adopt towards her late enemy is an impertinence that could not be described in polite language.'

Jules Furthman (1888–1966) – and since he became one of the masters of screen-writing, their exceptional quality may be due to him.

Paramount's major contribution to the war film cycle – triggered off by the success on Broadway of 'What Price Glory?' in 1924, with its emphasis on disillusion – was **Wings** (1927), directed by William A. Wellman (1896–1975), an ex-flyer. He staged his action beautifully, be it the craft in flight or the humans milling on the ground – in both respects superior to the later *Hell's Angels* (q.v.), his screenplay is by John Monk Saunders (1905–40), whose individual and acrid view of the Great War and its aftermath would be the basis for a number of even more pungent pictures (q.v.). In a conventional tale about two student pilots (Richard Arlen, Charles 'Buddy' Rogers) are moments still fresh: the realisation by the students that their cadet elder (Gary Cooper) will not return to finish his Hershey bar; a dying pilot scratching his neck; the RFC flyer who flinches as the medal is pinned on his chest; and all the scenes in Paris, where the men on furlough are going beyond the pursuit of loose women – including a lesbian or so – and drinking themselves into oblivion. These scenes shocked puritan America – while titillating those to whom drunkenness was supposedly a memory; and worse was to

come when the nice American ambulance driver (Clara Bow) allows herself to be taken to a hotel room.

The war films were much praised – and did little to disturb the Hollywood equilibrium. This one won the first Best Picture award presented by the Academy of Motion Picture Arts and Sciences (founded by Louis B. Mayer in 1927 in an attempt to prevent unionisation of actors and studio-workers) – and it is symptomatic of almost all those films associated with the Academy's prizes, subsequently called Oscars, being serious, prestigious, entertaining, spectacular and artistically above average. The war films also brought sex back across the Atlantic, having shown the doughboys indulging in Europe's old fleshpots. Until then Hollywood had found it prudent to set stories of sin and adultery in the Old World, thus emphasising the more homely and democratic virtues of the native land. Towards the end of the decade, however, newspaper headlines made it plain that sex was as common in the U.S. as bootleg gin – and the continental hooker made way for the college flapper, with Europe again relegated to the favoured setting for period romance.

This is not to say that American stories were about contemporary problems: until the advent of the gangster film, a concerned and shriven U.S. was only

From left to right, William Austin, Clara Bow, Jacqueline Gadsdon and Antonio Moreno in *It*. Miss Bow sells gloves in Moreno's store, and in reel One she sets her cap at him – which is more difficult than Mr Austin will believe. 'She's a ripping sort really,' he says, 'She's absolutely heavy with "It"!'

reflected in tales of flappers and jazz-babies – and they were innocuous enough. Social problems came with a laugh – as with **Are Parents People?** (1925), directed by Mal St Clair, one of the first films about divorce; and we know when the daughter (Betty Bronson) gets to work on Mum and Dad (Florence Vidor, Adolphe Menjou) what the result will be. The subject of a young couple (Lois Wilson, Warner Baxter) saddled with an appalling widowed father would seem to require more nerve, and the old boy does go into a home: but **Welcome Home** (1925), directed by James Cruze, had already been a successful Broadway comedy, by Edna Ferber and George S. Kaufman – and that was why Paramount wanted to film it.

Clara Bow (1905–65) was the quintessence of what the term 'flapper' signifies, according to F. Scott Fitzgerald, and since she was fully developed as such

before she arrived at Paramount, we may look at an enjoyable earlier film, made for one of the independent companies, **My Lady of Whims** (1926), directed by Herman Raymaker. It embodies the same myths as other flapper films – that, for instance, Greenwich Village is sinful, and peopled by sculptresses with names like Wayne Lee and lecherous artists who smoke Turkish cigarettes. A party is 'a rumpus' – and though described as 'wilder than an old maid under the mistletoe' it looks most decorous to the modern eye. It would be too much to claim that the sculptress is keen on Miss Bow, but hints are laid in that direction; she is rescued, anyway, from the triple temptations of literary aspirations, the Village and vice.

'Why, she'll flirt as long as she lives' says Ernest Torrence of Bow in **Mantrap** (1926), the sole subject of which is Bow flirting. Reputedly based on a novel by Sinclair Lewis, the title in fact refers to a small mountain town: when Joe (Torrence) leaves it for Minneapolis, the first one he notices is Bow, tripping from a taxi to a swell hotel. She's manicurist in the barber shop, but in no time she's Mrs Joe, and making eyes at a vacationing lawyer. Photographed entirely on location by James Wong Howe, and directed with a fine disregard for its implausibilities by Victor Fleming (q.v.), this enterprise considerably entertains. Bow is delightful. At the beginning as she moves towards the hotel she turns and winks; she primps her hair whenever a man hoves into view. Even when bored, insulted or misused, she is never woebegone for long, since she knows there's a new man round the corner. There is nothing subtle about her: she's attractive and she knows it. She wants to give a man a Good Time, in its most ample and admirable sense. Watch her when the lawyer arrives, or when Joe is preparing a party: she is hither, thither and yon, restless and eager to go. She's still primping at the end, incorrigible: reunited with Joe and in his arms, a new young Mountie appears and her eyes light up.

The quintessential Bow film – if only because of its title –is, inevitably, **It** (1928), directed by Clarence Badger. Madame Elinor Glyn (as she is billed) appears, to define 'it' – 'a quality possessed by some which draws all others with its magnetic force'. 'If ever I saw It, that's It,' says one male on sight of Clara. 'Hot socks, here's our new boss,' says her chum, at once sarcastic when Bow says she plans to marry him. 'Let's have a double wedding. You and him, and me and the Prince of Wales,' – to which Bow retorts, 'I'll soon take the snap out of your garters.' Because she has It, she does marry him, but not before some misunderstandings on a yacht – and since a yacht also provided the climax for *My Lady of Whims,* it was presumably the right place for girls of this kind.

Miss Bow's fame lives on. Raymond Griffith (1894–1957) has only recently been recognised as one of the great screen clowns, perhaps because audiences were spoilt then, and partly because so few of his features survive – and in none of those is he, like the other clowns, the whole show. His gags are not as individualistic as those of Keaton or Chaplin, and his

dude outfit is modelled on Max Linder; but he is inventive and endearing – and because he signals his irrepressible optimism with such glee he is more likeable, even, than Lloyd. He started with Vitagraph in 1914, and worked with Sennett as gagman and direct, but seems to have made his acting debut as a supporting actor in features – he has a small role in *Open All Night,* as a permanently drunk New Yorker hoping to be the next screen sheik. We note a cad's mannerisms but an eagerness to please (not the audience, but the suckers in the film), button-bright eyes and the physique of a mouse. **Paths to Paradise** (1925) is an enjoyable crook comedy, a forerunner of that staple of the Thirties, the elegant couple in uneasy alliance to con someone – and ending up in love. She (Betty Compson) poses as a maid and he as a detective, and there is some inventive business trying to steal a jewel, and a final slapstick chase. Clarence

Raymond Griffith, right, with Betty Compson in *Paths to Paradise,* one of his few extant films. Griffith has only recently taken his place with the great Silent clowns – though not because, as has been suggested, others overshadowed him. Except for Chaplin, they were all forgotten or half–forgotten till James Agee's famous essay in 1949. The fact that Agee did not mention him can only mean that he had not seen him.

Badger directed both this and **Hands Up!** (1926), in which Griffith is an inefficient but nimble Confederate spy. He's ingratiating when smiling to hide his guilt, or doing a double-take at realising one of his own mistakes; but the fun·is up and down till a roaring climax. In this film Robert E. Sherwood considered him ahead of the other comedians 'in point of ingenuity, imaginativeness and originality'. Talkies were difficult for him because he hardly spoke above a whisper (among those he made was *All Quiet on the Western Front*, playing the dying French Soldier); he later became a producer.

Paramount's other Silent comic (if we except Lloyd) was W. C. Fields (1879–1946), whose greater fame in Talkies has obscured the merit of his early films. These are just as disorganised as the Talkies, indicating on the studio's part a consistent tolerance towards the eccentricities of a particular talent. They also include many sequences and gags subsequently found in several of the Sound films. **It's the Old Army Game** (1926) trades on his old sketch, 'The Pharmacist' (filmed as a short by Mack Sennett in 1933) and has two sequences carried over intact into *It's a Gift* (q.v.). Since from his later films we know his clowning as a combination of misanthropy and a sense of damnation we may most treasure his delicate movements, to the extent that we may be tempted to place him with Lloyd and Keaton, though in the end his work is – inevitably – more improvised. Eddie Sutherland directed, lacking the firmness of Gregory LaCava (1892–1952) on **So's Your Old Man** (1927). The latter is rather thin, about a mild man who changes under hypnosis, but the earlier film finds him on form as Samuel Bisbee, glazier: 'See the world through Bisbee's windows'. Amidst bouts with his drinking colleagues, he invents an unbreakable windscreen – but mishap brings ignominy till a Spanish princess arrives to impress the snobs of the town in his favour. There also arrives a senator and a policeman, at the sight of whom he runs – for, like Keaton, he always expects to be outside the law. At the end, successful, he waves wife and princess goodbye, settling down to two weeks' vacation, drinking with his cronies. This is absolutely the Fieldsian universe – he remade it as *You're Telling Me* (q.v.) – and the original lacks only his murmured epithets. He is a very great man indeed, though contemporary audiences did not appreciate it. Paramount partnered him in his last three Silents with Chester Conklin in the hope of repeating the popularity of their teaming of Wallace Beery and Raymond Hatton.

Paramount also had a female droll, Bebe Daniels (1901–71), making strictly formula comedies. She had once been Harold Lloyd's leading lady, and had also played sultry ladies for deMille. She doesn't, in fact, seem funny so much as game. In **She's a Sheik** (1927), directed by Clarence Badger, she is chieftainess Zaida, rejecting the advances of wicked chieftain William Powell and kidnapping Foreign Legionnaire Richard Arlen for a strictly pure amour. As slapstick or parody it is tame. Better – because of La Cava's lighter touch – is **Feel My Pulse** (1928), in which she plays a molly-coddled, hypochondriac heiress who learns that her private sanatorium is being used as a base for rum-runners. Arlen is the sympathetic smuggler who is also a reporter, and Powell (b.1892) the gang boss. In both ventures William Powell's facial expressions are the best thing: though not yet immaculate, he has that eye to the main chance which he so well displayed in his Talkies' role of sauve charmer.

Richard Dix, who succeeded Wallace Reid as the studio's leading leading man, alternated comedy and drama. Jowly, even as a young man, he was suitably dressed in white tie and tails, high on bootleg booze until inevitably the right girl comes along to make him settle down. As such, he was in the tradition of the youthful John Barrymore, and **Let's Get Married** (1926) was a remake of Barrymore's 1914 *The Man From Mexico*. The 'right girl' is Lois Wilson, and by far the best performance in the film is Edna May Oliver's portrayal of a hymnal-seller with a taste for racy speakeasies. Dix is an Indian boy brought up as white in **Redskin** (1929), an action-filled tract made mainly in Technicolor, directed by Victor Schertzinger, from a story by Zane Grey; 'the greatest gift is not oil but tolerance' proclaims a worthy intertitle at the end.

Not then, or later, was Paramount interested in social problems, but the company made a notable move in the trend towards gangster studies with *Underworld* (q.v.) – which is also significant in the career of Josef von Sternberg (1894–1969). He was Viennese-born, Jewish, and an immigrant at the age of seven. More or less self-taught, he drifted from one job to another till he realised his capacity as an artist, which brought him into films. His first picture, **The Salvation Hunters** (1925), was the result of an arrangement with George K. Arthur, a British comic having difficulty repeating his native success in the U.S.: they made it for only $4,800, filming among the derelicts of the San Pedro waterfront. Its visual style is as unpretentious as the story is not. Each image is held until the significance of what is happening is properly understood; and the foreword makes it quite clear that: 'There are fragments of life which have been ignored by the motion picture because they concern the Thought and not the Body.' This Thought, or concept, is poverty, being down, out, despairing: but the story is trite in the extreme. It is one of the first 'arty' American films (contemporary with Nazimova's *Salome*, though that is arty in a theatrical way), and much impressed Fairbanks and Chaplin – it being seemingly impossible then, as now, for Hollywood to make the distinction between the arty-honest and the arty-phoney. They appreciated affinities with the German cinema. Suggestions that von Sternberg had worked there were not denied by him; they also arranged for United Artists to distribute it. Then he was engaged to direct Mary Pickford. She had second thoughts when he proposed another picture on poverty, perhaps because she took a second look at *The Salvation Hunters*. Chaplin also had second thoughts: he not only suppressed the film von Sternberg later made for him, but repudiated him by saying that he had only wished to test public acceptance of his opinions.

Despite the commercial failure of *The Salvation Hunters*, and two aborted films for M-G-M, B. P. Schulberg of Paramount took on von Sternberg, and put him on a story by Ben Hecht (1894–1964), which was troubling another director, Arthur Rosson. Hecht was a newspaperman, the first of many to flourish in Hollywood as audiences demanded contemporary stories. He had worked in Chicago, and his script for **Underworld** (1927) incorporates not only the killing of Dion O'Bannion in a flower shop in 1922, but a police siege and shoot-out of the sort he had often witnessed – though the film is less about what we think of as gangsters than derelicts, a couple of whom happen to be armed. This deliberate deglamorisation means that these robber chiefs dispute not so much over hooch or territory as over the plan of one to rape the girl of the other (George Bancroft) – a lady called 'Feathers' (Evelyn Brent). The film was much admired, and three years later the National Board of Review said that it had substantiated its director as 'an experimentalist whose work would sooner or later parallel in its creative aspect the work of artists in other fields and mediums of expression.' Its influence was strongest among the young French directors, but except for the shots of George Bancroft asleep among the carnival streamers, it has little of von Sternberg's visual flair.

The Last Command (1928) was also written by von Sternberg, from an incident told by Lubitsch of a movie director looking over the extras for a Russian officer 'type'. This one (Emil Jannings) had been a Russian general, and the director (William Powell) had been a revolutionary; the film flashbacks to their earlier activities, till, as an intertitle puts it, 'The backwash of a tortured nation had carried still another extra to Hollywood.' The Russian sequences are melodramatic, but the Revolution is imaginatively sketched in, and the Hollywood scenes are rightly frenetic, with some viciousness. Neither *The Dragnet* (1928) nor von Sternberg's last Silent, *The Case of Lena Smith* (1929), are known to survive. The latter was a Viennese story about a peasant girl's fight to regain her son from her husband's aristocratic family; and the former was a follow-up to *Underworld*, with Miss Brent and Bancroft – 'an emphatically mediocre effort' according to *The New York Times*. If so, **The Docks of New York** (1928) is at the other end of the scale. These docks are permanently wreathed in fog, and the clapboard houses look like anywhere but New York, but the story must be typical of any dockside at any time – if one overlooks the old fiction of the drunken night-time wedding, forgotten or regretted the following morning. Jules Furthman wrote the script from a story by John Monk Saunders, and they are entirely accurate on the violence, the casualness and licentiousness of the milieu; while the settings – the dark, crowded bar, the bare apartment-rooms – indicate that von Sternberg was approaching his peak as a visual stylist. Bancroft is the ox-like stoker and Betty Compson the frail he marries, bedraggled and all apprehensive glances, with an underlying hardness foreshadowing Dietrich in *Der Blaue Engel*.

Paramount's last Silent was **The Four Feathers** (1929) – last, because it took so long to make that it wasn't ready till every other screen was all-singing and all-talking. Its instigators were Merian C. Cooper (1893–1973) and Ernest B. Schoedsack (1893–1979), who had been, respectively, a flyer and a cameraman. Backed by Paramount, they went to Iran to make a film in the manner of Flaherty, *Grass* (1925) a 'vivid record' (Rotha) of the Baktyari tribe's twice-yearly migrations in search of grazing land. Its reception encouraged a further expedition – to the jungles of Northern Thailand, from which emerged *Chang* (1927), a story of a Lao tribesman and his battles with the jungle. However, little of the ethnic material brought back from Africa found its way into this version of A. E. W. Mason's novel, and the presence of a third director, Lothar Mendes, suggests that Paramount had no faith in their ability to handle fiction. The film is almost rousing: the shots of the Fuzzy-Wuzzies and the climactic battle are as good as in any Hollywood movie about the British Empire – proof always of how much Americans were in awe of that mighty, mystical concept. Like *Beau Geste*, the story begins in an English country house before moving to Africa, where the hero (Richard Arlen) redeems himself after accusations of cowardice: his bravery is super human, and if, also, so is his way with a dagger, all was permissible for Queen and Empire. Two intertitles are of interest: 'I promise you help is coming. Has a British officer ever failed you?' and 'Steady, men. Remem-ber that all Ney's cavalry at Waterloo could not destroy the British square.' The film follows the book in its awe of military mystique, and that has dated far more than reverence for the Empire.

At Fox, the theatrical demise of Theda Bara brought them to tales of home-spun virtues, mostly set in the West or mid-West. These films are notable mainly for their indication of change, as the wagon-trains gave way to the Model-T Ford and the great trains rushing through; most of them starred the company's two biggest stars, Buck Jones and Tom Mix.

Jones (1889–1942) was a man of the West, who liked fishing and idling: 'the idol of youths, the bane of the elders' as one intertitle has it. Both **Just Pals** (1920) and **Lazybones** (1925) show him winning gloriously over suspicion and distrust. In the former, directed by John Ford, he befriends a rootless boy and is suspected of stealing the school funds; in the latter, directed by Frank Borzage, he risks opprobrium by bringing up Zazu Pitts's son as his own – and, incidentally, the sequence where that lady is horse-whipped by her mother remains shocking.

Tom Mix (1880–1940) was described as 'that gun-toting cyclone on horseback' and another intertitle referred to 'The fastest gun, horse and smile of any man in the West'. He wore a skin-tight white outfit with gloves to match, but unlike the similarly accoutred cowboys who followed, he was the real thing – a former Texas Ranger, U.S. cavalryman, rancher and deputy marshal. As to his qualities as an actor, there is little evidence, but as a stunt performer he was a marvel: he jumped on and off horses, trains and stages; he wrestled beneath them and battled on top of them; on ropes he forded rivers and ravines, moving from precipice to valley and back again. His horse, Tony, was as enterprising as he – as swift as an eagle and as accurate as a homing pigeon. In **The Great K and A Train Robbery** (1926), the huge expresses are manoeuvred as easily as a toy, and just as easily Mix rounds up the gang, single-handed. In **The Last Trail** (1927), also directed by Lewis Seiler, he

The Last Man on Earth is one of those films so freakish that one can only question the mentality and motives of its makers. Earle Fox is the man, and, as an intertitle put it, 'There hasn't been so much interest in a man since the late King of England visited New York in 1924 – when he was Prince of Wales.' Clearly, this was science–fiction – of sorts.

brings up his pal's orphaned son, taking over from him as sheriff of the town, and defeating the dastardly outlaws in both battle and a chariot-race for the local Express concession.

Away from such sure-fire stuff, the Fox films faltered. In **The Silent Command** (1923) Edmund Lowe gets publicly disgraced in order to infiltrate a foreign power planning to blow up the newly-built Panama Canal. J. Gordon Edwards directed, and his film has two moments worth contemplating: the crew refusing to abandon ship, 'Beg pardon, sir, we'd rather go down with colours' and Bela Lugosi listening to a conversation miles away with a bugging device. Henry Otto directed **Dante's Inferno** (1924), which begins with both an imaginative evocation of Gustave Doré's illustrations designed for the text and a foreword claiming that much thought has gone into this version of a classic, implying that we would all enjoy it more because of the modern section – though that turns out to be a rehash of 'A Christmas Carol', with Dante and visions of hell replacing the visitations of the Christmas ghosts in the Dickens story.

Even more bizarre is **The Last Man on Earth** (1924), directed by John G. Blystone, which starts in 'the flip-flappering summer of 1940' with the men in dinner-jackets and jodhpurs, and the women in brief hooped-skirts and frilly pantaloons. Hattie (Derelys Perdue) tells Elmer (Earle Fox) that she wouldn't marry him if he were the last man alive – which is what he is about to become: the world is swept by a mysterious disease called 'masculitis' – fatal to males over fourteen years of age', as Dr Lulu Prodwell puts it. Ten years later, the women go around hand-in-hand, pantaloons abandoned for sequinned shorts. Only Greenwich Gertie of the Teahouse Gang knows where Elmer is – among the redwoods of California, and how her plane gets down in the midst of them is something only Fox could explain. Elmer is put up for auction, 'the most momentous sale in history', but it attracts only eight people, plus Dr Prodwell, who bids on behalf of her government. In her clinic, invalids

Reunion in the trenches: in *Four Sons*, two brothers (James Hall, left, and George Meeker) are fighting on opposite sides, and one hears the other, dying, cry 'Mutterchen'. He *hears* it, for the synchronised score is interrupted by just this one line of dialogue, an experience found 'disquieting' by *The New York Times* – whose only experience of Talkies hitherto had been *The Jazz Singer*.

throw away crutches to chase him – though the chief pursuer is the doctor's daughter, now a raging nymphomaniac. The aim is presumably Swiftian satire, and if the achievement is unsettling, it is for different reasons.

It is a relief to return to the Western, and it was **The Iron Horse** (1924) which made the reputation of John Ford (1895–1973), former propman and stuntman. He later suggested that a 'simple story' was stretched when Fox saw the location shots, but it is far more likely that Fox sought to emulate the success of *The Covered Wagon*. A foreword promises accuracy, and Ford has precisely caught the pioneering spirit: there is real pride in the statement that due to the enthusiasm of the workers the two transcontinental lines met seven years earlier than Congress had anticipated. This makes for a marvellous ending – as in deMille's *Union Pacific* (q.v.), in which the construction of the railroads is a backdrop to an equally trite story. In this case it concerns a buck-skinned leader (George O'Brien) who wins the boss's daughter (Madge Bellamy) from his treacherous aide. The Indian attacks against plains and distant mountains (photographed by George Schneiderman, assisted by Burnett Guffey) are handled in a way we recognise as Fordian, and **Three Bad Men** (1926) is even more stuffed with themes to which this director would return in film after film. Its images of the

Dakota Gold Rush of 1877 are even more consistently impressive than those of Cruze's film, as three desperadoes (J. Farrell MacDonald, Tom Santschi, Frank Campeau) adopt a fatherless heroine (Olive Borden) and find for her a husband (O'Brien). This couple could be John Wayne (q.v.) and Maureen O'Hara, and aficionados will also welcome the masculine camaraderie (tough old buzzard in tears after a farewell), slapstick (the dude getting a going-over to see whether he's a suitable husband) and sentiment (the prayer in the chapel).

Ford remained under contract to Fox till well into the Talkie period, occasionally getting his teeth into subjects that interested him: the reiteration of favourite themes suggests alternately playing it safe and a degree of independence not granted to his colleagues. **The Shamrock Handicap** (1926) has moments of hilarity – an Irish baronet so changed by U.S. democracy that he digs ditches till his horse can enter the big race; and one of meanness – the black valet who holds a razor-blade, just in case, during a changing-room fight. Two other films reflect Ford's Irish antecedents: **Hangman's House** (1928), a thriller with some horse-racing, a number of Celtic crosses, and Victor McLaglen as a local patriot bent on revenge; and **Riley the Cop** (1927), the adventures of an Irish cop (J. Farrell MacDonald) both on his beat and among the fleshpots of Europe. The latter manages a minor variation on an old theme: young America vs. old Europe, with a decided attempt to make boozing (then, of course, outlawed in the U.S.) attractive.

Sentiment also rides high in Ford's **Four Sons** (1928) – less an account of the four brothers involved than of Mother Bernle (Margaret Mann), the most lovable, most smiling, whitest-haired *mutter* of all. Three sons fight for the Kaiser; the other, remembering a slight by a German officer, leaves his New York delicatessen to fight against him. A hideously sentimental epilogue concerning Mother's arrival in New York is accompanied by the relentless grinding of two songs, 'Little Mother' and 'The Sidewalks of New York' – and as a whole the film sticks to the stereotypes of Griffith's war films.

Fox had already managed a more realistc view of the War in **What Price Glory?** (1926), though that had not been filmed till well after the Broadway success of the play by Laurence Stallings and Maxwell Anderson – and then only because *The Big Parade* (q.v.) had cleaned up for M-G-M. The play itself had not been produced till a year after completion, for not until rehabilitation was somewhat complete was it possible to look back at that mudbath of slaughter and suffering, and reflect that it had actually happened – and, even more incredibly, that some had survived it. Remarque in 'All Quiet on the Western Front' was the first to question its values and motives, and the Second World War was to come and go before a flood of books examined it: the tenor at this time was expressed in this film – 'What price glory now?' as the dead and dying are brought in. Another inter-title runs, 'The world must be in a bad way if the earth has to be wet down by the blood of boys like these every thirty years,' and others refer to the stench of death: but the piece mainly concerns the comic feud between Captain Flagg (Victor McLaglen) and Sergeant Quirt (Edmund Lowe). The front-line sequences have little to do with them, and indeed of all the war films from *Civilization* to the version (q.v.) of Remarque's novel only *The Big Parade* tackles the battles head on. The rest, overwhelmed or under budgeted – the Marne taxis in *Seventh Heaven* (q.v.) are particularly unconvincing – settle for montage; passion here is dissipated in the antics of Quirt and Flagg and their pursuit of Charmaine (Dolores del Rio) – who, like most of the ladies in these films, is no better than she should be.

The director was Raoul Walsh, who had come to Fox from Triangle and stayed, except for a brief spell at Paramount, for twenty years – though he made his best-known Silents elsewhere, e.g. *The Thief of Bagdad, Sadie Thompson* (q.v.). **The Red Dance** (1928) is, however, a good example of Hollywood influenced by Europe, with an orgy borrowed from *Die Liebe der Jeanne Ney*, and indications of sexual variety including lesbianism – which suggests more sophistication in Fox films than in the hayseed audiences for which they were usually

intended. It was considered essential to stress the decadence of Europe, but also by this time the American film, having reached technical perfection, was trying to translate the complex temperament of mankind. Unfortunately the plot is a simple-minded thing about the pure love of a Grand Duke (Charles Farrell) and a peasant girl (Dolores del Rio); the Imperial family is sympathetically portrayed, and the Revolutionaries are the stereotypes of the Soviet films themselves – from which are copied a number of the action shots. Ben Carré's art direction is elaborate. Walsh's direction is fluid, and the film easily reflects America's attitude to Soviet Russia – a mixture of fear, wariness and grudging admiration.

Also handling a number of Fox's more worldly products was another director destined to be one of the long-serving craftsmen of the American screen, Howard Hawks (1896–1977), a former racing-driver whose occasional ventures into the industry had led him to the scenario department of Paramount. Two years later Fox gave him the chance to direct – a film now lost, and no deprivation if we judge it by his second, **Fig Leaves** (1926), which he also wrote, yet another facetious look at primitive times, plus a hackneyed modern story about a mannequin (Olive Borden), her jealous husband (George O'Brien) and her employer (André de Beranger). It is hard to sit through today, though the vestigial reward of all early movies is an indication of the way people lived then – best exemplified in the work of directors considered 'great' at the time, like Henry King and Frank Borzage, because they were allowed freedom of interpretation. Setting out only to divert, a minor industry director like Hawks is especially dependent on this material. **The Cradle Snatchers** (1927) is a light-hearted romp about three unfaithful husbands, three neglected wives, and the students they employ to make their husbands jealous. **Paid to Love** (1927) is a drama about an apache dancer (Virginia Valli) employed by an American financier (J. Farrell MacDonald) to attract a penniless Crown Prince (George O'Brien) away from his automobiles. **Fazil** (1928), an adaptation of a French play which was one of the many imitations of *The Sheik,* concerns a French girl (Greta Nissen) who marries an

No matter what critics thought of the imaginative powers of the German directors, Hollywood tended to think of them only in terms of their best–known films: so Paul Leni was called upon by Universal to recreate the sinister aspects of the film we call *Waxworks*. Here is Laura La Plante being menaced in perhaps the classic 'old dark house' tale, *The Cat and the Canary*: the disguised gentleman has claims to the same inheritance.

The acquisition of Frank Borzage (1893–1962) strengthened Fox's roster of directors. A former stage actor, he had worked with Ince and had directed for Triangle. By the time he joined Fox in 1925 his films were billed 'A Frank Borzage Production' in letters as big as the stars' names. The best of those extant is **The First Year** (1926), based on Frank Craven's play about newly-weds, played here by Kathryn Perry and Matt Moore; that it is diverting for half its footage is due to the couple's disastrous dinner-party. Borzage's *Seventh Heaven* was once described as 'the Silent picture which nine out of ten people recall with most pleasure' and I shall recall it at the end of this chapter. However, it might be mentioned here that a barrier to present appreciation is the synchronised score, consisting almost wholly of a refrain we know as 'Diane', and clearly sister to the equally omnipresent 'Charmaine' of *What Price Glory?*

Arab prince (Charles Farrell) and finds, imprisoned in his harem, that never the twain shall meet; but she still loves him, and they die together like Romeo and Juliet. That *Paid to Love* is actually enjoyable is probably due to one of its three scenarists, Seton I. Miller, who would contribute to some of Hawks's best Talkies. Its deliberately risqué title is justified by the plot, which also includes a rape by the Prince – permissible, as it turns out, since love is mutual and democracy permits its victim to become Queen. **A Girl in Every Port** (1928) is said to be seminal, because Hawks later made several more films in which male friendship proves more enduring than fickle heterosexuality – but the presence of McLaglen reminds us that the situation had already been used in *What Price Glory?* Robert Armstrong is the other merchant seaman, Louise Brooks the girl, and the piece is boisterous and amicable. **Trent's Last Case** (1929) is the second of three film versions of E. C. Bentley's 1913 detective story (the other two were British), and it captures some of the book's ingenuity; Donald Crisp is the millionaire who plots his own death, and Raymond Griffith is the amateur detective. (A Sound version was made, but now appears lost.)

Like Fox, Universal lagged behind in the race to acquire theatres; there was greater financial acumen at Paramount and M-G-M. The rivalry between them was intense, and if exhibition was now considered far more profitable than production, it behoved studio chiefs to shore up exhibition with films the public wanted to see. Universal's founder, Laemmle, remained supreme, though briefly he handed the reins to the producer boy-wonder, Irving Thalberg (1899–1936), whose tenure of office coincided with Von Stroheim's battles; and if the latter's extravagance virtually impoverished Universal, he was also to an extent responsible for its remaining a major force. Apart from his films, almost the only ones the studio made which are still remembered – and the only ones greatly successful in their time – were two historical-horror stories with Lon Chaney; ironically, Chaney's best work was for M-G-M, with whom he was associated for most of the decade.

Lon Chaney (1883–1930) was the son of deaf-mute parents; he had done almost every job in the theatre when he started in films as an extra. An extraordinary facility with make-up brought regular employment, but he did not begin to achieve his great popularity until he played a sham cripple in *The Miracle Man* (1919) at Paramount. Often bereft of features or limbs, he became known as 'The Man of a Thousand Faces', a Caliban-like creature, more to be pitied than feared. Under contract to Universal, he played Fagin in *Oliver Twist* (1922), as well as cripples, crooks, mad scientists and those eternal bogeymen, Orientals. His burning eyes and the humps and limps make his Quasimodo in **The Hunchback of Notre Dame** (1923) a pathetic figure, but you may feel the make-up is excessive. The film is also notable for its replica of the cathedral itself, though the backlot construction did not go much above the doors; Wallace Worsley directed this simplification of Hugo's novel, but Rupert Julian was put in charge of **The Phantom of the Opera** (1925) – though replaced during the shooting by an uncredited Edward Sedgwick. This one reduces Gaston Leroux's nineteenth-century thriller to the relationship between a singer (Mary Philbin) and the mysterious creature (Chaney) whose obsession with her brings him up from the catacombs where he hides his hideous face from mankind. Prima donnas are noted for vanity rather than common sense, but it is hard to know why this one insists, when her life is in danger, on singing Marguerite and going to the *bal masque* – a sequence, incidentally, photographed in Technicolor.

As works to chill the bone, neither film can compare with **The Cat and the Canary** (1927) Paul Leni's first film in the U.S. John Willard's old play about the reading of a will is not as funny as the 1939 version (q.v.), but it has Laura La Plante as the pretty victim, and Creighton Hale as the cowardly cousin who helps to unmask the murderer. The director's work can be described as follows: 'By an ingenious use of shadows, lights and photographic angles Mr Leni has created the eerie atmosphere necessary in a house where sudden death and sinister happenings occur' – that is *The New York Times*, in fact discussing *The Chinese Parrot*, which no longer exists. In contrast, **The Man Who Laughs** (1928) is merely another historical, with Universal hoping that both this version of Hugo would repeat the success of *The Hunchback of Notre Dame,* and that it had

acquired another Chaney in the imported Conrad Veidt – who on this occasion is just another clown-hero of the time. **The Last Warning** (1929) returns Leni to his shadows, a thriller set entirely inside a theatre – and no one ever had so much fun with the sinister aspects of an empty theatre. After a flat exposition, the tension mounts: indeed, this is one of the most accomplished and enjoyable of all Silent thrillers – its small reputation due to its advent just as cinemas were wired for Sound, and possibly also to Leni's early death.

Universal's other prize European acquisition was E. A. Dupont, who retired to Europe after just one film, *Love Me and the World Is Mine Tonight.* The liaison between the studio and the Hungarian Paul Fejos (1897–1963) was more profitable but little more agreeable. He had studied medicine, but after contact with the theatre during military service took it up full-time, and made his first film in 1920. In the U.S. he found independent backing for *The Last Moment* (1927), now lost; it caused Laemmle to offer a contract and give him freedom on *Lonesome* (q.v.), the critical reception of which encouraged Universal to put him on one of their first big Talkies, *Broadway* (q.v.). Indeed, to make that Fejos and Hal Mohr, the cinematographer, were taken off **The Last Performance** (1929), which limped into cinemas a year later, its added Sound sequences of no benefit among the all-Talkies. The Fejos flair is always apparent in this tale of a stage illusionist (Veidt) and his obsession with his ward (Miss Philbin), but audience indifference may also have been due to over-familiarity with these black-rim eyed and sinister supermen. Fejos moved, after some uncredited work, to M-G-M, where he was removed from one film and otherwise kept idle. He returned to Europe, to make at least two interesting films (q.v.); but it is because of *Lonesome* that he has an honourable place in film history: it calls for separate discussion, which you will find at the end of this chapter.

Universal's most skilful native director was Clarence Brown (b. 1890), formerly assistant to Maurice Tourneur – and their *Foolish Matrons* we have already admired. Two of his Universal films are

Reginald Denny wearing just half of *Skinner's Dress Suit*, and the joke was a popular one in Silent days, starting with a close–up, and the camera drawing back to reveal – well, lack of respectability. His wife, Laura La Plante, had been mending the pants; and in their subsequent junketings it will take them a long time to realise that the dowdy, out-of-town couple they meet at the dance could be the saviour of his career.

romance is of more interest today than the drama of mother–love; and it was because of this aspect that Brown was engaged to direct *The Eagle* (q.v.) for Schenck, whose manager had caught it one evening in a cinema, and having missed the credits, had assumed – not unreasonably – that it was the handiwork of Lubitsch.

Finally at Universal we might pause at the comedies the company made with Reginald Denny (1891–1967), the British-born character actor who at this time was a star comedian, playing well-meaning young men forever getting into scrapes – as precise but not as elaborate as those of Lloyd, his nearest counterpart. William A. Seiter directed most of his vehicles, and particularly delightful are his versions of two older films, **What Happened to Jones?** (1926) and **Skinner's Dress Suit** (1926): what happened to Jones was that he got trapped in his shorts at the ladies' night in the Turkish Bath, but Skinner's trouble was due to his fondness for the charleston, spending sprees, and his inability to get to work on time.

Of the first studios, only Pathé survived; of the second wave Universal, Fox and Paramount were going strong, with the last named under Zukor as the industry's acknowledged leader – till challenged by Marcus Loew, whose theatre chain, Loew's Inc., had been one of Paramount's chief customers. When Loew decided, in 1920, that it was imperative to control production and distribution as well as exhibition, he acquired the newly-formed Metro Company, then under the aegis of a Vitagraph alumnus, George D. Baker. Metro's chief asset, if a hidden one, was June Mathis (1892–1927), a scenarist; her belief that filming was a collective job meant following Ince's rule of a detailed shooting script – preferably 'Written and Supervised by June Mathis', which was the credit-line on her films. Were there any doubts about her methods, the towering success of **The Four Horsemen of the Apocalypse** (1921), stilled them, though credit also went to the director, Rex Ingram. To *The New York Times* it was 'an extraordinary motion picture' and in *Life* Robert E. Sherwood commented that 'the grandoise posturings of David Wark Griffith and Cecil B. deMille appear

impressive: **Smouldering Fires** (1924) and **The Goose Woman** (1925) – the latter written by one of Goldwyn's Eminent Authors (q.v.), Rex Beach, who summed up that experience thus: 'As an author, I say that it is bunk that you want more and better authors . . . What you want is more mush and slush, pre-digested pap.' Both these films could be described as 'mush and slush' were they not redeemed by the direction. Both are vehicles for ageing actresses of considerable skill: *Smouldering Fires* concerns the strict boss (Pauline Frederick) of a factory who falls for one of her employees (Malcolm MacGregor), twenty years her junior; *The Goose Woman* is about an ex-opera singer (Louise Dresser) who reattracts world attention when she has the vital clue to a murder – in which, alas, her son (Jack Pickford) is involved. The spring-and-fall pale and artificial in the light of this new production . . . [which deserves] more than any other picture play that the War inspired – to be handed down to generations yet unborn, that they may see the horror and futility of the whole bloody mess.' Audiences liked it more than *The Birth of a Nation,* also concerned with war in spectacular manner; and apart from *The Singing Fool* (q.v.), its box office records would be held until *Gone with the Wind* – with which, in fact, it has a number of affinities. Both concern the disintegration of a pleasure loving society, its reduction to chaos, and its recovery. The riders of the title intrude in metaphysical manner in what is a Victorian tale of regeneration – that of a shallow playboy (Rudolph Valentino). The intertitles plug away at the Old World tearing itself apart in hatred while, by implication, the New World is serene. Actually, apart from a few newsreel shots and a muddy trench in which the playboy is heroic, the depiction of war is little different to that in other films of the time, being virtually limited to shots of the vicious Bosch marching or cavorting drunkenly. The long years of senseless carnage are ignored, and as towns and villages in France, Belgium, Britain and Italy were putting up memorial crosses to their fallen, Hollywood, with the aid of a Spanish novelist – Vicente Blasco-Ibañez – was perpetuating the myth that it was a glorious thing to die. That fitted the public's concept, as decreed by the press during the previous years. Also, war might be deadly, but mainly it was inconvenient. War brought out the best, even in gigolos.

This was Valentino's first important role and he was crucial to the film's success. He had not yet discovered that neurotic intensity which later made him such a foolish lover, and he was magnetic: women were undoubtedly thrilled by the 'free' life he lived in Paris. Give or take historical figures or an occasional immigrant, the only permitted foreign heroes had been British, noble Empire-builders all – possibly more courtly in the boudoir, but less exciting. With his brillianteened hair and cigarette-holder, Valentino represented much that was smart and sinful in the new century, with its changing morals ; and, of course, he was good underneath. To a great many American

men he was both effete and decadent, contentions ably proved when he played in a modernised **Camille** (1921) – or at least the film was, as produced by the starring Nazimova, with stylised decor, following the even more foolish *Salome.*

Traditional values were available in **Happiness** (1924), one of the three films made for Metro by Laurette Taylor, and, like the first, *Peg o'My Heart,* based on a play written for her by her husband, J. Hartley Manners. Indeed, after the phenomenal success of the original *Peg,* he had written a whole series of pieces in which she played waifs – and, personally, if there is anything less appealing than miserable waifs, it is happy and resourceful ones. However, Miss Taylor, forty and plumpish, overcomes most reservations, and King Vidor, directing, was clearly happy with her, her companions, and the Brooklyn milieu.

Meanwhile, the estimated \$4½ million earned by *The Four Horsemen* had enabled the acquisitive Loew to buy the Goldwyn Picture Corporation, originally founded by Sam Goldwyn (1882–1974) on leaving Jesse Lasky's company when it amalgamated with Famous Players. His financiers were Du Ponts and the Chase National Bank, and his partner Edgar Selwyn – hence the name, though wags noted the alternative combination, Selfish, since Sam at the time had not yet changed his name from Goldfish. Throughout his career, Goldwyn's only instincts as a producer were to copy and/or buy success, and thus he formed Eminent Authors Inc., which aimed to bring to the medium the same prestige as had the Famous Players. The scheme was a failure, but another Goldwyn instinct was to persevere (if not for long) and he hired Elmer Rice for **Doubling With Romeo** (1921), to collaborate with Will Rogers (1879–1935) – his biggest star, but one far from duplicating his stage success. As directed by Clarence Badger, the film is an inventive satire on how Hollywood had changed young ladies' ideas about love-making, but Rogers' humour, winning when personally delivered, seems clumsy in intertitles, viz. 'She speaketh but like a politician sayeth nothing.' After one more film, Goldwyn gave up on him. A profusion of intertitles also wrecks **Sherlock Holmes** (1922),

directed by Albert Parker, with John Barrymore in the title-role, Roland Young as Watson, Gustav von Seyffertitz as Moriarty, William Powell, Reginald Denny, some location shots of Baker Street, and complicated plot which has little to do with either Conan Doyle or William Gillette. Goldwyn was no luckier with *Caligari,* which he imported: few exhibitors would book it after New York audiences booed and demanded their money back. He learned the satisfaction — of inestimable value for the future — of having an artistic success, but his stock-holders were less happy and he was ousted; later in 1922 Loew took over the company in a stock exchange deal. Goldwyn started again as an independent, leaving as legacy for the new Metro-Goldwyn company a roaring lion

wanted, to manage a motion picture studio, he looked around for a surrogate. His eye alighted upon Louis B. Mayer (1885–1957), a former exhibitor and distributor whose fortunes had started with the local franchise of *The Birth of a Nation*. Mayer had been briefly involved in the founding of the Metro company, then called Alco, in 1915, and had started his own production company three years later, when he enticed the popular Anita Stewart from Vitagraph on an exclusive contract. Like all the moguls, he had a reputation for ruthlessness and double-dealing. Filching major stars from rivals remained a major activity among them; but from Miss Stewart's point of view it meant a higher salary and the proposition that the new company was devoted to her popularity and abilities. Mayer made an agreement with First National to distribute, and at a time when a good gross for a film was $250,000 that company offered a guarantee of $125,000 –and though Mayer's films usually cost more than that, they were profitable. Consequently Metro approached him with a request to make four films a year for them, in addition to his commitment to First National, and that brought him into contact with Loew, who was to find himself saddled with two failing companies – for Metro had begun to flounder when June Mathis left for Paramount with Valentino, indignant that the latter's salary request had been refused. Loew and Mayer signed an agreement for Mayer to manage both studios, in April 1924, and Metro moved to the Goldwyn lot at Culver City. The name Metro-Goldwyn-Mayer was not used till a year later; for the moment Louis B. Mayer – prominently – presented Metro-Goldwyn pictures.

Mayer was production chief, but the brains of the outfit was Irving Thalberg, recruited from Universal a year earlier, and who with the merger became second vice-president and supervisor. Within the industry, during his lifetime and for some time after, he was regarded as a 'genius' – even by the normally sceptical scenario-writers. That he had drive, ingenuity and a far-sighted commercial acumen there is no doubt, but the verdict on the films he produced and supervised cannot be so positive: most of them can

'The world was dancing. Paris had succumbed to the mad rhythm of the Argentine Tango,' says an intertitle in *The Four Horsemen of the Apocalypse*, but the film soon proved that it had other matters than tangoes on its mind. The war–torn French villages may not look so convincing to modern eyes, but audiences at the time were stunned.

(then mute) and a slogan, '*Ars Gratia Artis*', which, except for a brief spell of 'modernisation' in the Sixties, have opened every M-G-M film from then to the present.

The Goldwyn company was deeply in debt, but its assets included the studio at Culver City – built by Ince, and purchased from Triangle by Goldwyn – and since Loew neither knew how, nor only be judged in commercial terms. It is impossible to admire Mayer even to that extent; he may have made decisions which made the accountants happy, but his creative demands were, in Lady Bracknell's words, 'of more than usually revolting sentimentality'. He was a bigot and a hypocrite, once described thus by *Variety*: 'One does not remember his achievements so much as his monumental pettiness, his savage retaliation, the humiliations he heaped on old associates.' If his name is synonymous with that of M–G–M in its heyday it is because he loved publicity – while Thalberg eschewed it; and because the creative team built up by Thalberg was to remain at Culver City till long after his premature death.

The relationship between the two men was to be an uneasy one, developing into a complete rift during the Thirties. At this point they were too busy solving the two major headaches willed them by the Goldwyn company. One was *Greed*, which we have already discussed, and the other was **Ben-Hur** (1925), also taken on by the company as a prestige item after Sam Goldwyn's departure. General Lew Wallace's novel about a Jewish nobleman at the time of the Roman Occupation of his country had been the biggest-selling book since the Bible – from which it purloined a number of its episodes; the theatrical firm of Klaw and Erlanger had presented a stage spectacle based on the book in 1889, and as its popularity never dimmed the film rights were eyed longingly by the movie industry from the 1907 pirated version by Kalem onwards. In 1921 Erlanger arranged with the Wallace estate to offer those rights for $600,000, and then formed a consortium with two other impresarios, Ziegfeld and Dillingham. which bought them for that sum and offered them to the industry for $1 million. The Goldwyn company could not afford that, but it offered the syndicate fifty cents from every dollar earned by the film: that the film would be hugely profitable neither side had any doubt, for Lubitsch's German spectacles were currently proving again that huge expenditure was justified at the box office – as was, also, *The Four Horsemen*. And June Mathis, having now defected from Paramount (without Valentino), would

also be in charge of *Ben-Hur*. It was she who decided that the film must be made in Italy, that the director should be Charles Brabin and the star George Walsh: in conditions of chaos, caused partly by the Italians – both the authorities and the crew – and partly by an inadequate script, filming proceeded. After viewing the rushes, Mayer and Thalberg replaced Brabin with Fred Niblo and Walsh with Ramon Novarro; Mathis was also dropped, and after further erratic shooting, production was transferred to Hollywood, with only about ten per cent of the Italian footage retained. The final cost was just under $4 million, and the worldwide gross around $9 million; that it went into the M–G–M ledgers at a loss of $700,000 was due entirely to the percentage paid to Erlanger's group – however, reissued in 1931 with a synchronised score and sound effects it took somewhat more than that figure, which was a very good gross indeed.

That may seem surprising, since the Silent film was then dead, but the world had loved *Ben-Hur* – and it is easy to see why. Like all good Silent spectacle, it moves ahead with conviction and aplomb, and neither the sea battle nor the chariot race disappoints. The intermittent use of Technicolor and the groupings in such sequences as the Birth of Christ and the Last Supper (after da Vinci) indicate the care taken; and if the film not unreasonably takes its pictorial quality from nineteenth-century religious painting it is still much less Victorian in image and sentiment than the 1959 remake (q.v.). It is much more entertaining, and therefore a far better film: its qualities were certainly recognised by the makers of the new version, which uses identical set-ups in the chariot race and for Christ carrying the Cross.

Thus *The Four Horsemen* and *Ben-Hur*, neither of which had originally anything to do with Mayer or Thalberg, created the M–G–M image – of uplift and literary origins, of larger-than-average budgets (approximately one-third higher than at other studios), and, following Valentino and Novarro, of 'more stars than there are in heaven'. That was one boast of the publicity department, which more consistently than that of other studios maintained superlatives – and we can

The wicked Roman, Messala (Francis X. Bushman), hardly plays fair with his former childhood friend, Ben-Hur (Ramon Novarro), in the 1925 film of that name. There were several uncredited directors, and it was Reeves Eason who was responsible for the still-exciting chariot race, for which forty-two cameras were used. Though clearly they did not construct the whole stadium above ground level, the sheer size of what we see on the screen still takes the breath away.

agree that M-G-M product was the classiest. Later, it was often the most pompous, but as long as Thalberg was alive Leo the Lion had both teeth and guts. Two other films of M-G-M's first year – both instituted and shown as the company struggled with *Ben-Hur* – helped it take the industry's crown of leadership from Paramount. Both cost above the average, were commercially and artistically successful, and starred John Gilbert (1897–1936). One was Von Stroheim's *The Merry Widow*, and the other **The Big Parade** (1925), commissioned by Thalberg from Lawrence Stallings, co-author of 'What Price Glory?' – the Broadway success of which proved that the public was ready for another war subject, more realistically treated than *The Four Horsemen,* but not, finally, less romantically. It is structured like a symphony: the opening – the wealthy dilettante (Gilbert) who is so taken by a patriotic tune that he joins the army; the long middle section, the coda – the frolics of the hero and his buddies in the French village, and his wooing of a local Marianne (the aptly-named Renée

Adorée); and, finally, the battle. The actual plot emerges in an epilogue, when the hero, now crippled, returns to search for his beloved in an impossibly sun-drenched countryside. The facts of army-life and duo-national romance are glossed over, but the more important war scenes are handled by the director, King Vidor, with a skill that remains astonishing. He also ensures that Gilbert, for all his charm and authority, retains till the end some of his initial arrogance: unlike Valentino's earlier soldier hero, this is no cardboard toy.

Star and director, with Lillian Gish, shared another success with **La Bohème** (1926), quite rightly described by *The New York Times* as 'virtually flawless', before adding 'and one that will do its share to bring the screen to a higher plane.' Such could not be said of **Bardelys the Magnificent** (1926), based on a swashbuckling novel by Rafael Sabatini, but it is great fun. If all three films confirmed Vidor as one of the most accomplished of directors, posterity may give equal place to Monta Bell (1891–1958) – at least on the strength of **Upstage** (1926) and

Sjöström's *He Who Gets Slapped* was based on a popular play, 'a circus allegory', in Brooks Atkinson's words, 'that no one understood but everyone loved.' The film is only too understandable: the rejected scientist (Lon Chaney, right) who becomes a clown, the bare–back rider (Norma Shearer) he secretly loves, and the partner (John Gilbert) she loves but cannot marry. It made the reputations of Shearer and Gilbert, and enhanced that of Chaney.

Laugh (1928), directed by Herbert Brenon, who only three years earlier had been offering *A Kiss for Cinderella*. In that film, the camera of James Wong Howe had simply recorded the action, but now it contributes to it; so does the editing, and the sets and locations really look like Italy. And the acting is naturalistic, even if one hesitates before the mellifluent style of Lon Chaney. This version of 'Pagliacci' is based on a 1923 play by David Belasco and Tom Cushing, and the clown (Chaney) has melancholia: he is assigned to a Count (Nils Asther), whose 'spells of uncontrollable laughter are due to a life of self-indulgence', for a mutual cure, but it is still a question of *cherchez la femme*, a bare-back rider (Loretta Young) – whose attentions to the lascivious Count are further evidence of the increased sophistication in films during these years.

The films of Lon Chaney are a footnote to the taste of the Twenties, but merely as a thriller **The Unholy Three** (1925) is remarkably accomplished – and it is not to be judged by the 1930 Sound remake, also with Chaney, directed by Jack Conway. The trio of the title are a dwarf, a strong man, and a ventriloquist (Chaney) who is disguised as a dear old lady; their business is burglary and their cover a parrot shop. It is an ingenious story, economically and tensely told by Tod Browning, an old acquaintance and frequent director of Chaney, whose career had been bedevilled by drink up to this time. Brought to M-G-M by Chaney, together they embarked on a series of grotesqueries, usually involving the star as a pitiable-ghastly outcast of society bent on revenge for some past wrong, real or imagined. At its worst, the formula resulted in **The Unknown** (1927), in which Chaney is a supposedly armless knife-thrower who has his arms amputated in a scheme to destroy the lover (Norman Kerry) of the girl (Joan Crawford) he adores; and at its best, in **West of Zanzibar** (1928) in which he is a severely crippled trader whose revenge on his enemy (Lionel Barrymore) includes the use of voodoo and the reduction of the latter's supposed daughter to a drink-crazed whore. There are, of course, degrees of acceptability, and Browning, always (at this time) a vivid storyteller, works best when he can gloat over the whole paraphernalia of evil,

Man, Woman and Sin (1927), among his few films to survive. He had been one of Chaplin's assistants, and had directed his first film in 1924, *Broadway After Dark*; apart from producing *West Point of the Air* for M-G-M in 1935, he retired after the conventional *The Worst Woman of Paris?* (q.v.) two years earlier. Contemporaries never placed him with Vidor, nor were his films the sort to elicit exceptional attention – simply conventional tales of love and melodrama. Bell was able to apply both wit and tension to every sequence; he used imaginative but not arty set-ups, and was marvellous on the detail of the milieu – the vaudeville theatres and offices of *Upstage,* and in *Man, Woman and Sin* moving from newspaper-office to embassy-ball to suburban bordello. In the latter film Gilbert is the adoring cub-reporter used by the paper's society editor, played by an already legendary stage actress, Jeanne Eagels, with a natural ease and elegance. Gowned in chiffon, slightly bored and irritated, and occasionally amused, she treads her way through life with casual indifference to those around her. Bell cannot elevate this to tragedy, but his mixture of romance and realism makes this one of the best Silent dramas of them all.

Hardly inferior is **Laugh, Clown,**

as opposed to exploring the byways of sado-masochism.

Chaney's first film for M-G-M had been the amalgamated companies' first success, **He Who Gets Slapped** (1924), based on a popular play, and 'a shadowy drama so beautifully told, so flawlessly directed, that we imagine that it will be held up as a model by all producers' said *The New York Times*. Chaney is supported by John Gilbert and Norma Shearer, and the role is also that of a clown; however, Leonid Andreyev's variation of 'Pagliacci' offered the director, Victor Sjöström, only tentative opportunities for the sort of group portrait – i.e. the circus – which had been so taking in his Swedish films. An earlier film of Sjöström's, made before the amalgamation, has not survived, nor a number of the later ones, but **The Scarlet Letter** (1926) and **The Wind** (1928) are glowing testaments to his happy collaboration with Lillian Gish. The former begins with a sequence Sjöström had made notably his own – going to church on Sunday morning ; the interiors of the cottages and the images of meadow and stream have the calm beauty and authenticity we expect of him – but also of the superlative M–G–M art direction of the period. It is clear that it is not his *Scarlet Letter,* but that of Frances Marion, who did the adaptation, scenario and intertitles. For one thing, the protagonists simply do not have the complexity of those of his Swedish films, but Lillian Gish, as Hester, has a directness about her emotions, and an ability to project thought and feeling through the camera to the audience which is miraculous. It is not an easy role. The most interesting aspect of the affair is the conception of the child: the father is, after all, a priest – and she knew she could not marry him. All we are allowed to see is a discreet kiss, but Gish manages to suggest a decent woman so deeply in love that she gives way to one indiscretion.

Nathaniel Hawthorne's novel had been filmed before – there were two versions in 1917 – but by this time it had become a proscribed book; the Hays Office gave in to Miss Gish's pleas, partly because she was Miss Gish, and partly because she pointed out that it was a classic. She also initiated *The Wind,* a story by Dorothy Scarborough, and she says that Thalberg,

Miss Marion and Sjöström all shared her enthusiasm. She describes it thus: 'Its main character is a wind which constantly blows sand, indoors and out, and finally drives the heroine to madness. It is the story of a gently bred Southern girl who goes to Texas, marries a Texan, is violated by a man she met on the train, murders the man, and goes mad.' With that ending, everyone concerned 'thought it was the best film we had ever done.' But the company shelved it: 'Irving explained that eight of the largest exhibitors in the country had seen it and insisted on a change in the ending . . . The heart went out of all of us, but we did what they wanted. Marion told me that it was the last film to which she gave her heart as well as her head.' The ending is the least of the faults today – all of which have to do with the character of the vile seducer. At first the husband is one-dimensional, but Lars Hanson – so wild-eyed in *The Scarlet Letter* – is soon giving a performance to match the marvellous one by Miss Gish; we begin to feel an understanding between this couple after their disastrous beginning. Sjöström offers the set-pieces which were his speciality – the town dance, the cousin's dinner party – but also reaches his best

Lillian Gish and Lars Hanson in *The Wind* – with William Orlamond, right, glimpsed admiring Miss Gish, the mail-order bride. Sjöström directed, and Miss Gish herself said that she never worked with anyone she liked more – probably because they were very much at one in wanting honesty on the screen, that is, not only truth, but dimension and the wholeness of life.

The success of *Our Dancing Daughters* led to two sequels, of which the first, surprisingly, was Silent – since the most effective moment in the synchronised score and sound effects of *Daughters* was its one line of dialogue, a yelled invocation for Joan Crawford 'ti strut her stuff.' In *Our Modern Maidens* she (centre), Josephine Dunn (left) and Anita Page (right) are resting from the charleston and their manifold marital problems – which, as in the earlier film, are caused by their desire to have as wild a time as possible before the long married twilight.

level with the two most difficult scenes, the wedding night and the killing. This couple, on their wedding night, simply do not know how to react, and we are reminded of the relationship between Ingmar Ingmarsson and Brita. The film is the only one of Sjöström's surviving American work to stand with his native masterpieces, but, said Lewis Jacobs in 1939, his refusal to compromise and his 'propensity for psychology, realism and the rendering of the characters of people close to the soil' mitigated against either influence or popularity. And, he went on, quoting Robert Herring, that though Sjöström's films may not be true, pure cinema 'the cinema there in them is pure, and their own, which is why they breathe a nobility unlike any other films' nobility.' We may suppose that in this respect Sjöström found Miss Gish his ideal interpreter; and since she had taken over from himself as his problem-beset protagonist, we may further suppose that in this gifted woman he found an extension of himself. The film's complete failure

with the public resulted in her leaving M-G-M – and the virtual end of her screen career.

Miss Gish was an old-fashioned heroine; Norma Shearer (b. 1904), then married to Thalberg, was acceptable as both ginghamed heroines and silk-clad sophisticates. Her most notable Silent is probably **The Student Prince** (1927), for which Lubitsch went to M-G-M, nobly orchestrating: the romance between her, the tavern wench, and the prince; the massed choruses of the students, to be accompanied by the pit orchestra; and the scenes of palace protocol. And there was Joan Crawford (1906–77), M-G-M's answer to Clara Bow – after they had starred her as a flapper in **Our Dancing Daughters** (1928), directed by Harry Beaumont. Crawford was to prove remarkably consistent throughout her long career – for here she is already Misunderstood, all glitter and glamour on the surface, but suffering underneath. She is 'wild' or 'dangerous' Diana, and she can't even stop dancing the charleston as she pulls on her panties. The result, said a British trade paper, the *Kinematograph Weekly*, is 'entertainment of the smartly scandalous kind', though, it warned, 'sympathy is impossible for anyone, and the tone will always brand this type of film as a foreign one by its treatment; there is not a lady or a gentleman in the story as understood by British people' – which is doubtless why it was so popular, in Britain as well as the U.S. The freer morality of the young jazz set is both questioned and exploited, albeit always in euphemism: 'Before I met you – and knew what love means – things happened.' The speaker (Dorothy Sebastian) thereafter has a marriage whose happiness will be always clouded in doubt; the girl (Anita Page) who uses her virginity to win the man (John Mack Brown) is finally exposed and falls to a drunken death; and 'decent' Diana eventually triumphs. The plot, withal, is over-familiar, but Crawford's vivacity impresses: suffering, she looks fierce rather than noble, suggesting a better actress than she subsequently became.

Marion Davies (1897–1961) is a rather different case: virtually forgotten even before she quit films, she was remembered during later years, if at all, either as a joke or as the original of the mistress in *Citizen Kane* (q.v.) – a fact indeed which has restored her to fame. That film, and most comment on her relationship with William Randolph Hearst, the millionaire newspaper proprietor, is unsympathetic, but on his side at least this was a case of great devotion. She was merely acquiescent towards his belief that film stardom was the ultimate achievement, but he found an unexpected ally in Mayer. Although no newspaper even hinted at her position as Hearst's mistress – though it was a known fact in the industry – Mayer had noticed that her name appeared with monotonous regularity in each issue of Hearst's twenty-two newspapers, invariably accompanied by superlatives. Hearst was persuaded to move his Cosmopolitan Productions – then releasing through Paramount – to Culver City, to be financed by M-G-M, which would also pay Miss Davies the immense sum of $10,000 per week: in return for which the Hearst press was expected to pay similar

attention to other M-G-M players. To those *au fait* with the situation, regarding Davies as a joke played on a gullible public, Hearst offered fuel when he cast her in films like **Zander the Great** (1925), as a demure, ringleted orphan, if also a playful one. George Hill directed, with a number of Arizona locations, and the plot concerns a Mary Pickford type meeting a William S. Hart type. It is not, however, a scenario-writer's concoction, but a Broadway imitation of such, since it had seen service first in New York. The Hollywood-Broadway borrowings were not all one-way.

The Patsy (1928) had its source in a popular Broadway play of the period, and Davies is delightful in it – as she is in **Show People** (1928), though that is partly because her tendency to mug was in both cases checked by King Vidor. After his films with Gilbert, Vidor made *The Crowd* (q.v.), and perhaps it was because he wanted to make further 'uncommercial' subjects like that that he decided to put his then immense prestige at the service of Hearst, who had Mayer's ear. Certainly between these two comedies and another with Davies he did another risky subject, *Hallelujah!* (q.v.); and he showed no interest in comedy during his long Talkie career. *Happiness*, however, had indicated a flair for comic situations, and those in these two films were clearly promising before he set to

The stage career of Beatrice Lillie was so long and so rewarding that her brief period at M–G–M has been overlooked. She only made one film for the company – but no one who has seen *Exit Smiling* is ever likely to forget it. Samuel Taylor directed this tale of a small–time theatrical troupe in 1926, and Miss Lillie's inimitable clowning has marvellous scope as its meanest member. She gets to don a vamp–outfit, and the way she carries on not only bewilders Harry Myers but is as funny as anything in the whole canon of Silent comedy. Note that Bea is eyeing her ankle-watch.

Donald Crisp in *The Viking* (1928), a box-office failure, despite being one of the very few pictures of the time in Technicolor – and the first in the 'improved' process. Technicolor, the supreme colour system for at least two decades, from the inception of the three-tone process in the early Thirties, was the only one extensively used by Hollywood during the Silent period. It was the invention of a former college professor, Herbert T. Kalmus (1881–1963), who formed the Technicolor Company in 1912. In 1918, he produced his first film, a one-reeler, *The Gulf Between*, to no great acclaim; in 1922 he tried again, with the full-length *The Toll of the Sea*, a Chinese 'Madame Butterfly' with Anna May Wong and Kenneth Harlan, which Metro distributed; the following year deMille filmed the prologue to *The Ten Commandments* in colour, and in 1924 there were two films with Technicolor sequences, *The Uninvited Guest*, made by Metro-Goldwyn, and Sam Goldwyn's *Cytherea*. That year, also, Paramount made a feature completely in the process, *Wanderer of the Wasteland*, with Billie Dove and Jack Holt; in 1925 that company inserted Technicolor sequences into *The King on Main Street* and *Stage Struck*, while Universal used it for part of *The Phantom of the Opera* and M–G–M for sections of *Seven Chances*, *The Big Parade* and *Ben-Hur*.

Douglas Fairbanks made the third wholly-Technicolor film, *The Black Pirate*, but the system, despite the success of that film, was still confined to a handful of single sequences and shorts – for the simple reason that Technicolor reels tended to buckle when projected. Kalmus had developed in 1919 a practicable system, by which a beam-splitting device was fitted into the camera, allowing two negatives to be made – which were then printed on to positive film, coated with gelatin and cemented

together. An advance was made in 1928, whereby the dye images were transferred from a matrix film, with a relief im to the final print. Joseph Schenck felt that Technicolor was finally feasible for the industry and advised Kalmus that if t latter would produce a feature M-G-M would undertake to release it: in the event Thalberg liked the result so much tha persuaded the company to buy it. It proved to be one of his poor commercial decisions, for the public decided that it wa interested in Vikings – at least, not in this manifestation.

The subject had been sensibly chosen, for it disguised the limitations of the Technicolor palette under the two-tone system, being strong on the reds and browns of the Vikings costumes, and not too noticeably inaccurate on the hues of s and sky. The trouble is the story, concerning internecine str and a hellcat princess (Pauline Starke), and the direction, by William Neill, who quite rightly spent most of his subseque career making low-budget films.

Kalmus later blamed the film's failure on the public's preference for Talkies, but it was first shown in November before the rush began. Certainly its failure retarded the exte use of Technicolor, which except for Warners did not begir year later when that company had a big success with *Gold D of Broadway*. Warners had entered into an agreement with Technicolor, having decided that the company which had le way into Talkies should do the same with colour, and had e released *On With the Show* – often cited, so complete was th failure of *The Viking*, as the first Technicolor feature since Fairbanks's film. All the same, industry acceptance remaine guarded, even after the first three-tone Technicolor feature, *Becky Sharp* (q.v.) in 1935.

work – with what is equally clearly great affection. *The Patsy* is domestic comedy with Davies as a Cinderella pushed into the background by her mother (Marie Dressler) in favour of her prettier sister; in *Show People* she plays a Hollywood hopeful who forgets her dreams of drama when given a chance in slapstick – till signed by another studio, when she goes high hat and forgets the top banana (William Haines) who has given her her first chance. This is satire without cynicism, featuring a number of Hollywood personalities of the time, with a number of in-jokes, and in fact based loosely on the career of Gloria Swanson – whom Davies mimics at one point, as in the earlier film she had done devastating impersonations of Gish, Pola Negri and Mae Murray. At such times she justifies her stardom; but if in *Show People* she is warmly matched by Haines as the faithful swain, it must be said that *The Patsy* is taken by Dressler, vinegary as the ghastly snobbish mother.

The girl who became the greatest star of the era – and indeed of all eras – was not only acquired by chance, but they did not know what to do with her: Norma Shearer had turned down the role, and Greta Garbo was cast, since as she was both European and naturally girlish it was considered that she could encompass both aspects of the role, that of a peasant who becomes a famous diva. The film was **Ibañez's Torrent** (1926), the title indicating the studio's respect for the original writer. As it happened a novel by Ibañez was the source of Garbo's second American film, **The Temptress** (1926), which even more strongly indicates why he provided almost perfect Silent-screen material, offering many intrigues that can be illustrated visually, so that audiences were completely involved by the time the explanations came in the intertitles. The first film, directed by Monta Bell, has a plot not unlike those of the Italian 'divismo' movies, its mid-way spectacle – a flood – merely one of those popular at the time; its significance is that it permits its sophisticated, scandalous heroine to become playful again – on being reunited with her childhood sweetheart (Ricardo Cortez) – and there was no doubt which aspect of Garbo M-G-M felt was most commercial. She was rushed into *The Temptress,* with Mauritz Stiller directing, till replaced by Fred Niblo after a few days of shooting. It begins with a masked ball, two lovers in the garden, love – undying love – at first sight, and an idyll at dawn. The she (Garbo) is revealed as married, and he (Antonio Moreno) as an old friend of her husband: repulsion, and then expulsion, when she is further revealed, *à la* Theda Bara, as one who has ruined her husband and driven her host to suicide before his guests. Haughty still, she follows Moreno to South America to distract him from dam-building; two men die of love for her, his rival shoots her husband, and in a storm the dam collapses. He will rebuild: at the gala reopening she returns to claim him as he talks about the woman who inspired him. That, at least, was the American ending; for European audiences she walked the streets of Paris. It is curious now to reflect that M-G-M could only see Garbo as a scarlet woman. She was incredibly beautiful, which meant that she must break hearts; and it was a beauty both sensuous and angelic, hence enigmatic. She could be all things to all men. A limited acting range was at its best with anguish: hence, she must suffer.

During the period of her first contract – the customary seven years, with options in the studio's favour – she was to play virtually the same role, and her first fifteen minutes in **Flesh and the Devil** (1927) are almost a recapitulation of the opening of *The Temptress.* Clarence Brown directed, from a story by Sudermann, one of his tales of adulterous passion in provincial society, and the film is a splendid example of Hollywood apeing the German cinema to recreate Germany. Garbo plays Felicitas, who deceives her husband with a young officer (John Gilbert), eventually wrecking all around her when, married to yet another officer (Lars Hanson), she attempts to get him back. Growing as an actress, she plays the woman as completely self-absorbed except when in love – and the love scenes, with Garbo hungrily kissing Gilbert, were considered sensational at the time. That is why they became lovers again in *Love* (1927) directed by Edmund Goulding (1891–1959), which is 'Anna Karenina' modernised and reduced to 'Love Conquers All' – but on that level intelligently

If Garbo herself remains endlessly fascinating, so does the image that M-G-M created of her – usually making this slip of a girl into the most passionate of courtesans. RIGHT, she is adulterous with John Gilbert in *Love*, and, FAR RIGHT, unmarried for once, she still flouts society by running away with Nils Asther in *The Single Standard*, because she wants 'life to be honest – and exciting.' Audiences interpreted that, as they were meant to, as meaning that she wanted sexual freedom.

set up to satisfy audiences whose main object was to see Garbo loving Gilbert. As he, Vronsky, attempts to compromise her, her lack of anger suggests temptation; dancing together, their animation attracts attention. Her husband (Brandon Hurst) asks her to be mindful of her reputation, and as she looks at him she is comparing him unfavourably with Vronsky. The matching is inevitable with Gilbert's smouldering looks and flashing grins alternating: no member of the audience could blame her for preferring him. She refuses to see him till the races – and when he falls, she flails her arms in anguish, as if trying to swim to him through the crowds, or to duplicate his pain. It is at such highly-charged moments that Garbo's instinctive ability shines; throughout her performances

there are such gestures – which other actresses dared not attempt and no director taught her. Half the time she was using herself, using what she knew to be effective on the screen, 'inventing' herself; for the rest, her directors simply let the cameras catch the simplicity and spontaneity of her personality – that unforced and yet often huge response to any situation, frequently tactile. She needs less intertitles than any other Silent player. In this film, Vronsky does not tire of Anna, but she has resolved to leave him for the honour of the regiment. As he prepares to leave her, summoned by the Grand Duke, they are both emotional: 'Even death cannot part us,' he tells her, and her suicidal intention is startlingly clear. She can suggest fatalism better than any other tragedian. Their parting, as she wipes away

tears, is without intertitles – an exquisite, indescribably subtle piece of acting. All, perhaps, in vain: a tacked-on ending for the American version has Anna, a recent widow, discovering that her son's riding-master is none other than Count Vronsky.

The Divine Woman is among the missing films, which is sad, for it was the only time during the Silent period that she worked with an indisputably great director, Sjöström. The plot reads no better than that of **The Mysterious Lady** (1928), in which she is Tanya, a Russian spy, but this is directed by Niblo with not only fine regard for matters military but the language of the Silent screen. Indeed, the events do not seem too egregious after a superb opening in which she, encountered at the opera, invites into her apartment a young officer (Conrad Nagel): her magic never dims, but this is one of the sequences which allow it full rein, so overwhelming audiences that it follows them from the cinema. Since she was the screen's supreme exponent of eroticism, perhaps we should not complain that she did not take on the great parts, or the varied parts she asked in vain to play. What she does with these *soignée* but suffering *femme fatales* has to be experienced, since she gives mood, emotion and vitality where surely none existed in the script. Because of her **A Woman of Affairs** (1929), then considered unworthy, is an exceptional entertainment. The source was Michael Arlen's 'The Green Hat', as play and novel so notorious that M-G-M tried to conceal the fact; and the original cause of the heroine's shame – syphilis – has become embezzlement. The idea is attractive, concerning a woman who prefers dishonour to shaming her dead husband, and Garbo is moving. Looking correctly English county, in cardigans and tweeds, she had become not only intuitive but clever, as in the scene where she is reunited with her true love, Gilbert. Clarence Brown directed, and Sidney Franklin did an equally impeccable job on **Wild Orchids** (1929), one of the will-they, won't-they seduction stories of the time. Garbo, because she dominated her leading men, was seldom as girlish, partly due to the costumes designed for her on this occasion by Adrian, partly to the effective

performance of Lewis Stone as her elderly husband. Also, she does not react to the attentions of her would-be lover, a Javanese prince (Nils Asther), as the worldly woman of her other films, but what she does do with the flimsy sexual psychology makes it seem real and even startling.

The elderly 'protector' (or husband)–young aspirant formula was temporarily abandoned for **The Single Standard** (1929), though the title indicated that Garbo would, as usual, challenge the rules governing society. Like Norma Shearer in *A Free Soul* (q.v.) her idea of excitement is driving at 70 mph; other women cannot see what men find in her. This film, in its way, offers something more than her, and something more than a feeling for its time: there was a general mood of restlessness – Noël Coward wrote 'World Weary' in 1928 – and the film embellishes it. The lights of ships in the harbour, the sun-baked Southern shore; the urge to travel, to get away. Moments of tranquillity and moments of speed; the urge to escape. There is an urgency in this film consciously put there by the director, John S. Robertson, and by Josephine Lovett, who adapted the novel by Adela St John Rogers.

Long after other stars spoke, Garbo remained mute: M-G-M were afraid that Sound might destroy their most precious asset, as it had done other accented actresses. As late as November 1929 appeared her last Silent, **The Kiss** – in which she played a murderess and an adulteress. 'The kiss' was bestowed on her by an amorous schoolboy (Lew Ayres), and how could she, the Garbo, amused and flattered, refuse him so small a moment of happiness? Her husband, elderly once again, arrives suddenly, and in consequence she finds herself in court, defended by her lover (Conrad Nagel).

The director was Jacques Feyder, to whom she felt sympathetic because he was European, but she also liked Brown, and was to work with him again. Perhaps all of them helped her towards making these films seem more adult than they basically are, but it is also a matter of her vibrancy, grace and talent.

The end of the Silent film coincided with that of one of the major studios, First National, which had been founded in

1917 by a conglomerate of exhibitors in resistance to the policy of block-booking – objections to which were so widespread that there were no fewer than twenty-seven representatives of the circuits on its board. It was originally a distribution organisation, inviting independent producers to co-operate; Triangle was the first important company to join, and Paramount, alarmed at the growing strength of First National, began to buy its own theatres. First National countered by buying and running its own studios, but the real struggle was for the control of distribution, which could govern both production and exhibition – without the responsibility to either. Eventually most of the other production companies owned their own cinemas, and as the three branches of the industry aligned, block-booking was again forced on both the circuits and the few exhibitors who remained independent.

One of the purposes behind the formation of United Artists had been to control distribution – as it was for Ince and his Associated Producers, whose merger with First National brought to that company a store of talent, though significantly the general manager now appointed was Richard Rowland, who had had considerable experience of distribution. He had been one of the founders of Metro Pictures, and by claiming 'personally' to have produced *The Four Horsemen of the Apocalypse* was deemed able to run a studio; he was not however, able to hang on to much of the talent. Already, Chaplin and Pickford had passed through; a lesser coup was the acquisition of Charles Ray (1891–1943), defecting from Triangle, where he had established his perpetual role of country boy – the male equivalent of all the heroines in gingham. The most popular of his films was **The Old Swimmin' Hole** (1921), directed by Joseph de Grasse among sunny streams and meadows, and detailing the misadventures of Ray, the coquettish, beribboned Myrtle (Laura La Plante) and the pig-tailed girl (Marie Prevost) who worships him. The one flaw in its almost total charm is Ray, who acts delicately, but could not hide his years. Audiences soon tired of him; in 1922 he began to move from company to company, and in the Talkie era he worked

mainly as an extra.

One reason for his decline may be the comparisons made with other rustic heroes – like Lloyd Hughes, under contract to Ince and remaining with First National after Ince's death. He plays a Cajun in **Scars of Jealousy** (1923), one of the vastly complicated rural melodramas reinstituted after the success of *Way Down East*, and produced by Ince himself in an attempt to recover his fallen stock. Its director was Lambert Hillyer, who really fails to get much sense into it. Easily the best of such films is **Tol'able David** (1921) and the best of the barefoot boys was Richard Barthelmess (1895–1963), despite his 'city' face. He had left Griffith at the instigation of a businessman, Charles H. Duell, to form in partnership Inspiration Pictures, under the aegis of First National – and for their first film they were indeed inspired to choose Henry King (b. 1892), recently come to prominence after a decade as actor and director. Joseph Hergesheimer's then famous novel was a variation of David and Goliath, the 'Goliath' being the escaped convicts who have billeted themselves on David's sweetheart and her grandfather; family honour depends on young David, and one cares enormously what happens to him. Ernest Torrence is such a villain as to make Gustav von Seyffertitz seem like Prince Charming, bringing a look of congenital idiocy to a fearsome mug; and the film is a compendium of exquisitely-wrought moments, as when David's sweetheart pulls down her hat to hide her tears, or he surveys his home as conveyed in the intertitle, 'A wave of love swept over David – a love for everything and everybody that made his home.' King also directed Barthelmess in *Sonny* and *Fury*, both of comparable quality; and when Inspiration collapsed – due to Duell's chicanery – Barthelmess remained with First National, the company's leading male star for the rest of the decade.

Its chief lady star was Colleen Moore (b. 1900), at her worst and best respectively in **Irene** and **Ella Cinders**, both directed in 1926 by Alfred E. Green. The former had been the longest-running Broadway musical in 1919, and that, plus the seventeen road companies, could have been its only recommendation: without

Irene, with Colleen Moore and George K. Arthur. You might call Mr Arthur a prehistoric Franklin Pangborne, but Mr Pangborne was around at the time; you would certainly call Miss Moore a deft comedienne, but like all her breed she had an obligatory scene where she's left alone and whiles away the time by miming the sort of heroine she isn't, i.e. a vamp. At such times it is clear why audiences turned with relief to Garbo!

the music the story is thin, making us wonder today why audiences never tired of romances between rich boy and poor girl. Miss Moore's unstoppable cuteness mitigates against any enjoyment, but George K. Arthur is funny as a couturier, all bright eyes and quick movements – with a fashion-show in Technicolor. The star, however, gives a delicately-shaded performance in *Ella Cinders*, and Mr Hughes, flat-footed in *Irene*, is fine in the combination role of Buttons-godmother-Prince. Its motivation is not an invitation but a movie-talent contest, and Cinders ends not in a palace but on the spacious lawns of Hollywood – the appropriate end to a modern fairy-story: indeed, the film is deftly funny both about the small town thralldom to movies and movieland itself.

Playing himself in a guest role is Harry Langdon (1844–1944), First National's first clown. Vaudeville-trained, he made a number of shorts and one feature for Sennett, from whom he brought Harry Edwards and Frank Capra (q.v.). Edwards directed, and Capra helped to write, **Tramp, Tramp, Tramp** (1926), a quite funny film about a cross-country race. Capra had been appalled when he learnt that Sennett intended to make Langdon a star: 'Only God could help this creature'

he decided – and that became the basis for Langdon's screen character, whey-faced, titchy, gracefully birdlike, a child who hasn't discovered the rudiments of coping with the world; at one point he's discovered throwing rocks at a cyclone in an effort to persuade it to go away. He shows courage, rescuing the heroine from a wavering house, but not for him the flights of invention of Lloyd or Keaton. His best film is **The Strong Man** 1926). due less to him than to Capra's manipulation of the audience and his direction of an inventive screenplay by Arthur Ripley. Langdon is a Belgian ex-soldier looking for his pen-pal, Mary Brown. When in New York a thief, Broadway Lily (Gertrude Astor), drops some money into his pocket she has to take him to her apartment to retrieve it, and a succession of exceptionally detailed gags has him eventually fighting for his honour and she for the coat. He finally finds Mary, and we are not told whether he knows that she is blind – which leads to a shot of the blind leading the blind, when *he* falls over the stone in their path. By the time shooting started on **Long Pants** (1927), Capra loathed him, which is perhaps why he made him both a creature of lust and homicidal, which with his hopeless idiocy and no hint of character is an appalling combination. He is neither funny nor pathetic – and pathos was now what Langdon wanted to do. The acclaim for these three films convinced him that he was a genius, and he dispensed with Capra and Edwards on *Three's a Crowd* (1928) and the two that followed, after which First National annulled the contract. Hal Roach took him on for two-reelers, and he worked occasionally during the Talkie period.

First National's most famous film remains **The Lost World** (1925), directed by Harry O. Hoyt and the brainchild of Willis O'Brien, who had already featured models of prehistoric animals in a couple of movies. Unhappily these models are now derisory, as are most of the special effects – though the climax, a dinosaur at loose in London, has its moments; the situation would be reprised in *King Kong* (q.v.) on which O'Brien also worked. Wallace Beery is excellent as the Professor in what is not, withal, a typical First National product.

The company's pictures were stylish and well-crafted, but in general too slight to have great success. Typical are **Heart to Heart** (1928), directed by William Beaudine and ringing some pleasant changes in its theme of a princess (Mary Astor) in a small American town; and **Yellow Lily** (1928), a romance between a cold but lecherous archduke (Clive Brook) and the village doctor's noble sister (Billie Dove). The director was Alexander Korda, working from a story by Lajos Biro which would certainly have appealed to both Lubitsch and Von Stroheim, respectively the most successful and notorious of Hollywood's European directors – as Korda was surely aware. He had had one success with the company, **The Private Life of Helen of Troy** (1927), based on a novel of that title by John Erskine, and Robert Sherwood's play 'The Road to Rome' – though its real source is surely Offenbach's 'La Belle Hélène'; however, the treatment of ancient people in modern idiom needs spoken dialogue, and First National was not, in any case, as economic as other studios in its use of intertitles, which could be a reason its films found disfavour.

For eight years the other companies had nibbled away at its theatres; at its inception, Zukor had bought stock in the hope of killing it from within. In 1928, Warner Bros., riding high with Sound, negotiated a bank loan which enabled it to buy a controlling interest, and in 1929 the remaining circuit owner, Fox West Coast Theatres, sold Warners its own shares for $10 million. For ten years Warners produced pictures under the First National banner (literally: a flag was its logo) but they were Warner pictures in all but name.

Ironically, First National had released the first attempt at film production by the Warner Bros., *My Four Years in Germany* (1918), based on a bestseller by a former U.S. ambassador to the Kaiser. The Warners were the sons of an immigrant Polish-Jewish cobbler, and, starting with nickelodeons, were established with their film-exchanges before the battles with the Trust. The four brothers who entered the film business edged into distribution and then production, often writing and acting themselves. After the profitable *Four*

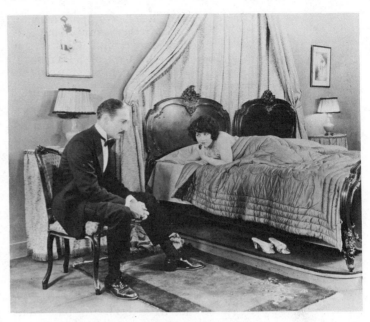

Years in Germany, they restricted themselves to serials till 1922, when they began to produce on a regular basis. Jack L. Warner (1892–1978) was in charge of the West Coast studio, and within two years he had been joined by the two men who would eventually be most responsible for that special quality of Warner Bros. movies, Hal B. Wallis (b. 1899), originally in the publicity department, and his predecessor as production chief, Darryl F. Zanuck (1902–79), a former salesman and writer who in 1924 was engaged to write the films of the studio's first star, a dog called Rin-Tin-Tin.

But if it was 'Rinty', as the dog was fondly called, which put Warners on the map, it was Ernst Lubitsch who first gave the company prestige, when it astutely offered him a contract after his experience with Mary Pickford; and since he·was far more famous than the Warners he was able to forgo the historical spectacles which had brought him U.S. renown, to return to the marital comedies he had so enjoyed making in Germany. He had not made a comedy since *Die Bergkatze*, and he had not then seen deMille's *Forbidden Fruit*, with a sequence he always claimed influential, in which a social climber hesitates as to which fork to pick up: his own refined visual skill is apparent in the opening sequence of **The Marriage**

Adolphe Menjou and Marie Prevost as husband and wife in Lubitsch's first American success, *The Marriage Circle* – at least, the critics liked it, and though the public stayed away that didn't prevent it from being much imitated – by Lubitsch himself, among others.

Circle (1924), when Adolphe Menjou finds his sock-drawer empty but his wife's stocking-drawer full. Clearly this is a Lubitsch summary of a marriage, its source a play remembered from his Berlin days.

The film's reception caused other studios to pour forth imitations, and Lubitsch imitated himself: **Three Women** (1924); *Kiss Me Again* (1925), now lost; **Lady Windermere's Fan** (1925); and **So This is Paris?** (1926). They are much of a muchness, whether set in Paris, Vienna, London or New York; they reflect the interplay between the sophisticates of the *beau monde* (Menjou, Irene Rich, Pauline Frederick, Monte Blue, Florence Vidor, Lew Cody) and the more playful younger generation (Marie Prevost, Mae McAvoy), all of them both mendacious and flirtatious – and if any of them had told the truth at the beginning, there would have been no plot. The scenarios were usually based on well-known European plays, and most of them are the work, partly or wholly, of Hans Kräly, Lubitsch's old collaborator. In the Talkie era, Ernest Vajda and Samson Raphaelson would replace him, but by that time he had helped formulate the famous 'touch'. Here is another example: the night one lover defects, Catherine the Great is consoled by another, and as was customary, he is promoted; later he has a chance to plead for the other man's life, 'Spare this boy! Thanks to him' – cut to Catherine anticipating the next words – 'I became a general'; and as that was not what she expected to hear, she signs the warrant. The sexual innuendo is what Lubitsch used so brilliantly in his Talkies, but which is largely absent in his Silents – and indeed this instance is not from his Catherine film at Paramount but *The Eagle* (q.v.), which Kräly wrote for United Artists. In fact, the American Silent comedies of Lubitsch lack the sparkle of both the earlier and later ones. The critics raved, the public was indifferent, and both reactions stemmed from the source material: the critics were favourably disposed towards the sort of respectable risqué plays which Lubitsch used, and the public disliked lengthy explanatory intertitles and talking heads. The visual points in *Lady Windermere's Fan*

have mainly to do with society's curiosity about Mrs Erlynne; Lubitsch wisely eschews the epigrams in the intertitles for a light, bantering tone; but he still has to tell a rather soppy story of a mother's sacrifice. In *Three Women* he tantalises us by omitting the intertitles in what is clearly an important conversation: but he still has a lot of plot – as much as deMille in his similar comedies of a few years earlier.

A European director who fared less well in Hollywood is Benjamin Christensen, brought over on the strength of *Häxan*, when the mood was for the weird and Lon Chaney was beginning to hold sway. After three films in that vein for M-G-M, none very successful, he turned up at Warners-First National for one last one before returning to Denmark, **Seven Footprints to Satan** (1929), a banal creepy-house tale which runs out of steam after the tenth or so trick. However, Michael Curtiz (1888–1962) remained to become Warners' most prolific director during their great period. Hungarian-born, he had been a colleague of Korda's at Sascha-Film in Vienna, making his name with two ancient-and-modern tales after the manner of Korda's *Samson und Delilah* – *Sodom und Gomorrha* and *Die Slavenkönigin*. Warners brought him to the States for another, though he directed several other films for them before it was ready – **Noah's Ark** (1929), from a story by Zanuck; either inspiration or money ran out, since it ends abruptly with the information that both ancient and modern goodies lived happily ever after. The modern part is set during the War, and concerns an Austrian dancer (Dolores Costello), a Russian agent who wants to rape her, and two American youths who befriend her; and if nothing much happens in the other part, the relevant disaster is eminently watchable – and a tribute to the co-operation of the Los Angeles water-board. Miss Costello is also in peril in **Old San Francisco** (1928), as a senorita fancied by a Barbary Coast boss (Warner Oland) who has betrayed his Chinese blood by affecting Christianity. Alan Crosland directed this anthology of San Francisco mythology, including its Spanish past and the earthquake, whose first tremors are felt just as things are blackest for hero and heroine. It had a synchronised score and sound effects – and, indeed, *Noah's Ark* was also available in a part-Talkie version: for during this period Warners had completely changed the dimension of film.

On the subject of spectacle, deMille was by now the acknowledged suzerain, and in **King of Kings** (1927) he gave the dying Pathé a last whopping success – and, indeed, it was still touring the church-hall circuit till comparatively recently. It was then important enough to open in London at the Royal Opera House and for *The Times* to give it a leader, but the mooted 'controversy' was mainly in the minds of the publicists. The religious advisers to deMille were on one occasion closeted with some new footage from the Holy Land (not that any is discernible in the film) when the actor playing Christ, H. B. Warner, was found *in flagrante delicto* with a young lady whose object was blackmail. This episode, though hushed-up, seems to me symptomatic of the whole hypocritical enterprise: 'This is the story of Jesus of Nazareth' says an introduction, whisking us to a Roman banquet modelled on one of the more worldly paintings of Alma-Tadema. Mary of Magdala, as she is called here, has become the mistress of Judas Iscariot, who has become ambitious – joining Jesus because he thought he would be king 'and reward him with money and high office'. Thus the most enigmatic figure in history has become just another Hollywood villain, but what astonishes is that, with its phoney provenance for quotations, the film should have received the endorsement of the clergy.

Its success justified deMille's departure from Paramount, after complaining of front office interference. From Ince's widow he bought the Producers Distributing Company, which amalgamated with Pathé in an attempt to keep both afloat; as the Sound revolution rocked the industry, and Pathé was absorbed in turn, he accepted an offer (q.v.) from M-G-M – but found that he disliked Mayer even more than Zukor, and returned to Paramount with a guarantee of autonomy. However, at P.D.C. and Pathé he did sponsor a number of other directors, including Donald Crisp,

Paul Sloane and William K. Howard. Crisp's **Dress Parade** (1927) is a genial comedy about the cocky newcomer (William Boyd) who learns to love West Point traditions; and Sloane's **The Blue Danube** (1928) is a Von Stroheim-like tale, with some sharp touches, about a baron (Nils Asther) whose passion for an innkeeper's daughter (Leatrice Joy) does not run smoothly. Howard's **White Gold** (1927) – the title refers to sheep – was another familiar story, about the woman (Jetta Goudal) marooned in a man's world: threatened with the inevitable seduction or rape, the extent of her complicity is withheld by the intertitles – which caused the piece to be critically acclaimed, though it flopped so badly that for years no print was thought to survive. The one that did proves it lacking the intensity of the Soviet *By the Law* and the honesty of the even more similar *City Girl* (q.v.). Pathé at this time gave refuge to another Paramount alumnus, James Cruze, whose **On to Reno** (1928) is an engaging marital farce with Marie Prevost and Cullen Landis as young marrieds whose hopes for a reunion are more cheerful than those of an older couple, Ned Sparkes and Ethel Wales.

Under Joseph Schenck, United Artists also provided a haven for other players anxious, like its founders, to escape the tyrannies of the big studio moguls. In 1925 he was joined by Sam Goldwyn, who had been releasing through First National since his break with the Goldwyn Co., and the three to four annual Goldwyn productions were to be extremely important to the distribution arm. Both Schenck and Goldwyn were ardent believers in stars, though the stars under contract to them did not have the freedom of Pickford and Fairbanks. Films were made committee-style, so although **Stella Dallas** (1925), directed by Henry King for Goldwyn, displays the director's usual sympathy and lucidity, its dual purpose was to exploit the personality of its star, Belle Bennett, and the narrative qualities of Olive Higgins Prouty's original bestselling story. As such, it was marvellously successful: advertised as 'The Greatest Mother-Love Picture Ever Made' it was indeed loved more than other mother-love movies, as Miss

Marceline Day and John Barrymore in *The Beloved Rogue* – who was François Villon. Of all the screen Villons, there was not one less attractive: forty–four at the time, equipped with ill–fitting wig and two whiffs of up–pointed moustache, Barrymore really appals, but atones somewhat with his agility, especially in a Rumpelstiltskin–like dance.

Bennett, acting superbly, snaps up a man (Ronald Colman) from a higher social sphere and is too foolish to change – slatternly at home, over-dressed in public but always good-hearted. **The Winning of Barbara Worth** (1926) bases its appeal on Goldwyn's 'love team', Colman and Vilma Banky, and Harold Bell Wright's 'famous' novel – according to the credits – for which Goldwyn paid the record sum of $123,000. It was also Goldwyn's bid in *The Covered Wagon* stakes, beginning with a desert sandstorm and concluding with a flood; but King's direction cannot disguise the clumsiness of the screenplay by Frances Marion, who, nevertheless, was on the way to becoming the industry's highest-paid scenario writer. In the original novel the lady of the title, played by Miss Banky in the film, does not appear till the end: here she is sought throughout by Colman, as an engineer out West, and Gary Cooper, the local man – till the latter is summarily dropped. Ronald Colman (1891–1958), English-born, and Cooper (1901–61), of English parentage, became two of the most enduring of stars.

If the appeal of both remains strong, that of Valentino again proves elusive in the two films he made for Schenck before his sudden death. However, **The Eagle** (1925) is probably his best film, as directed by Clarence Brown, taking his tone from Kräly's buoyant scenario, based on a story by Pushkin, about a Queen's guardsman who is loved by her (Louise Dresser) but prefers to help his beloved (Vilma Banky) by adopting a Zorro-like existence. **Son of the Sheik** (1926), directed by George Fitzmaurice, is as much like its predecessor as to be indecent, reminding us that nothing emphasises the gulf in taste between then and now than Valentino's two sheik films.

The constant reiteration of themes, scenes and situations is apparent in the three films John Barrymore made for Schenck. He played François Villon in **The Beloved Rogue** (1927), already filmed in this romanticised fashion in 1920 as *If I Were King,* with the addition now of the 'Court of Miracles' sequences as copied from *The Hunchback of Notre Dame.* Alan Crosland directed, and Conrad Veidt's gleeful, satanic Louis XI outclasses Barrymore's athletic hero. In view of the latter's reputation, it is perhaps a pity that he only once played a weighty role in films before drink impaired his capabilities: that was Captain Ahab, but of the rakes and roués whom he did play, his Beau Brummel, also for Warners, is splendid in his moments of pride. He is certainly well cast in **The Tempest** (1928), as a peasant-born dragoon who rises from the ranks, responds to the princess's whipping with a kiss, and goes to sleep drunk on her bed. One of his colleagues likes to stub out cigarettes on the necks of rankers, and another likes girlie magazines – in which touches we note the hand of Von Stroheim, who wrote it, but was contractually prevented from playing the lead and directing. The film is credited to Sam Taylor who, working again with photographer Charles Rosher, has made a film as technically good as *My Best Girl,* with superb art direction by William Cameron Menzies. If Schenck vacillated over the leading lady before settling on his own close friend, newly arrived from Germany, Camilla Horn, so he did on the director, and several eminent names are reputed to have worked on it. Lubitsch had been approached, and he did direct Barrymore and Miss Horn in another portrait of old Europe, **Eternal Love** (1929), in which they are Swiss patriots and lovers during the Napoleonic Wars. Kräly wrote it, his last film for Lubitsch, and there are echoes of their two Bavarian comedies; but in returning to a serious subject Lubitsch has emulated Sjöström. He uses snow as Sjöström used sand in *The Wind*; the affectionate interiors recall the latter's Swedish work, and the portrait of the prejudiced community is similar to that of *The Scarlet Letter*. Its climax apart, it is to be regretted that it got 'lost' in the rush to Talkies.

Gloria Swanson's most successful film with United Artists was **Sadie Thompson** (1928), based on Somerset Maugham's short story, 'Rain'. Although a dramatised version had been a wild success the world over, the Hays Office refused to sanction a movie till confronted with the determination of Swanson, and probably also that of her backer and lover, Joseph P. Kennedy. Sadie, the whore, still seduces the preacher, but so much else has been bowdlerised as to make it a distinctly foolish piece of fiction. Attention has shifted from the preacher, less hypocritical than smug, to Sadie, and though she has become a cipher, Swanson inevitably attempts to fill in the gaps – laughing with the marines, listening eagerly to the phonograph, or cheeking the preacher and his prim wife. She is immeasurably aided by Raoul Walsh's fluid direction, and William Cameron Menzies' art direction is again one of his best, a dark and storm-swept Pago Pago. The film is one more witness to the accomplishment of the American Silent screen as it was about to die.

Though critics lamented, audiences couldn't have cared less about its death. *Eternal Love* was not the only film lost in the crush, and there were others – among which were some which might have changed the course of American movie entertainment. The moguls demanded exoticism and melodrama, but Frank Borzage was one director esteemed enough to withstand demands, and his preference for dramas of plain people led eventually to **Seventh Heaven** (1927), and a follow-up also with Janet Gaynor

and Charles Farrell, **Street Angel** (1928). The first film is part *Broken Blossoms,* part *The Big Parade,* with a chunk of 'La Bohème' and the ending of 'Jane Eyre'. As usual, the girl is a *poule* – if only by wicked chance – and the boy a sewer-rat who leads her to true love, which means grinding his coffee or snuggling under the quilt: what *Picturegoer* called 'their unspoken need for each other and their unquenchable spirit' was something that appealed mightily to cinemagoers, as well as to the industry's Academy, which voted Oscars to Gaynor, Borzage and Benjamin Glazer for his scenario, based on a play by Ernest G. Palmer. *Street Angel* is based on a play by Monckton Hoffe, and though its borrowings are less eclectic, its subject is that old favourite, the Price Paid for a Moment of Sin. Equally sentimental, there is a new element to the Great Love – sexual obsession, and its presence is as traceable to German influences as are the settings. Equally stylised in both films, the Paris of *Seventh Heaven* is merely cardboard,

Gloria Swanson and Raoul Walsh, who also directed, in a version of Maugham's short story, 'Rain', rechristened *Sadie Thompson*, since the Hays Office refused to sanction the original title – which didn't matter, since everyone knew who Sadie was. The Rev. Davidson was no longer allowed to be a man of the cloth, and in all printed sources has been renamed Oliver Miller (but in the only extant copy – at Eastman House, with the last reel missing – he is Davidson in the intertitles, suggesting that it was never publicly screened).

while the Naples of *Street Angel* is the city of any of the German *street* films.

Both are far from realism, but that *Street Angel* is a mite rawer and tougher is due to Murnau's **Sunrise**, made at the same studio in the interim. Murnau had arrived in the U.S. with a copy of *Der Letzte Mann*, but the Hollywood companies had ignored him till that and then *Tartüff* were praised by reviewers; Fox then wanted him so badly that it accepted both the scenario – by Carl Mayer, from a story by Sudermann – and the set designs for a film he was about to start shooting. Consequently *Sunrise* was Germanic, causing Fox to add a foreword to the effect that the tale could take place anywhere and *The New York Times* to observe that Murnau could 'do just as fine work in Hollywood as he ever did in Germany.' Murnau's ability with narrative in images was at a new height, if marred by artiness – just as the tale becomes too melodramatic when 'The Man' (George O'Brien) becomes so sexually enslaved on a trip to the big city that he attempts to murder his wife (Janet Gaynor).

That city adventure brought a new vitality to American cinema, and the film's success encouraged two other studios to sanction tales of ordinary folks without star names. At Universal Paul Fejos directed **Lonesome** (1928) and at M-G-M King Vidor **The Crowd** (1928), both showing the German influence in such matters as montage and mobility of camera; both are about New Yorkers and include long Coney Island sequences. *Lonesome* is simplicity itself: a lonely factory-worker (Glenn Tryon) meets a telephone operator (Barbara Kent), loses her and meets her again. Vidor's film is more ambitious, taking its hero (James Murray) from birth onwards, his life is motivated by a conversation on the Staten Island Ferry, 'You gotta beat that crowd,' to which he replies, 'Maybe. All I want is the opportunity.' He loses a job, a child, and suffers a deteriorating marriage – matters not to be seen again in American movies till 1939 in *Made for Each Other* (q.v.) and then in 1952 in *The Marrying Kind* (q.v.), both influenced by Vidor's film. Audiences for it were enthusiastic, and its above-average cost, $551,000, made a small profit, but neither Vidor nor

Fejos was on principle encouraged to undertake another immediate 'personal' film.

At Fox, however, both Borzage and Murnau were allowed to try again; unlike Fejos and Vidor, but like Sjöström and von Sternberg at this time, they were after an amalgam of reality and romance, of the everyday and the erotic, but once again the people are supposed to be us – the audience. Borzage's **The River** (1928) and Murnau's **City Girl** have pulsing, realistic accounts of the daily grind, and work and sex go hand in hand, man's prime motivations. All other national cinemas followed this rule, even the British and the unknown Japanese: it was only in Hollywood that pretty little stories existed in a vacuum. In this group of films there are degrees of frustration and deprivation, and in these particular two the frustration is partly sexual. The girl in both is the strong-willed Mary Duncan, and the boy Charles Farrell; in *The River* she is a flirt, possibly a whore, who fritters away her time with a besotted country boy while her man is away for the winter; in *City Girl*, he brings home a Chicago waitress, to face the hostility of his family. From the fragments of *The River* that remain (almost an hour), Borzage clearly intended a documentary account of dam-labourers, and Murnau as surely intended something similar in his account of the lonely farm in the wheatfields. With one reel dubbed with Sound, *City Girl* was belatedly released, in 1931, to perish instantly in the All-Talking world. *The River* simply disappeared, though its banning by several states may be one reason why there is also virtually no written record of it. Borzage was permitted by Fox to do another realistic drama in the Sound period, *Bad Girl* (q.v.), since he still trailed the glory from *Seventh Heaven*; but Murnau quarrelled with Fox before *City Girl* was finished and departed with Robert Flaherty for the South Seas.

Flaherty's own quest for realism belonged to the same side of the coin. Since *Nanook* the studios had courted him, and Jesse Lasky told him that he would back him to the hilt if he could make another film equally interesting. Flaherty chose to go to Polynesia, as a nice place to take his family, and he spent three years

Scenes of Daily Life: Barbara Kent, looking at the camera, in *Lonesome*, ABOVE, and Mary Duncan and Charles Farrell on their way from Chicago to country in *City Girl*. Both these films were part of a movement away from nightclubs, newspaper offices and marble halls towards the actual environment of the ordinary joes in the audience. It was a feeling shared by directors in other countries around this time, but even when tarted up with a little sex the films found audiences sparse.

making **Moana** (1926). Since the Samoan people were contented with Western ways, and were ruled over by a New Zealand-appointed German governor, Flaherty had to recreate the idyllic past, though the film is supposedly set in the present. The subject is the coming of age of Moana, played by Ta'avale, who required a huge sum to submit to the tattooing of the initiation ceremony – a practice long obsolete on the island. It is ironic therefore that the word 'documentary' (from the French *documentaire*) was coined by John Grierson (q.v.) to describe this film, which is otherwise only important because Flaherty used Kodak's new panchromatic stock, resulting in glowing blacks and whites.

Despite a publicity campaign directed at the most prominent citizens of each town where the film was booked, it flopped, unhelped clearly by the naked breasts on view. Nevertheless Thalberg decided that M-G-M could market a similar film, though he insisted on Flaherty accepting W. S. Van Dyke (1889–1943) as co-director, to prevent the squandering of time and money, and to ensure a more commercial product; in 1931 Murnau interested Flaherty in an independent production to be made in the South Pacific, to be released by Paramount. Flaherty quarrelled with both Van Dyke and Murnau, and departed, thus receiving no credit on Van Dyke's **White Shadows of the South Seas**, and only a writing credit on Murnau's **Tabu** – which does not make either, as has been suggested, inferior to *Moana*. *White Shadows* has white traders, and an unconvincing story; and Murnau's native lovers are much to be preferred. The three films remain very beautiful and their approach is more paternal than patronising, but though one cannot doubt the sincerity of purpose, there is something

anomalous about high-priced talents making films about the 'simple' life; at all events none of the three is very riveting. *White Shadows* in particular was successful enough to cause M-G-M to send Van Dyke to Africa for the fictional *Trader Horn* (q.v.), and then to North Alaska for **Eskimo** (1933), a considerable film in its own right and a huge advance on *Nanook*. John Lee Mahin wrote this tale of a huntsman and the wife who is raped by a drunken white crew, and the Eskimo's dialogue has been turned into intertitles, but since the language has no first or third personal pronouns these become 'One' – and 'One leaves his wives in the same kramit' must be the most obscure intertitle in film history. There are difficulties with ethnological films, not the least of which is doubt of audience response – which in this case was minimal, thus causing Hollywood to turn to the things it better understood.

Murnau died in a car crash before they premier of *Tabu*, which had only a music-track and therefore went as unnoticed by mass audiences as *City Girl*. The public, after all, wanted excitement, and except for a coterie their needs were backed not only by the moguls but most journalists of the period, claiming that people did not go to the cinema to see themselves or their neighbours and workmates. This brief flirtation with realism does leave a partial record of the life of the average American in pre-Depression days, but it is otherwise a footnote to the era of wonderful nonsense. To an extent both realism and the ethnological films continued the cinema's experimentation – both as to what the medium could do, and what the public would pay to see. By the time the furore of Talkies was over the studio factories were confident of the answers, and for the next thirty years provided only entertainment.

8

The Twenties:
Britain and France

IT WAS AMERICAN films that cinemagoers preferred the world over. Neither the British nor the French industries recovered from the War, losing the dominant positions they had held in the world market. In Britain the influx of American films was strengthened from an odd source, the antagonism of the wartime government and the military authorities towards the home industry, which curtailed production and resulted in a placatory spate of patriotic dramas – with titles like *Boys of the Bulldog Breed, Boy Scouts be Prepared* and *A Munition Girl's Romance*. The films that were made had difficulty getting shown, for the American companies, now opening distribution offices in London, had foisted the system of block-booking on British cinemas, many of which booked product for a year ahead. In 1921 the industry called a meeting to decide whether to abandon production – during which William Friese-Greene, the pioneer, was found to have died, some minutes after making a plea for its continuance. In the same year the British National Film League was formed, campaigning ineffectually till 1927, when the Cinematograph Act – usually known as the Quota Act – was passed, decreeing that cinemas must show 5% of local product, rising to 20% ten years later. The effect on production was immediate.

Under the prevailing conditions, most of the films, not surprisingly, were of poor quality – since the entrepreneurs were not in cut-throat competition as were their American counterparts. They were mainly dilettantes and theatre showmen, including both managers and actors, though there were sound businessmen behind the most successful companies, which were Stoll, Ideal, G. B. Samuelson, Gaumont, the team of Thomas Welsh and George Pearson – the latter an alumnus of both Samuelson and Gaumont – and Hepworth, the sole pioneer to be still a force in the industry.

Hepworth, however, was forced out of business as he prepared to meet American competition, his last film ironically a remake of his greatest success, **Comin' Thro' the Rye** (1923), a Victorian tale of the sort popular in the lending-libraries – with a tomboyish heroine (Alma Taylor, the only one of the Hepworth stock company to play the same role in both versions), a handsome wealthy hero (Shayle Gardner), and the scheming rival who wants to take one from the other. The plot depends on the convention that a woman once kissed can only appeal to what the intertitles call man's 'worst part'– which becomes so enflamed after a glass of wine and the sight of some lovers embracing that its owner goes a-ravishing. This combination of tears and lust is no more retarded than in other films of the time; Hepworth's decision to remake it was prompted by a forthcoming film festival, but illness delayed production and by the time it was completed he had been declared bankrupt, as a result of trying to enlarge his Walton-on-Thames studio. He directed one more film, as an employee of Arnold Nettlefold, and spent the rest of his life making trailers, i.e. previews of coming attractions. As his stock of films was melted down for chemicals at the time of his bankruptcy, too few survive to make any assessment of his contribution to the medium, but this particular one is

187

technically as good as any of the era. The single most important development in films at this point was the progress from illustrating a dramatic situation to the telling of it in images: few in Britain were aware of this, but Hepworth is one who was.

We may not say the same of the also-prolific Adrian Brunel – to judge from **The Man Without Desire** (1923), considered, he says in his memoir, a masterpiece by the critics – though he himself didn't agree. A dopey piece about a lover (Ivor Novello) who wakes after two hundred years to face the sexual predicament of the title, it was admired because some of it was shot in Venice (unimaginatively) and authentic costumes were borrowed from private collections, which would explain why costumes in British historical films seemed to be falling apart with age. Although there were contemporary subjects, usually concerned with love or crime, the preponderance of costume romances indicates a dependence on novels and the West End stage rather than an attempt to emulate the German spectacles. In 1923 alone, the studios offered Novello as Bonnie Prince Charlie, Fay Compton as Mary Stuart, Lady Diana Manners as Elizabeth 1, Henry Ainley as Oliver Cromwell and Sir Frank Benson as Becket.

Such subjects were thought more exportable than local comedies of manners, and among their most enthusiastic promoters was Herbert Wilcox (1892–1977), a former film-renter whose ruthlessness and drive would not have disgraced an American producer. Turning director, he began a long career, and also like deMille, his early films are by far his best. He was innovative for he thought in international terms, as a producer bringing from Hollywood Mae Marsh, even if her popularity was fading; as a director he went to Berlin, co-producing *Decameron Nights* (1924) with Erich Pommer. The stars were Werner Krauss and Lionel Barrymore, though the latter's box-office appeal was insufficient to attract an American distributor – Ufa handled the film in the U.S. four years later, when for a brief period it had its own American company. Undeterred, Wilcox negotiated with First National's London office to handle *The Only Way* (1925), a version of the celebrated stage adaptation of 'A Tale of Two Cities' with its original exponent, Sir John Martin-Harvey. The American distributing companies in Britain were not otherwise involved in production, but First National's local success with this caused United Artists to pick up the American rights. Emboldened by this, Wilcox engaged another American star, Dorothy Gish, to appear in *Nell Gwynne* (1926), again made in conjunction with First National; but when money ran out, an American producer, J. D. Williams, helped to complete it. Adolph Zukor was so impressed that he offered one million dollars for three more films with Miss Gish – *London, Tiptoes,* which co-starred Will Rogers, and **Madame Pompadour** (1927), the first film to be made at Elstree Studios, built with optimism and Paramount money by Williams and Wilcox for their company, British National. It was also the last under this regime, since Williams' ways with money were chaotic, and Wilcox left to set up his own British & Dominions company.

He had engaged eminent foreign help on *Pompadour*: Frances Marion was the scenarist, E. A. Dupont, at a fee of £1,000 a week, was the 'Supervising Director', and Antonio Moreno crossed the Atlantic to co-star. Since popular tradition has made of royal mistresses – except Mistress Gwynn – painted harpies, dramatised editions have to reconcile that view with a sympathetic heroine; a formula had been found to satisfy audience expectations, whereby the lady is haughty at court, but simple-hearted and generous when her fancy is caught by a handsome peasant or guardsman. This screenplay does manage to surprise, but it is aided by Miss Gish's vivacious performance; and there is a good villain by Gibb McLaughlin, in the Restoration tradition of effeminate lechers.

With such exceptions, British films were not of the standard required by American audiences – or, indeed, those at home. American domination, financial crises, poor quality – these were the bugbears of the British industry, as they have been ever since. Another producer who survived them over the years was Michael Balcon (1896–1977), who also fought back by raising quality and looking realistically to the American market. Undeterred by the current industry crisis, he moved from making advertising films into production, with two partners, one of them Victor Saville (who later became a director). They hired space – alongside Wilcox – in Islington Studios, just vacated by Paramount after a short-lived attempt at local production (the films proved unsaleable in the U.S.); and they engaged as director Graham Cutts, formerly with Wilcox, and widely believed to share with him something of the American know-how. Emulating Wilcox, they brought over a popular American star, Betty Compson, at £1,000 a week, and gambling further they purchased a popular play, *Woman to Woman* (1923), the film of which got the new company off to a flying start. But when a second film with Miss Compson failed, their distributor refused an advance, and Balcon founded a new company, Gainsborough Pictures, whose product would be released by Gaumont-British. The first venture starred another American, Alice Joyce, and for the second, *The Blackguard,* Balcon obtained a co-production agreement with Ufa. Otherwise, he proceeded slowly and cautiously until **The Rat** (1925) provided the company with its first huge success. The star was Ivor Novello (1893–1951), whose signing was a coup for Balcon, since Novello had hitherto been his own producer, and was known in the U.S. by virtue of a starring role in Griffith's *The White Rose*; renowned also as composer, playwright and matinee idol, this was probably his finest hour, as the only British film star of international fame. This particular film was based on a play written by himself and Constance Collier, under a pseudonym, and he has the title-role, an apache king of ravenous sexual appetite – except for the girl he truly loves (Mae Marsh), queen among waifs. Comes slumming a rich man's mistress (Isabel Jeans): 'I gave in because you are nevertheless a child and irresponsible', to which his response is 'You smell nice.' 'I am bothering to talk to you,' she says, 'because you are my sort . . . In your world you rule. In my world I rule,' but when they quarrel the intertitles become disappointingly prosaic, 'I wish I'd thrown your rotten note out of the window.' Her lover, impatient, selects a new mistress, the waif, and when she refuses his advances he decides upon rape . . . The film's popularity was such that there were two sequels, *The Triumph of the Rat* and *The Return of the Rat,* and I count myself fortunate in not having seen them.

Balcon's chief screenwriter, sharing his predilection for contemporary subjects, was Alfred Hitchcock (1899–1980), who had entered films writing intertitles. From *Woman to Woman* onwards, he was one of Cutts's small unit, sometimes doubling as art-director; but as Cutts's professional jealousy increased, Balcon determined to promote Hitchcock to director. In so doing, he found someone not only able to enhance the value of his stars, but capable of drawing attention to himself as director – by virtue of an exceptionally flashy technique, and a number of other devices, all borrowed from Germany; fortunately Hitchcock's studies had also taught him how to make the narrative move compulsively forward. He had watched Murnau on an adjoining set while working with Ufa, and he returned to Germany for another co-production, **The Pleasure Garden** (1925), with the obligatory American star, Virginia Valli. She plays a chorus girl who marries a Britisher (Miles Mander) from the East; joining him there, she finds him with an under-age mistress and a bad case of D.T.s The husband's true character is withheld for a while, and the theatre scenes are lively, but Hitchcock did not find his way – there was an intervening film, now lost – till **The Lodger** (1926). Rushing from image to image, largely eschewing intertitles, he creates a portrait of London racked by a series of murders. 'A Story of the London Fog' is the film's subtitle, and as the lights of the Embankment fade, a girl is murdered: there is a montage of headlines and shocked people listening at their crystal-sets, while all the time a sign flashes, 'Tonight – Golden Curls'. The rest, however, is trite and unconvincing, neither faithful to Mrs Belloc-Lowndes's novel about a middle-class, middle-aged couple who come to suspect that their lodger is Jack the Ripper, nor to the facts of the case. In the title-role Novello acts suspiciously, beyond the call of reason, though always making sure that he is

Alfred Hitchcock came into prominence directing star vehicles for such popular British figures as Isabel Jeans, Betty Balfour and Ivor Novello. In *Downhill*, as the sweetshop cutie (Annette Benson) accuses Novello, right, of being the father of her child, the true culprit (Robin Irvine) stays mute. Novello stands by the schoolboys' code – though at thirty–four much too old for the role – and stays silent. After that, he goes from chorus boy to gigolo to unnamed degradation in Marseilles, and Hitchcock couldn't resist a symbolic 'downhill' to start it all off, as Novello goes down an Underground escalator.

photographed well; June, the heroine, is far less pretty than he, an early instance of dreadful leading ladies. However, it is presumably not his fault that at the last minute his mysterious behaviour is explained while the real murderer is arrested off-screen. Hitchcock, who did the adaptation with his then regular collaborator, Eliot Stannard, himself explained later that it was impossible at that time to cast a star as a killer; and the distributor had apparently demanded revisions.

The film's reception established Hitchcock, encouraging him to more batteries of arty shots in **Downhill** (1927) and **Easy Virtue** (1927) – though neither is remotely static, like most British film versions of plays. *Downhill* was another from the pens of Collier and Novello, and its U.S. release title, *When Boys Leave Home*, gives an idea of the plot, which is heavily misogynist. Its best sequence finds Novello as a miserable dance-partner in Paris, gradually aware that the motherly lady talking to him has sexual designs – during which, in Ufa fashion, her make-up gradually becomes more garish. Isabel Jeans, as a stage star, is

another who uses this unfortunate young man, and *Easy Virtue* was a vehicle for her, as hacked from Noël Coward's Pineroesque play. By removing the sub-plots and offering more of the heroine's life it emerges as bland nonsense, though still having to do with a family's hostility to the son's new wife. Coward's plays were shocking to West End audiences, and the idea doubtless was to let them be seen by the less sophisticated in Wigan or Dumfries. Balcon also bought **The Vortex**, and admitted later that he had been wrong: 'We followed trends and did not try to make them. It was doubly a mistake to lean on stage plays because we were making Silent films . . . both were financial failures.' As directed by Adrian Brunel, *The Vortex* makes incomprehensible Coward's tale of drugs and sex among the smart set, but the failure is also one of nerve: to make Miss Jeans sympathetic in *Easy Virtue,* she becomes ill-treated, wronged, and unjustly accused, a glamorous innocent in the mould of Irene Rich or Pola Negri – and this was the age of Clara Bow. British censors passed both Miss Bow's antics and the equally bold behaviour of Coward's stage characters, but here the latter have been handled – and it is true also of *Downhill* – with a sense of morality both smug and, compared with American films at this time, outdated.

Hitchcock left Balcon for British International Pictures, newly formed by John Maxwell, an exhibitor, in light of the Quota Act; Maxwell shortly afterwards allied the company and its studio (Elstree, not long vacated by Wilcox and Williams) to the Associated British circuit; and about the same time Gainsborough was absorbed into Gaumont-British, also developing its circuit interests – so in fact Hitchcock moved from one to the other of what were now the two biggest film companies. **The Ring** (1927) he regarded, after *The Lodger,* as the second 'Hitchcock picture', and the influence of *Variété* is again all over it, even to the story (written by himself), which concerns the rivalry between two boxers over the same woman. **Champagne** (1928), however, was 'probably the lowest ebb in my output,' though he neglected to add that it was a vehicle for Betty Balfour, whom the readers of the *Daily Mirror* had recently voted their favourite British star – probably the reason it apes the Hollywood vehicles of such as Colleen Moore, the story of a tomboyish heiress who toys with the advances of a roué (who, as with *The Lodger,* turns out to be not at all as we'd thought). The acquisition of Hitchcock and Miss Balfour indicates Maxwell's ambitions, and he also filched from Gainsborough two popular players, Jameson Thomas and Lillian Hall Davis; Hitchcock directed their second co-starring effort for B.I.P., **The Farmer's Wife** (1928), but it is less a vehicle than a straightforward version of Eden Phillpotts' long running play about the Devon widower who woos three spinsters before realising that his house-keeper is the ideal mate. For the mainly West country aphorisms, Hitchcock has tried to substitute visual humour, but if there is a satirical edge it is more Shaftesbury Avenue than Yelverton, and the film is certainly not to be compared with contemporary Hollywood comedies of small town life. **The Manxman** (1929) is another rural tale, based on Sir Hall Caine's old novel: 'What shall it profit a man if he gain the whole world and lose his soul?' is the foreword to this tale, as to many others – all to be preferred to this intense triangle drama, with its particularly tedious trio, Carl Brisson, Malcolm Keen and Anny Ondra. Dully made, it proves that as he curtailed his tricks Hitchcock was less interesting than in his derivative days. Like many other film-makers more interested in celluloid than people, he passed by every opportunity to comment on his era – except in *The Ring,* which, like its prototype, is rich in its portrait of its milieu.

Except perhaps in that film, Hitchcock's borrowings do not arise naturally from the situations but are imposed upon them: and the same is true of the films of Anthony Asquith (1902–68), the only other British director of the period to attract serious critical attention – though it helped to be well connected, and indeed he was the son of a former prime minister. He was able to study filming in America and Germany, and was taken on by British Instructional, a company which specialised in documentary reconstructions of battles. On his first film, **Shooting Stars** (1928), he was associate producer, editor, writer and director – though John Orton and A. V. Bramble (the latter a veteran of the industry) are respectively credited with the last named functions. This is yet another derivation of *Variété,* with the triangle drama set this time in a film studio, and ending on an ironic note, with the rejected husband (Brian Aherne) becoming famous and the unfaithful wife (Annette Benson) a nobody. Asquith had not sloughed off the German influence by the time he made **Underground** (1928), this time credited as director – and indeed he brought over Karl Fischer to do the lighting. More than the earlier film, it is an exercise in style, which is just as well in view of the plot – about the rivalry of an underground guard (Aherne) and an electrician (Cyril McLaglen) for a shop-girl (Elissa Landi). It is affectionately done – though it is clear how little Asquith knew of the lower orders, supposedly living in drab little rooms and going for picnics on Hampstead Heath. At the time, however, it was much praised – since most other films on British working-class life were either patronising or comic.

The director of *Variété,* E. A. Dupont,

was also at B.I.P., having fled Hollywood after his disastrous film for Universal. His five-picture contract included two Silents – and both follow *Varieté* in being triangle dramas with show business backgrounds; and though both were photographed by an old collaborator, Werner Brandes, and the second of them was designed by Alfred Junge, both brought to Britain from Germany (Junge remained, to become the doyen of British art directors), neither film is as derivative as the Hitchcock or the Asquith. **Moulin Rouge** (1928) is set in a Paris night club (despite Paris locations, a London night club was used), and concerns a star (Olga Tschechowa) who discovers that her daughter's fiancé has fallen in love with her; **Piccadilly** (1929), set in a London night club, is about a star (Gilda Gray) who discovers that its owner, her lover (Jameson Thomas) has fallen for the new attraction (Anna May Wong). Her dilemma is that she does not know whether or not she has committed a murder, a situation common in movies at the time, and on this occasion devised by Arnold Bennett, one of the very rare major writers to accept a commission to write an original screenplay. The polish of both films belies their origin, but they also reflect Dupont's uneasiness away from his native land; with the advent of Sound, he directed three Anglo-German dual language films: **Atlantic** (1929), based on the sinking of the Titanic; **Two Worlds** (1930), a story of Jewish life in Vienna during the War; and, more disappointingly, **Cape Forlorn** (1931), a heavy triangle drama set in and around a lighthouse. He then went back to Germany, and by the time he returned to Hollywood in 1933 was regarded as a spent force.

Another German director, Arthur Robison, was at Elstree making **The Informer** (1929), which unlike John Ford's later version (q.v.) is merely a tale of doom and atonement. We may be sure Ford saw this, since his studio-created Dublin is identical, but Robison of course had been one of the major influences of the Ufa style, as copied abroad for 'art' movies. His stars here are Lya de Putti and Lars Hanson, the latter in his usual pursuit of being haunted and hunted, a figure of destiny. These were not the only Continental artists in British films, since the local entrepreneurs had begun to raid European studios both to increase their export market and to improve the quality of their product – while the artists themselves saw Britain, because of the common language, as a step nearer Hollywood. The period was brief, and ended when British studios wired for Sound.

In France, those film-makers who believed in the film as an art considered that it should deal with real life – by which was understood the artisan class. Their leader was Louis Delluc (1890–1924), a young aesthete who was among the first of his countrymen to give the film more than serious consideration; he founded a magazine called *Cinéma*, whose every issue carried the injunction, 'The French cinema must be *cinema*; the French cinema must be French.' This conviction was the result of his enthusiasm for the three leading national cinemas, the American, the Swedish and the German.

Unhappily, the French cinema of the Twenties – far richer than the British – is far from accessible, its lack of representation in archives outside France serving to confirm how little impression it made, though enough is available for us to note its respect for its audiences. For instance, **L'Agonie des Aigles** (1921) is eloquent demonstration that historical subjects were free of the conventions imposed by Hollywood – and effortlessly superior to such as *Orphans of the Storm*, not an inapt comparison since the period featured is close enough, in this case the aftermath of Napoleon's reign. There is no love affair, beyond the machinations of a conniving dancer (Gaby Morlay); and the hero is an ageing duellist, played by Maxime Desjardins with all his Comédie Française expertise. The director was Dominique Bernard-Deschamps, who made just a few commercial films during a twenty-year career, being otherwise collaborator with Henri Chrétien on scientific films (a pattern not uncommon in the French film industry), and the source was a novel by Georges d'Esparbes, 'Le Demi-Solde'. The commercial cinema was happiest with literary adaptations; Delluc and his followers made their working-class-films; and the avant-garde artists went their own way.

The set-up of the industry was very much as it is today: there were the studios and the distributing companies, and between them the producers or production companies who rented space at the former and hired the completed film to the latter. The only major companies with a hand in all three branches remained Pathé and Gaumont, though known by the end of the Silent period as Pathé-Natan-Cineromans and Gaumont-Aubert-Franco-Films respectively. Ownership in each case shifted, as financiers from time to time considered that either company or both could, or should, monopolise the industry. It never happened, and one reason was that the industry was bedevilled with fly-by-night or dilettante producers – though many of these were not averse to finding backing for the eclectic works of the directors.

Chief of the film-makers grouped around Delluc was Marcel L'Herbier (1890–1979), a former poet and dramatist who arrived in films as a scenarist; his early films were experimental – and are now lost. The Silent films which survive are poor entertainments, but witness to a talent absolutely obsessed with the medium. **L'Homme du Large** (1920) follows Delluc's taste for working-class tales and has a number of good sequences, including a town fête and an evening in a low dive, complete with fondling lesbians; but this free adaptation of a story by Balzac, 'Un Drame au Bord de la Mer', about a father's grief over his wastrel son, is too much like *Terje Vigen* for its own good. In emulating Sjöström at every turn, L'Herbier simply fails to understand his purity; and by using artifice in theatrical manner, i.e. framing, fretworks, maskings, his overall images are in violent disharmony with the Breton settings. Even more does **Eldorado** (1921) represent the cinema aesthete thinking and working overtime, with great care given to set-ups, cutting, the use of people in landscapes, distorted images to express emotions: but as L'Herbier bundles in the whole paraphernalia with no sense of style, it is also clear that he confused the pictorial possibilities of film with those of the theatre and the decorative arts. He was certainly trying to find a route for the medium, and his ingenuity is often fascinating. However, ludicrous emoting and confused narration help neither this film nor his most famous one, **Feu Mathias Pascal** (1924), based on Pirandello's novel about a man (Ivan Mosjoukine) who begins a new life when reported dead. It organises a number of Pirandellan themes, including a dream sequence which disdains to make apparent what is truth and what is fantasy, as in *Aelita*. The locations, Rome and San Gimigniano, are refreshing, but L'Herbier makes little of Granada in the earlier film, which mainly concerns the tribulations of a dancer (Eve Francis, the wife of Delluc, and leading actress for the films of his group) over her sick bastard son.

Between the two, L'Herbier made *Don Juan et Faust*, now lost, with designs by Claude Autant-Lara influenced by *Caligari;* and with **L'Inhumaine** (1924) L'Herbier experimented again with decor, employing with Autant-Lara also Fernand Leger, Cavalcanti and Mallet Stevens (and Darius Milhaud also composed a score). The idea behind the film was to show the advances France had made in modern design – thus like a great many later French flop-movies, it was made to impress the Americans. It was commissioned and partly financed by its star, the singer Georgette LeBlanc – who plays a diva with an entourage of admirers, very much in the manner of the Italian 'divismo' films of a decade earlier. Indeed, L'Herbier, like Hitchcock and Asquith, was so besotted with the medium that he borrowed and copied slavishly. **L'Argent** (1928) is plundered from the Soviet films, from *Greed,* from *Dr Mabuse* – and in filming Zola's novel, now modernised, L'Herbier was probably emulating Renoir's *Nana* (q.v.). This film is even longer, running over three hours, telling mainly of the rivalry between two financiers (Pierre Alcover, Alfred Abel). The decor is again often extravagant, but the film is frequently striking to look at, notably the scenes in the stock exchange: you may prefer the cool, perfected, visual interpretation by this time in force in Hollywood, but L'Herbier's work is often dynamic – and in its turn was influential, certainly the inspiration for Feyder's *Les Nouveaux Messieurs* (q.v.). L'Herbier's Sound films (q.v.) would move towards

The Sound films of Marcel L'Herbier are stolid affairs, but in the Silent period he was forever experimenting – ceaselessly borrowing, and being borrowed from. This is Brigitte Helm in *L'Argent*, and it is almost certainly from her that von Sternberg got the idea for his Hollywood Dietrich.

conservatism, and indeed *L'Argent* spelled the end of the Delluc movement dubbed 'impressionist': the intellectuals who had originally praised the attempts at experiment had gradually cooled – and they had in particular disliked *L'Inhumaine*.

The accomplishment of Jacques Feyder (1887–1948) is much more sound. Belgian-born, this former actor with Feuillade directed his first film in 1915, and had his first commercial success with **L'Atlantide** (1921), Pierre Benoît's story of exploration in Atlantis – and ludicrous today as the Queen pounces on her romantic prey with wild eyes, flailing arms and golliwog hair; but of the two films which established him abroad the only surviving one has not dated at all – **Carmen** (1926). The medium had advanced since *L'Atlantide*, but this revitalisation of *Carmen* is vastly superior to Renoir's contemporary *Nana*. No one since Merimée, nor in later versions, has tried to interest us in the *characters* of Carmen and Don José, as opposed to their

fates, and Feyder does this by presenting them as thoughtful people. Louis Lerch, overall too boyish, does suggest a man buffeted by fortune; Raquel Meller (whom Feyder used against his will) does some of the conventional poses but is not the customary cardboard. Despite the meticulous detail throughout and the inclusion of more Merimée than we usually get, the vigorous approach makes this long *Carmen* seem short – Spain, for instance, has never been better used, and even today some of the shots are breathtaking. It is one of the glories of the Silent screen, which makes all the sadder the loss of *Thérèse Raquin* (1928) – especially as it was the more admired at the time. Particularly praised in this similar tale of obsessive love was the performance of Gina Manès and the evocation of atmosphere, indicating Feyder's primary allegiance to his source material. **Les Nouveaux Messieurs** (1929) has dated somewhat, since we are no longer shocked to find that ballerinas have elderly, rich protectors, or that they prefer them to idealistic young workers; we are familiar with the view that such idealists on attaining power may become as corrupt as those they denounce. With Charles Spaak, Feyder adapted this satire from a popular boulevard comedy by De Flers and De Croisset ; the title refers to trade unionists getting into government; but though the three leading characters offer chances in the matter of their morals, mores and motives, the film takes none of them. But it does confirm Feyder's mastery of the Silent language – now to be transferred to Hollywood; angered by local reaction to *Les Nouveaux Messieurs* he signed a contract with M-G-M.

By this time, the fame of René Clair (1898–1981) had eclipsed that of both L'Herbier and Feyder. The son of a wealthy soap merchant, he moved from journalism to acting in films which included two of Feuillade's serials. He also became film editor of *Le Théâtre et Comoedia Ilustré,* which published this manifesto on the occasion of his first film as director: 'If the cinema has any aesthetics of its own, they were discovered at the same time as the camera and the film, in France, by the Lumière brothers. They are summed up in one word: movement. The external movement of objects perceived by the eye, to which we will now add the internal movement of the action.' The film was **Paris Qui Dort** (1924), and it certainly looks back – not to Lumière, but to Clair's boyhood idols, Méliès and Zecca: a sardonic trifle about an invisible ray which, turned on Paris, immobilises life and movement – to the glee of some people safely beyond its effect, on the Eiffel Tower. **Entr'acte** (1924) was commissioned by the Ballets Suédois to accompany one of their ballets, to music by Satie and a 'book' by Francis Picabia – who also designed the decor. Picabia was a Dadaist, and appears in the film with other members of the group, including Marcel Duchamp and Man Ray: as with their aims, it is bizarre, inconsequential, designed to shock. Clair, though this is the only one of his French films for which he did not provide his own screenplay, took his chance: imagery, super-imposition, quick cutting and some 'in' jokes; but he was not really drawn to the avant-garde.

On neither film was the equipment more than amateur; and neither was destined for more than a limited public. His first full-length film and the first destined for commercial cinemas was **Le Fantôme du Moulin Rouge** (1925) – and the title, while not dishonest, was clearly meant to appeal at the box office. A man, disappointed in love, meets at the Moulin Rouge a doctor who can separate spirit from body: while his spirit haunts Paris, the doctor is accused of his murder. Clearly, this plot suits Clair's own dictum that a film should be above all visual; in his own words, this is 'a fantastic story based on superimposition' – but the superimpositions are poor, and the jokes (stealing clothes from a cloakroom, driving away in an empty taxi) both schoolboyish and scanty. **Voyage Imaginaire** (1925) is again *un homage à Méliès*, concerning a bank-clerk's dream: unlike the *Fantôme*, it was not successful, nor was *La Proie de Vent* (1926), an adventure story with a number of visual effects. For Clair's gift lay not in impish fantasy but in delicacy of comic situation, where the joke absorbs the plot or vice versa, coalesced, inseparable, as at the end of *Le Fantôme*: as the police prepare an autopsy, the ghost, now wanting to live, desperately needs to get back into the body before the first incision; and when he comes round, he glares at the surgeon for having nicked him.

Clair's flowering was **Un Chapeau de Paille d'Italie** (1927), based on a farce by Labiche and Michel which first saw the light of day in 1851; since he was among those who believed that adaptations from the stage and the novel had no place on the screen, he accepted the project only for the opportunity it gave to recreate the chase comedies of his youth, and thereby changing from a scientist with a camera to a puppet-master. To his existing skills – for balletic movement, for swift and pointed editing, for visual wit – he added that of satirical comedy, with a portrait of a wedding group of quite awesome awfulness. His plot, in fact, is ideal: a young man (Albert Préjean), on his wedding morn, has the misfortune to cross a ferocious army officer and his mistress, when his horse eats her hat; and needs must that he haplessly replace it before, during, or after the ceremony, whichever is soonest. Though the film was not popular in France, it made Clair's name with the metropolitan critics and internationally, and he stayed with Labiche and Michel for **Les Deux Timides** (1928), which he modernised, extending the original one-act play with some themes from a serious scenario, abandoned when the Censor refused to pass it because it was based on a recent crime. The gentlemen of the title are a meek lawyer (Pierre Batcheff) and the father of the young lady he would like to marry, both in frequent confrontation with the bigger and bullying fellow suitor. The two films run as merrily as a clockwork train, magically re-wound after losing speed on a bend; and though the visual tricks remain original and brilliantly funny today, much of the rest is derivative. Perhaps because these were not the sort of comedies Clair *wanted* to make, he borrowed – in *Chapeau de Paille* from Sennett, Zecca, Chaplin and Linder; in *Timides* from Lloyd and Keaton – and, indeed, its hero even looks like Buster. Clair's own genius would not be revealed till his Sound pictures, and it should be noted that he loathed the thought of a Sound cinema even more than most creative people in film at the time.

If, however, his reputation was already

made, that of Jean Renoir (1894–1979) had already settled on that seesaw where it was to remain till universal acclaim greeted him in old age. The son of the painter, his profession was ceramics and his passion the American cinema – a passion he shared with his wife, who had been a model of his father's; she looked, he considered, so much like the great American female stars that he was determined to make a film star of her – a project she regarded with indifference. He intended to be only the financier (his wealth, such as it was, was inherited from his father), but he could not resist collaborating with the friend whom he had commissioned to write the scenario, Pierre Lestringuez. The plot of **Une Vie Sans Joie** (1924) is obviously inspired by some of Mary Pickford's films, having to do with a waif (Catherine Hessling, as Madame Renoir had been rechristened) loved by a tubercular youth, and a former benefactor who risks scandal for her sake; and the influence of the American cinema may be found in its portraits of local dignitaries and – direct from *Intolerance* – do-gooders. Successful as a satire on small town life, it is otherwise ineffective, as Renoir – like Clair – started with one purpose and found himself better at another: his talent was not for the star vehicle (though he tried again later in his career), but for the by-play of society – never obscured by his dislike of the bourgeoisie. The director was Albert Dieudonné, who found his interference intolerable; and Renoir could not wait to be in sole charge. Their quarrels were in vain: the film was not publicly shown though, re-cut by Dieudonné – who also played the invalid – it achieved a few showings three years later, retitled *Catherine*.

Undeterred, Renoir embarked on **La Fille de l'Eau** (1924) – the title-role to be played by Miss Hessling; and though he may have entered films for her sake, he said that he became intoxicated by the medium after seeing Chaplin: 'For Catherine and me the cinema was a medium of expression that deserved a life of its own . . . [We] dreamed of developing a French cinema free of all theatrical or literary encumbrances. We also hoped to foster an American style of action, derived more from the direct observation of nature than the French style was.' Accordingly, this film was born 'of the strange juxtaposition of Catherine Hessling and the Forest of Fontainebleau' – and, we might add, other juxtapositions: his love of improvisation and his loathing of being dependent on a story, plus his belief that filming was merely technical and actors only machines. In the case of Miss Hessling, he was right, and her story – the tribulations of a parentless barge-girl – is banal; but its glimpses of village and village life are worthy of Sjöström. It was filmed entirely on location, and had it been unsigned you would still know that it was by the same hand as *Partie de Campagne* (q.v.).

It was also rejected by exhibitors, because of a dream sequence, but that – unknown to Renoir – had been extracted by Jean Tedesco to show with some avant-garde films at the Vieux-Colombier; his indignation dissolved when the audience, recognising him and his wife, applauded – which gave him the courage to try again. 'I stopped foolish criticism of the public's so-called lack of comprehension, and contemplated the possibility of reaching them by treating authentic subjects in the tradition of French realism' – and he chose to do Zola's story of the courtesan **Nana** (1926). As with Clair, he had earlier refused to contemplate an adaptation from another medium, but this one – selected partly because of the general enthusiasm for *Foolish Wives* – would allow him to change direction *and* make a 'commercial' film, thus enabling him to enter the industry proper. Of that change of direction, he was to say much later: 'The consistency that I hate so much – and which film critics are always demanding, because otherwise they get confused – also causes people who are creative at the beginning to start copying themselves,' and he may have been thinking of François Truffaut (q.v.), who claimed for him 'characteristic themes . . . the love of spectacle, the woman who chooses the wrong vocation, the actress trying to find herself, the lover who dies of his sincerity, the distracted politician, the showman.' Continuing, Truffaut is on surer ground: 'In short, *Nana* rhymes with *Elena*'. *Elena et les Hommes* (q.v.) has been described by Renoir as 'un homage à la puissance de la femme et la faiblesse de l'homme' – and so

Jean Renoir went into films because he believed his wife, Catherine Hessling, deserved to be a big star. When his first efforts failed, he went for broke in an expensive and grandiose version of Zola's *Nana*. Miss Hessling is here being adored by Jean Angelo who, along with Werner Krauss, outacted her. Renoir had got the message; and the marriage didn't last either.

is *Nana*. Its major flaw – again – is Miss Hessling, playing, as he says, like a marionette – her posturing emphasised by the superb performances of Werner Krauss and Jean Angelo, both aware that loving Nana is no easy thing. Unlike the later Goldwyn version – or any other film about a courtesan that I know – Renoir brings out the curious aspect of the 'system', that men in high places were content to share these women, unconcerned that their motives were primarily monetary. There is, however, no sensuality, for in following Von Stroheim he achieved merely a coldness – and he was moralising, hoping that audiences would be, as with Stroheim and deMille, equally scandalised and satisfied. At the premiere, he was both hissed and applauded; the film failed, but it had been anyhow 'a mad undertaking', with a budget of of a then unprecedented million francs, due partly to the fact that to get Herr Krauss for the role the interiors were filmed in Berlin.

Again, he left films, and in 'a gesture of farewell' he took the unused footage from *Nana* to make a short, **Charleston** (1926), a celebration of dance so joyous that one hardly notices that the two dancers never get around to dancing together. For the second time, the reception to an 'avant-garde fragment' kept him in films, and he accepted a purely commercial venture, *Marquitta* (1927), offered by his sister-in-law and written by Lestringuez, who had deliberately loaded it with clichés. For that reason, perhaps, the result elicited no further offers, but he scraped up enough money to make a shortish version of a Hans Andersen story for one of Tedesco's avant-garde seasons; he chose **La Petite Marchande d'Allumettes** (1928) because of its opportunities for fantasy, but although no camera-trick is missed, it is today, like Clair's early fantasies, creaky. **Tire-au-Flanc** (1928) is also amateurish; compared with any American comedy of the time it looks like a home movie, and is surely the worst of the four versions of this old vaudeville (the last in 1961), chosen because of its presumed popular appeal. He had capitulated to the commercial cinema: in the expressive phrase of the film historian, Georges Sadoul, 'partly from necessity, and partly in an attempt to learn, by these despised methods, how the heart of the general public was to be won.'

For a company called Société des Films Historiques, he made **Le Tournoi dans la Cité** (1929), a melodrama of the days of Charles IX, and **Le Bled** (1929), intended by its sponsors to be an 'epic historical fresco.' The former – at least in the truncated version which is all that exists today – makes little of its

Carcassone locations, but *Le Bled* makes marvellous use of Algeria. In this case government money was involved, for the film was to celebrate the centenary of that country's annexation by France; but apart from one sequence emphasising the closeness of the two countries, this is an increasingly preposterous melodrama – in the manner of the early Douglas Fairbanks films, starting with comedy and moving on to romance and high adventure. Had Renoir stayed with comedy, he might have made a small masterpiece, and in the early part, too, he responds to the terrain and the people with his individual sense of wonder. He said that he took on these films as chores, but began to like what he was doing – which would suggest that *Le Bled* was filmed backwards; we can see that the best of this and of *La Fille de l'Eau* would be echoed in his later *Toni* (q.v.).

The French film-makers of this time, influenced by cinematic advances in other countries, copied and experimented, playing with film as boys play with Meccano or Plasticine; hence, Renoir and Clair flirted with what is called the 'avant-garde' – and we keep the name for those film-makers who never managed to appeal to the public at large. The art of the film owes something to these experimenters, but most of their films are now difficult to watch with pleasure. Perhaps the most tolerable is **La Chute de la Maison Usher** (1928), directed by Jean Epstein (1897–1953), a journalist of Polish origin who came to films encouraged by Delluc. His best film is probably *Le Coeur Fidèle* (1923), a triangle set among the criminal classes, representing for him the artisans; he was drawn towards natural settings, but it was with this version of Poe that he first claimed serious attention. It does boast a staggering number of superimpositions, strange juxtapositions and speeding shots, and there is an effective sequence of nails being hammered into a coffin inter-cut with frogs copulating; but it is theatrical, and with the impact made in Paris by the Soviet films Epstein's interest in trickery faded.

Also associated with Delluc was Germaine Dulac, whose **La Coquille et le Clergyman** (1928) was another admired warhorse among film societies:

written by Antonin Artaud, its 'surrealism' is now – and probably always was – impenetrable. It was rejected by the British Board of Film Censors, as 'so cryptic as to be almost meaningless. If there is a meaning, it is doubtless objectionable.' Dulac gave up directing the following year to work in newsreels.

A similar progression may be noted in Luis Buñuel (b. 1900), a Spaniard whose interest in films had brought him to Paris, where for a while he assisted Epstein. **Un Chien Andalou** (1928), a fifteen-minute short, was co-directed with Salvador Dali, a countryman and fellow-Surrealist. It is difficult to discuss perhaps because 'it is impossible to translate completely into ordinary language the complexity of this poem – for poem it is, and not a fable or an allegory' – or so wrote Freddy Buache in his book on Buñuel. Reading about it, however, is as interesting as seeing it, which can be true of few films – especially one with the inconsistency of a dream. This dream begins with a human eye being dissected by a razor-blade, the shock of which is to rid the mind of associations and therefore capable of accepting on its own terms the film that follows – one in which, in the words of its creators, 'nothing means anything.' Its purpose is clear, its meaning obscure, its images repellent: the priests being drawn across the road by donkeys, the dead horse on the piano, the crowd looking at the hand in the road, the man whose sudden beard is made of woman's arm-pit hair. It is too ugly to care about, to care what it means – if it means anything.

Another disciple of Delluc's was Abel Gance (1889–1981). He had started in films as early as 1911 and had had a success with his anti-war *J'Accuse* (1919) before coming under Delluc's influence. He continued to work until the Sixties, but is best known for his five-hour **Napoléon** (1927), whose ambitions included the use of a triptych of screens, which proved possible only on its premiere at the Paris Opéra and in a number of other major cities. M–G–M, which had bought foreign rights for a huge figure, experienced so little interest during its New York run that release was delayed for a year, when the film, now in a single-screen version, suffered its second American failure. The Talkie revolution had by then arrived, but it is only too easy to see why Anglo-Saxon audiences rejected this piece, since this is a banal run-through of the French Revolution and the life of the young Bonaparte, told with all the narrative finesse of D. W. Griffith, i.e. in primitive manner and completely without tension. Some twenty minutes are technically of interest: the opening sequence at school, with the camera at the heart of things in snowfight and pillowfight, tricked out with superimpositions and the screen split into multiple images ; and the intercutting of a storm at sea with angry scenes at the Convention – a sequence called by Gance 'Les Deux Tempêtes', and calling for the two extra screens and projectors, brought into use also for three later sequences. The raising of the siege of Toulon takes an hour, and further time is wasted with a fictional character – a girl whose passion for the Emperor exceeds that of Stendhal's Sorel; indeed your only moment of pleasure is likely to be when, as Napoleon embarks for Italy, you realise that the thing has come to an abrupt stop.★

Also delving into history was Carl Dreyer, who arrived in France to make **La Passion de Jeanne d'Arc** (1928) – with which we may conclude this brief catalogue of disasters. The mystery of its acceptance as the summit and one of the summations of the Silent film was finally cleared up by Penelope Gilliatt in her film column in *The New Yorker* in 1973. She did not mention it, but was expounding on the subject of Great Art – which, Leonard Woolf had apparently once told her, was bound to be a little boring : Bach and 'Hamlet' were both 'a bit boring' and 'War and Peace' was 'often very boring' – opinions unquestioned by Ms Gilliatt, who used the premise to prove that the film she is reviewing is 'not art, because it signally fails to bore.' The prevalence of this attitude must surely explain why so much rubbish has cluttered our screens (and theatre stages), enabling audiences to feel elevated after watching something

without a single intellectual fibre. *Jeanne d'Arc* aroused admiration because it was 'austere', because it was on a religious subject, because there was no last-minute rescue, and because, as Mr Rotha put it, it demanded concentration. Dreyer chose a subject, dear to the heart of every Frenchman (the last day of Joan's life, the final trial and the burning), and he filmed it – over an eighteen-month period – in that pompous ascetic way often associated with religious art. Falconetti *looks* tremendous, with big peasant bones and eyes, but you cannot call it a performance, because she has nothing to express but eminent thoughts, except for a moment of dementia before the taunts of her oppressors. The camera searches her face and theirs for revelation, but finds none because it is clumsily placed; instead, towards the end of the film, it begins to offer images of startling vulgarity – a close-up of a shouting mouth, soldiers viewed from overhead – and that is because Dreyer, denied his last-minute rescue, substitutes action equally emotive. Thus, the shaving of Joan's head is intercut with carnival performers and her burning with rioting soldiers – in slavish imitation of Eisenstein, which was another reason for contemporary enthusiasm. The subject is not very filmic, and Dreyer made it clear that he would have preferred to use Sound, one of the few film-makers to welcome the change. It is ironic that, in general, the directors who most understood and best used their medium dreaded the innovation and, at best, declared that Talkies wouldn't last.

An image of surrealism: *Un Chien Andalou*, prepared together by Salvador Dali and Luis Buñuel, with an eager desire to shock – though the opening image, of an eyeball being pierced by a razor–blade, was supposed to prepare us for everything that followed.

★ Mainly due to the exertions of the film historian Kevin Brownlow this film was shown for special performances in London and New York – at Radio City Music Hall – during the winter of 1980–1 with a full-scale orchestra, the presence of which virtually transformed the film as an experience. However, as Bruce Goldstein observed, with a symphonic orchestra playing the Marseillaise any entertainment is off to a flying start.

9

Talkies!

IN 1926, Warner Bros, made **Don Juan**, 'inspired by the greatest lover of all the ages,' and claiming to be based on the poem by Byron. It is not so much about love as about innocent maidens hounded by would-be ravishers, one of whom, the Don himself, is played as a college-boy tease by the ageing John Barrymore; as directed by Alan Crosland, these would-be seductions take second place to duelling, torture and Western-like posses, but the result is 'A Warner Bros. Classic of the Screen.' The film is, in fact, a landmark – the first feature to be issued with a soundtrack.

Both Edison in the U.S. and Gaumont in France had, during the first decade of films, experimented with Sound, and many others had also tried to find a solution to the two chief problems, synchronisation and amplification. Before World War One, Lee De Forest solved the latter difficulty, and sold the patent of his system to the Bell Telephone Co., whose engineers continued to experiment with Sound-on-disc, to be synchronised to the film. They had developed a new turn-table and accompanying long-playing records, of thirteen to seventeen inches in diameter, capable of lasting a reel, and Sam Warner agreed to try the system for *Don Juan*. Exhibitors had shown reluctance in booking Warner Bros. films, which accordingly played the smaller theatres: by encouraging these to wire for Sound, Warner hoped to attract patrons away from the large cinemas – while his exhibitors would be compensated by cutting out the orchestras deemed a necessity in any city theatre. Vitaphone was formed by Warners and Western Electric – Bell's parent company

– in co-operation, and in the Vitaphone process the New York Philharmonic recorded the score of *Don Juan,* to which were added the sounds of bells, of knocking, and (muffled and faint) the clash of swords. Its premiere in New York, in August 1926, followed a series of Vitaphone shorts – featuring Mischa Elman, Martinelli and Eddie Foy – and a spoken message from Will H. Hays.

Since the large theatres provided not only orchestral accompaniment but Sound effects, the public was not impressed, but as Warners instituted a policy to record scores for their important films, a number of theatres – and not only the small ones – wired for Sound. The shorts were another matter, and by the end of the year Warners had put a hundred into distribution – a figure they doubled in 1927. Lee De Forest had continued his experiments, evolving a system of photographing sound on the film itself, and for some time already he had been touring his Phonofilms – records of vaudeville acts. The only Hollywood mogul interested was William Fox, and then not until he knew that Warners were negotiating with Western Electric; Fox also bought the patent of a German system of Sound-on-film said to have pre-dated that of De Forest, and his engineers developed the system, eventually known as Movietone. With *What Price Glory?*, Fox began adding scores to their films, and as Fox Movietone shorts began to rival those of Vitaphone, it was noticed that theatres showing them were doing excellent business: Warners took a gamble, and **The Jazz Singer** (1927) was born.

Among the artists featured by Vitaphone had been George Jessel, a vaudeville player who was having a success in some of Warners' Jewish comedies, including *Private Izzy Murphy*: that was to have been followed by a film of his stage success, 'The Jazz Singer', but when Warners decided to add some songs – reputedly at the suggestion of Darryl F. Zanuck – Jessel demanded $10,000 in addition to his $30,000. When he insisted on written confirmation, the role was offered to Eddie Cantor (who declined, thinking it imprudent to follow Jessel), and then to another artist of the Vitaphone shorts, Al Jolson – who asked and got $75,000 for his services, plus Warner stock. The rest is history – though ironically the Sound-on-films proved more satisfactory than synchronised records, and Warners soon went over to it; *The Jazz Singer* that survives is a re-processed one. Seen today, the film is over-sentimental, as directed by Crosland, and so slight as to have difficulty achieving its 89 minutes. Its hero is a rabbi's son who prefers vaudeville to his father's profession, a dilemma captured in one intertitle ('The show must go on') and a transition from 'Kol Nidre' to 'Mammy'.

If we ignore the shorts the first voice ever heard from a screen is that of Bobbie Gordon, who plays Jolson as a child. After the lachrymose 'Dirty Hands, Dirty Face' Jolson speaks one line, 'Wait a minute, you ain't heard nothing yet,' and later, between two songs to his mother, he does a mother-love spiel, in both cases improvising as he did on stage – and it was Sam Warner who decided to leave in these impromptus. It has been said that the effect would have been less impressive with a less electric performer, and certainly Jolson's personality provided an additional crackle. The film took over $3½ million, and the fact that his next film took even more is indication that he and the Talking picture started out sensationally together.

Meanwhile, Fox had added Movietone to his newsreels, and equally extraordinary to audiences had been the sound of Lindbergh's plane taking off, in the spring of the year, and President Coolidge greeting him on his return from Paris; in November the Prince of Wales could be heard – and seen – speaking. In February an agreement had been signed between Paramount, M-G-M, First National, Universal and P.D.C. to disregard Sound till a common – and cheaper – system could be found, and they appointed a committee to investigate. The Warners themselves hesitated: *The Jazz Singer* ran on and on for months at cinemas which usually changed their programmes weekly, and it was not till the end of March, 1928, that the second 'Talkie' opened – *Tenderloin*, a rowdy melodrama, which had one reel of dialogue. Its star was Dolores Costello, considered by the studio a good speaker, and she was heard again a month later in an historical romance, *Glorious Betsy*. With the equally audible Lionel Barrymore – playing a financier – *The Lion and the Mouse* had two reels of dialogue, and in July Warners offered the first 'All-Talking' picture, *The Lights of New York*, intended as a short till its director, Bryan Foy, suggested he turn it into a feature for an extra $15,000. This tale of an innocent involved with Broadway gangsters was heralded by *The New York Times*, 'Seven Reels of Speech', and of *The Terror*, with Edward Everett Horton, it said 'A Titleless Talking Film'. The quality of speaking and recording was too clumsy to advance the cause of Sound, and of Warners' rivals only William Fox was preparing to add dialogue to films – till Jolson, in a part-Talking film, made them change their minds; the fact that **The Singing Fool** (1928) did not come along till almost twelve months after *The Jazz Singer* indicates the Warners' own caution.

The film itself manages the considerable feat of being even more maudlin than the earlier one, at unhappily greater length, with Jolson as a fond husband deprived of his child (Davey Lee) by an unloving wife; the child dies, and after a few bars of 'On with the Motley' Jolson sings 'Sonny Boy' – a song written for him in cod mood by Brown, de Sylva and Henderson, and the year's biggest hit. Both sexes were seen to shed tears listening to it, and partly because of it the film took more money at the box office than any hitherto, with a domestic gross of $5½ million.

The studio's profits rose from just over $2 million in 1928 to over $14 million the following year; on a bank loan it acquired a circuit of two hundred and fifty theatres

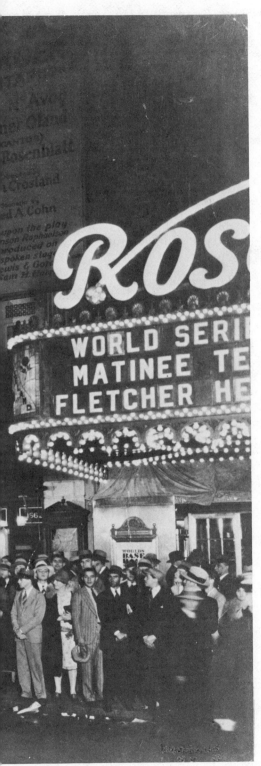

as well as the services of some of Jolson's stage colleagues – Fanny Brice, Texas Guinan, Sophie Tucker, Ted Lewis, Marilyn Miller – but none was to have more than a fleeting career in pictures; similarly, with *The Desert Song,* in May 1929, the company began a series of operettas but, despite Technicolor, each did progressively less business than the last. Jolson was on display again in **Say it with Songs** (1929), another tale of father-love, and **Mammy** (1930), a story of injustice against a minstrel show background; both were predicated on the idea that he was a great entertainer, and he does not miss an emotion familiar to the heroines of Victorian melodrama. As audiences tired of these screen-hogging antics, Warners tried to revive interest with **Big Boy** (1930), which he had done on stage: he is in blackface but hardly more entertaining, partly because the piece is no more than a filmed record of the original and, from the evidence, a third-rate original at that.

By this time, audiences were weary of movies which were little more than filmed plays or surfeited with talk. The early American Talkies are, indeed, extremely wearying; poorly staged, over-acted, and de-lib-er-ately spoken. We recognise them further by thuds which are too loud, gun-shots which are muted, and speeded-up action scenes, clearly filmed Silent. Footling little stories which might have passed muster in the perfection of the late Silent screen become, in such circumstances, insupportable. The first of them were made at panic speed, the accumulated skills of the cameraman subservient to 'king mike'; indeed, he and his equipment were installed in a sound-proofed booth, and freedom with the microphone only came with the invention of the boom. The confusion was apparent on the screen, as technical qualities fluctuated from month to month, from studio to studio.

During 1928 important pictures were increasingly released with synchronised score and sounds, but not till Jolson sang for the second time did the studios commit themselves to dialogue, amidst mutterings of it being a passing fad. The public proved otherwise: in 1927 there was an average 57 million admissions to

The Jazz Singer opened in New York on 6 October 1927. It could not be said that the movie business was never the same again, since most Hollywood studios thought the 'Vitaphone', as Warners' system was called, was only a passing fad. Alone, Fox and Warners persevered, and it wasn't until early 1929 that the industry decided that Talkies were here to stay. The most enthusiastic of the Warner Bros. for Sound was Sam, who died of a cerebral haemorrhage the day after *The Jazz Singer* was premiered.

Talkies!

U.S. movie theatres every week, which had risen to 110 million in 1930, despite the Depression. As lines formed for anything that spoke, dilatory theatre owners quickly ordered conversions, and dialogue sequences were added to films already in production. Throughout 1929, though the revolution had been accomplished by the end of the previous year, the 'part-Talkie' was much in evidence; for cinemas not yet converted, the studios prepared Silent prints of all their features, but the practice was gradually dropped during 1930.

Fox remained just a step behind Warners in the rush to Sound, and from that company emanated 'The First Outdoor All-Talkie', **In Old Arizona** (1929), for which cameras were hidden in bushes and which contains a celebrated close-up of sizzling ham and eggs. Raoul Walsh was directing and playing the lead when he lost an eye in an accident, relinquishing the former job to Irving Cummings and the latter to Warner Baxter – who won an Academy Award; he played the Cisco Kid, betrayed by the leading lady (Dorothy Burgess) to the law, as represented by Edmund Lowe. Such treacherous women were always of foreign extraction and usually of dusky skin, and an even more heinous example was to be found in John Ford's **The Black Watch** (1929), a glamorous female Mahdi (Myrna Loy) who dreams of conquering India. A sequence of the regiment leaving a London station was 'without a doubt the most realistic thing' achieved by Sound, said Mordaunt Hall in *The New York Times*, also noting 'giggles and chuckles' in the audience – which is not surprising since the film manages the amazing feat of combining the 'Arabian Nights' with *What Price Glory?*. A sequel to the latter appeared, **The Cockeyed World** (1929), commissioned from the same writers, and again directed by Walsh. Quirt and Flagg chase girls and fight in various corners of the globe, and those who had admired the earlier film (there would be several more sequels) were offered a sop in the form of a tame anti-war speech; the dialogue is shouted throughout, but audiences found its slang a welcome change from the theatrical speech of most current films. In fact they adored it, but they liked even

more **Sunny Side Up** (1929), directed by David Butler, which has pretty tunes, the popular team of Janet Gaynor and Charles Farrell, and the standby plot of stage musicals for a decade – Long Island rich boy falls in love with poor girl from the East Side. Still today somewhat entrancing, the dance routines and soaring fountains would heavily influence Busby Berkeley. **Hearts in Dixie** (1929), directed by Paul Sloane, is also a musical, intended to capitalise on the popularity of spirituals – though introduced, all the same, by a gentleman explaining that people were the same the world over, regardless of the colour of their skin. The camera certainly moves, and the soundtrack erupts, but the public did not like this serviceable study of negro life.

The public queued to hear the voices of their favourite stars. Ronald Colman spoke in **Bulldog Drummond** (1929), and a few months later in **Condemned** – though the improvement in technique makes it seem like years; the difference may be that its director, Wesley Ruggles, was a real film man and his skill makes the tale acceptable – an unwilling love affair between a prisoner (Colman) on Devil's Island and the warden's wife (Ann Harding). Colman's microphone technique is the *only* virtue in the creaky Drummond film: he thus became Goldwyn's sole asset, as Sound had killed the career of Vilma Banky, with her thick Hungarian accent. The Brooklyn-Jewish accent of Norma Talmadge did not fit the public image of her, and she departed after two Talkies: the title-role in **Du Barry, Woman of Passion** (1930) would seem to have been a careful choice, for she was also somewhat older than studio biographies maintained – but the public would have none of her, or this historical nonsense, atrociously written and directed by Samuel Taylor. Newcomers poured in from the stage, and, also at United Artists, Roland West directed a batch of them in **Alibi** (1929) – though it had been made originally Silent and was hurriedly re-shot, at night, on the set of another film (*Coquette*). The story is a remarkably silly one about an open-faced young man (Chester Morris) who marries a cop's daughter (Eleanor Griffith) and is revealed halfway through as a paranoic killer; but it has a niche in film-history because it is the first film to use Sound imaginatively. In his only other Talkies, *The Bat Whispers* and *Corsair* (q.v.), made in 1931 and both thrillers, respectively of the genres creepy-old-house and gangster, West makes his casts seem even more amateurish than this one – but he makes much here of the noise made by criminals and cops, clanging truncheons, marching feet, police-whistles; he also seems to have been the first film-maker to realise that the public would welcome musical numbers to punctuate the action. A night club is also the setting of **The Great Gabbo** (1929) directed independently by the once-mighty James Cruze, a thin story about a ventriloquist (Erich Von Stroheim, in the only work he could get – as an actor) and the assistant (Betty Compson) he tries to win back. This tale – Ben Hecht, astonishingly, wrote it– serves only as a peg on which to hang the production numbers, filmed months after those in *Alibi* but less imaginatively: audiences undoubtedly wanted the sort of entertainment vaudeville offered, but Cruze's work is a good example of why the phrase 'All Singing All Dancing All Talking' was soon used so derisively.

Audiences no longer were served Clara Bow's speech in intertitles, but could hear her say 'She knows her onions', 'You dumb bunny' and 'You've got Gil on the beam' – even if she was a little developed to play a schoolgirl, a bad lot who is really a good joe and finally able to indulge her crush on the professor (Fredric March) – in **The Wild Party** (1929), directed by Dorothy Arzner. The film is technically way ahead of other Paramount films of the same season: **Chinatown Nights**, directed by William A. Wellman, about a society lady (Florence Vidor) who falls headlong for the boss of the Chinese underworld (Wallace Beery); **The Mysterious Dr Fu Manchu**, directed by Rowland V. Lee, about a wily Chinese philosopher (Warner Oland), carrying out vengeance on his enemies while his ward and dupe (Jean Arthur) falls for one of his victims; and **The Hole in the Wall**, directed by Robert Florey, about a gangster (Edward G. Robinson) operating a fake clairvoyant racket, with the aid of a nice girl (Claudette Colbert). Better than this tawdry trio is von

Sternberg's melodrama about a miscarriage of justice, **Thunderbolt**, even if it is technically rough, with noises drowning out the dialogue, and its star, George Bancroft, enunciating thus: 'I've had . . . a lot of . . . time to think . . . *things* over.' Otherwise, the editor has lapped the Sound between sequences, a new sophistication. **Gentlemen of the Press** has Walter Huston (1884–1950), in his first film, as a dedicated journalist who finds that he has to make compromises when he takes on a job as publicity consultant: but this promising theme, as handled by Millard Webb, is too much a play and not much of a film. Huston and Gary Cooper shared the first famous exchange of Talkies: Huston (the villain): 'You long-legged-sonova –'. Cooper: 'If you wanna call me that, smile.' Huston: 'With a gun in my belly, I always smile.' The film is **The Virginian** (1929), the director is Victor Fleming, and it is a seminal Western if no longer an entertaining one.

Paramount's contribution to the craze for musicals was Maurice Chevalier (1888–1972), a Parisian of considerable and saucy charm. Ernst Lubitsch was invited to direct him, on the usual principle that they were both European – and he remained at Paramount for the next decade. A string of sparkling comedies began with **The Love Parade** (1929), and though Lubitsch subsequently made very few musicals, his delight in the form could have been predicted from the ballroom sequences of his early German comedies. **Monte Carlo** (1930) is indeed mainly notable for his staging of 'Beyond the Blue Horizon', sung by Jeanette Macdonald in a train, its music synchronised to the train's movements and those of the peasants in the fields – who join in with the singer. As the count who poses as a valet – to be near that lady – Jack Buchanan is no substitute for Chevalier, the ideal exponent of Lubitsch's conception of witty and charming male lust. *The Love Parade* was a critical triumph for both, and the director's visual sense particularly delighted at a time when words had taken precedence over pictures, as in the sequence where the Queen (Miss Macdonald) has to reprimand an officer (Chevalier) for a sexual indiscretion, and though she looks scandalised she rushes over to a mirror before receiving him. He becomes her husband, and deprives her of marital favours till she acknowledges that he is the boss – and since his satisfying the Queen is made of such concern, it might be imprudent to revive this film in countries prone to coronations and royal weddings.

An equally sophisticated view of sex was offered by the Russian-born Rouben Mamoulian (b. 1897) in **Applause** (1929), when an ageing burlesque queen (Helen Morgan) lets her men ill-use her, to the extent that she sacrifices herself rather than see her daughter suffer life upon the wicked stage. The magnificent Miss Morgan was one of the stage stars acquired by Paramount, but her puffy features, presumably, prevented a screen career. Mamoulian also came from the stage – one of several directors brought in to handle the new medium; some worked only as dialogue coaches, and others were forced on established film directors as assistants – but his reputation enabled him to study other film-makers, learning 'what not to do.' On the evidence of *Applause* he had also studied the most recent films from Germany and Russia (always seen in Hollywood, privately, but the New York cultural climate in which Mamoulian moved would have been far more receptive to their advances): it looks like a European film, with slanting shots, shadow shots, overhead shots and unexpected close-ups – indeed, it runs close to that line where innovation becomes pretension, and the fact that it doesn't is due to a flair for the apt image. Mamoulian is notably good on the theatres, offering a downbeat, nay, frowsy realism that is right for this particular story; the tragic ending is a European habit which Hollywood seldom allowed. The Sound is variable, and indeed the film is technically inferior to *Condemned*; but it has been held to be the film which got the cameras moving again.

Another claimant is King Vidor's **Hallelujah!** (1929). He reputedly borrowed the staging of the prayer meetings from Mamoulian's Broadway production of 'Porgy'; and certainly the story he wrote for it derives from that and the other famous white interpretation of negro life, 'The Emperor Jones'. Its sincerity and sympathy may not, however, be doubted, and its assumptions about the connection between religious mania and sexual excitement are not offensive. The huge praise it invoked overlooked the stereotypes and concentrated on its documentary-like fervour, while its use of spirituals and jazz (Irving Berlin wrote two new songs) contributed, and still do, to its power as entertainment. It fared no better with the public than Fox's negro film, but M-G-M were compensated by **The Broadway Melody** (1929), which cost almost $380,000 and made a profit of over $1,600,000. It is the original backstage musical, of strife and heartache between a small time sister act (Bessie Love, Anita Page), and a hoofer (Charles King) who makes it to the Great White Way, but after an exhilarating opening – a montage of the lights of Broadway against the title-song – neither Edmund Goulding, who wrote the story, nor Harry Beaumont, who directed, were inspired. However, Miss Love's warm and vital performance remains a pleasure.

Several aspects of the plot, and that of many other early Talkies, could also be found where they originated, in **Broadway** (1929), a melange of bootleggers and show people which George Abbott and Philip Dunning had written for New York's prize director, Jed Harris. The popularity of the play had been such that Universal decided that people would want to see it again if lavishly done – hence Charles D. Hall's vast art deco night club set, with Hal Mohr's camera swinging around in it: here, Paul Fejos's direction is lively, but backstage it slackens, with Glenn Tryon a dull hoofer and Evelyn Brent surprisingly subdued as a chorus girl whose fiancé is murdered.

It was M-G-M who came up with **The Hollywood Revue of 1929**, in which most of its contract players appeared in sketches, or sang and danced, such activities being now *de rigeur*, even for artists not competent at either. Warners followed with their stars in **The Show of Shows** (1929), but it is memorable only for a brief appearance by Beatrice Lillie. Not bothered by what must have been intense audience irritation and boredom – now that the novelty had worn off – Fox offered its stable in *Happy Days* (1930), which was intrepidly followed by *Paramount on Parade* (1930). Universal,

Since Talkies came in with a song (one of Jolson's), that seemed to be what the public wanted, and every star had to open up and give vent to melody. 'All–Talking! All–Singing! All–Dancing!' was the come–on line, and Technicolor was in on the act, usually only for certain sequences. But the two–tone Technicolor of the time was not an audience attraction, and even the three–tone system would take some years to win approval. This scene is from *The Broadway Melody*, and the trio in the front are, from left to right, Anita Page, Charles King and Bessie Love.

having few stars of its own, bolstered its revue with Technicolor, and brought John Murray Anderson from Broadway to supervise it – **King of Jazz** (1930). The title referred to Paul Whiteman, and because of his contribution and that of his Rhythm Boys (who included Bing Crosby), it is marginally the most bearable of the group. Amidst all this frolicking, a little 'class' rears its head: in *The Show of Shows,* John Barrymore appears as Shakespeare's Richard III, and in the M-G-M effort, Norma Shearer and John Gilbert run through the balcony scene from 'Romeo and Juliet'. Audiences were indeed soon to be offered a whole film of a Shakespeare play.

For years fans had clamoured to see 'Doug' and 'Little Mary' together, but the illustrious couple waited till Sound – and then chose **The Taming of the Shrew** (1929), as much a token of their exalted status as a desire (on her part at least) to change their image. In both New York and London it opened on a reserved-seat basis, but flopped despite kind reviews. It is less Shakespeare than slapstick, and

Sam Taylor demonstrates again that he was no director for Talkies. Fairbanks' Petruchio, all thrust and swagger, is certainly more to modern taste than Barrymore's Crouchback, but Miss Pickford is probably as bad as she feared she would be. Filming was marred by quarrels between them, and the famous marriage would soon be over; neither would have a career in Talkies, partly because audiences associated them with the trivial, pre-Depression decade just gone.

However, if their only film together was not the event of the season, then **Anna Christie** (1930) was – and with Hollywood so soon following Shakespeare with Eugene O'Neill it did indeed seem that the industry was growing up. 'Garbo Talks!' said the ads – a phrase that lives on down the years, witness to the potency of her legend and the skill of the publicity department. Much rested on it, since she was M-G-M's chief asset, and the public was proving fickle – for instance dooming John Gilbert's career by responding with laughs and jeers to his light baritone. Garbo's voice was intelligible and attractive, and O'Neill's heroine was of Swedish extraction. Audiences and critics were enthusiastic, not yet tired of tales of regeneration or questioning why sailors and whores were so bothered with pasts. Garbo's past this time is even less exalted than usual, but if uneasy with the slang she is good as a tired woman eager to start anew; she is prodigal with that frown – that crinkle between the brows – and also with that nervous half-laugh which unexpectedly ends in a chuckle: but Anna, in such circumstances, may have over-reacted. Otherwise, there is a superfluity of acting; neither of the male leads does it engagingly, but Marie Dressler's old toper convinces, with her weird challenging stares and slurred speech. Despite its customary self-boosting, M-G-M were among the technically retarded of the Talkie era, especially in treating stage material; but under Clarence Brown's direction, William Daniels does compositions of ship, sea and dockside which are almost as much of an asset as Garbo.

A German version was made simultaneously, with Garbo, directed by Jacques Feyder. Hollywood had panicked at losing the various European and Latin American markets, and it became the practice for important films to be made also in French, German, Spanish, or any one or two of these languages – usually with different artists, many brought to Los Angeles for the purpose; but even in only two versions the scheme proved uneconomical and was soon abandoned – except in the case of Maurice Chevalier, warranted a big enough star to make French versions until he left Hollywood in 1935.

Amidst the traumas and flurries and soul-searching, one great film emerged: **All Quiet on the Western Front** (1930), directed by Lewis Milestone with visual disregard for the microphone – Arthur Edeson's fluent camerawork was a revelation after so many static films – but employing it to pick up natural sounds and overhead conversation. Erich Maria Remarque's novel had been read by millions, which was why Universal bought it – and the huge $2 million cost of the film was justified at the box office. It was reissued in 1939 with a commentary pointing up the horrors of war, and again in 1950 – when Campbell Dixon in the

(London) *Daily Telegraph* summed up Remarque's creed: 'that all the fury and the agony were meaningless, a tale told by an idiot signifying nothing.' The screenplay (by Maxwell Anderson, Del Andrews, Milestone and George Abbott) keeps this firmly in view: the waste and disillusion; all the dead, and nothing accomplished; the glory at home, the misery of the battlefield and the fatalism of the soldiers – boy recruits, accepting and then adopting the cynicism of the veterans. When the hero (Lew Ayres) visits his old teacher, still holding forth on military glory, his response is: 'We live in the trenches. We fight. Sometimes we're killed and sometimes we aren't . . . Up there we know we're done for whether we live or die. We've had three years of it now.' And the film offers no bravery to counteract the futility: the old sergeant (Louis Wolheim) dies when straffed on a foraging mission, the hero dies reaching from a trench for a butterfly, shot down by a lazy sniper. At the end, more recruits are marching, superimposed upon a vast field of crosses, and as each turns towards the camera their eyes reflect only bewilderment. The Russian-born Milestone (1895–1980) would never again make a film as good.

Among the first German Talkies was Pabst's similar **Westfront 1918** (1930) based on a novel by Ernst Johannsen, 'Vier von der Infanterie'. It lacks the impact of the American film, and must already have seemed dated. Zuckmayer's play, 'Der Hauptmann von Köpenik', which also dates from 1930, depicts pre-war events in a way more representative of contemporary mood, and is much more scathing on the subject of German militarism; but this film gathers force, notably in the sequence when Karl (Gustav Diessl) goes home on leave to a populace not beginning to understand life at the front: the irony doesn't let up, and we, as much as Karl, are glad to get back to the camaraderie of the trenches and the graphic picture of life in a field hospital. After Karl has died, a Frenchman clutches his hand: 'Camarade . . . pas ennemis . . . de l'eau . . .' The film ends thus: 'ENDE?!'

Technically, the film shows its age with the explosions: the microphones picked up the bangs less well than the sound of falling earth nearer to them. When Pabst turned to a musical, **Die Dreigroschenoper** (1931), Sound techniques in Germany had not advanced sufficiently to do justice to Kurt Weill's score. The film is a synonym of Berlin at the time – though ostensibly set in Edwardian London – lit with a glare of desperate gaiety, and admitting to the principles of George Grosz while embracing the patterns of John Gay – for this is 'The Beggar's Opera', as adapted by Berthold Brecht, who unsuccessfully sued Pabst for misinterpretation. Weill might rather have sued over the removal of songs, less easily spared than elementary plotting and feeble attempts at humour, but those that remain are splendidly handled by Ernst Busch (as the streetsinger) and Lotte Lenya. As Mackie Messer, Rudolf Forster has the same sort of barbaric splendour as the London designed by Andrei Andreyev.

Pabst returned to the theme of 'All men are brothers' in **Kameradschaft** (1931), specifically addressed to French and German workers, and a co-production between the two countries, though the French version, *La Tragédie de la Mine*, is said to be considerably less radical. The setting is a small border town where a mining disaster causes the German workers to go to the rescue of Frenchmen – despite the frontiers, protocol, old wounds and international tension. The subject was a sensitive one, with the question of Alsace-Lorraine still in contention and when, because of the Depression, German resentment towards France was reaching a new peak. It is an uncluttered film, fresher than the majority of most subsequent mining dramas, but the people for whom it was intended were not interested, while its final note of warning – the authorities replacing the barriers – was removed by the distributors. Pabst learnt his lesson, and turned to escapism: **Die Herrin von Atlantis** (1932) or *L'Atlantide*, filmed on location in North Africa in German, French and English versions – all of them presumably superior to Feyder's old version of the tale, but it remains mumbo-jumbo despite Pabst's attempts to suggest a kingdom where all normal emotions are upended, from its Queen

(Brigitte Helm) downwards.

The film was surely too cynically undertaken to find a public, either, and it was not, in any case, the sort of escapism craved by German audiences who, after a decade of economic misery, were either basking in musicals or memories of the Prussian past – and indeed in a poll in 1931 they voted *Die Drei von der Tankstelle* (q.v.) their favourite film, and **Das Flötenkonzert von Sanssouci** (1930) third. This was the latest of the 'Fridericus' films, in this case directed by Gustav Ucicky but as usual starring Otto Gebühr, whose resemblance to Frederick the Great provided him with the means to a successful career. The series began in 1919, in the aftermath of the War, and this was the first Talkie 'Fridericus': the flag-waving apart, it is of the level of the George Arliss historicals (q.v.) which were its contemporaries – and a sad come-down for Ufa. It was exactly the type of film favoured by the company since its take-over by Hugenberg – even if, under his presidency, the new managing director, Ludwig Klitzsch, did persuade Pommer to return. Others also returned, since Ufa faced the problem of the American studios, of retaining its share of the markets in those countries which did not speak their language. The solution was held to be simultaneous ver-

Since the Silent picture was considered wholly international, it is curious that G.W. Pabst, hitherto a somewhat cynical chronicler of the malaise of society, should have chosen the coming of Talkies to preach international understanding. Both *Westfront 1918* and *Kameradschaft* (illustrated) are very fine, and if the propaganda in both is a little obvious, they remain remarkably realistic portraits of their time.

sions, but few of the English-language versions made headway in their intended countries, though the Germans continued to film in French throughout the Thirties. And the results are confusing, so that an international name like Conrad Veidt – who played in English versions in Hollywood and Britain – might turn up in both German and English, or in one or the other, in English sometimes dubbed and sometimes not. The engineers quickly became ingenious at combining dubbing and direct sound.

One such film overshadowed all the others, **Der Blaue Engel/The Blue Angel** (1930), marking a return to prestige for Ufa and a rare co-operation with an American company, Paramount, who were returning their German actor, Emil Jannings, and sending with him, to direct, Josef von Sternberg. The reputation of these two artists, and that of Pommer, was sufficient to cow Hugenberg, who disliked the socialist tone of Heinrich Mann's original novel, 'Professor Unrat'. It was Jannings's decision to eschew the latter part of it, in which the professor rises to become a pillar of society, in favour of his earlier lapse – when he becomes obsessed with a déclassée cabaret singer, Lola-Lola. This role was played by Marlene Dietrich (b. 1901), hitherto a minor star but immortal as this modern Carmen. Less entrancing than Louise Brooks in Pabst's two films, she is more her own mistress, not so much cruel as tough. We learn about her from her songs – 'Falling in Love Again', as haunting the thousandth time as the third, 'They Call Me Naughty Lola', 'Those Charming, Alarming Blonde Women', with its hints of bi-sexuality, and 'A Man, Just a Regular Man'. Sex is not only her business but her pleasure: the teasing, insolent smile will give way to open encouragement. Even her clothes tease. They conceal and reveal: a crinoline has no back, a skirt curls upwards to reveal a cancan panty and suspenders. For the professor, Lola-Lola's world is just out of reach, and her garters, which should be, are revealed to the world. She gives of herself, leaning back, hands on hips, white thighs gashed – and Dietrich was never more flesh-and-blood. The professor is the other paradox: the pleasure of her acceptance of him is the

first step towards public humiliation and the straitjacket. They are not even man and wife, except in his eyes. His fate is the last thing he expected. Jannings is brilliant, too self-conscious to draw tears, but as he rampages around screaming 'Cock-a-Doodle-Do' he evokes a deep hurt.

The film was a success everywhere, for many people the definitive film portrait of big city decadence in the Weimar Republic – but that was mainly because foreign distributors rejected other contemporary stories as either too depressing or too left-wing; the film's theme was tried and true, it had an international name, Jannings, and Paramount backing it. Pommer was capable of returning to that theme – without similar success – but in making multiple language versions he wisely chose subjects likely to be of first interest in the home market. Widely successful throughout Europe – but not in the U.S. – was the musical, **Die Drei von der Tankstelle** (1930), directed by Wilhelm Thiele (1890–1975) with a popular team of the Silents, Lilian Harvey and Willy Fritsch. Pommer had chosen Thiele for the first Talkie of the pair, both because he was Viennese and because he had studied Sound techniques: but the success of both *Liebeswalzer* and its English version, *Love Waltz*, was only relative. It was an old-fashioned operette, but this second film looked rather to *Sous les Toits de Paris* (q.v.), moving its similar theme from the city to, literally, the open road – where three young men (Fritsch, Oskar Karlweiss, Heinz Rühmann) counter bankruptcy by opening a garage. Audiences adored it because the music counterpointed the mime of the players, any of whom, at any given moment, is likely to break into song and dance. It instituted a series of proletarian musicals, of which **Ein Blonder Traum** (1932), directed by Paul Martin, touched less obliquely on the Depression by putting its equally improvident heroes into a converted railway carriage, in a meadow outside the town – as we find also in *Kühle Wampe* (q.v.), and by implication in *A Nous la Liberté* (q.v.). Lilian and Willy were expected to be only gay and light-hearted, and on this occasion they were joined by Willi Forst, the other major German musical star, before he turned to directing. Miss Harvey, for me, makes

words like 'coy' and 'arch' inadequate, and watching her pulling her skirts to her armpits and literally kicking her heels, smiling all the while, is as resistible an experience as cinema has to offer. Both films are so packed with *gemütlich* 'charm' that it is a shock to find that the second one was penned by Billy Wilder (q.v.) and Walter Reisch. Both, of course, went to Hollywood, as did Miss Harvey, though she was quickly returned when the American public failed to respond. Born in England, she remained a favourite in Germany till war was imminent, when she retreated to France, and thence to Britain, where she retired.

A number of the English versions were co-produced with the British studios, such as *Sunshine Susie* (q.v.), but the operettes which Pommer continued to make found more favour in France. Ufa's biggest success of all was made with both English and French versions, reflecting Pommer's belief that the 'book' of **Der Kongress Tanzt** (1931) was stronger than that of most operettes. The Congress concerned is that of Vienna, where Metternich (Veidt) schemes while the Czar (Fritsch) dallies with a shopgirl (Harvey). Erik Charell directed, another example of a director who made his only notable film under Pommer, and we might have preferred Lubitsch, whose staging of 'Beyond the Blue Horizon' is echoed in the film's most notable sequences, a song passed from customer to customer in a *heurigen*, and *'Das gibt's nur einmal'*, taken up by villagers and children as the shopgirl's carriage takes her to her lover.

The optimism of the Willy-Lilian musicals may have been inspired by *Menschen am Sonntag*, but whose freshness is testament to Pommer's wisdom in signing its chief instigator, Siodmack, to a contract. Inasmuch as it was made

Emil Jannings in the grip of one of the cinema's favourite themes, sexual obsession – happily led downwards from the moment she – Marlene Dietrich – slips off her panties on the stairs and drops them on his shoulder. She laughs when he proposes, but is flattered; later, when he is reduced to rolling on her stockings, she enjoys his humiliation. The film is *Der Blaue Engel*, made simultaneously in English as *The Blue Angel*, and the lady on the right is Rosa Valetti.

by young enthusiasts, it has been called avant-garde: it was certainly an attempt to bring realism to the cinema, and at Ufa Siodmack continued so to do, in **Abschied** (1930), a resolutely simple tale of life in a Berlin lodging-house. The characters are often funny – the morose maid, the man who borrows on the strength of becoming compère at a cabaret, the sister dance-team longing either for work or a date, the young jazz musician whose piano-playing is virtually the film's only music; and Siodmack makes something touching of the salesman (Aribert Mog) whose love is genuine enough while seducing but unlikely to survive on transfer to another town. **Voruntersuchung** (1931) is the more familiar world of German realism, opening as it does, and brilliantly, in a tenement populated by whores, as the lover of one of them, a student (Gustav Frölich), is implicated in her murder – which brings him in time to the enquiry of the title as conducted by a friend's father; in that role Albert Basserman is in the massive tradition of actors who do little to achieve the utmost effect, and if at that point the plot is conventional, the film is infinitely superior to any contemporary American crime film. Indeed, it bears witness to the maturity of the German cinema at this point, soon to tumble as people like Siodmack and Pommer were driven away after the Nazi rise to power.

The predominant artist of the new regime had already begun to direct – the actress Leni Riefenstahl (b. 1902), who broke away from her mentor, Fanck, and used much of her own money to make **Das Blaue Licht** (1932). It calls itself *ein Berglegende*, and is splendid on that level – the tale of a peasant girl who fatally draws handsome young villagers to the mountain peak whenever there is a full moon. She in turn is destroyed by materialism in the shape of an idealist (Mathias Wieman); and since he is German and the setting is Italy the dialogue is minimal. The views are beautiful, but as in the lady's more celebrated films, grandiloquent.

Studying Thiele's methods at Ufa, and taking advantage of his knowledge, had been René Clair, who had earlier called the Sound film 'a redoubtable monster, an unnatural creation': in the interim he had taken a trip to London to see the monster, as shipped from Hollywood, and it was because he was particularly taken with *The Broadway Melody* that he incorporated songs into **Sous les Toits de Paris** (1930), originally designed for score and only occasional dialogue. He therefore relied, as of old, on visual means to tell his story, and though to him that seemed natural he was widely regarded as a genius. Writing in *The Nation*, Alexander Bakshy said, 'He has produced a picture that is in many ways a little masterpiece, and he is lucky enough to be the first artist in a field that has been dominated by Holywood robots. Indeed, so great is one's relief and delight at seeing a fresh mind, unencumbered with hollow conventions and equipped with taste, subtle wit, and imaginative insight, apply itself to fashioning a work of art that [its] shortcomings inevitably recede.' Clair's achievement – and he was the first to do it – was the welding of three elements, dialogue, music and image, each commenting on the other from the first delirious moment when the camera pans down from the chimney-pots to the streetsinger (Albert Préjean). It was not a success in Paris, but launched by Tobis in Berlin with attendant publicity it soon repeated its German triumph the world over. Today, the charm lingers: its chief shortcoming is a plot so wispy that it blows away as you watch it – but without the compensating high spirits of the Clair films which followed.

For him, it was a trial run; **Le Million** (1931), converts a play by Berr and Guillemaud into 'une comédie musicale' – which means, in Clair's case, not a narrative that stops occasionally for a song, but one to which song is so integral that everyone sings: creditors pursuing the hero, cops chasing a crook, inevitably the opera-singers who provide the climax – and if neither of the heroes sings, there are unseen choirs to advise, warn or berate them. Clair removed chunks of the original dialogue, replacing them with his own lyrics; he injected the rhythm and created a fantasy which is not only effervescent but very, very funny. **A Nous la Liberté** (1931) has the same insouciance though his purpose was serious – 'to attack the idea of the sanctity of labour when it is not interesting or serious.' He later said he regretted using the musical comedy form, but the songs are integrated, and the material moves gracefully from satire to fantasy to all-out farce. The message has dated – that the greed of capitalism reduces men to machines – or, rather, it seems more a fancy of the age than a philosophical conviction: but it is less self-consciously delivered than in Chaplin, whose influence may also be felt in the plot, about two little men, tramps, whose friendship eventually survives the brief and accidental period when one becomes a millionaire.

Quartorze Juillet (1932) is both a tribute to Paris and France's national holiday, and, quite appropriately, gaiety is all – a wonderful feeling of being alive and belonging to the human race, even if Clair's people are puppets, to be manipulated by him in the cause of heartbreak as well as happiness. There are grave moments, as if Clair felt the responsibility of being a world-admired artist, probably the reason he turned whole-heartedly to satire in **Le Dernier Milliardaire** (1934) – though in the event the result, despite felicities, is long-windedly facetious. The screenplay was originally about a banker and a casino, but as Clair developed it, it became a treatise on dictatorship and royalty. Hitler, of course, had come to power, and Tobis, to whom it was contracted, refused to produce it. French backing was found, and further events confounded production – or, at least, distribution – when the King of Yugoslavia was assassinated in Marseilles, hardly a suitable prelude to Clair's feeble jokes. The actual idea of the plot is brilliant: a bankrupt principality woos back its one successful expatriate, a banker, promising a royal marriage, and it has no option but to accept his absurd laws after an accident has turned him into a buffoon. The film's references to the Stavisky affair, by implication critical of the authorities, caused disturbances during the Paris run and the film's subsequent failure in France caused Clair to accept an offer from Korda in Britain. He would not make a film in his native land again until after the War.

Clair's connection with **Prix de Beauté** (1930), often said to be written by

him, is slight. The scenario was submitted to Pabst, who thought it more suitable for Clair, but the latter liked only the final twist, and wrote a new script, incorporating it: for various reasons he never made it, and the idea passed to the Italian director, Augusto Genina, who wrote it and directed – memorably. Once again Louise Brooks is magical, this time as a stenographer who moves via a beauty contest to film stardom – but also to tragedy, as she lies shot by a jealous husband, and her image on the screen continues to sing, '*J'ai qu'un Amour, c'est Toi.*' The irony intended is representative of the film as a whole, but its lack of subtlety is matched by the pace and an astonishing variety of images – in such violent contrast to Genina's earlier work as to suggest that he was inspired by his star and the challenge of Sound, which he has mastered by ignoring it.

Typically, Marcel L'Herbier was drawn to that challenge, using the screams and bumps of an old dark house, and the winds howling round it, but **Le Mystère de la Chambre Jaune** (1930) is technically inept, and in this version Gaston Leroux's story is infantile to a degree; a sequel, **Le Parfum de la Dame en Noir** (1931), though pleasingly set in an art deco Côte d'Azur villa, shows only a mild advance in handling Sound, and the direction is hardly less amateurish. French cinema at this time, in contrast to the German, often seemed determined on puerility, and **On Purge Bébé** (1931) is only minor Feydeau, with jokes about chamber-pots and purgatives, bearable only for Michel Simon as a Feydeau man urbanely coping with the unexpected. Jean Renoir made it, to prove that he could work economically, since he wanted backing to film a novel by Georges de la Fouchardière – which the film's popularity obtained for him. **La Chienne** (1931) proved that when not working quickly and cheaply he could respond to the requirements of Sound, as with the piano being practised across the courtyard, or the gabbling of the crowd as the murderer slips away. The story does resemble that of *Der Blaue Engel*, at the same time more endearing and more misogynist, since *l'homme obsédé* is played by M. Simon, given both a nagging wife and

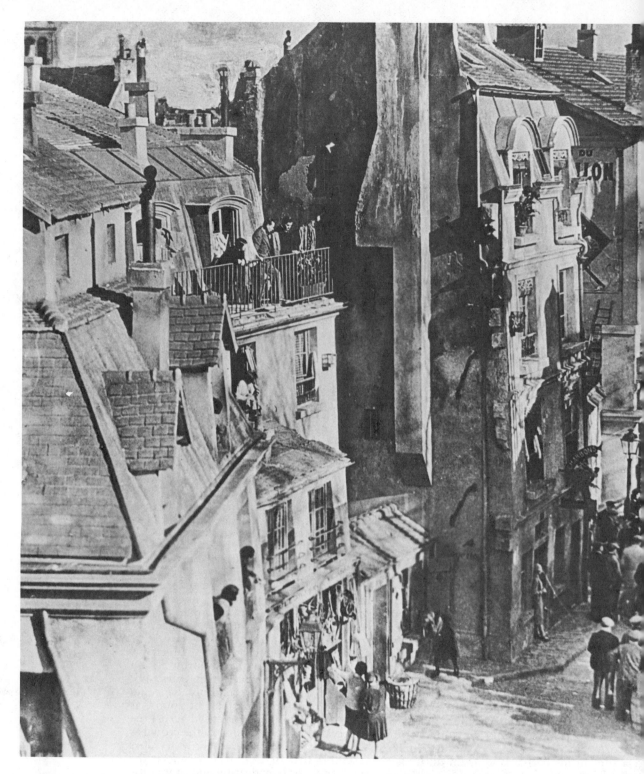

Almost alone René Clair brought a touch of springtime to the Talkies – for while all around stultified, he brought not only grace and gaiety but almost immediate command of the new medium. ABOVE, *Sous les Toits de Paris* – though its success also owed something to its haunting title tune, and to its portrait of one quarter of Paris. Orson Welles once observed that any fool could take a camera into the streets of Paris, but Clair created his own – as aided by his designer, Lazare Meerson. ABOVE RIGHT, *Le Million*, most Parisian of comedies, with a happy ending for René Lefèvre and Annabella, with, far right, Raymond Cordy watching them. RIGHT, *A Nous la Liberté* and what is perhaps the best-remembered scene in all Clair, when the wind scatters the money and then the silk hats of the nobs and nabobs, unable to resist the swirling bank-notes.

The Paris of René Clair

Talkies!

The Provençal charm of Pagnol's *Marius* trilogy remains strong, though the story of the first two films can be briefly put: Marius, the son of a saloon–owner, César (Raimu), dreams of faraway climes; he loves Fanny, daughter of Honorine (Alida Rouffe) who keeps the shellfish stall, but hesitates – and she, pregnant, marries Panisse (Charpin), a kindly, elderly widower. Raimu, right, in *Fanny*, with, from left to right, Robert Vattier, Mihalesco, Charpin, Paul Dulac and Mlle Rouffe.

a final joyous shot which is a prelude to *Boudu Sauvé des Eaux* (q.v.). These people are trapped in their environment – the pimps' bar, the commonplace flat of the fancy lady, the heavily draped apartment – and the film's producers found that they neither liked that nor Renoir's handling of Sound, so that he was initially barred from the cutting-room. Complicated wrangles followed before the film broke records in Paris, the one fact cancelling out the other so that Renoir had difficulty setting up his next project.

French producers, as unimaginative as any anywhere, were further stifled by foreign competition and foreign intervention, being forced to pay steep prices for Sound equipment – controlled by either Western Electric of the U.S. or Tobis in Germany. Tobis made French films in Berlin, and to their credit, opened a studio near Paris – as did Paramount, chief among the Hollywood companies unwilling to allow their French market to drain away. Its studio, said Sadoul, resembled a tower of Babel, as it

attempted as many multilingual versions as was economically possible. The majority of these were hardly more than photographed plays of appalling quality, but the distinction of **Marius** (1931) is immediately clear, as adapted by Marcel Pagnol (1895–1974) from his popular comedy-drama of life on the Marseilles waterfront. This ex-school teacher wrote with feeling, sly observation and great good humour, and, as on the stage, his interpreters were Pierre Fresnay in the title-role, Raimu as his father, and Charpin as his father's friend. Since its appeal was supposedly parochial, Paramount sanctioned no other language versions, though the director was one of the several Europeans returned from Hollywood for such purpose, Alexander Korda. Pagnol himself produced the sequel, **Fanny** (1932), choosing Marc Allégret to direct – though the direction of both films is as perfunctory as their contents are memorable. Pagnol himself directed **César** (1936), the only one of the trilogy written expressly for the screen, and it is not to be mentioned in the same breath – though that is because of the screenplay, mechanical and even more verbose. The characters have become bourgeois, and worst of all, César-Raimu (q.v.) has lost his magnificent rages and hypocrisies to become a powdered-hair cupid.

Owing to exhibitor indifference and censorship it was not until 1949 that Anglo-Saxon reviewers and audiences became familiar with the trilogy, falling in love with it and thus aligning themselves with the French public rather than the French critics, who had sneered – and it has remained a repertory item. Conversely, forgotten today is the one French Talkie – apart from Clair – to make a popular breakthrough abroad, **Le Rosier de Madame Husson** (1931), directed by Bernard-Deschamps and adapted from a story by de Maupassant (and the source, incidentally, of Britten's opera 'Albert Herring'). Its appeal remains apparent: a rollicking tale of small town hypocrisy, with those 'real' faces we associate with French movies. The town council, unable to nominate anyone to receive Mme Husson's annual cheque to the most virtuous woman ('Ah non, elle habite tout près de la caserne'). suggest a man, who, armed with cheque and new-found confidence, sets out to make up for lost time. Fernandel is this youth of divine imbecility, and Françoise Rosay (q.v.) is hardly less funny as the narrow-minded donor – with a particularly low view of the cinema.

Had she gone to it, she would have been incensed by Buñuel's **L'Age d'Or** (1930), which he said later was 'a deliberate seeking of scandal, dedicated to attacking the representatives of "order" and ridiculing their "eternal" principles.' The time, he thought, called for such a spirit; hence the ironic title, and it was 'the only film in my career conceived and created in a state of euphoria and enthusiasm' – which may be why it lashes out in all directions, anxious to hurt and shock as many spectators as possible. It has satire (mitres on skeletons), black comedy (a blind man kicked), eroticism (a girl sucks the toe of a statue while the Liebestod plays), heresy (Christ as the Marquis de Sade, or vice-versa) and a deep approval of lust. Audiences today, hipped-on to Buñuel's loathing of Church and State, laugh knowingly and applaud, in depressing contrast to his own after-thought, in 1965, 'How is it possible to shock after the Nazi mass murders and the atom bombs dropped on Japan? I feel today that the use of scandal is a negative action. L'Age d'Or, which in its day was a militant film aimed at raping clear consciences – and was therefore scandalous – is now a harmless work.' We might, however, still reflect on the responsibility of Church and State in regard to the concentration camps and nuclear warfare. At the time, many of its shafts found their targets, and their recipients retaliated: an alliance of the Jeunesse Catholiques, the Ligues des Patriotes and the Ligue Antijuive attacked the cinema, attracting the right-wing press, which promptly denounced the film. The censor stepped in with a complete ban – which was to remain in force in France for over twenty years.

Like *Le Chien Andalou*, it had been financed by the Vicomte de Noailles, whose money also permitted an indulgence to Jean Cocteau (1889–1963), swept away by Buñuel's experiments in putting surrealism on the screen. Made in 1930, **Le Sang d'un Poète** was not shown till two years later, because it was reshot when some of the relatives of the aristocratic performers objected to their applauding a funeral, and because the de Noailles family wanted the fuss over *L'Age d'Or* to die down. The title during filming was *La Vie d'un Poète*, but Cocteau thought up one with more reverberation, whose pretension he then had to justify: a fan of quite simple films, he could not bear to make one himself, and this one announces itself as dedicated to certain Renaissance 'painters of enigma'. A mish-mash of recollection, dreams and images, the film is only interesting as a forerunner for the later more responsible and organised films – *Orphée* (q.v.), with the same mirror through which the hero must walk, and *Les Enfants Terribles* (q.v.), though the snowball episode had already been used in the book of the name. 'Etonne moi', Diaghilev had said to him, but when a man says *'merde'* several times it is hardly in the same league as Buñuel's attempt to shock.

The Vicomte had thrown away his money to scandalise a few, and declined to do so again, while Buñuel discovered, as he said later, that surrealism had shown him that 'in life there is a moral direction man cannot but follow' – and thus returned to Spain to make a documentary study, **Las Hurdes** (1932), also known as *Land Without Bread*. He realised that the desperate lives of the Hurdanos did not need nor could suffer the indignity of 'interpretation'. 'Lack of nourishment, lack of hygiene and intermarriage' notes the commentary, as the camera settles on the face of a thirty-two-year-old woman who looks sixty. The region is not far from Salamanca, fifty-two villages with a population of 8,000, living on beans and potatoes except when supplies dry up and they go to the hills to forage for unripe cherries. The churches contain the wealth, and though Buñuel restricted his reference to one plain edifice, that was enough to have the film banned in Spain. Such conditions – the later commentary explains – brought the Civil War, and it was not till then that the film achieved its first public showings, in France. Buñuel had by then emigrated to the U.S., and when he eventually resumed filming, the plea for pity and care that is *Las Hurdes* would be more typical of his work than his two avant-garde films.

In Britain, the film-makers remained immune from such preoccupations, and just as certainly they were unprepared for Sound – despite a number of experimental shorts, starting with a sequence from Shaw's *Saint Joan*, produced by Lee De Forest, and featuring the play's first interpreter, Sybil Thorndike. That was available at the time of *The Jazz Singer*, but it was not till 1929 that the first Sound feature-length film appeared, **Kitty**, directed by Victor Saville and based on a novel by Warwick Deeping, about a tobacconist's daughter (Estelle Brody) whose romance with a soldier (John Stuart) is blighted by his war wounds and aristocratic mother. Trade-shown as a Silent, the reactions were sufficiently positive as to cause its producers, Saville and B.I.P., to send its principals to New York to refilm the last three reels with Sound, duplicating the interiors and replacing the Thameside locations with hastily painted back-cloths. Herbert Wilcox also hurried to the U.S., to produce for his own company the All-Talking *Black Waters*, a melodrama with an American director, Marshall Neilan, and a number of American players including its stars, James Kirkwood and Mary Brian. It had been predicted that the British would not understand American dialect, but Hollywood financial interests ensured that its films were shown, and when audiences indicated that, dialect or not, they continued to prefer them to their native product, British studios wired for Sound. At B.I.P., Alfred Hitchcock was preparing **Blackmail** (1929), and Maxwell agreed to convert the last reel to Sound – till panic hit the industry, and it was decided to re-film a number of the earlier sequences. Since certain scenes already filmed could be 'played' with only sound effects, the star, Anny Ondra, was retained; but as her Czech accent rendered her dialogue unintelligible, in reshooting she mouthed the words while another actress, Joan Barry, spoke them into a microphone behind the scenery. The combination of the heavy histrionics of the one and the 'refained' voice of the other makes this heroine one of the most

tiresome on record – though it is admittedly hard to sympathise with one who has agreed to pose for an artist late at night and then is surprised to find that the sight of her step-ins drives him wild. That she refuses to tell her Scotland Yard boyfriend (John Longden) that she has murdered, and that he, once arriving at the truth, behaves as suspiciously as she, is reason enough for Hitchcock to dismiss the story as 'rather simple' – but it is recognisably a film of this director: the chase through the British Museum, his first use of a famous building for climax; the blackmailer whistling 'The Best Things in Life are Free' as the detective hands over the cash; the camera swooping down on the knife during the struggle behind the curtains; and the famous scene as the heroine hears nothing but the word 'knife' as the silly neighbour gossips. The last of these is the Sound equivalent of the close-up of the mouth in *Sunrise*, and there are borrowings from *Geheimnisse einer Seele* (the recurring image of the knife) and *Varieté* (the off-screen murder): but they were, not unreasonably, much praised – though in the U.S. this could not persuade the public to sample them. In Australia, the public was denied the opportunity, presumably because the murderess did not pay the price.

The qualities of this confused melange of Silence and Sound helped to enshrine it as 'Britain's First Talkie', thus obliterating the claims of *Taxi for Two*, simultaneously on view, a Michael Balcon production directed by Alexander Esway, no longer available for verification – and which, incidentally, destroyed the career of its star, Mabel Poulton, who was found to have a harsh cockney accent. There is nothing cinematic about **Juno and the Paycock** (1929), as adapted from Sean O'Casey's play by Hitchcock and his wife, Alma Reville, a regular collaborator during the next decade. Filmed because the Abbey Theatre cast had recently been successful in New York, the players include a number from the original Dublin and London productions five years earlier – Sara Allgood, Maire O'Neill, Sydney Morgan and Barry Fitzgerald, the latter demoted to 'orator'; Edward Chapman, brought in to play 'Captain' Jack, is not of the same quality, and the piece which in the theatre can be exhilarating – cf. Laurence Olivier's National production in 1966 – is merely cramped and dowdy. Hitchcock had been handed the assignment as Britain's leading director but the impetus gained by *Blackmail* was lost in a number of atrociously directed films – photographed plays stagily acted, and occasionally intercut with arty shots. **Murder** (1930) is a whodunnit with a famous actor-manager (Herbert Marshall) turned amateur detective, and a trapeze-artist (Esme Percy) revealed as the murderer – incredibly misunderstood by François Truffaut to be transvestite, and therefore the film a treatise on homosexuality – on which Hitchcock didn't demur, since this made him a 'daring' director of the period. **The Skin Game** (1931) is indeed retarded, as adapted by the director and his wife from Galsworthy's play about a warring squire (C. V. France) and a nouveau riche industrialist (Edmund Gwenn); and although **Number Seventeen** (1932) is more of a film, with bumps in the night and a railway chase, it is also surely one of the silliest ever made. However, **Rich and Strange** (1931) is an exceptionally pleasing picture, about a bowler-hatted clerk (Henry Kendall) enabled by a kind relative to achieve his dream of seeing the world: he and his wife (Joan Barry, the first of Hitchcock's blondes) go to the Folies-Bergères and get drunk in Paris, enjoying a flurry of shipboard flirtations on the classic route to Empire – Port Said, Colombo and Singapore. Lacking in sophistication despite moments of irony, the piece nevertheless offered proof that Hitchcock might become a good director if he ever became as interested in people as he was in film-form.

Hitchcock was connected with one other disaster during his spell at B.I.P., **Elstree Calling** (1930), an all-star revue in which he directed a couple of sketches, and which was shot in twelve days at a cost of £13,000 – which doesn't explain why it is even worse than the Hollywood revues with which it hoped to compete. It may be endured, however, for the sake of the two songs by Lily Morris, the music hall comedienne. 'Shows Hollywood how to do it,' said Iris Barry, then film critic of the *Daily Mail* – and that is an early example of the xenophobic film 'criticism' which was to bolster the smug local industry through another thirty years of mainly dreadful product.

Michael Balcon's first Talkie, **Journey's End** (1930), was also made in the U.S. R. C. Sherriff's play about the trenches had, after an initial Sunday-evening performance, taken London by storm – to the extent that the film rights were sold for the then hefty sum of £16,000, an amount eventually shared by Balcon and his chief contender, Welsh Pearson. Since the latter had no studio and Gainsborough was not wired for Sound, a deal was done with one of the lesser Hollywood studios, Tiffany, with James Whale directing, as he had in London and New York, and Colin Clive from the West End production again in the lead. In Britain the film was a considerable success, but Tiffany were not too happy, despite *The New York Times* view that it was 'absorbing' and contained scenes 'undoubtedly far better than any other glimpses of warfare that have come to the screen.' These interpolated sequences on the battlefield are comparable to those in *All Quiet on the Western Front,* but the rest of it is a photographed play, despite Whale's attempt to provide visual variety; the acting is of theatrical intensity, totally unsuitable on film to this grim, purposeful slice of life.

Tiffany also provided facilities for Victor Saville, who wanted to do a quick Talkie remake of *Woman to Woman*: Balcon was also involved, and Saville returned to work with him after a last co-production with Maxwell, **The W Plan** (1930), an adventure story of startling fatuity, directed by Saville at snail's pace, and starring Brian Aherne as a British officer behind the German lines. It has often seemed that the British cinema has been dominated by war films, but those of this period were triggered off by the surprise success of Sherriff's play – thus very much paralleling the Broadway-Hollywood situation with regard to the genre. However, one company, British Instructional, specialised in reconstructions of the battles of the War, and could be expected to provide a good Gallipoli in **Tell England** (1931), as adapted from Ernest Raymond's novel – which had indeed been the most popular book on the War. The producer, Bruce Woolfe, had previously made *Zeebrugge* and *Mons*; he had also fostered the career of Anthony

Talkies!

Annabella and Gustav Fröhlich in Paul Fejos's comedy of the Depression, *Sonnenstrahl* – which translates as 'Ray of Sunshine', though we know it not by that title since there were no takers for the English version made simultaneously. Its view of the Depression is an often moving account of the era: and if its optimism is a little too facile it at least was what audiences needed.

Asquith, who wrote the script and co-directed with Geoffrey Barkas, writer of *The Somme* for this company. Their point of view is resolutely that of the 'officers and gentlemen', which makes absurd many of the scenes in the Mess and, more surprisingly, the earlier sequences of the public schoolboys and their tea-gowned mothers in the Grantchester-like calm of peace. Equally surprisingly, the film turns into a searing indictment of the fact of war. As one battalion dismounts, each man is mown down by machine-guns, and for them the counter-order came too late: 'It is inadvisable to send any more men ashore as conditions are unfavourable.' Asquith uses a dynamic Russian-style cutting and at least for fifteen minutes the film is as good as *All Quiet*. The (London) *Evening News* thought it 'one of the two or three outstanding British Talkies made so far,' but that, of course, is not saying much.

Other countries took longer to adapt to Sound, and for most of them dual-language versions, at least, became briefly a fact of life. As European directors returned from Hollywood, they saw their chances in charge of these films. Paul Fejos tried Britain, without success, and went to France to direct a new version of *Fantômas*; then in his native Hungary

he arranged a Franco-Hungarian co-production, **Tavaszi Zápor/Marie – Legende Hongroise** (1932). English and German versions were also made, but in fact there is little speech, and the characters too often gesture when words would be more appropriate – in keeping at least with the embarrassing naivety of the story, concerning a pregnant maid cast out by her employers and her odyssey to an ending which recalls 'Liliom'. There are haunting images of white cottage and steeple, and the flower-like face of Annabella conveys the right sort of dotty passion: but it is not surprising that British and American distributors thought it unsuitable for their publics. However, it is sad that they turned down the English version of **Sonnenstrahl** (1933), made also in French and German, in Vienna, also with Annabella, who with Gustav Frölich forms a couple who meet at the point of suicide and survive the vagaries of unemployment in that city. Adolf Weith's photography, much of it on location, is sparkling, and the soundtrack is freshly used: indeed, it is a film of great skill and charm – too much so at times, as the couple mime in a travel-office, or join in the song at the cab-drivers' ball. The unlikely happy ending recalls *Lonesome*; and it is a pleasure after *Marie*, grimly facing the world, to find the world helping the young couple. Fejos would not be the only one to use a fairy-tale approach to help audiences through the Depression, and it is sad that his own career declined – that after moving from country to country in search of commercial projects he finally turned to anthropological films.

Victor Sjöström directed the first Swedish Sound film, **The Markurells of Wadköping** (1931), made also in German as *Vater und Sohn*. He had directed a Talkie at M-G-M, *A Lady to Love,* which hasn't survived, and was in fact planning to resettle in Sweden when offered an assignment because of his experience with Sound. He chose a novel by his old collaborator, Hjalmar Bergman, and wrote the screenplay together with him, an Ibsen-like tale of a proud man who learns that his beloved son is not his own. The man is both mean and exuberant, unloved by the townsfolk, completely wrapped up in both his family and vindictiveness towards a man who wronged him years before. Unlike the character in the original, Sjöström – also acting the role – makes him likeable enough for audiences, convincing us that the discovery of his son's real parentage is his greatest tragedy. The last section of the film is solely concerned with his anguish: at first, disbelief and doubt; then anger and bitterness. He takes off his coat and puts it on continually; when his anger and bewilderment have calmed he takes refuge in despair – until, like a true Sjöström hero, he finally finds compassion and adheres to the word of God. The performance is equal to the role, and though Sjöström remains an uninventive technician, he gives the film a sobriety rare for the time; it is not a film like those of his heroic period, but is equally uncompromising. Its timing was wrong, for it failed, and Sjöström retired from directing, apart from a British historical adventure in 1937, *Under the Red Robe,* which clearly didn't interest him. He returned to the stage and acted also in other people's films, an ironic fate for the greatest film director of his era.

In the Soviet Union, film-makers welcomed Sound since it gave propaganda a new dimension. At least, the first Russian Sound films indicate a turning away from social drama to outright propaganda, and it was the director of *Bed and Sofa*, Abram Room, who made the first one, *Plan of Great Works* (1930), albeit that it has a track of music and effects, with a few agit-prop speeches. Its subject was the Five Year Plan, told in documentary fashion, and Dziga-Vertov's **Enthusiasm, or Symphony of the Donbas** (1931) would seem to be a companion picture, though its peasants and coal miners do take time off to dance a measure or storm the churches. Vertov was clearly so pleased with the sounds of plant, mine and factory that music is secondary. The first Sound dramatic picture was *The Earth Thirsts* (1930), with a plot about canal construction, but the first Russian Talkie seen widely in the West was **Road to Life** (1931), directed by Nikolai Ekk. In his review, Forsyth Hardy quoted a friend who claimed 'There are two films and only *two*: the Charlie Chaplin comedy and the Russian propagandist films, no

matter if red as hell, fierce, exaggerated in method, unlikeable in aggression, but dammit, purposeful.' The rest, he thought, were rubbish, and I wonder whether he could have seen this film, purposeful to no purpose. It deals with a real problem, those children left homeless by the Revolution. Sent to a school for rehabilitation, they learn boot-making, till come the winter floods, and they are idle. Are they put to drill or gymnastics, theatricals or painting? No: they build a railway, a real railway – those, that is, who have not returned to the drinking-dens of the non-Soviets. One expects to find that camel from another Road film, *Road to Morocco*, who commented, 'This is the screwiest picture I was ever in.'

Western intellectual fervour for such Soviet movies may be seen in the context of those Cambridge undergraduates who later spied for the Russians; and presumably some indulgence towards naivety had lingered, ensuring a belated welcome, over forty years later, to **Happiness**, directed in 1934 by Alexander Medvekin. Medvekin, a former Red Cavalry officer, believed absolutely in the party dictum of the importance of film, and turned a train into a film studio, travelling throughout the country to film the people and show them the end product. None of these films survive, but the work, he said in 1971, inspired him to make this film, which is anti-capitalist propaganda so simple-minded as to be of interest only to those who believe in anti-capitalist propaganda for the simple-minded. It is a theatrical burlesque in the style of Méliès but lacking his inventiveness and wit. It is also Silent, and that perhaps had something to do with its kindly Western press reception. Now, as then, the Silent screen has its advocates. It was the general public which so decisively rejected it. When the Talkie revolution started, the medium retrogressed to the equivalent of baby-talk: by the time it was complete, cinemagoing was a habit far more ingrained than it had ever been before. For millions the world over, life was inconceivable without the weekly or twice-weekly visit to the cinema, and so it would be for the next two decades.

10

Japan: The First Masters

THE JAPANESE cinema, though as wedded to studio control and the star-system as any other, has always been reliant on a chain of directors, some of them among the greatest ever to work in the medium. One reason for the early excellence of Japanese films is the fact that, unlike most Western countries, the cinema was almost immediately respectable, accepted both by intellectuals and the groundlings. Its first films were the expected street scenes and records of the Kabuki theatre, and indeed for years Japanese cinema was dependent on the Kabuki, with female impersonators and the *benshi*, who narrated the Silent films as they unfolded. Nevertheless, occasional attempts were made to 'free' the cinema, and the pioneer Norimasa Kaeriyama both filmed on location and introduced women to play the female roles. The greatest changes, however, were brought about by the earthquake of 1923, which devastated the studios in Tokyo. By the time that production was, shakily, resumed in Kyoto (the other film-making centre), exhibitors had had to turn to foreign films as programme-fillers, and the popularity of these persuaded Japanese film-makers to modernise their product. Additionally, the shock of the earthquake caused audiences to demand subjects more relevant to the times than Kabuki tales.

Two great directors emerged during this period, Yasujiro Ozu (q.v.) and Kenji Mizoguchi (q.v.), though their work would remain unknown abroad for another thirty years. By chance, the only director known earlier in the West was Teinosuke Kinugasa (b. 1896), justly, perhaps, since he was one of those most susceptible to Western influences. He was particularly drawn to experimentation, to which he

gave full vent in **A Page of Madness** (1926) – which by strange coincidence finally arrived in the West in 1973 concurrently with another aged curiosity, the Soviet *Happiness*. Such story as is discernible in Kinugasa's film concerns an old seaman now working in an asylum where his wife is incarcerated, and its inspiration is *Caligari* – about which Kinugasa had only read, since it had not been shown in Japan at the time. Kinugasa had been a female impersonator in the Kabuki and, as such, had entered films with Nikkatsu in 1917; when that company began hiring actresses, in 1922, he took part in the consequent strike and moved to another company, Makino, for whom he directed as well as acted. He was directing as late as 1967, but of the hundred films he made in just over fifty years only two are, or have been, widely known in the West. One is *Gate of Hell* (q.v.), one of the first Japanese films to arrive in the wake of *Rashomon* (q.v.), after the revelation provided by that film in 1951; the other is **Crossways** (1928), one of the few Japanese movies seen in the West prior to that. It is a typical Japanese 'family' subject, about a no-good rip whose adoration for 'a painted beauty' leads to his losing his sight, and his loving sister, who prostitutes herself in order to help him. As in *A Page of Madness,* a confusion between past and present is indicated by furious intercutting – a sophistication of expression unknown, or at least unused, in the West till the nouvelle vague in the early Sixties.

If we knew only these three films by Kinugasa, we might jump to many wrong conclusions. We would be correct in supposing from *Gate of Hell* that the Japanese make superb historical films, but we would be wrong in attributing a strong Germanic influence – also apparent in *Crossways,* gloomier and darker than many similar Japanese films and suggesting that Kinugasa was emulating such films as *Die Strasse.* Japanese directors were fascinated by foreign film-makers, and their films of the Twenties and Thirties abound with references, particularly to Hollywood: but their work does not seem to have been unduly influenced. A characteristic of the pre-war Japanese cinema is its neutrality. The traditions of the country's art and literature had decreed that it must be decorative, small-scale and civilised. It might move towards thundering melodrama or harsh social criticism, but it avoided the big gesture: there was no Eisenstein, no Griffith, Carné (q.v.), Dupont or Borzage. The films were divided into *gendai-geki,* or modern subjects, or *jidai-geki,* which in principle meant stories set before the abolition of feudalism in 1871. They could be divided then again into stories of the family, of the theatre, of the geisha, the samurai, the student and, occasionally, of the soldier or the criminal – with, as in *Crossways,* some overlapping. The contemporary dramas tend to be static, with little movement either of gesture or camera – in both of which respects the historical films go to the other extreme. Yet there is an overall modesty, certainly justified on those occasions when shooting seems to have started without an organised screenplay – a drawback of many of the period films. The modesty was not justified: many Japanese films of this time have a maturity of subject and viewpoint in advance of the movies of the West.

Even so, a number of the more placid dramas require from the Western viewer some degree of patience – and I am thinking of two Silents by two of the masters, Gosho's **Dancer of Izu** (1933) and Shimazu's **Okoto and Sasuke** (1935). The former concerns a spendthrift brother and his sister, the student who loves her and the mine-owner who is cruel to all of them; the latter, also slow and virtually incomprehensible, features a blind musician, her faithful servant and her playboy seducer. The story was filmed again by Kinugasa in 1961, to remind us how much the Japanese cinema, already repetitious in choice of subject, relies on remakes.

The *shomin-geki* (a modern working-class subject) is said to have been virtually invented by Yasujiro Shimazu (1897–1945), who made approximately one hundred and forty-four films during his twenty-five-year career, most of them for the Shochiku company; he was assistant director on one of the most celebrated early films, *Souls on the Road* (1921), and was the mentor for another generation of directors, including Gosho, Toyoda, Yoshimura and Kinoshita. (The traditional master-pupil relationship in Japanese art became axiomatic in the film industry – as, also, in France and Italy.) Heinosuke Gosho (1902–81) made around one hundred films, and *Dancer of Izu* gives little indication of his capabilities – just as *Okoto and Sasuke* does not compare with Shimazu's earlier *Our Neighbour, Miss Yae* (q.v.), which is a Talkie. The coming of Sound to the Japanese cinema was a prolonged affair, and indeed Gosho had directed the first Talkie, *The Neighbour's Wife and Mine,* in 1931.

Clearly, no hard and fast conclusions can be drawn, but from out of the vastness of pre-war Japanese cinema unknown to the West the works of two great directors have fortunately been made available. Yasujiro Ozu (1903–63) studied at Waseda University and entered films as assistant to Tadamoto Okuba at Shochiku in 1923. He directed his first film in 1927, but the first to survive is **Days of Youth** (1929), the chief interest of which is its indication of a director of talent, but one still in search of a personal style. He admired Chaplin and Rex Ingram, and said once that he became a director because of Ince's *Civilisation.* His interest in Hollywood is apparent in his early films, invariably featuring American movie-posters as part of their interior decor; all of them reflect a fascination with the Westernisation of Japan, as for instance when girls in modern dress mock young men in traditional costume. His preferred subjects for study were petty crooks and students – the former basing themselves on the gangsters of Hollywood movies, and the latter looking to the West for enlightenment and entertainment. The student rituals in **I Flunked, But . . .** (1930) have been copied from *The Freshman;* and the hero common to both this film and *Days of Youth* – played by Tatsuo Saito – is indeed based on Harold Lloyd. Between the two films, Ozu developed his style – a combination of that of his master, Okuba, when he handled comedy, and of the Shochiku house style, which was formed from a belief that what the public wanted was to leave the cinema contented from an adroit mixture of laughter and tears.

This style of Ozu's is not that of his better-known later films. There are quick bursts of action, usually handled with a travelling camera, and the detail is more telling. All Silent directors had learnt to use what we may summarise as the 'guttering candle' image, to suggest the passage of time, but Ozu repudiated symbolism in favour of the banal, everyday object – a hand closing a briefcase, a doll abandoned on a chair, a stubbed-out cigarette, an alarm clock being switched off. In *Days of Youth* a student carefully hangs up trousers and socks by their supporters; in *I Flunked, But . . .* a shirt bearing the exam answers is sent to the laundry; in *The Lady and the Beard* (1931) a nervous student pulls the stuffing out of his chair during an interview. In images and anecdotes Ozu offers a portrait of Tokyo circa 1930 which is in itself an invaluable record.

Walk Cheerfully (1930) has a familiar plot – the man who reforms for a good woman – but it also has a vivid picture of a small section of Japanese society: the girl's mother, worried about her losing her job; the girl's boss, smug and dapper in a tail coat; and the *gens de milieu,* hanging out in boxing gyms and cheap bars, the girls with sulky painted faces, the men apeing American gangsters in their dandyish clothes. The contrast between this fringe of the underworld and the office workers of Tokyo is made again in **Dragnet Girl** (1933), also written by Takeo Ikeda, and Ozu's last film in the genre; a reformation is again effected at the end, and themes from other films recur, such as the girl who pays for her brother's education and the girl whose idea of goodness is to knit her boyfriend a pair of socks. With Ozu, only gangsters are allowed girlfriends, adding to their glamour; for students, women are either sisters or mothers or the idealised unattainable. He never married, and lived all his life with his mother. His work suggests that he was an amused and loving observer of the human race, as exemplified in **That Night's Wife** (1930), about the growing sympathy between pursuer and pursued – the man who has robbed a bank for the sake of his sick baby, and the detective who has chased him to his apartment.

Tokyo Chorus is Ozu's twenty-second

film – the sixth to survive – and the third he made in 1931: his art is clearly deepening in this tale of a student, with a wife and children, who is sacked from college on a point of principle. The children do not understand, and if the relevent sequence is extraordinary in its insight into family life we may divine that for the director himself the break from college was one of the most profound of experiences. The next two surviving films, **I Was Born, But . . .** (1932) and **Where Now Are the Dreams of Youth** (1932), take up the same themes in deliciously comic manner, the latter made in an enforced delay during the production of the earlier film. It concerns a student forced to leave school and take over his father's company, and is a minor film but unique in Ozu's work by virtue of a sequence of physical violence – when the hero repeatedly strikes an old and unprotesting friend.

I Was Born, But . . . is about two small boys and their realisation that their father is not the 'big' man they thought. The underlying assumption that all men are not equal – which, as the mother says, is something with which they must learn to live – often recurs in Ozu's films about children. Though still a young man, he constantly strove to recapture his own past in his films. Of this one he said that he had hoped to make it cheerful but it turned out very dark and sad. Indeed, he now began to move towards studies of poverty, which to him – as to Renoir in the West – was neither ennobling nor sad. His people are cheerful and well-intentioned, often mistaken but resilient, with problems that are universal. The fact that in his own country Ozu was thought the most Japanese of their directors, unexportable long after *Rashomon,* would seem to indicate that they judged Western taste by the West's own films. The War with Japan would have happened regardless of whether or not we had known Ozu's work, but many Westerners would have found it difficult to reconcile his gentle characters with the view of the nation as then propounded in news bulletins.

Ozu's popularity with film goers had been assured by his first dozen films, but Shochiku was so uncertain of *I Was Born, But . . .* that release was delayed: however, it went on to win the country's leading film award, the *Kinema Jumpo's* first prize – which Ozu subsequently won for three consecutive years. There was no pressure on him, therefore, to turn to Sound; he wanted to explore the possibilities of Silents before they were discontinued. We can see now that his late, ossified style was beginning to evolve – he has just dispensed with the dissolve – but in brevity of expression he foreshadows Antonioni (q.v.). He is so contemporary in feeling that the films, were they in any degree 'bigger', would be astounding. As with Sjöström, he worked within the native tradition, which is why his achievement is so different – concise and delicate: together with Keaton, they understood the medium's capabilities and drawbacks more clearly than other Silent directors.

His additional reason for holding out against Talkies was that he had promised his cameraman, Hideo Shigehara, to wait until the latter had perfected the Sound system that he was developing. The suspicion that Ozu's art did not need Speech is borne out by the comparative dullness of his first two Sound films, **The Only Son** (1936) and **What Did the Lady Forget?** (1937), both badly paced, and with dialogue serving as verbal intertitles. *The Only Son* is a mother-love story, less effectual than his father-love stories, and it is no surprise to find that Ozu's exercises in this genre – known as *haha-mono* – were less popular than those which other directors made for Shochiku. *What Did the Lady Forget?* is a study of a bossy wife, her gossiping friends, her husband and his niece. The best that can be said of both is that they are honestly observed portraits of certain circumstances at a certain time.

Between 1937 and 1947 Ozu directed only two films. After finishing *What Did the Lady Forget?* he was drafted and sent to China; on his return he prepared a script based on this experience, but the censor rejected it. Instead, he made **The Brothers and Sisters of the Toda Family** (1941), avowedly influenced by McCarey's *Make Way for Tomorrow* (q.v.): instead of parents being shuffled between their children, Ozu has a mother and daughter in like predicament. The fabric of the family is minutely examined at the moment when it is disintegrating, and none of these good people knows how to prevent it falling apart. His spare story makes McCarey's seem like blazing melodrama, but unlike McCarey he could not resist a happy ending. Donald

Richie, in 'Ozu: His Life and Films', declares that every one of Ozu's films is about the disintegration of the family, which is demonstrably untrue: but this one is. The same book calls **There Was a Father** (1942) 'one of Ozu's most perfect films', but we are more likely to agree with the director himself that it could be improved. (He had started it before leaving for China, and had reworked it several times.) It deals once more with a father and son, from a well-to-do background, and how they get to know each other after years of separation. The father is played by Chisu Ryu, the gentle actor who might be said to be surrogate for Ozu himself in his films from now on, but although there are moments to savour – such as the men at the club playing games and drinking saki – the cryptic quality of Ozu's best work is absent. The film has neither melodrama nor life, and because of his now-rigorous style, it has no vitality either.

The other great Japanese director of the period is Kenji Mizoguchi (1898–1956). He was born into poverty and studied art and design, both Western and Eastern; he joined the Nikkatsu company in 1920, and got a chance to direct as a result of the 'actress' strike of 1922. His first fifty films are lost, and the first to survive, **White Threads of the Waterfall** (1933), indicates that while he had a body of work behind him similar to Ozu's he was not the master that Ozu was at this time. The film displays two particular characteristics – the restless, searching camera, and the concentration of isolated detail – and beyond those a few moments of passion such as we shall find again in his late masterpieces. It also embodies two favourite Japanese subjects – the adventures of a theatrical troupe and the woman who pays for her man's education. Played by one of the most famous of Japanese actresses, Takako Irie (who also produced), the woman is an actress, and her protégé a rickshaw man; later, he is defending counsel when she is on trial for murder, and there is a superb moment when their real relationship reasserts itself. Similar themes are covered in **The Downfall** (1934), not surprisingly since it too is adapted from a novel by Kyoka Izumi. The woman this time is mistress of a gangleader and the man the gang's runner, for whose tuition at medical school she pays. Mizoguchi himself thought the film 'failed to

225

The World of Ozu

Hideo Sugahara and Tokkankozo in *I Was Born, But . . .* , one of his stories of family life ABOVE LEFT (and not a first version of his later *Ohayu*, as has been claimed). BELOW LEFT, Takeshi Sakamoto and Mitsuo Koji in *A Story of Floating Weeds*, (1934), which he did remake, and his only extant film of theatrical life. ABOVE, Yoshiko Okada and Kazuko Kojima in *An Inn in Tokyo* (1935), one of his tales of slum life. BELOW, Michiko Kuwano, Sumiko Kurishima and Tatsuo Saito in *What Did the Lady Forget?*, in which Ozu moved socially upwards to what we call the bourgeoisie.

227

When the British magazine *Sight and Sound* 'introduced' Japanese cinema in 1957. Mizoguchi's *Sisters of the Gion* was 'considered the best pre-war Japanese film.' Yoko Umemura and Isuzu Yamada as the geisha sisters with contrasting ideas on their profession, balanced against the attempts of the latter to keep away from the failed businessman that the other one truly loves.

evoke the quality of the original work', and indeed it never lives up to the promise of the opening sequence, on the platform of a suburban railway station, where the now-aged couple, not recognising each other, independently remember the past. This was Mizoguchi's last Silent, and was said to be his first 'pure' Meiji-period (1852–1912) film.

Oyuki, the Virgin (1935) goes further into the past, to 1878 and the Seinan War, taking as its starting point de Maupassant's 'Boule de Suif'. Two prostitutes are reviled by their fellow passengers, even though it is known that one of them (Isuzu Yamada) has offered herself to the foreign commander (Daijiro Natsukawa) in place of the young girl he coveted. Mizoguchi himself dismissed the film as 'badly written', but if the earlier sections are confusing it is also one of his most physically beautiful films (only one poor, mutilated print is extant), with excellent performances by the leads, his favourite players at the time. In the same year, as a change from the period films with which his name was associated he made **The Field Poppy,** a tale of young people's marriage prospects – very much a subject dear to Ozu and, like Ozu's own stories in his later period, seemingly drained of life.

Mizoguchi was thirty-eight when he made **Osaka Elegy** (1936), but according to the French film historian Georges Sadoul it was this film of which he was thinking

when he said, late in life, that he only found his true voice after he was forty. Sadoul adds that the main thread of his work then began to appear – 'the depiction of society and the condition of women within that society' – but it is truer to say that, working for the first time with Yoshikata Yoda, who would write most of his subsequent scripts, he found the voice he needed. All Japanese films depicted society, but Mizoguchi had been making films especially angled to women because, as he explained, his mentor at Nikkatsu had done the masculine films.

His training in art had led him to historical subjects and stories about the theatre. Though the only previous contemporary subject to survive, *The Field Poppy,* shows little concern for anything, the chief concerns of *Osaka Elegy* – the unity of the family, the exploitation of women – are to be seen in the earlier films, as they are in most Japanese films, but for the first time there is bitterness: a young woman, a telephonist (Miss Yamada), allows herself to be kept by the boss because her family is in financial difficulties. In **Straits of Love and Hate** (1937) a hotel maid (Fumiko Yamaji) is seduced by the master's son and, abandoned by him, sinks into prostitution. Both are stories from Victorian melodrama (though the former also surfaced in Britain at this time as a contemporary tale, 'Love on the Dole'), but what makes these films superior to the versions still being made in the West is their conviction: the combination of psychological truth and telling detail, done with an assured narrative drive which knows exactly what to omit – a quality still rare in Western cinema – constitutes masterly film-making. The theatre troupe of the later film (the heroine joins it to escape from harlotry) is engagingly observed, and I prefer both films to the more highly regarded **Sisters of the Gion** (1936). The Gion is the red-light district of Kyoto (and, like the *scena* of Mizoguchi's historical films, a world of narrow alleys and wooden houses), and Mizoguchi, a great frequenter of geishas, suggested the idea to Yoda – about the traditional, older geisha (Yoko Umemura) and her younger, more ambitious sister (Miss Yamada).

The struggle for economic survival is always near the surface with Mizoguchi's people, and indeed **The Story of the Last**

Chrysanthemums (1939) is the study of a career – that of the famous Kabuki actor of the Meiji period, Kikunosuke Onoe. Its sobriety compares favourably with the Warner Bros. biographical films of the same period, and its chief interest is Mizoguchi's increasingly inventive use of *decoratif*, foreshadowing his later masterpieces. Assisting him at this time was Kaneto Shindo (q.v.), who summarised Mizoguchi's career by observing that he had become good after a poor start, and 'in the middle of his career he became bad again for a long time. Just before his death he was so good he became superb.' Given that his work of this period can be only partly glimpsed – only four of the ten films he made between 1938 and 1946 survive, though his *oeuvre* is complete from then on – it is hard for a Western observer to agree that he was bad for a long time. Nevertheless, it is difficult to feel kindly towards the two-part **The Loyal 47 Ronin of the**

Genroku Era (1942), which we also know under its original title, *Genroku Chusingara*.

This story of the loyal samurai corps which eventually avenges the suicide of its master was a Kabuki favourite, and a perennial in the Japanese cinemas till the present, occasioning as many as two versions within a year – invariably long and expensive, with the purpose of this one partly political. Shochiku – to which company Mizoguchi had moved a year or two earlier – was in debt and had been promised government aid if it would come up with yet another version, to glorify the 'bushido' spirit. Mizoguchi avoided this – the piece consists of endless parleys and conversations – and indeed lost interest in the project on being commanded to make a 'loyalist' statement; his friends also thought him disheartened by the Japanese aggression in the Pacific and the further shock at this time of his wife's mental breakdown, apparently caused by syphilis – for which, despite

Mizoguchi's *The Story of the Last Chrysanthemums* is one of the many Japanese films based on theatrical people – many of them, again, based on fact. Shotaro Hanayagi as the Kabuke actor, Kikunosuke Onoe, and Kakuko Mori as his mistress – both charming players, but like some of their colleagues so bland that we long for some spirit.

Yasujiro Shimazu was the mentor for several of the best-known Japanese directors, and it is a pity that we know so little of his work. *Our Neighbour, Miss Yae* is as complete a record of a world long gone as anything in Ozu: the story of two families. Here is the son of one, Den Ohinata – according to the plot a dead-ringer for Fredric March – and the daughter of the other, Yoshiko Okada. It so happens that she is married, and has returned home when relations with her husband have soured: so her relations with this young student become a little complicated.

blood tests to the contrary, he blamed himself. Mizoguchi did not like action or violence – violence of emotion was something else again – and went unwillingly to work on two short samurai films intended by Shochiku as morale boosters, **The Swordsman** (1944) and **The Noted Sword** (1945). His distaste is apparent, but the genre required the restoration of his once-probing, gliding camera, and the settings, against a background of unrest and conflict, are again a portent of his greatest work. The eponymous warrior of *The Swordsman* is Miyamoto Musashi, also the subject of innumerable films: both films, however, have sword-wielding heroines – but less from a concern for women than as a statement on Japan's desperate condition at this late stage of the War.

Ozu and Mizoguchi were masters. Of some of the other directors we can only make a tentative statement. It is clear from the Silent films available that all of them regarded the camera as more than a mere recorder; moving on to the Sound period, we find in Kinugasa's interesting **An Actor's Revenge** (1935) and Mansaku Itami's **Kakita Akanishi** (1936) an aston-

ishing number of glides and overhead shots, not one of them pretentious or incorrectly juxtaposed. *An Actor's Revenge* is a version of the novel by Otokichi Mikami, most famously filmed by Ichikawa (q.v.), and its popularity is such that this three-part film was reissued, edited down to normal feature length, as late as 1952. Itami's film is also concerned with derring-do and righting wrongs, one of a series he wrote for their star and producer, Chiezo Kataoka, who plays an all-too-human hero – the comic samurai role which Toshiro Mifune (q.v.) would inherit. The two films also share, beyond their themes, the director Daisuke Ito, who wrote the first with Kinugasa and who was the mentor of Itami. Ito was also the mentor of Hiroshi Inagaki, whose **The Rickshaw Man** (1943) was written by Itami – an old-fashioned tale about a family retainer who brings up his yong master, and known to us best in Inagaki's own, better-developed remake of 1958, with Mifune.

Kajiro Yamamoto (1902–74), though best remembered as the master of Kurosawa (q.v.), also made a number of engaging films. Outstanding among them is **The Loves of Tojuro** (1938), a historical tale of an actor (Kazuo Hasegawa) who, challenged by a newcomer, tries to recapture his audience with a new play written for him by Chikamatsu: that play turns out to be about two lovers who had committed suicide a year earlier, and the actor only finds his way into the role after his leading lady (i.e. a female impersonator) has impersonated an old love. There are notions here of art being stronger than life, and of anything, even tragedy, being grist to the artist's mill: but Yamamoto's strength lies in his suggestion of psychological ambiguity – an ability he shares with Shimazu, whose **Our Neighbour, Miss Yae** (1934) is one of the best of all *shomin-geki* films. It is a gentle study of two families living in a grassy lane on the outskirts of Tokyo. The men drink saki together, their wives gossip, and a schoolgirl daughter and the boy next door may be in the process of turning friendship into love; an unhappily married daughter arrives but the disruption is only temporary. This is the world we know from Ozu, complete to the visits to American films, but Shimazu exercises more humour than Ozu in his family films, showing a faintly ironic detachment which

Sukezo Kuketakaya, Chojuro Kawarazaki and Kanemon Nakemuro in *Humanity and Paper Balloons*, a remarkable film directed by Sadao Yamanaka – and the only one of his films extant. It is not unlike 'The Lower Depths', but perhaps both funnier and more powerful: since Kurosawa admired Yamanaka greatly, his later version of Gorki's play may be a homage to him.

almost recalls Jane Austen. Beside it, **The Whole Family Works** (1939), directed by Mikio Naruse, and former assistant to Shimazu, is lacking in spirit. The family in this case is lower on the social scale but, again, we join them at the point when one of the sons has to make the enormous decision between going to college or starting a career. The film is based on a novel by Sunao Tokugawa, a Marxist writer who took to writing about the poor when Marxism was proscribed in the Thirties; Naruse (1905–69) had been born poor, and had had no formal education; he made his name with slapstick comedies, but turned to serious themes as soon as he was able.

Akin to the family films were those centred on children, and the most successful director working in that genre was Hiroshi Shimizu – though he had been making films for fourteen years before his first notable one, **Children in the Wind** (1938). It is slight, but its virtue is that a situation of almost tragic gravity – the sacking from his job of a father and his (wrongful) imprisonment – is seen through the eyes of a child. Parental love is again propounded as a supreme virtue, but in

Children of the Sun (1938), directed by Yutaka Abe, we move closer to social melodrama – a film that may have been inspired by *Boys Town* (q.v.). The setting is a Roman Catholic orphanage in a remote part of Hokkaido, and the piece begins with the arrival of a certified delinquent; it changes with the introduction by one of the teachers of his new wife, formerly sold by her father into prostitution, who has feelings of inadequacy in this environment – but the stilted direction is unable to weld the two themes together.

On the evidence of **The Blossoms Have Fallen** (1938), Tamizo Ishida was not among the most inspired of directors – though the fault may lie with the screenplay of Kaoru Morimoto, at twenty too young, clearly, to tackle the complexities of geisha life. Outside, a rebellion or war is raging; inside the girls moon about their own and the others' problems, wondering what will happen when they are older. Though the film is admired by some, Ishida lacks both the humour and the emotion which Mizoguchi brought to his studies of geisha life.

Another favoured genre was the war film, and Tomotaka Tasaka's **Five Scouts**

(1938) is one of the pre-war Japanese films known in the West – though in view of the differing opinions pronounced it is doubtful whether, in fact, all the commentators have seen it. It is neither a defence of Japan's presence in China nor an apologia; the style is documentary without the fascination of authenticity, and the film seems to have no other purpose than to represent the Sino-Japanese conflict to a local audience, with no sympathy being shown either way. However, if neutrality were the keynote of most Japanese films of this time, **Humanity and Paper Balloons** (1937) reveals its director, Sadao Yamanaka (1909–38), as one of the most committed of film-makers, and one of exceptional talent. Of the twelve films he made, only this one survives (apart from a mutilated copy of one other), but his contemporaries were no less admiring than we. Since this particular film, though set in the eighteenth century, depicts authority as corrupt, uninterested and unjust, it is certain that he upset the military government, which, as a measure of repression, drafted him to the Chinese front, where he died. He was, in fact, a militant left-winger; he specialised in the *jidai-geki,* and was, according to certain commentators, a pessimist and a searcher for truth – either of which may have led him to the same conclusion. But although this film is about a working-class *quartier* of Edo, and the indignities inflicted upon the poor, it does not dwell on misery. It is a film of vivid life, portraying a community sharply divided between the privileged and the oppressed – among whom are Unno (Chojuro Kawarazaki), a *ronin* (i.e. an unemployed samurai) and Shinza (Kanemon Nakemura), who runs gambling parties against the wishes of the local 'Mafia'. Unno merely wants a favour from the local lord, but the same forces destroy both him and Shinza.

Yamanaka's co-producers were the Zen-shin-za, a well-known progressive group, backed by the Toho company – at this time locked in bitter rivalry with the other giant of the industry, Shochiku. Toho and Zen-shin-za were also responsible for **The Abe Clan** (1938), which sets out to show the life of a samurai at a feudal (1641) court. Life is a matter of honour, betrayal, poison, loyalty, carnage, and as the film builds from its – confused – beginnings to its powerful climax it does not hide its contempt for the samurai system. That must surely have been in defiance of the government, and it is significant that the film's director, Hisatori Kumagai, was among those named to the Americans at the end of the War as one of the industry's Class B criminals – among whom were a number of other prominent left-wingers.

On the evidence of this one film it is difficult to assess Kumagai as clearly as we can Yamanaka. What links Yamanaka, alone of his contemporaries, to the later, great generation of Japanese film-makers is his emotional power – though both Mizoguchi and Naruse would acquire this in time.

The abiding characteristic of the Japanese cinema of the Fifties and Sixties is the examination of both the feudal past and the nature of contemporary society – and both themes were tentatively present in the Thirties. The value of these older, lesser films resides in their portrait of the times, for which we have so few equivalents in the West that we perforce are reminded of Tchekhov, supreme chronicler of the everyday. If the historical films aspire towards the epic, the modern subjects tend to the reverse, and in contrast were filmed on location as much as possible. They demanded tranquillity of style, and the sudden interruption of that by a flurry of intercut montage almost always (and significantly) indicates change – the changing of the seasons or of a man's daily routine. The consistency of this style may not be remarkable, given the modesty and interdependence of these early film-makers, but perhaps when we can see more of their work we shall be able to attribute an individual style – as we can with Ozu and Mizoguchi. What we can already see is an abiding honesty and humanity, in complete opposition to the German film industry, which also was at work in a country preparing for war. In the aftermath of that war, and of the Japanese defeat, their cinema would rise to new heights – though, had we known these early films, its pre-eminence would not have so astonished us.

11

Sex, Crime and Booze: Warner Bros. in the Thirties

AUDIENCE enthusiasm for the Talking Picture was such that the Depression, arriving simultaneously, had little effect on cinema takings. Some producers felt it inappropriate to fill the screen with luxury, but as long as performers opened their mouths and sound emerged the public did not care whether they were in a palace or a hovel, on the prairie or the Place de la Concorde. There was a tendency, therefore, towards simple, cheap settings, the more so because at this volatile time Hollywood was unsure whether the good pickings would endure. There was also a halt to those large endeavours which have always bedevilled the progress of the American film – enterprises mainly characterised by their attempts at moral uplift and often also by their expense.

The films of this time are concerned, rather, with social realism and with gangsters, both subjects often interlocking and frequently described by the publicity department as 'Torn from Today's Headlines'. Not all these films are especially good, though they did recreate a recognisable world of second-rate people; their shortcomings are mainly due to over-haste – or they were made on two-to-three-week schedules in order to bring out more than one film a week. The directors scurried from film to film; the writers might be working on ten films at once, so that *six of them might be credited on any one project. They were not attempting to shake the world, nor did they strive for art; but despite their penchant for melodrama they

caught absolutely the ambience of their time. The War might not be mentioned, but one knew the men had been through it; the Depression made too obvious a background, yet there had to be a reason why a smart girl like Joan Blondell needed to make it rich before striking back to the mid-West. Everyone was making a fast buck, from the big-time racketeers and bootleggers to hoboes with loaded dice. It was a world of travelling salesmen, dance hostesses, show girls and con-men, each man mauling his mate – where the drinking is heavy and an advancing camera reveals that the singer of a song about 'our cottage small' is a raddled twenty-year-old. From time to time they showed soup queues, but there was no need to do so; one bare, dusty room told at once its tale of dingy passion. Points were made unobtrusively and with speed, and to their economy was added a vitality, a sense of reality and a feeling for the vernacular which make these films, as a body, unique in film history. The factory was humming, and none of the production lines worked more efficiently than that at Warner Bros.

If any one person deserves the credit it is not Jack Warner, who was in charge of production – or if so he was radical for only a brief period of his long tenure. The guiding force would seem to have been Darryl F. Zanuck, production chief from 1929 to 1933, and young and brash enough to have seen the virtue of reflecting the concerns of his audiences. 'Everyone,' said Joan Blondell later, 'got everyone else's juices going', and that probably started in the writers' department, where inspiration came easily and they worked fast (the synopses provided by Publicity often differed considerably from what was on

---

*In Hollywood, several names on the writing credit less often means a collaboration than that the project has been passed from one to the other till the producer is satisfied. In later years the credits were often determined by arbitration by the Screenwriters' Guild.

screen). Sometimes credited with the original story and sometimes with the finished script were such as John Bright, Kubec Glasmon, John Monk Saunders, Joseph Jackson, Maude Fulton, Wilson Mizner (subject of a hundred legends), Kenyon Nicholson and W. R. Burnett. They were obviously people who had knocked around a lot: the one consistent quality of their films is their cynicism.

They were also down to earth. *One Way Passage* starts with a sedate trio, each irritated that one of the coins tossed to them has gone in the spittoon, and the soprano interrupts 'If I Had My Way' to hiss 'Third door on the left'; the hero, when arrested, observes to his captor, 'Still on the garlic?' In *Blessed Event* columnist Lee Tracy always refers to crooner Dick Powell as a 'pansy', while Humphrey Bogart says in *Big City Blues,* 'The old town ain't what it used to be. Cops pick up a man, got two guns and a butcher's knife in one pocket, and a powder-puff and lipstick in the other.' In the same film the one sober chorus girl assuages her obvious boredom with 'The Well of Loneliness'. As Dorothy Mackaill sashays through the lobby in *Safe In Hell,* the loungers move their legs to let their crotches 'breathe'; in *Three on a Match,* a magnifying mirror finds Edward Arnold pulling hair from his nostrils. Says Aline MacMahon in *The Mouthpiece,* 'Forget it, kid, it's all in a day's work, as the road-sweeper said to the elephant.'

Even so, a spade was not always called a spade. The girls were 'broads' or 'dames', but there were euphemisms for the words the Hays Office would not permit: 'You had her on a thirty-day trial offer' says James Cagney in *Blonde Crazy,* and 'She's been sister-in-law to the world' observes Mary Astor in *Little Giant.* The women sat around with cigarettes in their mouths, in scanties and rolled stockings, unnecessarily unfrocked, which didn't prevent their men from undressing them mentally and putting their hands in forbidden places. They could be heard squealing in the next room during some pre-breakfast sexual routine; they had grapefruit (memorably) stuffed in their faces, they were kicked and thrown on the floor, only to return for more – provided the pickings were good, the diamonds real. They were unashamedly grasping, and in their musical apotheosis they stripped for the delectation of their

men – if only in silhouette and with iron-clad scanties . . . and even then the men equipped themselves with can-openers. Nor was it a one-way traffic: Ruby Keeler could burst into Dick Powell's dressing room to find him in his B.V.D.s, and though this couple is not otherwise obsessed with sex – unlike their colleagues in this particular film, *42nd Street* – she neither withdraws nor does he grab his pants with undue haste. The end justified the means: Vivienne Osborne in *Two Seconds* bribes the J.P. who thinks Edward G. Robinson too drunk to get married, and that same lady, in *The Dark Horse,* suggests strip poker to Guy Kibbee in order that he lose the election. Death was the next best thing: Frank McHugh perches on a coffin in *I Am a Fugitive From the Chain Gang;* Lew Ayres in *Doorway to Hell* gets a plastic surgeon to work on the corpse of his kid brother for his debut in the morgue. Sex, crime, booze: in Prohibition America they went hand in hand, and Warners celebrated all three. In *Public Enemy* the passing of the Volstead Act is signalled by liquor stores besieged by staggering customers; a couple goes by, the woman carrying the baby since the pram is stacked with drink; and when a bottle is dropped from a limousine an evening-gowned beauty steps out and tries to gather up the pieces.

Then there were the players – those dear dames and those tough mugs. Outstanding among the latter are Edward G. Robinson (1893–1973) and James Cagney (b. 1899), both from the New York stage. Writers and directors were fascinated by their dynamism, and expected audiences to be: and they were. The two men played tough guys, good and bad, with little deviation from film to film, yet they interest us all the time. Watch Cagney after a successful flirtation, and note his cocky little dance step: he had airiness, and Olympian confidence and vitality. Robinson's screen character was more readily defined – vain, dandified and presumptuous. Both were fetching braggarts because they had style and wit. Both would prove themselves masters of many moods, but this was not what Warners asked of them. Their directors include a number of now well-thought-of names as well as some whose post-Warner work is without interest: none at this point shows an individual style, and Roy del Ruth was then the equal of Michael Curtiz. Thematically even the musicals blur into the underworld thrillers, and therefore the following films are discussed in approximate chronological order.

The Dawn Patrol (1930) was directed by Howard Hawks from a story by John Monk Saunders, based on incidents from the latter's own war service. The pair of British boots, from a dead pilot, dropped by the Germans; the gramophone with one record; the young pilot shattered when his friend is killed; the booze, the jagged nerves, the quick camaraderie: such matters were to recur in other films written by Saunders (q.v.). Sadly, the acting – Richard Barthelmess, Douglas Fairbanks Jr – is so much that of the poor early Talkies that the 1938 remake (q.v.) is possibly preferable.

Doorway to Hell (1930), directed by Archie Mayo, is based on a story by Rowland Brown (later a director), 'A Handful of Clouds' (when you are shot 'a handful of clouds grabs you'). Many of the guys *are* shot – by gangland boss Lew Ayres, who is obsessed with Napoleon, all things military, his kid brother and himself, in reverse order. This performance is hysterical rather than neurotic, and the film was completely overshadowed by a more accomplished variation on the same theme, released a few days later, **Little Caesar** (1930), directed by Mervyn LeRoy. The boss is again Italian, but the subject is gang warfare, so popular at the time than Robinson's rise to power from his beginnings as a grab-happy little tough with a preening love of ostentation. The Mafia is not mentioned, but the clues are there; and those who knew enough of Al Capone, the source of Edward G. Robinson's 'Rico', might guess at his homosexuality from the latter's attitude towards his former dancing partner (Douglas Fairbanks Jr). W. R. Burnett wrote the novel on which the screenplay was based.

Burnett and John Monk Saunders were responsible for the original story of **The Finger Points** (1931), directed by John Francis Dillon. Here Barthelmess, spectacularly miscast, is the crusading journalist who turns to his assailants when his newspaper refuses to pay his hospital expenses, and thus becomes the tool of the underworld – as represented by Clark Gable in spats and bowler hat. Before the year was out Gable (q.v.), together with James Cagney, would transform the accepted

The superiority of *Little Caesar* over other gangster pictures was explained by Richard Watts in *The New York Herald Tribune*: 'by pushing into the background the usual romantic conventions of the theme and concentrating on characterisation rather than plot, there emerges not only an effective and rather chilling melodrama, but also what is sometimes known as a Document.' And, he added, 'Chiefly it is made important by the genuinely brilliant performance that Edward G. Robinson contributes to the title-role.'

image of the Hollywood leading man.

Cagney has one of the most enlivening moments in all cinema when, directed by William A. Wellman, in **Other Men's Women** (1931) – also known as *The Steel Highway* – he arrives at a dance hall, sheds his oil skins, chats up the hat-check girl, and then moves across the foyer with a hop, skip and a jump, his arms in the air, grabbing his girl as he reaches the dancers. The film itself is an engaging marital drama, set among railroad workers, with Mary Astor as the suburban wife and Grant Withers as the lodger, a high-spirited and amorous drunk, both of them lying to her husband (Regis Toomey) as to their feelings for each other.

The Public Enemy (1931) was also directed by Wellman, who observed later, 'The thing that made it a success was one word – Cagney.' Written by Glasmon and Bright, formerly reporters in Chicago, the film detailed the rise of an all-American

235

The scene in *The Last Flight* where the four dedicated drinkers – John Mack Brown, Elliott Nugent, David Manners and Richard Barthelmess – meet Nikki (Helen Chandler). The champagne-glass contains the false-teeth of someone who said 'he was going out to biff somebody', which seems reasonable to them. Nikki's response to most things is 'I'll take vanilla' or 'It seemed like a good idea at the time.' They all agree on booze: 'It'll make you laugh or cry.'

gangster (Cagney) from his days as trouble maker at a boys' club. To Andre Sennwald in *The New York Times*, it was 'just another gangster film', a view seldom echoed now. For much is memorable: Cagney and his pal, Edward Woods, tiptoeing to peer into their friend's coffin; their fear when caught on their first job; Woods being gunned down, the noise of machine-gun fire being drowned by a coal delivery; the final image of Cagney, a corpse, swaying in the doorway before falling towards his beloved mother. Then there are their women including Jean Harlow (q.v.), who says, not altogether carelessly, 'Oh Tommy, I could love you to death', which tells us something about the women who loved these gangsters, and something about the audiences which went to revel in this new breed of anti-hero.

The Maltese Falcon (1931), directed by del Ruth and the first of the three Warner versions of Dashiell Hammett's detective novel, was much admired by contemporaries for its fidelity to the original.

Aficionados of the 1941 version (q.v.) will note that Sam Spade sleeps with Ruth Wonderly, and that his relationship with his partner's wife is equally unambiguous. Ricardo Cortez, with insolent smile and hooded eyes, is Spade; Bebe Daniels is brittle but clearly guilty as Ruth. As Gutman, Dudley Digges is seedy, but not as threatening as Sydney Greenstreet.

Smart Money (1931), directed by Alfred E. Green, concerns Nick the Barber (Robinson), a small-town gambler whose syndicate sends him to the city to take on the big boys: double-crossed and double-crossing, he soon owns half the gambling joints in town, half of high society, and all of the D.A. Cagney is in support, in the only film he made with Robinson, and it is a pleasure to see them together.

Night Nurse (1931), directed by Wellman, has Barbara Stanwyck (q.v.) in the title role, a Depression-hit girl who badly needs a job. She also tends bootlegger Ben Lyon, rooms with knowing and once-eager Joan Blondell ('I was afraid the hospital would burn down before I got here. Now I have to watch myself with matches,') and who takes on the real villain, the chauffeur (Gable). She also, in this darkest of Warner films, nurses baby girls while their mother, drunk or drugged, lolls on a bed with her equally stoned lover.

The Last Flight (1931) was directed by William Dieterle (1893–1972), who, as we have seen, had moved from acting to directing; perhaps as it was his first film in English – under his Warner contract – the delivery is stilted, but that hardly weakens the superb screenplay by John Monk Saunders, based on his novel 'Single Lady' and identical with incidents in Hemingway's 'The Sun Also Rises'. Saunders's expatriate drinkers are led by Cary (Barthelmess), and there tags along with them Nikki (Helen Chandler), trading flippancy for flippancy, and Frink (Walter Byron), who, like Hemingway's Robert Cohn, is based on Harold Loeb. Except for the last-named – a member of the Wandering Hands Club, as they explain – their attitude towards her is asexual. On a whim they troop off to Portugal – the obvious choice, since they had so often wondered what was 'doing there tonight' – and one of them is wounded in the bullring: 'I'm glad I wore my new blue shorts. I'll be a big success in hospital.' Another is mortally wounded, still another shoots the unspeakable Frink and disappears. Left alone with Cary, Nikki makes what might almost be a declaration of love. 'Without them, nothing's left,' he replies. 'Comradeship. That's all we had.' The attitudes expressed would not find their way into films again till the Sixties, though the ineffable flippancy is echoed in *Laughter* (q.v.), written by Donald Ogden Stewart, who coincidentally was the prototype for another character – in 'The Sun Also Rises'. One can only speculate on how much is autobiographical. It is a portrait of people in a vacuum – and the most authentic study we are ever likely to get of the lost generation, infinitely more significant and enjoyable than the Hemingway novel. At the time its failure was complete: had it been a success the history of movies might have been very different.

Audiences undoubtedly found it easier to relate to **The Star Witness** (1931), about an ordinary family caught up with gangsters, and the film's throb of indignation concerning these innocents caught in the crossfire still seems genuine. **Love is a Racket** (1932) has a spendthrift nymphomaniac heiress (Frances Dee) throwing herself at an unprincipled columnist (Fairbanks Jr). She is encouraged by her aunt (Cecil Cunningham), and hindered by a gangster (Lyle Talbot), who hopes to muscle in. Wellman directed both films. His most sophisticated offering at this time is **Safe in Hell** (1931), from a play by Houston Branch which is one of several copies of 'Rain'. The loose, lost lady is Dorothy Mackaill, making a living, as she puts it, 'the only way I could', as the one white woman in a Caribbean hotel patronised by men as frustrated as they are crooked. Wellman also managed exotica – Chinese-style – in **The Hatchet Man** (1932), set in San Francisco at the time of the Tong War, and based on the old Belasco play, with Edward G. Robinson in the second of his usual two roles, the decent man driven to murder.

After *Little Caesar* Robinson's most famous early role was in **Five Star Final** (1931), as a newspaper editor, a tough old hand who claims that 'ideals won't put a patch on your pants'. He learns otherwise, of course, after victimising an innocent family: Mervyn LeRoy's sloppy direction foreshadows his later, sentimental work at M-G-M (q.v.). Nevertheless, Robinson has fun with the editor's cohorts: his secretary (Aline MacMahon), whom he has never thought of as a woman, let alone a sexual object; his unctuous handyman reporter (Boris Karloff), a one-time divinity student now as lecherous and as unprincipled as his boss; and a Jewish reporter (George E. Stone) of simple zeal.

The title of **Two Seconds** (1932), directed by LeRoy, refers to the amount of time Robinson has to relive his life as he sits in the electric chair – a mundane life till Shirley (Vivienne Osborne) comes between him and his buddy (Preston Foster). She soon drops claims to gentility and culture – 'Since when did you ask a dollar who was his father?' – and is the ideal denizen of the rooming houses and dance halls of this masterpiece of sleaziness. Robinson did a variation of the same plot in **Tiger Shark** (1932), directed by Howard Hawks, a film mainly notable for its setting – the San Diego waterfront – and its more forthright intimations of homosexuality, e.g. dying, Robinson has a caress for his pal (Richard Arlen), but none for the wife who has actually deceived him.

Cagney also strutted his stuff in vehicles designed for that purpose. **Blonde Crazy** (1931) and **Taxi!** (1932) were both directed by del Ruth. The former concerns a bellboy who moves from getting bootleg gin for guests to the shakedown game, making a bid for the big time by teaming up with one of its leaders (Louis Calhern): 'Honest men are scarcer than feathers on a frog' he says when double-crossed. The latter film concerns a cab driver whose marriage – to Loretta Young – is threatened when he becomes involved in a war between rival cab companies. In del Ruth's **Blessed Event** (1932) Lee Tracy replaced Cagney (currently fighting with his bosses over salary) in the role of a Winchell-like columnist who specialises in news of pregnancies and wages war against a crooner (Dick Powell) while a racketeer wages war against him. Like most Cagney vehicles, it is a ramshackle tale, notable for its minor characters, dovetailed in for laughs or thrills. The constant repetition of themes is best exemplified by Hawks's **The Crowd Roars** (1932), which thereafter Warners remade endlessly, with variations: in this original version a racing driver (Cagney) tries to keep his kid brother (Eric Linden) away from the horses and the dames which the tracks attract.

If Robinson and Cagney were the studio's most popular stars, its prestige actors remained John Barrymore and George Arliss. The latter, after a popular replay of an earlier stage and screen success, *Disraeli* (1929), continued in new versions of roles he had performed in his youth, and thus was sixty-three when he played the title role in **Alexander Hamilton** (1931), a gentleman who, at the time of the action actually was in his early thirties. The film is mainly notable for Alan Mowbray's performance as Washington, one of the few times the first President has been portrayed on the screen. Acting for Arliss consisted of twitching watery eyes to express cuteness – called for, its seems, at all times – and moving his mouth like a ventriloquist's dummy. He is fairly restrained in **The Man Who Played God** (1932), as a world-famous pianist whose sudden deafness takes him through atheism, philanthropy (towards Depression-hit couples in Central Park) and finally to reconversion to Christianity. Arliss's credited director on these and most of his films was John G. Adolphi, but according to Bette Davis (q.v.), the intense young ingenue whose career began to flower when cast in this film, Arliss was really his own director.

Barrymore, too, had a success with an old melodrama, **Svengali** (1931), directed without inspiration by Archie Mayo. Michael Curtiz directed the superior follow-up, **The Mad Genius** (1931), and both films are notable for Anton Grot's extravagant decor. The early Warner Talkies owe much of their distinctive look to Grot. That look was predominantly sour, but sourness and extravagance, when applied to tenement stairs and attics, can be memorable. Curtiz's style is still basically European, very much at home in such settings, and he places his camera imaginatively – and too briefly to be considered pretentious. *The Mad Genius* is further notable in both rehashing the plot of the earlier film and using as its basis factual material – both favourite ploys in the Warner writers' department, and much approved of by their bosses. Though nominally based on a play called 'The Idol', its central situation is recognisably the relationship between Diaghilev and Nijinsky, in which role Donald Woods is far from convincing.

Union Depot (1932) is one of the forerunners of *Grand Hotel*, a dioramic study of a railroad terminus in Depression America. Passing through the terminus are two hoboes (Guy Kibbee and Fairbanks Jr) an inebriated gentleman (Frank McHugh), an out-of-work dancer (Joan Blondell), the aged, crippled sex maniac (George Rosener) who is pursuing her, and every ethnic group in the U.S. The film was directed by Alfred E. Green who that same year also made a bright political satire, **The Dark Horse**: after deadlock at the gubernatorial convention a man (Kibbee) of sublime stupidity is nominated, and his hustling campaign manager (Warren William) is sprung from jail to launch him. Not daunted by the choice, he declares of his candidate, 'Every time he opens his mouth he subtracts from the total sum of human knowledge . . . We're going to convince the voters that they've got someone of their own level.'

Ruth Chatterton (q.v.) was one of the former Paramount stars acquired by Warners via an underhand deal with an agent;

the others were Kay Francis and William Powell, and none of the three quite fitted into the Warner Bros. world. The studio decided to go into something with more tone – **Jewel Robbery** (1932), set in Vienna, with Powell as a thief and Francis as a (married) Countess. The director, Dieterle, was, however, no Lubitsch – a fact doubly proved when Lubitsch issued a similar tale a few months later, *Trouble in Paradise* (q.v.).

With the same co-stars, **One Way Passage** (1932) is the story of a doomed shipboard romance, he a convicted murderer and she dying of an incurable disease, drinking Paradise cocktails and leaving the stems of their broken glasses intertwined on the bar. This dotty idyll is directed with conviction by Tay Garnett, its stardust counterpointed by Miss MacMahon as a phoney Countess, formerly known as Barrelhouse Betty, and Frank McHugh as a larcenous drunk. The critic Kenneth Tynan once observed of the movies of this time that 'with the passage of time, the profundities peel away and only the basic trivialities remain to enchant us', and *One Way Passage*, never profound, is enchanting – along with *The Last Flight* and *Hard to Handle* (q.v.) the best of all the unsung movies in this group of films.

Also among the more relishable of these Warner offerings are **The Mouthpiece** (1932), directed by James Flood and Elliott Nugent, and **The Strange Love of Molly Louvain** (1932), directed by Curtiz. The former is one of the most immoral of these many moral tales, set in the usual milieu of deviousness, fraud, fooling and booze – and the story itself is the familiar one of the idealist who finds he can make it big once he compromises. Warren William is the assistant D.A. who finds that juries are less impressed by truth than by cajolery, as a consequence of which he becomes New York's most celebrated lawyer – with a strictly criminal clientele; Sidney Fox is his secretary, matching guile for guile as she wards off his attempts at seduction.

In the second film, the strange love of Molly Louvain (Ann Dvorak) is that for her illegitimate child. Deserted by his father, she accepts an invitation to try on some silk stockings, and soon she is soused on a combination of beer and champagne, her heart breaking as she bangs out a wild rendition of 'Penthouse Serenade'. How-

ever, she decides to enjoy her new status, reckoning without the medical student (Richard Cromwell) who dumbly worships her, and the reporter (Lee Tracy) who recognises her as his sort: 'You're one of the tinsel girls,' he says happily.

The critics of the time were less appreciative than we might be today: 'Tedious and distasteful', said Mordaunt Hall in *The New York Times,* in fact discussing **Three on a Match** (1932), which follows the fluctuating fortunes of three girls, Blondell, Davis and Dvorak. The latter leaves her stuffy husband (Warren William) for a gangster, takes to drink, and comes to her senses when her child is kidnapped. (Kidnappings were big news in 1932.) **Big City Blues** (1932), about the hick (Eric Linden) who learns about life fast on his first trip to New York, evoked no warmer response from the press, but the director of both these films, LeRoy, aroused widespread admiration with **I Am a Fugitive From the Chain Gang** (1932) – and certainly on this occasion, if no other, he was the equal of any director then working. Based on a novel by Robert E. Burns, in turn based on fact, the film caused sufficient outcry for Congress to revise the penal laws relating to chain gangs. A returning doughboy (Paul Muni), rather than go back to his routine job, decides to use the engineering skills he learnt in the army: but the job doesn't last. In a doss house he meets a man who makes

Paul Muni, right, in perhaps the best of the 'Social Concern' movies made by Warner Bros., *I Am a Fugitive From the Chain Gang* (1932). He has in fact just escaped, and is welcomed in Chicago by a former colleague on the chain gang, Allen Jenkins. The double bed was a standard fixture in Hollywood films of this period, and if it was never seen in use the dialogue made clear that it had been or would be: indeed, the blonde, Noel Francis, is a kindly gesture on Jenkins's part to a man in need of relaxation.

This aggressively eupeptic juvenile and this coy little chorine are not what one remembers best from Warners' Depression musicals: or are they? – their very awkwardness is part of the charm of the pieces, and an effective contrast to the very knowing show business types who surround them. Dick Powell and Ruby Keeler in *Gold Diggers of 1933*, and, yes, her outfit is made of metal: the solution to *that* is provided by a 'baby' (Billy Barty), who turns up with some equally lewd ideas in the 'Honeymoon Hotel' number in *Footlight Parade*.

him the innocent instrument in a stick-up: and that gets him twelve years on a chain gang. He escapes to become eventually one of Chicago's leading citizens, but though he has been promised a pardon he has unfortunately talked to reporters about the system . . . The script is very clear on the divisions of society, on the haves and the have-nots: the former are corrupt and the latter victimised. The film became a rallying cry during the Depression. It remains often subtle, and always powerful, to its unforgettable, hammering finish.

Cabin in the Cotton (1932) handles the same theme, the exploitation of the poor by the rich, but in this case the poor are the cotton pickers of the South. Barthelmess is the educated peasant who is both pawn and arbitrator till the corruption of the landowners becomes evident. Curtiz directed, and in **20,000 Years in Sing Sing** (1933) he handled a plea for prison reform, putting forward a case for humane and reform-

conscious wardens. Davis is the moll who kills in self-defence, and Spencer Tracy (in a role meant for Cagney) the guy who takes the rap – a miscarriage of justice which in real life even the most backward jury would never have perpetrated. Curtiz also showed gusto on **Doctor X** (1932), occasioned by the success of Universal's horror films, and **The Mystery of the Wax Museum** (1933). In both Lionel Atwill plays a mad professor in a pleasing mixture of Victorian gothic and gadgetry.

Employees Entrance (1933), directed by del Ruth, is a study of life in a department store, and of the manager (Warren William) who drives himself and his staff beyond reason, relaxing only to give a bed to a girl (Loretta Young) badly in need of a meal – thus bringing into the open the inference of all these films , that sexual favours may be traded for a full stomach; later, however, without that motivation – since she has married in the meantime – she elects to stay the night, even if, to appease the Hays Office, she is supposedly drunk.

This view of man as predator and woman as victim was sustained in Wellman's **Frisco Jenny** (1933), a typical Ruth Chatterton vehicle and in fact a rehash of her most famous film, *Madame X*. Warners, however, were finally prepared to admit that women might be as sexually motivated as men, and as the chorus girls assemble to audition in **42nd Street** (1933), directed by Lloyd Bacon, they gossip about such matters as the friend who earns $45 a month but sends $100 home to her mother. The studio had first put such young ladies on the screen four years earlier, in *Gold Diggers of Broadway*, but as they revived them, in this film and in **Gold Diggers of 1933**, directed by LeRoy, they were considerably more mercenary. In the interim Warners had virtually killed off the film musical with its series of operettas – but after an absence of a year or so the genre was resuscitated by these two immortal movies. Both concern the putting on of shows, the lecherous 'angels', the driving producers, the temperamental stars, and the boys and girls who hoof all day and night rather than join the breadline. *Gold Diggers* concludes with a mawkish but moving tribute to the ex-doughboys who had not avoided the breadline , 'My Forgotten Man' – one of the flamboyant, vulgar and enjoyable production numbers devised by Busby Berkeley in

Mary Brian, Ruth Donnelly and James Cagney with two unnamed actors playing detectives in *Hard to Handle* – a title that reflected Warners' relations with Cagney rather than anything in the film. The best thing in the film – better even than Cagney – is Miss Donnelly. Miss Brian is her daughter, and their similar costumes represent not only a common hedge against the Depression, but their like-mindedness in matters concerning money and Cagney: they are as covetous of the one as they are suspicious of the other.

conjunction with the composer, Harry Warren, and the lyricist, Al Dubin. The other songs may be read as invitations to sex – 'I'm Young and Healthy', 'Shuffle Off to Buffalo', 'You're Getting to Be a Habit With Me', 'Petting in the Park': but then in both films, sex is as much a preoccupation as money. However, as befits the demotic approach, the two films are also built round hard work, with attendant sourness and disillusion. The total effect is exhilarating: both films are sharply-paced, and one could not cut a line from either without spoiling them.

Apart from the occasional stock, we see neither 42nd Street nor Broadway – in contrast to the boardwalks and alleys where Cagney operates in **Hard to Handle** (1933). However, it is the same venal world. He runs (literally: to escape from his victims) from promoter of dance-marathons to New York advertising and P.R., all gall and guts, with a host of

ingenious ideas as to how bright have-nots like himself can beat the Depression. To his prospective mother-in-law (Ruth Donnelly) he *is* the Depression, and her waxing and waning towards him, as his fortunes fluctuate, contribute towards virtual non-stop hilarity. LeRoy's direction emphasises both the satire and the sanity of the script. However, Roosevelt had been elected, and conditions were improving: Cagney became the crusading warden of a reform school in **The Mayor of Hell** (1933), directed by Mayo and inspired by the Soviet *Road to Life,* and in **Little Giant** (1933), directed by del Ruth, bootlegger Robinson decides to retire and acquire culture – only to find that Santa Barbara high society isn't quite ready for him. Prohibition was a dead duck, and this charming comedy begins with a montage of reactions to the new President.

Nevertheless, conditions in the country could not improve overnight, and like

241

In view of the plethora of money-grabbing heroines in the Depression era movies, we must assume that audiences found them at least half-admirable – though what Barbara Stanwyck was up to in *Baby Face* must have been in the mind of Will H. Hays when he strengthened the Production Code later in the year. Stanwyck, here in a factory-workers' speakeasy (with Nat Pendleton), is a part-time hooker to start with, and she has absolutely no intention of remaining in this milieu.

Cagney in *Hard to Handle* Barbara Stanwyck in **Baby Face** (1933) has a very personal way of overcoming them. Her method is to climb the ladder of success wrong by wrong – a not inappropriate expression, since her tale is the movie equivalent of the tabloid confession. She never stops to justify her conduct, be it the lie large or the look carnal – both of which are small weapons in her armoury. She ends back where she started, though she will surely try again: as directed by Alfred E. Green, this beguiling little tale deserved a sequel.

And yet these films are so much alike that they form a sequence. Their consistency is astonishing. Born out of star vehicles, the need to keep the distribution offices busy and the capitalist urge, they offer a pungent and mainly truthful account of America at a low point in its history. As we shall see in the next chapter, the other studios achieved nothing comparable. Warners did not set out to chronicle the Depression, nor did they ever quite abandon the concept of a varied batch of entertainments, but from their first Talkie successes – *The Dawn*

Patrol, Little Caesar – was born a concern in accord with the editorials of most of the nation's newspapers. Consequently the studio gathered a group of writers able to give voice to that concern and a team of players more at ease in bar rooms than in marble halls. Success bred success, and since Warners throughout its history was prone to repeat itself, it was providential that it had perforce to abandon the gangster movie just when those same editorials accused Hollywood of glamorising crime. On behalf of the studios, the Hays Office pointed out that the films themselves proffered the message that crime did not pay; the leader writers retorted that Hollywood's only solution to the Depression was crime or fantasy, at which point most of the studios chose to forget the whole business. Warners, however, continued to look the matter squarely in the eye, be it in a modest entertainment feature like *Employees Entrance*, or in a self-confessed document like *I Am a Fugitive From the Chain Gang*; then, with something like genius, the studio made three further musicals designed to cheer patrons without letting them forget the soup kitchens round the corner. It was the success of *I Am a Fugitive . . .* and those three musicals which brought to a close this remarkable series; concern with social conditions the studio may have had, but it was also anxious, in a time of recession, to report good returns to its stockholders.

Heroes for Sale (1933) poses the problem of Tom Holmes (Barthelmess), an ex-doughboy with steel splinters in his back, an affliction which leads first to morphine addiction, and then to theft. Cured in hospital he is able to make a new start in a factory, and after many vicissitudes becomes successful; but there is labour unrest in the city, and this encourages the anti-Red squad, whose members recall Tom's Communist affiliations during previous agitation. He joins the freight-hopping, jobless, but combats pessimism: 'Did you read Roosevelt's inaugural speech? . . . It takes more than one blow to knock out twenty million people.' Because of this note of hope, the ending is the opposite of that of *I Am a Fugitive . . .*, but where that film indicted a system, but no individual and no class, *Heroes* accuses the capitalists, or what we now call the Establishment. The director, Wellman, and the writers, Robert Lord and Wilson Mizner, may have been *commercially* indignant, and they certainly hedge their bets on Communism by making Tom's Red friend (Robert Barrat) both 'daffy' and 'a maniac'; they also leave a large hole in the plot, but they are entirely honest in their depiction of the world of the dispossessed.

Wellman went on to make **Wild Boys of the Road** (1933), about children from good homes who take to the freights to avoid being a burden on their impoverished parents. He avoids melodrama, managing a portrait of the rootless, shifting stowaways, living in a world of rape, and easy murder, one in which no head is turned in protest, a world in which the youngsters search for that reward best expressed by Judy Garland (q.v.), when the Depression was over, in 'Over the Rainbow'.

Wild Boys was admired but *Heroes for Sale* was an outright failure. The history of the American film is littered with films which so much offended the right-wing, asking it to face unpalatable facts about itself, that they were thrown on the scrapheap – both adversely reviewed and unable to get bookings. Since so much in this particular film

still astonishes – the Establishment plotting to destroy a worker, the anti-Red squad shown as bully-boys – we may be sure that such was its fate. Barthelmess, moreover, had lost his popularity, and that fact could not have helped two further films concerned with injustice, **Massacre** (1934), directed by Alan Crosland, and **A Modern Hero** (1934), Pabst's only American film. The serious nature of Crosland's film is emphasised by the fact that it was shot almost entirely on location. Barthelmess plays an Indian-born rodeo star made suddenly aware of the ways of his people, and cruelly exposed to their exploitation by white officials; Ann Dvorak is the Indian girl he meets, educated at the Haskell Institute, and long resigned to such facts. In Pabst's film, Barthelmess is on the other side, a bare back rider in a circus who, by virtue of a lucky investment – and a number of compliant women – becomes a successful manufacturer. Both Pabst and Warners were fond of sexual frankness and adept at seedy detail; the basic subject, on this occasion as taken from a novel by Louis Bromfield, was typical of both, but the revised Hays Code was beginning to bite and Pabst, loathing the compromises, refused to work in Hollywood again. That subject was similar to Fox's *The Power and the Glory* (q.v.), and as that foreshadows

James Cagney, Allen Jenkins and Alan Dinehart in *Jimmy the Gent*, directed in 1934 by Michael Curtiz, with Cagney as enterprising as ever in the usual precarious job – in this case an entrepreneur who makes his money finding heirs to fortune. The girl, alternately loving and sceptical, is Bette Davis, at the start of her long career as one of the screen's outstanding actresses.

Sex, Crime and Booze: Warner Bros. in the Thirties

The Busby Berkeley girls in the 'By a Waterfall' number in *Footlight Parade*. Since the patterns that Berkeley made with girls are *sui generis*, there is every reason why his name above all should be associated with the Warner Bros. musicals of this time. However, since he merely copied – if sometimes elaborating upon – the routines he had already done for Goldwyn and M-G-M, the extent of his creative contribution may be questioned, as it has, indeed, by other Warners alumni, who have claimed that the numbers were the result of collaboration between the whole production team.

Orson Welles's first American film, so does this his second, *The Magnificent Ambersons* (q.v.): all four films concern the corrupting effects of power.

Warners' third Depression musical was **Footlight Parade** (1933), directed by Bacon, and where his *42nd Street* took its tone from Warner Baxter as the producer, driving and hard-faced, so this takes its tone from Cagney in the same role, driving but chipper, quippy and optimistic. There is Blondell as his neglected, ever-loving secretary ('You don't like *anybody*' he snaps. 'If only you knew' she sobs); Ruth Donnelly as the impresario's wife, promoting her latest gigolo ('He's waiting outside, ready and eager to start his career'); Claire Dodd as a scheming vamp; Frank McHugh as the hard-working dance director; and, again, Kibbee as the impresario and Ruby Keeler and Dick Powell as the ingenues. The film, like its predecessors, is alive to the glamour of show business, with a chorus for ever rehearsing in the background, a pianist trying out the songs, and someone – usually Cagney – barking out orders; there is the same approach to morals ('Outside, Countess – as long as there are sidewalks you've got a job'), but perhaps a heightened vulgarity in Berkeley's numbers. 'Shanghai Lil', a melange of opium dens, tinsel blondes, sailors and red-white-and-blue patriotism – not the least of it in Cagney's dance – is pop-art at its most enduring.

Wonder Bar (1934), directed by Bacon, stars Al Jolson in his stage role of night club M.C. – a venue, it seems, for tourists to rub shoulders with gigolos and dance hostesses, slipping in and out of melodrama. It is also a centre for various kinds of love – adulterous, unrequited, deviant, criminal and, above all, purchasable. This one bypassed the new Code (though a blackface song, 'Goin' to Heaven on a Mule', offends taste), but **Dames,** directed by Ray Enright, did not. Warners advertised it as their 'Gold Diggers of 1934', but the new Code had drawn the studio's fangs. Since their movies had 'exposed' the same inequalities in the American system that the press picked upon, Hays could point to it as the most responsible of the studios, and he tightened the Code to curb the Misses Harlow and West rather than these gold diggers. Joan Blondell was the Warners' symbol of the Depression – never fazed, never down for long. She was a smiler and a soft touch, but clear-eyed. In *Dames,* as a scheming showgirl, her heartlessness has gone. The earlier gold diggers were motivated by mercenary considerations, but now they acted for society or 'the show'. Hugh Herbert is the puritan converted to boozing, gambling and showgirls, a consistent theme in these films; but where *Gold Diggers of 1933* offered such men as dupes, discovering a new life style, Herbert is merely a harmless clown. The Warner era of venality and venery was over.

It was not merely that the new Code was in force and that Zanuck had moved on to found 20th Century Pictures (q.v.); it was not merely that the studio bosses – the brothers Warner themselves – now looked towards the literary adaptations which spelt prestige at the other studios. Warner pictures would, indeed, retain demotic themes for many years yet. But the most notable thing about the Warner product between 1930 and 1934 is that no one knew at the time how good most of it was.

12

Hollywood before the Code

WARNER BROS. did not have sole prerogative on proletarian subjects during the Depression – they were simply the most insistent. Other studios continued with a mixture of wish – fulfilment and films which reflected the problems of their audience. The coming of Sound meant – words being a prerequisite – an even greater dependence on novels and plays, many of them written for a public more sophisticated than the old movie audiences. The stage players flooding into Hollywood were not geared to interpret the usual mindless entertainments, being in many cases too mature in age, and the new writers brought in were not interested in penning them. The Western and the swashbuckler, their spirit of adventure at odds with the mood of the time, went into decline. The young still went to the cinema, but, unlike later generations, *en famille*: while their parents waited for the latest gangster film, they were entertained by the increasingly diversified supporting programmes.

The only other studio besides Warners to show consistent interest in the working class was Paramount – even if their characters seldom stayed long at the counter or the work bench. An exception was Clara Bow in **The Saturday Night Kid** (1929), a remake of *Love 'em and Leave 'em*. She was meant to provide someone with whom all the footsore shopgirls of the world could identify; hence the title. As directed by Edward Sutherland, she is a clerk sacrificing everything for the sake of a conniving younger sister. Audiences had indeed increasingly identified with Bow, to the extent that her popularity fell away when headlines disclosed that she was in life much like the scandalous Clara of her early films.

Paramount saw the more mousy Sylvia Sidney as a replacement, defending her mobster father (Guy Kibbee) in **City Streets** (1931), directed by Rouben Mamoulian. 'What have your ideas got you?' she asks her boyfriend (Gary Cooper), who works in a funfair, 'Racketeers are smart, not dumb like some people.' Duly admonished, he joins the mob – not reforming till the fade-out.

Working Girls (1931) focuses on two out-of-town sisters (Judith Wood and Dorothy Hall) out to find jobs while fighting off men, and is set in one of the all-female rooming houses so common in films at this time; the director was Dorothy Arzner (b. 1900), to date the most successful of Hollywood's handful of women directors. Her **Honor Among Lovers** (1931) does have a heroine (Claudette Colbert) who keeps a maid on a secretary's salary – but she is an executive secretary. Her boss (Fredric March) is a philanderer, and the opening sequence – an office picnic lunch, with him advancing and her keeping him at bay, but both with mutual respect – is among the wittiest in films of this period.

Carole Lombard (q.v.) and Nancy Carroll also played working girls. In **No Man of Her Own** (1932) Lombard is a small town librarian, plucky but unlucky enough to marry a gambler (Clark Gable): 'A rather usual sort of melodrama,' Mordaunt Hall commented in *The New York Times*, but though without exceptional direction – by Wesley Ruggles – it is unusually entertaining today. In **Dangerous Paradise** (1931) Carroll is a woebegone singer with a particularly butch ladies' band and Richard Arlen is the lone trader who mistakenly believes her a whore. This very loose adaptation of Conrad's 'Victory' has direction by William Wellman which makes much of moonlit verandahs, low dives, desperation and a fine covey of villains. In **Hot Saturday** (1932), directed by William A. Seiter, Carroll is a suburban working girl torn between her hard-working geologist sweetheart (Randolph Scott) and the wealthy local representative (Cary Grant) of the post-jazz generation, spending Saturday afternoons picnicking with bootleg gin.

Fast and Loose (1930), a remake of *The Best People,* directed by Fred Newmeyer, indicates impatience with the irresponsibility of the young rich, and gold diggers are 'exposed' in **Girls About Town** (1931), in which two of them (Kay Francis, Lilyan Tashman) entertain visiting firemen for large fees. George Cukor (b. 1899), a Broadway director new to Hollywood, was unable to reconcile the comic and romantic elements, but he did better with **Tarnished Lady** (1931), about an impoverished member (Tallulah Bankhead) of the Four Hundred who marries for money and lives to regret it, through motherhood, street walking and store clerking before coming to her senses. And it might be said that **Devil and the Deep** (1932) also indicts the follies of the rich, as Miss Bankhead leaves her paranoid commander husband (Charles Laughton) to spend a night in the desert with his new second in command (Gary Cooper); Marion Gering directed.

Chief among the ladies who sinned and suffered for Paramount was Ruth Chatterton (1893–1961), who brought warmth and a degree of truth to the roles she was required to play – in what were then considered sophisticated entertainments by the trade, critics and audiences alike. However, **Sarah and Son** (1930) is merely a mother-love drama, with Chatterton as a German-born vaudeville hoofer who becomes a famed diva in order to fight for her son; in **Anybody's Woman** (1930), also directed by Arzner, she is an out-of-work chorus girl married to a drunken lawyer (Clive Brook). Dozens of films were predicated on this situation (the nuptials taking place while one of the parties is too drunk to comprehend) but this one does offer a convincing portrait of the subsequent marriage: two ill-suited people trying to adjust and making each other unhappier all the while. In John Cromwell's

Unfaithful (1931), Chatterton discovers that her husband is just that, so she drinks cocktails, sings 'Mama's in the Doghouse Now' in her frillies, and flirts with a nice artist (Paul Lukas). This film is unusual in that she starts wealthy and stays wealthy. Society had a remarkable mobility in Paramount's films, and, in general, the higher anyone moves the more venal the crowd. There were, in real life, stockbrokers on the dole and bootleggers in the penthouse, but if this portrait of a society in flux carries its own conviction that was not, necessarily, the prime motive: Paramount sold dreams, and it was *de rigeur* that the female star change her cotton frocks and cotton stockings for satins and silks. The Warner ladies often managed without – just as their movies sometimes managed without happy endings: in perhaps just a couple of these Paramount films is a happy ending actually justified.

A happy fade-out is not anticipated in **Behind the Make-Up** (1930), directed by Arzner and Robert Milton, an unpretentious story of two show business figures, the 'giver' (Hal Skelly, as type cast in his few films) and the 'taker', who makes off with wife, act and savings. The role of the taker was played by William Powell (b. 1892), who became a star in **Street of Chance** (1930), in which he is a big time gambler who sacrifices himself so that his younger brother shall not go the same way; in **For the Defense** (1930) he is a shady lawyer who prefers Sing Sing to seeing the woman he loves embroiled in a scandal. David O. Selznick produced both, Oliver H. P. Garett contributed to the screenplays, and Cromwell directed (q.v.); Lothar Mendes replaced the latter on **Ladies' Man** (1931), which ends with gigolo Powell thrown to death by the husband of one of his mistresses. If you mixed the reels of these films you would be mystified but not disconcerted – for you would recognise the same street corners, the same bars, the same hotel rooms and lobbies, both luxurious and threadbare; the leading ladies and the supporting players, when not the same, are interchangeable. Powell wears the same clothes, he plays the same role – the dapper, proper man of the world, whose connections, at the very least, are shady; to himself, however, and to his friends, his honour is as unimpeachable as his cravat. Audiences might let him die – he was too suave, too flippant, to be allowed to live – but they could admire him along the way.

Fredric March (1897–1973) was less rigidly typed, but he was also the urban man of the time, decent but hard-drinking. He is a columnist-dramatist in Arzner's **Merrily We Go to Hell** (1932), which is also explicit on what Americans in the Prohibition era were doing behind closed doors. In this case, his wife (Sylvia Sidney) is trying to get as drunk as he, and when that fails, she matches him infidelity for infidelity. The film is sharp on manners and morals, and in that same manner **Laughter** (1930) is very nearly a masterpiece. It starts with an attempted suicide and, later, when another attempt is successful, it plunges into melodrama; but between whiles it operates on the same frivolous level as *The Last Flight*. Watching March and Nancy Carroll in this film is an odd experience, as if the characters of Evelyn Waugh or Coward had sprung back into life – American versions of the Bright Young Things, callous, deprecatory, bantering. Like Helen Chandler

in the Warner film, Miss Carroll is dry, acerbic, in full control of her wit and laughter Harry d'Abbadie d'Arrast (1893–1968), a director of few credits, made it, and Donald Ogden Stewart helped to write it.

The grimmer elements in *The Last Flight* may be found in **The Eagle and the Hawk** (1933), also written by John Monk Saunders – saluted by Mordaunt Hall in *The New York Times* for a screenplay 'devoid of the stereotyped ideas which have weakened most of such narratives'. Credit for the direction is divided between Stuart Walker and Mitchell Leisen (1898–1972), the latter just graduating from art direction, but if we look at the other films which Saunders had a hand in writing – they include *Wings* and *The Dawn Patrol* – we will find his the controlling voice, thus invalidating once again the director-as-auteur theory. Despite different directors, these films have an astonishing consistency, being based on Saunders's own wartime experiences, and he is more realistic than other writers on the night-time

Fredric March and Nancy Carroll in *Laughter*: she is the young wife of an ageing man (Frank Morgan), competing with her stepdaughter for the attentions of a suicidal sculptor – till March comes upon the scene, persuading her to return to the laughter of the past, in a relationship devoid of morals or emotion.

248

drunkenness and the death-or-glory philosophy. *The Eagle and the Hawk* is the blackest of the four films. March (who is tremendously good) plays a man bewildered and embittered, particularly savage on the question of 'citations . . . they're broken bones and flesh, and blood'; in London, he is disgusted by talk of tactics and bravery. It is as if Saunders compensated for the Hollywood gold by being more ruthlessly honest than any other writer of his time; and this film remains moving, even if the Hays Office ordered the removal of the most passionate antiwar scenes – as well as cutting the sequence with Carole Lombard, as the 'beautiful lady' who offers March a pillow during his furlough in London, and the original ending, which had Cary Grant (q.v.), the irresponsible colleague and now a hobo, looking at a plaque commemorating March's heroism. Saunders later went to Britain to work on a semi-documentary, *Conquest of the Air* (q.v.), for Korda, and he committed suicide in 1940, at the age of forty-four.

Most of these films were of medium budget, and when in 1932 Paramount went into receivership it was due not to failure or over expenditure but to the fall in value of its stock. The Long Island studio was closed, and production concentrated in Hollywood. Jesse Lasky, the overall production head, was ousted, and so was B. P. Schulberg, manager of the California studio: neither quite recovered from the blow, though both managed to produce independently at other studios. Despite attempts by creditors to relieve him similarly of his duties, Zukor survived, and was made chairman of the board in 1935.

The crisis year coincided with the release of two of the company's best-remembered pictures, both from much-read novels. Robert Louis Stevenson's **Doctor Jekyll and Mr Hyde** (1932) has a whopping climax to which, after a slow start, the director Mamoulian imaginatively works; but the leading players, including March in the title-roles, are colourless, thus pushing into abeyance the matter of Jekyll's dual sexuality – in the context of Victorian London the most interesting aspect of the tale. On the other hand, Borzage's **A Farewell to Arms** (1932) has a poor ending, with Death, Wagner's Liebestod and the Armistice all fighting for attention –

though we should be grateful that they did not use the alternative 'happy' ending which had been shot. Till that point, however, this adaptation of Hemingway is instinctively right, with a dreamlike intensity from the moment Lieutenant Henry (Gary Cooper) spots Catherine (Helen Hayes); the War recedes, as it did with them, and their love story is very touching. It is also quite outspoken (the love scenes were pruned on reissue, by decree of the Legion of Decency – the Roman Catholic watch committee set up just after the Hays Code was tightened), but we may recognise the film as one of the magic artefacts that the dream factory then threw up from time to time.

Modern novels of quality were of no interest to the studios unless (a) suitable for star players, (b) the public had indicated a predilection for the work in question, or (c) there was a high sex quotient – which meant, even at this time, battles with the Hays Office. A few years earlier Hays had refused to sanction the filming of 'The Constant Nymph', which led indirectly to the Authors' League getting an agreement that offending properties could be filmed provided that the title was changed and, in some cases, the names of the chief characters. The most famous fish to slip through this net was William Faulkner's 'Sanctu-

Gary Cooper and Helen Hayes in Frank Borzage's *A Farewell to Arms*. Cooper is allowed his share of mooning and, like other Borzage heroes, tears, but a movie hero who likes boozing and brothels can take us with him: Borzage knew that if the hard facts of life are there, audiences will swallow the rest.

ary', which became, under the direction of Stephen Roberts, **The Story of Temple Drake** (1933), about a girl (Miriam Hopkins) of good family who, imprisoned in a whorehouse, finds later that she has no regrets for the life she led. However, despite the atmospheric photography – by Karl Struss – lust becomes fairly risible with dialogue, viz. 'You, Temple Drake, in a place like this! Are you – ? Did he – ?' Another oddity derived from a notable novel is one of Paramount's contributions to the horror cycle, **Island of Lost Souls** (1933), messily directed by Erle C. Kenton; its source is 'The Island of Dr Moreau' by H. G. Wells, who disliked the film intensely – and was not sorry when the British censors refused to let their countrymen see this tale of a mad scientist (Charles Laughton) lording it over a menagerie he is turning into human beings.

All was not grim at Paramount, which had acquired the services of a popular radio singer, Bing Crosby (1901–77), taking a number of jokes at his own expense – he plays himself – in a scatty farce, **The Big Broadcast** (1932), directed by Frank Tuttle. The cast also included Burns and Allen, the Mills Brothers and the Boswell Sisters, and its success initiated the practice of guest appearances from radio and vaudeville, former enemies of Hollywood, throughout the decade. The company's best comedy of the period – Lubitsch apart – is **Three-Cornered Moon** (1933), directed by Elliott Nugent from a play by Gertrude Tonkonogy about a well-to-do Brooklyn family hit by the Depression. Coping with the situation, without sentiment, is an almost perfect cast: Mary Boland as the fluttery mother unused to nickels and dimes; Claudette Colbert (q.v.) as the sensible puss who saves them all from starvation; and Richard Arlen as the family doctor, waiting for her to see through the budding novelist she thinks she loves.

One director determined to say something on contemporary problems was Cecil B. deMille, with a film called **This Day and Age** (1933), in which the idealism of the young triumphs over the corruption of the old, or, rather, the high school gang beats the big racketeers: plagiarised are *Road to Life*, 'Emil und die Detektive', any number of gangster films and *M*, even to its camera set ups. **The Sign of the Cross** (1932) is the antithesis, a Roman story

involving a sadistic, fiddling Nero (Charles Laughton), a nymphomaniac Poppaea (Claudette Colbert), an intense captain of the Guard (Fredric March), and a Christian (Elissa Landi). The subsequent fame of this film seems due to Poppaea's bath in ass's milk; it cannot even claim spectacular decor, and was not particularly successful in its time. However, it marked deMille's return to the company he had helped to found, and confirmed his bent for antiquity. A colloquial approach to Plutarch, **Cleopatra** (1934), contains some splendid lines, e.g. 'You took advantage of my uncle's body on the funeral pyre to win support for yourself – you with your "Friends, Romans, Countrymen"!' In the title-role Miss Colbert looks as if at a fancy-dress party, but the photography by Victor Milner won an Oscar, and there is a moment, when the giant oars of Cleopatra's barge move into action, worth the whole of the 1963 *Cleopatra* (q.v.).

DeMille, earlier, had been the company's most respected director, and he would later be its most commercial one: but in both regards it was Lubitsch who at this time dominated the Paramount lot – and the affections of the reviewers. 'All the shrewd delights that were promised in *The Love Parade,*' said Richard Watts in *The New York Herald Tribune*, 'are realised' in **The Smiling Lieutenant** (1931), which he went on to compare with *Le Million*; however, Clair's film is a lark, and *The Smiling Lieutenant* is an exercise in operetta, even if the evening's plot is founded on a wink. Maurice Chevalier has the title-role, forced to leave his mistress (Miss Colbert) for a princess (Miss Hopkins); he was reunited with his best partner, Jeanette MacDonald, in both **One Hour With You** (1932) and **Love Me Tonight** (1932). The former is a remake of Lubitsch's second American picture, its emphasis changed from the divorcing couple to the happily married one – happiness pointed up by the wife's whispered conversation with her girlfriend, whose sole comment is an incredulous 'He can?' The skill and grace of the leads are matched by Charlie Ruggles, who has designs on her, by Genevieve Tobin, who has designs on him, and Roland Young, who has designs on the maid. *Love Me Tonoght* is less surefooted in its approach to matters sexual, of which there are considerably more: a young widow (MacDonald) has melancholia which can only be cured by marriage – to a tailor (Chevalier) made to masquerade as an aristocrat. The songs are by Rodgers and Hart, staged in over-contrived manner or derived from Clair, but the film is still a box of delights: its director, as any buff will tell you, is not Lubitsch but Mamoulian. The direction of *One Hour With You* is credited to Lubitsch 'assisted' by George Cukor, who has however said that he alone directed it and that he had to threaten a lawsuit to get his name on the screen at all – which suggests that Lubitsch was highly satisfied with his work.

The leads of both **Trouble in Paradise** (1932) and **Design for Living** (1933) lack the ebullience of Chevalier and Mac-Donald, but in the first film Herbert Marshall and Kay Francis have nonchalance to spare as a jewel thief and his wealthy dupe; in the second Fredric March and Gary Cooper are miscast as Bohemian rivals for Miriam Hopkins – a lady common to both films. *Trouble in Paradise* is Lubitsch at his most sophisticated, but the Hays Office clamped down on the *menage à trois* situation of *Design for Living* as it had been treated in Noël Coward's play. Now it is explained that the characters resist sexual temptation in order to save 'time, trouble and confusion', and Ben Hecht's screenplay famously rejected almost all of Coward's dialogue for weak jokes such as 'Let's talk it over quietly like a disarmament conference'; a further liability seems to be that Lubitsch misunderstood the English puritan tradition against which Coward was rebelling.

In the midst of these films Lubitsch made an antiwar tract, **The Man I Killed** (1932) – or *Broken Lullaby,* as it was retitled after its New York premiere, when the public, as the studio had feared, failed to respond to rave notices. Its power remains discernible, despite some poor performances – Phillips Holmes, Lionel Barrymore – and the phoney German setting; the source was a French play about a guilt-ridden soldier (Holmes) who infiltrates himself into the rabidly anti-French family of a soldier he has killed. Since Lubitsch's concern, if untypical of his work, is implicit in every line, he was perhaps pleased to contribute to a film which, influenced by current economics, is as pessimistic as any ever

made. **If I Had a Million** (1932) is built round a millionaire who gives his fortune to names picked at random from the telephone book; its later fame was due to the all-star cast and the rarity of episode films, but it was a failure at the time. It also suffered cuts, on moral grounds, and lost at one time was the episode where the whore (Wynne Gibson) takes a hotel suite and discards with fury the second pillow. Another sequence finds George Raft in a flophouse, but the harshest of them is the final one, with May Robson as the inmate of an old people's home. The dark vision may be that of the uncredited producer, or it could have been caused by the collective conscience of the eighteen writers and eight directors who, sitting on their California lawns, put it together.

Those eight directors do not include Josef von Sternberg, which may be deliberate, since Selznick, then a producer at Paramount, recognised that his forte was for artificial people in artificial situations. Von Sternberg apparently conceived his mission as creating the right ambience for Marlene Dietrich. Because in *Der Blaue Engel* she had driven at least one man to destruction, Paramount decided that her appeal was akin to Garbo's – more tawdry, a little brasher, but again in the tradition of

Jeanette MacDonald and Maurice Chevalier in the Lubitsch-Cukor *One Hour With You*: 'What a Little Thing Like a Wedding Ring Can Do' is a song they sing in the bedroom – and if their joy being in bed together is not apparent, Chevalier is inclined to share his directly with the audience. It is indication of his considerable charm that he gets away with it.

Marlene Dietrich prepares to face the firing squad in *Dishonored*, refusing the blindfold offered by the lieutenant (Barry Norton) in charge of the firing party. 'Death is only another exciting adventure. A perfect end to an imperfect life,' she says. The films she made with Josef von Sternberg are imperfect; see the early ones, before he turned her into a dummy.

sophisticated European vice. M-G-M's inability to see Garbo as other than a courtesan was favourable to Dietrich, who proved to be unconvincing in any other role; as an adventuress she was more likely than Garbo, and she could read a witty line with more equivocation. She played a cabaret singer again in her first American film, **Morocco** (1930), written by Jules Furthman, from a play by Benno Vigny, with a clear distinction as to the varying kinds of love. 'Every time a man has helped me there has been a price. What's yours?' she says to Adolph Menjou, artist and man of the world, prepared to marry her with the knowledge that she can never be his. She entertains his advances, but gives her key to legionnaire Gary Cooper, to prove that her promiscuity is tuned to looks rather than wealth. He goes to her room, but they do

not even kiss – for if their passion is to be a lasting one they cannot do anything so cheap as to jump into bed. The extent, after that, of their relationship is unclear, but their individual independence prevents their love from running smoothly – an independence that is part of their sexuality, inseparable from his masculinity and her knowledge of where her body has led her in the past. In **Dishonored** (1931) she can be found plying her trade on a Viennese pavement, before being inducted into the Secret Service to seduce a Russian colonel (Victor McLaglen). She can therefore redeem herself by patriotism, if not love; and as the firing squad prepares to aim, a young lieutenant cries out against the injustice of killing beauty, to which she responds by applying a lipstick – an effect of crushing banality, entirely in keeping with what has gone before.

In contrast, von Sternberg made **An American Tragedy** (1931), abandoned by Eisenstein – lured by Paramount to Hollywood – after half a million dollars had been spent in preparation; the rights to Dreiser's novel had cost the corporation a huge $150,000 and von Sternberg was requested to achieve something on a reduced budget. He professed himself uninterested, but while never managing the resonances of the later version, *A Place in the Sun* (q.v.), his has both a stronger narrative drive and a more authentic feeling for the milieu. What is on screen hardly amounts to tragedy and is certainly not an indictment, as was the novel (Dreiser disliked the film, and unsuccessfully tried to sue); but it does make one wonder about the Clyde Griffiths of this world – this one a bounder (Phillips Holmes) who was lucky for a while. A former bell hop, he chances to meet a wealthy uncle, he chances to meet both the factory girl (Sylvia Sidney) he seduces and the rich girl (Frances Dee) who takes him up; by chance there is a newspaper headline about a drowned girl, but his downfall is not due to chance. He was not clever enough to start with.

Von Sternberg returned to Dietrich – and that breath-catching first moment of **Shanghai Express** (1932), when she advances along the platform trailed by Anna May Wong, 'and both of them rotten' as a bystander observes, 'Anyone can see they're out in search of victims . . . Why, she's wrecked a dozen men.' Among her fellow passengers is an old acquaintance (Clive Brook) who asks her tersely, 'Married?' 'It took more than one man to change my name to . . . Shanghai Lily' she replies. They are on the observation platform, she in feathers and he in full mess kit. Was the oldest profession ever so glamorous? It was certainly easy to make an entertaining 'train' movie with a writer like Furthman and a photographer like Lee Garmes – von Sternberg's invariable support – but it is the direction which provides the superb imaginary Orient, with its sinister face beneath the smile. Von Sternberg himself provided the story of **Blonde Venus** (1932), of a housewife who descends to whoring and 'uses man after man' before being a celebrity in a white satin tux in Paris; he later claimed that there was nothing of himself in the film, but at the time he fought the studio

for a happy ending – a reunion with the husband (Herbert Marshall). Paramount considered it immoral – not to say unconvincing – but gave in since star and director were ostentatiously preparing to leave. However, when box-office takings were disastrously below the $3 million earned by *Shanghai Express* – admittedly an outstanding amount – they were firm in separating director and protégée, putting her into the hands of Mamoulian, whose version of Sudermann's *The Song of Songs* effectively hides any quality in the original.

The Scarlet Empress (1934) is not only a demonstration of Selznick's comment on von Sternberg, but the latter's justification; it could only have been made by a vulgarian of genius. No writer is credited, but it lays claim to be based on Catherine the Great's diary, to which it stays close. It establishes her (Dietrich) as a virgin, out of her depth in the barbaric court, at odds with her imbecilic husband (Sam Jaffe) and her mother-in-law, the drunken Czarina (Louise Dresser); when the latter dies she succeeds to the throne because the army is on her side, she having, it is implied, taken a leaf from the old Empress's book and slept with most of its officers. Catherine thundering into the palace at the head of her army has such grandeur – despite or perhaps because of a soundtrack fusion of 'The Ride of the Valkyries' and the '1812 Overture' – that for a second one wonders whether it would have been a good film with a real actress; but then, without her, it wouldn't have been what it is. In one sequence, in a pique, she allows herself to be picked up by a young officer: given that it is instantaneous, that she is young and pretty and he magnificently caparisoned and handsome, the scene must rank high in erotic fantasy. The Hays Office would not have passed it a month or so later. In fact, the Code had been tightened before the film appeared, but that was because Paramount withheld it, fearing comparisons with Korda's British film about Catherine (q.v.). The comparisons were made, and were adverse; and it is possible to see, given the climate of the time, why that antiseptic piece was preferred to this carnival.

When few cinemas were prepared to book the film, Paramount permitted von Sternberg to try just once more: **The Devil is a Woman** (1935), based on 'La Femme et le Pantin' by Pierre Louys, later filmed by

Hollywood before the Code

Julien Duvivier with Brigitte Bardot, and later still by Buñuel. Despite that provenance, it was old-hat then – a triangle story in the manner of *Der Blaue Engel* and *Morocco,* concerning the obsessed middle-aged man (Lionel Atwill), his younger rival (Cesar Romero), and a trollop, if one may so describe the glittering but dummy-like *femme fatale* played by Dietrich. The public cannot be blamed for rejecting this film as completely as it did; audiences mistook plenty of synthetic blather for the real thing, but taken to this length it has all the excitement of a gift-wrapped bauble – which is often what it looks like. To achieve this sort of artifice is no mean achievement, but unlike the other great *décoratif* director, Max Ophuls, von Sternberg lacks heart and mind and gaiety; Ophuls's similar artificial stories are for adults, but von Sternberg's only intermittently – and then in cod fashion. He departed from Paramount, while Dietrich continued to hold her own in kitsch: once a breath of real air is let in, she withers and dies.

While von Sternberg turned this once-earthy fraulein into little more than a statue, Paramount was joined by the most glorious expression of the unabashedly amoral, Mae West (1893–1980). She arrived to play an old flame of night club owner George Raft in **Night After Night** (1932), directed by Archie Mayo, and in fact a Raft vehicle. It defines the Raft image: the backstreet boy who has made it to the top – legally, just. He is tough; he carries a gun when treating with rivals, but is loth to use it. He is a slick dresser and a ladies' man, but a nice guy at heart. As an actor, however, he is inexpressive, and it is a relief to turn to West, who, asked if she believes in love at first sight, replies, 'I dunno, but it sure saves time.' Her reception in this role proved to the studio that it might risk a starring vehicle for this actress associated with *risqué* stage plays, usually written by herself; such was the notoriety of her biggest success, 'Diamond Lil', that the film version was retitled **She Done Him Wrong** (1933). She first appears looking bored, but lights up when recognised and begins to purr as men doff their hats. Descending from her carriage, she pats a child on the head: 'You're a fine woman, Lady Lou' says the child's mother, and Lady Lou agrees: 'Finest woman who ever walked the streets.'. The film itself is a thrown-together thing, though directed by

Lowell Sherman with a fine eye for plush Bowery saloons; what matters is Mae, the honey pot round which the bees cluster. It remains refreshing to experience her unbridled and luxurious enjoyment of men, sin and diamonds – not necessarily in that order; it is not difficult to see why she shocked so many – for here was a lady who went after the men she fancied without a single inhibition. There were men in her past, and there would be men in her future; we never saw her in bed with one, but she had a habit of receiving in her bedroom. 'I'm meeting all comers this evening' she says in **I'm No Angel** (1933), adding, 'I like sophisticated men to take me out.' The man protests that he is not really sophisticated: 'You're not really out either.' she responds, and any way you consider the line its meaning is sexual. Her humour depends on a play on words to give that sort of meaning; it was outrageous most of the time, and sometimes witty. 'When women go wrong men go right after them.' she counsels in *She Done Him Wrong,* and her protégée (Rochelle Hudson) cannot wait to whip off her Quakerish dress and follow her advice.

This lady is virtually the only ingenue in a Mae West film. The star penned her own scripts, at least at first; she was not interested in writing for other women, and indeed disliked writing scenes in which she wouldn't appear. Hence the rickety nature of the vehicles; they are all quite short, and if they seem long it is because the material is often just enough for a revue sketch. The star's act – superb as it is – cannot sustain a full-length film: she merely sashays through it, throwing off remarks solely about sex, jewels and her easy going nature. The fact that the other characters are merely adjuncts further limits her, plus the insistence that she – invariably playing a vaudeville star – is 'the greatest star of the century'. It is remarkable that the films remain so entertaining, but they are progressively less so, and you may care to go no further than *I'm No Angel*, directed by Wesley Ruggles, and *Belle of the Nineties* (1934), directed by Leo McCarey (q.v.).

The Code proved almost fatal. The fury with which the custodians of the country's morals greeted *She Done Him Wrong* was only equalled by the public's curiosity. Paramount issued a formal statement to the effect that its profits had not only prevented

254

its creditors from selling out to M-G-M but the company's 1,700 theatres from closing – which only made it worse: she not only preached that sex was fun, profitably, but the country revelled in it. The far from silent majority directed their wrath against the Hays Office, and though other factors were involved in the tightening of the Code, Miss West was the chief one.

Her four subsequent films for Paramount are mainly notable for the bowdlerisation of her original character: she remains predatory, but now men come a good second to diamonds. The invariable sameness of her delivery becomes monotonous when the lines delivered are not funny; was she only capable of humour when it was a question of gender, or had the earlier films used up the jokes stored during the years on the stage? **Goin' to Town** (1935), directed by Alexander Hall, has her marrying for social position, singing Delilah in Saint-Saëns' opera, and getting her own back on uppity upstate New York society. In **Klondike Annie** (1936), she starts as San Francisco Doll, mistress of a Chinaman; deported, she sets her sights at the Captain (Victor McLaglen), but once in Nome gets involved in a Mission – but at least, as directed by Raoul Walsh, we have glimpsed the original Mae. The public lost interest, and we can only conjecture whether this was because she could no longer shock or, in fact, had been a nine days' wonder in the first place. Paramount was not inclined to renew her contract, but an independent producer, Emanuel Cohen, put her into two films for that company to release: **Go West, Young Man** (1936), directed by Henry Hathaway, in which she is a movie star who upsets a mid-West household when her car breaks down; and **Every Day's a Holiday** (1937), directed by Edward Sutherland, and only enjoyable for the performance of Walter Catlett, in a dry run for Disney's Honest John.

As it happened, Paramount had a monopoly of the great screen clowns of this period. W. C. Fields returned to play a king in **Million Dollar Legs** (1932), directed by Edward Cline. The title, as far as can be ascertained, refers to the athletes the king intends to enter in the San Francisco Olympic Games: but it is not a film in which to look for meanings. Fields headed a further cast of clowns in the also impenetrable but less hilarious **International House** (1933), directed by Sutherland, and was Humpty Dumpty in **Alice in Wonderland** (1933), as unrecognisable as were Gary Cooper as the White Knight, Cary Grant as the Mock Turtle, Edna May Oliver as the Red Queen, Edward Everett Horton as the Mad Hatter, etc. The Tenniel drawings were copied, but there is nothing of the mad but logical progression of the books, and even the most famous opening in English literature was turned inside out as directed by Norman McLeod in this pointless and rather nasty picture.

Paramount was returning to a vein they had mined in the Silent days, the children's classic, clearly intending a film with reissue potential. Conversely, Fields's other films were usually second features, designed to support the main attraction. Cinemas were more highly competitive than ever, offering comedy two-reelers, cartoons, a newsreel, general interest shorts, a theatre organ, live stage shows – and the competition had been intensified since the country capitulated to the Talkies. Then it was that the Hollywood companies began to oblige with supporting features, or B-pictures, approximately one-third shorter than the main feature – though in certain situations, notably the large cities, a Fields' film could top the bill. Anyway, **Six of a Kind** (1934), a factory-line Paramount B, directed by Leo McCarey, is a film for all time. It concerns a couple, Mary Boland and Charlie Ruggles, who decide to go West on a second honeymoon; to share expenses, she has advertised for a couple to accompany them, and they are landed with George Burns and Gracie Allen. Mr Burns had long learnt, if not to cope with Miss Allen, to accommodate her, but this was not something Mr Ruggles could do on such short acquaintance: thus, in disarray and confusion, they journey West. Mr Fields and Alison Skipworth do not appear till towards the end – to give the lie to the title, for they are as fly as the others are naive. It could not be said that with their entrance the film gets funnier: *that* would be impossible.

Nor does Fields appear till towards the end of **Mrs Wiggs of the Cabbage Patch** (1934), based on a sentimental old play about poverty and directed by Norman Taurog, with the mellifluous Pauline Lord in the title-role; but when he does, greeting his mail-order bride (Zasu Pitts) with

W. C. Fields in *It's a Gift*, with Kathleen Howard as his dragon of a wife, flanked by Tom Bupp and Jean Rouverol as their children. If Alison Skipworth made Fields a marvellous partner in duplicity, Miss Howard in this film and *The Man on the Flying Trapeze* was the ideal antagonist, magnificent in scorn and suspicion. A Prometheus sometimes – in stubbornness and cunning – he will always admit defeat when faced with this formidable lady.

'Madame, did you have dreams of connubial bliss?' and drinking without removing his cigar, the whole enterprise is redeemed. **It's a Gift** (1934), directed by Norman Z. McLeod, and **The Man on the Flying Trapeze** (1935), directed by Clyde Bruckman, are for those who want the man's genius neat and undiluted. In both, a thread of plot serves to support a series of calamities of which he is cause, butt or victim; with resignation and a touching awareness of inevitability he faces life's hardships. He alone is the good, kind man in a world peopled with nagging wives, rowdy children, inefficient assistants and rude neighbours – a good, kind man, with enough deceit to make life bearable and a flask to help when that proves deficient. He says yes and no to his wife's questions, offering for the explanations she demands the one she is (a) most likely to believe, (b) most eager to hear, or (c) least able to refute. It cannot be wrong to prefer Fields the put-upon paterfamilias to Fields the showman, as in *The Old-fashioned Way* and **Poppy**

(1934) – though in the latter he sells a talking dog which announces, as he exits the saloon, that it has given up talking. The film itself, a remake of *Sally of the Sawdust* directed by Sutherland, clearly reveals a double in some sequences; alcoholism kept Fields from films for two years, and he left Paramount after a rather tired appearance in *The Big Broadcast of 1938*.

Another survivor from the Silent era was Harold Lloyd, who scrapped the original, Silent **Welcome Danger** (1929) – at a cost of $400,000 – when he realised that the public wanted Sound, a challenge he met with typical ingenuity, staging a fight in almost total darkness, with the noises to amuse us. The public was sufficiently curious to hear him speak to make this spoof of Chinatown one of his more popular films, but when he returned to the top of a skyscraper, in **Feet First** (1930), it was not appreciative. Since he was a millionaire several times over, one can only marvel that he had chosen to do this again, but in his subsequent films he eschewed

such feats in favour of gags that any competent comic could have utilised; there are some good ones, however, in **Movie Crazy** (1932), an unacknowledged rehash of Harry Leon Wilson's novel, 'Merton of the Movies', the rights to which Paramount owned. All three films were directed by Keaton's former gag-writer, Clyde Bruckman. Lloyd's voice – high and slightly breathless – ideally suited the persona he had established, and he concentrated on character in the best of his Talkies, **The Cat's Paw** (1934), playing a dupe of the mob in this tale by Clarence Budington Kelland, who later provided the original of *Mr Deeds Goes to Town* (q.v.). Lloyd here might be cousin to Mr Deeds, and he is supported for the first time by a strong cast (Una Merkel, Grant Mitchell, Warren Hymer, Nat Pendleton, Alan Dinehart,

George Barbier, Edwin Maxwell); Sam Taylor directed, and the film was in fact made for Fox on a one-picture deal. Lloyd said later that he had been uncertain whether to play the story straight or use it as a prop for gags, and had only settled on the former after flipping a coin; uncertainty of approach is apparent in his last two films for Paramount, **The Milky Way** (1936), directed by Leo McCarey, and **Professor Beware** (1938), directed by Elliott Nugent. The latter is the more amusing, but its humour is of an earlier era: Lloyd, aware of this, retired from the screen, except for *The Sin of Harold Diddlebock* (q.v.).

The credits of **The Cocoanuts** (1929) are done over negatives, and it is entirely appropriate that the Marx Brothers should arrive on screen with everything turned inside out. They were a vaudeville team : Groucho (1890–1977), with the leer and fake moustache; Harpo (1888–1964), voiceless, larcenous, lecherous, an ensemble topped off with pink curls and a motor-hooter; Chico (1887–1961), with his fractured vowels and misinterpretations; and Zeppo, the juvenile, who left the act when their Paramount contract expired. Like Fields and Mae West, their self-absorption permitted little consideration of others, and none at all for the mores of the time: 'I'm Against It' is the title of Groucho's song in **Horse Feathers** (1932). Allowance was made for Margaret Dumont, the majestic dowager so often the object of Groucho's attentions, a relationship summed up by a line in **Animal Crackers** (1930): 'You've got beauty, style, money . . . You have got money, haven't you? – if not we'll stop right now.' In a deluge of puns good and bad, of malapropisms and innuendo, they insulted those about them; in a series of lunatic pursuits and misunderstandings they carried deceit to a new low; with sublime self-confidence they carried anarchy to the edge of destruction.

Paramount, understandably, approached them gingerly. *The Cocoanuts,* with direction credited to Robert Florey and Joseph Santley, is no more than a cameras-in-the-stalls account of a musical comedy of the period – on this evidence, a mediocre one – and no harbinger of Marxian antics to come. *Animal Crackers* they had also done on stage and as directed by Victor Heerman, little further effort had been made to open it out. Both plots have to do with larcenous activities, in hotel and country house respectively. **Monkey Business** (1931), directed by Norman McLeod, was written expressly for the screen, and casts the team as stowaways; their attempts to get past immigration by imitating Maurice Chevalier rank high in the annals of delirium. McLeod also directed *Horse Feathers*, set in a college, but like its immediate predecessor it suffers, in my opinion, from the absence of Miss Dumont.

In **Duck Soup** (1933), as the richest widow in the nation, Dumont chooses Rufus T. Firefly (Groucho) as its president – an appointment which no one thinks odd, least of all the gentleman himself, though he has fleeting doubts. Harpo and Chico are spies, changing sides so frequently that their competence – and interest in the job in hand – is merely academic. Indeed, the plot-line is so cussed, so sheerly irreverent, that it is soon non-existent, buried under an avalanche of gags – including a number of parodies of Hollywood films of the period. Allen Eyles has called this one 'mint-fresh and almost timelessly funny', but it was not much admired at the time. Groucho blamed Leo McCarey, who directed, but as the years advanced and it became accepted as their best film, he did an about-face and credited McCarey for its 'political satire'. As Gavin Lambert observed, 'It was probably the only time the Marxes worked with a comic talent equal to their own' – his point being – 'and they didn't like it.' Many well-known names – Morrie Ryskind, S. J. Perelman, George S. Kaufman, Irving Berlin, Kalmar and Ruby amongst them – wrote either directly for the Marx Brothers movies, or had their stage material adapted for the screen, but Groucho, in later years, tended to denigrate the more famous participants. There can be no question but that the Marx Brothers were their own invention.

At M-G-M the emphasis was, as ever, on star vehicles and expensive properties. The tandem partnership of Thalberg and Mayer was deteriorating, but their films continued to take a larger percentage of the box-office than those of other studios – and, significantly, to attract more critical attention. With Garbo, that is understandable. Despite the success of *Anna Christie,* the studio made no plans to put her into 'contemporary' situations. **Romance** (1930) was based on Doris Keane's old vehicle, already filmed in 1920; the hoary plot concerns an opera singer (Garbo), her ageing 'protector' (Lewis Stone), and the young parson (Gavin Gordon) who refuses to believe the truth about them; his love brings to her a new morality, and she is thus disillusioned when he asks to spend the night with her. In **Inspiration** (1931), also directed by Clarence Brown, it is she who makes that approach – within minutes of the film opening, and within seconds of meeting the young student (Robert Montgomery) whom she desires. We cannot blame her: 'How *yong* you are !' she says wistfully when he tells her he is twenty-four, and what heartbreak is in her voice when she says to her friends, when he has left her, 'He was all my life'! The film,

though set in the present day, is a version of *Camille,* set in the Bohemian circles of Paris, where the men are all grey-haired and their women all very young. Love and lovers are their sole topics of conversation, and marriage is only spoken of in connection with the heroine and her unnatural preference for a young man.

If she transcends such material, as she did throughout her Silent career, the early sequences of **Susan Lennox: Her Fall and Rise** (1931) are as miraculous as she is, for the man is Clark Gable, protecting her after attempted rape by her intended fiancé. Since he is Gable and she is Garbo, his will towards something similar and her submission must follow after an idyllic day fishing and laughing: but consequent events will then keep them apart till the last reel. Once again more sinned against than sinning, she is found whoring – and for the record this is the only film in which she is; she rises to the world of the demi-mondaine – and once again everyone on view is bereft of morals – and must sink to the level of his degradation

before they both may be redeemed. In all the films they made together William Daniels never photographed her more brilliantly; and it would be a mistake to underestimate the direction of Robert Z. Leonard (1889–1968), of whom I have never heard a good word, or a bad one.

In view of M-G-M's attitude towards her screen personality, it is no surprise to find her in the title-role of **Mata Hari** (1932), a flickering effort which only rises at the end to the level we expect for her – high tosh, but tear-jerking. 'Here are your eyes,' she says to the blinded Ramon Novarro, pressing her hands to his face. George Fitzmaurice directed, and had better material in **As You Desire Me** (1932): in a bleached bob, Garbo is a cabaret entertainer in Budapest, drinking to forget an already amnesiac past and perhaps her protector (Erich Von Stroheim), whom she kisses with passion but without an iota of affection. This is her familiar role, and equally familiar is her longing for a new life – in this case achieved, when a Count (Melvyn

Of *Grand Hotel*, the English critic C. A. Lejeune wrote, 'I remember nothing to equal the curiosity, excitement and impatience with which London prepared to sample [it].' The reason was the all-star cast, which included Greta Garbo and John Barrymore.

Douglas) claims her as his wife. Von Stroheim schemes to get her back – which provides a 'third act' of some suspense, due presumably to the source, a play by Pirandello: in the matter of Garbo vehicles this is more mature than most. One constant about her is that – *Mata Hari* excepted – she is always better than she was before; she always surpasses expectations. Superb as the singer, she is breathtaking later, playing with keen humour a woman rid of the past and unexpectedly loved. There is a beautiful, erotic sequence when she goes to the Count's room for a light for her cigarette, and in the final scene she acts with a common-sense confidence which is miraculous.

Grand Hotel (1932) was based on a book by Vicki Baum, a study of some half-dozen guests in a Berlin hotel, in the manner of *Menschen Untereinander,* and it had become an international bestseller: but what caused unprecedented public interest was M-G-M's daring step of casting the five leads with five stars – at a time when it was exceptional to find a second star billed above the title, and in this case only Lionel Barrymore was not accustomed to solo top-billing. Garbo is unsuitably flamboyant as a Russian ballerina who falls for the (phoney?) baron who means to rob her – John Barrymore. Brother Lionel is Kringelein, a bookkeeper who has checked in knowing he has an incurable disease; and Joan Crawford is the 'fast' stenographer who decides to enjoy his last days with him. The best performance – and the only attempt at a German accent – is by Wallace Beery, as the industrialist who desperately needs a big deal. The sensitive Edmund Goulding directed, but it is typical of the M-G-M approach that it tries to graft on to an American product the rather brittle quality of German cinema, falling between both stools; however, then it was the year's highest grossing picture and an Oscar winner – as best Picture.

Anticipation was almost as keen when the Barrymore brothers were joined by sister Ethel for **Rasputin and the Empress** (1932). John, less twitchy than usual, is Prince Chegodieff, a character based on Youssoupoff; Lionel is Rasputin, and the familiar rasp emitted through all that hair would be risible in any case. Ethel is every inch a Czarina, but she cannot listen to a sentence of three words without raising an eyebrow. The director, Richard Boles-

lawski (1889–1937), was a Pole who had worked in the New York theatre, and had been a dialogue director since the inception of Talkies. He was chosen for this film because of his background, managing some striking effects within the rather bland decor and some drama from Charles MacArthur's flatly-written screenplay. The royal couple are portrayed as dignified and humourless, he (Ralph Morgan) care-worn and decent, she as caring only for her children. The film starts with news of revolt, moves swiftly to the time the Czarevitch falls and is helped by Rasputin, brought in by a disciple, Princess Natasha (Diana Wynyard). One M-G-M executive decreed that Rasputin would be a blacker figure if he attempted to rape this lady, and it was on that technical ground, since she could be confounded with his wife, that Youssoupoff sued for libel in the British courts – and was awarded £25,000 plus huge costs. Ironically, his surrogate in the film kills the monk in self-defence – gruesomely and convincingly, however, and the film further redeems itself with its vignettes of the Romanovs in captivity; honourably, it is Hollywood's first serious attempt to explain the motivations of the people of history.

Dinner at Eight (1933), as adapted from the play by George S. Kaufman and Edna Ferber, was another exercise for an all-star cast, in this case tracing the fortunes of some guests at a dinner party. The hostess (Billie Burke) is a vapid woman, unaware that her husband (Lionel Barrymore) is dying and that his business is failing. The other strands of the plot are equally contrived, but are redeemed by their protagonists, each a monster of selfishness or self-pity: the daughter (Madge Evans), neglecting her fiancé for a matinee idol (John Barrymore), himself ruined by Talkies and bent on self-destruction; the businessman (Beery), out to ruin the host, and locked in mutual loathing with his wife (Jean Harlow), who is amusing herself with their philandering doctor (Edmund Lowe); and the now-penniless actress (Marie Dressler), ditching the host when he cannot loan her money. This is a New York item, shrewd and cruel, unpopular at the time with audiences outside the big cities. This cast makes any revival of the play unthinkable, and even John Barrymore is superb – perhaps because the performance is autobiographi-

cal. Miss Dressler, dripping with foxes and pearls, sails through each scene like a galleon, mugging, and letting not a laugh escape her; and Harlow, in form-fitting satin, is mesmerising, nibbling on a chocolate and then diving under the bed for an even bigger box. The producer was David O. Selznick, Mayer's son-in-law, arriving unwillingly from R.K.O. Radio (q.v.) when Thalberg's protracted ill health suggested a replacement was needed, and Selznick borrowed George Cukor from R.K.O. to direct.

M-G-M's specialist in filmed plays was Sidney Franklin (1893–1972). **Reunion in Vienna** (1933) had begun with Robert E. Sherwood's view that the events of 1914–18 could not stop schmalzy plays about that city, so he had written one in which the old romantics were shown replaced by the new city of Freud, attempting to be flippant about both. On the screen John Barrymore and Diana Wynyard replaced that theatrical team known as the Lunts, whose thrall was such that even a film version persuaded critics that this material was better than it was. Thalberg had persuaded the Lunts themselves to record one of their stage successes, Molnár's **The Guardsman** (1931). 'It is a pity,' said Mordaunt Hall in *The New York Times,* 'that there are not more Fontannes, Lunts and Molnárs ·to help out the screen, for then this medium

of entertainment would be in a far higher plane.' Alfred Lunt is a resourceful light comedian, but Lynn Fontanne, as on the stage, is less actress than hostess. The film, long unseen, answers the once-debated question as to why they made no others. They were both approaching forty, and despite the soft focus in her case, it shows; but chiefly she was no match for established screen actresses like Ann Harding (q.v.) and Ruth Chatterton, and he, for all his briskness, cannot hide a touch of effeminacy. Hall is also wrong about the play, which emerges as a witless piece wholly concerned with marital infidelity.

Franklin directed another disputing couple in **Private Lives** (1931), a straight forward adaptation of Noël Coward's comedy, with Norma Shearer and Robert Montgomery. Shearer manages to approximate the quicksilver delivery of Gertrude Lawrence, but the magic of the original – distilled in the excerpts from it that Coward and Lawrence recorded – is entirely missed. Franklin also directed Shearer in a new screen version of an old Broadway tearjerker, **Smilin' Through** (1932), concerning the bride shot on her wedding morn, and the niece destined to fall in love with the murderer's son (Fredric March) in England to fight in the War: the least that may be said is that it is done with conviction.

Norma Shearer (b. 1904) was only a

fraction lower than Garbo in the astral
hierarchy of the studio, and that was partly
because she was married to Thalberg, who
in Silent films had caused her to alternate
between demure virgins and women of the
world. With Talkies, she settled mainly for
the latter, and Thalberg sagely cast her as
the post-flapper woman – or as the title has
it, **A Free Soul** (1931). The story and
Clarence Brown's direction are undistinguished, but the attitudes are more provocative than those in Warners' similar tales.
Clark Gable kisses her and she says 'That'll
be all, thanks', but when his sole response to
her leaving their love nest is 'Your stuff's
still hanging in the closet, baby' she quickly returns.

Miss Shearer, however, baulked (as did
Joan Crawford) at playing the title-role in
Red-Headed Woman (1932), such was

the notoriety of Katherine Brush's novel.
According to Samuel Marx, at the time the
studio's story editor, the book was considered too 'racy', but it had sold so well that
no studio could afford not to bid for the
rights; he also says that it was primarily
responsible for the tightening of the Production Code, but in fact it only opened the
way for the flood of similar tales which
would eventually bring that about. Sex
unsanctified by marriage had been advancing its cause since Clara Bow, but Harlow
in this film is something else again. Anita
Loos wrote the screenplay, and her first line
has Harlow intoning 'So gentlemen prefer
blondes, do they?': she dons a see-through
dress, snaps a picture of a man in her garter
and goes to put the theory to the test. 'A girl
is a fool if she doesn't get ahead,' she says.
'It's just as easy to get a rich man as a poor

man.' 'Love?' says her prey, Chester Morris, 'Why don't you call it by its real name?' As directed by Jack Conway, when she follows Morris into a telephone booth her appeal is that of a quick-time whore. She ends, the richest woman in France, with an aged 'companion' and a young 'chauffeur' (Charles Boyer). Loose ladies before had sometimes ended happily, but never triumphant, and in the year that followed several others suffered assault on their nether regions and lived to laugh about it – and it was in that climate that Mae West was permitted to transfer her stage persona to the screen.

M-G-M asked Miss West, vainly, to write dialogue for Jean Harlow (1911–37) – partly because they were not entirely happy at having a major star typecast as a sinner, and partly because she was inadequate as an emotional actress. It is as a comedienne that she is to be cherished, at her best with Clark Gable (1901–60), at this point her male counterpart. The ideal male of the 20s wore an Arrow collar and was comforting over the tea cups, but for the Depression he wore no tie and swore at his women over the whisky bottle. In **Red Dust** (1932) Gable yells at Harlow, 'I'm not a one-woman man, I never have been and I never will be', and he doesn't realise that she is his kind till she says 'Mind if I get drunk with you?' His sex appeal is emphasised when he is lusted after by both her and a very proper newly wed (Mary Astor), a problem he takes in his stride. The film plays safe by setting its melodramatics in the jungle, it being a recognised fact that in the steamy topics everyone gets steamed up about sex. Gable's initial reaction to Harlow is a bored 'I've been lookin' at her kind since my voice changed', but at the end his hand creeps up her skirt as she reads him a sick-bed story about 'Little Molly Cottontail'. For its attitude to sex and for Victor Fleming's tick-tock direction, the film should be as vividly alive a century from now.

Also imperishable, also directed by Fleming and written by John Lee Mahin, in this case joined by Jules Furthman, is **Bombshell** (1933), still the wittiest satire on Hollywood. *The bombshell of the title

*I have seen this film in both New York and London and it plays better with native audiences. In New York, the laughter is virtually nonstop, perhaps because audiences are more relaxed, at ease with the crackling dialogue; in London the response was more hesitant, possibly because spectators feared they might miss something.

is Harlow, a poor little movie star, who supports: a drunken, cadging father (Frank Morgan); a moronic, cadging brother (Ted Healy); a conniving and graft-taking secretary (Una Merkel); a staff of servants including a maid (Louise Beavers), whose day off, in Harlow's words, 'sure is brutal on your lingerie'; the marquis she plans to marry; and, last but not least, three gigantic dogs. She also supports the studio, as represented by her director (Pat O'Brien) and publicity man (Lee Tracy), whose job it is to keep her on the front pages, while she attempts to escape and find freedom – the standard 'dumb blonde' plot, as used notably in *Born Yesterday* (q.v.).

Gable remained cheerfully amoral in his other films of the period, bedding women or slapping them around. He concedes his mistress (Myrna Loy) to the assistant district attorney (William Powell) in **Manhattan Melodrama** (1934), but then the latter had been a boyhood chum. This plot device, of two kids growing up together, one going to the good and the other to the bad, became a Hollywood perennial, and it is easily handled here by W. S. Van Dyke. Gable in fact becomes a casino boss and gangster, his several murders finally paid for in the electric chair at Sing Sing; but his charm and occasional gallantry make crime very appealing. Despite its later stately image, M-G-M at this time was as ready as any studio in Hollywood to portray the world as a place of fast boozing, casual sex and no morals in any direction – though both Mayer and Thalberg personally preferred the sort of movies which most appealed to the distaff half of audiences. In 1930 the studio offered **The Big House**, a conventional prison drama with an excellent performance by Chester Morris as the con who goes straight, and an interesting one by Robert Montgomery as a drunken driver whose prison term proves him to be despicable in every way. Under the direction of George Hill, it was a huge box-office success for the company, but there was no attempt to repeat it.

The Beast of the City (1932) is notable as one of the studio's few gangster pictures, though the emphasis is on the police force, as represented by Walter Huston. His brother (Wallace Ford) is also a policeman, but corrupted by a gangster's moll (Harlow whose conversation promises a number of unrefined pleasures. The direction

Moonlight was the *sine qua non* of Hollywood love scenes for over fifty years, but before the strengthening of the Hays Code, it could be – to quote Noël Coward – cruelly deceptive. In *Bombshell*, ABOVE, Lee Tracy is using romance to bring Jean Harlow into line. *Manhattan Melodrama*, LEFT, Myrna Loy is in the process of walking out on Clark Gable in favour of his best friend. It was a virtue of both films that audiences could not be sure who would end up with whom come the final clinch.

266

Walter Huston and
Karen Morley in the
final sequence of
*Gabriel Over the
White House*, a
film which caused a
rift among M-G-M
executives. The
ending originally
shot was hardly
suitable for U.S.
audiences, with its
cynical suggestion
that any good done
in the White House
was due to temporary
aberration and/or
divine intervention.

by veteran Charles Brabin indicates why he would soon be moved to B pictures, and the plotting, by John Lee Mahin from a story by W. R. Burnett, becomes desperate; but the ending is curious, as a demoted Huston, despairing of police protection, gathers some like-minded vigilantes to take the law into their own hands, both sides being wiped out in the process. There is a foreword pleading for less glamorisation of crime by the then-president, Herbert Hoover, who was a crony of Mayer; but the impetus for the film may have come from William Randolph Hearst, whose Cosmopolitan outfit nominally produced the film.

A year later Cosmopolitan offered **Gabriel Over the White House,** which also propounded America's ills and offered its own solution. A completely corrupt president (Huston) is brought back from the dead – another popular plot device of the period – to have a complete change of heart, and by firm action solving (a) the unemployment caused by the Depression (b) the problem of the big-time gangsters, and (c) the situation of a rearming Europe. If not a profound film, it is prodigal with ideas, including the conception of the 'reformed' president taking on the physical aspect of Lincoln; it was also potentially uncommercial, since the public had shown no great

taste for whimsy, or for politics or the Depression. The producer was Walter Wanger (q.v.), brought from Columbia, and like Selznick an anticipated replacement for Thalberg; he had chosen the director, Gregory LaCava, and the writer, Casey Wilson, who was from Thalberg's team. When Wanger arrived at M-G-M, Thalberg had advised him to ignore Mayer; Wanger accordingly sent the story direct to Hearst, who loved it, and contributed to the dialogue. Mayer knew little about the film until the preview, when his objections were supported by Will H. Hays and Nicholas Schenck (brother of Joseph, and since 1927 Chairman of Loew's Inc.), also Republicans. Since the film by implication attacked those presidents now being criticised in his papers, it served to alienate him from Mayer; Mayer thereafter distrusted Wanger, so that the latter soon moved on. A new ending was shot, whereby the president dies while reverting to his old self; however, the original remained for Europe, impressing critics with its power – and it would not have done for American audiences, with its cynical suggestion that any good done in the White House was caused by temporary aberration and/or divine intervention. The film was finally shown in the U.S. not long after the inauguration of President Roosevelt, who reportedly loved it.

Hearst's actual departure from M-G-M came about when Thalberg managed to get two properties for Miss Shearer, *The Barretts of Wimpole Street* (q.v.) and *Marie Antoinette* (q.v.), which Hearst had coveted for Marion Davies. Miss Davies in Talkies seldom showed the nimble comic wit of her Silent movies, and was often terrible, as in **Going Hollywood** (1933), though the blame in this case may be due to Raoul Walsh, making every mistake of which a director is capable. She is certainly better as handled by Edmund Goulding in **Blondie of the Follies** (1932), a supposedly typical showgirl story commissioned by Hearst from Frances Marion, with dialogue by Anita Loos. People within the industry were amused because it was in fact a thinly-disguised account of the relationship between Davies and Hearst – except that she is rescued from a life of sin by a handsome young millionaire (Robert Montgomery).

Joan Crawford had become one of the studio's most important stars, and her early Talkies indicate why she fascinated audiences for so long: she had authority and intensity, with eyes like hard-boiled eggs stuck with black olives. She clearly believed in her roles, doing everything with them – indeed, overdoing everything, as in **Paid** (1931), a version of Bayard Veiller's play 'Within the Law', already filmed in 1917 with Alice Joyce and in 1923 with Norma Talmadge. It presupposes that a girl, wrongly convicted, will revenge herself on society by a series of confidence tricks, strictly within the law, plus marriage to the son of the man who sent her up; Sam Wood directs, for a sort of dotty conviction. If Crawford is ridiculous in **Today We Live** (1933), this is only partly because she is miscast as an aristocratic Britisher engaged to another (Robert Young) but in love with an American (Gary Cooper), helping them to fight World War I. Her role, made the chief one, was written into the script at Thalberg's request, but there is little consolation for admirers of William Faulkner, on whose story it is based, since he also contributed to the ludicrous dialogue. The director is Howard Hawks, currently acquiring a reputation with *The Dawn Patrol* (from which the only convincing details are filched) and *Scarface* (q.v.): the presence of Cooper may remind us that his

previous film was also a war romance, *A Farewell to Arms* – and the two films underline the vast difference between a creative director and a hack like Hawks.

However, Crawford's best film of the period owes much to the unsung Robert Z. Leonard – **Dancing Lady** (1933), a musical, produced by Selznick, and quite the gutsy equal of the best shows over at Warners. Crawford's ambitions in later movies are strictly ersatz, but here she manages a nice, wry appreciation of her own aspirations, pleased when they like her singing and dancing – though the way she shrugs and turns down the corners of her mouth indicates that only mugs do not try for the big time. The cast includes Clark Gable as the harrying director, Robert Benchley, Franchot Tone and Ted Healy; Nelson Eddy makes his screen debut and so, more appreciated, does Fred Astaire, as 'himself' in a couple of numbers.

The career of John Gilbert was ending, reputedly due to the enmity of Mayer and an inadequate voice for Talkies – both certainly factors, though the timbre is merely light-tenored and uninteresting. As his face became lined, he became rather weedy – physically an absurd figure in **Downstairs** (1932) with ill-fitting double-breasted jackets. He contributed the story, which Monta Bell directed, about the new chauffeur seducing every lady in sight, including the ageing, plump cook – an idea perhaps borrowed from Von Stroheim. The film's main offering to the audience is a mild suspense – how long will it take him to break down the resistance of the butler's new bride (Virginia Bruce)? That also is the central situation of **The Barbarian** (1933), directed by Sam Wood (q.v.), one of the last vehicles of Ramon Novarro, whose career was also faltering with Talkies. In this case, the amoral hero is an Egyptian dragoman, and the lady (Myrna Loy) a British heiress. At one point he delivers her from peril in the desert to a more powerful and lecherous pasha (Edward Arnold), to whose silent handmaidens she gushes 'This is real hospitality' as they shepherd her into a massive pool filled with petals. She does not know what is in store for her, and the off-screen cries we hear seem to have been due to whips rather than rape; Novarro's seduction, after that, is more gentle, but the ending leaves us breathless, as she prefers sensuality on the Nile with him (obviously

at her own expense) to marriage with her stuffy fiancé (Reginald Denny). The role disguises Novarro's inadequacy as a Talkie actor, and clever direction, by Jacques Feyder, also does so in **Daybreak** (1931), from a Schnitzler romance about a guardsman and a music teacher (Helen Chandler). Given Schnitzler's cynical view of love – that it is never what it should be, especially as here, when it crosses class barriers – the happy ending seems unlikely. The film contains an odd scene in which Novarro's valet clandestinely wears his undershorts and coos 'Ooh, they are beautiful' when discovered.

Such decadence cannot be found in the films of Wallace Beery, former comic and Silent villain, who joined Gable in projecting for the studio a much more masculine hero – though in his case both bulk and

looks prevented him from being a romantic lead. He originally came to M-G-M to take Lon Chaney's place as the toughest convict in *The Big House,* and he proceeded to win a Best Actor Oscar (tying with Fredric March's Dr Jekyll) for **The Champ** (1931), directed with understatement by King Vidor – wisely, since this is an old-fashioned, maudlin tale of a child (Jackie Cooper) yanked out of poverty into a life of abject luxury. Fighting over him are an ex-champ (Beery), hoping for a comeback, and his charming ex-wife (Irene Rich), so wealthy that she has her own private suite on the railroad; it is to the former, however, a drunk and a gambler, that we are supposed to extend our sympathies: but then this film, like many another, insists that poverty makes people loving, considerate, open-hearted and understanding. It must

Dancing Lady is not only a splendid musical but a magnificent demonstration of the talents of Joan Crawford (right). Ever determined, she plays a showgirl of steely will 'fed up with burlesque, I'm going up to where it's art' – i.e. moving from the Bowery to Broadway. She has a temporary set-back due to a misunderstanding by the police.

269

be said that ten-year-old Cooper, with his young-old face, is worth jerking a tear over.

Beery's most popular films were the two he made with Marie Dressler, **Min and Bill** (1930) and **Tugboat Annie** (1933), and they are most remarkable for the comic skills of that lady. Miss Dressler (1869–1934), her vaudeville fame long gone, had arrived at M-G-M after some years of hardship, rising quickly from supporting actress to leader of the popularity polls. She and Beery were instantly 'lovable', and equally given to twitching eyes, mouths and facial muscles to keep audience attention from the other; she wins with her swivelling, darting looks of disgust and suspicion, but also because she conveys a wondrous sense of love triumphing over her experience of his failings – which have mainly to do with the bottle. Directed respectively by George Hill and Mervyn LeRoy, both are set on the waterfront, cleverly blending comedy and sentiment; Miss Dressler is the equal in artifice of their writers, but she always suggests a real woman with real problems.

Success type-cast Beery, thereafter given cute Wally Beery scenes, usually including one to draw tears from the stoniest heart; there are other minor flaws in **Viva Villa!** (1934), but this is with reason one of Selznick's own favourites among the films he produced while at M-G-M. Despite his status as a folk hero, Pancho Villa was an unusual choice of subject for an American movie, joining the Romanovs as one of the few recent historical figures so treated, and one of the few not noted for either loves or scandals. The screenplay by Ben Hecht manages a number of ambiguities – again rare in films of this period; and the device of a fictional American reporter (Stuart Erwin) to act as commentator was used again, notably in *Lawrence of Arabia* (q.v.). The photography by James Wong Howe and Charles G. Clarke is impressive, but so much like that of other films set in Mexico that we may suppose that that country imposes its own style. Its virtue is in the location-shooting, but that was as fraught as it was costly, dissuading Hollywood from using far-flung locations except when unavoidable for more than a generation. A quantity of exposed film was destroyed when the plane carrying it crashed; Villa's own son was to have played his father as a

young man, but became ill, and the sequences had to be dropped; the Mexicans objected to the casting of Beery – and were additionally upset when he rejected local hospitality to fly back to the capital every night; and, worst of all, a drunk Lee Tracy urinated from a hotel balcony onto the Mexican army. The director, Howard Hawks, left Mexico to try to defend him from the wrath of Louis B. Mayer, who was instrumental in preventing Tracy from ever again playing the lead in an A picture; the actor was replaced by Erwin, and Hawks by Jack Conway.

Location difficulties also plagued **Trader Horn** (1931), begun in fact by Van Dyke as a Silent, not long after his success with *White Shadows in the Blue Seas*. He was sent to Africa to film this semi-autobiographical story, with microphones and generators sent on when Sound became necessary – though according to sources at the time, most of it was reshot on the back lot and in Mexico. That is not evident, and if it surprises today, what must the film have seemed like then? There is a rhinoceros charge, an escape down a crocodile-infested river, an operation to steal meat from a lion, all bound into a typical jungle tale of a search for a white girl (Edwina Booth) brought up by cannibals. It owes much to the relaxed playing of Harry Carey in the title-role, but we may feel as warmly towards the manifold writers and cameramen as audiences did at the time. Across the years, I salute them.

Its success encouraged the purchase of Edgar Rice Burroughs' **Tarzan of the Apes** (1932), with a former Olympic swimming champion, Johnny Weissmuller, as the tree-hopping, somersaulting, all-conquering jungle hero. Van Dyke directed, but the sequel, **Tarzan and his Mate** (1934), was directed by the studio's art director, Cedric Gibbons – appropriately, for it is so packed with back projections, glass-shots and rubber animals (the chimp, Cheetah, is at one point played by an actor in a monkey-skin) that the planning must have taken longer than the actual filming. Tarzan's mate (Maureen O'Sullivan) is a well-bred English girl, which may be why she treats him maternally. In one of the later sequels they were put through a marriage service to appease the puritans, and in 1942, when M-G-M dropped the series, it was picked up by R.K.O.

M-G-M's own further entries in the penny-dreadful stakes included **The Mask of Fu Manchu** (1932), directed by Charles Brabin from the characters invented by Sax Rohmer, already picked over by Paramount. Boris Karloff is the Oriental overlord who manages to have Nayland Smith (Lewis Stone) bound to a plank above an alligator pool filling with water; to have Smith's associate await death at the connivance of two slowly-closing spiked doors, and his daughter prepared for sacrifice; and to have the almost naked hero injected with the serum which will make him a zombie-like slave and the desired of Fu Manchu's daughter (Myrna Loy).

It was an M-G-M director, Tod Browning, who had revived the horror movie, when loaned to Universal for *Dracula* (q.v.); when its follow-up, *Frankenstein* (q.v.) also did spectacular business, Thalberg reputedly asked Browning to 'out-horror' it, and the result was the well-titled **Freaks** (1932), a tale of the circus world – of the pinheads, the bearded lady, the man-woman, the armless or legless or both. Even among the cheapjack horror movies of the present, you could not imagine anyone similarly using, say, thalidomide victims, and it is as well that much of the playing is amateurish, for it might otherwise be unbearable. The studio was not happy with it, and appended an apologetic introduction; their London office was not sorry when the censor banned it – till 1963. Browning's subsequent Talkies are negligible, with the possible exception of **The Devil-Doll** (1936), written by Garrett Ford, Guy Endore and Erich Von Stroheim, in which an ex-convict (Lionel Barrymore) revenges himself on his enemies by reducing them to two inches in height.

Another survivor from the Silents was Buster Keaton, whose first Sound vehicle, *Free and Easy* (1930), took in more money than any of his films in years – which convinced the studio anew that he should not return to creative control. Edward Sedgwick directed this and all Keaton's M-G-M Talkies except **The Sidewalks of New York,** when he was replaced by Jules White and Zion Myers. This was so bad that release was delayed for two years, and Keaton himself particularly despised it; but it has moments of clowning – such as serving the duck – reminiscent of his great

days. The other Talkies indicate no understanding of his qualities – and if a leap onto a train in *Free and Easy* was to demonstrate his agility, it is bungled, since the crucial action is not shown. Perhaps he was too drunk to do it; alcoholism, unreliability and increasing audience apathy caused his contract to be annulled in 1933, and he entered that dark period from which he would not really emerge for more than two decades, when his Silent work began to be appreciated.

Cecil B. deMille also failed at M-G-M at this time. He arrived at the studio after his period of independence, and made **Dynamite** (1929) and **Madam Satan** (1930), both starring Kay Johnson, an actress new to the screen. Her assets were an attractive voice and a brittle comedy style, the latter certainly needed but in fact wasted in the cheerless circumstances. As critics of the time observed, both films blended deMille's specialities – sex and spectacle, with both scripts indicating humorous minds at work. Unfortunately, the serious lines in both are even funnier than those intended to be, and *Madam Satan,* with its climax of fancy-dressed partygoers parachuting from a stricken zeppelin, redefines that quality called by a later generation 'camp'. When a remake of *The Squaw Man* also flopped, deMille returned to Paramount, never again daring to attempt the marital society comedies of which these are the last examples.

Madam Satan was also a musical, a genre so overworked in 1930 that this particular studio abandoned no less than four already in production. After Warners re-established it, Thalberg invited Lubitsch and Chevalier to M-G-M for a new version of **The Merry Widow** (1934), reuniting both with Jeanette MacDonald, now under contract to the studio. She replaced the Metropolitan diva, Grace Moore, who refused to take second billing to Chevalier – a fact for which we must be grateful, since the existing partnership was never more entrancing – nor, with barely a kiss between them, more erotically charged. It is a triumph even by Lubitsch standards, brilliantly designed in blacks and whites, and as light and insubstantial as a dream.

Like his previous film for the company, *The Student Prince,* the cost was so high that a profit was unlikely – but this being M-G-M, no one minded too much. With the exception of *Ben-Hur,* the company had

271

never spent as much on a picture; *Trader Horn,* and more recently *Viva Villa!, Grand Hotel* and *Queen Christina* (q.v.) had all proved that a huge cost could be justified at the box-office – as would *Mutiny on the Bounty* (q.v.) in 1935. The budgets might be higher than at other studios, but when cinema attendances took a sudden tumble in 1932, M-G-M alone stayed in profit, with six of its productions listed in the *Motion Picture Herald* top ten grossing films. Warner Bros. lost $14 million, Paramount $16 million, and Fox exceeded both at $17 million, but M-G-M showed a profit of $8 million. That fall in attendances proved temporary; but if, in 1934, M-G-M remained the most lucrative of the studios, with a net profit of $7½ million, the losses at Warners, for instance, continued for the fourth year running – amounting to more than $2½ million, despite a paring of budgets.

Universal managed to stay afloat on the success of its horror fims – and like much in film history, that success was unexpected. In 1929 Carl Laemmle had appointed his son general manager – and it was Junior Laemmle (as he was usually known) who had instigated *All Quiet on the Western Front.* He had also bought a 1927 play, based on a novel by Bram Stoker, as a studio reunion for Tod Browning and Lon Chaney – but the latter died, and Browning had to substitute in the title-role of **Dracula** (1931) the Hungarian-born actor who had played it on Broadway, Bela Lugosi. With gleaming shirt-front and equally gleaming stare, he stalks through a fog-bound London in search of his prey – except when his bat-like cloak shelters him all too literally, and he flies. With Karl Freund on camera, the film bears witness to Browning's flair for the genre, but Universal gave the follow-up **Frankenstein** (1931), to James Whale, and a small-part actor, Boris Karloff, replaced Lugosi, who had quarrelled with the studio. James Whale (1896–1957) had successfully directed one film for the studio, *Waterloo Bridge* (q.v.), and as a European he was automatically, by the usual criterion, suitable for this version of an old but not classic novel, by Mary Shelley. It created an even greater furore than its predecessor, and remains the most viewable of vintage horrors – partly because of the masterly and famous make-

up, and partly because Karloff contribut[ed] so much, such as the splayed walk and th[e] animal groans. Nevertheless, the e[n]counter between the monster and th[e] child is somewhat embarrassing ('Who a[re] you? I'm Maria. Will you play with me?') but the sets, in which Whale took a speci[al] interest, are typical of his enterprise as [a] whole.

Freund himself was one of the Europea[n]s recruited by Universal to direct the[se] movies. **The Mummy** (1932) has Karlo[ff] in a double role, as the perfidious, hypnoti[z]ing priest, and his own ancestor, th[e] resuscitated 37,000-year-old mummy. ['Is] there a view anywhere like this in th[e] world?' asks someone, gazing on th[e] Sphinx and the Pyramids from a Cair[o] nightclub. Freund directed a few oth[er] films, including *Mad Love* for M-G-M, [a] remake of *Orlacs Hände,* with Peter Lorre a[s] outstanding villain, his head like a malev[o]lent egg. Universal pitted Karloff an[d] Lugosi against each other in **The Black C[at]** (1934), directed by a new director fro[m] Germany, Edgar G. Ulmer, and includi[ng] a Black Mass, which was not in Poe['s] original story and which caused the film [to] be banned in Britain and other countrie[s]. Alas, what had been allusive in his stor[y] **Murders in the Rue Morgue** (193[2]) becomes only too explicit as directed by th[e] veteran Frenchman, Robert Florey. Also [to] this series belongs **The Mystery of Edwi[n] Drood** (1935), directed (as was a version [of] *Great Expectations*) by Stuart Walker, [in] decline since leaving Paramount; one of i[ts] writers was the successful dramatist, Joh[n] Balderston, a contributor to most of the[se] scenarios, and among its players are Clau[de] Rains, as a very wicked John Jasper, a[nd] Francis L. Sullivan (in training for his rol[e] in David Lean's two Dickens films, q.v.) [as] Mr Crisparkle.

It was Whale who made the best [of] Universal's horror films, though the[se] would not include **The Old Dark Hou[se]** (1932), adapted by Benn W. Levy from [a] novel by J. B. Priestley about som[e] stranded strangers subjected to the o[dd] behaviour of its sinister inmates. Despi[te] enjoyable performances from Charl[es] Laughton (q.v.) as a newly rich Northern[er] and Karloff as a deaf-mute butler, lechero[us] and dangerous when drunk, the film seem[s] to despise even those audiences who sha[re] its jokiness. However, **The Invisible Ma[n]**

933) is amusing and faithful to Wells, as
apted by R. C. Sherriff in a happy reunion
ith Whale. The effects are outstanding,
d though the supporting performances
e terrible, Claude Rains beautifully
eaks the title-role – meant for Karloff,
ho had in turn quarrelled with the studio.
he Bride of Frankenstein (1935) solves
e knotty problem of a sequel by propos-
g that the monster was not, after all, dead,
it living by an underground lake.
nother curiosity is that this sequel, being
scussed by Mary Shelley in a historical
ologue, is nevertheless in modern dress.
his time Frankenstein (Colin Clive again)
tempted to create a bride (Elsa Lanches-
r) for the monster, who, rejected by her,
es on a rampage and destroys, *inter alia,*
the scientific apparatus: but this time a
ay was left open for a sequel. It came, in
39, as Universal relegated its horror
oduct to the lower half of double bills;
d Whale did not direct it.

His other early films are charming.
aterloo Bridge (1931) is a World War I
ecdote about a prostitute (Mae Clarke)
d a soldier (Kent Douglass), closely
apted from the play by Robert E. Sher-
ood and depending for its effectiveness on
e boy being too naive and love-sick even
suspect her true profession. **The Impa-
nt Maiden** (1932) disposes cleverly of
other artificial situation, this time caused
the Depression, as a stenographer (Miss
arke) allows herself to be kept by her boss
ohn Halliday) though in love with a
ident doctor (Lew Ayres). Nor is likeli-
od the strong point of **A Kiss Before the
irror** (1933), but it is refreshingly mat-
-of-fact on marital relations: a lawyer
rank Morgan) is defending a friend (Paul
kas) for the murder of his adulterous wife
nen he has cause to suspect his own
ancy Carroll). Morgan's innate good-
ss gives the film a centre, and the torment
the principals is thrown into relief by the
laxed playing of Charles Grapewin as his
cretary – proof that Grapewin was later
asted, type cast as a yokel. Without losing
s sense of realism, Whale moves easily
to the world of the wealthy Viennese
urgeoisie, but that is not the only reason
at *Motion Picture Magazine* found 'this
licately woven drama more like a fore-
n-made picture'. It remains extraordi-
ry, far better than Whale's own, Am-
icanised remake, *Wives Under Suspicion.*

Universal's horror films were part of the
Laemmles, makeshift policy, which consisted of the churning-out of programmers,
plus an occasional pre-sold popular novel
or play. Thus their major comedy of the
period, **Once in a Lifetime** (1932), is a
literal transposition of the Kaufman-Hart
play about the coming of Sound to Hollywood, with Aline MacMahon, Jack Oakie
and Russell Hopton as a vaudeville team
which takes itself to the studios to teach
voice. As directed by Russell Mack, Oakie
offers a portrait of stupidity unequalled in
films for more than a generation, and
Louise Fazenda is funny as a vapid gossip
columnist: but the piece belongs to Miss
MacMahon, cool-headed and conniving.

Not surprisingly, the Universal policy
did not attract talent, which usually arrived
on loan-out or short-term contract. Thus
John Ford arrived to make **Air Mail** (1932),
written by a specialist in such tales, Frank
Wead, offering little new, even then, in
squabbling flyers (Pat O'Brien, Ralph Bellamy) or in airfields with particularly
bad weather conditions. However, the
Laemmles did belatedly discover that they
had under contract a front-rank director,
William Wyler (1902–81), a distant relative, who had been turning out mainly
two-reel Westerns for them since 1925. He
established his mastery with **A House
Divided** (1931), since the subject was the
familiar – and artificial – one of the mail-
order bride. He made it both touching and
seemingly fresh, filming almost all the film
in a small fishing village; and there has never
been a more terrifying storm at sea on film
than the one that forms the climax. Walter
Huston gives his usual consummate performance as the groom and Helen Chandler
and Kent Douglass are superb as the
youngsters; Walter's son John (q.v.) gained
his first screen credit for the dialogue.
Wyler was further admired for **Tom
Brown of Culver** (1932), approaching
that institution with documentary vigour.
His sheer intelligence in planning and
execution is immediately evident in **Coun-
sellor-at-law** (1932), after he had battled
with the Laemmles to restrict the action to
the lawyer's offices, as in Elmer Rice's
Broadway play, using swift editing and a
battery of close-ups to disguise the fact. His
model was Capra's *American Madness*
(q.v.), and the result, said *The New York
Times,* was 'incisive and compelling' – not

273

Frank Borzage's *Little Man, What Now?* is one of the formidable Hollywood romances of the Depression era, in which the hero and heroine suffer prettily, sometimes amusingly and without rancour. Their garret is picturesque, and she, Margaret Sullavan, is wearing a sequinned evening-gown the day he is sacked. However, she is a realist, and knows exactly how to cope with her mother-in-law's lover, Alan Hale, seen admiring her here.

adjectives automatically applied to Rice's work – with one of John Barrymore's more rounded performances.

John M. Stahl (1886–1950) had been directing for over a decade when he found his forte with **Back Street** (1932), showing justified confidence both in Fannie Hurst's sentimental bestseller about a woman (Irene Dunne) who elects to spend her life as the unacknowledged mistress of a prominent banker (John Boles); and Miss Dunne (q.v.), plays the role with that blend of grace and light heartedness which was her own secret. Both this and the 1941 version (q.v.) appear miraculous beside a later one, directed in 1961 by David Miller and throwing away every aspect which makes them admirable. Margaret Sullavan (1911–60), the star of the second version, is Stahl's heroine in **Only Yesterday** (1933), pert and 'forward', like Dunne reacting to her woes with levity and never asking for emotional charity. The screenplay is supposedly based on a book of the same name, 'an informal history of the Nineteen Twenties', and it starts on the eve of the Wall Street crash as Boles receives a 'letter from an unknown woman'. Anyone who has seen Ophuls's film of that name (q.v.) will recognise Stefan Zweig's story, here uncr[edited], and this version is the more faithf[ul] despite the transposition of the setting [to] the U.S. and World War One.

Also directed for romantic intensity [at] full pitch, in this case by Frank Borzage, [is] **Little Man, What Now?** (1934), though [it] lacked the edge of the original material – t[he] novel by Hans Fallada which had caught t[he] imagination on both sides of the Atlant[ic] and had in fact already been filmed [in] Germany. Universal remembering its su[c]cess with another German bestselle[r] bought the rights, and cast as the coup[le] coping with the Depression Miss Sullav[an] and Douglass Montgomery – the Ke[n] Douglass of *Waterloo Bridge*. (That this a[c]tor reverted to his Broadway name wh[en] playing leading roles is indicative of t[he] failure of his earlier films.) However, he i[s a] prig, and his mother runs a bordello; the g[irl] sees things clearly and there is a chill in t[he] air, as in the other Borzage views [of] Europe, from *Seventh Heaven* to *The Mor[tal] Storm*. (q.v.)Political unrest is represent[ed] by two briefly seen rallies and a starvi[ng] couple who function as a Greek chor[us] talking of people of 'our faith'. No o[ne] mentions the Nazis or Communists, b[ut] at, in view of the whole Hollywood hema of the time would have been perfluous. The best scene in the film is set und a huge satin-quilted double bed, as e couple chat with the lecherous lodder lan Hale); it was also, almost certainly, e last time a couple were seen in a double d in an American film for many years.

t Fox, Winfield Sheehan ran the show, ice the founder had been forced out in •29 after an unsuccessful attempt to take er M-G-M – though the matter was mplicated by the Wall Street crisis and illiam Fox's own incapacity as the result a car crash. One of his last actions had en to endorse a wide-screen process, and s all-star revue, *Happy Days,* had been leased both in that and standard gauge. So as **The Big Trail** (1930), and since there as also a German-language version each ene was filmed three times, at a total cost over $4 million – though contributing to at figure was inadequate pre-planning for cation-shooting, something which the dustry coupled with M-G-M's troubles Viva Villa!. The film was so long ooting that M-G-M's wide-screen *Billy e Kid* preceded it, but the public would ve nothing to do with either. Its star any years later claimed that was because x withdrew the wide-screen version too ickly, but the truth was that the public d tired of endless versions of *The Covered agon.* The star concerned is John Wayne 907 –79), in his first leading role, gauche d inexperienced, doomed by the film's lure to spend the ensuing decade in B ovies. The director, Raoul Walsh, sponded more keenly to **Yellow Ticket** 931), adapted from a play for John rrymore had done in 1914, about a ussian Jewess (Elissa Landi) who procures e passport allotted to prostitutes in order circumvent racial laws: her manifold ventures involve a British journalist aurence Olivier), a prince (Walter yron), and the latter's uncle (Lionel Barmore), motivated equally by lust and spect for the aristocracy.

Sheehan's interest in European affairs, wever, was mainly concerned with peating the success of the Fox war films of e Twenties; thus he elected to make **rrender** (1931), already filmed by Universal in 1921, from a novel by Pierre enoît about a French prisoner of war

(Warner Baxter) and a German aristocratic family. 'What's Beethoven after the Big Berthas?' cries the only surviving son (Alexander Kirkland), as the old Count (C. Aubrey Smith) raves about the country's glories. The director is William K. Howard, moving his material at breakneck speed, as also in **Transatlantic** (1931), the usual shipboard potpourri – con-men, crooks and infidelity, and **Sherlock Holmes** (1932), a long way from Conan Doyle, with Clive Brook in the title-role, Reginald Owen, most masterly of character actors, as Watson, and Ernest Torrence stealing the piece as Moriarty.

The Power and the Glory (1933), was, in the words of C. A. Lejeune in *The Observer,* 'a courageous film, which has dared to break new ground in the very heart of the commercial cinema'. The funeral of the opening scene turns out to be that of the protagonist (Spencer Tracy), about whom there are divisions of opinion, and the film subsequently examines him as he changes from idealistic illiterate to ruthless autocrat. The thesis was not new even then – Tracy would do a later version in *Edward, My Son* (q.v.) – but the distinction lies in the fact that this man's life is not followed in chronological order. In that we recognise the genesis of *Citizen Kane* (q.v.): that this is not notably inferior is due less to Howard's direction than to the dialogue, by Preston Sturges (q.v.), then best known as a Broadway dramatist, and to Tracy's performance which, as gauche young man or unloved tycoon, always has an underlying humour. Colleen Moore plays the schoolteacher who becomes his – eventually embittered – wife.

Spencer Tracy (1900–67) is Fox's most interesting actor of the period. He came from the stage remarkably assured, but was too young – or so they thought at Fox – for the type of authoritative roles played by Walter Huston; since leading men were slotted into categories, he was cast tough and cocky like Gable and Cagney, though in his case resource and thought gave his roles more colour than was in the writing. He is superb as a confident, warm-hearted cop in **Me and My Gal** (1932), especially in his slanging matches with the girl concerned (Joan Bennett), which include a parody of *Strange Interlude*. It is an 'anything goes' tale, obviously, to do with racketeers; Raoul Walsh directed, with a certain zest,

275

Hollywood before the Code

The most enduring of the films directed by John Ford are probably those which he made for Fox in the early Talkie period – unpretentious studio productions, sometimes made with great feeling. *Pilgrimage*, OPPOSITE, features Henrietta Crossman, centre, a distinguished stage actress who made too few films, seen here with Robert Warwick. *Doctor Bull*, BELOW RIGHT, is one of the three films in which Ford directed another remarkable artist, Will Rogers – allowing him to rephrase the dialogue as he thought fit, which may be one reason why the actor's homely philosophising, difficult now to read, are delightful in practice.

but the blackness of the Warner films is lacking – the situation of the paralysed witness (Henry B. Walthall) seems to have embarrassed everyone but the actor concerned. However, as directed by Rowland Brown, **Quick Millions** (1931) is among the best gangster films. At the beginning Tracy is a truck driver but, as he says himself, he's a man with a ton of brain, too nervous to steal, too lazy to work; as a big-time racketeer, his life style is summed up by a statement to his moll (Sally Eilers), 'And before we get blotto, I'm gonna make another suggestion.' He falls for a 'high-class dame' but, double-crossed, attends the wedding only as a silk hat thrown from a limousine, whereupon a spokesman says that society has been cowardly, and blames the press for glorifying the dying words of gangsters. In fact, in this respect Hollywood and the press were locked in a mutual embrace of praise and rebuke. Thus, Tracy's first opponent in this film is in striking contrast to him, a contractor (John Wray) forced to pay protection money – ageing, bald, with wing-collar and pince-nez, a poor sap with whom no one in the audience would want to identify.

Born Reckless (1930) predates the Warner gangster movies. Edmund Lowe is a small-time crook who goes straight after becoming a war hero, but lets loyalty draw him back to crime – though as its victim. Unlike later examples of the genre, this one tries to suggest causes, but it is a minor film. John Ford directed, but was more at ease with **Seas Beneath** (1931), a conventional sea story which, without pitching and tossing, gives a more vivid impression of life at sea than any other film I can recall. Both films were written by Dudley Nichols (1895–1960), starting his long association with Ford. Their partnership is better exemplified by **Pilgrimage** (1933), about a mother (Henrietta Crossman) who enlists her son (Norman Foster) rather than have him marry the girl (Marian Nixon) she considers a tramp. The greatness of the film lies in its middle section, when she goes to France to see her son's grave, her guilt counterbalanced by the prestige of being the only bereaved mother in her county. Ford had caught beautifully the professional concern of social workers, and he manages well the sticky final sequence when the old lady in Paris, finds a surrogate son. Miss Crossman, keeping the woman's

humanity and odd humour dead centr gives one of the screen's great perfor ances.

Ford handled another consummate art in three movies – Will Rogers, who h come into his own with Talkies and w now the studio's chief male star. In **Doct Bull** (1933) he expresses the commonsen and homely wisdom expected both of country doctor and himself, without po posity and throwing away at least one li in six. He is a shy man, uncertain of success with women; he has a quiff and t button eyes of Little Orphan Annie. doesn't think he is a very good doctor – b he doesn't think much of the townsfc either; his enemies are stuck up, intoleran full of cant; and family audiences of t Depression welcomed his frank approa to such matters – not dissimilar from that Marie Dressler, equally middle-aged a popular. His humour is different from her if just as sly, observing that he lik delivering Italian babies because he is giv a glass of wine, or asking 'What you doin' here ? Someone git out?' to a gro looking into a grave. In this film Ford tak him close to emotion, but keeping him o of camera range or with his back towar us. **Judge Priest** (1934) is based on son memory pieces by Irvin S. Cobb, abo small-town rivalries: it is a movie suffus with love and affection, as is **Steambo 'Round the Bend** (1935), in which Co himself appears, as the rival riverbo captain. Appearing in both films, alas, Stepin Fetchit, a black actor who epito ised the idle and thick-headed qualit supposedly found in 'niggers'.

By the time audiences saw the bc steaming round the bend, Fox had amalg mated with 20th Century Pictures (q. and Rogers had died (like Miss Dressler, the height of his popularity), killed in an crash. Of his earlier films, **A Connectic Yankee** (1931) based on Mark Twain, h him offering homilies to the dunderhead knights of the Round Table, a one-jo film, neatly handled by David Butler. **N Skitch** (1933), directed by James Cruz concerns a family dispossessed by t Depression, and though it is pleasing tod to see this national hero with an eye to t fast buck, it could not have been of mu benefit to audiences of the time. **Lightni** (1930) is an account of Frank Bacon's vehicle (both as star and co-author), in

276

The foreword to Henry King's *State Fair* notes that such fairs are ephemeral, which, together with the film's short running time, suggest only a diversion. That it is much more than that is due to these four players – Norman Foster, Louise Dresser, Janet Gaynor and Will Rogers. The movies have seldom offered a more convincing family.

time (1918) the longest-running Broadway play, at 1,291 performances, and already filmed by Ford for Fox in 1925; as rewritten by S. N. Behrman and Sonya Levien the role of the divorcees' hotelier makes for 'a really enchanting one man show', as the British *Film Weekly* put it.

The director was Henry King, starting that contract which would make him Fox's leading director for the rest of his career: during the Zanuck period he would be associated with many of the company's most important films. Unlike Ford, who was tempted towards 'statements' like *The Informer* (q.v.), King never believed in film as an art; and where Ford tended to like certain situations, e.g. those involving masculine camaraderie, King was content with any believable one. The more honest the writing, the more realistic his handling, as critics had noted with *Tol'able David* and *Stella Dallas;* he brings warmth even to **Merely Mary Ann** (1931), a popular waif tale, already twice filmed and this time chiefly a vehicle for the team of Janet Gaynor and Charles Farrell – now nearing its end, as Farrell's high-to-rasping voice would soon relegate him to supporting roles. **State Fair** (1933), based on Phil Stong's novel, is worth both the – musical – remakes (q.v.) put together; unlike the 1945 version it does not try for charm, but it has it effortlessly. King's imaginative touches are not in the remakes: pa (Rogers) placing a

rug round ma's shoulders as they drive the fair; ma (Louise Dresser) pulling her e lobes as she hears she has won the pick prize; the son (Norman Foster) pulling t closet door to muffle his phone convers tion; the daughter (Miss Gaynor) and h reporter in the doorway of his flat, examin ing each other in the light from the street

Though the film re-established King reputation, he was assigned to **Mar Galante** (1934) merely as a reliable handl of players – for the female lead was Ke Gallian, a French girl who was Fox's ent in the Garbo-Dietrich stakes. Having ca her, like them, as a fallen woman in exotic locale, Fox then lost nerve, for t crimson heroine of Jacques Deval's nov had become, said *The New York Times,* virtuous and extraordinarily naive gir The story does not, therefore, make mu sense. Spencer Tracy is convincing as government agent trying to prevent t sabotage of the Panama Canal, but M Gallian, attractive at first, soon proves lesser figure than Helen Morgan – who two songs prove again that she was immensely poignant interpreter of wor and music.

One More Spring (1935) was mc congenial to King, but perhaps because conclusions are dishonest it is no more th pleasant – certainly a lesser work th Borzage's similarly-themed *Man's Cas* (q.v.). Everything, it says, following thr lovable derelicts in Central Park, will be A Right if we only love one another; it – t Depression – was nobody's fault; the go ernment is bound to help – but the be palliative is a convenient millionai Robert Nathan's novel had been publish in 1933, and things had begun to lo decidedly better by the time this film reach the world's screens. Bowdlerisation mea that the musician Rosenberg (Walter Woo King) is Jewish of feature and gesture onl and the hooker has become an out-of-wo actress (Miss Gaynor): the appeal to Fox l mainly in the co-starring chances for two its biggest – but fading – stars. Miss Gayn was finally becoming old-fashioned, b she could still put her imprint on a fil Warner Baxter was ever able to confron desperate situation with fortitude, but o cannot but come to the conclusion that to down-and-out at his age would not ha permitted the least levity.

Edwin Burke wrote the screenplay a

With one exception, the extant Silent pictures of Erich Von Stroheim concern the *recherché* sexual practices of the European nobility or military set, with an occasional American victim from a similar social order. The answer to how he might react to an American urban working-class milieu is *Hello, Sister!* – and it is clear that at this stage Minna Gombell and Terrance Ray had nothing to learn from any European. Though Von Stroheim's name is not on the credits, they were surely tutored by him.

also that of Borzage's **Bad Girl** (1931), from a novel by Vina Delmar. Borzage won an Oscar for his direction, and *The New York Times,* not always so perceptive, included the film in its list of the year's best. Its critic, Mordaunt Hall, was understandably puzzled by the title – for Dorothy (Sally Eilers) is a good girl. Since the plot is much like that of *The Crowd,* it is not surprising that she meets the boy, Eddie (James Dunn), on a steamer returning from Coney Island. He works in a radio shop, and dreams of owning his own; when at the end he refers to the new baby as 'the future president of the United States' the remark is not risible but a further indication of the stubborn faith in democracy. Earlier, the goodnight conversations on the stairs have a truth seldom found in American pictures, and there is a remarkable study of the relationship between Eddie and the girl's best friend (Minna Gombell), moving from mutual dislike through bantering insult to respect. The film is also notable for the rare use of overlapping dialogue, sentences half-heard and slang (elsewhere usually restricted to gangsters and reporters); and if there are a few jarring notes, it is eloquent proof that Hollywood's flirtations with realism in the late Twenties subsequently bore at least one fruit.

Unlike its predecessors it was popular, but the only result was a series of films co-starring Dunn and Eilers; although he is

279

terrific here, playing unforcedly and with natural gosh-oh-darn ability, none of his other films with Eilers is worthy of note except one which we may consider a companion piece, **Hello Sister!** (1933), with direction credited to Alfred Werker. However, it had started out as *Walking Down Broadway*, directed by Erich Von Stroheim; and though said to have been completely re-shot, this seems unlikely from internal evidence. 'All you gotta do is walk down Broadway and act like you're not clean-minded' is the advice of the much-married Mona (Miss Gombell) for Millie (Zazu Pitts) and Peggy (Boots Mallory); but after they're picked up by Jimmy (Dunn) and Mac (Terrance Ray), nothing again is quite so simple. The bumpy road to love is complicated by sexual needs – not to mention some climactic street explosions, which would seem not to have been part of Von Stroheim's film. Gone from his original are a bawdy love scene between Mona and Mac, and the hero's seduction of the heroine, watched by the frustrated Millie; the tampering has made the lovers little more than ninnies, and Millie behaves oddly, even for her. Nevertheless Mona, a whore in the original, remains more convincing than most of the broads of the period, and Mac's crude approach is singularly believable: it is a typical Von Stroheim touch that he should attempt rape after a successful bout with another woman. We may be sure that this sequence is his, and the visit to the gynaecologist (with its religious symbolism), as well as the Coney Island swapping which sets the prevailing mood of cheap sexuality – quite unlike that of the other films of the period. The conversion, in fact, was clearly half-hearted: it was due to a producers' row within Fox, involving Sheehan, and had nothing to do with Von Stroheim's extravagance – yet it was regarded as another of his failures, sealing his career as a director.

It has in common with **Call Her Savage** (1932) hardly a thought above the navel. This was designed for Clara Bow, whose career Fox hoped to resurrect, playing a half-Indian heiress discovered whipping her pal Moonglow (Gilbert Roland) – practising, as she explains, for marriage. She does marry, after two headline-making years at finishing-school, a man who only wanted to get even with his mistress; disowned by him, she gambles away her

allowance till he tries to rape her while supposedly dying; in New Orleans, she takes to the streets, to buy medicine for the baby. There is a fire, a death and a legacy, all at once, and she returns to New York to 'get even with life', which means becoming betrothed to a gigolo: but he leaves her after she has a public brawl with her husband's mistress, whereupon she takes to drink in a skin-tight white lamé gown. Since two effeminate waiters have a fond duet about sailors, we may say that only female homosexuality is missing. Miss Bow, bright-eyed and plump as a squirrel, makes us wonder how she might have been with a great director – which John Francis Dillon certainly was not. The film did not succeed in restoring her to public favour.

Still exploiting the femme fatale, Fox offered **The Worst Woman in Paris?** (1933), directed by Monta Bell with none of his earlier brilliance, a lugubrious drama about a notorious beauty (Benita Hume) who is a real joe at heart, sacrificing her true love to help a friend (Helen Chandler). As escapism, you might prefer **Chandu the Magician** (1932), based on a nightly radio serial, and the studio's only contribution to the fantasy-horror fad. Under the dual direction of Marcel Varnel and William Cameron Menzies, poor Chandu (Edmund Lowe) finds his magicianship limited, unable immediately to defeat Roxor (Bela Lugosi), who is planning world domination from his underground palace high above the Nile: 'This death-ray in the hands of Roxor means the end of all that is good, all that is sane . . .'

Of similar innocence is **Zoo in Budapest** (1933), set entirely inside the *tiergarten* and telling of the idyll between animal-loving Zani (Gene Raymond) and orphan Eve (Loretta Young), hiding from the humans who are hunting them. The director, Rowland V. Lee, and the photographer, Lee Garmes, make pretty patterns with birds, beasts and leaves, and the screenplay is nicely against cages, orphanages, fur coats, the evil and the ugly. There never was a heroine more winsome than Miss Young, but one loses patience with Raymond and the whimsy both. Jesse L. Lasky produced, his first assignment on leaving Paramount.

Fox's most important picture of the time – and for years afterwards – was **Cavalcade** (1933), despite or because of its being

obstinately British in every respect. Notwithstanding its success at Drury Lane,
Coward's play had not been seen in New
York, so a Movietone News crew was sent
to record the London production, in order
that it might be faithfully reproduced in
Hollywood. The film, therefore, preserves
the exact nature of British theatre of the
time, and if it is this which, by virtue of stiff
acting, harms it, it is also what makes it
enchanting – the inserts of the musical
comedy and the end-of-pier show. It is a
tale of 'upstairs and downstairs' – the
Marryots and their servants, the Bridges.
As the senior Marryots, Diana Wynyard
and Clive Brook cope with every well-bred
emotion which is their lot; as their children,
Frank Lawton and Ursula Jeans skirt passages that sound like self-parody ('But it
was *fun*, wasn't it?', 'Are you going to miss
me *des*perately?'); as the Bridges, Herbert

Mundin is fine but Una O'Connor goes
over the top. However, all that is maudlin
gets forgotten in the care taken to realise the
whole; all that is superficial – it is as accurate
a picture of British life as 'Peter Pan' – is
forgiven in the conception. The five-
minute montage of the War is magnificent,
given the emotive power of 'Tipperary' and
'Keep the Home Fires Burning': one strain
of 'Yankee Doodle' is thrilling in its brevity. As a gesture of American friendship,
the film is in itself moving; at the New York
premiere the audience stood and cheered – a
pattern repeated during its subsequent
career. In the domestic market alone it took
$3,500,000 – as much as any twelve Fox
movies put together, and it won Oscars as
Best Picture and for Frank Lloyd – whose
replacement of Borzage early in the filming
lost Fox one of its best directors.

Sheehan tried to repeat the success with

Cavalcade recaptures
the heartbreaks of an
era. Though its
jingoism has now
become quaint what
remains regrettable is
Noël Coward's
opposing attitudes
towards the upstairs
and downstairs
families – the
Marryots, played by
Diana Wynyard and
Clive Brook, centre,
and their servants,
the Bridges, played
by Herbert Mundin
and Una O'Connor: he
is in awe of the
former, patronising
towards the latter.

The World Moves On (1934), and was indeed so proud of it that he took producer credit (most Fox films of the time carry none). He commissioned Reginald C. Berkeley – author of a recent Broadway success, 'Lady with the Lamp' – to write a *Cavalcade* with an American slant. Berkeley's convoluted story begins with a New Orleans family in 1824, and mainly concerns its British, French, American *and* German branches in 1914, concluding in a dilapidated mansion just after the Wall Street crash. 'Everything's gone,' says Madeleine Carroll. 'Not everything,' says Franchot Tone, as the camera pans to a crucifix. John Ford directed: 'I pleaded and quit and everything else, but I was under contract and finally had to do it . . . It was really a lousy picture.'

At United Artists, Mary Pickford did her own version of *Cavalcade* – with a touch of *Cimarron* (q.v.) – called **Secrets** (1933) and based on a 1922 Broadway play by Rudolf Besier and May Edginton. A first version was scrapped, at a loss of $300,000, but after *Kiki* she returned to it, bringing in Borzage, who had directed the Silent version with Norma Talmadge, and a new leading man, Leslie Howard (q.v.). It opened, she recalled 'in twenty-five key cities on the day President Roosevelt declared the bank holiday. Very few people were spending money on entertainment in the weeks that followed, and while the film was well received, it was a financial disaster.' In any other circumstances it would still have been a disaster. The original is, obviously, a series of one-act plays concerning the same people, taking the heroine from elopement to distinguished old age via an ambush in a log cabin and her husband's infidelity. As a film from Borzage's richer period, it is particularly disappointing; he was adept at making romance both credible and touching, but he is handicapped by his star. She had a good speaking voice, but it is one without character – and that is true of her performance as a whole. In 'Act III' she plays a matriarch, the only time during her later career that she played her own age – and that is the closest she comes to being remotely interesting She did not film again.

In his role as American hero, Douglas Fairbanks decided to help vanquish the Depression, playing a stockbroker who loses his fortune in **Reaching for the Moon** (1931): but the suggestion that the solution is to marry an heiress (Bebe Daniels) is, if appealing, not very practical. Edmund Goulding directed, which may be why there are a number of misunderstandings concerning men embracing, less naively handled than was usual at the time. Distressed with the film's failure and his waning marriage, Fairbanks offered **Around the World in 80 Minutes With Douglas Fairbanks** (1931), co-directing with Victor Fleming, who also appears in it. He infuses it with his usual energy, whether clambering up Angkor Vat or doing a spot of calisthenics on deck. But he was no longer so lithe, and since Talkies were hardly the medium for his pantomime, he no longer knew what films to make. He did not care to return to Westerns nor invade the underworld, so he protected his image with **Mr Robinson Crusoe** (1932), directed by Edward Sutherland, jumping ship in the South Seas and playing at desert island, with mechanical devices as enterprising as anything in Disney.

Clearly, with Chaplin taking years to prepare one film, United Artists needed product, and since the only one of its producers supplying this with frequency was Sam Goldwyn, he assumed increasing importance within the company. When regarded by the press as either its head or its spokesman he was not inclined to contradict. His imaginative contributions were, as hitherto, confined to vehicles for his stars, but he did assign John Ford to direct Ronald Colman in **Arrowsmith** (1931), adapted by Sidney Howard from the novel by Sinclair Lewis. The direction, apart from some over-emphatic close-ups, is subtle, and Colman is at his Galahadish best as the young doctor who manages, just, to hang on to his ideals through indifference, quackery, official bungling and, most importantly, love of publicity. There are also good studies by Helen Hayes as the wife, and Myrna Loy as the New York sophisticate who comforts Arrowsmith when he is widowed.

It is the only interesting Goldwyn film of the period, unless you are addicted to the over-enthusiastic clowning of the vaudevillian Eddie Cantor (1893–1964). Certainly the black-face minstrel show in **Kid Millions** (1934), also with Ethel Merman, is invigorating as directed by Roy del

Ruth, and the musical finale – set in an ice-cream factory and one of the last instances of two-tone Technicolor – has a weird splendour of its own. The Busby Berkeley musical sequences of **Roman Scandals** (1933) contain only the five or six basic ideas and routines that he had been using for years, confirming later claims that his more elaborate later work at Warners was collaborative, but the film as a whole, if no more enterprising, indicates the Goldwyn approach – with George S. Kaufman and Robert E. Sherwood providing the story, and Sherwood and the equally well-thought-of William Anthony McGuire the screenplay. However, if they came up with anything beyond anachronistic jokes for Cantor – an old Goldwyn favourite – the direction by Frank Tuttle disguises the fact, though the chariot race was later plagiarised for *A Funny Thing Happened on the Way to the Forum* (q.v.).

Mention should also be made of Anna Sten, exquisite in European films but a failure for Goldwyn. When Garbo's appeal was found intensified by Sound, Hollywood's acquisition of continental beauties was stepped up and many embarked, never to be heard of again. Goldwyn, with greater belief than most in his own infallibility, persisted, and during the two years that Miss Sten laboured to learn English and whatever else was thought would make her the greatest star in the world, he announced grandiose plans. He finally settled on **Nana** (1934), to be directed by von Sternberg, supposedly experienced in the ways of accented glamour, but in the event it was directed by Dorothy Arzner. Further, the film was only 'suggested by' Zola, now having elements of Gloria Swanson's old ersatz imitation, *Zaza,* so that Miss Sten could sing à la Dietrich. There is no marked difference between her Nana and her Grushenka in *Der Mörder Dmitri Karamazov* (q.v.), except that, in English, she is merely another arch coquette – and audiences had had their fill of such ladies and their final-reel repentance. Goldwyn tried twice more before giving up, and there is a certain plodding worthiness about **The Wedding Night** (1935), as directed by King Vidor; Miss Sten is a country girl who catches the attention of a happily married writer (Gary Cooper).

One who found a haven at U.A. was Howard Hughes (1905–76), a wealthy playboy with an obsessive interest in films. **Hell's Angels** (1930) had started three years earlier, but his idiosyncratic methods meant that much of it had to be refilmed with the coming of Sound – travail that today seems wasted, despite the aerial sequences – though audiences enjoy (not without derision) Jean Harlow's performance as an English girl fought over by doughboys Ben Lyon and James Hall. Hughes, wisely, thereafter contented himself with producing only, and **The Front Page** (1931), as directed by Lewis Milestone, is an account of the Hecht-MacArthur play about crime reporters as fast-talking as it was influential. A superb cast is headed by Adolphe Menjou, appropriately weasely as the editor, with Walter Catlett, Edward Everett Horton and Frank McHugh among the newsmen; as Hildy, Pat O'Brien is likeable but indefinite, which is why in a long career he never achieved the stature of his friends Cagney and Tracy.

Hughes co-produced, with its director, Howard Hawks, **Scarface: Shame of a Nation** (1932), based on a novel by Armitage Trail, adapted by Ben Hecht, with a screenplay by Seton I. Miller, John Lee Mahin and W. R. Burnett – whose *Little Caesar,* like Tony Camonte here, had also been based on Al Capone. Since this is one of the most celebrated gangster films, it is curious how many of its aspects, if founded on fact, had already been used: the flower-shop killing in *Underworld;* the illuminated sign, 'The world is yours', in *Public Enemy;* the whistle before the murder in *M;* and the obsession with a sibling in both *Doorway to Hell* and *Born Reckless* – and as in the latter case it is a sister (Ann Dvorak) longing to get in with her brother's pals, but now the obsession is incestuous. Paul Muni (q.v.) as Camonte-Capone is both stupider and vainer than Edward G. Robinson, more open with the laugh and bonhomie, and, finally, more craven – the coward the Chief of Detectives had always claimed him to be. Originally, he was to have been killed by a rival gang, but the Hays Office insisted on his being hanged: a compromise was reached by which he is mown down by the police. Hughes fought all attempts at censorship: stories of what was excised or changed ensured the film notoriety before it opened, and it was that which caused its contemporary fame – plus the fact that it was more violent than its predecessors, and audiences had a field day recognising references to actual events.

The previous year at U.A. Roland West had made **Corsair,** deservedly his last film, about a college boy (Chester Morris) who joins the rackets to get even with his girlfriend's father – and in rejecting it the public had made it clear that it disapproved of the notion that gangsters were ordinary people. *Scarface* was more obviously crusading, contemptuous of the gangsters, with a preface from the Police Commissioner of New York demanding the control of fire arms, and the conclusion 'Let's get wise to ourselves. We're fighting organised murder.' The contribution such films made was to insist that new laws were needed, and to point out that the inability to enforce the existing ones was evidence of large-scale corruption (crooked lawyers, hung juries, suborned witnesses). That the public responded to the morality of *Scarface* naturally convinced the Hays Office that it had been right to fight for it, which reinforced a growing suspicion that a Code should be drawn up for the 'guidance' of the industry; the antics of Hughes were as much responsible as those of West and Harlow, on screen, for proving that the existing rules were insufficient.

Hughes turned his attention to other matters, aviatory and amatory. Hawks began his ill-fated tenure at M-G-M, but Milestone remained at United Artists to make **Rain** (1932) and then to take over as production chief, both moves at the behest of Joseph M. Schenck, who, despite Goldwyn, still ran the company. Milestone said later of the film that it 'had no surprise, no novelty and [Joan] Crawford wasn't up to it'; her too-blatant Sadie apart, he might have mentioned Walter Huston's fine moment of sexual tension, glint-eyed as if in the midst of a seizure. Schenck also brought Al Jolson to the company, convinced that he could restore him to favour after the failure of his last Warner films, and he assigned Milestone to direct **Hallelujah, I'm a Bum** (1933) when Harry d'Abbadie d'Arrast couldn't get on with Jolson. The film eventually cost $1¾ million – the equivalent of Jolson's equally astonishing salary – and that was partly because the actor insisted on the removal of Roland Young and Milestone, to be succeeded respectively by Frank Morgan and Chester Erskine, the latter uncredited. It was Miles-

tone who chose Rodgers and Hart to supply the songs and the rhyming dialogue; S. N. Behrman's screenplay about hoboes in Central Park bears a couple of references to the boulevard play which inspired it, and many more to the central relationship in *A Nous la Liberté* – since Milestone, like his fellow Russian Mamoulian, was alive to cinema in Europe. This weird combination of French comedy and Soviet imagery he certainly claimed as his film, and when the Depression audiences for whom it held a message failed, understandably, to find it or even to care, Schenck laid the blame on him: he was relieved of his post with the company, and was not replaced.

The history of the American cinema is littered with attempts to move away from formula: variously applauded in their time, few of them now seem superior to the well-tooled factory product. Their inception was most common when the studios had no strong yea-and-nay men, and United Artists was exceptionally vulnerable, still reeling from exhibitors' recriminations as it offered **Emperor Jones** (1933), directed by Dudley Murphy, whose previous experience, not coincidentally, had included some all-negro shorts. The title-role was played by the great negro artist, Paul Robeson (1898–1976), who had turned down the original stage production but had played it in Europe and also on revival, for financial reasons; it was because of a spiritual which he sang in it that he became singer as well as actor. His original objections to Eugene O'Neill's play had lessened when it had been pointed out that it did not follow conventional form; and it was the first serious play since 'Othello' with a black protagonist. In nine short scenes – and except for the first and the last, the Emperor Jones is alone on stage – the audience learns from his hallucinations how he fled his own country and became, with the aid of a local trader, head-man of a Caribbean island. O'Neill intended a comment on white exploitation in the area, as well as an allegory on the rise of Jean-Christophe in Haiti – a matter rendered topical by recent events in Germany. In the film both factors are virtually ignored, the latter in favour of a new first half, depicting American negroes in accepted fashion as feckless – whoring, shooting crap and knifing each other – a *coup de grâce* administered to Robeson after he had signed the contract. Once the film joins O'Neill, some purpose can be perceived, as Jones, accoutred like a marshal of Napoleon, becomes a strutting, arrogant, thoughtless oligarch, but whatever sense remains in the screenplay by Dubose Heyward (author of 'Porgy') is destroyed by Murphy, as reckless as any first-time amateur. In the circumstances, Robeson's performance, powerful and confident, cannot clarify the character; it was historically too early for films to utilise his tremendous talents, and he appeared in films fitfully and seldom to advantage. Like *Hallelujah!* this film was accepted as 'art' by a lot of people who should have known better.

The installation of a production chief had been Schenck's reponse to the demand for more films from the managers of the distribution offices and theatres in the growing circuit he had created – a problem solved when Darryl F. Zanuck entered the fold after a dispute over control at Warners. With Schenck he formed 20th Century Pictures, based on the simple expedient of formula pictures enhanced by known talent – consisting of the major independent directors and players (initially contracted for two films each), and by borrowings which were secured by the combination of Zanuck's reputation for sound film-making and Schenck's financial resources – which for this purpose would include brother Nicholas, the president of Loews. Therefore, for 20th's first film, **The Bowery** (1933), came Wallace Beery and Jackie Cooper, and from Paramount George Raft. It was a rollicking start: Zanuck's dynamism brought from a variable director, Raoul Walsh, his occasional vigour, and matters stayed bullish with **Blood Money** (1933), directed by Rowland Brown with the speed and authenticity he had brought to *Quick Millions*. An ex-lawyer (George Bancroft) makes a living going bail for the town's criminals, helped or hindered by his girlfriend (Judith Anderson), a tough Britisher who runs a speakeasy, and a society dame (Frances Dee) with a yen for low life and, as it turns out, an inexhaustible capacity for being pushed about. Like Walsh, Brown had just left Fox, and it was at this time that he reputedly crossed one of the industry's bigwigs, with the result that he had no major credits after being replaced in Britain on *The Scarlet Pimpernel* (q.v.).

Gregory LaCava directed two films for Zanuck, **Gallant Lady** (1933), notably well-acted by Ann Harding as an unfortunate mother and Clive Brook as her drunken-outcast admirer, and **The Affairs of Cellini** (1934), a historical charade with Fredric March as the sculptor, Constance Bennett (q.v.) as his noble prey, and Frank Morgan as her jealous husband – a role he had played in 1924 in the Broadway production of the original, 'The Firebrand'. Zanuck's requirements of gusto and a sometimes misplaced sophistication were also to be found in the two historicals for which he had brought George Arliss from Warners, **The House of Rothschild** (1934), directed by Alfred Werker, and **Cardinal Richelieu** (1935), directed by Rowland V. Lee. The former impressed contemporaries, with its intimations of anti-semitism and complex financial dealings, but indulgence now is needed towards such matters as Nathan's blessing of the romance between his daughter (Loretta Young) and a gentile officer (Robert Young), or the reaction of Wellington (C. Aubrey Smith) to Napoleon's escape, 'Aaah, that blasted little Corsican is back!' The screenwriter was Nunnally Johnson (1897–1977), a former columnist, beginning a long association with Zanuck.

Johnson also wrote **Bulldog Drummond Strikes Back** (1934) for Ronald Colman, greatly superior to the latter's previous Drummond film. Stylishly directed by Roy del Ruth in London fog and lavish interiors, Colman gives Sapper's paste-board a romantic twinkle and debonair ex-army bearing. 'India should be a sacred trust' he cries in **Clive of India** (1935), based on a chronicle play which ran a year at London's Wyndham's Theatre – and the film could not have cost much more than the stage production, since major events are covered by explanatory titles or take place at night, leaving the imaginative direction of Richard Boleslawski to paper over the cracks.

The success of these films ensured Boleslawski and writer W. P. Lipscombe a bigger budget on **Les Misérables** (1935). The Valjean of Fredric March on this occasion justifies Hollywood's faith in him as a 'costume' actor, but the film belongs to Charles Laughton's Javert, moving finally when his inhuman sense of duty yields to pity. Two other popular actors to arrive were Maurice Chevalier

The Western, usually considered a staple of Hollywood fare, has hardly been that in the Sound period: during the five decades since the coming of Talkies it was only popular during the Forties and Fifties. During the Thirties the poverty row studios turned out Westerns, but the major companies lost interest after *Cimarron*. One reason was that the huge success of that film caused so many inferior imitations.

(before returning, disgruntled, to France) and Clark Gable, courtesy of M-G-M. Chevalier had virtually a one-man show in **Folies Bergère** (1935), directed by del Ruth, which despite the title and the production numbers by Dave Gould (who won an Oscar for them) has less to do with the Folies than with a complicated scheme filched from *The Guardsman* – a husband who tests his wife's fidelity by impersonation. The Hays Office had frowned on the plot, but did allow the surprisingly explicit relationship of Gable with Miss Young in **Call of the Wild** (1935), which in other ways, too, violates Jack London's story. However, William Wellman directed, and like all his best work it has unexpected quirks and revelations, as in Reginald Owen's pebble-bespectacled villain, an irresistible impersonation of Laughton.

At this point 20th Century amalgamated with Fox, thus completing the pattern of Hollywood studios that would remain stable for the next thirty years. Columbia (q.v.) was still emerging as an important studio, and the start of the decade had seen the formation of the other major of the period, R.K.O. Radio. Its founder was Joseph P. Kennedy, whose involvement in the industry predated his liaison with Gloria Swanson. Soon after World War I he had invested in a circuit in New England, and in 1926 he purchased the Film Booking Office of America Inc. (F.B.O.), A British-owned producing and releasing company which conentrated on low-budget features. He was disinclined to change that policy as he waited for the results of the Talkie revolution. Others, he reckoned, would want a stake in the film industry's new fortune, presenting as it did a market for new equipment and a threat to live theatre and radio. He was therefore the prime instigator of a series of mergers whereby the Radio Corporation of America (R.C.A.), in conjunction with two other electronics giants, Westinghouse and General Electric, absorbed the Keith-Albee-Orpheum circuit, the last great vaudeville chain – which, converted to cinemas, could be supplied by Kennedy's studio interests. The consequent amalgamation called itself uncertainly R.K.O. or Radio before settling on the redundant R.K.O. Radio (i.e. Keith-Orpheum flanked by two references to R.C.A.).

Put in charge of production was William Le Baron, a former journalist, dramatist and associate producer (for Paramount), who had also been vice-president of F.B.O. for some years. His first two stars were Bebe Daniels and Richard Dix, both dropped by Paramount, and individually appearing in the two films which got the company off to a flying start – Miss Daniels in **Rio Rita** (1929), based on the Broadway musical and co-starring Wheeler and Woolsey (teamed by Ziegfeld for that event and to continue successfully at R.K.O.), and Dix in **Cimarron** (1931), with Irene Dunne (b. 1904); she too was from the stage and would also become a box-office attraction for R.K.O.

Cimarron was based on Edna Ferber's massive pioneer novel, made extensively and expensively on location under the direction of Wesley Ruggles, and notable today mainly for the sincerity of its leading players. The Academy voted it its best Picture Oscar, and the profits from it enabled Kennedy to add to the conglomerate two ailing studios, the Producers' Distributing Co. (P.D.C.) and Pathé – the troubles of the last named being caused less by only marginally successful films than by lack of a chain of cinemas in which to show them. However, Pathé provided not only the space and appliances of a major studio, but talent of the order of director Gegory LaCava and stars Constance Bennett and Ann Harding – as well as Pathé News. This nucleus of players dictated to a large extent the R.K.O. product, which was quite unlike that of the other studios at this time – high-toned, semi-sophisticated and verbose, often set in Britain. Coincidentally or not, such subjects were precisely of the kind to appeal to David O. Selznick (1902–65), who replaced Le Baron in 1932, brought by Kennedy from Paramount, where his acumen had made something of a mark. Although motivated by a desire to revenge his father's rejection by the industry, he had allied to his energy far more taste than his fellow moguls and an almost faultless judgment of talent.

The films made under his aegis bear witness to his attention to detail. Although *Photoplay* thought **The Conquerors** (1932) only 'a worthy successor' to *Cimarron,* it is in fact much superior, as written by Robert Lord (from a story of Howard Esterbrook) and directed by William Wellman. It gives, said *Photoplay,* 'a pretty definite idea of everything that has happened in this country since 1870 – shows you its progress, defeats, victories, indomitable courage' – all in eighty-four minutes, including the Depression. Indeed, there are three bank crashes in all – done in Eisenstein-like montage, but a good deal wittier – and if the final one is resolved only by a message of hope that was doubtless why 'it makes you proud to be an American'. Dix, and Edna May Oliver, were retained from *Cimarron,* joined by Miss Harding and Guy Kibbee.

Though Dix's films were directed at the male half of the audience, **Hell's Highway** (1932) is a most untypical R.K.O. film as directed by Rowland Brown, a bleak, location-shot piece set among the chain gangs. **The Lost Squadron** (1932) is chiefly notable for Erich Von Stroheim, playing with relish but not humour a film director very much like himself. The director of this film is George Archainbaud, and Mary Astor is a star, Follette, who has sacrificed Dix for her career. He, Joel McCrea and Robert Armstrong play stuntmen of mutual esteem: 'He's a *grand* fellow' and 'He's a *swell* guy' they constantly exclaim.

Friends and Lovers (1931) concerns Indian Army officers, Adolphe Menjou and Laurence Olivier, both in love with Lily Damita, married to Von Stroheim – complaisant till, pushed too far, he takes a whip to her. The two officers are finally convinced that they are better off without her – a denouement considered typically British, part of the stag party syndrome wherein army camaraderie has more worth than the opposite sex. It is just possible to admire the direction of Victor Schertzinger, but there is nothing to be said for the work of Herbert Brenon on **Beau Sabreur** (1931). Returning to the author, and cadre, of *Beau Geste,* he proves incompetent in Talkies; after two further films for the company, he finished his career in Britain.

Critics did not like Wheeler and Woolsey, but they filmed regularly till 1937, when illness split them. Bert Wheeler has curly hair, a boyish face and no distinctive style ; Robert Woolsey has Harold Lloyd specs, a Groucho cigar and a way of saying 'Whooooeee' at moments of stress. **Hold 'em Jail** (1932) has them involved with a prison football game: Norman

Taurog directed, S. J. Perelman was one of the writers, and Woolsey's wooing of Edna May Oliver, a prudish but game spinster, is not unmindful of Groucho's tactics.

Occasionally R.K.O. made a gangster film, such as **Bad Company** (1931), a complicated tale as co-written and directed by Tay Garnett, with Harry Carey as the police chief and Ricardo Cortez as the gang leader – with his bust of himself, his statuette of Napoleon, his paranoia about food and cats, and his habit of flicking his cigarette stubs on the carpet for his servants to pick up (borrowed from Charles Ray during his period of glory). The film, however, was a vehicle for Helen Twelvetrees, inherited from P.D.C., a lady whose speciality was crying. Since she was not very good at that, or indeed, any of the requirements of a star, she was soon dropped. Such was not the case with Irene Dunne and Ann Harding, meeting every reversal with a smile. Though both were too ladylike to have traffic with gangsters, their vehicles were curiously similar to those of Miss Twelvetrees. In **Consolation Marriage** (1931), directed by Paul Sloane, Miss Dunne marries on the rebound and takes several reels to realise that she loves her husband (Pat O'Brien); in **If I Were Free** (1933), directed by Elliott Nugent, she leaves her caddish husband (Nils Asther) but takes just as long to find happiness with the English lawyer (Clive Brook), who has given her life a new meaning.

Ann Harding (1902–81) was beautiful, serene, and only occasionally conscious of being a big star: she played with exceptional lightness, using inflexions and pauses which make most of her contemporaries seem common place. R.K.O. made her a 'new' woman, frank about sex, but determined to do nothing about it unless the band is on her finger. A spinster in **Devotion** (1931), she sets her cap at English barrister Leslie Howard; married for the second time in **Westward Passage** (1931), she finds herself attracted again to first husband Laurence Olivier. Robert Milton directed both films, and his frequent attempts at banter are keyed to his star's performances.

The motif in all these films is female sexuality. The lady who did not resist temptation was Constance Bennett (1905–65). Considered, by her fans at least, the epitome of glamour, and having had a great success as an unmarried mother, in *Common Clay,* she was kept at sinning. In **The Common Law** (1931), directed by Paul L. Stein, she falls in love with a young artist (Joel McCrea) who discovers her past before she can confess it, and there is many a reversal before she becomes his common-law wife (as we assume from the title), which is only one step to the 'approved' ending.

These frequent glimpses of sin must have made many a spectator wonder whether the path of virtue was the right one. The Silent cinema had weakened the still-prevalent Victorian moral code, but hypocritically the images of wickedness – ankle or champagne-glass – were often contradicted by intertitles. With the coming of Sound, the onus of sexual demand sometimes passed to the ladies. A Gable might be frank, or even a gentlemanly actor like Brook or Howard, but if that frankness was put into speech, he would be at best unlikeable and at worst a degenerate. It could still be pretended that women did not really enjoy sex; alternatively, the stories were based on the old myth that their bodies were their sole means of survival – so that exploiting them, or lying and cheating, was permissible behaviour. Not the least of the hypocrisies on display was the notion that even the wickedest woman could be regenerated by the love of a good man. Regeneration was less pernicious in Silents: the unhappy wives, seduced servant girls and whores from deprived backgrounds had all been made to see the error of their ways before 'The End', but now the pursuit of luxury was an end in itself. After her earlier roles it is no surprise to find Miss Bennett as a reformatory school girl desperate for a **Bed of Roses** (1933), but it is hard to believe that she could be redeemed by the love of humble river captain McCrea. She is technically pure, since her system is the common one (in movies) of getting the man (John Halliday) so drunk as to be incapable, and then climbing into his bed. Her friend (Pert Kelton) has no such qualms, and there is always the possibility – ambiguity never being absent – that McCrea's body eventually appeals more than Halliday's gewgaws.

The director was Gregory LaCava (1892–1952), whose R.K.O. work is varied. **Laugh and Get Rich** (1931) was one of several Hollywood attempts to find a co-starring team to rival Dressler and Beery: the couple here are suspicious, strict Edna May Oliver and woozy Hugh Herbert, running a boarding house. **Age of Consent** (1932) can stand with the Warner record of this period, perhaps as accurate a portrait of campus life as we have. The boys sit around in their shorts discussing girls, to the disgust of Michael (Richard Cromwell), unaware then that his own frustration will lead him into the toils of a 'friendly' waitress. **The Half-Naked Truth** (1932) is an irreverent farce with Lee Tracy as a quick-scheming P.R. man, Frank Morgan as a Broadway producer, Lupe Velez as a fake princess and, best of all, gravel-voiced Eugene Pallette pretending to be a eunuch.

LaCava's **Symphony of Six Millions** (1932) ranks with *Bad Girl* as an account of working-class life, but it is also the first serious portrait of American Jews – assuming its predecessors to have been primarily comic or sentimental. Jews in the first movies were patterned on Shylock, moneylenders or pawnbrokers – a stereotype broken when a stage player Sam Bernard, made a popular success as 'a rich, overpowering Jew', a Mr Hoggenheimer. Bernard became one of Zukor's Famous Players, around which time Broadway was laughing at the antics of Potash and Perlmutter, based on *The Saturday Evening Post* stories by Montague Glass. It was not till Goldwyn's film version ten years later, *Potash and Perlmutter* (1923), that Jews first appeared on the screen in full and admirable light – and that was due to the success of 'Abie's Irish Rose', beginning its long run the previous year. That also paved the way for *The Cohens and the Kellys* at Universal and *Kosher Kitty Kelly* at F.B.O., both in 1926, and Bernard's old success, *Friendly Enemies,* with Weber and Fields – Jewish comedians who made occasional films, as did Smith and Dale. The anomaly is that the film industry was predominantly Jewish, churning out sequels for the Cohens and Kellys but not highlighting the intensely Jewish theme of *The Jazz Singer.* The title *Symphony of Six Millions* suggests a portrait of New York, and if not applicable to the film it was doubtless justified by Fannie Hurst's original novel, in part based on her own experience. The opening sequence, in which the still-young parents discuss the futures of their children in European accents, must have struck a chord with many Americans.

The lead was played by a Jewish actor, Ricardo Cortez, so renamed because he was intended as a successor to Valentino. (It was not till the end of the decade that any studio engaged a romantic lead associated, via his stage work, with Jewish roles; he was John Garfield and the studio Warners, which had, however, had two important Jewish stars in Edward G. Robinson and Paul Muni). Cortez plays Felix, a doctor whose family persuades him to move from the ghetto to Park Avenue, to the neglect of his crippled girlfriend (Irene Dunne); unlike most screen doctors, his ideals are not in question, but LaCava, if less perceptive than Borzage, makes the most of the family gatherings and glimpses of ghetto life – matters not to be seen again in American films for almost forty years. During that time, less than half a dozen characters would be overtly Jewish, and the reasons must be speculative: I assume it to be because the Nazis brought anti-semitism to the fore and the Hollywood moguls decided – subconsciously perhaps – not to remind audiences of the differences, real or supposed, between Jews and gentiles. It could not have been because of the German market, since only Warners and R.K.O. withdrew at the time of the Nazi takeover, and Universal in 1936 – and none of the three closed their Austrian offices which could handle German distribution till after the Anschluss, at which time United Artists broke with Bayerisches-Film, which had been handling its product; Paramount, M-G-M and 20th Century-Fox maintained some form of distribution till forced to close their German offices in 1940/1.

Among directors, George Cukor was brought from Paramount and assigned to **What Price Hollywood?** (1932), after Selznick had fought front office claims that movies on this particular subject were seldom popular. Its five writers were old Hollywood hands, but it would be reckless to speculate on their sources – though, as metamorphosed into *A Star is Born* (q.v.), Colleen Moore would recognise incidents from her own life. This film is less vicious, and it is not a tragic love story, since the one who goes on the skids is not the husband of the star (Constance Bennett), but her mentor (Lowell Sherman); it does offer a portrait of a sybaritic town, peopled with parvenues prone to absurd expenditure and the values of the fan magazines. Sherman's own career, as actor and director, was ruined by drink, so he is well-cast as the unfortunate director: but the self-ironies, bragadaccio and fatalism were moulded (once again) on John Barrymore. Since the film is a compendium of all that was wrong with Hollywood in its *Photoplay* heyday, its deficiency is its avoidance of sex. There is no reference to the casting couch or the hundreds of hopefuls prepared to trade flesh for a 'chance': R.K.O. would let them admit anything but that.

It was Cukor and Selznick who brought Katharine Hepburn (b. 1909) from Broadway, for **A Bill of Divorcement** (1932), based on Clemence Dane's theatrical discussion on the problems of having a mentally sick father (John Barrymore). Hepburn is young, eager, and teetering between gaucherie and archness, yet in the often disastrous films that followed she saved the day with her directness of emotion. With misplaced confidence she would throw herself across the screen, fiddling with hair, sleeves, anything – but that same nerviness could be touching when her eyes strayed, embarrassed or hurt, looking for another focus.

In **Christopher Strong** (1933) she is the first woman to fly round the world, stealing from his wife (Billie Burke) a diplomat (Colin Clive), till then the happiest man in London. 'If I were the usual man . . . If you were the usual girl . . . We could have had our love affair and . . . not taken the thing so desperately seriously,' he says, to which she responds, 'If you were the usual man . . . If I were the usual girl . . . We could have had our love affair . . . and not taken the thing so *desperately* seriously.' She commits suicide by taking off her oxygen mask, thus transformed into the Victory of Samothrace, feathers sprouting from her arms. Because it is about an independent woman engaged in a masculine profession, this film has been requisitioned as a monument in the Women's Lib movement – but while both Hepburn and the director, Dorothy Arzner, may have held strong views on the subject it would be unwise to attribute any to Selznick, who produced, or Gilbert Frankau, who wrote the original novel.

Morning Glory (1933) starts with Hepburn wandering into a theatre lobby, and you can see that she is stage-struck by the back of her head. 'I shall never be wonderful like them,' she says, gazing at portraits of Ethel Barrymore, Maude Adams and Sarah Bernhardt, 'but I have something wonderful inside me' – and one experiences an odd frisson, since in the years since the film was made her fame has outstripped theirs. Her Eva Lovelace is magnanimous and pretentious, not qualities alien to this actress, but she has a wry humour; prattling on like a wound-up phonograph she says, 'Of course, I shall die at my zenith', and the audience roars, as the director, Lowell Sherman, intended. This dated tale remains amazingly fresh, thanks also to Adolphe Menjou as the producer who takes advantage of Eva's ambitions, and Douglas Fairbanks Jr as the dramatist who might have saved her from that fate.

Cukor's **Little Women** (1933) also remains in pristine condition, one of the few adaptations likely to please all admirers of the original novel; Hepburn is Jo, with Joan Bennett, Frances Dee and Jean Parker as her sisters, Spring Byington as Marmee, Douglass Montgomery as Laurie, Paul Lukas as Dr Bhaer and Edna May Oliver as Aunt March. The film brought Hepburn a new army of admirers, but few remained after **Spitfire** (1934) and **The Little Minister** (1934). In the former, directed by John Cromwell, she is Trigger Hawks, living in a log cabin, saying 'git' instead of 'got' and 'cain't' instead of 'can't'; in the latter, directed by Richard Wallace, she is Barrie's Lady Babbie, saying 'It's harrd fo' a lassie to keeeep up wi' a mun' – but at least the ads warned prospective customers, claiming 'something more than a motion picture – a Christmas gift for your heart'.

John Cromwell (1888–1980), a former actor, was also brought by Selznick from Paramount, and like Cukor was adept at the sort of subjects the producer favoured. He had already directed the Broadway production of Sidney Howard's **The Silver Cord** (1933), also with Laura Hope Crews, whose performance is a revelation to those who know her only from her amusing, later caricatures. the film betrays its origin by rarely straying from the family manse, and we may well wonder why everyone talks in loud voices in the hall, likely to be overheard – and the talk is dangerous, concerning a possessive mother (Miss Crews),

exposed and ousted by her daughter-in-law (Irene Dunne). Audiences are on tenterhooks to see how long it takes for the gullible to see through its monster; this is not a penetrating entertainment, but the arguments pertinent to the situation have been logically marshalled. When Miss Dunne finally turns on the old lady, calling her 'a self-centred, self-pitying, son-devouring tigress, with unmentionable proclivities on the side', it is doubtful whether all audiences understood, but the film so incensed one London suburb that it had to be withdrawn after a single performance, causing the *Daily Telegraph* to observe that it 'requires for its appreciation a certain knowledge of psycho-analysis'.

The reference is too guarded to be shocking. Since sexual frankness now constituted more than rape and seduction, how was the cinema to cope with subjects being aired in the novel and 'modern' drama? By this time the craze for Talkies was spent, Miss Harlow had given her all, and new ways were sought for enticing audiences. The executives were cautious: it was one thing to regard sex as a commodity, and another to attempt new ways to market it. The directors and writers were susceptible both to their bosses and to audiences – and in view of the apparently blameless lives of most spectators, caution was needed. But the climate was there for hints of strange psychologies and recherché habits – recognisable to the knowing, and to them part of the glamour of movies. Film-makers had become adept at suggesting odd perversions, and Cromwell made a widely-accepted version of **Of Human Bondage** (1934). Maugham's novel was no longer sensational, but by reducing it to the infatuation of a medical student it offered an experience alien to most spectators. Looked at coldly, Philip's obsession with Millie is masochistic and, to all but himself, tiresome; with Maugham's portrait of late Victorian London entirely gone, the film has to depend on the interpreters of the two roles. Bette Davis, borrowed from Warners, made her name as Millie, a self-centred harpy who refuses to see herself as other than 'a lidy': she has a flirty giggle for her other admirers, and an indifference, vehement and coquettish by turns, for Philip. However, the actress's love of detail is insufficient to counterbalance a cockney accent horrendous by today's standard. As

Philip, Leslie Howard is too commonsensical, hoping to convey passion with pensive looks. Withal, enough remains: this novel, boned, still makes an absorbing film.

The Fountain (1934) was based on a novel by Charles Morgan, whose reputation at this time perhaps exceeded Maugham's. The London *Times* – whose drama critic Morgan then was – observed that the cinema could not convey the quality of his prose, but 'the material outlines of the story remain intact': a British officer (Brian Aherne) is billeted by his German captors on a Dutch family, of whom he had known Julie (Miss Harding) while at Oxford; they fall in love again, a situation fraught with tension when her German husband (Paul Lukas) returns; but the two men find 'a peace too strong to be broken in upon by any human need'. Cromwell's direction uncovers a humourless portentousness which is apt for this particular writer, and he gets a particularly good performance from Aherne as the pipe-smoking Englishman who cares more for Keats than war: it is a character performance, but I do not think the actor knew it.

R.K.O. worked Miss Harding in such high-minded stories that the public – foolishly – began to tire of her; and the studio also borrowed Diana Wynyard for several similar items, which put *finis* to her Hollywood career. Neither was there to bail out **Jalna** (1935) – though one of the leading roles was taken by the equally sympathetic Kay Johnson, who was married to Cromwell. He tries hard with this synthetic family saga, by Mazo de la Roche, its members called Renny, Finch, Wake, Alayne, Pheasant, Eden and so on, who go about in riding boots because they're farmers. It is not surprising that R.K.O. spent most of the decade staving off bankruptcy.

The company was saved by some strokes of luck. One was the teaming (q.v.) of Fred Astaire and Ginger Rogers; another was John Ford's **The Informer** (1935), his second film for the company. Neither project interested his employers, Fox, though he had so much wanted to make **The Lost Patrol** (1934) that he had waived his salary – which suggested to the film historian Lewis Jacobs that he had 'awakened from his indifference and intended to make films about which he cared', adding that it proved he 'could make a film from the barest of materials provided

he was moved by it'. Today it is impossible to say why, or even whether, Ford was moved: the tale of men under duress has been done so often and in this same superficial way – a British cavalry unit consisting of: the idealist (Douglas Walton) who wanted to serve in the ranks because he loves Kipling; the public school drunk (Reginald Denny); the music hall artist (Wallace Ford); the religious maniac (Boris Karloff), etc. Dudley Nichols wrote it, and he also adapted *The Informer* from the novel by Liam O'Flaherty, Ford's cousin, which Ford preferred to the Western he had been offered. When Joseph Kennedy relinquished control of R.K.O., the project was abandoned, but was restarted by the new bosses on the principle that the participants were already on salary: the film was made in three weeks, at a cost of just over $200,000. Few evinced further interest till it was taken up by the New York critics, when it went on to win five Oscars, including Best Actor (Victor McLaglen) and Best Director. Ford's still-hovering reputation was finally made, and four years later Jacobs considered it 'one of the most important contributions since Sound'. All the leading American directors (Borzage, King, LaCava, Milestone, Wellman, Vidor, Capra) had made at least one such contribution – a picture of serious intent, its commercial potential of secondary consideration – but the point about *The Informer* is that there was no other American film quite like it. It is a tourist's view of Dublin – of boozy pubs, a brothel, not to mention a church or two. It is the story of a man who sells his pal to the peelers for the price of two steamship tickets – a tale of weakness and retribution, enlivened by whiffs of politics and religion. There is only a hint of romance – there was none in *The Lost Patrol* – and that was sufficiently rare as to be very impressive.

Unfortunately, like Ford's other ambitious projects, it exposes his weaknesses. There is no concern or passion, but there are the most arty of borrowed clichés:* the blind man looming in the fog; the poster blown across the street to flap at McLaglen's leg; the client done up like Mackie Messer in *Die Driegroschenoper* (q.v.). The

*Ford liked to think of himself as a 'plain' director, and when late in life a mutual friend saw him emerging from a Los Angeles art-house – he had been to see a film by Ingmar Bergman – Ford was clearly embarrassed. 'Got to keep an eye on the opposition' he growled.

The beast is, of course, King Kong in the film of that name, and the frightened lady Fay Wray. Since the film was largely composed of process shots, the stills look somewhat artificial (illustrations from films are in fact called stills since they are shot separately, frame-enlargements from the celluloid film itself never being wholly satisfactory); but at least on the screen itself this now-aged movie continues to thrill audiences. Those of the time, if they read the show business journal *Variety*, would have seen the accompanying advertisement, indicating that Kong was a cure for the Depression blues.

ending is particularly pretentious. But though the insights are no greater than those of, say, *Public Enemy*, the combination of lofty intent, low life and Ufa lighting made them seem so. Ford himself admitted that it lacks humour, but it lacks humour precisely because of its ambitions.

Considering its heavy irony, it is only fitting that modern audiences should prefer **King Kong** (1933). The credited directors are Ernest B. Schoedsack and Merian C. Cooper, but it was masterminded by Willis O'Brien, who had worked on the monsters of *The Lost World*. Shortly after the inception of R.K.O. he was employed on a project to utilise similar processes, to be called *Creation*. Money, however, was lacking; when Selznick took over production he asked Cooper (they had worked together on *The Four Feathers*) to inspect the studio's finances, and Cooper saw what existed of *Creation* – a script and a test reel: since returning from Africa he had been trying to set up a film about gorillas, and O'Brien 'bought' it. They set to work: the screenplay is credited to James Creelman and Ruth Rose, from a story by Cooper and Edgar Wallace (whose contribution was minimal); Selznick's main contribution was to scrape money from other budgets for the cost, $650,000. Apart from pre-production work, the actual filming took fifty-five weeks. It was premiered in New York simultaneously at that city's two massive cinemas, Radio City Music Hall and the Roxy, to instant success. It is far-fetched, this tale of a film crew whose leading lady (Fay Wray) is stolen by a giant gorilla: her screams remain a byword, and her reactions are in both senses of the word hysterical. But once Kong appears, after three-quarters of an hour, the excitement doesn't let up. Kong himself was only eighteen inches high (though parts of a 'real'-size Kong were used for some sequences) and the Wray he carries was an animated doll. I cannot say that all the process work is exceptional, or that you cannot see the joins, but the tricks are loaded with imagination and the editing is particularly brilliant. We shall not see its like again, or so I said some years ago – since when the 1976 remake has come, gone and been forgotten.

There was a sequel, **Son of Kong** (1933), which, hurriedly made, is much inferior. For a follow-up, try **The Most Dangerous Game** (1932), filmed simultaneously in the same studio jungle (actually 'planted' earlier for *Bird of Paradise*), using many of the same processes. The screenplay is by Creelman, and the directors are Schoedsack and Irving Pichel. An alternative title is *The Hounds of Zaroff*, and Leslie Banks manages to be both hammy and scary as the baron whose game is hunting human beings – Miss Wray and Robert Armstrong. It is a far cry from *Chang* or *Grass* – ersatz certainly, but wholly individual.

The success of *King Kong* was instrumental in the appointment of Cooper and Schoedsack as joint production chiefs when Selznick left for M-G-M, but it must be said that R.K.O.'s most astute producer then and for some years was Pandro S. Berman (b. 1905), a protégé of Selznick. Cooper and Schoedsack did nothing else notable as a team. The latter directed, and Creelman

helped to write, **The Last Days of Pompeii** (1935) – which in fact, as a foreword admits, has nothing to do with Bulwer-Lytton's novel. It has the usual Ben-Hurish story, a historically inaccurate eruption, and a Pompeii rendered only by glass shots and some wobbly back projections. If *King Kong* is the dream factory at its most persuasive, this film is old Hollywood at its considerable worst. As both are innocuous tales, we cannot blame the Code, but it is symptomatic of the dampening of spirits discernible in the post-Code films.

The public hardly noticed, having generally regarded anything that happened on screen as occurring in some never-never land with little or no relation to real life. (In any case, *Red-Headed Woman* was regarded as much less 'real' than *Little Women,* the film most often cited as both popular and healthy entertainment.) Comment, even in the trade press, was rare; the Hays Office published its 'recommendations' in June, 1934, and the films then in production were merely toned down, with the sharper writing and directing talents continuing to try to circumvent restrictions. Nevertheless, as we shall see, the studios soon began to return to the big-budget prestige productions which drew attention to the institution of cinema-going.

With the exception of M-G-M, the studios had eschewed these during this period, having sufficient troubles with the coming of Sound, the Depression and its accompanying financial losses, and the heart-searching over censorship. One factor remained constant – the star as the keystone of the industry, but even that certainty had taken a jolt when the creatures had to talk. Old favourites had disappeared with scarifying rapidity, but the fact that they were as quickly replaced by new ones meant that they offered no real threat to the power of the moguls. Nor did the directors. Except for the rise of the cinema circuits, which only increased the power of the front offices, the industry was fundamentally unchanged since 1915, and since the recent convulsions had been so easily – in retrospect – surmounted, the mood was set fair for the future.

Now that cinemas are again as small as the original
nickelodeons, we may feel nostalgic about the
palaces of the late Silent and early Talkie period, ever
more sumptuous and ornate. Audiences, marshalled
by squadrons of ushers, entered ankle-deep in
carpet. The gardens of the Alhambra were
reproduced on the walls of the auditorium and the
fountains of Tivoli in the foyers; ceilings contained
whole galaxies and dripped chandeliers; while in the
matter of gilt and marble the Paris Opéra looked
dingy in comparison. Two New York theatres were
the culmination of the vogue, the Roxy and, situated
a block away, Radio City Music Hall (illustrated).
The Roxy opened in 1927, named after the most
enterprising of movie showmen, S. L. 'Roxy'
Rothafel, and it was he who was called in to manage
Radio City which, if slightly less lavish, was even
bigger. R.K.O., the owners of Rockefeller Center
and its entertainment complex, intended the Music
Hall, seating 6,200, for live entertainment – to be
provided by the Metropolitan Opera, which wasn't
interested – while a smaller auditorium, seating a
mere 3,400, would offer movies plus the supporting
live show thought essential. Radio City opened with
vaudeville in 1932, and promptly flopped, reopening
in January 1933 with a screen-stage policy – and
since the first film on the bill was *The Bitter Tea of
General Yen* it is clear it was not intended to be the
family cinema it later became. In March 1933 it
played *King Kong* simultaneously with its smaller
brother (about to change its name from the 'New
R.K.O. Roxy' to the 'Center Theater'), and the
following month it programmed *Cavalcade* at
regular prices after its reserved-seat engagement: but
not till it began to have financial troubles in the
Sixties did it again show any movie that was not
first-run and exclusive – and even then, long, long
after other cinemas had dropped them, it retained its
supporting stage-show, highlighted by its
high-kicking and justly acclaimed chorus, the
Rockettes.

   If, in theory, the Music Hall showed films from all
the major studios, there was originally a bias
towards the films of R.K.O., and Disney's *Snow
White and the Seven Dwarfs* was one of its biggest
successes. Most films ran for only a week,
necessitating up to fifty-two different stage shows
every year, but towards the end of the Forties the
average run was four weeks – and M-G-M seemed
to have a virtual monopoly on the films supplied. In
the Sixties, with the Music Hall firmly established as
a tourist attraction, it became difficult to find
sufficient family films – a situation that became
desperate in the Seventies. In 1973 *Mary Poppins* was
the Music Hall's first revival, and two years later it
played for a week each four of the most popular
films in M-G-M's history, *Gone with the Wind*, *2001:
a Space Odyssey*, *Singin' in the Rain* and *Doctor
Zhivago*. A number of films from the Thirties were
revived (for one day only) to emphasise the Art
Deco interior – but Radio City finally shuttered in
1978. However, it was clear that New York would
not let it die and it reopened in 1979, supported by a
trust fund – the aim being flexibility of programme,
which may be a one-performance rock concert or a
six-week revue. Film shows survive, usually only as
morning revivals, and no longer supported by the
Rockettes. However, that institution happily
survives, along with the Music Hall's Symphony
Orchestra and such seasonal events as 'The Glory of
Easter' and 'The Spirit of Christmas'.

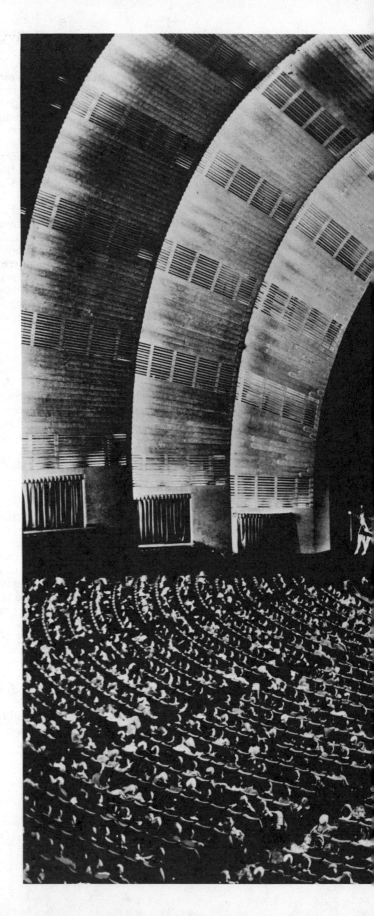

13

Film in the Third Reich

AS HOLLYWOOD settled down again after its own financial and moral crises, the situation in Europe deteriorated, till the prospect of another world war passed from a possibility to a certainty. Since most of the American movie moguls had been born in Europe and had relatives still there they occasionally allowed into their films a comment on conditions in Europe, but it would be seldom more than a comment – a pinprick of criticism directed at Germany. Few Hollywood writers felt themselves equipped for more trenchant opinion, but what Hollywood could do was provide escapist entertainments, increasingly expertly executed, to relieve a world increasingly in need of them. A desire to alleviate the world's troubles was not the prime intention of the American film-maker, nor, emerging from their Depression, did the American cinema-goer care to look too deeply into problems, his own or those of others: the front pages of the newspapers were gloomy enough.

The European situation was remote to most Americans and, however much the politicians warned, the official Nazi policies of expansion, rearmament and racial persecution seemed unlikely to result in another world conflict. But the Nazis themselves were fully aware that their immediate neighbours did not warm to their policies and methods, and the cinema was regarded as a way of dampening criticism. The leaders of the Nazi party not only adored the cinema as entertainment, but regarded it as the most powerful of all propaganda weapons. The German cinema would preach to the world the Nazi scheme of things, and the world, presumably, would understand. The leaders – or at any rate Goebbels who, as head of Nazi prop-

aganda, was officially in charge of the film industry – quickly realised, to their chagrin, that they did not have film-makers of world quality, able to compete with Hollywood; they thought, however, that by controlling the industry they could achieve this. That was typical of Nazi mentality. It is doubtful whether Goebbels, even at his most despondent over the films he commanded, ever regretted the promulgation of June 1933 – four months after Hitler was granted dictatorial powers – which forbade Jews to work in the industry. Many continued to work under pseudonyms; many had already left. A number of left-wing film-makers and others who realised that freedom of expression would be severely limited voluntarily departed also.

The German studios had been flushed with confidence as they settled down again after the disruption caused by the advent of Sound. There appeared to be an endless supply of talent to replace those directors, writers and players who had departed for Hollywood and elsewhere – a great many of whom were now being forced to return, though at least with 'international' reputations which would prove useful. With so many English-speaking people in the German studios, multilingual productions posed no problems; finance presented no problem either, for, in common with local audiences, those foreign distributors who imported German films were not looking for Hollywood-style lavishness but for tales of the everyday – provided, that is, that they were embellished with music and were mainly concerned with criminals.

Fritz Lang bowed to the current demand, and eschewed – for one film – master-criminals in favour of one despicable little murderer; but **M** (1931) was admired pre-

Fritz Lang's *M* remains one of the most famous films in the art-house repertory – partly because the direction remains startling, even today, with its clever use of sound and symbols. The title refers to the letter chalked on the shoulder of the murderer's coat – *Möder* in German – by one who suspects him. The 'M' in question is Peter Lorre, whose performance has been justly famous for fifty years.

cisely because it was recognised as a successor to those typical Lang Silents in which men were driven by unnatural impulses. Lang and von Harbou had originally planned a film on the worst crime they could think of, which they considered the writing of anonymous letters, but they then switched to child-murder; von Harbou was in fact finishing the script as the police hunted for Kürten, the Düsseldorf child murderer. The town in the film is recognisable as Berlin, whose underworld leaders co-operate with the police, baffled by lack of motive and clues. Routine checkups bring to attention a former mental patient (Peter Lorre), who in time is cornered in an attic by the underworld – and it is now difficult to take very seriously a story in which this particular subject is linked to such antiquated fictions as underworld confederacies and armies of beggars. The kangeroo court climax is too studied, with its sudden outbursts of cynical laughter, and Lorre's performance is of excessive virtuosity – though one is unlikely ever to forget his pudgy pale face and cumbersome bulk. At a time when movie villains were one-dimensional, his suggestion of inner torment evoked much praise, and Lang's

imaginative opening remains impressive: a child's balloon floating free, a toy rolling downhill, the whistling of 'Peer Gynt' on the soundtrack, and a shot of a blind beggar. Pare Lorentz in *Vanity Fair* was struck by the way dialogue was used, 'how Lang puts the audience right into his scenes by never showing the speaker – or, by thrusting his camera into a group of people, and making them so absolutely natural that the audience feels it, too, is actually seeing and hearing with the cast'. Despite its faults, the film indicates why it has remained one of the most popular items in the cinema repertory. There was a foolish American remake in 1951, directed by Joseph Losey, of which Lang remarked that it had brought him the best notices of his career.

Otto Wernicke plays Lohmann, the detective who tracks down the murderer, and Lang incorporated both actor and role in **Das Testament des Doktor Mabuse** (1933), sequel to the 1922 film, and another elongated tale of assorted skulduggery – abductions and time bombs and tick-tacky car chases. It is the antithesis of *M,* and there is nothing in the film to support Lang's later claim that he and von Harbou intended an allegory on the Nazi system of tyranny,

299

though he may be referring to a line which says, in effect, that mastery of crime is possible when mankind is ruled by terror. The film had been made as the Nazis prepared to seize power, and Goebbels refused to allow it to be released in Germany (it was shown in Austria, and the French version was smuggled into France); when he sent for Lang to offer him the leadership of the German film industry and made no reference to the ban, Lang decided that it was time he left Germany – leaving behind his wife, who became a Nazi.

Other directors of the Silent period kept up the tradition of the grotesque, and they must have felt the subjects more topical since the Nazi Party, formerly a sinister fringe group, was now a power in the land. Richard Oswald remade his own **Unheimliche Geschichten** (1932), the source for which is several stories by Edgar Allan Poe and one, 'The Suicide Club', by Robert Louis Stevenson. Here they are reduced to a Mabuse-like confrontation between a madman (Paul Wegener) and a detective; however, the scene where it is apparent that the patients have taken over the asylum can still produce a frisson. Robert Wiene remade **Der Andere** (1930), a success of 1913, based on 'Dr Jekyll and Mr Hyde' via a play by Paul Landau. Its protagonist (Fritz Kortner) is not a mere lawyer but the state prosecutor, holding forth on humanity and one's debt to society – but, as it turns out, he is overworked to the extent that in the evenings he tears off his collar and tie, frequents whores in low bars and becomes involved in burglary and attempted murder. Kortner, a great actor, is given too little to work with to make the transformation believable, but nothing mars his performance in **Der Mörder Dimitri Karamasoff** (1931), directed by the former Soviet film-maker, Fedor Ozep, and edited by Pudovkin. Nevertheless, it is not Russian in feeling but German, and it is another reduction, using Dostoevsky to produce a ten-a-penny tale of a man who loves a whore. The style, however, is agreeable, as if von Sternberg in his later style had attempted one of the 'street' movies, making it glitter with chandeliers, guttering candles and gleaming wine bottles. As powerfully emotional as Kortner's Dimitri is the Grushenka of Anna Sten.

Nor is **Berlin Alexanderplatz** (1931) the equal of Alfred Döblin's novel, though he himself worked on the screenplay. However, if the darker anecdotes have gone, the film removes those that remain from the pretentious and consciously Joycean text to offer, if not a study of the deprived of Berlin then of its underworld. Franz Biberkopf (Heinrich George) leaves prison determined to start a new life; he becomes a street pedlar, and in the film no longer wonders whether to sell the Nazi newspaper, the *Völkischer Beobachter,* to Jews. After the pianist has casually flashed her stocking tops at him, she moves in, and just as he is drawn to felony so he gradually returns to the kind of *crime passionel* which had sent him to prison in the first place. The film was made by Phil Jutzi and it is a remarkable successor to Lamprecht's portraits of Berlin, not to mention his own *Mutter Krausens Fahrt in Glück.* Lamprecht himself deserted such subjects to make **Emil und die Detektive** (1931), and its success almost equalled that of the phenomenally popular novel by Erich Kästner on which it is based. Billy Wilder wrote the screenplay, and the film, made almost entirely on location, is shrewd, though the story itself, about a country boy who persuades a crowd of Berlin children to help him tail a crook, now seems thin. Among its virtues is another of Fritz Rasp's relishable villains, wearing his bowler hat even in bed.

Niemandsland (1931) harks back to the Silent era in its plea for peace, as directed by Victor Trivas from the rather woolly ideas of Leonhard Frank. They establish the unlikely situation of a German, a French and a British soldier joined in companionship by a deaf-mute Jewish tailor. Trivas's style, borrowed from the Soviets, is eloquent with the message that he is pushing, and his battle scenes are as forceful as those in *Westfront 1918.* The film, much discussed in its day, is now largely forgotten; but **Mädchen in Uniform** (1931) remains famous, as directed by Leontine Sagan from Christa Winsloe's play on the heady passions of pupils and teachers at an all-female academy. Sagan, a theatre director, moved to films to make this under the supervision of Carl Frölich, and she manages her overheated subject with skill and subtlety. Although the film was originally banned by the New York state censors, few reviewers had the courage to say that they recognised lesbianism in it. There is an amazing ambiguity in the performance of Dorothea Wieck as the teacher suspected of corruption, a sensual and ageing woman who keeps her own council and is perhaps unwilling to give in to her emotions.

Also highly regarded abroad was **Ariane** (1931), a drama which deals as charmingly and truthfully with the battle of the sexes as any other movie I have seen. Scripted by Paul Czinner, the director, and Carl Mayer, it bears out all the claims that have been made for the latter; while the basic sourness of its view of love is presumably that of Claude Anet, who wrote the original novel. It concerns an affair between an experienced older man (Rudolf Forster) and a student (Elisabeth Bergner) which, since his motives are entirely selfish, goes wrong: and when it does neither knows how to handle the situation. Their silent last sequence would be one of the finest emotional passages in all cinema if it had been a little less studied – a fault of Miss Bergner's performance generally, though she is much more touching than might be imagined from her later performances in English.

After the superb *Abschied* and *Voruntersuchung*, Robert Siodmak disappointed his admirers with **Der Mann, der seinen Mörder Sucht** (1931), which was in fact made before the latter. Heinz Rühmann plays a would-be suicide who, unable to take his own life, commissions a petty crook to kill him – till he changes his mind after meeting a girl and then has to trace the man. The screenplay by Ludwig Hirschfeld, Curt Siodmak (the director's brother) and Billy Wilder is inventive, but the piece falls between several different comedy styles. **Quick** (1932) fails to be satirical on its twin settings, a health clinic and a theatre, and is basically a vehicle for the leaden charms of its stars, Lilian Harvey, as a lady who falls in love with a clown, and Hans Albers (q.v.), as the clown. But Siodmak made one of the best films of the period – or any period – in **Brennendes Geheimnis** (1933), a perceptive and subtle version of a story by Stefan Zweig. Set in a hotel on the Swiss lakes at the end of the season, it examines the effect on a 13-year-old boy of adultery between his mother (Hilda Wagener) and a wealthy philanderer (Willi Forst). The boy is all the more disillusioned since the man had in the first instance used him to strike up acquaintance, and in deciding that his mother should

choose either the man or himself – not to mention his absent father – he almost destroys himself.

Die Koffer des Herrn O.F. (1931) is one of the better German attempts at satire, but it was directed by a Russian, Alexis Granowsky. It does, however, decline once past its premise – which concerns a sleepy little town that decides to transform itself into an international centre on the basis of its one hotel housing a V.I.P. – who is in fact imaginary. **Ich bei Tag und du bei Nacht** (1932) is, as the title implies, a Box and Cox tale, with Käthe von Nagy and Willy Fritsch as the flat-sharers, hating each other before they fall in love. Cut into the film are excerpts from a florid movie musical playing next door to their lodging house – and it was precisely such a film which made the reputation of the director, Ludwig Berger. He had just returned from Hollywood, where Paramount had hoped he would be a second Lubitsch. Unfortunately, after this

Paul Czinner made his reputation in Germany with a number of fastidious Silent romances; in Britain in the Thirties he directed some vehicles for his wife, Elisabeth Bergner – mainly unwatchable because their chief aim was to show off her undeniable but mechanical talents. *Ariane*, however, has a more sensible aim and this scene from it shows Rudolf Forster and Miss Bergner in the virtuoso final sequence, both of them silent as audiences wonder on the outcome of their affair.

In cinema, the plays of Arthur Schnitzler will always be associated with Max Ophuls, who, born in Saarbrucken, was directing them (and other plays) at the Vienna Burgtheater in the late Twenties. One of his first films was *Leibelei*, which featured Magda Schneider as the poor girl who falls in love with a careless young officer, Wolfgang Liebeneiner. Years after Ophuls was able to recommence his career in Hollywood because people would recall this film – and among those he later made was a further adaptation of Schnitzler, *La Ronde* (q.v.).

comedy he returned to operetta, with *Walzerkrieg* (1933), about the rivalry between Strauss and Lanner.

Operetta was at first the speciality of Max Ophuls (1902–57), who had been dialogue director for Anatole Litvak, and who was given a chance to direct by Ufa. **Lachenden Erben** is a starring vehicle for Heinz Rühmann, and also a celebration of the grape, since it concerns the heir to a wine firm who falls in love with the heiress to a rival company. It is, appropriately, as light as most German comedies are heavy – and it may be because it is untypical that Ufa delayed its release for two years. In the meantime Ophuls satirised the waltztime musicals in which audiences wallowed as the Weimar Republic shuddered to its close – though **Die Verliebte Firma** (1932) is chiefly a comedy on the film industry, concerning an Alpine telegraph girl whom a daft film unit think they can turn into a star. The film has great panache, which is what also redeems **Die Verkaufte Braut** (1932), although it reduces Smetana's opera to a typical German musical of the period; the hero and heroine are horse-faced and singularly lacking in dash but, like their rotund and supposedly comic elders, they conform to the local taste of the time.

Ophuls made his reputation with **Liebelei** (1933), based on the play by Schnitzler and set in the Vienna of cunning little alleys and tinkly cafés, of dragoon officers and their ladies – in this case Fritz (Wolfgang Liebeneiner), who tries to disembarrass himself of his noble mistress for the sake of Christine (Magda Schneider), daughter of a violinist at the Opera. It ends sadly, though the original has been much softened, to become a peg for 'Viennese' themes, romantic ardour and youthful high spirits. Ophuls's fascination with opera houses and faithless young officers, the poignancy of railway stations or falling snow, the chivalry and stupidity of duelling would appear again, but he could become only a little more accomplished than here. The film is enchanting, from Mozart at the beginning to Beethoven at the end and with the waltzes in between.

At Ufa, Erich Pommer continued to be more successful, relatively speaking, than his Hollywood counterparts in the matter of multilingual productions. His costs were lower, his ambitions less, and his understanding of European markets somewhat greater. He did not try to ape Hollywood, and a science fiction tale, **F.P.1. Antwortet Nicht** (1932) was, because of its novelty, expected to sell in those foreign markets where Ufa was not strong. Hans Albers (1892–1960) had become a star under Pommer's guidance, and here he plays a hard-drinking, hard-loving aviator who sacrifices himself for the F.P.1, which is a landing stage set down in mid-Atlantic: personally, I prefer the French version with Charles Boyer (q.v.) or the English one with Conrad Veidt. The screenplay is by Walter Reisch from a story by Curt Siodmak, and the direction by the Austrian Karl Hartl – the only one of the three still to be in Germany for the semi-follow-up, **Gold** (1934), in which Albers is a German scientist kidnapped by a mad British scientist who wants to transmute base metals into gold. It has been suggested that the unfavourable portrait of the Britisher is indicative of the increasing nationalistic fervour of films under the Nazis but it is more probably due to the fact that in the meantime English-language versions of German films, in competition with Hollywood, had become unprofitable and had been dropped. French versions continued to be made; *L'Or* starred Pierre Blanchar.

Der Tunnel (1933), though made by a rival company, was also regarded as a follow-up to *F.P.1*, as based on Bernhard Kellerman's novel about the building of a tunnel under the Atlantic, with, predictably, speculators ensuring sabotage. The director was Kurt (Curtis) Bernhardt, who had already fled the Nazis; he was preparing the French version in Paris, and his backers there arranged a passport for him to return to Munich to make the two versions. The German one was banned after the War by the Allied Military Government because some of the villains were American.

Bernhardt and Lang were not the only ones to flee the Nazis; by 1934 virtually all these directors were working in France. Ophuls, since he was born in the Saar, was able to opt for French citizenship in 1934. Like Bernhardt and Robert Siodmak (who left the country when Goebbels criticised the 'dubious morals' of *Brennendes Geheimnis*) he became successful in the French film industry before departing when it became clear that the Germans would declare war on France; Richard

Oswald also left France at that time, but did not have the same success in the U.S., where he became a producer. Both Wiene and Granowsky died in France before the outbreak of war; Berger had a great success in that country with *Trois Valses* before joining Korda. Czinner and Leontine Sagan joined Korda almost immediately, the latter to make just one other (unsuccessful) film before moving to South Africa, where she remained, working in the theatre. Trivas also went to Hollywood; and among the impressive list of refugees – almost all at least temporarily domiciled in France – are the directors Karl Grune and Anatole Litvak, the animator Lotte Reiniger, the actors Peter Lorre, Ernst Deutsch, Fritz Kortner, Albert Basserman, Francis Lederer, Anton Walbrook, Oscar Homolka and Conrad Veidt, the producers Erich Pommer and Seymour Nebenzal, the composers Frederick Hollander and Franz Waxman, the cinematographers Eugen Schüfftan and Franz Planer, and the writers Walter Reisch, Carl Zuckmayer, Billy Wilder and Curt Siodmak. (The last-named paused on his way to Hollywood to work on a British version of *Der Tunnel* (q.v.). Reisch in fact wrote *Maskerade* (q.v.) in Vienna, and Jutzi worked in Vienna and Poland before abandoning direction for cinematography in 1938, shooting a few minor films before leaving the industry in 1942. Of the eminent pre-Nazi directors only Gerhard Lamprecht remained, to occupy himself with the founding of the German film archive in Berlin and a number of innocuous musicals and literary adaptations, including an uninspired *Madame Bovary* (1937) with Pola Negri.

Only one other film-maker of note remained, Werner Hochbaum (1899–1946), though the half-dozen films he made under the Nazis are seldom better than mediocre; however, of his earlier four features at least one is a masterpiece. He was dancer, actor and journalist before going into films, editing for others and reputedly making some experimental shorts before producing and directing **Brüder** (1929), about the Hamburg dock strike of 1896/7, one of the several semi-amateur left-wing movies of the late Silent period. Like the others, this one was inspired by the Soviet cinema, centring on one striking worker and his family. It tells us nothing of the trade unionism of the Kaiser's Germany, but is permeated by a feeling for socialism as it became a recognisable ideal – 'the last cry of individual man, the last movement among the masses on behalf of individual liberty, the last hope of living unregulated' as Barbara Tuchman put it in 'The Proud Tower', and in discussing this particular aspect of German history her tone is remarkably like that of Hochbaum in the film. However, it is possible that Hochbaum's prime motive was a portrait of Hamburg as potent as that of the capital in *Berlin: die Symphonie einer Grossstadt*. When the film failed to find a public it was offered to the Social Democrats, which body commissioned two propaganda shorts, of which I have seen **Zwei Welt** (1929), a persuasive exhortation to vote, amidst contrasting portraits of the poor and wealthy.

Razzia in St Pauli (1932) is arresting from the opening shot, of an accordion being played against a harbour wall, followed by the glittering sea and the superimposition of dancing feet. This is in fact a prologue, a montage celebration of a particular city, Hamburg, where we might live, laugh and love, at least for a while – to use the film's own faded romantic phrases. Its gaiety is shot through with melancholy, but it is a film above all abundantly, vividly alive. Workers arrive in a barge; a drunk stumbles home; Chinese restaurant workers blink in the dawn; and the orchestra in the Reeperbahn café starts playing at ten a.m. every day. In a room, a girl (Gena Falkenburg) adjusts a stocking while a man – client, pimp or lover? – knots his tie. He is there the following morning, too drunk to undress, and in the meantime she, Else, has had a brief fling with Matt (Friedrich Gnass). As she settles down again to sleep Hochbaum makes his point: the workers work, exploited but dedicated, and the dreaming Matts and Elses, similarly trapped, surrender to the circumstances around them. Hochbaum aligns himself with the great humanist film-makers, and because he documents rather than dramatises this is one of the best studies we have of low life. In Else's hang-out, the Kongo Bar, the bored tarts play cards, the lavatory attendant waits, and the first influx of dockers arrives, including two men who dance together (not portrayed as effeminate, as in most films of this period). They are far more believable than any other dockside people

in movies, less 'symbolic' than those in the two films which may have influenced Hochbaum, *The Docks of New York* and *Jenseits der Strasse*. He himself influenced no one, for hardly anyone saw his best films, which are the early ones. Of the several attempts at this time to get unvarnished life on the screen this late one is a culmination: Ozu was unknown, yet the similarities between Hochbaum's film and Ozu's own studies of the poor are startling, particularly in the relish of detail within rooms – and if Hochbaum is the more invigorating, that is perhaps because his images are choreographed to the score. Like Lamprecht and Siodmak, Hochbaum planned to rob the cinema of melodrama, going further than either in his portrayal of the ambiguity and unpredictability of life. It is one of the curiosities of film history that, as with the American 'realist' films, some should have been forgotten while others made or maintained their directors' reputation. It is understandable that Siodmak's *Menschen am Sonntag* appealed to contemporary audiences and has continued to be shown, but not that this exhilarating *Razzia*, once rediscovered, did not immediately join it in the international repertory.

The production company, Orbis, had financed it, since low-life tales were usually popular, and it now summoned Hochbaum to take over **Schleppzug M17** (1933) when its star and co-director, Heinrich George, quarrelled with Willy Döll, also the film's writer (and co-author of 'Mutter Krausens Fahrt ins Glück'). George, rotund and no longer in his first youth, was one of the several character players made stars by an adoring public; in this instance he accepted less than his usual fee to play a tugboat captain because that was what he had wanted to be as a boy. As a communist he welcomed the chance to work with Hochbaum, though when the Nazis came to power he changed sides with alacrity and soon joined the Party – an event which caused a hold-up in the shooting, partly due to the exodus of Jewish workers. Hochbaum took only five days to complete the film – two on location and three in the studio, but it is recognisably by the hand that had fashioned *Razzia*, with a number of similar sequences: the getting-up routine; the visits to the dives and bars; and the relationships of the captain with his wife and a whore (Betty Amman). The most

Werner Hochbaum was one of the two outstanding directors working in Germany in the Thirties. A fervent socialist, his early films had so little success that he remained virtually unknown when the Nazis came to power – and was therefore not forced to flee, like other left-wingers. Because of their failure, it is impossible to find stills for reproduction, so this picture is from his first – and only – international success, *Die Ewige Maske*, a strong psychological drama with Mathias Wieman and Peter Petersen.

remarkable sequence is a promenade through Berlin, the captain and his family contrasted with the pseudo-classical statues a mite self-consciously, but executed with a verve which was not to be seen again till the nouvelle vague.

What audiences there were, despite Herr George, found the plot lacking in incident, and Hochbaum was hardly likely to please them with **Morgen Beginnt das Leben** (1933), since the plot is even thinner than those of his earlier films. It starts with the same situation as in *Berlin Alexanderplatz*, that of a man (Erich Haussmann) leaving prison, but Germany's economic situation, not to mention Hochbaum's temperament, indicated a much less gloomy story. By mischance the man's wife (Hilde von Stolz) fails to meet him, and Hochbaum follows their subsequent adventures as he examines their individual fears before their eventual reunion. Again he offers a graphic portrait of the German capital, and if the film is less skilfully handled than those which preceded it, with a number of showy sequences, the couple in question have an ambiguity of character very rare in films of this period. The analogy with Ozu again arises, for the repeated shots of factory chimneys reinforce the view that he and Hochbaum were kindred spirits.

The film was again unpopular, and Hochbaum was professionally idle till invited to Austria to make **Vorstadt-varieté** (1934), set in and around a suburban music hall. The Austrian film industry was heavily dependent on Germany for both talent and distribution of its wares, but at the same time many of the films regarded as 'Viennese' subjects, such as *Liebelei*, emanated from Berlin. The secondary woman's role in that film had been played by Luise Ullrich, and *Vorstadtvarieté* is primarily a vehicle for this charming actress, playing a singer torn between an honest young draftsman and a dashing officer. As in all Hochbaum's films the leading characters are trapped by their circumstances, but as with the Ophuls film the original material – it was a play by Felix Salten banned for some years because of its anti-military stance – has been reworked to make it more palatable for a mass audience. Salten's bitter ending has now become a happy one, but the film continues to view the authorities with a cold eye and the world of the *heurige* with affection.

Hochbaum had a brief flutter of international recognition when **Die Ewige Maske** (1935), a Swiss-Austrian production, won one of the major prizes at the Venice festival. Otis Ferguson in *The New Republic* referred to it as 'the new *Caligari*, very intense and strange', but it is closer to *Geheimnisse Einer Seele,* also about a nervous breakdown. The victim is a hospital doctor whose principal refuses to sanction a serum he has perfected during an outbreak of meningitis, thereby sending him from depression to schizophrenia. Films on such subjects were seldom offered to lay audiences, and Hochbaum hoped to entertain them with his documentary account of the daily routine of the hospital. He also invests the subject with some of the eeriness of the German 'grotesque' films, while in adapting a novel by the Swiss writer, Leo Lapaire – with the latter's co-operation – he retains his feeling for the ordinariness of his characters.

Returning to Germany he also returned to his light vein, with *Leichte Kavallerie* (1935), a circus story whose main purpose was to introduce Ufa's new star from Hungary, Marika Rökk, and **Der Favorit der Kaiserin** (1936), a period comedy in the manner of Lubitsch, but hampered by inhibited playing. Both indicate Hochbaum's willingness to stay with subjects of no great passion, but **Schatten der Vergangenheit** (1936), made in Austria, and **Man Spricht über Jacqueline** (1937) are heavy-breathing melodramas. The first concerns twin sisters, both played by Miss Ullrich, the bad one impersonating the good one, an idea plagiarised by *A Stolen Life* in Britain a few years later. The second details the exploits of a foolish femme fatale (Wera Engels), as based on an English novel filmed five years later in that country under its original title, *Talk About Jacqueline*. The Hochbaum of the early films is only intermittently recognisable, but he compromises less in **Ein Mädchen Geht an Land** (1938), obviously happy to be back in the waterfront cafés of Hamburg. As of old he refuses to paint his characters in simple black and white, and if the put-upon heroine has little dimension as played by the pleasing but bovine Elizabeth Flickenschildt that is because the latter quality is essential to the role – since she is known to her family as 'the stevedore'. She leaves the family home – a freighter – for a series of adventures which includes a relationship with a man who is after her savings. His moral equivocation, as well as that of some

of the other characters, did not go unnoticed by Goebbels, who was only too aware of Hochbaum's past and his propensity for straying from official supervision.

Hochbaum was, in consequence, commanded to make **Drei Unteroffiziere** (1939), which, as the title implies, is a study of life in a small garrison town. Three NCOs put loyalty to each other above anything except the regiment itself, till both loyalties are tested by the inevitable woman, an actress. As if realising that this would be the last film he would make Hochbaum imposes on this uncongenial material a vision that is entirely his: each of the three soldiers reflects his usual perplexity when confronted with goodness, uncertain of its value in a world usually tipped against it. The one true quality of value is love, barrier against all the world's ills, and the soldier who falls in love does so as obsessively as all Hochbaum lovers. The doomed relationship between the beloved and her elderly protector is another familiar theme, but on this occasion the hero does not sink into morbidity or rebellion because of it, since the optimistic, militaristic ending was forced on Hochbaum. To that point he had only half-heartedly endorsed the military code at the centre of the film's subject, concentrating instead on such mundane dramas as the first date made and the first date broken: and not since his early films had he celebrated so keenly the lack of glamour of dingy teashops, barracks and dusty theatres. He did not succeed, as he had hoped, in ingratiating himself with Goebbels, and although the film received the official seal of the Predikat Commission the grant which traditionally went with it – the *kunsterlische wertvoll* – was withheld.

While preparing his next film Hochbaum was officially forbidden to work in the film industry, on the grounds that in 1923 he had offered his services to the French for espionage, a charge almost certainly without foundation. After serving for a while in the army he worked pseudonymously on scripts and was preparing *Der Tanz in der Nacht* for Defa in East Germany when he died in 1946. Doubtless he had been amused to find that *Drei Unteroffiziere,* not much liked by the Party, was banned by the Allied authorities.

As the Weimar Republic died there was one left-wing film, **Kühle Wampe** (1932), which caused the stir that Hochbaum had wanted for his own similarly-inclined works – and as open Communist propaganda it was only permitted to be shown after a number of cuts. Attempting to examine the obviously common situation of a jobless family, it finds the younger generation more embittered than its elders – the boy takes his own life, but the girl, after becoming pregnant, is saved from further misfortune by the joys of worker solidarity. A mixture of arty juxtapositions and stilted dialogue, the film was initially a labour of love and later the subject of litigation among its participants, including its director, Slatan Dudow, a Bulgarian much influenced by the Soviets, and Berthold Brecht, its writer, who subsequently claimed that it was the only film with which he had been associated of which he approved. The music, by Hanns Eisler, is the sole feature of the piece to indicate either talent or professionalism.

The films with which the Nazis hoped to convey *their* message could only be better, but any improvement might escape the casual viewer. The first with which they may be associated is **Morgenrot** (1933), since Hitler ostentatiously attended the Berlin premiere only two days after becoming Chancellor. This melodrama about U-boats proclaimed the merit of dying for the *Vaterland* – though directed by an Austrian, Gustav Ucicky: however, since a mother is seen to weep for the bereaved of the other side, this is not wholly a Nazi film. Ucicky no longer had such humanist touches when he made **Flüchtlinge** (1934), whose theme was one always popular with the Nazis, the persecution of a German minority by the Russians. The Party itself distributed **Friesennot** (1935), directed under an alias by Willi Krause, a tale of oppressed Germans who rise against their Russian masters during the Revolution and return to Germany.

Communists were more likely than Jews to be found as villains, on the assumption that a Jew could not be a worthy opponent for a German; Jews usually made brief appearances as venal capitalists. Other subjects for disapproval include the previous régime, shown to be a period of racial impurity, economic instability, drugs and suicide. **S. A. Mann Brand** (1933) concerns the enmity of the Bolsheviks and the National Socialists during that time, with the Communists shown as brutal and mean-spirited – except for their leader, who is wealthy and effete. They manage to get the Nazi Youth uniform banned, just as the widowed mother of our young hero has saved up to buy him one. He is consoled, however – in what must be the funniest moment in all cinema – by a framed photograph of Hitler, given by the boy next door. Perhaps spectators were rare because they feared they would laugh: they would have seen a handsome production, due to the Nazi money poured into it and the skilled photography of Franz Koch rather than to the direction by Franz Seitz, hitherto associated with Bavarian farces.

The second Nazi film proper was a biography of Horst Wessel, the sleazy pimp whose murder was celebrated in the song the Party had adopted as its anthem. Since the facts were unsuitable, its story bore little relation to the truth, with those responsible for the murder categorised as Communists. Till the dread deed, the idealistic Wessel (Emil Lohkamp) had been in the process of converting them by preaching the higher ideals of National Socialism, and it is because of his success that he is put out of harm's way. The only considerable talent involved is Paul Wegener, as the Communist leader, and the uninspired director is Franz Wenzler. Previewed as *Horst Wessel* (1933), it was hastily re-edited and re-titled, emerging a few weeks later as **Hans Westmar, Einer von Vielenein Deutsches Schicksal aus dem Jahre 1919,** but the public took no more notice of it than it had of *S.A. Mann Brand*.

Somewhere between the standard of both films is **Hitlerjunge Quex** (1933), directed by Hans Steinhoff, with which Ufa, albeit unwillingly, joined the Nazi bandwagon. Again the plot was based on a real-life murder – of a youth killed in 1932 by Communists, though for the film's purposes he has become a boy, bewildered both by opposing political forces and weak parents – these played by Heinrich George and Bertha Drews, repeating their teaming from *Schleppzug M17*. The boy was played by an unnamed member of the Nazi Youth, an organisation presented in this film as boisterous and robot-like: but just as the unfolding events reveal the Communists to be child-murderers rather than merely slovenly, drunken and promiscuous, so the Nazis prove to be loyal, steadfast and stalwart. However, their first loyalty is

The hero, played by an unnamed member of the Nazi Youth Movement, in the closing sequence of *Hitlerjunge Quex*, one of the films with which the Nazi party hoped to awaken the German nation to its virtues. The films are resolutely simple-minded, and after January 1933 the propaganda became considerably more insidious – with little more success till the war years, when in patriotic fervour audiences did flock to a number of pictures condemning Germany's enemies.

future: but with virtually every first-class film-maker forced out of the industry it was not easy to see how these achievements could be transmitted in film.

A solution was found with the documentary, which did not require much imagination, and the occasion presented itself with the 1934 party rally at Nuremberg. At Hitler's request an approach was made to Leni Riefenstahl, a former actress who had made a formidable start as producer-director with a starring vehicle for herself, *Das Blaue Licht*. That and the subsequent films she directed indicated a penchant for handling natural phenomena, and with **Triumph des Willens** (1935) she succeeded beyond Hitler's wildest dreams. The subject genuinely fired her imagination, as she photographed and then edited the images of the Nuremberg rally – as stage-managed by the party's favoured architect, Albert Speer, under the influence of *Metropolis*: huge columns, huge swastikas on huge flags, the central podium for the speakers and party members – and the multitude within this gigantic arena an impressive witness both to the solidarity of the nation and the co-operation between Party and Government. 'The purpose of the film was twofold.' says David Stewart Hull in 'Film in the Third Reich'. 'To show the solidarity of the Party, particularly following the divisions caused by the Röhm affair; and to introduce the leaders, many of whom spoke a few words, to this pre-television society. Another, more subtle, purpose was to impress foreign audiences, and at the same time to scare the hell out of them. The film succeeded on all counts.' It is an object lesson in image-making, as banners unfurl, men march, or at camp line up for food or comb each other's hair. Their faces shine with eagerness, and it is with the same eagerness that they assemble into ranks; but as the object of their fealty becomes clear, and as the film increasingly pleads for the end of the individual – beyond the chosen few – it becomes more than mildly repellent.

always to Hitler, man and leader – and as an official creed it is witness to their mentality. The only overt propaganda in the film is the montage of Nazi marchers which concludes it, but it is worth noting that though foreign Communists are evil incarnate German Communists are either misguided or composed of the dregs to be found in any society.

With the attainment of power, proselytising by the Nazis was no longer necessary – or prudent, since it could not be suggested that the ruling party actually needed converts to its cause. Nor could the state be shown to harbour any 'dregs' stupid enough not to see its virtues – or, if they existed, they were unworthy of notice, just in case someone, somewhere, identified with them. Undoubtedly Goebbels wished that his film-makers had some revolutions to draw upon, as the Soviets had had. Instead the Nazis would celebrate the present – and, they did not doubt, the

A peculiar mystique, however, has grown up around this film and its companion piece, **Olympiad** (1938), a record of the Games held in Berlin in 1936 and a glowing rebuttal of the director's claim that she was not a Nazi but a film-maker. As a spokesman for the Third Reich she has a footnote in history – though it is now difficult to know to what extent: the original negatives and German copies of the Nuremberg film no longer survive, and it is possible that the 'export' versions which remain were shorn of anti-Jewish propaganda (because of the high proportion of Jewish cinema proprietors who might have refused to show it). The original version of *Olympiad*, at 3 hours 40 minutes, may have included even more footage of a benignly smiling Hitler; it does have a few shots of the black runner Jesse Owens, obligatory because of his triumphs, but it is primarily a celebration of Aryan physical endeavour. The celebrated prelude – the mists of antiquity and the Greek sculptures – is now kitsch, and the handling of the opening ceremony does not begin to compare with Ichikawa's in *Tokyo Olympiad* (q.v.). In the 1972 Games, a British runner, Dave Bedford, observed that the difference between him 'and so many others is that I'm here to win, they're here to compete', but it is unedifying to watch a film permeated with the same ideal, constantly reminding us that Germany won more medals than any other country. The shots of the athletes relaxing and the symphonic arrangement of most of the other sports retain a mild virtue; Riefenstahl took eighteen months to edit the film, originally selecting the best images of fit, marshalled young men, but eventually became carried away by the rhythms she could create.

Both films, though recognised for what they were, were successful abroad, which could be said for few others made under the Nazi régime. In recent years there have been revivals of some of those directed by Detlef Sierck, as a consequence of the cult-following for the Hollywood melodramas he made after changing his name to Douglas Sirk – a following, incidentally, which both amuses and amazes him. The best of his German films is **Stutzen der Gesellschaft** (1935), a version of Ibsen's 'The Pillars of the Community' which is only adequate in direction and production values but does avoid being either literary or stagey. A dreadful, interpolated prologue shows Johan with the cowboys in the U.S., but Heinrich George is superbly cast as Consul Bernick, enduring a number of emotional ordeals as his past catches up with him. More typical of Sierck's work is **La Habanera** (1937), a vehicle for the Swedish singer popular in Germany, Zarah Leander, who has three unlikely songs in the midst of some junketings about a grandee's ill-treated wife who conspires with a brave young compatriot to cure an outbreak of fever. Gerhard Menzel, author of *Morgenrot*, provided the plot, clearly fashioned after the current Hollywood models, but in handling it Sierck manages none of their occasional wit or drama.

In the matter of foreign success, that of *Liebelei* was soon overshadowed by that of **Maskerade** (1934), in which the Hapsburg Empire again crumbled to the strains of waltztime. As so often, the wits and gossips found in their midst an unexpected true love – that of the roué (Anton Walbrook) and the damsel demure (Paula Wessely). The London *Daily Telegraph* called the film 'superb – intelligent as to story, wittily written, magnificently acted and directed', and though contemporary opinion attributed its success to Miss Wessely, she is a little calculating in the Viennese manner.

As an actress Leni Riefenstahl had been associated with the mountaineering melodramas, so beloved by the Nazis since they emphasised courage, nationalism and the open-air life. After they came to power she was asked to direct the official records of the 1934 party rally at Nuremberg and the 1936 Olympic Games in Berlin. The latter, *Olympiad*, persuaded only the gullible that she was more interested in celebrating the human body than the party.

Another player, Willi Forst, went behind the camera to direct, and *Maskerade*, the second film he made in that capacity, has a lightness he never again achieved. The story, if delightful, was only too typical of Viennese romances, as the gossips find in their midst an unexpected true love, as the roué (Anton Walbrook), becomes enslaved of the damzel demure (Paula Wessely).

Rather it is a triumph for Walbrook, both haughty as the amorist and touchingly human as the man in love. The story is unremarkable, but serves for the expected ironies, wittily written by Walter Reisch, whose Hollywood chores would include a remake, *Escapade;* and it was photographed by a superb craftsman, the Czech-born Franz Planer, whose long and distinguished career in German films would be followed by another in Hollywood. He had photographed *Liebelei* – and would work with Ophuls again on *Letter From an Unknown Woman* (q.v.) – and though this film is stagey and slow in comparison we may suspect considerable help by both Planer and Reisch since it is so superior to the other films directed by Willi Forst.

It was his second film in that capacity, and henceforth he acted only occasionally,

instead often contributing to the scripts he directed. **Mazurka** (1935) was a vehicle for Pola Negri, who had temporarily resumed her career in Germany. She plays a singer who wrongs her husband and, many years later, shoots her seducer since he is about to compromise her daughter and she does not wish history to be repeated. The actress thought her own performance outstanding, but there is nothing to detain anyone but devotees of soap opera – beyond the fact that it was first shown in London at the (original) Curzon Cinema, built by the Nazis as a showplace for their films. It opened there in 1937, one month before the Germans insisted in a new agreement with the Austrian film industry that they would only accept its product if no Jewish talent was involved. Elsewhere abroad, the Nazis were not always inclined to show their hand, and so little was known of their ownership of the Curzon that some British reviewers supposed it an Austrian film.

Forst did make most of his films in Germany, but **Bel Ami** (1939), like *Maskerade,* was made in his native Austria. A credit claims it a celebration of *belle époque* Paris, but de Maupassant's tale is merely a pretext for froufrou, all of it dowdy. As a director Forst is frivolous; excellent on occasion – in *Brennendes Geheimnis* – his own performance in the title role is poor. His anonymity is such that he could enter or leave a room without anyone noticing him, though in the case of this film one's energies are devoted to trying to follow the plot. Partly because of the setting it was one of the films the Germans foisted on the French during the Occupation; the French loathed it, but took unwillingly to the theme song. Forst was now established as a director of musicals, despite the equally lumpish *Operette* (1940), a tale of squabbling lovers: with it, he decided to give up acting, though it was because of his earlier popularity in that capacity that this was finally imported into the U.S. in 1949, to be quickly dismissed.

Reinhold Schünzel was another (former) actor who specialised in movie operettas, and the success of **Amphitryon** (1935) brought him an M-G-M contract (he directed three films for them, and made a subsequent living in Hollywood from acting). The French version, *Les Dieux s'Amusent,* made simultaneously, may well have given Giraudoux the inspiration to write his play 'Amphytryon '38'; there is a long tradition of re-telling this old Greek myth – and this particular version is only for those who believe (cf. *The Private Life of Helen of Troy*) that the Greek gods and heroes carried on like us – with such merry conceits as a Mercury on rollerskates. Willy Fritsch plays Amphitryon and Jupiter, and is rather good as the latter.

One genre had disappeared from the German cinema – the grotesque, because Goebbels knew how often these films hinted at subversion. The old tradition of the German cinema did surface for one last time with **Fährmann Maria** (1936). Death and his black-coated cohorts pursue an escaped convict, who is saved by the love of a lonely ferry-girl (Sybille Schmitz): the suggestion was whispered that this theme represented the defeat of the Nazi creed – and Goebbels, unsure, had the distribution curtailed rather than ban the film outright, which might have aroused curiosity. The director is Frank Wysbar, who also went to Hollywood, where his sole credit is a low-budget, inferior remake, *Strangler in the Swamp* (1945).

If *Fährmann Maria* is one of the more interesting films of the Nazi period, there is at least one fine film among the variable works of Helmut Käutner (1908–80), who, as with most German directors, arrived via the theatre and cabaret. His first two films are derivative, **Kitty und die Weltkonferenz** (1939), a modern tale in the tradition of *Der Kongress Tanzt,* and **Kleider Machen Leute** (1940), some variations on the theme of Zuckmayer's 'Der Hauptmann von Köpenick'. That play was anathema to Goebbels, and this film claims to be based on motifs in Gottfried Keller's 'Die Leute von Seldwyla' – both works, in any case, being akin to Gogol's 'The Government Inspector'. Käutner successfully resisted pressure to incorporate Nazi propaganda in his films while attempting to make light-hearted films on serious subjects – in both these instances, the bureaucracy of politicians, international and local. Despite his glancing touch, the humour remains pompous and Germanic, and *Kleider Machen Leute* deliberately avoids contemporary relevance, being set among the puppet-like citizens of a hundred years earlier, as drawn by Wilhelm Busch. The lead is played by Heinz Rühmann, who eventually played Zuckmayer's captain in Kautner's 1956 remake (q.v.).

Romanze in Moll (1943) is based on a story by de Maupassant, 'Le Bijou', and it is at least a great improvement on *Bel Ami;* since de Maupassant so disliked the Germans it is amusing to find that Käutner attacks his subject here in the manner of the Alsace-born Ophuls – mirrors, melodies and sweeping cameras – but he is not the stylist Ophuls was. He is even more superficial than Ophuls, and this tale of a bourgeois housewife (Marianne Hoppe) attracted to a successful composer and philanderer seems at times just out of mothballs. Fräulein Hoppe, though pleasant, does little but bring a roguish smile of triumph to the love scenes. The playing is also wan in **Die Grosse Freiheit Nr 7** (1944), but then no one is allowed to outshine its star, Hans Albers, playing an old sea-dog who sings for a living in a St Pauli bar and returns to the sea after being rejected by a much younger woman. The people are passionless and their emotions uninteresting – the besetting sins of the German films of this period; but the details of Hamburg life are lively and the colour is delightful.

Agfacolor had been first used for films in 1941, before it was fully developed, at Goebbels's behest: this is the fourth or fifth film in the process, the uncertainty coming from the fact that the film's premiere was delayed and finally given in Prague – Goebbels having commissioned the film as a tribute to the German navy and then, not surprisingly, disapproving of the result (Albers's huge popularity enabled him a measure of defiance; he had kept his Jewish wife with him till prudently deciding to send her to London).

If it compares with *Razzia in St Pauli*, **Unter den Brücken** (1945) is also strongly reminiscent of *Schleppzug M17,* being photographed almost entirely on the canals of Berlin. Almost certainly conditions in the studios were too chaotic at this stage of the War to allow filming there to proceed other than slowly: but the high percentage of shots of an unblemished Berlin may have been meant as a morale-booster to the rest of the country. Unfortunately the film was only ready as the Third Reich was about to collapse, and it disappeared till 1950 (a fate shared with Käutner's first film, withdrawn after its premiere because it seemed like a comment on the world situation; it did not reappear for over a decade). What audiences would have seen was the old German favourite of two men in love with the same girl, with not a semblance of inspired variation.

Less successful in resisting Goebbels's insistence that every script embody some aspect of Nazi ideology was Herbert Selpin. **Wässer fur Canitoga** (1939) features Hans Albers in familiar guise as a hard-drinking, bawdy mining engineer, breathing Teutonic warmth, as cutely set up as Shirley Temple ever was; his qualities of leadership are not necessarily Nazi, nor his self-sacrifice – but the martial tribute sung to him after death is by a group proudly identifying itself as composed of old soldiers. The setting is Canada at the turn of the century – a fact of little significance since Selpin considered that he was making a

Western, though at this time Goebbels was increasingly concerned with criticising British imperial power, in the hope of neutralising it.

Titanic (1943) was one of his pet projects, since he considered it a chance to show the British at their most craven and greedy. Selpin was assigned to it, because he had made two other sea stories – though he preferred light comedy, with which he had made his name. His usual writer, Walter Zerlatt-Olfenius, was a fanatical Party member, and a violent quarrel between them during location work was followed by Selpin's criticism of the officers acting as extras, because they regarded filming as of less importance than dalliance with their female counterparts. He refused to retract when called to account by Goebbels and was disposed of: photographs were prepared of him hanging in his prison cell, but on sounder consideration it was thought that the public might have difficulty in accepting yet another suicide in the film industry. However, since word did leak out the film was suppressed – though an additional reason was that the scenes of panic might remind audiences too forcibly of the effect of the R.A.F. bombings; to help recoup costs it was premiered in Paris late in 1943. These facts are of more interest than the film itself, though its tedium may be relieved by a laugh or so at the expense of the German couple in steerage who show themselves so much more heroic than anyone else on board.

Goebbels was particularly keen to encourage historical subjects, since in them Jews could be exposed as capitalist plotters – and the chances of exalting military might would be less gratuitous than in *Wässer fur Canitoga.* **Das Herz der Königin** (1940), a foolish romance concerning Mary, Queen of Scots (Zarah Leander), statically directed by Carl Frölich, has points to make on the perfidy of England; **Bismarck** (1940) shows Germany's most brilliant leader outwitting the rest of Europe – in a film that is cleverly accurate, despite its omissions, though that fact cannot disguise an abysmally stodgy director at work, Wolfgang Liebeneiner, the former actor. In the sequel, **Die Entlassung** (1942), Paul Hartmann has been replaced as Bismarck by Emil Jannings and Werner Krauss is one of his enemies, von Holstein, taking as of old any honours going for this partnership. In

both films Werner Hinz plays the crown prince, and in this one he also plays his own son, who becomes Kaiser Wilhelm II, depicted as effeminate or worse in his passion for uniforms. It is even duller than its predecessor, but does show Nazi propaganda in full flood – at the end Bismarck meditates on the future of the Reich, a concept greater than any man: it will outlive him, he says, and will need another great man to take on his mantle.

A great director, Pabst, returned to Germany to make two mediocre historical films for Goebbels, **Komödianten** (1941) and **Paracelsus** (1943). As a European war became imminent he had announced that he intended to leave France and take American citizenship; he was in Austria to sell some property and collect his mother when the fall of Poland prevented him getting an exit visa. His subsequent behaviour is puzzling, and work on a number of projects, helping other film-makers, has been ascribed to him. He was later evasive on his activities; however, it should be borne in mind that not only had he snubbed the Nazis by

refusing to work for them till now, but almost every film on which his reputation rested had been at odds with National Socialist doctrine. *Komödianten* is mainly a vehicle for the accomplished Käthe Dorsch, playing Karoline Neuber who, by virtue of carting her troupe around eighteenth-century Germany, is regarded as the founder of the German theatre. That Pabst won the Best Director award at the 1941 Venice Festival can only be due to politics – or the fact that only the Axis and its allies were competing. The film is relatively harmless, but *Paracelsus* is undoubtedly nationalist, with its sixteenth-century toasts to the concept of the German Reich. Both films have a dedicated protagonist, triumphing – at least spiritually – over the petty machinations of ducal families, ignorant merchants and busybodies. They are people of destiny, rejecting 'power, wealth and honour' in the service of honour – itself to be placed with the *volk* of Nazi ideology. Since Paracelsus (Krauss) was Swiss, he is identified in this film as an empassioned promoter of the German

The Nazi historical films are among the more rewarding of the films produced in Germany at this time – at least to historians, since the stories are basically accurate, and pleasure may be taken in finding the distortions, often minor in themselves, which aim to spread the Nazi creed. The approach, otherwise, is uninspired, and they are not recommended to seekers of entertainment. Among the better ones is *Bismarck*, with Friedrich Kayssler as the Kaiser Wilhelm I and Paul Hartmann as the Chancellor.

tongue. Apart from an astonishing apparition of Death, the direction indicates no directorial interest at all: one must assume that Pabst had no control over the script, or had become entirely cynical about his own work and the Nazis. *Der Fall Molander* was made in Czechoslovakia as the Russian armies advanced, and abandoned, though shooting was completed: it was never publicly shown, and is reputedly destroyed. After the War Pabst worked for several years in Austria, but without regaining his international reputation.

One German director did make very happily the nationalistic epics beloved of Goebbels, working with a skill and passion that exposes without mercy the banal talents of his confrères. Luis Trenker (b. 1893) came from the German-speaking section of the Italian Tyrol, a mountain guide discovered for films by Dr Arnold Fanck, who gave him a leading role in *Der Heilige Berg* (1926). After several years working solely as an actor, Trenker collaborated on **Berge in Flammen** (1931) with Karl Hartl, who co-directed and wrote the screenplay from a story by Trenker – who also played the lead in this tale of Austrian-Italian enmity in the Tyrol. Universal liked the film and asked Trenker to remake it as *The Doomed Battalion,* using much of the same spectacular mountain footage and with Cyril Gardner co-directing. Then, with a subsidiary of that company, Deutsche-Universal, Trenker made **Der Rebell** (1933) in collaboration with Kurt Benhardt, playing a young Tyrolean hero who defies Napoleon. There was also an English version in which Vilma Banky replaced Luise Ullrich as the heroine. It could not be said that then or later Trenker was an attractive hero, being tightlipped in appearance. Despite the fact that these two films were in English he made no headway with American audiences, who preferred their action heroes to be more homespun: his full-blooded romanticism and obvious national pride were also incompatible with the mood of the time.

Those same qualities sat very well with the Nazi Party: Hitler and Goebbels publicly saw the film and the latter recorded his appreciation in his diary: 'Thus I could imagine the film of the future, revolutionary in character, with grand mass-scenes, composed with enormous vital energy.' That was presumably not known to Sieg-

fried Kracauer when he came to write 'From Caligari to Hitler' in 1947, but he categorises Trenker as a Nazi director, partly on the eloquent use he made of flags. There is, however, apart from coincident ideals, no evidence that Trenker returned the admiration of the Nazis.

His next two films were mainly set and partly filmed in the U.S., and if he were indeed of the Nazi mentality it seems unlikely that he would have sought financial backing from Tobis, a company which was at this point financed from Amsterdam. A curious sidelight to the filming of the second film is that Trenker only had $30,000 available for the extensive location work, and that he was encouraged by Paul Kohner, the head of Deutsche-Universal, a company otherwise not involved: since its American owners had dropped Trenker it is ironic that their version of the same subject – *Sutter's Gold* (q.v.) – should be so infinitely inferior. Indeed, both these films are among the most remarkable of the period, and **Der Verlorene Sohn** (1934) was recognised as such at the Venice Festival, where it was awarded the Grand Prix. Despite that, and the fact that its long central section is in English, it has never been publicly shown in Britain or the U.S. This section concerns the adventures of a Tyrolean guide in America where, having failed to track down his girlfriend (Marian Marsh), he finds himself increasingly crushed by the Depression before returning home. **Der Kaiser von Kalifornien** (1936) is hardly more optimistic, concerning the ideal leader, enterprising and patriarchal, laid low by greed and political forces. If Trenker manages a happy ending to both – in this film an allegorical tribute to modern America, with the ghost riders in the sky from *Der Rebell* – it is because the romantic side of his nature always triumphed over the realistic. He was producer, director, sole writer and leading actor – and on the evidence of these two films a great film-maker, both of them towering above the majority of Hollywood's respective Depression tales and screen biographies. His films are at least visually magnificent, with some stunning montages and settings eloquently used.

However, returning to the subject of his first films as a director, alpine warfare, in **Condottieri** (1937) a number of images now begin to seem cliché – the fields of waving corn, waving flags, the mountains. Trenker, eyes and teeth agleam, preaching nationalism and love of the *Vaterland*, is a laughable figure; and though the nationalist cause came naturally to most Tyroleans it is hard not to regard this film as a sop to the Party. In fact it marked the end of the mutual enchantment, if there were any on his side: the Pope had recently issued an encyclical which had been interpreted, as intended, as a criticism of the Nazi régime, and Trenker's sequence in which his medieval hero is blessed by the Pope was regarded by Goebbels as not only gratuitous but an implied endorsement. It was cut, and the film withdrawn after a week's run in Berlin.

Trenker had begun to challenge the Nazis in *Der Kaiser von Kalifornien,* with its clear warning that self-made dictators can well end up powerless and lonely. At the time of its production he had remarked privately that he had turned down Hollywood offers because he feared for his German wife and children; now he sought foreign financing, perhaps Jewish, and he certainly had German-Jewish refugee collaborators on **The Challenge** (1938), made simultaneously with its German version, *Der Berg Ruft*. Gunther Stapenhorst produced for Korda, with a screenplay by Emeric Pressburger based on a German film of 1928, *Der Kampf ums Matterhorn,* concerning the first ascent of that mountain in 1865. Korda's cinematographer, Georges Périnal, joined forces with Albert Benitz, Trenker's usual collaborator, to bypass on this occasion the clichés of mountain photographers – and their achievement is superb, despite a limited budget of £80,000; but the scenes in the various hostelries are literally grounded, at least in the English version as co-directed by Milton Rosmer. In that, the hero is played by Robert Douglas, with Trenker as his Italian guide.

Like this film and *Condottieri*, **Der Feuerteufel** (1940) is a second-rate film made by a first-class film-maker – one with complete understanding of the possibilities of his medium. Like them, it is likeable and unforced, bringing a touch of humour to this deliberate attempt at a heroic tale. It also is much like *Der Rebell*, concerning an Alpine woodsman who leads a rebellion against Napoleon, but this time Trenker was playing with fire, since it was open

encouragement for all occupied countries to rise against the aggressor. The hero advocates peace over war, and speaks of the rights of individual nations to control their destiny. Although Napoleon, like Trenker's Sutter, is depicted as a man of some humanity, Goebbels this time could not overlook the implications, and the film was banned – except for showing to the armed forces, amongst whom it could do no harm. Trenker was immediately blacklisted, although he was allowed to act in the anti-British *Germanin,* after which he went to Italy, where he made a number of documentary shorts and a few features before returning briefly to the German industry in 1955, with *Der Flucht in die Dolomiten,* partly scripted by Pasolini (q.v.). Unlike those other veterans of the mountain film, Fanck and Riefenstahl, he had never been active in the Party, and

Luis Trenker in typical garb, playing an Alpine guide and looking very heroic against a mountain background. This picture is in fact from *Condottieri*. As an actor he is passable, but as writer-producer-director and cinematographer he achieved greatness on at least two occasions.

it is particularly ironic that he was banned with them and a number of other film-makers when in 1945 the Allies examined the probable guilt of the German film industry in supporting the Nazis. If they had looked at all his films they had not looked hard enough – nor, obviously, examined the facts. Trenker remains an enigma: branching out from the genre films which were clearly his favourites he made two magnificent films, only to retreat again. The fact that he worked in Nazi Germany perhaps inhibited him and certainly silenced him. We do not know whether he felt called upon to criticise the Nazi leadership from disillusionment or from love of humanity – though from moments in *Der Verlorene Sohn* we may suspect the latter.

Among others banned from the film industry by the Allies were Emil Jannings and Werner Krauss (Heinrich George died while interned in a Russian concentration camp), and the directors Gustav Ucicky, Wolfgang Liebeneiner and Veit Harlan. Krauss, like Trenker, was unjustly treated: his son's wife was Jewish, which was why he surrendered to Goebbels's pleas to appear in *Jud Süss* (q.v.) – the experience of which so distressed him that two years later he refused to play the lead in another propaganda historical, *Der Grosse König*. Ferdinand Marian, who played the lead in *Jud Süss,* was so riven with guilt that he committed suicide not long after he had been de-Nazified by an Allied committee. That particular film became the focal point for Allied interest in the Nazi film industry, and was banned after the War as 'the most obvious anti-semitic propaganda imaginable'. It was also the cause of its director being twice tried for Crimes Against Humanity – though he was acquitted for lack of evidence.

He was Veit Harlan (1899–1964), a former stage actor and director most noted for his soap operas, usually starring his third wife, Kristina Söderbaum, of Swedish origin. Typical of them, and of Nazi notions as to heroic and romantic ideals, is **Opfergang** (1944), concerning the re-action of Octavia (Irene von Meyendorff) when she discovers that her husband (Carl Raddatz) is having an affair with the woman (Söderbaum) next door. The wife wears tea gowns and plays Chopin; the mistress, also blonde, behaves alternately

as mermaid and Diana, and then horse-woman-in-silk-hat and kitten-among-the-cushions – all the time supposed to be a 'free', close-to-nature woman. Harlan also directed a number of historical films, including **Das Unsterbliche Herz** (1939), based on a 1913 play by his father, Walter Harlan, and concerning the medieval watch maker Peter Henlein (Heinrich George); and **Der Grosse König** (1942), the last gasp of the Fridericus films, again starring Otto Gebühr and surprisingly hinting at the monarch's homosexuality. Both are unabashedly Nazi: Peter Henlein prefers work to sex, he is an idealist – unlike the merchants around him – and he wishes to die in the saddle, like the soldier with whom he compares himself, offering his life for his country. Behind the dedicated figure of Frederick in the other film is that subtle theme of Nazi ideology, that every nation is weakened when there is no strong government to stand against dissidents.

That creed is openly expounded in *Condottieri,* but it is particularly insidious in Harlan's films and certainly in **Jud Süss** (1940), where by dissidents we understand Jews, by implication a completely grasping race. The anti-semitic films did not really start till 1939, preparatory to formulating the Final Solution, and as the Germans conquered Europe these films went with them, to create a climate in which innocent people could be taken from their homes and destroyed. *Jud Süss* is accordingly vile – all the more so since it is both handsome and well-made. Harlan was at best a plodding director, but he was aided by the high traditions in art direction which remained in the German studios. He is well served here by Krauss, in a double role as the Rabbi Loew and Süss's familiar, and magnificently by Herr Marian in the title role. It is an odd experience to be confronted with a great performance of a villain, knowing that we are not supposed to hate superficially, as with most screen villains. Marian's Süss has pride, cunning, greed, intellectual power, the ability to survive personal humiliation and prejudice; unlike the earlier, creaky British version (q.v.) we meet him first as a Jew, and he is sympathetic. But he becomes loathsome. Jewry was not in 1940 what it had been in 1733 (in Stuttgart), but the film is an incitement to hate all its members.

Goebbels himself revised the script,

eventually deleting Süss's final tirade against his enemies because it included a prophecy that their cities would be destroyed by fires from heaven. It is easy to believe Harlan's later claim that none of the principals wished to be associated with the project, claiming on his own behalf that all the characters were negative; however, he was also associated with **Kolberg** (1945), the apotheosis of Nazi film-making. Goebbels intended it to rival *Gone with the Wind* (q.v.) – and as that film had provided sustenance to British audiences during the War so this was similarly intended. Kolberg was a small Prussian town which had withstood the forces of Napoleon; as Goebbels wrote to the director, the film was to demonstrate that 'a *people* united at home and at the front will overcome any enemy' – and thus, as with Trenker's films, a people's army was extolled at the expense of the official servicemen. Goebbels initiated the project in 1941 and filming began two years later, with a budget of Reichsmark 8½ million. The statistics in Hull ('Film in the Third Reich') include more than 10,000 costumes, 6,000 horses and more than 187,000 people 'involved at one time or other'. These included troops diverted from the front, while one hundred railway wagons of salt were conveyed to the location to provide snow. As usual, Goebbels declined to tamper with history, since the propaganda content was the less suspect; but the French had finally overwhelmed Kolberg, hardly a fact to stir audiences after the reversals of 1943 and 1944. The ending, often left vague during preparations, was constantly changed – and footage to the value of RM 2 million removed: it was finally clear that the only message that the film could convey was that to capitulate is to destroy a nation. Many of Goebbels's own speeches were put into the mouth of the resistance leader (Heinrich George), reiterating that the story of Kolberg is a demonstration of the popular will. La Rochelle was chosen for the premiere because it was then under siege: cans of film had to be dropped by parachute for the

Veit Harlan's *Jud Süss* must be one of the most famous of all unseen movies, renowned as anti-semitic propaganda, and therefore seldom revived. It is offensive but the one reason to see it is the performance of Ferdinand Marian in the title role. It is an odd experience to be confronted with a great performance of evil, knowing that we are not supposed to hate superficially, as with most screen villains. Marian later committed suicide, reputedly from guilt because of his association with the film – but that was only after the Allied authorities had interrogated him on the matter.

appointed date, 30 January, the anniversary of the Nazis coming to power. Virtually the only cinema still open in the ruins of Berlin was assigned to show the film, but was allowed to withdraw it after a few days. A week before the War ended Goebbels screened the film for his staff, and in the accompanying speech told them that in a hundred years' time they would be the subject of a similar film. It was revived in 1966, with newsreel footage added to point up the propaganda, but when pickets appeared outside cinemas it was soon withdrawn. It is as dreary as it is unimpressive. It is appropriate that not only is what Goebbels considered his greatest epic so completely hollow, but that few people have ever seen it.

14

Frank Capra, the Name above the Title

COLUMBIA Pictures owes its major status to one man, Frank Capra; his pictures for the company overshadowed all other American films of the Thirties. They were not necessarily the best, but contemporary reviewers were far more concerned with his work than with that of any other American film-maker. They noticed him first as an excellent craftsman and then as a maker of exceptional comedies; by the time he was dealing with matters of social conscience he was putting his personal stamp on each of his films. The adjective 'Capraesque' was coined quite early. He was the only director of the time widely recognised by the public: the fan magazines of the period – still less trivial than their later counterparts – rarely featured articles on any other director. He knew the value of publicity, but then the fan magazines knew the value of directors.

Until he got into his stride, Columbia was a poverty row studio, seldom signalling that it would ever be anything else. The head of production – and part-owner – was Harry Cohn (1891–1958), by general agreement the most crass of all the film tycoons, and loathed quite as much as Louis B. Mayer. He was, like the others, of immigrant stock, and had also had a variety of early menial jobs, including a stint in vaudeville. In 1918 he went to work for Carl Laemmle, who was already employing his brother Jack. With another Laemmle employee, Joe Brandt, they formed the C.B.C. Sales Co. in 1920, which became Columbia Pictures four years later. Its output consisted of low-budget programme fillers, none of note till Capra made his first film for them.

Capra (b. 1897) was a Sicilian immigrant who originally intended to be an engineer. In his autobiography, 'The Name above the Title', he recounts that he drifted into films after the War, achieving some slight renown as gag-writer for Hal Roach and then Mack Sennett. He moved to First National with Harry Langdon, as writer and director, and for that company directed *For the Love of Mike* (1927), which failed – due, he thought later, to the script. Columbia was the only studio willing to give him a job: he made **That Certain Thing** (1928) for $20,000, and Cohn to his delight was able to sell it separately and not merely as one of a parcel of Columbia features. It has a not unusual story of rich boy and poor girl, with the thesis that money does not bring happiness but that industry and enterprise will be amply rewarded. Most films of the time held to such morals – if less attractively – and certainly Capra's later films also did.

Whether or not Cohn was pleased with its success, he kept Capra working on 'quickies' till he assigned him to one of the company's rare high-budget ($150,000) productions, *Submarine* (1928), to replace Irving Willat. Its success occasioned two more formula adventures with the same starring team, Jack Holt and Ralph Graves, *Flight* (1929) and **Dirigible** (1931), the latter a story by Graves and Capra himself which remains quite gripping, about an airship force landed at the South Pole.

Cohn had given Capra a contract worth $25,000 a year after *Submarine*, with **Ladies of Leisure** (1930), Capra gave Cohn the company's biggest success to date. The film's heroine, in her first important film appearance is Barbara Stanwyck (b. 1907), and she is a party-girl who finds true love with an artist (Graves) till his father breaks up the affair. Though based on a 1924 play the note of disillusion – and final hope – was exactly what Depression audiences were seeking; and though critics praised Capra's sophistication he himself thought the film's quality was due to the screenplay of Jo Swerling, a former newspaperman. Director and writer formed a happy collaboration on Capra's next four films – till, in fact, Capra found a writer that he liked even more. The first of these movies was a musical, *Rain or Shine* (1930), with Joe Cook, in his only film appearance, repeating his Broadway success, and the last of them was **Forbidden** (1931), another starring vehicle for Stanwyck. Capra provided Swerling with the original story, '99.44% soap opera' as he later termed it, admitting that much of it was borrowed from 'Back Street' – not at that point filmed, but critics noticed resemblances to *Possessed*. They again praised the direction, and the sheer lack of sentiment remains astonishing, even if the first half is the best, as Stanwyck leaves her dreary job to blow her savings on one spectacular holiday – during the course of which, on board ship, she meets the high-ranking politician (Adolphe Menjou) who returns, temporarily, her love. Meanwhile Capra made his first considerable film, **Miracle Woman** (1931), based on a play by Robert Riskin and John Meehan which aimed to stir the public into questioning the preachings of Aimee Semple Macpherson. The screenplay also included some borrowings from Sinclair Lewis's novel on the same subject, 'Elmer Gantry', including the rascally promoter and the climactic fire, purloined because Capra, in his own words, went soft: 'The thought of a wicked evangelist milking poor, adoring suckers for money in the name of Christ was just too much for my orthodox stomach. I weaseled. I insisted on a "heavy" to take the heat off [Barbara] Stanwyck the evangelist. *He* cons her into it. *He* gets wealthy. She becomes his flamboyant stooge. Did she or did she not herself believe those "inspiring" sermons . . . ? I didn't know, Stanwyck didn't know, and neither did the audience.' That is one of the reasons the film seems so modern today. He also anticipated many later (usually feeble) film-makers by stopping the film with a cataclysm because he had no ending, 'the cheapest trick in dramaturgy' as he put it. However, the film moves so convincingly that its basic melodrama is disguised: Can She Be Saved by the Love of a Good Man? He is a blind war

hero, very well played by David Manners; and as the lady who may or may not be a fake Barbara Stanwyck is also excellent. Capra makes touching their relationship and that, apart from the suspense, is his real achievement.

The chief significance of the film for him was that he met the writer who would be his alter ego, Robert Riskin (1897–1955). Indeed, a couple of the films that Riskin wrote without Capra are so much what we recognise as Capraesque that it is possible that his was the major influence. Riskin wrote only the dialogue of **Platinum Blonde** (1931), which is not a typical work; but there are details recognisably theirs – apart from the fact that the hero is dubbed 'The Cinderella Man', as Mr Deeds would be later. The blonde of the title is a debutante (Jean Harlow) who snares, marries and tries to tame a reporter – played in brilliant detail (wry and ebullient, realistic but happy – perhaps a study of Capra himself) by Robert Williams. The match

Frank Capra at the time he was everyone's idea of a great director. The industry admired him because his films were successful, the critics liked him because his films tried to say something, and the public trusted him because his films were so entertaining. Even now there is hardly one among his pictures which is not vastly entertaining.

p.320
Nils Asther and
Barbara Stanwyck in
*The Bitter Tea of
General Yen*,
a devilish bit of
Chinoiserie which
must confound
anyone who thinks
of Frank Capra as
a purveyor of
sentiment and
idealism.

Thing, poverty, success with the box lunches, reconciliation with papa; in *Dirigible,* a crash, a broken marriage, a letter that isn't read; in *Miracle Woman,* a confession, the fire, new hope; and in *Lady for a Day,* the suddenly whimsical behaviour of New York's upper crust. Mr Deeds, on trial for insanity, is saved by a confession of love; in *American Madness,* the president's marriage and his bank fail, or seem to at the same time – till the miraculous reversal. Not for nothing is one of Capra's later films called *A Pocketful of Miracles* (q.v.).

Capra and Riskin are always capable of humour, if sometimes lacking seriousness. *American Madness,* like *Miracle Woman,* moves into plot contrivance after a startlingly naturalistic start. Capra is good on the day to day activity of the bank but, even allowing for the emotional climate of the time the scenes of panic are exaggerated. He himself claims some notable firsts for the film – such as attempting to express the urgency of the bank's problems by hastening the pace faster than life, moving the performers at speed in and out of the heart of a scene, and omitting the then-current dissolve to indicate change of time or locale. Overlapping dialogue had been used before – in *Bad Girl* – but we may note a rare ability to combine humour and idiosyncrasy for greater credibility rather than less in, for instance, the characters of the piggish detective and the squeaky-voiced man at the directors' meetings.

Now, Capra decided, he wanted an Oscar: 'I would make the artiest film they ever saw ... Walter Wanger [then at Columbia] happened to be preparing a picture from Grace Zaring Stone's novel ... To me it was Art with a capital *A*.' In outline, **The Bitter Tea of General Yen** (1933) sounds not unlike *The Sheik,* but in practice it is a brave, romantic picture, far ahead of its time – or so one might suppose, except that it was booked into the gigantic Radio City Music Hall, and was the first film to play there. As Capra boasts, it is as much about miscegenation as eroticism; it also casts a queer light on one of the sacred cows of the era – mission work. Stanwyck plays a missionary rescued and imprisoned during a riot by a Chinese warlord (Nils Asther), and whose hostility towards him evaporates in the strangeness of her new surroundings: Beauty and the Beast interpreted in simple Freudian terms but subtle

goes awry, when, among other things, she insists that he wears garters, even if with solid gold attachments. Unhooked from her, he unhooks them and gives them to a passing hobo, who promptly demands his socks as well. The ungrateful bum was a Capra-Riskin speciality; their society people would always be, as here, stuffed shirts, and their journalists cynical but ultimately human.

When they are the heroes they will also be finally happy. Capra has an incurable belief in happy endings. If, in his own words, he and Riskin were as 'opportunist as Hearst reporters' in concocting their Depression fable, **American Madness** (1932), they at least ensured that their bank president hero (Walter Huston) 'is filled with youthful optimism and a cheerful trust in men'. All Capra's films are basically fairy stories, some by admission. All of them take their heroes to a desperate pitch before a final twist smooths things out: in *That Certain*

cinema language. Von Sternberg expressed eroticism by look; alone among players, Garbo expressed it by thought. Thinking people were rare in films, but the warlord and the missionary may be seen at least to ponder, even if, like Feyder's Carmen and Don José, their musings are closed to us. Further disrespect towards mission work is indicated in Walter Connolly's perform-ance as the warlord's Machiavellian finan-cial adviser, and it is not surprising that the film was banned throughout the British Empire, thus becoming – with *Miracle Woman* – Capra's only Columbia picture to lose money.

Reunited with Riskin, he again demons-trated his originality by being the first to bring one of Damon Runyon's stories to the screen, **Lady for a Day** (1933), a tract for the times concerning a Broadway pedlar, Apple Annie (May Robson), and telling how Dave the Dude (Warren William) helps her maintain the pretence, for the sake

of her daughter, that she is in society. We may take it that Apple Annie is a victim of the Depression, so it is comforting that not only the pool sharks but the high-ups show their sympathy–as does Capra, his mood closer to the Hollywood Christmas-round-the-fire of the Forties than to the gold diggers currently at Warners.

His reputation was now such that Thal-berg invited him to M-G-M – in exchange for a star to be loaned to Columbia; but the project, *Soviet,* was cancelled by Mayer while Thalberg was in Europe. Capra and Riskin went back to a story in *Cosmopolitan* magazine by Samuel Hopkins Adams, which came to the screen as **It Happened One Night** (1934). Robert Montgomery turned it down because he had just made a similar tale, and M-G-M substituted a re-bellious Clark Gable. Myrna Loy, Miriam Hopkins and Constance Bennett refused, though the last named offered to buy the script. Claudette Colbert (q.v.) accepted,

Anyone who went to the cinema in the Thirties could not escape whacky heiresses, and there were even more to be seen after the success of *It Happened One Night.* In this case the lady is Claudette Colbert, and pursuing her is Clark Gable, who sees in her a headline story. Her initial reaction is of icy contempt, but their relationship finishes delightfully if predictably. With them is Mickey Daniels.

Jean Arthur and Gary Cooper, the incomparable partnership of *Mr Deeds Goes to Town*, which starts by reversing the situation of *It Happened One Night*. She is the reporter, he the wealthy man whose story she is already selling to her paper, which is mocking him – hence the sneers of passers-by and her own apprehensive look.

because, according to Capra, it meant $50,000 for four weeks' work, happily coinciding with her vacation from Paramount. No one would ever turn down a Capra picture again.

The contemporary reviews were warm but not ecstatic, and it was word of mouth which made it a success, as exhibitors found on rebooking. In Hollywood, also, audiences were captivated, enabling Capra to more than achieve his ambition: this was the first occasion one film took a clutch of Oscars, and till 1976 the only time any film gathered what are conceded to be the five most important – Best Film, Best Director, Best Actor, Best Actress, Best Screenplay. An Academy Award is a distinctly unreliable guide to merit, but even if this is not the best American film of that particular year it is certainly the best of the twelve nominated by the Academy (the number was later reduced to five).

Its plot was already familiar (beyond the basic idea, which, as Capra has pointed out, is 'The Taming of the Shrew'), and has been subject since to endless variants: the pursuit of an heiress by a hard-up reporter who sees her as his next meal ticket. There were whole sequences which audiences took to their hearts: the passengers in the bus joining in a spontaneous 'Man on the Flying Trapeze'; Gable failing to stop a car with his vaunted thumb technique and Colbert succeeding with her leg; and 'The Walls of Jericho', when he hangs the blanket between the two motel beds. It is a picaresque tale, and Capra keeps the eccentricities unpretentious; the pace is fast and the playing joyous. Gable manages to suggest not only an old-sweat journalist but a 'parfit gentle knight', not giving a damn whether his lady will join him in eating raw carrots but finally touching in his stewardship; under her hoity exterior, she finally warms to a bum who is worth more than her aviator husband.

Capra borrowed both Myrna Loy and Warner Baxter for **Broadway Bill** (1934), and Baxter, often stodgy, is here a very dull dog indeed. The role is crucial, for he plays a son-in-law who turns his back on all the tycoonery for his first love, the race track; by the end he has won over his father-in-law (Walter Connolly), as well as the nice daughter (Loy). All is for the best in the best of all possible worlds. The world rejected is Higginsville, appropriately named for father-in-law: this is the first Capra-Riskin sketch of small town stuffiness, and the film furthers their search for memorable minor characters – here played by such actors as Raymond Walburn, Lynne Overman and Margaret Hamilton.

Mr Deeds Goes to Town (1936) is the crowning achievement of the partnership. If I had to choose one film to be both the best and most representative of the decade, this would be it. Graham Greene thought it Capra's 'finest film . . . and that means it is a comedy quite unmatched on the screen. For Capra has what Lubitsch, the pretty play-boy, has not: a sense of responsibility, and what Clair, whimsical, poetic, a little precious and *à la mode,* has not, a kinship with his audience, a sense of common life, a morality: he has what even Chaplin has not, complete mastery of his medium.' In the U.S. a left-wing critic, Robert Stebbins, writing in *New Theatre,* found the film 'astounding . . . a tremendous advance' for Hollywood, yet the scene he most admired, the meeting between Mr Deeds and a Depression-hit hobo, is the one which modern audiences find hardest to take – because its crusading heart is on its sleeve.

Up to that point Riskin has written a comedy of manners to stand with any in the language: of all the variations on the theme of the innocent amid the city slickers – from Ben Jonson onwards – it is the most satisfying. Mr Deeds (Gary Cooper) is no guileless bumpkin upsetting the sophisticates by chance, but a plain, honest man; his pleasures are simple (writing greeting card verse, playing a tuba, following fire engines), and he may be halfway duped: but he is a man with a sense of rightness, of resource and of pride. Cooper, by nature no one's fool, gives one of the great screen performances. The hard-boiled sob sister who both befriends and exploits him is beautifully taken by Jean Arthur (q.v.); the role may be a cipher but that is remedied by her playing. The discovery of her duplicity is followed by Mr Deeds's decision to surrender his fortune to the unemployed, and here we are in a different film – a Steinbeck 'We and Them' tale. It is not inconsistent with what has gone before, and the final court room sequence welds the essential component of comedy and social concern.

Capra won his second Best Director Oscar for *Mr Deeds,* though he thought that 'if anyone deserved Oscars Cooper and Riskin did'. Riskin, he said, wrote what he himself wanted to say, and the film's success increased his belief in what he called 'one man, one film', which the industry was prepared to accept – but only provided he was the man. He was not, as he asserts, the first American director since pioneer days to have his name above the title, for Vidor, Milestone, Borzage and deMille already had, but it is probable that only he and deMille had their names emblazoned on the marquees of cinemas. Even if statistics were available, they would be unable to prove *Mr Deeds* to be the most popular American Talkie till *Gone with the Wind,* but I think it true to say that it was both the best-thought-of and the most loved among all levels of brow.

Cohn, not a man prone to initiative – though he knew what he didn't like – had been content to let Capra have his head, and since he found himself the employer of the most admired man in the industry he agreed to buy for him a novel by James Hilton, and to allocate it $2 million, which would have paid for twenty normal Columbia features. The resulting film did not take at the first public preview, so Capra threw out the first two reels. Thus **Lost Horizon** (1937) begins in China, where Conway (Ronald Colman) 'England's man of the East, soldier, hero, diplomat' is superintending the evacuation of some Britishers: their plane is mysteriously hijacked, and they find themselves in a peaceful valley in the Himalayas called Shangri-La – for Conway, as it turns out, has been chosen to be its new ruler. He is unsure whether he wants to be, and when his final decision is not yet known in London, 'May he find his Shangri-La', they drink to him in his club, 'May we all find our Shangri-Las'.

You would have to be very cynical not to find in *Lost Horizon* the qualities of *Mr Deeds* – that it is possible to rediscover an essential beauty and goodness to life, both

Shangri-La as it appeared in *Lost Horizon*. The visual concept has dated somewhat, as has the film's view of Utopian ideals – which seemed particularly attractive in the Thirties. The film remains entertaining, because of Capra's exceptional narrative skill and Ronald Colman's charismatic performance.

bludgeoned out of existence by man in his thoughtlessness. The film offered hope in the form of fantasy. Age-old truths were to be found in Shangri-La: if not eternal life, eternal youth, and all the precepts – though it is never mentioned – of Christianity. The idea of a country without crime or war was meant to be considered against the background of events in Europe, but I cannot help feeling that cinema-goers were being sold a dud bill of goods – in theory if not in spirit. The decor by Stephen Goossens is often unfortunate, as in the interiors of the palace, looking like one of the grander Spanish *paradors;* and such things as the Utopian glade, with ducks on every pond and a squirrel to warn the bathing heroine of Conway's approach, are excruciating.

There can be no question of Capra's sincerity – though in time it would be questioned. The film was greeted with an avalanche of praise, though the more judicious critics found it expedient to ignore the metaphysics in favour of the spectacle. 'It is the second outstanding picture of the season' said *The New York Times* – the first being 'of course' *The Good Earth* (q.v.). Capra's sheer set-em-up skill is astonishing, but if even the most jaundiced must be hoping that Conway will return to Shangri-La, that has much to do with the actor concerned, 'beautiful of face and soul, sensitive to the fragile and gentle' as Capra put it. Colman's shrug as he contemplates becoming the next Foreign Secretary is an easy thing to do, but his achievement here is to listen to the High Lama (Sam Jaffe) with the intensity that must cloak the rest of the film. But not even he, nor critical praise, nor huge audiences (the film was one of the dozen or so of its time to be road-shown) could provide the miracle needed to enable Columbia to recoup its investment.

A Broadway comedy allowed Capra to plough the same furrow – Kaufman and Hart's **You Can't Take It with You** (1938), which had won the Pulitzer prize – an award that was justified, said Frank S. Nugent in *The New York Times,* not by the original but by this film version. The one-set-three-acts had become a flowing narrative; the one-dimensional characters had been clothed in flesh and blood; and it had become more serious. Nugent's review presumably pleased Capra, who had not wanted to make 'a laugh riot' but 'something deeper, something greater . . . an opportunity to dramatise Love Thy Neighbor in living drama. What the world's churches were preaching to apathetic congregations, my universal language of film might say more entertainingly to movie audiences'. The result won the Best Picture Oscar and the Best Director Oscar.

Time has proved Capra wrong, not to mention his writer Riskin, Mr Nugent and the Academy voters – even if one could still tolerate the visions of Grandpa Vanderhof as expressed by the sententious Lionel Barrymore (Henry Travers, who played the role on the stage, was surely better). He is spokesman for a household devoted to eccentric pursuits, and he himself is struggling with a capitalist (Edward Arnold) planning to enlarge his munitions factory at the expense of the family home. When the film chooses to be funny, it is hilarious; when it is serious, it is a parody of better

Capra pictures. There are, appropriately, two small salutes to Walt Disney (q.v.), for Capra's admiration for Disney transcended the usual studio rivalries; the two were certainly beholden to each other.

The heroine is Jean Arthur (b. 1905), partnered with James Stewart, and they would play together in Capra's next film, where he was perhaps a substitute for Gary Cooper. These heroes were good men but hesitant, and Miss Arthur, who had co-starred in *Mr Deeds,* was their perfect counterpart, on the surface confident and wise in city ways, but equally – or at any rate finally – devoted to the cause of right. She was Capra's favourite heroine and one of the magical comediennes of the Thirties, equally sure but delicate in drama, with a voice that is indescribable (like butter being churned, if butter had a voice) and with that warmth which seems to have died with the actresses of her generation. (Capra also adored Barbara Stanwyck, as did all the directors who worked with her.)

Miss Arthur's presence in **Mr Smith goes to Washington** (1939) is only one reason I consider it a moment in cinema comparable with *Mr Deeds,* and reviewers at the time were similarly affected. Yet there were some who noticed a deterioration, and in *The New Republic* Otis Ferguson recalled that at the time of the earlier film another critic, Alistair Cooke, had said that Capra had 'started to make movies about themes instead of people'. Ferguson himself thought *Lost Horizon* an aberration, adding that in *You Can't Take It with You* Capra 'had forgotten about people for good'. However, Graham Greene found in *Mr Smith* 'the delight – equal to the great Russians – in the ordinary human face' and considered it 'a great film, even if it is not a great story'. Capra thought the story – 'The Man from Montana' by Lewis R. Foster – both good *and* important, but it was certainly not new: Meyer Levin in *The Nation* pointed out that it was Christ and the money changers – while we may see it also as an old plot, that of the worm that turned. The screenplay is by Sidney Buchman, since Riskin had been lured away by Goldwyn, for whom however he did no credited work. Riskin's few, subsequent, non-Capra credits are not in fact very interesting, but they are still better than those of Buchman, who wrote such dire

films (q.v.) as *The Howards of Virginia* and *A Song to Remember* – the latter a cherished project of Capra's; we can only speculate what it might have been like in his hands.

Buchman's screenplay for *Mr Smith* concerns a newspaper tycoon (Edward Arnold) and a senior senator (Claude Rains) in cahoots with the Governor (Guy Kibbee); they have a land deal going, and need a junior senator who is either corrupt or a stooge. In Jefferson Smith (Stewart) they think they have the latter, till he is taken in hand by a Washingotn secretary (Miss Arthur) who, like Babe in *Mr Deeds,* rallies to him when she realises that he is a David up against the Goliath of the Senate. Capra was naive enough to think that Washington would approve of this; he believed he had struck a blow for democracy with his portrait of an idealistic senator – while Washington was only concerned with the unflattering picture of itself as a place of graft and corruption. 'Liberty is too precious a thing to be buried in books,' says Mr Smith, the lone idealist. But Capra himself is just such an idealist – the personification of the American dream, from penniless immigrant to world acclaim: he believes in the U.S.A., the land of the free. Mr Smith, like Mr Deeds, is him.

Beyond any ideas the film may have of putting the world to rights, it is marvellously well made and has an outstanding cast, even by the standards of the day; as always with Capra, each member of it has far more to express than the dialogue. Note three scenes in particular: Rains and Arnold regarding each other after they have agreed to let loose in Washington this Lincoln-Jefferson-spouting 'patriot'; Miss Arthur responding to him – part impressed, part amused; and the Press Club interviewing him, sending him up ever so slightly. No one is painted black or white; with the exception of Rains, all the villains offer a touch of humour. Mr Smith seems too naive and bumbling but, as Capra once remarked, 'Gary Cooper *is* Mr Deeds, just as Stewart is Mr Smith.' He has also said that this is his best film.

It was also his last for Columbia, and he had no intention of renewing his contract, since there still rankled (among other matters) that occasion when Cohn had taken advantage of his absence in Europe to pass off another director's film as his. Foremost among those who offered him autonomy

Claude Rains and James Stewart in *Mr Smith Goes to Washington* which was popular everywhere, except in the capital. Its timing was perfect, as when there enters the chamber 'two representatives of dictator powers who have come to see what they cannot see at home – democracy in action'. Since this turned out to be Mr Stewart rebelling at the chamber's lack of principle, Washington's reaction is not surprising.

were Goldwyn and Selznick, independents themselves, but he refused to commit himself beyond one picture at a time – and the only producer to whom that restriction was acceptable was Jack Warner, described by Capra as, 'the one non-conforming, irrepressible spirit among the studio heads'. Warner's sole stipulation was that Capra and Riskin, once again partnered, should invest $100,000 of their own money, with no requirements as to budget or subject. Capra admitted he chose his subjects to please reviewers, and had been peeved that when the New York critics' ten-best lists were combined his last three films were not included.

Meet John Doe (1941) was brought to him by its original writers, Richard Connell and Robert Presnell – the story of an out-of-work baseball player manoeuvred into becoming a national figure by preach-

ing the people's cause in a newspaper whose proprietor, a fascist with a private army, intends by this means to achieve the Presidency. As with *Mr Smith*, it seemed vitally important at that time to give a warning against fascism, but Capra and Riskin were trying to say more than that – and they were saying again what they had said better in earlier films. John Doe is the Miracle Woman, preaching Christianity for personal gain; he is Mr Deeds, innocent and unthinking; he is finally Mr Smith, rallying his intellectual resources to fight the evil which had been manipulating him. He is also played by Cooper, and the fascist yet again by Edward Arnold. Miss Stanwyck is the self-interested doll who finally, again, rallies to him, but both players, increasingly at sea with the motivation of their characters, fall back on mannerism – rare in a Capra film. His own flair leaves him, and he settles for a series of unfilmic duologues of no great interest. By that time he must have known the ending would not work: five different ones were shot, and audiences liked none of them. In his memoir, he implies that had he found the right ending he would have had a masterpiece – though he admits that he does not know whether this story ever had an ending.

Most critics liked the picture, but it was a box-office failure and Capra modestly determined to surrender some independence. By forming a company with Selznick he intended to become a fourth owner of United Artists, joining Pickford, Chaplin and Korda (q.v.). Had he been prepared to surrender all independence he could have written his own terms anywhere in Hollywood; as it was, the agreement with Selznick came to nothing since, believing that war was imminent, he joined the army. While waiting for his call-up papers he saw a play he wanted to film – one so meticulously constructed that it could not be cut without damage, and had therefore to be filmed as it stood. He envisaged a four-week schedule and a large salary to keep his family while he was away. Warners owned the rights, and Jack Warner was amenable to holding the film in storage, because it could not be released before the end of the Broadway run. **Arsenic and Old Lace** was in fact shot in December 1941, and did not premiere till almost three years later. As filmed theatre it is an exemplary job, as fast as *American Madness* and gloriously funny except where the humour has dated. No one by then could have been unaware of the subject: two dainty ladies – maiden aunts – who have made a habit of poisoning lodgers and burying them in the cellar. For all

Capra's skill and the good lines (Joseph Kesselring bore the credit for the play, but its producers, Lindsay and Crouse, are now known to have been chiefly responsible), it owes most to Cary Grant (b. 1904), playing the dramatic critic who – on his wedding day – discovers that his aunts are mass murderers slipping poison into their home-made elderberry wine. There was no actor better able to cope with the situation; William Powell or Melvyn Douglas would surely have turned the old dears in eventually, but Grant is manic enough to adjust. The Hays Office would not allow the famous last line to be used*: but if you know it, you can imagine the expression of Edward Everett Horton's face as he listens to it.

It is appropriate that the first phase of Capra's career should end thus, for he was primarily a wonderful entertainer. When he chose to be funny, which was most of the time, he was very funny and his humour has proved ageless. He also chose to demonstrate what he considered American virtues. Some have spoken of 'Capra-corn', but the seriousness of his films is more provocative of thought than are most serious films of the era. He was as much a cynic as an idealist, and the conflict which that implies is one reason that his films retain their vitality. He was not perhaps a great intellect but he was a great film technician. Do not misunderstand: I love and revere him. He has been patronised: 'Oh Capra! Of course . . . ' but he is beyond patronage. He is a giant in American cinema: it was he who taught Hollywood to think.

*Which concerns the offer of a glass of poisoned elderberry wine.

15

Clowns and Korda

NOT ALL BRITISH films of the Thirties were bad, but to native cinema-goers of the time it often seemed so. The Quota Act of 1927 had worked only too well, and production rose from thirty-one features the previous year to seventy-six in 1928. A number of new companies brought into being because of the Act folded in the shake-up caused by Sound, but in 1932 British studios offered over a hundred features, together with another two score or so for the 'supporting programme'. The latter were known as 'quota quickies', brought in for as little as £4,000 – as opposed to the £30,000 which was the average cost of the very few 'first-class' first features – and many of them were backed by the American companies. Second-rate or slipping American talents arrived to 'help out' the native industry – much as they would do in Italy in the Sixties – and everyone deliberately overlooked the fact that the Quota Act had been initiated to prevent American films predominating in British cinemas.

By this time the leading Hollywood companies had abandoned local renters to establish their own distribution companies, with in some cases production facilities as well. Paramount was notably active in British production, while some local entrepreneurs made exclusive arrangements with the American-owned distributors. The latter were not very discriminating, but when a company called Real Art sold successively to Fox, First National, Radio, M-G-M and United Artists, it was still relieved that it did not have to descend to the locally-owned distributors. The structure of the British industry had reached the state of its American counterpart twenty years earlier – and with as much in-fighting. What talent there

was, however, was more mobile: though most of the entrepreneurs were temperamentally like their American counterparts – European-Jewish, though of more recent extraction – the local climate had softened them to the extent that co-operation was more readily possible.

The wholly British side of the industry remained dominated by the two rival conglomerates, B.I.P. and Gaumont-British. The founder of B.I.P., John Maxwell, had gathered into his fold not only Pathé and First National, distribution offices no longer wanted by their new American owners, but the important A.B.C. circuit – or Associated British Cinemas. From the end of 1936 onwards his companies were whittled down to one name, the Associated British Picture Corporation, or A.B.P.C. On his death in 1941 Warner Bros. bought his shares – cannily, to protect its position as a leading supplier to the circuit, and at a time when, because of the War, American interest in British industry had receded; but despite this twenty-five per cent ownership A.B.P.C. was never a vital force in British production.

Fearful of the competition provided by Maxwell, or perhaps following his example, C. M. Woolf added to his growing Gaumont circuit a number of production companies and distributors, eventually amalgamated into Gaumont-British – though the Gainsborough logo was kept out of deference to Michael Balcon, who became Woolf's Director of Productions in 1932. Balcon realised that the only British films the British public really wanted to see were those with the popular comics of stage and radio, but his recognition and encouragement of talent enabled him to make a

328

few modestly successful more serious pictures, an achievement seemingly denied to other local producers till the advent of Alexander Korda.

Among Balcon's better films are those directed by Victor Saville, including **Hindle Wakes** (1931), the third film version (Saville had produced the second, in 1927, directed by Maurice Elvey) of Stanley Houghton's 1912 Lancashire play, the deliberately Victorian tale of a mill girl (Belle Chrystall) seduced by the boss's son (John Stuart); he wants to marry her but she has different ideas. For all the shots of terrace houses and factories, the film is stagey, while **Michael and Mary** (1932) is even closer to Shaftesbury Avenue, with Herbert Marshall and Edna Best repeating their stage roles. He is a novelist who writes books with titles like 'Sighing Wind' and

'Dream Child', and his cosy world is shattered when a visiting blackmailer, once married to his wife, falls in a struggle and fatally hits his head. An air of smugness is increased by the dachshund charm of Frank Lawton as their son, and his habit of calling his mother 'Bubbles' and his father 'Binks'. A. A. Milne wrote the original play, and Saville achieves a certain atmosphere in the Boer War flashbacks. The professionalism of this then-popular husband and wife team, Marshall and Best may also be found in **The Faithful Heart** (1932); he courts her in a montage of flowers, Gilbert and Sullivan and an evocation of misty moonlight nights along the waterfront. She is a barmaid and he a cocky First Mate: come two wars, and he is high-ranking in the Army, having to choose between their illegitimate daughter (also played by Miss

Victor Saville's charming film of the bestselling novel, *The Good Companions,* is about three non-professionals who join a concert party and have a fine time among the footlights and make-up sticks. From left to right, Denis Hoey, Margery Binner, John Gielgud, Percy Parsons, A. W. Baskcomb, Mary Glynne, Edmund Gwenn, Jessie Matthews, Viola Compton and Richard Dolman.

Jessie Matthews performing the Rodgers and Hart number 'Dancing on the Ceiling' in *Evergreen*. She was famous as a dancer, but it is her personality which now most pleases, with her expression of petulance when she smiles, at which time her chipmunk teeth both ruin her face and enhance it.

the pet projects of Isadore Ostrer, one of Woolf's partners, who so admired the Ufa originals that several co-productions were ordered.

Saville's best film is **The Good Companions** (1933), based on the novel with which J. B. Priestley successfully revived the picaresque tradition. Almost every literate person in Britain had followed the adventures of its three protagonists: Jess Oakroyd (in the film, Edmund Gwenn), a Yorkshire factory worker who loses his job and leaves his nagging wife; Inigo Jollifant (John Gielgud), a teacher at a dank private school in the Fen Country who sets out on his travels after insulting *in vino veritas* the principal's wife; and Miss Trant (Mary Glynne), a spinster who plans to see Britain before her miserable inheritance gives out. Their fortuitous involvement with the Dinky Doos, a stranded concert party, is handled with real affection, the occasional gaucheness part of the charm. Saville catches the atmosphere which is the lot of such troupes, such as the desperation when hot weather keeps customers away and the dressing room camaraderie. The film also reminds us of that time when houses had no electricity and the Great North Road was hardly double-track.

In **Friday the Thirteenth** (1934) a London bus crashes into a shop window and, emulating Thornton Wilder's 'The Bridge of San Luis Rey', the film examines how some half dozen people came to be on it at the time. The omnibus-story film was rare: the trouble with this one is that it is increasingly apparent which of the passengers will be the predestined victims. Featured in both films is Jessie Matthews (1907–81), a toothy, leggy star whose la-di-da accent disguised her humble background. Saville also directed her in the best British musical of the period, **Evergreen** (1934), which had earlier been a success for her when Cochran produced the stage version. As a chorus girl who tries to become a star by impersonating her grandmother, she expresses such determination, together with a surprising seam of sarcasm, that her curious talent is disarming. Her tap dancing is pleasant, but her high kicks and slow-motion jerks, to let the ospreys flow along her arms, now look absurd. Yet when she breaks into the best of the songs she is a pure spirit, certainly more effective on the screen than her rival, Evelyn Laye,

Best) and his fiancée, as in the original play by Monckton Hoffe. The charming period sequences of both films are the invention of Saville and his writer, Robert Stevenson, released from the confines of West End acceptability. However, their confidence fails with **Sunshine Susie** (1932), adapted from the German *Privatsekretarin*. Trying to unite Teutonic cheeriness and that of British musical comedy, they fall between the two stools, with Owen Nares and Jack Hulbert depressingly representing the latter and Renate Müller as the former, plump, willing and obtuse, forever emitting little tinkles of laughter. There were a number of these Anglo-German musicals,

Cedric Hardwicke, Conrad Veidt and Eliot Makeham in *Rome Express*, the quintessential train movie. Since Hardwicke's make-up gives him the appearance of the British publisher Victor Gollancz it is more than likely that the character, a phoney philanthropist, is also based on him.

though the latter was prettier and a better singer. At least, Saville could get little from this lady in **Evensong** (1934), charting the rise and fall of a diva among archdukes and temperamental managers, and based on a bestseller by Beverly Nichols, who had been secretary to Dame Nellie Melba.

I Was a Spy (1933) has a foreword by the then Secretary of State, Winston Churchill, assuring us that what follows is true: a Belgian nurse (Madeleine Carroll) finds war so intolerable that she is drawn into a spy ring with a German orderly (Herbert Marshall), plotting against a German officer (Conrad Veidt). Miss Carroll performs sanctimoniously, and though this is an implausible farrago the readers of *Film Weekly* voted it the best film of the year. And since *Picturegoer* stated categorically that **Rome Express** (1932) was 'the best British film yet made', double confidence was expressed in Woolf's new studio at Shepherd's Bush under Balcon's leadership. The director of this patent copy of *Shanghai Express* is Walter Forde (b. 1896), rattling it along at the pace the engines are

stoked: among the passengers whose paths cross and criss cross are an American film star (Esther Ralston); a suburban couple (Harold Huth, Joan Barry) escaping from their respective spouses; a golf-club bore (Gordon Harker); a philanthropist (Cedric Hardwicke) whose private life is as mean and petty as his public one is showy; and a shifty-eyed fugitive (Donald Calthrop) pursued by two mysterious men (Conrad Veidt and Hugh Williams).

Most of these films were aimed at the international market, and Balcon was encouraged to spend £120,000 – the highest budget for a British film to that time – on **Jew Süss** (1934), partly because Leon Feuchtwanger's novel (under the title 'Power') had been a sensational success in the U.S. In *The Observer* C. A. Lejeune commented that 'it could hardly have been done better', while regretting that the money had not been spent on 'a film of British industry, British agriculture or British mining' instead of one set in a German muncipality two hundred years ago – when Josef Süss Oppenheimer (Conrad Veidt) leaves the ghetto to become financial adviser to Duke Karl Alexander (Frank Vosper) of Württemberg. The complex issues of the novel – not to mention history – are reduced to a simplistic tale of a man too proud to avert his own destruction. Despite simultaneous premieres in London, New York and Toronto the defects were too numerous for transatlantic audiences, unable to accept comic-opera costumes, ludicrous emoting by all the cast except Cedric Hardwicke (as a rabbi), and the snail's pace handling of Lothar Mendes, a Ufa-trained Hollywood director.

If, despite Balcon's demands, the quality of Gaumont-British product was insufficient to ensure bookings overseas, little was to be expected from the other studios. Foreign talents appeared to succumb to the general lethargy; and since their work in Britain is so undistinguished, perhaps it was lack of confidence which caused some refugees to eschew Hollywood, where the standards were more exacting. The producer and director of *Die Strasse*, Max Schach and Karl Grune, made **Abdul the Damned** (1935) with the services of two other compatriots – all were originally from Vienna – Otto Kanturek, who photographed it, and Fritz Kortner, playing the title-role. Abdul Hamid was until Hitler the outstanding tyrant of modern times, and an analogy was clearly intended; ideas and intelligence abound, even if Abdul finally becomes the familiar megalomaniac of the German Silents. But not even Herr Kortner could surmount ineptitude as wholesale as *Jew Süss*.

Thus, though executives of the British film industry welcomed a number of cosmopolitan film-makers from Europe, whose Jewish backgrounds were often similar (albeit more sophisticated) to those of their opposite numbers in Hollywood, they were no more successful in moulding the British film for the foreign market. They found British studios lacked the intense enthusiasm of the German, probably due to the fact that only Balcon and later Korda really cared for the medium, as opposed to using it to make money. So the newcomers settled for mediocrity, compensating themselves with the artistic life of London, so much more substantial than that of Hollywood, which after the shakeup of Talkies, had again transformed the world into its own cultural suburb and,

even before *Cavalcade*, had proved itself able to make a better British film than the British. The Hollywood moguls, we might pause to consider, favoured such tales because they felt so near and so far from the velvet lawns of Empire. They were immigrants and parvenues, yet were attracted to the British (whose manners they aped in their Spanish-colonial drawing rooms) by ambition, a common language and by a taste for wealth. After Korda's first international success more American talent arrived, but they were unable in the event to help the British export either their strictly local product or their manifold imitations of Hollywood.

'British' films poured forth from Hollywood, and though packed with solecisms and accents to match were actually closer to the aspirations of British audiences than the indigenous films of the period, which mostly evoked a country of sporty gentlemen and their servants; all foreigners and the entire working class were irredeemably comic – a view also to be found in the bound volumes of *Punch*. Roy Boulting (q.v.) was once asked why he and his brother chose the cinema as a career, and he gave an answer no American or European would dream of giving. 'It was our nanny, actually' (it turned out that she had taken them to see Valentino). He gave, in fact, the *Punch* view – despite having made some of the worst-ever British movies, as late as the Seventies. The possession of a nanny does not preclude an understanding of audience requirements; George Orwell, after all, came from a household with servants, but the Britain he portrayed in 'Keep the Aspidistra Flying' and 'Coming Up for Air' is nowhere to be found in the films of the time. Concocted by immigrant and dilettante, hack and opportunist, they were as trivial in subject matter as their budgets were small.

The leading players of **No Funny Business** (1933) are three people who were three-quarters of the New York cast of 'Private Lives', one of the funniest comedies of the decade: Gertrude Lawrence, Laurence Olivier (q.v.) and Jill Esmond. Yet this tale of a divorce-bent wife and two professional co-respondents must be the unfunniest film ever made, marooning both Miss Lawrence's gift for comedy and the actors themselves – since they are usually photographed from the calves upwards, playing in uncertain profile to someone just off camera. Its producer-directors, Victor Hanbury and John Stafford, offered another Hollywood name, Victor McLaglen, in the title-role of **Dick Turpin** (1933), flailing about in a hopeless attempt to make the script comprehensible. **The Return of Bulldog Drummond** (1934) is insulting, since it turned up around the same time as Ronald Colman's second Drummond film. This one involves Drummond (Ralph Richardson) in the question of European rearmament till descending to a plot that would seem puerile even to admirers of *Fantômas* or James Bond. Walter Summers directed for B.I.P., but that company brought over an American director and players for **I Spy** (1933) – Ben Lyon to be mistaken for a secret agent, and Sally Eilers; but although Allan Dwan hurries matters along the limits of the genre are extended till they snap.

If such films were written off by spectators beforehand the thrall of cinema was such that few considered arriving only for the main feature – whose starting times were not featured in adverts, though 'Continuous Performance' was. It was not till the Fifties (in the U.S. and Britain) that audiences finally shook off the nickelodeon habit of dropping into a cinema with no regard for continuity – hence the expression, 'This is where I came in'. Among the few British films to play main attractions – other, that is, than in what the trade called 'indiscriminating halls' – were those starring the popular comic artists of the day. Both Gracie Fields and George Formby came from Lancashire, to be perplexed in their films by 'daft' city ways: it was perhaps because they did not betray their origins that they became national heroes (also in the Commonwealth, but they remained 'foreign' to Americans). Never before – and radio was also responsible – had the British been as aware of the diversity of their countrymen.

Gracie Fields (1898–1979) was unquestionably the most beloved entertainer the British have ever produced. After an amazingly successful career in music hall she made **Sally in Our Alley** (1931), directed by Maurice Elvey, from a play, 'The Likes of 'er'. The new title took advantage of her theme song, and it is no surprise to find her the darling of the *quartier,* with a bustling North Country common-sense and con-

fidence. Her boss wants to marry her and put her name above the café: 'It might look nice up there,' she agrees, 'but not down here,' and her pause before the qualification is beautifully timed. When a waiter is sacked for dancing with her at a charity ball, she offers to share her fee but does not insist when he refuses. As a screen actress she tends to play to the gallery, but has a warm sense of humour, often directed against herself, and – it is a quality rare in film stars – a huge liking for people. Basil Dean, the powerful theatre manager who also ran A.T.P. – Associated Talking Pictures – put her under contract while trying to make up his mind whether her forte was clowning or romance, her dentures and broad face being something of a dampener for the latter. She loathed filming, and simply did her duty for the audiences of the Depression with **Looking on the Bright Side** (1932), directed by Dean and Graham Cutts, the adventures of a manicurist in show business, and **Love, Life and Laughter** (1934), directed by Maurice Elvey, the adventures of a barmaid in love with a foreign prince (John Loder). Borrowing badly from Lubitsch and Clair, Dean later admitted that he grew tired 'of the caustic references by critics to the poverty of the material dished out to Britain's "£2-a-minute star" . . . the fact that much of the criticism was justified only made matters worse.'

He persuaded J. B. Priestley to write the stories for her next two films, which he himself directed, and of them **Sing As We Go** (1934) is at least ingratiating. As an unemployed millgirl forgetting her troubles in Blackpool, Miss Fields made the title song an anthem of the Depression especially with audiences in the most distressed areas who normally took their own holidays in Blackpool. Dean used extensive location footage, and although he enjoyed filming what he called *les actualités* he seems not to have realised that it was that, and the star in a recognisably demotic background, which was the reason for the film's great popularity.

Five writers were employed to assemble **Queen of Hearts** (1936), and a former Hollywood gagman and director, Monty Banks – whom the star later married – was brought in to impart Hollywood gloss; but the film is merely a long-winded farce about a seamstress with a crush on a matinee

Clowns and Korda

The singer and stage star Gracie Fields, centre, was a British institution in the Thirties, and consequently the films she made were enormously popular in the domestic market – if few of them were very good. The best is unquestionably *Sing As We Go*, and here she leads her fellow factory-workers to end the film on a high note – singing the title-song, which became an anthem for British workers during the Depression.

idol (John Loder). In two earlier films with this actor Fields had lost him to other ladies, but this time, between a number of comic routines – and an admirably perfunctory rendering of the title song – she was glamorous enough to aspire successfully. Although none of these films had been shown in the U.S., one American mogul, Darryl F. Zanuck, decided that Fields could reach an American audience, and he paid her an enormous salary to do it: but when her first film for 20th Century-Fox, *We're Going to Be Rich,* failed to impress his compatriots he was only prepared to spend miniscule amounts on her two subsequent British-made films for the company.

If bad films prevented Gracie Fields from finding American acceptance, there was little chance for George Formby (1904–61), who replaced her as A.T.P.'s chief asset. He also came to films from the halls; he played the ukelele, he had a soppy-but-happy grin, and his humour was strictly knockabout. His songs, if not his dialogue, were thick

with sexual innuendo, accompanied by a leer intended to convey to audiences that their interpretation is not his. By the time he made his first film for Dean, **No Limit** (1935), the latter had learnt the lesson of *Sing As We Go,* assigning the screenplay to another leading dramatist, Walter Greenwood, and virtually duplicating the story – by sending the star to a seaside resort, in fact the Isle of Man for the T.T. races. Banks directed, but most of the A.T.P. Formby films were made by Anthony Kimmins, who also wrote them in conjunction with Austin Melford, plus a number of other writers – many of whom would work on the later Ealing comedies (q.v.). In humour seemingly borrowed from Donald McGill's saucy postcards, they put him through the usual paces – bus conductor, airman, store clerk, invariably clumsy and stupid but inevitably besting the pompous high-ups who have the mischance to cross his path; he also manages to wrest the leading lady from his rivals – usually public school smoothies like Guy Middleton in *Keep Fit,* or in most of the other films the dangerously apoplectic Garry Marsh. The Formby vehicles, if simple-minded, have energy; the best is probably **Trouble Brewing** (1939), in which George, after creating havoc at a society party – dislodging by accident a girl's skirt and on purpose, or intending to, the garter of the very grand Martita Hunt – takes a somersault across the kitchen that is worthy of Keaton.

Jack Buchanan (1891–1957) was an upper-class Formby, to the extent that they were embroiled in similar situations. Remembered as an elegant song-and-dance man, he was in fact a poor dancer, as he well knew, though his light, slightly nasal tenor can still give pleasure, as in two of the most charming songs of the period, the title tune of **Goodnight Vienna** (1932) and 'Fancy Our Meeting' from **That's a Good Girl** (1933). Herbert Wilcox directed the first of these films, laboriously, and it was he who signed Buchanan for his British & Dominions company. Since Buchanan was a Broadway star and had made two Hollywood features, Wilcox was encouraged to seek American distribution, and made a commitment to United Artists. With *That's a Good Girl,* which Buchanan also directed, established a team, to include an experienced Hollywood writer, Ralph Spence, and an American music director, Van Phillips. For **Brewster's Millions** (1935) he imported from Hollywood Lily Damita and Thornton Freeland, who had directed *Flying Down to Rio* (whose most famous number was here plagiarised as 'The Caranga'); Fay Wray arrived to make **Come Out of the Pantry** (1935) and **When Knights Were Bold** (1936), and though both were directed by a Britisher, Jack Raymond, the former is significantly set in New York. Not only were some of these films based on old farces which had been as popular in the U.S. as in Britain, but the pacing was as fast as American audiences demanded. However, those few actually submitted to the latter were instantly rejected – with good reason, for they are of poor quality. Buchanan himself is hardly an asset: unflappable, insouciant and given to facetiousness, he is much too forced, as if trying to atone for the weakness of the material.

Nevertheless, he did produce one outstanding film, unjustly overlooked (by, for instance, *Film Weekly,* which referred to the succeeding, abysmal film – **The Gang's All Here** (1939), one of his *Thin Man* imitations, directed by Freeland – as 'just about the best' Buchanan made.) René Clair directed **Break the News** (1938), having suggested to Buchanan this remake of *La Morte en Fuite*. He had not intended to make it himself, but in view of the uncertain financial climate he agreed to do it in place of the two films for which he was contracted. The material he has not only transformed into a more typical film than *The Ghost Goes West* (q.v.), but one infinitely better; its twisting narrative is genially satiric at the expense of some of his customary targets – the press and the theatre. He is most inventive at the beginning, as two chorus boys battle for the attention, professional or amatory, of the star (June Knight), a shallow publicity-hunting bitch: and it remains joyous as well as surprising when one of them, supposedly murdered by the other, becomes involved in a European revolution – one of the few truly comic revolutions of the movies. Cole Porter provided one song, and with Maurice Chevalier as co-star, almost yanking Buchanan to his level, this was the latter's best bet in his avowed attempt to win over the U.S. – but when it opened there three years later, released by Monogram, the stars were old hat and the critics grudging.

Buchanan's films were not what Joseph P. Schenck had had in mind when he contracted with British & Dominions in his desperate need to find a flow of product for United Artists (after his own Artcinema group had proved unsuccessful) – and Buchanan in this period moved first to Woolf and then to Maxwell, amicably placating Wilcox by making a guest appearance in one of his musicals, *Limelight.* Earlier, when Woolf had lost the B & D franchise, he had ordered Balcon to hire at any cost its chief assets, Buchanan and the team of farceurs, Ralph Lynn and Tom Walls, associated with film versions of plays in which they had rocked audiences at the Aldwych Theatre. Lynn and Walls succumbed, the latter continuing to double as director, at which he became reasonably proficient after an unpromising start. Lynn, over fifty at this time, continued to play juveniles, and a further deterrent to laughter is the complacent playing of both actors: but the real trouble is the material, as was usual with adaptations by Ben Travers of his own plays or when written directly by him for the screen. Audiences today are only likely to enjoy the misanthropic boom of bald, put-upon Robertson Hare in supporting roles, but just bearable is **Cuckoo in the Nest** (1933), with Lynn locked trouserless in a hotel bedroom with another man's wife, and the rest of the cast on its way to discovering that fact. Because its American director, Tim Whelan, was more amenable than Walls to Balcon's dictum on pacing, **It's a Boy** (1933) is far funnier; it also has a much more accomplished team, Edward Everett Horton and Leslie Henson, playing respectively an ageing bridegroom and a conniver who claims to be his son. Balcon hoped, vainly, that the film's reception would prove to the overweening Walls that the Aldwych team was not indispensable.

Balcon was also having trouble with a far more formidable figure, Robert Flaherty, who, unable to find backing in his own country, was working for the Empire Marketing Board (q.v.). **Man of Aran** (1934) was intended to silence those critics who regarded Gaumont-British as capable of little more than farce and melodrama. There is no plot; the only dialogue is heard in the distance; it is virtually an abstract film, an impression of the endless sea – and it is better to regard it as such, for its documentary value is nil. The climactic fight with the basking sharks was a reconstruction, for it was sixty years since the islanders had engaged in that activity – and as they had had electricity for years they did not need, as the film maintains, oil for lamps. Nor is there any mention of the twin causes of the poverty – the landlords, who escalated the rents whenever there was even a half-good seaweed crop, and the Depression, which had curtailed the subsistence money sent by relatives in the U.S. As usual, the critics called Flaherty a poet and a visionary, a view only half-shared by Balcon, who noted sourly in his memoirs that the film cost twice its original appropriation. Business was so bad on the Gaumont circuit that it took several subsequent changes of programme before receipts returned to normal.

The word 'documentary' had been coined by John Grierson (1898–1972) when discussing Flaherty: and if Flaherty was the Christ figure of the documentary movement, said John Mortimer, the dramatist (*New Statesman,* 4 May 1979), Grierson was its St Paul. The British documentary movement began in 1928, when the government set up the Empire Marketing Board under Sir Stephen Tallents, who included among its forty-five departments a film unit, organised by Grierson. Fascinated by the potentiality of film to educate, Grierson had earlier approached Tallents with a scheme to make films 'in the national interest' – by which he meant also in the Soviet manner. Certainly **Drifters** (1929), a study of the herring fishing industry, was cut to Soviet patterns and conformed to a belief in the common man. Its reception was such that Grierson persuaded Tallents to expand the unit and invite Flaherty to join it. Flaherty began **Industrial Britain** (1933), but despite a larger budget than usual was removed from the project while photographing the traditional crafts which were to provide the contrast to the 'new' Britain; Grierson completed it, assembling thirty minutes of well-composed images. The commentary, however, is only too typical of the British documentary movement, running from the trite ('You cannot afford to think of industrial Britain without thinking of its steel-works') to the chauvinistic ('It will take some other country a generation to catch up with our quality').

The Empire Marketing Board did not long survive, but the film section was transferred to the Post Office where, as the G.P.O. Film Unit, it continued to train young film-makers. The best-known of them worked on **Night Mail** (1936), produced by Grierson, directed by Basil Wright and Harry Watt, with Cavalcanti (a Brazilian who had designed and directed in the French film industry) responsible for the recording of the music by Britten and words by Auden. It is an account of the night mail from London to Edinburgh, well-edited and unpretentious, but it cannot be said to be more revealing than the documentary passages of *Rome Express*. Paul Rotha, another leader of the movement, made **Today We Live** (1936), 'A Portrait of Life in Britain Today', which contrasts in a perfunctory way villages coping with the Depression in the Rhondda valley and Gloucestershire. Rotha later observed that Grierson 'produced very good film technically but the people in them were mostly the men behind the machine; you knew nothing about them'. Nor, with one exception, did the makers of these pictures, their *de haut en bas* attitude revealed only too clearly by their commentaries, written with patronage and usually spoken with a monotonous solemnity.

It may be significant that only one of this group tried to use the spoken word as little as possible and he, Humphrey Jennings (1907–50), is its one major figure. 'Let's go down and see Humphrey being nice to the common people,' said Grierson, as recalled by a colleague, Denis Forman, who went on to remark that Jennings 'had in every sense an aristocratic mind, his sympathy not so much with the refinements of culture as with the sturdy, vigorous and romantic virtues of English working people. He had no personal contact with them and no experience of their ways from the inside and yet, like Lord Shaftesbury in an earlier century and another sphere, he was passionately sincere in his admiration for their qualities.' This interest and admiration are exemplified best in Jennings's wartime documentaries (q.v.), but his fifteen-minute **Spare Time** (1939) is a warm-hearted and eloquent study, without one false note, of the urban British at their leisures. His colleagues disapproved of it, claiming that it was not educational.

The claims made on behalf of the other British documentarists have always been extravagant, partly because many of them were also writers on film, locked in mutual admiration. They were also either unable or unwilling to work within the commercial sector of the industry, which is not necessarily to their discredit. Technically inventive, their films, partly because of the commentaries, rendered numb all but spectators interested in such aspects. Later, when the requirements of the War turned documentary into propaganda, Grierson's claims for it were rendered even more hollow★. Mortimer, who worked with him then, said, 'How wrong he was! In fact the truth told about wartime in England by documentary films was far less, and even less courageous, than the truth told about

1930s America by the box office movies which Grierson despised . . . We falsified the whole feeling of a great period of history.' With the exception noted, the comment stands against the British documentarists as a whole.

They did not lie in presenting Britain as having great gulfs in wealth and class, but it was a view which they offered unwittingly: their Britain is remote, unlike that of the Balcon films, where it is, more accurately, predominantly cosy. The Britain of the foreigner, Alexander Korda, is one of traditional values. It may be said of Korda that the British film industry needed him as much as he needed it – which was considerably. Though Britain was one of the few leading production centres in which he had not yet worked, he was an Anglophile, convinced that with a galvanising spirit like himself the British could produce movies as much in demand abroad as their other goods. His reasoning, however, had a vital flaw – and it undermined the quality of every film he made. The best Hungarian film he had ever seen, he said, was *L'Image,* made in Vienna by the Belgian-born Feyder: he may be forgiven for thinking that he and the motley-languaged crew he gathered about him could make better films than the British, but he seems never to have taken cognisance of the fact that the Feyders of this world are thin upon the ground and that, when found, work best undisturbed. His interference was partly the result of making a phenomenally successful film almost immediately: the fact that it was what he considered a wholly British subject only augmented his self-deception.

After making *Marius,* he was sent across the Channel by Paramount, dissatisfied with its British operation. Of the two contracted films one was abandoned, but the other, *Service for Ladies,* a comedy with Leslie Howard, was sufficiently liked for the company to enter into an undertaking with London Film Productions, which Korda had formed with mainly City money. Five failures left Paramount uninterested in the prospect of another, and a sixth, part-financed and released by Woolf – **Wedding Rehearsal** (1932), a supposedly frothy society comedy with Roland Young – meant that he too passed when offered **The Private Life of Henry VIII** (1933).

★'. . . [It] can achieve an intimacy of knowledge and effect impossible to shim-sham mechanics of the studio and the lily-fingered interpretations of the metropolitan actor.' ('Grierson on Documentary').

Charles Laughton in the film that made him world-famous, *The Private Life of Henry VIII.* He was one of the few character actors to become a major star in both American and British films, and one of the few stars constantly to change his appearance, probably emulating Werner Krauss and Emil Jannings and certainly, like them, seizing on 'show-off' roles with gusto.

It was intended as a vehicle for Charles Laughton (1899-1962), then making his American reputation, and his wife, Elsa Lanchester – a keyhole biography of the monarch, as written by Lajos Biro and Arthur Wimperis in the style of Korda's Hollywood film on Helen of Troy. Laughton's salary was the largest item in the budget which, despite extraordinary economies, escalated to a final cost of £59,000. Paramount, which held Laughton's American contract, passed again when asked for completion money, despite the offer of *The Rise of Catherine the Great* (q.v.) in outright sale. United Artists, urgently in need of quality product, invested in both, after Schenck and Goldwyn had both read the revised script – but only after assent had come from Herbert Wilcox, who had exclusive rights to supply that company with British films. A

final, desperate bid obtained a sum from Ludovico Toeplitz de Grand Ry, a former engineer who had been financing films in Italy, but his interference was such that in settlement he was offered ownership of either the finished film or that of *The Girl from Maxim's*, just completed in Paris: by choosing the latter he deprived himself of the half-million pounds that *Henry* made on its first release.

There are several reasons for the film's success of which the only interesting one is Laughton, even if he plays Henry as a crusty old buffer with a heart of gold rather than the syphilitic despot he was becoming at the time the film opens. When it announces that we shall not meet Catherine of Aragon, 'a respectable woman and therefore not very interesting', we recognise the tone not of the *Helen* film but of '1066 and All that'. Less agreeably modern – with the exception of Lanchester's Anne of Cleves – are the queens and court ladies, badly directed by Korda; the sets by his brother Vincent, though elegant, seldom resemble those Tudor residences left to us. Public concern with royal wedding and bedding – indicated by extras with warming pans – should certainly be mentioned as additional factors in the film's popularity, breaking records at Radio City Music Hall; and Laughton's Best Actor Oscar was a further distinction undreamed-of for a British film. A preview so impressed Douglas Fairbanks that United Artists rewrote its contract with Wilcox so that Korda could supply, with financial participation, sixteen further films for American distribution.

The same formula was used for Fairbanks himself, and as written by Wimperis and Frederick Lonsdale it is much more erudite: **The Private Life of Don Juan** (1934), directed by Korda, makes much play of the great lover's reputation and his middle-aged response to living up to it – but the star is unimpressive, and when the film failed he decided to retire from acting. His son, Doug Junior, misunderstands the Grand Duke Paul in **The Rise of Catherine the Great** (1934), playing him as a petulant rake, and if the china-doll Catherine of Elisabeth Bergner is hardly less likely, neither character is really suitable to the keyhole approach. Claimed to be based on the same source as *Forbidden Paradise,* the two films have little in common but the character of Catherine, this one striving, as in Von Sternberg's film, to make her an acceptable heroine. As with many Korda films, it is eventually neither one thing nor the other; his insistence on taking over so much of the direction from Paul Czinner resulted in both Czinner and Bergner refusing to work with him again. Toeplitz was also involved, and for his first film as an independent, **The Dictator** (1935), he emulated Korda by choosing an historical subject and Hollywood-British names for the leads, Clive Brook and Madeleine Carroll. His meddling caused Victor Saville to make his worst film as a director, and even the supposedly topical title is a mistake, since Benn Levy's script has nothing pertinent to say about the Hamburg doctor, Struensee (Brook), who became a protégé of an eighteenth-century Danish king (Emlyn Williams) and later cuckolded him with his English-born queen.

Korda himself, seeking that American public which had proved unresponsive since *Henry*, offered **The Scarlet Pimpernel** (1934), from an eternal bestseller by a compatriot, Baroness Orczy, which had somehow been missed by the film companies; and he brought in a team of Americans – Roland V. Brown to direct, though he was replaced by another American, Korda's editor Harold Young; Robert E. Sherwood and S. N. Behrman to assist Wimperis and Biro on the screenplay; and Harold Rosson to photograph it, instead of the customary Georges Périnal. The result is oddly anaemic: the film's success was almost certainly due to its story – a good one of its kind, about an English milord who saves French aristos from the guillotine – and the performances of Leslie Howard (1893–1943), light of eye as the foppish Sir Percy, and Raymond Massey as the spider-legged villain. As the Prince Regent, Nigel Bruce has a reference to contemporary events: 'But if a country goes mad it has the right to commit whatever horror it chooses within its own walls.'

Sherwood stayed on to write **The Ghost Goes West** (1935), and two American players, Jean Parker and Eugene Pallette, supported Robert Donat (q.v.), who had recently made his Hollywood debut; the director was René Clair, offering a notably unfunny prologue – how a laird's son loves war less than the lassies. The laird's descendant (also Donat) offers some mild fun

trying to stave off creditors, and though there are some satiric notes on the American love of publicity, matters become too desperate for a film which had announced itself as fantasy. Korda reshot much of it: enthusiastic reviews placated Clair, but when they could not agree on material two further contracted films were not made and Clair moved on to Jack Buchanan.

However, if another director from France, Jacques Feyder, was below his best for Korda, that may have been due to the exigencies of the star, Marlene Dietrich. Also crossing the Atlantic for **Knight Without Armour** (1937) was Frances Marion, to help Wimperis and Biro on the screenplay, based on a novel by James Hilton. Graham Greene, noting the budget (over £300,000, of which a huge slice went to Dietrich) anticipated 'the traditional Denham mouse' but found 'a first-class thriller has emerged', citing one scene to rank with the Odessa Steps sequence in *Potemkin* – that in the deserted railway station, reverberating with the eerie vastness of Russia, its railways a link in isolations made worse by revolution. Feyder and his art director, Lazare Meerson, convey the confusion, but in the midst of the ruins is Dietrich, as a Grand Duchess carried to safety by an English spy (Donat), opening her eyes wide to express fear. At one point, in an army outpost, she finds and dons a ball gown which must have cost almost as much as her salary.

There are no such weaknesses in **Rembrandt** (1936), which Korda himself directed, over-reverently, and which Laughton plays with too much virtuosity. Miss Lanchester and Gertrude Lawrence are the contrasting women in the painter's life, which is not to say that this is the usual Korda view of historical personages. Carl Zuckmayer's 'Scenes from the Life of an Artist' screenplay finds the painter in decline. With Laughton's concurrence the portrait is closer than most in suggesting the artist's absorption in his work.

The film failed with the public, but **Things to Come** (1936) raised Korda's prestige to its peak. He persuaded H. G. Wells to write the screenplay, and brought back from Hollywood William Cameron Menzies to direct. Later it was said that Wells prophesied the outbreak of World War II, which could not have been difficult at that time; here it begins in 1940 and lasts twenty years. In 1966, a newspaper – price £4 sterling – headlines the 'Wandering Sickness'; in 1970, the world is putting itself to rights and another dictator – played grotesquely by Ralph Richardson – is put down by an organisation for World Peace. We move forward to the City of the Future, in 2036 – and to what is most memorable about the film: the art direction of Vincent Korda, one of Alex's two brothers. Time has wrecked many of the concepts; there is an absence of ideas when it comes to plot, and the dialogue is didactic and naive – but the combination of sets, special effects (by Ned Mann and Co.) and Périnal's photography remains stunning. Naivety is also the keynote of **The Man Who Could Work Miracles** (1936), adapted by Wells from one of his own stories, with a Hollywood director, Lothar Mendes, and Roland Young in the title role – a draper's assistant who calls the world's leaders together to harangue them on the chaos they have created. Young, dropping his aitches, is not well cast, and Richardson is again disastrous, as an ageing alcoholic colonel.

If both films were widely discussed they still needed paying patrons, and *Things to Come* at least was too costly to be profitable. Nonetheless, to the outsider Korda had succeeded beyond all expectations: this one-time Hollywood dropout was publicly welcomed into United Artists, even if its principals knew privately that he was buying in on deferred terms. His other chief backer, the Prudential Assurance Co., had built him a new studio complex at Denham in Buckinghamshire, but by the time it was officially opened, in 1936, the company's losses had swelled from £30,000 the previous year to £330,000. It was not simply a question of unprofitable films; there were scripts commissioned that were never used, and actors under contract similarly idle – which was true of the Hollywood studios also, but at least they were run efficiently. Denham was not – filming seldom began before midday – and at the end of 1938 the Prudential relieved Korda of the task of running the studio. Earlier he had made a half-hearted effort to utilise its resources by doubling his output. He said that he could not make 'bread-and-butter pictures', so apart from renting out the seven sound stages to other companies he arranged for certain independents to work under the London Films banner.

Chief among these is Victor Saville, though he started with what was obviously a Korda project, **Dark Journey** (1937), an unconvincing spy story by Biro and Wimperis, relying for its appeal on its cosmopolitan background and the uncertain star teaming of Conrad Veidt and Korda's new discovery, Vivien Leigh (1913–67). She is also in **Storm in a Teacup** (1937), another hybrid, an Austrian comedy reset by James Bridie in his native Scotland, concerning a crusading journalist (Rex Harrison) who exposes the bullying of the provost (Cecil Parker) and battles for civic responsibility. This Capra imitation, co-directed by Ian Dalrymple, virtually introduced 'social concern' into the British film, and if Saville went further in **South Riding** (1938) it is because its source, 'an English landscape by Winifred Holtby', had been a bestseller. A posthumous tribute to her at the beginning is ironic, since her left-wing bias has gone, and the thrills of the Council Chamber, as promised, are abandoned for the romance between an impoverished squire (Richardson) and the new schoolmistress (Edna Best). Saville considered this his best film, but the social contrasts, if typical of their time, are objectionable: the lady bountiful (Marie Lohr) who arranges for a home help so that the brilliant, motherless young girl can write essays, thus proving that the family's dedication to the community survives after four hundred years; and the asthmatical Labour member (John Clements), stupid enough to be taken in by scoundrels, being magnanimously pardoned.

Korda did make bread-and-butter films and they are typical of the very mediocrity against which his operation was, in theory, dedicated, further demonstrating what happens to normally efficient Hollywood talents away from home. **Men Are Not Gods** (1936), directed by Walter Reisch from one of his own screenplays, offers Miriam Hopkins in a battery of close-ups as a fan caught between an Othello-playing actor (Sebastian Shaw) and his Desdemona and wife (Gertrude Lawrence); **The Squeaker** (1937), directed by William K. Howard from a novel by Edgar Wallace, has Edmund Lowe and an appallingly well-bred ingenue, Ann Todd, in a London exclusively populated by toffs in evening dress, underworld characters and Scotland Yard men. Another American, Tim Whelan, struggled with poor material in a supposed comedy, **The Divorce of Lady X** (1938), a remake of one of Korda's Paramount quickies, and **Q Planes** (1939), a thick-ear job that was part of Korda's new deal with Columbia, enabling them to meet quota requirements and him his large weekly payroll. Its cinematographer was Harry Stradling, whose credits included *La Kermesse Héroïque* (q.v.), but more importantly both films waste the talents of two actors making considerable stage reputations at the Old Vic Theatre, Laurence Olivier (b. 1907) and the variable Richardson – both playing however with authority and a seemingly effortless comic skill which few young actors today can match.

Korda also gave chances to artists like Robert Donat (1905–58), Flora Robson and John Clements, but his promotion of Merle Oberon, though understandable since he eventually married her, does not redound to his credit. Because of her, Technicolor was used for **Over the Moon** – only the second British picture in that process – and *The Divorce of Lady X*, though it failed to entail the success of either. In fact the former was a disaster: an attempt at sophisticated comedy by several Korda writers, including Wimperis, Biro and Robert E. Sherwood, and directed by Thornton Freeland (and the uncredited and by now alcoholic Howard). It was shelved – so that technically it could remain a financial asset rather than a liability. Released on the instructions of Korda's creditors in 1940, as London Films was being wound up, it was accompanied by two other films with Olivier, the equally old and dire **Twenty-One Days** and the even older **The Conquest of the Air,** the latter started in 1936 and in fact never completed. As a semi-documentary – part-written and directed by John Monk Saunders – it was, however, releasable, even if few saw it; and few saw the mayhem that is *Twenty-One Days*, despite the current popularity of Olivier and his co-star, Vivien Leigh. One who did was Graham Greene, who noted in his *Spectator* review that the screenplay by himself and Basil Dean, who directed, was culled from a particularly unfilmable story by Galsworthy. He did not make excuses, but significantly had praise only for Hay Petrie, an exceptional character actor, playing a former priest turned vagrant.

Korda's most celebrated disaster was **I, Claudius,** with Charles Laughton as the Emperor in this adaptation of Robert Graves's novel. Josef von Sternberg directed, – at the suggestion of Marlene Dietrich, who accordingly waived the last instalment of her fee for *Knight Without Armour*. When Oberon, the female lead, was injured in a car crash, Korda negotiated for the insurance due on the film, probably settling for a sum in excess of what he expected it to earn: but a secondary reason would certainly have been the lack of any rapport between Laughton and von Sternberg. Because of their reputations, this remains the most famous of the many hundreds of abandoned films in cinema history. The reputation of its producer is also involved in this interest – and the anomalies which contributed to it. Korda's love of cinema and his will to make good movies were recognised by even those colleagues who deplored his methods – and though he achieved less than his few respected Hollywood counterparts he is the only European producer to have made a similar impact on world audiences.

That fact is all the more remarkable in that the only enduring entertainments of his pre-war output are his tributes to the British spirit. Like many another naturalised citizen, his patriotism was excessive, and it must be said at once that his first 'Empire' film, **Sanders of the River**

The multi-talented Paul Robeson – law student, football player, singer and actor – made less than ten films, all but two unworthy of him. It is pleasant to hear him sing Mischa Spoliansky's authetically-based melodies in *Sanders of the River*; not so the spectacle of a great artist rigged out as a comic cannibal king, humble before the superior British.

(1935) has only historic value. This tribute to that 'handful of white men whose everyday work is an unsung saga of courage and efficiency' was adapted from a novel by Edgar Wallace, admired by Korda for its portrait of a supposedly ordinary District Commissioner – though only remnants remain in this tale of the two rival rulers whom he (Leslie Banks) sorts out. He tells Bosambo (Paul Robeson) that the secret of the British is that their kings are not feared but loved, which brings a sung tribute from Bosambo to his wisdom. Robeson deeply regretted making the film, having only agreed to participate on the strength of the ethnographic material – which is also what had attracted the director, Zoltan Korda (1895–1961), Alex's brother, who was making only his second film. With typical Korda inefficiency two units were sent to Africa to obtain background material, both working from different scripts. Zoltan and his co-director, Robert Flaherty, shot endless location footage for **Elephant Boy** (1937), with more ordered results, despite the dissension seemingly inevitable on a

Flaherty project. The version of Kipling ('Toomai of the Elephants') agreed upon became a whittling down of usable footage, plus a plot filmed among the luxurious new jungles of Denham. It is not helped by blacked-up white actors, but there are enough ravishing shots of elephants bathing, and the like, to hold the attention; and Sabu, in the title-role, is an admirable young hero.

Fire Over England (1937) belongs to this group of films, despite a German producer (Erich Pommer), an American director (William K. Howard) and photographer (James Wong Howe), a French designer (Meerson), and a Russian (Sergei Nolbandov) as co-writer with Clemence Dane. The source is a novel by A.E.W. Mason, chosen because Korda wanted to make a film about Henry VIII's daughter. As Elizabeth I, Flora Robson is as avuncular as George Arliss but this is no irreverent look at royalty: it is an excuse for the swashbuckling of Olivier, as perky and determined as a young eagle. Because of expense, the Armada has to be disposed of

Korda the Imperialist

in three minutes flat, but it is anyhow only a *raison d'étre* – for Elizabeth's speech at Tilbury – meant to be relevant to current European rearmament.

The Drum (1938) is also based on a novel by Mason, a story of trouble on the North-West frontier, which on this evidence has as many holes as a piece of Gruyère. The film is unfortunate in a number of other ways: an ersatz India, with Wales doing duty for the Himalayas; direction by Zoltan Korda as stilted as the dialogue; a hero called Carruthers (Roger Livesey), who says 'Good grief, that's torn it' when his marriage proposal is accepted, and a heroine (Valerie Hobson), who wears silver lamé to a Government House reception. However, it has a rousing spirit: what matters is the skirl of the pipes as the army marches through the green hills. the following year *Gunga Din* (q.v.) would use such ingredients even better, but it does not have Technicolor.

The colour, both literal and figurative, is again superb in **The Four Feathers** (1939), partnering the same author and director,

though Zoltan's work has become more assured. The subject is conscience and Imperialism, specifically about a man who does not want to fight – by definition a man unwilling to protect the Empire. Harry Faversham (John Clements) makes the mistake of putting his own estates above Empire, and though his atonement – facing a million perils disguised as a native bearer – is excessive, few would have questioned his error in 1902, when the book was published, or, more importantly, at the time this film was made – when, it should be said, this view of military ethics did not seem as nostalgic as it essentially was. Neither film, of course, reflected revisionist thinking on Empire, which remained populated with either cannibalistic fuzzy-wuzzies or benevolent white traders and soldiers, united in their divine right to rule and protect the more docile of the former's kinfolk.

The success of *The Four Feathers* came too late to restore Korda's position with his financiers. **The Thief of Bagdad** (1940) is of the same quality, despite chaotic

The Drum ABOVE was set on the North-West frontier of India and in sheer excitement rivals the many Hollywood movies with that setting. In this picture villain Raymond Massey, second from right, confers with his cohorts.

343

changes. Ludwig Berger was replaced by Michael Powell and Tim Whelan, all of whom are credited, but the direction was also undertaken by Zoltan, Alex and William Cameron Menzies. However, from the first shot of sun-caught galleons, magic abounds. Using, with consent, the Fairbanks subtitle, 'An Arabian Nights Fantasy', this has little else in common, Biro having contributed a marvellous pastiche of such tales. One might wish less fustian in the dialogue of Miles Malleson, and a more virile hero than John Justin, with his Gielgudesque delivery; but Sabu is cute in the title-role, and Rex Ingram ★ does lots of ho-hoes as the djinni fifty feet tall. The Oscars awarded to Vincent Korda for Color Art Direction and to Périnal were richly deserved. The film was, finally, an American production, Korda having announced that since wartime conditions prevented the location-shots needed in Africa, he had transferred filming to Hollywood. In truth, with the outbreak of war and the loss of the European market, the Prudential had finally decided to cut its losses, and only with the customary Hollywood control was United Artists willing to continue with Korda's services.

That Korda's achievements, if often illusory, overshadowed those of Michael Balcon did not surprise Balcon, since he was neither interested in credit nor personal publicity. They may be regarded as the founding fathers of the British film industry, certainly with more varied and interesting pictures to their credit than the only other claimant, Herbert Wilcox.

Balcon himself said later that his programme at Gaumont-British fell into six categories: 1. the Hitchcock pictures; 2. the Jessie Matthews vehicles; 3. the Anglo-German films; 4. the comedies for home consumption; 5. the George Arliss vehicles; 6. the 'epics' made with an eye on the American market. The last two categories may be regarded as the same, for Arliss was a Hollywood star – if a fading one, which was why Balcon signed him only under protest. Gaumont's American subsidiary, distributing **The Iron Duke** (1935), must have been discouraged to find it relegated to the back pages of *Photoplay* and dismissed as

★The American black actor, not to be confused with the M-G-M director of the Silent Period.

'worthwhile' – which it certainly is not now: a weak romantic intrigue set around a dingily-staged Waterloo. directed by Victor Saville, with Arliss even less convincing, if possible, than in previous historical manifestations.

Among the 'epics' are **The Clairvoyant** (1935) and **The Tunnel** (1935), fast-paced but clumsy in Maurice Elvey's direction. The first, about a phoney mind-reader (Claude Rains) uses for climax the elaborate sets of the second which, predictably, makes a plea for Anglo-American unity (unlike its German original); but the presence of several Hollywood players, including Richard Dix and Walter Huston (as the U.S. president), can hardly have overcome its defects for American audiences. For them, only the title of **Non-Stop New York** (1937) could have been appealing, since it is a silly thriller with a Scotland Yard man (John Loder) climbing on the roof of an out-of-control airliner over the Atlantic. Robert Stevenson directed, and he made a much better job of **King Solomon's Mines** (1937), despite poor integration of the material shot in the studio and on location: none of the five leading players (only their doubles) went to Africa, and since the film concerns their journey through desert, bush and mountain, that is a handicap. They include Cedric Hardwicke, Roland Young, and, as their guide, Paul Robeson, singing some Spoliansky songs, as he did in *Sanders of the River*. This film is better than both that one and M-G-M's later version (q.v.) of the Rider Haggard tale.

Also, ever since *Evergreen* had played Radio City Music Hall the Jessie Matthews films had been angled towards American audiences. That particular film was emulated by **First a Girl** (1935) and **It's Love Again** (1936), both directed by Saville, concerning respectively a shopgirl who becomes a star by pretending to be a female impersonator (a remake of the German *Viktor und Viktoria*) and a stage aspirant who hopes to get ahead by impersonating a big-game hunter, Mrs Smythe-Smythe. Both are afflicted by the comic Sonnie Hale, the star's husband at the time, who was to direct her later films. In this capacity he proved no more talented and, in fact, by failing to draw out the charm that Saville had found, lost her whatever appeal she had had in the U.S. Almost all the other 'lighter' stars of stage and radio made movies, and Balcon was also successful with a husband and wife team, Jack Hulbert and Cicely Courtneidge, singly and in partnership; however, their limited but larger than life clowning, when unharnessed, is only too predictable.

The best of Balcon's clowns was Will Hay (1888–1949), if lacking in agility for American audiences. A formula was found for him with **Windbag the Sailor** (1936) when given companions equally venal, fat young Albert (Graham Moffat) and the ancient Harbottle (Moore Marriott). He lies, bluffs and cheats, and they are on to every subterfuge, openly contemptuous except when it is to their advantage. Often cast – as in his stage act – as a schoolmaster several degrees more ignorant than his boys, his finest hour was in **Oh, Mr Porter!** (1937). As the station master, he worries about the iniquities of Harbottle and Albert in giving tickets (in exchange for edibles) for trains that do not exist, and about his own sale of tickets for an 'excursion' to a gang of gun-runners who will not pay for them anyway. No British film of the decade is as worth preserving. Hay's usual writers were Val Guest, Marriott Edgar and J.O.C. Orton, and his directors William Beaudine, on the earlier films, and Marcel Varnel, on the later ones: though both were old Hollywood hands, they unquestionably slackened the pace for British audiences.

Varnel, however, took **The Frozen Limits** (1939) at full tilt, causing Graham Greene to call it 'the funniest English picture yet produced, bearing comparison with the Lloyds and Keatons of Hollywood'. Hay's writers and Moore Marriott, as an ancient prospector, are on hand, causing between them whatever hilarity is now to be had. Greene called the billed stars, The Crazy Gang, 'that rather repulsive troupe', and it must be acknowledged that they – three music-hall teams of two – do not clown at all; they twitter and squeak, thinking themselves no end of fine fellows because they don't stand on dignity. They, surely, want to make us laugh, and will try anything; but they know nothing of matters like timing and delivery.

The distribution organisation which Woolf had set up in the States never attempted to sell the British clowns (Korda, seeking world markets, did not bother with

them): but it discovered that it had a more attractive commodity than either Arliss or Matthews – a director, Alfred Hitchcock. His return to Gaumont-British after his stint at B.I.P. was not auspicious: he directed Jessie Matthews in a musical about Johann Strauss, **Waltzes from Vienna** (1934), which was not, apparently, a happy experience for anyone concerned – and that would certainly include audiences on its infrequent revivals. However, returning to crime with **The Man Who Knew Too Much** (1934), he discovered the rich vein which would make him one of the most successful directors of his generation. Most of his British films of this period are enjoyable, and having found his formula he was seldom to depart from it with profit – the apparently ordinary object which turns out to have sinister significance, and the extraordinary setting for the usual mayhem. This film begins in St Moritz, with the last words of a dying man, and ends with a gun-battle based on the Sydney Street siege;★ in between, an innocent couple (Leslie Banks, Edna Best), searching for their kidnapped child, are involved in a revivalist meeting which turns out to be a haven for crooks, and a concert at the Albert Hall which may be lethal for a visiting politician.

★Of 1911, when a small group of foreign anarchists, centred on the East End of London, took on the police and the army rather than surrender.

Graham Moffat, Moore Marriott and Will Hay in *Oh, Mr Porter* (1936), some comic adventures at a decrepit railway station. As the express approaches, they are still arguing whether the end of Official Summertime means that it is due now or in two hours' time; as the next one comes, Hay is struggling with the wheel that operates the level-crossing gate, which doesn't work: 'Why didn't you tell me?' he yells, and Marriott screams back, a refrain throughout the film, 'You never asked me.' The logic is irrefutable, the humour imperishable.

Hitchcock the Master of Suspense

Robert Donat in *The Thirty-Nine Steps*. A classic moment, perhaps, but it is hard to disagree with Graham Greene, who, introducing a collection of his film criticism in 1973, thought the story 'inexcusably spoilt' by Hitchcock. He also reiterated his earlier comments: 'His films consist of a series of small "amusing" melodramatic situations . . . very perfunctorily he builds up to [them] (paying no attention on the way to inconsistencies, loose ends, psychological absurdities) and then drops them: they mean nothing, they lead to nothing.'

The five writers who helped Hitchcock find his niche were reduced by two to fashion **The Thirty-Nine Steps** (1935) from John Buchan's novel, and if both films begin with the assassination of what turns out to be a secret agent, that at least was Buchan's device. There are other good ones: the uncurtained flat (it is being redecorated), the incessant ringing of the telephone, the figures at the corner phone booth, the revelation of the carving knife: who, with this genre, would be so ill-mannered as to ask why, if the killers got into the flat, they didn't polish off Hannay (Robert Donat) at the same time or why they were so careless as to leave that map in the victim's hands? —and what was she doing with it, anyway, in the middle of the night? Andre Sennwald in *The New York Times* thought the film superior to any Hollywood thriller, and virtually every critic liked the addition of a woman (Madeleine Carroll) to bicker with the hero in the Hollywood manner. Also more Hitchcock than Buchan are: the escape

from the train on the Forth Bridge; the interlude with the puritanical, suspicious crofter (John Laurie) and his kindly wife (Peggy Ashcroft); the Sunday pre-luncheon drinks party, with its surprising revelation; and the political rally from which the only escape is to pose as a visiting celebrity.

There is even less left of Somerset Maugham's Ashenden stories in **Secret Agent** (1936), and it is no longer a spy story, though mysteries abound—the body at the organ in the deserted church, the eeriness of the visit to the chocolate factory — and the last reels are borrowed from Lang's *Spione*. Hero (John Gielgud) and heroine (Miss Carroll) banter through the set pieces and what is supposedly Switzerland; Hitchcock later prided himself on including such 'Swiss' ingredients as chocolate and the Alps — the obvious choices of any hack Hollywood writer. Conrad's similarly-titled novel became **Sabotage** (1936), and working for the only time in his career on material by a major

346

Nevertheless, most cinemagoers will have cherished memories among Hitchcock's situations, such as that in *Young and Innocent*, when the camera sweeps down to the drummer to put into close-up that facial tic which reveals him as the murderer. In the same film, Hitchcock (in cap) appears as an extra – which he did in all his films, since this most cunning of self-publicists knew that he would be recognised.

347

The Lady Vanishes
– the best of
British Hitchcocks,
with, behind, Cecil
Parker and Linden
Travers, and then
from left to right,
Naunton Wayne,
Basil Radford,
Dame May Whitty,
Margaret Lockwood
and Michael
Redgrave.

writer, it is significant that Hitchcock makes no mention of the fact in his extensive, published conversations with Truffaut. The action has been brought forward to the present day, and there are a number of other changes, such as the transference of the episode of the time bomb from Greenwich Park to Trafalgar Square; but it is an intelligent adaptation, valid in its own right, very well played by Sylvia Sidney and by Oscar Homolka as her husband, the owner of a seedy cinema, cover for his nefarious activities. **Young and Innocent** (1937), reputedly Hitchcock's own favourite among his British films, eschews agents and anarchists for rural murder, with the Chief Constable's daughter (Nova Pilbeam) helping the wanted man (Derick de Marney) retrieve the clue which will establish his innocence. The central difficulty of

such tales – why the police don't apprehend the real murderer – never seems too relevant; and there are virtuoso sequences, such as the children's tea party fraught with menace, and the revelation of the real murderer, with its long tracking shot to close-up.

International fame invigorated Hitchcock: **The Lady Vanishes** (1938) is his most exhilarating British film, a far cry from the juvenilia of a few years earlier. When the lady vanishes, we are again in sinister Europe: only Margaret Lockwood has seen her, and apparently only Michael Redgrave believes her when she says so – though others have their reasons for feigning ignorance, such as the adulterous couple (Cecil Parker, Linden Travers) and the cricket enthusiasts (Naunton Wayne, Basil Radford) anxious to get home for the Test

Match. They are all monstrously sure of what they are doing, a rare quality in British films of the period. Through all the twists and loops – of which the best, surely, is that the hero and heroine do actually drink from the poisoned glasses – it remains cosy: but it is a film of stature which can even get away with a line like Wayne's during the final shoot-out: 'I'm half-inclined to believe there's a rational explanation for all this.'

The original novel, by Ethel Lina White, is not exceptional, and since the screenplay by Frank Launder (b. 1907) and Sidney Gilliatt (b. 1908) is brilliant, we may well ask how much, overall, Hitchcock owed to them. An answer of sorts is provided by their first script collaboration, **Seven Sinners** (1936), a remake of *The Wrecker,* a Gainsborough picture of 1929. The banter of the leads (Edmund Lowe, Constance Cummings) is obviously based on *The Thin Man;* and the fact that both *Seven Sinners* and *The Lady Vanishes* are set in and around trains is a coincidence. But both films are more tightly constructed than the preceding Hitchcocks, with each mystifying sequence leading directly to the next – though Hitchcock managed the transitions with more ease than the uninspired Albert de Courville. From this film, and in the same manner, Hitchcock used in *Dial 'M' for Murder* (q.v.) the vital clue hidden in a photograph of a reunion dinner, and there are elements of *Strange Boarders,* scripted by Gilliatt in 1938, in *Saboteur* (q.v.). To the acknowledgement that the roots of Hitchcock's 'art' lay in the British programme pictures of the period, may be added a kinship with Launder and Gilliatt, not least in a shared sense of humour.

That Hitchcock could flounder once away from his chosen genre is evidenced by **Jamaica Inn** (1939), a fact which he acknowledged by refusing to countenance any retrospective of his work which included it. He accepted the assignment between leaving Balcon and taking up his contract with Selznick, and we know from Selznick's memos that around the same time he and his British collaborators were busily engaged in destroying the same author's 'Rebecca' in their screen adaptation, till ordered to stick to the original. Daphne du Maurier's Cornwall, in the former tale, is a place of damp and mists, of hidden villages, of moors and rugged coasts; she also has a serviceable plot about a girl's growing awareness of her uncle's complicity in the wrecking of ships for booty – replaced in the film with conventional misdeeds, including a Silent screen finale in which the villain, now mad, abducts the girl and climbs the ship's rigging. Responsible for this travesty were Gilliatt and Hitchcock's usual collaborators, Alma Reville and Joan Harrison, plus J. B. Priestley, called in by Charles Laughton who wanted his part blown up – not surprisingly, for it is not in the original. In the book, the identity of the mastermind comes as a revelation, but Laughton, so obviously villainous from the start, further adds to the ruin of the film. As with *Young and Innocent*, there was a reluctance to go near the Cornish cliffs, a decision as detrimental as it might have been had John Ford decided to reconstruct Monument Valley in the studio for *Stagecoach* (q.v.). The inn itself, however – designed by Thomas N. Morahan – is considerably more picturesque than the original on Bodmin Moor, and it performs its sinister task better than do the actors.

The film was one of the three coproduced by Laughton and Erich Pommer after they broke with Korda. Of these, **Vessel of Wrath** (1938) details the events, as originally told by Somerset Maugham, which follow when a prissy spinster missionary (Elsa Lanchester) gets a fixation on a drunken beachcomber, Ginger Ted (Laughton). It retains the author's kick in the tail, 'My sister is a determined woman, Mr Gruyter. From that night they spent on the island he never had a chance,' but matters to which he merely referred – Ginger Ted's native women, the wrecking of the Chinaman's shop – are demonstrated in full splendour. Pommer directed, on locations so expensive that the film had little chance of recouping its cost.

Although Tim Whelan directed **St Martin's Lane** (1938), the look and feel of Pommer's Silent pictures has been so recaptured as to be uncanny. The combination of German romanticism and prewar London theatreland gives an odd patina to this tale of a busker (Laughton) who takes as his partner a cockney sneak thief – a role with which Vivien Leigh has trouble identifying herself. True, she goes on to become a star – selfish, vain and abnormally ambitious, with which facets Miss Leigh is quite at ease. Laughton is at his best, boasting, scheming, down and out, optimistic, and always with that ingratiating, timid beam of a smile. Clemence Dane wrote this fairy story, claimed in slightly changed form by Chaplin for *Limelight* (q.v.).

As with Korda, the combination of war and insufficient returns sent Laughton and Pommer on to Hollywood. In the meantime, Hollywood had begun to come to Britain. By 1937, when Korda and Hitchcock had proved that there was a world market for movies made there, the industry was in crisis. The two local conglomerates, Associated British and Gaumont-British, both posted losses on production, the latter to the extent of £100,000. This, already the most vulnerable branch of the industry, was further threatened when M-G-M announced the setting up of full-scale quality production in Britain, with its own studio; and there was no knowing when the other American companies might rival the better native product by moving upward from the currently sponsored quota quickies. United Artists was already heavily involved, since it distributed both London Films and those made by Wilcox's British & Dominions, and furthermore United Artists money was helping Oscar Deutsch to build up his Odeon circuit. American companies already dominated British distribution, and with their stars and know-how could certainly do so in local production if they so chose.

Britain was Hollywood's biggest market outside home territory: buying cinemas or investing in their building was not only easier and cheaper but wiser – since moves were already being made to divorce home exhibition from production and/or distribution. 20th Century-Fox had also acquired a considerable interest in the British industry, by virtue of a controlling interest in the Metropolitan & Bradford Trust, which was the majority shareholder in Gaumont-British – a fact which may throw light on the latter's decision to sell its distribution arm to pay off its production losses. The buyer was a consortium calling itself General Film Distributors, making a higher bid than Maxwell of Associated British, and consisting of Woolf, revenging himself for his forced resignation from Gaumont-British; Wilcox, who believed that United Artists was trying to oust him from his own company; Richard Norton, who had had interests in both that outfit and Korda's; and J. Arthur Rank, the only one

without industry experience, and the eventual survivor.

Rank (1888–1972) was a devout man who used the profits from his flour mills to finance religious shorts; in 1935 he joined Lady Yule, another philanthropist who believed in the 'uplifting' power of films, in backing a bucolic melodrama, **The Turn of the Tide,** directed by Norman Walker, about rival Yorkshire fishing families. It was distributed by Gaumont-British, whose unenthusiastic handling Rank blamed for its failure (seeing it today, it is hard to blame them). That whetted his appetite for battle, and since he was as patriotic as he was religious, he felt bound to prevent American financial infiltration into Britain. He was also sufficiently wise – and wealthy – to beat the foreigners at their own game, and had purchased twenty-five per cent of Universal Pictures when that company was in difficulties (q.v.) in 1936, a move that enabled G.F.D. to handle Universal's films. The G.F.D.–Gaumont agreement gave Rank not only access to Gainsborough Pictures, which had taken over all Gaumont's production commitments,* but to Gaumont's cinemas. And with the outbreak of war, when the Americans decided to withdraw their investments, he gained control of both these and Deutsch's Odeons, as well as Paramount's much smaller chain.

In the meantime, he had built a studio complex at Pinewood, not far from Denham (which he subsequently took over). Wilcox directed the first film to go on the floor, **London Melody** (1937), one of a series designed to build Anna Neagle – later Mrs Wilcox – into an international star. In it, she is discovered as a gypsy dancing in the streets and ending up, after some tussles with the diplomatic set, a big nightclub attraction. Such displays did not suggest to the principals of G.F.D. that Miss Neagle could or should play Queen Victoria, as Wilcox proposed: Woolf turned down the project, and Wilcox left G.F.D. He reached an agreement with R.K.O. to distribute, which brought in some cash from that source and by sinking his own and Miss Neagle's money into it he raised £100,000 of the budget; another £50,000 was needed, and Korda, generously, for Wilcox had

*e.g. the Will Hay films and *The Lady Vanishes* – the latter, however, distributed by M-G-M. 20th Century-Fox claimed others to fulfil quote requirements.

refused him participation, offered that amount of credit at Denham.

The result, **Victoria the Great** (1937), rode in on the fervour attached to a new outbreak of royalty, starting with a long coronation ceremony for those not surfeited with the authentic event earlier in the year. James Agate complained that beyond a glimpse of the Corn Law riots it gave no idea of Victoria's Britain, but what did he expect so soon after London had gone wild over Laurence Housman's series of playlets? – imitated here in such scenes as the quarrel, with thumpings on the bedroom door: 'It's me, the Queen . . . It's Victoria . . . It's your wife.' There is a gratuitous scene – clearly to please R.K.O. – with Abraham Lincoln divining that the intervention of the royal couple has prevented war with the U.S. The one triumph is Anton Walbrook's Albert: too romantic, no doubt, too much Strauss and too little Stockmar, it is still an interesting portrait, suggesting both the painful reserve and the quibbles of irritation, not to mention his eventual dominance. Indeed, with a signal exception, the acting is fine – H. B. Warner as Melbourne, Felix Aylmer as Palmerston, Walter Rilla as Prince Ernest – but that exception is crucial: Miss Neagle's coy and suburban Victoria. The film is so authentic-looking that it is visually indistinguishable from the sequel, filmed, by invitation, in the royal palaces, and with the embellishment of Technicolor. Agate had prophesied that the film would be popular, and it was – which may be why Wilcox did not see fit to employ an entirely new set of anecdotes. Although C. Aubrey Smith was brought in to play Wellington, **Sixty Glorious Years** (1938) gives an entirely new dimension to the expression *déjà vu*, and Walbrook's Consort, faced with Miss Neagle a second time, merely nods and pretends to listen. R.K.O., however, were so pleased that they called Wilcox and Neagle to Hollywood to film there.

In unequal exchange, Britain received various personnel from M-G-M, mounting its major operation on the outskirts of London. Louis B. Mayer cajoled Michael Balcon from Gaumont-British to head production – and then, according to Balcon's memoirs, treated him as a long-distance lackey. Certainly the project did not go as planned, for only three films emerged. The first of them, **A Yank at Oxford** (1938), directed by Jack Conway, is rightly considered an example of Anglo-American movie co-operation, and as such is treasured by all students of transatlantic interchange: it is the key film of the movement. Its most telling moment has Robert Taylor stroking the Oxford crew to victory in the Boat Race, but its prevalent tone is best expressed by an exchange between Taylor and his tutor: 'I want to major in American history' – 'There hardly seems enough of that to keep you occupied for three years.' The impact of the brash and bumptious Taylor on Oxford is followed by the realisation that we are all brothers under the skin, 'not such bad fellows after all' – which sentiments help one to overlook the fact that except for a brief shot of Magdalen Tower (which puts Taylor's college somewhere in the garden of St Hilda's) and another of the barges, it might just as well have been filmed at Culver City. As the don, C. V. France offers a superb portrait of Oxonian dottiness, and Vivien Leigh is very funny as a bookseller's wife with a set-line in vamping students.

The Citadel (1938) is based on a novel of a doctor's odyssey by A. J. Cronin, a former doctor who had seen too many doctor movies. 'I'm not going to be influenced by ignorance and superstition,' says this one (Robert Donat), struggling single-handed against both. Alas, he goes to Harley Street, but gets his ideals back in the last reel, just in time to upbraid his fashionable fellows: 'Have you heard of Louis Pasteur?' Audiences had, or so M-G-M hoped: had he not been Paul Muni (q.v.) a couple of seasons back? It is impossible to tell from this movie why the book had been so popular and widely admired: the best that can be said of it is that its clichés and half-truths have been lovingly rendered on to celluloid by King Vidor and its writers. Because of the mining sequences, the film was said to mark Vidor's return to the standard of his early films: they are not however 'equal to those in *Kameradschaft*', as Basil Wright claimed in *The Spectator*, but this section is the most successful, apart from Rosalind Russell, confusing her portrayal of the wife with Florence Nightingale.

This was, let us admit, the popular idea of a fine picture. It was as near to the truth as the majority of film-makers cared to go – and so was **Goodbye, Mr Chips** (1939), as organised by the director Sam Wood, the writers of the screenplay, R. C. Sheriff, Claudine West and Eric Maschwitz, as well as Victor Saville, who had replaced Balcon when he resigned. When the world said goodbye to Mr Chips it was also bidding farewell to a type of movie which disappeared during the War. The next study of a public school teacher, Terence Rattigan's 'The Browning Version', would take a distinctly bitter view of his lot, and when that writer was commissioned to work on the remake (q.v.) of this particular film, he could not bring himself to make his Mr Chips an honoured and much-loved old fellow. The War killed many forms of sentiment, hence increasing that of nostalgia: today we may be fond of the film precisely because it is sentimental about Chips – and the First World War, though certainly treated as if another was imminent. In James Hilton's novel, it is the war which brings Chips from retirement to achieve his ambition of becoming headmaster; there is no marriage, but that is the happiest of inventions. He meets his bride on a cycling tour, and before you know it he is in tails and she is bejewelled in a white gown (both kept, presumably, in their knapsacks): but what follows is genuinely delightful – the masters goggle-eyed that the dull Mr Chipping has caught so stunning a beauty, and she making him more approachable by asking the boys to tea and getting him to crack jokes. *Mr Chips* has heart, common sense and pathos; it manages to set its events against the background of the great world outside, e.g. 'Won't it be funny to have a king' and 'Stinks has gone to South Africa to fight the Boers' – and, worst of all but artlessly rendered, that response to a question as to what's in the papers, 'Nothing much. An Austrian archduke has been murdered in some foreign part.'

Donat, again, is much responsible for the success – he took the Best Actor Oscar that year – even if as the aged Chips he and the make-up move into caricature; as the wife, Greer Garson (q.v.) has the spirit for a girl to be found on an Alp and the graciousness to find life as a teacher's wife appealing. M-G-M was well-pleased, but in the uncertain European climate, future projects were postponed indefinitely or transferred to Hollywood.

The three productions which 20th Century-Fox made, through a subsidiary, New World, were more modest. They all starred the French actress Annabella, en route to take up a Hollywood contract: **Wings of the Morning** (1937), with Henry Fonda, and *Dinner at the Ritz,* both directed by Harold Schuster, the latter a romantic thriller with Paul Lukas and David Niven; and *Under the Red Robe,* directed by Sjöström, with Conrad Veidt as Richelieu.

Only the first is of interest, and that is because it is the first British feature in Technicolor, incorporating a brief snatch of the coronation procession. Fox had filmed the story before, in 1919, a jape about a Spanish gypsy (Annabella) disguised as an Irish stable lad – recalling 'As You Like It', obviously to its detriment. The title refers to a horse, and the cast includes 'the distinguished Irish artist and world personality', Count John McCormack, singing while the camera quite sensibly leaves him, to roam around Lake Killarney.

As it happened, 20th Century-Fox distributed Paul Czinner's **As You Like It** (1936), of which the first thing to be said, said James Agate, 'is that it has all other film versions of Shakespeare beaten to whatever is the elegant word for a frazzle'. He was an admirer of Elisabeth Bergner, though he had reservations about her Rosalind; but the reviewer in *The Illustrated London News* found that she had moulded the role 'to her own very definite personality, as every great actress has a right to do'. Those of us who are not admirers will admit that she does quite well by the text, managing the Ws with ease, faltering only on an occasional 'chepherd' or a line like 'Ah, how wery are my spihits'; but actual acting is restricted to sticking out her chin and smiling – a gallant, pixieish little Rosalind. Lazare Meerson designed appropriate settings for her: the duke's vasty castle with black-mirror floors, icing sugar walls and swans in art deco pools, and an Arden with sheep, hillocks and thatched cottages in the Raphael Tuck manner. Returning to Agate, we find him asking 'What of Shakespeare?' and the answer is that he is buried, or, rather Barried, for that eminent dramatist gets a huge credit for 'suggesting' the treatment, which presumably means that he approved the textual cuts – clearly selected to emphasise the plot at the expense of the poetry, which is not a good idea with this particular plot. However, we may

Clowns and Korda

Four British star-players in two of the few films of the Thirties which made the world aware that there was a British film industry. ABOVE, Robert Donat and Greer Garson in *Goodbye, Mr Chips*, and BELOW, Leslie Howard and Wendy Hiller in *Pygmalion*. M-G-M produced only the former, but released both in the States, its interest in *Pygmalion* due partly to Howard, who was a box-office star in both countries. So was Donat, though he made only one film in Hollywood. His failure to return there led to legal wrangles with M-G-M to whom he was under contract.

enjoy Leon Quatermaine as Jacques, and Laurence Olivier, sensibly playing this Orlando as half demented.

The M-G-M trio aside, Britain's biggest international success in the second half of the decade was a version of Shaw's **Pygmalion** (1938), produced by Gabriel Pascal, who had succeeded where others had failed – for he had not only persuaded the dramatist to sell the screen rights, but also to co-operate in the filming. Pascal was Hungarian, but where his compatriot, Korda, could by general consent charm the birds off the trees, he always had a bad press. However, he also persuaded Leslie Howard to return from Hollywood to play Higgins, and to co-direct with Anthony Asquith (who since his early successes had made only one major film, *Moscow Nights*, for Korda). It does not actually seem to have been directed, but the editing by David Lean moves it faster than most British films. Apart from Shaw's words, obviously, it is the acting which counts – and above all Wilfred Lawson's incomparable Doolittle; Howard's is his standard performance of an arrogant egotist, but none the worse for that. Wendy Hiller's Eliza is particularly good at the beginning, when her apple cheeks and salty personality project her character through the Covent Garden grime; later, she retails well the doll-like speech patterns, but heavy make-up and (as far as I'm concerned) the modern clothes work against her.

Pygmalion was the first film backed by G.F.D., which next sponsored **The Mikado** (1939), still convinced that such cultural events were what world audiences wanted. So Woolf told the trade press, mentioning the years of negotiation with the D'Oyly Carte Opera Company (which held the rights), and the enthusiastic trade reception. Press and public felt otherwise, and indeed the film is a grim experience, Gilbert's humour disintegrating completely amidst the deliberately stagey sets – although the colour cinematography did win an Oscar – and the tentative direction of Victor Schertzinger, imported from Hollywood along with the Nanki-Poo, Kenny Baker.

With the outbreak of war, the importation of American directors would cease, and with the exception of the three M-G-M films, there is no evidence that they were more beneficial than most local talents – nor is there evidence that Whelan, Freeland and Herbert Brenon were more efficient because they were Hollywood-trained. Balcon, moving to take control of A.T.P. after a brief spell as an independent, turned his back completely on America. Hitherto, the films made under his aegis indicate neither a precise knowledge of audience taste nor an ability to convey to posterity the forces which had moulded that taste. Like many of the Hollywood tycoons, he didn't always know what he did want, but he always knew what he didn't want. At this time he knew that what he wanted were wholly indigenous movies, and eventually something remarkable would emerge. Meanwhile, his first for A.T.P. was **The Ware Case** (1938), a 1915 play already filmed in 1917 and 1928, concerning an impoverished baronet (Clive Brook) who murders his wife's nasty brother. Horribly old-fashioned, it still has – under Robert Stevenson's direction – its wits about it, which is more than can be said for **The Four Just Men** (1939), a loose rendering of the Edgar Wallace novel, directed zestlessly by Walter Forde.

Both men would make better films for A.T.P., though in the meantime Balcon had begun to encourage a number of younger talents, including Pen Tennyson, who was, unfortunately, killed in action a few months after making **The Proud Valley** (1940), a tale of mine disaster and unemployment in a Welsh village. Tennyson treats courteously the situation of the black American (Paul Robeson) welcomed to the village, and if the second half is muddled – the men marching to Downing Street to complain of their treatment – that is because it was filmed during the autumn of 1939, when no one knew whether or not government actions should be criticised. Nevertheless, the setting is a Britain recognisably from life and not from earlier movies, and where the weekly pay packet is a matter of much importance; the same may be said of Stevenson's **Return to Yesterday** (1940) and Forde's **Cheer, Boys, Cheer** (1939), comedies romantic and social respectively. Stevenson's film, based on a play by Robert Morley, concerns a seaside repertory theatre, the machinations to close it down, and an incognito Hollywood star (Brook) revisiting the past to find out why life has gone sour on him. Forde's film concerns a small independent brewery threatened with takeover by the aggressive manufacturer of an inferior brew. The one looks back to *The Good Companions;* the other, with its Toby-jug-collecting brewer (C. V. France) and his rival (Edmund Gwenn), pencil-moustached, reading 'Mein Kampf' and cowed by his son (Peter Coke), is a smiling forerunner of the Ealing comedies (q.v.) – and within the next year Balcon would drop the name A.T.P. in favour of Ealing Studios.

Stevenson followed Hitchcock to Hollywood, also on a Selznick contract, and with Saville departed to produce for M-G-M – not to mention the Korda family – Britain had lost its less-than-a-handful of reliable directors. One possible replacement was Thorold Dickinson (b. 1903), whose experience of most branches of theatre was an advantage; another – rare to non-existent in the British film industry – was a combined knowledge of and enthusiasm for the medium. He made his first film, **The High Command** (1937), at the instigation of Gordon Wellesley, another writer and like himself an A.T.P. alumnus. The film is a mere rigmarole – treachery in the mess, false accusations, infidelity in the jungle – but the audience half-believes it, and the images are blended with flair, another rarity in British cinema. That is, however, a quality also to be found in **Midshipman Easy** (1934), which Dickinson had produced at A.T.P., the first film directed by Carol Reed (1906–76), based on Captain Marryat's boys' story, but otherwise spoilt by Hughie Green's smug performance in the title-role. Reed's second film was a version of J.B. Priestley's **Laburnum Grove** (1936), which pleased the critic of *The Spectator*, Graham Greene: 'Nine out of ten directors would simply have canned the play for mass consumption: Mr Reed has made a film of it.' Despite that, and an interpolated excursion taken to the West End, we get but a cursory glimpse of Britain in the Thirties, and Laburnum Grove itself is the usual studio set. Reed certainly keeps the film fast moving and is well served by his stars, Edmund Gwenn, as the mild suburban man claiming to be a counterfeiter, and Cedric Hardwicke, outrageous in loud plus-fours as the shifty, hypocritical brother-in-law who is either sponging or boasting of life back in the East.

Reed, illegitimate son of the actor Herbert Beerbohm Tree, had started humbly on the studio floor; like Dickinson, he was movie crazy, and by the time he made **Bank Holiday** (1938) was recognised as Britain's most promising young director. The film itself has no pretensions to be other than a composite picture of the seaside pleasures of the English: the beauty queen (René Ray), the cockney family (Kathleen Harrison, Wally Patch), the young couple (Margaret Lockwood, Hugh Williams) bent on a 'dirty weekend' – a double room with bath, at 18/6d a night – because they cannot yet afford to marry . . . (needless to say, she changes her mind). **A Girl Must Live** (1939), a comedy about a schoolgirl (Lockwood) fallen among show people, too strenuously apes Hollywood patterns, but **The Stars Look Down** (1939) deals with recognisable problems – as encountered by a miner (Michael Redgrave) who manages to achieve college and go on to be a Labour M.P. It is not an adventurous film; it is happier with the college boy's disastrous marriage than with politics; its account of miners' conditions calls for public ownership but is otherwise as perfunctory as that of *The Citadel* – and indeed, this film is also based on a novel by A. J. Cronin. The comparison this time with *Kameradschaft* was made by Graham Greene, not to Reed's disfavour, and he wondered whether this was not the best British film yet made.

It was not – by a long chalk, since it respects Cronin more than its audience, though that was a fault of the times. But if the British cinema remained bound to the bestseller, to literature, it was at least coming down from Cloud Cuckoo Land. The films of the clowns, and above all, Will Hay, had proved that it could be demotic and entertaining; *The Lady Vanishes, Pygmalion* and *The Four Feathers* had given it confidence, and though *Bank Holiday* was not an international success on their scale, its British reception had given Reed encouragement. If, under wartime conditions, film production were to continue, it was clear to observers that it would be in the hands of the usual bunch of mediocrities, plus himself, Balcon, and the team of Launder and Gilliat. There was no tradition to fall back on; but half a dozen films in the late thirties had given the British cinema, for the first time – *The Private Life of Henry VIII* always excepted – something of which to be proud.

355

16

Russia and France: Argument and Art

OF THOSE European film industries which had contributed to the 'art' of the cinema, only the French and Russian continued to hold sway in the Thirties. In the few cities where foreign-language films were exhibited there was always at least one French film to be seen – and indeed many buffs would later consider this the golden age of the French film. The Russian cinema, though second, was a long way behind, and the rest came nowhere – with the exception of Germany, and that was a special case since the Nazis were energetic in disseminating their films abroad. As the Soviets were also very propaganda-conscious, it might be supposed that they would have done the same: they tried, but to their surprise there was an audience resistance to films about tractors. The jokes made about the Russian films of the Thirtiess have basis in fact, and few of them can be recommended other than to the most ardent admirers of the Soviet régime.

It is sad that the interesting directors of the Twentiess now devoted themselves to reinforcing the faith of the masses in this régime, especially as, to judge from the results, they seem to have regarded their audience as simpled-minded to a man. Boris Barnet's **Thaw** (1931) carries a final intertitle warning its audiences to beware of reactionary forces still in their midst: otherwise this Silent is as stultifying as Dovzhenko's *Earth*, its meandering narrative subservient to the carefully composed images. Barnet was, presumably, instructed to emulate Dovzhenko – no information on this matter is forthcoming in Jay Leyda's 'Kino' or in the Russians' own histories of the period – but some of his old talent as social satirist returned with **Outskirts** (1933), which he wrote with Konstantin

Finn, based on the latter's novel and concerning the response of a small provincial town to the events of 1914–17. After an inventive and amusing start, however, Barnet, like many another, gets bogged down in propaganda, losing his sense of humour when it comes to politics. His second Talkie, **By the Bluest of Seas** (1936) is amateurish, apart from some stunning shots of the swirling Caspian; a tentative plot concerns a girl loved by two shipwrecked sailors, whose clowning is merely embarrassing.

Equally banal is **Alone** (1931), directed by Kozintsev and Trauberg, a Silent with added sound effects and a score by Shostakovich, about a Leningrad schoolteacher sent to the Altai in Siberia, where her example is such that the peasants decide to live by Soviet principles. At one point she gets frostbite and is rescued by an aeroplane – 'thanks,' says an intertitle, 'to our marvellous socialist state.' The director-producer team, not surprisingly, went on to make a trilogy about a typical party worker. Kuleshov was not so fortunate. His first Sound film, *Horizon*, about a Russian Jew returning to his native land from the U.S. was, according to Leyda, 'a fiasco'; he thereupon returned to contemporary American literature, which had provided him with *By the Law*, and came up with **The Great Consoler** (1933), based on a story by Al Jennings. Its protagonist is O. Henry, during his days in prison, and Kuleshov attempted an examination of the creative impulse by contrasting that environment with a bright spoof of one of his stories. As before, Kuleshov's admiration for the American cinema is self-evident, and in 1935 he was denounced by the Congress of Cinema Workers, ostensibly

Boris Babotchkin in the title-role of The Vassiliev Brothers' *Chapayev*, a pleasingly human hero. Since the Soviet takeover of Russia, the film industry was dedicated to propaganda, which presented the problem of heroes with weaknesses – and, if they had any, they must be very small ones. Chapayev, recently promoted to corporal, had only the failings of the 'new' Russians, being all for the new regime, but not entirely certain why.

for a film on which he was artistic supervisor. He was, however, able to make three films during the war years, and through the intervention of Eisenstein to become head of the Moscow Film Institute.

As a copy of an American genre, **The Jazz Comedy** (1934) is inept; directed by Grigori Alexandrov, Eisenstein's former collaborator, it co-stars Lyubov Orlova, who married the director – and attained a degree of popularity in his musicals – and Leonid Utyosov, who had his own 'jazz collective' in Moscow. The Russian title translates as *Jolly Fellows,* by which it was sometimes known in the West – where it was widely seen. About a shepherd who becomes involved in Moscow theatre life and society, it only serves to make Barnet's Silent comedies even more momentous in Russian cinema.

The other Soviet film widely seen in the West was **Chapayev** (1934), and in fact it became the one seemingly obligatory foreign film in the annual ten-best list of *The New York Times*. It is the only notable film of its directors, Georgi (1899–1946) and Sergei (1900–59) Vassiliev, known as The Vassiliev Brothers though they were not, in fact, related. It was a project of Lenfilm, for whom they usually worked (Sergei became the company's head in 1943), and was based on the memoirs of a widow, cleverly reconstructing the last forty-eight hours of her husband's life. He is one of Russia's new men, a cool and cunning Red commander during the Civil War which followed the Revolution, knowledgeable on Garibaldi and Suvorov but not on Alexander the Great, since he had only learnt to read two years before. He has an N.C.O.'s moustache and drinks tea from his saucer; criticised for sloppy dress, he upbraids a junior officer for the same reason. He is against Capitalism; asked whether he's for the Bolsheviks or the Communists, he answers slyly that he's for the International – and confused as to which, the second or third, he opts for whichever one Lenin is for. He is a lovely hero, very well played by Boris Babotchkin.

The plot is perfunctory, the battle scenes well-photographed but thin, and the scenes between the guerillas marred by 'meaningful' looks. Yet it is clear why the film was so acclaimed – how refreshing it must have seemed after such absurd war films as *Today We Live*! It was a huge success in the Soviet Union, where response to its hero meant a farewell to the idealised heroes of Dovzhenko and the mass-heroes of Eisenstein – much to the satisfaction of the oscillating Central Committee, which had decided to condemn both directors (as well as Pudovkin) for pursuing their art at the expense of the audience.

Chapayev influenced every Russian film till the War, not excluding **Lenin in October** (1937), directed by Mikail Romm (1901–71) – quickly, to please Stalin, who commissioned it to celebrate the 20th anniversary of the Revolution. Lenin (Boris Shchukin) is found to be a nice, dear man, either writing manifestos or thoughtfully striding about, hands on hips. His landlord–bodyguard Vasili (N. Okhlopkov) is awfully nice, too – full of humour and loving care. So, come to that, are all the workers, as they plot and plan for the great day: they may not be as handsome as the workers of Eisenstein's films or the young Nazis of the films that Fräulein Riefenstahl was then making, but they have the same idealistic gleam in their eye. The Kerensky government looks exactly like the Csarist governments of other films, with Kerensky himself featured as weaselly and hesitant; one of its members, a particularly devious man, is made up to look like Trotsky. As Trotsky had been exiled (in 1929) and was not part of Kerensky's provisional government, this might merely be an *aide-memoire,* associating him with the losing side. Stalin appears briefly, smiling broadly behind Lenin as Lenin, the man of destiny, strides to take power. The storming of the Winter Palace is a reminder of past cinematic glories, and there is a cheering sequence when the military joins the workers: as hagiography this is both handsome and well-constructed – perhaps the best of the dozens of films on Lenin, few of them of more serious content than Germany's *Fridericus* cycle.

Another of the better films extolling recent heroes is **Baltic Deputy** (1937), directed by Alexander Zarkhi and Josif Heifits (b. 1905), who had studied film together, and who, as a team, directed from 1928 to 1950. The picture is dedicated to K. Timiriazev, the subject of the film though for no apparent reason given a different name – a professor of plant physiology who sided with the Bolsheviks in 1917 and thus became caught up in the great events. He is played by Nikolai Cherkassov (1903–66), who often worked with this team, but his role is merely peripheral: interest is concentrated on two ex-students – the one against him vindictive and humourless, the one for him, bearded, bespectacled and hearty. There is a further hero, a sailor (A. Melkinov), impish and bluff, a solid man of the people. The roles are nicely played, art direction and photography are superb, and in no other film has the confusion caused by the Revolution been so well caught.

Perhaps one is clutching at straws, but the propaganda of the Russian cinema, except in some literary adaptations, is so all-pervading that the films seem accompanied by the creaking bones of cowed spectators. Equally depressing is the reaction of committed left-wing audiences, laughing at every feeble anti-capitalist joke, and applauding the more heavily the more intently the piece sticks to the party line. Taken for granted most of the time is belief in the solidarity of the workers, the satisfaction of life in the commune and the beastliness of life under the Czars.

As a boy born into poverty, Maxim Gorki knew at first hand about this last, and there can be no reservations about the propaganda content of the trilogy based on his memoirs, as directed by Mark Donskoi (1901-81). Donskoi had studied with Eisenstein; he made his first film, in collaboration, in 1927. He began these films after discussions with the writer himself, who, initially uninterested, later became enthusiastic. Discussing the first of the trilogy, **The Childhood of Maxim Gorky** (1938), Catherine de la Roche wrote in *Sequence* that 'socialist realism . . . became the official aesthetic of the Soviet Cinema in the Thirties – a concept of art aiming at the expression of a constantly evolving socialist society and its ideals, wherein the artist finds self-fulfilment through participation in the life of the community.'

Donskoi does not let us lose sight of the fact that life was hard and bitter, nor of the individual's place in that society: but its importance is its evocation of time – events recalled by Alexei (i.e. Gorky) of his childhood with his grandparents. He cannot recall his mother, because she had little

meaning for him, but he remembers incidentals – a cat by the hearth, a day by the
river – and such matters as his grandparents
begging and the professorial neighbour
chained to other convicts, being led to what
strange destiny. The archaic subtitles are
part of the film's charm, viz: 'On Fridays
when grandfather went to Vespers, a life
amusing beyond all description broke out
in the kitchen.'

When the film opened in London,
Richard Winnington in the *News Chronicle*
thought it one of the three best films ever
made, but I find it a mite self-conscious,
taking its tone from the performance of the
boy, Alyosha Lyarsky. I would not, however, argue about any superlatives garland-
ing the second part, **My Apprenticeship**
(1939). The prim little boy has grown as
expected into a man of integrity. In Part I,
he observed; in Part II, he reads. The stupid
people he encounters are particularly con-

temptuous of books; and in both films there
is the seemingly chance association of
books and prisoners, as if knowledge were
imprisoned in Czarist Russia. One day, in a
book, Alexei may find the answers to the
problems puzzling him – problems about
the nature of Russia itself, its vastness, the
poverty of his own family, the viciousness
of the family to whom he is apprenticed.
The screen writer was I. Gruzdov, but **My
Universities** (1940), like Part I, was written in collaboration with Donskoi: it is not
only less good than either, but tedious by
any standards. Perhaps Donskoi had tired
of the project, or perhaps the War overshadowed the filming: conditions were
surely affected, for there are few exteriors
and the broad rivers, a motif in the earlier
parts, are never glimpsed. Admittedly the
action takes place in the city of Kazan,
which clearly interested Donskoi less than
the towns and villages featured hitherto.

Mark Donskoi's
three films based on
Maxim Gorki's
autobiography,
though of unequal
merit, comprise
a remarkable
experience, effortlessly
invoking a past time
and a distant place.
This scene is from the
best of them,
My Apprenticeship.
Donskoi considered
the trilogy the
culmination of his
own apprenticeship
in cinema. He
planned it with
Gorki, but Gorki
died two years before
the first was
completed.

Also, N. Valbert has replaced Lyarsky, and a certain quality has gone. The story is a conventional one of tyrannical bosses and striking workers, with a particularly banal ending, as waves thunder and Alexei helps a woman give birth. 'It's coming,' he says, meaning the Revolution, and it is hard to believe that the director was the same man who shot the brief sequence in *My Apprenticeship* when a remote town learns, with a sense of awe, of the assassination of the Czar. Nevertheless, to see the three parts of the trilogy consecutively is one of the most rewarding experiences the cinema has to offer.

Russia's most famous director remained Eisenstein, so great had been the impression made by his Silent films. From that time on he was never to be professionally very happy, and except for a few hesitant intervals remained in official disfavour for the rest of his life. Stalin's disapproval of *Old and New* was followed by a European tour and, as we have seen, an abortive trip to Hollywood. Paramount was so anxious to be rid of him that the date of his departure was announced to the press, but Eisenstein left instead for Mexico, persuaded by a conversation with Robert Flaherty on the desirability of creative independence as well as correspondence with the painter Diego Rivera on the possibility of a film on Mexican life. The project became a vast panorama on present-day Mexico and its history, with financing provided – at Chaplin's suggestion – by the left-wing American novelist Upton Sinclair. However, Sinclair was unprepared for the film, now called **Que Viva Mexico!**, to become vaster day by day, and after shooting had dragged on for over a year he cut off his financial support. Since Eisenstein had been refused a visa to the U.S. he left for Russia, but with the understanding that the material he had already shot would be sent to him for editing. Sinclair, however, refused to part with it, issuing some of the footage as *Death Day,* and selling some to Sol Lesser, who used it as *Thunder Over Mexico* (1933). The best-known version is *A Time in the Sun,* assembled by Marie Seton, an Eisenstein disciple, who tried to stay as close as possible to the original plan – but her footage, culled from thirteen months' intensive filming, lasts a mere hour. The assembled film is a series of images, accompanied by guitars, of Aztec temples, cacti and mountains, a bullfight and a wedding. At one point there is a semblance of a story, with a peasant girl taken by a landowner and her young man tortured and killed – and also some references to revolution. The mood throughout is sensuous; one is always aware of the sun – though probably only someone from a cold northern country would have been so taken with the fronds of palms.

In 1935 Eisenstein began *Bezhin Meadow,* on the subject of Soviet policy for the peasants, but it was abandoned and condemned 'for its formalism and its political and sociological inadequacy'. He made a public *mea culpa,* and was later permitted to proceed with **Alexander Nevsky** (1938), deeply patriotic and topical – as one could not fail to note from its final warning, 'Those who come to us with the sword shall perish with the sword'. The invaders in the film are the Teutonic knights, in 1242, and it tells how the fisherman prince (Cherkassov) rose to defeat them before turning back to stave off the encroaching Mongols. The screenplay, by the director and Piotr A. Pavlenko, is as formalised as a primitive epic, though not without propaganda, since the rich are depicted as willing collaborators. Critics at the time thought the film a retreat to the static processional images of Lang's Nibelungen saga, but it became admired, to the extent that Richard Griffith was to write in 1948, in 'The Film Since Then', that though as spectacle it was 'nearly indistinguishable' from the work of deMille or Curtiz, it benefited from 'Eisenstein's discriminating taste and his supreme mastery of crowd scenes, and the absence of Errol Flynn'. Few today would prefer this mortician's job to the best Curtiz-Flynn movies. The battle scenes have a mechanical brilliance, but though the Teutonic knights are striking grotesques, in close-up they are seen to be mounted on rocking horses. The film is rabble-rousing, negligible as entertainment and only just redeemed by the Prokofiev score, though even that is punctuated by patriotic songs of extreme banality. Cherkassov is unconvincing as the prince, except for a brief moment as he claims he 'will not let these dogs set foot on Russian soil'.

The film silenced Eisenstein's critics, and he was appointed head of Mosfilm; in 1941 he began what was to be his final work,

Ivan the Terrible, planned in two parts and expanded to a trilogy as his enthusiasm grew. The third part was never shot, since the second, finished in 1946, was banned by the Central Committee – along with several other historical films – in case audiences drew a parallel between the characters of Ivan and Stalin. With the subtitle *The Boyars' Plot* Part 2 was offered to Western audiences in 1958, and reading the reviews one would not know how aptly titled is this *Ivan the Terrible*. Many critics were defensive, and writing in 'Kino' of Part 1 Jay Leyda observed that 'the film that does not conceal its maker's calculation has always been the least popular anywhere in the world . . . The rare film artist who defies the spontaneous, to show that the medium can invent as well as mirror, has as much to contribute to the future of cinema as do all the great artists . . . who treasure the *effect* of calculation.' He goes on to quote Eisenstein's words on this calculation: 'The grandeur of our subject called for a monumental means of presentation' and in rejecting the attempt to make Ivan accessible in modern fashion Eisenstein found 'a different tone. In him we wished chiefly to convey a sense of majesty, and this led us to adopt majestic forms.' 'Majestic forms' turn out to be a spectacular kind of village pageant, with actors congealing beneath a profusion of ruffs, baubles, cowls, cloaks, jewels and elaborate head dresses: called upon occasionally to perform, they emote in a manner considered old-fashioned even when Eisenstein was an apprentice in the industry. This is a dark, brooding film but of no serious worth. Eisenstein had had years of enforced silence, and either could not, or would not, go back to his exhilarating films about the proletariat. At least *Nevsky* moved, but in *Ivan* in searching again for historical grandeur, he confused it with the theatre – and dead theatre at that. From time to time the immense pains he took to get these posturing effects catch the imagination; but never for long. It is sad that the man who had once been the single most vital and powerful creative force in all cinema could find no better expression of his talents.

One film curio that emanated from Russia at this time was **Kämpfer** (1936), made by a group of refugees from Germany headed by Gustav von Wangenheim

(1895–1975), whose identification with left-wing theatre was such that he fled when the Nazis came to power. He wrote and directed the film, and on this evidence cinema was not his metier, for it is virtually incoherent. Nevertheless, it repays interest – as much, anyway, as any propaganda movie with no other aim. Its background is the Reichstag fire and the subsequent trial in Leipzig of a Communist named Dimitrov, who later found a haven in the U.S.S.R. He and all the 'lefties' are noble, handsome and community motivated, as in *Kühle Wampe,* while the Nazis, when out of uniform, look like the capitalists of Soviet Silent cinema; the sameness of left and right propaganda is furthered by the Maryan insistence of motherhood, and the boyish figure and hairdo of the heroine. The film, moreover, has shots of a Nazi orgy, suggesting that the men would be sexually involved with each other were they not dead drunk.

Some of the most memorable images in all cinema are provided by Eisenstein's *Ivan the Terrible,* but the film as a whole provides little in the way of entertainment or instruction. Eisenstein had been an innovative force, yet in attempting a new approach to this historical subject he made a film as rewarding as a visit to the waxworks. Cherkassov played Ivan.

361

It was presumably made for distribution in Austria and Switzerland and, perhaps, for the German-speaking population of the U.S. (where it was shown as *Der Kampf*). The progress of foreign-language films between the coming of Talkies and the War, when there were only a few art houses, is curious. Almost every other country exported a film or two, but none of those I have seen – Greek, Portuguese or Finnish – deserves recalling. The most famous continental film of the decade – beyond any French or Russian Movie – was Czech, **Extase,** shown in New York in 1937. It was not seen publicly in London till 1950, yet it was known the world over to millions, and for the same reason – its leading lady, Hedy Kiesler, appeared in the nude, a fact even more widely disseminated when she reappeared in Hollywood as Hedy Lamarr. Only in stag movies, made strictly for private consumption or men's conventions known as 'smokers', did anyone appear nude on the screen, and by such standards – or those of today – Miss Keisler's appearance is chaste indeed, fleeting and hidden by trees. The shape to be discerned is undoubtedly that of an unclothed human female and her dash through the woods was to many, as Howard Dietz put it in his memoirs, 'refreshing'.

The director, Gustav Machaty (1901–63), had had a success in Germany in 1929 with *Erotikon,* but his other Czech films had not been shown abroad: that this one was has much to do with the naked gambol, but a combination of sparse dialogue, incessant and pulsating music, and accessible symbols – rearing stallions, etc. – conferred a spurious artistic respectability. A young girl marries an old man, bald and pince-nezed as usual, who falls asleep in the bathroom on their wedding night; later, while she is swimming, her horse bolts and is stopped by a lusty young lover . . . None of it was new – Woman, deprived of Satisfaction at the hearth, seeks it with a Stranger – but Machaty made of it a masturbation fantasy, schoolboyishly romantic, a hymn to primeval love.

In France, at a time when the country was increasingly unsure of itself, the industry turned out a great number of films astonishing in their confidence, all of them – and it is not paradoxical – a reflection of those times. As it became clear that dual language productions were not economic, foreign interests departed, to be followed by an incursion of refugees from Germany: in that condition of flux, the industry was exceptionally vulnerable to the country's financial crisis of 1934, which resulted in the majority of production companies being declared bankrupt. In the consequent independent atmosphere there was freedom to move away from formula, with autonomy handed to the directors, who tended to be reflective, meticulous, quasi-romantic and vitally concerned with the possibilities of the medium as an expression of narrative. Though sensibly commercial in their intentions they aimed to please the public without condescension and they also respected each other's ability. The French cinema of the Thirties is a complete body of work, its influences self-contained. Accepting that Clair's first Talkies provided an astonishing prelude, his immediate successors were of little account, but they include one enormously sympathetic figure.

Jean Vigo (1905–34) came from a journalist/anarchist background, which may have led him to avant-garde cinema. The already established director Germaine Dulac helped him, as did his father-in-law when he financed **A Propos de Nice** (1930), made in collaboration with Boris Kaufman (b. 1906), brother of Dziga-Vertov and much later a distinguished Hollywood cinematographer. This Silent, hypnotic three-reeler is an impression of Nice, and if the juxtaposition of wealthy tourists and slum dwellers no longer has much force (because it has been overused), the sum is impressive: facades, a cemetery, a game of *boule,* the Promenade des Anglais with strollers muffled up in high summer. **Zéro de Conduite** (1933) is also a short film, and impressionistic, as deeply personal as it was innovatory – recalling Vigo's own schooldays in a blend of fantasy, private jokes and public ridicule, culminating in a sequence (borrowed from the much less lethal *A Nous la Liberté*) where the boys shoot at their masters. The censors thought it subversive, and until 1945 it was banned, except for film societies.

Vigo's backer was Jacques-Louis Nouñez, who persuaded him to take on something more conventional, **L'Atalante** (1934), a scenario by Jean Guinée, which Vigo adapted with Albert

The most famous foreign-language film of the
Thirties was *Extase* (1933), an anecdote stretched to
ninety minutes about a young and frustrated wife
who meets a handsome young surveyor after taking
a dip in an old swimming-hole. Perhaps he saw her
like this, which was really more than audiences saw
of her, since for most of the time the camera stayed
well back behind the trees as she dashed through the
woods. She is Hedy Kiesler, whose husband later
attempted to buy up all copies of the film. Later still
she went to Hollywood and became Hedy Lamarr.

Jean Vigo died young, leaving only a handful of shorts and one remarkable feature, *L'Atalante* (1934). The title refers to a barge, on which a young bride, Dita Parlo, arrives, to start a life which is not quite what she expected. Michael Simon is the old deckhand whose cabin she finds so fascinating.

Riéra. Its subject is the relationship of a newly wed couple (Jean Dasté, Dita Parlo), and the bride's reactions to her monotonous new life on the canals and rivers of France. The husband is mean-spirited but conscientious, likeable despite bouts of jealousy, while the wife, shy and bewildered, is thrilled by the prospect of Paris and flattered by a smooth-talking pedlar. These people belong in this landscape of desolate *quais* and factory chimneys – since described variously as 'realistic' and 'lyrical'. And if realism is attention to detail we can only say that Vigo has got it marvellously right. I am less sure of the passages labelled 'expressionist' – the search for the bride under water and the sequence in which he and Kaufman try to indicate sexual longing in images: but the rest is flawless. As *Le Chaland qui Passe,* retitled thus after exhibitors applauded a featured song, it was a commercial failure; as *L'Atalante* it was first shown publicly in 1940 – to become a rallying cry for a later generation of directors. Its most immediately striking qualities – the use of location, the blending of the gay and the melancholic – were established ones in French films; but it is darker than those that preceded it, due

almost certainly to Vigo's background and the leukemia which was shortly to kill him. Some have regarded his films as expressions of a social conscience, but since there are only four – the other is a short on swimming – it is more proper to regard them as experiments in self-awareness.

Vampyr, ou l'Etrange Aventure de David Grey (1932) has also been admired by cineastes, in part because Carl Dreyer adopted the formula of Universal's horror films and tried to avoid showing anything specifically horrific. But the plot is anaemic, and the film's failure prevented Dreyer from making another for ten years. Another foreigner, Fritz Lang, also had a commercial failure, **Liliom** (1934), but that, he himself thought – I think correctly – was due to the nature of the piece, which turns abruptly from drama to whimsy. The source is the Mólnar play which, set to music by Rodgers and Hammerstein, became *Carousel* (q.v.): but in Lang's version, at least, the second half is the better, being both funny and infinitely less sentimental. His first half is also good, establishing the romantic aura of the fairground, the vigorous bully of Charles Boyer

(1897–1978) and Madeleine Ozeray's touching loyalty to him.

A wistful, put-upon heroine and a sense of destiny and time passing may also be found in **La Maternelle** (1933), the most admired French film of its time. The director was Jean Benoît-Lévy (1888–1959), who spent his career alternating between educational films for schools and commercial movies, with Marie Epstein a frequent collaborator, as here. Their situations, taken from a novel by Léon Frapie, are familiar and sentimental, but their setting is realistic: Rose (Madeleine Renaud), a nursery school skivvy, adopts young Marie when her mother, the inevitable *putain,* goes off with a new man; but then Marie has a further problem when Rose receives a proposal from the school doctor. The cluttered apartment, the poorly dressed children on the stairs, even Rose scrubbing the floor, are depicted with both compassion and vitality.

Equally romantic and even more influential was **Le Grand Jeu** (1934), Jacques Feyder's first film after returning from Hollywood, written with his compatriot, Charles Spaak (1903–75). A soldier (Pierre-Richard Willm), stationed in North Africa, is struck by the resemblance between a lost soul he meets there and the coquette he left behind – both roles played by Marie Bell, though dubbed by another actress for one of them, an innovation which elicited much praise. He loves the one only as long as he can cast her in the role of the other, uncertain where the dream stops and reality begins – beautifully and erotically expressed by Feyder in a scene where Willm, thinking her asleep, removes her shoes and bends to kiss her tenderly, only to find her in command, whereupon he throws himself upon her body, luminous between her black underwear and a feathered peignoir. The accompanying realism in this case is the seedy, bug-ridden hotel kept by Charles Vanel and Françoise Rosay (1891–1974), Feyder's wife, in one of the best of her often magnificent performances. She has the eyes of a woman who has seen everything, and who would clearly rather be anywhere else; her black silk dress and her habit of spreading her legs are anything but ladylike, but her poise suggests having come to terms with the hand that life has dealt – and on the subject of the cards she is an expert. **Pension Mimosas** (1935) is closer to melodrama than tragedy, loosely adapted by Spaak from 'Phèdre', with Mlle Rosay as the woman who falls in love with her adopted son. Otherwise the two films are much alike: instead of North Africa, the Côte d'Azur; instead of the legionnaires, a milieu of petty crooks; instead of the cards, the roulette wheel.

Feyder's remarkable evocation of atmosphere was achieved with the help of Lazare Meerson, his art director, and Harry Stradling, his photographer; with Spaak, they reassembled to make **La Kermesse Héroïque** (1935), the antithesis of both films – accepted then as a masterpiece and for at least two decades the yardstick by which historical films were measured. If its light-hearted approach is so much less facetious than that of Korda and Guitry (q.v.), those of us who love it must allow that the argument has faded somewhat. In a small Flemish town the Burgomaster (André Alerme) and other dignitaries await with unease the encroaching Spanish army; the Burgomaster feigns death in the hope that the Duke (Jean Murat) will pass by in deference to the mourners, but his wife (Rosay) takes command – and is too sensible, surely, to turn down the solicitations of the handsome duke. A statement is made, obviously, on the equality of women, and though few spectators then cared that the real subject of the film is the advisability of collaboration between oppressors and the oppressed it was later welcomed as such by the Nazis. It may also be said to be anti-clerical, in the person of the duke's chaplain (Louis Jouvet), a man of little faith but much appetite for gold and wine.

Since both French and German versions were made in France, Feyder decided – after *Knight Without Armour* in Britain – to make both versions of *Fahrendes Volk*/**Les Gens du Voyage** (1938) in Germany. The title refers to circus people, and Feyder's view is the usual one of the cinema – of incestuous passions, bitter rivalry, low morals, a milieu close to the underworld. Mlle Rosay is indomitable as the lion tamer, rich in humour and long-suffering wisdom; as her husband, a fugitive from justice, André Brûlé is weak, and it is possible that Hans Albers makes more of the role in the German version. The loss of Spaak is felt, for the story is trumpery. Feyder's creation of atmosphere is as vivid as ever, more

Jacques Feyder's *La Kermesse Héroïque* (1935) was once among the most famous of all films, cited by critics for its fidelity to period and its ability, then rare, to portray the people of history without either undue reverence or being patronising. Françoise Rosay, on the left, is leading the women of the town in obeisance to their temporary conquerors.

interesting than in rival movies, but we do not expect to have to make comparisons, for in the past he has towered above other directors. **La Loi du Nord** (1939) is equally disappointing; and *Une Femme Disparaît* (1942), with Rosay, is only a partial return to form. This last was made in Switzerland, where he spent the war; his last years were occupied with working in the theatre and supervising the film projects of others.

A former assistant of Feyder, Jean Grémillon (1902–59), observed of him that even when he seemed to care only for the purely plastic qualities of film, 'one can feel him tormented by a need to offer total reality. [He needed] *to make live* the drama – with the greatest force, with the greatest presence – to make it part of the life of the

spectator.' The same may be said of Grémillon himself, though significantly he had been making indifferent movies for nine years till Spaak wrote for him – from a novel by André Beucler – **Gueule d'Amour** (1937). The chief of several resemblances to *Le Grand Jeu* is the obsessive soldier lover (Jean Gabin), an N.C.O. in the Spahis. In the telegraph office at Cannes he meets the woman (Mireille Balin) who takes all his money, shuts the door in his face and later, when he has left the army, is unable to make up her mind about him. She becomes engaged to his unprepossessing best pal (René Lefèvre), and he has to choose between sexual love for the one and amical love for the other. Since Grémillon regarded the film simply as a commercial chore he was surprised by the subsequent acclaim. This merely adequate *femme fatale* tale does always seem more profound than it really is – despite in this instance the somewhat statuesque performances of the leads. Jean Gabin (1904–76), who managed to be in almost every notable French film of the period, was often a presence rather than an actor. Here, called upon to play a man desperately in love, a man desperate in desertion, one distracted enough to murder, he manages no more than his usual gloomy expression – but it is, as on other occasions, adequate.

Working again in Berlin for the Alliance Cinématographique Européen, the grandiose name adopted by Ufa for its French-language films, and again with Spaak – who wrote the dialogue, on a scenario by Albert Valentin – Grémillon achieved his best film, **L'Etrange Monsieur Victor** (1938). M. Victor (Raimu) is a respectable shopkeeper who allows another man (Pierre Blanchar) to go to prison for a murder he himself has committed; conscience, however, causes him to pay a stipend to the man's wife (Viviane Romance) and the matter becomes even more complicated when the man, escaped from jail, turns to him for help. Grémillon slips easily from drama to comedy, but what is most striking is that the film throbs with life. The location shots of Toulon blend with studio reconstructions – the photographic blow-up of the harbour used far more skilfully than in M-G-M's *Port of Seven Seas* (q.v.): people tumble out of bars, a girl accosts a sailor, women gossip behind clotheslines, disgruntled customers wander into M. Victor's overstocked emporium. Grémillon, like his master, believed that the care he took would be appreciated, and he *moulded* his films accordingly. In Hollywood, a few directors had managed to achieve similar results – and William Wyler was currently working with similar aims. However, part of the vitality here is provided by Raimu (1883–1946), who was temperamental, not handsome, nor renowned for intelligence; but he understood as well as any actor the demands of the camera.

Spaak worked only on the additional dialogue of **Remorques** (1941), though the screenplay was by the even more prestigious Jacques Prévert: the uneven result of this teaming may have been caused by the cessation of filming on the outbreak of war

and its resumption several months later. Gabin is a seaman with an obsessive love, this time for a lady (Michèle Morgan) who happens to be married to another. Grémillon seemed more involved than ever in his setting, a small Atlantic port, and was veering towards the non-fiction feature: in the post-war period he planned a number of semi-documentaries, with government aid, on such subjects as the Revolution of 1848 and the Munich settlement, but none came to pass. He did make several short documentaries, and the few features he subsequently made proved that he had lost interest in fiction.

Jacques Prévert (1900–77) came to films via a three-reeler, **L'Affaire est dans le Sac** (1932), written in collaboration with his actor brother Pierre, who also directed. Like other amateur ventures into films it is self-admiring but also amiable, its humour deriving from the Paris music hall; a barely discernible plot concerns the many suitors of an heiress, and the best of it features a hatter who runs around Paris stealing hats in the hope of drumming up custom.

Between them Prévert, Spaak and Henri Jeanson (1900–70) worked on every important French film at this time, so it is possible the consistency of mood or vision

Jean Grémillon's *L'Etrange Monsieur Victor* teems with life. It has one of the complicated murder plots popular in the Thirties and uses a common device of the time – a man accused of a murder he did not commit was so drunk on the evening in question that he has no memory of it. Pierre Blanchar, right, who plays the accused man, escapes from prison and turns for help to Monsieur Victor (Raimu), who unbeknownst to him – but not to the audience – is the real murderer.

Jean Gabin and Michèle Morgan as the doomed lovers in Marcel Carné's *Le Quai des Brumes* (1938), seemingly so representative of France at the time, both to foreigners and to the French themselves. At this stage of his career Gabin invariably played an outsider or a deserter, more honourable despite his status than the cheats and crooks around him who had turned the world into a place of petty corruption.

was theirs. There is reason to believe that the films of Marcel Carné (b. 1909) owe more to Prévert than to Carné himself, as Carné's work declined sharply when their collaboration ceased. Yet Carné's pre-war films are extraordinarily strong in atmosphere – which may be more the 'creation' of the director than the writer. He is the central figure of the pre-war French film-makers, and they form a school as certainly as any group of painters in art history. As a young man, before becoming assistant to Clair and then Feyder, Carné was an influential film critic. It was Feyder who enabled him to become a director by obtaining backing for **Jenny** (1936), with Rosay in the lead – that of a somewhat weary nightclub proprietress who tries to keep her profession from her priggish daughter. The role was not unlike the one she had played in *Pension Mimosas,* and Carné realised that a familiar plot would only bear retelling if exceptionally well-handled – which meant in the style of *L'Atalante* and of Feyder, by presenting the seedy suburbs of Paris in a lyrical style. His art director, Alexander Trauner (b. 1903), helped him reset that style; he had been assistant to Meerson on the films

which the latter had designed for Clair and Feyder, and he had also worked with the Préverts on *L'Affaire est dans le Sac.* Incidentally, both Meerson and Trauner were foreigners (Meerson was born in Russia and Trauner in Bulgaria), which may be one reason why Trauner's studio-built Paris is such a memorable distillation.

Conversely, he made little attempt to provide a convincing London in **Drôle de Drame** (1937), and this second Carné-Prévert collaboration, though crazy in the manner of *L'Affaire est dans le Sac,* was to prove untypical. It was an original, the first *comédie noire,* derived from an English mystery novel – 'His First Offence' by J. Storer Clouston – turned into boulevard romp with murder rather than amour the motif. The French were delighted with this attack on British snobbery – and so were the British – but today the film seems small beer compared with the best of its few descendants, *Kind Hearts and Coronets* (q.v.), being also concerned with murder in high places (though strictly speaking there is only the semblance of a murder, the matter being complicated by the presence of a self-proclaimed homicidal maniac). Pratfall follows joke follows inanity, and, given the leading players, it is a pity the film looks more to event than character. They form a tremendous triumvirate: Michel Simon as an orchid-fancier who writes lowbrow thrillers under a pseudonym; Françoise Rosay as his all-gracious and all-cunning wife; and Louis Jouvet (q.v.) as their priggish episcopal cousin, a match for either in his hypocrisy.

Prévert's screenplay for **Le Quai des Brumes** (1938) has a delicate duality, assuming a contemporary urgency for a romance as mythic and as enduring as that of Tristan and Iseult. His source was a novel by Pierre MacOrlan, originally set in Montmartre in 1914 – and he has changed the hero, played by Gabin, from hoodlum to army deserter. Gabin's frequent association with uniform seems less a matter of typecasting than a continual quest for a meaning in the contemporary climate of French politics and opinion: if there was anything worth running away from it was the army, but there proves to be no matter or manner of loyalty to replace it. Without it, the will to survive is weak, and Gabin can only manage a grunt of surprise for an act of kindness. The film's title is not a quasi-romantic description of Le Havre, but the name the locals have for a particular part of it. There, Jean (Gabin) meets Nellie (Michèle Morgan), ward of the beastly Honoré (Michel Simon), who slobbers over her among the picture postcards and souvenirs of his little shop; for her, unsurprisingly, Jean gives up a passage to Venezuela. He says that were he a painter, he would paint a drowning man rather than a swimmer – to which the barman responds, impassively, 'A quoi ça sert?' – and Nellie is equally fatalistic, confessing, as she falls in love, 'Chaque fois le jour se lève, j'espère quelque chose nouvelle, quelque chose frais'. In her lover's arms she says 'C'est difficile à vivre', and she is only seventeen.

He, the stock Gabin figure, humourless and stoic, and she, with waxen features and false eyelashes, convincing neither as waif nor streetwalker, underline the film's duality – both schematic figures in an antiromantic fantasy and yet by some alchemism real human beings. Their one night of happiness owes something to Murnau and von Sternberg, both admired by Carné and Prévert, and here there are shadows both figuratively and literally.

Hôtel du Nord (1938) is less committed, but that is part of its charm. That it is lighter is due to the substitution of Jeanson for Prévert – though the adaptation of Eugene Dabit's novel was made by Jean Aurenche (b. 1904) who would become one of the most respected writers in the industry. Though typecast, both Louis Jouvet (1887–1951) and Arletty (b. 1898) are at their most inimitable, he as the shifty fugitive from justice, with a fingernail hold on respectability and elegance, and she as his mistress, good-humouredly accepting her lot – which is, physically, one cluttered room in a no-star hotel on the Canal Saint Martin. Jean-Pierre Aumont and Annabella, as the suicide-bent lovers, do not hold the same fascination, but there are François Perier, as the young man who prefers the company of other young men to that of Annabella, and Bernard Blier, inheriting Arletty from Jouvet and startled to find that she doesn't accord him a jot of the same respect.

Perhaps Trauner's is the major contribution to **Le Jour se Lève** (1939): one might forget the story, but one could never forget the sets – the small square on the outskirts of town, dominated by the one high building in which Gabin rooms, and the lane between the railway line and the factory. Nor could one ever forget the way Gabin looks, holed up throughout the long night, chain smoking because he is out of matches. This simple tale of love and jealousy was written by Prévert from a story by Jacques Viot, but its true subjects are the humdrum, the failed and the feeble. The arch-seducer, Jules Berry, is too weak to kill Gabin, his rival, but he does goad Gabin into killing him – in itself a sign of weakness. Gabin himself is pitiable. Life has been, he says, like waiting in the rain for a tram which, when it comes, is full. The two women have fared no better: both are promiscuous (each in her fashion) and both are somewhat pathetic – at the beginning because they are tied to Berry, at the end because they have lost Gabin. Whether such pessimism – here, as in *Quai des Brumes* – was intrinsic, endemic or acquired, the film remains remarkable for the inter-relationship between these four people. Berry is superb, with his fur collar, the cheap little brooches he gives to his girls, the wheedling, eavesdropping and fake dandy airs. Jacqueline Laurent is wilful and feminine, given to teddy bears and foolishly content to enjoy the admiration of both men. Gabin is his customary self, his relationship with Arletty an unusual one for the cinema at this time: when he proposes leaving her she responds, frowning, that they are not in love – then adding on a note of regret that with him she is able to 'breathe' a little.

The profound disillusionment was not lost on the Daladier government, which banned the film for export. A copy was, however, smuggled to North Africa, from which it reached the Allied countries in Fifties – when, because of the prestige of French movies, then denied us, it perhaps seemed better than it was. Long withdrawn because R.K.O. remade it as *The Long Night* (q.v.), its reputation growing thereby, it did not, when it resurfaced in the 50s, seem the masterpiece it was widely assumed to be. One reason was that people remembered Carné's films as being profound rather than artistic, as allegorical rather than melodramatic (or had read about them as such); they had thought them progressive and they found them dated. There were doubts as to the extent of Carné's fatalism, which was originally thought to have conveyed the spirit of the time. And, of course, we had hindsight: by

There have been at least three cinematic attempts at Jules Renard's novel *Poil de Carotte* (1932), but the only one ever recalled is Julien Duvivier's second version (he had made it as a Silent). One reason for this is the magnificent performance of Harry Baur, left, with Robert Lynen in the title-role. They play father and son, and in this scene Baur realises how appallingly the boy has been treated.

1939, with the exception of the ultra-romantic *Les Enfants du Paradis* (q.v.), Carné's best work was behind him.

His reputation has, however, suffered less than that of Julien Duvivier (1896–1967), once considered his equal. Duvivier had been assistant to Marcel L'Herbier and Louis Feuillade before directing his first film in 1919, but he had to wait till 1932 and **Poil de Carotte** to really establish himself. He had already done a Silent version of this Jules Renard novel, the title of which refers to the nickname given to the youngest Lepic child (Robert Lynen); his sister Ernestine is flat-faced and deceitful, his brother Felix is mother's pet, smug and stupid and a petty thief to boot. Father (Harry Baur) is a withdrawn, unobservant man; he hasn't spoken to his wife (Catherine Fonteney) for years, and he gives her plenty of opportunity to bully the youngest boy. 'Pourquoi ça?' he whispers, when he finds the boy attempting suicide – and Harry Baur (1881–1941), a great actor, was never more moving. His strength in the reflective sequences with the boy★ atone

★Both were victims of the Nazis: Lynen was shot for his work with the Resistance, and Baur, a Jew, died mysteriously after being confined to his apartment.

for Duvivier's attempts to wrench a tear; and if the director also seems uneasy with Renard's misogyny, he clearly cherishes the deeply rural setting.

With **La Bandéra** (1936), written by Spaak, Duvivier showed that his command of his medium had become firmer, and their collaboration on **La Belle Equipe** (1936) resulted in one of the most entertaining films of the decade. Spaak's story grows from themes in Clair's films, gathering a dustier, darker veneer in the less optimistic European climate: five layabouts, living in a run-down hotel, win 100,000 francs in the Loterie Nationale, which they invest in an inn on the banks of the Marne. Their solidarity is threatened when the wife (Viviane Romance) of one (Charles Vanel) makes a play for another (Gabin): however, the latter sends her packing by saying, 'Un copain est vaut mieux que toi', and with that sentence actually spoken this has to be the strongest of all the movies about male friendship, including Spaak's own *Gueule d'Amour*. What delighted the public was the friendship between the five men, the équipe itself, and this was one of the few non-comic demotic subjects to be widely liked: the film is an expression of the government coalition of left-wing parties called the Popular Front, and its hopeful ending would surely have been tragic if made a year later, when the political climate had worsened.

Duvivier turned to escapism, firstly with a new version of **Le Golem** (1936), made in Czechoslovakia, notable mainly for Baur's performance and the decor, and then with **Pépé le Moko** (1936) – though it was not regarded as such by contemporaries. It again posed a number of popular themes: the North African colonies as places of intrigue and mystery, and the gangster-outsider as hero. The detective Ashelbé wrote the orginal novel, Jeanson the perfectly-geared screenplay. Pépé le Moko (Gabin), wanted by the police, hides out in the Casbah which he wants to leave as much as he longs for Paris, for the Place Blanche. He meets a beautiful woman (Mireille Balin), for whom he finally quits the Casbah, and is shot down as her ship leaves for France. The ending has a number of resonances, and if the rest is hardly subtle Duvivier's handling is both fluid and imaginative. 'Perhaps', said Graham Greene in *The Spectator*, 'there have been pictures as exciting on the "thriller" level as this before, but I cannot remember one which has succeeded so admirably in raising the thriller to a poetic level.'

Un Carnet de Bal (1937) was as warmly received, but has not aged well, disappointing its original admirers on its infrequent revivals, which is ironic, for its theme is Never-Go-Back – the story of a widow who finds an old dance programme and seeks out her partners of that night. Richard Griffith noted sourly later that it impressed the 'intelligentsia', and one turns to Basil Wright, again in *The Spectator,* to discover why: he found 'a wonderful sequence depicting a crazed mother who won't believe that her son died twenty years ago, and lives in hourly self-deception awaiting his return'; the other scene he liked, featuring Pierre Blanchar as an abortionist, now seems self-consciously arty. Marie Bell's performance is so devoid of character as to make one doubt that she would be remembered after two years, let alone twenty; but a supporting cast that includes Rosay, Jouvet, Baur, Raimu and Fernandel would

Jean Gabin and Viviane Romance in Duvivier's *La Belle Equipe*, whose title refers to five friends and colleagues. Gabin is one member of the equipe and Mlle Romance, clearly trying to split them up, plays the wife of another. Romance was an excellent actress, often associated with roles – and apparel – like this.

371

outshine most stars. The contrived nature of the piece – Jeanson was one of the three screenwriters – left the French public indifferent, despite the players and a popular theme tune, 'the Valse Grise'.

Duvivier signed a Hollywood contract, but he had an unhappy time making *The Great Waltz* (q.v.), returning to France for another collaboration with Spaak, **La Fin du Jour** (1939). Its setting is a home for retired thespians, coping with old age and each other; Jouvet is ill at ease, while Duvivier's variable response is only at its warmest with Michel Simon, as an old man with a fondness for teenage boys. His last prewar film is **Untel Père et Fils** (1940), the saga of a French family from 1870 to the present day, which had the backing of the government – presumably overlooking the fact that its characters, like most of Duvivier's protagonists, ended up dead, defeated or settling for second best.

Among other French film-makers then much admired is Sacha Guitry (1885–1957), although he was primarily a man of the theatre – the son of an actor and an actor himself as well as playwright and impresario. Coming late to the cinema, he began a prolific screen career as actor-director-writer, and since his films, whether adaptations of his stage plays or original works, were mainly to display his own talents, he infuriated a minority of observers. Abroad he was regarded as the epitome of French sophistication, so that his disregard for film convention passed for daring. He acquired international screen renown with **La Roman d'un Tricheur** (1936), and it remains his most entertaining film. As the title indicates, it is a biography of a cheat, and told almost entirely in commentary. As its hero a boy, stole eight sous, and is punished by being denied the treat of a mushroom dinner: a few hours later he is the sole survivor, not knowing whom to mourn, since, as he says, he has an *embarrass de choix*. Having decided that he owes his life to dishonesty, he embarks on a career of trickery, his actual exploits less rewarding than the bonbons: Frehel singing to army recruits; a description of Monaco, with the palace guard marching forward – and backward; a montage of lovers in a window, with discordant music when they quarrel; himself coming through a permanently revolving door in many disguises; and visual speculation on

his bride in various guises – a device used later in *On the Town* (q.v.). Guitry's younger self is played by two other actors, and when at the second transition he observes, 'I had to resign myself to the fact that although I was only thirty-four I looked forty' it is impossible not to enjoy him.

Les Perles de la Couronne was made to celebrate the coronation of 1937, an agreeable contribution to the Entente Cordiale. Italy is also heavily involved in the plot, neatly suggesting that France lies not only physically but culturally between the two countries – and in the English and Italian sequences those languages are spoken, which was then unusual. Indeed, the conception is so civilised and the narrative so freewheeling that one looks beyond the facetious tone for something which might illuminate the events mirrored: disappointingly, and typically, there is nothing. Nor is there much real wit; and, equally disappointing, the historical pageant gives way to some frippery about missing jewels. **Ils Etaient Neuf Célibataires** (1939) pinpoints Guitry's faults and virtues more engagingly. It has a funny premise, indulgently carried out. It also has a huge part for himself, but it uses the medium well, keeping several plots going simultaneously. He plays a confidence trickster who takes advantage of a new decree expelling foreigners to arrange for nine aged and improvident bachelors to accommodate wealthy foreign women who will pay heavily for husbands. One woman is furious to discover that she has married a man she once turned away as a beggar, till she finds that as an accountant he can fiddle her tax returns: we could be happy together, she says, to which he replies, 'Why not? We've never been in love.' For the most part, however, the piece is not so much cynical as simply heartless.

If Guitry's following abroad could be described as a coterie, Marcel Pagnol eventually acquired a foreign reputation which seemed about to take his films beyond the confines of the art-houses. Also from the stage and taking a primarily comic view of his fellow countrymen, he both wrote and directed, after taking a keen interest in the filming of his plays by other hands. These include not only the first two of the 'Marius' trilogy, but **Topaze** (1933), his most popular piece, handled stagily by Louis Gasnier,

a one-time Hollywood director, with Jouvet as the mild mathematics teacher who, given the opportunity, becomes a financial genius. About the same time Pagnol set up his own studio in Marseilles, since his aim was to make films of Provençal life – usually from his own material but also remodelling the novels of Jean Giono till they seemed like his own work. As director he began with assurance: **Angèle** (1934), after Giono, concerns a farm girl (Orane Demazis) seduced by the fast-talking stranger who, after their child is born, persuades her into prostitution; the family handyman (Fernandel) is sent to bring her home, and her outraged father locks her in a shed while her destiny is being resolved. That takes an excessive amount of talk – and Pagnol's refusal to contemplate 'pure' cinema earned him, in France, a similar disdain to that accorded Guitry.

However, the sun of Provence shines bright; and Pagnol's celebration of that region of France would become, in **La Femme du Boulanger** (1938), quite marvellous. There is a dead dog down a well, and there are elms preventing the sun ever getting to a neighbour's spinach; the curé is quarrelling with the schoolteacher over the remark that Joan of Arc had *thought* she heard voices. It is also the day when the new baker (Raimu) will bake his first loaves, and the villagers turn up in expectation – including the marquis (Charpin) and his shepherd, Dominique (Charles Moulin), who will collect the bread twice a week for the chateau: and when the first look passes between the handsome Dominique and the baker's young wife (Ginette Leclerc) it is a *coup de foudre*. When Dominique comes serenading, the wife slips out; and as the baker gets quickly drunk on Pernod he

Marcel Pagnol's tales of Provençal life are not as highly regarded as they once were, and he admittedly was not averse to melodrama. When his humour and powers of observation prevailed his films could be splendid, as in *La Femme du Boulanger*. The lady of the title has gone off with a young man, and her husband, the baker, has gone on strike. Discussing the matter are the squire, Charpin, left, and the cure, Robert Vattier.

makes one thing clear – that there will be no bread made till she returns. The story is predictable and some sequences are over-stretched, but the film preserves a way of life which disappeared first with the advent of the automobile and then with television; nowadays it is unlikely that the matter would be settled by a triumvirate of the marquis, the curé and the schoolteacher. The curé exults in his own tact; a lone spinster waits on the road to see the sinners return; and one man is desperately anxious to establish that the couple he saw on a horse seemed only a *semblance*. There are few richer films, and that is its justification: no one now could care whether this is 'pure' cinema.

Abroad, the film joined *La Kermesse Héroïque, Mayerling* (q.v.), *Un Carnet de Bal* and *La Grande Illusion* (q.v.) in encouraging new audiences for the foreign-language film. Flushed with such successes, the French film industry contemplated a larger share of the world market. Its output was only one-fifth that of Hollywood, but lower costs – the average expenditure per film was the equivalent of only $75,000 – meant higher profits; and the mainly trans-ient producers began to think in bigger terms than local product and co-produc-tions with Germany or Italy. The majority of these entrepreneurs regarded France as a stopping-off place on their journey from Eastern Europe to America, thus hardly contributing to a settled industry, and their manifold liaisons with local film-makers had resulted in the industry being frag-mented, with production and distribution companies almost equalling the number of cinemas. The trade papers of 1938/9 announced ambitious plans, to feature internationally-known names; few of them, however, were definite projects, and the declaration of war put paid to those that were.

Though it was by chance that the struc-ture of the industry enabled directors to control their own product, they took advantage to an extent not possible in most other countries at the time. Thus the German refugee directors were able to contribute substantially to the French cinema, even though most of them were heavily indebted to the Russian-born Ger-man producer, Seymour Nebenzal (1899–1961), who had produced the last German films of Pabst and Lang. He had set up a French operation before the Nazis came to power, to enable Pabst to make the basically French *L'Atlantide,* but his biggest success in France was **Mayerling** (1936), directed by his compatriot, Anatole Litvak (1902–74), who too had found himself no longer welcome in Germany. The film is a highly romanticised account of the nineteenth-century Hapsburg tragedy; while not afraid to hint at some of its more sordid undertones, it is pictorially hand-some and drenched in atmosphere. At its centre are the lovers, the crown prince and his mistress, vividly and touchingly por-trayed by Charles Boyer and Danielle Darrieux (b. 1917). It is reputed to have inspired a number of suicide pacts among the romantically inclined, and caused Hollywood to send for Litvak.

Thus Pabst inherited **Mademoiselle Docteur** (1937), his first film in three years, but it is impossible to see why the piece should have interested two such eminent directors, unless it was the cast – Jouvet, Pierre Blanchar, Pierre Fresnay, Charles Dullin, Viviane Romance, Jean-Louis Barrault and, in the title-role, Dita Parlo. It is a trashy tale, set in Salonika during World War I, in which almost everyone turns out to be a spy. It was perhaps the uneasy European situation which raised a crop of espionage tales. French audiences had also shown a fondness for stories of faraway places, and Pabst made **Le Drame de Shanghai** (1938), as if to prove that drama in Shanghai was equally as witless as in Salonika. It concerns a Hong Kong-educated schoolgirl (Elina Labourdette), the daughter of a nightclub singer (Chris-tiane Mardayne) who is also a spy and in the power of a scar-faced member (Jouvet) of a spy ring called Le Serpent Noir. The sequences of the rallying Chinese were clearly inspired by Malraux's novel 'La Condition Humaine', but they neither raise the level of the piece nor indicate any keen interest on the part of Pabst.

Robert Siodmak, a lesser director, fared much better in France, starting with **La Crise est Finie** (1934), produced by Nebenzal. It is of a wondrous gaiety, belying the fact that both men had recently been exiled from their own country. Though the title specifically refers to a theatrical troupe which survives by putting on its own show, it also refers to the Depression – and the cast reprises the title song, clearly intended to mean in France what 'Who's Afraid of the Big Bad Wolf?' had meant in the States. The direct connection is only made when two of the troupe dress up as *flics* to recruit some men on the dole working as street musicians – which is a more definite comment on the Depression than the film's model, *42nd Street*. The finale tries for a Berkeley-like spectacle, using imagination rather than size. Till that point, Siodmak had taken Clair's style as well as his leading man, Albert Préjean, but since the piece is so entertaining it would be invidious to speak of derivation.

Both **Cargaison Blanche** (1936) and **Mister Flow** (1936) emulate Hollywood models less successfully. The former, though supposedly based on a recent magazine *reportage,* uses white slave trading as a background for the adventures of two in-and-out-of-love journalists, Jean-Pierre Aumont and Käthe de (von) Nagy; the latter is a comedy in which an aristocratic master-crook, Edwige Feuillère, gets herself involved with an innocent young advocate, Fernand Gravey. As with most of Siodmak's films, whether made in Berlin, Paris or Hollywood, subsequent events fail to measure up to the intriguing opening, which includes Jouvet fawning and cringing as an imprisoned valet who is not quite what he seems. Similarly, the best of *Cargaison Blanche* is sustained by the villainy of Jules Berry and Charles Granval.

Mollenard (1938) is virtually two different films lurking inside one. Siodmak's penchant for free spirits led him to this classic example of the anti-bourgeois film, with Harry Baur as the rumbustious, adventuresome sea captain, Justin Mollenard, and Gabrielle Dorziat as his prim, narrowminded wife. Unfortunately the skulduggery in Shanghai is no more mature than that in Pabst's movie, despite such denizens as Pierre Renoir and Dalio; and there is something about Baur's crabbed face which indicates that he could never really be a gun-runner in a B-movie. The Dunkerque sequences are very different, with a real bite, but they have difficulty in surviving the first half. Setting aside *La Crise est Finie*, this is the best of Siodmak's French films, with distinguished contributions from Eugen Schüfftan

The German director Robert Siodmak, who had been making some very fine films was forced to flee when the Nazis came to power. He settled in France – till the Germans invaded – and directed a mixed batch of films, of which *La Crise est Finie* is the best. It concerns a theatrical troupe in difficulty. Here the leading lady, Danielle Darrieux, allows herself to be taken to dinner by Marcel Carpentier, one man who could certainly help. He outlines his conditions over champagne, and Mlle Darrieux feels them too compromising.

and Henri Alekan, who trained their cameras on sets by Trauner; and from Darius Milhaud, who wrote the score, and Spaak who wrote the screenplay with the author of the original novel, O-P. Gilbert.

Pièges (1939) opens well, and for much of its length is 'French-good' – melo-dramatic and mysterious: but too often it is 'French-poor' – mock *Carnet de Bal*. Maria Déa is the taxi-dancer who agrees to be a police decoy to attract a mass murderer, a killer who meets his victims by advertising in the personal columns of the journals; Maurice Chevalier is the man whom the police suspect, and Pierre Renoir is his partner, suspected by audiences. There is little of the sexual obsession that American reviewers thought had been censored when the film was shown there, and modern audiences are unlikely to be titillated by just two shots of Mlle Déa's legs.

Edouard Corniglion-Molinier, the producer of *Mollenard*, was another refugee from Germany, he had earlier backed **Mauvaise Graine** (1934), written and directed by the Hungarian, Alexander Esway, who had been his assistant some years before, and also Billy Wilder, in his first attempt at direction. As in the case of *La Crise est Finie,* these exiles produced a cheerful little film, in this case borrowing from Clair (and the German musicals) the central theme of male friendship. One of the two, Jean-la-Cravatte, goes around stealing neckties – which we may recognise as a Wilder touch; and the film states bluntly that gentlemen rich enough to afford cars deserve to have them stolen, at least by such a merry and enterprising gang of thieves. This is not the only film of the period to suggest, at the end, that a new life waits overseas, a solution to the evils of Europe. Esway remained there, at one point becoming a producer in Britain, while Wilder (q.v.) went on to Hollywood.

The most successful of the emigré directors was the naturalised Frenchman, Max Ophuls, who began his French career with a new version of *Liebelei*, subtitled *Une Histoire d'Amour,* which is in fact the German film, recut and dubbed, a number of its scenes uninterestingly reshot with French principals. The German original was admired by the Italian publisher, Rizzoli, who reunited Ophuls with its writers, Hans Wilhelm and Curt Alexander, to adapt a novel by Salvator Gotta, **La Sig-nora di Tutti** (1933). Its heroine is a schoolgirl, Gaby Doriot (Isa Miranda), and its subject her involvement with the Nanni family – with the father (Memo Benassi), an academic, who has made her his mistress, and the son, who would like to make her his wife: when the mother dies girl and father resume their relationship, till guilt over-whelms her. The film was obviously congenial to Ophuls, for if the opera montage and the lavish use of music – by Daniel Ampitheatrof – recall *Liebelei,* certain aspects would reappear in his later work: *Letter From an Unknown Woman* (q.v.) would also feature a decent young girl caught up in a passion beyond her, and *Lola Montes* (q.v.) would use a similar framing device, for, like Lola, Gaby becomes an actress. While this is the second Ophuls film to be set in and around the film studios, **Divine** (1935) moves him to the world of live theatre, as represented by a sub-Folies Bergère outfit in Paris – his heroine is an innocent but far from divine chorus girl (Simone Berriau), whose involvement with drugs reeks of Silent melodrama: doubtless there were drug addicts in the tatty music halls of Pigalle, but the handling is absurd, due not least to the screenplay – partly contributed by Colette, on one of whose stories it is based.

Invited to the Netherlands to make **Komedie om Geld** (1936), Ophuls allowed his instinct as social satirist to take command – and the film, if uneven and often overemphatic, has extraordinary bit-terness: it is the only film made by any of the emigrés which suggests that they were working off anger at their treatment by Germany (as opposed to criticising its new régime). It is possible to see analogies, as the capitalist system it attacks is represented by bankers and industrialists presumably similar to those who financed Hitler; its hero is a little man, a cashier (Hermann Bouber) whom they use and then destroy. The changes in his fortunes reflect *A Nous la Liberté, Der Letzte Mann* and *L'Argent,* but Brecht was also influential in both theme and structure; and a compère similar to that of *Dreigroschenoper* appears from time to time to sing about money.

The structure of **La Tendre Ennemie** (1936) is almost top-heavy for its hour's running time, and André-Paul Antoine's play, 'L'Ennemie', has been softened by taking some of the blame from Man's

In *Sans Lendemain*, Edwige Feuillère hires a house to impress a nice Canadian doctor so that he will agree to bring up her son. In this shot, however, she is returning to her real home. The novelletish plot is lifted by the admirable performance of Mme Feuillère and by Max Ophuls' direction – and in fact this is one of the most memorable of his tragic romances.

natural enemy, Woman, and placing it on fate. There are vestiges of Ophuls's talent for regarding society, but **Yoshiwara** (1937) demonstrates that other aspect of it, the lushly romantic. It is adapted from a popular novel by Maurice Dekobra and concerns a Russian officer (Pierre-Richard Willm), a high-born geisha (Michiko Tanaka) and the coolie (Sessue Hayakawa) who loves her madly. No better and no worse than other French romances of the time, with its uniformed men and helpless ladies, treachery and death, it at least marks a new assurance in Ophuls's work.

He later considered that he had betrayed his revered Goethe (a copy of 'Faust' was by his bedside when he died) in **Werther** (1938), which he and Wilhelm adapted for the producer Nebenzal. It is not a satisfying film since the story has been much prettified, but it is the first time, even including *Liebelei*, that all his particular qualities reach maturity – his intellect, his decorative flair and his instinct for irony and romance. Goethe's autobiographical tale concerned a young man, Werther (here, Willm) who falls in love with the fiancée, Charlotte (Annie Verney) of his best friend, Albert. When she learns of this she is both flattered and angry, and when both

Werther and she realise that they cannot change he, after taking to drink, commits suicide. In the film he does not know of the engagement, and the character has been downgraded to a shuffling Dostoyevskian official. But as the film moves further from its source and the simplicities of the first half it becomes a stronger emotional drama than most films of the time. Charlotte becomes a victim of fate, not destined for real happiness, and when the betrayed Albert confronts Werther with the dossier of his dissipation both men are almost submerged by the experience. As the moral issues grow so M. Willm gets increasingly lost, except for a brilliant moment when Werther's poetry is mocked in a brothel. There is also one quite remarkable sequence of a musical evening which in its visual handling and understanding of the past is as unspectacularly satisfying as anything in the history of cinema.

Sans Lendemain, released in the spring of 1940, must have struck a chord with French audiences, for it tells of a Woman with a Past – one who, like France, had not managed her affairs too well and thus might be said to have seen better days. She is a faded stripper who works in a Montmartre nightclub in order to bring up her son;

377

when an old lover (Georges Rigaud) reappears she puts herself in hock to a gang-boss for an assumed existence, and the latter sees her actions as a conscious move towards his empire of prostitution. It is more novelettish than Ophuls's films either side of it, but he is more at ease than in either, both with the sleazy settings and the chief protagonist. As played by Edwige Feuillère, who never before or again came so close to a Garboesque evocation of a doomed lady sick with love, she is one of his most affecting heroines. The film was not shown in London till 1948 (it was not released at all in the U.S.), by which time it seemed old-fashioned; we may now see it as we see Le Jour se Lève, where no reality impinges on the false reality which is its romantic essence.

The success of Litvak's earlier film provided the raison d'être for De Mayerling à Sarajevo, which despite its title limits its subject to a portrait of the morganatic marriage between the Archduke Franz Ferdinand (John Lodge) and the Countess Sophie Chotek (Feuillère). That an heir to the throne insisted against all odds on marrying the woman of his choice still had a certain topicality when this film went into production – but filming was postponed owing to events more pressing, and the film was finally premiered the day the Germans invaded Belgium and Luxembourg. A foreword disclaims factual accuracy, but the treatment of the romance is intelligent, even if, as is customary in such ventures, the writers – who include Carl Zuckmayer and Curt Alexander – adopt the ironic approach. 'What a pretty name!' declare the children on hearing that their parents are visiting Sarajevo, whose citizens in their loyal address express the hope that the royal visitors will find the day memorable. If the direction shows a weakness for the chandeliers of throne rooms and the drapes of boudoirs, it also manages sympathy for the humans beneath the braid – notably in Sophie's encounter after fifteen years with the emperor's head of protocol, when he assures her that he would not let pass this first chance to do her a favour, and in her first meeting with the archduke's mother who was well-practised in coping with royal amours. In this role Gabrielle Dorziat steals the film. Lodge makes less of the archduke, but he is pleasant enough, if not much like the real Franz Ferdinand.

The film opened in Paris in May 1940, six weeks before that city fell to the Germans, and clearly it was to audiences then only of limited interest. Louis Jouvet helped Ophuls after he had escaped to Switzerland, where Jouvet was acting after the fall of France, and they began to make a film of L'Ecole des Femmes, in which Jouvet was appearing on the stage. But there were romantic complications – both were in love with the same lady – and Ophuls left for the U.S. where he later resumed his career. Later still he returned to France to make another group of films, work that would make him world famous. Few of those made at this time were seen outside France, but they contribute to an astonishingly rich body of work.

Marcel l'Herbier had become a specialist in historical reconstruction, and his films of this time are as solid and satisfying as the sets for them designed by Eugène Lourié, who also worked with Ophuls, and the veteran Andreyev. Nuits de Feu (1937) is the first of three films set in Russia, an adaptation of Tolstoi's play, 'The Living Corpse', about the state prosecutor (Victor Francen) who stages his own murder when he learns that his wife (Gaby Morlay) has fallen in love with a younger colleague (Georges Rigaud). The wife loves both men but differently, and though the theme is therefore that of Shaw's 'Candida' this is merely a thumping melodrama of suspicion, injustice and revenge. La Citadelle du Silence (1937) concerns the daughter (Annabella) of a revolutionary who marries a prison governor (Pierre Renoir) in order to free her lover (Bernard Lancret); La Tragédie Impériale (1938) is a version of the fall of the Romanovs, concentrating on Rasputin (Harry Baur) and a young couple (Willm, Carine Nelson) who are the first to disdain him.

The French taste for royal romance at this time occasioned a remake of Le Joueur d'Echecs (1938), moving further back in Russian history to the Court of Catherine the Great (Françoise Rosay), whose patronage of the robot-making Austrian baron (Conrad Veidt) leads to mayhem; Jean Dréville directed. Raymond Bernard, who had made the 1928 version, remade a scrupulous Les Misérables (1933), its five hours originally shown in three separate parts. Charles Vanel brings few histrionics to his steely Javert, and the drive needed by

Jean-Louis Barrault and Viviane Romance in Jeff Musso's *Le Puritain*, which, if not as good as was thought at the time, does not deserve the semi-oblivion into which it has fallen. This seems to be the fate of films made by directors who were not prolific or who did not distinguish themselves in any other way. Musso himself made only two other films apart from this one, which is supposedly set in Dublin.

this long event is provided by M. Baur as Valjean. Baur is also the incomparable Porfiry of **Crime et Châtiment** (1935), relaxed and good-humoured, but of terrible determination. Pierre Chenil directed, drawing from Pierre Blanchar his best screen work as Raskolnikov.

These literary, historical films, made by directors equally adept at thrillers and action tales, were the commercial corner-stones of the French cinema, despite or because of their underlying pessimism. Their directors are skilful, experienced craftsmen, often veterans. Among their successors is Jean Delannoy (b. 1908), whose **Macao, l'Enfer du Jeu** (1939) is a superb example of the genre film. The basic material – from another 'exotic' novel by Maurice Dekobra – is the usual nonsense about *femmes fatales* and gunrunners, but whereas Pabst despised *Le Drame de Shanghai*, Delannoy clearly enjoys every second. The plot, which has more twists than a bedspring, involves a large cast of characters, including a stranded showgirl (Mireille Balin), a German adventurer (Erich Von Stroheim), a French journalist (Roland Toutain) and the Chinese owner (Sessue Hayakawa) of a luxurious gambling den. Marc Allégret (b. 1900), after

Fanny had specialised in farces and then melodramas, of which **Entrée des Artistes** (1938) is a good example: involved in a murder at drama school are two of the students (Odette Joyeux, Claude Dauphin), a journalist (Carette) and the professor (Jouvet).

Christian-Jaque (b. 1904) at this time seemed headed towards an interesting career; after assisting Duvivier and Guitry (uncredited, he directed most of *Les Perles de la Couronne*), he scored an international success with **Les Disparus de Saint-Agil** (1938), brilliantly invoking the enclosed, somewhat unhealthy world of the boarding school. This is not, however, a French, male version of *Mädchen in Uniform*, but a straightforward mystery, involving a drunken art master (Michel Simon) and a cordially-disliked foreign teacher (Von Stroheim): unfortunately, the plot is foolishly resolved – a fault so common that most ordinary Hollywood thrillers revive better than their more 'atmospheric' European counterparts.

The Dublin of Jeff Musso's **Le Puritain** (1937) is so Parisian as to be disconcerting: the source is a novel by Liam O'Flaherty which begins as a crime story and moves into (not very profound) psychology. A

379

religious fanatic and journalist (Jean-Louis Barrault) is in the habit of knifing prostitutes and then demanding that his paper indict society. He arouses the suspicion of the police inspector (Pierre Fresnay) while attempting to test his virtue with a whore (Viviane Romance). That he is motivated by suppressed lust seemed daring at the time, and was one reason the film was admired; this was the first feature made by Musso, who had come to films by way of writing music, and the only one of the three he made which was successful.

Far from such fictional gloom is **L'Espoir,** the one film made by André Malraux (1901–76), the novelist, historian and essayist. He began it in 1937, adapting it from his book of the same name, which details his experiences in Spain with the International Brigade. It was backed by Corniglion-Molinier, who had helped to form the air squadron attached to the Brigade. Unfinished and apparently unsatisfactory at the outbreak of war, the film was hidden away by one of the Paris staff of Pathé. When finally shown it was a failure: after the Liberation the public was in no mood for a feature-length documentary, especially one on other people's troubles. But though it is awkward, with an air of improvisation and an amateur structure, it is not only worth more than most movies on war but is an important film in its own right – not because it is anti-fascist but because its makers thought it was, as vitally certain of their cause as the great Russian Silent film-makers were of theirs. Here too amateurs play all the roles; there is no one hero with whom to identify, but a group of them; and the narrative follows no precise line but is a pattern of struggles, with newsreel footage of the Civil War intelligently blended with the material shot in Teruel. Like the film *For Whom the Bell Tolls* (q.v.), it is about the blowing up of a bridge. Dynamiting is difficult, since a machine-gun post guards the route, and bombing is no easier, as there is a fascist air base between the target and the Loyalists, who have only two slow, ancient bombers. When one plane crashes the wounded and dead are brought down from the mountains, to be joined by a trickle of sympathisers which becomes a crowd and then a multitude: it is a moving sequence precisely because up till then the film had regarded its subject with the nonchalance

associated with its heroes.

While Malraux was working on this film the French cinema was being praised for one of the few significant movies on war, *La Grande Illusion* (q.v.), which was Jean Renoir's only great success of the decade. His work is uneven, but his films of the Thirties can now be seen as the most impressive, in sum, of any of his contemporaries. After the financial failure of *La Chienne*, he chose as more commercial **La Nuit de Carrefour** (1932), the first of Simenon's novels to be filmed. Commenting on it, Jean-Luc Godard calls it Renoir's most mysterious film, but then spoils his point by observing that Simenon has affinities with Balzac and Dostoyevsky. So he has, but this mild, tinny Maigret thriller cannot sustain such cultural respectability. However, on its way to a dénouement concerning a hoard of cocaine and some stolen jewellery there are agreeable accompaniments: the desolate crossroads and the misty country byways; the incongruity of the doctor, in white tie and tails, tending a wounded man in an oily service station; a heroine with fondness for an old Italian tune and a gauche eroticism; and Maigret (Pierre Renoir) himself, with his little black moustache and dejected countenance. The director financed the film from his own resources, and though it was released with some reels missing (lost, apparently, by Jean Mitry, who acts in the film and was later a critic) this did not prevent its being mildly successful.

Boudu Sauvé des Eaux (1932) is not a mile away from Balzac. Boudu (Michel Simon) is crossing the Pont des Beaux-Arts when he is spotted by an antiquarian bookseller, M. Lestingois (Charles Granval), who sees in him, as he says, a very successful *clochard*. He rescues him from drowning and gives him a home, which Boudu accepts with reluctance and regards with contempt, till, weeks later, his anarchic habits have brought Madame to a state of hysteria and Monsieur – who is having an affair with the maid – to sexual frustration. Madame, however, fancies Boudu, who reasons that if Monsieur can avail himself of both ladies so can he. The source material, a boulevard comedy by René Fauchois, saves the situation with a lottery ticket and a marriage, but Renoir returns to the Seine, into which Boudu throws his new bowler hat, symbol of the middle class. The film finishes with one long, last pan of the river, not at this point particularly attractive, but restful. Boudu's choice may be admirable, but is he, a man who boasts of never having said thank you to anyone, better than his benefactor, a purely disinterested philanthropist? The film's ambivalence disconcerted contemporary audiences, few of which would have preferred penniless arcadia to a comfortable bourgeoisie. It was not seen abroad publicly till the Sixties, when it became one of Renoir's most popular films. It is nice, incidentally, to learn towards the end, at his wedding, that this cuckoo in the nest is called Priapus. Priapus Boudu.

Chotard et Cie (1933) had been a stage success and its author, Roger Ferdinand, invited Renoir to film it, working with him on the screenplay. Charpin repeats his stage role as Chotard, a Marseilles grocer, whose daughter (Jeanne Boitel) dithers between two suitors, a pompous gendarme (Louis Seigner) and a dreamy poet (Georges Pomiès), who proves a disaster as a shop clerk. Renoir ruins his chance to say something about the nature of the artist and his calling by encouraging Pomiès to give the same balletic performance he gave in *Tire-au-Flanc*. This film is hardly funnier than that, but since Renoir proves – again – adept at small town satire, he may be said to be partly successful in his aim, which was to make a comedy in the American style.

Increasingly convinced that adaptations could become good cinema, he envisaged **Madame Bovary** (1934) as 'filmed theatre' – and that was what the public wanted. But in Renoir's own terms it meant a series of dialogues in long takes, allowing the performers and the material to rise to the dramatic heights of which both were capable. The screenplay he wrote from the book is exemplary, but he fails to convey the stultitude of provincial life. Nor is he helped by his Emma, Valentine Tessier, unable or unwilling to portray any taste for fantasy or hatred of her environment. With so much of the central character missing, the piece could not totally succeed, but it is good on Emma's affair with Rodolphe and her eagerness to begin a second liaison, and it has a small triumph with its Bovary, a lost, lorn, loving man as played by the director's brother, Pierre. The original ran over three hours, but was cut by the distributor to just over a 100 minutes.

A foreword to **Toni** (1935) explains that all races meet in this particular part of the Mediterranean, and it was Pagnol who enabled Renoir to make the film, at his own studio in Nice and on nearby locations. Carl Einstein helped Renoir with the scenario, based on material supplied by a friend of Renoir's who had been police commissioner at Martigues. Toni (Charles Blavette), an Italian immigrant worker, falls in love with Josefa (Céla Montalvan), who is Spanish; they are forced to marry others, but neither marriage is happy, and Toni is drawn into the affairs of Josefa, her drunken bully of a husband, and her cousin-lover Albert. These people – fortunately, given the ending – live and breathe; they follow the creed that the world is divided into the haves and have-nots, a creed which in Renoir's best work is expressed in terms of weakness versus personal dominance (as opposed to wealth and influence). He takes us gently into this rural corner of the world and he illuminates it.

Murder in the artisan class is also the subject of **Le Crime de Monsieur Lange** (1936), and it is committed when M. Batala (Jules Berry) returns to claim the publishing house which he had left in debt. In the meantime a workers' co-operative had made it profitable, and M. Lange (René Lefèvre), believing Batala dead, decides to keep it that way. His surname is a play on *l'ange,* and he looks angelic – meek, a dreamer, vague: the only positive actions he makes are to shoot Batala and to follow a buxom prostitute who accosts him when his girl has run off – both actions of which the director clearly approves. Renoir has returned to the mocking style of *Boudu,* but has become more confident in indicating his affection – for the magazine workers, their neighbours in the laundry and even for his villain, but that may be because Berry was one of the most relishable bad men in the business.

La Partie de Campagne celebrates love, youth, beauty, tranquillity and the countryside. Henriette (Sylvia Bataille) feels, she tells her mother (Jane Marken), an *espèce de tendresse* for the trees, the sky, the fields. She and her mother are gay, lively, attractive, while their men are dullards, imperceptive and, in the case of M. Dufour, gross. The canoeists who offer to entertain them while their men are fishing clearly deserve them as much as the ladies in turn

381

Jean Renoir is now regarded as a great director, yet during the Thirties his international reputation was established by only two films, *La Grande Illusion*, ABOVE with Erich Von Stroheim to the right of the staircase, and *La Bête Humaine*, ABOVE RIGHT, with Simone Simon and Jean Gabin. Most of his other films were not seen outside France, while *Partie de Campagne*, RIGHT, with Jean Marken and Georges Saint-Saëns, was left unfinished, and *La Règle du Jeu* FAR RIGHT, with Roland Toutain and Renoir himself, was cut to ribbons after a disastrous Paris showing. When the remains of the one were assembled and the complete version of the other finally restored, both were seen to be among his greatest works.

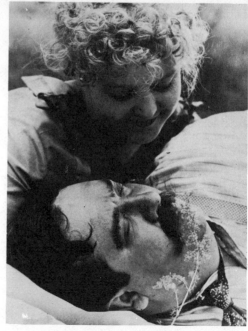

382

deserve them. But as this world goes, it cannot last. The film seems beyond analysis, or rather, should be: if not Renoir's masterpiece, it is surely flawless. It is also unfinished. Renoir wrote this adaptation of de Maupassant in 1936, and filmed it in the summer of that year, on the banks of the Loing, near Montigny – but rainy weather held up shooting till the date he was contracted to start his next film. Renoir always claimed that the piece was complete, that he had always intended to make only a 50-minute film, which was all the material could stand: but it lasts only thirty-seven minutes and has two long titles to explain points essential to the narrative. On the other hand, the producer, Pierre Braunberger, is supposed to have asked Prévert to write a full-length script featuring Renoir's material – but by the time he was ready the cast had grown too old to use. It seems unlikely that Braunberger would have backed so short a film, and one so difficult to market: at all events, it was not publicly shown. It was destroyed by the Germans during the war, but Henri Langlois of the Cinématheque Française had saved a copy of the uncut negative. This was reshaped by Marguerite Renoir and Pierre Lestrinquez and shown in Paris in 1946 as one section of a three-part film – as it was in New York, in 1950; London first saw it, without its other two parts, in 1948.

The project for which Renoir had abandoned it was **Les Bas-Fonds** (1936), based on the play by Gorki. He persuaded Charles Spaak to work on the screenplay with him, and if they have a stronger narrative than the original they do not depart too seriously from its characters: the thief (Gabin); the baron (Jouvet), embezzler and gambler; the alcoholic actor (Robert Le Vigan); the mistress (Suzy Prim) of the dosshouse; her cruel and feeble-minded older husband (Vladimir Sokoloff); her sister (Junie Astor); and the whore (Jany Holt). They do not seem Russian, and when the film was shown in London for the first time Dilys Powell in *The Sunday Times* compared it unfavourably with Donskoi's Gorki trilogy: 'theatrical, almost flimsy, a superficial comment from a different society'. Certainly life in these particular lower depths is not degrading or particularly harsh, and there is hope and understanding: when the whore lies about her past, lifting incidents from a book she has just finished

reading, the baron observes, 'It is not what she says, but why she says it.' Renoir himself described the film as a realistic poem on the loss of human dignity.

He had made it when thwarted in his wish to film *La Belle Equipe,* whose screenplay he had loved, and it should be noted that he had been drawn to *Le Crime de Monsieur Lange* because of the co-operative idea it expressed. His sympathy for the less affluent classes had not gone unnoticed by the French Communist party, which invited him to direct **La Vie est à Nous** (1936). Later, living in America, he explained his ('delighted') acceptance as an attempt to combat Nazism, but at the time, under the Popular Front, his action needed no excuses. His collaborators included Jacques Becker, Jean-Paul Le Chanois and Henri Cartier-Bresson, working under his supervision, and his own responsibility did not extend to the editing, which is significant, for the finished film is largely a compilation of newsreel material. It starts with a teacher (Jean Dasté) giving schoolchildren an impressive series of statistics on France, and then moves back to offer a history of working people in the matter of strikes, protest marches and poverty. The villains are picked out – the French fascists, stirring up trouble; the equivalent of the Hitler Youth louts, attacking a vendor of the newspaper *L'Humanité.* The answer to these and other evils turns out to be the Communist party, seen labouring on behalf of the workers in three episodes, each purportedly selected from the letters of three grateful members. A modern foreword to the film claims that it was a tremendous success, which is not suprising, since its showings were private and restricted to dedicated Communists. Its view of the party is the usual one of the great provider, but it also manages to imply that the party had failed to come up with an operative system. However, the criticism is so slight that it would not have redeemed the picture for the Nazis, who were said to have destroyed it: it survived, and was first publicly seen in Paris in 1969.

La Grande Illusion (1937), written with Spaak, was based loosely on Renoir's experiences in the War. Its setting is a P.O.W. camp, and its central characters are two officers, De Boeldieu (Pierre Fresnay), from a military family, and Maréchal (Gabin), who has risen from the ranks;

indeed, the only other officer of De Boeldieu's own class is the German commandant (Erich Von Stroheim). Class, however, is less the subject of the film than the distinctions made by temperament and tradition, as expounded in the commandant's admission of singular trust in De Boeldieu. 'For the people it's a bad thing to die in a war,' he says. 'For you and me it's a good solution.' The great illusion is that men must hate each other in war. The film's pacifism was immediately admired but not completely understood, for it was claimed that Renoir intended a plea for France and Germany not to go to war, whereas, by making one of the characters (Dalio) a wealthy and sympathetic Jew, he ensured that it would not be shown in Germany. In France it was the year's most popular film, and after running an unprecedented six months in New York it was voted the Best Foreign Film by the critics of that city. Till then, although Renoir had been respected within the industry, filmgoers, if they thought of him at all, would probably have connected him only with *Le Crime de Monsieur Lange* and *Les Bas-Fonds,* the only films of his for which they had shown any great fondness.

If, by Renoir's own confession, he longed for recognition, he could hardly have hoped to find it with **La Marseillaise** (1938), subtitled *Quelques Faits Divers sur la Chute de la Monarchie.* Made as a co-operative venture under the influence of the Popular Front, it attempted to find parallels with a return to reason in government. The aristocracy is beastly, and the workers, as Renoir himself put it, 'very simple, good-hearted people', but both are treated simplistically – the one by quibbling over dance steps or similar fripperies, and the other with cosiness. In modelling the film on *October* and *The End of St Petersburg,* Renoir saw fit to add levity; his hesitancy may have been due to the divergence of his own opinions and the more truly demotic experience of his collaborators, but certainly the end result is an inadequate response to the most momentous event in his country's history.

Renoir's second great success came with another collaboration with Spaak, **La Bête Humaine** (1938). He chose Zola's novel as being 'commercial', and perhaps hoped to emulate the pessimism so much admired in many of his confrères. However, the film remains somewhat below the level of *Quai des Brumes,* despite the expectation aroused by a foreword to explain the mental condition of Lantier (Gabin). That character is no longer, as in Zola, a passive victim of fate, and with all passions brought to the surface little is left beneath. Nevertheless Lantier's involvement with the minx Sévèrine (Simone Simon) and her older, jealous, scheming husband (Fernand Ledoux), makes for melodrama as gripping as that of the not dissimilar *La Chienne*. But the film's main strength lies in its setting, the Paris-Le Havre railway line. Renoir's realism is less poetic than Carné's, but equally memorable: the cheerless little station, the hut by the railway line where the mackintoshed lovers consummate their *amour maudit,* and the workers' dance with its haunting song, 'Le Petit Coeur de Ninon'.

La Règle du Jeu (1939) was described by Renoir as only a divertissement, and it could be somewhat autobiographical – since he plays Octave, kindly and muddled, and the character may be based on himself. Octave is one of a number of people, rich and pampered, at a house party which may be the last for all of them. Their adventures are prefaced with a quotation from Beaumarchais, to music by Mozart – actually and appropriately from 'The Marriage of Figaro'. Like that, this is a gavotte for servants and masters; it is also a masterpiece. The party is given by the marquis (Marcel Dalio), a Jew, whose wife Christiane (Nora Gregor) is Viennese, and it is perhaps because of their backgrounds that they are lightly patronised by their guests, who include the marquis's mistress, Geneviève (Mila Parély), and a famous aviator, André Jurieu (Roland Toutain), nourishing a hardly secret passion for his hostess. During the weekend, on the evening of masquerade (i.e. fancy dress), he will ask her to runaway with him, and will brawl with another suitor. Below stairs, the new servant, an ex-poacher, Marceau (Julien Carette), has fallen for the wife, Lisette (Paulette Dubost), of the gamekeeper Schumacher (Gaston Modot). He flirts, she returns his interest; and Schumacher storms through the house with a gun. Above stairs, the game is played to different precepts. It is Octave, the onlooker, who points out to André and then to Christine the rules of high society. This is a society which has codes of

One reason many people treasure the French films of the Thirties is that they contain a number of memorable performances, and of the six players on this page the adjective 'great' can safely be applied to at least three, if not all, of them. The lady is Françoise Rosay, in *Le Grand Jeu*, and the actors are, CLOCKWISE from Mme Rosay: Louis Jouvet in *Hôtel du Nord*, Harry Baur in *Crime et Châtiment*, Pierre Renoir in *Pièges*, Michel Simon in *Drôle de Drame* and Raimu in *Le Femme du Boulanger*.

behaviour but no principles: they are not vicious people, or unkind, but they are unthinking. So absorbed are they in themselves that they hardly notice Schumacher and his gun – although when the marquis apologises for the behaviour of his servants the fat lady replies, 'The poor have a right to be happy too.' The action below stairs is considerably less decorous, because its denizens do not know the chief rule of the game, which is to lie. When Christine discovers that Geneviève was her husband's mistress before her marriage, she objects to living a lie: but, Octave points out, everyone lies – government, newspapers, the radio, even the cinema. And at the end, after Schumacher has shot André – because Christine has borrowed Lisette's cloak and he mistakes them – that becomes a lie, despite the victim's eminence: a victim of fate, shot by Schumacher in mistake for a poacher. Society – this society – shrugs, and moves on to the next game.

The film had no success with spectators accustomed to the literal interpretation of all dialogue and action, but some were sharp enough to recognise its anti-fascism. Showings on the Champs-Elysées were interrupted by right-wing rioters, and the distributor, alarmed, made cuts before withdrawing it completely a few days later. The censor banned it when war broke out; the Germans ordered it destroyed. For years only hacked-about copies were in circulation, and it was in an abbreviated form that the film found its way to New York in 1950 and to London a year later. F. Maurice Speed commemorated it in his 'Film Review': 'Rather jerky little French film about a house party at which the guests behave with cruelty and complete lack of morals. All rather confusing and silly.' Such was the general reaction. It was not till the late 50s that the complete version, some of it miraculously rediscovered, was painstakingly reassembled.

The film imposes itself not because of what it says, which is unexceptional, nor because of its quasi-literary style, but because it is, withal, a personal statement in a medium which up to that time had offered very few; it has the wit, wisdom and love of humanity which inform all of this director's best work. Renoir was more richly endowed with these qualities than his contemporaries, and this film can be seen as the culmination of a remarkable period in French cinema. Technically French films had become the equal of those of Hollywood; and in the matter of maturity – of approach and subject – they surpassed any other national cinema except perhaps Japan.

This was due not to executive encouragement, except in the case of a few imaginative producers, but to an assembly of creative individuals quite as extraordinary as that working in Germany during the Silent period. There were great screenwriters, Spaak and Prévert; great art directors, Meerson, Trauner, Lourié; and great actors, Jouvet, Baur, Raimu, Pierre Renoir and Françoise Rosay. If we have an idea how much the Prévert-Carné films owe to the writer it is also clear that the Spaak scripts usually became the best work of their respective directors. Perhaps, in the end, the films said very little that is positive, always excepting the man's love of life and friends and women, as exemplified in Renoir and Pagnol; we do not doubt the cynicism of Ophuls and Guitry, so perhaps we should not doubt the pessimism that distinguishes almost every other French film-maker of this era. That is a reflection of France herself, or so we like to think, after the collapse of the Popular Front; that this pessimism was often achieved by the creation of 'atmospheric' romances and melodramas is immaterial. With or without hindsight this period of French cinema remains, as a cinema-going experience, extraordinarily potent.

17

Hollywood's Golden Age:
R.K.O., Paramount and 20th Century-Fox

THE AMERICAN movies of the late Thirties remain, by and large, vastly entertaining – expertly-wrought artefacts reflecting the confidence of the industry which produced them. Darryl F. Zanuck spoke for all the moguls when he told Henry King, his leading director, 'Henry, we have three thousand four hundred at this studio. It's my responsibility for those people to know that they have a job and it's permanent. So that's where you and I come in; we share the responsibility to give audiences substantial entertainments. We're not going to give them a lot of doctrines. We're making pictures to keep the theatres open and not to sell a lot of patent medicine.'

The convulsions which had shaken the industry at the beginning of the decade soon seemed as distant as the flickering Silents, now regarded by the trade press as items for mockery or, at best, as quaintly nostalgic. With the exception of Chaplin, all the great names of that era had been forced into retirement, belonging as much to the past as Tiffany lamps and bootleg gin; admittedly Garbo and Ronald Colman found even greater popularity in Talkies, but most of the Silent stars who elected to go on working were reduced to accepting bit roles. After the influx of stage stars and well-known stage players came a new generation of movie stars. Thus Norma Shearer and Gary Cooper had been featured above the title in the Silent era, but it was in Talkies that they became beloved; Myrna Loy, Jean Arthur, Carole Lombard and William Powell had played only supporting roles in Silents; Clark Gable, James Cagney, Spencer Tracy, Bette Davis, Katharine Hepburn, Humphrey Bogart, James

Stewart, Margaret Sullavan and Henry Fonda all came from the stage, but they were hardly names to conjure with till they appeared in movies; while from vaudeville or radio came such stars as Bing Crosby, Bob Hope, Judy Garland and Alice Faye. The studios were geared to turning out star vehicles and were interested in virtually no other sort of film. Each studio had its stable of stars, with one producer assigned to any handful: he selected the properties that would best exploit their talents and chose the writers to assemble the script. The public might not know the names of the producers, but the stockholders certainly did.

The new studio, 20th Century-Fox, counted itself fortunate indeed in acquiring Shirley Temple; Universal would almost certainly have gone out of business had it not been for Deanna Durbin; while Warner Bros. told Bette Davis that the profits from her films enabled them to build a third sound stage. Such attractions were the strongest card in the industry's battle against the rival menacing its prosperity – the radio networks. R.K.O. Radio was financially linked with N.B.C., and Paramount, in response to such heavy new investment at the start of the Talkie era, had put money into N.B.C.'s young rival, C.B.S. That percentage of the population not inside the movie houses was almost certainly tuned into the wireless, and just as the movie studios had raided Broadway so they began to poach from the radio stations. It could not, however, be said that they were either displeased or disconcerted when many radio stars – Fibber McGee and Molly, Amos n' Andy, Kate Smith among them – flopped on the screen. As late as 1938 Paramount was exhorting exhibitors, especially those in small towns, to book its films because it had stars like Bing Crosby, Bob Hope and Jack Benny, who were 'radio personalities'. And Hollywood used radio in reverse, its stars ostensibly 'guesting' in variety shows while in fact promoting their current vehicle. Until 1938 when Orson Welles (q.v.) was invited to do radio drama for C.B.S. virtually the only serious plays on American radio were recreations of movies on the 'Lux Radio Hour', with the original stars or others of like renown.

Fan magazines detailed every aspect of the stars' lives, real and imaginary, and they sold by the million. The only discordant noises came from exhibitors, who sent in contributions to the *Motion Picture Herald*'s grouse corner, 'What This Picture Did for Me', and, of course from critics – like the writer in *The New York Times* whose praise for one particular film, *The Great Waltz* (q.v.), did not preclude it from being 'a bit of a bore' – it being understood, he went on, that M-G-M 'makes the most beautiful bores in the world'. The public did not agree, keeping track of the most highly-touted films till their long-awaited local arrival. Seldom were they disappointed, and withal critics were impressed with almost as much frequency. For instance, in 1937 distributors were encouraged to road-show a total of nine films in New York (i.e. at advanced prices, running from three to fifteen weeks instead of the usual one week), and the majority of these are good on their own terms.★ Favourable notices, though welcome, were of little value beside the industry's own estimation; and as poor notices seldom kept spectators from the box-office, who needed critics? Critics in the metropolitan areas wilfully encouraged the highbrows to patronise the latest European movie – though since the end of the Silent era that was less than ever a commercial threat. Hollywood no longer aped the continental film, though it did purchase remake rights to a few. Apart from waning stars and the difficulty of finding the right vehicles for popular ones the only problem for producers was

whether the additional cost of Technicolor was justified.

The improvement in the Technicolor system was unquestionably the most important technical advance of the decade, but was regarded with almost total indifference by most people in the industry; and only cursory consideration, if that, would have been given to using it for the nine films listed in the footnote. Nowadays, because almost all of the films of the period were in black and white, television networks prefer to air them, if at all, at off-peak times, thus banishing a whole generation of exceptional talents – players, writers, directors, designers and cameramen.

If the over-riding flaw of the films of this period is lack of realism, we may yet admire the simulation of Paris or Venice on the studio lot; William Wyler said that it never occurred to anyone involved with *Dodsworth* (q.v.) to film the European sequences *in situ*. The only contemporary subjects were taken from novels or plays already successful, and reconstructions of the past were as far as Hollywood was prepared to go towards what was often its declared aim, to 'elevate' the medium and educate audiences. Forgotten along with the Silents were the sex stories of the pre-Code era and the modestly-budgeted conversation pieces (and it had always been clear which conversations were most worth catching), to be replaced by films of the utmost respectability. Hollywood, which had once offended the nation's morals, was now its spokesman on such matters. Banished from movies was a vast spectrum of American life – factories, drinking-dens, the poor: in movies, immigration was no longer a factor, and not to be mentioned were the ethnic origins of any of the characters. Faced with the gentle realities of suburban or rural life, they had all been American for generations; and indeed the only part of the American past to be mentioned – bar a trip or so to the Barbary Coast – was the time of the pioneers. As the decade reached its halfway point Hollywood again could afford to finance the pioneer tales and historical epics which had been the surest crowd-pullers in the Silent days.

So although the pre-Code films tell us much about American life at the time,

★*The Good Earth, Lost Horizon, Captains Courageous, The Life of Emile Zola, The Hurricane, The Firefly, Souls at Sea, The Road Back* and *High, Wide and Handsome*.

those that followed were set in some sort of idealised land, of lawns and mansions, of spacious and clean tenements – a land where stenographers had a change of attire for every scene, and very often a maid as well. Racial tension, like sex, was virtually non-existent, and after an era of unemployment, near-starvation, large-scale crime and civic corruption the palliatives served up were welcome to a population trying to regain an even keel. The American films of the late Thirties tell us little beyond what audiences liked, or were thought to like. The U.S. recovered, but the rest of the world darkened. Europe rearmed, while the U.S. remained in isolation; but even in Europe cares were momentarily stilled as audiences watched Mickey Mouse and Garbo and Fred and Ginger. Entertaining audiences was what the studios understood, and as one examines the films they made one can see how seldom they deviated from the star vehicle. And what stars they were! They captivated audiences then, and they have captured the imagination since. Of all the stars who have emerged since the War, perhaps less than a dozen have left any lasting impression. Their films have become more realistic, as they were bound to do, but I doubt whether posterity will regard them as fondly as those of the Thirties.

R.K.O. was the studio responsible for the immortal musicals which Fred Astaire made with Ginger Rogers. Astaire (b. 1899) had been a Broadway star; Miss Rogers (b. 1911) had come from Broadway to play second leads in pictures. R.K.O. put them both into **Flying Down to Rio** (1933), directed by Thornton Freeland, planning to bolster a star who was not shining as brightly as the studio had once hoped, Dolores del Rio: they were merely accessories – he a buddy of the male lead, Gene Raymond, and she a brassy-tongued band singer. But they had one speciality dance together, 'The Carioca', and on the strength of rave notices for that they were teamed in **The Gay Divorcee** (1934), adapted from Astaire's most recent New York and London success. There were misgivings about his looks, not deemed to be sufficiently romantic, but it was hoped to duplicate his stage popularity in films. In the case of

Rogers, it was *faute de mieux*: she could sing and dance, if in neither case with his style, and had an aptitude for the sassy dialogue required of such pieces. This one, concerning marital misunderstanding, was typical stage fare, and remained such as directed by Mark Sandrich (1900–45), a former gag-man who would go on to handle half the Astaire-Rogers films. The Cole Porter score was jettisoned, with the exception of 'Night and Day', but one of the new numbers, 'The Continental', won the newly-designated Oscar for Best Song. Also from the play came Eric Blore and Erik Rhodes, respectively as a leering waiter and effeminate professional co-respondent, to be joined as comic relief by Edward Everett Horton, dithering as Astaire's best pal, while Rogers's sidekick, Alice Brady, is an ageing lady 'on' to men. (These three actors would support Astaire in other films of the series, but Miss Brady's role would be reinterpreted by Helen Broderick or Luella Gear.) Despite vast sets with which Van Nest Polglase turned Brighton into a science fiction version of Palm Beach, the effect is intimate, and that became the keynote of the films that followed.

It was not intended as a series, but **Roberta** (1935), a starring vehicle for Irene Dunne, had two other roles of equal importance, a bandleader and a showgirl who poses as a Polish countess. Astaire and Rogers were cast, and Jerome Kern's score was rich enough to allow them some numbers, including 'I Won't Dance'. Randolph Scott is the American bandsman who helps Miss Dunne revive her Paris couturier-house – a matter handled by William A. Seiter more seriously than warranted, probably because the original had been a Broadway success, but Dunne and Astaire are individually so captivating that the twin romances sit easily together.

There would be, with one exception, no more dual love stories. Thereafter the films devoted themselves to Astaire wooing Rogers in flippant and debonair manner, her recalcitrance keeping him at elbow length till the last reel – except for the dances, proof to us and to him, if not to her, that they were meant for each other. These dances – among the supreme pleasures of the cinema – adhere to no formula, sometimes taking place on stage or on dance floor, but also in natural surroundings when arising directly from the plot. The stories and dialogue are weak, but the charm of the principals is such that we are restless only when the numbers are few and far between – as in **Top Hat** (1935), though when they appear they are superb: 'No Strings', which starts as a simple expression of high spirits; 'Isn't This a Lovely Day?', the greatest wooing dance in movies; the title song, with Astaire immaculate before a male chorus; and a balladic pas de deux, 'Cheek to Cheek'. Since at this stage the studio wished only to repeat the success of *The Gay Divorcee,* the plot is homogenised farce: Mark Sandrich directed, Irving Berlin wrote the score, and both did better with **Follow the Fleet** (1936) – Berlin if only because he contributed seven songs instead of five. Two of them are sung by Harriet Hilliard, as Ginger's sister, and we might like them and her more – not to mention Scott as Astaire's sailor buddy – if they did not keep us from the main couple.

Swing Time (1936) is the only occasion when Astaire and Rogers had a first-class director, George Stevens (1904–75), and it is the peak of their partnership. Both the settings and Miss Rogers's gowns have been simplified, so that she entirely complements Astaire instead of diverting attention from him, and it is the only film of the series with an elegance to match his own. We find him, dapper and white-tied, against a black marble floor, and as he finishes 'Never Gonna Dance' he and Rogers go into 'The Way You Look Tonight' and reprise 'The Waltz in Swingtime', changing styles and rhythms, offering more of their skills, and for longer, than in any other of their films – proving in this case that one cannot have too much of a good thing. Jerome Kern wrote the superlative score – only for Gershwin perhaps to surpass it in **Shall We Dance?** (1937), directed by Sandrich. In this case 'They All Laughed', 'They Can't Take That Away from Me', 'Let's Call the Whole Thing Off', and the rest divert attention from a particularly tedious plot about a musical comedy queen and a ballet dancer reported to be married. Miss Rogers had continued to make straight films, and for almost as long Astaire had fretted about being merely

half of a partnership. At first R.K.O. felt that the team was too great an asset to be disbanded, but finally they agreed to let him make a film without her, **A Damsel in Distress** (1937). The Gershwins wrote another superb score and Stevens again achieved visual elegance, for an inconsequential plot (from a novel by P. G. Wodehouse) about an American stage star hired as an under-footman to woo, for the sake of a bet, a British heiress (Joan Fontaine). It is admirably suited to Astaire's throwaway style of acting, the self-conscious charm of which is rescued by the modesty and uncertainty often evident in great performers (in his case betrayed by the nervous twist of his hand at an emotional moment or the pause at a sentimental phrase in a song); Fontaine dances only a few twirls, so that audiences could not make comparisons, and the comic team of Gracie Allen and George Burns were the billed co-stars. It is a film oddly neglected, for surely no one looks at Ginger when Fred is on screen.

Reunited in **Carefree** (1938), they managed to live up to the title despite the internal evidence of R.K.O.'s ever-faltering finances, the too infrequent dancing and a lumbering plot about a psychiatrist, Astaire, trying to cure the vacillating fiancée, Rogers, of Ralph Bellamy (who as usual loses the girl). Sandrich directed, and the Berlin score has two strong numbers: 'Change Partners' and 'I used to Be Color-blind'. For the first time no special score was commissioned for **The Story of Vernon and Irene Castle** (1939), which also differs from the others in being a show-business biography and having a sad ending, causing Frank S. Nugent to remark in *The New York Times* that the stars were so identified with light comedy that this was 'practically as disconcerting as it would be if Walt Disney were to throw Mickey Mouse to the lions'. The separation of the team, announced before the film appeared, further obscured its merits, which include a lively ragtime sequence and H. C. Potter's lighthearted direction. Astaire's contract was due to expire and he planned to freelance; but he told R.K.O. that if he returned to the studio it would not be for a resumption of the partnership.

That partnership had been largely responsible for the survival of the

391

The Screen's Great Dance Team

Roberta, RIGHT, followed *Flying Down to Rio* and then came *Top Hat*, ABOVE RIGHT, which, if not the best of the Astaire-Rogers musicals, is the most famous since the title immediately brings to mind Astaire's ever immaculate appearance. The invigorating dances culminate in 'The Piccolino' which a huge chorus repeats several times until the camera cuts to Fred and Ginger – first to their feet, till, drawn inexorably by the rhythm, they rise tip-tapping to the camera. They appeared next in *Follow the Fleet*, ABOVE, one of the best remembered of their efforts and which was succeeded by their best film together, *Swing Time*, FAR RIGHT.

company, at the peak of its popularity with *Top Hat* and *Follow the Fleet* bringing it into profit – $684,000 – for the first time since 1930. That was in 1935, when Floyd Odlum bought a half-share in the company, convinced that there could be further profits if there were more business sense at the top; with Sam Briskin in charge of production profits rose to almost $2 million two years later. However, the other co-owners, R.C.A. and Rockefeller Center Inc., did not care for the policy of B-pictures and a few quality films. In the search for more prestige, they brought in George Schaefer as president and Pandro S. Berman became head of production, encouraging major talents to come to R.K.O. – a policy that continued after Berman had left for M-G-M in 1940, with Joseph I. Breen in charge of production and Sol Lesser as executive producer.

Unfortunately R.K.O.'s finances seldom permitted the major talents to remain for long. There was only one important director under long-term contract, George Stevens, and he rose by merit from B-movies to some of Hollywood's most memorable entertainments. Other leading directors came and went, as was the case at Columbia – often seeking a temporary berth after disaffection at Paramount, M-G-M or 20th Century-Fox. A similar situation prevailed with the stars: of the chief R.K.O. stars only Astaire, Rogers and Katharine Hepburn were under exclusive contracts, while others, such as Irene Dunne, Cary Grant (b.1904) and Barbara Stanwyck, were free to film elsewhere. These particular three were so much in demand that they did not need the protection of a long-term contract, but whereas at Columbia Harry Cohn avoided such binding terms from meanness, the R.K.O. management was in a constant state of insecurity, undoubtedly due to Odlum's indecisive leadership.

The studio publicity department explained the breaking-up of Astaire and Rogers as due to her desire to be known as a dramatic actress. As such, she was really only competent at playing working-class girls, even if in **Having Wonderful Time** (1938) she does not attempt a Bronx accent – but neither does Douglas Fairbanks Jr, in the role John Garfield had played on stage. Arthur Kober, adapting

his own play, was required for the film to eliminate the Jewishness of these working folk on vacation in the Catskills; but, as directed by Alfred Santell, it is still a more truthful account of working-class life than was customary. The **Fifth Avenue Girl** (1939) is Miss Rogers: it is a Cinderella story, but that role is assigned to Walter Connolly who, discovering that his family could not care less whether he is alive or dead, decides to pass off an out-of-work shopgirl as his 'companion'. The writer, Allen Scott, worked on some of the Astaire-Rogers musicals but none of his other credits suggest a film as interesting as this. The script is very funny but it is Gregory LaCava's direction which adds distinction: unlike the other tales of mad Park Avenue families, this one is aware that the rich *are* different; their lovable eccentricities are more kindly handled than the communist-spouting speeches of the chauffeur, but there is no doubt which side LaCava was on.

He and Scott approach the very different family of **Primrose Path** (1940) with appropriate wit – Pa (Miles Mander), one-time classics professor and now a hopeless drunk; Granny (Queenie Vassar), whose vicious tongue is directed at Pa; and Ma (Marjorie Rambeau), an easygoing woman whose Goodtime Charlies make up for Pa's shortcomings. The film does move towards fairy tale in the manner of such predecessors as *Man's Castle* (q.v.); but LaCava never loses sight of the quotation from Menander which prefaces the action, 'We live not as we wish to, but as we must.' His source was a play by Robert L. Buckner and Walter Hart, acted on Broadway by Betty Field, an actress of far more range than Miss Rogers, whose chief contribution is a new brunette hairstyle. She won an Oscar for **Kitty Foyle** (1940), but there is nothing in the film to explain why: she gets a vast number of close-ups, and is always pretty enough to justify them, but neither in performance nor accent does she suggest a girl from the wrong side of the tracks – which is what the film is supposed to be about. Since the flashbacks – just then a wildly popular device – give no indication of the period, which was the early Thirties, the film falls even flatter, and is not helped by Sam Wood's direction or the emasculation wrought by Dalton

Trumbo on Christopher Morley's novel.

As we have seen, R.K.O. was happiest fashioning vehicles for its female stars. If, to the studio, Miss Rogers (away from Astaire) was at one end of the social scale, Katharine Hepburn was at the other. In **Alice Adams** (1935) she is not best pleased that the Adams family is not well off. Alice is 'a pushing sort of person', as someone puts it, and when her mother says of her that she has been 'snubbed and picked upon by every girl in town', we can hardly blame them. There is no doubt that Hepburn understands Alice: she shows her as pretentious and artificial but she also brings out her fundamental loneliness and bravery; Fred MacMurray, as her wealthy suitor, is somewhat awed by her, which is not, even with Hepburn, the way one expects the rich to react to shabby gentility. The dinner party scene, with Alice desperately delving into French to divert attention from the slatternly maid (Hattie McDaniel) is so funny as to make Booth Tarkington's original (unhappy) ending unthinkable. Hepburn had been determined to film this book, but found no R.K.O. director interested except George Stevens, stuck till then with Wheeler and Woolsey comedies: by insisting that he direct, she started him on his fine career – and if here he indulges her a little we can hardly blame him.

It was George Cukor who suggested to her a film of Compton Mackenzie's picaresque novel, **Sylvia Scarlett** (1935), and star and director are self-indulgent to the point of embarrassment, presumably hoping for a modern 'Twelfth Night'. The wayward story slips from comedy to melodrama, but most of it is for connoisseurs of the bizarre, notably the moment of Hepburn's decision to play a boy, and her chunks of dialogue with the curly-headed, pipe-smoking artist (Brian Aherne) with whom she has fallen in love. Cukor has said that he and Hepburn were so appalled by the reception at the preview that they offered the producer, Pandro S. Berman, to do a film for no salaries – to which he responded tersely that he wanted neither of them ever to work for him again.

R.K.O. would have been better off – at least financially – without the next three Hepburn films. **Mary of Scotland** (1935) falls into every pitfall available to the historical film: it is reverent and anachronistic (it offers tartans long before they were known and the sound-track throbs with Jacobean melodies), and though it distorts and simplifies it manages to be both confusing and dull. The source is a play by Maxwell Anderson – his blank verse eliminated by Dudley Nichols, whose companion play about Elizabeth I was to make a better film (q.v.) for Warners. Hepburn merely postures and John Ford bungles even the big scenes, handling the confrontations with Knox, the murders of Rizzio and Darnley and Mary's trial both perfunctorily and pretentiously. 'I'm a sight tonight and I wanted to look my best,' are Mary's first words on entering Holyrood; 'Ah, Darnley, still hanging on?' asks Bothwell – and with such dialogue Fredric March's interpretation is clearly ludicrous. The fact that the characters behave like modern people also mars **A Woman Rebels** (1936), which concerns a strong-minded Victorian 'gel' who becomes a crusading journalist – an interesting idea in an area neglected by film-makers, but the writers, Anthony Veiller and Ernest Vajda, have burrowed into Victorian fact and fiction without understanding either. However, Hepburn more than makes up for her earlier Mary Stuart: as directed by Mark Sandrich, here she is always charming, and as she ages she looks remarkably like herself twenty years later (a rare occurrence in the annals of movie make-up).

She flutters and sobs energetically enough in **Quality Street** (1937), but in view of the nature of the piece – a James Barrie sub-'Cranford' trifle – her obvious pleasure in her own pantomime is disconcerting. No one else so misjudges their roles, yet despite her overplaying and the ceaseless background music one is always aware of a civilised and even cultured director at work – George Stevens – though his skills are really more than the film deserves.

The American public, remembering the last Hepburn expedition into Barrie, was not tempted, but her box–office standing was temporarily restored by **Stage Door** (1937), considered by most reviewers to be even better than its Broadway original, by Edna Ferber and George S. Kaufman, as adapted by Morrie Ryskind and Anthony Veiller. The setting is a theatrical boarding house where the girls lounge

Adolphe Menjou with Ginger Rogers and Katharine Hepburn as stage hopefuls in Gregory LaCava's *Stage Door*, which remains a delight at least to those who relish bitchy wisecracks. Rogers, reverting to her 'Anytime Annie' persona, gets the best lines, such as this one to a girl – not Hepburn – about to dine with a producer, 'Don't eat the bones and give yourself away.'

between auditions, into which coven comes Miss Hepburn, a wealthy daddy's girl, kind and clear-sighted despite her affectations. Unexpectedly she does not fall on her face but becomes a star – this at the expense of Andrea Leeds, fretting about losing the role she considered herself born to play. The ardour of both these characters is nicely balanced by the cynicism of the three other leading girls in the boarding house, Ginger Rogers, Lucille Ball and Eve Arden. Leeds was nominated for a Best Supporting Oscar, proof that that sort of 'sobbing woman' playing was prized above the splendid work of the Misses Ball and Arden; and the director, Gregory LaCava, was reported as crying whenever in later years he watched her suicide scene. He shot as few takes as possible, which accounts for the honesty and high spirits, as well as an occasional unconvincing moment.

In **Bringing Up Baby** (1938) Hepburn is a 'madcap heiress' (as they were usually described), with Cary Grant a palaeontologist who has the misfortune to get in her way; their joint adventures culminate in jail for singing 'I Can't Give You Anything but Love' to a leopard at midnight in a neighbour's garden. Hepburn's manner alone carries off the illogicality of it all, while Grant gallantly plays straight man. Obsession is their métier: she with him, he with an ancient bone – and obsession can be very funny in comedy. Their playing has brought the film some status in recent years but at the time it was not particularly well received by either press or public. Eileen Creelman wrote with some fairness in *The New York Sun*: 'The film is rather frantically funny, relying on improbable situations and slapstick. Mr Grant and Miss Hepburn, when in doubt, fall flat on their faces, fall over logs, knock each other down. Once was enough . . . The film is much too long, stretching its title joke to 102 minutes.' Howard Hawks directed, and the film was Hepburn's last for the company, which was conscious of the fact that two comedies in a row had failed to reinstate her in public favour.

In view of the fact that Hepburn had always been a thorn in their flesh, it is probable that the R.K.O. executives regarded her most fondly for having promoted George Stevens. After *Alice Adams* he made **Annie Oakley** (1935), Barbara Stanwyck's first vehicle under her R.K.O. contract. A foreword warns that the true story of its heroine is more incredible than most films, but the events of this one are virtually negligible, as if waiting for the Irving Berlin score to liven up matters (the 'book' of 'Annie Get Your Gun' is so similar as to suggest the same source material). Stevens has settled for good performances and an impeccable period atmosphere: the meticulousness which was always the centre of his craft is particularly apparent in the sequence of the group photograph – and in making Annie when famous somewhat blowsy. His work on *Swing Time*, *Quality Street* and *A Damsel in Distress* established his position as the studio's best contract director, and **Vivacious Lady** (1938) confirms his gift for comedy. A college professor (James Stewart) is reluctant to admit that the showgirl (Ginger Rogers) with him is his newly-wed wife: they have difficulty, therefore, in consummating the marriage, and though that is never mentioned, it is proof that by this time Hollywood writers were exhausting every situation in which a handsome young couple might find themselves. Miss Rogers is light of touch without ever becoming a comedienne, which throws most of the burden on to Stewart, who fortunately can cope with it.

Stevens was assigned to the studio's most expensive production to date, **Gunga Din** (1939), which uses Kipling's poem only as a starting point. Ben Hecht and Charles MacArthur came up with a story about three army buddies (Cary Grant, Douglas Fairbanks Jr and Victor McLaglen) and their Indian bearer (Sam Jaffe). Stevens's handling is exemplified in the two ambush sequences, one wittily choreographed and always entirely possible, the other particularly exciting. Those were what made it a popular success; but as with *Cavalcade* one wonders what Americans made of its Imperial concepts. At this time Britain was increasingly looked to as the one free and strong country in Europe, and it may be that Hollywood only wanted to express admiration: these and similar films imply that because the British Empire was so admirable Americans should follow the noble precepts which had helped to build it. Bluntly put, these were that white is right and black is not – which was something most Americans could accept. The faithful Gunga Din is the representative of all those millions to whom the British were paternal, and bets were further hedged by making the group-villain a sect devoted to killing.

'British' subjects were usually given to Hollywood's most prestigious or sensitive directors, and Stevens does excellently on **Vigil in the Night** (1940), which R.K.O. hoped would duplicate the success of *The Citadel,* also based on a novel by A. J. Cronin. 'The world's most famous doctor rips the veil from the hidden lives of bitter women who knew men too well,' said the publicity department, ill-preparing us for a tale of a doctor (Brian Aherne) who sports a pipe, three-piece tweeds, a dashing but comforting moustache and a twinkle in his eye when confronted by eager young nurses. It is he whom Carole Lombard sends for after a bus crash, and afterwards over cocoa – she refuses the sherry offered – he talks to her only of his plans for the new hospital, which may seem strange conduct for a

man alone at night with this particular actress, even though she enacts the role as if she were a reincarnation of Florence Nightingale. Yet if Stevens cannot make his stars flesh and blood, he is good elsewhere: rare among American directors of the time he allows no caricatures of the British, and he shows an understanding of their national character; and since the life of the hospital is as convincingly portrayed as in any movie then or since, the whole is preferable to the film of *The Citadel*.

With a title like **Penny Serenade** (1941) the battle is half won, and it matters not whether it refers to the sentiment on display or the adopted child at the centre of the story. As Irene Dunne recalls, with the aid of phonograph records, the ups and downs of her marriage with Cary Grant, Stevens tries for a blend of comedy and real-life hurt and pain, never getting far from the promise of the title: but the balance he achieves, with Morrie Ryskind's adroit screenplay and the tact of his players, is still miraculous.

The film was in fact made at Columbia, and for a number of reasons – not least the presence of Miss Dunne – we may pair it with Leo McCarey's **Love Affair** (1939).

Douglas Fairbanks Jr as one of the three comrades-in-arms who keep the Union Jack flying in India in *Gunga Din*. It is a splendid adventure film, though its attitudes are now somewhat bewildering, as when Cary Grant says ''Ow can I get a nice little war going?'

Irene Dunne and Charles Boyer in Leo McCarey's *Love Affair* which magically succeeds as romance while played in a comic vein which ought to have deflated it, as when she says, under the stars, that her father's philosophy was 'Wishing will make it so. Just keep on wishing, and cares will go. Dreamers tell us dreams come true,' adding, after the briefest of pauses, 'Of course, my father was a drunk.'

In *Penny Serenade* Stevens had treated his more serious sequences with the rigour of the best French cinema of the time, but both he and McCarey attained 'that genius of sentimentality' which Stravinsky noticed in 'La Bohème', 'so perfectly matched to the dramatic substance and so superbly deployed that even I leave the theatre, when I can get a ticket, humming my lost innocence.' *Love Affair* is one of several good films of the time concerned with great and difficult romances, with a screenplay by Delmer Daves and Donald Ogden Stewart. The film begins as an amusing shipboard romance between Miss Dunne, a sophisticated New York 'kept woman', and Charles Boyer, playboy of two continents. Parted after their journey, they do not meet again till she is hopelessly crippled: he does not know that was why she did not keep their rendezvous, or indeed of her accident – and since she is seated, and with no intention of telling him, the audience is reasonably on tenterhooks for a happy ending. (And it was said, incidentally, that the Hays Office allowed Miss

Dunne to play a kept woman since the accident could be seen as just retribution.) Of course the playing helps: Boyer's combination of the debonair and the doglike was never more attractive, and if Miss Dunne flutters and gurgles and arches her eyebrows over every misfortune there still isn't a single consonant or vowel that she cannot elevate into a whole continent of wit.

John Cromwell was also adept at making doubtful material believable, and the playing of Carole Lombard and Cary Grant in **In Name Only** (1939) further helps it on its way. As a married man and the woman for whom he wants a divorce, their reactions are always right – hers of frequent despair and his of encouragement and frivolity. Graham Greene in *The Spectator* noted that this was one of the few American films in which the 'other woman' was the heroine, admiring also the picture of misery engendered by divorce and such moments as the seedy hotel manager suggesting a cigarette or a drink or something more with Miss Lombard. Such matters, however, cannot quite rescue the material from soap opera: even in movies the course of true love was seldom more bumpy.

R.K.O. found an interesting director in Garson Kanin (b. 1912), a minor Broadway figure brought to Hollywood by Goldwyn, who did not use him. At R.K.O. he directed a B-movie, *A Man to Remember* (1938), which was sufficiently well-received for him to do **The Great Man Votes** (1939). The screenplay by a contract writer, John Twist, concerns politics, for which reason the budget was restricted to $200,000; but as the 'drunk old bummer' who holds the crucial vote and is therefore promised the job of Commissioner for Education ('If it's good enough for the mayor's brother-in-law, it's good enough for you'), Kanin was allowed to use John Barrymore – persona non grata at the studio since his disappearance in mid-film some years before. Barrymore's histrionics overwhelm an otherwise pleasing combination of political satire and 'Little Orphan Annie', but Kanin's next two films, **Bachelor Mother** (1939) and **My Favorite Wife** (1940), proved 'Hollywood's youngest director', as *Photoplay* called him, adept at handling light-hearted situations – classic comedy built on deceit and predicament. The protagonist is put in an impossible situation, which entails lying, and that leads to further intricacy. In the first of these a shopgirl (Ginger Rogers) is landed with an orphan baby which no one will believe is not hers; in the second a newly-married husband (Cary Grant) is unable to pluck up courage to tell his second wife that his first (Irene Dunne) is back from the dead. Delicate situations are handled surely but in the airiest manner, and the playing is considerably more inventive than the dialogue. In view of the fact that Kanin did not direct after the War (apart from two failures in 1969) it is sad that neither of his other films of this time quite works: **They Knew What They Wanted** (1940), from Sidney Howard's once famous play, already filmed in 1928 and 1930, with Lombard now as the mail-order bride, and **Tom, Dick and Harry** (1940), with Miss Rogers beset by suitors. Both heroines are so mercenary that their last-reel conversion to true love is unbelievable. Censorship wrecked the Howard piece, reducing the mutual attraction of wife and foreman (William Gargan) to one night of passion followed by contrition; the unpleasing suggestion that love rests solely on physical attraction remains, despite the ending, perhaps because Charles Laughton is tediously Italian and hence unconvincing as the husband. Miss Rogers as the small-town girl determined to marry a millionaire – presumably an admirable goal in the post-Depression U.S.– plays even a calculating hussy with too much calculation; marrying the boss's son (David Niven) in *Bachelor Mother* she is perfect, but that is New York fairy tale.

So is **The Devil and Miss Jones** (1941), and Jean Arthur is also perfect. She plays a store clerk who meets an old man (Charles Coburn) at Coney Island, and feeling sorry for him encourages him to get a job in the store, not knowing that he is the boss. That is the sort of situation Hollywood talents could make workable – in this case including Sam Wood (1883–1949), directing without pretension just before embarking on more ambitious projects.

A lesser director, Leigh Jason, nevertheless made one of the quintessential movies of the time, **The Mad Miss Manton** (1938), an inconsequential and inventive murder mystery, with the pleasing team of Henry Fonda, as a New York editor, and Barbara Stanwyck, as the sleuthing but empty-headed heiress who is, till the last reel, the bane of his existence. Many of the star pairings of this era are marvellous, but William Powell hardly hits it off with Ginger Rogers in **Star of Midnight** (1935) and not at all with Jean Arthur in **The Ex-Mrs Bradford** (1936), both *Thin Man* (q.v.) imitations directed by Stephen Roberts; the second is particularly poor. We may wonder what Depression audiences made of the impeccably-tailored Powell in these enormous apartments in glass and white. It was probably the aftermath of the Depression which caused so many movies like **Joy of Living** (1938), which questioned material values; there were also too many with this particular plot, about the poor little rich girl who starts to wake up and live after just one night's binge. In *Joy of Living* she is Irene Dunne, supposedly Broadway's greatest star, teaming neatly with free-living Douglas Fairbanks Jr; the songs are by Jerome Kern, and the direction by Tay Garnett emphasises how much the best screwball comedies owed to the McCareys and LaCavas.

The customary cross-pollination between the poor and the wealthy is less in evidence in **Lucky Partners** (1940) and **My Life with Caroline** (1941), perhaps because both were based on French originals by, respectively, Guitry, and Louis Verneuil and Jacques Barr. They also mark a turning point in American film comedy: the careless spirit of the Thirties lives on, but the wit has gone. Ginger Rogers is in the first, involved in complications over a lottery ticket. A British actress, Anna Lee, is in the second, a rare instance in a Hollywood film of an inadequate star player. Both films star Ronald Colman as a man of affairs, in the process making him somewhat tiresome, but it is hard to feel sorry for him since he had not long before turned down both *Rebecca* (q.v.) and *Intermezzo* (q.v.). He also co-produced, with the director, Lewis Milestone, who observed that these were movies 'you did if you hoped to stay in pictures, in the expectation that the next film might give you a chance to redeem yourself'.

Perhaps the R.K.O. comedy most revived is that which the Marx Brothers made between assignments at M-G-M. This is **Room Service** (1938), a successful Broadway play for which the studio, in its erratic policy, paid the then-record sum of $225,000, and for which the Marxes were paid $250,000 for four weeks' work. The history of the film is confusing, from Groucho's claim that R.K.O. needed them because there were no suitable players under contract, to the statement that it was intended as a vehicle for them. They were not players easy to fit into existing material, and as Morrie Ryskind's screenplay adheres faithfully to the original, that may have been written with them in mind (its authors, John Murray and Allen Boretz, had not long since arrived at R.K.O. under contract). Groucho is the frantic producer of a theatrical troupe stranded in a hotel, Chico the show's director and Harpo a handyman. Weaknesses in the supporting cast indicate late budget restrictions, as does the fact that, under William A. Seiter's unimaginative direction, it is little more than a filmed play.

Another newcomer to the studio was Lily Pons, acquired during the Hollywood onslaught on American opera houses after the success at Columbia of Grace Moore (q.v.). It finally gave up hopes of her with **Hitting a New High** (1937), a title in no way descriptive of the film as directed by Raoul Walsh. She reveals no reason to indicate why R.K.O. tried once, let alone three times in all, yet the obvious desperation is interesting: having failed with her in romance, they dropped her in to farce, as a cabaret singer pretending to be a Rima-like bird-girl in an attempt to get a chance in opera, with considerably less footage allotted her than to supporting players Eric Blore and Edward Everett Horton.

Also welcomed to Hollywood were the Britishers, Herbert Wilcox and Anna Neagle, whose two films on Queen Victoria had been successful for R.K.O. However, directed by Wilcox in **Irene** (1940), Neagle, like Anna Lee, proved deficient in the star personality expected in such glossy Hollywood products. Since her singing and dancing are amateurish, and since a fine supporting cast has nothing to support, it is not surprising to find *The New York Times* later lamenting: 'Miss Neagle has now appeared to very dubious advantage in screen versions of *Irene* and *No, No, Nanette*, and they say that she is next to play the late Marilyn Miller's role in a translation of *Sunny*. If she continues at this rate, the fine nostalgic flavor of American musical comedy will soon be completely dissipated. It is all very depressing indeed.' After similar notices for *Sunny* the pair returned to Britain.

Another English player, Charles Laughton, was signed to an R.K.O. contract, and in **The Hunchback of Notre Dame** (1939) he is a more memorable Quasimodo than Lon Chaney, acting with one eye (the other is in the middle of his cheek: his make-up man deserved an Oscar), limping and making the guttural sounds of a deaf mute. He evokes pity, whether in the pillory or gazing at Esmerelda – less a fiery gypsy dancer than a shy Irish colleen as played by Maureen O'Hara, who must have dismayed William Dieterle; but he moves the old tale at a fast clip. Later offered a producer-director contract under a new studio policy to encourage well-known names to join it, Dieterle made **All that Money Can Buy** (1941), sometimes known as *The Devil and Daniel Webster* after the story by Stephen Vincent Benét upon which it is based. It concerns a man (James Craig) who sells his soul to the devil (Walter Huston), and for once, intoned the English critic James Agate, 'Hollywood has boldly ventured into something that is neither vulgar nor silly'. He and others were undoubtedly impressed by the artistic approach, which includes the title credits, not designating the actual functions of any of the personnel, and lighting effects which were common when the director was working in Germany, often on similar plots. This one is Americana, and is therefore whimsical rather than eery – but it is equally humourless and lacks the twist in the tail which might justify the malarkey. Craig, a nice man who otherwise played mainly leads in Bs at Metro, can spark no interest, and sin for him is merely a bad attack of thoughtlessness and a mistress (Simone Simon).

Of the two films directed by Rowland V. Lee for R.K.O. **The Toast of New York** (1937) is also concerned with matters financial and moral, but both he and the writers (Dudley Nichols, John Twist and Joel Sayre) demonstrate the usual Hollywood confusion at having to deal critically with capitalism: they are detailed but not explicit on the financial finaglings of Jim Fiske, demoting him from one of the most evil of the robber barons to a mere scoundrel. Fiske's penchant for uniforms and his private army are treated as harmless eccentricities, and although he Pays at the End he is played by Edward Arnold, specialising then in 'lovable' tycoons. Later, when Hollywood managed to condemn a capitalist, it made him primarily a fascist, as in two of the characters Arnold played for Capra; and though the film sets out to show that Fiske's quest for power was as unprincipled as that of modern dictators, it is clearly less interested in that than in his relations with the actress (Frances Farmer) who is his 'protégée'.

Among the few other R.K.O. films of serious content is **The Plough and the Stars** (1936), which John Ford remained to make after *Mary of Scotland*: and since both films share with *The Informer* an impression that everything happens at night we must assume that to be Ford's approach to his more important endeavours. Despite the success of *The Informer*, this version of Sean O'Casey's play was completely compromised: in return for being allowed to import some Abbey Theatre players, Ford was compelled (or so he claimed) to use a star, Barbara Stanwyck, and though she agreed to wear no make-up, it must be said that her accent is uncertain. A happy ending was tacked on, and, after Ford had left, the studio removed all references to the fact that the Clitheroes (Stanwyck, Preston Foster) were married. Dudley Nichols's screenplay has chopped the play into three separate entities – the comic Irish (Barry Fitzgerald), the romantic Irish (Stanwyck) and the fighting Irish (Arthur Shields) – while Ford's poetic Dublin looks even more precious than hitherto when intercut with newsreel footage of the 'Troubles'.

R.K.O. had another way of using existing material, which though not uncommon in Europe was rarely a Hollywood practice – and that was to buy up foreign productions and intercut their most spec-

tacular scenes with newly-shot material. **The Woman I Love** (1937) is therefore mainly *L'Équipage*, complete to the Honegger score, with the same director, Anatole Litvak (whom the success of *Mayerling* had brought to Hollywood); but whereas Annabella, Jean-Pierre Aumont and Charles Vanel had made something touching of this wartime triangle drama, it becomes merely coarse as enacted by Miriam Hopkins, Louis Hayward and Paul Muni. **The Soldier and the Lady** (1937), trade-shown as *Michael Strogoff*, is a revamp of a French-German co-production of the previous year, with the same star, Anton Walbrook. When he swiftly left Hollywood R.K.O. lost interest in the film, since his performance was its strongest asset; the trade was unimpressed, knowing that all the genuinely spectacular sequences had been bought – if matching the new material directed by George Nicholls Jr.

R.K.O.'s most signal failure of the decade was its involvement with Technicolor. In 1932 the Technicolor Corporation had finally achieved the three-colour process which offered the whole prism. One of the few industry executives interested was R.K.O.'s head of production, Merian C. Cooper, who failed to get the New York office either to invest in the Technicolor Corporation, then ailing, or to film *Flying Down to Rio* in the system. As distributors, however, they were to handle a Disney 'Silly Symphony', **Flowers and Trees** – for which Disney had enthusiastically scrapped the existing black and white footage to re-do it in colour. R.K.O. had not been encouraging, and Disney only proceeded when Sid Grauman, after a minute's trial, agreed to book it into his Los Angeles theatre to support *Strange Interlude*. Probably everyone at the premiere had seen an experimental colour short, either in (two-tone) Technicolor or in one of the other myriad colour processes; but the enthusiastic reaction to this 'Silly Symphony' indicated that future Disney cartoons in monochrome were inconceivable: the Silly Symphonies went into colour immediately, and Mickey Mouse followed two years later.

Meanwhile, Disney failed to get backing from his usual distributor, United Artists, for a full-length cartoon version of *Babes in Toyland*, and he appealed to Cooper, who was unable to persuade the R.K.O. board that a full-length cartoon was a viable proposition. Cooper remained one of the few powerful industry figures farsighted enough to agree with Disney about colour, and in order to exploit the process he formed Pioneer Pictures – in conjunction with John Hay Whitney and Cornelius V. Whitney, with some financing from Technicolor. The Technicolor Corporation had granted Disney exclusive rights to three-tone Technicolor, partly from pique at industry indifference, and it was not until July 1934 that Pioneer tried out a short, **La Cucaracha**. That won an Oscar as the year's best short subject, but the industry waited to see audience reaction to Pioneer's first feature, and that had to be delayed till Cooper's R.K.O. contract was up. Nevertheless, as with *La Cucaracha*, R.K.O. distributed, the nominal producer was an R.K.O. man, and the studio's penchant at the time for English literary tales was reflected in the material.

The film, rechristened **Becky Sharp** (1935), found audiences siding with the industry. They had not long adjusted to Sound and were content. Insufficient patrons were curious to see the film, and since the popularity of the Disney shorts was enormous it was clear that colour should be confined to animation. It could not be said that *Becky Sharp* is the better because of it. It begins imaginatively, after white and grey titles, with a girl's head popping through a grey curtain, but otherwise the sole sequence of note is that in which the officers hurry from the Duchess of Richmond's ball, their red cloaks swirling. Rouben Mamoulian (who took over direction when Lowell Sherman died, reputedly throwing out a month's footage) may have given thought to the pallette, but he reveals no understanding of what is one of the greatest novels in the language. We look vainly for Thackeray's amusement at the foibles and follies, the superficialities and snobberies of that high society he christened 'Vanity Fair', finding instead the pallid progress of a saucy gold digger. Becky was not subtle, but Miriam Hopkins signals every scheme and manoeuvre as if she were a lighthouse, less an adventuress than a spoilt young woman with a yen for men.

This actress's brittle manner fitted her best for roles of bitchy persuasion, but she insisted on playing for sympathy, and in the most predictable way, alternating half-smiles and half-tears – using so much effort that she was incapable of making any one line relate to another, ruining Becky as a comic character. Cedric Hardwicke's Lord Steyne, cold and grey, is a major performance, with such authenticity of feeling that he overshadows Nigel Bruce, as Jos, and Alan Mowbray, as Rawdon, both otherwise capable. Alison Skipworth has some moments as Miss Crawley and William Stack is good as Pitt, but Frances Dee as Emmy and Colin Tapley are not, predictably, Thackeray's ninnies at all. But then the twenty years of his novel have been reduced to just eighty-three minutes.

Pioneer and R.K.O. tried again with **The Dancing Pirate** (1936), but if the lack of star names was a contributor to its failure it seemed to confirm that colour in itself was not a box-office attraction – and it was also still very costly. At 20th, Zanuck used it for the ending of *The House of Rothschild* and one reel of *The Little Colonel* (1935), while *The Trail of the Lonesome Pine* (q.v.), in fact the second Technicolor feature, was a mild success for Paramount. By virtue of having become Disney's distributor R.K.O. handled the first really successful Technicolor attraction, *Snow White and the Seven Dwarfs* (q.v.), but that was regarded as a freak, and it was not until audiences had endorsed Warners' *Adventures of Robin Hood* (q.v.) that most studios began to abandon caution. R.K.O. was not among them: twice bitten it remained shy, holding out till well after the War.

At Paramount there were recurring threats of bankruptcy and boardroom shuffles. On returning from M-G-M and *The Merry Widow* Lubitsch was appointed head of production by the new management, till it was decided that the films made under his supervision, while successful enough, were more costly than necessary. He was succeeded in 1936 by William Le Baron, reckoned to be the company's most astute Associate Producer (since his return from R.K.O. in 1932), and under his skilful control Paramount's financial troubles receded.

During that period Lubitsch had prepared one film, **Desire** (1936), borrowing Frank Borzage from Warners to direct it – and it is apparent from the outset that it has affinities with *Trouble with Paradise*. The opening is pure Lubitsch: Marlene Dietrich (released from Von Sternberg at last) glides into the Place Vendôme in quest of a pearl necklace for which she has no intention of paying. Having accomplished her coup, she has to get the necklace past Customs, and behind her is Gary Cooper, an engineer from Detroit, an all-too-convenient innocent: but it is one thing to slip the necklace into his pocket and another to retrieve it. Nothing in the film is as good as its opening scene – and if a reformed Dietrich settles for Detroit, that is part of the general fantasy. Borzage leaned more towards the romantic than Lubitsch, and the stars complement each other as dreamily as in *Morocco*, she self-assured in Travis Banton gowns, he ingenuous in double-breasted suits, and in awe of Europe.

A world of make-believe was the whole *raison d'être* – a point missed by C. A. Lejeune in her celebrated put-down of **Angel** (1937): 'The first moment that Miss Marlene Dietrich sweeps up to the reception desk of a Paris hotel, you feel sure that you are looking at a mystery woman. It is something about the highlight on her lip-rouge, the way her eyes peek from side to side, and the dashing way in which she tosses off the signature "Mrs Brown" in the register. You know, of course, that she isn't Mrs Brown, but beyond that you have no notion who she may be, except possibly Miss Marlene Dietrich, practising acting. In point of fact, she is the wife of a British Cabinet Minister, who is currently representing his country in Geneva. Oh, you move in exalted circles in *Angel*, and meet the most wonderful people.' This critic was not the only one to quote one of the more fatuous exchanges: 'What's worrying you, darling?' asks Dietrich, 'Is it France?' He shakes his head. 'Jugoslavia.' Lubitsch knew that this was risible: the jig is to keep us entertained by a tale which never reaches the far borders of probability. He not only takes advantage of Hollywood convention but piles it on. Thus the country mansion has, as Lejeune says, 'yards of mullion round the windows', and the

lady's wardrobe surpasses most in lavishness and tasteful tinsel. Dietrich is more puppet-like than ever; Herbert Marshall and Melvyn Douglas, as husband and would-be lover respectively, were never more urbane or gentlemanly.

Lubitsch made **Bluebeard's Eighth Wife** (1938) to fulfil a promise to Claudette Colbert, whose special gift for hesitant or unexpressed scepticism was seldom better exploited. It also demonstrates why he preferred directing Gary Cooper to any other actor. Cooper plays one of the richest men in the world, wanting, in a Côte d'Azur store, only the top of a pair of pyjamas, while she wants only the pants: that is the start, and the scene ends with her cure for insomnia – spelling Czechoslovakia backwards. As with such references in *Angel*, audiences were expected to contrast the facetiousness with the situation current in Europe: and in treating in equally unmindful fashion the real theme of the film – which is

Lubitsch grew so weary of being praised for his famous 'touch' that he branched into new forms of comedy on leaving Paramount in 1939. His later Paramount films are notable for their artificiality, as might be guessed from this scene from *Angel*, with Herbert Marshall, Marlene Dietrich and Melvyn Douglas.

Carole Lombard. In her playing of comedy, beauty and elegance were matched by a perfect sense of movement, timing and delivery – and as much might be said of Irene Dunne, Jean Arthur, Claudette Colbert, Myrna Loy, Constance Bennett and, on occasion, Katharine Hepburn and Barbara Stanwyck. They were real, they were unreal, they were extraordinary: few actresses since have approached them in skill – and whether they acquired it or were born with it, why are today's actresses so much less blessed?

the non-consummation of a marriage – Lubitsch was playing for time, till the real issues had to be faced. On *Angel* his writer was, as customary, Samson Raphaelson, working from a play by Melchior Lengyel, who would collaborate on *To Be or Not to Be* (q.v.); *Bluebeard's Eighth Wife* was written by Billy Wilder and Charles Brackett – teamed for the first time – but equally clearly Lubitsch dictated the tone (so different from Sam Wood's 1923 version of the same tale, with Gloria Swanson). However, the finale, in a mental home, may be recognised as the sort of thin ice on which Wilder would skate for the rest of his career. Later both he and Lubitsch made films about the War which were both more realistic *and* more entertaining than most films on the subject; before that they would collaborate on *Ninotchka* (q.v.) which, if still shirking the real issues, took a pungent enough look at Russian communism. Lubitsch was canny: when *The Man I Killed* failed to make anything like the same impact as

Milestone's *All Quiet on the Western Front* he stuck to furbelows and baubles, retaining control of his career while the eclectic Milestone was forced to take industry assignments. *Ninotchka* was made at M-G-M because he wanted to make a film with Garbo; he did not return to Paramount.

That company's penchant for comedy may be explained by the presence among their star players of Miss Colbert (b.1905) and Carole Lombard (1908–42). Colbert was equally adept at dither or serenity when faced with impossible situations, whereas Lombard was possessed of an uncontrollable impulse towards the erratic and the extravagant. They were respectively in the two films said to have begun the memorable cycle of Thirties comedies, *It Happened One Night* and *Twentieth Century* (q.v.), both made at Columbia. This cycle has been variously described, but *Webster's* definition of 'screwball' provides the only appropriate adjective: 'One conspicuous for dizzily fantastic ideas or wildly irrational behaviour' – which surely describes Colbert in that particular movie and Lombard in most that she made. The films have been called 'sophisticated', since their normal milieu is boudoir or night club, and 'slapstick', because their characters take pratfalls; but though their *attitudes* are sophisticated, there is a paucity of verbal wit. To judge from audience response, the funniest moments are those which do not translate into print, as when, in Leisen's *Easy Living* (q.v.), Jean Arthur boasts that the boys' magazine for which she works has a million readers and Edward Arnold riposts pompously, 'You haven't got me' – and that is a particularly successful example of a screenwriter working in the much-admired tradition of *The New Yorker* magazine. Though the spectacle of debutantes and lounge lizards acting crazy can be dispiriting when poorly done, the fact that the best of these films have not yet received the recognition that is their due★ is probably because we cannot quote from them as we can from Mae West or the Marx Brothers.

Mitchell Leisen was Paramount's best comedy director after Lubitsch. While an

★ I once saw on the same day Coward's oft-revived play 'Present Laughter' and LaCava's totally neglected *She Married her Boss* (q.v.), which is at least five times as funny.

artisan seldom crosses a Lubitsch drawing room, in the films of Leisen the penniless are in constant conflict with the well-to-do. After making his debut on *The Eagle and the Hawk* he achieved both commercial and critical success with **Death Takes a Holiday** (1934), an Italian piece of whimsy revamped by Maxwell Anderson, whose artificial situations made it the *L'Année Dernière à Marienbad* (q.v.) of its day. Leisen increased in confidence, and **Hands Across the Table** (1935) is a delightful film. When Lombard first sees Fred MacMurray he is playing hopscotch in a hotel corridor; told they cannot enter a nightclub in day clothes they start to strip; and, discovered trouserless in her apartment, he claims he is her husband, which she caps by denying it. It is a tale of like meets like: both are intent on marrying money. The first millionaire she meets is a crippled aviator (Ralph Bellamy), but both his lust for her and his physical condition are ignored by the director. Leisen tolerated no experiments in taste or sentiment, such as we associate with his best-known writers after they turned director, Preston Sturges and Billy Wilder. Because of their later renown, and because they provided him with his two masterpieces, **Easy Living** (1937) and **Midnight** (1939) respectively, it is tempting to suggest that he was only as good as his material – yet we are aware of a sureness of control comparable to that of Lubitsch.

In *Easy Living* a typist (Jean Arthur) is riding on the top of a Fifth Avenue bus when a fur coat drops on her head, and soon the whole of New York has jumped to the conclusion that she is the mistress of the thrower, a tycoon (Edward Arnold). In *Midnight* an American showgirl (Miss Colbert), having left her last bangle in a Monte Carlo pawnshop, arrives in Paris looking for a millionaire; she had one once, she tells the cab driver (Don Ameche), till his father offered to buy her off. 'Didn't you hit him?' he asks. 'How could I?' she replies. 'My hands were full of money.' Miss Arthur's Cinderella, to her astonishment, finds herself installed in New York's best hotel; Miss Colbert's finds herself posing as a countess so that John Barrymore can woo away his wife (Mary Astor) from her latest 'admirer' (Francis Lederer). Both

Mitchell Leisen's two great comedies of the Thirties, *Easy Living*, LEFT, with Luis Alberni and Jean Arthur, and *Midnight*, ABOVE, with John Barrymore, Don Ameche, Rex O'Malley and Claudette Colbert. Neither was particularly well received: *Variety* said of the former, 'Slapstick farce, incredible, and without rhyme or reason, is Paramount's contribution to the cycle of goofy pictures', while *Midnight* was disregarded, overshadowed by events in Europe. Both films were the product of a Hollywood looking askance at the world, and compelled to lighten it in its own manner.

films are heartless and convoluted, and may be seen as tracts for the times: but whereas there was no longer the need for the obligatory reference to the Depression by the time *Midnight* was made, in the earlier film we may compare the bums' invasion of the automat with the seventeen trunks the tycoon's wife takes to Florida.

Leisen directed Lombard and MacMurray again in **Swing High, Swing Low** (1937), a new version of 'Burlesque', partly written by Oscar Hammerstein and partly reset in Panama. The playful first half is well balanced by the dramatic second, whose shots of MacMurray stumbling about a back-projected Manhattan prefigure a number of later movies featuring drunken jazz musicians. Leisen failed with the team of Jack Benny and Gracie Allen (plus George Burns) in **The Big Broadcast of 1937** (1936), despite a large team of writers, but with an equally ordinary screenplay he transformed **Artists and Models Abroad** (1938), with Benny leading a cast which seems to be happily improvising. The plot concerns a third-rate theatrical troupe stranded in Paris, and the musical numbers include two, in street and hotel room, which achieve spontaneous group outbursts into song, usually thought to be absent from musicals till *On the Town* (q.v.). We may also thank Leisen – fashion conscious though he was – for realising that most movie-goers were bored by fashion parades, and that consequently the best way to treat such occasions was to send them up. **Remember the Night** (1940) is the last screenplay by Sturges that he did not direct himself, and its tone is close to his subsequent films (David Chierichetti's excellent book on Leisen indicates that he shot considerably less than Sturges wrote.) Barbara Stanwyck plays a girl who not absentmindedly leaves a jewellery store without paying for the goods and is prosecuted by MacMurray; he gets her out on bail for Christmas, and a series of surprisingly credible circumstances has them spending it together.

Audiences took this stream of comedies for granted: Wesley Ruggles made one after another, written from **The Gilded Lily** (1935) onwards by the adept but uninspired Claude Binyon (till he left for Columbia in 1940). This is a superficial romantic comedy, justified by the presence of Miss Colbert. She is a stenographer at first, but she gets to be a famous cabaret singer – which was exactly what audiences expected. They went to see the Colbert fashions, the Colbert figure, the Colbert smile; they went to see Colbert sad and Colbert witty; they wanted less to appreciate than to revel in the familiar and much-loved Colbert personality. This film actually calls for nice Claudette to go high-hat, but the dénouement is so fixed that audiences will go on loving her. Miss Lombard worried less about wardrobe – and less about being loved: in **True Confession** (1937) she plays a girl who confesses to a murder she didn't commit in order to throw the limelight on her husband (Fred MacMurray), an unsuccessful lawyer. Recognition for the films themselves was not lacking: Graham Greene later described this one as the 'year's funniest film' and *The New York Times* placed **I Met Him in Paris** (1937) among the year's best films. The latter, a revamp of *Design for Living*, leaves Colbert, Melvyn Douglas and Robert Young stranded with witless material, so that *True Confession* is, despite a weak ending, the only one of Ruggles's later films that can now be strongly recommended.

Leo McCarey's reputation for comedy could rest solely on **Ruggles of Red Gap** (1935), from the novel by Harry Leon Wilson (who also wrote 'Merton of the Movies') which had been filmed twice in the Silent era. The conversion of the perfect (British) servant, Ruggles, into his own (American) man was said to be a psychological study or a comment on democratic values, but the film is now best regarded as a vehicle for several star comics – which McCarey, emulating his own *Six of a Kind*, surely intended. And though Charles Laughton gives a performance of resource and delicacy in the title-role, stoically accepting the vulgarity of his new employers, he almost loses the film to Roland Young, whose bemused aristocrat, tempted by ladies, booze and the habits of Mr Floud, is a lovely creation. Equally good are Charles Ruggles as Floud, a simple man of the frontier, Mary Boland as his socially ambitious wife, forever bearing down and forbearing his peccadilloes, and Zazu Pitts as the widow who courts the manservant.

The film's reception encouraged McCarey to produce and direct another piece for several middle-aged players, **Make Way for Tomorrow** (1937). A penniless elderly couple (Beulah Bondi, Victor Moore) must be separated till their five children can club together enough cash to buy them a new house. The New York son is played by Thomas Mitchell and his wife by Fay Bainter, both adept at portraying likeable, dependable people, and they remain likeable, more or less, as she grows increasingly irritated by Ma's ways and he comes to the decision to put her in a home. Frank S. Nugent in *The New York Times* praised the film's 'humanity, honesty, warmth', but the situation is contrived: five children – one with a maid – and not one spare double room? – and surely Pa, not senile, could have found a job? Nugent also thought the film 'courageous' to provide no final solution, but if that was meant to leave no dry eye in the cinema McCarey and his sensitive screenwriter, Vina Delmar, elsewhere refuse to milk tears. The sentimental journey taken by Ma and Pa to their honeymoon hotel is perhaps excessive, but there is a Jewish character, rare in films at this time, a friendly storekeeper (Maurice Moscovitch). Nugent listed the film as among the year's best, alongside *The Life of Emile Zola, The Good Earth, Stage Door, Captains Courageous, They Won't Forget, I Met Him in Paris, A Star Is Born, Lost Horizon* and *Camille*: in other words, Hollywood entertainment at its most appealing. McCarey's is the only film on the list to reflect ordinary life, since the others are set in either an unusual milieu or an exceptional one – except *They Won't Forget* (q.v.), which is too melodramatic to be taken seriously.

That *Make Way for Tomorrow* also reflected credit on Paramount was of no consequence when it failed outside the urban centres, and McCarey was sacked. Paramount's stockholders were more interested in deMille, whose films continued to be expensive but profitable. One of them, **The Crusades** (1935), was described by *Film Weekly* as 'alternatively thrilling and inept', but the thrills are confined to the taking of Acre, which takes up less than ten minutes of the film's two hours. Needless to say, it features the Coeur-de-Lion (Henry Wilcoxon) of

legend (if mildly misogynist), finally inspired by the Moslem concept of peace – clearly meant as a message for audiences of the time. This could possibly be the most historically inaccurate film ever made. At least any superlatives applied to deMille's next film, **The Plainsman** (1936), should be complimentary. Graham Greene thought it 'perhaps . . . the finest Western in the history of films.' The form had been in abeyance for some time, except for the poverty-row Westerns churned out for addicts, and these were so despised that Paramount's attempts to revive the genre with King Vidor's *The Texas Rangers* and Frank Lloyd's *Wells Fargo* were carefully categorised as 'pioneer epics'. In returning to the Western deMille made his first good film in more than a decade, and we may echo Greene's surprise, also wondering whether the for once excellent dialogue was an accident and whether deMille was not inspired by players of the quality of Gary Cooper and Jean Arthur – as a Wild Bill Hickock and Calamity Jane helping to make the frontier safe. In the lesser **Union Pacific** (1939) Barbara Stanwyck and Joel McCrea aid the joining together of the two transcontinental railroads in Utah; and with **Northwest**

Beulah Bondi and Victor Moore in Leo McCarey's *Make Way for Tomorrow*, one of his rare serious films and an unusual one for Hollywood, since its subject is old age.

Mounted Police (1940) deMille, despite a move into Technicolor, was back to his now customary low standard, with Cooper helping the British to suppress the rising of Louis Reil – a subject chosen to indicate solidarity with the Empire.

Apart from *The Texas Rangers*, Vidor's other film for Paramount was also an exploration of America's past, **So Red the Rose** (1935), a Civil War story about a Southern belle (Margaret Sullavan), coquettish and self-willed like all such ladies in fiction. Her adventures are banal, but Vidor responds when a chance is offered – the reading of a letter from the Front, a mother searching for the corpse of her son on the battlefield. The screenwriters included Lawrence Stallings and Maxwell Anderson, and since, like Vidor, they had made memorable cinematic statements on war much was expected of this film. Its failure became legendary, and later comforted those who had passed up or missed the chance to buy the rights to *Gone with the Wind* (q.v.). When that film became successful the industry remembered *The Birth of a Nation* and decided that the public was only interested in the Civil War as an epic. This one is notably confused on the crucial issue, the freedom of the slaves, who move rapidly from Massah-lovin' to rabble rousing and are then quickly forgotten. It is as if the harsh truth must not intrude on the daydream which this film really is – more Louisa M. Alcott than Stephen Crane – and audiences resented its dishonesties more than those on more trivial subjects.

Frank Lloyd, after *Wells Fargo*, again delved into American history for Paramount: **Maid of Salem** (1937) tells of the seventeenth-century witch trials in Massachusetts – perfunctorily handled, with more attention paid to boy-meets-girl. Fred MacMurray is miscast as a devil-may-care Irishman, and Claudette Colbert is too modern as one of the accused; it is also difficult to accept the strictures on her bonnet frills when her face is caked in make-up. At the end, his evidence frees her, and the judges merrily declare that the whole business has been a temporary aberration – a view compounded by Lloyd, who never achieves a persuasive picture of hysteria and panic. Lloyd's once-high reputation plunged still

further with **If I Were King** (1938), the screenplay for which – by Preston Sturges – was of little help in reviving the oft-told tale of François Villon (Ronald Colman).

Paramount's best action director was Henry Hathaway (b.1898), who progressed from B-Westerns to some of the studio's most important films. His first A-feature was **Now and Forever** (1934), which is fine as long as it concentrates on con man Gary Cooper and his mistress (Carole Lombard), but not so good when it shifts to his child (Shirley Temple). **Lives of a Bengal Lancer** (1935) was described by *Photoplay* as 'one of the best [films] ever to come out of the Paramount studios' – reviewing it after *Clive of India*, *The Good Fairy*, *Ruggles of Red Gap* and *David Copperfield*, which prompts the reflection that two tributes to the British Empire in one month seem excessive, especially among the assorted studies of British eccentricities. As a portrait of the Raj it is romanticised, and the climax – the siege and the tortures – belong to a lesser film; but the barrack scenes – the bantering hostility between Cooper and Franchot Tone, their fathering of the new recruit (Richard Cromwell) and their mutual interdependence – reflect with affection the peculiar psychology of regimental life.

Hathaway's inclination towards romanticism was allowed full play in **Peter Ibbetson** (1935), from George du Maurier's novel about two lovers who, though parted, see each other as young and together only in their dreams – an unusual subject for this time, though Paramount had filmed it in 1921 with Wallace Reid. The studio rebought the property in 1931, after Deems Taylor had turned it into an opera for Jeanette MacDonald, who did not play it; the film then became a (straight) vehicle for Fredric March, but he left the studio before production started. Robert Donat and then Brian Aherne both accepted but did not take up the role, which Hathaway eventually persuaded Gary Cooper to play; during these delays Irene Dunne ceded the lead to Ann Harding, whose ethereal presence immeasurably aids Hathaway's purpose. As against its complete rejection by the American public, it had a cult following in Paris, where it was quaintly described by André Breton as 'a triumph of surrealist thought'. It is likeable if absurd, with such solecisms as a railway station called 'London', and a shot of Tower Bridge, unfinished when the novel was published – and in any case the film is set a quarter of a century earlier.★

Hathaways's **The Trail of the Lonesome Pine** (1936) was Paramount's first Technicolor film, and it is difficult to say whether the subject was chosen to fit the colour or vice-versa; James Fox Jr's novel had been filmed before, in 1916 and 1923, and it must have been old hat then – with hill families feuding, like the Hatfields and McCoys, till the railroad comes and the handsome stranger (Fred MacMurray) steals the girl (Sylvia Sidney) from the mountain boy (Henry Fonda). The colour – mainly outdoor – gave it a cachet, but the unwieldy Technicolor cameras seem to have inhibited both cast and director to the point of petrification. Hathaway was clearly much happier returning to black and white with **Souls at Sea** (1937), with Cooper and George Raft, and **Spawn of the North** (1938), with Fonda and Raft: but his vigorous handling of squalls and brawls does not entirely compensate for script deficiencies.

Technicolor was supposed to enhance **Men with Wings** (1938), which William Wellman returned to Paramount to direct – and this lachrymose, longwinded and fictionalised study of the early days of aviation needed all the help it could get. Though it was not a return to the form of *Wings*, Wellman did manage to get back into form with another film from that era, **Beau Geste** (1939); his remake follows the Silent version to a T, improving on the sinister opening, though losing perhaps a little with the mutiny. Its most significant difference is the substitution of Gary Cooper for Ronald Colman – the latter the ideal Beau, whereas Cooper is the ideal Cooper, which is not the same thing. Wellman directed Colman in another remake, **The Light that Failed** (1939), also a tale of British heroism, but of such pessimism that it was curious of Paramount to offer it as Britain prepared for war. It was based on Kipling's first novel, and one representing his own

★ Conversely, the Customs House in *Desire* is a replica of the one that still stood there, on the French-Spanish border, as late as 1962.

attitude towards literary London: Helder (Colman) returns to London from the Sudan, and becomes corrupted as his war paintings make him famous. The heroics at the end suggest that Paramount wanted another *Bengal Lancers*, but the pessimism of the book is too strong for them. The miscasting of Colman accentuates the unsatisfactory nature of the piece: Helder drinks like Sidney Carton and is similarly disillusioned (on the wound that caused his blindness, 'If a man starts cutting you across the head, don't duck, let him keep cutting'), but he cannot convince you that he is a man without integrity. What he could do, movingly, is a line like the one on learning of his blindness, 'We've got it badly, little dog, just as badly as we could get it.'

Lewis Milestone's stint at Paramount included **Anything Goes** (1936), a fast-moving musical farce with Bing Crosby singing a score somewhat different from the Broadway original: the jettisoning of the old in favour of the new was common practice in filming musicals, but when the original songs are among Cole Porter's best it becomes ludicrous. When Paramount offered no further assignment, Milestone got hold of **The General Died at Dawn** (1936), and secured for the screenplay Clifford Odets, who had just made his name with 'Waiting for Lefty'. Lubitsch, then head of production, was not enthusiastic, but Milestone was allowed Gary Cooper in the lead – and Cooper was the company's most popular male star. As a soldier of fortune he meets up with Madeleine Carroll, a lovely lacquered lady who is to lead him to his doom on an Oriental train. As it chugs through the rain to its meeting with machine guns it is reminiscent of the Shanghai Express that Dietrich once took, and these intrigues need the vitality of the earlier film. Milestone does manage some good atmospherics, notably in a Shanghai hotel where several seedy schemers (Dudley Digges, Akim Tamiroff, Porter Hall, J. M. Kerrigan) clasp each other as birds of a feather. Odets's dialogue is quite wrong for the matters in hand, as when Cooper says to Carroll, facing death: 'We could have made beautiful music together. We could have made a circle of light and warmth.'

Rouben Mamoulian made one film for

409

Paramount during this time: **High, Wide and Handsome** (1937), which many think of as the 'pipe-laying musical' – telling as it does of the Pennsylvania farmers who, having discovered oil (in 1859), lay a pipeline rather than see the railroad tycoons take their profits. Kern (music) and Hammerstein (words) wrote it in the same celebration of Americana which had resulted in 'Show Boat' and 'Sweet Adeline' – from the film versions of which came Irene Dunne, to play a circus girl who marries a farmer (Randolph Scott). Her song 'The Folks Who Live on the Hill' is staged with wrinkles in the backcloth and fake apple blossom; and the film as a whole fails to substantiate claims for the director's reputation.

Fritz Lang went to Paramount for one film, **You and Me** (1938), his third in the U.S., but failed to repeat the critical success of the first two (q.v.). That he made so few films at this time was due to his determination to select his own material – but on this occasion he chose badly. He wanted to make a film following Brecht's method of *Lehrstück* – 'a play that teaches you something' – and the resulting message is certainly simple-minded, with Sylvia Sidney proving to a bunch of crooks that 'only the biggest saps in the world think crime pays dividends'.

The success of Ben Hecht and Charles MacArthur as suppliers of material to Hollywood was such that their agent, Leland Hayward, arranged a unique contract with Paramount – to write, produce and direct four films, albeit on limited budgets, with complete independence. Lee Garmes, one of the studio's most experienced cameramen, was sent to help them – for the Long Island studio had been reopened for the purpose. The general impression, however, of **Crime without Passion** (1934) is one of amateurism, and while fashion still demanded a 'European' look and patina for self-important subjects, it is startling to find that the two newspapermen who wrote 'The Front Page' have gone so wild. Their film begins with three ladies in flowing robes pretending to be Furies, and concludes with them after they have brought Nemesis to Claude Rains. Pretension proliferates: a close-up of a drop of blood, a *boutonière* grasped as a victim falls to her death . . . Contemporaries,

however, were impressed: it was thought to be witty, presumably because of Rains's high-handed approach to women and to his profession, the law.

The second film, **Once in a Blue Moon**, was so bad that release was delayed for two years; **Soak the Rich** (1936) was an even greater flop. Reviewers, however, were for a second time favourable – to **The Scoundrel** (1935), doubtless because Noël Coward at last deigned to make his film debut and the eminent critic Alexander Woollcott agreed to be in the supporting cast, both playing members of New York's literary set. Coward is a publisher loathed by his authors, and he himself has no illusions, planning to marry 'the only person I've ever met who is emptier and more superficial than I am'. Obviously this is not the poetess (Julie Haydon), for she is offered 'one month of happiness and six months of farewells'. 'I'm old-fashioned,' she tells him. 'You're the dawn of time,' he reassures her, but she is soon just another life he has wrecked. He dies in a storm at sea, but returns like the Flying Dutchman – and for the same reason. This mixture of cynicism and the supernatural eked out a miserable week at Radio City Music Hall, but later, with *Caligari*, it became the life-blood of New York's art cinemas. British audiences break up when Coward has a plain if emotional line, e.g. 'Julia – *don't* – be tiresome', and it must be said that when he reappears as a spirit his clipped delivery makes every line seem even more banal.

Paramount's experiment with Hecht and MacArthur confirmed the impression left by Griffith years before, that creative film-makers, however talented, could not be left without supervision. Lubitsch had made a firm bid against that industry rule, but Hecht and MacArthur managed to lose all the ground he had gained. Studio control of the stars was no less onerous, yet most of them could say that at Paramount at least their talents were well displayed. As we have seen, the popularity of Cooper and Colbert was maintained by their work under the studio's leading directors, and before we leave this studio we might glance at four performers who did not command those of the first rank.

To move from Coward to Shirley Temple (q.v.) is not quite to move from the sublime to the ridiculous; she was far more famous than he, and their renown, like that of Garbo and Chaplin, far transcended the show business gossip column. She made two films for Paramount as that fame was beginning – and in **Little Miss Marker** (1934) received solo star billing: but it has little in common with her later films for Fox and does not even seem designed for the same audience. Its source is a story by Damon Runyon, and it is a Damon Runyon picture before it is a Temple vehicle: Runyon – according to Garson Kanin – was the only contemporary writer respected by the Hollywood moguls, and this film, directed by Alexander Hall, is certainly respectful of him. It is about a bookie called Sorrowful Jones, who finds himself saddled with someone else's small child; the bookie is expertly played by Adolphe Menjou, with Lynne Overman, Charles Bickford, Dorothy Dell, Warren Hymer and Sam Hardy among the lugheads looking after the child.

There are three star players whose names will always be associated with Paramount: Bing Crosby, Bob Hope and Dorothy Lamour. Miss Lamour's speciality was the jungle romance, a genre for which Paramount thought Technicolor especially suited. The studio's second film in the process was **Ebb Tide** (1937), a dull version of the South Seas story by Robert Louis Stevenson and Lloyd Osbourne, directed by James Hogan. Frances Farmer in fact wore the sarong in this, but in just one film – her first, *The Jungle Princess* (1936) – Lamour had made that garment her own, and she donned it again for **Her Jungle Love** (1938), with Paramount venturing into colour for only the third time. If you can follow the film attentively, which is difficult, you will find that it cannot decide whether it is set in Malaya or the South Pacific. George Archainbaud directed. Another Silent veteran, Alfred Santell, made **Aloma of the South Seas** (1941), a later demonstration of studio cynicism, with shoddy special effects and dialogue which refers to the ocean as 'the big water' and a volcano as 'the fire god'. As a primitive native girl Lamour says 'Oh pooh' in times of crisis, and is otherwise the only person involved who has her tongue in her cheek. She made some half dozen of these films,

which raises the question as to whether any other woman in film history was set to such idiotic tasks.

Bob Hope (b. 1904) came from vaudeville and Broadway; he was primarily a gag-man, but his expressions of cowardice and self-delight carried him through a large number of films. The public adored him, to the extent that by the end of the War he was already a national figure, although without achieving much critical regard – in which respect he is unlike most of the major screen clowns. His early films revive extremely well. They have funny lines and situations, suggesting that his writers enjoyed inventing for the vain scaredy-cat whom he plays so superbly; and they are, unlike most vehicles for comics, extremely well made – one might compare those that Paramount produced with W. C. Fields. For instance, consider the art direction, of the pathetic *Aloma of the South Seas* alongside that of **The Cat and the Canary** (1939) or **The Ghost Breakers** (1940), whose creepy old dark houses are masterpieces of the designer's skill. The former is a straightforward remake of Paul Leni's funny-creepie – made funnier now, because Hope, as a vaudeville performer, is allowed some jokes – and it is just about the best film with which to experience secret passages and sliding panels and portraits with removable eyes. Elliot Nugent's direction allows no burlesque, and the same is true of George Marshall's work on *The Ghost Breakers*, also with Paulette Goddard, and also the remake of a Silent film. **Louisiana Purchase** (1941) is based on a stage musical with book by Morrie Ryskind, who ten years earlier had been one of the writers of 'Of Thee I Sing', the first musical to win the Pulitzer Prize – despite which the movie companies had always avoided it, since its subject is political corruption. So it is here, but this was filmed because Buddy de Sylva, who had produced it on Broadway, had since become Chief of Production at Paramount (in succession to William Le Baron). From the show came Victor Moore, as the incorruptible senator, and also Irene Bordoni and Vera Zorina to aid Hope (replacing William Gaxton, who had teamed with Moore in both the stage shows), who is blackmailed into corrupting him. Aided by Irving

Cummings, who in any case always directed at a plod, de Sylva decreed a literal version of the show, even to the 'business' for the lead comics. Eliminating most of Irving Berlin's score is inexcusable: to keep the book and throw out the songs* was one of the many unfathomable decisions which litter Hollywood history.

Bing Crosby always gave the impression of being one of the nicest fellows ever to step before a camera. He sang in a relaxed manner, called crooning to distinguish it from the stentorian voices of the ballad-singers who were prevalent when he started. Gradually he found complete audience acceptance in the light comedies he made for Paramount in the Thirties, his songs interspersed throughout the love-doesn't-run-smoothly plots. Perhaps because of his lazy manner they have little impetus; his clowning is game rather than accomplished, and he tried whenever he could to offset the soulfulness of most of the songs he was given to sing. He enjoyed working with comics and wisely handed **Doctor Rhythm** (1938) to Beatrice Lillie, in fine fettle as a woman who hires him, a medic posing as a cop, to prevent her niece (Mary Carlisle) from running off with a fortune hunter; Frank Tuttle directed, supposedly from a story by O. Henry. **The Birth of the Blues** (1941), ostensibly about the formation of the first all-White Dixieland band, is not really about jazz, nor the event mentioned in the title: however, it is unpretentious and is one of the first features that not only acknowledges but clearly likes what it refers to as 'darkie music' – perhaps because the director, Victor Schertzinger, was also a composer. Crosby's admiration for Louis Armstrong had got that player included in two earlier Crosby vehicles, and it is a pity he is not in this (except in a montage); Edward 'Rochester' Anderson is the only coloured entertainer on hand, as a caustic family retainer. The leading lady is Mary Martin, briefly under contract to Paramount – and her failure to find popularity in films is astonishing: she now seems, after Judy Garland, the best female in musicals of the time – so much warmer, more vibrant, more pure fun than the Grables, Huttons

and Lamours. She, Crosby and Jack Teagarden have a number together, 'The Waiter, the Porter and the Upstairs Maid' which, though indifferently staged, is as delightful as anything in the genre.

The conditions prevailing at 20th Century-Fox were happier than at R.K.O. and Paramount, and since there were no financial troubles as the industry recovered from the Depression, there were no executive shifts. Darryl F. Zanuck was the youngest head of any of the major studios, and considered the most enlightened; but his policy was no different from that of any of the other tycoons, for it also revolved round the stars. However, virtually all the studio's most important pictures were directed by either John Ford or Henry King, filmmakers of proved accomplishment. Significantly, they were also veterans, having wielded the director's megaphone for almost a decade before the coming of Talkies. The industry, including Zanuck, was not a great believer in youth – at least, behind the camera; and one of the reasons Hollywood and its films changed so little between the end of the Depression and America's entry into the War was its lack of interest in new blood. Indeed, between the arrival of theatre directors with the coming of Talkies and the graduation of directors from television almost three decades later only a handful of important new film-makers arrived – usually from Broadway or abroad.

John Ford's Oscar for *The Informer* gave him more clout at 20th Century-Fox, his home studio, and in **The Prisoner of Shark Island** (1936) he made one of his best films, handling with quiet verisimilitude sequences of great tension. Nunnally Johnson wrote the screenplay, and as in many another good film the story is from the byways of history, concerning the Dr Mudd (Warner Baxter) who splinted the leg of John Wilkes Booth, broken as he fled the scene of his crime. Mudd was convicted in the hysteria which followed Lincoln's assassination and sentenced to life imprisonment on what, so a title informs us, is the American equivalent of Devil's Island. The facts have been simplified, omitting both Mudd's recognition of Booth and the savage treatment he received before

---

* Berlin's Hollywood contracts thereafter gave him total control over the use of his material.

his trial; but the cinema has rarely done so well by its old standby, the miscarriage of justice.

Zanuck's most pressing need was for suitable vehicles for Shirley Temple, an unexpected gift to film-goers and his stockholders. Thus, after returning to R.K.O. for his Scottish and Irish pictures, Ford directed her in **Wee Willie Winkie** (1937), which changed the sex of Kipling's young hero to accommodate her. She brings peace to the North-West Frontier between some red-blooded scenes concerning the sergeant (Victor McLaglen), and Ford's portrait of Frontier life is as romantic and heroic as the American West of his later films. He responds to India as Hathaway did in *Lives of a Bengal Lancer,* but again away from his home lot **The Hurricane** (1937) confirms a new mastery in his approach. The camera is placed with a clear eye for the strongest possible evocation of time and place, and in such a way as to enhance both players and subject. Bert Glennon was the cinematographer and in fact, working for Goldwyn, Ford was able to use a number of his preferred collaborators, including Dudley Nichols (who adapted a story by Nordhoff and Hall). The film was one of the expensive 'natural disaster' movies of the time, and it remains watchable: a slight tale of colonial injustice holds our interest till the winds start to blow – concerning a separated native couple, Jon Hall and Dorothy Lamour, who are expertly supported by Mary Astor, Raymond Massey and Thomas Mitchell – and the climax itself is tremendous.

If, on such occasions, Ford begins to justify such hyperbole as 'the indomitable poet of the American cinema' (Gavin Lambert and Lindsay Anderson in *Sight and Sound*), he is anything but on either **Four Men and a Prayer** (1938) or **Submarine Patrol** (1938). The former concerns four brothers (Richard Greene, David Niven, George Sanders, William Henry) trying to discover why their father (C. Aubrey Smith) was cashiered from the Indian Army; in the second a playboy (Greene) joins the Navy as a grease-monkey, and it does have a certain bite when confined to the activities of the crew. War films were reckoned to be anathema at the box-office, but, said the *Motion Picture Herald,* with 'war on the front pages of every newspaper showmen shouldn't be afraid of this one'.

Ford's irritation with both assignments increased when Zanuck would not approve his next project, a Western script he had bought (nor would Selznick, so Ford never made the contracted film with him); but Walter Wanger, producing independently for United Artists, agreed to do it. The film was **Stagecoach** (1939), and it was a watershed. Gary Cooper had turned down the leading role so Ford cast John Wayne, an actor from B-Westerns – and with Wayne he was restricted to a medium budget. Nevertheless he went to Monument Valley for locations (for the first time), and if the film in that regard and others now seems stale, that may be because it is one of the most imitated films ever made. Wayne became a leading star, and Westerns again became the staple they had not been since Silent days. This one was not exactly new, for Ernest Haycocks had based his novel on Guy de Maupassant's celebrated tale, 'Boule de Suif'. It is the tale of a mixed group of people suddenly thrown together, including a prostitute (Claire Trevor) hounded out of town, a drunken doctor (Thomas Mitchell), a pregnant woman (Louise Platt), and a pompous bank manager (Berton Churchill) absconding with the cash. Nothing much happens till the Indians attack, and then, as Ford later admitted, the film would have ended if they had had the sense to shoot the horses.

Ford's next project, **Young Mr Lincoln** (1939), was sanctioned by Zanuck because a play on the subject ('Abe Lincoln in Illinois') had been a Broadway success; Ford wanted to do a story foreshadowing Lincoln's later greatness, and worked closely with Lamar Trotti on the superficial script, which is almost saved by the likeable portrait by Henry Fonda in the title-role. The images have been so carefully composed as to be almost petrified. Ford was ever prone to preciosity, especially when he took it upon himself to be 'artistic': there is a huge difference between the shots of shutters in *Wee Willie Winkie* and those in *The Fugitive* (q.v.), one commercial and the other ostensibly 'art', and in the same way the evocation of the American past is much less pretentious in *Stagecoach* than in *Lincoln,* on

John Ford's tendency towards artiness when confronted with a 'serious' issue was effectively curbed on *The Grapes of Wrath*, which stands as the peak of his career. The film is impressive not because it is about people on the starvation line but because it never patronises them, and only rarely makes concessions to melodrama or to sentiment. The players are Jane Darwell, Henry Fonda and Russell Simpson.

which Ford made the same distinctions. There are elements of both in **Drums Along the Mohawk** (1939), where the conventional early Technicolor shots of banked clouds are preferable to the self-consciously 'Fordian' compositions; similarly the piece is strongest on such matters as the Indian attacks, weakest when attempting a statement on war. Trotti and Sonya Levien wrote the screenplay, from a novel by Walter D. Edmonds, and the besieged pioneer couple are Fonda and Claudette Colbert.

However, these films had increased Ford's standing to the point where, if unable to select his subjects as freely as Capra did, he could at least select from the properties available those with which he felt the closest affinity. Zanuck's offer of **The Grapes of Wrath** (1940) enabled him to prove again that he was a fine director given a good script and under the right conditions – and that Hollywood could make a great and serious film if it had the right book upon which to build. John Steinbeck's novel had been a best seller: but in view of Nunnally Johnson's superb screenplay we need not consider studio motivation. It stands today, four decades after it was made, as a document of social history, and presents an America that would not be seen on the screen again for another two decades. The novel starts

in the Oklahoma dust-bowl, and the film opens as an anonymous 'they' have sent in tractors to mow down the shacks serving as homesteads. In reality, the sharecroppers had farmed their lands unwisely and when the droughts came were forced to mortgage everything they had; whereupon the banks forced them out because they considered they knew more modern ways to farm the land. Actually, the film is not about Oklahoma, except to start the Joad family on its odyssey, but about the exploitation they found in California. The migrants there were not treated as human beings; and they hardly regarded themselves as such.

One of the achievements of the film is its avoidance of a statement on human dignity. The Joads do not particularly suffer, or smile through their tears; all they ask is for work in order to eat. The famous ending, with its affirmation of the refusal to be 'licked', comes a mite falsely, but it is the right sentiment, and a better ending than Steinbeck provided. I cannot see in the film any indignation or concern on the part of its makers, but that was not then considered part of their job – which was to make *us* concerned. At the end, the Joads arrive at a decent camp administered by the Department of Agriculture. 'Why aren't there more like it?' asks Tom (Fonda), and the caretaker (Grant Mitchell) replies 'You figger it out. I can't.' Fonda's grave face and his loping walk were never better used; as Ma, Jane Darwell's strength and smile are perhaps too comforting, but her eyes convey her suffering and her indifference to it now. She won a Best Supporting Oscar, and the Academy also voted one to Ford as Best Director; but they did not like the film enough to place it above *Rebecca* (q.v.) or the lightweight *Philadelphia Story* (q.v.), which were voted respectively Best Picture and Best Screenplay. Nevertheless, the controversy it stirred up was entirely favourable to Hollywood, even if the industry's conversion to current affairs was a little tardy, and as ever based on prior acceptance in another medium.

Ford returned to Wanger and United Artists to make **The Long Voyage Home** (1940), a modernisation by Dudley Nichols of four one-act plays by Eugene O'Neill, set on a homeward-bound British merchant vessel. The photographer was Gregg Toland, whose uncluttered, clear images for *The Grapes of Wrath* here give way to Ufa-style artiness, a weakness to which Ford was prone. However, this is still the best American film about life at sea. It is meandering: whores come aboard and smuggle in liquor; there is a raid by a German aircraft and a funeral at sea; the whores are paid off and the men get drunk – a flawed sequence, but redeemed by its feeling for the fragmentary and romantic nature of such occasions. The captain is Wilfred Lawson, and the motley crew includes two Svenskas (John Wayne, John Qualen) and inevitably several Irishmen (Thomas Mitchell, Barry Fitzgerald, Arthur Shields). The use of Irish airs in Ford's Irish films is oppressive, but he makes the shanties work; and if the use of 'Harbour Lights' is anachronistic this song surely expresses the sweet-sour oil-salt smell of ships and ports and being at sea.

Tobacco Road (1941) as a play – by Jack Kirkland, adapted from the novel by Erskine Caldwell – had, as a foreword tells us, opened in New York City in 1933 and was still running. The chief reason for that – and some said the only one – was its sexual content, and the Hays Office allowed only hints of that in the film, as when young Pearl runs away from Lov (Ward Bond), who 'wasn't doin' nothin' to her but tiein' her up with some rope' and he replaces her with a sister (Gene Tierney) too grown-up for his tastes. People sit around scratchin' and arguin', as one might expect in a film in which Charley Grapewin gets top billing: the burden of it falls on him and Elizabeth Patterson, as his wife, making sympathetic comedy out of 'poor white-trash'. Ford, reflecting the original play, finds nothing in poverty but quaintness.

His supposed sympathy for the proletariat brought Ford to **How Green Was My Valley** (1941). 'The majesty of plain people and the beauty which shines in the souls of simple, honest folk are seldom made the topics of extensive discourse on the screen' was the way Bosley Crowther began his review in *The New York Times,* going on to describe it as 'one which may truly be regarded as an outstanding film of the year'. It went on to win a handful of Oscars, including Best Picture and Best

Director. Richard Llewellyn's novel had been read by millions, and it cost a packet to build his Welsh village on the backlot. The only Welshman in the cast is Rhys Williams, in a minor role, but despite only occasional attempts at the right accent by the rest of the cast you know where you are because – this being a Ford movie – the soundtrack throbs with appropriate airs. Philip Dunne's adaptation of the novel – which is of the 'trouble-at-t'-mine' school – retains its framework, that of a middle-aged man recalling his boyhood in such phrases as: 'For singing is in my people as sight is in the eye.' The boy is played by 'Master Roddy McDowall'; Donald Crisp is the father, Sara Allgood is the mother, Maureen O'Hara the daughter, and there is a heap of sons, all of whom work down the mine. Since the material is so inferior to the Steinbeck – though it was not thought so at the time – it is interesting to find Ford descending to its level, if effectively, as in the sequences calculated to invoke family love. He is at his best with the boy (as movies often are), but this family defeats even his loving treatment, much too self-satisfied despite a generation-gap quarrel over socialism and the daughter's improbable marriage.

Until Ford came into his own Henry King had been Zanuck's automatic choice for his prestige pictures. King made the studio's first Technicolor feature, **Ramona** (1936), which was the fourth screen version of that old and highly sentimentalised account of the plight of an Indian couple – and if the first part (fiestas and such) is artificial, it improves mightily once the drama begins, partly as a result of the expansive performance of Jane Darwell, and partly because it is not till then that King responds to both the drama and the colour, making them, as they should be, inseparable. Loretta Young in a black wig is Loretta Young in a black wig; and we do wonder why the Christian and Westernised Indian chief (Don Ameche) doesn't simply don Western dress to avoid trouble. King remade two other famous films (both inferior to his best films of that time), **Way Down East** (1935) and **Seventh Heaven** (1936), and though the material was equally dated, his response, when stirred, is sound, going for full-blooded romance by way of exquisite framing and romantic lighting. But you wonder why they bothered – especially in the latter case, with the Hays Office requirements making equivocal the profession of the heroine, played by Simone Simon with overmuch sophistication. It is also hard to accept James Stewart as a Parisian sewer-rat; but if the lecherous C.O. at the end has become a shining (if wounded) subaltern, there is gain in the role of Chico's chum (J. Edward Bromberg, chameleon among character actors), whose love of cats and hatred of Diane suggests some darkling thought.

Lloyds of London (1937) was one of the factual historical dramas of which Zanuck was so fond, and is mainly notable for the revelation of a new leading man, Tyrone Power (1913–58), who became after Shirley Temple the studio's most important property: willing rather than gifted, he was put into the studio's biggest projects and therefore continued to benefit from King's expertise. Miscast as an ambitious schemer buying politicians in **In Old Chicago** (1938), King simply gets him offscreen as quickly and often as possible. The role was meant for Clark Gable (the advent of Power meant that Zanuck became less dependent on Metro when he had a male lead to cast, and an additional blessing was the advent of Alice Faye, playing here the role intended for Jean Harlow), and the film itself is a part-copy of *San Francisco* (q.v.), with a similarly contrived plot, to be resolved by a disaster – the Great Fire – which also provides a spectacular climax. It is, however, a gutsy, gusty entertainment: the Chicago of 1871 knee-deep in mud, carriages tearing through, pretty ladies with parasols, and men with walrus moustaches in lush, over-padded interiors – all this, and Mrs O'Leary's cow.

The same three players, Power, Faye and Don Ameche, were reunited for **Alexander's Ragtime Band** (1938), and it has been suggested that their obvious liking for each other is one reason for its almost-total success; but King himself claimed credit for responding warmly to his material – a show-business story built around people he had known in New York. Two dozen or so songs by Irving Berlin, old and new, dictated the form of the story, a panoramic one from ragtime

to radio, via the First World War. The form was innovatory for a musical, the combination in this genre of comedy and drama had been untried for several years; and more than any film so far it confirmed the reputation of what was then Hollywood's youngest studio.

King's craftsmanship and always responsible approach to his material are further evident in both **Jesse James** (1939), another excursion into Technicolor, and **Stanley and Livingstone** (1939), both confirming Zanuck's penchant for the historical spectacular. There are considerable distortions of fact in both films – particularly regrettable in the case of Nunnally Johnson's screenplay for *Jesse James,* for the James brothers were virtually the only ones among the famous outlaws to have had any degree of political importance; indeed, Johnson uses none of the horrifying facts (even the details of the assassination are wrong), offering a bland tale of injustice and turning the James boys into Robin Hood-motivated badmen. 'He ain't a knight fightin' a bad railroad,' someone says, 'he's a wild animal.' But as played by Mr Power the only animal he resembles is a domestic cat. In *Stanley and Livingstone,* Spencer Tracy and Cedric Hardwicke play the famous explorers, journalist and medical man respectively, and both are on their best form: no audience would ever snigger at the manner in which the famous line is spoken. When the piece sticks to the facts, it is dull, and when it telescopes and hypes them, towards the end, it becomes banal; but all in all, as B. R. Crisler said in *The New York Times,* it 'represents rather a fine renunciation of cheap dramatics by a studio which occasionally in the past has shown an inclination to overindulgence'.

Zanuck next came up with **Little Old New York** (1940), whose title and the presence of Alice Faye (q.v.) were meant to suggest a follow-up to *In Old Chicago.* The less than robust rivals for her favours are Fred MacMurray and Richard Greene, the latter as Robert Fulton, who built the first steamboat in 1807. King's handling of the boat-building sequence attests to his response when enthused, as he was throughout two better studies of the American past, **Chad Hanna** (1940) and **Remember the Day** (1941). The former, in Technicolor, is a tale of circus folk in the 1840s, written by Nunnally Johnson from a story by Walter D. Edmonds, with Fonda, Darwell, Guy Kibbee and two conventional Hollywood ladies, Linda Darnell and Dorothy Lamour; the latter is one of several films spawned by the success of *Goodbye, Mr Chips,* with Claudette Colbert as the aged teacher remembering earlier days and the sportsmaster (John Payne) who went to war and did not come back. It belongs in the vanguard of memory films of the time, all touching on the First World War (it was released at the time of Pearl Harbor): with girls in gingham dresses strolling on lawns, the first Model T Ford, and stern or benign fathers in wing collars.

Henry Hathaway joined 20th and made **Johnny Apollo** (1940), a film untypical of both, about a college boy (Power) who turns mobster after considering the disparity between the prison sentences handed out to his father (Edward Arnold) and another gangster (Lloyd Nolan). In this case, both period detail and Power were poor – the film was a deliberate attempt by Zanuck to put Power into the sort of role which had made Cagney famous. To that end one of the writers of the screenplay – the other was Philip Dunne – was Rowland Brown, who had made two of the best gangster films: undoubtedly we owe to him the chilling details – the stiletto kept inside the trouser-leg, the sequence in the mortuary – which make this less an attempt to revive an old genre than the first *film noir* of the Forties. Of **Brigham Young** (1940), Hathaway said later, 'It was a very difficult film to make – all those goddam wagons.' The word *Frontiersman* was added to the title to forewarn audiences that they could not expect a film about legalised harems – and though Young (Dean Jagger) admits to twelve wives, we see only one (Mary Astor). Unhappily also visible is a completely untruthful tale of the Mormons' trek to escape religious persecution, the usual pallid romance, between Power and Linda Darnell, and a repeat of the climax of *The Good Earth* (q.v.).

Its writer was Lamar Trotti, whom Zanuck considered an expert on the American past. He was also responsible for the screenplay of **Hudson's Bay** (1940), which Irving Pichel directed, concerning two French explorers (Paul Muni, Laird Cregar) and the Court of Charles II (Vincent Price). Muni displays misplaced enthusiasm with dialogue like this: 'Before yoy take a contri wiz your hand yoy most take eet wiz ziz' (placing hand on heart); while John Sutton asks, quite seriously, 'How's Nell?' Zanuck's historical films are among the most useless ever made. Scott Fitzgerald thought **Suez** (1938) would put the cinema back three years, and that seems an optimistic estimate. Zanuck's penchant for building pictures round a concept – event, place, person – was never more foolhardy than here, as de Lesseps (Power) loses his beloved Eugenie (Loretta Young) to Louis Napoleon (Leon Ames); just about everyone turns up, from Disraeli to Liszt and Victor Hugo. The director, Allan Dwan, said he was drawn to the film for its 'human story. Whether the canal was built or not was of no importance to me.' He also mentioned that the de Lesseps family sued, in France, but the case was thrown out because 'this picture did such honour to France'. France, possibly; 20th Century-Fox, decidedly not.

It is not surprising that the majority of these films concerned the New World, since there was a revulsion in the U.S. towards events in the Old one, as war threatened once again. As the subject became increasingly discussed, Hollywood produced a number of films on World War One, but the public did not want to see Zanuck's **The Road to Glory** (1936), based on a four-year-old French film which he had bought, *Le Croix de Bois.* Howard Hawks returned to direct, and eventually a new screenplay was commissioned from Joel Sayre and William Faulkner, borrowing much from Humphrey Cobb's novel, 'Paths of Glory'[*] (and the line about blindness from *Mata Hari*). Warner Baxter and Fredric March are entirely serious, but the finale with white-bearded Lionel Barrymore, meant to represent a last act of supreme heroism, founders in bathos. Indeed, although this film is much grimmer than Hawks's *The Dawn Patrol,* it is not in the same league.

The purpose of **The Mark of Zorro** (1940) was not so much to recreate old

[*] 'Some Time in the Sun' by Tom Dardis confirms that Faulkner had owned a copy.

417

California as to allow Tyrone Power to swashbuckle, which he does with zest, unembarrassed by the tight pants and the necessary show of effeminacy. Basil Rathbone is, for once, conventional as a villain, and the film belongs to J. Edward Bromberg as the greedy and incompetent governor, strutting about like a turkeycock. Gale Sondergaard★ is his vain wife and Linda Darnell an effective heroine. Rouben Mamoulian's direction is almost flawless, but another remake of a famous Silent, **Blood and Sand** (1941), is overlong and unduly earnest. Power has Valentino's role, and the women in his life are Miss Darnell and Rita Hayworth, the latter particularly decorative in Technicolor – which seems to have taken most of Mamoulian's attention.

Since most of Mamoulian's later films are unsatisfactory, the sheer excellence of *The Mark of Zorro* may be due to the team built up by Zanuck, or to the man himself in his capacity of taskmaster, examining every inch of film and chivvying everyone around him. Another poor director, Bruce Humberstone, made an exceptional film at this time, **I Wake up Screaming** (1941), based on a murder novel by Bruce Fisher. With *The Maltese Falcon* (q.v.) this film launched the vogue for what we now call the Hollywood *film noir* – an overstudied but enjoyable series. As with *Johnny Apollo,* the studio created an exceptionally sleazy New York – the allnight cinema, a florist's shop, the bare precinct; and the often shifty detectives of the old gangster films become in Laird Cregar a figure of such sadness and evil that Humberstone does not need the camera to emphasise the huge expanse of waistcoat, the Oscar Wilde lips and hooded eyes. Elisha Cook is the cringing, fawning lift-boy with a hang-up on the dead girl (Carole Landis), a former hashslinger whose heart of stone had finally put the ticket to Hollywood in her purse – but the film is even more enjoyable if you wonder exactly what she had done for him and Cregar. The keynotes of the *film noir* – pathology, seediness and melancholy – were merely revivals from the gangster film era, to be noted and enjoyed now that the pace of films had so slowed down.

★ Ten years later, both artists were among those blacklisted for supposed communist affiliations; Bromberg's family believe he died because of it.

The studio also had a brief fling with the most famous detective of all, and **The Hound of the Baskervilles** (1939) is the most taking of the Holmes stories, with the ghostly cur roaming Dartmoor baying for blood. This was the sixth film version, and the first time Basil Rathbone and Nigel Bruce played Holmes and Watson, but what most concerned Fox was that it provided an English gentleman role for Richard Greene, unconvincing as anything else. Graham Greene noted a number of changes from the book, including the fact that Holmes had been given a sense of humour, and its welcome prompted a sequel (the later B-series with Rathbone was made by Universal), **The Adventures of Sherlock Holmes** (1939), with Alfred Werker replacing Sidney Lanfield as director; both films, though medium budget, are handsome and reasonably intriguing.

Under Two Flags (1936) was another much-filmed piece, with Frank Lloyd this time in charge of Ouida's novel. In a Foreign Legion station, 'the white man's most distant outpost', a tough major (Victor McLaglen) is in love with the local bar-owner, Cigarette (Claudette Colbert) till the advent of a sergeant (Ronald Colman). 'Do you speak Arabic?' someone asks him. 'Oh, fairly well,' he says, with familiar nonchalance. Lady Venetia (Rosalind Russell) arrives on the scene, displaying a most unladylike desire to inspect the barrack room. She falls for the sergeant, certain that she has met him before, and without batting an eye goes on to discuss 'one of the most popular officers in the Guards' who shielded his younger brother and disappeared.

The subject of the British abroad also featured in **The Rains Came** (1939), from a more recent best seller, by Louis Bromfield, and Clarence Brown was borrowed from M-G-M to direct. No one gets the accents right, including Marie Ouspenskaya and Tyrone Power as Indians, and though the Indian character and the British presence are much discussed, the film actually says nothing, while the plot, about a bored socialite (Myrna Loy) finding redemption in healing, is tired. However, the flood and earthquake are impressive, as huge pieces of masonry hurtle about the screen: and if, for the director's convenience, the special effects generally take place at night, the disasters are all the more frightening for taking place in darkness.

With the outstanding exception of *The Grapes of Wrath,* that was the closest 20th came to a serious film on a contemporary subject, but mention might be made of **Dante's Inferno** (1935), directed by Harry Lachman, and **It Had to Happen** (1936), directed by Roy del Ruth, both concerned with a backstreet boy whose ambition turns sour on him at the end. In the former Spencer Tracy is the carnival barker who tramples on everyone till he is a powerful entrepreneur; in the latter George Raft is the immigrant who becomes one of the underworld powers behind the governor. That a wealthy and married society lady (Miss Russell) stands by him when he is indicted with fraud is one of the interesting themes which this film merely plays with. The other film is notable for its recreation of Dante's hell, building from the sequences of the Silent film of the same name to create a Bosch-like splendour.

The success or failure of most 20th Century-Fox films had become relatively immaterial with the rise of Shirley Temple (b. 1928). Her popularity in fact began during the Fox regime, after her singing one song in **Stand Up and Cheer** (1934), a musical intended to make audiences feel less despondent about the Depression. Presumably it did, for the public took her to its heart, and for the next three years she surpassed even Clark Gable as the biggest box-office draw in films – a fact which makes even more curious much of the dialogue of her early films, nudging audiences by constantly referring to her as adorable, lovable, cute, etc. 'Curly Top, you're a bundle of joy-/Curly Top, you're like a wonderful toy/You're so full of sunshine, folks all agree,' sings John Boles in **Curly Top** (1935).

Her pictures were often new versions of the Silent vehicles of Baby Peggy and Mary Pickford, but instead of growing up to adolescence in the last reel for the fade-out kiss Temple was usually given an elder sister to take care of that department; because audiences liked to see the tot sing and dance, many of her films are concerned with show business. She was constantly surrounded by ageing vaude-villians, and her movies are sometimes

worth seeing for them or for the equally ageing supporting players. Some are worth viewing for themselves, at their best when proposing the Dickensian view of a child struggling against a malevolent universe, and at their worst when she is restoring happiness to others or melting stony hearts – including on occasion Honest Abe and Queen Victoria. **Captain January** (1936), directed by David Butler, is one of the former, while – were it not for little steelheart of the golden locks – **Heidi** (1937) would rank with the very best films made for children. Taken from Johanna Spyri's popular tale, the child suffers a vicious aunt (Mady Christians), a crabbed old hermit of a grandfather (Jean Hersholt) and, with her crippled companion (Marcia Mae Jones) a governess (Mary Nash) of such double-dyed villainy that she plans to sell Heidi to the gypsies. The director was Allan Dwan, working with Raymond Griffith

The entire world in the Thirties seemed to agree with 20th Century-Fox that Shirley Temple was the most adorable child on earth, but today audiences find her an acquired taste. It was inevitable that she would play *Heidi* and that by any standard is an admirable film.

as producer, and Dwan paid him this tribute: 'He understood pictures because he had been in them and knew all the problems. And he was excellent at gags . . . He had an effervescent attitude.' They also worked on **Rebecca of Sunnybrook Farm** (1938), which is enjoyable, due mainly to the presence of Helen Westley, magisterial in pince-nez and floral prints, bridling at each suspected infringement of her dignity. This actress also decorates **Stowaway** (1936), as does Alice Faye, but more prettily; and as directed by William A. Seiter the excitement promised by the title is still conveyed to every child in the audience.

Of the other Temple films, two are worth seeing for their villainesses: Jane Withers in **Bright Eyes** (1934), a pampered, vicious infant who delights in pulling dolls apart, and Miss Nash again, as the headmistress in **The Little Princess** (1939). Neither the addition of Technicolor nor the fact that Temple, approaching adolescence, had become an adequate actress could prevent the film from falling below expectations. Zanuck had refused to lend her for *The Wizard of Oz* (q.v.), thus doing the world an enduring favour; but when that film triumphed he put Temple into a similar Technicolor fantasy, **The Blue Bird** (1940), with Walter Lang as director. The story is less engaging, but there is a tremendous sequence of a forest fire raging amid a huge storm, and it is only inferior in one great respect – its heroine, who lacked not only the wistfulness but almost everything else that made Judy Garland so effective. **Young People** (1940), directed by Dwan and inspired by *Babes in Arms* (q.v.), reminds us that Garland had arrived in films, although Temple, leggy now, was no better a singer or dancer than she had ever been. The public refused to flock to either film, and though the studio defensively attributed the well-known failure of *The Blue Bird* to its exorbitant cost, only a tentative step was taken towards renewing the child's contract. Her run had been phenomenal – and that is the right adjective in both senses: she appeared when Hollywood and audiences needed her, in reaction to the sleazy sex stories washed away by the new Code, and with a smiling confidence which suggested that if she had heard of the Depression it did not bother her. But the fact that the public deserted her almost overnight on the advent of a more talented youngster – not to mention Deanna Durbin (q.v.) – suggests only a freak attraction.

In the same category belongs Sonja Henie, an Olympic skating champion who came into films and skated. Years later Zanuck observed that 'stars confine you to the standard thing,' but if in deploring the star-system he contradicted much of his career he had demonstrated, with these 'standard things', that he knew plenty about packaging a young lady who, once she took off her skates, was devoid of interest. Her early films have ridiculous plots – mere opportunities to get her on to ice – and an excellent array of supporting talent whose excessive fondness for the Sonja character was also borrowed from the Temple films. Henie's two best movies are both with Tyrone Power and directed by Sidney Lanfield; **Thin Ice** (1937), in which, for once, the skating is imaginatively staged and choreographed, and **Second Fiddle** (1939), with its half dozen songs by Irving Berlin – and if he was not at his most inspired who could blame him, since neither artist could sing or dance? The War might have revitalised Henie's career, since her Norwegian accent enabled her to play a refugee in **Sun Valley Serenade** (1941), directed by Bruce Humberstone in an uneasy compromise between the wholly visual and the wholly aural – because its rival attraction is Glenn Miller's orchestra, for whose sake it is occasionally revived today.

Judy Garland made her feature debut at 20th in **Pigskin Parade** (1936), directed by David Butler, a college musical only otherwise remarkable for the presence of a left-wing student (Elisha Cook Jr) – who is, of course, an object of scorn. The leading players are Stuart Erwin, Patsy Kelly and Jack Haley. Garland, billed ninth, does sing three songs, but the studio was not sufficiently interested to ask M-G-M – who did not know what to do with her – whether it could keep her; nor was it then interested in the lady billed sixth, Betty Grable, who later became one of its biggest stars.

The singing star at 20th Century-Fox

was Alice Faye (b. 1915), whose popularity soared once Zanuck decided she need no longer look like Jean Harlow; indeed, the more gentle appearance suited one of the screen's most amiable personalities and the best of the light vocalists. She did not have to be packaged like Temple or Henie, but her films – unpretentious, undemanding entertainments – show a similar care: **King of Burlesque** (1935), directed by Lanfield, with Warner Baxter reprising his role in *42nd Street* and Faye and Jack Oakie in the roles they would play again in *Hello, Frisco, Hello* (q.v.), a partial remake; **Sing, Baby, Sing** (1936), directed by Lanfield, in which Faye is a singer promoted by a no-good agent (Gregory Ratoff) because she's supposedly being wooed by a drunken movie-star (Adolphe Menjou, parodying John Barrymore); **On the Avenue** (1937), directed by Roy del Ruth, singing the Irving Berlin score and, according to the billing, 'supporting' Dick Powell as a Broadway composer-producer star and Madeleine Carroll as the richest girl in the world, who is lampooned by him; and **You Can't Have Everything** (1937), directed by Norman Taurog, as an aspiring playwright whose work is pinched by a musical comedy writer (Don Ameche). Indeed, she is not only a playwright, but an intense young intellectual – a role never played less convincingly nor more charmingly, while Ameche responds with pleasing insouciance. They are an underrated team, he enthusiastic and sometimes unfeeling, she loving and patient. In **Hollywood Cavalcade** (1939) he is a prop-boy who becomes a director after discovering her, and she later gives him the chance of a come-back, directing her first Talkie. The Mack Sennett reconstructions, directed by Mal St Clair, are accurate, but otherwise only the old tunes provide an authentic period touch; the rest is sluggishly directed by Irving Cummings, wasting a good idea, a good title, Technicolor and Buster Keaton, cast as a custard-pie-throwing Silent comic (which he emphatically was not).

This was one of the panoramic musicals engendered by the success of *Alexander's Ragtime Band* (though audiences waiting for Faye to become a *singing* star were disappointed), another was **Rose of Washington Square** (1939), directed by

Gregory Ratoff. Intended as a dramatic musical, it concerns a stage star (Faye) in love with a gambler (Tyrone Power). Al Jolson appears as the heroine's confidant and 'the greatest star Broadway's ever known', singing yet again a medley of his famous songs, and giving a real charge to Nunnally Johnson's dialogue: 'The only girl on Broadway who'd rather listen to her own voice than her own heart!' and 'This is your song. It was born just for you. Sing it and they'll never forget it or you.' The song is 'My Man', and no one could have missed the allusion to the woman who had made it famous in the U.S., Fanny Brice. Song and situation recur in *Funny Girl* (q.v.), when they were so poorly rendered that no one could say, as here, 'It's like taking her heart in her two hands and holding it out in front of her.' Also to the same formula, and as

Tyrone Power and Alice Faye in typical mood when they were the biggest stars on the Fox lot: *Rose of Washington Square*. Since the film was recognisably based on the life of Fanny Brice, the usual disclaimer in the credits of 'any resemblance to real persons' is writ large instead of being tucked away at the bottom of the screen.

421

genial as they are predictable, are **Tin Pan Alley** (1940), directed by Walter Lang, and **The Great American Broadcast** (1941), directed by Archie Mayo – indeed, the plots and casts are virtually identical, though the World War One footage in the former is stridently pro-British.

Zanuck was as adept at copying others as himself, and **Swanee River** (1939) was an attempt to repeat the success of M-G-M's Strauss musical and Paramount's *The Great Victor Herbert*; moreover, he realised that the Old South and the Negro minstrel shows would look splendid in the Technicolor he was increasingly using – and they do, partly because the Technicolor Corporation insisted on supervising, restraining the palette to pastel shades. Otherwise, as directed by Sidney Lanfield, the story of Stephen Foster (Ameche) is reduced to 'And then I wrote . . .', blaming his alcoholism on his frustrated yearning to be a serious composer rather than on his being a Northerner writing in Southern idiom at that time of conflict. Jolson, appearing as Christy the minstrel man, is given one self-indicting line, 'If there's anything I hate in a man it's an inflated ego,' while Ameche, not an actor of much resource, has charm to spare and a light touch. His d'Artagnan is the one saving grace of **The Three Musketeers** (1939), a 'musical comedy version' directed by Dwan, though the songs of that otherwise unfunny team, The Ritz Brothers, playing the lackeys, have a certain daffy splendour.

Ameche's screen partnership with Miss Faye was interrupted with **Down Argentine Way** (1940), when illness necessitated her replacement by Betty Grable, who plays an heiress with a bare midriff given to singing in Manhattan bars. This otherwise dreary racetrack tale, directed by Irving Cummings, was also notable for introducing the Argentinian-born Carmen Miranda, even if her numbers were filmed in New York and interpolated into the completed film. Beyond her elaborate costumes, nothing in the film justified the use of Technicolor, at this point only used in Hollywood for subjects considered of pictorial beauty. Public response supported Zanuck's faith in the system, and he stepped up production to one Technicolor film a month, often with subjects which did not, by the standards of the other studios, seem to require it. Within two years Technicolor was synonymous with the 20th Century-Fox musical, though with the increase in colour films the Technicolor Corporation was no longer able to supervise each production as it would have liked. The system was no longer discriminately used, as may be seen in **Moon Over Miami** (1941), where the by now *de rigeur* night club settings are part paint-box and part chocolate-box. The film itself, directed by Lang, is the 'standard thing', the second version of the studio's perennial about three fortune-hunting girls – and quite the dullest, apart from a few minutes by Ameche as a drunk millionaire and a bright song-and-dance at the beginning, choreographed by Hermes Pan, whose work with the studio would be much less distinguished than that with Fred Astaire, either before or later.

422

18

Hollywood's Golden Age: Universal, Warner and M-G-M

AT UNIVERSAL the problem was less to find the right star vehicles – the studio had no major names – than to keep the bailiff from the door. Not paying huge star salaries kept the overheads down, but it also meant that exhibitors were not inclined to book Universal pictures – which was one reason the studio continued, reluctantly, to make the potentially profitable horror films. Amongst these, and its programmers, Universal leavened each season with a couple of big pictures; and the Laemmles' assets included two or three directors capable of drawing leading players from other studios.

The success of earlier four-handkerchief efforts by John M. Stahl brought Claudette Colbert to the studio for **Imitation of Life** (1934), and Irene Dunne returned for **Magnificent Obsession** (1935), both of which make the earlier films seem as austere as legal textbooks. The first is taken from a novel by Fannie Hurst on racial integration and the second is based on an 'inspirational' novel by Lloyd C. Douglas. Neither would seem to appeal to anyone of mature mind for more than a few minutes – and that certainly applies to the remade versions of the Fifties – but Stahl works lightly and directly, keeping well back at the tricky moments and having sensible, humorous people (Ned Sparkes, Charles Butterworth) to support the stars. *Imitation of Life* concerns the partnership between a young widow (Colbert) and her coloured maid (Louise Beavers) who become wealthy as co-owners of Aunt Delilah's Pancake Mix. They live together, but one sits beside the chauffeur and the other behind; one goes downstairs and the other

up, and while the one upstairs throws a party the one in the basement sits listening to the noise. Presumably such conventions would have been observed, even if the film had had a stronger basis in reality, and it is sympathetic towards its lovable, stereotyped mammy and the daughter who, wanting to pass for white, is comforted with the dry philosophy: 'You've got to get used to it, so you might as well start now.' Everyone is desperately keen to do the right thing, which is also true of *Magnificent Obsession,* with its drunken playboy (Robert Taylor), accidentally responsible for the death of a doctor and the blinding of his widow (Miss Dunne). Taylor, his bounce kept down, is convincing except when, having redeemed himself, he is revealed as a Nobel prize-winner; while Dunne, though she is seen reading Braille with only one hand, actually did so herself after several weeks of instruction by experts. In **When Tomorrow Comes** (1939) she is equally convincing whether bending to examine a magazine while warbling the Liebestraum or delivering the one good line, 'I'm so hungry I'd eat anything that didn't bite me first'. The plot, however, is strained – about a waitress involved in a *coup de foudre* with a pianist (Charles Boyer), before discovering he is married – and showed that Stahl had lost conviction. He had left the studio after the change of management and had been assigned to a programmer on his return; he left again after this film, and continued to decline.

As did James Whale, an erratic but often talented director. Stahl was at one time capable of the same kind of alchemy as Borzage and McCarey, and the achievements of this small group contrasted sharply with the results of the Warner craftsmen, who could only hope their zest and attention to detail would paper over any cracks. Whale, like Mamoulian, belongs to a third group who, capable of mismanaging and misjudging their material to a degree, are yet by virtue of their taste and a penchant for copying directors with a strong personal style able to make an occasional good film. However, even in Whale's best films there is little evidence of strong control. *Photoplay* praised the direction of **By Candlelight** (1934), but its fairground sequence is taken from von Sternberg and the rest is pastiche Lubitsch. Hans Kräly's name appears among the four screenwriters (working from a German play adapted by P. G. Wodehouse), and the idea is Lubitschesque: a valet (Paul Lukas) masquerades as his master in order to emulate his philandering, not knowing that the lady concerned is in fact the lady's maid (Elissa Landi). But Whale misses the point, which is that two nice people make a fairy tale come true by emulating two not very nice people, and the rout is completed by the stars, he elephantine in a role ideal for Boyer (not then a star) while she seems to be playing exclusively for audiences in Shaftesbury Avenue.

Whale was one of the few homosexual directors to fail with actresses, but in **One More River** (1934) Diana Wynyard is an exception. With her aristocratic tones and delivery she at first seems only of the period, but then she advances ahead of her time, throwing away words and stepping on those of others, changing tempo within speeches as her thoughts change and using her whole body to convey meaning. She cannot, however, pull the film through: from a portrait of the English as forelock-tugging yokels it descends to domestic trivia, going to extreme lengths to put the wife (Miss Wynyard) in a compromising situation – in a broken-down car near Henley – and then keeping her chaste. R. C. Sherriff wrote the screenplay from a novel by Galsworthy, and the film was presumably meant for those who followed the headlines-making society divorces of the period.

Showboat (1936) was Universal's second version of the Kern-Hammerstein operetta, based in turn on Edna Ferber's novel about the old Mississippi and the showboat daughter (Irene Dunne) who marries the gambler (Allan Jones). Whale clearly enjoyed recreating old-time melodramas, and in general the anachronisms – e.g. those shots illustrating 'Ol' Man River' – can be forgiven as the cast sweeps into Kern's almost intact score. 'Ol' Man River' is sung by its greatest interpreter, Paul Robeson, for whom Kern wrote a new song, 'I Still Suits Me'. From the original cast Helen Morgan does her incomparable, moving 'Bill' and 'Can't Help Lovin' dat Man'. Only Mr Jones is poor: if it were a perfect world, the ideal man would have been Howard Keel from the later M-G-M version (q.v.). That gave us a better ending, and Technicolor; this is at its best with the moonlit river and the lovers on the top deck singing 'You Are Love': they don't do the verse, but then it's not a perfect world.

The Road Back (1937) was suitable for Universal inasmuch as its source was a novel by Erich Maria Remarque, taking off from *All Quiet on the Western Front*; its screenplay is by another war veteran, R. C. Sherriff, with Charles Kenyon, and, like the earlier film, it has a non-star cast. It starts in the trenches, and moves via the Armistice to the Revolution, which it handles gingerly; devolving into a study of post-war restlessness, it takes on a seriousness which the propagandist fervour of the earlier reels lacked. The art direction makes a convincing Germany, and reminds us that decor was Whale's strength. Whale copies Pabst for the murder; and though the subsequent trial turns on the old plea that the boys were taught to kill, it remains powerful, concluding with a montage of Europe rearming: it would be two years before another American film acknowledged that fact.

The film was a failure, thus not redeeming the situation at the studio, whereby the new management was hostile to most of the people who had worked for its predecessor. At Warners, Whale made **The Great Garrick** (1937), with Brian Aherne in the title-role and described as 'a play for the screen by Ernst Vajda' – and though derived from 'She Stoops to Conquer' closer in spirit to the period farces which still cluttered the world's stages. The credits also boasted

'A James Whale Production', a distinction granted by the studios only to directors of eminence, e.g. Capra, Lubitsch – but the film itself gave no reason why Whale retained it. He had no recourse but to take on two Bs at Universal before moving to M-G-M on a three-picture contract negotiated before Thalberg died. It was Thalberg's intention that he make *Goodbye Mr Chips,* but he was put, instead, on **Port of Seven Seas** (1938), a condensed version of Marcel Pagnol's *Marius* trilogy, which someone had seen as a vehicle for Wallace Beery: acting his head off, he never comes within a million miles of Raimu. As the film consists mainly of the wrangles with Panisse (Frank Morgan) it is clear that the screenwriter, Preston Sturges (chosen because he spoke French), wanted to preserve the original, but the finished film indicates no understanding of it. It is not all Whale's work, for Sam Wood did some re-takes; Whale's contract was annulled, and he went to United Artists for a fair version of *The Man in the Iron Mask* (q.v.), returning to Universal for **Green Hell** (1940). Frank Nugent called it 'the worst picture of the year', confident that the succeeding eleven months would provide none worse; in Britain, C. A. Lejeune, somewhat kinder, thought it 'the funniest melodrama since *Her Jungle Love*'. As Joan Bennett wears a series of gowns more suited to a Buckingham Palace garden party the film does not live up to its name, offering in fact, an all-too-desirable jungle. 'Funny, it's the little things you remember,' says John Howard, preparing to die. 'It must be spring now in Devonshire,' says George Sanders. In Devon then the people were accustoming themselves to likely invasion. Whale's war drama, *They Dare not Love* (1941), indicated further that he was no longer in touch with this planet; he retired on its completion.

William Wyler belongs to the contrasting school of directors, a group of strong and meticulous craftsmen capable of forging films at least technically perfect. He left Universal mainly due to the management troubles there; his last film for that studio, **The Good Fairy** (1935), is an excellent example of his work, but has a flaw that a director of his temperament could not disguise. That flaw springs from the nature of the material, a play by Molnár about a marvellously innocent girl whose desire to do good leads her into a variety of situations with men whose own desires are primarily sexual. The Hays Office refused to sanction the material as it stood, and the adaptation by Preston Sturges was necessarily extensive: but if it was not to give offence, and the girl's naivety retained, there was no alternative but also to retain the excessive verbiage used by Molnár to set up his situations – at least, there was no alternative for Wyler, though he responds best to the Sturges interpolations and to the star, Margaret Sullavan. Since Wyler married her (however briefly), we need not wonder about the perfection of her performance. In no other film, however, does she so well demonstrate her ability to find that point at which she could express her own personality or star quality while still offering maximum fidelity both to the script and the rules of human behaviour. This is true of all the best performers and some, like Clark Gable, found that truth without it being anything but their star quality and were hence effective even if not greatly gifted. It was and is a delicate balance, poised between elements of personality, technical knowledge, exhibitionism and a gift for acting – which is perhaps why Miss Sullavan, then in her early twenties, demonstrates it so well. Some performers upset the balance as they age, if their technical mastery increases or their personality strengthens with success – and then they need a strong director. Bette Davis is one such example, with her tendency to demonstrate that she definitely is *not* coasting through her role. Another is Katharine Hepburn, anxious always to flaunt the admired Hepburn personality. The balance may have been achieved instinctively or with the help of directors. Miss Sullavan did not lose her understanding of it as she aged: but if in some cases it was due to youth that would be ironic, since cinema-goers of the time thought of the Hollywood stars as ageless.

Another of the magical names, Carole Lombard, made two films for Universal, playing in both a wilful, tantrum-throwing, zany, rich girl. **Love before Breakfast** (1936), directed by Walter Lang, has a story-line described by *The New York Times* as 'thin to the point of emaciation' and that is part of its charm; it is not one of the great screwball comedies, but it is the one most about nothing. **My Man Godfrey** (1936) is one of the classics of the genre. William Powell is the derelict, 'a forgotten man' in the film's parlance, dragged from his shack under the Queensborough Bridge to be Lombard's trophy at a society scavenger hunt. Taken on as the butler, he has to cope with her lovesickness, the schemings of her sister (Gail Patrick), the non sequiturs of her mother (Alice Brady), and mother's simian 'protégé' (Mischa Auer); Eugene Pallette is the bewildered father. To see Miss Lombard pursuing Godfrey – she is a lady to whom nothing has been denied – is to see heaven, but the film's serious implications are best ignored, as devised by the director, Gregory LaCava, and the writers, Morrie Ryskind and Eric Hatch. By now the worst of the Depression was over, but the film cheats: the derelict turns out to be the scion of one of the best Boston families, gone to pieces after his marriage failed, and *his* cure for the times is to turn shantytown into the ritziest nightspot in town.

The film was a great success, but was finished a few weeks too late to save the Laemmles. During 1932 and 1933 the company had chalked up losses of over a million dollars, and after a small profit in 1934 – mainly due to *The Invisible Man* – it went into the red again in 1935 to the tune of $677,186. The situation was not helped by the year's major productions: *Magnificent Obsession,* though popular, had been expensive, and *Showboat* was delayed in production; while the public did not care for **Diamond Jim** (1935), despite its excellences, which include the vitality of Edward Sutherland's direction and a screenplay without extreme blacks and whites by Preston Sturges. No film better captured the vulgarity and achievement of the nineteenth-century tycoons and, as Diamond Jim Brady, Edward Arnold has the requisite dynamism. However, he was a burly, middle-aged character actor, whom, unaccountably, most Hollywood studios thought a star, and he would soon appear on the exhibitors' list of those they considered box-office poison. Unfortunately he was cast in **Sutter's Gold** (1936), on which the Laemmles placed their chief hopes.

This epic on the man who had discovered gold in California – the subject also of Trenker's *Der Kaiser von Kalifornien* – was based in part on Blaise Cendrar's novel 'L'Or', which Eisenstein had planned as his first American film and which Universal had bought from Paramount. The Laemmles made a second mistake in offering the direction to James Cruze, on the ground that he had made a 'classic' pioneering epic, *The Covered Wagon.* However, his more recent films had been potboilers, and his work on this one is of such ineptitude that long explanatory titles are needed. During production, Laemmle negotiated a loan of $750,000 from an investment group headed by the Standard Capital Corporation and Charles R. Rogers, offering as collateral his controlling stock and the films currently in progress. A further $300,000 was negotiated a few months later, as delays extended the shooting of both *Sutter's Gold* and *Showboat,* and one month later, in March 1936, Rogers decided to exercise the option, thus purchasing Universal for himself and Standard Capital for a mere $4,500,000. Laemmle not only lost the theatres and distribution companies throughout the world but also the studio – not too great a deprivation, for he was nearing the end of his life. Junior Laemmle was less expectedly ousted, having been held responsible for all the company's successful films since *All Quiet on the Western Front.* Rogers, however, had had considerable experience as a producer, if only of programmers (for Paramount and R.K.O.), and automatically was appointed vice-president in charge of production. He was replaced two years later – a contributory factor was the ambitious *Top of the Town* (1938), usually referred to as 'Flop of the Town' – by Cliff Work, from the R.K.O. circuit, who owed his appointment to Universal's new president, Nate Blumberg, arriving from the same source. It is, however, a child of fourteen who was finally responsible for taking the studio out of the red.

Deanna Durbin (b. 1921), Canadian-born of British parents, had a remarkable soprano voice and, this being the high era of the studio talent scout, had appeared in a short for M-G-M, with Judy Garland, and had sung on radio. She was brought to Universal by producer Joe Pasternak and director Henry Koster, both formerly with the company's now defunct European branch and started in the U.S. with the medium-budget films with which Rogers hoped to keep the studio ticking over. **Three Smart Girls** (1937) featured a bevy of popular supporting players, including Alice Brady and Mischa Auer in virtual repeats of their roles in *My Man Godfrey,* and is a comedy about divorcing parents reunited by their children: Miss Durbin was the youngest of these, and after a few days' shooting her part was built up and the original budget of $150,000 doubled. On first release the film took $2 million at the box-office, and when her succeeding star vehicles did as well, or better, Rogers's cares were over.

Miss Durbin occurred when not only Universal but the audiences of the world needed her; they responded with an affection afforded few stars since Mary Pickford – another innocent – and it was the last time they would be cheered and heartened by innocence. In the U.S. the Depression had weakened belief in the old fundamental values; Europe was seething with refugees, with racial intolerance, and with the unthinkable prospect of populations destroyed by aerial bombardment. The movies offered a panacea, allaying both the miseries of the past and the horrors to come. Innocence was not really endemic to Hollywood and audiences understood this: that was part of the fascination. The films that Koster and Pasternak fashioned for Durbin were fairy tales, but no one thought they were made up by dreamers or mystics. If today they are not better known it is perhaps because those who have seen only the later work of Pasternak and Koster are disinclined to investigate the rest. Deanna was not, as Graham Greene pointed out, 'the innocent centre', but 'everything is innocent all round her'; she was (in her own words, later) a 'Little Miss Fix-It', but unlike Pickford or Temple she was a meddling, bossy brat who in other circumstances would be a pain in the neck. Those around her either fawned on her or distrusted her and, just as they are observed with asperity, so her misplaced sense of charity saves her from winsomeness. That her meddling was in the interests of others, and carried out with such verve, was one reason she seemed to audiences

the ideal daughter or sweetheart; and if the time was right for her extreme self-confidence it was also right for the smattering of popular classics she sang – all of which conveyed a picture of wholesomeness; indeed, for the cinema-goers whom J. P. Mayer interviewed when researching his 'Sociology of the Film' she was the most consistently admired and emulated star.

In **One Hundred Men and a Girl** (1937), directed by Koster, she finds work for on the dole musicians, an endearing entertainment but for Stokowski's stilted performance as himself; Adolphe Menjou is her father, saying 'Fairy tales never come true', and at one point we find her rushing through a song she didn't want in the first place while glancing hungrily at the food she had had to abandon: 'Don't go, you're too original and charming,' coos Alice Brady, but the response of her husband, Eugene Pallette, is 'Shut up, you brat'. In **Mad about Music** (1938), directed by Norman Taurog, she finds and pesters a surrogate father in the shape of Herbert Marshall; in **That Certain Age** (1938), directed by Edward Ludwig, she is a pest to a journalist (Melvyn Douglas) till she hears of his

Of the many films in which Deanna Durbin appeared the one most fondly remembered is *One Hundred Men and a Girl.* That a fifteen-year-old child should have had such a clarity in singing and masterly musicianship was remarkable, but matched by a similar instinct for acting is nothing short of miraculous.

427

experiences in the Spanish Civil War and develops a crush on him. In **Three Smart Girls Grow Up** (1939) she is involved in her sisters' romances, and in **First Love** (1939) she is a modern Cinderella. These two are the best of the Durbin vehicles, with Koster confidently in command of the make-believe and the reasonably witty scripts. Indeed, the latter is something of a triumph, since a modern 'Cinderella' is not very appealing, but from *Ella Cinders* to whatever is the latest version of the Perrault story, this is easily the best: and I would match its crazy family with any other zany movie family of the time.

Koster's crisp approach, particularly on these last two films, contrasts with that of William A. Seiter, who simply refuses to find any comedy inherent in the pleasant scripts of **It's a Date** (1940) and **Nice Girl?** (1941), so that apart from the star's presence they are chiefly notable for Pasternak's astuteness in weening her into adult roles. In the former she develops a crush on a man (Walter Pidgeon) of her mother's age, resolutely refusing to see that he prefers her mother (Kay Francis); in the latter, tired of being taken for granted by the boy (Robert Stack) next door, she again throws herself at an older man (Franchot Tone), intending to lose her virginity – though the word is never mentioned. Now in romantic roles, she was to be plagued by dull leading men till she retired, but she has Charles Laughton as co-star in **It Started with Eve** (1941); he is supposedly dying, so for his sake she poses as the fiancée of his son (Robert Cummings). Koster directed, and the situations are well explored by the writers, Norman Krasna and Leo Townsend. An 'Ambersons-gloom' mansion counterbalances Durbin's sunniness and Laughton's cuteness, but it was the last time Pasternak found the balance for her: he could not agree with Universal how the adult Durbin was to be handled, and moved to M-G-M.

The Rage of Paris (1938) is the one picture under her Universal contract made by Danielle Darrieux; pert and roguish, she is suspected of being a gold digger by her fiancé's friend, Douglas Fairbanks Jr. Pasternak produced and Koster directed, confirming his light touch at this time, and it was written by Bruce Manning and Felix Jackson, both of

whom worked on the Durbin films. They also wrote the exemplary screenplay which is the basis of the second version of **Back Street** (1941), directed by Robert Stevenson. It is the story of the Other Woman from a different angle – hers. Helping to jerk the tears so expertly are Charles Boyer as the man, handsome and loving but unwilling to give up his career, and Margaret Sullavan as his mistress, who starts out flighty and self-possessed but ends up lonely and bitter.

It was Pasternak who revitalised the career of Marlene Dietrich, returning her to Blue Angel mood, vulgar and hoydenish, in **Destry Rides Again** (1939), prototype of all those Westerns with heroes slow on speech and quick on the draw. Universal had filmed Max Brand's novel with Tom Mix in 1932; this time Pasternak decided to capitalise on the opportunties for comic relief. It is the first comedy Western, parent of the facetious Westerns with us to this day and superior to all of them. In a long career George Marshall never elsewhere achieved such mastery – moving the story at a fast pace, balancing the fun and the tension, and single-mindedly embellishing the evils of Bottleneck. As the town's real boss, the saloon queen Frenchie, Dietrich has a genuine mocking nastiness and cheap allure, surprisingly well matched by James Stewart as Jefferson Destry, the 'innocent' gunman – in its own right a fine performance. Equally well partnered by John Wayne, as an easy-going all-American lieutenant, she does for the South Seas in **Seven Sinners** (1940) what she had done for the Old West: but where that was satirical this is parody, cheerfully tossing in all the clichés of the genre. The director, Tay Garnett, has fun at the expense of von Sternberg, with a camera style that finds the shadows of shutters over everything (though that is true of all Hollywood excursions into Maugham territory) and Dietrich as of yore decked in sequins and ostrich feathers. In no other post-von Sternberg film is she allowed to do her thing so much and so well, whether striding along the waterfront in black lace which looks like a petticoat or descending the stairs in naval drag intoning, cigarette in lips, 'You Can Bet the Man's in the Navy'. Garnett's handling is as confident as Marshall's, and both films are superior to anything made by either Howard Hawks or Raoul Walsh, who in recent years have monopolised most discussions of the Hollywood action film – which is doubly odd, because both Marshall and Garnett made films just as awful as the worst of Hawks and Walsh.

The other memorable star player at Universal at this period was also a Paramount alumnus, W. C. Fields, returning to films, after a long illness, and a new popularity due to a radio programme he shared with Charley McCarthy, the dummy, and Edgar Bergen, the ventriloquist: they are with him in **You Can't Cheat an Honest Man** (1939), but though the Fields–McCarthy feud offers little Fields is often very funny – disguised as Buffalo Bertha, a bearded bare-back rider, confessing to the bailiffs that his real name is Gretchel Schickelgruber, or meeting the Bel-Goodies (glorious Fieldsian name!) and telling an interminable story about his exploits at Lake Titicaca, proceeding unperturbed each time his mention of snakes sends Mrs Bel-Goodie into hysterics. Fields himself provided the film's story, under a pseudonym, and the credited director is George Marshall – though when he could no longer control his antipathy towards Fields he was replaced by Eddie Cline. Cline directed the rest of the comic's films for Universal, but fared no better; as Fields's biographer, Robert Lewis Taylor, remarked: 'With the hapless Cline he set marks of high-handed truculence that the movie industry may never see equalled.' The famous collaboration with Mae West can be seen not working in **My Little Chickadee** (1940), when the camera catches her unhappiness. Beyond that, they are an ill-suited team, she as studied as he is casual. The screenplay, credited to both of them, mainly concerns her marrying him after being compromised by a masked bandit, and his wan but not hopeful attempts to consummate the marriage. The best of it are his asides, ad-libbed on set in an attempt to steal the film from her.

'What is he up to now?' is the first line of **Bank Dick** (1940), spoken by Fields's film mother-in-law (Jessie Ralph), who despises him just a bit more than does his wife (Cora Witherspoon); the latter could not be less interested when he becomes a hero by capturing a robber – and then is

actively annoyed, for she has a grudge against the bank concerned. His elder daughter (Una Merkel) for her part reacts to praise of him with indifference tempered by surprise, but the younger one makes with mother and grandmother a trio united in loathing. 'Shall I bounce a rock off his head?' she asks: 'Respect your father,' says mother, adding quickly, 'What sort of rock?' That Fields knew he was best in domestic situations is clear: his most-admired earlier films, *It's a Gift* and *The Man on the Flying Trapeze*, are among the half dozen for which he provided the stories: *Bank Dick* is his only solo writing credit (his first screenplay credit is the one with Miss West), and it is prodigal with humour. Misanthropic in life he may have been but as an entertainer he saw comic possibilities in everything – most of all in the role of a tippling middle-aged man who alone regards himself as a success. His pseudonym on this occasion was Mahatma Kane Jeeves, which should have prepared some for the surrealist capering of **Never Give a Sucker an Even Break** (1941), lurching as it does from non sequitur to outright implausibility. It starts in a film studio, that much is clear; later, when his whisky bottle falls out of a plane, Fields dives after it and lands in a mountain eyrie, where a girl tells him she has never seen a man before – which spurs

It seemed like a good idea at the time to team W. C. Fields and Mae West in *My Little Chickadee,* and both magnificos co-operated on the script. During the filming the antipathy between them increased to the extent that they had to be photographed separately whenever possible – and as a result the picture is spotty and devoid of both genuine humour and spontaneity.

him into instant action. He had courted widows and spinsters for money but never girls, for the odds were too great: but this he can't resist, inventing a kissing game appropriate to her age and the occasion, called 'Squiggleum' – which is funnier than it sounds, as is a further Pooh-like hum, 'Chickens Have Pretty Legs in Kansas'. There is a descent in a basket, a scene in a Russian village, a fight with a gorilla and, as in *Bank Dick,* a hilarious Keystonian chase at the end – though this time it has no connection with the plot.

Arriving temporarily at Universal was Alice Faye, for **You're a Sweetheart** (1937). With her Zanuck sent director David Butler, for a pleasant musical about a Broadway star and a waiter (George Murphy), with whom she becomes involved in a publicity stunt. Butler returned to helm the two films Bing Crosby made for Universal, and, as with Miss Faye, suited the material to the star's usual style rather than that of the studio. **East Side of Heaven** (1939) is also agreeable, despite a homosexual *double entendre* rare at this time, when Joan Blondell sobs at hearing the Crosby-Mischa Auer lovey-dovey dialogue, not knowing they are talking to a baby.

Among Universal's other light fare is **The Boys from Syracuse** (1940), which throws out several Rodgers and Hart songs but is otherwise a reasonable facsimile of the Broadway original. The studio's scant faith in it is indicated by the short running time and the lower-case cast headed by Martha Raye and Allan Jones – but then it is based on 'The Comedy of Errors'. Shakespeare also looms over **Tower of London** (1939), the story of Richard III (Basil Rathbone), plus a sinister headsman (Boris Karloff) purloined from Harrison Ainsworth's novel of the same name. It is no worse than, say, *Suez,* but more irritating because it edges towards both the swashbuckler and the horror film, worthier forms than the feeble retelling of historical fact. Both films cannot hide budget limitations. The directors were, respectively, Edward Sutherland and Rowland V. Lee. Lee also made the much better – and more serious – **The Sun Never Sets** (1939), directing and producing, with Douglas Fairbanks Jr and Basil Rathbone as two British brothers devoted to the Foreign

Service, who manage to outwit a man planning to dominate the world by undermining the Empire. His nationality is not given, nor is he played with an accent by Lionel Atwill but his name is Hugo Zorif, which has a Germanic ring, and most spectators could have guessed the nationality of those likely to be involved in scientific research in Africa. The heroes' grandfather is C. Aubrey Smith: indispensable in such tales.

'Three hours of Entertainment that was Three Centuries in the Making! Since there has never been a motion picture like [it] its exhibition to the public will differ from that of any other screen attraction . . . Premieres of these engagements will not only be outstanding events in the film world, but significant civic occasions': thus Warner Bros. announced **A Midsummer Night's Dream** (1935) – which in fact lasts just 132 minutes. Renowned for their introduction of Sound, and recognised for their social dramas, the Warners felt it incumbent on them to advance the art of the cinema once more – offering the Bard, no less, in the first of his plays to be filmed since the Pickford-Fairbanks *Shrew.* Max Reinhardt, a legendary theatre man, was brought to direct – with the aid of the film-experienced William Dieterle, a fellow-countryman: the result is like one of those funfair machines with a mechanical hand manipulated to pick up objects visible within the glass case – useless things stuffed in because they're supposed to be pretty, or because people are supposed to want them. The film's visual conception, meant to be charming and impressive, is now just dowdy, be it a Court of Athens more suitable for chorus girls or the cobwebby, dewdropped forest peopled with the biggest army of fairies ever to escape from the pictures of Arthur Rackham, prancing in muslin, gliding in waist-length peroxide wigs – often viewed through Vaseline (on the lens) to pick up extra highlights. There is one magical moment: Oberon riding off at dawn with his black cloak billowing out behind him – and if there is anything else to admire it must be the confidence apparent in the whole mistaken enterprise, plus the irreverent, capable way the verse has been chopped up into four-word sentences. The text was mangled partly to use

Mendelssohn's score; but the cast cannot manage even these speeches: like many American players in Shakespeare they intone so carefully that their depleted energy allows only two expressions – a frown to denote anger and a mouth turned up at the corners to signify happiness. Victor Jory's stern-jowled Oberon is capable; the hysterically-giggling Puck of Mickey Rooney (q.v.) is at least bearable. As Snout, Hugh Herbert over-uses his giggle, but the best of the rustics is Bottom as tackled by James Cagney – bombastic, cheery and light of foot.

Despite the failure of reviewers to echo the publicity department, the film found sufficient public for M-G-M to proceed with *Romeo and Juliet* (q.v.). Warners, with prestige still in mind, offered **The Green Pastures** (1936), a not particularly courageous act in view of the play's 640 performances in New York and no less than five national tours. However, foreign returns were uncertain – in Britain the play was unknown because the Lord Chamberlain had banned it – so the film was so budgeted that its cost would be recovered by reasonable patronage in the U.S. The play had won the Pulitzer Prize, and *The New York Times* had pronounced it 'Marc Connelly's naive, ludicrous, sublime and heartbreaking masterpiece'. The film, said the same paper, 'still has the rough beauty of the home-spun, the irresistible beauty of simple faith'. Its subject is heaven, and it consists of selected events in the Old Testament as pictured in the imagination of a piccaninny Sunday School. It was the first all-Negro film since *Hallelujah!*, and there is no other quite like it. But apart from the performance of Rex Ingram as De Lawd, authoritative and with an uncanny glow of holiness, it is now difficult to see why the piece was so much admired. It is no longer possible to appreciate the Bible in *faux-naïf* terms, an interpretation by a professional playwright of the slangy idiom of the Southern negro. Warners thought Connelly so important that he was given co-director status with William Keighley, but the actors are not so much directed as marshalled.

Both films are listed among the credits of Hal B. Wallis, who had risen from publicity director to Executive Producer in Charge of Production, replacing Zanuck, in 1933. Though answerable to Jack L. Warner, he was allowed reasonable autonomy and was probably responsible for all the best Warner films of this period, either in his executive capacity or as individual producer of many of them, notably including most of the Bette Davis vehicles (q.v.). The studio owed its greatest prestige to him, as producer of the series of biographical films directed by William Dieterle, usually starring Paul Muni (1895–1967). After working together on **Doctor Socrates** (1935), a likeable and fast-paced piece about a kindly small-town doctor 'used' by gangsters, star and director were reunited for **The Story of Louis Pasteur** (1935), for which Muni won an Academy Award. Muni's zest and penchant for impersonation convinced many that he was a great actor, and it was to find something worthy of him that Warners had undertaken the project. It was, for the time, sober and conscientiously done, as the press recognised, but few liked **The White Angel** (1936), with Kay Francis impersonating Florence Nightingale. However, **The Life of Emile Zola** (1937) pleased everyone, winning also a Best Picture Oscar. Muni is Zola; Gale Sondergaard and Joseph Schildkraut are the Dreyfuses, all teeth and tightness respectively; Robert Barrat is the puzzled Esterhazy; and Henry O'Neill, Picquard. For a while it is as trying as *Suez* – Cézanne as Zola's best friend, Zola meeting his inspiration for 'Nana', Anatole France flitting across the screen – but as a brief guide to the Dreyfus affair it is altogether admirable. The ads called it 'One of the few great films of all time', a claim taken seriously by the press – and today we might still admire the concise attempts to pierce the mentality of the General Staff. We may writhe when the defending attorney says 'Once before the centuries reversed the judgment – that too was a closed case' but the use of Anatole France's statement, 'He was a moment in the conscience of time' is still moving.

Juarez (1939) can hold its own with any historical film yet made: it also telescopes and distorts, but the screenplay – by John Huston, Wolfgang Reinhardt and Aeneas MacKenzie – knits its various strands into a dramatic whole, all the more remarkable in that it divides our attention between Juarez (Muni) and Maximilian (Brian Aherne), without even an engineered meeting. The dialogue is archaic but never absurd; the writers have positively embraced the whys and wherefores, and the exposition is good drama and goodish history as it outlines Louis Napoleon's reasons for intervention and the situation in Mexico. After the fantastic establishment of a Hapsburg palace on that alien shore, the situations become more conventional, with on one side the growing misery of the head that wears a crown and on the other the idealist dreaming of unification. Dieterle is as assured with the intermittent battles as with the confrontations, and Tony Gaudio's photography is memorable, notably in the shot of the hunched and victorious Juarez with his supporters, or the final shot of a slumped Carlotta (Bette Davis). Miss Davis has the least of the three major roles, but from the start she conveys both great love and her desperation; her eyes really do seem to shoot balls of fire when she berates Napoleon (Claude Rains). Aherne's Maximilian is correct – weak, well-intentioned – but not a very resourceful performance; nor is Mr Muni's unsmiling but benevolent 'father of the people'.

Despite the customary praise from the critics, the film did only fair business. The Warners were unwilling to abandon a series which had brought them so much prestige, and virtually every figure in modern history had become a candidate for the studio's treatment. Beethoven was one of them, but the project was cancelled after the returns were in on *Juarez* – and as a result Muni left the studio. Edward G. Robinson replaced him in **Dr Ehrlich's Magic Bullet** (1940) and **A Despatch from Reuter's** (1941), in the former as the German doctor who discovered a cure for syphilis and in the latter as the founder of the news agency. In returning to the humanist-scientist origins of the series, *Ehrlich* has a certain weight, and would have been better if it had been less mealy-mouthed both as to the nature of syphilis and the faith of Ehrlich, especially as the postscript is a reprimand to his countrymen for the treatment of modern Jews; but if *Reuter's* indicated that Warners had lost courage both in subject matter and treatment, it found Dieterle also disin-

terested, concluding the series on a conventional note.

These film biographies had been particularly pleasing to the Warner board, satisfying its craving for respectability and its preference for star vehicles. Warner Bros. advertised itself in the trade press as the studio of stars, whereas that, as far as the public was concerned, was M-G-M. Warners was the only other company with which the public associated a particular commodity, and that commodity was the 'social conscience' drama. Wallis was not particularly interested in the form, though he had produced *I Am a Fugitive from a Chain Gang,* and while the studio did not entirely abandon it the message conveyed was usually subsidiary to displays of star personality and the customary ingredients of 'action' drama.

As we have seen, Warners' crusading films had begun to fail at the box-office, and **Black Fury** (1935) did little better, after Hays Office interference had made a butchery of the original script, on the grounds that it might cause anarchy in the Pennsylvania coalfields where the film is set. The subject is trade unionism, but after establishing that a rabble-rouser (J Carroll Naish) arrives to create a strike at the behest of a company of professional strike-breakers, the rest, under the direction of Michael Curtiz, is incomprehensible. The dissatisfied star, Paul Muni, referred to the result as 'Coal Diggers of 1935', and as Radek, an ebullient Slav miner, he is saddled with lines like 'Joe Radek, he like everybody and everybody like Joe Radek'.

Since Warners so longed to be M-G-M, it was able to return to the genre after Metro's prestige success with *Fury* (q.v.). **Black Legion** (1936) concerns a nice guy played by Humphrey Bogart (1900–57) who becomes bitter when passed over for promotion, allowing his resentment to grow till he is sucked into the Ku Klux Klan. An attempt is made to examine his mentality, and in the film's most revealing moment he poses before the mirror with his new gun: but the conclusion seems to be that he and his fellows are petty and cowardly, less fanatics than mere tools of the racketeers who run the Klan for profit. Archie Mayo directed, and Mervyn LeRoy both produced and directed **They Won't Forget** (1937), which also sets up its situation with skill before falling apart – and only partly because, as in most Warner movies, detectives are incapable of detecting and doctors of performing autopsies. It is the more ambitious of the two films and is set recognisably in the South – which indeed is its *raison d'être*. Two Northerners, a man accused of murder and his lawyer (Otto Kruger), find that they are no match for Southern bigotry, particularly as practised by an ambitious district attorney (Claude Rains), who rather than ride to glory on a 'Nigra' prefers a white suspect to a black one. The film's refusal to disclose the guilt or innocence of the accused is its trump card, for it demands that audiences respond instead to the prospect of his being lynched; but the clues that he is in fact guilty become increasingly hysterical. There were similar faults in LeRoy's early films, but his direction on this occasion is sloppy and the acting dreadful – with the exceptions of Clinton Rosemond as the Negro janitor and Elizabeth Risdon, who provides a fine portrayal of tragic grief as the accused man's mother. Robert Rossen and Abem Finkel wrote the screenplay, from a fictionalised account of the Leo M. Frank affair – which is why the disclaimer as to 'any resemblance to persons living or dead' appears before the studio logo. Lincoln's claim, 'A nation conceived in liberty and dedicated to the proposition that all men are equal' provides a foreword, but the film, despite contemporary admiration, is unworthy of it.

The next few Warner films in this genre are best considered as crime films or star vehicles, but **Confessions of a Nazi Spy** (1939) proved that the old crusading spirit was not dead. Jack L. Warner had been the only Jewish studio head to support the industry's Anti-Nazi League, and his view is stressed in this film: 'In six centuries the world fought its way from Medieval barbarism. In six short years the Nazis have darkened it again.' He ran no risk of Warner films being banned in Germany, for by this time few American films reached there, but there was the possibility of this one being banned by countries not wishing to offend Germany, and it became the subject of a dispute between the U.S. Government and the German Embassy. The Government stressed Hollywood's right to free speech, and pointed out that the film was based on a trial in which three people were convicted of spying for the Germans.

The small interest that occasioned has become in the film 'blazing headlines' and the hectoring, laughable commentary is grandiloquent in its chauvinism, rabidly anti-appeasement and anti-isolationist: but the film's exciting account of espionage and justice is matched by another of inter-related Nazi propaganda activities, and the intolerance they helped to promote. Technically it manages to be both derivative and adventurous, borrowing from the newsreel approach of 'The March of Time' and M-G-M's 'Crime Does Not Pay' series, against a background of the annexation of Austria and Czechoslovakia. Anatole Litvak directed, from a screenplay by Milton Krims and John Wexley, based on articles by a former F.B.I. agent, Leon G. Turrou – played here, under a different name, by Edward G. Robinson. It is heartening to see a Jewish actor in this role, holding the tension between the factual and the melodramatic without histrionics. His opponents are headed by Paul Lukas, as a fascist fanatic; by George Sanders, moving into Teutonic caricature; and notably by Francis Lederer, as a shifty little man who dreams of glory.

It cannot be termed 'social concern', but **Oil for the Lamps of China** (1935) is as good as any film that ever came from Warners. 'This fine, sincere story of an idealist's unwavering faith in his job will remain long in your memory,' said *Photoplay,* and if that was all there was to it it would deserve the neglect into which it has fallen. It is a tale of a working-life – admittedly a remarkable one – spent in China. The epidemics and revolutions of other movies about China are kept in the background, and the piece mainly progresses by way of the colleagues, good and bad, of the central character (Pat O'Brien), and if he is sometimes foolishly loyal that is because he has a wife and child and therefore needs a salary. Alice Tisdale Hobart wrote the original novel and the film is not free of 'bestsellerdom' – such as O'Brien's meeting with the woman (Josephine Hutchinson) he marries; but there is such common sense and such lack of 'rigging' that it commands

433

Pat O'Brien, left, in *Oil for the Lamps of China*, based on a popular book of the Thirties. It was because of the It was because of the book's success that Warners filmed it, but there is no other film quite like it in Hollywood history, for it is simply an account of one man's career: and although the setting is exotic, what happens to him is very much what happens to professional men in Oshkosh or New York.

Both these films were among the few made at Warners which were aimed at both men and women. So were the films of Errol Flynn (q.v.), but by and large the studio's product could be divided into vehicles for Kay Francis and Bette Davis, destined for the women, and the vehicles for Robinson, Cagney and O'Brien, meant for the men. At the end of the decade the pattern changed slightly, with the loss of Francis and O'Brien and the arrival of both John Garfield (q.v.) and George Raft; and the percentage of male dramas increased when it was clear that the studio would have to give in to critics and public and no longer confine Bogart to support-ing roles. The masculine films are the more stereotyped, featuring the know-it-all-kid, the learned-it-the-hard-way philosophy and the fight-against-the-odds finish. They were churned out so quickly that many of the scripts are cannibalistic, but a number of them remain enjoyable, such as **San Quentin** (1937), directed by Lloyd Bacon, in which O'Brien is a prison governor whose 'psychological' approach to inmates is tested when he has to handle Bogart, who happens to be the brother of his girlfriend (Ann Sheridan). The plot is virtually the same as that of the earlier *Mayor of Hell,* of which **Crime School** (1938) is a straightforward remake, made by Warners' B-unit and directed by Lewis Seiler, with the Dead End kids (it was a vehicle for them) and Bogart, in fine form as the humanitarian governor. A few months later M-G-M's *Boys Town* (q.v.) was to make the country aware of the problem of juvenile delin-quency; this film shows as much concern and has as little credibility.

Several of Robinson's films are notable for more than his performances in them, and both **Bullets and Ballots** (1936) and **Kid Galahad** (1936) remain effective melodramas. The former, directed by William Keighley, has nothing to do with elections, proving perhaps that the title had found favour. Robinson is an under-cover man who infiltrates the rackets – and if this does not give a true picture of such matters the myths remain satisfy-ing. The plot is less so, but the villain is Bogart, embarking on his career of needling Robinson and Cagney, his lot here being one of constant frustration. His thunderous expressions are to be

admiration. LeRoy proves on this occa-sion that he could direct, and O'Brien my contention that all good actors have an especially fine performance in them. Miss Hutchinson at first seems to be one of those actresses whose sole virtue is the smile that relieves her plainness, but she has a contained emotion that is increas-ingly telling.

White Banners (1938) also belongs to the unsung near-masterpieces in Warners' past, and even when it comes apart at the end (like *Magnificent Obsession* it is based on a novel by the sanctimonious Lloyd C. Douglas) it remains likeable. The direction by Edmund Goulding is exemplary, ini-tially teasing in its account of a school-master (Claude Rains), his family and the stray old lady (Fay Bainter) they take into their home. Since he makes them as or-dinary as they are amusing, Goulding demonstrates remarkable skill at superior soap opera.

savoured, and he and Robinson cross notably in the opening sequence of *Kid Galahad*: handy with gun and flick-knife, he shows off by cutting off the pants of a bellhop (Wayne Morris), who promptly slugs a prizefighter – whereupon Robinson resolves to promote the boy into a champion. 'He don't want no girl,' snarls Robinson, predictably furious when the boy falls in love with his sister (Jane Bryan) but remarkably understanding when his own moll (Bette Davis) also falls for Sunny Jim. Michael Curtiz directed this best of Thirties boxing movies.

A Slight Case of Murder (1938) is based on a play by Damon Runyon and Howard Lindsay. It had not been one of the glories of the American theatre: that the film *is* one of the glories of the screen reflects credit on the scriptwriters, Earl Baldwin and Joseph Schrank. Robinson is a one-time bootlegger settling into respectability when his house-party is intruded upon by the bodies of four late enemies. The farce that ensues is not, as it has been said to be, a satire on gangster movies, but Robinson is certainly guying *Little Caesar*, with boundless vanity and occasional sneers and elegant flicks of the cigar. His wife is the marvellous Ruth Donnelly, uncertain in her bid for 'class', and also in gratifyingly large roles are Edward Brophy and Allen Jenkins, as Robinson's henchmen. Not to be overlooked is the daughter's fiancé (Willard Parker), a six-foot-plus state trooper who quails at the thought of confronting the corpses. Lloyd Bacon directed, and in his **Brother Orchid** (1940) Robinson is again a mugg who wants to go straight – to get 'class' in 'London, Paris, Rome, all them places'. Dunned and broke, he returns to find his ever-lovin' broad (Ann Sothern) the owner of a nightclub, and his Number Two (Bogart) in charge of his gang. Self-preservation later finds him in a monastery, where he gets the rackets going again; but despite felicities this is not quite as funny as the earlier film.

As far as James Cagney was concerned, **G–Men** (1935) was his best picture since *The Public Enemy* – according to *Time Magazine,* while *Liberty* thought it 'as masculine as a bank robbery'. He plays a failed lawyer who becomes a government agent to avenge a pal's death: his quarry is Barton MacLane, burly villain of every other Warners movie and seen here at his best. En route to the climactic shoot-out there is some Warner crusading in the form of a police plea for Senate help (to make bank robberies federal offences, to have G-men armed), and as directed by William Keighley it is a fast ride. That steam-engine Warners pace was soon to be lost, but Howard Hawks uses it in **Ceiling Zero** (1935), one of a series of films teaming Cagney and Pat O'Brien, the former as treacherous but lovable, finally coming to heel, and O'Brien equally dynamic but nevertheless pugnacious and longsuffering. In this one they spend most of their time in the control room, an indication that the original Broadway play was of that slice-of-life school popularised by Elmer Rice: Frank Wead wrote both that and the screenplay, borrowing from *Air Mail*, on which he also worked.

In view of the lack of originality prevailing at Warners at this time and the fact that he was required to make half a dozen similar movies every year, it is not surprising that Cagney walked out on his contract. Because the Warner stars were the most rebellious, Jack L. Warner was forced, eventually, to be the most magnanimous of the tycoons – which may not have been difficult for him, as he was considered as charming outside the studio as he was dictatorial – and ignorant – within it. Cagney duly returned for **Boy Meets Girl** (1938), directed by Bacon from the Broadway play by Sam and Bella Spewack about two scriptwriters; it was one of his happiest teamings with O'Brien, playing mutually dependent kidders, moving in a whirlwind of wisecracks in what was a thinly disguised sketch of Hecht and MacArthur. The result is less satiric than *Once in a Lifetime,* despite a baby star who is a has-been at eight months and a vain cowboy star (Dick Foran) also suffering from audience rejection. Ralph Bellamy is a studio executive, doubtless recognised by some – painstakingly tolerant of his writers, servile and sycophantic to those above him, hostile to those below, dedicated, moronic, self-conscious, referring to 'we intellectuals' and occupied in trying to edit out chunks from a film, 'Young England'.

In **Angels with Dirty Faces** (1938),

Humphrey Bogart, all gritted teeth and nervous glances, is a superb villain in *Angels with Dirty Faces,* and James Cagney, as a good guy gone to the bad, is even better. The New York critics named him the year's Best Actor, presumably because he is so alive, so true, and so thrilling to watch.

Cagney and O'Brien are East Side buddies as kids: grown up, the former gets in with Bogart, a crooked lawyer who is in cahoots with George Bancroft, in turn in league with every corrupt V.I.P. in town. Meanwhile O'Brien has become a priest, with a trilby that he sports over one eye or, on important occasions, carries. He is tolerant of Cagney, as is Ann Sheridan, their mutual old flame, but then she too has been through the mill. Also on hand are the Dead End kids from *Dead End* (q.v.), and dull delinquents they are, but Cagney's handling of them is enterprising. He agrees to go to the Chair as a craven coward so as to dampen their hero worship, and if the morality is dubious it may be said that Curtiz tears through the tale with little pause for reflection.

There are also assumptions about law and order in **The Oklahoma Kid** (1939), with Cagney as a bad man who is acceptable as a hero because he's on our side, for which reason he may also take the law into his own hands. This is the first of the two Westerns he made during his career, and neither he nor Bogart, in black as the villain, is at home on the range. Lloyd Bacon directed, and Rosemary Lane, in the expected gingham, is a rather more

spunky heroine than usual. **The Fighting 69th** (1940), directed by Keighley, was at least smartly timed, and the American public responded as to no other war drama in recent years. It is based on fact – on a New York regiment also known as 'the fighting Irish' – and the plot involves two of its most famous sons, the poet Joyce Kilmer (Jeffrey Lynn) and Father Duffy (O'Brien), whose statue stands near Times Square – and which appears at the end of this film, with O'Brien and Cagney superimposed upon it. The latter plays his customary braggart, hot-headed and undisciplined: 'I don't go for that Holy Joe stuff,' he tells Father Duffy, who of course becomes his best friend. Dying, he tells him, 'Father, I just been talking to your boss.'

He plays a boxer in **City for Conquest** (1940), risking his sight in the ring so that his kid brother (Arthur Kennedy) can play his concerto at Carnegie Hall – *the* concerto, one that 'captures the hum of a great city'. The kid waxes emotional over the sacrifice, but there is some atoning tension in the scenes between Cagney and Sheridan, as the dancer he loves, and Sheridan and Anthony Quinn, as the rotter she takes up with. Elia Kazan is an East Side boy who becomes a mobster, muttering 'I never figgered on this' as he lies shot; and the studio's virtues are in evidence, as well as its occasional vice of sermonising. As directed by Anatole Litvak, it was considered one of the best pictures made about New York – a feat it manages solely by means of back projection, plus no doubt the borrowings from *Dead End* (q.v.) and *Golden Boy* (q.v.).

Before looking at Cagney's partnerships with the other tough-guy stars, and some of their films, we might pause at **The Strawberry Blonde** (1941), a remake of a Gary Cooper vehicle, *One Sunday Afternoon,* made by Paramount in 1933. The new film was occasioned when the Broadway success of 'Life with Father' again indicated interest in the days when the century was young. The gentle story gets lost among the bustles, sleeve-garters and barbershop quartets, but that is mainly because Raoul Walsh handles it as though it were farce. When a dentist (Cagney) loses the belle he loves (Rita Hayworth) to his buddy (Jack Carson), he marries on the rebound but continues to nurture his passion through years of marriage: but with Olivia de Havilland at her most appealing as the wife this seems nonsense, and the point is further weakened because the Hays Office would not allow Cagney to be unfaithful, even in thought.

The British version of **Each Dawn I Die** (1939) has a foreword explaining that the conditions depicted therein are not those of British prisons – but those conditions, apart from the usual humane governor (George Bancroft) seem not unlike those of a holiday camp. Nor does the title seem appropriate, for far from each day being a living death there is a thrill a minute as directed by Keighley. And, of course, the screenplay cheats, since the convicted hero is innocent: 'Framed! – because they knew I was going to show them up for the grasping rats they are!' – and he is framed, incidentally, with a whisky bottle and a crashed car, a device of earlier gangster films and still being used as late as *The Thomas Crown Affair* (q.v.). George Raft is the fellow con sworn to bring Cagney's enemies to book because he is the first man not to want moolah for a favour rendered.

Cagney is not in **Invisible Stripes** (1940), but Raft is, playing – as so often – an ex-con up against it. Forced unwillingly back into crime, he robs banks to buy a garage for his kid brother (William Holden), to prevent him joining the numbers racket. In time he and Bogart are mowed down in the garage, and there is an epilogue in which the kid renames the garage in commemoration. 'Who's the brother?' asks a passing cop. 'A sort of silent partner?' 'You could say that,' replies Holden. Warners must have hoped that audiences had forgotten that the garage was financed by hold-ups in the mid-West: thus crime does pay if you have a considerate elder brother. Bacon directed.

Such topsy-turvy moralising was sanctioned by the Hays Office, whose requirements had compromised the gangster film proper: however, the success of *Angels with Dirty Faces* dictated another attempt – and, of course, the era of Chicago warfare was now history. At the time **The Roaring Twenties** (1939) attracted little attention, but if actually not the best of the cycle, it does pack the most in, with its marvellous montages of booze,

bottles, bootlegging and bombings, of old cars, gangs, revelry and shoot-outs (many pinched from earlier films). It starts in the trenches, with Cagney, Bogart and Jeffrey Lynn, and follows their fortunes till Black Tuesday and after: Bogart is all bad, Lynn is all good, and Cagney would be good if bootlegging weren't so congenial a way to earn a living. Priscilla Lane as a would-be singer does some songs of the period, which is otherwise poorly evoked; but the dialogue is superb. It was written by Jerry Wald, Richard Macaulay and Robert Rossen, whose intermittently romantic view is shared by the director, Raoul Walsh. The epilogue this time has Cagney dying on the snowswept steps of a church, cradled in the arms of a raddled cabaret singer (Gladys George), who answers the inevitable passing cop: 'He used to be a big shot.'

Raft and Bogart are long-distance truck drivers in **They Drive by Night** (1940), based according to the credits on 'Long Haul' by A. I. Bezzerides but borrowing much from *Bordertown* (q.v.), with Ida Lupino as the floozie wife who murders her husband (Alan Hale) in a vain bid to win the hero. As directed by Walsh, this is formula film-making at its best, its quality partly due to the playing, notably Ann Sheridan as an itinerant hash-house waitress, and partly to the outstandingly slangy screenplay by Wald and Macaulay – which gives her the best lines. 'Classy chassis,' says one trucker, and another ventures that he would be prepared to pay in instalments. 'You couldn't even afford the headlights,' she tells him.

It is not an agreeable experience to watch Bogart support Raft, a much inferior actor. Since he had returned to films in 1936 in *The Petrified Forest* (q.v.) – he had made his reputation in the Broadway original – Humphrey Bogart had been one of the most critically admired of the Warner players. He finally became a star in **High Sierra** (1941): the crook as tragic hero, never more *purely* done than in this adaptation of a novel by W. R. Burnett, scripted by him and John Huston and directed by Walsh. The role was turned down by Paul Muni because he was angry over the abandonment of his Beethoven project, by Raft because he did not want to die at the end, by Cagney because he resented being asked third, and

Humphrey Bogart and Mary Astor in John Huston's exemplary screen version of *The Maltese Falcon*, the third and best of Warner's attempts to film Dashiell Hammett's novel. It was one of several films of that time which Bogart made by default, the roles having been turned down by other actors: but reading Hammett's description of Sam Spade, it is difficult to believe that the role was intended for anyone else, for Bogart had established a screen character equally rueful, unsurprised and cynical.

by Robinson because he didn't care to do the location work. None of them could have been as good as Bogart, part-Galahad, part-Capone, preparing from his mountain cabin what will be his last caper: a good man gone bad going to his end. There is an edge, a force, a danger to him that Raft always lacked.

It is also not an agreeable experience to see Bogart in a film as poor as **The Wagons Roll at Night** (1941). The wagons roll quickly under Ray Enright's direction but otherwise it is tired, perhaps because it had first seen service as *Kid Galahad,* swopping the boxing arenas for a circus tent, with Bogart as the boss. **Manpower** (1941), a vehicle for Edward G. Robinson, is a ragbag of bits from two of his early films, *Tiger Shark* and *Two Seconds,* now set among a crew of high-voltage cable repairmen. He is again the unlikely candidate for marriage, proposing to a penniless girl (Marlene Dietrich), and Raft is the buddy who falls in love with her: once more he is the decent man who gets drunk and goes mad at the end. However, the credits note an 'original screenplay', by Wald and Macaulay, of the same zesty level as those they did for

The Roaring Twenties, They Drive by Night and *Torrid Zone,* in which Cagney and Sheridan cross wits with each other. Wald produced and Macaulay wrote *Across the Pacific* (q.v.), also notable for the punchy dialogue, but as their credits before and after their collaboration are of little interest we must assume this a specially felicitous union, especially when, as here, they had Walsh to hand over their material in good shape to the cutting room.

That particular film reminds us that Warners' tough guys would soon be fighting Nazis and Nippons; but as this series of crime melodramas died it produced its one undisputed classic, **The Maltese Falcon** (1941), Huston's version of Dashiell Hammett's novel. John Huston (b. 1906), the son of Walter Huston, was first assigned to screenwriting by William Wyler when directing his father, but did not make his mark till he joined Warners and worked on *Jezebel* (q.v.). He wrote the screenplay for this third version of the Hammett book, staying faithful to it, and was assigned to direct it on a modest budget. He says that nervousness caused him to sketch a plan for every shot, and as we know that most American film-makers prepare a project by screening anything made earlier that may be relevant to it we may suppose his sketches were made after viewing Paramount's 1935 version of another Hammett private eye novel, *The Glass Key,* directed by Frank Tuttle. After noting that both films were tailored for the same star, George Raft (who refused this one) and that the 1942 version of *The Glass Key* (q.v.) is different in feel and appearance – if better – than the earlier one, it is apparent that both Huston and Tuttle had the sense to allow Hammett's style to dictate theirs, so that spareness of setting and camera movement counterbalances the intricacy of plot and the deviousness of everyone involved in it. Bogart leads a magnificent cast: Mary Astor as Miss Wunderly, consciously lady-in-distress, girlishly anxious but for a suggestion of greed around the lips; Peter Lorre as Joel Cairo, frizzy-haired and smelling of gardenia, as querulous as he is treacherous; Elisha Cook Jr as the 'bodyguard', overcoated to the floor; Jerome Cowan as the murdered partner, somewhat shifty; Gladys George as the falsely-grieving widow; Barton MacLane and Ward Bond as the cops; Lee Patrick as the loving secretary; and Sydney Greenstreet, above all, as Mr Gutman, vast, jovial and deadly, though minus the black ringlets with which Hammett endowed him.

Warners had another tough star in John Garfield (1913–52), acquired from Broadway. A gutter-brat vitality suggested an heir to Cagney, but while he often played the same big-headed punk he was less a man of action than a chip-on-the-shoulder guy caught in the crosswinds. He made his film debut in *Four Daughters,* based on a novel by Fannie Hurst, which was so successful that it spawned a number of sequels; **Daughters Courageous** (1939), also directed by Michael Curtiz, utilised much of the same cast for a not dissimilar story, based on a Broadway play. Garfield is a young bum, as penniless as he is uncouth, but he is acceptable as a suitor in this democratic bourgeois family till the daughter concerned (Priscilla Lane) realises that he is a younger edition of her returned prodigal father (Claude Rains). That respectability triumphs is the sole concession to reality.

The advent of Garfield gave Warners another chance to recycle old material, but both **They Made Me a Criminal** (1939), directed by Busby Berkeley (promoted from his role of choreographer), and **Castle on the Hudson** (1940), directed by Anatole Litvak, are inferior, sanitised versions of their progenitors, *The Life of Jimmy Dolan* and *20,000 Years in Sing Sing* respectively. However, in the former Garfield is more convincing than was Douglas Fairbanks Jr as an unprincipled prizefighter, and the opening sequences show his involvement with a fast-living crowd with the old panache; but once he has been framed for murder and is on the lam the film becomes conventional. He is also on the run for most of **Dust Be My Destiny** (1939), but the director, Lewis Seiler, is unable to disguise the fact that Warners' later protest movies have become flaccid. No couple ever behaved as foolishly as Garfield and Miss Lane do here – but then even Warners seldom stacked the chips so high. When retribution comes she pleads: 'If you convict him I'll have to believe the way he does – that there's no hope for people like us.' Two scenes prove the old realism not quite dead: tramping the highways has so frayed their nerves that they quarrel, agree to part, then cannot go through with it; and, marrying for the money before a movie audience, they are hustled and ignored the instant the ceremony is over, and he is ordered to get out of them (striped) pants pretty damn quick.

Garfield lacked Cagney's charm but his wry, alert expression suggested that he would be well cast as the aspiring, ordinary guy and in **Saturday's Children** (1940) he dreams of becoming an inventor or of voyaging to the Orient. The piece has other points in common with *Bad Girl* – Maxwell Anderson's original play had won the Pulitzer Prize in 1927, and First National had filmed it two years later – but in the intervening period poverty in urban areas was no longer so desperate (if it ever was) that a man would maim himself for the compensation money. Warners deserve credit for acknowledging that there were people who led humdrum lives; the only other studio to do so was R.K.O., but their 'plain folk' films were comedies in the Capra manner. Both studios showed that they could be serious on such subjects, but *Saturday's Children* does not indicate that either Warners or the director, Vincent Sherman, were very interested.

Before leaving the films designed mainly for the men in the audience we should look at two of the studio's occasional horror movies – in the case of **The Walking Dead** (1936) for its enterprising plot. A syndicate of businessmen pin the murder of a judge on a man (Boris Karloff) he once convicted, first ensuring that he has no alibi; he is charged and found guilty, but as he is electrocuted defence witnesses come forward and a doctor (Edmund Gwenn) brings him back from the dead to seek out the guilty. The tale is superbly packaged by Michael Curtiz, who makes its sixty minutes pass as ten. He was not normally a B-picture director, but was given this assignment because of his success with *Doctor X*. A sequel to that finally appeared, **The Return of Dr X** (1939), again a combination of reporters, sinister doctors, unexplained deaths and urgent operations, this time directed by Vincent Sherman. Humphrey Bogart despised his role as the bloodsucking doctor, but with scarred white face and pincenez, and a white streak in his hair, he is an alarming figure.

The outsider in Warners' menagerie of stars is Errol Flynn (1909–59), and it is tempting to think that his films were designed for the small boy in all of us. He was often felicitously teamed with Olivia de Havilland (b. 1916), as delicate and beautiful as he was dashing and handsome. When he played Robin Hood to her Maid Marian he said 'I do love you, you know,' and we did not need to be told years later that he meant it. He was born in Australia of Irish parentage and after some years as a small-part actor arrived at Warners just as the studio despaired of getting a British lead for their version of Rafael Sabatini's pirate tale, **Captain Blood** (1935). His looks were still cloddish, his dash less than he would muster thereafter, his Australian accent intermittently apparent and harassed by 'Heaveho m' hearties' dialogue. As the heroine, Olivia de Havilland is not as pretty as she would later become, and as the villain Basil Rathbone is only a shadow of what he could be: indeed, it is a stale piece except for the battles. It is impossible to

say how many set-ups were used, and how much stock footage (e.g. from the Silent *Sea Hawk*) was incorporated, or how much is owed to the editing: but the screen is alive with action at every corner and, like all of Curtiz's action films, stirring. The Curtiz-Flynn romances as a whole are the most enduring of screen spectaculars: they have wit and brawn and glitter; they deploy their crowds with a vigour and a prodigality we are unlikely to see again; they are devoted to action and adventure and have no desire to be other than a showcase for Flynn's gallantry.

He lost his gaucheness without gaining much in thespian ability, but most of the time that didn't matter: in **The Charge of the Light Brigade** (1936) he is a dedicated soldier, far-sighted, resourceful and steely-minded. These are the things that matter in a film which positively dotes on the military and the panoply of Empire (even if, as C. A. Lejeune noted, nine times out of ten the Union Jack is upside down). It was harshly thought of at the time for distorting history, but the foreword explains it is fiction. Was it the Charge that prompted its making? – or had Warners looked at the profits of *Lives of a Bengal Lancer* and commissioned an Indian Army epic of their own? Or did they rummage through Imperial history for a subject, find two, and decide to combine them? The plot owes much to G. A. Henty, and has the ring of Victorian adventure, building splendidly from India to that insane assault on the Russian cannon. Tennyson's poem is naively superimposed on the images, and the effect is oddly moving – not just because the battle is magnificently re-staged but because the old ringing phrases retain their power. Miss de Havilland is again the heroine, unaccountably preferring Flynn's brother (Patric Knowles) to him.

The Adventures of Robin Hood (1938) is even better: indeed, it is the Curtiz-Flynn masterpiece, though to be accurate the direction was shared with William Keighley. The cinematography was also shared: Sol Polito, who worked so memorably on these films, was joined by Tony Gaudio, and they used Technicolor – with spectacular result. It is Hollywood English; some of the chases are reminiscent of B-Westerns; and even

Seen today on television, *The Adventures of Robin Hood* is merely good entertainment, but in the cinemas for which it was designed it is magnificent, frequently bringing forth cheers and applause. Here are Olivia de Havilland as Maid Marian and and Errol Flynn as Robin.

this subject might take a little more sophistication; but I still think it one of the most splendid entertainments ever devised. If Flynn's bravura is a little gauche, he has nonchalance, nobility and a concern for the Saxons that we take for real. Miss de Havilland's Maid Marian melts before him, and to these best among heroes and heroines one must add the best, or worst, of villains: Basil Rathbone as the terse, humourless Sir Guy; Claude Rains as the smiling, devious Prince John; the boastful, cowardly Sheriff of Melville Cooper; and the merriest of men: Eugene Pallette as Friar Tuck, Alan Hale as Little John, Herbert Mundin as Much, the miller's son, Patric Knowles as Will Scarlet. Carl J. Weyl won an Oscar for the decor, and an award might as well have gone to whoever devised the magical duel at the end.

The climax of **The Sea Hawk** (1940) is equally magnificent, with Henry Daniell, most underrated of villains, replacing Rathbone; and if elsewhere Brenda Marshall is no substitute for de Havilland she *looks* Spanish, which is the point. Technicolor is absent, but this is again a perfect schoolboy romance, with the Queen Elizabeth of such tales – this is another adaptation of Sabatini – animated with vivacity by Flora Robson. When he proposes to rob the Spanish treasure troves she says, 'You go with the express disapproval of the Queen of England but take with you the grateful affection of Elizabeth,' but matters move differently at the end, when she speaks of 'the ruthless ambition of one man,' adding that England will fight tyrants now 'and for generations to come' – which we may regard as Hollywood's equivalent of Bundles to Britain, reassuring and touching, if of little use to the War Effort.

Flynn is badly cast in two Westerns, **Dodge City** (1939) and **Virginia City** (1940). Both have splendid shots of movement across the wide open spaces, the former, photographed in Technicolor by Sol Polito, being one of the first films to demonstrate how liberating that process was to imaginative cameramen. It also has perhaps the most spectacular barroom brawl on record, plus Miss de Havilland. *Virginia City* is a story of espionage during the American Civil War, with uneasy performances by Miriam Hopkins as a dance hall queen and

441

Humphrey Bogart as a half-caste bandit. Like Flynn, both are miscast, and we might also note the backstage loathing between Flynn and Curtiz, and that of both towards Miss Hopkins – while Bogart despised Flynn, a fact that had much to do with his opinion of Flynn's prowess in such parts. Like his rival *jeune premiers,* Tyrone Power and Robert Taylor, Flynn was not a natural man of the West. As a swashbuckler he has dash and fervour, but his other heroics look false, particularly in the egalitarian world of the Western. 'I quite understand your point of view, men,' he says in **Santa Fe Trail** (1940), but he patently doesn't; he was never one of the 'lads', as he called them, which was why Warners realised that he could not be an everyman hero as Gable or Cooper could. Warners made him quizzical, mocking, polite but amused in lovemaking, and one remains conscious of the real Flynn, wanting to be ruthless, arrogant, drunken. *Santa Fe Trail* is also a Civil War Western, and in both that and **They Died with Their Boots On** (1941) he starts out as a West Point cadet. Indeed, in the latter he is General Custer, given to extravagant uniforms, self-glorification and, between the War and Little Big Horn, liberal drinking. In the earlier film Ronald Reagan plays Custer, and the abolitionist John Brown (Raymond Massey) is a subsidiary character. Flynn and his colleagues are supposed to be sympathetic towards his cause, but it is Miss de Havilland who puts it into words: 'Why can't they free the slaves before it's too late?' These were her last two films with Flynn, and this one was his last with Curtiz. They quarrelled, and Raoul Walsh directed *They Died with Their Boots On* – which is equally vigorous, suggesting that those really responsible for the Warner action films were the men in the cutting room.

Curtiz had also directed Flynn in two comedies, **The Perfect Specimen** (1937) and **Four's a Crowd** (1938). This studio was not strong in comedy, but both begin on that Hollywood premise of the period, the eccentricity of the very wealthy – respectively, an old lady (May Robson) bringing up her son (Flynn) to be the perfect specimen, and a bad-tempered tycoon (Walter Connolly) who becomes involved in the schemes of a P.R. man (Flynn). The former is a variation of *It Happened One Night,* with Joan Blondell as a reporter; Rosalind Russell is the obligatory reporter in the other film, with de Havilland and Knowles making up the 'crowd'. Connolly has the best line, 'Posterity. What's posterity ever done for me? Why should I do anything for posterity?'

In **Green Light** (1937) Flynn is an agnostic young surgeon who, after taking the blame for the death of a saintly old lady, goes to the wilds to research a cure for spotted fever and when the real culprit flies out to save his life finds God. None of the Warner virtues is evident, as directed by Frank Borzage, and the film's sole point of interest is its inferiority to *White Banners,* taken from what is presumably an equally mawkish novel by the same writer.

Flynn appears only intermittently in **The Prince and the Pauper** (1937), Mark Twain's twee story of a guttersnipe who invades a Tudor palace and changes places with Prince Edward – roles played by the young Mauch twins. The film was a vehicle for them, but Warners also clearly wanted to show the world a British coronation ceremony when that was the topic of the day: it is inadequate, however, and William Keighley's direction lacks all sense of fantasy. Edmund Goulding directed **The Dawn Patrol** (1938), and while his sensitivity confined him otherwise to women's pictures, the scenes here of the mess indicate that quality – and with Flynn, Rathbone and David Niven all superior to the players in the original version, this is much the better film. However, critical prejudice against remakes and public indifference meant that it failed at the time. Warners remembered that when Britain's entry into the War started another spate of war dramas, and did not put Flynn – who usually played Britishers – into any of them. However, in acknowledgement of the War, Flynn cast away his doublet and hose after *The Sea Hawk,* and was called upon to be more responsible thereafter.

The European War persuaded Warners to back a pet project of Jesse L. Lasky, an independent producer since leaving Paramount, and **Sergeant York** (1941), a biography of the World War I hero, was very popular. As the film has it, he (Gary Cooper) is a drunken layabout till he has a vision and finds God: refused deferment as a conscientious objector, he one day has another vision which enables him to go ahead and kill lots of Germans; a coda at the end suggests that he wanted more than glory. Ploddingly directed by Howard Hawks, this mixture of hayseed drama ('Figger on goin' to thet there shindig nex' Sat'dy ev'nin', Miss Williams?'), heavenly choirs and shoot-outs is now only bearable for one of Cooper's best performances.

On Warners' lighter side was Joe E. Brown, a likeable comic but never a major one. His chief asset was his face – a huge mouth and a bemused expression. Most film comic roles, from Max Linder onwards, were about inefficient people who succeed only by luck, but Brown was often cast as a man of some eminence, proclaimed by dandyish clothes – loud checks and stripes, Argyle socks, glaring bow ties. Indecision and naivety, however, did not correlate with his position, and he could be put upon and manipulated. He had a gift for knockabout, and his films are generally persuasive. Two of his best are **Alibi Ike** (1935), directed by Ray Enright, from Ring Lardner's tale about a star baseball player who cannot help lying, prevaricating or just making excuses; and **Bright Lights** (1935), directed by Busby Berkeley, in which he is a burlesque star who neglects his wife (Ann Dvorak) to court an heiress.

Jolson returned, with wanton single-mindedness, to make two pictures as himself, in both of them a Broadway headliner trying for a comeback. In **Go Into your Dance** (1935) he has to conquer a reputation for unreliability and excessive ego, and in **The Singing Kid** (1936) he has lost his voice. The first, directed by Archie Mayo, is the better, somewhat resembling *Wonder Bar,* with an excellent cast including Helen Morgan and Ruby Keeler (then Jolson's wife); the second, directed by William Keighley, is notable for a large and unusual production number which begins on stage and finishes amid the traffic. Jolson loathed doing it, complaining that the other artists had too much footage; and refused to make the third film for which he was contracted. As ever, he is referred to as 'the world's greatest entertainer'. 'From what I hear,' says Miss Keeler, 'in more

ways than one.' One cannot imagine Fred Astaire passing either of those lines; Chevalier might have sanctioned both, but never in conjunction. Jolson seems to have believed that arrogance and vanity were virtues, and in his case perhaps they were.

The other Warner musicals are not up to their predecessors. The fortune hunters of **Gold Diggers of 1935** (1935) are not girls, but Adolphe Menjou, Glenda Farrell and Grant Mitchell, out to fleece Alice Brady, Hugh Herbert and other rich suckers. The setting is a hotel at a luxury resort, but there are no jokes about honeymooners: sex is no longer a laughing matter. The film does, however, have Busby Berkeley's best work (he also directed): the opening number, bright and cynical, tossed around by the hotel staff; an Astaire-Rogers-type duet for Dick Powell and Gloria Stuart; and two huge productions at the end, one with crinolines, candelabra and a hundred gliding grand pianos, and the other the 'Lullaby of Broadway'. Berkeley is a vulgarian, but these vignettes of Broadway are hypnotic – a clock going round, the milkman on his way, the 'babies' preparing for bed, and that gigantic night club with its serried rows of pounding feet.

The success of the Astaire-Rogers films however was proving to the studio that the effort and lavish expenditure needed for such numbers was unjustified, and the numbers in **In Caliente** (1935) and **Gold Diggers of 1937** (1936) are very simple. The former has 'The Lady in Red' and 'Muchacha' ('Muchacha, I've gotcha, and I'm hotcha for you'), and the latter some casual numbers for Powell and Joan Blondell, plus a finale, 'All's Fair in Love and War', which marks a nadir – though perhaps Berkeley was not responsible for the notion that bombs and guns are amusing. Lloyd Bacon directed both films on the principle that at 90 m.p.h. such nonsense is mildly diverting, and in both Miss Farrell is a gold digger. *In Caliente* is again set in a luxury hotel, and has a farcical plot about a hard-boiled New York editor obsessed with a dancer (Dolores del Rio). *Gold Diggers* starts out with stranded showgirls and vintage lines ('When they start shelling out jobs in a men's washroom a new day is dawning' says one blonde), but turns out to be about putting

Fredric March and Olivia de Havilland in *Anthony Adverse* (1936), which is what happened to Warners after it abandoned stories of the everyday for the bestseller. That said, it is a treat, galloping along under Mervyn LeRoy's direction, and cramming in as much as possible of Hervey Allen's widely discussed novel of a foundling who has a thousand and one adventures before coming into his rightful inheritance.

on a show. **Varsity Show** (1937), directed by Keighley, is some travail about collegiates putting on a Broadway show with the help of alumnus Dick Powell – whose co-stars are, according to the billing, 'Fred Waring and his Pennsylvanians'. Berkeley's finale is ingenious, and the film contains a stunning black speciality act, Buck and Bubbles.

Hollywood Hotel (1937) is also rubbishy, but it is cheerful, often funny and gleamingly professional as it charts the progress of Mr Powell from sax player with Benny Goodman to his apotheosis as singer on Louella Parsons' radio hour. Berkeley directed the film and arranged the numbers, functioning in the latter capacity only on **Gold Diggers in Paris** (1938), which Enright directed. The stars are Rudy Vallee and Rosemary Lane, not backed by the usual splendid supporting cast; it is but a pale, pale shadow.

Warners lost interest in musicals and released only one, *Naughty but Nice* (1939), in the period 1939–42. They bought **On Your Toes** (1939), and tossed out the superb Rodgers and Hart score

with the exception of 'Slaughter on Tenth Avenue' and its hit tune, 'There's a Small Hotel', the latter heard only in the background. The result, as directed by Enright, is an odd comedy about a hoofer (Eddie Albert) caught up with the exponents of Russian ballet. Another curiosity with music is **Blues in the Night** (1941), clearly meant to be significant since Anatole Litvak's direction and Robert Rossen's screenplay attempt both realism – only Priscilla Lane has conventional movie looks – and dimension. Excited by negro jazz, some white boys (Richard Whorf, Billy Halop, Elia Kazan) form a combo, making an odd buck or so, and while they are 'giving' with a number called 'Hang on to Your Lids, Kids' we cannot guess that they're about to meet up with wild and woolly melodrama in a New Jersey roadhouse, with the hero (Whorf) finally stumbling around Times Square, unshaven and begging for a drink. That was not so much a cliché then: in 1946 Richard Winnington referred to this as 'the only swing [sic] film I've ever liked'. The only memorable ingredient is Harold Arlen's title tune, sung by a negro chorus; the hero later turns it into a piano concerto.

Among the Warner Bros. ladies Kay Francis endured some heart-pulsing melodramas, after unashamedly playing Lenin's secretary in **British Agent** (1934), directed by Curtiz, a weird concoction fashioned from the memoirs of H. Bruce Lockhart, 'our man' during the Bolshevik Revolution, played here by Leslie Howard. **Living on Velvet** (1935) concerns a flyer (George Brent) who becomes a charming eccentric after killing his family in a crash; one enchanted evening he spots Miss Francis during a party and whisks her away from Warren William to live on Long Island, where he converts their back yard into an airstrip – which for her is the last straw. Frank Borzage directed under his Warner contract, and it finds him again at low ebb. **Stolen Holiday** (1935), directed by Curtiz, is based on the Stavisky affair, and if it is possibly surprising to find that as the basis for a story of love and self-sacrifice it *is* surprising to find the Eiffel Tower lurking just behind Le Bourget. Miss Francis as usual wears some four dozen creations by Orry-Kelly, with the excuse this time that she is head of a fashion house, financed by the man (Claude Rains) whose mistress she probably is. When his empire crumbles she signs away her every penny to pay the people he swindled, and is comforted by a nice British diplomat (Ian Hunter).

Hunter and Errol Flynn are her leading men in **Another Dawn** (1937), and William Dieterle directed this modern division of the Bengal Lancers movie in which Flynn, as flirtatious as he is daring, makes a pass at the Colonel's lady. 'But I wish I was Judy O'Grady,' she says as she kisses him. Caught in a sandstorm, she observes, 'We can't go on meeting like this,' and later she cries to her husband, 'There must be some solution'. 'Yes, there is. To play the game according to the rules.' She decides to leave them both: 'You will go on, building a nation . . .'

Miss Francis is a pitiful figure in Hollywood history, her prolonged decline engineered by Warners while the fan magazines speculated on how long she could cling on. She hardly deserved to be a major star, being less an actress than a clothes-horse, smiling and self-conscious; in the three consecutive films she made with George Brent it is depressing to watch him trying to be devil-may-care and her attempting to match him flippancy for flippancy. Her comic approach consists of opening her eyes wide and speaking quickly: in **First Lady** (1937) she is the soft centre. She is also a far cry from dowdy, beloved Eleanor – a not irrelevant point, since the film's source, a play by George S. Kaufman and Katherine Dayton, had been occasioned by the acute interest in Washington caused by the arrival of the Roosevelts. Central to the plot is the enmity between Francis and Veree Teasdale, whose husband (Walter Connolly) is also running for the presidency – and this ill-matched couple have one of the longest and funniest sequences of the decade, as he attempts to listen to his favourite soap opera during one of her tirades. The director is Stanley Logan, who made only a handful of films, and the screenwriter Rowland Leigh, but the tone is recognisably that of Kaufman.

It was one of two stage comedies – from a rich Broadway season – that Warners filmed at this time. Jacques Deval's

Tovarich (1937) had been anglicised by Robert E. Sherwood, and Casey Robinson wrote it for the screen: it still concerns a White Russian couple (Claudette Colbert, Charles Boyer) in Paris, subsisting by light-fingering at the *charcuterie* till forced into domestic service, which they tackle happily if not skilfully. Their employers, a pompous banker and his scatterbrained wife, are deliciously rendered by Melville Cooper and Isabel Jeans; Miss Colbert is at her considerable best and Boyer, if not the world's most natural light comedian, has grace and wit. Directing, Anatole Litvak demonstrates how quickly a European film-maker could subdue his own style to that of the Hollywood factory.

Warners' great female star was, of course, Bette Davis (b. 1908), a New England girl who was managing a modest career on stage till signed for pictures; she played conventional leading ladies – unconventionally when possible – up to *Of Human Bondage*. She has an equally colourful part in **Bordertown** (1935), directed by Archie Mayo – that of the young wife of a middle-aged café proprietor (Eugene Pallette), relieving her boredom with a Mexican lawyer (Paul Muni). She loathed most of the films she was called upon to do – but is, for instance, stylish in **Front Page Woman** (1935), and much more convincing than in *Of Human Bondage*, despite the fox furs and flower-pot hats easily suggesting the drive of an ace reporter. As the rival with whom she is in love George Brent is lively for once, Curtiz directs as if matching the rhythm of the typewriters in the newsroom and that, with some goodish lines, helps him to disguise the film's essential triviality.

It is Davis who is **Dangerous** (1935), discovered as a haggard tramp on the sidewalk. 'Say, weren't you Joyce Heath?' asks someone. 'What a vitally tempestuous creature she was!' says someone else, and since she *is* Joyce Heath, and since a young architect (Franchot Tone) remembers her – 'Only two people could have played that part, Jeanne Eagels and Joyce Heath' – he sets out to rehabilitate her. The yarn has surprises, and Alfred E. Green's direction an attention to pertinent detail, but contemporary interest was centred on Miss Davis, who won an

Oscar for her performance: she puts an intensity and an equivocation into the role that it hardly deserves, missing nothing of the woman's destructiveness or her callousness. Thus she revolutionised star acting in Hollywood. If the great comediennes were arrogant and indifferent to their audiences that was the basis of their style; and those who played bad ladies, such as Crawford and Shearer, were incapable of shadings: Davis was arrogant, but instead of demanding audience love or loathing she asked for understanding. Character actors of genius who were also stars – Werner Krauss, Charles Laughton – had tapped this vein, but most stars were encouraged to be relatively unambitious: the instinct and intelligence of a Cagney or Garbo enabled them to put flesh and blood on thin characters, but Davis went further, by continually – almost perversely – rejecting the standard ways of expressing emotions, and by deliberately giving those emotions greater and more varied play. She established a personality with strength, drive, a sense of reality and a brittle sense of humour – and over the next forty years she continued to utilise these qualities, with the added ability of being able to subdue them and substitute others less admirable, as Hepburn, for instance, would not or could not subdue her hauteur and 'radiance'.

In **The Petrified Forest** (1936) Davis transformed herself into an adolescent; the drive is there in the form of an ardour for literature, but the dreaminess is new. She can make credible a line like 'You know, that guy' – François Villon – 'writes wonderful stuff.' She has changed herself, whereas Leslie Howard, no less convincing despite equally sticky lines, gives his usual performance – part quizzical, part lost, filling out the unlikely role of a vagabond philosopher. The third memorable player is Humphrey Bogart, his theatrical entrance reminding us that the role was not new to him; but he understood the medium well enough to throw away the rapping comments of contempt and sarcasm. Also excellent are Genevieve Tobin and Paul Harvey, finding in adversity – they are held up in an Arizona gas station – a mutual marital loathing. Indeed, the performances are the saving of Robert E. Sherwood's drama, directed by Mayo as filmed theatre.

Satan Met a Lady (1936) is *The Maltese Falcon* revamped, and nothing in it prefigures the marvellous remake of four years later; the falcon itself has become a hunting horn, and Mr Guttman has metamorphosed into Alison Skipworth. Warren William is as much Casanova as private eye, for matters are entirely frivolous, the heavy pantomiming suggesting that Dieterle did each scene in one quick take. Davis, soignée and crisp, takes her reversals with a smile.

Like Cagney, she quarrelled about scripts, and after her walk-out returned to make **Marked Woman** (1937), which is certainly better than most of her films up till then. Like many another Warner melodrama this was concocted from fact, the long-delayed arrest of Lucky Luciano, on sixty-one charges of compulsory prostitution: the girls under his control turned against him, and two of them penned their confessions for *Liberty Magazine* – the basis of the screenplay by Robert Rossen and Abem Finkel. However, the film was closely watched by the Hays Office, which insisted that the girls become dance hostesses, and for further safety made them share an apartment. The only time money changes hands it is due to a misunderstanding on the part of Davis's innocent sister (Jane Bryan) – the ever-present sibling of Warner movies. It is left to the cast to suggest the unspeakable, and to Lloyd Bacon to supply the pace, which he does; the best scenes are those between Davis and Bogart, particularly forceful as an attorney, a character based on Thomas E. Dewey.

A reformed gangster's moll whose past comes back to haunt her is the subject of Davis's next film, **That Certain Woman** (1937), written and directed by Edmund Goulding from *The Trespasser*, which he had made with Gloria Swanson in 1929: his evident fondness for the dated material cannot really excuse it. Well received in its time, **It's Love I'm After** (1937) seems thin today, with insufficient laughs in Casey Robinson's script and too heavy a touch in Mayo's direction; as the spatting theatrical lovers Bette Davis and Leslie Howard are never flamboyant enough. Davis's performance, however, is unlike any of her others before – puffing on a cigarette (a mannerism for the future), icily sarcastic but humourless. Howard is believable as a philanderer, but not as an overweening egotist. The film is anyway stolen from them by the relatively inexperienced Olivia de Havilland, as a dewy socialite with a crush on Howard, and then from her by Eric Blore as Howard's valet. It would have benefited – a rare fault at Warners – by tighter editing.

Jezebel (1938) is a magnolia-scented tale about a spoilt Southern girl (Davis) who schemes to get back the fiancé (Henry Fonda) she has lost. The standard plot is nevertheless enjoyable, since we can never anticipate Davis's reactions, always one of her virtues, if unquestionably helped on this occasion by the director, William Wyler. He takes perhaps too much care over this portrait of antebellum society, with its fads and duels and codes of honour and de darkies singin' on de old plantation, his majestic style now seeming too rich for an intrinsically meretricious tale. As Buck – Rhett to Davis's Scarlett – George Brent has all the animation of a penguin, but Fonda is fine as the obstinate, determined beau. Fay Bainter won a Best Supporting Actress for her performance as the aunt and Davis, consecrated by a second Oscar, settled into a decade of unrivalled admiration with critics, with the public, and within the industry.

The vehicles Warners fashioned for her, however, are essentially second-rate if beautifully carpentered and written above the average – qualities inherited from their sources, usually well-meaning lending library fiction. Litvak directed **The Sisters** (1938), a family chronicle that takes in a number of political rallies, the 'Frisco 'quake, a bordello sanctioned by the Hays Office and run by Laura Hope Crews, and the failing marriage of Errol Flynn and Davis, the latter as a determined woman hopelessly in love. 'There's a kind of quiet assurance about you which bewilders me,' says he, a remark which sums up both characters and both players. Edmund Goulding directed and Casey Robinson wrote both **Dark Victory** (1939) and **The Old Maid** (1939), the latter from a novel by Edith Wharton – one of the very few to be filmed, after a Pulitzer-prizewinning Broadway version. *Dark Victory* concerns a rich bitch who falls in love and goes blind, acquiring niceness and bravery with marriage and

knowledge of The End. This was a property which had been around Hollywood for years, and Davis fought to play it. The result 'turned out to be my favorite and the public's favorite part I have ever played'. In the other film, she is the Old Maid, an independent girl who brings up her own child in the orphanage she runs, pretending to the child and the world that she is the daughter of her flighty and malicious cousin (Miriam Hopkins). Goulding is particularly at home here, the camera gliding among the plush and crinolines, but the film would be nothing without Davis. She takes every scene from Hopkins, though that lady, as usual, does everything but chew the scenery.

Davis's approach to her work is apparent in **The Private Lives of Elizabeth and Essex** (1939), even if her claim (in her memoirs) to have studied 'the Holbein portrait of the Queen' does not invite confidence in her research. She shaved her head and plucked her eyebrows, and also against studio advice insisted on farthingales of the correct width. She was thirty, and Elizabeth was in her sixties; she is short not tall; and she has the wrong-shaped head. Nor does she have the

Bette Davis, left, in *Jezebel*, at the time audiences were discovering that they loved her wilful or downright wicked. She is a Southern belle who shocks the town and loses her fiancé, Henry Fonda, by wearing red to the season's most important function; also shocked is Fay Bainter, as her giddy but worried aunt.

Queen's long fingers, but she uses her hands to brilliant effect, fondling her fan or the gewgaws at her neck, at moments of emotion helplessly clawing the air. She is glimpsed first as a shadow and even thus conveys the blazing sun the Queen was to her court and the endless source of mystery to her people. The Technicolor sets and costumes (Anton Grot and Orry-Kelly respectively) are, if not accurate, resplendent, and that is the other reason the film is memorable. Apart from some mistaken malarkey in the Irish bogs Michael Curtiz keeps the series of conversation pieces moving briskly; and if Warners chose to simplify a relationship which has intrigued historians from that day to this they were only following in the steps of a formidable number of novelists. The source, in fact, is a blank verse play by Maxwell Anderson, which the Lunts had once done – and it would seem to have been a very bad one. Or perhaps the screen writers are to blame for the climax, in which the Queen secretly visits Essex (Errol Flynn) in the Tower (offering the throne, which he gallantly refuses because his 'ambitions might harm the people'), or for the dialogue, which descends from the authentic to such lines as 'As a queen, yes, but as a woman? – do I mean nothing to you?' Flynn's stock schoolboy hero is useless here. Davis had unwillingly accepted him as co-star and neither she nor Curtiz seems to have given him the slightest help.

However, in **All This and Heaven Too** (1940) she for once has a leading man to her measure, Charles Boyer. Their skill and magnetism lead us through a wayward plot about a nobleman (Boyer) who murders his unstable wife (Barbara O'Neill) because he is in love with the governess (Davis). Casey Robinson adapted the popular novel by Rachel Field, based in turn on an incident in the family which owned the chateau of Vaux-le-Vicomte. Anatole Litvak handles the period detail with ease but is defeated by the framing story – which concerns marriage with an American pastor (Jeffrey Lynn), but a future with Mr Lynn can be no one's idea of bliss, least of all Miss Davis's.

The ending is also the weakest ingredient of **The Letter** (1940), and as Nemesis waits in the moonlight, imposed by the Hays Office, it is the only weak aspect of the film. Warners again borrowed Wyler from Goldwyn, and he does disguise the fact that Maugham's play, from one of his own stories, is one of the old warhorses – originally performed by both Gladys Cooper and Katharine Cornell in 1927 and filmed two years later with Jeanne Eagels: it could never have been done as well as this version. It is one of Maugham's studies of infidelity in the Malay peninsula, and in Howard Koch's brisk screenplay might be called serious fun: towards the climax we anticipate a trenchant statement on the nature of love and death (why she killed her lover, why she loved him, why she deceived her husband, whether she should die), and that is because Davis continually suggests that this is more than melodrama. It is one of her great performances – a woman of both abiding respectability and sensuality, of calculation and sensibility. Wyler gets her to use long silences and mordant stares, with an occasional blink of the big eyes, and she is never likeable or pitiable. The equivocable relationship with her defending counsel (James Stephenson) is brilliantly done; and other equally good performances include Herbert Marshall as the husband (he was the lover in the 1929 version) and Bruce Lester as that particular type of earnest young Englishman found in the Colonies. Amidst the studio jungle – with the moon as his motif – Wyler offers a vivid and correct impression of British Malaya, stiff and snobbish; and when confronted with Chinatown and the Eurasian wife (Gale Sondergaard) he soft-pedals. That he should view this society with more bite than the not dissimilar one in *Jezebel* is proof of Maugham's superiority, if sometimes only slight, to the majority of writers adapted for the cinema.

The Great Lie (1941) is also a film with class, which is clear because it starts with the thunderous chords of the Tchaikovsky Piano Concerto in B Flat Minor. It caused such a run on records and sheet music that this piece was featured in several films thereafter – and it opened up American films to the use of classical music. Mary Astor is a concert pianist; she is also a bitch. 'I hate her' are Davis's first words on the subject, and the film gives us plenty of opportunities to share that feeling, as they squabble over George Brent and a baby. Davis is all urgency and intelligence; Astor, behind the vanity and gay laugh of a spoiled career women, suggests someone desperately unhappy with herself. The latter has only featured billing, but Davis allowed her as many close-ups as herself. Goulding's direction is exactly right for the screenplay by Lenore Coffee – above average for this writer – from a novel by Polan Banks; and did it occur to anyone that there never would have been a Great Lie if Mr Brent had demanded to see the birth certificate.

Pausing between such histrionics Davis did two comedies, **The Bride Came C.O.D.** (1941) and **The Man Who Came to Dinner** (1941), both directed by William Keighley. The former proved that though she and Cagney could play slapstick they needed material worthy of them. The latter is not great art, but is a reminder of the golden age of Broadway comedy, for the material has been but little adapted. Kaufman and Hart's play is the apotheosis of the comedy of insult, as personified by Monty Woolley (in his stage role), bon vivant and litterateur, rude and insufferable. The character is based on Alexander Woollcott; the vain and bad-tempered actress on Gertrude Lawrence, though a miscast Ann Sheridan makes her into a vamping Hollywood blonde; Banjo (Jimmy Durante) is Harpo Marx; and Beverly Garland (Reginald Gardiner) Noël Coward. Also subject to Woolley's whims and insults are his dedicated secretary (Davis), the apoplectic and increasingly unwilling host (Grant Mitchell), the latter's wife (Billie Burke), and, best of all, the frozen-faced nurse (Mary Wickes). Woolley, often dull in films, is here roaringly good.

'Til We Meet Again (1940) is about a heroine with an incurable disease. Also like *Dark Victory*, it was directed by Edmund Goulding, with George Brent in the male lead. The heroine is not Davis but Merle Oberon, whom Jack L. Warner had contracted in expectation of replacing Davis as the studio's chief dramatic lady – which is one of those industry misjudgments to take the breath away. Goulding gets from her at least an approximation of acting, and indeed this is a good entertainment for those who like to listen to consistently elevated dialogue, viz. 'You can find eternity in a moment' and 'Everything you say has a note of farewell in it'. At moments of desperation Merle is prone to rush out and plead with the sky, 'Not just yet'. She wears some sumptuous gowns and looks healthy, if pale. Pat O'Brien is a detective; as the Countess, Binnie Barnes isn't a patch on Aline Mac-Mahon in *One Way Passage*, of which this is a remake. Nor is anything else.

That Warner Bros. abandoned their sharp social documents for glossy romances has much to do with the account ledgers at M-G-M. In 1934 the Warners restricted themselves to carefully budgeted films, yet still managed to end in the red for the fourth successive year. M-G-M, after spending lavishly on what went on the screen, managed the highest profits of any of the Hollywood companies. Until the War M-G-M outstripped its rivals at the box-office, reaching an unprecedented $14½ million in 1937 – which was even better than the sum racked up in the Talkie boom year of 1929. To get more, M-G-M spent more: when the average cost of a programme picture was $100,000 Loews might designate a budget of one million dollars or more for a vehicle for Garbo or Gable. Thus, as the other studios prepared their spectacles, so M-G-M more than ever eschewed the sort of subject which excited controversy but no action at the box-office; in 1935, two M-G-M films of social concern did manage to slip through, but they were the last. Neither, significantly, looks or feels at all like an M-G-M production.

Robin Hood of Eldorado (1935) is based on a novel by Walter Noble Burns, who had earlier provided the basis for the studio's film *Billy the Kid*: that had not been a success, but this one had affinities with *Viva Villa!*, and that recommended it to the company. Its subject is the dispossession of the Mexican population when the Americans overran California, and it is offered with a real sense of grievance; it was William Wellman's first film for the company, and the fact that his name appears on the writing credits – when it was commonplace for directors of his calibre to work on their screenplays anyway – indicates more than the usual involvement. It is a true story – subsequently retold in a number of minor films

– of Joaquin Murieta (Warner Baxter), who becomes an outlaw after the Americans rape his wife and steal his smallholding. His plight is charted from a sunny fiesta to a final welter of blood, and with one exception – Bruce Cabot as his pursuer – the Americans are portrayed as crafty, scruffy and dirty. The violence, circumspectly handled, is more effective than in many films of the Seventies; there are some weaknesses, however, in the latter section, notably the performance by Ann Loring as the revolutionary leader. Mr Baxter merely looks old and troubled. He was cast in this role because of his popularity as the Cisco Kid, but that fact did not recommend this more serious film to audiences; nor did the title.

Fury (1936), on the other hand, commended itself by its cliff-hanging plot, about a nice young man (Spencer Tracy) arrested on circumstantial evidence and the victim of mob violence. This was Fritz Lang's first film for the studio, after a year on salary, working from a story by Norman Krasna; he wanted it to look like a newsreel, which it frequently does, but after the quiet construction of the trap around Tracy in the first half the latter section seems overpitched, with huge close-ups of the citizenry and Tracy behaving like a manic Emil Jannings. It was its Germanic quality as much as its indictment of mob rule that brought it contemporary renown; today it is easier to react to the statement by the district attorney (Walter Abel) that in the last forty-nine years there had been 6,010 outbreaks of violence, and that only 675 people had been brought to justice. According to Lang, Louis B. Mayer was initially puzzled by the film and its press reception, then began to loath its positiveness, furious at the inference that the U.S.A. was not composed of decent family men. Despite the réclame, the film was never reissued. Wellman paid for his aberration by being assigned to a routine love story, **Small Town Girl** (1936), and then went to work for Selznick; Lang, brought originally to M-G-M by Selznick, was punished by having his contract abrogated – and he also went to work for one of the independents, Walter Wanger (q.v.).

That Selznick was at M-G-M was partly to do with the fact that the Mayer-Thalberg relationship was disintegrating. It was considered that Thalberg's quest for quality, together with his knack of estimating box-office potential, were mainly responsible for the pre-eminence of M-G-M: accordingly, Mayer was anxious to appease him; but as time went by Thalberg hankered to be free of anyone who in the final resort had the yea or nay – and, for Mayer's part, Thalberg's failing health was a source of anxiety. Thalberg approached Nicholas Schenck with a view to forming his own company, the films to be released, like the M-G-M films, through the parent company, Loews. Schenck agreed, though insistent that Thalberg complete his contract first – but Thalberg died of pneumonia before that was achieved. It was against this background – Thalberg's health and his quarrels with Mayer – that Mayer approached Selznick to join Metro. Though unrestricted, he was, as he predicted, unhappy at Culver City, though the films he produced for the company were prestigious and generally held in esteem. His two versions of Dickens were notably successful.

His conscientious approach to **David Copperfield** (1935) is typical. From R.K.O. he brought George Cukor, who had directed *Little Women* for him, and from Britain he summoned Hugh Walpole to do the adaptation and Freddie Bartholomew to play the boy David – in resistance to Mayer, who wished to cast Jackie Cooper. Lord David Cecil has described the book 'not as a clear, shapely whole, but as a gleaming chaos', and it is that chaos which Selznick and his collaborators appreciated, cramming in as much as possible. The 'gleam' is partly M-G-M, but it is also partly 'Phiz', from the opening onwards – a shot of a determined Betsy Trotwood stumping through the windy garden of Mrs Copperfield. As in the original, the best part is David's childhood, and if Creakle's establishment and the friendly waiter have both gone the Orfling is there in the person of Elsa Lanchester, and there are superb minor interpolations, such as that sinister moment when Mr Murdstone wheels away David's mother as she tries to wave goodbye to her son. The second half concentrates on David's first marriage and the Wickfield-Heep-Micawber machinations, held together by Frank Lawton, a usually uninteresting actor. To call the casting inspired is to underrate it (cf. the 1969 version, with half the British acting aristocracy): W.C. Fields as Micawber; Edna May Oliver as Betsy Trotwood; Basil Rathbone as Mr Murdstone, an unfeeling man rather than a villain, and Violet Kemble Cooper as his sister, venting her feelings with 'Of all the boys in the world I believe this one is the worst'; Jessie Ralph as Peggotty; Roland Young as Heep; Herbert Mundin as Barkis; Lennox Pawle as Mr Dick; and Maureen O'Sullivan and Madge Evans as David's two loves, respectively and rightly fluttery and insipid.

A Tale of Two Cities (1935) is similarly blessed: Miss Oliver as Miss Pross; Walter Catlett as Barsad; Henry B. Walthall as old Manette; Donald Woods as Darnay; and Reginald Owen as Stryver. Mr Rathbone is, alas, a lip-smacking St Evremonde and Blanche Yurka a ludicrous Mme Defarge but there is great good fortune in the Carton. The charm and the noble gesture come naturally to Ronald Colman; any competent actor might have managed the drunkenness and the manner of *laisser-aller*, but he invests both the poseur and the disinterested friend he pretends to be with a dignity which makes the final sacrifice very moving. Jack Conway directed; the clever adaptation is by W.P. Lipscomb and S.N. Behrman. 'For more than two hours it crowds the screen with beauty and excitement,' wrote Andre Sennwald in *The New York Times*, overlooking the fact that the crowds seem to be Silent film footage and Paris is a matter of process-shots.

The two films differ little in quality: one was directed by a man who has a great number of fine films to his credit and the other by one who made a handful of good ones and many mediocre ones – and that is a tribute to the M-G-M production machine. When M-G-M lost by death and defection (for Selznick soon left) its two boy wonders the machine should have foundered, but in terms of subject matter, quality and technique there is little to choose between the Metro films of 1933 and those of 1940. Both Thalberg and Selznick had negative as opposed to positive creative ability; they seldom knew what they wanted, unless in terms of an existing film, but they knew what they didn't want, and left it to their writers, directors and craftsmen to find the solution. A young writer from Paramount, Joseph L. Mankiewicz (b. 1909), became, as a producer, one of the heirs of Thalberg: when much later he became a writer-director his films have both consistency and intelligence, but one must search for these qualities in the earlier films he produced, which range from the untypical *Fury* to *Reunion in France*, a Joan Crawford vehicle which is bad even by the standards of Joan Crawford vehicles. Little more individuality is evident among the directors – Clarence Brown, Sam Wood, Victor Fleming, King Vidor, Robert Z. Leonard, Frank Borzage, W. S. Van Dyke, Richard Thorpe, Cukor and Conway, who were all associated with M-G-M at this time. We can say that Thorpe's films were seldom interesting, and that Van Dyke's usually were: both were notable for printing the first take, but whereas in Van Dyke's case his films have spontaneity and vigour – he was known as 'One-Take Woody' – the reverse is true of Thorpe. Lubitsch made two films at Metro which are undeniably Lubitsch films, but where in the case of Borzage are the qualities of his early films? Julien Duvivier came from France to make *The Great Waltz* which if in no sense personal at least has the same imaginative approach of his other films – except that the best stuff in it (according to Selznick's memos) was shot, uncredited, by Fleming.

In this context, we might look at one of the studio's most successful films, **The Good Earth** (1937), a tale of a Chinese peasant couple through poverty, wealth, famine, revolution, marital disorder and death. Thalberg bought Pearl S. Buck's highly-regarded best seller in 1932 (the film is dedicated to his memory). The credits list a play based on it, and just three of the writers who worked on the screenplay in the intervening years – Talbot Jennings, Tess Schlesinger and Claudine West. Frances Marion also worked on it; her ex-husband, George Hill, was originally scheduled to direct, and when he was sent to China to get footage she was sent to keep an eye on him (he was an alcoholic: back in the U.S., aware that he was to be removed

Paul Muni in *The Good Earth*, in the California valley M-G-M leased for the film's production. Karl Freund deserved the Oscar he won for his photography, his spare and beautiful images often compensating for the lack of heart in the performances.

effect and Paul Muni is 'strong' without being interesting. It would be impossible now to accept Hollywood stars pretending to be Chinese peasants, and we would jib at the superficiality; but that it works at all is what the magic of the movies was all about.

The reason for the subservience of producer and director is simple: the most important element in a film was the star, and M-G-M boasted they had 'more stars than there are in heaven'. More, they were, according to M-G-M publicists, the public's favourites. The public went to see M-G-M films because M-G-M stars were in them, and those films had to be good enough to ensure that the fans stood in line the next time Clark Gable or Myrna Loy turned up at the local Bijou or Strand. A star was worth, according to Joe Pasternak, ten million dollars, and on the title page of the monthly magazines a cartoon Leo glowed with pride at the success of M-G-M players in M-G-M films. Both Thalberg and Mayer were ardent believers in stars; and the greatest of theirs remained Garbo. Her films of this period are those we know best, and some of us have watched them countless times, embarked on what is always a voyage of rediscovery.

She was cast in **Queen Christina** (1933) at her own insistence, the first time she hadn't played a lady with a past. It is hard to say whether, coming from that long line of courtesans, she had the measure of Christina, but it is clear that – with the exception of Bette Davis – she is light years ahead of her contemporaries in the matter of royal interpretation. When she tells the mob that it is her business to govern one does not question it; one notes the dignity with which she receives her lover before the court, a secret smile playing at her lips; and one wonders, in her abdication speech, to what extent she is sincere. However, in view of her projection of love, one sympathises with the studio's reluctance to cast her as anything but the amorous lady. The celebrated scene in which she memorises the room in which she has slept with her lover is hauntingly beautiful, but note the subsequent scene where, vaguely impatient and pleased to have her lady-in-waiting see that she is happy, she is otherwise locked in a private exultation that we cannot

from the project, he shot himself after a story conference). Victor Fleming took over, but when he became ill was replaced by Sidney Franklin, the credited director; and, according to *The Hollywood Reporter*, Sam Wood was working on crowd scenes and Fred Niblo – the studio's once-supreme director, now retired – had returned to get the 'atmosphere' shots. Franklin was much less interested in directing than producing – he did not direct again for more than twenty years – and it may be that he merely assembled the actors, checked their make-up, and turned them over to be photographed by Karl Freund, who was returning to cinematography after directing some half dozen features.

Credit must also be due to the special effects man, Arnold Gillespie, who simulated the plague of locusts by photographing ground coffee swirling in a glass tank; to Margaret Booth, champion of editors, and to her protégé, Slavko Vorkapich, who did the impressive montages. However, the leads deserve little praise, though Luise Rainer uses her two expressions, smiling and woebegone, to good enter. To say that she is playing a woman who has discovered love and happiness is, in view of the image she presents, to reduce her performance to triteness. With genius or at least good judgment Rouben Mamoulian keeps her at the centre of the film, but otherwise fails again to justify his reputation – the crowd scenes would not do justice to a third-rate fit-up company. Cora Sue Collins as the child queen could not have grown up as Garbo's stand-in, let alone Garbo, and John Gilbert's pop-eyed, insipid lover works only at room temperature. The high-style romanticism is of its era, but despite lapses the dialogue remains good – at least it seems so as spoken by Garbo; the cadences of her voice, the way she alights on one word or syllable, ignoring others, are unmistakably modern and right.

Although the expensive *Christina* made a handsome profit Garbo's popularity in the U.S. had begun to fade. Loews studied her American reviews and her undiminished European popularity in conjunction with her salary; they sighed, and not very happily continued to carry her as a prestige asset. In return for letting her play the Swedish queen she was thrown back into the sort of story from which she sought to escape: **The Painted Veil** (1934), Maugham's tale of adultery in Hong Kong, more than somewhat transformed. For her the trip to the cholera-infested town becomes an act of regeneration rather than retribution; there is a happy ending, but most to be regretted is the elimination of the bitchy, accurate study of local society – the book's *raison d'être* – and the flashbacks, indicating why the Colonies were populated with these particular people. To accommodate Garbo, the wife has become Austrian; Maugham's opening, one of the most striking in all his work, gives way to her meeting with the man she will marry. As the film takes off into the upper realms where Garbo was made to dwell, there is no point in considering it on any realistic level; M-G-M's Chinese festival is to the real thing as Cartier to a Woolworth brooch. She takes the advances of her lover (George Brent) in playful manner, a woman of sunny disposition and common sense; but there remain darker corners, as in the multi-syllabic 'No' to her husband's question as to whether she had

slept, the reply of a woman who has spent the time deep in her own thoughts. The dialogue is simple, alone an echo of Maugham; these people talk intensely but rationally, usually in one long take. Richard Boleslawksi's direction is exemplary: The film could be shown to students to demonstrate how to make this kind of story.

The original also overshadows **Anna Karenina** (1935), making of it a parody of real life, never entirely false but also never exact. As an example of M-G-M film-making it can hardly be faulted, with Clarence Brown's discreet set-ups, with its featureless, elegant Cedric Gibbons decor, and with some sterling performances – Reginald Denny as Yashkin, Reginald Owen as Stefan, May Robson as the Countess Vronsky; but though a couple of the later scenes between Anna and Vronsky come off the only true echo of Tolstoy is in the two sequences where Anna visits Stefan and Dolly. The dialogue (Clemence Dane, Salka Viertel, S. N. Behrman) is passable. Garbo's Anna is her least endearing performance but fascinating not only in its revelation of range but for the economy with which she makes her points. She smiles indulgently at Stefan, sadly at Kitty, reassuringly at Dolly; her second look at Vronsky records complaisance, her greeting to Karenin that the marriage is dead. The great care taken – over, for instance, pronunciation – is dissipated by the playing of the men in Anna's life. As the son, Freddie Bartholomew is beyond redemption; as Karenin, Basil Rathbone acts with a permanent sneer and no dimension; and though Fredric March, with Prussian haircut and moustache, is good as Vronsky the soldier, he is lost as a lover. Consequently Garbo hardly lavishes as much love on him as on some of the others, with the result that this film is not high in the Garbo canon.

Handicapped by the well-meaning, semi-sensitive dolts who planned her career or, rather, marketed her as merchandise, she existed serenely in their centre, trying to put love and spirit and 'body' into the grand passions in which they embroiled her. **Camille** (1937) is often said to be her best film, and certainly George Cukor was more tasteful and tactful than her other directors. The sets, of quilted satin, are vulgar even for a demi-mondaine, and the same may be said of Laura Hope Crews and Leonore Ulric as the cronies of this one, Marguerite Gautier (Garbo); while Robert Taylor's Armand is of such unworthiness as to give the old drama an extra poignancy. However, as the baron, Henry Daniell is invaluable: there is little here but good speaking and style, but his coldness counterbalance's Taylor's puppyish warmth; and of the players one must also except Jessie Ralph, whose Nanine provides Marguerite's only prop in a fickle world. Garbo herself is more yearning, more sardonic, more world-weary than ever, projecting the feeling that she knows she owes her place in the world to the bestowing of physical favours: she can give up Armand because she is accustomed to losing men. *Camille* has the most exultant love scenes of her Sound films, as for instance when she grasps Taylor by the shoulder-pads to draw his lips hungrily to hers; and it is this quality of love which makes her death scene so memorable.

When she has other people on the screen to whom she can respond, her whole body is aglow: her humanity reaches out to them and consequently to us. If one sometimes becomes aware of her limitations when she is acting to the camera alone she is sublime with a partner, and in **Conquest** (1937) Charles Boyer is one of her best (in the Sound period, only Gable is as strong, though Melvyn Douglas complements her admirably). The film itself is one of the stranger Hollywood manifestations, costing over $2 million at a time when Garbo was a box-office risk. Anti-climactic and over-ambitious, both a love story and a study of Napoleon, it is satisfactory as neither, and would be forgotten along with *Suez* and *Marie Antoinette* (q.v.) were it not for the presence of the stars. Everyone has worked conscientiously – Garbo's films were regarded more critically than those of any Hollywood artist except Chaplin and Capra – but the result is like an early nineteenth-century memorial tomb, heavy and intricately decorated. Nevertheless, the stars move through M-G-M's marble halls as to the manner born, and contemplating either of them our spirits lighten, particularly in the ballroom scene which is their second meeting

– when he and we glimpse her in the throng, alone of the ladies in translucent white, throwing her head back to laugh. Her most sombre mood is one of resignation, not the desperation of Anna Karenina or the shame of Marguerite Gautier. As Marie Walewska, Polish mistress of the Emperor, she is less at ease than as some of the loose ladies she had played in earlier films; and on this occasion Clarence Brown cannot quite hide her occasional gaucheness. Boyer is magnificent: the film retains Napoleon's paunch, but nothing could have prevented this actor from projecting the romantic aura that was uniquely his at the time. His eyes have a manic glitter, his gestures the pettiness of egotism, but he carries the 'destiny' and can, when required, evoke the great man foolishly in love; without help from the writers, he manages to suggest in the final sequences that Walewska's love has now only little but practical value. Few American films of the Thirties offer so rounded a performance.

American audiences, however, proved indifferent, which gave M-G-M pause. Garbo herself had made it known that she wanted to play comedy – she had asked to do both *Tovarich* and *Idiot's Delight* (q.v.) – and Lubitsch that he wanted to direct her: **Ninotchka** (1939), the result, commissioned from Billy Wilder, Charles Brackett and Walter Reisch, starting from the premise that three Soviet commissars, in Paris to recover some White Russian jewels, are so taken with Western hedonism that another commissar (Garbo) is sent to fetch them back. The anti-Russian, anti-Communist jokes are at best good-natured, but it is otherwise virtually flawless, *au fond* the old story of the plain Jane country cousin first at odds with, and then succumbing to, the glamour of the big city. Lubitsch manages few of his visual jokes – and they are mostly to do with the reactions of the three commissars to compliant cigarette girls – but then this is primarily a vehicle for Garbo; and this time her predominant, enthralling quality is her vulnerability. Arriving in Paris, she is sceptical, caustic and supremely self-controlled; but we know that she is in a lion's den. Wisely, the writers do not predicate a character change (or if they did she doesn't play it),

Garbo in the Thirties

Garbo in two of her historical warhorses which made audiences weep in the Thirties – and still do. UPPER LEFT, with Ian Keith in *Queen Christina*, LOWER RIGHT, with Robert Taylor in *Camille* and, LOWER LEFT, a glimpse of her dancing the Chica-Choca in *Two-Faced Woman*, the 'gayer GRANDER *GREATER* Greta' promised by the trailer.

and she smiles little after she surrenders. 'Garbo laughs' was the slogan, but we remember less the one scene of laughter than the mordant way with the caution 'Don't make an issue of my womanhood'. Melvyn Douglas's suave *boulevardier* is the perfect counterpart; accustomed though we are to the two top-billed players ending in a clinch, there is still something startling about this man falling in love with this woman, and Douglas, an underrated actor, is clearly as surprised as we.

There was at the time a poignancy about the Paris of *Ninotchka*. Throughout the decade Hollywood purveyed a city – albeit via back-projection – in which glamour and romance were the *sine qua non*, but by the time this film came out the real Paris was at war; by the time it had completed its release Paris was Occupied. The European market was closed to American films, and since there was little prospect of a Garbo picture recovering its cost in the U.S. alone M-G-M relinquished a long-held plan to turn her into Madame Curie; moreover, *Ninotchka* had been her most popular film in years, proving not only that she could play comedy but that this was the way the public wanted to see her. Hoping for a Lubitsch-like lightness, Behrman, Viertel and George Oppenheimer adapted an old play by Ludwig Fulda (filmed in 1920 as *Her Sister from Paris*, with Constance Talmadge), and **Two-Faced Woman** (1941) was introduced to cinema patrons thus: 'Who is the screen's rhumba queen?' – 'Who is still your favourite top-ranking star?' – 'Who no longer wants to be alone?' – 'A gayer GRANDER *GREATER* Greta . . . Every other inch a lady – with every other man.'

This trailer, if she saw it, must have confirmed her view – which was not without foundation – that M-G-M wanted to kill her off. *The New York Times* called her 'as gauche and stilted as the script' and referred to her 'obvious posturings, her appallingly unflattering clothes', while *Time* magazine found it 'almost as shocking as seeing your mother drunk'. The film itself does not deserve such abuse but because its reception signalled her desertion from us we may regard it no more favourably. She is consistently good, but is, however, diminished by the total effect of the

Chica-Choca, the negligees, the candid man-poaching and lines more suitable to Joan Blondell, e.g. 'I like men. Especially rich men.' Her co-star, again Melvyn Douglas, later said she 'didn't have an ounce of humour in her', but that in *Ninotchka* Lubitsch had utilised her 'utterly charming sense of childish play . . . all her *eccentricities*, if you like, for comic effect'. This was something George Cukor now failed to do, as Garbo attempted to recapture her straying husband by impersonating her sister; and what fun there is is lessened by the scene – interpolated to appease the Legion of Decency and others – in which Douglas accidentally learns of her plan. He is good, as are Roland Young, Ruth Gordon and Constance Bennett – a lady who must bear some responsibility for the loss of Garbo from the screen, for the latter trusted her to choose her wardrobe for her, and Bennett ensured that her own chic gowns would easily upstage Garbo's. Garbo originally retired only for the duration of the War but, ever timorous, lacked the courage to face the cameras again: as new generations discovered her in revivals, it mattered less. In 1940 Malcolm Muggeridge wrote (in 'The Thirties'): 'It is difficult to realise that ten years hence Greta Garbo will seem as sadly strange as Lillian Gish does now': it says much about both Garbo and the evolution of the cinema that that has never happened.

If Garbo stood supreme and apart, it was generally conceded that Norma Shearer was the Queen on the M-G-M lot. The reverse of Garbo, all technique and no feeling, she set her seal on some varied heroines – Elizabeth Barrett Browning, Shakespeare's Juliet and Marie Antoinette. Eyes glistening with tears of joy or happiness, she ought in every case to be inappropriate, but in fact she tackles all three roles with perception as well as high-spirited charm. Two of the three films are surprisingly durable. **The Barretts of Wimpole Street** (1934) had been a highly successful Broadway and London play – by Rudolf Besier – and no film ever did less to hide its origins. Sidney Franklin's direction, however, like the playing, is animated by its own dynamism: whatever the quality of the material, it is impossible to look away – for every member of the audience must be waiting for the monstrous father to get his come-uppance. In that role Charles Laughton is a master of morose expressions, testiness and forbidding silences; as the impetuous Mr Browning Fredric March is as self-conscious as he is debonair. **Romeo and Juliet** (1936) is remembered for its over-age lovers, but at least this best of the pre-Olivier Shakespeare films can be discussed seriously, as its rivals could not. Leslie Howard is Romeo, and whether by coincidence or design the lovers' contemporaries are all played by actors who had been in films since the early Twenties. The director, Cukor, has said 'It's not desperate enough. Zeffirelli got that very well' (i.e. in his later version, q.v.); he also said that neither he nor Oliver Messel fought the art department strongly enough, and indeed Messel's designs are coated with M-G-M icing sugar: the Capulet and Montague retinues suggest unlimited time with needle and thread. We long for simplicity; but there is compensation in the vigour of the handling.

As romance – Hollywood's equivalent of the historical novel – **Marie Antoinette** (1938) is not quite boring, and the dialogue (by Claudine West, Ernst Vajda and Donald Ogden Stewart, based 'in part on the book by Stefan Zweig') not actually laughable, but that is all. The first part does touch on the ramifications of dynastic marriages, the peculiar milieu of the Court of Louis xv and the anomalous position of the King's mistress. Later, Marie Antoinette is seen to meddle in politics to a minute degree, and she is given a conscience – on being offered the famous diamond necklace: 'What, when people are starving?' Yet she purchases it, and thus causes the Revolution! Robert Morley plays Louis xvi as a booby, and makes the character touching. John Barrymore is excellent as Louis xvi and Tyrone Power dull as Fersen, the Queen's lover; others include Joseph Schildkraut (indispensable in Hollywood historicals) as the Duc d'Orleans and Gladys George as the Dubarry. William Daniels's camera takes the chill off the marble halls without diminishing their grandeur, and when he has a difficult scene – as when the mob arrives to cart off the king and queen – he shoots it from slightly above, the only way to do it. The

director was W. S. Van Dyke, a last-minute replacement for Sidney Franklin, reputedly because he shot faster. However, the move was seen by some as an attempt to dishearten Miss Shearer, who by virtue of being Thalberg's widow controlled a huge portion of Loews stock. It was seldom thought that Thalberg – this film had been one of his pet projects – indulged his wife, for her popularity was enough to justify her own whims; but despite that popularity and because of executive hostility she made plans to retire.

Of her five last films two were highly successful versions of Broadway plays. **Idiot's Delight** (1939) was written by Robert E. Sherwood in 1936, and visualised a Europe on the verge of World War Two. Brooks Atkinson has called the play 'a playfully highminded antiwar comedy', and it won a Pulitzer Prize; but *Time* magazine – on the film – comes closer: 'The fact that [it] has nothing very important to tell its audience by no means indicates that it is bad entertainment.' Between the highmindedness – a debate between a pacifist (Burgess Meredith) and an armaments manufacturer (Edward Arnold) – there is a plot about the latter's Russian mistress (Shearer) and the American hoofer (Clark Gable) who swears she once played the bill with him in Omaha. Sherwood's screenplay does away with the play's mystery by offering that past time as prologue – either because audiences were not expected to take a whole film of highmindedness or because Miss Shearer wanted to look and behave naturally before donning the blonde page-boy wig and accent as used by Lynn Fontanne in the play – she rather saw herself as the Lynn Fontanne of the screen. As directed by Clarence Brown, this half hour is delightful, with Laura Hope Crews as a tippling clairvoyant and Gable having the time of his life as a third-rate vaudevillian. M-G-M had bought the play for Garbo – attracted by highmindedness again: but it does provide one of the studio's rare excursions into the contemporary world.

Not so **The Women** (1939), as presented, say the credits, 'for 666 performances of its triumphal run at the Ethel Barrymore Theatre'. Clare Booth Luce's all-woman play is two hours of bitchiness and sentiment, and of doubtful value; but

457

from the first good line – 'I hate to tell you, dear, but your skin makes the Rocky Mountains look like velvet' – it takes wing. Cukor takes his cue from what he sees as the key character, Sylvia (Rosalind Russell), for it is her machinations and gossip which move the plot about; and she is very funny. Shearer is so soignée, so generous-hearted and 'lovely' that it is hard to believe in her as a mouse-like creature who loses her husband; but she has two or three telephone calls with him – after his defection – which deserve to be anthologised. As Crystal, the perfume-counter clerk who steals him, Joan Crawford, like Russell, overdoes it, and one correspondingly enjoys her eventual discomfiture. Among the others are Mary Boland, as the much-married countess, hopefully crying 'L'amour, l'amour toujours l'amour'; Paulette Goddard as the predatory, wisecracking showgirl; and Joan Fontaine as a little ninny.

Shearer plays a Countess in **Escape** (1940), becoming involved with Robert Taylor, who has come to Germany to look for his mother (Nazimova), who has disappeared inside a concentration camp. After *The Mortal Storm* (q.v.), this was the studio's second comment on the evils of Nazism, and it further deserves respect as a superb example of the Hollywood production factory, as directed by Mervyn LeRoy. The plot, from a once-famous book by Ethel Vance, is not without coincidence, but is a cliff-hanger nevertheless.

Joan Crawford had waited more than a decade to step into Shearer's shoes, and it is therefore ironic that just at the time Shearer left, Crawford's contract was not renewed. Her films of this period are as delirious as those of her other periods, but **Forsaking All Others** (1934), directed by W. S. Van Dyke and written by Joseph L. Mankiewicz from a failed Broadway play, proves that she could not play comedy. Around her, Clark Gable and Robert Montgomery do the daffy things of screwball comedy, but she, steely-jawed, is merely game. There is at least one convulsive moment in **The Bride Wore Red** (1938), directed by Dorothy Arzner: Crawford, a Trieste cabaret singer, has been offered a vacation by a mysterious benefactor, but despite the newly-acquired virginal veil she is lonely – when

along come the villagers, in Tyrolean dress, to serenade her with one of their Neapolitan songs. At that instant you may appreciate the full force of the slogan in the ads, 'The Kind of Glamorous Production Only M-G-M Makes'. More than the other Crawford films, this one reveals Mankiewicz as the complete cynic. There are her vehicles, and there are movies, and though the two seldom resemble each other the gap is narrowed by **A Woman's Face** (1941), adapted by Donald Ogden Stewart and Elliot Paul from a play, 'Il Etait une Fois' by François de Croisset (already filmed in Sweden, with Ingrid Bergman (q.v.)). For one thing, Cukor has kept the star under control: given her head, she gives her all, but here she is almost as sober as her supporting cast – Melvyn Douglas, Conrad Veidt, Albert Basserman and Reginald Owen. The story is incredible, but everyone behaves logically, though the two halves of the film still refuse to make a whole: the business of this woman's face has nothing to do with her later role as a governess – except that we're asked to believe that a woman once badly scarred can loathe the world so much that she could turn child-murderer. But that is M-G-M: they would let Crawford blackmail (as here), they might let her play Lady Macbeth, but they would never let her murder a child – even this one (Richard Nichols), who fully deserves such a fate.

By the time M-G-M let Shearer and Crawford go they had found a new 'lady' star, Greer Garson (b. 1914), an Irish-born London stage actress, who after her appearance in *Goodbye, Mr Chips* was rushed to Hollywood to star in **Pride and Prejudice** (1940). It is a truth universally acknowledged that M-G-M's Olde England has little in common with the world of Jane Austen: at the time the two collided the life of a film was reckoned at ten years, but since television became the circulating library of old movies Miss Garson remains Elizabeth Bennett to many who have never read the book. She spars neatly, but if her words are not coquettish her manner is – to the extent that we may not be entirely grateful that it is she rather than Miss Shearer who, fancying herself in crinolines, had persuaded M-G-M to buy Helen Jerome's stage version. Darcy was originally intended for Clark Gable, but he refused to consider another costume role and Laurence Olivier was eventually chosen. The strictures applied to his co-star emphatically do not fit him – darkly, smoulderingly handsome and if arrogant and distant, not unlikeable, despite his refusal to use an ounce of charm. He is one of the players Miss Austen might have acknowledged, along with Edmund Gwenn's Mr Bennett and Melville Cooper's pompous Mr Collins. Mary Boland is a vulgar Mrs Bennett, even for Mrs Bennett, but she is marvellous: and we may think similarly of Edna May Oliver's too-broad Lady Catherine. The screenplay by Aldous Huxley and Jane Murfin is a clever condensation of the book, with stretches of the original dialogue, and since the film gets so much right – Mr Collins shooing away the chickens as he rushes to see Lady Catherine – one may forgive it such conventions of period movies as ladies chattering behind fans. The producer, Hunt Stromberg, and the director, Robert Z. Leonard, had done service on the MacDonald-Eddy movies (q.v.), but on this occasion they clearly warmed to their task.

Anyone not put off by the title, **Blossoms in the Dust** (1940), deserves to actually watch the film, which consists of one hundred minutes of treacly Technicolored uplift. Miss Garson plays Edna Kahly, who turns into a society gadfly, laughing on the outside and crying on the inside, after losing her child; and though she remonstrates when her husband sneaks a replacement into the house in no time at all she is running an orphanage. Bankruptcy is later threatened, but since the outcome is not vouchsafed us we may assume that it interested neither the writer, Anita Loos, working from a supposedly true story, nor the director, Mervyn LeRoy – the same Mervyn LeRoy who had once made *Little Caesar*.

Fortunately for sanity, the Marx brothers were also working at M-G-M – due to the enthusiasm of Thalberg, who supervised **A Night at the Opera** (1935) but died during the preparation of **A Day at the Races** (1937). However both, at his suggestion, were tried out as stage shows – so that what went into them was not necessarily what the Marx brothers did best, but what the public best liked

them doing. These preparations also enabled the director, Sam Wood, to shoot their routines in one take. Groucho considered these their two best films because they were the most commercially successful, and for the same reason he defended Thalberg's insistence on the songs and sub-plots for the juveniles – which buffs are united in deploring. Even at their lowest ebb – a song called 'By Blue Venetian Waters', danced amidst fountains by one Vivien Fay – they are worth bearing, for Groucho still has more insults to throw at Margaret Dumont – who never loved him more. In *A Day at the Races* she is in full bloom, a hypochondriac bridling with pride as she announces 'Dr Hackenbush tells me I'm the only case in history. I have *high* blood pressure on my right side and *low* blood pressure on my left side.' There are those who doubt his qualifications – he is in fact a horse doctor – but she never does.

A Night at the Opera is the more brilliant of the two films, with the Marxes' most celebrated sequence, the cramped cabin, and Groucho interpreting Harpo's horn-blowing as 'Two more hard-boiled eggs', one of their unspoken conspiracies. Running amok during 'Il Trovatore' Harpo is a wild sprite defying the pursuers who would encage him; but the old anarchic spirit is missing, later to decline still further; and it is hard to identify the one-time sex maniac with this pied piper to a bunch of piccaninnies in *A Day at the Races*. In **At the Circus** (1939) one cannot imagine him stealing cutlery, let alone sporting a blackjack. The film comes alive only when Groucho's insults are recognisable Marxist theory; the butt of them, Miss Dumont, does get fired from a cannon, and at the end of the film an orchestra floats out to sea – which is, with good reason, the only thing people remember about it. The writer was Irving Brecher and the director Edward Buzzell, who were also responsible for **Go West** (1940), which is the Marxes' 'Timon' or 'Cymbeline'. They no longer create anarchy, lords of their own domain, for the script suggests that Brecher had been studying The Three Stooges. If he had seen any of the Marxes' previous movies it could only have been the one he wrote – on this evidence he simply would not have understood *Duck Soup*. The final chase is aboard a train, to remind us that Buster Keaton was a gag-man at M-G-M at this period: but, he recorded, the Marx brothers failed to connect with him. Bad notices and their concomitant, increasing studio indifference, determined them on retirement. One last film is a partial return to form: **The Big Store** (1941), directed by Charles Reisner. It is not particularly Marxian – the chase might have been written for any comic team – but it does cast Groucho as a detective, and he is more or less at his best, despite unmemorable lines; also, Miss Dumont – absent in the previous film – returns for a last measure of derision. Tony Martin sings 'The Tenement Symphony', which is schmaltz of a certain order.

While the Marx brothers were then of limited appeal, Jeanette MacDonald and Nelson Eddy were the world's singing sweethearts. Mention them today and strong men faint while others smirk: and confronted with their all-too-public declarations of love – 'Ah, Sweet Mystery of Life!' – who can blame them? That song features in their first film together, **Naughty Marietta** (1935), a version of an old Victor Herbert operetta which finds the director W. S. Van Dyke at his least enthusiastic; but he also handled **Rose Marie** (1936), an enjoyable film by any standards. Also from an old stage piece, it has the definitive version of the 'Indian Love Call', warbled by the lovers on a lake in the Rockies. Later she sings it as he, a Mountie, escorts away her brother (James Stewart), and strains of it interrupt her interpretation of Act III of 'Tosca'. Finally they carol it reunited on her sick-bed. Louis B. Mayer was so impressed by Grace Moore's success at Columbia that both these films had originally been planned for her – so the famous teaming was accidental, since MacDonald was cast in both by default. The title role of *Rose Marie* had been adapted to suit either – and had therefore become a temperamental and self-centred opera singer, and it is at her expense that Van Dyke offers the first number. He keeps the proceedings light and airy, and MacDonald abets him gleefully throughout, never demanding sympathy: even the cumbersome Eddy cannot dampen the fun.

There are excellent moments to be found in these films – though not in all of them, and certainly not in **Maytime** (1937), which concerns a penniless singer (Eddy) in Paris, a prima donna (MacDonald) and her Svengali-like mentor (John Barrymore). More cloying than the plot is a sub-plot which frames it – set in a cherry orchard of such ostentation that if you missed the credits you would still know it was an M-G-M film. It finishes with petals falling thick and fast, while ghosts of Eddy and Jeanette warble 'Will You Remember?' – the only song left from Sigmund Romberg's original score. Frank S. Nugent in *The New York Times* called the movie, 'the most joyous operetta of the season, a film to treasure', but then he liked the opera fashioned from Tchaikovsky's Fifth. The film does feature a chunk of 'Les Huguenots' – one of the few times that Hollywood, ransacking the classics for their 'heavier' singers, used a rare opera. **The Firefly** (1937) is also based on an aged piece and its 131-minute running time is witness to M-G-M's confidence in it: but instead of concerning a yachting trip to Burma, as in Friml's operetta, it is about a runaway prima donna who becomes a double agent during the Peninsular War. Eddy has been replaced by Allan Jones, not quite an improvement, but he has 'The Donkey Serenade' – if not the best song then the best *handled* song in the series. Snatches of it break into the action, swelling against the images, till finally he gives vent to voice: it may not be the song one most wants to hear (again), but the skill with which it is deployed is undeniable.

Robert Z. Leonard directed both films and also two other warhorses, **The Girl of the Golden West** (1938) and **New Moon** (1940) – the latter remembered as the one in which Eddy and chorus press on through swampland, oblivious of conditions, singing, 'Give Me Some Men Who Are Stout-Hearted Men'. The former, from Belasco's play, already filmed three times, boasted not Puccini but a new Romberg score. *New Moon* was his 1927 operetta (filmed by Metro in 1930), with the stars more judiciously cast – French countess and freedom fighter, as opposed to (untutored) saloon queen and dashing bandit. They are a husband and wife team on modern Broadway in **Sweethearts** (1938), utilising an old Victor Herbert score and Technicolor, the studio's first film in that process. **Bitter Sweet** (1940) also has Technicolor and Van Dyke's direction, plus a certain respect for Noël Coward's songs, even if these are no longer distributed throughout the cast. MacDonald, otherwise increasingly arch, kicks up her heels to recall her Lubitsch days in 'Ladies of the Town'. Despite barely diminished public response the formula was shifted with **I Married an Angel** (1942), a Rodgers and Hart modern fantasy from Broadway, directed by Van Dyke, but the decision had already been made to discontinue the series, owing to all-round personal differences. The two stars had given great pleasure to cinemagoers, few of whom would have dreamed that one day their films would be considered greatly inferior to those of that other popular musical couple, Astaire and Rogers.

Of the same genre is **The Great Waltz** (1938). 'See this film for its musical charm, its infectious lyrical quality, and its joyous spirit,' said *Film Weekly*, doubtless deluded into finding these qualities in a film claiming the 'spirit' of the music of Strauss the younger. The musical sequences are cleverly staged, in particular the crowds drawn to the empty restaurant where Strauss is conducting one of his waltzes, and the drive through the Vienna Woods, where the clip-clop of the horses inspires him to a certain composition . . . The score is played with such verve, with the editing choreographed to it, that the sheer contrivance is disarming. The rest is distinctly not 'joyous' – operetta plot No. 1, in which the marriage of composer (Fernand Gravet, as rechristened) and waiflike wife (Luise Rainer) is threatened by the bounteous diva (Militza Korjus, pronounced 'gorgeous' said the ads): what makes it especially trying is that 'Schanni' isn't even moderately considerate to his wife – yet it turns out that *she* was his inspiration, for as the Viennese sing back at him, on the balcony of Schönbrunn, it is her likeness which is superimposed over the belvedere. The credited director, Julien Duvivier, is absolved from blame, for most of the film is known to have been by other hands.

As the title implies, **The Great Ziegfeld** (1936) was the other mighty M-G-M musical, though it was originally a Universal project, sold because of financial difficulties. Billie Burke was to have played herself, Ziegfeld's second wife, but Myrna Loy replaced her: William Powell is Ziegfeld, and Miss Rainer his first wife, Anna Held – and, except in her celebrated telephone scene, excellent, with all the characteristics associated with a great and silly lady of the theatre. The splendid cast also includes Fanny Brice and Frank Morgan; but the film lasts just over three hours – the longest Sound film made up to that time – and as directed by Robert Z. Leonard it seems like it. Nevertheless, it made a profit on substantial expenditure, and won a Best Picture Oscar. There is only one song in the last hour, and the famous number, 'A Pretty Girl is Like a Melody', with the kitsch and classical interpolations, is really the climactic moment.

Customarily the M-G-M musical *ended* with the spectacular number – in terms of size dwarfing those of other studios and often built around the Terpsichorean talents of Eleanor Powell. **Rosalie** (1937) replaced Gershwin's 1928 score with a new one by Cole Porter while retaining the 'book' (but then the film's producer and writer, William Anthony McGuire, had contributed to that), a fable about a Puritanian princess and a West Point cadet. Miss Powell and Nelson Eddy make a deadly duo, he wooden and she twinkling her perception of the joke to every member of the audience – presumably because Van Dyke did not give her the same attention as her other directors.

As with their early Talkie progenitor, neither **Broadway Melody of 1936** (1935) nor **Broadway Melody of 1938** (1937) has much to do with the real Broadway – no exteriors, no grit and grin, no hint of the harshness of *42nd Street*: just two more backstage tales with excuses to get into white-tie-and-tails for the big numbers. The songs again are by Arthur Freed (q.v.) and Nacio Herb Brown. The director of both is Roy del Ruth, and in both Robert Taylor is a Broadway producer and Miss Powell a stagestruck youngster. The first of them wastes Jack Benny; it has an excellent 'impromptu' number danced by Buddy and Vilma Ebsen on a Manhattan rooftop, and another as magical as any in movie musicals – 'I've Got a Feeling You're Fooling', tip-tappy toes on a night club floor, all

461

Irving Berlin's song, 'A Pretty Girl is like a Melody', as featured in *The Great Ziegfeld*. It is absurd, of course, but it is impossible not to feel a frisson as the camera finally moves back to reveal this set, decorated in its moving kitsch.

join in and everybody sing. In the second film two of the numbers foreshadow the best of the musicals which Freed later produced: a dance in a rainstorm (done by George Murphy) and an ad-lib dance in a freight car very much like the 'Good Morning' sequence also in *Singin' in the Rain* (q.v.). Coming between the two, **Born to Dance** (1936) has the same writers as the earlier film, the same director, and so many of the original players – Powell, Una Merkel, Ebsen, Frances Langford and Sid Silvers – that the decision not to call it 'Broadway Melody of 1937' is inexplicable. Cole Porter's score includes 'I've Got You Under My Skin' and 'Easy to Love', the latter crooned by an unembarrassed James Stewart as the sailor hero. These films, if not easy to love are easy to take – and if we are fonder of **Broadway Melody of 1940** (1940), it is because of Fred Astaire, more precise and more ethereal than ever. The score is again by Porter, the direction by Norman Taurog, and the construction even smarter than Astaire's R.K.O. movies, keeping the dancing couple – she is Miss Powell, and Murphy is his partner and rival – romantically but not choreographically apart till the finale.

The chief joy to be found in these pictures is, however, the youngster billed eighth in *Broadway Melody of 1938*, a stagestruck child being promoted by her grandmother (Sophie Tucker); she has an extraneous number built around a photograph of Clark Gable, 'You Made Me Love You', whose lyric contains the words 'As far as I'm concerned you'll always be the top' – which is the way many Hollywood-watchers feel about *her*: Judy Garland (1922–69). The daughter of vaudeville parents, she had been with M-G-M, idle, till Roger Edens, of the studio's music department, arranged the Gable song for her to sing at a party for the star. She was to be profitably teamed with Mickey Rooney (b.1920), another child of vaudeville, in movies since childhood, as he climbed to a popularity which would outstrip even Gable's, always playing the know-it-all wise guy with the tender heart, junior version. **Thoroughbreds Don't Cry** (1937), directed by Alfred E. Green, was designed to demonstrate the opposing talents of him and the studio's other boy actor, Freddie Bartholomew – replaced, in the event, by Robert Sinclair. As the girl trying to attract their attention Garland is a miracle: dumpy, plain, given to puppy-fat, her playing is relaxed and her singing has a sense of self-mockery remarkable in a child. 'I'm going to be a great singer, I'm going to be a great actress,' is her second line, and she plays it for laughs.

Stage-struck again in **Everybody Sing** (1938), she gets into a show with the family chef, Allan Jones, and the Russian maid, Fanny Brice; and her duet with the latter, though a poor song, makes clear that you are watching two of the century's legendary artists. 'Are all families as crazy as this?' she asks, and the answer is No, only in movies. Edwin L. Marin directed this one.

The family in **Love Finds Andy Hardy** (1938) is something else. The Hardy family started in a B-picture, *A Family Affair* (1937), with Rooney, and Lionel Barrymore as the father; in *You're Only Young Once* (1938) Lewis Stone and Fay Holden took over the roles of the older Hardys, which they would play in all the sequels. Family series – the Joneses at 20th, Blondie at Columbia – were common on the lower half of double bills, but Louis B. Mayer so loved these two films that the budgets were increased to A-picture level, and the public responded warmly for some years. The Hardys hopefully reflected America to itself: they were comfortably off – father was a judge – and both parents were founts of wisdom and virtue. Andy (Rooney) got into scrapes, but father's advice prevailed in the end; he flirted with other girls, but always returned to Polly (Ann Rutherford). There was a touch of humour, a touch of sentiment, always well handled by George B. Seitz, an unobtrusive director. In this case, William Ludwig's screenplay is both funny and sympathetic – and Rooney is unquestionably a most gifted performer. Several strands of plot include Garland's crush on him, which, of course, he doesn't notice. She is, admittedly, appealing, but her delicacy of approach, with an instinctive use of the right glance and the right inflexion, constitutes a formidable talent – never more than in a haunting and witty lament, 'In-between'.

Her own 'in-between' stage presented a problem, for she was too young for

Judy Garland as the world fell in love with her. ABOVE in *The Wizard of Oz*, having proceeded far enough along the yellow brick road to meet the Scarecrow, Ray Bolger, and not suspecting the troubles in store, which include the Witch (Margaret Hamilton). RIGHT, in *Babes in Arms*, with Mickey Rooney, one of the series designed to showcase their talents in every direction.

romance and too old for the customary child-star roles, though she did have a Shirley Temple-like role in **Listen, Darling** (1938), directed by Marin, bringing romance to mother, Mary Astor, in the shape of Walter Pidgeon. Then came **The Wizard of Oz** (1939), for which Mayer had wanted Miss Temple: in fact, Goldwyn sold the property – Frank L. Baum's book – because he too had been unable to wrench that child from Zanuck. As fantasy was a risky proposition (there had been earlier versions in 1910 and 1925), it is clear that Loews were persuaded by the takings of *Snow White and the Seven Dwarfs* (q.v.); but it was the intention of Arthur Freed to launch Garland as a star – it was his first film as producer, though the official credit went to Mervyn LeRoy, who supervised. Victor Fleming directed – until taken off to complete *Gone with the Wind* (q.v.), at which point King Vidor (uncredited) filmed the Kansas sequences, including 'Over the Rainbow'. The screenplay stays close enough to the book, with witches, flying monkeys, and those equally fantastic figures who are the companions of Dorothy (Garland) on the journey to Oz – the Scarecrow (Ray Bolger), the Tin Man (Jack Haley) and the Cowardly Lion (Bert Lahr). The start is only middling, and the move into Technicolor not magical; but as Dorothy breaks into a gay little dance, 'We're Off to See the Wizard', it achieves enchantment. Garland seems to believe in the magic, which is complete but for the decor – notably Oz, the Emerald City, an art-deco monstrosity with fake glitter, and the calendar-art land of the Munchkins. Frank Morgan is the wizard, Billie Burke and Margaret Hamilton the good and bad witches respectively, and the score is by Harold Arlen and E. Y. Harburg – all factors in its being, apart from Disney, the most popular film for children ever made; it was a huge success then, and in terms of re-issues and television showings the most successful film M-G-M ever produced.

Babes in Arms (1939) had been a Rodgers and Hart Broadway musical about the offspring of touring vaudevillians putting on a show of their own: with the score trimmed and the book reworked into a sentimental valentine to show business, it remains a very taking film, justifying two follow-ups, **Strike Up the Band** (1940) and **Babes on Broadway** (1941), also both produced by Freed and directed by Busby Berkeley. Their purpose is to exploit the talents of Garland and Rooney, with wistful ballads for her and clowning for him, impromptu duets round a piano, or the two of them leading a well-drilled chorus in the slam-bang finales. They appear to be enjoying themselves hugely, and so does the audience (though when these films were shown in post-war France, the critics were appalled by their popularity, certain it was undermining French culture); the plots, virtually indistinguishable, fill the spaces well enough, and if there is a flaw it is their smugness: 'Gee, it's more than just a show. We're doing it for all the kids in America,' says Rooney. We might jibe at some patriotism – a song called 'God's Country' – but what to make of the last of

the trio, with its message of love for Britain? James Agate found it 'patronising', but there is a lump in my throat as Garland sings 'Don't give up, Tommy Atkins . . . There's a whole world behind you shouting, "Stout fella".'

She pined for Rooney again in **Andy Hardy Meets Debutante** (1940), and while M-G-M was not the studio to resist public demand – hence the dependence on teams – her growing popularity and Freed's desire to showcase her talent found her solo in **Little Nellie Kelly** (1940), George M. Cohan's old play, which Freed bought for her. Audiences may have loved this tale of feuding New York Irish in 1922, but it was stale by this time. Garland has a double role, mother and daughter: touching as mother, she is just another cutie as the younger Nellie – at least as directed by Norman Taurog. She is better served by Robert Z. Leonard in **Ziegfeld Girl** (1941); the studio had debated a Ziegfeld sequel for years, but this has little in common with the earlier picture, less a backstage story than a woman's magazine serial punctuated with songs. It focuses on three hopeful showgirls, and the lacquered personalities of Hedy Lamarr and Lana Turner throw Garland's talent into relief. She was certainly well-versed in playing stagestruck girls, and one may wonder how much these roles – longing for the big time, to play the Palace – contributed to the confused state of her later life.

At about this time there arrived at M-G-M another of the nonpareils, Margaret Sullavan. 'Hers is a shimmering, almost unendurably lovely performance,' said Frank S. Nugent in *The New York Times* of her work in **Three Comrades** (1938), for which she also won the New York critics' Best Actress Award. Following *Little Man, What Now?*, this was the second German subject in which she was directed by Frank Borzage. The source is a novel by Erich Maria Remarque, about three war veterans (Robert Taylor, Robert Young, Franchot Tone), one of whom falls for a girl (Sullavan) dying of tuberculosis. 'I'm not alone any more,' she says, giving to such lines an extraordinary poignancy for all their sentimentality: 'There are so many drifters. We may all drift together and some day we may find pleasant seas.' Borzage takes an equally romantic view. 'Get drunk, get very drunk and love your comrades,' says one of them, but perhaps there we recognise the hand of F. Scott Fitzgerald, whose only screen-writing credit this is (shared with Edward E. Paramore). He considered himself betrayed by the producer, Mankiewicz, but while the latter indeed rewrote his dialogue it was because Miss Sullavan could not speak it and because the front office had decreed that the Nazi angle be soft-pedalled – to the extent that the word 'Nazi' is not mentioned, nor the hoodlums identified.

Despite the altered European situation **The Mortal Storm** (1940) also hedges: says the wife (Irene Rich) of the professor (Frank Morgan) whom we understand to be Jewish: 'Now that these people have come to power, what about people who think differently – people who are . . . (pause) non-Aryan?' Germany is portrayed as a nation of thugs, where people are carried off and never seen again – and as in the case of *Confessions of a Nazi Spy* the German Embassy again protested. The film was much admired perhaps because it was made in a neutral country, and it was cheering to those Americans with relatives still in Germany; but if mild compared with the truth it is still too melodramatic. Miss Sullavan is the professor's daughter, in love with a young man (James Stewart) brave enough to defy the storm troopers. The source is a novel by Phyllis Bottome – and Borzage's participation, despite the credits, was minimal. Victor Saville took over production from Sidney Franklin, who left to prepare *Mrs Miniver* (q.v.). He found Borzage, he said, 'in great difficulties', and directed all but a week of it, refusing credit since, as a British Jew, he feared he might be thought parti pris. Yet Loews, of course, was a Jewish firm. Because both films are so mealy-mouthed – and because the settings are so patently false – it is impossible to find them impressive on contemporary problems, though *Three Comrades* is a touching romance. Even on their appointed subjects, sincerity is not enough.

The Shopworn Angel (1938) is an enjoyable attempt to tell a conventional story in realistic fashion. H. C. Potter directed, Mankiewicz produced, Waldo Salt wrote the screenplay, and one would not have to know their later work – Salt wrote *Midnight Cowboy* (q.v.) – to see this as a wry tale for sophisticates, 'La Dame aux Camélias' updated. The 1929 version starred Nancy Carroll and Gary Cooper. Like Carroll, Miss Sullavan specialised in suffering, and Metro regarded James Stewart as their answer to Cooper – but this version is hard and sharp, and very different to the earlier one in mood. The lady is a hard-boiled dame, and her protector (Walter Pidgeon) very understanding; she is selfish, dissolute and greedy, and it is her unwillingness to love the soldier (Stewart) that gives the piece conviction.

Sullavan's special qualities are particularly apparent in **The Shining Hour** (1938), for she is pitted against Joan Crawford. Of stardom, Clive Brook said once, 'We became rubber stamps – trademarks – recognised as Clive Brook, Ruth Chatterton, Ronald Colman, or whatever trademark we are sold under;' and as Crawford was trademarked as the Tough Go-It-Alone Girl, so was Sullavan as the Little Woman Bravely Coping. Like Fay Bainter, here playing her sister-in-law, she could be artificial; but even then she at least resembles a real woman, which Crawford never did. The latter plays a dancer from the wrong side of the tracks who marries a Wisconsin farmer (Melvyn Douglas), with catalytic effect upon his family (Sullavan, Bainter, Robert Young). Mankiewicz produced, Borzage directed, allowing us nary a glimpse of the cattle about which we hear so much (the Borzage of *The River* had long gone); the original play was by Keith Winter, adapted by Jane Murfin and, of all people, Ogden Nash.

For Miss Sullavan and **The Shop Around the Corner** (1940) the Culver City sound stage was turned into the Budapest of dreams, cream pastries and gypsy violins; and though peopled by Hollywood actors its conviction, unlike *The Mortal Storm*, is complete. Lubitsch was the alchemist responsible, together with Samson Raphaelson, who wrote the screenplay from a play by Miklos Laszlo. The result does not belong to any tradition of screen comedy: the only movies it at all resembles are other Lubitsch films, but in leaving innuendo behind he continues to regard his characters with delighted anticipation – the hero (James Stewart) and heroine (Sullavan) working in the same shop, mutually antagonistic, both of them, unknown to the other, dreaming of a pen pal. Frank Morgan plays the boss, a sad figure when he loses his wife and a ferocious one when he fires people. It is the film's underlying sadness which prevents this caprice from outstaying its welcome, but then it was made by the most adroit judge of effect and taste in Hollywood history.

Innocence – of a sort – is also at a premium in **Waterloo Bridge** (1940): 'Such things don't happen!' says her friend when Vivien Leigh tells her that her husband (Robert Taylor) has returned from the dead to save her from a life of sin – and it is the best possible comment on the whole film. The British at war wallowed in it, not minding such solecisms as Gloucester Cathedral doubling for a Mayfair parish church. As directed by Mervyn LeRoy the film is vastly inferior to the earlier version, and the subject has slightly shifted – to that of a particular English society and a dancer destroyed as she seeks to enter it. That she becomes a whore from expediency is hard to believe, what with the demand for chorus girls in the shows for the boys on leave, but there she is, welcoming the boys at Waterloo in beret and black silk dress, Taylor is in such a state of euphoria that he does not notice her outfit, and the game is only up when his C.O. (C. Aubrey Smith) tells her she will be an honour to the regiment. 'Has there been anyone else?' asks her fiancé's mother (Lucile Watson), in response to her tears, and we are cheated of the obvious reply ('Hundreds') by a cool line, 'Oh Lady Margaret, you are naif!' She would not have been the first lady of the manor who had been a lady of the evening, but for American audiences, even at this time, British hypocrisy had to triumph over true love. Miss Leigh suffers prettily against 'Swan Lake' and a medley of British airs: as an actress she was only technically accomplished, but she has a springlike aura stemming from the knowledge that she was beautiful and very clever.

Waterloo Bridge is one of the few Robert Taylor vehicles that has not slid into oblivion. Another of his films, **Stand Up and Fight** (1939), is a nineteenth-century

adventure tale with a note of seriousness – about setting the slaves free: 'People have been arguing that point for years. Maybe there'll be a war about it one day.' There were graver problems at Metro than the questioning of historical attitudes – the problem of Taylor, for instance: how to package this handsome and wooden star so that he appealed to men as well as women. Thus this particular formula movie: he as a ne'er-do-well growing up in the two-fisted milieu of the old West, with Florence Rice in a crinoline and Wallace Beery as the gosh-darn-it manager of her stage line; Van Dyke, directing, was clearly not interested in the narrative. **Billy the Kid** (1941) is a remake in Technicolor by David Miller of the early Talkie, again romanticising the saga: Billy (Taylor) has a grudge against society because his father was shot in the back; when treated kindly he becomes an upstanding citizen – till compelled to revenge his benefactor (Ian Hunter). Gene Fowler's screenplay tries for the frontier feeling – an awareness of sudden swift death, a loyalty to friends and benefactor. The effect, for a film of the time, is liberating, but Taylor and Brian Donlevy (as the Pat Garrett character) were both dull actors.

Johnny Eager (1941) was another attempt to give Taylor a more robust image, for he plays a tough gangleader –

Margaret Sullavan and James Stewart, right, in Lubitsch's enchanting *The Shop Around the Corner*. To call her vulnerable and skittish, or him gawky and down-to-earth, is to underrate them both; it is easier to 'place' Frank Morgan, centre, as the boss, crusty but with a heart of gold.

William Powell and Myrna Loy with Asta the dog in *The Thin Man*, the first of a popular series. Their diamond-hard playing still delights: Miss Loy said later that she based her characterisation on Lillian Hellman, the mistress of Dashiell Hammett, on whose novel the film was based.

and if this is odd casting, it is less so than that of Lana Turner as a sociology student. We may understand her leaving her staid life for love of him, but her claim to a knowledge of 'Cyrano de Bergerac' is one of the least convincing speeches in screen history. Mervyn LeRoy directs this good example of the late gangster film, well performed by Edward Arnold, Barry Nelson and Glenda Farrell. Van Heflin plays Taylor's self-pitying friend and lodger with a crush on him a mile high and a mile wide – the first overt Hollywood portrait of a deviate, presumably slipping past the notice of Louis B. Mayer (and winning for Heflin a Best Supporting Oscar).

Mayer did not like Westerns or gangster films, and **The Last Gangster** (1937), despite its title, is basically a mother love drama. Edward G. Robinson plays a hotshot gangster who loses his wife (Rosa Stradner) to a smarty-pants reporter (James Stewart) while in jail and has to see her again when their son is kidnapped. Edward Ludwig directed, from a screenplay by William A. Wellman and Robert Carson, suggested by events in the life of Al Capone. As with Capone, Robinson is caught for tax evasion, and Capone's

rumoured homosexuality expressed by Robinson's complete indifference towards his wife.

In **The Earl of Chicago** (1940), Robert Montgomery is also a gangster – one who inherits an English peerage and begins to take his tenantry seriously. Richard Thorpe directed, from a screenplay based, say the credits, on the 'philosophy' of a book of the same name; according to the producer, Victor Saville, Montgomery was responsible for both style and story. The 'philosophy' is contained in a speech by the valet (Edmund Gwenn): 'Our class never let yours down, and your class never let ours down.'

Montgomery had played the role at his own insistence, as he had earlier played the psychotic in the film of Emlyn Williams's play, **Night Must Fall** (1937), directed by Thorpe. Presumably as a relief from comedy parts he acted both roles in the same odd manner, repeating the performance yet again in **Rage in Heaven** (1941). This is another picture which, as directed by Van Dyke, has particular reverence for M-G-M's England, and is clearly one of the psychological dramas which flowered in the wake of *Rebecca* (q.v.). But are the intimations of homosexuality in the original novel by James Hilton, or are they the invention of Christopher Isherwood, who with Robert Thoeren wrote the screenplay? The presence of this theme in yet another M-G-M film suggests a concerted effort in the writers' bungalow to offer an affront to the front office and the moralising Mayer – but in this case less hidden than usual, since Montgomery pushes his best friend (George Sanders) at his wife (Ingrid Bergman) after secretly gazing at a photograph of him and then goes, literally, mad with jealousy. The result is a very curious melodrama.

The studio's leading light comedian was William Powell, his career given a new impetus by the film for which Van Dyke is best remembered, **The Thin Man** (1934). While directing Powell and Myrna Loy in *Manhattan Melodrama* he envisaged them as Nick and Norah Charles, Dashiell Hammett's amateur private detective and his wife, and since Powell had played Philo Vance several times the studio thought this a safe enough investment. Van Dyke was given a B-picture schedule of sixteen days, and that was all he wanted. 'We managed to achieve,' said Miss Loy later, 'what for those days was an almost pioneering sense of spontaneity.' Today the film is just another murder mystery, but Powell and Loy are nonchalant, debonair, take-it-or-leave-it – and it is startling to realise that their chief interests are sex, money and booze: she says, surveying the drunks at their Christmas party, 'I love you because you know such lovely people,' and he explains thus his refusal to take up a murder case, 'I'm much too busy making sure you don't waste the money I married you for.' Albert Hackett and his wife, Frances Goodrich, added a few such lines to Hammett's, and the result is a film much more modern than the 1950s T.V. series based on it.

For much of its length **After the Thin Man** (1936) is better still: the banter is light, the plot pleasingly complicated and the work of Powell, Loy and Van Dyke as accomplished; but it goes on too long – 110 minutes as opposed to ninety-three. In **Another Thin Man** (1939) the red herrings are as compulsively confusing, but as the weaker plot indicates the Hacketts have based their screenplay on the second of the series rather than on Hammett. The credits of both films insist that they are based on 'an original story' by that writer, but the pretence is not kept up in **Shadow of the Thin Man** (1941) – nor from now on do the titles acknowledge that the 'thin man' of the original was the actual murderer. This is a shadow indeed: the Hacketts have ceded to Irving Brecher and Harry Kurnitz, who do not observe whodunnit rules. Later, in **The Thin Man Goes Home** (1944), directed by Richard Thorpe (Van Dyke had died), and **Song of the Thin Man** (1947), directed by Edward Buzzell, Norah and Nick would be bowdlerised, partly because the studio traded on Miss Loy's image as 'the perfect wife'.

Reckless (1935) was planned by Selznick as a Joan Crawford vehicle in the manner of *Dancing Lady*, a basically serious tale told in wisecracks; Powell was set to co-star, and at the last minute Crawford was jettisoned in favour of Jean Harlow, whose romance with him was very much in the public eye. Opportunism was further rampant in that the plot was based on the case of Libby Holman, a Broadway star widely suspected of having murdered her husband. In the film the star's career suffers when her playboy husband (Franchot Tone) shoots himself; Powell is the old standby. It is more enjoyable than **Wife vs Secretary** (1936), which, as directed by Clarence Brown, is no more than a vehicle for Loy, Harlow and Clark Gable – names which promise more than they actually deliver. Harlow's popularity had grown to the extent that her old image no longer suited M-G-M, so her hair was darkened for her to play the perfect secretary. Gable is tempted by her in a Havana hotel room, but resists while Loy foolishly suspects the worst. The credits of **Libeled Lady** (1936) are preceded by a shot of Powell, Loy, Harlow and Spencer Tracy walking towards us, a sign of Metro's prodigality in the matter of stars. Loy is the lady of the title, Tracy the libelling editor, Harlow his fiancée, Powell the colleague Tracy persuades to marry Harlow, with the object of getting her to sue Loy for alienation of affection. Jack Conway's direction seems confident that the players will make the oscillating fun seem more homogenous than it is.

The Powell-Loy comedies were inevitably about marital relations. He was the more gifted of the two, an accomplished farceur; her personal charm tended to disguise the fact that she was really only effective at one sort of cool, guarded, sarcastic humour. **I Love You Again** (1940) and **Love Crazy** (1941) are both screwball comedies, directed by Van Dyke and Conway respectively. In the former Powell, recovering from amnesia, is appalled by every facet of his past life except his wife (Loy), whom he persuades not to divorce him; in the latter, to prevent her from divorcing him he feigns madness – which requires him at one point to don female attire. Because of this impeccable drag act and its more inventive slapstick, *Love Crazy* has the edge. It also has the advantage of Gail Patrick as an old flame, Jack Carson in one of his best big-headed roles and, above all, Florence Bates as the mother-in-law, eyes agleam with venom.

In common with other late screwball comedies **It's a Wonderful World** (1940) has tremendous contrivance as written by Ben Hecht and Herman J.

Mankiewicz (q.v.: Joseph's brother), going to great lengths to keep hero and heroine scrapping till the last reel. Van Dyke must take much of the credit – if not for his pacing, as fast as ever, then for the inventiveness of the playing: James Stewart as a private eye out to establish his innocence, and Claudette Colbert as the poetess unwillingly involved with him, companions in loathing, one or other of them clinging to the other, by turns, like leeches. The prototype is *It Happened One Night*, and the middle part is a good deal funnier, even, than that: as ever Miss Colbert's eyes are glazed when there is news she doesn't wish to hear, but she reveals a stronger determination than ever to turn everything to her own advantage.

The film is certainly wittier than M-G-M's most renowned comedy of the period, **The Philadelphia Story** (1940), a version of 'The Taming of the Shrew' – or, rather, the prig. At the time it broke records at Radio City Music Hall, and resuscitated the career of Katharine Hepburn. She had scored a personal success on Broadway in Philip Barry's original play and had cannily purchased the screen rights. Warners offered $225,000 for them, but that did not include her; M-G-M took a chance, offering her $175,000 for the play and $75,000 for her services. Clark Gable was supposed to have propped her up at the box office, but refused the assignment. Cary Grant replaced him, on condition that he got top billing and that his fee of $137,500 was paid to British War Relief. In the subsidiary role of the snooping reporter James Stewart won a Best Actor Oscar (clearly a compensation for not having won for *Mr Smith Goes to Washington*). George Cukor directs with the utmost discretion, using mainly two-shot, and letting relaxed playing give the maximum to the lines and situations. The point is supposed to be that Tracey (Hepburn), a Philadelphia blue-blood, is humanised after some digs from her ex-husband (Grant), a drunken romp with the reporter and a lecture from her playboy father: but we are shown no transformation. Much is said about her, but beyond one aside (correcting 'my house' to 'our house' for the sake of her fiancé) there is no indication that she has changed an iota. The strength of Hep-

burn's personality disguises the fact that her role hardly exists, and the few real laughs go to lines devoid of wit, like her description of Philadelphia, 'It's an interesting place, full of relics, and how old are you, Mr Connor?' and the rest of the dialogue consists of such flat aphorisms as 'The prettiest sight in the world is watching the privileged classes enjoying their privileges.' Donald Ogden Stewart won an Oscar for his screenplay – having, in his own words, merely copied out Barry's text, and from neither is there a hint of comment: from Fairbanks Sr's two-reelers to *Fifth Avenue Girl* Hollywood had promulgated a satiric view of the rich, but beyond the bemusement of the reporters there is none here.

Hepburn wanted to stay at M-G-M, and it was Garson Kanin who provided the excuse, having, as he said, 'discovered the formula for a Hepburn success . . . a hoity-toity girl is brought down to earth.' **Woman of the Year** (1942) concerns a woman political pundit and a sports columnist (Spencer Tracy). Kanin was drafted, so handed the idea on to his brother, Michael, whose subsequent screenplay with Ring Lardner Jr won an Oscar. Other civilised talents involved included Joseph Mankiewicz, as producer, and George Stevens, brought in to direct. It is a film which doesn't pall, and in this, the first teaming of the stars, they were never better – she priggish and self-centred, he the rough diamond, practical and tolerant. Married, he moves in: 'I won't be much trouble,' he tells her maid, who agrees: 'Yes, that's what she said.' War-time sentiment dictated the subsequent descent into bathos; the writers should have found something stronger than the words of the wedding service to trigger Hepburn's inevitable act of repentance. That takes the form of a maladroit attempt to prepare breakfast, under Tracy's baleful gaze, and it is one of the classic sequences of screen comedy.

Tracy's progress at M-G-M had been cautious. As the Portuguese fisherman in **Captains Courageous** (1937), after an uncertain start, he takes over the film, giving it a grandeur in the dull middle reaches which reverberates after his death and makes the film oddly touching. Instituted as a result of the success of *Mutiny on the Bounty* (q.v.), Kipling's story offers

Harold Rossen a chance for some fine seascapes and Victor Fleming the opportunity for a robust adventure; with some years lopped off his age, the spoilt brat regenerated by the sea becomes Freddie Bartholomew, and he is finely supported by Melvyn Douglas (as his father), Lionel Barrymore and Mickey Rooney.

For the performance Tracy received a Best Actor Oscar – and the chore of partnering two of the studio's lady stars, Luise Rainer and Joan Crawford, in **Big City** (1937) and **Mannequin** (1938) respectively. The director of both was Borzage, much below the form of an earlier film with Tracy, *Man's Castle* (q.v.). Tracy is a cab driver involved in a taxi war in *Big City*, written by Dore Schary and Hugo Butler, probably after first planning the trailer – a mixture of fisticuffs and Luise 'soffering'. She also does a reprise of her telephone scene from *The Great Ziegfeld*, and since she plays Tracy's immigrant wife he tries to pretend that he is in love with her; in *Mannequin* he tries to persuade us that he is dotty over Miss Crawford. The writers (story by Katherine Brush, screenplay by Lawrence Hazard) aspire to nothing higher than displaying the slender talents of this lady – though there are signs that they also wanted to entertain anyone who might have simply stepped out of the rain: they have given Tracy a good role, but sadly the presence of Tracy in a Crawford film does not guarantee depth or intelligence. To anyone not reared on the Hollywood movie it must be an odd experience to see these two together, both working conscientiously to give some semblance of meaning to the script, he emerging as reasonably real and she as her usual unreal self. He is the shipping magnate who loves her truly; Alan Curtis is the rotter she marries. The title is inaccurate: she starts out as a factory worker (the opening is reminiscent of *Bad Girl*), and subsequently becomes a chorus girl. (Connoisseurs may argue whether this is the first movie appearance of the rose-covered cottage so memorable in *Random Harvest* (q.v.).)

After such films **Boys Town** (1938) seemed fresh, and since M-G-M seldom produced anything with any contemporary significance they made quite a fuss about it. Norman Taurog directed, very

simply, this tribute to one of the country's most admired men, Father Flanagan, who had founded a home for stray boys in Nebraska. In that role Tracy won his second consecutive Oscar, and he uses a sardonic and quietly self-righteous sense of humour on dialogue which must have been difficult to speak. 'How much time I got?' asks a condemned man: 'Eternity begins in forty-five minutes,' says Tracy Flanagan, ineluctably. Such matters inspire him to turn his home over to derelicts and to start saving boys: 'It's worth a shot, isn't it?' Yes: but since the screenplay (by Dore Schary and John Meehan, from a story by Schary and Eleanor Griffin) can think of nothing to say about either Flanagan or Boys Town it offers instead (a) his greatest critic financing his scheme, and (b) the rebellious Whitey (Mickey Rooney) reforming and leading the boys of Boys Town to capture the crooks.

It was singularly popular at Saturday matinees, but the same could not be said

Woman of the Year marked the first appearance together of Katharine Hepburn and Spencer Tracy, whose opposing qualities made them very effective. It was pleasing to learn, years later, that they appreciated these qualities in each other, or at any rate perhaps behaved together in private as on the screen: at any rate their off-screen devotion to each other added another folk-tale to the many that surround Hollywood.

of **Northwest Passage** (1940), which concerns Rogers' Rangers, an expeditionary force attached to the British army (the time is 1759), and their efforts to destroy a band of marauding Indians. They suffer starvation, mosquitoes and sickness; they carry their boats overland and form a human chain to cross a river – and so on. There is only one good actor in the cast – Tracy as Rogers – and even he cannot fill 125 minutes with little to do but look authoritative. Nor is there distinction in King Vidor's direction – a deficiency little helped by his own comment: 'We only filmed the book's first part, which was really a prologue to the main action in Part II. The second part was never made because of the producers' lack of courage. In the first part Rogers was a tremendous hero, but the second part showed his going to pieces, his disintegration, and I guess they feared that audiences of that time wouldn't accept it. Anyway, we kept enlarging the first half so much that it became a full-length picture, and it was always anticipated that I would continue on to the second part.' Jack Conway shot the truncated ending; Laurence Stallings and Talbot Jennings wrote the screenplay, from Kenneth Roberts' best-selling novel. The location shooting, in Technicolor, was a considerable undertaking for the time, and Vidor, in priding himself on the lack of process-shots and backdrops, could only do so by forgetting the back-projections and studio sets.

By this time Tracy was held in the same esteem as Paul Muni at Warners, whose biographical format M-G-M bettered by simultaneously making *two* films on Thomas Edison, **Young Tom Edison** (1940), directed by Norman Taurog, with Mickey Rooney in the title role, and **Edison, the Man**, directed by Clarence Brown, with Tracy struggling to surmount cliché, hagiography and an acreage of face-whiskers. Unlike the Rooney film it was a success, but cynics noted that the Associate Producer was called Orville O. Dull. Tracy otherwise resisted the sort of prestige roles associated with Muni. He even fought against doing **Dr Jekyll and Mr Hyde** (1941), and was mortified when both film and performance were badly received by reviewers, it being axiomatic that remakes were inferior to the earlier versions. That was not in fact

so in this case, and, as directed with astonishing force by Victor Fleming from a screenplay by John Lee Mahin, it is superior both in setting forth Jekyll's theories of moral ambiguity and in its atmosphere. The intimations of sadism and the erotic fantasies during the transformations would have been daring in Hollywood in 1931, when the far less restricted Mamoulian version was made; while this is M-G-M's best London, a place of railings and beckoning steps, vistas of lamplight and damp trees dripping in the fog through which Hyde flashes like a bat. It is not till late in the film that we actually witness the transformation of Jekyll into Hyde, which, as it turns out, is dramatically the right place for it. Except that he does not attempt an English accent, Tracy is perfect: as Jekyll, he has only a demoniac glint and a twist to his mouth; as Hyde, he is all make-up, barnstorming to blazes, which is really the only way to play the part. Ingrid Bergman is inviting enough as the light lady, and forlorn later, if never a Cockney drab. As the ingenue, Lana Turner has to listen to a fellow diner who asks 'Has anyone read that poem by that new chap, Oscar Wilde?' and she deserves no better.

The failure of *Young Tom Edison* gave M-G-M an unpleasant jolt, since at that time Mickey Rooney was, according to American distributors, an even more potent box-office draw than Gable. At first the least of the studio's three boy stars, he soon overtook the other two – Jackie Cooper and Freddie Bartholomew – in popularity. He was top-billed with them in a vehicle for the trio, playing New York schoolmates in **The Devil is a Sissy** (1936), an early example of studio shamelessness, directed by Van Dyke. Rooney's great popularity sprang from the Andy Hardy films and his partnership with Judy Garland, but he also made the best of the several screen versions of **The Adventures of Huckleberry Finn** (1939), directed by the otherwise uninspired Richard Thorpe. Mankiewicz produced, with fine Missouri locations and a likeable cast – Elizabeth Risdon as the widow Douglass, Rex Ingram as the slave Jim and Walter Connolly and William Frawley as the two rogues; the role of Huck fits Rooney like a glove, by turns rebellious, mischievous and enthusiastic.

Rooney also appeared in **Ah, Wilderness** (1935) as the younger son, with Lionel Barrymore and Spring Byington as his parents, Wallace Beery as tippling Uncle Sid and Aline MacMahon as Cousin Lily. The older boy (Eric Linden) returns home drunk, but that would seem to be the only vice around these parts, since his left-wing leanings are merely a reflection of youth's rebelliousness. M-G-M had earlier filmed two of Eugene O'Neill's more sombre plays, so this one was a natural for the studio; Louis B. Mayer loved such subjects, and Clarence Brown proves his skill as a director at this time – as he would illustrate again in **Of Human Hearts** (1938), a less cheerful look, despite the title, at America's past. It is Americana, and it is significant that no other country has a similar word – though doubtless a number of them could produce a similar body of work. The word suggests pride and cosiness, and yet for most of its length the plot here concerns either poverty or ingratitude. Walter Huston is the poor parson and Beulah Bondi his wife, settling on the Ohio River, the views of which recall Silent photography at its peak. James Stewart is the son, forgetful of his mother while at war. By the time Lincoln (John Carradine) reminds him of his filial duty the film has started to fall apart. But then perhaps it was a little too compromised and conventional to begin with.

H. M. Pulham, Esq. (1941) also concerns the American past, but is, in keeping with the changed attitudes of the last two or three years, more nostalgic and consequently not entirely faithful to John P. Marquand's original book, despite its physical presence under the credits, complete with dust jacket 'by the author of "The Late George Apley"'. The earlier book was an anatomy of a man's life, but this is merely an account of a Boston gentleman (Robert Young) forced by family pressures to leave the hurly-burly of a Manhattan advertising office and the girl (Hedy Lamarr) he loves. Bostonian philosophy is expressed rather vaguely by his father (Charles Coburn): 'You get it in a good book. In Scott. In Thackeray. In what I understand of Shakespeare.' As directed by King Vidor the film is better than *Kitty Foyle*, but much inferior to *The Magnificent Ambersons* (q.v.), also manifes-

tations of American interest in its old families.

It is a film to suit M-G-M's changed image; **China Seas** (1935) is more typical of the studio's more raffish reputation while Thalberg was alive. Clark Gable is the captain, hard drinking ashore and at sea given to reminiscing about the rivers of England. 'Limey' he is called by China Doll (Jean Harlow), who has pursued him to this corner of the East. He becomes engaged to a patrician English widow, Sybil (Rosalind Russell), but finds that he would rather wait for China Doll to come out of jail than leave the China seas for Sybil and his beloved English rivers. There is a pirate attack and a mutiny, a subplot about a stolen necklace involving Akim Tamiroff and Ed Brophy, and such ballast as Robert Benchley as a drunk writer, Lewis Stone as a one-time coward, and C. Aubrey Smith as the captain. As the villain Wallace Beery for one does not mug nor is he lovable, while Gable, still boyish, dominates the action and justifies his huge popularity. The director was Tay Garnett and the writers were Kevin McGuinness and Jules Furthman – whose hand we recognise in the rich irrelevancies, including the lady who has 'sailed the China seas for thirty years and never lost a spangle' and the cheery farewell of the maid (Hattie McDaniel): 'Goodbye Miss Dolly. You sho' been mighty good to me even if they does hang you.' *Photoplay* thought the film 'not sufficiently adroit in its handling to make coarseness and brutality even slightly palatable' – the sort of high-handed reaction which prevented this highly enjoyable entertainment from receiving the recognition it deserved.

There were no such reservations about the studio's other lavish sea drama, **Mutiny on the Bounty** (1935), which made a million dollars' profit on an investment of almost two million – the studio's most costly project since *Ben-Hur*; it also won a Best Picture Oscar. There was respectability here – and history, as taken from the popular books by Charles Nordhoff and James Norman Hall. 'It is superlatively thrilling' said *The New York Times*, not without reason, of the adventures of H.M.S. *Bounty* and the clashes between First Mate Fletcher Christian (Gable) and the inhuman Captain Bligh

San Francisco, not without reason, is one of the most self-absorbed of cities, and it relishes the movie which M-G-M made of the famous earthquake and fire of 1906. Still today, in the revival houses, when the organ breaks into the song that Jeanette Macdonald sang in the film, the whole audience joins in without prompting. Clarke Gable and Spencer Tracy spend the last part of the film looking for that lady, and at this point seem to be climbing Twin Peaks, where they will find her comforting the displaced population with a hymn.

(Charles Laughton). But neither the screenplay – by Talbot Jennings, Furthman and Carey Wilson – nor Frank Lloyd's direction can disguise the fact that the tale is anti-climactic. It is not surprising that the inferior remake (q.v.) had difficulty in finding an ending.

Because of that remake the film remained for years as hidden as *China Seas*, but there never was a close season for **San Francisco** (1936), so that Judy Garland could years later bring down the house when she did a take-off of Jeanette MacDonald singing on amidst the ruins. The earthquake sequence is as stunning as the Odessa Steps sequence in *Potemkin*, due to editor Booth and effects man Gillespie, who devised magnetic rods to support the buildings, which fell apart when the current was cut off. The plot, however, does not evoke *Potemkin*, an on-again off-again affair between a saloon owner (Gable) and a singer (MacDonald), which could have been on-again or off-again many more times (or less) without anyone giving a damn, but it swings forward with confidence under Van Dyke's direction. 'Magnificent and vulgar' says a title in the film of the Barbary

Coast, and we may feel the same way, as Gable spars with his dog-collared boyhood buddy (Spencer Tracy) or strides through the ruins, trouser leg coyly ripped, bow tie askew, a smudge of blood on his forehead, looking for Jeanette, who is finally found trilling 'Nearer My God to Thee' as the population resolves to build a new – and greater – San Francisco.

Saratoga (1937) is Harlow's final film with Gable, with a script so complicated that it gives them no chance for their treasurable slanging matches – though by this time the Code was working with a vengeance, forbidding the old sexual tangling. She looks tired; perhaps knowledge of her imminent death cast a pall on the proceedings – she is said to have died suddenly, but in one scene Walter Pidgeon helps her to a cigarette and when three or four fall out he ignores them: the fact that director Conway did not retake it suggests that speed of completion was of the essence. The stand-in who completed her part is so obviously that (back to the camera, hidden by dark glasses or picture hat) that it is difficult to concentrate. The plot, naturally, is about horses, with Gable as a bookmaker with an eye to the main chance. **Parnell** (1937) became famous as Gable's only flop of the period, but it certainly did not deserve the critical lambasting that it received. John M. Stahl directed, from a reasonably accurate and well-constructed screenplay by John Van Druten and S. N. Behrman, based on a recent Broadway play. Since at this time public opinion still held that the private lives of public figures should be above reproach,* the film withholds some important details: but after constantly referring to Parnell as 'the uncrowned king of Ireland' it has him echoing Edward VIII in speaking of 'every man's right to have the woman he loves standing beside him'. The chief weaknesses in the film are its leading players, allowed to be in awe of playing Victorian Britons: Gable lacks his usual fire and Myrna Loy, as Kitty O'Shea, performs in equally restrained and dignified manner.

Another Gable vehicle, **Test Pilot** (1938), was once admired for its aero-

* A number of British politicians resigned after scandalous revelations in the 1960s; in the U.S. in 1980, ten years after the Chappaquiddick affair, Senator Edward Kennedy gained widespread support in his bid for the Presidency.

nautics: in *The Nation* Mark Van Doren confessed that he staggered out of the cinema, unable to persuade himself that some of the aerial sequences were faked: 'there is no use denying it, [this is] a terrifying affair; and since that is what it tried to be it must be acknowledged a success'. Today it is notable for the curious and heated courtship of Loy by Gable, her devotion to him and that of Tracy as his mechanic; the latter's presence and Victor Fleming's direction give it class. 'Entertain me! Thrill me!' says Walter Connolly at the start of **Too Hot to Handle** (1938): he is the boss and Gable a newsreel cameraman – one not averse to faking shots, which is nothing to what Special Effects get up to here. In fact, the fakery is so evident and the climax up the Amazon so far-fetched – even for this sort of tale – that it fails to thrill. But it entertains, as crackingly handled by Conway and played by Gable, Loy and Pidgeon as his rival.

Since Gable spent most of 1939 on loan to Selznick making *Gone with the Wind* (q.v.) it is a pity that his return was marked by **Strange Cargo** (1940), a film which marked his final teaming with Joan Crawford. The producer, Mankiewicz, Frank Borzage and Lawrence Hazard (adapting a novel by Richard Sale) had last worked together on a Crawford vehicle, and that is what this chiefly is, if not typical. The first scene, set on the quayside of Devil's Island, is stupendous: Gable is a convict who dreams of Paris, and Crawford, though referred to as 'one of the girls from the café', a whore from Marseilles; she carries a parasol and has a cigarette hanging from her mouth. Later they are involved in an escape attempt, with Albert Dekker and Paul Lukas – and Ian Hunter, a stranger beatifically smiling among the convicts. For a while it seems that we are watching an adventure story into which someone had the taste – bad or good – to add God; and when we reach a thirty-minute patch in an open boat without drinking-water, it is clear that something is being said about the human condition. There is much talk of death,

Hunter is the Conciliator, and when they die they die happy. As Joan says, 'When it came to their end, they suddenly found *sumthen tuh hang on tuh.*'

In fact, Gable's presence in *Gone with the Wind* seems to have confused M-G-M, for the films he made immediately following it are all poor. He has his Rhett Butler status of entrepreneur in both **Boom Town** (1940) and **Honky Tonk** (1941), plus his old image of ladies' man, a bit of a heel (who'll reform) and a hell-raiser. Rivalry among the oil fields with Tracy makes the former picture bearable for a while, but its sermonising on capitalism – of which it definitely approves, despite the evidence presented therein – is inept; and Hedy Lamarr is tiresome as the industrial spy who tries to win him from Claudette Colbert. *Honky Tonk,* also directed by Conway, has Lana Turner as a sparring sex partner, but she is not even a grade school imitation of Harlow; as the saloon queen who loses him, Claire Trevor is much more his sort of woman – and of course a better actress.

Gable is more his old self in **Comrade X** (1940), directed by King Vidor from a script by Ben Hecht and Charles Lederer and based on an original by Walter Reisch, who had worked on the similar *Ninotchka*. The cracks here are less funny and more vicious – for at this time the U.S.S.R. was fair game (Russia had a non-aggression pact with Germany): 'The problem of taking the masses from boogie-woogie is a difficult one,' says Lamarr as a tram driver, a poor substitute for Garbo. Gable is a fearless American correspondent, involved at one point in a chase more suitable for a comic. Gable took pratfalls; he played con men; he was brusque and short tempered; he lied and cheated; in this film his fedora is seldom worn correctly and his braces dangle from his pants. He was not without vanity, but he was the most human of the great romantic stars – which was something that of those who came after him only Burt Reynolds (q.v.) understood, and Gable, in direct contrast, was far more instinctive.

19

Hollywood's Golden Age:
Columbia and United Artists

COLUMBIA in the Thirties was, as we have seen, mainly notable for the films of Capra, bringing that studio to the point where it joined Universal and United Artists as the lesser of the eight acknowledged majors. Harry Cohn was even more of an opportunist than the other tycoons, and liked to employ waning stars and directors or those in dispute with the other studios, for he was then able to pay them less than their usual salaries. He offered only short commitments, which satisfied both parties. Few either stayed or returned, for Cohn – known as White Fang – was the most foul-mouthed and abusive of the studio dictators, and those who clashed with him did not, if they could help it, do so again. His only important star at this time was Jean Arthur, though both Irene Dunne and Cary Grant signed non-exclusive contracts, the advantage to them being that with less competition they got the pick of the star roles. Columbia did attract a number of leading directors, for the successful ones tended to be the most independently-minded; and they had noted Capra's claim that once he had convinced Cohn that a particular project was the one he wanted to make, and the only one, he was allowed to proceed without interference. And that was rare in Hollywood.

Before Capra's rise to fame one leading director, Howard Hawks, had already tested Cohn's non-intervention, and he was to make three more films for Columbia during the decade. After his success with *The Dawn Patrol* at Warners Cohn invited him to direct **The Criminal Code** (1931), one of the studio's rare attempts then to escape from supporting features; it was also more serious than most Columbia films, but Cohn hoped to emulate M-G-M's success with *Big House*. Based on a Broadway play by Martin Flavin, it concerns a humane prison warden (Walter Huston) and a prisoner (Phillips Holmes) whom he puts on trust. Hawks handles it over-deliberately, and its quality is due mainly to Huston, a little theatrical but as ever confirming Stanislavsky's opinion that he was one of the best living actors.

Hawks's next Columbia film, **Twentieth Century** (1934), belonged with a number of recent plays exposing and exploding the egos of show folk. Himself parodied in 'The Royal Family of Broadway', John Barrymore here parodies Jed Harris, producer of 'The Front Page', the authors of which, Hecht and MacArthur, wrote this screenplay (though using as their source an unproduced play). Barrymore's hamming, for once conscious and therefore enjoyable, is well complemented by Carole Lombard as a bitchy actress whom he discovers and puts into a dreadful Southern play (all dreadful plays in movies are set in the South); the years pass and she has a bad case of her Master's temperament as they squabble on the Twentieth Century Express among a motley group which includes a religious maniac (Etienne Girardot). The introduction of this character is so clumsy as to suggest a new plot starting, and though Hawks juggles his people in and out of staterooms the pacing is frenetic but not assured.

More nonsense has been written about Hawks than any other figure in Hollywood history. At Columbia he made his two best pictures – not because he needed to express some 'Hawksian ethos' but because he had the sort of material to which he could respond. **Only Angels Have Wings** (1939) was written by Jules Furthman and concerns a group of American flyers in a banana republic. They are joined by Jean Arthur – and what would she be doing down there if she wasn't a stranded showgirl? Their boss is Cary Grant – finding new levels of charming boorishness – whose henchmen include Thomas Mitchell, not prepared to acknowledge that his flying days are over, and Richard Barthelmess, more hangdog than ever as a one-time coward hoping for a new break; the latter's wife is Rita Hayworth, a relic of Grant's past and the only anaemic player in the film. It is otherwise a confident piece of film-making; the aerial shots vary, but otherwise the atmosphere is very strong. Hawks has a dangerous control over the witty script, but it is Miss Arthur who lifts it, as the seemingly tough, confident girl who finds that she is neither when she realises that she is carrying a torch for the tough, confident man.

His Girl Friday (1940), Hawks's masterwork, was written by Charles Lederer from 'The Front Page', and evolved from an attempt by Hawks to demonstrate to friends that the play had the best modern dialogue ever written, when, since no actor was available, a girlfriend read the part of Hildy. Thus in the film Hildy has become the ex-wife (Rosalind Russell) of Walter Burns (Grant), who not only wants headlines from her but to have her back in his arms. No lie or trick is too low: Grant offers two dozen expressions and they all mean deceit. The marvellous quality about their playing – and neither was ever more adroit – is her cold-eyed acceptance of his cunning, which in itself amounts to a *rapprochement*. What is also there, whether consciously or not, is the glamour of people like Hildy and Burns: they are one step ahead, the haves – as opposed to the have-nots, such as the stolid fiancé (Ralph Bellamy) and the condemned man; and the other reporters also are absolutely true to that generation of American humorists. The timing throughout – unlike that in *Twentieth Century* – is brilliant.

Superlatives may also be applied to **Man's Castle** (1933), Frank Borzage's first independent production. The pub-

licity stressed its resemblance to *Seventh Heaven,* and love now flowers in a shantytown on the Hudson instead of in a Paris garret. Borzage takes his customary romantic attitude towards life among the down and outs, probably in this case because no other was suitable in view of the Depression: yet when Bill (Spencer Tracy) meets Trina (Loretta Young) starving and contemplating suicide he subtly suggests that for women at least there is an alternative to the river. Tracy's gifts of warmth and caring were never better used, and it is surprising that Cooper, Cagney and Muni were all considered for the role before him. Miss Young never again acted so delicately, and they are beautifully supported by Glenda Farrell, Walter Connolly and Marjorie Rambeau. Jo Swerling wrote the screenplay, from a play by Lawrence Hazard, and its wry/funny dialogue includes the same endearments for the girl as in *Bad Girl,* 'whozis' and 'stoopid'.

Loretta Young and Spencer Tracy in *Man's Castle,* directed by Frank Borzage. 'From these characters and this background the Old Master charms something like beauty and when it is all over and you are out in the street you wonder how he has done it' said *Picturegoer.*

Irene Dunne and Cary Grant in *The Awful Truth*, one of the insouciant screwball comedies of the time. It was in films like this (to take a phrase associated with a later movie, the lugubrious *Love Story* of 1970) that being in love means never having to say you are sorry.

Swerling also wrote **No Greater Glory** (1934) for Borzage, from Ferenc Molnár's 'The Boys of Paul Street', and we may well wish that they had left this 'immortal novel' – as the credits have it – between its covers. This tale of boys engaged in their own messy war games had been filmed in Hungary in 1928 and had a renewed topicality with the Nazis in power and the U.S. apparently terrified of a Communist takeover: hence the strong anti-militarist tone, with its deliberate echo of *All Quiet on the Western Front*. 'A film with a propagandistic flavour,' said *The Times* (London). 'The objections to it are many and obvious, but [it] is a quite magnificent film, sure of its approach' – presumably meaning that it hammers away at the obvious, like many another well-intentioned Hollywood 'message' film basically unsure of its audience. Harry Cohn's objections were many and obvious and when the public apparently agreed with him the film had no prospect of recovering its slight investment – especially as several countries, including France, banned it. Borzage left Columbia in such disgrace that in signing with Warners he had to forfeit the independence he had had for almost a decade.

It was the other way round with Leo McCarey and **The Awful Truth** (1937), remade as a vehicle for Irene Dunne. Arthur Richman's 1922 play had been filmed by P.D.C. in 1925, and then by Pathé in 1929 with its Broadway star, Ina Clair; when Pathé was in turn absorbed by R.K.O. all its story properties were sold to Columbia for a mere $35,000. Capra was at loggerheads with Cohn, who sought out McCarey to prove to Capra that in the matter of comedy Columbia was not dependent on him alone – to the extent that he found himself paying McCarey not the peanuts he expected (because of the failure of *Make Way for Tomorrow*), but $100,000 (as opposed to Miss Dunne's $50,000 and Cary Grant's $40,000). McCarey brought in Vina Delmar to improve Dwight Taylor's existing script; he made the film under budget; and won the 1937 Oscar for Best Direction. The film itself is arguably the supreme example of the 'life is a game' school of comedy. Grant and Dunne are both rich, pampered and handsome; they are also relentlessly facetious, with no objective in life other than to trump the other's ace as they embark upon an improbable divorce. 'You didn't hurt both hands?' she says, only to look disappointed on learning that he had not; or, having expressed regret at picking up the phone – it was his fiancée – doing so again with alacrity and a smile broader than a Cheshire Cat's.

She Married her Boss (1935) is also clever and delightful. The title refers to Claudette Colbert, and her boss is Melvyn Douglas; the marriage she so much desired brings with it, however, his self-dramatising sister (Katherine Alexander) and his spoilt brat of a child (Edith Fellows). Sidney Buchman wrote it, getting his biggest laughs from what is left unsaid – such as non sequiturs and interrupted sentences. The director, Gregory LaCava, responds at such times but loses control whenever Buchman's invention fails him. Buchman is credited on the screenplay of **Holiday** (1938), along with Donald Ogden Stewart, but according to George Cukor, who directed, the latter alone was responsible for this version of Philip Barry's play. Filmed originally by Pathé in 1931 with Ann Harding, the property was another which Columbia purchased in its job lot, and Katharine Hepburn came to the studio because she wanted to make it, bringing her cronies with her. Cary Grant partners her again, and as with *The Philadelphia Story*, which would reteam them with Cukor, the screenplay is as verbose and superficial as the direction is unobtrusively skilful. The subject is the intrusion of a poor man (Grant) as fiancé into a wealthy family and, joined by Jean Dixon and Edward Everett Horton as his bohemian friends, the bemused attitude towards the excesses of the rich is better expressed than in the later film: but in neither do Barry, Cukor or Stewart have anything pointed to say on the subject.

John Ford also made one film for Columbia, **The Whole Town's Talking** (1935), for which the studio borrowed Edward G. Robinson, in a double role as meek clerk and infamous gangster – and as each impersonates the other at various times (and we are never in doubt as to his identity) it calls upon all his ingenuity. The twists outnumber the laughs, and the plotting is so ingenious – screenplay by Swerling, from a novel by W. R. Burnett – that it would be churlish to point out a gaping hole at the climax. A good cast includes Jean Arthur as the girl.

Lewis Milestone's one film for the studio is **The Captain Hates the Sea** (1934), so much like *Transatlantic* as to support the adage that most American films were copies; but in this case the passenger list is more colourful and the director more proficient. It isn't, in fact, the sea that the captain (Walter Connolly) hates, but the passengers: a tippling writer (John Gilbert); an ex-cop turned detective (Victor McLaglen); a nouveau riche lady (Alison Skipworth); an ex-whore (Wynne Gibson), whose husband is paranoic about her past; a South American general (Akim Tamiroff); a lady (Helen Vinson) posing as a Boston librarian; and a number of assorted crooks.

Rosalind Russell and the director Dorothy Arzner arrived at Columbia to make **Craig's Wife** (1936), based on a play by George Kelly which was later remade with Joan Crawford. Its subject is a houseproud wife, and the best of her several moments of comeuppance occurs when the husband (John Boles), finally exasperated, smashes her favourite vase.

In this version it is an act of defiance, and Miss Russell accepts it as such; in the other, it is an act of rebellion, and in one of the best sequences in all Crawfordiana one waits for the lady to descend the stairs and spot the breakage. Cool and unruffled as Russell is, she is not quite as enjoyable as Crawford.

The film has dated less than the once-admired **Golden Boy** (1939), based on Clifford Odets's play – which was, said Brooks Atkinson, 'a metaphor of cultural corruption in a materialistic society'. It was mauled on its way to the screen, but Odets cannot be exonerated, for, though uncredited, he did actually write the film version, according to Rouben Mamoulian, its director. William Saroyan also worked on it at one point, and might thus share the blame for such lines as 'Poppa, you don't understand. I gotta do what I gotta do' and 'I'm good for only one thing – slugging. Slugging my way to the title.' 'Music and fighting don't mix,' says Joe Bonaparte (William Holden), and at the end he faces a future without either, untainted by his contact with the underworld but taking with him the girlfriend (Barbara Stanwyck) of his promoter (Adolph Menjou) – and no one has a tear for *him*. Due partly to Lee J. Cobb's over-the-top performance the scenes of home life are particularly embarrassing.

Incredibly, the plays of Odets and the others presented by the Group Theatre were considered to be too highbrow for cinema audiences, and when Ben Hecht imitated Odets in **Angels Over Broadway** (1940), he diluted his message with Runyon-flavoured whimsy. A clerk (John Qualen) embezzles $3,000 and then decides to commit suicide, so he elects – as we all might – to spend his last hours in a night club where he falls in with a penniless con man (Douglas Fairbanks Jr), an unemployed dancer (Rita Hayworth) and a drunken playwright (Thomas Mitchell). Hecht's ideas of dramatists' dialogue make Odets seem reticent: drunk? – 'an understatement by three bottles and a thousand tears'; his wife? – 'The only place I felt at home was in your heart. You were the only light that didn't go out on me.' Fairbanks tries for an Allen Jenkins accent from time to time, and has one sentimental speech: 'What happened to the Poles, the Finns, the Dutch?

They're little guys. They didn't win,' to which Hayworth replies, 'They will, some day.' Hecht wrote and directed, with Fairbanks as associate producer, and with Lee Garmes again on camera – as in Hecht's earlier ventures with Charles MacArthur: it is also incredible that he was undeterred by neither those nor this, and tried yet again with the even more pretentious *The Specter of the Rose* (1945), a ballet story.

Josef von Sternberg made two films for Columbia, signed at the behest of B. P. Schulberg, who had found a temporary home there after being ousted from Paramount. It was Schulberg who assigned him to **Crime and Punishment** (1935), which had the misfortune to open in most cities just after the French film of the same novel. Graham Greene called it 'this gleaming lunch-bar chromium version' and, warming to his theme, 'vulgar as only the great New World can be vulgar,' but it is not that bad. Its virtues are negative ones: the lack of music, except for an occasional violin; the simple sets (clearly reflecting the budget); and the direct way with the plot – which, though cut to eighty-eight minutes, is still too long. As Raskolnikov the too-old Peter Lorre repeats his performance in *M*; Edward Arnold is no more than capable as the Inspector; and as the whore Marian Marsh seems to have wandered in from a B-Western. There are echoes of von Sternberg's better dramas, but he eschews, alas, chiaroscuro – not that light and shade is the way to interpret Dostoevsky, but darkness can at least evoke gloom and evil, both needed here. Also miscast is Grace Moore as a teenage princess, in **The King Steps Out** (1937): von Sternberg had been invited to embellish her few natural charms when audiences failed to respond to her second Columbia film as they had to her first, *One Night of Love*. Star and director, both noted for their unruly temperaments, worked in mutual antagonism, but despite her performance, which lacks the required daintiness, this is a good example of farce-operetta, with music by Fritz Kreisler – one of several tales of the youth of the Empress Elizabeth, here wooed incognito by Franz Joseph (Franchot Tone). As an apoplectic innkeeper Herman Bing is very funny, and Raymond

Walburn has perhaps the only explicity homosexual line in an American movie in three decades: after telling the ballet girls not to flirt with the soldiers he adds, to the startled ballet master, 'And I trust you won't, either.'

The receipts of neither film endeared von Sternberg to Cohn, and his Hollywood career was almost over, as was that of Schulberg, though the latter produced a handful of films for Paramount and again for Columbia before he also was rejected by the industry. Another former Paramount glory, Frank Lloyd, arrived, having persuaded Cohn that a remake of a famous Silent film, **The Howards of Virginia** (1940), could constitute Columbia's reaffirmation of its faith in democracy – a statement thought necessary in view of the War. Unfortunately Lloyd agreed to direct, proving that *Cavalcade* was long in the past. Adapted from the first part of Elizabeth Page's 'The Tree of Liberty', it starts with Cary Grant as a shabby backwoodsman and never gets more likely – nor does it miss a cliché as it moves him, via the War of Independence, from log cabin to colonial mansion.

The dramatist Robert Sherwood was another who resided temporarily at Columbia, to produce just one film, **Adam Had Four Sons** (1941) – which he had no hand in writing. This is another family saga, indifferently directed by Gregory Ratoff and this time concerning the viper in its bosom. She is the bad girl (Susan Hayward), whom everyone thinks is good, while the good girl (Ingrid Bergman) takes the rap. Being clearly so sensible, Bergman is well cast; beyond the fact that she must be the nicest governess four boys ever had, she has the instinct of her compatriot, Garbo, for the right gesture – as with her hunched-up stance over the banisters during the operation on the mother (Fay Wray). Archer Winston commented in *The New York Times*: 'Miss Bergman is such a wholesome and healthy-looking individual that it seems too much to hope that she could be an actress of taste and sensitivity also. But that is what she establishes . . . beyond any question.' This was the second American film of the Swedish-born Bergman (b. 1915), and with the acquisition of this refreshingly natural actress Hollywood reached a milestone in its progress to maturity. She was not under contract to Columbia, and it was a star at the other end of the scale, Rita Hayworth (q.v.), who would help Cohn complete the transformation of Columbia into a major studio.

At United Artists Chaplin was the only founder member still active, and the gestation period of his films had increased to almost five years. **Modern Times** (1936) was over a year on the studio floor, and the final budget reached $1½ million. Though it was patently derived from *A Nous la Liberté*, Chaplin claimed at the time 'an impulse to say something about the way life is being standardised and channelised, and men turned into machines', while in his autobiography he takes pains to claim credit for his 'original idea'. Critics pointed out the resemblances to Clair's film, but few dreamed of finding fault, and the Tramp's adventures with the automatic feeding machine and the conveyor belt were considered satiric rather than anti-capitalist. The film's original introduction, an equation of 'humanity' with a flock of sheep, was revealingly removed by Chaplin from the reissue prints; and since the film is no longer either pointed or funny it is fortunate in having a sustaining element in the relationship of the Tramp and the gamin, played by Paulette Goddard, with whom Chaplin was at that time living and had supposedly married. In the film she is a minor, and if they behave as man and wife there is nothing to which the Hays Office might have taken offence: it is possible that the relationship is a kind of autobiographical comment on Chaplin's sexuality (not unknown to the public, after the revelations of his first two wives) – though it is certain that the sentimental aspect of two derelicts protecting each other also appealed to him. At one point they are sitting on a grass verge in a cosy suburb when a policeman moves them on – the poor never win; yet the triteness of this is counterbalanced by the fact that till he meets the girl his dearest wish is to return to prison, where the police keep him well fed and comfortable. His ambivalent attitude towards the rich is extended to Authority, and it is a strength which helps the film survive – plus the Tramp's beautiful movements, skilfully choreographed from the tip of his hat to the open ends of his boots.

As Thornton Delehanty said in *The New York Post*, there was no doubt that the film was 'the season's motion picture event' – but that was as nothing to the advent of **The Great Dictator** (1940): 'No event in the history of the screen has ever been anticipated with more hopeful excitement,' wrote Bosley Crowther in *The New York Times*. 'No picture ever made has promised more momentous consequences.' Not only was Chaplin to *speak* on the screen for the first time (*Modern Times* had one gibberish song among the music and sound effects) but he had taken on no less an adversary than Hitler. In a dual role, he plays a Jewish barber, a man very like the Tramp, and Adenoid Hynkel, dictator of Tomania – a vain little man, given to protocol, vainglory, ranting and bluster; he has an aide, Garbage (Henry Daniell), and a fellow dictator, Benzino Napaloni (Jack Oakie) who, like him, is planning to invade Osterlich. When he finally does so the Jewish barber is mistaken for him: forced to make a speech, he makes a plea for freedom and an end to tyranny. That speech was Chaplin speaking to the world, and it was the object of much admiration: it is long but patently sincere – which is its justification. Chaplin had been told so often that he spoke for all mankind: one cannot decry him for taking this opportunity to prove it. The film is today often poorly received, since its attempts at both sentiment and humour are grotesquely over-contrived; but at the time Chaplin's courage in offering a political tract in comic strip form only confirmed his supposed genius.

Of the other original United Artists, Mary Pickford did emerge from semi-retirement to produce two films for a company she formed with Jesse L. Lasky, but neither was successful. Her relative inactivity and that of Chaplin left them free to interfere with board decisions, and the comings and goings at United Artists – beyond the major suppliers, Korda, Goldwyn and Selznick – were as frequent with this company as at R.K.O. and Columbia. Among the motley crew welcomed was Arnold Pressburger, an emigré attempting a foothold in Hollywood and bringing a fresh eye to bear on

Fredric March, Margaret Sullavan and Glenn Ford in *So Ends Our Night* (1940), directed by John Cromwell for producers David L. Loew and Albert Lewin, and released by United Artists. Based on a novel by Erich Maria Remarque, the film gets as close as Hollywood dared to the situation in Europe, following a group of people hounded from their native land because their race, religion or creed did not suit Hitler. The script uses the word 'Jew' instead of the expression 'non-Aryan', which Hollywood preferred when dealing with this subject. When Ford says, 'Let's drink to the beauty of the world, we have a right to that,' Sullavan replies, 'We have no rights to anything, we are refugees.' And there is a moving gesture a moment later, when a stranger offers them a cake because he hates what is happening in his country.

The Shanghai Gesture (1941). The source was a play by John Colton, a specialist in the exotic (he had dramatised 'Rain'), and in the sixteen years since its Broadway presentation it was reputed to have been turned down by the Hays Office thirty-two times, in as many adaptations. The setting of the original was the Shanghai brothel of Mother Goddam, whose main attraction is her half-caste, drug-addicted daughter Poppy. As adapted by the director, Josef von Sternberg, and his collaborators, this has become the gambling den of Mother Gin Sling (Ona Munson), among whose thrill-seeking clientele is Victoria (Gene Tierney), who finds 'it has a ghastly familiarity, like a half-remembered dream'. She is really Poppy, and she makes a play for her mother's lover (Victor Mature) by quoting 'Omar Khayyam' at him, to which he responds with the information that he was born under a full moon near the sands of Damascus. Every character is either corrupt or equivocal, and the best of them is Walter Huston, in the impossible role of the girl's English father. It was not, with reason, a film that appealed to either the industry or the public, and since that was increasingly true of von Sternberg's films Hollywood producers were no longer prepared to countenance his arrogance. An exception was Howard Hughes (q.v.), and von Sternberg did contribute to other people's

films without credit till **The Saga of Anatahan** (1952), which he wrote, produced, directed and photographed in Japan: its failure was complete, and his later involvement with film was confined to teaching the subject in California.

Another Silent veteran berthed briefly at U.A. was Ernst Lubitsch, who remade his own 1925 *Kiss Me Again* as **That Uncertain Feeling** (1941), with a script by Donald Ogden Stewart, who had thought of nothing to help this tired tale of a wife (Merle Oberon) who leaves her husband (Melvyn Douglas) for an egotistic musician (Burgess Meredith). Of the principals, only Douglas has the required style. Korda was to an extent involved in the production, as he was married to Miss Oberon and was establishing himself as an American supplier to U.A. He and Lubitsch co-produced *To Be or Not To Be* (q.v.) before the latter moved on to 20th Century-Fox, and meanwhile he designed **Lydia** (1941) primarily as a vehicle for Oberon. The director was Julien Duvivier, exiled from France because of the War, and though its inspiration was clearly his *Carnet de Bal* the only points in common are a ball in the past and a woman who recalls old lovers: instead of visiting them she dreams of youthful romances in flashback.

Another veteran producer, Edward Small, made some uneven films for U.A., but there is some merit in his four versions of Dumas. **The Count of Monte Cristo** (1934), was directed by Rowland V. Lee and has a cheering performance by Robert Donat in the title role. **The Man in the Iron Mask** (1939) suffers from Louis Hayward's colourless performance in the lead and from James Whale's faltering handling, but the combination of Lee and Hayward is pleasing in **Son of Monte Cristo** (1940): as ersatz Dumas, its plot resembling the current crop of European resistance movies, it has no right to be the most successful of the three movies. Small persuaded Douglas Fairbanks Jr to finally take on the mantle of his father in **The Corsican Brothers** (1941), and in his first full-blooded swashbuckling role the actor proves himself a true heir, handsome and dashing; but Gregory Ratoff, directing, is less at home than Lee with the conventions of the genre.

Yet another Silent veteran, Hal Roach,

eventually arrived at United Artists, but since he kept autonomy during the years in which M-G-M in fact distributed his product it is not unreasonable to consider him with these other independents. Roach was not the only producer to try to keep alive the spirit of Silent comedy, but he was the most successful, turning out two-reelers with, among others, Charley Chase, 'Our Gang' (a group of children) and Laurel and Hardy. Stan Laurel (1890–1965) was born in Lancashire and gravitated to films via the British music hall and American vaudeville. Oliver Hardy (1892-1957) was born in Georgia and had started in films as a bit player before his bulk typed him as a villain – it being the fashion for fat men to be the butts in the comedies which he mostly made. They were both under contract to Roach and had appeared together before *Putting Pants on Philip* (1927) teamed them for the first time. Their Silent shorts contain their most brilliant work; speech slowed them up, and the years took toll of their inspiration, which was mainly that of Laurel, the creative partner. Their early shorts are variable, but **Laughing Gravy** (1931) triumphantly supports the view that they were great screen comics. James V. Horne directed these misadventures set in a grim boarding house and their private world was never better exemplified as they try to protect their beloved mutt from a weasely, hard-hearted landlord. No matter how much Stan's woolliness infuriates Ollie or how much they bicker and fight, at times of crisis their delight in each other is a stirring thing. They were seldom more in accord than in that orgy of suburban destruction, **Big Business** (1929), while Ollie's exasperation with Stan is best sampled as they manoeuvre a piano up a vast flight of stairs in **The Music Box** (1932).

Pardon Us (1931), directed by James Parrott, was one of their spoofs on other movies, in this case *Big House*, whose set was still standing on the M-G-M lot. In return, Metro demanded a feature, so a compromise length was reached of fifty-five minutes. Their second full-length film, **Sons of the Desert** (1934), is better sustained as directed by William A. Seiter. Adapted from one of their Silent shorts, *We Faw Down* (in itself a remake of an earlier Roach short, *Ambrose's First False-*

hood), it has them living it up at a masonic convention, on the lam from their wives – and when they are married, the ladies concerned make the spouses of W. C. Fields seem like angels of sweetness and light. **Bonnie Scotland** (1935) does begin in that country, but as a take-off on *Lives of a Bengal Lancer* most of it is set on the North-West Frontier: hardly more organised than *Pardon Us*, it should be seen for their dance to 'A Hundred Pipers', which is touching, graceful, inventive, absurd and marvellous. The best thing in **Way Out West** (1937), also directed by Horne, is their soft-shoe shuffle to 'The Trail of the Lonesome Pine'. They were comic relief in a number of feeble operettas, the best of which is **Swiss Miss** (1938), in which they are mousetrap salesmen; the same director, John G. Blystone, also made the most integrated of their features, **Blockheads** (1938). Borrowing from several of their early shorts (and those of Harry Langdon, who worked on the script), it makes them old war buddies, reunited – too late, for Ollie has just married Minna Gombell, his 'dove' and 'cooey lamb', nice enough but suspicious. 'How often have I told you not to bring your tramp friends around here?' she asks, to which he replies 'But Toots – Stan is different.' Of course: how could she have understood their special relationship?

That was their last picture for Roach

Laurel and Hardy in *Laughing Gravy*, a two-reeler which alone would justify their immortality. The dog in Stan's arms provides the title, for that is his name – and it is the sort of whimsical touch with which their best films are studded.

Constance Bennett with Alan Mowbray in *Merrily We Live*, one of the many comedies of the time dealing with crazy families. They were invariably wealthy, and audiences were doubtless greatly relieved to find the rich viewed as completely irresponsible.

and M-G-M. Laurel had been increasingly unhappy, demanding more creative control (to placate him, some of the later features were labelled 'A Stan Laurel Production'); but after **Flying Deuces** (1939) for Boris Morros, released through R.K.O., they returned to Roach – now releasing through United Artists – for two further features. When they could not get backing for an independent feature they signed contracts with M-G-M and 20th Century-Fox – but were allowed no creative say in the eight remaining American films they made. Their personal relationship was always cordial, but in the Roach days there had been the possibility of a split. In that eventuality Langdon was cited to take Laurel's place, and Roach did team him and Hardy in **Zenobia** (1939), the latter as a kindly doctor who unties a knot in an elephant's tail and is therefore sued by Langdon for alienation of affection – a promising idea suffering from a lame script and poor production values; Gordon Douglas directed.

Roach's cavalier approach to production values was less apparent in his first feature without Laurel and Hardy; but because two leading stars were involved M-G-M was more concerned with **Topper** (1939) than with most Roach products. Its source was a novel by Thorne Smith, and its subject ghosts – as impersonated by Cary Grant and Constance Bennett, materialising to the embarrassment of the Toppers (Miss Burke, Roland

Young). Comic ghosts appealed to Roach, while the racy tone of Smith's humorous novel had caused other producers to neglect it. Unfortunately the adapters found nothing to substitute for the raciness, nor do they explore the potential of the situation. However, it is funnier than **Topper Takes a Trip** (1938), which lacks more than Mr Grant. Both films were directed by an old comedy hand from Paramount, Norman Z. McLeod, but **Topper Returns** (1941) was done by Roy del Ruth. Miss Bennett was gone – replaced by Joan Blondell – and so had the spirit of Thorne Smith: it is another 'old dark house' comedy-thriller in the manner of *The Cat and the Canary* – and as such, not unsuccessful. McLeod also directed **Merrily We Live** (1938), and that has affinities to *My Man Godfrey*, with another scatty woman (Billie Burke) trying to help the down and outs by making one of them (Brian Aherne) her chauffeur. He tames her temperamental daughter (Miss Bennett), and turns out to be a novelist. The film, though not one of the half dozen best screwball comedies, has foolishness and fun.

Foolishness is all with **One Million B.C.** (1940): the idea of making a serious film set in pre-history was then so outlandish that it could only have come from a former gag-writer like Roach (who had employed D. W. Griffith at the planning stage, till they quarrelled). There is a background of Montague and Capulet-like warring tribes – with Victor Mature and Carole Landis as the lovers – and to sustain interest the dinosaurs are wheeled on: the special effects man was king, but his effects, if numerous, are derisory.

Roach produced one excellent serious picture, **Of Mice and Men** (1939), but only in lieu of paying damages to Lewis Milestone, who had successfully sued him over a contract. Like many other people, Milestone had been impressed by John Steinbeck's novella and the Broadway play made from it; the screenplay – credited to Eugene Solow, though Milestone claimed it as his own work – is remarkably faithful, beginning in gloom and foreboding and then courting tragedy as it studies some itinerant farmworkers during the Depression. Within the dual themes of the deeply loyal friendship between the simple-minded Lennie (Lon

Chaney Jr) and bright-as-a-button George (Burgess Meredith), and the relationship between the boss's son and his bored wife (Betty Field), there is an honest portrait of life down on the farm: the camaraderie in the bunkhouse; the gossip in the washroom; the silent, vast meals; the beer-swilling Saturday night hops in town. Lonely old men spend their affection on dogs, and the crippled, bespectacled Negro (Leigh Whipper) long ago became accustomed to being denied the bunkhouse. Milestone's love of the piece is apparent and it is his best film after *All Quiet on the Western Front*. Meredith and Chaney never had better roles, and Miss Field is the definitive floozie – not loose, just bored and empty-headed, courting disaster by hanging round the men.

Of the other independents Walter Wanger (1894–1968) was reputedly the best-liked and best-read of Hollywood executives, and one of the few of his generation with a college background; he gained theatre experience with, among others, Harley Granville-Barker. Jesse Lasky brought him to Paramount in 1929 in charge of production, and after brief spells at Columbia and M-G-M he returned to that company, which at that time was so desperate for producer talent that they acceded to his terms – to work within the company as an independent. The first of the ten contracted films was **The President Vanishes** (1934) which, despite its source in a Rex Stout story, is less a thriller than an attack on fascism, profiteering and war-mongering as directed by William Wellman. A President does vanish, rather than be drawn into a European war. However, we suspect the complicity of the Greyshirts, and it is they who provide the chief interest, along with their crazed leader (Edward Ellis), who was prophetically christened Lincoln (George Lincoln Rockwell would be the American Nazi party leader in the Fifties). But the film is far from its prototype, *Gabriel Over the White House*, as a political statement.

Wanger invited LaCava, his director on that film, to rejoin him for **Private Worlds** (1935), one of the few serious movies of the time to lose little over the years, even if Claudette Colbert is described as 'one of the finest doctors in the country'. Written by Lynn Starling and LaCava, from a novel by Phyllis Bottome, it does not shrink from the details of life in a psychiatric clinic – and if these now seem mild none is notably dishonest. A later film on the same subject, *The Cobweb* (q.v.), goes further in suggesting that the staff are as dotty as their patients, but their problems engage us: for Colbert, it is frigidity and overwork; for Charles Boyer, the new head, prejudice against women in medical work and how to cope with his neurotic sister; and for Joan Bennett, her own inadequacy in relation to her husband (Joel McCrea).

When United Artists decided that it needed product an offer was made to Wanger, recognised as one of the best 'quality' producers; as an incentive he was promised larger budgets and complete autonomy unless he wanted to spend over $750,000. His first film for the company was **You Only Live Once** (1937), and he offered the direction to Fritz Lang – an obvious contender, since *Fury*, for another 'social protest' movie. Its stance is simple: ex-convicts have the dice loaded against them. It has been suggested in recent years that the film is a version of the Clyde Barrow-Bonnie Parker saga, but there are only fleeting resemblances – at the end, when Jo (Sylvia Sidney) and Eddie (Henry Fonda) are fugitives, living in a motor car. Lang does not substantiate Eddie's claim of innocence, but the film does demand our sympathy – puzzlingly so, for surely the Hays Office would not have allowed the sentimentalisation of a couple of killers? The film is clearer in its portrait of a society which cannot forget or forgive, even if it allows us only two incidents of prejudice. Fonda's performance is no help in clarifying the intentions of its makers – intense and passionate, but hardly suggestive of a criminal mentality. Thus the film works best as a tragic love story, at what Lang called the theme running through all his work – 'this fight against destiny, against fate'. His direction has moments of Germanic showiness (prison bars and their shadows; swirling fog for the confrontation with the padre) not inappropriate to the preposterous material. Yet Lang's view of the U.S. is mordant, and in a sense he made the only real Depression films: in them, the country is like a soft-centred chocolate which, when bitten into, turns out to be rock hard and sour. America did not like this view of itself for, despite glowing notices, the film was a commercial failure.

History Is Made at Night (1937) is the quintessential Thirties movie, with its dotty title, which Publicity ensured was equated with the *Titanic* disaster: spectators not drawn to it would surely have been converted by the shipwreck footage in the trailer for forthcoming attractions. Then there are Jean Arthur and Charles Boyer, in evening dress throughout, though in his case the wayward plot has him posing as a head waiter. Since neither was ever better, and since Frank Borzage achieves a unifying romantic mood in episodes melodramatic or facetious, the story does not matter. The cinema has become more realistic in the intervening years, but posterity may prefer lovely confections like this to the entertainments currently offered. The writers were Gene Towne and Graham Baker, also responsible for *You Only Live Once*; they also wrote **Stand-In** (1937), from a story by Clarence Budington Kelland, and Tay Garnett directed. 'Howling laugh-material for the movie colony's selected few,' said *Photoplay*, 'But will probably mean little to the average audience.' Audiences seeing it today, clued in on Hollywood, greet it with roars of approval – but then *Photoplay* found Leslie Howard 'never so colourless': I think him brilliant here, as a wizard accountant sent out to save (or sell) an ailing Hollywood studio. His unexpected aides are a confident stand-in (Joan Blondell) and an alcoholic director (Humphrey Bogart); the latter's 'In Hollywood, when you turn the other cheek, they kick it' is virtually the only critical line, for the humour is affectionate, deriving from three main sources: Howard's ignorance of movies, Blondell's worldliness ('Life has only one great moment left for me – when they make Shirley Temple president of a bank'), and the pretensions of the star, Cherie ('Why, even I was a cigarette girl in a night club in Dallas – would you believe that?).

Blockade (1938) is a story 'of adventure and love' says a foreword, 'not intended to treat with or take sides in the conflict of ideas' – for its subject is the Spanish Civil War. And these words were added by Wanger to answer criticism that the film trivialises that war. This paltry account of spies and counterspies was ineptly written by John Howard Lawson (later blacklisted), and directed similarly by William Dieterle – though he gets a half-decent performance from Madeleine Carroll as a White Russian. Henry Fonda almost convinces one that he's the one Spanish farmer able to quote Byron. Deliberately more escapist is **Algiers** (1938), the first important American remake of a renowned European film of the Talkie period, causing much less outcry and derision than later examples – partly because Wanger bought the U.S. rights to Duvivier's *Pépé le Moko*, so comparisons could not be made (it was not shown in the U.S. till 1941). John Cromwell, directing, insisted that the original could not be improved, and settled for a carbon copy: footage of the Casbah was freely borrowed, and a new one was built on the Goldwyn lot. The casting was as close as could be with, for instance, the police informer (Charpin) played by an equally roly-poly actor (Gene Lockhart). The intensity of Boyer and the beauty of Hedy Lamarr make the love scenes agreeably exaggerated: she is exactly right, even if, as Cromwell maintained, she was no actress (the performance was apparently put together in the cutting room). Lawson wrote the screenplay, and James Wong Howe photographed; the final effect is mechanical and, like most copies, disjointed.

Slightly Honorable (1940) was an attempt to add a serious note to a whacky murder mystery in the shape of corrupt senators and a war-trained killer, but director Tay Garnett is at a loss with the shifts in the material. **Sundown** (1941) is marvellous hokum, a horse opera set in Kenya, where George Sanders tangles with native Gene Tierney and dies for King and Country, and with an epilogue in a bombed London cathedral. Henry Hathaway directed, emphasising the absurdity of the dialogue. The film was financially very successful, but was released after Wanger had left United Artists following long battles with the board over money. His early films for the company had been deemed too costly, and certainly there were large losses on the Technicolored *Vogues of 1938* – though these were more than made up for by the significant earnings of *Trade Winds,*

Algiers and *Stagecoach*. His next few films were unsuccessful or, like *The Long Voyage Home* and *Foreign Correspondent* (q.v.), slow to turn a profit. The company declared Wanger $300,000 in debt to it, while he himself reckoned that at least $1 million due to him was frozen abroad because of wartime currency restrictions. Finally the board purchased his unit for $100,000, eventually making good profits on his more recent films. He was permitted to take with him the pre-production plans for *Eagle Squadron*, which the company did not wish to make, and the screenplay of *Arabian Nights* (q.v.). Both films were undistinguished but profitable, which may explain why less than a handful of Wanger's subsequent films are of interest.

In the quarrels between Samuel Goldwyn and United Artists the dissatisfaction was mainly on the part of the producer. In 1937 he and Korda, whom he considered the only other producer contributing to the company's profits, were thwarted of buying out the interests of the founders. Goldwyn subsequently charged the new president, Maurice Silverstein, with sanctioning too many poor pictures, thereby damaging the prestige of his own and defeating the very purpose of the company as originally defined. Those who worked for him have assured us that he wanted only the best; but he was said by others to have been vain, vindictive, publicity-seeking, devious, arbitrary, petty and tyrannical. He once told Garson Kanin: 'Directors are a dime a dozen. You know how many directors are in Hollywood? And most of them looking for work. But executives, producers – real producers, not these jerks [who] call themselves producers . . . Don't you see that when you're a producer, you *hire* directors. Producers hire directors, and sometimes they *fire* directors. Did you ever hear of a director hiring a producer? Did you ever hear of a director *firing* a producer?' In 1935 he hired a director, William Wyler, whose eight films for him are virtually the only Goldwyn products worth serious consideration. After the critical success of the earliest of them Wyler was allowed almost complete autonomy – which included the producer's absence from the set during shooting. Goldwyn recognised

Wyler's standing with the critics and hence assigned him to his more important projects – Wyler's first three films for him were based on much-admired Broadway plays – though his acumen in acquiring properties was due less to an understanding of them than his ability to keep his ear to the ground. His male stars (Colman, Cooper, Cantor) were all proven successes, while his female stars (Sten, Hopkins, Oberon, Virginia Mayo) do not inspire confidence in his judgement. Leaving aside the Wyler films, it is clear that his own taste ran to Americana or grandiose projects like **The Goldwyn Follies** (1938), in fact planned since Ziegfeld's death, and an attempt to establish himself as the movie equivalent. George Marshall directed Ben Hecht's witless script, set in a film studio, and the jumble of artists on display, presumably reflecting Goldwyn's own taste, include the Ritz Brothers, Edgar Bergen, Kenny Baker and Vera Zorina – whose 'classical' ballets, choreographed by her then-husband, George Balanchine, are at best embarrassing. George Gershwin contributed the score, unfinished when he died, and one of its best songs, 'I Was Doing All Right', is relegated to the equivalent of a bit role.

The Adventures of Marco Polo (1938) was originally the idea of Douglas Fairbanks, planning a lighthearted film on the famous traveller. Unfortunately Goldwyn commissioned a script from Robert E. Sherwood, who had no gift for the form required. John Cromwell directed for one week, and Wyler refused to take over after reading the script and seeing the rushes: Archie Mayo finally directed, dully, and Gary Cooper is Polo. When Goldwyn found that Oberon was not succeeding with the American public and wanted to find a vehicle for her to be teamed with Cooper, Leo McCarey cynically rehashed 'The Taming of the Shrew' and sold it to him for $50,000: and twenty-seven writers in all worked on **The Cowboy and the Lady** (1938), including Robert Ardrey, Frederick Lonsdale, Robert Riskin and Dorothy Parker. McCarey had refused to direct and Wyler, who unenthusiastically began it, was replaced by H. C. Potter – himself replaced (since he had another assignment) by Stuart Heisler, at that time an editor. Both films are amongst the worst that Cooper ever made.

487

Barbary Coast (1935) and **Come and Get It** (1936) are better, and typical Goldwyn concepts, tying flimsy stories to re-creations of America's past. The former was turned into a screenplay, for a daunting sum, by Hecht and MacArthur, and is about a saloon queen (Miss Hopkins), her boss-man lover (Edward G. Robinson), and an idealistic young prospector (Joel McCrea). The second film was in fact adapted from a novel by Edna Ferber by Jane Murfin and Jules Furthman, a story of Wisconsin timber men set over two generations: an ambitions foreman (Edward Arnold) lets go the girl (Frances Farmer) he loves, only to fall much later for her daughter (also Miss Farmer). In both there is compensation in the mise-en-scene of Howard Hawks, notably his Barbary Coast, a city of permanent mists, gaslight gleaming malignly and the hulls of ships looming threateningly above scurrying figures. *Come and Get It* is credited to both Hawks and Wyler, after Hawks was forced off the set, because Goldwyn, who had been in hospital, objected to what he had shot – on the principle, apparently, that he had rewritten some scenes and was not an accredited writer. Wyler – who was working on *Dodsworth* (q.v.) – resisted the assignment, but there was nothing in his contract to protect him. He did not consider it one of his films, and observed that the first half hour – all Hawks – is the best of it, citing also the superb logging sequence directed by Richard Rosson.

Wyler's films for Goldwyn, along with the Capra movies, were regarded as the summit of Hollywood achievement in their time; and though their seriousness now seldom seems justified, his fastidious and instinctive direction remains a pleasure. Any individual scene is correct as to tempo, imagery and intensity, slotting easily between those preceding and following it. Like Cukor and George Stevens, his art lies in his response to his material rather than any insistence on individual themes or idiosyncrasies, and, indeed, his chief pleasure was to tackle something he had not done before. As with most people in the industry at that time, he believed the material the most important element in the constitution of any movie. Since, therefore, his own personality cannot be found in his films, they

have been decried, and it has been claimed that he was immeasurably aided by Gregg Toland (1904-48); but Toland's photography varied, and was always at its best under the stronger directors. He was expected to contribute as much to the end result as the cast, and it is significant that both photography and playing are of high standard with Wyler, Stevens, Cukor, Fleming and Capra, while they are variable with Borzage, LaCava, McCarey, Vidor, Ford and Hawks, who were less interested in psychological detail (as rendered by players or visuals) than in mood and pacing. All had in mind the same result: to take the audience into the heart of the matter, and send them out content.

Wyler's first film for Goldwyn was **These Three** (1936), adapted by Lillian Hellman from her own Broadway play, 'The Children's Hour' – and bought by Goldwyn, reputedly, not recognising nor understanding the subject of lesbianism. But since its real subject is scandal and the havoc created by the lies of a vindictive child it was easy enough for the screenwriters to change the accusations to heterosexual fornication – though robbing the piece of some of its force, it being unthinkable that a child could have imagined her teachers locked in embrace. In the film the child (Bonita Granville) accuses one teacher (Hopkins) of having an affair with the fiancé (Joel McCrea) of the other (Oberon). The Hays Office had no intention of passing the play for the screen, and it is doubtful whether exhibitors or audiences would have tolerated it. 'I have seldom been so moved by any fictional film,' wrote Graham Greene. 'After ten minutes of the usual screen sentiment, quaintness and exaggeration, one began to watch with incredulous pleasure nothing less than a life: a genuine situation, a moral realism.' I cannot imagine anyone today being moved by this transference to the screen of a well-made play, which continues to bury its situation in sentiment and exaggeration. Wyler removed that when he remade it, with the original title (q.v.), but with that Hollywood scaffolding gone all credibility went too, revealing the piece as soap opera with pretensions to tragedy.

Goldwyn's reputation rests more firmly on **Dodsworth** (1936), though he had shown no interest in Sinclair Lewis's novel till Sidney Howard's dramatisation had been successful in New York. Sam and Fran Dodsworth are wealthy products of the mid-West who find their marriage falling apart during their first trip to Europe. His complacency receives a jolt, but his common sense and receptivity see him through. Fran, however, her ambitions hitherto stifled by the ethics of the country club set, finds herself so enchanted by what she conceives to be continental sophistication that she loses Sam to another woman. Movie audiences had not been asked to contemplate the prospect of middle-aged people finding each other attractive since the days of the deMille comedies, and this film was far from lighthearted: indeed the bedtime row while husband and wife undress may be the only time a man in his garters has been used for drama instead of farce. Wyler, afraid perhaps that audiences would not be interested in such material, takes it at a speed of knots, so that today it seems melodramatic, sustained for a while only by Walter Huston's portrait of Sam, a friendly, uncomplicated man, alternately exasperated and amused by Fran's surrender to all things European. Ruth Chatterton surprisingly fails to give Fran dimension, and she emerges as a conventional villainess, while Mary Astor as Sam's comforter looks wistful or understanding on cue. However, the material eventually rises to Huston's level, and this remains one of the most entertaining dramas of the period.

On the other hand, **Dead End** (1937) has dated as badly as all the other sociological studies which arrived in Hollywood via Broadway. Since the film was crusading in purpose – with every one of the $140,000 that Goldwyn had paid for the rights – it was safe for *The New York Post* to editorialise, informing Congress that it should have been shown to the committee that crippled the Wagner Housing Act. Critics praised, and Miss Hellman's screen play misses none of the excitement which had endeared Sidney Kingsley's play to theatregoers. It might be more acceptable had Wyler been allowed to film on location, as he had wanted, but Richard Day's famous set remains an emotion in itself, portraying that part of Manhatten where the apartments of the wealthy look down upon the deprived. A would-be architect (Joel McCrea) takes many words to realise that he loves not the rich girl but Drina (Sylvia Sidney) from his own block; she is footsore from picketing, and it is typical of the film's approach that we know not why. Babyface Martin (Humphrey Bogart) is a Dead End Kid gone wrong, and his girl (Claire Trevor) has become a lady of the streets (in the original she also had syphilis). 'What chance have they got against all this?' says McCrea of the kids, but unlike the more romantic *Man's Castle* the film finally tells us nothing about the Depression.

It was because of Miss Sidney that Wyler directed a film of Emily Brontë's masterpiece, **Wuthering Heights** (1939). Wagner had planned a version for her and Charles Boyer (both of whom knew they were wrong for the roles), and had commissioned a screenplay from Hecht and MacArthur – which he was not sorry to sell, at Wyler's insistence, to Goldwyn. Although the latter was to claim it his favourite film he would not let work proceed till persuaded that it was an ideal vehicle for Merle Oberon. The resulting film uses only the first half of the book, omitting the vengeance worked out on a second generation. There is something of Heathcliff in every wild-spirited romantic hero created since then, but the original is a complex man – finally motivated by a dual emotion, consuming love for Cathy and deep hatred for Hindley. Laurence Olivier manages both emotions effortlessly, though without touching on one whole side of Heathcliff, that coal-black, earthy, surly, dangerous eagle spirit. He attempts at the outset a touch of Mummerset; as the gentleman Heathcliff, he speaks with an Old Vic accent, if softly – but was even then an actor of such persuasion that a frown suggested self-torture and a sardonic smile a bent for physical cruelty. Wyler had continually to hold him in check; had he not, Miss Oberon would have been swept away. Her declaration, 'I *am* Heathcliff,' is done with all the elocuted passion of a deb on her first day at finishing school. The lack of the Yorkshire Moors is almost as detrimental, but Wyler and Toland cleverly use the California mock-up. It is a measure of the film's success that a British

Geraldine Fitzgerald and Laurence Olivier in William Wyler's *Wuthering Heights*. Olivier himself has said that the only thing that stands up is the Isabella of Miss Fitzgerald – no one could say it of Merle Oberon's Cathy – but the whole is watchable and intermittently powerful.

version, made in 1972 *in situ*, in colour and with the right accents, neither challenged this nor made a dent in the cinema consciousness.

Wyler had begun as a director of Westerns, and the successful resurrection of the genre caused him to go back to his roots – plus the fact that **The Westerner** (1940) was a suitable vehicle for Gary Cooper, playing a stranger 'from nowhere in particular' bound for 'nowhere special'. He meets a rascally self-appointed judge (Walter Brennan), and their confrontation, mutually wary, suspicious and respectful, is a classic Western situation. The judge is a historical character of little note called Roy Bean, later impersonated by Paul Newman (q.v.): both films dwell on his passion for Lily Langtry and his arbitrary manner of justice, and this one, essentially more serious, is also funnier – but the story (by Stuart N. Lake, written for the screen by Jo Swerling and Abe Burrows) is weak enough to suggest that it was considered secondary to the setting. Experienced action directors, when in doubt, would accelerate the pace, but Wyler is so deliberate that possibly he hoped the film would seem more signifi-

cant than it is. Brennan is not an opponent to the measure of Cooper, but Academy voters may have been so surprised not to see him in his usual country bumpkin role that he won his third Supporting Oscar in successive years.

Wyler's most commercially successful films had been the two he made at Warners with Bette Davis, but directing her in **The Little Foxes** (1941) was 'a gamble', according to *Life* magazine, since she was its sole box office asset. The *Life* article went on to discuss the studios' few prestige pictures, which must have pleased Goldwyn mightily – but since the piece is merely puff we may suspect that it was written in conjunction with his publicity department, which traditionally stressed that he was more interested in art than in money. In fact, Miss Hellman's much-praised play was basically the sort of melodrama which movies had done since they began, though disguised by sombre and long-winded comments on the nature of greed. The characters divide into those that are evil (the Hubbard family) and those that are good (everyone else), but they speak intelligently, and the expected stabs-in-the-back and worms-turning are handled with ingenuity. Wyler excelled at strong emotional situations, and Toland's gliding camera finds many of them happening on the circular staircase which Wyler decided to make the pivot of the action (as Welles would do, with the same photographer, a few months later, in *The Magnificent Ambersons,* q.v.); and if the mansion is too grand – it should be decaying, as Davis herself pointed out – that is because Goldwyn interfered. From the Broadway production Patricia Collinge, Dan Duryea, Charles Dingle and Carl Benton Reid give memorable performances. As the husband Herbert Marshall could not be bettered, finding strength at last to pay back Regina for a lifetime of misery. As Regina Miss Davis is the only point of controversy: Wyler wanted the character to have 'great charm, humour, sex', but Davis, having reluctantly seen Tallulah Bankhead's stage performance, believed that that was the only way to play it – inhumanly. As she watches her husband die (the situation had been used in *Gabriel Over the White House*) her face expresses malevolence, satisfaction and fear – such as no other actress could have achieved. It may be, however, that Wyler was right, since the film's ending goes for little: Regina's self-absorption does not even suggest that she will notice her loneliness much.

The film made a great deal of money – but not because of an interpolated romance between the daughter (Teresa Wright) and a reporter (Richard Carlson): it is presumably because of this new sub-plot that Miss Hellman has said that she dislikes the picture, and we may suppose it the work of Arthur Kober, Dorothy Parker and Alan Campbell, who are credited with additional dialogue (though Wyler does not recall anyone but Hellman working on the screenplay).

The director, said *Photoplay*, 'plays restraint against shopworn dramatics for magnificent effect [and] the film rolls from the cameras as almost perfect cinema, telling the story with direct and brutal simplicity' – but the magazine was speaking not of Wyler, of whom it would also be true, but King Vidor. The film in question is the remake of **Stella Dallas** (1937), and the adapters, realising that the material had dated, have made father and daughter a good deal more sensitive, and Stella, at the beginning, merely a dreamy girl. Of its type, it is good; this is not the way people behave together, but there are a number of felicities on the ways of soap opera people, as at that moment when daughter takes over from mother the business of re-dyeing the parting in her hair. Barbara Stanwyck is Stella, splendid in the part – and as always under a good director avoiding cliché.

She and Gary Cooper almost salvage **Ball of Fire** (1941), which is enjoyable rather than particularly funny – as was its intention. Stanwyck plays a burlesque queen and Cooper one of seven professors – since the starting point for the writers, Billy Wilder and Charles Brackett, was *Snow White and the Seven Dwarfs* (q.v.). Unfortunately the sages are a cute bunch, at their worst in Richard Haydn's standard performance, and Howard Hawks gets little more fun from the gangsters – though as their chief Dana Andrews was not the man to help him. Instead Hawks concentrates on the stars, and Stanwyck is wonderfully believable as a hard-boiled dame in love with the last man she would

have dreamed of, while Cooper, if over-doing his 'shucks, me' act, gives the impression of being a very nice man indeed.

R.K.O. Radio released both this film and *The Little Foxes*, since Goldwyn had finally broken away from United Artists; after a series of court battles he sold his stock to the board for $300,000 – only half of what it was worth, since he wanted to be rid of his contract to supply pictures. Among the producers likely to replace him the company looked to Sol Lesser, but in 1941 he also left to join R.K.O., where he returned to an old pastime, that of producing Tarzan pictures. In fact he produced only one notable film during his time at United Artists, **Our Town** (1940), one of the so-called prestige pictures noted by *Life* magazine, but of less value than any Tarzan movie. The people of *Our Town* are meant to be ordinary – 'no one very famous ever came from here, least, as far as we know'. As the commentator drones on about 'something eternal here, and it has something to do with human beings . . . there's something eternal about every human being' it is clear that on screen Thornton Wilder's dialogue becomes even more banal, Mom-and-applepieist. The result is a soppy version of Andy Hardy despite Sam Wood's direction, which has a number of grace notes in its Hollywooden way.

A greater blow to United Artists than the defection of Goldwyn was the loss of David O. Selznick, when he ceased production in 1940. (In fact he signed a new agreement in 1941, buying a quarter interest in the company for $1,200,000, and later there was litigation between him and the board, which objected to his selling properties for which it had forwarded the preparation money.) He had arrived there in 1936, finding a natural berth for his independent company, Selznick International. His first backers were Thalberg and Norma Shearer, but the bulk of the financing came from the Whitney family. John Hay Whitney (chairman) had also backed Merian C. Cooper when he formed Pioneer Pictures to exploit the use of Technicolor; Cooper now joined the new company, and although the name 'Pioneer' was dropped that company owned both *A Star is Born* (q.v.) and *Nothing Sacred* (q.v.), which were part of the programme of Selznick International. As Whitney also owned stock in Technicolor Inc, Selznick was expected to give a lead in that direction to other studios whose attitude was, at best, hesitant. A Technicolor programme was drawn up, but financial requirements indicated a first film to be issued with the least possible delay, so that **Little Lord Fauntleroy** (1936) was after all made in monochrome.

John Cromwell directed and, shorn of Mary Pickford's curls, the story is endurable: a small American boy becomes heir to an English earldom and melts the heart of the old earl (Sir C. Aubrey Smith) who greatly resents his American mother (Dolores Costello Barrymore, as she is billed). It is worth remembering that its author, Frances Hodgson Burnett, was a true Anglo-American (born in Manchester and brought up in Tennessee, and later resident for long periods in both countries): a reappraisal of her work in recent years has indicated that the little lord is not that contemptible – and the only note that jars in this version is the tugging of the forelocks, though that is historically correct. Selznick's partiality for the story was conditioned by the fact that his young Copperfield, Freddie Bartholomew, was considered a draw at the time, and that his priggish good manners and smug behaviour are just what is required here. And Sir C. Aubrey played aristocratic curmudgeons so often that one takes him for granted, but he is quite touching in his conversion.

To Selznick's generation the novels of the Victorians and Edwardians (like their paintings) were the height of respectability. **The Garden of Allah** (1936), was based on one by Robert Hichens, its ingredients including mysticism, self-sacrifice, religious preaching, cardboard characters and the sort of dialogue better engraved on tombstones. The fact that the film is at all watchable is due to the Technicolor ('designed for the screen by Lansing C. Holden'), and the spectacle of Marlene Dietrich (Garbo refused the role) and Charles Boyer mooning about in the desert. Since both are fleeing from monastic propriety it is impossible to believe in either character or their Great Love – but at least Boyer endeavours to invoke some conscience and feeling as directed by

Richard Boleslawski. Dietrich, auburn-haired, a deathshead with her plucked eyebrows, is as rewarding as ever.

Equally romantic but a brighter prospect is **A Star Is Born** (1937), Selznick's return to the theme of *What Price Hollywood?*, here credited to William Wellman, who also directed, and Robert Carson, with a screenplay by Dorothy Parker, Alan Campbell and Carson. The 1954 version (q.v.) improves upon it, but the second halves of both films are much alike, with certain key scenes – the visit of Niles to the sanatorium, the encounter at the race track, the night court – virtually identical. The weakness of this earlier version is at the beginning, when Esther (Janet Gaynor) announces her intention of becoming a movie star, and is taken so seriously that her grandmother provides the rail fare to California – though, once she arrived there, this fairy tale turns sour. She eventually gets a job as a waitress at a party given by a drunken director (Owen Moore) and meets an equally drunk big-time star (Fredric March), who gets her a screen test because he is both drunk and sentimental. They fall in love, but as her career waxes his wanes. Miss Gaynor is merely sweet and touching and quaint; it is curious that both she and Judy Garland played this role towards the end of already long screen careers. March is excellent in a role probably based on Owen Moore,★ underplaying, and here more of an actor and less of a star than any of his peers. There are two improbabilities – that the press agent (Lionel Stander) should be so rude to him while his wife is the studio's leading star, and that March's suicide stems from believing her stardom more important than their happiness. That, of course, is a Hollywood point of view, as is the slapstick honeymoon in a trailer, predicated on the assumption that movie stars are simple people at heart, longing to get away from fame and the Cocoanut Grove. Otherwise the film underlines the cruelty of Hollywood, only hinted at in earlier films on similar subjects. Like the remake, it is worth seeing; the 1976 version is not, and not merely because its milieu has been changed from movie studio to rock-concert platform.

★ However, as Colleen Moore recognised this as partly her story, the character may be based on her first husband, John McCormick.

A Star Is Born was Selznick's third movie and only the sixth in Technicolor. Its cost was $1,400,000 and that of *The Garden of Allah* $2,700,000. Since a year later *The Goldwyn Follies* cost $2,100,000 against the estimated $1½ million it would have cost in black and white we may conclude a round million for a monochrome *Star*, and even at that price it was a doubtful proposition. Selznick's subsequent Technicolor ventures, *Nothing Sacred* (q.v.) and a very likeable version of Mark Twain's *The Adventures of Tom Sawyer* (1938), directed by Norman Taurog, likewise caused no stampede to the box-office, and the tide did not begin to turn till four colour films – *The Goldwyn Follies, Robin Hood, Kentucky* and *Sweethearts* – were listed among the top ten grossing films of 1938. But in the meantime Selznick had abandoned colour, thus exemplifying the perversity of Hollywood: of his first six films, only two were in black and white – and they were the two which would have benefited most from colour.

We can get some idea of what **The Prisoner of Zenda** (1937) would have been like in Technicolor, since M–G–M's remake is a carbon copy – though this version will be around long after the latter has rotted away. Selznick said that he purchased Anthony Hope's 'old-fashioned fairy tale and melodrama' partly because he believed the public to be ready for 'a great and clean love story', rendered topical by the romance of Edward VIII and Mrs Simpson, but mainly because Ronald Colman was under contract. He may never have made a more prescient move, for Colman is perfect as the gallant English gentleman forced by chance to impersonate the dissolute Ruritanian king. (The concept of this mythical Balkan kingdom originates in Hope's novel.) The others in the cast are his equal, this being a film in which each role is marvellously cast: Madeleine Carroll, meltingly beautiful as the princess; Douglas Fairbanks Jr as Rupert of Hentzau, the jesting soldier of fortune; Raymond Massey as Black Michael, unable to hide either his superciliousness or his furies; Mary Astor as his mistress, serenely but desperately plotting his overthrow; Sir C. Aubrey Smith, the epitome of proud-backed, aged counsellors; and David Niven as the carefree young

Madeleine Carroll and Ronald Colman in Selznick's version of *The Prisoner of Zenda* – and this was exactly the sort of still taken in the hope that it would grace the covers of fan-magazines around the world. So it should have done, for this is one of the magical films of which Hollywood was then capable.

aide. The screenplay is by John L. Balderston, the photography by James Wong Howe, and the sets by Lyle Wheeler, but the supreme achievement is that of the director. John Cromwell brought intelligence to some pleasant romances and here achieves what Selznick intended, a fine, holding tale of love and derring-do, no more serious (hence its strength) than Hope's novel. Nevertheless, W. S. Van Dyke was brought in to restage the duel, and George Cukor (thought the best man to handle it) did the renunciation scene – lopped from Rex Ingram's Silent version because exhibitors then refused an unhappy ending.

Nothing Sacred (1937) has a golden reputation among fanciers of Thirties comedies, and the idea is fancy enough: poor little poor girl Carole Lombard gets a trip to New York and achieves fame by her flamboyant bravery in the face of what she claims to be imminent death. It might be a companion picture to *Mr Deeds Goes to Town*, being one of the few comedies of the era to justify the adjective sometimes applied to them, 'satirical', but Capra's film is funnier and warmer. Ben Hecht* wrote the script, William Wellman directed, and they must take the blame for

---

* The profusion and variable quality of Hecht's output was later thought to be due to his employing a team of ghost-writers.

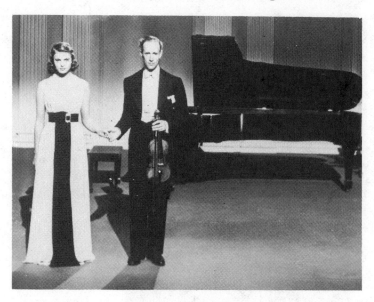

Ingrid Bergman and Leslie Howard in *Intermezzo: a Love Story*. Miss Bergman had appeared in a Swedish version of this story, which Selznick bought, he said, in his belief 'that a duplicating job on it could be done, with a somewhat faster tempo . . .'

sequences which fail to build. But the real weakness is Fredric March as the opportunistic reporter, offering only a general willingness in place of the wit and style of William Powell or Don Ameche. In contrast **The Young in Heart** (1938) is admirably written, by Paul Osborn, from a novel by I.A.R. Wylie, and well directed by Richard Wallace. Its sentimentality is deplorable, but the comic moments, if few, are treasurable. Its moral values seemed correct at the time, and if we may now prefer confidence tricksters to be unregenerate, the reformation of this group is the whole point. They are played by Roland Young, almost startlingly in command of his technique, Billie Burke and Douglas Fairbanks Jr, equally good, and Janet Gaynor, too obvious a candidate for reform.

Made for Each Other (1939) was written by Jo Swerling and directed by Cromwell: *Time* magazine didn't know whether to credit them, Selznick or the stars (Lombard and James Stewart) 'for the indisputable fact that this mundane, domestic chronicle has more dramatic impact than all the hurricanes, sandstorms and earthquakes manufactured in Hollywood last season . . .' He is a young New York lawyer called John; she is called Jane; and their problems include a nagging mother, a cancelled honeymoon and dinner for the boss after the maid has walked out. Years later, Garson Kanin

and Ruth Gordon, remembering this picture, sat down and wrote *The Marrying Kind* (q.v.), also about the trials and tribulations of the first year of marriage (a frequent subject in the Silents): but they got it right; this film does not. There *is* a hurricane, or at least a snowstorm; the marriage has fallen apart, baby is ill with pneumonia, and wouldn't you know that the only vaccine is in Salt Lake City and all the planes are grounded?

Intermezzo: a Love Story (1939) is the remake of a Swedish picture, recommended to Selznick by his story editor, Kay Brown, together with its female lead, Ingrid Bergman. He dallied with Loretta Young; Ronald Colman and then William Powell turned down the male lead, and he planned to start it with Miss Young and Charles Boyer; but he came back to Bergman. Leslie Howard took on the male role because Selznick allowed him to be Associate Producer – in fact an appeasement for Howard's reluctant involvement with *Gone with the Wind*. Wyler was to have directed, but there were delays and *The Westerner* intervened. Since the result is so much better than any other film directed by Gregory Ratoff we must acknowledge the photography by Gregg Toland (Wyler's choice) and Selznick's own painstaking concern. The American film is twenty-two minutes shorter than the Swedish one, and it is much to Selznick's credit that he thought it sufficient thus – at sixty-six minutes, the shortest major Hollywood picture in thirty years. A celebrated violinist (Howard) asks his daughter's music teacher (Bergman) to accompany him on tour: extemporising after a concert, he tells her they should have been playing 'Rustle of Spring', and it is an apt analogy, for Miss Bergman is springlike. This radiant, sensible, demure girl is the most innocent of home-breakers. We do not smile that they have separate rooms in that unlikely Riviera hotel; we do not demur when, like Camille, she renounces him for love. Of course it is dishonest, with the understanding wife (Edna Best) waiting to welcome him home. Audiences fantasised with the lovers, grew sentimental, later, when they heard the theme tune on the wireless, and welcomed, reassured, the downfall of adultery.

These romances, like Hollywood's

494

screwball comedies, did not survive the war, and few later attempts to imitate them were successful. Almost the last of them was **Rebecca** (1940), which although directed by Alfred Hitchcock – his first American film – is primarily a love story. It does, however, have suspense and a murder, though that was changed to an accident to conform to the Hays Office regulations (which by insisting that all crimes must be expiated before the final fade-out would in this case have necessitated an unhappy ending). Daphne du Maurier's novel had taken both Britain and the U.S. by storm, and since many people can quote, still, its opening line, they probably agree with James Agate that it is not well written but impossible to put down. It is a story both preposterous and endearing, though it has dated now, for we have lost our fascination with stately homes and the rich who live in them. Yet the girl who marries into one is the perennial Cinderella (she is also Jane Eyre); the hero's dead first wife and her faithful (living) housekeeper are the ugly sisters, and he, Prince Charming, is revealed as a murderer. This Cinderella is discovered on the Côte d'Azur, the mousy companion to a vulgar, celebrity-hunting American (Florence Bates). That lady's reaction when she learns that the girl has nabbed one of the best catches in England makes one of the most entertaining sequences in all movies, and from then on audiences are hooked. Joan Fontaine was born to play the girl, and Laurence Olivier manages shading as the moody, aloof husband. With the exception of the bounder, played by George Sanders, no other character has any existence outside this genre, but at least they are well-acted – except for Judith Anderson's too villainous housekeeper.

Hitchcock's summons to Hollywood was further evidence of the revived prestige of the director, coinciding as it did with the rising eminence of Wyler and the re-emergence of Ford, all of them being accorded the respect shown to Capra. Though others had wielded power on occasion, the producer remained god, and the film that is Hollywood's masterpiece is a demonstration of Selznick at the peak of his powers.

The making of **Gone with the Wind** (1939) is a consistently interesting affair.

Margaret Mitchell's novel about the Deep South and the Civil War, modelled on 'War and Peace', had been published in 1936. Encouraged by Whitney, Selznick bought it, still in galley, for $50,000 – a record price for a property not an established success. Jack L. Warner had taken an option, as a subject for Bette Davis, but had dropped it when she left for Europe. Other producers watched curiously – aware that the film would have to be very expensive – and thinking Selznick less and less foolish as the book became the rage of the nation. Its success solved the major problem, since it became increasingly clear that the public would insist on seeing *all* the story, thus entailing a commitment to a very long film. At one point a two-part movie was contemplated; the final running-time was 3 hours 43 minutes, plus intermission. This meant – with the essential re-creation of Atlanta in the 1860s – an unprecedented cost, which finally totalled $4,250,000. The Selznick publicity fanned the flames, and by the time the film was ready a Gallup poll had certified that over fifty-six million Americans could not wait to see it.

The premier choice for Rhett Butler was Clark Gable, but Mayer, still smarting from Selznick's defection, was considered unapproachable. Goldwyn refused a bid for Gary Cooper; Warners, approached for Errol Flynn, offered him

Joan Fontaine and Laurence Olivier in *Rebecca*, and this is one of the more memorable moments from a memorable film. It is deeply romantic, but she has just mistaken his proposal of marriage, assuming he wanted only a secretary.

495

in a deal to include Bette Davis, who desperately wanted to play Scarlett – but not to Flynn's Rhett. Selznick returned to Ronald Colman, actually announced for the role because he was under contract, and also dickered with the idea of Warner Baxter; but it was progressively more apparent that the public would consider no Rhett but Gable. Mayer refused every overture till May 1938 when he offered to buy the property, plus all pre-production work and Selznick's services as producer. The matter was resolved thus: it remained a Selznick International picture, but M-G-M contributed Gable and an investment of $1¼ million (Selznick, short of money after his expensive and unprofitable programme, was tempted to sell outright, but Whitney supplied the extra finance needed) – for which they got fifty per cent of the profits and distribution rights. As Selznick's contract with United Artists did not run out till the delivery of *Made for Each Other*, he was not anxious to begin production – and à propos of that there was the vexed and popular matter of the casting of Scarlett O'Hara.

The first name announced was Tallulah Bankhead. Miriam Hopkins was also considered, but the only serious early contender was Norma Shearer – till she canvassed her fans and found that they did not want her to play this baggage. Other established actresses considered were Carole Lombard, Irene Dunne, Claudette Colbert, Margaret Sullavan and Joan Crawford (Mayer's choice); among the unknowns and little-knowns were Paulette Goddard, Ann Sheridan, Lana Turner, Susan Hayward and Lucille Ball. By the time production was due to start – at the end of 1938 – the choice had levelled down to Joan Bennett, Jean Arthur, Loretta Young and Katharine Hepburn – the last-named the choice of George Cukor, signed at the start to direct the film (she was also, almost certainly, the actress the author had in mind when she wrote her final draft); but neither Selznick nor Gable wanted Hepburn, and nor, to judge from the response to her recent films, did the public. At the last minute, as the cameras started turning – on the burning of Atlanta (which was the left-over set of *King Kong*, needing to be cleared so that other sets could be constructed) – Selznick's brother, Myron, an agent, turned up with the English actress, Vivien Leigh, whose tests were to prove so exciting – because, as Cukor recalled later, 'there was an indescribable wildness about her,' as if 'possessed of the devil'.

She was signed in January 1939 (noticeably, in the flight across the burning Atlanta, Scarlett either has her head turned from the camera or her arm across her face; but the close-ups are marvellously integrated). Filming proper began at the end of that month and stopped two weeks later with the removal of Cukor due to 'disagreements'. Elaborating many years later Selznick said that Cukor could not respond to the spectacle, but speculation within the industry at the time centred upon Gable's dissatisfaction. He had been unwilling to play the role and since the failure of *Parnell* was apprehensive of donning period costume; he was also said to be unhappy that Cukor was paying less attention to his performance than those of Miss Leigh and Olivia de Havilland, though Cukor is on record as saying that Gable made no complaint direct to him.★ Of the four M-G-M directors mentioned to take over, Jack Conway, Robert Z. Leonard, King Vidor and Victor Fleming, the last-named was the obvious choice, since he had had two recent 'spectacle' successes, *Captains Courageous* and *Test Pilot*, the latter with Gable, who regarded him as a friend. He was, however, working on *The Wizard of Oz*, at that point the most important Metro film in production, but Gable's preference prevailed. (Vidor took over that film for the final weeks of shooting and in this game of musical chairs Cukor went to M-G-M to make *The Women*, thus releasing Lubitsch to begin *Ninotchka*.) All that Cukor shot is in the film: the birth of Melanie's baby; the marauding soldier at Tara; and the death of Bonnie. Sam Wood directed, according to Selznick, 'three solid reels' when Fleming was felled by overwork and these are dotted throughout the film. Although the sole writing credit went to the dramatist Sidney Howard, others who contributed, apart from Selznick himself, were Oliver

★ Cukor later said privately that he believed that he had a moral advantage over Gable, since he knew that Gable as a young man in Hollywood had been the lover of one of the best-known leading men of the day; and they did dispute once on the set – when Cukor insisted on Rhett's crying at the death of his child.

Garett, Ben Hecht, John Van Druten and Scott Fitzgerald. Ernest Haller is the credited photographer, but Ray Rennahan and Lee Garmes also worked on it.

But the glory for this Hollywood monument should finally go to Selznick, Cukor and William Cameron Menzies, credited as Production Designer. They spent two years preparing it, and because the film is so consistent in its alternation from close-up to long-shot (much more so than in most films of the time) we may assume they 'blocked' the script in this way. Menzies was given carte blanche on the physical look of the film, as we know from his detailed story-board designs, but it was presumably in consultation with Cukor that he decided to set so many conversations before windows, beyond which Atlanta burns or merely raindrops fall. And of course anything that Selznick did not suggest he had to approve, down to the smallest detail.

The film remains visually splendid, but its silhouette-and-sunset pannings back to Tara – complemented by Max Steiner's pounding musical theme – more than anything else now render it old-fashioned. Another factor that keeps the film of its time is the character of Scarlett, but that is mainly because she was the prototype of every subsequent soap opera heroine of any ambition. Just as Miss Mitchell took from Becky Sharp elements of her character she most understood – such as her scheming – so later writers have quarried Scarlett for her most sensational aspects: her dealings with men, her wilfulness, her taking to drink, her denial of the marriage bed to Rhett, her losing her child by falling downstairs. It is clear, however, why the adventures of Scarlett enthralled a generation of readers and picturegoers: in war, she grew from silly girlhood to capable womanhood. First glimpsed as a girl whose sole realities are the total admiration of beaux and having her own way, she is deprived of both at once when Ashley Wilkes (Leslie Howard) tells her that he is to marry another; she reacts by marrying the man who happens to be nearest to her, his early death, later, in battle, being of no consequence. She still pines for Ashley, but is pursued by Captain Butler – best described as an adventurer, if not a war-profiteer, but always very gallant,

especially where Mrs Wilkes, Melanie, is concerned. He knows Melanie to be worth a dozen Scarletts, with her courage, understanding, kindness and gentleness – as opposed to Scarlett's one admirable quality, her tenacity. Nevertheless he marries Scarlett, but cannot tame her or control her; even more clear-sightedly, at the end he walks out on her.

If audiences were satisfied that Scarlett gets her just deserts they were fascinated to find that even Gable could not tame this shrew – just as they applauded her vow not to let war defeat her, and sympathised when she, as a volunteer nurse, refuses to help at the amputation of a leg. *Gone with the Wind* is, in fact, two films: although the war between the States is its *raison d'être,* and it was this which helped it towards its enormous popularity that is only the background to Scarlett's adventures – and if we question the worth of the characters the film's portrait of war becomes its greatest achievement. This is not very well done, despite the dead and dying in hospital or in the square outside, despite the gunfire, the fires, the deserters, the casualty lists, the destruction everywhere. But an odd sentence touches the nerve, as when Rhett says, 'Take a good look, my dear. One day you can tell your children how you saw the South disappear in one night,' or Aunt Pittypat's sad 'It's like the ending of the world.' What is moving is the very breadth of the tale, its attempt to show the end of an era – and Hollywood's faith in itself as a chronicler of such things. For compulsive viewing the first half will stand with anything put on film. It is also, quite often, funny – modern audiences love Scarlett's disdain for her widow's weeds at the ball, and Prissy's claim that, after all, she 'don' know nuthin' 'bout birthin' babies, Mssss Scarlett'.

The second half is the Reconstruction. After an opening which retains the broad canvas of the earlier part it devolves into a study of an incompatible marriage. I do not think Miss Mitchell understood much of such matters as the refusal of marital rights; and that we remain attentive says much for the first part and the superb performances of the four principals – two of whom had not wanted to be in the film in the first place.

No film has caught the popular imagination as *Gone with the Wind* did, and it continues to do so. ABOVE, Scarlett running through the grounds of Tara. BELOW, Scarlett with her 'Mammy', Hattie McDaniel, ABOVE FAR RIGHT, Scarlett and Melanie as nurses in the hospital of Atlanta. BELOW FAR RIGHT, Olivia de Havilland as Melanie with Leslie Howard as Ashley Wilkes, her husband.

Leslie Howard was as uninterested as Gable was unwilling, which does not contradict Olivia de Havilland's statement years later that everyone concerned embarked upon the film as upon no other, with the thought that it would be their one claim to immortality – a touching belief, as well as telling us much about Hollywood at the time. She herself brings so much warmth and beauty to a character too good to be true that we cannot despise her as Scarlett does. As for Miss Leigh, apart from an invincible spirit she has a cat-like beauty in repose, both disarming and inscrutable. Despite her later claim that she could find nothing of herself in Scarlett, biographical accounts suggest a number of common qualities – ambition, wit, selfishness, temperament (it was her differences with Fleming which led to his near-nervous breakdown), loyalty, and a coquettish way with men. She overdoes the 'Fiddle-de-dee' Scarlett of the beginning, but the mature Scarlett deserves all the praise showered upon her. She won the Best Actress Oscar; the Best Supporting Oscar went to Hattie McDaniel for her splendid Mammy, Scarlett's unimpressible nurse. As Scarlett's father, Thomas Mitchell was similarly honoured, and the film took the expected fistful of Oscars.

Its achievements are thrown into relief when one starts to enumerate its faults – and length is not one of them, despite longueurs in the second half. Apart from the tale itself, which will be ever tinged with purple, there is only one major flaw – the large number of shots through glass and other trick shots, too many of them unconvincing (late in production Selznick realised that much more of the film should have been filmed on location). The movie has been castigated for taking no stand on the race problem, but that is beside the point; more pertinently, as some contemporary critics pointed out, it did nothing to illuminate the events which were essential to its telling.

Of the several accounts of the filming there have been no less than three full-length books, one by Gavin Lambert (which is ironic, for at the time – the early Fifties – he was editor of *Sight and Sound,* and it was a film which his contributors, if they mentioned it at all, despised). What vexed those who regarded themselves as the guardians of 'serious' cinema is that both the industry and the public regarded it as 'the greatest film ever made' – yet it could be advertised as such on its revivals in the Seventies without fear of contradiction. In 1975 David Robinson in *The Times* pointed out that truth, noting that no one says that it is the *best* film ever made. Certainly none of the later colossi so beloved of the industry (*Quo Vadis?, Ben-Hur, Doctor Zhivago,* q.v.) is ever likely to win such universal respect; and it requires no prescience to say that there will never be another film quite like it. It was for many years the most financially successful film ever, only dropping down the lists when the rise in seat prices automatically increased the profits of more recent films; but recent adjustments, bringing 1939 seat prices into line with current prices, indicate that it has still been seen by more people than any other film to the present day. And that is without taking into account its first American telecast (in November 1976, on two nights, with an estimated seventy-nine minutes of commercials), when it broke all viewing records. In 1978, when it was leased to T.V. for a twenty-year period for $20 million, it was already the only film, with the exception of Disney's cartoons, to be consistently and successfully reissued as a major movie world-wide – on some occasions saving M-G-M from bankruptcy. (Selznick had sold his interest in the film to Whitney during the War to profit from capital gains; Whitney sold it to M-G-M in 1944.) Its only notable failure was in Paris, in 1950, when it arrived at the end of the backlog of Hollywood movies which had piled up during the war years, and it had perhaps been too keenly awaited for too long; but it subsequently became as firm a favourite in France as elsewhere. For a great many people it was part of their War; it ran in London throughout the Blitz, and for four years thereafter. Its timing was right. It is old-fashioned now, but still powerful entertainment. It is the Sistine Chapel among movies, with all the weaknesses, virtues and vastness that that implies. It is the apotheosis of the Hollywood film.

Clark Gable and Vivien Leigh in the second half of *Gone with the Wind.* The film has virtually never been shown without an interval, dividing the story at the obvious point, and most people seem to think the first half the better. The strength of its situations – the coming of the War between the states – and the conviction with which they are told, carry us through to the very end of the film, as well as, today, lulling us into acceptance of their essential melodrama.

INTERMISSION

IN 1978, a writer in *The New Yorker's* 'Talk of the Town' column (issue of 6 March) decided that 'any inventory of the things that have stuck in a nation's collective mind is going to be odd and unpredictable', citing as examples 'the movies of certain decades (the Thirties and Forties) but not of other decades (the Fifties and Sixties) . . . our present decade might have very little to contribute.' We might therefore look at an American newspaper poll of a few months earlier, when readers voted on their ten best American films of all time. The final list read:

1. *Gone with the Wind*
2. *Star Wars*
3. *The Wizard of Oz*
4. *The Sound of Music*
5. *Jaws*
6. *The Godfather*
7. *Ben-Hur* (1959)
8. *Rocky*
9. *The African Queen*
10. *One Flew Over the Cuckoo's Nest*

That the list includes five films from the Seventies does not necessarily mean that the public has a short memory; but how many of those five films will be in a similar list in ten years time? More revealing is the poll of October 1975, when the Broadcast Information of the U.S. asked industry executives and their spouses for their favourite films, which turned out to be, in order, *The Best Years of Our Lives* (which tells us much about them), *Casablanca*, *Gone with the Wind*, *All About Eve* and *The Wizard of Oz*, none less than thirty years old. Is, incidentally, *The Wizard of Oz* genuinely more loved than *Snow White and the Seven Dwarfs*, or is its annual presence on T.V. a factor in its popularity?

As the golden years of Hollywood died, one New York cinema polled its patrons as to their favourite movie. The result:

1. *Mrs Miniver*
2. *Gone with the Wind*

3. *How Green Was My Valley*
4. *Goodbye, Mr Chips*
5. *Rebecca*
6. *Wuthering Heights*
7. *The Good Earth*
8. *Boys Town*
9. *The Philadelphia Story*
10. *Mr Deeds Goes to Town*

The same year, 1942, in Britain, the readers of *Picturegoer* came up with their list:

1. *Goodbye, Mr Chips*
2. *Mrs Miniver*
3. *Gone with the Wind* (not then seen outside first-run theatres)
4. *Rebecca*
5. *How Green Was My Valley*
6. *The Good Earth*
7. *Citizen Kane*
8. *Snow White and the Seven Dwarfs*
9. *Wuthering Heights*
10. *Ben-Hur* (1925)

In 1951, when *Picturegoer* conducted a second poll, the only pre-war film to figure on the list was *Gone with the Wind*, which was first: but then, such statistics depend on local factors, and it is doubtful whether, at that time, more than a handful of *Picturegoer* readers had seen the Silent *Ben-Hur*. Around the same time – in 1950 – *Daily Variety* polled its readers to commemorate a half-century of films. The best Sound film, said its readers, was *Gone with the Wind*, followed by *The Best Years of Our Lives*. Asked specifically for Silent films, they chose *Birth of a Nation*, followed by *The Big Parade* and *The Kid*.

Since these may well have been the only Silent films they remembered, we should turn to one of the best critics of the time, Richard Winnington, who listed his choice of the world's 'greatest films', worked out in conjunction with Gavin Lambert and Lindsay Anderson. There were nine; they couldn't agree on a tenth: *The Childhood of Maxim Gorki*, *The Grapes of Wrath*, *Earth*, *Road to Life*, *Zéro de*

Conduite, Le Jour se Lève, Ladri di Biciclette, Un Chapeau de Paille d'Italie and *City Lights*. In 1958, the organisers of the Brussels Film Exhibition polled 117 film historians in twenty-six countries for their selection of the twelve greatest films ever made:

1. *Battleship Potemkin*
2. (equal) *The Gold Rush*
   Ladri di Biciclette
4. *La Passion de Jeanne d'Arc*
5. *La Grande Illusion*
6. *Greed*
7. *Intolerance*
8. *Mother*
9. *Citizen Kane*
10. *Earth*
11. *Der Letzte Mann*
12. *Das Kabinet des Dr Caligari*

The list is as relevant as if a list of the best plays in English was found to consist of pre-Shakespearian drama, and the 1952 *Sight and Sound* poll of critics and film historians also did little but indicate the extent of reputation:

1. *Ladri di Biciclette*
2. (equal) *City Lights*
   The Gold Rush
4. *Battleship Potemkin*
5. (equal) *Louisiana Story*
   Intolerance
7. (equal) *Greed*
   Le Jour se Lève
   La Passion de Jeanne d'Arc
10. (equal) *Brief Encounter*
    Le Million
    Le Règle du Jeu

Ten years later, the *Sight and Sound* poll retained only a few of the pre-war titles: *La Règle du Jeu*, *Greed* and *Potemkin*, but had added two more from that period, *Citizen Kane*, which was first, and *L'Atalante*. Ten years on, in 1972, *La Règle du Jeu*, *Potemkin* and *Kane* all remained, the last named still in first position; *La Passion de Jeanne d'Arc* had returned to the list, and *The General* had found its way on to it.

Any reader who has borne with me to this point may suspect that I am more partial to the public's choices than to the critics'. They are certainly more honestly chosen: I understand a liking for both *Mrs Miniver* and *How Green Was My Valley*, much as I dislike them, but I cannot understand a taste for *Earth* or *Road to Life*, which seem to me equally worthless as representations of life in this century. It is certainly true that critics and some buffs prefer to look back on the elevating, the innovative and the socially-crusading. They have tended to despise the merely entertaining, and are certainly subject to fashion, so that neither Clair nor de Sica commands the admiration they once did; they find it safer to vote for *Potemkin*, kept firmly in the repertory for many years.

Fortunately, at the present time, film appreciation is under constant scrutiny, with the Hollywood entertainment film at last receiving its due – and often very much more than its due. I have watched friends stumble glassy-eyed with boredom out of *Intolerance* and *Caligari*, and have found veterans, once enthralled by Pudovkin and Chaplin, puzzled as to why they should now appear so dowdy and dull. To me, the supreme artists of the Silent era are Keaton and Sjöström, whose work I am confident will still engage attention a century hence; and I trust posterity will continue to find excitement in the work of Eisenstein and Pudovkin, of Pabst and Lamprecht, of Ozu, and enjoyment in much of Von Stroheim and Harold Lloyd. Posterity, I think, will find richness from the first decade of Talkies: Lubitsch, Clair, Carné, Renoir, Trenker, Ophuls; much of Ford, Hochbaum, Borzage, Feyder, LaCava, Grémillon, Wyler, Siodmak, Cukor, Hitchcock, Duvivier, McCarey, Henry King, Wellman and Hawks; a number of screwball comedies and some Hollywood romantic pictures; the early Warner melodramas; above all, in the presence of a generation of players which has not been equalled since.

Few of these films represent their period accurately in terms of what it was, but they reflect the aspirations and hopes of the people who watched them, if not always of the people who made them, and they have an emotional vitality recognisable to the patrons of the Renaissance painters, or the first readers of Dickens, Thackeray and George Eliot. The Lumières had only recorded, but Méliès entertained, and since then the chief function of the film has been to entertain. Between Méliès and *Gone with the Wind* a mercifully large body of films managed to achieve something more: the record may be incomplete, the portrait uncertain, the light it throws on humanity somewhat biased – but the richness of human behaviour and misbehaviour had been trapped in celluloid.

And then came 'Rosebud'.

21

Kane and Other Citizens

IN AN INDUSTRY geared to the star system there was little real place for any other creative force except the actor – unless its name was Capra or Lubitsch. As for the writer-director that was a concept not unknown in Hollywood but unacceptable to its executives, at least until the new decade, when the situation in Europe indicated both a lessening of foreign markets and growing local intolerance of trumpery melodramas. Foreign invasion was no longer outside the bounds of possibility, and indeed a vast number of citizens thought it had arrived one evening in 1938, as they listened to C.B.S. radio. The panic was caused by a documentary-like version of H. G. Wells's novel, 'The War of the Worlds', and Hollywood promptly sent for the man responsible.

Orson Welles (b. 1915) came to movies after a sensational career in radio and theatre – and with a determination to live up to his reputation. Recommended to R.K.O. Radio by one of its founders and chief stockholders, Nelson Rockefeller, he asked for and was given terms commensurate with that reputation: $100,000 for one film a year, to be produced, directed, written and performed by him, on a subject of his own choosing, with no artistic interference, and the right to refuse executives access to the film till completed. The industry gasped, but according to Welles's then-partner, John Houseman, in his memoir 'Run-Through', 'R.K.O. was a maverick operation . . . its present interim and insecure boss – a former sales manager named George Schaefer – had little to lose and a lot to gain by putting many of his eggs into the hands of the Wonder Boy of Broadway and radio, who might just come up with a

winner for him.' After six months, during which announced plans came to nothing, R.K.O. made it known that, till a final script emerged, salaries would be deferred to the Welles unit, which consisted mainly of personnel with whom Welles had worked in New York. These included an experienced screenwriter, Herman J. Mankiewicz (1897–1963), who relieved Welles of a difficult situation when he came up with an idea called *American*. The screenplay of **Citizen Kane** (1940), as it was eventually called, is credited jointly to them, but according to Houseman and Mankiewicz's biographer, Richard Meryman, it was written by Mankiewicz, assisted by Houseman.

Welles's reluctance to give Mankiewicz credit was due to the fact that Mankiewicz's reputation was at a low ebb in Hollywood – he had only recently been sacked by M-G-M. He was also a production-line writer and therefore his participation might tarnish a glittering occasion. Ever short of money, Mankiewicz had been writing some scripts for Welles's radio show – though the credit went to Welles – and he agreed initially to work on the film uncredited. Mankiewicz poured into the script experience from his days as a journalist, including some autobiographical touches. Mankiewicz said of Welles, 'There but for the grace of God goes God,' which was capped by Dorothy Parker, a friend from the days of the Algonquin Round Table: 'It's like meeting God without dying.' The exact authorship of *Kane* is worth establishing, since Welles's later work – after he left R.K.O. – is so disastrously inferior. He would never lose either imagination or flair; and if Houseman allows the glory of *Kane* to Welles, so

RIGHT: Orson Welles
as the young Charles
Foster Kane in
Citizen Kane, before
he has acquired
Xanadu, ABOVE,
the vast mansion
based on Hearst's
San Simeon.
In it Dorothy
Comingore, as
his mistress and
eventual second
wife, spends most of
her footage being
miserable.

may we, but not without noting that his cinematographer was another great professional, Gregg Toland.

The film is the study of a tycoon; but whereas its model, *The Power and the Glory*, is a conventional tale of a man's thirst for power, this is, as Welles intended, sociology. In the earlier film the posthumous enquiry into the nature of the tycoon is done as a series of recollections, but here it is quite literally an enquiry, as pursued by a reporter. If the build-up in this case (the newsreel obituary on Kane's death; the attitudes assumed by Kane's friends) is extraordinary, it is Welles's own performance which gives the film momentum – gilded youth personified, insolent and self-assured, and still powerful when acting less interestingly as the older Kane. The character was known to be based on William Randolph Hearst, whose relationship with Marion Davies is paralleled here by Kane's relationship with his mistress, whom he promotes, despite critical ridicule, as an opera singer – and it is at that point, in the second part of the film, that it begins to weaken. Not only is Dorothy Comingore poor in the role but, like the discarded wife (Ruth Warrick), she appears only to illustrate some facet of Kane's megalomania. There is nothing to suggest that he has either affection or sexual feeling for her, or that she might tolerate the world he has created. Why is she sitting gloomily doing jigsaws if there are hundreds of guests in the west wing? Why is their home, Xanadu, so hideous and thunder-racked? Is this what Welles wished on Hearst, or is it supposed to be the fate of tycoons? It is, in its gothic manner, effective. We learn about Kane only in dazzling fragments – the dancing with the show-girls, the shrugging-off of responsibility – and the portrait has eventually no more depth than that in *The Power and the Glory*: in both films the underlings are baffled and bemused as they begin to loathe the boss, but coping with the whims of powerful paranoics is not as simple as that. The film is stuffed with irrelevant detail, much of it showing-off on the part of its director. The final effect is one of youthful enthusiasm accompanied by intensity and vitality – qualities not usually then seen in the so-called 'serious' film.

Although in the furore that followed the preview Welles denied that the character of Kane was based on Hearst that gentleman's past had certainly been researched by Mankiewicz: not only do Kane's political ambitions follow the general outline of Hearst's but his speeches and the newspaper headlines that we see are subtle parodies of Hearst's endeavours. Both Hearst and Kane were expelled from Harvard; and if the Comingore character were not based on Davies the source would be Sybil Sanderson, an early mistress of Hearst, whose operatic debut was saluted extravagantly in his *San Francisco Examiner*.

The first person outside the studio to identify Kane with Hearst was Hedda Hopper, the gossip columnist who was the rival of Louella Parsons, Hearst's own Hollywood correspondent. Hopper forced her way into a preview, and her subsequent behaviour was undoubtedly an attempt to persuade Hearst that she would be better in Parsons's job than she was. Both ladies, the one vindictive (Hopper)

and the other stupid, were enormously influential: they believed, not without truth, that they could make or break careers and they now set out to break a film. Parsons told Nelson Rockefeller, a major creditor of R.K.O., at that point in receivership, that she would print an unpleasant story about one of his relatives. Louis B. Mayer intervened, and his boss, Nicholas Schenck of Loew's, offered to refund Schaefer the negative cost, plus all expenses incurred to that time, $842,000. Schaefer declined to suppress the film, but its booking at the company's flagship, Radio City Music Hall, was cancelled. Hearst himself threatened a series of exposés of Hollywood morals in his papers and banned all R.K.O. advertising. When Hearst failed to take legal action, on the grounds that he could not go into court and admit that he recognised himself in the role of the unpleasant Kane, R.K.O. threatened anti-trust suits against the circuits which refused to book the film. Those mainly independent cinemas which did show it took care of the demand to see it which, despite the publicity and warm reviews, was not excessive. The film was nominated for several Academy Awards, but the industry's nervousness about Hearst and renewed resentment against Welles – now that he had lived up to his reputation – ensured that it won in only one category, that of Best Screenplay.

This pattern was to an extent repeated with **The Magnificent Ambersons** (1942), though this time Welles himself was partially to blame. He did not seem to care whether or not his work appealed to a mass cinema audience, which he respected as little as he did the Hollywood system. Houseman has pictured him as a man of whim and great indecisiveness, a genius in a hurry, with quickly waning enthusiasms; and he apparently lost interest in *Ambersons* as filming proceeded and his next project began to occupy his thoughts. He was attracted to Booth Tarkington's novel because it allowed him to re-explore the terrain of *Kane* – the surging, evolving America of the previous half century. Again, there was precedent, in Vitagraph's 1925 version of the novel, *Pampered Youth*, and the similar presentation of a number of sequences suggests that Welles had seen it. The material is a not particularly distinguished family saga, but the film nicely

541

sets the tone: 'In those days, they had time for everything. Time for sleigh-rides, and balls, and assemblies, and cotillions.' The ball is sumptuous, like everything about the Amberson mansion, and the set was constructed to allow the camera to keep moving from room to room. The decor (by Mark-Lee Kirk) – or at least the use that Welles puts it to – alternates between the ornate and the very plain; similarly the camera of Stanley Cortez sweeps and pounces, and then remains stationary, as in the famous kitchen scene between Aunt Fanny (Agnes Moorehead) and George (Tim Holt). If the work has even more bravura than *Kane*, the finished product is more consistent – except for the three scenes at the end not directed by Welles, easy to spot because they entirely lack his combustive energy.

The direction is at its most striking in the interplay between Morgan (Joseph Cotten) and his daughter (Anne Baxter) and that within the Amberson family – which may be because Moorehead and Cotten had been members of Welles's Mercury company in New York. She, with her pinched, unhappy face and that dry, querulous voice has more dimension than most movie spinsters. 'Really, George, I don't think being an aunt is the great career you think it is,' she says, part-fretful and part-malicious. Cotten is the faithful suitor, authoritative in some matters but amiable enough to let a whippersnapper like George put him in his place. Holt's weak looks are right for the role, and he suggests an incipient Fascism: a more dynamic actor might have been better in the part, but this is very much a movie which does not need a centre or a focus of attention.

In this case, the trouble started with the previews. Schaefer had been dismissed, and the new management demanded the running-time be reduced from 148 minutes so that the film could be programmed on double-bills. Welles, on location in Brazil for his next film, telephoned a number of suggestions; other hands were called in to make deletions and insertions, and to clarify the plot, since (it was said) Welles had left a number of points unexplained. Perhaps most regrettable is the loss of two reels of panoramic documentary; at 88 minutes the film satisfied R.K.O., who finally released it to support *Mexican Spitfire Sees a Ghost*, one of a series with Lupe Velez, designed ordinarily to play the lower spot.

Welles, who did not appear in *Ambersons*, was meanwhile acting in but not directing the third film of his contract, **Journey into Fear** (1942). American entry in the War and the box-office failure of *Kane* had made his position in Hollywood uncertain, so he needed to complete another film quickly. The sets used were those constructed for the abandoned *The Heart of Darkness*, from Conrad's novel, which had been announced as his first film venture; as director he chose Norman Foster, because he both admired the Oriental atmosphere of Foster's B-movies and was employing him already on pre-production work for the South American venture. Welles had chosen to make a thriller, taking as his source one by Eric Ambler. The plot involves a man in a vast political trap from which he cannot escape: but at that point in Ambler, when the nightmare builds in complexity, the movie simply disintegrates. It is a heavily atmospheric film but gives the impression of having been made in a hurry – for Foster was not given to the endless retakes undertaken by Welles. The film exists in two versions, since Welles on his return from Brazil was appalled by the 69-minute one first released. He re-cut it, and shot a new final sequence, adding thirteen minutes. The faults this time are more clearly his: the screenplay, credited to him and Cotten, picks up ideas and drops them, characters are not developed and the story leads nowhere. Neither does either of them emerge with credit as performers: the Turkish police chief of Welles is sketchy, and Cotten, supposed to be frantic, looks merely frustrated.

The South American adventure ended in debacle. Rockefeller believed that the world situation required America to emphasise its closeness to its Southern neighbours, and he encouraged Welles, in a picture additional to his contract, to journey south with that in mind. Welles envisaged a three-part film, to be called *It's All True*, but had to stop shooting when the new management abandoned the project. Welles's three films had proved him 'uncommercial', but it was due to his extravagant working methods that he was viewed with bitterness. Like Von Stroheim before him, he could only work in Hollywood as

actor – at least for a while. The later
films (q.v.) he directed have flair, but only
intermittently do they suggest that Hollywood let go a great film-maker. Yet *Kane*
and *Ambersons* are indelible achievements.
It is a sad comment on the Hollywood
system that it could not accommodate a
maverick, however self-indulgent and undisciplined. These were precisely the qualities which the studios' editors should have
been capable of curbing, or using to their
advantage – since overshooting would
give the team in the cutting-room much
more with which to work: which may be
why *Kane* and even the mutilated *Ambersons* are so very good.

There was already one eminent writer-
director in Hollywood as Welles began
Kane, and he was to have an equally difficult time. In the Silent era a number of
scenario-writers had turned director, invariably relegating the scripting to others.
One writer, Preston Sturges (1898–1959),
did not care for the treatment that other
directors had meted out to his scripts, and
he decided to do something about it. Like
Welles, he came from a background both
wealthy and intellectual, and had been
educated, if somewhat bizarrely, in
France, Germany and Switzerland. His
satiric attitudes may just be discerned in
one of the first films he wrote, *The Big
Pond*, but are largely absent in the others to
which he contributed over the next ten
years. The most interesting of them is *The
Power and the Glory*, and although Sturges
disliked what Mitchell Leisen had done
with his screenplays for *Easy Living* and
Remember the Night, they are still recognisably Sturges's work, certain that the world
is divided into the haves and have-nots.

He persuaded Paramount to let him
direct **The Great McGinty** (1940), partly
by selling them the script for only $10,
partly by agreeing to the severely restricted budget of $350,000 – necessitated
in any case by its commercially risky subject, political corruption. A foreword informs us that two men have met, one who
did one dishonest action in an honest life,
and one who did just one honest action in a
dishonest life: it doesn't matter in the end
who did which, since both end up down-
and-outs in a South-of-the-Border bar.
'Everyone lives by cheating everyone
else,' says the Boss (Akim Tamiroff),
while the Politician (William Demarest)

claims, 'They forget that if you don't have
graft you'd have a low type of person in
politics. Men with no ambition.' McGinty
(Brian Donlevy) marries for the sake of his
image, and it is a marriage quite as spurious as that of Citizen Kane; however, he
eventually falls in love with his wife, but
giving up the Good Life for a Good
Woman is not a satisfactory Sturges
dénouement.

The films of Capra had created a climate
in which Sturges was permitted to express
his fierce anti-capitalism. **Christmas in
July** (1940) concerns a slogan competition
for a coffee manufacturer, Maxford
House, with a clerk (Dick Powell) conned
into believing that he has won. Says his
boss (Ernest Truex): 'I *think* your ideas are
good because they seem good to me. I
know they're good because you won the
contest over millions of other people.'
Sturges's general view of human greed and
frailty becomes more particular in **The
Lady Eve** (1941), as two card-sharpers
working the North Atlantic, father
(Charles Coburn) and daughter (Barbara
Stanwyck), prey on a Harold Lloydish
young man (Henry Fonda), heir to the
Pike's Ale fortune. All is discovered, and
in the course of time she turns up at the
Pike mansion, posing as a British society
girl – and her revenge is one that the
changing moral standard has now rendered very tame. However, the freshness
and ingenuity for which the film was
praised still delight, and it is perhaps the
last good example of a dying breed, the
screwball comedy.
Sullivan's Travels (1941) is dedicated
to 'those who made us laugh . . . the
motley crew, the clowns, the buffoons'.
Sullivan (Joel McCrea) is an idealistic
movie director, weary of turning out trivia
like 'Ants in the Pants of 1939' and therefore researching a social treatise called 'Oh
Brother Where Art Thou?'. In the course
of his travels he has the experience of
watching Mickey Mouse with an audience, and changes his mind. 'There's
something about making people laugh. It
isn't much, but it's all some people have.'
He also learns that poverty does not en-
noble, as he had thought, and the film
becomes oddly poignant when this intelligent man has for his audience only one
pathetic and aged half-wit. Sturges's overall view is not as serious as the one Sullivan

The world of Preston Sturges: Joel McCrea and Claudette Colbert, RIGHT, feuding husband and wife in *Palm Beach Story*, and FAR RIGHT, Eddie Bracken, centre, the little man caught up in situations too big for him, in *Hail the Conquering Hero*. Both McCrea and Bracken were actors whom Sturges admired and used more than once, but the two with Bracken appeared in virtually every Sturges film and were essential to his world – left, the effeminate busybody Franklin Pangborn, and the marvellously gruff William Demarest.

intended, since the film is often hilarious: but then throughout the film he seems to be crying out for the best of all possible worlds.

Palm Beach Story (1942) has no such preoccupations, being content to chart the amorous adventures of a millionaire (Rudy Vallee, made up to look like John D. Rockefeller III) and his sister (Mary Astor) with a divorcing husband (McCrea) and wife (Claudette Colbert). Among marital comedies there is none better, with dialogue not so much notable for its wit as for its bite and discrimination. Sturges catapults ideas one after the other, as in the superb scene when Vallee is explaining his penny-pinching ways to an artlessly enquiring Colbert. And the slapstick – notably when Colbert is adopted by the Ale and Quail Club – is merely incidental to the comedy, unlike, say, *Bringing Up Baby*, where it is essential to it. In the same tradition, neither McCrea nor Colbert plays for sympathy, and in fact their roles are hardly admirable, have-nots no better than the haves. Yet the lack of any moral centre is one of the film's most invigorating features. James Agee, remarking upon the evasions and cynicism of **The Miracle of Morgan's Creek** (1944), suspected that 'Sturges feels that conscience and comedy are incompatible,' adding that 'it would be hard for a man of talent to make a more self-destructive mistake.'

That talent was in fact evolving: Sturges's first films (i.e. as director) look

back to the social comedies of the Thirties, while both *The Lady Eve* and *Palm Beach Story* are in the tradition which stretches back to Wilde, or even Restoration comedy. But both *Miracle* and **Hail the Conquering Hero** (1944) are contemporary tales, built around the reaction of small-town America to the War, as represented by the military in its midst. *Miracle* encapsulates that period when G.I.s were on the loose for loose girls, and girls were glad to be that way. Possibly the Hays Office insisted that this particular girl (Betty Hutton) marry her G.I., but the wedding is the only event of one wild night that she remembers. The audacity of the resulting situations is encouraging but, apart from the breakneck pace, all that I find to admire is Sturges's view of a world where all well-meant schemes go wrong and opportunists wait on every corner. If *Conquering Hero* looks back to *Christmas in July*, with its protagonist caught up in plots not of his own making, its comment on American gullibility is freely borrowed from *Nothing Sacred*. Woodrow Lafayette Pershing Truesmith (Eddie Bracken) is recognised by a marine sergeant (William Demarest) as 'Hinky Dinky's boy', i.e. the son of an old comrade-in-arms, so he and his buddies phone Woodrow's mother to tell her that he is a hero, which, as someone says, is the least you can do for a mother. The town goes ecstatic, but the squirming Woodrow refuses to wear uniform till someone points out that his grandfather wore his Civil War uniform as long as he lived, so that we could never forget that brother fought brother – which is the most extreme example of Sturges's cynicism. His second half is predictable, as if Sturges, having poked fun at both the cults for military heroics and Monism, was afraid to go any further. However, the film provides Demarest's biggest role in films, and for that it is notable; Raymond Walburn and Franklin Pangborn are also at their best, the other constants of the Sturges stock company – the realist and the two dreamers.

Despite its faults, the film confirms Sturges as far ahead of his peers in light comedy, and **The Great Moment** (1944) proves him level with them in more serious matters – though a number of comic sequences indicate that, long before films like *M*★*A*★*S*★*H* (q.v.), he found humour in pain. Here the hero is W. T. G. Morton, the nineteenth-century dentist who claimed the discovery of the anaesthetic effects of ether, and he is played by Joel McCrea, Sturges's favourite leading man. Biographies of such figures were generally accorded the greatest respect in Hollywood but Sturges's own interest in Morton, began because he had been a man who had benefited society but had been so little thanked, remembered or admired. In fact Morton's claim was much disputed, and the disappointments of his life would have made a much more ironic – and indeed a more Sturges-like – ending than the happy one the film provides. That is Sturges's own ending, as referred to in the title, but the original structure of the film, as suggested by *The Power and the Glory*, did not attempt a strict chronology. Paramount disliked much of the film, which included in the first frame a shot of Morton's grave, followed by one of a modern operation; Sturges, tired of his disputes with the company, left the recutting to his usual editor, Stuart Gilmore – after which the film sat on the shelf for two years, finally being released in 1944 to almost complete indifference. There is no doubt that it is less than we might expect from one who has been called a genius by some, and though still weighty in comparison with the films on Pasteur, Ehrlich, etc. the writing is similarly conventional.

In *Sullivan's Travels*, when Sullivan tells his bosses that he wants to make serious films, one of them observes, 'Something like Capra, I suppose?' to which Sullivan flashes back, 'What's the matter with Capra?' The film answers the question: nothing, but Sturges lacked Capra's belief that there would always be someone to speak up for the 'little man'. As Capra went to war, Sturges rose, to blaze like a comet, and not till Billy Wilder made *The Apartment* (q.v.) would any American director equal the balance of comedy and seriousness of *Sullivan's Travels*. With Sturges's decline, Wilder, the other great cynic of the American cinema, had emerged as a bright new talent. Like John Huston (q.v.) he was encouraged by Sturges's success to turn director. Sturges's decline was quick. He had become very expensive: whole towns had to be constructed and hundreds of extras employed. He wrote at night, slept mornings, which meant that shooting did not start till the afternoon; and though he shot with few retakes, the longer schedule increased the budget. He had also become autocratic, demanding a place in the commissary for his stock company on a par with deMille's. Nevertheless, when he left Paramount at the end of 1943, and while that company pondered on the box-office appeal of three unreleased films, he was asked to come back. He refused, also rejecting an offer from M-G-M, and with an old friend, Howard Hughes, formed California Pictures. Hughes's interest in the company was the promotion of his latest protégée, Faith Domergue.

He believed that she could become a bigger star than Jane Russell (for whom he had fashioned *The Outlaw*), but the costume film he planned for her, *Vendetta*, with Sturges as producer and Max Ophuls directing, had to be postponed (it was eventually released in 1950, with the direction credited to Mel Ferrer). Hughes's interference and vacillation drove both men 'to distraction', according to Hughes's biographer, Noah Dietrich, but with Hughes's money and independence Sturges 'went wild'. His contract with Hughes called for two more films as producer-director-writer and he conceived the idea of making a film with Harold Lloyd, whom he admired because he had achieved a long career with complete independence. He inveigled him out of retirement (Lloyd had found the fun had gone out of filming while making *Professor Beware*), and **The Sin of Harold Diddlebock** (1947) begins with the last reel of *The Freshman*, for its purpose is to examine the college hero later in life. We find little has changed: he was an accountant and has remained one. However, he is suddenly sacked, and with his savings has his first alcoholic drink, which sends him on a binge, during which he buys an eccentric check suit and wins and loses a fortune – losing it mainly by acquiring a circus. It is a very poor film indeed, and the charge against Sturges is not that he misuses Lloyd, though he does, but that he does not begin to understand him. It is grievous to see the irrepressible young Harold become a failure – the man who surmounted so many plights and dangers now facing the same yet virtually turning away. He is saved by chance and not by his own skill.

Lloyd, Sturges and Hughes were the strangest of bedfellows, and Lloyd, who had been persuaded that the film would be an attack on smugness, loathed it. So did everyone else. After previews it was re-titled *Mad Wednesday*, as which it limped around the U.S. for a while, not surfacing in New York till 1951. Its artistic and commercial failure shattered Sturges, as well as the deal with Hughes. Sturges never recovered, and his drinking did not help his later work.

As we saw, Sturges, like Capra before him, paid tribute to the one true independent, Walt Disney (1901–66). His is one of the industry's great success stories, perhaps because he was the antithesis of Welles and Sturges – of artisan stock, lowbrow, very much concerned with pleasing his audiences. Like them, however, he put his 'art' before financial consideration, which is not contradictory, for his taste was far closer to audiences than his advisers understood. He made the animated cartoon into an art for the masses, which is why David Low, the British newspaper cartoonist, called him 'the most significant figure in graphic arts since Leonardo'.

He was born in Chicago; a talent for drawing took him into commercial art, and in Kansas City, with Ub Iwerks (1901–71) he began making animated shorts for cinemas. In Hollywood he found buyers for a series of short cartoons called *Alice in Cartoonland*, and with Iwerks started a series of shorts for Universal called *Oswald the Rabbit*. He, or they, created Mickey Mouse in 1928, beyond which it is difficult to determine to what extent Iwerks was the creative force at the Disney studios. He received credit for the early cartoons, which remain by far the most inventive ever to emanate from Disney, though Disney disliked giving credit – till persuaded to do so for the feature-length cartoons, which were issued with such extensive lists of names that the public only remembered his. He may have been a kindly employer, as has been claimed, but the publicity department created a mystique about him, as though he created the films single-handed. Iwerks left in 1931 and did not return for many years, his work for other companies reputedly suffering from his lack of narrative sense and also, as an independent, the financial acumen of Disney's chief adviser, his brother Roy Disney. It is more than likely that Iwerks had left a durable mark on the Disney team: the quality of the shorts had begun to decline before the end of the decade (and production had by then started on the early feature cartoons, even those released as late as 1943).

The first Mickey Mouse short was **Plane Crazy** (1928) and the second **Steamboat Willie** (1928), to which was added, after completion, a synchronised score. Their immediate success led to Columbia reaching an agreement with Disney to release his films, starting with the synchronised *Plane Crazy*. To anyone who knows only the later, epicene Mickey, these early works are astonishing: he could put his anatomy to amazing use, and he could be ferocious and randy. The screen is ablaze with action, everything is animated, including inanimate objects – usually involved, like the casts of animals, in questionable play. In **Karnival Kid** (1929) the hot dogs are obviously phallic, and one has pants like a foreskin for Mickey to peel back to tan his behind. The anal and the phallic humour were quickly banished – perhaps when the implications were pointed out to Disney; a harsher cinema climate dictated the end of such commonplaces as yowling alley cats and flying chamber pots. The pre-Code Disney films could be called Rabelaisian, but the term does not apply to those made later.

In 1929 the first 'Silly Symphony'

appeared, **The Skeleton Dance**, in which amazing things happen to rattling bones. The series went into colour in 1932, and the first in Technicolor, *Flowers and Trees*, so impressed the Academy of Motion Picture Arts and Sciences that it introduced a new category in its annual awards – Short Subject: Cartoon – which Disney then won annually till the end of the decade, despite his several imitators. This Oscar, however, went only to the Silly Symphonies, and then usually to the winsome rather than the raucous – **The Three Little Pigs** (1933), *The Tortoise and the Hare* (1934), *Three Orphan Kittens* (1935), *Country Cousin* (1936), *The Old Mill* (1937), *Ferdinand the Bull* (1938) and *The Ugly Duckling* (1939). The cartoons, however, were not particularly profitable: when in 1932 Disney moved to United Artists they were guaranteed an advance of $20,000 each from that source, to be set against the manufacturing cost of around $27,500, which almost doubled with the making of prints and shipping. Despite their popularity, their average gross during the first year in release was only $80,000; *The Three Little Pigs*, however, took $125,000 in that time, and twice as much again before being withdrawn. Its phenomenal success bewildered Disney, and since its theme tune, 'Who's Afraid of the Big Bad Wolf?', and the film itself, seemed to mean so much to Depression-hit America, he is said to have screened it constantly to find out why – but there was no discernible message, only a tale of two improvident pigs and their wise brother, whose brick-built house keeps out the salivating wolf (who was at some later point redrawn and re-recorded to remove the characteristics supposedly typical of Jewish pedlars). At the end of the year *The New York Times* 'safely' ventured that it had been 'shown at more theaters simultaneously than any other film, short or feature length'. It temporarily reintroduced the industry's practice of bicycling prints.

As box-office attractions the Disney shorts outdistanced any other item on the bill except the main feature, and audiences roared their approval when the first titles flashed upon the screen. The Mouse, already joined by Minnie, Pluto the Dog and Goofy, went into colour in 1934, the same year that the bad-tempered bird, Donald Duck, made his debut – and he proved so popular that he later 'starred' alone. The public mania for the menagerie meant a flood of comic strips and subsidiary rights of all kinds, from towels to toothbrushes; and highbrow and lowbrow alike had no reservations about Mickey.

Disney's decision to make a feature-length cartoon was born less from a desire to capitalise on this success than from ambition: it had not been done, therefore he would do it – which he did, against almost total opposition, and in addition to foregoing the financial security which would have been his at the time. When the contract with United Artists came to be renegotiated in 1936 the Disney brothers not only insisted on retaining television rights – a good indication of their farsightedness – but wanted to include the feature cartoon already in production. The directors of United Artists were not interested, and a deal was made instead with R.K.O., which took the shorts at better terms – advancing the total cost of production, with a promise of 50% of the gross receipts when that investment had been recouped – but insisted on a separate agreement for the feature. Virtually Disney's only ally was the manager of Radio City Music Hall, who booked it sight unseen; by the time it premiered there, five years from its inception, the cost had escalated from the original estimate of $250,000 to over $1,700,000, partly as a result of Disney's augmenting his staff to make it. Disney's survival did not depend on it, but many expected him to be crippled with debts for years: the film, however, was a triumph for him, both within and outside the industry.

The film is, of course, **Snow White and the Seven Dwarfs** (1937), and the Disney Organisation has reissued it since at seven-year intervals, to new generations of children, though few can have experienced the same enchantment as those who saw it earlier. I do not believe that it has been bettered in the intervening years, but I have to say that to my own generation it was a completely new experience; many of us had never seen a film, and certainly not television. It is a story with terror and hope, deception and romance, with a special magic in the sequence when the dwarfs entertain Snow White – simply because audience pleasure is balanced by the knowledge that the Queen is planning

Disneyland

The artwork for *Snow White and the Seven Dwarfs*, ABOVE RIGHT, was the basis for the original advertising campaign, and has been used in moderated form for most of the reissues – sometimes in inferior manner, which is curious for a company which specialises in design. RIGHT, *Pinocchio* and ABOVE, Mickey Mouse, of course.

further witchery. Sentimentality is kept at bay by Grumpy – murmuring 'Mush' while Snow White warbles 'Some Day My Prince Will Come' – and the comic stuff remains funny still because the dwarfs are so richly characterised, atoning for the saccharine heroine and the operatic posturing of the Prince. If the animals of the forest are most kindly regarded as being in the taste of the time, the film survives marvellously on its visual qualities, both in its evocation of the Brothers Grimm and the colours of its palette: the luminosity of Snow White as she runs through the forest, the predominantly crimson, fawn, ochre and brown of the dwarfs' clothes and the velvety shimmer of the Queen's gowns and the witch's cloak. The concept of these two ladies – though they are in fact the same – is genuinely astonishing, with the magic mirror, the huntsman's shadow, the transformation scene and the vultures circling as the dwarfs pursue the witch up the rain-wet rocks. (Recent reissues have lost the witch kicking the prone skeleton as she proceeds to her Stygian boat.) These effects were reached by committee – although David Hand is credited as supervising editor – but there must have been elements in the climate of the time for something so imaginative and terrifying to emerge.

Disney's faith in feature-length cartoons was so strong that he had already begun work on **Pinocchio** (1940), which is also peculiarly sinister. From *The Skeleton Dance* onwards, through Pegleg Pete, Mickey's enemy, and such shorts as *The Mad Doctor*, a spoof of Frankenstein, the studio had been practised in the gruesome; and Carlo Collodi's fantasy was ideal material, concerning an innocent in a malevolent universe. On the side of the puppet-come-to-life-Pinocchio are his loving but ineffectual 'father', the insect appointed to be his conscience and the formidable Blue Fairy. Against him are a series of monsters and freaks progressively more terrifying: Honest John the fox and his simple but vicious assistant, Gideon; Stromboli, the puppeteer; the stupid Lampwick, who will lead Pinocchio into corruption and vice; the Coachman, who manages to make Stromboli's greed and malice seem almost virtuous; and Monstro the Whale. The film may be a bastardisation of the book, but it is a black masterpiece, with one sequence – that in which the boys are metamorphosed into donkeys – as terrifying as any ever put on film.

Fantasia (1940) was begun in the wake of the acclaim for *Snow White*, and was a bold undertaking. The Silly Symphonies had demonstrated Disney's interest in the marriage of sound and image; The Sorceror's Apprentice was planned as a short, but Stokowski expressed a wish to conduct the score and suggested a full-length cartoon on similar lines. Disney saw himself as a populariser, and bringing music to the masses became his dream, as it was Stokowski's avowed intention 'that [its] beauty and inspiration must not be restricted to a privileged few.' Whether more than a few would be receptive was another matter, and as it turned out they decisively were not. The critics, however, were fascinated, if polarised between those who considered 'great' music demeaned and those who, like Bosley Crowther, of *The New York Times*, told readers that 'history was made last night.' More cautiously, Frank Hoellering in *The Nation* called it 'a promising monstrosity' and in Britain James Agate found it 'magnificent and trivial, inspiring and commonplace, exciting and tedious'. Today one might wish for the animators to have departed more frequently from the Disney style – at its worst in the interpretation of Beethoven's Pastoral, with sexless centaurs and cute cherubs. The Dance of the Hours is a dullish satire on ballet, with hippopotami and other animals in tutus, and The Nutcracker Suite is variable, at its best in the Thistle cossack dance and that of the Chinese mushrooms. The introduction, abstract patterns to Bach's Toccata and Fugue in D Minor, soars; The Rite of Spring, curtailed and rearranged, astonishes with its vomiting volcanoes and shuddering mountain-quakes, and The Sorcerer's Apprentice, with Mickey Mouse, is equally effective; while The Night on a Bare Mountain does have the quality of Bosch, and in sheer drawing technique is more advanced than the rest of the film – though it is followed by an interpretation of 'Ave Maria' more suitable to a nursery wall. The film cost $2,300,000 and was made under great financial pressure when the profits from *Snow White* were exhausted and the banks refused credit. If Disney had expected it to

Mickey Mouse's most popular rivals were Betty Boop, BELOW, drawn by Max Fleischer for Paramount, and Tom and Jerry, ABOVE, drawn by Hanna and Barbera for M-G-M.

make money it was because he had confidence in all his judgments, as he had every right to have – at least, from the commercial standpoint. But in this case the public was not ready for serious music, and though that situation would change within a few years the first reissues were tentative; not till a decade later did the film start to enjoy a wide popularity, and it is difficult, today, to reconcile it with its former reputation as 'highbrow'.

Meanwhile **Dumbo** (1941) did much to restore Disney's financial standing. Taken from a run-of-the-mill children's story, it was originally intended to be a Silly Symphony and cost only $700,000. Disney resisted pressure to make it longer than 64 minutes and, despite comparatively simple animation, the film is packed with a number of splendid items: the flying elephant himself; the circus train, chugging away in the manner of the Silly Symphonies; 'Pink Elephants on Parade', an arabesque for elephants; and the song of the crows, 'When I See an Elephant Fly', in which the view of Negroes as flash dandies is alleviated by the joyousness of the number itself. **Bambi** (1942), three times as expensive and much longer in preparation, is technically a much more accomplished work. The story of a baby deer and his growing up, from the novel by Felix Salten, its hold on sentiment, when necessary, is equally sure; and the treatment of the forest glades in lightly Impressionist manner indicates an artistry seldom found

thereafter in the studio's work. Indeed, this enchanting film is Disney's last major work.

The decline of the short cartoons had already begun, and it is possible that Disney's artistic judgment faltered under pressure. The popularity of *Bambi* hardly offset its cost, and his losses were such at the time the U.S. entered the War that he was only too happy to take commissions from the government, which realised the propaganda uses of the animated film. Most of the resulting shorts were for showing on service installations; a feature, *Victory Through Air Power* (1943), with Donald Duck, was released to cinemas. Also as part of the war effort Disney toured the southern continent on behalf of the U.S. State Department, and made, with **Saludos Amigos** (1942) and **The Three Caballeros** (1944), hotchpotch assemblies of animated Latin-American travelogues and unrelated short cartoons, linked by the presence of Donald Duck. The second of the two used both drawings and humans, of which supposed innovation the publicity department made much, overlooking the fact that Disney had done that at the start of his career, in the *Alice* cartoons. The method here is a little more sophisticated: settings for humans who are made to look like cartoons, some back projection and some painting on the finished film. The final sequence, as a real girl sings inside an animated flower, has a few abstract designs which recall the best of *Fantasia*.

Disney's fading pre-eminence in the short cartoon was indicated in 1940 when the appropriate Oscar went to M-G-M's Tom and Jerry, the malicious but hard-done-by cat and his cheeky rodent adversary; and though Disney took the award again in the two subsequent years it went to Tom and Jerry five times during the next six years (and on the other occasion to Warner Bros.). Until that time most of Disney's rivals had followed his lead, including the team of Hugh Harmon and Ralph Ising at M-G-M with their 'Happy Harmonies', though they claimed to have used both Sound and serious music (a Strauss waltz) before Disney. Their reign in Fred Quimby's Shorts Department ended as Tom and Jerry rose, giving way to Joseph Barbera (b. 1911) who had started the cat and mouse as a magazine strip, and his partner William Hanna (b. 1920). The two hundred cartoons they turned out over the twenty-year period are seldom as inventive as the Iwerks Mouse, but good enough to supplant the Disney characters as popular favourites. Of the others, perhaps only Bugs Bunny and company at Warners were serious contenders – and probably the Terry-Toons at Fox were the least likely. Most of these rivals were created by defectors from Disney, and Hanna and Barbera are unusual among animators of the time in that they never worked for him.

However, Disney's most serious rival was flourishing when he joined the industry. Max Fleischer (1889–1973) made 'Out of the Inkwell', a series combining live action and animation. With his brother, Dave, as his administrator, he had a success in the early Thirties with Betty Boop, a sexy little flapper, and later a more pronounced one with Popeye, the bellicose but soft-hearted sailor. Paramount distributed, and after the success of *Snow White* agreed to a feature, **Gulliver's Travels** (1939), which uses the first section of Swift's novel for a pantomime about a helpful giant in a warlike kingdom. The film is technically often impressive, but like the Capraesque **Mr Bug Goes to Town** (1941) too slight to do more than mildly amuse. The second film was a complete failure, since Fleischer had never been able to enter the world of children as Disney had, and that was something, apparently, that even adult audiences wanted from full-length cartoons. He did not attempt another, leaving that field free to Disney, who was to have no further rival during his lifetime.

There were in Hollywood at this time four foreign directors who managed to preserve artistic control over the films they made – if only at the cost of moving from studio to studio. Easily the most successful was Alfred Hitchcock, under contract to Selznick, whose reduced activity allowed him to 'loan out' Hitchcock for projects that they both considered suitable. After *Rebecca* Hitchcock made the more characteristic **Foreign Correspondent** (1940) for Walter Wanger, who was more willing to appreciate his particular talent than Selznick. Wanger's interest in foreign politics had led him to buy the memoirs of Vincent Sheean, 'Personal History', to serve as a basis for a tale of an American reporter in Europe; but the early scripts were abandoned as the European situation changed, and it was turned over to Hitchcock to make the film to his British formula – in his own words, 'the innocent bystander who becomes involved in an intrigue'. His starting point was the superb sequence of the assassination in the rain, followed by the windmill hideout. Equally memorable are the scenes where the hero (Joel McCrea) is at the top of Westminster Cathedral with a professional assassin (Edmund Gwenn), and that in which McCrea escapes his own would-be assassins along the hotel parapet in robe but no pants – a suitable garb for a reporter to work in in the privacy of his own room but leading, once down from the parapet, to farcical complications. This is one of Hitchcock's funniest films, as it is one of the most ingenious, and plotted as cleverly as any of Graham Greene's political thrillers. The screenplay is credited to Hitchcock's old associates, Joan Harrison and Charles Bennett, with dialogue by James Hilton and Robert Benchley. Benchley is also in the cast, which is a splendid one: Albert Basserman as a statesman considered able to prevent war; Herbert Marshall as head of the Universal Peace Party; George Sanders as a reporter; and Laraine Day as the heroine. Unfortunately, the last sequences have dated: the shooting-down of the clipper over the Atlantic seems a last-minute idea to remind audiences of the seriousness of war, and McCrea broadcasting to the U.S. – while bombs fall around him in London – now seems banal.

Hitchcock directed **Mr and Mrs Smith** (1941) as a gesture to Carole Lombard, who co-stars with Robert Montgomery. They play quarrelling spouses who philander ostentatiously after parting: Hitchcock claimed that he did not understand the characters, so filmed the Norman Krasna dialogue as written. The sole funny sequence – that in which Lombard struggles into an old dress – therefore may be his. Returning to crime, he was no happier with **Suspicion** (1941), accepting a foolishly simulated England of thatched manor houses. Presumably, however, he was responsible for the screenplay – by Miss Harrison, Alma Reville (his wife) and Samson Raphaelson – which does scant justice to the original novel, 'Before the

The fifty-year film career of Alfred Hitchcock has a number of highs and lows: the late Thirties and the Fifties are certainly high points, and he also made some of his most enjoyable films in the first half of the Forties. RIGHT, the assassination in the Netherlands which sets off the events in *Foreign Correspondent*.

Fact' by Francis Iles. That was about a woman who gradually realises that her husband plans to murder her, but who is so much in love that she does not mind, whereas the film is a dotty cat-and-mouse tale, leading to a chase sequence rendered ludicrous by a happy ending. Cary Grant is the cat, and Joan Fontaine, who won an Oscar for the role, the mouse. Hitchcock explained the film's artistic failure by saying 'the producers would have refused' to let Grant be a murderer.

The producers of both films were at R.K.O., but finding another independent producer – Frank Lloyd at Universal – Hitchcock again hit his best form, providing the scenario from which Peter Viertel, Miss Harrison and Dorothy Parker wrote the screenplay. **Saboteur** (1942) significantly is to formula, about a man (Robert Cummings) who flees because he thinks no one will believe his innocence. The crime committed is sabotage in a Californian factory, which leads to the unmasking of a spy ring in New York, on the way to which are such diversions and/or set-

pieces as a seemingly deserted shanty town near Boulder Dam, a chase through Radio City Music Hall and another on the crown of the Statue of Liberty. **Shadow of a Doubt** (1943) gained a reputation as Hitchcock's own favourite among his films, but if he gave that impression, he said later, that was because it caused the least dissatisfaction to those who complained of implausibilities in his plots. The situation is that of a murderer (Joseph Cotten) living in a family, and what happens when his adored and adoring niece (Teresa Wright) finds out. What she does *not* do is go to the local police (when she cannot contact her detective boyfriend); but otherwise this is a clever screenplay as written by Thornton Wilder, Sally Benson and Alma Reville, from a story by Gordon McDonnell, a novelist married to the head of the Selznick story department. Wilder had been invited to participate because he had written 'Our Town', and this particular small town – Santa Rosa, California – has such ordinariness that the presence there of an evil man is the more powerfully felt. It was unusual at the time to go on location when simulation was possible on the back lot; and the film was further admired for the intimations of the murderer's psyche, though these, like the heavy ironies, now seem jejune.

Hired out again, to 20th Century-Fox, Hitchcock made **Lifeboat** (1944), proceeding from a desire to produce a motion picture from limited material – in this case a party adrift at sea, a 'microcosm', as he himself put it. John Steinbeck was invited to write the script, but his efforts proved inadequate and the screenplay was eventually credited to Jo Swerling. On the lifeboat are Kovac (John Hodiak) and other crew-members (William Bendix, Hume Cronyn and the black Canada Lee) of the torpedoed ship; a nurse (Mary Anderson), a millionaire (Henry Hull) and a lacquered and be-minked journalist (Tallulah Bankhead), complete with typewriter. In time they pick up another woman (Heather Angel) with a 'biby', as she calls it, and a German captain (Walter Slezak), whom they christen Willy. They let Willy guide them, and each time he glances surreptitiously at his compass the audience's tensions and suspicions mount. He is, of course, the representative totalitarian, controlled, efficient and calm-in-an-emergency, while the others – a spectrum ranging from the Fascist millionaire to the Communist-inclined Kovac – are in disarray, panicky, self-pitying and self-absorbed. Hitchcock said later that he wanted to show that 'while the democracies were completely disorganised, all the Germans were clearly headed in the same direction. So here was a statement telling the democracies to put their differences aside temporarily . . .' which is an improvement at least on the only other political statement he made in a film – in *Saboteur*, to urge good Americans to look for Nazis in the woodpile. His other comments on the film are as pompous as his direction is expert; he permits no sense of studio-tank or back-projection and although Miss Bankhead is incongruous, both she and Hitchcock know it.

Jean Renoir, less classifiable, had a much harder struggle than Hitchcock. As the maker of *La Grande Illusion* and *La Bête Humaine*, he had no difficulty getting a contract – with 20th Century-Fox, which offered him the 'class' subjects, historical or European, which Hollywood associated with esteemed directors. He was not interested, especially when he realised that the results would have to conform to the studio's standards – which meant abandoning those methods which had led to his reputation in the first place. Determined to tackle an American subject, he came upon the screenplay of **Swamp Water** (1941), written by Dudley Nichols from a novel by Vereen Bell for John Ford, who had turned it down. Renoir was allowed to go to the Okefenokee region of Georgia to do location work. The film itself indicates that he thought it worthwhile to tell of plain folks against their genuine background, but the screenplay is unequal to the occasion, contrived and, until the climax, blindingly obvious. Even Walter Huston fails to make his character come alive, and Dana Andrews and Anne Baxter are not the screen's most sympathetic lovers. Renoir was at one time removed from the film, when shooting went over schedule, and he was not permitted to do his own editing, which he regretted. He did not work for Zanuck again, and in his memoir sadly quoted Zanuck's opinion of him: 'Renoir has a lot of talent, but he's not one of us.'

In that same memoir Renoir did not mention his experience at Universal, which gave the industry good reason to think again about employing him. The studio had decided that what Deanna Durbin needed at this stage in her career was a European-type movie, and Renoir was given virtual carte blanche, the sole proviso being that she be the central character. He began the film that eventually became *The Amazing Mrs Holliday* (q.v.), concerning Durbin in charge of some Chinese refugee children, but after some weeks of filming he decided that he was dissatisfied with it. He would prefer, he said, to make a modern version of 'The Taming of the Shrew', set in and around a Texas gas station. Both the star and Universal liked the idea, if unsure whether she would be credible as a gas-station attendant; but Renoir himself quickly found that he disliked this idea too and reverted to the original project – which he could not finish since Dudley Nichols had arranged a joint venture at R.K.O. Universal, after six months' filming and no vehicle in sight for its most popular star, were glad to see him go. One of Miss Durbin's writers, Bruce Manning, was given the task of salvaging what he could of the first story. Renoir had, of course, behaved similarly in France over *Partie de Campagne*.

The R.K.O. film, written and produced by himself and Nichols, was **This Land Is Mine** (1943), 'intended to show that life for the citizen of a country occupied by an enemy power was not so simple as Hollywood seemed to think.' That country – unnamed in the film but clearly meant to be France – is at first affected only when teachers are required to tear pages from history books, but when supplies for Germany are blown up hostages are taken. Interest centres on two teaching colleagues (Charles Laughton, Maureen O'Hara) and he, a coward, is forced into bravery. When the Gestapo finally comes for him he is declaiming the Declaration of the Rights of Man – a forgivable ending for local audiences, but when French audiences saw it after the Liberation they laughed, and Renoir was ridiculed by former advocates of his work. Worse errors are the Hollywood-style close-ups of Miss O'Hara and the scenery-chewing performances of Una O'Connor as Laughton's mother and Walter Slezak as the German governor. Laughton, basing his characterisation on Renoir himself, cannot save the film, since Renoir, dis-

trusting his audience, is constantly overstating in an already melodramatic tale – in sum one much inferior to the not dissimilar *The Moon Is Down* (q.v.). The sole indication of subtlety is, surprisingly, the performance of George Sanders as a patriot determined to make concessions to the invaders.

After another long period of inactivity Renoir restored his reputation with **The Southerner** (1945), backed by Robert Hakim and David L. Loew at United Artists, which loathed the film and only took it because Loew had interests in other of their projects. Hakim had offered the screenplay to Renoir, who disliked it; but he admired the book of short stories on which it was based, 'Hold Autumn in Your Hand' by George Sessions Perry, and proceeded to write his own script. It is a wresting-a-living-from-the-soil story, reminiscent of John Ford's rural movies. The touches of melodrama are more in keeping with American taste of the time than with Renoir's French work, but the real failings are elsewhere. The story concerns people who are grindingly poor, but Renoir feels no indignation at their plight. He offers instead affection, a lovely quality but not the one needed. He hardly shows us the anxiety of the young couple (Zachary Scott, Betty Field), but emphasises instead their love and mutual respect for each other. It was not enough to use non-stars and deglamorise them further, though Miss Field is moving as a young woman who has reflected on her lot and come to accept it.

The film won First Prize at the first postwar Venice Festival, and its critical success enabled Renoir to set up **The Diary of a Chambermaid** (1946), envisaged as a vehicle for a friend, Paulette Goddard – whose husband, Burgess Meredith, co-wrote and co-produced with Renoir, as well as performing in the film. It occasioned little interest then and, as with Renoir's other American films, was execrated in France. It has been rehabilitated since, and if flawed by the obvious studio exteriors – even though designed, as with *This Land Is Mine*, by Eugene Lourié – is otherwise among his best work. Octave Mirbeau's novel had long been dear to Renoir, who had echoed it in *La Règle du Jeu*, in the scenes of the servants aping their masters. Celestine (Miss Goddard) is a

Renoir's *Diary of a Chambermaid* gives the chambermaid, Paulette Goddard, a number of piquant adventures – mainly amorous. Here she is between the two chief men in her life – left, Hurd Hatfield, her boss by virtue of his being his mother's son, and right, Francis Lederer, a companion of hers from below stairs.

Paris-born maid whose situation with the family Lanlaire involves her with the vicious Joseph (Francis Lederer), the valet, and the whimsical captain (Meredith) next door. The screenplay follows a dramatised version once done in Paris, and Buñuel's later film (q.v.) follows Renoir's, both of them incorporating Celestine's recollections of earlier employments, but using different ones. In Mirbeau a grandmother encouraged Celestine to amuse her tubercular grandson. Here, Madame Lanlaire (Judith Anderson) wants her to look pretty enough to keep at home her wandering, wayward son, Georges (Hurd Hatfield).

The film begins as a satire on the bourgeoisie: the dominating mistress of the house, whose relationship with the valet is perhaps more intimate than it should be; and the useless master (Reginald Owen), who is sent out on walks or to prune the roses, and is not allowed a word or a penny of his own, although he carries on a petty feud with the retired officer next door. This latter gentleman, lecherous and eccentric, is mothered by his servant (Florence Bates), though if it suits him he locks her up. This playful mood is abandoned when Celestine settles for the valet, his ambitions of more consideration to her than the fact that he is a murderer; and the mood turns black when he uses his whip on the villagers. It should have ended there, with the two lovers riding on, ambition achieved but outcast. However, Celestine turns tail, for a tacked-on 'happy' ending as unconvincing as any in Hollywood history. Somewhere between Mirbeau and Miss Goddard Renoir compromised.

When the film failed Renoir again found himself casting around for work.* It was now possible for him to return to France, but he wanted to stay in Hollywood – he resided in Los Angeles for the rest of his life – and therefore approached R.K.O. with a view to making low budget films of quality. He found a sympathetic producer there, and R.K.O. offered them a starring vehicle for Joan Bennett, **The Woman on the Beach** (1947); but Renoir had to cope on his own when the producer died, and the original novel – 'None So Blind' by Mitchell Wilson – proved more intractable than he had hoped. The result is a very

*Another project had foundered in 1944, when R.K.O. cancelled *The Temptress* after Jean Gabin had insisted that Marlene Dietrich replace Louise Rainer as his co-star.

ordinary melodrama about a bored, trampy wife (Miss Bennett), her blind, bigoted and selfish husband (Charles Bickford) and a moody marine officer (Robert Ryan). It is not Renoir's worst film, but one without a shred of his character, except that the central situation reflects the pessimism of his previous film. He had reason to be pessimistic, since he would not find work in Hollywood again.

René Clair was more successful in America, by the industry's own standards; but the four films he made there are not among his best. Disillusioned with his experiences in the British studios, he had returned to France in 1939, and had begun work on *Air Pur*, a story of slum children in a summer camp – an idea which had come to him when meeting his own small son at the Gare de Lyon. Shooting was abandoned in August 1939 and most of the unit was mobilised. By the time it would have been possible to resume filming most of the children in the cast had grown too much. Meanwhile Clair signed a contract which called for him to make a film in Hollywood for either R.K.O. or Columbia, and the Ministry of Information discussed with both him and Julien Duvivier the possibility of making French films in Hollywood: that project became impossible after France submitted to Germany's terms, but the two directors were allowed to leave for the U.S.

The first film made by Clair was in fact at Universal, where Joe Pasternak thought he might be the ideal director for Dietrich. Clair was attracted to Norman Krasna's screenplay, since it is set in the then French city of New Orleans, in the nineteenth century, and his sense of irony is apparent in the otherwise wan **The Flame of New Orleans** (1941). He capitalises on Dietrich's lack of range by allowing her to use her best expression – a look of surprise. Here it indicates her astonishment that her imposture (as a countess) should be accepted so easily; and he photographs her as did von Sternberg, with veils.

The film's failure left Clair free to instigate his next project, **I Married a Witch** (1942), based on Thorne Smith's last, unfinished comic novel, 'The Passionate Witch'. A chance remark to Preston Sturges brought him and the project to Paramount, who thought it ideal for its new star, Veronica Lake – whom Clair accepted on Sturges's urging. In the event the studio disliked the finished film and sold it to United Artists when that company was desperate for product. Presumably both were aware of the film's commercial worth – i.e. not much, since whimsy was usually unsaleable, though the names of Lake and Fredric March were. In fact whimsy began to enjoy a vogue during the war years, and like Duvivier's *Flesh and Fantasy* (q.v.) this film was highly regarded. Since the March character is candidate in a gubernatorial election a political aura is established, but the promised satire does not materialise and we are left with the tiresome tale of a respectable man pursued by a sexy vamp. Since she had been a witch and is now a ghost the film recalls Clair's earlier excursions into the supernatural, *Le Fantôme du Moulin Rouge*; the level of humour is little higher.

United Artists were sufficiently pleased with the result to ask Clair to stay, and he made **It Happened Tomorrow** (1943), which he himself thought the best of his American films. Of the three comedies it has the soundest basic idea – a newspaper reporter (Dick Powell) magically finds himself the recipient of the next day's paper, which enables him to make some wonderful scoops and become very rich via his bets at the race track. The early editions continue, but on the third day he reads of his own death and nothing, it seems, can prevent him from being at the appointed place at the appointed time. Powell's smugness harms both the tension and the humour, and as written by Clair and Dudley Nichols the screenplay is superior to the direction. Nichols led Clair to an independent company releasing through 20th Century-Fox, and he wrote the screenplay of **And Then There Were None** (1945), based on the most celebrated of Agatha Christie's thrillers, 'Ten Little Niggers'. Since the story is taller than tall – ten guests are mysteriously killed during one night at an island mansion – some humour is injected, without the characters being any less flat than as left by Mrs Christie. The voice of the dead host on a record is that of Alfred Hitchcock, an in-joke which few filmgoers of the time could have appreciated. However, the humour is not taken far enough: thus when the doctor (Walter Huston) observes 'but this knife I removed from the back of the victim means only one thing' everyone concerned seems to be in dead earnest. Clair returned to France, and although R.K.O. had a financial interest in his next film, *Le Silence est d'Or* (q.v.), he never seriously considered working in English again.

Fritz Lang had been long enough and successful enough in Hollywood for the industry to consider him 'one of us', though his reputation had dimmed since the days of *Fury* and *You Only Live Once*. He worked for two years on a Western saga, which he saw as the New World equivalent of the Nibelungen, to be called *Americana*; and when the project was abandoned Zanuck, having noticed Lang's interest in the old West, offered **The Return of Frank James** (1940), with Henry Fonda repeating his role of the younger James brother, and then **Western Union** (1941), with Robert Young and Randolph Scott leading the expedition into Indian Country to wire up the cables. Both are unpretentious and pleasing in their background authenticity – in Technicolor; the latter has more exuberance and a much better script, by Robert Carson.

Both films might have been made by any good Hollywood journeyman, and Lang's next three films are shaky contributions to the war effort. The worst of the three is that on which he had complete autonomy, **Hangmen Also Die** (1943), backed by Arnold Pressburger at United Artists. As a Resistance story it starts with an excellent theme – German reprisals in Prague after the assassination of Reichsprotektor Heydrich, known as 'the hangman' – but, as Theodore Strauss put it in *The New York Times*, 'as it tries to echo the anguished heroism of a captive people it fails badly both in the script and the performance.' The script, which contains the classic film-Nazi expression, 'Ve haf vays of making you talk,' is by Lang and 'Bert' Brecht, who were both indignant when the American Screenwriters' Guild (after arbitration) insisted on sole credit going to John Wexley, a German-speaking writer whom they had brought in to help them with the English. One would have thought that they would rather have been glad to let him take the blame. Both **Man Hunt** (1941) and **The Ministry of Fear** (1944) are set mainly in London, and though they were made respectively for 20th and Paramount it is a London even more phoney than usual. The films also have in common particularly uninteresting leads – Walter Pidgeon and Joan Bennett in the former, Ray Milland and Marjorie Reynolds in the latter – and their source in exceptionally strong writers – Geoffrey Household's 'Rogue Male' and the 'entertainment' by Graham Greene. Lang, returning to the thriller genre, is at least at ease, and both films are entertaining. *Man Hunt*, made before the U.S. entered the War, has an anti-Nazi fervour missing from *Hangmen Also Die*; its subject is a Nazi pursuit of a big game hunter who had intended to assassinate Hitler at Berchtesgarten. The film introduces a prostitute, the role played by Miss Bennett – her profession, of course, is never mentioned, though we can tell from her outfit and the saucy way she holds a cigarette – and has many new adventures for the beleaguered hero in London. Lang ensures that the very air of the city holds menace, and that is true of the film of Greene's novel, even though the portrait of a weary wartime London has gone: the best of the film is, however, from Greene – the fête, the seance, the organisation called 'Mothers of Free Nations', which is clearly up to something more sinister. Lang, who accepted the assignment after making an offer himself for the novel, disliked the changes made by the producer-scenarist, Seton I. Miller, but Greene proves stronger than both Miller and Lang.

Lang in turn retrieved his reputation with **The Woman in the Window** (1944), also a thriller, and the only reservations in the reviews concerned the ending, when the nightmare situation in which Edward G. Robinson finds himself turns out to be just that, a dream; but Lang later defended the denouement by claiming that the plot developments would otherwise have been implausible. He fought the producer-scenarist, Nunnally Johnson, over it, and managed to incorporate the apt little coda suggesting that the dream would come true. The film is more typical of Lang's best work than Johnson's, his misanthropy seldom better expressed than when Joan Bennett says off-handedly about searching the corpse, 'It had to be done, didn't it?' Bennett smiles and smiles and plays the villain memorably, while Robinson's skill at playing mild, trapped men should not be taken for granted. They

would play similar roles for Lang in *Scarlet Street* (q. v.), produced independently; this film was made by a new company, International (q.v.), releasing through R.K.O.

The postwar rush to independence began with the small group of individuals working during the War. It must be said that Disney stands apart, and of the others of this period only Hitchcock was a success by industry standards. Wilder would be similarly regarded; the former prestige of Capra and Sturges would be remembered by other producers and directors anxious for autonomy, and they would recall what had happened to Welles, one of the most gifted men to work in Hollywood. Directors did not necessarily do their best work when granted independence, but they often managed to assert in it their individuality; as critics praised *The Woman in the Window* and *The Southerner*, they reflected on the comparatively recent feeble work of two directors once greatly esteemed. The industry might not want Renoir, Welles or Sturges, and it never cared greatly for Lang; but about this time studio executives began to concede that Chaplin and Capra were not the only directors who might be permitted to mould their films as they saw fit.

The high regard in which Fritz Lang is now held was not his during much of his career, and he had been some years in the critical wilderness when he made *The Woman in the Window*. Edward G. Robinson is a professor accosted by a model, Joan Bennett. 'I'm not married, I've no designs on you. One drink is all I require,' she says, and in her apartment he is equally matter of fact, 'I was warned against the siren-call of adventure.'

557

22

The British at War

THE BRITISH cinema grew up during the War and, as has doubtless been remarked elsewhere, it needed to. In the gravity of the situation – the proximity of the enemy, the Blitz, the successful invasion of most of Europe – audiences demanded either better escapism or more reflective content, and as far as the latter was concerned, the industry began to answer their needs when it re-adjusted after the Blitz. Although Hollywood met the challenge of the War more immediately, it was not until 1945 that it produced any contemporary subjects of lasting worth: yet it is one of the curiosities of film history that American films, when they seem to change with the passing of the years, become either better or worse, while on re-examination British films, if they change at all, only become worse. The tendency of British critics to overpraise local product, as the only mass-cinema alternative to the almighty Hollywood, was natural enough in peacetime, but under wartime conditions the tone became shriller and more urgent. A great many British films were overpraised, but a great number of hitherto promising talents were thereby encouraged to do their best work (as it turned out).

Though the declaration of war in September 1939 closed cinemas for fear of air-raids, they were soon re-opened in the cause of maintaining morale – and the increased attendances, to continue throughout the War, proved the justification for this move. Work in the studios was also temporarily interrupted, to the chagrin of Korda, who on his enforced departure for Hollywood left as legacy **The Lion Has Wings** (1939), conceived on 2 September, the day after the Germans marched into Poland, and released just two months later. Three directors, Michael Powell, Brian Desmond Hurst and Adrian Brunel, worked simultaneously, and Korda, uncredited, directed Ralph Richardson, as an R.A.F. officer, and Merle Oberon, as his wife who joins the Red Cross. The G.P.O. Film Unit was engaged to shoot documentary material, and the newsreel companies were raided, along with *Fire Over England*, for Elizabeth 1's Tilbury speech, and a 1937 short called *The Gap*, which imagined an air-raid on London. The plot – dog-fights in the sky and tensions in the Ops Room – is dull, but the long introduction is a valuable example of propaganda, contrasting Britain and Germany, with Hitler ranting while the King and Queen sing 'Underneath the Chestnut Tree', and German pilots being briefed 'in striking contrast to the friendly atmosphere which is Britain's way'. The film cost £30,000, and Korda used his last life insurance policy to complete it; the British were not grateful, but the Americans were, doubtless because it was so much more immediate than newspaper reports.

There was no other serious approach to the War for a while, though there were a good number of Nazis to be seen on British screens – played by the familiar villains of British comedies, and indeed in their customary roles, revealed in reel ten to have swastikas on their underwear. Scriptwriters reworked the same old plots, only our heroes rounded up fifth columnists instead of gangsters, and that was, as they put it, one in the eye for old Hitler! In Walter Forde's **Sailors Three** (1940), Tommy Trinder captures a German battleship; in Forde's **The Ghost Train** (1941) Arthur Askey captures gun-runners, who have become Nazis since the original play and earlier film version; in Marcel Varnel's **Let George Do It** (1940), George Formby rounds up a spy ring in Norway; while in John Paddy Carstairs's **Spare a Copper** (1941), he uncovers a sabotage plot in Liverpool; and in Varnel's **The Ghost of St Michael's** (1940), Will Hay discovers that the ghost is really a Nazi agent. Hay, turning director, worked with Basil Dearden on **The Black Sheep of Whitehall** (1941) and **The Goose Steps Out** (1942), respectively finding spies in a nursing-home and being parachuted into Germany to steal a secret weapon. These harmless comic-cuts were made either by Ealing, where Formby had been joined by Hay and Trinder, the latter a brash newcomer from the music-hall, or by Gainsborough, which hoped that the diminutive, chirpy Askey would take the place of the defecting Hay. Askey's best film is **Charley's (Big-Hearted) Aunt** (1940), directed by Forde, a distant cousin of the play by Brandon Thomas, while the best wartime films of Hay and Formby also had nothing to do with the War – respectively **My Learned Friend** (1943), directed by Hay and Dearden, with Hay as the intended sixth victim of a homicidal maniac, and **Turned Out Nice Again** (1941), directed by Varnel, with Formby as overseer in a ladies' underwear factory.

Cottage to Let (1941) concerns an unworldly inventor (Leslie Banks), who lives in a Scottish village which turns out to be a hive of espionage activity: everyone behaves suspiciously, and Anthony Asquith always cuts away before we learn why. Carol Reed does something similar with **Night Train to Munich** (1940), taking it at express speed. The Nazi agents include Felix Aylmer as a Hampstead dentist and Rex Harrison as a German officer, except that he is really on the British side. Their concern is a Czech scientist whom the Nazis want to recapture, and like *The Lady Vanishes*, also written by Launder and Gilliat, the climax takes place aboard a train. As in that film, Margaret Lockwood is the bewildered heroine, while Basil Radford and Naunton Wayne are again the foolhardy Britishers abroad.

The formula was quickly set: **Pimpernel Smith** (1941) also has a British mastermind who is not what he seems, and who at times dons Nazi uniform. Its other ingredients include doltish and Achtung-ing

German officers; a trap to be evaded in the last reel; and a propaganda message for Allied audiences. There is much to be said against turning war into a Richard Hannay-type adventure, but this one is as disarming as it is witty, due in no small part to the direction of Leslie Howard and his playing of the seemingly woolly-minded professor. Howard had disliked being a Hollywood leading man, and had returned to Britain to participate in the war effort. His presence in the British studios gave a lift to the entire industry, while his popularity in the U.S. ensured a hearing there for the propaganda contained within his films. However, **The First of the Few** (1941) has to work hard for contemporary relevance since it is a tribute to R.J. Mitchell, the designer of the Spitfire aircraft, who had died in 1937. Accordingly it features a sequence in which German industrialists in 1934 boast of their supremacy and of the new Chancellor, Herr Hitler. Howard again played the lead and directed, but he served only in the latter capacity on **The Gentle Sex** (1943), bringing deft Hollywood-learnt skills to this composite portrait of the women's army, the A.T.S. The film takes lightly the heartache and bloodymindedness but is otherwise honest (i.e. without comic stereotypes or false heroism), and it has performances to match the title by Rosamund John, Lilli Palmer, Joan Greenwood

The wartime Resistance thrillers were all much of a muchness, but *Pimpernel Smith* is an exception. Its subject is the spiriting away of prisoners from the Nazis in the summer of 1939. Few films of the period knew how to end, since the conflict that was their backdrop continued, but in this one Pimpernel simply disappeared in a cloud of smoke, his voice on the soundtrack assuring the Germans that he would be back. Here Leslie Howard, who also directed, is on the verge of disappearing.

and Joyce Howard. Leslie Howard speaks the commentary and may be seen in the opening shot – which was a last glimpse for audiences, since, after a government-sponsored lecture tour of Spain and Portugal, his plane was shot down over the Bay of Biscay.

Posthumously shown was **The Lamp Still Burns** (1943), solely credited to Maurice Elvey, who had worked on *The Gentle Sex* – and this is similarly a recruiting poster. It is based on an autobiographical book by Monica Dickens, 'One Pair of Feet', and concerns a young woman (Rosamund John) who gives up a lucrative job as an architect for a life of drudgery as a nurse. The War is hardly mentioned, and the plot chiefly concerns the nurse's rebellion against hospital discipline; her dedication eventually triumphs, with no suggestion that she will marry the winsome Stewart Granger when the War is over. Nevertheless the film is typical of Howard's approach, and the sober style is his rather than Elvey's, which tended towards the vulgar and pedestrian. Together the four films demonstrate that the former Hollywood matinee idol might have become an important force in leading the British cinema towards greater honesty and realism.

Howard also appeared in **The 49th Parallel** (1941), along with Laurence Olivier, Raymond Massey, Anton Walbrook, Eric Portman 'and the music of Ralph Vaughan Williams'. Although dedicated to the people of Canada it was aimed at American audiences, and was the most ambitious of the films to do so. Retitled *The Invaders* and distributed by Columbia, unfortunately it was not seen in the U.S. till three months after the War was over. It was a jinxed film from the start, for the Ministry of Information, having been allotted half a million pounds for such ventures, withdrew after an expenditure of £60,000 (and its experience resulted in it spending but little, and gingerly, in future). Part of the trouble was that the female lead, Elisabeth Bergner, after filming locations in Canada, declined to return for the interiors in Britain, preferring the safety of the U.S. Glynis Johns replaced her, after the completion money had been advanced by J. Arthur Rank, who thereby again moved towards production. Michael Powell directed, from a screen-

play by Rodney Ackland and Emeric Pressburger, and there is probably no more rabid propaganda movie in existence. This propaganda is sometimes cleverly contrived – as, for instance, when the 49th Parallel is referred to as 'the only undefended frontier in the world'. A group of Nazis, inhuman, Führer-fixated – in fact, a stranded U-boat crew, led by their even more fanatical commander (Portman) – journey across Canada. There they meet a carefree French-Canadian trapper (Olivier); a Hutterite leader (Walbrook), who refuses to declare for Hitler by pointing out that his community left Germany for racial and religious tolerance; and an Indian expert (Howard), who chatters on about a tribe whose barbarities remind him of the Nazis.

Michael Powell (b. 1905) had begun in films with Rex Ingram at his studios in Nice, and he had directed over twenty quota-quickies in Britain before *The Edge of the World* (1937) brought him to the attention of Korda. Because of the similarity of setting he was assigned to **The Spy in Black** (1939), set in the Orkneys, and to help with the script Korda brought in a fellow-Hungarian, Emeric Pressburger (b. 1902), thus initiating a partnership that was to endure for over fifteen years – with joint credit as producers, writers and directors, though Powell usually functioned alone as director. This, their first collaboration, was a far-fetched espionage drama, set in the First World War, and their second, **Contraband** (1940), was more of the same, also with Conrad Veidt and Valerie Hobson but set in contemporary London. *The 49th Parallel* was their first prestige film, but it was **One of Our Aircraft Is Missing** (1942) which made the reputation of the team – incredibly, for this is a 'Boy's Own' adventure about the Dutch Resistance helping a grounded R.A.F. crew, consisting of the usual spectrum of British types. That a country fighting for its existence should offer such lunatic fictions almost beggars belief.

Michael Balcon's Ealing Studios offered two even worse films, both naval dramas. **Ships with Wings** (1941) was directed, ineptly, by Sergei Nolbandov, a former writer who otherwise only produced a few films for the company. This one concerns a disgraced civil pilot who joins a run-down airline on a spy-ridden Mediterranean island, and who in wartime redeems himself by bombing the German dam – a model so atrocious that Noël Coward regarded it as one of the laughs of the War. The film purports to be a tribute to the Fleet Air Arm, while **The Big Blockade** (1942) hopes to be a semi-documentary account of the British Navy's blockade against Germany. As directed and part-written by Charles Frend, it attempts vignettes of life under the Nazis. 'A fantasy for us – a hideous reality for the conquered nations,' says the commentator, journalist Frank Owen, but the whole film is fantasy. The American journalist Quentin Reynolds also appears, to assure the British that the U.S.A. is with them one hundred per cent – and to remind us that those films not aimed at the Americans were meant to cheer up local audiences.

Ealing had a better moment with **Went the Day Well?** (1942), directed by Cavalcanti from a screenplay by John Dighton, Diana Morgan and Angus MacPhail, all of whom added so much to the original story, by Graham Greene, that the latter refused credit. Perhaps his true reason was that as directed the story simply strains credibility. It is possible that the situation did not seem so improbable then, when 'Careless Talk Costs Lives' was an everyday expression, and quislings were thought to be lurking under every bush but, assuming that a group of Germans could take over an English country village for forty-eight hours, how did they ever get there in the first place? They, of course, are beastly, but the film is interesting in that it takes a while for the British to become heroic, and also because it is accurate in sentiment, as in its comment by one evacuee (Harry Fowler), 'We won't 'arf give those blinkin' jerries the works.' The producer, Michael Balcon, later expressed surprise that it had never been recognised as the important film he believed it to be.

Pastor Hall (1940) deserves a mention as a tale of the Resistance in Germany. Poor in every department, including the direction of Roy Boulting, and solidly British despite the 'herrs' and 'fräuleins' of the dialogue, it nevertheless demands attention for sincerity and for the performance of Wilfrid Lawson in the title role, a priest whose opposition to Nazi doctrine leads him to a concentration camp and death. The source is a play, based on fact, by Ernst Toller, a socialist who left Germany in 1932, and who committed suicide in 1939, just before a translation appeared, by Stephen Spender (who is not credited on the film). Asquith made **Freedom Radio** (1940) on the same subject, specifically concerning Hitler's doctor (Clive Brook) who runs a clandestine radio station to apprise Germans of the truth, and who until the last minute is misunderstood by his wife (Diana Wynyard), an actress who stage-manages Hitler's rallies. Sober and well-made, it is nevertheless much less effective than *Pastor Hall*.

As far as the other European nations are concerned, it would seem in retrospect that Britain and Hollywood were in competition to see who could make the most idiotic Resistance film. The ingredients were almost interchangeable: the goodies (the occupied people) versus the baddies (the Germans); an ammunition dump to be blown up; a pilot to be smuggled across the lines; hostages to be sacrificed; and quislings round every corner. The British tended to like a note of hope: **Tomorrow We Live** (1942), set in France and directed by George King, and **The Day Will Dawn** (1942), set in Norway and directed by Harold French. In the latter the hostages, in prison, listen for the sound of the firing squad. But what is this? Boats bounding across the sea? A British commando raid? Naturally. The villains are shot, and our British heroes and the entire population of Lungefjord decamp, to spend the rest of the War in Britain.

A year later a note of reality had crept in: 'The truth is that a nation will live only as long as it has people ready to die' are the last words of **The Silver Fleet**, directed by Vernon Sewell and Gordon Wellesley with the co-operation of the Royal Netherlands government and the Royal Navy.

The public, at least, loved **Dangerous Moonlight** (1941), if mainly for the 'Warsaw Concerto', composed by Richard Addinsell with no illusions as to its merits but which was nevertheless a huge factor in the wartime expansion of interest in 'serious' music. The star is Anton Walbrook, with his lionlike but soulful presence and hint of temperament – and the conjunction of him and the music suggests a great romance; but this is a numb, small film, typical of its director, Brian Desmond Hurst, and of Terence Young, who wrote the story and the screenplay. Walbrook plays a shell-shocked pilot and pianist, remembering both Warsaw and an American journalist (Sally Gray); later, in New York, she tries to convince him that he can serve his country better by hammering away at that concerto than by joining the Free Polish Air Force.

This England (1941) is a panorama of English life – retitled *Our Heritage* for Scottish cinemas – as described by squire (John Clements) and labourer (Emlyn Williams) to a visiting American (Constance Cummings). The magic of cinema takes them back to 1066, 1588, 1805 and 1918, but there is not much magic in what happens, as Clements and Williams overact their forebears and Miss Cummings variously impersonates their ladies. Williams wrote the dreadful script, and the direction by David Macdonald is of the same level. **The Demi-Paradise** (1943) is an affectionate account of the British at war as viewed by a visiting Russian engineer (Laurence Olivier) and as written by a Russian, Anatole de Grunwald, who also produced. It is pleasing enough on its Home Counties upper-crust level, but is neither informative nor satiric – except about a village pageant, which has Margaret Rutherford and Joyce Grenfell as eager participants. Olivier has a discreet romance with a shipbuilder's daughter (Penelope Dudley Ward) and makes a speech in which, as Richard Winnington put it, 'he gives us just that line we love, a deprecatory statement of our national faults, as a prelude to the big boost which is the absolute peak of inverted smugness.' Since the film was designed as propaganda for the U.S.A., if not the U.S.S.R., it is a shame that it is another which did not arrive there till well after the War, meaninglessly retitled *Adventure for Two*. Anthony Asquith directed. As defiantly English, though not about the War, is his **Quiet Wedding** (1941), adapted and opened out by de Grunwald and Terence Rattigan from a matinee play by Esther McCracken. Margaret Lockwood and Derek Farr, as the couple thwarted of a quiet wedding, are colourless, but rendering the mild humour are Marjorie Fielding as the impervious, managing mother, and such players as Athene Seyler, Peggy Ashcroft, Roland Culver, David Tomlinson, Martita Hunt and Margaret Rutherford.

Thunder Rock (1942) proves that better the approach patriotic than the approach philosophic. Robert Ardrey's play was first presented in New York, by the Group Theatre, but it was its success in London which led to its being filmed, with Roy Boulting directing and M-G-M participating. A young man (Michael Redgrave) has taken refuge on a lighthouse in the Atlantic, having failed to make either the British public or its newspaper proprietors aware of the dangers of Fascism. Holed up, and away from the apathy of his countrymen, he conjures up spirits from the names he finds in an ancient ship's log-book – drowned people fleeing from the tyranny of Europe, as represented by the Industrial Revolution, medical bigotry in Vienna and anti-women's suffrage. The spirits realise that they should have stayed to fight, which makes Redgrave resolve to return. This actor gives his usual performance when faced with a moral or emotional dilemma, which is to gaze soulfully at some object just out of camera range; but there is a good, brief appearance by James Mason, as an old friend, and a better and longer one by Frederick Valk as the Austrian doctor. Mr Valk was Jewish, and we are reminded that Ardrey ignores the more important issue of racial prejudice; but what renders the piece meretricious is that though it aches with concern it is of the wise-after-the-event kind.

We would not expect it to compete with **Major Barbara** (1941) in brilliance of ideas but nor would we expect this film of Shaw's play to be one of the most stimulating of the war years, since his truths stand revealed as those of a late nineteenth-century reformer. These concern economics rather than politics, as expressed in his preface: 'to wit, that the greatest of our evils, and the worst of our crimes is poverty, and that our first duty, to which every other consideration must be sacrificed, is not to be poor.' Eventually the armaments manufacturer, Undershaft, is revealed as one of the privileged who has accepted the world's values in order to provide for the other half, while his daughter Barbara, in a plea for Shaw's new morality, is encouraged to find 'the way to life through the factory of death' rather than through organised religion. In all of Shaw's plays the confrontation of the upper and lower orders provides some of the best fun and the best argument – even if, on examination, the latter seems specious – and unfortunately here the poor are played with too many a nudge and a wink by Emlyn Williams and Robert Newton, as respectively the hypocritical repentant and the genuine one. It is not an easy piece to handle, with its diverse moods and locations – bound only by the author's rhetoric – and if the scenes with the Undershaft family emerge as the best that is not entirely due to the acting, since it is of many styles. Rex Harrison as Dolly and David Tree as Charles, both playing in impeccable Shaftesbury Avenue manner, at least belong on the same 'stage' as Marie Lohr as Lady Brittomart. Sybil Thorndike is outstanding as the warm and wily Salvation Army general. Along with Mr Newton, the calamity is Robert Morley's Undershaft – the actor was not only too young for the role but played it as a white-bearded, fanatical evangelist. Wendy Hiller as Barbara entirely misses the humour of her priggishness. To blame is Gabriel Pascal who, after the success of *Pygmalion*, got backing again from the Rank-owned General Film Distributors, plus an investment of £20,000 from Shaw himself. Pascal decided to direct, and indeed takes credit, though most of the work was done by David Lean, as then untried, and Harold French who, returning after having been fired, was therefore able to demand minimal interference. The original ten-week schedule doubled, as did the cost – due also to the fact that French brought in Harrison to replace the original Dolly (Andrew Osborne) and to constant air-raids; finally the film did miserably at the box office.

A filmed play much admired was **Gaslight** (1940), from Patrick Hamilton's long-running thriller about a long-time spinster now adrift in an increasingly unhappy marriage and uncertain whether she is going mad. In the role of the scheming husband Anton Walbrook is basically manic, but Diana Wynyard is distracted rather than distraught; moreover the piece loses its effectiveness because the atmosphere of claustrophobia has been lost to make it cinematic, and the wife has become much younger, to accommodate the box office. Thorold Dickinson, directing, has unfortunately concentrated on Victoriana at the expense of tension.

Conversely, **Kipps** (1941), despite dreadful studio exteriors and somewhat excessive Cecil Beaton costumes, is otherwise excellent. The theme of Wells's novel, that kind hearts are worth more than coronets, has dated now, despite the fact that the snobbish Walsinghams are sympathetically treated. Michael Redgrave does not have the right levity for Kipps (and his plebeian accent wobbles), but he is good when trying to improve his knowledge and learning to move into society. As the girl he hopes to marry Diana Wynyard looks and plays like the goddess he thinks she is. Carol Reed directed and Edward Black produced – from a script by Launder and Gilliat – for 20th Century-Fox, one of a series of films this team made for Fox under the auspices of Gainsborough.

Another is **The Young Mr Pitt** (1942), occasioned by the success of Korda's Hollywood film about Nelson, *That Hamilton Woman* (q.v.). It has the gall to start with the elder Pitt defending the American Revolution, and does not stop proselytising till the end, when Pitt makes his last public speech: 'Let us hope that England, having saved herself by her energy, may save Europe by her example.' In between Launder and Gilliat are nothing if not partial: Pitt is meant to be Churchill, and his accession to power to parallel Churchill's in 1940, with the obvious conclusions to be drawn between the belligerent Pitt and the mediocre Addison. This does more than justice to Churchill, whose position in politics before Munich was not comparable to Pitt's, and it does less than justice to Pitt, who cleverly kept England out of European involvement for some years. Nothing is shown of Pitt the appeaser, or of his treaties with Russia and Prussia; at no point is it suggested that Britain is not alone against the devouring might of Napoleon. Such single-mindedness extends to Robert Donat, who makes of this Prime Minister a well-meaning, self-confident and honourable man, with only his cynicism to represent the vices and shortcomings noted by contemporaries. The wartime coalition dictated no mention of Whig or Tory, so we are left to guess at the beliefs of 'Mr Pitt's party' and 'Mr Fox's party' – except that Robert Morley's flamboyant, petulant Fox is portrayed as untrustworthy. As the vain aspirant to Pitt's heart, Phyllis Calvert is toothsomely cloying, but there are good performances by Raymond Lovell as George III; Max Adrian as Sheridan, a snake-tongued charmer; and Albert Lieven as Talleyrand, as Talleyrand ever is in movies – sly, smart and transparent. Most notably, Reed's direction is both economic and elegant.

Among the other historical propaganda films are **The Prime Minister** (1941), Thorold Dickinson's sober study of Disraeli, with John Gielgud in that role, and Diana Wynyard as his wife; **Atlantic Ferry** (1941), also produced by Max Wilder for Warner Bros., directed by Walter Forde, with Michael Redgrave building the first steamship to cross the Atlantic for the eventuality that 'Britain and the United States should be united against a common enemy'; and **Penn of Pennsylvania** (1941), sincere but foolishly scripted, directed by Lance Comfort with Clifford Evans as Penn.

Another British historical, **The Great Mr Handel** (1942), was Rank's second whole-hearted involvement in production. He wanted to make a religious film, but did not want to lose money, the evident concomitant. Having, therefore, no clear aim other than to raise the tone of the cinema, he consulted Norman Walker, director of his previous venture, *The Turn of the Tide*. A contributor to that had been L. duGarde Peach, best known for his radio plays for children – and one of these, transcribed, would provide uplift, thought Walker, with himself directing and Wilfrid Lawson, star of the earlier occasion, playing Handel. The result is effortlessly superior to the European attempts of the previous decade to make romances from the lives of Schubert, Beethoven and Tchaikovsky. These films have in common a protagonist who loves music so much that everything else is subsidiary; but in Handel's case the consequent woes are not amatory, but concern royal displeasure, lack of commissions, debts and personal unpopularity – and these matters are handled with more tact, taste and truth than were usually found in the movie lives of the great. Contemporary appraisals concentrated on the music, the art direction by Sidney Gausden, the colour photography of Claude Friese-Greene and Jack Cardiff, and Lawson's lovable-bear-at-heart Handel. Business at home was good, and in the U.S. above average for a British film, though Rank, in deciding to use Technicolor and two players with reputations – if small – in America (Elizabeth Allen played Mrs Cibber), had hoped for more.

The script takes pains to point out that, though born a German, Handel preferred the British way, and something similar is the sole proposition of **The Life and Death of Colonel Blimp** (1943) – incidentally, the second of Britain's seven wartime features in Technicolor. Messrs Powell and Pressburger are again very certain of the beastliness of the Hun, if allowing a few good ones, represented through three generations by Anton Walbrook. 'You are fighting for your very existence against the most devilish invention of the human brain – Nazism,' he tells Colonel Blimp (Roger Livesey) in the third part of this chronicle. The first episode, set just after the Boer War, has at its base a good idea, with Blimp in Berlin to negotiate a lessening of anti-British propaganda, but the two that follow prove pointless. Powell and Pressburger juggle with such intriguing matters as the nature of the British, Anglo-German relations and the mentality of the professional soldier, but without having anything to say about any of them. The length (163 minutes), the settings by Alfred Junge, the connection with David Low's newspaper cartoon Blimp – though limited to the physical – and an impression of seriousness, brought a modicum of approval.

In trying to explain the British to themselves and others the documentarist Humphrey Jennings could say more in five minutes than Powell in as many hours. **The First Days** (1939) is a typically perceptive and wide-ranging account of Britain at war, starting with that sunny Sunday when Chamberlain announced the beginning of hostilities, and concentrating on London's preparations for the coming bombardment. Though the direction is credited to Cavalcanti, he was in fact only the producer and Jennings's imprint is stronger than that of his two co-directors, Pat Jackson and Harry Watt. Also in two reels, and apparently co-directed with Stewart McAllister, **Listen to Britain** (1942) is a medley of sounds and pictures meant to illustrate twenty-four hours of life in wartime Britain for American audiences. Munitions workers, miners, servicemen and teachers go about their daily tasks, and a Londoner walks to his office past bomb-damage. Their routines are set to the tunes which Jennings used so eloquently in most of his films, from 'Roll Out the Barrel' at the Palais de Dance to soldiers on a train chorusing 'Home on the Range'. In the factory lunch-break Flanagan and Allen sing 'Round the Back of the Arches' while, at the National Gallery, Myra Hess plays Mozart, her pages turned by an airman while the Queen and Kenneth Clark look on. Mozart continues over views of Trafalgar Square, factories and a field of waving corn till replaced, in diminuendo, by 'Rule, Britannia'. (Jennings's fellow-documentarists did not approve. Their work, John Grierson had stated in 1937, arose not so much from an 'affection' for film but from 'an affection for national education', and one of their number, Edgar Anstey wrote – in *The Spectator* – that 'it will be a disaster if [*Listen to Britain*] is sent overseas'.)

The record that Jennings left of that war is the best available to us – from any film maker, from any country. He saw his job as a morale-booster, but his patriotism was subservient to his interest in people. His portraits of Britain indicate that it was a good place in which to live, but his genius is precisely in the selection, the juxtaposition and the length of his images. His work for the B.B.C. – at the time he began in films – eventually gave birth to **Words for Battle** (1940), an attempt to match the appearance of wartime Britain with spoken sentiment. Laurence Olivier speaks the verse, which moves from Milton and Browning to Blake, with 'Jerusalem' accompanied by evacuees first being herded away and then playing in 'England's green and pleasant land'. London devastated by the Blitz is accompanied by Kipling's poem to the effect that the British have learnt to hate, and the Gettysburg Address by tanks moving past the Lincoln Memorial in Parliament Square.

London Can Take It (1940) is not a documentary about the Blitz, but a celebration of the British spirit at the time. It shows people walking to work through the rubble and broken glass, clearing up the debris, Civil Defence workers being trained in salvage operation. It is not a film

about nobility but sweetness, not about bravery but doggedness. **Heart of Britain** (1941) is a companion piece, set in the North and Midlands at the time their cities were being bombed, and it emphasises two of Jennings's beliefs – that the obligatory, morale-boosting shots of the King and Queen must be as brief as possible, and that in the midst of chaos orchestras must be seen to play and choirs to sing. At 36 minutes **The Silent Village** (1943) is longer than most of his films, and they are among the most moving in the history of cinema.

The village concerned is in the Welsh valleys, and it is a mining community – and so, a foreword tells us, was Lidice, the Bohemian village obliterated by the Germans in revenge for the assassination of Heydrich, the Nazi governor. Jennings does not identify the enemy, which, beyond a few uniformed men briefly seen, exists only as a loudspeaker on a car. Similar reticence is applied to the villagers, and destruction amounts to a burst of gunfire, a burning building and a stream littered with furniture.

A Diary for Timothy (1945) is a companion piece to *The First Days*, being an anthology of events in Britain and Europe from D-Day to Christmas 1944, when the outcome was no longer in doubt. The less emotional (I speak of effect, not of intention) and evocative films still indicate skill and sympathy of a high order: **The Eighty Days** (1945), the story of the Flying Bomb, and **A Defeated People** (1946), an essay on the British zone of Germany. **The True Story of Lili Marlene** (1944) becomes, with its concluding shot of the grave of the Unknown Soldier, a plea for an end to wars; it is nevertheless interesting as documentary, but the 'acted' scenes do not indicate that Jennings could have moved towards the fiction film. As much may be said of **The Cumberland Story** (1947), though in this case his participants are mining and union officials playing themselves. The film itself is eloquent on the long-lasting divisions within that industry, and it is clear, despite the supposed objectivity, where Jennings's sympathies lie. Perhaps, after the Socialist government took office in 1945, he felt he needed a breathing space. He eventually decided to move his film-making career in a different direction, and was scouting locations in

Humphrey Jennings was the only major film-maker to emerge from that misguided movement, the British documentarists. His one feature-length film *Fires Were Started* is a tribute to firemen, whose bravery is all the more moving because they are unaware of it: they are not even particularly aware of saving London, but are merely 'doing their bit'.

Greece when he died on Poros in a fall in 1950. It was appropriate, since he had hymned Britain so brilliantly, that his last film, commissioned for the Festival of Britain, should again be on that subject. **Family Portrait** (1951) has a modest commentary; its choice of men to exemplify the country's quality consists of engineers rather than poets; and the images are as much of town as of country. The ending does not eschew cliché, but transforms it, suggesting a world civilisation, since the British came from many parts of Europe and their truths from Greece, Italy and Israel.

Jennings left one feature-length documentary which, if not the best film made in Britain during the War, is unequivocally the best portrait of the British at war. **Fires Were Started** (1943) (there was an earlier, shorter version, *I Was a Fireman*) was the official tribute to the Auxiliary (then National) Fire Service, and it now has a resonance unconsidered at the time – a record of ordinary people doing extraordinary things. They are not even particularly aware of saving London, but are merely 'doing their bit'. Only one brief scene is out-of-synch, when a telephonist dives under the table at the sound of a close bombing, to emerge and say into the

phone, 'Sorry for the interruption.' It is not that this is phoney – wartime conversations were full of stories like it – but that it exemplifies the stiff-upper-lip platitudes of commercial films to which Jennings never otherwise resorts. The earlier part of the film concerns one particular unit – not the usual liquorice allsorts cross-section – quartered in a converted school and welcoming a new recruit, played by William Sansom, the writer. At night, they wait for the Blitz to start, sing 'Please Don't Talk About Me When I'm Gone' and someone reads Sir Walter Raleigh's dissertation on death. This is dockland, and the ships stand idle. The German quarry is a factory in Trinidad Street, and the unit at first fails to quell the fire started by incendiaries. One man is killed, and his wife, unknowing, listens to the News, 'Fires were started . . . casualties light.'

The Bells Go Down (1943) is also about the Fire Service, the training of three men (Tommy Trinder, Philip Friend, Mervyn Johns) and their (literal) baptism of fire. Basil Dearden's direction and the screenplay are so abysmal that the climax – two men sharing a last cigarette on what is left of the thirteenth floor, as they wait for the building to cave in – is bizarre rather than moving. The film's sole redeeming feature is James Mason's performance as the disciplinarian who trains the recruits. This was a production of Ealing Studios, where Michael Balcon was trying to build a new team to provide the more serious films he thought the times demanded. To this end he brought Cavalcanti in from the documentary movement, specifically to supervise contemporary subjects. Another such is **The Foreman Went to France** (1942), directed by Charles Frend, who had made *The Big Blockade*, and the three films make an appalling trio. In this case J.B. Priestley provided the original story, based on fact, of a foreman (Clifford Evans) who before the Fall of France was sent to prevent some valuable machinery from falling into German hands. His progress to the coast, accompanied by a Cockney tommy (Trinder) and a stranded American (Constance Cummings), features every possible cliché, including that one in which the British C.O. (John Williams) is really a Nazi in disguise.

Balcon also brought Harry Watt from documentary films, and at the very least

Nine Men (1943) is not a betrayal of that movement. Watt wrote his own screenplay, ostensibly from a story by Gerald Kersh but more probably from a Russian picture, *The Thirteen*, which was also the basis for Columbia's *Sahara*. All three films concern a small band of soldiers stranded in the desert; in this version their exploits are related in flashback, a device which looks like padding, since the entire film runs only 68 minutes. The scenes of barrack-room life are admirably done, and the desert sequences made without undue heroics. It is more honest than the major effort of the Crown Film Unit* itself, **Western Approaches** (1944), a feature-length account of a boatful of torpedoed merchant seamen adrift in the Pacific. Pat Jackson, a stalwart of the Unit, directed.

The first really good British war film was made by a consummate and complete man of the theatre. Noël Coward had evinced no interest in the cinema since *The Scoundrel*, and when Lord Louis Mountbatten suggested a film about the Navy at war he said that he would be agreeable if it was based, at least in part, on Mountbatten's own experiences. Coward wrote, produced and acted in **In Which We Serve** (1942), and since he was inexperienced as a director he looked for a collaborator, choosing the inexperienced David Lean (b. 1908), on the basis that the films edited by Lean moved faster than most British films. Ronald Neame was hired as cinematographer. As far as reviewers were concerned, the result was the 'best' (Dilys Powell in *The Sunday Times*) or 'finest' (*Newsweek*) film of the War. 'There have been rumors that a truly great motion picture was coming to New York,' wrote Howard Barnes in that city's *Herald Tribune*. 'They are triumphantly confirmed . . . It is a masterpiece of film-making, a stirring testament to men of good will, in whatsoever age they may have loved, fought and endured.' We do not have to disagree, today, to also understand why most naval men saw it with an embarrassment bordering on shame. 'This is the story of a ship,' says the foreword, and as the ship is launched a copy of the *Daily Express* lies sodden in a pool, its headline claiming 'No War This Year' (which is one reason its proprietor,

*As the G.P.O. Film Unit was rechristened, making wartime propaganda movies.

Lord Beaverbrook, pursued Coward and Mountbatten with such hatred through the years). Shipwrecked, the Captain (Coward) and two others reminisce – the Chief Petty Officer (Bernard Miles) and a rating (John Mills) – on the role of the Navy in their lives. On Christmas Day the rating's family joke about the Navy and the Marines in a gorblimey way and toast both; the Chief Petty Officer and family toast the ship itself, H. M. S. *Torrin*; and the Captain toasts the King, while his wife (Celia Johnson) makes an eloquent toast to her rival, the Senior Service. Film critics, but surely not servicemen, might agree with Coward's sentiments at the end '. . . for if they had to die, what a grand way to go, for they lie with the ship we loved so much.' Away from the battle-front sang-froid, the film belongs to the cosy artefacts of the period, but is accurate, for instance, on the grin-and-bear-it attitudes of the Blitz. Reservations are further lessened because of the performances, especially those of Miss Johnson, Miles, Joyce Carey (Miles's wife), Kathleen Harrison and Kay Walsh (respectively Mills's mother and sister), and including Coward's own stiffly self-conscious portrayal. Also admirable is the film's composition, from the first shots of the rivets being driven in to the final view of the surviving officers disappearing into the darkness of the dock at Alexandria.

It was also the most influential film since the outbreak of War. Though the documentary movement had for the first time impinged on the public consciousness with such features as *Target for Tonight* (1941), directed by Harry Watt, and *Coastal Command* (1942), directed by Jack Holmes, only Ealing had responded, though it was hard to tell as much from the results. Coward's film proved to both British and Hollywood producers that the lives of servicemen and their loved ones at home were sufficiently dramatic without Nazi agents and fifth columnists. Its influence can be clearly felt in Anthony Asquith's **We Dive at Dawn** (1943), in its portrait of a submarine crew on leave, and its sober account of the voyage to the Baltic to sink a German warship. The screenplay, by Val Valentine, J. B. Williams and Frank Launder, avoids stereotype by giving the Captain (John Mills) an address book of popsies, and by making its representative

567

The British at War

Noël Coward, right, with John Mills just behind him, shipwrecked in *In Which We Serve*, and it is while clinging to this raft that the men reminisce, via flashback, to happier days. Although the film was accepted on the Home Front as an accurate portrait of service life, the troops themselves thought its respect towards the Navy exaggerated, and wondered where Coward had found his portrait of uncomplaining cameraderie.

On the other hand, Carol Reed's *The Way Ahead* is much better on the boredom of service life, as it follows a group of recruits from training to induction in battle. Here, looking suitably fed up, are from left to right, Leslie Dwyer, Jimmy Hanley, Raymond Huntley, James Donald and John Laurie.

rating (Eric Portman) particularly sour. But then it loses its nerve and opts for a ridiculous climax, with the latter dressed as a German officer and keeping Hitler's entire army at bay with one machine-gun.

Carol Reed had directed a short for the Army Film Unit, *The New Lot*, showing the induction of one group of civilians into army life, when he and the actor David Niven fell to discussing the possibility of a film on the wartime Army such as Coward's on the Navy. Thus emerged **The Way Ahead** (1944), based on *The New Lot*, one of whose writers, Peter Ustinov, was joined on the new film by Eric Ambler. By a fortuitous stroke of timing it opened in London on the day of the Normandy landings, and if it was in the fervour of the moment that C. A. Lejeune called it 'one of the splendours of the British cinema' the remark is no less true today. We may not now feel, as she did that these actors are so good that we do not think of them as such, especially as many of their faces became over-familiar, usually above a uniform. As with *In Which We Serve* barrack-room banter was never as discreet as this; but this is the Army as seen by the Army, a necessary and benevolent institution, and on its own terms the film's sole mistake is the Chorus of two Chelsea pensioners, representing Tradition. The men do curse and grumble, and if their Sergeant (William Hartnell) is a disciplinarian, underneath he is as fond of them as is their officer (Niven). The men adjust to the food, to beds without sheets; they are invited to a local home, and attend a camp concert that would be of singular ghastliness were it not so typical. The broadest and best portrait is of Davenport (Raymond Huntley), who had 'quite an important job, really', in charge of officers' kit, and thus was accustomed to meeting 'them' on equal terms; disillusioned, he later becomes almost happy, and nothing in a basically true film is better than his joining in with the others as Tessie O'Shea sings 'If You Were the Only Girl'. Having shared such common relaxations as well as common boredom, they share common danger, and we leave them as they disappear in the gunsmoke of battle in North Africa. Reed's mastery is complete: he was a director who lived films, and saw as many as he could, but no particular influence is discernible here. The film is all the more moving a tribute to the men who humbly helped to play their part in saving Britain in that it sets out merely to record.

It was Anatole de Grunwald who decided that there should be a comparable film for the R.A.F. **The Way to the Stars** (1945) was directed by Anthony Asquith, his usual collaborator, and written by Terence Rattigan, who had been in that branch of the services. It did not come out till the War was over, which may have helped its popularity, for it already looked back to that time as deeply romantic – and the R.A.F. was, in any case, the most romantically regarded of the three services. Dilys Powell said, 'I can only say that now, at this end of a moment in history, the piece is to an ordinary citizen inexpressibly moving,' but it no longer is, precisely because that is what it so wants to be. It is all here: the briefings, the camaraderie of the local pub (as prominent in the story as the airfield), the transient wartime romances, the Yanks who came over and went on to bomb the hell out of the Ruhr, and the people who waited, sometimes in vain. One has the suspicion, as the Yanks take over the film as well as the airfield, that it was made for the American market – an impression confirmed when a huge title, 'August 17th', interrupts the action, followed by a note to the forgetful that that was the date of the 'First U.S. Raid on the Nazis'. The comic misunderstandings between British and Americans are merely coy; the corrective balance of the great romantic films is here common farce; and the direction, though 'sensitive', drains away what life there is in banal two-shots for the endless dialogue. And where *In Which We Serve* has a sufficiency of stiff-upper-lips and *The Way Ahead* has Niven's eternally charming officer, this film is awash with stiff upper lips on the faces of charming officers. John Mills, terribly decent and terribly nice, bears the brunt of the clichés. Trevor Howard, as the brisk C.O., too soon killed, and Michael Redgrave, as another doomed flyer, do manage a bit of personality, if only their own, but Mills has nothing but sincerity to offer. The widow (Rosamund John) is allowed only the wisp of a romance with the American flyer (Douglass Montgomery). It is possible that time may restore the qualities which once endeared this film to audiences – and it was far more popular

Gordon Jackson and Patricia Roc in Launder and Gilliat's *Millions Like Us* – 'and millions like you' say the credits, after the cast list. Since this could hardly mean workers in Delaware or Detroit, no American distributor was interested in taking the film, which was a shame, for it was honest (and sometimes funny) on what the War was like for the average Briton.

than Coward's film, or Reed's: but where those are, above all, about people, this is the home equivalent of the films about the Empire, being mainly concerned with such sentiments as love and bravery.

It is better, however, than **Journey Together** (1945), written and directed by John Boulting from a story by Rattigan, and it is perhaps because the sponsor was the R.A.F. Film Unit that only the uniforms reconcile us to the fact that it is about the R.A.F. – it is not even comparable to the already doubtful R.A.F. of the other film. The title refers to both the co-operation given by American and Canadian instructors to the service and the friendship between a Cockney corporal (Richard Attenborough) and a college graduate (Jack Watling). The Cockney flunks his flying test and, like John Garfield in *Air Force* (q.v.), is made bitter and twisted before becoming a hero. The chief interest is the brief presence of Edward G. Robinson as one of the American instructors, having donated his services after an approach from the British Ministry of Information.

The other aspect of the War, the home front, receives its due in **Millions Like Us** (1943) which is, with *Fires Were Started*, the outstanding record of what it was like to live in Britain at this time. The writing team of Launder and Gilliat, after directing a short, *Partners in Crime*, were given the

chance to produce and direct a feature – and in an interesting dual career they did nothing more accomplished. The Ministry of Information suggested the subject. After establishing, in the manner of Jennings, the atmosphere of August 1939, the film follows the fortunes of Celia (Patricia Roc), who longs to be a W.A.A.F. or a Landgirl but is shunted into a Munitions factory by an overworked official. So is the haughty Jennifer (Anne Crawford), who has an inconclusive affair with the foreman (Eric Portman). The stories intertwine, but Celia's is the more remarkable precisely because it is the more mundane, and her romance with and marriage to a young R.A.F. sergeant (Gordon Jackson) is handled with extraordinary simplicity. Miss Roc, never thereafter as good, has a grace in her ordinariness, providing ample reason why she could turn no man's head while considerably interesting viewers. There are also vignettes in the Jennings manner: the Home Guardsman who slips off for a pint; the stories of queueing, of 'before the War'; the air-raid; and, at the end, a 'Workers' Playtime' concert which conveys better than any other film the 'oneness' of Britain at the time.

Launder and Gilliat decided after this experience never to co-direct again, but they continued to co-produce, each usually directing his own script. **Two Thousand Women** (1944) was written for Hitchcock, who accepted it till Launder was persuaded to direct it himself. It might, for box-office purposes, have been called 'Two Thousand Women and Three Men', being about British women interned in France, in a former luxury hotel, and the airmen they are trying to smuggle to waiting Resistance forces. Launder later said that he should have treated the subject more seriously. As it is, this is a good-to-fair thriller, with Miss Roc, Phyllis Calvert, Flora Robson and Co. coping with dialogue some notches below *The Women*.

In **Waterloo Road** (1945) Gilliat, writing and directing from a story by Val Valentine, examines the consequences when a soldier (John Mills) goes A.W.O.L. in search of a spiv (Stewart Granger) who has seduced his wife – only he hadn't really: she was simply fed-up with the cramped quarters of her in-laws. The slot-machine arcade is an art director's paradise, and if the raffish atmosphere of that part of London is missed Gilliat gets instead something of the quality of the Blitz – the nights in the tube, the sea of uniforms changing trains, the shortages, the sense of change and flux.

This batch of films emanated from two companies: *In Which We Serve*, *The Way Ahead*, and *The Way to the Stars* from Two Cities; and *We Dive at Dawn* and the Launder and Gilliat films from Gainsborough – and by the end of the War these were recognised as the two leading British studios. Two Cities had been founded in 1937 and had received a boost two years later when Paramount had agreed to co-operate on its production of *French Without Tears*, from Rattigan's play to which it owned the rights, and it had also contributed Ray Milland. Legal adviser to the company was Filippo del Guidice (1892–1961), brought in by one of its founders, fellow-Italian Mario Zampi, later noted as a comedy director (q.v.). Del Guidice was instrumental in raising the money for *In Which We Serve*, including an extra advance from the distributor, British Lion, when funds were exhausted. Two Cities films were thereafter handled by either Eagle-Lion or G.F.D., both owned by Rank, and it was Rank who provided additional finance when needed during the filming of *Henry V* (q.v.), which gave him a degree of control over the company, now in fact managed by del Guidice – who, a keen entrepreneur, was also associated with Powell and Pressburger, and would take on Launder and Gilliat when they left Gainsborough Pictures. Gainsborough was also coming into the orbit of Rank, via his relationship with C.M. Woolf within G.F.D. – and it was well worth having, since under the management of Maurice Ostrer and the production initiative of Edward Black it had become the most financially successful studio ever to operate in Britain.

Its run of phenomenally popular films began with **The Man in Grey** (1943), directed by Leslie Arliss (son of George Arliss and formerly a writer specialising in comedy) and adapted by him and Margaret Kennedy from a period romance by Lady Eleanor Smith. Without exactly intending to, it challenged Hollywood where it was strongest – in the areas of escapist entertainment and star performances. Though Margaret Lockwood, Phyllis Calvert, Stewart Granger and

James Mason (b. 1909) had all been in films for some time, only Miss Lockwood might have been termed a star; seen today, only Mason is at all good, and it was his suave villainy which carried the film to success. His part hardly begins to exist – a grim, grey Regency rake who marries a ninny (Calvert) for the sake of heirs and then has an affair with her best friend (Lockwood) – but he is a supreme example of an actor who has merely to enter a room to dominate it. Screen villainy took a new turn as he sneered at Calvert, sniffed round Lockwood and finally took a horsewhip to her. Lockwood, given to frigid smiles and moods of envy, plays a girl of unamiable ambition, and the film is as good as any of the subsequent movies about scheming women, British and American, to which the success of this one gave rise.

Fanny by Gaslight (1944), directed by Anthony Asquith, is based on a much better novel, by Michael Sadleir, a man fascinated by the Victorian underworld – both by the gilt and plush brothels, where overdressed milords over-drank and over-ate till they sank into stupor, and by the hypocrisy, whereby the Church Commissioners preferred not to know that the rents they collected came from harlots living at poverty level. This is the richest of Sadleir's three novels on the subject, but Doreen Montgomery has extracted from it merely a conventional romance, about the

The auguries for *Fanny By Gaslight* are not good, since it was directed by the variable Anthony Asquith and produced by Gainsborough, whose period romances so infuriated British critics. Some of them, however, stand up well, and this one particularly – partly due to James Mason, who is glowering at Stewart Granger to the left. Phyllis Calvert and Jean Kent watch in alarm.

illegitimate Fanny (Miss Calvert), the high-born swell (Granger) who defies his family to go and live with her, and the evil Lord Manderstoke (Mason), whose footsteps dog their fate – but it works, nevertheless, as well as some of the best Hollywood love stories. Enough of Sadleir remains; and this is the only film ever made to look at the sexual underworld of Victorian Britain, its brothels and dance-halls. The handling of the duel scene would not have disgraced Ophuls, and in both this film and *The Man in Grey* the superb sets give no sign of wartime austerity.

That was part of their attraction, and audience enthusiasm was such that the more homely Lockwood and Calvert were preferred to all but a handful of Hollywood stars. Critics moaned, but despite buzz-bombs and black-out audiences queued for **Love Story** (1944), directed by Arliss, in which a doomed pianist (Lockwood) falls in love with a dashing R.A.F. pilot (Granger), whose sight is failing. The background is Cornwall, the music the 'Cornish Rhapsody' (cousin to the 'Warsaw Concerto'), the outcome, inevitably, that Love Conquers All, even a scheming Patricia Roc.

Although a foreword to **Madonna of the Seven Moons** (1944) assures us that its 'facts' are known to the medical world the plot belongs to the world of Grand Opera – and Italian opera at that, for though Roland Pertwee's screenplay is based on a British novel, by Margery Lawrence, the ingredients include gypsies, fiestas and assorted Latin passions. A convent girl (Calvert) has Something Awful happen to her in a wood. Though happily married – says her husband, Giuseppe (John Stuart), gazing at her, 'Pity Botticelli isn't alive' – and with a grown-up daughter (Roc), all within the space of seconds, she has a mysterious illness which causes her to disappear. When Sandro (Peter Glenville) turns up at a ball, she grabs her jewel-case, snaps a dagger in her garter and takes a one-way ticket to a 'slum' called San Gimignano. There she enjoys an idyll with Nino (Granger), till Sandro tries to rape her daughter. Sandro knifes her and she stabs him, at which point Nino realises the reason for her long absences: but, as she told him earlier, 'A love like ours can't be measured by time.' The direction is credited to Arthur Crabtree who, like every-

one concerned with this production, seems to have aimed it for amateur night at the village hall.

From there Gainsborough could only go up, and C. A. Lejeune of *The Observer* – whose weekly column was the *sine qua non* for all self-respecting British movie buffs – was so startled to find a film from this company which she liked that she called **A Place of One's Own** (1945) 'a fine piece of work'. It is a tale of a girl possessed by a spirit, clearly filmed because of the success of *The Uninvited* (q.v.), but the director, Bernard Knowles, failed to understand the importance of atmosphere in such stories. Distinguished contributors include Rex Whistler, credited with 'additional designs', and Sir Osbert Sitwell, author of the original story, who co-operated on the production – surprisingly, in view of its disregard for the niceties of late Victorian society. Miss Lockwood is the girl; James Mason (who asked for the role) plays the elderly Yorkshire grocer whose wife (Barbara Mullen) engages her as a companion.

Ealing also offered a ghost story, **The Halfway House** (1944), directed by Basil Dearden. It is derivative – and finally trite – and yet quite unlike any other film. Its forebears include 'Outward Bound' and J. B. Priestley's Time plays. The War had created among certain film-makers a more than usual interest in the might-have-been and the hereafter, and it is precisely the War which has created all the problems for these people stranded in a remote inn in Wales. They include a naval wife (Françoise Rosay), a black marketeer (Alfred Drayton), and an officer (Guy Middleton) who has absconded with the mess funds. Angus MacPhail and Diana Morgan wrote the script which, however misguided, did provide evidence of the ideas British cinema was now prepared to tackle.

For audiences satiated with war, Ealing offered **Champagne Charlie** (1944), a fable about the popular Victorian entertainer George Leybourne (Tommy Trinder) and his rivalry with The Great Vance (Stanley Holloway). It is pleasing to find a Hollywood formula – in this case, the backstage story – being used for indigenous factors, and instead of chorus-girls we get the songs straight, the booze-boasting ballads of the era. There is no love affair for George, while the juveniles are dull, and what matters above all are the theatres and bars, marvellously recreated by the director, Cavalcanti, the art director, Michael Relph, and the photographer, Wilkie Cooper. Richard Winnington called Holloway's 'a delicious performance by an actor who is Britain's best film discovery of the war years'; apart from the fact that Holloway had been in films for years he is right.

Only the prologue of **On Approval** (1944) mentions the War, and only then to remind us how remote it is. The film is a valediction by Clive Brook, whose acting career had been faltering since he left Hollywood in 1934. He produced, directed and adapted Frederick Lonsdale's play, doing none of these things well, but it is still a droll piece. That is due to the sharp playing, by himself and Googie Withers (as the couple who go off to Scotland for a trial marriage), and to the sublime performances of Roland Culver and Beatrice Lillie as their scornful chaperones. Miss Lillie is a permanent termagant whose level glare indicates constant affront and suspicion; it was about this time that she turned down a seven-year M-G-M contract – to be near her son – and film history is the poorer because of it.

Another play filmed was **This Happy Breed** (1944). Noël Coward had decided that what the times needed was another of his patriotica, but as the mood had shifted since the days of 'Cavalcade' he wrote not of upstairs and downstairs, but of one South London family, against a background of the Armistice, the General Strike and the Abdication. There can be no question that his heart was in the right place, and that the dialogue, purposely mundane, is often entertaining; but it gives pause when Miss Lejeune approvingly quotes a Flying Officer in the Balkan Air Force who said he had seen the film on three consecutive nights, with Dominion and Allied troops, 'who were seeing England, the real England, for the first time'. *Cavalcade* worked so well because it was part fantasy, and we all knew it; this piece works less well because it is so determined to be on 'our' side. Even so, the film removes much of what was so condescending in the play, Coward having left it in the hands of the creative team of *In Which We Serve*, now assembled as Cineguild, an off-shoot of Two Cities. The screenplay is credited to Ronald Neame,

Anthony Havelock-Allen and David Lean. The latter also directed, sensitively, in Technicolor. In the thankless and demanding role of the mother Celia Johnson is called upon to register as many emotions as any actress since films began, and she never fails us; as the father Robert Newton is less mannered than usual; and Stanley Holloway is a tower of strength as the next-door neighbour.

In the matter of patriotic drama, the major event was **Henry V** (1944). The studios had left Shakespeare well alone since the three attempts to film his plays almost a decade earlier; the incentive this time came from Dallas Bower who, on hearing Laurence Olivier in a radio excerpt of the play, was impressed with its potential as propaganda. The man determined to make the project a reality, however, was del Guidice. As well as playing the title role Olivier agreed to direct when no one else he trusted was able or willing, and in his hands the filming of Shakespeare was revitalised. Wartime economy caused the particular and imaginative shape of the film so that it starts in 'this wooden O', the Globe Theatre, moving on to an equally theatrical Harfleur, based on the Duc de Berri's *Book of Hours*, and thence to 'the vasty fields of France', which are indeed fields. Then, having opened out completely, the film folds again, like the petals of a flower. The budget was huge, just under £500,000; the Battle of Agincourt was re-enacted in Ireland – to avoid aircraft – but these still plagued shooting, as did bad weather. It is an exciting and colourful battle, deploying the full panoply of medieval heraldry and armour. It is not perhaps much like the real Agincourt, for the movie did not aim at naturalism but wanted to show little England overwhelming the immense forces of the foe – and it is that nationalistic interpretation, now often under-emphasised in stage productions, which limits the film today.

It concentrates on Henry's great rallying cries, plus the battle and the reflective sequence which precedes it. 'If the cause be just,' says the English soldier, and in 1944 it seemed so; but in the interim we have come to believe less in the right of kings to go a-conquering. Olivier plays for laughs the sequence concerning the Salic law, as he also plays down the insult of the gift of tennis balls; but we may still feel

that Henry's invasion of France is committed for the most trumpery of reasons. Olivier's own force of personality holds the film together. He plays the king as a correct English gentleman, and only in the exquisite wooing scene does he allow a touch of humour. The acting throughout, in what we may call the Old Vic style, is exemplary – with Leslie Banks as the Chorus, Renée Asherson as the Princess, Esmond Knight as Fluellen and Leo Genn as the Constable. Paul Sheriff's artwork is outstanding, as are the costumes of Roger Furse; and Robert Krasker's camerawork never allows a banal image – which would have been easy among the stylised settings. William Walton's music borrows an air or so from the Songs of the Auvergne, and is thrillingly matched to the images. I have indicated that Olivier's concept is imaginative and, though the final impression is of solid craftsmanship, that is the way – with constant invention – that he led his team.

Understandably, given the moment – and the previous poor screen versions of Shakespeare – the film was widely hailed as a masterpiece; and since it brought much prestige to Mr Rank he had high hopes of **Caesar and Cleopatra** (1945), which Gabriel Pascal had chosen as the third of his Shaw films, this time without directorial help. With two stars who were names in the U.S. market, Vivien Leigh and Claude Rains, he persuaded Rank to provide a budget of £470,000, with the expressed aim of making a dent in the international market. Despite the War, a unit was sent to Egypt to shoot locations, and the cost began to spiral, eventually stopping at £1,300,000, making it the most expensive film yet made. Filming was an unhappy experience for all concerned, and Claude Rains, for one, appalled at Pascal's incompetence, ceased speaking to him. Rank, some months after the premiere, spoke of 'a disastrous loss', and cancelled his contract with Pascal, who was told formally by the Association of Cine-Technicians that he would not be allowed to work again in Britain, except under the most stringent restrictions. Rank could not even comfort himself with prestige, for the film was slaughtered by the British press, and though in America the critics were kinder it did, in contrast to *Henry v*, almost no business there. Shaw had written an intimate comedy, with great historical charac-

ters portrayed as matter-of-fact people: the film is not comic but facetious, and it is certainly not intimate. The action sequences, moreover, are atrociously staged, and when ever anyone moves the camera seems to be in the wrong place – which can hardly have been the fault of Robert Krasker, F. A. Young, Jack Hildyard or Jack Cardiff, since individually on other occasions each showed himself a master of his craft. Oliver Messel's sets are dull, and, in a film costing so much, folds in the backcloth are even less forgivable than usual. Mr Rains and Miss Leigh are efficient; Stewart Granger is a boisterous Apollodorus, about as Sicilian as a Henley coach; Basil Sydney is a spirited Rufio, while Flora Robson, as Ftatateeta, and Cecil Parker, as Britannus, struggle to enliven Shaw's jokes on, respectively, the difficulty of pronouncing her name and woad-wearing Britons.

Mr Rank's wrath may have been assuaged by a modest – but also Technicolored – stage adaptation, **Blithe Spirit** (1945), directed by David Lean for Cineguild. Coward's play, as all good comedy should be, is funny, ingenious and callous. It is also a re-working of 'Private Lives', inasmuch as both pieces concern a man beset with two wives, the second of whom turns up – in this case in spirit form – to bicker with him over what went wrong with the marriage. Rex Harrison is the husband, and his clubman *persona* makes the exchanges even more brusque than they need be; Constance Cummings is Ruth, the second wife. From the stage production come the two definitive portrayals: Kay Hammond as the spectral first wife, petulant, sulkily drawling, delighting in Ruth's discomfiture; and Margaret Rutherford as Madame Arcati, the medium, with her brisk manner, hockey-sticks slang and over-reaching enthusiasm.

Coward's play, though it ran in the West End throughout the War, made no reference to the conflict. Its success was the reason that it was filmed, but unlike, say, *Quiet Wedding*, it was not meant as a relief from ration-books and the air-raid sirens; the War was receding. From 1943 on there are no diatribes against 'old Hitler'; but there were a number of films about England, as if in relief that it was no longer on the brink of extinction. This was not a case of militant patriotism: there was a greater

Laurence Olivier in *Henry v*, offering a straight reading of the role, attempting for instance neither power-complex nor divine mission. One imagines him behaving similarly on the set, for the film gives the impression of having been cared for by all its participants.

The British at War

awareness of the diversity of the country since people visiting evacuees and doing military service were travelling to parts of the country they had not seen before. In escaping into rural Britain the film-makers were questioning materialism and traditional values. That was the starting-point for Powell and Pressburger in making **A Canterbury Tale** (1944), which is about three young people going to Canterbury for variously idealistic reasons – a Landgirl (Sheila Sim), an army sergeant (Dennis Price) and a G.I. (Sgt. John Sweet of the U.S. Army). Throughout the film, for every good idea there is a daft one – such as the misogynist J. P. (Eric Portman) with a penchant for pouring glue over the heads of young ladies in the black-out. Indeed, as one of the film's admirers wrote to the weekly *Time & Tide*, the plot is 'doolally'; and for all that the native cinema would be poorer without Powell and Pressburger, this film is no exception to the rule that most of their films are terrible.

Tawny Pipit (1944), also celebrates the rural landscape. Charles Saunders and Bernard Miles wrote and directed this kindly film about a rare bird which has laid its eggs in a cornfield, which must therefore be protected from Ministry ploughs and

army tanks by the villagers, including a nurse (Rosamund John) and a convalescent pilot (Niall McGinnis). Lejeune observed, 'It is just for the right to enjoy such things, the film suggests, that we are fighting; and, although conceivably mad, that is the way we are.' In other words, the film celebrates the cuteness of the English.

So too does **Don't Take It To Heart** (1944), written and directed by Jeffrey Dell, a comedy about a stately home and the place of the aristocracy in a changing world. Both films, from Two Cities, are the germs from which Ealing comedy (q.v.) grew.

Ealing itself remained serious, and **Johnny Frenchman** (1945) offered a new slant on the Englishness of the English by contrasting it with the Frenchness of the French – as represented by those age-old rivals, the Cornish and the Bretons. However, the similarities between these peoples is reduced to a latter-day Min and Bill by the writer, T. E. B. Clarke (q.v.), with Françoise Rosay as French Min and Tom Walls as Cornish Bill, and their children as Romeo and Juliet. Paul Dupuis is good as the French boy, but Patricia Roc's Mayfair accent negates her flat heels and pinnies. Charles Frend directed this 'hands-across-the-Channel' effort.

Ealing, for all its postwar reputation, still lagged far behind del Guidice's Two Cities as purveyors of entertainment, but both companies shared a resolve to avoid their old formulae. No longer did the British studios ape Hollywood, or try to make the musicals they did so badly. The comics had been unceremoniously dumped, and gone, too, were the asinine thrillers and tabloid newspaper stories. It was therefore a very changed industry to which Alexander Korda returned, and one much more to his liking – but it was not one to which, with his record, he could gain easy access. To all intents and purposes it was owned by Rank, who in his benevolence would have welcomed Korda: but Korda decided that if he were to be responsible to anyone he would prefer that person to be far away, and he approached M-G-M, anxious to re-activate its British operation. To the mutual gratification of himself and Louis B. Mayer, therefore, London Films and M-G-M-British amalgamated, but after a two-year association and an expenditure of £1 million only one film emerged: **Perfect**

Strangers (1945). The idea for the film was Korda's, despite the fact that some of Metro's money had gone to such esteemed writers as Evelyn Waugh, Graham Greene, James Bridie, James Hilton, A. E. W. Mason and Robert Graves, all put under contract by Korda. Virtually the sole satisfaction afforded Mayer was that it utilised Robert Donat and Deborah Kerr, both under contract but not required under those contracts to work, at that moment at least, in Hollywood.

The film starts at breakfast-time: she (Miss Kerr) is drab, with a sniffle, he (Donat) meticulous, wing-collared and Something in the City. When he joins the Navy she joins the Wrens, and since their leaves are cancelled or do not coincide, and he is torpedoed, they do not meet for three years – by which time neither is sure that they like their old selves, and both are pretty sure that they do not like each other. Though it could be a great deal better – the eventual reunion is much too prolonged – this is a valuable and important film on a subject no other tackled. Hollywood made the most successful film on homecoming, *The Best Years of Our Lives* (q.v.), but this one, far less sober – indeed, it is a romantic comedy – has far more to say, since its subject is the changes wrought by the War upon individuals. Wives changed not only because they joined the services, but because many went out to work for the first time; the experience of going abroad and the rigours of personal combat changed many men; and both sexes had their first chance to mix with people from other social classes. In this film both husband and wife are allowed a discreet romance, and it should be said that the success of the film owes much to these players, who, never notably glamorous, do not have to try too hard for plainness. Clemence Dane, one of the many people to work on the screenplay, won an Academy Award for Best Original Story. Wesley Ruggles was to have directed, but was frustrated by Korda's constant interference with the script, so that Korda himself took over the job.

The last impressive British war film was **The True Glory** (1945), released as the War in the Far East was ending: a British-American co-production, sponsored by the U.S. Office of War Information and Britain's Ministry of Information. Carol Reed and Garson Kanin co-directed this distillation of all the newsreel footage – said to be 6½ million feet – taken between D-Day and V.E.-Day, almost a year later. Thus the Invasion and the battle for Europe is told in newsreel images, but what puts the film ahead of the other war documentaries – except those of Jennings, whose influence is clearly felt – are the troops' voiced impressions of what is happening. The dialogue is spoken by professionals (at least, one recognises certain voices, such as Celia Johnson and Leslie Dwyer), but the credited writers – Eric Maschwitz, Arthur Macrae, Jenny Nicholson, Gerald Kersh and Guy Trosper – surely collected it rather than invented it. An American speaks of Belsen in a neutral tone, 'It was the worst thing I ever saw in my life and I wouldn't have missed it for anything,' and in the ruins of a German town a British soldier comments, 'A German woman said to me, "If only you'd given up in 1940 none of this need've happened." ' It is seldom brave and comfortable dialogue, and it is not free of criticism and complaint, speaking of the Boche without either bitterness or magnanimity, but rather with compassion. Basically the film is a tribute to the common soldier, and above all it offers a more compelling insight into what can only be described as 'history' than any other movie on record. The score, by William Alwyn (who contributed so memorably to *Fires Were Started* and *The Way Ahead*), is here bombastic enough to emphasise the banality of the images, though perhaps that is its purpose. Two of those images are particularly memorable in capturing the moment: the shot of the Fleet steaming across the Channel, and the shot from inside the barge as the men prepare to disembark on French soil to rid the world of Nazism.

23

Hollywood's War Effort

HOLLYWOOD's preparations for war had not gone unnoticed. The War Department was delighted with those films which encouraged recruitment, but the anti-Nazi films provoked less favourable reactions among non-interventionists. In August 1941 Senators Gerald P. Wye and Burton K. Wheeler accused the film industry of having brought the country to the brink of war, as a result of which a Senate investigatory committee was set up. It had not proceeded far when the Japanese attacked Pearl Harbor, at which point – in fact, the very next day – it was disbanded. The Hollywood studios threw themselves into the war effort with vigour, loaning facilities and equipment to make training films, and sending out stars for Defense Bond tours and U.S.O. camp shows. Meanwhile the Motion Picture division of the Office of War Information suggested that Hollywood build its product round one or more of six basic principles:

1. The Issues of War:
   what we are fighting for, and the American way of life
2. The Nature of the Enemy:
   his ideology, objectives and methods
3. The Allies
4. The Production Front:
   supplying the materials for victory
5. The Home Front:
   sacrifice and civilian responsibility
6. The Fighting Forces,
   including the job of the man at the front.

The whole-hearted response of the studios was due partly to guilt at being so far from the field of battle and partly to their customary sense of responsibility as providers of the world's leading communications medium. They were little affected by wartime shortages, for the government recognised the cinema as a prime means of maintaining morale – and indeed during the war years more Americans were regular cinemagoers than at any other time in the industry's history.

Production remained at full throttle to meet the demand, and it was not necessary to mention the War in *every* film despite government decree – for many war-weary spectators would be glad to forget it for an hour or two while watching comedies and musicals. As in Britain, the film companies welcomed new themes and new stories, even if many of them were old ones in disguise. As far as the British were concerned, Hollywood's heart had gone out to them at the time of the Blitz; and after Pearl Harbor the whole of America felt even closer to them in their beleaguered isle. Sentiment was to play a large part in the reception of many wartime films.

Since M-G-M remained the leader of the industry, it was appropriate that it produced the one film which seemed to everyone to represent the common experience of war – if not quite their own experience of it. 'Perhaps it is too soon to call this one of the greatest motion pictures ever made,' said Bosley Crowther in *The New York Times*, 'but certainly it is the finest film yet made about the present war, and a most exalting tribute to the British, who have taken it so gallantly.' He went on, 'One cannot speak too highly of the superb understatement and restraint exercised throughout.' In truth, since the film is **Mrs Miniver** (1942), one cannot speak of them at all. As it happened, Jan Struther's stories of a British family coping with the War had been published in *The New York Times*: Sidney Franklin bought the rights and assigned four writers to the script, including the novelist James Hilton. William Wyler was borrowed from Goldwyn to direct, his last film before joining the U.S.A.F. – which took him to Britain, where he soon realised that the film was inadequate to its subject. In their annual poll the New York critics affirmed the superiority of *In Which We Serve*, but in Hollywood Oscars were showered on the Minivers: Best Film, Best Direction, Best Actress (Greer Garson), Best Supporting Actress (Teresa Wright), Best Screenplay from Another Source and Best Cinematography (Joseph Ruttenberg). Today the two actresses concerned are handicaps in what at least was an honest endeavour, the one relentlessly noble and the other dimpling prettily throughout. The film took at least $5½ million in admissions, the highest-grossing M-G-M film up to that time. Since then Miss Garson rounding up a German flyer in her garden has become a cinema joke. Mr M. (Walter Pidgeon) had taken his little boat to Dunkirk, and it is just after turning in the German that Mrs M. sees it returning in the pretty river at the end of the garden. Doubtless the studio's heart was in the right place, but the war was not like this – even remotely (there is no mention of rationing, which was what concerned the British most after the bombing). However, Winston Churchill said in Parliament that the film had done more for Britain than a flotilla of destroyers.

It was only one of several M-G-M hymns to Anglo-American understanding. The company had always been Anglophile and, since the American public had indicated a weakness for spires and cloisters in *A Yank at Oxford* and *Goodbye, Mr Chips*, it was to be hoped that it would not notice the solecisms of similar films made on the Culver City lot. **Random Harvest** (1942) has the same writers as *Mrs Miniver* and also Miss Garson, as a music-hall star who meets and marries an amnesiac officer (Ronald Colman). The time is Armistice Day, 1918, and the film follows their benighted fortunes till the reunion under the cherry blossom. Mervyn LeRoy directed, but it is Colman's conviction which keeps us watching – and interested – while our intellect is assaulted. It is inferior to the great prewar romances, and one does wonder why 'Loch Lomond' accompanies the sequences in the West Country; but, at least, unlike *Mrs Miniver*, it does not have exalted ideas of its own importance.

The White Cliffs of Dover (1944) does not feature the wartime song of that title, since presumably it was not classy enough for the occasion: instead the soundtrack throbs with every well-known British air except 'Loch Lomond'. Clarence Brown directed, from a screenplay by two of the *Miniver* writers, Claudine West and George Froeschel, joined by Jan Lustig; and this came from an unlikely but popular source, a long poem by Alice Duer Miller, about an American girl (Irene Dunne) who marries an English baronet (Alan Marshall) and loses both him and their son in the two World Wars. She moves only in the best society – Sir C. Aubrey Smith and the like – and sheep graze in all the country exteriors. While the couple enjoy a holiday idyll in a Dieppe hotel, thousands of men were dying just down the line – but typically there is no indication of that in this gauzy-glamorous film. The plot makes much of the British delight at the U.S. entries into both wars, and the point was not lost on the British that though they may have taken American girls into their aristocratic families, when it came to fighting they needed American men.

Irene Dunne plays lightly, making lines passable which in the mouth of Miss Garson would seem like lead. Of **A Guy Named Joe** (1943), which again stars Irene Dunne, I can do no better than quote a letter I once received from a friend, Donald Wayne Hunt: 'Honest to God, the plot goes like this: Spencer Tracy is a fighter pilot who loves Irene Dunne, a ferry pilot. He gets called to the heaven of dead pilots where God, played by Lionel Barrymore, sends him back to earth assigned to student pilot Van Johnson, who meets and falls in love with Irene. Tracy is invisible, even to her, though the way her eyes mist up we know she *knows* he's there. When Van draws an assignment to bomb a munitions dump, she knows that his number is up because he pulls at his eyebrows the way Spence used to pull at his: so she steals out and takes the plane up, and Tracy is there with her showing her how to work the guns, and her eyes are all misted up. Then he sets her free to marry Van, because a love like theirs shouldn't wither away. One nice thing: she sings

Spencer Tracy in Fred Zinnemann's excellent *The Seventh Cross* (1944), made somewhat surprisingly by M-G-M, a company also responsible for some of the worst films about the War. The public discriminated, but not always wisely, and seem to have been put off this by critics commenting that it showed a number of Germans in a favourable light.

"I'll Get By".' Dalton Trumbo wrote the screenplay, a perfect demonstration of Dwight Macdonald's comment that the Hollywood 'Unfriendly Ten' (i.e. those blacklisted in the late Forties) were by and large the Untalented Ten. Blame must also be apportioned to the director, Victor Fleming, for permitting the painted backdrops that masquerade as airfields in the film.

'A highly placed American officer with whom I discussed the matter said that wartime Hollywood had become a pain in the neck to all decent-thinking Americans, and that the boys themselves, meaning the troops, were not amused,' wrote James Agate in 1943. One film they may have had in mind is **The Cross of Lorraine** (1943). The Marseillaise thundering out over the credits announces its intention, and Tay Garnett directed these adventures of a group of Frenchmen from Conscription to Resistance. Gene Kelly represents all those who wanted to fight on while the rest capitulated; Jean-Pierre Aumont pretends treachery in the cause of heroism; Hume Cronyn is the prospective collaborator; Peter Lorre the German sergeant; and Cedric Hardwicke the senior member of the Church. The film concludes with the Germans temporarily vanquished, and the villagers marching to a hide-out in the mountains singing you-know-what.

M-G-M atoned with **The Seventh**

Cross (1944), which shares with the prewar anti-Nazi films a sense of responsibility, as if its makers too understood the significance of handling totalitarianism. Helen Deutsch wrote the screenplay from a novel by Anna Seghers, and even the title takes us into mystical areas to which movies seldom aspire: it begins in a concentration camp – the time is 1936 – where the film's hero, George Heisler (Spencer Tracy) has been imprisoned for crimes described as 'political'. We follow the story of his escape and the pursuit, and very few thrillers then and since have dealt so honestly with their audience. Wounded, Heisler goes to a doctor (Steven Geray) who says, 'Before I treat you the law requires me to tell you that I am a Jew,' a sentence that can still send a chill down the spine. The only fault in an otherwise flawless film is a touch of romance at the end, though the climax itself is more subtle than was customary. Comment at the time indicated that the film was premature in showing good as well as bad Germans: what impresses now is that the evident brutality of the bad ones is not underlined, and that the good ones are more rounded than most movie people of the period. Tracy, grim and haunted, gives his best performance in his best serious film. At the time, he astonished the M-G-M publicity department by offering to meet the press to praise his company. The Viennese-born director, Fred Zinnemann (b. 1907), had worked with Robert Flaherty in Germany in the early Thirties on a documentary which was abandoned: what he learned from that experience he put into practice in a semi-documentary about fisherfolk made in Mexico in 1935, *Redes* (or *The Waves*). It was unusual to find a filmmaker with a penchant for realism at M-G-M, but in *The Seventh Cross* he achieves, with the aid of his art director, Leonid Vasian, a Germany that looks like Germany. He succeeds far better than Lang, Renoir and other European directors who handled similar themes at this time; the film has infinitely more dimension and individuality than any other M-G-M war movie and, since Zinnemann carried far less clout than Wyler, Brown or LeRoy, that is no mean achievement.

Keeper of the Flame (1942) was also topical, and its screenwriter, Donald Ogden Stewart, reckoned it 'the picture

I'm proudest of having been connected with – in terms of saying the most about Fascism that it is possible to say in Hollywood'. He also thought it daring to have made it under the nose of Louis B. Mayer, but in fact the possibility of Fascism in America had been discussed far more boldly in *Meet John Doe* and *Confessions of a Nazi Spy*. In view of the current U.S. hostility towards Hitler, it was not courageous to suggest that a man aiming at a similar degree of power should be destroyed. This potential dictator had been a national hero till he took to preaching anti-Semitism: but since he is dead before the film starts any potential argument is stifled. Some interest is engendered when a reporter (Spencer Tracy) attempts to meet his widow (Katharine Hepburn), but matters soon descend to the level of turgid gothic mystery with an insane old mother hidden away and a glowering cousin who swaggers about in riding boots. It is possible that I.A.R. Wylie, who wrote the original novel, and Cukor, who directed, were so entranced by the underlying theory – that idealism can turn to Fascism – that they felt they might find a wider audience by indulging in melodrama. Resemblances have been noted to *Citizen Kane*, but Cukor finds 'no conscious echoes . . . [they] were just an accident. There was something in the air; it was simply the result of the prevailing political climate'; at the time the film was compared, unfavourably, with *Rebecca*.

Coming back to haunt Mayer later was **Song of Russia** (1943), one of a number of American films extolling the Russians made at the height of Allied co-operation. A naive propaganda piece, greeted by the armed services with 'one long howl of laughter' (according to *Time* magazine), it was quickly forgotten till resurrected by the House Un-American Activities Committee in the late Forties: Mayer managed to imply that it had slipped out while he was not looking, and its star, Robert Taylor, testified that he had made it under protest. The Soviet's own movies are not more ardent in their fervour for the Collective way of life: working in the Collective fields, training with the Collective machine-gun, listening to the Collective radio or marching home after a hard day's work with their hoes over their shoulders and their voices raised in song. There is

even an Eisenstein-like close-up in a montage, but on this evidence the director, Gregory Ratoff, had never heard of his distinguished predecessor.

Having foisted this film on to defenceless audiences M-G-M came up with the equally foolish **Dragon Seed** (1944), feeling it incumbent upon them, as makers of *The Good Earth*, to inform the world exactly how the Chinese were coping with the Japanese occupation – or, rather, overcoming it, as Katharine Hepburn, impersonating a Chinese peasant, disposes of the entire Japanese garrison by putting poison into the duck sauce. Under the same slant-eyed make-up are Aline MacMahon and Walter Huston, mouthing such dialogue as 'Wait five hundred heartbeats and then go to her'. Pearl S. Buck again wrote the original novel; Jack Conway directed, with Harold S. Bucquet replacing him when he became ill; and Lionel Barrymore speaks the unbelievably condescending commentary.

Wartime propaganda also turned up in **Madame Curie** (1943), since its aged heroine (Miss Garson, now the studio's biggest star) at the end makes a plea for international understanding. Planned for Garbo, this respectful tribute might with her presence have taken fire, but Garson seems to move in a cloud of sanctity, smiling quizzically to indicate intelligence. Paul Osborn and Paul H. Rameau have taken the facts from Eve Curie's biography of her mother; Mervyn LeRoy, directing, never finds the requisite spirit. The scientific work is well explained, and her private life – there is no mention of her real-life lover – depicted as idyllic till the accidental death of Pierre (Walter Pidgeon). To be savoured is an incredible moment when Van Johnson turns up claiming to be a reporter from Grenoble.

In **Gaslight** (1944) the Swedish Ingrid Bergman, the Frenchman Charles Boyer and the American Joseph Cotten all pretend to be British, Bergman as the frightened wife, Boyer as the sadistic husband and Cotten as the Scotland Yard man still on the trail of her aunt's disappearance. Patrick Hamilton's original play,* a study in morbid psychology, had been reworked – by John Van Druten, Walter Reisch and

*The British film version had been held up pending the Broadway production, which was so successful that M-G-M bought the rights.

John L. Balderston – into a conventional murder mystery with Victorian trimmings, and Cukor, directing, was unable to evince from Bergman the requisite panic and terror. Her Best Actress Oscar was presumably an expression of Hollywood's fascination with her at this time, and could certainly not be justified when Barbara Stanwyck was nominated for *Double Indemnity* (q.v.).

Also set in Victorian London, **The Picture of Dorian Gray** (1945) marked a return to the studio of Albert Lewin, a former Associate Producer who had made *The Moon and Sixpence* (q.v.) for United Artists. His second excursion as writer-producer-director finds Wilde's novel filmed with three virtues: the decor, excessive but splendid; the inserts of the portrait in Technicolor, a rarely used device; and Angela Lansbury as Sybil Vane – a 'vaudeville' performer in this incarnation – plaintively singing 'Goodbye, Little Yellow Bird' in her perky hat while paper snow is thrown over her. As the immaculately silk-hatted Dorian looks at her in the East End dive we know that he will destroy her, and we enjoy a slight *frisson*, contemplating his catalogue of crimes – but they, often left ambiguous in the book, are hardly more explicit here. Drinking in a Ufa-influenced dockside den, listening to his favourite Chopin prelude, or climbing up the rickety stairs, he is without joy. However much Wilde privately flouted Victorian morals, his book upheld them, so doubtless Lewin was correct in showing sin as mirthless – not that Mayer or the Hays Code would have permitted him to do otherwise. And by not specifying the reasons for Dorian's hold over a number of young men Lewin may have been dropping a hint that only one in a thousand of the audiences at the time would pick up. As Dorian, Hurd Hatfield not only reveals no wrinkles but no discernible emotion at all; as Lord Henry, George Sanders is permitted to mouth a number of epigrams borrowed from other of Wilde's works.

Equally an expression of Metro's love affair with Albion is **Lassie Come Home** (1943), directed by Fred M. Wilcox, and the apotheosis of the boy and dog movie, throbbing with sentiment, aglow with Technicolor, and with an ending that James H. Fitzpatrick could not have bettered. It was adapted from a novel by Eric Knight, a Yorkshireman who survived the First World War but died in the Second as a major in the U.S. Army – or so a maudlin introduction tells us. Roddy McDowall plays the boy who loses his dog and never sheds a tear, obviously to accommodate the wartime notion of the British as a titanically stoic race; as for Lassie, she makes her way back from Scotland via Big Sur, Colorado and the swamps of Georgia, not to mention that vast river (a heavenly choir accompanying) which, explains Dame May Whitty,[*] separates Scotland from England. Nigel Bruce is the squire, and Donald Crisp gives his stock performance as the boy's father. And then there is Lassie: what can one say in view of the fact that it took no less than three canines to play the role, all of them male? The question becomes even more confused in **Son of Lassie** (1945), directed by S. Sylvan Simon, which is really Lassie Goes to War, only it is the son, Laddie . . . and like James Cagney in *The Fighting 69th* he doesn't learn the meaning of discipline till the last reel. Canada this time does duty for both Yorkshire and Norway; and the grown-up McDowall is Peter Lawford, as an R.A.F. sergeant in a blue previously unknown to the R.A.F. *Lassie Come Home* is not anyone's idea of a good movie, but it had a certain drive and sincerity: this has neither.

Of the same lineage is **National Velvet** (1944), lifelessly directed by Clarence Brown from Enid Bagnold's whimsical tale about a little girl determined to ride her horse in the Grand National. The film has achieved some fame, partly because it is the only one from Elizabeth Taylor's childhood which anybody remembers. It is also tawdry; the California coast poses grandly as the Sussex downs, and the back-lot village is painted and garish; the quality of hope in the book has become gooey sentiment, except in the performance of the mother by Anne Revere, who rightly won a Best Supporting Oscar. Angela Lansbury offers a pleasing study of adolescence, and Jackie 'Butch' Jenkins is a *Saturday Evening Post* cover child come to life – not English, but not bad; Taylor plays honestly and spontaneously – qualities she never showed as an adult –

---

[*]Her husband, Ben Webster, plays exactly that here, and it is odd to think of him (the original wearer of Wilde's green carnation, before his days as Shakespearian actor-manager) being in the same film – her first – as Elizabeth Taylor.

confirming the truth that some children have a natural talent.

Another talented child actress was Margaret O'Brien, who was the antithesis of Shirley Temple and therefore popular with many critics. She could indeed perform with emotion, if a little too knowingly as time went on. She is pleasing in **The Canterville Ghost** (1944), directed by Jules Dassin and, as updated from Wilde, an uncertain mixture of slapstick, whimsy and homilies on Anglo-American co-operation. Robert Young heads a G.I. platoon and Charles Laughton is 'the most fearsome phantom in all England'. **Our Vines Have Tender Grapes** (1945), as directed by Roy Rowland, is an affectionate study of a Norwegian community in Wisconsin – O'Brien and her cousin (young Jenkins) quarrelling over roller skates and getting lost in the spring floods, and father (Edward G. Robinson) taking her into town in the night to see the circus pass through. C. A. Lejeune was so taken by the child that she thought the film 'one of those rare hours in the cinema that leave you wondering if the thing may not grow into an art some day'.

Such films – the family Americana – were dear to the heart of Mayer, and in the presumptuously titled **The Human Comedy** (1943) they reach an apotheosis. It was written by William Saroyan, whom the producer Arthur Freed had introduced to Mayer, who was so impressed with his conversation that he offered him a contract. Freed also persuaded Saroyan to write the story on which this film was based. Mayer purchased it for $60,000 and gave Saroyan $1,500 a week to be groomed as producer-director, but Mayer then became disenchanted after seeing a short Saroyan made, *The New Job*, so the direction was given to Clarence Brown, Metro's prime exponent of the American way of life. He was seldom more sensitively employed. The subject is the War as seen from a small Californian town, and there are at least a dozen superb scenes, including all those with Frank Morgan as a tippling newspaperman. As it happens, drink is the town's sole vice. Everyone is nice and kind; no one lies or loses his temper, which hardly atones with my idea of the human comedy. Saroyan's view is not merely cosy but dripping with sentiment, and the final sequence, where Mickey Rooney recognises the uniformed stranger as his dead brother's best buddy, lays fair claim to being the most embarrassing moment in the whole history of movies. Time has not changed it, since C. A. Lejeune spoke for all the critics when she said: 'Have you ever seen a film that irritates you, embarrasses you, and yet moves you so much that you stiffen at the criticisms of other people equally irritated and embarrassed?'

It was reputedly Mayer's favourite movie. He did not like **An American Romance** (1944), the third part of the war-wheat-steel trilogy proposed to him twenty years earlier by King Vidor, who claims that the studio ruined it. *The Big Parade* and *Our Daily Bread* (not made at M-G-M) were now ancient history; Vidor was allowed Technicolor, but not the promised stars, Spencer Tracy, Ingrid Bergman and Joseph Cotten – and Brian Donlevy, Ann Richards and Walter Abel are dull replacements. The picture is part documentary and part fiction, and when the first cut called for pruning, the studio started lopping at the main story, whereas Vidor would have preferred losing some of the shots of fields and mills. In fact, these remain the film's sole justification; the rest is garbled stuff from better movies – such as the schoolteacher wife and illiterate husband in *The Power and the Glory*, or the Cotten/Able role, an amalgamation of those Cotten played in *Ambersons* and *Kane*.

One veteran director did provide M-G-M with a good film, and indeed **They Were Expendable** (1945) is one of the best contemporary films about the War. It was John Ford's first film since leaving the navy, and his first for the company since *Flesh* in 1932; it would also be his last for M-G-M. Robert Montgomery, also returning from naval service, plays a character based on Lieutenant Johnny Buckley, who pioneered the use of the P.T. boat in combat, and Frank Wead adapted from a book by William H. White. Since there is little plot the mood is all: the film is a tribute to wartime camaraderie – to the men's attitudes to fighting, to dying and to each other, and the sentiment is more honest than in most of Ford's films. Montgomery and John Wayne are excellent, though the latter's heroics are in the conventional mode.

Judy Garland and Robert Walker, right, in *The Clock*, their romantic mood momentarily shattered by a drunk, Keenan Wynn. The critic James Agee paid the film the rare tribute of believing it would be remembered in fifty years' time.

From M-G-M, too, came the best wartime romance, **The Clock** (1945), the story of a G.I. (Robert Walker) and the girl (Judy Garland) he meets and marries on a two-day pass. The director, Vincente Minnelli, used New York, as he said, as a 'third character' when he took over from Fred Zinnemann (whom Garland found unsympathetic), largely abandoning a script in which the characters mouthed banalities instead of what they really thought – a device for which he thought audiences were not ready. Despite some back-projection, the Manhattan of this film is alive, and the comic relief – Keenan Wynn as a drunk, James Gleason as a friendly milkman – forced but accurate. For once in a movie the lovers do seem to care for each other, and Garland handles a number of non-movie emotions, as when her room-mate berates her for letting herself be picked up, or when she experiences the panic and self-pity of not feeling married at the wedding feast. This is an infinitely better (both more interesting and more honest) performance than the one which won Joan Crawford an Oscar that year – and those given by the other nominated ladies.

Garland's other wartime films were musicals, and with the advent of Minnelli M-G-M was to attain a form in this field which demands a chapter to itself. However, we might glance here at **Thousands Cheer** (1943), since it almost shakes with emotion for all things military. The ambiguous title might suggest the army or 'the M-G-M star parade', or the former cheering the latter at the concert which provides the film's climax – a form of self-congratulation pioneered by Paramount with *Star Spangled Rhythm* (q.v.). But apart from songs by Garland and Lena Horne there is little to cheer over. The pre-concert story concerns Kathryn Grayson as the pride of the regiment and Gene Kelly as the rebellious G.I. for whom she falls. Soon involved is Mother (Mary Astor), who had left Father (John Boles) years before because he loved the army more than her – an unconvincing assertion in view of the fact that he is seen to do nothing but fuss about the romance. Kelly eventually learns that teamwork and discipline are as essential to life in the army as they were to his trapeze act – a glimpse of which offers a revealing detail of G.I. life, that they shaved their armpits. It also convinces him: 'I want to be the most important man in the world – a private in the United States Army,' he says, after which it is left to Miss Grayson and a massed choir to sing 'Make Way for a Day Called Tomorrow' before the flags of the Allies.

The United Artists contribution to the all-star wartime film was **Stage Door Canteen** (1943), the brainchild of Sol Lesser as written by Delmer Daves, who later provided the identical story for *Hollywood Canteen* (q.v.). The institutions celebrated served the forces with food and entertainment, as provided by thespians high and low; since U.A. had no contract list Lesser used Broadway players who had appeared at the Canteen and Hollywood stars currently without affiliation – thus we are offered such as George Raft and Alfred Lunt in aprons, Katherine Cornell doling out hamburgers, and Tallulah, cigarette in hand, growling to a G.I. 'You do your job well, and remember, we'll do our job well.' Among the few bearable turns are Yehudi Menuhin playing 'The Flight of the Bumble Bee', Ethel Merman belting out 'We'll Be Singing Hallelujah as We're Marching Through Berlin', and Benny Goodman playing 'Why Don't You Do Right?', with Peggy Lee as his vocalist.

Between turns we are offered some budding romances, such as that between a G.I. called 'Dakota' (William Terry) and an aspiring actress (Cheryl Walker), who after a tiff sit watching the dawn come up over Washington Square, saying things like 'I like hot baths on cold nights' and 'Do you like dogs?' – an apt question with this particular film. Finally the young actress is given a pep talk about doing her bit by no less than Katharine Hepburn: clever lady, she waits till the end and gets the best scene. The once estimable Borzage directed.

One of U.A.'s more memorable additions to the war effort was **That Hamilton Woman** (1941), a pro-British movie released some months before Pearl Harbor; American audiences actually applauded when Nelson (Laurence Olivier) says of Napoleon, 'There are always men who for the sake of insane ambition want to destroy what other men have built up.' It was virtually a British film: Korda produced and directed, and the writers were R.C. Sherriff and Walter Reisch, who had both worked with him at Denham. It was made in six weeks on a low budget, with some improvisation, and was constantly revived over the next few years. It ran throughout the War in the Soviet Union, and Churchill, who loved it, had special screenings for visitors. Today it stands as another of those romantic dramas which betray the truth of human behaviour yet manage, by virtue of dramatic intelligence, to remain moving years after the audiences for which they were made have passed on. As usual, this has something to do with the players, and with this barely-written role Olivier completes his quartet of Hollywood heroes (Heathcliff, Maxim, Darcy), playing each for full-blooded romance in four quite different ways. Here, on his first appearance, he is direct with Sir William and gauche with milady; he even manages to suggest that he is wall-eyed. Later, lacking arm and eye, he establishes himself as a figure grown in authority, but subject to a passion which he tries not to show. Gladys Cooper is the bitter Lady Nelson, and Alan Mowbray has the best role as the cuckolded Hamilton. Vivien Leigh's Emma hardly manages a Cockney accent, and she is too naive; but she is pert and pretty and vital; no wonder the two men refuse her nothing! In the later stages,

listening to Hardy as he tells her of Nelson's death with one unchanging expression of disbelief, she is also moving. The Hays Office insisted that she pay for her sins, so the story was framed by a sequence with her as a derelict in Calais – removed by Korda for later reissues. We are otherwise not shown her darker side – one of her qualities captured by Terence Rattigan in his 'A Bequest to the Nation'. In fact, the 1973 film based on Rattigan's play borrowed and tinted the battle sequence from this film, despite the fact that the ships were obvious models.

Korda continued his Sabu vehicles with **The Jungle Book** (1942), directed by his brother Zoltan, with his other brother, Vincent, providing sometimes superb decor. Its chief demerit is the presence of white actors in dark make-up, but Sabu is a natural Mowgli. Kipling's stories do not too readily lend themselves to adaptation, and Lawrence Stallings's screenplay leans heavily on Edgar Rice Burroughs.

Before returning to Britain – where he was engaged on secret war work for two years – Korda co-produced **To Be or Not To Be** (1942) with Lubitsch, who directed. In Britain, in *The Spectator*, Edgar Anstey observed that they 'here and there abandoned their buffoonery to commiserate with the Poles and Jews, and to make some return for their Hollywood comforts with sequences which they no doubt hope may prove to be anti-Nazi propaganda'; and in the U.S. *Life* magazine sniffed, 'In years to come the fact that Hollywood could convert part of a world crisis into such a cops and robbers charade will certainly be regarded as a remarkable phenomena [*sic*].' Lubitsch was upset when accused of bad taste – notably over a line spoken by Sig Rumann as a German, of Jack Benny as a 'great' Polish actor, 'What he did to Shakespeare we are now doing to Poland.' It is true that his original intention (he wrote the story with Melchior Lengyel; Edwin Justus Mayer turned it into a screenplay) was to show that actors remain actors whatever the circumstances. In the event, the heroic antics of this theatre troupe are neatly balanced against the rottenness of the Nazis, and indeed the latter are so menacing that the advent of Rumann as a cretin is a relief. It should have been clear that Lubitsch's approach was preferable to the daft exploits of the now-proliferating Resistance movies – on which this, if a mite prematurely, is a sharp satire. Benny – who should have made more films – is superb, as is Carole Lombard as his wife (it was her last film; she was killed in an air crash while travelling across the country to sell War Bonds).

With the departure of Korda (and Goldwyn) the company was so desperately in need of product that it bought a group of B-pictures from Paramount, plus two A-features, *I Married a Witch* and *The Crystal Ball*. It flirted increasingly with Rank, and had big-city successes with *In Which We Serve* and *Henry V*, but there was acrimony over the failure of *Caesar and Cleopatra* – and Rank, anyway, was becoming financially involved with Universal. Of the established U.A. producers, Edward Small continued to turn out usually modest products, including **International Lady** (1941), directed by Tim Whelan, one of several current films concerning espionage and intrigue in London, Lisbon or the North African cities, with in this case the uninteresting team of George Brent and Ilona Massey. For Small, Allan Dwan directed **Abroad with Two Yanks** (1944), which concerned two marines (Dennis O'Keefe, William Bendix) in London, and a sequence of lively comedies based on old stage farces, **Up in Mabel's**

Room (1944), **Brewster's Millions** (1945) and **Getting Gertie's Garter** (1946). O'Keefe is the bright but not brilliant farceur in the trio, of which the best is the middle one, since Eddie 'Rochester' Anderson is on hand as his valet. Benedict Bogeaus started badly with the company with **The Bridge of San Luis Rey** (1944), an intolerably slow version of Thorton Wilder's novel as directed by Rowland Lee, but he picked up with **Dark Waters** (1944), a frightened-lady-in-the-old-dark-house situation, beautifully directed by André de Toth, who never again came anywhere near this form; the dreariness of his leads, however – Merle Oberon and Franchot Tone – detracts from the atmosphere he creates.

A concurrent attempt at gothic melodrama was **Guest in the House** (1944), produced by Hunt Stromberg, the most promising of the newcomers to U.A., since he had given M-G-M some of their biggest successes, including *The Great Ziegfeld* and the MacDonald-Eddy musicals. This one is more typical of his work for U.A., being indifferent in all respects but the supporting performance by Aline MacMahon. John Brahm directed, and it includes a number of quintessential Forties ingredients, including pounding surf, the house on the storm-beaten cliff, and the scheming woman (Anne Baxter), thought by all to be the flower but to be revealed as the serpent under't. Stromberg's health was in fact being undermined by drugs, but he had started well as an independent with **Lady of Burlesque** (1943); his director was William Wellman, who was more than able to evoke the tawdry bustle of backstage life. Barbara Stanwyck is the bump-and-grind star who goes sleuthing, and she has three amusing buddies, Iris Adrian, Marian Martin and Gloria Dixon – not that they're very close: Stanwyck was ever a cat that walked alone, and here she is more catlike – and laconic – than ever. The source was a novel by Gypsy Rose Lee, 'The G-String Murders', a title which the Hays Office refused to sanction.

Also at U.A. Wellman directed **The Story of G.I. Joe** (1945), for Lester Cowan, described by him as 'a bastard', and an otherwise undistinguished producer. Agee observed that Wellman and his colleagues – the writers are Leopold

Atlas, Guy Endore and Philip Stevenson – 'did not regard their job as an ordinary one. They undertook a great subject. It is clear that they approached it with a determination to handle it honestly and to make a masterpiece' – and if it was not that, he concluded, 'I cannot help resenting those films that are.' Its subject is the ordinary soldier foot-slogging it from North Africa to the road to Rome, as witnessed by Ernie Pyle, the war correspondent, who died not long after the film came out and is played in it by Burgess Meredith. 'I have loved many men,' he says at one point, 'but C Company most of all,' and the incidents he describes comprise the film; the doling-out of mail or Christmas chow; the young soldier so alarmed at what he has seen that he bursts into tears in the telling; the rock-like sergeant who succumbs to battle fatigue; the enemy seen only as shadowy figures or as gun bursts. 'But the G.I. lives so miserably and dies so miserably,' says Pyle to the captain (Robert Mitchum). The final sequence Agee thought 'a war poem as great and as beautiful as any of Whitman's': the men, veterans now, sit by the road as other units move on, and the captain's body is brought down the hill at twilight to be laid in a field of new white crosses. As with *They Were Expendable* and *The Clock* it was not until the cessation of hostilities that movies portrayed the serving man with any honesty: Wellman's fine film is the best contemporary American tribute we have in this medium.

In contrast is **Since You Went Away** (1944), produced and written by David O. Selznick – whose inactivity had been of serious concern to his partners in United Artists. In 1941 he had signed a contract with Pickford, Chaplin and Korda for a quarter-share in the company, and had in the meantime toyed with a number of projects which he had sold off to other companies. Looking for something important enough to follow *Gone with the Wind* he came up with what the foreword calls 'the story of that unconquerable fortress – the American Home Front, 1943'. We follow a year on the home front from the departure of Father to the cablegram announcing that he is, after all, not killed. It takes 170 minutes and though smoothly directed by John Cromwell there is hardly one of those minutes which I do not find offensive even now. The American home front was probably the least affected of all the countries involved in the War, but the insult lies in the inference that the events depicted are typical. 'You are what I thought America was,' Mother is told by a refugee (Nazimova), but she isn't, for she is Claudette Colbert, photographed without a wrinkle though she has a grown-up daughter (Jennifer Jones). Apart from taking in a paying guest (Monty Woolley) and praying – to the strains of 'Ave Maria' – she seems unaware of the War – though she does go into a munitions factory at the end. 'I thought we might try out those new hairstyles from *Vogue* tonight,' says Colbert, but Jones refuses. 'Do you mind, Mother, I want to try out those treatments for third-degree burns.' Love plays a great part in their lives, since Mother has an old admirer (Joseph Cotten), sporting a dazzling array of uniforms, and daughter a shy young G.I. (Robert Walker). They are a liberal family, and gladly entertain a fellow-officer (Keenan Wynn) of Cotten's called Solomon. The maid (Hattie McDaniel) has been let go, but wants to work without pay. 'I couldn't let you do that,' says Colbert, but sho'nuff Miss McDaniel is soon waiting at table and dispensing Hattie McDaniel-type philosophy. Relief is provided by Agnes Moorehead as a cocktail-lounge gossip who takes the War lightly, and Colbert, as capable as ever, does manage to make quite moving the scene where she tells Jones that her fiancé is missing: it seems almost like an accident.

The film's cost of $2,900,000 was justified at the box office, and Selznick gave the company another success with *Spellbound* (q.v.); but he left U.A. soon afterwards. There was a third film for United Artists at this time, **I'll Be Seeing You** (1944), directed by William Dieterle, a wan and ridiculous romance about the mutual help given by a shell-shocked soldier (Cotten) and a thief (Ginger Rogers) on parole.

Albert Lewin, in conjunction with David L. Loew, gave the company an odd prestige movie in **The Moon and Sixpence** (1942): M-G-M had owned the movie rights to the novel while Lewin had been scenario editor there, but had not seriously considered wrenching a screenplay from it. We may thus assume a labour of love in Lewin's screenplay and direction – by its fidelity to the original, as far as was

From left to right, Jeanne Cagney, James Cagney, Joan Leslie, Walter Huston and Rosemary de Camp as the Cohan family in *Yankee Doodle Dandy*. Its patriotism may now seem excessive, but James Cagney's ebullience keeps the film, most of the time, several feet off the ground.

possible. Deprived of Maugham's speculations on the Gauguin-Strickland character, the story is thin; and though in that role George Sanders is convincing as bounder and cynic, he is an unlikely painter. Herbert Marshall plays Maugham; and Lewin's respectful treatment brought appropriately respectful notices.

United Artists also provided a haven for James Cagney, tired of haggling with Warners over contracts. Again the idea seems to have been an attempt at less standardised fare, but there is little to be said for **Johnny Come Lately** (1943) and even less for **Blood on the Sun** (1945), both produced by his brother William, and with himself as a tough reporter on both occasions. In the former, directed by William K. Howard, he helps an old lady (Grace George) revive her newspaper, and takes on corrupt politicians; in the latter he tackles what seem to be the entire Japanese army, government and police force. His contempt for all things Japanese may have brought cheers from Allied audiences,

long immune to the presentation of the enemy as one-dimensional villains; but Cagney's behaviour is intolerable, and Frank Lloyd's tired direction does not help. As Cagney returns at the end to face death, for the sake of democracy, and Sylvia Sidney – on our side, after all – sails off with Japan's plans for world conquest, one may conclude that if a nation's intelligence is indicated by its film industry, the U.S. would have been, till recently, in the dunce's corner. Only fourteen years separate *Blood on the Sun* from the first part of Kobayashi's *The Human Condition* (q.v.), but it seems like centuries.

In the last days at Warners, Cagney had been in two more efficient propaganda pieces: **Captains of the Clouds** (1942) and **Yankee Doodle Dandy** (1942), both directed by Michael Curtiz, and respectively waving the Union Jack and Stars and Stripes. The former has a lumbering plot borrowed from earlier Cagney movies; it is in Technicolor, and its setting would be evident to a blind man, since the soundtrack thunders with 'The Maple Leaf Forever'. Cagney hears on the radio Churchill's speech, 'We shall never surrender', and wants to join up ('Now there's a guy who knows how to issue an invitation'); but is refused. 'Why don't you go back where you came from?' he snarls to the examining officer, who replies, 'I can't, Mr MacLean. My home was in Coventry' – a line which is touching in that audiences were trusted to get the full import. *Yankee Doodle Dandy* is the story of George M. Cohan, as told in a ghastly framing device to an invisible Roosevelt, and its prevailing tone is set by an early remark, 'I guess I was born with an American flag in my hand.' Cohan's songs are marvellously staged and sung, or whipped into a plethora of montage sequences (arranged by Don Siegel), and the dialogue is mercifully sparse (when the *Lusitania* is sunk, Cohan says, 'And we were worried about the success or failure of our show. Now we've really got something to worry about.') Though the writers (Robert Buckner, Edmund Joseph) do provide correctives – via some characters who despise Cohan's chauvinism – the schmaltz can be overpowering. Cagney's George M. won him Best Actor citations from the New York critics and the Hollywood Academicians, and the film was the first hugely successful show business biography since *The Great Ziegfeld*. If we accept the two early Jolson Talkies as special cases, only five American films had taken more money – *Gone with the Wind*, *The Birth of a Nation*, *Sergeant York*, *The Big Parade* and *Mrs Miniver*. They were all war stories, which may or may not be coincidental.

Bogart also went to war. With snappy direction, by Vincent Sherman, and an excellent cast (Peter Lorre, Conrad Veidt, Ed Brophy, Frank McHugh, William Demarest, Wallace Ford), **All Through the Night** (1942) is watchable; but after a promising start it descends to high jinks about rounding up Fifth Columnists in New York, with Bogart seemingly uninterested in the anti-Nazi speeches he has to make. In **Across the Pacific** (1942) he single-handedly saves the Panama Canal★ from Nippon sabotage but, till then, the piece has much of the savour of *The Mal-*

★Hawaii in the original script, but shooting was overtaken by events.

tese Falcon – understandably, since John Huston again directed and Mary Astor and Sydney Greenstreet repeated their performances as mysterious lady and genial if menacing adversary. The screenplay by Richard Macaulay (from a novel by Robert Carson) has the bantering, slangy dialogue he had been providing in films like *Torrid Zone* and *They Drive by Night*, to remind us how much more febrile was Miss Astor than the other independent dames.

Bogart has another memorable partner, Ingrid Bergman, in **Casablanca** (1942) which could never have attained mythic status had it starred the lesser Warner players previously announced. It starts like a B-picture, and by planting a nightclub in an 'Oriental' city it collects at once two staples of movie melodrama; but since the War is on, the situation is more than usually tense, since most of the *dramatis personae* are desperate for American visas. It is their interplay which first indicates that the film is a unique one: Claude Rains, as the corrupt and wily police chief; the fawning Lorre, with the stolen visas – 'Now are you impressed with me?'; Veidt, as a visiting German officer; Greenstreet, owner of a rival bar and, by his own admission, 'leader of all illegal activities'; and, at their centre, Bogart as Rick, the American with the successful saloon, drinking too much, a former gunrunner and Loyalist fighter who now declines to 'stick his neck out for nobody'. His black pianist (Dooley Wilson) plays 'As Time Goes By' and in walks Ilsa (Miss Bergman), wife of a Resistance worker (Paul Henreid) but Rick's beloved in prewar Paris. Till then, the film had hurtled along; now it pauses, to give marvellous expression to his pessimism and her divided loyalties. The role of Ilsa is written as a *femme fatale*, which Bergman ignores: she is simply superbly right in every way that has to do with beauty, youth, warmth and lack of sophistication and conventional glamour. It is the contrast between the personalities of Bogart and Bergman which makes their scenes so captivating: the Paris flashbacks of their long ago love affair are tinged with heartache. The love scenes were written by Casey Robinson, uncredited, after Bogart refused the script as penned by Julius J. and Philip G. Epstein and Howard Koch (based on an unproduced and apparently poor play); that was why they had no

Humphrey **BOGART** · Ingrid **BERGMAN** · Paul **HENREID**

A HAL B. WALLIS PRODUCTION

"Casablanca"

CLAUDE **RAINS** · CONRAD **VEIDT** · SYDNEY **GREENSTREET** · PETER **LORRE**

Directed by MICHAEL CURTIZ

ending until the last day of shooting – and it was the producer, Hal Wallis, who contributed the famous last line. No one involved thought the film exceptional till it won Academy Awards for Best Picture, Best Direction (Michael Curtiz) and Best Screenplay. The reviews had indicated merely that it was above average of its kind, and it had been fairly but not sensationally popular. It was not till the Fifties that it came to be regarded as the best-loved Hollywood melodrama; it is extraordinary that material basically so artificial should become so holding and so moving.

It was typical of Warners to produce a number of imitations, including **Background to Danger** (1943), directed by Raoul Walsh, with George Raft, set in Ankara, and **The Conspirators** (1944), directed by Jean Negulesco, with Hedy Lamarr and Paul Henreid, set in Lisbon. The contract list was expanded to include several European actors suitable for such tales, including Victor Francen, Philip Dorn and Helmut Dantine – who, together with the inevitable Lorre and Greenstreet, supported Bogart in **Passage to Marseille** (1944). The presences of Rains and a European beauty – Michèle Morgan – plus the flashbacks, further the resemblance to *Casablanca*; Curtiz again directed, from a screenplay by Robinson and Jack Moffit. Bogart is an exponent of Free France, 'a greater patriot', in the words of another patriot, 'than we can ever hope to be'. We first meet him imprisoned on Devil's Island, and his adventures subsequent and previous (i.e. in the flashbacks) are ridiculous even for a Resistance tale. Much better is **To Have and Have Not** (1944), freely adapted from Hemingway's novel by William Faulkner and Jules Furthman, who have introduced into it the Free French and the Vichy French. The setting is Martinique, and Bogart is the neutral observer, an American who runs a fishing boat for wealthy visitors. Much of the action again takes place in a saloon, and Hoagy Carmichael has replaced Dooley Wilson at the piano. Howard Hawks is far too strong a director merely to recreate the atmosphere of *Casablanca*, and he has a whole new cast of characters, headed by Dan Seymour as the fat, effete Vichy inspector, with Sheldon Leonard and Aldo Nadi as his co-thugs. The woman drifter common to most of these movies is like the one Furthman wrote for Hawks in *Only Angels Have Wings*, plus some of the insolence he had written for Jean Harlow in *Red Dust* – and with Bogart responding in the same rueful manner as he had to Astor in *Across the Pacific*. This one is baby-faced, as played by a novice Lauren Bacall, and very self-assured. 'Anyone got a match?' is her first line, lounging in the doorway of his room. The scenes between them have not dated a jot. She: 'I'm hard to get. All you have to do is ask me.' It is not simply their rapport and pleasure in each other (in life, they fell in love during the film and married), or that she is as cynical as he, but that the characters they created remain so vivid. At such times Bogart seems the best of all screen actors; his impatience of cant was never better expressed than in his response to an official asking his nationality: 'Eskimo,' he says.

The Mask of Dimitrios (1944), like *Background to Danger*, is based on a novel by Eric Ambler, but in this case Frank Gruber's screenplay retains its civilised tone and sinewy quality. The exposition is stunning: the body washed up on the shore of Turkey, supposedly that of Dimitrios, and the interest shown in it by the writer Leyden (Lorre), increasingly troubled by glimpses of the mysterious Mr Peters (Greenstreet). As Dimitrios, Zachary Scott looks right but does not sound it; and despite a ludicrous impression of Paris, a 'European' flavour is well maintained in Negulesco's controlled direction. It revives better than one of the Warners' few sober accounts of War – **Action in the North Atlantic** (1943) – which is about the Merchant Navy's role, with Raymond Massey as a commander and Bogart as his executive officer – but then, Lloyd Bacon's direction cannot conceal the clichés.

For Warners, Errol Flynn also went to war, but the films concerned were the subject of much derision: for years people remembered his gall at the end of **Desperate Journey** (1942), crying, 'Now for Australia and a crack at those Japs!' Raoul Walsh directed, as he did **Northern Pursuit** (1943) and **Objective Burma!** (1945), the former a conventional story of Nazi infiltration into Canada, with Flynn as the Mountie they hope will turn traitor. Since we know he won't, it makes dull viewing. *Objective Burma!*, on the other hand, is a very good film, and it is ironic that jokes about Flynn capturing Burma single-handed should have haunted him to the end of his life. The screenplay makes clear that he is leading a small American group, but the lack of any significant British participation so incensed the British that the film had to be withdrawn a few

days after its London premiere. It was the straw that broke the camel's back, for the newly-liberated European nations were being flooded by the backlog of movies bragging of American heroism. In fact *Objective Burma!* is for the most part a realistic portrait of fighting men, foreshadowing both *A Walk in the Sun* (q.v.) and *The Story of G.I. Joe* – and indeed the character of the war correspondent (Henry Hull), aware of age and fallibility, is based on Ernie Pyle. Two sequences are first-rate in their depiction of men at war; the troops in their planes on the way to the target, and the fear in the night of the survivors, anticipating an attack. But courage fails Walsh and his writers, Ranald MacDougall and Lester Cole, who, trying for the full horror of war, lack conviction: one need not have seen similar sequences in Japanese films to find ludicrous the one here in which the men find their colleagues dead and dying. Walsh, otherwise, does a superb job, confirming that most of his later work was cursory: he keeps the camera low, and drives most of the action towards it, achieving dynamism without pretension.

Flynn's limitations were such that there was little that Warners could do but cast him as the intrepid hero of such films. War films were usually new variations on old shoot-em-ups, and the studios, it seems, were much less interested in informing a public avid for information on the War than in keeping their coffers filled via the usual star vehicles. Thus Flynn is typically grim and purposeful, if an unlikely Norwegian patriot in **Edge of Darkness** (1943), which, as directed by Lewis Milestone and written by Robert Rossen (from a novel by William Woods), attempts to be a serious Resistance epic. While long, it has a hard edge, and looks more closely than most films at the reactions of Occupied and Occupiers. The Norwegians are found to be cautious, and subject to conscience, human error and frailty, while the German invaders (for once, three-dimensional) have that jocular coarseness and lack of feeling which characterised many of them. A wholly American cast does not help; and as the heroics become increasingly far-fetched it is clear that the suffering that was endured and the bravery achieved should not be reduced in this way. Eventually, with Nancy Coleman becoming a whore

591

Hollywood's War Effort

By now, Bette Davis has had a longer screen career than any other star actress – lasting for fifty years – and one reason is the series of superior melodramas she made for Warner Bros. in the early Forties, astonishing audiences with her range and attack. The films were also so popular that she was once called 'the fourth Warner brother'. RIGHT, with Mary Astor in *The Great Lie*, discussed in Chapter 17; FAR RIGHT, with Claude Rains in *Now, Voyager*; and BELOW, with Walter Abel and Rains in *Mr Skeffington*.

and Ann Sheridan getting raped, war becomes simply a nasty business.

Away from the War, Flynn was James J. Corbett in **Gentleman Jim** (1942), the bank clerk who became one of the famous figures of the fight game. Ward Bond is John L. Sullivan, his rival, Jack Carson his sidekick, and Alexis Smith the haughty lady to whom he aspires (in life, Corbett had three wives); in general the care and thought put into this piece place it way ahead of most films about sportsmen. Walsh directed.

Walsh's companion in favour, Howard Hawks, directed **Air Force** (1943), a project instigated by the Army Air Corps, and the lack of histrionics does again suggest seriousness: it is clear that the aim was to show what it was like to be part of a bomber crew – in the Pacific, at that particular time. But on the screenplay Dudley Nichols was neither inspired nor informed: there is no evidence that he had ever heard any G.I.s talking, and his hero is the usual chip-on-the-shoulder underdog (John Garfield), a gunner resentful because he flunked pilot training – and who of course single-handedly brings down the crate with its undercarriage gone. Hawks is as good an action director as he ever was, but the film is nevertheless a well-intentioned slog until the last reel, when it veers dangerously out of control.

Warners had the temerity to offer not one but two of the patriotic all-star musicals: **Thank Your Lucky Stars** (1943) and **Hollywood Canteen** (1944) are respectively the best and worst of them. David Butler directed the first, chiefly remembered for Bette Davis's sung lament, 'They're Either Too Young or Too Old', but there are other good moments: Ann Sheridan instructing a sorority house that 'Love Isn't Born, It's Made'; and Hattie McDaniel exhorting 'Ice-Cold Katie' to marry that soldier. The score by Frank Loesser and Arthur Schwartz helps; a plot about young hopefuls trying to get into show business does not. One of these is Joan Leslie, and one of the idiocies of *Hollywood Canteen* is that a G.I. (Brian Hutton) chooses her when offered as a prize an evening with any star in Hollywood. Another is that this film city equivalent of the Stage Door Canteen is devoid of any stars but Warners': maybe the other studios were jealous, or maybe

they had read the script – by Delmer Daves, who also directs. The shamelessness of one scene became famous: a G.I. (Dane Clark) dances with a girl who looks like Joan Crawford, and when she confesses that she *is* Joan Crawford, he falls down in a faint; later, he finds that because of that dance he no longer needs a stick, and says, 'All those big shots being friendly . . . That's democracy, all them big guys talking to little guys like me.' Warners produced this memento because Bette Davis had been a prime mover in founding the Canteen; she plays herself without embarrassment, a considerable feat in this film.

This actress has one of her rare 'normal' roles, that of a loyal wife in **Watch on the Rhine** (1943), based on Lillian Hellman's play. Ostensibly about the nature of Fascism, that word and 'Germany' are bandied about, with one fleeting reference to thugs smashing up a local fête as explanation of how Nazism came about. A famous German anti-Nazi (Paul Lukas) and a party sympathiser (George Coulouris) are fellow guests in an 'ordinary' American home, but since there is neither discussion nor confrontation it seems strange, to say the least, that the original play was given the New York Drama Critics Award. The screenplay is by the author and Dashiell Hammett (Hellman's lover), and the director, Herman Shumlin, had done the New York production, as is evident from the film's staginess. Lukas, also in the stage version, won both an Oscar and the New York film critics' award for his performance, and if the thing has any merit it is in his eventually gritty portrait of a man who puts duty before personal safety.

Watch on the Rhine is the only Davis film of this period not to revive well – ironically, since it was well received, at least in the U.S., while the others were usually dismissed as 'women's pictures'. It so happened that I saw **Now, Voyager** (1942) at a press show – in 1972 – and the audience not only broke into applause at the end but cheered at that moment when Davis revolts against her selfish mother (Gladys Cooper). Davis is splendid as 'poor Aunt Charlotte', tense and bruised, a frump in sensible shoes who smokes in the secrecy of her room. Taken in hand by Claude Rains, 'the foremost psychiatrist in the country', after listening to the Whitman lines which give the film its title, she

'The Fourth Warner Brother'

becomes glamorous and *soigné* – but Davis from the start sensibly had signalled the qualities of strength and gaiety now established in the character. Paul Henreid is the man she meets on her recuperative cruise, and they fall in love over Old-Fashioneds, to Max Steiner's theme song, later reprised each time they look at, or think of, each other. Irving Rapper directed this worm-that-turned tale, which is perhaps more enjoyable than the better-constructed **In This Our Life** (1942), credited to John Huston, but since he and Davis disagreed on the handling Raoul Walsh directed most of her scenes. Howard Koch wrote the screenplay from Ellen Glasgow's strong novel about a small Virginia town and the family that dominated it. The film is not, as the book was, an indictment of the conditions that arise when the rich are careless of their privileges but, in the words of *The Sunday Times* of London, 'that one about the self-centred girl who wrecks lives and, ultimately, cars.' She is Stanley (Davis), and the film's success is in always making us doubt whether or when the others will see her for the bitch she is. Olivia de Havilland, playing in flippant style, is just the sort of woman to attract the same men as she; and Dennis Morgan and George Brent are foolish enough to go from one to the other.

Miss Davis's ability to give life to these melodramas was not lost upon the public, which had conferred on her a popularity unprecedented in Hollywood for a serious actress. She gave value for money while never misjudging her effects, and it is a pleasure to see her take **Old Acquaintance** (1943) from Miriam Hopkins, an actress who never does a half-gesture when she can do a whole one. The formula is that of the haves-and-have-nots, and, as in *The Old Maid*, she has it not while Hopkins is the successful one who has it and loses it. They are both novelists, Davis the respected one in modest tweeds and Hopkins the flashy bestselling lady. As adapted from the play by John Van Druten, the piece retains its theatricality – but then audiences looked forward to the inevitable 'confrontation' scene of the Davis movies. In **Mr Skeffington** (1944), also very well directed by Vincent Sherman, she is on the receiving end, as a spoilt society beauty who uses those about her.

The film retains the ending of the original novel, by 'Elizabeth', in which the now-blind Mr Skeffington – Claude Rains at his best – continues to think of Fanny as a young woman, and the fact of his blindness was resented by some critics. But it is not for nothing that he is called Job, with patience to match his biblical namesake. Both films are not entirely dishonest as to how certain American ladies conduct their careers and emotional lives, and indeed *Mr Skeffington* is often very funny on the subject of women who place physical appearance above all else, or who take to psychoanalysis because they have nothing else to do. Davis never loses sight of Fanny deep down, who is just like Fanny on top – coquettish and vain, a woman brought up without regard for the realities of life which, when pointed out to her, could not interest her less. It is a superb interpretation of that phenomenon, the famous and fading beauty.

Another well thought of stage play was the source of **The Corn Is Green** (1945), one of the lesser Davis vehicles – and not just because she hardly has a field day as the English teacher who founds, against all odds, a school in a Welsh mining village at the turn of the century. The screenplay relegates to the background the social forces of Emlyn Williams's original, which is further reduced by becoming a tale of inspiration and idealism, with the star pupil (John Dall) going, not like Cinderella to the ball, but to Oxford. Irving Rapper directed, and was presumably not responsible for the reproduction of the village, which marks a nadir in Hollywood's attempts to reconstruct other places and other times. Davis is excellently supported by Rhys Williams and Mildred Dunnock as her colleagues; in the difficult role of the budding Shakespeare Mr Dall has a variable accent; as the Cockney slut who almost brings him down, Joan Lorring almost brings the film down as well.

It is possible that the enterprise might have fared better had Hal Wallis still been at the studio. Casey Robinson – credited for the screenplay with Frank Cavett – is on record as saying that Wallis was responsible for the high quality of the Warners pictures at this time. Wallis had been at the studio since the amalgamation with First National, as producer and then executive producer, and having to make thirty pictures a year, as Robinson put it, he 'needed any help he could get – the type of writers who could prove their worth on the screen . . . And so out of this peculiar circumstance of Jack Warner's pecuniary stinginess' – he refused to pay for rewrites and reshooting – 'and Hal Wallis's need and recognition of talent, there grew up the greatest staff of writers that ever existed in the history of the motion pictures.' Warners had been the most misogynist of studios but, with the rise of Bette Davis, vehicles for the lady stars were needed, and amidst the often tear-jerking formulas can be found qualities common to virtually all the films in which Wallis had a personal hand – sourness, hardness and cynicism.

Wallis meanwhile was determined to leave Warner Bros. He had stepped down from head of production to make a handful of films annually with virtual independence, but found Jack L. Warner both uncooperative and interfering. The last straw was when Warner bounded down the aisle at the Academy Awards ceremony to collect the Oscar for *Casablanca*, since it was one of Wallis's films. Wallis could have gone to any Hollywood studio, and J. Arthur Rank asked him to name his own terms to take over his British operations; but Wallis chose to go to Paramount with complete autonomy over his productions.

A monument to him, to Robinson, and to Sam Wood who directed, is **King's Row** (1942), adapted from a virtually intractable novel by Henry Bellamann – a small town exposé, again set in the early years of this century: but out of this 'trash', as Robinson called it, he found his theme: 'the struggle of young people to grow into manhood and womanhood'. The film has a quality unlike any other small town film, with its cross-currents, the assumption by some of superiority, and the whispers on all manner of things from insanity to self-righteous sadism. Claude Rains is a tortured doctor, and Charles Coburn a brisk one, with little outward sign of evil; Ann Sheridan is the girl from the other side of the tracks, as warm and understanding as any legless man could want for support; and Betty Field is a wounded bird of a girl, desperate for company. As the joint heroes, Ronald Reagan and Robert Cummings are unexpectedly good; but the virtuosity and James Wong Howe's camera-

work cannot disguise the fact that King's Row is a painted town.

The Hard Way (1942) also had excellent construction, a strong narrative drive, and was well thought of then, when it won for Ida Lupino the New York critics' award for the year's Best Actress. Personally, I feel that any film which begins with her committing suicide is off to a good start, but the rest is flashback as she ruthlessly pushes her sister (Joan Leslie) to stardom – 'the John Dillinger of the one-night stands', as Dennis Morgan puts it. Jerry Wald wrote the story, after talking to a certain star's ex-husband following his suicide attempt, and the director, Sherman, admitted that it was based on a famous star and her mother. The screenplay by Irwin Shaw and Daniel Fuchs

At one time the small town movie constituted a genre in its own right, but this sunny picture from *King's Row* is not entirely typical, since the film took a somewhat misanthropic view of its eponymous setting. The stars were Ann Sheridan and Ronald Reagan: he turned to politics as his film career faltered, eventually becoming President of the United States.

drops a hint or two that the lady concerned was Ginger Rogers.

On the lighter side – which the company seldom was – the most cherishable of their comedies is **Larceny Inc.** (1942), with Edward G. Robinson, 'flannel-brain' Broderick Crawford and Ed Brophy as three ex-cons who want to go straight, but need cash and therefore buy a shop next door to a bank. Lloyd Bacon directed, sharply, which is more than can be said of William Keighley's work on **George Washington Slept Here** (1942): despite Ann Sheridan and Jack Benny this is a dull version of the Kaufman-Hart play about a couple buying a dilapidated country home – the first of several movies on this theme. **The Male Animal** (1942) raises a serious issue, when a professor (Henry Fonda) wants to read to his pupils a letter written by Vanzetti but is opposed by another (Eugene Pallette), who sees a red under every bed; but it is more concerned with the triangle between him, his wife (Olivia de Havilland) and a superannuated ball-player (Jack Carson). Elliott Nugent directed, from the listless play that he wrote with James Thurber.

The studio's two most important morale-boosters were both entrusted to Michael Curtiz after his success with *Yankee Doodle Dandy*. **This Is The Army** (1943) was based on the stage revue devised and produced by Irving Berlin, with songs by him. Meant to promote good relations for the army and featuring entertainers currently in battledress, its metamorphosis into film now included a storyline linking it to a Berlin show of the First World War, and since its every sequence is drowned in patriotism it is perhaps appropriate that the father and son leading roles are played by George Murphy and Ronald Reagan, both of whom later took up political careers. The film beams good will, and so, in a different way, does the other film, **Mission to Moscow** (1943), one of the oddest Hollywood contributions to the War. It is an account of Joseph E. Davies's relations with the Soviet Union from his appointment as Ambassador in 1936 to his tub-thumping on its behalf after Hitler attacked. The film was instigated by the Office of War Information, which chose Warners to produce it on the strength of *Confessions of a Nazi Spy*. Recalling the public response to

that, Warners were not enthusiastic and the initial praise turned sour when the handling of the subject matter was attacked. The reservations which Davies had expressed in this autobiographical book were ignored in Howard Koch's screenplay, and Davies himself was criticised for appearing in the film to vouch for its integrity. The distortions include: blaming France and Britain for appeasement, and suggesting that the U.S.S.R. distrusted Fascism, being driven into its arms – the Soviet-German pact – by the conduct of those two countries; Davies visiting a prescient Churchill in 1939, whereas in his book he mentions merely meeting him two years earlier; myriad references to Japanese aggression – whereas a Russian-Japanese non-aggression pact was still in force when this film came out; and a complete falsification of the Moscow trials. The trials were featured in the film because Davies had referred to them in his book, being now intended as implied criticism of the régime to counterbalance the admiration shown for the May Day parades, etc. But where the film Davies (Walter Huston) speaks of 'the integrity and honesty of the Soviet leaders' the real Davies was already privately aware of Stalin's purges. The combination of documentary footage and reasonably re-enacted accounts of Davies's work in Russia, plus Huston's performance, make the film persuasive; and Curtiz and the editing department move the film to a climax where none really exists. Since its purpose was to make Americans understand the Soviets and love Uncle Joe, it may be said to have succeeded.

Adolph Zukor continued to lead Paramount, though the titular chief was a former Georgia showman, Y. Frank Freeman, who according to John Houseman (in his autobiography) was 'respected in the industry, where he had a reputation for "fairness" and financial know-how. In my experience I found him ignorant, bigoted, reactionary and malignant' – notably in trying to ensure that no negroes appeared in Paramount pictures. The Chief of Production remained B. G. (Buddy) de Sylva, who (as we have seen) had succeeded William Le Baron. The latter moved on to 20th Century-Fox to produce mainly musicals and light comedies – which were precisely the genres of films preferred by de Sylva, whose team included many experienced talents in those fields. With some reason Paramount projected the friendliest image of the studios, and it may be seen in **Star Spangled Rhythm** (1942), the first of all the films about Hollywood doing its bit for the troops. A sailor (Eddie Bracken) has both a father (Victor Moore) and a girlfriend (Betty Hutton) working at Paramount, and he accordingly persuades the entire contract list to put on a show for the boys. George Marshall directed, and among the less-dated turns are 'Hit the Road to Dreamland', sung by Mary Martin and Dick Powell, and an old chestnut of a sketch, 'If Men Played Cards as Women Do', acted by Ray Milland, Franchot Tone, Lynne Overman and Fred MacMurray. Bing Crosby sings a long patriotic number, 'Old Glory', before a painted Mount Rushmore, while several ethnic groups (despite Mr Freeman) explain why they are proud to be American.

The 'Road' pictures which Crosby made with Bob Hope have turned out – surprisingly, I think – to be ageless. **Road to Singapore** (1940) had been originally planned as a vehicle for Dorothy Lamour, with Fred MacMurray as a wealthy boy fond of the roving life and George Burns as his sidekick. MacMurray decided that he wanted no part of this jungle lore, and the script was seized upon by Hope and Crosby, whose verbal sparring on the golf-course had persuaded them that they should make a film together. Hope's role was built up; as a team they were not yet free-wheeling, but under the same director, Victor Schertzinger, they took off in **Road to Zanzibar** (1941). It was this which established the pattern for the series: they are carnival performers who, forced to flee, find themselves in an exotic spot where they encounter Miss Lamour, for whom – and perhaps some buried treasure or merely a quick buck – they are prepared to double-cross each other and anyone else in sight. In *The New Republic*, Otis Ferguson decided that this was 'the funniest thing I have seen on the screen in years', and in the course of a long analysis on screen humour observed that it 'still has the free and happy air of the spontaneous, the best vein, the laughter shared and mounting'. With **Road to Morocco** (1942), directed by David Butler, they

added sight-gags, puns in abundance, and jokes about Hollywood and themselves for which posterity may need a glossary. The films were easily the most popular screen comedies since Chaplin's peak: the Forties would not have been the same without them. Hope and Crosby take us into their idiot make-believe world, conning and cheating and chasing the girl, and they do it with teamwork that is a high spot in film history; no other film comics ever approached their mutual understanding, and of other screen teams only Hepburn and Tracy matched their timing. It is a nice act to start with, beyond the pleasant personalities founded on greed and lust: the beauty is in the ad-libs and throwaways. The films themselves are not smart or anarchic, and they offer no vision of the world; at the worst, they are amiable, and at the best uproariously funny. The daffiest is *Road to Morocco*, the most inventive narrative the Alaskan adventure, **Road to Utopia** (1945), directed by Hal Walker, and the best gags are in **Road to Rio** (1947), directed by Norman Z. McLeod. The writers are various, and the fair-to-excellent songs by Burke and Van Heusen.

Bing Crosby and Bob Hope in *Road to Utopia*. Much earlier, before the 'Road' films became a series, the *Motion Picture Herald* called Crosby and Hope 'the most successful pairing of comedy talents brought forth upon the screen since Hollywood memory runneth not to the contrary.'

Ingrid Bergman and Bing Crosby in *The Bells of St Mary's* directed by Leo McCarey and a sequel to *Going My Way*, also with Crosby. It takes a high place among the 'spiritual' films turned out at this time, which, if one refers to the earlier film, is a weak compliment; however, the disparity in quality was not remarked upon at the time.

Irving Berlin wrote the score for **Holiday Inn** (1942), which increased Crosby's already huge popularity. Berlin had been trying to build a revue around the American holidays, and when the project did not materialise he sold it to producer-director Mark Sandrich as a vehicle for Crosby, with the possibility of Fred Astaire as co-star. The War had just started, and Paramount, uncertain of its effect upon the box office – in fact, audience numbers increased enormously – only agreed to the salaries involved by economising on the leading ladies, the little-known Marjorie Reynolds and Virginia Dale. If the point of a musical is to be a showcase for the talents of its contributors, this is a great one, as the screen's best dancer and its most popular singer share Berlin's lilting songs, including 'White Christmas', introduced herein. Ease is both the keynote and the manner in which the stars handle an inconsequential plot about amorous rivalry and a country club. It matters not that there are musicals with more zest.

Leo McCarey conceived a film for Crosby, but it was not till he arrived on the Paramount lot that Crosby learnt that he was to play a priest in **Going My Way** (1944), a film which today seems merely an extended P.R. job for the Roman

Catholic Church. Father O'Malley is more Crosby than Crosby, a temple of all human virtues who wears casual clothes, sings popular songs, and enjoys a tot of whisky and a round of golf; Barry Fitzgerald is the irascible Irish elder priest who is converted to his ways – and my own attitude towards both actors is for once reversed, since the latter's grumpiness is welcome in a film whose 'holier than thou' stance is virtually intolerable. Both actors won Oscars, and the New York critics agreed with the Academicians over Fitzgerald, over Best Picture and Best Director; McCarey also won an Oscar for Best Story, and Frank Butler and Frank Cavett for Best Screenplay. Public response made it the most successful film yet made, after *Gone with the Wind*, till overtaken by its sequel, **The Bells of St Mary's** (1945) – which for contractual reasons was made at R.K.O. It is mercifully less sentimental, and both more confident and less insistent in its treatment of religion. The screenplay by Dudley Nichols is more subtle, and Crosby, who in the earlier film rarely seemed human, is very winning here. This time his priest is pitted against a hidebound nun (priests were not new in movies, but nuns were, except in small roles) and to that role Ingrid Bergman brings a discretion which equals Crosby's. At ease in both films, he underplays the better material of this one, and the farewell scene between him and Bergman is touching, despite the arc-lights trained on her nose. The popularity of both players had much to do with the film's success, but the reviews were universally good: Howard Barnes in *The New York Herald Tribune* called it 'inspiring, in the best sense of the word'.

After Crosby and Hope, Paramount's most popular star was Alan Ladd, an inexpressive, slight-of-stature tough guy. Of his many films, less than half a dozen are memorable, but those that are include the first two in which he starred, though made by directors whose other work is largely undistinguished. Frank Tuttle handled **This Gun for Hire** (1942) and Stuart Heisler was responsible for **The Glass Key** (1942), but we may suppose the films' qualities emanate from their original novels – respectively by Graham Greene and Dashiell Hammett (the former with a screenplay by Albert Maltz and W. R. Burnett, and the latter with one by Jonathan Latimer). In the case of the Greene, the book is pictured under the credits, usually an indication of respect: the dialogue and plot are virtually intact. It concerns a hired gun (Ladd) searching for the man who betrayed him; but whereas Greene's Raven had a hare-lip and was hired by a doddery old Jewish millionaire who wants an assassination to start a war in order to grow rich on armaments, in the film he has an injured wrist and is employed by a manufacturer who aims to sell gas to the Japs. What was original in Greene has by a trembling of a leaf become movie-conventional; what was moving – Raven's probing towards a relationship with the girl (Veronica Lake), his comments on his past – often seem glib. Most to be regretted is the substitution of Los Angeles for Greene's shabby, cold Midlands town with its grimy grand hotels, its ABC cafés, the Industrial Revolution railway yards and its one run-down music hall. Notably good are the portraits of the old master-mind (Tully Marshall), and the fat and cowardly connoisseur of chorus girls and candy (Laird Cregar) – both characters to reappear revamped in the American *film noir*. If *The Glass Key* lacks the gallery of characters that made Huston's *Maltese Falcon* so satisfying, here is William Bendix, whose ape-like features, stupidity and Brooklyn accent nicely underscore his deadly endearments, 'You mean I don't get to smack baby?' and 'Little rubber ball does all right, doesn't he?' Veronica Lake again plays Ladd's female foil, and it is difficult to believe that her screen persona was not dreamed up by these writers, for her golden mane and little girl insolence suited this genre as no other.

Another undistinguished director, Lewis Allen, made **The Uninvited** (1944), which, to start with, looks more like Cornwall than do most films loc-ationed at Carmel. The art directors, Han Dreier and Ernst Fegte, managed an exceptionally good haunted house – a house in which the new tenant (Ray Mil-land) is woken by a sobbing woman, the cat refuses to go upstairs, there is sudden cold, a scent of mimosas in the air, and in the attic a bouquet of roses shrivels. Like all such establishments, it has a malevolent influence on a beautiful girl (Gail Russell), but the film still comes across as one of the best of its type. **The Unseen** (1945) is one of the worst, with an unconvincing Lon-don, two children borrowed from 'The Turn of the Screw', and a father (Joel McCrea) whose daft behaviour menaces the children's young governess. The first film has a good screenplay, by Dodie Smith and Frank Pártes, from a novel by Dorothy McCardle, the second an absurd one by Raymond Chandler and Hagar Wilde, from a novel by Ethel Lina White; and Allen has reacted accordingly, the direction of the one being as assured as the other is sloppy. Miss Russell is in both films, and the producers were Charles Brackett for the first and John Houseman for *The Unseen*, whose first film this was in that capacity.

The direction of **For Whom the Bell Tolls** (1943) was entrusted to a freelance, Sam Wood, though originally announced for deMille. It is possible that the author, Hemingway, vetoed deMille, since we know that he recommended the stars, Gary Cooper and Ingrid Bergman – but his advice was not taken in the case of the latter till executives saw the rushes of Vera Zorina in the role. The already huge bud-get was extended to a publicity campaign of like proportions, and the film lasts almost three hours – during which it is mute on the causes of the Spanish Civil War. Indeed, were it not for the cast (com-posed of every nationality except Spanish) and the weaponry at the end, one might take it for an episode in the history of the Hatfields and McCoys. A further quota-tion from the Donne sermon follows the credits, 'Any man's death diminishes me', which provides a moving statement on the existence of the International Brigade, of which Cooper is its chief representative, while Bergman represents the Spanish peasantry. The front office had emascu-lated Dudley Nichols's screenplay, and although the Hays Office had sanctioned Cooper's farewell line to her – 'I am you and you are me. You're all there'll be of me' – audiences had to grasp at its mean-ing. However, sex on the screen did ad-vance when she agreed with a cheery grin that she was shameless. Bergman is odd casting, tall and blonde,* for a character

*Her cropped hair was a deliberate policy on Paramount's part to counteract the popularity of Veronica Lake's long tresses. In emulation of Miss Lake many women on war work were getting their hair caught in the machines, and Paramount was held responsible.

naively conceived in the first place, and we may find her Maria hardly more real than the surprisingly poor process work; but as Wood subjects her to a battery of smiling close-ups, as if unable to accustom himself to an actress so natural, we may at least, all these years later, understand how he felt.

DeMille's two wartime spectacles are dreadful even by his later standards. **Reap the Wild Wind** (1942) has a tale of amorous rivalry against a background of sailing ships, a battle with a giant squid, and some of those pointless discussion/courtroom scenes which then characterised the more ambitious historical films. It also has a high-spirited heroine who scandalises society; Paulette Goddard's performance only reminds us how much better Vivien Leigh and Bette Davis were in like circumstance. The awfulness of **The Story of Dr Wassell** (1944) is more serious, since it was based on the true story of the doctor who insisted on staying on Java to care for the stretcher cases after the Japanese had landed. Gary Cooper copes with the situation in a way that reduces our memories of Mr Deeds, but the film turns out to be less interested in that than in his youth, settling for a long and cliché-ridden flashback about trying to find the cause of some dread tropical disease in China. The art direction is ghastly; and deMille's vulgarity was never better demonstrated than by the cut from a hospital being bombed to cute Chinese children singing on a small humped bridge.

Paramount had in fact the distinction of being the first studio to make a film about American participation in the War, and **Wake Island** (1942) came out while other studios were still offering hokum like *Across the Pacific*. It tells, 'as accurately and factually as possible', of the first American feat of valour, when a small group of Marines held out against repeated enemy assaults on a former Pan American fuelling base. That they eventually surrendered was known to every American, and the difficulty of ending films on the War by the depressing truth was solved by a commentator assuring audiences that the Marines would return to exact a 'terrible' vengeance. Bosley Crowther saw it on a Marine base, where it was received 'with thunderous applause' – and reported that it would 'bring a surge of pride to every patriot's breast'. It is hard to watch today,

especially for those familiar with the clichés of the First World War movies purloined by W. R. Burnett and Frank Butler for their screenplay: the Quirt and Flagg relationship of the buddies (Robert Preston, William Bendix), the dedicated commander (Brian Donlevy), and the jabbering enemy – who are glimpsed being elated or disconcerted as the case may be. The polished direction is by another variable talent, John Farrow,★ who managed beautifully with an even less promising war story, **You Came Along** (1945). Ivy Hotchkiss (Lizabeth Scott) is selected to chaperone three Air Force heroes on a bond-selling tour, and she falls for the one (Robert Cummings) who has leukaemia: 'Promise me one thing, never grieve for me,' he says as he proposes, and they thank God for every day they have together. When his time comes, he gets his buddies to look in on her: 'Here's to the four of us' they say, a lachrymose *menage à trois*, as the camera pans to a sky of silver linings. There is a glutinous theme song and an unattractive cast apart from Miss Scott, showing in her first film the warm and genuine spirit she had before they turned her into a cut-price Lauren Bacall. There are also sequences of charm and humour, as in the other soap operas of Hal Wallis, whose second 'independent' production for Paramount this was.

Mitchell Leisen also made a film about flyers, **I Wanted Wings** (1941), taking over from J. Theodore Reed, and thus saving its producer from certain disaster. It is watchable, which is an achievement in view of the fact that it has the standard plot of all service movies, i.e. the ups and downs of some rookies: the know-it-all rich boy (Ray Milland), the dumbbell (Wayne Morris) and the grease monkey (William Holden). Made before the U.S. entered the War, it has an extraneous prologue assuring Los Angeles that in the event of a blackout the Air Force is standing by. The War in Europe provides the springboard for **Hold Back the Dawn** (1941), one of the last great Hollywood romances, written by Wilder and Brackett for Leisen, their third film for him. They gleefully pursue a sure-fire plot, from a semi-autobiographical story by Ketti

★'John [Farrow] combined the distinction of being a Papal Count with a reputation for sadism practised professionally and individually on the persons of male and female performers' (John Houseman in 'Front and Center').

Frings, starting pleasingly in a Hollywood studio with Charles Boyer as a down-and-out putting a touch on Leisen himself. He, Boyer, turns out to be a former gigolo domiciled in Mexico who nabs the first virginal schoolteacher (Olivia de Havilland) to cross his path, because he needs an American visa – and how blithely she ignores the little indications of the truth of the matter! As the besotted and then disillusioned woman Miss de Havilland was never more winning; Boyer in the second half has little to do but look stricken at his lack of scruples – partly because Wilder and Brackett wrote him out when he refused to play a scene with a cockroach.

After some bland comedies, Leisen succumbed to Paramount's plea that he helm **Lady in the Dark** (1944), part-persuaded by the fact that he had not worked in Technicolor before. He helped design the costumes and, though the Hacketts are credited, wrote the screenplay – from Moss Hart's 'play with music' which had startled New York in 1941. That had concerned a fashion editor undergoing psychoanalysis, but the subject had deterred the Hollywood studios, together with the difficulty of replacing Gertrude Lawrence in the role and staging her dream sequences. Korda had bought the rights, and when Ginger Rogers insisted on doing this film under the terms of her contract, he parted with them for the then-record sum of $285,000.★ A difficult shooting schedule included much temperament on the part of the star – she refused to do the requisite bumps and grinds for the song 'Jenny', because they did not fit her image – and also the jettisoning of much of the Kurt Weill–Ira Gershwin score, including the indispensable 'My Ship', because it was despised by B. G. de Sylva. As offered here, the story is neither comedy nor drama, nor anything between: the problem of the woman's romantic choice is of no interest, and her dreams are merely tastefully vulgar. But then, as C. A. Lejeune observed, the film was 'variously described as the Song of Songs of Every Woman; the Last Word in Beauty, Spectacle, Colour, Music, Romance; the Girl of the Moment with the Loves of the Year in the Picture

★Korda made a huge profit, taking advantage of Miss Rogers's intransigence; but in general Broadway successes had more value than best-selling novels. Paramount paid $150,000, for *For Whom the Bell Tolls* the previous year and that was then a record sum for a novel.

of a Lifetime; the Startling Story of a Woman's Secret Love; the Minx in Mink with a Yen for Men; and – rather breathlessly – the Most Beautiful Thing in the World of Motion Pictures from Paramount. Who says so? Guess who.'

Frenchman's Creek (1944) was also expensive, at $4 million the most costly American film made to that time (though concurrently at M-G-M reshooting on *Ziegfeld Follies*, q.v., would push it to that sum). This one suffered a number of mishaps (such as fog during location shooting), but Leisen was also prone to extravagance. He thought Daphne du Maurier's novel 'as dull as dish-water' and the picture 'lousy', and he is not wrong; but in lushness and silliness it reminds us of the days when movie-going was fun. The middle reaches – when the aristocratic concubine dresses up as a cabin boy – are brackish, and that is partly because as her pirate lover Arturo de Cordova lacks any romantic aura; but Joan Fontaine is playful and artificial, just what the enterprise needs. Memorable is another Cornish mansion, created by Dreier and Fegté, for which they won an Oscar.

Dreier's recreation, with Walter Tyler, of eighteenth-century London in **Kitty** (1945) is also outstanding. Leisen was fascinated by the period, and this was one project for which he cared: a tale about a Cockney guttersnipe (Paulette Goddard) who ends up a duchess – from a novel by Rosamund Marshall which combined 'Forever Amber' with 'Pygmalion' – in which role, foppish and elegant, Ray Milland is excellent. Those situations not already exhausted are diverting: 'How will I find her?' asks Kitty, arriving to take tea with Lady Susan (Constance Collier). 'Drunk' is the laconic reply of the butler (Eric Blore), masterful beneath his powdered wig. Cecil Kellaway is superb as Gainsborough, and Reginald Owen gives a magnificent display of decrepit lechery. Miss Collier was seldom better than as the tippling beldame, her bearing masking a complete lack of scruples. The script tentatively suggests that Kitty is the true lady, since she lacks the deceits of society, and her progress is closer to American democratic ideals than the skeletons in the cupboards of the British aristocracy.

The film temporarily halted the decline in Leisen's work which had begun after

Hold Back the Dawn, and with the death of Lubitsch in 1946 there were few other practitioners of the comedy in which they had been supreme. Billy Wilder (b.1906) had written for them both, and like Preston Sturges he turned director as a result of Leisen's cavalier treatment of his scripts.

Wilder adored the films of Lubitsch, but his own films were more surely shaped by his familiarity with what Sturges had achieved at Paramount – as well as by his experiences as a child and a young man. Born in Vienna to a family of hoteliers he learnt quickly the facts of hotel life; in Berlin during Inflation he was a dance partner, his cynicism increasing as he sought work as a journalist or in films. As we have seen, he emigrated to Paris when the Nazis came to power, and a fellow expatriate, Joe May, helped him to get a writing job in Hollywood. His career really began when he was teamed with Charles Brackett on *Bluebeard's Eighth Wife* in 1938, and their great success was another reason that he turned director with **The Major and the Minor** (1942), encouraged against studio opposition by the lady for whom it was written, Ginger Rogers. She plays a country girl who, after twenty-seven jobs in New York, decides to pack it in; but the only way she can afford the fare home is to disguise herself as a small girl. The screenplay is much less witty than the one Wilder and Brackett had written for *Midnight*, and superficially the film is conventional. However the first half contains a number of incidents influenced by Sturges: the lecherous client (Robert Benchley) chasing Rogers round the room; the guy who pricks her balloon; the stumblebum who pinches her change; while the second half contains a number of typical Wilder preoccupations, such as the continuation of the masquerade (by Rogers). Two subjects which most interested him, however, had to be treated with deference to the Code: the 'Lolita' situation, whereby the Major (Ray Milland) is attracted to the 'child', and the sexuality of the adolescent cadets whom he teaches.

The film was based on a *Saturday Evening Post* story and an unrelated, unproduced play. Wilder's sources would often remain unusual – *Sunset Boulevard* (q.v.) grew from a proposal that *The Royal Family of Broadway*, to which Paramount owned the rights, might be adapted to suit a Hedda Hopper-type gossip columnist – and **Five Graves to Cairo** (1943) is a remake of *Hotel Imperial*, as suggested by Lajos Biro, who wrote the play on which that film was based. It takes only the bones of the original – the inn, the maid, the fugitive and the occupying army – which is perhaps why, at the time, no one noticed the resemblance, though there had been a remake in 1940. The fugitive (Franchot Tone) is now English, the army is headed by Rommel (Erich Von Stroheim) and the inn is in the desert. Other ingredients include an impersonation, a body in the cellar, a secret map, a manhunt – and Wilder handles them as though he had been directing thrillers for a lifetime. The wittiest lines go to Von Stroheim, but the Englishman is, as ever, gentlemanly and resourceful; the German lieutenant (Peter Van Eyk) humourless and efficient; and the French girl (Anne Baxter) shrewd and bitter, is prepared to bargain her body for her brother's life. The Egyptian (Akim Tamiroff) is confused and sycophantic, and the Italian general (Fortunio Bonanova) an opera addict and a hopeful lecher; the latter is the butt of several jokes in a thoroughly enjoyable tale.

Double Indemnity (1944) was written by Wilder and Raymond Chandler, who later wrote, 'Working with Wilder . . . was an agonising experience and has probably shortened my life, but I learned from it about as much about screenwriting as I am capable of learning, which is not very much.' Their source was a novel by James M. Cain, a devilish thing about a proposal for accident insurance which snowballs into the perfect murder. Its efficacy depends on its twists, but the best sequence is still the tone-setting first meeting between the insurance agent (Fred MacMurray) and his client's bored young wife (Barbara Stanwyck), with his professed admiration for her ankle-bracelet and her riposte to his 'pass', 'There's a speed limit in this State' – her cheap perfume and the smell of that hot, dusty room permeate the rest of the film. The star players here are murderers with no regrets – Wilder had difficulty in finding willing players and commented that he knew he had a good film when George Raft turned the role down. Mac-Murray has the facile charm, the shifty eyes, the hail-fellow-well-met attitude which does not disguise an iron will as

Barbara Stanwyck, Fred MacMurray and Edward G. Robinson in Billy Wilder's *Double Indemnity*, the latter as the cant-hating insurance man investigating the death of the lady's husband. Robinson later observed, 'It might have been a classic if Wilder had had just a little more heart,' but to most of us it is a classic as it is.

strong as the lady's – to be intermittently observed in the smiling eyes beneath the cheap blonde page-boy of a transformed Stanwyck.

At Universal the career of Deanna Durbin survived the debacle of **The Amazing Mrs Holliday** (1943). Studio executives placed her future in the hands of Felix Jackson, but it hardly endured beyond her marriage to him, since only the first films he produced satisfied the public devoted to the now grown-up Deanna. This venture was popular – the tale of a girl who, to find a home for Chinese evacuees, claims to be the widow of an aged naval commander who is not, as she thought, dead. However, as credited to the writing team of Frank Ryan and John Jacoby, and directed by Bruce Manning, the result is a synthetic and somewhat tasteless mixture of comedy and wartime sentiment. The same combination does work pleasantly in **Hers to Hold** (1943), directed by Ryan, which resurrects only the youngest of the *Three Smart Girls* so that, as headstrong as ever, she can pursue a handsome flyer (Joseph Cotten). At one point she sings 'Say a Prayer for the Boys Over There' to her fellow workers in a munitions factory, but

for all that these are pictures less grovellingly patriotic than most of the period.

There is nothing of the War in **His Butler's Sister** (1943), one of the last Hollywood fairy tales, agreeably directed by Frank Borzage. Pat O'Brien is the butler and the film's best invention has his Park Avenue peers (Akim Tamiroff, Alan Mowbray, Frank Jenks, Sig Arno and Hans Conried) all vying for the hand of the new maid, Miss Durbin. Only her employer (Franchot Tone) takes till the last reel to realise that she is Broadway's best bet in years – but he had missed hearing her topical medley of Russian songs. One reason to like the film is that Walter Catlett has a large role, as a lecherous producer.

'Deanna Goes Dramatic' was Universal's publicity line on **Christmas Holiday** (1944), which is Maugham's novel diluted. He wrote of a confident, bourgeois young Englishman whose values are shattered by a visit to Paris and a meeting with a White Russian prostitute, married to a convicted murderer. 'I've learnt,' he says – as transcribed in the screenplay by Herman J. Mankiewicz – 'a hundred years of living in the past twenty-four hours.' On screen he has become a nice young lieutenant (Dean Harmes) in the U.S. Army, the setting is

New Orleans, the brothel has become a roadhouse and the lady its resident singer. She still has her reminiscences to tell and Mankiewicz, following his work on *Citizen Kane*, has chosen not to relate them in chronological order. Suffice to say that she meets a bounder (Gene Kelly) while listening to the 'Liebestod', and marries him. As both the B-girl listlessly waiting for her man to be released and the sensible, strong young woman too nice to ask all the right questions, Durbin holds both sections of the film together – despite the fact that, according to the director, Robert Siodmak, she 'wanted to play a new part, but flinched from looking like a tramp; she always wanted to look like nice, wholesome Deanna Durbin pretending to be a tramp'. Siodmak (who had known the producer, Jackson, when the latter was a writer with Ufa), does so well with the atmospheric centrepieces which were his speciality, that we hardly notice when the film falls apart towards the end – as Durbin has to cope with a confrontation and declaration of love which would have defeated even Duse herself.

The result, however, pleased all concerned, including the public, but the star decided to return to more obviously escapist fare. Jackson had the good sense to commission Jerome Kern to compose the songs for **Can't Help Singing** (1944) and they were the best she was ever given. She plays a senator's dizzy daughter who pursues her lover to California, taking her pratfalls with a will and acting without any concession to 'charm' or sentiment. A crisp script is plentiful with misunderstandings and subterfuges, bowled along with zest by the director, Ryan. The Grand Canyon and Durbin were photographed in Technicolor for the first time, but with make-up as harsh as any Goldwyn Girl it does not flatter her. **Lady on a Train** (1946) is similarly marred, an otherwise neat whodunnit, from a novel by Leslie Charteris, nicely directed by Charles David (best known, otherwise, as the producer of *Drôle de Drame*), who later became her third husband. In view of the personal relationships, one must assume that both producer and director complied with her own wish to look like a blonde cutie, singing 'Give Me a Little Kiss, Will You, Huh?' in the finger-snapping style of Betty Grable. Given that she intensely disliked

her screen image, her decision to change it is understandable. On the other hand, her fans were not pleased, and since, according to *Picturegoer*, 'more than most stars her private life has been her public's concern', a second divorce – from Jackson – did not help matters. Both on screen and off, the child to whom the world had given its heart was, after all, just another Hollywood star.

Universal took firm action, and returned to its early formula, an unglamorised Durbin in light comedy with songs, but few people liked **Because of Him** (1946). Richard Wallace directed airily, but there is not a single laugh in this tale of a stage-struck girl (Durbin) who cheats a ham actor (Charles Laughton) into helping her achieve her ambition. One does not necessarily have to recall *All About Eve* (q.v.) to recall how good Hollywood could be on the morals and mores of Broadway. The star herself retained that impulsiveness which had made her so fetching as a child star, and it now suggested the sort of roles that Carole Lombard had once played – or Margaret Sullavan, since **I'll be Yours** (1947), directed by William A. Seiter, was a remake of *The Good Fairy*. The Preston Sturges script was used again, but neither the leading man, Tom Drake, nor two usually excellent supporting players, William Bendix and Adolphe Menjou, were of much help to the star.

The film was seen after Universal amalgamated with International Pictures (q.v.), whose owners, Leo Spitz and William Goetz, had made the deal with the primary aim of acquiring Miss Durbin's services. She remained, as she had been since arriving at the studio, its only major box-office star. She had made the transition to adult roles with ease; she could play both comedy and drama; she could be demure or glamorous; she could sing anything within a range from opera to swing. She was in fact a better actress and a more effective screen presence than Betty Grable or Rita Hayworth, who were worth fortunes to their studios, respectively 20th Century-Fox and Columbia. But the public which had deserted Miss Durbin after *Lady on a Train* were not reconverted by the two subsequent films. Spitz and Goetz hired Johnny Green, the musician, to salvage her career but soon lost heart: they had purchased a Broadway show for her, **Up in Central Park** (1948), but filmed it in black and white when the other studios were using Technicolor for musicals. Durbin herself, aware that Judy Garland – they had appeared together in their first film, *Every Sunday*, a short – never stepped before a camera without being surrounded by M-G-M's best talents, pleaded for better material but instead was offered a raise in salary. In 1947 she was the highest-paid person in the U.S., but Universal now claimed, paradoxically, that her fee was too great to accommodate either colour or more popular co-stars. It turned out to be ill-advised penny-pinching; the lady retired to live in France with M. David, and has remained amused but otherwise silent about the whole episode.

In her last poor films her natural but effervescent personality remains as attractive as ever, though one sometimes senses her impatience with the inadequate material. Like Alice Faye she refused to continue struggling with poor scripts and turned her back on the business rather than start again at another studio (for twenty years more her old mentor, Joseph Pasternak, begged her to come to M-G-M). It is sad to see talent driven out by studio executives (other stars – Garland and Marilyn Monroe q.v. – were instrumental in their own destruction), but Miss Durbin had a sweet and satisfying revenge – if we are to believe the constant reports from radio and television stations which deal with requests from the public: for she invariably heads every list.

Universal had acquired another box-office attraction – Abbott and Costello, a former vaudeville team. Bud Abbott is the straight man, wholly without charm, and Lou Costello, short and tubby, the comic. He is a creature to whom things happen; he exists in the middle of slapstick, not contributing. Universal set them to the usual tasks allotted screen teams: they joined the navy, played detective, and so on. They lacked the ability to create their own lunatic universe in the manner of Laurel and Hardy; timing and wit they knew not of. Their real popularity was brief: by the end of the War their films were double-bill fare, but they kept going till the mid-Fifties in a series of 'creepy-funnies' in which their co-stars were ghosts, Frankenstein, the Invisible Man and other

Deanna Durbin in 1948, smiling despite the terrible films she was required to make for Universal.

phenomena. If posterity draws a blank with Abbott and Costello, it warms slightly to another vaudeville team, Olsen and Johnson, and that is because of the three films they made the first is **Hellzapoppin** (1941). The pair had struck lucky with a Broadway revue of this title in 1938, with 'improvisations' which included a gorilla dragging a woman member of the audience from a box, a tout trying to sell tickets for another show, and a man and woman undressing in the stalls. It ran for over three years, and Universal bought the film rights – at least, they bought the title and its two stars, then commissioned from Nat Perrin and Warren Wilson a script to satisfy anyone who had heard of it or them. It starts, literally, with a merry hell that turns out to be a film set, and moves on to a Long Island estate for a conventional musical comedy plot – but H. C. Potter, directing, pushes through the gags at reckless speed: Martha Raye, an overgrown vaudeville star, has only to see Mischa Auer, a phoney Russian count, to start chasing; Frankenstein's monster steps in to give a helping hand; dogs talk, also photographs, and the players to the audience; the film itself slips from its sprockets, part of it is censored, and one reel supposedly gets mixed up with that of a Western. It is a lively experience, and one that must have influenced the 'Road' comedies; what would have been interesting is a filmed record of the original show.

Chief among the studio's other players were Jon Hall and Maria Montez, who starred in a number of Technicolor adventures which found wartime audiences at their most indulgent. Walter Wanger, now a contract producer at the studio, produced the first of them, **Arabian Nights** (1942), clearly inspired by Korda's *Thief of Baghdad*; the credits are promisingly done over a simulation of Persian prints, and they list as writer Michael Hogan, who had worked on some reasonable movies, including *Rebecca* and *The Prime Minister*. He has tried to be light-hearted, but gets no help from the director, John Rawlins – his only A-feature in a career directing Bs – or the two leads. The woodenness of both Hall and Montez may be the reason that the subsequent films in the series are so awkward and inept – astonishingly so among major studio productions. **Ali Baba and the Forty Thieves** (1944), directed by Arthur Lubin, does have a mite of spectacle, and a plot that is one half 'Robin Hood' and one half Resistance drama. **Cobra Woman** (1944) has Montez in a double role, and was directed and part-written by two men who should have known better, Siodmak and Richard Brooks. The former called it 'silly but fun. You know, Maria Montez couldn't act from here to there, but she had a great personality and believed completely in her roles: playing a princess you had to treat her like one all through lunch, but as a slave girl [her dual role here] you could kick her around anyhow and she wouldn't object – Method acting before its time, you might say.'

Siodmak, in his own words, 'had been in Hollywood for three years, doing what work I could get. Then Universal sent me the script of **Son of Dracula** (1943): it was terrible...' His wife persuaded him to take it, in the hope that it would lead to something better, and though there is nothing in it to indicate the major talent responsible for such films as *Abscheid* and *Brennendes Geheimnis*, Universal were sufficiently impressed to offer a seven-year contract. It was not *Christmas Holiday* – much less

Cobra Woman – which re-established his reputation, but a lesser film, **Phantom Lady** (1944), perhaps because it is more obviously redolent of his European work. Some Ufa-like settings and lighting indicate Siodmak's actual control over the material, but that, alas, is poor, despite a good start in which a man (Franchot Tone) whose wife has been murdered seeks to find the woman who can provide an alibi. In the original novel by William March the murderer is not revealed till the end, but he is disclosed here much earlier – and in that role Tone tears at the scenery. The situations are again preposterous in **The Suspect** (1944), though the central idea is also promising: a mild-mannered tobacconist (Charles Laughton) does away with his nagging wife (Rosalind Ivan) and is blackmailed by a neighbour (Henry Daniell). That apart, the tale owes as much to Francis Iles's novel 'Malice Aforethought' as that owes to the case of Dr Crippen. Edwardian London is the usual foggy metropolis, but Siodmak has made the house of murder exceptionally sinister. Both films are handicapped by a pretty but inept actress, Ella Raines – she is particularly incongruous in the Ethel Le Neve role – and at this point only *Christmas Holiday* reveals Siodmak at his best, particularly in the sequences in the all-night café, the too-roomy roadhouse and the punters' bar.

Another European director, Julien Duvivier, also found a haven at Universal, if less permanently than Siodmak, but at least he fared better on Hollywood's own terms than his compatriots Clair and Renoir, as his prestige increased during his time there and theirs did not. Both **Tales of Manhattan** (1942) and **Flesh and Fantasy** (1943) were regarded as 'different' and therefore superior to most American films. The former – made in fact for 20th Century-Fox – like Duvivier's earlier *Carnet du Bal* consists of a series of sketches with a common motif, in this case a tail coat passed from hand to hand. Ten writers are listed as having contributed to story and screenplay, including Molnar and Ben Hecht, but the unacknowledged source is a German film, *Der Frack*, as recalled by Billy Wilder and Walter Reisch. It had been recommended by them to the producer S. P. Eagle, who had not long arrived in Hollywood after a varied career in Europe – he was to have a distinguished one in the U. S. under a new name, Sam Spiegel. Eagle invited Duvivier to do the film, and one of its star players, Charles Boyer, asked Duvivier to join him at Universal, where he was moving on an actor–producer contract (which proved short-lived). Together Boyer and Duvivier produced *Flesh and Fantasy*, which is composed of three disparate stories of the macabre. One is 'Lord Arthur Saville's Crime', modernised and its outcome hardly in doubt since Edward G. Robinson was one of the few stars acceptable as a murderer; another depends for its effectiveness on a mask resembling a face. The creation of the supernatural is unhappily too literal; as in *Tales of Manhattan* the events on screen are artificially treated and not pithy enough in their own right. Despite their all-star casts both films failed to find a large public, so that although the Hollywood moguls admired Duvivier they were not thereafter anxious to employ him.

Lacking as it did any truly creative filmmakers, Universal chose to turn to its own past. Of several remakes the most enjoyable is **The Phantom of the Opera** (1943), though poorly performed under Arthur Lubin's direction by Susanna Foster as the diva and Nelson Eddy and Edgar Barrier as the smirking rivals for her hand. (They sing excerpts from the operas 'Martha' and 'Amour et Gloire', the latter consisting of morsels of Chopin to which someone has laboriously set a French text). The Technicolored backstage sets look exactly right for the Palais Garnier, while the wronged violinist is Claude Rains, whose silky tones invoke the appropriate pity and terror. **The Spoilers** (1942) is the fourth of five screen versions of Rex Beach's novel, produced by Frank Lloyd, as ever showing his fondness for the 'big' picture. The setting is Nome in 1900, where a gold prospector (John Wayne) vies with the crooked commissioner (Randolph Scott) for a dance-hall girl (Marlene Dietrich); as directed lightly by Ray Enright, the famous marathon fight starts in her bedroom and ends some miles down the street. Wayne and Dietrich complement each other in the manner of the best screen teams – he relaxed, steadfast and teasing, she painted, fickle and humourless. She was said to have been considering retirement at this time, perhaps because she had

to wear the same costume in three different scenes.

Broadway (1942) was remade because Warners had had a success with *The Roaring Twenties*, but despite the vintage songs it has not the slightest feel for that particular era. William Seiter's direction has to contend with the fact that George Raft plays himself as a younger man – a hoofer and good egg, true to some idiotic George Raft code that prevents him co-operating with the cop (Pat O'Brien) trying to prove his innocence. He played himself again, more or less, in **Follow the Boys** (1943), 'Show Business's Tribute to Show Business'. There may be no more embarrassing sequence on celluloid than that in which the stars, coyly batting eyelids, volunteer to entertain the armed services. They are all Universal players (with Miss Durbin and Abbott and Costello more gainfully employed), plus a couple freelancing, a scattering of vaudeville names, and the usual bandleaders. The only one to emerge with credit is Dinah Shore, with two suitable songs, 'I'll Walk Alone' and 'I'll Get By'. The 'turns' were mainly done on the back lot, though intercut with location footage when such as Sophie Tucker and the Andrews Sisters were entertaining the troops – and it is a shock now to see the black servicemen bunched together in the audience. Universal was clearly in agreement, since the one black performer, Louis Jordan, is seen playing for an exclusively black unit, though Raft magnanimously joins him. The object of this and similar films was to remind the world of the film industry's contribution to the war effort, but the list of names at the end, headed by Carole Lombard and Leslie Howard, merely adds insult to injury: apart from a few performers who did travel extensively to entertain the troops, the War hardly intruded upon the lawns and orange groves of Beverly Hills.

The executives of Universal should have felt particularly ashamed, since apart from having Abbott and Costello join the Army, the Navy and the Air Force, they virtually ignored the War. If we discount Hitchcock's *Saboteur*, the company's sole war film of distinction is **Corvette K-225** (1943). Some critics at the time considered it superior to *In Which We Serve*, and it can now be seen to be one of the handful of fiction films to give a true indication of what the War was like. The production, by Howard Hawks, and the direction, by a veteran of B-movies, Richard Rosson, utilise newsreels, back-projection and some unconvincing models, but these are subservient to a very fine screenplay by John Sturdy, a lieutenant in the Royal Canadian Naval Reserve. His focus is an escort ship, and though his incidents parallel those of *Action in the North Atlantic* he had had experience denied to the writers of that film. He knew that among the hazards faced by a small craft are the heavy seas that sweep into every cranny; that after a Luftwaffe attack below-decks becomes a make-shift sick-bay; that junior officers may not follow the example of a disciplinarian captain (Randolph Scott); that the tension of living in cramped quarters can be so extreme that even such a small thing as the repeated playing of a phonograph record can cause a row; and that a floating lifeboat may not contain living survivors. The Canadian source is the reason why the corvette and its crew are of that nationality – which is why the film was retitled *The Nelson Touch* for Britain and its then territories.

Columbia also failed to cover itself with glory during the War. The loss of Frank Capra found Harry Cohn at a low ebb, till the public discovered Rita Hayworth and he promoted her into the studio's leading star. Miss Hayworth (b. 1918), a former dancer, had played small roles at 20th Century-Fox before moving to Columbia. She was wondrous to look upon but not much of an actress, so Cohn put her into two musicals, **You'll Never Get Rich** (1941), directed by Sidney Lanfield, and **You Were Never Lovelier** (1942), directed by William A. Seiter. The studio scored a triple coup by bringing in Fred Astaire (not then greatly in demand) and for the scores respectively Cole Porter and Jerome Kern, both of whom loved working in films. In the former, Astaire joins the army and persuades a Broadway producer (Robert Benchley) to put on a show for the troops. In the much better second film – it also has the more memorable songs, including 'Dearly Beloved' and 'I'm Old-Fashioned' – Astaire is an American dancer employed by a South American tycoon (Adolphe Menjou) to woo his frigid daughter (Hayworth). Miss Hayworth observed in

1970 that these were the only two films she made that she could watch without laughing – 'the only jewels in my life' – but presumably she overlooked **Cover Girl** (1944). Astaire turned down the project because he did not want to be again associated with one particular partner; Gene Kelly (q.v.) was brought in, and it must surely be one of the jewels in his life. He has said that by the time he came to the project Cohn was so desperate for a leading man that he acceded to his request to do his own choreography. To assist him on this Kelly brought in Stanley Donen (q.v.), and though neither is credited – Sidney Buchman, also uncredited, produced and Charles Vidor directed – it was Kelly's contribution, as was immediately recognised, which made this one of the great musicals. Of a range of imaginative numbers, composed by Kern, there are such highlights as 'Put Me to the Test', with its impromptu clowning, and 'Long Ago and Far Away', the first ballad since the Astaire–Rogers series to indicate falling in love; but it is the zingy 'Make Way for Tomorrow', with its seeming vivid spontaneity, which opens the way for *On the Town* (q.v.). Kelly is sympathetic, though required to play the usual boorish producer (Bing Crosby was almost the only star actor in musicals never required to be boorish), and Hayworth is the usual model who forgets him and her antecedents when she becomes famous. Because it is in colour, this film is her apotheosis, and the crude tones of Technicolor at this time make it absolutely of its period. Despite that, and its routine book, it revives well.

Flushed with its success, Vidor and Buchman – the latter as writer only – embarked upon a one-time project of Capra's, **A Song to Remember** (1945), a life of Chopin. It should be a camp classic, with Merle Oberon as George Sand in pantaloons and rakish top hat, and with that memorable moment when Technicolor blood drops on the piano keys; but it is arduous to watch, partly because this Chopin (Cornel Wilde) is a dead fish. As his professor, Paul Muni donates enough acting for the two of them, attempting a spectacular impression of S. Z. 'Cuddles' Sakall, and Oberon is merely absurd. 'I hope you like Paris, Monsieur Chopin. I'm sure Paris will like you' she says on her first entrance, accompanied by Liszt and de

Musset – who will be joined on the cast list by other celebrities, including Balzac, Paganini and Delacroix. Columbia was apprehensive of a movie with 'classical' music, and only occasionally is Chopin allowed to play more than a few bars: but the movie public's discovery of his music is the chief reason why this film is so popular.

It was a rare 'class' offering from this company. Miss Hayworth apart, Columbia concentrated on medium-budget comedies. Typical are **They All Kissed the Bride** (1942), directed by Alexander Hall, and **What a Woman!** (1943), directed by Irving Cummings. Both concern career women whose hearts are melted by, respectively, a charming reporter (Melvyn Douglas) and a flip professor (Brian Aherne). In the case of the reporter, his task is eased when the lady (Joan Crawford) takes to jitterbugging and getting drunk at the firm's dance – after which she yearns for simple things like knitting and babies. The moral was salutary at the time when women were increasingly needed for men's jobs, but both films were merely vehicles for important female stars. Crawford, borrowed from M-G-M when Carole Lombard was killed, still could not play comedy; but Rosalind Russell, in the second film, could make palatable such masochistic roles. Given half a chance, as in her drunk dancing scene, she is formidable.

An even better comedienne, Jean Arthur, was in a position to refuse such stereotyped roles; she played in two films directed by George Stevens, which, like *Woman of the Year*, were primarily comedies but indicated a new seriousness. In **The Talk of the Town** (1942) Miss Arthur is a schoolteacher who lets her house to a professor (Ronald Colman), and then discovers a suspected arsonist (Cary Grant) hiding in her attic. The three become allies as the town works itself into a lynching mood, which causes the film to say something pertinent on civic corruption and social duty. Funnier, but less likeable, is **The More the Merrier** (1943), one of several films about a Washington overcrowded because of the War; frenetically sharing a room with Miss Arthur are Joel McCrea and Charles Coburn.

The War otherwise hardly impinged on Columbia's films. An exception is **Destroyer** (1943), but it is at the opposite end

of the scale from *Corvette K-225*. William A. Seiter directed, and Edward G. Robinson plays an ex-Navy man restored to his command on the outbreak of war – despite opposition and the distrust of his men. They are led by the Chief (Glenn Ford), who nevertheless woos and wins Robinson's daughter, while Robinson wins over the men by single-handedly repairing the torpedoed ship.

R.K.O., after the collapse of its dreams of glory with Orson Welles, again relied upon Disney and Goldwyn to keep its distribution arm in profit. The studio itself returned to its former policy of programmers and B-pictures interspersed with an occasional A-movie. Its leading director, Leo McCarey, was united with its principal stars, Ginger Rogers and Cary Grant, for the misleadingly titled **Once Upon a Honeymoon** (1942). McCarey had said earlier, 'I'll let someone else photograph the ugliness of the world. It's larceny to remind people of how lousy things are and call it entertainment,' but at this juncture he decided to remind people of the dreadful conditions in Europe in the form of entertainment. This is one of several films in which a nice American girl (Rogers) unwittingly marries a Nazi (Walter Slezak). A reporter (Grant) chases her all over Europe to apprise her of the truth, whereupon she gives her passport to her Jewish maid and in a supposedly comic scene gets herself and Grant arrested as Jews. They are imprisoned in a Jewish transit camp till the U.S. ambassador turns up to rescue them, and the sequence would be offensive even if the film were not operating at that level where Rogers can crack the Nazi cabinet's secret code and later push her husband overboard (to prevent him from converting the U.S. to Nazism). Except for its patriotic fervour, audiences were not expected to take all this seriously, but as a piece of film-making it is as inept as McCarey's previous film, *Love Affair*, was controlled. He would recover some prestige with his 'priest' films starring Bing Crosby, but would never recover his old form.

It was apparently difficult for the American film industry to come to terms with Nazism, and **Hitler's Children** (1943), though more responsible in content is considerably more hysterical in

609

approach. It is one of the few movie dramas – as opposed to thrillers – set in the Germany of the Third Reich, and as adapted from 'Education for Death' by Gregor Ziemer it examines the effect of Nazi ideology on an American girl (Bonita Granville). When she refuses further indoctrination she is threatened with sterilisation, and that brings a member of the Nazi Youth (Tim Holt) to his senses. The film, made on a small budget, was not meant for major consideration, but it became a freak success when taken up by the public (its domestic gross of $3½ million represented a return on investment of just under 1,000 per cent). Its director, Edward Dmytryk, was forthwith promoted to major projects.

Despite the profits from that film, R.K.O. was as usual in the red, and it was suggested that some musicals with Dick Powell might prevent the company going into receivership – an odd proposition, since Powell was no longer a box-office name. Powell himself declined to sing again on screen, fancying himself as a tough guy – and it was agreed that he would play private detective Philip Marlowe in a version of Raymond Chandler's 'Farewell, My Lovely', to be directed by Dmytryk and retitled **Murder, My Sweet** (1944) in case the conjunction of Powell's name and the word 'lovely' suggested a musical. R.K.O. owned the rights, having filmed it with changed names to fit into a B-series as *The Falcon Takes Over* just two years earlier ('The Falcon', played by George Sanders and then by his brother Tom Conway, was a debonair fixer of crime mysteries) – but Chandler's reputation had grown in the interim. Chandler himself thought Powell the best of the screen Marlowes – perhaps because his performance is anonymous throughout. He glowers, but brings neither the character nor tension which Bogart was to bring to *The Big Sleep* (q.v.), but, once that is accepted, we may enjoy the respect accorded the material (as scripted by John Paxton). As the dangerous Mrs Grayle, Claire Trevor fails to measure up to Mary Astor or Barbara Stanwyck in similar roles, but the others are good: Mike Mazurki as the slobbish, beastly Moose Malloy; Esther Howard as the drunken Mrs Florian; and Otto Kruger as the silky psychiatrist quack, Jules Amthor.

Another attempt to make R.K.O. solvent was to invite Val Lewton (1904–51) story-editor with Selznick, to form a new B-unit producing thrillers to take the lower half of double-bills. Lewton decided to utilise budget restrictions by limiting himself to unseen phenomena – to what he called 'dramatisations of the psychology of fear'. He made eleven such films, and the cult admiration that exists today may have begun with James Agee's comment after seeing the first half-dozen, praising Lewton's team 'because for all their unevenness their achievements are so consistently alive, limber, poetic, humane.' On the other hand I find the films disappointing. A B-picture is always a B-picture: the studio's first requirement was not that it should be entertaining but that it should be brought in as quickly and as cheaply as possible. The imaginative touches in Lewton's films are invariably derivative, while there are inadequacies in performing which tend to emphasise the perfunctory nature of the action. The first of them, **The Cat People** (1942), has an ingenious story by DeWitt Bodeen about a man (Kent Smith) whose wife (Simone Simon) believes, with reason, that she turns into a panther at night; but apart from one set – in fact left over from *The Magnificent Ambersons* – the film lacks completely the necessary atmosphere as directed by Jacques Tourneur. An R.K.O. executive, hoping for a sequel, came up with the title **The Curse of the Cat People** (1944), but Lewton refused to capitalise on the earlier film, which is of the 'horror' genre – however mild. Bodeen contributed a story about a child bewitched by her ghostly mother (Mlle Simon), but he admits that the film is really Lewton's work, since Lewton put into it all his ideas on child psychology. Gunther Fritsch and Robert Wise (q.v.) directed. The result is not unlike *The Uninvited*, but if that film is a supernatural feast, even perhaps vegetarian, this is a stale cucumber sandwich. **I Walked with a Zombie** (1943) does manage a passable reconstruction of a Caribbean island, and Frances Dee is a sympathetic heroine; but Tom Conway is poor in a role based on Charlotte Brontë's Mr Rochester and the final effect is only too trivial as directed by Tourneur.

Also brought in to help the studio out of its difficulties was Damon Runyon, but only one film resulted, **The Big Street** (1942), directed by Irving Reis and written by Leonard Spigelglass from what is described simply and modestly as a *Colliers* magazine story: immediately recognisable are the customary muggs with the heart of gold, the two-timing dames and the firm belief that magic can happen in a nightclub. Eugene Pallette (as Nicely Nicely Johnson), Agnes Moorehead, Sam Levene, Louise Beavers, Ray Collins, Millard Mitchell and Marion Martin are likeably Runyonesque; Henry Fonda is kindly and intense as 'Little Pinks', the bus boy 'stuck' on the boss's foul-mouthed doll – a difficult role, and only once before the end does Lucille Ball show any feeling. She is so expert with the cracks that she is engaging without ever being sympathetic. She made one more film at R.K.O. before going to M-G-M for *DuBarry Was a Lady* (q.v.) and her performance here almost compensates for her poor work for Metro.

In another attempt at box-office success R.K.O. brought back Fred Astaire, but **The Sky's the Limit** (1943), directed by Edward H. Griffith, is a mere husk of former glories. Astaire plays a 'flying tiger' with lots of Japanese planes to his credit, a fact not disclosed to Joan Leslie, who tries to fix him up with a job till her boss (Robert Benchley) plays cupid, and she gazes skywards with misty eyes as 'his' plane whizzes past – the end, it would seem, of every other wartime movie. Harold Arlen's score includes 'One for My Baby', the *pièce de résistance* as sung by Astaire in three different bars and concluded by a drunken tap dance.

The songs in **Show Business** (1944) are old ones, used to deck out an affectionate and unpretentious tale of loving and war-ring vaudeville couples, directed by Edwin L. Marin and produced by Eddie Cantor, who also stars, with the equally agreeable George Murphy, Constance Moore and Joan Davis. Miss Davis was a horse-faced comedienne – described here as looking like 'an umbrella with a broken handle' – with considerable attack; she is very funny with a good line, thus, 'Listen, show me a way to earn folding money and I'd do a fan-dance with a fly-swatter.' Among the minor pleasures here is a montage of railway trains and billboards.

The Enchanted Cottage (1945) is also more successful than it has any right to be.

This late play by Pinero (1922), called by him a 'fable', had been filmed by First National in 1924 with Richard Barthelmess and May McAvoy, and it belongs to that era. Resurrecting it while the War was still on appeared foolhardy, since its subject is a man (Robert Young) embittered by his war scars. He marries a 'homely' girl (Dorothy McGuire), and under the spell of their honeymoon cottage they become beautiful, which his meddling mother (Spring Byington) and her equally insensitive husband cannot understand. When the couple meet they are photographed alternately as they are and as they think they are, leaving us to wonder whether they will hold on to their illusions. Owing to the dedication of the director, John Cromwell, and the skills of DeWitt Bodeen and Herman Mankiewicz, who wrote it, this is one of the few pieces of Hollywood whimsy that works. Miss McGuire is here the best of those unglamorous, breathy actresses who linger on the last words of a sentence, even if her transformation does only prove that all she needed was an hour in a beauty parlour; and Young is good simply because he has no false romantic aura. They are beautifully supported by Mildred Natwick as the householder who cedes her place – rather dopily – to maid McGuire, and by Herbert Marshall as the blind friend.

Sam Goldwyn's major contribution to the war effort was **The North Star** (1943), a hymn to the gallant Russians. Russian-born himself, he insisted on compatriot Lewis Milestone as director, though Milestone disliked the script commissioned from Lillian Hellman. When she refused to change a word, Goldwyn sided with Milestone, and an uncredited Edward Chodorov worked over her screenplay. As shot by James Wong Howe, the result looks both epic and European, but in sum is absurdly pretentious, its comments on war emerging as piffling. Among the better situations is that of the humane town doctor (Walter Huston) provoked into killing the German C.O. (Eric Von Stroheim), after telling him that the intelligent Germans are more guilty than the Nazi puppets; while the introduction into the plot of the fact that the Germans took blood from Russian children for their own wounded soldiers is more plausible than most of the atrocities Hollywood dreamed up for them.

611

They Got Me Covered (1943) is a salutary reminder of the time when every other beauty parlour in Washington was a front for a Gestapo spy ring. This particular ring is rounded up by Bob Hope, playing an otherwise incompetent journalist, and he has quips about such other wartime hazards as the blackout and air-raid wardens. He was borrowed from Paramount, in a deal which included Dorothy Lamour and the director David Butler; when Hope and Butler returned to Goldwyn for **The Princess and the Pirate** (1944) the package included some of Hope's usual writers, Don Hartman, Melville Shavelson and Everett Freeman. Both films are burlesques, a form neglected from the Silent period to the second 'Road' movie with Hope and Crosby – and Hope was to work memorably in this field in the postwar period, with such films as *The Paleface* (q.v.). It suffices to say that *The Princess and the Pirate* is one of Hope's most brilliant films, both fond and funny beyond the knowingness which is all that some recent practitioners have brought to the genre. Clearly, it is a spoof on pirate adventures, and one reason it is so good is the glee with which it re-creates its world of easy death: the bleaker and blacker the milieu, the funnier Hope's craven behaviour.

The only studio constantly to treat the War with comparative responsibility was 20th Century-Fox. Joseph Schenck resigned as chairman in 1941, after being jailed for tax evasion and for bribing film unions during the industrial troubles a few years earlier; the following year the company's president, Sidney Kent, died, to be succeeded by a former exhibitor, Spyros Skouras. Both men had been instrumental in merging 20th Century with Fox, along with Darryl F. Zanuck and William Goetz. When Zanuck joined the army his assistant, Goetz, became his deputy – though Schenck was able to resume a certain amount of power. Both of them were responsive to talent (unlike Schenck's brother, Nicholas, the power at M-G-M), but Zanuck's lieutenant-colonelcy in the Signal Corps did not prevent him from continuing to make his voice heard at the studio. Unlike the other two dynamic studio heads, Harry Cohn and Jack Warner, he brought creative ability to the making of films. He knew how to construct films and had the ability to spot weaknesses in a script; he appreciated intelligence in subject matter and dialogue, while distrusting motivation to the extent that he would have preferred his films to consist chiefly of action. His first instincts were good: his poorest films were often those he worked upon longest and hardest. He was absent, in fact, at war for only eighteen months, until May 1943, when he found his patriotic fervour somewhat less than that for movies, and he asked to be put on the inactive duty list. Any assessment of his work must take into account the fact that although Fox musicals became increasingly stereotyped they were preferred by the troops to those made by any other company.

One of his personal productions, **This Above All** (1942), was directed by Anatole Litvak from a novel by Eric Knight which, like many another bestseller, undoubtedly embodied a number of fine thoughts and unimpeachable values. Joan Fontaine plays a wealthy English girl so earnest about the War that she joins the W.A.A.F.s, quickly falling for a working-class bloke (Tyrone Power) who hates the aristocracy and deserted after Dunkirk. She gives him one of those eulogies on England ('the sound of taxi-horns, the dignity of our ancient cities') of which Hollywood was so fond at this time, and if it is an odd England, it is an even odder W.A.A.F. service: 'Can you get leave?' he asks and she replies unhesitatingly, 'Of course I can, darling.' No wonder that she is fairly ludicrous in uniform. Power makes no attempt at a British accent, but tries hard to suggest a man beset by both neuroses and left-wing yearnings; in support Alexander Knox is a one-armed, pipe-smoking, dog-collared figure of compassion.

Son of Fury (1942) and **The Black Swan** (1942) both prove that Power could not swash a buckle as blithely as did Errol Flynn. John Cromwell directed the first, from a novel by Edison Marshall, about an orphan – played as a boy by Roddy McDowall – cheated of his inheritance in Regency England, and consoled by both a two-faced blonde (Frances Farmer) and a Polynesian beauty (Gene Tierney) encountered on his travels. Henry King directed the other, adapted from Rafael Sabatini s novel by Ben Hecht and Seton I. Miller, a teaming which promised something considerably more lively. Leon Shamroy won an Oscar for his colour cinematography of some obvious model-galleons in full sail against resplendent sunsets. Power, Laird Cregar, a one-eyed Anthony Quinn and a red-bearded George Sanders are the pirates. The heroine is Maureen O'Hara, who plays with 'no more feeling than a load of clams', as fellow crewman Thomas Mitchell says scornfully.

Power's departure for the Marine Corps left Betty Grable and Alice Faye as the studio's chief assets, and they proceeded to make the same film under various titles. When neither was available, as in **My Gal Sal** (1942), Rita Hayworth was borrowed. The film was directed by Irving Cummings from a reminiscence by Theodore Dreiser of his brother, Paul Dresser, 'whose own career was as flamboyant and extravagant as the era he set to music'. As detailed here, it follows the familiar progress of the struggling songwriter (Victor Mature) and his stormy affair with a Broadway leading lady, while Dresser's own songs are supplemented by no less than five new ones by Robin and Rainger. The numbers are mounted with extravagance, if not flamboyance, and during wartime austerity the costumes were a tonic – the ladies in osprey headdresses, candy-striped bustles and diamonds, and the men in duds equally dazzling. Public response to this sartorical display convinced 20th to cover Miss Grable's legs with long skirts for most of **Coney Island** (1943), directed by Walter Lang, in which she is fought over by rival saloon-owners, and **Sweet Rosie O'Grady** (1943), directed by Cummings, in which she bags an English duke while pretending to be a 'class' artiste. Both films are inferior to *My Gal Sal*, though that has nothing to do with the playing; in both Miss Grable is a wised-up showgirl who is at heart a good Joe. The troops adored watching her, especially the famous legs – when they had the chance – and were indifferent to her limited talent. The famous pin-up picture of her is seen under the credits of **Pin-Up Girl** (1944), directed by Bruce Humberstone, an otherwise dim piece in which as a secretary in Washington she dons specs so that the naval hero (John Harvey) will not recognise her. She does have one dance number – with an apache, whose clothes,

bearing and postures would reappear in Gene Kelly's developed style.

The Gang's All Here (1943) is a dire film, but it has an impressive place among the myths and memories of the era, with its G.I. sentiment ('Hearing from you every day would make me feel as though you're marching with me at the head of the column'), Miss Faye sighing gently to the stars, and Carmen Miranda in her fruit cocktail headpieces, bare midriff and platform shoes. The director is Busby Berkeley, whose production numbers have won a belated fame, though at the time 'The Tutti-Frutti Hat' was noticed by *The New York Times*, which thought that 'if interpreted [it] might bring a rosy blush to several cheeks in the Hays Office'. This has much to do with the raising and lowering of giant bananas by a line of scantily-dressed chorus girls, and what it tells us of Berkeley's subconscious hardly bears contemplation.

Two or three seconds of 'Daisy, Daisy', sung on a trolley car in *My Gal Sal*, may have inspired the best number in *Meet Me in St Louis* (q.v.). Certainly the success of the latter inspired Fox to remake **State Fair** (1945), as a musical, and the only one of the time with any claim to originality. Since the piece always was Americana, Zanuck hired the new heroes of that form, Rodgers and Hammerstein, to write the songs, which resemble those of 'Oklahoma!' – updated, perhaps, and made palatable to front office taste. They are splendid, of course, but unenterprisingly done apart from 'It's a Grand Night for Singing'. As directed by Walter Lang, the rest is Forties kitsch. Jeanne Crain's sugary breathlessness has dated as badly as the dirndle skirts and bouffant sleeves she wears, and as her brother Dick Haymes plumbs new depths of charmlessness. The self-conscious air of niceness affects Charles Winninger and Fay Bainter as their parents, as well as Donald Meek and Percy Kilbride, also representing the older generation.

Zanuck, the first to realise how much Technicolor enhanced musicals, would not use colour for **Stormy Weather** (1943), but it is the one most worth preserving, offering as it does the talents of Lena Horne, Cab Calloway, Fats Waller and a sensational dancing team, the Nicholas Brothers. Andrew L. Stone produced and directed this all-black musical, sanctioned after the critical reception given to M-G-M's *Cabin in the Sky* (q.v.), and it is a pity that no white person is ever seen in the night clubs which provide the film's setting.

The best of the studio's pieces of Technicolor escapism is **Heaven Can Wait** (1943), directed by Lubitsch and adapted by Samson Raphaelson from a play by Lazlo Bus-Fékete called 'Birthday', in which, apparently, the hero's birthday was an excuse to reminisce about amorous gambols in his past. It could never have been a distinguished piece, but its wild humour has an air of breathless gaiety which sits well on period comedy. The pleasures of Henry (Don Ameche) range from the French maid in boyhood to the night nurse in his dotage; his wife is Gene Tierney, and she was never again as good – which is true also of Charles Coburn as Henry's indulgent grandfather, Laird Cregar as Old Nick in the framing sequence, Eugene Pallette and Marjorie Main as a couple who communicate only through their servants and Anita Bolster as the lady who at Henry's funeral sings 'Now Is the Closing of the Day' – something he had managed to avoid while alive. The chief joy is Ameche, taking the role of a lifetime and giving one of the great comic performances of the American cinema.

This film and **Cluny Brown** (1946) reveal that Lubitsch was tired of both the famous 'touch' and the eternal triangle. The latter movie, written by another regular collaborator, Samuel Hoffenstein, with Elizabeth Reinhardt, is a straightforward version of Margery Sharp's novel – taking, indeed, its wry tone from that source. Lubitsch had always been amused by protocol, and *Angel* had demonstrated his fascination with the British upper classes; but *Cluny Brown* is, rather, about British snobbery, both above and below stairs, and he could not bring himself to be cruel enough. His Hollywood British cast do not play with sufficient edge, and his leads – Jennifer Jones as a parlourmaid, Charles Boyer as a Czech refugee renowned for his anti-Nazism – are not the first names that come to mind as comedy players.★ These were the only two films Lubitsch completed under his contract with 20th. He prepared a remake of *Forbid-*

★She was cast at the insistence of Miss Sharp, who refused otherwise to sell the rights.

den Paradise, called *A Royal Scandal*, but ill health caused him to hand it over to Otto Preminger; and the latter was the studio's choice to replace him when he died while making *That Lady in Ermine* (q.v.).

Preminger had been a sometime actor and theatre director in Vienna, who had directed his first American film in 1937, at 20th, but did not do so again till the same company asked him to re-stage *Margin for Error* which he had directed on Broadway. Zanuck disliked him, and relegated him to the B-unit, but agreed to let him produce a screenplay by which Preminger held much store – **Laura** (1944), written by Jay Dratler, Samuel Hoffenstein and Betty Reinhardt, from a novel by Vera Caspary. Rouben Mamoulian was to have directed, but Zanuck asked Preminger to replace him after a few days' shooting. His direction is not as ponderous as his later efforts; and the film's unique quality springs both from David Raksin's haunting theme tune, and the acidulous dialogue given to the *bon vivant* Waldo Lydecker (Clifton Webb). When the lady of the title is found murdered, a detective (Dana Andrews) interviews those who knew her – her aunt (Judith Anderson), her fiancé (Vincent Price) and Lydecker, whose protégée she had been. As we move into flashback, an ordinary mystery takes on a certain fascination. Lydecker is a compendium of Alexander Woollcott, George Jean Nathan and other holy horrors. 'In my case,' he tells Laura (Gene Tierney), 'the self-absorption is total.' The film does not divulge the extent of their relationship, but anyone acquainted with Manhattan society will recognise the suave bitchiness of both Lydecker and the fiancé as more than likely homosexual in origin. The acclaimed sophistication of this film is in truth a little simple-minded, but taken as a whole it remains enjoyable.

There is murder, but little mystery, in **Roxie Hart** (1942), the first of three films made at 20th at this time by William A. Wellman; Nunnally Johnson wrote it from Maurine Watkins' play 'Chicago', originally filmed by Pathé in 1928 with Phyllis Haver. That had concerned a travesty of justice when a murderess wins the sympathy of an all-male jury by pretending to be an expectant mother. To pass the Code, the film is about a showgirl who confesses to a murder to get her name in lights –

though she does invent a pregnancy when her thunder is stolen by the more notorious Two-Gun Gertie (Iris Adrian). The evocation of the period is weak, and Ginger Rogers is self-conscious as Roxie. She is at her best chewing gum and with legs ready to shimmy, but not in the same class as Stanwyck in Wellman's *Lady of Burlesque*. Adolphe Menjou is good as the defending lawyer, mainly preoccupied with cash and manipulating the jury, and there is a memorable moment when Roxie's Paw gets back to his rocking-chair and says laconically, 'They're gonna hang Roxie,' to which Maw replies, undisturbed, 'Whatud I tell ya?'

Most of **The Ox-Bow Incident** (1943) is memorable. Certainly its genesis is. A writer, just sacked from 20th, had asked Wellman to read Walter Van Tilburg Clark's novel about a small-town lynching, with a view to turning it – 'You won't believe this,' said Wellman – into a vehicle for Mae West, in an interpolated role as a singer who entertains the cowboys. Since the writer had been unable to interest anyone in Hollywood in either the idea or the book, Wellman was able to buy the rights for $6,500 – and when he too could find no interested producer, he contacted Zanuck (according to him, they had not spoken since a quarrel during the filming of *Call of the Wild*), who said that it would not make a nickel but that it was the sort of movie with which his studio should be associated. After Zanuck was drafted, his deputy, Goetz, cancelled it, but allowed Wellman to remind Zanuck of their agreement.

Thus the film was made, from a screenplay by Lamar Trotti; and after a preview in the presence of the principals, Mrs Zanuck observed loudly that the studio should be ashamed. The entire front office concurred: but Zanuck was able to return to his initial enthusiasm once the notices were in. Audiences, however, by their absence, agreed with Mrs Zanuck, since at that time they were ill-prepared for a subject so uncompromisingly 'depressing', or even a serious subject not bathed in 'uplift'. Two years later, when the War had brought a new seriousness to the cinema, they might have taken it in their stride.

The setting is a small town in Nevada in 1885, where the men gang up to murder someone – anyone – because they are bored. Questions of guilt are secondary. It is a world and an era where nothing is certain: Carter (Fonda) and his companion ride into town to meet with automatic suspicion, but their motive in joining the lynch party is probably to see justice done. Other reactions are equally ambiguous, and since the faces are so much more eloquent than the dialogue it is a pity that the final moralising is so explicit and that there is never any doubt of the innocence of the doomed men (Dana Andrews, Anthony Quinn, Francis Ford). However, there is enough subtlety to counterbalance the self-righteousness, and it is not of great import that the lighting in the night scenes emphasise the film's aspirations to art – though the European influence was no longer Ufa but Marcel Carné.

Buffalo Bill (1944) was one of the studio's recurrent looks at old American heroes, undeterred by the fact that they all led boring lives – boring, that is, as generally rendered. The film has none of Wellman's usual vitality or questioning, and when occasionally the script begins to suggest that Bill Cody may have been a charlatan it quickly veers away to safer concepts. Joel McCrea plays the likeable but uninspiring man of action; Miss O'Hara is incongruous as the enamelled girl he marries.

In **The Immortal Sergeant** (1943) this actress describes herself as a pianist, and one apparently with unlimited clothing coupons. She is remembered in the desert by a British corporal (Henry Fonda), since this was the first film on the Libyan campaign, hastily adapted from John Brophy's novel by Trotti when 20th decided it must make some sort of a bow to the British war effort. Brophy had written about a shy young man who found himself influenced by a rough N.C.O. from the working class – the character of the title, played by Thomas Mitchell in an 'inspirational' glow. These soldiers' adventures resemble the events in a Foreign Legion movie; and the feeling of unreality is increased by poor lighting – the men often have *two* shadows apiece in the desert, a rare fault in a major Hollywood movie. The director was John M. Stahl, who specialised in British subjects for the company.

Holy Matrimony (1943) is a version of the only Arnold Bennett novel which has interested Hollywood, 'Buried Alive' (it had been filmed by Paramount in 1933 as

His Double Life), but neither Stahl nor his writer, Nunnally Johnson, has quite the measure of it, for only once does it offer the moral knot which Bennett provided so generously. Monty Woolley is the artist who takes the place of his own valet (Eric Blore), when the latter dies; Laird Cregar is his dealer; and Gracie Fields, not at all at home, is the woman he marries.

Stahl worked with the writer George Seaton on **The Eve of St Mark** (1944), adapted from a Broadway play by Maxwell Anderson – somewhat drastically, one imagines, since it falls into three sections: home front sentimentality just before Pearl Harbor; stress under fire in the Philippines; and barrack-room badinage. The barrack-room scenes are reasonably authentic, demonstrating that though 20th Century-Fox's war films are not overall better than those produced at other studios, they did try harder.

Stahl was not the director he once was, but was assigned to one of Zanuck's more ambitious projects, **The Keys of the Kingdom** (1944) – working this time with a distinguished producer, Joseph L. Mankiewicz, who had just arrived from M-G-M. Mankiewicz also worked on the screenplay with Nunnally Johnson, but it omits the whole point of the novel, by A. J. Cronin, on which it is based. That concerned a priest who, after a lifetime in China, was more Chinese than Scottish, his Christianity imbued with the teachings of Confucius – which was why his Church failed to understand him: but as played by Gregory Peck he is merely a sincere and questioning individual with a penchant for talking to God. There is an excellent scene where an aged Mother Superior (Rosa Stradner) tells the aged priest what his friendship has meant to her, but the other representatives of the Church are either twinkle-eyed or disagreeably worldly. The film makes several moral judgments, but like most religious films of this period it is not religious at all.

It followed the standard procedure for bringing bestsellers to the screen: dignified advertising, a longish running time and a cast of major character players. There was also a standard trailer, in which the camera tracked along a shelf of successfully-filmed books to pause at *this* one, described in such terms as 'the novel the world has thrilled to becomes the mighty motion picture it cannot wait to see'. The sales and borrowings of books did rise considerably during the War, and there was a reawakening of interest in the works of the Victorian novelists: but the decision to remake **Jane Eyre** (1944) – there had been a version with Virginia Bruce ten years earlier – was probably caused by Goldwyn's successful reissue of *Wuthering Heights*. Hollywood was obsessed with the British and their land of mists and shadows; so after many imitations it made sense to go to one of the prototypes of all romantic fiction. The model adaptation, by John Houseman, Aldous Huxley and the director, Robert Stevenson, deviates from the original with poignancy by having Jane (Joan Fontaine) return to Aunt Reed (Agnes Moorehead) rather than stay with the Rivers'. Stevenson and his photographer, George Barnes, approach their subject with relish, and though they used the studio lights at full tilt the film stays in the memory while the locations for the matter-of-fact 1971 version have faded. It has been claimed that this pictorial style was influenced by *Citizen Kane* because Orson Welles heads the cast: it could be said with more certainty that he was permitted control of his performance, which suggests a Mr Rochester as mad as his incarcerated wife. With Peggy Ann Garner as the child Jane, Henry Daniell as Mr Brocklehurst and Miss Moorehead's complacent, unfeeling Aunt, the first part of the film captures superbly the eerie quality of the novel at that stage, but the remainder is not an anti-climax.

Jane Eyre was one of the films planned by David O. Selznick and sold to 20th Century-Fox, along with its star and director (Stevenson's contract with Selznick was one reason for his inactivity in Hollywood – unlike his compatriot Hitchcock, who both awed Selznick and was in demand elsewhere). Another such deal was done with **Claudia** (1943), together with the services of Dorothy McGuire, who had played the title role in Rose Franken's original play on Broadway. In an attempt to re-create the press interest over the casting of Scarlett O'Hara, Selznick had pretended that he had had no intention of using Miss McGuire, and several important stars were reported as having tested for the role, including Margaret Sullavan – on whose screen image the role was mod-

616

lled, intentionally or not. Claudia wears lat shoes and a cardigan, her hair is untidy nd she slouches or lolls when in a chair; ut it is made clear – or as clear as the Hays Office would allow – that her slightly-lder husband (Robert Young) finds her exually irresistible. She is therefore an nteresting character to find in movies at his time, since Zanuck was apparently iercest in the belief – shared by all the tudio heads – that women were either vhores or chaste. The film otherwise is a mug comedy, set in a never-never Con-ecticut peopled with comic neighbours: hat would be much imitated, but the pple-pie girl who was also sexy would ot be common in movies for some years – f ever. The director was the veteran Ed-nund Goulding – his first film for the tudio in which he was to eventually end lis career.

The director of **The Lodger** (1944) and **Hangover Square** (1945) was John Brahm, who was German-born, but be-ore arriving in Hollywood he had worked n Britain – a fact which has a certain elevance, since the mists swirling in both ilms are London fogs. The films also have n common Laird Cregar in sinister roles nd George Sanders as Scotland Yard stal-varts; they were produced by Robert Bassler from screenplays by Barré Lyndon - whose other work, like that of the direc-or, is of little or no distinction. The re-reation of Edwardian London, by James Basevi and John Ewing, is outstanding, nd the second of the two films is at least xtremely well made: in that, Linda Dar-nell gives real edge to her usual movie role t this time, a floozie, but Brahm managed o similar miracle with Merle Oberon in he first. She plays niece to the folk who nouse the lodger of the title, and his in-ended final victim: and as he had seen her on stage doing her version of the can-can we may feel his thoughts of homicide justi-ied. Lyndon follows Hitchcock's Silent version in adding such frills to this story of ack the Ripper; but the mangling of Pat-ick Hamilton's novel, for the second film, s more serious, beginning with the trans-osition of the action from the present day. Gaslight (based on a play by Hamilton) and The Lodger itself may have proved that London was more frightening some years arlier, while The Phantom of the Opera ossibly dictated the change of the protag-

onist's profession from motor-car sales-man to composer. Bernard Herrmann's concerti for him are impressive, but, as Richard Winnington observed, 'It's al-ways safer to make a homicidal maniac an artist.' With his soft voice and lumbering frame, Cregar is particularly remarkable in this role as a schizophrenic. His powerful personality had helped to promote him to stardom, but since he was hardly leading-man material the studio considered him as its Chaney or Karloff. He so resented the alterations made to Hamilton's novel that he submitted himself to a slimming course so as not to be typed; and it killed him.

Another actor surprisingly to be found at Fox was Jean Gabin, and much care was taken over his American debut, with the eminent John Steinbeck retained to write the screenplay (from a novel by Willard Robinson). But **Moontide** (1942), like The Ox-Bow Incident, proved Holly-wood's over-readiness to ape Europe

Edwardian London, with its fogs and hansom cabs, had a fascination for movie-makers from the Silent days until the Fifties, usually for stories of murder and mayhem. Two of the best were offered to wartime audiences, *The Lodger*, illustrated, and *Hangover Square*, both starring Laird Cregar, a versatile actor who was exceptionally effective being sinister.

when attempting seriousness: the title is reminiscent of *Sunrise*, and not for nothing are there endless *brumes* engulfing these California *quais*. Gabin is a drunken migrant worker caught between a would-be suicide, Anna (Ida Lupino), and his best friend (Thomas Mitchell) – whose love for him is so extreme that he plans to rape Anna rather than arouse other suspicions in the audience. The film does, at least, begin well: a riverside bar, 'Remember?' on an old phonograph echoing across the bay, and a drunken montage – perhaps the contribution of Fritz Lang, who directed for four days before being replaced by Archie Mayo.

The actual contribution of individual directors under the studio system has always been difficult to assess: **The Moon Is Down** (1943) and **Guadalcanal Diary** (1943) may be added to the list of good films made by mediocrities, the first by Irving Pichel and the other by Lewis Seiler. In each case the original material was superior to most and adapted with respect – the former from Steinbeck's play by Nunnally Johnson, the latter from the book by the war correspondent Richard Tregaskis by Lamar Trotti. *The Moon Is Down* is better than most Resistance films in striving to explore the relationship between opposing nations and ideologies trying to live together, even if Steinbeck misunderstands Nazism; the characters spout attitudes at each other, but the dilemmas of the mayor (Henry Travers) and the German commander (Sir Cedric Hardwicke) are reasonably presented – and the film ends with muted heroism instead of the usual idiocies. Death in *Guadalcanal Diary* also seems not squalid, not quite necessary, and needing courage to confront. The film's strength is that it seems to have been filmed wholly on location; its overriding fault is that its squadron of Marines contains only stereotypes: the kindly chaplain (Preston Foster), the scared kid (Richard Jaeckel), the conscientious sergeant (Lloyd Nolan) and the Brooklyn bruiser (William Bendix). Richard Conte and Anthony Quinn represent the underprivileged ethnic groups, but there are no blacks to be seen.

Lloyd Bacon directed two films about the home front, neither free from cliché, but **The Sullivans** (1944) is as good as **Sunday Dinner for a Soldier** (1944) is

poor. The Sullivans were an Iowa famil[y] who lost five sons at Guadalcanal, and th[e] film is a tribute to such 'typical' people[.] The family in the other film lives in a shac[k] and is bone-shakingly cute: when the gir[l] (Anne Baxter) speaks of their poverty th[e] soldier (John Hodiak) tells her that they ar[e] the richest family he knows, 'You hav[e] the sort of wealth no one can destroy.' [A] British critic, Winnington, found '[a] warmth of honest sentiment that is irre[-]sistible', but in the U.S. James Agee fe[lt] 'embarrassment rather than simple ange[r] because most of the people who worke[d] on [it] appear to have loved it, believed i[n] it, and had great hopes for its originalit[y] and worthiness'.

Lewis Milestone's two war films for th[e] company are also polarised in quality. **Th[e] Purple Heart** (1944) was based on a[n] actual incident, when a bomber crew, sho[t] down in Japan, were subjected to a civilia[n] trial in Tokyo for allegedly strafing non[-]military targets. From the few availabl[e] facts Zanuck (under the pseudonym o[f] Melville Crossman) devised a story abou[t] the bravery of the crew and the beastlines[s] of the Japanese – and though most of th[e] torturing takes place off-screen, the film was censured in the press for marking [a] new depth in the depiction of cruelty[.] Today, despite the sobriety of the direc[-]tion, the film is merely absurd. As th[e] Japanese general, Richard Loo seems t[o] have strayed in from a Silent yellow-peri[l] melodrama; the crew is the usual cros[s] section – Dana Andrews as the fearles[s] commander, Farley Granger as 'the kid'[,] Conte as the Italian, Sam Levene as the Je[w] – though as in *Action in the North Atlanti*[c] his Jewishness extends only to his name.[*] The soldiers of **A Walk in the Sun** (1945[)] have greater individuality, but this was [a] further example of superior source ma[-]terial – a novel by Harry Brown, writte[n] for the screen by Robert Rossen (q.v.). [A] simple plot follows a platoon from it[s] landing in Italy to the taking of a farm[-]house, its men glad of 'butts' (cigarettes) o[r] any minor diversion as they are decimated[;] under the guidance of their sergean[t] (Andrews) they are merely doing their job[.] Milestone produced and directed indepen[-]

*I do not mean to imply that any such quality exists, but tha[t] Hollywood, incapable at this time of showing any ethni[c] group without stereotyped mannerisms, was sensitive on th[e] Jewish issue.

dently, and showed the finished product to Zanuck, who 'raved about it . . . and enthusiastically recommended it to his principals in New York. He accordingly got the release, and the rest is history' – an ambiguous remark, since the film initially failed. 20th did not open it in Britain, but sold it six years later to a minor distributor, who opened it to exceptional notices just after a revival of *All Quiet on the Western Front*.

As hitherto, Zanuck's major projects were assigned to Henry King – and there was none more major than **The Song of Bernadette** (1943), based on the best selling novel by Franz Werfel, a Jew, about the French peasant girl who claimed that the Virgin in person had directed her towards the discovery of a spring with healing properties. It is a handsome film reminiscent of the prints of the period – 1858 – and King creates a not especially reverential mood around the religious controversy engendered by the child's claim. 'For those who believe in God, no explanation is necessary. For those who do not, no explanation is possible' runs the famous foreword, but I think it immaterial whether Bernadette saw the Virgin – the Roman Catholic Church, who made her a saint, obviously believes she did – since the story is strong enough anyhow: one girl's faith against the combined scepticism of the townsfolk and the clerical establishment. George Seaton's dialogue dwindles into a series of discussions in a dusty room, and though King strives for variety by staggering the tempo and changing the groupings he cannot sustain the film over 156 minutes. We cannot blame him for the heavenly choir, but the effect is banal whenever Bernadette sees the Virgin: there are highlights on the young girl's face, while the Lady, surely better unseen by us, is played by Linda Darnell (uncredited) and shimmering like a Rockefeller Center Christmas tree. Jennifer Jones, hitherto unknown, as Bernadette is just a young girl with a piping voice; and the other mistake in an otherwise fine cast is Vincent Price, doing his usual supercilious job as the Imperial prosecutor. There are some poor lines ('So you're the urchin every idiot in France is talking about?'), but it is easy to see why the studio spent its largest advertising budget to this time – despite the fact that starless films seldom did well –

and to see why the public responded so warmly.

Its success encouraged Zanuck to embark on another venture without the guarantee of star players, and indeed at $5,200,000 **Wilson** (1944) was the most expensive film made in the U.S. up until then. It too lasted two and a half hours. The minds of movie moguls are unfathomable, and one cannot imagine what Zanuck hoped to gain other than an Oscar from this study of the chilly twenty-eighth President of the United States, remembered as the man who reluctantly led the U.S. into the First World War and who later sought to rid the country of its isolationist stance by promoting the League of Nations. The War had brought renewed interest in such matters, so at least we can understand Zanuck's claim that if the film failed he would never make another film without Betty Grable. (It did, and he didn't.) Trotti's screenplay reduces any political issues to a magazine summary, while the characters are dummies, carefully made up to resemble the originals, wheeled on and then off after saying their piece. Both Mrs Wilsons smile all the while, but as the President Alexander Knox is admirable, never playing for sympathy. King seems overwhelmed, unable to convey the sense of flux and change and inner struggle which were available in a not dissimilar tale, *The Magnificent Ambersons*.

Zanuck's belief in American democracy was given full play in **A Bell for Adano** (1945), taken from John Hersey's topical novel about the rehabilitation of a defeated people after the War – specifically about the impact of a handful of American soldiers on a small Italian town, left in ruins and without food after the Germans and the Fascists deserted it. It is the task of Major Joppolo (John Hodiak) to accustom them to peace, and he spouts to them of American democracy – mainly to the peroxide blonde Tina (Gene Tierney), who understands what he means by his Bronx upbringing: 'My dark hair was my Bronx. I wanted something very different.' The film becomes banal and anachronistic whenever she appears; Hodiak, however, is excellent, with his Clark Gable moustache, army haircut, incipient double chin and his little boy smile of enthusiasm coping with the preachiness. In

Hollywood's War Effort

Darryl F. Zanuck firmly believed in message movies, especially if they were based on bestselling novels or longrunning plays. *A Bell for Adano* remains one of the most interesting, partly because of its setting, a small Italian town to which the American military personnel are bringing their concept of democracy. The chief spokesman, happily, is the excellent John Hodiak, centre, with William Bendix, left. Among those playing the locals is Monty Banks, the Italian-born Silent screen comic (and Gracie Fields's husband).

the U.S. at least the arguments would have had a reassuring effect on a public shaken by the War. Today we may admire King's smooth direction and the studio-constructed town, meticulously researched, and photographed by Joseph LaShelle in a manner – cobbled squares shown from high above, crowds massing – which was to deeply influence the Italian film-makers themselves.

In return an Italian film, *Roma, Città Aperta* (q.v.), would help to pave the way for a more realistic cinema in America – something that was felt to be urgently required as the War ended. Some of the films we have looked at had brought the industry renewed respect, and it is these which are the valuable records of the time. They were seldom what people wanted, but despite the fact that audiences increased enormously under wartime conditions public taste was growing closer to the critics: on the home front, at least, many,

busy with war jobs, became selective about what they wanted to see. The troops felt differently, and we should perhaps be indulgent towards the escapism which for an hour or so diverted them. Nevertheless, Hollywood had become more schizophrenic than ever about its responsibilities. The tinny, cliché-ridden musicals and daft Resistance thrillers were manufactured to keep the wheels turning and the stockholders happy; on the other hand, many within the industry felt that, with the world situation so grim, the cinema-going public might be conditioned to think more than hitherto about the quality of the wares. In the meantime, the studios counted record profits, not really alarmed that a few critics in the big cities were for the first time preferring a number of British films to the home product. But it was only a mild threat to the American film industry's supremacy; and there were no others to be seen on the horizon.

24

Italy: The Tradition of Realism

FOR MOST FOREIGN audiences the Italian cinema died after the early spectacles. It had apparently produced nothing of interest since – that is, nothing that foreign distributors wished to handle. Therefore, when the first postwar Italian films were seen abroad, they were as startling as Minerva springing full-grown from the brow of Jupiter. They were regarded as revolutionary, with their apparently makeshift location shooting and their unactorish or seemingly amateur players; they considered the vitality of the medium and the worth of ordinary people of primary importance and were therefore to be preferred to the expensive product of Hollywood. 'Shoestring masterpieces' Richard Winnington called them in 1949, also saying, 'Since Rossellini (q.v.) shook the screens of America, France and Britain over three years ago the prestige of the Italian cinema has come to be the highest in the world, equivalent to that of France in the period before 1939.'

The film with which Rossellini shook the screens of America and Britain was *Roma, Città Aperta*, known as *Open City*, but it had impressed neither the Italian nor French critics who had seen it at the first postwar Cannes Festival.* France had been seeing Italian films regularly throughout the Thirties and the War years so there was nothing new in the film to excite them. In the debate that followed between British and American critics and film historians the French remained silent, though Georges Sadoul in 1953 confused the issue (in 'French Film') when he said,

erroneously, that Renoir's *Toni* 'can be traced as the source from which springs the modern Italian school of Rossellini and de Sica'. This movement was called neo-realism, and it was said to have been started by Visconti with his *Ossessione* (q.v.), tantalisingly unseen after the War because it was based on James M. Cain's 'The Postman Always Rings Twice', and M-G-M, which owned the rights, quite justifiably banned showings. *Ossessione* was screened under club conditions at the National Film Theatre in London in 1957, when critics again wondered at Visconti's 'discovery' of the miracle of neo-realism. They were reflecting an article in *Sight and Sound* of the previous year in which Giulio Cesare Castello made such claims for Visconti, and he was supported by Gianfranco Poggi, writing in *Film Quarterly* in 1960. Both can be dismissed as more than partial to the work of Visconti, and the truth became further obscured a year later, when in his book 'Il Cinema Italiano', the director Carlo Lizzani claimed that virtually all the films made under the Fascist regime were worthless.

Thus was the myth of neo-realism established, and even if the prefix does indicate a re-birth, there was only a very brief period during which Italy abandoned the realist tradition, started by the Neapolitan film-makers with such films as *Assunta Spina* in 1915 – and indeed, these were only in accord with the *verismo* school of painters (Segantini, Pellizza) and musicians (Puccini, Mascagni), working to the tradition of peasant drama. At the same time another myth was perpetuated, that of the *telefono bianco*, supposedly the essential prop of the chiefly frivolous comedies or trivial melodramas of the Mussolini

---

*It was in fact the first ever Cannes Festival, having been postponed from September 1939 due to the outbreak of War: it had been initiated in protest at the rigging of the voting of the Venice Film Festival, begun in 1934 at the behest of the cinema-orientated Mussolini government.

Italy: The Tradition of Realism

period. The postwar film-makers did not deny this, perhaps because they preferred not to look back to that time, and it was not until 1975, when the Pesaro Festival featured a number of Italian films of the Thirties, that their true quality was available for rediscovery.

The leading realist of the Thirties was Alessandro Blasetti (b. 1900), a former film critic, who in 1928 formed Augustus, a co-operative, intended to alleviate the appalling state of the Italian film industry, bankrupt after the remaking of *Quo Vadis?* by the producer Giuseppe Barattolo. The pioneer Palermi followed that extravagance with a new *Gli Ultimi Giorni di Pompei*, as disastrously expensive. The directors with some reputation – Genina, Gallone – left to work abroad, and in 1926 the government, alarmed that cinemas had only foreign films to show, set up a commission. Blasetti was a supporter of the regime, and the subject of his first film, *Sole* (1929), now partially lost, was the draining of the Pontine marshes south of Rome, a project initiated by Mussolini. It was Blasetti's desire to return to the principles of the Neapolitan school, including shooting on location, which was not new since technicians were accustomed to using sunshine instead of arc-lights; but after a peasant drama, *Terra Madre*, Blasetti turned to more theatrical material, including **La Tavola dei Poveri** (1932), which bears the influence of René Clair.

Both **1860** (1934) and **Vecchia Guardia** (1935) show the influence of the great Soviet propaganda films, and indeed the hero of *1860*, like that of *The End of St Petersburg*, is clearly meant to represent the whole Italian nation. In the same way as the Russian heroes are viewed at some distance from the leaders of the revolution, so Garibaldi is much discussed but not seen. The film superbly encapsulates the major issues concerning the Risorgimento: its inevitability, the people's determination that it could only be achieved with Garibaldi, and their speculation about the government of the country when the fighting was over. A simple story takes a Sicilian partisan to Civitavecchia to make contact with revolutionary forces, and then home again, where he takes part in a battle. The film abounds in a sense of history, and patriotism, and in documentary technique; the leading roles were played by amateurs, post-dubbed, sinc Blasetti insisted on using natural light an hence avoided the limitations then im posed by sound equipment. Post-dubbin; became general in the Italian film industry with professionals doubling for botl amateur players and stars – to the exten that the true voices of many stars were no known to the public – but with *Vecchi Guardia* Blasetti used natural sound. Hi purpose was again semi-documentary showing the rivalry and occasional battle between small town socialists and Fascists and if the death of the boy Fascist i deliberately modelled on the Nazi propa ganda films, Blasetti is by no means vi cious, as they were, about his opponents Indeed, the film is only moderate propa ganda, and the sole reason given for thi family being Fascist – and it is offered witl a shrug – is the fact that the father serve in the War. There is a finale involving the March on Rome and military songs but the film's group heroics and discurs ive nature are unsatisfactory. The Italia: public of the time avoided it.

Also a complete failure was **Il Canale degli Angeli** (1934), directed and co written (with his brother) by Francesco Pasinetti (1911–49), whose writings had been the inspiration for Blasetti, and whc was to be described by Vittorio de Sica (q.v.) as 'our conscience'. Vitally impor tant as teacher and writer on cinema, and later screenwriter and director of shorts, this sole feature allowed him to put his ideas into practice – though the film itsel bears a debt to other attempts at realism, notably *Lonesome*. It is lyrical, as were all films on the working classes except Lam precht's – a simple tale, concerning a young wife and mother tempted to run off with a sailor; it is performed by amateurs (Maurizio D'Ancora, who plays the sailor, later founded the firm of Gucci) and was entirely filmed on location, in Pasinetti's native Venice. The cost – which was not high – was supplied by the government, since Pasinetti, though himself well-to-do, took advantage of the special grant for dubbing, initiated to protect the language.

The directive was really aimed at foreign films, which began trickling through again (after a hiatus with the coming of sound) once they had been dubbed – and a tax on this dubbing was ploughed back into the local industry. This duty saved one of the ldest and in theory one of the most owerful companies, Cines, whose new hief, Emilio Cecchi, decided to film a tory by Luigi Pirandello, the only Italian uthor with an international reputation; nd to increase its chances of success broad he brought in a German director, Valter Ruttmann. **Acciaio** (1933) has ittle dialogue and, like Pasinetti's film, the implest of working-class stories – of a oung man (Piero Pastore), who returning rom conscription, finds his girlfriend (Isa Pola) engaged to his best friend (Vittorio Bellaccini). As may be expected of the man vho made *Berlin: die Symphonie einer Grossstadt*, Ruttmann in this refreshing ilm views the inhabitants and sunny treets of Terni with fondness; he includes he almost obligatory fairground sequence nd allows one-third of his running time to he steel-works where the two men work.

Also working at Cines at this time was Mario Camerini (1895–1981), whose films or the company were aggressively working-class. He had entered the industry as an ssistant to his cousin, Genina, and had tarted directing in 1923. His Silent films vere a mixed bag but, influenced by the vriting of Blasetti, Pasinetti and others, in 1929 he made *Rotaie* in the realistic tradition. *Rotaie*, a stark title, was no more ikely than *Sole* to appeal to a basically rural nd uneducated population, and the titles of both **Gli Uomini, che Mascalzone . . .** 1932) and **T'Amerò Sempre** (1933) deliberately set out to attract the least ophisticated cinemagoer: beneath both hese titles, however, lurk remarkably good films, and as far as the second is concerned the title is ironic – since the heroine (Elsa de Giorgi) is not loved for ever, as she discovers to her sadness in the maternity home. A traditional tale of orphan girl and wealthy seducer develops into an equally conventional tale of an unwed mother, but one transformed by charm and a gift for *verismo*. In an almost extraneous sequence the heroine is invited to a party at the home of her new, bourgeois, suitor (Nino Besozzi), and it is a sequence of extraordinary freshness, reminiscent of scenes in earlier films by Stiller, Von Stroheim and Clair. In this film Camerini offers a vivid portrait of the heroine's working-day, in a hairdressing salon, and *Gli Uomini, che Mascalzone . . .* is very much centred on the jobs

of its lovers – chauffeur and shopgirl. He (Vittorio de Sica) spots her (Lia Franca) as she leaves for work, and follows her tram on his bicycle through the streets of Milan: the film merely portrays the mainly comic ups and downs of their relationship till he proposes.

Vittorio de Sica (1902–74) came to the fore in Camerini's comedies, and he was particularly funny as a working-class man, underplaying to the extent that a slack jaw was his prime comic gift. In **Il Signor Max** (1937) he is a newsvendor courting the maid (Assia Noris) by day, and at night a fake-millionaire courting the mistress. Camerini said that he intended a satire on the petit bourgeois, as represented by de Sica, but that the film was liked because it was seen as a satire on the aristocracy. Despite his customary geniality it is second-rate; so is **Darò un Milione** (1935), despite a brilliant Clairish beginning in which a millionaire (de Sica) changes places with a tramp. The press takes up the story and everyone in town becomes generous to down-and-outs. The film degenerates into junketings in a circus, and is a particular disappointment as the first screen credit of Cesare Zavattini (b. 1902), who was to be so significant in de Sica's career as a director (q.v.).

Camerini also made a mirthless version

Lia Franca and Vittorio de Sica in Camerini's charming *Gli Uomini, che Mascalzone . . .* The tune they are dancing to, and the film's theme song, helped the film become a big success in France, from where the song passed to the U.S. and Britain as 'Love's Last Word is Spoken, Cheri'. Its popularity did not enable the film to be seen in either country.

623

of the old Spanish tale, now transferred to Italy, **Il Cappello a Tre Punte** (1935), primarily a starring vehicle for the Neapolitan comic team of Eduardo and Peppino De Filipo, who had been appearing in a stage version, the former as the governor and the latter as the miller. Since the film mocked authority, several sequences were censored, and the film was excoriated in the magazine run by Mussolini's son, Vittorio: Vittorio Mussolini (at least unofficially) controlled the film industry and was involved in the production of many of its propaganda films.

Two of the most famous, **Lo Squadrone Bianco** (1936) and **Scipio l'Africano** (1937) were directed respectively by Augusto Genina and Carmine Gallone, veterans recently returned to work in Italy. Each film has in common a fervour for Italy's intervention in Africa, either from historical right or sheer love of the desert, and a deadly dullness. Genina wrote his film with Joseph Peyre, from the latter's novel about the French Foreign Legion – here Italianised, but since it is Foreign Legion plot Numero Uno, they need surely not have bothered. Rejected by a woman, Mario (Antonio Centa) joins the Legion, where he becomes a hero under the stress of fire and because of the tuition of an admired disciplinarian captain (Fosco Giachetti) – the latter very much a required figure in the Fascist cinema; and we may note that the lady concerned, like any good Fascist, relents when she knows that Mario is in Africa. In the other film, it is not till the final reels that Scipio actually crosses the Mediterranean – but if the events concerned are presented somewhat incoherently they are, as in the Nazi historical films, in accordance with the true facts. The heroine is based on deMille's Cleopatra, and both the crowd scenes and battle scenes were intended to out-Hollywood Hollywood.

Since these films lack the venom of the Nazi propaganda films, it is difficult to feel about them in the same way: Nazism and Italian Fascism were as different as the character of both countries, and a rare 1959 showing of Genina's pro-Franco *L'Assedio dell'Alcazar* (1940) caused the French director Yves Boisset (q.v.) to note a true heroic style and that 'the appalling suffering of the besieged families is communicated with moving restraint.'

However, it is easy to dislike the heroic of two of the films directed by Goffred Alessandrini, a former member o Blasetti's co-operative, who at one tim had helped M-G-M dub its movies int Italian. **Luciano Serra, Pilota** (1937), wit Amadeo Nazzari in the title role, stresse Italian patriotism, as we may suppos from the participation of Vittorio Musso lini, who provided the idea for it, combin ing his love for movies with that of avia tion; it was the most popular film in Ital during this period. **Cavalleria** (1936 stresses the glory to be gained from dying for one's country in battle when th cavalry-officer hero (Nazzari) joins the ai corps; throughout, the film positivel dotes on young men in uniforms and shin boots, but in the matter of handling hi turn-of-the-century bitter-sweet romanc Alessandrini proves himself no threat to Max Ophuls.

Nevertheless, the film paved the way fo a series of period romances, and film makers turned to them gratefully as ar alternative to dealing with contemporary Italy, where Mussolini was increasingly endorsing Hitler's policies. Blasetti, after glorification of the navy in **Aldebaran** (1936), turned first to fantasy, in *La Contessa di Parma*, and then to history, in *Ettore Fieramosca*. In the latter, the Soviets again provided the inspiration, in this case, that of *Alexander Nevsky* – and the same influence lingers on in **La Cena delle Beffe** (1941), a tale of medieval Florence as taken from a dramatic poem first published in 1909. Presumably Blasetti was attracted to it as a compendium of what is expected in medieval tales – revenge, cruelty, lust and rivalry, encrusted with torture, madness and murder. It is a difficult film to like, since the entire dramatis personae is unsympathetic, including the chief protagonist, Nazzari; and as his opponent Osvaldo Valenti is monotonous.★ Clara Calamai, Dietrich-like as the woman who goes from one to the other, has at one point a breast-baring scene, apparently the first in Italian, if not world, film history. The influence of Eisenstein's film is felt also in the earlier **La Corona di Ferro** (1941), another distillation of the old legends, with their intrigues and turns of fate. There are

★In this case life imitated art, since Valenti known for his activities in torturing anti-Fascists, was shot by partisans in 1945.

other influences – *Maciste*, Lang's *Nibel-ungen*, the Fairbanks *Thief of Baghdad* – but Blasetti and his writers tried to create a legend of their own: they have a magnificent tournament in the middle, after which the action is sufficiently ludicrous as to be riveting.

One of Blasetti's writers was Mario Soldati (b. 1906), master of the period film proper. A successful novelist, he scripted several movies, often for Camerini, regarding the cinema as a means of making money in order to pursue his true occupation. However, turning director, he allows no indication of condescension in **Piccolo Mondo Antico** (1941) – indeed, no better film of the period exists. As with Max Ophuls's *Werther*, which may have influenced it, it tries for a real insight into the way people lived; it is not a romance, but it is romantic, inasmuch as most of the characters are fired by the thought of the Risorgimento – which eventually separates Franco (Massimo Serato) from his

wife (Alida Valli). The latter role is exquisitely played, and Ada Dondini, playing Franco's grandmother, is a magnificent villainess. There are also such matters as a secret marriage and a suppressed will, to remind us that the source is the nineteenth-century novelist, Antonio Fogazzaro; the final section, when the couple are separated by grief, is both literary and lacking the momentum of the rest but nevertheless absorbing. With **Malombra** (1942), Soldati turned to an earlier novel by the same writer – and an inferior one, being pseudo-gothic with intimations of Ibsen. Like the other film, this is one detailed, elegant and surprising, but though there are some first-rate sequences towards the very end, Soldati loses interest halfway through the long running time. One handicap is Isa Miranda, a far better actress than most of the Italian ladies of this time but playing passion conventionally and looking more like a modern glamour queen than a nineteenth-century orphan. The role is

The early films of Mario Soldati are notable for their exquisite recreation of period detail. Both *Piccolo Mondo Antico*, with Alida Valli, and *Malombra*, ABOVE, were based on novels by Antonio Fogazzaro and set in and around Lake Garda.

625

that of a self-willed girl so determined to re-live past events that she is prepared to destroy both those who stand in her way and others innocently involved. Andrea Checchi is her major victim, perhaps the natural son of her guardian, and the adaptation seems uncertain as to whether he or the girl should be the chief protagonist. Both films have in common the setting of the Italian lakes, lovingly photographed, and art direction by the brilliant Gastone Medin, responsible for that of every major Italian historical film of the period. Of the two, this is the lesser, but Soldati's quest for realism in this particular subject has resulted in a film like no other – one more taking, but less satisfying, than any Hollywood gothic romance of the time, and far ahead of its French counterpart, *L'Eternel Retour* (q.v.).

One of Soldati's writers was Renato Castellani (b. 1913), who had also worked with Blasetti and Camerini: he in turn made his directing debut with **Un Colpo di Pistola** (1942), with Soldati among his writers. This school of film-making had by now been termed 'calligraphic', meaning that as much attention was paid to the method of telling as to plot, and this particular film, based on a story by Pushkin, is extremely literary, depending for its suspense on two separate if linked episodes told to a French novelist by the chief protagonist. He (Fosco Giachetti) is a Russian officer who thinks he has lost his fiancée (Assia Noris) to his best friend (Antonio Centa), and their separate dilemmas are almost ruined by Miss Noris, who, correctly coquettish in the first half, merely poses as the desperate heroine of the second. She was one of the several somewhat artificial film stars thrown out of work by the return to realism in the postwar period; as the solo-billed star we may regard her as less than an asset to Castellani, whose direction is academic and lacking the spirit of Soldati.

Ferdinando Maria Poggioli (1897–1945), another disciple of Blasetti, came to prominence at this time, after working on short documentaries. **Addio Giovinezza!** (1941) is based on the play by Sandro Camasio and Nino Oxilia which had been filmed at least three times before (twice by Genina). By concentrating on the Torino locations and period detail Poggioli robbed it of much of its senti-

mentality. Unfortunately, Maria Denis was another actress identified with a certain cinematic behaviour, in this case suffering; she is certainly never wholly bad, and in the first half is delightful as the shopgirl who attracts a student lover (Adriano Rimoldi), only to lose him temporarily to a woman of the world (Clara Calamai) – and then permanently as a result of her jealousy. **Gelosia** (1943) starts brilliantly, with a murder, and it turns out that the killer is the Marquess (Roldano Lupi), jealous of the man he forced his mistress (Luisa Ferida) to marry: their eventual fates never involve us overmuch, since Signor Lupi is weak in a role needing the young James Mason, but the evocation of rural Sicily in the nineteenth century is splendidly done. **Sissignora** (1941) is set in Genoa, and recounts the adventures of a serving-maid (Miss Denis), after she has attracted the attentions of her spinster employers' favourite nephew. This is probably the most ingratiating of Poggioli's films, notable for its sequences in market and dance-hall. Every room in a Poggioli film is richly characterised, and **Sorelle Materassi** (1943) offers a particularly interesting villa just outside Florence, where impoverished spinster sisters, again played by Irma and Emma Grammatica, sew to restore the family wealth. This threatens to be devoured by a completely amoral nephew, played in appropriately sullen fashion by Massimo Serato, whose misadventures, financial and sexual, are faithfully rendered from Aldo Palazzeschi's popular novel: but the hero's final pursuit by a wealthy Argentinian (Miss Calamai) belongs to any crass minor comedy, as if the homosexual Poggioli had no interest in seeing his stud hero settle into domesticity.

Another historical subject to be tackled was **La Tosca** (1940), which Jean Renoir was invited to direct. He accepted, because he wanted to 'experience the complicated magic of Italian baroque', and because the French authorities wished to do everything possible to keep the friendship of Italy. The subject was apt: a French play (by Sardou) with an Italian setting, but Renoir had shot only the opening sequence – the galloping horses – when the French ambassador recommended that he leave. Rome was increasingly full of Germans, and the Italian police were turning a blind eye to their strong-arm tactics. Renoir handed over the film to Carl Koch, a colleague who had worked with him in France (and the husband of Lotte Reininger). Obviously, it was safer in the hands of a German, for no one could have missed the analogy of Rome under a foreign-appointed governor – especially with Michel Simon's Scarpia, as petty as he is arrogant. Puccini's music is used in the background, and the only weakness is Imperio Argentina in the title role, always too frisky and inadequate in the emotional moments. Renoir said later that it was a pity that Koch never directed another film, which on this evidence it is; however, the film's most striking feature is its use of the Castel St Angelo and the streets and churches of Rome.

One reason for the sudden crop of period films was the existence of Cinecittà, built by Mussolini, and opened in 1937 with the intention of rivalling Hollywood. After the decrepit studios in France, Renoir and his colleagues were amazed by it, while Italian film-makers were only too easily seduced into availing themselves of its facilities. **Via delle Cinque Lune** (1942), though ostensibly set near the Piazza Navone, was filmed entirely within Cinecittà, despite its being a production of the progressive film school, Centro Sperimentale di Cinematografica;* indeed the director of the film, Luigi Chiarini, had founded that in 1935, with Mussolini's blessing. It is an entertaining film, from a sound Balzacian novel by Matilde Serao, about a dragonish woman (Olga Solbelli) who is sexually drawn to her prospective stepson – and the attraction is not only reciprocated, but after the affair has begun he becomes as rapacious as she. In this role, Andrea Checchi once more demonstrates his versatility, and the scenes of the two of them together with the lady's familiar indicate Chiarini's delight in villainy. The film, the best of the half dozen that he made, is another brilliant evocation of the last century, despite a rather ponderous style. Chiarini (later a critic), who became the first professor of film in Italy and director of the Venice Film Festival during the Sixties, was already at this time a theoretician of film. He had published a book on the subject with Umberto

*The prospect of lecturing to its students was another reason Renoir had come to Italy.

Barbaro – who was, with Pasinetti, his fellow writer on this film.

These were the apostles of neo-realism: Chiarini and Barbaro propounded their ideas both in a magazine called *Cinema* and as lecturers at the Centro Sperimentale. **La Peccatrice** (1940), scripted by Pasinetti and Chiarini for the director Amleto Palermi, was considered a step in the right direction, since it was a contemporary story with an implied social criticism. Palermi's *Cavalleria Rusticana* (1939), based on Verga, was also admired, and he himself is a key figure, since he too chose to work with Zavattini, Barbaro and Aldo Vergano. It is not surprising that Barbaro and Vergano, both Marxists, returned to the principles of Blasetti, since they had belonged to his pre-Talkie collective. Students and critics emerging from the Centro Sperimentale, such as (q.v.) Antonioni and Giuseppe De Santis, both future directors, were scornful of the calligraphic school, claiming that its conjuncture of cinema and literature was arid, and at a time when cinema memories were short, such films as *Il Canale degli Angeli* and *Vecchia Guardia* seemed to belong to prehistory. In fact, the essential tradition of Italian films had been maintained, with only a few exceptions, for the working lives of their characters were considered as relevant to the plots as their emotional problems. The demand for a 'new' cinema was not only exaggerated, but the movement must be considered in the light of political frustration. Those mainly concerned disliked both the War and the government, yet, unable publicly to express their feelings about either, knew that the solution for the industry did not lie with period romances. Paradoxically, they admired both the writings and the documentary-like work of Francesco De Robertis (1902–59), who remained as staunchly Fascist as Blasetti and Chiarini had been.

De Robertis, a former naval officer and theatre producer, was appointed head of the naval film service, for which he wrote and directed **Uomini sul Fondo** (1941), an account of a submarine stuck on the ocean during routine manoeuvres. It is entirely staged, or re-enacted, by amateurs picked from the service, and what humour there is is derived from the reaction of the men, while the drama arises from their

Italy: The Tradition of Realism

The importance of the Italian neo-realist movement overshadowed all other discussions of international cinema in the postwar period, and since foreign critics saw so few of the films the origins of the movement were wrongly attributed – and were certainly not found to have taken root during the War. One early film of the movement is Blasetti's *Quattro Passi fra le Nuvole* with Adriana Benetti and Gino Cervi. Among other matters, it is set in the milieu of working people, and to the protagonists their means of earning are essential to the plot, as would be true of all the neo-realist films.

anxiety and the mechanics of rescue. When the last men are finally raised from the sea, the waiting fleet gives vent to a show, recalling *Potemkin*, with the crews clustered in similar picturesque fashion on the rigging. De Robertis later supervised *La Nave Bianca*, the first film made by Rossellini, his assistant on *Uomini sul Fondo*, and after the fall of Mussolini organised the remains of the Fascist industry till Venice was taken by the Allies.

Meanwhile, those hoping for a new cinema were also encouraged by de Sica's third film as a director, **Teresa Venerdi** (1941). Though the title refers to the orphan girl (Adriana Benetti) who wins her hero in 'Daddy Long Legs' fashion, the true subject is the love life of the hero, a penniless young doctor, played by de Sica himself. His mistress is a volatile music-hall star (Anna Magnani), and she and her seedy milieu are portrayed as amusingly as are the guardians of the orphanage, while the sympathy extended to the unfortunate girls prefigures the later films that Zavattini, here uncredited, wrote with de Sica.

Zavattini is responsible for introducing satire and feeling into the Italian cinema. Neither quality had been entirely absent, for both were encompassed within the affection Camerini and Poggioli felt for their characters; but other leading film-

makers had tried to be detached, avoiding the cheap tricks by which the makers of slapstick comedies and sentimental dramas hoped to find their audiences. Moreover, Zavattini believed that these qualities sprang from the everyday, a theory that he was able to put into practice in **Quattro Passi fra le Nuvole** (1942), which Blasetti directed and helped to write – and the result may be considered creatively theirs, since the customary plethora of Italian screenwriters is often suspect, i.e. they are often friends or relatives of the producer, and should only be considered seriously when they have other credits. In this case, the film is much warmer than Blasetti's other work, almost certainly because Zavattini contributed to both story and screenplay. His stated intention throughout his career was to build a film round one day in the life of an ordinary man. Such films had been attempted before, and they all begin, as this one does, with the ringing of an alarm-clock and someone rising from bed. Paolo Bianchi (Gino Cervi) is almost aggressively ordinary, a salesman dependent on commission, in his mid-thirties and with a nagging wife. He sets out for his usual working day, but by a series of circumstances, each of them slight yet detailed, he finds himself by the end of it pretending to be the husband of a pregnant girl (Miss Benetti) and spending the night with her in the family home. The title, the 'four steps in the clouds', refers to his sensation at returning to the country, and the movie, charmingly filmed in the open-air, is light-hearted, clever and refreshing. Since it was hailed as a triumph of neo-realism when shown in Britain and the U.S. in 1948 – the only Italian film of the war years to reach either country at that time – it is worth noting that the scene of the coach-passengers all singing in a bus is indebted to *It Happened One Night*.

The most significant of all neo-realist films is, however, **Fari nella Nebbia** (1942), directed by Gianni Franciolini (1910–60), who was associated with the avant-garde during most of his stay in France. He had returned to Italy to direct one documentary and just one feature prior to this one. Apart from tenuous connections a decade later – one section of a dim, episodic film, *Siamo Donne*, to which Visconti and Rossellini also contributed, and as director of a Zavattini script,

Buongiorno Elefante! – he has no link with the movement, nor have any of the several writers who worked on the script. Violently demotic, set in and around Savona, it tells of the broken marriage of a truck-driver, and how the wife is tempted by a flash-Harry, while the husband (Fosco Giachetti) takes up with the 'fast' Piera (Luisa Ferida). This may well have been the first time European filmgoers – Hollywood's delicacy in such matters was all-pervading – had seen adulterous lovers in bed together, and Franciolini is equally honest with his settings, moving from cluttered rooms to doleful bars to the ramshackle trucking offices. His direction fails, however, to inject momentum, and his ending is particularly poor.

Its significance is in its influence on a much greater film, **Ossessione** (1943), with which Visconti introduced an element of subversion into the neo-realist movement. Mussolini was shown the film privately, and the censors banned it because they disapproved of the protagonists, a grubby couple who murder the lady's older husband in order to continue fornicating. Visconti may have begun his preparations before seeing Franciolini's film, and he may have shot some material before the authorities interrupted shooting; but the credited photographer is Aldo Tonti, who had shot *Fari nella Nebbia*, and the two films have much more in common with each other, both as to tone and visual quality, than Visconti's does to his source (its plot-line apart).

Luchino Visconti (1906–76) was of the ducal family, more interested in horses and couture till Coco Chanel introduced him to Jean Renoir, who took him on to the production team of *Partie de Campagne*. He had stayed with *La Tosca* after Renoir's departure, by which time he decided that he wanted to be a director. It was Renoir who recommended Cain's novel – already filmed in France* – and Visconti had started work on it, without benefit of permission, when the censor refused to sanction his first project, an adaptation of Verga. Visconti's ambitions determined him to undermine complacency in the cinema, but as a Fascist he did not set out to challenge authority; he did not become a Marxist, at least openly, till it was safe to

*As *Le Dernier Tournant*, from which Visconti also borrowed details.

do so. In his version James M. Cain's taut, legal thriller has become an updating of Boccaccio, though with only two scenes which could be described as erotic – the first quick, sudden mating, and the later reconciliation on the sands of the estuary. Giovanna (Clara Calamai) is tired, bored with her husband and with drudgery: she wastes no time when she sees Gino (Massimo Girotti) and by the following day is not only rejuvenated but in thrall to sexual passion. In the book, their relationship falls apart under the strain imposed by the investigations; Visconti burdens Gino with the guilt of a Macbeth and, though he did not realise it, recedes into convention.

Gino, having persuaded Giovanna to run off with him, immediately finds her an encumbrance, and falls in with an itinerant actor (Elio Marcuzzo), in a relationship which ends in violence, as would several such relationships in Visconti's later films (q.v.). He may have believed that destruction was an element of homosexuality, or at least a way of making it acceptable to audiences at the time: the implication is gratuitous, but confirms what the brilliance of Calamai's performance (the role was meant for an even stronger actress, Magnani, who was pregnant) almost disguises – the inference that Visconti was romantically inclined towards his leading

Massimo Girotti and Clara Calamai in *Ossessione*, the film with which the aristocratic Luchino Visconti hoped to challenge the Fascist regime, since its subjects are infidelity and murder – social evils which the government claimed to have eradicated (which is one reason, since they are the staples of fiction, Italian film-makers had been concentrating on period films). The film was promptly banned, but was shown when Italy was liberated a few months later; for copyright reasons it was not seen publicly abroad till fairly recently.

male character. Everything about Gino is approved of to the point of inconsistency: his rolling-stone disposition; his preparation for the sexual act, posing like a figure in Grand Opera; and his reaction to the permanence of his relationship to his mistress – drinking, and leaving her for bed after a busy day at the inn, with a solitary meal and the debris in the kitchen to be tackled. The film is visually memorable – the small trattoria on the bank of one of the tributaries of the Po, the straight road disappearing into the marshes, and the interiors of the inn, like an opera-set and larger than those in *Fari nella Nebbia*. Against the realistic sound of the amateur concert at Ancona, there are the pseudo-Puccini fugues of doom on the soundtrack. Visconti would both explore the tenets of neo-realism, and become a director of Grand Opera; his films would in themselves represent the eternal dichotomies of the Italian cinema – the realistic on the one hand and the epic and grandiose on the other.

De Sica's **I Bambini ci Guardano** (1944) also examines the consequences of an illicit affair – from the point of view of a small boy (Luciano de Ambrosis). We only glimpse matters which he does not comprehend, such as the furtive sexual relations of other grown-ups which impinge upon his life, or his mother's fascination with her lover. At one point the child's parents are reconciled and spend a vacation in Alassio – which has the same liberating effect on de Sica as the Po estuary had on Visconti, allowing him to make witty comments on the pleasantries in the dining-room and the festivities on the beach. In apportioning no blame to the grown-ups, the screenplay retains the traditional detachment, but it introduces to the pre-occupations of the neo-realists that of responsibility, as the title indicates. It was the first film directed by de Sica in which he did not appear. He became a director, he said, from vanity – and a sense of righteousness, after the press had criticised a performance he had given under Gallone's direction and Gallone had refused to listen to his own comments on that performance. In this case he had decided to film a novel by a friend, 'Prico' by C. G. Viola, and he had sought Zavattini's collaboration because of his dissatisfaction with the original screenplay. They had not

known each other at the time both had worked on *Darò un Milione*, but had later met socially, at which time de Sica had been impressed with Zavattini's views on screenwriting.

Nevertheless, Zavattini was still engaged in such trite exercises as **Il Birichino di Papà** (1943), directed by Raffaello Matarazzo, a vehicle for fifteen-year-old Chiaretta Gelli – Italy's Deanna Durbin – and the film's sole virtue is to indicate how well Zavattini understood the construction of the early Durbin films, even if, with these collaborators, he was unable to duplicate it. In June 1943 the word 'neo-realism' had just been coined by Barbaro in an appreciation of *Ossessione*, but feeling that it should lead to the rejection of the light comedies and calligraphic films in favour of Italian films in the manner of *Quai des Brumes*. Meanwhile, shut off from the rest of the world's films other than the French and those of Nazi Germany – which were ignored – Soldati was imitating more recent and far more interesting French cinema. **Quartieri Alti** (1944), a version both of an Italian novel and of Anouilh's play, 'Le Rendez-vous de Senlis', owes much to such films as Autant-Lara's *Douce* (q.v.), with its clever, but artificial, conversations and intrigues.

Inevitably such films were swept away by **Roma, Città Aperta** (1945), which the Italian public liked as much as their critics had disliked it: but would the furore it created abroad have been quite the same had British and American critics known that Rossellini's two previous films, *Un Pilota Ritorna* and *L'Uomo della Croce*, had been, at best, mediocre tributes to the Fascist war effort? Roberto Rossellini (1906–77) had started in films as an amateur, and had been welcomed into the industry as a writer by Vittorio Mussolini; he had assimilated the documentary technique he had learnt with De Robertis, to the extent that *Roma, Città Aperta*, a study of the city during the last days of the Occupation, was said by some foreign critics to have been filmed surreptitiously at that time. Its improvised appearance – due to the shortage of equipment – and its formlessness were considered a virtue; it is certainly facile and often self-conscious, but it is deservedly a monument, as engrossing and exciting now as when it came out. It follows the fortunes of the hunted

Resistance leader (Marcello Pagliero) and a pregnant widow (Anna Magnani), whom one of his colleagues hopes to marry and who is shot down in the street. The film's ingredients also include a kindly priest (Aldo Fabrizi) and a consideration of the German authorities, together with a lesbian collaborationist, and the silly young tart (Maria Michi) led into their circle for the sake of a fur-coat. Whatever its reception at Cannes, the film was rapturously received in Paris; critics everywhere were united in preferring the peasant-like Anna Magnani (1908–73), with her power and humour, to the songs of Bernadette and Betty Grable.

They also preferred **Paisà** (1946) to the well-meaning *Bell for Adano*; like its predecessor, *Paisà* is less a tale of battle than a portrait of Italy at war. One is about the Germans leaving; the other is about the Americans arriving, and it follows them from Palermo to the Po, in a series of anecdotes with anti-climaxes and no easy solutions: an Italian girl leads a group of G.I.s on a night sortie, who sneer when she is killed by German snipers; in Naples, a drunken negro soldier has his boots stolen by an urchin; in Rome, a G.I. (Gar Moore) tells a prostitute (Maria Michi) of the sweet and pure girl he had met on his last visit, failing to recognise that they are the same woman; in Florence, an Italian-speaking American nurse and a partisan move through the beleaguered city with the cool acceptance of death we noted in *Roma, Città Aperta*; in the Romagna, three padres, Catholic, Jewish and Protestant, are received in a remote monastery – the best and only comic episode; and in the marshes of the Po, when the O.S.S. and the partisans are finally routed by the enemy, the former are spared under international convention but the partisans are dumped summarily into the river, bound, gagged and presumably still living. The film fades on this image, and like the one which began the sequence, it offers the most emotional comment on how the Italians felt about the War. The impact of this film remains extraordinary, though to a greater degree than *Roma, Città Aperta* it arouses the suspicion that its virtues are largely due to necessity and chance. Both are tremendous films, and given the jagged nature of Rossellini's contribution, it would be unwise to suggest, as did many observers at the

time, that the major creative force was that of screenwriter Sergio Amidei (b. 1904): yet the brilliance, particularly of *Paisà*, is in the concept and the dialogue.

Amidei worked with Zavattini and de Sica on **Sciuscià** (1946), but the essential contribution seems to have been that of Zavattini, for de Sica, offered the subject by an Italian-American producer, Paolo William Tamburella, initially found it too theatrically treated, particularly since it was based on fact. Like Rossellini's two films, it created a sensation abroad. James Agee found it 'different from almost any other movie you care to name [because it concerns] the ultimate absoluteness of responsibility of each human being' – and it is a responsibility far deeper than that of de Sica's earlier film about childhood, *I Bambini ci Guardano*. De Sica said later that the most urgent necessity of the time was to 'redeem our guilt' for the Fascist years, and as we can read into that film some criticism of a guilty couple – and in the Rossellini films that of a foreign power – *Sciuscià* is unquestionably an indictment of all society. It is therefore a vital addition to the premises on which neo-realism was founded. With its amateur cast, its sour, grim locations and uncommercial subject,

It is now curious to read the contemporary British and American review of *Roma, Città Aperta* and *Paisà* – because, for instance, many critics insisted that all the players were amateurs, which they were not. The director, Rossellini, was widely said to be a genius, a fact disproved by his subsequent films, though these two remain extraordinarily impressive. This is a scene from *Paisà*, with a part-time whore (Maria Michi) taking home a drunken soldier (Gar Moore), who only wants to talk about the girl he had encountered when last in Rome.

Italy: The Tradition of Realism

Andrea Checchi and Vivi Gioi in *Caccia Tragica*, De Santis's haunting study of rural Italy in the aftermath of war. Set in Piedmont, it begins in the muddy lanes and fields where the peasants hope to earn a few lire for food; it ends as shown here, with two criminals trapped in their hide-out, and the director moves easily between realism and melodrama. There are, incidentally, good reasons why this still is reminiscent of the one of *Quai des Brumes*.

de Sica was able to get backing only on the strength of the world reception of *Roma, Città Aperta* – and, as with that film, *Sciuscià* picks its characters from the streets of the capital, the fourteen-year-old orphan Pasquale (Franco Interlenghi), and the younger Giuseppe (Rinaldo Smordini), equally rootless but with an older brother, whose black market dealings will entice them away from shining the shoes of G.I.s and eventually land them in a reformatory. The film is not an object-lesson in what happens to homeless children, but it is about the prison gates that close as adulthood approaches. From the first sad, chance involvement in crime, the boys lose the freedom that is the right of all children, till in jail they are coarsened and lose their sustaining feature, the friendship of their earlier lives. The film allows few culprits: the police are harassed and the school authorities without imagination. A breezy old doctor observes of one chronically sick boy that his solution lies not in prison or in sanatorium but in vagrancy, for then he would have the chance to survive. The lawyers, possibly representing that section of society which should know better, are depicted as mercenary, shifty and doddery, while the boys are sometimes treated in the sentimental manner of 'Emil und die Detektive'; and it is surely a mistake to use the horse, owned by the boys, as a symbol of the soul – if by no means as blatantly as in *Viva Zapata!* (q.v.), whence it was copied. De Sica's approach was again dispassionate, or seemingly so, and that was what made *Sciuscià* revolutionary among polemical films: the indignation of de Sica and his colleagues was so palpable that they had no need to guide audiences towards the desired reaction.

It is precisely that passion which **Il Sole Sorge Ancora** (1946) lacks. A rural version of *Roma, Città Aperta*, it is a vivid portrait of one small Italian town from the Armistice in 1943 to the rising against the Germans in 1945. The characters are divided into the partisans and their supporters, and those who collaborated with, or tolerated the German occupiers, chief among whom is Major Heinrich, played with monocle and cropped haircut by Massimo Serato. The film is also conventional in other ways; the hint of lesbianism may have been inspired by Rossellini's film, and the opening scene, of the hero (Vittorio Duse) in a brothel, may be a borrowing from or a homage to, the opening of *Acciaio* – since the bordellos in both are incidental to the events that follow. The portrait of the collaborators is the most unflattering yet, which may be a reason why export was discouraged – though the film received some recognition, as *Outcry*, when shown in New York in 1949. It is the best film directed by Aldo Vergano, who had written *Sole* for Blasetti: he believed himself unjustly neglected at the expense of his colleagues, and wrote a bitter autobiography before he died in 1957.

His co-writers on this film included Carlo Lizzani and Giuseppe De Santis (b. 1917), the latter having moved directly from film criticism – he notably savaged Rossellini's *L'Uomo della Croce* – to working on the screenplay of *Ossessione*. He made an impressive start as a director on **Caccia Tragica** (1947), which is even more valuable than *Il Sole Sorge Ancora* in its portrait of the chaos and confusion of postwar Italy. Based on fact, the film follows the consequences when a group of *banditi* have stolen the annual payroll of one of the newly-formed workers' co-operatives. This act was born of desperation, and when the co-operative sets out to pursue the thieves, they come across service veterans marching to protest against the lack of work and bread. The *banditi* themselves, whom we assume at first to have strayed in from a superior gangster picture, turn out to be an assortment thrown together by the times – a German ex-soldier, a girl (Vivi Gioi) called Lili Marlene since she had been a collaborator, and her lover (Andrea Checchi), a victim of the German concentration camps. It is increasingly clear that these two are meant to represent the guilty of Italy, and that they are modelled on the doomed couple of *Quai des Brumes*: Barbaro, who looked to that film for inspiration in defining neo-realism, is one of the writers of this, together with the director, Lizzani, Michelangelo Antonioni and Zavattini. This is perhaps the key film of the movement, with all its strengths and weaknesses. At the same time it is an honest and socialist-inspired portrait of the working classes, and a thriller which can as easily encompass 'grotesque' cinema, as when the hero (Massimo Girotti) finds himself surrounded by children in masks.

Alberto Lattuada (b. 1914), a former screenwriter who had begun directing in the calligraphic style in 1942, took advantage of the new and freer shooting methods to make **Il Bandito** (1946), while aiming for tragedy, though both here and in **Senza Pietà** (1948) the effect is often closer to melodrama. Both films are further portraits of Italy in the aftermath of war, the former concerning the returning soldier (Amadeo Nazzari), who is appalled to discover the falling-away of morals in his native town but is eventually another contributor to this – as driven by his wife (Anna Magnani). *Senza Pietà* is set in Livorno, where a number of American deserters had settled to form a small colony – inevitably of social outcasts – and one among them, a negro (John Kitzmiller) falls in love with a prostitute (Carla Del Poggio). Lattuada's handling, supposedly detached, like that of de Santis recalls Carné: his obvious sympathy for the lovers created problems for its American distributor.

In **Vivere in Pace** (1946) Luigi Zampa returns to the war years and brings comedy to neo-realism. The setting is a village the War has passed by, though that does not mean that its inhabitants believe the local Fascist when he claims that his side is winning it. Two escaped American prisoners arrive, one of whom can be passed off as a local to the solitary German corporal; the other, however, is a negro (Kitzmiller), and must be kept hidden. The inevitable confrontation goes not as expected, since the local wine has had its effect on both belligerents, but it underlines Zampa's purpose throughout, which is the absurdity of war.

The fragility of neo-realism was apparent in Rossellini's **Germania, Anno Zero** (1947), written with Lizzani, and, for the German dialogue, Max Kolpet. The attempt was to portray the former ally and enemy coping in the aftermath of War, and devastated Berlin was to provide the contrast with the well-preserved Italian cities. The protagonist is again a child, Edmund Köhler (Edmund Möschke), the family breadwinner, except for what his sister makes by being friendly to the occupying forces. Father is sick in the apartment which is shared with another family; the brother has never registered, so cannot work. A pederastic teacher (Erich Gühne) uses the boy to sell a record of a Hitler speech to some G.I.s, and he also persuades the boy to dispose of his father, since as an invalid he is useless to society. The boy duly administers poison and then commits suicide, clearly atoning for German guilt, a matter otherwise mentioned only in passing. As Hitler on the record boasts of victory, the camera roams across the ruins of Berlin, and that is virtually all that Rossellini has to say about Germany in the year zero. As Adam Helmer observed at the time in *Sequence*, 'its pessimism, the so-called tragedy . . . is false and concocted, a manoeuvre rather than a conviction.'

It is now clear that **Il Miracolo** (1948) is no improvement. At the time consideration of its merits was overshadowed by its content and the consequent censors' edicts; after being banned outright in Britain, it was, wrote Dilys Powell, 'being talked about as if it were a cross between the works of the Marquis de Sade and the First Epistle to the Corinthians'. The story was

Italy: The Tradition of Realism

By 1948 the Italian cinema was beginning to exhaust the War and its aftermath as a subject, but for many life remained a struggle against poverty, which was what Visconti wished to show in *La Terra Trema*. The actors were amateurs, the *pescatori Siciliani* so proudly announced on the credits: this one played the film's chief protagonist, seen here with his brother in the film.

written by Federico Fellini (q.v.). It tells of a stranger who plies with wine and makes pregnant a shepherdess (Anna Magnani) – she only too willing, since she sees in him a dead ringer for St Joseph, with the consequent belief that the child she carries is the Messiah. As the villagers cast her out, an allegorical point is made, but the piece is merely an anecdote, a vehicle for Anna Magnani, as is clear from the dedication, which is to her 'art'; it was originally part of a longer film called *Amore*, but the other section, a version of Cocteau's 'La Voix Humaine', was lopped off by Rossellini and has hardly been seen since. Certainly Magnani is one of the few actresses convincing as a peasant, and the views of village and sea accorded to the principles of Italian cinema at the time. **La Macchina Ammazzacattivi** (1948) is set in a small

seaport south of Naples and is about a photographer who finds that his camera has magic powers: as he photographs snapshots in his studio, their subjects expire in another part of the town, and he embarks on a scheme to kill the wicked, the greedy and the corrupt. Eduardo De Filippo, with Fabrizio Sarazani, provided the story of this rural whimsy, but in Rossellini's hands it is neither *comédie noire* nor the sunny comedy suggested by the setting. It is merely undisciplined and completely unfunny: Rossellini later referred to it as 'an isolated experiment' and in fact it went virtually unseen. There were some isolated showings★ four years after completion, in 1952, and despite his international reputation it was not considered of sufficient merit to be exported.

Had the neo-realist movement depended on Rossellini, it would have died with these two films, the one artificial and the other quite pointless. However, Visconti was already at work on **La Terra Trema** (1948), which he envisaged as a great new opening for the movement. Indeed, he was so determined to make the most of neo-realism that the dialogue was recorded in the Sicilian patois of its fishermen characters, all of them played by amateurs. That fact limited its commercial reception in Italy, and when Visconti, with aristocratic disdain, refused to re-dub, showings were confined to the film societies. He was also unable to film the other two episodes of what was to have been a trilogy: this one bears its original subtitle, *Episodio del Mare*; the source is Verga's 'I Malavoglio', which Visconti had abandoned before *Ossessione*, and the other two parts were to have concerned the sulphur mines and farming. The running time of just under three hours is as ambitious as the title, with its echoes of revolution: indeed, it was meant to be a revolutionary manifesto, proclaiming in a foreword the truth of the conditions depicted as 'true of all countries where men exploit men'. At the centre is the Valastro family, of Aci Trezza in Sicily, living and working as they have done for generations. They are kept poor by the wholesalers, in an agreement not to offer competitive terms: 'Ntoni Valastrato decides to confront them by going direct

★According to some commentators it was never publicly seen.

634

to the retailers, and the family support him by mortgaging the house. The elements defeat him; his girl will not speak to him, and his brother is lured away by a stranger in plus-fours who hands round Lucky Strikes. Home gone – squalid enough, goodness knows – and head bowed, he goes to work for the mocking wholesalers. The men and the buildings, the sea and the sky, marvellously photographed by G. R. Aldo, with Gianni di Venanzo as his cameraman, coalesce into one gigantic fresco – a word used advisedly, since the characters are one-dimensional. Visconti's response to the poverty of fishermen was intellectual: they are found to be stoic, long-suffering, hard-working and tolerant – and thus without the anger and greed of the characters of de Sica and Zavattini. If we note that the men are far better looking than the women, and prey to them (according to the commentary) that is not necessarily untrue; in general the film is free of Visconti's operatic graces, and is made with such imaginative grasp that it is powerful for its entire length. It is a rigorous film, and of great purity; it is one of the twin peaks of neo-realism.

The other is **Ladri di Biciclette** (1948), which is also probably the greatest film of the movement. While *La Terra Trema* languished in the vaults, this film of de Sica's opened up vast new audiences abroad for foreign language films. Considered then a great film, partly because it concerned poverty, its sometimes clumsy technique was also admired, though curiously the word most often occurring in reviews is 'flawless'. It is the least formidable of great films; it is transparently honest. Zavattini wrote it from a story by Luigi Bartolini, and as a Marxist he was perhaps grinding an axe; de Sica seems merely to have been content to illuminate a small corner of existence. Its reputation has dimmed, since most people cry during at least part of it and remember it as sentimental – which it is not, even remotely. It is harsh and hard and cold-eyed. Antonio (Lamberto Maggiorani, a non-professional, as were all the cast) gets a job as a bill-sticker provided he has a bicycle, and his wife sells the sheets to get that out of pawn. On the first day it is stolen, and the police are indifferent – an intimation of bureaucracy which accounts for much of the film's success with post-war audiences. With his son (Enzo Staiola), Antonio combs Rome for the thief, who goes into an epileptic fit, which is probably faked, when caught. Before a hostile crowd, Antonio speaks to another indifferent policeman: 'If you knew what this meant to me,' and it must be the most understated plea in the history of films. The boy watching his father's eventual humiliation provides one of the most pessimistic of all endings, and it is odd that Richard Winnington, who admired the film inordinately, should have allowed his left-wing viewpoint to suggest to him that Antonio would get help because he had friends. Discussion is academic: poverty may not have gone from Rome, but the city has changed out of all recognition – this is a mean provincial town, with hardly a car in sight. There are few trees and little cement, since de Sica used locations near the Tiber; he filmed in odd days, often Sundays, over a long period, and the total cost was the equivalent of $25,000 or £9,000, supplied by a consortium of three businessmen after de Sica had failed to get backing from the film industries of Italy, France and Britain – having journeyed in desperation to Paris and London, since *Sciuscià* had been successful in both cities.

Despite the prestige accruing from its foreign success, the Italian film industry continued to loathe it. It rejoiced instead in the success abroad of **Riso Amaro** (1948) – a success which was to damage the industry to the present day, so that it is always looking for ways to recapture the world market. That success was made by the stills of Silvana Mangano, up to her calves in the rice-fields, with huge thighs above black stockings which looked infinitely worth the parting. Sex is certainly provided by the story, during the course of which Mangano divides her attentions between a police sergeant (Raf Vallone) and a small-time thief (Vittorio Gassmann), and the melodrama drives out any serious comment intended on the exploitation of the migratory female workers in the Po Valley rice-fields. Giuseppe De Santis directed, having made a conscious decision to abandon the principles he had preached as a critic and had demonstrated in *Caccia Tragica*. Paradoxically, he said about this time that the Italian contemporary he most admired was Visconti, since he alone refused to consider the world market when making a film – and yet he deliberately

Italy: The Tradition of Realism

As the neo-realist movement began to die, it started to turn back to the traditional Italian tales of bucolic rape and murder. De Santis's *Riso Amaro* tried without success to be a serious portrait of a rural community. Sex was prominent – one reason the film was so popular in Anglo-Saxon countries – and its chief exponent was Silvana Mangano.

aimed *Riso Amaro* at the local audiences which had shunned the later films of Rossellini and de Sica. Yet even as a 'commercial' film, this is a swift descent from *Caccia Tragica*, almost always sacrificing probability for effect; realism has gone, to be replaced by a phoney melancholy which would be copied by others, including Fellini, in the next decade.

De Santis may have argued that sex was not incompatible with neo-realism, since it had been an essential ingredient of peasant drama – and he might have added that the movement did put grave limitations on material. Audiences, in reaction to the Fascist past and postwar confusion, made it clear that they did not want frivolous subjects. Blasetti tried to return to the epic of antique times in *Fabiola*, which was a resounding failure, but audiences were also no longer responding to tales of deprivation among the working people. In October 1949, for instance, they were presented with **Il Mulino del Po** and **Ciello sulla Palude**, both good films, but hardly cheerful entertainments. The former is directed by Alberto Lattuada and is set in 1876, adapted from a novel by Riccardo Bacchelli concerning labour unrest when the trade unions come into conflict with the local *padrone*. Lattuada keeps an admirable balance between the principals, the family running the mill on the Po, and the peasantry at large, and if, as a portrait of the past, it lacks the intensity of Sjöström it is virtually as convincing. *Ciello sulla Palude* also concerns the past, as a destitute family roams the marsh country looking for a roof. The director is Genina, whom we may consider the Vicar of Bray of the Italian cinema, but he takes to neo-realism as a duck to water, superbly guiding his amateur cast and conveying the tale in images of great simplicity. The screenplay is by Suso d'Amico Cecchi, daughter of Emilio Cecchi, and Fausto Tozzi, based on the 'life' of Maria Goretti: clearly she did not have much of a life, with little recourse but to pray whenever rape was threatened (she was later canonised, for forgiving her attempted rapist and murderer on her deathbed). That rape and violence arise from poverty and ignorance is a plea the film convincingly makes: and their circumstances are as banal as the final crime, which I intend as a compliment. We may in both films enjoy the photography, of Aldo Tonti and G. R. Aldo respectively; and a visit in each to the local fiesta only underlines the quality of sameness.

Contemporary problems were examined in **Il Cristo Proibito** (1951), but audiences had been subjected too often to its twin themes, the difficulties of the returning war veteran (Raf Vallone), and his attempts to sort out exactly what went on in his absence between the collaborators and his partisan brother; some doubted that any sort of realism was really achieved when peasants are so beautifully grouped and photographed. It is the only excursion into cinema of the novelist Curzio Malaparte, who wrote and directed, and it is an absorbing movie – of a genre almost unknown in the Anglo-Saxon cinema, the serious melodrama. On a personal level, the film becomes an examination of the futility of war, and like all good Italian films a celebration of Italy, done with love, pride, wonderment and more than a touch of cynicism.

These qualities are also to be found in two marvellous films directed by Renato Castellani: the aptly-named **E Primavera** (1949) and **Due Soldi di Speranza** (1952). Castellani, after his first two films, embraced neo-realism with *Mio Figlio Professore* in 1946. After one more film, he attacked *E Primavera* with what Gavin Lambert in *Sight and Sound* called an almost boundless vitality: it is apparent in his locations, his non-professional performers, and in the screenplay which grew from conversations with several conscripts on the advantages of amatory adventures when away from home territory. In this particular case, one (Mario Angelotti) takes, with conceit and charm, a wife in Milan and another in Sicily. Castellani's view of his countrymen is to paint them warts and all, and the villagers in *Due Soldi di Speranza* are greedy and grasping. The youthful members of the Communist party are in direct contrast to the priest, who is fat and slothful, and their conflict reflects Italy's greatest dilemma since the War. The setting is a village on the slopes of Vesuvius, and the protagonist is Antonio (Vincenzo Musolino), just back from the War, and without a job to support his two sisters and self-dramatising mother: he would like to work for his future father-in-law, but the old man cannot stand the sight of him. He is enterprising in getting work, and the fact that it turns out to be always temporary is never actually his fault. The title refers to his marrying the girl without either a job or her father's approval, which make for a denouement slightly at odds with the honesty of the rest of the film. Both movies are as funny as they are furiously inventive. Castellani's reputation was such that he persuaded the Rank Organisation to back **Romeo and Juliet** (1954), ravishingly photographed, in Technicolor, in and around Verona. It was, however, not a success, since he failed to get even adequate performances from an amateur, Susan Shentall, his Juliet, or his Romeo, Laurence Harvey. Discouraged, Castellani returned to writing for other directors, and the occasional films he directed are of indifferent quality.

Meanwhile, de Sica and Zavattini had also brought comedy to neo-realism, though the key sequence of **Miracolo a Milano** (1951) is near the beginning, when a small boy is left alone in the world. Later, on leaving the orphanage, all his possessions are stolen from him. Even so, he has a 'Buon Giorno' for everyone, and finds friendship in a shanty-town on waste ground outside the city. With his simple goodness, he turns it into a real village, and is much loved: but after the miracle of the title occurs, there is little love anywhere, since the derelicts turn out to be as covetous as the tycoon who owns the land. They cannot win against him, and the piece concludes as they fly on broomsticks over the cathedral to a land where 'Good Morning really means Good Morning', on the bitter theory that there is hope for the poor only in heaven. This most cunning of film fantasies has prepared us for this ending, with its deliberate references to *A Nous la Liberté*. It had started with the credits superimposed over images from Hieronymous Bosch: there is little Bosch in Clair, but there is much here – the pained despair, the physical ugliness, the greed, and the hopeless fêtes and fairs. De Sica made the film as a favour to Zavattini, whose screenplay was based on one of his own novels and one of which he was particularly fond. For his next project he asked Zavattini to write a screenplay on the subject of old age.

Umberto D (1953) is in fact about an old man's hopelessness, and that is all there is to it. Umberto (Carlo Battisti, in life a university professor) lives in a respectable apartment, albeit in one room, and is neatly dressed; he is proud and querulous, and is unable to make up the difference between expenditure and income. He tries to sell his watch, and his books, and he campaigns for a raise in pensions outside the Ministry concerned; he gets himself packed off to hospital in order to save a few days' food. We do not know whether he is widower or bachelor; his only friend is the pregnant scullery maid, though whether by the soldier from Napoli or the one from Firenze she does not know. That is her lot, together with the truckle-bed in the hall, the cockroaches above the sink and the letter home. Her relationship with the old man is based on a common loathing of the landlady/mistress, and he is sustained otherwise only by his love for his dog.

637

De Sica's Compassionate Films

De Sica's reputation has been hurt by his greatness, since people remember being moved by his films (the good ones, that is) and recall them as sentimental. They are not: they are cries of despair that the world is a cruel place for the poor and deprived – though that is not entirely true of the young hero, Luciano de Ambrosis, of *I Bambini ci Guardano*, RIGHT, though his parents disregard him as they pursue their own selfish ends. This film crept into the cinema consciousness, via showings at film societies after the furore caused by *Ladri di Biciclette*, BELOW, when it first appeared outside Italy. As *Bicycle Thieves* in Britain and *The Bicycle Thief* in the U.S. it ran for months, establishing undreamt-of records for art-house showings. With its successors, *Miracolo a Milano*, FAR RIGHT, a comedy, and *Umberto D*, BELOW RIGHT, it established new criteria for foreign-language films.

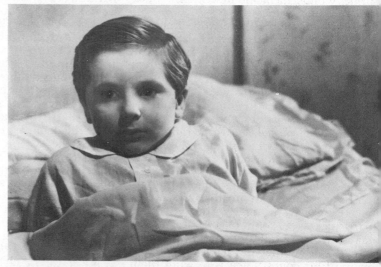

The players in all four films were amateurs. They are Lamberto Maggoriani and Enzo Staiola in *Ladri di Biciclette*, an unnamed boy, the hero as a child, in *Miracolo a Milano*, and Carlo Battisti (in life, a university professor) and Maria Pia Casilio in *Umberto D*, which de Sica dedicated to his father, whose name was Umberto. These three films were disliked by Italian critics as giving a false picture of Italy, which partly explains why *Umberto D* was the peak of de Sica's career and why he began to decline thereafter.

Italy: The Tradition of Realism

When suicide seems the only solution, this love may save him. The film is a masterpiece, but like *Ladri di Biciclette* it has suffered from being remembered wrongly – as a story of a man and a dog. Zavattini had wanted to write a film about a man to whom nothing happened, and here he had written about a man to whom nothing much happens, with the enormous exception that poverty is constantly allied to death – though it is very doubtful whether the old man comprehends that.

When this film came out, we felt that there was nothing the cinema could not do, that there was no facet of human behaviour which even merely gifted men could not use to make us understand ourselves and our planet better. After *Ladri di Biciclette* and *Miracolo a Milano* we had expected greatness: we could not have guessed that it was the summit of de Sica's and Zavattini's work both together and individually. Still less could anyone have realised that the humanist film would die, except for such practitioners as (q.v.) Ermanno Olmi and Satyajit Ray. However, it was perhaps not surprising that de Sica and Zavattini became professionally cynical. They struggled to make these films, and though they were artistically and commercially successful abroad, they were execrated at home, either for presenting a false picture of Italy or exaggerating a problem which hardly existed. The future prime minister Giulio Andreotti was among several leading public figures who roundly and publicly condemned them, which made it difficult for them to get further backing. Rizzoli had financed *Umberto D* in the hope of persuading de Sica to direct *Il Piccolo Mondo di Don Camillo* (q.v.) and its total failure in Italy did not encourage that company to try again. De Sica refused the Don Camillo film, and he is reputed to have refused Selznick's proffered backing for *Ladri di Biciclette*, with Cary Grant playing the leading role as part of the deal. De Sica did finally agree to work with Selznick, on *Stazione Termini* (q.v.), and was forced into a series of compromises which were soon to have a disastrous effect on his work. He and Zavattini remained proud of these three films, but they surely could not have been surprised by their failure in Italy, for despite their humour and an implied compassion in attempting to record the imbalance of society, the overriding mood of each is despair.

Neo-realism was only marginally a humanist movement. It was important technically, in removing the encrustations that increasingly burdened film since the cameras were first taken out into the streets of Paris – the artificiality, the 'glamour', the synthetic tree or mountain which was not as convincing as the real thing. It removed the Italian cinema from the confines of Cinecittà, but its importance inside Italy was relative, since the *verismo* tradition was so strong. Nevertheless, the few postwar Italian films shown abroad had an influence on other cinemas comparable only with that of the Soviet films in the late Twenties. Their value to Italy, and to the rest of the world, lies in their record of a particular time in the country's history – set down with as much fidelity and honesty as was possible at that time.

25

French Cinema during
Occupation and Readjustment

FILM PRODUCTION in France halted and hesitated during the early months of the War – a handful of movies was abandoned, first temporarily and then permanently – but once the German Occupation was established the studios returned to full activity. The number of French-language films made in Germany prior to the War is evidence of Dr Goebbels' interest in French cinema. With the Occupation, the offices of Tobis and Ufa in Paris were reopened, and their activities enlarged; the Germans also took over a number of industry properties either Jewish-owned or controlled, including cinemas. Approximately one-third of the industry was German property for the duration of the War. Production recommenced in the 'free' zone, in the studios at Nice, sooner than in Paris, but there, too, Jews were among the early victims. Following a decree by the Vichy government in October 1940, the Comité d'Organisation Cinématographique headed by Raoul Ploquin – producer of *Gueule d'Amour* and *L'Etrange Monsieur Victor*, among other films – issued a list of specific Jewish personnel who could not be employed.

Jewish players were also cut from the reissues which cinema-managers programmed during the film shortages caused originally by the (temporary) closure of the studios and then by the banning of British and American films. Some films, accordingly, no longer made much sense, while *Macao, l'Enfer du Jeu* was partially reshot with Pierre Renoir in the role played formerly by Erich Von Stroheim. As German films replaced American ones as the big attractions on the Champs-Elysées, Goebbels took an interest in their reception – but that, in general, was poor. Fore-seeing similar resistance to French films emanating from Tobis and Ufa, Goebbels set up a 'French' company, Continental, reputedly recommending it to only produce films which were *'légers, vides et si possible stupides'*. Ostensibly, however, Continental allowed artistic freedom to those it employed; a request for the services of a particular player was in fact a command, and many artists spent the war years finding good reasons to be unavailable – usually by pleading retirement or overwhelming prior commitments.

There was indeed no vestige of freedom. All scripts and the finished product itself were examined by both the German censor and that of Vichy – the novelist Paul Morand. Otherwise the industry might be regarded as healthy. Activity increased, to the extent that eighty-two films were produced in 1943 – almost twenty more than the prewar average, and twenty more than were produced in Germany that year. Given the limitations on subject matter – an edict had forbidden any more than forty per cent of the running time being devoted to adultery – it is not surprising that of the 225 films made between 1940 and 1944 only a few had any quality. A great many were thrillers, and the remainder almost all in full flight from reality.

That is in direct contrast to many made in the period immediately before and we might pause for a moment to look at **Menaces** (1940), shown six months before the Germans occupied Paris and containing a riveting portrait of the period September 1938 to September 1939. The director, Edmond T. Gréville, was usually mediocre, but his fellow writers on this occasion were Pierre Lestringuez, who had worked with Renoir, and Curt Alexander, who had worked with Ophuls. The setting is a small hotel near the Panthéon, and at the obvious level this is conventional drama, some way below *Hôtel du Nord*. But most of the guests come from abroad, from a Europe which is clearly disturbed; one of them, a German professor (Erich Von Stroheim), is a refugee from Hitler, and after reflecting on peace and war – he wears a mask to hide wounds received in World War One – he commits suicide. The characters are all pitiable or lost, except for one guest who is French, Denise (Mireille Balin), who is engaged to an English journalist (John Loder) – and the handling of that relationship is clearly symbolic. Guests and staff are increasingly apprehensive as they listen to Hitler on the wireless, and the film ends with the hotel closed for the duration as planes thunder overhead. Gréville changed the script as filming proceeded, and then had to begin again after the original negative was destroyed by fire; the second version was completed as the Germans invaded Poland.

Goebbels found it expedient to forget which film-makers had expressed anti-German sentiments. With the exception of Marcel Carné, France's best-known directors were in Hollywood – Clair, Duvivier, Renoir; and they were joined after the Occupation by Jean Gabin and Michèle Morgan, claiming either prior contracts or leaving by the devious route of 'Free France' and North Africa. (The great actor Louis Jouvet spent the War in South America, after taking a theatre troupe into neutral Switzerland.) To this day controversy surrounds some of the artists who remained: Maurice Chevalier did not make any films, but he did sing to German audiences – though it was later established that that was in return for the protection of Jewish friends; Danielle Darrieux worked for Continental and went on a goodwill tour to Germany with other members of the industry, but in 1942 she retired for the duration.

Marcel Pagnol was making **La Fille du Puisatier** (1941) in Nice when the Germans moved into France, and in the confusion he lost one of his players, Betty Daussmond. He replaced her with Line Noro, and inserted a sequence in which Raimu, Fernandel and Josette Day listen to Marshal Pétain's radio announcement of the end of hostilities – though the artists concerned had already concluded their work on the film. Later, the radio speech was replaced by one by General de Gaulle, and that was the version which was so warmly welcomed by British and American audiences after the War. Some critics felt that Pagnol now tended to emphasise the 'Frenchness' of his characters, and others, with more reason, that the piece lacked the humour of *La Femme du Boulanger*. In France it was said that he had told this particular story once too often – of the pregnant girl (Miss Day) and her angry father (Raimu) – but there are some pleasant variations on it as told in *Fanny* and *Angèle*. She is one of six unmarried daughters, and her father turns her out because of the effect of her influence on the younger ones; her lover (George Grey) is a dashing, well-heeled young man who leaves her to join the airforce. The scenes between Raimu and Charpin, as the boy's father, make up for longueurs elsewhere; and Fernandel is enjoyable as the girl's vain suitor.

Many newcomers entered the film industry. Sadoul has observed that the best film-makers retreated into 'brilliant fantasy' but I think a better term might be 'black whimsy'. It can certainly be applied to **L'Assassinat du Père Noël** (1941), directed by the veteran Christian-Jaque. The action is literally cut off from what was happening elsewhere, being set in a snowbound village in the mountains of Haute Savoie. The characters are crippled emotionally, mentally or physically, and all are involved in personal missions of despair, fantasy or obsession. There is little reality in their everyday lives, but they try to escape from whatever there is. The man who is called Père Noël (Harry Baur), a globe-maker by profession, treats the children to fantastic stories of a Chinese bandit while his daughter Catherine (Renée Faure) makes dolls. The Baron (Raymond Rouleau) insinuates that he has leprosy, though that is only a device to keep people away. Catherine takes pity on his loneliness, and it flowers into love. Pity often merged into love in the films made during the Occupation, but love, when it came, was passionate, perhaps not to last, and these emotions were often associated with dusty baronial halls, candlelight and archaic costume, as in this case. The general mood is fey and uneasy, thus able to encompass the hooded figure who stomps through the village – for it is, despite the trimmings, a thriller. Unfortunately, the direction becomes as banal as the story. The film does, however, demonstrate the French cinema in both its glory and the guise it wore at this time; and it is likely that the crippled boy urged to walk again was meant to represent France itself.

Marcel l'Herbier's **La Nuit Fantastique** (1942) could surely have appealed at no other time. It asks us to accept Fernand Gravet (almost forty) as a student: those who know him only from his two Hollywood films will be relieved to find that in his own language he has a certain charm, if perhaps whimsical – not a disadvantage in these circumstances. He dreams of a white lady, and when he thinks he sees her (Micheline Presle) he follows her, his illusions shattered when he finds her with her father (Saturnin Fabre) and cadaver-like fiancé: and of this grim trio, she, silly and giggling, is perhaps the worst. With the illogicality of dreams, a farce backstage at a magic show is followed by an escape from a madhouse; a love scene set on the rooftops of Paris is followed by a trip to the Caveau des Illusions; the comfort of being drunk or looking at beautiful women is shattered by mental patients clutching at prison bars or by a bicycle race. L'Herbier and his writer, Louis Chavance, may have intended a homage to Méliès, but for all the levity and promise of a happy ending, despair and tragedy lurk round the corner.

This film, together with *Les Visiteurs du Soir* (q.v.) and **L'Eternel Retour** (1942), was one of the three great successes during the Occupation. In the two last named films may be seen the influence of the current films of Blasetti, notably *La Corona di Ferro*, which for some months engaged the attention of artistic circles in Paris. *L'Eternel Retour* was written by Jean Cocteau, his first work for the cinema since *Le Sang d'un Poète*. It is a revamp of the story of Tristan and Isolde (the dramatist Jean Anouilh was currently enjoying success with 'Eurydice', another tragic myth become doomed love story) and this was not the first time that Cocteau had turned to the old legends for inspiration. His avowed reason on this occasion was to make a movie star of his protégé and lover, Jean Marais, who is kitted up in a stunning wardrobe of sweaters and riding breeches;

directed by Jean Delannoy, Marais appears in often identical shots to the Prince in *Snow White and the Seven Dwarfs*. Cocteau succeeded beyond his wildest dreams: Marais became the desired of every other woman in France, and audiences by the million fled their hardships with this gloomy tale – not to the dismay of the Occupiers, who approved both of the source of the film, which could be said to be Germanic, and of the blond Aryan good looks of the lead players. Even in wartime audiences were unlikely to swallow the business of the love potion, so Isolde (Madeleine Sologne) has a pal who specialises in herbal medicines; and the fate of the lovers is sealed by the meddlesome *méchant nain* who is part of the fetid household. Unfortunately, when Isolde observes that matters have become so absurd that she refuses to believe them, she is speaking for modern audiences. Contemporary comment was almost entirely favourable, and even as astute a critic as William Whitebait wrote, for the *New Statesman*, 'a mature work of art that embodies civilisation as surely as do Eliot's "Four Quartets", Britten's Michelangelo Sonnets, and Henry Moore's shelter drawings'. That was in postwar London; a later generation would find it adolescent fantasy and homosexual to boot. It has no sympathy for women: the heroine is as warmly conceived as the plaster cast which her face resembles, and the other women are either malicious or predatory. Only a homosexual, I think, would want to '*boire énormément*' when left alone with the woman he supposedly loves,★ while Marais's response to getting engaged is not to embrace his fiancée but to throw himself on the bed in a mock battle with her brother. We are meant to understand that the brother has a crush on him, since to know Marais was presumably to grovel at his feet.

Le Baron Fantôme (1943) also looks back to Blasetti, as well as to Marivaux; it is linked to *L'Eternel Retour* by a breathlessly romantic sleepwalking sequence and, though a box-office failure, would lead Cocteau to *La Belle et la Bête* (q.v.). He wrote it (and also plays a supporting role) but the scenario is credited to the director, Serge de Polignac. It is set in 1826 in a

★The situation is repeated in John Osborne's play 'A Patriot for Me', in which the hero tries to persuade himself that he can become heterosexual by getting drunk.

haunted castle, and each time it comes dangerously close to being a fairy story, it throws in something humorous, macabre or cynical – the cynicism is so often directed at the film's central characters, a quarrelsome quartet of lovers, that they thereby avoid becoming tiresome.

Les Visiteurs du Soir (1942) is more sprightly than most of the escapist films; it suffers, however, from the presence of Alain Cuny, an unsuitable romantic lead. Marcel Carné decided to emulate *La Corona di Ferro* when the censor turned down each of the contemporary subjects he submitted, and Pierre Laroche and Jacques Prévert provided a script about two of the Devil's creatures sent up to the medieval world. They are Gilles (Cuny) and Dominique (Arletty), *en travestie*, and when each becomes romantically involved with a human, the Devil (Jules Berry) manifests himself. The lovers, Gilles and Anne (Maria Déa), are separated, but their love is so strong that they manage a 'Peter Ibbetson' kind of relationship, and when the Devil, who represents Hitler, turns them to stone their hearts continue to beat – an allegory not lost on French audiences at the time. This is the familiar Carné–Prévert duel between good and evil, the hopeful and the corrupted, but the only good reason for seeing it is Arletty, with her infinite grace and Giaconda smile, the most enigmatic of Devil's envoys.

The influence of the Italian calligraphic films can be seen in **Douce** (1943), which even opens with the panning shot of rooftops as in Poggioli's films. Recourse to a period subject was natural to its director, Claude Autant-Lara (b. 1903), who had worked with both l'Herbier and Clair as art director. Directing infrequently for a decade – including two French versions of Buster Keaton comedies for M-G-M – he had not been successful till *Fric-Frac* in 1939, a polished version of a famous comedy about crooks, with Arletty and Fernandel. *Douce* was adapted – from a novel by Michel Davet – by an experienced screenwriter, Jean Aurenche, and a new one, Pierre Bost (1901–79), who would thereafter work almost exclusively together, and indeed usually for this director. Its subject is three generations – the imperious Countess (Marguerite Moreno), her ineffectual, crippled son (Jean Debucourt) and his perverse, wilful daughter

(Odette Joyeux); their relationships with the governess (Madeleine Robinson) and the groom (Roger Pigaut) provide a certain satire, though we are offered a welter of emotions instead of the clean irony of *La Règle du Jeu*. The characters are enjoyably rounded, speaking in civilised tones, which as we saw in the last chapter was a facet of French cinema much admired by contemporaries in Italy.

The two countries collaborated on a handsome new **Carmen** (1943), vigorously directed by Christian-Jaque, with Viviane Romance in the title role and Jean Marais as Don José: the version to see is the (dubbed) Italian one, in which Don José has a more suitable bass voice. The supreme French evocation of the past is in a film begun clandestinely during the Occupation, **Les Enfants du Paradis** (1945) – and it is the past of Balzac and Eugène Sue, the Paris of theatres and sideshows along the streets and byways. The courtesan Garance (Arletty) and the mime Debureau (Jean-Louis Barrault), meet and fall movingly in love, though she is bound to Lacenaire (Marcel Herrand), a man of doubtful tastes and activities; she is also loved by the actor Lemaitre (Pierre Brasseur) and is the mistress of a nobleman (Louis Salou), but it is for Debureau alone that she feels emotion, an emotion which is part maternal and part concupiscent. Like its predecessor, the film owes much to Arletty's bewitching performance, but it is flawlessly conceived and realised, by Carné and Prévert, on a vast romantic scale. It is a masterwork, and it is to the French cinema what *Gone with the Wind* is to the American – and the peak of Carné's career. It was a tremendous success in France and in every country where it was screened – one of the first French films to be shown abroad after the War.

Prévert's brother, Pierre, had meanwhile made his first film since 1932, **Adieu, Léonard** (1943), and like *L'Affaire Est dans le Sac* it is larky – but professional. Léonard (Carette), a salesman of novelties, turns to crime to maintain his wife's pretensions, and is therefore the blackmail victim of Bonenfant (Pierre Brasseur), who wants him to murder his wife's cousin Ludovic (Charles Trenet). Ludovic is a simple philanthropic soul and an incurable optimist, quite unperturbed at being thought mad and by Léonard's attempts to

Arletty, with unnamed player and Jean-Louis Barrault, seated, in *Les Enfants du Paradis*. The fact that it so richly recreates the Paris of the 1820s has somewhat obscured the fact that its theme is the same of the other memorable romantic films of writer Jacques Prévert and director Marcel Carné – of the brevity of happiness and the frustrations of love in an imperfectly designed universe. It is the masterpiece of this team and in 1979 was voted by the French Academy of Cinema Arts as the greatest French film ever made. The runners-up were, in order, *La Grande Illusion*, *Casque d'Or*, q.v., *La Regle du Jeu*, *La Kermesse Heroïque*, *Pierrot le Fou*, q.v., *Hiroshima Mon Amour*, q.v., *Les Jeux Interdits*, q.v., *Quai des Brumes* and *Le Salaire de la Peur*, q.v.

murder him: he eventually triumphs, however, in a quasi-Clair ending that is as pathetic as Trenet's performance. The piece, inventive without being surprising, would have been better if it had all been as sharp and blustery as Brasseur's performance.

Autant-Lara's **Sylvie et le Fantôme** (1945) also needs more asperity; with that quality and its château setting, it might have passed for one of the *pièces roses* of Anouilh. The château is saved by selling the painting of the White Hunter, who leaves behind a ghost (Jacques Tati); Sylvie (Odette Joyeux) loves the White Hunter as if he were real, and matters are complicated by the professional ghost hired from Paris – her father's birthday gift. For such conceits, this film was much admired: William Whitebait thought it audacious to add farce to a wistful tale of a girl's love for a ghost. Alfred Adam, influenced by Giraudoux's 1933 play 'Intermezzo', wrote the story; the direction is as light as air. Mlle Joyeux's co-star is François Perier, but the successful rival for her hand is Jean Desailly, a featured player: that co-stars did not always fall in love was one

reason why French pictures held more surprise than those from Hollywood.

Les Anges du Péché (1943) is one of the rare screenplays by Giraudoux, with dialogue as studied and formal as the film's appearance. The director, Robert Bresson (b. 1907), had been assistant to Clair on his *Air Pur*, abandoned on the outbreak of war, and had directed one unsuccessful film nine years earlier. He had also been an art photographer, and he knew exactly what he wanted when he stepped inside this particular cloister. Convent life is clearly a way of escaping contemporary problems, but other problems arise, and as expressed here – the pride of one nun, and her rivalry with another – they are far more fervid than the austere style at first suggests. Despite its complete lack of humour, the film can just be taken seriously, which is more than can be said for **Les Dames du Bois de Boulogne** (1945), written by Cocteau and Bresson from a story by Diderot, 'Jacques le Fataliste', which had also served D. W. Griffith for *Lady of the Pavements*. The tale is an early example of two of the chief themes of French literature, revenge and destruction of the young by cynical elders, but this modernised version is merely lurid melodrama. Moreover, Bresson's Paris belongs to no known world, and the characters move like puppets through carpetless, echoing rooms: the chic woman (Maria Casares), bent on vengeance, in pearls and black skirts that sweep the floor, contrasting with the girl (Elina Labourdette), in felt hat and raincoat. In the original story the latter is manipulated into prostitution, but here she only does a solo rumba in a cabaret before rushing home where, skirtless, she helps mother entertain young men in white tie and tails with champagne. That hardly makes her unworthy of the man (Jean Marchat) in love with her – and perhaps explains why the film was disliked when it appeared.

Sharing Bresson's misanthropy was another new director, Henri-Georges Clouzot (1907–77), who had been assistant to Anatole Litvak and E. A. Dupont. He had worked in Germany on French-language films; and because of his right-wing views he was not unwilling to work for the German company, Continental, initially as writer on *Le Dernier des Six* (1941), adapted from a detective novel by S. A. Steedman, and directed by Georges Lacombe, with Pierre Fresnay. His adaptation of a novel by Simenon, **Les Inconnus dans la Maison** (1942), was notably well received; a story of a lawyer (Raimu), long past his better days and heavy with drink, who returns to his profession at the behest of his daughter and her lover – a Jew, whose criminal tendencies had caused her to stray from the straight and narrow path. As directed by Henri Decoin, its atmospherics and social criticism made it seem in the prewar tradition, though it did not escape attention that Raimu's summing-up speech quoted, in Sadoul's words, 'favourite catch-phrases of the Vichy Press'. Raimu, whose presence at Continental was considered a coup for the company, asked his agent to find him immediate work elsewhere to prevent him from staying, but Decoin was to make several more films for Continental.

Clouzot adapted another novel by Steedman, **L'Assassin Habite au 21** (1942), and Continental gave him the chance to direct. Few directors made a more brilliant start – literally, since after an opening sequence in which a series of grisly murders is discussed in a bar the camera follows one of its patrons along the street and it is gradually clear to the audience that he is being followed by the killer. Subsequently the detective in charge (Pierre Fresnay) goes to stay in a boarding house where everyone is suspect: they, the guests, are droll, and Fresnay himself has some Hollywood-style sparring with Suzy Delair, his mistress, who has decided to do some sleuthing on her own.

Le Corbeau (1943) is also a whodunnit, but harsher and darker, leaning even more heavily on the style of the late German Silents. In a small town where children play in the sun and the curé is a leading force, a series of poison-pen letters provoke suspicion and unrest: as they mount into hundreds, few people escape – and most of them blame a doctor (Fresnay), accusing him of being an abortionist and a lecher. The doctor's relationships with the spiritual but married Laura (Micheline Francey), and the sexually ravenous – and crippled – Denise (Ginette Leclerc) are unusual, and the latter's attempts to seduce him are strong by the standards of the time: it is nice to be able to reveal that lust wins.

The film was disliked in France for its unflattering portrait of provincial life, which was one reason that the Germans ensured that it was shown in other Occupied countries. It was not, however, shown in Germany, since the authorities there decided that it might cause outbreaks of anonymous letters with which the Gestapo could not cope. That fact was utilised after the War by Clouzot and the film's writer, Louis Chavance, when they were indicted for having contributed to anti-French propaganda; and Chavance was able to prove that not only had he not specifically written the film for Continental but that the screenplay – based on some actual events which happened in Tulle – had existed as early as 1933. However, both he and Clouzot were forbidden to work again in the film industry.

The order was later rescinded, and both men returned with films which were among the greater successes of the postwar period. However, it was with Jean Ferry that Clouzot adapted yet another novel by Steedman, **Quai des Orfèvres** (1947) – and they falter in their task only at the end.

The film's absorption in its chosen milieu is as comfortable as a glove – prewar Prévert superimposed onto postwar Paris. And memorably so: who could ever forget the seedy Menilmontant music hall, filled with tobacco smoke, and Suzy Delair 'avec son tra-la-la', with her toothy smile, or the way she looked in her black underwear? – or Charles Dullin's definitive dirty old man or, above all, Louis Jouvet's wily, tired but relentless detective, coping with a running cold? It is a tale not only of murder but of pimping, ambition, jealousy and passions not then usual in films: when the detective realises why Dora (Simone Renant) has risked so much for Jenny (Delair) he observes that, like himself, she has not been particularly lucky with women.

Jouvet was also in the film which allowed Chavance to work again, **Un Revenant** (1946) – written in co-operation with Henri Jeanson and directed with Christian-Jaque. Jouvet plays a successful choreographer who returns to his home town and is reminded of a youthful love affair. The woman concerned (Gaby Morlay) obliquely suggests a manner in which he can take revenge on those who destroyed their love: eventually, however, he abandons his plans to do so and his cynicism gives way to reflection – and both qualities are, nicely, found within the film.

As with Clouzot, the first feature of Jacques Becker (1906–60) was also a thriller, **Dernier Atout** (1942). He had directed some short films, and had been assistant to Renoir; in 1939, he had started a feature, *L'Or du Cristobal*, but the money ran out and he disowned the result as finished by other hands. *Dernier Atout* concerns American gangsters in an imaginary Latin American city, and it was specifically designed to appeal to those who felt deprived of American films; the plot is overcomplicated, but Pierre Renoir is a sour, glowering villain and the tone light enough to be called felicitous. Becker's second success was **Goupi Mains Rouges** (1943), with story and screenplay by Pierre Véry, who had provided the similar mysteries and black humour for *Les Disparus de St Agil* and *L'Assassinat du Père Noël*. In this case a large and self-regarding provincial family closes ranks when one of its members has been murdered. Becker regards them with detachment and one

suspects that his fascination is due to the unchanging ways of country folk – as is demonstrated in the final sequence.

Naïs (1945) is also bucolic melodrama, and yet another modernisation, in this case of Hugo's 'Naïs Micoulin': it concerns the love of a hunchback (Fernandel) for the beautiful Naïs (Jacqueline Bouvier), and how he comes to her aid after she has been seduced by a wealthy wastrel (Raymond Pellegrin). The director is Raymond Leboursier, but the Provençal locations and the approach indicate that Marcel Pagnol was the writer and producer; amidst the clichés there remains his awareness of the complexity of life, and the acting – with the exception of Mlle Bouvier, who was his wife – also contributes to the film's effectiveness. However, Pagnol's time had passed, and the few films he subsequently made aroused little interest.

Le Ciel est à Vous (1944) also offers a convincing portrait of provincial life, in an uncertain tale of a married couple so obsessed with aviation that their home is almost destroyed by it. Begun and abandoned in 1939, the film was finished in 1943, and apparently the dedication of the couple had significance in the final days of the Occupation. Charles Spaak wrote the screenplay from a story by Albert Valentin, and it is the last film of any consequence directed by Jean Grémillon. He planned a number of semi-documentaries, with government aid, on such subjects as the Revolution of 1848 and the Munich Settlement, but none was made. He did make some documentary shorts, and the fiction films he produced revealed only too clearly his loss of interest in that form.

Martin Roumagnac (1946) is also set in a small provincial town and, as stolidly directed by Georges Lacombe, is notable for its assembly of attitudes from prewar Gabin films. Gabin himself plays a builder who falls for a lady known locally as *la veuve joyeuse* (Marlene Dietrich), supposedly an Australian: she marries in name only a diplomat (Marcel Herrand), and after Gabin has been acquitted of strangling her, he is shot by her latest admirer (Daniel Gélin). The film was a failure, but was at the time notorious as the vehicle chosen by the two stars after the debacle of **Les Portes de la Nuit** (1947). Since *Les Enfants du Paradis* had confirmed the ability of Carné and Prévert to provide the French film industry with international success, a great deal of money was invested in *Les Portes de la Nuit* – 80 million francs, or a quarter of a million dollars. Dietrich left the cast after deciding that her role was too small, and Gabin was sacked after complaining about the script and quarrelling with her replacement. Though the public cast Gabin as the villain, Carné's own primadonna temperament and extravagance – he meticulously reconstructed great areas of the Boulevard de la Chapelle in the studio – had made him many enemies, and when this film failed with both public and critics he was cast into a wilderness from which he never really returned. It is not difficult to see why the film was disliked: its gloom and fatalism were only too reminiscent of prewar days, and by wallowing in these qualities as a new era was supposedly dawning Carné and Prévert were either showing themselves reluctant to change or throwing out a challenge to the public. On the evidence available within the film they may have felt that any salute to the new era must wait till the recent past had been examined. Their miscalculation was compounded by having the fatalism personified – by a *clochard* (Jean Vilar) who claims he is destiny itself – and by the unholy mixture of dated romanticism and references to wartime collaboration.

Today the film is as hugely enjoyable as any that Carné made, and it certainly has nowhere to go but down after a dazzling opening – the Métro at Barbes-Rochechouart during the rush hour. Opposed, for the purposes of the plot, are two friends (Yves Montand, Raymond Bussières) and a father (Saturnin Fabre) and son (Serge Reggiani), whose activities have moved from collaboration to the black market; to Kosma's song 'Les Feuilles Mortes' Montand falls in love with a married woman (Nathalie Nattier), daughter of his enemy, while two younger lovers moon and dream on the periphery of the story.

The film's failure caused the abandonment of the next Carné–Prévert film *La Fleur de l'Age*, and they did not work together again. Carné was reunited with Gabin, for **La Marie du Port** (1949), but with his usual team – Kosma for the music, Trauner to do the art direction and with

the addition of Alekan on camera – he failed completely: beyond the locations, in Normandy, there is nothing to suggest that this film was not made by a hack. Carné and Louis Chavance had adapted a novel by Simenon, but fail to capture the atmosphere created by that writer – a dusty, flaked-out people, dying a little each day in their dull little towns. With the exception of *Hôtel du Nord* Prévert had written all of Carné's films, and since from *La Marie du Port* onwards Carné's work would comprise only one above-average film, *Thérèse Raquin* (q.v.), we may well conclude that it was indeed Prévert's influence which made the best Carné films so atmospheric, romantic and teeming with life.

A new hero among directors was Jean Delannoy, and when in 1947 the magazine *Cinémonde* and Radio Luxembourg, Europe's most popular commercial station, asked for votes on the most popular film of recent years, an easy winner was **La Symphonie Pastorale** (1946); it also won the Grand Prix at the first postwar Cannes Festival and an acting award for Michèle Morgan, portraying blindness by giving one of her expressionless performances. Much better is Pierre Blanchar as the pastor who self-indulgently and secretly loves her. The screenplay (by the director and Aurenche and Bost) trivialises everything that was admirable in André Gide's original tale by attempting to turn it into a tragic romance. For **Les Jeux Sont Faits** (1947) Delannoy was able to command the services of Jean-Paul Sartre, an even more impressive cultural figure, in this case writing his first screenplay. Sartre's existential quest caused him to question man's relationship to God and the universe and the film attempts to do likewise, foolishly aiming its half-formed theories at the audience like rockets. The chief question is whether there is life after death: in a fictional country run by a Fascist usurper two people are fantastically reprieved: a wealthy woman (Micheline Presle), poisoned by her husband – one of the dictator's underlings – and a factory worker (Marcel Pagliero), assassinated while attempting to overthrow the régime. They fall in love before dying again, and the difference in their social positions is handled as soap opera rather than sociology. There is a love scene, fully clothed, which is remarkably erotic by the standard of the day and unusually imaginative for Delannoy. Another question raised is whether love and lust are more important than loyalty to comrades, and after the recent work of the Resistance it was presumably an important one.

The reasons for the pessimistic fantasies of the French cinema at this time are obvious, and we may include among such films **La Belle et la Bête** (1946), though that is of more enduring enchantment. Cocteau follows Mme Leprince's tale faithfully, but I do not think you would be wrong to find allegory in this rendering, since Cocteau was always prone to autobiography in his work. At this time homosexuals were pariahs, like the Beast; they were not thought to have feelings, and certainly conventional people were not supposed to fall in love with them. Perhaps that is why the triumph of the film is the Beast, his appearance and character, and the sepulchral tones which emerge from him: he is a carnivorous monster, and you may never forget his anguish after he has killed for food. It is all the more ironic that at the end he is transformed into a golden-haired fairy prince, but we should not mind, since Beauty (Josette Day) clearly does not. The influence of *Snow White* is again obvious, but Cocteau employed Christian Bérard, a designer of genius, whose contribution he warmly acknowledges in his diary on the making of the film. Also unforgettable is the château, with the flambeaux held by magical arms, and the caryatids of the chimney with their moving eyes. Henri Alekan, the photographer, suggested slowing down or increasing the camera speed, which had not been done since the Silent days. Yet the guiding hand was always that of Cocteau: he wrote the screenplay, and as the credited director became the new golden boy of French cinema.

According to an interview published in *Sight and Sound* in 1950, the real director was René Clément (b. 1913). Clément had been a gag-writer (with Jacques Tati), and a maker of documentary shorts; he had started in features as assistant to Yves Allégret, and while 'assisting' Cocteau on *La Belle et La Bête* was concurrently making a full-length documentary on the Resistance, **La Bataille du Rail** (1946). The documentary marked a return from the unreality which had by necessity afflicted the French cinema since the fall of France. A large number of Resistance dramas poured from the French studios over the next few years, to the embarrassment of French critics, who did not know whether to be more incensed by them (because they looked to the past) or by the Hollywood versions which were now arriving. As far as posterity is concerned it is another matter, and nothing in this genre is as funny and as moving as a slight scene in Clément's film when two men in a café watch the retreating Germans and one says, '*Ça arrange, ça arrange*'. With France divided, the railways were the only link between the two zones, and Clément, who also wrote the scenario, shows how men were smuggled across the frontier, how messages were conveyed and how acts of sabotage were carried out. Sabotage is the business of this movie, often done by amateurs growing into professionals – and nothing in it is as stirring as that growth, as the men co-operate with the Maquis, the real professionals. The Germans, except for one sequence when they wait for a derailed train to be righted, remain shadowy, or present only via their signs and posters – and indeed, the film begins with one such, to the effect that Jews are not permitted to cross into the Occupied zone. One of Clément's achievements is to involve us in situations instead of with people – with a revolt always gathering force as the railworkers try to prevent German supplies from reaching Normandy after D-Day. A portrait emerges of a nation under stress, co-operating secretly and silently for its freedom. Clément does not theorise between some marvellous shots of trains, being content to show the ingenuity of the Resistance workers and to admire them.

Inevitably Clément's subsequent films were less impressive, but **Les Maudits** (1947) is interesting, if only in its ambitions; it is an allegorical tale of the Nazi collapse – in panic and recrimination after an abortive attempt to found a new Nazi state somewhere in Latin America. France is represented among the Fascist refugees by a collaborator and by the hero, a country doctor (Henri Vidal) who has been shanghaied to tend a wounded man on the submarine in which the Nazis are escaping; the Nazis are uninteresting, except for their leader (Jo Dest), and that is because he is given an acolyte (Michel Auclair) who is obviously something closer than that. There are no other instances at this time of any leading character being overtly homosexual – and this is a particularly unpleasant one, revenging himself sadistically on his friend for a momentary flirtation elsewhere.

The success of *Bataille du Rail* tempted another documentary director, Georges Rouquier, to make a feature, **Farrebique** (1947), which takes its title from a farm in the Massif Central. It invites audiences to spend a year with the inhabitants of the farm, and they play themselves – which is perhaps why we do not get close enough to them. They make bread and they harvest; the children go to school, with packed lunches; in the evening they sit around the lamp, the silence broken only by the ticking of the clock. They want electricity, but must share the cost with an unwilling neighbour; there are bigger dramas when the eldest son falls off the hayrick and when it becomes necessary to share out the farm after the old man dies. For the exquisitely wrought intimation of his death, Rouquier deserved both his Cannes Grand Prix and the Grand Prix du Cinéma Française. He misses a certain dimension – we do not see the family in the bistro or at the market – but his film is worth all the fictions and falseties of his acknowledged influences, Flaherty and Dovzhenko. One sequence beautifully and notably foreshadows television documentary, as the old man uses maps, postcards and old photographs to illustrate his words. Later there would be a place for films like this on television, but there was none, then, in cinemas, despite the warm reception given this one and also to Clément's film in France and elsewhere; distributors regarded them as freak successes, and Rouquier had to abandon plans to make similar features on the workers of Paris and the natives of North Africa. In the Fifties, he made two unsuccessful fiction features and eventually moved over to television.★

Another documentary to be noted is **Paris 1900** (1950), a pioneering assembly of early film by Nicole Védrès. Earlier searchers in the vaults had used their finds

only facetiously, but Mlle Védrès set out to portray an era in this delightful piece. Since the available material was not plentiful she cheats a little, with detail, for instance, of an Art Nouveau Métro station and a sequence or so from some of Zecca's fictions. She offers La Belle Otero dancing and the Seine overflowing, Bernhardt in *La Dame aux Camélias* and the blowing up of a gangster's hide-out; here are Chevalier and Mistinguett, Colette and Willy, Renoir and Monet, Tolstoi and Andrew Carnegie. Here, too, as young women are Yvonne de Bray and Gabrielle Dorziat, whom audiences had seen recently in *Les Parents Terribles* (q.v.) – and to see them now in this film is to be offered an awesome glimpse into the way in which cinema changes historical perspectives: for the Paris of the *belle époque* seems to be closer now than when Mlle Védrès set out to put it into perspective for us in this collage.

Like Rouquier, she remains famous for one film, and the same was true for many years of Roger Leenhardt, who made just two fiction features in a lifetime of making shorts. **Les Dernières Vacances** (1948) was a promising debut; and it is, as the title indicates, a film about growing up. It contains another traditional aspect, for it looks mockingly at a bourgeois family; it is also sunny as well as sad, indications that the French cinema was finally leaving its postwar gloom. Unfortunately the performances are both colourless and strident, making us wonder about the director's sensitivity – but it is on the whole a likeable sensitivity.

Jean-Pierre Melville (1917–73) also found difficulty following his first feature, **Le Silence de la Mer** (1949), based on the novel by Vercors which had been published clandestinely during the Occupation. A lover of film, Melville had directed as an amateur, and this feature, financed by himself, was filmed entirely on location with a small crew over a two-year period. Again, it is very much of its time, with its wintry exteriors, extended commentary and air of melancholy. The latter is certainly appropriate, for the subject concerns an elderly Frenchman (Jean-Marie Robian) and his niece (Nicole Stéphane) during the Occupation and their reactions to the German officer (Howard Vernon, a Swissborn actor who specialised in such roles) billeted on them. The situation is artificial,

★As this book goes to press, he is making, with American money, a sequel to *Farrebique*.

Jean-Pierre Melville is best-known for his thrillers of the Sixties, and that is partly because his early films were not very successful – including the first, *Le Silence de la Mer*, based on a clandestine bestseller of the Occupation; but that, by 1949, was something that the French preferred to forget. The film, however, is an eloquent if romantic reminder of that time, with Howard Vernon as the German Officer trying hesitatingly to communicate his love of their country to the household with whom he is billeted.

for surely if the two of them welcome the German's visits to their room – which they will not admit – they would have melted before his ardent francophilia: but it is most touchingly done, and with its companion picture, *Léon Morin, Prêtre* (q.v.), proof that Melville's true forte was romanticism.

Maurice Cloche made dozens of films, to be renowned only for **Monsieur Vincent** (1947) – since he was incapable otherwise, said Sadoul, of making a good one. With that in mind, and the strange fact that it was almost wholly financed by parish collections, it may be that Cloche was, literally, inspired. Working from a screenplay by Jean Anouilh and Jean-Bernard Luc, he presents St Vincent de Paul (Pierre Fresnay) as the first social worker of the modern world, while always keeping in mind the underside of hagiography, in this case the do-gooder as masochist. Vincent, the priest, was not well born, but chance brought him into contact with those who were, and he used that relentlessly on behalf of the poor. Setting out to discover the misery caused by poverty, he is appalled, though it still has to be demonstrated to him – which the film shows in such a way as to make socialists of every member of

the audience. '*Je n'en savais rien*,' he says with tears in his eyes. An oddity of the film is its double ending, consisting of Vincent's reflections with Anne of Austria on the differences between their lives' work and his passing on of his creed as he lies dying. For such matters the film was praised – to the mortification of its detractors, irritated by the simplifications and its open proselytising. In that respect, it fulfilled its function: the audiences who flocked to it everywhere were impressed to find a film about dedication and selflessness. For myself, I was moved only once, when Vincent takes the place of a galley slave – for despite the diseased faces and bodies on display, it is, in the end, a comfortable film: yet the audiences were right, for it has a rare humanity.

The readers of *Le Film Français* voted it the best film of the year, while those of *Cinémonde* reversed the position with that of the runner-up, **Le Diable au Corps** (1947), directed by Autant-Lara and adapted by Aurenche and Bost from the novel by Raymond Radiguet – relevant again at this time, since it concerns a married woman who carries on an affair while her husband is at the front. Distancing made it palatable: the time is the First

It is not altogether surprising that a new generation of critics and film-makers should sweep away the literary adaptations which had been a staple of the French cinema since its inception – and it may have been for the best. On the other hand, some of the Thirties and Forties versions of the classics contain both solid craftsmanship and solid entertainment values – like Christian-Jaque's long but fast-moving version of *La Chartreuse de Parme*. Gérard Philipe is Fabrice and Maria Casares the aunt whose attitude towards him is always so equivocal.

World War, with the young man (Gérard Philipe) the most charmingly heartsick of students, and the woman (Micheline Presle) as lacking in conscience as he. The scenes between them have a tenderness rare even in the French cinema.

Gérard Philipe (1922–59) was the first actor of his generation noted for his stage work in the classics. In films, he was drawn to adaptations from literature, and is memorable as Dostoevsky's Prince Myshkin in **L'Idiot** (1946), directed by the otherwise undistinguished Georges Lampin. Charles Spaak's screenplay follows a tortuous route, always aware of matters greater than itself, but by picking the flesh off the bones it concentrates on aspects which best demonstrate Dostoevsky's genius. Philipe is entirely what the latter intended, moving in an odour of sanctity like a half-baked evangelist, but destroying because he fails or refuses to understand that other people are ruled by greed and vanity. Meek of mien and proud of bearing, there is a demonic gleam in his eye. The billed stars are Edwige Feuillère and Lucien Coëdel, whose sketch of Rogogine, the merchant, indicates a man of strong inner momentum. Mlle Feuillère is,

of course, Nastasia Philippovna, now more accessible as relegated to a demimondaine, of which the actress offers a traditional portrait – generous, capricious and undoubtedly Garboesque.

Philipe is also an excellent Fabrice in **La Chartreuse de Parme** (1948), playing him with an air of perpetual surprise but suggesting a man tempered by good humour. The film has that quality, too, and at almost three hours' running time is always an enthralling entertainment; the story is unharmed by its being built round the matter of Fabrice's imprisonment and replacing Stendhal's irony with a vaguely sardonic tone. Maria Casares is rightly haughty as the aunt, Gina, and there are splendid performances by M. Coëdel as the conniving police chief, Rassi, by Louis Salou as the tyrannical prince, and Tullio Carminati as the weak-minded prime minister. A weakness is the Clélia of Renée Faure, then married to Christian-Jaque – who directed on Italian locations – but the rococo decor adds to the felicitous result.

If by now the Italian cinema had become the most admired by the press, the foreign-language picturegoers in the English-speaking world still remained loyal to the French. The films of Jean Dréville enjoyed a wide popularity, and though some critics dismissed them, quite rightly, as having too much artifice, for their specialised public they were – it was often said – films which only the French could make. **La Ferme du Pendu** (1945) was particularly attractive, for one of its leading characters was insatiable in his sexual desires – which intrigued a great many Anglo-Saxons and confirmed a number of others in their opinion of the French. The so-called sex maniac (Alfred Adam) comes, rightly enough, to a sticky end, while his elder brother (Charles Vanel) eventually dies so that this provincial family shall not lose its land. The conjunction of sex, death and devotion to the land was further appealing, as was the very plot of **Le Visiteur** (1946), which concerns a famed lawyer (Pierre Fresnay) who evades a murder rap by hiding out in the orphanage of which he is the benefactor; since the boys hero-worship him he must not disillusion them when the police come for him. **Copie Conforme** (1946) is an ironic comedy in which Jouvet plays several roles, but mainly those of an unambitious little man who accepts employment with a prominent con-man – who uses him as his alibi when carrying out his jobs.

The later films of Dréville show a marked decline, but there seems no good reason why these particular ones – like many discussed in this chapter – should have lost their place in the international repertoire. The films of Jean Cocteau are usually available, and the best of them surely deserve to be. Most of the others seem to me to be no more than representative of the French cinema of this time, being claustrophobic, fantastical and usually superficial. Contemporary reviewers noted that Cocteau was poet, novelist, dramatist, designer, film-maker, a public figure and even an architect – and thus to some a Renaissance man reincarnate. Few suspected that he was drawn to the studios chiefly to further the career of Jean Marais – and there could be no other reason for making **Ruy Blas** (1948), one of Victor Hugo's lesser plays which Cocteau rendered even less by replacing the verse with flat modern dialogue. The director was Pierre Billon and the designer Georges Wakhévitch, whose triumph it is, since apart from a church and a market-place he had to achieve visual elegance with confined spaces and a small budget. Marais has a double role, as student and nobleman; Danielle Darrieux is the damsel in distress, a Queen of Spain; and Marcel Herrand is the chief of police who would like to trap them both.

Cocteau himself directed **L'Aigle à Deux Têtes** (1948), of the same species, with splendid barbaric decor by Bérard, and Marais in lederhosen as a would-be assassin. His intended victim is a Queen (Edwige Feuillère) till revolutionary fervour turns to love which allows some spectacular emotions, since the piece was designed solely to display the talents of its two stars. They had done it on the stage, and the play had subsequently been received with respect in translation in London and New York. Feuillère at least was worthy of the attention; and was never more Garboesque. The role might have been written for that actress – the royal widow who casts off her weeds for a brief, doomed happiness – but where Garbo's allegiance was to her script and herself, Feuillère's was to her art: in this case that

was not entirely the wrong approach.

Les Parents Terribles (1949) is meretricious and its author-director is at his most coy when one character remarks that if there were not situations like this there would be no plays. Cocteau had originally written it as a stage vehicle for Marais, based on the latter's hectic relationship with his own mother – a role destined for Yvonne de Bray, who declined it for the stage but accepted for this film version. The mother is furious at the engagement of her son to a young girl (Josette Day) who happens to be the mistress of his father (Marcel André), a gentleman for whom aunt Léo (Gabrielle Dorziat) has long nurtured a secret passion. Both play and film were regarded as a critique of the bourgeoisie, and Cocteau was rightly congratulated for retaining the restricted settings but avoiding the semblance of a photographed play. He may also be complimented for his cast, acting away like mad, but interestingly so.

He declined to direct **Les Enfants Terribles** (1949), based on his old novel, and assigned it to Jean-Pierre Melville on the strength of *Le Silence de la Mer*. The result he considered the best of his films, and certainly Melville has made the most of this material, which considers the odd relationship between Paul (Edouard Dermithe) and his sister Elizabeth (Nicole Stéphan), who live, eat, wash and sleep in the same room, in a state of permanent disorder. Paul is hit in the chest by Dargelos (the name and the incident also occur in *Le Sang d'un Poète*), and has to stay in bed, after which each invites a schoolfriend of the same sex to move in. These newcomers are tolerated only because they provide an audience for the quarrels and tantrums without which the others cannot function, till Elizabeth suddenly marries a wealthy American Jew, who is conveniently killed on his wedding night, for (says the narrator) she had married him for his death. Cocteau himself referred to the piece as 'the no man's land between life and death', and as such it is wryly amusing from time to time. Had he been more honest about the sexual orientation of the pair it might have been more than a diversion: instead we pick our way among a series of hints, such as Paul's pin-ups of boxers and male movie stars, all with the same sulky expression as himself. Der-

653

Cocteau's Fantasies

From youth onwards Jean Cocteau moved at the centre of the artistic life of Paris, his contributions to it seemingly in accordance with Diaghilev's command to astonish everyone. He loved the cinema, and in typical manner toyed with it until 1946 when he wrote and co-directed *La Belle et la Bête*, with Josette Day and Jean Marais, RIGHT. His published diary of the making of the film indicates much hard work, much teamwork and a conviction that the finished result would be a major achievement, but it does not dispel the impression of Cocteau as a dilettante. However, the film is important and it has lost little of its power to astonish.

The penchant for modernising ancient legends has been widespread among French writers for centuries, but it received a new impetus during the war years and just after – when it was triumphantly manifested in Cocteau's *Orphée*, BELOW, Maria Casares, with Edouard Dermithe, being carried by two motorcyclists, and Jean Marais. It deals fairly with its source, is richly autobiographical, and its cinematic tricks remain as rewarding as those in *La Belle et la Bête*.

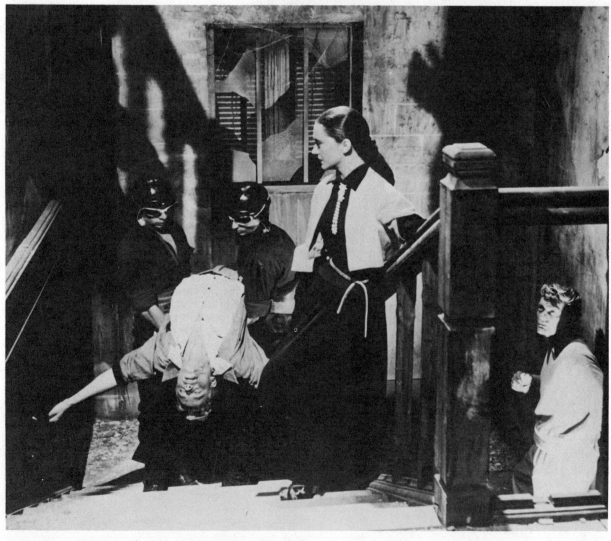

mithe had replaced Marais in Cocteau's life, and the characters (according to Janet Flanner) were based on one of Cocteau's former lovers★ and his sister. The film leaves an acrid taste, to remind us that its original English title was *The Strange Ones*, and its novelty was accentuated by the innovatory use of baroque music – by Vivaldi – on the soundtrack.

Although **Orphée** (1950) was also based on his youthful material, a play, Cocteau regarded it as the summation of his life's work and 'the fulfilment of those ambitions which once drove me to attempt *Le Sang d'un Poète* with no experience and insufficient technical means. Here, I felt, I wanted to express something that could not be expressed through any other medium . . . and this is to my mind the real task of the film.' As a foreword acknowledges, this is a retelling of an old myth, but it is a great improvement on *L'Eternel Retour*; and has its own unique flavour. When Cegeste (Dermithe) is killed during a café brawl by Death's outriders, Death – the Princess (Maria Casares) – takes instead Orphée (Marais), but allows him to return home in the company of Heurtebise (François Perier), who will fall in love with Eurydice (Maria Déa). Orphée has already fallen unwillingly in love with the Princess, who steals Eurydice to entice him back: but she relents and releases them provided he does not look at his wife; unfortunately, he sees her by accident in a car mirror. Heurtebise, from love of her, agrees to take Orphée back to the Underworld to rescue her, but he himself and the Princess are arrested for failing to conform to the standards of the Netherworld – for allowing Life to go free.

It is a film which lends itself to meanings, all of them clear to anyone with even a perfunctory knowledge of Cocteau's work, such as the '*étonnez-nous*' spoken during the café fight, implying that to astonish is more important than to quarrel: it is the prerogative of the artist. Later, Death says to Orphée, '*Il ne faut pas comprendre. Il ne s'agit de quoi,*' and we may understand the artist's fascination with death, death as a mother figure, mother as a muse, death as a muse – as well as the artist's need to travel into the unknown, his right to stimulation and his awe at his own dispensability. The film is a marvellous experience, because of its deliberately unreal level of fantasies and passions, and the trickery with which they are executed: the throbbing of drums during the fight and the invasion of the Bacchantes; the motorcyclists, deliberate reminder of Fascist authority, as emissaries of Death; the use of negative on the road to Hades, and the concept of a mirror as an entrance to hell. D'Eaubonne, with an assistant, is credited with the sets (the film is dedicated to Bérard, who died while it was being prepared). The film haunted me for months when I first saw it and it may be a film to see when young. There are films more enriching than this glittering basket of '*étonnez-nous*', these Chinese boxes, but I would wish everyone a film to discuss and argue over and dream about – one which, as Cocteau intended, is timeless.

Clouzot's **Manon** (1949) is, on the other hand, a tract for the time – though set in 1944, which was a convulsive year for France. Just as the heroine of Prévost's 'Manon Lescaut' could not help being a trollop, neither can this one as written by Clouzot and Jean Ferry. There is little to choose between the two ladies as Manon (Cécile Aubrey) moves from collaborationist in Normandy to black marketeering in Paris; but whereas the original Des Grieux was an honest man who accepted degradation because his beloved was wedded to her profession, here, as played by Michel Auclair, he has no quality at all – beyond having been heroic with the Maquis. Both of Clouzot's lovers are absurdly childlike – perhaps the reason he drops the love story some way into the narrative; but there is no compensating insight into the matters taken up instead, which include the Liberation, illegal immigration and the Jewish-Arab War (which provides the desert setting for the finale). *Greed* was as much an inspiration for Clouzot as Prévost, with Manon dying of thirst and exhaustion after days in the desert. The sequence was much criticised as sadistic and it caused much trouble among the world's censors. Today it looks overblown, an early example of the modern trend to visual extravagance offered in the hope that audiences will read significance into it – and only the cynical may be

---

★The man was Jean Bourgoint, introduced by Cocteau to drugs, and who later became a Trappist monk; Bourgoint's sister contracted gonorrhoea on her wedding night and shortly afterwards committed suicide.

unsurprised that this film was awarded a Grand Prix at the Venice Film Festival. Elsewhere, some were shocked, such as Leonard Mosley in England's *Daily Express*, who could 'not recall a more horrible film . . . everywhere touched with evil'. Reputation preceded it even before its Paris opening, when the police were called to prevent hysterical crowds from fighting; it subsequently flopped, and except for its few and vague comments on corruption, it deserved to do so.

Clouzot followed the customary pattern in such cases, and with Ferry adapted **Miquette et sa Mère** (1950), in fact the third Talkie version of a revered boulevard comedy. The plot is traditional, and concerns the passion felt by young Urbain (Bourvil) for a shopgirl (Danièle Delorme). Because of this, he is sent away by his uncle (Saturnin Fabre) on a theatrical career – with a touring actor (Louis Jouvet) of the fifth or sixth rank. The delights of the piece are less in its mechanics than in the glimpses of backstage life, with the climax set against an absurd historical play concerning Richelieu at La Rochelle: Clouzot was, all the same, happier with the sinister theatre of *Quai des Orfèvres*, but the whole film is as disarming as the bows that the cast takes at the end.

Helping to lift the gloom of French cinema was Christian-Jaque, who first tested public mood with **Souvenirs Perdus** (1950), one of the first of the portmanteau films which would prove so popular with French (and Italian) producers over the next two decades. Inspired by the British *Quartet* (q.v.), these four stories are linked by items in the lost property office, and they are respectively, sentimental comedy, comedy of situation, melodrama and farce. This director also attempted a fairy tale, **Barbe-Bleue** (1951), but all is heaviness surrounding Pierre Brasseur's pleasingly facetious playing of the title role. Also in the film's favour is the castle designed by Wakhévitch, though its splendour is diminished by the limited palette of Gevacolor (this was one of the first French films in colour). The sunny landscapes of **Fanfan la Tulipe** (1951), as photographed by Christian Matras, are an asset, as is the deadpan commentary, written by Henri Jeanson: for this is a comic swashbuckler – another genre to be endlessly repeated in

France and Italy – and an inventive and ingratiating one, with Gérard Philipe as adept with a sword as he is, we assume, in the haystacks and fourposters with the ladies. He helped Christian-Jaque towards his last great success both in France and abroad, and from then on this director declined with a series of historicals and sex comedies.

Occupe-toi d'Amélie (1949) could be termed sex comedy, and when a suitor explains the absence of his trousers to Amélie as a way of saving time, the British censor was so outraged that he refused to pass the film; that a number of local authorities did permit it to be shown hastened the introduction of the X certificate, applied to 'Adults Only' films, of which most of the first batch were French. This film introduced to British and American audiences the work of Georges Feydeau, farceur supreme of the *belle époque*; and they were reminded, for the first time since the strengthening of the Hays Code, that the pursuit of sex can be gloriously funny. Autant-Lara directed, sometimes using theatrical settings and retaining the proscenium arch, at the same time indicating a fondness for both the decor of the period and Feydeau's artlessly simple complications. Danielle Darrieux, Jean Desailly and the rest of the cast have precision and are funny without being vulgar, which, taken together with the breathless pace, so impressed the critics that the film did in fact advance the cause of sex in the Anglo-Saxon cinema.

Occupe-toi d'Amélie and *La Ronde* (q.v.) made the recent work of René Clair seem old-fashioned. Returning from Hollywood, he had made **Le Silence Est d'Or** (1947), set against a background of filmmaking in the Silent era, on which subject he is witty and affectionate. However, he is not at his best with the central situation, that of a young girl, an innocent at large in Paris, attracted to its less orthodox opportunities but prevented from enjoying them by her guardian (Maurice Chevalier), who falls in love with her but unwittingly hands her over to his rival (François Perier). Unashamedly a middle-aged comedy, its melancholy is misjudged because there is no compensating charm in the crucial corner of the triangle – the girl, who is poorly played. **La Beauté du Diable** (1950) is a retelling of Faust – a subject which might well have suited

Gregoire Aslan, trouserless, in *Occupe-toi d'Amélie*, a situation which most of us today would recognise as stemming from Georges Feydeau. There is no such scene in the original play, but when the director Claude Autant-Lara did send his characters out into the street the camera was just as likely to draw back to reveal that street behind a proscenium arch. This film therefore retains the theatricality of French farce while pretending to dress it up in cinematic manner, which means for audiences the best of both possible worlds.

Clair, but he strains for both jokes and significance, though agreeably without pretension. Gérard Philipe is Faust and Michel Simon the mischievous Mephistopheles; the film was made in Italy, for Clair had run into trouble setting up the project. That difficulty was not unconnected with the relative failure of the previous film, one of the first postwar foreign-language films distributed by an American company, in this case R.K.O. It may have been compensation for Clair that in both cases the critics were kinder than the films deserved.

As he began to recover his old form with his next film, so did Carné, for the last time, with **Thérèse Raquin** (1953). The script he wrote (with Charles Spaak) distorted Zola's original story almost as much as it modernised it. Instead of Zola's sweaty animals, Carné offers the usual illicit couple, living now in Lyon, and the man has become an Italian truck driver; he does not murder from lust for Thérèse, but in anger; they no longer live under the eyes of the paralysed Mme Raquin, but guiltily till reunited by the threat of blackmail. Their fate is therefore achieved by circumstance rather than faults within themselves, as in earlier Carné films, and if we compare this one with those we can see

that his narrative skill is as sure as ever. The initial situation is both faithful to Zola and beautifully handled: Thérèse (Simone Signoret) has married in gratitude her cousin (Jacques Duby), a snivelling, petty clerk who cheats at the card game he plays every Thursday with his cronies and his doting mother, who is implacably hostile to Thérèse. In the circumstances, the audience palpably wants Signoret to fall in love with Laurent (Raf Vallone), who looks dependable and handsome – and almost the best aspect of the film is her realisation of the nature of passion. As of old, Carné is helped enormously by his settings: the stuffy apartment above the shop and the deserted suburban dance hall where the lovers meet.

Another reason that the film was poorly received in France was that Carné was supposed to be sustaining a pessimism he no longer felt, and this particular film is best regarded as an excellent thriller, made at a time when the French film industry was beginning to change. The pessimistic mood prevailing in French films for the early postwar years was said by critics to have been dictated by producers, hoping to repeat their prewar successes, but the French had perhaps better reason to make despairing films after the War than before:

657

A number of reputations crumbled in the postwar French cinema, as local critics objected to the continued spate of pessimistic films, suggesting that film-makers were trying to cling to the themes which had made them renowned initially. Abroad, with the promised return to prewar conditions still some way off, critics were much kinder to these films – and since Yves Allégret's *Une si Jolie Petite Plage* remains so enjoyable, Allégret's motives in making it seem unimportant. Also, of course, foreign audiences found the problems of Gérard Philipe somewhat more important than those bothering Cary Grant or Gary Cooper.

the traumas of recent history were not shaken off overnight with the Liberation. In any case, the instability of the industry was hardly conducive to a run of bright comedies; added to that was the uncertainty induced by the failure of *Les Portes de la Nuit*, on which so many hopes had rested. Sadoul attacked the 'postwar imitations' for 'repeating endlessly such faults as [the earlier] films had had, usually in the form of a convention for apeing a "naturalism" far removed from actual life.' He cited as typical two films directed by Yves Allégret, **Dédée d'Anvers** (1948) and **Une si Jolie Petite Plage** (1949). They both are indeed in the tradition of *Quai des Brumes* and *La Bête Humaine* – emotional drama posing as social realism. The Italian neo-realists demanded that audiences consider injustice in society, whereas French cinema really offered escapism – inviting audiences to forget their own difficulties in experiencing the highly romantic problems of their characters who, though ostensibly working class, were not at all like themselves. Nevertheless, these films of Allégret are very entertaining. Both *Dédée d'Anvers* and **Manèges** (1949) feature his then-wife, Simone Signoret, respectively as a prostitute finding brief happiness with an Italian seaman in the dusty cafés of Antwerp, and a perverse, restless wife in French château country. They are mechanical but memorable films, and it is impossible to forget the images of *Une si Jolie Petite Plage* – the ill-assorted guests gathered in the bar of

the ugly resort hotel in winter to discuss a recent *crime passionel*, and Gérard Philipe as the fugitive from justice, wandering gloomily among the rain-sodden dunes and beach huts. Allégret's best work is forceful, and the dingy emotions with which he dealt, usually relating to love and/or sexuality, were refreshing then when considered beside the more anodyne problems of the English-speaking cinema.

Two films at least proved that the lovers caught in the web of fate had had their day. **Les Amants de Vérone** (1949) is set against the filming of a new version of Shakespeare's play, and the lovers (Anouk Aimée, Serge Reggiani) are alone exempt from the universal cupidity and amorality. They, and everyone else, have supposedly been conditioned by the War, so the film presents, among others, the once-famous attorney (Louis Salou) whose wartime associations have made him a drunken, half-crazed hermit, and his war-maddened gun-crazy cousin (Marcel Dalio). Jacques Prévert wrote the screenplay for André Cayette, and though the piece is as melodramatic as, say, *Caccia Tragica*, it is not redeemed by any honest observation of the society which it is criticising. Nor does it have the romantic aura of the Carné–Prévert films – and it was precisely that which was sought by the neo-realist writer, Zavattini, and the director of *Bataille du Rail*, Clément, in their collaboration, **Le Mura di Malapaga/Au delà des Grilles** (1949), made in Italy in both Italian and French versions. The story is a concoction about a seaman (Jean Gabin) who, wanted for murder, jumps ship in Genoa and falls in love with a waitress (Isa Miranda): extensive location work did not rescue the film from seeming old fashioned.

Clément made an indifferent star vehicle with Michèle Morgan and Jean Marais, *Le Château de Verre*, before succeeding with **Les Jeux Interdits** (1952), which the British Film Academy voted 'The Best Film from any Source' and the American Academy its Best Foreign Language Film.★ For a few years thereafter it consistently

★Until 1956, when the American Academy committee established the Best Foreign Language Film as a separate category, with five nominations, this was an honorary or special award, in response to members' admiration for developments abroad, starting with an award to Laurence Olivier for *Henry V* in 1946. The other awards, prior to 1956, were to *Sciuscià* in 1947, *Monsieur Vincent* in 1948, *Ladri di Biciclette* in 1949, *Le Mura di Malapaga* in 1950, *Rashomon* in 1951, *Gate of Hell* in 1954 and *Samurai* in 1955.

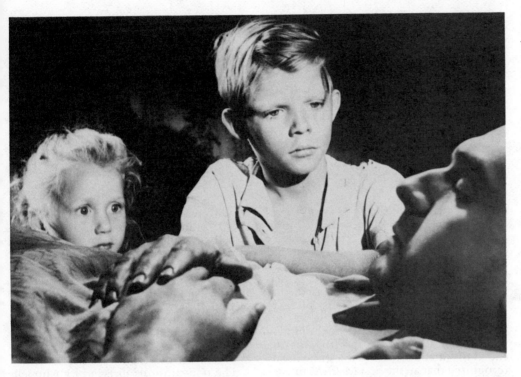

By the time René Clement made *Les Jeux Interdits* the French cinema had been knee-deep in gloom for almost two decades, but all was exorcised by this one film. It was not the most horrifying film that could be made on the subject of war – which was only peripheral to its central plot – but it was a genuinely strange piece, some of its eeriness springing from the fact that it stressed not only the sufferings of the innocent but the way in which their minds can be twisted. The innocents concerned were Brigitte Fosey and Georges Poujouly, both remarkable in their roles.

headed students' lists of the greatest film ever made – probably because they, like the film's protagonists, had been children during the War. A prologue establishes the flight from Paris in June, 1940: German planes swoop down with machine guns, and a child (Brigitte Fosey) is left an orphan. As she chases after her dog, floating dead in a river, she meets a boy (Georges Poujouly) slightly older than herself, and his peasant parents give her a bed. The boy's friendship enables her to accustom herself to her new surroundings, and then they invent their secret games, which consist of burying the dog, and then mice, chicken and insects, with crosses – after they get ambitious – stolen from the local churchyard. The title puts undue stress on that aspect of the story, since what interested Clément most was the situation of the little girl, suddenly bereft of parents and set down in an alien world. Working from an adaptation by Aurenche and Bost of the novel by Jean Boyer, he directs with humour, sensitivity and sympathy.

The film was admired for such touches as the lovers in the hay, the fat old priest cuffing the boy, and the flies that settled on faces – the appurtenances of realism. But, like a great many other films which the public found significant, its realism merely disguised – despite the chilling ending – a throbbing romanticism. Within France, the significance was much more real. It was the last film which was really close to the experience of the War. Those that came later, whether nostalgic or bitter with re-criminations, were historical reconstructions. It also ended, perhaps because it was like no other film, that obsession of the French cinema with doom and gloom which had begun with appeasement and continued through the guilt of the war years and during the shame of the aftermath. As we have seen, comedy was returning to French films, and the tradition of pessimistic drama could not be broken by one film, however cathartic; but the French film-makers at this point lost interest in allegory, symbolism and message. For the rest of the decade they returned to the primary business of entertaining audiences.

26

The M-G-M Musical

THE SUPERIORITY of the M–G–M musicals in the postwar period is now an acknowledged fact; they used better talents, better directors, better songs, orchestrations and even better colour than other studios. It was with *On the Town* (q.v.) in 1949 that both industry and critics realised that something exciting was taking place at Culver City, and the excitement was repeated a number of times before the Hollywood musical began to die towards the end of the next decade. By that time it was recognised that all the best M–G–M musicals prior to *On the Town*, as well as those made after, had been produced by Arthur Freed (1894–1973). Since most of them are of enduring quality, and have delighted successive generations, we may speak of him in the superlative – as the most gifted producer in the history of Hollywood. The adjective is well deserved by the man who fostered, encouraged and used to the best advantage the abilities of Judy Garland, Fred Astaire and Gene Kelly.

A former song-writer, he had been with M–G–M since the early days of Sound, and was an early advocate of Garland's talents, one reason why Louis B. Mayer promoted him to producer. Freed initiated *The Wizard of Oz*, and produced the first three Garland–Rooney musicals. Later in his career he produced four non-musical films, and he did eventually become, in theory at least, an independent producer, releasing through M–G–M. He was the first to admit that he was neither creative nor intellectual, but he knew how to choose the talents he needed, and he was wise enough to give them artistic freedom. These were essentially musical talents, and include most notably Roger Edens (1905–70), musical supervisor and later Associate

Producer, and Vincente Minnelli (b. 1906), a director whom Freed found on Broadway and trained for two years before putting him in charge of a film. If Edens's contribution can never be properly estimated, Minnelli's work is on screen, signed, and with the exception of his second film, *I Dood It*, all his M–G–M musicals were made for the Freed unit. If Minnelli wanted a particular composer or New York designer, Freed, it seems, was always amenable.

The non-musicals directed by Minnelli are discussed in a later chapter, but they were mainly produced by Pandro S. Berman, who produced two musicals for Metro, one of them *Ziegfeld Girl*. The achievements of the Freed unit are thrown into relief when one compares the musicals created at this studio by other hands, who had the same pool of talent upon which to draw. Also associated with this form at Metro were Joe Pasternak – who had moved from Universal after a disagreement over the handling of the adult Deanna Durbin – and Jack Cummings, a nephew of Louis B. Mayer, whose earlier films had included the *Broadway Melodies of 1938* and *1940*.

It was Edens who, years later, described Garland as 'the biggest thing to happen to the M–G–M musical', something which he and Freed believed from the moment they heard her sing. They nurtured her during the transition from child star to adult player: as a grown-up she came into her own with **For Me and My Gal** (1942), which also marks the screen debut of Gene Kelly (b. 1912), a dancer and, later, choreographer who had achieved Broadway stardom in 1940 in 'Pal Joey'. Busby Berkeley directed for Freed, and though the film is dedicated to all vaude-villians past and present, it is a bit short on the vaudeville side, being heavily involved with the First World War, like *Tin Pan Alley* two years earlier. As the U.S. was now in the War, the film tends towards the patriotic and sentimental. The Freed unit is shown at its best with the first number, the title song, in which Kelly talks Garland into joining him in a dance, and in a medley of World War One songs when Garland responds to the audience (as opposed to the camera). If you look closely you can see her young face crossed with lines, but her acting is perfect. Kelly's natural charm helps him through a role that requires him to be determined heel in the first half and, despite the plot, a determined hero in the second; also likeable is George Murphy as the guy who loses Garland to him.

Minnelli's first film was **Cabin in the Sky** (1943), based on an all-black Broadway show. Freed was given a budget of $600,000 ($200,000 less than that for *For Me and My Gal*, and only half the cost of each of his next two films – though these were in Technicolor) since he had convinced the front office that it would be a prestige success. M-G-M had had such a success with the all-black *Hallelujah!*, yet in the intervening years nothing had been done to remove the element of gospel singing from negro entertainments; but this one has a cheery plot about the struggle of Little Joe (Eddie 'Rochester' Anderson) between his ever-lovin' Petunia (Ethel Waters) and his weakness, Georgia Brown (Lena Horne). Miss Waters, one of the greatest of all entertainers, can wring your heart with lines like 'Lord, why you let me love him so much he can hurt me so bad?', and her fellow artists – who include Louis Armstrong, Rex Ingram and the Duke Ellington Orchestra – also help to make the material palatable. Freed usually made his own decisions regarding the music, and though he often jettisoned good Broadway songs for new and inferior ones, in this case he kept the best by Vernon Duke and John Latouche – the title song, 'Taking a Chance on Love' and 'Honey in the Honeycomb' – while commissioning three from Arlen and Harburg which are better than those unused. Minnelli's staging is happier with those in the jazz idiom, and only occasionally does he revert to stage patterns.

Norman Taurog directed **Presenting Lily Mars** (1943) for Pasternak and **Girl Crazy** (1943) for Freed. The former, from a novel by Booth Tarkington, is much like Pasternak's Durbin pictures, with Garland playing with great aplomb a stage-struck brat and having one enchanted sequence, on a darkened stage, when she and a stage-sweeper (Connie Gilchrist) do an improvised 'Every Little Movement'. *Girl Crazy* was the last teaming of Garland and Mickey Rooney, whose functions Freed had now defined – when she is not singing, he is clowning: his wide-ranging talent is at its best as he plays a young city slicker bested by the rubes. The source was an old Gershwin show, with the plot – about a co-ed school in the wilds of Nevada – and the score both left more or less intact. The stars have a song, 'Could You Use Me?', which may well be the best comedy duet in films, and it was filmed on location: this was one of the first musicals to go extensively outside the studio. The finale is a long extravaganza by Busby Berkeley, and he was also to have directed till replaced at Garland's request – the first recorded instance of her temperament.

On the other hand, Freed mangled both *Lady, Be Good* and *Panama Hattie*, by dropping songs, turning the 'books' inside out and adding guest stars: M-G-M badly needed a leading lady in the Ethel Merman mould, and cast Ann Sothern, a B-picture star, who was good, but in neither film quite good enough. So M-G-M signed Lucille Ball, another B-picture star, and put her in both **Best Foot Forward** (1943) and **Du Barry Was a Lady** (1943), directed respectively by Edward Buzzell and Roy del Ruth. Perversely, Freed kept the undistinguished Broadway score of the first, while throwing out most of the Cole Porter songs of the second. Ball is poor in both, and in *Du Barry* neither she nor Red Skelton are substitutes for Merman and Bert Lahr, whose teaming had been the main raison d'être of the original. That had also been rather risqué, and despite the fact that it had pleased Broadway for over four hundred performances, the Hays Office demanded considerable alterations – and the fantasy sequence which gives the film its title is abysmal. For solace, look to the third-billed star, who is Kelly, though then an indifferent dancer in white-tie-and-tails still seeking his individual style.

661

At the last minute he and Virginia O'Brien move in to prevent Ball and Skelton from ruining a splendid song, 'Friendship'.

Broadway Rhythm (1944) is also based on a show, and though as 'Very Warm for May' it was one of Broadway's more memorable flops, that seems little reason for retaining only 'All the Things You Are', with a brief sending up of the other songs from the Kern-Hammerstein score. Originally, like *Babes in Arms*, concerned with some kids putting on a show, the piece now has a clichéd plot about a Broadway producer (George Murphy) caught between a search for 'art' and a big Hollywood star – played by Ginny Simms, a plastic, podgy radio singer who was a protégée of Mayer. It is difficult to decide whether she or the ingenue, Gloria De Haven, is the less talented. Five minutes of dialogue as if by clockwork alternate with five minutes of song, all taking place in night clubs, theatrical agencies, theatres and hotel rooms, to emphasise the fact that, like *Born to Dance*, the film is a *Broadway Melody* in all but name: as was the case with the later Broadway Melodies, del Ruth directed for Cummings, and the otherwise dire guest list includes Lena Horne.

Cummings produced **Bathing Beauty** (1944), one of the first features directed by George Sidney (b. 1916), a former studio all-purpose man with a long experience in short subjects. It was also the first starring picture of Esther Williams, hard-faced and unsympathetic, not yet the smiling girl – she never could act – of her later films. Metro executives, in their wisdom (rightly as it turned out), thought this professional swimmer could be a star attraction, and for the next decade producers and writers were required to fashion stories set around swimming pools. In this one Miss Williams is a teacher at a girls' school, and Red Skelton, also from the downmarket end of the studio's players, is her ex-fiancé and a deviser of water pageants. The finale, conceived by John Murray Anderson, has great fountain leaps to rival the masturbatory fantasies of Berkeley in *The Gang's All Here*.

Clearly, none of these films prepared audiences for **Meet Me in St Louis** (1944), and it was not a project favoured by the front office. Freed had wanted to buy 'Life with Father', but had lost it to War-

ners, and was persuaded instead to buy Sally Benson's stories of turn of the century St Louis, which had also appeared in *The New Yorker*. Mayer agreed to what he regarded as a period Andy Hardy-type film: one jazzed-up screenplay was abandoned when Minnelli, Freed and Garland protested – though she in any case had at first not wanted to appear in the film. Later, she was very proud of it, as were all the participants and the front office as well, since apart from *Gone with the Wind* it was M-G-M's biggest grossing film up to that time. Garland's own magic contributes – as do the sets, designed by Cedric Gibbons,[*] Jack Martin Smith and Lemuel Ayers: George Folsey's camera moves through them, timed to the music, in what is the most entrancing co-ordination since *Le Million*. The film is, as James Agee pointed out, a love story between a family and their way of life, and that is beautifully expressed in the opening sequence: Mother (Mary Astor) is in the kitchen making ketchup with the maid (Marjorie Main); Grandfather (Harry Davenport) is singing the title song, and the two older girls (Garland, Lucille Bremer) take up the refrain before mooning about the boy (Tom Drake) next door; the two younger girls (Margaret O'Brien, Joan Carroll) are following the ice cart, while Father (Leon Ames) returns home hot and bad tempered. They are all agog over the romantic phone call expected from New York, and there is a reference to young Lonnie (Henry H. Daniels Jr) going to Princeton. The dinner-table conversation is funny and unforced: every line of the confident screenplay, by Irving Brecher and Fred F. Finklehoffe, adds to our knowledge of and liking for these people. No musical since *Swing Time* had been handled with such grace and sensitivity, but then, there had been no musical like this one: a sole reservation might be that Minnelli allowed Garland to sing 'The Trolley Song' with vivacity but no joie de vivre – and perhaps a second one would be that the finale at the St Louis Fair seems to need a song.[†]

---

[*]Though Gibbons was credited as Art Director on almost every M-G-M film for over thirty years, at this stage he presumably only approved the work of the others, who were working to the specifications of Freed and Minnelli.

[†]It originally had one, 'Boys and Girls Like You and Me', which Freed had bought from Rodgers and Hammerstein when it was cut from 'Oklahoma!', but it was also omitted here when the film was thought overlong.

Judy Garland and Lucille Bremer in Minnelli's enchanting *Meet Me in St Louis*. The film's visual elegance was not reflected in the studio's publicity material, which reflected great uncertainty as to whether the public would respond to a period musical. That material included the advertisements and sheet music covers, for there was no soundtrack album, but when Garland's record company, Decca, was successful with studio recordings of her songs M-G-M negotiated for Decca to release songs taken directly from the soundtrack of her next film (*The Harvey Girls*). Hitherto only Disney had licensed his soundtracks but in 1946, with *Till the Clouds Roll By*, M-G-M founded its own company to issue recordings from its films. It was not for another ten years that the other studios began to see the advantages of soundtrack recordings, but meanwhile almost all the great M-G-M musicals were commemorated on disc.

Despite the general standard of screen musicals, the fact that *Meet Me in St Louis* was no more than warmly received by reviewers suggests that they were less spoilt than imperceptive; it is equally hard to credit that **Anchors Aweigh** (1945) was overall better liked, but at least most critics recognised that Gene Kelly was becoming a creative force in film musicals. As directed by George Sidney for Pasternak, this one is stuffed with songs and dances, but in a lucky dip manner, since for each good thing there are several duds – the latter including José Iturbi graciously playing himself, as well as 'The Donkey Serenade' and the 'Hungarian Rhapsody' accompanied by an army of pianos, and Kathryn Grayson, whether singing, acting or trying to be charming. Isabel Lennart's laboured screenplay has to do with some sailors meeting Kathryn Grayson in Hollywood, but it is punctuated with

Kelly's dances. Because of his success with *Cover Girl* he was allowed to do his own choreography, and not long into the film he and Frank Sinatra bid farewell to their buddies in a marvellously freewheeling number; later his solos are proof that he regarded movies as fantasy bait: obviously he believed that dancing on film could be enhanced by the use of dreams and cartoons – and most people remember this movie for his dance with Tom and Jerry.

For Freed and Minnelli, the success of *Meet Me in St Louis* had been followed by *The Clock*, also with Garland, and the first straight film for all of them. In addition they were euphoric at having coaxed Fred Astaire into a long-term contract, but in proving that he could also dance in balletic style they made a mistake, which is entitled **Yolanda and the Thief** (1945). The leading lady is Lucille Bremer, 'a protégée of one of the studio bosses', said Minnelli later, 'and quite unsuitable'. He also referred to 'the insane plot' – taken from a story by Jacques Théry and Ludwig Bemelmans, about two American con men (Astaire, Frank Morgan) involved in the affairs both of a mythical kingdom and a fey, convent-reared heiress. The attempt of the decor to reproduce Bemelmans' paintbox colours is merely vulgar, while the hillocks and flowers swamp Astaire. He and Bremer do have one halfway good dance, 'Will You Marry Me?', but it is School of Agnes deMille, which does not suit him. This was the first Freed production to lose money, and was perhaps instrumental in Astaire's decision to retire – which, fortunately for the cinema, was later rescinded.

He had already filmed his sequences in the Freed–Minnelli **Ziegfeld Follies** (1946), and their reception must have been a consolation to all three of them: 'This Heart of Mine', in effect his first film ballet, a gay piece about a jewel thief, with Bremer; 'Limehouse Blues', a part-theatrical piece of chinoiserie, also a ballet with Bremer; and 'The Babbitt and the Bromide', the Gershwins' old number, teamed with Gene Kelly. Also in the region of the sublime is 'A Great Lady Has an Interview', giving Garland's wit full rein as a gracious movie queen – and with added piquancy if you know that it was written for Greer Garson. Freed had long cherished the idea of another film celebrating Ziegfeld (M-G-M held the rights to the name), and finally came up with the first purely revue film since the early Talkies, and the last created specifically for film.* In heaven, Ziegfeld (William Powell) looks down and murmurs something about 'so many wonderful people remaining and so many wonderful people coming along in the meantime': the only Ziegfeld star on display is Fanny Brice, and her sketch is somewhat less unfunny than others with Red Skelton, Keenan Wynn and Victor Moore; a number of other sketches were tossed out during a troubled production history which brought costs to an almost unprecedented $3¼ million. Started in

1943, the film was delayed because its ostentation was thought to be at odds with the wartime mood; it was previewed at the end of 1944, in a three-hour version, and again with cuts and changes the following year. Minnelli, despite being solely credited, directed only the Garland and Astaire numbers and the florid staging of the 'Drinking Song' from 'La Traviata'. George Sidney, whom he originally replaced, directed the opening number, 'Here's to the Ladies', with Lucille Ball and Virginia O'Brien, and many hands worked at the finale – Kathryn Grayson's ballad amid the floating foam – but it cannot be worse than the one originally intended, with Astaire, Bremer and James Melton. We may also wonder about an artistic judgment which threw out an Astaire solo but kept the Esther Williams water ballet. The film did, however, make a handsome profit.

After Roger Edens had seen 'Oklahoma!' he wanted to make a Western musical, and **The Harvey Girls** (1946), intended as a straight vehicle for Lana Turner, became a musical for Garland. The latter had become, according to Gallup, America's favourite female star, after Ingrid Bergman and Bette Davis, and that was partly because of Meet Me in St Louis: so that although Freed did not like repeating a formula, he allowed the numbers to be influenced by that film – the wistful love song, the waltz for the girls, and the marvellous opening, 'The Atchison, Topeka and the Santa Fe'. He had always liked unusual performers, but had slotted them into his films usually as specialities till Minnelli (in Cabin in the Sky and Meet Me in St Louis) had shown that each could have his moment or be part of the ensemble – and George Sidney, directing on this occasion, goes further by integrating into the whole the contrasting talents of Virginia O'Brien, Ray Bolger, Cyd Charisse and Kenny Baker. Nevertheless, it remains Garland's film. Her private difficulties are beginning to show – she is a peaky, unjolly heroine; but her smile, when it comes, could melt the snows of Everest. Her role is that of a mail-order bride-to-be who arrives in a small Western town and joins the Harvey Restaurant girls in their battles with the saloon hussies, led by Angela Lansbury.

Till the Clouds Roll By (1946) was

---

*Such wartime films as Thousands Cheer had proved the form viable, but they had 'books', as did Warner's 1952 Starlift. The independently produced New Faces (1954) was a record of a Broadway revue, and some compilations of television comedy series have found their way to cinemas.

Freed's first bid in that breed known as the biopic, and it is as dreary as any of the others. The composer maligned here is Jerome Kern (Robert Walker), especially when he looks at the Mississippi and is inspired to compose 'Show Boat', or when he says 'I'd rather hear her sing my songs than anyone else in the world,' referring to Lucille Bremer, who in this narrative becomes a big M-G-M star. Real M-G-M stars sing the songs, including two by Judy Garland as Marilyn Miller, which were directed by Minnelli, to whom she was now married. Richard Whorf, a former actor, is credited with the direction, but Sidney handled the finale, a bland potpourri of Kern's songs (for which Sidney cannot be blamed) and the majority of the other numbers were the work of Robert Alton; the opening medley from 'Show Boat' at least starts the film well.

Pandro S. Berman produced **Living in a Big Way** (1947), written and directed by Gregory LaCava, who had not made a film for five years – and he would live for five more without making another. He had become an alcoholic, and though the film is lively and well made, it was a flop. Gene Kelly was persuaded into making it because the studio hoped to turn his co-star, Marie McDonald, into another Lana Turner, but he found her 'a triple threat who couldn't sing, dance or act'. He also thought the script dated, and it is certainly mushy on the subject of war veterans; but LaCava is to some extent his old self on a favourite theme, the impoverished citizen (i.e. an ex-G.I.) who becomes embroiled with a wealthy family. Kelly's numbers include a spectacular dance on the rafters of an unfinished house. The film was in black and white, otherwise abandoned for musicals by M-G-M in 1943, which could be one reason for the public's indifference.

Summer Holiday (1947) was also a director's first film in five years and a disaster: he is Rouben Mamoulian, and the producer was Freed. Its source is O'Neill's 'Ah Wilderness!', but it might just as well have been called 'Andy Hardy Gets Drunk': Mickey Rooney is merely brash as a precocious student with a deep love for a poem he calls 'The Ballad of Reeding Gole'. The elders – Walter Huston, Selena Royle, Frank Morgan and Agnes Moorehead – are obviously suitable, but Gloria De Haven is null as Rooney's puppy love and Marilyn Maxwell only a small-time Mae West as the chorus girl alternative. Mamoulian himself liked the sequence where the latter's dress changes from pale pink to scarlet as she and Rooney sit drinking, but here and elsewhere the use of colour does not prevent the film from being vastly inferior to Clarence Brown's earlier version of this play: nor does the passing of song from person to person help it approach the quality of *Meet Me in St Louis*, even if Mamoulian had done that successfully in the past (in *Love Me Tonight*).

The period detail – the time is the Twenties – is somewhat sporadic in **Good News** (1947), but the film is lively, as directed by Charles Walters (1911–82), promoted by Freed after having choreographed for his unit for some years. The cast breaks into song and dance as if it were the most natural thing in the world, and the songs are mainly those of Brown, deSylva and Henderson, whose old college musical has been rather vaguely followed. The students are led with predictable charm by June Allyson and Peter Lawford. She obviously was directed to sing her two ballads with the wistfulness and gestures of Miss Garland.

Garland herself was reunited with Kelly in **The Pirate** (1948), one of their less popular films – for on this occasion Minnelli and Freed were galloping too fast for public taste. Albert Hackett and Frances Goodrich wrote this cod tale of Caribbean romance from a play by S. N. Behrman, originally a divertissement for the Lunts. It is fun but not funny: a daydreaming orphan (Garland) is torn between her chosen fiancé (Walter Slezak) and a strolling player (Kelly), who pretends to be her idol, a notorious pirate. Garland's grasp of the form required is surer than Kelly's, for she only hints at parody, while his attempt to mix the styles of Barrymore and Fairbanks is too broad – which may be why he regards the film as a failure while Minnelli does not. The settings are theatrical without the preciosity of *Yolanda and the Thief*, and the Cole Porter songs include 'Be a Clown', to provide a rousing finale.

The same principals were originally involved in **Easter Parade** (1948), but Freed replaced Minnelli with Charles Walters, since he thought that the Garland–Minnelli marriage, now under strain, might mend if

height, and given to disappearing when lyrics were urgently needed. No hint is given of Rodgers's defection to Hammerstein during the last months of Hart's life, nor of the latter's taste for low-life pickups – and his unrequited love is naturally heterosexual. The ending originally had a drunken Hart watching his old flame (Betty Garrett) in a dive where she is singing 'It Never Entered My Mind', but it was cut, presumably as being too strong after the blandness which had preceded it. The numbers are zestfully staged, whether as party pieces or the usual stage routines, and the success of a ten-minute ballet, 'Slaughter on Tenth Avenue', danced by Gene Kelly and Vera-Ellen, was further impetus to the Freed unit to experiment with the musical form.

Kelly and a frequent collaborator, Stanley Donen (b. 1924), provided the original story for **Take Me Out to the Ball Game** (1949), and it is immediately clear that their aim was to use the ultra-masculine world of baseball as an occasion for song and dance. They also choreographed and directed the musical numbers, favouring (apart from one vaudeville duo) 'spontaneity' in natural settings, and an exhilarating collection they are. 'Don't go home yet' sing Kelly and Frank Sinatra to the audience at the end, explaining that the romantic complications have yet to be solved – and their action is an acknowledgment that we did not come to the cinema to see a musical about a baseball team, but these particular people entertaining. That we are more interested in them than in the plot derives from the Hope and Crosby films, but Kelly and Donen would use the concept to bring the film musical to its richest form. This one was directed by Busby Berkeley, and Esther Williams (as owner of the baseball team) does not have a swimming ballet, though she does take a turn or two around a hotel pool.

The Barkleys of Broadway (1949), though in no sense innovatory, does indicate that the Freed unit had become even more confident after its recent successes. The film musical still counted for less than the Broadway musical, though by this time *Meet Me in St Louis* had been recognised as the best since the films of Astaire and Rogers. Since 'Oklahoma!' the Broadway musical had been experimenting in

The *sine qua non* of the musical is a likeable cast, and that the M-G-M musical usually boasted. Beyond that the studio had three stars who were almost certainly the greatest ever to work in the genre – Judy Garland, Fred Astaire and Gene Kelly. She made three films with Kelly, but only one with Astaire, which is why *Easter Parade* is precious. She proved herself no mean dancer, and she could pick up steps immediately – but the purpose of 'A Couple of Swells' was, as can be seen, comic.

they did not work together; and when Kelly broke an ankle, Astaire was persuaded out of retirement. Thus the film stars two nonpareils, and is generally worthy of them – at least, to see it now is to marvel at their talents, and that of Irving Berlin, whose songs, old and new, are bountifully melodious. The staging of the numbers, by Walters and Robert Alton, ranges from the good to the magnificent – in the case of a montage of ragtime done by the stars; and the book, by Goodrich and Hackett, is a serviceable tale of a dancer and his two partners – the other of whom is Ann Miller.

The score of **Words and Music** (1948) is also exceptional, since the title refers to the work of Rodgers and Hart, whose collaboration provided Freed with a more refreshing film than the one on Jerome Kern. The story, as directed by Norman Taurog, is bland. So is Tom Drake as Rodgers, presumably out of deference to the composer; as Hart, Mickey Rooney is merely cocky, self-conscious about his such matters as plot and atmosphere, and its Hollywood poor relation also dropped the traditional comic supporting players, while often remaining lighthearted. In reuniting Garland and Astaire, Freed wanted to capitalise on her way with a comic line, and also to reintroduce the comedy element from Astaire's prewar pictures. A suitable script was commissioned from Adolph Green (b. 1918) and Betty Comden (b. 1919), a team of New York writers whom he had brought to the coast for *Good News*. Like much of their screen work, this one has an element of the biographical, concerning as it does a dancing team which splits up when the distaff half wishes to go dramatic. Ironically, the ailing Garland was replaced by Ginger Rogers – and also ironically she is the reason that the result is hardly funnier than *Easter Parade*. The new ladylike Ginger is not a patch on the young Ginger: tackling a recitation in French of the 'Marseillaise', she does it absolutely straight, for all the world as if she had seen another Oscar in her crystal ball. As a result this film lacks the careless rapture of the films the team made for R.K.O., but as an entertainment it did not disappoint the many cinemagoers who came to see this already legendary couple.

Since the failures of *Yolanda and the Thief*, *Living in a Big Way* and *Summer Holiday*, M-G-M had been reluctant to sanction musicals that did not involve theatre folk, and since **In the Good Old Summertime** (1949) concerns the romance of two shop assistants, its four songs – there is also a lullaby – are bunched in twos, as if removable. Garland sings them all, two at the firm's party, and two in the shop – for fortunately the shop sells music and musical instruments. This is an otherwise straightforward remake of *The Shop Around the Corner*, now set in Chicago in the 1900s, and as directed by Robert Z. Leonard for Pasternak not quite achieving the marzipan tone of the Lubitsch original. Both directors took their cue from their star, and Garland – looking healthier and happier than in the films made either side of it – is very funny as she tries to prove her worth in the shop while mooning about her pen-friend, Van Johnson. (The piece was intended to be one of his teamings with June Allyson, who was pregnant.) The supporting cast includes Buster Keaton, till recently a gagman at the studio – and he has one pratfall which can bring the house down.

On the strength of *Take Me Out to the Ball Game*, Freed allowed Kelly and Donen to direct **On the Town** (1949), and though one of its heroines is a dance student, none of the other principal characters has any connection with the theatre. It is the great liberating musical of the American cinema. M-G-M had bought the property before its Broadway opening because of the enthusiasm of a member of Mayer's staff, who happened to be a friend of the composer, Leonard Bernstein. Mayer and his fellow executives so loathed it, however, that when Comden and Green arrived under contract they were advised to remind no one that they had written the book. George Abbott had directed it on stage, and when Freed invited him to make a film of his choice he chose this – though the project was taken over by Kelly and Donen within hours of Freed's assent. Kelly considers the result his greatest contribution to the film musical, and I think we may assume that the achievement is mainly his. The film recounts the adventures of three sailors in New York; it begins in the Brooklyn Navy Yard as they leave ship at 6 a.m. – and break into song and dance in anticipation. The scene was filmed on location, and the song continued in recognisable parts of New York – if not in fact very many, for M-G-M was nervous about something so novel, and ordered the company and crew to return before they had finished: but the opening is one good reason why the film bowled over every critic who reviewed it. The staging of the numbers was another, and the key to their success lies in Kelly's view: 'If you make it look like hard work it's no good. You've got to make the public believe they can go out and do it themselves.'

In *Anchors Aweigh* there is a moment when Kelly and Sinatra are escorting the girl home, and there is a kidding gaiety about them, because they have had a marvellous evening together: it is a feeling that recurs throughout *On the Town*. Each number seems to be improvised and impromptu – and this was the first time an entire film had been built around this concept. Previous examples had seldom had as much exuberance and hilarity, a feeling of

The Screen's Other Great Dancer

By 1949 Gene Kelly had gained creative control over the musicals he made, bringing the genre to its peak. Together he and Stanley Donen directed *On the Town*, ABOVE, which raised Kelly's speciality, seeming spontaneity, to a new art, and here are, clockwise, Betty Garrett, Ann Miller, Kelly, Alice Pearce, Jules Munshin and Frank Sinatra entertaining impromptu the customers of a Coney Island bar. Minnelli directed *An American in Paris*, ABOVE RIGHT, with Kelly and Leslie Caron in the climactic ballet – the artiness of which was reflected for a brief moment in *Singin' in the Rain*. ABOVE FAR RIGHT, The lady is Cyd Charisse, more rewardingly employed in another sequence, RIGHT, from the same exhilarating number.

Howard Keel in
Annie Get Your Gun,
based on Irving
Berlin's Broadway
musical. When in
1974 M-G-M issued
its compilation film,
That's Entertainment
it was not permitted
to include a sequence
from this particular
musical since Berlin
held the rights and
was smarting from
the cancellation – by
another manage-
ment – of a project
built round his
songs, and one on
which he had
worked for years.
However, he
relented in view of
the film's enormous
popularity, and there
is a scene from *Annie*
in *That's
Entertainment Part 2.*

nice people liking each other – of just being
alive on a night like this – and it was never
more invigoratingly done than in the
anticipatory title song, as rendered by the
sailors and their girls, starting at the top of
the Empire State Building and continuing
into the street. It is one of the new numbers
written by Comden and Green with Roger
Edens, and good enough almost to justify
the rejection of much of Bernstein's score,
which Freed did not like. Bernstein's ballet, 'Fancy Free', which inspired the show,
received homage from Kelly in the form of
a new ballet to Bernstein's music, 'A Day
in New York'. It was recognised as far
more modern and cinematic than the only
other ballet then conceived for the screen,
the British *Red Shoes* (q.v.).

The admiration accorded *On the Town*
tended to obscure the fact that it was an
adaptation, and indeed the original had run
only just over a year on Broadway, while
really successful shows ran for several. The
price of the film rights had therefore escalated and deterred the Hollywood companies from purchasing them, while the whimsical nature of many musicals prevented

them from reaching the screen.* **Annie
Get Your Gun** (1950) may be considered
the first film version in several years of a
Broadway musical, and it was a second
consecutive triumph for Freed, who had
persuaded the studio to pay a record
$800,000 for the rights as a vehicle for Judy
Garland. Unfortunately, he assigned Busby Berkeley, whom she loathed, to direct.
When her personal difficulties led to her
removal, his footage was thought unusable and he was replaced by George Sidney. Sidney agreed with Freed that he
should approach it as one of Broadway's
great shows, with a strong book by Herbert and Dorothy Fields, and a marvellous
score by Irving Berlin. It has been filmed as
if for a stage audience, with the songs
belted at the camera – and it is certainly
the right decision, in view of the over-
emphatic and enthusiastic approach of
Betty Hutton, Garland's replacement. She
so clearly wants to be loved and admired
that she eventually succeeds, while Howard Keel is a tower of strength as Annie's
big-headed beau. It is a carnival film, never
losing sight of the milling circus crowds,
the galloping horses, the balloons and the
banners.

The skills of the Freed unit were appearing in the studio's other musicals, and
Three Little Words (1950), directed by
Richard Thorpe for Cummings, could be
the definitive 'And then I wrote . . .'
movie, detailing the collaboration between song-writers Bert Kalmar (Astaire)
and Harry Ruby (Red Skelton). Astaire
brings attention and style to very little in
the way of plot and choreography, but
really needs a sharper partner than Vera-
Ellen to make the most of his remarkable
qualities. The pairing of Garland and Kelly
in **Summer Stock** (1950) is perfect, despite the fact that she is stoutish – and was
having so many problems in her personal
life that sometimes she did not know what
she was doing, or so said the director,
Charles Walters. Pasternak, the producer,
noticed that these did not show in the
finished result, and when she finally takes
the lead – as we knew she would – in the

*M-G-M bought Lerner and Loewe's 'The Day Before
Spring' for $250,000 in 1945, and never filmed it; the much
more successful 'Brigadoon', also a fantasy, was purchased
by the company for only $120,000 – but not until three years
after its Broadway opening, and filming did not start till three
years after that; Walt Disney bought 'Finian's Rainbow' but
did not film it.

show which Kelly has been rehearsing in her barn, he says with exceptional feeling, 'You're wonderful – everything I ever hoped for in a leading lady.' In each of the films prepared for her since *The Pirate*, a comic duet had been planned, but she did only one, 'A Couple of Swells' with Astaire in *Easter Parade*; Astaire did others with Ginger Rogers and Jane Powell, while her absences during the shooting of this particular film caused Kelly to do this number with Phil Silvers. When Garland left the studio by mutual consent after this film, the front office was relieved, but her colleagues – tried though they had been by her behaviour – acknowledged that the M-G-M musical would never be the same again.

Certainly Esther Williams was no replacement, swimming – and singing – in the *sea* in **Pagan Love Song** (1950), and even if she and Howard Keel do little else for the 76 minutes' running time, that is part of the film's charm, along with its songs and bounteous South Seas locations. Unfortunately the missing plot is telescoped into the last five minutes, destroying the audience's relaxed mood. Robert Alton directed, one of his two films in that capacity, after Miss Williams had complained to Freed that his first choice (Donen) had no belief in her talents. Donen's direction of **Royal Wedding** (1951) and his staging of the numbers is so dire that we may confidently credit Kelly with the energy and inventiveness of the films they made together. Indeed, apart from the contributions of Astaire and the composer, Burton Lane, the film is disastrous, perhaps because Freed had conceived it for two doubtful British acquisitions – some Technicolor footage of the last British royal wedding, and Moira Shearer, the dancer of *The Red Shoes*. Astaire found her an unsuitable partner, and she was replaced by the even less suitable Sarah Churchill, daughter of Winston, and a sometime actress. The screenplay has Astaire falling in love with her while in London with his sister and vaudeville partner (Jane Powell), and as written by Alan Jay Lerner the script is witless.

At the lower end of the studio's musicals are those with Mario Lanza, a temperamental tenor whose career was entrusted to Pasternak. Lanza made two films with Kathryn Grayson, which the public wisely avoided, but 'Be My Love', a song from the second of the two, had been much played on juke boxes. The studio accordingly embarked upon **The Great Caruso** (1951) hesitantly, since a film of operatic excerpts was considered a risk. However, these were by no means unfamiliar to the public, and the box office benefited from a hit song, 'The Loveliest Night of the Year', based on an old waltz, 'Over the Waves', sung to Caruso at his birthday party in one of several borrowings from *The Jolson Story* (q.v.) Lanza's arias are curtailed (unlike this particular song), but confidence in the project is not instilled by the very first shot (Naples with Vesuvius to its north). The real Caruso was short, stout and inordinately vain, though managing a spectacular career before dying after a long illness in Milan at the age of forty-eight. In the film he dies on the stage of the Metropolitan, appropriately so, since it is made to appear the only opera house of any importance – and as played by the bull-like but otherwise negative Lanza it is not a moment too soon. The memoir by Caruso's much younger American wife was the basis for the screenplay, and it comes as no surprise to find that she publicly dissociated herself from the film.

Commercially, at least, the M-G-M musical was at a peak. This film joined *Annie Get Your Gun* to become one of the most profitable the company had ever made, while Freed's next two productions also appeared in the list of the year's highest-grossing films. **Show Boat** (1951) is very handsome: George Sidney's films, including his non-musical ones (q.v.), were increasingly pleasing to look at, and this, with its notable shots of the show boat as it moves down the Mississippi, has felicitous contributions from Charles Rosher, the cinematographer, and the designer, Jack Martin Smith. The orchestrations are by Adolph Deutsch, and though the score has been curtailed the songs seem to come up at five minute intervals, while the rest of the time they may be heard behind the action – which is sometimes choreographed to them, most agreeably when Magnolia and Julie break into their gay little dance. Despite the presence of Miss Grayson as Magnolia, it is the way Kern's music is used which makes this the best of the three film versions – and it has Howard Keel to sing his share of the lyrics.

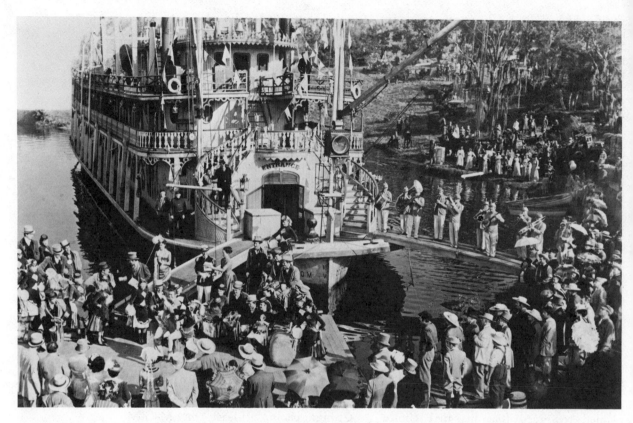

Those with fond memories of Universal's 1936 version of *Show Boat* did not expect the M-G-M remake to be quite as good as it is – which was almost certainly a challenge to Freed's team. They capitalised on two factors – its incomparable score, splendidly arranged and recorded even when relegated to the background, and Technicolor. It may have been the easiest decision to have the show boat itself move down the (back-lot) Mississippi to the strains of 'Ol' Man River', but it is enormously effective.

Ava Gardner is a magnificent Julie; Marge and Gower Champion have two witty dances; and Joe E. Brown and Agnes Moorehead are the Wilkes. The book has also been better compressed – by John Lee Mahin – than in Whale's version, and Sidney makes it move along with a certain charm.

Equally popular and much more admired, **An American in Paris** (1951) has dated badly, though we may consider it beyond good and evil because Minnelli, the director, and Kelly expected audiences to share their enthusiasm for Paris and modern French art. No one involved seems to have got closer to Paris, re-created in the studio, than any two-day tripper, and Alan Jay Lerner's screenplay about an ex-G.I. (Kelly) staying in the city to paint is exceptionally thin. The staging of the songs, from the Gershwin library, is as self-conscious as it is confident, but the numbers are nonetheless memorable – especially the cheerful 'Swonderful', as sung by Kelly and Georges Guetary, the romantic 'Our Love Is Here To Stay', as

danced by Kelly and Leslie Caron, and 'I'll Build a Stairway to Paradise', a luscious and affectionate parody of Ziegfeld production numbers, sung by Guetary. The final dream ballet, too much influenced by the one in *The Red Shoes*, now seems studied and over-zealous, with its prancing around the mock fountains of the Place de la Concorde. It was filmed last – at a cost of over half a million dollars, just under one-fifth of its total budget – because the studio had reservations: ironically, it was the one musical number (if I may so term it) which the industry most admired* and it helped the film towards its several Oscars, including Best Picture and a special award to Kelly for his choreography.

On the other hand, the unappreciated **The Belle of New York** (1952), directed by Walters, retains its charms. Freed had been preparing it as a vehicle for Astaire

*In the 1974 compilation of numbers from M-G-M musicals, *That's Entertainment*, the commentary still spoke of the ballet as their major achievement. As a celebration of these films, this one was enormously popular, but a sequel, *That's Entertainment 2*, was, despite the linking material provided by Astaire and Kelly, dismissed – quite rightly – as a rip-off.

and Garland when Astaire announced his retirement in 1945: there were script troubles – the film has only a slight connection with the old stage musical of the same name – and they were hardly solved when the project was re-activated. Freed's musicals had been moving towards a loose, inconsequential structure, but the plot – a man about town (Astaire) meets and woos a Salvation Army lass (Vera-Ellen) – found little favour. Astaire said that he is 'mad' that it failed as it is one of his favourite films, and it was fun to make: it is fun to watch, mainly because the numbers show him and the Freed unit at their best, especially in 'The Bachelor Dinner Song', 'Oops', done on a streetcar, and the Currier and Ives number.

By common consent **Singin' in the Rain** (1952) is the masterpiece of the Freed unit, and probably the best musical ever made in Hollywood – the gayest, the funniest, the most affectionate, the most insouciant. Freed had wanted to build a film about the songs he had earlier written with Nacio Herb Brown for the first Talkies, which gave Comden and Green the idea of a Hollywood story about the coming of Sound; and Howard Keel was originally to have starred as a Silent actor adjusting to speech. The film has a silly, entrancing plot about a Silent swashbuckler being converted into a Talkie, with Gene Kelly as its hero and Debbie Reynolds as the chorus girl, whom he wants as his leading lady; Jean Hagen is Lina Lamont, his actual co-star, who reads all the fan magazines and consequently believes that he loves her as much in life as on the screen. Since Lina's voice does not, to put it mildly, match her looks, the moment when she opens her mouth is overwhelming. Miss Hagen's performance is one of the funniest ever put on film, as she ardently and triumphantly quotes the magazine which called her 'a shimmering, glowing star in the cinema firm-a-ment'. As directed by Kelly and Donen, the film is never serious for more than a fleeting second, with good jokes at the expense of Hollywood and that era of wonderful nonsense. Kelly, Reynolds and their cohort Donald O'Connor are captivating together, especially in their 'spontaneous' numbers, while Kelly's usual song and dance to denote his falling in love, this time in the rain, is probably the most beloved sequence in the history of film musicals. Most of the film has a deliberately drab look, coming vividly to life whenever it celebrates show business, as in the 'Beautiful Girl' number which heralds the coming of the 'All-Singing All-Dancing All-Talking movies', and the ballet, with its scarlets, greens, yellows and whites. The ballet, a salute to old Broadway, is described by Kelly to the producer (Millard Mitchell; the role is based on Freed), who says, *after* we have seen it, 'That's all very well, but I'll have to wait till it's visualised on screen.' The film is replete with such touches, which is one of the reasons few people ever tire of it. It did not, as it happened, get tremendously good reviews – certainly not as good as those for the more innovative On the Town and the arty An American in Paris, but the public loved it.

Metro's acknowledged supremacy in musicals resulted in the purchase of a number of old Broadway shows, few of which were filmed. **Lovely to Look At** (1952) is one that was, a remake of *Roberta*, and the worst that may be said of it is that it entailed the suppression of the earlier film for two decades. As produced by Cummings and directed by Mervyn LeRoy – except for the fashion parade at the end, which Minnelli directed – it may be enjoyed for the deployment of its score, almost intact, and its handling by Keel, Ann Miller and the Champions. Something similar may be said of **The Merry Widow** (1952), equally sumptuous, for the Danilo of Fernando Lamas is surprisingly effective; he looks very romantic, even if he lacks the charm or comedy sense of Chevalier. Pasternak produced this third M-G-M version of the Lehar operetta, and it was directed by Curtis Bernhardt who, like LeRoy, is not the lightest of directors, in this case foolishly allowing Lana Turner (in the title role) to set the tone.

Lili (1953) was directed by Charles Walters, whose own favourite picture it was: 'We certainly had problems on that one – including two dull leading men – but it all worked out marvellously.' As adapted by Helen Deutsch from a story by Paul Gallico, this film is about a waif (Leslie Caron) who, taken into carnival life, is torn between the magician (Jean-Pierre Aumont) and an embittered puppeteer (Mel Ferrer) – a matter she resolves after a couple of

673

One of the reasons that Fred Astaire's career at M-G-M was so rewarding was that Freed was determined to show even more of his extraordinary talent than had been revealed during his days dancing with Ginger Rogers at R.K.O. He was pushed towards the balletic, and in *The Band Wagon* was engaged in an enjoyable number taking off thick-ear private eye thrillers. The lady is again Cyd Charisse, going from brunette to blonde and back again to prove herself deadly to the male.

dream ballets. With the exception of Miss Caron, the cast – which also includes Zsa Zsa Gabor and Kurt Kasznar – is not one to be employed when attempting winsome charm; the puppet scenes are cute; the one song is plugged to death; and the settings are the worst kind of Hollywood France. Caron's performance has honesty and a quiet vitality; against all studio advice she insisted on drab clothes, and by not playing for sympathy she almost makes this film bearable. Walters and Deutsch must have agreed with the interpretation, for the Cinderella Caron plays for them in **The Glass Slipper** (1955) is described as 'not exactly an amiable child', and the hostility shown to her is understandable. For such reasons this is one of the better films for children, but they – and indeed, anyone – would be bored by the dream ballets choreographed by Roland Petit. The producer of both films was Edwin H. Knopf, who also came up with a new version of *Waterloo Bridge* with Caron, the ghastly **Gaby** (1956), directed by Curtis Bernhardt.

Meanwhile, since Astaire's only two failures for M-G-M had been without a show business background, Freed commissioned a theatre story from Comden and Green. **The Band Wagon** (1953) is cousin to *Singin' in the Rain*, since it is also about turning a flop entertainment into a success, and is also built round some old songs, by Arthur Schwartz and Howard

Dietz (who was a 'house' man, in charge of the studio's publicity). The characters played by Nanette Fabray and Oscar Levant are based on Comden and Green themselves; the theatre director *wunderkind* played by Jack Buchanan is based on Minnelli; and Astaire plays a washed-up Hollywood song and dance man who had once starred in 'Swinging Down to Panama'. Some of his lines reflect his unease at still playing in musicals in middle age, and while in-jokes, rare in movies at this time, proliferate (there is a parody of the auction scene in *The Star* q.v.) the darts are not particularly well aimed. The musical numbers are among the best ever put on film, whether 'improvised' or as part of the stage show. Astaire is in incomparable form, and when Cyd Charisse wraps her arms and legs around him as they dance you may forgive her for seeming to read her dialogue from cue-cards. As directed by Minnelli, everything about the film has style.

That is not a word to be used about a new version of **Rose Marie** (1954), as produced and directed by Mervyn LeRoy, whose attitude seems to have been that people who like operetta will like anything. In this case they were offered neither the original plot nor score, though the new songs are an improvement on the old ones omitted. They are sung by Keel, Ann Blyth, Fernando Lamas and Bert Lahr, but are so poorly staged as to minimise both singer and song. The original setting of the Canadian Rockies remains, since the studio found the subject suitable for its first CinemaScope (q.v.) musical, but the location work only emphasises the painted studio mountains which alternate with it. Another CinemaScope remake, **The Student Prince** (1954), directed by Richard Thorpe, is sometimes revived, presumably since it features 'The Singing Voice of Mario Lanza'. Relations between Lanza and the studio had reached a point of no return, the star having given the word 'temperament' a new meaning, according to Pasternak. M-G-M owned the songtracks, already recorded, and replaced him in front of the camera with Edmund Purdom, who does little to improve matters. Towards the end he goes into the cathedral to sing, with Lanza's voice, 'I'll Walk with God' (a number of religious songs had been getting into the hit parade), and you

would be well advised to walk out of the cinema – if, by chance, you are still there.

Though *The Student Prince* is handsome in the M-G-M fashion, it is hard to believe that it and *Rose Marie* were in production at the same time as **Kiss Me, Kate** (1953) and **Seven Brides for Seven Brothers** (1954), since these are among the best M-G-M musicals – and they were produced by Cummings. *Kiss Me, Kate* was made in 3-D, like CinemaScope then being used in an attempt to prevent audiences from defecting to T.V. A three-dimensional effect was achieved by having each spectator wear special glasses, and the system was exploited by ensuring that a fair number of things were hurled at the audience. The decision to make this property in that gimmicky process may be one reason why Freed was not involved – for he was a friend of Cole Porter, whose greatest stage success it had been. The show was unsatisfactory only because the Sam and Bella Spewack book lacked wit, and Dorothy Kingsley's screenplay is little improvement. A famous acting couple, once married, are reunited for a musical version of 'The Taming of the Shrew' – of which we see a potted version between their bickering and other backstage nonsense. As most of the content consists of a stage performance it can only transfer uneasily to film, and George Sidney directs with no firm control. However, the musical numbers make it a feast if not a banquet – at least to admirers of Keel and Cole. Keel is notably good with the point numbers, and his Petruchio is a luscious piece of braggadocio. As the virago of a leading lady, Kathryn Grayson improves mightily over her simpering soubrettes, but is an inconsiderable artist and insufficiently stylish. Ann Miller has five numbers, including two duets and two excellent dances shared with Tommy Rall, Bob Fosse and Bobby Van – 'Tom, Dick and Harry' – and the interpolated 'From this Moment On'. 'Brush Up Your Shakespeare', done with amateur buck and wing by Keenan Wynn and James Whitmore, is still a show-stopper, despite some bowdlerisation of the lyrics.

Seven Brides for Seven Brothers was made in CinemaScope, and at this point it may be said that its extra cost and its temporary achievement as a box-office attraction caused some studios to avoid Technicolor

for a cheaper colour system. M-G-M owned Anscocolor, and used it for this film, which, with painted backcloths, makes it often visually depressing, though, when Keel breaks into 'Bless Yore Beautiful Hide' it is clear that Stanley Donen, the director, has found a style to match the hope of the song's lyric, the jauntiness of its music, and the masculine strength of the singer. The screenplay was written by Albert Hackett, Frances Goodrich and Dorothy Kingsley, working from a story by Stephen Vincent Benét. Keel plays a mountain man who takes a wife (Jane Powell, in her best screen work), whereupon his six brothers are encouraged to emulate the rape of the Sabine women by forcibly abducting their chosen brides. Keel has a song about that event, 'Sobbin' Women', and Powell has a similar one, 'Goin' Courtin''', which whirls itself into a joy we seldom see; but the film's tour de force is the virile, balletic square dance, as exhilarating as any sequence ever put on film.

Though Donen's work on this occasion achieves something as good as his films with Kelly, he plummeted again with **Deep in My Heart** (1954), one of the two films produced by Roger Edens (independently of Freed). There is in theory no reason why two supposedly forward-looking artists should involve themselves

Seven Brides for Seven Brothers is another landmark of the M-G-M musical. It was the last one which was critically admired and hugely popular – with the exception of *Gigi*, which was recognised as a late flowering. The end of the M-G-M musical is one of the mysteries of cinema, for the financial return on *Seven Brides* was enough to offset the two or three failures that followed. A planned follow-up, with Howard Keel as a singing Robin Hood, was cancelled: Keel is virtually the only one of the leading players not in this picture, and it is Matt Mattox whom the others are admiring.

with a biography of Sigmund Romberg, even if that composer was not then well out of fashion, but this humourless enterprise damns both of them. The guest turns, notably those of Ann Miller, Gene Kelly (and his brother Fred), sometimes help, but the film is mainly a bonanza for José Ferrer as Romberg: he is presented not only as dedicated composer but prankster, lover, dancer, high liver, conductor and idealist, at one point miming a whole musical comedy in the manner of Danny Kaye.

Also unsuccessful were Minnelli's **Brigadoon** (1954) and **Kismet** (1955), both in CinemaScope, a process which robbed musicals of their intimacy and which he himself disliked. He was not interested in transferring Broadway musicals to the screen, and only did the second one in return for receiving assent to his proposed film on Van Gogh, *Lust for Life* (q.v.). He had disliked *Brigadoon* on stage, and it is with incredulity that one learns that Alan Jay Lerner objected to the changes that Minnelli and Kelly proposed making to his daft, solemn book. On stage it had been billed as 'a whimsical musical fantasy': two Americans stumble on a small Scottish town which materialises only once every hundred years, and one of them falls in love, thus willing the town to reappear. Kelly had liked it on stage but lost interest when it was decided to film it in the studio; at the time Freed said, in a widely-quoted remark, that he had gone to Scotland and found nothing that resembled Scotland, while a further plan to shoot on location at Big Sur was abandoned in an economy drive. However, the sets – a brave attempt by Preston Ames at lochs and hills – are the least of its failings. The cast, which includes Cyd Charisse and Van Johnson, was clearly of no help, and Minnelli misuses Kelly's particular talents, as he admitted; and most reviewers found the performance forced. Helping to reduce the whimsy in the original show was the male chorus dancing – increasingly important in Broadway musicals and hence a heavy influence on *Seven Brides* – but the wedding reel in the film is glum. Agnes de Mille's final chase ballet was restructured for film, but comes too late to save the situation. Furthermore, for the first time in his career Minnelli often positions the camera in the wrong place, as he does again in *Kismet*.

With the exception of the Caliph's wedding procession – 'Night of My Nights' – and 'Baubles, Bangles and Beads' the numbers in *Kismet* are not so much staged as merely delivered. Keel and Dolores Gray perform with verve, but Ann Blyth and a sluggish Vic Damone slaughter 'A Stranger in Paradise', in a garden set which looks like a Macy's window display, while 'And This Is My Beloved', shorn of its multiple rhythms and voices, is a mere shadow of its old self.

Kelly also gave Freed two consecutive musical failures, but **It's Always Fair Weather** (1955), directed with Donen, revives better than contemporary opinion suggests. The starting point was *On the Town*: Comden and Green wondered what had become of the three sailors – who became soldiers when Frank Sinatra refused to be part of the project – and decided that civilian life had made them cynical, smug and hypocritical. This is a musical of disillusion and disenchantment, and to everyone involved 'most friendship is feigning, most loving mere folly.' It does show talent evolving, and also on the credit side are the use of the wide screen and Kelly's solo dance on roller skates, using passers-by as props, as he once used a rainstorm. Against these must be set the muddy colour, a weak score by André Previn, some broad satire at the expense of television and advertising, and the fact that alone of the cast Dolores Gray is good, playing a phoney, schmalzy T.V. star; as Kelly's old buddies, Dan Dailey and Michael Kidd are well cast.

Kelly's original intention with **Invitation to the Dance** (1956) was to salute American dancers, but the studio, having cautiously agreed to an all-dance film, insisted that he himself appear in it and then, to keep costs down, that it be made in Britain. Production began in 1952, and though the delay in completion was due to the fact that one sequence required animation, the studio so disliked Malcolm Arnold's score for 'Ring Around Rosy' that Previn wrote a new one, working from the images on the screen. Another sequence was abandoned because Freed disliked the rushes, but as a tribute to Tin Pan Alley it would surely have been more 'commercial' than what remained. These are: 'Circus', a commedia dell'arte romp, with Kelly as a white-faced clown and some splendidly energetic male dancing; 'Ring Around Rosy', a version of Schnitzler's 'La Ronde', which is neither as funny nor as sophisticated as it should be; and the animated 'Sinbad the Sailor', which alternates between failure, as in Kelly's pas de deux with the cute princess, and success, as with the witty and fantastic harem guards. Kelly himself thinks the film failed because there was too much dancing to absorb, but the reviews were universally bad. It had cost almost $1½ million, and in the U.S. took only $200,000.

Also finding little degree of acceptance were the low-budget experimental musicals produced by Cummings, usually with the studio's lesser talents. The dancing of Marge and Gower Champion saves Donen's **Give a Girl a Break** (1953), but there is no redeeming feature in Richard Thorpe's weird **Athena** (1954), about a nice young lawyer (Edmund Purdom) who becomes involved with a family of California cultists and a Mr Universe contest. The huge success of *Seven Brides* restored studio confidence, leading directly to **Jupiter's Darling** (1955), produced by George Wells, a studio writer and producer of three minor musicals. The props and costumes from *Quo Vadis?* were in store, and the studio owned Robert E. Sherwood's 'The Road to Rome', an historical spoof adapted here by Dorothy Kingsley without wit; the score is also poor. The result is pleasing, partly because George Sidney makes the most of the costumes and spectacle, and partly because the players seem to be enjoying themselves – Esther Williams, the Champions and Keel, who, as Hannibal, has a self-glorification song copied later in 'A Funny Thing Happened on the Way to the Forum'.

The film failed, while Pasternak's conventional musicals found favour, at least with the public. **Hit the Deck** (1955), directed by Roy Rowland, is based on an old Broadway show, and though the subject matter is not dissimilar to that of *On the Town*, the discrepancy is wide – a fact not unassociated with the standby cast, including Jane Powell, Debbie Reynolds, Tony Martin, Vic Damone and Russ Tamblyn. There is also Ann Miller, tapping away in the finale in front of hundreds of sailors, as Eleanor Powell once did: the song is 'Hallelujah!' and if the choreography of Hermes Pan is unworthy of it,

the score as a whole – taken from several shows by Vincent Youmans – atones for much.

Recent failures had made the M-G-M management unreceptive to musicals, but there was no hesitation in producing **High Society** (1956), because it united so many fine talents and indeed this remake of *The Philadelphia Story* is a drawing-room comedy interspersed with songs. If the performance is of no more than of repertory standard that is because Walters's direction seems non-existent. The four leads are otherwise solid gold, with Bing Crosby and Frank Sinatra offering lazy charm instead of the rather frenzied approach of Grant and Stewart; Grace Kelly (q.v.) has eagerness and coldness where Hepburn was extravagant and disdainful, but her presence is refreshing; and Celeste Holm, though given too little to do, is quite delicious. Louis Armstrong has two guest turns, including a duet with Crosby, 'Now You Has Jazz', one of the four superb songs slapped into the centre of the film. There are not many others, but they are all by Cole Porter, and if they do not seem directed either, this is one occasion when leaving well alone★ achieves gratifying results.

The director of the original, George

Grace Kelly was one of the nicest things to happen to M-G-M in the Fifties – if briefly, since she had been only five years in films when she went off to become Her Serene Highness Princess Grace of Monaco. She didn't exactly happen to the M-G-M musical, but she did sing a few notes with Bing Crosby in *High Society*, earning herself a Golden Disc in the process when the soundtrack recording of 'True Love' had sold over a million copies.

★Too well, since this is the only Hollywood film I know where the microphone may be glimpsed; it was made quickly to allow Miss Kelly to marry her prince.

Cukor, made **Les Girls** (1957) for the same producer, Sol C. Siegel, responsible for musicals good and bad during his tenures at Paramount and 20th Century-Fox. On this occasion Cukor's handling of Porter's songs (it was his last score) and the backstage scenes is as assured as those in his version of *A Star Is Born* (q.v.), while one number in particular, 'Ladies in Waiting', has a panache which – as rarely in their screen treatment – belongs completely to Porter's world of musical comedy. However, like *High Society*, this is less a musical than a story punctuated by songs, concerning as it does a libel trial at the Old Bailey, and what may or may not have happened among some members of a dancing troupe in Paris. Vera Caspary wrote the original story and John Patrick did the screenplay, making nothing out of much. A subdued Kelly is the head of the troupe, in dispute between Taina Elg, Mitzi Gaynor and Kay Kendall. Miss Kendall (1926–59) is gorgeous, with those intimations of civilised zaniness which so beautifully recall Carole Lombard, and as long as she is front and centre the film is fine.

Kelly requested a release from his contract, which was granted; and, since musicals were now frowned upon, Howard Keel was allowed to go. Though both continued to work in films (and elsewhere), the great days of their careers were over, even if at this stage they may have been more popular than those stars important in box-office statistics (Rock Hudson, Yul Brynner, Burt Lancaster, Glenn Ford and William Holden): they are certainly more fondly remembered. Kelly may have been drained artistically and marked by both the failure of his ballet film and the traumas of its making. He had also at one point been making a musical version of *Huckleberry Finn*, which was abandoned, and Donen has said of their last collaboration that it was 'one hundred per cent nightmare. Gene didn't get on well with anybody. It was the only picture during which the atmosphere was really horrendous.' Since *The Band Wagon* had been made in similar conditions – partly due to Astaire's worry over his wife's illness, and Jack Buchanan's nervousness at working with him – the personal factor should be considered in the decline of the M-G-M musical, a reason perhaps why the talents involved agreed with the bosses that it was

dying. The artistic failure of several of these films may have sapped confidence, and indeed the safe, unimaginative treatment of Broadway musicals at other studios was proving more satisfactory to the public.

Then there were the performers. Apart from Doris Day, none of the other women stars still under contract at the studio was worth building a musical around, and she made only *Love Me or Leave Me* (q.v.) for M-G-M at this time – though she returned to Warners, where Donen co-directed her in *The Pajama Game* (q.v.). The male stars were ageing, a fact taken into account by Edens as he prepared **Funny Face** (1957) for Astaire and the much younger Audrey Hepburn (b. 1929) – and she, significantly, was not known as a singer or a dancer, though she had sung and danced on the London stage before arriving in Hollywood. This was Edens's second film credited as producer – and his last, despite its success. It was planned at M-G-M but, when the Gershwin score that Edens wanted was sold by Warners to M-G-M, the whole package was bought by Paramount, who owned both Hepburn's contract and a commitment from Astaire. Donen directed, and unlike the other film he made for Edens, this is, or was, considered chic. What was then thought to be imaginative in the pictorial treatment has long since been assimilated into movies, and you may blanch at the juxtaposition of tourist Paris and fashion plates. Neither Astaire nor Hepburn could be less than entrancing, but Donen has refrigerated the air around them – though Kay Thompson's occasional asides warm the whole self-conscious enterprise. Leonard Gershe's screenplay is feeble, supposedly poking fun at the fashion world and people talking intently in left-bank cellars – and Hepburn is merely playing a new version of the classical-music-playing dame who takes off her specs and starts to jive. When she dances with Astaire in the Pré Catalan they are surrounded by turtle doves and primroses, which are unnecessary embellishments for artists of this quality. You would, however, not want to miss a second of him singing the title song, her version of 'How Long Has This Been Going On?', or the two of them joining Kay Thompson to rejuvenate that business of singing in the streets, 'Bonjour Paris'.

Astaire danced on the screen for the last time in **Silk Stockings** (1957), but in spite of this and the Porter score it was another nail in the coffin of the M-G-M musical. This is *Ninotchka* by way of Broadway, supposedly more topical than ever, but the anti-Russian jokes give an impression of mindless superiority. The stockings of the title replace the hat to which Garbo succumbed; Ninotchka is now sent to Paris to retrieve three composers retained by an American film producer. Freed chose the Russian Rouben Mamoulian to direct, against the advice of his unit (remembering the failure of *Summer Holiday*), and a degree of misplaced confidence is obvious – on the part of Mamoulian, for instance, in discovering 'satire' in the script by Leonard Gershe and Leonard Spigelgass, from the Broadway book by George S. Kaufman, that gentleman's wife and Abe Burrows. Mamoulian supposedly wanted to tell the story through dance, which simply does not happen: people lumber on from one side of the (wide) screen and go off the other, behaving as though trapped in Greek tragedy. Since Hermes Pan's choreography seems to be serviceable, the lifelessness of Astaire's numbers with Charisse must be blamed on both directorial incompetence and her lack of presence. Foolishly, she attempts Garbo's accent while speaking Garbo's lines. Astaire does a rock 'n' roll number which both he and Porter loathed (it was commissioned for the film in a panicky effort to attract 'modern' audiences), but there are isolated pleasures, as when Astaire breaks into the lyrics or sings 'Stereophonic Sound' with Janis Paige, playing a dumb movie star anticipating her first non-swimming role.

Gigi (1958) was a last success for the team of Freed and Minnelli, aided by the co-operation of Lerner and Frederick Loewe, whose success with 'My Fair Lady' brushed off on this film – with the M-G-M management, the public and Academy voters, who awarded it nine Oscars, including Best Picture. Its achievement is undeniable, and if it is studied and heartless these are qualities not alien to the subject, for Gigi, after all, is a little girl being trained to be a *poule de grand luxe*. The only interests of its characters are money, gossip and *l'amour*, in that order, and when the film was praised for its charm, it was the charm of a Paris motivated by three ruling

passions – by money, gossip and *l'amour*. Lerner's screenplay, based on Colette's story, attempts Wildean epigrams ('Bad table manners, my dear Gigi, have broken more households than infidelity'), but, as usual, his lyrics are smart; Loewe's music mines the same Viennese seam he used for 'My Fair Lady' – less melodically, but efficient in context. Cecil Beaton's costumes and decor are exquisite, and graceful use is made of the Palais de Glace, Maxim's and the Bois: the piece evokes the painters and writers of the era, so that Gigi in the Bois is Proust's Albertine, and the beach scenes are Boudin. Attempting all this has defeated Minnelli, who misses when he strives for insouciance in 'The Night They Invented Champagne'. Filming in Paris was fraught with difficulties, and when he remained there to work on another film, Walters re-shot in Hollywood a number of scenes which had been disliked at previews. Leslie Caron is the most adorable of little girls, and Louis Jourdan's wooden good looks blend into the fabric of the whole; the major asset is Maurice Chevalier, a practised charmer in such situations – and it was significant to observers of the musical form that he was the only real singer in the cast and though Caron can dance, she was not called upon to do so (and her singing was dubbed).

The film proved to be the one exception to the industry rule that the public would only 'buy' film versions of Broadway hits – a rule typically self-protective and self-

Gigi was the final triumph of Freed and Minnelli – at least statistically, for it made a lot of money and won a fistful of Oscars. However, some of it seemed forced, and the sum was less than the parts – the latter notably including a nostalgic duet for Hermione Gingold and Maurice Chevalier, 'I Remember It Well'.

deceptive, since audiences had liked both *Seven Brides* and *Funny Face*. M-G-M laid claim to one Broadway success, **Bells Are Ringing** (1960), because the book was by Comden and Green. It is a daffy piece about a meddling telephonist, and was written for their old colleague, Judy Holliday (1922–65), with lyrics by Sammy Cahn and an excellent score by Jules Styne. Both Cahn and Comden have said that the film should have been much better, and Cahn said of the leading man, Dean Martin, 'He blew it away. They should have got a better singer or a better actor.' The CinemaScope camera sits before obvious sets, recording too-broad performances, and as we watch them we may decide that the real culprits are Freed and Minnelli. After the failure of *Kismet*, they should have realised the pitfalls of playing to non-existent footlights. In that film at least there were vestiges of Minnelli's penchant for smart decor and his ability to handle ambitious numbers, but the big ones here are reduced to dowdiness – while three of Holliday's best numbers in the show have gone. She was unhappy during filming, and wanted to buy herself out – and she is certainly badly treated on screen, coiffured and dressed as no telephonist ever was. That she remains marvellous is no credit to anyone but herself.

Minnelli directed no more musicals for M-G-M, while Freed spent the last years of his life planning *Say It with Music*, to have been built round Irving Berlin's songs, a project which was cancelled during the several changes of management in the late Sixties. Edens was Associate Producer on what are, in effect, the last M-G-M musicals, **Billy Rose's Jumbo** (1962) and **The Unsinkable Molly Brown** (1964), both directed by Charles Walters, getting the utmost from the material, and both at times worthy of the heyday – especially in the production numbers for *Jumbo* (Billy Rose managed to get his name in the title because he had presented the original show on Broadway). This has a Rodgers and Hart score, and because of its circus setting had been at first bought by Freed as a possible follow-up to *Annie Get Your Gun*; the project was resurrected because Doris Day, then the reigning box-office queen, had indicated that she would like to sing again and owed a commitment to M-G-M. She is fine, but Stephen Boyd, an exceptionally dreary leading man, sinks the enterprise. The powers that be, however, decided that the film failed because audiences did not want to see Day in musicals and *Molly Brown*, bought for her, went to Debbie Reynolds. Miss Reynolds throws herself about like a dervish, clowning, singing, dancing, and even emoting heavily, but is as interesting as a slice of stale angel cake. This time there is a stalwart leading man, Harve Presnell, but the fortunes of the piece, as on Broadway, were not increased by a banal score by Meredith Willson, who had seen in the leading character, a late nineteenth-century eccentric, a promising subject to follow his success with 'The Music Man' (the film, q.v.).

The M-G-M musical had really died with *Bells Are Ringing*, and it was an unexpected way to go – mishandling an above-average Broadway show and its star. It is sad to reflect that Freed and Minnelli, responsible for so many triumphs in the musical field, should have seemed with that project as tired as any of the hacks who had ever toiled in Hollywood's poverty row. No excuses have ever been forthcoming, nor, I think, could there be. All the great and good things had been done, and all the good things in this particular Broadway show had been copied from M-G-M musicals – which is surely why Minnelli showed so little interest in transferring them to the screen. His influence, and that of Kelly, would continue to be felt: there would be half a dozen goodish musicals in the decade to come. They would not, however, have Kelly, or Garland, or Astaire.

27

Postwar Hollywood:
The Directors in Their Brave New World

THE FILM-MAKERS who had served in the War returned to California very much changed. They had discovered honesty and reality, and they wanted to make films that were honest and real. William Wyler had served in Europe and had also made two documentaries on the Air Force's contribution to the War, *The Memphis Belle* and *Thunderbolt*. He found the subject of **The Best Years of Our Lives** (1946) in a verse novel by MacKinley Kantor, which he asked Goldwyn to buy – though the publicity maintained that the idea came from Goldwyn himself and Mrs Goldwyn. Its subject is service veterans readjusting to civilian life, and the first half hour remains moving, especially the sequences involving the young sailor amputee – a role played by Harold Russell, who had lost his hands, and whose only previous acting experience was in an army documentary. (In the original story, the character was a spastic on the verge of alcoholism, but Wyler considered that a spastic was both too difficult and too easy to portray.)

A film which offers such a situation is not spun of the usual web of dreams and there are impressive passages: the sergeant (Fredric March) discovering that his children have grown up while he was away; the bombardier (Dana Andrews) becoming disillusioned with the wife (Virginia Mayo) he knew for only twenty days. She sings in the usual Hollywood-sized night club and like the sergeant's wife (Myrna Loy) is positioned to catch the highlights on her face and well-coiffed hair; the sergeant – a bank teller in civilian life – lives in a mansion-sized apartment, indicating that Wyler's desire for honesty and reality was either insufficient or curtailed by

Goldwyn. The film, in any case, settles for triteness – as when the sailor rejects his fiancée because he fears pity, a situation already used in the British film *The Captive Heart* (q.v.); and it is hard to believe, for instance, that the bombardier, reduced to his old job of soda-jerking, would be sacked for defending the amputee in an argument with a civilian blowhard.

Few reservations were expressed at the time and the film was widely received as proof of the new maturity expected of Hollywood. It won seven Oscars, including Best Picture, Best Direction and Best Screenplay (Robert E. Sherwood), and there can be no doubt that it spoke more directly to Americans than any film yet made. After the turmoil of war it was encouraging to find that the country had not changed – if only in the Hollywood scale of things.

Frank Capra also offered reassurance, reiterating his vision of America in **It's a Wonderful Life** (1945). He had spent the war years on a series of documentaries called *Why We Fight*, and this new film was intended to be an extension of the arguments put forward in those documentaries, as it hymns a regular guy (James Stewart) saved from suicide by a guardian angel and his nursery version of Donne, *viz.* 'Remember no man is a failure who has friends' and 'Each man's life touches some other lives.' Capra found his fable on a Christmas card, where it was called 'The Greatest Gift', and R.K.O. had already commissioned several other (unused) scripts – since by coincidence it owned the poem. To his delight, it was offered to Capra – who is credited with the screenplay with Albert Hackett, Frances Goodrich and Jo Swerling. According to his memoirs, he considered the result not only his best film, 'but the greatest anybody ever made' – and it remains his (and Stewart's) favourite. But critics and public liked it much less than Wyler's more topical treatise, not appreciating their similarities – for both kept intact the myth of an America that was cosy, understanding and loving. Capra borrowed situations from his earlier films too readily (John Doe's contemplated suicide, Mr Deeds's 'sharing out'); the film was old fashioned, and whimsy was at odds with the postwar mood – which accounts for its failure. In Europe, and especially in Italy, filmmakers were reasserting the central belief of the realistic film, that the meek shall not inherit the earth – a view untenable in Hollywood, even if already tentatively expressed by Preston Sturges. Capra certainly was not making a realistic film, though he too was trying to indict the system, with one man's restored idealism shown as the only alternative to the evils of capitalism. The latter is represented by a honky-tonk town of dives and strip joints, which, apart from the assumption that ordinary people disapprove of booze and sex, demonstrates a failure by Capra and his hero to face up to the world. This particular sequence is an antidote to the sweetness and light of the rest of the film. As the good time girl turned whore Gloria Grahame is virtually the only Hollywood player allowed to be explicitly so since the tightening of the Hays Code in 1934.* The prevarications at the heart of the film are the more insidious because it is so entertaining and beautifully crafted; it has a superb cast, and James Stewart was the best possible choice to play Mr Goody Two-Shoes.

Capra had returned from the War more than ever imbued with the idea of 'one man, one film', convinced that the public was hankering for quality after the 'anything goes' policy of the industry during the war years. Since the three most successful films in more than a generation – *Gone with the Wind*, *The Bells of St Mary's* and *The Best Years of Our Lives* – had each been produced by an independent, almost every Hollywood figure of importance was forming his own company. With Samuel Briskin as secretary-treasurer, Capra had formed Liberty Films, and Wyler and George Stevens were invited to join, each with autonomy as producer-directors; a deal was made with R.K.O. for nine films, with facilities to be advanced in exchange for distribution rights. When, in industry terms, *It's a Wonderful Life* was 'less than a smash', R.K.O. baulked at the high budget ($2,800,000) of **State of the Union** (1948), which Capra intended for Gary Cooper. M-G-M, however, picked up the project because Spencer Tracy coveted the leading role, an aircraft tycoon, chosen as presidential candidate by a Republican newspaper proprietor (Angela Lansbury). He deceived himself that he can win, despite the political chicanery of his sponsors and their opposition to such demands as universal Medicare, more housing and more internationalism. As written by Anthony Veiller and Myles Connolly, the film is witty and apparently sharper than the original Pulitzer Prize-winning play by Howard Lindsay and Russell Crouse; it has little remarkable to say about political immorality, but on that subject a restatement of the obvious is always welcome.† Tracy's final stand, reunited with his estranged wife (Katharine Hepburn), may echo other Capra dénouements, but the film is a fresh departure for Capra and proof, despite the weaknesses in the material, that he believed in 'worthwhile' subjects.

The volatile public mood had again veered towards escapism and though it was ready to accept a number of 'serious' films, the reception for this one proved little warmer than for other political films in the past. The wind blew bitterly towards Liberty, and a decision was made to sell the company to Paramount, with the properties it had acquired and the services of its directors. Stevens was against the deal and was proposing to join Leo McCarey, when he discovered that McCarey was also considering the sale of his company to Paramount. The disintegration of Liberty was undoubtedly regarded by the studio bosses with

---

*The Hays administration finished in 1945, and the Breen Office, as it then became known, was later officially titled the Motion Picture Association of America or M.P.A.A. Hereafter I shall refer to it as such, and to the Hays Code by its official designation, the Production Code.

†I saw it at the height of the Watergate scandal, and Tracy's line, 'I forgot how quickly the American people smell out double-dealers and crooks,' brought a prolonged round of applause.

satisfaction. Others who surrendered their independence at this time, after virtually only one film apiece, included Fritz Lang, Mervyn LeRoy, the Cagney brothers, Frank Borzage, Garson and Michael Kanin, and Gary Cooper. Wyler and Stevens settled in at Paramount, but Capra, in his own words, 'drank the hemlock of champions: the bitter, souring realisation that part of what made [me] great was dying'. The loss of his independence was made even more painful by an edict from Barney Balaban, the studio's head, that no film should cost more than $1½ million. Balaban could point to the fact that attendance figures in the U.S. had dropped from eighty million patrons weekly in 1946 (an all-time high) to only sixty-two million in 1948, but we may suspect a certain wish to humiliate the fugitives now once again under control.

Among the properties Capra could not make for the required sum were several which became successful for other directors – *Roman Holiday* (q.v.), *Friendly Persuasion* (q.v.), *Westward the Women* and *A Woman of Distinction*. He thought a new version of *Broadway Bill* could be kept within the budget – though that is why **Riding High** (1950) has a rather inadequate leading lady. He had had reservations about the original, because Warner Baxter had been afraid of horses, and Bing Crosby, who loved them, was, like himself, under contract to Paramount. Since Crosby was the more ingratiating actor, the result, as Capra claims, is an improvement, with Crosby's songs fitting easily into Robert Riskin's original screenplay, kept more or less intact. In their original roles are Raymond Walburn, Margaret Hamilton, Clarence Muse, Douglas Dumbrille, Ward Bond and Frankie Darro, while what Capra called 'the greatest collection of time-saving, sure-fire entertainers ever assembled in one film' also includes Charles Bickford, James Gleason and Oliver Hardy.

A warm reception did nothing to alleviate Capra's unhappiness. He was offered **Here Comes the Groom** (1951), another Crosby vehicle, and took it, intending a spectacularly entertaining swan song. He should have scrapped the opening (as he did with *Lost Horizon*), where Crosby sings to a bunch of orphans in Paris something about hanging 'the dreams you want as pictures on the wall'. Once Crosby arrives in the U.S. to recapture his ex-fiancée (Jane Wyman) the fun is lively – and it includes 'In the Cool, Cool, Cool of the Evening', as sung by them strolling round an office desk and down into the street. The number sparkles, which Capra thought partly due to his refusal to pre-record the songs, then a long-standing practice; it makes one regret that he never attempted a real musical. He made no further fiction films for a decade, working much of that time on scientific documentaries for the government.

Meanwhile, Wyler took years to find a subject to follow *The Best Years of Our Lives*, and in contemplating its lack of contemporary relevance it should be borne in mind that at that time versatility was an even more prized quality. **The Heiress** (1949) is a faithful version of Henry James's 'Washington Square', as written by Ruth and Augustus Goetz from their own Broadway adaptation. The story is theatrical – the shy, clumsy Catherine (Olivia de Havilland) is courted by a man (Montgomery Clift) whom her father (Ralph Richardson) believes is a fortune hunter – and so are the effects: she waits for the carriage that never comes, and slowly puts out the lights at the end. The crisp, ironic lines which punctuate an already good text – 'Father, talk to him about me – you know me so well, it will not be immodest of you to praise me a little,' and 'Cruel? You forget, aunt, I have been taught by masters' – require master players, and Richardson, cold, gently ironic, self-centred and unfeeling, never gave a better performance. The role of Catherine has many subtleties – for example, the possibility of her knowing that Morris is rotten, and not caring since her real aim is to get away from her father – and Miss de Havilland won an Oscar for it; she is particularly good in the later scenes, where uncertainty has hardened into a never defined vindictiveness. She was, I think, greatly helped by Wyler, whose usual quest for perfection caused him to exceed the Hollywood average of takes per shot – but his attention to detail helps to make this an enduring entertainment. He could do little with the far too modern Clift (q.v.), who is not a man you could ever imagine buying real chamois gloves.

Wyler changed genres again with

683

Detective Story (1951), also adapted from a Broadway success – of the genus 'Street Scene', in which audiences are invited to witness a series of actions in a supposedly realistic milieu. Adapted by Philip Yordan from Sidney Kingsley's play about life in a police precinct, this was stale stuff even then; Kirk Douglas is a tough detective who has to cope with a couple of burglars, a shoplifter (Lee Grant), a suspected abortionist (George Macready) and his own, hysterical wife (Eleanor Parker). The complete absence of background music was considered an asset at the time.

Returning to period drama, Wyler made **Carrie** (1952) mainly for the opportunity to portray an interesting time in American history. Hollywood had long flirted with Theodore Dreiser's novel, but had hesitated, since its protagonist is a loose woman who suffers no retribution after one man has ruined himself because of her. The screenplay by the Goetzes makes Carrie (Jennifer Jones) reluctant to become a kept woman and at the end she feels such remorse that she searches for Hurstwood (Laurence Olivier) in the hope of taking care of him. Dreiser wrote of the new, teeming cities, and of the girls seduced by carriages and restaurants, so much to be preferred to damp tenements and tramways, but Wyler, whatever his motives, has merely made a version of All for Love, or the World Well Lost – yet this, because of Olivier, is a moving document. His Hurstwood is elegantly mannered and attired, with only an occasional pinched look to indicate an unhappy marriage: when he meets Carrie he reacts like a thoroughbred puppy, but his sadness returns fleetingly when he is not with her. Technically, this actor is always a marvel, revealing Hurstwood's degradation by the slope of the shoulders, a pulled down Homburg, and unkempt moustache and blank, dead eyes. In the generally dire reviews this great performance was noticed by only a few critics – and did nothing to prevent box-office failure, for audiences, if occasionally approving of sad endings, tend to avoid films which move downhill all the way. That fact further emphasises the novel's limitations as screen material: to say that they are not overcome and that this is, nevertheless, one of Wyler's best pictures is to demonstrate his position among film-makers. Like Dreiser himself, he is a first-rate artisan; and though his attachment to verisimilitude, to the details of the commonplace and the minutiae of personal behaviour sometimes blinds him to the larger passions, he cared greatly for both his stories and the intelligence of his audience.★

Of the three Liberty directors, George Stevens took the longest to return to work; when he did, it was on loan to R.K.O., which owned a popular play which he wanted to film. This was **I Remember Mama** (1948), which John Van Druten had adapted from a memoir by Kathryn Forbes about her Norwegian family. Van Druten was too old a hand to persuade himself that the material was fresh, but no one was more adept at artfully presenting everyday activities in a way which would delight Broadway audiences. There are no family eccentrics – with the possible exception of fearsome Uncle Chris (Oscar Homolka); father is neither lovable drunk nor improvident inventor and there is no juvenile romance. Rightly, therefore, the qualities which Stevens brings are also negative – reticence and discretion; the result is arguably the least cloying family film since *Meet Me in St Louis*. It has charm, inevitably, since Mama is played by Irene Dunne. Barbara Bel Geddes is the girl remembering, and her well-scrubbed face is as pleasing as anything in movies. Also refreshing are the views of San Francisco, with its clapboard houses and steep streets with the cable cars sweeping up and down, while women climb the hills slowly, the wind ruffling their hair and feather boas. Stevens otherwise uses the standard 'quality' approach to stage material – one large set comprising all the cluttered rooms, and a mobile camera to follow the family from one to another.

Thus did Hollywood's brave new world offer sentimental valentines to the American past. On the other hand, George Stevens's **A Place in the Sun** (1951) was considered an important film in America, and it was thought significant when Chaplin, in a rare public statement, pronounced it 'the best film ever to come out of Hollywood'. It went on to win four Oscars, including Best Direction and Best Screenplay from Another Source – the source

★Wyler later cited this film as one he regretted making 'because it didn't make a penny'.

being Theodore Dreiser's 'An American Tragedy'. The story has been reset in the present and, like Wyler's treatment of this writer, has been reduced to a 'tragic' love story. Moreover, this adaptation sins even more grievously, for in removing Clyde's antecedents, and therefore his reasons for wanting a place in the sun, it also does away with all of Dreiser's comments on materialism. Montgomery Clift as Clyde – renamed George Eastman – is both the film's greatest asset and biggest liability. He plays with intensity and sensitivity, a rare combination in American actors at this time, but he suggests neither a seducer nor a pushy young man: if the American tragedy is a will to succeed at all costs, including murder, then this lugubrious film is not an example of it.

The most interesting change makes the victim shrill instead of stupid, though in the performance of Shelley Winters she remains pathetic; as the rich girl for whom she is dumped, Elizabeth Taylor suggests one of no intellect at all. In the book she refuses to have anything more to do with Clyde after the murder, but here she turns up in prison in a chic outfit to assure him that she will always love him – while to Franz Waxman's relentless and swelling 'love-theme', close-ups of their kisses are superimposed over the image of his face as he walks to the Chair. Abroad, the film was at least admired for its visual style, but in fact the slow dissolves and cunning use of shadow were derived from von Sternberg's long-unseen version of this tale, as Stevens privately acknowledged. Had the film adhered to the spirit of the novel, the M.P.A.A. need not have worried so much about the situation of sex outside marriage: this was permitted for the sake of 'art' and Hollywood maturity, and the film's reception did in fact result in further relaxations.★

Among the younger directors permitted a certain choice of material was Billy

Wilder, also at Paramount, and that was because of **The Lost Weekend** (1945), a project for which he and his producer and co-writer, Charles Brackett, had overcome front office opposition. It went on to win the chief Oscars – Best Picture, Best Direction, Best Screenplay/Adaptation and Best Actor – and was widely regarded as one of the films which helped Hollywood grow up. Certainly it is one of the rare dramas of the period which may be taken as seriously now as then. Agee thought it 'unusually hard, tense, cruel, intelligent and straightforward', but we would agree with him that it does not enter deeply enough into the world of the alcoholic, failing to examine the hurt caused by the majority of alcoholics. In Charles Jackson's novel, an attempt was made to probe into the childhood of Don Birnam (Ray Milland), and the conclusion was drawn that his trouble was caused by a refusal to accept homosexual tendencies; Wilder and Brackett settled for the most obvious censor-free motivation, that he is a writer without inspiration. Since writers are prone to drink, it is a good premise, though we are not encouraged to believe that the talent is a major one – nor does Milland suggest a character basically flawed. Certain sequences remain unsurpassed – the trudge along Third Avenue trying to sell the typewriter, the theft of the handbag, the exchanges with the sour bartender (Howard da Silva). Wilder had insisted on the then rare luxury of New York locations, and audiences were impressed by the sight of an apartment that was for once small and cluttered.

Turning about, Wilder decided to emulate his idol, Lubitsch, and **The Emperor Waltz** (1948) has a delicious framing device and a role for Joan Fontaine modelled on the young Jeanette MacDonald – that of a countess, prim at first, who succumbs to an uncontrollable passion for the leading man. He (Bing Crosby) is no Chevalier, so Brackett and Wilder have given him a randy mongrel who sexually assaults the countess's prize poodle – which at this time was somewhat outrageous. The studio shelved the film for over a year, even though Crosby was its leading box-office star. Wilder was actually too sophisticated to make a vehicle suitable for this actor, and the film, little liked when it appeared, is hardly more likeable now.

★Up to this time, the situation had, as if statistically, been limited to one film a year, and then only when germane to the plot, as in (q.v.) *The Sea of Grass, To Each His Own* and *Letter from an Unknown Woman*, each of which is set in the past, when supposedly different values prevailed – but even so assumed merely one lapse, and the woman clearly suffers because of it. *Johnny Belinda* (q.v.) concerns a rape, and *Not Wanted* an unmarried mother: the M.P.A.A. recognised serious purpose in both films, and the latter, an independent, low-budget film, was thought likely to pass unnoticed by sensation-seekers – as indeed happened. Cases where audiences presumed illicit sexual relations were, of course, something else again.

Three lost Hollywood souls in Billy Wilder's *Sunset Boulevard*: Gloria Swanson as the forgotten Silent star dreaming of a comeback, William Holden, centre, as the screenwriter who accepts her hospitality as the bailiffs close in, and Erich Von Stroheim as her one-time director, now her chauffeur, who writes the fan letters she still expects to receive daily. Holden looks uncomfortable, for heroes even in Wilder films were not expected to become gigolos.

It is doubtful whether many today would agree with Agee that much of **A Foreign Affair** (1948) is 'in rotten taste'. Wilder laid his comedy among the ruins of Berlin, and a jeep speeds through them as the soundtrack offers 'Isn't it Romantic?'. At the Brandenburg Gate, the troops are engaged in activities unthinkable on Main Street, such as purchasing each girl in sight with one candy bar or a pack of Camels. It was not until the arrival of Preston Sturges that the American film had satirised others than the rich and famous: Wilder was to go much further, and this study of the occupying armies and the defeated is his first flowering. 'Sometimes I wonder whether it wasn't a waste of money to import eleven thousand ping-pong tables for you men,' says the General (Millard Mitchell), reprimanding the hero (John Lund) for his affair with a singer (Marlene Dietrich); and after explaining to a committee of visiting congressmen that four million Displaced Persons had been re-settled, he adds that on the day the gas was reconnected there were 160 suicides. Wilder and his co-writers Brackett and Richard L. Breen also refurbish the cliché of the plain jane who takes off her glasses and falls in love – in which role Jean Arthur takes top billing, the man and the film from Dietrich.

Its topicality was not much admired, as that was not then considered a requirement of the American screen, despite recent successes such as *Mrs Miniver* and *The Best Years of Our Lives* – not to mention the excitement currently engendered by the Italian cinema. Indeed, Wilder's greatest critical success to date was set in a Hollywood even less in touch than usual with the contemporary world or indeed anywhere but itself. **Sunset Boulevard** (1950) begins with a body in a pool, and the body tells the story. He (William Holden) is just another minor screenwriter in a sports jacket, fleeing the bailiffs – after which Hollywood fact Hollywood fantasy takes over, as he finds refuge in the mansion of a dotty and singularly humourless Silent picture queen, Norma Desmond (Gloria Swanson). 'You were big once,' he says irreverently. 'I am BIG,' she replies, 'it's the pictures that got smaller.' She dreams of a comeback, but hates 'that word. It's a return – a return to the people who've never forgiven me for deserting them.' She has written a script, 'Salome': 'They'll love it in Pomona,' he observes, to be interrupted with 'They'll love it everyplace.' She projects for him her old movies (among them *Queen Kelly*, one of the few Swanson Silents not made by Paramount, but directed by Von Stroheim, here playing the butler); plays bridge with cronies (Buster Keaton, H. B. Warner and Anna Q. Nilsson); the young man stays and they tango on the floor where Valentino danced. 'As long as the lady's paying,' says the tailor's salesclerk, and for an instant Wilder's subtlety deserts him. 'Twenty press-agents working over-time can do terrible things to the human soul,' says Cecil B. deMille, as himself, recalling that at seventeen Norma had 'more courage and wit and heart than you could possibly imagine', but in the film she is always pathetic. If Holden merely suggests an all-American boy going to seed, Swanson is magnificent, assuming the gestures associated with the Silent screen but vulnerable beneath the snake-like exterior and imperious manner. The woman is a shell; under the bombast there is nothing but hurt. She is not of the stature of Lady Macbeth or Cleopatra – and similarly the movie is classic but not a masterpiece. It has dated only in the most perfunctory way; and its strongest quality, permeating the entire film, is its veneration for an earlier age of motion pictures.

The screenplay was written by Brackett

and Wilder (with D.M. Marshman Jr) and the severance of their partnership at this point was not connected with the film's commercial failure. It was, nevertheless, unexpected – at least by Brackett, who moved to 20th Century-Fox and never recovered from the break. Wilder chose Lesser Samuels and Walter Newman as his co-writers on **Ace in the Hole** (1951), sometimes known as *The Big Carnival*; it was rechristened after its initial failure – a failure that again was gratifying to those who regarded Wilder as attacking their professional ethics. The profession in this case was journalism, and there were few good reviews. Unbiased critics recognised it as one of a number of superior films then being made which combined the thriller form with a glancing thrust at American society: in this, with the exception of a newspaper proprietor (Porter Hall), everyone is avaricious, particularly one journalist (Kirk Douglas). Learning that a garage man has been trapped in a cave-in, he turns it to his advantage. The facts of the film are reminiscent of the Floyd Collins case of 1925 (Collins had won a Pulitzer Prize for his coverage of a mine disaster). Among other things, the journalist persuades the victim's bored, sluttish wife (Jan Sterling) to remain at the site. 'I met a lot of hard-boiled eggs in my time, but you, you're twenty minutes,' she says, and as much might be said of the touts and hucksters who flock in to prey on the tourists.

Only a mite less misanthropic is **Stalag 17** (1953), which was much liked only in the U.S., where the Broadway original – by Donald Bevan and Edmund Trzcinski – had prepared audiences for a view of P.O.W.s which found them anything but noble. As in *A Foreign Affair*, the soldiery are a conniving bunch, headed by Sefton (William Holden), who runs a black-market trade and appears to be in cahoots with the Germans. Wilder likes the film as much as any he has made, 'perhaps because there were eight minutes which were any good' – and he may be thinking of the Christmas party, where the men dance together; he liked to ignore Hollywood taboos and he does so on this occasion with wondrous tact. In the matter of taste, there is also the one-legged prisoner who stores contraband in his empty pants-leg – further compensation for the soft ending,

a fault only avoided in Wilder's films of this period by *Sunset Boulevard*.

Sabrina (1954) is soft to start with, and Wilder chose it as his last film for Paramount because it gave him a chance to direct Audrey Hepburn. Its source is a comedy by Samuel Taylor, apparently influenced by *Sunny Side Up*, and as written for the screen by the two of them, with Ernest Lehman, it has ideas of democracy as naive as the fairy tale which surrounds them. As Sabrina, the chauffeur's daughter, Broadway audiences had loved Margaret Sullavan, and Miss Hepburn is just as enchanting, with grace and a sombre, little-girl intensity. That she attempts suicide in an eight-car garage is a typical Wilder touch, as is the younger scion (Holden) having the debris of champagne glasses picked from his rear. Humphrey Bogart, playing the elder son, disliked both players, Wilder and the film; he is too old for his role, and though too good an actor to be miscast, this was not his finest hour. When the piece came out, it seemed too long and big for its frail little tale, but it pleases intermittently today.

Among other directors pleasing audiences – if less often – was John Ford, who fulfilled his commitment to 20th Century-Fox with a Western, **My Darling Clementine** (1946), notable mainly for Henry Fonda's tight-lipped performance as Wyatt Earp, though the relationship with Doc Holliday – mistrust ripening into cagey friendship – would be more interesting with a better actor than Victor Mature. That relationship is based on one in *The Westerner*, as is the barn-dance sequence; and in returning to the Western for only the second time since the Silent days, Ford also borrowed from Renoir's *The Southerner*. **The Fugitive** (1947), another of his attempts at the Great American Art film, was influenced by Eisenstein's Mexican material – though the photographer, Gabriel Figueroa, may be exonerated, since his later work for Buñuel has none of the pretension apparent on this occasion. The screenplay by Ford and Dudley Nichols follows its source, Graham Greene's 'The Power and the Glory', and succeeds now and again on the level of elementary suspense. Dolores del Rio is allowed Madonna close-ups which are more spectacularly lit than those in all the churches in Rome. She is not, as in the Greene novel,

John Ford directed many excellent movies, but he was also as opportunist as any who ever toiled in the Hollywood vineyards, making a number of disastrously arty films and then, when they failed, incorporating 'Fordian' sequences in his more honest enterprises. He did not coin the adjective, but when certain admirers drew attention to aspects of his work, he repeated them for effect – rewardingly in, say, the recreation of a certain atmosphere, but foolishly, as in the repetition of funeral sequences. One such appeared in the otherwise splendid *She Wore a Yellow Ribbon* with, in the foreground, Ben Johnson, John Wayne and Frank McGrath.

living with the priest (Fonda), nor would the M.P.A.A. allow him to be alcoholic – which eliminates any point in making the film. The retention of the original ending is nullified by the standard of the whole (an alternative 'happy' ending still precedes Greene's conclusion in the final print) and though Mexico is credited for providing production facilities, the story is no longer set there. Whatever religious or political pressures were put on Ford, he himself claimed that 'It came out the way I wanted it to – that's why it's one of my favourite pictures – to me, it was perfect.'

Critics and public thought otherwise and the film was a dismal beginning for Argosy, the independent company Ford had formed with Merian C. Cooper, with whom he had worked at R.K.O., which distributed the film. Its failure, and the arrival of Howard Hughes as boss, caused Cooper to make an agreement with Republic, whose owner, Herbert J. Yates, used the company mainly to promote to stardom Vera Hruba Ralston, whom he later married. Since *My Darling Clementine* had confirmed renewed popularity for the Western, Ford concentrated almost exclusively on that genre for Republic – and indeed for the rest of his career. His Westerns of this period, underrated then and subsequently overvalued, are nevertheless – with the exception of *The Grapes of Wrath* – his most enduring films. Heroes are good

for the nation, he observed, and these films are tributes to the pioneers. You will not find an authentic portrait of the Old West, and you may be disappointed by the puppet-like characters (why else would he have used Maureen O'Hara?), by the gleaming neatness, and by the 'Sons of the Pioneers' singing on the soundtrack. Many spectators see only the clichés and the mawkishness. His expositions are often weak, his climaxes careless, and his situations – reflective of sentiment, camaraderie and dalliance – often ritualistic.

Fort Apache (1948), written by Frank S. Nugent from a story by James Warner Bellah, is a Cavalry vs. Indians tale, set in a stockade in Monument Valley commanded by a Patton-like Fonda; John Wayne is his second-in-command, Pedro Armendariz the Spanish-speaking sergeant and Shirley Temple and John Agar the tiresome juveniles. **Three Godfathers** (1948) was made by Argosy for M-G-M, which owned the rights, having done the last of the four previous versions in 1936; Ford himself had made one of these in 1919, with Harry Carey, to whom the 1948 version is dedicated. Harry Carey Jr is in this film, with Wayne and Armendariz, and they are three bank robbers lumbered with a baby in the Mojave desert. The naivety and Christian symbolism belong to an earlier age, but it is a film to be experienced, as filmed on unearthly locations by Winton C. Hoch, in colour – Ford's second venture in that process. Hoch's Technicolor photography for **She Wore a Yellow Ribbon** (1949) was based on Remington, and won an Academy Award, but the story by Nugent and Laurence Stallings, again from a novel by Bellah, is of less interest. As the Indian-fighter captain, nearing retirement age, Wayne is an asset, but the reverse is true again of the juveniles – Agar, Carey Jr and Joanne Dru – and you must be Ford-indulgent to enjoy the shenanigans of Victor McLaglen as the fist-happy, softhearted and hard-drinking Sergeant Quincannon, a character common to several films in this group.

When Willie Comes Marching Home (1950), an assignment at 20th Century-Fox, concerns a small town boy (Dan Dailey) who becomes a local hero when he is the first to enlist, only to become an object of scorn when he fails to get an overseas posting; as written by Mary

688

Loos and Richard Sale from a story by Sy Gomberg, this is a long way after *Hail the Conquering Hero* and Ford's not dissimilar comedies with Will Rogers – and, except for William Demarest as the boy's father, indifferently cast.

Ford himself provided the self-indulgent storyline of **Wagonmaster** (1950), which concerns two horse-traders (Carey Jr, Ben Johnson) taken on by a Mormon leader (Ward Bond) to guide a wagon train heading West. **Rio Grande** (1950), together with *Fort Apache* and *She Wore a Yellow Ribbon*, is said to complete Ford's cavalry trilogy, and the setting is once more Monument Valley at the end of the Civil War. Wayne is again in command and again untypically moustached (seemingly a badge of office for those in charge in Ford's films), coping with Indians, an estranged wife (O'Hara), and a son (Claude Jarman Jr) expelled from West Point.

However, the ambivalence we feel towards Ford's writers does not extend to his superb photographers – not only Hoch, but Bert Glennon and Archie Stout, either individually or in pairs – or to Wayne, who was seldom more authoritative and relaxed. Despite the occasional presence of Wayne, who was finally achieving huge popularity after almost twenty years in films, all these movies were at best middling successes at the box office, or, in the cases of *Three Godfathers* and *Wagonmaster*, outright failures – as was a remake of the Silent **What Price Glory?** (1952) at 20th Century-Fox with James Cagney and Dan Dailey. It was planned as a musical, but Ford declined to use the score – which could only have improved it.

He felt no such inhibitions about the soundtrack itself of his films, and **The Quiet Man** (1952) pounds away with every overfamiliar Irish air. Ford, observed Richard Winnington, 'enthusiastically joins the great company which, aided by the Irish themselves, insists on viewing Ireland's aimlessness, poverty and disease through a mist of begorras and blarney . . . this must be the work of any good Hollywood hack.' Elsewhere, astonishingly, it was called 'Shakespearian' (by Lindsay Anderson in *Sight and Sound*), presumably because it attempts the lyrical and has recognisably Irish versions of Beatrice, Benedick and Dogberry. Even a better

film would have been ruined by these studio exteriors, and close-ups which jar with their surrounding shots. Ford is unhappily trapped between a misty-eyed obsession with the auld country and the quest for a heroic concept such as he had already attempted in *The Informer* and *The Fugitive*. Most of the cast is Irish distilled in Hollywood, including McLaglen as the squire, Barry Fitzgerald, and Ward Bond and Arthur Shields as rival priests. Only Wayne is at ease as an American returning to his native land to woo a pre-Raphaelite O'Hara, for whom he engages in a donnybrook borrowed from *The Spoilers*.

That battle was instrumental in the film becoming the biggest success in the twenty-five-year existence of Republic (which abandoned production in 1957, with Miss Hruba Ralston as far from popularity as ever). Ford followed it with a 'little' picture – a policy, he claimed, which enabled him to relax. **The Sun Shines Bright** (1953) is a return to the 'Judge Priest' stories, of which three were gathered into a screenplay by Stallings. Ford later cited it with *The Fugitive* and *Wagonmaster* as 'coming closest to what I wanted to achieve', and it certainly demonstrates his handling of mood and composition; it also resembles rather closely other Ford films but not much, as usual, real life. Among several strands of plot is one where the judge (Charles Winninger) coolly turns away a mob hunting a black boy accused of insulting a white girl; in another he arranges for a madam 'a funeral with all the trimmings', though it puts his re-election in jeopardy – and virtually the only moment of genuine sensibility is that when her 'ladies', in black bombazine, sit upright in their carriage to counteract the indignation directed at them. The film was unsuccessful, but since it was 'personal' it endeared itself to those about to drag the *auteur* theory into film criticism. Ford was on the verge of achieving a recognition such as he had never known – and he was ready for it, growling out a macho, no-bull philosophy which, as with a number of American writers, contrasts with the inherent sentimentality of his work.

Alfred Hitchcock was another to benefit from the *auteur* theory. Aided by a 'concerto' by Miklos Rozsa and a dream sequence designed by Salvador Dali, he had another big success with **Spellbound**

689

(1945). He told a disappointed Truffaut, who admired the film, that it was 'just another manhunt story wrapped in pseudo-psychoanalysis', but in claiming to be the first to put psychiatry on the screen he clearly did not think of Pabst. Credited to Ben Hecht, from a novel by Francis Beeding, the screenplay is about an amnesiac (Gregory Peck) only able to clear himself of a suspected murder if he can recall his past – which he cannot do because of a traumatic incident in childhood. Leo G. Carroll is the head of the clinic, Ingrid Bergman is the doctor trying to help Peck, Rhonda Fleming is a nymphomaniac who hates men, and Wallace Ford a man in a hotel lobby who pesters Bergman sexually – understandably, we may feel. She, as so often, provides the main interest: a severe hairdo, glasses and a concentrated expression can neither hide her beauty nor suggest 'a dedicated scientist', but she admirably portrays a woman in love.

She is less convincing at the start of **Notorious** (1946), having turned to men and martinis because her father was a traitor – but the plot makes her atone when a government agent (Cary Grant) recruits her to infiltrate the household of one of her father's friends (Claude Rains). The relationship of the three has piquancy: Rains, the older man uncertain of his luck in getting a beautiful bride; Bergman, caught between love – for Grant – and duty; and Grant, deeply resenting the claims of the latter. Indeed, this is a classy example of the thriller, and its key sequence – Grant's stealing away from a reception to get into the wine cellar – is one of Hitchcock's finest essays in suspense. The two stars also have a kiss which broke records in screen length – and that, as its publicity-minded director intended, made the film very famous at the time.

It had been prepared by Hitchcock and Selznick, but was sold by Selznick before production to R.K.O. for $800,000 and half the profits – which were again considerable. The two men collaborated for the last time on **The Paradine Case** (1948), with a screenplay credited to Selznick. He had once persuaded M-G-M to buy Robert Hichens's novel as a vehicle for the Barrymore brothers and Diana Wynyard, later purchasing it himself for another star – but as one of his memos sadly states, 'Miss Garbo has always had an aversion to the story'. This film proves her to have been right: a happily-married lawyer (Peck) falls in love with his client (Alida Valli), believing in her innocence despite the enmity of her murdered husband's valet (Louis Jourdan), later revealed to be her lover. This is the sole enigma in a two-hour plod which stops abruptly when it is announced that the valet has done away with himself (in exactly those words) and the beautiful client confesses her guilt. Most of the cast is ill-equipped to breathe life into it: of the stars only Charles Laughton, as the judge, is good, and only Valli – whom Selznick fancied as a new Garbo – is forgivable, since it was only her second film in English. John Williams can be spotted in the courtroom, with never a line of dialogue : later, in Dial 'M' for Murder (q.v.) Hitchcock would give him his first major screen role – and we may suppose that had he thought (or been allowed) to cast him in the part played here by Peck, this would not be so unreservedly Hitchcock's own worst American film.

Despite its reception, Hitchcock was in a better situation than most to become independent, and he formed Transatlantic Pictures with Sydney Bernstein, an old acquaintance of his British days, head of the Granada circuit in the U.K. Preserving his autonomy and most of the profits, he supplied the talent and Bernstein the money; the subjects were chosen with special attention to the company's name. There is no other good reason why the action of **Rope** (1948) should have been transferred from Britain to the U.S., even if Patrick Hamilton's play had been inspired by the Leopold–Loeb murder case. As restaged in a palatial Manhattan penthouse, the piece loses much of its fetching grisliness – as well as (because of censorship) Hamilton's hints at the exact relationship of these degenerate young students (John Dall, Farley Granger) who 'killed for a thrill'. That the piece survives is due to the acting – though not that of James Stewart, miscast as the professor who guesses their horrible secret – and the dialogue: it is almost all dialogue. For this film, Hitchcock used the much-touted 'ten-minute take', purportedly to allow sequences to build to a dramatic climax. He assuredly had fun devising the camera movements, but otherwise the technique resembles that of the early Talkies – or of T.V. drama, with which audiences were then becoming familiar. In fact, the only thing that prevented the film from looking like television was Technicolor; and it is perhaps because of television that Hitchcock dropped the device after one more film.

This was **Under Capricorn** (1949), and the publicity 'push' was not the ten-minute take, but that he was returning to Britain with the biggest star of the time, Miss Bergman. Hitchcock's own attitude to this homecoming with Bergman he later categorised as 'childish', and it was presumably that which caused him to choose a subject suitable to neither – though the dramatist James Bridie, working from a novel by Helen Simpson, almost makes it work. The setting is Sydney in 1831, and as on past occasions the director is unhappy with a historical subject. Equally ill at ease are Joseph Cotten as Sam Flusky, ex-convict, and Bergman as his wife, an Irish aristocrat turned alcoholic. Since she attempts an Irish accent on top of her Swedish one, the casting is one of the reasons why people find this film preposterous. Margaret Leighton, as the evil housekeeper, drops one H in three – and reminds us of *Rebecca*, as does the crux of the film, when Bergman confesses that she is a murderess. The piece is not at all bad on such matters as ladies who marry beneath them and on the difficulties for a once-convicted man to acquire respect; there are also several sequences of the sort Hitchcock always does with relish (e.g. dinner parties) and, overall, we may find the result somewhat more enjoyable than contemporary opinion allowed.

Warner Bros. released both films, and their failure found Hitchcock working out a contract made directly with that company. He remained in Britain to make **Stage·Fright** (1950), based on a novel by Selwyn Jepson, which he later admitted had attracted him only because several reviewers had observed it to be suitable for a Hitchcock film. A drama student (Jane Wyman) helps a man (Richard Todd), who tells her that an actress (Marlene Dietrich) has murdered her husband and involved him, whereupon she poses as a maid in order to investigate on his behalf. Hitchcock partly blamed Miss Wyman for the film's failure, claiming that she refused

to deglamorise herself for the impersonation – a remark which quite understandably bewildered that lady. In fact, the film has only two frail strands of suspense – when will the police put a stop to the girl's snooping and how long will it be before they discover that the actress is the real killer? More crucial to our disappointment is the fact that Hitchcock cheats. When Agatha Christie in an early mystery novel broke a similar rule, her audacity surprised her readers – but the camera should not lie, even in flashback. The suspect roles are uninteresting as rendered by Dietrich and Todd; Wyman and Michael Wilding, as the detective, are pleasing; Alistair Sim, as so often, brightens the proceedings – but when Truffaut told Hitchcock that he disliked the performance, Hitchcock replied, 'Here again is the trouble of shooting a film in England. They all tell you, "He's one of our best actors; you've got to have him in your picture."'

Strangers on a Train (1951) was the long-delayed return to form – and the plot at least is a classic one, written by Raymond Chandler and Czenzi Ormonde from a novel by Patricia Highsmith. On a train, Bruno (Robert Walker), wealthy mother's boy and psychopath, proposes to Guy (Farley Granger) that they exchange

Like John Ford, Alfred Hitchcock decided early on that he wanted to be noticed as a director, and he was also sufficiently gifted to realise what he could not get away with. But after he had succeeded in Hollywood in a way no other British director had done, he began to make bad movies. One was so poor (*The Paradine Case*) that the two independent pictures that followed could only be improvements: but they were hardly better liked, and Hitchcock returned to the cleverly-plotted thriller which had made him famous, *Strangers on a Train*, with Robert Walker as the killer. His victim was played by Patricia Hitchcock, the director's daughter.

murders, as each wants someone out of the way. Guy does not take the matter seriously, but since this is a set-up for the perfect murder it is tempting to regard the film as the perfect murder story. It does not, unfortunately, repay close examination, but the set pieces are among the director's best: Bruno, losing self-control during his demonstration of strangling at a party; the tennis match that Guy must win in order to get away to the scene of the crime (why didn't he just throw the match?); the murder itself; and the finale – the fight on the carousel. For Hitchcock himself, the flaws included 'the final script', and 'the ineffectiveness' of the leading players. Walker's performance is generally regarded as brilliant, suggesting neuroses beneath a level-headed charm, while Granger's indication of weakness satisfies the spectator's need for logic, explaining why he does not go to the police.

To consolidate the renewed interest in his work, Hitchcock spent a long while preparing **I Confess** (1953). The locations were filmed in Quebec, a city of dark mansions and gloom as seen by him – which pleases those of his commentators looking for a sense of guilt which they say can be traced to his Jesuit upbringing; we might remark instead that his only early successful films were those dealing with crime, and that he therefore developed an interest in stories within that genre. This particular one first saw the light of day in 1902 as a play by Paul Anthelme – and it was recommended to Hitchcock by Louis Verneuil. Discussing it, Hitchcock observed that 'most of the material submitted to me is generally wrong for me' – and it is surely significant that, working within what is in itself a second-rate field, he avoided the first-rate within it (Chandler and Hammett). He was really only interested in displaying the Hitchcock 'genius'; nothing was allowed to get in the way of that. This is technically one of his most brilliant films, with every shot precise and well judged. The premise is appealing: a murderer confesses to a priest (Montgomery Clift) who, later accused of the crime, is unable to break his vow of silence. He does behave, as the detective (Karl Malden) puts it, 'with too much mystification', and though that is later justified, the course is strewn with the usual red herrings of pulp fiction, including missing clues, a wrong police diagnosis, and a confession by an old girlfriend – played by Anne Baxter, forced on Hitchcock by Warners in place of Anita Bjork (whom he had already signed), and acting so badly as to detract from the priest's dilemma.

Movies in this genre usually trade probability for tension, and Hitchcock was certainly aware of the pitfalls in his branch of the trade; moreover, he did not take himself as seriously as some of his admirers do. He could be very entertaining, as he is here, but given that he had more freedom of choice than most Hollywood directors it is sad that all the expertise was not expended on something more worthwhile. After watching all his films again at close intervals for the purposes of this book, I was only too aware of the tricks, lies and cheating involved in creating that tension: but perhaps, in the end, it is enough that a dozen or so of them do repay watching a second time.

After earning his living for four years as an actor, it was with a Hitchcock-like thriller that Orson Welles returned to directing. He was engaged to play one of the leads in **The Stranger** (1946), which John Huston had written and was planning to direct; but Welles persuaded Sam Spiegel to let him direct it as well. Huston departed amicably, and the screenplay is credited to Anthony Veiller: whoever wrote it, it is deeply rooted in years of Hollywood junk. A good prologue introduces Edward G. Robinson as an agent tracking down Nazis in the U.S. – and this actor subsequently holds the film together; it also 'establishes' a small Connecticut town, in wintry sunshine, and Russell Metty's photography would later serve Welles's increasingly flashy style. Welles himself plays a Nazi, disguised as a professor, 'till the day we strike again'; Robinson recognises him when he claims 'Marx wasn't a German, he was a Jew', and the pursuit that follows includes his new wife (Loretta Young) watching newsreels of Auschwitz, but otherwise behaving with the illogicality of most film heroines by deliberately courting death. Welles looks so panic-stricken and wild-eyed that he gives himself away in the first reel.

Even worse is **The Lady from Shanghai** (1948), which Welles had talked Harry Cohn into letting him make, claiming that he could bring in a class film on a low budget. He was also at the time married to Rita Hayworth, Cohn's biggest star, and as the marriage was already on the rocks, Cohn felt that a professional collaboration could not worsen the situation. Cohn loathed the rushes, and when the cost reached $2 million, shooting was hastily wound up; Welles had nothing to do with the final print, into which badly-matched close-ups of Hayworth had been inserted to justify its existence. On this admittedly doubtful result, Welles's earlier films seem flukes: not only does this thriller not thrill, but when it is straightforward it is unbelievable and for the rest of the time incomprehensible. It has to do with a mysterious blonde (Hayworth), the Irish sailor (Welles) she encounters while being mugged in Central Park, her crippled, older husband (Everett Sloane) and his partner (Glenn Anders), who also has a crush on her. Redeeming features are the naturalistic trial and the famous shoot-out in the hall of mirrors.

Further persuasion by Welles found Republic financing **Macbeth** (1948), on a budget of $800,000 – roughly the cost of a Vera Hruba Ralston vehicle (which seldom made a profit anyway). It was shot in the summer of 1947, in three weeks, but due to dubbing problems not shown till late 1948 – and in a few cities only; withdrawn for re-dubbing, it did not open in New York till the end of 1950. Despite ignominious reviews it has survived, usually defended as visually imaginative – since no other claim can be made for it. The opening sequence promises well, with swirling mists, but they clear too soon, revealing the backlot sky. Macbeth's castle, all papier-mâché cliffs and stairs that go nowhere, has puddles on its black marble floor; the equally pretentious costumes (Welles designed those of the men) include a series of headgear for Macbeth purloined from *Alexander Nevsky*. Aurally, the occasion is even less rewarding. The dialogue was recorded in Scottish-English, in British-English, and in Transatlanticene: what was finally used seems to be a blend of all three. It hardly matters, for the text has been so mutilated as to suggest that the screenplay was compiled from a dictionary of quotations, with interpolations which are pure doggerel. The cast, which includes Welles in the title role, is abysmal.

Undeterred, he did an **Othello** which borrows from Olivier's *Hamlet* (q.v.) by beginning with its hero's funeral: other comparisons are supposedly allayed by Welles's own description, 'a motion picture adaptation'. He began the planning in Rome, while making another film there, and started shooting with inadequate funds. He sank his own money into it, and any more he could beg or borrow – the bulk of it coming from a financier in Casablanca (which is why the film has Moroccan nationality) where he had made *The Black Rose* (q.v.). Filming was not only interrupted by his work on other films, but by a nervous breakdown and a London production of the play (under Olivier's management). The film was premiered at the Cannes Festival in 1952 and won the Grand Prix, but United Artists did not release it in New York till 1955. Lea Padovani, Cecile Aubrey and Betsy Blair had all had a go at playing Desdemona, but were either fired or frightened away; Suzanne Cloutier, who finally acted the role, was French-Canadian. The influence of Eisenstein is apparent, especially in the opening scene, with black-cowled monks against the sky. The Venetian scenes are hurried through – the Ca d'Oro and the Bovolo staircase for Desdemona's home, the Miracoli for the wedding, the Scala dei Giganti for the conclave with the Duke; the rest seems to have been photographed at the fortress in Mogador. There are two good sequences: Iago planting the seeds of suspicion in Othello's mind as they are pacing the battlements, and Roderigo's attempted murder of Cassius in a Turkish bath. But though Welles has worked out the action in film terms, it is clear that without the aid of the Hollywood cutting rooms he has no sense of narrative. His gifts as an actor should have been sufficient to make up for deficiencies elsewhere, but he makes matters worse by offering an Othello with only one pained expression. The net result is a dreary one-dimensional tale, moving in fits and starts to an improbable ending. In the circumstances, Michael MacLiammoir is an acceptable Iago; Fay Compton is an execrable Emilia.

Welles provided Chaplin with the idea of **Monsieur Verdoux** (1947), and the latter seems to have been attracted to Landru, the French Bluebeard, for his 'message' value – for Verdoux's murders, the film claims, are hardly worse than the mass murdering done by nations; at his trial – supposed to take place in 1938 – Verdoux claims that the gains from his crimes are as nothing to those to be made in the forthcoming conflict. Verdoux is a meticulous dandy, with a voice so high-pitched as to be androgynous. His rapport with people and the scrapes he gets into are entirely those of Chaplin the Tramp – and considering how ruthless the Tramp could be it is no surprise to find Chaplin only physically transformed; he kills solely for the sake of his crippled wife, though with the added incentive of revenging himself upon a society which had sacked him after thirty years in the same job. The best scenes are those involving Martha Raye, who distrusts him as much as his other wives but will forgive everything for some slap and tickle – or more: in no other film of the period does a woman so lust after her man. There is also a waif (Marilyn Nash, perhaps the most amateurish of all Chaplin's discoveries), and his dialogues with her are the essence of later Chaplin – naive philosophies passed on as truths, e.g., on death, 'I guess if the unborn knew of the approach of life they'd be just as terrified.' In his memoir, Chaplin claims this to be 'the cleverest and most brilliant film I have yet made', and though it is muddled, overlong and sometimes mistaken, he is probably right. Most American critics took the view of Howard Barnes in *The New York Herald-Tribune*, that it was 'something of an affront to the intelligence'. In cinemas, the debacle became a rout: catcalled in some, it was withdrawn in others. The intelligentsia was pro-*Verdoux*, either on its own merits or because Chaplin could do no wrong, while a number of people, especially in the industry, were determined that the public should not see it. His personal stock was near to zero. A much-publicised morals trial, though it acquitted him, had harmed his image, and the situation was not helped by his marriage to the very young Oona O'Neill and the objection to the marriage by her father, the playwright Eugene O'Neill. Chaplin's pro-Soviet stance during the War was recalled to make him a target for rightists. In short, a great number of Americans regarded *Verdoux* as subversive – a view which could be sustained only if they had not seen it.

In Britain, which had a Socialist government, the political bent of the film was hardly remarked upon; in France, the left-wing weekly *L'Ecran Français* returned to it constantly with newer and better superlatives. The situation had changed little by the time Chaplin offered **Limelight** (1952), for though on this occasion American reviewers approved, hostility in other quarters had hardened: the State Department made it clear that if he left the country to attend the film's British premiere there would be no guarantee of re-entry. (He had remained a British citizen.) Chaplin went to London, and then settled in Switzerland with his young family; his personal situation may have been one reason why the film was ecstatically received in Europe. If anyone saw it as evidence of decline, which it surely is, it was not mentioned.

The plot is slim: Calvero (Chaplin), a once-famous clown, saves from suicide a young dancer (Claire Bloom) whom he nurtures into success; she helps him to one last triumph, and goes on dancing, his creation, as he dies. As with *Verdoux*, the screenplay is a compendium of a lifetime's reflections – on such matters as audiences, success, love, art, fame and poverty. One is momentarily intrigued when Chaplin's own face appears from behind the mask inadvertently, as in the situation of the girl's love for a much older man. This parallels his own life at this time, but of course young girls are better box office than old girls. And though the decline of Calvero cannot be autobiographical, it is presumably a musing on what might have happened had Chaplin not left Fred Karno's company. When Calvero is a success with the same act he once flopped with, we assume audiences to be conditioned by factors (time, place, publicity) which have nothing to do with talent or the essential being of an artist – but the point is made so unobtrusively (unlike most of the film) that I am not sure that Chaplin was aware of it.

Limelight reaffirms Chaplin's belief in the innate goodness of mankind: the realisation of this vis-à-vis Chaplin's own situation undoubtedly affected reviewers then, but it should not blind us now to the fact that this is all the picture has in common with his earlier films. It soon soured in the memory, with its cheeseparing sets and the glutinous theme tune, composed by Chaplin, ubiquitous on the airwaves for a year afterwards; and then Chaplin withheld the film from us for twenty years. It was indifferently received when revived – a pleasant enough 135 minutes but unexceptional, except perhaps in the music hall act with Buster Keaton. Some observers find it hard to forgive Chaplin for cutting, as we now know, Keaton's footage in this scene, but one had remained a star while the other had not – and Keaton was glad to work. In the interim we had had the chance to assess the achievements of them both, and the film now sours not afterwards but while watching it.

A King in New York (1957) was made in Britain and, on Chaplin's orders, not shown in the U.S. Considering that his purpose was to attack that country, this was self-defeating; doubtless he thought that deprivation would be some punishment for its treatment of him. It was because of that treatment that much was expected of this riposte: the reaction of the British press was one of baffled disappointment. It was finally shown in the U.S. in 1971, when it was generally ignored. Chaplin himself passed over it in his autobiography, but is reported as saying 'I was disappointed in the picture. I meant it to be so up to date and modern, but perhaps I didn't quite understand it.' He was sixty-eight when he made it, and obviously out of touch. Television commercials are such easy game that he cannot be congratulated on being amusing in that direction; but he is not funny on movie trailers, rock 'n' roll and such old targets as social climbers, plastic surgery and room service. Where he should be sharpest, on the then-American obsession with reds in their midst, he is feeble; and the views of democracy put into the mouth of a schoolboy are only too infantile. When he had made *Modern Times* he had said, 'There are those who always attach social significance to my work. It has none. I leave such subjects to the lecture platform.' This is ingenuous; it might just be true of his films till then, but it certainly is not true of those that came afterwards. The message of this one, such as it is, might not be so diminished were the film not so appallingly executed, with its ancient stock shots and London landmarks standing in for Manhattan.

Preston Sturges is equally disappointing with **Unfaithfully Yours** (1948), the first of two films he made for 20th Century-Fox. Unlike Chaplin, Sturges was an accomplished satirist, but this screenplay is devoid of wit. A bad-tempered musician (Rex Harrison) is given cause to think that his wife (Linda Darnell) is unfaithful: while conducting – Rossini, Wagner, Tchaikovsky – he fantasises on her infidelity and his revenge. The uneasiness is not lessened by Darnell and Barbara Lawrence in roles which required players of the calibre of Constance Bennett and Ina Claire. Perhaps Lucille Ball was needed for **The Beautiful Blonde from Bashful Bend** (1949) – but it has Betty Grable, as a brassy saloon singer, rather too quick on the draw. 'Nice clean world,' she muses, 'no drunks to roll, no salesmen to listen to,' but it is not her line, nor was she adept at knockabout comedy. Zanuck, stung by the terrible reviews her films received, had made an effort to find her better material: Sturges wrote and directed from a story by Earl Fenton, cribbing wildly from 'L'il Abner'. The result is not good Sturges, nor a satire on Westerns, but its sly humour is at least a partial return to form – though it fared no better with audiences than did its predecessor.

Many of the later films of Fritz Lang found little more favour. After the success of *The Woman in the Window* he formed a production company with Walter Wanger and Joan Bennett, and in **Scarlet Street** (1945) they set about emulating that film. Edward G. Robinson is again the infatuated older man and Bennett the woman who embroils him in her affairs; once more they are supported by Dan Duryea, up to no good. Dudley Nichols, who had written *Man Hunt* for Lang, did the screenplay, from the same novel which had been the basis of Renoir's *La Chienne*. Lubitsch had held the rights for years, but could not get a workable script; Lang felt that it would be possible if Greenwich Village were substituted for Montmartre. That it is not is the fault of the Production Code: *The Woman in the Window* had been just a murder mystery, but this is a study of relationships – made implausible right from the start since the Bennett character cannot be designated an out-and-out prostitute. The M.P.A.A. did not, for once, mind the hero getting away with murder, but he has to suffer from guilt instead; the ending is mere bathos, whereas Renoir's was an ironic twist. **Secret Beyond the Door** (1948) was based on an old script that Wanger had in his files, and the project, dogged by ill fortune, wound up the Wanger-Bennett-Lang company. Lang had no good word for it, and it is surely one of the worst of the many Forties films about murderer-husbands. This particular one collects rooms where famous murders occurred, and the title refers to a replica of the heroine's own bedroom. Michael Redgrave has tried hard to find a motive for the man's behaviour, but the role defeats him.

Lang's reputation did not recover with the films he made for other companies. **Cloak and Dagger** (1946) is a Hitchcockian adventure about a mid-Western professor (Gary Cooper) sent into Switzerland during the War to discover whether or not the Germans are developing the atom bomb. Lang said that Warners would not permit any comment on the latter, but his attempt to make something more than a Resistance thriller was foiled by an absurd script by Albert Maltz and Ring Lardner Jr. Equally contrived is **House by the River** (1950), made at Republic, as adapted by Mel Dinelli from the novel by A. P. Herbert. Louis Hayward is both colourless and unsubtle as an unsuccessful author who finds involvement in murder a sure way to sell his books, and Lang responds to his material only in the courtroom climax and in his handling of the gloomy Edwardian mansion in which most of the mayhem takes place. **An American Guerilla in the Philippines** (1950) concerns Tyrone Power and Tom Ewell hiding from the Japanese occupiers, frequently reminding each other that MacArthur promised to return: when he eventually does, someone says, 'He said he'd return.'

'Hate, murder and revenge' is said, or rather sung, throughout **Rancho Notorious** (1952), to remind us that it set new standards for violence in a Western; it is also a precursor of later Westerns in keeping its tongue firmly in its cheek. It did not prove influential (apart from a theme song integrated into the action, a device immediately copied by *High Noon*, q.v.), nor was it an attempt to extend the range of the Western – for this tale of an ageing dance hall girl and an old gun-hand was conceived as a vehicle for Marlene Dietrich.

Since Lang found her 'very, very disagreeable' on the set, it seems apt that she should be its chief weakness, masklike and humourless – yet at the same time she gives the piece a flavour, dealing cards with a cigarette dangling, or intoning a song. As a gun-slinger, Mel Ferrer has an insolent smile but is as likely as Pegleg Pete waiting table in a gay bar, and Arthur Kennedy is not the most convincing actor to play a relentless avenger. But in dealing with matters which include rape and wholesale slaughter, Lang works with greater confidence than in years. This renewed vigour is also apparent in his second film for R.K.O., **Clash by Night** (1952), adapted by Alfred Hayes from a play by Clifford Odets – and though Jerry Wald, the producer, admired Odets, it is difficult to see why he thought this tired eternal triangle situation worth another whirl. It entertains by its sheer awfulness, as when a jaded Barbara Stanwyck returns to her home town, observing 'I don't remember a lot of things.' Knowing that she had done this sort of role too often, she plays down the histrionics; as the dull man she marries, Paul Douglas does a deal of teddy-bearing but is convincing in the harsher moments; and Robert Ryan was seldom better than as the smart-ass pal she falls for. In the play, the husband killed the lover, but in the film the wife finally discovers the husband's True Worth. The film also transferred the action from Staten Island to Monterey; it was Wald's idea to use a fishing village, and the documentary material that Lang shot gets the film off to a good start. Later scenes of pounding surf and scudding clouds indicate that he knew the level of his material, but with a stronger milieu than he had had since *Fury*, he responds magnificently: the Sunday afternoon dance, the beer halls, the shore, the quayside.

There are some promising foggy exteriors in **The Blue Gardenia** (1953), but it is otherwise stale. A girl (Anne Baxter) goes to a man's apartment while drunk, and then thinks she has murdered him. When an esteemed director takes on such tales, it is either for the twists or for opportunities with *mise-en-scène*: but since neither is apparent, we may suppose Lang still nourished a desire for independence – which he had retained, in the main, over his recent films, despite the involvement of the major companies as distributors. Lang would not be the first or last to equate independence with a vague but cynical notion of what the public wanted, the result in this case being a film of no quality at all. Its failure, and the consequent blow to what was left of his reputation, caused him to move to Columbia for a programmer, **The Big Heat** (1953) – and ironically it was that which restored him to critical favour. A cop (Glenn Ford) investigating a suicide begins to suspect that it was murder; as he probes deeper, an attempt is made on his life and his wife is killed – then he discovers a nest of corruption which includes a number of high police officials. Civic corruption in movies had, since Capra, only been hinted at, and it was refreshing to see the subject handled again at this time, from a story by Sydney Boehm, who also contributed some crude but excellent dialogue. The film's violence was much commented upon, especially that directed at the gangster's moll (Gloria Grahame). Lang's response was intense, and this is, simply, a superb thriller, looking more intently at the roots of crime than any other film of the time.

Human Desire (1954) was Lang's second attempt at remaking one of Renoir's films, and the idea was Wald's, since he had loved *La Bête Humaine*; it was originally to have been made with the same stars as *Clash by Night*, but Wald took the property with him to Columbia, who cast Ford and Grahame. Renoir's film is a black, engulfing drama; Lang's is a footling little melodrama about adultery. He has reacted well to the grey industrial town where it takes place, the bar where the husband (Broderick Crawford) goes to drink, the suburban home with television and flying ducks on the wall, but the story does not work in this American setting. Glenn Ford fails completely as both a potential murderer and a man motivated by an *amour fou*, and in his role Crawford has neither the necessary guile nor the intelligence.

Moonfleet (1955) was produced by John Houseman, British-reared and therefore familiar with the hundred and one boys' adventure stories on which it was modelled; since it has little in common with J. Meade Faulkner's half-forgotten classic of the same name, we may assume that the writers, Jan Lustig and Margaret Fitts, poured into it every breathtaking

convention of the genre. Lang disliked the story (though he was flattered to be asked back to M-G-M), but brought to the film the strong atmospheric qualities that Houseman hoped for. As the boy hero, Jon Whiteley is a huge asset, grave and courageous, unflinching at revelations of his idol's villainy; in the part of guardian and smuggler chief, Stewart Granger found his best screen role; George Sanders is a milord; Joan Greenwood his treacherous wife; and Viveca Lindfors is the common-law wife from the Indies. M-G-M loathed the film and threw it away as the lower half of double bills – to the indignation of many, savouring (for what would be the last time) the director's old panache.

While the City Sleeps (1956) and **Beyond a Reasonable Doubt** (1956) are both pulp thrillers, needlessly well made. The first has a newspaper background and a cast including Dana Andrews, George Sanders, Ida Lupino, Vincent Price and Thomas Mitchell; the second has a more intriguing plot about a husband who has theories about a murder which are turned against himself, and it has Andrews and Joan Fontaine. Lang may have had no illusions about the basic value of his material, nor qualms about the way these films too were thrown away by R.K.O., a company then in its death throes. He was no longer interested in working in Hollywood; he said later that as old age approached he was certain that it was no longer worth the ulcers.

At this time, Lang's reputation was outstripped by that of Robert Siodmak, who had had fewer setbacks with his own strongly atmospheric melodramas. After the success of *The Suspect*, Universal bought for him another English period melodrama, by Thomas Job, **The Strange Affair of Uncle Harry** (1945), but as adapted by Stephen Longstreet it was now set in the present day in New Hampshire. Siodmak is able to make little of 'the typical small town' promised in the foreword, but he clearly enjoys the cluttered mansion which is the setting for Harry (George Sanders), a mild draughtsman, and the neurotic sister (Geraldine Fitzgerald) whose passion for him threatens his engagement. There is another large house in **The Spiral Staircase** (1946), and the time is again the turn of the century. Written by Mel Dinelli from a novel by Ethel Lina White, this is less a whodunnit than a who'lldoit: several physically handicapped girls have been murdered, and a deaf mute (Dorothy McGuire) is expected to be the next victim. A shadowy figure spies upon her as she leaves for the house where she is a servant, and is later glimpsed within it. 'Oh, it's you,' says Blanche (Rhonda Fleming) to someone we cannot see in the cellar, 'You quite frightened me.' In time the deaf mute is alone in the house, and a storm rages without . . . The art direction is appropriately splendid, and the film was rapturously received. Selznick produced, and this was one of the films he sold in pre-production to R.K.O.

Returning to Universal, Siodmak made **The Killers** (1946), which disposes of Hemingway's story in so tense and eerie a ten minutes as to make the remainder an anticlimax. There are ninety-five more to go, and their substance was devised by the producer, Mark Hellinger, in conjunction with Anthony Veiller and John Huston. (As with *The Stranger*, Veiller gets sole credit, but in this case because Huston's contract with Warners forbade mention of his name; Veiller later worked on some of Huston's own productions.) An insurance investigator (Edmond O'Brien) is called upon to examine the past of the murdered man (Burt Lancaster) and his involvement with a gang boss (Albert Dekker), a detective (Sam Levene) and a two-timing dame (Ava Gardner). Lancaster, in his first film,

performs in a manner which suggests that he learned his lines phonetically; but he is not ineffective.

The Dark Mirror (1946) permits Siodmak no atmospheric shots, since the action is virtually restricted to an apartment and a consulting room. That also suggests both considerations of cost – the film was made for International (q.v.) while in the process of amalgamating with Universal – and a belief that the story is sufficiently strong. It concerns seemingly respectable twin sisters, both played by Olivia de Havilland, one of whom is suspected of murder – and the plot is engrossing till it is obliged to reveal which one of them is guilty: from that point Siodmak and his producer-writer, Nunnally Johnson, try to sustain interest by such devices as Miss de Havilland handing articles to Miss de Havilland or embracing herself with both profiles to the camera.

Siodmak dismissed most of his subsequent films as potboilers, but connoisseurs of the *film noir* of the Forties cherish **Cry of the City** (1948), made for 20th Century-Fox, and **Criss Cross** (1949), made for Universal. Both are imitative of old Warner Bros. thrillers, but are deficient where their prototypes were strongest – in their leading men. In *Cry of the City* Richard Conte and Victor Mature are uninteresting as gangster and detective respectively. There is, however, a superb job lot of supporting characters: a shyster lawyer (Berry Kroeger), a psychotic jail-cleaner (Walter Baldwin), a sadistic guard (Roland Winters), a friendly hooker (Shelley Winters), a tough nurse (Betty Guard) and a bull-dyke masseuse (Hope Emerson), who is revealed to be the Miss Big of the operation at the heart of the plot. *Criss Cross* concerns a guy (Burt Lancaster) who turns crook when he discovers that his wife (Yvonne de Carlo) has moved in with a bounder (Dan Duryea). In this case it is less the subsidiary characters who are memorable as the settings: it begins in a car park outside a dance hall, soon revealed as a tacky room behind a long, low and smoky bar; by day sunlight filters into it while cars bake in the Los Angeles heat. 'There's so much you can't control,' said Siodmak to explain his loathing of shooting on location: but you would not know it from his use of it.

He was invited to go to M-G-M to take

Yvonne de Carlo and Burt Lancaster in *Criss Cross*, a conventional crime story of the sort now seen nightly on television. What distinguishes the film is the direction by Robert Siodmak, whose reputation fluctuated from his first film in Berlin in 1929 to his death over forty years later. That was why his material was often undistinguished, but there were occasions, such as this one, when his handling made it seem much better than it was.

over **The Great Sinner** (1949), with a screenplay by Ladislas Fodor and Christopher Isherwood – but with no credit offered to Dostoevsky. Gregory Peck plays a nineteenth-century Russian writer who becomes involved with, among others, a countess (Ethel Barrymore) based on the countess of 'The Gambler' and a pawnbroker (Agnes Moorehead) from 'Crime and Punishment'. M-G-M was not a natural habitat for Dostoevsky, as Siodmak discovered when he tried to cut a screenplay which would have run for six hours. He managed to bring in a three-hour version, but it was 'heavy and dull', mainly due, he thought, to Gregory Peck, whose normally slow speech became even slower, so overawed was he by acting in Dostoevsky. 'Now the story didn't even make sense. By the first preview we had cut it down to two hours ten minutes . . . At that point I washed my hands of the film, and heard nothing until a message came that they – at M-G-M it was always "they" – had decided that what was needed was a new and stronger love story.' Since Siodmak refused to return, Mervyn LeRoy did the reshooting, and though Siodmak claimed that he did not recognise the finished result, it retains a European feeling. It is set around the Casino in Wiesbaden, and the action gathers momentum whenever we get to the tables: the dozens of films featuring roulette and chemin-de-fer were to the taste of industry executives rather than audiences, and this one was rare in making these scenes exciting. The rest of it is hardly Dostoevsky but not despicable. Ava Gardner is miscast as a Russian countess, and some other performers are left floundering – Walter Huston as her father, Melvyn Douglas as her fiancé, and Frank Morgan as an inveterate gambler.

Like *Criss Cross*, **The File on Thelma Jordan** (1949) has a brilliant opening, and it is placed in palm-lined California, where all motives are ambiguous and even the oranges are sour. Thelma (Barbara Stanwyck) is new in town; it is possible that she may not be all she seems to be when the Assistant D.A. (Wendell Corey) kisses her goodnight and she is then pulled into the shadows by a mysterious stranger. Corey, with his bow ties and wintry smiles, is the decent man embroiled in the machinations of a scheming woman – who protests her

innocence seemingly without guile. Ketti Frings wrote the screenplay (from a story by Marty Holland), and Hal Wallis produced for Paramount; without being particularly convincing, it is always interesting – and that is due entirely to Siodmak. With the exceptions of *The Spiral Staircase* and *The Dark Mirror*, both carefully plotted, he was dealing with material with few ideas but with characters who were perverse or criminally-minded: building upon that, he found contradictions and tensions not only in these people but in the bars and apartments they inhabited. Today his unpretentious films are preferred to some of the stuffed albatrosses of the period: but at that time content was all, and by specialising in crime stories Siodmak not only failed to enhance his reputation but virtually ruined it.

Like Melville in France, he remained at heart a romantic, and welcomed the offer to make **The Crimson Pirate** (1952) for Burt Lancaster's company. That actor appears before the credits, advising us to believe only half of what we see, and Siodmak moves easily between spoof and the lightheartedness of the best old swashbucklers – and the climax is a straight steal from *The Black Pirate*. Roland Kibbee wrote the screenplay, and the action is inventive and high-spirited, as Lancaster and Nick Cravatt, his old circus partner, do their stunts; the cinematographer, Otto Heller, manages to convey the tang of the sea in his images. Though set in the Caribbean, it was filmed in the Mediterranean, and Siodmak remained in Europe to work; after a remake of *Le Grand Jeu* in France, he filmed mainly in West Germany. Like Lang, and for the same reasons, he abandoned Hollywood, but of the dozen or so films he made at this period, including three in English, I can find little of interest. Presumably he, too, found the German film industry temperamentally sympathetic but artistically stultifying.

As Siodmak moved towards the end of his American career he helped Max Ophuls begin his – with **The Exile** (1947). Ophuls had arrived in Hollywood, via Switzerland, in 1941, and he had been one of the directors working for Howard Hughes on *Vendetta* before being fired. Siodmak recommended him to Douglas Fairbanks Jr, then preparing his second film as producer – and it is a pity that Fairbanks did not choose his writer with the same discrimination. He had written the screenplay himself, a trifling episode of Charles II's Dutch exile, but wisely left the visual aspects to Ophuls, who combined his knowledge of Dutch painting (including the costumes in the portraits) and flair for the *decoratif* to produce remarkable results.

The film's visual beauty, if nothing else, attracted attention, enabling Ophuls to direct **Letter from an Unknown Woman** (1948), as instigated by Howard Koch, remembering *Liebelei*. Koch wrote the screenplay from a story by Stefan Zweig (filmed earlier as *Only Yesterday*), and it became a labour of love on the part of both of them and John Houseman, who produced. It is a synthesis of old Vienna, and that is all. A girl (Joan Fontaine) falls in love with a pianist (Louis Jourdan) in the same tenement: they are separated, and she has his baby to cherish till they meet again . . . You might say that she is a silly little ninny, but you would be reckoning without Miss Fontaine, who is exquisite, in one of her three great screen performances. And you would be reckoning without Ophuls, and his love of an idealised past – of champagne and chandeliers and horse-drawn carriages, of the gleam of gaslight and jewellery, of waltzes and romance and heartbreak that is almost, but not quite, a game. In a railway carriage in the Prater, painted scenes of Venice flash by; at a last dance at dawn, the all-woman orchestra is impatient to go home; and in a small square in Linz an engagement is celebrated to the oom-pa-pa of the local band. Franz Planer photographed, as he had done for *Liebelei*, and Alexander Golitzen's sets include a narrow circular stair with iron railings: it is looking down the stairwell that the young Fontaine sees the pianist bringing home a girl, and we see it from the same angle when it is she whom he has brought home.

In the U.S. the critics deplored the film, and the public avoided it, suspecting escapism (then unfashionable), rather than the romantic film it is – or so thought Houseman. In Britain, Universal sold it off to a minor distributor, who booked it into a suburban hall, and there it was tracked down by Richard Winnington, whose notice began its rehabilitation.

As Ophuls's reputation began to be slowly restored, the newly-formed Enterprise Studios (q.v.) offered him the direction of **Caught** (1949), a triangle story written by Arthur Laurents (then, a promising Broadway playwright who had just done the screenplay for *Rope*), from a novel by Libbie Block. Another dreamy heroine (Barbara Bel Geddes), marries a millionaire (Robert Ryan) and regrets it – especially when trying to start a new life as receptionist to an East Side doctor (James Mason). 'The film,' said Ophuls, 'goes off the rails towards the end. Up to the last ten minutes, though, it wasn't bad,' and he is probably referring to the handling of the girl, the tycoon and their motivations, all carefully worked out. As the camera rakes every banister of the millionaire's claustrophobic mansion, we may be reminded of James Mason's words on Ophuls's technique:

A shot that does not call for tracks
Is agony for poor dear Max,
Who, separated from his dolly,
Is wrapped in deepest melancholy,
Once, when they took away his crane,
I thought he'd never smile again . . .

Mason also had some pertinent remarks to make about Walter Wanger, who produced the last one of Ophuls's four American films: he was 'a man who wanted to be a European. He didn't know how to be a European, so this was the kind of film – I suppose, like *Brief Encounter* (q.v.) – that he wanted to make.'

The film concerned was **The Reckless Moment** (1949), and it was to have been another alliance between Wanger and Jean Renoir. The latter, however, was anathema to Harry Cohn – Wanger was now with Columbia – and Ophuls was brought in instead. 'It was just another magazine story, not very well written,' said Mason of this tale of a woman (Joan Bennett) who covers up for a near and dear one, directing suspicion to herself because she thinks a murder has been committed; Mason himself plays a blackmailer. Bennett is exceptionally good, chain-smoking distractedly while not finishing some sentences and not hearing others: the overall portrait of family relationships, so different to that of *Caught*, is nevertheless similarly honest. Both films are evidence of Ophuls's mastery, and this one was sufficiently successful for Wanger to get independent backing for a version (to be filmed in Europe) of *La Duchesse de Langeais*, with

Mason and Garbo; but when it became clear that Garbo did not have the courage to resubmit herself to the scrutiny of camera, Ophuls accepted a French offer to direct *La Ronde* (q.v.), the start of the brilliant climax to his career.

The misshapen career of Robert Flaherty finished with **Louisiana Story** (1948), the story of a boy of the bayou. 'His name is Alexander Napoleon Ulysses Latour' says a Voice Over, and you might as well leave if you do not fancy another 76 minutes of poetry. Men arrive to disturb nature with their oil wells, and when Father sings to them they laugh, in the forced manner of T.V. interviewers. The public remained indifferent, despite the usual furore among the critics: 'Films like Robert Flaherty's don't turn up often enough in the lives of film-critics to keep flexible their personal standards of what is worthwhile in the cinema,' (E. Arnot Robertson in 'The Penguin Cinema, 1950'). Of course, it was a change from Vincent Price and Lynn Bari; and had not Flaherty so often tried to compromise with the industry to no avail? And had he not obtained financing for this one from Standard Oil and then shown the oil companies in an unflattering light? At least Virgil Thompson's music is splendid.

A good film about children is **The Search** (1948), directed by Fred Zinnemann for M-G-M and Praesens of Zurich. M-G-M's unlikely involvement in European production was due solely to the enthusiasm of Arthur, one of the younger members of the Loew family: thus, Loews distributed *Goupi Mains Rouges*, the first continental film shown in the States after the War. The company later promoted *The Last Chance*, a Swiss film made partly in English, about a British-American team of soldiers helping refugees cross the border. The producer was Lazar Wechsler and though M-G-M International was short-lived (since it had been started only under sufferance), Wechsler persuaded Loews to co-operate on *The Search*, an original screenplay by Richard Schweizer, with additions by David Wechsler and Paul Jarrico.

For those who judge a movie on content or intent it is a great film; in subject matter at least it dwarfs virtually every American film of the period – for it concerns the rehabilitation of the children who survived the concentration camps. Less pure than *Sciuscià*, it is equally an essential footnote to World War Two. In an UNRRA camp in ruined Germany an American woman (Aline MacMahon) is wearily interviewing children, including a Czech boy (Ivan Jandl); he panics and flees, but is eventually befriended by a G.I. (Montgomery Clift), who takes him under his wing. The introduction of the boy's mother (Jarmilla Novotna) brings an element of suspense (will they be reunited?); and there is a ghastly moment when the boy asks, 'What is a mother?' As against that, there is a moving sequence of the child lost, wandering among the rubble, bewildered by another small boy behind a wire fence; the words 'German' and 'Nazi' are never used, and the war and the concentration camps mentioned only in passing. For its creators, including Zinnemann, this film may be a way of thanking the Americans, as represented by two people – a middle-aged woman and a carefree young G.I. – for their unselfishness in the aftermath of war. Miss MacMahon is never tearful or indulgently smiling, and Clift is better than any other screen G.I. that I have seen – chewing gum, shirt bulging from his pants, sprawling (never sitting) in a chair.

Notable in Zinnemann's **Act of Violence** (1948) are characters more rounded than was usual, including the protagonists – a good bad man (Robert Ryan) and a bad good man (Van Heflin), respectively a killer with a justified vengeance and a decent man with a guilty war secret. A gun before the credits and the nebulous title indicate a thriller; as such, it has its moments, especially when Heflin and his wife (Janet Leigh) are cowering in the darkness, listening to Ryan's gimpy foot moving round the house. Both the actors are excellent (Ryan in particular), but the best thing in the movie is Mary Astor. Hollywood had not allowed a whore in a leading role since before the Code, and hers is superbly realised: she has a heart of gold, but she is middle-aged and sad, cheering herself up with lines like 'I got my kicks. I got along.' Robert Surtees's photography includes some notable views of downtown L.A. at night, deserted except for a wind-tossed newspaper – which was not yet a cliché.

The Men (1950), like *The Search*, is a

701

The Films of Fred Zinnemann

As a contract director at M-G-M Fred Zinnemann
began to make interesting pictures as soon as he was
permitted and his first films as an independent were
notably courageous. *The Men*, RIGHT, was a study of
war-wounded paraplegics, notable for its sobriety
and the performances of Everett Sloane, right, and
Marlon Brando, the latter reminding us how he
revitalised American acting – though it must be said
that none of his rawness and vibrancy rubbed off on
Teresa Wright. Those who were moved were not
many, and Zinnemann had to wait till *High Noon*
FAR RIGHT for his first big popular success – and that
too has dated little, as its frequent revivals testify. In
the centre of the picture are Grace Kelly and Gary
Cooper, and no one who has seen the film will need
to be told at what point this scene occurs. However,
The Member of the Wedding, BELOW, with Julie Harris,
Ethel Waters and Brandon de Wilde, is Zinnemann's
favourite among his own films.

study in rehabilitation, in this case G.I.s handicapped by paralysis. It concentrates on one ex-officer (Marlon Brando) whose bitterness has to be eradicated before he will agree to marry his fiancée (Teresa Wright). It was partially filmed at the Birmingham Veterans Hospital near Los Angeles, where preliminary studies had been done, and Zinnemann insisted on his cast being thoroughly rehearsed in the subject. It is clear that the film means to be more honest than most hospital films – as the doctor (Everett Sloane) lectures to the patients' wives on the malfunctioning of bladder and bowels; he turns out to be unlike other movie doctors, being salty-tongued, gritty in his humour and capable of being testy. The hospital scenes are hard and edgy, for example, using little dialogue to indicate the way in which the sullen hero responds to his fellows. Unable to compete in sexual frankness with the much later *Coming Home* (q.v.) this film nevertheless moved its audiences more – but the wedding night sequence (picked out for special praise by Richard Winnington in *Sight and Sound*) is now crude in forcing emotion, partly due to the writing and partly to the equally conventional playing of Teresa Wright. The brilliance of Marlon Brando (b. 1924) only serves to emphasise her inadequacy. This was his first film after his Broadway success, and to see it now is to be reminded how he changed the course of American acting, with his shifts of moods and darting energy. The film falters in other ways, as in its opening plea for pacifism, but it is always free from the weaknesses of *The Search*. Both were foremost among the films which gave Hollywood renewed respect in itself; and since Stanley Kramer, the producer, and Carl Foreman, the writer, though often serious minded, did little of worth outside their work with Zinnemann, we may suppose the achievement to be mainly his.

Despite the protestations a few years earlier, Zinnemann seemed now the only Hollywood director concerned with contemporary problems, and with **Teresa** (1951) he attempted to study the adjustments needed to be made by the G.I.s' foreign wives. Returning to M-G-M and producer Arthur M. Loew Jr, he persuaded them to allow him foreign locations, still a rarity, and a cast of unknowns.

Louis B. Mayer had been ousted in favour of Dore Schary precisely because Schary had been associated with contemporary subjects; but *Teresa* is only too typical of the customary approach to such matters, and too much action is piled into it because many of those involved had no confidence in a simple subject. Alfred Hayes, with firsthand experience of the army in Italy, wrote the story with Stewart Stern, but the latter's screenplay enmeshes its mixed-up hero (John Erickson) in swathes of war guilt and family guilt which were not exactly typical of those G.I.s and their brides who did have difficulty in readjusting and settling down. Zinnemann, unlike most of his confrères at the time, believed that the way to involve audiences was to suggest that it was filmed as it happened, but Stern's screenplay seems to have unnerved him. Zinnemann makes *Teresa* 'better' than most American films of the time, but only by emulating de Sica or Emmer – two of the players here were in *Domenica d'Agosto* (q.v.) and the bride, Pier Angeli, was discovered in a film made by Leonide Moguy.

Zinnemann returned to form with **High Noon** (1952). The conjunction of the theme music and the railroad stretching into the distance is an indelible cinema experience; you know that something will happen when the train arrives at high noon. Gary Cooper is the friendless sheriff who waits to confront the killers out of his sense of duty, and the Code of the West was never expressed with less pretension. In Zinnemann's own words, it is about 'a man's crisis of conscience'. Foreman wrote the screenplay, and because he was blacklisted thereafter, political references have been read into it; there was certainly dissension between him and Zinnemann on incidentals, and Zinnemann himself thinks the prime contributions are those of Floyd Crosby, who photographed and Dimitri Tiomkin, who composed the score. It was not until Tiomkin had persuaded Frankie Laine to record the song that U.A. lost their reservations about the film. It was an instant classic: 'quite on a par with *Stagecoach*' said John McCarten in *The New Yorker* – and it has not dated nearly as much.

The Member of the Wedding (1952) confirms Zinnemann as a man of taste and meticulous craftsmanship, but the fact that it is his own favourite amongst his films tells against him as a film-maker, for it is in the Broadway-American literary tradition of tales about people to whom life has not been particularly kind – and Carson McCullers's fragile novel had been successful in a stage version. As on Broadway, Julie Harris's performance deserves superlatives, but the theatre still clings to it; the backcloth of this child's backyard looks like a backcloth with imported Spanish moss. The best sequence was not in the play – when she is picked up by a drunken boy G.I.: suddenly the book's central subject, adolescence, is presented without coyness, and Zinnemann's feeling for the terror and romance of night-time America comes across with force. Harris's precocious, wayward and loquacious tomboy is accompanied by the black servant (Ethel Waters) and the solemn younger boy (Brandon de Wilde): together on screen, they move the film towards magic – but it is the magic of the theatre, even when transcended by Waters singing 'His Eye Is on the Sparrow' before what must be the Second Act curtain.

Zinnemann had persuaded Kramer to buy the play – to the disgust of Columbia, whose contract with Kramer allowed them no control over his material. The film's complete failure was one of the reasons why Kramer returned to United Artists. Zinnemann remained at Columbia to direct **From Here to Eternity** (1953), grateful for the chance to 'go commercial', as he put it. James E. Jones's novel had Tolstoyan ambitions; he did not write well and he wrote too much, but the cumulative effect was of something torn from life – a bitter tale of the peacetime army, the ox-like regular servicemen, their limitations and the degradations inflicted upon them. Since the situations and language were then considered 'raw', the industry had hesitated; Daniel Taradash finally came up with a workable screenplay, but it is a glossy summary of some aspects of the book, over-explaining, and without understanding. The affair between the officer's wife (Deborah Kerr) and the sergeant (Burt Lancaster) has become real love, despite the still-famous clinch amidst the foam; and Lancaster is given the impossible task of both loathing his officers to the point of self-destruction and making glowing tributes to Service life. Lorene (Donna Reed) is no longer a whore, but is

allowed Madam's sitting room and sofa for the long *conversations* she has with men. The stars remain stars, and in that respect are almost all inferior to the players in the 1979 T.V. adaptation; an exception is Montgomery Clift as the rebel, his thought processes getting in the way of a man who worked on instinct, but undoubtedly strong. All the artists billed above the title were nominated for Oscars, and the film collected a bevy of awards; it was popular everywhere, but not much admired critically outside the U.S. Nevertheless, it helped to break down taboos in the American cinema, and Zinnemann managed some aspects of Service life beautifully: the aimless wandering around the barrack room, the high spirits as the men prepare for a night out – a motley group, with small aims and vices, an aptitude rather than a taste for drunkenness and an apathetic attitude towards each other.

Like Capra, Stevens and Wyler, John Huston's war service included a number of government-sponsored documentaries, sufficiently touted for him to return to Hollywood with reputation enhanced. **Let There Be Light** (1946) remains an impressive study of the rehabilitation of soldiers mentally scarred in battle. His first postwar work was writing for other directors. He returned to directing with **The Treasure of Sierra Madre** (1948). Most of it was shot on location in Mexico, with Humphrey Bogart urging Huston on to film as he liked; Warners viewed the result with distaste, and released it with indifference – to be surprised at its pattern of praise and awards: Best Motion Picture and Direction from the New York critics; Best Screenplay and Direction from Academy members. The film was liked for being unconventional, by implication because the leading players were unshaven and unheroic; and because greed and other chicaneries plague the progress of these treasure hunters it was thought to have some significance. It is dated today by Max Steiner's thundering score, dissipating the tension built up by the direction; the studio sets, though few, do not help, and Huston's screenplay – from the novel by B. Traven – needs humour. For virtually the only time in his career Bogart lacks conviction; as the seedy, suspicious and small-minded Fred C. Dobbs he has to disintegrate – literally – before our eyes, and he seems to have been unnerved by the prospect. In any event he would have been outclassed by Walter Huston, as the wily old prospector who talks in gusts, in his own shorthand – a character realised as we are seldom privileged to see on the screen.

Key Largo (1948) was Maxwell Anderson's rejigging of the *The Petrified Forest*, and James Agee thought the Huston–Richard Brooks screenplay an improvement on the Broadway version; but he added, 'Some of the points Huston wanted to make were cut out of the picture after he had finished it, and I rather doubt anyhow whether gangsters can be made to represent all that he meant them to – practically everything that is wrong with postwar America.' The film seems to me, rather, to pose the gangster as an anachronism in the postwar period – Johnny Rocco (Edward G. Robinson), boasting of the time he bought and sold state officials, is a stale survivor: at the end, when he is dead, Lauren Bacall opens the shutters to (aaagh!) let the light in. Opposing the gangster is a disillusioned war veteran (Bogart, repeating his role in *Dead Reckoning* q.v.). Huston's flair for depicting eccentricity of character is exemplified here by the gang: the bullying and deceptively friendly Curly (Thomas Gomez); Toots (Harry Lewis), baby-faced and capable of a torture that hints of castration; Angel (Dan Seymour), moon-faced and observant; and the moll (Claire Trevor), doing a rotten job on 'Moanin' Low' for the price of a drink – probably the first lady lush in Hollywood history actually to be well dressed and made up.

Huston's first film as an independent – he had formed a company with producer Sam Spiegel – was a failure. **We Were Strangers** (1949) is a story of revolutionary activities in Cuba, and in this way an unlikely couple (John Garfield, Jennifer Jones) are brought together. Trying to say too much, the film says little, and in the matter of illegal motives Huston is much happier with the petty criminals of **The Asphalt Jungle** (1950). He wrote the script with Ben Maddows, from a novel by W. R. Burnett, and directs with a strong feeling for time and place – a small mid-Western town, where a German doctor (Sam Jaffe), a drifter (Sterling Hayden) and a shady lawyer (Louis Calhern) combine for a heist. We had not seen mascara

running in movies before, which happens here with the pathetic tramp (Jean Hagen), nor for years a relationship like that of the lawyer and his baby-faced girl (Marilyn Monroe, q.v.), given the difference in their ages and her pouting note of sexual anticipation. For that matter, the dénouement – the crooks falling out and apart – was a revelation, and if that has dated, like the cop's earnest comment on his role in society – this remains one of the best of all crime films.

It was made for M-G-M, after Huston had begged release from *Quo Vadis?* (q.v.), which had originally interested him as an allegory on modern dictators. He remained at Metro for **The Red Badge of Courage** (1951), which provided an experience as disastrous as his involvement with *Quo Vadis?*. Louis B. Mayer loathed the project from the start, but Huston and Dore Schary (q.v.) had the backing of Nicholas Schenck in New York. Mayer seemed to have been proved right when the preview audience catcalled, and in panic the film was reduced to a mere 69 minutes, with an explanatory commentary, and touted as a version of an American 'classic'. What remains surely catches the feel of Stephen Crane's strange evocation of the near past and one frightened young man's experience of war; nor does Huston betray Matthew Brady, whose photographic record of the War he emulates without pretension. The cuts do not show, but with a longer running time – and hence more cumulative force – the film might have become the masterpiece it has sometimes been said to be. The press perhaps reacted to the accounts of the production as published in *The New Yorker* (and later in book form, as 'Picture') by Lillian Ross, who had decided that it might be an interesting one to follow. None of the principals involved emerged with much credit, but Gottfried Reinhardt, the producer, correctly assessed the film's failure: 'We do not have a great picture. There is no story because we do not show what the youth is thinking. It is not in the script. John said he would put it on the screen. It is not on the screen.

Huston missed the later quarrels, having gone to Africa to shoot **The African Queen** (1951) for his own company: location work was both difficult and uncomfortable (because of heat and insects). A further drawback was that the only box-office factor was the presence of Bogart, which represented for Huston the sort of risk he liked to take. C. S. Forester's novel had been bandied about for some time – once as a starring vehicle for Bette Davis and John Mills – so it is worth remembering how well the film endures.★ It is classic adventure stuff – a crazy trip down an African river because the spinster (Katharine Hepburn) is determined to do something for the British war effort, to its wild, illogical ending. The book concludes more reasonably, but Huston could not kill off his stars. Neither the novel nor, according to him, the screenplay (by himself and James Agee) originally had much humour, and that only arose after he had suggested that Hepburn model her role on Eleanor Roosevelt. An additional factor was that Hepburn and Bogart realised that they enjoyed working together.

A love affair between a stubborn spinster and a feckless, drink-sodden Cockney (Canadian in the film) had been originally done by Maugham (in 'Vessel of Wrath'), but here it is accompanied by their growing also – in daring, in understanding – into heroes; their love is bound up in their acceptance that they are unlikely to come out alive. His grudging 'Yes, miss' becomes 'Of course, Rosie', but he catches her determination just as she learns from him dependence and humility in the face of privation. Whether sitting on the porch with dry tears for the death of her brother (Robert Morley) or pouring away her partner's gin, she has us mainly on her side; when she says, 'Dear, what is your first name?' no one in films could match her look of apprehension, but he has several different looks of apprehension. There is no other screen romance as rich as this.

Moulin Rouge (1952) was further proof of Huston's eclectic taste. Its justification could well have been that no one had yet made a film of an artist's life that was not risible. However, the basis for the screenplay – by himself and Anthony Veiller – was a novel by Pierre LaMure of incredible banality, and the worst of it has not been entirely banished: 'I have a friend, maman, he is a painter. His name is Vincent

Van Gogh,' says Lautrec (José Ferrer). The film does ask compassion for Lautrec as artist and cripple: he was not, in fact, an outcast from the society into which he was born, but the concept of him as an embittered and misanthropic dwarf is valid enough. His relationship with one woman is borrowed from 'Of Human Bondage', and another, with an older woman, is platonic: thus he is driven into brothels to satisfy his needs, and thus the great movie public is supposed to forgive him. The famous opening of the film, in the Moulin Rouge, does suggest very strongly that in this milieu this man finds both inspiration and companionship and the piece overall is most successful in its visual representation of the belle époque, as photographed by Oswald Morris. Ferrer's technical achievement (walking on his knees) results in a bloodless performance, but he is his usual self in doubling as Lautrec's father.

Again changing direction, Huston offered **Beat the Devil** (1954), written with Truman Capote from a novel by Claude Cockburn, a quirky black comedy of a type that became popular later. Its detractors (Bogart, the star, was one) hoped for a thriller, and complained with more justice that the plot was not clear: what matters is both the upending of the usual rules in stories of mayhem and the eccentricity of the characters – a British couple (Jennifer Jones, Edward Underdown), seemingly veddy County, though

John Huston's predelections led him to more full-blooded and gritty adventure stories than were common in Hollywood at the time. Perhaps the most admired – and most loved – of all his adventure films is *The African Queen*, with Robert Morley, Humphrey Bogart and Katharine Hepburn.

★In 1967 readers of the *Los Angeles Times* voted it their favourite film, and four years later those of the (London) *Sunday Times* considered it the one they most wanted to see again.

707

she is a congenital liar; an American adventurer (Bogart) and his Italian wife (Gina Lollobrigida), obsessed with all things British; and his associates – fat, cowardly, *toujours la politesse* (Robert Morley), foppish (Peter Lorre), and the minute, bowler-hatted ex-Indian major (Ivor Barnard), ever ready with a knife. The film's wry humour is entirely typical of Huston – though we had seen it only infrequently at this point. This was his third film in Europe; and only when interior shooting is necessary has he since returned to the American studios (except for *Annie*, q.v.).

Elia Kazan (b.1909) came to the fore during this period. A graduate of the Group Theatre, his reputation was such that 20th Century-Fox negotiated a contract that stipulated only an occasional film. The first was **A Tree Grows in Brooklyn** (1945), from Betty Smith's best-selling novel about a Brooklyn family in the earlier years of the century. Hard up working-class people seldom found their way to the screen: the novel had conveyed the sense that they were only one remove from fact, and that was a quality kept by Kazan and his writers, Tess Slessinger and Frank Davis. That the film is moving, when the feckless father (James Dunn) dies of alcoholism, is due chiefly to the performance of Peggy Ann Garner as the daughter. In Kazan's own words, 'she was not pretty at all, or cute or picturesque, only true'; he said, rightly, that Dorothy McGuire was miscast as the working-class Catholic Irish mother, but it is a pleasing performance within the conventions of the time, and there are some excellent supporting performances, especially Lloyd Nolan as the local cop and James Gleason as proprietor of the bar the father frequented.

Kazan's handling of material which could have been rendered sentimental is admirable, but he did not distinguish himself when he took on **The Sea of Grass** (1947) for the chance of working with Spencer Tracy and Katharine Hepburn (the back-projection work, on the wheatfields which give the film its title, had already been done by the time he arrived on the project). They and he seem depressed by this nineteenth-century saga about a land baron and a wife so bored that she slips into sin with his mortal enemy (Melvyn Douglas); the son from this liaison grows up to be so dissolute that his antics bring her back to the neighbourhood and, for an unconvincing finish, into her husband's arms. Kazan loathed the material (and Metro), and immediately took on **Boomerang** (1947), one of 20th Century-Fox's factual series which had begun with *The House on 92nd Street* (q.v.), using real locations in Stamford, Connecticut. In Richard Murphy's screenplay the accused man (Arthur Kennedy) is innocent, despite the number of eye witnesses who declare him guilty; but the D.A. (Dana Andrews) is on his side. Kazan has said, 'I think it's a good film. I thought everything *worked*. It was a piece of mechanism, a fairly effective piece of story-telling mechanism.' Not everything works now – nor did it work then, for the accused man is a war veteran, and it would be some time before a veteran could be shown as anything but perfect. The real culprit is laughably obvious, but against that, Kazan has given fresh thought to the methods of the police and the reporter (Sam Levene). The film's reception by the press secured Kazan's reputation, which leapt further when his next film won Oscars for Best Film and Best Direction.

The Academy Awards of the postwar years seemed to Hollywood to confirm its new social conscience. There remains merit in *The Lost Weekend*, and at least it is possible to see why contemporaries admired *The Best Years of Our Lives*; but **Gentleman's Agreement** (1947) is based on a false premise, and audiences today find it, at best, quaint. It is difficult to accept Gregory Peck's Galahad of a reporter – so high-principled, so dedicated, so charming – and even harder to believe that he could have reached his age without any awareness of anti-Semitism, especially as his oldest friend (John Garfield) is a Jew. He seethes with indignation and starts research for an article to be called 'I Passed for a Jew for Six Months'. The original novel was by Laura Z. Hobson, and Zanuck – the only Gentile among the heads of the major studios – was much praised for acquiring it. The screenwriter, Moss Hart, was a Jew, and also too intelligent (on other evidence) to have penned these platitudes without intending to satirise Hollywood's crusading heroes. He does have a moment or so of honesty: Dorothy McGuire trying to persuade Peck to drop the pretence for his first visit to her sister; June Havoc hiding her Jewishness under a Gentile name; Sam Jaffe as a professor much amused by his Jewishness; and Garfield deciding to move his family to Connecticut because someone has to break down the barriers. (The outstanding performance is that of Celeste Holm, as a breezy and understanding fashion editor.) In fact, the barriers had been down for years: anti-Semitism, rife enough in the States by the Twenties, began to fade as news filtered through of Hitler's Germany and was dealt a severe blow when wartime conscription revealed the extent of prejudice and discrimination against blacks. Hollywood was, as ever, years behind, but Zanuck caught up somewhat with his own film on that particular racial problem, **Pinky** (1949), about a black girl so light-skinned that she could pass for white: again Zanuck compromised, by casting a white actress, Jeanne Crain – or so said Kazan, who does not regard this as one of his own films, since he took it on when John Ford fell ill after a few days' shooting. The writers, Philip Dunne and Dudley Nichols, working from a novel by Cid Ricketts Summers, offer their heroine an identity crisis but refuse to deal with racial prejudice; the film's only superiority over the other racial dramas of the time – *Lost Boundaries, Home of the Brave* – is in its half-decent depiction of the Southern black's miserable lot.

Kazan found his style with **Panic in the Streets** (1950) – or was helped to it by Joseph Macdonald, the photographer. Macdonald and Norbert Brodine between them had photographed almost all 20th Century-Fox's 'factual' movies, and Kazan used their skill dynamically, adding to the city's chiaroscuro harsh natural sound and furious editing, suggesting a corner of life as experienced by someone with raw and jagged nerves. It was a style entirely suited to the subject – the search for a murderer with bubonic plague. It is a chase story, pure and simple, well written by Richard Murphy and well acted by Paul Douglas as the police officer in charge of the case, Richard Widmark as the city medical officer, and Barbara Bel Geddes as his wife.

Kazan had directed **A Streetcar Named Desire** (1951) for Broadway: 'The Pulitzer Prize-Winning Play and recipient of the New York critics award' say

the credits, by way of preparing audiences for what was then unusual cinema fare. Both film and play for once deserved that favourite adjective of publicists, 'sensational': Blanche duBois (Vivien Leigh), a seemingly well-born teacher, is revealed as frequenting the infamous Flamingo Hotel not merely for money, and her brother-in-law Stanley (Marlon Brando), having discovered this, ravishes her the night his wife Stella (Kim Hunter) gives birth to their baby. It no longer shocks, now that rape and nymphomania have become commonplace on the screen: as they were, of course, though in more decorous fashion, before the Hays Office clamped down. In this instance the M.P.A.A. bowed to the play's reputation, resisting only Blanche's brief reference to her husband's homosexuality and insisting that Stanley be punished for his uncontrollable lust. As it happened, screen audiences were not immensely taken with *Streetcar*, perhaps because of Tennessee Williams's baroque, poetic approach; but the matters with which it deals could then only be found in textbooks on psychology. Its greatest truths are in the relationship between Stella and Stanley. The warm, practical Stella and the ape-like, self-possessed Stanley *enjoy* each other – the way the other looks and talks – and when they kiss, you can sense the sexual pleasure; it is in direct contrast to Blanche's sleazy past and Stanley's donning of his best pyjamas when he has decided to take her.

Brando and Miss Hunter are wonderful, and their performances move into a region which takes no account of concepts of 'theatre' or 'cinema'; from the Broadway production, Karl Malden – as the hoped-for suitor – is almost as good, but most of his scenes are with Blanche, and she is a very theatrical lady.

At the last minute Kazan decided to film the play as written, jettisoning a free adaptation, a wise decision, since both Stanley and Blanche are larger than life; though the cinema can absorb without difficulty his half-articulate slobbishness. Blanche is a coquette of airs and graces, her speech remembered from cheap novels and primers on etiquette: she represents something of the author's fascination with Southern belles and sex for sale, but she is also a very real character – and one going mad. To have put both her and the gradual

Early in his career as a director Elia Kazan made a handful of films which remain as powerful as contemporary opinion maintained. Among them are *A Streetcar Named Desire*, RIGHT, with Marlon Brando, Vivien Leigh and Kim Hunter all repeating their stage performances, and *Viva Zapata!*, BELOW, with Brando. Kazan understood exactly how to harness Brando's personal magnetism to the brutish Stanley of *Streetcar* and the rebel leader in *Zapata* – and this leader was certainly unlike heroes played by Cooper, Gable or Tracy.

insanity into acceptable screen terms would surely have destroyed the qualities of the original; instead, her artificiality is emphasised by dressing her in fussy nets and tulles, so at odds with the clothes of Stella. Miss Leigh is the only Blanche I can ever imagine or ever want to see. Kazan says that she was so imbued with her theatrical interpretation (as directed by Olivier for the London production) that he had difficulty in getting her to act for the camera – unsuccessfully, one imagines, since she is constantly in the middle of a speech, or even a word, when the camera angle shifts slightly via a cut, suggesting that the performance was assembled in the cutting room. The film is nevertheless a masterwork in some indefinable middle ground which is neither quite stage nor screen. Kazan uses huge close-ups, he uses a jazz soundtrack (by Alex North, the first time jazz had been so used in a dramatic film), he shows cluttered interiors and peeling exteriors; out of mist appears the woman selling flowers for the dead, and when Blanche tells Mitch of her past, mist shrouds the light across the bay. The style is the right one, and Williams has paid tribute to Kazan's creative contribution to his work. There is no more *filmic* record of an American play than this one.

Another admired writer provided the screenplay and, alas, the 'poetic' dialogue of **Viva Zapata!** (1952). The project grew from a conversation between Kazan and John Steinbeck. (Since Zanuck had achieved much prestige with *The Grapes of Wrath*, this, too, became one of his 'personal' productions.) Their view of the brigand who became President of Mexico was romantic, and though not solving the enigma he represents in the history of his country, this film appeared to aim for greater veracity than most Hollywood biographies. While it was true that few people outside Mexico could question the accuracy, it could be claimed that Zapata had to be made into an acceptable revolutionary hero.

His indiscriminate killings and pillaging, and his twenty-six bigamous marriages are omitted; but the most serious simplification is the suggestion that he relinquished the presidency after a few months, to return to country life (in fact, he ruled jointly with Villa for eight years, and his reasons for leaving were far more complex). However, the film was courageous by Hollywood standards and extraordinarily exciting to all who saw it; some sticky symbolism is one reason it revives less well, but with virtually no competition it remains the best cinema study of revolt between *October* and *La Battaglia di Algeri* (q.v.). Taking liberties, chances, and sometimes leave of its senses, it offers the contrast between an illiterate and inert peasantry and a vicious militia – and between the dead lives of the former and the battles and intrigues of the latter; Kazan moves incisively, claiming that he learnt from *Paisà* 'to jump from crag to crag, rather than going all along the valleys'.

For once, the tensions of a revolutionary's life are understood, and Brando plays him as the inarticulate underdog, as in his earlier films, and the man of destiny which he would often play later; he has both personal magnetism and a sullen expression, disguising his surprise at being caught up in these events. The film was designed to expose the ineffectiveness of idealistic revolutionaries. Kazan has explained, 'I believe that democracy progresses through internecine war, through constant tension – we grow only through conflict. And that's what democracy is. In that sense, people have to be vigilant, and the vigilance is effective. I truly believe that all power corrupts . . .' Such is probably the thinking behind every 'political' film made in Hollywood.

The comment (though made years later), and the film itself, were meant to justify Kazan's co-operation with the House Un-American Activities Committee, investigating Communist affiliations with the film industry.

To emphasise his fitness to be part of a de-Communised film industry, Kazan accepted a political subject from Zanuck, **Man on a Tightrope** (1953), the story of a circus in conflict with the State, specifically Czechoslovakia. The commissars complain that the clowning of Cernik (Fredric March) lacks commitment; and although the point is hammered home that under Communism no artist is allowed freedom, the film was regarded merely as an indifferent chase thriller by contemporary critics – who commented adversely, if at all, on the dialogue by Robert E. Sherwood (working from a novel by Neil Paterson). To this high-flown script Kazan brought 'European' direction – Ufa lighting and groupings from *Varieté*, which had had a not dissimilar story: despite or because of that he attains a singular conviction in his deployment of the circus itself and the (German) locations. For anyone with a taste for irony there is the arch right-winger, Adolphe Menjou, at his best as a left-wing commissar, moustache drooping seedily and his front speckled with cigarette ash.

Kazan's films (though *Streetcar* was made for Warners) contributed much to the reputation of 20th Century-Fox as the boldest of the studios. So, increasingly, did those made by Joseph L. Mankiewicz, whose stint as a writer for Paramount had been followed by what he called 'the black years', producing for M-G-M.★ Only cynicism can explain his Joan Crawford

★He left after a row with Louis B. Mayer over his relationship with Judy Garland. His contract, which had some time to run, was assigned to Fox, then being run (Zanuck was in the army) by Joseph Schenck, who was so pleased to get Mankiewicz that in a unique deal for the time he was allowed to produce, direct and write, or any one or two of the three.

vehicles, and though he also made such films as *Three Comrades* and *Woman of the Year* few could have forecast his achievements at Fox. His contract guaranteed him the opportunity to direct and, sidetracked into producing and writing *The Keys of the Kingdom*, he had worried over Stahl's handling of it. Although he disliked the derivative novel (by Anya Seton) on which **Dragonwyck** (1946) was based, he agreed to direct and script it as he would be working under the supervision of Lubitsch, his friend and mentor at Paramount. (The novel had been purchased for Lubitsch as a change from comedy, but after the heart attack which had caused him to relinquish the direction of *A Royal Scandal* he had decided to accept the less strenuous job of producing only.) Mankiewicz stresses the American-Dutch elements of the setting in order to play down the pseudo-Gothic plot, but as soon as we see the mansion illuminated by lightning we know the new governess (Gene Tierney) will take up the candelabrum for a midnight prowl; as soon as the nice young doctor (Glenn Langan) opposes the mysterious master of the house (Vincent Price) we know which one will be holding her in his arms at the end. At least Mankiewicz gets Tierney and Price to resemble real people.

As far as Mankiewicz was concerned, he was acquiring an unobtrusive directorial style. **Somewhere in the Night** (1946) is a melodrama about an amnesiac army veteran (John Hodiak) – and by a process known only to Hollywood, amnesia can turn a nasty guy into a nice one.★ He sets out to find his identity in the familiar world of *film noir*: a dusty rooming house where a hooker lurks in the hall; a Turkish bath with a surly attendant; a fortress-like mental home. There is also the girl, played by Nancy Guild with the looks, voice and talent of a combined Tierney and Veronica Lake, proving again that no star ever made it who was a copy of just another one – or two. She has to say 'Things don't happen like this,' which does not excuse Mankiewicz or his fellow screenwriter, Howard Dimsdale.

The next three films were written by Philip Dunne, whose screenplays for them are verbose but – at least as far as the first two are concerned – intelligent: in both

★The idea, however, had been used earlier by Jean Anouilh in 'Le Voyageur sans Bagage'.

respects they reflect Mankiewicz's later, more personal work. **The Late George Apley** (1947), adapted from the play by John P. Marquand and George S. Kaufman (from the former's novel) is an aimless comedy about a Boston blue-blood (Ronald Colman) who in middle age has to learn that there are values other than his own. **The Ghost and Mrs Muir** (1947), adapted from a whimsical novel by R. A. Dick, concerns a widow (Miss Tierney) who falls in love with a deceased sea captain (Rex Harrison). Neither is promising material, but by treating them as witty observations on social behaviour and putting justified confidence in the charms of his leading men Mankiewicz makes elegant entertainments of both. Rex Harrison, as it happens, persuaded Zanuck to sanction **Escape** (1948) for him, as he had admired the 1930 film version of Galsworthy's play with Sir Gerald du Maurier: shooting on location on Dartmoor gave the company an opportunity to use funds 'frozen' by the British government and to use two British contract-players (the other was Peggy Cummins) whom American cinemagoers were not exactly taking to their hearts. The plot hoarily supposes that an escaped convict (Harrison) can easily find a car to steal, a hut to hide in, a spirited girl (Cummins) to help him, and so on: it is accompanied by dialogue in which are embedded some nuggets of wisdom, equally dated, and though Mankiewicz handles all matters in a smooth style there is nothing to suggest that his next film would be so very good.

A Letter to Three Wives (1948) established Mankiewicz as a brilliant director and screenwriter – it won him Oscars in both capacities – and as a social comedy it has dated hardly a jot. As a director he relies much on good faces and good furniture, and as a writer he has an aptitude for lines both funny in themselves and able to illuminate the quirks and whims of character. His subject is marriage: three ladies ponder on theirs, as the voice on the soundtrack (Celeste Holm, uncredited) informs them that she has run off with the husband of one of them. Mankiewicz is not particularly interested in the country-club couple (Jeanne Crain, Jeffrey Lynn) and their wartime marriage, but he dotes on the others – whose stories to an extent intertwine. They are a soap-opera writer

(Ann Sothern), her poetry-pop-quoting husband (Kirk Douglas), and the girl (Linda Darnell) from the wrong side of the tracks who is using every wile to get her boss (Paul Douglas) to the altar. A dinner party involving the four of them, plus a slovenly maid (Thelma Ritter) and a monstrous sponsor (Florence Bates), is as funny as the similar sequence in *Alice Adams*.

The film's producer, Sol C. Siegel, interested Mankiewicz in **House of Strangers** (1949), adapted by Philip Yordan from a chapter of a novel by Jerome Weidman: Mankiewicz rewrote the script but declined to share the credit with Yordan and was consequently denied any by the Screen Writers Guild. The story, derived from the biblical tale of Joseph and his brethren, concerns an Italian barber (Edward G. Robinson) who becomes a bank tycoon by managing the affairs of other immigrants, all the while singing the praises of spaghetti and opera, and finally allowing his favourite son (Richard Conte) to take the rap for embezzlement. The piece itself is not unoperatic, but there is a feeling that it should have been about a Jewish family* rather than an Italian one and indeed Jewish talents were involved. The film was a box-office failure, but Mankiewicz's twin Oscars were a contributory factor in Zanuck assuming the producer credit on Mankiewicz's next three films. This was an usurpation of command, but Zanuck did institute **No Way Out** (1950), which he considered, rightly, a more creditable addition to the brief cycle of racial dramas than *Pinky*. For Mankiewicz it was a belated return to the mood of *Fury* (which he had produced), and similarly a good crime story is buttressed with indignation at social injustice. But if Mankiewicz and his co-writer, Lesser Samuels, start with some impeccable and understated points about the behaviour of blacks in the face of racial prejudice their young doctor (Sidney Poitier) is, in the end, too noble, too impervious to danger. 'Maybe someday some autopsy can analyse that mind,' says the head doctor (Stephen McNally) of the thug (Richard Widmark) determined to kill Poitier. Sidney Poitier (b.1924) would become the first black movie star since Paul Robeson,

*Weidman's novel had originally concerned a Lower East Side Jewish family but he had changed it before publication to an Italian one after criticisms of his treatment of the Jewish community in 'I Can Get It for You Wholesale'.

and though not required to play 'Sambo' roles he would, for most of his career, play a number of fellows so noble that they have little dimension.

Meanwhile, Mankiewicz wrote and directed **All About Eve** (1950), which was popular at the time – at least with the carriage trade – and now causes most people to stay home whenever it is on television. Its durability confounds those who thought it too talky and too static. The exposition is swift, the dialogue smart, the characters appealing – theatre-obsessed, egotistical, virtually incestuous in their loves and hates. Mankiewicz set out to examine – with no conclusions drawn – the psychology of a successful actress; he ended with a symposium on the theatre as witty as it is deflationary, encapsulating all one might care to know on the subject. His comments are put into the mouths of people with the rare virtue of having a life independent of what they are doing on the screen – with the exception of the critic, Addison de Witt (George Sanders), whose function is not unlike that of the Greek chorus, and his 'protégée', Miss Caswell (Marilyn Monroe), 'a graduate of the Copacabana School of Dramatic Art'. However, the film's ace is in its portrait of the actress concerned: actresses have always revelled in playing actresses and for more than two generations Bette Davis's rendering of this one, Margo Channing, has been definitive.

The events recounted in Mary Orr's original story happened to Elisabeth Bergner. The star originally contracted was Claudette Colbert, who broke her back, and it was then offered to Gertrude Lawrence, whose agent wanted her to sing a song in the party sequence – a suggestion Mankiewicz declined. Davis, by a quirk of fate (she had broken a blood vessel in her throat and was forced to speak in a lower register) discovered that everyone thought she had based her portrait on Tallulah Bankhead; she has said that Margo is not like herself, but there must be something personal to explain the sense of heartbreak, which is as sure as any put on film. Margo's suspicions, her need for comfort and reassurance, her realistic attitude towards her job, all lead to a number of clashes with her entourage. That is one situation; the other tells how Eve (Anne Baxter) schemes to take over her friends, her man

Joseph L. Mankiewicz had been writer, then producer and finally director before handling all three functions on some films fondly remembered – and in the case of *All About Eve*, still much admired. Its subject is the theatre, and for a while its clever remarks are those one might expect from a bright Hollywood boy who had been an occasional observer of the Broadway scene. That it becomes something more is due partly to the portrait of an ageing actress by Bette Davis, seen here with Gary Merrill.

(Gary Merrill) and certainly her next role. Margo is as wary of her as of everybody, and though there have been aspiring actresses as vulpine and unscrupulous as Eve, I find it hard to believe that even sentimental theatre folk would be taken in by her as played by Miss Baxter. The years have done nothing to diminish Davis, Celeste Holm and Thelma Ritter (as best friend and dresser respectively), but Baxter now seems just another plastic puss, unable to convey shades of meaning: only the drive of Davis even off-screen prevents Baxter's scenes from falling apart – yet Davis's is, if marginally, the lesser role. Mankiewicz reflects the general belief of the time that audiences were more intrigued by smart little schemers than ageing actresses – which is why it is all about Eve and not all about Margo.

With fistfuls of Oscars and other awards, it was inevitable that his next film would be an anti-climax, and **People Will Talk** (1951) was not popular. The acclaim had been such that he had nothing to con-

sider but his own talent, and he put it at the service of doctors as *Eve* had put it at the service of actresses. His source was an old German play and film, *Dr Med Hiob Praetorius*, by Curt Götz and it was used, as Mankiewicz explained in an interview, to prove that 'psychiatry is as necessary to the doctor as anatomy itself, and that medicine should be more than pills, serums, and knives.' The minimal plot concerns a humanitarian, all-wise doctor (Cary Grant, who never had a better chance to express himself) who marries a pregnant girl (Jeanne Crain) and triumphs over a jealous colleague (Hume Cronyn) who has been sniping at him; but the plot gives Mankiewicz the chance to air such topics as free medication, quackery, the idiocies of habit, the decline of standards and academic backbiting – the last of these being a reference to the current H.U.A.C. witch-hunts. In its form it is an unsatisfactory film. It proved to Hollywood that Mankiewicz could make a serious film with the sort of intelligent dialogue for which he was now noted; he uses Brahms and Wagner to prove that good music is as essential to civilised living as good conversation. As for the heroine's pregnancy, that was a challenge to the childishly restrictive M.P.A.A. Mankiewicz claimed that without that situation the film could not have been made, but the plot would not have suffered had the girl been a widow instead of unmarried. Like all of Hollywood's leading talents, Mankiewicz wanted movies to be more realistic: so Miss Crain, who had not bothered to get married, is not punished but rewarded – with Mr Grant.

Mankiewicz had one film left under the terms of his contract. He had no intention of renewing it, since he disliked Zanuck's helping himself to the producer credit; Zanuck, though he felt it vital to the company's prestige to keep Mankiewicz, disliked his status as 'producer' being so obviously subservient to a now-renowned writer-director. Mankiewicz found a way out of the impasse by suggesting **Five Fingers** (1952), scheduled for Henry Hathaway, as his last assignment – and since the project already had a nominal producer and a writer (Michael Wilson) Mankiewicz would relinquish credit for both activities, though he did virtually rewrite the script. In the event he again proved himself at ease in a milieu – the diplomatic set – which had often defeated film-makers. The diplomats are for once played by the correct nationalities, and the locations are those of the original incident – Ankara in 1944, when the Albanian-born valet of the British ambassador sold secrets to the Germans for what turned out to be counterfeit money (among the documents he photographed were the plans for the Normandy landings, which the Germans ignored). The facts were set down by L. C. Moyzisch, a former German attaché, in 'Operation Cicero', a book published in 1950, and the film starts with the British government's admission of its accuracy. Wilson's addition of an impoverished countess (Danielle Darrieux) was resented by some critics, but her verbal sparring with the valet (James Mason) is of an urbane level – and so superior to Wilson's other efforts as to confirm Mankiewicz's hand. Darrieux plots secretly and pouts deliciously; Mason is superb, both proud of his wit and humble calling, if not much like the shifty and shabby original. That gentleman was alive when the film came out, and never told his own side of it: I doubt whether that would include the final chase from Ankara to Istanbul, which provides a perfect climax.

As with Mankiewicz, the films of George Cukor are civilised, if not sophisticated. He also brought to above-average material the correct furnishings, photographing them (whether faces or props) without pretension and keeping most of the action in medium close-up. He was fastidious over his choice of material, and it was four years after *Winged Victory* that his name appeared on a film – since in the interim he refused a credit for his work on **Desire Me** (1947), which starred Greer Garson as a Breton war widow whose first husband turns up after she has remarried – a situation taken in this case from Pirandello. (Among others who toiled on it was Mervyn LeRoy, but it went out without a director credit, the only major Hollywood production to do so between the Silent era and the present.) Cukor would not have been foolish to have also disclaimed credit on **A Double Life** (1948) and **Edward, My Son** (1949), two superficial studies of paranoia. He admitted that he could not direct melodrama, and he chose in both cases a style that is of the theatre but not

theatrical. The former, in fact, concerns the theatre, and was written by Garson Kanin and his wife, Ruth Gordon. It was one of the postwar bids for independence, produced for Universal by Kanin's brother Michael – and since Kanin had no wish to return to directing, Cukor (who had worked with Miss Gordon on *Two-Faced Woman*) was borrowed from M-G-M. When Kanin calls the film 'terrible', he may be thinking of its central idea – that some actors are so overwhelmed by an emotional part that they allow it to affect their private lives. This one (Ronald Colman) is currently playing Othello,* but no further suggestion is forthcoming for his Jekyll and Hyde behaviour. Colman, as Cukor said, had no sense of the demonic, being merely moody and uncharacteristically wild-eyed; the Oscar he was accorded for this performance may have been due to sentiment, or to the voters' customary admiration for anyone in a double role – or capable of speaking Shakespearian verse. Nor is Spencer Tracy at his best in *Edward, My Son*, though reverting to his old role of the self-made tycoon who destroys all about him: his wife (Deborah Kerr) becomes an embittered alcoholic and his son a wastrel. These tired themes had been rejigged into a British play by Robert Morley and Noel Langley which had a mild success on Broadway, suggesting to Metro an ideal way to use funds blocked in Britain. Donald Ogden Stewart's screenplay retains the gimmick of the original, which never allowed us to meet the Edward so much talked about.

Adam's Rib (1949) was written by Kanin and Gordon for Tracy and Katharine Hepburn, drawing upon characteristics of all four of them – and it is a movie which inspires affection for its leading players, partly because the affection between them is manifestly there. As a team their characters had been established in *Woman of the Year* (which Kanin, uncredited, had initiated): they have a greater number of domestic scenes here, and the same professional rivalry – they are lawyers, he prosecuting and she defending Doris (Judy Holliday), who had shot at her unfaithful husband (Tom Ewell); they are opposed,

---

*Othello's offstage homicidal tendencies had already been examined in a Matheson Lang vehicle, 'Carnival', filmed in 1921 and 1931, and *Men Are not Gods*.

Postwar Hollywood: The Directors in Their Brave New World

The early Fifties were clearly a happy time in Hollywood, with the directors gaining more power and the studio bosses not yet panicking as television began to eat into cinema attendances – or so we may suppose, for George Cukor was yet another director whose work of the time is both confident and relaxed. Though mainly associated with drama, he concentrated on comedy with the aid of some very bright scripts by Garson Kanin and his wife Ruth Gordon. *Adam's Rib* was written for Spencer Tracy and Katharine Hepburn, right, but it contained a large supporting role for Judy Holliday, centre, who had scored a Broadway hit in Kanin's play 'Born Yesterday'.

equally wittily, over what is now called women's lib. Miss Holliday (1922–65) had appeared on Broadway in Kanin's 'Born Yesterday', and there was a conspiracy to throw scenes her way so that Columbia could not avoid putting her in the film version (q.v.) of the play; these scenes – her deposition and appearance on the witness stand – are notable for the unselfishness of the other players and her own skill. The supporting cast includes David Wayne, singing a ballad by Cole Porter.

After directing Hepburn and Holliday, Cukor turned to the vacuous Lana Turner: Isobel Lennart's screenplay for **A Life of Her Own** (1950) was ordinary, he once admitted, but bearing in mind that it was a star vehicle, he thought he could do a useful job. It is quite lively, especially on the practical difficulties and mechanics of a model's life, accepting the sort of facts which good movies (let alone soap operas) were still ignoring – that girls who take up this career are ambitious but not too bright, and that the men who take up the girls are likely to be elderly. The subsidiary characters similarly have more life than we

might expect – the sour-faced pianist acknowledging an offered drink with a nod, the bustling fat concierge turning the men out of the mezzanine of the hostel, the fashion editor with the cigarette holder and exaggerated English accent. What Cukor could not manage was to get a good performance from Turner, but she is not – for once – a dead loss. Preview audiences disliked her suicide at the end, so that was changed; but the same fate was allowed to Ann Dvorak, stunningly good as a girl who knows the score yet is pathetically involved with a playboy.

Judy Holliday did get to repeat her stage role in **Born Yesterday** (1950), and Cukor, borrowed from M-G-M, once again used unobtrusive skill in translating high quality theatrical dialogue – reworked from his own play by Kanin, though for various reasons he let credit go to a lesser writer who had worked on one of the drafts. This story of an education is sometimes sententious, since the education begins with lectures on Tom Paine and Jefferson, and there are even indications that we are meant to see Billie (Miss

716

Holliday) as a free democratic spirit escaping from the tyranny of Brock (Broderick Crawford) the scrap dealer who keeps her. In fact, Billie is one of the great comic creations, moving between the two moods learnt from experience – suspicious and defensive, with a matching armoury of phrases. Her philosophy is summed up thus: 'If he don't act friendly, I don't act friendly. As long as I know how to get what I want, I'm all right.' To watch Holliday begin to learn, understand and warm to her tutor (William Holden), is a wonderful thing; and to that extent the story is a combination of Cinderella, Pygmalion and the worm that turned. Holliday's performance, touchingly vulnerable, childishly triumphant, is to be endlessly studied and savoured, from her surprised 'What d'ya know!' to her crumpled 'I did look it up and I still don't know.' Brock has only two things to say to her – 'So shut up' and 'All right, I'll buy it for you' – and Crawford is bull-like, lacking the vestigial charm Paul Douglas brought to the role on stage. Perhaps it is as well that there seems no sexual attraction between them – though that is an odd omission in a piece about a kept woman. Nor is there any sex when she says to her tutor, 'Are you one of those talkers or would ya like a little action?', which is the creed of a woman who owes her wellbeing to her body.

It is clear that Cukor and/or the Kanins were happier with domestic love: **The Marrying Kind** (1952) was written expressly for Holliday and this, the third of their comedies together, is more serious than the theatrical froufrou of the earlier two. Its roots lie in the American working-class comedies of the early Thirties, and there is in it a quality of hurt which would not be found again in an American comedy till Billy Wilder's films of the early Sixties. Florence (Holliday) and Chet (Aldo Ray), are in the process of divorce, and flashbacks fill us in from their meeting in Central Park to the present: an anniversary that goes wrong, an accidental death, a radio quiz show, hospitalisation, interfering relatives and, in the end, too many rows. We see the past as it was, while each remembers only what most favours themselves: the laughter is wrought from reality. Only the dream sequence grates and it confirms a suspicion that the Kanins worked with their heads and memories of other movies

rather than with their hearts. The breakup of a marriage needs more compassionate handling than it gets here. Cukor supplies the balance, and Holliday and Ray go a long way towards supplying the missing dimension. She is again incomparable, funny and touching in every line and gesture; he, especially in a too-large lounge suit, is never like a movie star, while a gravel voice and a certain reticent eagerness make him equally likeable. Neither player makes us feel that this is a great love match, but this tale of two nice ordinary people who marry and are happy and then unhappy is a big achievement among the movies of the time.

Meanwhile Kanin and Gordon had written **Pat and Mike** (1952) for Tracy and Hepburn. He plays a dubious sports promoter and she an all-round sports-woman who resists his 'advances' till she contemplates life with her dull fiancé. Despite the success of *Adam's Rib*, M-G-M hesitated over the material – not surprisingly, since there is no plot, and thirty of the ninety-three minutes' running time are taken up with a golf game. Cukor himself seemed disinclined to develop the authors' tentative situations and was clearly happier on **The Actress** (1953), written by Miss Gordon from her autobiographical play, 'Years Ago'. It is about the desire of Ruth Gordon Jones (Jean Simmons) to go on the stage – after seeing 'The Pink Lady' with its star, seen by her and by us as a remote

After Judy Holliday made the film of *Born Yesterday*, *The Marrying Kind* was fashioned for her, to prevent her from being typecast as a dumb blonde – though as Aldo Ray's wife she was not exactly supposed to be an intellectual genius.

717

deity, which is the sort of right, elegant touch one expects from Cukor. The setting is a small town before the First World War, and he rescues it from the morass of sentimentality, Technicolor and Jeanne Crainisms that we had met hitherto; family life has not only affection but meanness and smallness. The interiors are cluttered and cramped, the exteriors wintry – and the final effect is similar, despite the charm of Miss Simmons, in her best performance up to that time. She is a sloppy, starry-eyed dream of adolescence, her constant high spirits somewhat mocked; as her sea dog father, Tracy never plays for sympathy, but his softhearted conversion to her ambition makes for longueurs in the second half.

In **It Should Happen to You** (1954) July Holliday's ambition to be 'somebody' inspires her to hire a huge sign in Columbus Circle to spell out her name, 'Gladys Glover'. Kanin's screenplay, from his own story, falters towards the end, and well before that it is clear that he could not decide whether he wanted a satire on mini-celebrities (which is what Gladys becomes) or a Holliday vehicle. It is often witty and charming, and this actress justifies his every word, whether handling an ad agency with varying expressions of wariness, or gazing at her poster in a state of euphoria. She is hurt and bewildered when Jack Lemmon (b.1925), in his first film, yells 'What sort of fruitcake are you?' – and at the same time indignant, 'No sort of'. The sequences between these two players are among the most likeable in the whole canon of American cinema. In the admittedly inferior *Phffft!* (q.v.) they are less effective together, thus emphasising Cukor's usual careful tension between the cinema's ability to charm and entertain and its responsibility to truth.

This balance between entertainment and truth can be found in the work of all these directors, but since it is not necessarily the right balance for serious drama, it is the comedies which wear best; and as Cukor and Mankiewicz made the most accomplished comedies it is ironic that some of their films, with no discernible directorial flourishes, should best represent that age when the American director was for the first time in thirty years being recognised as the prime creative force in film-making.

The modesty of Mankiewicz and Cukor is endearing – *Adam's Rib* even uses a puppet theatre to disarm criticism of its theatricality – but then they were content to stay within their fields of social satire, while other directors had statements to make. The other memorable films of the era – *Letter from an Unknown Woman*, *A Streetcar Named Desire*, *The African Queen*, *The Asphalt Jungle*, *High Noon* – represent different movie conventions; though it must be said at once that Billy Wilder as ever is *hors série* and *The Search* is an almost wholly successful attempt to emulate the European movie. Most of the directors at this time were influenced by, or at least interested in, what was happening in Europe; they, too, wanted to startle with their 'art'. And the most admired films of the time were those that did so – like *A Place in the Sun*, which seemed to reviewers to presage Hollywood's snatching the crown from Europe, that America, after years of stagnation, complacency and Production Code stifling, would once again make the most exciting movies in the world. Contemporaries were wholly right to admire Stevens and Wyler rather than, say, Cukor, since he was conservative and they were trying to expand the boundaries of cinema – though not, as we have seen, towards the contemporary realistic dramas anticipated in the immediate postwar period. That expansion is the keynote to this time: spurred on by the example of Europe, praise from critics and commercial success, the leading directors were challenging the ever reluctant executives to make the sort of films which they wanted to make – and there is hardly a film discussed in this chapter which was not debated intensively by people who took the cinema seriously. Time has reversed a number of judgments, and may do so again. Meanwhile, we may note that Cukor and the Kanins did not work together again (and the latter were unable for some years to sell scripts in Hollywood), and that Cukor left M-G-M, as did Hepburn and Tracy. The much-desired independence, after a false start in the late Forties, was becoming a necessity a few years later; for the first time since the Twenties the structure of the industry was changing.

28

Postwar Hollywood: The Studios

BY LOOKING FIRST at the leading directors we have covered most of the important American films of the postwar period – if by 'important' we mean those which contemporaries regarded most highly; yet the less prestigious names pointed Hollywood towards its most significant direction of the time – the return after two decades to filming in the streets.

Since the beginning, the cinema had been in the thrall of literature and the stage – which is why it was considered an art form subsidiary to both. For years it had been thought suitable mainly for the frivolous, as the novel had been. In England and America, Dickens, with his social purpose, made the novel virtually essential reading, and the greatness of the Victorian novelists generated a century of fiction. Novel-reading reached a peak during the War, and it could be argued that with the end of the War the decline of the novel began. Escapism became less important, realism more so. The Italians, as we have seen, were the first to respond to the new mood. In Hollywood this happened before American critics began praising de Sica and Rossellini, though few noticed at the time.

Henry Hathaway, the veteran director, was mainly responsible, and he did it without much support from 20th Century-Fox, his studio. He came across the script of **The House on 92nd Street** (1945), to be produced for the company by Louis de Rochemont, one of the founders of 'The March of Time' (a series for the cinema which had been examining current affairs since 1934) – and since these formed part of the supporting programme, Zanuck was confident that the same distinctive approach could only be used for B-movies. The lone predecessor in adopting the 'March of Time' technique (*Confessions of a Nazi Spy*), had not been successful, and the script that Hathaway pleaded to do was also concerned with German espionage activities in the U.S. – in this case seeking the formula for the atomic bomb. The F.B.I. vouched for the film's authenticity and gave full co-operation, which was a coup; but Hathaway underlined the 'authenticity' by shooting on location – as he said, the 'feel' of the script demanded it, and in any case he had always done so with Westerns. The critical reception was such that Hathaway used the same approach for **13, rue Madeleine** (1946): which again included a foreword vowing truth, the shots of filing cabinets, maps and briefings as prelude to a tale of American spies training for action in Nazi-occupied Europe – and despite the presence of James Cagney as chief instructor, a film quite unworthy of its forerunner.

Meanwhile, Hathaway had made **The Dark Corner** (1946) in conventional Hollywood fashion, an excellent thriller about a private eye (Mark Stevens) confronting the New York art world as represented by Clifton Webb and his thuggish aide, William Bendix. Resemblances may be found to the ambiguities of *Laura*, and under the titles we note the presence of 'Street Scene', an orchestral piece to be repeated in the other Fox thrillers of the period. The spy lode could not be mined indefinitely, but the F.B.I. framework was too valuable at the box-office to be thrown aside. The reviews of *Boomerang* once more proved to Zanuck the value of actual locations – and memories of his days at Warners prompted him to commission a 'social conscience' screenplay from Ben Hecht and Charles Lederer for Hathaway to direct. In **Kiss of Death** (1947), the F.B.I.'s quarry is its old enemy, the gangster. Victor Mature is the kid from the back street who just cannot help going to the bad; Richard Widmark (in his first film) is naturally evil, pushing a crippled old lady downstairs; and Brian Donlevy is the lawman convinced that Mature can go straight. The title has no relevance unless it is meant to refer to Mature's performance.

The F.B.I. paraphernalia was, as yet, of more importance than the filming in natural surroundings, but as Hathaway came up with **Call Northside 777** (1948) – with James Stewart as a reporter trying to prove the innocence of a convicted killer – Universal released the first 'imitation', *The Naked City* (q.v.), filmed almost entirely in the streets of New York.* The press called them 'semi-documentaries' for want of a better word, and was so overwhelmingly favourable that there was no going back. The postwar mood was right for the thriller, and with a large number of petty crooks in the news, the public was appreciative of seediness and intimations of weakness in the screen's larger-than-life gangsters: they would not have supported the return of the flashy paranoiacs, but they responded to Richard Widmark in **The Street With No Name** (1948), as a sniggering weakling with nasal inhaler and floor-length overcoat. Zanuck's acquisition of Widmark was good enough reason to revive the underworld film, but in any case this one would have justified the revival. William Keighley, another veteran, directed and, despite having made no recent films of interest, rallied vigorously to the style set by Hathaway. His work is taut and tense, and he positively revels in this portrait of a dull small town, with its pool-halls, gymnasiums, seedy hotels and run-down all-night diners. J. Edgar Hoover, the head of the F.B.I. himself, presents the introduction, indicating that on occasion his organisation needs to send in an undercover man (Mark Stevens): the film then follows the complicated business of manufacturing a fake criminal career, after

*The title of Universal's film was taken from a best-selling book of photographs by the photo-journalist 'Weegee', whose pictures of seamy life were a great influence on all these films.

which it deals in suspicions and tip-offs till the final shoot-out in a deserted factory.

The battle, if battle it was, was won: except for interiors, the days of studio shooting were numbered. When Jean Negulesco arrived at 20th Century-Fox (from Warners) he was offered **Road House** (1948) because Zanuck had noted his flair for location; and the small town atmosphere is excellent. When Cornel Wilde tells Ida Lupino, 'There's small pickings in this town,' you know it is true: as manager and chanteuse, they fall in love amidst stale cigarette smoke, beer-guzzling and bowling – people still young, but with sapped spirits, making a last effort to shake off spiritual isolation. 'All I want to do is hang around someone on Sunday,' she says. As the cashier, Celeste Holm suggests another sort of loneliness, that of a nice girl who simply wants company; as the owner, Widmark is another lost soul – till he turns psychopathic at the end, a disappointing development.

Jules Dassin came from Universal to make **Thieves' Highway** (1949), thrown away on double bills but a good deal fresher than his lauded *Naked City*, with a feeling for night-time San Francisco beyond the scene of the immediate action: the fruit market, where a truck-driver (Richard Conte) is out to get the Big Man (Lee J. Cobb) who ruined his Pa. By this time night scenes were obligatory, but these have a dusty, melancholy quality, achieved without either menace or mood music. There is also an understated rendering of the life of a trucker, as might be expected from A. I. Bezzerides, who had written *They Drive by Night*, and his dialogue again crackles, till the advent of the rather woebegone whore (Valentina Cortese). With her we see the European influence being at last felt in Hollywood: not Rossellini, but prewar Carné.

Fourteen Hours (1951), from a screenplay by John Paxton and a story by Joel Sayre, is based on an actual event when a would-be suicide stood on the ledge of a skyscraper. Some of the incidents in the crowd are box-office trimming, but others are pleasing: the cab driver, annoyed at first at the delay, laying bets on when the man will jump; the reporters, fed up with the mother's hysterics, getting some 'man-in-the-streets'; the hotel guests adjusting to the disruption of service with irritation and grim curiosity; and the exasperated police chief (Howard da Silva) reacting to telephoned advice from his superiors. There is not much merit to the psychological interpretation – that the man (Richard Basehart) has a dominating mother (Agnes Moorehead, seizing her showy moments with sharp judgment) and a weak father (Robert Keith); but once the film starts gently to send up the enthusiastic psychologist (Martin Gabel) it deserves nothing but praise. Especially good is Paul Douglas, as the traffic cop who happens to be first on the scene and gains the man's confidence.

The subject of Hathaway's next film was even more difficult: **The Desert Fox: the Story of Rommel** (1951). Germans were still unpopular, and a sympathetic portrait was a box-office risk; the difficulty of screen biography increases when names like Goering and Montgomery are bandied about by actors pretending to be their contemporaries. Nunnally Johnson based his screenplay on the biography by Desmond Young, cunningly introduced (and played by Michael Rennie) as a man honourably interested in Rommel's mysterious death. The story proper starts with Rommel (James Mason) receiving instructions to hold out at El Alamein, and details his various periods in hospital, including the crucial one when the ex-mayor of Stuttgart (Cedric Hardwicke) tries to warn him that Hitler is paranoic. The exchanges between the two men are literate and thoughtful, as are those with von Rundstedt (Leo G. Carroll, who is particularly good) – and yet sufficiently sparse. The sobriety of Hathaway's approach works beautifully as we move towards Rommel's disgrace – to the extent that Churchill's panegyric, quoted at the end, is oddly moving.

The Snake Pit (1948) contributed further to the esteem in which 20th Century-Fox was held. It followed *The Lost Weekend* and the studio's own *Gentleman's Agreement*, seeking to interest the public in a pressing social problem. Perhaps critics, in praising these rare Hollywood excursions into life's darker side, were clutching at straws, and it may not be irrelevant that all three films were adapted from middle-brow novels (*The Snake Pit* is based on one by Mary Jane Ward). Nevertheless *The Spectator* spoke for many people when it called *The Snake Pit* 'a memorable and profoundly disturbing film', for none before had attempted a serious portrait of conditions inside a mental home. Inside, Anatole Litvak's direction is sober, careful and concerned to a degree, but when dealing with the heroine's past it is often heavily over-emphatic (like the music). The famous process shot of the inmates viewed as in a snake pit no longer impresses. The film's real subject is a nervous breakdown, and when its causes are finally revealed they are the expected business of an over-loving father and an antagonistic mother. The jolly analyses made by the psychiatrist (Leo Genn) are dramatically weak, and it does not help that he, the understanding husband (Mark Stevens) and the other doctor (Glenn Langan) are merely ciphers. The heroine's confession of love to the last-named is only a device with which to finish: the film ought to have ended with the beautifully-observed dance sequence and its moving rendering of 'Going Home'. Olivia de Havilland's role is one of the most demanding in the history of films, and she always has it under control, excellently supported by Celeste Holm, Ruth Donnelly and Beulah Bondi.

Another sombre enterprise, **Twelve O'Clock High** (1949), begins with an ex-U.S.A.F. officer (Dean Jagger) hearing ghostly choruses of 'Don't Sit Under the Apple Tree' and 'Bless 'em All' on a deserted East Anglian airfield. He recalls the young C.O. (Gregory Peck) whose belief in discipline caused his officers en masse to ask for transfers – till he himself proves his valour on a bombing mission. Unfortunately, as written by Sy Bartlett and Bierne Lay Jr the action takes place in a vacuum: there is a reference to the awful weather, but none to Betty Grable or the local pub. The only character with any dimension is Jagger's moderator, and he won a Best Supporting Oscar; but reviewers of the time took the film at its own valuation.

Henry King's direction cannot hide a certain smugness, but together with **The Gunfighter** (1950) it brought his reputation to its highest point since making *Tol'able David* thirty years earlier. Zanuck regarded *The Gunfighter* as suitable only for prestige, and allowed King to take his own time in evoking the atmosphere of a sleepy little town, galvanised by the presence of Peck as a has-been gunfighter (at

721

thirty-five) – an object of disapproval by the town's matrons, of awe to the children, and of aggression to punks who fancy themselves as his equal. When he is killed, one of them will take his place – and a rotten tradition will have been passed on. It is a thesis too pat for a film otherwise more complex than most Westerns of the period; when the busybody ladies appear – a device favoured by John Ford – it is clear that King has achieved more feeling and more suspense than is available in any Western that Ford ever made.

Yellow Sky (1948) and **Rawhide** (1951) are also good examples of the genre, with William Wellman and Hathaway responding to sound, unpretentious material. Both films concern innocent victims in the clutches of bank robbers, and the former has the nastier villains – Widmark, John Russell and Henry (later, Harry) Morgan – with only Jack Elam to match them in *Rawhide*. Wellman's film can also boast more blood and guts than was usual at the time, as well as Joe Macdonald's photography of a ghost town in Death Valley. Both films are unfortunate in their leads: Peck is conventional in *Yellow Sky* as the bank robber with decent feelings, and as the prisoners in *Rawhide* neither Tyrone

Power nor Susan Hayward is able to create tension.

Peck was not under exclusive contract to the studio but had become Zanuck's first choice for almost every leading role, including **The Razor's Edge** (1946). Zanuck, however, changed his mind and it became Power's first postwar film. It needed an actor of more ability than either to give meaning to Somerset Maugham's hero Larry, who leaves a comfortable life and his fiancée (Gene Tierney) to seek in Europe and elsewhere his own holy grail. He does not find it, but Maugham – played, as in *The Moon and Sixpence*, by Herbert Marshall – concludes, 'Goodness is after all the greatest force in the world.' But if that was what the book was about, the film keeps it a secret. George Cukor was to have directed from a screenplay by Maugham himself, but when Zanuck found it unusable Edmund Goulding replaced Cukor, with a revised screenplay by Lamar Trotti, the best of which is in the commentary, a prolonged series of opinions and asides taken directly from the book. In uttering these, Maugham appears as an idealist, and his dislike of his nouveau riche friends remains discernible, but the original text is otherwise unrecognisable apart from Clifton Webb as Elliott Templeton, the Europeanised all-American snob. Marshall is good, and would seem even better if everyone did not say 'Mr Maugham' as though *he* were the holy grail. Goulding uses very long takes, directing – according to the cinematographer, Arthur Miller – as if for the stage, though his camera moves subtly among the cast; Miller also recalled that he unsuccessfully implored Zanuck to change the appalling backdrop in the Indian scene. This was another film in which *Life Magazine* took a special interest – in return for which 20th Century-Fox advertised it heavily in that journal.

A lesser novel, by William Lindsay Gresham, provided a better film for Goulding and Power, as written for the screen by Jules Furthman. **Nightmare Alley** (1947) reaches into terrain where Hollywood seldom ventured – murky areas of cruelty and ambition, the occult and religious sensibilities. Stan (Power) is an orphan who has wandered into the job of carnival barker, and when you see him watching the geek in the first scene you

In the postwar period 20th Century-Fox made a series of thrillers which found urban America a grim, seedy place. The studio also made a number of more serious pictures with an equally pessimistic view, the most interesting of which is *Nightmare Alley*, with Tyrone Power and Joan Blondell and directed by the veteran Edmund Goulding.

know that that is how he will end up. (A geek is a man who eats live chickens because he is in an advanced state of alcoholism and that is apparently the only way to get his bottle a day.) He starts out by using Zeena (Joan Blondell), half of a phoney mind-reading act, and moves onwards and upwards till he meets his match in Lilith (Helen Walker). She is quite as unscrupulous as he, but unfortunately portrayed as the usual movie predator, with bags of self-confidence and a chic wardrobe. Nor is Power good enough; having returned from the War with a new seriousness, he begged for the role and plays conscientiously: but in place of ambition he offers only deviousness, and for blarney only a fast-moving dimple. Goulding keeps the carnival scenes tacky, and at its best this film is reminiscent of the German Silent studies of low life; it is a pity it is not better, for it is Goulding's last important film and also the last important one that Furthman wrote.

Henry King directed Power in **Captain from Castile** (1947) and **Prince of Foxes** (1949), historical extravaganzas based on the imaginings of Samuel Shellabargar – and the first since Silent days to make extensive use of locations, the former among the Aztec temples and volcanoes of Mexico, and the latter among the towers of Volterra, though Volterra, because of the cost and comparative failure of the earlier film, did not rate Technicolor. Power is the captain from Castile and, as in *Son of Fury*, he sails away from injustice to seek his fortune, followed by a laundress (Jean Peters): 'You'll join the women with the army,' Cortez (Cesar Romero) greets her, 'hoping to find a husband?' – which is Hollywood's way of dealing with one of the more awkward historical facts. Power survives tropical disease and an embarrassing fandango to marry her – because, after all, they are in the New World, home of democracy. The thirty-seven companions who helped Cortez conquer the Aztecs have become a huge concourse of extras. The title of *Prince of Foxes* refers to Cesare Borgia (Orson Welles), and Power here is one of the followers who turns against him when ordered to drive a wedge between the fair Camilla (Wanda Hendrix, pathetically miscast) and her elderly husband (Felix Aylmer).

With **Fallen Angel** (1946) Power's erst-while co-star, Alice Faye, gave up the battle against typecasting and retired. She did on this occasion play, and very well, a timid spinster whose insistence on marrying a blackguard (Dana Andrews) prompts him to plot both a getaway with her money and the murder of her rival, a hash-house waitress (Linda Darnell). The script, by Harry Kleiner from a novel by Marty Holland, has a degree of frankness rare at the time, if only in implying Andrews's lust for Darnell and Faye's for him. A better director than Otto Preminger might have made more of this, but aided by Joseph La Shelle's photography he does achieve a keen portrait of a one-horse town; Ann Revere offers an intriguing study as Faye's sister, recognising the man for what he is and trying to adjust to that fact.

A more conventional look at the mysterious husband and the frightened wife was available in the first of two films for the company directed by Robert Wise (b. 1916), an editor with R.K.O. before becoming a director with Val Lewton's unit. In **The House on Telegraph Hill** (1951) the wife (Valentina Cortese) is an impostor, having taken a friend's place in Belsen (a situation treated so unpretentiously in the prologue that it is quite acceptable). Arriving in San Francisco, she is confronted by a hostile governess and a room into which her husband (Richard Basehart) forbids her to go. Wise's other movie for Zanuck at this time is **The Day the Earth Stood Still** (1951) – the day in question being that when a messenger arrives from another planet to warn of the dangers of a nuclear war. Michael Rennie plays the role, and as he seldom seemed human it is good casting; as the boarding-house neighbour who befriends him Patricia Neal is too good for such storm-in-a-teacup melodrama. But both films, particularly the first, are good examples of the Fox movies at this time. Between 1946 and the advent of CinemaScope in 1953, the studio made some of the most visually satisfying of all movies, in crisp blacks and whites, with locations simply but expressively used. The scenes are, for the most part, shot in medium close-up; the settings were seldom ornate or mannered; the performances were not overburdened with technique, and as a result plots like the basically daft one of *The House on*

723

Telegraph Hill seem better than they are.

Not in this category is **Leave Her to Heaven** (1945) – if only because it was one of the few melodramas of the time to be filmed in Technicolor – as adapted by Jo Swerling from a novel by Ben Ames Williams. C. A. Lejeune's review reminds us that its sponsors described it as 'the sum total of human emotions . . . You will know you are in the presence of a great moment in screen history,' but she felt, rather, that 'the entertainment lies in seeing what new sin the lady can get up to.' There is just one variation on the other wicked lady dramas of the period, in that it takes Gene Tierney an hour to show her hand. The principals – the others are Cornel Wilde, Jeanne Crain and Vincent Price – are not the ones to portray 'a great moment in screen history', and the director, John M. Stahl, once adept with such material, was clearly dispirited.

As a work of fiction **Forever Amber** (1947) towered above such pieces, having garnered in book form a notoriety which had made it an enormous bestseller. The Legion of Decency led the organisations militant at the thought of a film version, and the chances of getting a workable script were remote. Shooting eventually began under Stahl, with the wildly unsuitable Peggy Cummins in the title role (unlike Scarlett O'Hara, it was a role no one wanted to play): both were dropped by Zanuck after the expenditure of two million dollars, and replaced by Otto Preminger and Linda Darnell. (Zanuck preferred Darnell to Preminger's choice, Lana Turner, because he was unwilling to make overtures to M-G-M for Turner's services.) Zanuck also refused to concede Preminger's point that the material should be mocked because its mediocrity matched its reputation; the result amply demonstrates Preminger's own claim that he was otherwise not interested. Nor were there enough patrons to justify the final $6 million cost, and it may be said that those who did turn up were disappointed. As eviscerated by Philip Dunne and Ring Lardner, Jr, Kathleen Winsor's heroine is still a forward hussy, and if almost forgotten now, it would then not have been necessary to remind anyone that her adventures were conducted in and around the court of Charles II (George Sanders). 'I've been fire-fighting all afternoon down at the docks . . . Perhaps my guests might be interested. It's been such a dull season,' he says to indicate why he was called the Merry Monarch. He (of course) becomes one of her conquests, though she continues to pine for her first love (Cornel Wilde); in the end she is deserted by all, a moral lesson to us and an echo of Scarlett O'Hara.

Zanuck's persistence with such stuff is an enigma: under his aegis Fox was now turning out a higher proportion of good movies than any of the other studios, but it was also perpetrating some which could not possibly have looked good, even on paper. Unlike Warner, Cohn or Mayer, he was a creative producer, capable of going far beyond an assent or refusal to the ideas put to him, and in addition he had a great deal of practical experience behind him. However, he also believed as much in quantity and variety as in excellence. Since the system demanded a biblical 'epic' from time to time – and having studied the profits of deMille's *Samson and Delilah* (q.v.) – he decided to make **David and Bathsheba** (1951). Indeed, it was one of his personal productions, with a superior director, King, and with a writer, Philip Dunne, capable of rising to the occasion: since part of the exercise was to outsmart deMille, they stuck to the Old Testament, with dialogue unrhetorical though also flat and predictable, except for a moment when David is described as 'exposing himself to the enemy'. King seems to have decided that the only way to film it was to move the people in and out of the (excellent) sets like puppets, and his attitude may have been induced by watching Gregory Peck and Susan Hayward reverentially enunciate what they seem to regard as holy writ. He, she and the script deserve each other, and it is noticeable that the climax succeeds well without them, as King does an imaginative job on a flashback of the boy David slaying Goliath.

When Hollywood had need of one of nature's aristocrats it sent for Peck. He is miscast as the hero of **The Snows of Kilimanjaro** (1952), based on Hemingway himself – as he would later be miscast as F. Scott Fitzgerald in *Beloved Infidel*. Peck looked Ivy League, but is unconvincing as a writer since his expressions are so consistently bland – and indeed becomes quite ludicrous (which was not his fault) by banging on about bullfighting and big game hunting while never leaving the soundstage. The film's popularity is unfathomable, unless the Second Unit material deceived audiences into believing that Hollywood was moving out into the world (it was, but this film was a regression). Hemingway's original story was of a man (Peck) critically ill who recalls his misdeeds: Casey Robinson's screenplay gives him plenty of flashbacks deriving from the Hemingway ethic – as well as one cherishable line, spoken to Peck, sick on safari, by Susan Hayward, 'I'm going to shoot some game. The larder's almost empty.' Towards the end, he says, 'I had it all and what did I have? My picture in the papers'; in the interim all *we* have had is Ava Gardner, till she disappears to Madrid where 'that wretched Civil War is on'. She is the love of his life, the only indication he shows, beyond his tweed suits, of good taste – and the only person to emerge from this thing with credit; certainly King, the director, does not.

Anna and the King of Siam (1946) is based on the novel by Margaret Landon, described on the credits as a biography, and in fact based on a memoir by the English widow who in the 1860s went out to teach English to the sons of the Siamese king. Because of this film and the musical – *The King and I* (q.v.) – based on it, most people know the tale, but it was an unusual subject for the cinema then: as the magazine *Time* said, it 'flies in the face of established Hollywood precedent by ignoring young love, and it proves that a movie can be lively entertainment even if boy doesn't get – or even meet – the girl'. There is much that is spurious – the settings, the starlets as Siamese wives, Rex Harrison's make-up as the king – and you may feel your emotions being manipulated; but it is also entertaining and, for a moment or two, touching. That has much to do with Irene Dunne, as conscientious in trying an English accent as preparing for a close-up, and performing with what I can only call a loveliness of spirit. The film keeps Anna's difficulties in sight – being publicly humiliated, summoned at all hours of the night, treated as one of the harem – and they have been rendered with a degree of truth by the writers, Talbot Jennings and Sally Benson. The direction offers one of the last chances to appreciate the sensi-tivity of John Cromwell, resisting, he recalled, requests to jazz it up: 'D.F.Z. was wondering whether you couldn't punch up the love scenes, inject a little more comedy . . .' It is funny, however, despite Harrison's lack of ease – querulous where Yul Brynner would be insensitive; as his aide, Lee J. Cobb hams, but does suggest a complicity with Anna in dealing with the complex character of the king – which is one of many happy touches.

Zanuck's admiration for the British movies based on Somerset Maugham's short stories (q.v.) resulted in **O. Henry's Full House** (1952), introduced by John Steinbeck, whose reading of a few snatches indicates why Henry does not translate into film terms – though few of this cast are able to render him effectively. The best of the five stories is 'The Ransom of Red Chief', directed by Howard Hawks, with Fred Allen and Oscar Levant as kidnappers of a ghastly small boy; but it is enjoyable less because of Allen and Levant than for the parents' quiet acceptance of their son's enormities. Allen, a unique radio comedian, made too few films; however, he did appear for Fox in what is also the best episode of **We're Not Married** (1952), with Ginger Rogers, as radio stars whose private life is very different from the one projected. Edmund Goulding directed all the episodes – which are predictable from the film's title. The public reception of both films – remarkably inexpensive despite the casts – put into serious doubt the concept of omnibus films in Hollywood.

20th Century-Fox remained literary with **Les Miserables** (1952), tautly directed by Lewis Milestone, who said that he regarded it merely as a job; he also proves to be one of the few directors able to prevent Robert Newton – playing Javert – from hamming. Richard Murphy's screenplay is not overly burdened with fustian, and of all the screen versions (there have been at least ten since 1909; this is the ninth) it could be the best. Michael Rennie plays Valjean directly, never resorting to that raised-eyebrow charm he used in his British films, and is supported by Edmund Gwenn as the bishop, Elsa Lanchester as his housekeeper and Sylvia Sidney as the unfortunate Fantine.

Titanic (1953), another period piece, is not to be despised, as directed by Jean Negulesco and written by Charles Brackett, Walter Reisch and Richard Breen, fresh from their success on *Niagara* (q.v.). On this occasion they bring too much taste and too few details to the tragedy of the *Titanic*, though the actual sinking is as well done as expected. The long fictional frontispiece chiefly concerns a failing marriage, with an American wife (Barbara Stanwyck) taking her children back to the States to rid them of the values learnt in the salons of the old continent: that it works so well is also due to Clifton Webb as the husband, really showing his mettle in a serious role. Some actual names are used – the 'Molly Brown' character is there, played by Thelma Ritter – but the only one of the now legendary incidents used is that concerning the elderly Jewish couple who refused to be parted: perhaps because we know it to be true, it is the only moving moment.

I Can Get It for You Wholesale (1952) is a contemporary drama about the garment industry, based on a novel by Jerome Weidman which had been around for some time. The decision to film it had much to do with *All About Eve*, in which an ambitious schemer tramples her way to the top: common to both films is George Sanders to tempt the lady concerned. She is played by Susan Hayward, a better actress but less mesmerising than Joan Crawford in such roles. Only in Marvin Kaplan's performance as the cocky young clerk is there a strain of the Jewish comedy which, I imagine, was such a feature of the book. The screenwriter, Abraham Polonsky, and the director, Michael Gordon, were both to be victims in the McCarthyism then raging in the industry.

The Star (1953) concerns another dominant lady, and its own star, Bette Davis, recognised Joan Crawford as the source – as its writer had once worked for that lady. In the film, as produced independently for Fox distribution, she has become a has-been, played by Miss Davis quivering with intensity. 'Come on, Oscar, let's you and me get drunk,' she roars at her statuette, but beyond this storm at the film's centre it is a quiet piece. Stuart Heisler's pacing is weak, and he makes his performers seem awkward, including Sterling Hayden as the man the star finds she would like to come home to. The film tries to find something unsaid in *Sunset Boulevard* and *All About Eve* on the loneliness of stardom and the difficulty of ageing, but while it may be nearer the truth it is not in the same league as either.

20th Century-Fox's own leading star remained Betty Grable, still heading all the box-office polls. In her first postwar film she and June Haver played **The Dolly Sisters** (1945), the Hungarian immigrants who in real life had become the rage of New York, London and Paris for their vaudeville act. The film had been planned for Grable and Alice Faye, who had played a sister act in *Tin Pan Alley*, and it comes as no surprise to find this history of the Dollys is merely a rehash of the equally dire Fox musicals of that time, even to having John Payne join the army. Neither Grable nor Haver look remotely like their originals; nor do their talents appear comparable. Irving Cummings directed (his penultimate film) and clearly he was tired. However, with the troops now demobilised, Zanuck realised that the Grable vehicles needed an injection of originality if audiences were to leave their homes to see them. **The Shocking Miss Pilgrim** (1947) used four unpublished songs by George and Ira Gershwin and a story about a demure but feisty stenographer in old Boston: and if the result is hardly more attractive than Grable's other films this is due to the direction by George Seaton. **Mother Wore Tights** (1947) tells, with the aid of flashbacks, of a vaudeville couple trying to combat their daughter's snobbery. The vaudeville stages still have Fox's polished glass floors and shimmering curtains, but the milieu was reasonably unfamiliar – as were musicals with plots comparatively as strong: the public discerned in it qualities concealed today and under Walter Lang's direction it restored Grable to favour after the failure of *Miss Pilgrim*, as well as providing her with a regular screen partner in Dan Dailey.

There are two Grables in **That Lady in Ermine** (1948), one the captive hostess of an Hungarian commander (Douglas Fairbanks, Jr) and the other an ancestress who descends from a portrait on the wall: for this is operetta, directed by Lubitsch, no less, and scripted by his old collaborator Samson Raphaelson. Lubitsch died during shooting and the film was completed by Otto Preminger, leaving an impression of some agreeable fantasy but basically poor material. It failed, as did *The Beautiful*

Blonde from Bashful Bend, already discussed, and Zanuck returned Miss Grable to clichés as her appeal gradually faded.

There were other occasions when the musicals of this studio attempted to get out of the rut, but they were usually copies of those being made at M-G-M. **Centennial Summer** (1946) is so modelled on *Meet Me in St Louis* that it is hard to believe that it was originally planned as a straight film. The songs (by Jerome Kern) were added, claimed the publicity, because of the success of *State Fair*: but when this family (Dorothy Gish, Walter Brennan, Jeanne Crain, Linda Darnell) sings 'Up With the Lark', passing it around in the manner of the Smiths of St Louis, they only prove that they are not a family you would care to sing along with. The plot has them anxious about the visit of an aunt, and as she is played by Constance Bennett audiences may echo Gish when she wonders 'whether she's still as stunning': but she is not, and we are left to wonder which of her nieces will fall to her 'companion', Cornel Wilde. The fair in this case is the one held in Philadelphia in 1876 (footage of which turns up as the Chicago World's Fair in *Wabash Avenue*) and the director is Otto Preminger.

Margie (1946), therefore, is all the more surprising, being as good as those two films are bad. Henry King's direction never strives or is self-conscious in this affectionate, sketched-in picture of high-school life in a small town in midwinter: the tale of a girl (Miss Crain) who has a fumbling boyfriend (Alan Young) and a crush on the new French teacher (Glenn Langan) in the days of the Stutz Bearcat and the Charleston. This was the first post-contemporary Hollywood film about the Twenties to look like the Twenties; the songs of the period – this is not really a musical – are used delightfully, and so is the star: in King's hands she remains winsome but is for once very appealing.

The level of Zanuck's musicals did not rise when Danny Kaye was imported to play two roles in **On the Riviera** (1951), a revamp of that plot which had seen duty as *Folies Bergère* and *That Night in Rio*, with a good many of its *double entendres* surprisingly intact. Kaye could not have been inspired by his leading ladies – Corinne Calvet and Gene Tierney – but he does have one very bright number, 'Popo the Puppet'. The film was directed by Walter Lang, who was also responsible for the studio's most popular musical of this period, **With a Song in My Heart** (1952), based on the life of Jane Froman, the singing star who was permanently crippled in a wartime air disaster. Susan Hayward plays the role conventionally, but the songs were dubbed by Miss Froman herself – and I trust it is the warmth and richness of her voice which move me, momentarily, as she sings, towards the end, a medley of 'Back Home' songs to the troops at the front.

Lang also directed **Call Me Madam** (1953), sensibly keying the proceedings to Ethel Merman, its star, who had made the original a Broadway hit. On the film's release she observed that at last she was a success in Hollywood, and planned to stay, but it did not work out that way. She is both what is right and what is wrong about this film: vital and vivid, very much a star, but theatrical in gesture and timing, always playing to the gallery. Lang has had to slow the whole thing down to suit her; one admires her button-bright eagerness, even if her charm is as tightly corsetted as her figure. In addition to her role – that of a vulgarian Washington hostess appointed by President Truman to the embassy of a small European country (based on fact: the hostess was Pearl Mesta and the country Luxembourg) – the show has a good Irving Berlin score and a lively book, combining Ruritanian nonsense and some heavy satire on American aid to Europe.

The Fox comedies of the period are no more endearing than their musicals; in the most famous of them, **Miracle on 34th Street** (1947), an elderly eccentric (Edmund Gwenn) insists that he is Kris Kringle and is hired for Macy's Thanksgiving Day parade; kept on, his recommendation of Gimbels and other rival stores makes him either a goodwill asset or a candidate for Bellevue. Such things may recall Capra, but there is an almost clinical impersonality about this film, and the only one of the players to match Gwenn's lightness is Thelma Ritter (in her film debut) as a satisfied mother. Gwenn's old-world charm is hard-pressed to sustain **Apartment for Peggy** (1948), as a widowed professor who finds new reason for living after being inveigled into letting his attic to a G.I. couple, William Holden and Jeanne

Crain. She, jabbering enthusiastically, is meant to carry the film, which sometimes goes beyond cosiness to wisdom, as when Gwenn speaks about teaching: 'You make a lot of people through the years a little more enlightened. You have contributed something.' Both films were written and directed by George Seaton.

There are similar homilies in his **Chicken Every Sunday** (1948), and in **Cheaper by the Dozen** (1950), directed by Walter Lang, two more of the seemingly endless family reminiscences started off by 'Life with Father': the former has Dan Dailey as an impractical dreamer, Celeste Holm (who is excellent) as the managing little woman, and Colleen Townsend as the girl who wrote it all down; the latter has Clifton Webb as the eccentric efficiency expert who carried his business ideas into his home, Myrna Loy as the managing wife, and Miss Crain as the young authoress. It also rated Technicolor and a sequel, **Belles on their Toes** (1952), directed by Henry Levin and equally innocuous. Clearly these entertainments met public demand – most of them are adapted from popular books – for in a fast-changing society, audiences wanted to be reminded of a time when families coped only with gentle changes, such as the excitement of the first automobile and the first phonograph; it is no coincidence that most of them depicted a stern father unwilling to accede to new ideas.

In the same mould are **Mr 880** (1950), directed by Edmund Goulding, with Edmund Gwen as a lovable counterfeiter and Burt Lancaster as the eventually-disarmed F.B.I. man, and **The Jackpot** (1950), directed by Lang, with James Stewart as a suburbanite who wins a quiz-show. One of the most popular of Fox's comedies was **Sitting Pretty** (1948), directed by Lang, about a middle-aged bachelor (Clifton Webb), who becomes an unconventional nurse to the bratty child of Robert Young and Maureen O'Hara. Dreary as many of these family films sound, it should be explained that the public mood five years after the War was different from that which had given rise to Jean Harlow and Carole Lombard.

Come to the Stable (1949) concerns two nuns (Loretta Young, Celeste Holm), one of whom is noticeably wearing lipstick. They are French, and have turned up in the U.S. since they swore during the war years to build a church there; having no money but much faith, they win over a bishop (Basil Ruysdael), a gangster (Thomas Gomez) and an embittered songwriter (Hugh Marlowe). The film sells Christianity, but with more humour than is customary in such circumstances; it also has Dooley Wilson, a mastiff called 'Orson' and Elsa Lanchester as something out of 'Mother Goose'. It is necessary to experience them, and the brisk Miss Holm, to understand why this is one of the movies' more bearable ventures into religiosity. Henry Koster directed, and the artful writers were Oscar Millard and Sally Benson, from a story by Clare Boothe Luce.

The less sentimentally-minded will prefer **I Was a Male War Bride** (1949), which returns comedy from the parlour to the bedroom, an analogy not disqualified by its being the first American comedy filmed extensively on European locations. Its mainspring is that old kick-off, non-consummation of marriage – as suffered by a lieutenant (Ann Sheridan) in the W.A.C.S and an officer (Cary Grant) in the U.S. army. He is called Henri Rochard, and as the screenplay, by Charles Lederer, Leonard Spigelglass and Hagar Wilde, is based on a story by someone of that name we may assume a basis in fact. It sags towards the end, when Grant is looking for somewhere to lay his head in Bremerhaven, but otherwise he runs the gamut of expressions, as usual when directed by Howard Hawks, while Sheridan was one of the few actresses of the Forties who could appear to be having a ball. The plot of **Monkey Business** (1952) involves a rejuvenation formula invented by Grant, which takes him and his wife (Ginger Rogers) back to adolescence and then childhood. The writers are Lederer, Ben Hecht and I. A. L. Diamond, all of them, like Hawks, experienced enough to know that crazy comedy either works at once or never. It makes one wonder why they did not abandon this one during production. Ignored at the time, it achieved a slight fame later because of the presence of Marilyn Monroe (1926–62), in a small role as Charles Coburn's secretary. She has only five lines or so, but the camera lingers on her primping and glowing, because it was clear that this woman had an extraordinary appeal. Zanuck could not see it, but said that she could be shoved into any movie which could use a sexy blonde.

When finally convinced that she was not a nine days' wonder he gave her star roles in **Niagara** (1953), and **Gentlemen Prefer Blondes** (1953), films he judged to be as cheap and vulgar as her appeal. The difference between them, however, is infinite, and *Niagara* is one of the great cod melodramas, as directed by Henry Hathaway and produced by Charles Brackett, who wrote it with Walter Reisch and Richard Breen, two other former associates of Billy Wilder. The way Monroe walks (photographed from behind) and dresses (skintight, and obviously without underwear), and the way she half-closes her eyes and half-opens her mouth at moments of passion seemed sensational; and the writers had concocted a story to indicate that on her honeymoon she is already carrying on with another man – and she is egging on the new man to kill her husband (Joseph Cotten). Overall, she is effective, but not really good; but in *Gentlemen Prefer Blondes*, perfectly cast as Lorelei Lee, the Cinderella of gold-diggers, she proves that with a good line she can move mountains. Jane Russell is her partner, and Zanuck's contempt is indicated by an extremely poor cast, with the exception of Charles Coburn as Sir Francis of the roving eye. The film has only a tenuous connection with Anita Loos's book, being catapulted from the Twenties into some contemporary limbo; and it has little more to do with the 1949 Broadway musical version, retaining just three songs and hardly more of the lines. The new songs are poor, unevenly distributed, and staged with the pointless rushing-about and flouncing of skirts characteristic of Fox musicals: as directed by Howard Hawks this ranks among the most crass films he ever made.

Between Zanuck and his best directors – Mankiewicz, Kazan, King and Hathaway – 20th Century-Fox did respond to the postwar mood with a more mature range of subjects than the other studios. Paramount, however, obliged only by making its melodramas a little more weighty. This studio had always prided itself on being purveyors of 'entertainment', but with the shining exception of Wilder's *A Foreign Affair* did not choose to reflect contemporary problems. The War, however, remained useful for romance.

To Each His Own (1946) starts during the London blitz, as a middle-aged Olivia de Havilland reflects on her small town American past, which turns out to be a combination of *Back Street*, *Only Yesterday* and, later, *The Old Maid*: the First War takes her lover, and the Second brings back her illegitimate son. **Golden Earrings** (1947) also adopts flashback, to show a British colonel (Ray Milland) on the run from the Nazis in 1939, though it is less a thriller than a comedy drama about a stuffy Britisher humanised by an earth mother – a gypsy (Marlene Dietrich). Mitchell Leisen directed both films, and if Charles Brackett's script for the first had a little more humour it would be a classic of its kind; the second is high tosh, and the start of Leisen's run of increasingly poor films. He insisted upon casting Dietrich, against Paramount's wishes, since he wanted a really glamorous woman under the make-up to make the romance work. She may say that she has garlic on her breath and cod liver oil in her hair, but she remains Dietrich with an unusual Max Factor job.

Leisen's last decent picture was **Dream Girl** (1948), based on a play by Elmer Rice which had been a stage vehicle for his wife, Betty Field. In her role, that of a wealthy girl with aspirations to culture, Betty Hutton is miscast and monotonous; as the reporter who persuades her that the world would be a better place if we stopped dreaming and started living, MacDonald Carey does not provide the colour she lacks. It could have been satiric on either New York intellectuals or pseudo-intellectuals, but a novel called 'Always Opal' is the height of its satiric daring, and it is much less pointed on the foibles of the rich than almost any prewar comedy. With these reservations, there are reasons for seeing this film: some small bite in the dream sequences; some funny lines given to the bride's mother (Peggy Wood); and a delicious cameo by Zamah Cunningham as her singing teacher. The film failed to duplicate the play's success, and its failure with the public hastened the departure from the studio of both Hutton and Leisen.

William Dieterle, another of Hollywood's better directors, was also involved in a romantic war melodrama. In **Love Letters** (1945), written by Ayn Rand from a novel by Chris Massie, a soldier (Joseph Cotten) goes in search of the girl (Jennifer Jones) to whom he wrote the letters, finding her both an amnesiac and the murderess of the man she *thought* wrote the letters. He marries her, despite the enigmatic comment of her aunt (Gladys Cooper), 'I interfered once and lived to regret it' – which is no help in untangling the plot, described by James Agee as 'factitious'. The word for Miss Jones's performance, said *The New York Times*, is 'fatuous' and that Selznick thought her 'absolutely sensational' is proof again that love is blind: the role, however, is impossible, all giggles and walking on walls. So is the portrait of England, with Nelson's Column looming just outside the window of an apartment, and a wedding in the ruined church (other quaint notions include rationbooks for porridge and dropping in on the nearest bishop whenever you have a problem) – and indeed, all the studio exteriors are painful.

In that respect there was a change when Dieterle came to make **September Affair** (1950), among the first American films made extensively on European locations, its Cook's Tour taking in a bit of Naples, a *trattoria* on the slopes of Vesuvius, and much of Florence. The lovers lease what must have been the largest *palazzo* in that city, the M.P.A.A. leaving unclear whether or not they have separate rooms – and the film is exactly what cynics might expect of a Hollywood version of *Brief Encounter*, with Joan Fontaine as a celebrated concert pianist and Cotten a very wealthy, unhappily married, engineer. Homage to the British film may be intended in the use of the same Rachmaninoff Piano Concerto, often enterprisingly blended with Neapolitan airs and/or Kurt Weill's 'September Song'. This song is also intelligently used, the verse as well – firstly as the lovers listen to Walter Huston's recording, and again as it is taken up in a restaurant by a rather drunken G.I. (Jimmy Lydon) – and that, together with the locations, explains why many people have a weakness for this film.

It is one of a series of highly artificial stories produced independently by Hal Wallis, each of them characteristic of this period inasmuch as infidelity was allowed to go unpunished, but not to end happily, and Freudian explanations were tentatively offered for such matters as possessiveness, mother-domination, buddy-buddy crushes and even criminal mentality. They were inspired by the Bette Davis melodramas which Wallis had produced at Warners, and usually starred two other 'strong' actresses, the veteran Barbara Stanwyck and the young Lizabeth Scott. You will not believe a word of either **The Strange Love of Martha Ivers** (1946), directed by Lewis Milestone, with Stanwyck, Scott, Kirk Douglas and Wendell Corey, or **Desert Fury** (1947), directed by Lewis Allen, with John Hodiak, Mary Astor, Burt Lancaster, Wendell Corey and Miss Scott – the words in both cases supplied by Robert Rossen, a former Warners writer – but just try to look away. Wallis's men are a new breed – Douglas and Lancaster, with restless energy, to be later joined by Charlton Heston, sharing with Lancaster a new Hollywood anomaly of broad shoulders and asexuality.

Wallis brought to Paramount an old Warners colleague, Anatole Litvak, to make **Sorry, Wrong Number** (1948), which may remind you of that *New Yorker* cartoon of a theatre patron observing, 'If this is supposed to be a realistic play, how come the telephone always works first time?' The sole character of Lucille Fletcher's celebrated thirty-minute radio play is an invalid who, chancing on a crossed line, hears a murder plot whose victim she has reason to believe is herself. In opening out the play, Miss Fletcher's screenplay is less faithful to the original than to what audiences expected of Stanwyck, playing a rich bitch ('When I want something I fight for it and usually get it') who pursues poor boy Lancaster ('What's a dame like you want with a guy like me?'). The second half loses impetus, as is true of **Dark City** (1950), where murder also stalks, on account of an out-of-town salesman (Don Defore) who has committed suicide after gambling away a cheque for $5,000. Heston is the gambling-den boss, out to foil these murders, and his light-toned virility is neatly counterpointed by Scott, crooning 'I Don't Want to Walk Without You' in an almost-baritone. Dieterle directed, and both films manage that Forties ambience we noticed in those of Siodmak: lonely, rainy streets at night, over-furnished rooms with parties going on, pay-telephones in grimy diners, and men in shirtsleeves sitting around in bare rooms.

Most of these films of Wallis belong to what was later recognised as the American *film noir* (and for its first scenes, *Dark City* is as good an example as exists). A masterpiece of the genre is **The Blue Dahlia** (1946) which was also greeted only politely when it appeared. John Houseman produced and George Marshall directed Raymond Chandler's only original screenplay: a South Pacific veteran (Alan Ladd) returns to find, firstly, his wife (Doris Dowling) flaunting her relationship with another man (Howard da Silva), secondly, her corpse, and thirdly, himself as the prime suspect. He tries to get the murderer before the police get him, a favourite plot of the time, remoulded for Chandler's sour, disjointed world, and populated by such as the cool-as-cucumber heroine (Veronica Lake), the seedy hotel dick (Will Wright), the boarding-house proprietor (Howard Freeman), and the veteran's buddy (William Bendix), liable to uncontrollable rages. One of these was not the villain intended by Chandler, and it is worth quoting him on the film's chief weakness, 'Ladd is hard, bitter and occasionally charming, but he is after all a small boy's idea of a tough guy.' With Ladd and Lake one hardly cares what happens to them: for this material really to take off, another team was needed (and that team – Bogart and Bacall – was at Warner Bros.).

It is also difficult to feel anxiety for the man on the spot in **The Big Clock** (1948), for he is both smug and self-sufficient – qualities often inherent in the acting of Ray Milland, who plays him: however, Jonathan Latimer's screenplay thoughtfully refers to the first quality and the plot requires the second. Milland is the editor of a crime magazine, part of the publishing empire of Charles Laughton, who is autocratic, bad-tempered, ill-mannered and pathetic because, as is pointed out to him, he has not a friend in the world. When his mistress (Rita Johnson) is murdered, Milland's situation will remind you not only of *The Blue Dahlia* but of Graham Greene and Hitchcock, with a dash of Hammett and Ambler: the race for the truth, the formidable opponent, the eccentric minor characters. Moving everything at a fast clip, John Farrow confirms the impression of *You Came Along*, that his interest could

be kindled by a comic barman or a crowded restaurant.

Farrow's best film is **Two Years Before the Mast** (1946), and if Agee thought the screenplay – by Seton I. Miller and George Bruce – falsified Dana's contempt for his fellow-seamen, these have not been reduced to stereotypes – with the exception of Barry Fitzgerald in his *Sea Wolf* performance as the Irish cook. Dana (Brian Donlevy) sets out to investigate life at sea, and is duly shown keeping a journal indicating that it consists of flogging, speed and scurvy; the inevitable mutiny is, of course, led by the shipowner's shanghaied son (Ladd). This is not the sort of script that actors can do much about, jogging up and down on some corner of the Paramount lot, and Ladd, after a good start as the cocky young swell, finally becomes a very wan fellow indeed; but the excellence of the film stems directly from the delineation of Captain and First Mate. As the former, Howard da Silva is not so much wicked as content in isolation; William Bendix is the unblinking, unquestioning Mate, a man whose subservience to the Captain goes to the bottom reaches of his soul. Once on dry land, the story tails away with references to Dana's 'scandalous' book, as if the writers could not

There have been books written on the American *film noir*, a genre to which its practitioners did not know they were contributing. Nevertheless, there is a certain similarity between several Hollywood crime films made between 1940 and the late Fifties, even if the same elements may be found in the faster-paced thrillers of the pre-Code era. Many of the later films were influenced by the novels of Raymond Chandler, who wrote the original screenplay of *The Blue Dahlia*, which starred Alan Ladd, seen here escaping from the clutches of Don Costello.

731

decide how to handle the question of the reforms it occasioned, and the climate at Paramount was not conducive to the discussion of serious matters.

As a result of the film's success, Farrow was assigned to **California** (1946), which was the studio's idea of 'serious'. It hymns, as the title suggests, the State Of, starting with several postcard views in Technicolor and a eulogy, one of several sickly songs, including 'Gold', which accompanies Eisenstein-like shots of greedy faces. Barbara Stanwyck does her own singing, and plays her usual wilful but essentially good woman; Milland can be no one's idea of an action hero. You know from the start that it will be a concocted story, and Farrow clearly shows his lack of interest.

They might as well have handed the subject to deMille, whose **Unconquered** (1947) is about the men 'who push ever forward the frontiers of man's freedoms', as represented by a dour Gary Cooper and a gauche Paulette Goddard. Incidentals include da Silva, excellent again, as the villain; Mr Mason, Mr Dixon and George Washington chuckling at the thought that Pittsburgh, 'this little village . . . will sprout into a city of maybe four or five thousand folk'; a waterfall rescue pinched from *Our Hospitality*; and a climax which gives Goddard a big moment as the Scottish pipes are heard, 'It is! It is! Chris got through!' For all its awfulness, the film demonstrates that reaffirmation of the principles of democracy deemed necessary after the recent world conflict – to which extent it differs from deMille's earlier pioneer dramas which, like his biblical epics, offer a more Victorian view of the triumph of the virtuous over the wicked.

He revived that genre with **Samson and Delilah** (1949), and since the tale had almost no relevance in the postwar world, we may assume its audience was attracted by the prospect of sin and spectacle. It broke every record except those held by *Gone with the Wind*, and yet its vulgarity is transcendent but dreary – except when Samson (Victor Mature) fights the lion, in close-up a moth-eaten old rug, while in long-shot the Samson does not remotely resemble the actor concerned. Since he was claimed to be Hollywood's beefiest man, and Hedy Lamarr its most beautiful woman, casting was thought to be ideal, but as her sister, Angela Lansbury alone of

the cast reassures. The collapse of the temple provides a climax, if a dim one.

The time had not yet come when the contempt of critics could harm such highly-publicised films and when deMille's next film garnered good notices – the first in a decade – it, in turn, became the second most profitable film ever made. **The Greatest Show on Earth** (1952), obviously a circus tale, also won a Best Picture Oscar – presumably since little was expected of deMille. Barnum and Baileys and the Ringling Bros. had just amalgamated, but that was not enough for deMille, who offers documentary footage and several parades – which are fine for those who like decorated floats. The plot concerns primarily a trapeze artist (Betty Hutton), the surly manager (Charlton Heston), and the guest star (Cornel Wilde), professional rival of the one and amatory rival of the other, muttering '*Nom de chien*' in lieu of a convincing French accent. Then there is Buttons (James Stewart), a murderer – a *good* one – hiding out in clown's make-up and redeeming himself by performing an emergency operation after a train crash (the coaches crumble like match-boxes, and one's concern is lessened by a jolly voice calling, 'Here's another corpse'). The film then finishes with the Show Going On, as they put it, 'under God's big top', by which time 153 minutes have passed, seemingly like hours. DeMille's final film, *The Ten Commandments* (1956) lasts 222 minutes, and I have never had the courage to see it. The public queued as before, and even in this age of television other studios were encouraged by its success to invest in projects equally grandiose: it was reasoned that other film-makers could do better, given big budgets and with a minimum of effort – and such indeed was the case.

Paramount's aversion to seriousness was traditional; one of its few topical films was based on a Broadway comedy, Norman Krasna's **Dear Ruth** (1947), as adapted by Arthur Sheekman and directed by William D. Russell. The situation set forth concerns a lieutenant (William Holden) who arrives to woo his pen-pal (Joan Caulfield), only to find that the letters were in fact written by her younger sister (Mona Freeman). Audiences presumably enjoyed Billy de Wolfe as the stuffed-shirt fiancé, and were titillated by the fact that the correspondence was reportedly 'hot', but today it is hard to see why the piece ran so long on Broadway or why the film was popular enough to give rise to two sequels.

Paramount's most important stars remained Bing Crosby and Bob Hope, overwhelmingly everyone's favourites in the postwar era. Since Hope's later films would be so poor, he needed to be rediscovered by a yet later generation – and he almost certainly benefits by putting his comic persona in the context of the War. He is frequently clumsy and cowardly when confronted with death, and his mock-heroic behaviour was probably a relief to audiences when the War was over, as in dazed reaction they wondered how they had coped. His popularity was enormous, and rather like that of Harold Lloyd, but unlike Lloyd his films tell us nothing about his time. A string of gags was built around his vanity and cowardice by, most notably, Jack Rose, Melville Shavelson, Don Hartman, Edmund Beloin, Melvin Frank and Norman Panama; his was a limited talent, and one of the joys of his films is that it is utilised to the full. He never doubts – such is his uncertain place in the world – chicanery all about him; advancing into middle age, he remains desperately anxious to be liked and is never fazed by innumerable rebuffs to his vanity and denigrations of his sex-appeal: one of the reasons he is so good with Crosby is that the latter's simple cunning is too subtle for such an innocent.

As we noted with his two wartime films for Goldwyn, *They Got Me Covered* and *The Princess and the Pirate*, Hope's writers had discovered that he was particularly effective in burlesque. In his prewar films it had been established that he was funny when faced with sudden death, but it was not until *The Ghost Breakers* that an element of spoofing was introduced, in that case on the 'old dark house' genre. The second 'Road' film was a burlesque of adventure films, and about the same time audiences laughed at a send-up of *The Thirty-Nine Steps*, *My Favorite Blonde*, which he made with Madeleine Carroll. He did two more in this splendid series, **My Favorite Brunette** (1947), directed by Elliott Nugent, with Dorothy Lamour, and **My Favorite Spy** (1951), directed by Norman Z. McLeod, with Hedy Lamarr. Miss Lamour is the brunette, a mysterious woman whose sanity is doubted by, *inter alia*, Peter Lorre, a deadly knife-thrower boning up on his examination for naturalisation, and Lon Chaney Jr, parodying his own performance in *Of Mice and Men*. Hope himself plays a baby photographer with aspirations of becoming a private eye: 'I'd rather be caught dead,' he exclaims, before realising what he has said. In *My Favorite Spy* he is set down in a singularly glamorous and inaccurate Tangier, to constantly dodge marksmen lurking behind doors, double-crossing women or even simply eavesdroppers. He plays a comic impersonating a master-spy – and if the description of the latter sounds like Ian Fleming planning the creation of James Bond, the film itself can be seen as a send-up of *Casablanca* and its imitations.

In **Where There's Life** (1947), directed by Sidney Lanfield, Hope is the target of a number of assassination attempts since he is the unwitting heir to a revolution-torn European kingdom; in **The Great Lover** (1947), directed by Alexander Hall, he is the butt of the boy scouts he is supposed to be squiring on an ocean liner, the panting aspirant for the love of a beautiful woman (Rhonda Fleming), the dupe of her impoverished father (Roland Culver), and best of all, the prey of a homicidal maniac (Roland Young). 'I always wanted to be a man about town' is his response to the prospect of dismemberment, and the line is from one of the two Damon Runyon films, **Sorrowful Jones** (1949) and **The Lemon-Drop Kid** (1951), both directed by Lanfield. Shyster and braggart, he fits absolutely into Runyon's world: 'You never heard my courage questioned,' he says to Lucille Ball, who shoots back, 'I never heard your courage mentioned' – and because she is a more forceful lead than Marilyn Maxwell, the earlier film is better. Both are remakes of films Paramount had done in the Thirties – the first as *Little Miss Marker* – and these late versions are, against the odds, sharper-eyed and harder-faced than their predecessors.

Monsieur Beaucaire (1946) puts Hope into Valentino's old swashbuckling role, and is rich in both incident and invention as directed by George Marshall; but the same director's **Fancy Pants** (1950) is a strident remake of *Ruggles of Red Gap*, not improved by the introduction of Miss Ball as a hoydenish heiress. This particular film

733

owed its inception to an earlier Hope excursion to the old West, **The Paleface** (1948), his most celebrated burlesque and his biggest success after the 'Road' films. He plays a dentist who discovers, as he says 'What Horace Greeley meant' on encountering Jane Russell. He is funny discovering that he is a hero, and there is an amusing sequence in a morgue (and a good song, 'Buttons and Bows'); but the plot thereafter lacks development. One of its writers, Frank Tashlin, blamed the director: 'I'd written a satire on *The Virginian* and it was completely botched. I could have killed that guy,' but Tashlin himself made a hash of the sequel, **Son of Paleface** (1952). Hope was instrumental in Tashlin becoming a director after shooting some sequences, uncredited, on *The Lemon-Drop Kid*. Earlier, Tashlin had worked on Warners' cartoons, and he tries to turn Hope into Bugs Bunny, making him skid through a series of doors, to emerge flattened, and so on. The film is crazy – but not in the manner of, say, *Million Dollar Legs*, which preferred its ineluctible view of the universe to a gag for its own sake.

Later, *Blazing Saddles* (q.v.) would try both approaches; Tashlin's jokes prefigure Mel Brooks, as when Roy Rogers says he prefers horses to women and Hope looks askance and steps aside. In failing to understand the nature of Hope's world and his persona, Tashlin did nothing to halt the decline of screen comedy: indeed, if the sequel is compared to *The Paleface* it may be said rather that he accelerates it. For Woody Allen (q.v.) a weekend 'of pure pleasure . . . would be to have half a dozen Bob Hope films and watch them, films like *Monsieur Beaucaire*.' In the light of the films made by Allen and Brooks, most of Hope's middle-period films can indeed be viewed with 'pure pleasure': it is a treat to see comedies so highly tooled, in which everything works.

Crosby's postwar films are not, on the other hand, a happy lot. In its time, **Blue Skies** (1946) wowed audiences: Crosby, Astaire and twenty Irving Berlin songs – plus Technicolor – were enough, since musicals were expected to have mindless plots. Like an earlier Berlin musical, *Alexander's Ragtime Band*, this one is about a romantic trio over the years, and like *Holiday Inn*, much of it is set in night clubs: but

with little period detail and nothing in the way of humour we are left, between songs, to study the familiar contours and colouring of the stars. Crosby is so much more interesting and charming than Astaire (Joan Caulfield's preference is quite understandable) that we may suppose Astaire was directed – by Stuart Heisler – so as to pose no real threat to Paramount's chief asset; Astaire, freelancing, is certainly given less to do. He announced his retirement while making this film, perhaps because he was only getting offers like this, as Bing's side-kick; M-G-M made him change his mind, and he never again appeared to such disadvantage.

Crosby's next few films owed much to *Going My Way*, including the two in which he was again teamed with Barry Fitzgerald: **Welcome Stranger** (1947), directed by Elliott Nugent, as rival doctors against a background of small town politicking *à la* Capra, and **Top o' the Morning** (1949), directed by David Miller, a dire tale about the theft of the Blarney Stone. In the Thirties Crosby's songs – 'I've Got a Pocketful of Dreams', 'Pennies from Heaven' – suited both him and the times, but as Father O'Malley he had delved deeper into the realm of homespun philosophy, 'In the Land of Beginning Again', 'Aren't You Glad You're You?'; thus, after the credits of *Welcome Stranger* he's enjoining us to 'Smile Right Back at the Sun', and in **A Connecticut Yankee in King Arthur's Court** (1949) he is found telling a crowd of children what to do 'If You Stub Your Toe on the Moon'. This film is clumsily directed by Tay Garnett, and hideously decorated, destroying any lingering fantasy in Mark Twain's old tale. Attempting to take on Will Rogers's mantle was not wise, and Crosby reverted to a more natural role as a Broadway star of his own age in **Mr Music** (1950), a loose remake of *Accent on Youth*, with Nancy Olsen as the younger girl with a crush. Standing apart from her and taking its tone from Crosby's easy manner, Richard Haydn's direction is sluggish and the staging of the numbers so tired and over-deliberate that one of Bing's best scores (by Burke and Van Heusen) remains unknown to this day. Crosby seems to have been not so much a poor chooser as a modest one, perhaps leaving too much to the Paramount team, which over-calculated: on the other hand, his musicals of the Thirties remain simple and pleasing.

Paramount's most important female star at this time was Betty Hutton, whose popularity surprised the front office: taken on as a singer and character comedienne, she soon graduated to leading roles. She is remembered for three show business biographies, and indeed it was the popularity of the first of them, in conjunction with *The Jolson Story* (q.v.), which opened the floodgates for films in which stars of the past were revived against a background of their songs, a largely fictional summary of their unhappy love lives, and a usually sketchy portrait of their times. In **Incendiary Blonde** (1945) Hutton is Texas Guinan, nightclub queen of the gangster era; in **The Perils of Pauline** (1947) she is Pearl White, Silent serial star; and in **Somebody Loves Me** (1952), Blossom Seeley, speakeasy singer. She loves and is ill-treated by three dull leading men – respectively Arturo de Cordova as a gangster, John Lund as an actor, and Ralph Meeker as a nonentity trying to get on in the business. As directed by George Marshall, the first two films have a certain gusto, and an affection for the days of tatty touring companies and Silent serials. *Incendiary Blonde* was the first film to treat the subject since *Hollywood Cavalcade*, and its other embellishments were also then rare, including an unhappy ending which is comparable only with that of the Astaire-Rogers film about the Castles, and much better judged. The star herself can be appealing when she sings, either noisily or wistfully, and as an actress her eagerness and enthusiasm are initially touching; but she cannot, for instance, sit in the gallery and watch one of Lund's performances without making moues of approval all the time. Nor was she anything like the ladies she portrayed – for old films reveal Guinan and Seeley to have been tough old birds. The three movies do not represent a trilogy, since that suggests a certain dynamism, and the last of them, as written and directed by Irving Brecher, is exceptionally tired. It demonstrates Paramount at its most commercial, unimaginative and opportunistic, since Hutton was also scheduled to play Mabel Normand, Sophie Tucker, one of the Duncan Sisters, and so on; but she quarrelled with Paramount over her next director and walked out. Her appeal was probably exhausted, since she did not make a career in television, as did Hope and Crosby when their film popularity waned. Apart from one programmer for an independent she did not film again, evidence that defiance of the studio ruined her career, probably the last example of such an outcome, since the studio system itself was crumbling.

The stars themselves now began to realise that they did not need long-term contracts to survive; they could earn more by moving around, and perhaps prolong their careers by choosing freely (the major grievance was not being tied *per se*, but being forced into uncongenial projects or loan-outs on which the studio made huge profits on their fees). In their turn, the studios found, as audiences deserted them for television, that they were paying players whose actual drawing power was small. At Warners, during the late Forties, around thirty of them could expect to have their name above the title but a mere handful could be called popular. In 1945, almost all studio activity centred on these – Davis, Bogart, Flynn, Lupino, Crawford, Sheridan and Garfield: most of them had been there since 1938. But by 1952 they had left – and already gone or going were those who had come up in the meantime – Doris Day, Kirk Douglas and Jane Wyman.

The dominant figures were Davis and Bogart: her success mesmerised the front office, which had under contract a number of similarly 'strong' actresses – to associate Warners in the public mind with 'women's pictures', and to take over the scripts that she turned down. Bogart was less easy to replace: Cagney and Robinson, the obvious choices, were reluctant to return. Thus the majority of Warner films were vehicles for their women stars.

A Stolen Life (1946) was originally written by Margaret Kennedy to allow Elisabeth Bergner the chance to show her talent as twin sisters. Davis chose it as her first 'independent' production under a new contract. The sisters are rivals in love, the men in their lives including a surly painter (Dane Clark) and a ferryman (Glenn Ford), whose sudden promotion to a business career in Chile is the sort of leap that only films like this can make. What makes it interesting is Davis, as the impostor, encountering classic situations as in the

735

later *Dead Ringer* (q.v.), not knowing which door to use, the dog not recognising her. As directed by Curtis Bernhardt, she tries no great feat of differentiation, being reasonable and straightforward as the heroine and hardly less so as her shallow rival. **Winter Meeting** (1948) confirms her as the best actress of her time. In her imperious moments she is mannered, but in her quieter moments there is no one as relaxed or as able to suggest a thinking woman. She plays a spinster publisher involved with a naval hero (Jim Davis) – a relationship probably futile, since he wants to be a priest. This actor's lumbering integrity is very convincing, but at the time he shared in the opprobrium cast upon the film by reviewers, possibly bewildered by a suggestion of depth and an almost complete lack of melodrama. The ending is trite, but under Bretaigne Windust's direction the film is sharp on certain strata of New York society, and Catherine Turney's dialogue (as in *A Stolen Life*) avoids clichés.

The vibrant intelligence of Davis could make endurable, if not save, a film as bad as **Deception** (1946), directed by Irving Rapper: so we cannot therefore disregard his claim that in fact she directed the films on which they worked together. This one is about good music, and at Warners, where good music was concerned it was class all the way. Just before Joan Crawford romanced John Garfield in the ritziest of apartments in *Humoresque* (q.v.), Davis shot Claude Rains on the grandest of grand staircases in *Deception*. Since her penthouse must be the biggest in New York, the emotions on display are of the same size. She has deserted the world-famous conductor (Rains) for an old love, a violinist (Paul Henreid); when the former turns up at the wedding reception, Davis says feebly – if that adverb could ever be applied to her behaviour – that there had not been time to send an invitation. With poise, she continues to eat her meal, while he observes that the caviare is over-chilled: but they do not ignore the situation. 'Have one husband, have eight,' says Rains in his matter-of-fact fashion, 'but you'll come back to me.' Memorable moments in movies have often nothing to do with life, but the pleasure of this one is that, while it is wholly artificial, there is the nagging thought that this woman, having deceived

both her men, might just continue to wolf down her smoked turkey as if nothing had happened.

The director of **Beyond the Forest** (1949) is the once-great King Vidor, and it is a long way behind its contemporary films, such concurrent items as *The File on Thelma Jordan* and *The Reckless Moment*, surely equally synthetic on paper. Davis must take some of the blame – for the absurd décolletage, the hip-swinging and the Charles Addams hairdo. It was she who had started the 'wicked lady' cycle, and this was the last in a decade rich with them: a better actress than others who played these ladies, her performance of this small-town tramp compounded the miscasting. She loathed Vidor and the whole production, believing herself too old – and not the person to hesitate if she wanted to go to Chicago (a device on which the plot hinges); she also thought Eugene Pallette would have been more suitable than Joseph Cotten as the cuckolded husband. 'You're something for the birds, Rosa,' says one of her victims, and so is the film. It ended (by mutual consent) her eighteen years with Warners. Perhaps only the association between M-G-M and Garbo has left a more worthwhile record of an actress and her art.

Writing at the time, Jympson Harman is the London *Evening News* would appear not to agree: 'Nothing seems to happen to disturb my impression that Joan Crawford is the best dramatic actress on the screen today. Bette Davis is a fine runner-up, but her performances are always impregnated with the B.D. personality' – and you wonder how and why he could ever have imagined that the Crawford roles were not 'impregnated' with the 'J.C.' personality. Curtis Bernhardt, the director of the film in question – *Possessed* (q.v.) – observed that it took Crawford twenty minutes to emerge from any given expression after a take, and I must say that that sounds more like her. Her limitations are legendary, and may today be mesmerising – for instance, in the curious way she speaks to domestic servants in her films, as if incredulous that she is not in their place. But was it for such reasons audiences went to watch her play the same monstrous woman in what must often have seemed like the same film? After leaving M-G-M she sat around at Warners for a couple of years before

The melodramas that Joan Crawford made for Warner Bros. provide a field day for lovers of the genre. She was often found, as here, with a gun in her hand and a mink over her shoulder – the mink usually having been earned the hard way, since that had been the subject of her first Warner film, and these were strictly formula pieces. The one with the nearest connection to real life – which is not saying much – is *Flamingo Road*, which also boasts the presence of Sydney Greenstreet, who for most of the film tries to get her out of town. Hence the gun, for Joan was not a girl to be treated that way.

making **Mildred Pierce** (1945), playing a woman who works her claws to the bone for the sake of her daughter (Ann Blyth), who gets meaner by the minute. As written by Ranald McDougall from a novel by James M. Cain, there is a certain fascination in the vicissitudes of these two ladies, and Michael Curtiz gets excellent performances from Warners' not-always-reliable second-stringers, Jack Carson, Zachary Scott and Bruce Bennett. As Crawford's employer and friend, Eve Arden is much more alive and interesting than she is, but nevertheless Crawford won an Oscar as Best Actress and entered a new period of popularity.

In **Humoresque** (1946) she is a bored society dame and John Garfield is a violinist. 'He's rather what you find in a Van Gogh painting,' she says, 'a touch of the savage.' She tells him, 'I have the reputation of knowing about good clothes, good food and good wine,' adding, 'Do you like martinis? They're an acquired taste, like Ravel.' Clifford Odets (reworking an unused screenplay he had written for *Rhapsody in Blue*, q.v.) and Zachary Gold pro-

vided these words, or mined them from a novel by Fannie Hurst; Jean Negulesco directed, failing to persuade his 'strong' star team that they were acting in the same film. It is not that their styles are different, but Garfield has little to do but look dedicated to his violin, and she little but to look dedicated to him: since clearly neither of them felt that way it is a very ho-hum humoresque. While he plays a transcription of the 'Liebestod' – called here 'the love music from "Tristan" ' – she walks out of her beach-house into the sea, just like Norman Maine except for the shimmering evening-gown. Why, is not clear, but as Oscar Levant had put it earlier, 'She's as complex as a Bach fugue.' The last word is Levant's, and it comes early in the film: 'Schmaltz? You want schmaltz?'

In the course of **Possessed** (1947) Crawford tries desperately to cling to a man who doesn't love her, marries a man she doesn't love and tries by fair means and foul to prevent her step-daughter from seeing her old flame, and when that doesn't work, shoots him dead. As the film starts she is in a catatonic trance, and as she recalls her

737

past we discover that she has suffered from hallucinations, brainstorms, persecution mania, homicidal mania, schizophrenia, paranoia, and traumas, not to mention various attacks of jealousy and false accusations of guilt – all in ankle-strap shoes and the Adrian shoulder-pads which she herself thought as passé as 'the improbable corn' of **This Woman Is Dangerous** (1952). She left Warners because of *This Woman Is Dangerous*, but it is difficult for most of us to find any distinction between her films of this period. In this one, directed by Felix Feist, she is a high class gangster's moll and criminal mastermind, and it has to be admitted that she does try for a new expression – a sort of agonised apprehension appropriate for someone on the verge of reformation. Yet she can be surprising: as a housewife in R.K.O.'s *Sudden Fear* (q.v.) she is hard-bitten, but as a cooch-dancer in **Flamingo Road** (1949) she is demure. Flamingo Road is the local version of Nob Hill, to which cooch-dancers can make it if ambitious enough; with a good villain (Sydney Greenstreet), a touch of civic corruption and some of Curtiz's best-paced direction, this is the most reasonable of Crawford's Warner melodramas.

Ann Sheridan was promoted from light roles to similar parts. In **Nora Prentiss** (1947) and **The Unfaithful** (1947), the warmth of her personality almost nullifies the most grotesque wardrobes and coiffures ever landed on a queen of soap opera. Vincent Sherman directed both, using the streets of San Francisco and Los Angeles respectively in the way demonstrated by 20th Century-Fox – if only tentatively – and realism extends no further: both are excellent examples of films where no one makes the obvious remark or asks the obvious question. Warners, unrivalled in recycling old material, surpassed themselves on both occasions: the screenplay for the former, by N. Richard Nash, borrows from 'Sister Carrie', *The Blue Angel*, Dr Crippen, *Phantom of the Opera* and *Brief Encounter*, being about an unhappily married doctor (Kent Smith) who falls for a nightclub singer (Sheridan) and tries to start a new life; the latter, though boasting an 'original screenplay' by David Goodis and James Gunn, is recognisable as *The Letter*, the infidelity in this case caused by the separations of war.

War was a useful ingredient in these women's pictures, reminding the still-serving G.I. audiences of the problems of their women at home. Warner writers did not forget the War as quickly as those at other studios, revealing a residue of that old social conscience; and it is probable that their strong, managing heroines struck a chord with those returning servicemen who were having difficulty in adjusting. Barbara Stanwyck drew two of the lighter assignments. In **Christmas in Connecticut** (1945) she is a phoney cookery expert whose editor (Sydney Greenstreet) demands that she entertain a wounded veteran (Dennis Morgan) for the festive season; but as directed by Peter Godfrey matters deteriorate after a promising start. In **My Reputation** (1946) she is a war widow who changes her mind about remarrying after meeting a major (George Brent), though assuring her sons that she will never forget their father. She is seen going into the major's hotel room, but again, as directed by Curtis Bernhardt, the distance from real life is enormous, and there is no suggestion that anyone had ever heard of a bed: it must seem bizarre to a generation not reared on such films.

Ida Lupino never reached the stature of the other Warners ladies, but for those sufficiently perverse she may be enjoyed in **Devotion** (1946). Richard Winnington wrote: 'As one who has spent hours pondering on the aching enigma of the Brontës in front of Branwell's badly painted and beautiful portrait of them in the National Portrait Gallery, I found *Devotion* painless. It never got nearer to the subject than names and consequently didn't hurt.' Here, Charlotte (Olivia de Havilland) learns the bitter truth from Thackeray (Sydney Greenstreet), that 'Wuthering Heights' was created from Emily's frustrated love for the Reverend Arthur Bell Nicholls; here, Charlotte is a self-centred, scheming coquette, revelling in the attentions of London society (whereas in fact she was so shy that she became physically ill). Here the three sisters dress not in drab parsonage clothes but in magnificent crinolines for the ball. Lupino plays Emily, another fate Emily did not deserve; the unbending and unattractive Nicholls is played by the 'charming' and unattractive Paul Henreid, with an Austrian accent – while Branwell (Arthur

Kennedy) has an American one. When the truth is so astounding and heart-breaking, why could they not have used it? The chief culprits are Keith Winter, who wrote it, and director Bernhardt, who later compounded his crime by saying, 'This is the kind of film I like to do. I'd always been interested in the Brontës.'

It would be nice to think that Warners had doubts about the film, for it was one of several whose release was delayed for a couple of years. Another was **Saratoga Trunk** (1945), made by Gary Cooper and Ingrid Bergman on completing *For Whom the Bell Tolls* at Paramount, with Sam Wood again directing – and refusing to take seriously this pseudo-epic of the early days of the railroad. Edna Ferber's novel about a Creole adventuress had been bought in the hope that Vivien Leigh would play it, and certainly Bergman is not as good as she – or Bette Davis – would have been, for she was not a 'scheming' actress. However, her scenes with Cooper work – he seeing through her plotting, and she knowing that he does – partly because of his sure sense of comedy. Like the Warner films of another era, this one is always prepared to sacrifice probability for humour. It played in army camps in 1943, but was withheld from public exhibition till audiences were flocking to see Miss Bergman in *Spellbound* and *The Bells of St Mary's*, presumably on the assumption that they could then better appreciate her versatility.

Warners though that in Viveca Lindfors they had found a new Bergman. She was Swedish also, and **Night Unto Night** (1949) was intended to make her a big star. She is discovered, clearly disturbed, in a house in Key West, when Ronald Reagan comes along: 'I'm a scientist,' he tells her pal – Broderick Crawford as a kitsch William Blake. 'One of those atomic-bomb fellas?' asks Crawford, but it turns out that he is on the side of humanity – creating, not destroying. He too, is sick, subject to 'low-grade epilepsy', which means that he has seizures; Crawford has an exhibition of his paintings, and Lindfors has a nymphomaniac sister (Osa Massen), who, like all such ladies in movies, is also a drunk. The direction is by Don Siegel (b. 1912), former chief editor for the studio – in which capacity he was responsible for some of its most renowned montage sequences.

From the ranks of Warners' second leads, Jane Wyman found a huge popularity with **Johnny Belinda** (1948) as a deaf-mute victim of a rape. It seems to me a sober and decent picture, despite the melodrama and a self-conscious attempt at poetry. Warners had bought the play by Elmer Harris, and assigned it to producer Jerry Wald and director Negulesco, both of whom recognised its true worth but felt that with tact a good movie could be wrested from it. Jack Warner loathed the result so much that he shelved it and sacked Negulesco, which indicates that working on location (in California), Negulesco did things very much his own way: certainly this Nova Scotia community is tenderly evoked. Charles Bickford and Agnes Moorehead are believable as people who have spent their lives tilling the soil; as the rake turned rapist, Stephen McNally is rightly just a village bully, and Jan Sterling is his complement as the girl who marries him. Lew Ayres makes an admirable centrepiece as the doctor, and Miss Wyman blessedly underplays (she studied for the role at a school for the dumb, and used wax in her ears on the set). She won a famous Oscar and, if not giving evidence of overwhelming talent, succeeds marvellously in what I think with anyone else would have been a lesser picture. It is worth adding, because it is seldom revived, that it was in its day a great success with both critics and public.

At Warners Miss Wyman made only one other worthwhile film, **The Glass Menagerie** (1950) the screen version of Tennessee Williams's first stage success. It was poorly received, and I have never come across anyone with a fondness for it apart from myself. As Williams knew, the mood was Tchekhovian – well-meaning people but forlorn, saturated in yearning, frustration and faded dreams. If the actors can only show their concern for each other, where appropriate, the piece plays itself, as it does here under the direction of Irving Rapper. As the painfully shy and lame Laura, Miss Wyman smiles meekly, speaks in a whisper, and betrays occasional panic: she is very likeable, which may not be said for Arthur Kennedy as her brother or Kirk Douglas as the consciously charming Gentleman Caller, but the piece does not depend on them for its effectiveness. As the mother, the role in which Laurette Taylor had made her celebrated return to the stage, Gertrude Lawrence made one of her rare screen appearances, and it was not difficult for this actress to suggest a woman who once had great charm before she lost heart.

Warners' interest in Broadway brought them **Life with Father** (1947), based on Clarence Day's reminiscences of his stern and eccentric father as published in *The New Yorker*; the dramatised version by Howard Lindsay and Russell Crouse had opened in 1939, and Warners were forbidden to release their film till its run finished, which is still a Broadway record for a straight play. The late appearance of the movie did not affect its popularity in cinemas, but there were too many imitations for it to be of much interest today. Cosy, unadventurous, it offers family drama and comedy but, despite the direction of Michael Curtiz, not enough of either. Its chief pleasures are the performances of William Powell and Irene Dunne; and if he plays with the twinkle necessary for sympathetic audience reaction she, commendably, does not.

Broadway was also raided, after a fashion, for **Rhapsody in Blue** (1945). George Gershwin had been dead for only seven years but, as an acknowledged folk hero, was a sure subject for film treatment – which in this case includes a laudable concentration on his serious music, though apart from this audiences must endure a long movie of stupefying banality. After a fair portrait of a vaguely Jewish family, it depicts Gershwin's career as the usual toss-up between jazz and serious music, with his off-duty moments split between the chorus girl (Joan Leslie) who is his one endearing love, and the society beauty (Alexis Smith) who dallies with him at the height of his fame. He is portrayed as inordinately vain, but it is hinted that this is only a passing phase: certainly as played by Robert Alda he has no more character than have the two ladies. Ferde Grofe, who worked with Gershwin, did the arrangement of the Rhapsody, and Walter Damrosch and Paul Whiteman appear to conduct the pieces as they had originally done. Jolson appears as himself, to be thanked sycophantically for singing 'Swanee', and the original Bess (Anne Brown) is made to sing 'Summertime', which is not one of Bess's songs in 'Porgy and Bess'; more questionable is Oscar Levant's appearance as himself, since he was supposed to be a friend of Gershwin.

On the lighter side, Warners offered **Always Leave Them Laughing** (1949), a saga of a big-headed and second-rate vaudeville comic, played by Milton Berle, who had been in vaudeville and who was otherwise known for supporting roles in a few movies. In 1948 he went into T.V., the new medium, and became known as 'Mr Television'; his popularity was the alleged reason for the upsurge in the sale of sets (numbering around 190,000) by the end of that year. Much care went into packaging him for the cinema public. Roy del Ruth directed, and Melville Shavelson and Jack Rose wrote the screenplay, which leaves no facet of Berle undemonstrated. He might have had a longer cinema career had they done otherwise; the quick failure of this film caused the other Hollywood studios to look askance on T.V. 'stars' for at least another decade.[*]

Warners did not have a female star for musicals of their own, though that did not prevent them from turning out several musicals every year, often with the duo of Dennis Morgan and Jack Carson, who were some light years behind Crosby and Hope. A band singer, Doris Day (b. 1924) eventully arrived, with pretty, healthy looks, a natural smile and a fetching gawkiness, as well as a singing voice which was not only very much in the fashion of the time but relaxed and increasingly versatile. Warners could only see her as a surrogate Betty Hutton, and thus she was in her first film, **Romance on the High Seas** (1948), an attempt by Curtiz (producing and directing) at a Lubitsch-style marital musical. Immediate public response enabled Day to get away from the Hutton curls, and she appeared to advantage in **Tea for Two** (1950) and **Lullaby of Broadway** (1951), both directed by David Butler. In the wake of M-G-M's success, Warners had realised that the public was tiring of the backstage formula, and if both films are better than most of their predecessors, they are still not good enough. *Tea for Two* uses some songs from 'No, No Nanette' and is set in the Twenties, but apart from a mild Charleston makes nothing of the period; we can,

---

[*]Warners had another failure with a T.V. name, Liberace, in *Sincerely Yours* in 1955.

however, recognise that Harry Clork's screenplay aspires to 'musical comedy'. *Lullaby of Broadway* also has several old songs, comedy relief, and a fair screenplay (by Earl Baldwin) on the subject of a girl (Miss Day) suspected of being an old man's darling. Gladys George is her mother, and Gene Nelson was promoted from the earlier film to leading man, but although a good dancer he lacks star quality as an actor.

I'll See You in My Dreams (1951) is one of the last and best of show business biographies as written by Shavelson and Rose and directed by Curtiz, as ever providing pasteboard characters with some dimension. Its subject is Gus Kahn, and it was observed that since Hollywood had run out of composers it was turning in desperation to the lyricists. His life apparently differed little from the composers, and one would have liked more on his collaborators – who included Gershwin – and perhaps greater honesty on his 'managing' wife (Miss Day). Danny Thomas plays Kahn as a schnook, but for all that the film is low-keyed and affectionate.

Young Man with a Horn (1950) was adapted from Dorothy Baker's novel based on the life of Bix Beiderbecke, who died at the age of twenty-eight with a reputation as one of the great white jazz musicians. As renamed Rick Martin (Kirk Douglas), he moves from a jazz-obsessed childhood to a society marriage to alcoholism – from which he is rescued by a band singer (Day) and 'Smoke' (Hoagy Carmichael), an experience which makes him 'a bedder person' as 'Smoke' confides to the camera. It is a good film, except for the interlude with the society girl, superficially written and then misinterpreted by Lauren Bacall. Douglas is not entirely taking, especially when reeling down Third Avenue at dawn – the inevitable ending of such tales, already featured in *Swing High, Swing Low* and *Blues in the Night*. Curtiz makes the major contribution; he always placed his camera for the utmost effect and in this case he uses it for the expression of the music, honing in on, or moving away from, dance halls, jazz-joints and Village bars. The music includes more great songs than in any other movie I can think of, for instance, 'Someone to Watch Over Me' and 'Can't We Be Friends'. They are not reproduced in the manner of the period –

Harry James ghosted the trumpet – but for once it does not matter.

'At fifteen,' says Miss Day in **The West Point Story** (1950), 'I was singing with a band, one-night stands. At seventeen I had a Hollywood contract. I'm a commodity now, not a woman,' but after this promisingly harsh start the story turns into a compound of those of *Varsity Show* and *Flirtation Walk*. James Cagney repeats his role in *Footlight Parade*, that of the hustling show director who, when crossed, becomes a bouncing ball of fury: but the pugnacity sits less easily on a thick-set, middle-aged man. No one could resist his younger self, but here he is for admirers only. Roy del Ruth directed, and apart from Day and Gordon MacRae he and Cagney lack the skilled co-players of their great days at Warners.

Cagney had returned to Warners for **White Heat** (1949), which was occasioned by Zanuck's imitations of their own early gangster films. Twenty years later a gangster's life has become more difficult, and Jody Garrett (Cagney) is reduced to hiding out in a cold, tacky bungalow with his gang: Ma (Margaret Wycherly), his cheap wife (Virginia Mayo), his aide, Big Ed (Steve Cochran) and a man whose face is a mess of bandages. As directed by Raoul Walsh, the mood is sour and grim; the prison sequences are the best that Warners ever did, and it is impossible to forget Garrett's epileptic fit or his final shriek as the police snipe at him above the oil tanks, 'Top of the world, Ma, top of the world!' It is an ironic postscript to *Public Enemy*. The mother in that film was motherhood sanctified, but the one in this is even more demoniacal than Cagney; his wife gets only a kick in the butt when she takes up with Big Ed – because 'All I ever had is Ma.' This Oedipus complex was Cagney's own idea: in his memoir he is insistent that most Warner scripts were 'the same old thing', and that he did what he could to give them individuality* – in this case conceiving the idea of modelling the gang on Ma Barker and her boys. Miss Wycherly is superb, and the others are good, including Edmond O'Brien as an undercover man and Fred Clark as a criminal

---

*I once came upon a copy of *L'Express*, reviewing this film on a Paris revival in 1963 and devoting its flattery to the director: ironically in its two-page review it did not see fit to mention Cagney's name.

After emerging as the biggest star on the Warner Bros. lot Humphrey Bogart never quite forgave his employers for keeping him so long as a supporting actor. And it was hard to blame him, for they seemed incapable of finding a worthy vehicle after *Casablanca* – except for three that he made with Lauren Bacall, *To Have and Have Not*, *The Big Sleep* and *Key Largo*. There was a fourth, *Dark Passage*, illustrated here because this picture conveys something of their appeal as a team.

mastermind: but one comes away pondering on the appeal of the star, here at the end of a lifetime of crime.

The writers for *White Heat* were the team of Ivan Goff and Ben Roberts, who also wrote **Come Fill the Cup** (1951) for Cagney. He plays an alcoholic reporter rehabilitated by an 'ex-alkie' (James Gleason), asked in turn by his boss (Raymond Massey) to help his nephew (Gig Young), a composer, whose drinking prevents him from finishing his concerto; the latter is also married to the reporter's ex-girlfriend (Phyllis Thaxter) and the climax has a gangster forcing the two men to get drunk at gunpoint. Virtually every review evoked *The Lost Weekend*, but here the intelligent beginning gives way to matters more lurid. It remains well directed, by Gordon Douglas; Cagney is at his most subdued and humorous – probably the most likeable of his later performances.

He moves close to self-parody in **A**

Lion Is in the Streets (1953), as uncertainly directed by Walsh. Cagney is at the same time the film's strength and weakness, playing with characteristic intensity and attempting gestures that a lesser actor would not dare. The role is not easy: it is that of a pedlar with an obsessive interest in law whose ambitions – not credibly deployed – lead to the governor's mansion. Adria Locke Langley's original novel, like 'All the King's Men', was based on the career of Huey Long and is reputedly more accurate; Columbia, which had made a film of that book (q.v.), sued Warners for plagiarism (it is surprising that the Hollywood studios were not suing each other all the time), but the films are dissimilar except in outline. The Columbia film was in newsreel style and this is in Technicolor – both to attract audiences which had seen that and to present the story in appropriate picture-book manner: the American dream gone sour, Huck Finn grown up and gone bent.

Apart from the films he made with John Huston, Humphrey Bogart also fared uneasily during his last years at Warners. He is at his peak in **The Big Sleep** (1946), returning to his most satisfying incarnation, the private eye. There may be distinctions between Sam Spade in *The Maltese Falcon* and Philip Marlowe in this film, but Bogart is superb as both: each film is so strong that it is impossible to confuse them. The confusion that arises in *The Big Sleep* has to do with the narrative. The director, Howard Hawks, said that no one could follow it; the author, Raymond Chandler, when appealed to, could not enlighten him; and William Faulkner, Leigh Brackett and Jules Furthman, writing the screenplay, were unable to clarify it. Whatever the convolutions – and I have never heard anyone express the least dissatisfaction with this film – the result is recognisably Chandler. It may not be visually distinctive, but there is nothing equivocal about the environment or, except where necessary, the characters: the multi-millionaire (Charles Waldron), living in an orchid hothouse to survive; his vulpine daughters, the thumb-sucking nymphomaniac (Martha Vickers) and the insolent divorcée (Lauren Bacall); the bland and cringing bodyguard (Elisha Cook, Jr); the pince-nezed librarian (Dorothy Malone), a rare Forties example of the quick lay; and the various black-mailers and scroungers, all-American footballers gone to seed. Bogart has some searing dialogue, notably his exchange with John Ridgely which builds to the latter's 'I could make your business my business,' and Bogart's rueful response, 'You wouldn't like it, the pay's too small.' The rather déclassé savoir-faire, the sardonic humour, the hunch-backed acceptance of these appointments with fear: Chandler might have created Marlowe for him.

Bogart and Bacall make a self-mocking, inexorable team, but the studio clearly had no idea how good they were together: reunited in **Dark Passage** (1947), she has a role that could have been played by any contract actress, and they are simply not given the teasing dialogue which was a feature of their earlier films together. The source, a novel by David Goodis, is clearly inferior, and Delmer Daves, writing and directing, is merely ponderous. The story concerns a convicted man trying to prove his innocence; Bacall attempts to help him, and Agnes Moorehead is her silly, loquacious sister. The latter takes whatever honours are going, but Bogart is hardly eligible, being seen only in longshot or shadow for the first thirty-five minutes, and then in bandages for the next twenty.

Returning to villainy, he was even less interesting. Capable of a wide range from pettiness to paranoia, he was not a natural wife-murderer, though Warners, having failed with him in **Conflict** (1945), had him at it again in **The Two Mrs Carrolls** (1947). The first, directed by Curtis Bernhardt and adapted from a story by Robert Siodmak and Alfred Neumann, has Bogart bewildered as mounting evidence suggests that the wife is alive after all; the second film sins more grievously, since the wife is Barbara Stanwyck and this is the only time she and Bogart appeared together. The teaming should have left us some tough, slangy drama instead of this cheerless enterprise, drawn from a West End thriller already over a decade old. In the original, there is some doubt as to whether Mr Carroll had murdered the first Mrs C., but this version throws away even that mild bit of suspense. Peter Godfrey directed but, unlike his work on *The Woman in White*, fails to offer a plausible England.

The Enforcer (1951) was Bogart's last film for Warners, and as with Cagney in *White Heat*, an excellent return to beginnings. The British title, *Murder Inc.*, is more telling – and, I should have thought, more enticing to prospective patrons. Notably well constructed – despite flashbacks within flashbacks – it starts on the night before an important trial, with the Assistant D.A. (Bogart) protecting his only witness – a vital one. Raoul Walsh apparently directed most of the film, though the credited director is Bretaigne Windust. A largely unfamiliar cast add to the authenticity, but we may also enjoy some actors we know: Everett Sloane is the mastermind, Zero Mostel the one who cracks; and Bogart is admirable, despite his claim that he had played the role so often that he did it mechanically.

Errol Flynn, another Warner veteran, continued his career in mainly indifferent vehicles. Among the more ambitious is **Silver River** (1948), directed by Walsh. It is set in the West, but Flynn wears silk hat rather than Stetson, since this is one of the many tales of nineteenth-century cattle barons and their ambitions. Ann Sheridan is Bathsheba to Flynn's David, an analogy given emphasis in the script by Harriet Frank Jr and Stephen Longstreet, from his novel. The film did not halt Flynn's waning popularity, so it was courageous of Warners to pour money into **The Adventures of Don Juan** (1948), another example of the studio returning successfully to a particular genre after a long break. The settings are among the most lavish ever, and the costumes among the most sumptuous – owing much to Velázquez, though internal evidence places the action between 1558 and 1603. Vincent Sherman directed, lightheartedly, and the merely serviceable plot provides multiple opportunities for action and intrigue. The writers were Harry Kurnitz and George Oppenheimer, who said 'It's like a piece of Venetian glass,' to which Jack Warner replied 'To hell with that. You know Flynn, he's either got to be fighting or fucking.' Sherman has said that Flynn was no great swordsman, but that he could appear so, adding that he was 'an incipient homosexual' (he designed his own costumes, insisting upon unnaturally tight tights). Sherman also observed that Flynn was more conscientious than he pretended to be, and one can sense behind the breezy charm a sad man – his drinking problem was now extreme – trying to do his job. That is the nearest the film gets to Mozart's opera, from which Max Steiner borrows some of his themes; just as the duels borrow from Olivier's *Hamlet* (q.v.).

Peter Lorre, a deceptively timid villain, and Sydney Greenstreet, jovial and menacing, had become a star team – much to the credit of Warners, even if their films were allotted only medium budgets. In **The Verdict** (1946) it was clearly expedient for Don Siegel – in his first film as a director – to shroud Edwardian London in a fog even thicker than was usual, since that prevented the expense of exterior settings. Greenstreet is a Scotland Yard man with a guilty secret, Lorre is a hard-drinking artist – and Joan Lorring is a music-hall artist for whom Frederick Hollander has provided songs which are more Dietrich than Marie Lloyd. **Three Strangers** (1946) is also fogbound, with Geraldine Fitzgerald joining Lorre and Greenstreet to form a curious trio holding a sweepstake ticket; John Huston wrote the genuinely weird screenplay, and Negulesco takes it to a certain pitch.

Also set in a phoney London is **Confidential Agent** (1945) which Graham Greene thought the best American film of one of his novels – not necessarily a good adaptation, but an interesting film in its own right. Robert Buckner, the producer and writer, has kept the original premise – it could have been adapted to conventional espionage – that a Spanish republican (Charles Boyer) arrives in London to prevent the supplying of coal to the opposite side. I find, even in this painted Britain, the plangent Greene notes: the hotel skivvy whom the Spaniard befriends; the languages school for a form of Esperanto, where he meets Lorre; and the aristocratic girl (Lauren Bacall) too drunk on first meeting to prevent his being beaten up. She does not attempt an English accent – and Boyer, Lorre, Victor Francen and Katina Paxinou are hardly Spanish. Under Herman Shumlin's direction the result is crude, but not negligible.

Greene's novel, though set before the War, could have provided a platform for a discussion of contemporary problems. No more than the other companies were Warner Bros. interested in such matters –

buoyed up as the industry was with the box-office returns for the mindless entertainments which predominated as the War ended. As we have seen, certain directors toyed with postwar problems, but as far as the front office was concerned these were usually to be considered in terms of genres acceptable to the managers of the circuits. It is in this context that we should consider **Storm Warning** (1950). Warners' social reform melodramas had petered out, though Zanuck had remembered them and had recently emulated them. It was his films which prompted Jerry Wald to institute this one, based on a script by Richard Brooks and Daniel Fuchs which had been lying around for some time. It roundly condemns the Ku-Klux Klan as 'a group of wicked men' and with equal lack of subtlety offers a portrait of a town too self-absorbed, as in *Black Legion*, to be aware of the canker in its midst. The members of the Klan are merely 'a lot of hoodlums dressed up in sheets', as the D.A.'s deputy says, admitting that he had once been one of them. To this reasonable presentation – the town appears to have no racial problems – is added the situation of a model (Ginger Rogers), who witnesses a murder while visiting her sister (Doris Day) and recognises her brother-in-law (Steve Cochran) as the killer. She does the obvious thing – rare in such films – and tells her sister, but has a crisis of conscience on the witness stand. Her dilemma is foolishly resolved: we had noticed certain situations borrowed from 'A Streetcar Named Desire' and the film dallies with others from that play as it rushes downhill. Stuart Heisler's direction borrows from its prototype, *Fury*, and is further interesting in subduing Miss Rogers, who 'acts' less than in most of her straight roles, with a consequent gain in credibility.

King Vidor, once concerned with social questions, turned up at Warners, for whom he made three of his late quartet of melodramas: *Beyond the Forest*, already discussed, **The Fountainhead** (1949) and **Lightning Strikes Twice** (1951). 'Perhaps no other director has gone off the rails quite so spectacularly,' observed Gavin Lambert of the fourth, **Ruby Gentry** (1952), made independently and released by Fox. Though Vidor himself disliked *Lightning Strikes Twice*, which is about a girl (Ruth Roman) who refuses to believe that a dour Britisher (Richard Todd) is a wife-killer, he thought the others constituted 'a trilogy of modern American life'; and he scribbled on the script of *Ruby Gentry*, 'Motion pictures are an art form', to which Selznick retorted that this one at least was a commercial enterprise. *The Fountainhead* was written by Ayn Rand from her own novel, with dialogue as high-flown and fly-blown as the plot: an idealistic architect (Gary Cooper) is the object of a smear campaign waged by a newspaper tycoon (Raymond Massey) and a journalist (Patricia Neal) – who seduces the architect but marries the tycoon. On trial for blowing up one of his own buildings, the architect, like Mr Deeds, refuses to defend himself till the last minute, whereupon Massey realises that his wife loves him and shoots himself after one last commission: 'Build it as a monument to your spirit – which could have been mine.' The film ends with Neal symbolically going up in an elevator on the building-site where Cooper is symbolically waiting.

Ruby Gentry concerns a girl (Jennifer Jones) from the wrong side of the tracks who wears tight sweaters and jeans to indicate her wild spirit. The love of her life is Boake (Charlton Heston), who says, 'No woman like her – fightin', scratchin', next moment sweetest woman alive,' but marries another. Ruby, in the manner of her forebears Scarlett and Amber, cannot reconcile herself to losing him, so in revenge accepts the marriage proposal of her foster-father (Karl Malden): 'You and me's the sort of people . . . We're mongrels.' He is soon lost at sea, and the rumours grow till a crowd assembles outside her mansion to scream 'Murderess' – which provokes her to vindictiveness towards all and sundry, especially Boake, who understandably refuses to become her lover again, but later rapes her in revenge for having flooded his land. This director, let it be reminded, once made *The Crowd*.

Vidor's film with Gary Cooper is typical of Cooper's vehicles of this period, which include almost a dozen more unhappy ventures for Warners. **Distant Drums** (1951) is set in Florida, with Cooper as an Indian fighter commissioned to clear the Everglades of the Seminole. The screenplay by Niven Busch and Martin Rackin makes him even more monosyllabic than ever, and his lack of interest was surely increased by Mari Aldon, his leading lady, an ex-ballerina. She starts almost every scene leaning on a palm tree and gazing at the moon, presumably on the direction of Raoul Walsh, whose work here is of definitive ineptitude. In his long career there was only one period when his work was consistently good, from 1939 to 1945, his first few years at Warners – during which time the studio had probably the most proficient script department in Hollywood and the most skilful editors. This film, however, is completely without tension – the action scenes unroll as if by chance – the sort of hack job which made many people lose interest in Hollywood in the late Forties.

The matter of apportioning blame and credit in most studio films is a vexed one. Walsh 'signed' *White Heat* at a time when all his other films were mediocre, while Curtiz reached a last peak before he too declined – coinciding with his departure from Warners; but if it was the Warners' cutting-room which bailed out Curtiz, why did the editors not do the same for Walsh? All that is certain is that **The Breaking Point** (1950) is the best screen Hemingway since Borzage's *A Farewell to Arms*. Warners played down the Hemingway connection, since this was a remake of *To Have and Have Not* – though as faithful to the novel as the earlier film was not. It tells of a fisherman forced into transporting illegal immigrants; one major change from the novel is the substitution of California for Florida. A line of white-painted inexpensive bungalows shelters under a stormy sky, the first of Ted McCord's memorable compositions of harbours and boats, a large deserted waterfront restaurant, smoke-filled bars. Ranald McDougall's screenplay manages at times to parody both Hemingway and the star, John Garfield – for example, 'A man alone ain't got no chance.' The film is slick, but always pleasurable: the credit may not be due entirely to Curtiz, but some is certainly attributable to the good-time girl of Patricia Neal, taunting and confident, leaving the other vamps of the time at the starting-post.

Speaking of vamps, Columbia had one: 'There never was a woman like Gilda!' said the ads. 'Blimey! there never was,' said C. A. Lejeune, noting that after a while

745

It is now a little difficult to appreciate that Rita Hayworth in *Gilda* represented the height of Hollywood eroticism, though she was certainly very effective singing 'Put the Blame on Mame' – or, more correctly, mouthing it, since her singing voice was dubbed.

there is 'a suspicion, subsequently confirmed, that nothing is going to happen except Miss Hayworth'. Richard Winnington thought that to anyone uninterested in that lady 'it will look like one of the worst films in living memory'. Yet **Gilda** (1946) lives on, despite a director, Charles Vidor, and writers, Marion Parsonnet and Jo Eisinger, whose other credits show little else with a claim to immortality. The plot is a wild thing, consisting of skulduggery in and around a Buenos Aires nightclub, but in what is essentially a triangle drama the two men concerned seem to have been more than room-mates. The relationship is unprecedented in an American film, and that it then went unremarked may be attributed to the fact that most people were unprepared to consider the implications of the dialogue. 'You've no idea how faithful and obedient I can be,' says Glenn Ford to his boss (George Macready), and it must be said that this actor, with his bright

boy-gigolo manner, is unable to suggest ambiguity. When the boss – based on the Clifton Webb character in *Laura* – returns from distant parts with a wife (Rita Hayworth), the relationship between the two men changes – ostensibly because Ford had been in love with her years before, but clearly because the boss demands the return of the key to his bedroom. The role of Gilda was supposed to prove Hayworth a serious actress, and though most critics were unimpressed, she does project – for the last time on screen – a sort of silky earthiness. Her hair was ever her most alluring feature: she makes her first appearance from the bottom of the screen shaking it and later caresses her scalp as she sings 'Put the Blame on Mame'.

By the time she made **Affair in Trinidad** (1952) her charms had flown. This was *Gilda* revamped – an attempt to re-establish her after her years in Europe, loving and losing Aly Khan amidst great publicity. Ford is her co-star and Alexander Scourby is the suave older man; a sole back projection may be Port of Spain, but the film offers the standard South-of-the-Border nightclubs and mansions. The only interest is provided by a foreshadowing of the Cuba crisis: Scourby plans to establish rocket bases which 'will make Pearl Harbor seem like a slap on the wrist'. In *Gilda*, Macready schemed to master the world, and it is only too typical of Hollywood to have taken the worst of that film for this new edition: there is nothing in Vincent Sherman's direction to show that he knew what the worst of it was.

Salome (1953) boasted the cinema's love goddess in Technicolor as one of history's infamous women – no matter that the love goddess was by now too old and that the biblical Salome could hardly provide a full-length film. DeMille had turned Hedy Lamarr into Delilah, so Harry Cohn made Hayworth into Salome, even commissioning one of deMille's writers, Jesse Lasky Jr, to provide the story – which interestingly reveals that it was in fact Herodias (Judith Anderson) who demanded the head of John the Baptist (Alan Badel), so annoying Salome that she runs off with her Roman lover (Stewart Granger), a Christian, to listen to the Sermon on the Mount. The conception of Salome as a misunderstood and well-meaning young lady could have been funny, but Miss Hayworth's interpretation is no laughing matter. William Dieterle directed as though he had a respectable script, which was a mistake, and a good (British) supporting cast follows his lead: Cedric Hardwicke (Tiberius), Basil Sydney (Pontius Pilate), and Charles Laughton, whose Herod is not as rich as was his Nero.

Columbia's dependence on Miss Hayworth is almost all there is to say about the studio at this juncture. However, **The Jolson Story** (1946) was the company's biggest success at that time. It was the project of Sidney Skolsky, a newspaperman, who braved the indifference of the film industry and eventually sold the idea to Harry Cohn. Jolson wanted to play himself, so it was much to his chagrin that they chose a contract player, Larry Parks, to play the role. The movie uses only cliché as he goes from boyhood to the break-up of his marriage to Ruby Keeler, here called 'Julie Benson', since Miss Keeler refused to allow her name to be used; Evelyn Keyes's manicured performance is little like the original. Alfred E. Green directed, but was replaced by Henry Levin on **Jolson Sings Again** (1949), though that belongs less with the original than to something like *Freaks*. It starts with Jolson as half-forgotten (though only he himself is permitted to refer to his faded popularity) and describes his restitution via a film of his life. Parks plays himself as well – a mite less convincingly than his ungalvanic impersonation of Jolson – and undreamed-of heights are achieved when he goes with Jolson (Parks) to a preview of *The Jolson Story*: though if Levin had tried harder he could have got three Jolson/Parks on the screen at the same time – the two in the audience watching the one in the film. That might have been preferable to what seems to be a total reprise of the songs from the earlier film – yet the Jolson songs and the Jolson voice were the ingredients which made these two films so popular.

All the King's Men (1949) was the studio's first responsible film since Capra; it was written, produced and directed by Robert Rossen (1908–66), a former screenwriter, whose second film as director, *Body and Soul* (q.v.), had received much praise. This one is based on the Pulitzer Prize-winning novel by Robert Penn Warren, and is based on the life and times of Huey 'Kingfisher' Long, Governor of Louisiana, but with as much interest in the myth as in the man, and also with a few backward glances at Mussolini. During filming Rossen improvised in an attempt at spontaneity. He was unable to get everything in and unwilling to leave anything out, and the result is chaotic. Such conventional characters as the discarded wife and the dissolute (foster-)son (John Derek) are less rewarding than the members of the demagogue's retinue, including the reporter (John Ireland) who degenerates into an acolyte, and the vicious, equally cynical secretary (Mercedes McCambridge). Indeed, the keynote is cynicism, with too much hysteria and too little analysis – though we may enjoy the manipulation of the crowds ('You're a hick and I'm a hick. We're all hicks') and their blind faith in Huey, here rechristened Willie Stark. Willie's rabble-rousing, his contempt for public ethics and his black book of enemies also provide fascinating material, but eventually the cliché-ridden commentary and lack of organisation put the film far below its model, *Citizen Kane*. Unlike that film, this appealed to the industry, which voted it a Best Picture Oscar; Broderick Crawford's bull-headed but empty performance as Willie also won an Academy Award. Hollywood's approval of Rossen was short-lived, and he was blacklisted when he refused to admit past membership of the Communist Party to the House Un-American Activities Committee. He did return to filming in the mid-Fifties, with uneven results (q.v.).

Meanwhile foreign critics did not receive *All the King's Men* with the rapture of their American colleagues. Today it seems hardly superior to a programme picture like **Bad for Each Other** (1953), 83 minutes of vacuous good intentions about an ex-army doctor (Charlton Heston) who dallies with a mine-owner's daughter (Lizabeth Scott) before realising that his place is with the miners. This echo of *The Citadel* was written by Horace McCoy (author of 'They Shoot Horses, Don't They?') and Irving Wallace, later a bestselling novelist. Irving Rapper directed, and the film was developed but not produced by Hal Wallis, who imposed the property and the two stars on Columbia as part of his price for releasing Burt Lancaster to do *From Here to Eternity*.

Miss Scott may also be seen in **Dead Reckoning** (1947), with Humphrey Bogart: 'He set the pace. He would arrive on the set totally unprepared at nine. He would then proceed to learn his lines before his martini and lunch. Then he would work till five and leave, the scene completed or not . . . These were his rules and although I was equally the star of the picture, I abided by them, as did the crew, the director, the producer and the studio.' Bogart made several films for Columbia (choosing the company to handle his independent productions as a deliberate snub to Warners) and this is the best of them, concerning a tough hero, a double-dealing dame and various heavies. The *films noirs* of the Forties are ritualised, and in this one the writers (Oliver H. P. Garrett and Steve Fisher) hold our attention by the lengths to which Bogart will go in challenging the very dangerous villain. John Cromwell, better known for romantic dramas, times each sequence for the utmost tension; it was his last film before he was blacklisted for suspected left-wing sympathies.

Bogart is also superb in **Knock on Any Door** (1949), as defence counsel for the pleasant youth (John Derek) who is indeed the killer he says he is not: but the touted suggestion that there is one like him in every home is typical of the film's approach – and of the equally superficial juvenile delinquent stories set off by its (albeit mild) success. Nicholas Ray directed, a new man whose work at R.K.O. at this time (q.v.) also indicated a modicum of skill; but **In a Lonely Place** (1950), after a good beginning, proceeds downhill at an alarming rate, unhindered by Ray's handling. For once it is difficult to enjoy Bogart, since as a Hollywood writer suspected of murder he behaves in so guilty a fashion as to forfeit all patience.

The United Artists were foundering; of its originators, only Chaplin and Pickford were left. The postwar surge to independence should have benefited the company above all others, and that it did not may be due to what Selznick in 1945 referred to as the 'insupportable tyranny' of the Chaplin–Pickford faction; both he and other spirits bent on independence found a warmer berth at R.K.O., and by 1951 U.A. was operating deeply in the red, due to the dearth of product and the low profits

on what there was. The financial squabbles between Chaplin and Pickford were increasingly acrimonious, and for this reason they both sold the majority of their holdings to a syndicate in 1950. When *The African Queen* and *High Noon* had made the company prosperous again, they took the opportunity to sell their remaining interests.

Few U.A. films of the period are of more than passing interest, and with a couple of exceptions their producers were at best undistinguished. Miss Pickford herself produced **Sleep, My Love** (1948), a thriller which almost revels in its lack of suspense as directed by Douglas Sirk. Claudette Colbert is the bride whose marriage brings hallucinations, and Don Ameche is the suave husband; a third performer is their Sutton Place mansion, if second-best to the one in *Gaslight* where such antics started.

Benedict Bogeaus, a former real estate dealer, and Burgess Meredith, co-producers of *Diary of a Chambermaid*, were reunited for **On Our Merry Way** (1948), one of Hollywood's rare episode films. Two of the three stories were directed by King Vidor, who described the result as 'a synthetic hotchpotch'; the third and best was directed, uncredited, by George Stevens, from a story by John O'Hara about two musicians (Henry Fonda and James Stewart) who, down on their luck, plan to 'throw' a contest to the mayor's son. Leslie Fenton directed the prologue, in which a wife (Paulette Goddard) urges her husband (Meredith) to write a story about the influence of babies in people's lives. It is laboured, as is the tale of movie extras (Dorothy Lamour, Victor Moore); the final story plagiarises O. Henry's 'The Ransom of Red Chief' and is about two con-men (Fred MacMurray, William Demarest) who manage to get themselves kidnapped by a horrible child. That the anecdote could soon reappear in *O. Henry's Full House* is evidence of this film's failure.

Somewhat more successful is **Champagne for Caesar** (1950), though it was less so at the box office, since the stars later sued the producer, Harry M. Popkin, for their deferred fees. They are Ronald Colman and Celeste Holm, usually joyous in comedy, but struggling to make bricks without straw under the direction of

In Europe the episode film, i.e. one consisting of short stories either tenuously linked or not at all, has long been popular, but there are probably less than half a dozen in all Hollywood history, partly because most of those failed. The depth of the failure of *On Our Merry Way* can be gauged from the fact that it was retitled *A Miracle Can Happen* while in release, and it is still today known under both titles. Its failure was three-parts deserved, but the fourth part was a very funny tale about two unemployed musicians, incisively but casually played by Henry Fonda and James Stewart.

Richard Whorf. The film is notable, however, in being one of the first to recognise Hollywood's new rival, television, though its real target is quiz-shows, which were outstandingly popular on both T.V. and radio at the time. Colman plays a mastermind who enters a quiz-show, and Vincent Price is very funny as its pretentious and humourless sponsor.

The Marx Brothers had more or less retired as a team after *The Big Store*, but David L. Loew tempted them back with the incentive of a cut of the profits. **A Night in Casablanca** (1946) is at least funnier than their last film for M-G-M. It is a spoof of wartime spy stories, with Sig Rumann as one of several people in search of Nazi treasure in the Hotel Casablanca, of which Groucho is the new manager. Chico is first discovered running an outfit called 'Chameaux a Piloter Soi-Meme'. Archie Mayo, usually a careful director, approximates the ramshackle atmosphere of their early films, and they appear glad to be back

in it. Harpo has a good comic duel, and when he is kissed one realises that Disney's Dopey was based on him – both the coyness and fierce determination. Harpo cannot, however, sustain **Love Happy** (1949); since dumbness is basically unfunny – a fact the other films managed to hide. Harpo, who (according to Groucho) saw himself as a creative genius, wrote the story, which gives him the leading role as a tramp (the script's word for him) who steals food for an impoverished theatre troupe and has the baddies after him because a sardine-can contains the Romanov diamonds. Chico joined the project because he needed the money, and Groucho was enlisted when no backer proved interested in a film with only two Marx Brothers. Groucho has less than ten minutes of screen time – memorably with Marilyn Monroe, then unknown, who complains that she cannot stop men following her. The screenplay is by Frank Tashlin and Mac Benoff; David Miller directed; and Miss Pickford and Lester Cowan produced, accumulating extra cash by selling advertising space★ to companies whose names may be seen on the neon signs in the final sequence. The film was not well received or at all popular – and is surely only revived for fans curious to know why this is so.

Red River (1948) was U.A.'s only spectacular at the time and, with the exceptions already noted, its only popular success, though high production costs involved in the location shooting cut the profits. It is entertaining but completely unsurprising; its appeal to admirers of the director, Howard Hawks, must be because they recognise familiar themes, especially the relationship between the ageing John Wayne and his protégé, Montgomery Clift: 'You really love him, don't you?' says the spunky heroine (Joanne Dru) to one or other of them from time to time. There is much talk of loyalty and man's inheritance, and lots of wide open spaces: but no amount of cattle stampeding or unshaven faces can make us believe the Old West was like this – and Clift (1920–66), a Broadway actor in his first film, does not give the impression that he was the sort of guy to enjoy sleeping rough.

This film and *Arch of Triumph* (q.v.), made by Enterprise (q.v.), were the only major United Artists films of 1948, by which time it was operating on a mere dozen or so releases annually. The new management did increase this to over a score by 1952, but, with the exceptions of the producer Stanley Kramer and John Huston, whose work has already been discussed, the company's reputation deterred other important independents from joining. Consequently the only other U.A. film of this period of interest is **He Ran All the Way** (1951), produced by Bob Roberts for John Garfield – they had earlier made two films (q.v.) at Enterprise – and directed by John Berry. The title is a misnomer, since the 'he', a small-time hood (Garfield) runs only at the beginning, spending the rest of the time holed up with the family of a girl (Shelley Winters) who had befriended him. Like Berry's earlier *From This Day Forward* (q.v.), this was intended to be a rare account of proletariat

New York, but the Winters menage is rather like that of Joan Crawford in *Mannequin* – close to the truth but not close enough. Garfield, who had complained of type-casting under contract, chose to give his usual chip-on-the-shoulder performance. This particular film was made under stress, since the principals were under investigation by the House Un-American Activities Committee. Roberts and Berry were subsequently blacklisted, while Garfield's fatal heart attack at the height of McCarthyism has been attributed to tension caused by Hollywood's rejection; Roberts made no more films, but Berry continued his career in France.

Two new companies were set up in the Forties to challenge the established major studios – the first attempt to do so since Zanuck and Joseph Schenck had founded 20th Century Pictures. International Pictures was the first, and since it was formed in 1944 it preceded the postwar trend to independence. The founders were two alumni of 20th Century-Fox, Nunnally Johnson and William Goetz, together with Leo Spitz, an ex-president of R.K.O. That company was to release International's films, originally intended to be two a year.

The first was **Casanova Brown** (1944), produced and written by Johnson from a play by Floyd Dell and Thomas Mitchell, already filmed as *Little Accident*. Gary Cooper plays a professor who, on the verge of marrying, learns that he has become a father by a previous marriage. The sequences of his going gaga over the baby are not very winning, but this actor knew how to use his personality to make a comic point and he has some funny scenes under the direction of Sam Wood (their fourth film together in two years). Frank Morgan is as ever superb as the prospective father-in-law, scornful that his pal Cooper must marry the daughter he loathes and resentful that though he himself had married for money he has hardly seen a penny of it.

When International's second film, *The Woman in the Window*, did well, production was stepped up, but there was short welcome for both *It's a Pleasure*, with Sonja Henie, and *Belle of the Yukon*, with Dinah Shore and Randolph Scott. Commendably the company attempted a drama supposedly topical in the postwar world, but **Tomorrow Is Forever** (1945), as written

*The practice became prevalent in the Sixties, when airlines became particularly susceptible to seeing the characters of a film fly in one of their planes.

by Lenore Coffee from a novel by Gwen Bristow, is only 'East Lynne' with pretensions. Orson Welles is a soldier so scarred in World War I that it is not till after the Anschluss that he returns to Baltimore and his wife (Claudette Colbert), now remarried and unable to recognise him. Miss Colbert, though over-gracious, remains likeable, and perhaps for that reason the film is not quite loathsome with its earnest conversations about militarism going on in a house where the French windows are always open and the children quote Patrick Henry. Irving Pichel directed, and Welles, in beard and heavy glasses, gives what Dilys Powell in the London *Sunday Times* found 'a performance of such sensitivity that I cannot believe the make-up is of his own choosing' – but we know better (cf. *Confidential Report*, *Histoire Immortelle*, q.v., both directed by him).

Welles's *The Stranger* was the last International film released by R.K.O. The company's last two films, *Temptation*, directed by Pichel, with Merle Oberon, and Siodmak's *The Dark Mirror* were released by Universal, which became Universal-International when that ailing company was taken over by International.

Enterprise was not so fortunate. Its chief founders were Charles Einfeld, formerly head of publicity at Warners, and David Loew, of Loew's Theatres, who had also produced some films for United Artists. That company was to distribute the Enterprise films domestically, and M-G-M overseas (because David's brother, Arthur Loew, was the head of M-G-M International), but Enterprise did not intend to be merely a supplier for long: with the help of $10 million in revolving credit from the Bank of America, huge premises were commandeered in Los Angeles and a grandiose programme announced, including the return to the screen of Norma Shearer. That did not happen, nor did the projects for other names like Joan Crawford and Ginger Rogers, attracted not by independence but a share in the profits – a practice which had been becoming reasonably common for major talent just before the War and was being revived.

The first Enterprise film was a Western, *Ramrod* (1947) with Veronica Lake and Joel McCrea. The second was a melodrama, **The Other Love** (1947), produced by David Lewis, who had just moved over from International. He had earlier produced *Dark Victory*, and clearly liked heroines dying from unmentionable diseases. She (Barbara Stanwyck) is a concert pianist, and as she tells the clinic's chief doctor (David Niven), 'There have been many men in my life – Bach, Brahms, Beethoven.' 'Your music belongs to the world,' he responds, 'you've got to get better for that.' When later she finds herself deceived she flees to Monte for one last fling with a racing driver (Richard Conte) but comes to her senses after an attempted rape by a croupier (Gilbert Roland). We leave her with neither hope nor despondency about the future, and such endings, supposedly honest, had become common in the postwar period – usually for dreadful films. The painted mountain backdrops place the setting as Switzerland; the superior score is by Miklos Rozsa, and André de Toth directed from a story by Erich Maria Remarque, as written for the screen by Ladislas Fodor and Harry Brown.

Lewis had a fondness for Remarque, which was to prove fatal to Enterprise. A huge budget of $4 million was set for **Arch of Triumph** (1948) and because of his success with Remarque's *All Quiet on the Western Front*, Lewis Milestone was set to direct. The script credited to him and Harry Brown was overlong, he said later, but the Enterprise executives refused to shorten it since they had paid a vast sum for the rights, and had contracted two important stars. In addition, they hoped to duplicate the success of *Gone with the Wind*, which had just been reissued. The book was a portrait of refugees at a time when France was uncertain both of its future and its attitude towards appeasement, whereas the film is only about a doomed affair between a German refugee surgeon (Charles Boyer) and a lady (Ingrid Bergman) of little virtue. It manages to hint that he scrapes a living by performing abortions, and there were further M.P.A.A. restrictions imposed on *her* problem, which was whether she should live in poverty with the man she loves or in luxury with several men she doesn't – an unsympathetic dilemma, made no more palatable by dressing Bergman as the usual movie *poule* (in mac and beret) or her inability to express coquetry. When the public decisively rejected the film, it was

751

said that it chose not to see Bergman in such a role; but the film itself is glib and gloomy, and disappointingly short on Paris. Milestone managed some sequences well, particularly those in hotel rooms, but it seems that he and Enterprise had different films in mind.

Though the trade reviews were favourable, the studio chiefs had doubts about the film. They were contracted to deliver to United Artists, which threatened to sue if they did not. As far as United Artists was concerned, the quarrels between Chaplin and Pickford had resulted in many banks withdrawing backing. Added to a ten per cent drop in admissions at home was the virtual closure of the British market (boycotted by the American film industry in retaliation for the seventy-five per cent *ad valorem* duty imposed by the financially-troubled Labour government). Enterprise in turn could not afford to delay release while legal problems were settled, as almost all its capital was bound up in the film. The writing was on the wall since only one of Enterprise's first half dozen films had shown a profit.

This was **Body and Soul** (1947), directed by Robert Rossen and produced by Bob Roberts as a vehicle for John Garfield, who plays an unscrupulous prizefighter. The writer was Abraham Polonsky, whom Roberts promoted to director on **Force of Evil** (1948), which Polonsky scripted with Ira Wolfert, author of the original novel, 'Tucker's People'. Garfield is an ambitious young attorney involved in the numbers racket and though, like the earlier film, it has a rough and edgy texture it is again too stereotyped to hold the interest. It was shown as Enterprise closed its doors, and it was one of the three films to be released worldwide by M-G-M – in return for a small injection of cash, which had been managed because of the Loew family connection. The seventh film due to United Artists under the original agreement was never made, and Enterprise returned its studio to its owners, though the lease had not expired. It was announced that the company would be restarted if its last three films were successful, but the public showed no more interest in *No Minor Vices* (1949), a comedy with Dana Andrews and Lilli Palmer, directed by Milestone, than it had in *Force of Evil*. Hopes held out, after previews, for

Ophuls's *Caught*, but it proved the eighth failure out of nine films. It is a pity; the director Robert Aldrich (q.v.), who worked at Enterprise, said that it was a particularly happy studio, with probably a better *esprit de corps* than elsewhere; it had 'everything in its favour except one thing: it didn't have anybody in charge who knew how to make pictures.'

The situation at Universal was little happier, since the studio was turning out more than its fair share of failures. When, in 1954, the Bank of America sold the entire Enterprise output to General Teleradio Corporation – a subsidiary of General Tires – for television transmissions (for $2,350,000) it added twenty-one other films which had not repaid their loans, almost all from Universal and R.K.O. (and one or two each from Republic, Eagle-Lion, International and United Artists).

Among the few Universal films that the public did want to see was **The Egg and I** (1947). Betty MacDonald's account of the experiences of herself and her husband in running a chicken farm was less a bestseller than a publishing phenomenon; and audiences presumably went to this film to revel in their favourite incidents – each predictable, even to one chancing upon them for the first time, and ranging from the funny (the yokels and Claudette Colbert at the village hop) to the sentimental (the neighbours rallying round after the fire). The dilapidated farmhouse had done service in *George Washington Slept Here*, but audiences like the tried and true – which included the stars, who indicated that they had been doing this sort of thing for far too long. The husband is a war veteran, which at this time meant that a number of ageing actors – here Fred MacMurray – could get up to a number of tricks for which they were much too old; Miss Colbert, who had just played June Allyson's mother, wears bouffant sleeves and has a baby. Chester Erskine directed, and the support includes Marjorie Main and Percy Kilbride as Ma and Pa Kettle, she slovenly and raucous but good-hearted, and he slyly borrowing articles which he has no intention of replacing. These two artists later appeared in a B-series built around these characters.

Two further exceptions to Universal's

The studios relentlessly copied each other, as it was their business to do if they were to provide the varied entertainment required by the exhibitors who hired their films. Throughout the Thirties, however, Warner Bros. alone was associated with prison melodramas, but when they lost interest Universal came up with one of the strongest, *Brute Force*, with Howard Duff and Burt Lancaster.

run of failures were **Brute Force** (1947) and **The Naked City** (1948), both produced by Mark Hellinger and directed by Jules Dassin. The former is a late example of a once-popular genre, the prison melodrama, with the usual cross-section – the rebel (Burt Lancaster), the honest Joe, the squealer, the psychopath – shuffling for our attention till the breakout at the end. The director and the equally promising writer, Richard Brooks, strive for greater realism but only make matters nastier and more jejune – as in the character of the guard (Hume Cronyn). He has taken upon himself a Nietzschean mantle, and for a spot of beating-up is half-undressed, with Wagner on the turntable and a print of one of the Michelangelo slaves on the wall. The M.P.A.A. would not have permitted anything more explicit, but this is an instance of Hollywood's gradual return to the often sleazy realism of its pre-Code melodramas. *The Naked City* was much praised for advancing the cause of realism in the matters of New York locations and the notion that its subject, an ordinary

crime, is taken from police files. Indeed, Hellinger introduces the film in self-congratulatory tone by claiming that New York is its 'star' The piece is dull indeed till the climactic shoot-out on the Williamsburg Bridge, and as with *Brute Force* the direction is always sharper than the material: Dassin is to be particularly congratulated on having kept Barry Fitzgerald, as the detective, under control – to his obvious irritation.

Conversely, both **All My Sons** (1948) and **Another Part of the Forest** (1948) are stagey, studio-bound presentations of Broadway plays, the former by Arthur Miller, a study of a war profiteer (Edward G. Robinson) directed on screen by Irving Reis; and the other by Lillian Hellman, a tale of Southern greed with Fredric March as the paterfamilias, directed by Michael Gordon. Both suffered additionally from inadequate performances among the younger players – Burt Lancaster as Robinson's son and Ann Blyth as March's daughter, a role played earlier by Bette Davis (in *The Little Foxes*, which covers the *later* fortunes of this particular family). It was partly because of these two films that Universal's losses continued to mount, but also pushing the company into the red in 1948 were the late, lacklustre Deanna Durbin films, *Letter from an Unknown Woman* and some of the films produced by Walter Wanger.

Only **Canyon Passage** (1946) proves that Wanger had not quite lost his touch – and that is mainly due to the Technicolored Oregon locations and the snatches of Hoagy Carmichael's song, 'Ole Buttermilk Sky'. Jacques Tourneur, the director, once observed that William K. Howard on his deathbed advised him not to make his own mistake of turning down so many scripts – and he has not: 'Indeed, how is one to know what can be done with a script?' But there is no indication that Tourneur did more than tell the actors which chalk lines to stand on. As a pioneer drama this is no better or worse than most, though the exposition is notably long-winded; Dana Andrews is a sullen hero and Susan Hayward flounces to negative effect. (A credit, 'Introducing Patricia Roc', remained in the British release print, though she was one of Britain's most popular stars; her presence in the film was due to pressures by Rank, then a large stockholder in Universal, who wanted to get his own contract artists better known in the U.S.)

The worst Wanger film for Universal-International (as it now was) is **The Lost Moment** (1947), based on 'The Aspern Papers' – which few could ever have imagined as a vehicle for Susan Hayward and Robert Cummings. There is a further bad omen in that it is the only film directed by an actor, Martin Gabel. It was the first screen version of any story by Henry James, though in Leonardo Bercovici's screenplay only the central situation remains. Miss Tina (Hayward) has become young, beautiful, sensual and schizoid – a situation cured after a visit to a 'funiculi-funicula' dance hall with a nice American (Cummings). John Archer plays the man after the letters and Agnes Moorehead is the elder Miss Bordereau: the film's publicity centred solely on the rubber mask used to make her into a centenarian.

It is hardly surprising that at this stage the studio abandoned any project that smacked of class – with the exception of the films of James Stewart, who arrived with a financial agreement often said to be unique, which it was not, but which was certainly not as prevalent as it was to become in the Fifties. Universal had always been plagued by its lack of box-office stars and with audiences now beginning to shrink it was financially unsound to have stars under long-term contracts. So, Stewart, who usually commanded $200,000 per film, was offered, as the studio's official history puts it, '50 per cent' of **Harvey** (1950) and *Winchester '73* (q.v.), the latter the first of a series of successful Westerns this actor made for the company. *Harvey*, directed by Henry Koster, was a big success, as had been Mary Chase's Broadway play on which it was based. Its subject is an amiable drunk (Stewart) whose best friend is an imaginary six-foot rabbit, and your attitude towards it will depend on your taste for whimsy, if leavened with an occasional funny line. In any case the piece is only made bearable by Stewart's underplayed performance and that of Cecil Kellaway, as the head of a sanitorium increasingly unwilling to believe that Stewart belongs inside it.

Otherwise Universal-International concentrated on low-budget action films, usually in Technicolor, and the series with Francis, the Talking Mule (who co-starred with Donald O'Connor) and with Ma and Pa Kettle. As can be seen from his work with 20th Century-Fox and his later independent productions, such films were not to the taste of William Goetz, who had been production chief since the merger; he and Spitz moved out in 1951 after selling their shares. The purchaser was Decca Records, who the following year acquired the controlling interest by buying the shares of J. Arthur Rank. Milton Rackmil became president of both companies. Over several years Rackmil cautiously instituted a programme including only eight pictures with large budgets, up to $1 million, eventually bringing to an end a dark period in the company's history.

In the immediate postwar period several memorable films were made, such as *Letter from an Unknown Woman* and those directed by Robert Siodmak which were also looked at in the last chapter. To them I would tentatively add **Take One False Step** (1949) and **The Senator Was Indiscreet** (1947), two vehicles with

William Powell. The former is a comedy-thriller, the genre in which Powell excelled, and he plays a professor suspected of murdering a blonde (Shelley Winters) with whom he had had a tumble during the War. The film is often implausible, but it entertains as directed by Chester Erskine from a screenplay by him and Irwin Shaw. The other film was an independent production by Nunnally Johnson, who persuaded George S. Kaufman to direct – his only film in that capacity. 'The people we call satirists now,' Dorothy Parker once remarked, 'are those who make cracks at topical subjects and consider themselves satirists – creatures like George S. Kaufman and such who don't even know what satire is.' This piece is assuredly satire – though Kaufman did not write it; Charles MacArthur did – his first screen credit since 1940 – from a story by Edwin Lanham, and it concerns an exceptionally pinheaded senator (Powell) who loses his diary. That brings to his side his opponents while causing other politicians to prepare for flight to Outer Mongolia or the other two countries with which the U.S. does not have extradition treaties. After noting that Kaufman himself was once entrapped by the revelations of Mary Astor's famous diary, we may say that this film is choppy and self-indulgent; but it is refreshing and it is comforting to know that the senator's claim, 'There's a rule in our state – if you can't beat 'em, bribe 'em,' caused Senator Joe McCarthy to denounce the film as 'traitorous' and 'un-American'.

At R.K.O. the situation was also gloomy. In 1946 the film industry achieved a record turnover of $1,692,000,000.* Wartime conditions had increased dependence on the cinema as the country's major leisure pursuit, and it remained so for returning servicemen and their families. That it might fall back to its prewar position worried no one, for that had also been astoundingly healthy. The ten local television stations which had been closed for the duration in 1942 resumed operations, but these were enjoyed by only a minute fraction of the population – and it occurred to only a few in the film industry that the programmes might one day improve. More worrying was the Justice Department's

*The figure was not approached again till 1974, and that was mainly due to much higher seat prices.

order for the severance of the film companies from their theatre chains – a situation to be examined in more detail when we come to consider M-G-M at this period, for the simple reason that Loews fought longer and harder against the decree than any other of the companies.

Under the management of Floyd Odlum, R.K.O.'s precarious financial position had finally steadied, and the deliberately unambitious production schedule of Charles M. Koerner had put the company modestly in profit as the War ended. However, then R.K.O. made a huge sum from its release of The Bells of St Mary's and when Koerner died in 1946, his successor, Dore Schary (1905–79), a former screenwriter, was instructed to woo those talents capable of bringing in similarly successful films. Existing agreements with Goldwyn and Disney (and International) boosted the receipts of the distribution arm and, since the R.K.O. circuit would eventually have to be hived off, the health of what was left of the company would be more sound if it handled other successful independents. Hence the agreement with Liberty Films and the flirtation with Selznick.

R.K.O. seldom made a profit from distributing Disney's films, despite their popularity – which was one reason for persevering, since exhibitors appreciated R.K.O.'s links with Disney. The high cost of the films themselves kept the Disney studio in a parlous financial situation (not to be ended till he entered the field of live action films, which enabled him to form his own releasing organisation, Buena Vista, in 1954). During the War, only government contracts for national purposes had kept the studio open, and though in no doubt of the value of re-issuing the full-length cartoons Disney hesitated to embark upon more. He compromised by offering **Make Mine Music** (1946) and **Melody Time** (1948), assemblies of short cartoons linked by music, to be split up should the public not respond. Both films may be regarded as collections of Silly Symphonies or Fantasia re-done for the original child audiences of Snow White and Pinocchio, tentatively thought of as adolescents with no interest higher than popular music. Neither has ever been reissued, but my unfond memories of both were confirmed when I was able to see Make Mine Music recently. It is by turns

755

saccharine, vulgar and cute, with relief from the unimaginative draughtsmanship provided by only two numbers, 'After You've Gone', an abstract on piano keyboards to the playing of Benny Goodman, and 'The Whale Who Wanted to Sing at the Met', a narrative sung by Nelson Eddy, which is vintage Disney.

Indecision also brought about two features divided into two, **Fun and Fancy Free** (1947), about a circus bear called Bongo, followed by a version of 'Jack and the Beanstalk' with Mickey Mouse and friends, and **The Adventures of Ichabod and Mr Toad** (1949), based on stories by Washington Irving and Kenneth Graham. The Graham tale is, of course, 'The Wind in the Willows', in as nasty a betrayal of a classic story as the cinema has yet achieved. The *Ichabod* half was a version of 'The Legend of Sleepy Hollow', narrated by Bing Crosby, with the Headless Horseman himself worthy of vintage Disney 'terror' – perhaps because Ub Iwerks did the special effects.

For years Disney had been considering live action films, but with **Song of the South** (1946) he hedged his bets: announced as the first of a series of films combining animation and actors, it has a slight and unexceptional framing story, directed by Harve Foster and prettily photographed by Gregg Toland, in part about a small boy (Bobby Driscoll) and the black Uncle Remus (James Baskett). The latter's stories are illustrated, and though Brer Bear sounds like Lennie in *Of Mice and Men*, he, Brer Fox and Brer Rabbit are interchangeable with any other cartoon animals of the period; even the Tar Baby is disappointing. Public acceptance was sufficient for Disney to offer a wholly live action picture, *So Dear to My Heart* (1948) and then *Treasure Island* (q.v.), both with Master Driscoll – who would die, unDisneylike, a drug addict at thirty-two.

Samuel Goldwyn's postwar efforts, apart from *The Best Years of Our Lives* and other more coquettish attempts to probe the spirit of the American home, were directed towards the star vehicles of Danny Kaye, a former Broadway and nightclub comic. Kaye has a daft smile, a gift for mimicry, an undoubted ease with a gibberish song but no recognisable comic weakness. **The Secret Life of Walter Mitty** (1947) remains his most celebrated

early film partly because it is based on James Thurber's masterly anecdote and partly because it gives Kaye opportunities to do several impersonations, including an intrepid R.A.F. flyer and a Mississippi gambler. The original tale has been enlarged and glamorised under the direction of Norman Z. McLeod, and brightly it shows that those close to Mitty either despise him (his boss) or despair of him (his mother). But stuck in the sort of situations in which Bob Hope often found himself – pursued, for instance, by a homicidal maniac (Boris Karloff) – Kaye has none of Hope's resources and is simply bland and energetic.

The only other Kaye/Goldwyn film often revived is **Hans Christian Andersen** (1952), a long-cherished dream of the producer who, uncertain of his approach, finally settled for 'a fairy tale about this teller of fairy tales'. Charles Vidor directed, from a screenplay by Moss Hart and a story by Myles Connolly, and to these usually estimable names we may add those of Richard Day, who provided the blowsy, cheap-calendar decor, and Frank Loesser, whose inventive songs do sometimes catch the spirit of Andersen. But otherwise this seems to me one of the nauseous mixtures ever concocted. A British film with an Andersen connection, *The Red Shoes* (q.v.), had been such a success in the States that Goldwyn decided also to incorporate ballet into his film, with the same star, Moira Shearer; and when she became pregnant her role went to the current rage of Paris, Renée Jeanmaire, whose husband, Roland Petit, tagged along to do the choreography. The result, eagerly categorised by the publicity department as a magic mixture of Broadway, Hollywood, Paris and Copenhagen, is deeply dispiriting.

David O. Selznick also devoted most of his attention to one star, Jennifer Jones, whom he eventually married. For her he fashioned **Duel in the Sun** (1946), adapted from a novel by Niven Busch, on which he himself took screenplay credit. The credited director is King Vidor, with whom he quarrelled, and so most of it was done by William Dieterle who (inexplicably) wanted credit; other sequences were handled by Sidney Franklin and Josef von Sternberg, the latter unofficially employed as colour consultant. It was Selznick's first production since *Gone with the Wind*, and he employed similar methods, but without much conviction that he could surpass himself. The critics soon informed him that he had fallen far short, but the public, led to expect something steamy, made it the biggest money-maker in cinema history, apart from its predecessor and *The Best Years of Our Lives*. Indeed, Selznick capitalised on its reputation – it was widely known as 'Lust in the Dust' – and dropped the original 'dignified' ads for something more lurid. Miss Jones plays a half-caste, Pearl, sent by her father (Herbert Marshall, the first actor in history to get star-billing for a three-minute role) to live with an old flame, Laurabelle (Lillian Gish), her husband (Lionel Barrymore), and their two sons – the noble Jesse (Joseph Cotten), who realises that he loves her only after she has been frequently ravished by the lecherous Lewt (Gregory Peck). It may be the l'il old debbil bequeathed by her maw, but Pearl sho' is a puzzle – wanting to be a lady like Laurabelle, but wearing off-the-shoulder blouses guaranteed to give any man ideas. Apart from Miss Gish and Walter Huston (as an evangelist, a role cut to pieces after protests by religious groups) the film is vilely acted and today it tends only to amuse – particularly when one extremely bilious studio sunset evokes the comment, 'What a strange light this evening.'

Selznick, disappointed by the critical onslaught, was further confused by the reception for **Portrait of Jennie** (1948), based on Robert Nathan's wistful novel, about an artist (Cotten) who falls in love with the strange girl (Miss Jones) he meets in Central Park. Miss Jones is appropriately fey, but where in the original she was unreal here she remains a Hollywood star. Miss Gish is a Mother Superior and David Wayne is Cotten's pal – a good instance of artists in movies always having garage mechanics as pals instead of other artists. Dieterle directed; originally there were sequences in sepia and Technicolor, while at the end the screen grew bigger and was tinted green – in a few of the few cinemas which booked it. Due to bad weather on location and Miss Jones's absences due to emotional problems (she was still married to Robert Walker) the cost had mounted to a huge $4 million, and after the original screenings Selznick spent another abortive

$250,000 refilming the storm sequence. Both this and *Duel in the Sun* were in fact distributed by the Selznick Releasing Organization, which he had set up just after the War, and which was now forced to close. The company had always been plagued by lack of product – though he had turned down the chance for it to handle *Red River* on the ground that that was just another Western: his self-confidence was further shaken when it made a fortune at the box office. Apart from *The Third Man* (q.v.), the only films in which he was subsequently involved were a handful with Miss Jones, ending with *A Farewell to Arms* (q.v.) in 1957.

Four of his other projects had been sold to R.K.O., all successfully. We have already looked at the two thrillers, *The Spiral Staircase* and *Notorious*; the other two are comedies – and the comedies of the Forties are not to everyone's taste: fires burn in the grate, breakfast is in bed, lamps are dotted round the room and Ethel Barrymore looks more knowing than the wise old owl. They tend to the mechanical, like both **The Bachelor and the Bobby-Soxer** (1947), directed by Irving Reis from a script by Sidney Sheldon, which has Cary Grant and Shirley Temple in the title roles with Myrna Loy as a judge, Temple's sister, who cures her of her crush on Grant; and **The Farmer's Daughter** (1947), which has Miss Barrymore as a politicking matriarch whose maid (Loretta Young) stands against her own candidate, and who is revealed to be a Fascist by omniscient Ethel, having encouraged him to get drunk in order to expose him. We are not required to condemn her for having hitherto been wrong, but are supposed to be indignant about a bigot in our midst and then amused when, Capra-style, he is exposed. H. C. Potter directed, cosily, and presumably Miss Young won her Best Actress Oscar for her maintenance of a Swedish accent.

Magic Town (1947) is a Capra film without Capra, produced independently for R.K.O. release and written by Robert Riskin, clearly in the hope that Capra would direct. William Wellman, a close friend of Capra and a good substitute, took on the project, but the result indicates how much vitality the genre had lost since the War – perhaps because of it – for the small-town myth was fading, as Capra's own *It's a Wonderful Life* had already suggested. When this one is found to be the most 'typical' town in the whole country, a city slicker (James Stewart) arrives to exploit it, but has a change of heart when he realises that this is also the intention of the town bigwigs; so with the aid of the local teacher (Jane Wyman) he sets out to prove that they are ruining it. The film is crowded with incident but awash with cliché and sentimentality, demonstrating just how far Riskin was dependent on Capra.

Leo McCarey's **Good Sam** (1948), written by Ken Englund from McCarey's own suggestion, concerns a disarmingly kind man (Gary Cooper) sucked dry by leeches, but again it is really a copy of Capra, leavened with the superficial 'do good' ethics of McCarey's two Father O'Malley movies with Bing Crosby. All comes right after Cooper gets drunk in a downtown bar, to remind us that Capra-esque heroes, unlike the rest of us, only get drunk in moments of desperate depression. McCarey's decline is further indicated in one of the several subplots, in which Cooper and his wife (Ann Sheridan) are impeded in their desire for 'marital relations'. This situation, long familiar in farce, had now invaded domestic comedy – and would notably feature in *Room for One More*, with Cary Grant – and there is no reason why it should seem so much more distasteful except that in this case McCarey cannot resist a smirk, taking advantage of the amiability of his star players.

Another theme which McCarey treats is the dream home, undoubtedly a matter of interest to many postwar couples: but his are not in their first youth, nor is that couple (Grant, Myrna Loy) of **Mr Blandings Builds His Dream House** (1948), which describes some misadventures of a New York family settling in Connecticut and is quite nonchalant about mortgages and escalating costs. H. C. Potter directed, from a lively screenplay by Norman Panama and Melvin Frank, based on a book of 'The Egg and I' school. Nevertheless, it all seems to belong to the prewar world, as does the scatty lady novelist, always good for a laugh in Thirties Hollywood: in **Without Reservations** (1946) Claudette Colbert is such a one, and John Wayne is the marine flyer she pursues because she wants him for the film of her book.

Mervyn LeRoy directed for Jesse Lasky – who was attempting another come-back – and he tries briefly to be serious about postwar conditions; in particular, the plight of Mexican immigrants.

The Long Night (1947) does reflect the contemporary unsettled mood after the war years – paradoxically, for it is a remake of *Le Jour se Lève*. It is by no means as inferior as was thought at the time, though that had much to do with the (false) claim, which infuriated critics, that all copies of the original film had been destroyed. This version suggests a postwar disillusionment, a world where all is not black or white; the transference to a small American coal town works quite well, and the only major changes are taken care of in the casting, with the girl (Barbara Bel Geddes) quite innocent and the man (Henry Fonda) going off at the end to face his trial with hope. His dilemma becomes a smaller one – a mulish inability to distinguish between kinds of love; otherwise the screenplay, by John Wexley, and the camera set-ups are virtually the same as in the original. Anatole Litvak directed for Raymond and Robert Hakim, producers who had left France when the Nazis arrived. Earlier, they had done a more thorough plundering job on Decoin's 1939 *Battement de Coeur* (in itself the remake of an Italian film made a few months earlier), even pillaging footage: **Heartbeat** (1946) is a hybrid as directed by Sam Wood (there is no screenplay credit, though Morrie Ryskind is named as adapter), but these exploits of a teenage pickpocket among the diplomatic set might just amuse for their ingenuity, were it not for the miscasting of Ginger Rogers. Far from being artless, she was the knowingest dame in movies, far too old, and no substitute for Danielle Darrieux in the original.

The most important among other independent productions handled by R.K.O. was **Joan of Arc** (1948), produced by a company owned by Walter Wanger, Ingrid Bergman and her doctor husband. The film was based on Maxwell Anderson's 'Joan of Lorraine', which Bergman had earlier played on Broadway. She admitted to a fixation on Joan, and had asked William Wyler to direct to no avail; the result suggests a vanity production, recalling other occasions when the star's husband, also amateur, interfered – it is certainly not as professional as we should expect of Wanger, or Victor Fleming, who directed. It cost $5,600,000 and needed to take $8 million to break even, but according to *Variety* it grossed only $4,100,000, and in her memoir Joan Bennett, Wanger's wife, records that she resumed her career to help pay off the debts incurred. Miss Bergman worried for years that the film hastened the deaths of Fleming and the photographer, Joseph Valentine, neither of whom long survived its completion. In such circumstances it would be nice to find something to praise, but all is disaster: Anderson's screenplay is flat, the production garish and the playing one-dimensional. Bergman's honesty and fervour are not enough.

A comparable decision almost wrecks **From This Day Forward** (1946), since Joan Fontaine is an unlikely working girl from the Bronx, wife of a lathe-operator (Mark Stevens). As a returning serviceman, he looks back on their marriage, their numerous in-laws and the uneasy employment market of the late Thirties. John Berry directed, and Garson Kanin did the adaptation, with less insight than he put into *The Marrying Kind*, Hollywood's next important attempt to portray working-class life. This one does show husband and wife in bed together – by special dispensation of the M.P.A.A. which was beginning to realise that the War had changed the popular view of the cinema's priorities. **Crossfire** (1947) is also about servicemen, in this case drinking and wandering aimlessly in a town strange to them, Washington, till brought up short by the knowledge that one amongst them is a murderer. In Richard Brooks' novel the victim was a homosexual, but since the M.P.A.A. would not sanction that he has become a Jew (Sam Levene), thus providing this film with its reputation as the first to attack racial intolerance. As a polemic, it is infinitely better than *Gentleman's Agreement*, and it remains a good thriller, despite the fact that the detective (Robert Young) seems modelled on Hammett's fictional Nick Charles. John Paxton wrote the screenplay, Edward Dmytryk directed, and it is well acted by Robert Mitchum and Robert Ryan as two of the G.I.s, Ryan as the confident Jew-hater, with an odd look of panic in his eyes in unguarded moments.

The reception of both films, especially that for *Crossfire*, encouraged Dore Schary to put into production **The Boy with Green Hair** (1948), the adventures of an unfortunate war orphan (Dean Stockwell) among a lot of twinkly-eyed Americans. Whichever way you look, there's a message: war is bad, racial intolerance is wrong, and so on, rather predictably. There is no reason why such matters should not be wrapped in whimsy, but this one is too heavy-handed, as written by Ben Barzman and Alfred Lewis Levitt and directed by Joseph Losey. Losey later admitted that he had been unable to deal with the 'unrealistic scenes' but claimed more surprisingly, 'I'm not ashamed of it.'

Many of the talents fostered by Schary fell foul of the House Un-American Activities Committee. Dmytryk was found guilty in 1947 of Communist affiliations and jailed for a year, after which he directed two films in England; in 1951, again before the Committee, he incriminated Adrian Scott, the producer of *Crossfire*, who then left the industry, and John Berry, who went to Paris. Losey was also blacklisted at this time, and he made a new career in England. Dmytryk's imprisonment had been an embarrassment to Odlum, whose dissatisfaction with R.K.O. increased when, at the end of 1947, it was found to have lost $2 million, a large sum, since the company had been in profit for the preceding four years. (The biggest contributors to that loss were Ford's *The Fugitive*, and Dudley Nichols's appallingly stagey version of O'Neill's *Mourning Becomes Electra*, which attracted only minimal audiences.) To add to the imminent divorce of studio from circuit and the growing threat from television was the fact that several foreign governments, including Britain (at that time Hollywood's best foreign market) had frozen American earnings. Odlum decided to sell R.K.O., and he found a buyer in Howard Hughes, whose fascination with the film industry had been unaffected by the failure of *The Outlaw*. He paid $9 million in May, 1948, and Schary soon returned to M-G-M (where he had once been a writer), to the relief of both men; he and Hughes had quarrelled incessantly.

Schary believed in uplift and Hughes in entertainment, and during Hughes's regime at least every other R.K.O. release was a melodrama. Schary had established a series of such films as they could be made cheaply and were usually profitable. **Out of the Past** (1947) is about a private eye (Robert Mitchum), now working in a garage in Lake Tahoe, a paranoiac millionaire (Kirk Douglas), and the latter's missing mistress (Jane Greer). After a good start it falls apart, as written by Geoffrey Homes (also known as Daniel Mainwaring) from his own novel; Jacques Tourneur's otherwise skilful direction shows a touching devotion to cliché. Nevertheless, the film is often cited as a good example of that accidental form, the *film noir* – which **They Won't Believe Me** (1947), despite some claims, definitely is not. When the commentary speaks of seedy, hideaway bars, they turn out to be Hollywood's customary plush nightclubs. Irving Pichel directed from a screenplay by Jonathan Latimer which has more twists than a corkscrew and concerns a playboy (Robert Young) with one woman too many. The most engaging of them is Miss Greer, whose tremulous, lived-in young face and clear tones should have made her a much bigger star than she was.

Also to be classified as *film noir* is **They Live by Night** (1948), which Hughes disliked so much that it was shelved for a while. Nicholas Ray, the director, had been brought to the studio by John Houseman, invited to produce a film of Edward Anderson's novel 'Thieves Like Us', and its quality was recognised when it was released to play some B dates. The protagonists are a deprived and inarticulate young couple (Farley Granger, Cathy O'Donnell), and though they move through what Richard Winnington called 'a haze of bank robberies, cheap hideouts and stolen cars', the film concentrates less on crime than on their doomed romance. That it no longer moves us may be due to Mr Granger, whose character does not suggest years of hardening in prison; we may enjoy the action sequences and the depravity of the rest of the gang. Ray's work on occasion was masterly, as this is evident from the action-atmospheric opening of **On Dangerous Ground** (1951), his sixth picture, again produced by Houseman. The film was a failure, owing perhaps to the fact that the public had just seen a fist-happy cop hero in *Where the Sidewalk Ends*, though this one (Robert Ryan) is not so much violent as disillusioned. There is another impressive sequence where he sets out in the snow to find the child-murderer, but the tiresome nature of the rest of it is due to Ida Lupino's playing of a blind girl, gazing blankly at anything but Ryan and the camera, and looking as if she were party to the wisdom of ages.

According to Josef von Sternberg, the credited director, Ray directed almost all of **Macao** (1952), to which Hughes had assigned von Sternberg as a peace offering after the debacle of *Jet Pilot* – which, begun in 1949, was subjected to so many revisions by Hughes that it did not surface till after he had closed the studio. Von Sternberg was removed from *Macao* after a few days' shooting, and Ray presumably used his set-ups, for the film is visually strong – which is just as well, for the story needs all the help it can get. Robert Mitchum and Hughes's protégée, Jane Russell, were meant to rival Bogart and Bacall, but only he can handle the slangy – if inferior – dialogue. When she asks him whether he caught her nightclub act, 'I didn't exactly fracture the people, did I?', we do not blame the people.

Angel Face (1952) is among the most attractive melodramas of the Hughes regime, due mainly to the performance of Jean Simmons (q.v.) in the title role, a woman not so much vicious or scheming as living in a sad little world of her own. Otto Preminger, the director, called her 'wonderful in the film', and his work on this occasion is both astringent and economical; he had been borrowed from Fox because Hughes knew he could work quickly and Simmons was available for only eighteen days during a six-week period, because of litigation over her contract. Rank had sold that to R.K.O. without consulting her, after previously loaning her to the studio for **Androcles and the Lion** (1952), which provided a disastrous and protracted start to her Hollywood career. Gabriel Pascal, unable to work in Britain, had persuaded Hughes that films of Shaw's plays would give R.K.O. a touch of class, but with the incompetence of the one and the interference of the other, filming turned into a two-year ordeal. James Donald (signed to play the captain) got fed up waiting for filming to start and returned to Britain, to be replaced by Victor Mature (Harpo Marx and Frank Sinatra tested for the role of Androcles; both Rex Harrison and George Sanders turned down the role of the Emperor). At least Pascal did not direct: Chester Erskine did that, and also wrote the script, but the material is lifeless as rendered by a seemingly bored cast – which also includes Alan Young and Elsa Lanchester as Androcles and spouse, and a palpably stuffed lion. There is hamming by Maurice Evans as the Emperor and Robert Newton as the convert Ferrovius, against painted backcloths and between inserts culled from *The Last Days of Pompeii*. The result was universally unappreciated, and Pascal, spurned by the film industry, spent the last years of his life peddling a musical 'Pygmalion' to Broadway producers.

Hughes's other attempt at grandeur (his *King Kong*) was **The White Tower** (1950), a mountaineering drama, a species Hollywood had always left well alone. It was unprecedented for an R.K.O. team to photograph on foreign locations (around Mont Blanc), and this was only the fourth studio production in colour.* Ted Tetzlaff, a former photographer, directed, from a screenplay by Paul Jarrico based on a novel by James Ramsay Ullman, and their characters are strictly from stock: the girl (Alida Valli) wanting to revenge her mountaineering father's death; the cynical ex-G.I. (Glenn Ford); a British scientist (Cedric Hardwicke); an alcoholic French writer (Claude Rains) and a Nazi bigot (Lloyd Bridges). Given that there remain too many backcloths and the fact that the downward journey is done in less than a second, the film did not live up to Hughes's expectations.

The studio reported a loss of just over $4 million in 1949. In desperation Hughes brought in Norman Krasna, a writer, and Jerry Wald, the successful Warners producer, at large salaries and with promises of complete autonomy. Of the twelve productions announced by this new team, only four were made, including *Clash by Night* and **The Blue Veil** (1951), the latter an effective remake of *La Maternelle*,

directed by Curtis Bernhardt, with Jane Wyman in the Gaby Morlay role. It is a wonder that any films emerged at all, given the reigning chaos at the studio: those that did were given short shrift by critics and public, and the distributing arm had to draw comfort from an occasional independent production. Among these was **Sudden Fear** (1952), directed by David Miller, which is about a wife (Joan Crawford) who learns of her husband's plan to murder her: it defeats belief that she never even considers going to the police, but the film achieves a certain panache when she fights back in her own way. In **The Thing** (1951) a group of isolated Arctic scientists is threatened by the creature of the title; the film is remarkable for Charles Lederer's naturalistic dialogue and the unforced direction, reckoned to be by the producer, Howard Hawks, rather than the credited Christian Nyby.

By juggling with the figures, Hughes managed during these years to show that the company made a small profit. In 1952 he sold his interest to a five-man syndicate whose sole concern seems to have been to sell off the backlog of films to T.V. When the deal was leaked to the press and their credit disallowed he was left with only their $1½ million downpayment. By 1954 he was unable to disguise losses totalling over $40 million, and with production down to thirteen features, he arranged to buy out all other stockholders – at $2 more per share than had been the price when he had taken over the studio. Therefore he paid over $23 million for the sole ownership of the company which he had single-handedly demolished – and that, industry observers felt, was twice as much as its assets were worth. However, he was thought to have made a $10 million profit when in July the following year he sold the company for $25 million to General Teleradio which, as we have seen, had entered the film industry by buying a bunch of unprofitable films and selling them to television. Six months later the new company, now called R.K.O. Teleradio Pictures, sold the T.V. rights of over 700 R.K.O. films to C & C Cola for $15 million. It also announced full-scale production, but those films still in release – including *The Conqueror*, with John Wayne as a Mongol warrior, begun by Hughes and eventually costing over $5 million – performed so

*Since the end of the War, the other major studios had allocated Technicolor to twenty-five to thirty per cent of their product, usually musicals and historical subjects. R.K.O.'s sole Technicolor films to this time were *The Spanish Main*, *Sinbad the Sailor*, produced by Douglas Fairbanks, Jr, and *The Boy with Green Hair*.

disastrously that the programme was abandoned. Those in development likely to make money, such as *The Naked and the Dead*, were made and handed over to Universal-International for distribution. The studio itself was dismantled and the premises reopened for television; in 1958 it was purchased by Desilu Productions, a T.V. outfit owned jointly by Desi Arnez and his wife, Lucille Ball – who had once been an R.K.O. bit player.

M-G-M was also having trouble, but this was not, for the moment, caused by unsuccessful films. The difficulties began in Washington, where for a long time there had been unease at the situation whereby a single organisation controlled production, distribution and exhibition, resulting in such restrictive practices as block-booking. The companies owning the circuits had a considerable advantage over those which did not – and Universal, United Artists and Columbia continued to fight for the bookings they wanted. In 1938 the Department of Justice had begun an investigation which was interrupted by the War; and the anti-trust suits instituted when it was over were as much an incentive to independence as was frustration with the hide-bound methods in operation at the major studios. Films were not automatically booked into thousands of cinemas but were to be bid for on merit – except for the moment in Loews' theatres, for that company fought on till the end, not bowing to the inevitable till 1952. Loews decided then to keep its cinemas and divested itself of M-G-M.

Although, as we have seen, M-G-M's distributing company was concerned with some films with which members of the Loew family were connected, it put on a fiercer front against the independents than any of the others. Louis B. Mayer was utterly opposed to independence of any sort, and Metro continued to operate as it had always done. With Clark Gable back on the lot, it was almost as though the War had never been; but after four years fighting for his country M-G-M showed its gratitude by clobbering him with **Adventure** (1945) and a slogan he loathed, 'Gable's Back and Garson's Got Him'. As a gift for the world's first postwar Christmas the film was 'one of the most outstanding pieces of twaddle in a month

of Sundays' as C. A. Lejeune put it. Gable's return to M-G-M was as momentous as that after his absence making *Gone with the Wind*, and just as that was followed by *Strange Cargo* he was again required – obviously due to his pre-eminent status – to be part of a muddled statement about God's importance to mankind. Portents of this eventual message appear in the early part of the film, which mainly concerns the bickering of seaman Gable and librarian Garson – a sure sign that That Slogan represents the plot. They fall in love under a bush while stealing a neighbour's chicken, which at least allows her to be other than bossy, bad-tempered or tearful. Under Victor Fleming's direction Gable does not show how dispiriting he reportedly found acting with her, but he never really recovered from this film: he stayed off the screen for eighteen months and never again played a devil-may-care adventurer.

Admittedly, he starts that way in **The Hucksters** (1947), but he finishes as an executive with integrity: and the postwar Gable no longer prefers the Harlow kind of woman, charmingly played by Ava Gardner, but the prim widow (Deborah Kerr). In Frederic Wakeman's novel this lady is an unfaithful army wife, so hot for the hero that she is happy to be with him in a hotel little better than a whore-house – a situation turned about in the screenplay by Luther Davis, so that she leaves him flat because he has unfortunately chosen such a hotel. As in the book the romance is dreary and all the commercial sequences splendid, their detail on the advertising world as directed by Jack Conway making this one of the better postwar films. Gable plays a service veteran attempting to re-establish himself in his old profession, and Sydney Greenstreet is his monstrous client (a character based on Walter Hill of American Tobacco).

The starry cast (it also included Adolphe Menjou, Keenan Wynn and Edward Arnold) was an indication of the studio's hope of repeating the era when its films were the talk of both industry and cinemagoers, and there was another such backing Gable in **Command Decision** (1948) – Van Johnson, Walter Pidgeon, Brian Donlevy, John Hodiak, Edward Arnold and Charles Bickford. In charge of both this and *Homecoming*, Gable's previous film, was Sidney Franklin, the studio's most valued producer, another indication of Gable's continued standing. *Command Decision*, directed by Sam Wood and based on the Broadway play by William Wister Haines, has far more guts and intelligence than the not dissimilar *Twelve O'Clock High*. Gable plays a high-ranking officer undecided as to whether the bombing of German factories (known to be manufacturing a new long-range aircraft) is worth the heavy casualties among his own men.

When the public failed to appreciate this further contemporary situation Gable was put into lighter fare, with former co-stars, ladies of his own generation, and you would have thought, considering their ages, that they would not have waited till the last reel to get married. **To Please a Lady** (1950), directed by Clarence Brown, casts him as a famous midget-car racer and Barbara Stanwyck as a needling journalist; **Key to the City** (1950) has Gable and Loretta Young as rival mayors at a convention. In one scene he is locked out of his hotel room searching for his trousers in a Little Lord Fauntleroy suit – a situation which implies that the hotel has no extra keys nor he extra pants, and which would have been far more suitable for someone like Joe E. Brown. George Sidney directed.

Another formula was needed, and **Across the Wide Missouri** (1951) and **Lone Star** (1952) were Gable's first Westerns since joining Metro over twenty years earlier. Mayer had never cared for the genre, but was persuaded that *Across the Wide Missouri* was an epic of the pioneers – of the days when their Technicolored Eden was marred only by marauding Indians. Gable is a trapper, seemingly the only American; his best friend (Adolphe Menjou) is French, and there are innumerable Scotsmen, including one (John Hodiak) who has taken up both Indian costume and their way of life – and when Gable does the same, we may acknowledge a rare example of the pro-Indian film. As directed by William Wellman, it is one which loves the wide open spaces and the people who move through them so clearly aware of their splendour. Their unconventional behaviour and the film's length – a mere seventy-eight minutes – indicates that the cutting-room made the best of a bad job of Wellman's free-and-easy location work. *Lone Star* has a story

and screenplay mainly by Borden Chase, co-founder with Howard Hawks of the Motion Picture Alliance for the Preservation of American Ideals – some of which may be hazily found in this tale of tempers running hot at the thought of Texas joining the Union. There are some fair scenes between Gable, in a replay of Rhett Butler, and Ava Gardner, as a newspaperwoman militant against annexation; Broderick Crawford is a cattle baron and Lionel Barrymore, in his penultimate screen appearance, is Andrew Jackson (as he had been in *The Gorgeous Hussy*).

Gable made three more films for the company, including *Mogambo* (q.v.), which reawakened the company's interest in him, but he knew that the front office had planned to drop him, and he left in bitterness. Few filmgoers could remember a time when there had been an M-G-M without Gable.

Greer Garson left about the same time: with Gable and Judy Garland, she had been one of Metro's most popular stars in the immediate postwar period, but by the time of **Julia Misbehaves** (1948) her lustre had dimmed, and the film was titled in this way in the hope that everyone would know that a new Greer was on display. The trouble was, there wasn't: she has a chic wardrobe and tells lies for the fun of it, but underneath she's just the same old Greer with the same old problems. Based on Margery Sharp's light-hearted novel 'The Nutmeg Tree', the film is not funny, nor is she, nor Walter Pidgeon, as the husband she re-meets at her daughter's wedding. When a number of sentimental dramas with Pidgeon failed to find a public, M-G-M tried another comedy, **The Law and the Lady** (1951), based on Frederick Lonsdale's 'The Last of Mrs Cheyney', which it had filmed twice before. The new prologue, which is quite long, works better than what is left of Lonsdale, since the director, Edwin H. Knopf, cannot handle a comedy of manners; Miss Garson, raven-haired as the jewel-thief, is arch, and no match for Michael Wilding as her accomplice, who (seemingly undirected) floats into view, says his lines effectively and floats out again.

A decade later almost all remakes would become musicals – a thought that may occur as you watch a reworking of *Grand Hotel* called **Weekend at the Waldorf**

763

(1945), 'suggested by a story by Vicki Baum'; Guy Bolton as adapter and Sam and Bella Spewack as the writers are content simply to disguise the source. There is a sad little film star (Ginger Rogers), so busy making movies and money that she has had no time to live, and a sad little soldier (Van Johnson), so badly shot up – apparently (or, rather, not apparently) – that his hospital treatment is a matter of life and death. Will they find love and happiness during this weekend at the Waldorf? Yes, but not with each other: M-G-M have picked for her an ace war correspondent (Walter Pidgeon) and for him a peachy-looking stenographer (Lana Turner). The smaller roles are excellently played, and Robert Z. Leonard marches the cast on and off the sets with his usual dexterity: unfortunately the two central situations are awash on a sea of absurdity. The plot is more faithful to the original than it sounds, but the chief virtue of that was its misanthropic view. This film has no point of view at all, unless it is opportunism or postwar sentimentality – as when Johnson has the band play a tune by his dead buddy for the folks back in Iowa.

Thus did the postwar world impinge upon M-G-M, but since the other studios did no better it did not need to feel ashamed. Indeed, its defenders could point to *The Search* and **The Beginning or the End?** (1947), the latter a study of the development of the atom bomb, a subject, as directed by Norman Taurog, more interesting than the relationship between the scientists and service personnel involved. M-G-M had retained its sense of responsibility, but its primary commitment was towards heavyweight bestsellers, such as the films of **Cass Timberlane** (1947), by Sinclair Lewis, and **B.F.'s Daughter** (1948), by John P. Marquand. Both concern social inequality in marriage. In the former, a judge (Spencer Tracy) marries a poor girl (Lana Turner), to the consternation of his country-club friends, and the marriage is predictably endangered when one of them (Zachary Scott) makes a play for her during rehearsals of 'The Barretts of Wimpole Street'. The characters include a war veteran (Tom Drake), who drinks both because he cannot settle down and because his father's firm has benefited from crooked business during the War. 'At the time we thought we were making a

great picture,' said the director, George Sidney, '[but] on television it comes over like soap opera.'

War looms larger in *B.F.'s Daughter*, because war-work separates wife (Barbara Stanwyck) and husband (Van Heflin), an assistant professor at Columbia. In view of his pronounced, indeed infamous, socialist stance it is, to say the least, insensitive of her to purchase a Connecticut palace without consulting him – but then he is not too proud to object to her allowance from her father (Charles Coburn). In one sequence the couple prefers to go to 'Hamlet' rather than the latest Broadway musical smash, and awe at their daring is made apparent by all concerned, including the director Robert Z. Leonard.

Head and shoulders above M-G-M's other serious films is **Intruder in the Dust** (1949) which, as directed by Clarence Brown and photographed by Robert Surtees, has an intensity and harshness quite untypical of the studio at this time. This is William Faulkner's novel, scripted by Ben Maddow with some speciousness but much suspense, about some townsfolk bent on lynching and the stand against them taken by an old negro (Juano Hernandez) and his stalwarts – a boy (Claude Jarman Jr) and his lawyer uncle (David Brian), an indomitable spinster (Elizabeth Patterson) and the victim's one-armed father (Porter Hall).

'My favourite picture ever, though, is **The Yearling,**' (1946) Brown has said. He directed from the novel by Marjorie Kinnan Rawlings about an Everglades family haunted by poverty. Mother is unfeeling, and the boy, Jody, is closer to Paw – for he has just started to hunt and tend the crops, and when Paw is took sick with a snake-bite, he takes over his duties. M-G-M had tried to film the book in 1941, with Spencer Tracy and Anne Revere, directed by King Vidor, who was replaced after a month by Victor Fleming: according to Brown, the footage was 'lousy', but as far as I am concerned the adjective is too kind for his version, with its Technicolor cloudscapes and heavenly choir. Jane Wyman as the mother looks plain and careworn, but is permitted a tear and a smile when no one is looking; no amount of corn-pone dialogue ('Leave off, Maw. Aint 'nuff trouble fallin' out the sky without the family quarrellin'?') can make

Gregory Peck (Paw) other than ludicrous. Claude Jarman Jr as the boy is capable, but, like Peck, directed for charm. Paul Osborn's screenplay decks every scene in irony, jokiness and sentiment: this is not the simple tale of a boy and his pet, a fawn, but a multi-million dollar investment. It was successful and well-liked at the time, while *Intruder in the Dust* had difficulty getting bookings – and not only in the South. It is difficult to believe that both films were made by the same man.

M-G-M continued to make pictures starring Lassie the collie, but the canine's career had begun to falter when he, she or it supported – how are the mighty fallen! – Jeanette MacDonald in **The Sun Comes Up** (1949). Both were under contract, as was young Jarman, so for them the author of *The Yearling* concocted a plot about a dog-owning singer who does not want to adopt the boy who hangs around the country home where she Has Gone to Forget. At the end dog rescues boy from fire, and as directed by Richard Thorpe this is one of the most renowned of those films demonstrating that M-G-M had no shame.

Miss MacDonald had returned to the studio under a two-picture contract at the behest of Joe Pasternak, the producer; and doubtless the title **Three Daring Daughters** (1948) will remind you of his earlier *Three Smart Girls*: instead of daughters trying to unite parents, they are trying to separate mother from her new husband, José Iturbi (as himself), and who could blame them? The director is Fred M. Wilcox, responsible for a number of Lassie pictures and one very good film, **The Secret Garden** (1949). As adapted by Robert Ardrey, Frances Hodgson Burnett's novel for children provides a field day for those who like tales of old houses with secrets and severe housekeepers and noises in the night, but the director makes enough of all this and the Yorkshire moors to suggest that on this occasion he was the one inspired. The sequences in the garden itself are in colour, and a good cast includes Herbert Marshall as the misanthropic guardian, Gladys Cooper as the housekeeper, Elsa Lanchester as the maid, Reginald Owen as the gardener, and, as the children, Margaret O'Brien, Dean Stockwell and Brian Roper.

Little Miss O'Brien's intensity is well used in **The Unfinished Dance** (1947), as an obsessed ballet student whose crush on the premiere dancer (Cyd Charisse) leads her into planning an accident to the visiting ballerina (Karen Booth). This is an inferior remake of Jean Benoit-Levy's 1937 *La Mort du Cygne*, based on a story by Paul Morand. The producer and director, Pasternak and Henry Koster, had once brought us Deanna Durbin's arias, but are less courageous with ballet: the big number is based on 'Holiday for Strings', danced on glass floors like no stage outside a sound-stage. The scenes with the children are good, because they are all so precocious: though, like Miss O'Brien's performance, I am not sure that it was what was intended.

It is a relief to turn to **Lady in the Lake** (1946), one of the best attempts at filming Raymond Chandler – and perhaps almost too faithful as rendered in Steve Fisher's screenplay, for there is so much plot that the direction concentrates on that at the expense of the necessary atmosphere. A good cast includes Audrey Totter as the magazine editor who commissions Marlowe, Leon Ames as its owner, and Lloyd Nolan and Tom Tully as cops; Robert Montgomery is Marlowe, and (with the exception of George Montgomery in *The Brasher Doubloon*) the least of the screen Marlowes, beaming smoothly whenever we see him. This is not often, for this is the famous occasion where the 'I' is the camera, with Marlowe seen only in mirrors except when speaking directly to the audience. This was Montgomery's own idea, directing a film for the first time, but Chandler does not need gimmicks.

Another classic thriller met a worse fate: that **The Postman Always Rings Twice** (1946) has occasionally been named as one of the best *films noirs* of the period – presumably by people who have never read the novel – is a tribute to James M. Cain's novel, which is taut, atmospheric and riveting; the film, faithful only in outline, is full of holes. As the husband victim, Cecil Kellaway ambles through his role, and Lana Turner, though she has a trashy, cheap quality, is no better under Tay Garnett's direction than she was under anybody else's. As the lover-accomplice, John Garfield is, for once, hardly more expressive: just when we should be most concerned about their fate, there arrive Leon

765

Ames and Hume Cronyn, two real actors, as the opposing lawyers.

Under Louis B. Mayer, the studio continued to show little orientation towards thrillers or action films, but his days as prime arbiter were numbered. Since the death of Thalberg, everything had to receive his assent; as the old guard left – the more vigorous-minded producers, like Hunt Stromberg and Joseph L. Mankiewicz – M-G-M films were increasingly a reflection of Mayer's taste, and he was a man of formidable likes and dislikes. When, in 1946, Loews, Inc., made a record net income of $18 million, Mayer's position was unassailable; but two years later the figure had shrunk to just over $4 million (the lowest figure since 1933) and the studio was operating at an estimated loss of $6½ million. With the loss of the theatres imminent, the front office panicked, and decided that what was wanted was a new Thalberg. The job was offered to Arthur Freed, who declined it, and then to Dore Schary, who arrived in July 1948: the individual producers were to be responsible to him rather than Mayer, and he was to be responsible not to Mayer but to New York – not a situation congenial to him, because of Mayer's reaction, and even less congenial to Mayer. At this uneasy juncture, the company celebrated its twenty-fifth anniversary.

The anniversary films were lavish and Technicolored. Mervyn LeRoy's **Little Women** (1949) is inferior to Cukor's version, but you may become reconciled to it if you accept that the Jo of Miss June Allyson is as anxious to be liked as that of Katharine Hepburn was not; there is, however, good representation of the older generation – by Mary Astor (Marmee), Lucile Watson (Aunt March), C. Aubrey Smith (Mr Lawrence), Leon Ames (father) and Elizabeth Patterson (the maid). **The Three Musketeers** (1948) also suffers from uneven casting: on one hand Gene Kelly, a marvellously agile D'Artagnan, Frank Morgan and Angela Lansbury as the King and Queen, and Keenan Wynn as the valet; on the other, Van Heflin a too-sober Athos, Miss Allyson a sugary Constance, Vincent Price a too-knowing 'President' Richelieu (in deference to Catholics he was not allowed cardinal's robes) and Lana Turner, a void as Milady. Kelly's avowed inspiration was the elder Fairbanks, and

the decorators have provided him with sets evocative of the Fairbanks version of this story – narrow Paris streets, rose-covered inns, marble ballrooms; the duels are both ingenious and funny, but there is no sense of respect for the material. Fairbanks knew better, but the chief trouble is Robert Ardrey's screenplay, which has not succeeded in taming a long novel, and under George Sidney's direction the film flies off at every angle.

The anniversary line-up was led by **That Forsyte Woman** (1949) – appropriately, for it is the quintessential M-G-M film: stately, star-studded, sumptuous and pointless. It continued the studio's love affair with Britain, for it is, as the credits clarify, 'Part One of John Galsworthy's "The Forsyte Saga"', a study of the late Victorian moneyed classes. The Forsytes prided themselves on being exactly what they were, on thinking exactly as they thought, and doing exactly as they wished, but as Soames, their chief representative, Errol Flynn is merely gruff and grim, and as Irene, Greer Garson is all suffering graciousness; the true relationship between this ill suited couple is beyond either performer. As the two others who challenged the complacency of the Forsytes, Walter Pidgeon as Young Jolyon is a conventional black sheep, and Robert Young as Bosinney is twenty years too old and completely without Bohemia in his soul. Whether the novel had more merit than other family sagas filmed in the Forties is not clear from the screenplay, by Jan Lustig, Ivan Tors, James B. Williams and Arthur Wimperis, or the direction by Compton Bennett, a Britisher – on loan from the Rank Organisation – who prided himself that he never raised his voice on the set.

Schary was fully aware that the studio's reputation depended on such entertainments. Some thought was given to remaking *Trader Horn*, but it was decided that **King Solomon's Mines** (1950) would make a stronger African adventure. Rider Haggard's story provides only the framework: a wife or widow (Deborah Kerr) hires Alan Quartermain (Stewart Granger) to go into dark unexplored regions in search of her husband. Helen Deutsch wrote the screenplay, leaving out the business of the eclipse (perhaps because it had recently turned up in *A Yankee at*

King Arthur's Court) and making it just another trek through the jungle. The film was very popular, so the studio must have thought their money well spent. Like *Trader Horn*, it was filmed in Africa, and, unlike the Gaumont-British version, it uses a real African tribe; the climax among the Watusi is memorable – and Umbopa, the guide who turns out to be a king, was played by a real one, Siriaque. As against this, audiences roared with laughter when Miss Kerr, having washed her hair in the jungle, looked as though she had just popped out of the studio beauty parlour – which may be the fault either of Bennett, again on loan to M-G-M, or of the second-unit director with whom he was compelled to share credit, Andrew Marton.

Stewart Granger, according to Bennett, was 'monstrously difficult' to work with, but this British acquisition was ideal material for Schary's plan to remake two of the company's silent successes, **Scaramouche** (1952) and **The Prisoner of Zenda** (1952) – and Lewis Stone, who had had leading roles in them, was again featured as a sentimental gesture at the end of his long career. The writers of *Zenda* were John L. Balderston and Noel Langley, the first of whom had worked on the 1937 Selznick version – of which, frame by frame, this is a copy, a fact obscured by Richard Thorpe's plodding direction and the addition of Technicolor. With the exception of James Mason's bullet-headed and insolent Rupert, the cast is inferior: as the King, Granger is arrogant and overweening, and as Rassendyll he has British Imperial integrity and a good profile – but as was proved again by the 1973 *Lost Horizon*, Ronald Colman films should not be remade without Ronald Colman. Nor could Granger manage the laughter of Rafael Sabatini's Scaramouche. The other leads are again weak, including Mel Ferrer as the smiling villain – the hero's brother and not, as in the earlier version, his father. There is only an approximation of seventeenth-century France, but George Sidney's approach is even more spirited than on *The Three Musketeers*, perhaps because he has a better screenplay, by Ronald Millar and George Froeschel: the sequences in the Assembly and the Commedia dell'Arte are splendid, as are the swordfights – and the climactic duel all over the theatre, all seven minutes of it and devoid of any

sound but the clash of rapiers, may well be the best ever put on film.

Sidney's films were usually fast-paced and visually handsome, but his name appears on **Young Bess** (1953), which is neither. Margaret Irwin's novel had been owned by the studio for some time, and this film was rushed into production after the accession of Elizabeth II – an M-G-M candy for the Coronation. Clumsily adapting the book's viewpoint, but ignoring its comment on the nature of Seymour's ambition, the film presents Elizabeth (Jean Simmons) as a teenager with a crush on one of the male teachers, watched tolerantly by her grown-up rival, Catherine Parr (Deborah Kerr). Seymour becomes, in Stewart Granger's handling, the usual Granger hero, but with one memorable line, 'I wish that Italian fellow were alive . . . Leonardo. He knew how to paint a woman like you.' At such moments it is clear that the Hollywood historical was determined not to grow up: there had been vast advances in education since such dialogue was common, and the Tudor period is so alive with death-tinged intrigue that there was no need to add or subtract anything. The writers were Arthur Wimperis and Jan Lustig, the former one of the writers of Charles Laughton's Henry VIII, and in repeating that role Laughton improves upon it by indicating the king's cruelty.

As puzzling as Sidney's unevenness is the work of the cutting-room, and we can only conclude that the editors of *Young Bess* were not supplied with the material to bring it anywhere to the level of *Scaramouche*. Similar assumptions may be made about **Kim** (1950), which is credited to Victor Saville, though there is no internal evidence of its having been directed. The camera merely records the actors speaking their lines and their actions, the pieces then being assembled to form a narrative. Without the essentials which made up Kipling's novel – its mixture of mysticism, high adventure and feeling for India – the editors evidently had no chance to make a decent movie. Dean Stockwell has spirit in the title role and, what is rarer among child actors, intellect; in the smaller role of Red Beard, Errol Flynn is lively.

M-G-M's historicals include *Ivanhoe* (q.v.), made in Britain, which proved again that the profits were commensurate with the cost. Since the company was, in

At the time Vincente Minnelli was an incomparable maker of musicals he also made some good serious films, including *Madame Bovary*, with Jennifer Jones. She was so perfect that it was no surprise to learn from Minnelli's autobiography that she herself was partly Emma.

financial terms, only limping along, it looked again to its past – specifically to *Ben-Hur*, but the chance to remake that was passed over in favour of **Quo Vadis?** (1951), from an equally venerable novel which the studio had owned for some time. With Schary's approval it was given to producer Arthur Hornblow and John Huston. Mayer argued against their 'intellectual' approach in favour of a deMille spectacle, going over their heads to Nicholas Schenck in New York. Accordingly the project passed to producer Sam Zimbalist and Mervyn LeRoy, with the then stupendous budget of $10 million – to be spent in Italy, where costs remained lower than in California. Eventually the film was only just behind *The Greatest Show on Earth* among box-office successes, but in spite of a number of reissues it had earned only $12½ million before being sold to T.V. Now that the days of the monster biblicals have gone, it is hard to regret the expenditure. What is to be regretted is the script, by John Lee Mahin, S. N. Behrman and Sonya Levien, with its religiosity and a wishy-washy romance between a feebly acted Roman general (Robert Taylor) and a Christian (Deborah Kerr). There is a Jewish Paul (Abraham Sofaer), a Scottish Peter (Finlay Currie), and a host of other British players, including Peter Ustinov, whose Nero almost saves the occasion – exuberant, larger than life, petulantly and naively in awe of his own genius. This is another Metro film which seems to have been assembled rather than directed, but, unlike the later attempts in the genre, the climactic moments do not fail: the two decades of experience were not lost in filming the scenes in the arena.

With M-G-M's pool of talent to draw upon, Schary instituted a scheme he had been fostering at R.K.O., which was to encourage directors to make low-budget films of their own choosing. The directors concerned were veterans, like William Wellman, who made *The Next Voice You Hear*, the next voice being God's – in a radio broadcast – or newcomers, like John Sturges, whose *The Magnificent Yankee* is a biography of Oliver Wendell Holmes (Louis Calhern). As the series proved unsuccessful, it turned towards the thriller, and one of the last was Sturges's **Jeopardy** (1953), as unpretentious as the title, a tense little tale about an escaped convict (Ralph

Meeker) and a woman (Barbara Stanwyck) whose husband (Barry Sullivan) is trapped as the tide is rising.

One of the best serious M-G-M films of the time came from Arthur Freed, who had admired the work of writer Richard Brooks and brought him to the studio for **Crisis** (1950), which, with the compliance of Cary Grant, Brooks directed, from his own screenplay. Its credited source was a story by George Tabori, about a surgeon (Grant) forced to operate on a foreign dictator (José Ferrer): a British film with an identical plot was simultaneously on view, *State Secret* (q.v.), and the fact that there was no report of litigation may be because the situation had already been used in a little-known play by Karel Čapek, 'Skeleton on Horseback'. Both films are thrillers, and the American one is more sober; the British one, by identifying its setting as a Balkan state indicates a Communist dictator, but this film is more cagey – unwilling to admit that there might be a Communist state in the Western hemisphere, even though the setting is South of the Border. (Prophetically, the dictator wears a Castro-like beard.) There are implausibilities, but *Crisis* is carefully worked out; Grant, in one of his last serious performances, is excellent and Ferrer is amusing, self-congratulatory and prone to tantrums.

Freed's most famous protégée, Vincente Minnelli, did poorly with his first serious film, **Undercurrent** (1946), produced by Pandro S. Berman and renowned at the time as Robert Taylor's first postwar film. Taylor plays a deranged captain of industry who marries an unworldly girl (Katharine Hepburn) and decides to murder her when she proves a gauche hostess and over-curious about his brother (Robert Mitchum). There are a number of the customary, infallible scenes, such as the one where she tries to flee and the car will not start, but the result is high tosh, for which Taylor was singularly unequipped.

Berman also produced **Madame Bovary** (1949), since he wanted to make a film about adultery, in the manner of current European films, and had been advised that a version of a 'classic' was more likely to be passed – with the M.P.A.A. helpfully adding that it stood a better chance with an actress like Jennifer Jones rather than Lana Turner. To appease the censor even more the film has a prologue and epilogue in which Flaubert (James Mason) defends his work and attempts to justify Emma's behaviour. The unexpected triumph is Miss Jones's Emma, exactly the sort of girl who has fed her adolescence with tales of romantic love and marries the first man to come along. The screenwriter, Robert Ardrey, and the actor (Van Heflin) have missed the point of Charles Bovary, who was not merely an affectionate nonentity but devoid of imagination; Louis Jourdan is a tired fop rather than the uncouth, selfish squire; and Christopher Kent – Sweden's Alf Kjellin renamed – is simply awkward. The film omits the sexually-charged airings in a closed carriage, but none of the changes damage its purpose. The critic of the *Manchester Guardian* observed that it used 'exceptionally fine material to add yet another competent film to the many competent American films which are made just as easily from novels of much less literary worth', which is absolutely true, so it is a comment on the relative strengths of the two media that there are scenes in the film which must be memorable even to the least attentive spectator: the ball marking Emma's debut in society, with the camera holding her giddy, gliding excitement; the coach for her planned elopement moving past, leaving her stranded; and her ineffable appreciation of the opera at Rouen. Minnelli's overall understanding is remarkable, as is the transformation of Metro's famous village★ into Normandy.

Minnelli directed **Father of the Bride** (1950), which is a chronicle of the funny things that surround a wedding, scripted by Frances Goodrich and Albert Hackett from a book of comic essays by Edward Streeter. Matters are entirely predictable, from father's realisation that his dove is about to flee the nest, to his contemplation of the guest list: 'It's no longer a question of insulting people, but of survival.' The direction is heavy, and Minnelli cannot make the young couple (Don Taylor, Elizabeth Taylor) anything but ninnies. However, all is right when Spencer Tracy is on screen, talking to the audience in a

★Recognisable by its stream and humped bridge, despite often drastic work by the art department, it featured in virtually every M-G-M film of this period which was set in Europe, e.g. *Till the Clouds Roll By* (English), *The Green Years* (Scottish), *Desire Me* (French again).

wry, not-to-be-defeated tone. This actor is reputed to have had doubts about every film he accepted, so it is hard to understand why he made **Father's Little Dividend** (1951), which is living, or rather, dead proof that sequels are seldom good. Its subjects is an expectant mother, and there was nothing in it, incidentally, to offend *Picturegoer*, which a few months earlier had complained that the continental tendency to show pregnant women as pregnant was extending to the U.S. – a 'disgusting' practice which, it was hoped, would not spread to British films.

The Bad and the Beautiful (1952) is perhaps Minnelli's best non-musical film, and it is the cinema equivalent of the *roman-à-clef*, stuffed with Hollywood folklore as it recounts the exploits of an all-time heel. Charles Schnee wrote it from a story by George Bradshaw, John Houseman produced it, and its structure is the same as the most famous film on which he worked, *Citizen Kane*; in it a producer (Walter Pidgeon), a director (Barry Sullivan), a star (Lana Turner) and an author (Dick Powell) each remember a former colleague (Kirk Douglas). The film picks at its victims, refusing to dig beneath the surface – which is perhaps why the industry did not loathe it as it had loathed *Sunset Boulevard*. It is circumspect, for instance, on sex, with just one representative dame to be nice to producers, with just a hint of men passing on their women: one extra complains to her boyfriend that getting on 'depends who you *live* with' (my italics). Oscars went to this movie for costume design, set design and Robert Surtees's cinematography (as well as to the screenwriter), evidence of Minnelli's flair for the visual: the camera rakes across a studio floor, catching details in pools of light, and it trails the guests at a cocktail party, catching snatches of conversations. The film is even more enjoyable if one knows its victims: the Turner character is mainly Diana Barrymore, daughter of John, and part Turner herself, 'wooden, gauche and artificial' as described by Leo G. Carroll, playing a very British director; while the Douglas character is mostly Selznick, part Thalberg, and a little Val Lewton – though his faults all seem to stem from Broadway's Jed Harris. Among the extras may be spotted a dead-ringer for Lubitsch, a plaintive chantoosie looking like the 1948 Judy

Garland, and a Joan Crawford-like star who speaks lovingly of her fans; collectors of trivia may care to note that the film in this movie called 'The Proud Land' can be seen on a 42nd Street marquee in Minnelli's next film, *The Band Wagon*.

'Jealous – in London! Forbidden – in Rome! Dangerous – in Paris!' read the ads for **The Story of Three Loves** (1953), and though at least two of the three adjectives are lies, you know what sort of film this will be. Sidney Franklin produced it, after searching for a vehicle for the new continental actresses under contract, Leslie Caron and Pier Angeli; not coming up with anything, he put them in two separate stories and added a third, with Moira Shearer. Minnelli directed the Caron sequence only, in which she plays a governess loathed by her charge (Ricky Nelson) till he visits a witch (Ethel Barrymore) who tells him that if he gets up to some jiggery-pokery at bedtime he can turn into Farley Granger. The direction flounders in whimsy, and the whole enterprise was far from being the equal of the European art movies intended.

It was not a success, nor was *Crisis*; it is no wonder, then, to find the studio panting for the return of Joan Crawford, directed in **Torch Song** (1953) by Charles Walters: 'When you make a Crawford picture you've got to go all the way. *She's* the picture and she dominates. I remember stealing ideas from her personal life to fit the character in the picture . . .' John Michael Hayes and Jan Lustig wrote the script, and Crawford must surely have recognised that of all the bitches she played this one at least was based on herself – though of course it is hard to tell, since she had a humourlessness that bordered on the bizarre. She plays a song-and-dance girl, still holding up her skirt as she did in *The Hollywood Revue of 1929*. 'You're the times in Times Square, you're the broad in Broadway,' says her agent, but she is bored. So bored. After glowering at her blind pianist (Michael Wilding) for ten reels, she discovers that before his accident he wrote of her 'gypsy madonna hair' and the film ends with her arms around him, less protectively, I thought, than as if she were about to devour him.

We may wonder why such films hung on so long, anachronisms in the postwar world. Hollywood was slow to acknowledge that a considerable portion of its audience was spilling over into the art houses, to see films like *Ladri di Biciclette* and *La Ronde* (q.v.) – and the industry's attitude is understandable when much-praised films, *and* in English, were failing to attract more than minimal audiences. When these films lost money, the industry and M-G-M could not decide whether it was because they were the wrong films or because the publicity representatives – and hence, exhibitors – were flummoxed when faced with what they considered to be films untypical of M-G-M. Of the films for which Schary was personally respons-ible, only one was enormously successful – *Battleground* (1950), a World War II drama, directed by William Wellman – and it was in the wake of that that Loews Inc. re-affirmed its faith in Schary by finally forc-ing Mayer from the company he had helped to found. Mayer's belief that films should be made for the entire family had been successfully challenged by Schary, who had reintroduced Westerns and action films, but it is doubtful whether he be-lieved in them. If he believed in anything at all, it was the 'message' film in rather chi-chi form – in violent contrast to Zanuck, the most astute studio head at this time, who believed in 'message' only if the 'entertainment' ingredients were right. Arthur Freed certainly believed in his musicals, and so popular was the M-G-M musical at this time that it kept profits

buoyant and prolonged Schary's regime.

Mayer's reactionary stance was neither more nor less reprehensible than Schary's inadequate attempt to break new barriers: however far apart they seemed to each other, they were at heart commercially-minded industry men. The film industry itself had been stable for so long that it could not comprehend the changes which were about to be wrought upon it. Audi-ences were falling and the threat of tele-vision was growing. Such things were understood, and each studio was not un-willing to dispense with the huge number of players under contract. The business-men and executives had refused to under-stand the drive for independence by crea-tive talents – who in turn had not under-stood its failure. At the heart of the matter was the volatility of audiences, restless after the War, who were finding new calls on their leisure time. Critics and public had had little impact on each other in the Thir-ties, but their views were seldom far apart – though paradoxically their preferences grew further apart as more and more cinemagoers turned to reviewers for guid-ance. A trend had begun, which would continue till the late Sixties, for poor films to attract crowds and good films to pass unnoticed. The majority of the box-office successes of the postwar period are not worth a dime either on television or at revival houses, while many of the failures have passed into folklore.

29

Production in Austerity Britain

IN BRITAIN, the end of the War meant the end of air-raids and the black-out; servicemen returned to Civvy Street, but conscription continued. So did the rationing of petrol, fuel, clothing and most foodstuffs. In the bitter winter of 1946–7 the government forbade the cinemas to open before four p.m. because of the fuel crisis. At the same time, the television service resumed, for the few thousand sets which had been in operation before the War. Despite the poor quality of the programmes transmitted by the B.B.C. (then a monopoly) the service made much greater headway than in America, partly because of the televising of Princess Elizabeth's wedding in 1947 and of the Coronation in 1953: during that time there was a significant falling off in cinema attendances. The person most concerned was J. Arthur Rank, who owned two-thirds of the nation's cinemas and its leading production and distribution companies. The resurrection of Alexander Korda's London Films presented competition but no rivalry, since Korda was a creative producer and Rank mainly a financier, dipping into the profits from his flour-mills to retrieve his film interests where necessary – which happened frequently, owing to the poor economic health of both the country and the film industry. The government had imposed an Entertainment Tax, on cinema admissions, so that the industry was crippled where it was traditionally strongest, in exhibition. Someone once observed that Rank's family motto should have been *Panem et Circenses*, and his ambitions with regard to the latter caused him to make repeated expensive forays into the American market.

Unfortunately Rank did not understand cinema – nor, incidentally, have any of his successors at the Rank Organisation to this day. The creative force in the company at the end of the War was Filippo del Guidice, who had gathered there the most talented film-makers in Britain. Rank allowed them creative freedom, but del Guidice's position was weakened as, one by one, they deserted to Korda, impressed by his immense personal charm, and a greater enthusiasm for the medium than Rank possessed.

Del Guidice was eventually ousted, not long after giving Rank **Hamlet** (1948), which received praise unprecedented for a British film. It won awards throughout the world – including Oscars in Hollywood for Best Picture, Best Direction and Best Actor, overshadowing the prestige gained by *Henry V*. Since that time del Guidice had been cajoling Laurence Olivier into undertaking another Shakespeare film, and it is typical of Olivier's career that he should take on the challenge of filming what many consider the greatest play ever written. He rejected 'Macbeth' and 'Othello' because Orson Welles had expressed an intention of doing both; as far as the box office was concerned – and exhibitors quaked at the thought of programming Shakespeare – *Hamlet* was marginally the best known of the three titles. Alan Dent's adaptation chopped away many of the play's complexities, to leave a firm story-line and to allow Olivier to develop this 'tragedy of a man who could not make up his mind' – a statement which prefaces the film, together with the 'So oft it chances in particular men' speech. Olivier as the prince is less interested in his contemplative moods than his sardonic humour.

Physically, it is not easy for him to look vacillating, so he starts as a student withering away in aimlessness, but when the ghost directs him to his destiny he becomes misanthropic and suspicious, a focus for the court around him. As director, he imparts an atmosphere of danger and propels the narrative towards its powerful and exciting climax, the duel; and there are other elements as impressive as they are harmonious – the music by William Walton, the photography by Desmond Dickenson and the cavernous sets designed by Roger Furse. It was clear then that Olivier and his collaborators understood the Bard better than any of the others who had attempted to present him on screen – and if we extend the remark to include Olivier's own *Richard III* (q.v.), it takes care of all other efforts in the meantime. Roman Polanski, later to film *Macbeth* (q.v.), is only one of several filmmakers to have spoken warmly of the influence of *Hamlet*: and its position today,

after some years during which the initial reaction was thought excessive, is unassailable. It is a very satisfying film, because it takes very great material and interprets it with honour, imagination and intelligence.

It marks a peak in postwar British production, as does *The Best Years of Our Lives* in American cinema. Neither, as different as they are, was typical: the British studios showed as little interest in classic plays as basic material as their Hollywood counterparts did in contemporary subjects. As far as the latter were concerned, the demand for topical material declined sharply with the end of the War. It had been easy enough to construct thrillers around the gangsters of the Depression era and the Resistance fighters of the War; but relief that the War was over prevented anyone from suggesting that there might be discord within the current mood. Nevertheless Britain could not return to the trivial thrillers and comic cut-ups of the prewar

The praise accorded Olivier's three Shakespeare films, especially *Hamlet*, indicated that they were regarded as important cultural artefacts, with the result that their reputation has fluctuated over the years. They have always been popular on revival – when they can be judged for what they are, superbly-crafted versions of classic plays. Olivier as Hamlet is in the chair, with Eileen Herlie as Gertrude and Basil Sydney as Claudius; to the right is Terence Morgan as Laertes.

years. European critics, seeing British films for the first time in five years, were astounded by the improvement, while the American cinema seemed virtually unchanged – a fact gradually dawning on some American critics, who used British cinema as another stick with which to beat Hollywood.

The new Labour administration was undoubtedly the inspiration for making **Fame Is the Spur** (1947), based on Howard Spring's novel about a Socialist politician (played in the film by Michael Redgrave) – a thinly-disguised Ramsay MacDonald, the first Labour prime minister. Nigel Balchin's screenplay has in common with *Goodbye, Mr Chips* the early death of the wife and the protagonist's lonely if honoured old age: but since it leaves vague the extent to which he regrets his betrayal of his youthful ideals the result is hardly more than a rags-to-riches story. The accompanying attempts at 'art' and significance, as directed by Roy Boulting and produced by his brother John, are typical of the time.

Moving from Rank to Associated British, the Boultings brought similar ability to **Brighton Rock** (1947) or **The Guinea Pig** (1948), but these are, nevertheless, distinctive films. The former was scripted

by Graham Greene from his own novel (the credits claim as co-writer Terence Rattigan, who said that his contribution was small and that he did not work with Greene), and this is possibly why the film is agreeably raffish, with seedy seaside streets, tacky cafés, deck-chairs on the promenade – a world of Woolworth teacups, bottled ale and wind-up gramophones. The cast fits splendidly into it, except for the boy killer (Richard Attenborough), either posed or posing, and the direction always signals the action. Roy Boulting also directed *The Guinea Pig*, a further copy of *Goodbye, Mr Chips*, and more reasonably, since it is based on Warren Chetham Strode's public school play. The subject was topical, in that the Labour government was expected to abolish these seats of privilege, and it specifically concerns a grammar-school boy sent to one of them. His dilemma is treated in a patronising half-hearted way, and for a climax the film has the effrontery to offer his tobacconist father (Bernard Miles) arriving to say that the house system is partly responsible for Britain's greatness. The boy – played by Attenborough on one note of quivering lip – has the impudence to use the word 'arse' to a master, and much fuss was made because the censor let the word pass.

The British public was otherwise indifferent, preferring undisguised fictions, and indeed, as the War in Europe finished, it was watching James Mason drive Dulcie Gray to drink in **They Were Sisters** (1945), unperturbed that Dorothy Whipple's novel had been falsified to further Mason's popularity as a villain. Gainsborough's romances now exuded the confidence brought by success, and this one catches well the British upper bourgeoisie of the Twenties, as three sisters (Phyllis Calvert, Anne Crawford, Miss Gray) marry diversely; it is also a vast improvement for Arthur Crabtree, who had directed *Madonna of the Seven Moons*. **The Wicked Lady** (1945), again demeans its source, Magdalen King-Hall's pastiche account of one of the eccentric seventeenth-century miladies, who in this case takes to larceny on the king's highway. The writer-director, Leslie Arliss, added elements of 'Vanity Fair' and 'Forever Amber', but also some wit, moving it through gracious settings at a tremendous

Margaret Lockwood, *The Wicked Lady* herself, could not resist going to the hanging of the lover and partner that she has betrayed: but in the view of the letter handed to her by Ivor Bonard, left, she clearly wishes that she hadn't. The critics loathed the film, but the public loved it, while it was the other way round with *Brief Encounter*, OPPOSITE. The public soon reversed its judgment, but if *Brief Encounter* has become one of the most beloved of all films, *The Wicked Lady* is really not that bad at all.

clip. He certainly provides a field-day for Margaret Lockwood, flashing her eyes and curling her lips with wild improvidence – indeed she owed much of her popularity to the fact that English lady stars had not hitherto been allowed such high-flown passions. Audiences recognised in her the Hollywood heroines who had thrilled them in like manner, but the only other of the major players not gauche is Mason as a highwayman. Any other faults escaped the notice of the public. It was the most popular British film up to that time; in the U.S. market, despite much refilming to meet M.P.A.A. requirements over the matter of Miss Lockwood's cleavage, it failed to make the least impression.

Brief Encounter (1945) opened in London the same day, to the reverse reception – critical praise and indifference from the audience. Now it is constantly revived while *The Wicked Lady*, though undeniably a junk classic, is half-forgotten. It did not take long for *Brief Encounter* to become loved – and imitated – though none of the subsequent cinema encounters have been as touching (and many of them have dated far more). Noël Coward adapted it from his one-act play, 'Still Life', viewing the situation only from the outside – the difficulties of meeting, the fear of what neighbours might think – but thereby matching his characters, who are middle-class Britishers. Laura Jesson and Alec Harvey are not frustrated or despairing; they have all their lives done the 'decent' thing, and they respond to each other when they laugh at the inmates of the station buffet, the Donald Duck cartoon and the pince-nezed lady in the Kardomah coffee-house. He has a Galahad quality: she is left breathless by his insistence on seeing her again and by his quixotic solution, which is to emigrate. Celia Johnson and Trevor Howard generously fill in the emotions between the lines; the comic passages – Stanley Holloway and Joyce Carey in the buffet – are by no means as far-fetched as they may later seem; and David Lean's direction is exemplary.

At this point he and his collaborators at Cineguild – the producer Ronald Neame and associate producer Anthony Havelock-Allen – turned from Coward to Dickens for further examples of the British ethos for world audiences. Both **Great Expectations** (1946) and **Oliver Twist**

(1948) are superb, from the mystery and disquiet seen at the outset to their galloping finales. (Both have been done again, in colour and with music,* though the addition of songs to Dickens's teeming plots must be at best superfluous.) Lean has absolute faith in his author, with Guy Green on camera and John Bryan, the designer, integrating and exploring every aspect of their crafts – even to a slight overheating, but that is exactly the sort of virtuosity required. Of the other Dickens films, only Cukor's *David Copperfield* approaches the excellence of this pair, partly because his casting, too, was near-perfect. As the grown-up Pip and Estella, John Mills and Valerie Hobson are no more appealing than Dickens made them, but as children they are well played by Anthony Wager and Jean Simmons; Martita Hunt the memory-haunted, nocturnal Miss Havisham; Freda Jackson and Bernard Miles are the Joe Gargerys; Finlay Currie is Magwitch, most alarming of convicts; Ivor Bonard is Wemmick, Hay Petrie Uncle Pumblechook, O. B. Clarence the Aged P., Alec Guinness Herbert Pocket and Francis L. Sullivan is Jaggers. Sullivan

*In the case of the 1974 *Great Expectations* the songs were, however, cut from the release print.

Celia Johnson and Trevor Howard in *Brief Encounter*. The prestige of J. Arthur Rank was at its peak; he was the financier, a benevolent despot to the film-makers working in the companies he controlled. Gainsborough Pictures, making melodramas like *The Wicked Lady*, OPPOSITE, brought in huge profits, while Cineguild – an offshoot of Two Cities – reaped fine notices and awards. In 1946 the New York critics voted Celia Johnson the best actress for *Brief Encounter* and Laurence Olivier best actor for Two Cities' *Henry V*, the first time they had cited players for films not made in Hollywood.

Production in Austerity Britain

In retrospect, the praise meted out to British films in the Forties does seem justified. No one has filmed Shakespeare as well as Olivier, and no subsequent version of Dickens has been a patch on the two made by David Lean – and this is *Great Expectations*, with Jean Simmons and Anthony Wager as the infant Estella and Pip, and Francis L. Sullivan as Jaggers. Film-makers today leave the handling of such classics entirely to television, which may or may not be a pity.

is Mr Bumble in *Oliver Twist*, so well matched by Mary Clare in their early sequence that it is a joy to see them unhappily wed; Ralph Truman is the mysterious, brutish Monks; Gibb McLaughlin and Kathleen Harrison are the Sowerberrys, with Diana Dors as the drudge and Michael Dear as uppity Noah Claypole; Henry Stephenson is the kindliest of Mr Brownlows and Anthony Newley the most artful of dodgers; Robert Newton is a frightening Sykes, and in the title role John Howard Davies is a little too well-spoken and self-effacing. Alec Guinness enjoys himself as Fagin, whose presentation in this tale, though unavoidable, caused high blood pressures in the Jewish-dominated American film industry, necessitating some cuts and a three-year delay in its being shown in the U.S.

Lean's run of fine films ended with **The Passionate Friends** (1949), H. G. Wells's 1913 novel modernised by Eric Ambler, who also produced. 'The important thing is the situation,' he said of his adaptation, 'and that could have happened at any time.' Yes; but not, surely, like this. The happy ending is a violation of Wells's intention, and far from there being a suggestion of free love, we are not party to Mary's sexual relations with either husband (Claude Rains) or lover (Trevor Howard): if they are more than friends, passionate or otherwise, why does Mary (Ann Todd) show not an iota of feeling? C. A. Lejeune suggested that the box-office failure of *Brief Encounter* made Lean have his characters 'wear dressier clothes and move in smart settings' but I suspect that he wanted (it is not uncommon among European directors) his star, who was also his wife, to be shown off in Hollywood-like glamour. Neither the Swiss locations nor her extensive wardrobe are objectionable, but her mask-like face gets many a glistening close-up and gives nothing in return.

The Cineguild team had split by this time, and Neame and Havelock-Allen, together and separately, tried to turn the clock back with some thrillers only too depressingly reminiscent of prewar British programme-fillers. However, **The Small Voice** (1948), produced by Havelock-Allen and directed by Fergus McDonell, is a well-paced and well-cut piece about convicts keeping a lonely household prisoner – a situation common in Silent Westerns, and to be used again in several films of the Fifties. Neame turned director, and a prosaic one, bringing to his subjects neither vulgarity nor vigour. Two literary adaptations are agreeable: **The Card** (1952), written by Ambler from Arnold Bennett's novel, and **The Million Pound Note** (1954), by Jill Craigie from Mark Twain. The former does not catch the flavour of the Five Towns, but is better than most British comedies because Bennett was more resourceful than most people who write comedies for Alec Guinness (b. 1914). This is a vehicle for Guinness, a stage actor then establishing himself in a series of mildly eccentric screen frolics. He is likeable, if not pushy enough, as the deceivingly inventive Denry, well-abetted by Glynis Johns as a conniving minx

and Valerie Hobson as a democratically-minded countess. The Twain tale has Technicolor, Joyce Grenfell as a society hostess, and concerns an unusual banknote offered by two clubland pranksters to a penniless American – played by Gregory Peck, brought across at great expense by Rank in yet another belated attempt to break into the American market.

The decline and disintegration of Cineguild is symptomatic of the British film industry at that time. During the War and just after, Lean and his colleagues had made a handful of films worthy to set with the world's best; also under the Rank umbrella, other bright talents were making the films which were recognised as having greater vitality than those arriving from Hollywood. Inevitably among those tackling unhackneyed subjects were Powell and Pressburger – though in the case of **I Know Where I'm Going** (1945) an old one was tricked up to make it seem like new. Their first film together had been set in the Hebrides, and they returned to the Isles for this story of a girl (Wendy Hiller) who finds that love is more important than money. She learns her lesson through the Islanders and their customs, including Highland reels and falconry; and she is also subjected to the kilted charm of the laird (Roger Livesey).

The producer of Lean's Dickens films was Ronald Neame, who himself shortly thereafter turned director and in *The Card* turned an Arnold Bennett novel into a pleasing Ealing-type comedy. Alec Guinness, seen here with Glynis Johns, was already associated with Ealing comedy and the public relished his ability constantly to change his appearance. He was the first star daring enough to do so without the benefit of an outsize personality, like Laughton or Olivier.

Production in Austerity Britain

It is a slight and charming film, but the three films which followed it are remarkable for the courage of their excesses. Powell and Pressburger claimed that their films were entirely collaborative efforts, and it was not disclosed till later that Powell was the actual director and that Pressburger contributed little once the film was on the studio floor. More than their earlier films together this bizarre trio calls into question the nature of their collaboration, and an examination of the films they made before they teamed up suggests that Pressburger is a writer of European sensibility while Powell may be relegated to the ranks of work-a-day directors. (After the team split up he made an almost appallingly silly horror film, *Peeping Tom*, but even that had a moment or two of visual flair.) Yet the faults of **A Matter of Life and Death** (1946) are so thorough that there is no apportioning blame. It is as platitudinous as it is ambitious. There is no other film quite like it, even if it follows the European tradition of whimsy (e.g. *Death Takes a Holiday*) and borrows some dim ideas from a dim picture – the dead pilots' receiving room in heaven from *A Guy Named Joe*. While a pilot (David Niven) struggles for life under anaesthetic, his doctor (Livesey) – after mounting an endless staircase leading to a heavenly courtroom – pleads for his life before a Jewish judge (Abraham Sofaer). Many of the arguments concern the differences between Britain and America (their cultural values represented respectively by broadcasts of a cricket commentary and 'Shoo Shoo Baby') – the excuse being that the pilot has fallen in love with an American girl (Kim Hunter). The prosecuting counsel (Raymond Massey) is an American, and though there is evidence of Powell and Pressburger's customary pride in Britain the specious arguments set forth show much kowtowing to the country on the other side of the Atlantic. There were economic reasons for that and for the presence of Americans in the cast: the film cost so much that only with American acceptance could Rank get his money back. He did not get it. It was treated with great earnestness – a fact that must give pause to anyone coming upon it now for the first time. For that reason it has a minor place in the history of postwar Britain – along with the fuel crisis of 1947 and the 'Britain Can Make It' exhibition – and also because it was selected for the first Royal Film Performance.

'One is starved of Technicolor up here' is typical of the humour, since the trial scenes are in monochrome; but Powell and Pressburger elsewhere seldom starved audiences of Technicolor. **Black Narcissus** (1947) is visually ravishing as photographed by Jack Cardiff and designed by Alfred Junge; it was filmed entirely in Britain and the process work simulating the Himalayas may be described as miraculous. The setting is a convent and the screenplay is quite faithful to Rumer Godden's novel as it charts the quarrels and rapports of the nuns (headed by Deborah Kerr and Flora Robson) with two princes, father (Esmond Knight) and son (Sabu), and their British agent (David Farrar). Our doubts may arise when the jealous nun (Kathleen Byron) doffs her wimple for a spot of raving nymphomania, but this time I intend an unqualified compliment when I say that there is no other film quite like it.

The same is not entirely true of **The Red Shoes** (1948), with its formula backstage plot – a dancer torn between composer and a Svengali-like impresario;★ it also manages to parallel the Hans Andersen tale – which itself turns up in the climactic ballet. And as the first English-language film to deal almost exclusively with ballet it attempts several large statements on the nature of art and the artistic impulse. As the dancer, the Sadler's Wells star Moira Shearer is gazelle-like, badly made-up and completely without humour; Marius Goring is the dullest of composers and Anton Walbrook the most demonic of impresarios; the presence of Massine, Robert Helpmann and Ludmilla Tcherina helps to lend authenticity to the backstage scenes. The combination of the familiar and the fervid made the piece popular in the U.S., where the profits made up for the losses on *Stairway to Heaven* (as *A Matter of Life and Death* had been retitled). Indeed, the film's success in America was greater than that of any other British movie of the time, thus encouraging Rank's ambitions in that direction – ironically so, for at one point during shooting, when the budget was exceeded, overtures were made to Korda

★The inspiration was, like the 1931 film, *The Mad Genius*, the relationship between Diaghilev and Nijinsky.

to take over the project. Korda declined, but in view of Rank's trepidation it is not surprising that Powell and Pressburger made their next films for Korda.

Frank Launder and Sidney Gilliat also followed their wartime successes with one equally interesting film, **The Rake's Progress** (1945), which they wrote and Gilliat directed. It 'anticipates the first British satire of the screen' thought Richard Winnington, contemplating this study of a typical playboy (Rex Harrison) of the Thirties – from being sent down from Oxford (for placing a chamber-pot on one of the dreaming spires) to killing his father (Godfrey Tearle) in a drunken motor accident. His first job, as befits the black sheep, is with the British in South America, where cricket is more important than work, and attendance at the club more important than either – a condition satirically handled, but a poor reason for his cynicism and philandering. He marries an Austrian half-Jewish girl (Lilli Palmer) to help her escape the Nazis – a situation used to dramatic advantage and also interesting since the plight of European Jews had mainly escaped the attention of filmmakers. His kindness is short-lived, but at the end he is redeemed by the love of a good woman – after which, in the epilogue, he becomes a war hero. C. A. Lejeune was one of several reviewers who objected to the implication that this was 'the type who won the War': today we are more likely to agree with her contention that the film shirks 'the responsibility of a really rotten hero'. Apart from bogeymen, the screen would not see a wholly reprehensible protagonist till Wilder's *Ace in the Hole* (q.v.).

Launder and Gilliat returned to roots with two thrillers, but as we may expect from the writers of *The Lady Vanishes*, both are superior examples of the genre – and, indeed, **I See a Dark Stranger** (1946) has a number of similar twists as it charts the progress of an Irish girl (Deborah Kerr) from her spying for the Nazis to her conversion by a British officer (Trevor Howard); Launder directed from their screenplay. Gilliat directed **Green for Danger** (1947) based on a novel by Christianna Brand – which is classic, inasmuch as a great number of skeletons are dragged from cupboards as each of the major characters is suspect in turn after murder in the

operating-room. The suspects (Howard, Leo Genn, Sally Gray, Rosamund John, Megs Jenkins, Judy Campbell) wear their uniforms as though striding the wards for years, but it is Alistair Sim, smug and infuriating as the Scotland Yard man, who transforms a good thriller into a remarkable one. Gilliat was much less skilful in **London Belongs to Me** (1948), reducing to stereotypes the inhabitants of Norman Collins's South London boarding house – for this is a version of that author's Grand Hotelish bestseller.

It was becoming clear that Launder and Gilliat were unlikely to fulfil the promise of *Millions Like Us* and *The Rake's Progress*. **Captain Boycott** (1947) takes an engrossing subject, the landlord (Cecil Parker) who drove the nineteenth-century Irish peasantry to extremity, but since it portrays him as merely misguided the film suffers from a lack of conflict. It was further compromised by Stewart Granger, in a narcissistic performance as the Errol Flynn-like hero; the fact is that it was rewritten thus after he had expressed an interest in playing the role. Admittedly without him Rank would not have backed the venture, since it required expensive location work. So did **The Blue Lagoon** (1949), which was also primarily Launder's film. 'Crusoe-and-soda' Claude Cockburn described de Vere Stacpoole's antiquated bestseller, and because of

One particularly admired British partnership of the time was that of Launder and Gilliat, who had begun – as writers – modestly on quota quickies in the Thirties and would become disappointing journeyman film-makers in the Fifties. *The Rake's Progress*, however, with Rex Harrison and Lilli Palmer, is one of several Launder and Gilliat films of the Forties which revives strongly.

watchful censorship boards it was even sillier on screen: the couple (Jean Simmons, Donald Houston) stranded on a desert island are no longer cousins, and before the baby is born they read to each other the marriage ceremony as found in a convenient-to-hand book of etiquette! As intended, the palmy beaches and sunsets did help to lighten the gloom of postwar Britain, but the country's critics ungratefully termed the film more than usually irrelevant. Americans for once proved uninterested in desert island romance, and since it had been financed with more than an eye on the American market it was Launder's second failure for Rank. He and Gilliat also departed to work for Korda.

Carol Reed followed *The Way Ahead* with **Odd Man Out** (1947), and as the earlier film had established him as the country's leading director it was both fitting and typical that he should choose as his source F. L. Green's novel: it was clear to this movie buff film-maker that the bleak, sad story of a hold-up in an Irish city could provide affinities with certain classic films, e.g., *The Informer, Quai des Brumes*. For most of its length, it is very fine indeed as a straightforward thriller: but when it deserts the streets for the decaying mansion – where a mad, drunken artist (Robert Newton) wants to paint the eyes of the dying Johnny (James Mason) – it splurges into the surreal. Reed then tends to lose control and move towards pretension, but in that respect the film is more subtle than most of its contemporaries. It was certainly regarded as unreserved proof that the British could make a 'great' picture.

Reed's first two films for Korda consolidated his unrivalled position. **The Fallen Idol** (1948) and **The Third Man** (1949) were both written by Graham Greene, the former from his published story and the latter from a novella written expressly for screen adaptation. *The Fallen Idol* is about a small boy (Bobby Henrey), the son of an ambassador whose butler, Baines (Ralph Richardson), is his idol and surrogate father; Mrs Baines (Sonia Dresdel) is the embassy Carabosse – and the child's mainly innocent world darkens further with the discovery of adultery and a death. The Belgrave Square locations remain vividly in the memory. For *The Third Man* Reed used what seemed like most of Vienna, a city of ruin and shadows harbouring felons more sinister than usual – cold-war opportunists and black marketeers. It is a second tale of disillusion, this time experienced by a writer (Joseph Cotten) in search of a mysterious friend, Harry Lime (Orson Welles), now a profiteer. Assisting the writer is a laconic British major (Trevor Howard) and not helping him is a ballerina (Alida Valli), with strong convictions about the Harry she once loved. Enhanced by its haunting zither theme music, the film was a great success the world over – though less so in the U.S. It was a co-production between Korda and Selznick – for the Americans were resuming their prewar interest in the British film industry.

Both films retain their powerful individuality, even though *The Third Man* was imitated, conspicuously by Reed himself (see below); but, after three critical successes, Reed disappointed all the more with **An Outcast of the Islands** (1951). The cinema has seldom tackled Conrad, and William Fairchild's screenplay reveals that he was the wrong man for the task, since after an uneasy exposition nothing much happens. The rigours of filming on location (Ceylon, not the Malaya of the novel) may be one reason why Reed accepted some dreadful performances: Robert Morley, a buffoon as Almayer; Richardson (who was superb in *The Fallen Idol*), orotund as the captain; and George Coulouris and Kerima, who as natives seem to have strayed from a Maria Montez epic. Only in Trevor Howard's Willems and Wendy Hiller's Mrs Almayer are there intimations of the film that might have been. Its failure forced Reed to backtrack. He had once told an assistant, Guy Hamilton, 'When in doubt, do a comedy-thriller. You may lose some of the laughs and some of the thrills, but you'll get something': but there is little of either in **The Man Between** (1953). The script commissioned from Harry Kurnitz is reminiscent of *The Third Man*; but Reed's snowbound Berlin has none of the eeriness of his Vienna, and James Mason, as the enigmatic Ivo, cannot escape from the shadow of Harry Lime.

Reed then made a more serious mistake in tackling something new. Both he and Korda believed that that was the business of film-makers, but Korda had doubts about **A Kid for Two Farthings** (1955), written by Wolf Mankowitz from his own short story. A patronising concoction of

Carol Reed's Shadowland

We may also feel that the later films of Carol Reed are not so good, but the promise of his prewar films was more than fulfilled by his films of the Forties, including *Odd Man Out*, ABOVE, with James Mason and F. J. McCormick, and two versions of Graham Greene, *The Fallen Idol*, ABOVE RIGHT, with Bobby Henrey, and *The Third Man*, RIGHT, with Orson Welles. Reed was the first film director to be knighted, and whether or not one agrees with the British honours system that is indicative of the prestige he brought to the native industry. He is also the only British film director to be so honoured to date, if we accept Olivier and Richard Attenborough as primarily actors and Chaplin and Hitchcock as American film-makers – and both of them were knighted towards the end of their lives.

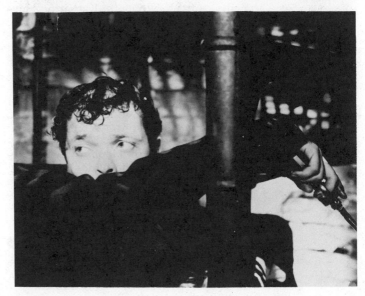

Petticoat Lane philosophy, humour and fantasy, it is played by a bunch of show business Cockneys bearing as much resemblance to the real thing as Christmas tree glitter to snow – an analogy I use to give some indication of the decor. Few major directors ever miscalculated so horrendously.

David Lean's films for Korda also show a falling-off – though at the time **The Sound Barrier** (1952) was much admired and actually voted by the British Film Academy as superior to, q.v., *Rashomon*, *The River* and *Casque d'Or*. The film opened at the time the first jet passenger plane, the Comet, made its early flights, and was therefore bang up to the minute, with its discussions on the conquest of space and its then-unprecedented aerial photography. Terence Rattigan's screenplay toys with the idea that scientific idealism is compatible with human sacrifice, but is otherwise soap opera, with its fanatical aeronautics tycoon (Richardson), bravely-waiting little woman (Ann Todd) and phlegmatic test pilots.

Lean, like Reed, turned about, unearthing **Hobson's Choice** (1954), Harold Brighouse's old play. It concerns the cobbler's daughter (Brenda da Banzie) who sets about marrying the meek employee (John Mills) and unseating pa (Charles Laughton). The photography of the exteriors is a celebration of Edwardian Salford, but its fussiness in the cramped interiors is communicated to both the screenplay and some of the performers. Nevertheless, Lean's direction seems more personal than in his two previous films and in the one that followed.

That is **Summer Madness** (1955), a mating of two wonders, Katharine Hepburn and Venice – and Lean seems to have been content to let his camera stare starry-eyed at both. It has subsequently proved impossible for many to be a tourist in Venice without recalling this film (if only because the quintets in the Piazza San Marco still perform its theme tune) – and, of course, few cities have a better claim to be captured in colour for the screen. It is seen through the eyes of a hopelessly enthusiastic tourist, played by Hepburn – who despite some actressy tricks makes touching a woman's loneliness and what may be both her first and last affair. The screenplay, by Lean and H. E. Bates, is not with-

out wit and acerbity, as based on Arthur Laurents's Broadway play, 'The Time of the Cuckoo'; the film's American title is *Summertime*; Ilya Lopert and United Artists joined Korda in backing it. Lean's career henceforward was to owe more to Hollywood than to Britain.

American interest proved fatal to Powell and Pressburger; they had made **The Small Back Room** (1949), for them a rare excursion into monochrome, which Powell believes is his best film. Unfortunately, Nigel Balchin's novel of the darkest days of the War featured two aspects already hackneyed – meddling civil servants and an embittered war hero (David Farrar), a scientist with a tin leg who wants to go back on the booze. There followed, in Powell's own words, two 'disastrous films', **Gone to Earth** (1950) and **The Elusive Pimpernel** (1950), for which Korda had welcomed the participation of Selznick and Goldwyn respectively. Selznick's excessive interference in the former was due to the fact that Jennifer Jones was in the lead, while Goldwyn was involved in the latter because the other star, David Niven, was under contract to him. Powell later observed, 'If you're making a film between Goldwyn and Alex Korda . . . you get ground to powder.' *The Elusive Pimpernel* had been planned as a musical, and 'it never went right,' according to Powell, 'because there were relics of the musical idea still in it.' Whoever was responsible, direction, acting and writing are of an appalling level, despite the excessive cost of £450,000, which became half a million with the retakes demanded by Goldwyn, who, in the end, decreed it below the standard necessary for the U.S. market. (A small independent outfit managed to get it a few dates there four years later.) Selznick felt the same about *Gone to Earth*: the British premiere was delayed by the insertion of close-ups of Miss Jones, while the American version, rechristened *The Wild Heart* and shortened by twenty minutes, was extensively re-shot and re-cut by Rouben Mamoulian. In this instance the difficulties were partly due to the source material, a novel by Mary Webb, reduced to a sex triangle between the wicked squire (Mr Farrar), the new minister (Cyril Cusack) and a fey girl (Miss Jones) who keeps a pet fox.

To retrieve their reputation, Powell and

Pressburger accepted a suggestion from the conductor Sir Thomas Beecham, who had helped on *The Red Shoes*, to film **The Tales of Hoffman** (1951). At that time Italy was exporting a number of black and white opera films, with the camera seemingly set in the stalls; Powell, of course, went to the other extreme. The prologue and the Olympia sequence are often imaginative, but vulgarity – always just at bay in his work – sinks the Giulietta sequence beneath its pink Venetian waters, while the Antonia section, placed last, is a dull and muddy anti-climax. The special effects are inspired by Cocteau, while the decor by the variable Hein Heckroth, Powell's invariable collaborator, only renders Offenbach's masterpiece as Festival of Britain kitsch. The film's comparatively low cost was not enough to endear Powell and Pressburger to the industry when the public failed to respond, and they were absent from the studio till Associated British backed **Oh . . . Rosalinda!!** (1955), a modernisation of 'Die Fledermaus' influenced by Peter Ustinov's play 'The Loves of Four Colonels' – an attempt at satire on the Allied powers occupying Vienna. The level of the humour is exemplified by the Russian colonel claiming that a book entitled 'Five Thousand Ways to Say No' is a standard work in his country, while the performances, aspiring to the 'naughtiness' suggested by the new title, are bloodcurdling – with the definite exception of Anton Walbrook as the bat and the possible one of Anthony Quayle as the Russian. Indeed, as a catalogue of disasters this is an *embarrass de richesses*, though *The People* newspaper proved that chauvinism was not dead by declaring, 'This film puts British musicals on the map at last!' That map did not include the U.S., whose distributors refused to handle it after studying the other reviews and the domestic receipts. Nor does it appear in that curious phenomenon of the present day, Powell retrospectives.

It is ironic that despite the more benign atmosphere reigning at Korda's studio none of these film-makers managed to maintain the standard of their earlier work. Since not one of them (I exclude Laurence Olivier, a special case) has a better film in his future we may conclude that the confident days of the British film were over. Launder and Gilliat started the period well

but were spent forces by the end of it. It should be noted that though their first two films for Korda are excellent, neither is exactly forward-looking. **State Secret** (1950), written and directed by Gilliat, has a plot not unlike those they tackled in *The Lady Vanishes* and *Night Train to Munich*, involving a man (Douglas Fairbanks Jr), whose life depends on crossing the border to a free territory; he is now in one of the iron curtain states, and as in the concurrent *Crisis* he is a surgeon who has operated on a dictator.

The Happiest Days of Your Life (1950) concerns the billeting, due to a Ministry blunder, of a girls' school on a boys' school. As directed by Launder and written in collaboration with John Dighton (the author of the play), the consequent chaos is worked out logically and is wonderfully played, from Alistair Sim and Margaret Rutherford downwards. They are the head teachers, and their battle is titanic – she lips-pursed determined, righteousness personified, blissfully unmindful of her eccentricities and those of others; and he abandoning his armoury of pouts and nervous giggles to shudder before a new onslaught perpetrated by her or her girls, his eyes quivering like fried eggs. In any other film Joyce Grenfell and Richard Wattis, getting a laugh with every line, would be called scene-stealers: this is one of the funniest of all screen farces.

Gilliat was engaged on an ostensibly more lavish Korda production, **The Story of Gilbert and Sullivan** (1953), which was issued to celebrate the twenty-first birthday of London films. The account of the famous partnership is limited to the pompous Englishness of Gilbert (Robert Morley) and the yearning of Sullivan (Maurice Evans) to write serious music; but the excerpts from the operettas are so abundant and so charmingly presented that the flatness of the rest of it becomes unimportant.

Launder returned to the schoolroom with **The Belles of St Trinian's** (1954), but where *The Happiest Days of Your Life* galloped towards an organised chaos, here only confusion reigns. The screenplay by himself, Gilliat and Val Valentine catches the macabre note of Ronald Searle's cartoons, with girls competing with mistresses (Miss Grenfell, Hermione Baddeley, Irene Handl, Joan Sims, Beryl Reid

783

and Mr Sim – in drag) in monstrousness; but the joke becomes wearisome. It was popular, and Launder and Gilliat made a number of sequels as their joint careers faltered. At that time what turned out to be their last film for Korda was **The Constant Husband** (1955), directed by Gilliat from a screenplay by himself and Valentine, with Rex Harrison playing a confirmed bigamist. That it is so much worse than any of Launder and Gilliat's previous films may be due to the speed with which it was assembled. Korda sold it to American T.V. for its world premiere, claiming it was a bold experiment but in fact evidence of his financial troubles. *Variety* commented kindly that it was unlikely to do much for the cause of British pictures in the U.S.

The Boulting brothers were also with Korda for one film, and it is their best. **Seven Days to Noon** (1950), directed by John from a story by Paul Dehn and Anthony Harvey, concerns a professor (Barry Jones) who threatens to blow up central London with a nuclear bomb unless the premier (Ronald Adam, chosen because he resembled Attlee) bans the manufacture of such weapons. It begins as a thriller and ends part–documentary as London prepares for devastation; the final scenes are a pastiche of wartime moods and situations, from the evacuations of children to 'crisis' speeches, justly borrowing from Humphrey Jennings for an effect both powerful and moving. There is a touch of moralising, and of course implausibility, but the casting is superb – the heroine (Sheila Manahan) looks, for instance, more like a duck than a starlet: and most notable is Olive Sloane as the ageing soubrette who unwillingly shelters the professor. The players are also fine in a follow-up, **High Treason** (1952), directed by Roy Boulting for Rank, which is a story about Scotland Yard's efforts to prevent the destruction of Battersea Power Station by a group of Communist saboteurs.

Korda's first production after the War was **A Man About the House** (1947), but despite the foreign (Sorrento) locations, then a rarity, he found it unworthy to launch his postwar programme and it was released without the London Films logo. The producer was Edward Black and the director Leslie Arliss, who, as fugitives from Gainsborough, knew how fond British audiences were of the past – not the Imperial past or the historical past, both of uncertain advantage despite the recent victory, but that specific period of prosperity and safety which began in the reign of Victoria and ended with the First World War. Audiences were constantly offered ladies in bustles going about the business of adultery or murder – but in this case it is the Italian husband (Kieron Moore) who is suspected of poisoning one of the two schoolteachers (Dulcie Gray, Margaret Johnston) from North Bromwich. Adapted from Francis Brett Young's novel, British superiority fades under Italian resource and British frigidity succumbs to Italian charm: that the film even partially succeeded is mostly due to Mr Moore who, though a failure later as Korda's much-touted new star, is impressive here as the enigmatic Italian peasant.

Thus **An Ideal Husband** (1947) reintroduced London Films, and it was also Korda's farewell as a director. The Englishness of the Irish Wilde particularly appealed to him, though this was a less happy choice for filming than either 'The Importance of Being Earnest' or even 'Lady Windermere's Fan', both of which had recently enjoyed successful revivals. Cecil Beaton designed the costumes, which are shown to advantage in Technicolor. Bedecked in a number of them is Paulette Goddard, to whom Korda owed a commitment – and Mrs Cheveley is probably the only character in Wilde for which she was suitable. She plays her nevertheless as an absurdly obvious schemer – in direct contrast to Michael Wilding, whose superb, underplayed Lord Goring did not apparently please Korda, perhaps because he was trying to approximate a stage production. Once that is accepted, the other performances may be enjoyed, especially those of Diana Wynyard and Hugh Williams as that insufferably priggish pair, the Chilterns.

Vivien Leigh, like Miss Goddard, was a close friend of Korda, and he talked her into doing a new **Anna Karenina** (1948) – against her better judgment, as she later admitted. She does provide a centre, but it is of the nature of Dresden porcelain. The justly drubbed Vronsky (Kieron Moore) could have been of no help to her, but confronted with Ralph Richardson's excellent Karenin she proffers only well-bred prettiness. Far more of the story is retained than in the M-G-M version, which seems crude beside this one – except, of course, that it was transformed by Garbo's intensity: at best this is just another triangle drama in a handsomely reproduced Russia. Jean Anouilh's original screenplay had relocated it in the Paris of the *belle époque*, which Korda would not sanction, but the script was eventually credited to Anouilh, Guy Morgan and the director, Julien Duvivier. Duvivier and Korda had worked quite harmoniously on *Lydia*, but their quarrels on this occasion were so fierce that Korda himself had to take over on those days when Duvivier refused to go on the set. Despite these crippling circumstances the major scenes have dramatic pitch, and presumably both decided to keep the camera off Vronsky wherever possible – a positive virtue.

Korda had reverted to his prewar policy of employing the best British talent available and attracting any names which had any meaning for American exhibitors. He brought from Hollywood the director Gregory Ratoff, who seldom made a good film – but who could be relied upon in turn to attract American stars unwilling to be handled by British directors whose work they did not know. A further ploy was to offer the stars pleasing locations. Thus resulted two dreadful films: **That Dangerous Age** (1949), in which Myrna Loy, in Capri, is attracted to a man who is not her husband, and **My Daughter Joy** (1950), with Edward G. Robinson, in San Remo, obsessed by his daughter to the point of paranoia. Also common to both films are Richard Greene and Peggy Cummins, British-born players who had starred in some American movies.

Also from Hollywood came two Britons, David Niven and director Robert Stevenson, contracted for **Bonnie Prince Charlie** (1948), which became the greatest disaster of Korda's career. Stevenson had worked on the project for eighteen months and directed for just over one when he left after a quarrel with Korda, who took over before assigning Anthony Kimmins, the credited director. The credited writer is Clemence Dane, but she was only one of many. The hapless prince (Niven) was doomed not to leave the studio at Shepperton, whose rocks and crags ill match the unit photography; the film, which in fact cost a fortune, looks as though it had been made by a fly-by-night Wardour Street operator hoping to make a quick buck. Disjointed and dull, it is a contender for the worst film ever made, and – if it is not a contradiction in terms – one of the least profitable.

Still, at this time Kimmins did provide Korda with one of the few London Films to get good notices. The critic Richard Winnington considered **Mine Own Executioner** (1947) fit to be bracketed with *Great Expectations*, *Brief Encounter* and *Odd Man Out*, only missing 'as in the book from which it is taken, an overriding poetry'. It seems to me that what is missing is plausibility, intelligence and craftsmanship, not to mention seriousness – though that is the one quality its makers clearly thought they had. This film stands with its contemporary, *Spellbound*, as the two major movies to deal with psychiatry, and it was customary for the British to congratulate themselves on handling something soberly which Hollywood had treated romantically. In this case Nigel Balchin's screenplay, from his own novel, would appear to have been penned after perusal of a magazine article on the subject, and his plot ('Physician, heal thyself') seems taken from something similar.

Anthony Asquith, who had directed some of Anatole de Grunwald's successful films, was reunited with him for **The Winslow Boy** (1948), and it is one of London Films' enduring entertainments. De Grunwald had originally commissioned the screenplay from Terence Rattigan after *The Way to the Stars*, and when he rejected it Rattigan refashioned it for the stage – where its success enabled him to ask much more for the screen rights. It is not an exemplary film, because it is all talk – and sententiously so in discussing British fair play; but the acting is satisfying and the material somewhat more than that. It is based on the Archer-Shee case of 1910, when a Dartmouth cadet was expelled for a petty theft: one advantage over similar dramas is that this one is less concerned with injustice than the process by which the boy was vindicated in law. As the advocate, based on Sir Edward Carson, Robert Donat nobly heads a cast including Cedric Hardwicke, Margaret Leighton and Kathleen Harrison.

785

Production in Austerity Britain

Donat was also a participant in one of Korda's less fortunate schemes, when three leading actors were invited to turn director on modestly-budgeted projects of their own choosing. **The Cure for Love** (1949) had been one of those regional farces – in this case by Walter Greenwood – that used to take root in Shaftesbury Avenue. Donat repeated his stage role of the returning soldier trapped by the tarty and rapacious blonde (Dora Bryan) who wants to marry him, and the nice girl (Renée Asherson) he wants to marry. The camera reveals him too old for the role and also exposes the painted sets. Similarly, most of **The Last Days of Dolwyn** (1949) occurs in the open, but it never uses a location when it can opt for a painted set. Emlyn Williams, as accomplished an actor as writer, starts off with the excellent idea of a Welsh village about to be flooded in order to provide a reservoir for the English; its inhabitants are to be rehoused and recompensed, but the chapel caretaker (Edith Evans) refuses to go, after discovering that she owns her cottage in perpetuity. Unfortunately, Williams's own performance as an erstwhile villager bent on vengeance is as wildly melodramatic as the motivations of his characters. Ralph Richardson, like Donat, also selected one of his stage successes, **Home at Seven** (1951) about a clerk who finds himself suspected of a double murder committed during his twenty-four hour amnesia. R. C. Sherriff's play could never have made a good film, but it just might have provided an interesting picture of suburban life. Shooting was done in fifteen days, for this is one of several low-budget films instituted by Korda during 1951–2 in the hope of offsetting his losses. He himself supervised while Jack Hildyard, one of the credited photographers, planned the shooting; Richardson restricted himself to giving tips to the actors. All three films seem equally directionless.

Korda's fortunes, as parlous as ever, were temporarily restored by **The Wooden Horse** (1950), directed by Jack Lee, a former documentary director who had made one minor film for Rank (like Anthony Asquith, he subsequently declined to work for Korda again). The film, from a novel and screenplay by Eric Williams, concerns a break-out from Stalag Luft III: but as recounted here this true

happening becomes a schoolboy jape – and one with little tension. Nevertheless the British public lapped it up, and when Rank had a similar success with *The Blue Lamp* (q.v.) it was officially declared that there was no longer any urgent need to angle films for the American market. Doubtless Korda was sincere in agreeing with the statement – and doubtless he had to, since the British Film Production Board (q.v.) was no longer prepared to countenance his extravagance. Even so, the American market remained tempting, especially after the success there of **The Captain's Paradise** (1953), which featured one passé Hollywood name, Yvonne de Carlo, and one art-house attraction, Alec Guinness. Certainly there was little merit in the film itself, good American reviews notwithstanding – a comedy, directed by Kimmins, about a sailor with wives (the other is Celia Johnson) in two ports.

Korda accordingly approached 20th Century-Fox for participation in **The Deep Blue Sea** (1955), though the initiative in this case came from Vivien Leigh, who had implored him to find a film for her – and he acceded to her request for this particular property, though he thought it wrong for her. So did Kenneth More (1914–82), at that point becoming Britain's most popular star. He was repeating his stage portrayal of the breezy ex-R.A.F. type attempting to extricate himself from a love affair gone sour, and the film is only notable for its preservation of that performance. Fox insisted upon Anatole Litvak as director and the use of CinemaScope (q.v.), which factors, plus the miscasting of Miss Leigh as the older woman, all but destroyed Rattigan's intimate drama. Like *Summer Madness*, also a coproduction with Hollywood, the film failed at the box office.

Hardly more popular were two African stories, but both are honourable and interesting – as superior to most of Korda's postwar output as the Imperial adventures among his prewar films. In both cases the superiority is due almost entirely to the source material. It should be noted, however, that with **Cry, the Beloved Country** (1952) Zoltan Korda was permitted, to his satisfaction, to be more realistic than on previous African excursions. The country of the title is South Africa, and the film is a plea – as written by Alan Paton from his own bestselling novel – for racial integration. That plea nests easily within the framework of the plot, which chiefly deals with a black priest (Canada Lee) whose son has gone to the bad, and a bigoted white man (Charles Carson), who disapproves of his own son's efforts on behalf of such people. Since the film would have no point did he not see the error of his ways, it is to its credit that the conversion is more subtly done than in most didactic films – despite naiveties elsewhere. John McCarten noted in *The New Yorker* that 'the picture is obviously more interested in getting the problem on record than in providing a hard-and-fast solution'; it does provide a dossier on the huge unbridged gap between the black shanty-towns and the comfortable white suburbs.

George More O'Ferrall (the first British director recruited from T.V.) brought little more distinction to **The Heart of the Matter** (1953), but it is a reasonable condensation, by Lesley Storm and Ian Dalrymple, of Graham Greene's major novel. Set in an East African township during the War, among the traders and the British community, it observes one man (Trevor Howard), the deputy police commissioner, as he so compromises his professional and private lives till suicide is the only solution. It is Howard's understanding of the role which makes the film worthy of its original: only a resonance in his declaration of love recalls his doctor in *Brief Encounter* and only his bearing that of the officers he played elsewhere: for this is the complete Scobie, 'the typical second man', and one of the best performances ever recorded on film.

The same may be true of Laurence Olivier's interpretation of the title role in **Richard III** (1955), and that was the intention. His career was, by his standards, in the doldrums, so he sought to put on record his much-praised, definitive performance. The play was renowned as a vehicle for great actors, but was not entirely suitable screen material – and Korda's backers would not underwrite the battle sequences★ as Rank had once lavishly financed Agincourt. A foreword notes that this is one of the 'legends' that surround the English crown, and the crown is always central to the piece, offered by Olivier, if not Shakespeare (there is no

★They were filmed in Spain as an economic measure.

screenplay credit, but it was Olivier's decision to incorporate interpolations by Colley Cibber and Garrick, and to start with the Coronation scene which concludes 'Henry VI, Part 3'), as a prize which perverts and corrupts all those subservient to it. Utilising Otto Heller's camera and Roger Furse's sets (cf. *Hamlet*) to underline the intrigue – and with William Walton's score emphasising the melodrama – Olivier's direction is full of master touches (even if most of them are to enhance his own performance): this wittiest of actors sees Richard as the wittiest of villains, delightedly sinning his way to the throne. He is a compendium of perfidy – jealous, hypocritical, petty, scornful; and as demanded by the text he is a whole menagerie of animals from the dark side of the moon. Yet by looking into the camera he makes us share his arrogance and delight in his own scheming, so that at the end we pity him, alone and helpless, as he fights on to the finish. Three other actor-knights support him: John Gielgud looking apprehensive as 'false, fleeting, perjured' Clarence; Cedric Hardwicke, a benign Edward IV; and, most notably, Ralph Richardson as Buckingham, a blandly-smiling, secret opportunist. Claire Bloom is the Lady Anne; the termagant Margaret has been sensibly removed and Jane Shore has been added – with only one line, but in the tantalising person of Pamela Brown.

The film restored Olivier to his pre-eminence among British actors. He went on to play Macbeth at Stratford – which in common with most people who saw it I consider the greatest of all his performances. He spent a great deal of his own money on preparation for a film version, but backing was not forthcoming, though he had gone cap-in-hand to Rank, to the American companies and the British government. Korda had just died; *Richard III* had been his final financial wave-of-the-wand, composed partly of $500,000 from N.B.C. Television for its American premiere, in a complicated deal which included a repayment of $300,000 if earnings in cinemas exceeded $350,000. But *Richard*, though as warmly reviewed as *Henry V* and *Hamlet*, was not as popular as either and therefore could not help London Films survive the death of Korda.

Though Korda's postwar regime produced more worthwhile films than the prewar one, it had been equally disastrous financially: it would be easier to list the films which had made money than those which lost it. At the outset the losses on *An Ideal Husband*, *Bonnie Prince Charlie* and *Anna Karenina* were such that when the government set up the British Film Production Fund in 1949 it immediately allocated one million pounds to settle Korda's debts. Another two million followed from the same source, as *The Third Man* proved that he could produce a money-making film, but both the sum and the film only staved off disaster; nor were the coffers filled from the proceeds of those movies made to keep the studio ticking over. Closure was only avoided by the sales of the Olivier and Rex Harrison films to American T.V. and the prewar London Films library to the new British independent television channel. That no other British producer had a large collection of films to sell may be a fitting epitaph to Korda's achievement.

Financially these years were no better for J. Arthur Rank, and they were calamitous artistically – though that was not something which interested him too much. He was sufficiently chauvinistic for us to suppose that he would have found some way of holding on to those talents which had made him internationally famous had Korda not been there to take them on. But Rank was primarily a financier, and as owner of two cinema circuits he knew that cinemas could be filled with run-of-the-mill product. Chauvinism was his downfall: just as he could not see that lavishly assembled British films could not compete with Hollywood on its own terms, so he failed to appreciate that it was Hollywood's packaging that made ordinary stories so attractive. He began the period with two producers who did understand such matters – Filippo del Guidice at Two Cities and Edward Black, working under the auspices of the Ostrers at Gainsborough; but they were replaced by people much less expert.

Admittedly at that point his chief task was the administration of the studios, production companies and distributors which, though nominally independent, were under his financial control. The rational solution was for them all to be brought under one umbrella, the J. Arthur Rank Organisation. The distribution arm remained known as General Film Distributors, at least for the present, since it was with that company that Universal had signed an agreement for the release of its product in Britain. G.F.D.'s involvement with Universal encouraged Rank to buy Universal shares, till at one point he was the largest individual shareholder with twenty-five per cent. One outcome of this was the proposal for a jointly-owned American circuit so that Universal could compete with those companies which owned their own, but the plan was unfeasible with the government's anti-trust laws pending. Instead, in 1945, Rank and Universal announced the joint formation of United World Pictures, with an annual distribution programme of eight British and eight American productions. The American films were not to come from Universal, but from a new company, International (then releasing through R.K.O.) – and the attractiveness of International's offerings were to compel American theatre owners to take the Rank films as well. But since, as we have seen, the new laws were designed to prevent the practice of block-booking, this project was also aborted. United World was disbanded, and Universal and International amalgamated – though Rank was appeased by a new agreement by which the Universal-International distribution offices would annually handle twelve of his films. He was convinced that since British cinemagoers had long learned to love American films, the reverse would ensue once Americans were accustomed to British accents, and therefore the Universal-International dozen would be insufficient for American requirements. In the event that company failed to find a dozen it thought suitable for its audiences – which left Rank with another American outfit that he had optimistically started, Eagle-Lion.

The name came from what was to have been a worldwide distribution organisation started in 1944 but absorbed by G.F.D. in Britain two years later: it was applied to a now defunct American company, Producers Releasing Corporation, specialists in B-movies – and once again the initial programme was to consist jointly of American and British product. Under its American management, Eagle-Lion was also to produce films, but since these were little better than the rock-bottom

B-pictures made under its former name, it was hardly a prestigious outlet for Rank's British-produced movies (Rank eventually closed it in 1950). A further attempt to reach American cinemagoers was made in a deal with R.K.O. based on the theory that they would learn to love British stars by seeing them acting alongside their R.K.O. favourites. Accordingly, R.K.O. sent Edward Dmytryk to Britain to direct an Anglo-American cast (including John Mills, Trevor Howard, Richard Carlson and Martha Scott) in **So Well Remembered** (1947), based on James Hilton's novel about a small-town newspaper; but there were no successors. Rank was able to develop a circuit in Canada, but below the border had to content himself with a New York showcase, the Winter Garden, because of the decree divorcing exhibition and distribution. With the exception of Olivier's Shakespeare films and *The Red Shoes, The Seventh Veil* (q.v.) was the only British film to rouse American audiences during that period which finished with the announcement that Rank and Korda would no longer try to woo them. In 1951 *Variety* reported that both impresarios hoped to build upon the unexpected popularity their old films were finding on American television (then as yet without any significant Hollywood competitors).

Rank's obsession with the American market began during the War, when critics on both sides of the Atlantic observed that such films as *In Which We Serve* and *Henry V* not only equalled but surpassed those emanating from Hollywood. Thereafter Rank constantly put his faith in the wrong projects; after *Caesar and Cleopatra*, which failed to appeal despite star names and spectacle, he aped Hollywood with a musical, **London Town** (1946). Wesley Ruggles had come to Britain to work with Korda but had quarrelled with him, and therefore he proposed this film to Rank, to star a West End comic, Sid Field. The plot, about an understudy waiting for his chance of stardom, managed to include Field's best-known routines. Ruggles brought over a number of his colleagues from Hollywood, including the songwriters Burke and Van Heusen. The numbers are staged with definitive incompetence, often moving between a variety of styles, and Ruggles's work as producer and director was such that he could not find work again after

returning to the U.S. The film was eventually shown there, much cut and retitled *My Heart Goes Crazy*, in 1953: it was said in the meantime to be the greatest item in Rank's posted loss in 1946 of £1,700,000.

Also contributing to that loss was **Men of Two Worlds** (1946), which was directed by a proven talent, Thorold Dickinson. Dickinson was allowed £600,000, three years, location-shooting and Technicolor to make this an examination of the British responsibility to its Empire, as exemplified by a district commissioner (Eric Portman), a doctor (Phyllis Calvert) and an educated African (Robert Adams) trying to come to terms with the primitive nature of his people. Dickinson's first film had been a high-pitched African melodrama, and this was an attempt to make amends; but it is as patronising as earlier British films which sent Paul Robeson to battle with the witch-doctor – and even dumber and duller. The crêpe-paper banana-trees may have contributed to its delay in reaching the U.S. – in 1952, retitled *Kisenga, Man of Africa*. Another contemporary subject was poorly handled in **School for Secrets** (1946), written, directed and co-produced by Peter Ustinov. It involves back-room scientists or boffins (a word much bandied about at the time) and their difficulties in developing radar – the boredom of which is only relieved by that bugaboo of early wartime movies, the secret raid into Germany led by Ralph Richardson.

Both films were considered important, but two romantic films adapted from second-rank novelists proved more durable, even if interpreted by directors of lesser stature (both promptly disappeared) – Stanley Haynes with Compton Mackenzie's **Carnival** (1946) and Charles Frank with Sheridan Le Fanu's **Uncle Silas** (1947). *Carnival* concerns the doomed romance between a Cockney dancer (Sally Gray) and a dilettante artist (Michael Wilding), and though neither player has quite the romantic aura found in the best Hollywood love stories, she has a sweet toughness and a springlike look when her hair is down, and he has the *désinvolture* which explains his irresolution. The film's chief contribution comes from Paul Sheriff, whose sets are a far better reproduction of Edwardian London than was customary. The standard of British art direction – certainly in historical films – was outstanding at this time, perhaps reaching a peak in Laurence Irving's Gothic mansion for *Uncle Silas*, which he also produced. Irving's illustrious career in the theatre had left him little time to work in films, where his efforts had been confined to the design of two films for Fairbanks Sr and *Pygmalion*. The screenplay credit on this occasion is unexpected, being Ben Travers, the writer of the celebrated Aldwych farces. Le Fanu's tale, of an heiress (Jean Simmons) terrorised by uncle (Derrick de Marney) and governess (Katina Paxinou), makes an entertaining film in its particular genre.

These films were produced by del Guidice, clearly in emulation of the Gainsborough melodramas, which remained profitable for Rank: those made between 1943 and 1946 earned twice their cost, but by 1946 the Gainsborough management had changed. Edward Black had left after a quarrel with Maurice Ostrer, joining first M-G-M and then Korda; it was he, just before he died, who instituted the *Bonnie Prince Charlie* which caused Korda so much grief. As the Rank-owned companies grew closer together, Ostrer resented the interference of del Guidice and resigned. He subsequently produced **Idol of Paris** (1948), a melodrama in the Gainsborough mould, and left the business forthwith, since its reception indicated no other course. Del Guidice remained till the end of the decade, when Rank compared his extravagance with the tight economies practised at Balcon's increasingly successful Ealing Studios (q.v.). A replacement was found for Gainsborough, Sydney Box, who with one film proved himself adept at making the sort of 'women's pictures' for which Gainsborough was noted.

That film was **The Seventh Veil** (1945). 'BRITISH – and a WINNER all the way,' said the *Daily Mirror*, an attitude which helps to explain the popularity of certain native films. This one was unusual, as written by Box and his wife Muriel, since it suggested that a disturbed mind might be cured by psychoanalysis; it also flattered audiences that they could be attentive to 'good' music; and it was James Mason's moment. The film is now, initially, tedious and unattractive, but just as you are about to reach for your hat it takes on a grandeur, composed of the melodramatic elements of 'Trilby', 'Jane Eyre' and 'The Constant Nymph'. That effect was

accidental, happening only after Mason replaced the infinitely less romantic Francis L. Sullivan: as the guardian, Mason suavely suggests a misogynist drawn towards his ward (Ann Todd), and simultaneously the impresario drawn to his protégée. Audiences loved his sadism (*Deception* and *The Red Shoes* would confirm this particular view of the practitioners of classical music) and clearly the ingredients were right for both the time and the director, Compton Bennett, perhaps the most assured of the second-rank local directors. His aspirations were clear when he and Box made **Daybreak** (1946), but the film was not released until 1948 due to censorship problems over the love scenes and its indictment of capital punishment. It again stars Ann Todd, who looks like Michèle Morgan, and the film, a triangle drama chiefly set on a barge in the Thames, resembles several prewar French ones: but Bennett was much less successful in this respect than Reed had been with *Odd Man Out*.

As head of production for Gainsborough, Box's position was strengthened by **Holiday Camp** (1947). Holiday camps were a postwar phenomenon: petrol was still rationed and few people could afford to go abroad; war had both staled the memory of boarding-houses and accustomed much of the population to live in regimented fashion. Like *Bank Holiday* this film looks at a cross-section, but, unlike that, it always opts for the cheapest emotion, the easiest laugh: it was clearly put together for people who love holiday camps by people who would not be seen dead in one; Ken Annakin directed from a story by Godfrey Winn. Its huge popularity resulted in three more films built around its leading characters, Mr and Mrs Huggett (Jack Warner, Kathleen Harrison), who had caught the imagination of the public. The intention was a British equivalent of the Hardy family but more down-to-earth, since that is how the British saw themselves in comparison with their American rivals. In the event, the press reception for the first of these follow-ups ensured a speedy end to the series – except that the assembly-line production methods forced upon Box meant that the third film was already shooting.

The industry was in serious trouble, which began with the dollar shortage. Since Britain was both impoverished (because of the War) and Hollywood's best export market (in 1947 over $18 million went to the American film companies) the Exchequer was rumoured to be considering a twenty-five per cent *ad valorem* tax on all American films arriving in Britain. The Hollywood companies hastily suggested leaving their earnings in Britain to finance production – which Rank regarded as a threat to his virtual monopoly while also fearing retaliation in his attempts to market his films in the U.S. The government listened to neither side and levied a tax of seventy-five per cent. The American companies immediately withheld their films, leaving their British subsidiaries to dig into their small stockpile and make attractive packages of reissues (neither, of course, subject to tax); but if the cinemas themselves were to survive, British studios had to fill the gap. The government did not want them to close, since it extracted a large revenue in Entertainments Tax.★ Rank was asked whether his studios could supply the demand, and with over two-thirds of the country's 2,100 cinemas of his own to be programmed he arranged for bank loans of over £9 million. In November 1947 a programme of forty-seven films was announced, but that was insufficient for his ambitions since as distributor and exhibitor he knew how much Hollywood earned from the supporting programme. He had already started an animation unit with David Hand, a Disney alumnus, in charge, as well as a British equivalent of 'The March of Time' called 'This Modern Age' – but when a year later a loss of £3½ million was announced on production alone it was clear that neither would survive. Under the Ostrers, Gainsborough had delivered a handful of films annually; the reviews were marginally better for most of Box's twice-monthly films, but few appealed to the public.

The only success – at least, critically – of the Box regime was **Quartet** (1948); four Somerset Maugham short stories adapted by R. C. Sheriff for four different directors. The short story form had been virtually neglected by the screen – and none of calibre equal to Maugham's had appeared

in their original, abbreviated form. The Old Party himself conferred his imprimatur by introducing them, but neither here nor in the two sequels, **Trio** (1950) and **Encore** (1951) were the best stories included – perhaps because he wished to reserve those as likely to be the basis of a full-length film. The treatment of the ten stories in these three films does not begin to compare with any of the series made later by British television, but the changes wrought upon the texts tell us something of the mentality of those who made them. All opportunities for comic pantomime are zealously taken; sex is as resolutely erased – 'The Facts of Life' and 'Gigolo and Gigolette' have become meaningless titles – although British censorship was much more relaxed than American. The whole point of 'The Alien Corn' is lost, since the family is no longer either Jewish or nouveau riche; but it should be said that 'The Colonel's Lady' is almost intact, tersely directed by Annakin and lovingly acted by Norah Swinburne and Cecil Parker.

Box's Gainsborough saw the rise and fall of David Macdonald, originally considered Rank's most distinguished director after the defection of the best of the others to Korda. Macdonald had made some respectable thrillers before the War and had come into prominence with a number of wartime documentaries. His first postwar film, **The Brothers** (1947) was adapted from a novel by the worthy L. A. G. Strong and beautifully photographed under the glowering skies of the Hebrides: it benefited from having an unusual subject – or so it seemed, for in fact it embodies almost every cliché of bucolic melodrama, including rape – and that the heroine (Patricia Roc) and the rapist (Maxwell Reed) secretly loved each other conformed to British movie ideals of the time. So did the mainly seedy set of characters on display in **Good Time Girl** (1948), which follows the downward path of a teenager (Jean Kent) through Soho hat-checking to reform school to a liaison with – final degradation! – two American G.I. deserters.† Critics' doubts about Macdonald became certainty with **The Bad Lord Byron** (1949), whose wisely-uncredited screenplay culminates in the revelation

★ In 1948 'from a net box-office receipt of £70 million the British producers were left with £7½ million. But since production costs had amounted to nearly twice that (£14 million) the tax was taking from the film industry nearly ten times as much money needed to enable it to break even.' ('The Great British Picture Show' by George Perry, London 1974.)

†The film was inspired by the case of Betty Jones, who eventually, with an American deserter, went on trial for murder.

that the celestial judge appointed to examine the life of Byron (Dennis Price) is none other than the poet himself. By the time the film had insulted the intelligences of critics and the few spectators who had ventured to see it Macdonald was in the midst of shooting **Christopher Columbus** (1949), Rank's latest expensive intended-assault on the American box office. To that end Fredric March and Florence Eldridge were brought over, she to play Queen Isabella and he to suffer every indignity available to the historical film: 'You'd never see a civilised man doing that,' he says on seeing Indians smoking – and since critics ridiculed this and other dialogue, written by the Boxes (with Cyril Roberts), Rank's disenchantment was complete. Box left, but the films of Two Cities, Gainsborough and the Rank 'independents' became, if anything, even more standardised.

Those covered in the next few pages seem to me symptomatic of the ills of the Rank Organisation – or, much less numerous, of interest for their own sake. The latter do not include **Trottie True** (1949), a Technicolor musical. The failure of *London Town* still rankled, and this film was meant to prove that the lesson had been learned – for, like the much-praised *Champagne Charlie*, it did not ape Hollywood in telling its tale of an old-time music hall star. In that role Jean Kent proves that she would hardly have made it to the chorus in an American film; its total lack of success is also due to the perfunctory direction of Brian Desmond Hurst.

Hurst was one of the most trusted of the Rank directors, as was John Paddy Carstairs, who specialised in films of Shaftesbury Avenue comedies. **The Chiltern Hundreds** (1949), written by William Douglas Home (of the political family), attempts to come to grips with the 1945 General Election, one of the watersheds of modern British history. Home was bright enough to realise that there was a new flexibility among the classes, and offers a number of pro-left jokes. His plot and conclusion are, however, depressingly prewar: the scion (David Tomlinson) of an aristocratic family decides to stand as a Socialist, while his butler (Cecil Parker) opposes him as a Tory – till the latter realises both that he would rather buttle and that it is part of the appointed order

that a milord should represent the county. **Fools Rush In** (1949) is of the *Quiet Wedding* genus, with an uncertain bride (Sally Ann Howes), a reprobate father (Guy Rolfe), and the bridegroom who forgets his pants – a joke Carstairs felt so funny that it is repeated in **Tony Draws a Horse** (1950), which prefigures 'Equus' inasmuch as a boy needs psychiatric treatment because of a horse fixation.

Psychiatry is also the subject of **The Astonished Heart** (1950), adapted from the short play by Noël Coward, who replaced Michael Redgrave in the lead during shooting. Coward had earlier written that the play concerned 'the decay of a psychiatrist's mind through a personal sexual obsession', but the film is simply an arch triangle drama, with Celia Johnson as the wife and Margaret Leighton as the mistress. All concerned were thoroughly ashamed of it, with good reason. The co-directors, Terence Fisher and Anthony Darnborough, also collaborated on **So Long at the Fair** (1950), based on the classic mystery of a disappearance at the 1889 Paris Exposition. David Tomlinson is the one who vanishes, and his sister is Jean Simmons, the only reason for seeing the film. 'I would say, without hesitation,' said C. A. Lejeune, 'that England has never had a nascent film star and I stress the word *star*, which is not necessarily synonymous with actress – of her quality.'

Roy Baker was one of the more promising directors who came to prominence with Rank. **The October Man** (1947) has atmospheric sets designed by Vetchinsky – a Home Counties common with a shabby-genteel boarding-house on the edge of it; it is also notable for its heroine, played by Joan Greenwood, generous with feeling. Train whistles screech in the night and a distraught John Mills – suffering from amnesia and suspected of murder – is inexorably drawn to bridges overlooking the tracks. But, since the police pursue their investigation in the usual dim movie manner, this is not the best screen work of the usually admirable writer, Eric Ambler, who also produced. In **Morning Departure** (1950), a submerged-submarine drama, Baker has Mills, Kenneth More and others sport upper lips so stiff that one suspects rigor mortis; and Richard Attenborough, the coward, is similarly afflicted after a pep-talk.

Public approval of these naval heroics replenished Rank's coffers, and since G.F.D. released Ealing's films Rank was also the beneficiary of the enthusiasm for police work demonstrated in that studio's *The Blue Lamp*. The much-vaunted 'realism' of both gave rise to **White Corridors** (1951), though many would regard the British movie tradition of steely devotion to duty as another cliché. This portrait of hospital workers has Googie Withers and James Donald as doctors who put romance second; nor is it significantly more authentic than the American *Vigil in the Night*. It is well directed, by Pat Jackson, whose work in the documentary field had brought him an M-G-M contract – but he made only one programmer during the five years he languished in Hollywood. *White Corridors* seemed to presage a new career, but subsequently he did little of note.

It is also a film with an original screenplay, and that is the virtue – if virtue it is – of almost every film made at the time by the Rank Organisation. Certainly adaptations of well-known novels were few, but the two films produced by the actor John Mills for Two Cities are versions of H. G. Wells and D. H. Lawrence, **The History of Mr Polly** (1949) and **The Rocking-Horse Winner** (1950) respectively. Mills's own self-conscious performances, as the dreamy draper's assistant and the Cockney groom, are not endearing, and the direction by Anthony Pelissier reduces the material to a plod. But the selection of the stories does credit to Mills. Wells's collection of minor eccentrics is admirably realised, and Megs Jenkins is touching as the homely innkeeper with whom Mr Polly finds bucolic tranquillity; in the Lawrence, there are good performances by Valerie Hobson as the mother and John Howard Davies as the boy with a knack for picking the horses.

Even Anthony Asquith abandoned his apparent plan to film the Complete Works of Terence Rattigan (including his screenplays) for an original by an unknown writer, John Cresswell, **The Woman in Question** (1950). Though an unexceptional whodunnit, it does have an interesting central idea – of tracing the varying viewpoints of a woman (Jean Kent), now dead, by five people who knew her. The camera as a seeing-eye with different points of view had been used by the Ger-

man and Russian directors who had so influenced the young Asquith, but it had not before been the basis of an entire film (coincidentally Kurosawa was doing something similar in *Rashomon*, q.v.). Asquith returned to Rattigan for **The Browning Version** (1951), which the dramatist himself extended to feature-length from his one-hour play, about a middle-aged schoolteacher whose career and marriage are simultaneously revealed as failures. The mechanics are apparent, but the piece does not lack pity, as when the wife's lover (Nigel Patrick) berates her for her treatment of her husband. 'I think he's been as deeply hurt as a human being can be.' (The similar dialogue in 'Death of a Salesman', across the Atlantic, reminds us that both compassion and the failed hero were late in coming to English-language modern drama.) As the dry, apparently insensitive teacher, Michael Redgrave is as imposing as was Eric Portman on the stage (and he was superb), but the casting of Jean Kent removes the original's poignancy, since this is no longer the question of an embittered middle-aged woman throwing herself at a younger man. Miss Kent is not only too young, but plays in conventional 'wicked lady' manner; and, as befits a Rank star, her clothes are more suitable for Ascot than for Open Day. Otherwise Asquith, sensitive, if often bumbling, is at his most professional.

The Rank Organisation had a number of box-office successes in the Fifties – though few in proportion to what emerged from its studios – yet it is difficult to find respectful reviews, let alone admiring ones. *The Kidnappers* (1953) is an exception, though its director, Philip Leacock, who began as a documentarist, did little else of note. Neil Paterson wrote it, from his own story, and it concerns two young boys sent to live with their fierce granpappy in the Nova Scotia of the 1900s. His dialogue for the adults was much less good than that for the children, who were played winningly by Jon Whiteley and Vincent Winter (Whiteley is the taller one).

He attempts only filmed theatre with **The Importance of Being Earnest** (1952), and in the opening sequence Redgrave and Michael Denison aim their dialogue at some non-existent balcony. Edith Evans's famous Lady Bracknell, perfect on the H.M.V. recording, is so given to overemphasis that both accent and character are vulgar. Asquith simply will not leave Wilde's lines to the players but constantly cuts for reaction shots – so that Gwendolin and Cicely share their tea-party with the butler's raised eyebrows. However, there are two perfect pairings: Margaret Rutherford's Miss Prism, enchantingly scatterbrained, with Miles Malleson's urbane Chasuble; and Joan Greenwood's splendidly jaded Gwendolin with Dorothy Tutin's Cicely, superficially as 'simple, unspoiled' as Lady Bracknell considers Gwendolin, but in fact equally coquettish and grasping. In view of these four performances, this version might be said to be nearly definitive; interestingly, though by far the best of Wilde's plays, it was the last of them to reach the screen.

The Young Lovers (1954) concerns a cold war Romeo and Juliet – a U.S. embassy official (David Knight) who meets a Soviet bloc ambassador's daughter (Odile Versois) at Covent Garden: but with this premise established the screenplay has nowhere to go – one reason why Asquith's respectful handling is disappointing. It leaves *The Importance of Being Earnest* and *Genevieve* (q.v.) as the last interesting films from Rank for many a year.

Rank himself by now relinquished the running of the organisation to John Davis, an accountant, who decreed that profits were the first of his priorities – and that meant popcorn in the cinema foyers (those that were not closed down) and less films on the studio floor. The trouble with Davis was not that he made fewer films but that those that he sanctioned were formula pictures involving mediocrities both fore and aft of the camera. The Rank films of the Fifties were among the dreariest ever made, which is why some people in the industry do not have fond memories of Davis. The government was not much help. The discriminatory tax against American films was so clearly a mistake it was lifted after a few months – and those that flooded in from Hollywood did nothing to benefit the British industry when, as a result of American pressure, the forty-five per cent quota requirement (to show British films) was lowered to forty. The Entertainments' Tax was reduced slightly: and to counter criticisms of the amount that the government took from the industry a system of loans and subsidies was established by which, as we have seen, £3 million went to Korda. Harold Wilson, then President of the Board of Trade, made that decision, refusing all other applicants – including del Guidice, who otherwise might have continued independently in films. In 1950 the quota was adjusted again, to the more sensible thirty per cent, and money was taken 'voluntarily' from exhibitors to go into a pool from which producers could borrow. All the while some independents worked on without attracting the headlines that accompanied the problems of Korda and Rank.

The most successful – by far – was Herbert Wilcox. He had been promoting his wife, Anna Neagle, with varying degrees of success for over a decade, till, in the later war years, there were no takers; then he found a story with the right ingredients to re-establish her, **I Live in Grosvenor Square** (1945), for which he found financing without recourse to Maurice Cowan, its author, who was to have been a partner on the production. It concerns an English girl (Neagle) torn between the British and U.S. armies as represented by Rex Harrison and Dean Jagger, and it was followed by **Piccadilly Incident** (1946), with Michael Wilding as the man Neagle loves and loses in the chaos of war. The British loved that and, equally unexpectedly, found they loved the stars, who were therefore teamed in a series of curious films (all with London place-names in their title) – snobbish, sentimental, cliché-ridden and, with one exception, inept. Since they were also old fashioned their popularity may have had something to do with the wish of audiences to escape from the realities of postwar Britain. Miss Neagle, like Joan Crawford, impresses by her very lack of talent: never as wholeheartedly absurd, she as ardently believes in her tinny stories, flashing her regal airs but unbending now and then to offer a little song or two. She wears elbow-length gloves and picture-hats, and on one memorable occasion was to be found with a large hat *and* flowers in

794

her hair, sipping Cassis through a straw. Towards her Mr Wilding adopts a tone of light-hearted gallantry or downright frivolity, having decided that that is the only way to treat the lady: you cannot call it a technique, but he is the saving grace of these films – apart, that is, from some unintentionally funny lines, such as when Neagle says, 'Father, are you subject to apoplexy? – I'm thinking of going on the stage.'

The line occurs in **The Courtneys of Curzon Street** (1947), which repeats *Piccadilly Incident* in that the stars marry, are separated and reunited while she is singing to the troops, but the rest of it is so much like 'Cavalcade' that Coward might have sued for plagiarism had he felt so inclined. **Spring in Park Lane** (1948) is for many the only watchable Neagle film, and certainly the only Wilcox film of this period to be well received by the press. A trifle about a young milord posing as a footman, it has an unexpected gaiety, but when Wilcox remade it in Technicolor, with borrowings from his earlier *Irene* and now titled **Maytime in Mayfair** (1949), he substituted facetiousness for what had been occasional wit. He left Wilding aside for **Elizabeth of Ladymead** (1949), in which Neagle is discovered as a young aristocrat waiting for a returning husband in 1946: since Wilcox was so quick to borrow, one ought to have expected something from *The Best Years of Our Lives*, but instead she is whisked back to 1854, 1903 and 1919, when each soldier husband returns to find her a Different Woman. In 1919 she is a flapper, and when the husband finds Ladymead deserted, you know – with relief – that she will not sing to him; but she does not deny us a few sedate steps of ragtime.

Returning to her prewar urge to play the famous women of history, she had the title role in **The Lady with the Lamp** (1951). Lytton Strachey's study draws a comparison between the Florence Nightingale of popular conception and the lady of fact, concluding that the latter was the more interesting – which of course is not the one Neagle attempts. Warren Chetham Strode's script, from Reginald Berkeley's 1929 play, is reasonably accurate in outline; the film is too genteel to get to grips with the horrors of Scutari, but the matt-work is notably good; so is the supporting cast, which includes Wilding as Sydney Herbert. Sybil Thorndike (who played another famous nurse, Edith Cavell, for Wilcox in 1928, in *Dawn*) is Miss Nightingale's secretary at the end, and it is curious to see a good, aged actress playing scenes with a poor one pretending to be old.

In 1953, for the Coronation, Neagle had appeared in a stage enterprise entitled 'The Glorious Days', in which she had reprised her Nell Gwynn, Queen Victoria and various musical comedy actresses, cobbled together with other situations from her films, with songs. The press reception – Kenneth Tynan's review was one of the wittiest ever penned – did not prevent Wilcox from filming it, as **Lilacs in the Spring** (1954), with no screenplay credit and Errol Flynn imported to play the male lead, his Hollywood professionalism having appropriately disappeared en route. The result is a film for connoisseurs, a camp classic, but for Wilcox, it was no laughing matter – the first of a series of box-office disasters which were to lead to the bankruptcy courts. Other ageing film-makers have been luckier: they were only employees, and merely faded away. But there was no public sympathy for Wilcox: lively and innovatory in the Twenties, he had since simply followed in the wake of others, borrowing and repeating, finally unaware of the changing taste of audiences.

He sought redemption with **The Beggar's Opera** (1953), but not without a degree of opportunism, since the star was to be Laurence Olivier and the director Peter Brook, the most discussed man of the theatre of his generation. Brook had not made a film before, and no one involved had any experience in filming eighteenth-century musicals. Whenever Macheath (Olivier) launches into action or a song it is clear that the sequence has been choreographed for maximum visual effect – but unfortunately the strain shows, and the high spirits intended are often dampened by Macheath's obvious doubts as to the life he is leading. The uncertain grasp of the material also extended to Dennis Cannan, who adapted John Gay's libretto, with additional dialogue by Christopher Fry. The score, arranged and conducted by Sir Arthur Bliss, is marvellously sung – and dubbed, except by Olivier and Stanley

795

Holloway, singing for themselves. The exceptional cast also includes Dorothy Tutin as Polly, Daphne Anderson as Lucy, George Devine and Mary Clare as the Peachums and Athene Seyler as Mrs Trapes. The decor by Wakhevitch uses primary colours against the drab grey of the prison walls and they positively glow. However, the film was dismissed by a number of critics as looking like an animated Yardley's perfume ad and its faults stressed – so that what is withal a hugely entertaining film became a total failure; the industry, uneasy with such 'highbrow' subjects, sent *enfant terrible* Brook back to the theatre and returned to its inane light comedies and war films.

Associated British, apart from backing Wilcox's first two 'London' films, had been more or less quiescent, its few A-pictures falling by the wayside. Production was stepped up after the success of **My Brother Jonathan** (1948), produced by Warwick Ward, the former actor, and directed by Harold French from Francis Brett Young's 1928 saga about the trials and tribulations of a young doctor. It has a homely British quality, and were it possible to believe in it for an instant it might make us fonder of qualities such as self-sacrifice and the will to fight hypocrisy as personified by Michael Denison – whose sincerity certainly benefits the film. The company made a bid to become a major force in film-making with **The Dancing Years** (1950), directed by French (to his admitted shame), a Technicolor version of one of Ivor Novello's Viennesy stage musicals. In Novello's own role, Dennis Price's embarrassment communicates itself to the audience – though any members persevering will find pleasures not dissimilar to those of *Lilacs in the Spring*. Associated British did better commercially with **Angels One Five** (1952), a title bearing tones of *Twelve O'Clock High* and set on an airfield existing in a similar vacuum. If it says little about the Battle of Britain, its portrait of the R.A.F. is less risible than usual, and the direction by George More O'Ferrall has a certain energy.

With **The Queen of Spades** (1949) Associated British achieved a critical success. The film's instigator was the playwright Rodney Ackland, who hoped to direct, but he received only a co-writing credit in the end and Thorold Dickinson

directed. As designed by Oliver Messel, photographed by Otto Heller and finely cut, it is a handsome film, but it is also boring. Much of the point of Pushkin's tale is lost, since we are shown matters which he only implied: Herman stakes his all on either a ghost or a figment of his imagination – it matters not, since he is mad: but he does not become mad in this film. In that role, Anton Walbrook is miscast, and in a rubber mask Edith Evans is uninteresting as the old countess.

For Associated British J. B. Priestley contributed a rare original screenplay, **Last Holiday** (1950), but it went unnoticed, on the assumption – thus was the cinema regarded – that if he had considered the material important he would have made a novel or a play from it. This is a typical piece, overly concerned with the 'little man' (Alec Guinness) and convinced that all would be right in this world if the running of it were left to him: in this case the man has a fatal illness which gives him new courage to help his fellow holiday-makers. They are variously eccentric, or conventional types, but Priestley sees them in the round, so that when they co-operate to get dinner we may smile at this ingenuous Utopian view, but we may also find it attractive. As directed by Henry Cass, Kay Walsh brings memorable warmth to the role of the caretaker, and Guinness vaults easily from timidity to life-and-soul of the party.

Cass also directed **Young Wives' Tale** (1951), about two couples sharing because of the housing shortage. The situation is hardly original, but it has Audrey Hepburn in one of her first roles, Athene Seyler as the most indulgent of nannies, and Joan Greenwood, who, recognising the material as rightfully hers, floats as confidently through it as she had surely done on stage. She creates her own world, as did Keaton and Beatrice Lillie, a world in which her fantasies sustain her as her good intentions are misunderstood, her dinners burn and her nannies are always taking umbrage. **Laughter in Paradise** (1951) also features two players who could enrich any comic situation: Alistair Sim, as a self-effacing writer who publishes lurid fiction under several pseudonyms, and Joyce Grenfell, as his gawky naval fiancée. He is one of a number of heirs required to do uncongenial jobs before they can inherit a fortune: the opening sequence is reminiscent of *If I Had a Million*, but the jokes that follow are strictly British, even if ordered by an Italian, Mario Zampi, who directed several British comedies with similarly strong basic situations. In Britain this was the year's most popular film.

British National offered one film of interest among its entertainments for middle-aged ladies, **No Room at the Inn** (1948), directed by Daniel Birt from a screenplay by Ivan Foxwell (who produced) and Dylan Thomas, not then earning much from his poetry. Since Joan Temple's play about evacuees was seriously regarded, it should be noted that the film is like a dark, charcoal version of 'Hansel and Gretel' – preposterous, yet extraordinarily vivid. There were indeed people like Mrs Voray (Freda Jackson), a hard-drinking good time girl who accepts a houseful of kids for the money they brought in. The core of the story concerns the refined little girl who might eventually be corrupted by her or by her other charges – and since the role is priggishly played it is hard to sympathise; yet one experiences a shock, if cheaply motivated, when the child's father proves less interested in her complaints than in Mrs Voray's sexual advances. Miss Jackson at times finds a sense of humour in this woman, but in rendering her monstrous almost chews the scenery; her neighbour, a gin-soaked harridan as grasping as any in Dickens, is played by Hermione Baddeley, who, as ever in the business of overplaying, spurts home an easy winner.

Renown, hitherto best known for its sponsorship of the Old Mother Riley comedies, made three versions of classic novels. The first, **Tom Brown's Schooldays** (1951) was filmed mainly *in situ*, at Rugby, but the director, Gordon Parry, mismanages the scenes of bullying by making them both unpleasant and trivial; he gets a good shot from Robert Newton as Dr Arnold. Still, I suspect the film was made mainly to exploit the prepubescent charms of John Howard Davies, who had been David Lean's Oliver Twist. Both **Scrooge** (1951), directed by Brian Desmond Hurst, and **The Pickwick Papers** (1952), directed by Noel Langley – who had a hand in the screenplay of all three films – only serve to recall the superiority of Lean's Dickens films. As Scrooge Alistair Sim sets his face into a scowl, resembling nothing but a nice man with a bilious attack. Nor do the members of the Pickwick Club – James Hayter as Mr Pickwick, Nigel Patrick as Mr Jingle, James Donald as Mr Winkle – leave much impression; but headed by Kathleen Harrison as Miss Wardle, the Pickwick ladies come off somewhat better: Miss Grenfell as Mrs Leo Hunter, Miss Baddeley as Mrs Bardell, Athene Seyler as Miss Witherfield and Hermione Gingold as Miss Tomkins.

Just about everybody is in **The Magic Box** (1951), the industry's collaborative effort to celebrate the Festival of Britain. Ronald Neame produced, John Boulting directed, and Eric Ambler wrote it, immediately soothing a contentious matter by claiming in the preface that its hero, William Friese-Greene, is but 'one of the inventors of cinematography'. Robert Donat plays Friese-Greene, and like the film is likeable without having much fire; his wives are Maria Schell, smiling through her tears, and Margaret Johnston. The sixty or so stars are listed only at the end; the one everyone remembers is Olivier, who turned down the lead but accepted the plum among the other roles – that of the Holborn policeman who was the first in the kingdom to see moving pictures.

By this time the American companies had begun to return to Britain. 20th Century-Fox had honorably led the way as early as 1946 with *Meet Me at Dawn*, with two second-rank stars, William Eythe, an American, and Hazel Court, a Britisher, but it was not a success. During its quarrel with the British government, Hollywood's expressed desire to help the British industry resulted in no more than a handful of films, but as audiences everywhere began to shrink, if slightly, by the end of the decade it was realised that filming in Europe was cheaper – and British technicians spoke English.

Before that Warner Bros. released **They Made Me a Fugitive** (1947), having retitled it – the original novel was called 'A Convict Has Escaped' – to remind audiences of their old movies (for the U.S. they renamed it *I Became a Criminal*). It was claimed to be Britain's first gangster film, since the crooks in prewar movies were usually forgers or race-track 'fixers'; but during the War, and hardened by it, the black market attracted the criminal element. The story is about a disaffected R.A.F. type (Trevor Howard) who joins a black-market operation; but the film is neither a realistic portrait of the London underworld nor a good thriller, and the direction by Cavalcanti is lumberingly slow, making the American-type wisecracks in Noel Langley's script even worse.

Night and the City (1950) attempts the same tack, its Soho seen by an American writer, Jo Eisinger – adapting a novel by Gerald Kersh – and an American director, Jules Dassin. Dassin moved about town for locations, but his is merely a film about ugly people – a club boss (Francis L. Sullivan), his wife (Googie Withers), and a dreary little con (Richard Widmark). There is also Gene Tierney, doing little, but included for the sake of the U.S. box office. The producer was 20th Century-Fox, the most active of the major studios in Britain, sending over a number of important directors and stars: among them was Irene Dunne, and as Queen Victoria, being phlegmatic with her cheeks stuffed with cotton wool, she is not to be believed in **The Mudlark** (1950), directed by Jean Negulesco. And it is a shock to find James Stewart living in a council house in **No Highway** (1951), even if he is the archetypal absent-minded scientist and described as having lived in Britain for some years. This version of Nevil Shute's novel was directed by Henry Koster, and it was thought to be a mature film because Stewart shows no romantic interest in either airhostess Glynis Johns or fellow passenger Marlene Dietrich (who, facing certain death when she hears their plane has metal fatigue, is as unbelievable as Stewart). Another Fox miscalculation is **The Black Rose** (1950), in which two Saxons (Tyrone Power, Jack Hawkins) set out on the road to Cathay and, like Hope and Crosby, acquire a girl, Cecile Aubrey. Aware that audiences had grown up since mindless swashbucklers like *The Mark of Zorro*, Fox offered a real historical background, some serious implication, e.g. racial intolerance, and numerous locations – among which the director, Henry Hathaway, was overwhelmed.

It was the American acceptance of Disney's **Treasure Island** (1950) which warmed the Hollywood companies to the British studios. Disney was using blocked funds, but it made sense to him to make a British classic with British players. This was his first wholly live action film, directed by Byron Haskin, and it offered the two most familiar ingredients of his cartoons, incident and visual beauty. Alas, today, the painted backcloths are all too visible; and an otherwise good cast starts horrendously with Robert Newton overacting as Long John Silver, and cutely with American Bobby Driscoll as Jim Hawkins. **The Sword and the Rose** (1953) is a Disney remake of *When Knighthood Was in Flower*, with Glynis Johns in Marion Davies's old role of that playful princess, Mary Tudor, who was forced to marry the aged Louis XII by her brother, Henry VIII – in which role James Robertson Justice roars and winks to the point of alienation. The hapless hero, Richard Todd, was also cast in the title role of **Rob Roy** (1953), with the same co-stars, but Disney this time made amends – for at least this is a stirring version of Sir Walter Scott's novel as directed by Harold French.

M-G-M also had a success with its version of Scott, **Ivanhoe** (1952), scripted by Noel Langley and directed by Richard Thorpe, with Robert Taylor uneasy in the title role. The performance by Elizabeth Taylor is justly famous, but, as Rowena, Joan Fontaine is almost as bad – and hers is the more serious fault, for she could act when she tried. **Never Let Me Go** (1953) stars the other ageing Metro idol, Clark Gable, as an American correspondent in Moscow who marries a Russian dancer (Gene Tierney), an unimaginative idea which under Delmer Daves's direction amounts to little. Of the cast only Kenneth More, as Gable's English confrère, is able to get away with the anti-Russian sentiments.

Warners used their frozen funds for **The Hasty Heart** (1949), though in Britain it was released as a production of Associated British, a partially owned subsidiary. It was a splendid example, at least commercially, of Anglo-American harmony. The original Broadway play was by an American, John Patrick, who had based it on his wartime experiences with a British ambulance unit. Warners sent over a director, Vincent Sherman, and a writer, Ranald MacDougall, both adept at handling superior soap opera, which this is; they were accompanied by Patricia Neal, to play a Canadian nursing sister, and Ronald Reagan, to play 'Yank' – both inmates of a British field hospital in Burma. A relatively-unknown British actor, Richard Todd, played superbly the leading role, that of an arrogant and embittered young Scots corporal who does not know that he is dying. He gets the backs up of the men in his ward, and since the piece concerns the breakdown of mutual hostility it should be pointed out that it only does so by ignoring or transgressing virtually every rule known to any Medical Corps in any army; but the scene in which the black African with no English shows that he likes the Scot provided a comforting message to the postwar world.

Bette Davis crossed the Atlantic for the British-backed **Another Man's Poison** (1951), though insisting on an American director, Irving Rapper. With flaring nostrils, those wide eyes widening, a cigarette in one hand and a riding-crop in the other, she strides about in jodhpurs, commits double murder, tries to send a man to his death in a jeep without brakes, steals her secretary's boyfriend, and has a fixation on a horse called Fury. Incredulity sets in within a minute of the credits. You might feel similarly about **Pandora and the Flying Dutchman** (1951), produced, written and directed by Albert Lewin, apparently under the influence of 'Omar Khayam', though one might probably be grateful to him for bringing Ava Gardner with him, to be as lovingly photographed by Jack Cardiff in Technicolor as the Spanish locations. She is Pandora, a nightclub singer; the spirit who loves her is a glowering James Mason.

Hollywood's tentative and self-interested foray into the British cinema did not stem the overall decline in quality, yet as the decade turned the films from Ealing Studios continued to improve – as they needed to, from their dreadful but well-meaning productions of the war years. The War had given Michael Balcon's company a sense of direction. Until then he had had no policy such as he had had as head of production at Gaumont-British, but by 1945 Ealing consisted of a dedicated group identifying itself with its native hearth. The lessons of documentary had been learned, and are charmingly pleasant in a slight tale of life on the barges, **Painted Boats** (1945), directed by Charles Crichton, and made as a supporting feature. Nevertheless there remained for some years a fallacy at Ealing that good films resulted from taking the camera out into the open, preferably the streets of the East End: it was only by studying Hollywood that Ealing realised that a strong story was also needed.

Eschewing for the moment the sunny fields and dark satanic mills, the studio came up with **Dead of Night** (1945), a compilation in the manner of Julien Duvivier's *Flesh and Fantasy*. The directors were Crichton, Cavalcanti, Basil Dearden and Robert Hamer (1911–63), working from a number of writers including H. G. Wells and E. F. Benson. The most truly macabre is the tale of the ventriloquist's dummy who takes over his master (Michael Redgrave), but for those who have seen *The Great Gabbo* it is as predictable as the rest. One sequence recalls *Friday the Thirteenth*, which Balcon had produced, and he ordered a revamp of that, **Train of Events** (1949), in which four assorted flashbacks explain why these people are travelling on this particular train; but as directed by Dearden, Crichton and Sidney Cole they make negligible entertainment.

For the moment Ealing stayed with artificial drama, though **Pink String and Sealing Wax** (1945), based on a popular stage play, has more on its mind than the murder at its centre. Hamer, directing, intended a compendium of Victoriana – the gin-palace, the heavy father, concerts on the pier. The dramatic construction is weak, and the sets, though attractive, are very obviously sets. Accordingly Charles Frend manages slightly better another period piece with the same actress, Googie Withers, **The Loves of Joanna Godden** (1947), skilfully photographed on the Romney Marshes. Miss Withers plays a tough lady farmer, and the film's chief flaw – which is not the fault of the actress – is that by failing to communicate her feeling for her land, sheep or men, the story creeps into inertia. Notwithstanding that the film is set in Edwardian England, it does reflect the fact that women could play a more important role than hitherto in British society. It has been suggested that this may also be found in the Gainsborough melodramas, but the roles played

Production in Austerity Britain

The British film industry, like many another, was incapable of putting working people on the screen without mixing them with criminals. Ealing's *It Always Rains on Sunday* was no exception, but the details of working-class life were not only accurate for once but observed without condescension. The man hiding is John McCallum, army deserter and crook, seeking refuge with old girlfriend, Googie Withers, now a respectable East End mum – who is clearly apprehensive that his presence will be discovered by her stepdaughter (Patricia Plunkett).

by Margaret Lockwood and Phyllis Calvert are basically imitations of those played by Hollywood's important female stars – and apart from Gracie Fields the British had not before had any popular lady movie stars. Miss Withers's following was not in the same league; and as their films prove, the talents at Ealing were more alive to contemporary feeling than those at Gainsborough.

Nicholas Nickleby (1947) had the misfortune to be released while Lean's *Great Expectations* was fresh in the memory; it is not one of Ealing's successes. John Dighton's screenplay brought some order to the long and disorganised plot, and Michael Relph's decor is impeccable. But Cavalcanti's direction often makes the distinguished cast look awkward – even Cedric Hardwicke as Ralph Nickleby and Stanley Holloway as Mr Crummles. As Nicholas and Kate Nickleby, Derek Bond and Sally Ann Howes are well cast, being players without discernible personalities: but that does not help the film at all.

Turning to a contemporary subject, in fact the War, **The Captive Heart** (1946) followed the adventures of some P.O.W.s in Germany and their homecoming: the actual scenes of their ship docking, a sequence not (as far as I know) duplicated in any other fiction film of the time, is very moving. The central character is a Czech (Michael Redgrave) who has successfully till now impersonated a British officer –

and though the situation is *ersatz* it is nicely directed by Basil Dearden. The other P.O.W.s are, however, strictly from stock: they include Basil Radford, Mervyn Johns, Jimmy Hanley, Gordon Jackson (as a sensitive young Scot afraid that his fiancée will not want him now that he is blinded, cf. *The Best Years of Our Lives*) and Jack Warner (as a Joe Blunt Cockney). These particular actors appeared so often in Ealing films as to suggest they represented certain kinds of Britishness to Balcon, though a doubt persists that Ealing ever cared much for either performers or the characters necessary to its stories.

That Warner's reassuring middle-aged persona turns out to be a traitor in **Against the Wind** (1948) indicates that the film was meant to be more honest than others on the work of Resistance fighters and those who were parachuted into Europe to help them. But the other characters, who include a Belgian woman (Simone Signoret) and a partisan priest (Robert Beatty) are conventional, and their adventures are pallid beside *Bataille du Rail*, though the film has aspirations in that direction. Crichton directed, from a screenplay by T. E. B. Clarke (q.v.), who was so important in the development of Ealing comedy.

'Would *you* take Frieda into your home?' asked the advertisements for **Frieda** (1947), directed by Dearden from a West End play. It concerns an ex-officer (David Farrar), his German war bride (Mai Zetterling), and the various reactions to this viper in the nest. His sister (Glynis Johns), who lost her husband in the War, is compassionate; his aunt (Flora Robson), about to stand for parliament, is a kind woman, but uncertain whether there is anything in the German character to be kind about – a view apparently confirmed when Frieda's Nazi brother (Albert Lieven) turns up, to send Frieda rushing down to the weir like Rebecca in 'Rosmersholm'. Till then the film is serious; and audiences approved of the scene where Frieda insists on watching the newsreels of the Nazi concentration camps in order to share German guilt.

Despite its topicality, the film, with its small-town setting, fails to reflect the austere Britain of Sir Stafford Cripps, the Chancellor of the Exchequer. That can be found in no film of the period – in the way that *Millions Like Us* reflects wartime Britain – but **It Always Rains on Sunday**

(1947) takes us back to the time when Dad put on three-piece suit and watch-chain to go to the pub on Sunday and a bunch of daffs could be bought for half-a-crown. Young men could not take girls to their rooms, records spun at 78 r.p.m. and, more germane to the plot, petty spivs operated in the arcades and dance-halls of Bethnal Green. They are less East Enders than West End actors pretending, and there are occasional notes of archness between the opening (raindrops at dawn near the railway-arch) and the hackneyed climax (a chase at night through the railway yard). The virtues include Miss Withers, as a married woman whose former lover (John McCallum), a convict on the run, wants to hide in the air-raid shelter, now a tool-shed, and the dialogue, adapted from Arthur La Berne's novel by Angus Mac-Phail, Henry Cornelius and Hamer, whose direction has gusto. As with *Dead of Night* and *The Captive Heart* the notices were warm, and it was, in addition, Ealing's first great popular success.

All the same it is not to be compared to *The Street with No Name*, and it was the 20th Century-Fox films of that school which taught Ealing much about filming in the streets. London is splendidly used in **The Blue Lamp** (1950), a tribute to the Metropolitan police, directed by Basil Dearden. It was enormously popular, but it is difficult now to say whether it was once a good film. There is a scene in which a couple quarrel about a film they have just seen, and he says that the only laugh he had was when the baby died: and some of us may feel that way about the scene in which the young P.C. (Jimmy Hanley) has to inform a stoic police wife of the murder of her husband (Jack Warner). For like most Ealing films, this one insists on whimsical, unsentimental niceness. All the bobbies on display are cheerful and understanding, with a quip for a small boy, a helping hand for an old lady, and their choir carols 'Nymphs and Shepherds'. The film exudes moral fervour, but is closer in tone to *Rebecca of Sunnybrook Farm* than *The French Connection* (q.v.) – or, to take, more suitably, a contemporary, *The Asphalt Jungle*.

The same troubles beset **The Cruel Sea** (1953). Ealing's prestige was such by this time that Rank, as distributor, was happy to find the huge financing needed for the rights to Nicholas Montserrat's whopping bestseller. During the period of austerity and the junketings of the Festival of Britain the War had been partly forgotten, but Montserrat's book began a nostalgia for the War years, as if it were time to take stock. That did not include the brothel scenes, missing from the film, though a vital element in the book's success, and Eric Ambler's screenplay turned personal reminiscence into the clichés of the wartime movies – so that one officer has a flighty, faithless wife and another a very nice one, who accompanies him for the inevitable picnic on the downs. As directed by Charles Frend, the characters are complacent and bloodless, as might have been surmised from Frend's earlier study in British heroism, **Scott of the Antarctic** (1948). The screenplay by Ivor Montagu and Walter Meade refuses to acknowledge that Scott's expedition was at best foolhardy and mismanaged, and it chauvinistically plays down the fact that Amundsen had beaten Scott to the Pole. Its dispassionate tone is demonstrated in the shots of feet tramping in the snow, offered in lieu of any explanation of how the men coped; and even in the location shots there is no steam on their breath (to show this in his run-of-the-mill *Dirigible*, Capra caused the actors to suck dry ice – and one of them lost three teeth and part of his jaw). As Scott, John Mills is just another kindly C.O., his motives unexplained, while Christmas in the Antarctic turns out to be just like Christmas in a P.O.W. camp in any British P.O.W. movie; nor is there the slightest sense of adventure.

It was made in Technicolor, as was **Saraband for Dead Lovers** (1948), and the simultaneous release of these two expensive productions was intended to demonstrate that Balcon now considered Ealing a studio of world class. *Saraband*, like Cineguild's earlier *Blanche Fury* – also with Stewart Granger – was yet another attempt to demonstrate to Gainsborough that at least one British studio could treat an historical subject with both flair and accuracy. The source was Helen Simpson's novel on the amours and intrigues of the Hanoverian court, and as directed by Basil Dearden it was with some justice critically trounced.

It is nevertheless more watchable than Ealing's three 'Commonwealth' adventures, the first of which, **The Over-**

landers (1946), was much praised. Balcon and Harry Watt had discussed a film paying tribute to Australia's war effort, and Watt pointed out that reconstructed documentaries had been rendered obsolete by the several features composed of newsreel footage, such as *Desert Victory*. He was also struck by the fact that that 'huge, exciting, hard country' had not been used by filmmakers, and his determination to utilise it himself was strengthened when an official of the Ministry of Information mentioned an incident which could provide the basis for a film combining fact and fiction in equal measure – specifically, the driving of 100,000 head of cattle across the country in 1942. Unfortunately, Watt and his writers deal with this situation only in thundering cliché. Among others, Richard Winnington had reservations, but he was excited about the prospect of the Commonwealth being used as Hollywood had used the great spaces of the American West. So was a South African conglomerate, which approached Ealing for a similar film on Africa. After a preliminary sortie, Watt suggested a film based on the work of the Kenyan conservationist, Mervyn Cowie. Three writers are credited with the script of **Where No Vultures Fly** (1951), but their ideas on conservation are on the level of a vapid Shaftesbury Avenue thriller. It was chosen for the annual Royal Film Performance – an institution about to fall into disrepute, due to the kind of dish the industry saw fit to set before the King – and was popular enough to necessitate a sequel, even more stilted, **West of Zanzibar** (1953). Neither is in the same league as the M-G-M *King Solomon's Mines*, which they hoped to emulate.

The actors concerned, not in the first place of the highest quality, clearly received little help, and a study of all three films does nothing to solve the mystery of why Watt was considered one of Britain's leading directors. A similar enigma surrounds Thorold Dickinson, despite his apparent intelligence and love of the medium. The best of his handful of films is **Secret People** (1952), though by an odd circumstance it shattered his reputation. Simultaneous with the premiere there was published a book about the production, 'Making a Film', written by Lindsay Anderson with such admiration that the critics lost their balance – a view at least

tenable after a re-reading of the reviews, which are negative and almost totally untrustworthy. For instance, Valentina Cortese's performance, far below her best work, was much praised, while most complained that the film was incomprehensible – which, for all its faults, it is not. Gavin Lambert's review in *Sight and Sound* speaks constantly of 'style' – which is wholly lacking, despite some action sequences so well achieved that they make up for the gaucheness elsewhere. The subject is terrorism, as practised in London by some foreigners hoping to assassinate a Fascist dictator, and Dickinson's script (written with Wolfgang Wilhelm from his own idea) says unequivocally that those who resort to violence, from whatever motives, are thugs. Yet Winnington thought the message only 'tentative'; he is on surer ground concluding that since the innocent (Cortese) caught up in the scheming is in no sense politically active the film had no point, and 'Sir Michael Balcon was much perturbed over this vital flaw.' In the final analysis this is a fair attempt at a political thriller, less tense than Hitchcock's not dissimilar *Sabotage*, but more mature.

Significantly, Dickinson was the only outside director invited to work at Ealing, whose films in general made little out of much. Balcon's team approached interesting ideas in a prissy, pussyfooting and peculiarly British way. **Lease of Life** (1954) wears its Englishness like a halo. It is a study of a country parson (Robert Donat), directed by Frend from a screenplay by Eric Ambler, and it has points to make on ecclesiastical promotion, mortality, the interdependence of a middle-aged couple – even village busy-bodies. Donat plays with the correct blend of humility and theatricality; the film, though sincere and likeable, suffers from a lack of guts. Ealing's basic trouble was that it made its films by committee. Old hand Balcon encouraged his bright young men to throw out ideas, and they hammered at them until all individuality had gone. To Balcon the image of the studio was more important than the ideas of any particular filmmaker, and as a result it is impossible to distinguish the work of one Ealing director from another.

That was exactly what was intended. It was not a writer's studio either, as we may see by examining the Ealing films written by Jack Whittingham (b. 1910), whose previous work, including (especially) *The Dancing Years*, was of little account. His first film for Ealing was no better – **Cage of Gold** (1950), with which Balcon hoped to please Mr Rank, since it was a vehicle for Jean Simmons, playing a girl caught between a respectable doctor (James Donald) and a rotter (David Farrar), the usual former R.A.F. officer adrift in the postwar world. Dearden directed, clearly depressed by the screenplay, so it is a surprise to find that **Pool of London** (1951), made by the same team, is one of the most successful of all Ealing pictures. (The writer John Eldridge conceived the idea and was working on the script with T. E. B. Clarke, but Clarke found himself handling the seemingly obligatory 'criminal element' as a joke. His ideas were developed into *The Lavender Hill Mob*, q.v., and he was replaced by Whittingham.) It follows, in the manner of *Grand Hotel*, some merchant seamen during one summer weekend, especially the quick-talking, philandering Dan (Bonar Colleano) and his Jamaican chum, Johnny (Earl Cameron): the latter falls in love with a cinema cashier (Susan Shaw), quite discreetly, but this is nevertheless the first inter-racial romance in an English-speaking film.* The 'crime' ranges from the smuggling of nylons to a diamond heist; and the piece is not without coincidence. But I know no more vivid portrait of London – its pubs, its trams (soon to be done away with, as someone says), its music halls (one grand and one seedy) and the silent empty streets of the City and Dockland.

A similar formula is applied to probation officers in **I Believe in You** (1952), directed by Dearden and written by him, Whittingham, Nicholas Phipps and Michael Relph, who also produced. Relph was one of the stalwarts of Ealing, as art director, Dearden's usual producer and in the case of this film son of the actor George Relph, who gives a touching performance alongside Celia Johnson, Godfrey Tearle and Cecil Parker as the other probation officers. The piece is conventional both on their dedication and the delinquency of their charges. **The Divided Heart** (1954) is even more high-minded, and as modest in conception as it is lofty in aim, i.e. it

*Always excepting, that is, the dusky maidens who enslaved white men in such jungle melodramas as *White Cargo*.

denounces war with particular attention to the havoc it wreaks on the innocent – to whom it refuses a happy ending. Whittingham's story and screenplay, based on an actual event, concern a war orphan (Michel Ray) whose foster parents, a Bavarian couple, discover that a Slovene woman (Yvonne Mitchell) has applied to the Allied High Commission for custody in the certainty that he is her son. By concentrating on the court case the film hopes it avoids sentiment; but as directed by Charles Crichton it is sometimes arch and occasionally plodding.

Its inspiration is obviously *The Search*, just as there are echoes of *Ladri di Biciclette* in **Hunted** (1952) in the relationship of a murderer (Dirk Bogarde) on the run and unwanted small boy (Jon Whiteley). Crichton and Whittingham balance that relationship with the 'chase' element, and tug neatly at our emotions when the boy – the performance is as worthwhile as any in movies – recites 'The Owl and the Pussycat'. C. A. Lejeune said, 'This is a film with a great deal of heart for its small size, and I think it should command affection.' It also commands respect, but it was not made for Ealing, since the crowded production schedule would not permit it; it was made by one of Rank's production companies. But it is of the Ealing level, workmanlike and well-meaning. Only two of Ealing's directors made considerable films elsewhere, Henry Cornelius with *Genevieve* (q.v.) and Alexander Mackendrick with *Sweet Smell of Success* (q.v.). Balcon was paternal and protective: the outside world was very cold.

The Ealing comedies reflect this, being insular, if in the best sense, with a sharp eye for the foibles of the British – even if they are reduced to such stock types as plucky Londoners and cunning country-folk. The scripts are *gemütlich*, but are, in general, inventively developed. The films are the British cinema's most original and influential body of work – too influential, which is why they revive variably. The first of them, **Hue and Cry** (1947), was less a comedy than a boys' adventure with laughs, an unusual film to make in the climate of British cinema at the time: it cost little, and had it failed it could have been expected to recoup its cost at children's Saturday matinees. Crichton directed and the script by T. E. B. Clarke (b. 1907), by

The Ealing comedies came as a tonic to austerity Britain – and indeed the world, notably finding a new audience for British films in the U.S. The cuter, more homely ones were so much copied that some of them seem dated today, leaving as the peak *Kind Hearts and Coronets*, a stylish black comedy perhaps too good to be imitated – a proposed remake in 1976 was cancelled after a storm of protests. Almost certainly they could not have found players to match the originals, including Joan Greenwood and Dennis Price.

far the most individual of Ealing's writers, started by reworking 'Emil und die Detektive' against London's blitzed buildings: a gang of Cockney kids sets out to trap some black marketeers, with a timid writer (Alistair Sim) of blood-and-thunder stories caught between them. Encouraged by the film's reception, Balcon initiated work on three more comedies rooted in national and regional life, and they each opened in London a week apart: **Passport to Pimlico** (1949), directed by Cornelius from an original screenplay by Clarke; **Whisky Galore!** (1949), directed by Alexander Mackendrick (b. 1912), an American-born former scriptwriter for the company, from a screenplay by Angus MacPhail and Compton Mackenzie, from the latter's novel; and **Kind Hearts and Coronets** (1949), directed by Robert Hamer, and written by him and John Dighton from an Edwardian novel by Roy Horniman.

It is significant that both MacPhail and Dighton had worked on scripts for George Formby and Will Hay, and *Passport to Pimlico* takes its basic idea from *Look Up and Laugh*, which Gracie Fields had made for A.T.P., Ealing's predecessor. Updated, it provides a bombsite and an old charter to prove that one area of London belonged to Burgundy – a fact seized on by its inhabi-

tants, anxious to be free of ration books and other restrictions imposed since 1939. The spirit of the blitz prevails: 'It's because we are English that we're sticking to our rights to be Burgundians' used to get the biggest laugh. For later audiences, perhaps, the fun has faded – bureaucratic bunglers, lend-lease parcels, postwar spivdom; but it remains a sweet film, winningly performed by everyone, from Stanley Holloway (owner of the local hardware store) and Margaret Rutherford (the historian authenticating the charter) downwards. On the other hand, *Whisky Galore!* wastes Joan Greenwood, the most endearing of English comediennes. The film itself is an under-nourished account of a shipwrecked cargo of whisky which disappears, and the efforts of the red-tapebound authorities to prise it from the locals. As *Tight Little Island*, it was a particularly big hit in the U.S., presumably with those who find crafty Highlanders hilarious in themselves.

Kind Hearts and Coronets is the best of the Ealing batch, the only one with a claim to greatness. I can only think of one movie like it – Carné's *Drôle de Drame*, and that, in contrast, is less an ironic comedy than farce. Guitry used irony and irreverence towards the matters handled here, families and murder, but nothing in British cinema prepares us for it except perhaps *On Approval*; Lonsdale and his peers might have created its hero – flippant, imperturbable, unable to speak except in epigrams. Every other line has a double meaning, whether known to its speaker or not, and though a certain elegance is attained, the visual style is not always of an equivalent standard; nevertheless after several viewings the film manages to surprise, and it keeps before us a cast of characters who, when they are not sublimely foolish, are selfish, self-centred and heartless. As the young man who murders the family which stands between him and a dukedom, Dennis Price is good enough to make one regret that his screen career gave him no other similar chance; Alec Guinness, in a celebrated tour-de-force, is several members of the family; and Miss Greenwood and Valerie Hobson are their women, a match of scheming cupidity and condescending stupidity.

Ealing did not try to duplicate *Kind Hearts and Coronets*, but the chorus of praise for all three films resulted in **A Run for Your Money** (1949) and **The Magnet** (1950), where the incipient larkiness and cuteness of *Passport to Pimlico* and *Whisky Galore!* have been somewhat extended. The regional interest pertains to Wales and Liverpool respectively, and though both films are more modest and less amusing, they are, as directed by Charles Frend, immensely likeable. *A Run for Your Money* follows two Welsh miners up for the international rugby match at Twickenham, and it has that Ealing device of most of the cast haring over most of London. It has excellent contrasting performances by Donald Houston, desperately wide-eyed as one of the miners, and Guinness, as the gardening correspondent reluctantly accompanying him, a meek man whose assertiveness is limited to his moustache. The best scene involves Joyce Grenfell as an excruciatingly gauche dressmaker, and it is too good to be spoilt by Moira Lister, playing her usual role of a gold-digger with all the subtlety of a ten ton truck. *The Magnet* concerns a small boy (William Fox, who changed his Christian name to James as a grown-up actor) who covets a magnet belonging to an even smaller boy, and who, having deceived to get it, is ashamed, and unable to dispose of it as he hopes. T. E. B. Clarke wrote it, and the film is one of the best ever made for children.

Clarke's most celebrated script, for **The Lavender Hill Mob** (1951), directed by Crichton, starts with a plan to rob the Bank of England by a staid, humble bank clerk (Guinness), but he can think of no way to hide the bullion till a manufacturer (Stanley Holloway) of geegaws comes to live in the same boarding house . . . Alas, the film is now almost threadbare. Making mugs of the police in comic chases goes honourably back to the Keystone Cops; but although the ploy had been intermittently used it became a cliché with this film. So did the situation of Cockney criminals and/or lovable eccentrics planning and executing a heist: no other Ealing comedy was as much copied.

For that reason it revives less well than **The Man in the White Suit** (1951), directed by Mackendrick, in which Guinness amused us at about the same time. It is no longer particularly funny, but alone of the Ealing comedies it remains relevant (if any of them were) – for it is a comedy of the boardroom, and like *The Solid Gold Cadillac* (q.v.) it is one of the few films to stray in that direction. The prospect of an everlasting dirt-free fabric might then have been a gleam in a boffin's eye – which may be why the single-mindedness of Guinness, as its inventor, is still so effective. The spectacle of the manufacturers uniting to suppress the cloth is revealing, and the concern of the workers about redundancy a real one. The screenplay by Dighton and Roger Macdougall, from an unproduced play by the latter, rightly withholds from both sides the fact that they want the same outcome: and if in other ways it is careless (as good American comedies never were) it juggles its complications inventively.

Though it is easy in retrospect to pinpoint weaknesses in all these films, the first time contemporary critics did so was with **The Titfield Thunderbolt** (1953). Britons at the time were chuckling over Emmett's cartoons of whimsical railways in *Punch*, and since these were dedicated to the notion that machines were quaint a union was inevitable, since the Ealing comedies felt the same way about people. Clarke's screenplay repeated the view of *Passport to Pimlico*, that when the British are up against it they lose their reserve and with cheery optimism team together in opposition. In this case, faced with the closing of a branch line, they combine to operate a railway – led by the vicar (George Relph), delighted to indulge his life-long passion for steam-engines. There are felicitous incidents and, this time, Technicolor, but the qualities peculiar to Ealing comedy are used without restraint. These are not evident in **The Love Lottery** (1954), also directed by Crichton, though the idea is typical: a movie star (David Niven) is offered as first prize in a lottery. A Hollywood writer, Harry Kurnitz, was brought in to polish up a script attempting satire on big business and movie stardom (in particular the 'sexy Rexy' aspect attached to Rex Harrison's image): together with the international star name (Niven) and exotic locations (the Italian lakes) this represents the company's one excursion into mainstream comedy, and it is a disaster.

The participation of Americans in *The 'Maggie'* (q.v.), on release simultaneously, was essential, but meanwhile American interest was helping to destroy Ealing. The popularity in the U.S. of the comedies,

Genevieve was not strictly speaking an Ealing comedy, but the director, Henry Cornelius, had worked for the studio, and the screenwriter, William Rose, would subsequently do so. Since its four leading-players were little known, there was no advance publicity and the critics were as surprised as they were delighted. Kay Kendall and Kenneth More both became stars – and the film itself still holds the record for reissues in Britain: *Gone with the Wind* has played the circuits more often, but not in such a concentrated period.

especially those with Guinness, revived Balcon's competitive spirit, recalling the inroads made into the American market during his tenure at Gaumont-British. He was cautious since he appreciated that Ealing's success depended on its parochial approach, but increasingly Rank tried to dictate policy – and the more successful and ambitious Balcon became the more he was dependent on Rank's financial support. The accountants who had taken over at the Rank Organisation had stultified production at the studios already controlled by them, and they attempted to prevail at Ealing without having the least understanding of Balcon's creative policy. As Balcon capitulated, Ealing's films became indistinguishable from those of the Rank studios, and his position was weakened by the increasingly indifferent reception accorded them – and by the inevitable defection of the members of his team. In 1955 Stephen Courtauld, who had managed Ealing's financial affairs since the arrival of Balcon, decided to retire. Balcon resolved to finance the immediate projected batch of Ealing films from the National Film Finance Corporation – as Harold Wilson's production fund was now called (as a member of the board he had not wanted to call on it before). In order for the loan to be repaid

he accepted an offer from B.B.C. television for the Ealing studio itself, for £350,000, on the understanding that the two new soundstages being built at Pinewood were to be for the exclusive use of the Ealing unit. For John Davis, the situation provided an opportunity to bring Balcon even further under Rank control, for Balcon was to petition for studio space at Pinewood like any other Rank producer. Balcon accordingly dissolved the 1945 agreement by which Rank distributed his films, and he signed a new one with M-G-M, which recognised Ealing as a company with a world-wide reputation. But Ealing, to all intents and purposes, was dead; a disheartened team made some films for M-G-M as weak as the later ones for Rank, including the final Ealing comedy, *Barnacle Bill* (q.v.). In 1959 what was left of Ealing became Michael Balcon Productions, though briefly, and he himself later served in advisory capacities with Bryanston (q.v.) and British Lion. The Ealing catalogue passed to Associated-British – a more valuable item than its own.

If we except *Barnacle Bill*, the comedies ended on a high note, though the best of them, and the most spectacularly successful, **Genevieve** (1953), was made directly for Rank when (as in the case of *Hunted*) the

Ealing schedule was too full. The script was by an expatriate American, William Rose (b. 1918), who had hitherto contributed to some nondescript British films; the director, Henry Cornelius, had served as editor and writer at Ealing but was otherwise only known for his handling of *Passport to Pimlico.*★ The film has such Ealing characteristics as a quaint central idea – the Old Crocks' rally to Brighton and back – and an amused but affectionate view of such local types as obtuse policemen and kindly but unhelpful landladies. What Rose added was malice and sex: it has a bite which recalls the Hollywood comedies of the Thirties – not least, as Richard Winnington pointed out (in one of the unanimous rave reviews), because it was unique among British films in regarding its main characters as sexual beings. They are a husband (John Gregson) and wife (Dinah Sheridan), their best friend (Kenneth More) and the model (Kay Kendall) he hopes to bed when they arrive in Brighton. In appearance and attitudes they are, for the first time on screen, the affluent postwar generation; and though the marital squabbles are beautifully managed, it is the other couple who take the screen. More, with his desire to combine the London-Brighton run with 'a really beautiful emotional experience', goes further than Gregson in arrogance and adolescent delight in old cars; and the film was the first to exploit the gift of Kay Kendall (1927–59) for remaining soignée while being bumped or slapped around. None of these players had been well known hitherto: but they were seen frequently as the film had an unprecedented number of circuit re-issues over the next few years. Abroad its reception was rather 'caviare for the general', but it is constantly revived the world over.

Rose's next two screenplays were written for Ealing, and **The 'Maggie'** (1954), like *Genevieve* and his later *It's a Mad, Mad, Mad, Mad World* (q.v.) is about getting from one place to another – in this case as

★Balcon's excuse for not finding studio space for *Genevieve* was apparently that Cornelius was no longer on the payroll.

experienced by an American (Paul Douglas), who wants some £4,000-worth of equipment transported to his new island home in the Highlands. The concept came from Rose's fellow-American, Mackendrick, who also directed, and like his *Whisky Galore!* its chief subject is Scots canniness – in this case more than a match for American ingenuity. Both aspects are handled with charm and discretion, as when Douglas discovers that he enjoys both the open life and the battle of wits. Perhaps because the cast includes so many dour Scots it lacks insouciance, but the second Rose-Mackendrick collaboration, **The Ladykillers** (1955), can hardly be faulted. Like *Genevieve*, it builds inventively; like *Kind Hearts and Coronets*, it is *comédie noire*; and like all the Ealing comedies its keynote is a coy irony. As with *The Lavender Hill Mob* its band of comic, incompetent crooks (Guinness, Cecil Parker, Peter Sellers, etc.) would be much copied, yet they are both too original and too much indebted to the cartoonist Charles Addams (with acknowledgment: cf. Guinness's make-up) to be entirely equalled. And no one could use again the enchanting situation of the lavender-and-old-lace landlady (Katie Johnson) who innocently proves more than a match for them.

This film was on release when the break with the Rank Organisation was announced. For M-G-M, Balcon, Frend, Clarke and Guinness made **Barnacle Bill** (1957), about a retired sea-captain who takes charge of a seaside pier, but it only proved that confidence had crumpled; the dispersed team of Relph and Dearden made the infinitely better *The Smallest Show on Earth* (q.v.), with a script by Rose, for British Lion, and with it the age of Ealing comedy was over. By that time, for the first time in almost three decades, Balcon was no longer a force in British film-making. Korda, his rival of the prewar years, had died while Balcon was negotiating his escape from the Rank Organisation – which was left, alas, as the only potent force in the British film industry.

30

Luis Buñuel and his Followers

TILL THE END of the Forties most of the foreign-language films shown around the world were French, with a smattering from Italy, Russia and Germany. The situation began to change in 1950, when the Mexican *Los Olvidados* (q.v.) and the Japanese *Rashomon* (q.v.) were warmly received at the Cannes and Venice Film Festivals respectively. The Mexican film was the work of a name then hallowed only in film societies, themselves few in number: Luis Buñuel.

He had lost interest in making films after *Las Hurdes*, but rather than live on family money he returned to Paris to supervise the dubbing of Paramount's films for the local market. He went on to do the same for those of Warner Bros. in Madrid, and was also executive producer on some minor Spanish films. On the outbreak of the Spanish Civil War he offered his services to the Republican government in Paris, who sent him to Hollywood to advise on any movie project favourable to its cause: he did work on one such project, at M-G-M, but it was abandoned when it was clear that Franco would be the victor. Iris Barry got him a job at the Museum of Modern Art in New York, supervising Spanish versions of American films for Latin America; and when he was forced to resign – because someone discovered that he had directed the still-scandalous *L'Age d'Or* – he found similar work with the U.S. Army. That too was terminated when a report appeared that Salvador Dali had described him as an atheist. Warners either did not know or did not care, for they took him on to dub their pictures for the Latin-American market, and at one point considered assigning him to the direction of *The Beast with Five Fingers*. His preparatory work on the film revived his taste for filming, and he went to Mexico to prepare a version of Lorca's 'La Casa de Bernardo Alba', to be shot in France, but the necessary financing was not forthcoming. A Mexican producer, Oscar Dancigers, offered him a straightforward commercial job, **Gran Casino** (1947), starring two popular singers, but when it failed to confirm their reputation Buñuel received no further commissions. However, he had established a good relationship with Dancigers, who encouraged him to submit an idea for a film for children. Instead, Buñuel suggested a film *about* children, which became *Los Olvidados*; Dancigers promised him 'a degree of freedom' if he would first do a comedy of the type popular in the Latin-American market.

This was **El Gran Calavera** (1949), based on a play, with a screenplay by Luiz Alcoriza, who was to work on many of Buñuel's subsequent films. Its subject is a family versed in deception and headed by an ageing widower (Fernando Solar) who gets drunk every night, to the indifference of his sponging relatives – who are, in fact, the reason for his drinking. When they eventually realise that he may drink away his fortune they trick him into believing that he has lost it. To get his own back, he is faced with the necessity of reform, which he miraculously achieves overnight – undoubtedly to the amusement of Buñuel, a dedicated and unrepentant alcoholic (by his own admission, but possibly not at this particular time). Till that point in the plot the film is a celebration of drink, but Buñuel's expressed aversion to the bourgeoisie is otherwise confined to giving the prospective mother-in-law a not inconspicuous moustache.

His contempt for middle-class values is the abiding theme of his career, but it is nevertheless absent from **Los Olvidados** (1950), which reintroduced him to cinema-goers who remembered him only as the director of two much earlier surrealist films. That contempt would not have been amiss, if only as a side-line, for Buñuel here is concerned with the state of the poor – which he discusses in terms as compassionate and pessimistic as in *Las Hurdes*. Unlike that film, this is fiction aimed at the mass market, for since de Sica's *Sciuscià* there had been several much-discussed and popular films on juvenile delinquency. Buñuel's foreword is unoriginal ('the problem is left to the city . . . and the progressive forces of our time') and the whole is not without some moralising in the manner of *Boys Town* as it ranges through the underside of 'a certain Mexican city', finding overcrowding and promiscuity the essential accompaniments to poverty – together with religiosity, superstition and violence. The children are corrupt and devious – a far cry even from de Sica's protagonists; but it is not till the end, when the blind man they have robbed is revealed as no longer pitiable but lecherous and vindictive, that the film becomes more than a careful and well-photographed study. At that point we recognise the voice that is uniquely Buñuel's, mordantly convinced of human weakness.

Before the film achieved its success at Cannes he had embarked on another purely commercial chore, which, like those that immediately followed, was not expected to travel far beyond the Mexican border. Later he sometimes pretended to forget their titles – while remarking that of his entire output there were only two or three films that he did not like. On another occasion he said, 'I have always been true to my surrealist principles: "The need to eat never excuses prostituting one's art." In the nineteen or twenty films I have made there may be three or four which are frankly bad, but in no way have I infringed my moral code. To have a code at all is childish to many people, but not to me.' That code is discernible in these films, clumsy as they are and often poorly acted, for they picture bourgeois families emotionally crippled by religion and tradition. Their members quarrel and scheme against each other, as the plots slide from melodrama to farce;

and these stories usually depend on that great divider, sex, rendered never as tenderness but as lust and jealousy, always ambiguous and usually farcical as well. **Susana** (1951) is a rural tale of the cuckoo in the nest – the new maid who agitates all the male members of the household in turn. The piece is not without its ironies, as when someone observes, in fact wrongly, that the name Susana means 'charity' – for charitable she is not, and anyone taking her deserves all he gets. She, like the film, is not subtle, but it is interesting as a blueprint for the more mature *Le Journal d'une Femme de Chambre* (q.v.); it would also have been improved, as Buñuel himself observed, with a different ending, presumably one in which she is not simply forgiven for her sins.

La Hija del Engaño (1951) is a remake of one of the films Buñuel had produced in Spain, the 1935 *Don Quintin el Amargao*. Don Quintin (Fernando Solar) casts his wife out on discovering her infidelity, and she retaliates by screaming that their child, a daughter, is not his. Later, when he has become the successful but embittered proprietor of a gambling den, she tells him

Luis Buñuel – seen here with shooting script and parrot – had the strangest career of any major director, so that we are fortunate to have the masterpieces of his late middle-age. After establishing a reputation with *L'Age d'Or* in 1930 it was almost two decades before he directed again. *Los Olvidados* re-established him in 1950, but he was to spend most of the subsequent decade working on commercial Mexican films – though as handled by him they are not routine. Here he is on the set of another of his important films of that time, *The Adventures of Robinson Crusoe*.

Luis Buñuel and his Followers

Subsequent to *Los Olvidados*, few of Buñuel's Mexican films were intended for audiences abroad, and most of them have only been seen at retrospectives of his work. Of the few that were widely screened overseas at the time *El* was perhaps the best received, and it remains a powerful study of an obsessional jealousy. Arturo de Cordova played the husband so afflicted, and, as you may have guessed, it is he on the right of the picture.

that she lied – and he learns that the girl has fled the peasant family with whom he deposited her, because of their cruelty. The film is an odd mixture, at its most acrimonious and comic in the gaming sequences, which contain the only really characteristic Buñuel touch. A young clerk is suicidal because of his gambling debts, but later he becomes a confirmed addict: the irresistible attraction of vice was something that Buñuel would feature in many later films.

Subida al Cielo (1952) has for its hero a young bridegroom who succumbs much too soon to the advances of a whore. It is Buñuel's most personal film of this period, with its haunting, surrealist dream sequence and a cast of characters – passengers on a bus – mainly corrupt or treacherous. The film merely follows their antics, and those of the bus itself, as it travels from one place to another. 'This is the other Mexico of the tropics,' wrote Tony Richardson in *Sight and Sound*, 'with its rich fruitfulness and lazy Indians, and it has never been so spontaneously caught as in this enchanting film.' However, it is too crude and uneven for complete enchantment. **Una Mujer sin Amor** (1952) must surely be one of the

films that Buñuel dislikes, rambling from the predicament of a young mother who loves another man then later to the two grown-up sons who quarrel as a consequence: the bourgeois family torn apart by dissension is a typical theme, here muted by exceptionally poor playing. The source is a story by de Maupassant, 'Pierre et Jean', adapted by Jaime Salvador, who also wrote *Susana*.

The flimsy construction of all these films contrasts sharply with the intense narrative drive of **El Bruto** (1953) and **El** (1953), both written by Buñuel himself and Alcoriza, the second from a novel by Mercedes Pinto. They are unquestionably melodramatic, but the difference between a Buñuel film and one made by anyone else on the same subject is that he pushes every aspect to its limit (or that permitted by the censors) while never overstepping the bounds of probability. Against his will, *El Bruto* underwent lengthy script changes, but it remains fascinating. Pedro (Pedro Armendariz) is the brute of the title, a slaughterhouse worker who becomes the willing tool of a tatty but ruthless old landowner (Andres Soler); and the abattoir and butcher's shop provide the background for a tale of lechery and senility, of opportunism and exploitation of the poor. The film is particularly critical of the landowner's degenerate family, but on this occasion the relationship of the brute and the waif does not seem to have interested Buñuel. Such relationships had provided movies with a theme since the time of D. W. Griffith – and Buñuel would also return to it, but his later lechers would be much less gross than on this occasion.

In *El* the situation is reversed, since the man is in thrall to a woman. He is the 'el' of the title – Don Francisco (Arturo de Cordova). The woman is again the more innocent, the weaker of the two: but his strength is destructive, for he is jealous to the point of paranoia. Despite his belief in his own infallibility he is neither vicious nor irredeemably vain, and when, finally, he has no one to turn to but his valet, we see that he is essentially pitiable. Doubtless comforted by a foot fetish, he has nevertheless missed so much in life: people who only half-live, suggests the film, do not live at all. Which is, we may suppose, only to be expected of an aristocracy vitiated by centuries of self-indulgence and God-worshipping. Both the glimpses of a priest-ridden society and the charting of Don Francisco's relationship with his wife demonstrate a new energy in Buñuel: unlike *El Bruto* this film has a visual sense as striking as its narrative drive, and both qualities were seldom to disappear from Buñuel's work.

Not till he returned to Europe – and not always then – would he have the advantage of first-class working conditions, but **The Adventures of Robinson Crusoe** (1954) was made in Spanish and English versions, in colour and with an American actor, Dan O'Herlihy, as Defoe's desert-island hero. The international success of *Los Olvidados* had proved to Buñuel's producers (including Dancigers) that Mexico could make a film for world markets, but he himself was unenthusiastic when this project was suggested to him, till he realised that his subject could be solitude, accompanied by despair. Dealing with Crusoe alone as he conditions himself to life on the island and to loneliness, Buñuel finds an almost intoxicating purity of tone but, with the advent of Friday (Jaime Fernández), the film becomes perfunctory, only hinting at equivocation in the master-servant relationship. Buñuel ignores the implications of how two men from entirely opposing cultures can learn to live together, while Friday vacillates between being the 'noble savage' and just a nice guy.

Begun prior to *El*, *Robinson Crusoe* was not premiered until Buñuel had made two more films for local consumption, one of which, **Abismos de Pasión** (1954), transposes the plot of 'Wuthering Heights' to a Mexican setting. The other, **La Ilusión Viaja en Tranvia** (1954) is a pleasant film and, though not typical of Buñuel's oeuvre, has a companion piece in the darker **El Rio y la Muerte** (1955), since both look critically at contemporary Mexican society. Indeed, the earlier of the two films admits in a foreword that its view is 'sincere and somewhat trivial'. It is an urban comedy about a tram, due to be scrapped, that is taken on a final pirate ride by its maudlin driver and conductor. The second film, a rural melodrama, concerns feuding families, and it is only slightly superior to its European contemporaries about peasant vendettas. Both films reach the same conclusion, that man is the product of his immediate society. The driver and conductor rebel, run amok, but must finally conform; and so must in the other movie, the doctor from the city, despite his intellectual rejection of the primitive rules of the village.

Man retarded by his environment was the true subject of *El*, the archetypal Buñuel film of this period, and therefore the one to be seen at all costs; but there are a number of witty variations in what might be the second choice, **Ensayo de un Crimen** (1955), which is best known by its English title, *The Criminal Life of Archibaldo de la Cruz*. The 'crime' of Archibaldo (Ernesto Alonso) is his compulsion to murder, from which he is invariably prevented by fate. Rodolfo Usigli's black comedy provided Buñuel with one of his most congenial subjects, but what matters is the startling way in which he has worked it out, interweaving boyhood traumas and fetishism into a tale of sex and death, and including one splendid scene in which an army officer, a priest and a government official go into orgies of self-rapture about the patriotism involved in all ceremonials – including funerals. The film's triumph, as with *El*, is in its leading character, self-absorbed and selfish, again a representative

811

of all that is wrong in bourgeois society. He may be impotent, but more than any other film I know this one is a masturbatory fantasy. We find him at one moment fondling a brassière and silk stockings: we do not know why, but it does not matter.

A year or so earlier Buñuel had remarked that he would like to film in France, because 'it is easier to make good films there'. The international acclaim accorded *Los Olvidados* and *Robinson Crusoe* gave him the chance to return to make **Cela s'Appelle l'Aurore** (1956). With Jean Ferry he adapted a novel by Emmanuel Robles, and the film, which is poorly shaped, concerns a doctor (Georges Marchal) who begins an affair with an Italian woman (Lucia Bosè) while his wife is away. He also becomes involved again with a peasant friend (Gianni Esposito) of the war years, who has been evicted by his landlord. According to Freddy Buache (in his 1970 monograph on Buñuel), the film 'advocates subversion and makes statements that are very rarely to be heard in the cinema', and he further notes that the title is drawn from the final line of Giraudoux's 'Electre', with its reference to day breaking and everything pillaged or lost – and so ends this otherwise unremarkable film. It is a solid commercial venture very much of its period; de Sica's *Umberto D*, for instance, is far more subversive, and that is only part of its purpose. One sequence, however, is reminiscent of de Sica (and Renoir): two peasants, the sacked one and his replacement, make the best of the cruel situation – one brought about by (of course) the self-opinionated, hedonistic *petits bourgeois*. The film's chief theme is loyalty, be it marital, amatory, patriotic, local, between old comrades or employer and employee. The acting of Marchal, a fading matinee idol, and Bose, who was pretty but of no great ability, is of little benefit: Buñuel did not return to France first-class.

La Mort en ce Jardin (1956) and **La Fièvre Monte à El Pao** (1960) were Franco-Mexican productions, and so inferior to the intervening *Nazarin* (q.v.) as to emphasise that both were again purely commercial chores – though they do share resonances with it. The setting in each case is a squalid, totalitarian banana republic, but since in melodramas like these such

matters as police brutality, political imprisonment and injustice are used for routine dramatic effect the moral point is lost – along with Buñuel's own interest, if it can be judged by his indecisive approach and the sagging narrative shared by the two films. *La Mort en ce Jardin* concerns a small mining town run by the French, and the loyalties that divide when the militia arrive; and although the prostitute (Simone Signoret) parading in the jungle in evening gown and jewels may be a comment on the follies of human behaviour in adversity – anticipating *El Angel Exterminador* (q.v.) – the sequence might as well belong to any down-market jungle movie. The second film is 'Tosca' with twists, and its main interest lies in its leading characters – the governor's lady (Maria Félix) with the instincts of a whore, the president (Jean Servais) who has abused his revolutionary ideals, and the Cavaradossi figure (a miscast Gérard Philipe), whose idealism is of wrong-headed and muddled as that of the protagonist in *Nazarin*. The last-named is prefigured in *La Mort en ce Jardin* by the character of the priest (Michel Piccoli), who responds to the laws both of the jungle and those made by man (often in the name of Christianity) with his own daft interpretation of Christian ethics – which, when lost in the jungle, is ridiculous. At that point in the plot there is a hint of Ingmar Bergman's favourite theme, the refusal of God to reveal himself: the fact that it is only a hint may reflect Buñuel's indifference or his confusion. Nevertheless he was steeling himself for a confrontation with the subject of Christianity.

That comes in **Nazarin** (1959), which is a masterpiece. Like Bresson's earlier *Journal d'un Curé de Campagne* (q.v.), it is the study of a failed priest, but, as adapted from a late nineteenth-century novel by Benito Pérez Galdós, is more complex. The screenplay by Buñuel and Julio Alejandro has transferred the action from Spain to Mexico, and some important shifts in emphasis may be explained by Buñuel's own comment, 'As a young man I was able to glimpse something that, on the spiritual and poetic plane, goes far beyond Christian morality. I'm not so presumptuous as to want to make the world over . . . It is possible to be *relatively* Christian, but the *absolutely* pure, the *absolutely* innocent man – he's bound to fail. He's licked before he starts.' Don Nazario (Francisco Rabal) is absolutely pure and absolutely innocent. In the ranks of the church he is of the lowliest, existing in abject poverty, without a parish or permanent post. Anticipant of charity, he is stoical because he has gone hungry before and most likely will again; he deflects abuse; he endures. He is a Christian penitent who receives a pittance substituting occasionally for the fat-cat Father Don Angel, even rolling his cigarettes for him. There ought to be better ways of being a priest than this – servile and parasitic, one of society's failures. Don Nazario faces each fresh humiliation and insult with the Gospel prescription to love, unprepared to discover that there are other forms of love – mainly profane ones. Those who duly laugh at Buñuel's anticlerical references – and there are several sharp ones here – will find that this film is essentially a questioning of that 'love', though Nazarin's humility may be preferable to the smug self-assurance of Don Angel. As in de Sica and Preston Sturges, the meek shall definitely not inherit the earth. We leave Nazarin – unlike the original novel – moved because charity has been given to him as a man rather than as a priest, and we cannot know what that act has done to his faith. Many of Buñuel's endings are open to various interpretations, and of this film as a whole he remarked that it is 'strange and ambiguous. The style is ambiguous and that's what interests me. If a work is obvious, as far as I'm concerned it's finished.'

The Young One/La Joven (1960) starts keenly, as a boat puts in to a small tropical island: a Negro (Bernie Hamilton) gets out to meet Miller (Zachary Scott), the island's warden, as well as the newly-orphaned Evalyn (Kay Meersman), all three of them very conscious that she has just passed puberty. It is an open question which one of these honourable men will seduce her. It is Miller who does so: but that his own sexual conduct is unlawful does not prevent him from joining in a false assumption that the black man is a rapist. The film by this time has fallen apart, and since the black man is being chased through the swamps by a nigger-hating Fascist, we have to seize on small matters – such as the character of the prim, well-meaning priest – to remind ourselves that we are not watching a steamy Holly-

wood B-movie. The racial overtones extend our knowledge of Buñuel, but the quality of debate is distressingly trite. One often suspects that this director plays down to his audience, and the fact that this film was made in an English version, that is, for wider consumption, may be one reason it lacks the bite or ambiguity of even his least Mexican film. It was not a success, and Buñuel remained a shadowy figure outside the Spanish-speaking world, known only for his early films and *Los Olvidados* and *Robinson Crusoe*, plus the three French films which few had liked (*Nazarin* had not yet been seen outside Mexico).

It was **Viridiana** (1961) which permanently re-established him, and those who had hoped for the return of his anarchic spirit, as evidenced in *L'Age d'Or*, found it stronger than ever. The film itself is a virulent attack on Christian ethics, and

Francisco Rabal in *Nazarin*, Buñuel's complex study of the priesthood – a subject whose success is not assured, but is perhaps explained by Buñuel's own remarks on the film: 'The style is ambiguous and that's what interests me. If a work is obvious, as far as I'm concerned it's finished. As for the religious problem, I'm convinced that the Christian, in the pure and absolute meaning of the word, has no place on earth.'

Luis Buñuel and his Followers

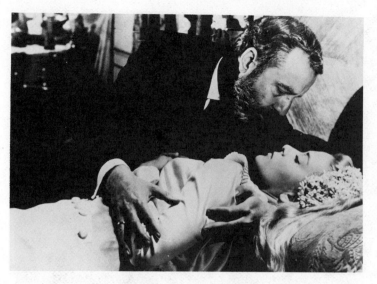

Fernando Rey and Silvia Pinal in *Viridiana*, which re-established Buñuel. He made it in Spain, invited back by the government, but in anarchic spirit chose a subject of which he could hardly have expected the government to approve, for it not only questions Christianity but throws rocks at it.

because it was made in Franco's Spain many were astonished – not least Buñuel himself, and the whole episode appealed mightily to his sense of humour. A young Mexican producer had proposed a co-production with Spain to Buñuel, who consented only because some young filmmakers, such as Luis Berlanga (q.v.), were trying to wrench Spanish cinema free from the stranglehold of cheaply-produced musicals and melodramas. The censor in Madrid duly asked for some changes in the screenplay, and when Buñuel agreed the Spanish government dropped its guard. Buñuel moved to Paris to complete his editing of the film, which he was invited to take to the Cannes Film Festival, since he was attending in a personal capacity. Spain had not entered a film for the competition, and the assumption that *Viridiana* was an official entry gained credence when a government spokesman failed to deny that it was. It was awarded the Palme d'Or, but the government earned no consolation from the implication that the film revealed Franco as more tolerant of 'free speech' than was generally thought: for everywhere it proved impossible to discuss the film without reference to the facts that it was banned in Spain and that the government had been hoodwinked. The film's effect on audiences and critics was – to use correctly for once the most-abused word of movie publicists – sensational.

As I said, *Nazarin* had not been seen in Europe, so it was not recognised that

Viridiana was a progression from that film. Viridiana (Silvia Pinal) is soul-sister to Nazarin – an ex-nun whose belated 'education' is the subject of the film. Alejandro again wrote the screenplay with Buñuel, from their own original story – but we may assume that Galdós was at least an inspiration, for its plot much resembles that of *Tristana* (q.v.), another of his novels that Buñuel filmed. There are also echoes of earlier films, notably *El*, in that a man (Fernando Rey) is obsessed with a young girl, though in this case it is because she can be persuaded to re-enact the eroticism of his dead wife. When he dies, Viridiana devotes herself to charity and self-sacrifice, only to be brutally awakened to the realities of life by his bastard son (Rabal). She submits to his way of life, though whether from carnality, self-knowledge or a sense of futility is unclear: the only finality, the only solution, is sin. Goodness is equated with smugness, hypocrisy and destruction. Viridiana destroys; her victims include both the beggars she tries to help and the old man – destroyed as much by her as his own fantasies. The son is realistic and survives: he knows that religion is no substitute for a rich, full life.

Viridiana, even more than *Nazarin*, underlines the paradox in Buñuel's approach to Christianity. The more violently he attacked the Church, the more his 'religious' characters are shown to be subject to the temptations of the flesh and the devil. It is as though he recognised in some people a natural aptitude towards holiness and sanctity, which he found himself compelled to defile. *Viridiana* was accused of blasphemy, whereas what Buñuel himself considered debasing is the divorce of the Christian religion from many of the things which make life worth living.

This passionate enquiry into the nature of clericalism is continued in **El Angel Exterminador** (1962), made in Mexico. Alternatively, the film may be regarded as a wry look at a fatuous aspect of human endeavour and aspiration: the society dinner party. It opens as the party ends, when the guests find themselves incarcerated in the dining room, apparently overcome by lassitude and cowardice. They remain for several days, discussing their dilemma and agreeing that it is not logical, and all the while their hold on their morals and emotions is ebbing away. The situation is

treated as both ordinary and extraordinary, the clues to Buñuel's purpose emerging as pinpricks: 'A key is anything that opens the door to the unknown,' says someone. As 'society' breaks down it becomes vicious, an attitude adopted by many satirists before Buñuel, and what happens at the end should hardly be of much relevance to those brought up in the freer-thinking Protestant tradition. On repeated viewings this allegory retains a horrible fascination, and nothing in it is entirely alien. Buñuel's own reflection on the film is found in his remark that 'people always want an explanation for everything. It's the logical result of centuries of bourgeois education. And when they can't explain something, they end up by turning to God. But what good does that do them? They then have to explain God.'

Buñuel returned to Spain after completing the film; the government indicated that its difficulties with *Viridiana* were forgotten, and that it would like him to make another Spanish film, but at the last minute permission to shoot *Tristana* was withheld (he was not to make it till 1970). Accordingly he went to France to find backing for **Le Journal d'une Femme de Chambre** (1964), from the novel by Octave Mirbeau which had been the source of Renoir's film of 1946. In the history of screen remakes there is no parallel case of two great directors using the same source material, each moulding it to his whim – though as David Robinson has pointed out, *âpre* (bitter, harsh, violent) was Mirbeau's favourite word, and the quality is as much to be found in Renoir's version as, more expectedly, in Buñuel's. The original story is related in the first person by Célestine, a housemaid newly employed

There is no other film quite like *El Angel Exterminador*, whose meaning is not yielded until the final sequence. Meanwhile, these dinner guests have lingered on. 'We are all victims of a joke in bad taste' says one of them, and that turns out to be a comment on two thousand years of Christianity.

Luis Buñuel and his Followers

Jeanne Moreau and Georges Géret in *Le Journal d'une Femme de Chambre*. The same novel had provided a film for Jean Renoir, and though there are other cases of good directors using identical material, in no other instance can the results be said to be so outstanding.

by a wealthy bourgeois couple. Each film uses different incidents from her past to embellish her progress in this household. Buñuel's screenplay – written with Jean-Claude Carrière, collaborator on all his French films thereafter – is the record of a girl determined to make headway in the world of her 'betters'. Jeanne Moreau's performance beautifully suggests a woman of limited imagination but unlimited experience – and very much her own mistress. She guardedly but obediently obeys the instructions of madame, and deftly parries the amorous advances of monsieur (Michel Piccoli); she gamely reads to madame's father and wears the boots as required by him; she is repulsed but yet attracted to the gamekeeper (Georges Géret), who may be a child-murderer and is certainly a great patriot and religionist. Finally, she marries the neighbouring captain (Daniel Ivernal) who is no better than any of them. The bourgeois, in fact, get a thorough beating: these people writhe like maggots in their own deceit and pettiness in the pursuit, usually, of sexual fulfilment, but having to settle for *certaines caresses* – which, as madame admits to the prurient priest, is all that she permits to monsieur. What Célestine sees and deplores, she inevitably becomes. Buñuel's irony was never more effective, but he had never before directed actors of this quality. Technically the film is superior to even his most polished

previous work – adroitly shaded visually and psychologically.

Buñuel returned to Mexico to make **Simón del Desierto** (1965), an anecdote about a man who emulates St Simeon Stylites. In all the annals of hagiography there can be – even according to the precepts of the time – few more ridiculous figures than a man who spent the last thirty-seven years of his life on the top of a pillar, and he inspires Buñuel to some donnish jokes. His Simón (Claudio Brook) is, like Nazarin, a foolish figure, one of society's rejects, while his theory that asceticism is the bridge to God is regarded with bemusement. Only in relation to the people below does he have any stature – figuratively and literally – but they are unhappily ungrateful for his act of devotion, while the Church, also to his dismay, sees in him a threat to its own power. The Devil appears, in the guise of both Christ with a lamb and a typical Buñuel heroine, exposing her stocking-tops: and when Simón succumbs to her, he is transported to a New York *boîte*, where the world frugs and twists without heed or need of his sacrifices or those of any other saint. The film is short – 45 minutes – and the ending is abrupt and unsatisfactory: despite the low budget, the money ran out, thus robbing us of another full-length portrait of one of Buñuel's lame-duck protagonists.

Among the pleasures of **Belle de Jour** (1967) is its portrait, unlike that in any other film, of a brothel. The film stands chronologically between the old, romantic view of such matters, as in *La Viaccia* (q.v.), and the realistic attitude of *The Last Detail* (q.v.). Whether or not Buñuel shared what seems to be the universal fascination with the oldest profession he depicts it here with relish. The brothel concerned is situated in a small street near the Opéra, and it is clinically furnished – not unsuitably, since we see it only during the equivalent of office hours: for it is then that Belle (Catherine Deneuve) slips away from married respectability and memories of a Catholic childhood. The subject – an upper middle-class wife who turns to whoredom – must have appealed to Buñuel, though he disliked Joseph Kessel's original novel (published in 1929). The critic John Simon, admitting an aversion to Kessel, wrote, 'I gather the dream fantasies are Buñuel's, as is that elusive ending. So, too, is a daydream in which an ageing, crazed duke performs on Belle de Jour a mock ceremony involving incest, necrophilia, onanism and sacrilege; perversity coupled with anti-Catholicism is as dear to Buñuel as to de Sade.' But, Simon concluded, 'Buñuel or Kessel, it is all trashy because superficial' – and I would agree only inasmuch as fantasy and perversity were to provide the starting-point for Buñuel's worst film, *Le Fantôme de la Liberté* (q.v.). As a documentary on the activities of a brothel, *Belle de Jour* is both audacious and reticent; Buñuel works with wit and clarity on what may be considered the opposite of these qualities – the ambivalence of human behaviour. Certainly, as narrative it touches a number of nerves – will the husband (Jean Sorel) find out? How will she react when, inevitably, a friend of his appears? To what degradation will she sink?

Since the ending, with Belle punished, is moral, we look in vain for a trace of Buñuel the anarchist: the producers (the Hakim brothers) eliminated some minor details and the film had virtually no trouble with censors anywhere in the world – undoubtedly due in part to Buñuel's reputation. He himself called it 'pornographic . . . by that I mean *chaste* eroticism', and though we might prefer him to have provided unchaste eroticism, his purity of style is remarkable. It is the perfect counterpart to Mlle Deneuve, as glacial as ever: unable to express much beyond a slight wonder, her thoughts remain for us to guess; her white underwear and long blonde hair are both virginal and sensuous at the same time. It is this balance, maintained throughout the film, which is Buñuel's finest achievement. We, the cinemagoers, are forced more than by most films to be voyeurs, and just at the point when we are enjoying it most Buñuel asks us to take a moral view of what Belle is doing. The result is one of his most enjoyable and accessible films, and though in France the critics did not like it, the public did. Undoubtedly it was its subject, as with *Never on Sunday* (q.v.) which brought it a popularity beyond the art house the world over; and since Buñuel was now commercial the industry itself could finally regard him as a 'great' director on the lines of Bergman

and Fellini – the irony of which could not have been lost on the old surrealist.

He retaliated, typically, by offering **La Voie Lactée** (1968), whose deliberate obscurity – except to the initiated – endeared it to neither critics nor public. The Voie Lactée is the route taken by pilgrims to Santiago de Compostella, and as two *clochards* journey south they are involved allegorically with the six central 'mysteries' of Catholic doctrine and the heresies which have grown up around them. The concept is too cerebral, but some of the incidents find Buñuel at his most brilliant and dexterous; for example, the argument between the Fascist policeman and the priest who turns out to be mental, and the two sixteenth-century students who arrive

Francis Blanche, impatient client, and Catherine Deneuve, whore, in *Belle de Jour*. She is a respectable wife who does not have to do this for a living – which is, as it happens, the subject of the film.

in the present day and are befriended by a priest whose interest is more than fatherly. Elsewhere the piece lacks buoyancy, leaving the audience uncertain whether to regard Catholic teaching as mumbo-jumbo or God's truth – and that cannot have been the intention.

The Spanish government finally granted Buñuel permission to film **Tristana** (1970) – in Toledo, the quintessential Spanish city, and one virtually unchanged for centuries. Since the film's themes are familiar throughout his work, we may suppose that it was the Spanishness of Galdós's novel that most appealed to Buñuel and therefore the reason he did not, as with *Nazarin*, transfer the action to another country. He has, however, brought the action forward to the Twenties. Its subject is the relationship between Tristana (Mlle Deneuve), an orphan, and Don Lope (Fernando Rey), an impoverished but fiercely independent middle-aged gentleman. She is not essentially his opposite, though she is devout, unworldly and young. They are drawn together – she for protection and he from lechery – and presumably a symbolic bond is intended by successive close-ups peering over the tops of her stockings and the garters on his socks. His attitude towards her is alternately paternal and conjugal, the implication being that this can only happen because they are Spanish or, rather, that because this is Spain it is the sort of thing that happens. He destroys her by gradually draining her of freedom – not that she was free in the first place, but she could, as she says, choose which of two streets to walk down. Seducing her and then not permitting himself to marry her is a violation of her Spanishness, as is the decision by the young artist (Franco Nero) to marry her though she is not a virgin. Don Lope must therefore marry her to keep her in his power: she survives him, to become bitter, crabbed – and amputated, a situation which seems to have little to do with the film's arguments, except that no one can again spy at her stockings (and it is a reflection of the fate meted out to Belle de Jour). In Buñuel's Mexican films the men survive, but in the later films it is the women who confront us at the end – and we cannot tell whether they (Viridiana, Célestine, Belle, Tristana) are the happier for it.

Everyone survives in **Le Charme Dis-cret de la Bourgeoisie** (1972), despite its background of anarchy and revolution: gunned down, these remnants of *El Angel Exterminador* – bishops, ministers, ambassadors and their wives – perk up again, which we may suppose is the prerogative of their class. With sangfroid, they continue their rituals and chit-chat, their insistence on the importance of good food and good manners, backed up by the unholy alliance of Church, state and the military (the police are so long entering the scene that it is almost a relief to find that Buñuel had not forgotten them – and, of course, they prove as adept at violence as the others). The film slips into its myriad fantasies with deceptive ease, calmly accepting the chaos it conveys – and that we may take to be Buñuel's prerogative in his old age. He fails to build to a climax of any sort, but huge audiences nevertheless delighted in seeing him take pot shots at the bourgeoisie and its sacred cows – though the laughter, plentiful to start with, is later sparse. The film won an Oscar for Best Foreign Language Picture, and did very well for 20th Century-Fox, who released it in most territories. Fox happily handled **Le Fantôme de la Liberté** (1974), but though Buñuel had become too fashionable to reap the poor notices the film deserved, it was shunned by the public. It was, noted the critics, surrealist and subversive, and though Buñuel had said that he would never attempt another *L'Age d'Or* (since world events had proved to him the emptiness of his attempts to be outrageous) the similar 'shocks' of *Le Charme Discret* had found a whole new audience for him. I believe that this *Fantôme* was flung contemptuously in the face of the public – that public which did not patronise his better films. It contains a ragbag of favourite themes, offered without surprise or wit, filled out with bad taste jokes borrowed from lesser directors – Godard,[*] Polanski, Bertolucci – and with a perfunctory salute to contemporary terrorism.

Urban terrorism of many varieties is present in the background of **Cet Obscur Objet du Désir** (1977), causing some observers to consider it relevant to its central theme – which, once again, is the nature of obsession. Having failed with *Le Fantôme*, Buñuel abandoned the shocks

*For Buñuel's opinion of Godard see page 1019.

Luis Buñuel and his Followers

Buñuel's last film, *Cet Obscur Objet du Désir*, returns him to a favourite theme, that of sexual obsession. Fernando Rey, at the left, is the man obsessed, and Angela Molina is the object of desire, not too obscurely: her plan, at this point, is to increase his frustration by making love with a man of her own age, David Rocha.

and fantasies of his last two films for a relatively straightforward tale which he had long wanted to film. This was Pierre Louys' 'La Femme et le Pantin', and at one point he had been the proposed director of the 1959 version which Julien Duvivier eventually made (earlier, von Sternberg had filmed the story as *The Devil is a Woman*). Fernando Rey is again the man obsessed, though dubbed by Michel Piccoli, a popular and eminent actor who had already made four films for Buñuel: playing a Frenchman, Rey cannot have a Spanish accent, but the casting also suggests that Buñuel regarded Rey as his alter ego (as von Sydow was to Bergman). The Spanish ambience of the original has been retained by setting the film partly in Seville; and the object desired is played by two actresses, one Spanish and one French – which is not especially gimmicky, though the actresses, contrarily, are not required to represent different aspects of the character. Neither is very interesting, and though she, Conchita, perversely leads on Rey and then repulses him there is little variety in her provocation. Rey's gnawing frustration is not, therefore, interestingly drama-

tised and when, at the end, he becomes violent as she taunts him by having sex with another man before his eyes, the effect is disappointingly mild. It is ironic if the one director always so far in advance of usual movie concerns should be overtaken by younger men often emulating him, but had this film been made by anyone else it would not have caused a ripple.

For at least ten years Buñuel had been proclaiming his intention to retire – an intention circumvented by Serge Silberman, the producer of his last three French films; and during that time the cynicism often apparent in his work had become more and more obtrusive, culminating in *Le Fantôme*. *Cet Obscur Objet* is more insolent, and indeed its refusal to offer denouement, climax or even ending is breathtaking – for, like the work of many inferior film-makers it does not conclude but simply stops, with an explosion. Even in *Tristana* the old master had begun to lose interest before the end; but then, when left to himself – i.e. not working from a novel – in all his later films he is inclined to disintegrate, being wayward, jokey, and hitting out at his old favourite

819

targets with both an obvious symbolism and with private jokes. It is probable that the jaded polemics of *Le Charme Discret* will delight audiences as long as those of *L'Age d'Or*; but I believe that his most lasting monument will be his studies of man's illusions – *El*, *Nazarin*, *Viridiana*, *Le Journal d'une Femme de Chambre* and *Tristana*, films as good as any ever made. Buñuel died in 1983.

Apart from Buñuel, the Spanish cinema has made little impact on the international scene. Once in every half dozen years a Spanish film enjoys success in other parts of Europe and in the U.S., offering evidence of a national cinema of some vitality. In the Fifties, while Buñuel was in Mexico, both Luis G. Berlanga (b. 1921) and Juan Antonio Bardem (b. 1922) enjoyed a measure of international acclaim. Serious Spanish cinema may be said to begin with them, as they chose to move away from the stereotyped musicals and melodramas which had emanated from the studios in Madrid.

They trained together at the Instituto de Investigaciones Cinemátograficas, and collaborated on a number of shorts before writing and directing their first feature, **Esa Pareja Féliz** (1951). Its acknowledged influences were Becker's *Antoine et Antoinette* and the writings of Zavattini, but it also owes a debt to Clair and Capra. The title is ironic, since the couple are happy neither before nor after they are chosen by a soap company offering them Madrid at their feet for a day. The prospect is exciting for them, but almost everything goes wrong and they end the day in a police station. Their adventures are almost charming and sometimes funny. The film's lack of ambition is to be admired, as is its assurance that everything about Madrid – especially its entertainments – is second rate. Berlanga and Bardem then wrote **Bienvenido Mr Marshall** (1952), which Berlanga directed. It was sent to the Cannes Film Festival in 1953, after which it enjoyed a success in most countries – and it remains Berlanga's best-known film. The setting is a small town in Castile, where the only excitement is the weekly cinema showing of an old Western – till, that is, news arrives of the impending advent of Marshall Aid. For a while, everyone is greedy; then the townsfolk decide that they should welcome the Americans – whom they expect in person – with

appropriate fanfare. They elect to transform the place into the traditional Spanish town, even to the extent of erecting false façades and building a bull-ring. The film strongly bears a resemblance to Ealing comedy, as do Berlanga's next films, though in each case there are also other influences at work: in **Novio a la Vista** (1953) there are shades of *Les Dernières Vacances* and in **Calabuch** (1956) there are traces of *Seven Days to Noon*. *Novio a la Vista*, set in a small resort town in 1918, deals with a group of children who revolt against their parents and go to live in a separate camp: they include the tomboy, who at the end of summer opts for adulthood and romance. *Calabuch* proposes an atomic scientist so ashamed of his researches that he goes into hiding – in a small Spanish fishing village, where he becomes involved in making fireworks for the local celebrations. The professor is played by Edmund Gwenn, and the romantic leads are Franco Fabrizi and Valentina Cortese, both stars in their native Italy: but the film, with good reason, did not repeat the success of *Bienvenido Mr Marshall*.

Indeed, that was a freak success. Berlanga's films to this time are pleasant, but too local in interest. Another influence is Pagnol, but Berlanga lacks Pagnol's humour. He changed course with **Plácido** (1961), undoubtedly influenced by the writer Rafael Azcona, who was to collaborate on all his future scripts. *Plácido* elaborates on the theme of the earlier films – the provincial town transformed by commercial interests – but it has a blacker satirical thrust. A firm of soap manufacturers is bringing a trainload of film stars from Madrid for the Christmas Eve festivities, which also include the poor being invited into the homes of the rich for a meal: but as with *Esa Pareja Féliz*, nothing goes as planned. **La Boutique** (1961) was an ambitious project, filmed under inadequate conditions in Argentina. Its interesting central situation involves a philandering husband (Lautaro Murua) who decides to indulge his mild little wife (Sonia Bruno) on learning that she has not long to live: she decides to open a boutique, allows herself to be seduced by its designer and is soon making her husband feel unimportant.

El Verdugo (1963) enjoyed some international success. It is based on the lively notion of a young man (Nino Manfredi), who takes on the occupation of his father-in-law, that of public executioner, only for the sake of the new apartment that goes with it: he intends to retire at the prospect of the first garrotting, but that is to be in Palma, and his wife has always wanted to holiday there – and, says her father, the man is bound to be reprieved. The film is an attack on capital punishment, its satiric intent weakened by Manfredi, who plays the hero, a vain and fraudulent Latin type, for sympathy. Sitges is the setting for **Vivan los Novios!** (1970), and as bikini-clad tourists stare at a black-garbed funeral procession Berlanga and Azcona are making their own comment on the old and the new Spain. Both the middle-aged hero (José Luis López Vázquez) and his bride-to-be (Lali Soldevilla) represent the old Spain, but he, with so many blondes about, is tempted to try the new Spain. The film otherwise is a rather strained black comedy, and I do not think **Grandeur Nature** (1974), also known as *Life Size*, is any more successful. It concerns a dentist (Michel Piccoli) who becomes obsessed by an inflatable life-size plastic doll; he loses his wife, and it becomes clear that his obsession can end only in madness or death. It is a film about loneliness and fetishism – about 'masturbation de luxe', in the words of Jean-Claude Carrière, who wrote the screenplay from an original story by Berlanga and Azcona. Carrière's contribution may be one reason the film is richer than Berlanga's other films; and it may be why Buñuel (or a semblance thereof) appears in its final shot. Buñuel certainly approved of fetishism: but this film is as much a condemnation of the Spanish mentality as is *Viridiana*. Like *El Angel Exterminador* it does not reveal its meaning until the end – when the dentist's Spanish servants and their friends (the film is set in Paris) are revealed as crude, animalistic, and so stupid as to treat the dentist's aberration as normal (so does his mother, but Buñuel never showed much affection for mothers, either).

The film, made in France, was not shown in Spain till censorship was relaxed after the death of Franco. Berlanga was expected to be one of the most vocal critics of the Franco regime, and **La Escopeta Nacional** (1978) is virtually a compendium of the faults, vices and stupidities of the ruling classes. It lacks the subtlety of *Furtivos* (q.v.), without being any less derivative than usual: it is no more than a mixture of *La Règle du Jeu* and *Le Charme Discret de la Bourgeoisie*. It is also noisy, frenetic and scatological – all reasons why it was not seen outside Spanish-speaking territories, although it was one of the biggest successes ever shown in Spain. That fact called for a sequel, and Berlanga and Azcona had the excellent idea of bringing its leading characters, the decadent marquis and his family, into Madrid in the hope of breaking into court life. The earlier film was set in the last days of Franco, and **Patrimonio Nacional** (1980) in the first days of King Juan Carlos. There is every reason to suppose that these two social satirists should have made one of their best films, but on the contrary this is an anything-goes farce, and a rather tired one at that. Both films indicate that Berlanga, despite years of trying otherwise, had become strictly a local director.

His old colleague Bardem elicited some international interest after their collaborations. **Muerte de un Ciclista** (1955), Bardem's third film as a solo director, was one of the revelations of the Cannes Festival. It was more accomplished than Berlanga's films to this time, and seemed more impressive than it was, since few outside Italy at that time had seen Antonioni's *Cronaca di un Amore* (q.v.), its inspiration. In both films Lucia Bosè is an adulteress, and it is the accident of the title, caused by her and her lover, which occasions the guilt and consequent reassessments of the corrupt society around her. The society of **Calle Mayor** (1956) is provincial, as the title indicates: a gang of pool-punters plan to trick a plain spinster (Betsy Blair) into believing that she is to be married – and the elected fiancé (José Saurez), not the brightest of schemers, finds the situation far more difficult to get out of than he had expected. Bardem was in the middle of shooting this film when the authorities, disliking *Muerte de un Ciclista*, found an excuse to jail him, and he was there when it won the Critics' Award at Cannes. The foreign success of both films established him as Spain's leading director, but **La Venganza** (1958) was so mutilated by the censor as to become only a travesty of what had been intended. The export of his

821

Luis Buñuel and his Followers

Among Spanish directors, Carlos Saura is among the best known outside his own country, perhaps because many of his films feature Geraldine Chaplin, who has an international reputation (if hardly that of her father, Charlie). Here she is in *Peppermint Frappé*, with another of Saura's favourite interpreters, José Luis López Vázquez. The film itself is reminiscent of the work of both Buñuel and Resnais, but Saura's work, when not highly individual, is clearly emulating only the best.

films was discouraged, and a film magazine that he had founded was banned after nine issues. As the prime figure in bringing Buñuel to Spain for *Viridiana* he again angered the government, and it would seem that these battles sapped his creative energy. A co-production in English, **Les Pianos Mécaniques** (1965), with James Mason and Melina Mercouri, was poorly received.

Virtually the only other Spanish film of this period seen widely abroad was **El Cochecito** (1959), after scoring a success at the Venice Festival for its Italian-born director, Marco Ferreri. He had undertaken various jobs in his native film industry before a Spanish producer decided to finance this venture. It was in fact his third film, written in collaboration with the author of the original novel, Rafael Azcona, who had not at that point linked his fortunes to those of Berlanga. The film purports to be a black comedy, as an old man (José Ibert) discovers that he lacks the love and honour which should accompany old age, and that his troops of friends are the cripples of the streets. He decides that he would like a motorised wheelchair like his friends, but this promising material – the setting (Madrid), the bourgeois family – is reduced to a cipher. Ferreri returned to

Italy to make a series of films on equally eccentric situations – *L'Ape Regina*, *La Grande Bouffe* (made in France with Azcona), *L'Ultima Donna* – but lacking point or narrative form.

Carlos Saura (b. 1932), like Berlanga and Bardem, studied at the Institute of Cinema Research in Madrid, and his first feature, **Los Golfos** (1959), is as blighted as those films of the academically-trained directors of the Soviet bloc, though it is far from an endorsement of this equally totalitarian regime. Indeed, its portrait of a group of young, impoverished drifters from the outskirts of Madrid is an implied criticism – and its form self-confessedly influenced by the Italian neo-realists. There is, however, no discernible personal statement, and Saura was to re-examine his approach after meeting Buñuel – still *persona non grata* in Spain – when *Los Golfos* was sent to the Cannes Festival in 1960. For the next few years Saura taught at the Institute in Madrid, until his contract was allowed to lapse. His scripts were all turned down by the censor, but in 1964 he deliberately set out to make a purely commercial film, *Llanto por un Bandido*. That enabled him to make, for the producer Elias Querejeta, **La Caza** (1965), an account of four gentlemen rabbit-hunting, each old enough for their vague references to 'the War' to have a meaning. The film is a parable of the Civil War, if examined closely enough, and was described by Buñuel as the most completely achieved work he had seen in a while; it is clear, however, why his words were not warmer, for the film has talent and energy but insufficient discipline or imagination. It won prizes at both the San Sebastian and Berlin Festivals, and at Berlin **Peppermint Frappé** (1967) won for Saura a Best Director award, a consideration echoed by the Spanish Screenwriters Guild, who also voted it Best Script: but in fact neither film was seen widely in Spain – though government policy encouraged their export, to indicate how liberal the regime had become. Neither film was more than tentatively subversive – and *Peppermint Frappé* is chiefly notable for its slavish imitation of Buñuel, to whom it is dedicated. As it is a successful imitation, with suspense and some wit, it entertains considerably, and is beautifully acted by José Luis López Vázquez as the forty-ish, bald, celibate doctor from Cuenca who

becomes obsessed with two women, one of whom, his nurse, he attempts to re-mould in the image of the other. Both women are played by Geraldine Chaplin, who became Saura's chief interpreter and wife.

La Prima Angelica (1974) is dedicated to 'Charlie and Oona'. In it Miss Chaplin plays the present-day Angelica and, in the flashbacks to 1936, her mother; in **Cria Cuervos** (1975) she plays the present-day Ana and *her* mother. Much of *Peppermint Frappé* revolves round memory, and these later films are devoted to that subject. They are both more complex, reminiscent of the gothic puzzles of Leopoldo Torre Nilsson (q.v.). Significantly in *La Prima Angelica* the leading character, a Barcelona businessman (López Vázquez), considers Proust and the madeleine as he takes a journey into the past while in Segovia to bury the ashes of his mother: he recalls the outbreak of the Civil War and, bemused by memories of his cousin Angelica as she was, and is now, he leaves without being able to reconcile past and present. *Cria Cuervos* is set in a well-to-do suburb of Madrid, with the grown-up Ana recalling incidents before the death of her parents – which have mainly to do with the infid-elities of her military father. Saura, writing a screenplay unaided for the first time, has worked diligently, though it is difficult to find his own personal despair in the film. It may be found in the superior *Angelica*, but the weakness of the later film really lies in the infant Ana, played by an intense child called Ana Torrent. Saura admitted that he was fascinated by her, and is, I think, rationalising wildly when he claims that she, he and we are 'victims of modern society'.

Mama Cumple 100 Años (1979) stars Miss Chaplin, who had recently appeared in Altman's *A Wedding* (q.v.) – of which this is a rehash, plus the inevitable borrow-ings from Buñuel (*El Angel Exterminador*) and in this case Berlanga (*La Escopeta Nacional*). Family gatherings, if they can-not be original, should at least contain either likeable or amusing participants. **Deprisa, Deprisa** (1981) is a return to the milieu of *Los Golfos*, and it is one of Saura's best films. It charts the progress of three young thugs, from stealing cars to robbing banks: they are joined by Angela, the adolescent mistress of one of them, who in Franco's Spain would have been a virgin and attended church daily. Now she em-braces drugs, guns and the accompanying thrills – and I would like the film more if it did not imply that such appurtenances are essential to youngsters today anxious to break the monotony of daily life. It is one thing to be objective, but there is no great film-maker, including Saura's idol, Buñuel, who was not also a moralist. The particular quality of the film is due partly to the locations: the suburbs of Madrid and the scrubbish countryside around Segovia. The brilliant photographer involved is Teo Escamilla, who also worked on *Mama Cumple 100 Años* and Saura's **Bodas de Sangre** (1981), a brief account (72 mi-nutes) of a dance version of Lorca's 'Blood Wedding', as adapted and choreographed by Antonio Geddes. The producer, Emi-liano Piedra, had so admired Geddes's flamenco ballet that he commissioned Saura to film it, and Saura, uninterested in filming the production, has restaged the work in a rehearsal room. He observed that he disliked adaptations, 'as they rep-resent a kind of betrayal', an odd re-mark from one whose work has been so derivative. But the film is exhilarating.

Saura's usual producer is Elias Quere-jeta, who has been responsible for some of the most distinguished Spanish films, in-cluding **El Espiritu de la Colmena** (1973) – *The Spirit of the Beehive* – directed by Victor Erice from a screenplay by Fran-cisco J. Querejeta. It takes place in 1940, in a remote village of Castile, and recalls another first feature about childhood, Truffaut's *Les Quatre Cents Coups*. As Erice is another film-maker obsessed with movies, the action devolves round the visit of the child (Ana Torrent) to Whale's *Frankenstein*. It has an air of mystery which many films on childhood lack, but that mystery seems borrowed from other cryp-tic films rather than observed from life; it thus destroys the faint comment it proffers on the country after the Civil War.

It has in common with all the films produced by Elias Querejeta an allusive quality. His influence may be judged by **A un Dios Desconocido** (1977), since he wrote the screenplay with its director, Jaime Chavarri. It purports to examine the dilemmas confronting a middle-aged homosexual (Hector Altiero) in contem-porary Spain. The Argentine-born Altiero

823

Luis Buñuel and his Followers

The death of Franco effectively released the Spanish film industry from its shackles – which had restricted it to safe themes and certainly no criticism of the regime. The best films since have examined this recent Fascist past, or attempted to make a statement on the division between right and left which still exists in the country. Among these is *Furtivos*, directed by José Luis Borau, who also played a supporting role as a provincial governor. Once again the film is so good as to make one regret that we have since seen too little of a clearly revitalised industry.

won a Best Actor award at the San Sebastian Festival for his performance, but it consists of little but allowing a singularly glum expression to break into an occasional smile. It is difficult to sympathise with him – but that is also because the script is less interested in him than in its symbolism. It begins with the death of Lorca, but the man's obsession with Lorca, an interesting theme, is hardly developed. At the same time the piece works best in those sequences, perhaps influenced by Saura, in which the past impinges on the present.

Sexual irregularity is also discreetly handled in **Mi Querida Señorita** (1972), the tale of a middle-aged spinster (López Vázquez) who attempts, unsuccessfully, to come to terms with the sex 'she' was born with, i.e. male. The director, Jaime de Armiñan, treated another unusual subject in **El Nido** (1980), the relationship between a fifty-ish widower, a landowner (Altiero), and a twelve-year-old village girl (Miss Torrent). It is an accomplished film, with luminous photography by Escamilla; but the spirit of Buñuel lies heavily over both films. These were not subjects which attracted him, but his influence descends via Berlanga and Bardem to Saura and José Luis Borau – and Borau produced and wrote *Mi Querida Señorita* with de Armiñan before becoming a director himself. These films have Buñuelesque

qualities: a far-fetched story, usually one of passion, told in such a manner as to seem reasonable; a critical look at Spanish society, especially its authoritarian aspects; and if not an unhappy ending, a sense of impending doom. Generally lacking, however, is his sense of humour.

There is humour in Borau's **Furtivos** (1975) – *The Poachers* – which became the most popular Spanish film seen abroad after *El Espiritu de la Colmena*. Borau's voice, amused and acrid, is recognisable in *Mi Querida Señorita*, and that piece is to be preferred to his own first directorial effort, **B. Must Die** (1973), incautiously aimed at the international market – though its humour makes it rare among its breed, that of the political thriller. It is set, ostensibly, in a South American country, where a Hungarian truck-driver (Darren McGavin) comes up against the system and winds up dead; en route he lives with a plain, ageing widow (Patricia Neal), and is persuaded by a fellow boarder (Burgess Meredith) to seduce the mistress (Stéphane Audran) of an industrialist troubled by labour unrest. There are ruthless police and anarchist bombers, but the film offers insufficient parallels with Spain for it to have worried the authorities. However, the censor, though by this time more liberal, refused at first to pass *Furtivos* without cuts, allegedly because of its erotic content. The plot is darkest bucolic, not too far from 'Maria Marten' – the faithful husband, Angel (Ovidi Montllor), the flighty wife (Alicia Sanchez), the jealous mother-in-law, the bandit lover who suddenly turns up – and it sometimes seems saved only by the luminous photography of Luis Cuadrado (who later went blind), also responsible for *La Prima Angelica* and *El Espiritu de la Colmena*; but, like them, it sets its figures surely in a landscape, and bears its double meaning with ease. To Borau himself, the film is summarised by the sequence in which the governor emasculates Angel – who is also his foster-brother – by making him a game warden, punishment for having shot the stags he wanted to bag himself. Buñuel had left – in his Mexican films and *Viridiana* – a tradition of the clerical and bureaucratic haves, as against the peasant have-nots, but Borau has refined it; this governor, played with wit by Borau himself, is fastidious, shallow, self-important and above all, petty –

and there is a great, suppressed cry for freedom emanating from Angel, from his wife, mother, the bandit and the governor, locked as they are in degrees of fear, possession, position, rivalry, ingratitude and several sorts of love. 'Spain is a cruel mother who devours her children,' said Borau, and *Furtivos* is a cruel film. There was a chance that it would not be publicly shown in Spain, and the censor only relented when it was chosen as the country's official selection for its own festival at San Sebastian, where it carried off the Grand Prix. It subsequently became the most successful Spanish film ever shown in its native cinemas. Borau refused to see it as a turning point; he did, however, concede that there was a new movement headed by Erice and Saura.

The film's popularity benefited from the death of Franco, since in the new, immediate, freedom there were no restraints on either showing or publicising it. **Camada Negra** (1977), a product of the post-Franco era, caused an uproar, because it deals with a situation labelled political; and I fancy it would have done so in any country alive to the threat of the extreme right to the progressive left in this era of youthful terrorists. The film is quirky, violent, and vastly entertaining; it says little that is controversial and nothing profound, partly because it is woven with fantasy, adopted for once with humour: but there are dazzling intellects behind it – those of Borau and Manuel Gutiérrez Aragón. They had also written *Furtivos* together; Borau this time acted only as producer, and Aragón directed. Their thesis centres on a group of young men who sing publicly as a choir and clandestinely plan to destroy any manifestation of the left: their first target is a left-wing bookshop – and the location used was a bookshop savaged by rightist hooligans some months before this film started shooting. The fiercest of these Fascist partisans is one too young, in fact, to join the clan, the angelic-looking Tatín (José Luis Alonso), whose sex life is as impotent as it is brutal. A director who plays with symbolism to the extent that

this film does should be fast and subtle, and Aragón is.

His limitations were revealed, however, in **El Corazón del Bosque** (1979) and **Maravillas** (1981), co-written with and produced by Luis Megino. Escamilla's contribution to the former is paramount, since his photography gives the film a dreamlike quality. Nevertheless, the film would be better were its style keyed to its essentially simple plot, concerning a hunt for a guerrilla leader who has been hiding in the mountains of Asturias since the end of the Civil War. *Maravillas* is a black comedy about an adolescent girl in present-day Madrid. Once again in a Spanish film the piece consists of quirkish behaviour, constant allusion – often to the Civil War – and borrowings from Buñuel and Berlanga.

Earlier Aragón had been the co-writer on the successful **Las Largas Vacaciónes del 36** (1976), with its director, Jaime Camino. It was made before Franco died (which coincided with the conclusion of shooting), and was the first film to deal both overtly and at length with the Civil War. Camino described it as a memory piece, dealing with the War seen by the children of two Catalan families, but despite a number of sickening sequences the title's closeness to *Summer of '42* (q.v.) is not inapt, for what begins as a record of unusual times becomes gradually the usual adolescent chronicle of sexual encounter. For all that, it is a vast improvement on **Jutrzenka** (1970), the only other of Camino's films that I have seen, a stultifying account of the Chopin-George Sand affair.

My attitude is undoubtedly ungrateful, since *Jutrzenka* is one of the few Spanish films I have seen not bearing the influence of Buñuel. He was, as I have said, a great director, but these few of his compatriots have demonstrated sensitivity and skill to the extent that they should be able to turn in other directions. Perhaps the Spanish cinema is too young to be assured, despite *Furtivos* and *Camada Negra*, films of astonishing maturity.

31

A Picture of India: The Films of Satyajit Ray

INDIA PRODUCES A vast number of films every year, almost all of them for local consumption. Those we see in the West are usually quiet stories of village life, with occasional excursions to Bombay and Calcutta. They are hardly representative of Indian production, which likes to cram several lifetimes and a couple of continents into one film. One of these extravaganzas was seen in the West when offered to distributors by its producer, emboldened by the fact that it was the first Indian film in colour and the knowledge that the West enthusiastically accepted *Rashomon*. In this case the press and the public regarded the film as a curiosity, and to this day it is the only film of its kind to have been widely seen.

Its title is **Aan** (1952), sometimes known as *The Savage Princess*, and it was directed by Mehboob, one of several Indian film-makers who start with an outline and let the plot develop during shooting. Although set in the distant past, 'when civilisations rose and fell', there are motor cars on view and a villainess who wears jodhpurs and a hacking-jacket. She, the savage princess, comes between a peasant boy (Dilip Kumar) and his sweetheart, while her brother usurps the maharajah's throne. They act out their adventures in a farrago of duels, chases, murders, assassination attempts and intervals of song and dance, as they move from palace to gypsy camp to torture chamber to lion's den. They do not kiss, since the censor forbids the touching of lips, but they embrace; and there are several left-wing messages in the 180 minutes running-time (150 minutes on its original Western showings).

The musical numbers were in Indian films since the coming of Talkies, when it

was discovered that audiences mutinied if they were not included. Earlier Indian films are accordingly less extravagant than *Aan*. The father of the Indian cinema is reckoned to be D. G. Phalke (1870–1944), who gave it his first success, *Raja Harishandra*, in 1913. Only one reel now survives, but I have seen *Childhood of Krishna*, made six years later, and Phalke's daughter as Krishna is not the only reason that the film seems like a very bad home movie. **Light of Asia** (1926) is an enormous advance on this, as made by Himansu Rai and his German co-director, Franz Osten (who remained to film in India till 1935). The film's source is a once-popular Victorian poem about the life of the Buddha, who is played by Rai. The credits on the existing English print inform us that what follows is 'as seen at Windsor Castle by Royal Command' – which may be the reason it ran for ten months in the Philharmonic Hall and was voted the third Best Film of the year by the readers of the *Daily Express*.

Up until 1955 ten per cent of Indian films were Bengali made. From the beginning they were largely based in the Bengali literary tradition, rather than song and dance epics ubiquitous in the rest of the subcontinent. Since the popular novels tended to be vacuous and the films themselves inert, there was a movement that began in the Thirties towards making 'social issues' cinema which faltered, only to be resumed in the Fifties. If to Western audiences Indian cinema means the films of Satyajit Ray (b. 1921) that is not necessarily an injustice, since he towers over his contemporaries. The son of the writer, painter and photographer Sukumar Ray, Satyajit Ray was educated at Calcutta University. He started his career in the

826

A Picture of India: The Films of Satyajit Ray

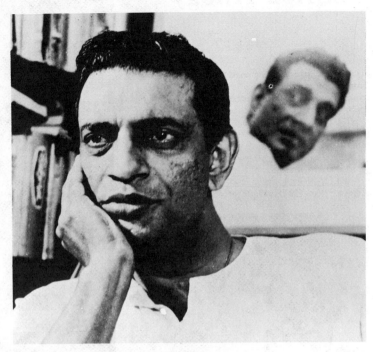

Calcutta branch of a British advertising agency, and developed an interest in film while living in London as a young man. He says that he liked the films of Wyler, Ford, Capra and Stevens, and thought himself fortunate in London to catch up with the work of Clair, Duvivier and Renoir. On his return to India he founded the Calcutta Film Society, and engineered a meeting with Renoir when he was in the country to make *The River* (q.v.). He cites Renoir and de Sica as the governing influences on his own work, along with a fellow Bengali, Bibhuti Bhushan Bannerjee, whose autobiographical novel he had illustrated for publication. It was after seeing *Ladri di Biciclette* that he determined to make a film of Bannerjee's book, which he eventually started with his own and his wife's money. Just when it seemed that he might have to abandon it, Monroe Wheeler of New York's Museum of Modern Art, visiting India to prepare an exhibition of Indian art, saw some stills and promised to premiere the film at the museum in conjunction with the exhibition. In the climate of Indian cinema, Ray knew that foreign showings were essential for the film's acceptance and for his own financial wellbeing. The government of West Bengal were sympathetic to his aims, and gave him further money. The film, **Pather Panchali** (1955), went on to triumph at Cannes, and Ray decided to make two more from the same source material, **Aparajito**/*The Unvanquished* (1956) and **Apur Sansar**/*The World of Apu* (1958), for which he was able to obtain private financing.

We know the three films as 'The Apu Trilogy', from Apu, their hero. *Pather Panchali* means 'Song of the Open Road', but it is this film which should have been called 'The World of Apu', for it is about the world of a young boy, centred on the derelict home with its fine courtyard, except when his sister (Uma Das Gupta) takes him across the cotton fields to see the trains. His father (Kanu Bannerjee) picks up a job here and there, between dreaming and writing plays; his mother (Karuna Bannerjee) is thrifty and perpetually worried; Auntie (Chunibala) is an old crone tolerated rather than loved, surviving poverty and infirmity by retreating into her fantasies. Apu (Subir Bannerjee) goes to school, watches a play, raids his sister's toybox; his aunt and then his sister die, and

his mother only gives way to grief when his father returns from the city. As they leave to live in Benares a snake weaves its way into the deserted house, and as they huddle in their wagon they look out at the rain but do not see it. Ray loves his people, but never patronises or sentimentalises them. He lingers on a moment of humour, on a faded hope, on reeds on the lake, the wind ruffling the water-lily leaves, the boy dawdling on the way home from school, the sweet-seller jogging by the river. There is a timelessness which evokes the dead lightness of time in the tropics, of everything suspended listlessly in the warm air; and with it is conveyed a series of perceptions that come to us all as we are growing up. It is my view, although aware that the analogy is not particularly apt, that the Apu films are to cinema what Proust is to literature: they are simply richer and more universal than most films ever made.

Aparajito begins with Apu (now played by Pinaki Sen Gupta) in the train to Benares. In the village he had played with bow and arrow, but in the city he reads, choosing a book about Livingstone, who at that time – 1920 – was a gigantic figure in the Empire saga. He sleeps in a room with an electric light, he has a toy globe on which he can locate Calcutta; eventually he

Satyajit Ray, the first Indian film-maker to have gained a world-wide reputation. A lover of movies from his youth, he determined to make films in Western style – that is, without the spectacle and songs expected by local audiences. His films are therefore too austere for India, and few of them have been overwhelmingly popular there. Some also appear too austere for the West – at least, they have not always received the acclaim that should rightfully be theirs.

The Apu Trilogy

It was the praise for the Apu Trilogy at film festivals in the late Fifties which gained Ray recognition. The three films are among the noblest works of the cinema, which has few experiences as absorbing or richly rewarding as following the progress of Apu from boyhood to manhood. The fact that he is, inevitably, played by several different actors passes unnoticed. BELOW, Subir Bannerjee as the boy Apu in *Pather Panchali*. FAR BELOW, Pinaki Sen Gupta, who shared with Smaran Ghosal the role of the growing Apu in *Aparajito*, and, RIGHT, Soumitra Chatterjee in *The World of Apu*.

is able to explain to his mother the workings of the heavens. The boy's awareness in the earlier film is partly replaced by doubts and a growing sense of responsibility, in particular towards his widowed mother, who needs his love and protection. In this respect the film is more perceptive than any other study of adolescence that I know. Ray's calm and subtle method of charting the boy's progress allows the spectator to become aware of the most important moments in Apu's life; for instance, that his ailing mother will not see him again, and that the acquisition of learning is the most important goal in life.

Nevertheless, in *Apur Sansar* he is forced to leave college without graduating. Encouraged by his friend Pulu, he tries to make a living as a writer, and it is for the sake of Pulu's family that he replaces a chosen bridegroom who has been discovered to be mentally sick. His marriage is idyllically happy until his wife (Sharmila Tagore) dies in childbirth. He refuses to see his son and loses all interest in the world until finally prevailed upon to see the child. *Pather Panchali* ends in defeat and *Aparajito* in death, but in echoing their closing sequences *Apur Sansar* ends in hope: this is 'The Unvanquished'. Despite the physical dissimilarity of the three Apus (in *Apur Sansar* played magnificently by Soumitra Chatterjee, who would become Ray's favourite interpreter) one becomes more than ever involved in Apu's world: as in childhood, the dingy room with the flapping curtain to keep out the rain; the train whistle, symbol of his (and India's?) progress; and his love of Wells's 'Outline of History' because he finds it revelatory. When he speaks of the novel he is planning he says of his hero, 'His hardship, his education broaden his mind and sharpen his wit. He feels the seed of greatness within him . . . The whole point of his life is facing up to life, not turning his back on humanity.' That, modestly offered, is the philosophy behind the trilogy, since Pulu laughs, not impressed, and Apu shrugs, seeming to agree. The comment is at once touching and ridiculous, symptomatic of Ray's approach throughout, which is to appear detached while being tremendously involved.

By the same token – and Ray is aware of this – *Apur Sansar* does not have the purity of the earlier films. He made it after their world-wide success, which he must have wanted to emulate. He makes no concessions, but after the gentle opening, with its references to the past, he moves to a more exotic India, with the wedding ceremony and the consequent melodrama revolving around the mad bridegroom. Other works about growing up come to mind, whose authors remembered their childhood with artless fidelity but recalled their adult life somewhat less convincingly. The portrait of Apu, with his hopes, aspirations, sorrow and striving, is matched by those of the people around him. They are caring and kind. So is Ray. He has said that he considers himself by instinct and education caught between East and West, but that being a Bengali and working in that country have given him an ability to understand it. In 'The Apu Trilogy' he evinces a love of his homeland and his fellow-countrymen unequalled by any other director.

While working on the trilogy, he made two films designed primarily for domestic audiences, **The Philosopher's Stone** (1957) and **Jalsaghar**/*The Music Room* (1958). Ray's love of children's stories led to the first of these, from a tale by Parasurum about a sacked bank clerk who finds a stone that can turn metal to gold but does not bring happiness with it. It was Ray's love of music which caused him to make *Jalsaghar*, from a Chekovian story by Tarashankar Bannerjee, about an impoverished landowner or *zamindar* (Chabi Biswas) who has mortgaged his decayed palace to the local Lopahin. His last three hundred rupees are spent on a musical entertainment, after which, at dawn, he goes to a drunken and bravura death on his trusty steed. Both films, despite their simplicity, are somewhat clumsily constructed – for instance, the early death of the wife and daughter in *Jalsaghar* renders much of the subsequent action anti-climactic: but it is still a haunting, elegiac piece.

The Philosopher's Stone was not seen much abroad, but *Jalsaghar* was successful in most countries, confirming Ray as one of the greatest living directors; but in my opinion **Devi** (1960) is even more remarkable. He adapted a story by Prabhat Kumar Mukherjee, based on a theme by Tagore, which deals with a man who loses his wife to a god; a foreword to the film remarks that in India it is not uncommon for a woman to suppose herself to be the reincarnation of the goddess Kali. The time is that of the Raj, when cultured Indians were adapting themselves to the West and awakening to the world outside India. 'Why is it so important to learn English?' someone asks, but although there is no answer, the husband (Soumitra Chatterjee) is happily adapting, while his wife (Sharmila Tagore) is drawn towards the past. As a rational man, he rejects reincarnation, but his inability to take a firm line with her proves fatal; she is encouraged by his father who, unlike him, is part of the fabric of old India (and like the old man in *Jalsaghar*; the same actor plays both), and, similarly, takes a long time a-dying. Even more than the trilogy, *Devi* reveals Ray's preoccupations with British influence on India and the Indian temperament, which he finds by turns vain, vacillating, bad-tempered and foolish. Mr Chatterjee's performance as the weak but amiable husband is unforgettable, as are the views of the wide river and the religious festivals, the clanking verandahs of the palace and the scenes of the 'goddess' receiving her flock.

Ray's involvement with Tagore, who was a family friend, has enriched the medium, not least in a documentary, **Rabindranath Tagore** (1961). The government commissioned several artists to contribute works to celebrate the centenary of Tagore's birth, but hesitated before approaching Ray because he was not a historian. It was Nehru who insisted that Ray be asked, but Ray found himself hampered by the contract, which called for an hour-long film to send abroad and a two-reel condensation for local consumption. In this hour Ray combined still-photographs, newsreels, views, interviews and re-enactments of Tagore's youth in a way which would become standard procedure in television documentary. His aim was to prevent the result from being static, and he believes that he worked harder on it than on any three of his features. He stresses Tagore's well-born origins, his stance as a man of peace, and his belief in the importance of the dialogue with the West while treasuring all that is best in Indian life; he emphasises that Tagore, city-born like himself, grew to love the country, which he claimed he himself hardly knew until he came to make *Pather Panchali*. He has also said 'uniqueness and universality are what I try to convey through my films', and these are qualities found in both the subsequent films based directly on Tagore's stories.

The first of these, **Three Daughters** (1961) contains three separate tales. It lasts three hours, and it is advisable to adapt to its pace, containing as it does the slowness of life itself, the meticulous selection of incident and a fond look at our follies. There are again scenes from provincial life, about good intentions, hopes too brave and love which does not quite work out. In 'The Postmaster' Nanda (Anil Chatterjee) arrives from Calcutta, hangs the family group photograph on the wall and starts to stamp the letters. He is drawn to his housekeeper, Ratan (Chandana Bannerjee) – an eleven-year-old who is in some ways already a woman – and she to him: but despite that, and their loneliness, they are unable to help each other. 'Monihara' is a ghost story, though we may accept it as another of Ray's studies of a marriage. He himself excised it for showings in the West, but the film is richer for being a triptych. Phanibhusan (Kali Bannerjee) brings his wife to the house that he has inherited, but the marriage disintegrates as she frets over her childlessness and fears that his family do not like her. *Devi* is recalled even more strongly in the last

The riches of Ray's films seem sometimes inexhaustible, and his adaptations from Tagore are equally as enthralling as the Apu Trilogy. *Three Daughters* (1961) is an 'omnibus' film, with three separate stories. All are good, but the first, 'The Postmaster', is outstanding. Chandana Bannerjee is the new maid, and Anil Chatterjee the postmaster himself, trying to adjust to rural ways.

story, 'Samapti', with Soumitra Chatterjee again as its Westernised hero, complete with a portrait of the King and Queen on the wall, a watch-chain on his waistcoat and suspendered Argyle socks and brogues under his dhoti. Amulya, his examinations passed, has returned to his remote village home on the Ganges, but refuses to accept the dumpling of a girl his mother chose as his bride. If he must marry, he says, he will have the village tomboy (Aparna Das Gupta): but, having rejected an arranged marriage for himself, it has not occurred to him that she could do the same. He spends much of their hilarious courtship angrily stomping through the mud to see her before she changes her mind.

Kanchenjungha (1962) was Ray's first original screenplay, and where certain other great film-makers (Renoir, Bergman, Antonioni) only came into their own when working from their own material, Ray had already established his mastery. There is nothing startlingly original about the film's theme, which is that of a group of people whose lives are changed by a catalyst within their society and an outside event. They, gathering on the hilly paths of the town, include a daughter who is trying to avoid an arranged marriage; her sister, whose arranged marriage has come apart; their brother, a philanderer; and the outsider, Ashoke (Arun Mukherjee), with his B.A. degree and cheerful disposition. As Ray himself said, the cinema can be the place for a conversation piece, provided the conversation is good: 'The quality of a good wordy film does not consist in the words alone, but in the way the words are combined with significant action, details of behaviour.' *Kanchenjungha* is as such satisfying, and if it lingers in the memory it is because of the use made of Darjeeling, the town the British built as a summer retreat across the valley from Kanchenjungha. However, the location shooting seems to have impaired his players (Anil Chatterjee, superb in *Three Daughters*, is awkward as the philanderer) and Ray's usual cameraman, Subrata Mitra, was inexperienced in filming in colour. For these reasons the film may have been neglected; it was not publicly shown in Britain until more than ten years later, when it appeared on television. It was seen in the U.S. in 1966, due to the enthusiasm of an elderly distributor, Edward Harrison, whose constant belief in Ray's work was never affected by the indifference of American audiences.★

Abhijan (1962), virtually unknown in the West, was a huge success in Bengal. At 150 minutes it may move too slowly for Western audiences, but while that is by no means a fault, it does emphasise what seems to me the flaw in Ray's talent – that he cannot make a narrative point (as opposed to an emotional one) with economy. Like *Jalsaghar*, the source is a novel by Tarashankar Bannerjee, suggested to him by a producer: Ray agreed to write the script, but only decided to direct after he had seen the locations, a plain scattered with gigantic rocks. Soumitra Chatterjee again demonstrates his range, as Narsingh, the member of a high-caste family in reduced circumstances and now a cab driver. His mournful mien and monotonous life only lighten when overtaking other cars on the road, until he is befriended by both a Christian family and a prostitute, people of goodwill who are anxious to love him. They live in a village very different from those in Ray's other films, with its miserable drinking den and poorly-lit restaurant, where there is talk of trafficking in drugs and whores: life for these people is only alleviated by a visit to a film-show or a twopenny circus.

Waheeda Rehman, who plays the whore, was a star in her own right, drawing a fee of 250,000 rupees (approximately £18,600) a film – which had been more than the total cost of each of Ray's films before he made *Kanchenjungha*. Ray has said that all of his films except *Aparajito* have been profitable, but obtaining the financing has not always been easy, coming from various orthodox production companies, philanthropic institutions and wealthy individuals. He has turned down numerous offers to work abroad. (Asked whether he would make a film about an Indian family living in Britain, he said he would do so only if convinced there was no British Indian able to make it.) He works for a flat fee, a remarkable decision in view of his creative participation, which ranges from writing and directing to

---

★This is one example – we shall examine others – when the influential opinion of *The New York Times* was wholly destructive, since Bosley Crowther did not like Ray's films, starting with *Pather Panchali*, which he thought 'so amateurish that it would barely pass for a rough cut in Hollywood'.

Charulata is another version of Tagore, serving Ray again for a study of a marriage and of a Westernised Indian, here played by Sailen Mukherjee, with Madhabi Mukherjee as his wife. She appears neglected, and is: but the film is about much more than that.

composing the music (Ravi Shankar had provided the scores for his first few films) and later doing his own camerawork. He is also his own producer, inasmuch as he initiates his projects and selects all the creative elements and the locations: but he does not think of himself as a producer, because he is not interested in the bureaucracy involved in arranging distribution and foreign screenings. In the matter of locations, incidentally, he says that he is primarily a studio director, and the fact that so few people can notice when a sequence moves from a real city street to a simulated one is a tribute to his photographers, designers and lighting directors.

In the early Sixties four of his films were financed by a producer new to the business, R. D. Bansal, with help from the government-funded Film Finance Corporation. At least two of those films are flawless (*Kapurush-O-Mahapurush* and *Chiriakana* have never been seen in the West, and Ray does not intend that they ever shall be). **Mahanagar**/*The Big City* (1963) and **Charulata** (1964) are both about marriage, but that is all they have in common. *Mahanagar*, taken from two stories by Narendra Nath Mitra, concerns a wife (Madhabi Mukherjee) who breaks with tradition and takes a job because her husband (Anil Chatterjee) cannot make ends meet on his salary as a bank clerk. He

is a graduate, and a recurring theme in Ray's work is that teaching and the university degrees are of little aid to advancement. Once again he presents a detailed but selective picture of 'earning a living', and again this is a study of change, as the timid wife adjusts to both life in the office and selling knitting-machines door-to-door. She is helped by a jazzy colleague (Vicky Redwood), an Anglo-Indian, 'that race left by our ex-rulers' says the boss, as he sacks her. *Charulata* is from a story by Tagore, in which the husband is Bhupati Dutt (Sailen Mukherjee), a well-off Calcutta man whose passions in life are local politics and those abroad, which involve Mr Gladstone, one of his heroes. As the publisher of an influential journal of small circulation which takes up most of his time, he provides company for his wife (Miss Mukherjee) by arranging for her brother and sister-in-law to live with them; but it is a cousin, a character based on Tagore himself, the student Amal (Soumitra Chatterjee), who furnishes the company she needs, and as he teaches Charulata to write she falls in love with him. The sequences in which this happens are among the most delicately observed in all cinema, and they are entirely of Ray's making, for the love is only hinted at in the original. The fact that the story was autobiographical and that the lady concerned did commit suicide may have inspired Ray to emphasise her emotions, almost at the expense of Tagore's study of a British-orientated literary-political society. Less positive than the conclusion of *Mahanagar*, *Charulata* ends on a note of hope, instead of bleakly as in Tagore's novel. Charulata, Amal and Bhupati join Ray's gallery of beautifully-realised characters, but it is Bhupati who most interests him, a man completely Anglicised but deeply conscious of being Indian: it is typical of him that he celebrates Mr Gladstone's victory with a concert of traditional local music.

Charulata is Ray's own favourite among his films, because 'it has the fewest flaws'. It was the twelfth he had made in the first decade of his work in the industry, and at least nine of the films are masterworks – which constitutes a record perhaps only equalled by Bergman. Leaving aside the two films he refuses to be shown abroad, it may still be said that his next two films are minor. **Nayak** (1966) is a pleasant enough tale of a movie star (Uttam Khumar) and of his brief acquaintance, on a train journey, with a young student reporter (Sharmila Tagore); interwoven with their conversations are amusing flashbacks to the star's usual routine and vignettes of their fellow passengers, most of whom wish to return to the days of the Raj. **The Adventures of Goopy and Bagha** (1968) is Ray's adaptation of a folk-tale by his grandfather, Upendrakishore Roychowdhury, which takes its two ne'er-do-well heroes from the granting of three wishes to a 'Gulliver's Travels'-like conclusion. Despite some stunning locations, it soon becomes stale; every creative director is allowed one mistake, and this is Ray's.

He has said that his major films exhausted him, and that he was learning to relax with less demanding material: accordingly, while making *Goopy and Bagha* he was gearing himself for **Days and Nights in the Forest** (1969), based on a novel by Sunil Ganguly. It is a study of four wealthy Calcutta men who spend a week's vacation in a forest lodge, with no ambition other than to laze away the days and drink away the evenings – till, that is, they become involved with a Calcutta family of their own class and with the villagers, whose women drink and work 'just as in Western society'. The men do not really communicate, even between themselves, since their only common bond is an obsession with money. The symbols are not writ large, and the restating of old themes – chiefly of people whose lives touch for a while – has here a new-found pessimism. That quality is even more apparent in **The Adversary** (1971), based on a book by the same novelist. The title is ironic: the protagonist, a failed medical student, Siddhartha (Dhritiman Chatterjee), has a friend who is an anarchist, but if he himself is opposed to anything it is bureaucracy – or, subconsciously, a society which does not need him. His life is a round of futile interviews, gossiping with friends and meandering, until he finally takes a rotten job in a fly-blown small town outside Calcutta. The forlorn ending may come from the original novel, but we are a long way from *Il Posto* (q.v.), which Ray surely had in mind. Ray is always less lighthearted than Olmi, and our sole consolation is that Siddhartha is a younger version of the

usual Ray protagonist: he has the same preoccupations as the most sensible of the young men in *Days and Nights in the Forest*, he is a modern Apu, the movie star in *Nayak*, the various husbands: overdog or underdog, they may sin and accept defeat, but they are all for life, understanding and compassion.

They are also, even the young Siddhartha, throwbacks to the Raj. The young men in *Days and Nights* pride themselves on their deft English phrases, and try to imagine that they are vacationing on the French Riviera: they ape the Britishers of the past or their movie heroes, but the young protagonist of **Company Limited** (1971) is entirely of 'the new India'. He is Shyamal Chatterjee (Barun Chanda), a personable young executive with large glasses. Like his predecessors, he sighs for what might have been (in his case continuing his earlier vocation as a schoolteacher in Patna), but he knows that the good things in life are in Calcutta. His past and present take on renewed vividness when he is visited by his wife's sister: he asks her twice whether she thinks that he has improved as well as changed, and neither time does she answer. He drinks whisky, and copes with office problems: he confronts crises by combining a native cunning with Western notions of unions and strikes – and since the result consists of no

Sharmila Tagore and Soumitra Chatterjee with, between them, Robi Ghose, another favourite interpreter of Ray's, in *Days and Nights in the Forest*. The two men are among a party of Europeanised friends enjoying a week's vacation, and Miss Tagore is a widow, also from Calcutta, with whom they become involved. Here they are visiting the village fête as it winds down towards the grey evening.

833

red ink in the ledgers and a directorship, it is a good conjunction. He does not really comprehend the moral surrender involved in the inevitability of Europeanisation, a process which Ray views as inescapable, with reverberations of the India that was and the one that is to come.

The Middle Man (1975), like *Company Limited*, is based on a story by the novelist Shankar, and with *The Adversary* they make an unintentional trilogy about life in contemporary Calcutta. Ray has observed that all three films were based on 'second-rate' novels but with fascinating elements 'which were retained and then the rest was transformed in the process of writing the screenplay.' The middle man is Somnath (Pradip Mukherjee), another young graduate who cannot get a job and therefore engages himself in buying unneeded goods to sell to uninterested parties. He is not a very special fellow, and he bends with the wind, eventually turning to pimping, a matter which troubles him only because the girl concerned is the sister of a friend. Ray regards the conclusion as pessimistic but essential since 'the main mood is one of cynicism: it deals with corruption.' Yet while clearly condemning the bartering of flesh for contacts, he is aware that it is a step up for Somnath, preferable to driving taxis. One reason for Ray's superiority over virtually every other director working today is his ability to take a moral stand, and yet be both sympathetic and humorous – qualities necessary in portraying such people as Somnath, occupied with his own useless company as a status symbol and finding that doing business, if not reliable, can be agreeable.

These three films were made in answer to those Indian critics who constantly accused Ray, as the country's leading film-maker, of avoiding contemporary issues – and that may be why he worked from three sources for which he had no great respect. He has since said that he is only really interested in making films about the problems of the rural areas, in which respect he is echoing Gandhi, who observed that those who want to know the real India must go to the villages. In the midst of making the three Calcutta stories, he turned again to Bannerjee, the author of *Pather Panchali*, for **Distant Thunder** (1973). The setting is a remote village in 1943, and the title refers to the War –

something which no one understands, beyond the fact that King George is fighting the Japanese. The fact that Singapore has fallen is regarded as a grave matter, except that no one knows where it is. The schoolmaster hero (Soumitra Chatterjee) says that it is in another province, which might have ended any speculation on war till rice becomes scarce and, as a result, law and order break down. An astounding final shot is followed by a title epilogue with the information that over five million people died in what became known as the 'man-made' famine in East Bengal in 1943. I believe that this film was also made as a reply to Ray's critics, but that, once away from the city, he found himself incapable of the requisite harshness. He does not flinch from portraying the ugly mood in the latter part of the film, but his customary humour and affection are apparent whenever he contemplates the teacher, feckless and kind, with his odd little white lies and innate decency, and his wife, touchingly loyal and kind. He pauses for a sudden expression on their faces, as he does for a shot of a flower, of a field with a bank of clouds over it, of a stream flowing through a wood or a snatch of overheard conversation. Thus he shares with us some images from one man's small existence.

It was Ray's first film in colour since *Kanchenjungha*, and he was to use colour with each film from **The Chess Players** (1977) onwards. This was Ray's first film in Hindi and made in Bombay ostensibly because it required a larger budget than usual and Hindi films are more widely distributed than those made in Bengali. In fact, Ray's autocratic attitude had made him unpopular with the self-regarding Calcutta film industry, but he could point to the fact that the original story, by Munshi Premchand, was in Hindi. Its subject is two chess-playing nabobs, and there is a sub-plot about the East India Company trying to manipulate the abdication of an effete ruler. The latter is but a pawn in the game of taking over India, and we may assume that his lack of will and the indifference of the nabobs were contributory factors in India becoming a red mass on the map of the British Empire. However, the film is decorative rather than political, and when it attempts to explain it does so in primer-style, filling in the background with long duologues between the British commander (Richard Attenborough) and his aides. Ray had one of his greatest successes in the West with this film, but I find that it neither flows nor breathes. More surprisingly, the relationship between the nabobs (and their wives) lacks shading – that shading which had hitherto made his work so infinitely rewarding. In his studies of married couples, of Calcutta businessmen, of students and graduates he had always conveyed the minute pressures, the small compromises, the growing (or receding) consciousness which constitute for all of us ways of coping with life.

The Chess Players seems to me less good than the three children's films that he made at this time. The first of them, **The Golden Fortress** (1974) is two and a half hours of enchantment, and while I appreciate the difficulties involved in programming long, subtitled films for children, I do not understand why this one has not been seen in the West outside the festivals. Based on a serial Ray wrote for the children's magazine which he edits, it is the reverse, let it be said, of *Goopy and Bagha*. When its young hero, Mukul (Kushul Chakravarty), is seen reading Tintin, we know what to expect; like Tintin, Mukul sets out on his adventures with some motley friends, including a bodyguard detective (Soumitra Chatterjee), and there is many a cross and double cross before the villain is unmasked in the golden fortress itself, Rajasthan. **The Elephant God** (1978) is an enjoyable sequel, and **The Kingdom of Diamonds** (1980) consists of the further adventures of Goopy and Bagha, which are considerably more colourful than those in the earlier film. Ray's feeling for his characters and for the vastness of India – particularly strong in *The Golden Fortress* – are among the reasons these are some of the very best films for children.

They were extremely popular on their home territory, and Ray has observed that his unit had great fun in their making. During this time he also made some documentaries, but none of this work does he consider as major. That he has been so much less prolific in recent years is due to his refusal to undertake any project which does not interest him wholeheartedly. He has recently made two short films, one for television in France (a country in which his films are having a belated success), and it is

heartening to know, as I write, that he is embarking upon *The Home and the World*, from a story by Tagore which he had originally intended to make before *Pather Panchali*.

Ray was a great admirer of Ritwik Ghatak (1926–76), whose first film, **The Citizen** (1952), pre-dates *Pather Panchali*. Ghatak was born in that part of Bengal which eventually became Bangladesh, and the Partition haunted him all his life. He started writing plays at college, and joined the Indian People's Theatre Association, but decided that as a Communist – and, like Ray, prompted by *Ladri di Biciclette* – films offered a greater platform for his political views. Ray, paying tribute to him after his death, said that his most valuable and distinctive characteristic was that he was 'a Bengali director in heart and soul, a Bengali artist'; he also said that he admired him for there was nothing of Hollywood in his work, despite the fact that these were almost the only foreign films seen in India during their formative years. Ghatak had, apparently, seen the Soviet Silent classics, and Ray detected the influence of these in Ghatak's films, along with 'theatre, in the dialogue, content and conclusions of his films'. *The Citizen* is theatrical, in the manner of the Group Theatre, and understandably so, since Ghatak's work in the theatre had involved him in American left-wing plays. Unlike de Sica, Ghatak in *The Citizen* tempers realism with poetry, in the repeated symbol of the pavement violinist. Its few scenes in Calcutta bars and offices are lively, but he is less intense and less sensitive than Ray in dealing with the poverty-stricken family at the centre of the film. Prostitution beckons for the girls; the family's hopes are centred on Ramu (Satindra Bhattacharya), alternately optimistic and depressed as he regards his university degree, which he finds is no passport to employment. That is only one of the several themes in this film which was to turn up in Ray's later work, but that may be because poverty in Calcutta is unchanging.

Ray may not have seen the film. It was an entirely cooperative effort, made with friends (many of the players became important stars), and a revolutionary project for India: the studio, the laboratory and the supplier of film stock all contributed, but though passed by the censor the film came into the hands of a dishonest businessman and was not seen publicly till after Ghatak's death. Following Ray's example with *Pather Panchali*, Ghatak applied to the government of West Bengal for the financing of **The Mechanical Man** (1958), which became a great favourite with local audiences. It was submitted to the committee of the Venice Film Festival, which turned it down, thus denying Ghatak an opportunity to win international fame and the attendant benefits – and world audiences of seeing a superb film. In a series of gently amusing episodes it deals with Bimal, a rural, drunken cab driver, and his even more unreliable but beloved taxi, which has, to put it mildly, seen better days. The ending of the film is undeniably sentimental, but technically this film is so accomplished that it should be required viewing in film schools.

None of Ghatak's other films is as satisfactory, starting with **The Runaway** (1959), about a small boy who flees to Calcutta for a series of adventures of varying quality. The film has a dreamlike quality and Calcutta has no reality: for the boy, it is, like dreams, by turns benign and disturbing, and absolutely nothing turns out as he expects – at least in human terms, as adults are revealed as anything but what they seem at first. Consequently the boy's perceptions are both heightened and limited, evidence enough that the film itself is more perceptive than most films on childhood. Ghatak's next two films seem to me unsatisfactory, partly due to the performances of Supriya Choudhury in the leading roles. **The Hidden Star** (1960) is not unlike *The Citizen*, about an impoverished family dependent on the daughter (Miss Choudhury). She loses her amiable fiancé to her sister and subsequently finds after all her sacrifices that she has a fatal illness. The film is beautifully made, but the autobiographical **E Flat** (1960) tries to say too much, and it does not say it well. Its subject is the rivalry between avant-garde theatre groups, to which is attached the relationship between the idealistic chief (Abanish Bandyopadhyay) of one and an actress (Miss Choudhury) in the other. Both of them are victims of Partition, and are drawn together because of it.

Partition is the subject of Ghatak's most complex film, **Subarnarekha** (1962), which manages to combine some bravura passages, both beautiful and melodramatic, with much social criticism, directed mainly at the methods of small-minded businessmen. The film's central characters have been left stranded by Partition: Ishwar is helped by an old friend to get a job at an iron foundry in the country, and he takes an abandoned small boy whom he educates. The boy, grown-up, wants to marry his foster-sister, but as he is thought to be of a lower caste the bosses intervene, and the young couple run away to Calcutta, where she is eventually forced into prostitution. The tale of these three people culminates in violence, but the film's ending is of hope, not unlike *The World of Apu*. Ishwar himself is a tragic figure, but like many another protagonist in the Indian cinema so weak that he can be easily destroyed by stronger forces.

The film was not shown till three years after it was made. A number of other projects were begun and abandoned, partly because Ghatak's reputation as an alcoholic and as undependable frequently prevented him from getting backing. He did make *A River Named Titus* in Bangladesh not long before he died of tuberculosis and chronic alcoholism, and he knew that he was dying when he made the autobiographical **Reason, Debate and a Tale** (1974). He himself plays the leading role, that of a man whose career and marriage have been ruined by drink. With some equally aimless companions he goes to visit his wife, before becoming involved with some terrorists. Ghatak's inspiration was Fellini's *8½* (q.v.), and for a while it is more pointed; but, like much of the work of alcoholics, it is self-pitying, boring and eventually incoherent.

Ghatak's preoccupation with Partition is shared by M. S. Sathyu, whose first film, **Hot Winds** (1975), is sufficiently like *The Citizen* as to suggest a homage to Ghatak. Sathyu, coming from the theatre, is an uninspired but careful craftsman, and the achievement of *Hot Winds*, which is considerable, lies in its screenplay by Kaifi Azmi and Shama Zaidi, from an unpublished story by Ismat Chugtai. It focuses on the plight of one Muslim family left in Calcutta after Partition, the increasing hostility around them, the difficulty of continuing in business (they own a small shoe factory) and the temptation to join other members of the family who have

A Picture of India: The Films of Satyajit Ray

emigrated to Pakistan. Emotional problems caused by Partition drive the daughter to suicide, which seems a dramatic device rather than a matter deeply felt, but the ending, in which the remaining members of the family find that they cannot leave India, is superb. The film was much reviled and discussed when it came out, but was popular with audiences. It was seen at the Cannes Film Festival and deserves to be more widely known.

The most political of Indian filmmakers is Mrinal Sen, whose didacticism has sometimes alienated even those who share his left-wing views. His early films were influenced by Brecht and the *nouvelle vague*, and by the time of his third movie, *Akash Kusum*, in 1965, his work was dismissed by Ray, who can be a severe critic of the films of his colleagues. It is ironic therefore that Sen had an enormous popular success with **Bhuvan Shome** (1969), though it should be noted that it was made in Hindi rather than his native Bengali, unlike his earlier films. This one was backed by the Film Finance Corporation, and was so profitable that the government entered the film business on a large scale, to

the extent that the country's annual output was doubled (India made 396 films in 1970, which had risen to 742 in 1980, many of them made for the linguistic minorities, hitherto accustomed to Hindi films with subtitles). *Bhuvan Shome* is little more than a character study of the eponymous hero, a railway official who learns to relax and become more human on a hunting trip. Chiefly responsible for his conversion is the fiancée (Susasini Mulay) of one of his employees, a man to be sacked or reprimanded for taking small bribes. Miss Mulay is reason enough for seeing the film.

For Western viewers, it has a Godardian friskiness which is tiresome, and the exposition is clumsy, a fault Sen has not always managed to overcome in his later, better films. Among these are **The Royal Hunt** (1976) and **The Outsiders** (1977), both rural tales in which the villagers are harassed, harried and deprived of any real livelihood by the landowners or their representatives. The first film concerns the headman's son, a hunter, and his friendship with the white district officer whom he considers a god. When the landowner's

837

agent kidnaps the hunter's wife for sexual purposes he murders him before telling his white friend – a rather unconvincing denouement in view of the latter's fondness for the couple. The outsiders of the second film are an unruly old man and his son, whom he encourages to be idle and to steal, like himself, rather than submit to the iniquitous system imposed upon the other villagers. Again, the climax is ridiculous, as the young man sits by and lets his wife scream during the labour pains that kill her, but Sen makes a point from that, as the two men beg for the fees for the funeral. Something is wrong with a society that has money for death but not for life: it is a powerful ending if you take the cynical view that Brecht and others have taught us that the message must be simple-minded.

And Quiet Rolls the Dawn (1979), Sen's only film to be widely seen in the West, was criticised for its didacticism, but if it is occasionally nudging it is subtle enough as a feminist tract. Based on a story by Amalendu Chakravarty, it is, like Ghatak's *The Citizen*, in the tradition of tales about families living in poverty in large decaying tenements (once mansions) in Calcutta. As in the earlier film the rest of the family depends on one member, the daughter Chinu (Mamata Shankar), for its livelihood, and the action solely concerns

the one night when she does not return. There are fears that she has had an accident, and the elder son (Tapan Das) goes to the police station, the morgue, a hospital; the suspicion that she may have been with a man becomes a certainty, if to her family but not to audiences, and yet again the ending lacks conviction. Overall this is a sweet, unpretentious film, with some telling vignettes of the family, of neighbours, of officials – all of them, as is usual in Sen's films, beautifully acted.

Sen lacks the intellectual rigour of Ray and Shyam Benegal (b. 1934), though Benegal shares his indignation, particularly in regard to conditions in the rural areas. All three of them are trying to tell us about their country, but where Sen makes his habitual condemnation Ray and Benegal ask for an understanding to be extended. Ray wants us to love his people as much as he does, finding chinks of hope; Benegal seems dismayed that conditions remain so feudal, and does not express much hope in change. He has, like Ray, stated his preference for filming in what he calls 'the remote corners of our land. The glitter and glamour of the few cities that most of us are a witness to are not in reality our way of life.' His first four films form a remarkable quartet.

He is a Hindi, born in Hyderabad, where he also attended university. He worked on documentaries before turning to fiction with **Ankur**/*The Seedling* (1974) – a fiction, however, based on events that he had witnessed as a student, about a young man, Surya (Anant Nag) who is sent to oversee a remote corner of his father's estate and finds that he cannot cope. **Night's End** (1975), also based on an actual incident, is set in 1945 and concerns the abduction of the new schoolteacher's wife by the family of the *zamindar*, one of whom is sexually attracted to her. **The Churning** (1976) is founded in events told to Benegal while making one of his documentaries, about the efforts of some city-dwellers to bring a cooperative to a backward village. **The Boon** (1978), conversely, is whimsical. Its hero, Parasuram (Mr Nag), believes that he has been granted divine powers, which prove to have terrible consequences when he is forced to use them.

The themes of the four films are interchangeable, but whereas *The Boon* concen-

The films of Shyam Benegal are too little known, and the best of them are worthy to rank with those of Ray. *The Churning* concerns a city man, marvellously played by Girish Karnad, right, who attempts to persuade a rural community to adopt more modern methods. He is a kindly man, but that was not the quality required and he retires at the end defeated.

trates on the effect of superstition and the misuse of religion its most brilliant sequences concern the family of the *zamindar*. The iniquities of the *zamindars* provide the most sustained of the themes throughout the quartet: they are greedy, self-indulgent and indifferent to the wrongs they do, while the police who support them are lazy and corrupt. The peasants are slothful and resigned, unlikely to respond to the teachers and townsfolk who want to help them and who in any case have their own shortcomings – pomposity, divided goals, lack of money and an inability to overcome centuries-old prejudices and mores. In *The Seedling* Surya's 'kindness' to his housekeeper, a woman of lower caste, leads to his complete isolation, as do the teacher's rightful claims for his wife in *Night's End*. In Benegal's films violence and rapacity are always in prospect, which is one reason we could never confuse them with Ray's.

The first two of the quartet were backed by Blaze Enterprises, a successful producer of advertising shorts run by two journalists. *The Churning* was financed, the credits inform us, by '500,000 farmers of Gujarat', that is by the milk cooperatives of that province, each member of which provided two rupees towards its making. Since milk production creates the staple income in most smallholdings, the government formulated its plans on the cooperatives in an attempt to end the exploitation of the peasants by the landowners: but from the radio broadcasts heard in the film it is clear that Benegal does not think the government entirely blameless. This is a true socialist film, if less vehement than Sen's similar tales, more contemplative and richer and more honest. It is the best of the quartet, of which only *Ankur* has been publicly seen in Britain.

Ironically, two of Benegal's lesser films have been publicly shown in London. **Bhumika**/*The Role* (1977) is too long at 140 minutes for its content – which is close to soap opera, despite the director's claim that 'it is about the problems of women in our society, the search for their own identity, their desire to achieve independence'. He himself contributed to the screenplay, based on an autobiographical book by Hansa Wadkar, a film star of the Thirties. This film begins then, but mainly concerns the years of success of the star,

Usha (Smita Patil), and her manipulation by her husband (Anant Nag), who is also her manager. Unfortunately Benegal does not let us know to what extent the man controls Usha's career and instead offers some affectionate satire on the Indian movies of the time. Escaping her husband, the woman has casual sex with a stranger and goes to live with him, finding the domesticity she always craved but an even greater restriction on her freedom – and it is at this point that the film at last becomes powerful. **Junoon** (1979) has an even stronger situation, but Benegal is simply overwhelmed by it. Its source is a nineteenth-century story, 'A Flight of Pigeons', by Ruskin Bond, about the plight of an Anglo-Indian family at the time of civil disorder. The actor Shashi Kapoor produced, on a large budget, and plays the lead, that of a Pathan nabob obsessed by the daughter of the family. Benegal lacks the courage to be full-bloodedly romantic, as demanded by the subject, and makes instead small and tactful points about British rule and Indian submission which in the end amount to very little.

Ascending Scale (1982) would seem to confirm that Benegal is at his best dealing with contemporary issues. His subject is once more the power of the landowners, which was hardly shaken by the government decree of 1967 that the peasants must be given three out of every five shares of land. That power, and local superstition, plus an inefficient bureaucracy and an often corrupt judiciary, are all evidenced in this film, and it is therefore almost startling to find that it was sponsored by the government of West Bengal, using the cinema's powers of persuasion as they had seldom been used since the Soviets at the time of Eisenstein. There are parallels in the portrait of the effete landowners, and the solidarity of the workers (at the elections; during the Great Bengal Flood of 1977), while the main plot concerns the ten-year struggle, often in the courts, of Hari (Om Puri) to claim the land that is rightfully his. Two subplots concern relatives who because of poverty go to Calcutta where one, Hari's brother, becomes involved with crooks and anarchists, and the other, a girl, becomes a kept woman before going mad. Her story in particular is melodramatic, but that is possibly because unsophisticated audiences could hardly be expected to be wholly taken up with Hari's legal battles – and the film was clearly made *pour encourager les autres*. It is an important, powerful and absorbing one, and if it firmly establishes Benegal as a polemic film-maker he remains primarily a humanist.

One reason that Mr Kapoor had produced *Junoon* was that as one of India's leading film stars he had become disillusioned with the 'rubbish' that was being offered him – and the word is that of his wife, Jennifer Kendal, whom he had met and married while acting with other members of her family in *Shakespeare Wallah* (q.v.). He produced **36 Chowringhee Lane** (1981) as a starring vehicle for her, and in it she plays an Anglo-Indian teacher living in Calcutta. She is a spinster, and lonely because her niece has recently married an Australian; she befriends a young couple (Debashree Roy, Dhritiman Chatterjee), who respond in order to be able to use her cluttered apartment to make love, and she is consequently disillusioned when marriage means that they no longer need her. This is a delicate, touching film, and all praise is due to those concerned, which include the Film Finance Corporation (the cost was two million rupees, or the equivalent of £117,000, as opposed to six million or £350,000 for *Junoon*). There are jejune touches, such as the shots of the Calcutta poor against 'Silent Night' on the soundtrack, and Miss Kendal's otherwise lovely performance is spoilt by a tendency to over-react: but perhaps Aparna Sen did not care to 'direct' the producer's wife. Miss Sen also wrote the screenplay, performing both functions with the blessing of Satyajit Ray, for whom she had made her screen debut in *Three Daughters*. The Indian censor, incidentally, passed the nude and the usually-banned kissing scenes on the grounds that this was an 'English' film: in fact, the lovers speak Bengali to each other, and certain other scenes seem to have been filmed in that language and dubbed.

Since America has been inhospitable to Ray, we do not need to ask why Benegal's films have only been shown in that country at festivals. As far as Britain is concerned, the praise of a handful of critics who have championed Indian cinema is offset by the others, who have been mainly indifferent – with art-house audiences apparently agreeing, as explained by one distributor who had failed several times with the work of the Singhalese director, Lester James Peries (b. 1921). The same distributor observed that he had made losses on a couple of Ray's films – and Ray, said Peries, 'is a far greater director'. This is true, but that might still mean that Peries is a very good one. There are a number of interesting films among his work, but his first film, **The Line of Destiny** (1956), is not one of them – despite its acclaim at the time in Sri Lanka (then Ceylon). At that time the available 'Singhalese' films were made in Madras, by Tamils, with painted scenery and no knowledge of Sri Lanka except for the language. They were very long, with musical episodes. Peries, a former journalist (like Ray, he had worked in London for some years), was engaged on filming documentaries for the government, and he asked two colleagues to join him on a true Singhalese film, which, incidentally, went into production as Ray was finishing *Pather Panchali*. He wrote the screenplay himself, since there were no suitable works for adaptation (those available were either didactic or in the style of nineteenth-century melodrama), and it is about a small village boy who is thought to have magic powers, which turn against him when the area is afflicted by drought.

If *The Line of Destiny* fails to illuminate village life, Peries had become much more accomplished by the time he made **Gamperaliya** (1964), his third film. It is the story of an arranged marriage in a village in southern Ceylon just after the turn of the century, and, with reason, it won the Grand Prix at the Delhi Film Festival. I am not sure that it reveals 'the inner life' of its characters, which Peries claims is one of the virtues available to those who make films. The otherwise interesting **Between Two Worlds** (1966) fails on that account, as it follows the doubts of a wealthy playboy (Tony Ranasinghe) when he knows that his family intend that a servant should take the blame for a hit-and-run accident for which he is responsible. Peries's slow pacing is tiring (as Ray's is not, for his films are more richly detailed) and **Five Acres of Land** (1969) is overlong at 132 minutes. Otherwise it marks another advance for Peries, both in the skill with which it is made and the material itself, which is built round a young man (Milton Jayawardena) who is being educated at a college in the city. He is a nice young man, lonely at first, and conscious of the sacrifices being made by his humble family: yet he falls in love with the bourgeois girl with whose family he is lodging and loses his chance of bettering himself.

The title of **The Treasure** (1972) refers to both a human being and gold, insofar as it exists. The hero's confusion between the two is one reason why this is a very appealing story. The hero is Willie (Gamini Fonseka), a penniless landowner. He has a dream of becoming rich: legend says that treasure is buried in a deserted temple in a forest, but can only be unlodged by someone sacrificing a virgin. Willie dreams about a virgin with certain birthmarks, sees her in the flesh, and offers marriage. He treats her as father rather than husband, till he realises that he loves her, but Willie is caught up in a train of consequences which lead to tragedy. A framing device gives dimension to this somewhat dubious story, written by G. B. Senanayake; the screenplay is by Tissa Abeysekera, Peries's usual collaborator at the time, and M. S. Anandan's photography is as luminous as it was for *Five Acres of Land*. Fonseka's detailed performance is magnificent, as is that of Malina Fonseka as the bride. She is as meltingly beautiful as Madhabi Mukherjee in *Charulata*, to which Peries pays homage in one scene. Despite the shortcomings of the plot, this is a film of almost the same quality.

The Eyes (1972) confirms that Peries came into his own by this time. A simpleminded village man (Joe Abeywickrema) marries a blind girl (Srijani Amarasane), and is then not sure whether he wants her to be cured by the holy man (Ravendra Randenija). **Enchanted Island** (1976) is a simple tale of a youth so wild and destructive that he alienates his parents and the kindly schoolteacher (Mr Abeywickrema) to whom he is sent for correction. He cultivates a desert island so successfully with a friend that the crown agents allow them to keep it. **White Flowers for the Dead** (1976) somewhat resembles *The Treasure*, and within its complex past-to-present structure is an affectionate portrait of a doctor (Mr Ranasinghe) whose bitterness after his wife's death is lessened as he becomes caught up once more with the members of her family. Peries's direction,

after the confidence of *The Treasure*, becomes hesitant again, a fact somewhat disguised by his superlative team of players and a series of photographers of the same quality.

Peries did make two expensive and unqualified failures. **The God King** (1974) was financed by a Briton, who offered him the subject, an historical fresco set in the fifth century, and the largest budget ever offered by the West to an Asian director (Ray had failed to make a projected film with Peter Sellers; Kurosawa had walked off *Tora! Tora! Tora!*). Peries was so flattered that he ceded control over casting (three British actors were blacked-up to play Singhalese) as well as script and editing (his wife's cut was not accepted). The Rank Organisation, which was due to release the result, lost interest, as did the minor British company which took it up after a test engagement in Liverpool for the Indian and Pakistani population, who quite reasonably were not interested in a Singhalese film. The failure of **Rebellion** (1978) is Peries's own, indicating that he has no aptitude for the epic form (I cannot say the historical film, since his second film, *The Message*, was historical and so popular that the negative and all remaining copies were worn out, so that it does not exist for valuation). The film's subject is Veera Puran Appu (Mr Randenija), the Singhalese outlaw and patriot who led a revolt against the British in 1848. Local critics disliked the film because of its

Like most Asian directors, Lester James Peries has been influenced by Satyajit Ray, and they have a common goal, to depict the everyday life of ordinary people. When Peries has been more ambitious he has sometimes failed, and his best films have all concerned wealthy bourgeois families in his native country, Sri Lanka. His best film is *The Treasure*, a study of a strangely motivated marriage between a landowner (Gamini Fonseka) and a girl (Malina Fonseka) from another class. Both players, who are not related, are superb.

A Picture of India: The Films of Satyajit Ray

unpatriotic climax (the revolt had been unsuccessful), but the anti-British stance of it is both justifiable and well expressed. Elsewhere Peries seems to have no control, but it is interesting for once to see British colonials as the villains.

British Ceylon is the background to **Village in the Jungle** (1980), based on Leonard Woolf's novel of the same name, published in 1913. Its subject to an extent resembles that of *Ankur*, for it finds a weak landowner's son banished to a remote village as overseer, but who himself contributes to the greed, superstition, prejudice and depravity that he finds there. A comparison of the two films shows Peries unable to make his characters as full-blooded as those of Benegal, though he is equally critical of rural life. As with Ray, Peries is found wanting by some local critics who claim that his films are not sufficiently political; left-wing Indians and Singhalese who recognise both directors as powerful communicators are heartened by the demotic subjects they choose but are disappointed by the end product. Although Peries has echoed Ray in saying that the only material which really interests him concerns the conditions in the rural areas, he has returned to the bourgeoisie of *Gamperaliya* for his most recent work. When he set out to make that film he was unaware that the original novel, by Martin Wickremasinghe, was the first part of a trilogy, 'The Changing Village'. The popularity of *Gamperaliya* in Germany encouraged one of the country's television channels to finance the further two parts, of which the first, **Kaliyugaya** (1981), has already been shown. The circumstances of its being made clearly restored Peries's confidence, for this is his most masterly film since *The Treasure* and *The Eyes*. It takes up the fortunes of the family of *Gamperaliya* some twenty years later (with flashbacks, which of course are in monochrome), and finds them now living in the city and somewhat more affluent. Its chief theme is the alienation of the son, who went to live in London when the family disapproved of his chosen bride: at the end of the film he breaks off all communication with his widowed mother, leaving us to wait for Part Three to know whether this family solves its difficulties.

We may also regard the American, James Ivory (b. 1930), as a disciple of Ray.

He studied film in California, where he was born, and as a documentary filmmaker was sent to India by the Asia Society of New York. There he met Ismail Merchant, who became his partner and who operates the commercial end of their production company, tapping various unlikely sources for financing in many countries. One reason for this is the uneven quality of Ivory's work – and hence its eventual reception at the box office – but his first film, **The Householder** (1963), is good and the second, **Shakespeare Wallah** (1965), something more than that. Ivory's co-writer was the German-born[*] novelist, Ruth Prawer Jhabvala, who was to receive sole billing for the screenplays of most of Ivory's later films. *The Householder*, based on one of her novels, is reminiscent of both *The World of Apu* and *Mahanagar*, being a study of the first year of marriage of a city couple (Shashi Kapoor, Leela Naida). It is slight and unspoilt, even if derivative. From an indigenous couple Ivory turned to an English family in *Shakespeare Wallah*, a band of actors in an India that no longer really wants them. They had come out years before, as idealists, trailing across the subcontinent to play Shakespeare in halls, gardens, private homes, till interest has dwindled to an occasional princeling, an indulgent school and the British who have remained. The film is a tender postscript to the British love affair with India; the Darjeeling that we see is not that of *Kanchenjungha* but of British hotels, damp and decaying. It is a film of resonance and nuance, not least because Geoffrey Kendal and Laura Lidell were virtually playing themselves; at the end their daughter Felicity leaves for England – as she did in life, later to become one of Britain's brightest stars of stage and television. Her portrait of adolescence is as touching as that in Renoir's *The River*, and this is, like that, a special film, one for which many people have a fondness.

It is clumsily and often amateurishly made, faults not always eradicated in Ivory's subsequent and more expensive films. **The Guru** (1969) was also made with love and it also has some acute perceptions about the British in India – the modern, young British, that is, for it con-

[*]Her parents were Polish; she was educated in England and married an Indian architect.

cerns a pop-singer (Michael York), who comes to study the sitar. 20th Century-Fox were the backers – this was not long after the world-wide success of *Un Homme et une Femme* (q.v.) – but they did not, in view of the returns, care to repeat the experience. An Indian businessman financed **Bombay Talkie** (1970) and Ivory's first American feature, **Savages** (1972). *Bombay Talkie* proposes an engaging new version on the theme of East versus West, and on real emotions as opposed to pretended ones, since its leading characters are all engaged in the media. A much-married and bestselling American novelist (Jennifer Kendal) is attracted to both a penniless and honest poet (Zia Mohyeddin) and a good-natured but vain film star (Mr Kapoor): the opening sequence between the three of them is especially well balanced. Thereafter the film moves downhill to a conclusion which is anything but. For sheer pointlessness and melodramatic idiocy it would be hard to

equal it, but Ivory managed this in *Savages*, which follow a group of primitive beings as they invade a deserted mansion, become civilised and then regress to their original state.

The film needs, but does not have, the cinema's twin bogies, sex and violence, which is also true of **The Wild Party** (1975), a pastiche tale of Hollywood in the Twenties, with James Coco as an Arbuckle-like clown. Its source is a melodramatic narrative poem by Joseph Moncure March, its emphasis weakened by overstatement. The backers this time were American International Pictures, whose version was refuted by Ivory in letters to a number of leading critics, claiming that many of his discarded sequences had been inserted in 'a cheap attempt to over-exploit everything exploitable'. Since not one single scene worked on screen, the film only served to underline Ivory's position as a dilettante among film-makers. However, **Roseland** (1977), three separate

The director James Ivory made his best film at the beginning of his career, *Shakespeare Wallah*, about the adventures of a group of strolling players, seen here arriving in a small town in the hills.

843

A Picture of India: The Films of Satyajit Ray

stories of lonely people drawn together at New York's famous dance-hall, finds him in finer form than at any time since *Shakespeare Wallah*. This film and that have in common some lonely, unwanted people in a somewhat faded and déclassé setting, and perhaps that is where Ivory's sympathies really lie.

Returning to India, he made **Hullabaloo Over Georgie and Bonnie's Pictures** (1978), financed by a British T.V. company. The subject is fascinating. An aristocratic English collector (Peggy Ashcroft) and an American dealer arrive to prise away from a bankrupt young maharajah (Victor Bannerjee) his inheritance, a group of paintings the two con-artists believe would be of more benefit on gallery walls. Eventually both the Englishwoman and the American discard their selfishness and find new values, but that theme, apart from being an unoriginal one, is hardly explored. Turning to Henry James, Ivory reveals in **The Europeans** (1979) a lack of narrative sense or rhythm, thus failing to do justice to the material. He seems to believe that camera movement and editing can make a movie, which perhaps in the days of the studio system they could; but his players, if likeable, have no life beyond the set, and since this is a costume picture one readily imagines them taking their clothes from wicker baskets just before parading in front of the camera. The experienced Lee Remick acts at best moderately well, and only Lisa Eichhorn seems deeply immersed in her performance. As beautiful as both ladies are the yellow and red leaves of the New Hampshire Fall. James did not call for these, but his story is just strong enough to survive.

Perhaps because of his own life in India or his peripatetic adventures as a film-maker Ivory has been drawn to tales of people adapting themselves to strange environments, to expatriates, to people passing through, and this penchant led him to the Anglo-American colony in Paris in the Twenties, in **Quartet** (1981). Its source is Jean Rhys's cynical, autobiographical novel, founded on her relationship with Ford Madox Ford. The characters based on the two of them are played by Isabelle Adjani, whose limitations are of no help to the piece, and Alan Bates; his wife is played by Maggie Smith. The characters around them are somewhat more interesting, with their double options and conflicting, if usually selfish, emotions. The Paris of the time is as attractively caught as the Hollywood of the Twenties in *The Wild Party* was not. And, unlike *The Europeans*, Ivory has not betrayed his source material.

Anyone who cares for civilised cinema – particularly as it seems to be disappearing – would want Ivory to succeed as well on every occasion. Returning to India he did so, with **Heat and Dust** (1982), the first time that Ms Jhabvala has adopted one of her novels for Ivory since their collaboration began with *The Householder*. Side by side it examines the India of today, as a British woman (Julie Christie) seeks information on the life of her great-aunt, and the India of the Raj, when that lady, as a young woman (Greta Scacchi), first arrived to join her husband. Christie finds an India of teeming people, fake American pilgrims, bus-rides and offices; Scacchi's India is of elegance, idleness, ceremony, of dressing for dinner and of picnics with a romantic nawab (Shashi Kapoor) distrusted by the British. The film is too schematic and has moments of over-emphasis, but Ivory's handling shows a confidence missing from some of his recent films. His best work has always been that which reflected a more glorious past or that in which two cultures try to come to terms with each other. There is no one theme in the film, which is, as the title implies, about India – and it is one of the most loving and accomplished on that huge subject ever made.

It reminds us that in his first two films he also added to our understanding of India. Ray, incidentally, had been instrumental in their production, lending members of his unit and his photographer, Subrata Mitra. Perhaps he influenced them more than we know. Bengal, Peries and Sen have acknowledged their debt to Ray, who has also been an inspiration to other realist, humanist film-makers in Third World countries or those few who work with honesty while mired in an industry dedicated largely to inanities. But Ray's greatness as a film-maker goes beyond his influence. The moral complexities of his characters and the notion of 'right living' may be found in the great writers of the world, from Jane Austen to Tchekhov; but in very few film-makers.

32

Hollywood in the Age of Television: The Directors

THE AMERICAN FILM industry had not expected cinema attendances to hold to the record level of 1946. Its major preoccupation in the years that followed was in learning to accept the separation of exhibition from distribution and production, thus ending those practices which made the majority of films profitable. But once the smoke had cleared, it was evident that the decline in audiences could not be halted, for they were becoming selective. Increasingly the public began to echo the age-old cry of critics that Hollywood films were inferior to those from Europe; and television was proving itself a more formidable rival than the industry had ever considered. The large companies were horrified at the thought of leasing or selling their films to television,* but the small independent companies had no such qualms. The laughably low quality of old British films on television did not seem so funny when patrons were being lured away from their sets to see the latest Ealing comedy – if, as yet, only in the big city art-houses. Other television entertainment might also be derisory, but the living-room armchair began to take precedence over the effort required to see the latest Betty Grable vehicle. The habits of a lifetime were being broken, and Hollywood was vulnerable for the first time since the Depression.

Its answer was three-fold. The most important and least remarked upon was the greater autonomy allowed to individual film-makers – a move that the

moguls regarded with magnanimity, having crushed or frustrated the postwar desire for complete independence. The least significant, at least for the moment, was the poaching from television of product and talent. The other, inevitably much publicised, was the use of devices denied to the pocket-sized black-and-white screen in the corner of the living room.

In the graveyard of important but half-forgotten old movies is a tombstone called **The Robe** (1953) – a noteworthy tombstone, since it was the first film made in CinemaScope. This system, invented by Professor Henri Chrétien (1879–1956), replaced the customary box-shaped screen with one of panoramic proportions. The image projected was two and a half times as wide as it was high, an effect achieved by compressing a wide angle of vision on to a strip of 35mm film and expanding it again as it moved through the projector. The system dated back to 1927, when Chrétien had adapted the distorted lens he had devised during the First World War for tank periscopes. The following year Claude Autant-Lara had used it for a short, *Pour Construire un Feu*, but Hollywood had passed it over when making its own handful of wide-screen (70mm) films in 1930–1, and it had lain dormant till brought to the attention of 20th Century-Fox in 1952, amidst speculations in the industry about films requiring several projectors and/or special eye glasses for three-dimensional effects. CinemaScope was relatively simple, but there remained the possibility that exhibitors would refuse, as they had twenty-two years earlier, to make the necessary expensive conversions. Darryl F. Zanuck and Spyros Skouras, by now convinced that CinemaScope was the sole solu-

---

*It has been claimed that Walt Disney was the only producer in the prewar period whose contract specified the possibility of television showings, but Paramount's lawyers seem to have been equally farsighted, if not sanguine, about that ever happening.

845

Hollywood in the Age of Television: The Directors

With the growing popularity of television, Hollywood decided that colour alone was insufficient to combat the public's fondness for the new medium. The home screen was small and in black and white, so it could easily be put to shame by the industry's new systems – the third-dimensional film, the wide screen and stereophonic sound. The first 3-D film most people saw was *House of Wax*, TOP RIGHT, but the use of special glasses was a barrier to really wide acceptance, and the industry moved over to the wide screen when 20th Century-Fox introduced CinemaScope a few months later. BOTTOM RIGHT, you can see how they advertised the new techniques, and this piece of promotion material was issued to emphasise how much more audiences were getting for their money. As it happened, *The Robe* did not use the wide screen well.

tion to the problem of declining audiences, decided to minimise the risk by offering a biblical spectacle, always a certain crowd-puller. *The Robe* was based on an 'inspirational' bestseller by Lloyd C. Douglas; the novel's triteness and mawkishness have been retained with awesome fidelity in Philip Dunne's screenplay. 'When it comes, this is how it will start – some obscure martyr in some forgotten province' says the Emperor Tiberius (Ernest Thesiger) as a Roman centurion (Richard Burton) is converted to Christianity for the sake of a childhood sweetheart (Jean Simmons). Vast numbers of people found in the film exactly what they knew, or wanted to know, about Christianity, undeterred by the fact that the director, Henry Koster, had adopted a camera-in-the-stalls approach.

It was considered that the public would accept neither close-ups nor imaginative cutting in the use of the wide screen, a timidity comparable with the cinema's early days and the coming of Sound. This was in accord with the reverence required by the subject, but studio executives were so excited by the early rushes that the green light was given for a comedy in Cinema-Scope, **How to Marry a Millionaire** (1953). Jean Negulesco directed this re-tread of Fox's familiar tale of three girls in search of wealthy husbands, having regard to the new system by stringing his stars – Marilyn Monroe, Lauren Bacall and Betty Grable – across the wide screen, for example by making them lounge horizontally in their penthouse apartment. Despite Monroe's short-sighted dumb blonde and Bacall's stylish divorcee, the film is only mildly amusing today, but its popularity confirmed that CinemaScope was not a flash in the pan. The profits of 20th Century-Fox rose to a record level, and though it was tempting to retain Cinema-Scope for its exclusive use (the company owned the patent), it did not do so because that would have been contrary to the interests of exhibitors. They were expected to install Stereophonic Sound, the essential accompaniment to the wide screen – although Skouras later capitulated on that requirement. He also announced that all Fox films would be in 'Scope and colour (thus ending the particularly rich but unpretentious visual aspect of its monochrome films of the time), and other

studios jumped on the band wagon till they began to develop wide-screen systems of their own. Skouras balanced the increased budgets by eschewing Technicolor and using a cheaper colour system, De Luxe; the other companies acted similarly, but it was admitted later that Warnercolor and M-G-M's Anscocolor and Metrocolor were merely versions of Kodak's Eastmancolor. Only Paramount stood aloof, retaining Technicolor and using its own patented VistaVision, which used depth of focus in something like the old ratio, so that the exhibitor had the option of increasing the size of the projected image without loss of clarity. The action was restricted to the centre of the ribbon, so that the film could be projected on screens of any width. However, as the standard screen ratio was changed at this time to accommodate exhibitors with screens of variable length, Paramount decided that VistaVision was redundant. Although Technicolor Inc. introduced Technirama, its own wide-screen process in 1957, by the mid-Sixties all films intended to benefit from a panoramic image were using the more economical Panavision.

Like the wide screen, the three-dimensional film had been given experimental showings in the early Talkie era, and in 1953 M-G-M reissued some old 3-D shorts in a package. The wearing of special glasses (disposable, with one cellophane eye green, the other red) did not appear to be offputting – indeed the profits reaped by the first 3-D feature, **Bwana Devil** (1953), a meretricious jungle drama written and produced by an independent, Arch Oboler, were highly encouraging. To even larger and more appreciative audiences Warners offered a remake of *The Mystery of the Wax Museum*, **House of Wax** (1953), directed by André de Toth and starring Vincent Price. These audiences, cowering under an onslaught of ping-pong balls, the legs of can-can dancers, and other missiles, moved on to ooh and aah their way through a few better films, including *Dial M for Murder* (q.v.) and *Kiss Me Kate*. But later films made in 3-D were issued 'flat', to no public protest, and the trade turned its attention to CinemaScope – except, that is, those who believed that the answer to television was Cinerama.

Since Cinerama required the wholesale and costly conversion of a cinema, it was

OLD STANDARD SCREEN

CINEMASCOPE

only selectively adopted and never really looked like the road to salvation. Invented by Fred Waller, it called for a wrap-around floor-to-ceiling screen to take slightly overlapping images from three separate projectors. Its sheer size and the obvious joins limited its use for showing fiction, and the travelogues which clogged the converted cinemas for years on end – they had to, if a profit was to be made – were more effective on scenic railways and runaway trains than on visits to the Vatican. There were some thrilling trips above and across the world's terrain in the series of spectacles which began with **This Is Cinerama** (1952), but a decade later diminishing returns led the Cinerama Company into an agreement with M-G-M for two narrative films. *How the West Was Won* (q.v.) seemed to indicate that there was a future for the process, with takings of $23 million, but at the same time *The Wonderful World of the Brothers Grimm* managed to earn only a meagre $6½ million. While its failure proved that Cinerama was not in itself a box-office attraction, hopes for improving the system were pinned on a single-lens system, used initially for *It's a Mad, Mad, Mad, Mad World* (q.v.). However, though the images were exceptionally well-defined across the giant curved screen, the screen itself detracted from the film's merits (few as they were). Once the size of the screen was reduced, Cinerama became just another wide-screen process and was abandoned after another failure, *The Greatest Story Ever Told* (q.v.).

Cinerama had only ever been a practicable attraction when confined to one theatre within a large catchment area: the requisite higher prices and advanced booking added to the circus-like sense of occasion, causing some showmen to recall the infrequent cinema 'road-shows' which had begun with the early Italian epics and continued till *Gone with the Wind*. Some dozen films a year were exploited in this manner – at least in the big cities – and when the practice was abandoned it was because of the War. A Broadway entrepreneur, Mike Todd (1907–58), decided that the time was ripe for its revival, and persuaded Rodgers and Hammerstein to partner him in filming *Oklahoma!* (q.v.), an epoch-making musical for which they had so far refused all film offers. The 'wide open

spaces' of the stage original were resplendent in a wide-screen system called Todd-AO, and certainly the public's response was sufficiently encouraging for Todd to embark upon **Around the World in 80 Days** (1956). Jules Verne was chosen to emulate the Cinerama travelogues, and among the locations selected (by William Cameron Menzies, the associate producer) were Paris, the temples of Rangoon, the bull ring in Almeria and Mount Fujiyama. James Poe, John Farrow and S. J. Perelman wrote the screenplay, and the director was Michael Anderson, a hitherto little-known Briton. He handles the travels of Phileas Fogg (David Niven) as though they were a stroll around the block, and although he may have been taking his tone from the relaxed manner of his star, the great enterprise is thereby reduced. The film does, however, use its guest stars amusingly. The practice of cramming several names into one movie had been abandoned after a Korean war re-run of the all-star revue – Warners' excruciating *Starlift* – but Todd revived it for publicity purposes. The first guest contracted was Noël Coward, on the correct assumption that if Coward sanctioned the project, others would follow, for less than their customary fees. The range of names goes from Marlene Dietrich to Fernandel and includes, most enjoyably, Buster Keaton as a railroad conductor, Beatrice Lillie as a Salvationist, John Gielgud as Fogg's valet, and Ronald Colman as an Indian railway official (and what a Fogg he might have been!). Todd's gift for publicity was rewarded at the box office and, cynics might think, by the Academy of Motion Picture Arts and Sciences, which voted this the year's Best Film.

The film's success mesmerised the industry. Musicals and biblicals were one thing (deMille's *The Ten Commandments* came out around the same time), but the public was now prepared to pay high seat prices for other spectaculars, most of them requiring a whole evening to see. By the early Sixties about half a dozen films were opening annually, on an advance booking basis, and complete with 'Overture', interval and souvenir programmes. Since 'more' seldom means 'good', the arrangement only survived by virtue of a few huge public successes. The most memorable of these were musicals – the screen versions of the Rodgers and Hammerstein Broadway shows – and it may be rewarding to examine them as a group.

The composer and lyricist were involved in the productions of **Oklahoma!** (1955) and **South Pacific** (1958), which may be why neither seems to have lost a syllable or a note from the original. Both are canned theatre, despite the balmy breezes ruffling the real corn sheaves and palm trees that were only painted on Broadway. *Oklahoma!* has the better director, Fred Zinnemann, and the better cast, headed by Gordon MacRae as the cowboy and Shirley Jones as the girl. Zinnemann handles his material sensitively, but seems to have overlooked the fact that everything that had been innovatory about it in 1943 had in the interim been surpassed on the screen by the M-G-M musical. On the other hand, Joshua Logan treats *South Pacific* as earnestly as if he were handling Greek tragedy – doubtless because he had also directed it on the stage. Logan and Rodgers and Hammerstein had only themselves to blame for the dreary Mitzi Gaynor and Rossano Brazzi in the roles played originally by Mary Martin and Ezio Pinza. As the American nurse who falls in love with a French planter, Miss Martin had provided the show with its greatest charm, though there were those who appreciated the robust chorus of half-naked sailors of whom Logan seemed so fond. Tossing off 'There Is Nothing Like a Dame', they provide a sturdy opening to the film, but when it arrives at the song about Bali Ha'i the screen turns magenta and puce; as cued by a line in the lyric, 'A Cock-Eyed Optimist' is photographed through a filter of canary yellow – and similar procedures are followed till the end of the film. Consequently one longs for the songs to finish so that natural colour will be restored. Nevertheless, the film ran for months in some cities – and for five years at one large London theatre.

The hallmarks of Rodgers and Hammerstein – the unusual choice of material, the ineluctable welding of song and book – did impress anew in **Carousel** (1956) and **The King and I** (1956), both filmed by 20th Century-Fox, who owned the plays on which the shows had been based. As directed respectively by Henry King and Walter Lang, each film is an admirable reflection of Hollywood craftsmanship at its most skilful. The texts are, again, over-faithful, but there is compensation in the Maine harbour settings of *Carousel* and the studio Siamese palaces of *The King and I*, photographed in CinemaScope 55, a high-definition process so expensive that it was immediately abandoned, despite the popularity of both films. The yachts bob on the water and there is an elaborate mating dance to 'June Is Busting Out all Over', which is just one of the songs in a score that I have seldom found less than entrancing. Gordon MacRae and Shirley Jones splendidly head the cast, but *Carousel*, like its source, 'Liliom', concludes in whimsy, which is rendered here with an arty and saccharine ballet likely to destroy the goodwill of all but the most indulgent audiences. The leads are also admirable in *The King and I*, based on *Anna and the King of Siam*: Deborah Kerr is basically theatrical but sincere as the indomitable governess, while Yul Brynner as the king shows warmth, humour and authority, qualities that were rarely apparent in his later screen work.

When Rodgers and Hammerstein's *Flower Drum Song* was converted from mild Broadway success to outright film failure by Universal, in 1952, Rodgers wisely decided – his partner had died – that **The Sound of Music** (1965) would be more safely berthed at 20th Century-Fox. As creative spirits and entrepreneurs this partnership had dominated the musical taste of Broadway for two generations; their taste coincided with that of the public to a marked degree, flattering it in subject matter and never shattering its complacency (even with the then-unusual anti-racialist song in 'South Pacific'). *The Sound of Music* was based on the last of their Broadway shows, which had been disliked by most reviewers. The true story of the von Trapp family offered a certain novelty, featuring nuns, Nazis and a handful of troublesome children, but as interpreted it was undeniably schmaltzy. In an attempt to counteract this, 20th Century-Fox offered the direction in turn to Billy Wilder and William Wyler,★ without success. The screenplay was entrusted to Ernest Lehman, also considered one of the more sophisticated men working in films; his

---

★Wyler in fact accepted, but then decided that he would prefer to do *The Collector* (q.v.).

The Sound of Music was seen by more people than any other film for more than a generation. One reason was Julie Andrews (with her arm raised); another was the direction of Robert Wise, who beyond the 'favourite things' and the Do Re Mes had audiences panting with Austrian patriotism at the end of a mediocre song called 'Edelweiss'. Here is the inevitable 'Do Re Me' that Miss Andrews is singing, accompanied by Charmian Carr, far left, and the other children.

partner on *West Side Story* (q.v.), Robert Wise, turned down the direction three times, and each time the offer of profit participation was increased; yet he accepted only when the illness of Steve McQueen (q.v.) caused the postponement of *The Sand Pebbles* (q.v.). The result is awash with common sense, good advice and 'inspiration'. It has not dated an iota, because it was already old fashioned – with a story similar to several that Mary Pickford did; at one point, as she leaves the convent, Julie Andrews even looks like Pickford.

Julie Andrews (b.1934), is the film's great good fortune, carrying it through the quagmires of taste by seeming thoroughly to enjoy herself and making every half-funny line count for far more than its worth. She lights up the screen in a proverbial manner, the more so because she is surrounded by a lacklustre cast. Christopher Plummer plays the baron with a smug chill rather than what was needed – the charm of the young Anton Walbrook. As the countess who hopes to win him – Blanche Ingram to Julie's Jane Eyre – Eleanor Parker overacts with every eyebrow and elbow, and Richard Haydn is auntish as the family friend. After Miss Andrews, what matters is Salzburg slumbering in the sun, and the lakes and mountains which surround it. The helicopter shot that starts the film, moving

from the crags to the mountain field where the young novice is singing her head off, is one of the great moments in films – and is typical of the care that went into its planning. Many of the other songs are carolled all over the environs – mimed, in fact, to be fitted together later: but instead of being mechanical, Andrews and the children give them an air of spontaneity. We have her word and that of the director that every line of dialogue was examined several times before shooting, and if there are still times when the unwary feel like crawling under their seats that is in the nature of the beast. As far as the industry was concerned, someone did something very right, for the film was to supersede *Gone with the Wind* as the most financially successful film yet made. Unlike the films that overtook both movies a decade later, this was a considerable achievement, for seat prices in the Sixties were not significantly higher than those for Selznick's film on its initial high-price release.

Hollywood itself regarded *The Sound of Music* as a miracle film, voting it six Oscars including Best Picture and Best Direction. Not the last part of the miracle was that an expenditure of $8 million had, by 1969, brought in over $115 million. There were two subsequent reissues in the U.S., and a television showing, before the film was licensed to N.B.C. for a twenty-year period – which would bring a further $25 million – in all, over 1,750% return on investment. The myriad expensive attempts to find the same market failed, but then *The Sound of Music* was an anachronism – it was the last melodious musical, and the children who first saw it grew up to prefer a very different sort of tune.

Despite the felicities in these Rodgers and Hammerstein packages, especially in *Carousel* and *The Sound of Music*, with each of these films the cinema died a little. With the wide screen, the American film became stultified, at least for a time – as will be seen in the next chapter, which takes up the continuing fortunes of CinemaScope. The quality small film – economically budgeted, without star names, in black and white – also made its appearance. The cycle began with **Marty** (1955), which won the most important of the year's Oscars – Best Picture, Best Director, Best Actor, Best Screenplay – and proved that there were big pickings to be had from the simplest ideas. It was written by Paddy Chayevsky (1923–81) from his television play. The play had been seen by someone at the Hecht, Hill and Lancaster organisation who thought that a large screen version would provide both prestige and a means to submit a tax loss in order to offset excessive profits. There was little reason to suppose that it would appeal to more than a minority, since in its own parlance it deals with a couple of 'dogs': an amiable and aimless mother-dominated thirtyish bachelor butcher (Ernest Borgnine) and a painfully shy and awkward spinster (Betsy Blair) whom he meets in a Brooklyn dance hall. With a sympathy rare among writers, Chayevsky observed the nuances of speech, the uncertain interplay of characters not brought up to command the world. Admittedly *On the Waterfront* (q.v.) had already introduced an inarticulate hero, but for the first time in films Brooklyn and Bronx accents were no longer confined to floozies and cab drivers.

Since Chayevsky's style – 'What'ya doin' tonight, Marty?' – was so much parodied, it is astonishing how well his films revive, and I like even better **The Bachelor Party** (1957), made by the same team which included Delbert Mann, who had also directed both television versions. He moves the action from poky flat to Greenwich Village loft to subway to a men's toilet; we had never seen them before, at least not like this, and what most impresses is the delineation of the daily grind. Four accountants accompany a fifth on a bachelor party – away from wives and night school – yet despite the occasion their individual worries are never quite suppressed. These are best summed up by the oldest and most respectable of the group, Walter (E.G. Marshall), who, drunk, is more than ever conscious of his doctor's recommendation to move to Arizona: 'What does it all mean? . . . "Sound and fury" . . . yeah, I read a book. You think I ain't read a book? Everyone thought I'd be the first Catholic president.' The morning after the bachelor party, nothing has changed: we are a great remove from Clifford Odets, since these people are as far as ever from knowing what they want from life.

The success of *Marty* encouraged a slew of television dramas refashioned for the large screen until, low costs and high praise notwithstanding, they failed to arouse much activity at the box office. Many of them were worthy, but lacked Chayevsky's affectionate yet pessimistic attitudes. His effect upon the choice of subject matter was strong, but too often the films emerged as fictionalised versions of agony-column problems – infidelity in *Strangers When We Meet* (q.v.) and abortion in *Love with the Proper Stranger* (q.v.). Chayevsky's real influence was not truly to be felt till the Seventies, when young talents coming into the industry tried again to treat everyday problems with more honesty.

The American cinema stagnated during the Eisenhower years. At their onset, McCarthyism was so harrying the industry that few could consider it calmly enough to turn it to dramatic account (even in allegorical form), and by the time the country was reflecting upon the consequences of the Korean War, Hollywood was engrossed in its contest with television. Later, the assassinations of John and Robert Kennedy and Martin Luther King were too terrible to be assimilated quickly, and as the nation began to absorb the horrors of Vietnam and political corruption, Hollywood occupied itself with its own collapse – the staggering losses, and struggles for control over the faltering studios. The television-inspired small-budget dramas – there is no generic name – were, during this period of confusion and false calm, the sole exemplars of responsible cinema – that is, apart from the works of the major directors.

Given the autonomy then granted to this group of film-makers, in retrospect the results can be seen to be not nearly as good as they should have been. The battle against crass producers had been fought and largely won. There is a significant line in *The Big Knife* (q.v.) stating that the only reason for being in films is to work for 'Wyler or Wilder, Stevens, Kazan, Ford or Zinnemann'. Such directors were, in the main, intelligent men working on projects aimed at intelligent audiences. They were still hampered by censorship, but they undertook their work with the responsibility which was Capra's legacy to them. They tried to make films which, if not of any marked social import, were more entertaining than the studio products –

and the growing number of discerning filmgoers looked forward to these movies and discussed them avidly afterwards. Still, the tastes these directors displayed were almost as limited as those of the moguls thirty years earlier – precisely because it was at that time that most of them had started to work in films. There were probably few brighter or younger film-makers than John Huston or Joseph L. Mankiewicz, and they too had been in films since the early Thirties.

That statement in *The Big Knife* should certainly have included Mankiewicz, who, when he left 20th Century-Fox, in 1953, was admired as no other film-maker since Capra. He moved to M-G-M to direct **Julius Caesar** (1953) for the producer John Houseman, who had persuaded the company that a Shakespeare film could be made comparatively cheaply (the *Quo Vadis?* costumes in Rome had only to be shipped across). Houseman did not want the drama to be swamped by production, so he refused the offer of Technicolor, but though adopting the contemporary 'black and white of newsreel and television screens' the film refuses to draw political parallels. Mankiewicz, renowned for his handling of dialogue and players, was an ideal choice. Despite all the care taken in selecting the cast, he thought its members sufficiently disparate to insist upon three-weeks' rehearsal (almost unheard of in Hollywood) – during which time, apparently, John Gielgud's expertise and encouragement set the tone of the production. It is a film of quiet excellence, faltering only in the later moments when budget restrictions hampered the handling of the battle sequences. As Brutus, James Mason is somewhat self-consciously noble, but his scenes with Gielgud's superb Cassius are particularly splendid, negotiating the verse as in no other Shakespeare film to date except Olivier's, and as effortlessly projecting thought and feeling. The Antony of Marlon Brando is astonishingly convincing and there are sound interpretations of Caesar and Casca by Louis Calhern and Edmond O'Brien respectively. Greer Garson (Calphurnia) and Deborah Kerr (Portia) were cast to bolster the film's box-office chances. It did extremely well, and though some Hollywood companies have been involved in the occasional Shakespeare films made since

then, none has been made in America as a major studio production.

Mankiewicz failed to agree with M-G-M on the two other projects for which he was contracted, and so United Artists agreed to finance two films which he would write and direct for his own company. Since he had made a wise and witty film about a Broadway star, *All About Eve*, there was considerable interest when it was known that **The Barefoot Contessa** (1954) was about a movie queen. As with *Eve* Mankiewicz used a favourite device, the flashback, to tell the tale with the wisdom of hindsight. The story chiefly involves three people: the star (Ava Gardner) – a role based partially on Rita Hayworth – with peasant beginnings, sensuality, a kind heart and a complex about men; her director and discoverer (Humphrey Bogart), an ex-alcoholic who finds that he can be bought – by a Howard Hughes-like producer – when confronted with lies and innuendo; and the European aristocrat (Rossano Brazzi) whom she marries. The result, however, is an overlong thesis on movie stardom, its parts not relevant to the whole nor referring to each other. 'In a nutshell,' as Bogart puts it, 'the plot is that life louses up the script' – which is clever, since Mankiewicz points to the confusion experienced by such people. As Mankiewicz moves from movie people to international society he appears to pursue gossip for its own sake, but in his own opinion the second part of the film is weakened by the casting of Brazzi (James Mason turned down the role) and the fact that he could only hint at the character's impotency.

To an extent **The Quiet American** (1958) is a very good film. The Saigon of Graham Greene's novel, with its seedy restaurants and apartments, is superbly conveyed, and much of Greene's dialogue has been retained. 'Twenty-two million people: all they need is to survive,' observes the Englishman (Michael Redgrave), obstinate but vague in conscience, pitting himself against the American (Audie Murphy), all puppy-eagerness, patronising and devious. The Englishman betrays him to the Communists, supposedly from jealousy, at which point the film makes nonsense of what has gone before and of Greene's powerful criticism of entrepreneurs like the American and his countrymen's intervention above and below the line. Greene's furious letter to *The Times* irredeemably damaged the film's chances in Britain, where success might have compensated for its failure in the U.S.

The Barefoot Contessa had failed equally, and after both instances Mankiewicz surrendered his independence, working respectively for Sam Goldwyn and Sam Spiegel. Goldwyn had outbid all competitors for Frank Loesser's Damon Runyon musical, **Guys and Dolls** (1955), and added to the then-record price of $800,000, plus residuals, he set a budget of $5 million. It was his first film in three years, and just as Mike Todd had hired Zinnemann for *Oklahoma!* he engaged a director associated not with musicals but with prestigious films. Mankiewicz, who wrote his own screenplay, enjoyed working with Goldwyn, but between them they made two errors. A musical is not, or should not be, a story punctuated by songs, but a celebration of a time when life is cosier and happier – and the only way to express yourself is to burst into song. This film is more respectful of Runyon than Loesser, even dropping three of the songs (including that incomparable expression of dawn in Manhattan, 'My Time of Day'). The settings are largely plastic-abstract, except for Miss Adelaide's nightclub, where Hollywood's usual lavish decor replaces the cheerful tattiness it had onstage. At least Vivian Blaine's Miss Adelaide and beaming, chubby Stubby Kaye's Nicely Nicely Johnson are retained; and as the Salvation Army lass, Jean Simmons also shows that she was having a wonderful time. Marlon Brando's* way of playing comedy is to raise a supercilious eyebrow, and Frank Sinatra, lacking all the gutsiness that Sam Levene had in the role, is simply bland.

Spiegel, who regarded himself as a latter-day Goldwyn, had bought a one-act play by Tennessee Williams, who wrote the screenplay with Gore Vidal. So, for the first time in a decade, Mankiewicz worked on a film only as director (he had fashioned the screenplay of *Julius Caesar*): **Suddenly Last Summer** (1959). Not for nothing is

the exposition set in a hothouse, complete with Venus flytrap, but the direction is always in control of the excesses. The play had been a study of hysteria, of the suppressed emotions apparently common to many people; there may have been no need to add cannibalism to incestuous love and neurotic imbalance, but it is not dramatically invalid. Unfortunately, the film shows in flashback what the play only mentioned and, as the hysteric, Elizabeth Taylor discloses so little feeling that we do not care whether her outburst is a quest for truth or mere vindictiveness. Before witnesses, she and the mother (Katharine Hepburn) of the dead Sebastian argue over the suspicion that his passion for young men led to his being eaten on an African beach. The M.P.A.A. had refused to allow the Brazzi character in *The Barefoot Contessa* to be homosexual, and had in the interim refused similar implications in the film of Williams's *Cat on a Hot Tin Roof* (q.v.), but it was permitted in this instance.

Mankiewicz then began moulding Lawrence Durrell's Alexandria Quartet into a screenplay, until called upon to rescue **Cleopatra** (1963) – the making of which is considerably more interesting than what finally emerged on screen. Two books have been written on the subject, one by Walter Wanger, who was returning to large-scale production. Wanger first announced the project in September 1958 as a modestly-budgeted spectacle starring either Joan Collins or Dana Wynter, but then decided that he preferred Elizabeth Taylor – whose agent put her fee at one million dollars. Both she and 20th Century-Fox liked the attendant publicity so much that neither cared that the contract drawn up stipulated much less – that she did earn much more was due to expenses and huge fees when shooting went over schedule. That began in September 1960 at Pinewood, on a budget of $6 million, with Rouben Mamoulian directing, Peter Finch as Caesar and Stephen Boyd as Antony. When Mamoulian abandoned it the following spring – with Taylor's illness a contributory factor – $7 million had been spent, with only twelve minutes of film to show for it, which Mankiewicz, taking over, considered unusable. Filming recommenced in Rome, with Finch and Boyd replaced in turn by Rex Harrison and Richard Burton. Eventually Wanger was

*For the role Goldwyn had wanted Gene Kelly, who wanted to play it, but his contract was held by M-G-M, whose boss, Nicholas Schenck, harboured grudges against both Goldwyn and Mankiewicz. Ironically, a deal was made for M-G-M to release the film.

sacked, Spyros Skouras fired as head of 20th Century-Fox, and as the final cost came to around $37 million, Mankiewicz was taken off the film. He could not therefore oversee the editing, but was later permitted to carry out some minor adjustments at Pinewood in the spring of 1963, two months before the film's premiere. There were a number of million-dollar lawsuits over the film, but all were dropped or settled out of court. One of them accused Taylor and her paramour, Burton, of devaluing the film by their behaviour – but the charge itself is debatable, since Taylor's defection from her then husband, Eddie Fisher, provided a bonanza of publicity. However, the fact remains that while this dull film might just have been acceptable with another actress, it was doomed when she was cast. For almost four hours we are subjected to the whims, ambitions, amours, tantrums and follies of the Egyptian queen, yet not for an instant does she command interest or sympathy. 'You have broken out of your nursery to irritate the adults' says Caesar – and that is fair comment.

Mankiewicz did not like sharing the screenplay credit with Ranald MacDougall and Sidney Buchman, who had worked on it before he arrived: but equally they must share the blame for some jarring modern idioms – which, since Mankiewicz wrote and rewrote, often on the set, he had neither the will nor the stamina to avoid. His direction is so graceful, however, that it seems unfair that the film's reception should have dented his considerable reputation. 20th Century-Fox had persevered with this project after a series of flops, hoping that it would do for them what *Ben-Hur* (q.v.) had done for M-G-M's finances, but it did not turn a profit till sold to television, and has proved to have no revival value.

Mankiewicz once commented that the film was 'conceived in a state of panic, shot in confusion, and wound up in blind panic', but he has since refused to discuss it publicly. He is equally unhappy about **The Honey Pot** (1967), with which he returned to independence, since the distributor, United Artists, insisted on removing the framework of the original script (in which an American theatre owner discusses aspects of the script with the film's leading actor), and then almost twenty minutes were cut after the London premiere. It remains much too long, a protracted joke about a modern Volpone (Rex Harrison) who sends for three former mistresses to tell them that he will leave one of them his fortune. They are inexpertly played by Susan Hayward, Edie Adams and Capucine, but even the scenes between Maggie Smith (as the secretary of one of them) and Harrison are strained, despite some typically civilised dialogue. As the Mosca character, a former gigolo (though the reference to this is no longer in the present version) and the actor who is stage-managing the deception for Harrison, Cliff Robertson was encouraged to impersonate Mankiewicz himself. The film is much richer than either the (modern) play or the novel on which Mankiewicz based it, but nevertheless it confirms that he was in love with his own talent. He had every reason to be: but he was a better film-maker when he was less so.

His experiences on both films convinced Mankiewicz not to direct his own scripts again – and with **There Was a Crooked Man . . .** (1970) it is interesting to see him at the service of a strong screenplay by David Newman and Robert Benton. It was their first credited work after *Bonnie and Clyde* (q.v.), and their purpose was the same: to destroy the old myths while creating new ones – in this case that of the Old West. The men stink downwind and have no loyalties except unto themselves. The film, much aided by Henry Fonda's performance as the corruptible governor, is more subtle and polished than the similar *Cool Hand Luke* (q.v.), also backed by Warners, with Mankiewicz's cynicism providing a neat gloss to the enthusiastic script. **Sleuth** (1972) was written by Anthony Shaffer from his long-running play, and any cynicism would have destroyed its simplistic cat-and-mouse twists. The play's renown was reason enough to attract Mankiewicz, together with the casting of Laurence Olivier and Michael Caine as cat and mouse respectively. Apart from their participation however there was no good reason to go and see it. Mankiewicz's subsequent retirement has not been voluntary, but among the projects he has turned down is *The Front Page* (q.v.), which Wilder took on after Mankiewicz decided that the material had lost its freshness.

With more reason, the reputation of George Stevens did not survive this period intact. Riding on the crest of his success with *A Place in the Sun* he made **Something to Live For** (1952), which failed, though in my opinion it is better than the earlier film and those he made thereafter. Its lush Victor Young score and Dwight Taylor's screenplay imply that soap opera was intended, as a husband (Ray Milland) is tempted to leave his wife (Teresa Wright) for an actress (Joan Fontaine). The lovers teeter on the edge of a precipice, not because of infidelity but because of their shared alcoholism, a terror which Stevens conveys with understanding. He also understands both Manhattan, pictured alternately with acrid realism and glamorous virtuosity, and his stars, stripping from them the fossilised and film-starry mannerisms they had learnt to use under other directors. Few films better illustrate the changes that can be wrought on sub-standard material by sensitive and polished direction.

Shane (1953) was acclaimed as a classic Western from its first appearance. Two aspects separated it from other essays in the genre: its deliberately mythic treatment of the stranger (Alan Ladd) who rides in, stays to help, and then moves out again into the blue, and the related viewing of events through the eyes of a child (Brandon de Wilde). Stevens was much congratulated on choosing a 'superior' Western novel – by Jack Schaefer – to which was added an excellent script by A. B. Guthrie, Jr, and 'picturesque' photography by Loyal Griggs, who was awarded an Oscar for it. What the film lacks is momentum, and one gets the feeling that life has been crushed out of it by its production values. The suspicion that Stevens gave precedence to producing over directing was confirmed in **Giant** (1956), a formless version of a novel by Edna Ferber. The title refers to Texas, but if Stevens had any feeling about the way the discovery of oil had coarsened and changed its society, it is lost in the welter of themes – commerce vs. agriculture, racial prejudice, female emancipation, the *nouveau riche*, the emptiness of ambition . . . As the central couple, Elizabeth Taylor and Rock Hudson are not players of sufficient calibre to engage our attention for three hours (the over-long running time), and as they age, their hair becoming bluer, they hardly resemble real people. The role played by James Dean – in youth the outsider, in middle-age the magnate – is poorly motivated and interpreted. *Shane* at least has an innate simplicity and a spirit of adventure; *Giant* has neither, and having raised a large number of questions, it suddenly stops, as if hoping that sheer length has bludgeoned audiences into approval.

Shane had been Stevens's last film for Paramount; *Giant* was to have been the first of several projects for Warner Bros. Both studios regarded him as a prestigious director, whose invariably warm notices were reflected in the box-office takings; but the profits of both films, though considerable, were eroded by his increasingly fastidious production methods. Accordingly he moved to 20th Century-Fox to make **The Diary of Anne Frank** (1959), working, alas, from the stage version by Frances Goodrich and Albert Hackett, who also wrote the screenplay. They have added a commentary, from the young Dutch girl's own words, but even with that addition the film is pallid. It merely plods through the routines and small events of the Frank and Van Daan families hidden away at the top of the warehouse in Amsterdam, and in the process destroys an earlier inference that they are meant to represent all the Jews marked out for elimination. The use of Cinema-Scope, albeit in black and white, contradicts the fundamental feeling of claustrophobia and intimacy, and a more serious error was the casting of Millie Perkins as Anne. This ex-model was chosen, sensibly, so as not to associate Anne with a known actress, but Miss Perkins has a jarring accent (even to American ears) and the gamine looks fashionable in 1959. The direction is expectedly careful and tasteful, but again lacking in feeling: a book which haunts all who have read it has become a forgettable film.

The same accusation may be levelled at **The Greatest Story Ever Told** (1965). It was Stevens's not unambitious intention to chronicle the Gospel better than the admittedly poor previous screen attempts. Since his screenplay, written in collaboration with James Lee Barrett, was based on Fulton Oursler's bestseller, critical expectations were not high, even with Carl Sandburg as artistic adviser. As costs

855

rose during the years of preparation, 20th Century-Fox lost interest, and sold the project to Cinerama, who arranged with United Artists to share the eventual budget of $24 million. It was the second most expensive film (after *Cleopatra*) made by a U.S. company, and at 225 minutes the longest since the days of Von Stroheim.

Stevens had gone for broke and lost: faced with disastrous notices, the 'exclusive' Cinerama showings were abandoned – in favour of Ultra Panavision 70 – in an effort to recoup costs before the public realised how bad it was. United Artists began whittling away at the length, eventually arriving at 141 minutes, thereby removing some of the guest stars – but not, alas, John Wayne's centurion, whose delivery of his one line ('This truly was the sahn of Gahd') is of staggering banality. Many of the others are hardly better. In Max von Sydow the film has an austere, sincere Christ; and in taking pains to duplicate nineteenth-century religious paintings Stevens presumably achieved his object in giving the least offence to most people. But the film is as dull as it is reverent, with a particularly crass ending: 'The fuss will all be forgotten in a month's time' says someone, and the answer comes back quickly, 'I wonder . . .'

The resounding failure of this film affected Stevens far more than that of *Cleopatra* had hurt Mankiewicz, since at least a number of patrons had turned up to see *Cleopatra* out of curiosity. But it was the star of that film, Elizabeth Taylor, who enabled Stevens to work again by insisting that he direct one of her films, thereby proving as loyal to her colleagues – she had similarly tried to help the actor Montgomery Clift in his sad last years – as she is uninteresting on screen. A former child player, she had stayed in the public eye by virtue of good looks and a number of highly publicised marriages and divorces. Her film appearances made considerably less impact on the public until she began to have some isolated box-office successes just before and after *Cleopatra*; yet her films had already begun to fail★ by

★The paucity of female stars was one reason that Hollywood hoped Taylor would remain popular. The industry was similarly blinkered with the equally untalented Natalie Wood and Debbie Reynolds, also being paid huge salaries long after the public had lost interest. Earlier, scripts passed from Taylor to Audrey Hepburn to Marilyn Monroe to Shirley MacLaine (or vice versa), and it is hard to imagine four more disparate personalities or talents.

the time 20th Century-Fox agreed to let Stevens direct her in **The Only Game in Town** (1970). Her ability to create headlines apparently meant more to this studio than the notices of critics, which had seldom been kind. The terms granted her on this occasion were even more farcical than usual, starting with the $500,000 20th Century-Fox paid for Frank D. Gilroy's original play before it opened on Broadway (where it ran for one week). Despite the evidence of its own *Cleopatra*, the company decided that Taylor's presence in the film would help it recoup its investment and a deal was worked out whereby she and Richard Burton, now her husband, were to share $2½ million for her appearance in this and his in *Staircase*. At their request, and despite the fact that the settings were respectively Las Vegas and London, the films were to be made in Paris – at much extra cost (as was pointed out at a stockholders' meeting) since everything down to door handles had to be imported. Eventually *The Only Game in Town*, with a cast of only two and having virtually only one set, cost $8 million. The studio disliked the result so much that it was kept on the shelf, with not even a token showing to qualify it for the Academy Awards. When at last it did open it took a meagre $1½ million; that at least was considerably more than the earnings from *Staircase*.

Such plot as there is concerns an ageing, aimless showgirl and her relationship with a compulsive gambler (Warren Beatty). Stevens, who had hitherto coaxed two reasonable performances from Taylor, on this occasion only ensures that she does not fluff her lines. She remains a dull, shrill woman, her dead eyes giving no reason why she had chosen this particular profession. Apart from this, the piece seems very well directed, with the smooth mixture of intimate detail and bravura that distinguished *Something to Live For*: it is pleasing to see an old master return to such form in his last film.

Concentration and confidence were also the qualities most evident with William Wyler, who made one of his best late films with an actress of a different quality, Audrey Hepburn (b. 1929), making her Hollywood debut after some small parts in Britain. The film is **Roman Holiday** (1953) – a reversion to that old movie staple, royalty travelling incognito. Ian

McLellan Hunter and John Dighton wrote the screenplay, and Wyler's touch is neither light nor in any other way reminiscent of Lubitsch; that the piece serves romance better than comedy is due to this actress of heartbreaking enchantment. Miss Hepburn won a Best Actress Oscar as the princess escaping from protocol, grave, wistful and unworldly but very sure of herself. As the American reporter who doesn't let on because he wants her story, Gregory Peck is at his best. Wyler was equally dependent on his leading players in **The Desperate Hours** (1955), but the requirements were vastly different. Humphrey Bogart, in one of his gratifying appearances as a man with no redeeming quality, is one of a criminal gang which holes up with an ordinary suburban family, headed by Fredric March. The material, as adapted by Joseph Hayes from his Broadway play, is not otherwise very effective, and its inferiority to most that Wyler handled reveals his shortcomings at this stage of his career. Despite his attempt at realism, there is nothing beneath the surface: the characters behave convincingly but cease to exist once the cameras stopped turning.

Wyler's shortcomings are also evident in a better film, **Friendly Persuasion** (1956), his first independent production, made under the auspices of Allied Artists, formerly known as Monogram. The name had been changed in 1953, and two years later Walter Mirisch, the company's vice-president, courted three of Hollywood's most admired directors in an effort to move into the major league. He was unsuccessful, although, in the end, Wyler's film was not as great a failure as Wilder's *Love in the Afternoon* (q.v.) – after which the company decided not to proceed with John Huston's *Typee*.

Friendly Persuasion also created a number of problems. Jessamyn West's novel about a Quaker family in the Civil War had been originally – like *Roman Holiday* – one of Capra's projects at Liberty Films. A law suit was brought by Michael Wilson, claiming that the current screenplay – by Jessamyn West and Wyler's brother Robert – was based on the one he had prepared earlier at Capra's behest. As Wilson had been blacklisted in the McCarthy purges of 1951, Allied Artists counterclaimed that his name was a commercial

liability – and so the film went out without a screenplay credit. The budget had risen to double the $1½ million originally estimated, and the film looked like being a disaster, until it won the Grand Prix at Cannes. Business improved further when Pat Boone's recording of Dmitri Tiomkin's title song charmed its way into the hit parade. Mr Boone's voice accompanying the credits is part of Wyler's calculated assault on audience sensibilities. As with Stevens and Capra, the failure of Liberty Films influenced each decision Wyler made thereafter, but in striving for popularity he has made this family, under their sombre garb, as saccharine and cuddlesome as the Hardys. Gary Cooper and Dorothy McGuire are pleasing enough players and the social milieu is more interesting than in many American films of the time: but it might have been just as well to leave the Quakers to themselves instead of turning them from plain to fancy.

William Wyler continued to hold his pre-eminent position during his later career, choosing his subjects with care and handling them with skill and affection. If his work became overly academic it is because his pace is in direct contrast to his early films. *Roman Holiday* would have benefited from that speed, but it is nevertheless engaging, partly because of Audrey Hepburn, as a princess befriended by American journalist, Gregory Peck.

857

Given Wyler's attitude, it is no surprise to find that **The Big Country** (1958) is only too aptly named. Inside this long, inert and grandiose movie is a small, short and entertaining story about earnest pioneers and greedy cattle barons. Its major defects are its pretentiousness and the performance of its star – elements which come together in the person of Gregory Peck, who co-produced with Wyler (a relationship which ended in bitterness). In Wyler's only major sound Western, *The Westerner*, Gary Cooper allowed himself to be used: the stars of Peck's generation consented only to being handled. Peck is well cast in *The Big Country* as an Easterner, a man of good will who tries to bring peace to the big country, but his nobility is, as always, tiresome. There are also too many close-ups of him appearing wise and given to philosophies which are at once self-aggrandising and much too modern for the film's supposed period. As his opponent, Charlton Heston is given very few close-ups or homilies.

The bigness of **Ben-Hur** (1959) was a different matter. When financial tremors shook M-G-M in the late Fifties, its new president, Joseph R. Vogel, promised shareholders a new *Ben-Hur*. Thinking big usually brought commensurate results: the company had done so with *Quo Vadis?*, whose producer, Sam Zimbalist, was assigned to this project. To direct he wanted Wyler, who resisted, but because of the chariot race (though already under way with the second unit, headed by Andrew Marton and Yakima Canutt) finally accepted; as he said later, 'Basically, of course, it was an adventure yarn.' The chariot race *is* tremendous, but otherwise an 'adventure yarn' is treated as holy writ, making heavier weather of its nineteenth-century moralising than the infinitely superior Silent version. One might have supposed it directed at Sunday-school teachers – though of course the plot ensures the Jewish vote. By what seems like mischance, Wyler keeps the heavenly choir silent till the final shot, and he did bring in Christopher Fry (to whom the Screen Writers Guild would not allow a credit) to make decent language out of Karl Tunberg's screenplay. However, some people were impressed, among them those who vote for the Hollywood Oscars, of which it won eleven, including Best Actor

(Charlton Heston), Best Picture, Best Director and Best Supporting Actor (Hugh Griffith). The $15 million investment (until the advent of *Cleopatra* it was the most expensive film made) had yielded a profit of approximately the same amount by the time it was sold to television. Vogel had been justified. Others were merely grateful that the *nouvelle vague* was now rising: it was not to drown dinosaurs like this, but it would keep them in their place.

It was in the wake of such films – not to mention those of Antonioni and Bergman – that **The Children's Hour** (1962) was foisted upon audiences. Wanting to do a 'little' film after *Ben-Hur*, Wyler chose to remake *These Three*, restoring the lesbian theme. The property was purchased from Goldwyn for $350,000, and Lillian Hellman, author of the original, was engaged to write the screenplay – but upon the death of Dashiell Hammett the job was assigned to John Michael Hayes. Miss Hellman loathed this film, and Wyler respected her reasons: 'I had been too faithful to the original and made no attempt to modernise and bring it up to date.' Her stage play, like many of the time, depended on confrontations, hidden secrets and revelations, with characters to root for and characters to detest: consequently *These Three* is enjoyable, but this film version, slow and serious, only emphasises the meretricious nature of the material. Wyler was initially hurt and surprised by the film's reception, feeling that he had been brave in filming a story about a community shocked by the discovery of lesbianism in its midst, but neither the play nor this film goes further than *thoughts* of deviant love on the part of one of the teachers. Shirley MacLaine plays this decent, ordinary girl. As the other, Audrey Hepburn looks like a model, and as the man who walks into their relationship James Garner looks less like a doctor than someone advertising beer.

Wyler tried to make amends with **The Collector** (1965), again demonstrating care but little regard for the sensibilities of modern audiences. He had found himself 'fascinated' by the unsolicited screenplay sent to him by Stanley Mann and John Kohn, based on John Fowles's novel, in itself an English variation on the Proust-Albertine situation. The result, with little resemblance to Fowles, rests uneasily between suspense story and contemplative melodrama, while the casting of little-known players – Terence Stamp, Samantha Eggar – is insufficient proof of integrity. **How to Steal a Million** (1966) was written by Harry Kurnitz, and is ample demonstration of Kenneth Tynan's observation that his real-life wit seldom found its way into his screenplays. Once, memorably, Wyler took Audrey Hepburn to Rome, but here they are forgettable in Paris – except that she is, as ever, a pleasure to watch, if hardly varying her inevitable comedy role, the wide-eyed innocent. As her co-star, Peter O'Toole is, in the words of the critic John Gillett, 'more winsome than winning'.

Having turned down *The Sound of Music*, Wyler accepted a second offer of a screen version of a Broadway musical, **Funny Girl** (1968). The producer of the show and the film was Ray Stark, whose (deceased) mother-in-law, Fanny Brice, was the funny girl of the title. It is a meat-and-drink role: a ghetto girl who becomes a Ziegfeld star, in the process getting hooked on a no-good gambler. Fanny is (as in life) undoubtedly and unashamedly Jewish, and thus in the film becomes the first Jewish heroine (since the Silent era) to express herself in the East Side dialect. Her quick, put-down humour is marvellously conveyed by Barbra Streisand (who had played the role on Broadway) and that, coupled with the razzmatazz numbers in Jules Styne's superb score, makes the first half of this long entertainment quite enjoyable; but her moping in the second half is wearing. Acting straight, Streisand is so completely without feeling that by the time she gets to her *pièce de résistance* – 'My Man', rightly interpolated – one could not care less, even if her squealed rendition were not far below Garland, Faye, Mistinguett and Miss Brice herself. Almost all the songs not done by her in the original have gone (including the marvellous 'Who Taught You Everything You Know?'), while others have been elaborated to make her shine even more brightly. The battles between her and Wyler during shooting were due, it was said, to her experience of audience reaction to her best effects, and they are in the film for all to see – glaringly.

The film's popularity heartened Wyler, but its reception by reviewers confirmed the impression that he was *passé*; trying to rectify that, he did a tale about a contemporary social problem, **The Liberation of L. B. Jones** (1970), based on Jesse Hill Ford's novel on racial prejudice in southern Tennessee. Since Stirling Silliphant had recently won an Oscar for his not dissimilar script for *In the Heat of the Night*, he was assigned to this one. In its excellent exposition L. B. Jones (Roscoe Lee Brown) wants a divorce, and since his wife wants alimony, he is forced to cite a white cop (Anthony Zerbe) who, together with his lawyer (Lee J. Cobb), is determined to prevent this. The result increasingly resembled overheated melodramas like *The Chase* (q.v.) and, when it was dismissed as old fashioned, Wyler decided to retire. However, the film has merit, and he had proved, like Stevens and Mankiewicz in their very last films, that his old skill and sensitivity remained intact.

Frank Capra also found himself redundant and made his exit, though in his case he refused to compromise or submit to the exigencies of the stars concerned. He had been engaged on scientific documentaries for some years when offered **A Hole in the Head** (1959) in partnership with its star, Frank Sinatra. Arnold Shulman adapted his own Broadway play about a small-time Florida wheeler-dealer, but at the insistence of star and director the characters were changed from Jewish to Italian – and given a happy ending. Whether Sinatra plays Jew or Italian is immaterial, since he acts in his own leading-man style – i.e. with quizzical, casual charm – which is hardly what this particular wheeler-dealer needs. Capra did manage the sentiment and comedy adroitly, and virtually for the first time humour seemed compatible with the wide screen.

The film made a small profit, but since it did not, in Capra's opinion, re-establish him, he embarked upon a remake of his *Lady for a Day* (paying Columbia $225,000 for the rights, as opposed to the $15,000 originally paid to Damon Runyon). **A Pocketful of Miracles** (1961), as the film was called, is pleasant, but unnecessarily attenuated, being half an hour longer than the earlier version. Glenn Ford is bouncy, though not miscast as Capra implies in his memoir; Bette Davis makes the same mistake as May Robson – after the transformation the old lady is too regal.

Thomas Mitchell and Edward Everett Horton are among the veterans in support, and Peter Falk – Capra's 'joy, my anchor to reality' – has Ned Sparkes's old role of right-hand man. He is also the anchor of the film. Capra had looked upon it as a gamble, because the subject was old fashioned, and considers that United Artists did not market it properly. 'My people,' he said, 'did not come' – because he had compromised: 'this was not the film I set out to make; it was the picture I chose to make for fear of losing a few bucks. And by that choice I sold out the artistic integrity that had been my trademark for forty years.' He goes on, 'When Glenn Ford made me lick his boots – I had lost that precious quality that endows dreams with purport and purpose.' Earlier Capra had bowed out of a filmed life of Jimmy Durante when he realised that his stars, Frank Sinatra, Bing Crosby and Dean Martin, had reserved the right to co-produce so that all decisions were subject to the agreement of all parties. Later he left *Circus World* when John Wayne preferred another script to the one that he had prepared. But his memoir makes clear that it was his experience with Glenn Ford which scarred him.

Capra's old idol, Walt Disney, became richer as his films became worse. In 1954 he began the first of his hugely successful forays into television; the following year he opened Disneyland in California (Walt Disney World was opened in Florida in 1971, five years after his death). Disney also increased his live-action programme to some half dozen or more films a year – many of them popular, if negligible as entertainment. His catalogue of feature-length cartoons proved literally invaluable, as it became clearer than ever that they could be reissued at intervals to new generations of children – a mixed blessing, since the later cartoons are as poor as the early ones are good. Stylistically they wander from self-plagiarism to strip cartoon, and seem to have little care for colour or the integration of the cute and coy creatures set to gambol in the foreground; mediocre songs are simply thrown in (no less than seven people adapted Tchaikovsky for *The Sleeping Beauty*) amidst the tired whimsy and uninspired knockabouts. Singularly objectionable are Disney's half-hour cartoons based on

A. A. Milne's Winnie-the-Pooh stories, since the animation vulgarises Ernest H. Shepard's original illustrations.★

In over thirty years only two of Disney's full-length cartoons have been well received: **The Lady and the Tramp** (1955) and **One Hundred and One Dalmatians** (1961), both with largely canine casts. I for one find the former highly resistible on the whole: no advantage is taken of the wide screen, the settings are cheapest Woolworth Christmas card, and the romantic leads, a spaniel and a mongrel, absolutely deserve the future they were to have as miniature china ornaments. The film does have an occasional *frisson* of horror and two amusing songs, written and sung by Peggy Lee – one as two haughty Siamese cats and the other as a blowsy blues singer. Such moments of taste and invention occur gratifyingly often in *One Hundred and One Dalmatians*, which, along with *Alice in Wonderland*, is the only Disney cartoon since *Bambi* worth preserving. Extra care may have been taken because of the remarkably bad reviews for *The Sleeping Beauty*, or possibly the Disney team was inspired by Dodie Smith's story, the strongest plot line since the heyday of the studio, concerning the kidnapping of some puppies and the subsequent chase over half the English countryside. The villainess is loathsome in the right way, and wittily drawn; and there are rare touches of satire – as in the Osbert Lancaster-inspired London, replacing the particularly insipid one which had appeared in *Peter Pan*.

Mary Poppins (1964) is live action except for one animated sequence, of the customary visual level, seemingly influenced by the British adverts for Babycham. The film's source is another stout English original – P. L. Travers's stories of the flying governess who, in her own words, is 'practically perfect in every way'. As crisply delivered by Julie Andrews, the line brooks no argument, and indeed she is irresistible as the self-confident nanny who offers her charges a life of enchantment. Directed by Robert Stevenson, the film is a mite heavy, but like *One Hundred and One Dalmations* it demeans neither its subject nor its audiences – which may be why it was the most

★Which under a licensing agreement the Disney organisation now controls, and while not suppressing them is able to flood the book market with its own inferior imitations.

financially successful of all the Disney films.

Another veteran entertainer, Alfred Hitchcock, increased his hold on the public, who in the Fifties again felt that his name guaranteed an evening of enjoyable mayhem. Many of his admirers find this his richest period, but I find almost all of his later films lumbering, literal and not nearly as clever in evoking thrills as they think they are. In fact, seeing his films of the Fifties again has been for the most part a disappointment, except for the presence of Grace Kelly (1928–82), the cool, elegant blonde for whom he had been subconsciously searching for years. In **Dial M for Murder** (1954) she is an intended murder victim who turns the tables on the assassin (Anthony Dawson) hired by her husband (Ray Milland). Aided by a crisp performance by John Williams as the Scotland Yard man, the film's twists are enjoyable – despite a cheap back-projection London and the fact that it is no more than a filmed play. Frederick Knott wrote it – and sold it to Korda for £1,000 before it became a success on both sides of the Atlantic; his chagrin when Warners bought it from Korda for a much larger sum was presumably mitigated when he was hired to write the screenplay.

Hitchcock moved to Paramount – with an unusually advantageous contract – taking Miss Kelly with him. In **Rear Window** (1954) and **To Catch a Thief** (1955) she has to radiate sexual attraction for James Stewart and Cary Grant in turn. Since she was both subdued and intelligent, the dialogue perforce required a certain sophistication, and Hitchcock found in John Michael Hayes the man to write it. What goes on around it is of the usual confected order, and *To Catch a Thief* concerns an outbreak of cat burglary on the Côte d'Azur – views of which considerably help its purpose as a smart entertainment. *Rear Window*, after an exceptionally plodding exposition, is eventually light-hearted about a morbid interest in murder. Stewart, chairbound with a broken leg, is convinced that one of his neighbours across the courtyard is a killer. His nurse (Thelma Ritter) relishes gore, creating a combination of the funny and the macabre, unusual at the time. Stewart is, after all, a voyeur, and he sees some suspect goings-on – usually of a sexual nature

– featuring the honeymoon couple, a frustrated spinster who picks up a man, and a 'Miss Torso' constantly entertaining men. These are only minor aspects of the script, but their acceptance by the M.P.A.A. demonstrates the influence of Hitchcock's impish sense of humour on Hollywood's growing-up. An additional factor in that respect is the 'atmosphere' between Miss Kelly and her leading men.

There are views of London and Marrakesh (replacing St Moritz) in the remake of **The Man Who Knew Too Much** (1956), with Doris Day and James Stewart as the parents who get caught up in international espionage. Hitchcock has extended the set pieces of his earlier version, such as the projected assassination in the Royal Albert Hall, and as a result the film dies. In **The Trouble with Harry** (1956) it is Harry who is dead – buried in a New England wood in all its autumn glory. The film's irreverent attitude to beds and bodies found little appreciation at the box office, though an additional reason may have been the nice, but unstarry cast – Mildred Dunnock, Mildred Natwick, Edmund Gwenn and the then-unknown Shirley MacLaine (as Harry's widow). There is no other film quite like it. It was followed by **The Wrong Man** (1956), which is, conversely, one of the most humourless films ever made. Hitchcock made it for Warners, partly because he felt that he owed them a film (having given them three failures of the five movies he made there, he took no fee), and partly because they owned the property – based on the true story of a man wrongfully arrested that he had read in *Life* in 1952. Maxwell Anderson and Angus MacPhail turned it into a screenplay, Henry Fonda plays the man, and Hitchcock used the actual locations where possible. His long-held fear of the police was one reason he was attracted to the subject, and the film is detailed on police procedure: but the result, as he said himself, is one of the 'indifferent' Hitchcocks.

He returned to the rich and glamorous in **Vertigo** (1958), but with John Michael Hayes no longer on hand the laughter is against the film rather than with it. The screenplay is by Alec Coppel and Samuel Taylor, from a novel by Boileau and Narcejac, who wrote it with Hitchcock in mind after learning that he had liked *Les*

Hollywood in the Age of Television: The Directors

Hitchcock, the old master of suspense, hit a winning streak again in the Fifties, virtually never faltering in his choice of material and its execution – though we might accord a nod to fortune, who so obligingly supplied him with the ideal Hitchcock heroine in Grace Kelly. And there must have been a slight element of luck in finding in Robert Bloch's novel *Psycho* the perfect horror story for him. Anthony Perkins stands on the steps and the house still stands on the Universal lot – and of all the old dark houses in movie thrillers it is probably the most memorable.

Diaboliques (q.v.). The plot is a mighty con job, but may be enjoyed by those not knowing the twist; however, 128 minutes of James Stewart and Kim Novak mooning around San Francisco is self-defeating. He is fine as the ex-cop hired to study her strange behaviour, but ludicrous when supposed to be in the grip of an *amour fou*. The film has a dreamlike quality, but also much flashy use of colour and camera. The reviews were uniformly poor, which may be why Ernest Lehman apparently made an intensive study of the more successful early Hitchcocks before writing the screenplay of **North by Northwest** (1959), which they made at M-G-M. The mistaken-identity victim comes from *The Man Who Knew Too Much*, the hero-in-a-trap from *The Thirty-Nine Steps* and *Saboteur*, the climax on the national monument from *Blackmail* and *Foreign Correspondent*. In any case Eva Marie Saint is a more acceptable substitute for Grace Kelly (by now Princess of Monaco) than all the other actresses Hitchcock hoped would be. As one of the villains, James Mason is stylish; as the hero Cary Grant muggs somewhat.

By this time Hitchcock sponsored a television series, 'Alfred Hitchcock Presents . . .', some episodes of which he directed. His spoken introductions made him a household name which, with his gift for self-publicity, he exploited to the hilt each time one of his films was to be launched upon the world. This weekly television series caused him to move away from accepted 'Hitchcock' material, to try a cinema essay in that admittedly grubby genre, the horror film. He admitted that his approach to **Psycho** (1960) was as to a television film, but he took particular delight in matters unlikely to be sanctioned for television in a million years (or so it seemed then). He was attracted to Robert Bloch's original novel – based on a newspaper item about a man who kept his dead mother in the basement – because of the early, sudden murder in the shower.★ Being murdered in some unknown stop-off place by a stranger runs second only to the nightmare of having dared to commit embezzlement and being discovered at it.

★The designer Saul Bass planned and edited this famous sequence, a fact not generally acknowledged until after Hitchcock's death.

The film then shifts into different gear, but is always nasty, skilful and self-consciously clever. The plot is preposterous and is rounded off with an absurd piece of amateur psychology, but the film grips even on repeated occasions, which is no mean achievement when its initial impact depended on the element of surprise (it was not uncommon for members of the audience to scream).

It was Hitchcock's last film for Paramount. His agent, M.C.A., was associated with his television series and still, at that point, affiliated to Universal, with whom a deal was made stipulating that he was not required to seek approval for any film budgeted at $3 million or less. As it turned out, **The Birds** (1963) was his last estimable film. Evan Hunter wrote the screenplay, transferring the action of Daphne du Maurier's short story from Cornwall to California, and considerably fleshing it out – since attacks by birds on people would hardly sustain a two-hour feature. Those attacks required much planning and pre-production (as well as a budget of more than $3 million). The film is smoothly entertaining, and Rod Taylor is a tower of strength as the hero.

The heroine, Tippi Hedren, was an ex-model chosen because Hitchcock thought he could mould her into another Grace Kelly. In **Marnie** (1964) she plays a kleptomaniac and Sean Connery a man with a compulsive desire to bed her – the element of the plot which appealed to Hitchcock on reading Winston Graham's novel. Neither player is up to the demands of the film, which dallies with an *amour fou* in the manner of *Vertigo* before drifting into matters reminiscent of another of Hitchcock's worst films, *Spellbound*. Deservedly, it failed, and he returned to stars and more familiar material in a Cold War thriller, **Torn Curtain** (1966). On this occasion, the earlier films plundered included *Psycho*, *North by Northwest* and *The Lady Vanishes*, plus two not by Hitchcock, *State Secret* and *The Man Between*. The credits nevertheless claimed an 'original' screenplay – which makes it the first that Hitchcock had directed since *Notorious*. He subsequently dismissed its writer, the novelist Brian Moore, as the wrong man for the job, and also in public was less than gracious to his stars, Julie Andrews and Paul Newman.

Since *Torn Curtain* did only a little better than *Marnie* he determined never again to work with stars – who did, after all, deflect attention from him. Just as he had given up John Michael Hayes for some lesser screenwriters (though, to be fair, Hayes's other credits are of unequal quality), so he relinquished Bernard Herrmann, whose music had contributed to so many of his films. Without the cost of stars he did not need to seek budget or subject approval, though it was Universal which suggested **Topaz** (1969) when he could not settle on a property. Whatever the merits of Leon Uris's original novel, based on a true espionage affair, the film emerged as a showy exercise in Hitchcockism, moving its setpieces from Harlem to Copenhagen to Cuba to Paris. The last two films are equally mechanical and much more old-fashioned than such concurrent formula films as *Dirty Harry* (q.v.). **Frenzy** (1972), about a London sex killer, was based on a novel by Arthur La Bern, who wrote to *The Times* denouncing the film. **Family Plot** (1976), written by Ernest Lehman from a novel by Victor Canning, is set in California and involves two pairs of crooks (William Devane and Barbara Harris; Bruce Dern and Karen Black) whose paths cross, with fatal results for the less cunning of them.

Although Hitchcock in old age expressed discontent over the projects which, he said, his backers would not sanction, he failed to take any of the risks open to the world's most famous director. Because of his position, his decline was less inevitable than most, and it is probably no coincidence that his films became less interesting as his fame increased because of television and the over-lauding of some cinéastes. Daniel Gélin, working with him on the remake of *The Man Who Knew Too Much*, reports that Hitchcock used to chuckle over the *Cahiers du Cinéma* theories, for ever claiming unwarranted complexities in his films, but there is sad evidence that the old man eventually began to believe them. A disservice had been done to an entertainer whose long career encompassed some enjoyable films.

Another veteran, George Cukor, made one of the most enduring films of the period, **A Star Is Born** (1954), intended as a showcase for the talents of Judy Garland by her (second) husband, Sid Luft,

Personal difficulties kept Judy Garland off the screen for four years before *A Star Is Born*, and although it was among the biggest money-making films of 1954 reports of her temperament – denied, however, by her director George Cukor – marked her as a star best avoided: a loss both to the industry and cinemagoers. One of the themes of this particular film is star quality, as explained by James Mason in the film, 'That little bell that rings inside your head, that little jolt of pleasure . . . You've got that little extra something that Ellen Terry talked about.'

whose inexperience as a producer contributed to the film's excessive budget. Another cause of overspending was the decision by Warners to scrap the initial shooting and recommence in Cinema-Scope. CinemaScope had not till then been used with imagination; here the opening sequence, a Hollywood premiere, is handled by Cukor as a whirling bubble of self-importance and hysteria, while Garland supplies the intensity dissipated elsewhere by the wide screen. This is intimate drama, and she plays the star who rises while her husband (James Mason) wanes. Reworking the screenplay of the earlier version, Moss Hart considerably strengthened the satire of the first half, while leaving intact the tragedy of the second. Cukor handles both with virtuosity, understanding the glamour and viciousness of Hollywood, and knowing that as a show-business tale it is entitled to wear its heart on its sleeve. The faults are minor: alcoholism is pictured as not disagreeable while the kindness of the studio head (Charles Bickford) and the malignancy of the press agent (Jack Carson) each seem

exaggerated (would the latter have been quite so nasty to the husband of his most important client?). Of the two leading players, Mason may be the better, since he submits himself to the material while Garland dominates it. But that is half the point: her acting is allowed greater range than hitherto, and her handling of the songs – particularly 'The Man That Got Away' – unparalleled in Hollywood history. Mason and Cukor observed that the film was better without the twenty-minute song sequence, 'Born in a Trunk', interpolated after Cukor had moved on to his next project; and they and others who saw the original three-hour film have testified to its superiority over the two-and-a-half hour version which was put into release.* There had been no longer American film since *Gone with the Wind*, but Warners got cold feet when it was clear that it would not do commensurate business. In the event, it turned a small profit.†

Cukor's years with M-G-M concluded with a more orthodox musical, *Les Girls*, already discussed, and **Bhowani Junction** (1956), produced by his old colleague, Pandro S. Berman, from John Masters's novel about the plight of Anglo-Indians at the time of the British withdrawal. This was clearly a more responsible view of the Raj than Hollywood's prewar adventures, and the locations again demonstrated Cukor's mastery of the wide screen. But, in his own words, 'the story went wrong'; it succeeds neither as political thriller nor action tale, and it is hard to like or understand the characters in the foreground, who include Stewart Granger as the C. O. and Ava Gardner as an Anglo-Indian subaltern. We may feel the same way about those in **Wild Is the Wind** (1957), since they include Anthony Quinn as a son of the soil, Anna Magnani as his mail-order bride, and Anthony Franciosa as the adopted son with whom she falls in love. These players provide no justification for disinterring this revamp of *They Knew What They Wanted*.

Cukor's response to the theatre sequences in *Les Girls* was repeated in the de-

*In 1983 most of the lost footage was restored and the reconstituted version was endorsed by critics and audiences.

†Warners did not proceed with the next two pictures called for in their contract with Garland, presumably because her unreliability and Luft's inexperience were given more weight than the film's good business and her glowing personal notices.

lightful re-creation of nineteenth-century drama in **Heller in Pink Tights** (1960). He was attracted to the subject, a theatre troupe in the old West, and although he admitted that there was no real story, he felt that it would be serviceable. It is hard to believe that the troupe's leading lady (Sophia Loren) would prefer her morose fellow-thespian (Quinn) to the attractive outlaw suitor (Steve Forrest, on this occasion transformed from his usual dull screen self). Or that, in this metier, she would experience such remorse at promising sex – in return for favours – that she would flee from each aspirant. Restrictions had recently been lifted on depicting such matters, so perhaps Cukor was working from an old script; it was the last one written by Dudley Nichols (with Walter Bernstein, from a novel by Louis L'Amour). The exteriors are imaginative and the interiors authentic in a way which was unprecedented. Cukor was always anxious to praise Hoyningen-Huene, credited as 'colour co-ordinator' on several of his films at this time – and it is for their visual quality that they are memorable – as opposed to the urbanity of most of his earlier work. There is little of either quality, however, in **Let's Make Love** (1960), a supposed satire on theatre people written by Norman Krasna. Cukor seems to have been depressed by the presence of a British 'pop' singer, Frankie Vaughan, playing a Broadway star, while both Yves Montand and Marilyn Monroe are wan as a multimillionaire and the singer he falls for.

20th Century-Fox made the film, and later threatened to sue if Cukor did not fulfil his other contracted commitment to them. He solved the problem by agreeing to make **The Chapman Report** (1962), based on Irving Wallace's novel about a Kinsey-like examination of selected Californian women. Cukor had always claimed to be a commercial director, and he later defended this rather salacious film by observing that the novel 'presented something contemporary (at the time) about outwardly respectable women who were frigid and took lovers and went to psychiatrists'. Zanuck, returning to the company as head of production during the troubles with *Cleopatra*, stopped work on all projects, including this one – but he nevertheless produced it, under an agreement with Warner Bros. This meant two

front offices making cuts and changes – and the censor also interfered. Blaming them for the resulting version, Cukor said 'I know one always talks this way when a picture doesn't turn out, but in this case it was definitely so . . . The picture did have some virtues.' As it stands, its chief virtue is Jane Fonda, even if her inexperience shows as a young widow troubled by her frigidity (a subject only elementarily handled). Shelley Winters is conventional as a married woman with a passion for a man who regards her as just a passing fancy, and Glynis Johns is lamentable as an arty wife who seeks experience with an unlikely beach boy (Ty Hardin) – thus ruining the intentionally comic section of the film. Claire Bloom punishes herself for her nymphomania by committing suicide after being gang-raped – a situation new to American films. Such words as 'foreplay' and 'frequency' (of orgasm, a word not mentioned) are bandied about, but few commented on the film's frankness. Conditioned by *Peyton Place* (q.v.), whose source was an even more meretricious novel, the public seemed to think that it was time Hollywood accepted the facts of life.

Few of Cukor's films since *A Star Is Born* had made much public impact, but his reputation remained high – and it rested chiefly on movies which made him, in his own phrase, a 'wise choice' for **My Fair Lady** (1964), based on the most successful musical in Broadway history. Unfortunately, Jack Warner insisted on a replica of the stage show, insofar as it was possible, and he had, after all, paid an unprecedented $5 million for the rights. The Shaw Estate apparently refused any further excisions in what had once been 'Pygmalion', and not only was Alan Jay Lerner disinclined to cut his own libretto, but he even added to it, drawing on Shaw's additions to the 1938 movie. Consequently, the material was both overfamiliar and too thin for a three-hour film, a fact undisguised by Cukor's mobile camera and command of the big screen. He said that they were aiming at a fairy-tale London, but it is heavy and graceless, while Cecil Beaton's celebrated costumes are too theatrical for the screen. Still, these are offset by Rex Harrison's definitive Higgins and Audrey Hepburn – even if, like most Elizas, she is not too comfortable before the transformation and over-enthusiastic after it.

Cukor took over **Justine** (1969) in mid-production. 20th Century-Fox had struggled for ten years to fashion a screenplay from Lawrence Durrell's Alexandria Quartet. After the debacle of *Cleopatra* Mankiewicz was not invited to return to his version; one by Durrell himself was turned down, and the film eventually went ahead with a script by Lawrence B. Marcus. The original director, Joseph Strick, had been chosen as the result of two art-house semi-successes, *The Balcony* (q.v.) and *Ulysses*, but when the company disliked the footage arriving from Tunisia, Cukor was asked to replace him – and he reshot as much as possible. Since the chief virtues of the four novels were descriptive, it is rewarding to see Alexandria as it should be, with teeming streets and houses with hot, untidy, dirty rooms. It may not be quite as Durrell portrayed it, but it is a clever updating of that old Hollywood hunting ground, the cosmopolitan city of intrigue, now populated by transvestites, trollops and deviates. They – French, English, Greek, Jewish, Coptic Egyptian – move from brothel to embassy, united only in contempt for the native population and each other. Trying to pin down something of the original, the plot flies off in all directions, with Cukor racing through such setpieces as the carnival in bravura style. An unusually uneven group of players revived his reputation as an actors' director: Anouk Aimée as the mysterious Justine, Dirk Bogarde, Anna Karina, Philippe Noiret and John Vernon. If the exposition remains clumsy, Cukor's overall rescue job is a triumph, unrecognised by the press for the achievement it is. Audiences today are no longer concerned whether Durrell has been betrayed, caring more for a director at the peak of his form.

Nevertheless, Cukor's style was unable to make amends for a poor screenplay fashioned from Graham Greene's novel **Travels with My Aunt** (1972); and a miscast Maggie Smith, who replaced Katharine Hepburn at the last minute, does not improve matters. Nor did Cukor emerge with much credit from **The Blue Bird** (1974), except that he seems to have been the only one of the American principals to have had any regard for their Russian co-workers. This first Soviet-American co-production was the brainchild of Edward Lewis, a former writer who had produced for the companies of actor Kirk Douglas and director John Frankenheimer (q.v.). Reports on the shooting suggest that very few of those concerned had a good word to say for Lewis (several of the more catastrophic films of this time were produced by independent operators). The hapless studio involved was 20th Century-Fox, but much of the $15 million budget was put up by the Russians, who also provided production facilities in Leningrad. A prime mistake was the choice of Maeterlinck's dated play; the two child actors involved are uninteresting, and Elizabeth Taylor is a banal presence. Unfortunately, she has three roles, and in the most important, the Fairy Light, lacks beauty and magic – though Jane Fonda, as Night, and Ava Gardner, as Luxury, are little better. Luxury's party reveals some of Cukor's old flair, but there is one scene, as Light waves her wand to bring on various balletic elements, which is exactly like parents' night at the local dance school – an effect emphasised by dialogue in rhyming couplets.

Cukor's civilised talents were more suitably engaged in **Love Among the Ruins** (1975) and **The Corn Is Green** (1979), both with his old friend Katharine Hepburn, who is a little too consciously radiant for the circumstances. The first is an autumnal teaming with Laurence Olivier, giving a witty performance as a one-time lover now defending her in a breach of promise case. James Costigan's screenplay (written for the Lunts) would have benefited from the old Hollywood treatment, resulting in more point, humour and body than it presently has. The second film is a remake for Warners of their old movie, superior because of its views of Wales, a sensible attempt to improve the dialogue and the performance of Ian Saynor as the miner-student.

Both films were made for television, following the disastrous reception of *The Blue Bird*. With the outstanding exception of *My Fair Lady*, Cukor's movies of his last two decades were unsuccessful, so it said much for his standing within the industry that he became, at eighty-two, the oldest director ever to be entrusted with a major film, **Rich and Famous** (1981). It was the second Bette Davis film that he had re-made in a row, for it had once been *Old Acquaintance*; but more importantly, it was another rescue operation, with Cukor brought in after Robert Mulligan (q.v.) had not seen eye to eye with the producers, who included Jacqueline Bisset, one of the stars. She plays the highbrow novelist, Candice Bergen the friend who writes trashy bestsellers, and David Selby the man who marries the one but wishes he had married the other. Gerald Ayres's script was, said Cukor, 'witty, intelligent' and therefore 'irresistible', but despite that there were glib references to Yeats and Eliot and some cheap touches, such as Bisset allowing a nineteen-year-old pick-up to make love to her (in the Algonquin). It was another commercial failure, perhaps because it remained too much like the films Cukor had made on first arriving in Holly-wood; but overall it bore impeccable witness to the unobtrusive skills he had acquired in the fifty years' interim.

The late films of John Ford, another old master, bear witness to all that he had learnt in a similar period, but unlike Cukor, his energy, if not his craftsman-ship, diminished as the years went by. **Mogambo** (1953), a remake of *Red Dust*, is one of his brightest pictures, but perhaps because M-G-M paid handsomely for African locations the flora and fauna take precedence over John Lee Mahin's screen-play. The bantering, taunting dialogue be-tween Clark Gable and Ava Gardner is less amusing and outrageous than that Gable shared with Jean Harlow, but both players are superb.

Mister Roberts (1955) is one of Ford's finest achievements, or so it seems after examining the contentious shooting his-tory, which ended with the Directors Guild insisting on a shared credit with Mervyn LeRoy. Thomas Heggen's novel had been adapted and produced for Broad-way by Joshua Logan, whose contract specified the direction of any eventual film. Since he owned twenty-five per cent of the property, he ceded to Ford, who was Warners' choice, agreeing that the result was likely to be more profitable thereby. John Patrick wrote the screenplay, but Ford brought in Frank S. Nugent (the former critic, his son-in-law and a regular collaborator since *Fort Apache*) to make further changes to what he always referred to as 'a homosexual play'. Thus the contin-gent of nurses in the original was increased from one to six, but Henry Fonda, who had earlier played the title role on Broad-way, felt that the changes vulgarised the material. After an altercation between the two, Ford got drunk and, according to Logan, stayed drunk. The actor Ward Bond directed some sequences before LeRoy was called in, and Logan himself directed some – for which he was consoled with a writing credit. But the visually magnificent exteriors which comprise most of the film are superior to the forced comedy of the scenes inside the ship, and they are all Ford's work. Fonda is excellent as the exceptionally nice officer beloved by the crew, as is James Cagney as the vicious captain; William Powell is the doc and Jack Lemmon the amorous ensign – and it is pleasing to see together these two supreme light comedians of different generations. The American public loved the film, with its portrait of service life as a mixture of boredom, horsing around, drunkenness and petty-mindedness. The British critics were scandalised almost to a man, a telling comment on the dishonesty of British movies on service life.

Ford continued on form with **The Searchers** (1956), written by Nugent from a novel by Alan Le May about the early settlers and marauding Comanches. There are flaws and irrelevancies, but once John Wayne sets out on his dual mission, of revenge and quest for his captive niece (Natalie Wood), the film's epic ambitions are sustained. This was the level at which Ford was expected to work, now that he was no longer restrained by crass pro-ducers; but neither **The Wings of Eagles** (1957) nor **Gideon's Day** (1958) are of the standard of his early commercial chores for Fox. The former, based on a true story, deals with a dedicated naval man, Frank Wead (Wayne), who takes up writing screen-plays, including *Ceiling Zero* and *Hell Di-vers*, after being crippled. *Gideon's Day* is a half-hearted account of a Scotland Yard man (Jack Hawkins), which was produced in London by Lord Killanin (who was also responsible for Ford's Irish venture, *The Rising of the Moon*). John Creasey's novel was adapted by T. E. B. Clarke, writer of *The Blue Lamp*, which shares with this film the obvious premise that the police are as human as the rest of us.

867

The Last Hurrah (1958) was the last spurt of an old runner. As no American film on politics had succeeded at the box office since *Mr Smith Goes to Washington* (and this was to prove no exception) it was surprising that Columbia wanted to film Edwin O'Connor's novel. As the 'engaging rogue' who stands for re-election, Spencer Tracy was never more richly human. He had not worked with Ford since his first film, and the occasion snared some of the great character actors among their contemporaries: Pat O'Brien, James Gleason, Wallace Ford, Frank McHugh, Basil Rathbone, Basil Ruysdael and Edward Brophy. The material might have yielded better results in the hands of a more sensitive director, but no one could have treated these people – both the roles they play and hence the subject itself – with more affection.

Ford continued making films for another ten years, each one worse than the last. As with Hitchcock and Cukor, some buffs held him in an admiration which amounted to idolatry, but where Cukor justified it by stretching his talent, Ford, like Hitchcock, fell into self-parody. He made John Ford movies, each lethargic, often plotless, with cardboard characters bashing away at one another in a manner meant to be light-hearted. Admirers claimed that he had earned the right to be self-indulgent, but others were bored by these formless melanges of masculine camaraderie and sentimentality. **The Horse Soldiers** (1959) and **Two Rode Together** (1961) both treat the over-familiar rivalry between old hand and young upstart. These are played by John Wayne and William Holden in the first, and by James Stewart and Richard Widmark in the second. **Sergeant Rutledge** (1960), set in cavalry days, yet again, more interestingly concerns a black (Woody Strode) on trial for rape and murder – though never for a moment is it doubtful that he is blameless. It is evident that Ford, with customary cynicism, saw the theme as a way of establishing himself with a new generation as a liberal, caring film-maker – whereas, equally clearly, he was not really interested. **The Man Who Shot Liberty Valance** (1962) – which marks, incidentally, a last return to black and white – has Wayne in his usual role, Stewart (unbelievably, given his age) as a

novice in the West, and Lee Marvin as the villain. Wayne and Marvin fight each other over a number of beaches and bars in **Donovan's Reef** (1963) – this is an Hawaiian *Quiet Man*. Like *Liberty Valance* it is tired to the point of dropping, and both films were made worse by sequences with cute native kids.

Ford, Henry Hathaway and George Marshall shared the direction of the M-G-M Cinerama Western, **How the West Was Won** (1962), with its several episodes and thirteen star names – the whole, as scripted by James R. Webb, adding up to an anthology of pioneering clichés. Of its various spectacles, only one succeeds★ – the train robbery – and that is due to Eli Wallach's gleeful little bandit rather than the speeding train on the triple-panel screen. Said Hathaway: 'That god-damned Cinerama . . . Cinerama was a joke anyway. I laid out that film; it was my conception to break it into four sections. I shot "The Rivers" and "The Plains" and then I had to reshoot most of George Marshall's stuff, "The Trains". I didn't touch John Ford's Civil War stuff even though it looked a little stagey. He shot the whole sequence on a sound stage and it was no good, frankly. It looked shabby. It was the most expensive film I've ever made: nearly ten million dollars.'

Its producer, Bernard Smith, went into partnership with Ford, and despite Ford's poor box-office record in recent years, found backing for what turned out to be his last two completed films. The first, **Cheyenne Autumn** (1964), was very expensive, its appeal like *Sergeant Rutledge* predicated on a liberal point of view. Webb wrote it, from a novel by Mari Sandoz, and it is about the return of the Cheyenne in 1868 to their native territory – a journey of 1,500 miles – escorted by a squadron of cavalry. Not only is it pro-Indian, but the cast includes some Quakers to plead the pacifist cause, asking such questions as, 'Does it matter who fires the first shot?' No one concerned seems to have been remotely interested in the answer, and the film is hindered by a number of familiar faces lurking under the wampum beads and warpaint. Cuts were made in the original running time of 170 minutes, but it was still a flop. **Seven Women** (1966)

★Perhaps I should say succeeded, since Cinerama is no longer with us.

might have been acceptable if made thirty years earlier, but as it is, audiences were reduced to giggles when the agnostic doctor (Anne Bancroft) saved the ladies of the lay mission by swallowing poison and 'giving herself' to the Chinese warlord. It was 'a hell of a good picture' commented Ford later, in his sad decrepitude.

Earlier illness had forced him to cede **Young Cassidy** (1965) to Jack Cardiff, the former cinematographer, whose direction complements a script superior to most that Ford worked with. It was written by the dramatist John Whiting, from Sean O'Casey's first volume of memoirs, 'Mirror in My House', and it conveys well O'Casey's instinctive protest against the poverty around him. It is ambivalent on the subject of the patronage of Lady Gregory (Edith Evans) and Yeats (Michael Redgrave), but clever with regard to its effect on him. Accordingly it ranks high among films about writers; its re-creation of Dublin at the time of the Troubles is outstanding; and though 'A John Ford Production', it is his one 'Irish' film in which the soundtrack is not weighted down by the most hackneyed Irish airs. In the title role, Rod Taylor is not only physically the antithesis of O'Casey but more sympathetic.

Almost everything that may be said about Ford's last films may be said about those of Howard Hawks. An epic of antique days, *Land of the Pharaohs* (1955), was, with some reason, so badly received that Hawks took several years off to contemplate 'how we used to make pictures'. That did not include the provision of plot, as Leigh Brackett observed after being commissioned to write **Rio Bravo** (1959) with another old and valued colleague, Jules Furthman. What plot there is derives from *High Noon*, but since John Wayne had loathed that film (because no one had come to Gary Cooper's aid) he is given three assistants plus a girl (Angie Dickinson) in the vein of earlier Hawks heroines – when they were so much better played by Jean Arthur or Lauren Bacall. **El Dorado** (1967) 'could have been called "Son of Rio Bravo Rides Again" ', said its writer, Miss Brackett. Its easy superiority over *Rio Bravo* is partly due to the casting of Robert Mitchum, both a more likeable drunk than Dean Martin and a more challenging partner for Wayne. The casual bantering tone

of Hawks's early work reappears with ideal interpreters, and this is his best film in two decades. Sadly, Hawks's other late films are negligible – *Hatari!* (1962), *Red Line 7000* (1965) and *Rio Lobo* (1970); there was also **Man's Favorite Sport?** (1964), with Rock Hudson, who later said 'He'd made very many brilliant films. But it was like he'd given up. And therefore it was quite disillusioning. All the jokes and comic sequences in that film were repeats of things he'd done in his various other films.'

The later films of John Huston are more eclectic, including some as uninspired as lesser Ford and Hawks but many which are, at least, satisfactory entertainments. His most ambitious project to that point, **Moby Dick** (1956), ended up between the two extremes. With his photographers, Oswald Morris and Freddie Francis, Huston evolved a colour scheme approximating that of old whaling prints, but despite extensive location work at sea we are all too often aware of the studio tank – not to mention the synthetic Moby. The film manages some fine moments in Nantucket and aboard the *Pequod*, but Melville's thundering mysticism has become an occasional eeriness, and that is partly because of the portrayal of Ahab. Huston favoured Laurence Olivier, but accepted Warners' suggestion of Gregory Peck, a sounder box-office name for what was a risky venture; and since he had coaxed a performance from Audie Murphy (in *The Red Badge of Courage*) he was confident that he could do the same with Peck. But Peck is neither pitiable nor indomitable; he is never vengeance incarnate. Leo Genn's Starbuck is no more interesting, and Richard Basehart is a bland Ishmael. The screenplay is credited to Huston and Ray Bradbury, who has claimed that it was his work alone.

Despite its shortcomings, the film added to Huston's reputation for making 'art' movies, but with forethought he knew that a failure with a similar project would leave him vulnerable. To prove that he remained at the service of the industry rather than vice-versa, he signed a contract with 20th Century-Fox for three films. The subjects were not necessarily of his choosing, but he was to have autonomy during shooting. **Heaven Knows, Mr Allison** (1957) follows the adventures of an American marine (Robert Mitchum) and an Irish nun (Deborah Kerr) on a Pacific atoll in wartime. It has the enchantments of other coral island stories rather than those of *The African Queen*, of which we are initially reminded; and since the central relationship raises the issue of romance, which it then avoids, we may see this as an example of Huston's ability to take an unlikely or unlikeable subject and convert it into a reasonably sophisticated entertainment. He directed **The Roots of Heaven** (1958) for Zanuck, whose independent company produced for 20th Century-Fox release. After quitting as head of production, Zanuck made his headquarters in Europe and turned out films usually featuring one of his several French mistresses – in this case Juliette Greco, who can sing, in her fashion, but cannot act. This one, Huston admitted, 'wasn't a very good picture', but if it achieves the dubious distinction of being the best of Zanuck's batch that is due to Trevor Howard's sincere and energetic performance as a man fanatically opposed to the destruction of elephants. The script, by Romain Gary and Patrick Leigh-Fermor, from Gary's novel, was an acknowledged mess when shooting began, and it suffered the further indignity of having chunks omitted when the African locations proved too arduous or when Errol Flynn was too drunk to remember his lines and improvised.

Many of Huston's films were battlegrounds: he worked with many stars who were roisterers or difficult, as later in the cases of Marilyn Monroe and Montgomery Clift. He and John Wayne detested each other on **The Barbarian and the Geisha** (1958); Wayne was as professional as he was popular, and relations deteriorated as he realised that Huston, a recognised maverick, was making a semi-documentary instead of a star vehicle. The 'barbarian' of the title is Townsend Harris, accepted under duress in 1856 by the Japanese as the first American consul, after two centuries spent avoiding European influence. The screenplay sidesteps all the issues and opts instead for pretty panoramas. That there is a genuine feeling for the Japanese past probably stems from the participation of the veteran director, Teinosuke Kinugasa, credited as 'script supervisor'. The result is not an enthralling entertainment, though it does not provide

evidence of the decline spotted by contemporaries, admittedly with *The Roots of Heaven* fresh in their minds.

After these far-flung American adventures, Huston decided to return to American roots, if not to Hollywood (and he avoided shooting there for another two decades). The experience of his last two films had taught him that he needed good screenplays, and two were at his disposal, both set in the West. **The Unforgiven** (1960) was adapted, by Ben Maddow, from a novel by Alan Le May, in which he reversed the situations he had used in 'The Searchers': in this case it is the Kiowa Indians of Texas who want the return of a girl they consider their own. As the girl, Audrey Hepburn is miscast but nevertheless an asset; Burt Lancaster (whose company produced) is the man of the house; and Lillian Gish the matriarch. Franz Planer's Panavision photography greatly aids what is essentially an attempt at the epic, but if the result is sometimes self-conscious Huston, typically, has 're-thought' the West: he offers the necessary neighbourliness (when possible) and the logistics of living so close to Indians in an area of almost supernatural vastness, with incandescent days and long nights of vaulted, fearful darkness.

The second film with a Western setting was **The Misfits** (1961), written by Arthur Miller for Marilyn Monroe, to whom he was married at the time. Great coverage was given in the press to the troubled shooting, due in part to the break-up of the Monroe-Miller marriage and culminating in the death of her co-star, Clark Gable, a few days after filming finished. The character of Roslyn, naive and caring, was based on Monroe herself, but Miller was not writing exclusively about her: this was a New Yorker – not a Westerner – looking at the land beyond the Rockies and the sort of people it produces, and wondering why and how it differs from the old West and its myths. These misfits find odd pockets of compassion for each other. Gable is beautifully cast as the man with two kids somewhere, nothing guiding him beyond the hatred of a nine-to-five job and a longing for the days when the hills were full of mustangs. Montgomery Clift, so weak as a Westerner in *Red River*, easily manages the aimless, simple-minded Pete, obsessed with loathing for his stepfather; Eli Wallach is Guido, a former bomber pilot; and it is only Thelma Ritter, the divorcee, who allows her past to catch up with her, forcing her to desert her new-found friends. The rounding-up of the mustangs accelerates the break-up of the party, till its violence gives way before the spirit of Roslyn. As this poignant creature, Monroe gives no hint of the comedienne – which to this point she was considered to be. The film itself has grown in stature with the years, justifying Huston's faith in the screenplay, which was not generally admired.

The filming of **Freud** (1962) was also fraught with trouble. Huston and Charles Kaufman had wanted to make a movie on psychoneurosis since 1946, the year they had made *Let There Be Light*, a documentary for the War Department. By 1957 Wolfgang Reinhardt and Jean-Paul Sartre had joined the project. Sartre's proposed screenplay would have run to ten hours' screen time, however, and the one eventually used is credited to Reinhardt and Kaufman, from a story by Kaufman. Universal backed it, since at that time the company was making an effort to return to 'quality' films, but difficulties with Clift (Universal sued him, and he countersued) sent the budget and shooting schedule soaring. A 240-minute print was whittled down to 139 minutes, and then to much less on release. According to Robert LaGuardia, in his biography of Montgomery Clift, this film was Huston's 'dream of a lifetime', but his inability to understand the subject was 'embarrassing' – or so Kaufman told him. Apparently Huston approached the subject in ignorance, and later 'puritanically' took out much that was best in the script. The result is very much like the screen biographies Warners made when Huston was a writer with them: it is craftily made, dark, handsome and sober, with no serious anachronisms. Freud's thirteen documented cases are reduced to one and a half, but his growing understanding of the troubles of that one patient (Susannah York) makes interesting enough entertainment. The dream sequences renew one's respect for Huston, but there are some sentences of the 'Siggy, you're working too hard' variety, and the film eventually disappoints because its 'revelatory' climax on sexuality in children is no revelation for the great majority of its audience.

After an inadequate joke-thriller, **The List of Adrian Messenger** (1963), Huston tackled a play by Tennessee Williams, and after *A Streetcar Named Desire*, **The Night of the Iguana** (1964) is the best film of a Williams drama. In reworking his short story for the stage, Williams had moved close to self-parody, but Huston's screenplay (written with Anthony Veiller) eliminated those facets of Williams with which he had no sympathy. Gone is the half-squeamish fascination with decadence, in favour of what had attracted him ever since *The Maltese Falcon* – the interplay of assorted individuals: the drunken ex-priest (Richard Burton), grandiloquent and sardonic; the warm-hearted innkeeper (Ava Gardner), with her young male escorts; the untalented but resolute spinster (Deborah Kerr); the lesbian chaperone (Grayson Hall); and her young charge (Sue Lyon) who cannot wait to jump into bed with the priest. The images – palm tree, shore and shutters – are as heady as the text, but as photographed by Gabriel Figueroa they manage to remain a knife edge away from cliché.

Huston accepted the challenge of **The Bible . . . in the Beginning/La Bibbia** (1966) offered by Dino de Laurentiis, who intended it to be the culmination of the recent spate of religious epics. Originally several other film-makers were to have been involved, each with artistic control over their own sections – Robert Bresson (for The Creation), Orson Welles, Fellini and Visconti – but there were quarrels over Christopher Fry's draft screenplay. Even with a sole director in control, the project seemed one of the most risible in cinema history, but Huston, mindful of his reputation – since with it went his independence – approached it with care and vigour. The result is one of his finest achievements. A series of episodes from the Old Testament, visually impressive, is accompanied by a text which is an excellent pastiche of the King James Version. Solutions have been found to virtually insurmountable problems, marvellously so in the cases of the Flood (Huston himself played Noah) and the Tower of Babel; but unfortunately the ninety-minute story of Abraham, rounding off the second half, is no more than a scripture lesson. There are, too, occasional banalities, but also few shots which do not carry the mystique of

871

Of the major American directors, only George Cukor had a longer career than John Huston, and Huston's career is the more interesting, since he has shifted from genre to genre with frequency, even to finally making a musical, *Annie*. His films of the last three decades have not been uniformly good, but he has succeeded with some notoriously difficult subjects – not least with the overheated world of the novelist Carson McCullers, *Reflections in a Golden Eye*. Here he converses with Marlon Brando, the film's leading actor.

the text, if in the manner of Victorian illustrations: to that extent it is superior to Wyler's *Ben-Hur* and Stevens's *The Greatest Story Ever Told*, but if you had read the reviews you would not have supposed it so much better. Stevens's film was instrumental in lessening public interest in the genre, but this one found its own – rapt – audience.

Nor were American reviewers kind to **Reflections in a Golden Eye** (1967), but it was liked elsewhere. Carson McCullers's novel, a quadrille for two army couples, contains risky matters for the screen, and the screenplay by Chapman Mortimer and Gladys Hill, Huston's secretary,★ adds yet another – the officer horsewhipped in front of guests by his flighty wife. Huston ignores the difficulties and brings his sardonic humour to bear on three interrelated studies: the sickly, withdrawn wife (Julie Harris) and her camp, sycophantic houseboy; the colonel (Brian Keith), engaged in an affair with the major's wife (Elizabeth Taylor); and the major (Marlon Brando), with his fixation on an enlisted man. The major gazing at a photograph of a nude statue or applying rejuvenation cream seems a naive approach to homosexuality, and no more

★There is no doubt that Huston contributed to virtually all the screenplays he directed, whether credited or not, but by this time Miss Hill so clearly understood his requirements that he was happy to let her take sole credit for most of the writing they did together.

than in *The Night of the Iguana* does Huston seem sympathetic to the preoccupation of the Williams-McCullers school in such matters; but he had decided, irrespective of what other film-makers were doing, that it was time they surfaced in films – hence, similarly, Freud's identification as a Jew in that movie, at a time when Jewish characters were rarely recognised as such in films. For the deficiencies in both films Huston atones in this one with a superb scene in which Brando waits for the soldier, as tense as one of Buñuel's shoe fetishists, irrevocably committed to a meeting he knows is foolish. Brando's performance is the definitive study of a military man – a hopeful martinet everywhere but in his own home, where he uncertainly accepts humiliation. Brian Keith is equally good because he is equally stupid underneath his virility, and Julie Harris completes a trio of excellent performances.

Huston said later that he had made 'only three good films in the last decade', citing this one, *Fat City* (q.v.) and *The Man Who Would Be King* (q.v.). He liked, he said, 'to jump around in life and in films . . . Perhaps my greatest contribution has been that of keeping certain films from being mediocrities instead.' He blamed the failure of **Sinful Davey** (1969) on himself, explaining that he had lost interest before filming began – which is not surprising, given the derivative script by James R. Webb for this Scottish *Tom Jones* (q.v.) and the inadequate casting of the then unknown John Hurt in the title role. **A Walk with Love and Death** (1969) also has deficiencies in the script and leading performances – Assaf Dayan (son of the Israeli statesman) and Anjelica Huston (the director's daughter); the setting, however, is well realised. The challenge of recreating Moscow may have attracted Huston to **The Kremlin Letter** (1970), or he may just have wanted to try his hand at a spy thriller. He wrote the screenplay with Gladys Hill, from a bestseller by Noel Behn, and it has that rueful humour and ruthlessness that we recognise as his hallmarks. The basic plot, about a team of experts operating behind the enemy's lines, is as old fashioned as Phillips Oppenheimer, if decorated with such elements as Cold War commissars, perversion and drugs.

By this time Huston was much in

demand as an actor – having been invited to make his debut in Otto Preminger's *The Cardinal* in 1963. One may have supposed that his career as a leading director was behind him, and the last three films tended to confirm this. Nothing, even in his best films, prepared the public for **Fat City** (1972), as freshly observed as if made by a newcomer. None of his contemporaries had managed to come to terms with the changed cinema of the Seventies in the same way. Huston had taken Leonard Gardner's naturalistic novel and tossed it around in the fashionable fragmentary style, but, more importantly, he imbued the film with all the perceptions that are fascinatingly possible in life but that were not available in movies when Huston started his career. It consists of a series of vignettes in the lives of two small-time boxers, one (Stacey Keach) already over the hill at thirty, and the other (Jeff Bridges) just starting on the same path. They hang out in Fat City – Stockton in Northern California – in grubby bars and sweaty little halls, doing deals over hamburgers or the pool table. The youngster marries the girl he has got pregnant, and is probably as happy as the next man – but, if that man is Keach, playing marvellously, he keeps his thoughts to himself. The public had never cared for films about losers, however compassionately treated, and despite rapturous notices this was no exception. Aware of this, Huston had agreed to direct two films with Paul Newman. Both **The Life and Times of Judge Roy Bean** (1972) and **The Mackintosh Man** (1973) feed on old movies, written in the first case by John Milius and in the second by Walter Hill (from a novel by Desmond Bagley), both newcomers who were later to become directors. Neither film was well received, and the $400,000 paid for the screenplay of the former, about lovable eccentrics in the old West, was not money well spent. *The Mackintosh Man*, a man-on-the-spot tale in the Hitchcock mould, manages both tension and surprise, with the director's humour surfacing as he follows the rules of the game.

It was Newman's partner, John Foreman, who found the financing for **The Man Who Would Be King** (1975), an expensive project Huston had planned twenty years earlier for Humphrey Bogart and Clark Gable. Kipling's well-nigh-unfilmable short story had been turned, by Gladys Hill and Huston, into a long (130-minute) screenplay, which is remarkably faithful in spirit, though that is not enough to make it work. It is not remotely mysterious, despite or because of the mountain locations (Morocco deputising for the Khyber Pass); and what in Carnehan's recollection is elusive or fantastic becomes only too literal on the screen. The fault lies in the stars: 'I use actors with strong personalities, ones who are like the characters they play,' Huston said, of Sean Connery as Dravot and Michael Caine as Carnehan, adding that he marvelled at Olivier, but 'that's a kind of virtuosity that does not serve my purpose'. Connery, however, has everything for the role but the one essential quality – recklessness – and Caine, on this occasion, is quite hopeless.

The film, though not a gigantic success, restored the industry's confidence in Huston, but instead of the major projects he was being offered, he chose to make **Wise Blood** (1979), the first time in his career he worked without a major studio or distributor behind him. That, and the film itself, would be remarkable in any Hollywood director; it is even more remarkable in one of his generation. The producers were amateurs, friends of Flannery O'Connor, whose novel provides the source, and the producers' son, Benedict Fitzgerald, wrote the screenplay, which is mainly about Hazel Motes (Brad Dourif), who may or may not be a lay preacher. Motes is volatile, basically bruised and introspective, but he cannot be said to be stupid, as everyone else is. I am not sure that Huston has conveyed Flannery O'Connor's questioning views on Southern religion, but as in *Fat City* he has gone to a forgotten part of America, where the buildings are bleak and the roadways seem endless, where there is a deadness in the air except in the almost gothic rooming houses.

Huston's next two films, **Phobia** (1980) and **Victory** (1981), indicated no great interest on his part; the first, a Canadian horror film, was an assignment done at a time when his health had deteriorated to such an extent that no insurance company would accept him as a client during the usual shooting schedule. He had obviously recovered by the time he made **Annie**

(1982), into which producer Ray Stark and Columbia poured some $25 million, including $6½ million for the screen rights – the highest sum ever paid (the reported figure was $9½ million and a final cost of $40 million, but these were the 'hype' sums, according to Columbia's president, Frank Price). Clearly it was hoped that *Annie* would repeat the success of *The Sound of Music*, but the score is poor, and the book, based on a comic-strip about a cute little orphan in the Thirties, includes such dubious conceits as a singing F.D.R. There are past examples of prestigious directors failing with the musical form, but Huston had always shown himself able to learn from past mistakes, his own included. In addition, he had recently proved himself to be as much in tune with the times as any film-maker fifty years his junior – if that was what was needed. What he has done to *Annie* is a matter of conjecture: he has tried to treat its dull 'book' lightly – and Carol Burnett gives an outrageous, but funny, performance as the orphanage gorgon. Ann Reinking handles some songs and dances with ease, but as 'Daddy' Warbucks Albert Finney lacks the necessary villainy and geniality. Huston observed that since this was his first musical he would leave the handling of the numbers to those expert in such matters. The numbers, however, are memorable only for the inefficiency with which they have been staged, with the camera constantly cutting away as they try to work up steam. One, 'Let's Go to the Movies', takes place in Radio City Music Hall,★ with its platoon of ushers and the Rockettes; but it is even niggardly in using them. Columbia in desperation advertised the film as 'The musical of Tomorrow' – a reference to its only known song – but it assuredly was not.

Huston's reputation as a maverick and his record of occasional box-office (and artistic) failures has not prevented him from almost uninterrupted employment with the major Hollywood studios. Orson Welles, on the other hand, has not been prolific; he worked frequently as an actor for Zanuck, who on other occasions expressed the warmest regard for Welles's work. Welles's reputation in fact grew as

Citizen Kane retained its stature in the eyes of each new generation of movie buffs. He began innumerable projects, usually in Europe, often with distinguished participants, but the money either ran out or the film was abandoned, temporarily and then permanently, when Welles accepted an acting job. 'I started at the top' he observed in 1982, 'and worked downwards' – and the films he did make prove that he has only himself to blame. He persuaded a consortium of Swiss and Spanish businessmen to finance **Confidential Report** (1955), the shooting of which took cast and crew to Munich, Juan les Pins, Tangier, London, Chillon, Segovia and Paris (the action takes place in another half dozen exotic cities, but the regional shots were, presumably, from stock). The film is a rehash of *Citizen Kane*, with some mayhem thrown in; it has the same intricate structure, but the tycoon whose life is examined is European – perhaps based on Kruger, the match king. But in Europe, Welles is just a tourist: his script has nothing to say about wealth, international business or indeed anything. As the tycoon he looks ludicrous, and acts no better than anyone else in the cast. Warner Bros. bought the film for American distribution, but did not open it in the U.S. until seven years later, as *Mr Arkadin*.

Universal employed Welles as director on **Touch of Evil** (1958), apparently at the insistence of the star, Charlton Heston, who refused to believe that Welles had been hired only to act in the film. Welles's own performance, as a crooked district attorney, is, as usual, weird – and his direction of like quality. A simple thriller has been given an extraordinary surface: as ever, Welles is able to achieve striking visual effects, but only at the expense of the plot, which is often obscure. The version released was not Welles's own conception: a different management kindly issued that in the late Seventies, but it did not prove to be superior. To date, Welles has not directed another film for a Hollywood studio.

In France he made *The Trial* (q.v.), and then again with Swiss and Spanish backing he directed **Chimes at Midnight/Falstaff** (1966), which he adapted from both parts of 'Henry IV', plays that have been regarded as the greatest celebration of England and Englishness ever penned. The

---

★Which is playing *Camille*, which was not shown there, one year before it opened. The montage of scenes from that film is another of this one's miscalculations.

film has been so affected by the gaunt, cold walls of Castile, where it was filmed, that Welles hoped to fend off criticism by calling it 'a lament for Merrie England'. The plays have been savagely cut, but, unlike his earlier Shakespeare films, cut with understanding. John Gielgud is the old king, and Welles wisely left it to this admired exponent of the Bard to carry every scene in which he appears; elsewhere, much redubbing was necessary to bring the film to the level of the occasion. The battle sequence is magnificently conceived, outstripping in effectiveness that in *Richard III*, but its purpose seems less to honour Shakespeare than the film's producer-director-star. As Falstaff, he is not very merry, and he lacks heart. Keith Baxter is an excellent Prince Hal, and Norman Rodway a lusty Hotspur, though the role has been much reduced. All the performances are superior to those in Welles's *Macbeth* and *Othello*. In sum, the film was encouragement to those who wished to believe, despite evidence to the contrary, that the Welles of *Citizen Kane* was not dead.

Although *Kane* and *Ambersons* remained in the repertory of many art-houses, there was little interest in Welles as a director. In the mid-Fifties interesting film-makers were working in Hollywood, and those people who a decade earlier had looked to Welles to make the best films now turned above all to Elia Kazan. Rightly or wrongly, *Man on a Tightrope* was quickly forgotten, and the man who had made the acclaimed earlier films could still tackle anything that appealed to him. He himself was certain that *Panic in the Streets* was his best film, and he set to work with the playwright Arthur Miller on a not dissimilar subject – and one much to the fore at the time, about the troubles in the Longshoremen's Union in New York. Columbia was to have produced but Miller lost interest and the script was finally written by the novelist Budd Schulberg (b. 1914), the son of B. P. Schulberg, the founder of Paramount. Schulberg's screenplay for what became **On the Waterfront** (1954) was based on some magazine articles by Malcolm Johnson; it was to be filmed in New York, partly because the locations demanded it, and partly because Kazan, like Huston, Mankiewicz and Zinnemann, believed

that the atmosphere of Southern California was detrimental to his work. He was still angry about the cuts Zanuck had insisted on in *Man on a Tightrope*, but nevertheless *On the Waterfront* was destined for 20th Century-Fox until Zanuck decreed that audiences were not interested in labour problems. The project was taken on by the independent producer, Sam Spiegel, who arranged a deal with Columbia, and whose help in all ways was 'tremendous', according to Kazan.

The film reunited Kazan with Marlon Brando, whose performance as Terry Malloy, ex-pug and longshoreman, is one of the best ever recorded on celluloid. A foreword claims that the film 'will exemplify the way self-appointed tyrants can be defeated by right-thinking people in a vital democracy', thus avoiding the main problem, which is how tyrants achieve power in the first place. Malloy defeats them not by persuasive convictions about democracy but by the old movie standbys, revenge and the strength that comes from love. The film's rich texture and dialogue disguise the fact that Malloy is activated by a familiar maxim, 'A man's gotta do what a man's gotta do', but, as Brando makes clear, he is not accustomed to thinking. As events crowd in on him he uses his hands

A familiar face looks at us from a Spanish film – or at least one filmed in that country: and perhaps it is wisest not to enquire where Orson Welles gets his financing or why he films – as a director, that is – in so many different countries. We should pass discreetly over the films begun and to date not completed, leaving this one, *Chimes of Midnight*, the sole triumph of his later career – or, if it comes to that, the only wholly successful film he has directed since *The Magnificent Ambersons* over twenty years earlier. He played Falstaff; the lady behind him is unnamed in the cast list.

Eventually Elia Kazan's *On the Waterfront* falls into most of the traps lurking to ensnare film-makers of reforming zeal, but its virtuosity is undeniable – be it the words unheard under the ship's hooters or the shuffling conversation in the taxi, devices which were then new in films. The film, though often imitated, still retains its power, not least in the taxi scene, where Marlon Brando, right, tells his brother Rod Steiger that he coulda been a contender.

desperately in gesture or is forced back on an insolent grin; he under-reacts in contrast to the admittedly striking histrionics of Rod Steiger as his brother, of Lee J. Cobb as the corrupt Union boss and a rather dotty Karl Malden as the local priest. Brando is most memorable in the love scenes with the equally impressive Eva Marie Saint, playing the neighbourhood girl who encourages him in a quietly bantering way which effectively contrasts with the excitement of the rest of the film. It can be enjoyed as a thriller about corruption – at least, till the denouement, when Malloy becomes a Capra-like hero and testifies before the Crime Commission, and is ostracised by his colleagues – but rises from a beating-up to martyrdom and atonement. The subject is emotional and volatile, filmed in a style appropriate to the occasion; Leonard Bernstein's score is theatrical, but offset by Boris Kaufman's photography of Hoboken across the river, white with winter mists and steam drifting from the manholes.

The film's seven Oscars included awards to Kaufman, Brando, Kazan for direction and one as Best Picture. Its popularity re-established Kazan after the box-office failure of his previous two films. He identified with Malloy ('he felt proud and ashamed of himself at the same time. He wavered between the two, and he also felt

hurt by the fact that people – his own friends – were rejecting him. He also felt that it was a necessary act'). ★ And he chose his next film, **East of Eden** (1955), for autobiographical reasons – he had always felt that his father preferred his brother to himself, and he found a similar theme in John Steinbeck's novel. As O'Neill turned to the Greeks, so Steinbeck turned to the Bible, resetting the Cain and Abel story in the Salinas Valley of California during the early years of the century. Adam (Raymond Massey) is of a Bible-punching righteousness, but the behaviour of Cal (James Dean) would alienate the most patient of fathers, being fey, attention-seeking, erratic, vindictive, selfish and otherwise tiresome. Cal finds that his brother's girl (Julie Harris) enjoys being with him, but the pangs of despis'd love worsen when his brother, like his father, turns against him; he eventually gets revenge on his brother by taking him to visit their mother (Jo Van Fleet), thought dead, who runs a brothel in Monterey. Kazan disliked Dean, but used every facet of his 'unpredictable' behaviour for the role. Nevertheless, Dean is too cute for Steinbeck's pretensions, which were otherwise followed in the screenplay by Paul Osborn, commissioned by Kazan. The use of colour and CinemaScope complete the impression of trivial situations being treated in epic proportions.

With the equally meretricious *Splendor in the Grass* (q.v.), *East of Eden* was Kazan's last commercial success, but with good reason his next two films were much admired. His reputation and that of Tennessee Williams enabled **Baby Doll** (1956) to be made in defiance of the Code, but denunciations by the Roman Catholic church proved detrimental at the U.S. box office. Kazan constructed the film from two of Williams's short plays, and though Williams is credited with the original screenplay it would seem to have been their joint work. When Archie Lee (Karl Malden) burns down the cotton-gin of Vacarro (Eli Wallach), the latter sets out to seduce his virgin child-bride (Carroll Baker). The mixture is familiar: the Deep South is still deep in decadence, with

★Many left-wingers regarded the final sequence as Kazan's own comment on having given evidence before the House Un-American Activities Committee, which many former colleagues had refused to do.

mansions crumbling and leaves falling, but there is probably normal life continuing beyond the central trio playing their own cruel sex game. At least, they seem to be playing a game, although in fact the bride is a case of arrested development, Archie Lee is unaware of what is going on and Vacarro is motivated less by sensuality than revenge. The situation is dramatically effective, since it involves suspense and the promise of a cataclysmic change in relationships if Vacarro succeeds in his aim – but those elements have more to do with the audience's own erotic expectations than anything in the film, which is one reason why it is so powerful.

Kazan worked with another former collaborator on **A Face in the Crowd** (1957) – Budd Schulberg, whose screenplay was based on his own short story about a popular television personality who develops megalomania.* There have been a number of films on this theme, including *Citizen Kane* and *Network* (q.v.), as well as *The Great Man* (q.v.), which preceded Kazan's film by a few months – and we should note a new urgency in the subject, as television was creating a new breed of demagogue. Lonesome Rhodes (Andy Griffith) is an Arkansas hillbilly singer who moves from local radio in his home state to television success in Memphis and eventually national fame in New York: the adulation is such that his advice is sought not only by advertising agents but by a senator with presidential ambitions – and since the girl who discovered him, Marcia (Patricia Neal), realises that he is virtually a Fascist, she determines to destroy him. Her sexual fascination with him, which begins only with his climb to power, is one strand in a film rich in detail – and these include references to Nixon's 'Checkers' speech and Will Rogers, a Marilyn Monroe look-alike model, 'This is Your Life', a sycophantic Sammy Glick-type agent (Anthony Franciosa) and Walter Winchell (the number of unpleasant people playing themselves in cameo roles may be an in-joke). The voice of conscience is a cynical writer, played by Walter Matthau, then little-known, and since he is plain and bespectacled and the closest the film comes to a romantic hero much of what he has to say may be forgiven. Kazan himself says

*Schulberg wrote the story after discussing the television star Arthur Godfrey with William Roland, his producer.

that the film is 'over-explicit' and equally correctly it had remained in my memory as somewhat hysterical; the ending, borrowed from a film Schulberg's father produced with Emil Jannings, is grandiloquent. Nevertheless, in humour and intelligence this film is probably the best on this particular subject.

These movies, and those that Kazan made up to and including *The Arrangement* (q.v.) were released by Warners, but **Wild River** (1960) completed his contract with 20th Century-Fox, whom he blamed for its failure, since they hardly bothered to promote it. The film, 'one of the one or two purest I've made', arose from a desire to say something about the work of the Tennessee Valley Authority. After trying his hand at his own script, Kazan again commissioned one from Paul Osborn based on two novels, 'Mud on the Stars' by William Bradford Huie and 'Dunbar's Cove' by Borden Deal. The result unfortunately reflects the disparate sources, combining a romance between the T.V.A. agent (Montgomery Clift) and a Dogpatch-like lady (Lee Remick), and some community-conscience sequences about an old woman (Jo Van Fleet) to be evicted in the course of building the new dam. The piece meanders so much that it is eventually hard to care about the fate of the old lady, despite Miss Van Fleet's affecting performance.

Usually categorised as poet or realist, Kazan used **Splendor in the Grass** (1961) to demonstrate that he was, rather, someone who went to the heart of any subject that interested him, which in this case was the conflicting moralities of the Twenties. He has been at pains to point out that the film is not just about the traumas suffered by a boy (Warren Beatty) and girl (Natalie Wood) because they cannot sleep together, but as no other point is discernible it would seem that he did not get to the heart of this particular matter. The erosion of moral standards may well give rise to tragedy, but William Inge's original screenplay – the recipient of an unaccountable Oscar – is merely the forerunner of later, more opportunistic movies which were to encourage the younger members of the audience to 'do their thing'. The film's reception diminished Kazan's reputation, which was not restored by two ventures, **America, America** (1963) and

The Arrangement (1969). Both are based on autobiographical novels he had written: the first follows the adventures of a young Anatolian Greek immigrant (Stathis Giallelis) at the turn of the century, and the second recounts the various breakdowns endured by a middle-aged man (Kirk Douglas) because of his family, his adultery and his high-powered job in advertising. *America, America* begins with a portrayal of racial intolerance in Turkey, which colours the rest of the film and its hero's desire to escape; the individual sequences are powerful and possibly more effective now than then. On the other hand, *The Arrangement* is merely top-heavy with ideas which do not coalesce into a whole; and it is a pity to see this master film-maker borrowing the flashy cutting from the *nouvelle vague*. Further, the film is not helped by the fact that the Douglas character is drawn with self-loathing but is designed to elicit sympathy. (The film might have been better with Brando, who at the last minute relinquished the role.)

Experimenting with 16 mm, and with a cast and crew of friends, Kazan made **The Visitors** (1972), about some Vietnam veterans, but the result suggested that he had not regained his creative force, a view confirmed by **The Last Tycoon** (1976). He had been invited back to Hollywood by Sam Spiegel, but there was no echo here of their collaboration on *On the Waterfront*. Neither the direction nor Harold Pinter's screenplay shows the least understanding either of Hollywood or Scott Fitzgerald's unfinished novel. It must be the most po-faced film ever made about the movie industry, at the same time rejecting Fitzgerald's outline for the continuation and conclusion of the plot in favour of cliché. Its box-office failure may be added to what Kazan called his 'six colossal disasters' since *On the Waterfront* (the exceptions being *East of Eden* and *Splendor in the Grass*, which were popular, and *The Visitors*, which did not try to be). It is a sad comment on someone who had given Hollywood a handful of its most memorable movies.

Fred Zinnemann, unspectacularly, weathered the years better. Having risked – and almost lost – his reputation with *Oklahoma!*, he had another close shave with **A Hatfield of Rain** (1957), based on a sensational and specious Broadway play about drug addiction by Michael V. Gazzo, whose screenplay, written with Alfred Hayes, is no improvement on the original. The grainy photography of a wintry New York was then rare, and the players are convincing as ordinary people in extraordinary circumstances: Don Murray as the 'junky', Eva Marie Saint as his wife and Lloyd Nolan as his father.

The Nun's Story (1959) is based on Kathryn Hulme's bestselling autobiographical novel and much of the 151-minute running time is a documentary account of convent life, so organised as to let us draw our own conclusions about the system. Elsewhere we are invited to examine the conscience of Sister Luc (Audrey Hepburn) during her struggles for humility, the back-breaking work and the decision, reached after much heartache, that she is not suited to the calling. There are contrivances in Robert Anderson's screenplay, and Franz Waxman's insistent score is appropriate to Zinnemann's style: with a lesser director the result would be pompous or ponderous, but this one respects his subject and his audience. He wanted to use monochrome for the Belgian sequences and colour only for those in the Congo, but Warner Bros. decreed the use of Technicolor throughout. Miss Hepburn was the one actress of her generation who could convey intelligence and dignity, and Zinnemann uses her personality to intensify the script's intentions – as do the other actresses, most memorably Peggy Ashcroft and Edith Evans as Mothers Superior of limited imaginations.

At the time **The Sundowners** (1960) was regarded as the best Australian picture yet made, if, in principle, it should be difficult to accept Robert Mitchum and Deborah Kerr as denizens of the Outback. They act so attentively that their portrait of a happy marriage has freshness, while their relationship to this terrain – the film's chief theme – is achieved by the meticulous and optimistic Zinnemann despite a sprightly Tiomkin score, such expected fauna as kangaroos and koalas, and a Cockney saloon owner, carelessly played by Glynis Johns. The casting is central to the failure of **Behold a Pale Horse** (1964), a fact that Zinnemann realised too late, after casting Gregory Peck as a Spanish guerrilla leader and Anthony Quinn as a captain in the

Guardia Civile. In the circumstances Zinnemann's sympathies for Spain* in the aftermath of the Civil War went for little.

The subject of **A Man for All Seasons** (1966) is the intransigence of Sir Thomas More. Robert Bolt, adapting (and improving upon) his very successful play, had more on his mind than the king's bedding and wedding, though both are relevant to More's quarrel with the king. At the centre of these matters is Paul Scofield's exquisite portrait of More, a man of sweetness and strength, thinker, reader and unwilling courtier, with unbounded faith in his own intelligence and integrity. Watching his destruction – and his efforts to prevent this without compromise – make the film a compelling experience, despite some simplifications in the characters of Cromwell (Leo McKern) and Wolsey (Orson Welles); and purists may have preferred Henry VIII as the physically bloated, middle-aged man that he then was to the golden, youthful figure that Robert Shaw makes of him. Given aptly presented confrontations audiences will enjoy history and religion, but the film was also helped to success by six Oscars (including Best Picture, Best Direction, Best Actor and Best Screenplay) – and it was a deserved success, for Zinnemann has placed More beautifully in his time and setting; the Thames runs at the foot of his garden and is depicted in all its moods, especially those of night and twilight, times of contemplation.

This film and *The Nun's Story* are rare demonstrations among Hollywood artefacts, if so we may term them, of good intentions not gone awry; if we add to Zinnemann's record just *The Search* and *The Men* it is evident that this most modest of film-makers felt that he had much to live up to. After several years' pre-production work on *The Old Man and the Sea* (q.v.) and *Hawaii* (q.v.) he was dissatisfied, and left both to be made by other directors. In 1969, on the morning that shooting was scheduled to begin, the new management of M-G-M cancelled *Man's Fate*, based on the novel by André Malraux, on the grounds that it was unlikely to recover its considerable cost. Zinnemann also

*The Spanish government did not feel the same sympathy: the film was banned in that country, and as a mark of displeasure Columbia's films were refused distribution in Spain for several years.

worked for some years with various writers in an attempt to find a way to film *The French Lieutenant's Woman* (q.v.), also eventually made by another director. These four aborted projects were all based on popular books, but they are not contradictory to the themes most apparent in Zinnemann's work – courage, obsession, integrity held in the face of adversity. Since these subjects also interested Kazan, another liberal-minded director, we might note two further analogies between the two men: both disliked Hollywood (Zinnemann had lived in London since the Fifties) and both returned to commissioned work after more than two decades of acclaim. But whereas *The Last Tycoon* did not turn out well, **The Day of the Jackal** (1973) and **Julia** (1979) showed that Zinnemann had moved with the times. His former academic style had given way to one more elliptical but not otherwise influenced by current European fashions; with the exception of Huston, Zinnemann was the only one of his contemporaries to realise that modern audiences liked to draw their own conclusions.

The Day of the Jackal is a thriller, from Frederick Forsyth's novel, with Kenneth Ross's screenplay carefully examining the

Fred Zinnemann apparently abandoned the contemporary problems with which he had made his reputation – but we cannot tell for sure, since he worked on several projects which he left before their completion when he doubted the quality of the final result. His search for perfection has, however, served the cinema in a curious way, for he is another who has succeeded where other American directors have failed – with the re-creation of history, for example, *A Man for All Seasons*, with Paul Scofield as Sir Thomas More.

879

various people involved when a professional assassin (Edward Fox) is engaged to kill De Gaulle. *Julia*, written by Alvin A. Sargent from Lillian Hellman's 'Pentimento', a memoir of people she had known, is chiefly about that childhood friend whose passionate but illogical political beliefs – the role was well taken by Vanessa Redgrave – culminate in her disappearance while fighting Nazism in Berlin. The tale is padded out with references to the relationship between Hellman (Jane Fonda) and Dashiell Hammett (Jason Robards), to the success of her first play, and a train journey sequence familiar from movies like *Night Train to Munich*. The disturbing ending is partly the director's triumph, with Hellman's disquiet at a mystery unsolved, at events, a friendship, which she knew she should have handled better. Both films were made on myriad European locations, but **Five Days One Summer** (1982) is set chiefly in Switzerland, in the Thirties, for it is there that a Scotsman (Sean Connery) brings the girl (Betsy Brantley) who is ostensibly his bride. Zinnemann had long had an affection for Kay Boyle's original story, which on this evidence is rather slim. It is an old-fashioned film – a throwback to the German 'mountain' movies, but particularly pleasing in regard to the other films on offer at the time; it should have been more successful than it was.

Stanley Kramer (b.1913), who had produced three of Zinnemann's most distinguished early films, became a director, but is chiefly remembered for those movies and a handful of others emanating from his production company. A former film researcher and writer, he formed this company in 1948, releasing through United Artists, but with the exceptions of his second production, *Champion*, and *High Noon*, most of his films were failures, if honourable ones, like **Cyrano de Bergerac** (1950). Michael Gordon directed – one of the rare American attempts to film 'classic' European drama – on budget limitations reflected in the cast and settings. In the title role José Ferrer was awarded an Oscar but roundly trounced by British critics, who had lately seen Ralph Richardson play it on the stage. Ferrer can speak the verse, and he has panache and glee but no sense of pathos – nor of modesty, so that he is still showing off in his technically correct death scene.

For Kramer, Laslo Benedek directed **Death of a Salesman** (1951) and **The Wild One** (1953). Born in Budapest in 1907, Benedek worked in Germany as assistant to Joe Pasternak, who was later to give him a chance to direct, at M-G-M in 1948, with *The Kissing Bandit*, a musical with Frank Sinatra. Like Benedek's later American films, it is of no interest, but *Kinder, Mutter und ein General*, made in Germany in 1955, has quality, as have the two for Kramer. *Death of a Salesman*, from Arthur Miller's play, has Fredric March overacting as Willy Loman, the salesman, but is otherwise well performed, by players chiefly drawn from the original Broadway production; Mildred Dunnock's Mrs Loman is especially good. The permanent, composite set used on stage gives way to a cinematic device whereby Willy is able to walk into his past, which is quite powerfully done. *The Wild One* was called *The Cyclists' Raid* in production, and that is what it is about in John Paxton's factually-based screenplay, as two rival bands of motorcyclists gradually take over and terrorise a small town. Till the halfway point, the piece is frighteningly convincing, and as it becomes trite it becomes clear that the chief character's troubles are a ragbag of those listed later in the song, 'Gee Officer Krupke', in 'West Side Story'. However, Marlon Brando's performance

As a producer Stanley Kramer made a name sponsoring films attacking the evils of modern society, but when he continued to do so as both producer and director it became clear how much the earlier films had owed to their directors, particularly Fred Zinnemann and Laslo Benedek. Benedek, however, is a puzzle, for his first Hollywood films are poor, and so are the later ones he made; but *The Wild One* with Marlon Brando, centre, is splendid.

makes a lasting claim on our attention. This tin Napoleon is different from the hero of *On the Waterfront*: he has the same difficulty thinking and articulating, but what Brando conveys is the shifty mentality of the master-boy. 'What're you rebelling against, Johnny?' asks the town blonde, and he replies, 'What're ya got?', which to some makes him the forerunner of the rebels in all the youth films that followed. Fearing that young Britishers might emulate these gangs, the British censor banned the film, the first major American movie to be so treated since the early Thirties.*

The first of these two films was released by United Artists and the second by Columbia, for Harry Cohn was looking for 'quality' films to swell his company's product. An agreement was made with Kramer for thirty films, each with complete autonomy and a budget ceiling of $980,000 unless Cohn agreed to further expenditure. As each flopped (the worst was a musical fantasy, *The 5,000 Fingers of Dr T*, which returned only $249,000 of its $1,631,000 cost), Cohn's disenchantment grew, and Kramer's contract was annulled after only ten films. Kramer was determined to make one last film a success, and in fact **The Caine Mutiny** (1954) wiped out the accumulated deficit, making a gross of $11 million on an outlay of $2½ million. Cohn had agreed to the budget because Herman Wouk's novel had been a bestseller, and Stanley Roberts's screenplay is an exemplary model of how to cut a long text – even if it still allows too much time to the priggish young ensign played by Robert Keith. Edward Dmytryk directed, and the film itself is a fine entertainment from the mutiny onwards. Humphrey Bogart's performance as the disciplinarian Captain Queeg, shifty-eyed, weak-jawed and finally paranoic, is one of his most notable achievements. The film's foreword claims that there had never been a mutiny in the U.S. Navy, but subsequently one such commander, carrying discipline to idiotic lengths, was court-martialled during the Vietnam War.

Disbanding his production team and turning director, Kramer arranged distribution through United Artists and chose another bestseller, **Not as a Stranger**

*The ban was lifted in the mid-Sixties.

(1955), about the medical profession, with a hero (Robert Mitchum) so ambitious that he destroys a number of people in his path. So much goodwill was felt towards Kramer that the film was dismissed as merely disappointing, so that it was not until **The Defiant Ones** (1958) that he was taken seriously as a director – at least in some quarters. The plot involves a prejudiced white man (Tony Curtis) with an understanding black (Sidney Poitier), because they are convicts chained together; their eventual concord is one of those messages always worth restating, but the path to it is strained, not least in the introduction of a lonely young widow (Cara Williams) who seems neither to know nor care that there are dangerous escaped convicts in the neighbourhood. The physicist Dr Linus Pauling told Kramer that he had saved the world with **On the Beach** (1959), an adaptation by John Paxton of Nevil Shute's novel in which atomic fall-out brings about the end of humanity – clearly not with a bang but a whimper, as a naval commander (Gregory Peck) moons over a dipso nympho (Ava Gardner). At the end, vistas of deserted streets (the film was made in Australia) and an abandoned banner, reading 'There is still time . . . Brother', only serve to remind us of the superiority of *Seven Days to Noon*.

Inherit the Wind (1960) starts with the disadvantage of having a subject inherently without tension: 'The Monkey Trial' in Tennessee in 1925, in which a teacher was tried for instructing his pupils in Darwin's theories of evolution. This circus became a Broadway play by Jerome Lawrence and Robert E. Lee, well-intentioned and with no (obvious) concessions to public taste, and as such was a logical subject for Kramer. In re-creating a similar cause célèbre in *Ace in the Hole*, Wilder used satire, but Kramer fights his old fight with earnestness but no insight into either the town concerned or the era. Of the opposing attorneys, Fredric March is in his element as the showy and pompous William Jennings Bryan, but Spencer Tracy takes the film as the more thoughtful Clarence Darrow (though neither of these names was used in the film). Kramer's inability to *construct* a film is one reason this film is so boring. **Judgment at Nuremberg** (1961) may be his most watchable film, because he had the unofficial assistance of George

Roy Hill (q.v.) who had directed the original television version. That was written by Abby Mann, whose three-hour screenplay is exactly double its length. Inevitably during that time it makes an occasional worthwhile statement on German war guilt, but they are mainly in the nature of notes for further study – such as the fact that there are 'good' and 'bad' Germans – and the Auschwitz newsreels have been doctored so that they are not too painful. The whole would be decent enough on some distressing matters had it not been stretched out, inflated and star-studded. There are thoughtful performances by Tracy as the judge, Maximilian Schell as the prosecuting counsel and Judy Garland and Montgomery Clift in cameo roles as victims of the Nazis. Richard Widmark is good, Marlene Dietrich is unlikely, and Burt Lancaster out of his depth as one of the elderly accused.

To prove his versatility, Kramer presented **It's a Mad, Mad, Mad, Mad World** (1963), typically planned as the biggest comedy ever made – 3 hours 12 minutes – in Cinerama (not in itself a disadvantage, but laughter and awe – at the all-enveloping views – are not suitable bedfellows). Everything goes on too long, and the Sennett-like destructions ignore what Sennett himself knew – that destructiveness for its own sake is not funny. That may have been in Groucho Marx's mind when he observed that one reason no one laughed at this film is because it is not about anything – other than greed and chasing about in cars – which reminds us wistfully of *Genevieve*, from which William and Tania Rose have cannibalised two or three gags. With Tracy heading the cast, and some genuinely funny men among the huge cast of 'comics' – Peter Falk, Terry-Thomas, Eddie 'Rochester' Anderson, William Demarest *and* Buster Keaton – the film was a box-office success, but it is doubtless significant that no one tried to make another three-hour comedy in Cinerama.

Ship of Fools (1965) lasts 150 minutes, not, apparently, having lost a comma from the Katharine Anne Porter novel on which it is based. She looked at the Old World as the Nazis came to power, believing that her account of it might help us all; and certainly Kramer and Abby Mann were the right people to put it on the screen. But unlike older movies about transatlantic liners, this is the most tedious of crossings. 'There are a million Jews in Germany. What are they going to do – kill all of us?' asks the Jew (Heinz Rühmann), who happens to be the most understanding, warmest and cutest little chap on board. The general overstatement is offset only by the relationship between the ship's doctor (Oskar Werner) and a drug-addicted countess (Simone Signoret); because the roles are interesting, these two non-English players are more at ease than anyone else in the cast. Vivien Leigh plays a woman regretting her fading beauty and a famous marriage that failed: 'We put up a wonderful front. In private it was different.' That she could say such autobiographical lines with no apparent feeling is another reason why this film is better forgotten.

If **Guess Who's Coming to Dinner?** (1967) does not deserve the same fate, it is because the stars are Katharine Hepburn and Spencer Tracy, in the last of their teamings. Kramer, to his credit, was the only producer to find work for the aged Tracy; in desperation, knowing that he had not long to live, Kramer turned to William Rose, who remembered an old, unproduced play in a drawer and turned it (just) into a screenplay (but later admitted privately that it was insufficient for the occasion). Hepburn and Tracy play a couple confronted with the prospect of a black son-in-law – the casting of whom, the improbably perfect Sidney Poitier, made the whole even more specious. The popularity of these three players ensured a great box-office success, about which Kramer declared, '[but] I don't think we made it with the intellectual idiot fringe because they were already ahead of us' – a remark symptomatic of his aspirations.

By the time he made this remark he was smarting from the successive failures he had had since that film. After he had discussed them on television one reviewer wrote: 'According to Mr Kramer, he didn't really make any mistakes. It was just that the American public, inexplicably, perversely, chose not to appreciate certain movies Mr Kramer thought would be good for them, those big-budget, big-idea jobs thrust upon us, like cough medicine for a sore conscience. Really, now, Mr Kramer *produced* some pretty good movies; he *directed* things like *The Defiant Ones, On the Beach, Judgment at Nuremberg* and *Ship of Fools*. All those big ideas – race hatred, nuclear war, evolution, genocide – running around in that tiny mind gives me cramps.' Interestingly, that appeared in *The New York Times* (in 1975, written by the paper's television reviewer, 'Cyclops'), but the films listed had all appeared in that journal's Ten Best of the Year lists, as chosen by its critic of the time, Bosley Crowther. After acknowledging that the period would not have been the same without Kramer's tombstone Messages to the World, it must be said that Crowther, as critic of the nation's most influential newspaper, could make or break any movie with any pretension to seriousness. Consciously or not, other reviewers followed suit. Since he supposedly represented the views of the New York intelligentsia, he often influenced the voters of the Academy Awards. He had a knack of liking the films which impressed the industry itself – including those of Otto Preminger, another mediocre film-maker whose reputation did not survive Crowther's departure from *The New York Times*.

Apart from *Laura*, Preminger's early films had attracted little attention and the fact that **The Moon Is Blue** (1953) did so had nothing to do with its quality. It traces the attempts of an architect (William Holden) to seduce a fey girl (Maggie McNamara), and is precisely the sort of comedy (one set, four characters) which twenty years later might be seen on television any night of the week. The Legion of Decency, knowing the Broadway original (which Preminger had 'produced'), threw up its skirts in horror, and the M.P.P.A., having seen words like 'virgin' and 'mistress' in the script, refused the film its seal – which in theory meant that no cinema in the U.S. could book it. It was Preminger's first independent production, and he went ahead courageously, if on a small budget: the reams of press coverage persuaded exhibitors to show it and the public to see it – thus taking the first steps towards the crumbling of the industry's own censorship.

Preminger returned to 20th Century-Fox, where he had been a contract director, to make two films in CinemaScope. **River of No Return** (1954) takes the situation of *The African Queen* to the Old West, but he was not the director to get sparks from these supposedly incompatible companions in danger, a gambler (Robert Mitchum) and a showgirl (Marilyn Monroe). **Carmen Jones** (1954) takes Bizet's opera to the Deep South, as adapted by Oscar Hammerstein II for Broadway. The film starts magnificently, as the sauntering Carmen (Dorothy Dandridge) goes into her Habañera – 'Dat's Love' – and taunts Corporal Joe (Harry Belafonte) by, at one point, brushing his pants, a peak of eroticism at the time; but from then on it proceeds at ponderous pace.

An all-black musical was still considered daring, and since with two of these three films Preminger had succeeded in drawing attention to his advanced thinking, he did so again with **The Man with the Golden Arm** (1955), sensibly retaining from his last film Saul Bass, whose posters and credit titles did so much to get Preminger's films discussed. In this case, a still rare jazz score – by Shorty Rogers – also helped. The subject, taken from Nelson Algren's novel, was drug addiction, which had been taboo in the movie industry since the era of *Broken Blossoms* – to which, most of the time, this film seemed to belong. Only for a brief moment, when its hero (Frank Sinatra) needs a fix, does it have the force or legitimacy of *The Lost Weekend*, which it was patently emulating.

Following previous example, **Anatomy of a Murder** (1959) introduced a number of banned words, such as 'contraceptive', 'rape' and 'spermatogenesis'. Respectability was triply confirmed by a Duke Ellington score, by the fact that the original bestselling novel had been penned by a judge (under the pseudonym Robert Traver) – who felt that the readers of fiction should for once be told the truth about real-life murder and trial – and by the casting of a much-respected lawyer, Joseph N. Welch, as the judge in the film. Wendell Mayes wrote the screenplay, and for Preminger this is an accomplished film, but 160 minutes is too long to attend to characters – lawyers, witnesses and the accused – for whom we could not give a damn.

Porgy and Bess (1959) is an ignominious step in Preminger's career, since, with the compliance of Sam Goldwyn, he virtually destroyed one of the major works of this century. Goldwyn, for what was to be his last film, had signed Rouben Mamoulian, who had directed the original stage production. The two could not get along, so Goldwyn substituted the director of *Carmen Jones*, who but gingerly moves his Todd-AO camera within the horrendously theatrical setting. Except for a picnic sequence which is derived from *Carousel*, the piece dies from inertia, its talented cast reduced to amateurs. I have seen William Warfield as Porgy and Leontyne Price as Bess on the stage, and in place of Warfield's soaring, majestic voice, a light tenor has been dubbed to Sidney Poitier's conscientious and dull performance; and where Price was a superb slattern, Dorothy Dandridge's dubbed Bess is a mere waif tossed on the breeze.

Although foreign critics, especially those in Britain, looked askance at Preminger's work*, *Porgy and Bess* was sufficiently applauded in the U.S. for him to acquire (or have bought on his behalf) the expensive rights to bestsellers. **Exodus** (1960) is an overblown account of Leon Uris's tale of Jewish refugees settling in Israel, but Allen Drury's novel, **Advise and Consent** (1962), provides the basis for what is by far Preminger's best film. Bass's credits promised to lift the lid off Washington, and certain observers recognised the characters' real life counterparts – as well as the juggling for power, the party rivalry and the skeletons in the closet. The skeletons turn out to be Communism and homosexuality, and if Wendell Mayes's screenplay has a fault it is its inability to see the comic aspect of setting up these particular bogies. Homosexuality as a fact of life had at last been acknowledged in a Hollywood film, after insinuations in a number of others, but this was the first to stage a sequence in a gay bar, and to portray a homosexual both overtly and sympathetically. He (Don Murray) is a happily married senator being blackmailed to do something of which he disapproves (we may find it difficult to believe that any politician would prefer suicide to

compromising his integrity). Given Preminger's opportunistic attitude towards the liberalisation of the screen, I do not think he deserves credit for retaining this element from Drury's novel, but he is to be acknowledged for telling his story plainly and rejuvenating the veteran cast of Lew Ayres, Henry Fonda, Franchot Tone, Walter Pidgeon, Paul Ford, Peter Lawford and Charles Laughton. This is Laughton's last film, and as the wily Southern senator he walks away with it under his arm.

The renown of these films, if somewhat self-engendered, served to obscure one resounding failure in their midst, a stolid version of Shaw's **Saint Joan** (1957), waywardly cut by Graham Greene, if we are to believe the screenplay credit. A solid English cast supports an American teenager, Jean Seberg, whose total inexperience is only too obvious. A few years later, Preminger's reputation ebbed to nothing – not overnight, but from *The Cardinal* (1963) via *In Harm's Way* (1965) to *Hurry, Sundown* (1967). With Hollywood censorship gone, there were no more taboos to break, and he was revealed more than ever as a lumbering showman drawn to overblown bestsellers. However, **Bunny Lake Is Missing** (1965) embodies, for the most part, the straightforward virtues of *Advise and Consent* and such early contract films as *Angel Face*. It is Preminger's contribution to the grotesqueries that followed *Psycho* and *Whatever Happened to Baby Jane?* (q.v.), and it finds him in charge of the two greatest names in the twentieth-century British theatre, Laurence Olivier and Noël Coward, one as a no-nonsense Scotland Yard man, the other as a witch-like landlord.

The eminence of both players seems to have protected them from Preminger's on-set rages. He did not, as the saying goes, run a happy ship, and many actors, having once worked with him, refused to do so again. Among his last films is **Such Good Friends** (1972), a comedy about smart and promiscuous New Yorkers which followed a number of others such. Louis Gold's reputedly autobiographical novel was the basis of the screenplay by Elaine May (q.v.) – under the pseudonym of Esther Dale – and the dialogue is as pointed as the situations are distasteful. It starts with the pleasing premise of a wife (Dyan Cannon) confronted with her husband's

---

*Goldwyn waited through the five years' London run of *South Pacific* to get the Dominion Theatre for *Porgy and Bess*, and in Paris he waited a similar period for a cinema caught up with *West Side Story* (q.v.); but *Porgy and Bess* failed to repeat the success of either film and after dreadful notices was withdrawn in a matter of weeks.

infidelities as he is dying; the scene in which she goes down on a doctor (James Coco) and he spatters on her nose shows Preminger unchanged with the years.

A more sincere seeker for significance was Robert Rossen, though the two films he made after *All the King's Men* both flopped – **The Brave Bulls** (1951), made in Mexico, and **Mambo** (1954). With the advent of CinemaScope, the studios took a renewed interest in epics, and Rossen persuaded United Artists to back **Alexander the Great** (1956), which with *Helen of Troy* (q.v.) is the best of a bad bunch – and coincidentally the only other Greek subject among a plethora of Romans. Both films use uncluttered texts and look impressive: in this case the veteran art director André Andreyev achieves a superb pastiche of Greek architecture with economy – but the harsh Spanish locations could persuade no one that they are in Macedonia or Asia Minor. Rossen's original three-hour script became, after intervention by U.A., only 135 minutes on the screen, in the end neither a comic strip nor the intended psychological study. Its only merit is its responsibility to the subject, and it might be less dull if Richard Burton, though graceful and authoritative, could suggest any complexity of character.

Rossen's commitment to substantial subjects was sufficient reason for Zanuck to engage him for **Island in the Sun** (1957), written by Alfred Hayes from Alec Waugh's novel about life in the British West Indies. The tenets behind the tale are sound – that it is time for the black people to take over government – but any interest that Rossen may have felt is deflected by the starry cast and exotic locations, seemingly the essential requirements of CinemaScope. The major problems touched upon in reel one are reduced to a couple of interracial romances. Harry Belafonte plays the key black role, a young lawyer and opportunistic labour leader – in fact, a nonsensical amalgamation of two characters in the book. His love scenes with Joan Fontaine, though confined to some hand-holding, were the subject of much comment in the press and were regarded by the industry itself as a great step forward in this area. Thus, yet again, a bestseller freed Hollywood from its Victorian morals – a point reinforced by the fact that no one commented (publicly,

at least) on the clinch, earlier in the film, between John Justin and Dorothy Dandridge, probably the first white-black kiss★ in the American cinema.

Independently Rossen made **They Came to Cordura** (1959), which attempts to examine courage and cowardice as it follows a trek across the desert. Led by Gary Cooper, in one of his late masochistic performances, it was, deservedly, a failure, and Rossen was planning to recut it when he died in 1966. If we ignore, as we should, his last film, *Lilith*, we find his uneven work capped by one excellent one, **The Hustler** (1961). Here he is marvellously in control of the script he had written with Sydney Carroll, faithfully based on a novel by Walter Tevis and concerning the small-time Charlies whose aspirations rise and die in the shadowy world of pool rooms. As a young man Rossen had written an unperformed play on the same theme, which is perhaps why he responds so well. It was a subject that films had ignored, at least in the U.S., and his portrait of the seedy night city stands alone between *Act of Violence* and *Fat City*. The film is memorable for the well acted performances of Paul Newman, George C. Scott, Piper Laurie, Jackie Gleason and Myron McCormick.

★There were of course occasions when white actresses played half-castes. However, the difference was that Dorothy Dandridge was black, and not a white actress in dusky make-up.

Jackie Gleason and Paul Newman in *The Hustler*, which finally fulfilled the promise of Robert Rossen's early movies. He had worked as a writer on some of Warner Bros. more distinguished melodramas before turning to direction in 1947. He made only a handful of films in that capacity, including *All the King's Men*, which established him as a major writer-director, but it was not till *The Hustler*, ten years later, that he found a subject as congenial to his talent.

The cinema's battle for audiences included a vast number of musicals and historical spectaculars, with many of Hollywood's leading directors tempted to work on them, as well as some of the lesser lights, like Anthony Mann, who directed *El Cid*, with Charlton Heston, left. The producer was Samuel Bronston, who supplied the apparent need for such films from Spain, where the costs were cheap – including those of the hundreds of extras needed for soldiers. After a while, however, the public decided that the reserved seats/higher prices/separate performances system was not worth the boredom of spectacle without content. Bronston went bankrupt, leaving *El Cid* as the one watchable film he made.

As a producer of epics Samuel Bronston achieved a brief eminence, and we might pause to look at the two directed by Anthony Mann, best known for such action tales as *Winchester '73* (q.v.). Mann began *Spartacus* (q.v.), but was replaced by Stanley Kubrick, and was thus free when called to Spain by Bronston for **El Cid** (1961). Bronston had produced one Hollywood film in 1943, and resurfaced in 1959 after a trip to Spain, during which he learnt that filming in that country was economical since wages were low, and that many American companies had funds there blocked for reinvestment. Both *John Paul Jones* and a new version of *King of Kings* had 'name' casts and were taken for distribution by the Hollywood companies, which encouraged Bronston to pay the star salaries demanded by Charlton Heston and Sophia Loren for *El Cid*. As Spain's legendary hero Heston has stature, but his comic-strip face is incapable of much emotion. However, he is involved in adventures which are the very stuff of boys' fiction, often detailed with visual imagination – especially in the final sequence, the battle on the beach and the siege. Public

response caused Bronston to embark upon the building of a studio near Madrid, and after the failure of *55 Days at Peking* he recalled Mann for **The Fall of the Roman Empire** (1964), whose harsh winter colours again confirm his visual flair. Not since *Intolerance* had so many individuals been seen in such grandiose settings but when they come to talking only James Mason among the leads is not reduced to a waxwork. Bronston had a second flop with *Circus World*, and when at the same time his principal financier withdrew, he left the industry in a flurry of lawsuits.

Neither Rossen nor Mann were familiar names to the public at large, nor was, or is, Robert Wise, despite the success of *The Sound of Music*. Wise is typical of this period in that he rose from contract director to independent producer-director, by dint of choosing above-average material; but his conscientious and often shrewd craftsmanship cannot – at least with hindsight – disguise the hollowness of much of it. **Executive Suite** (1954), for instance, has some quaint notions about big business, insisting that it is less interested in profits than keeping the workers happy and turning out good products. In this boardroom struggle for power, the issue is between two directors – young, idealistic William Holden, seen in overalls doing something unspecified on the factory floor, and ageing, avaricious Fredric March, who even before Holden's Capraesque speech is generally despised by the other members of the board. The film's precepts were hardly questioned, since it moved away from stereotyped areas of screen fiction – and it was much praised for dispensing with background music. Ernest Lehman scripted, from a novel by Cameron Hawley; and another presumably honest man, John Houseman, the producer, had brought Wise to M-G-M, who offered a contract.

Wise moved briefly back to Warners for **Helen of Troy** (1955), and it has to be said that with Homer to guide him he had an easier task than Rossen with *Alexander the Great*. However the dialogue does not strike a note equal to the high matters on display, and the leads – Jacques Sernas as Paris, and Rosanna Podesta as Helen – are etiolated. Nevertheless, helped by Harry Stradling on camera and the decor of Roger Furze, Wise attacks the big scenes with vigour and imagination, getting closer to 'The Iliad' than was appreciated by reviewers. More justifiably, the critics did not care for **Tribute to a Bad Man** (1956), which suffered from the substitution of James Cagney for Spencer Tracy during shooting. Tracy was by this time a gruff bear, but Cagney retained his bantam-like persona; for all his authority the piece really needed something of the godlike stubbornness that Tracy brought to *Broken Lance* (q.v.) – for this is a Western with conscience, needing an heroic centre. It was typical of the films produced at M-G-M under Dore Schary's regime, one of the last of which was **Somebody Up There Likes Me** (1956). It was one of several based on confessional bestsellers, in this case by Rocky Graziano, who assures us in a foreword that what follows is accurate, a comment at odds with the title song, which offers the sort of syrupy self-satisfaction that had remained the keynote of M-G-M. The locations used are strong and 'realistic', but the piece is bathed in a romantic glow to facilitate approval of the fact that an admired prizefighter (Paul Newman) had been a juvenile delinquent.

Ernest Lehman wrote the screenplay, and it is surprising to find that he considers it his best; he also regards the film itself – the second of the four he made with Wise – as the most satisfactory of those with which he has been connected.

Wise does not seem to agree: at least, when he came again to tackle a factual, contemporary subject – after three unexceptional, if pleasing, pictures – he allowed no compromise. **I Want to Live!** (1958) is the story of Barbara Graham, a small-time party girl whose life ended in a gas chamber in San Quentin in 1955, after being convicted of murdering an old lady during a burglary. Walter Wanger initiated the project, which was produced by Joseph L. Mankiewicz's company because his nephew Don (son of Herman) had written a screenplay from the material provided by Ed Montgomery, a Pulitzer Prize-winning journalist who had doubts about Graham's guilt. After Wise agreed to direct, the material was reworked by the novelist Nelson Gidding – who, Wise said, should have received a sole writing credit. The film's first hour sets out the details of Graham's grubby life, and the second follows her time in jail. A further half hour charts all the grisly minutiae necessary for Graham's death and is a harrowing plea for the abolition of capital punishment: if we accept the polemic and the fact that crime must be followed by punishment, this section causes the film to tower above the other crime dramas of the time. Instead of the types assembled in the gangster films of the Thirties, Wise cast players who resemble the people we meet in the street; and though he overstates elsewhere he does not do so when it really matters. He is let down only by his leading actress, Susan Hayward, who never tried harder but was incapable of portraying anyone but the usual movie broad – sharp-tongued and chip-on-the-shoulder. Because of her the film is not moving but only well-intentioned and gruelling.

Unlike Stanley Kramer, Wise did not take the film's favourable reception as evidence that more significance was needed in the cinema, but behind the heist thrills of **Odds Against Tomorrow** (1959), produced and directed for Harry Belafonte's company, is a plea for racial tolerance. Slater (Robert Ryan) has, as the film puts it, pre-Civil War ideas about blacks,

887

and the heist turns on the fact that one of his partners (Belafonte), accepted unwillingly, is black. This mixture of message, seediness and crime is as skilfully managed as that in *I Want to Live!*, but it is less well balanced – which may be why audiences were not interested.

Nevertheless, both films pointed to Wise as the logical choice for **West Side Story** (1961), given its attitude to the backstreet gangs which are at its centre. It had been a triumphant Broadway achievement directed and choreographed by Jerome Robbins (who accepted co-director billing on the film after initially refusing to go to Hollywood just to re-create his dances). Wise, who had not directed a musical before, observed after United Artists had sacked Robbins (for going over-budget and over-schedule) that the film remained their joint effort, since Robbins had rehearsed all the numbers with the cast. Robbins had shot the opening sequence, 'The Jets' Song', before leaving, and it is so electrifying that we are a long way into the film before realising that the rest of it is not exactly compelling. Certainly the moralising of the screenplay (by Lehman, from Arthur Laurents's original) is now tedious, the street gangs too much like chorus boys, and the Romeo and Juliet lovers cloying as played by Richard Beymer and Natalie Wood; but the choreography and much of Leonard Bernstein's score remain exciting. The film was as enthusiastically received as the original and went on to win Oscars for Best Film and for its two directors.

Wise followed with two modest black and white films, **Two for the Seesaw** (1962) and **The Haunting** (1963). The first had been a Broadway two-hander by William Gibson, coming to the screen virtually unchanged – and, alas, uncut – and therefore heavily dependent on its players, Shirley MacLaine and Robert Mitchum. The second film was based on a novel by Shirley Jackson, which on this evidence has a weak exposition ('What is a poltergeist?') and an even sillier denouement. This was Wise returning to sources, since he had directed his first film for Val Lewton; but in following Lewton's principles on horror, he raises never a frisson, unaided by mannered performances from Julie Harris as the frightened girl and Claire Bloom as a predatory lesbian.

The problem after *The Sound of Music* was to find another musical for 20th Century-Fox and Julie Andrews. The associate producer on that film and *West Side Story* had been Saul Chaplin, who is the credited producer on **Star!** (1968), a project mooted around Hollywood for two decades and by this time resolutely old fashioned. It is the story of Gertrude Lawrence, 'probably the most beautiful and entrancing creature who ever walked on the English stage', as she is described in the film by her famous partner, Noël Coward – impersonated by Daniel Massey with Coward's own (uncredited) intervention on his dialogue. The rest was penned by William Fairchild, a British writer with an undistinguished record. Opening with a newsreel in the manner of *Citizen Kane* (on which Wise had worked as editor), the screenplay brings not a modicum of wit or intuition to Miss Lawrence's fairly uninteresting life. Julie Andrews plays with style, clearly most at ease in those aspects which parallel her own career, which is why the first half is the better. She is also winning when the songs are done simply or in keeping with the period (as in the two excerpts from the Coward plays); but too often they are staged in the manner of this studio's musicals of the Betty Grable era. There was a particularly ugly advertising campaign, and Wise, reflecting on its failure, felt 'we had got ourselves mislaid somewhere along the way. There wasn't quite the documentary feeling about it that I had intended.' Others felt that the public did not want to see Miss Andrews as a bitch goddess, hard and lacquered. Wise has worked intermittently since, but with no marked degree of success.

Another R.K.O. alumnus who has enjoyed a long career is Robert Aldrich (b.1918), purveyor of the wittiest and most indiscreet interviews in Hollywood – and some of its worst films. He became a director in 1953, and came to the fore with two adventures for Burt Lancaster's company, **Apache** (1954) and **Vera Cruz** (1954), the latter chiefly notable for playing down Gary Cooper's ageing hero in favour of Lancaster's grinning villain. Aldrich's penchant for Hollywood stories was first apparent with **The Big Knife** (1955), filmed in the wake of *A Star Is Born* but, unlike that, bland and hysterical at the same time. James Poe's script goes further than Clifford Odets's original play in indicating an endless supply of blondes and booze, but if it is eloquent on Hollywood's ruthlessness it is weak on the search of one poor little star (Jack Palance) for integrity. Aldrich later admitted that it was difficult to feel sorry for a man making $5,000 a week; and the drama further suffers from the fact that the balance of power had changed so much since 1949, when the play was written, that few stars were still dependent on the whims of producers.

The film demonstrated no directorial style at all, unless it was over-emphasis at the more demanding moments, but it could be said that Aldrich had achieved a certain florid manner by the time he came to make his most famous film, **Whatever Happened to Baby Jane?** (1962). Obviously he saw in Henry Farrell's thriller a chance to make his own *Sunset Boulevard*, for its subject is two Hollywood stars (Bette Davis, Joan Crawford) after the glory faded. The camera pokes about their Santa Monica home for over two hours, which is a long time to watch two old ladies locked in depravity. Their environment is admirably conveyed, but the chief interest, as in the follow-up, **Hush . . . Hush, Sweet Charlotte** (1964), is in watching Bette Davis give point and meaning to the grotesques she plays. A third exercise in Grand Guignol was meant for Davis, **Whatever Happened to Aunt Alice?** (1969), but she was replaced by Geraldine Page, with Ruth Gordon as the other obligatory ageing star. Aldrich turned over the direction to Lee H. Katzin, whose flair for the genre atones for the absence of Miss Davis.

With a war film, **The Dirty Dozen** (1967), Aldrich had a success comparable to that of *Baby Jane*, and this seemed to confirm his view that he should never suggest when he could emphasise, especially when handling the more sensational aspects – in this case repeated violence. His handling was not perhaps detrimental to another Hollywood tale, **The Legend of Lylah Clare** (1968), but it was in any case a failure, for which he blamed himself. 'There are twenty-five cop-outs' he said, 'who cared about Peter Finch, and is Kim Novak a joke in her own time? . . . [but] if the director-producer can't, with no limitation on money, communicate to an audience what he wants them to be interested in, fascinated in and/or amused by, then he has failed. Then he shouldn't have made that picture.' The source was a television play about a lightly disguised Marilyn Monroe, but the film, in his words, involves 'an amalgamation of myths', which we recognise also as Dietrich, Joan Crawford, Harlow and perhaps Garbo. Unfortunately, they emerge less as myths than ideas – ideas desperately in search of a script. Novak is for once almost adequate trying to portray them, but Finch is absurdly miscast as a von Sternberg-type of director – and at this time looks absurd in only removing his shirt before throwing himself on the bed to make love. Even so, as thriller or Hollywood gossip, the film has something, which may not be said of another show-business tale, **The Killing of Sister George** (1968). Frank Marcus's original play had been both funny and touching as it followed a B.B.C. star of soap opera whose professional and private lives fall apart simultaneously. On the stage in London and New York, Beryl Reid as Sister George had been bad-tempered, selfish, piggish and particularly nasty when drunk (which she habitually is), yet somehow sympathetic: but in the film Miss Reid becomes simply another of Aldrich's grotesques. As her sullen, childish lover, Susannah York is negative, while as the B.B.C. official who comes between them, a mailed fist in a velvet glove, Coral Brown is only bitchy. These two ladies have a love scene – the first in a respectable industry film – claimed to be essential to the argument, though it had originally been at a different point in the script and between York and Reid – till the latter refused to play it.

Loud accusations of vulgarisation were levelled by the novelist Joseph Wambaugh after he had seen Aldrich's version of his tale of the L.A. police force, **The Choirboys** (1977). There was much talk of lawsuits and Wambaugh insisted thereafter on creative control of any of his novels bought for filming. We may assume Steve Shagan felt the same about **Hustle** (1975), since his hero (Burt Reynolds) is a younger version of the one he wrote for *Save the Tiger* (q.v), romantically-minded, aching with nostalgia and with a stubborn belief that chivalry and compassion can counter contemporary malaise. He is a cop and is constantly humiliated, for instance by listening to the conversations of his callgirl mistress with her clients. Whereas by this time even the least crime movie attempted subtlety, Aldrich reverted to the style of *Kiss Me Deadly*, explaining and then underlining; this is presumably why it was one of the few Reynolds vehicles to fail at the box office – as indeed did most of Aldrich's films of the Seventies.

It is agreeable, at least for a while, to turn to Stanley Donen, who seldom sought other aims than to divert us. After *Funny Face* he returned to directing in collaboration at the behest of Warners, who brought George Abbott from Broadway to re-stage **The Pajama Game** (1957) and **Damn Yankees** (1958) with the original casts – apart from the two leads who were replaced by Doris Day and Tab Hunter respectively in the interests of the box office. These are the best records we have of Broadway shows, since in spite of a mobile camera and much reshaping, often for the open air, their origins shine through, especially in the musical numbers. The effect is frequently exhilarating, and credit must be shared with Bob Fosse, reworking his Broadway choreography. The music and lyrics by Richard Adler and Jerry Ross (who died during the second show's New York run) often lack the 'heart' which is extolled in one of the best songs. Both books were based on the premise, then current, that the most suitable subject for a musical was the least likely – that is, a wage dispute in a pyjama factory, and 'Faust' with a baseball background; the latter has the advantage of Gwen Verdon's emissary from Below, 'a ravishingly beautiful witch', whose obvious and inept vamping is a high spot in the decade's musicals.

But musicals were going out of fashion and Donen turned to comedy. **Kiss Them for Me** (1957) was written by Julius Epstein from a play of the same name by Luther Davis, based on 'Shore Leave', a novel by Frederick Wakeman. The result is just another comic World War II movie (the spate of these was due both to nostalgia and to America's involvement in a rather more squalid war, in Korea) which tries to examine the attitudes of some participants and non-participants. The bitterness of the climax, however, is merely spurious, and Cary Grant is miscast as a giddy young rip. Despite the film's failure, Grant and

Donen formed their own production company, but the films it made (all comedies) – and those made by Donen without Grant – were equally badly scripted and often featured players with no gift for the genre (though in this case Jayne Mansfield and Suzy Parker were forced on Donen by 20th Century-Fox).

Donen was certainly no Lubitsch, but **Indiscreet** (1958) has its pleasures, not least of them Cary Grant making bricks without straw as a diplomat involved in an affair with an actress – played by Ingrid Bergman, whose smile alone compensates for the fact that she was not a natural comedienne. The setting is London, as scripted by Norman Krasna from his Broadway play. In **Once More with Feeling** (1960), Harry Kurnitz, adapting his own play, also relocated the action to London. The subject here, long absent from movies, is warring spouses, played by Kay Kendall and Yul Brynner. Brynner's only resource in comedy is to look bright and pleased with himself, and since Donen, aiming for the skittish, allowed Brynner's steamroller approach to dictate the tone, the film is almost a total disaster. With Grant in the cast, **The Grass Is Greener** (1960) is an improvement, but compares unfavourably with his prewar comedies – though it goes further than they could in suggesting physical infidelity, when a hitherto blameless wife (Deborah Kerr) is drawn to an interloper (Robert Mitchum). Cary Grant is the husband, Jean Simmons the other woman, and the setting is one of the stately homes of England – the country where Donen settled, though he continued to make Hollywood or Hollywood-style movies.

The best of these are **Charade** (1964) and **Two for the Road** (1967) – indeed they are among the best-remembered films of their era. In both Donen was working again with Audrey Hepburn, and once more he settles for chic; his confidence atones for a certain lack of subtlety. *Charade* is imitation Hitchcock, depending on European locations (mainly Paris), the twists in the plot (which are often good), and the playing of Grant and Hepburn (who are splendid – he quizzically underplaying and she having the time of her life). In *Two for the Road* Hepburn and Donen were allied with two more realistic Britons, Albert Finney and the novelist

Frederic Raphael, with results more rewarding than usual in such circumstances. Raphael had cleverly devised a study, fairly abrasive and in non-sequential order, of a deteriorating marriage set against the roads of France, where the couple first meet – and neither Miss Hepburn nor the Côte d'Azur was ever more appealing.

It is best to draw a veil over some of Donen's other films, which are closer in quality to *Once More with Feeling* than to *Singin' in the Rain*. Indeed, as each came along, one began to wonder exactly what his contribution to the films made with Gene Kelly and George Abbott had been. There was a singularly unfortunate musical, **The Little Prince** (1974), with music by Frederick Loewe and book and lyrics by Alan Jay Lerner – who in his memoir blames Donen's handling for the film's complete failure. However, **Movie Movie** (1978) is sheer delight, cleverly written by Larry Gelbart and Sheldon Keller. The spoofing of old movies had been a staple of television comedy, and sometimes in the Sixties there seemed to be half a dozen spoofs of old Hollywood musicals playing off-Broadway at the same time – all of them dreadful. *Movie Movie*, reasonably, looks back primarily at old Warner Bros. movies, one on boxing, 'Dynamite Hands', and then a musical, 'Baxter's Beauties of 1933' – and between the two is shown an equally sharp take-off of a trailer of the period. Donen and his collaborators are both affectionate and accurate, but not slavishly so – both sections, for instance, gain from the use of colour.★ *Movie Movie* lacks only heart and drive, qualities also missing from George C. Scott's performances as veteran boxing trainer 'Gloves' Malloy and Broadway producer 'Spats' Baxter. Audiences, not associating Scott with light entertainment, and having perhaps been 'bitten' by those off-Broadway shows, stayed away; it was their loss.

The very nature of *Movie Movie* reinforces my belief that many of the lighter entertainments prove more enduring than those sweating for uplift or message. There are some good serious films in this period, and those that failed did so not because of the temerity of producers and

★On its original cinema release 'Dynamite Hands' was in black and white.

distributors, as in the past, but because of the inadequacy of the talents tackling them. There was one director who remained light-hearted, but he is a social satirist of a high order. Billy Wilder o'ertops all other American film-makers at this time, and some half dozen of the films that he made then are likely to be around as long as there are screens on which to show them.

If one of them proves to be **The Seven Year Itch** (1955), that will be because of Marilyn Monroe, curiously thought to be 'too substantial for dreams' by the critic of *The New Yorker*, who added that she reduced the picture 'to the level of a burlesque show'. The level was hardly high to start with, being a Broadway farce of the same species as *The Moon Is Blue*, but much less smirking and twice as funny. Its author, George Axelrod, wrote the screenplay with Wilder, involving a grass widower (Tom Ewell) whose erotic thoughts wander to the girl upstairs. In the role of the girl, a combination of two comedy standbys, old and new – the innocent in the big city, and the kook – Monroe seems oddly cast at first glance: looking as she does, she is hardly likely to be either. But in a way that was hers alone – for she never seemed to have a particularly strong, definite personality – she makes the girl warm, funny and sexy, to the extent of overwhelming the little man with the seven-year itch. That may be just as well, since Ewell is over-reliant on leers and cunning grins.

For his second film as an independent, Wilder accepted Jack L. Warner's offer of **The Spirit of St Louis** (1957), based on the first solo transatlantic flight. In writing the screenplay with Wendell Mayes, from an adaptation by Charles Lederer of Lindbergh's memoirs, he found it difficult to 'reach' the flyer. The film was a challenge, since he had never tackled an 'outdoor' subject, nor could he rely on his sardonic humour. He resolved his difficulties triumphantly, by simply and soberly recreating the experience – the events leading up to departure and the flight itself, with its perils and wonders. Above all – with the aid of the superb images caught by Robert Burks and J. Peverell Marley – it is the awe that he has captured: of clouds, sea, mudflats, tiny planes in the distance; of mist and darkness and sunlight peeping into the

891

cockpit; of the crowds in Paris which take on the quality of a seething, roaring, unknown beast. At a cost of $6 million the film was the most disastrous flop in the studio's history; years later in his memoir Jack Warner was still pondering on the matter. A contributory factor may be the performance of James Stewart, over twenty years too old for the role, with hair waved and blonded, and seemingly daunted at playing a living hero. But the truth probably is that in the jet-age Lindbergh's flight was no longer of interest, especially as everyone knew the result.

Wilder's imagination and understanding were more expectedly on display in **Love in the Afternoon** (1957). These qualities were needed, since these post-meridian sessions overlooking the Place Vendôme are between a dewy-eyed student (Audrey Hepburn) and the middle-aged roué (Gary Cooper) whose amours preoccupy her private detective father (Maurice Chevalier). As is apparent from the gypsy band kept at hand to aid amorous conquest, this is Wilder again attempting the Lubitsch style, though the film is for much of its length a straightforward remake of Czinner's *Ariane*. Both versions are about double standards, but Wilder obscures that. In this, his first collaboration with I. A. L. Diamond (who was to partner Wilder on all but one of his subsequent scripts), they manage to suggest that the girl is quite compliant, but in not making the lover the cold fish that he is in the original – it was presumably important to retain Cooper's charm – they are conventional where Czinner was poignant. To keep Czinner's magical ending then requires an unconvincing line to the effect that all planes are grounded. When the public failed to find any virtue in the age discrepancy of the lovers, Wilder fell back on a thriller, **Witness for the Prosecution** (1958), based on Agatha Christie's courtroom play. The script, which he wrote with Harry Kurnitz, has added some necessary humour. Wilder's puckish approach is most apparent in the portrait of the testy defending barrister, splendidly hammed by Charles Laughton, but it is hard to care whether Tyrone Power is acquitted or convicted, and Marlene Dietrich is ludicrous both as a thirtyish singer and in impersonating a Cockney.

The Diamond connection obviously stimulated Wilder, and they started a splendid run with **Some Like It Hot** (1959), again a risky subject and again developed from an antique German film. It was, in box-office terms, the most successful comedy ever made, and it is one of the near perfect ones, the wit of its lines only exceeded by the bizarre quality of the situations – which involve, as perhaps the whole world knows, two men hiding in drag with an all-woman orchestra. Marilyn Monroe's band singer, with her realistic estimate of her voice and her yen for bootleg hooch and saxophone players, is one of the cinema's most endearing creations; Wilder matches the innocence he found in her with that of Jack Lemmon and Tony Curtis, from the first moment we see them disguised, purse-lipped and tottering on high heels. Unlike Curtis, Lemmon does not, for his own reasons, yearn to get back into men's togs, despite his lech for Marilyn; this actor's playing in most comedy is virtuoso but here it has to be, and indeed is, inspired.

Flushed with success, Wilder and Diamond mounted another assault on the accepted sexual themes permissible in the cinema. **The Apartment** (1960) concerns a nice young man (Lemmon) who lends his flat to his bosses for assignations, and a nice young woman (Shirley MacLaine) who willingly goes to such places with one of them (Fred MacMurray). She is, admittedly, made to suffer in the way of female transgressors, by being deserted and attempting suicide – but that enables Wilder to add poignancy to what was otherwise a conventional mélange of situation comedy and satire. Whether or not it was his intention, he gets closer in tone than hitherto – certainly closer than in *Love in the Afternoon* – to the bitter-sweet continental romances of the early Talkie period. And in that respect, he was aided, paradoxically, by a compendium of the relaxed but wary attitudes of New Yorkers – towards the office party, loneliness in a crowd, smart little bars in which to get blotto, assumptions about hit shows, and the tragedy in the neighbouring apartment. These, and more, are superbly expressed by Lemmon and MacLaine, both managing those odd curves between farce and pathos which make this film unusual. The source, Wilder has admitted, is *Brief Encounter*, since he began to wonder about that apartment which was almost used for adultery.

The source of **One, Two, Three** (1961) was a one-act play by Molnár, unrecognisable here as performed and directed *molto furioso*, with the jokes coming a dozen a minute. In the circumstances, it is not surprising that some do not work, and others hit obvious targets – e.g. Russia and Communism, Germany and its lack of war guilt, the U.S. and Coca-Colonisation; but most are smart (there are several cinema references), some utilise a knowledge of the famous international *sous-entendres*, and many of them are wonderful. The film is built around, and takes its frenetic speed from one of the great players, James Cagney, in his last film before retirement:* he plays a rough-and-tumble businessman up against it when his ward – a batty Southern belle, deliciously played by Pamela Tiffin – falls in love with a bare-footed and rabid red (Horst Buchholz).

After three superlative comedies – though the last of them was not particularly popular – Wilder tackled **Irma La Douce** (1963), which had been the first French musical in generations to become an international success. This was due to Marguerite Monnot's score and a book which celebrated the whores and pimps of Pigalle. Wilder jettisoned the score because he said that he could not make a musical, but that left him with a risqué story which censors would find hard to ban, since it had been acclaimed in several of the world's more sophisticated cities. The screenplay did try to appease Middle America by making Irma (MacLaine) turn from unrepentant whoring and by making Nestor (Lemmon) a pimp by accident. Doubtless Wilder was amused at making the first American film in which the baby is born on the altar steps, but it is only because this was the first major American film on prostitution in fifty years that it was popular. It was Wilder's biggest financial success, which amuses him, for he likes it least of all his films. In my view, it is as bad as any film could be that is directed by him and stars these particular players. Lemmon and MacLaine remain resolutely American, and though Wilder hired Alexander Trauner to design a studio Paris to match

*From which he emerged, twenty years later, to appear in *Ragtime* (q.v.)

the comic-strip humours, the Frenchness of the original eluded him.

Wilder had always taken care with casting, knowing that likeable playing is a palliative to outrageous behaviour: but in **Kiss Me Stupid** (1964) we are constantly invited to confuse the character played by Dean Martin – a smug, semi-alcoholic and lecherous singer – with Martin himself. Passing through a small, remote Western town, he meets two songwriters who will stop at nothing to have him sing one of their songs. They are two ordinary Joes so obsessed with the American dream that they resort to pimping – and that is but one of several frontal attacks on sacred cows: the image of the television personality; a climactic melée in which a wife and a hooker (Kim Novak) swop roles and like it; and an implicit suggestion that the only fun place in town is the local brothel – 'The Belly Button' – 'Drop in and get lost.' Since the line is typical, it is clear that the film is not greatly dependent on wit. Like all good farces – the source this time was an Italian play, 'L'Ora della Fantasia' – it depends on surprise or, in the case of Wilder and Diamond, the extent to which they dare go. The dialogue here is single-minded, concerned with the hopes and hypocrisies with which society surrounds copulation. Everyone is cheapening sex hereabouts, perhaps because that is in the nature of the beast. The message did not get lost; not since the heyday of Mae West had there been such an outcry against Hollywood's 'immorality', and United Artists hurriedly dissociated itself from the film by passing it to a minor distributor (in fact, owned by them, and used to handle foreign-language product). Wilder, to his eternal shame, issued a public apology. Elsewhere, the gaminess was remarked upon, but nobody got upset – but then, it was not their society that Wilder was satirising with such acerbity.

The Fortune Cookie (1966) is even denser and richer, a film of astonishing black humour. When Harry (Jack Lemmon) is hospitalised after being struck during a ball game, his brother-in-law, Whiplash Willie (Walter Matthau), is determined to sue everyone in sight: that brings to Harry's side his ex-wife (Judi West), as grasping as Willie, and the kindly Boom-Boom Jackson (Ron Rich), the ballplayer responsible for his troubles in

The Comedies of Billy Wilder

The first film that Billy Wilder directed was a comedy, but there were dashes of a mordant sense of humour in the mainly serious films he made after that. Since *The Seven Year Itch*, RIGHT, with Marilyn Monroe and Tom Ewell, he has concentrated again on comedy, but not without notes of seriousness, as in *The Apartment*, BELOW RIGHT, with Shirley MacLaine and Jack Lemmon, and *The Fortune Cookie*, BELOW, with Lemmon and Walter Matthau. When both films sidestep the laughs they offer some pertinent if pessimistic comments on human behaviour, and even in those films devoted solely to laughter Wilder seems uncertain whether he likes the human race. His most beloved movie is *Some Like It Hot*, BELOW FAR RIGHT, with Jack Lemmon and Marilyn Monroe, and his most brilliant is, perhaps, *One, Two, Three*, ABOVE FAR RIGHT, with Hanns Lothar, James Cagney, Horst Buchholz and Pamela Tiffin. Wilder is on record as saying that he enjoyed directing Cagney, and many of us would say something similar about watching these Wilder films, among the most endearing – and enduring – in the history of film.

the first place. 'The pressures on Wilder to help maintain the American dream are probably immense,' wrote Hollis Alpert in *Saturday Review*, but after chipping away for years this was Wilder's second full-scale assault on that dream. There is Willie, dedicated to dunning; the wife, moving from one crummy flat to the next for a chance in show business; Harry, hoping to be reunited with that awful woman; and Boom-Boom, sobbing and defeatist. It is Boom-Boom who at the end walks away with Harry into the sunset – a fact unremarked upon at the time, though Wilder was surely aware that he had made the first Hollywood love story between two men, or at least the beginning of one. Boom-Boom is also black, and, though rich and famous, happy to return to the black-white relationship of a hundred years earlier: when he cooks dinner for Harry and his wife it does not occur to them to ask him to join them – but we can be sure that that also occurred to Wilder.

Wilder may be a cynic, but his later films reveal a compassion absent from those he wrote and/or directed from the Thirties to the Fifties (with most Hollywood filmmakers, the reverse is true: their work reveals less feeling as they age). Lemmon and MacLaine are mere babes in the wood in *The Apartment*; in *Kiss Me Stupid* the cheap, sad hooker is battling against the forces of darkness which are the respectable townsfolk; the lovers in *Avanti!* (q.v.) have been repressed till the onset of middle age. The best that we can say for Wilder's other sympathetic characters (as against those played sympathetically) is that they are vacuous and unworldly – like Tiffin in *One, Two, Three*, or Monroe in *Some Like It Hot*. The boss in *The Apartment* is completely self-centred; others – Cagney in *One, Two, Three*, Matthau in *The Fortune Cookie* – are opportunistic, as were Holden in *Sunset Boulevard* and Douglas in *Ace in the Hole*. When Buchholz in *One, Two, Three* finally and joyfully opts for the capitalist way of life, it is just another joke: for its values, as depicted here and elsewhere, are as offensive – if more subtle and luxury-lined – as the Communist slogans he formerly spouted. Wilder is moralist as well as cynic, the cinema's heir to Voltaire: Candide would be at home in any of his films. But the American public, after laughing at *Irma La Douce*, turned its back.

The time was wrong, between the assassination of John F. Kennedy and Watergate, for a critique of American society.

Wilder turned away to the past, to pastiche. He had held the rights to Conan Doyle's characters since 1957, and he and Diamond wrote some new exploits for the famous detective (Robert Stephens) and Dr Watson (Colin Blakely) in **The Private Life of Sherlock Holmes** (1970). Only two of the four projected adventures reached cinemas, though all of them were filmed; the plot(s) may be as far-fetched as the films of Wilder's youth, but with a decreasing impetus. Filming on British locations seems to have put Wilder into a mellow mood, though he cannot resist a desire to shock, even slightly, with hints of drugs and sexual perversion. **Avanti!** (1972) is even more relaxed – and perhaps again Wilder succumbed to his setting, Ischia. A hyperactive American businessman (Jack Lemmon) finds himself surrendering both to old Europe and British rationality, in the person of an overweight, 'not very attractive' London girl (Juliet Mills), the daughter of his father's mistress. They have come to the island to claim the corpses of these parents, he at first shocked by the adulterous relationship of the deceased, and then re-enacting it. There are a few bad jokes, a few outrageous ones, and a touching sequence in the morgue; as the film works towards full-blown romantic comedy it is handicapped by the very ordinariness of Miss Mills, but the result is one of the rare pleasures among the films of the period.

Wilder's reputation for handling 'bad taste' caused him to be asked to remake **The Front Page** (1974), after the producer, Paul Monash, had seen a revival at the National Theatre in London. Raciness was considerably and pointlessly added; given that Wilder had been at one time a newspaperman, we may not find the four-letter words inappropriate, but the coarsening was often unfunny, as in making the fastidious Bensinger into a guy given to fondling young men and complaining that his toilet roll had been stolen. Lemmon and Matthau were the best possible choices for Hildy and Burns respectively, the latter gloomy and deadly, at times erasing memories of Cary Grant in *His Girl Friday*. Wilder knew that he had that film to beat but the chases – especially after those in *One, Two, Three* – reveal a man devoid of confidence. That may well have been the result of his string of failures: but this was the only one which deserved its fate.

Wilder could not get backing for **Fedora** (1978) in the U.S., and it was made in Munich – with little subsequent interest after a Cannes unveiling, though United Artists did later open it in the U.S. The instinct was to love this problem child, especially as it had become increasingly clear during Wilder's decade of bad luck that his earlier films – constantly revived – were amongst the most enduring ever made; but John Coleman in the *New Statesman* could not resist calling it 'old hat', and in a basically kind review pinpointed the trouble, '. . . I hardly believed in the brittle plot.' The source is a novella in Thomas Tryon's collection, 'Crowned Heads', and as presented here it concerns a desperate Hollywood producer (William Holden) confronting a series of Chinese boxes as he tries to persuade a reclusive Garboesque star to make a comeback and thereby get him the backing he needs. Some reviewers evoked *Sunset Boulevard*, and clearly Wilder had reasons for his jokes about the current state of the industry; the mood is rather that of *Avanti!*, and once you have swallowed the plot you may be entertained in the manner of *The Major and the Minor* or *Sabrina*. I cannot say how well it may stand up, but I can say that I would rather see it again than most of the films of this period.

Buddy, Buddy (1981) is another matter. Two producers at M-G-M, Alain Bernheim and Jay Weston, wanted to help Wilder off his losing streak, and Jack Lemmon said that he would always be there if the director needed him. Lemmon plays a would-be suicide (because his wife has left him) and Walter Matthau is the hit man in the room next door, unable to prepare for his killing because of Lemmon's antics. On internal evidence the script was hastily assembled and filmed while these actors went from one engagement to the next. Basically the film is a straightforward remake of *L'Emmerdeur* (q.v.), with few extra jokes – despite such targets (hotel life,

posses of police) as had delighted Wilder in the past. Some scenes in a sex clinic – it was an ordinary clinic in the original – fail completely, but otherwise this is one of the few unfunny comedies which is nevertheless pleasant. Diamond observed in an interview that Wilder had turned down *Victor/Victoria* (q.v.) because he hated to repeat himself, but much of *Buddy, Buddy* is reminiscent of *The Front Page*, including a final gag about someone running off with someone of their own sex.

If Wilder, in the end, is in decline, he is in good company: most of the leading directors of his generation had done their best work by the end of the Fifties – yet in the following decade he was to make some of the boldest and most mature films in the history of the American cinema. In this profession (or industry, whichever way you prefer to regard it) age seems to take a toll of talent. As the Fifties started, only Welles and Chaplin trailed clouds of critical glory, but though both were professionally active – at least in theory – for most of the following two decades they did little to justify their reputation. Some of the other admired American filmmakers made only one or two good films apiece: Stevens, Ford, Disney, Hawks, Wyler and Hitchcock, plus Capra and Rossen, whose output was severely limited. It may be that the academic films of Wyler and Stevens will look better in ten years' time; it may be that Hitchcock's films of the Fifties, which seemed so enjoyable then, will further diminish in effectiveness (even on their own chosen level). I would not want to be categorical about this, since I would not want to follow *Cahiers du Cinéma* with its 'pantheon' of admired directors. In fact, I start from a different premise, that as far as the American film industry is concerned the important directors were those who were willing to risk their reputations in making films above the average. By that token the modern American cinema was made by Kazan, Mankiewicz, Zinnemann, Cukor, Huston, Wilder and, to a lesser degree, Robert Wise. While the moguls worried and fretted about the size of screens, they strove to make movies for intelligent people.

33

Hollywood in the Age of Television: The Decline of the Studios

IN 1947 THE WEEKLY cinema attendance in the U.S. averaged 87 million, but this had dropped to a mere 15 million by 1969, the year when Hollywood faced its own Armageddon, with most of the major studios convulsed by their financial losses. By then the industry had accustomed itself to the fact that television had become the country's favourite leisure activity. In the Fifties Columbia and Warner Bros. had been the first studios to acknowledge the vitality of the growing rival by becoming suppliers of television programmes; 20th Century-Fox made potted versions of its famous movies for the new medium and Universal moved in via its acquisition by M.C.A. At the end of this chapter I shall list the more radical changes, since they are better discussed as applicable to the industry as a whole than to individual studios. For the last time we shall look at films which are primarily studio artefacts – either because they were typical or of more than passing interest. The studio system still operated so well that few of them were made, if planned, in panic, but they were designed to lure back those patrons who had succumbed to the small screen at home. The liberalisation of attitudes to sex was to play a vital part in the battle.

Although the introduction of Cinema-Scope had enabled 20th Century-Fox to dominate the industry, the system itself proved of only temporary benefit, partly because it was not well used. Audiences were often given the impression that they were watching as through a proscenium arch, with the entire cast lined up across the screen for longish periods. Almost all the contemporary subjects seemed to consist of people talking in rooms, with some token views (usually of New York's skyline) thrown in. **Three Coins in the Fountain** (1954) was no exception. This was the studio's perennial about three girls in search of rich husbands, but it had been re-set in Rome, with manifold picture postcard views of that city interrupting the 'action', if so it may be called. A title song destined to blare from every juke-box in the country helped it to a huge popularity, encouraging the studio to send the film's director, Jean Negulesco, on to Hydra for **Boy on a Dolphin** (1957), which offered underwater photography and some equally spectacular views of Sophia Loren in a wet dress. By this time the studio had become much less cautious about using CinemaScope, and Westerns, in particular, benefited from the photography of the wide open spaces.

Initially, because of the success of *The Robe*, the wide screen was thought ideal for historical spectacle and the courts of Napoleon (Marlon Brando) and Elizabeth I (Bette Davis) were on display in **Désirée** (1954) and **The Virgin Queen** (1955) respectively. As directed by Henry Koster, who had made *The Robe*, the two stars were below their best, but these were personalities able to overcome the staginess apparently inherent in filming in Cinema-Scope. The first musical in the process was **There's No Business Like Show Business** (1954), built, like the studio's *Alexander's Ragtime Band* of old, round a bevy of Irving Berlin's songs old and new. Strung across the screen is a show-business family – Ethel Merman, Dan Dailey, Donald O'Connor, Mitzi Gaynor and Johnny Ray – all of them resistible performers as directed by Walter Lang. Acting with them, Marilyn Monroe is patently amateurish, but in her case it matters little.

The archetypal professional, Fred Astaire, is in **Daddy Long Legs** (1954), which is also unappealing – or as much so as any film could be in which he appears. It had been planned for Dailey and Gaynor, but they were dropped and Leslie Caron was borrowed from M-G-M. Under Negulesco's direction she is relentlessly cute, and the old story is not improved by insisting that there is nothing a French orphan could want more than to be brought up in the U.S. The colour and settings are poor but, to compensate for two derivative ballets choreographed by Roland Petit, there is one splendid dance for Astaire, 'Sluefoot', and a pleasing song, 'Something's Gotta Give'.

The songs in **The Best Things in Life Are Free** (1956) are from the catalogue of deSylva, Brown and Henderson, who are impersonated in it by Gordon MacRae, Ernest Borgnine and Dan Dailey. Show-business biographies were going out of fashion – and not a moment too soon – but this one was made just after *Carousel* and *The King and I*: the extra care taken with them was reflected at the box office, so something similar was done in this case. Most of the numbers are stylishly handled, and the film marks a return to form for Michael Curtiz, whose direction had sometimes been slack since leaving Warners. José Ferrer directed **State Fair** (1962) and, according to Alice Faye – returning briefly to the screen to play the mother – he gave no help whatsoever to the cast, which may be why three of the four young players are so poor – Bobby Darin, Ann-Margret and Pat Boone. Pamela Tiffin is the other, but despite her and Miss Faye the apple-pie feeling of the 1945 version is missing; and it is grossly inferior to Henry King's original version.

The success of M-G-M's *Gigi* inspired 20th Century-Fox to film **Can Can** (1960), a Broadway musical which had not interested Hollywood when produced seven years earlier. That concerned an upright young judge who one drunken night finds himself loving the flesh-pots of Montmartre; the film script, by Charles Lederer and Dorothy Kingsley, substitutes smuttiness for sophisticated corruption and, though the characters have not become virtuous, they are dull in their vices. The seductress *d'un certain âge* is now the scrubbed, young, all-American Shirley MacLaine, while Louis Jourdain (the judge) and Maurice Chevalier repeat their double-act of *Gigi*, and Frank Sinatra his role from *Guys and Dolls*. Walter Lang's direction takes no advantage of the Todd A-O screen, which was preferred to CinemaScope on this occasion, and some of Cole Porter's score has been omitted to accommodate four of his most hackneyed songs. Since the same thing happened at Columbia on *Pal Joey* (q.v.), whose 'book' was also bowdlerised, we should note the presence on both occasions of Sinatra, who was certainly powerful enough to insist on changes (or prevent them). The can-can within the film cannot compare with those in the movies by Renoir and Huston, though it created a minor sensation during the filming when the Soviet premier, Krushchev, denounced it as immoral – somewhat ungratefully, as it was staged for him on his visit to the studio, Hollywood's official welcome during his American tour.

The film's failure, though deserved, was one reason why the studio took special care with another Broadway hit, **Hello Dolly!** (1969). The production and screenplay were entrusted to Ernest Lehmann, who had done both for *The Sound of Music,* and the direction to Gene Kelly, considered the most knowledgeable practitioner of the musical form. Together they strove to emulate the verve of the M-G-M musical in the production numbers, but at the same time the lack of originality suffocated the piece. The Broadway Dolly, Carol Channing, rightly thought it 'like a version of *The Sound of Music* only more ponderous. *Hello Dolly!* should crackle, snap, never stop moving.' The title song, on stage a *tour-de-force* for her, has in Barbra Streisand, her screen replacement, only a lank, mechanical pivot, while elsewhere this actress attempts to be an adenoidal Mae West. Less expectedly, Walter Matthau, as the object of her attentions, cannot disguise the fact that the material is less than brilliant. The cost was $24 million – including $2½ million for the reconstruction of New York's 14th Street on the back-lot – which made it the studio's most expensive film ever, apart from *Cleopatra.* Yet even as it was clear that the response was not warm enough for it to recover its costs, 20th Century-Fox was pouring $25 million into *Tora! Tora! Tora!*, a re-creation of the bombing of Pearl Harbor. This was yet another attempt to repeat one of the studio's past successes, and it was an even greater failure than either *Can-Can* or *Hello Dolly!*

The earlier film concerned is **The Longest Day** (1962), adapted from Cornelius Ryan's best-selling documentary account of the Normandy landings. At the time when Zanuck had quit the studio to become an independent producer, it had produced another film on this subject, *D-Day, the Sixth of June,* which had passed unnoticed. Nevertheless, from his base in Europe Zanuck decided that *The Longest Day* would crown his career, and he even directed the American interior sequences himself. The other credited directors are Ken Annakin, responsible for the British interiors, Bernhard Wicki, responsible for those with the Germans, and Andrew Marton, who filmed the American exteriors; Eric Williams was 'co-ordinator of the battle episodes'. It lasts three hours; it has a star, or at least a 'name', in fifty or so leading roles. (Most of them were paid $25,000 for two or three days' work, except John Wayne, who refused his role because of his experience at this studio on *The Barbarian and the Geisha*; he finally relented when offered $250,000.) The film is well organised, but suffers from presenting only stereotypes: the British are casual and stiff upper-lipped, the Americans democratic, somewhat cynical and given to reminiscing about the folks back home; the French are wily and excitable; and the Germans the same rule-book lugheads of the wartime Resistance movies. Zanuck himself was wrestling with a drink problem, and the film went over budget. It nevertheless made a huge profit – which was one reason why Zanuck was urged to return as production chief.

The film was made in black and white; the studio had originally relented on the question of monochrome with Cinema-Scope when the producer Charles Brackett considered colour unsuitable for **Teenage Rebel** (1956), a drama about the reunion of a mother (Ginger Rogers) and a daughter (Betty Lou Kim). Brackett and Walter Reisch wrote it, Edmund Goulding directed, but they had all become tired. So had Nunnally Johnson, writing and directing **The Three Faces of Eve** (1957), based on another best-selling book and also in

black and white: but the film was much discussed as one of the few contemporary American movies to deal with a situation based on fact. Its subject is the treatment by a doctor (Lee J. Cobb) of a schizophrenic, by turns a drab housewife and a whorish slut who, in either guise, still shrinks from sexual contact. When she is cured of both manifestations a third personality emerges – an Eve who resembles every other film heroine. In the role(s) Joanne Woodward fills in the gaps left by the inadequate handling, deserving her Oscar for Best Actress.

The Young Lions (1958) and **Compulsion** (1959) were also thought unsuitable for colour, the first because it is set in World War II and the second since it centres on one of the grimmer aspects of the Jazz Age. *The Young Lions* is Irwin Shaw's synthesis of the experience of war as set down in the ironic terms prescribed for best-sellerdom. The book is faithfully followed in Edward Anhalt's adaptation which resulted in a better film than *From Here to Eternity* (though that had better source material and a better director) because in the five years between the two the M.P.A.A. had lifted considerable restrictions on the portrayal of such matters. Edward Dmytryk's direction shows him unbothered by his many and far-flung locations and by the fact that the paths of his three chief protagonists will not cross until the final reel. Dean Martin and Montgomery Clift are the Americans and Marlon Brando the German – attempting to encompass in his performance a suggestion that the Germans were not the only guilty ones. The film's polemics manage to incorporate the word 'ovens' during the sequence of the concentration camp, but it is reticent on a subject which much concerned Shaw, anti-Semitism in the army. Indeed, it plays down the fact that the Clift character is a Jew. Similarly, the Jewishness of Leopold and Loeb is hardly referred to in *Compulsion,* but the M.P.A.A. permitted hints of their homosexuality; the emasculation of Meyer Levin's brilliant – and by its very nature sensationalist – book seems to have been the decision of the producer, Zanuck, since the film leans over backwards to be sober and respectable. As directed by Richard Fleischer and written by Richard Murphy, the gaps and flaws prove its undoing, and these include the lack of period sense, the book's pains-taking descriptions of the police investiga-tion and Levin's pervading sense of incre-dulity that this once had happened – that two wealthy young men (Dean Stockwell, Bradford Dillman) killed a young boy simply for the excitement of it.

That both **Peyton Place** (1957) and **From the Terrace** (1960) were also set in the recent past – the Forties – was clearly irrelevant to Mark Robson, their director. John Michael Hayes and Ernest Lehmann respectively wrote the scripts from novels by Grace Metalious and John O'Hara, with Hayes retaining at least some of the for-mer's 'profundities': 'Time should not pass: it should be used.' The film 'lifts the lid off' one supposedly typical Pennsyl-vania town to find everyone seething with sex – or the lack of it, as in the case of the heroine's frigid mother (Lana Turner). The book's enormous popularity meant further encroachments of the Production Code, as 20th Century-Fox persuaded its guardians to permit reference to mixed nude sunbathing and youngsters sending for one of those manuals which arrive in plain brown wrappers. The effect is pru-rient; but the three years elapsing before the equally meretricious second movie brought further frankness, enabling it to be matter-of-fact about the infidelities of the hero's wife (Joanne Woodward) and mother (Myrna Loy).

Robson also directed **The Inn of the Sixth Happiness** (1958), from another best seller, 'The Small Woman', based on the life story of Gladys Aylward, who spent more than thirty years as a mission-ary in China. Ingrid Bergman, who plays the role, is very obviously *not* small, and also references to her throughout as 'the Englishwoman' are inconsistent with her accent. But her saintly no-nonsense enthu-siasm sits well on this Gladys and as a more practical, older co-worker Athene Seyler is superb, and Robert Donat, in his last screen performance, is the mandarin. Wales doubles for China, whose people Robson clearly did not understand; but this is a pleasant, accomplished movie, even if the book should have yielded some-thing different.

The same stricture may be applied to **The Sun Also Rises** (1957) and **Tender Is the Night** (1962). *The Sun Also Rises,* written by Peter Viertel from Heming-

way's novel, was one of the films Zanuck produced independently. It may have been his decision to treat it with the reverence usually bestowed on classics – not a good idea, given these characters, a bunch of irresponsible drifters. As played by Tyrone Power, Errol Flynn, Mel Ferrer and Eddie Albert, they are the dreariest of drinking companions; Ava Gardner glit-ters but is wrongly cast as Lady Brett. Zanuck did a disservice to himself in asking Henry King to direct, for King re-sponds to neither the European locations nor the material. Since the reviews pointed this out, King did himself a disservice in tackling Fitzgerald's novel, as adapted by Ivan Moffatt. He starts Tender Is the Night well, with Jennifer Jones making a brave stab at Nicole and Joan Fontaine stagey but enjoyable as her sister; but as Dick Diver, Jason Robards lacks both charm and style in a story reduced to that of a dull man not knowing what to do for the best. The film brought King's distinguished career to a sad end.

M-G-M and then David O. Selznick had earlier owned the rights to 'Tender Is the Night', and Selznick had sold them to 20th Century-Fox with the proviso that Miss Jones play the lead. He relinquished them also because of the disappointing experi-ence of **A Farewell to Arms** (1957), which 20th Century-Fox released. Apart from *Stazione Termini* (q.v.), it was his first film in eight years, and the last he produced. In this case the rights to 'A Farewell to Arms' had passed from Para-mount to Warners (in exchange for *A Con-necticut Yankee*) when Warners had planned a version to star Humphrey Bogart and Ingrid Bergman as a projected follow-up to *Casablanca*; it was never made, and Selz-nick in turn obtained them in exchange for his rights in *A Star Is Born*. He commis-sioned a screenplay from Ben Hecht, and John Huston directed till receiving one of Selznick's longer memos, which con-firmed his gloomy suspicions that Selznick saw the film primarily as a vehicle for Miss Jones. Whether handled by him or his replacement, the opening battle scenes are good; but thereafter in re-creating the Italian campaign Selznick seemed to think that he was burning Atlanta over again. Hemingway's self-congratulatory lovers were tiresome enough on the page, but with Miss Jones's determined smile and

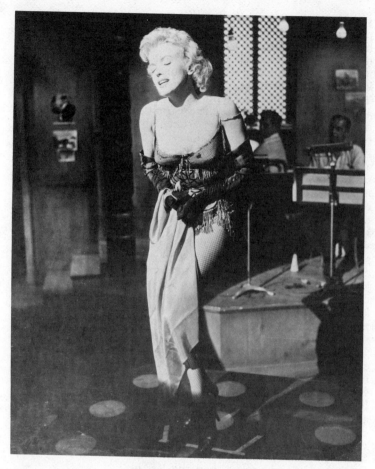

When Marilyn Monroe made *Bus Stop* she had been off the screen for a year, due to quarrels with the studio and personal difficulties. She returned with a new gift for pathos, playing a small-time show girl, eking out a living by wiggling her hips for cowboys and dreaming of being 'discovered' on the corner of Hollywood and Vine.

Rock Hudson's blankness they exhaust our patience early on; the film is twice the length of the earlier Borzage version, with none of its intimacy.

Another remake, **An Affair to Remember** (1957), is also inferior to, and longer than, the original, *Love Affair*, but in this case Leo McCarey was again in charge. The ease of Cary Grant and the delicacy of Deborah Kerr are no substitutes for Charles Boyer and Irene Dunne; and it ends mawkishly with children carolling 'There's a wonderful place called Tomorrowland, and it's only a dream away'. McCarey directed two more films, neither of distinction. In fact, he made only four films in the last twenty years of his life, which was summed up succinctly by Peter Bogdanovich (q.v.): 'A bright, happy first half of life that led to sadness, tragedy. A near-fatal auto accident. Drink. Drugs.'

Anatole Litvak, another veteran, directed **Anastasia** (1956), presumably chosen because he was Russian-born, but there is no internal evidence that he worked hard at the job. As written for the screen by Arthur Laurents, it is a study of the woman who claimed to have survived the massacre at Ekaterinburg and it finds its level with the Grand Duchess (Helen Hayes) playing cupid to her and the man (Yul Brynner) who trained her. As Anastasia, Ingrid Bergman reminds one that she was never the actress to suggest mystical inspiration; the several awards she won for this performance may have been tokens of pleasure at finding her back on the English-speaking screen after the scandal that began with *Stromboli* (q.v.).

With Bergman and Deborah Kerr (for *The King and I*) in competition that year for the Oscar (which Bergman won), 20th Century-Fox was not interested in promoting the chances of Marilyn Monroe, so that she was not even nominated* for a performance with more bite than either. The film is **Bus Stop** (1956), and though her vulnerability in the role now contributes to the legend, this was the first time audiences were aware of the full extent of it. Curiously, the part in William Inge's original play is much more like the naive vamp enacted in *The Seven Year Itch*, whose author, George Axelrod, wrote this screenplay. He is not one from whom pathos is normally expected and, as the film is more serious than the play, it is possible that he was inspired by qualities that Monroe had which had not yet been shown on the screen. She may also have inspired the director, Joshua Logan, as this is more surely handled than his *Picnic* (q.v.), also from an Inge play: it is equally diffuse, but more successful in being romantic about second-rate people. The view it offers of the U.S. – materialistic and seedy – was one seldom then seen in movies, but the situation, of the reluctant bride, is from classic comedy. As the brash cowboy who pursues Monroe, Don Murray achieves depths unsuspected on first encounter. There are also nice performances

*The studios are not supposed to be influential in either the nominations or the winners, but a certain amount of lobbying goes on, and the studios are allowed to remind potential voters of the nominees in their films by advertisements in the trade press. There is general agreement within the industry that certain performers won chiefly because of canvassing in the trade press.

by Eileen Heckart as Monroe's solicitous pal and Betty Field as the brassy proprietress of the bus-stop diner.

There is little to be said for the early CinemaScope comedies, but **Will Success Spoil Rock Hunter?** (1957) is the best of Frank Tashlin's career. It was directed and adapted by him from Axelrod's play, a satire on advertising and Hollywood – to which Tashlin constructively added television. Says the copywriter, 'What has success to do with talent? If it had, Brooks Brothers would go out of business, T.V. studios would be turned into supermarkets' – an unexceptional remark today, but not then. The tone is sour in the Manhattan manner and the piece remains hilarious. Jayne Mansfield, whom the studio hoped would replace the temperamental Monroe, plays the dumb blonde movie star based on Monroe, and the fact that Mansfield herself soon became a joke may be one reason that this film is denied the reputation it deserves. Tony Randall, accomplished as he was, later played roles which turned him into a poor man's Jack Lemmon, while Tashlin disappeared into a welter of Jerry Lewis comedies. Tashlin emerged only notably with an amiable farce, **Bachelor Flat** (1962), written by Bud Grossman from his own play. It has just two comic notions, girls popping out of cupboards and a man bereft of pants – in which role Terry-Thomas, as a British professor running around a Californian beach with rolled umbrella, is an inspiration to his countrymen everywhere.

Gene Kelly directed **A Guide for the Married Man** (1967), one of the first comedies to take advantage of the relaxation of the Production Code. Frank Tarloff's screenplay, from his own book, starts with a quotation from Oscar Wilde, 'The one charm of marriage is that it makes a life of deception absolutely necessary for both parties,' but that is its highpoint. Walter Matthau is the man desperate to be unfaithful to his wife, and Robert Morse is the neighbour only too anxious to help him. Both try to rise above the film's leering attitude towards women, as exemplified in the recurring images of wiggling bottoms. The view that all women are aching for a roll in the hay is at least put more wittily in **The Secret Life of an American Wife** (1968). As written and directed by Mr Axelrod, this is a variation on his theme in *The Seven Year Itch*, in which a man thinks about sex the moment his wife leaves for a vacation, an acceptable situation in the post-Kinsey era, and this film was only possible now that the Code was defunct. Here a Connecticut housewife (Anne Jackson) fantasises about sex with a movie star (Matthau) and sets out to put her dream into practice the instant her husband leaves for the office. Axelrod, a genuine satirist – he is very funny on the pandering to movie stars' whims – has much to say about the battle of the sexes, which puts his comedy on a higher level than those of the time which relied upon salacity for its own sake.

Sex had always been box office, and the denial of the M.P.A.A. seal of approval to *The Moon Is Blue* and the British-made *I Am a Camera* (q.v.) had not prevented American exhibitors from booking them. In the meanwhile the art-houses were doing turn-away business with the films of Brigitte Bardot (q.v.), and those turned away were returning the next day instead of making a bee-line to the circuit theatre down the street. Also withheld from the Hollywood companies was the money that could have been earned from those sitting at home before their television sets – and sex was something that T.V. did not have. In the face of falling attendances the studios and exhibitors were delighted at the gradual erosion of the Code, though few acknowledged the fact publicly, and in 1966 it was finally abandoned. Instead the M.P.A.A. substituted a series of ratings certificates meant to separate the men from the boys – except in such cases where 'Parental Guidance' was needed.

But if that meant that sexual conduct could be shown instead of merely implied – and few could have guessed that the M.P.A.A.'s new regulations would lead to the graphic depiction of sexual acts – it was not only needed in the cause of frankness. By this time people were reacting against the mindless, cosy domestic comedies which television stations had been transmitting for more than a decade – 'sitcoms' of such patent phoniness that they may be one reason why family life in the Sixties fell apart for many of the post-T.V. generation.

These changes were eventually reflected in a number of films celebrating the hippie movement, but they may be found in

903

more subtle form in **Pretty Poison** (1968), produced by 20th Century-Fox less because of any desire to reflect the general disorientation than because of the success of *Bonnie and Clyde* (q.v.). This chilling film concerns two youngsters caught in a web of fantasies which endanger a society misfit (Anthony Perkins) with arson in his past and a girl (Tuesday Weld) with matricide in her future. The setting is Massachusetts, its particular beauty at odds with the evil beneath the surface as the murderers go about their business as calmly as the citizens go about theirs. The film was written by Lorenzo Semple Jr from a novel by Stephen Geller, and directed by Noel Black, neither of whom was to repeat their achievement of this, their first film.

The graphic portrayal of violence marched hand in hand with the new sexual leniency. **The Detective** (1968) was one of the first films to employ both. Within seconds of its opening, a cop (Frank Sinatra) is stating 'Penis cut off', as you or I might remark on the weather (except that the actor's delivery is somewhat self-conscious). The victim is a homosexual and his killer turns out to be a married man – whose discovery of his sexual orientation might have been more credibly handled. But then the writer, Abby Mann, and the director, Gordon Douglas, are busy detailing such ingredients as semen stains on the sheets, a cop who 'won't lick ass' and an estranged wife (Lee Remick) who has galloping nymphomania. Sinatra is exceptionally kind to black cops until one (Al Freeman Jr) steps out of line, when he behaves ruthlessly. Such was the new realism; but, like its hero, this film flaunts 'concern', it does not feel it. It is preferable, however, to **The St Valentine's Day Massacre** (1967), a re-creation of the era of Al Capone (Jason Robards) and Bugs Moran (Ralph Meeker), directed by Roger Corman without flair.

This was virtually Corman's only film for a major company. His speciality was horror films on small budgets, some of which helped him gain a cult reputation. He was chief among some idiosyncratic movie-makers whom the major studio executives did not really understand and, when he failed to achieve a success for them, he was forced back into independence. It was symptomatic of the panic of this time that the studios were prepared to employ exploitation movie-makers while still deploring their work. After Corman's departure Russ Meyer was hired by 20th Century-Fox. He had begun making pornographic movies in 1959, and was the most successful practitioner in that field as more and more cinema houses, desperate for business, succumbed to demand. When the abolition of the Code led to the introduction of hard-core pornography, Meyer remained with soft-porn and was thus sufficiently respectable for 20th Century-Fox to take him on.

Beyond the Valley of the Dolls (1970) reflects no credit on him or its co-writer, Roger Ebert, a Chicago film critic, or the studio. *Valley of the Dolls,* based on Jacqueline Susann's sleazy best seller about young hopefuls, had been a box-office success, so the studio prepared a sequel. She was to have turned the outline into a book, but refused when executives balked at her demand of $1½ million for the rights to 'The Love Machine'. They were accordingly left with a title and an outline, which Meyer was required to turn into a 'non-Hollywood' film, i.e. one without star players and as much sex as the ratings system would allow (which would mean an X, so that no one under seventeen could be admitted). The cast includes a brazen nymphomaniac and several other women apparently with the same inclinations; a man who sports a German S.S. uniform and another in a leopard loin-cloth; while the sex includes much nipple-fondling and lingering kisses amongst the women and a weirdo homosexual trying to arouse another male. Halfway through, a harmonium erupts on the soundtrack, in a vain attempt to link the film to the unrealities of soap opera: like the bloody ending, the device seems desperate, and audiences laughed at the film instead of with it. When Meyer's second film for the company, *The Seven Minutes*, also failed, it was decided not to experiment further along these lines.

We have looked elsewhere at the M-G-M musical and there is little else of distinction to note as its forty-year reign over the industry drew to a close. Amid fluctuating profits and continual boardroom battles the studio chiefs never sank as low as 20th Century-Fox, but they too were desperate.

M-G-M was still clinging to the system of long-term contracts as the Sixties dawned, but few of its stars or directors were of more than passing interest.

Stewart Granger was one of their last stars, at one point specialising in remakes of Silent swashbucklers. **Beau Brummell** (1954) was based on an unvenerable antique by Clyde Fitch which had seen service for John Barrymore. It concentrates on the Beau's friendship with the Prince Regent, played by Peter Ustinov as a temperamental booby, but one with taste. Robert Morley is George III, and there was an outcry when this movie was chosen for the Royal Film Performance, thus ensuring that the Queen watched the antics of a mad ancestor on her annual public cinema outing. That, together with Curtis Bernhardt's direction and Elizabeth Taylor's performance, rather obscured the film's virtues, which are real. In leaving the behaviour and character of Brummell an enigma, Karl Tunberg's screenplay anticipated the coming trend in drama; but he was unwise to adhere to the foolish climax of the Fitch play.

The film was made in Britain, and M-G-M, the only company with its own studio there (since 1948), no longer gave the impression of a wealthy relation conferring a favour. The advantages were the relative cheapness of shooting, the army of high-quality supporting players and, when necessary, convenient locations. After *Ivanhoe* had shored up Robert Taylor's waning popularity, producer Pandro S. Berman and director Richard Thorpe sent him to Tintagel for **Knights of the Round Table** (1954) and to Chambord and Chenonceaux for **The Adventures of Quentin Durward** (1956). The settings cannot disguise the dullness of this actor, and *Knights of the Round Table* has in addition a wooden Arthur and a miscast Guinevere (Ava Gardner) – which may be why it reminds one of cut-out paper figures placed before a cardboard set; at the same time, this was the first 'British' film in CinemaScope, a process which seems to have terrified Thorpe. The veteran art director, Alfred Junge, tries to evoke the pre-Raphaelites here and more especially in *Quentin Durward*. That the last is the most entertaining of the trio is due to Robert Ardrey's screenplay and the presence of Kay Kendall as the lady in distress.

Another durable boys' adventure, **The Time Machine** (1960), also has good art direction and a superior screenplay, by David Duncan, as well as a likeable time-traveller in Rod Taylor. In this case H. G. Wells's London and future world were created in Hollywood, at the instigation of George Pal, who produced and directed. He was one of the few film-makers with a continuing interest in the cinema's capacity for fantasy, and had already produced some science fiction films, including *War of the Worlds* (q.v.); for M-G-M he also produced and directed *tom thumb*. Another semi-classic, **Green Mansions** (1959), emerged less convincingly as directed by Mel Ferrer. Selznick had originally bought W. H. Hudson's novel in 1931 as a vehicle for Dolores del Rio and M-G-M had acquired the rights in 1946 for the singer Yma Sumac. A version with Pier Angeli was started and abandoned in 1954, and it says much about the changes at the studio that like-thinking did not prevail on this occasion, with inadequate B-picture back projection and studio jungle. There are strange performances by Anthony Perkins as a revolutionary and Lee J. Cobb as the grizzled grandfather of Rima the bird girl – in which role Audrey Hepburn (then married to Ferrer) darts about like a Disney fawn. The music is by Villa-Lobos, except for one ditty sung by Perkins to a guitar, 'In this land of eternal spring/Where humming-birds can learn to sing/And green grow the mansions of love'.

M-G-M had disdained Westerns since the Silent era, but a number were made during the Schary regime, of which the best is **Escape From Fort Bravo** (1953). We may admire John Sturges's fresh handling of some old themes: the wilful, independent heroine (Eleanor Parker), travelling through perilous territory – Arizona – with several trunks of Helen-Rose-designed gowns; the captain (William Holden) whose sense of duty rankles with both his Union colleagues and the Confederates; the dance; and the prisoners crooning at night. The lengthy climax, with a party ambushed in the desert by Indians, moves this film to classic status. However, it was **Bad Day at Black Rock** (1954) which deservedly made Sturges's reputation. Like all his films, it has a simple aim, seeking only to entertain by creating great tension. He finds menace in a couple of deserted gasoline pumps or reflection in a plate-glass window, and he emphasises the smallness of his central figure against the Arizona mountains and the shacks that constitute Black Rock. That figure is a one-armed Spencer Tracy, arriving in this middle of nowhere on a government mission, to find hostility from everyone, especially Robert Ryan, Ernest Borgnine and, even more villainous, Lee Marvin.

It was Tracy's last film for the company; Clark Gable also left, but Gary Cooper arrived to make his penultimate film, **The Wreck of the Mary Deare** (1959), in which he and a taciturn Charlton Heston try to salvage a wreck in the Channel; those up to no good include Richard Harris as a sarcastic first mate. Eric Ambler wrote the screenplay from a novel by Hammond Innes, and Michael Anderson directed after Hitchcock abandoned the project.

Glenn Ford was the last important male star ever to be under long-term contract to M-G-M, but he was not one to fill the shoes of the great departed. He was assigned to several military comedies, made in a bid to attract diminishing audiences with nostalgia; but it is significant that in the Eisenhower years these films reaffirmed the message which the U.S. had given to its allies and defeated enemies ten years earlier. **The Teahouse of the August Moon** (1956) is set during the

American occupation of Japan, and the humour lies in the consistent outsmarting of the sophisticated Americans, led by Ford, by the primitive and resourceful villagers as represented by Sakini (Marlon Brando). What starts amusingly soon degenerates into maudlin sentimentality on the differences between East and West; among those responsible are Daniel Mann, who directed, and John Patrick, who adapted – with few changes – his own long-running and Pulitzer Prize-winning play, mined in turn from Vern Sneider's novel.

It was not only that CinemaScope was as much blight as boon in its first years, forever slowing down the action; there was a blight too in the artistic climate of the studios, so that films emerged trying to be all things to all men. **Don't Go Near the Water** (1957) strives to be comedy, spectacle and a vehicle for Ford; much footage is expended in establishing his niceness. He plays a sceptical junior officer who brings democracy to a far-flung Pacific island – in fact by blackmailing an odious reporter (Keenan Wynn) to get a native school built: but then in the cause of democracy anything is possible. The dialogue has real bite as written by Dorothy Kingsley and George Wells from the book by William Brinkley; Charles Walters directed. Ford is superbly supported in the first of these films by Paul Ford and in this one by Fred Clark, both playing superior officers with solid bone where the brain should be.

Walters worked almost exclusively in comedy, more reliant than most directors on the quality of his scripts. In **The Tender Trap** (1955) he is never incisive enough to surmount the excessive length, stagy settings, CinemaScope and the self-conscious charm of Debbie Reynolds. She plays a starlet bent on marriage, stealing Frank Sinatra from Celeste Holm, though it is made clear that he had only encouraged this older lady as long as she tolerated his philandering. With this one-time Broadway play Sinatra instituted a series of comedies about 'swinging' bachelors with large pads and large champagne glasses, and very soon he and rivals would not have to wed the girl to bed her. The prevailing mood was one of self-satisfaction, replacing the moralising inherent in previous Hollywood comedies on philandering, since they had always been derived, if

Among the spate of service comedies of the Fifties is *The Teahouse of the August Moon*, in which Marlon Brando, left, as a wily Japanese villager, outwits the American army as represented by Paul Ford and Glenn Ford (no relation). Their puritanism is overcome and the teahouse built: here they are on the site of it.

on occasion somewhat distantly, from Schnitzler and his contemporaries. Gone too was the mordant wit and repartee which had once enlivened American comedy, though an exception is **Ask Any Girl** (1959), about an innocent in New York, played with a battery of ingenuous expressions by Shirley MacLaine. She wins the sternest and strictest of her admirers (David Niven), while the two philanderers (Gig Young, Rod Taylor) end up on the shelf. Walters directed, and the superiority of this film is presumably due to its source, a book of comic essays by Winifred Wolfe.

Five years on, the innocent concerned rather wanted to lose her virginity, which is what makes this **Sunday in New York** (1964) different from the one spent by Judy Garland and Robert Walker in *The Clock*. Rod Taylor as the womaniser and Jane Fonda as the girl are pleasing company – she sharp and shrewd but, like Carole Lombard, able to assume naïvety when required. As directed by Peter Tewksbury and written by Norman Krasna from his own play, this is as funny as any of Krasna's scripts twenty years earlier. **Designing Woman** (1957) is a rehash of the idea behind *Woman of the Year,* but is directed lamely by Vincente Minnelli. Lauren Bacall has a stylish comedy sense rather than comedy technique, and Gregory Peck is not a light comedian of the quality of James Stewart, for whom the role was written.

The picture was personally produced by Dore Schary, and was his last film for the company. Joseph Vogel, the president of M-G-M, dismissed him with the explanation that he was disliked by the board, that he was unable to work as a member of a team and that he had too many political interests. But in fact they had clashed earlier when Schary had refused Vogel, then head of the Loews theatre chain, a private screening of an unfinished film. On that occasion Vogel had sworn that he would sack Schary if given the chance.

Designing Woman had been planned for Grace Kelly, whose films made on loan were so superior to the one she made at her home base, M-G-M – **Green Fire** (1954), a puerile adventure tale with Stewart Granger, directed by Andrew Marton. She had turned down many projects and did this one under protest – and its reception only exacerbated her discontent. Since the press took up the cudgels on her behalf the studio did prepare a number of more promising films, but most of them were made with other actresses after she went to live out her own Ruritanian romance. As she married Prince Rainier of Monaco audiences could see her in something similar, **The Swan** (1956). They were not, with reason, unduly appreciative, but seeing it now on television (i.e. robbed of its CinemaScope frame) it gains in intimacy to become one of the most pleasing comedies of the period. Based on Molnár's play about a royal wooing, it has a Lubitsch-style opening and if, after that, the director Charles Vidor fails to add much in visual terms he moves with ease among these European aristocrats – who include, apart from Miss Kelly, Alec Guinness and Louis Jourdan.

Miss Kelly's popularity was such that her loss was a blow to M-G-M, which had continued to uphold its tradition of fashioning vehicles for the leading female stars – at this point becoming an endangered species, which was why the practice was abandoned by the other studios. June Allyson made her last film for the company in 1956; Debbie Reynolds remained until the Sixties; Ava Gardner was unwilling to return to fulfil her commitment. M-G-M were delighted to have Doris Day on a non-exclusive basis, particularly after the success of her first film for them, **Love Me or Leave Me** (1955). Charles Vidor directed this biography of Ruth Etting, whose songs Miss Day sings in very different manner. Etting's old recordings were reissued as the film came out, and on the album cover she looks demure (with a voice to match her appearance); but in playing her Miss Day is hard and whorish, perhaps because Etting had been a dime-a-dance girl. With that exception – and that the small-time hood (James Cagney) she married made her a star – the facts in the film and those on the record sleeve bear little relation to each other. The situations are dramatic ones in principle, but the film muffs most of them, despite Cagney's cocky and oddly touching performance. The real Ruth Etting must have been either more ambitious or more naïve, and surely she could not have loathed her man quite so much.

Film biographies of the lost souls of show business proliferated, owing to the

907

success of **I'll Cry Tomorrow** (1955) as both book and movie. Lillian Roth's memoir followed her life from starring in the Follies to Alcoholics Anonymous, via two drunken husbands and a spell on the Bowery; but neither the script nor Daniel Mann's direction is able to illuminate the problems of alcoholism. Since Susan Hayward was not an actress to compensate for their deficiencies (and as she was not a singer, like Miss Day, there are few songs), the chief point of interest is Jo Van Fleet as a stage mother.

In theory this was the sort of 'thought-provoking' drama that Schary had been brought in to foster, but he became cautious as the profits on the studio's musicals showed the public in the mood for light entertainment: no more than during Mayer's regime was M-G-M regarded as a studio interested in social problems – and the few that were made were the work of the writer-director Richard Brooks, who was only sometimes adequate to the task. He adapted **The Blackboard Jungle** (1955) from Evan Hunter's novel about his teaching experiences in New York, but retained only a few nuggets of fact or genuine emotion in an often superficial essay. Glenn Ford is the teacher who refuses to accept the indifference of his colleagues and Sidney Poitier the most delinquent of his pupils, with a chip on his shoulder because of his colour. The film is mostly remembered for a song played by Bill Haley and the Comets, 'Rock Around the Clock', which was to lead to a radical change in popular music. Brooks only directed **The Catered Affair** (1956), which Gore Vidal scripted from Paddy Chayevsky's T.V. play, but with a note of contrivance more pronounced than usual in filming this writer. The title refers to a Bronx–Irish wedding, and the family quarrels it provokes sound truthful enough; but in emphasising that this is not the usual movie tale of young love Brooks makes heavy going of the bride's unattractive parents. They are played by Ernest Borgnine and Bette Davis, who, moving into character roles with a vengeance, is too broad for the setting.

In his pursuit of 'important' issues, Brooks wrote and directed **Something of Value** (1957), obtaining the endorsement of Winston Churchill, who appears to introduce it: but its portrait of British Africa

in its death throes is as cliché-ridden as its David and Jonathan relationship between white (Rock Hudson) and black (Sidney Poitier). Brooks turned to Dostoevsky, but if his own adaptation of **The Brothers Karamazov** (1958) is a fair summary of its events, it reveals little understanding of the concern behind them. In any case, the project was foredoomed by the casting of Yul Brynner as Dmitri and Maria Schell as Grushenka.

Nor did Brooks do justice to Tennessee Williams with either **Cat on a Hot Tin Roof** (1958) or **Sweet Bird of Youth** (1962), missing the cadences of passion and corruption in an attempt to provide 'adult' drama. At least *Sweet Bird* preserves Williams's tumbledown hotel and the Broadway performances of Geraldine Page and Paul Newman. As a has-been star Miss Page is even more flamboyant than Davis in *All About Eve* and Swanson in *Sunset Boulevard* – and she manages to convey the fear that lurks in every celebrity even better than they did. Newman is more workaday as the exponent of the American dream gone sour, returning to his home town not as the movie star he hoped to be but gigolo to another – and now less an ageing bisexual opportunist than a golden-beauty ne'er-do-well. The Production Code, still in operation, dictated that the castration become a beating-up and that the abortion be glossed over – changes which should in theory have improved the piece, but it is still often too lurid. *Cat on a Hot Tin Roof*, a better play, has become even more tawdry in Brooks's hands, with whipped-up hysteria and a camera constantly picking up meaningless images. Newman is Brick, managing well his scorn and self-pity as he sinks into alcoholism; Elizabeth Taylor spits out defiance but conveys neither Maggie's sexuality nor her frustrations. Williams observed kindly that she was not his idea of Maggie the Cat, and he loathed the film, which refuses to allow that Brick's affection for the dead Skipper had caused his impotence. Instead, that is blamed on Maggie's infidelity with Skipper, but it hardly matters since little of it makes much sense.

Such films, even with bowdlerisations, were boldly made in an effort to maintain M-G-M's domination of the industry. Similarly, at this time, this company was prominent in filming on location in

Europe. Making the transatlantic trip were Arthur Freed, for his last produced film, **The Light in the Piazza** (1962), and John Houseman, another of Metro's better producers, for **In the Cool of the Day** (1963). The setting of Freed's film is Florence, where Olivia de Havilland is uncertain whether to tell a wealthy and amorous Italian (George Hamilton) that her daughter (Yvette Mimieux) is mentally retarded. Guy Green's direction and Julius J. Epstein's script dilute some of the points which Elizabeth Spencer made in her novel, but ambiguities still remain. *In the Cool of the Day* is a combination of *Dark Victory* and *September Affair*, its lack of originality not disguised by the screenplay or the direction, by Robert Stevenson. Jane Fonda plays a fey creature who leaves her husband to disport herself over much of Delphi and the Acropolis with a British publisher (Peter Finch). The theme of Americans in Europe might still have provided valuable material, but Hollywood was impressed by the inroads into its audiences made by European films. The increase of tourism created audiences eager to relive their vacations; and the Duomo in Florence and the Parthenon were relatively new subjects for the wide-screen cameras to focus upon.

At the same time, in an exotic locale, M-G-M's fortunes were again in the balance. In the wake of Dore Schary's departure, the company suffered its first annual loss* since its inception and, as we have seen, Vogel saved the situation with the remake of *Ben-Hur*. Since that was happily filling theatres, the decision was reached to remake another of the studio's past successes, **Mutiny on the Bounty** (1962) and, on the principle that only the biggest stars are suitable for the biggest pictures, Marlon Brando was approached to play either of the two chief roles. After turning down the project several times – during which the salary offers rose to a final $500,000 against 10 per cent of the gross, plus $5,000 a day overtime if shooting continued beyond the specified schedule – he de-

cided that he might inject some message for humanity into the role of the hero, Fletcher Christian. He then realised that what interested him was the fate of the survivors on Pitcairn Island and, according to the producer, Aaron Rosenberg, was granted 'consultation rights on that part of the picture'. A dozen different endings were written and shot, and any of the other eleven must have been better than the one that was used. Till that point, the film is often entertaining, and the wide screen views are breathtaking even as it is clear that events are conforming to the jungle princess formula. The original writer and director, Eric Ambler and Carol Reed, distinguished British names, were replaced by old Hollywood professionals, Charles Lederer and Lewis Milestone, after two months' shooting, with only one sequence finished. The views of billowing sails and scrubbed decks were done by second-unit directors, but if most of the first half – the voyage out of the *Bounty* – is credit to Milestone's skill, we know from his own account that he gave up: 'Since Brando was going to supervise it anyway, I waited till someone yelled "Camera!" and went off to sit down somewhere and read the paper.' Accordingly Brando may be blamed for his own dreadful performance as an aristocratic fop who becomes tough and heroic under changed circumstances. It is an interesting concept, but he is never the equal of Trevor Howard's blunt and blinkered sea-dog, Bligh. Since this actor is given much less footage, the expected clash of eagles never occurs. The costs had mounted from $10 million to $19 million, but Technicolor and Ultra Panavision notwithstanding, the earlier version is preferable, as the returns indicated to M-G-M's book-keepers.

Vogel resigned the following year and was replaced by Robert O'Brien, who had been executive vice-president of Loews since 1957. His ignorance of the movie-making process was obscured when *Doctor Zhivago* (q.v.) gave the company a good year; and there were several reissues of *Gone With the Wind* to fill the coffers. During his tenure few worthwhile films emerged, and **The Comedians** (1967) is not among them, despite the fact that Graham Greene wrote the screenplay from his own novel. Mauritius and Dahomey deputised for Haiti, but for all the use made

*The situation had been so critical in 1957 that thought had been given to selling the company, which was saved by the popularity of a low-budget vehicle for the rock singer, Elvis Presley, *Jailhouse Rock*. It made up for the losses on *Raintree County*, a bland Civil War epic with Elizabeth Taylor and Montgomery Clift, instituted by Schary as a traditional M-G-M feature. Ironically, one of his first actions on arriving at the studio had been to cancel an earlier version based on the same novel.

of them the film might have been shot on the back-lot. With the local colour and the original sense of menace gone, the tale looks dangerously like self-parody, especially when a dour Richard Burton makes a reference to either faith or death. As his mistress, Elizabeth Taylor has no passion and substitutes an indefinable accent for the German one in the book. Greene said later that the experience was one which he hoped never to repeat, but as a former film critic he should have been wary of producer-director Peter Glenville, whose many poor films include another failure for M-G-M, an unfunny version of a Feydeau farce, **Hotel Paradiso** (1966), with Alec Guinness.

With such films did the once-mighty company wither and die. Its lingering self-respect was surely shattered with **The Singing Nun** (1966), the tale of a Belgian Dominican (a pertly pious Debbie Reynolds), whose singing brings her to the height of anyone's ambition – appearing on the Ed Sullivan Show. She had existed, but this attempt to repeat the success of *The Sound of Music* exists in no real world as directed by Henry Koster. Had it been made in the Forties, the time to which it spiritually belongs – when Hollywood's way with such tales was often as naive as opportunistic – it would still be one of the worst films ever made. Audiences recognised it for the anachronism it was and stayed away, as they did from most M-G-M films at this time.

Paramount survived much better the onslaught of television, though once again not with any consistent policy unless it was an insistence on light entertainment. Profits continued to be satisfactory, mainly due to the comedies of Martin and Lewis produced by Hal Wallis, whose other films were the studio's sole concessions to seriousness. After the departure of Wilder, Wyler, Stevens and Capra, Paramount made no attempt to attract the leading film-makers, apart from Hitchcock, whose films also helped to keep the company prosperous. So did deMille's *The Ten Commandments,* but with his death, and the withdrawal of Hope and Crosby, Paramount no longer seemed like Paramount.

The last films that Hope and Crosby made for the studio are not among their best but they themselves are not blameless, since they were to various extents involved in the production. **Road to Bali** (1952) is the only 'Road' in colour; a later one, *The Road to Hong Kong* (q.v.), was made for United Artists, and if either had been the first it is doubtful whether there would have been another. As directed by Hal Walker *Bali* is careless in both senses of the word, and its humour depends on how much you know about its predecessors.

It was 20th's musicals rather than the airy M-G-M product that Paramount followed for the style of two mechanical and incohesive films, **White Christmas** (1954) and **Anything Goes** (1956). As far as the ingredients are concerned, Paramount had also looked to its own past, for these are rehashes of previous Crosby vehicles. Maybe there were inhibitions, as he was by now virtually a national monument. Perhaps that is why he is again cast as a world-famous entertainer, even if one surrounded by some of the ugliest sets and costumes ever devised. The songs are by Irving Berlin and Cole Porter respectively. In fact the Berlin film was planned to reteam Crosby and Astaire, with a screenplay (by Norman Krasna, Norman Panama and Melvin Frank) which draws on the earlier films they made together, plus a dash of *This Is the Army*. Astaire read it and refused it, and when the second choice, Donald O'Connor, fell ill, Danny Kaye stepped in. As directed by Michael Curtiz, Kaye's 'look at me' niceness does not help an occasion that Scrooge might have cited to justify his attitude. O'Connor did co-star with Crosby in *Anything Goes*, which restores much of the score jettisoned in Paramount's earlier version, plus some new songs by Cahn and Van Heusen which are, again, inferior versions of numbers which Crosby had done with Hope. The sole connection with the original 'book' is the shipboard setting, and the new one, by Sidney Sheldon, is as damp as Robert Lewis's direction.

Crosby did make two decent pictures – in black and white since they were serious subjects – **Little Boy Lost** (1952) and **The Country Girl** (1954), both written and directed by George Seaton. The former was adapted from Marghanita Laski's novel about a journalist looking for the son he had left in France at the beginning of the War, while the latter was founded in a Clifford Odets drama about a drunken actor making a come-back – and with its show-business background the apparently obligatory songs for Crosby were less intrusive. Odets's theme was not new and his customary hyperbole might have passed in a metier where exaggeration is the accepted norm: but many of his scenes are ludicrous, such as that in which the play's director (William Holden) forces a kiss upon the actor's wife (Grace Kelly). However, Seaton's amendments are often telling and original and, if at first it is strange to see Crosby, an entertainer of legendary success, playing one having to audition and afraid of accepting stardom, there is not one emotional scene in which he is not thoroughly in command – even when the words he has to say are disproportionate to the feeling he brings to them. Miss Kelly's inexperience in a demanding role is a prime example of cardigan and glasses convincing the New York critics and Academy voters that they were watching a Best Actress.

Bob Hope's final movies under his contract are tired. Attempting to establish a more serious image, he remained with Paramount for two more films which he produced – **The Seven Little Foys** (1955) and **Beau James** (1957). Written by Jack Rose and Melville Shavelson, who also directed, these are factual tales whose protagonists have attributes not entirely distant from Hope's accepted screen persona, that of a wily opportunist. But it is also clear that the originals in both cases were extremely unpleasant and the sentimental approach further destroys promising material. Despite an attempt to make him charming, Eddie Foy in *The Seven Little Foys* can be seen to be a bad-tempered, misogynistic small-time comic, fussing about billing and exploiting his children until they mutiny and the case ends in court. Mayor James J. Walker in *Beau James* has become a lovable scoundrel whose downfall is brought about when he advances his mistress (Vera Miles) at the expense of his wife (Alexis Smith). The many distortions in this case are exasperating – Walker did not say 'So long, sweetheart' as he left New York for exile, but 'So long, suckers' – even allowing for the fact that the film's model is *The Eddy Duchin Story* (q.v.) rather than many predecessors on corrupt politicians.

Paramount envisaged the much less volatile Rosemary Clooney as a replacement for Betty Hutton, casting her as a brassy saloon singer in **Red Garters** (1954), originally planned as a spoof Western with Jane Russell and Danny Kaye, to be directed by Mitchell Leisen. After several false starts and cast changes it was clear that Leisen was no longer able to satisfy Paramount executives as he once had and he was replaced by George Marshall, who had had some great successes in this vein; but on this occasion his slow pacing only emphasises the double cuteness of the jokes and of the leading man, Guy Mitchell, a popular singer, in the role intended for Kaye. The stylised one-colour sets (inherited from Leisen) aroused some admiration but, considering that the film was a failure, it is a surprise that Paramount allowed something similar with **Li'l Abner** (1959). The antics of Al Capp's strip-cartoon hayseeds are assimilated into a bright book, mainly about the choice of Dogpatch, 'the most useless place in America', as a testing area for atomic bombs. There are references to Washington corruption and to the vanity and impotency of Abner, played by Peter Palmer with what might not be simulated naivety. Two Paramount writers, Norman Panama and Melvin Frank, had written the show for Broadway, where it had been very successful: they were allowed to return with most of the New York cast, vivacious and energetic on film, especially Stubby Kaye as Marryin' Sam and Julie Newmar as Stupefyin' Jones, a robot-like sex-object. They exult in a lively score, by Gene de Paul and Johnny Mercer (who had written *Seven Brides for Seven Brothers*), and some frenetic choreography, from Michael Kidd's original. Frank's direction unimaginatively reproduces the Broadway show, but at least he learnt from this mistake: when producing another comic-strip musical, *A Funny Thing Happened on the Way to the Forum* (q.v.), he got someone else to direct it.

Panama and Frank, like Shavelson and Rose, another team which had written for Bob Hope, provided Paramount with several old-fashioned comedies at this time. With such stars as Danny Kaye and Sophia Loren, these films prove these writer-directors no match for the LaCavas and McCareys, who understood that stars shone brighter when expressed through

In the days when Marie Dressler coped with a boozing husband, both she and the situation were comic: consequently the more realistic *Come Back, Little Sheba* was regarded as a new departure for Hollywood. Shirley Booth's magnificent performance won her an Oscar, while Burt Lancaster's first 'character' role gave his career a new impetus – a mixed blessing, as it turned out.

situation and dialogue rather than as personalities for their own sake. Another team at Paramount, William Perlberg and George Seaton, also produced several comedies, including two with Clark Gable, *Teacher's Pet* and *But Not for Me*. They were also responsible for one of the few contemporary films on the Korean War, **The Bridges at Toko-Ri** (1954), which Mark Robson directed. It concerns an admiral (Fredric March) with a weakness for young men who resemble his dead son, and a World War II veteran (William Holden) who fills that bill: during this new war Holden becomes less embittered at having had to don uniform again, after accepting March's thesis of the domino theory in South-East Asia. The bridges of the title are symbolic, intended to show the Communists that 'we' shall not give in, but on the evidence of this film James A. Michener's original novel was not useful propaganda.

Hal Wallis was otherwise, as I said, the sole guardian of Paramount's contact with the real world, and he only really liked that if filtered through Broadway. The post-Miller/Williams school of American drama was not entirely congenial to cinema-goers, and to the possible losses on film

versions Wallis could point to the success of his formula films with the rock singer Elvis Presley or those of Martin and Lewis, arguably the most excruciating comedy team in the history of cinema.

Nor, I think, will posterity be entirely grateful to Wallis for the films concerned. The one obvious exception is **Come Back, Little Sheba** (1952), directed by Daniel Mann, since it enshrines Shirley Booth's Broadway performance. Because she was neither young nor glamorous the film was regarded as a new direction in cinema: 'It is essentially *about* the sad business of making the best of a bad job' said *Sight and Sound*, mentioning 'the sort of relationship that carries on quietly in one corner of a Chekhov play'. Lola (Miss Booth) shuffles about in a dressing-gown, listening to soap operas, spying on the young couple in the parlour, and hoping that her husband will not relapse into alcoholism, and even if the character had been much copied, that does not detract from its truth. She does not understand what drove him to drink in the first place, but unfortunately we do – he abandoned his medical studies to marry her when she became pregnant. It is only too clear to us that he will again resort to the bottle, because of the antics of the pretty student (Terry Moore) and her beau (Richard Jaeckel), one of the Adonis-like creatures that tend to crop up in the works of William Inge (who because of this play was taken as seriously as Tennessee Williams and Arthur Miller). If Doc's alcoholism is tritely conveyed, it has an appropriate interpreter in Burt Lancaster, who is quieter even than Spencer Tracy at his quietest, but self-consciously so, always forcing himself on the audience's attention. Coupled with the film's refusal to offer even a fragmentary portrait of small-town life, we are left only with Miss Booth, heart-rendingly offering a portrait of a woman who has not made a success of being a wife.

Shirley Booth won an Oscar, and Wallis immediately cast her in **About Mrs Leslie** (1954), a curious and almost splendid film. It has the same director and the same screenwriter, Ketti Frings (in this case working with Hal Kanter, from a novel by Vina Delmar). The problem of finding a suitable vehicle for this dumpy, middle-aged lady was solved by involving her in a middle-aged love affair. She keeps a boarding house in Beverly Hills and he (Robert Ryan) is an executive who snatches a few weeks every year away from wife and boardroom. Ryan has just the right mixture of shyness and decency, while Miss Booth is good natured and humble (she is much too flattered to rebuff his first pass), having developed a sturdiness and a touch of waspishness after a number of life's knocks. The film failed with both press and public, so it was some years before Shirley Booth next worked for Wallis. In **Hot Spell** (1958) she plays a mother trying to cope, a conventional role that she tackles with her usual lack of self-indulgence. The piece itself is of the Inge-Williams school, written by James Poe from a little-known play by Lonnie Coleman. The film's failure in this case seems to be due to the fact that without a Broadway reputation to guide it, the public was not yet ready for dramas in which mamas and papas were not remembered fondly. There are faults here in writing and execution, but there is a rare harshness in the fights between father (Anthony Quinn) and son (Earl Holliman), as well as a funeral done without the usual movie sentimentality. Some humorous, but bit-

ter, scenes between mother and a friend (Eileen Heckart) are not at odds with the rest of the film. Mann again directed.

The cast includes Shirley MacLaine, who supported Shirley Booth again in **The Matchmaker** (1958), directed by Joseph Anthony from Thornton Wilder's play (itself derived from a nineteenth-century Austrian farce). It had been a success in London and New York for Ruth Gordon, whom I saw in the role. I have also seen it as transformed into 'Hello Dolly', and it had, apart from this version, struck me as a mediocre work. As farcical comedy it has little wit, but the situations spring mainly from the motives of the characters – who are wonderfully played: Paul Ford as the pompous and miserly merchant; Anthony Perkins and Robert Morse as his assistants; MacLaine dimpling prettily as the milliner; and Miss Booth in the title-role, her chins and cheeks permanently wobbling, her eyes darting hopefully from the merchant's face to somewhere beyond camera range. Her four screen performances are touched with magic because she works with that combination of truth and professional instinct which is the hallmark of all great players.

The film was produced by Don Hartman, a former comedy writer, who shared many of the principles and pretensions of Wallis. He was also responsible for **Desire Under the Elms** (1958), which is *not* notable for its performances – Sophia Loren as O'Neill's mail-order Phaedra, Burl Ives's over-ripe New England farmer and Perkins as his tic-afflicted son. Delbert Mann directed, unfortunately stressing O'Neill's sophomoric tragic values. The film was redundant in any case, since Wallis had recently produced another with the same situation, *Wild Is the Wind,* with Anna Magnani.

To capitalise on the Oscar that Magnani had won for that film, Wallis bought the rights to **The Rose Tattoo** (1955), a concoction that Tennessee Williams had written for her but which she had refused to do on Broadway. Williams was a good writer with the instincts of a hack and his screenplay contains a number of puerilities, not to mention two dream figures with little more dimension than photographs in a physique magazine, a young sailor (Ben Cooper) and an ageing but still hunky truck-driver (Burt Lancaster). The young lovers are, admittedly, supposed to point up mother's frigidity, which has to melt before the truck-driver, and Daniel Mann's direction accentuates the most attractive aspect of the piece, its pervading sexuality. In this respect, Magnani also contributes, despite the fact that she spends most of the time shouting at her daughter (Marisa Pavan), the neighbours and the whores; and at one point is seen struggling into a corset. Lancaster is more than willing in situations beyond him; he is his usual ineffable self in **The Rainmaker** (1956), as a peripatetic con-man who stops just long enough to teach an ageing virgin (Katharine Hepburn) the meaning of life. The then novice director, Joseph Anthony – he had staged N. Richard Nash's play on Broadway – allows this actress uncontrolled authority and tears; and he cannot hide the namby-pamby but derivative nature of the material. The obsession with sex in such plays (cf. the works of Arthur Miller) helped liberalise Hollywood, since the M.P.A.A. had difficulty in forbidding what sophisticated New York had applauded. If Wallis saw them primarily as vehicles for the 'strong' actresses he had long favoured, they were also regarded as among the more civilised entertainments to be seen in a cinema.

He was also partly responsible for the return to favour of the Western. That was due to a few good ones as opposed to the genre as a whole, and his **Gunfight at the O.K. Corral** (1957) is expectedly sound and vigorous. The script by Leon Uris – not then a best-selling novelist – retells the feud between the Earp family and Doc Holliday on one hand and Billy Clanton and his gang on the other – the latter bunch acted by some choice bad men, including John Ireland, Dennis Hopper, Frank Faylen, Lee Van Cleef, Lyle Bettger, Jack Elam and Ted de Corsia. As Earp, Burt Lancaster offers in physical bulk what he lacks in virile delivery, while as Doc Holliday Kirk Douglas conveys a real sense of menace, doubtless developed by the expert director, John Sturges. As Frankie Laine warbles a Dmitri Tiomkin ballad, we may be reminded of *High Noon*, a film that helped to redefine the Code of the West.

One-Eyed Jacks (1961) is a frontal attack on that ethos as produced by Marlon Brando and directed by him (after a dispute with Stanley Kubrick, q.v.). The hero (Brando) is stupid, cunning and vicious, finally shooting his enemy the sheriff (Karl Malden) in the back. It is a story of revenge at a time of rough justice, of racial prejudice, of no morals, set in a country where drab-looking girls wait in run-down, deserted saloons, where the desert is vast and lonely and where there is a whipping-post for the hero. That particular sequence may reveal masochism or an intimation of a Messiah-complex on the part of Brando himself; the whole film is an early example of the self-indulgence that was to run rife once the studio system had completely broken down. At the same time it is accomplished, clearly influenced by both John Ford and Kurosawa and, like *Viva Zapata!*, veering back and forth from the romantic to the realistic (the men wear duds as seen in the photographs of the time – 1880 – which movies had forgotten since Tom Mix had introduced his more photogenic outfits). That Brando has not been given another opportunity to direct may be due to the huge final cost, which was only just recovered at the box office.

Despite much publicity and comment, the film was far less influential than Sam Peckinpah's not dissimilar *Ride the High Country* (q.v.) a programmer of the following year. That moved the Western decisively away from Monument Valley and introduced both more violence and older, more robust characters. One of its descendants is **True Grit** (1969), to date the last really popular Western. Credit for its quality is due to the author, Charles Porteous, rendered so capably by Marguerite Roberts in her screenplay, and the veteran director Henry Hathaway. Other recent collaborations with Wallis, the producer, and the equally venerable cinematographer, Lucien Ballard, had not augured a Western of this quality, so we may suppose Hathaway by this time to be only as good as his script. A fat, ageing, one-eyed drunken marshal, Rooster Cogburn (John Wayne), a guileless, rather fey but wary girl (Kim Darby) and a sassy young Texas Ranger (Glenn Campbell) set out amidst yellow saplings and green firs to pursue a killer – and so disarming is their interplay that the villains, led by Robert Duvall, arrive with ferocious suddenness. Only the bad men – Richard Jordan, Anthony Zerbe – are good in an opportunist sequel, **Rooster Cogburn** (1975), directed by

Stuart Miller because Hathaway now considered himself too old for the location work. Wayne and Katharine Hepburn are parodies of their former selves in a pseudonymous script (Wallis and his wife were among the contributors), which is a Wild West version of *The African Queen*. Audiences were not interested in this first teaming of two legendary but aged stars and, unlike its two progenitors, this film was a box-office disaster – the last of several which Wallis had had with Universal, to whom he had moved after a quarrel (q.v.) with Paramount over a film with Richard Burton; and he forthwith retired.

From Paramount came also the Western programmers produced by A. C. Lyles in the early Sixties, and fancied by some buffs since they featured bevies of names from an earlier era, many of them now toupéed, corseted (or unfortunately not), with drooping jowls and, it would seem, in an advanced state of alcoholism. Also from Paramount was a Western musical, **Paint Your Wagon** (1969), persuaded into the project by Alan Jay Lerner, who had written the 1948 Broadway show with Frederick Loewe. After several failures the industry was chary of musicals, but this one offered the opportunity, as with *The Sound of Music,* of attractive locations; and there were leading roles for two of the biggest box-office stars, Lee Marvin and Clint Eastwood (though neither could sing) plus another, supposedly with a certain European clout to help it in that difficult market for musicals, Jean Seberg. Costs rose to over $20 million during the extensive location shooting – often due to difficulties with the director, Joshua Logan. He was a strange choice, since most reviewers had suggested that both *South Pacific* and *Camelot* (q.v.) would have been better with someone else in charge. On this occasion his vulgarity is restrained, despite the opportunities in the story – about sex-starved miners and a *ménage à trois*. Paddy Chayevsky wrote it when Lerner decided that his original book would not do, but he himself wrote the screenplay; when Loewe refused to write any new songs (because he had retired) André Previn contributed two, in a needless Sixties rock idiom. The money was at least well spent when the green valley comes alive with the miners carolling the title song and 'There's a Coach Coming

In'. The singers are self-conscious, but so is the film – including a farcical, destructive climax, pleasantly reminiscent of *Steamboat Bill Jr.*

The film was more popular in Britain than the U.S. (though that did not help it recover its cost), and so, unsurprisingly, was **Half a Sixpence** (1967), a musical version of 'Kipps' which had duplicated its success on Broadway and whose prime virtue, its star, becomes its chief liability on film. Tommy Steele substitutes teeth for talent: after 146 minutes of his grin in close-up, one cherishes all the more Buster Keaton's stone face. Steele has star quality but no reticence, compounding his exuberance with a nasal, grating singing voice and is all the more obtrusive since his leading ladies – Julia Foster as the humble Ann, and Penelope Horner as the haughty Helen – lack personality. Some of their elders (Pamela Brown, Cyril Ritchard) have the requisite style, but this enterprise is only saved from total disaster by the American director, George Sidney. He makes this perhaps the prettiest of all period musicals and has staged the poor numbers with skill and vitality. He is also alive (as the book is not) to H. G. Wells's original novel.

Wells also provided the basis for **The War of the Worlds** (1953). Except for some Z-budget serials, science fiction was ignored by Hollywood from the Silent era until 1950, when George Pal made *Destination Moon* for Eagle-Lion. The not dissimilar *Rocketship X-M* followed soon after, and, if we regard *The Thing* as primarily a horror item, Paramount was the first of the major studios to venture into the field when it financed Pal's Technicolor productions of **When Worlds Collide** (1951) and *The War of the Worlds*, directed respectively by Rudolph Maté and Byron Haskin, with B-picture casts playing dedicated scientists with virtually unspeakable dialogue. The budget for the live-action sequences of the latter was $600,000, an inconsiderable sum, but Paramount was sufficiently encouraged to allow $1,400,000 for special effects. These in their day were good, but the transportation of Wells's novel to contemporary California robs it of much of its appeal without adding to the thrills.

A very different war was the background to Paramount's first European co-production, **War and Peace** (1956), and it became involved because it had first call on the services of Audrey Hepburn. The film industry had always considered Tolstoy's novel too big and too 'highbrow' – with the not surprising exceptions of Korda and Orson Welles, who had planned a production during the War. David O. Selznick and then Mike Todd announced their own versions in the mid-Fifties, as did the Italian team of Carlo Ponti and Dino de Laurentiis, both of whom harboured ambitions outside Italy. They interested King Vidor and Miss Hepburn, the latter to play Natasha with her then husband, Mel Ferrer, as Prince Andrei. As she was so clearly the perfect choice the other producers hesitated, and Paramount agreed to support Ponti and de Laurentiis. The adapters have approached Tolstoy's novel about the French invasion of Russia as though it were *Gone with the Wind*, giving us most of the content, a little character, some motivation, but no complexity. The result is without crassness or sanctimoniousness and, if the characters hardly seem Russian, they are perhaps more alive than in most historical movies. Certainly Miss Hepburn is, whether mooning over the men going to war or revelling in a trip to the country. The other triumph is the photography by Jack Cardiff, with second-unit work by Aldo Tonti. The rest of the acting varies, from Barry Jones (Rostov), Jeremy Brett (Nicholas) and Henry Fonda (a thin and Omaha-accented Pierre), to Ferrer, John Mills (Platon) and Anita Ekburg (Helena) at the other end of the scale.

Hepburn made a number of enjoyable films for Paramount, including *Breakfast at Tiffany's* (q.v.), whose screenwriter, George Axelrod, also scripted **Paris When It Sizzles** (1964), based on Duvivier's *La Fête à Henriette*. She plays stenographer to William Holden, and they are joined by Noël Coward, Marlene Dietrich and Tony Curtis in guest appearances. There are in-jokes, a film within a film, echoes of *Funny Face,* and Eastmancolor, all advantages denied to Duvivier, but of no obvious help to the director, Richard Quine.

Holden was Paramount's primary male star at this time, taking the plum parts and leaving to the equally handsome and dull Charlton Heston the programmers made

for the studio by the production team of Pine and Thomas, who liked the tried, the true and Technicolor. Among the veteran stars who filmed for Paramount at this time is Spencer Tracy – and one of the reasons that he left M-G-M was its refusal, because of cost, to sanction **The Mountain** (1956), based on Henry Troyat's novel. In the interim he had made *Broken Lance* for 20th Century-Fox, from which he brought the director Edward Dmytryk and Robert Wagner. Neither actor makes a convincing French peasant in *The Mountain* and it is equally hard to accept Wagner, thirty years his junior, as Tracy's brother. The moral issues raised as they climb the mountain are simplistic, as rendered in Ranald McDougall's screenplay. He adapted **We're No Angels** (1955), in which another of the great stars, Humphrey Bogart, plays a Frenchman. The Broadway version of this French play goes unmentioned in the credits, but the direction by Michael Curtiz – Wallis's old Warner Bros. colleague – does little to disguise the source. As escaped convicts in an emporium on Devil's Island, Bogart, Peter Ustinov and Aldo Ray enjoy themselves and amuse us and, since this is a comedy, it comes as no surprise when at the end they elect to return to jail.

Comedy had never been Curtiz's forte, and he seems to have been chosen for **A Breath of Scandal** (1960) on the basis that, like its author, Molnár, he had been born in the Austro-Hungarian Empire. Molnár's play – 'Olympia' – is about a hussar officer who takes revenge on an arrogant princess who has spurned his advances. However, this adaptation (by Sidney Howard, who had died in 1939; there is no screenplay credit) concerns a haughty princess suspected of having an affair with an American car salesman. Sophia Loren is no one's idea of a Hapsburg princess, and neither she nor John Gavin are natural farceurs, leaving only Isabel Jeans, as Momma, with the right style, which suggests that Curtiz gave little help to two other experienced players, Maurice Chevalier, as Poppa, and Angela Lansbury, as Loren's jealous rival. Among his later films, only **The Scarlet Hour** (1956) is reminiscent of his Warner Bros. melodramas – made, like this, in black and white. It tells of an unfaithful wife (Carol Ohmart), the lover (Tom Tryon) who is an employee of her husband (James Gregory), and what happens to the two of them when they overhear some men planning a robbery. The night clubs are seedier than they used to be, the bars darker; and much of the action takes place in parked cars.

This sharp and unpretentious movie was not typical of the Paramount films of the time; nor did the company care to follow up its one excursion into filming an admired T.V. play, *Fear Strikes Out* (q.v.). One 'serious' enterprise deserves to be recalled, but only as an object of scorn. This is **The Buster Keaton Story** (1957). As far as Hollywood was concerned, Keaton was one of the derelicts of show business and therefore the fitting subject of a film. The producer-writers Robert Smith and Sidney Sheldon, who also directed, show not the least admiration for Keaton, reducing him to a silly little man and an unfunny minor comic. Their story-line is almost totally fictional, but what is most repugnant is that it violates everything for which Keaton stood. It must surely have saddened him to see some of his sublime numbers vulgarised by adding inane slapstick of which he was incapable. In fact, the film was too cheaply made to re-create his routines well, so that that of *Cops* uses only one set and ten cops. Acting as technical adviser, he was well paid for teaching Donald O'Connor to flap his arms. Keaton loathed the film and must have seen it as Hollywood's last attempt to do him in.

Later, as a novelist, Sheldon's model was to be Harold Robbins. Robbins's bestsellers were unlike those Hollywood used to film, being throw-away airplane reading – consisting often of glamorous beings in highly-charged sexual activities. Paramount's co-productions with Joseph E. Levine are among the more shameful moments in its history. **Where Love Has Gone** (1964) offers two hours with unprincipled and unpleasant people, with Susan Hayward as a sculptress, one of the most curious manifestations of Hollywood casting. 'In the field of sculpture', says someone, 'she's one of the greats.' She herself has such lines as 'I used sex as you used alcohol' as her marriage breaks up, and 'Oh Sam, the United Nations!' on receiving a commission from that source. Her husband, Michael Connors, later attempts to rape her fully-clothed, at which point you may decide that the once-excellent director, Edward Dmytryk, is as cynical as everyone else involved in the enterprise. He makes little attempt to disguise the fact that his film is a series of conversations, but these at least receive a charge whenever Bette Davis enters the luxurious settings – and she is some consolation as Hayward's snobbish mother. For those interested, Robbins's starting-point was the occasion when Lana Turner's daughter tried to stab her mother's gangster lover. Later movie attempts to duplicate Robbins's paperback sales produced only flops, till by the late Seventies Hollywood had lost interest in him and his imitators. **Sidney Sheldon's Bloodline** (1979) was a last lone flowering, its odd title meant by the author or his agent to remind the industry that one of its hacks had become a best-selling novelist. The film failed more abysmally than a predecessor, *Jacqueline Susann's Once Is Not Enough,* so Paramount soon reduced its ads to minute size, leaving only the title and, to meet contractual requirements, the name of the director, Terence Young. Hence the ads contained the two names likely to deter discriminating patrons, while omitting those of such popular players as Audrey Hepburn, James Mason and Ben Gazzara. Typical of the reviews was David Denby's comment in *New York Magazine*, that 'poor Michelle Philips gets her knees nailed to the floor for not paying her gambling debts. Paramount may have to do the same thing to get audiences to stay through this movie.'

Only one studio did not panic at this time, and that was Warners, whose television Western series were bringing in a reasonable income. Perhaps the prevailing calm is one reason why only Warner Bros. of the major companies offered a homogeneous group of films during this period, projecting the image of middle-class America – usually cosy, unless the requirements of the original, often a best-selling novel, decreed otherwise. Such had ever been Hollywood's intention, and at this time the films may reflect Jack L. Warner's taste more than at others during the company's history. Warners' great periods were moulded by Zanuck and then Wallis and, with the defection of Jerry Wald in 1951, there was no longer a strong or innovative producer at the studio: the only veteran was Henry Blanke, whose productions ranged from the dire (*Sincerely Yours*) to the noble (*The Nun's Story*).

Despite the failures of *Always Leave Them Laughing* and *Sincerely Yours,* Warner himself still believed that patrons could be induced to see their fireside favourites on the big screen, and Jack Webb was hired to direct and star in a cinema version of his T.V. series 'Dragnet'. It enjoyed a mild popularity, encouraging Webb to remain to make **Pete Kelly's Blues** (1955), again functioning in both capacities. The formula of this fondly-remembered film was simple – jazz and gangsters, the latter ever a speciality of this studio; it was the first film to re-create both aspects of the Twenties with any degree of fidelity, and it did so with a pervading melancholy then rare. Webb's own rather uninspired work includes his individual style of narration as used in 'Dragnet' (and parodied in *The Band Wagon*); Richard L. Breen's screenplay is sporadically witty, and the songs are sung by Peggy Lee (in a role which combines the second wife of *Citizen Kane* with Ophelia) and Ella Fitzgerald who, with hardly a muscle moving, sets the pulse racing with her version of 'Hard-Hearted Hannah'.

The Twenties were revisited by Warners for **The Helen Morgan Story** (1957), yet another standardised biography of a great star, palely impersonated by Ann Blyth. Had she used her own soprano voice, she might have managed an approximation of Morgan's style; she is ghosted by the richer voice of Gogi Grant and, because the songs are often superb, the film has its moments. Directing, Michael Curtiz is at his most professional, presenting in the bootlegging scenes an occasional echo of the old Warner gangster movies.

Act One (1963) is another show-business story, based on Moss Hart's memoir, a classic rags-to-riches account told wisely and wittily. Dore Schary, adapting, producing and directing – one of his few films after leaving M-G-M – has tampered only to cut, but his reverent approach destroys the exuberance of Hart's text. The matters dealt with are chiefly Hart's relationship with George S. Kaufman – leading to the triumphant first night of 'Once in a Lifetime' – and in that role Jason Robards rises above the treatment, as well as managing a good physical

resemblance. Hart is played by George Hamilton, whose gleaming good looks are not matched by his talent.

Hart's Jewish youth is played down; and when Warners insisted on diluting the essential Jewishness of Herman Wouk's characters in **Marjorie Morningstar** (1958) the screenwriter, Everett Freeman, sought (unsuccessfully) to have his name removed from the credits. Gutting the novel, he has concentrated on Marjorie's experiences as 'dramatic counsellor' at a summer camp in the Catskills and her fascination with Noel Airman *né* Ehrman (Gene Kelly), philanderer and little-theatre genius. Despite the changes, Natalie Wood's performance as the heroine and Harry Stradling's too lyrical colour photography, the film is better than some of the other novels filmed by Warners at this time. It is odd to see any of them on T.V. today, with only the clothes and the slowness of pace to indicate that they had not been made years earlier. Wouk's **Youngblood Hawke** (1964) is especially relishable, as rendered in Delmer Daves's screenplay and direction. The central character is based on Thomas Wolfe, and it is hard to know which is less convincing – the performance of James Franciscus, the palatial publishing offices, or his relationship with a scheming entrepreneur (Geneviève Page) who goes off to England, as she puts it, 'to look over some Shakespearian actors'. Wolfe's own romance with his mistress is bastardised, and the film's only contact with reality is in Mary Astor's original study of a kindly, but fading, Broadway star.

A more famous novel became a duller film, **The Old Man and the Sea** (1958), a co-production between its author, Ernest Hemingway, Leland Hayward (then a Broadway producer) and Spencer Tracy – whom they agreed should star. Fred Zinnemann began the filming in 1956, but left the project with little footage in the can, due to the difficulties of filming on the ocean. A great tank was constructed on the Warner lot (during which Tracy made another film), but the result, as directed by John Sturges, recovered little of its $6 million cost. Since its sole subject is the old man's pursuit of a giant fish, it depends much on Tracy, but even his skill cannot overcome the fact that the sky behind him is too often painted; and his

Among the brighter stars of the Fifties and Sixties was Doris Day, who was sunny, energetic and natural. These qualities were never better used than in *Calamity Jane*, probably the best film she made. Its makers saw the famous female gunslinger as a tomboy, torn between her fiancé, Philip Carey, left, and Howard Keel, right, playing Wild Bill Hickock.

speaking of the third-person commentary cannot rid it of its pretension.

Buying best sellers, Warners came up with **Sex and the Single Girl** (1964), Helen Gurley Brown's advisory essays. They have been transmuted into a comedy about a Helen Gurley Brown (Natalie Wood) whose best seller on sexual matters causes a battle with the publisher (Tony Curtis) of a scandal magazine. The roles require a technique which the players do not have, making it doubly sad to find superior artists in supporting roles as brawling neighbours. In the event, Henry Fonda and Lauren Bacall publicly repudiated the film, claiming that the director, Richard Quine, had reneged on his promise to build up their roles. The plot borrows from innumerable sources, as scripted by Joseph Heller, who wisely has not written a film since, and David R. Schwartz, whose only other worthwhile credit is a gangster spoof, **Robin and the Seven Hoods** (1964). Gordon Douglas directed and Frank Sinatra produced it to star himself and his 'clan', one of several films engendered thereby. It is brightened by Peter Falk, as a gang leader, and Bing Crosby, as a deceptively quiet do-gooder.

Crosby has the best song, 'Style', or, rather, he steals it from its fellow performers, Sinatra and Dean Martin. Elsewhere the Cahn-Van Heusen score is pleasantly satirical.

Warners had not been noted for their musicals since the early Thirties, so **Calamity Jane** (1953) was a surprise – all the more so, since it borrowed so heavily from 'Annie Get Your Gun' and 'Oklahoma!' As one critic put it, in the *Financial Times,* 'It manages the impossible by making a repeat performance seem as fresh and cheerful as its predecessors.' That is partly due to the stars, Doris Day and Howard Keel, and partly to the songs, staged with vivacity by Jack Donohue; David Butler directed. The film was enormously popular and still delights audiences on its rare revivals.

Miss Day later returned to Warners for *The Pajama Game,* the success of which – and the Rodgers and Hammerstein movies – dictated the style of **The Music Man** (1962) and **Gypsy** (1962). Both are theatrical in their new 'natural' settings, hoping thus to harness some of the energy which had contributed to their stage success. The first came to the screen with its Broadway star, Robert Preston, and director, Morton da Costa; in *Gypsy* Ethel Merman ceded to Rosalind Russell, and the direction was handed to Mervyn LeRoy. Both are, I think, great originals, with scores which in the Broadway cast albums remain enlivening. Meredith Willson wrote that of *The Music Man,* as well as the book, which follows the adventures of a fast-talking con-man in a mid-Western town. Jules Styne composed the music of *Gypsy,* with words by Stephen Sondheim, and a story based on Gypsy Rose Lee's memoir – which is mainly about her dominating, stage-obsessed mother. The thesis in *The Music Man* is that all should be forgiven those who bring life and happiness to those around them and, though da Costa has not solved the problem of restaging Willson's witty numbers, their work is infectious – if, that is, one can take folksiness in full flood and yet another return to the days when all men wore straw hats and the women carried parasols. Even if Preston was a mite old for the role, he is still wellnigh irresistible. In *Gypsy* the only good numbers are those – 'All I Need Is a Girl', 'Gotta Have a Gimmick' – featuring the original Broadway players. As Gypsy, Natalie Wood's striptease would titillate nobody and Miss Russell is broad and hammy: dubbed most of the time by Lisa Kirk, the singing lacks the thrilling urgency of Merman's. Sidney Lumet (q.v.), in explaining why he wants to remake this film, says, quite rightly, that it is a disaster: but without Merman,★ *Gypsy* is not *Gypsy*.

Despite favourable reviews, *The Music Man* failed outside the U.S., but Jack L. Warner still outbid the other studios for the rights to two other Broadway successes, both by Lerner and Loewe – *My Fair Lady*, discussed earlier, and **Camelot** (1967), directed for the screen by Joshua Logan. Noël Coward's remark (apropos the Broadway original) that it was longer than 'Parsifal' but without the laughs is a comment on Alan Jay Lerner's earnestness in fashioning a tribute to Goodness from T. H. White's pastiche of the Arthurian legends. As in the film of *Paint Your Wagon*, the theme is the love of two friends for the same woman, none of them wanting to hurt each other, and it is touchingly

★I have, however, seen it well acted with Angela Lansbury and magnificently sung by Dolores Gray.

rendered by Richard Harris as Arthur, who 'grows' beautifully from irresponsible youth at the beginning, by Franco Nero as Lancelot, and by Vanessa Redgrave as Guenevere – though she lacks the merriment of Julie Andrews's Broadway performance, which gave the piece an entirely different dimension. David Hemmings's Mordred is not one of the classic villains and the other knights only grasp at the English comic tradition. The castles are Spanish – the huge pile of Coca stands in for Camelot itself – and John Truscott's art direction, fusing Arthur Rackham and the Pre-Raphaelites, is so attractive that it distracts from the ponderous direction and the relentless chopping-up of the songs. For once, the money that went into these super-musicals was well spent, but the public was not overly appreciative.

Warners co-operated with the American Broadcasting Co. to produce **Mame** (1974), as that company was closing down its film-making operation. One of the reasons it was so short-lived was that A.B.C. always made the wrong decisions, and it never made a worse one than in casting Lucille Ball as Mame. Her singing is a mere croak and, since it has difficulty settling on the right note, it is hardly a pleasant croak; her dancing consists of a few whirls, and she has failed to grasp that Mame is an impulsive, spontaneous, eccentric lady, by turns bitchy and soft-hearted. She manages the bitchiness, but if she ever understood the other qualities she had forgotten them long since. Gene Saks's direction is of no help, and Robert Preston, as Mame's Southern beau, has too little to do to save the day. New York's fondness for Auntie Mame (hitherto heroine of a novel, a straight play, a film and the Broadway original of this movie) helped to break records at Radio City Music Hall during the first week of the run; but word-of-mouth drastically reduced its figures the following week. Elsewhere, the film's reception proved that few loved Lucy, and its failure was another nail in the coffin of the Hollywood musical.

Before *Camelot* and after his tentative attempt to save *Mister Roberts,* Joshua Logan had directed **Sayonara** (1957) for Warners. Paul Osborn wrote the screenplay from James A. Michener's novel about the American occupation of Japan and the servicemen (Marlon Brando, Red Buttons) who find themselves drawn into relationships with local women. In the book both romances end unhappily, but only one does in the film. The subject of mixed marriages conformed to the studio tradition of expounding liberal attitudes, and Logan underlines the significance; but since, as usual, he wants at the same time to be visually striking the only lasting impression is of pretty cherry blossoms. Some may prefer the only unambitious film that Logan directed, **Tall Story** (1960), a few college japes largely memorable for the performance of Jane Fonda (in her film debut) as a girl bent on marrying the star athlete, Anthony Perkins. Perkins appears nude, if rear-view and briefly, and was probably the first player to do so in a major American film.

The film was based on a Broadway play, as was **The Dark at the Top of the Stairs** (1960), adapted from William Inge's original by Harriet Frank Jr and Irving Ravetch, whose other pieces of Americana include *Hud* (q.v.) and *The Cowboys*. Robert Preston is father, a fast-talking travelling salesman, and Dorothy McGuire repeats, fifteen years on, her role in *A Tree Grows in Brooklyn*; Eve Arden plays in her usual style – which, however pleasing, would jar in a better movie; but the film is taken from them by Angela Lansbury as the husband's beautician friend. Delbert Mann directed this mixture of *Life with Father* and early Tennessee Williams; there are references to anti-Semitism and middle-aged sex (or lack of it), daring at the time, but the effort went unregarded.

The studio tradition of social melodrama was only really revived in **Rebel Without a Cause** (1955), a primary text on juvenile delinquency. The Warner approach to social problems had always been excitable, and the screenplay by Nicholas Ray, who directed, builds from *The Blackboard Jungle* and *The Wild One* (both recently approved of by adolescent patrons) to a dotty climax reminiscent of *The Song of Songs*. His characters are stereotypes, with the important exception of James Dean in the title role, perpetually intense, bewildered, shy-serious, by turns garrulous and inarticulate and with an odd mixture of foolishness and idealism in his adolescent defiance of society. With the

actor's death, the film was raised to cult status by sub-teenagers. It was also the first of many movies in which the young were sympathetic and the middle-aged either venal or contemptible or both. We knew that Andy Hardy and neat little girls in peep-toe shoes were not the truth about childhood, but neither was this lurid tale: nor is it any more on the side of youth than was Louis B. Mayer. At the time the film was either dismissed or considered inferior to Frankenheimer's more honest account of a bourgeois misfit, *The Young Stranger* (q.v.). The producer, David Weisbart, went on to make a number of teenage musicals at 20th Century-Fox.

After a change of management – Jack L. Warner sold his interest in the company to Seven Arts (q.v.) in 1967 – there appeared **The Sergeant** (1968), one of the first films on homosexuality: but in the event that is a subject on which the director John Flynn and the writer Dennis Murphy (working from his own novel) seem to have no opinions. This lack is emphasised by the almost non-existent plot, about a sergeant (Rod Steiger) with a hang-up on one of his men (John Philip Law). Apart from his loneliness and the fact that he had killed a German soldier during the War we are told nothing about him to put his 'weakness' into context. Rejected, the sergeant shoots himself and we are left only with an idle comment on the misuse of authority (the man had been seconded to the sergeant's office). The film is equally reticent on army life, but its portrait of a damp northern France – and Steiger's performance – suggest that the director might have had a more distinguished career.

Earlier, Warners had produced a film of Tennessee Williams's novel, **The Roman Spring of Mrs Stone** (1961), in conjunction with Seven Arts. Williams had apparently situated Rome deep in the Mississippi delta, but he had managed a perceptive portrait of a disillusioned and lonely American fascinated by the decadance of old Europe – represented, poorly, in the film by Warren Beatty's gigolo and the fawning but grasping countess of Lotte Lenya. Under the direction of José Quintero, from Broadway, each scene is designed as if for the stage, and an atmospheric, tenuous novel has become a rather obvious tale. As the lady who takes up with the gigolo, Vivien Leigh has not a

Roman spring, summer, autumn or winter, since she is either obviously doubled or works against a painted blackcloth. In an unbecoming blonde wig, she moves through the piece as if opening a bazaar, substituting a barely perceptible spark of malice for emotion. As in *Ship of Fools*, she presents a self-portrait of the former Lady Olivier, lonely and not liking the once-beautiful face which stares back from the mirror – and unnecessarily established in the tale as a rotten Shakespearian actress.

Also among the Warner grotesques is **Dead Ringer** (1964), with which Bette Davis returned after her success for the studio in *Whatever Happened to Baby Jane?* She plays twins in this second gobbet of Grand Guignol, which is sufficiently well-plotted to lend itself to admirers of the genre. Whether it is to be recommended to admirers of this actress is another matter: as directed by a former co-star, Paul Henreid, she is magnetic but bereft of her once subtle gift for establishing character.

The last Warner movie I think of, chronologically, as a 'studio' product – as opposed to a director's film made at Warners – is also in this category, and an unexpected success as directed by Terence Young from a run-of-the-mill stage thriller, by Frederick Knott. It is **Wait Until Dark** (1967), in which a blind girl (Audrey Hepburn) is beset by a gang of thugs (who include Alan Arkin). The twists of the plot are handled with efficiency; but it is because of one moment which always evokes screams from the audience that it belongs to the screen's most memorable thrillers.

Columbia had not only been astute in forming its television subsidiary, Screen Gems (q.v.), but had begun to distribute European films – not with any marked degree of success. There was no longer any doubt that Columbia was a major studio, but it could only continue to be so if there were enough leading film-makers to work for Harry Cohn. In 1953 he approached Jerry Wald, who had left Warners to form an independent company with Norman Krasna, its product to be released by R.K.O. Wald decided that on balance Cohn was preferable to Howard Hughes – especially as Cohn was to appoint him Vice-President in charge of production. After three unhappy years, Wald joined 20th Century-Fox – as did Buddy Adler,

who had been producing for Cohn since 1948. By the same token, Fred Kohlmar left that studio for Columbia in 1952 and was there when Cohn died in 1958. Between them, Wald and Kohlmar produced all the studio's memorable films at this time, with the exception of its most acclaimed and profitable film to date – *From Here to Eternity*. Adler was actually responsible for that, a fact which Cohn sought to minimise by adding his name to the publicity for the first time in the company's history.

The success of that film was followed by those of *On the Waterfront* and *The Caine Mutiny*, both produced independently within the organisation, demonstrating to Cohn the benefit of welcoming independent producers, and in that matter Columbia was second only to United Artists. But that was only for a brief period, since by the mid-Fifties it was clear that all the studios would have to follow their example.

Of the independent films, David E. Rose's **The End of the Affair** (1955) is yet another mangling of a novel by Graham Greene – as written for the screen by Lenore Coffee and directed by Edward Dmytryk. The piece is no longer about guilt, belief and several kinds of hatred, leaving only the skeleton – a tale of a woman (Deborah Kerr) who gives up her lover (Van Johnson) and his attempts to understand why. No less tolerable than Johnson are two British actors, Peter Cushing as the husband and John Mills as a detective. Belgravia is now the setting instead of that South London common – a loss almost too much to bear – and the atmosphere of wartime London is quite absent. The same is true of **The War Lover** (1963), produced by Arthur Hornblow. It was also filmed in Britain, but in this case with a British director, Philip Leacock. Its subject is American servicemen or, rather, one of them, a psychopathic airman, played by Steve McQueen with leers and smug grimaces. As with *Twelve O'Clock High* no interest is shown in placing these G.I.s in this alien setting, and it is difficult to learn whether John Hersey's novel had any point to make. Both films had been made because the originals had been much praised and popular, but have been so treated as to appeal to as many and offend as few as possible.

On the other hand, **The Strange One** (1957) retains the acrid qualities of the original novel, 'End As a Man', Calder Willingham's attack on military academies. Sam Spiegel produced – his only film between *On the Waterfront* and *The Bridge on the River Kwai* (q.v.). Book and film are different in plot, for Willingham's screenplay was based on a Broadway version as improvised by Actors' Studio personnel under the direction of Jack Garfein. He also made the film with the same actor, Ben Gazzara, as Jocko de Paris. Jocko is peculiar: where his fellow students wear track suits for such after lights-out activities as gambling, boozing and bullying, he disports himself in his cap, a Hawaiian shirt, black shorts, socks and garters and a long cigarette holder. He forces an egregious colleague on his girl-friend (Julie Wilson) and encourages a creepy young man with a crush on himself. These grown men touch each other and help each other to dress: in the book they were more obviously adolescent, which is why the film is the more disturbing. It falls apart at the end, with the kangaroo court, and it lacks depth. Gazzara, shiftily smiling in this film debut, remains its strongest feature. Seeing it again leaves unresolved the question why he never became an important movie star.

The Harder They Fall (1956) also offers an unflattering portrait of one aspect of American life: the fight game. In adapting his own novel, Budd Schulberg has harked back to his screenplay for *On the Waterfront* and allowed an exaggerated crusading attitude to overtake the action. Humphrey Bogart, in his last film, is the once-renowned columnist who succumbs to corruption until his integrity is restored. The boxing scenes are remarkable, as photographed by Burnett Guffey and directed by Mark Robson, who had made a somewhat better film on the same subject, *Champion*.

Wald was the producer, and it is to him that we also owe **The Eddy Duchin Story** (1956), which is romantic goulash, nicely photographed on New York locations by Harry Stradling. Tyrone Power is Duchin the pianist (his playing dubbed by Carmen Cavallero) and Kim Novak the first of his two wives. Sam Taylor's screenplay is dotted with the Statements that graced films at this time – for example,

'No one gets the big jackpot more than once' – and George Sidney directed. Sidney brings imagination and sympathy to **Jeanne Eagels** (1957), also an examination of one of the unfortunates of show business – but made in monochrome since *I'll Cry Tomorrow* had demonstrated that to be more suitable for alcoholism. Robert Planck's photography is always revealing and Daniel Fuchs's screenplay seems more accurate than in other cases (it provides a chance for Frank Borzage to play a Silent film director). Among Sidney's many borrowings is the ending from *Prix de Beauté* which, if inaccurate and sententious, is nevertheless pleasing in this context. He shows a genuine regard for Eagel's plight, while coaxing from Novak what is possibly her most acceptable film performance. Even so, she is less potent with speech than Eagels was when Silent; as her mentor and lover Jeff Chandler is more Yiddish than Italian and insufficiently volatile.

Sidney's forte at M-G-M had been musicals, but the two he made for Columbia are both betrayals of their Broadway originals – which is virtually criminal

Among the films of the Fifties which suggested a new order in Hollywood was *The Strange One*, which looked at life in a military school and didn't like what it saw. Here is Ben Gazzara, left, in the title role, with Paul E. Richards, taking advantage of the latter's crush on him.

in the case of **Pal Joey** (1957). When the original 1940 production had been dismissed as sordid by some critics, Hollywood had shown no interest until the 1952 revival not only rehabilitated it but reaffirmed its brilliance. Columbia, however, decided not to take advantage of the relaxations of the Production Code and removed what social comment there was, and the sexuality, reducing it to the tale of a heel and two ladies. Of Rodgers and Hart's dazzling score, gone are the daring, *intime* ballads ('What Is a Man?', 'Take Him', 'Our Little Den of Iniquity'), while the rousing songs written for the night-club production numbers have been relegated to background noise. There is no consolation to be gained from the four interpolated songs – only one of which is appropriate – and in any case we had heard Frank Sinatra sing them often before. Otherwise, cocky and brash, he goes some way to saving the day, not helped by Rita Hayworth as the older lady or Kim Novak as the younger one – and in that role her inadequacy quickly became legendary. **Bye Bye Birdie** (1963) also suffers from Ann-Margret, a cute, brash, ingenue, while Janet Leigh in a black wig is no more than likeable in the role in which Chita Rivera had been outstanding. The original had also had satirical points to make about show business and the hysteria surrounding pop singers (and in particular Elvis Presley's call-up): but it was now aimed at pleasing the very teenagers who were part of its original target; again the score has been savagely cut.

Kohlmar produced both films (returning to Columbia for the latter) and it was he who invited Joshua Logan to make **Picnic** (1955), as he had directed on stage. Logan's film experience was limited to one movie co-directed in 1938 and his work on *Mister Roberts*. In *Picnic* he tends to let his camera stand immobile while the players emote in the pretty mid-West locations. William Holden is too old and too withdrawn to play a light-fingered youth of braggart mentality, while Rosalind Russell is also miscast as a man-hungry spinster. The character she plays shares with Logan a penchant for bare chests, and her attempt to rip off Holden's clothes comes high on the list of risible movie moments. The film is over-pitched, though William Inge's small-town play was his most successful blend of Tennessee

Williams and Tchekhov. The ending is even changed for the film, allowing the heroine to follow Holden instead of relapsing into dull routine. She is Miss Novak, cherished in memory as she sways in tune to 'Moonglow' in a pink dress against a velvet night: actually she moves awkwardly and looks both bovine and heavily corseted.

For a brief period Novak became the glamorous star for whom Cohn had been searching since the defection of Rita Hayworth. His only other female star of note was Judy Holliday – and both ladies were rivals for Jack Lemmon in **Phfffft!** (1954), a sex comedy commissioned from George Axelrod after his success with 'The Seven Year Itch'. Holliday and Lemmon are much too likeable to play Axelrod's heartless and smart-alecky people; but comparing the several situations similar to those in Cukor's Holliday films it is clear that Mark Robson is a lesser director.

At one time Richard Quine seemed to be Columbia's leading director. After a long apprenticeship with the company he made his mark on loan to Universal for **So This Is Paris** (1954), a blatant and charmless imitation of *On the Town*, with Tony Curtis and Gloria de Haven. Its vitality encouraged Cohn to entrust Quine with an expensive musical, **My Sister Eileen** (1955). When Miss Holliday twisted her ankle, Betty Garrett substituted; other M-G-M alumni were Janet Leigh (borrowed for the occasion), Tommy Rall and Robert (Bob) Fosse, who also did the choreography. The numbers accordingly have the spontaneity and sunniness of those of the best M-G-M musicals and, if they have much in common with the Broadway musical 'Wonderful Town', that is because both pieces have the same source, Ruth McKenney's *New Yorker* stories about her sister Eileen (who was married to Nathaniel West and died with him in a car crash). Columbia owned the film rights to those stories and the play based on them, but Cohn was too mean to buy Leonard Bernstein's score for 'Wonderful Town'. He commissioned a new one from Jules Styne and Leo Robin, which did nothing to ensure the success of the film. Nevertheless, it is one of the best of musicals, and if it has only one premise – everyone's preference for Eileen over Ruth – Miss Garrett's way with a self-deprecatory line makes it always funny. 'Wonderful Town' remains unfilmed, and Betty Garrett's touching and often whacky talent was not seen again in a major movie because the industry looked charily at a lady married to Larry Parks, who was found by the House UnAmerican Activities Committee to have been a Communist.

Quine did direct Miss Holliday in **The Solid Gold Cadillac** (1956) and **Full of Life** (1957), both of which re-established her as a working-class American. At least in comedy, few screen heroines since Jean Arthur had actually been seen working: Miss Holliday in *The Solid Gold Cadillac* does work hard, but only after making a nuisance of herself in the boardroom. In adapting the play by George S. Kaufman and Howard Teichmann, Abe Burrows has changed the role from that of an old lady to a young one. Presumably we owe the view to all three writers that those who run large corporations are mainly concerned with making their piles and saving their skins. The film is often extraordinarily funny as Holliday bests the board with that blend of daffiness and singleness of purpose which was her movie stock in trade. As her chief opponents, John Williams and Fred Clark are joyous, though Williams's discomfiture is less rewarding than Clark's explosions of unsurprised disgust; Paul Douglas is the one honest board member. In *Full of Life*, Holliday is a pregnant wife – and pregnancy was a new subject for Hollywood comedy. With Richard Conte coping with her and his idiosyncratic father (Salvatore Baccaloni) the film tries to be original but is only sentimental.

Quine's reputation for handling this genre increased with a fast-paced army comedy, **Operation Madball** (1957), but promptly went in the other direction with **Bell, Book and Candle** (1958). The former pits Jack Lemmon, as the wiliest soldier ever, against the egomaniac and cunning captain of Ernie Kovacs; the latter film wastes Lemmon and gives Kovacs only brief footage as a world-weary alcoholic author. On the stage, John Van Druten's play about some modern witches had had charm and stylish playing by Rex Harrison and Lilli Palmer: any funny lines it had are not retained in Daniel Taradash's screenplay, which Quine has foolishly treated as a Manhattan love story in the manner of *The Eddy Duchin Story*.

Whatever allure or talent Miss Novak had shown in her earlier films had already gone, and James Stewart is miscast in Harrison's role.

There was a return to form with **It Happened to Jane** (1959), in which a businesswoman widow eventually routs a greedy tycoon (Kovacs). Since the community finally joins together to help the heroine – and the shenanigans concern a train – we may be reminded of Ealing comedy. We certainly think of Capra, though Norman Katkov's script is more obviously an amalgam of *It Should Happen to You* and *The Solid Gold Cadillac*. Judy Holliday was appearing on Broadway and so the heroine is played, incisively, by Doris Day. Lemmon is, again, the exasperated beau, and Kovacs's mean, satisfying villain emphasises Columbia's superiority in comic talents at this time. Quine's imaginative direction and the green Maine settings are also assets, but the public was not interested – even though it was to flock to the inferior Thirties-style comedies (q.v.) which Day was to make for Universal.

Quine's decline was quick, and it began with his first serious picture (there had been some programmers earlier), **Strangers When We Meet** (1960), in which Novak and Kirk Douglas inexpressively portray adulterous suburbanites. His excuse is that his wife (Barbara Rush) takes no interest in his work; hers is that her husband fails to react when she sends the kids away for the night and pushes down her blouse to reveal her bra. An effort seems to have been made to treat the subject in the frank manner of *Brief Encounter*, but Evan Hunter's script, from his own novel, is cliché-ridden. Tedium is averted by Kovacs as a writer in a perpetual state of nerves and by Walter Matthau as a malicious, lecherous neighbour.

We have already looked at Quine's *Sex and the Single Girl* and *Paris When It Sizzles*. **The Notorious Landlady** (1962) is equally disappointing, but **How to Murder Your Wife** (1965) is a partial return to form. Both are black comedies with Jack Lemmon, the former concerning American diplomats in a Hollywood England; the presence of Fred Astaire and his 'A Foggy Day' on the soundtrack hardly compensate for Miss Novak in the title-role. *How to Murder Your Wife* also has a weak leading lady – Virna Lisi – but the first hour, at least, is a good George Axelrod jape about a confirmed bachelor (Lemmon) who marries when drunk and regrets it. Axelrod produced (for U.A.), and it is possible that he curbed Quine's style, by now strident and limp – for this is the only one of his later films to recapture any of his early fluidity.

After Cohn died, Columbia did not invite Judy Holliday to make the last film of her contract (she was, incidentally, one of the few people with a genuine regard for him). She herself resented Hollywood's neglect at this time, feeling, quite rightly, that she was a better comedienne than Doris Day. Ironically, therefore, Columbia was imitating Day's Universal sex comedies with **Under the Yum Yum Tree** (1963) and **Good Neighbour Sam** (1964), both with Lemmon and directed by David Swift, from television (to which he soon returned). The first is particularly distasteful, since Lemmon is both lecher and voyeur; the second at least has a genuine comic idea – of a girl (Romy Schneider) who borrows another woman's husband (Lemmon) in order to inherit a fortune. One would wish for more asperity and less reliance on supposedly amusing decor and the beds – unlike earlier films, there is no doubt what these are for. Lemmon single-handedly tries to salvage both films. Best cast as a reasonable man in desperate circumstances, he often goes to the limit of his resources in order not to disappoint. If he were not the best light comedian we have, he would still be exceptional.

Divorce, American Style (1967), like the concurrent *A Guide for the Married Man,* took advantage of the relaxation of the Code while trying to be honest about the modern American ménage, consuming too many Martinis amidst too much gadgetry. Divorce lawyers and marriage counsellors wait to pounce; a colleague takes the husband to a call girl, and every Sunday there is confusion as to which kids have to be sent to their other mummies and daddies. Alimony is the name of the game. Debbie Reynolds and Dick Van Dyke play the divorcing couple and, under his Ivy League glow and her doll-like smile, they would seem to be fairly nasty people. With the exception of Jean Simmons, as the other woman, few of the principals have

charm, which may be one reason why the film is only mildly amusing – and therefore only a half-success for its writer, Norman Lear, and its director, Bud Yorkin. It is better than the other films made by this team, who were to make their reputations with some popular 'social' comedies on television.

Cat Ballou (1965) is one of the very few successful comedy Westerns and an isolated achievement for its director, Elliott Silverstein. He sometimes forces the pace and if Lee Marvin deserved his Best Actor Oscar for his double-act – the shambling dipso Kid Shelleen and steel-nosed gunman Strawn – he gets a close-up too many. Jane Fonda, returning from her European sojourn, is really the best of it, a round-eyed Alice in Wonderland, enjoying every moment of the derring-do. Her schoolteacher heroine has an eager naïvety which enables her to upset the Code of the West; and there is the double-act of the young outlaws (Michael Callan, Dwayne Hickman), cowards and college boys, who go from each other's arms to hers.

Among Westerns, **3.10 to Yuma** (1957) starts from *High Noon*, the point being not whether the killers will get off the train but whether this one (Glenn Ford) will get on it. The excellent screenplay is by Halsted Welles and the splendid black and white photography by Charles Lawton Jr. The film is directed, self-consciously but without frills, by Delmer Daves, who returned to his customary standard with **Cowboy** (1958). This is based on Frank Harris's 'Reminiscences of a Cowboy' and, since these were mainly apocryphal, they were a curious source for a film attempting a more authentic picture of the West than was usual. The book was foolishly adhered to, so that the film has no narrative drive. Jack Lemmon is likeable as Harris, but Glenn Ford lacks the necessary force as a drunken cattle-driver. Again, Lawton's (colour) photography is an asset, and the film, while not a critical success like *3.10 to Yuma*, brought Daves some prestige. After more than two decades in Hollywood, the success of these Westerns enabled him to become producer as well as writer and director; he then proceeded to make some overblown romantic dramas.

Among adventure tales, Columbia offered several films produced by Charles H. Schneer, who specialises in fantasy.

The credit for them rightly belongs to his special-effects man, Ray Harryhausen (b. 1920), who had been fascinated by *King Kong* as a boy and later worked with Willis O'Brien on *Mighty Joe Young*. Harryhausen's partnership with Schneer began in 1952 with *It Came from Beneath the Sea,* and their work includes many other equally unpromising titles. Mainly disregarded by the press and often with second-string players and directors, their films remain in the repertory as useful items for children's matinees. The acting is invariably wooden, the dialogue fustian, the situations closer to comic strips than their sources suggest, yet Harryhausen creates magic. Sometimes one can see the strings; not all his effects work well: but he cares not only for the cinema's capacity for fantasy but also for the mysteries that existed for the ancients. In filming Swift, Jules Verne, the Greek myths and the Arabian Nights he sends his heroes on sea voyages, to unknown islands where strange creatures lurk. He likes sails and decks, deep waters, awesome landscapes and, above all, monsters – who arrive at regular intervals. The Swift tale is **The Three Worlds of Gulliver** (1960), directed by Jack Sher, and the Verne **Mysterious Island** (1961), which is somewhat better: the director is Cy Endfield, blacklisted in Hollywood ten years earlier and whose first subsequent credit this was. He had been living in Britain, which became the headquarters for Schneer and Harryhausen, because of its proximity to Europe and lower costs. Among the dozen Harryhausen films to be enjoyed are **The Golden Voyage of Sinbad** (1973), directed by Gordon Hessler, and **Jason and the Argonauts** (1963), directed by Don Chaffey. The latter film began Harryhausen's collaboration with the British writer, Beverly Cross. Cross is married to Maggie Smith – who with the equally illustrious Claire Bloom and Laurence Olivier played Olympians in **Clash of the Titans** (1981), directed by Desmond Davis. Obviously this was no low-budget production: it was several years in the making, and in fact handled by M-G-M. The conception of Olympus is the usual one, of swirling mists and columns, and some effects, e.g. the Gorgon's head, are not as frightening as they could be. But there are some superb ingredients, such as the destruction of Argos, Perseus (Harry Hamlin) on the back of Pegasus, and the Kraken rising from the sea. If we regard *Superman* (q.v.) as filmed comic-strip we can claim *Clash of the Titans* as the best cinema fantasy since Korda's *The Thief of Bagdad*.

A less respectable but equally enjoyable action tale is **Diamond Head** (1963), a cross between *Aloma of the South Seas* and a Deep South novelette. Set in Hawaii, it concerns a white girl (Yvette Mimieux) whose love for a native boy (James Darren) arouses the wrath of her proud, landowning brother (Charlton Heston). Watching it, I was reminded of the minotaur's head which used to betoken opinions in the film reviews of *L'Ecran Français*, his expressions going from sheer joy to abject depression: he had one of surprised glee, which he would surely have used for this film, as the clichés mount without pausing for breath. The director was Guy Green, who was handed many more such banalities in **A Walk in the Spring Rain** (1970). In the words of Stirling Silliphant, who provided them, they were aiming for a new version of *Brief Encounter*, as Anthony Quinn, a middle-aged Zorba, pursues a still-radiant Ingrid Bergman. 'There's a lot of woman left in ya,' he exclaims when she protests that she is a grandmother. And he says quite seriously, 'A man's gotta do what a man's gotta do' when accused of adultery.

Middle-aged passion is also the theme of **Middle of the Night** (1959), as a garment manufacturer (Fredric March) becomes involved with a young employee (Kim Novak). Paddy Chayevsky wrote it, from his own long-running Broadway play and, as with *Marty* and *The Bachelor Party,* the director is Delbert Mann. Apart from these three films little of Mann's work is impressive, though as the writer-director Paul Schrader (q.v.) has pointed out the distinctive style of Chayevsky's films was contributed by Chayevsky.* The authenticity of the working-class dialogue is matched by the settings, but the final effect is as wintry as the bare trees frequently on view. Despite a tagged-on happy ending, a vein of pessimism runs through the piece, not least in the often moving performance of Mr March, which Chayevsky himself preferred to the more warm-hearted one

*The only other recent writer of such 'strength', said Schrader, was Neil Simon (q.v.).

given on Broadway by Edward G. Robinson. To acquire the rights, Columbia had been compelled to make **The Goddess** (1958), based on an original screenplay by Chayevsky, who insisted that John Cromwell direct (Cromwell had returned to Broadway after being blacklisted in 1951). When both films failed, Hollywood rejected Chayevsky's work for years – and it loathed *The Goddess* to start with, for it is about a girl (Kim Stanley) who becomes a star by sleeping with producers. She uses her body and anyone who happens to be handy, developing a protective shell that leaves her devoid of feeling. Eventually she is alone and alcoholic, having alienated everyone except her protective and probably lesbian secretary. The film is verbose and as unfeeling as its central character. Chayevsky labours too hard at the iniquities of ambition, corruption and self-destruction to permit a glimpse into the Hollywood system, thereby ending merely with a thesis. Miss Stanley is a Kim of a different hue from Miss Novak, going through every emotion, except love, that can be asked of an actress. She suggests, as few contemporaries did, an interesting woman – though one not much like Marilyn Monroe, Chayevsky's supposed model: certainly he used his knowledge of her, and of other stars who destroyed their careers – though Joan Crawford would seem the most likely candidate.

The question of source also arises at Universal-International, since the title of **The Great Man** (1956) refers to 'America's most beloved humorist'. As in *Citizen Kane,* the film is a quest for the true nature of someone whose name had been a household word: he did not say 'rosebud' as he died, but the sort of word then only found on lavatory walls. His vices were the usual ones – he is greedy and grasping and drives his wife to drink. The sharply idiomatic script is by Al Morgan, who wrote the original novel, and José Ferrer, who directed unimaginatively except in finding close-ups of his star – who is also himself. He plays a television reporter planning a tribute to the dead man, with a last-reel change of heart, so that he tells the truth – which so impresses the sponsors that, without a trace of irony, he becomes the dead man's successor. It is an ending which contradicts everything we know about the television industry, and it is a pity the film never has the courage to dissect media popularity. An excellent cast includes Ed Wynn, superb as the man who gave the great man his start, his son Keenan, Jim Backus and Dean Jagger. When Julie London mimes to her own record the film offers the quintessential feeling of the time – hard, gritty, the blues, not too bright.

This was virtually Universal's only serious film in more than a decade, and because it failed at the box office the company reverted to its policy of bland programmers. **The Man of a Thousand Faces** (1957) may be an exception, since it is a biography of Lon Chaney with James Cagney – Hollywood legend as Hollywood legend. This is an improvement on other sunshine-and-showers screen biographies, for it is reasonably accurate – except in suggesting that Chaney's sole motivation in life was frustrated father-love; but the direction by Joseph Pevney is rather heavy.

Among the few other large-budgeted films at Universal were those with James Stewart, all of which are Westerns except for the popular *The Glen Miller Story*. They and it were directed by Anthony Mann, and the Westerns at least show his fine visual sense. However, except for the first of them, *Winchester '73* (1950), the incidents are both ordinary and handled in similar fashion.

The producer Ross Hunter and the German-born director Douglas Sirk first worked together on two pleasing period films with stars no longer shining as brightly as they once did. **Take Me to Town** (1953) is a Technicolor musical with Ann Sheridan as a saloon singer of questionable virtue, and **All I Desire** (1953) shows what happens when a vaudeville star (Barbara Stanwyck) returns to the family she deserted years before. Then the still popular Jane Wyman, under contract for one film, insisted that it be a remake of **Magnificent Obsession** (1954). Sirk, unable to get through the original novel, asked for a treatment based on Stahl's film version, and he found 'a combination of kitsch and craziness and trashiness'. But, working with that in mind and without Stahl's lightness of touch, his film is not to be mentioned in the same breath. Rock Hudson is less bumptious than was Robert Taylor; the sympathetic Miss Wyman smiles too much, but that is part of the Hunter-Sirk approach. The locations, the colour, the fashions, the furnishings, the emotions are 'beautiful' – but plastic-wrapped, as attractive as sandwiches in an airport lounge. The film's success – it cost $800,000 and the gross profit was more than $12 million – encouraged Hunter and Sirk to continue making slushy soap operas. Audiences often laughed at them, and they still do.

Written on the Wind (1956) is about a playboy (Robert Stack) and his nympho-maniac sister (Dorothy Malone), both drunks, and their involvement with their surrogate brother (Rock Hudson) and a smart New Yorker (Lauren Bacall). The background of the Texas oil-fields clearly interested Sirk less than the two small towns of his first films with Hunter, and the piece is flat, slick and characterless, but not badly made. Sirk himself has observed that he is bewildered by the cult following these films have; asked about that, Miss Bacall observed that on the set he was uninventive in staging and unhelpful when the players demanded less unspeakable dialogue.

As public taste for Hunter's tearjerkers declined – there were several with Lana Turner – he found a new formula when a comedy with Doris Day and Rock Hudson, **Pillow Talk** (1959), proved extremely popular. As directed by Michael Gordon, it was an attempt to return to an earlier period of comedy; in it, and those that followed, Miss Day went to bat for her virginity, always in luxurious settings. The art of seduction had been bowdlerised but not banished during the enforcement of the Production Code: that it could return to movies, in terms of basic farce, had much to do with the magazine *Playboy*. These films are only too much like *Playboy*'s leering yet sanitised view of sex (as it was then), with orgasm promised more often than achieved. They offer candy-floss salaciousness instead of wit. Sex in *The Apartment* had been touching, cruel, desperate and funny, but the only desperation here is in the jokes – at rock-bottom level in **The Thrill of It All** (1963), when the ageing maid (Zasu Pitts) screams 'Rape' on seeing her kindly master (James Garner) in the doorway of her bedroom. An exception is the experienced Cary Grant in **That Touch of Mink** (1962),

directed by Delbert Mann (and the film is the antithesis of *Marty*, which made his reputation). Hudson is no more adept than Garner, but they are more interesting than Miss Day, whose natural charm gets lost in an artificial welter of hairdos and chic clothes to match the decor. As she continued to remain *virgo intacta* comment became derisive – poetic justice since the films raked in as figures of fun anyone who might ever have had a sexual thought. The writers ape the *Playboy* cartoonists, sometimes aspiring to Peter Arno, with no talent other than to exploit the new permissiveness. They underline the deterioration in American comedy when it was uprooted from New York and Chicago to settle in Californian comfort.

We have already looked at other comedies influenced by these. Universal made several with heroines other than Miss Day, and she, when advised by her manager-husband, moved to other studios to make similar movies. Ross Hunter, after two decades of popular films, had become one of the most powerful producers in the industry; yet when, in 1972, he elected to move to Columbia to make a musical version of *Lost Horizon* it was a flop of such proportions that – with absolutely no critical reputation to save him – he lost his position overnight and retreated into television.

It Came from Outer Space (1953) and **The Incredible Shrinking Man** (1957) are among Universal's more enduring films, both medium-budget science-fiction tales directed by Jack Arnold. His work does not, here or elsewhere, suggest more than journeyman talent. The first is adapted from a novel by Ray Bradbury, and the second was written by Richard Matheson – an eerie idea about a man who, caught in a radioactive cloud, contracts to the point where he battles spiders with pins and is thought by his family to have been eaten by the cat. Both films would have benefited from bigger budgets (an expensive 1981 revamp, *The Incredible Shrinking Woman*, with Lily Tomlin, was disastrously received), since such tales depend on their special effects. But at least the amorphous one-eyed monsters in *It Came from Outer Space* are imaginatively conceived – and the film itself gained from being originally made and released in 3-D. If it looks somewhat primitive that is because

Kubrick revitalised the genre with *2001: a Space Odyssey* (q.v.). The idea of 'them' taking over 'our' bodies was also used with variations in *Invasion of the Body Snatchers* (q.v.) – and it could be said that *Close Encounters of the Third Kind* (q.v.) is a loose remake of *It Came from Outer Space*. We are told that the bright young directors of the present day prefer to make the sort of films they enjoyed when they were growing up – and of course *It Came from Outer Space* is so much easier to improve upon than *All About Eve*.

In time, Universal's executives gave thought to the films the studio was turning out. With the growth of television the market for their anodyne entertainments (few of them, incidentally, shown to the press in Britain) was decreasing, and in 1958 a loss was announced of $2 million. The annual output of approximately thirty-six features was halved in 1959, and overtures were made to artists with their own production units who might contribute box-office films – most notably with Kirk Douglas and *Spartacus* (q.v.). In February 1959 the plant was sold to the Music Corporation of America for $11,250,000, with the right to rent back facilities for future production. M.C.A., once a talent agency, needed space for its T.V. subsidiary, Revue Productions but, when in 1962 it acquired Universal itself, it was forced by government decree to dispose of its agency. In fact, Decca had by that time become virtual owner of Universal, and it was the record business which interested M.C.A. Yet during the intervening three years the film company prospered mightily for the first time since the heyday of Deanna Durbin and Abbott and Costello. The reason again was comedy, especially Miss Day's. Lopping off the second half of the name Universal-International, the company embarked on a carefully-planned programme – few films of which are actually memorable.

One is **Lonely Are the Brave** (1962), an 'art' Western venture which more than half succeeds as directed by the usually undistinguished David Miller. Dalton Trumbo wrote it on the thesis that the world of freeways, jeeps and helicopters has little use for cowboys, as exemplified by one (Kirk Douglas) who is mistreated by the society that is served by them. The film's earnestness is endearing and not, as

is usual in such cases, tiresome, but when Douglas gets holed up in the mountains in the manner of Bogart in *High Sierra* he has better reason for being there and is more genuinely one of society's outsiders.

Like most of the leading stars of this era, Douglas had a hand in the production, as did Gregory Peck with **Cape Fear** (1962). Peck had recently worked with the director, J. Lee Thompson, on *The Guns of Navarone* (q.v.), perhaps the biggest success of both their careers, and he had also worked several times with both the producer, Sy Bartlett, and the screen writer, James R. Webb. It could be said that he selected talents on his own level, except that his co-star is Robert Mitchum – and any sensitive person would be rooting for Mitchum's mean villain rather than Peck's noble hero. The villain has sworn vengeance on Peck, a lawyer, by planning the rape of his wife and daughter. Thus an old-fashioned thriller takes advantage of the new permissiveness, its essential sleaziness not offset by a comment or so on the sanctity of the home. Rape is also threatened in **The Night of the Following Day** (1969), since one of the kidnappers (Richard Boone) fancies the English teenager (Pamela Franklin) whom they have locked up in a house on the dunes near Le Touquet. Other kidnappers include a blond, black-garbed Marlon Brando and a jittery, drug-addicted Rita Moreno. The director is Hubert Cornfield, who wrote the screenplay with Robert Phippeny, from a novel by Lionel White, and it is easy to see why he has not been more prolific – for he constantly misuses the camera. But his enjoyment of his setting makes this a thriller unlike any other. (The T.V. version shows even more of France, as this is one of the films which Universal padded to eke out its length: irrelevant detail, obviously filmed later, adds twenty minutes to the original running-time, while at the same time cuts have been made affecting Moreno's addiction and her relationship with Brando.)

Airport (1970), one of Ross Hunter's last productions for the company, was adapted from a cross-section novel by Arthur Hailey. The most fastidious of filmgoers may enjoy its organisation and its use of the artefacts of aviation to provide the excitement. That is presented in an assured and unpretentious manner, but the credited director, George Seaton, who wrote the script, fell ill and most of the film was directed by Henry Hathaway who, out of friendship for him, refused both billing and salary. Its popularity ensured a sequel, **Airport 1975** (1974), with Jack Smight directing and Charlton Heston succeeding Burt Lancaster at the controls. Jack Lemmon took over – the most thankless task of his career – in **Airport '77** (1977), and his passengers were the usual ageing stars and semi-names, cast on the assumption that familiarity with them will ensure our anxiety that they conclude their fraught journeys. The plot this time is borrowed from another 'disaster' movie, *The Poseidon Adventure*, with the unfortunate aircraft, a 747, lying on the ocean bed. It is a marvellous example of Hollywood knowhow – a thin, impersonal, wholly manufactured film, but providing a frisson or so that you will not find in, say, *Providence*.

Like Universal, United Artists prospered during this time. Mary Pickford and Chaplin had sold the company to a law firm representing an Eastern circuit of cinemas, and two lawyers with experience of the industry were put in charge, Robert S. Benjamin and Arthur Krim. They were assured of 50 per cent control if they could turn a profit in their first year – 1952–3 – and they took full control five years later, with an executive team which remained basically the same till they were ousted in 1978. Under their leadership United Artists, in my opinion, succeeded 20th Century-Fox as the company making the most interesting pictures; but it would be unwise to assume that Benjamin or Krim were creative managers, since for a long while they merely encouraged acknowledged talents to work for them. United Artists had always functioned that way, but after a decade of successfully choosing films for the company to distribute, and successfully counselling the producers of those films, Benjamin and Krim – or their team – began to initiate productions themselves.

For the first few years of the Krim-Benjamin regime United Artists continued to release low-budget films – with the exception of *Moulin Rouge* and some British movies. With *The Moon Is Blue* Otto Preminger began to supply the company with popular films, but the decisive

factor in U.A.'s rise to affluence was Burt Lancaster. With his partners, Harold Hecht and James Hill, he produced a number of money-making movies starring himself, including *Vera Cruz* and *Trapeze* (q.v.). The Hecht, Hill and Lancaster company also produced *Marty* and *The Bachelor Party* – the achievement of which is all the more striking when compared to **Separate Tables** (1958), also directed by Delbert Mann. If the two Chayevsky films were renowned for their honesty, this is as false as its Hollywood-constructed English resort hotel. Terence Rattigan's two one-act plays, a success in London and New York, have been dovetailed, and the material, thin to start with, loses theatrical contrivance with no consequent gain; and what had been a star turn for Eric Portman and Margaret Leighton, in two roles each, becomes – unlike Mann's earlier films – a star vehicle (for four stars). Burt Lancaster and Rita Hayworth (who was married to Hill, her fifth husband) are poor, and unlikely Americans to be in this particular hotel; Deborah Kerr is more successful as the plain and nervous spinster, but David Niven's performance is a mere shadow of Portman's. His Oscar for Best Actor was presumably due to the fact that he allowed himself to be cast unflatteringly, as a bogus major who molests women in cinemas; thus one more curious aspect of human behaviour was accepted into films with the help of an acclaimed Broadway play.

In this respect 1956–8 marked the watershed – with *Baby Doll, The Great Man, Lust for Life, Edge of the City* (q.v.), *Twelve Angry Men* (q.v.), *Fear Strikes Out, The Young Stranger* (q.v.), *Love in the Afternoon, The Strange One, Full of Life, A Hatful of Rain, A Face in the Crowd* and *Paths of Glory* (q.v.). Not all of them are good films and some of them are more superficial and immature than their makers thought they were: but the least of them is to be preferred to any *Magnificent Obsession*, since they are trying to say something about the human condition without the aid of film starriness or beautiful settings – or, for that matter, any of the traditional glamour of the American film. The statements made were not always new, but they had not been allowed in films since the immediate pre-Code days, when they had been expounded with the same gritty realism.

Hecht, Hill and Lancaster's **Sweet**

Tony Curtis and Burt Lancaster in what is probably the best film either made, *Sweet Smell of Success*, about the power of a gossip columnist. It made few Ten Best lists in the U.S., since columnist Walter Winchell remained powerful – and Lancaster's glasses were of course an allusion to Winchell's trademark. In the film he is sanctimonious, self-righteous, vindictive, petty and cynical, while Curtis's press agent is cringing and fawning, with just enough gut-sense to keep going.

Smell of Success (1957) is redolent of several Warner Bros. movies of that era, with its central character, a Broadway columnist, fixated on his sister – though that also provides a narrative thread, as he attempts to destroy the young man in love with her. As played by Lancaster, the journalist is modelled on Walter Winchell and recognisably so, which was only possible because Winchell's power was lessening – as, on the evidence of this film, it deserved to. It reveals a world without virtue: with everyone motivated by self-interest, corruption is rampant in night clubs and newspaper offices. The press agent (Tony Curtis) is sleazy, opportunistic and sycophantic, with no qualms about pandering his girlfriend to a client in his drive for success. The script by Ernest Lehman and Clifford Odets, from the former's novella, has contrivance but also sour, brilliant dialogue, and the British director Alexander Mackendrick took to night-time New York with assurance.

Mackendrick was expected to have a brilliant Hollywood career, but after starting **The Devil's Disciple** (1959) for Hecht, Hill and Lancaster he was replaced by Guy Hamilton. One of the virtues of *Sweet Smell of Success* was its refusal to allow Lancaster to be in the centre of the screen, but Hamilton apparently flinched at the prospect of directing his producer, for he does not seem to have done anything at all. Lancaster as Pastor Anderson and Kirk Douglas as Dick Dudgeon appear to be having a ball, perhaps because they had relegated to third billing and a supporting role an actor generally regarded as far superior – Laurence Olivier.* Since Janette Scott is inept as Mrs Anderson it is left to him to save the day, which he does – at his most stylish and authoritative as General Burgoyne. As this role has become slightly more important, few would complain that the play has been altered – and the film, admittedly made in Britain, is a vast improvement on the two previous American attempts to film Shaw.

Douglas's own company had a rousing and unexpected success with **The Vikings** (1958), a synthesis of the Sagas as given to children to read, half Eddas and half Li'l Abner. Portents appear in the sky (the daughters of Odin ride across the moon), men are thrown to the wolves, and the returning warriors dance on the oars as their ship comes to harbour in the fjords.

*Olivier had walked out of *Separate Tables* after Lancaster had tried to tell him how to play the role.

Some critics complained about the violence, surely more acceptable on this occasion than on some others; one could complain with more justice about the heavy American accents of Douglas, Ernest Borgnine, Tony Curtis and Janet Leigh. However, the director Richard Fleischer keeps their performances trim, and his triumph is shared by Jack Cardiff, whose photography emphasises the marine aspect of Viking life.

United Artists also benefited from the films produced by the Mirisch Company, for Walter Mirisch chose U.A. to handle his movies after Allied Artists – of which he had been executive producer – folded in 1957. Mirisch's most successful films for United Artists included several directed by Billy Wilder, including *Some Like It Hot,* and *West Side Story.* Also deservedly popular were two adventure films, **The Magnificent Seven** (1960) and **The Great Escape** (1963), admirably directed by John Sturges. The former transfers the plot of *Seven Samurai* to Mexico, but whereas in Kurosawa's film the seven were deadbeats down on their luck, here they are professional gunmen thirsty for adventure. Yul Brynner is the leader of a likeable bunch, including Steve McQueen, James Coburn and Charles Bronson. These three actors were reunited in the other film, among the British and Canadian P.O.W.s determined to tunnel their way out of the camp.

The Broadway producer Paul Gregory, after working with Charles Laughton on the stage, went to Hollywood to make **The Night of the Hunter** (1955), which Laughton directed (his only film in that capacity) and wrote, with James Agee, from Davis Grubb's novel. With the eagerness of novices they have loaded it with symbols and allusions, evoking the world of children's horrors. It is not coincidental that it is set during the Depression – West Virginia in 1930 – a land devastated by poverty and where terror stalks in the person of a preacherman (Robert Mitchum), who is prepared to kill two small children for some treasure he thinks they have (he has already married and murdered their mother, played by Shelley Winters). The river setting and the dead-drunk Uncle Birdie are from Mark Twain; the children begging for food are from Dickens, as is the spinster (Lillian Gish)

who takes them in; the children's song is pure 'Silly Symphony' and there are touches of the Bible, Grimm, Andersen and Aesop. The film has images as clumsy as they are striking, but it is also unique, an idiosyncratic mixture of black comedy and social comment; it was poorly received at the time, but its quality was soon to be recognised.

The director Alexander Singer had an isolated success with **A Cold Wind in August** (1961). Partly due to the exigencies of the star system, there were many movies about ageing men in love with younger women, but this one and *The Stripper* (q.v.) were virtually the only ones made in America in which an older woman is the predator.★ She (Lola Albright) is a stripper and he (Scott Marlowe) the janitor's boy, who leaves her as lonely as she was when he eventually returns to his own generation. The script has its weaknesses, but Singer's handling is so fresh – especially in two 'idyllic' sequences, in which he turns the mood to laughter – that several reviewers suggested that the American cinema might have a New Wave of its own.

Another one-of-a-kind film is **Lonelyhearts** (1959) and in this case it is just as well. Nathaniel West's story, like the better-known 'The Day of the Locust', is about the destruction of souls, but the producer-writer Dore Schary apparently felt the need to step in and save them – so that it is no surprise to find the film ending with the hero about to begin a new life (in the novel his death is a *coup de grâce*). Vincent J. Donahue, a Broadway director – who never made another film – manages for the first half hour to convey some of the hatred expressed in the original; as the Shrikes, Myrna Loy and Robert Ryan convey their mutual hostility well, while Maureen Stapleton is superb as the woman who paves the way for the hero's ruin. He is the gossip-columnist of the title, played by Montgomery Clift with unaccustomed exuberance, easily encompassing the problems of a man hanging on for a while with the hope of booze and sex. His sharp girlfriend (Dolores Hart) has been turned into a Florence Nightingale, and since, by the halfway mark, West's situations have been rendered conventional, the film

★ *The Graduate* (q.v.) is about sex, not love.

933

deserved its failure, adding yet another significant figure to the many mishandled by film-makers unequal to the task.

United Artists seemed chary of comedy, but Bob Hope found a niche there for two films, reunited with old colleagues from Paramount – Norman Panama and Melvin Frank (as writers, with Frank directing) and with Lucille Ball, in **The Facts of Life** (1961), which somewhat surprisingly catches both the charm and amiability of the comedies that he made at the start of his career. Its splendid notion is that a married man and a married woman set out to commit adultery but are plagued by difficulties at every turn. Panama and Frank also wrote, and Panama directed, **The Road to Hong Kong** (1962) which, if not as lackadaisical as *Road to Bali,* is still to be recommended only to the most fervent admirers of Hope and Crosby, at their best with the guest appearance of Dorothy Lamour, elsewhere replaced by an ineffectual Joan Collins as the girl they scrap over. Budget-consciousness seems to have been the

reason for making it in Britain and in black and white. Panama and Frank did not work again as a team, but each has a subsequent credit on a film for which the other was mainly responsible. Frank produced and directed **Buona Sera, Mrs Campbell** (1968), which has some good ideas, including the plot, about an Italian woman (Gina Lollobrigida) who has been receiving paternity cheques for the same child from three ex-G.I.s (Peter Lawford, Phil Silvers, Telly Savalas) – now returning to the scene of the conception. Since Lollobrigida had sabotaged Frank's *Strange Bedfellows* each time she had had a funny line we must wonder why he cast her. It is also unclear whether she is meant to be as unsympathetic as she is. The same is true of the tense and viperish Glenda Jackson in **A Touch of Class** (1975). She plays a British divorcee involved in an adulterous affair with an American (a manic George Segal) living in London: this is both a reworking of *The Facts of Life,* as nothing goes quite right, and an affectionate spoof of *Brief Encounter* (which the couple are found watching at one point). Frank advances from both those films by showing the couple actually fornicating (which provides a joke, since the man's back gives out at the first thrust), but the film is nevertheless schmaltzy and lacking in point.

While Frank persevered, with an occasional big success, George Axelrod made only *The Secret Life of an American Wife* after directing a failure, **Lord Love a Duck** (1966) – his first film in that capacity. He wrote it with Larry H. Johnson, from a novel by Al Hine. It is close to his own novel, 'Where Am I Now that I Need Me?', in its execration of almost every facet of contemporary American society – where all values are surrendered to youth, beauty, gadgetry, fame, success or wealth. The progress of Barbara Ann (Tuesday Weld) towards movie stardom is helped by a genie (Roddy McDowall), and perhaps it is the whimsy which alienated audiences: but Axelrod's satiric potshots, sometimes jaded in his book, are always well-aimed.

It may be that cinema audiences did not care for satire at this time, for **How to Succeed in Business Without Really Trying** (1967) signally failed to repeat its success on the stage. Based on Shepherd Mead's Christmas-gift 'funny' book, it is not satire of a high order, as David Swift,

Among filmed Broadway musicals *How to Succeed in Business Without Really Trying* holds a high place, being so invigorating that its theatricality did not matter. Here, singing a love song to himself, is Robert Morse, making his way to the top: it is uncertain whether he is funnier in glee at his success or in abject repentance when one of his tactics is exposed.

directing, realised. His comic-strip style works better here than in his previous films, and this is one instance in which a Broadway musical, preserved and encapsulated, is invigorating on the screen. Its virtues are those of the original, and chief among them are Frank Loesser's witty score and lyrics and Robert Morse, as the little guy who will literally stop at nothing to get to the top. Looking like a cross between the cover-boy of *Mad Magazine* and a benighted cherub, he has an armoury of glances, falsely humble towards his superiors and gleeful towards us, letting us share his double-dealing. His diminutive stature allows him to fawn on the executives in puppy fashion, in contrast to his equally sycophantic rivals, much more 'square' and much less gifted. As the chief of these Anthony Teague is all teeth and glasses above his Ivy League suiting; as the boss, Rudy Vallee has a dignity only exceeded by his fatuousness; as his secretary, Maureen Arthur looks like an auburn, simian version of Monroe and sounds like Carol Channing; and Michele Lee is warm and winning as the secretary determined to have our hero at any cost.

At Republic, on the point of extinction, **Come Next Spring** (1956) is another one-time movie, for in a long career R. G. Springsteen directed nothing else of note. It is set in Arkansas in the Twenties, with all the hallmarks of the rural dramas of the Silent era, including sentiment and a thrill a reel. After eight years, Matt (Steve Cochran) returns to his wife (Ann Sheridan), who is as sceptical as the townsfolk of his reformation. The central situation is whether, or when, marital relations will be resumed, and it is understated. Elsewhere, despite a tornado and a donnybrook, the material has been infused with enthusiasm and affection. Cochran is likeable and Miss Sheridan is brisk and severe without losing her underlying warmth.

Joan Crawford is at her most grandiloquent in **Johnny Guitar** (1954), a bilious Western directed by Nicholas Ray. The characters are cardboard, even if the women are tougher than the men, and the goodies turn out to be the baddies and vice-versa. An occasional bizarre moment – Crawford tinkling the ivories, the posse turning up dressed in black – hints at an attempt to make a gothic Western, but even on that level it is damply depressing.

As Republic gave up the ghost, its place as the foremost of the minor studios was taken by Allied Artists, the former Monogram, which had changed its name in an effort to redeem its past. Monogram had specialised in B-pictures and, however much these may have enthused the young Jean-Luc Godard, audiences in what the trade called the more discerning halls greeted its logo with groans. With unwonted perspicacity the executives of Monogram foresaw the B-film as doomed when television began to attract the mass audience, and they stopped using the name in 1952. They had been using the title Allied Artists since 1947 for their more ambitious product, but it took some years and the advent of Walter Wanger to produce one of note. Wanger's career as a major producer had ceased in 1950, when he was convicted for shooting at Jennings Lang, the agent who represented his wife, Joan Bennett, thinking him her lover. He found a haven at Allied Artists after his sojourn in prison – an experience which occasioned **Riot in Cell Block 11** (1954). The director, Don Siegel, has said that it is entirely Wanger's film. The mixture of action and well-meaning polemic is uneasy, and if the story is less rigged than in the old prison melodramas, it hardly digs any deeper. Ironically, it is most notable for the work of Siegel, hitherto an uninteresting director. Here he first displayed his grasp of narrative technique and incidental detail – qualities more strikingly to be seen in **Invasion of the Body Snatchers** (1956), also produced by Wanger. This is a low-budget science fiction, shot in eighteen days, mainly on location; its eerie fascination is partly due to its story – from a *Collier's* serial by Jack Finney – about a doctor (Kevin McCarthy) who gradually comes to realise that the erratic behaviour of his fellow townsfolk has its source in a mysterious extra-terrestrial invasion.

The Phenix City Story (1955) also attracted attention to Republic, as well as to itself, since there was some controversy as to whether its violence (exceptional for the time) was necessary. There was admiration for its portrait of a small town in which gambling and prostitution are big business, its council controlled by racketeers while the police look the other way.

Just as in France some film-makers were tired of industry film-making so was the actor John Cassavetes, who got together a group of friends to make *Shadows*: they improvised and he directed. It has natural (New York) locations, obscurely placed cameras, overlapping dialogue – and the roughness and readiness of life. Ruefully humorous on a certain milieu – the literary set, minor show-business figures – such plot as it has concerns a couple, Anthony Ray and Lelia Goldoni, whose love scene, discussing the loss of her virginity, was remarkably outspoken.

Even so, the film came somewhat tardily after its inspiration, Kefauver's Senate investigation and his subsequent book on the subject, 'Crime in America' (published in 1951). The director, Phil Karlson, did little else of note, but credit is due to him and his colleagues for a semi-documentary flavour. The locations are splendid: this is a featureless small town of great atmosphere, and as the crowds mill around in search of their evening pleasures one can almost smell the hot dogs. The bad guys include some interesting fatties and weirdies, while as the lawyer pursuing them Richard Kiley has a receding hairline and more intelligence than usual.

Among independent productions **Martin Luther** (1953) demands attention, not only because *The New York Times* thought it one of the best films of the year but also because it was the first time a predominantly Jewish industry had shown interest in a religious figure who was neither biblical nor Roman Catholic. Irving Pichel directed the chiefly British cast and Louis de Rochement produced, claiming accuracy and expecting controversy. It does whitewash Luther (Niall MacGinnis) and is hard on Catholics, headed by a fat and pettish Pope who complains, 'How we are to pay Michelangelo for the Sistine Chapel we don't know!' The commentary says of the 95 theses: 'None could know that this was to be one of the most widely read documents in all history,'

and that exemplifies the approach of this well-meaning picture.

There had always been groups prepared to back religious films, and those who invested in *Luther* could anticipate a continuing income from 16-mm showings in church halls. Otherwise minority cinema in English was not feasible till art houses multiplied and began to cater to wider audiences. At the end of the Fifties a number of young film-makers began to gamble on the cost of a film being recovered from this source. The surge to independence was also spurred on by the *nouvelle vague,* obviously working on minute budgets, and so there appeared three films with private investment: John Cassavetes's **Shadows** (1960), Shirley Clarke's **The Connection** (1961) and Joseph Strick's **The Balcony** (1963). John Cassavetes, an established film actor, used his own money and that of friends, till a mention on television of the project brought in enough to complete the cost of $30,000; Miss Clarke got her vital $167,000 from private sources on the strength of the original play's success in New York; and Strick, by virtue of having Shelley Winters in the promised cast, raised $165,000 from one backer, an art-house distributor, Walter Reade. Reade believed that the art circuit was ready for minority films in English, but when *Shadows* opened in New York nine months after its premiere at the National Film Theatre, it failed to repeat its London triumph. *The Connection* also did poorly in New York, opening eighteen months after its warm reception at the Cannes Film Festival.

In truth, Cassavetes's film is the only interesting one of the trio, both for its technique and its decent statement on black–white relations.* It grew out of a series of improvisations at the Variety Arts Studio in New York and involves a couple who sleep together but part when he discovers that she is black. *The Connection* spends its entire time with a group of junkies awaiting their fix in a derelict attic, and though it has merit – harsh black and

*Among his Ten Best of the year Bosley Crowther chose *A Raisin in the Sun,* a specious black family drama filmed virtually as a photographed play. The huge British acclaim for *Shadows* probably told against its reception in the U.S., and Hollywood at first only gingerly welcomed Cassavetes into its ranks of directors. However, the film was unquestionably influential in Britain and in Europe and, if inevitably it now seems slightly amateurish, it retains the freshness which gave it such an impact.

white photography, skilful direction, a jazz soundtrack – it so lacks insight into the characters that we could not have cared whether they were waiting for Godot instead of heroin. *The Balcony* takes us behind the scenes in Genet's brothel for a number of charades, perversions and fetishistic impersonations, while a revolution takes place outside; it is a hollow piece, indifferently filmed and demonstrating that adaptations of *outré* European plays were not the way forward for independent American cinema.

The choice of subject was ironic, since at the time – or so it seemed – American literature was experiencing one of its most vital periods; so too was the European cinema, for the first time since the 'neorealist' period in Italy. Clearly there had to be an American system which could rely on the stimulation of new ideas rather than glamour and spectacle – but the 'alternative' cinema offered often turned out to be lunatic avant-garde experiments like **Hallelujah the Hills** (1962) – an alienating experience written and directed by Adolfas Mekas.

David and Lisa (1962) and **One Potato, Two Potato** (1964) proved, particularly the first, that there was a public beyond the art houses willing to support no-star, small-scale, black-and-white movies without benefit of the ballyhoo of the major distributors. A number of Americans may have patronised *David and Lisa* simply because it represented a force against the Goliath of Hollywood. Frank Perry directed, from a screenplay written with his then-wife, Eleanor, and it is clear from internal references that they like the best museums and the best (foreign) movies. The piece is transparent in manipulating its central couple – a boy (Keir Dullea) and a girl (Janet Margolin) in a mental home – and, because of its setting, unpalatable. *One Potato, Two Potato* handles equally delicate material – the difficulties of a mixed marriage, specifically between a white factory-worker divorcee (Barbara Barrie) and a black white-collar worker (Bernie Hamilton). Friends are embarrassed, a cop calls her a hooker, and her ex-husband turns up, appalled that his child is to be brought up among blacks. Eventually Hamilton's performance and Larry Peerce's direction lose out to a screenplay bent less on conviction than making points about racial prejudice.

Both Perry and Peerce were invited to work in Hollywood, now alert to the tone of the individual artist. Earlier Raymond Chandler had written, 'The future of the motion-picture industry is in the hands of that small group of people who will break their necks to achieve something beautiful in the almost certain knowledge that it will be spoiled by vulgarians': but the small group was gaining ground and the vulgarians disappearing. In the past, successful European directors went to work in Hollywood, but in the Fifties the American companies began financing projects to be filmed on their home ground. After David Lean had made some extremely popular films for Hollywood, United Artists backed Tony Richardson's *Tom Jones* (q.v.) and M-G-M Antonioni's British-made *Blow-Up* (q.v.) – both to extremely profitable figures. Subsequent adventures with Richardson and Antonioni failed. As profits began to waver and fall for the first time in its history, large-scale failure became a fact for the industry to ponder upon. An industry which had always thought in big terms now learned to suffer on an appropriately grand scale. With television now the nation's chief diversion, it would not have survived had the massive number of flops not been offset by a few very successful films.

The *only* studio that was consistently successful was that of Walt Disney, its policy unchanged with his death. Its unambitious films for children and family audiences made money till the late Seventies, when their old-fashioned subject matter at last began to fail to attract potential spectators: but during the time the Disney films were popular, attempts by the other studios to emulate them only ended in losses. Since the major companies also failed at the other end of the scale with their tentative attempts at the 'adult' films which were coining money for the various independents (some of them little more than amateur efforts), they persevered in their own known territory, the middle ground. But, as one producer, Richard Zanuck (q.v.) put it in 1970, 'The rule book has been thrown away. Today almost anything goes. Frankly, I go on what pleases me personally because I just can't tell what pleases the audience any more.'

937

Hollywood in the Age of Television: The Decline of the Studios

Hollywood had survived two world wars and actually had thrived on them; it had survived the coming of Talkies and the growth of television – indeed the latter, once an enemy, became a friend, as each company formed a subsidiary turning out programmes or series for the networks. It was a way of using studio space and personnel, though it was not always as straightforward as that, as we noted when M.C.A. bought Universal. Alone of the big studios Universal continued to prosper and doubtless the reason it has been the most consistently successful of the majors was due to M.C.A.'s decision to have the studios move into the new medium.

Columbia was the first movie company to go into T.V. production, via its Screen Gems subsidiary in 1952; Warners followed in 1955, with cut-rate versions of movies like *Casablanca* (with Charles McGraw in the lead) and *King's Row* (with Jack Kelly); 20th Century-Fox followed with forty-five minute condensations of its most famous films, but often with star names. In fact, movies could already be seen on the home box: even in the late Forties you could have tuned in to such Silent pictures as *The Eagle*, or to Monogram's B-movies featuring the detective Charlie Chan. The networks bought packages of British movies and, in 1955, Republic sold its entire 1937–48 backlog. A year later, in November 1956, M-G-M allowed *The Wizard of Oz* a single airing on Ford Star Jubilee for the sum of $1 million – a cost justified by the viewing figures; the Wizard became a perennial, licensed only for short periods for similar fees, which has remained a popular television practice. By 1958 the networks would pay up to $100,000 for less exceptional fare, but the trade press thought it foolish to accept, since *For Whom the Bell Tolls* had taken $800,000 on its 1957 reissue. The studios were shortsighted: Warner Bros. sold its entire pre-1948 library for $21 million – a figure reached when the deal was done in the Twenty-One Club – to Associated Artists Production Corporation, which two years later sold it to United Artists. Two years later U.A. estimated that they had made $21 million from licensing the short cartoons alone. (In 1982 Warners was prepared to pay $95 million to recover its heritage, though the films concerned had seldom been away

from television screens; the figure was said to be a bargain, interesting only to U.A., since that company was in desperate financial straits – and the deal fell through as that situation ameliorated). In 1958 Paramount was reported to be considering an offer of $50 million from M.C.A. for its pre-1948 library, and Universal $23 million – though Universal wisely changed its mind. Not only did people stay at home when old movies were aired, but it stimulated an interest in the cinema's past then unthinkable outside film societies. Also in 1958, *Variety* reported that some post-1948 movies had been sold to T.V., including *High Noon* and *Moulin Rouge*: the trickle soon became a flood.

It was Harry Cohn's nephew, Jack Cohn, who founded Screen Gems by arranging to produce thirty-nine dramatic programmes to be sponsored by the Ford Motor Company, which contributed 75 per cent of the finance for one showing and an option for more; within five years Screen Gems was becoming as important a money-maker as Columbia itself. In time the production and distribution arms became subsidiaries of Columbia Industries Inc., and the studio, under production chief Michael J. Frankovitch, was for some years one of the most stable. But in 1971, as losses on unsaleable films began to mount, the studio property itself was sold and Columbia moved into Burbank alongside Warners – an extension of relations abroad, where the two companies shared distribution facilities. Hopes were pinned on a few expensive films, such as *1776*, *Young Winston* and the re-make of *Lost Horizon,* but when the public would have none of them, losses for 1972–3 were reported (in *Variety,* 29 August 1979) as over $82 million. In 1977, however, a gamble was taken with the expensive *Close Encounters of the Third Kind* (q.v.) and, when that proved justified, Columbia was itself again – at least for a while. Over the next five years there was only one success, but it was a big one, *Kramer vs. Kramer* (q.v.): but with that ratio of success to failure, Columbia continued to limp along with either few films in production or strict budget limitations on those that were.

CinemaScope did not help 20th Century-Fox for long, and its finances in the late Fifties were helped mainly by the discovery of an oil-well on the back lot. We have already looked at the company's losses on *Cleopatra,* its profits on *The Longest Day,* and the comings and goings of Zanuck. On returning to Hollywood in 1962 he became the company President with his son Richard in charge of production – and it was under their control that 20th Century-Fox enjoyed the unprecedented success of *The Sound of Music.* In quick succession *Doctor Dolittle* and *Star!* failed to recover much of their respective budgets of $18 and $10 million – though their failures were partially offset by the success of *Planet of the Apes* (q.v.). Then, when in 1969 it was clear that *Hello Dolly!* would not recoup its cost – $24 million, of which only $11 million were recovered at the box office – both the Zanucks were moved 'upstairs': Darryl becoming Chairman and Richard President. Both were forced to resign two years later, and Richard became a successful producer, but Darryl Zanuck, after almost fifty years of profitable film-making behind him, left in a welter of failure. The titles involved included *The Only Game in Town, Justine, The Great White Hope* (q.v.), *Staircase, The Kremlin Letter, Che, The Games, Hello Goodbye, The Magus* and *The Undefeated,* which individually lost sums of between $2 million and $7 million. In 1969–70 the company's losses totalled $101,637,000 and they were not unwarranted. A number of traditional entertainments subsequently helped the company to recover – *Butch Cassidy and the Sundance Kid* (q.v.), *The Poseidon Adventure* and **The Towering Inferno** (1974), the last named, incidentally, backed jointly with Warners, when it was discovered that both companies planned films on the same subject, a skyscraper on fire. Stirling Silliphant was commissioned to write a screenplay from the two novels concerned and obviously it did not matter what was rejected, for the fire was the chief element: it breaks out just minutes after the film has started, which is one reason why audiences preferred it, as directed by John Gillerman, to other 'disaster' movies of the time – since in most of them they had to wait till the climax for the thrills. This was the first such studio cooperation in Hollywood history, but that was to become a common practice as inflation pushed up budgets until they became too unwieldy for the financing banks to entrust them to a single concern.

As the number of independent producers and backers multiplied, turning to the old majors for distribution, the latter might take on the film concerned for certain territories only. As European investors, including Britons, financed or part-financed American production in return for distribution rights, films travelled abroad under varying logos. The companies were often eager for films to handle; distributors of foreign films began to handle American films. The proliferation is such that we may only note the earlier instances, such as American International continuing in its chosen field of 'youth'-oriented, low-budget films till the declining demand caused it to move upmarket at the end of the Seventies. Founded in 1955, American International began to make itself heard five years later, just as a former exhibitor, Joseph E. Levine, was heavily promoting an undistinguished Italian adventure which he had rechristened *Hercules Unchained*: from that he progressed to backing some Italian films starring Sophia Loren. Under the name Embassy, his American films were originally distributed by Paramount. Shortly after becoming his own distributor he was bought by the Avco Corporation, whose main business is insurance, and the company was renamed Avco-Embassy (it became Embassy again in 1982 when Avco sold its interest). The three U.S. television networks took advantage of the break-up of the power of the major studios to enter film production in the late Sixties; but none of them, after sustained losses, stayed long. A.B.C. began by buying the assets of the Cinerama Corporation, which had ended $18 million in the red; but even the success of *Cabaret* (q.v.) did not encourage it to continue. Profits on that film were, in any case, shared with Allied Artists – a company increasingly involved with television, though occasionally prepared to back a big film, such as *Papillon* (q.v.).

Avco was not the only giant company looking towards American films capable of vast profits, and with assets, such as property and subsidiary rights in music and records, to which could be added other resources like publishing companies. It was possible at last, by the late Seventies, for one company to control a film from its appearance in author's typescript via hardcover and paperback editions to the record of the film's score and its appearance on television. In 1966 Paramount was bought by the vast oil-based conglomerate Gulf+Western, and the intrusion of this outsider into the industry was almost as great a shock as that of losing ground to television, although that had been more gradual. In the event, Gulf+Western had little effect on Paramount's fortunes: at least that company had been modestly profitable for some years and when, in 1970, it produced some hugely expensive and unpopular films – *Darling Lili* (q.v.), *The Molly Maguires* (q.v.) and *Catch 22* (q.v.) – Gulf+Western absorbed the losses. At a mere $22 million Paramount's inventory write-down was much more modest than those of the other companies.

In 1966, Warners was bought by Kinney National Service Inc. – best known for its parking lots – though as we have seen, this was no longer the Warners' Warners. One of the first things Kinney did was to drop the Seven Arts which had been hyphenated to it by the Hyman brothers, Eliot and Kenneth. Eliot had been one of the first people to see the advantage of selling motion pictures to television; and among the films with which he had been associated were *The Misfits*, *Lolita* (q.v.), *Whatever Happened to Baby Jane?* and *Moulin Rouge*. Kenneth's credits as a 'packager' are less distinguished, but certainly it was by making films the public wanted to see that Seven Arts had grown big enough to swallow Warners. However, the programme inherited by Kinney consisted of a great many films the public did not want to see, including *There Was a Crooked Man*, *Flap*, *Rabbit Run*, *The Ballad of Cable Hogue* (q.v.), *Which Way to the Front?*, *Start the Revolution Without Me*, *Performance* and *The Last of the Mobile Hot Shots*. Warners was actually the first of the companies to go under, with an industry write-down of over $59 million in 1969, and the following year fifty-five out of sixty-two pending projects were cancelled at one fell swoop. The films begun by Kinney – now renamed Warner Communications – performed better and the company's standing within the industry was made clear when the new independents chose to be aligned: First Artists, part-owned by Paul Newman, Steve McQueen, Barbra Streisand and Sidney Poitier; Orion, a company organised by the former long tenants of

United Artists after their differences with the new owners; and the Ladd Company, formed by a group which had been successful at 20th.

Those former United Artists executives, Robert Benjamin and Arthur Krim, had finally faltered after two decades of success – and they no longer owned the company since, following the absorption of Paramount and Warners by conglomerates, they had sold it, in 1968, to the Transamerica Corporation, another insurance company which felt it might project a benign public image as owner of a Hollywood company. It was soon disillusioned as, almost two years later, in 1969, U.A. had had its own inventory write-off of $50 million. The titles responsible include *The Secret of Santa Vittoria*, *Gaily Gaily*, *The Hawaiians*, *Women in Love* (q.v.), *Ned Kelly*, *Leo the Last* (q.v.), *They Call Me Mister Tibbs*, *The Landlord* (q.v.), *Queimada!* (q.v.), *The Happy Ending*, *Born To Win*, *Doc* (q.v.), *The Private Life of Sherlock Holmes*, *200 Motels*, *Halls of Anger*, *Mrs Pollifax – Spy* and *One More Time*. Bolstered by a number of successes, including the James Bond (q.v.) goldmines, the company enjoyed an equable situation for more than a decade, when differences over policy between Transamerica and the company management sent the latter, as I have said, into the arms of Warners.

But it was the mighty M-G-M, the acknowledged leader of the industry, which suffered most – which, as Myrna Loy said, was something that no one had thought possible, even in their wildest dreams. Throughout the Sixties the company was beset with boardroom troubles, increasingly reflected in its films, until by 1969 all except a handful of Metro productions seemed wilfully unattractive. The battles to oust Robert O'Brien had begun in 1967, as it was clear that only David Lean's *Doctor Zhivago* (q.v.) and the reissues of *Gone with the Wind* had kept the company solvent. In 1970 Lean's *Ryan's Daughter* lost money for M-G-M, but meanwhile Edgar Bronfman of Seagrams Distilleries had acquired control, with O'Brien promoted to Chairman. Battle immediately ensued between Bronfman and Kirk Kerkorian, of Tracy Investments – whose chief interests were in Las Vegas hostelries – and Kerkorian won. He appointed James T. Aubrey, the former head of C.B.S., president – the third in eleven months – and losses were posted of $35,366,000, though that included some cancelled projects, among them *Man's Fate* and *Say It with Music,* on which the respective sums of $3 million and $1 million had already been spent.

Under Kerkorian's aegis, Aubrey began to dispose systematically of M-G-M's assets, including part of the studio grounds, sold for real estate, and the prop department and its contents, including costumes worn by Garbo and Judy Garland's ruby-red slippers from *The Wizard of Oz*. The British studio was closed and a ceiling budget of $2.3 million was put on every film – but these turned out to be even worse than those made during the O'Brien regime. In 1973 it was announced that M-G-M was going out of business except for its television interests, though there would almost certainly be some 'highly selective quality films and other leisure and entertainment activities' – the latter including the newly opened M-G-M Grand Hotel in Las Vegas, its walls hung with portraits of Garbo, Gable and Garland. M-G-M's remaining foreign cinemas were to be sold and its distribution offices closed – with its library and current product handled on home territory by United Artists and overseas by Cinema International Corporation, a company owned jointly by Paramount and Universal.

Looking back to the M-G-M films discussed in this chapter and remembering some of the horrors foisted on us over the years, few of us still cannot help feeling sad – and therefore glad when, in 1980, the company rose from the ashes. It had acquired a new President in Frank E. Rosenfelt, the first of the new moguls (or the old ones, for that matter) to believe in the value, artistic as well as financial, of the films lying in the vaults. By a judicious reappraisal of their worth and by licensing *Gone with the Wind* to television for a twenty-year period he was able to capitalise on the company's past, and in the best possible way, by restoring its glory.

In 1981 Rosenfelt announced that M-G-M was returning to full-scale production, and about the same time he revealed the acquisition of United Artists, its library, assets and projects, for $380 million. This was the fourth of the real industry thunderbolts, following the death of R.K.O., Paramount's absorption by Gulf+Western and the auction of M-G-M's props. As it happens, R.K.O. is currently returning to the film business, as are the American television companies – but I am anticipating, since these matters belong at the end of the book. So does the apparent end of United Artists and, for the moment, it may be said that that was brought about by the failure of one film. What had been threatened by *Cleopatra* and the 1962 *Mutiny on the Bounty* – the folding of one of the major companies – had finally been achieved by *Heaven's Gate* (q.v.). In the event M-G-M and United Artists amalgamated, and were said in 1982 to have debts to the banks of $650 million, due to a number of unprofitable films put in hand by both managements. *Heaven's Gate* had been written off, but the figure M-G-M paid for United Artists should be compared with the $722 million paid a few months later for 20th Century-Fox by the millionaire Marvin Davis.

When such figures appear in the press we are reminded more than ever that the cinema is an industry and that the people now in control are no longer creative. Doubtless among those calling themselves producers there are those who buy properties – since most of them are ex-agents. It was reported that when Krim and Benjamin were ousted from United Artists the new management bought Gay Talese's book, 'Thy Neighbour's Wife', for $2½ million to prove their clout. This was, it was said, to provide the basis for two films – even if most experienced movie people felt that it would not even provide the basis for one (and, in the event, nothing more has been heard of the project). The studios now exist as production facilities and offices to which talent – stars, directors and writers – take their projects, depending on their attitude to their occupants. The studios exist to do deals. When we return to Hollywood it will be to look at the films initiated by their directors. It may not, in fact, be evident that the demise of the studio system gave rise to better pictures.

34

Ingmar Bergman:
The Quest for Understanding

WHEN IN 1959, the Swedish Institute published an introduction to Swedish cinema, it needed only a few bridging paragraphs, referring to the 'artistic deterioration' of the Thirties, to pass from Sjöström to Ingmar Bergman – Sjöström's heir and the man who has dominated his native cinema for almost forty years. The intervening period was a time when serious films were out of favour, and there was a decade of tedious melodramas and unfunny comedies (Bergman has said that though they seemed bad at the time they are now rather charming). The best light films were made by Gustav Molander, a contemporary of Sjöström – but he also made the best serious films as well. Few were seen abroad (though one of them launched Ingrid Bergman on her American career), but when, during the postwar period, Swedish films began to trickle across the sea, they became synonymous with gloom and sex – frequently intertwined, since it was often the one night of passion which led to the unwanted baby.

Such, after all, has been the tradition of rural stories the world over, and Swedish films only reflected the national dichotomy of believing deeply in the pleasure of the sex act itself – but unwilling to cast off the puritan spirit. This was the theme of one of the first postwar Swedish successes, **One Summer of Happiness** (1951), in which the castigations of the pastor against a young couple (Folke Sundquist, Ulla Jacobsson) lead inevitably to tragedy. It was directed solemnly – by Arne Mattsson – which was absolutely what audiences expected; many of them had gone to see the nude bathing scene, though that survived intact in very few countries.

Prior to that, many had been impressed by **Hets** (1945), known as *Frenzy* in Britain and *Torment* in the U.S., which transposes a similar story to an urban setting, inasmuch as the student hero (Alf Kjellin) again finds sex irresistible. In this case, the girl (Mai Zetterling) is promiscuous, and the tormentor is the boy's teacher (Stig Järrel) who, since he is also her lover, is the professor of *The Blue Angel* in reverse. Alf Sjöberg (1903–80), the director, makes much of the atmosphere – the echoing school, the over-stuffed home of the boy's parents, the girl's squalid flat – but the result is melodramatic, despite what seems to be an effort on the part of both the director and writer to achieve something a little deeper.

Sjöberg, after making his first film in 1929, had spent most of the subsequent decade directing for the theatre, though he remained obsessed with movies. Few Swedish films were being made, but production was increased when the War isolated Sweden. Accordingly he was able to return to films in 1940. Two years later he attempted to revive the spirit of Sjöström's rural dramas with **The Road to Heaven**, visually influenced by the nineteenth-century primitive religious paintings. Most Swedish films looked back to an earlier era, partly because there was richer source material in the films and plays of the Twenties. *Hets* is, in fact, much more typical of that time than is *The Road to Heaven*: so it is ironic that it was regarded as a statement on behalf of the younger generation, rebellious at what they considered Sweden's inward and backward-looking predilection. It established Sjöberg as a figure equally important to the cinema as he was to the theatre, and he went on to make a number of accomplished films. **Iris and the Lieutenant** (1946) could not claim originality in subject matter, though it recounts the love affair between a servant girl (Mai Zetterling) and a young nobleman (Kjellin) with a warmth and tenderness rare in Sjöberg's work. His screenplay has only a hint of the satirical tone in Olle Hedberg's original novel but, with the collaboration of the author Ivar Lo-Johansson, he captured absolutely the cruel world of the novelist's much-admired **Only a Mother** (1949) – one of his series on the plight of exploited farm workers on huge country estates. Sjöberg was delighted with the film's success, since he believed in the cinema above all as a force for social change. Eva Dahlbeck is magnificent as the woman whose life story the film traces.

Though *Iris* (under that title) was seen briefly in London, Sjöberg was known abroad only for *Hets* when **Miss Julie** (1950) was awarded the Grand Prix at Cannes (jointly with *Miracolo a Milano*). Sjöberg's screenplay was recognised as a brilliant extension of Strindberg's play, introducing by way of flashback some scenes of Miss Julie's childhood and seizing the obvious opportunity to wander into the fields and gardens for the midsummer night's frolic – brilliantly photographed by Göran Strindberg (the playwright's grandson). That the film remains enthralling is partly due to Sjöberg's tenacious hold on the central relationship, from the time Miss Julie (Anita Björk) first humiliates the valet Jean (Ulf Palme) to their separate traumas as each broods on the consequences of their love-making.

The film's international success encouraged its producer, Sandrews, to invest heavily in Sjöberg's version of Pär Lagerkvist's novel **Barabbas** (1953), to the extent of filming abroad – rare for a Swedish film – in Israel and Italy. Despite Mr Palme's magnificent performance in the title role, the film was hardly seen outside Scandinavia: nor was **Karin Månsdotter** (1954), with which Sjöberg returned to Strindberg, basing the central episode on his play 'Erik xiv'. Inspired by his successful additions to *Miss Julie*, in this screenplay Sjöberg frames Strindberg's drama with other events known of the mad King Erik (Jarl Kulle) and his peasant-born queen (Ulla Jacobsson). The prologue, in colour, is a burlesque of Silent comedy

showing their meeting; the epilogue follows their adventures after the king has been deposed. At the start the film has a certain humour, but the tone has been set wrongly: the court intrigues are uninteresting, and the relationships between the king, queen and his commoner adviser (Palme) are marred by the two-dimensional playing and writing. The piece is visually striking, but did not appeal to audiences or critics. The same judgment was passed on Sjöberg's subsequent handful of films, leaving his international reputation to rest on *Hets* and *Miss Julie*.

Hets was one of Sjöberg's few films that he did not write himself. His commanding position in the theatre and the reception accorded *The Road to Heaven* had caused Carl-Anders Dymling, the head of Svensk Filmindustri, to invite him to make a film to celebrate the company's silver anniversary. *Hets* was considered suitable, even though the screenplay was by someone with no previous film experience – an ambitious young theatre director, Ingmar Bergman (b. 1918). He had based it on one of his own short stories influenced by his schooldays, and he so wanted to be in cinema that he accepted Sjöberg's offer and took on the lowly job of continuity boy. Some months later, when directing his first film, *Crisis* (q.v.), he was due to be sacked after three weeks because the results were so bad, and the movie was to be

Between the films of Sjöström and Stiller in the early Twenties and Ingmar Bergman in the Fifties only a handful of Swedish films were seen outside Scandinavia. The director Alf Sjöberg had two international successes, the second of which was a version of Strindberg's play *Miss Julie*, which effectively combines lyricism with as much eroticism as was permissible at the time. Anita Björk and Ulf Palme are the mistress and servant who too soon come to regret their moment of lust.

restarted by another director. But Victor Sjöström, as artistic adviser to Svensk, insisted that Bergman reshoot the work, and that he himself would assume full responsibility for its quality. Thus Bergman believes he owes his career to his two great predecessors. Always venerating Sjöström, he regarded Sjöberg as a friend and mentor until his death.

Bergman is the son of a Lutheran minister. While still a boy he had built several toy theatres for himself and by the time he was sixteen had read all fifty-five volumes of the collected works of Strindberg. He was educated at the University of Stockholm, where he was able to develop some of his theories on drama. He was artistic director of the theatre at Hälsingborg when Carl-Anders Dymling, impressed by Bergman's screenplay for *Hets*, offered him the direction of **Crisis** (1945). 'An out-and-out bit of whoredom', said Bergman later, referring to the fact that he disliked the play on which it was based ('Moderdyret' by a Dane, Leck Fisher) – and also perhaps because it was made as a star vehicle for Dagny Lind, a middle-aged actress who specialised in suffering. He also said that 'more than anything else I was longing to make films', but today he mildly approves of only one sequence – that in the beauty parlour. I think he underestimates its portrait of provincial life which, like those in the films of Stiller, is both chilly and amusing. The plot concerns Nelly (Inga Landgré) who, living with her foster mother (Miss Lind), is fascinated by her real mother (Marianne Lüfgren), a Stockholm beautician who is keeping company with a callow young actor (Stig Olin). Nelly finds him more seductive than the foster-uncle who is wooing her, and the rejection of her provincial 'family' prefigures later Bergman films where love will lose ground or go unrequited. With hindsight too, we can see that Bergman already had a predilection for wearing a hairshirt in films, so it may be that the young actor is a self-portrait. Lorens Marmstedt, a theatre owner and distributor, met Bergman while he was making *Crisis* and it was he who produced, and to some extent chose the material for, the next three films Bergman was to direct. **It Rains on Our Love** (1946) also introduced Bergman to the gifted young actor Birger Malmsten and the Stock-

holm drama critic and writer, Herbert Grevenius, who was to collaborate with him for the next few years. The film itself, based on a Norwegian play, is typical of Scandinavian cinema at this time – its theme is the plight of two lovers (Malmsten and Barbro Kollberg) with all the world, or most of it, against them. Their enemies and occasional friends are the grotesques who were so frequently to people Bergman's films for another decade: that none of them is tiresome is due to the confident handling, positiveness of dimension and the setting – a vacant summer villa. Allied to the fact that Marmstedt later gave Bergman the opportunity to direct one of his own screenplays, *Prison* (q.v.), Bergman was also grateful to him for constantly reminding him that he was not Carné nor Malmsten Jean Gabin.

This film is too Nordic for us to make a comparison, but the mark of Carné is on **A Ship to India** (1947) – as is that of Michael Curtiz, whose films Bergman was studying at the time. The film is a melodrama, but less of one than *Mildred Pierce* – for the characters here are much more convincing. What brings the film within reach of greatness, in my view, is its visual richness. The director of photography was Göran Strindberg, whose compositions are without parallel (until the Japanese took to the wide screen): but they are always, and only, used for dramatic effect. Briefly stated, the plot – taken from a play by Martin Söderhjelm – involves a war between father (Holger Löwenadler) and son (Malmsten). Father, a retired sea captain, operates a small salvage barge, but prefers to spend his days whoring, boozing and fighting; the son, a hunchback, dreams of going away to sea and, after one of their incessant fights, gets drunk and attempts to rape his father's mistress. The true tragic figure is the mother, who suffers the rows and the presence of mistress on board, and always forgives; but she is virtually ignored and is passed over completely in the prologue and the epilogue, set some years later, which puts the boy's youthful traumas into perspective.

'It was a silly little film, but my first popular success,' said Bergman of **Night is My Future** (1948) (the Swedish title translates more accurately and less sensationally as *Music in Darkness*). It is about blindness and, if it is not the best film on the subject, Malmsten's performance is the most convincing portrayal on film of a blind man. The ending, with its echo of 'Jane Eyre' and the suggestion that blindness is hardly an affliction if there is someone to care, may be why Bergman dismisses the film – passing over its interesting exposition and magnificent middle section. When Bengt (Malmsten) becomes blind, he stays with a family friend, and there is a chance that he will marry her maid's daughter (Mai Zetterling) – especially as her concern for him is accompanied by erotic feelings. His disappointment is twofold: he cannot marry her because class differences prove too great, and he is rejected by the Stockholm Academy of Music. He becomes a pianist in a small provincial café, where he is subjected to the bitterness of his violinist partner (Gunnar Björnstrand), the whims of the drunken proprietor and the depredations of the landlady's young son. The view of provincial power is darker than that of Stiller or *Crisis*, though we shall find the same view recurring as late as *The Touch* (q.v.).

Port of Call (1948) is set in Gothenburg and is a realistic account of an affair between a merchant seaman (Bengt Eklund) and a girl (Nine-Christine Jönsson) more sinned against than sinner. The romance does not go smoothly, because the girl is on probation – just one aspect of a fairly miserable existence. Love, in Bergman's films, is always a battlefield, but hitherto he had followed such dramatic convention as coincidence, misunderstanding or commitment to the wrong partner. Molander had just directed a screenplay written by Bergman along those lines, **Woman Without a Face** (1947), a straightforward tale of a man (Alf Kjellin) who deserts his wife for a floozie (Anita Bjork). *Port of Call*, however, brings social forces into play, reflecting Bergman's ever-ready ability, at this time, to assimilate what other important film-makers were doing: like de Sica, he believed that individual suffering was caused by the defects in society. At least that view is tenable in *Port of Call*, but he presumably came to believe that the ills of Italian society were not those of Sweden, for none of his other films blames poverty *per se* for the misery of people's lives.

The fault, suggests **Prison** (1949) – also known as *The Devil's Wanton* – lies with

ourselves and, since the film is autobiographical, it is as well to take into account Bergman's volatile nature. He had left home in his teens after a row with his parents; at thirty, his second marriage was in ruins; and the film industry was wary of, rather than impressed by, his energy, which was why he had written and directed films but had not been allowed to function in both capacities at the same time. Having established a good relationship with Svensk Filmindustri, Bergman returned to Marmstedt, who allowed him to direct his own screenplay. *Prison* begins in a film studio where a director (Hasse Ekman) and a writer, Tomas (Malmsten), discuss a film about evil with a reference to the atom bomb, thus reflecting Bergman's own uneasiness about Swedish neutrality (he had produced an anti-Nazi 'Macbeth' at the time Norway and Denmark were invaded). Tomas comes up with an idea for a film about a prostitute (Doris Svedlund) he had once interviewed, whose sister was in league with her pimp (Stig Olin)

Ingmar Bergman at the time of *Persona*. He had been directing films for almost a decade before becoming widely known outside his homeland – and since then his reputation has fluctuated at the dictate of newspaper critics, able to keep audiences away by writing of gloom and depression. The more serious critics – those, that is, who write in the specialist cinema magazines – have seldom wavered in their loyalty and at least twenty of his thirty-odd films are in the permanent international repertory.

945

to keep her working. Then he, Tomas, drinks himself into gloom and decides to put an end to the bickerings with his wife (Eva Henning) by murdering her and committing suicide. Instead, he meets up with the prostitute and they flee to a boarding house where, in the attic, he finds toys from his childhood, including a cinema projector. The final result of the film is undiluted *angst*, but it contains some unexpected diversions – the gaiety of the scenes with the projector, the comedy of the murder that isn't and the purity of the scenes of Malmsten by the river, contemplating suicide.

We can see now that the writer, the pimp and the director are all aspects of Bergman. *Prison* impressed a number of critics, but was regarded as a failure. Bergman accordingly turned again to Grevenius for a screenplay, and they settled on some short stories by Birgit Tengroth for what became **Thirst** (1949), in which Miss Tengroth herself plays a secondary role. That the two films have so much in common indicates the understanding between the two men (though they drifted apart later, when Grevenius was converted to Catholicism): both centre upon an unhappy married couple played by Malmsten and Henning, and crucial to their unhappiness is the loss of a baby. *Thirst*, like so many later Bergman movies, features a train journey, and as the train goes from Basle to Stockholm it traverses a Germany that prefigures the unnamed country in *The Silence* (q.v.), not merely in ruins but with a ghostly eeriness. Throughout the journey Rut (Henning) and Bertil (Malmsten) bicker, causing her to recall a supposedly happier relationship, with an army officer (Eklund) who did not tell her that he was married until she had informed him that she was pregnant. Rut's present and past troubles are interrupted by some simultaneous events back in Stockholm, concerning Viola (Birgit Tengroth), who is having an affair with a doctor (Ekman). He miscalculates the extent of her dependence on him, so that she is alone on midsummer's night when she meets Valborg (Mimi Nelson), a friend from Rut's days with the ballet. Viola realises that Valborg's need is for something beyond friendship, but at the testing moment she rushes out to wander, like so many Bergman protagonists, down along

the river. These episodes constitute not a narrative, but a thesis – that it may be hell being together but it is better than being apart. Viola's suicide has been unnecessary, for living is preferable to death, even if it means suffering a slippery philanderer or a predatory lesbian. Being single – lonely (as opposed to being merely alone) – is the one great impossibility; an unsatisfactory love is better than none. A similar view is found in the French existentialists, and Bergman has admitted that both this film and *Prison* were influenced by contemporary writing.

When shooting was finished, Malmsten and Bergman took a trip abroad, during which time Bergman began to feel romantic about 'my then marriage, that is to say the one I'd just taken extreme delight in ripping to pieces in *Thirst*.' He also became sentimental about the symphony orchestra he had worked with in Hälsingborg; consequently marriage and music are the twin subjects of **To Joy** (1950), whose hero is a mediocre practitioner of both (Bergman had begun to consider 'how I wasn't such a genius as I'd imagined'). The film centres on two members of a provincial orchestra, Martha (Maj-Britt Nilsson) and Stig (Stig Eriksson), who marry; the years pass and Stig takes solace in a sordid affair – till brought up short by the presence of a lodger (Malmsten), who is also in the orchestra. Stig decides that he is surrounded by mediocrity, and that he will try at least to make his marriage first-rate. Bergman calls the film 'suspect – but with some nice bits in it', and by that he is referring, I imagine, to the scenes of rehearsal, with Victor Sjöström playing the conductor – and offering, as of old, a character in which authority, sympathy and weakness are equally matched.

Otherwise the piece is unsatisfactory, partly because Bergman's fighting spouses were becoming tiresome. It is no less jejune and occasionally melodramatic than Bergman's other films up to that time, but it is interesting as a foretaste of one of the themes of his middle period: the responsibility of the artist. It also lacks the sheer zest of his other early films, which for all their faults still prove him to have been one of the most exciting directors working anywhere in the world.

Till he had achieved international recognition his films were largely confined to

Scandinavia. **Summer Interlude** (1950) is the first Bergman film to have entered the international repertoire with any permanency. Both this and **Summer with Monika** (1953) are about adolescent love affairs – the one to end in death, the other to founder because of the girl's perfidy. 'Has life any meaning?' asks the bereaved heroine (Maj-Brit Nilsson) in *Summer Interlude*, and the answer comes back, 'No, not in the long run.' Years later, when she is a successful dancer, the protagonist is entrapped between a sinister ballet master (Olin) and a boorish lover (Kjellin); similarly the increasingly impoverished and unhappy lovers (Lars Ekborg, Harriet Andersson) of *Monika* have finally the option of moving from one mouse-trap to another. Monika turns out to be both perfidious and sexually unfaithful, which Bergman's heroines, despite their failings, had not been hitherto. The film itself might be said to be the first screen presentation of his burgeoning misogynistic streak; and it is pertinent to remark that six marriages do not seem to indicate great emotional contentment.

Professionally, both films were important. In tackling the subject of a doomed love in a sylvan setting he was following Swedish film tradition, but in *Summer Interlude* he felt, for the first time in filmmaking, that 'it all worked', while *Summer with Monika* is one of his few early films that he likes and is 'always glad to see again.' The first marked the last time that he worked with Grevenius, and the second and virtually the last time that he worked with any collaborator or adapted from another source; he did later work on screenplays to be directed by Sjöberg and Kjellin, but increasingly he saw each film as a work wholly by Ingmar Bergman. He tended then, and now, to work as far as possible with the same team, once observing that twenty people crammed into one small space called for harmony.

He wrote the screenplay for **Waiting Women** (1952) while the Swedish film industry was idle due to dissatisfaction with its inadequate financing methods. He had been making commercials and wrote this, waiting for matters to right themselves, in 'bad temper, sheer temper . . . My finances were in shreds and my marriage badly frayed.' In common with most of his films at this time, it is built round a

Summer Interlude, ABOVE, and *Summer with Monika*, LEFT, have more in common than the similarity of their titles, for both concern adolescent romances, in which the couples concerned live their idylls among lakes and pine forests. Beyond that, they have little in common, for *Summer Interlude* is an early Bergman attempt to come to terms with the importance of artistic endeavour. She, Maj-Britt Nilsson, is a dancer, and the lover gazing at her is Birger Malmsten. *Summer with Monika* is only about an affair – and it is not idyllic for long – as may be seen here, for Harriet Andersson does not seem overwhelmed by the visit of Lars Ekborg.

947

series of flashbacks, with three women recounting to each other the particular moment when they saw their husbands in a new or different light. The first episode is about a wife (Anita Björk), whose casual infidelity with a friend (Jarl Kulle) leads her husband to decide, after his initial fury, that an unfaithful wife is better than none at all. The second concerns seduction – not this time by a Swedish lake, but in a Paris hotel – when a girl (Maj-Britt Nilsson), disenchanted by her G.I. fiancé, meets a romantic fellow-Swede (Malmsten); and the third involves a pompous, rather drunk man (Björnstrand) who, stuck in a stalled lift with his wife (Eva Dahlbeck), confesses to infidelity and then makes love to her. Bergman says he was delighted by the gales of laughter which greeted the film – presumably only the final, frivolous episode – but to non-Swedish ears the humour is only mildly funny.

Gycklarnas Afton (1953) – *Sawdust and Tinsel* in Great Britain and *The Naked Night* in the U.S. – was another film made, according to Bergman's own report, at a time he felt emotionally humiliated. It was also a film made for its own sake, a situation which has usually resulted in his less interesting work. It bears witness to its inspiration, *Varieté*, in an unappetising tale about a circus couple (Ake Grönberg, Harriet Andersson) trying to escape from their relationship, he to the wife he deserted long ago, she to an effeminate and possibly sado-masochistic actor (Hasse

Ekman). A flashback at the beginning – based on one of Bergman's own dreams – in which a husband is humiliated while his wife cavorts in the sea with some half-naked sailors looking on, accurately foreshadows the film as a whole: it is brilliantly done, but hollow.

The film's rejection by Swedish critics caused Bergman to run for cover and, recalling audience delight at the Dahlbeck-Björnstrand episode of *Waiting Women*, he fashioned **A Lesson in Love** (1954) for the same players. Most of it takes place on a train to Copenhagen, and the use of a journey to revive old memories is a frequent device. A number of the flashbacks are excellent, especially that with the aged parents which anticipates *Wild Strawberries* (q.v.), but slapstick is not Bergman's forte. The rest is ponderous and joylessly optimistic, proving that Dahlbeck and Björnstrand were unlikely ever to rival Hepburn and Tracy.

A similar pretentiousness is echoed in the opening sequence of **Kvinnodröm** (1955) – *Journey into Autumn* in Britain and *Dreams* in the U.S. – set in a photographer's studio; but it is quickly succeeded by one of Bergman's most virtuoso passages, a rail journey at night. The subsequent plotting is evidence of the textural richness of which he was now capable, and the dialogue is alternately ironic and tender. His personal preoccupations were also clearly stated: man's sexual subjugation to woman, the vain hope that love endures and the examination of its possibilities outside marriage.

Smiles of a Summer Night (1955) contrasts the sexual intrigues of the middle-aged with the idealism of the young rather in the manner of Jean Anouilh, though Bergman has claimed that his inspiration was the earlier dramatist, Marivaux. It was Marivaux whom Renoir had in mind when writing *La Règle du Jeu* and superficially the two films are alike.★ But, unlike Renoir (and Ophuls and Lubitsch – whose period comedies were an inspiration also) this film has little kindness; indeed, the screenplay is not only heartless, but defiantly so. Again Bergman had returned to comedy after a failure – *Kvinnodröm* – but, he says, 'head office told me it had been a dreadful

★Bergman thinks Renoir over-rated and one of the reasons he dislikes *La Règle du Jeu* is because he thinks it badly acted.

Jarl Kulle, Gunnar Björnstrand and Margit Carlqvist in *Smiles of a Summer Night*, a film neither smiling nor summery, but often quite pointed on the matter of sexual liaisons. It is a Nordic version of Anouilh's 'Ring Round the Moon', and it was that play Harold Prince and Stephen Sondheim had in mind when they began to prepare the Broadway musical that became 'A Little Night Music': when they were unable to purchase the Anouilh rights they bought those to Bergman's film instead.

miscalculation. The film wasn't funny. It
was stylised. It was too lame, and too long'
– all of which is true.

The film was, nevertheless, entered for
the Cannes Festival – though Bergman
says that Swedish films were then only
entered at festivals so that the producers
could enjoy a free trip. He was astonished
when it won the Grand Prix and it was this
that ensured it international distribution;
but it had no more success than had *Gycklarnas Afton*, earlier dismissed in both New
York and London as heavy and overdrawn. It was **The Seventh Seal** (1957),
finally, which made his world-wide reputation. The film's concept is impressive:
the knight (Max von Sydow) playing chess
with Death for his life; the chiaroscuro
both visual and dramatic – the contrast
between the knight's quest and the drunk-
en cavorting of the people, between religious experience and the harsh facts of
poverty and pestilence – indeed the whole
panorama of medieval life and superstition. The final effect is less of pretension
than of muddle – clarity sacrificed to a joke
or private image. It is a divertissement by
one whose father had been a preacher, a
series of abstractions remembered from
hours of boredom in church as a boy.

Many spectators who held out against
this film were converted by **Wild Strawberries** (1957). Its starting point is childhood or, rather, a search for the state of
childhood, which was triggered off by a
drive Bergman took to the town in which
he had grown up. His protagonist would
be 'a tired old egocentric, who'd cut off
everything about him – as I'd done': he is a
professor, and the film is a record of his
journey to Lund University where he is to
be honoured. With him is his daughter-in-
law (Ingrid Thulin), and they pick up three
students, one of whom is enacted by Bibi
Andersson, who also plays the old man's
childhood sweetheart. He reminisces, and
dreams of death; his regrets are those of
an old man who has spent his life compromising. If Bergman had any purpose other
than the cinematic equivalent of a sketch
for a portrait, it becomes fleshed out by the
fully rounded performance of Victor Sjöström, looking blinkered and misanthropic; but the contours of his face
nevertheless express contentment and
tolerance. Bergman found it 'marvellous,
having this inexhaustible wellspring to

hand every day', though he admits that the
lessons to be learned from Sjöström were
contained in the great films which he had
directed years ago – 'his incorruptible demand for truth, his incorruptible observation of reality. His way of never for a
moment making things easy for himself,
or simplifying or skipping things or cheating or settling for mere brilliance.' For the
first time Bergman expresses his love for
his country as Sjöström did, in a film richer
and more mature than any he had made up
to that time. Its reception consolidated his
reputation, though neither here nor in *The
Seventh Seal* is there much to suggest the
substance of the great films to come –
although in *The Seventh Seal* we may note
the knight's remark, 'I want God to show
Himself to me.'

Favourite preoccupations emerge in
what is otherwise a straightforward tale of
a maternity ward, **Nara Livet** (1958) (*So
Close to Life* or *The Brink of Life*): the
relationship of women away from the
world of men; the omnipresence of death;
the inconsequence and consequence of our
sexuality. Its source is a novel by Ulla
Isaksson, who is credited on the film itself
as sole screenwriter, though Bergman
elsewhere shares the credit. Released in the
same year, **Ansiktet** (1958) (*The Face* or
The Magician) is the most deeply personal
film he had yet made. 'Fraud is so common
that those who tell the truth are usually

Though *The Seventh
Seal* made Bergman
a name on the
art-house circuit it
was his next film,
Wild Strawberries,
which brought
respect into
admiration. He felt
similarly for
Victor Sjöström,
who played the old
professor in the film,
for Sjöström was not
only the mightiest
figure in the early
days of the Swedish
cinema but as artistic
director of Svensk
Filmindustri had
been greatly
encouraging during
Bergman's own first
films as a director.
With Sjöström here
is Bibi Andersson in
a scene from the film.

Ingmar Bergman: The Quest for Understanding

Naima Wifstrand, Ingrid Thulin, Max von Sydow and Åke Fridell in *Ansiktet* (*The Face* in Britain; *The Magician* in the U.S.) When it was first shown, Bergman was known only as a weighty film-maker, so it was a surprise to find him enjoying himself in creating the terrors of a horror film. It was immediately recognised that there was more to it than that, but it was only when we had seen more of his work that it could be seen as one of his most personal films.

branded as liars,' says the wife (Ingrid Thulin) of the magician (Max von Sydow). The film is about the nature of truth, and it is a homage to the artist who creates the illusion, as the only member of our society permitted overt concealment. Vergérus (Gunnar Björnstrand), foremost of the bourgeoisie in judging these charlatans and mountebanks, says 'It is distasteful if science has to accept the miraculous' and, later, 'You represent what I hate most – something I cannot understand.' The hypocrisy of his committee is contrasted throughout with the legerdemain of the actors – and though their leader is undoubtedly something of a fake, he is also something of the Christ, both in appearance and suffering. He fights the lonely battles of Jesus, who, like the artist, told the truth and was branded a liar; he dies and is resurrected; and is finally accepted when patronised by royalty – as Christianity was adopted by Constantine.

The film cheats us as much as the magician, Vogler, deceives his audience, since the terror in the attic is caused by cinematic trickery. 'Haven't I done everything to offer you a sensation?' asks Vogler, and that is also Bergman speaking. No earlier film better expresses his approach to directing: 'I make my pictures for use! They are not made *sub specie aeternitatis*; they are made for now and for use . . . Also, they are made to put me in contact with other human beings, to whom I give them and say, "Please use them. Take what you want and throw the rest away." My impulse has nothing to do with intellect or symbolism; it has only to do with dreams and longing, with hope and desire, with passion.'

By this time Bergman had achieved a fame outside Sweden that far exceeded that of any other Swedish director, including Sjöström, and his self-confidence permitted him a number of disquisitions on the silence of God – as in **The Virgin Spring** (1960), for example, where He does not step in to prevent the rape of a young girl. This film is a return to the medieval world, with a screenplay credited to Miss Isakkson, and described by Bergman as 'an aberration, a touristic, lousy imitation of Kurosawa'. **The Devil's Eye** (1960) he

950

described as 'my little game . . . My intention (if any) was to play, for the amusement of the beloved and feared audience' – but few were amused by this Nordic whimsy about Don Juan (Jarl Kulle) sent back to earth by the Devil to deflower a pastor's daughter (Bibi Andersson): 'One of hell's tiny triumphs is more significant than any great success of heaven's' as its final statement puts it. This was, incidentally, the last of Bergman's films to be photographed by Gunnar Fischer; since then his cinematographer has been Sven Nykvist, with whom he had worked intermittently before.

The next three films Bergman regards as a trilogy, since each defines more clearly his views on man's relationship with God. **Through a Glass Darkly** (1961) is about a man (Gunnar Björnstrand) who tells his son that God manifests Himself in love; in **Winter Light** (1962) a clergyman (Björnstrand) loses his faith and tries to believe that God is love; and in **The Silence** (1963), God has deserted the world. Since *The Virgin Spring*, critical esteem for Bergman had been ebbing, and the first two of these films were poorly received – rightly so, in my opinion, in the case of *Through a Glass Darkly*. It portrays a family of tortured souls ruminating beside a gloomy sea – and the love manifested is that of the seduction by a mentally sick girl (Harriet Andersson) of her younger brother. The family's rampant misery here seems shallow, but *Winter Light* springs from deeper doubts. The pastor cannot help himself; too late he has realised that his isolation from the real world began while working as chaplain in Portugal during the Spanish Civil War, and he has therefore no consolation for Jonas (von Sydow), whose melancholia is caused by the world situation. He cannot respond to the lumpy woman (Ingrid Thulin) who became his mistress after he was widowed, and who tells him that he will die in hate. The film makes a number of both oblique and trenchant comments on the Church, but were we to ignore Bergman's preoccupations this would still be a remarkable study of desperation; its events are as harsh as the landscape outside, where the snow is whipped furiously by the wind.

The Silence is set in a strange foreign city, where tanks pass through on their way to a probable war. In a deserted hotel

Gunnar Björnstrand in *Winter Light,* LEFT, and Jörgen Lindström and Gunnel Lindblom in *The Silence,* BELOW, which with *Through a Glass Darkly* Bergman regards as a trilogy, since each is an attempt to understand man's relationship with the Deity. *Through a Glass Darkly* was made first, and since it often verges on self-parody it was not well received – a fact which perhaps led to the undervaluation of *Winter Light,* which is masterly even by Bergman's own standards. Happily, *The Silence* was accorded the recognition its merits deserve.

two women express their obsessive, self-hating interest in the other, and their indifference to the child with them. One (Thulin) seeks solace in vodka and masturbation,* and the other in casual promiscuity. They may be sisters or lesbians; the hotel and the no-man's-land they are in may reflect that unreal state which can mark the onslaught of a nervous breakdown. Bergman had been using symbolism in his work for years, and since the advent of Antonioni and Resnais had furthered its use in films, he could push even further his own penchant for the allegorical.

The Silence marked a resurgence of overwhelming critical favour, doubtless because the film's mysteries were in tune with the current climate; and as its two predecessors had been dismissed or misunderstood, few commented on its title – though no one misunderstood its preoccupation with God's presence. Bergman himself said later that *Winter Light* was his last film on God: thenceforward 'We have nothing to do with each other.' However, a clergyman, the Rev. Robert E. Lander, writing almost two decades later in *The New York Times* on *Autumn Sonata* (q.v.), found him as 'hooked on God' as ever: 'Simply stated, [his] theme is the struggle of human beings to communicate love in a world in which God is silent. The meaning and value of that struggle are made precarious for Mr Bergman by the presence of death.'

In 1961 Carl-Anders Dymling became mortally ill, leaving the staff of Svensk Filmindustri without guidance. Bergman was among those on the committee to keep the Rasunda studio functioning and he devised **The Pleasure Garden** (1961) for Alf Kjellin to direct. It was basically a vehicle for Björnstrand and Sickan Carlsson, a rather beefy comedienne on the brink of middle age, who, to this time, had usually played teenagers (and who, according to Bergman, has not filmed since). Björnstrand plays David, a provincial school teacher, whose past catches up with him when a local columnist, Lundberg (Stig Järrel) reveals him as the author of a book of juvenile love poems. Both men have mistresses: David's is a waitress

(Sickan Carlsson) who confesses herself the mother of a twenty-year-old daughter (Bibi Andersson). David decides to be seen publicly with both – for which he is ostracised by the town, but defended by Lundberg's mistress, the local bookseller, who decides that his action is the logical progression from the feelings expressed in the poems. Local hypocrisy is further shattered when, though unknown to all but the audience, the young curate is so overcome by lust for the daughter that he would seduce her there and then. Otherwise, this young couple is idealistic, in contrast to the two older men, whose complacency towards their women is severely shaken. But most original is the role that is played by the book of poems: the film states that it is possible for our attitude towards a work of art to change under circumstances – that critics are fallible, that even a neophyte work can be valuable, that the meanest creative work should not be written off if it can find a response in one sensitive soul (i.e. the bookseller). The screenplay is by Bergman and Erland Josephson, who had played a small role in *So Close to Life* and who, at the end of the decade, was gradually to replace von Sydow as Bergman's preferred male interpreter (partly because von Sydow's fame as an international actor made him less often available for Swedish films).

The screenplay was publicly credited to the pseudonymous Buntel Ericsson, and some sources list this name as the author of **Now About All These Women** (1964) directed by Bergman. The two films have in common a number of comments on the critic *vs.* the artist, especially the 'littleness' of the former compared to the purity and dedication of the latter. 'Genius,' says the film several times, 'is an ability to make the critic change his mind.' The artist, as the film begins, is dead; a critic, Cornelius (Jarl Kulle) is so angry at not being granted an interview before he died and also at being unable to duplicate his success with women, that he plans revenge – to destroy the deceased's reputation. The piece is slapstick, with stylised mock baroque sets, and the women wearing pretty costumes of the Twenties. It was Bergman's first film in colour (though he had done some tests for *Through a Glass Darkly*). It is not a funny film, and it is – again – hard to disagree with Bergman, who described it

---

*Almost certainly the first time this had been shown – via the actress's expression – in a non-pornographic film. Bergman's reputation was sufficient for the censors of most nations to pass the sequence.

as 'glossy, sophisticated, swift, hard and poisonous'. It is mean-minded, partly because by this time he had established himself as so much greater than most filmmakers and therefore above his critics. His own voice speaks loud and clear, as ever, but what he is saying is unworthy of him.

The film was catastrophically received, and the welcome was not much warmer for **Persona** (1966), now regarded as one of his finest films. **Hour of the Wolf** (1968), he has said, is one of his most personal pieces. Its title refers to an hour at dead of night, and both this and the preceding film are protracted nightmares. The first concerns an actress (Liv Ullman) who has dried up, suffers a breakdown and finally turns to her nurse (Bibi Andersson), finding in her a mirror image. The film is of complex structure – partly in its choice of images – but its theme is simple: if we look too deeply at ourselves, or the world, the awfulness of both are such that they are intolerable to all but those able to turn away or find someone with whom to hide.

Johan Borg (von Sydow) tries to turn away in *Hour of the Wolf*, and he still has a nervous breakdown. In resuming the themes of *Ansiktet*, Bergman does so with bile, allowing the film to move nearer to Fellini in that no distinction can be drawn between reality and fantasy. Borg speaks for Bergman the artist in making a statement on his fears for his own creativity and his response to the society which has made an outcast of him: 'Nothing is self-evident in what I create – except the compulsion to create it . . . I feel megalomania waft about me, but I think I am immune.'

The Rite (1969) is a dissertation on Bergman's commitment to his art, his fellow artists and his audience – and the three actors undergoing examination by a judge are all aspects of himself. This is a jape, made for television in nine days, and Bergman has said of it that he is equipped with his own angels and devils. This time we cannot share them – perhaps because this was for television, and he did not care whether audiences understood or responded.

On either side of this minor piece he made the two films with which, at last, he takes his place as one of the great creative figures of this century. The title of **The Shame** (1968) refers to the experience of war, and its effect on people; it may also

refer to Sweden's traditional neutrality. Though the specific war is a civil one, and it is probably taking place in Sweden. The couple (Liv Ullman, von Sydow) whose fortunes we follow are called Rosenberg, which may not be a Jewish name in Sweden, but Bergman knows that to the world it is Jewish. They are concert violinists who became farmers when the war destroyed their living. As the conflict spreads to the remote island where they live, they are confronted with the multitude of shaming experiences that war can bring: from the inability to act in the name of humanity and the uselessness of any artistic credo in such circumstances, through the humiliation of killing, of compromising, of being forced to suffer propaganda . . . to the experience of sitting and waiting in an office in an overcoat. As they drift out to sea, in the end, with dead bodies floating around them, the wife speaks of a dream and says, 'I knew I ought to remember something that someone said – but I've forgotten what it was.'

This finale is used as a dream sequence in **A Passion** (1969), also known as *The Passion of Anna*, but then this film abounds in references to his other films, be it repeated names – Vergérus, Andreas, Winkelman – or the same Vietnam War report watched on television in *Persona*. The setting is the same desolate island of the last few films, and the countryside is uneasy, this time due to a maniac who attacks animals at night, to kill or to maim. Thus the central plot again takes place against unnatural events, for God's purpose is turned upside down. Eva (Bibi Andersson) says that she thinks she believes in Him, but she would not instruct her children to believe – a statement which is an urgent, unspoken desire for the Manifestation of God, as if that might put an end to the unhappy writhings and strivings. If Bergman's films are about the implacable silence of God, they are also a quest for the meaning of existence. At first sight, Winkelman (von Sydow) is a happy man, and Anna (Liv Ullman) is more immediately unhappy: starting a relationship, they are contrasted with a happily married couple, Elis (Erland Josephson) and Eva – but she is rootless and more deeply disturbed than she first appears. As the relationships deteriorate – even more painfully than those in the earlier films –

Ingmar Bergman: The Quest for Understanding

Liv Ullman and Max von Sydow in *A Passion*, with which Bergman confirmed his position as one of the greatest of contemporary directors – if not the greatest of all. Those who have followed his career with enthusiasm might be permitted to say that it is in decline, for this film has been succeeded by a number of lesser works; but such is its stature that they were almost inevitably lesser.

the lies grow larger, the undiscussed matters more menacing, the sense of needless waste and loss more overpowering. Winkelman, at one point a man caught by vultures, is finally free but lonely – aimless, stricken, not knowing which way to turn.

We may conclude that Winkelman is Bergman, to the extent that both believe in 'complications which will bring on mental disturbances which will bring on, in their turn, physical and psychical violence.' It is notable that at this time he only used von Sydow when his leading male character was sympathetic (at other times he used Kulle and Björnstrand), but that he rarely made him appear twice in the same guise. Interviewed on film, during the film, von Sydow tells us, the audience, that he has difficulty playing a man without expression – which is plainly untrue, both as regards the character and his own magnificent acting ability. The other three players are equally enigmatic, but the film itself is not. The allusions are there to grasp, while Bergman's technical mastery was by now extraordinary. 'What is this deadly poison which corrodes all of us?' cries Andersson, 'leaving only the shell' – which may be an expression of Bergman's personal dilemmas. If so, it was having the reverse effect on his work.

The Touch (1971) furthers this examination of the loneliness and littleness of man, though it also has affinities with the mood and theme of some of his early films, when some people did come

together, did try to achieve love and did then fail. A woman (Bibi Andersson) is only middlingly happy with her very nice husband (von Sydow), so it is easy for a foreign-born archaeologist (Elliott Gould) to come between them. He, David, is a Jew born in Germany and brought up in the U.S. Like the woman's husband, he is a kind man, and it is possible that the woman allows herself to be destroyed by him because, like Sweden, she remains neutral to the suffering of those around her – specifically that of her husband. She seems unaware of any predicament other than the mechanics and ruses involved in committing adultery. For the first time since *Summer with Monika* Bergman is not generous towards his heroine. His obvious fondness for the von Sydow character may be a valediction, since Erland Josephson would, from the next film onward, replace this actor as Bergman's chief male protagonist (as long as he remained in Sweden); and the film's attitude towards the Gould character is to the end undefined. The presence of Gould did not bring the attention or the audiences that the film deserved – despite the fact that its largely English dialogue is both apposite and idiomatic. American producers had been offering Bergman backing in exchange for world rights, and he had always turned them down, but he relented, and this was a co-production with ABC television, during its brief foray into making films for cinemas. It is also Bergman's second consecutive film in colour, which he would use henceforth.

Earlier, the success of *The Silence* had caused United Artists to make a deal to handle world rights for the next few films, a happy proposition for Svensk Filmindustri; but as the films involved had successively less appeal to the American art-house audience, the arrangement had come to an end with *The Shame*. As I have implied, the fluctuations of Bergman's reputation have been constant throughout his career, and I believe that to be because many critics failed to respond to or recognise the demands he made upon them. With the exceptions of *Now About All These Women* and *The Rite* he made what are to me a series of masterpieces between 1962 and 1971 – beginning with *Winter Light* and ending with *The Touch*, seven films in all. Yet it was the reception accorded **Cries and Whispers** (1972) that raised Bergman's reputation to the plateau on which it has remained since. The 'cries and whispers' of this family portrait are the usual preoccupations, but compared with the last few films this is chamber music to their tone poems – exquisitely wrought, but flawed. It is set at the turn of the century, with the past aspirations and present fantasies inexorably mixed; but sequences involving lesbian incest and sexual mutilation verge on self-parody.

It would have been surprising had Bergman not been drained after his great films, and perhaps significantly he worked in television for the next few years, where matters are usually dealt with on a smaller scale. He himself was fascinated by the technology of television. When asked years later whether his work could be seen as a force for social change he said 'Honestly, no', adding that he believed that television had usurped the cinema's position in this respect. His attitude does, I think, explain the nature of his subsequent films, since he observed that the cinema could help in personal matters: 'It is the director's job above all to reach out and touch people.' This is also true of his work for television.

Bergman wrote and directed two television series, the first of which he compared to 'Winnie the Pooh': A. A. Milne wrote his stories and found the world buying them, and 'it was the same with this. I wrote it just for fun and didn't know what to do with it.' Both series were shown in cinemas in different versions which we shall look at in a moment, but we should first note his production of **The Magic Flute** (1975), which was also released to cinemas. It is a small-scale delight, less theatrical than many screen versions of stage pieces, if using artifice to achieve the necessary magic but with the music as the unifying force.

Bergman also wrote a play for television, 'The Lie' – written in fact for Eurovision, which meant that it was telecast simultaneously in local productions in most of the Western democracies. It was an attempt to find the truth about a disintegrating marriage, and that is the subject also of **Scenes from a Marriage** (1974), which is not remotely like 'Winnie the Pooh'. Bergman has also said of it that it is very private, and we may suppose it to

be a distillation of personal experience. It should more aptly be titled 'Scenes from a Divorce', since after a long discussion on the complacency involved in a happy marriage it moves to even longer sequences of anguish and hurt. As played by Liv Ullman (who had lived with Bergman and borne his child) and Josephson, this couple, nice at heart, are stripped emotionally and, more cruelly, ethically before our eyes: the result is very much like a public expiation.

While planning **Face to Face** (1976) Bergman found himself suffering from anxieties which he could not pinpoint, so that there are parallels with his own life in this study of a psychiatrist (Ullman) moving towards a nervous breakdown. He sent a letter to members of his unit explaining that though the film concerned his usual subjects – life, death and love – he wanted to be more rigorous than usual. Without being as accessible as *Scenes from a Marriage* it is less baroque and allusive than the films which precede the two television series: in those Bergman seems to be speaking for humanity, but in these merely for himself. There are nevertheless enthralling sequences in *Face to Face*, notably Ullman's dreams, those of a would-be suicide, and her breakdown itself; but the inclusion of male homosexuality would seem to have been made as the one form of emotional behaviour with which Bergman had not previously dealt. It is surprising to find this humanitarian depicting the prancing, preening gays of films like *La Dolce Vita* (q.v.), and though they are supposed to be counterbalanced by the kindly professor (Josephson) the character is poorly defined. When the psychiatrist accuses him of wanting to seduce her, she is making one of the least of her mistakes, but a significant one, for she of all people is expected to understand emotional responses. Her failure to cope with herself means that the film is a variation on 'Physician, heal thyself', and we may see it as a cry of frustration on Bergman's part: for, like her, he was better equipped than most – after years of public psychoanalysis in his work – to expunge his personal devils and yet was still unable to do so.

Scenes from a Marriage was a six-part T.V. series cut to a movie of 168 minutes, that is, it contained just over half the original material. *Face to Face* was a four-part serial, but after the acceptance of the earlier film in theatres, its cinema version was prepared simultaneously. More debatably, it was shown abroad in some countries in an English version, with Bergman's consent (he had for years controlled the English titles of his films), but to no particular commercial advantage. At least Ullman and Josephson spoke their own lines, in rhythm to the original image, so the dubbing was less barbarous than usual. Bergman had been offered backing by Dino de Laurentiis in Hollywood, and his next film was made in English in conjunction with that producer, but under very different circumstances. In 1976 Bergman had been literally hauled out of the theatre in which he was working for alleged tax offences, and his passport was confiscated: while waiting for the necessary public apology he went into self-imposed exile. With the backing of de Laurentiis, he had his choice of the major film-making countries; he chose Germany, and the resulting film, on Germany in the Twenties, was one he had long contemplated. The leading characters of **The Serpent's Egg** (1977) are trapeze artists, indicating once again the influence of *Varieté* – and the film also contains several none-too-oblique references to Lang's *Dr Mabuse* films. Many reviewers raised the name of Kafka, and those who disliked the film mentioned *Cabaret* (q.v.); indeed, the stage version of that musical may have provided Bergman's starting point of a society drifting, inert, unaware. Both Manuela (Ullman) and Abel (David Carradine) are aliens, he the more so as an American Jew, and it is hard to understand why they remain in a Berlin increasingly hostile and potentially lethal for them. The nightmare eventually depends too much on *Caligari*. In fact the plot is rigged – to an extent unknown in Bergman since *Ansiktet* – and, as if this were a horror film, flesh is made to creep. Still, Bergman does transcend his material, if only once, when Abel goes berserk at the notion that it is because he is Jewish that he is (falsely) accused of several murders. At that moment Bergman reveals an understanding of the resentment that some Jews may feel at being Jews; and throughout he has a view of the Germans, who, with the possible exception of the inspector (Gert Froebe), emerge as a most unpleasant nation. Büchner's comment 'Man is an abyss and I turn giddy when I look down in it' was quoted by Bergman to justify the film, and if he had used it as a foreword he might have avoided the many unfavourable reviews he received.

Perhaps the strain of making films for over thirty years was beginning to tell: he had worked at the rate of one a year, with an intensity unknown in any other artist working in this medium. By this time he no longer pretended – if pretence it was – that his films were a summer diversion between his more serious winter work in the theatre, directing other people's plays. It would have been miraculous if he could have stayed at his highest level – miraculous if he could continue to dig deeply into himself every time. If the strain were to show, it would be preferable in an 'entertainment' rather than in one of the more personal films. **Autumn Sonata** (1978) is not personal, inasmuch as it was a vehicle for Ingrid Bergman, keeping a promise made to her some years earlier. Nevertheless, the customary themes are present – in his own words, 'the presence and absence of love, the longing for love, love's lies, love that is deformed and love that is our sole chance of survival.' The film's mother-daughter relationship springs from Bergman's feeling that this is a subject neglected by both literature and the cinema, but at the core of the piece is an argument on the consequences of choice – as experienced by a woman (Miss

Ingrid Bergman and Liv Ullman in one of Bergman's later and comparatively more mellow films, *Autumn Sonata*. Miss Bergman in her memoirs revealed the extent to which it uncomfortably reflected her own life and how the strong wills of herself and the director almost ground the project to a halt before shooting started. In the event all concerned found the filming a rewarding experience – as did audiences when they saw it.

Bergman) who put her career as a concert pianist before her children. The script is largely a duologue between mother and daughter (Liv Ullman), and after a mellow opening, promising reflection rather than dissension, the bitterness seems occasionally contrived. But there is a distinctive mood, unlike that of any other Bergman film, and the acting alone makes its thoughtfulness absorbing. Ullman is a great actress under Bergman's direction, and Ingrid Bergman, in her native tongue, emphasises how rarely her American films allowed her to display the full extent of her talent.

Aus dem Leben der Marionetten (1980), made in German, strikingly demonstrates Bergman's weaknesses when making a film for its own sake. *The Serpent's Egg* represented the first time that he had dealt extensively with crime (if we except *This Can't Happen Here*, a secret-agent thriller made 'for money' in 1950, which he declines to regard as one of his films), and this one begins with a particularly horrible crime: a successful fortyish businessman (Robert Atzorn) has murdered a prostitute and then committed anal intercourse upon the body. It is no surprise to discover that the cause is a latent homosexuality, as in *Il Conformista* (q.v.), among other films, and when the reason for this is revealed as being in his childhood, with an accompanying final shot of a boyhood toy, *Citizen Kane* springs inevitably to mind. Like *Kane*, this film is an investigation into the man's character and an analysis of his actions – a theme derived (at least) from Dostoevsky, but dealt with much in recent films, notably Imamura's *Vengeance Is Mine* (q.v.). Imamura's particular obsession with appearance and reality has also occupied Bergman, who here handles the series of interviews, examinations, dreams and reminiscences with a virtuosity which at least is not dependent on other films. The factors which prevent the man from recognising his homosexuality – a strict upbringing, a successful social life with his wife – suggest a more repressed time, earlier in the century. Bergman has certainly chosen a perverse way to acknowledge the bisexuality in all of us, and the counterbalancing figure of the gay man – the wife's partner and confidant – is no more satisfactory than the one in *Face to Face*. The actors concerned, like the screenplay, fail to convey the essence of the Bergman we have come to know through the artistry of Malmsten, von Sydow and Josephson – but, frankly, apart from the *angst*, I cannot find Bergman in this film. He had hitherto given more of himself than we had any right to expect, but by the same token we had not asked it of him.

The film was poorly received, meaning that only one of Bergman's three 'foreign' films could be counted a success. The Swedish government having apologised to him, he returned to make **Fanny and Alexander** (1982), with money provided by the Swedish Film Institute and the French company, Gaumont. As an expensive production, it was pre-sold to television in a five-hour version; the three-hour one available to cinemas shows Bergman again at his best. In the words of Derek Malcolm, 'It is a summing up devoid of all *angst*, but full of the old magician's most attractive tricks . . . drawing on the mastery of a lifetime'. The film starts with a family Christmas in 1907, perhaps influenced by *Il Gattopardo* (q.v.), for it celebrates a way of life, with no incident unrecorded. The Ekdahl's are an extrovert theatrical family, loving the good things in life, including food and sex; when one of its members dies, his widow (Ewa Fröling) remarries into a family which is the reverse – and the two young children of the title find life cruel. The new husband is a bishop, so here is the opposite side of the Swedish character – puritanical, spiritual, repressed, authoritarian. The children are spirited away by an ageing Jewish ex-lover (Erland Josephson) of their grandmother's, and with him appears the third influence on Swedish life and Bergman's work, also providing stimulus – the foreign and the fantastical. It is in this context – the old man and his nephews – that Bergman refers to *Wild Strawberries, Ansiktet* and *Persona*; the strain here is of the outsider, the one that moves between the other two, capable of profundity and yet unreal. Perhaps that is Bergman's final message, that he has spoken but we are not to take his words too seriously.

The Josephson character has something of Prospero, still capable of magic but intending to retire: perhaps this way, caught between the secular and the religious, Bergman wants us to remember him – for he had announced that this

957

would be his last film and was quoted (by *The Times*, London) as saying that the Bergman era was over – I trust with a sense of humour. It is doubtful whether most of us have thought of the past forty years in these terms, since he has been the least influential among great film-makers – because he is the most personal.

Nevertheless he overshadowed his Swedish colleagues, though Arne Sucksdorff (b.1917) enjoyed a brief degree of international fame. A former photographer, he had written, directed, photographed and edited some short documentaries, including **A Divided World** (1948), a study of the savagery of forest animals. He returned to this theme in the feature-length **The Great Adventure** (1953), though it is peripheral to the central story of a small boy and his pet otter. It enchanted one generation – admittedly a generation to whom animal documentaries meant either complete lack of imagination or Disney's jazzed-up 'True Life Adventures', but today the blending of fact and fiction looks very contrived. Though working deftly with colour, wide screen and stereophonic sound, **The Flute and the Arrow** (1957) was merely a hackneyed tale of a tiger which threatens an Indian village, and **My Home Is Copacabana** (1965) was a completely artificial study of homeless children in Rio de Janeiro. Indeed, Sucksdorff seemed to confirm the invalidity of the semi-documentary in comparison with fiction told with the insight that de Sica brought to *Sciuscià*.

Earlier, only a few people outside Sweden went to see **The Pram** (1962), the story of a girl and boy who make love too soon and pay the consequences; or **Raven's End** (1963), the tale of an adolescent growing up in the depressed Sweden of the Thirties. But Bo Widerberg (b.1930) achieved world fame with **Elvira Madigan** (1967), a remake of an earlier film and based on a true case towards the end of the last century, when an aristocratic soldier (Thommy Berggren) ran off with a circus tightrope walker (Pia Degermark). In the film they spend an idyllic summer, haunted by the plangent second movement of Mozart's 21st Piano Concerto (which made the hit parade as 'The Theme from *Elvira Madigan*'). Then their money runs out and they are reduced to

subsisting on berries. The film is visually exquisite, but, as George Cukor once observed, 'The moment you're aware of something, like the photography is great, it usually means something else is lacking.' Widerberg may be the most guilty of all current practitioners – certainly of those drawn to the more serious issues. **Adalen 31** (1969) and **The Ballad of Joe Hill** (1971) respectively concern a strike and strike breakers in a small Northern town in the early Thirties, and the Swedish immigrant (Berggren) who became one of America's early labour martyrs. Both are unsuitably pretty – which would matter less if Widerberg paid as much attention to the script as to the photography. He dumps an inadequate number of facts before us, and, with an abrupt statement, assumes that he has our sympathy because he is on the side of the people.

His friend and contemporary, Jan Troell (b.1931), has also been disappointing, after his beautifully realised first feature, **Here Is Your Life** (1966), which he adapted from Eyvind Johansson's novel about a boy growing up in the earlier years of this century. The boy goes from pillar to post, and he is the usual wistful, weak adolescent of such films, so that this picaresque story is of little originality; but the discoveries of adolescence have seldom been as sympathetically portrayed. Continuing his theme of an unsatisfactory life in **Who Saw Him Die?** (1967), a schoolteacher (Per Oscarsson) is unable to control his pupils, and Troell is as indecisive as his principal character. That he was happiest with images was borne out by **The Immigrants** (1971) and **The New Land** (1972), a two-part story of a Swedish couple (Ullman, von Sydow) and their adventures in America – and significantly it was only in the two countries concerned that the films were liked. Troell's American film, **Zandy's Bride** (1974), with Liv Ullman, was admired nowhere.

Bergman himself helped to produce **Summer Paradise** (1977). It was directed by Gunnel Lindblom, one of his actresses, who collaborated on the script with Bergman's former associate, Ulla Isaksson, on whose novel it is based. Centred on a middle-aged woman doctor (Birgitta Valberg), it examines both her not too satisfactory life and the members of her family during their summer vacation. The influence of Bergman lies no heavier on it than on other Swedish films, including those of the Finnish-born Jörn Donner (b.1933), who has written and lectured on Bergman, and who is married to Harriet Andersson. She and Berggren were the stars of Donner's first feature, **A Sunday in September** (1963), a study of marriage in its year of disintegration. This may have been the first non-pornographic film to show a couple in the act of copulation – if only from the waist up – but that guaranteed it few audiences outside Sweden.

And that brings us full circle, for apart from Bergman, the Swedish cinema continues to mean sex and gloom – though since 1963, or thereabouts, most nations have been producing their own sex films, and they are not interested in importing the gloom. The Scandinavian cinema as a whole has inclined towards rustic tales of everyday rape, only too often reminiscent of 'Cold Comfort Farm'. Also, since the populations of the four Scandinavian countries are comparatively small, so are the audiences and hence chances for filmmakers. Almost certainly the best Finnish film of this time, and probably ever, is **The Unknown Soldier** (1955), the tale of men at the Front during the Winter War of 1940. Its theme is their adaptability. Edvin Laine's direction is notable for its honesty and integrity no matter how much he may have borrowed from some famous war films and no matter that the narrative is weak and the steady tempo monotonous.

During this period Carl Dreyer made three films in Denmark (and one in Sweden, which seems to have disappeared), all adapted from plays: **Day of Wrath** (1944), **Ordet** (1954) and **Gertrud** (1964), and as offered, all entirely trivial. Poor Dreyer simply forgot how to direct in his decades between films. His admirers may invoke 'integrity' to excuse the paucity of his work, but he is plainly incapable of bringing his characters to life, or sustaining any degree of narrative force or rhythm; furthermore it was foolish to choose such blatant melodramas for which he clearly had no conviction. *Day of Wrath* is about seventeenth-century witch hunts, and *Gertrud* is Ibsen-and-water – from a play by Soderberg, a contemporary of Ibsen – clearly bereft of his intellectual fibre and his gift for plot. *Ordet* is another

matter: the subject is merely listless. But it was powerful enough in Molander's 1943 Swedish version – in which Sjöström played the paterfamilias, the rural Montague who, for religious reasons, refuses to allow his son to marry into the Capulets. The creator of this conceit was Kaj Munk, a Danish country parson, and the title means 'The Word' – *i.e.* the word of God. Both Bergman and Sjöström in their films felt the need to have God speak to them – an importunity which seems to be a quintessentially Scandinavian preoccupation.

The Swedishness of both Bergman and Sjöström we have already noted, and Bergman's debt to Sjöström, but whereas these two turned it to triumphant account, it has inhibited their fellow film-makers – most seriously those of Bergman's own generation and after. They seem to feel that there must be seriousness of purpose and seriousness of manner, which often results in a commonplace view of the mundane at a snail's pace. There is also a certain coldness, as if the directors at heart disliked the characters they are offering to us. So, perhaps, does Bergman; and though interviews indicate a cheery and good-natured man, his films would seem to intimate that he is disenchanted with himself. If so, he has turned that concept to magnificent, magisterial account.

He is unquestionably among the greatest film-makers, though that may be seen as a comment on some of the others, since the word 'great' is often applied to those who could better be described as purveyors of good entertainment. Clearly that is no mean achievement, but those whom I think most deserving of our admiration are those who have tried to illuminate our society. Bergman is not the first name that comes to mind in considering films on political abuses, the origins of war or the ills of the deprived, though he has touched on all these matters. He has, instead, cried out against the relationship of the sexes, against the demands society makes upon the artist, and the very nature of God. No one has better expressed our difficulties with each other or with the Deity, in the films that I referred to as masterpieces. But even some of the earlier, relatively journeyman pieces remain as stimulating as when they were first made: his is a unique and astonishing body of work.

35

The Japanese Masters

IT WAS SATYAJIT RAY who pronounced them 'the Japanese masters', and as there are few opportunities to see their films in India, he may have based his assessment on only a few of the titles that we shall be examining in this chapter – which are, in turn, only a small proportion of the total. In this book I have restricted myself in general to those movies shown throughout the world, but the Japanese cinema requires special consideration. Ever since Kurosawa's *Rashomon* appeared in the West – magical harbinger of a mighty film industry – most of his other films have been accessible outside Japan; some of those of Ozu and Mizoguchi have been shown commercially and entered the international repertory, as is true of a handful made by Ichikawa and Kobayashi. These are undoubtedly great film-makers – so good that we may assume that they tower above their confrères, tantalisingly unknown to most of us. Yet festivals and retrospectives arranged by such bodies as the Japan Film Council have indicated that Japan's cinema heritage is one of the richest in the world. For instance, Heinosuke Gosho made over one hundred films, not one of which has been shown commercially in the West: yet the few that I have seen demonstrate a skill and perception the equal of his internationally acclaimed colleagues. Further, the country's decorative tradition is so strong that even the most plodding of its film-makers is capable of work of a satisfying visual beauty. I am therefore going to discuss most of the Japanese films that I have seen.

I cannot imagine any true lover of the cinema missing an opportunity to see any Japanese film of the Fifties or early Sixties made in the wide-screen process – whether in colour or black and white. Unlike most Western directors, those in Japan mastered the new width immediately, deftly adhering to the graphic tradition of the *makimon* (i.e. the scroll paintings which unroll horizontally). The wide screen did not arrive – as in the West – at a time of desperation, for television did not become a threat to Japanese cinemas until the late Sixties; moreover, it came into use at a time when the country's leading directors were experimenting with film form. They did not think of themselves as innovators, and as soon as any new narrative form was introduced – as, say, the intercutting of past and present – it was immediately adopted by others. These film-makers considered themselves artists, still rigidly applying the rules of master-pupil relationships to themselves and their assistants or followers, but they were realistic enough to consider their own needs subservient to those of the industry as a whole. Audiences, unlike most of those in other countries, recognised the director as a factor when choosing the evening's entertainment, but the studios were sufficiently powerful to control even the most famous. There were constant pressures to maintain budgets and schedules, so that in the peak year of 1956 the industry produced 514 films. It says much for the Japanese temperament that under these factory conditions a number of outstanding films resulted – and the Japanese cinema of this period can be seen as one of the most impressive in the history of this industry. As we can date the major creative eras of other national industries, so this one begins *circa* 1950: then, as the major directors of this magnificent decade aged, so in the Sixties the quality declined. Their achievement may not be known outside

Japan, but many of them are among the greatest ever to work in the medium.

Some of the accolades for the later films of Yasujiro Ozu are, however, ill judged. By the time he and the century were in their early fifties his style had become ossified, and his camera, stationed knee-high at distances from four to six feet from the actors, *never* moved; worse, he appeared to be making the same film again and again. Nevertheless, his first two postwar films are very fine, reminiscent of his most reflective and delicate earlier work, stories of the poor and deprived told without sentimentality. Both **The Record of a Tenement Gentleman** (1947) and **A Hen in the Wind** (1948) deal with situations current throughout the country and many parts of Europe at the time, where daily life had been disrupted by the War. Respectively they deal with a child left homeless by the War, and the wife (Kinuyo Tanaka) whose husband returns to be confronted by her wartime infidelity. Despite the title and the fact that the tenement gentleman is played by Chishu Ryu – who remained Ozu's favourite interpreter – the central situation of the first film chiefly concerns a crusty old lady whose heart is melted by the boy. In the second, the wife prefers the pavement to the bread-line: the film makes clear that there was no government provision for the wives of soldiers who were missing, still trying to make their way home from those parts of the mainland where they had once been conquerors. Nevertheless, both films border upon nineteenth-century traditions of melodrama which Japanese cinema seemed reluctant to relinquish.

Late Spring (1949) is based on a story by Kazuo Hirotsu, and it must have been the tale for which Ozu had been searching all his life – for he remade it, with variations, many times. After a lapse of fifteen years he was reunited with Kogo Noda, who earlier had contributed to some of his screenplays; thereafter they collaborated on each of Ozu's films. Both this and **The Munekata Sisters** (1950) are unusual among his work, since they are not based on original screenplays, and in both cases Ozu found it difficult to cope with the author's intention and the moulding of it to his own interpretation. Yet, working thereafter from his own material, characters and situations became increasingly

two-dimensional. He also began to slacken his pace – most of his late films are over two hours long – and audiences can pick up his points faster than he realised. Both these films look at the marriage plans of young people and their impact on the family; and it is not too much to say that virtually the only difference between *Late Spring* and **Early Summer** (1951) is that the latter is thirty minutes longer and Mr Ryu plays Setsuko Hara's brother instead of her father.

It was not until **The Flavour of Green Tea over Rice** (1952) that Ozu eventually expressed an opinion on arranged marriages, by contrasting a middle-aged marriage grown stale with the attitude of the wife's niece, who resists the idea of the *o-miai* – the formal introduction to the chosen fiancé. Both in this film and **Tokyo Story** (1953) Ozu's feeling for people trapped in their environment is much revitalised, in the latter instance perhaps because of a change of subject: a middle-aged couple visit their children in Tokyo, only to be disillusioned, for they find their children no longer interested in them. But **Early Spring** (1956), another new departure, is lifeless. At least, it is not so much a new departure as a return to the studies of office life he made so brilliantly many years before: they had been shot in two weeks, and it is probably significant that he laboured three years over this. It was made under the influence of Kurosawa's *Living* (q.v.), and was clearly meant to be a definite statement on the life of an

The later films of Yasijuro Ozu give a new meaning to the expression 'much of a muchness', but his first two postwar films are remarkable. Both concern contemporary problems, *A Hen in the Wind* being specifically about a soldier's wife (Kinuyo Tanaka) who, having received no money from her husband during his absence, resorts to prostitution to pay the hospital bills of her small son. She sins but once, but is too honest not to tell her husband (Shuji Sano) when he returns – and, clearly, the matter causes a rift between them.

961

ordinary clerk. He said, 'I wanted to show the life of a man with such a job . . . his hopes for the future gradually dissolving, his realising that, even though he has worked for years, he has accomplished nothing . . . It is the longest of my postwar films, but I tried to avoid anything that would be dramatic and to collect only casual scenes of everyday life, hoping in doing so that the audience would feel the sadness of this kind of life.'

His own life may have been sad. He never married and lived with his mother all his life, so that these films about fathers might be a wish-fulfilment. Significantly – as in the case of several other directors who have worked out their fantasies or problems on film (Bergman is the outstanding example) – he has chosen the same actor, Chishu Ryu, to be his mouthpiece. Increasingly in these late films Ryu may be seen drinking with cronies in bars – for long sequences – pondering on their relationships with their children and the meaning of marriage. When, in contrast, the father has less admirable qualities, as in **Equinox Flower** (1958), Ozu's first film in colour, he is played by Shin Saburi. This film and **Tokyo Twilight** (1957) do glance at subjects other than arranged marriages, and **Ohayo**/*Good Morning* (1959) providentially focuses on a small suburban community and in particular on the two young boys in one family.

All these films, with the exception of *The Munekata Sisters*, produced by Toho, were made by Ozu for Shochiku, but a move to Daiei for one film only, **Floating Weeds** (1959), proved refreshing. This remake of his tersely constructed early film about tensions in a theatrical troupe is now much too long – and also unconvincing – but there are compensations, especially in the picture-postcard views that constitute his style on location. Daieicolor is a great improvement on the Agfacolor Ozu had been using, and instead of his usual photographer, Yushan Atsuta, he has Kazuo Miyagawa, who did amazing work with Kurosawa, Mizoguchi and Kobayashi. On the other hand, Ozu's last three films resume his old preoccupations, with an increasing staleness: **Late Autumn** (1960), **The End of Summer** (1961) and **An Autumn Afternoon** (1962). As the titles indicate, his integrity has now been combined with melancholy;

his formal visual style may still be deceptively subtle, but if we knew him only through these films we might regard him as a cold, academic director. Only rarely do we glimpse the marvellous observer of his Silent films – he had become either timid or obsessed to the point of eccentricity – but seeing his faithful players for the last time – Mr Ryu, Saburi and Miss Hara – is like saying goodbye to old friends.

If Ozu's vision contracted as he aged, the reverse is true of his contemporaries, though that has less to do with ageing than with the War. At a time when the country was at its most militaristic, a significant number of Japanese film-makers were trying to express humanist values. There is, I think, a schism in the Japanese character, a dichotomy – on the one hand there is the mentality which led to the conflict in the Pacific, and on the other the concern for human life and values which is reflected in virtually every Japanese film. Both may usually be found in the *jidai-geki*, or historical subjects, using the one to point up the other. Those film-makers who had attempted to criticise the regime felt themselves justified by its complete collapse, but they now had to consider the whole experience of War, the atomic bomb, defeat and Occupation. Mizoguchi said that his postwar films represented the working-off of 'a sense of resentment' which had been accumulating during the War, and even today these films remain astonishing (it was not till the Seventies that work of the immediate postwar period was seen in the West). As in the prewar years, he and his colleagues were still subject to the dictates of a military mentality – in this case those of the Americans, who as the occupying force, were quite definite about the films which the Japanese could and could not make. Subjects concerning rehabilitation and the democratisation of Japanese life were likely to be acceptable, but certain to meet with disapproval were any which glorified the military, the Empire and outmoded codes of honour. If we refer again to the prewar Japanese cinema, we can see that these rules did not put too heavy a burden on the best film-makers; they often met the challenge with great honesty and a searing power.

Mizoguchi's first postwar film was **The Victory of Women** (1946), hastily made for Shochiku, which needed product. The company had no other directors at its Ofuna studio and Mizoguchi worked from an already prepared script by Kogo Noda and Kaneto Shindo. It centres on the personal and professional relations between Hiroko (Kinuyo Tanaka), a female lawyer, and her Fascist-minded brother-in-law, also a lawyer. He was responsible for her fiancé's wartime sentence as a political prisoner, and now they are to fight in court, she as the counsel for defence, over a poor woman who has accidentally strangled her baby. Hiroko believes the responsibility for this act lies with the armaments manufacturer who had sacked the woman's husband, so it is clear that the film has a moral tone acceptable to the American authorities. (It also has an inconclusive ending which alone would put it ahead of most contemporary Occidental films.)

The Americans also approved of the fact that the chief protagonist was a woman in a profession usually associated with men, and Mizoguchi's next two films, **Five Women Around Utamaro** (1946) and **The Love of Sumako the Actress** (1947) are also about the emancipation of women. Yoshikata Yoda, reunited with Mizoguchi, wrote them under rather difficult conditions, since both are *jidai-geki* subjects, to which the Americans were opposed. However after much tampering with the scripts it was decided that, on the whole, the films would be beneficial. Both are biographical, but at the opposite end of the scale to such concurrent Hollywood products as *Devotion* and *Song of Love*. The painter Utamaro is portrayed as a man of the people with a modern attitude towards the rights of women; and Sumako was the actress who first played Ibsen's Nora in Japan. Despite Mizoguchi's training as an artist and his work with actors neither film is particularly strong on the artistic process, and *Sumako* is at its boldest in the relationship between the actress (Miss Tanaka) and her married professor (So Yamamura). *Utamaro* at least reflects its subject matter in being exquisitely beautiful, and contains memorable portraits both of the artistic life of Tokyo in the eighteenth century and of Mizoguchi himself – for Yoda based his characterisation of Utamaro on him.

On the other hand, **Women of the Night** (1948) is a cry of pain: like *Sciuscià*

and *Paisà* it is an unreasoned, instinctive outburst, blaming the War for the current chaos in the cities, yet aware that War should have blown the old system away. The first impression is of an unsettled population, struggling to survive, uncertain where loved ones are or whether they are alive; and some, haunting the bomb sites looking for pick-ups, are both desperate and vicious. When, at the beginning, the heroine (Kinuyo Tanaka) is told by an old crone that there are other ways to survive than by selling clothes, we are aware that the plot-line will be much like the German prostitute films of the Twenties (made also by a country in defeat). But this is not like them, nor like Mizoguchi's own geisha films; his vision is darker than it was – moving towards the misanthropy of his later masterpieces – and very much at the centre of the whore's life are such matters as pregnancy and syphilis. When the heroine bitterly talks of infecting her clients in revenge, we are not sure whether it is because her lover has slept with her sister or whether it is because he has given her a venereal disease. The double reasoning and the use of implication were present in Japanese cinema long before they were in ours and it is possible that in this case Mizoguchi avoided a factual statement because he did not wish to sensationalise the subject.

In **My Love Has Been Burning** (1949) the heroine is again played by Kinuyo Tanaka, and once more she is an exponent of women's rights. She is a liberal, and the film is remarkable as a portrait of society in an age of political turmoil, towards the end of the last century. It centres on a group of activists, with their printing presses, their attempts at solidarity with strikers, their imprisonment and subsequent election to power; but in contrast to his public views, the Westernised hero (Ichiro Sugai) is not so advanced in private, and Miss Tanaka, in an echo of 'A Doll's House', finds herself forced to leave him when she discovers that he has merely 'used' his other mistress. We may also note that it would have been extraordinary in a Western film of the time to hear a woman say that she enjoyed sex. Yoda and Shindo wrote it, from a story by Kogo Noda based on an autobiography by Hideko Kageyama, and it was Mizoguchi's last film for Shochiku, who had refused to back *The Life of*

O-Haru (q.v.). Shintoho agreed to do so, provided that Mizoguchi would first direct **Portrait of Madame Yuki** (1950), based on a popular novel. Madame Yuki (Michiyo Kogure) is an aristocrat, married to an uncouth, somewhat older man (Rijiro Yanagi) who flaunts his mistress before her: that she cannot bring herself to leave him is almost certainly due to sexual attraction. The film has an exceptionally beautiful end – as the camera tracks back and forth across the lake we are aware of a suicide – but it is essentially a hollow tale.

While waiting to make *O-Haru*, which was to be the first of his masterpieces, Mizoguchi made one very good film, **Miss Oyu** (1951), and another that is almost a great one – **The Lady from Musashino** (1951). The latter, set during the last days of the War, has a line to the effect that that event was caused by a panicky government in conjunction with mentalities left over from the Meiji period. *Miss Oyu*, set in the Twenties, is an examination of the effect of such mentalities on three people – a man and two women – whose defiance of the feudal laws governing sex and marriage leads to the destruction of their relationship. *Musashino* centres on a group of friends, scrutinising them like flies in amber in a way that recalls Virginia Woolf. They are worldly people but struggling for identity, voluntarily and involuntarily hurting each other as they try to settle emotional problems which are beyond their understanding. It is a rare achievement in cinema – one which Bergman later managed, but with a Nordic intensity rather than the elegiac feeling with which Mizoguchi endows the subject here. Later, Ray was also successful, and, in a different fashion, Antonioni (q.v.) – but before them Mizoguchi and his compatriots were using an allusive style then unknown in Western cinema.

Mizoguchi himself thought this film 'didn't quite work' because it dealt with too many themes – among them the uncertainties of the postwar world, the break-up of family life, the responsibility of arms manufacturers and the personal dilemma of a professor who is, significantly, an authority on Stendhal. It is the best of Mizoguchi's contemporary films, marred only by the ending – which, as is so often the case with this director, involves a suicide; moreover, in this instance it is only too predictable. The Musashino of the title is a region near Tokyo much loved by two of the characters, and we see it through their eyes. This is an example of style and content in perfect cohesion.

Mizoguchi's mature style first became apparent in *Utamaro*. That was the first time he had gone further back in history than the Meiji period, but the world portrayed was fundamentally tranquil and his treatment selective. Before the War, in *Oyuki the Virgin*, with its background of turmoil, he had used a more probing camera, and *My Love Has Been Burning* was another Meiji drama which required a style to match the turbulence of a time when violence, rape and revolt were apparently common occurrences. The camera sweeps up, past and down on crowds and groupings, whereas in *Miss Oyu* he returned to what we might call his contemplative style. There, his people are found in medium or long-shot, often still, in pools of light; he lingers on a moonlit garden, on the shimmering waters of a lake, mists rising from the fields. The two styles coalesce marvellously in Mizoguchi's four masterpieces, **The Life of O-Haru** (1952), **Ugetsu Monogatari** (1953), **Sansho Dayu** (1954) and **Chikamatsu Monogatari** (1954). These are, simply stated, stories of love and suffering in feudal times. Japan remained an oligarchy well into the last quarter of the nineteenth century, and if three of the four films are set in the early eighteenth century (to the West, of course, an age of elegance) they echo the more remote era of *Sansho Dayu*, set in the eleventh century. The foreword to that film states that it was a time 'when mankind had yet to awaken to his humanity'. The population, especially those people living in rural areas, had to be alert against the depradations of warriors, of marauding armies which could in minutes destroy their livelihood, burn their homes and rape the women. Mizoguchi's disposition led him not to tales of heroism, but to tragedy – except of course that tragedy, by definition, concerns the great – and his people are either the poor professional and merchant classes, or the impoverished nobility, families of disgraced samurai.

These historical tales, adapted for the screen chiefly by Yoda and/or Matsutaro Kawaguchi, have their sources in literature.

Chikamatsu Monogatari is searingly faithful to the then advanced drama by the eponymous eighteenth-century playwright. It lacks the tragic intensity of *Sansho* and *O-Haru*: it is 'Romeo and Juliet' to their 'King Lear', with the lovers thwarted by conditions and circumstances, while the protagonists in the latter films struggle on in a universally hostile and savage world. They struggle because there is hope: 'Compassion is what makes men human,' says the father to the son in *Sansho*. 'Be merciful even at a cost to yourself' (but he may say it because this film is the only one of the four to have its origins in a work of the twentieth century). O-Haru herself and the family in *Sansho* suffer – through deprivation, prostitution, injustice, rape, poverty, war, the ambition and greed of others and, indeed, all that flesh is heir to – but they have hope, compassion and varieties of love to sustain them. We may at times be tempted to think of Chekhov's Trofimov and his two-and-twenty misfortunes; the lot of O-Haru is so miserable that a positive reaction to the film can best be made by considering the content of its fellows.

Chikamatsu, since it is set in a time of peace, is the quietest of the quartet, and *Ugetsu* perhaps the most remarkable, since it most consistently blends its mysticism and beauty with barbarism and cruelty. It is also the most magical, especially towards the end, when its hero returns home, a Ulysses with hallucinations. When Mizoguchi died, Kurosawa commented that there were very few directors left able to view the past clearly and realistically, and we may add, in all its complexity. These films are richly satisfying experiences and visually magnificent: Mizoguchi's photographer was Kazuo Miyagawa, whose work we noted on *Floating Weeds*. Miyagawa's other films include *Rashomon*, with Kurosawa, and *The Human Condition* (q.v.) with Kobayashi; yet his films with Mizoguchi alone would proclaim him a genius in his field. The leading players in the four films include Kinuyo Tanaka, Masayuki Mori, Machiko Kyo and Eitaro Shindo.

Although **Shin-Heike Monogatari** (1955) and **The Empress Yang Kwei-Fei** (1955) are taken from traditional tales of feudal times, neither is of a similar quality. Kaneto Shindo, in discussing Mizoguchi,

commented that he had poured everything he had into *O-Haru*, and that these two films represented a decline, 'for he was in need of money at that time and was bent upon making some out of his last films'. They are both in (Eastman) colour, and it is perhaps superfluous to say that it is exquisitely used. It may be that Mizoguchi's energies all went into the design, for there is something relatively lifeless in the telling, as if he had no interest in the intrigue which surrounds the main threads of the plot – respectively about the son of a warrior searching for his real father, and an emperor (Mori) whose love for his favourite concubine (Machiko Kyo) is destroyed because of her family's ambition. (The latter, set in China, was a co-production with Hong Kong.)

During these years Mizoguchi made two more films on geisha life, **Gion Festival Music** (1953) and **A Woman of Rumour** (1954), which, while slight, take on added resonance when placed beside the

Unlike Ozu, Kenji Mizoguchi became more interesting as he aged, and just before he died he made some magnificent historical films. *The Life of O-Haru* features Kinuyo Tanaka, who worked for him often during her career. Here she plays a woman buffeted by fate. She is seen with Toshiro Mifune, who pays with his life for daring to fall in love with such a high-born lady.

965

rather better **Street of Shame** (1956), his last film. All three look with regret on the changes in the geisha world and on its downgrading in the years since the War. After the War many geishas became prostitutes, and *Gion* concerns one such (Michiko Kogure) fighting to retain her dignity. The film is not a remake of *Sisters of the Gion*, as has been claimed, but the situation is similar – with the elder geisha, trained in the traditional way, and her younger companion, of more fiery disposition. There are two women in *A Woman of Rumour* and, as in 'Mrs Warren's Profession', they are mother and daughter – the latter, incidentally, modelling herself on Audrey Hepburn. She falls in love with her mother's lover, a young doctor, who does not, in the circumstances, behave as admirably as we had reason to expect. *Street of Shame* has more in common with *Women of the Night*, since it is simply about prostitution. All these films infer, if not state, that these women have chosen their profession out of poverty; that their lives are being destroyed by varying emotional needs and that they will be available as men need them. The garish brothel in *Street of Shame* is called 'Dreamland', and the Yoshiwara we see outside shows the influence of the now departed G.I.s, with its glaring neon signs. Miki (Machiko Kyo), ex-mistress of a G.I., dresses and acts like an American cutie – a striking contrast to the gentle Michiko Kogure in *Gion Festival Music*. Miss Kogure – who was also Mizoguchi's Madam Yuki and is, perhaps, his most enchanting actress – also works in 'Dreamland', but only to support her family. Another inmate (Ayako Wakao) is a cheat and a money hoarder; her attempted murder is as near to violence as any instant in Mizoguchi's contemporary subjects except for *Women of the Night*. Unlike the kindly madam of *A Woman of Rumour*, this one is mercenary and vicious, and the customary male owner, often benevolent in earlier films, is hypocritical and greedy.

The prevailing bitterness in this film is not surprising, for Mizoguchi was a lifelong frequenter of geisha-houses and, as I said earlier, believed that he was therefore responsible for his wife's mental instability; he also knew that he was dying of leukaemia. The film itself is less hermetic than his others on this subject, and it is possible that at a time when Japanese films

were trickling through to the West he thought he could abandon his contemplative style.

Because of its subject matter, *Street of Shame* was seen in London not long after it was finished and in New York three years later. Initially both cities (and hence their respective countries) proved hospitable neither to Mizoguchi nor to Ozu. The first of the latter's films to arrive was *Ohayo*, which was put into commercial distribution in America some seven years after it had been made, and in Britain after another gap of seven years. *The Life of O-Haru* was, in fact, the second postwar Japanese film seen in the West when, following the success of *Rashomon*, it was sent to the Venice Festival in 1952, but it failed to reap the same acclaim. The following year the Japanese selectors submitted a contemporary subject, *Children of Hiroshima* (q.v.). After a festival showing in 1954, one New York distributor launched *Ugetsu* to an indifferent response. However, the French critics, right for once, began to praise Mizoguchi, and within a few years of his death in 1956, he became an established name in Paris art cinemas. In 1962, when the British magazine *Sight and Sound* published its international critics' poll of the best films ever made, *Ugetsu* was sufficiently known worldwide for it to be voted fourth, in a tie with *Greed* – whereupon a British distributor arranged for its first public showing in this country. It was not until the Seventies that as many as a handful of Mizoguchi's films were seen commercially in Britain. The situation is little different in the U.S., though a number have sneaked into art-houses and campus screenings without benefit of press shows. More recently the same has happened in America to the films of Mikio Naruse.

Naruse is an unassuming film-maker whose work becomes more appealing as it becomes more familiar. And, like Mizoguchi, he seems to have moved from early mediocrity to mastery towards the end of his career. He specialised in *shomin-geki* subjects,★ and with **Repast** (1951) re-established the theme of everyday lower middle-class life, which, apart from Ozu's films, had been out of favour since the

★As explained earlier, *shomin-geki* is a modern working-class subject and *jidai-geki* is a story set before the abolition of feudalism in 1871.

War. The subject – a failing marriage – is one that Ozu treated twice and the resemblance is heightened by the presence of his favourite actress, Setsuko Hara; but Naruse's film is at once more richly detailed and more deeply felt than Ozu's. Naruse, like Mizoguchi, was a pessimist, certain that none of us gets what we want in this world. His study of a family, **Mother** (1952), leaves us in doubt as to whether the mother, no matter how beloved, is truly happy; the young tour guide in **Lightning** (1952) decides against marriage after contemplating her sponging brother, her weak-willed brother-in-law and her sweaty suitor – though she is uncertain of the alternative; and the retired geishas in **Late Chrysanthemums** (1954) live only in regret. Naruse returned to this theme in **Flowing** (1956), which is even richer: his people as ever are trapped – making do, carrying on, locked in vain hopes and aspirations.

Perhaps because he uses the wide screen and colour in **The Summer Clouds** (1958), Naruse's world seems less glum – but that is partly because humour, a rare trait, is allowed to intrude. The film concerns the landowners who were dispossessed by the 1946 reforms, its heroine a war widow who accepts as her lot both her ungrateful mother-in-law and the fields she has to farm singlehandedly. Her family is drawn to the larger towns, while her affair with a married journalist suggests that she herself should grasp at any possible change in a life of poverty. The film contains a wonderful portrait of a rural community, even though the leading actress, Chikage Awashima, gets a number of starry close-ups, and a 'sad' ending which seems intended mainly to please her fans. Certainly Naruse envisaged **Her Lonely Lane** (1962) as a vehicle for Hideko Takamine, one of his favourite players, but her rather unforceful performance does not overly involve us in this character and her singularly unfortunate emotional life. It is based on a memoir by Fumiko Hayashi, whose work also provided the basis for *Repast*, *Lightning* and *Late Chrysanthemums*. Hayashi was the daughter of itinerant workers which was why Naruse, with his deprived childhood, was attracted to her work. Possibly his instinctive urgency had lessened by this time, and certainly he is at his most compassionate in

Flowing, the one film of his I have seen which can be set with those of his peers.

The films of Heinosuke Gosho are even richer. Like Naruse, he is sentimental, but the dusky pessimism of his characters is gently tempered by both humour and introspection. A pupil of Shimazu, he had directed his first film in 1925, and his style eventually became as formularised as that of Ozu, except that the vast number and composition of his images – aided by the occasional rapidity of his cutting – allow for greater fluidity. Those of his films that I have seen are more lovingly crafted than those of any other director I know – including his colleagues – and that in itself makes them very satisfying to watch. It is perhaps necessary to add that he uses his settings brilliantly – the industrial Tokyo of **Four Chimneys** (1953), and the hotel and its surroundings of **An Inn in Osaka** (1954). The former is a comparatively simple tale of a childless couple and someone else's unwanted baby, and the latter a study of a group of people who realise at last to what extent their lives have been changed by a guest in the hotel, Mr Mita (Shuji Sano). Hotel life was a particularly congenial subject for Gosho, for he liked to manipulate a dozen characters at the same time, contrasting their always different moral dilemmas.

He returned to a hotel setting in **The Fireflies** (1958). The plot involves a neglected wife (Chikage Awashima) and the inn's proprietor, who in middle age develops a passion, quite platonic, for a brave

Mikio Naruse is not one of the great directors of Japanese cinema, but he is only a little below them – which means that most of his work is very good indeed. His best film is *Flowing*, a haunting and penetrating study of life in a geisha house, which tells how modern changes are affecting an ageing geisha, who is also beset by financial difficulties. She is played by Isuzu Yamada, right, and to the left Kinuyo Tanaka supports Haruko Sugimara. All three actresses are among the best-known to Japanese audiences, and Miss Yamada, like Miss Tanaka, had a very long career as a star.

That the genre stories worked so well in Japanese films was due to the director. Gosho's *An Inn in Osaka*, adapted from a novel by Takitaro Minakami, is a complex study of life in a boarding house. Shuji Sano is the catalyst, and like many Japanese heroes he is a well-meaning man whose good intentions turn out badly. He helps a geisha, Nobuko Otawa, who drinks too much and is involved with a friend – but that does not stop her from falling in love with this Galahad.

young man (Miki Mori). Like Naruse's *The Summer Clouds*, this film could be regarded as another occasion for audiences to watch Miss Awashima suffering, but the embroidery is rich: the lazy husband obsessed with cleanliness; the sister who runs off with the travelling conman; and the mistress who hopes to make capital on the – false – claim that she is pregnant. Moreover, the brave young man, Sakamoto, is a liberal who was (in life) assassinated in 1867 for his attempts to overthrow the Tokugawa regime. Japanese audiences expected *jidai-geki* films to be connected with actual events. This one, though considerably less subtle than *An Inn in Osaka*, manages to suggest overwhelming forces determined to put an end to feudal Japan. The hotel receives samurai working for rival tribes, and the bloody struggle when they meet manages to be a comment on life as it is lived in this backwater. It also proves that Gosho, usually considered a miniaturist, was the equal of any in the handling of action sequences.

One of the miracles of Japanese cinema

is that these films, angled to appeal to every taste, could still be complex. However by the time Gosho directed **Our Wonderful Years** (1966) he was required to treat an equally vast canvas with more simplicity. It was one of the last films he made before retiring, and since television was making inroads into the once huge Japanese appetite for cinema, the producers were looking askance at the power wielded by the director. The industry had been founded upon the individual director and his attendant establishment, but that was something the producers had never been entirely happy about. Their attitude changed somewhat when Kurosawa proved that a foreign market existed for the work of certain directors, but by the mid-Sixties even Kurosawa found that the studios were using the threat of television to back only what they considered to be sure-fire successes. In Gosho's case, he was known abroad only for *Four Chimneys*.

Our Wonderful Years is typical of Gosho's work, in that it is an honest and unmelodramatic *shomin-geki* account of a large family. It is as pleasing as *The Summer Clouds*, with which it has a number of common elements: the action takes place on a farm near the sea, it is a tribute to a managing mother and it is set against recent events. Like many other Japanese films, it is based on a memoir, allowing for a nostalgic but not necessarily rosy summary of past happenings – in turn implicitly commenting on the changes in society, an essential of the *shomin-geki* films. The sameness of subject and treatment in Japanese films is remarkable – and would probably be insupportable in the hands of the myriad less gifted directors.

Like Gosho, Shiro Toyoda (1906–77) had benefited from the strict and intense teachings of Shimazu. He also began to direct in the Silent era and leaned towards the *shomin-geki*, dealing predominantly with women. However, whereas his contemporaries sometimes moved close to Western emotional dramas, in which women are tested and tortured by love and duty, he was always concerned with women's place in society. **Sweet Sweat** (1964) is a study of a prostitute, not unlike Fellini's earlier *Notti di Cabiria* (q.v.) but with considerably more realism and complexity. Unfortunately it is victim to the slightly mechanical quality which can develop in most veteran directors, and is certainly a minor work compared to **Marital Relations** (1955), which is less about the situation of women than the interdependence of men and women within society. The title is ironic, since the couple are not married, and that gives rise to most of their difficulties. It is the case history of a love affair, of its joys and its reversals – caused, not by the prejudices of society, but by the particular character of the young man (Hisaya Morishige). As his sister says, 'He has been pampered and spoilt, but he is still a very nice man.' In 1955 no Western film had been as perceptive on either family or adulterous relationships; indeed, I know of no Western film like it.

Another constant concern in Japanese cinema is the transitory nature of life: and in the films of Tomotaka Tasaka, who made *Five Scouts*, events end with journeys, usually by train, for life to start anew. Fortune is precarious and innocents may get buffeted, as in **The Maid** (1955), when the woman of the title is sacked for caring too much for the child in her charge, or in **A House in the Quarter** (1963), in which the lovers are separated when circumstances force the girl to work in a

Kyoto brothel. Tasaka works with the same sympathy and attention to detail as his contemporaries, but unlike many of them he is less adept at concealing the old-fashioned nature of the situations so frequent in the *shomin-geki* films.

Daisuke Ito continued to be sharper and more bitter, as in **The Chess Master** (1948), which is more persuasive and more reticent than Western biographical films of the time – though restraint is not a quality found in its star, Tsumasaburo Bando, who specialised in playing roguish working men. Ito was drawn to the historical epic, and **The Conspirator** (1961) is a tale of civil war and revenge as enthralling as any *jidai-geki* subject we have seen.

Even finer is **Killing in Yoshiwara** (1960) directed by Tomu Uchida (1897–1970), who, on this evidence alone, was the equal of Mizoguchi and Kinugasa, both cronies of his. Based on one of the *bunraku* (puppet) plays of Chikamatsu, it is a story of love betrayed: a wealthy merchant (Chiezo Kataoka) is rejected by the geishas because of his scarred face, but accepted by a whore (Yoshie Mizutani) – for whose ambition, to become a geisha, he sacrifices his fortune and, indeed, everything he has. By the early Sixties the

Tomu Uchida's *Killing in Yoshiwara* is one of the most splendid of all Japanese historical films, beautifully photographed in colour for the wide screen, and with a narrative of considerable intrigue. Traditionally the Japanese film moves at a sedate pace interrupted by small flurries of action – but action in the historical subjects can become prolonged and violent. In this particular film Uchida handles the battles brilliantly, as here, where Chiezo Kataoka, centre, fights off his enemies.

The Japanese Masters

The Japanese cinema of the Fifties and early Sixties can now be seen as one of the great periods in the history of the medium, though few of the films concerned reached the West till much later – which is curious, for many of those that arrived at the time were acclaimed and entered the international repertory. Among those is Kinugasa's *Gate of Hell*, which was particularly admired for its use of colour. Kazuo Hasegawa plays a samurai who, having gallantly rescued the wife, Machiko Kyo, of another, is reluctant to let her go.

West had shown a huge liking for *jidai-geki*, with its exciting duels and battles, so it is surprising that neither of these examples was widely distributed abroad. The reason may be that we did not much care for Toho's expensive version of an old perennial, **Chusingara** (1962) or *The Loyal Forty-Seven Ronin*, remade for perhaps the fortieth time, to celebrate the studio's fiftieth anniversary. This was another example of a Japanese film company misunderstanding the taste of the West: they had made the film very pretty – like an Edwardian production of 'Madame Butterfly' – but the potential audience in the West had become accustomed to the more austere beauty of the films of Kurosawa. Its director, Hiroshi Inagaki, although prolific, also tends towards the stolid; he is a mediocre film-maker and in Toho's view 'commercial' – so it is entirely understandable that a number of his samurai films have been put into distribution in the U.S.

A superior exponent of the genre is Kosaburo (or Kimisaburo) Yoshimura (b. 1911), whose **Tale of the Genji** (1951) was made to mark the tenth anniversary of Daiei. The writer was Kaneto Shindo – his usual collaborator before he also became a

director – who cleverly compressed the fifty-four volumes of the eleventh-century stories of the amorous Prince Genji. In its portrait of the period and its cinematic style it is so much like the subsequent historical films of Mizoguchi as to suggest that it was well studied. These directors did not baulk at borrowing, and to copy at this level is a matter of intelligence and taste rather than straight imitation. Shindo, after all, had worked with Mizoguchi as the latter's style matured – and the contribution of the photographer was also extremely important. If we knew Yoshimura's earlier films we might see what he had learnt from Mizoguchi; what may be said is that working with Mizoguchi's photographer, Miyagawa, and again with Shindo, his **Sisters of Nishijin** (1952) is disappointingly prosaic. Yoshimura was another of Shimazu's pupils and, like most of his colleagues, admired William Wyler's ability to move from one genre to another; but he seemed unresponsive to this modern subject, uneasily juggling its twin themes, the failing fortunes of an industrial family and its consequent difficulties with its workers.

The textile industry of Kyoto is the background of **Night River** (1956), known also as *Undercurrent*, and it is much more vividly detailed. Sumie Tanaka wrote the film from a novel by Hisao Siwano, and it weaves together beautifully the heroine's affair with a married man and her day-to-day existence – which is concerned with dyeing fabrics. Since colour is essential to the heroine's art, Yoshimura and Miyagawa decided to make the film in colour, even though the system they used was not entirely satisfactory.

The first Japanese colour film shown in the West was **Gate of Hell** (1953), directed by the veteran Teinosuke Kinugasa, using the Eastman system. Karel Reisz, then a critic, observed that colour 'is employed to better effect than perhaps ever before in a film'. As one of the early few Japanese films to arrive in the West, its savagery and splendour were overwhelming; even today, it remains impressive. The story, again taken from classical literature, is about a samurai (Kazuo Hasegawa) determined to have at all costs the lady (Machiko Kyo) he has rescued during a revolution, with the inevitable tragic results.

Among Kinugasa's modern subjects at this time is **Actress** (1947) made at the same time as *The Love of Sumako the Actress* and is perhaps even better than Mizoguchi's film. The subject of both is Sumako Matsui (played here by Isuzu Yamada), who, after two failed marriages decided to go on the stage and became renowned for her left-wing views. She is regarded as the first liberated Japanese woman – and all these aspects were dealt with in this film, which is notable for its constant use of nuance to make its points.

These veterans all shared very long careers. The second generation of Japanese directors began during the war years and their work is happily more accessible than that of Uchida, Yoshimura and Kinugasa. Of them, Miyogi Ieki seems the least inspired, and the quality of **The Half Brothers** (1958) may be due to the contribution of Yoda, Mizoguchi's writer, working with Nobuyoshi Terada from a novel by Torahiko Talmiya. The film follows the fortunes of a military man (Rentaro Mikuni) from the late Twenties to the Armistice in 1945. He rapes his maid (Kinuyo Tanaka) and, forced to marry her, continues to treat her with contempt, idolising his own equally militarist sons while the two he has by her are disappointments to him. The film sets out to demolish the standards by which he lives, and does so by virtue of some telling vignettes; it is also actually touching on the subject of this strange marriage, due partly to what may be Miss Tanaka's most brilliant performance. Ieki's early films were, by government decree, of an entirely opposing stance.

Tadashi Imai (b.1912), a former scriptwriter, also made militaristic films during the War and became a Communist when it was over. It should be axiomatic that left-wing directors in democracies are equipped to provide above-average films, since the capitalist bosses under whom they operate will put a brake on blatant propaganda, while being prepared, at the same time, to accept their more sophisticated skills than those of purely commercial film-makers. Imai is a film-maker committed to sympathetic studies of the poor and deprived, but his work is too often cerebral and misogynist. **And Yet We Live** (1951) is an account of a family on the bread-line, and a number of similarities reveal that it was prepared under the influence of *Ladri di Biciclette*. However, it lacks not only the compassion of de Sica's film but also the calm emotiveness of Ozu's prewar films about poverty. It was criticised at the time because its players had been selected from a theatre company – albeit a left-wing one. On other occasions it has been clear that because of his political views Japanese critics admire Imai above all his contemporaries.

Imai did realise a noteworthy humanist film with **Kiku and Isamu** (1959), the study of two children living with their grandmother, who makes a meagre living from silk-worms. Their mother is dead and their father (now back in America) was a black G.I., which is why other children regard them as freaks. Imai's best film is probably **Shadow in Sunlight** (1956), also known as *Darkness at Noon*, an enthralling account of police pursuit through the Tokyo underworld. The self-confessed murderer is bullied into implicating his gang, who are completely innocent – and Imai is clearly on their side against the law. He may have learnt from the Italian neo-realists how to be passionately partisan while, at the same time, appearing theoretically objective; and in adopting the thriller form for his purpose he predates the films of Costa-Gavras (q.v.). The story was based on fact, and the film caused a sufficient stir for the Supreme Court to order a re-trial in 1957.

Imai admitted that he was happier with contemporary subjects, and it was not until **Night Drum** (1958) that he tackled an historical theme, written by Kaneto Shindo and Shinobu Hashimoto from a play by Chikamatsu. It is set at the time the country was under the sway of the Tokugawa shoguns and it concentrates upon a minor court official (Rentaro Mikuni) whose wife (Ineko Arima) has been unfaithful. He is unwilling to exact the punishment demanded by society, but does so: he instructs her as she commits hara-kiri; equally reluctant he sets out to find the man who cuckolded him. An epilogue reveals him a ruined man and the final close-up shows him in anguish at having to bow to the absurd code. Imai uses a quiet, reflective style – unlike that of most of his modern stories – but cuts abruptly from past to present as the husband is faced with mounting evidence of his wife's infidelity (in view of Imai's misogyny, it is not surprising that she turns out to have been the aggressor). The varying accounts told to the husband indicate that the film is emulating *Rashomon*, but otherwise the abrupt time-shifts are much in advance of Western narrative technique. Since, outside Japan, such devices were first associated with the *nouvelle vague*, we may suppose that Resnais saw this film, or heard it discussed, when he was in Japan making *Hiroshima mon Amour*. Certainly *Night Drum* and Kinoshita's *The Snow Flurry* (q.v.) are the only precedents I know for *L'Année Dernière à Marienbad* (q.v.).

Imai returned to an historical theme with **A Woman Called En** (1971), based on the true story of a seventeenth-century woman who, after spending most of her early life in prison (she was forty-four when released), refused her lord's command to remarry and earned her living by her medical knowledge. The subject seems more a concession to local women's libbers than another traditional movie examination of women's place in society, but that may be because once again Imai seems rather remote from it. **Takiji Kobayashi** (1974) is a biography of the proletarian writer who died not long after being taken into police custody in 1933, and we may therefore suppose it to have more relevance to Imai. It was his most ambitious film for many years, but on this evidence he had lost his former passion.

Imai finally relinquished his own film company, set up in 1948, and went to work for Toho on **Mon and Ino** (1976), an odd choice for a director once noted for social concern. Also known as *Brother and Sister*, the tale had been previously filmed by Sotoji Kimura in 1936 and Naruse in 1953: a girl has been seduced, and her loutish brother turns on the gentle and gentlemanly student responsible. Hints of incestuous passion jostle awkwardly with the brother's old-fashioned notions of morality, and a comparison with Kimura's version reveals that the story no longer has much relevance. As a concession to the Seventies the family occupation has been changed from fishing to riverside catering, and in handling this environment Imai reveals fragments of his former skill. For that reason alone he deserved his Grand Prix at Delhi. As a result of the award the film was bought for British distribution – to no critical interest whatsoever. It was only the second of his films to be seen publicly in the West, more than twelve years after *Bushido* in New York in 1964.

It is even more to be regretted that the films of Keisuke Kinoshita (b.1912) remain largely unseen. Imai, when asked which of his contemporaries he most admired, named Kinoshita, adding that it was 'peculiar' that he was unknown outside Japan. None of Kinoshita's fifty-odd films has been seen commercially in Britain, but three have reached New York, including the first Japanese colour film, **Carmen Comes Home** (1951) – the Fujicolor used proves to have been, at the time, the truest colour system after Technicolor. Kinoshita wished to take advantage of the countryside around Mount Asami, and he himself wrote this light comedy of a returning showgirl and her effect on the villagers. It brings to mind the work of Pagnol in its affection and elegiac sentiment, but Kinoshita himself regarded it as a reflection of his admiration for René Clair. He had deliberately set out to restore satire and comedy of character – for both had been largely absent since early Ozu – and he is more successful with the second quality than the first.

Like Yoshimura, Toyoda and Gosho, Kinoshita was a pupil of Shimazu, and his work is further evidence of Shimazu's firm schooling. If a number of his first films are clumsily handled, it may be because their subjects were chosen for him by the government. He was still relatively unskilled when he made **A Morning with the Osone Family** (1946) which is nevertheless a fascinating film. It was designed to be palatable to the American occupation forces, dealing as it does with a liberal-minded – and, it is implied, Christian – family and its attitude towards the War. The film indicates that the country, in defeat, now shares the stance of the family – but that is of little consolation to them, as three of the sons have been killed. The Italians made movies about partisans, but not for twenty years would the Italian film industry allow films to examine the Fascist past; similarly after both wars the German cinema failed to examine Germany's role in the two conflicts; but this film is in the tradition of prewar Japanese cinema in its care for human values. The family is so affectionately and intelligently handled that it atones for the film's didacticism and the overdrawn portrait of the militarist uncle.

By the time of **A Japanese Tragedy** (1953) Kinoshita had become one of the masters of world cinema. The film is not dissimilar to *A Morning with the Osone Family*, being also an example of the *babe-mono* or 'mother-love' story, stunningly set against the events of contemporary history. This mother (Yuko Mochizuki) is rejected by both her children – the daughter preferring to live with a married English teacher, and the son with one of the doctors with whom he is studying. Likeable though they are, both are selfish, able to justify their actions by citing the loose life that their mother had been leading, but the true implications are clear: had there been no War there would have been no widowhood, and hence no 'immorality', no rejection and no final tragedy. The title is by no means pretentious, because the film is representative of Japan at a time of upheaval, showing the country as it moves decisively from the alternating moods of doubt and complacency. The material is sufficiently absorbing to start with, but what is remarkable is Kinoshita's handling, for he makes implications only – as opposed to statements – about his leading characters, pre-dating Antonioni, who introduced the form into Western cinema. He also pre-dates Western techniques by cutting swiftly into the narrative such background matters as the black market and student riots, often in time-shifts.

The intercutting of past and present was developed by Imai, as we have seen, in *Night Drum*, but Kinoshita used the technique even more brilliantly in **The Snow Flurry** (1959), employing it perhaps to add vitality to an otherwise lacklustre story. It is another tale of mother-love, set during the War years and their aftermath in a rural community, and it examines particularly the hardships wrought by the 1946 Land Reform Acts. Chiefly about the sufferings of a mother and son at the hands of a bourgeois family like themselves, the piece, unlike *A Japanese Tragedy*, is not without touches of sentimentality, but once again Kinoshita's selection of detail and incident is astonishing. He wrote the original screenplay, and if, because of the subject, the final effect is minor, it still

dwarfs most contemporary Western films.

The other two Kinoshita films seen in New York exemplify his fascination with stretching the possibilities of film as narrative. **She Was Like a Wild Chrysanthemum** (1955) is evidence of his strong attachment to Japan and the past, but, since his framework is unusual, he doesn't display both at the same time. The title refers to an old man's first love, as he revisits the town in which he grew up, and the flashbacks are enclosed within oval white frames to suggest photographs of the era. **The Song of Narayama** (1958) is set in a remote mountain area where the privations are so great that the people traditionally take their aged to the peak to die; one old lady (Miss Tanaka) is convinced that her time has come and has to persuade her son of it. Kinoshita decided that the exigencies of the subject, bordering on the mythic, required an absence of realism, and chose a style borrowed from the Kabuki, with 'magical' transformations of scenery in the theatrical manner. Since he is, above all, a stylist, the effect is hypnotic – but it is even more remarkable because he was working in wide screen and colour for the first time. In its visual qualities *The Snow Flurry* is even more accomplished, and both films disclose Kinoshita's revitalised creativity. I cannot consider this handful of Kinoshita's movies without being puzzled by their lack of recognition in the West – beyond the fact that those

Of the acknowledged Japanese masters, the least known outside Japan is Keisuke Kinoshita. Isolated showings of a handful of his films suggest that there are riches in the other fifty he has made. *A Japanese Tragedy* is one of the most distinguished of the films which attempted to chart the unrest that followed the Second World War, and comparable to the best of the Italian neo-realist movies. The title also translates as *The Japanese Tragedy*, and it is a particular story which reflects the lives of others in that troubled period – a tale concerning a family, with Yuko Mochizuki and Uteko Katsuragi as mother and daughter.

which reached America were subjected to a group of uncomprehending critics.

This is a vitally important question. If our ignorance of Kinoshita is, as Imai said, peculiar, our admiration for Akira Kurosawa (b. 1910) is justified. Kurosawa, as he has been the first to admit, has been much luckier – having had solid acclaim in Europe before his films were assessed by American critics. When the taste for Japanese prints began in the last century, American collectors, even before the French, led the world in their enthusiasm. But in general American taste-makers have been impervious to the Japanese cinema – despite the fact that New York, at least, has had more opportunities to discover it than any other leading city outside Japan. When in the late Fifties American distributors realised there was an art-house market for samurai films, they began importing subtitled prints, and most of these films have remained in the art-house repertory. Not all of them were reviewed; and during the two decades 1950–70, *The New York Times* – as I said before, the key to serious acceptance in the U.S. – included only four Japanese films on its Best of the Year lists. One was Kobayashi's *Kwaidon* (q.v.); the other three were directed by Kurosawa – and they appeared only when there was a separate category for Best Foreign Films and only after critical acclaim in Europe. Even today, many serious American filmgoers believe that the Japanese cinema begins and ends with Kurosawa – a fallacy which does not, of course, diminish his immense stature.

Having failed to make a living as an illustrator, Kurosawa joined P.C.L. studios as assistant to Kajiro Yamamoto, his only master – though he acknowledges the influence of Capra, Ford, Wyler and, later, Antonioni. He wrote scripts and while at Toho asked to direct the version of a novel by Tsuneo Tomita, **Judo Saga** (1943), a story of the rivalry between judo and jujitsu. It is also a study of the awakening of a young man who, like later Kurosawa protagonists, theorised, practised and did not act until he was fully prepared. Kurosawa made a sequel in 1945, and in the meantime had composed an almost documentary study of a number of factory workers, **The Most Beautiful**. He wanted to make an historical film, but horses were proscribed for movie pur-

poses under postwar restrictions and, further, he was allowed only one set. **Tora-No-O** (1946), also known as *They Who Step on the Tiger's Tail*, is a medieval anecdote, based on fact, and in the repertory of both the Noh and the Kabuki. The American authorities banned it, because of 'the feudalistic idea of loyalty expressed' and it was not shown until 1953. Then it was immediately bought by several Western distributors in the hope that it would appeal to the patrons of *Rashomon*; but it is by no means of equal interest (and since it runs less than an hour is not easy to programme). In the interim Kurosawa had made nine films, most of which are notable. **No Regrets for Our Youth** (1946) is based on the 'Takikawa Incident' of 1933, when a professor was dismissed from the faculty of Kyoto for alleged Communist leanings. The narrative is unsatisfactory – Toho exacted changes in order to differentiate it from a similar story being filmed simultaneously – and the action hazily focuses on the professor's daughter (Setsuko Hara). It does, however, reveal Kurosawa making his way towards his (to me) miraculous style, with its travelling shots and incisive cutting.

Drunken Angel (1948) marks Kurosawa's enfranchisement and, working with new confidence, he captures admirably the curious postwar mood as he examines the relationship between a local doctor and the hoodlum he treats for tuberculosis. The roles are played respectively by Takashi Shimura, a gentle, middle-aged actor, and Toshiro Mifune (b. 1920), who was making his first film. Mifune's sheer energy encouraged a more Western method of acting – and a more robust style was what would help Japanese films find acceptance overseas. There had been other 'rogue' actors in the Japanese cinema, but they would not, or could not, be disciplined in the way that Kurosawa was able to control Mifune. Mifune and Shimura became Kurosawa's preferred actors throughout his career, and at this time he featured them in three more films consecutively. In **The Quiet Duel** (1949) they play doctors, father and son, the latter adjusting to civilian life after some years in the army, and in **Stray Dog** (1949), they are detectives, with Mifune as the junior, searching for his stolen gun. Obviously a thriller, this film tries to put the younger man in the context of the postwar world.

More clearly in **Scandal** (1950) Kurosawa reverted to the social preoccupations of his previous films, this time attacking press ethics – which Kurosawa considered were degenerating as the Occupation came to an end – with a plot about a painter (Mifune) and a singer hounded because of an imaginary affair. He evokes Capra at the end when the lawyer (Shimura) puts probity above his career.

Kurosawa had wanted to make **Rashomon** (1950) for years, and in fact moved from Toho to Daiei to do so. In it, he perfected his technique – which so startled the West – with its gliding camera and dynamic rhythm. It was a style wholly dictated here by the film's source – two stories by Ryunosuke Akutagawa, one of which suggested the framing device, and the other, the central story. It is a study of conflicting testimonies concerning a rape and a murder, and as each version is re-enacted, the nature of truth itself is put in doubt (simultaneously, in Britain, Asquith's undistinguished *The Woman in Question* was predicated on the same theme). The situation belongs absolutely to a country riven by civil war, and with even more virtuosity than in Mizoguchi or Kinoshita, violence is contrasted with a transitory tranquillity – in this case the sylvan setting – and peace is more deceptive because in the undergrowth lurks the bandit (Mifune) bent on rape. The resultant horror is made worse since the deed is witnessed by the husband (Masayuki Mori) who, like us, cannot be sure that his wife (Machiko Kyo) did not enjoy it. The film is spellbinding and, like all great works of art, still holds its mysteries. Neither the executives at Daiei nor Japanese critics liked it, though audiences were sufficiently fascinated to make it financially successful. When Venice requested a Japanese film for the 1951 festival, *Rashomon* had not even been considered, but it was chosen by a representative of Italiafilm in Tokyo, and sent despite the opposition of Daiei. Kurosawa did not even know that it had been entered, and when it was awarded the Grand Prix he observed that he would rather have been honoured for a modern subject, mentioning *Ladri di Biciclette* as the sort of film he had in mind.

However, borne aloft by his prize, he chose not a subject of social awareness but

'art', and persuaded Shochiku to back a version of Dostoevsky's **The Idiot** (1951). Clearly meant to be no ordinary film, it ran to 245 minutes, but Shochiku, by this time agreeing with Daiei that *Rashomon* had been a fluke, cut it to 166 minutes. It was badly received both in Tokyo and on its first Western outing in New York, two years later. Even if it is intermittently powerful and fascinating, it is essentially unsatisfactory. Kurosawa transferred the action to Japan but attempted to express the story in Western terms and in so doing failed to distinguish between tragedy and melodrama. The result is an array of agonised expressions and histrionic confrontations, stagily contrived. As the Rogozhin character, Mifune over-reacts; Setsuko Hara as Nastasya, modelled on the Casares character in *Orphée*, assumes – even more foolishly – Joan Crawford mannerisms; and Mr Mori is simply ineffectual as Mishkin. Kurosawa used the northern island of Hokkaido because of the snow and its Westernised furniture. When he came to film Gorki's **The Lower Depths** (1957) he realised his earlier mistake and did not this time attempt to compromise; but in removing the action from its quintessential

Akira Kurosawa was the first Japanese director widely known to Western audiences, and he remains the best known – though he himself, and Japanese critics, regard both Kon Ichikawa and Masaki Kobayashi as of equal mastery. Indeed, they once teamed with the equally distinguished Keisuke Kinoshita in a doomed bid for independence from the powerful Japanese studios.

Russian milieu to one purely Japanese the piece eluded him even further.

Ikiru (1952) is generally known in English as *Living*, though at one time it was titled *Doomed*, not inappropriately, since it follows the reactions of a minor civil servant (Shimura) on discovering that he has only a few months to live. The theme is nothing less than an examination of Man's reason for living, and the last section consists of the long wake accompanying his funeral, in which all the ironies of his life are exposed. These become a series of anti-climaxes, and though the earlier part of the film lays emphasis on the man's vain dependence on booze and sex – he is a widower – and the lack of understanding between him and his children, these are not great discoveries for a film director to make. The portraits of bureaucratic life and of the Ginza are engrossing, but as a whole the film lacks the urgency and compassion of de Sica's *Umberto D*, with which it has a number of affinities.

These qualities are, however, to be found in **Seven Samurai** (1954), which was made expressly to entertain. It is also humorous, especially in Mifune's performance as the lowly born samurai, and has tremendous tension. The ambience is a primitive one of carnage, misery, self-interest and evil, in the midst of which is just one point of redemption – the honour and idealism of the samurai code. A singularly luckless village employs seven warriors to defend it against pillaging freebooters, though, as is apparent, these are samurai who have seen better days. Both sides fight with desperate courage, the samurai plotting and harassing till there is hope of victory – achieved strikingly in the same strategic manner as was used by the feudal warriors in the West, reminding us that we have no similar film. Our fondness for this led to a Hollywood interpretation as a Western, *The Magnificent Seven* (q.v.). The original version of 200 minutes is even more impressive than the 160-minute rendition usually in circulation.

Both films reflect Kurosawa's own acknowledged quest – to examine the reasons why mankind is incapable of living in harmony. In the wake of new nuclear experiments by the Russians and Americans he felt obliged to make **I Live in Fear** (1954), also known as *Record of a Living Being*, a study of an elderly industrialist

(Mifune) determined to emigrate to South Africa to escape the threat of atomic warfare. The film was Kurosawa's greatest commercial failure to that time, and though he himself thinks it is before its time – 'no one was thinking seriously of atomic extinction' – it is a deeply flawed work. Having elected a young man, Mifune, to play an old one, he prevents us from peering too closely, and as a consequence we never know the man. His fears are not dramatised. As a modern-day Lear he is the one sane man in a world gone mad, but beyond the fact of Tokyo in a hot summer, this world does not seem mad. His own descent into madness is merely verbose. Kurosawa observed that he intended to make a satire and found himself making a tragedy, but it is difficult to see what he is satirising unless it is the bickering, grasping family, representing a society on the brink of disaster.

Shakespeare was indeed in Kurosawa's mind, and **Throne of Blood** (1957) is based on 'Macbeth'. It is an infinitely more successful adaptation than *The Idiot*, but it also reduces its source, which, robbed of its poetry and argument, becomes a tradition-ridden, bleak adventure story. As the samurai warrior who plots to rule, Mifune does not develop; his wife (Isuzu Yamada) is small and baleful, and the weighty reasons for killing the overlord become simply 'Without ambition, a man is not a man.' The defeat of Macbeth in Shakespeare satisfies our desire for a return to law and order, but in Kurosawa it is merely the fitting end to a cautionary tale. This is ironic, in view of the magnificence of the conception. As in Shakespeare, civil war has destroyed the countryside and evil lurks at every corner – or rather, in the dark, damp huge· forests or within the swirling fogs and mists. The soundtrack uses the whinnying of horses – the sound of fear – and *musique concrète* to reinforce the searing deeds of this protagonist. Macbeth dies – in one of the most pulsating and terrifying climaxes ever filmed – in a flight of arrows, pinioned to the wooden walls of his castle.

Kurosawa's technical mastery was now complete. He said that he turned to *jidai-geki* because he thought most other such films 'historically uninformed', but almost certainly he preferred this form because it gave full rein to his powerful visual imagination. He did say that he resisted the use of colour to keep the feudal world in charcoal blacks and subtle whites, and whatever the narrative shortcomings of *Throne of Blood* it is a haunting film, eerie and unearthly. He used the wide screen for **The Hidden Fortress** (1958); and for the hero (Mifune) the world remains a grim, sinister place, with no succour from either the poor, who are cowardly, naive opportunists, or the powerful who are greedy and ruthless. Still, as with *Seven Samurai*, Kurosawa injects a degree of humour, resembling the films of Douglas Fairbanks in both the settings and the resourcefulness of Mifune – he even sweeps up the princess-heroine on to his horse as he rides past, to escort her through the enemy lines. However, this is the only scene where Kurosawa allows humour to relieve the tension of dangerous situations.

Despite the failure of *I Live in Fear*, Kurosawa was determined to devote his efforts to a contemporary story of 'some social significance' for his first production as an independent (releasing through Toho). **The Bad Sleep Well** (1960) is about corruption in big business, and the connection with Shakespeare this time is 'Hamlet', although the hero, Nishi (Mifune), has a sardonic humour rather stronger than that of the Danish prince. His revenge is directed not against a usurping uncle, but his father-in-law (Masayuki Mori) who, Nishi believes, was responsible, with his colleagues, for the death of his father. Company funds had been misappropriated, and no one will tell the truth since company loyalty is not so far removed from the old samurai loyalties. As a cat-and-mouse thriller, the film is superb, but such devices as ghosts and sleeping draughts seem at odds in a contemporary context, and the tragedy of the ending is unsatisfactory.

Mifune's understated performance is delightful, especially since the success of *The Hidden Fortress* with the Japanese public identified him with heroic roles. Elements of that film and Mifune's role in it were, therefore, incorporated into **Yojimbo** (1961), Kurosawa's second independent production. It too was phenomenally popular, and when Toho asked for a sequel, Kurosawa obliged with **Sanjuro** (1962), later observing that he considers only the earlier film a major work. The term *yojimbo* means 'bodyguard', and Sanjuro is the name of this master swordsman whom Mifune makes into one of the cinema's great creations. He is shabbily dressed, somewhat theatrical, cautious; and, though by no means a modern man, not unlike the uninvolved, sardonic heroes played by Humphrey Bogart. When underdogs are endangered, however, his innate chivalry comes to the fore. He is a professional, a killer, available to oppressors and oppressed alike, who, in terms of stupidity and evil, are a match for each other. Reunited with Miyagawa as director of photography for the first time since *Rashomon*, Kurosawa creates images like those of Goya's etchings, evoking a stench of rotten, decaying corpses and charred wood. *Yojimbo* has a precision, a sense of inevitability and a harsh beauty that we recognise as requisite to this director, while *Sanjuro* is shorter, and the opposing sides somewhat shallower. Mifune, still aloof, is allowed to blunder; when he eventually triumphs, he strides away, as in *Yojimbo*, spurning the congratulations of his fairweather allies.

High and Low (1963) is based on Ed McBain's novel 'King's Ransom' and is about the kidnapping of the young son of an industrialist (Mifune). Its long and detailed exposition, as the police enquiry gets under way, is reminiscent of Kurosawa's early films, but he continues to strive for the complexity of his recent work, especially in his account of Mifune's relationships with the police on the one hand and his colleagues on the other. As a social realist, Kurosawa makes the contrast between the rich and the kidnapper, who lives in a shanty town, and it is this aspect which gives the film its title, which in Japanese means 'Heaven and Hell'. Though a superb thriller, this is probably not among Kurosawa's greatest works, while **Red Beard** (1965) most assuredly is. Its canvas is vast, as, set in the nineteenth century, it seeks to delineate a bridge between the feudal world and the modern one. Mifune again plays a right-minded, noble spirit, living in the midst of squalor; he is a doctor, running his own clinic, and passing on his wisdom to a younger man (Yuzo Kayama) – a tradition which has been the theme of many medical dramas. If

978

Kurosawa's Japan: Feudal and Modern

These pictures celebrate not only Kurosawa's artistry but also his popularity in the West: LEFT, *Seven Samurai*; BOTTOM FAR LEFT, *Throne of Blood*, with Toshiro Mifune; BOTTOM LEFT, *Rashomon*, with Machiko Kyo and Mifune; BOTTOM RIGHT, *Red Beard*, with Terumi Niki and Yoshio Tsuchiya, and BELOW, *Ikiru*, with Takashi Shimura in foreground.

this has any affinity to a Western work, it is to Antonioni's studies of young men's self-discoveries, for the arrogant young doctor here learns that the old man has skills and an awareness of which he had not even dreamed. But it is also about a dedicated humanitarian who has chosen to live out his life among the flotsam and jetsam of mankind. The running time is over three hours, the aim being to 'push the confines of movie-making to their limits', and it is wonderfully designed and orchestrated. It is no coincidence that Kurosawa likes filming rain, for he prefers to compose in horizontals and verticals; but, unlike most Western directors whose images may be as forcefully or as carefully composed, his are never arbitrary, but always subordinated to the subject, often as a continuation of it.

As with all great directors, Kurosawa's films plead for involvement. **Dodeska-Den** (1970), in which he returns to a shanty town, similar to *The Lower Depths*, features derelicts no more appealing than those in the earlier film, and with fantasies even less so. The title refers to the noise made by the young hero as he pretends to be a tramcar, and the source is a story by Shugoro Yamamoto, whose work had also provided Kurosawa with *Sanjuro* and *Red Beard*. His first film in colour, Kurosawa brings to it the same warmth as Jean Renoir did when he began to use colour, but unfortunately the settings are theatrical. The film, initially, was to have been over three-and-a-half hours long and even at one hour less it drags: a monumental miscalculation. The public had never cared for tales of gutter survival or for stagy settings, and the combination was a disaster for Kurosawa, who had pooled resources with Kinoshita, Ichikawa and Kobayashi to make completely independent films, which Toho was to distribute. The complete loss of its production cost, and the annulment of his agreement with his colleagues following a quarrel with Mifune and the severing of their partnership, caused Kurosawa to attempt suicide.

During the next few years a number of projects fell through, partly because Kurosawa's attempt at independence had been viewed unfavourably by the industry. But Toho came to his aid after he had persuaded Mosfilm (of the Soviet Union) to back **Dersu Uzala** (1975), based on the books by Vladimir Klavdievic Arsenyev

which he had read years before. In 1902 Arsenyev had led an army unit making a topographical survey of the forest land approaches on Russia's Pacific seaboard, across the straits from Sakhalin, and in the course of his work he had met a hunter, a member of the forest-dwelling Goldi people, named Dersu Uzala. The title role is played by Maksim Munzik, and the army captain by Yuri Solomin; and probably the 'noble savage' syndrome was never more impressively expressed. The captain's admiration for the hunter is due to Dersu's many qualities, chief of which is his instinctive co-existence with the life of the forest, which the captain hopes to acquire himself. Since the man is alone and superstitious and his life is hard, the captain later gives him a home, throwing into relief the extraordinary forest scenes. In these sequences Kurosawa eschewed his swirling camera movement and virtuoso cinematic techniques for a stillness reflecting the nature of the forest: the stereophonic sound and the wide screen, which had never been better used, find us alert to any noise and unexpected movement. Kurosawa surpasses himself in the creation of tension, and the ending in particular reminds us that his films have always been richly imbued with humanity.

The Russians suggested a further project, but did not care for the subject of the script submitted to them. Another screenplay found no backers in Japan, but Toho agreed to a third, an historical film, **Kagemusha** (1980), but not to its estimated budget of $7 million, the highest of any Japanese film to date. Kurosawa, while on a visit to Hollywood, mentioned this to Francis Ford Coppola and George Lucas, and as a result 20th Century-Fox contributed $1½ million in exchange for world rights outside Japan.

At 159 minutes the 'international' version is twenty-two minutes shorter than Kurosawa's original, and although we have been assured that only battle scenes have gone, something more integral seems to be missing. *Kagemusha* is no more than a good historical story, like one of the lesser Mizoguchis; Kurosawa's own historical films usually dealt with power and the responsibility that goes with it, which is precisely what this film would seem to be about, but is not. The screenplay is based on fact – a sixteenth-century shogun named Shingen who used a double to deceive his enemies. In the film Shingen's double – the *kagemusha*, or shadow warrior – is a thief, and both roles are played by an unrecognisable Tatsuya Nakadai, who had played Mifune's foe in *Yojimbo* and in *Sanjuro*. After Shingen's death, the thief, aided by the ruler's brother, assumes the lord's role and in Kurosawa's brilliant exposition the thief, craven at first, begins to settle into the deception and to enjoy it. The dead man's illegitimate son, however, becomes restive on seeing his father's triumphs being enjoyed by so ignominious a creature. The story at this juncture promises a serious comment on the uses of power for good or evil, but nothing interesting materialises: the thief is booted out when he is no longer useful, but he so identifies with the lord's clan that he goes to his death after all the other members have been massacred. It is possible that Kurosawa lacked confidence after fifteen years of disappointments; for even *Dersu Uzala*, with all its critical acclaim, had failed to attract a large foreign audience. However, apart from some minor theatrical lapses, the film is visually magnificent and, because of 20th Century-Fox's handling, has probably been seen by more people than any other Japanese film hitherto.

In the West, the best known of Kurosawa's contemporaries is probably Kon Ichikawa (b. 1915), who was drawn to the cinema by the early films of Walt Disney. He wanted to be an artist and did become an animator, later studying filming under Yutaka Abe. He made his first film, with puppets, in 1946, but the American occupation forces refused to allow it to be shown. His second film was unfinished, but he began directing regularly in 1948 and the following year started his collaboration with the screenwriter Natto Wada, whom he married. They tended to concentrate on comedy, with satiric intent but a supposedly objective approach; their criticism of Japanese society, *i.e.* other people, is imperfect, the individual always commands respect, even if he himself may be no better than those around him. **Pu-San** (1953) was based on a contemporary cartoon and was made in response to Japanese re-armament (sanctioned by the Americans because of the Korean War). Ichikawa feared that public apathy would permit a resurgence of militarism and he

tries, not too successfully, to depict the country in a state of despair and flux – seen through the eyes of a bumbling schoolteacher who loses his job. The effect is rather as though Monsieur Hulot (q.v.) had stumbled into *Umberto D*, but the film is remarkable for its economy of detail, avoiding the irrelevant and concentrating on the informative. The Japanese cinema, as I have said, used omission tellingly, long before the West did, and **The Heart** (1954) not only omits for the sake of discretion, but because Ichikawa thought it unnecessary for us to know the precise extent of the two relationships at the core of the film. Yukio Mishima's 'Confessions of a Mask', had been published a few years earlier, and may have led Ichikawa to an older novel by Soseki Matsume – who died in 1926 – about a man confronting his homosexuality. The relationships concerned are those between Nobuchi (Masayuki Mori) and a friend, now dead, and between Nobuchi and a student. When Nobuchi's wife challenges him about the student he commits suicide (as in the contemporary novels which were timidly raising this subject in Western society), but not before advising the student to seek a happier life through self-knowledge. It is doubtful whether Nobuchi himself ever acquired this knowledge, a matter conveyed stylistically by Ichikawa, moving from the recticent present into flashbacks.

The small military unit at the centre of **The Burmese Harp** (1956), taken from

Kon Ichikawa first became known in Japan as a satirist, but the West became acquainted with him via *The Burmese Harp*, which recounts the odyssey of one young soldier stranded in Burma after the capitulation of Japan in 1945. Ichikawa ignores a number of important subjects – an army in defeat, another army coping with it, the needs of the native population – for one which he clearly considers even more vital, the futility of war; and by emphasising the camaraderie his film is romantic, and absolutely successful in its attempt to be epic.

an original story by Michio Takeyama, is treated elliptically and sentimentally by Ichikawa. There are a number of other flaws, such as the superfluous montage of suffering to indicate the agony of the hero, Mizushima (Shoji Yasui): but these are too minor to mar what is a very big film indeed, and one clearly meant to be epic. It is about a soldier making his way home through South-East Asia after the end of the War. He is a pacifist, and after donning the robes of a Buddhist monk he feels compelled to bury or burn the bodies of the dead. Unlike some stories in Western literature, the donning of the monk's robes does not change Mizushima, and his attitude to religion remains ambivalent: he is of a particular mentality, which Ichikawa constantly has to underscore in order to prevent the film from becoming an expression of a mystical experience – but it may still have become that for many of the audience.

Fires on the Plain (1959), also deals with a soldier after defeat, and concerns, not guilt and expiation, but survival. It is the harshest of all war films, and there is no more degrading shot in all cinema than that of its protagonist, Tamura (Eiji Funakoshi), with his mouth, chin and chest covered with human blood. The civilised world has been turned upside down and Tamura is co-existing with two others whose bestiality includes cannibalism: but he makes his final gesture for humankind – perhaps a useless one. In Shohei O-oka's original novel Tamura returned to Japan to enter a mental home, but in the film he dies; and that is his salvation, as Ichikawa once remarked. War is the greatest sin, he said, able to change the nature of man, and he contrasts what man has done with God's work – the calm beauty of the plains of Leyte. Where in *The Burmese Harp* he offered the spiritual peace of Buddhism and the singing of 'Home, Sweet Home', here there is the image of the cross on the deserted village church.

A third young hero in **Conflagration** (1958) reveals the extent to which Ichikawa differs from Kurosawa as a moralist: it is possible, according to Kurosawa, to struggle on into middle-age with hope for a better society, but in Ichikawa's view hope is destroyed in the young. The screenplay, derived from a novel by Mishima that was, in turn, based on fact, is set

not long after the War and concerns Goichi, the student priest who, deformed by a stutter and crippled by an inferiority complex, deliberately set fire to the Golden Pavilion temple in Kyoto. The temple represents to him all that he is not, and in burning it down he destroys not only his enemy but also himself. Ichikawa chose the subject as a means of showing the poverty, both economic and spiritual, of Japan at the time, again using flashbacks to indicate what led Goichi to the burning. His dispassionate style contrasts with the more partisan approach to social problems taken by Kurosawa and Kobayashi, and it seems to owe much to the photographer, Kazuo Miyagawa. This was the first film in the wide-screen process for both of them and they employ it to extraordinary effect; Ichikawa believed that the camera should take an active part in the action, but left the details to Miyagawa. They worked together on several more films at this time, but not altogether happily, since Ichikawa, far more interested in the directing of actors, was, according to Miyagawa, 'rather vague' about what he wanted.

Ichikawa's interest in the intellectual and mental sickness of society led him to **Kagi** (1959) or *The Key*, a deeper study of sexual irregularity than *The Heart*; in this instance it is not accompanied by love, which is part of the problem. Corruption surfaces in the dishonesty of a family and the young doctor (Tatsuya Nakadai) whom they involve in their relationships. But worse than corruption is their refusal to face up to the truth, acting as they do under a system of double and triple standards, yet still being considered by their fellows – and this is 'the key' – an integral family and ultra-respectable. As human beings, they were spiritually dead before they died; the ending, when the servant poisons the three survivors, was not in the original novel by Junichiro Tanizaki but is, said Ichikawa, his own judgment on them.

Two family dramas, **Bonchi** (1960) and **Her Brother** (1960), reinforce his expressed belief, already evident in *Kagi*, that each member of the family must respect the individuality of the others. A *bonchi* is the eldest son, and the film is an enquiry into one such person, set against a background of recent history, while *Her Brother* deals with the relationship of two siblings in prewar Japan. *Her Brother* is the slighter of the two films, but as the children have a self-centred, and Christian, mother, it is an even more virulent attack on a matriarchal society. **Being Two Isn't Easy** (1962) is, by contrast, a fond look at family life, just avoiding cuteness and false drama as it views the world through the eyes of a baby; one must assume that Ichikawa took it on as a challenge – as he was to with *Alone on the Pacific* (q.v.). Since that, and the two films made on either side of it, represent the art of the director at its most triumphant, I shall discuss them together below. Of his films made subsequently only a few have been seen in the West and they are not of great interest: **To Love Again** (1971) is a trite love story in the manner of *Un Homme et une Femme* (q.v.), dealing with a French boy and a Japanese maiden, and **The Wanderers** (1973) is a tale of the *toseinin* – an amoral brigand breed, runaway, peasant-born rogues – told in an anti-heroic manner. Both of these later films are, of course, well made, but watching them is almost an affront since the subjects are so unworthy of a great director.

Ichikawa was seldom attracted to the *jidai-geki* and **An Actor's Revenge** (1963) is more swashbuckler than history. Because the actor of the title works in Kabuki, Ichikawa was prompted to use a theatrical style, which means one highly stylised – cutting into elegant panoramas for detail, trailing through a stage copse, allowing lights to quiver or grow bright, and confining himself to horizontal and vertical movements throughout the whole. He uses a number of angles from Kinugasa's 1936 version, and the same actor in the lead, Kazuo Hasegawa (who had been known as Chojito Hayashi in the prewar film). The role is a dual one, that of a leading transvestite actor and of a thief, his guardian angel. The actor is seen only in female garb and is referred to as 'half-man half-woman', able to take on the characteristics of each. Hasegawa's interpretation of both roles is faultless. He is, in the role, an actor in life, on the stage and consciously a player acting for the camera, a symbol of deception as also celebrated by Renoir in *The Golden Coach* (q.v.) and scrutinised by Bergman in *Ansiktet*.

He is also the Ichikawa epic hero, the man obsessed with a difficult or impossible mission; and we might say that this film

and the two that followed it are studies in determination. In 1962, after several years' planning, the twenty-three-year-old Kenichi Horie crossed the Pacific in a small yacht, which had never been done, as he says, by a Japanese – and indeed should not have been done at all: in almost the first line of dialogue in **Alone on the Pacific** (1963) we learn that small craft are forbidden on the open sea. The film is based on Horie's logbook and its star, Yujiro Ishihara, also the producer, clearly saw in it an excellent role for himself. It starts with Horie's clandestine departure at night, moving backwards to his preparations. Past and present alternate until he is well into his voyage, and Natto Wada's screenplay, even by her own high standards, is marvellously crafted. Horie is obviously an otherwise unremarkable young man; he is not even articulate on his obsession and is, in the event, less well prepared than he thought. He anticipated the loneliness, but not the fear. The film, magically, gains in intensity as Horie becomes inured to poor winds, boredom and his inadequate diet. He cries, he gets drunk. He behaves childishly when spotted, once by a plane which he pretends to photograph so that its occupants should not think he is in need, and once by a tanker, whose offer of food is rejected out

Ichikawa's career reached a peak in the early Sixties, with three remarkable films, *Tokyo Olympiad*, a documentary, *Alone on the Pacific*, a re-creation of actual events, and *An Actor's Revenge*, an historical film as unlike them as they are unlike the rest of his work. All three are masterpieces and unique experiences. *An Actor's Revenge*, as the title implies, is a melodrama, about a Kabuki actor (Kazuo Hasegawa) determined to revenge himself upon the respectable merchants who drove his father to suicide and his mother to madness. Here he is with the chief of the villains, played by Ganjiro Nakamura.

983

of some notion of pride. As land is glimpsed through the mist, he decides to spend the night outside the Golden Gate, in the same mistaken pride which inspired the venture in the first place. In the early-morning light San Francisco – of which he is more terrified than the open sea – rises majestically: for an instant it seems wrong to show us its traffic, to lose, for the first time, Horie's point of view, until we realise how unsuspecting is the city of this transoceanic traveller – and that henceforth Horie's life will be an anti-climax. Ninety-four days at sea, and he is a hero for one day more.

Ichikawa views the man's fanaticism and odd practicality with the bemused detachment which he employs for the athletes in **Tokyo Olympiad** (1965); he also conveys the same sense of awe, and the film is even more extraordinary. Under Miyagawa's supervision over one hundred cameras were used to record the eighteenth Olympic Games, and Ichikawa edited the footage into 130 minutes' celebration of sport and the international spirit. The first, breathtaking section celebrates the carrying of the torch from Athens, tracked by a fluid camera through mountain passes and followed by a portrait of the idiosyncrasies of the nations at the opening ceremony: the final part records the marathon with such intensity and concentration that the closing ceremony is inexorably an explosion of exultation and joy. It is succeeded by these words: 'Night, and the fire returned to the sun . . . to meet again in four years' time. Is it then enough for us – this infrequent, created peace?' They emphasise what had been evident from the start, that Ichikawa was not interested in sport *per se*. His long middle section is an essay on the aspiration, the endeavour, the competitive spirit, the sanity, the magnification of working musculature, the beauty of movement and the fundamental brotherhood of man, and he has done it with great wit and the imaginative use of every single trick at the disposal of the film-maker. But that was not what was required by the Olympic Committee, which had commissioned it and thereby prevented it from being shown except in those countries which had contracted for the rights before the event. The version shown in the U.S., for instance, bears little relation to Ichikawa's and consequently Americans have not had the chance to see one of the masterpieces of modern cinema.

Fate seems to have meted out a like destiny for what, in my opinion, is unequivocally the greatest film ever made, **The Human Condition**, directed by Masaki Kobayashi (b. 1916), a film-maker of the same humanist persuasion as Ichikawa and Kurosawa. He is equally a great director, for it takes an exceptional film-maker to take and fill every second of over nine-and-a-half hours. The film consists of three parts, *No Greater Love* (1959), *Road to Eternity* (1960) and *A Soldier's Prayer* (1961), each over three hours long – in itself an obstacle to commercial distribution. In Japan they were shown separately over a period of years to great popular success; but when the first two parts were shown at European film festivals they were criticised for both length and content. However, enough British critics were sufficiently impressed to guarantee them a showing in London. Unfortunately the venue, a club cinema which had been recently experimenting with sex films, was unsuitable and they were largely ignored. In the U.S. only the first part was shown to the New York critics and, as Bosley Crowther of *The New York Times* disliked it, it quickly disappeared. (Today all three parts are in circulation in the U.S., but the complete work has been seen in Britain only at the National Film Theatre). In *Sight and Sound*, John Peter Dyer spoke of 'titanic journalism', but he also observed that 'no normal, informed person enjoys seeing films about slave labour camps and the inhuman practices of war. There is an understandably general feeling about such films that their message, since it is obvious, is superfluous.'

Were that so, the United Nations would never have been needed and the Nobel Peace Prize would have been discontinued long ago; and that award, in all justice, should have been given to Kobayashi for this film and to Jumpei Gomikawa, on whose six-volume novel it is based. The film, with a screenplay by Kobayashi and Zenzo Matsuyama challenges all normal – as opposed to literary – concepts of capitalism and militarism. It is an epic, or the word has no meaning, awesome in ambition and achievement – in subject matter alone ahead of any Occidental film to this day.

人間の條件 一

The Guinness Book of Records lists Kobayashi's *The Human Condition* as the longest film ever shown, though that source does point out that it was in three separate parts – shown originally in Japanese cinemas over as many years. The film has many another claim to fame, not least in its ambition, which on one level is to pay penance for Japanese aggression in the Thirties and Forties and on another to condemn fascism in all forms. Kobayashi's achievement is immense, so it is ironic that the only available illustrations are rather like this, showing its hero, Tatsuya Nakadai, in contemplation. This is a scene from Part One, as he considers the action to be taken against the cruelty of the guards towards the P.O.W. labourers.

Its hero, Kaji (Tatsuya Nakadai), endures privations which would have defeated Job, and he faces trials more arduous than those which confronted Hercules. Kobayashi understood that to keep us engrossed for so long a time we must love Kaji wholeheartedly; and Kaji is a dedicated humanist.

The Japanese historical film indicates that the humanity of its heroes, from *Sansho Dayu* to *Red Beard*, is alien to the characters who surround them, and we know from *The Human Condition*, which starts in the Thirties, that the word 'humanism' entered the Japanese language unaltered immediately after the War. Kaji lives in a world where he alone knows what it means. He is an avowed pacifist, the opponent of brutality in any form; he believes in the innate dignity of his fellow man, of whatever persuasion, and it is the affirmation of that belief which constantly brings him into conflict with his superiors and with society, and his obstinacy in pursuing his beliefs which makes him both fool and saint. Irony besets his life; he is always misunderstood when acting on behalf of the common good. As late as 1961, even to so perceptive a critic as Dyer, it seemed 'obscure' to present a hero of contradictions: but Kaji, to go no further back, is

like Buñuel's Nazarin, a man whose belief in the society around him constitutes his weakness. Like all of us, he is fallible – and he has the misfortune to be conscripted in 1943. We first meet him some years earlier working for the South Manchurian Steel Company, as labour supervisor at one of the company mines and determined to be compassionate to the six hundred prisoners of war who had been seconded there. He survives denunciation, just as in Part Two he survives barrack-room brutality and in Part Three defeat by the Russians and starvation. He is proud, clever and resourceful, which is why he is so long in succumbing to death.

Kobayashi's length in telling the story is as necessary as that of 'War and Peace', essential to encompass what has to be said: as it progresses, gathering force like a huge river, there is hardly an aspect of contemporary life on which it does not touch. A film that calls itself *The Human Condition* has to incorporate man's capacity for self-destruction, which, in the largest sense, always means war: the barrack room is a microcosm of the larger battlefield, and since the men cannot live in peace in one room it cannot be expected that they can do so elsewhere. Kobayashi, like Ichikawa, finds that war reduces men

985

Kobayashi's *Rebellion*, like many of the other great samurai movies, seems to have taken its cue from the films of Douglas Fairbanks – building tension slowly, with little action, till suddenly all hell breaks loose. It is also a brilliant picture of feudal life, literally concerning a rebellion, when one family pits itself against all those in authority over them. The cause is love, when a young wife is called to the castle now that her illegitimate son, by the deceased lord, has become an heir. Supporting her and her son is Toshiro Mifune, left, called upon to fight Tatsuya Nakadai, a friend in former happy times.

to beasts, but he goes further than Ichikawa or Kurosawa (whose war films are all set in the past): by concentrating on violence and cruelty he is attacking not only Japanese imperialism and aggression in the Thirties and Forties but Fascism in whatever form it is found. It is not profound of him to show that war and destruction degrade the human spirit, and he can be heavy when making a point, as with his one-dimensional villains; and subtlety is lacking, but that does not disqualify *The Human Condition* as a work of art – but I would state that after nine-and-a-half hours during which I have been awed, entertained, thrilled, harried and harrowed for every second my critical faculties are lowered. I have no doubt, however, that just as Kaji is the definitive hero of this century, so this powerful epic dwarfs every other film made up to the present.

Kobayashi had begun directing in 1952 and the following year made *The Room with Thick Walls* about war criminals. Shochiku delayed release for four years while Kobayashi made what he termed 'sweet domestic dramas' in the manner of his master, Kinoshita – but the eventual success of the 1953 film led to *The Human Condition*. Understandably, after that he made a comedy, **The Inheritance** (1962), and only at his most cynical could he claim

that its theme is the individual's response to the problem created by his environment, which he has said is the subject of all his films – since it concerns people whose worries are caused by the modern pursuit of money and materialism. It is not in the manner of Clair and Lubitsch, whom he so much admires, but is black comedy, not far in spirit from 'Volpone', involving a number of intriguers gathered around a dying man. The film holds one's attention, but is hardly funny.

Harakiri (1962) is Kobayashi's first *jidai-geki* film, and is magisterial. It moves the anti-militarist argument of *The Human Condition*, as well as the actor Nakadai, into a seventeenth-century feudal setting. Tsugumo (Nakadai), like Kaji, grows progressively more humane: as a samurai he accepted the code of *bushido*, but just as conditions exposed Kaji to a new set of values, so poverty changes Tsugumo, and he awakens to the code's absurdities. The Tokugawa dynasty brought peace to Japan after 250 years of civil war; but although some *daimyo* remained established in their castles, some samurai had lost both their overlords and their homes and were reduced to a state of ronin. Tsugumo arrives at the castle of Iyi clan and pleads for a corner in which to commit the honourable act of hara-kiri, only to face Saito (Rentaro Mikuni), deputising for the lord, who believes that some samurai have adopted this 'threat' as a form of begging. Just as *The Human Condition* shows the survival of the samurai spirit, so this film tries to destroy whatever lingering beliefs there were in its worth. In the final sequence the whole code is turned upside down, irony piled upon irony until its ethos is demolished. (There is even irony in the casting of Mikuni, an actor accustomed to playing heroic and, indeed, reasoning roles.) The great Japanese directors have always loved irony, but I suspect that what attracted Kobayashi here was the form of the film. It lasts 134 minutes and as the outcome is never in doubt he must have enjoyed filling them. There is much savagery (the film would be unthinkable in colour), but the style is austere, except for the justly celebrated duel on the heath.

Kwaidan (1964) is Kobayashi's first film in colour, his declared aim to make 'a gorgeous multi-coloured scroll painting based on the lines and tones of an Indian

Kobayashi's *Kaseki* begins in Paris, and few films have looked so lovingly at that city – indeed, the first half of the film is a superb exploration of European culture as experienced by a Japanese business-man, Shin Saburi. With him is Keiko Kishi as Madame Marcellin, the wife of a Frenchman and, as it turns out, the Shadow of Death – but as such she is realistic rather than malign or upsetting.

ink painting'. To that end he worked entirely within the confines of the studio to create the seas, forests and swirling mists, in a visual style of great intensity. The film is in four parts, each consisting of a ghost story derived from Lafcadio Hearn's versions of traditional Japanese tales; since a fair number of ghosts materialise magically it is clear that the cinema's capacities for fantasy and mystery are exploited to the full.

Kobayashi returned to the historical film with **Rebellion** (1967), a tense account of a samurai (Toshiro Mifune) who rejects a specific feudal code, is dishonoured thereby, and who waits, as ever, to revenge himself upon those who have cast him out. Chief among these is Kobayashi's own preferred actor, Nakadai, while Mifune, who produced for Toho, is at his most magnificent; it is no disservice to Nakadai to speak of the director and the actor-producer as a matching of giants.

That these three last films were available in the West would seem due to our fondness for samurai and ghosts; as *Rebellion*, in particular, was popular it might have been supposed that we would be shown Kobayashi's next films. However, there was in fact a gap until **Kaseki** (1974), whose commercial chances were reduced by its length (3 hours 40 minutes) and unsatisfactory colour – due to its being culled from a series made for television (with Pan American Airways as one of its sponsors). It is a return to the subject of mortality, and, as in Kurosawa's *Ikiru*, its hero (Shin Saburi) is a modest man. A manufacturer on business in Paris, he suffers the twin pangs of a thwarted love affair and intimations of death. He pauses to contemplate the Romanesque carvings of Vézelay and reflects on the French who have died for its fields – experiences which are absolutely relevant to himself and which help him to put order into what is left of his life. Kobayashi pauses, too, his pacing more apparent now that he avoids the virtuosity of his work hitherto. The mixture of European culture, Japanese big business, the supernatural and the acceptance of the inevitability of death does result in an unusual and enriching experience.

The greatness of these directors influenced many lesser ones, such as Kenji Misumi, whose rather plodding **Zatoichi Monogatari** (1962) nevertheless contains a certain pictorial splendour. He follows the standard formula of late *jidai-geki* – detailed exposition, with several strands of plot coalescing into one, and between the scenes of contemplation and dialogue only one flurry of action before the climactic battle. The author of the original story is Shugoro Yamamoto, whose work was used by Kurosawa. The hero, Zatoichi (Shintaro Katsu) is much like the swordsmen portrayed by Mifune, an outsider of exceptional skill and integrity, somewhat flamboyant, yet doomed to be employed by, and fight for, chieftains and clansmen much his inferior. As so often, the central struggle is between two leaders for local supremacy, and Zatoichi becomes friendly with the champion of the other side, once a great samurai from Edo, now fatally ill. Zatoichi himself, a gambler and masseur when not a warrior, is blind; and it is a measure of Katsu's abilities as an actor that we never doubt that his blindness is a terrifying handicap when fighting in battle.

Katsu has made a career of this role, later taking on both production and direction. (He was replaced by Nakadai in *Kagemusha* when he was found to be monitoring his performance on a T.V. set, since Kurosawa decreed that there was only one director on that project.) The popularity of Zatoichi has resulted in over thirty sequels, and there have been a number of T.V. series, but, unexpectedly, the very first one is reputed to be the best. **Zatoichi and a Chest of Gold** (1964), directed by Kazuo Ikehiro, is equally enjoyable, but memorable mainly for the visual compositions in wide screen and colour by the great cinematographer, Miyagawa. Zatoichi is only one of several legendary swordsmen beloved by Japanese audiences, but unique in having been invented expressly for the cinema. His predecessors include Musashi Miyamoto, based on a real person, whose distinction was that he preferred art and philosophy to fighting, and the fictional one-armed, one-eyed Sazen Tange. They have been the subjects of innumerable films, including trilogies – and which are known by the generic name of *chambara*, a colloquial expression for *ken-geki* or sword-theatre. We have already considered Mizoguchi's film on Miyamoto, *The Swordsman*, and there is at least one good film on Tange, called **Sazen Tange** (1953), directed by Masahiro Makino, which has a labyrinthine plot, intrigue conveyed by conversations interrupted by bursts of action, some social conscience, historical perspective and characters of complexity.

The great Japanese directors built on the groundwork of such films with ferocious virtuosity (including Mizoguchi himself, whose later work is superior to that of *The Swordsman*). In the Sixties two more series vied with Zatoichi for attention, and it is interesting to see vestigial evidence of high intent in even the least of these films, made by various directors usually associated with purely commercial products. Tange was not resurrected during this period, but like him, Kyoshiro Nemuri originated in popular modern fiction. Nemuri's singularity, apart from his reddish hair, was that he was born of an illicit affair between a Portuguese missionary and a lady of the court, from which springs his particular detestation of Christians. The *chambara* films go back to the earliest days of Japanese cinema, but owed this new lease of life to the success of *Yojimbo*. Toei, which had last featured Miyamoto in 1954, initiated a five-part series in 1961 for the company's most popular star, Kinnosuke Nakamura, and its best-known director, Tomu Uchida. Daiei followed suit with the prolific series based on Zatoichi and on Nemuri, who was the subject of eleven films between 1962 and 1969, originally starring Raizo Ichikawa, and, after his death in 1969, Hiroki Matsukata.

I have seen a number of both the Miyamoto and Nemuri films, and, in addition to their striking compositions and invincible heroes, they have a number of other features in common, including the always treacherous court officials and ladies. The scenarios have been constructed with care and flair – for instance, pitching the climactic battle in an unusual terrain. **Musashi Miyamoto: Duel at Ichijoji** (1964) follows the same plot as two earlier versions in trilogies directed by Inagaki. I have not seen them, but cannot imagine that the final battle is as inexpressibly exciting as the one staged here by Uchida – the hero, wielding a sword in each hand, takes on the odds of seventy-three to one in the lanes between the paddy fields. I also cannot imagine why all these films have not been more widely disseminated in the West – they are infinitely superior to the sword-and-sandal spectaculars then being made in Italy – but I must also add that, the action scenes apart, Uchida's handling on this occasion does not seem worthy of the director of *Killing in Yoshiwara*.

The first Japanese film dealing with a contemporary theme to be seen in the West was **Children of Hiroshima** (1953), made independently by Kaneto Shindo (b. 1912), a prolific screenwriter turned director. As a native of Hiroshima he hastened to make this film as soon as the American occupation ended. The Americans had prohibited publication in Japan of detailed photographs or documents of the destructions of Hiroshima and Nagasaki by the atomic bomb, and although everyone knew of the slaughter, little was publicised about the mutilated, burnt or diseased survivors. As a device Shindo uses a young teacher returning to her native city, to learn from survivors what happened the day the bomb fell; and the teacher also becomes involved with a former employer of her father, now a blind beggar, who is trying to find his small grandson. One does not need to be aware of the tremendous cries of rage later raised by Ichikawa and Kobayashi to find much of this too mild and rather picturesque. However, a more committed film on this subject might have been too horrifying to sit through, and we must admit at least that this one is grave and concerned.

Shindo had been assistant to Mizoguchi, but **Onibaba** (1964), his own adaptation of a folk story, does not have his master's distancing, his eeriness or his ability to transform historical fact into legend; nor does it bear out Shindo's claim that his class-consciousness causes him to concentrate on tales of ordinary people. In the tall reeds by a lake, at a time of civil war, two women, one old and one young, rob stragglers of their armour and leave their bodies to rot in a pit. The women grieve for the death of a soldier, son to one, husband to the other: but when a comrade-in-arms arrives, the younger woman throws herself at him while the older writhes in sexual frustration. The film is hysterical in manner and, whatever Shindo's claims, is close to (soft) pornography – which is why it had a certain success with Occidental audiences.

Although Shindo is not as profound as some of those with whom he had worked, there is some merit in **The Life of Chiku-zan** (1977), a biography of the famous, half-blind *shamisen* virtuoso, who appears in person to introduce it. Exquisitely photographed by Kiyomi Kondo, in win-try landscapes and on seashores, it balances grinding poverty and misery against joy in music, physical freedom and movement. Domestic audiences found the film tired and over-familiar, but even though Western cinema had achieved a sophistication equal to that of the Japanese, this was still a more mature biography than most made anywhere else at the time.

Shindo had continued to write occasional screenplays for other directors, such as **The Elegant Beast** (1962), a verbose attempt at social satire centring on a family of scroungers and set entirely in their apartment, which was directed by Yuzo Kawashima. Kawashima, who died the following year aged forty-five, was a strong influence on his contemporaries, among them Yasuzo Masumura, a former assistant to Mizoguchi and Ichikawa. Masumura had been directing for ten years when he made **The Wife of Seishu Hanaoka** (1967), written by Shindo from a story by Sawako Ariyoshi based on the life of a nineteenth-century physican. Accordingly, it follows *Red Beard*, but the films are not alike, this one being a sentimental family chronicle, with births, deaths, illnesses, etc., and just enough conflict for it to be considered a comment on human affairs. It is skilfully made, but is basically a vehicle for three immensely popular players – Raizo Ichikawa, Ayako Wakao and the veteran Hideko Takamine.

Shindo's left-wing views are also common among his contemporary filmmakers. Satsuo Yamamoto's most commercial films are always virulent propaganda, like **The Travelling Players** (1955), which centres on a Kabuki troupe who best their capitalist boss by adopting his principles. Among the other younger directors working in the great tradition, using sensitivity and observation, is Koreyoshi Kurahara: his **Flame of Devotion** (1964) is a beautifully crafted, but much too pretty film about two lovers separated when the boy is conscripted. **Shadow of a Flower** (1961), directed by Yuzo Kawashima, is the study of a bar hostess with too many lovers, which is both a critique of Japanese society and an event for ladies who like to cry in cinemas. The same could be said of **He and She** (1963), in which a housewife finds her suburban world of little account when she meets an improvident rag-picker. The role is played by Sachiko Hidari, the wife of the director, Susumu Hani; the film is principally a star vehicle for her. Much better is **Home from the Sea** (1972), written and directed by the less heralded Yoji Yamada, about a young seaman who is forced to give up his job and move to the mainland. Yamada clearly shares the boy's regret at changing values and handles with loving care the facts of his day-to-day existence.

Except for Hani, these directors are almost unknown in the West, but we have seen several films of their contemporaries, in which the posturing and posing, always present in Japanese cinema, have taken over completely: their films are visually striking, but incoherent to a degree. The artificiality of Yoshige Yoshida's **Coup d'Etat** (1973) destroys a potentially interesting subject, a study of a right-wing professor of the Thirties. A formalised visual splendour robs two historical subjects, **Double Suicide** (1969) and **Himoko** (1969), of any sense of human involvement. Both were directed by Masahiro Shinoda (b. 1931) who clearly hopes to throw off the yoke of the past by emphasising the image – but he does it at the expense of characterisation and theme. He adopts an intense theatricality in telling **The Scandalous Adventures of Buraikan** (1970). The diffuse screenplay by Shuji Tereyama concerns a layabout (Tatsuya Nakadai) who joins a theatrical troupe at the time of the Tempo Reformation in 1842. By setting each scene against paintings, tapestries and huge prints Shinoda does achieve a unity, but it is not an interesting one.

His work is at least polished – something that could not be claimed for the films of Nagisa Oshima (b. 1932). Like many equally ungifted European directors, he has experimented with explicit sex and violence. We may sympathise with his expressed desire to avoid the idioms and techniques of his predecessors, but they are surely better models than Godard and late Fellini. 'I try to start out with the problems of the individual,' he has said, 'and these problems should be meaningful to anybody in the world.' Presumably he was not referring to **Three Resurrected Drunkards** (1969), the clownish adventures of three students, a film which, two-thirds into its exposition, repeats its beginning and continues unchanged – not that the events are any more comprehensible the second time around. And it would be a rare person who could find anything 'meaningful' in the seemingly endless and mindless discussions of orgasm which constitute **Diary of a Shinjuku Thief** (1969). 'Sexual inadequacy,' said the director, 'is a political inadequacy in itself.' References in the film placing the protagonists in the upheavals of 1969 are not something, apparently, with which audiences are sympathetic, since this is a film always accompanied by the banging of seats being vacated. **The Boy** (1969), a traditional story of a child growing up in poverty, is for the most part professional, if frequently sacrificing conviction in pursuit of visual effects.

Fortunately, the post-Kurosawa generation of film-makers had an imposing exponent in Shohei Imamura (b. 1926). After a conventional start he went on to express a commitment to social reform with more intensity than any of his predecessors or colleagues. He had become an assistant to Ozu in 1951, but there is not the least influence of Ozu by the time he came to make his fourth film, **My Second Brother** (1959). This was a studio assignment based on a bestselling diary written by a young girl as she and her brothers and sister struggled against deprivation during the Recession of 1953/4. Magnificently photographed in monochrome by Masahisa Himeda, its portrait of a small seaside mining town in Kyushu is more eloquent than its narrative, proving that Imamura remained faithful to the traditions of treating sentimental stories with extreme harshness: like its contemporary, Imai's *Kiku and Isamu*, it has at once a softheartedness and a realism which should have value for posterity.

Hogs and Warships (1961) is a better example both of Imamura being a filmmaker before a polemicist and his penchant for working on a large canvas. It is stunningly organised and orchestrated, set in the port of Yokosuka where the civilians working with the U.S. Navy have local live-in mistresses and the sailors get drunk in the red-light district. The Americans supply drugs, and are presumably responsible for the fact that gang warfare is infinitely more vicious than at the time of early Ozu (Imamura was a boy when Ozu made his last gangster film). There are several Mr Bigs, and so many rivalries that the 'business' changes hands frequently: challenging the older mob is a bunch of young punks. The youthful hero hopes to escape poverty by resorting to crime; his pure girlfriend gives in to it, and is soon getting drunk and going to a hotel room with three American sailors. Imamura's rather heavy, sardonic humour (though on this occasion he had no hand in writing the script) is apparent as a small boy reads a book about Japan's unique culture still being able to absorb the finer aspects of Western civilisation.

Imamura's obsession with sexuality found clearer expression in **The Insect Woman** (1963) and **Unholy Desire** (1964) – though both are profoundly feminist – which, like many other important Japanese films of this time, reflect the changing role of the woman in marital relations. The title of *The Insect Woman* refers to the life of its heroine, Tome, grubbing like an insect to survive in postwar Japan. The action starts at the end of the First World War, and for a while is incomprehensible. It improves as Tome finds a way to earn a living by exploiting the contacts she made as a servant in a brothel. She loves her protector and is 'used' by him; her daughter sleeps with him and uses him – but ends unrepentant and happy. *Unholy Desire* describes the pitiful attraction a woman feels towards her rapist, a situation not dealt with (at least in Western cinema) since the Silent period. The man concerned is insignificant, a musician playing with a small combo; the woman is not extraordinary, and our emotions are manipulated as we increasingly loath her husband and his mistress, hoping that the wife will take advantage of her semi-infatuation for her own sake. The film is long, sumptuously photographed by Himeda, and in its combination of black humour and melodrama, typical of this period in Japanese cinema. Since it was also a period of greatness, it should be emphasised that this film is entirely worthy of it.

The Pornographer (1966) is less satisfactory, though that may be true only of the export edition which was prepared by Imamura's customary employer, the Nikkatsu Studio. The film is subtitled 'An Introduction to Anthropology', and claims the co-operation of the sex researchers, Phyllis and Eberhard Kronhausen. Its simple thesis is that the trade of pornography is corrupting and degrading. Plied by Subu (Shoichi Ozawa), a former vendor of medical instruments, it is not well paid; he is constantly harried by the police and rival gangs, and the porn film actors are indifferent and unreliable – so he turns his hand to pimping and the peddling of sex drugs. As always in the films of Imamura, the pressures of poverty lead to the disintegration of family life: his stepson makes off with mother's savings, his stepdaughter becomes a prostitute or worse (i.e. is prepared to offer herself for nothing). Subu takes an assistant, also a sexual misfit, uncertain whether he prefers sex with himself or unemotionally with his sister. Subu gradually withdraws from the world, but since he cannot withdraw from his job, he tries to manufacture a life-size doll, in order that men can function sexually without emotion.

The three films, with their common themes, constitute an unintentional trilogy: there are implications throughout that Imamura is becoming impatient of fictional narrative. Ichikawa had dispensed with it in two of his great films, and questioned the worth of it in *An Actor's Revenge*. Antonioni in *Blow-Up* (q.v.) had debated the function of the camera as an instrument of truth, and Imamura himself had begun to question this in *Unholy Desire*, as the mistress stalks the lovers with a camera, and in *The Pornographer*, in which, in the porn film being made, the viewer will see only what he wants to see – and, indeed, will command such movies to order, requiring even more than usual fabrication on the part of the pornographer. Imamura's musing on the subject resulted in **A Man Vanishes** (1967), which is solely concerned with the nature of truth. The man who has vanished has been charged with embezzlement, but that provides only one clue to his disappearance. At first we may suppose the enquiry is being pursued by the police, or by the press, but it turns out that the film itself is the investigation – a documentary. What we, the audience, thought was fiction was actually fact. But it makes little difference, for Imamura is so intent on examining theories that the film dies.

Aware of its failure, he moved to a new theme, or at least seemed to. **Legends** from a Southern Island (1968), also known as *The Profound Desire of the Gods*, is his initiation to colour, and is set on a tropical island almost untouched by civilisation. Its oldest family is primitive in a way that gives added meaning to the word – riddled with superstition, incest, nymphomania, supernatural cunning, mental deficiency and existing at a level hardly higher than animals. That is how they are regarded by the pasty-faced engineer from Tokyo sent to run the local factory. We may see them as akin to the characters of *Tobacco Road*, until Imamura decides to show them – and, eventually their surroundings too – through their own eyes, revealing the island as a paradise that should remain unspoilt. It does not, and the epilogue reveals the native family being endowed with a mythic status for the delectation of the tourists, a status in which truth and legend are mingled until they are indistinguishable.

Following this film, which is as haunting as it is ambitious, Imamura retreated to familiar themes in **History of Post-War Japan as Told by a Bar Hostess** (1970). Like *Hogs and Warships* it is set in the red-light district of Yokusuka; the title is reminiscent of the theme of *The Insect Woman* and like *A Man Vanishes* it consists of personal recollections of past events. Its form is a combination of newsreels and interviews, with Imamura himself on camera asking his bar hostess whether she is telling the truth. Her misplaced trust in her own destiny is contrasted with her cynicism towards such matters as the Imperial wedding and photographs of atrocities in Vietnam; both attitudes are contrasted with a more general portrait of society, seemingly forever disturbed by train crashes and revolutionary fervour. But the general and the particular aspects of this film do not really fuse, which is why I think it a pity that it is this director's only film to be widely seen in the West. It is much less riveting than **Karayuki-San** (1975), a relatively simple documentary about a woman who, kidnapped in her teens, has spent her life in a series of brothels in Malaya. It is part conversation with the old lady herself, part reconstruction of her past, and part dissertation on the subject of prostitution. Imamura made this film for television, his chosen medium at this time, finding it preferable for the

examination of a number of his preoccupations – and there were several further studies of the War and its aftermath.

Imamura returned to feature films with **Vengeance Is Mine** (1979), based on a novel by Ryuzu Saki, in turn based on fact, and once again his protagonist is formed by the environment, postwar Japan. Enokizu (Ken Ogata) is a multiple murderer with no redeeming feature except his sense of humour and, as in his earlier films, Imamura lays a number of unpleasant facts before the audience, inviting it to reach some conclusions of its own. He offers an explanation, since Enokizu suspects his wife of an incestuous relationship with his father (the incest frequent in Imamura's work is seldom between blood relations), and then withdraws it. He refuses to show compassion – the usual excuse for sex and violence on the screen – though he does detail the conditions, usually induced by poverty, which can produce a morally malformed character. Enokizu is captured and hanged, but there remains one murder unexplained by its perpetrator, his captors, or the events that we have seen: and the effect is chilling. Since I believe that Imamura had earlier inspired less talented directors to use sex and violence on the screen, his object may have been merely to show them how to use these ingredients. Indeed they are portrayed so graphically as to be indefensible, were it not for his consummate skill.

The film reaffirms Imamura's claim to be considered the principal heir to the Japanese masters, but his next film, **Eijanaika** (1981), signally fails to support this claim. It is his first exercise in *jidai-geki* – and Japanese film tradition and history are too powerful for the term to be avoided, even at this stage. The film is set immediately before the Meiji restoration and Imamura wished to draw comparisons with the situation then and that existing today. The title may be translated as 'What the hell!' and is the name given to the supposedly spontaneous riots of 1867, which occurred all over Japan in an attempt to overthrow the Tokugawa Shogunate, as many of the clans resented its fraternisation with foreigners. Imamura wonderfully conveys a society in flux: the 'invaders' with their import-export offices, the disillusioned samurai, the occasional national in Western dress.

The central character is Genji (Shigeru Izumiya), who returns to Japan with rudimentary English after being shipwrecked. His wife meanwhile has become involved with the criminal underworld, and the two of them are among a large cast of characters, all whipped on and off the screen so quickly that they remain shadowy. In this case Imamura's preference for a broad canvas defeats him: even at 151 minutes it telescopes both particular and historical events too much for comprehension. Himeda's photography has never served this director so well, but the chance has been lost – the chance, that is, to get a major film by Imamura into distribution in the West,★ where audiences have shown a preference for *jidai-geki* subjects.

I believe the film fails because Imamura tries too hard: even he finds it daunting to invite comparisons with a great generation of film-makers – despite the fact that his contemporary subjects demonstrated a revitalisation after the achievements of Ozu, Shimazu, Gosho, Naruse and Imai. Those film-makers had found that the restrictions of the genre film were an advantage – but when the bounds were breached by Kinoshita and Mizoguchi, all Japanese directors found themselves confronting greater truths in both modern and historical subjects, pointing the way for the great films of Kurosawa, Ichikawa and Kobayashi. When questioned, these directors have preferred to remain mute about their successors (I hope in the case of Imamura because they regard him rather as a contemporary), but they have been vocal enough on the subject of their industry, which they insist has never been more constricting and less adventurous. On both issues they must feel betrayed.

When Richard Griffith wrote 'The Film Since Then' in 1956, he had had but a glimpse of Japanese cinema and, helped by secondhand accounts from other writers on cinema, briefly noted some twenty-eight films. This was enough for him to think we were on the verge of making a great discovery. I have seen over two hundred Japanese films, but I would make the same observation. The Japanese cinema started moving towards greatness in the late Forties, to reach its peak in the Sixties. It is easy enough to list the Japanese masters – and let me make it clear that I regard Imamura as belonging with those mentioned in the preceding paragraph – but I have included, where possible, the work of other directors of whom our knowledge is incomplete. Almost the only Japanese film to enter the international repertory in the Seventies was Oshima's absurd, but sexually explicit, *In the Realm of the Senses*. Yamada, who made *Home from the Sea*, remains unknown outside his own country; Imamura is known mainly from festivals and retrospectives organised by the cinematheques.

But if we are forced back on those Japanese directors whose work we do know thoroughly there are still assessments to be made. They made masterpieces, and at the very least we can say that they never confused or misled audiences in the construction and composition of their extraordinary images. These are the great storytellers and the great stylists and it is with wonder that I recall the sheer density and excitement of their historical films. And it is with gratitude that I think of the humanity with which so many of the rest are imbued.

★As this book goes to press, *The Song of Narayama*, a remake of Kinoshita's film, won the 1983 Grand Prix at Cannes.

993

36

France: Before and After the Nouvelle Vague

After his Hollywood sojourn Max Ophuls returned to France to make his last four films. The last of them all, the ambitious *Lola Montes*, was unfortunately a failure with both the press and the public, but the three films which preceded it must be among most people's happiest cinema memories – witty, stylish and deeply cynical about the romantic world they invoke. ABOVE RIGHT, *La Ronde*, with Simone Signoret (and it is Gérard Philipe who is gazing down at her); BELOW RIGHT, the first episode of the three-part *Le Plaisir*, with Simone Simon; and ABOVE FAR RIGHT, Charles Boyer and Danielle Darrieux in *Madame De* .

TO THE POSTWAR generation, the foreign-language cinema meant predominantly the French. The Italians were impressive, but Anglo-Saxon importers remained wary – and, besides, art-house audiences were familiar with French players and directors. The French cinema was established as presenting a more civilised view of life than was to be found in most American and British movies. Its devotees were accustomed to films which would be uncommercial in English – but what was not readily apparent was that French cinema was moribund, decaying in imaginary gloom. With the hindsight of over three decades this becomes evident, especially because in the interim there was an explosion of talent which changed not only French cinema but all cinema. It was the nouvelle vague or new wave, supposedly washing away the established French film-makers. Most of those did become redundant, but not entirely with justice.

In movies at that time to be civilised meant, above all, to be witty about sex – and the supreme exponent of that was Max Ophuls, returning to work in France after his years in Hollywood. After the modest success of *The Reckless Moment*, its producer, Walter Wanger, tried to set up a production of *La Duchesse de Langeais* in Europe, with Ophuls directing Garbo and James Mason. But while the lady hesitated – which was why the backers eventually balked – Ophuls received an invitation from France to film Schnitzler's 'Reigen', with a glittering cast. Whatever the weaknesses of Schnitzler's text, **La Ronde** (1950) is a triumph from the instant the credits fade: Anton Walbrook, elegant, suave and blasé, strolls on to a set which is neither studio nor stage but a dreamlike

fantasy of how Vienna should have been. Jean d'Eaubonne designed it and Christian Matras photographed it, complementing the text, which if not high wit is at least in the tradition of such moralities. The characters are puppets as they act out their *vie amoureuse* – the whore (Simone Signoret), the soldier (Serge Reggiani), the chambermaid (Simone Simon), the student (Daniel Gélin), the married woman (Danielle Darrieux), her husband (Fernand Gravey), the *grisette* (Odette Joyeux), the poet (Jean-Louis Barrault), the actress (Isa Miranda) and the count (Gérard Philipe), who meets up with the whore to complete the circle. Since their sexual needs differ, the outcome of each relationship cannot be predicted. The loneliness, the frequent degradations and the lack of satisfaction have scarcely been transmitted by Ophuls, who in using period conventions could only function in this *décoratif* way. However, his obvious understanding of such matters provides the work with its unique texture, and its enchantment has not diminished with the years, even if its piquancy has gone. Audiences were not then accustomed to such sexual frankness, and it is doubtful whether the film could have played in Britain had the censor not recently introduced the X certificate for such fare. Denounced by the popular press and praised by the critics, *La Ronde* ran even longer in the West End of London than the unprecedented twelve months of *Ladri di Biciclette*. American distributors were reluctant to handle it, and when it eventually arrived in 1954 its sexual frankness was no longer a box-office factor. It was to be some years before Ophuls was recognised in America, despite his Hollywood films. In Britain, astonishingly, critics were

The Romantic World of Max Ophuls

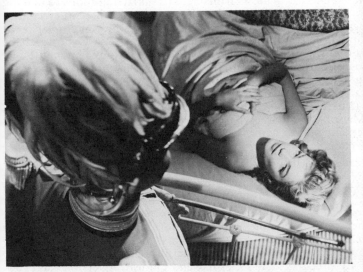

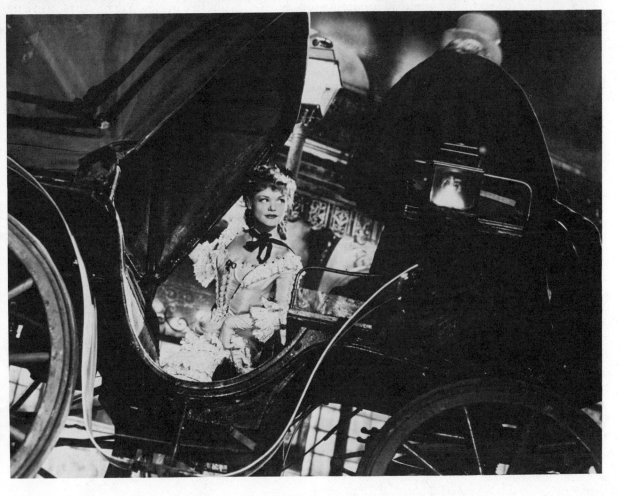

grudging about his next two films. Even with the success of *La Ronde* Ophuls found difficulty in getting backing for **Le Plaisir** (1952), which, following omnibus film versions of short stories by Maugham in Britain and O. Henry in the U.S., is made up of three tales by de Maupassant. 'Cynicism and sentimentality substitute for irony and melancholy,' noted Richard Winnington, but that is not true of either 'Le Masque', concerning a man who refuses to submit to old age, or 'Le Modèle', which follows the quarrels of an artist (Gélin) and his mistress (Mlle Simon). The long central story, 'La Maison de Madame Tellier', about a carriageful of whores who take an excursion to the country for a first communion, has a vivacity which defies criticism.

Madame de . . . (1953) is, wrote Karel Reisz in *Sight and Sound*, 'all stylishness . . . an uneven, often tedious film', but no matter how many times the camera of Matras glides full circle round d'Eaubonne's *fin de siècle* sets, the film is a masterpiece. These images are precisely correct for a wealthy, handsome society engaged in amorous intrigue, eventually more deeply snared by their hypocrisy than in any of Ophuls's other tales in the same vein. The character of Monsieur de . . . (Charles Boyer) is the archetype of his era, acknowledged to have a lover while his wife (Mlle Darrieux) may not; he allows her to flirt and lie, but because of his own double standard he is oblivious to the fact that she is playing with fire; and when she uses these deceits on the baron (Vittorio de Sica), in a love of genuine passion, he too rejects her. Thus society, frivolous and superficial, claims its victims, which is the theme of all of Ophuls's best films, from *Liebelei* through *Komedie om Geld*. Irony and melancholy are in *Le Plaisir* and *Madame de . . .*, as they are in *La Ronde*: but to find them you must perhaps be prepared to look beneath the surface.

Ophuls himself, working in an industry of vanities, was also a victim, his reputation constantly fluctuating. He was forced to return to Germany for what became his last film, **Lola Montes** (1955), the most expensive yet made on the Continent – and a failure of equal proportions. Like Paul Fejos, a quarter of a century earlier, a degree of success had made him (or his producers) overambitious, and the film

was made in three languages. Like Hitchcock with *Under Capricorn*, he was returning after many years to his native country with a subject which he admitted was unsuitable but which he felt was a worthy challenge. His initial objections to making a film about a nineteenth-century courtesan were silenced as he contemplated the romantic life of Zsa Zsa Gabor and the nervous disorders of Judy Garland. So he made the courtesan/star a victim, condemned to live out her life in the gaze of a contemptuous public, as indicated in the allegorical framing device of a circus, with Peter Ustinov as the ringmaster, 'exposing' Lola, but secretly sympathetic to her. This circus is as dazzling as anything Ophuls ever did, in itself a device similar to that used in *Komedie om Geld* and the compère introduced into *La Ronde*; but it so disturbed the earliest audiences of *Lola Montes* that the sequences were badly cut and reassembled at the end of the film by its producers, hoping to recoup their losses. The film failed equally in French, German and English. A version was eventually seen in New York in 1978, when the critic John Simon quite correctly observed that it 'sinks under the combined ballast of banality, sentimentality and pointlessness'. Ophuls retains only his visual style on this occasion; fatally lacking is his sense of humour, apparent even in such thankless chores as *The Exile*. Doubtless he was depressed by the wooden performance of Martine Carol, imposed upon him because she was supposed to be a popular star; he needed the wit of a Feuillère or Darrieux.

The French cinema was also the brighter for the return of another great film-maker, Jean Renoir, but in his case he went back reluctantly. His reputation, declining during his Hollywood years and with only *La Grande Illusion* then remembered from the earlier period, was restored when **The River** (1951) was acclaimed at the Venice Festival. He had, with her assistance, adapted Rumer Godden's novel about an English family living in Bengal, convinced that it would reopen the American studios to him. They wanted him to include either elephants or a tiger-hunt, as did Kenneth McEldowney, a Los Angeles florist who otherwise loved the book as much as he did; but the film went ahead without either after McEldowney had raised the money through his connections in India and in the

film industry. The film is in the form of a diary kept by an adolescent girl – played by Patricia Walters, who had never acted before – and it is an affectionate documentary and a tale of the pangs of youth, which include her crush on an embittered ex-G.I. (Thomas E. Breen). Some of it is trite but all of it is beautiful, as photographed in Technicolor on locations found by Renoir's customary art director, Eugene Lourié. This is the East that Occidentals know, the ordinary among the extraordinary, with no dividing line between dream and reality; throughout there is the feeling that when the British have gone life will go on as before.

Renoir continued to live in California till the end of his life, but he had to go to Italy to get backing for his next film, **The Golden Coach** (1953). It is based on a one-act play by Mérimée about a *Commedia dell' Arte* troupe in a Spanish colony, whose

leading actress (Anna Magnani) has to choose between three suitors, including the viceroy (Duncan Lamont). Simultaneous versions were made in Italian, French and English, but when the English one was only moderately successful Renoir commuted to Paris to make – in French – his last half-dozen films. **French Cancan** (1955) is the story of a showman (Jean Gabin) whose instincts for theatre take precedence over his love life, even though, as he admits, the two are inseparable. In **Elena et les Hommes** (1956) an impoverished Polish princess (Ingrid Bergman) is persuaded by her lovers – who include Jean Marais and Mel Ferrer – that their passion for her might change the course of France's politics. Gaiety and high spirits pervade all three films, recalling *La Règle du Jeu* – for in a world in which masters chase maidservants, the theatre is the only reality. Except, of course, that it is

The last films of Jean Renoir are uneven in quality, but in sum they represent his life's ponderings on love, on art and the other matters that had often preoccupied him. The 'art' in *French Cancan* is that of the theatre, and since there are many pretty girls around, most of the male characters are in love with one or the other of them, while Renoir clearly rejoices in the cancan itself, since it was designed to shock the bourgeoisie.

not: in 1957 Renoir observed (in an interview in *Cahiers du Cinéma*) that 'the more honest approach to what we call a work of art would include the recognition that art is transitory . . . I wonder if the idea we have of a work isn't more important than the work itself, and if in turn the importance of this idea is not based on the good that this idea can do for men: a good which is absolutely undefinable, and which I refuse to catalogue. I refuse to say "This is good, that is bad".'

Yes, but in *The Golden Coach* and *French Cancan* a number of facts and factors jostle in a roundelay – success, poverty, promiscuity, prostitution, talent, art, roistering, wealth, failure, ambition. All may be forgotten when the curtain goes up – in the most transient of all the arts. In *Elena et les Hommes* all difficulties are solved by love, and that is the greatest illusion of them all. In the decade that culminated with *La Règle du Jeu*, Renoir was starkly realistic; in these three films, with their often stylised sets, he is, respectively, romantic, frivolous and facetious. They are all four, to an extent, the same film.

Elena et les Hommes, dubbed and rechristened – *Paris Does Strange Things*, by Warner Bros. – was a failure and Renoir never again flirted with international names or was so ambitious. In 1955 in Paris he directed a play he had written, 'Orvet', and arising from that he decided to examine further the nature of good and evil. He made a very personal adaptation of 'Dr Jekyll and Mr Hyde', called *Le Testament du Docteur Cordelier*, which he directed for television in 1959. It was shown in Paris cinemas two years later, and on the large screen is insubstantial and amateurish in appearance. Jean-Louis Barrault plays the double-role, but Renoir is fatally unable to be explicit about the exact nature of his evil. He so liked the working methods of television that he chose to film **Le Déjeuner sur l'Herbe** (1959) with five simultaneous cameras and in chronological order (in twenty-four days), using his father's home, Les Collettes, near Cagnes. As the title implies, he tried to render in screen terms the spirit of the early Impressionists – their discoveries with light, nature and sensuality. The wind rustles the leaves of the silvery Provençal trees, the goatherd blows his pipe and some picnickers embark on a bacchanal; a *savant*

(Paul Meurisse), usually preoccupied with European plans for artificial insemination, forgets everything in the arms of a farmer's daughter (Catherine Rouvel). We knew from *Dr Cordelier* that Renoir detested modern science, and this clash between nature and science is balanced the way he wanted it; it is the thesis of an old man imparting the lessons of a lifetime. Like his published memoir ten years later, it is neither penetrating nor provocative, but it is full of love and old truths. It is his last wholly personal statement.

That memoir does not mention **Le Caporal Epinglé** (1962), the only film of his later years which he did not initiate himself – clearly offered to him because he had made the most famous of P.O.W. films. He said at the time that the distributor had cut it, thereby distorting it, but it is a good film, somewhat different from his recent work. Of course, detention camps are ugly, yet something precious comes out of the German incarceration of the French in 1940 – camaraderie. When the two friends (Jean-Pierre Cassel, Claude Rich) say goodbye at the end, Renoir has gone further than in *La Grande Illusion*, in which the absurdity of war created mutual understanding. He made this statement again in his memoir, when he spoke of his love for Jacques Becker, noting that only chance had made it a non-sexual one. Clearly, when sex was not involved, love was no longer an illusion. The theme is repeated in his last screen work, **Le Petit Théâtre de Jean Renoir** (1969), in the episode 'Le Roi d'Yvetot', when the mutual love between husband, wife and best friend is only spoilt by the sexual act – or what society assumes to have been sexual. This four-part film was made for television, and apart from this sequence is negligible, with a Christmas Eve fantasy and an extended sketch about a houseproud wife. Renoir did not retire and did not give up the hope of making another film until just before his death. Despite the failure of *Elena* – in France also – his reputation had continued to grow in the Fifties and the restitution of the original version of *La Règle du Jeu* confirmed his position. Three years later *Le Caporal Epinglé* proved him as capable as any of making a youthful film. I do not know why the nouvelle vague directors, who admired Renoir so much, were unable to persuade their financiers to help him as they aided each other. I do know that his late films seem even better now than when they were made.

The strain sometimes evident in René Clair's two post-Hollywood movies may be found again in **Les Belles-de-Nuit** (1953), a tale of an impoverished musician (Gérard Philipe) who seeks relief from frustration, bureaucracy and the day's noises (pneumatic drills etc) in dreams – going back each time to a different generation, only to find that 'the good old days' were not so good after all. His dream adventures are mainly amorous, and as they turn sour he is pursued from epoch to epoch neither amusingly nor inventively. However, there is a pleasing tendency for everyone to burst into song, and Georges Van Parys's score is witty even if Clair's screenplay is not. No one else could have made it, and some of the sequences of the musician with his friends recall Clair's early films, which means that some of it at least is magical.

Putting aside whimsy, Clair made his most touching film, **Les Grandes Manoeuvres** (1955), about a philanderer (Philipe) who wagers with his fellow-officers that he can make any woman fall in love with him – and the woman chosen is a divorcée (Michèle Morgan) who is also the local milliner. The plot* had seen valiant service in musical comedies, and the challenge to Clair was to make it work again, which he does in a splendid fusion of the players, the setting – a small garrison town before 1914 – and colour, predominantly pastel shades. The music of the period is wittily used and at least two sequences are of total enchantment. We had not seen Clair in this mood before, but **Porte des Lilas** (1957) has the same wistful quality – of chances lost and hopes unfulfilled. At the same time, like *Les Belles-de-Nuit*, it recalls the early films, for it shares a joy in the enterprise and loyalty of artisan chums – 'L'Artiste' (Georges Brassens) and the dreaming, drunken Ju-Ju (Pierre Brasseur), who shelter a gangster (Henri Vidal) on the run.

If none of these films has, when required, the gaiety of his early films they are nevertheless equally fresh, but with **Tout**

l'Or du Monde (1961) Clair was suddenly tired: some city-slickers, aided by the press and a publicity-seeking pop-singer, descend upon a village which they plan to turn into a skyscraper city – till it turns out that the country bumpkins are too smart for them. The targets are familiar ones from Clair's Silent films onwards, but his jokes have become laboured. In the interim Hollywood, and Ealing, had tackled the situation with more zest, but there are some minor delights, including Bourvil as three different generations of yokel. One further film, **Les Fêtes Galantes** (1965), with Jean-Pierre Cassel, was considered so inferior to all the numerous historical romps which had followed in the wake of *Fanfan-la-Tulipe* that Clair retired. However, as with Renoir and Ophuls, a mellow decade followed his unsatisfactory experience in Hollywood.

Certainly the three of them were luckier than some of their contemporaries. Julien Duvivier made, in Italy, **Le Petit Monde de Don Camillo** (1952), which was so successful that a sequel was called for, **Le Retour de Don Camillo** (1953), made in Spain. The second seemed unnecessary at the time, and the first has dated, despite the fact that its subject – the clash of Church and Communism in postwar Italy – remains a factor in European life. Taking its

René Clair had not made a contemporary tale of his beloved Paris for over two decades when he filmed *Porte des Lilas*, and instead of the joyous, studio-created city of *Le Million* he filmed in one of the shabbier quartiers, under glum skies. However, his mood had hardly changed, and this a jolly, affectionate film; his heroes, Pierre Brasseur and Georges Brassens, are quite as enterprising as those of his earlier films.

*Clair's source was a novel by Georges Courteline, but the best-known version, 'Captain Jinx of the Horse Marines', is by Courteline's American contemporary, Clyde Fitch.

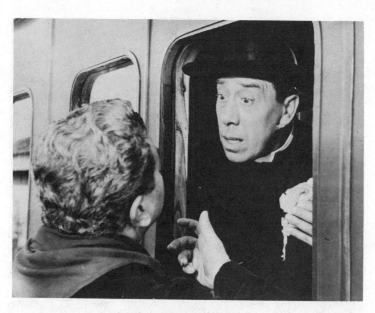

The comic actor Fernandel had been popular in foreign art-houses for many years, but it was *Le Petit Monde de Don Camillo* which brought him a wider popularity, to the extent that after that every film he made was imported into Britain and the U.S., though with diminishing results, since few of them were as good. This was one of the last good films of the once-estimable Julien Duvivier; with Fernandel is Gino Cervi.

tone from the original novel by Giovanni Guareschi it offers no more than a series of comic compromises between the priest (Fernandel) and the mayor (Gino Cervi). The virtual dismissal everywhere of **Pot-Bouille** (1957) was an indication that Duvivier was no longer taken seriously. It is a good film, or seems so now: he was never a great director, but had on occasion fine material. Since Zola's book was not betrayed in Henri Jeanson's adaptation, and since the film is wholly amused and cynical about the sexual habits of the bourgeoisie it gives much pleasure, except towards the end when everyone suddenly seems tired of the venture. Gérard Philipe is the young philanderer from Aix whose arrival at the boarding house – the *pot-bouille* of the title – only increases the adultery being conducted therein. Dany Carrel is one of his victims and the more-than-fleeting glimpse of her bare breasts is instance of France still leading the way in screen frankness.

Duvivier continued making films till his death, but the results were at best undistinguished. The half-dozen features made by Marcel Carné during this period – the last in 1971 – were no more kindly received, but **Les Tricheurs** (1958) was very successful on its home territory. It was accepted as an authentic portrait of the French *jeunesse*, their morals and mores, but by the time it arrived in Britain and the

U.S. it seemed dowdy and cliché-ridden in comparison to *Les Cousins* (q.v.), which had preceded it. **Trois Chambres à Manhattan** (1958) is handled equally flatly, but Carné has retained some of the spirit of Simenon's original story, and it is engagingly played by Annie Girardot, Maurice Ronet and Gabriele Ferzetti.

Claude Autant-Lara, never as celebrated as Duvivier or Carné, fared much better and made some interesting films in the Fifties – even if, as before, the interest was often chiefly in the decor. Both **Le Rouge et le Noir** (1954) and **Le Joueur** (1958) are prettily designed in pastel shades. Gérard Philipe is wonderfully at home in both films, his Julien Sorel perfectly partnered by Danielle Darrieux's Mme de Renal and his Alexei by Françoise Rosay's aged countess. These are attractive and intelligent entertainments, but to be worthy of their originals – Stendhal and Dostoevsky – they need wit, bustle, energy, detail and intellectual strength. Autant-Lara's customary writers, Aurenche and Bost, gave him one of their rare original screenplays with **L'Auberge Rouge** (1951), and they were all more deft on this occasion. The inn of the title shelters a coachload of travellers, including a monk (Fernandel) and his accompanying novice (Didier d'Yd), who learn, but cannot report, that the innkeeper (Carette) and his wife (Mlle Rosay) are mass murderers whose customers never complete their journeys. Many Anglo-Saxons first learnt the expression *comédie noire* because of this film, which remains superior to most later examples of the genre.

Autant-Lara was one of several directors, including Rossellini and Yves Allégret, who contributed to **Les Sept Péchés Capitaux** (1952), and his episode is the best as well as the longest. It concentrates on two ladies, Rosay and Michèle Morgan, who are proud and impoverished, so that they surreptitiously steal food at a society gathering. Autant-Lara's instinct for emotional situations served Colette well in **Le Blé en Herbe** (1954), her story about a woman – played in the film by Edwige Feuillère – who, to relieve boredom during a long, hot summer, initiates an adolescent (Pierre-Michel Beck) into the pleasures of love-making. In **En Cas de Malheur** (1959) the same actress suffers heartbreak when her lawyer husband (Jean

Gabin) falls passionately in love with a hussy (Brigitte Bardot, q.v.) half his age. With more forceful material Autant-Lara made one of his best films, **La Traversée de Paris** (1956), which takes as its starting point Paris under the Occupation. That was a subject the French cinema had not yet confronted, and the exigencies of this plot required reference to the black market – for it is because of that that a painter (Gabin) and an unemployed cab driver (Bourvil) have to smuggle a pig across Paris in the blackout. Their series of adventures are mainly of a comic nature; although in Marcel Aymé's original story one murdered the other in exasperation, the ending used here is unusually moving, and it makes its own comment on the Nazis and the Occupation.

Jacqueline Audry (b. 1908) is a small-scale Autant-Lara, insofar as she was attracted to literary adaptations, preferably set in the recent past. Unlike him, she had little technical skill, being content to set her camera down before two people talking. In spite of this, her three films of Colette stories have a certain charm. Danièle Delorme, 'discovered' for **Gigi** (1949), is the star of all three, and she is absolutely right. She is marvellously partnered in that film by Frank Villard, a somewhat pasty and paunchy Gaston, growing younger as he falls in love, while Gaby Morlay as her tightmouthed aunt and Yvonne de Bray as her grandmother are also splendid. Audry had had difficulty setting up the film, but its success led to **L'Ingénue Libertine** (1950), with Delorme and Villard as the couple whose marriage founders in infidelity and boredom till a really good bout of love-making – but that was something even the French could not convey at this time. Again with her husband, Pierre Laroche, scripting, Audry made **Mitsou: ou, Comme l'Esprit vient aux Filles** (1957), with the welcome addition of colour. It falters on its thesis that a soldier would expect a cabaret artiste and kept woman (Delorme) to be a lady of taste, but is otherwise charming. It arrived in New York one month before M-G-M's icing-sugar *Gigi*, to which all three films are preferable.

The adolescent emotions in **Olivia** (1951) are lesbian, and this is the first major film since *Mädchen in Uniform*, also set in a girls' school, to handle the theme. The author of the pseudonymous novel was later revealed to be Dorothy Bussy, Lytton Strachey's sister, and it is an autobiographical account of her girlhood at a French school, where she was presumably the object who comes between the graceful, understanding headmistress (Feuillère) and her peevish, coquettish lover (Simone Simon). The film offers no more than a hand squeezed to bosom or lip to brow, but only once does it indicate that the love – not sexuality – permeating the school is unacceptable to society. Ophuls's designer, d'Eaubonne, had replaced Audry's earlier collaborator, and had clearly stimulated her to a more fluent style. There is a lesbian (Arletty) in **Huis Clos** (1955), closeted in a déclassé hotel room with a failed revolutionary (Villard) and a vapid Parisienne (Gaby Sylvia). This is a version of the play in which Sartre proposed 'L'enfer, c'est les autres', and these three people are to irritate each other throughout eternity. By moving beyond the room in time and place, the film improves upon the play; but it is doubtful whether it is more worthwhile than adaptations of less distinguished dramatists.

It was still a long while after *Olivia* that the screen could suggest that schoolboys suffered similar passions, and **Les Amitiés Particulières** (1964) is based on a twenty-year-old novel of which producers had hitherto been wary. In the interim its author, Roger Peyrefitte, had become one of France's most respected writers – despite his hostility to the Church. Aurenche and Bost, who did the adaptation, have substituted for that a wry humour, though the picture of the Catholic seminary remains unflattering. Didier Haudepin and Francis Lacombrade are the unfortunate boys, with Michel Bouquet as an over-curious priest and Louis Seigner as the one whose meddling kindness leads to tragedy – the two of them as prejudiced as they are pious. The film indeed is an unexpected success, and a last major work by Jean Delannoy, whose historical films and literary adaptations had usually been inferior to those of Autant-Lara. However, he had directed two lively adaptations of Simenon, **Maigret tend un Piège** (1958) and **Maigret et l'Affaire Saint-Fiacre** (1959), both with Jean Gabin. He also made a visually exquisite but static version of **La Princesse de Clèves** (1961), with

Simone Signoret, centre, in *Casque d'Or*, Jacques Becker's romantic film, set in the Paris underworld just before the turn of the century. Much later this actress observed that it was the only *chef d'oeuvre* with which she had been associated and, if she is being unfair to the many other good films she has made, her pride in this one is understandable. On the left of her is Claude Dauphin and on the right Dominique Davray.

Marina Vlady and Jean Marais, thus resuming his collaboration with Jean Cocteau, who had prepared this version of Mme de Lafayette's novel some years earlier, but now felt disinclined to direct it himself.

Cocteau's own farewell to the cinema was **Le Testament d'Orphée** (1960), and in returning to the trickery of *Le Sang d'un Poète* he had come full circle. The reference in the title to his most celebrated work may be acknowledgement that it is the only one he created of lasting merit; the two films are not to be compared, despite the degree of cannibalism involved. Cocteau, whatever acclaim he had received, refused to see himself as part of the great world, since his penchant for fantasy and his private life were unsuited to it. His real-life lover, Edouard Dermithe, appears in that capacity and as Cégeste from *Orphée*; but although this is an arrogant film it resorts constantly to symbolism. George Steiner once wrote in *The New Yorker* that 'in Cocteau, homosexuality breeds ingenious tinsel', but the symbolism is far from ingenious. The film is a conceit, at once totally negative and totally narcissistic.

Among the younger French directors, Jacques Becker held the commanding place, though now it is hard to be amused by **Edouard et Caroline** (1951), which

made his name with Anglo-Saxon audiences. Marital, as opposed to bucolic, comedy was rare from France, inasmuch as the many similar French farces from the Thirties had not been exported; the quarrelling spouses here are Anne Vernon and Daniel Gélin, and the attempts at satire – at the expense of the bourgeoisie – are lacking in originality. Becker in fact is a puzzling talent, but he made one masterpiece, **Casque d'Or** (1952), and it is so perfectly crafted as to suggest that it was the only time he had complete control over his material. In taking this novel from the Thirties, based on a true underworld romance, his self-confessed task was to combine the worlds of Auguste Renoir and Eugène Sue; and quite probably the sequence of the lovers' rural happiness was inspired by *Partie de Campagne*. Much of it was filmed on location, in the wide cobbled streets of Montmartre and on the riverbanks of Arnet-sur-Marne; the art direction is by d'Eaubonne, surpassing himself, rendering his fine work for Ophuls and others as mere frou-frou. The details are unforgettable, such as Marie (Simone Signoret) knifing off slivers of cheese as she taunts her *mec* (Claude Dauphin), or her lover, Manda (Serge Reggiani), stuffing his casquette into his corduroy jacket as he prepares for the fight. Such moments are enveloped by Becker in a gathering narrative, like particles of dust shimmering in sunlight, triumphantly surmounting the major convention of underworld melodrama, in which the lovers cannot escape their tragic destiny. No praise can be too high for the playing: Signoret's hip-waggling, mocking whore is redeemed by an innate decency, and later transformed into a woman zealously in love, while Reggiani's meek, moustached carpenter finds sinew when that love is challenged. The film was poorly received in Paris and Brussels before winning golden opinions in London, as Mme Signoret recalled in 1973, when Paris flocked to a revival.

Touchez pas au Grisbi (1954) is a contemporary *Casque d'Or*, inasmuch as it is a gangster story; but this is more obviously B-picture material, if transformed by Becker's use of the milieu – plain little cafés, uncluttered hotel rooms. The movie re-introduced a theme of prewar French cinema, the undivided loyalty of two pals

(Jean Gabin, Lino Ventura), and it was one to be repeated in virtually every gangster film that followed – chiefly because of the success* of this one, though its popularity had much to do with a catchy theme tune. Of Becker's last four films, only **Montparnasse 19** (1957) was widely seen abroad – despite its failure in France. It is dedicated to Max Ophuls, for whom the screenplay had been prepared, and Becker took it over when he died. We had learned to expect more from both of them than this conventional biography of an artist. He is Modigliani, and at first Gérard Philipe seems to want to play him as he was, prickly, cynical, cruel to women and determined to drink himself to death. But Philipe soon settles into his own customary charm; Anouk Aimée, gazing at him with cow's eyes, hardly suggests Jeanne Hébuterne's fierce devotion, while Lilli Palmer as Beatrice Hastings affects a mocking smile and a long cigarette holder as though she had just strayed in from a spy spoof. Nevertheless in a series of episodes the film does convey at least an impression of the difficulties of this artist's life, notably in a cruel scene in which he is persuaded to visit a prospective (American) patron at the Ritz. One sequence is a homage to *La Ronde*, with Lino Ventura as a death-watch art dealer hovering over the sick 'Modi', and it is an artistic intrusion on the honest style of the rest of the film. There is no screenplay credit, as Henri Jeanson took his name off the film after quarrels with Becker over cuts in his dialogue.

Le Trou (1960) is about four men who dig a tunnel out of the Santé prison, only to be betrayed at the last minute by a fifth. José Giovanni (q.v.) wrote a novel based on this factual incident, and turned it into a screenplay with Becker and Jean Aurel. The result is one of the best films made about prison life, and throughout Becker emphasises its strange rituals: being marshalled for 'promenade'; watching a guard cut into every item of a parcel; sharing out the grub; and there is a scene as two of the men peer out of a manhole at the Paris dawn, and it is full of wonder for them. The relationship of the men is somewhat too sweet, and Becker does not make the dénouement convincing. Despite the

excitement of the escape sequences the film was not very popular, partly because it came out at the height of the nouvelle vague. He was even considered to be trying to adapt to the rising fashion, by using amateur actors (though three of them – Philippe Leroy, Michel Constantine and Marc Michel – all went on to successful film careers).

Like Becker, Henri-Georges Clouzot had a small output before a comparatively early death. He had two international successes to Becker's one, and they were of such proportions that they reached beyond the art-house audience, which tended to make reviewers both at home and abroad look askance at Clouzot, and may have in turn inhibited him. There is no doubt that **Le Salaire de la Peur** (1953) and **Les Diaboliques** (1954) succeed magnificently in their objective, which is to get the spectator on the edge of his seat – the first with events that are literally cliff-hanging and the second with some which are spine-chilling. *Les Diaboliques* is well named, for it is devilishly clever as adapted from the novel by Boileau and Narcejac. In a bleak boarding school, the headmaster (Paul Meurisse) ill-treats both his cowed wife (Vera Clouzot, the director's wife) and his confident mistress (Simone Signoret), who conspire to murder him; their scheme

Of the films so far illustrated in this chapter, *La Ronde*, *Don Camillo* and *Casque d'Or* were each notable in attracting new patrons to foreign-language films. The first two were particularly popular, but both were eclipsed by *Le Salaire de la Peur* – which had the advantage of very little dialogue for spectators unaccustomed to subtitles. The thrills they found were as unusual as they were plentiful, and here is one of the stickier moments for Yves Montand and Charles Vanel.

*Not repeated in the U.S. or Britain, since it arrived after Dassin's *Du Rififi chez les Hommes* (q.v.) and was generally written down as inferior.

following the Occupation there had been references to the social and moral climate in France, but after Clément's *Les Jeux Interdits* the French cinema buried its head in the sand. It was not expected to compete with de Sica's exceptional films, while it had achieved a level of artistry which raised it above the even more moribund British cinema; but, by the end of the Fifties, Hollywood was turning out more films of social relevance than France had once made, and with more vitality. Clouzot hoped to rectify the situation, with the added incentive that Raoul Lévy, the promoter of Brigitte Bardot, was looking for a vehicle to prove that she could act; thus with five others Clouzot wrote the screenplay for **La Vérité** (1960), which, in the guise of a murder trial, examined the lifestyle of one of today's young – Bardot. Unfortunately, she was not typical, and if the portrait of *le jeune Paris* is more accurate than that in *Les Tricheurs* and less baroque than that in *Les Cousins* (q.v.), it is equally superficial. In Paris it was widely discussed, but elsewhere dismissed as unimportant. Bardot, incidentally, did not pass the test as an actress, but then most young stars would have looked amateur in the company of such players as Vanel, Meurisse and Louis Seigner.

One director who might have tackled contemporary problems was René Clément, but after *Les Jeux Interdits* he aimed for an international career. He set up **Knave of Hearts/Monsieur Ripois** (1954) in London, with Gérard Philipe as a clerk who, tired of filling forms in triplicate, turns to philandering. His boss (Margaret Johnston) is won over by a bottle of Chamade and some compliments; a nice suburban girl (Joan Greenwood), encountered with a cold and a copy of 'Gone with the Wind', refuses to go to his room in Westbourne Grove because of what Mummy might say but changes her mind after an offer of marriage; and a smart lady (Valerie Hobson), taking French lessons, converts him from 'J'irai Cracher Sur Vos Tombes' to Mallarmé. The real love of his life is woodenly played by Natasha Parry, but Hobson and Greenwood compensate, especially the latter as a dear little silly; Philipe's charm is formidable, whether running about like a puppy in Hobson's apartment, or refusing to spend a wet Sunday in a museum – and we never doubt the

René Clément's work went into decline after he started to make 'international' films, but the first of them, *Knave of Hearts/ Monsieur Ripois*, made in London, seemed to prove the contrary. Gérard Philipe was the young Frenchman who considered every other English girl his natural prey, including Joan Greenwood. British morals have seldom been so well observed, despite what shocked British critics wrote at the time.

succeeds, until the body disappears . . . *Le Salaire de la Peur* starts in a sleazy Mexican village, where four derelicts (Yves Montand, Charles Vanel, Peter Van Eyck, Folco Lulli) agree to drive a consignment of nitroglycerine across treacherous mountain roads, for what – since only one of the lorries is expected to get through – is the paltry sum of $2,000. The journey is long – for once length is a virtue in a thriller – and you do not have to believe the premise, as taken from Georges Arnaud's novel, to find it full of tension. Because these people are exploited by greed and cynicism the film was regarded in some quarters as a comment on Capitalism.

Certainly that was as much as the French cinema wanted to say on any contemporary problem. In the years immediately heartlessness beneath the smiling surface. London had not by a long chalk been better used – but that did not stop the British press, sensing an affront to British womanhood, from denouncing the film as 'immoral'.

Its failure sent Clément back to France, for **Gervaise** (1956), which was Zola's 'L'Assommoir' prepared by Aurenche and Bost, and directed with a Daumier-like intensity of feeling for the underside of Paris in the Second Empire. The film teems with life: the wedding party and its visit to the Louvre; the fight in the *blanchisserie*; the heroine's birthday; and a certain underlying coldness is offset by the director's narrative drive. He said himself that it was not the social problems of the novel, drunkenness, which interested him, but the fate of Gervaise, played by Maria Schell. She had been imposed on Clément, who intended to dub her with a French actress, but the film went with the original soundtrack to the Venice Festival so that she might be eligible for Best Actress prize – which she won. Thus the producers refused to dub, and Clément went into litigation to no avail. Since Gervaise is a noble spirit reduced by poverty, Fraulein Schell misconceives the role, smiling through tears as she hobbles from one disaster to another. It is a far cry from Lillian Gish, and in my opinion, this truly appalling performance is one reason why this otherwise fine film is seldom revived. François Périer is excellent as the husband, who, crippled, turns to drink, and Susy Delair is vivacious, if too vindictive, as Gervaise's rival.

Clément's reputation began to disintegrate when Dino de Laurentiis provided Italo-American backing for **The Sea Wall/La Diga sul Pacifico** (1958), based on Marguerite Duras's novel of a colonial family in Indo-China – a family strangely consisting of Jo Van Fleet, Anthony Perkins and Silvana Mangano, with Richard Conte as the girl's admirer. The film was taken from them by Alida Valli as the wealthy courtesan who seduces Perkins, and Nehemiah Persoff as Mangano's foolish, unwanted admirer. The locations are splendid, but this is another hybrid of a growing, and generally unwanted, breed. **Plein Soleil** (1960) was written with Paul Gégauff, who was to collaborate with Claude Chabrol on his more hedonistic thrillers (q.v.), but neither he nor Clément seemed interested in putting flesh on the cardboard characters of Patricia Highsmith, on whose 'The Talented Mr Ripley' it is based. The portrait of aimless and cynical young people to be found in Mediterranean resorts is largely correct, but if this story of murder and impersonation offers a frisson or so, it is hard to accept Maurice Ronet and Alain Delon as Americans. The latter was also disastrously miscast as a young Italian rip in **Che Gioia Vivere** (1961), made in the peninsula, a rather glum comedy about the early days of Fascism. It was not a success, and Clément returned to the time and theme of *La Bataille du Rail* for **Le Jour et l'Heure** (1963), in which an ordinary housewife (Simone Signoret) conspires to help an American flyer (Stuart Whitman) over the border. In **Les Félins** (1965) two American women (Jane Fonda, Lola Albright), living on the Riviera, play cat and mouse with the vain, amatory crook (Alain Delon) who hides out in their mansion. Both were made in English versions – respectively as *The Day and the Hour* and *The Love Cage* or *The Joy House* – but without success. Both, purely as thrillers, deserved more, but **Paris Brûle-t-il?/Is Paris Burning?** (1966), which followed, was a misconceived, misdirected and overlong effort, based on a bestselling account of the last days of Paris under the Occupation. It was brought to the screen after the success of Darryl F. Zanuck's similarly structured *The Longest Day*. The screenplay by Gore Vidal and Francis Coppola has only a cursory connection with either the book or history, and substitutes confusion for complexity in an attempt to find cameos for its international cast – which includes Jean-Paul Belmondo, Orson Welles, Leslie Caron, Kirk Douglas, Jean-Louis Trintignant, Yves Montand and Simone Signoret. The credited French producer is Paul Graetz, who had backed Clément on the definitive film study of the Resistance, *La Bataille du Rail*. Between the two, Clément had had only two unqualified successes, *Les Jeux Interdits* and *Gervaise*; and certainly he deserved better with *Les Maudits, Knave of Hearts* and *Le Jour et l'Heure*. His decline is even more puzzling than that of de Sica (q.v.). In 1969 Clément resigned from an American film, *Play Dirty*, which would suggest that his principles remained intact, but he subsequently made two tales of skulduggery, **Passager de la Pluie/Rider on the Rain** (1969) with Charles Bronson and Marlène Jobert, and **La Maison sous les Arbres/ The Deadly Trap** (1971) with Faye Dunaway and Frank Langella – neither of which has the slightest merit. It would be too easy to say that he was left stranded by the nouvelle vague, but after using the movement's favourite photographer, Henri Decae, on *Plein Soleil*, he struggled against it, making the sort of films the new critic-directors had vowed to exterminate. It was foolish and self-destructive, for it is impossible to guess from these last two films that Clément had once been one of the best directors of his generation.

Of foreign directors who came to work in France, the most prolific was Jules Dassin, unable to work in Hollywood after the blacklistings of the early Fifties. After some years of silence he equalled his best Hollywood work with **Du Rififi chez les Hommes** (1954), based on Auguste le Breton's thriller about two underworld gangs who cross and double-cross each other for the sake of a fortune taken from the rue de la Paix branch of Mappin and Webb. The four thieves include Jean Servais and Dassin himself, acting under the pseudonym of Perlo Vita; and the thirty-minute heist sequence, done without music or dialogue – coming halfway through the picture – is rightly famous. The film's world-wide success enabled Dassin to film an ambitious allegory, **Celui qui Doit Mourir** (1957), from the novel by Kazantzakis. In Greece under Turkish domination the survivors of a devastated town arrive in a prosperous village where the only ones to welcome them are those about to take part in the annual Passion Play, and the man (Pierre Vaneck) playing Christ becomes a symbol of compassion. There are other symbols, but its points on religious intolerance could never be superfluous. Dassin's experience as a director of thrillers enabled him to push the film – brilliantly – in that direction.

Established as an art-house draw, he virtually destroyed his reputation with **La Loi** (1959), so that he was only able to raise a meagre $150,000 for **Never on Sunday** (1960), a star vehicle for his wife Melina Mercouri, the Greek actress who had been

in his last two films. Recognising his own inadequacy, he was nevertheless forced into playing the male lead, an American who falls for her, in her role of Piraeus whore – and she is the happiest whore who ever lived, slapping down his idealism and puritanism. Dassin's own screenplay is the customary concept of young America versus old Europe, with borrowings from *Born Yesterday*, but it is the first ever to treat a prostitute as a creature *for* life and love. Movies had always loved the ladies of easy virtue, but the only full-scale studies had been of the tragic ones. Mercouri in *Never on Sunday* is realistic and unashamed, and by the standards of the time the film was erotic – if less in the bedroom scenes (by virtue of Dassin's performance) than those in which Mercouri joins the sailors to dance the sirtaki. The music of Manos Hadjidakis was one reason audiences adored the film; another was the sunshine, however murkily photographed. *Never on Sunday*, for all its naivety, is one of the great liberating films. Quite astonishingly, the years have not withered it.

Its unfortunate consequence was that it enabled Dassin to make **Phaedra** (1962), one of the legendary bad movies, though alas too solemn to laugh at. Made in English, it was nevertheless premiered in France, on the premise that the French would know their Racine if not their Euripides – though by setting the tale among the jet set Dassin has been able to load it with chic. At the climax, Phaedra (Mercouri) is preparing for suicide in a sleeping mask, with the aid of her lesbian servant; her husband (Raf Vallone) is trying to assuage the grief of the black-veiled women whose loved ones have gone down in one of his tankers; and the son (Anthony Perkins) is speeding to his death round the hairpin bends yelling 'Escorted out by Bach. Johann Sebastian in person. . . . Goodbye, Greek light; goodbye, sea . . . She loved me.' The mismatching of Perkins and Mercouri may be classic and there is a weird fascination in Dassin's overestimation of his own and his wife's talents. Dassin temporarily retrieved his reputation with **Topkapi** (1964), another caper movie, based on a novel by Eric Ambler, with generous glimpses of Istanbul in Technicolor; the cast includes Mercouri, Maximilian Schell, Robert Morley, and, most notably, Peter Ustinov as an expatriate who – in the actor's own words – 'hovers between the more reprehensible columns of the *News of the World* and oblivion'. The film was a respite in the pretension which had been growing since *Celui qui Doit Mourir*, but Dassin abjured serious consideration with **10.30 p.m. Summer** (1966), written with Marguerite Duras from one of her novels, which may, or may not, be about a couple (Mercouri, Peter Finch) who need a third (Romy Schneider) to make their marriage work. A number of subsequent films, made in France, Greece and the U.S., have been no better received.

Sadder – because his was a much greater talent – is the case of Preston Sturges who, unable to work in Hollywood, made one last film in France, **Les Carnets du Major Thompson** (1955), from the book by Pierre Daninos. This supposed memoir by a pukka Briton about his experiences in France had been a gigantic bestseller, and the producers hoped that signing Jack Buchanan to play the major would attract the international market. Sturges wrote the script, taking a long time in setting up obvious targets and with no degree of asperity; it is not even well directed – but it was popular in France, if nowhere else.

The same is true of another work by a major American film-maker, Orson Welles, who found backing for a version of Kafka, **Le Procès/The Trial** (1963), absurdly casting Anthony Perkins, tense and squirmy, as Joseph K. The film might have worked if set in the costume of the period, when the cosy bourgeoisie was first threatened by secret police and concentration camps; but filmed in the defunct Gare d'Orsay, dwarfing, both figuratively and literally, the events described, it hints less at the horrors of Nazi Germany and Soviet Russia than at what happened *L'Année Dernière à Marienbad* (q.v.). There was a guarded, kinder welcome outside France for **Histoire Immortelle** (1968), made for television and based on an Isak Dinesen short story about an aged man (Welles) who employs a virginal sailor (Norman Eshley) to make love to an experienced woman (Jeanne Moreau); notions about corruption, old age and loneliness move in such small concentric waves that they are soon lost, and the slight conviction available is ruined by Welles's every appearance, preposterous in make-up, performance and photography.

In the matter of serious film-making, Robert Bresson stood alone. Silent since 1945, his earlier films had not prepared us for **Le Journal d'un Curé de Campagne** (1951), one of the best realised achievements of cinema. Based on the novel by Georges Bernanos, who wrote of anguish

The career of Robert Bresson has been one of the most curious in films. He made his reputation with two melodramas in the Forties, and in the last two decades he has made many films equally silly – though melodrama might have brought some life to them. However, in the mid-Fifties he achieved a number of magnificent films, *Le Journal d'un Curé de Campagne*, with Claude Laydu, being pre-eminent among them – a study in solitude as effective as it is austere.

France: Before and After the Nouvelle Vague

and doubt and torment, it is set in a hostile countryside – a bleak Normandy, where a lonely young priest (Claude Laydu) can die, unloved and forgotten, of consumption. Bresson imparts relevant images – a bottle of wine, a letter, a walk through the mud – to accompany the text of the diary, and he withholds what the diary withholds, thus not destroying the priest's delusions. This was, within its limitations, the first 'interior' movie. Remarkably, Bresson made a companion film, as absolute and austere, **Un Condamné à Mort s'est Echappé** (1956), whose source was a story by André Devigny, based on his own experiences in a wartime jail. The mechanics of the plan of escape, interesting in themselves and sprung with tension, are irrelevant to the record of this man's existence. If the film has a fault, it is too clinical, but in confronting the same subject for the third time – what Dilys Powell called 'the man who has to face a terrible predicament in human solitude' – Bresson has become romantic. In **Pickpocket** (1959) he feels no need to explain why his hero has become a thief, and invention runs no deeper than presenting a Dostoevskian inspector to play a cat-and-mouse game and a good woman for whom he reforms at the end.

If this film is banal but absorbing, the second adjective cannot be applied to **Le Procès de Jeanne d'Arc** (1962), which, like Dreyer and perhaps because of him, is based on the minutes of Joan's last trial. Although we had waited eagerly for the self-revelation that came to the country priest, the prisoner and the pickpocket, here we see only a burning, and an end to the mouse-like amateur actress whom Bresson chose because she looked like the only surviving portrait of Joan with any claim to authenticity. The film succeeds only in being austere to the point where passion is drained. One film later, Bresson returned to Bernanos with **Mouchette** (1967), the story of a gangling fourteen-year-old girl who finds salvation in heaven – to the strains of the Monteverdi Magnificat – leaving behind an alcoholic father, a dying mother, and the gamekeeper who rewarded her friendship with rape. Bresson fills in the detail of this poor child's world with his old unobtrusive skill, but the questioning and compassion of his earlier Bernanos film are missing. **Une Femme Douce** (1969) confirmed that,

like Dreyer, he no longer knew how people behaved. The first of two films based on Dostoevsky, it keeps to the plot, he says, while trying 'to communicate impressions that are mine and part of my experience' – which leads one to suppose that his impressions and experience belong to a world other than this. The plot is centred on an unlikely marriage, but at no point does Bresson come close to understanding either participant. **Lancelot du Lac** (1974) had been a pet project for years, but he had lacked financing: this reputedly cost $1 million, but Camelot consists of some smallish tents and an old castle wall, populated by the king and queen and approximately ten knights, all played by amateurs. Cinema, indeed, reached a nadir as the queen intoned such lines as '*Lancelot, tu es vivant et tu est là*' and '*Prends ce corps interdit*', to be followed by a tournament, which turns out to be a series of medium shots of horses's flanks, knights falling, the winner's flag being rung up, and a small section of the pavilion. Lack of funds need not be a drawback with a film-maker of skill and imagination, which Bresson had once been.

Since Bresson was never going to pander to the commercial dictates of the cinema, even his poor films have their admirers. There is also a coterie rooting for Jean-Pierre Melville, who similarly loved the medium but had difficulty in coming to terms with it. Having been branded an 'intellectual' director, he said, because of his first two films, he accepted **Quand tu Liras Cette Lettre** (1953) as a commercial assignment. It is a mediocre film, as taken from a story by Jacques Deval, but Melville responds warmly to the Nice bars and hotel rooms which are the natural habitat of his protagonist (Philippe Lemaire), a gigolo and would-be murderer, who is forced by a convent novice (Juliet Greco) to become engaged to her sister whom he has made pregnant. Earlier, Melville had planned a 'crook' melodrama on the Pigalle milieu which he knew so well, but he abandoned it after seeing *The Asphalt Jungle*, because of its similar plot. Huston's film, he always maintained, contained the nineteen elements (no more and no less) available to a cops-and-robbers story – and he was to use some of them in each of the crime films he wrote and directed. Some turned up in *Du Rififi chez les Hommes*,

Jean-Pierre Melville is another French director whose following might best be described as 'cult', though late in his career he made a number of popular gangster thrillers, such as *Le Samourai*, in which Alain Delon, right, played a hit-man.

which he was to have made – despite its resemblance to *The Asphalt Jungle* – before finding that its producers preferred Dassin; others appear in **Bob le Flambeur** (1956), the tale of an ageing gambler (Roger Duchesne) whose debts encourage him to return to his former life of crime, organising a heist from the casino at Deauville. Melville asked Auguste le Breton to write the dialogue because of the success of *Rififi* but later thought it dated; the film has an air of melancholy which distinguishes it from other thrillers. Melville's love of Hollywood movies is not immediately apparent, but that is evident in **Deux Hommes à Manhattan** (1959), as the title may imply. Indeed, beyond a comment on journalistic ethics – the plot concerns a reporter (played by Melville himself) and a photographer (Pierre Grasset) searching for a missing French diplomat – the film has nothing to express apart from its fascination with New York.

Both movies were an influence on the nouvelle vague directors, but since their own films had begun to appear *Deux Hommes à Manhattan* seemed old fashioned and it was a failure. Melville was only able to film again when Jean-Paul Belmondo (b. 1933), the key actor of the movement, enabled him to get backing for **Léon Morin, Prêtre** (1961). Like Melville's first

feature, it is set during the Occupation, and as written by him from a novel by Béatrix Beck the central situation is somewhat artificial; but it is blessed with life and two protagonists who are likeable and interesting. One is a young widow (Emmanuelle Riva), Communist, Jewish and atheist who, in the absence of young men from the town in which she lives, is sexually attracted towards a woman with whom she works; but after meeting a priest (Belmondo) who responds to her priest-baiting in kindly if idiosyncratic fashion, she tranfers her attentions to him. As in *Le Silence de la Mer*, a great deal is left unsaid, and the priest, finally, remains the more enigmatic of the two. In Belmondo's performance he is as appealing to us as to her.

It is a beautiful film, but the two that followed, both with Belmondo, are of only moderate interest. *Le Doulos* (1963) is a stealth-by-night gangster tale, and **L'Aîné des Ferchaux** (1963), relates the adventures of two Frenchmen as they travel from New York to New Orleans. One is a proud old man, a banker (Charles Vanel), seeking refuge from the police, and the other is a destitute boxer (Belmondo) who has taken on the job as his bodyguard; in their relationship the latter gradually assumes the dominant position –

and that is something which Melville views romantically, despite the film's source, a novel by Simenon, and the detail of life in motels and diners. Melville claimed that his films were as far from realistic as possible, and it was the romanticism he now brought to **Le Deuxième Souffle** (1966) and **Le Samourai** (1967) which make them so superior to *Le Doulos*. They are again basically formula stories of the underworld, but transformed into masterly expositions of the thesis that the criminal is loyal, lonely and eventually horribly dead. The first, from a novel by José Giovanni, involves a master-crook (Lino Ventura) in one last heist and gang warfare; the second, from an American novel by Joan McLeod, transposed to Paris, follows the final days of a professional hit-man (Alain Delon).

Melville returned to the Occupation in **L'Armée des Ombres** (1969), as portrayed in a novel by Joseph Kessel, but despite his cast – Ventura, Signoret, Jean-Pierre Cassel, Paul Meurisse – and careful filming, this tale of failing nerves and divided loyalties among the Resistance adds little to our knowledge of the subject. Nor are his last two films, **Le Cercle Rouge** (1970) and **Un Flic** (1972), as good as the two which preceded it; it is clear from the episodic nature of both that they were devised to utilise some of the 'nineteen situations' that he had not yet attempted. Delon is in each, in the first as a crook who meets and teams up with another, Gian Maria Volonté, and an ex-cop, Yves Montand, for a heist, and in the second as a world-weary police inspector. As *Le Samourai* had been designed primarily in shades of grey, so the predominant colour of *Un Flic* is blue: but the matching of colour to the prevailing mood does not seem pretentious when the set-pieces, chiefly bank-raids and escapes, are so flawlessly executed.

The French cinema was not, however, all misery, period frills and gangsters; Fernandel continued to be extraordinarily popular – and for a brief while, after the Don Camillo films, was exportable – while Bourvil and later Louis de Funès kept local audiences laughing. The one French funny-man consistently welcome abroad was Jacques Tati (1908–82), a former cabaret artist and actor who turned clown, producing and directing himself in **Jour de Fête** (1949), the selected adventures of a village policeman. His great success was **Les Vacances de M. Hulot** (1953), some adventures of a tourist in a small Channel coast resort. Much loving care has gone into the creation of Hulot – the *politesse* is Chaplin's, the hitched-up trousers are Larry Semon's, and the clumsiness that of any of the great Silent clowns without their nimbleness and wit. Most of Tati's gags are stolen from the Silents, but they come along slowly, without either the timing of the originals, or any relation to the gag before or the one after. Tati's quest for international attention is one reason why this film is so abysmal, for he tries to keep the dialogue to a minimum, making the action more self-conscious than is necessary. In the original, there was only one English couple at this Brittany pension, but in the 1977 re-issue print redubbing has made only the proprietor and Hulot French. The foreign market was important to Tati because of his high production costs: his later movies were unprofitable, and eventually his films (including this one) were impounded by creditors – thus restricting further income from them, which in turn would have enabled him to continue financing his own projects.

Pierre Etaix (b. 1928), a former assistant of Tati, also aped the Silent clowns. He made his debut with a short, **Heureux Anniversaire** (1961), written and directed with Jean-Claude Carrière (also beginning his own career as a screenwriter). This tale of the Parisian perils awaiting a little man hurrying home to an anniversary dinner is a total success. There are also some splendid moments in **Le Soupirant** (1963), the adventures of a young man pursuing a bride, whereas **Yoyo** (1965), the life story of a clown, only exposed Etaix's weaknesses. Etaix's physical resemblance to Max Linder was furthered by his sporting silk hats and spats in the earlier part of *Yoyo*, but he does not know how to use his appearance to make his loss of dignity funny; like Tati, he goes to elaborate lengths for gags which die in the process. Unlike Tati, he is good-hearted, but two subsequent features evidence a law of diminishing returns, as the gags became increasingly ponderous.

One other short should be mentioned, for it provides 36 minutes of pure pleasure:

Le Ballon Rouge (1956), a slight tale of a boy and his red balloon. Edmond Séchan photographed it, and Albert Lamorisse wrote and directed – not without a degree of obvious calculation – but the final moments, as the boy is wafted aloft by a bunch of coloured balloons over the grey roofs of Paris, constitute as pretty a time as may be had in a cinema.

Le Ballon Rouge and M. Hulot joined *Le Salaire de la Peur* and *Rififi* in moving out from the art-house circuit; but Brigitte Bardot (b. 1934) did more for the French film abroad than all four put together. She was the wife of Roger Vadim (b. 1928), a former assistant of Marc Allégret, and both Vadim and the producer Raoul Lévy recognised her potential as a sex symbol. Together they wrote **Et Dieu . . . Créa la Femme** (1956), from a news item Lévy found, '*trois frères, un village, une surprenante créature, un crime*', and with it Vadim was given a chance to direct. The brothers were to be played by Christian Marquand, Jean-Louis Trintignant and Curd Jürgens – the latter the 'name' imposed by Columbia Pictures if it was to finance colour and CinemaScope; but in the event Jürgens plays an American millionaire. The village became St Tropez and the crime never materialised (though a gun is waved about); the *surprenante créature* is Bardot. The film was sourly greeted in Paris, but went on to become by far the most successful French film yet shown in foreign markets. It is not a good one: despite occasional humour the direction is flat-footed, Bardot pouts, grins and sticks out her chest, but she is not much of an actress. Nevertheless she and Vadim changed the way we think about women in films – for by then most people had forgotten the equally blatant Clara Bow and Jean Harlow. Marilyn Monroe was reminding audiences of the female readiness to cooperate, but Bardot was even less inhibited, sunbathing naked, forgetting her wedding guests in her desire for her husband (Trintignant) and, a few days later, satisfying his brother (Marquand) in the rolling surf. If Vadim and Lévy were determined on eroticism, their attempt at myth-making is also evident in the plotting – and they did much for St Tropez, here a character in its own right.

Vadim and Bardot separated, privately and professionally, though he directed her

again when their careers needed a boost. He strove for a certain chic with **Sait-on Jamais?** (1957), a confused thriller set in Venice, with the Modern Jazz Quartet on the soundtrack, and **Les Liaisons Dangereuses** (1959), which uses the music of Thelonius Monk: but because of Vadim's complete lack of narrative sense both are dowdy. The latter is a modernisation of the eighteenth-century epistolary novel, otherwise faithful in outline except that the destructive protagonists are no longer lovers but husband and wife – of whom Jeanne Moreau has to carry the film since Gérard Philipe's range did not extend to profligacy. The government censor insisted on the addition of *1960* to the film's title to indicate its disapproval of the venture and banned it from export (though that was later rescinded) on the grounds that it showed the French diplomatic set in unflattering, i.e. promiscuous, light. Vadim's stock-in-trade remained sex through a number of pictures, including a

The makers of *Et Dieu . . . Créa la Femme* set out to exploit the nubile charms of Brigitte Bardot, and they proved delightfully exploitable. The director, Roger Vadim, had no hesitation in 'borrowing' the famous beach scene in *From Here to Eternity*, even if Bardot and her brother-in-law (Christian Marquand) could have fled to the bushes a few yards away. The point, of course, was that neither party could wait: and the screen's view of women would never be the same again.

remake of **La Ronde** (1964), flatly written by Jean Anouilh, and **Barbarella** (1968), a version of a science-fiction comic-strip, witlessly written by Terry Southern (and others), which starred his next wife, Jane Fonda. Vadim's direction is always vulgar, except in the matter of sex, when he may adopt any number of moods, from the frenetic to the limpid, though the love scenes in his films invariably emerge as quite asexual. And yet this meretricious film-maker was, if unwittingly, one of the precursors of the nouvelle vague, which revitalised the French cinema.

The nouvelle vague consisted of a number of young men, mostly acquainted with each other, who were besotted with films. Some of them were on the edge of the industry, some wrote film reviews, and several managed to make a number of shorts. Among the most vocal of them was Jean-Luc Godard (q.v.) who was to say much later (in 1980, to a reporter from *Variety*) that they did not have to become directors themselves to know that the so-called auteur theory was absurd: 'We invented it,' he said, 'to draw attention to ourselves.' Their rallying ground was *Cahiers du Cinéma*, an analytic buffs' magazine which, because of their subsequent success as working directors, was to have a disproportionate influence. They worshipped Hollywood and good commercial directors like Hitchcock; because their own first films were so impressive, it occurred to few critics to question whether their adulation for Hitchcock was not excessive. Most writers on film rejected their more idiosyncratic choices, but since we enjoyed Hitchcock – this then seemed his best period – we assumed that we had been missing something, instead of suspecting some perverse sets of values. On the subject of French directors the proponents of the movement were, understandably, more sound; they knew the tradition of French cinema had become stale. Certainly most film historians agreed with them that Renoir, whom they idolised, had been underrated – while Clair's reputation was unassailable. Chabrol once boasted that he had liked only *A Nous la Liberté* of Clair's films and Godard only *Quatorze Juillet*, while as far as he could recall Truffaut and Rohmer had not liked any – and these comments are worth contemplation in the

light of the evident superiority of Clair's work to any of theirs as film-makers. Autant-Lara who, like Clair, was cold-shouldered as the film industry embraced the nouvelle vague, vehemently dismissed as worthless all the films it threw up, which is not quite fair. Those who, like myself, originally supported these young critics against most of the older, academic film-makers could not have foreseen how badly their own films would date – nor how benignly posterity would view many of those of Autant-Lara and his confrères.

There was a fervour in the way these young turks set about destroying the complacency surrounding both the industry and the medium itself. They had established their own credentials in a number of shorts, fiction and non-fiction, none of them indicating their love of Hollywood and most of them showing more intellectual sinew than the features they supported. The most important of the short-subject directors are Georges Franju (b. 1912) and Alain Resnais (b. 1922).

Franju was one of the founders, in 1936, of the Cinémathèque Scientifique, along with Jean Painlevé, the documentary film-maker, and it was there that he made **Le Sang des Bêtes** (1949), about slaughter-houses. In 1952 he was commissioned to make a documentary on the **Hôtel des Invalides**, which startled its sponsors by disapproving of that institution and all matters military. It was these two films, plus **Les Charmes de l'Existence** (1950), a witty study by Jean Grémillon and Pierre Kast of 'academic' painting, which are the primal seeds of the nouvelle vague. Short films flourished, since cinemas were forbidden by law to show double features. When that law was abolished, in 1953, the *Groupe des Trente* was formed to keep the documentary alive – its members including Franju, Painlevé, Alexandre Astruc, Nicole Vedrès and Resnais. Resnais made a slight reputation in 1950 with *Guernica*, an essay built around Picasso's painting, and he consolidated it in 1956 with **Nuit et Brouillard**, commissioned by the Comité de la Seconde Guerre Mondiale to mark the tenth anniversary of the liberation of the concentration camps. Resnais took an Eastmancolor camera to Auschwitz, to photograph the red-brick ruins languishing under a blue autumn sky, and as the camera begins to probe the commentator falls silent. Both he and the colour give way, so that newspaper newsreels and clippings tell something of what happened there between 1941 and 1945. The film's title derives from the order to destroy human beings, which became known as the 'Night and Fog' decree. The film is one epitaph on the Thousand Year Reich. Another was spoken by Hans Frank as he was led to the gallows at Nuremberg, 'A thousand years shall pass and Germany's guilt will not be expunged,' though the film's own final comment, 'Je ne suis pas responsable' is equally moving in context. Resnais's shattering half-hour film is essential to anyone trying to understand this century, yet it is still inadequate.

These shorts and the arguments in *Cahiers du Cinéma* coalesced to form a cultural climate in which cinema had a leading place: Melville★ and Bresson were heroes, as was Vadim, because he was one of the young people to make a mark in an ageing industry. All three of them rejected the stultifying studio art direction in favour of location shooting, in the manner of one of the more inexplicable heroes of the *Cahiers* group, Rossellini. Working in documentary, the young directors looked further back to the early Soviet film-makers, and Georges Sadoul coined an expression, *cinéma-vérité*, as a method to be recommended, requiring absolute honesty, to result in an immediate contact with the spectator. What was to be expressed was another matter: neither the always crumbling French political system nor De Gaulle's return to power in 1958 interested them, but in 1954 Françoise Sagan had published her first novel, 'Bonjour Tristesse' and its enormous success revealed a public for moral and sexual disorientation among the young.

That such a subject could be communicated in a movie was proved by another young film-maker, Louis Malle (b. 1932), former assistant to Jacques-Yves Cousteau, the marine documentary director, and to Bresson, when he found backing for **Ascenseur pour l'Echafaud** (1958) and **Les Amants** (1958), both starring his current mistress, Jeanne Moreau (b. 1928), then a second-rank star. Malle said at the

★Although Melville became friendly with most of the nouvelle vague directors, he dismissed their films as 'amateurish'; his own heroes were William Wyler and Robert Wise, whom they disliked, while he abhorred many of their American favourites, such as Nicholas Ray.

time that watching films bored him, but that he enjoyed making them, and the paradox is evident, since he brought a fresh eye to everything – especially in *Ascenseur*, to Paris. Location shooting was to be a hallmark of the nouvelle vague, providing a contemporary portrait of Paris which would be virtually complete. *Ascenseur* also contained reference to current affairs – the troubles in Algeria and Indo-China; it had a first-class, if not airtight, thriller plot, from a novel by Henri Calef, about a man (Maurice Ronet) who murders the man who is both his boss and the husband of his mistress (Jeanne Moreau); and throughout it there broods the sexual intensity of Mlle Moreau. Such sexuality was the *raison d'être* of *Les Amants*, together with the love act itself. Louise de Vilmorin wrote the sparse dialogue for Malle's own adaptation of an eighteenth-century story about infidelity. This was the movies' most idealised version of a brief encounter; there is a reverie – in a garden, at night – before the lovers begin coupling, which was far less censored than predicted. By later standards the sequence is prudish rather than discreet, but what in fact made the film acceptable in the eyes of censors and critics was the witty manner in which Malle viewed his central triangle. Moreau decides that her husband (Alain Cuny) is odious and the prospective lover (Jean-Marc Bory) ridiculous: it is the ironic contrast of these three personalities which makes the film so entertaining.

Meanwhile, Claude Chabrol (b. 1930), a *Cahiers* critic, had used the inheritance of his (first) wife to make **Le Beau Serge** (1958), which he shortly followed with **Les Cousins** (1959). The first is a sombre and ultimately pointless bucolic drama about a wanderer (Jean-Claude Brialy) who returns to his roots to find that his old pal (Gérard Blain) has become a drunkard. The film bears two more hallmarks of the nouvelle vague – the arbitrary behaviour of its characters, and young acting talent. In *Les Cousins* Blain is the country mouse and Brialy the town mouse, or rather rat, whose Sorbonne set destroys his country cousin. The film is shallow but entertaining, and its ironic detachment was another new factor in movies. The point is made that Blain reads Balzac, neglected by all but provincial students, yet he is, in the end, as silly as any character within the

Balzac canon. André Bazin, so influential a critic for the nouvelle vague, had said that film-makers should learn from literature, and we ought to bear Balzac in mind when we learn that Chabrol's purpose, as he admitted, was to make us contemplate rather than identify.

Franju's first feature was **La Tête contre les Murs** (1958), adapted from Hervé Bazin's novel by an actor, Jean-Pierre Mocky, who had hoped to direct it himself. Mocky gives a surly performance as a high-living youngster committed by his father to a mental home, and the ambivalence of both characters, and of the chief doctor (Pierre Brasseur), gives a lift to an otherwise dull film. Franju never learnt to create mood or tension, which is why his Grand Guignol thriller, **Les Jeux sans Visage** (1959), confirmed him as one of the lesser members of the nouvelle vague. The most light-hearted member of the movement was Philippe de Broca (b. 1933), former assistant to Truffaut and Chabrol, whose company produced **Les Jeux de l'Amour** (1959), a rather old-fashioned comedy about a man (Jean-Pierre Cassel) who will neither marry his mistress (Geneviève Cluny) nor allow her to have a baby.

To an extent the nouvelle vague was a press invention, like the 'angry young men' in Britain two or three years earlier, but when three films by new or newish directors astounded the Cannes Festival in 1959, there was no longer any doubt that here was a vital new force in French cinema. One of the directors was Marcel Camus (1912–82) who hitherto and subsequently, in his few faltering films, showed little vitality. His first film, **Mort en Fraude** (1956), had been an uneven melodrama of a fugitive (Daniel Gélin) in Saigon; but the film that impressed at Cannes, **Orfeu Negro** (1959), if not really a nouvelle vague film, holds its charm better than some that are. It is set in Brazil at carnival time – the dialogue is in Portuguese – and as written by Jacques Viot, Camus and Vinitius de Moraes, from de Moraes's play, the screenplay is both simple-minded and strained. But that does not matter: if the picture were merely a travelogue with plot grafted on, its extended account of Rio and the carnival would justify its existence. The film is above all a celebration of both, with a score by

Antonio Carlos Jobim and Luis Bonfa which is one of the most haunting ever composed for a film.

The other two films at Cannes that year were Resnais's **Hiroshima Mon Amour** (1959) and *Les Quatre Cents Coups* (q.v.), directed by François Truffaut. Resnais's film was proposed by the Japanese, stipulating that it should be filmed in both countries. When Françoise Sagan refused the offer to write the screenplay, he turned to Marguerite Duras, who later said that both agreed that they could not imagine a film about Japan which did not deal with Hiroshima. But this surely cannot be why it starts with a prolonged bedroom scene, prelude to much musing by the lovers, a Japanese man (Eiji Okada) and a French woman (Emmanuelle Riva). Were you there, she asks. And he answers, Of course not. '*Une chance, quoi?*' she says, and he agrees. '*Une chance pour moi aussi,*' she replies, which may give you an idea of Mlle Duras' contribution. After that, you must accept that the film is not about Hiroshima at all, but about Riva's affair with a German soldier during the War, which branded her as a collaborator. This becomes, therefore, a film about memory and forgetfulness, and is minimal compared to *Nuit et Brouillard*, though it is, at least, beautifully constructed.

This method of combining past and present was new, since it was essential to the nouvelle vague to 'de-conventionalise' movies; but the theories of the movement were most effectively put into practice by Truffaut (b. 1932) in **Les Quatre Cents Coups**, significantly dedicated to André Bazin – who had bailed Truffaut out of reform school at the age of fourteen. One of Bazin's beliefs was that films should attempt the ambiguity and multiple levels of meaning to be found in literature – and it was this injection by the nouvelle vague which makes 1959 as important in cinema history as 1929 and the coming of Sound. In Italy, Antonioni (q.v.) was advancing in a more sophisticated manner, but though there was less scope in this simple autobiographical tale, Truffaut leaves conversations half heard or indeterminate, and reveals the inner identity of his young boy hero (Jean-Pierre Léaud) by a process of peeling off, like an onion skin, from reel to reel. The film is full of insights into the matters which pain a child, or amuse or bore him: his father hitting him in front of his classmates because he has lied; half-hearing a parental row when his mother gets in late; stealing a milk bottle at night from a Pigalle doorstep; being reminded to take down the garbage. If the film had not managed so complete a portrait of the world of this boy, the ending alone would have come as a revelation. As it is, it is simply perfect – the progression from the adventure with the stolen typewriter to reform school, and escape . . . The famous ending, by the sea, with the frozen frame. When Olmi uses it in *Il Posto*, it is more moving, since it suggests an even greater trap, but the point about *Les Quatre Cents Coups* is that the Bazin-dictated vocabulary was in full flower for the first time (not to mention a number of in-jokes). Truffaut himself said that the film was to be judged on its sincerity, rather than its technical quality, but it is a triumph on both counts.

Anything it lacked was available in **A Bout de Souffle** (1960), the last crest of the nouvelle vague, directed by Jean-Luc Godard (b. 1930), a fellow *Cahiers* critic of Truffaut, who ostensibly supervised the film. It is dedicated to Monogram Pictures, a sign of Godard's devotion to the American B-movies, which influence his young thug hero (Jean-Paul Belmondo), toting a gun, stealing money from his girlfriend's handbag, muttering 'Bogey' affectionately before a poster of Humphrey Bogart, facing death – as everything else – with a shrug. She (Jean Seberg) likes Mozart and Faulkner, and has a philosophy, 'Between grief and nothing, I would take grief.' They loaf about, play games, and since she is pregnant – a fact both refuse to face – we know that they have made love, but sex is second to their egotism. When she betrays him, it may be an *acte gratuit*, or mere practicality (to keep her work permit); or she may want to wake him from his lethargy. Godard's people say one thing and do another, they speak truth and deceive themselves at the same time. If life and people are wayward, Godard found an approach to fit: he said that he found it by cutting away everything not of prime importance, which is clearly not true, but if the jerky style is an accident, it is nevertheless a style. It was shot in chronological order, at a cost of approximately $100,000, and premiered just ten weeks after Godard met Belmondo,

whose passage to fame it was. Belmondo was certainly the most unusual and gifted of the nouvelle vague players – even if he moved into a star stereotype later – and his role here was said to characterise a generation. The film was described as 'anarchic' and 'challenging', but in fact it is highly moral. It is a superb analysis of the mentality of thugdom. It also communicates its love of the medium, and is as exciting to watch now as it was then.

It was not that the nouvelle vague was innovatory – at least, not consciously, as Antonioni was – but they were using with enthusiasm and intensity the tools which others had picked up and dropped, or used and only half understood. With one or two films each to their credit, Resnais, Truffaut, Godard and Chabrol were being discussed as eagerly as Eisenstein ever was. The French government stepped in: it was obvious that young film directors were beneficial for the industry, and in 1959 the decree called '*Avances sur Recettes*' was promulgated, with an 8,000,000 million franc fund (later enlarged), to be dispensed by a committee after consideration of the proposed script and budget, and with up to one million francs available for an individual film, though the average amount advanced was usually just under that. In addition, French producers lent a ready ear to anyone under thirty who wanted to make a film. Of the results, it was estimated that for each one which received a Paris premiere another languished on the shelf. At the beginning of 1961 *Le Film Français* listed no less than sixty-seven directors who had made their first features within the past two years. Less than twenty of them made another, and less than a handful subsequently enjoyed a career as a director – the most notable being (q.v.) Claude Sautet, Michel Drach, Claude Lelouch and Eric Rohmer, of whom only the latter was linked with the nouvelle vague movement. Clearly a new generation of *cinéastes* did not emerge – the important ones had already arrived – but the euphoria within the industry resulted in a number of memorable films.

Roger Leenhardt, one of the heroes of the new directors, made his first feature in fourteen years, and his last to date – **Le Rendez-vous de Minuit** (1962), a film for the *cinéaste* if ever there was one, a Pirandello-like confection, haunting and

The five films that
made the reputa-
tions of those five
directors which we
call the nouvelle
vague – and the
expression, 'the new
wave', indicates the
force with which
each film knocked
away the old stan-
dards of the French
film. ABOVE FAR
RIGHT, Louis
Malle's *Les Amants*,
with Jeanne Moreau
and Jean-Marc
Bory; ABOVE RIGHT,
Claude Chabrol's
Les Cousins, with
Juliette Mayniel,
Jean-Claude Brialy
and Gérard Blain;
BELOW FAR RIGHT,
Alain Resnais's
*Hiroshima Mon
Amour*, with
Emmanuelle Riva
and Eiji Okada;
BELOW RIGHT,
François Truffaut's
*Les Quatre Cents
Coups*, with Jean-
Pierre Léaud; and
BELOW CENTRE, Jean-
Luc Godard's *A Bout
de Souffle* with Jean
Seberg and Jean-Paul
Belmondo. Interest-
ingly, each of these
films remains virtu-
ally as impressive as
they did at the time,
while the later work
of their directors has
varied. Resnais and
Malle remain major
film-makers, but
Chabrol seems
determined to make
as many bad films as
good while Godard
and Truffaut have
gone steadily down-
hill. Ironically, the
work of many of the
film-makers whom
they as critics affected
to despise is now
more rewarding than
their own films.

1016

The Nouvelle Vague

intricate. A poor, lonely woman is fascinated by a film about a rich, lonely woman – both played by Lilli Palmer, who later appears, tantalisingly, as herself; the poor woman's suicidal plans are interrupted by another cinemagoer (Michel Auclair) and then contrasted to the life of the rich woman, whose problems with her lover (Maurice Ronet) are wholly artificial. Life is shown to imitate art, but it would be wrong, I think, to regard the film as more than a sprightly *jeu*. It is 'one of the films requesting from their audiences a new standard of literacy', as Penelope Houston put it in *Sight and Sound*, though she was in fact discussing **La Proie pour l'Ombre** (1961), directed by a friend of Leenhardt, Alexandre Astruc. Astruc, a former *Cahiers* critic and occasional film-maker (though with only one popular film to his credit, *Le Rideau Cramoisi*) did not have the deserved success with this one. Admittedly both dialogue and the basic situation are banal: but in presenting yet again the eternal triangle Astruc offers a woman (Annie Girardot), caught in adultery, who never admits or concedes that it may be her fault. Predating Women's Lib, that is the film's subject, and virtually alone of all these films Astruc has eschewed Haussmann's Paris for the city of auto-routes and tower-blocks.

The British theatre director, Peter Brook, making his first film since *The Beggar's Opera*, adapted a novel by Marguerite Duras – with Gérard Jarlot and the author herself – **Moderato Cantabile** (1960), meant, he said, to please her and its star, Jeanne Moreau. The particular qualities and talents of Mlles Moreau and Girardot may be one reason for the preponderance of adultery as a subject in these films, but in this case Moreau only contemplates it. The setting is a small, bleak town on the Gironde, a lost waste of countryside: there has been a *crime passionel*, and the woman's fascination with it brings her into contact with one of her husband's employees (Belmondo). It is a love affair not only without sex but with no ecstasy; we never question that their meeting is the single most important event of her life, and that she will henceforth be even more miserable than before. Inevitably reminiscent of *Les Amants*, the film is, in Brook's own words, 'an attempt to tell a story with a *minimum* of fictional devices by using and

relying on the actors' power of characterisation'. Both players are superb. There is a moment when Moreau leans against a tree and rubs her head against it – and when Belmondo responds there is no better expression in all cinema of the need of one human for another.

The central situation of **Une Aussi Longue Absence** (1962) is similar: in a dusty suburb of Paris the owner (Alida Valli) of a bistro becomes convinced that a local vagabond (Georges Wilson) is the husband who disappeared years before. As with Brook's film, there are heavy emotions in a quiet setting, a yearning for a life that might have been. The situation was handled with dexterity by Henri Colpi (b. 1921), a former editor with Resnais, who in fact made a few further films: the accomplishment of this one makes their failure all the more surprising.

Jacques Doniol-Valcroze (b. 1920) was once a critic – with Bazin he was one of the founders of *Cahiers* – and occasional actor and director. His films have created no great stir, but **Le Coeur Battant** (1962) seems to me one of the most enchanting of comedies – *L'Avventura* (q.v.) in reverse, as a man (Jean-Louis Trintignant) and a woman (Françoise Brion) first squabble and fall in love while waiting for her lover to turn up. The setting is a small seaside resort, affectionately used as only the French seem able.

Robert Enrico (b. 1931) wrote and directed documentaries for cinema and television during the Fifties, eventually breaking away with **La Rivière du Hibou** (1961), which won the Palme d'Or at Cannes and an American Oscar for Best Live Action Short Subject. Between the two awards Enrico incorporated it into a feature, *Au Coeur de la Vie*, with two accompanying sections also based on short stories by Ambrose Bierce. This has not been shown complete in the U.S. or Britain, but *Rivière*, as *Incident at Owl Creek*, may be found at repertory cinemas, often dwarfing the feature. The incident depicted is of the War between the States, when a partisan escaped the hangman. Enrico has filmed the story with great simplicity, but credit should also go to the photographer, Jean Boffety, and to Roger Jacquet, the pursued man, whose expression may haunt one for days. Enrico went on to commercial films, with Bardot and

Belmondo among others, but of those I have seen, only one has merit, **Le Secret** (1974), a thriller written with Pascal Jardin from a novel by Francis Ryck about the adventures of an unworldly couple (Philippe Noiret, Marlène Jobert) and a possibly homicidal intruder (Trintignant). Among enigmatic 'twist' thrillers, it holds a high place, moving with surprise and without pretension; and if its political message is trite, it is worth recalling how many unsolved murders in France are rumoured to be politically motivated.

Jacques Rivette (b. 1928) has also managed a career since his first feature, **Paris Nous Appartient**, begun in 1957, completed in 1960, and finally shown in Paris in 1962, with friends such as Truffaut and Chabrol endorsing, on the posters, the director's personal vision. The film seemed remarkable then: a study of a group of people in Paris in August, the dog days, unable to come to terms with themselves and a world that includes the Bomb and Fascism – a world of unanswered telephones, bare apartments, rumoured organisations, and endless discussions. It may now be found to be as self-indulgent as its characters; the finale, set in a deserted garden in the country, was *the* cliché of the nouvelle vague, and the film now seems a parody of the movement.

Essentially, the movement was a matter of individual talent; and it was a matter for each member of the audience, each buff, to decide whether he wanted to continue the love affair with the director concerned. Buñuel once said of Godard 'I'll give him two years more, he's just a fashion' – speaking to Satyajit Ray, who observed some years later (in 1968, to *Sight and Sound*) how accurate Buñuel's prophecy had been.

Godard's work is exemplified thus: Anna Karina cavorting in a room; a montage of book jackets, postcards, advertisements; references to movies – usually bad ones (*Some Came Running*, *Hatari!*, *Viaggio in Italia*); long duologues, the camera darting to and fro, to be replaced in time with long muttered monologues to the camera, of even more stultifying banality . . . '*La photographie, c'est la vérité, le cinéma, c'est la vérité ving-quatre fois par seconde,*' says Michel Subor in **Le Petit Soldat**, but in Godard's case it is not enough. That was his second film, made in 1960, but because

of references to the Algerian situation it was not shown till 1963. It is a jigsaw about an O.A.S. man trying to escape his nemesis, and falling in love with a waif, played by Anna Karina, who became Mme Godard. Both **Une Femme est une Femme** (1961) and **Vivre sa Vie** (1962) are odes to her, the former a semi-musical re-hash of *Les Jeux de l'Amour*, with ill-advised references to Lubitsch and Gene Kelly, and the latter a sort of sentimentalised diary of a whore. It is dedicated to American B-pictures, to remind us of the critic Peter John Dyer's prescient comment on *A Bout de Souffle*: 'So one ends with a vague sense of infantilism, partly due to the film's violent repudiation of feeling, partly due to its mythomaniacal devotion to a washed-up, B-picture world which never existed in the first place. [It] is riveting enough in style and picaresque subject, and blessed with sufficient local insight, to prevent it deteriorating into the sort of dishonestly blown-up quickie, such as *Kiss Me Deadly*, on which it is undoubtedly dependent for its inspiration. But by eliminating meaning and feeling, Godard has merely trapped himself in that artistic cul-de-sac – the film all dressed up for rebellion, but with no real tangible territory on which to stand and fight.'

Les Carabiniers (1963) is about fighting in a mythical kingdom – symbolised by a rubbish dump – where two stupid young men volunteer for the army,

Jean-Luc Godard threw so many artefacts into his films that it took some time before audiences realised that most of them were devoid of content. Another reason why some remained faithful was the presence in many of his films of Anna Karina, and he certainly conveyed his own fascination with her. Here she is in the best of their collaborations, *Vivre sa Vie*, with Sady Rebbot.

1019

dreaming of money, lust and power. A preface quotes from Borges, 'As times passes, I value simplicity more. I use the same metaphors . . .', but the film is less simple than nihilistic: there is little point in being anti-militarist and anti-capitalist if audiences are left as devoid of shock as the people in the film. It was an enormous failure, due, it was said, to its message being antipathetical to De Gaulle's France, but Godard's career was thought to revive with **Le Mépris** (1964), financed by Joseph Levine and produced by Carlo Ponti as well as Georges de Beauregard, who had backed several of the nouvelle vague films. Its source was a novel by Moravia, about the disintegration of a marriage within the movie industry, and Godard's consciously boring screenplay mocks his sponsors. He reduces Brigitte Bardot, Michel Piccoli and Jack Palance – as a Hollywood producer – to ciphers. The film failed everywhere, and may be best explained by Raoul Coutard, who photographed it, 'Godard is trying to explain something to his wife . . . It's a sort of letter – one that's costing [the backers] a million dollars.'

After that debacle, Godard disciplined himself to make three films which, if not as good as *A Bout de Souffle*, are at least as much fun as *Vivre sa Vie*. It might be that his good films were the result of some happy choices – in the case of **Bande à Part** (1964) the juxtaposition of the gazelle-like, sometimes incandescent Karina and the dreary suburb of Joinville, a hidden treasure and two impish, petty criminals (Sami Frey, Claude Brasseur). The reason for success with this *bande à part* may be found in a remark by Jean-Pierre Gorin, a later collaborator, 'With Jean-Luc and me, it was a love story; we really were deeply in love with each other, with no shame, no guilt. It was a deep, involved, sexual thing.' **Une Femme Mariée** (1964) – retitled from *La Femme Mariée* after the censor decreed it a slur on French womanhood – concerns adultery, with the smoky-faced Macha Méril as the lady concerned. The usual conceits are here, be they bursts of Beethoven, references to concentration camps or discussions on paradox, but Godard's style has become so beautifully honed that the film is a small pleasure. He moved from the white interiors of this to the harsh, cold boulevards

and towers of **Alphaville** (1965), a science-fiction caper that borrows from '1984', Cocteau's *Orphée*, Ian Fleming and Saul Steinberg – not to mention pulp fiction, as indicated by the subtitle, 'Une Etrange Aventure de Lemmy Caution'.

It was about this time that Godard made his oft-quoted remark that movies should have a beginning, a middle and an end, but not necessarily in that order – which did nothing to convince the increasing number of people who did not wish to stay to see the end of his films. Mindless confusion reigns from then on – anarchists, subversive agents, Hollywood references, high jinks, asides – through the next four films, each more trivial than the last. To an extent, **Weekend** (1968) is Alphaville revisited, a dream-fantasy of a brutal, technological future. It encompasses both the best and worst of Godard – the audacity, the insistence on breaking the rules, the witty, coruscating critic of a materialistic society who has no better answer for his failed revolutionaries than to have them resort to cannibalism. When he seesaws – dangerously, after the superb control in *Vivre sa Vie* – we must assume that he does it intentionally, though we may still find the blend of intelligence and irresponsibility irritating. Many artists have produced sloppy, uninteresting work when their technique has deserted them, but Godard is symptomatic of many in this period whose brilliance goes hand in hand with an equally startling childishness. Audiences will tolerate self-indulgence, but only while there are rewards, and it was at this point that they fell away – as did the financiers. Godard continued to make films, sometimes directed in collaboration, some on 16mm, but they attracted minimal attention. The early Godards, when they came out, were among the most stimulating experiences the cinema has ever offered me and, with reason, they influenced virtually every film-maker – certainly those of his own generation and younger.

The decline of François Truffaut has been much more gentle. After the achievement of *Les Quatre Cents Coups* he wrote a second film with Marcel Moussy, **Tirez sur la Pianiste** (1960), based on an American pulp fiction (a frequent source of his subsequent work). It sets a mild piano-player (Charles Aznavour) on the fringe of the underworld, whose denizens move in to destroy him – and the personality of the star, with his attractive combination of optimism and fatalism, gives, as Truffaut intended, a particular colour to what is a free-wheeling blend of satire, shoot-ups and *comédie noire*. **Jules et Jim** (1962) was designed for Jeanne Moreau, playing a 'free spirit' loved by, and loving two men (Oskar Werner, Henri Serre) simultaneously. The source was Henri-Pierre Roché's old novel, idiosyncratically observed by Truffaut, with an airy grace which finally degenerates into verbosity. It was one of the first films to emphasise the weaknesses of the nouvelle vague – its superficiality, as when the heroes watch a newsreel of Nazi book-burning, and its characters, often cases of arrested development: their individuality seems honest at first, but after a while one wonders why they cannot behave like other people. Moreau is particularly irritating – a selfish, wilful bitch, endowed by Truffaut with misguided charm.

The film was nonetheless for many years Truffaut's greatest success, both in France and elsewhere; but there was little liking anywhere for either **La Peau Douce** (1964), a grey tale of adultery between a podgy lecturer (Jean Desailly) and an air hostess, or **Fahrenheit 451** (1966), a mundane and finally embarrassing account of Ray Bradbury's novel, describing a society of the future in which the only surviving humanists turn themselves into books. It was one of several films Universal made in Britain at the time, of apparently highbrow interest or with prestigious names. Truffaut was so keen on the project that it was undertaken before his English was adequate to the task, but the result is so bad that it does not warrant making excuses. It was at about this time that Truffaut observed to Hitchcock that critics were unimaginative (which he did not think a bad thing) but that that lack of imagination 'might account for a predilection for films that are close to real life. On seeing *Ladri di Biciclette*, for instance, he's likely to think this is just the sort of thing he might have written himself, but that thought couldn't possibly occur to him in connection with *North by Northwest*.' This being so, he's bound to attribute all kinds of merit to *Ladri di Biciclette* and none whatever to *North by Northwest*.' In fact *Ladri di Biciclette* was admired not because it was 'close'

to life, but because it made relevant and, indeed, moving comments on life, and because it was a marvellous example of what a sensitive director might do with his material – as opposed to *North by Northwest*, which is engineered fiction with cardboard characters. Truffaut went on to imitate Hitchcock, but not profitably. In his best films, he emulated Renoir, certainly as good a model as de Sica, and **Baisers Volés** (1968) was his last entirely acceptable film. He had returned to his young hero of *Les Quatre Cents Coups*, Antoine Doinel, in a sketch-film, *L'Amour à Vingt Ans* – an amusing anecdote about the boy, again played by Léaud, visiting the parents of his girlfriend. With sympathy and gentle ironic humour *Baisers Volés* follows Antoine from the end of his military service through a number of love affairs and mediocre jobs; but two later adventures of Antoine, **Domicile Conjugal** (1970) and **L'Amour en Fuite** (1979), both made after other films had been poorly received, are mild indeed.

They are nevertheless preferable to the imitations of Hitchcock, **La Mariée était en Noir** (1968) and **La Sirène du Mississippi** (1968), both based on novels by William Irish. The first is about a bride (Moreau) who sets out to murder the several men she thinks responsible for her husband's death, and the second involves a wealthy tobacco planter (Belmondo) who falls for the mysterious mail-order bride (Catherine Deneuve) who may be feeding him rat-poison. In this case the film emulated is *Vertigo*, indicating that Truffaut preferred to copy bad Hitchcock rather than good. He returned to a humanist theme with **L'Enfant Sauvage** (1970), based on a true story of the late eighteenth century, about a wild boy of the woods and the struggle to civilise him and prove that he has a soul. Truffaut himself plays the doctor trying to help the boy, but the film is less effective than the not dissimilar *The Miracle Worker* (q.v.). **Les Deux Anglaises et le Continent** (1971) is based on a novel by Roché which reverses the situation of *Jules et Jim*, with Jean-Pierre Léaud as the young man in love with two women. If, as Truffaut insists, his films take their personality from the leading player, that may be why this one and the later Antoine pictures are negative. Certainly **Une Belle Fille Comme Moi**

(1972), designed for Bernadette Lafont, is much more lively; it also recalls an earlier film, but more positively, for like *Tirez sur le Pianiste* it combines differing qualities, moving from sociological treatise to burlesque and thriller.

If Truffaut is happiest with a star player, to deflect attention from himself, that may be, as he himself admits, because he knows more about movies than life. That knowledge went into the screenplay of **La Nuit Américaine** (1973), in which he himself plays a director much like himself, involved in incidents recognisable to those who have followed his career. Consequently this is another filmed collection of memories, but without the invention and charm of Leterrier's similar *Projection Privée* (q.v.). It was a success in Britain and the U.S. but not in France, where the local branch of United Artists financed most of his films, with the option of purchasing world rights – to no great financial risk, since Truffaut is an economical film-maker. Foreign appreciation of his work had always been kinder than at home, but it was a French critic, Jean-Loup Bourget, writing in *The New Review*, who described **L'Argent de Poche** (1976), as 'offensively bad, as untrue as it is condescending' – an ironic judgment on a man reputed to have walked out of *Pather Panchali* and who, as a critic, loathed Clément, whose *Les Jeux Interdits* is also an infinitely better film about childhood. Among his next few films, **L'Homme qui Aimait les Femmes** (1978) most exposes his weaknesses. The man (Charles Denner) concerned uses women to gratify his sexual urges, and writes a book about them to exorcise the memory of his mother, which prevents him from fidelity and the experience of love. The moral point is there, but lost in trite philosophising, while the enterprise desperately needs humour or at least some resemblance to real life – if we are not to find it distasteful.

Truffaut's standing in his native land was restored by **Le Dernier Métro** (1980), which was not only his greatest commercial success to date but the winner of virtually every available César award, voted annually by the French film industry. It may be regarded either as his attempt at *Les Enfants du Paradis* or a theatrical companion piece to *La Nuit Américaine*. It is set during the Occupation, among theatre people including a Jewish impresario (Heinz Bennent), who is hidden in the cellar; his wife (Catherine Deneuve), who is under consequent strain; a new young actor (Gérard Depardieu), a secret member of the Resistance; a homosexual director (Jean Poiret); a lesbian designer (Andréa Ferréol); and a collaborationist critic/censor (Jean-Louis Richard). Truffaut does absolutely nothing with this potentially interesting group, and it is astonishing that anyone could have preferred this film to Resnais's *Mon Oncle d'Amérique* (q.v.) or Pialat's *Loulou* (q.v.), two of the other nominated films.★ Resnais and Pialat are astute observers, which cannot be said of Truffaut, whatever his other gifts. **La Femme d'à Côté** (1981) is a singularly unconvincing examination of adultery among the well-heeled suburbanites of Grenoble. The *amour fou* of the lovers (Gérard Depardieu, Fanny Ardant) bears the influence of *Vertigo* again and *Marnie*; indeed the film seems to belong to that era, with such outdated devices as telling stares and conversations summarising the past for audience convenience. Chabrol had not long before remarked that Truffaut was now making exactly the sort of films which he had condemned as a critic. It is therefore ironic that these two films show him now to be an infinitely inferior film-maker to even Clément in his decline.

The career of Claude Chabrol has a more complicated history, partly because he had no popular success immediately after *Les Cousins*. **A Double Tour** (1959) is a prettily coloured, rather vapid study of a Provençal family and its hangers-on, which evoked only mild enthusiasm. Although **Les Bonnes Femmes** (1960) was liked neither in France nor elsewhere, it seemed to me both then and now one of the triumphs of the nouvelle vague. One of its virtues, as with the best of the films of the movement, is that it is impossible to tell in which direction it will go – though a clue is provided by the cherished memento kept by the cashier in her handbag. For this is a black comedy about four shopgirls, with a particularly acrid tone and some brilliant detail of the daily grind in an electrical shop near the Place de la Bastille.

★The other film of the four was Godard's supposed return to 'commercial' film-making, *Sauve Qui Peut*, which made little impression elsewhere.

An epilogue explains the violent climax, asserting that a few hours' real happiness is worth the rest of the day's drab happenings. Chabrol's writer on both films was Paul Gégauff, who had also contributed to *Les Cousins* and was later to become a regular collaborator.

Les Godelureaux (1960) is a more bizarre variation on the themes of *Les Cousins*, but its interplay of character was to lead Chabrol to two more fine films, **L'Oeil du Malin** (1962) and **Ophélia** (1962). If *Les Bonnes Femmes* is the first mature demonstration of the malevolent Chabrol universe, these two films show this realm to be situated rather near to the *haute bourgeoisie*. The settings are respectively the home of a successful writer and the country estate of a landed family, their curiously calm existence about to be shattered by young men who are dreamers rather than schemers. In the first case destruction comes from without, from a journalist (Jacques Charrier) who is over-possessive towards both wife and husband, and in the other it comes from within, wrought by the son (André Jocelyn) who insists on re-enacting the situation of 'Hamlet' inside the family circle. The nature of evil was to preoccupy Chabrol, whose studies of its effects were to take him far deeper into psychology than his idol, Hitchcock. He would far surpass him as a film-maker, but at this stage of his career he made one film which approaches the standard of Truffaut's Hitchcock imitations. This is **Landru** (1963), but then this study of the mass-murderer has a particularly specious screenplay by Françoise Sagan. Despite the magnetic performance of Charles Denner in the title role, and the presence of Danielle Darrieux, Michèle Morgan and Hildegarde Neff among his victims, the film failed to attract audiences. It was the most publicised of Chabrol's failures, causing him to turn to solidly commercial products.

During this period he contributed to three of the numerous French omnibus films, among them **Les Sept Péchés Capitaux** (1961), a wholly nouvelle vague affair which did not demonstrate, as intended, its superiority over the film of the same name made by the old guard a decade earlier. He also made a conventional war film, **La Ligne de Démarcation** (1966), and three cinema equivalents of comic strips – *Le Tigre aime la Chair Fraîche, Marie-Chantal contre le Docteur Kha, Le Tigre se Parfume à la Dynamite* – all aiming, without much success, at the tongue-in-cheek high spirits of de Broca's *L'Homme de Rio* (q.v.). **La Route de Corinthe** (1967) was a slight move upwards, if only for some ambiguity in the murders, but Chabrol returned to more congenial territory in **Le Scandale/The Champagne Murders** (1967) – to look at the wealthy world of party-goers, gigolos and ladies who are not quite what they seem to be. It is a film of dubious standing, certainly not offering evidence that he would escape from the doldrums with his next film, **Les Biches** (1968). This was written with Gégauff, and its faults may be attributed to the fact that Chabrol wanted to make a commercial movie, but one less derisory than those he had been making. In setting the film partly in St Tropez he may have had in mind *Et Dieu . . . Créa la Femme* rather than his own studies set among the smart set, rich and destructive. The malicious character in this case is also the strongest, a lesbian, played by Stéphane Audran, the sleek and sensuous actress who was the second Mme Chabrol; the weak sides of the triangle are taken by Jacqueline Sassard and Jean-Louis Trintignant.

It was as his own writer that Chabrol began his unparalleled studies of bourgeois crime – predominantly murder – often derived from pulp fiction but in a way never contemplated by Truffaut or Godard. On one level Chabrol borrows from the glaring headlines of the French popular press, and his movies also depend for their effect on other movies – i.e. we are conditioned to expect the conventional pattern of the thriller, which he then proceeds to ignore. He uses suspense rather than guilt, and is compassionate only intermittently: the curiosity about the nature of the crime is matched by his interest in the equivocation of motive – not only on the part of the murderer but frequently by someone close who has guessed at the crime. Since most of these films are set, vividly, in the country, they might be subtitled 'Scenes From Provincial Life', and are all eloquently photographed by Jean Rabier. **La Femme Infidèle** (1968) concerns a mild husband (Michel Bouquet) who murders the lover (Maurice

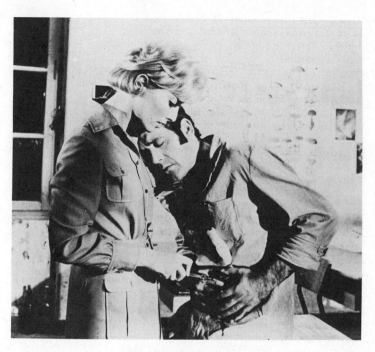

After a number of failures Chabrol became a purely 'commercial' director for a while, but emerging from what was clearly a trough in his career he embarked on a series of bourgeois murder stories which are among the most sustained group of films in all cinema – sustained, that is, when they are good, for there is at least one rotten apple in the barrel. Anyway, this picture is from the best of them, *Le Boucher*, with Stéphane Audran and Jean Yanne.

Ronet) of his wife (Stéphane Audran). **Que la Bête Meure!** (1969) centres on a journalist (Michel Duchaussoy) setting out to find the hit-and-run killer of his son. **La Rupture** (1970) is a group portrait of a Brussels family, Balzacian in its variety, its title referring to an L.S.D.-addicted man (Jean-Claude Drouot) who attacks his wife (Audran) and small son. **Juste Avant la Nuit** (1971) involves a successful businessman (Bouquet) who murders his mistress and feels bound to confess to both his wife (Audran), and his best friend (François Perier), husband of his victim – neither of whom wish to judge him. **Les Noces Rouges** (1973) reverts to adultery as its prime subject, with the wife (Audran) of the mayor (Claude Pieplu) sneaking off to the woods with a family friend (Michel Piccoli). Occasionally Chabrol uses a perfectly harmless object to create tension, manipulating his audience in the manner of minor directors of the thriller genre, but that he is capable of perfection is proved by **Le Boucher** (1970), a masterpiece depicting the relationship between the village schoolteacher (Audran) and the butcher (Jean Yanne), who happens to be a compulsive murderer.

The least pure and most conventional of the group is *Que la Bête Meure!*, and it is the only one on which Chabrol had a script collaborator – once again, Paul Gégauff. It is surely no coincidence that Gégauff worked with him on his one dreadful film of this period – **La Décade Prodigieuse/Ten Days' Wonder** (1971), a family saga from a novel by Ellery Queen, with any number of absurd undertones, including Moses and the House of Atreus, performed in a like manner by a cast including Orson Welles and Anthony Perkins. Gégauff also contributed to **Docteur Popaul** (1972), and that is not very good either. The ultra-chic furnishings of Chabrol's films, and their insistence on the 'games people play', often reveal a vulgarity just kept at bay. His instincts are invariably right on the films he makes alone, but when he pushes towards extravagance and excess that may be because the film concerned was designed as a lightweight entertainment. This one is *comédie noire*, the story of a philandering doctor (Jean-Paul Belmondo) whose marriage to a cripple (Mia Farrow) does not prevent him from bedding her sister (Laura Antonelli), with dire consequences to all concerned. When Chabrol creates his 'own' people, as it were, they are bitten by inhibitions and passions they cannot confess, but with Gégauff at this stage of his career they become no more than the cardboard figures of so many thrillers.

Gégauff's disastrous influence is borne out by **Une Partie de Plaisir** (1975), written solely by him and based on the break-up of his own marriage. The leading role was intended for Trintignant, but Chabrol felt that there was so much of Gégauff in it that he persuaded him to play it himself. His ex-wife plays his ex-wife, and their daughter their daughter; the premise is that Gégauff tells his wife that he is having an affair, and that she should feel free to do so, at which point the marriage falls apart – to his surprise and irritation. Gégauff offers a protagonist, trendy and wearing clothes twenty years too young, as dislikeable as any in movies. From Chabrol's point of view, this is another devastating attack on the bourgeoisie; but any other way it looks like the first major exhibitionist movie – of which there have since been a good number.

Gégauff was not, however, involved with two more 'game' stories, **Les Innocents aux Mains Sales** (1975), written by

Chabrol alone, and **Folies Bourgeoises/ Twist** (1976), written with Norman Enfield. The first, set in a large house in St Tropez, examines a disintegrating marriage; the second, set in equally glamorous Paris apartments, is about infidelity, real or imagined, among the literary set. It is clear in each case that Chabrol set out to make a mordant comedy, but the jokes are laboured, the plotting absurd and his handling miscalculated. The stars of the one are Romy Schneider and Rod Steiger, while among those in the other are Bruce Dern and Ann-Margret; even more than *La Décade Prodigieuse* the films prove that Chabrol should avoid attempts at 'international' cinema. Both were poorly received, causing Chabrol to abandon the assaults on the bourgeoisie which had been one of the staples of his career. Instead, he has floundered in all directions, making only four respectable entertainments over the past decade and a half.

Nada (1974), written with Jean-Patrick Manchette from his own novel, is about a political kidnapping. Chabrol claimed that the piece was apolitical, perhaps because those responsible include cynics, neurotics and anarchists as well as leftists and idealists; but the opposite side is led by a kill-happy, fascist – and eventually ridiculous – detective, clearly one for spectators to dislike. **Violette Nozière** (1978) was a commissioned piece, based on a screenplay by other hands and the only Chabrol murder story, with *Landru* and *Les Noces Rouges*, with a foundation in fact. In 1933 Violette (Isabelle Huppert) administered poison to her parents (Mlle Audran, Jean Carmet), and although she became a heroine to the Surrealists she remains in this film as mysterious as many other ladies of scandal. For some critics, **Les Fantômes du Chapelier** (1982) showed Chabrol on form again, but the story, after Simenon, has to rely on devices familiar from Hitchcock (a dummy posing as a body) and Agatha Christie (the extraordinary coincidence involving the victims). The setting, a small coastal town, reaffirms Chabrol's gift for atmosphere, and there can be no doubt of the quality of Michel Serrault's performance as a mass murderer, a smug, dandified tradesman. The three films, however, if better than those made around the same time, use elements of sensationalism unworthy of the director of *Le Boucher*. The fourth, **Le Cheval d'Orgueil** (1980), as a study of a Breton community in the manner of *L'Albero degli Zoccoli* (q.v.), suggests that his career might move in another direction.

Resnais was, and remains, the enigma of the nouvelle vague, his seven films since *Hiroshima, Mon Amour* being unequally daring and unequally rewarding. After that film he commissioned a screenplay from the novelist Alain Robbe-Grillet, **L'Année Dernière à Marienbad** (1961), which deals with a past either real or imagined. In a rococo grand hotel, a man (Giorgio Albertazzi) and a woman (Delphine Seyrig) touch and circle each other, with an effect at first hypnotic but soon soporific – a fact with which the expressionless playing is not unconnected. If Resnais and Robbe-Grillet intended allegory – we are Outward Bound, or in a womb, or a mental home – they should have offered something less bloodless, less redolent of the avant-garde films of the late Twenties. As written by Jean Cayrol, **Muriel, ou le Temps d'un Retour** (1963) is another riddle, but one of astonishing richness. It builds tension from the outset, as Seyrig waits at the station: the visitor is an old lover, the girl with him is a 'niece', and the boy at the subsequent dinner party is Seyrig's stepson. But as soon as the strands have come together, they are fragmented: images tumble on, days pass in a flash or are lingered upon. What matters is the disease and dissatisfaction of time passing – memories play false, and the newsreels from Algeria suggest that tomorrow promises no better. All that was here, is here, will be, are the cliffs and streets of Boulogne, divorced from thought and association – and even then, they deceive. The film exists because it exists, and this is what it chooses to say – in a manner as warm as *Marienbad* is frigid.

La Guerre est Finie (1966) confirmed Resnais as a full-blooded romantic. Jorge Semprun, a Spanish novelist living in France, contributed the screenplay about a Spanish exile (Yves Montand), half immersed in subversive activities relating to the Civil War, and uncertain whether or not he believes in the myths associated with it. Like *L'Avventura* (q.v.), the film is an insight into a man's soul, but where in that film each action sprang from the one before, the happenings of this film are arbitrary – as arbitrary as Montand's musings on his past, which may be imaginary. The enigma of memory was less agreeably worked over in **Je t'Aime, Je t'Aime** (1968), a science fiction, written by Jacques Sternberg, in which the hero (Claude Rich) is injected with a serum in order to make an odyssey into his past – which is also a search for the meaning of existence.

The film failed, and in 1971 a British project about the Marquis de Sade, with Dirk Bogarde, fell through. After a sojourn in the U.S., Resnais returned to France, where Semprun was preparing **Stavisky** (1974), mainly financed (without credit) by Jean-Paul Belmondo, who played the lead. It is not about the Stavisky affair, which began only with the death of the Russian-Jewish swindler: it is, said Resnais, 'a very sinister story about a crook . . . a fairy-tale, that's to say a cruel legend without any magic.' One expected more from this team: the film, as pretty as cake-frosting, is entertaining, but it constantly doles out historical facts without marshalling them. A subject more complex than *Citizen Kane* is made in the butterfly style of Ophuls, but without his control. Resnais is more dependent than most on his writers, and **Providence** (1977) by the British David Mercer, and filmed in English, is a melange of *Marienbad*, late Fellini and *Accident* (q.v.). According to one of its stars, Bogarde, no one in Britain wanted to show it, but after winning a number of French awards and golden opinions from some American critics, it opened to mildly respectful reviews. One American critic who disliked it was John Simon in *New York* magazine who called it Resnais's first unmitigated disaster. Mercer himself had explained 'I, myself, am bored with naturalism now, pissed-off with verisimilitude. As Francis Bacon said when someone asked him why he didn't paint realistic portraits, "I can do you one, but it would bore the arse off me" ' – a remark entirely in keeping with the content of the movie. The chief production company involved shortly afterwards went into bankruptcy.

Conversely **Mon Oncle d'Amérique** (1980) was Resnais's first popular success in France. Jean Gruault's screenplay evolved from Resnais's idea of a montage film, blending excerpts from old films with comments by Professor Henri Laborit, an expert in behaviour patterns (it was Gruault who had shown Resnais a number of American Silents, while Resnais and Laborit had already discussed a projected film on memory). The professor's comments, together with frequent shots of laboratory tests on rats, provide the framework, and clips of Danielle Darrieux, Jean Gabin and Jean Marais are shown to indicate the influence their screen activities had on the film's three chief protagonists (Roger Pierre, Nicole Garcia, Gérard Depardieu). The effect is amusing rather than serious, as the three characters explain themselves in terms of their childhood environment, in each case selective and becoming more detailed as they reach the present. Since what is shown to us is very much the real world, dealing in such matters as parental authority, infidelity and, most importantly, the choice of careers and the subsequent perils of earning a living, the professor's comments are often apposite, referring frequently to self-justification and self-protection. Despite the theorising this is not an intellectual film, though we may find it as clever as it is hypnotic. It serves Resnais's purpose better than any film since *Muriel*, for his aim has always been to question the nature of man and find what makes him behave in so mysterious a fashion. That questioning – which has led him into two disastrous movies – was never more explicit.

Like Resnais, it is only by an accident of timing that Louis Malle became associated with the nouvelle vague, and like him he was not to be greatly prolific or prone to any particular genre. **Zazie dans le Métro** (1960) is an adaptation of Raymond Queneau's novel of a small girl's crazy adventures in Paris: the outrageous puns and suchlike felicities are transcribed by a number of visual jokes, inspired, said Malle, by the Keystone Cops on one side and Buñuel and Dali on the other. In neither case does it show, and the film should be avoided except by those who like speeded-up photography and/or orgies of destruction. **Vie Privée** (1962) began as an M-G-M vehicle for Brigitte Bardot, and emerged as a film about her, i.e. a tale of a poor little rich little movie star. Bardot emerges as someone wanting only to be loved and admired, with no intellectual resources; but the views of Spoleto, photographed by Henri Decae, are splendid.

In both films the result was far from Malle's intention, but **Le Feu Follet** (1963) is one of the most perfectly realised of films. It is a cry of despair, and though there were to be many such in the years ahead, the only precedent was Antonioni. Like Antonioni's films, this is literary cinema, incisive and discursive, using the camera and a minimum of dialogue for the story – written in 1931 by Drieu la Rochelle, an imaginative account of a friend driven to suicide. La Rochelle later killed himself, and his own sexual torment is implied by Malle in the sequence where the hero (Maurice Ronet) returns for too long a young man's look in a *toilette* and leaves with sweat on his brow. The financial problems of the book have become a loan from a mistress; the drugs have become booze. The man is recovering from alcoholism and is bent on suicide; he says '*Demain je me tuerai*' and his visits to his old friends are an undertaking to find out why he should not; Ronet is as good in the role as Malle could conceivably have wished.

There is a golden rule that the quality of highly publicised movies is in inverse proportion to the publicity, and **Viva Maria!** (1965) was no exception. With United Artists money Malle directed two media favourites, Moreau and Bardot – and George Hamilton – in a burlesque set during a Mexican revolution. The musical numbers are charming, but the climactic battle has far less invention than the similar one in *The Beautiful Blonde from Bashful Bend*. **Le Voleur** (1967) has Belmondo as a turn-of-the-century burglar, in that always romantic French criminal milieu, but it was a second failure for Malle. He took a long while to prepare **Le Souffle au Coeur** (1971), a crafty, commercial, constructed film about growing up, about learning the variety of life and the importance of literature. It takes place in 1954, with many references to Dien Bien Phu, but as a background to more important matters, such as masturbation. To be fair, though, in this film the 'variety of life' in fact means sex, which means a session with mother, looking exactly like an Italian movie star – which she should, since she is played by Lea Massari. With the exception of the incest theme, the film is autobiographical, as Malle has admitted; the title refers to the boy's illness, a comparatively minor matter, and the film is, *faute de*

mieux, probably the best portrait we have of puberty. Lucien, in **Lacombe, Lucien** (1974), is somewhat older, a seventeen-year-old peasant who joins the French Gestapo; this is a study of him and his collaborators, and of a Jewish family living in hiding, paying dearly for the privilege of not being handed over to the Germans. Lucien is not intelligent – which is the whole point of the film. Collaboration was not a subject the French cinema had tackled before, and Malle's film was probably inspired by Marcel Ophuls's documentary, *Le Chagrin et la Pitié*. *Lacombe, Lucien* is an absorbing film, its only fault Malle's usual one of offering some minor point as though it were a great revelation.

After it, **Black Moon** (1975) is a particular aberration. Within minutes of it starting a series of enigmatic happenings and the presence of the military in a generally deserted countryside establish a cliché, for such matters had been used already as a metaphor for the world after nuclear destruction, usually by film-makers much Malle's inferior. Subsequent events, at an isolated house with a bedridden old lady and a brother and sister who may be her grandchildren, are resolutely obscure, and the final message, when it comes, is paltry. What little dialogue there is is in French, despite the title – not that either factor mattered, since the film was little seen.

Whether or not it was always advisable is uncertain, but Louis Malle is the only one of the nouvelle vague directors to have moved from genre to genre – proving in the process that he is at his best in the sort of intense, intimate dramas which at least to outsiders look more difficult to bring off than the burlesques he has also attempted. *Le Feu Follet* follows in perceptive detail the last days of a suicide, played by Maurice Ronet.

France: Before and After the Nouvelle Vague

Pretty Baby (1978) is Malle's first film in English, backed by Paramount, and its subject is child prostitution in New Orleans some years ago. The film sprang both from his love of jazz and his admiration for the photographs taken by E. J. Bellocq in the cathouses of the New Orleans redlight district *circa* 1917. The scenario, by Polly Platt, is an unsurprising one, detailing the relationship of a photographer (Keith Carradine) with the daughter (Brooke Shields) of a prostitute, a child who at twelve is only too eager to follow Mama's profession. Malle, claiming that his approach is that of a film-maker rather than a moralist, adopts a matter-of-fact approach to the child's joy at losing her virginity or joining Mama with a client, the drugging of the madame, or men buying two women at once. Clearly, such matters are a long way from all the French prostitute films of Malle's youth: but his approach is the same – deeply romantic. Photographed in hushed tones by Sven Nykvist, the brothel is splendid to look at, a box of delights for the child, and an amusing place for us to spend an evening.

Malle did not want to return to French cinema because, as he said, he no longer found it stimulating. He arranged to make a film in Canada, but left the project after the producer did a deal with Disney, who never allows the director the final cut. The Canadians did back **Atlantic City** (1980), which Malle suggested to them after visiting the city with the dramatist John Guare, with whom he had said he wanted to work. Guare's screenplay is that of a convoluted thriller, like that of Malle's first film, centred on a bag of cocaine which interests a number of people, including the hippie couple who had found it, as well as a waitress (Susan Sarandon) and a supposedly retired gangster (Burt Lancaster). He, like Atlantic City, has seen better days, and the eccentricities of the place are not ignored as Malle pursues his aim of creating the tension and surprises necessary to this genre. The film came out at the same time as *Mon Oncle d'Amérique* and is equally satisfying. It was rewarding to find both directors so much on form after two decades of film-making.

Georges Franju was the least adventurous of the nouvelle vague directors. His best film is **Thérèse Desqueyroux** (1962), based on the novel by François Mauriac, and written with Mauriac's son

Georges Franju became associated with the nouvelle vague directors because, like some of them, he had made short documentaries – and he moved into features about the same time. His early full-length films were thrillers, and then he did a very successful literary adaptation, *Thérèse Desqueyroux*, after Mauriac, with Emmanuelle Riva and Philippe Noiret: it turned out to be the high spot of his career.

Claude. This is another attack on the *haute bourgeoisie* and its stifling way of life, exemplified in the tale of Thérèse (Emmanuelle Riva), who marries her best friend's brother (Philippe Noiret) to be near her, and then, a modern Emma Bovary – she also hates the country – proceeds to poison him. The same measured pace was adopted for **Judex** (1963), a homage to the director Feuillade that is quite as trivial and, less inevitably, almost as boring as the original, and also for **Thomas l'Imposteur** (1965), written with Jean Cocteau – his last work for the cinema – from his early autobiographical novel. Thomas (Fabrice Rouleau) is a dreamy adolescent who makes his way to the trenches, along the way posing as the nephew of a general, and as such is taken up by the Princess (Emmanuelle Riva). It lacks the necessary theatrical flourish but is, for all that, a respectable entertainment. However, Franju's lack of invention, and his inability to 'build' a narrative, make only melodrama from **La Faute de l'Abbé Mouret** (1970), based on Zola's novel about the young priest (Francis Huster) who goes from religious to sexual mania when he meets the Eve-like Albine (Gillian Hills). It seems typical of Franju that the bitterness and realism of Zola have been reduced to something that is pretty, whimsical, and rather dull.

Jacques Demy (b. 1931) is another of the incurable romantics of the French cinema, and his first feature, **Lola** (1961), is one of the most irresistible of films. In Nantes, a number of lives touch tangentially – especially those of Lola (Anouk Aimée), a prostitute, who goes to bed with sailors because she likes the uniform and dreams of the father of her child returning; of Roland (Marc Michel), not long out of adolescence, who dreams of her and of the South Seas; and of a widow (Elina Labourdette), whose aspirations include a suitor for her daughter and a knowledge of English. Mother and daughter are facets of Lola, and the sailor and lover are facets of Roland. Demy understands Roland best, for this is a film made by someone discovering that the adult world is made of lost ideals and lost loves. A number of themes recur in **La Baie des Anges** (1963) – the mysterious beau (Paul Guers), the sailors, an adoring hero (Claude Mann), an aggressively glamorous woman (Jeanne

Moreau) who happens to be a compulsive gambler and whose ups and downs are all the film has to offer in terms of plot. Demy returned to the Atlantic coast for **Les Parapluies de Cherbourg** (1964), which, since its characters include Roland from *Lola*, also reintroduces his theme, extended by Michel Legrand for a complete score – to which all the dialogue is sung. Furthermore, the film is pretty, with decor to match the jacket of hero and skirt of heroine. He (Nino Castelnuovo) works in a garage, and she (Catherine Deneuve) works in the umbrella shop of her mother (Anne Vernon): they are parted by his *service militaire*, and the threatening sentimentality gives way to a fatalism essentially and irrevocably French. Demy catches life on the wing, events half-glimpsed and half-understood; he has grown up since *Lola*. The film, which should not have worked, won a Grand Prix at Cannes, and went on to win hearts all round the world.

Basking in that success, Demy was rewarded with American backing and the presence of Gene Kelly for a follow-up, **Les Demoiselles de Rochefort** (1967), clear proof, after Clément and Truffaut, that French directors get worse in proportion to the American investment. (Vadim, for example, never a good director, was even worse when he set his sights on the international market.) Hollywood musicals have become an important factor in

Another failed director associated with the nouvelle vague is Jacques Demy, as if confirming the jinx on the movement – that they begin with excellence and then work downwards (to say nothing of the myriad other young directors given a chance by the industry at this time, who after a mediocre first picture and a terrible second one were not given a third chance). Demy's first feature, *Lola*, remains a pleasure – not least for the performance of Anouk Aimée. The sailor about to enjoy her favours is Alan Scott.

French culture, but they were not made by putting a moving camera among moving people who sing and dance. Rochefort responds less well than Cherbourg to a fresh paint job; Legrand's score is poor, and the choreography sub-Jerome Robbins; as the *demoiselles* Deneuve and Françoise Dorléac are limited musical performers, Danielle Darrieux is wasted as their mother and Kelly was simply too middle-aged for bare-armed dancing and twinkly smiles. Despite the film's failure, Columbia backed **Model Shop** (1969), which relocates Lola as an L.A. callgirl, loved by a loafer (Gary Lockwood), and the film becomes increasingly like trying to fight one's way through candy floss. Two fairy-tales, *Peau d'Ane*, and *The Pied Piper*, were even less successful, and a comedy about a pregnant man, *L'Evénement le Plus Important depuis que l'Homme a Marché sur la Lune*, is a fiasco. Demy's career is a sad example of starting at the top and working downwards, and **Lady Oscar** (1979) did not reverse the pattern. A Japanese film, based on a Japanese comic strip, it is set at the court of Marie Antoinette, with a cast of British unknowns. To find a plot, Demy evolved 'the kind of picaresque structure . . . already used in *Lola*: a host of characters whose paths cross, diverge, reappear, diverge once more': it proved to be highly unsuitable and the film itself has to date not been seen in France.

In 1962 Demy married Agnès Varda (b. 1928), who had made her own first feature about the same time as *Lola*. **Cléo de 5 à 7** (1962) is not as beguiling or original, but it is not unworthy of a director who had been one of the most distinguished of the short film-makers. Cléo (Corinne Marchand) is a singer who believes that she has a serious illness, which causes her to look at Paris anew – thus this film is another nouvelle vague love affair with the city. It also has odd mood changes and unfamiliar faces: in comparison **Le Bonheur** (1965) looks very conventional. It tells of a young carpenter (Jean-Claude Drouot), who loves equally his wife (Claire Drouot) and his new mistress (Marie-France Boyer). Moving from one to the other – from Fontenay-aux-Roses to Vincennes – enabled Varda's photographers, Rabier and Claude Beausoleil, to photograph every brightly coloured wall in both suburbs, and every brightly coloured lorry which

plies between the two. The lingering, lyrical shots of sunny meadows and of limbs in the throes of love-making, are further evidence of the detrimental effects of the nouvelle vague, though in fact this film is only a half-way mark between the movement's original use of such matters and the subsequent T.V. commercials based on them. Varda then moved into an artistic wilderness, not unlike that of her husband, to emerge charmingly with **L'Une Chante, l'Autre Pas** (1977), a study of two women friends from 1962 to the present. Both more feminist and more contrived than *Cléo*, it is a reminder that she can be both fond and funny on the subject of rather tacky people.

Among the *Cahiers* set, Eric Rohmer (b. 1920) took much longer to gain renown, but that was partly because of the failure of his first feature, **Le Signe de Lion**, in 1960. He began his series of *contes moraux* two years later, but it was not until the fourth, in 1969, that he became internationally known. The first two, **La Boulangère de Monceau** (1962) and **La Carrière de Suzanne** (1963), were shot on 16mm in black and white, and originally shown on television; both are quite short. They concern the love-pangs of students, and throughout the series Rohmer was looking at life through the eyes of a much younger man. His men and women on the brink of adult relationships are either introverted or complacent, hesitant in love or confident. They exist in deliberately beautiful images, the books around them seem to encase them, and the results are inconclusive: the would-be, could-be, might-have-been are set amidst the minutiae of daily life, and an accompanying commentary constantly suggests the possibility of a God-ordained world. Rohmer constructs like a novelist, embroidering seemingly real situations, and though these are usually sexual, intercourse usually remains only a probability. **La Collectionneuse** (1967) is a variation on the triangle of *La Carrière de Suzanne*, inasmuch as two friends share one girl, though not at the same time – and it should be emphasised that the relationships in these anecdotes are far from the usual course of movie love (one difference between the two films is that this one is set in a villa near St Trop', instead of around the Boul' Mich, and that it is in colour – since it was made for cinemas). **Ma Nuit chez Maud** (1969) takes place near Clermont-Ferrand, in winter, and presents Jean-Louis Trintignant as a returned emigrant caught between two women, with one of whom (Françoise Fabian) he mainly discusses Pascal, Marxist theory and Christian doctrine. **Le Genou de Claire** (1970) finds Jean-Claude Brialy, in a Cézanne-like beard, on the shores of Lake Annecy, meditating on the nature of love. Like its immediate predecessor, the piece is over-verbose; but Rohmer returned to his earlier theme of choice in **L'Amour, l'Après-Midi** (1972), when Frédéric (Bernard Verley) is tempted by the predatory Chloë (Zouzou) to desert his wife. These are rich films, inevitably minor, but as good a gloss on one aspect of modern life as we have.

The series concluded, Rohmer turned to period drama, in the shape of a story by Heinrich von Kleist, **Die Marquise von O . . .** (1976), about the unfortunate noble lady who finds herself pregnant some years after her husband's death. Filmed in the ossified style of the new German cinema (q.v.) it was, said Russell Davies in *The Observer* – knowing only too well what he was saying – 'destined to be a feature of art house repertory for some time to come.' Those critics subjected to the scattered showings of **Perceval de Galles** (1978) were considerably less kind. Rohmer accordingly announced a series of 'Comédies et Proverbes', which is clearly intended to be a continuation of his *contes moraux*. The first of them, **La Femme de l'Aviateur** (1981) is equally honest but completely lacking wit and insight. It is an anecdote about a married man who involves a passing – female – stranger in his musings about an affaire his mistress may be having.

Also belonging to the central group of nouvelle vague directors is Philippe de Broca, who followed *Les Jeux de l'Amour* with two more comedies with Jean-Pierre Cassel. **Cartouche** (1962), an oft-filmed subject – a French Robin Hood – is as light-hearted and entertaining as any swashbuckler that comes to mind, and with the same actor, Belmondo, **L'Homme de Rio** (1964) is simply the best of its genre, the chase spoof. It is a super-Tintin, neglecting no element of the adventure tales which it parodies, be it the crawl along the wall of the skyscraper, the stolen Aztec statuettes, the car(s) coming at the hero in the midst of the desert, or the jungle temple climax. It is a once-in-a-lifetime film, as was proved by the less successful **Les Tribulations d'un Chinois en Chine** (1965), substituting Hong Kong and the Himalayas for Rio and Brasilia, and said to be based on a tale by Jules Verne. In the same year de Broca made **Un Monsieur de Compagnie** (1965), a facetious and sometimes frenetic farce, with Cassel as a man who lives by his amatory wits. It was followed by the even more disappointing **Le Roi de Coeur** (1966), a piece of whimsy set at the end of World War One, in which the lunatics who take over the town – Senlis – are clearly more admirable than the Germans and British fighting over it. Tricked out with a number of processions and dances, not to mention some underscored jokes, this allegory on the folly of war is depressing – not least because it became a cult film in the U.S., running several years in some cities. De Broca admitted that because of that he was regarded as a commercial director in France.

His next two or three films did not cross boundaries, and **Le Magnifique** (1973) seemed to confirm a decline: it is another re-hash of *L'Homme de Rio*, with the ingenious addition of Belmondo also playing the meek writer who dreams up the adventures for the gentleman of the title. With **Chère Louise** (1972), de Broca turned serious, for this is the tale of a divorcée (Jeanne Moreau) who falls in love with a teddy-bear of a man (Julian Negulesco) half her age. In fact, de Broca proved incapable of exercising the requisite discipline for a serious subject: but he remains so inventive and affectionate throughout that the film did not deserve the dismissal it generally received. But then, few of the reviews of **Tendre Poulet** (1977) – or *Dear Detective* as it was splendidly retitled – gave any indication that it was one of the most amusing films in years. It is contrived, but the gags are as fresh as they are funny, and they are bountiful. Annie Girardot and Philippe Noiret had on other occasions proved a felicitous team, and here she is a detective of the Sûreté and he an unworldly professor, meeting for the first time since youth. The thrills are of the parody sort, in the manner of *L'Homme de Rio*, and there had not been a film

Anouk Aimée and Jean-Louis Trintignant in a typical scene from Lelouch's *Un Homme et une Femme* – or at least an almost typical scene, for much of the time the windscreen-wipers were working, to make rainswept compositions. The film itself may not be the best there is on a romance, but it is the best there is on a romance between a scriptgirl and a racing-driver.

with such good humour since that time.

For good commercial entertainments, de Broca is rivalled only by Claude Lelouch (b. 1937), who started making amateur films as a teenager. His first success was **Un Homme et une Femme** (1966), which created a stir at the Cannes Festival, and went on to win an Oscar (Best Foreign Language film) and break records for a French movie in the U.S. The man of the title is a racing-driver (Trintignant) and the woman a scriptgirl (Anouk Aimée), both of them grieving over dead spouses. Lelouch clearly started with only the personal charm of both players, adding to them Francis Lai's pulsating score, some rose-tinted views of Deauville beach in winter and, thankfully, some improvisation (or what seems like it). The film's popularity resulted in a critical reaction against Lelouch, who, consciously or not, has continued to offer ammunition to his critics. **Vivre pour Vivre** (1967), a similarly glossy love story, is intercut with scenes of violence in Vietnam on the premise that the protagonist (Yves Montand) is a television journalist; his mistress (Candice Bergen) is a model, another of the jet-set occupations. As we watch this pretty film – the best sequences are in Amsterdam in winter, where the wife (Mlle Girardot) has planned a second honeymoon – we may feel that it does not provide an appropriate occasion to remind us that men are dying elsewhere in the world. **La Vie, l'Amour, La Mort** (1969)

is a study of a meek murderer (Amidou) and a plea for the abolition of capital punishment: it is dazzlingly well made. By this time Lelouch – who is his own photographer and, usually with Pierre Uytterhoeven, his own scenarist – had mastered the tools of his trade better than anyone in the business, whether the camera lurks or stares hard in close-up, whether he chooses to cut off the sound or move into monochrome, or ignore chronology or move into flashback. His people fit easily into their settings, but it is hard to feel much sense of involvement. Amidou is both this film's prize and its chief drawback; he is sympathetic, so we feel for him when the whores – his victims – humiliate him, yet he is impassive as he watches a T.V. newsreel on his crimes. But with all his technical mastery Lelouch's patent manipulation of audiences destroys this film as the document it sets out to be. On the matter of crime and punishment he is less persuasive than Chabrol, and by far the lesser film-maker.

But if Lelouch is second-rate his films are not only technically adroit but beguiling and often charming. **Un Homme qui me Plaît** (1969) involves a French film star, played by Girardot, and a French composer (Belmondo) who start an affair while engaged on a film in Hollywood. These artists are two of the most likeable and talented working today, and what makes their affair singularly convincing is that they are put into an alien environment, i.e. tourist U.S.A., as cunningly and wittily observed as we are likely to get it. **Le Voyou** (1970), with Trintignant as a crook, is too clever by half, with its time ellipses, and on crime again **La Bonne Année** (1973) is best described as ingratiating. It may be more ephemeral than most films, but as Lino Ventura takes the Cannes branch of Van Cleef and Arpels for a fortune, or sweet-talks the beautiful Françoise Fabian, that is no matter. It begins with a clip from the director's most famous film, *Un Homme et une Femme*, which is then promptly and disarmingly disparaged. But I have to say that the last of Lelouch's films that I have seen,★ **Si C'Etait à Refaire** (1978), justifies all that

★Since writing this I have seen several more of Lelouch's films, including Les Uns et les Autres *(1981), which was phenomenally successful on its home ground; it is hard to imagine a movie more ambitious and more banal.*

his detractors have claimed. It has flashbacks within flashbacks and a glossy surface; it has dialogue constantly suggesting that the characters are on the verge of discovering the secret of life; and an idiotic story about an ex-convict (Catherine Deneuve), her adolescent son and a friend of hers (Anouk Aimée) who decides to seduce him.

Still, at its considerable worst it is more entertaining than **Détruire Dit-Elle** (1969) and **Nathalie Granger** (1972), written and directed by Marguerite Duras, presumably for her friends, or as Françoise Giroud put it of their confrères in her 1975 memoir, 'for the people they expect to meet at dinner'. I could not tell you what the former is about, other than that the eternal dialogue is of ineffable banality and inconsequence; the second concerns two zombie-like women (Moreau, Lucia Bosè) and a travelling salesman (Gérard Depardieu). As V.S. Pritchett once said of a novel by Samuel Beckett, 'All significance and no content.'

If there has to be pretension in films, it is better found in such as Jean Gabriel Albicocco's **La Fille aux Yeux d'Or** (1961), since it is a quality which sits better with triteness than wilful obscurity. This is a modernisation of one of Balzac's three stories in L'Histoire des Treize, and it emerges here as a tale of gothic horror. Balzac's contempt for the young and the idle rich is dissipated; the implied lesbian relationship has become explicit and is now set appropriately in the world of Paris *haute couture*. The updated plot, of a man who realises that his rival is a lesbian, is not derisory. The soundtrack, of Corelli and guitar, and the Cocteauesque decor, were entirely to the taste of Parisians, but the film's lack of success elsewhere did not augur well for Albicocco. He had one further success, also photographed by his father, Quinto Albicocco, **Le Grand Meaulnes** (1967), based on Alain Fournier's novel, and written by the director with Fournier's sister, who had refused till then to part with the screen rights. As it turned out, this was one of the last of the French screen transcriptions of literature, and the old tradition died in high visual style, vaseline on the lens, arc-lights and distortion, but like the earlier film, consistent in effect. The film sets out to be a portrait of a village some seventy years

earlier, of its schoolchildren and the charismatic Meaulnes (Jean Blaize), of his meeting, possibly imaginary, with the girl (Brigitte Fossey), and of the narrator's hero-worship.

La Fille aux Yeux d'Or belongs to that euphoric time when the French film industry was suddenly young, and also to that period belongs **Les Dimanches de Ville d'Avray** (1962), or *Sundays and Cybèle* as it was called when, by some chance, it was premiered in New York before Paris. It was the French art film *par excellence*: a score compounded of Handel, Albinoni and Maurice Jarre; florid photography by Henri Decae, never taking the normal view if he can find a mirror or a steamed-up window; and with a plot about the friendship between an amnesiac ex-pilot (Hardy Kruger) and a young girl (Patricia Gozzi). The setting, as with many of these films, is a wintry village, and this one is the supreme example of the great romantic French movie tradition dying in the wake of the nouvelle vague. It also demonstrates something else: in *The New York Times*, Bosley Crowther wrote, 'Heaven knows for what rare virtue New York has been rewarded with the first public exhibition of a French motion-picture masterpiece. But it has. And, what's more, this work . . . is almost by way of being a cinematic masterpiece.' When the film opened in Paris, with that and other U.S. praise quoted in the ads, both press and public were bemused; in Britain unanimously bad reviews despatched it at once.

A similar situation arose with both Claude Berri's **Le Vieil Homme et l'Enfant** (1964) and **La Vie devant Soi** (1977), directed by Moshe Mizrahi – the films known respectively in the U.S. as *The Two Of Us* and *Madame Rosa*. Each concerns childhood and old age: Berri's film is about an anti-semitic man (Michel Simon) who during the War grows to love a Jewish child, while in Mizrahi's a Jewish prostitute (Simone Signoret) shelters an Arab boy. Clearly both films had great appeal to New York audiences, at least, and **La Vieille Dame Indigne** (1965), also with an aged leading player (Sylvie), again found favour in the U.S. but not elsewhere outside France. Its appeal to American art house audiences is only too apparent: it is 'unusual', anti-bourgeois and slightly complex – which in fact here means muddled.

The old lady behaves in unconventional manner on becoming a widow, and at the end we are informed that she finally blossomed after living her life as the chattel of another. The original story is by Brecht, but René Allio, the director, far from achieving any Brechtian alienation, attempts spontaneity. The result is merely careless; his later films are slapdash to the point of incomprehension.

Government intervention in the form of subsidy has brought forth a great many films from people who might be better employed making mindless commercial movies, but while there has been no restriction on subject matter in French cinema the brighter young film-makers continue to emulate the nouvelle vague – thus, for instance, the autobiographical films which pour out at the rate of half a dozen a year. It has become common in France in the last few years to say that the nouvelle vague was a disaster from which the French film industry has never recovered – and among those who have said so are Roman Polanski and the actor Daniel Gélin. In fact the movement revitalised the industry and it is only with hindsight that we might prefer the academic, historical and literary films which preceded it. It is also true that of the central nouvelle vague directors only Resnais and Malle have not declined. We have noted Chabrol's comment on Truffaut, of whom Godard dryly observed that he had forgotten all he ever knew about making a film, before adding that Chabrol had never known anything. He may be right, but Chabrol has at least a dozen fine films to his credit, which is more than Godard and Truffaut can muster between them.

So great, however, was the stir created by the nouvelle vague directors that despite decline or paucity of output they have overshadowed their successors, few of whom have established an international reputation. Though some have achieved both popularity and esteem within France, foreign audiences have seen only occasional films. From Clair's late Silents through Carné and Duvivier to the nouvelle vague, we have always been able to follow the careers of the leading French directors; but as the number of art houses has increased in the Seventies and Eighties so have the films imported from other film-producing countries. Now even the most ardent Francophile may have only a sketchy knowledge of recent French films.

He would almost certainly know that Maurice Pialat (b. 1925) is one of the outstanding directors of the present time, having worked in television before making his first feature, **L'Enfance Nue** (1978). Among his sponsors were Claude Berri and Truffaut, whose first features were also about childhood. François (Michel Tarrazon) is unwanted; he wets the bed, is vicious and wantonly destructive. One pair of foster parents return him to the authorities, who send him to an aged couple who between them – each had been married before – have a vast family of their own. They suffer under him, reaching out to him with love but not much understanding, because, as the old lady stubbornly puts it after he has been sent to reform school, 'Il a un bon coeur'. She, like the whole cast, is played by an amateur, Marie-Louise Thierry (and playing her husband is her husband), and she is memorable; but the boy, unlike those in *Ladri di Biciclette* or *Les 400 Coups*, could be any boy. The film is filled with moments of fresh observation, as when François instinctively gives the first foster mother a farewell gift. It is a rich piece, with as much insight and compassion as has been found since de Sica's great days.

Nous ne Vieillirons pas Ensemble (1972) portrays a couple (Jean Yanne, Marlène Jobert) whose six-year affair seldom looks less than temporary, and **La Gueule Ouverte** (1974) is about a family whose mother is dying. Like Chabrol's people, Pialat's are sexual beings; as in Renoir, life goes on; but more than any other director I can think of, Pialat finds humour in the grim facts of the everyday. Because both films refer to the same incidents, they may be autobiographical. In **Loulou** (1980), for the first time, Pialat is not wholly in command of his characters (it is therefore ironic that this was the first of his films to be publicly shown in Britain and the U.S.). He had said that he had a complex about starting to direct so late in life and then making so few films, which may be why he made this picture of a lout, nicknamed Loulou (Gérard Depardieu). It is an attempt to pin down today's young as rootless, shiftless, classless and apparently motivated mainly by sex, for example when the bourgeois Nelly (Isabelle Huppert) boasts to her rich cast-off lover of Loulou's prowess in bed. She patiently tolerates Loulou's constant drunkenness, his idiot family, occasional larceny, friends that move into their room to stay, even the termination of her pregnancy so that she can work to keep him. There have been hundreds of films about men obsessed with unworthy women, and the few taking the opposite as a starting-point have usually seen the men as either weaklings or philanderers. It is typical of Pialat that he takes a denser, more interesting approach: much is left mysterious or unexplained, but he does take us deep into the world of this sad couple.

It may be said that Pialat works in the tradition of Renoir, Chabrol and Rohmer in placing his characters in firm social context – as does Claude Sautet (b. 1924). A former collaborator of Franju, Sautet achieved a mild success with his second feature, **Classe Tous Risques** (1960), a *policier* in traditional manner, with Ventura and Belmondo as the loyal friends. It was not until 1970 that Sautet had a popular success, when he and Jean-Loup Dabadie – his usual writer – collaborated with Paul Guimard on an adaptation of Guimard's novel, *Les Choses de la Vie*, an unemotional account of events in the life of a man (Michel Piccoli), fatally injured in reel one. Still keeping to middle-aged reflections, Sautet offered **Vincent, François, Paul . . . et les Autres** (1974) and **Une Histoire Simple** (1978), the former built round a group of friends, including Yves Montand, Serge Reggiani, Stéphane Audran, Michel Piccoli, and the latter – which might have been called 'Marie et les Autres' – round Romy Schneider.

Sautet also contributed to the screenplay of **La Vie de Château** (1966), along with Jean-Paul Rappeneau, who directed, and Alain Cavalier, who has also directed his own scripts. This is a sunny comedy set during the Normandy landings of 1944, with Philippe Noiret as the squire and Catherine Deneuve as the wife who falls prey, in both senses, to a young hero of the Maquis. There is no other film quite like this, so it is a pity that Rappeneau's other films have been comparatively undistinguished.

Bertrand Tavernier (b. 1941) seems the most determined of his generation to inherit the mantle of his great predecessors, deliberately flouting the nouvelle vague

by choosing as his writers Aurenche and Bost. An adaptation of Simenon, **L'Horloger de Saint-Paul** (1974), about a mild-mannered man (Philippe Noiret) adjusting to the knowledge that his son is a murderer, was a quiet, and wholly assured, feature debut. However **Que la Fête Commence!** (1975), an historical romp looking at what we might call the worm under the Watteau, was reminiscent of the worst amateurish excesses of Allio's *Les Camisards*. **Le Juge et l'Assassin** (1976) is also historical, a study in contrasts between the judge (Noiret), who sees in the assassin a means to glory, and the murderer (Michel Galabru), who means, from stupidity or certified insanity, to achieve the same ends. Aurenche and Bost, with one of their rare original screenplays, have provided Tavernier with a plot in the manner of Costa-Gavras (q.v.), but without the passion – and the piece is ultimately pointless. Returning to the present-day, Tavernier in **Des Enfants Gâtés** (1977) indicated with irony, humour and emotion how a series of small events can illuminate the way society functions – the theme of the earlier films but far better expressed. This tale of a middle-aged film-maker (Piccoli) who leaves home to live in a tenement, and who finds himself involved both with a girl half his age and the indignant tenants, is a complete achievement.

Tavernier dedicates **Une Semaine de Vacances** (1980) to Aurenche, but the film is in the mainstream of contemporary French cinema, being realistic and civilised, but with too few of the insights which make Pialat so rewarding. In examining in detail the reasons why a young teacher (Nathalie Baye) should find herself on the verge of a nervous breakdown, Tavernier is often platitudinous, and only the sympathetic tone prevents it from being as irritating as those contemporary American films which similarly dispense their creators' wisdom. The setting is Lyon, but the picture postcard views which punctuate the action illuminate neither the narrative nor the characters. We knew from *L'Horloger de Saint-Paul* that Tavernier loves the city (he was born there), but when he re-introduces the protagonist from that film in a 'guest' appearance here, the effect is one of smugness – even if relieved by the pleasure of seeing

M. Noiret. When at the end the teacher asks her pupils whether they saw *Casque d'Or* on T.V. we are reminded of how much the French cinema has lost since then – and how strong the force of the nouvelle vague was that even so confident a director as Tavernier is uncertain of his aims.

Death Watch/La Mort en Direct (1981) is further proof that with Hollywood names and/or the English language French directors go to pieces. Tavernier, with David Rayfiel, adapted a science fiction novel by David Compton, and the first hour of this long film is both obscure and nonsensical. It poses a very shabby Glasgow as a city of the future, and it has an excellent concept – a journalist (Harvey Keitel) has a television camera in his head and is therefore allowing viewers to watch, unbeknown to her, the antics of a dying woman (Romy Schneider). The film does improve in the second half, as they flee to the Scottish countryside and he develops a sense of guilt; and it is eventually brought to a respectable level by the authoritative presence of Max Von Sydow, as the woman's ex-husband.

Tavernier's best film to date is **Coup de Torchon** (1981), based on an undistinguished American thriller set in the Deep South – but which has become tropical Africa in 1938. That was the setting of many prewar romances, to which this film pays brief and amusing homage: but this is what the Colonies were really like, with the natives cowed and people in authority who would hardly have been employed as roadsweepers back home. Chief among them is the weak police chief (Philippe Noiret), who turns a blind eye to the affair that his slatternly wife (Stéphane Audran) is conducting with her 'brother'. One day, after a pep talk by a fascist-minded fellow-cop (Guy Marchand), this worm turns and shoots two pimps who have been taunting him. After that he does not know where to stop, and since he and his equally unprincipled mistress (Isabelle Huppert) are the most sympathetic people in the film Tavernier's intentions are questionable: the justification he offers is that of *Le Juge et l'Assassin*, itself borrowed from *Monsieur Verdoux*. Until that point it is a surprising and often amusing black comedy.

Another director who has shown a fondness for Simenon's psychological studies is Pierre Granier-Deferre (b. 1927),

who with **Le Chat** (1971) and **La Veuve Couderc** (1971) made two of his best films. Simone Signoret is in both, in the first with Jean Gabin as her husband, locked in mutual loathing in a dreary Paris suburb, and in the second as a country widow who hides a fugitive (Alain Delon) from the police. More ambitiously, in **Une Femme à sa Fenêtre** (1976) Granier-Deferre tackled Drieu la Rochelle's novel of the diplomatic set and certain moral causes between the wars. Scripted by him with Jorge Semprun – in mood closer to *Stavisky* than *La Guerre est Finie* – the film is hardly more than a prettily-coloured kaleidoscope, moving from Delphi to Athens and eventually dwindling into an account of Romy Schneider's love life. She is, as ever, incapable of displaying much emotion, but Philippe Noiret and Victor Lanoux present differing studies in conscience. **Une Etrange Affaire** (1981) is much more successful, though it is hard to agree with Granier-Deferre's own claim that the story, based on a novel by Jean-Marc Roberts, breaks new ground. It was one of several puzzle pictures popular in French cinema at this time, the puzzle being why a young department store employee (Gérard Lanvin) allows his boss (Michel Piccoli) and his cohorts to take over his life to the extent that his marriage disintegrates. For much of its length the film is brilliant, notably in its portrayal of the anxieties of office life, but it is much less brilliant in hinting at sexual ambiguity and then simply stopping with the question unresolved. It would have been too easy to make homosexuality the key to the mystery, but no other is offered.

Michel Deville (b. 1931) began with a series of inconsequential comedies, of which the most taking is **Adorable Menteuse** (1962), about a young Parisian (Marina Vlady) whose fantasy world takes on a sinister turn when she mistakenly suspects a neighbour (Michel Vitold) of wrong doing. The most striking of Deville's later films is **Le Dossier 51** (1978), based on a book which would seem to be a combination of Kafka and Eric Ambler's 'The Intercom Conspiracy'. Deville has filmed it in an appropriately impersonal manner which is nevertheless riveting; it is a pity that at the root of the mystery, which involves espionage, is the old bugbear of sexual deviation.

Alain Jessua (b. 1932) made a second feature, **La Vie à l'Envers** (1964), of wit and style, telling as it does of a man (Charles Denner) who begins to withdraw from the world, to the extent that he is quite, quite alone. Jessua's other attempts at parable were much less original, till in **Les Chiens** (1979) he combined *Alphaville*, *Invasion of the Body Snatchers* and several movies demanding sympathy for the underdog. François Leterrier (b. 1929) is another variable talent. After acting in Bresson's *Une Condamné à Mort* he became assistant to Malle and directed his first film with **Les Mauvais Coups** (1961), one of the soulful 'quiet lives' dramas of the time, based on a novel by Roger Vailland, about a woman (Signoret) who throws a younger woman in the way of her husband, in an attempt to rekindle his love. However it hardly prepares us for the invention and high spirits of **Projection Privée** (1973), a film about making a film, with a nod to Pirandello in the script and a wryly satirical look at the focal point of most French movies, *l'amour*.

Les Violons du Bal (1974), directed by Michel Drach (b. 1930) is also autobiographical. It starts similarly, with Drach as a Jewish film-maker trying to interest a backer in a project about his family during the Occupation; he metamorphoses into Trintignant for the modern part of the film. Marie-Josie Nat, Drach's wife, plays both herself and his mother, i.e. mother of the small boy hiding from the Nazis. The film has the grace, the sense of humanity and the superb narrative line of the best French cinema, qualities less discernible in **Le Passé Simple** (1977), one of the *Marienbad*-Kafkaesque movies which represent the worst: but if one cares to follow all the strands of the plot, they coalesce with logic. Mlle Nat is the frightened wife and the supposedly sinister husband is played by Victor Lanoux.

Lanoux is also in **Servante et Maîtresse** (1977), which may be the best of all the 'puzzle' movies which proliferated at this time. It is a rather bankrupt genre, with little reward except that which the spectator awards to himself, but as with Drach's film this one eventually plays fair. The director, Bruno Gantillon, and his writers, Dominique Fabre and Frantz-André Buruet, neither bore nor offer fake enigmas. Lanoux and Andréa Ferréol play

– brilliantly – the couple involved, but their game of Genet role-reversals soon involves other people, with tragic results.

In the same area of decadence is Joël Seria's delicious **Marie Poupée** (1976), whose hero (André Dussollier) has a fetish for early Twentieth-century dolls – to the extent that he marries a girl (Jeanne Goupil) who looks like them. Forced to dress like them, she eventually rebels, one twist among many which are as witty as they are economically treated.

Claude Miller's **La Meilleure Façon de Marcher** (1976) indicates, at first glance, a healthier society, taking place as it does at a boys' camp. That one of the guardians (Patrick Bouchity) wears lipstick and skirts in his own room is offset by the fact that he has a girlfriend, but neither factor is of benefit in his relationship with his best friend (Patrick Dewaere). Matters come to a head at a fancy-dress ball, as dramatically ineffective as it is unbelievable: from a tale of adolescent torment we are swept into a Cocteau-like enigma, for if the man is not gay the piece is pointless. The relationship of the two men, always improbable, resembles that of many similar movies, since the French, sometimes prudish, will often allow no hint of sexual consummation. Miller had been assistant to Truffaut, and may have emulated him in losing contact with reality in moulding what may be a fragment of autobiography. Pascal Thomas's **Les Zozos** (1973) is a better film in the same vein: the sexual urge this time is undoubtedly hetero-, and it is handled with a sense of sly satire. It is clear that Thomas had in mind both *Zero de Conduite* and *Les Quatre Cents Coups*, but although his vision is even fresher than Truffaut's it cannot be as touching fourteen years later.

Anthracite (1980) also concerns adolescence. This first feature written and directed by a former actor, Edouard Niermans, is sure of its setting – a Catholic boys' boarding school – if not of its style. It is really a film about cruelty, meted out to a withdrawn boy by his fellow-pupils and to one of the staff, despised by both the boys and his fellow priests.

Diane Kurys is somewhat less bitter about school in **Diabolo Menthe** (1977), another first feature, and she, too, is often funny about her teachers. The film, set in the early Sixties, is clearly autobiographical, and is one of the few about female

Annie Girardot in Jean-Pierre Blanc's droll *La Vieille Fille*. She has the title role, a spinster alone on vacation who finds herself increasingly preoccupied with a more-than-friendly businessman of her own age – and Mlle Girardot's playing makes it clear why she has been the most popular female star in France for almost two decades.

puberty. Claude Berri's **La Première Fois** (1976) is set a decade earlier and is also about a Jewish family. Unlike Kurys, Berri stresses this aspect, quite openly offering the film as a tribute to his parents. The title gives a clear indication that growing up means having sex, and though Berri is somewhat prurient about it, he clearly believes that its pursuit finds us all at our most absurd. This theme recurs in **Un Moment d'Egarement** (1977), when an adolescent girl falls in love with the best friend (Jean-Pierre Marielle) of her father (Victor Lanoux), a potentially tragic situation which Berri treats cheerfully. He does not do so without strain, but the Côte d'Azur locations and the acting remind us of the great traditions of French cinema.

Jean-Pierre Blanc's **La Vieille Fille** (1972) is also resolutely old-fashioned and is also set by the sea, at a resort near the Spanish border. The spinster of the title, Annie Girardot, and a businessman, Philippe Noiret, find themselves placed at the same table; she keeps herself to herself while he is affable and insensitive – and the question is, after a while, will they or won't they? The two stars play marvellously together, the vignettes of hotel life are often funny, and the film is absolutely

successful on its chosen level. Jeanne Moreau, turning director, explored a similar territory, and it is pleasing to find her taste apparently unaffected by the increasingly arty movies in which she had been appearing. Her co-star in **Lumière** (1976) is Lucia Bosè, with whom she had endured *Nathalie Granger*, and they play actresses. The great heart of show business is found for once to be neither sobbing nor corroded, but a metier like any other. After this least egotistical of autobiographical films, Moreau, not this time appearing or writing her own screenplay, directed **L'Adolescente** (1979) with what was for the most part the same admirable objectivity. It is a tale of growing-up, in Pagnol territory, during the last summer of peace, in 1939. The film is even less ambitious, even more likeable than *Lumière*, and if Moreau blunders artistically in demanding sympathy for the Jewish doctor – beautifully played by Francis Huster – it is a fault on the right side.

Although a number of these films touch on social problems, they are clearly not the main preoccupations of French filmmakers. Tavernier once observed that to make good films one must be angry, yet I find less anger in him, even in *Des Enfants Gâtés*, than in Yves Boisset (b. 1939), whose films, though not distinguished, are nevertheless more closely related to contemporary France than many we have been discussing. **Dupont Lajoie** (1975) is a study of the average Frenchman – played by Jean Carmet – whom we see at his least attractive, on holiday in *le camping*. The film is much in the manner of *Bank Holiday*, observing a cross-section of holiday makers, until Lajoie becomes involved in a sex-murder, at which point the film veers towards Chabrol, and later, when local Arab workers are blamed, towards old Hollywood movies about racial prejudice. The film was enormously popular in France, and Boisset subsequently created a furore with **Le Juge Fayard Dit le Sheriff** (1977), because it suggested a connection between politicians and organised crime. It was based on a factual incident, and the young *juge* (Patrick Dewaere) who had discovered the connection becomes very dead. Boisset had earlier shown his expertise with the cops and robbers genre in **Folle à Tuer** (1975), an unpretentious kidnap drama. As one of the kidnappers, the usually amiable Victor Lanoux proves to be a villain as good as was Jules Berry; the other guilty parties turn out to be connected with big business and a charitable organisation.

L'Argent des Autres (1978) deals with a financial scandal and was directed by Christian de Chalonge from a screenplay written by him and Pierre Dumayet; unfortunately they were too clearly carried away with indignation at the fate meted out to the employee (Trintignant), who was forced to take the blame, to make their case watertight. The subject of a cover-up and the pursuit of truth had been the theme of *Cadaveri Eccellenti* (q.v.), and it is that film that de Chalonge has imitated. The grandiloquence of the settings on this occasion only serves to underline the banalities, but nevertheless, like *Le Juge Fayard Dit le Sheriff*, *Une Etrange Affaire*, *L'Horloger de Saint-Paul* and *Les Choses de la Vie*, this film was awarded the Prix Louis Delluc as the best film of the year.

Not one of them has repeated its success overseas – to many people the French cinema stopped with the nouvelle vague. In Italy and Japan a generation of great filmmakers similarly inhibited the succeeding one. In the case of France the nouvelle vague directors were less excellent than famous. Their successors drew the best from them – the 'fly on the wall' method of story telling, and slice-of-life stories that build neither to a flashy dénouement nor an anti-climax. Despite their faults these films are civilised and several have been very funny.

One of the two hugely successful French films of the Seventies, another Delluc prize-winner, **Cousin, Cousine** (1975), was directed by Jean-Charles Tacchella, his second film as director, after writing some of the more forgettable films of the Sixties. For audiences who loved *Un Homme et une Femme*, it was the same form of wish-fulfilment; those driven away by late Godard were now brought back. A nice woman (Marie-Christine Barrault) responds to her husband's frequent infidelities by taking a lover (Victor Lanoux), and they shack up cosily at every opportunity. This old situation of French farce is treated realistically, but at the same time we are supposed to sympathise with the lovers and, as of old, despise the bourgeoisie who disapprove; unlike previous

practitioners in the genre, Tacchella's manipulations of the plot and audience reaction are blatant.

The other greatly popular film was *La Cage aux Folles* (q.v.), directed by Edouard Molinaro (b. 1928), whose films have seldom lived up to the promise of his first, **Le Dos au Mur** (1957), a dark thriller with Jeanne Moreau as an adulteress. Whether tackling a cod thriller, **Arsène Lupin contre Arsène Lupin** (1962) or sex farce, **La Chasse à l'Homme** (1965), his approach is ponderous, and the success of **L'Emmerdeur** (1973) is mainly due to the situations of Francis Véber's original play, adapted for the screen by both of them. A contract killer (Lino Ventura) finds that he cannot carry out the job because of the antics of a sad sack (Jacques Brel) in the neighbouring hotel room. Their subsequent adventures may lack invention, but do offer suspense and amusement.

La Cage aux Folles (1978) has been more widely seen in Britain and the U.S. than any other foreign language film to the present time★ – a matter of some interest, since it is neither good, nor, one would have supposed, a subject of wide appeal, dealing with the menage of a middle-aged gay couple. It was written by Jean Poiret for himself and Michel Serrault, a frequent collaboration in the boulevard comedies of the Paris theatre. In the film Poiret's role is taken by Ugo Tognazzi, while Serrault repeats his role as the drag-star half of the couple, who runs a transvestite nightclub in St Tropez. When Tognazzi's son invites his prospective in-laws to dinner Serrault decides to turn up as his 'mother', which does provide some riotous moments. 'Obvious' homosexuality is a legitimate subject for comedy, but elsewhere Molinaro's tendency to sentimentalise the central relationship is misjudged in this context, and his handling of Tognazzi's serious scenes with son and ex-wife only add to the general impression of feebleness. Since there are several genuinely comic moments, the public acceptance is understandable: but like *Cousin, Cousine* it would seem that sexuality becomes sophisticated and hence appealing if in French –

★It played well into its second year in cinemas in both London and New York, though a sequel, *La Cage aux Folles II*, came and went with speed – proof either of the power of the critics, who unanimously thought it inferior, or that the first film had satisfied audience curiosity for the humour to be derived from gay liaisons.

for the level of humour in both films is unremarkable (and both adultery and homosexuality had during these years become a staple of situation comedy on television).

In Belgium, André Delvaux (b. 1926) made documentaries on several movie-directors, and was backed by the Ministry of Education and the state television service to make his first feature, in Flemish, **The Man Who Had His Hair Cut Short** (1966), an anecdote about a schoolmaster with a crush on one of his pupils, and what happens when they meet again when she is a famous actress. Its success enabled him to get French backing and players for his next two films, **Un Soir . . . Un Train** (1968) with Yves Montand and Anouk Aimée, and **Rendezvous à Bray** (1971), with Mathieu Carrière and Anna Karina. Both are puzzle pictures, but whereas attention is held in the first by the performances of the leads and the increasing nightmare of the plot, the second only confirms that Delvaux is less interested in emotions than in decor and camera angles. As far as can be ascertained its theme is the unexpressed love of one young man for another, just before World War I, but as the characters mope on and on, one may prefer the vulgarity of *La Cage aux Folles*.

Nevertheless, Delvaux's is a subtle, if derivative, talent. The same must be said of the two Swiss directors, Alain Tanner and Claude Goretta, who worked for the British Film Institute in the Fifties and co-directed a pleasing documentary, *Nice Time*. Their first features were made very cheaply, with the backing of Swiss television. Though German is the predominant language in most of Switzerland, filming in French is more economic there, because the films may play in France and Belgium (the German-speaking films, in Schwyzer-deutsch, have to be dubbed for Germany and Austria.) Tanner's **Charles Mort ou Vif?** (1969) which he wrote himself, is inclined to be discursive, but is an otherwise affecting study of a middle-aged man (François Simon) given a new lease of life. His collaborator on **Le Salamandre** (1971) was the English expatriate author, John Berger, draining him, apparently, even of his minor insights and surprises. The young lady of the film, played by Bulle Ogier, bedding any

nearby man, is clearly the antithesis of the Swiss ethos, a nation renowned for conformity. **Le Retour d'Afrique** (1973), equally cold and grey yet equally in favour of life, is a portrait of a young married couple and of their sitting around bored and waiting when their plans to emigrate to Africa fall through. The audience gets bored too, for there is a 30-minute gap in the middle of the film when nothing happens.

Goretta is inclined to be more cheerful, and to acknowledge his sources – which in the case of both **Le Jour des Noces** (1970) and **L'Invitation** (1973) is Renoir. The former, about a wedding party, is homage to *Partie de Campagne*, and the latter, about a country-house party, to *La Règle du Jeu*. Both are more fluent than Tanner's work, but neither anticipates the mastery of **La Dentellière** (1977), written with Pascal Lainé from his Balzacian novel, but without the desolation of the original. Beatrice (Isabelle Huppert) is seduced by François (Yves Beneytoun) and they subsequently set up house together. But what, in the squally days of autumn in Cabourg had been heady, is only distressing in Paris; she is a hairdresser, he a student, and as they realise that she cannot fit into his world, she is destroyed. Goretta, offered a subject with substance, responded with empathetic sensitivity.

Delvaux is not specifically Belgian, nor Tanner and Goretta specifically Swiss. Two of these nine films – *Rendezvous à Bray* and *La Dentellière* – were filmed in France and all of them are quiet and thoughtful, qualities to be found in almost all the post-nouvelle vague films. The directors concerned have, to an extent, rejected the fascination with Hollywood melodrama which gave early Godard its vitality, and they have looked as one man to Renoir. The exception to prove the rule is another foreigner, Constantine Costa-Gavras (b. 1933), whose polemic thrillers have an audacity lacking in his colleagues. He arrived from Greece at the age of eighteen to study at the Sorbonne and subsequently became assistant to René Clair and Yves Allégret. Later he was assistant director on both *La Baie des Anges* and *Le Jour et l'Heure*, and we may assume from his subsequent work that Demy was less congenial than Clément's thriller. His first film, **Compartiment Tueurs** (1965), was set up by a collective which included Yves Montand and Simone Signoret and many of the rest of the cast – Trintignant, Pierre Mondy, Claude Mann, Daniel Gélin, Françoise Arnoul, Michel Piccoli and Jacques Perrin. Costa-Gavras wrote the screenplay from a thriller by Sébastien Japrisot, and it is best not to regard it as a whodunnit, since the dénouement is a cheat – though the territory is rich in signposts if you know how to recognise them. But it is smashing entertainment, wittily played by the cast, especially Signoret as a less-than-successful actress, and Montand as a Sûreté officer – with a head-cold. The detail throughout is brilliant under the racing camera, and the clutter and bustle of the police station was to be echoed frequently, in such films as *Madigan* (q.v.).

It was Costa-Gavras' third film, **Z** (1969), which made him world famous, and it is one of the most exciting ever made. With his screenwriter, Jorge Semprun, he signs a foreword to the effect that any resemblance of the characters to living people is intentional: their source is a novel by Vassili Vassilikos, based on the Lambrakis case of 1963, when a left-wing Greek deputy was killed in mysterious circumstances. It is the contention of the film that he was murdered, albeit accidentally, as the result of several right-wing alliances, with the police and the army secretly supporting organisations of fascist-minded thugs. A young and dedicated public prosecutor resists pressure to withhold details involving officials, but in the subsequent trial the two leading thugs receive light sentences – reduced further by good behaviour – and the officials are reprimanded. The resultant brouhaha brought about the fall of the government, and rather than see a left-wing one succeed it the Colonels stepped in. This corollary is presented to the audience as a postscript, which also lists the writers banned in Greece since the Colonels came to power; even as other countries were applauding this film Mikis Theodorakis, who composed the score, was in fact being held in a Greek prison without trial. The film rushes at its audience – mixing subtlety, deviousness, a joke or two – and is built dramatically, propelled by tension rather than chronology. Outrageously, it offers some conventional thrills – a man fleeing a killer in a car – and a reference to an earlier

miscarriage of justice, the Dreyfus case. Above all, *Z* has a sense of urgency, a reflection of the prosecutor's determination to get to the truth. He is played by Trintignant, and the deputy by Montand; Renato Salvatore and Marcel Bozzufi are the thugs; the deputy's wife is Irene Papas, Charles Denner a party member, Bernard Fresson a committed man of the left, and Perrin an inquisitive photographer.

Costa-Gavras stated publicly that he wanted to reach a mass audience with films about oppression and injustice, and in **L'Aveu** (1970) he and Semprun found both in Czechoslovakia, where the conspiracy trials of the Fifties, intended to disguise the regime's disastrous economic policy, were carried out, with a strong anti-Semite basis, on Stalin's orders. The historical background remains elusive, but as a dramatic reconstruction the film works powerfully, with the director exercising imagination to bring a comparable restlessness to a subject far more static than his earlier films. Montand is the primary accused and Signoret is his wife; as the principal interrogator Gabriele Ferzetti conveys the intelligence needed for that job, with the single mindedness typical of a Party hack.

Montand is the victim again in **Etat de Siège** (1973). An attaché at the American embassy in a South American country –

The 'political thriller' was not new when Costa-Gavras made *Z*, but he gave it a new excitement, and not only because he took a completely partisan view of recent events in his homeland, Greece. It could clearly not be made there, but the supposedly fictitious country in which it took place had Greek number plates on the cars and posters for Fix beer. (It was actually made in Algeria.) Yves Montand is in the centre of the picture, with Charles Denner, left.

identifiable as Chile – he is kidnapped by a terrorist group, the Tupamaros, who officially do not exist. Santore (Montand) claims that he is in the country for a peaceful organisation, Alliance for Progress, upon which the Tupamaros ask why the organisation has supplied the police force with 300 patrol cars. When Santore claims that his aims are the same as theirs – the end of corruption, chaos and public theft – they declare that he wants to preserve inequality and defend privilege; they say they want to balance the social order, but he replies that they are Communists out to destroy Western, Christian, civilisation. The film covers what turns out to be the last week of his life, taking in a number of other matters, such as the local allies of the Americans who, except for a misguided idealist or so, are professional agitators. 'I don't see why we need stand by and watch a country go communist due to the irresponsibility of its own people' said Henry Kissinger, on 27th June 1970, at a meeting of the National Security Council's 'committee of Forty', and though the remark is not quoted in the film, it was surely the mainspring for Costa-Gavras and Franco Solinas, his writer. Since this film is an unabashed attack on American imperialism, someone obviously blundered in choosing it to premiere for a charity in Washington.

Section Spéciale (1975) completes Costa-Gavras' political quartet in France – the only one with a French setting – written with Semprun from a novel by Hervé Villeré. The title refers to the unit formed by Vichy France to select and submit scapegoats to the Gestapo after a German naval cadet had been shot in the Métro. The accused are all criminals, and the French, enthusiastically working to gratify the Occupying power, have chosen either Jews or known communists. The French are shown with less bias than is the director's wont – depressed, befuddled, trying to save their own skins – and as in *Z*, the sting is in the tail, with a printed comment that none of the parties involved was indicted or even accused in the collaborationist trials at the end of the War.

It is not only that *Section Spéciale* is set in the past which makes it the least of the quartet: there are times when Costa-Gavras' elliptical style overburdens the subject by incorporating flashbacks and tangential incidents. He can use the medium as eloquently as the Japanese directors, and sometimes does; that he is rabble-rousing is entirely to the point. It is probably because he has been so successful that he has been condemned by a minute coterie of critics,* one of whom – not unconnected with the New York Film Festival – explained his dislike to me by observing that the discussion of left-wing causes should be confined to left-wing magazines. And that is all the justification that Costa-Gavras needs. It must be discomfiting to such critics to find that the only French directors to have made any public mark since the nouvelle vague are Lelouch (for a while) and Costa-Gavras, and the public is probably right in both cases. The latter's political beliefs are of no importance: he tries to make films which might illuminate the events of the time in which we live – and he has been uniquely successful in achieving his aims.

As far as the whole of French cinema of this period is concerned the verdict is not yet in. The dust still has not yet settled after the explosion of the nouvelle vague. Most of the work of Malle and Resnais would seem to be permanent and some of the films of Chabrol; with the exception of Costa-Gavras no director has contributed a body of work as satisfying as that of the older directors, Ophuls, Clair and Renoir.

*However, there was virtually blanket praise for his first American film, *Missing* (q.v.).

37

Occasional Bulletins from the Eastern Bloc

EVEN AT THE height of the wartime *entente* with Soviet Russia, its Western allies were in no haste to import its films about tractors and merry peasants. The art-houses remained content with revivals of Eisenstein and Donskoi's Gorki trilogy until the Iron Curtain descended in the late Forties – and with that went the prospect of programming any Soviet film but the classics. The U.S.S.R. continued to send films to the film festivals, and when **The Cranes Are Flying** (1957) won the Grand Prix at Cannes it became the first Russian film widely seen in the West since the war years. It was said to be significant in Russian cinema because it eschewed ideology, but probably most people responded to it because of its traditional elements – it is a tale of unrequited love, of life continuing, of a weak husband, a letter that is not read. It is set during the war and its aftermath, with a sketch of tenement life in Moscow and a more detailed study of commune life in Siberia. The troubled heroine is sensitively played by Tatiana Samoilova, who somewhat resembles Audrey Hepburn, and whose habit of staring into space reminded some of Garbo; she is more plebeian than either, and the scenes with her have a warmth rare in Soviet cinema. The veteran director, Mikhail Kalatozov, manages a number of virtuoso sequences, including a rape during an air-raid, with gun-fire, blowing curtains, startled eyes and movement in the dark.

The break-through established, the Russians began to send us films about the War, in which patriotism and heroism intermingled, and shots of peasants outlined against the sky proclaimed that little had changed in Soviet cinema. The heroes were as comely and idealised as ever, we found, as the cameras raked their features before moving on to river and meadow, marsh and spinney. The Western filmgoer again became familiar with the vastness of Russia and with its rail links, as in **Ballad of a Soldier** (1959). The soldier (Vladimir Ivashov) requests a trip home to see mother rather than a medal for his bravery – because, for one thing, the roof needs mending. His wish is granted, and equally naturally, a pretty girl stows away on the same freight car: but this contrivance can be forgiven since the director, Grigori Chukhrai, so obviously cares for his characters. As it happens, his first film, **The Forty First** (1956), dealt with a less likely relationship, between a Red partisan and the White Russian officer who is her prisoner, derived from Protazanov's Silent film of the same name. It follows the adventures of a Red patrol in the Turkestan desert at the time of the Civil War, and if only competently handled, is handsome to look at. It had received a few sporadic showings in the West before Kalatazov's film, but that and *Ballad of a Soldier* were almost the only Russian films of the Fifties to which audiences readily responded.

There had, however, already been some showings of **The Grasshopper** (1955), directed by Samson Samsonov from his own dramatisation of Tchekov's short story, with Sergei Bondarchuk as the doctor whose cheerful wife prefers artists – any artist – to his own modest achievements. The film itself is modest, and delightful; it proved to be the forerunner of some literary adaptations which would be much more welcome than the war stories. **The Lady with the Little Dog** (1960) was commissioned from the veteran director Josif Heifits to mark the centenary of

The stream of films imported from Russia in the late Twenties had become a trickle by the war years, and even the wartime alliance did not improve matters, since the majority of the films concerned were of interest only to the most ardent pro-Soviet spectator. Only *The Stone Flower*, a fantasy – and the first Russian film in colour – made much impression in the decade following the end of hostilities, till *The Cranes are Flying*, RIGHT, made an impact at the Cannes Festival in 1958: one reason was the performance of Tatiana Samoilova.

OPPOSITE Another Russian film that Western audiences liked greatly was *The Lady with the Little Dog*, ABOVE, featuring Ya Savvina in the title role, and directed by the veteran Josif Heifits. This adaptation of a Tchekov short story was made to mark the centenary of his birth, and its success was such that Heifits followed it with another, *In the Town of S*, BELOW, with Nonna Terentieva and Anatoly Papanov. An equally rewarding and somewhat denser work, it has, surprisingly, remained much less well known.

Tchekov's birth. Since dissolving his partnership with Alexander Zarkhi in 1950 Heifits had directed some contemporary subjects; none of his previous work prepares one for the perfection of this film. In the dying summer at Yalta, a Moscow banker (Alexei Batalov) engages the attention of a married lady (Ya Savvina), whom he is destined to seduce – in one of the most delicately handled sequences in all cinema. The fidelity to the spirit and the letter of the original are remarkable, but in adapting 'Ionych', retitled **In the Town of S** (1966), Heifits takes a number of liberties. The original is a portrait of a country doctor – played in the film by Anatoly Papanov – who falls mutely in love with the daughter of some very social friends in the nearest town, and Heifits has extended it with some amusing vignettes of their various *soirées*: it is as if we, the audience, were eavesdropping, and as that is the impression we receive with the plays and stories, it may be said that Tchekov in cinema has had no finer interpreter.

The Duel (1973) is the first of these films in colour, but on this occasion Heifits

failed. This is one of Tchekov's Caucasian tales, based on the literary convention of conflict between two men of opposing principles: but whereas in the original each of their clashes has a precise order, in the film many seem arbitrary. The embellishments are a trifle vulgar and the duel itself is farcical rather than serio-comic. Heifits's feeling for people in their landscape is also evident in two contemporary subjects, **The One and Only** (1975) and **Married for the First Time** (1980). *The One and Only* is about a divorce – that of a truck-driver who returns from military service to find his wife unfaithful, and who cannot, even during a second, happy, marriage, get over her: but as he finally decides that where there's life there's hope, the propaganda for the Soviet way of life is again heavily with us. That, however, is absent from the second film, which follows an unwed mother from pregnancy to marriage – after a fortuitous meeting with her pen-pal, recently widowed. That takes place more than twenty years later, and the piece is often comic on the mother's difficulties and those of her daughter, who is

courted by an ambitious young man working in movies. These three films have achieved only minimal showings in the West, which is a pity; but *The Lady with the Little Dog* and *In the Town of S* are unlikely ever to leave the international repertoire.

A more unexpected literary success was achieved by another veteran, Grigori Kozintsev, whose earlier films, as we have seen, were also made in collaboration. His last work with Trauberg was in 1945, after which he devoted himself chiefly to the theatre for some years. After a *Don Quixote* in 1957 (which I have not seen, as the only available version is dubbed) he made what is usually referred to as 'the Russian **Hamlet**' (1964) to distinguish it from Olivier's version – and it was, with that actor's stage Othello, the supreme celebration of Shakespeare in the quattrocentennial year. Kozintsev takes his key from the 'something rotten in the state of Denmark', with an Elsinore that is fortress rather than

Anastasia Vertinskaya as Ophelia and Innokenti Smoktunovski as the Prince in Kozintsev's *Hamlet*, as clear and as noble a version as Olivier's film, from which it borrows a number of details, including the melody for Ophelia's lament. It was made to mark the quatercentenary of Shakespeare's birth, an event celebrated worldwide – but not by either the British or American film industries.

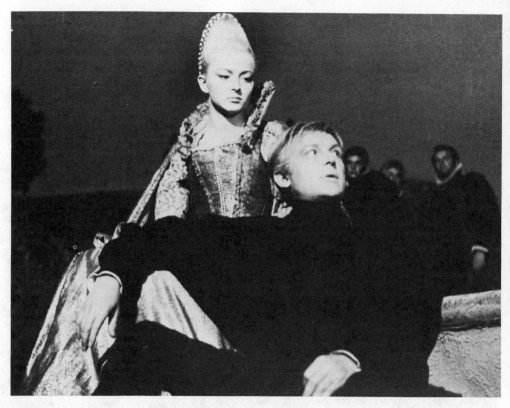

palace, its drawbridge up, guarded by stormtroopers corrupt and menacing: it is a place from which Hamlet can only escape by death. He (Innokenti Smoktunovski) suggests despair, an inability to deal with tyranny; I have never found more moving 'What a piece of work is a man' – which obviously has less to do with his delivery than his drawn appearance. Constantly Kozintsev adds to our understanding of the tragedy – not least with the steely Ophelia – but his **King Lear** diminishes it. Again the translation is Boris Pasternak's, and the spare but superb score is by Shostakovich; again the period is indeterminate, the landscape savage and the concept of kingship socialist. Taken out to the heath, Lear is merely a tetchy old man brought low by court intrigue. Further, with the exception of an Edmund of barnstorming villainy, all the leading roles are undercast. In this case, there was no Olivier for guidance – and Kozintsev acknowledged that he had borrowed details from him: but if Kozintsev's *Hamlet* sometimes soars his *Lear* is resolutely earthbound.

We have an American version of Tolstoi's greatest novel, which I understand is preferred in Russia to the **War and Peace** (1967) directed by Bondarchuk and featuring himself as – a rather over-age – Pierre. Reputedly the most expensive film ever undertaken – at the rouble equivalent of $100 million – it originally lasted 507 minutes. The state export service offered it in various versions – in France, for instance, virtually whole, in four separate parts, shown when possible on the Cinerama screen. The version shown in the U.S. and Britain has an average running time of 365 minutes, usually played in two parts. In the dubbed version★ the Natasha (Ludmila Savelyeva) has Hepburn-like cadences to remind us of what we are missing; the Andrei is dull and the rest of the cast assembled as if for the lids of chocolate boxes. They are not so much dwarfed by the spectacle as hobbled by the most eclectic battery of shots ever accumulated. We may hope, after literally hours of battle,

★Unlike *Don Quixote* this film has been available in both Russian and English versions.

that human values reassert themselves, but this is not really Tolstoi: a random thought or so is transcribed, as the film settles for love, sentiment, heroism and gallantry.

I have also been disappointed by the Russian versions of Tchekov's plays that I have seen. In Yuli Karasik's **The Seagull** (1971) all the characters except Trigorin (Yuri Yakovlev) seem to disappear into the scenery; in Andrei Mikhalkov-Konchalovsky's **Uncle Vanya** (1971) they moon about in a sinister mansion, victims of some period *angst* rather than their own frustrations – and that *angst*, if I understand the opening correctly, has to do with guilt over the starving peasantry.

Mikhalkov-Konchalovsky is from a family of artists and writers; his brother Nikita Mikhalkov (b. 1945) is better known to us, since his second film, **A Slave of Love** (1976), has been widely seen outside the Soviet bloc. Mikhalkov-Konchalovsky and Friedrich Gorenstein were the writers of this promising satire, about the reaction of an irresponsible film unit to the Revolution of 1917. The American reviews were encouraging, indicating that the Russian cinema was finally escaping from fifty years of didactic, moribund material. So it has; but I watched this film with mixed feeling, caught between admiration for the variety and appositeness of the visuals and distaste for them, since they have been achieved at the expense of plot and narrative. Nor is **Unfinished Piece for Mechanical Piano** (1977) any more effective, as adapted from several of Tchekov's works, including the play 'Platanov' – unrecognisable in this manifestation. The plot is difficult to follow, perhaps because the actors were encouraged to improvise; the screenplay is credited to Mikhalkov himself and Alexander Adabashian, whose further collaborations would include two substantial works.

Adabashian adapted **Five Evenings** (1978) from a play by Alexander Volodin (he also plays the hero's friend, engagingly, and was one of the art directors). It is a comedy of tenement life, written and set in the late Fifties, and Mikhalkov has filmed it in the style of the movies of that period, without any propaganda for the Soviet way of life; instead there is wry humour and a spirit of enquiry in this tale of an easy-going man, missing since the War,

who returns to confront his former fiancée, now a settled spinster and guardian of her student nephew. The collaboration of director and writer on **Oblomov** (1979) or *A Few Days of I.I. Oblomov's Life* is as successful as their Tchekov film was not. Aided by a commentary and a number of flashbacks, Goncharov's long novel has been compressed to show Oblomov's idyllic childhood and his youthful friendship with Stolz (Yuri Bogatyryov), devices which serve to demonstrate the sameness of life in old Russia. The film's length and pacing, with its limpid photography and meticulous period detail, also contribute to that effect. It is splendidly performed, especially by the three principals – Bogatyryov, Oleg Tabakov as the slothful Oblomov and Yelana Solovei as Olga, whom Stolz has designated to look after Oblomov, to the latter's surprised delight.

Autumn Marathon (1979) has an original screenplay by Volodin, concerning an academic translator who complicates his life by trying to share it with a mistress and a wife, who is unaware of the other's existence. The film has a few insights into the bureaucratic life which is the lot, apparently, of Leningrad's literary set, but it is bland – comment enough on the Soviet cinema since the director of this movie, Georgi Danielia, a Georgian, is reputed to be its leading satirist. The difficulty of commenting on the greatest factor of Russian life – those who control it – is partly overcome by the director Ilya Averbakh in **Declaration of Love** (1979), for the simple reason that it is set in the past. The source is 'Four Quartets', a novel by Evgeni Gabrilovich, a friend of Meyerhold and Eisenstein, and it follows the fluctuating love affair of Filippok (Mr Bogatyryov), a bespectacled bear of a man, and Zina (Eva Szikulska), a striking blonde with an illegitimate child. At their first meeting, before the Revolution, he claims to be an anarchist, and he later acquires fame for his studies of the collectives. The film presents only certain aspects of life during its fifty-year time span, but they are vividly portrayed – and if the final impression is of nostalgia, that was perhaps necessary.

Private Life (1982) deals with a middle-aged executive (Mikhail Ulyanov) in despair at suddenly being made redundant. The director is the octogenarian Yuli

Towards the end of his career the director Mark Donskoi returned to Gorki, whose autobiography had served him so memorably over three decades earlier. *The Orloffs* (1978) is the story of a drunken ikon-painter (Anatoly Semyonov) and his wife (Nina Ruslanova), and how their marriage disintegrates as she finds escape from poverty. That poverty is horrible was the theme of the earlier Donskoi-Gorki films, and if here Donskoi seemed keen to show off his knowledge of new cinema techniques he demonstrated too all his old feeling and ability to re-create the past.

Raizman, responsible for some of the great propaganda films of the Silent era, and it is interesting to see him managing not to question the Soviet way of life, yet give body and blood to the problem its bureaucracy has presented to his protagonist. Indeed, this group of films, considered with Heifits's two contemporary films and *Five Evenings*, do answer many of the questions most of us have about Russian life; and the warm sympathies expressed in them, coupled with impeccable craftsmanship, may mean that Russian cinema could be entering one of its richest periods. Curiously, **Moscow Does Not Believe in Tears** (1980) has much in common with *Married for the First Time*, following as it does the progress of an unmarried mother. It was awarded the Oscar for the Best Foreign Language film, and among the nominated entries it had not then been shown to the New York critics for their approval, usually a crucial matter for this particular award. I suspect that the Academicians liked it because it resembles several old Bette Davis vehicles. The director is Vladimir Menshov and Vera Alentova plays the leading character, whose life is detailed from her carefree days in a workers' dormitory to the stress of being a leading executive. As a young woman she is seduced while 'Bésame Mucho' plays on the turntable, by a man she regards as glamorous because he works in television; years later she is having an

affair with a married man when she meets a simple fitter (Alexei Batalov), who proves to her that though she may be a big wheel in the Union of Soviet Socialist Republics she is still a woman at heart. As in Davis's films, her fate is contrasted with that of some friends, while in middle-life she also has trouble with her daughter. It is a richly entertaining film, and was much liked in the U.S.; in Britain the title was changed to the less telling *Moscow Distrusts Tears*, and patrons showed their own distrust by not going to see it.

The British responded to *Oblomov* but not to *A Slave of Love*, both of which were relatively popular in the U.S. This leaves Andrei Tarkovsky (b. 1932) as the only Russian film-maker of the postwar period yet to gain any reputation in the West. In this regard the Americans have shown themselves wise in rejecting his films, some of which have been praised by European critics. His first feature, **Ivan's Childhood** (1962), also known as *My Name is Ivan*, is not only a paean to the Russian way of life, with heroism to match, but is filmed entirely according to the textbook theories of the film academies. It has exquisite photography which represents nothing but exquisite photography. Also, its story, the tutelage of a young boy by an experienced soldier, an old staple of films, has never been so unfeelingly projected. It was coolly received. So too was **Andrei Rublev** (1966) when it played in New York as *Rublyov* the year after it was made; but by the time it turned up in Britain in 1973 it was known that the Russians had banned domestic showings for some years. Its subject is a fifteenth-century ikon painter and his conflict between his art and his debt to society, told in eight seemingly interminable episodes from his life – episodes of pagan and Christian rites, of philosophising and merry-making, of battle and siege, during most of which gesticulating peasants are fleeing from cavalry. Despite this, the piece does not toe the Party line, but it is as barren of true content as its predecessor; for all the insight shown into the hero's art or times he might as well have been a gravedigger.

I am clearly not the person to criticise Tarkovsky, since I fled from **Solaris** (1972) after an hour, and was forced to leave **Mirror** (1974) even earlier. *Solaris,* which concerns a voyage to outer space, was originally shown in Britain to little favourable comment, but was revived after the success of *Andrei Rublev*; *Mirror*, in my opinion, was chiefly welcomed because it was also known that the Soviets had withheld its export for six years, either because they thought it decadent art, or because those examining it for subversion kept falling asleep. I could discern no plot in *Mirror*, nor the slightest resemblance to human behaviour or connection with imaginative thought. The soundtrack pounds with Bach and Pergolese, and at one point the film stops to examine a book of Renaissance prints. That Tarkovsky has a degree of culture should not fool anyone into supposing that he has an intellect. Of the film he himself has said 'There are no episodes to decipher like symbols . . . if one finds double meanings in it, that will be because we are not used to seeing truth on the screen.' I have read exhaustively Tarkovsky's interviews to try to find his intent, e.g. 'My objective is to create my own world and these images which we create mean nothing more than the images which they are. We have forgotten to relate emotionally to art.' I can only say that to move from the simplistic *Ivan's Childhood* through two mediocre movies to the impenetrable *Mirror* is progress of a peculiar sort.

Andrei Rublev may be compared with a magnificent film about an artist, **Pirosmani** (1971), directed by Georgy Shengelaya – though credit must surely be shared with the art director, Avtandil Varazi, since the film succeeds through being tableaux in slow motion. The difference between it and the earliest movies of all is, of course, enormous, and it should be said that Shengelaya adopted this form in an attempt to get at the truth behind the paintings, since they are virtually all we know of Pirosmani. He was an itinerant painter, a primitive – his subjects were usually animals and scenes of village life – and the film shows the hills of Georgia in which he wandered and the cafés of Tiflis in which he drank, as counterpoint to his work.

The film is so rewarding that I went to **The Eccentrics** (1974) because it was made by the director's brother, Eldar Shengelaya, but it is a filmed folk-tale of little distinction. The lively Georgian cinema is better represented by Otar Yossiliani (b. 1934). He made his first feature in 1967 and has made only two since: **A Thrush Once Sang** (1972) and **Pastorale** (1975), both with musical motifs. *Pastorale* is a mild group portrait of some youngsters who form a string quartet, with a slight narrative about their effect on the villagers with whom they are staying. It lacks the exuberance of the earlier film, which is about a young tympanist with the symphony orchestra in Tiflis, and what he does with those evenings when he has only a couple of drum-rolls. Yossiliani explains his inactivity in the studios by saying that he has difficulty in finding subjects agreeable to the bureaucrats who control the Soviet cinema, but he is more fortunate than his fellow Georgian, Sergei Paradzhanov (b. 1924), who has spent most of the past decade in prison (allegedly for incitement to suicide, homosexuality and currency offences). Both regard themselves as followers of Dovzhenko, but unlike his famous predecessor Paradzhanov is not patronising. The best known of his half-dozen films is **Shadows of Our Forgotten Ancestors** (1964), which is composed of extraordinary images – such as that of the farm-workers in their barn-like dormitory home, standing half-naked around the fire as they dry their shirts, wet from the rain which is literally cascading through the ceiling. The setting is that of a

There is only a handful of successful or even tolerable films on the lives of artists, and among the best of them is *Pirosmani*, made by the Georgian director Georgy Shengelaya, who followed both his father, Nikolai, and his brother, Eldar, into the film industry (all of them as directors). The beauty and simplicity of this film prove him a major film-maker and it is sad that we have had no further chance to sample his work.

Carpathian community in the early years of this century, and the story concerns a young man and his two women – the childhood sweetheart he loses to the river and the wealthy girl he unhappily weds. Paradzhanov's last film is **The Colour of Pomegranates** (1974), a biography of the Armenian poet Aruthin Sayadin; it may well be that Paradzhanov's real offence is in identifying himself with the traditional roots of Georgian culture, which is unlikely to be congenial to the authorities.

As I have implied, it is sad that we are not better acquainted with the films now being made in the Soviet Union. Other Russian bureaucrats, those at Sovexportfilm, have been assiduous in arranging weeks of Russian films, which are attended by the faithful, but with the exceptions noted art-house distributors have remained wary of those on offer. If the propaganda content has been drastically reduced in recent years, the subject matter remains limited. Melodrama is not permitted, as presumably too decadent, and the targets for comedy and satire are proscribed – which is a pity when we recall some of the Russian Silent comedies. Crime, the staple of much Western cinema,

is supposedly rare in the Communist utopias, but adultery★ and other forms of sexual behaviour are not to be regarded as common after more than fifty years of Communist inculcation. The behaviour of the authorities and their suppression of thought, independent culture and doctrine, etc., is potentially the richest imaginable subject – and clearly the most inconceivable.

The first Czech films we saw were the puppet films of Jiri Trnka, exported and welcomed precisely because of their lack of dogma. Karel Zeman (b. 1910) also began with puppet films, and moved into animation. With **Baron Munchhausen** (1962) he proved himself a true heir to Méliès, as live actors move against the Doré illustrations to Bürger's story, with animation to provide the special effects necessary to the fantasy. **A Jester's Tale** (1964) is repetitive and sometimes over-extended, but it is even more lighthearted and it has a sympathetic central character – the proverbial peasant caught up in the Thirty Years'

★The various seductions in the films I have mentioned are not destructive; as a general rule no one suffers because of them.

Milos Kopecky in Karel Zeman's version of *Baron Munchhausen*, a spirited rendering of the Baron's famous adventures. Although Gottfried Bürger's stories were published first in London they have never been as popular with Anglo-Saxon readers as on the Continent – and few of the several European film versions have found their way to our shores. However, it may be said with some confidence that none of them is as enchanting as this.

War; both films are breathlessly enjoyable. The fact that the latter is in black and white proved an obstacle, as *Variety* predicted, to Western appreciation, but that is clearly not the reason *Munchausen* is so little known. Though the original stories were first published in English (in 1785) none of the countless continental film versions has found an audience in the Anglo-Saxon countries; an animated version was begun in Canada in 1947, but abandoned. Zeman changed technique again in **The Tale of Honzik and Marenka** (1980), though I understand that he had used it earlier for *The Sorcerer's Apprentice*: his characters are cardboard cut-outs, wittily existing because they are two-dimensional. For a drawbridge that lowers, a dragon that turns, a winged horse, he uses true animation, and equally sparingly the camera rests on real water for a rainstorm or sea. The story, a synthesis of Czech fairy tales, is as captivating as Zeman's effects.

A more obvious inspiration for Czech film-makers is Kafka, and the unexpected aspect of **Joseph Kilián** (1963), a 40-minute feature directed by Pavel Juráček and Jan Schmidt, is that it approaches bureaucracy with a positive glee.. We do not know why the nondescript young man (Karel Vasicek) at its centre is searching for Joseph K., and anything and everything may have a double meaning – or no meaning at all, as in the sequence towards the end re-creating the inverted logic of an Escher drawing. A cat, literally, is let out of a bag, and two men discuss the difference between men and animals: 'Reasoning,' says one, but 'Obedience,' says the other. As bemused as this young protagonist are the guests in **The Party and the Guests** (1966), another gloss on the Communist state, and in simple-minded fashion the party of the title means the Party. The director, Jan Němec, was clearly influenced by Buñuel's *El Angel Exterminador*, which has wit, conviction, mystery and a blazing sense of what humanity is up to, qualities unknown to Němec. It was made during the Dubcek regime, when it was permissible to criticise the hold of Soviet Communism, and finished just before the Russians marched in to oust Dubcek. Němec's **Diamonds of the Night** (1964) is about two Jewish boys who have escaped from the train taking them to a concentration camp; different versions of

events are confusingly and boringly shown, but the film is a model of clarity beside Juro Jakubisko's **The Deserter and the Nomads** (1968), which tries to interpret the last two world wars and a future one in the style of folk painting. The cinema seems the wrong medium to attempt this approach, though such experimentation must seem laudable when subject matter is restricted; but as so often with obscure film-makers, the discernible message is trite. A subtitle wings across the screen: 'It is bad enough when people kill out of hate. It will be worse when they kill for the sake of killing.'

The aspect of war covered in **The Shop on the High Street** (1964) is the deportation of the Jews. The film was heralded from Prague by the critic Kenneth Tynan, who considered it 'the most moving film about anti-Semitism' that he had seen, before contemplating its fate at the Cannes Festival. In the event, the French critics considered it old-fashioned, which it is; but it is worth several of *The Deserter and the Nomads*. Tynan said 'The grand theme of the film – as of all good modern drama – can be simply stated: how much of a man belongs to authority and how much to himself? What demands can society legitimately make of a man without requiring him to sacrifice his selfhood?' The dilemma is that of a man divided between conscience and the demands of the state. He

Sometimes it seems that the only films imported from the Eastern bloc are, if not literary adaptations, about the War, but few of these on that subject have the quality of *The Shop on the High Street* or *The Shop on Main Street*, as it is known in America. Ida Kamińská and Jozef Króner were both memorable, she as the Jewish proprietor of a village shop, he as the 'Aryan controller' appointed to it by the authorities.

Of the three Czech directors who left their homeland to work in the West – the others are Ján Kadár and Ivan Passer – only Milos Forman has been greatly successful, a fact that may have been foretold by his early films, in which he brought freshness of observation to a number of every-day subjects. The dance-hall sequence of *A Blonde in Love* is both long and very funny; in fact the frustrations of these three soldiers in finding partners is extraneous to the main plot.

(Jozef Króner) is appointed 'Aryan controller' of a Jewish shop owned by a widow (Ida Kamińská) too senile to understand his function – let alone the turmoil wrought in this remote little town by the anti-Semitic insanity of a group of men living thousands of miles away. The film won the Best Foreign Language Oscar, which eventually severed the partnership of Ján Kadár (1918–79), the director, and Elmar Klos, the writer. After one more film together Kadár went to Hollywood from whence, after two indifferent films, he moved to Canada to make *Lies My Father Told Me* (1976), described by John Coleman in the *New Statesman* as 'benign, humorous, worldly and fraudulent'. The first three adjectives apply equally to *The Shop on the High Street*, and in view of its ghastly ending – in the manner of *Maytime* – the fourth and last is not surprising; but like all the best movies, it reverberates for days afterwards.

The Czech cinema received further impetus from Milos Forman (b. 1932), another director whose sense of humour survived film school training – not to men-

tion the death of his parents in a concentration camp. His first feature, **Peter and Pavla** (1964) recalls Olmi, and in particular *Il Posto*, since it is about a boy's first job – young Peter, working in a supermarket, is required to spot shoplifters. The blonde of **A Blonde in Love** (1965) goes to bed with a pianist she meets at a dance, and on a whim goes to his home in Prague where, finding him out, she spends a dull evening with his parents. The Saturday night dance of the first film becomes a 30-minute feature of the second, concentrating on three middle-aged soldiers who are doubtful of their chances with a hundred young conscripts as rivals.

This beautifully observed, hilarious sequence is developed into **The Firemen's Ball** (1967), a film which recalls another cinema commentator on the inarticulate, Humphrey Jennings; and, no more than he, does Forman require commendation for using physical characteristics as signposts to character. The difference between Jennings' firemen and Forman's is that the latter's are self-important and lecherous. They aim to dignify their dance with a 'Miss Fireman' conquest, and the degrees of vanity and ribaldry lead, to borrow a phrase, to 'a dithyramb of disaster'. Forman delights in walking on that knife-edge between truth and cinema convention; he is less instinctive and more impressionistic than either Olmi or Jennings, and he has, at the end of *The Firemen's Ball*, a vision blacker than either. Forman stated that he did not set out to make an allegory, but if the comedy was true it 'will automatically reveal an allegorical sense. That's a problem of all governments, of all committees, including firemen's committees – that they try and they pretend and they announce that they are preparing a happy, gay, amusing evening or life for the people. And everyone has the best intentions. And everybody's prepared to be happy, to help, but suddenly things turn out in such a catastrophic way.'

Since Forman left Czechoslovakia in the aftermath of the Russian take-over, we might digress to examine the genesis of *The Firemen's Ball*, as it provided him with his first important contacts outside his homeland. His first two films had been naturally state-funded, and they had so impressed Carlo Ponti that he offered Forman a project on American tourists. While preparing it with Ivan Passer and Jaroslav Papousek, his usual co-writers, they attended a firemen's ball which was 'such a nightmare that we couldn't stop talking until the next day about it.' They abandoned the American tourists and Ponti agreed to a film on the firemen, but only to approximately half its cost, i.e. $110,000. The contract specified a film of at least 80 minutes, and although Forman had shot 100 minutes of material, he felt that only 73 minutes of it would make a satisfactory film. It therefore became necessary to find a new sponsor, and he approached Claude Lelouch, who, like Ponti, had expressed a wish to sponsor a film of Forman's. Lelouch was unable to be in Paris for the screening of the material, but another French director, Claude Berri, arranged for the replacement of Ponti's investment. Passer, incidentally, followed Forman to Hollywood, where he was able to find work on the strength of *Intimate Lighting*, which he directed in 1966; but with the exception of *Cutter's Way* (q.v.), his American films were not as successful as those made by Forman (q.v.).

Hynek Bocan's **Private Hurricane** (1967) begins in the same way as Forman's early films, with a composite portrait of small town life, in this case the industrial town of Usti nad Laben. Contrast is established between a pretty factory worker, Bohunka, and her ox-like boyfriend, Standa, enjoying weekly sex while they wait to marry, with Standa's mild-mannered boss and his plump, pretty wife. In time the boss meets Bohunka, and his interest in sex is revived – at which point a pleasant 'slice of life' drama becomes black comedy, since Standa discovers their relationship and vows murder, though matters eventually turn to farce. The characters are small, ordinary and grubby, and their approach to sex and nudity is refreshing.

With this film and Forman's, and with Menzel's **Closely Observed Trains** (1966), the Czech cinema seemed to offer new impetus to proletarian cinema. *Closely Observed Trains*, based on a novel by Bohumil Hrabal and set during the War, also concerns a boy's first job – at a lonely railway station; it also relates his first fumbling attempts at sex, which are complicated by premature ejaculation. If we are startled that he seeks advice from the stationmaster's venerable wife, and sceptical when he eventually loses his virginity by an extremely glamorous Resistance heroine, we may rightly assume the director, Jiří Menzel (b. 1938), to be less able on the subject than Forman.

His **Capricious Summer** (1968), based on the novel by Vladislav Vančura – shot by the Nazis for his Communist beliefs – is centred on a freshwater bath-house, and concerns the effect of Anna from the circus on some local males. **Seclusion Near a Forest** (1976) takes a familiar situation, city folk renting a country home, and for much of its length simply represents the Czech equivalent of the events direly portrayed in *The Egg and I*. **Those Wonderful Movie Cranks** (1978) pours love and movie lore into a tale of the cinema's first days but is, unhappily, even less convincing than the films which preceded it. Several years' study at film school has apparently not quite equipped Menzel to portray the real world, which would seem to have been his mission in at least two of these films.

Reality hardly impinges on his best film,

Occasional Bulletins from the Eastern Bloc

hovered between the two approaches, but *Cutting It Short* shows him marvellously closer to Forman.

Our knowledge of the Hungarian cinema is no more complete, but it seems to me to be even more polarised between the watchable and the unwatchable – sometimes within the work of one film-maker. István Szabó (b. 1938) is one such. **Father** (1966) contrasts the battles between the partisans and the Germans in Budapest in 1945 with the uprising against Russian domination twenty-one years later, as experienced by one person, boy and man. It is clearly a personal film, with its grown hero perhaps finding maturity in his relationship with a Jewish girl whose parents died at Auschwitz – a matter to be set against his father's experience in fighting the Germans, with the inference that the present, Communist state, is the inevitable result of the War. The fact that the father's heroism turns out to be imaginary makes a discordant note, but this is an extremely well-crafted film. A certain flashiness points towards **25, Fireman's Street** (1974), which pictures for us the dreams of the folks living at that address. This being a movie from the Eastern bloc, the dreams have mainly to do with the war: but a dream is a dream is a dream, and the film was barely seen outside the festival circuit. **Confidence** (1980) presents the situation of a married man and a married woman living in one room, pretending to be husband and wife because of the War; it is just another artificial war drama of the many sent to us by the Eastern bloc, and less convincingly motivated than the similar *How To Be Loved* (q.v.).

In contrast, **Mephisto** (1981) has been enormously popular with Western audiences, and was awarded an Oscar for the Best Foreign Language Film. Szabó wrote the screenplay with Péter Dobai from the novel by Klaus Mann, which is biographical inasmuch as its central character is based on Gustav Gründgens, who married Mann's sister Erika. Mann made him heterosexual since homosexuality was a weakness in the Manns themselves; the book, though written in 1936, was not thought safe to be published until twenty years later. The content of the film is not exceptional, as it follows an ambitious young actor, Hendrik Höfgen (Klaus

'A film of contrived intensity' said David Denby in *New York Magazine* of the latest to date of István Szabó's films, *Confidence*, and that describes all but a handful of the films of the Eastern bloc that we have seen in the past three decades. One that is intense but not particularly contrived is Szabó's earlier *Father* – about a man's relationship with his son, played as a child by Dani Erdélyi, being pulled about here.

Cutting It Short (1980), although it is based on an autobiographical story by Hrabal, in this case about his own parents. Again they wrote the screenplay together, setting the story in a small rural brewery in the Twenties, managed by Francin (Jiří Schmitzer). The board of the brewery questions his competence, but its members adore his wife Marja (Magda Vašáryova) and her cooking. Apart from the arrival of his extrovert brother, little of real moment happens – Francin's motor-cycle side-car refuses to stop, Marja adopts the fashionable bobbed hair – but such details are beguilingly presented and Menzel's love of the countryside is given even more lyrical expression than in his earlier films.

He has also acted in some of the films directed by Vera Chytilová (b. 1929), whom he considers his mentor. To judge her from **Daisies** (1966) and **The Apple Game** (1976) she is relentlessly facetious, with social observation confined to movies she has seen. Czech cinema, as we know it, is devoted to a recognisable world, in which ordinary people, by virtue of pursuing a career or an obsession or sex, get caught up in extraordinary situations – but not impossible ones. They are situations such as Kafka might encounter had he to traverse modern Prague. Where Forman, observing human foibles, is affectionate and funny, Miss Chytilová is simply tricksy. For a while it seemed that Menzel

1054

Maria Brandauer), from a left-wing theatre group in Hamburg in 1929 to the position of favourite player of the Nazis. There are hints of sexual ambiguity as he cavorts with a black dancing mistress and marries the daughter (Krystyna Janda) of a professor, but he later refuses to flee with his wife to pre-Occupation France because he is achieving success at home. Hendrik supports the Nazis because they support him; he is an opportunist. Szabó's period detail is often sloppy, and some sequences recall the worst of his earlier work. Yet each possesses an inner momentum and the film as a whole, with its dynamic leading performance, has an energy reminiscent of the films of Andrzej Wajda (q.v.).

The first Hungarian film to be widely seen in the West in the postwar period – and indeed it was one of the first films from the Soviet bloc – was **A Sunday Romance** (1957), a period piece in the style of Ophuls, about a serving maid and the aristocratic journalist with whom she takes up, in the belief that he is the army private whose uniform he borrows to wear once a week. The director, Imre Fehér, in his first film offers the romanticism and irony we associate with the Budapest school of dramatists – he is also a playwright – leading us then to expect other, similar films from Hungary. It is a pity that we have not seen Fehér's subsequent work, and that we know so little of István Gaál (b. 1933), though neither has been prolific. Gaál studied at the Centro Sperimentale in Rome, which may be why he is more accessible than his colleagues, being one of the very few Soviet-bloc film-makers to put feeling before form. **Dead Landscape** (1971) is a slight tale of a young couple (István Ferenczi, Mari Törőcsik) who elect to remain on their farm when the neighbours move away because of the impending industrialisation of the region; in the isolation, they begin to drink and quarrel, leading to an unhappy arbitrary ending – which is offset by Miss Törőcsik's glowing performance.

Most film-makers of the Eastern bloc show in their work the difficulties of working within a totalitarian regime; yet most seem afraid to criticise the authorities, and they are equally reluctant to confer respectability by treating them favourably. Hence the number of films set in the past or in remote parts of the country – and István Gaál's excellent *Dead Landscape* seems deliberately to be set in a backwater far from contemporary events. The mourning couple are Mari Törőcsik and István Ferenczi.

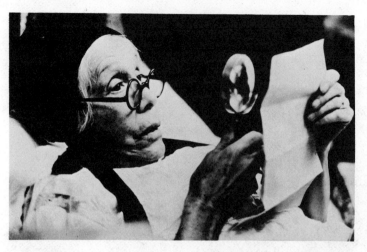

The bleakness of a socialist Hungary is a feature of Károly Makk's *Love* (1971), since this old lady lives either in the past or in dreams about her son, whom she believes to be a successful film director in America. The screenplay by the veteran novelist Tibor Déry is eloquent on the quality of love, as experienced by son, wife and mother. The latter is beautifully played by an actress of Déry's generation, Lili Darvas – in life the widow of Ferenc Molnár.

The best-known Hungarian director is Miklós Jancsó (b. 1921), whose powerful visual style is unaccompanied by any positive narrative. In his early films he took his camera to the lonely wastes of the great Hungarian plain, its grasses changing pattern as the winds move them – and somewhere in the distance, or swooping down towards us, is the cavalry. Judging from **My Way Home** (1964) and **The Round-Up** (1965), Jancsó likes men in uniform and on horseback; he also likes them out of uniform, and if for every bevy of nude men there is a naked lady or so she is usually being subjected to some indignity – such as running between ranks of soldiers as they whip her. The first film concerns some young conscripts straggling home at the end of World War II, and the second the rounding-up of revolutionaries after the suppression of Kossuth's rebellion against Austria. In *Sight and Sound* the Hungarian-born critic Robert Vas suggested that Jancsó's work is 'Kafkaesque', that he 'invites his viewers to throw away the pleasant, comfortable dream of Hungary's romantic-heroic past and face up to reality', but Jancsó's subsequent films, shown abroad to diminishing returns, do not show much interest in reality.

It is a sad comment that Jancsó's work has been available to us while that of Gaál, for instance, has not. Jancsó's wife, Márta Mészáros, is a feminist, and those who share her views may be responsible for the circulation of her films in the West. **Adoption** (1975) was awarded the Golden Bear at the Berlin Film Festival, which suggests that the feminist cause is more strongly supported than many suspected. In it, a forty-two-year-old widow (Kati Berek) adopts a baby when she fails to persuade her lover to father one; she also gives shelter to a younger woman, encouraging the girl's own romance to such a self-sacrificing extent that the movie becomes sentimental and unconvincing. **Nine Months** (1976), set in a small industrial town, confirms that Mészáros at least is interested in reality; but I am afraid that setting a romance in an iron foundry and having a plain, surly-looking heroine are no guarantee of honesty. She (Lili Monori) is pursued by the foreman (Jan Nowicki), who is somewhat perturbed to find that she already has a son; their miserable courtship is concluded by her giving birth to his child, in graphic detail. It is no surprise to learn that in the sequel, *The Two of Them*, they are unhappily married and he has become an alcoholic.

Similarly, I fail to share the enthusiasm for **Angi Vera** (1978), which has been praised by a number of critics, possibly because it portrays life under Communism as grim. Its heroine (Veronika Papp) is an assistant nurse selected by the State for special training, during the course of which she offers herself to a married instructor (Tamás Dunai) – daring behaviour for an eighteen-year-old virgin in 1948. However, she turns against him the following day in a public denunciation which leads to her further promotion. Pál Gábor, who wrote the screenplay – from a novel by Endre Vészi – and directed, says that the theme of the film is that society can only be manipulated to the extent that individuals are willing to be manipulated. However, he would have had a stronger case with a less inconsistent heroine. We assume that the girl is stupid enough to mix sex and politics because she lacks insight, but since Gábor himself is ambivalent on matters of human behaviour, sexual or social, we are unlikely to trust his views on political thought. He is talented, but the sequence of the social evening, influenced by Milos Forman, lacks Forman's humour and powers of observation, and as a critique of Communist rule the film is far less incisive than Wajda's *Man of Marble* (q.v.).

The weakening of the allegiance to the Warsaw Pact is not a subject confined to

Wajda and his Polish colleagues. **Duty Free Marriage** (1980), directed by János Zsombolyai, is on the surface less subversive than *Angi Vera*, but it reflects a fascination with the values and materialism of the Western democracies. It is a Hungarian-Finnish co-production, telling of a girl (Mari Kiss) who persuades a visiting Finnish businessman (Tom Wentzel) to propose marriage so that she can get out of Hungary and join her real boyfriend, who has defected. Once she and her girlfriends arrive in Finland the plot lacks direction, but the film is fresh and often funny, with an added charm for many of us, since its leading characters can only communicate in their limited English.

The joker of the Eastern bloc is Pál Sándor, whose best-known films, **Football of the Good Old Days** (1964) and **Improperly Dressed** (1976), are both set in the years following World War I. The first deals with sport and movie-going and the second, less promisingly, with transvestism, detailing the exploits of a young man who dons female attire to escape his enemies. Sándor is another film-maker not interested in probability or narrative form, which may be why his attempts at humour fail so completely.

We know even less of the films of Yugoslavia. Those that I have seen offer a generally unsavoury group of characters in an environment with which it is difficult to sympathise. They have been made with love and care, they are prodigal with conceits and concepts, but do not satisfy either as entertainments or works of art. Several of the films of Dušan Makavejev (b. 1932) have been exported, but the only one to make an impression is his second feature, **The Switchboard Operator** (1967), a slim story of a girl who ends up dead. She is picked up in a street in Skopje by Ahmed, the public ratcatcher. He leaves for a while and she, having as she says a passionate nature, gives in to a messenger boy. Ahmed returns, goes on a bender, and she is killed while trying to save him from suicide – it being an irony that he is arrested for her murder. Makavejev explained 'Men live their beautiful, wild lives quite close to magnificent ideas and progressive truths. My film is dedicated to those interesting, vague, in-between spaces.'

The photographer on this film was Aleksandar Petrović, whose third film as director, *I Even Met Happy Gypsies*, won the Grand Prix at Cannes in 1967, but that did not, in the event, qualify it for a successful international career. Emphasising Yugoslavia's independence of Russia, Petrović filmed **The Master and Margarita** (1972), Mikail Bugakov's posthumously published novel detailing his own frustration with the Soviet authorities. Since it is virtually unfilmable, this movie, a co-production with Italy and with Ugo Tognazzi as the maestro, was said to be based on 'ideas' contained within it. It wavers between satire, fantasy and polemic, failing at each because it connects with no known world.

Special Treatment (1980), directed by Goran Paskaljević, is a better example of the treatises so often offered by the Soviet bloc. It recounts an outing to a brewery of a group of patients of a sanitorium for alcoholics, guided by their doctor (Ljuba Tadić), who believes himself a liberal but is in fact a tyrant. The film is an allegory: thus any Communist regime, paternalistic but uncaring, its citizens seething with revolt but forced to be quiescent. The doctor's methods are supposed to liberate the patients, but in fact they do not have the freedom which is so much discussed.

Of all the countries behind the Iron Curtain, Poland is the only one which speaks to us directly – and frequently. Before the War the U.S.S.R. was the only Eastern European country to sell its films in the international market with any regularity. The establishment of film schools in the countries of the Soviet bloc brought about a confidence in producing and selling films, but there seems to have been a greater vitality at the academies in Cracow and Lodz than elsewhere. One man gave impetus to the Polish film industry, Aleksander Ford (b. 1908), who began making documentaries in 1928. His radical views and wartime military films with the Russians earned him the leading position in the state film industry when it was established in 1945; two years later he became production chief, and during the next two decades he made occasional films until 1968 when he quarrelled with the Party and emigrated to Israel.

Among his pupils is Andrzej Munk

(1921–61), best known for his last film, **The Passenger** (1963), a study of life in Auschwitz, and particularly the relationship between one of the overseers, a German woman, and one of the female prisoners. The film is told from the point of view of the German woman, twenty years later, a sequence told in commentary and still pictures as Munk had completed only the Auschwitz section when he was killed in an accident. Other Polish films seen at this time include **Mother Joan of the Angels** (1961), directed by Jerzy Kawalerowicz, an account of the incidents associated with the devils of Loudon but transferred to Poland, and a murky melodrama until it gathers intellectual strength towards the end, confident in its anti-clericalism; and **The Knife in the Water** (1962), directed by Roman Polanski (b. 1933), a sterile exercise in games-playing by a married couple and the hitch-hiking youth they pick up on their way to their yacht.

Polanski used the international success of the film to move to the West, and one of his co-writers subsequently followed – Jerzy Skolimowski, though he waited till he had achieved some success as a director, notably in 1966 with *Barrier*. In Belgium he made **Le Départ** (1967), borrowing from Godard his cameraman on *Masculin-Féminin* and his two leading players, Catherine Duport and Jean-Pierre Léaud, as well as his passion for photographing motor vehicles and some of his style. After his next Polish film was banned by the authorities he worked in Germany and Britain, usually in English, but with uneven results. Too often Skolimowski is careless and self-indulgent, but **Deep End** (1971) is a free-wheeling achievement of the sort one might expect of an admirer of early Godard. It is clear from its visual style and lack of humanity that it is the work of an obsessive film-maker. The plot, if it exists at all, is wayward, culminating in one of those senseless deaths which solve nothing; but along the way there are some good jokes and some refreshing improvisation. The setting is a convincingly antiquated London municipal swimming-bath (though the film was made in Munich), where the new assistant (John Moulder-Brown) develops a passion for his opposite number (Jane Asher) in the female section. Their adventures are dreamlike, bizarre and unpretentious in turn, with an adolescent sexuality of extraordinary intensity.

If Skolimowski's later films have been disappointing, those of his fellow expatriate, Walerian Borowczyk (b. 1923) have been disastrous – which may be no surprise to those unimpressed with **Blanche** (1971), which he made in France after moving there in 1958. After many years working alternately in animation, in which he was trained, and live action shorts, Borowczyk turned to features, but it was the third, *Blanche*, which brought him some reputation. It is based on a nineteenth-century medieval tale by another expatriate, Juliusz Slowacki, and since Borowczyk wrote, directed, edited and was responsible for the art direction, we may suppose him misguided, since it is a tale of purple passion needing a more vital approach. Using the same arid style for **Story of a Sin** (1975), made in Poland, Borowczyk manages to be as entertaining as he is irritating. Based on a 1908 Polish novel influenced by Zola, it is about a woman's emancipation while searching throughout Europe for her one true love; it is typical that that emancipation has become almost wholly sexual, with sequences which move beyond voyeurism to pornography. The decor is vivid and glowing, but ultimately pointless because the film violates all precepts about the people of that era, who surely did not behave as if on the stage of a modern strip-club. Nevertheless, on this occasion Borowczyk communicates a real zest for medium and material, however degraded.

The film includes one of the cinema's more convincing rape scenes, with the man holding down his victim with one hand as he tears his clothes off with the other, and it is similar to the one in **How To Be Loved** (1962), although it is hard to imagine a director more diametrically opposed to Borowczyk's methods than Wojciech Has (b. 1925). Has has a self-discipline so daunting that his work has perfection but little conviction. This particular film has a strong situation, as a middle-aged actress (Barbara Krafftowna) recalls the war years and the actor (Zbigniew Cybulski) who was hidden in her room throughout. The War also features in **Farewells** (1958), for it separates a student and the dance hostess with whom he has been frittering away his time. Has's most celebrated film is more florid, **The Saragossa Manuscript** (1964), based on the catalogue of stories by Jan Potocki, centring on the Peninsula War and first published in Poland in 1847. From the introduction to the prints in foreign distribution we learn that Polish audiences were as bemused as we are likely to be; but with at least fifty minutes excised, the claim that all will be clear by the end is not justified. The piece is a melange of intrigue, amour, duels, gothic miracles and stories within stories, insufficiently incisive to maintain a level more than beguiling. Has's star is again Zbigniew Cybulski (1927–67), whose exceptional talent and charisma brought him a following in the West until his accidental death.

On the strength of **Hotel Pacific** (1975), the talent of Janusz Majewski (b. 1931) is more positive. It is much like that of Forman or Olmi, gently amused at the minutiae of everyday life – and equally discreet, seldom venturing beyond the confines of the hotel itself and refusing to capitalise on the period setting, which is the Thirties. It is a 'grand' hotel and we see it first through the eyes of the new help, who begins by washing dishes, and we leave it as he quits it, on the point of becoming head waiter. I know of no better film on the subject of hotel life. Marek Piwoski's **Excuse Me, Is It Here They Beat Up People?** (1976) is set in and around a department store. It is a competent, minor thriller, notable in the admission that Warsaw contains some petty crooks; but although the title would appear to refer to the police, they are as avuncular and professional as one would suppose of a Communist country.

There is one director who, if we discount the veterans still working in Russia, towers above all the others in the Soviet bloc, Andrzej Wajda (b. 1926). The son of an army officer, he worked with the Resistance and then studied painting and cinema at the Lodz Film School before making **A Generation** (1954) under 'the artistic supervision' of Aleksander Ford. The generous title refers to the youth of Warsaw who struggled surreptitiously against the Germans; and clearly a new day is dawning as they have forsaken religion for the teachings of 'a clever old boy with a beard' as the subtitle archly puts it.

Tadeusz Lomnicki plays the lead; whether or not the film is autobiographical is difficult to detect, for it is academic and with little of the feeling Clément brought to *La Bataille du Rail*. **Kanal** (1956), a tale of partisans forced into the sewers of Warsaw during the uprising of 1944, is less demonstrative of their desperation than its own craft; but **Ashes and Diamonds** (1958), Wajda's third film on the Resistance – sometimes called 'The Wajda Trilogy' – is something else again. The skills learnt at film school have given way to borrowings – from German expressionism, *The Wild One*, *Richard III*, *La Belle et la Bête*, from Buñuel. The symbols are heavy – the moth in the interrogator's flame, the crucifix upside-down – but here for the first time is that vitality which characterises almost all of Wajda's work. It is both more immature and more literary – its source is a novel by Jerzy Andrzejewski – than the two earlier films, and it was artless to clothe the hero, Maciek (Cybulski) in the duds of Brando and James Dean so that he is not only a Resistance hero but a representative of the generation that followed. He is also a modern Hamlet, undecided whether to live or die because, with the War over, he no longer has a cause. Cybulski's playing deliberately disguises Wajda's refusal to make Maciek anything more than cynical and confused, despite experience of love and mortality and with his own death probable. Equally imminent is the struggle for power between Maciek's side, the freedom-fighters, and the Communists whose motives are no clearer, since their leader longs only for the good old days, fighting in Spain. Everyone talks in large statements, but it is a film for which all can be forgiven, since it is consistent and all-encompassing until the last couples dance drunkenly towards the dawn, to a Chopin polonaise played hideously out of tune.

It established Wajda's reputation in the West, ensuring at least a muted welcome for **Lotna** (1959), which is built around an incident in 1939 when a Polish cavalry unit charged the German tanks. Wojciech Zukrowski, who had written a novel about the event, worked on the screenplay with Wadja, but if either of them had deep feelings on this foolish act of gallantry they are not communicated. Nevertheless the images are memorable: a soldier with a rifle pumping an organ; a bridal veil caught on bushes near some corpses; a stuffed eagle smouldering after a fire; children rushing to pick up a German cap. **Innocent Sorcerers** (1960) was praised for the wrong reasons, but understandably so: as Dilys Powell said in *The* (London) *Sunday Times*, it was 'fascinating to learn that young people in Warsaw may carry on in much the same way as young people anywhere else – mad about jazz, eager for chance encounters.' The film was made under the influence of *Les Cousins*, but the milieu is less affluent and there is a happy ending (forced upon Wajda by Film Polski). Above all, it is a film of *copains* – with Lomnicki as the protagonist, a young doctor, Polanski and Cybulski as his friends, and a screenplay by Andrzejewski and Skolimowski. In similar mood, Wajda contributed to an episode film, **L'Amour à Vingt Ans** (1962): his section, about a wealthy girl (Barbara Lass) who temporarily adopts a local government clerk (Cybulski), is a worthy companion to Truffaut's, but the others (German, Italian, Japanese) are poor.

In a surprising about-turn, Wajda moved to melodrama – to a tale by Nikolai Leskow which Shostakovitch had used for an opera, some extracts of which are heard on the soundtrack of **Siberian Lady Macbeth** (1961), filmed in Yugoslavia. It provides proof that Wajda was capable of making a superb film in this manner, a declaration of huge passions which must be played out, before witnesses, to the inevitable, tragic conclusion; but more importantly what the film has in common with Shakespeare are its ambiguous motivations. Katerina (Ljuba Tadic), deserted by her husband and despised by her father-in-law, is seduced – after barely a look has passed between them – by an itinerant swineherd, Sergei (Olivera Markovic). Carried away by lust, they progress towards murder – he unwillingly, for he had planned to move on before becoming trapped in her malice. Like Macbeth and his lady, guilt alienates them from society, leading at least one of them to madness and self-destruction. Wajda uses the wide screen with the acumen of Kurosawa, whose *Throne of Blood* was clearly the inspiration. He is blessed with his male interpreter, for Markovic's Sergei is one of the great screen performances, vaulting many devious emotions with ease; Miss

Tadic is rightly plump, and ripe, but a little too equable as events overtake them.

Wajda's ambitions tempted him to the four-hour *Ashes* in 1966, but it was hardly seen abroad, while *Gates of Paradise*, an account of the Children's Crusade of 1212, made in English for a British company, seems never to have been publicly shown. On his return to Poland he made **Everything for Sale** (1968), dedicated to Cybulski, whose death inspired it – an attempt to define Cybulski's place in the Polish cinema as well as his attitudes towards wife, mistress and friends. A film actor disappears: his director, simply called Andrzej (Andrzej Lapicki) casts the actor's wife as his wife in the film he is making, and his own wife as the actor's mistress; he replaces the actor with another (Daniel Olbrychski), physically unlike him – but who will, he predicts, become like him in time. This is not a film about stardom and only marginally is it about fame: the myths about Cybulski are examined in such a personal way that they spread to Wajda himself, till the piece is also partly auto-analysis. The same themes are evoked in **Hunting Flies** (1969), in which a mild librarian (Zygmunt Malanowicz) is enticed from his wife by a glamorous, high-spirited student (Malgorzata Braunek), determined to turn him into a celebrity at whatever cost. The film has a dual ending – one of the few successful ones of the several attempted over the years – and both movies propound that mixture of personal fantasy and intellectualism on which other directors have foundered. Wajda succeeds because he has a hold on the real world and an ability rare in Western cinema – the Japanese can achieve it – of matching his images to the prevailing mood and yet against it at the same time. Where others lack self-control, he has a dozen ideas simultaneously; but he can fall into the same traps which await his inferiors, as in **Landscape After Battle** (1970), which gathers power to little purpose. Its setting is an army barracks, sheltering detainees just released from a concentration camp – who are, they tell themselves, a 'great moral force'. A bishop preaches platitudes; an over-emotional American officer makes promises; and a bookish young man (Olbrychski) meets a girl (Stanislawa Celinska), uncertain of her identity and her Jewishness. At the Cannes

Festival the film was dismissed, not unreasonably, as just another well-meaning statement on the aftermath of war.

The Wedding (1972) recounts the nuptials undertaken by a poet and a peasant girl in Cracow in 1908. What attracted Wajda to the piece was the opportunity to show 'class conflict . . . though this may not be clear outside Poland because of the local colour'. The drunken fantasies which intersperse the action may be saying something about Poland's bloody past, but this would seem to be a work unsuitable for foreign audiences. Its screenwriter, Andrzej Kijowski, claimed great popularity for the story in Poland – at least in the original play by Stanislaw Wyspianski. Wajda had directed that on stage, as he had **November Night** (1978), which he made into a television film, with Wyspianski's own collaboration. This darts back and forth between revolutionaries and Tsarist rulers in Warsaw in 1830, with a commentary by the goddesses of Ancient Greece and with startling imagery but not, I think, much content.

Land of Promise (1974) must also be ranked as a failure, a long and chaotic study of Lodz under Tsarist rule, its population consisting equally of Poles, Germans and Jews, with a protagonist to represent each. The Pole (Olbrychski) is an impoverished nobleman but is able to move into the new class of factory-owners and is last seen defying the striking workers and trampling their red flag in the mud. The film's source is a novel by the Nobel prize-winner, Wladyslaw Stanislaw Reymont, clearly on the side of the oppressed; Wajda clouds his own attitude by making his heroes exponents of gratuitous sex and violence, less gentlemen of the last century than contemporaries of ours. That said, Wajda's sheer energy, as always, animates his subject and the film is still compelling. Conversely, **The Shadow Line** (1976) is well-crafted but rather dull, due in part to Marek Kondrat's performance as the young writer. He allows us no glimpse into his soul, surely essential in filming this particular novel by Conrad. He was presumably chosen because of his ability to speak English, for this was a co-production – made in Bulgaria – with British television. However, the mysterious, nightmarish voyage is handled so well that it is a pity that it is not better known.

Wajda was later to claim that most of his early films were only made after battles with the authorities over either the material or his approach to it, which may be why at this stage he chose to work on uncontroversial subjects. Some young film-makers were not prepared to be so circumspect, among them Krysztof Zanussi (b. 1939), also a graduate of the Lodz Film School, who regards Wajda as the major influence on his work. His early films made little impression, including **The Catamount Killing** (1974), a German movie made in English, in Vermont, about a bank raid in a small town. International attention came with **Camouflage** (1977), a tightly constructed and complex study of master-pupil relationships. An idealistic young lecturer (Piotr Garlicki) finds himself in conflict with a cynical older one, and has to stand by while a student prize is awarded to an essay far less advanced and talented than the one by the rumbustious Raczyk (Eugeniusz Priwieziencew). The students had looked to the lecturer as the one uncorrupt member of the faculty and therefore resent him when he proves unresponsive, of necessity, to their demands for reform. The film's thesis is that society only survives by relegating those whose radical approach suggests changes to it. It had been approved because on paper it had appeared to be a comedy about the stupidity of university life, and therefore anti-academic, but when it was shown, in Zanussi's words, 'my actors looked like some real-life people, allegories intervened, a certain fuss arose. But then the Ministry of Culture, which was forced to defend the film because it was guilty of having produced it, ran up against the Ministry of Propaganda, which greatly disliked it. Eventually it was shown, but no one was allowed to write about it, and the posters were torn down two days before the screening – I couldn't have had a better publicity campaign.'

That Zanussi was a writer-director of power and perception was confirmed by **The Constant Factor** (1980), whose hero, Witold (Tadeusz Bradecki) is another young idealist. The son of distinguished parents, his job as electrician-administrator gives him opportunities to travel abroad. He is startled to find that bribery is needed to obtain a better hospital bed for his mother, and it is his integrity which destroys him, when he refuses to 'fiddle' his expenses during one of his trips abroad. The title refers to the Polish pre-deliction – or necessity – for compromise. In his spare time Witold attends a course in advanced mathematics and devises a quicker and more efficient solution than that proposed by the teacher, who explains to him that for some problems the longer, more circuitous methods are best. **The Contract** (1980) is overtly critical of Polish society only in its portrait of a government dignitary able to confer favours, but even more than *The Constant Factor* it looks constantly towards the West and never towards the East. All of the characters have a smattering of English, and one of them (Leslie Caron) is a visitor from England. She is a guest at a wedding, and Altman's film on that subject obviously inspired this. It is a comedy, not without symbolism, showing the guests' behaviour while awaiting the return of the bride, who has fled from the church. Most of them ignore the disruption of events and, indeed, the trouble between the young couple, which remains unresolved at the end. It is as though all of them are reluctant to admit that they are on the brink of revolution.

Both of these films were made as Poland seemed to be moving towards a freer society, coincident with the founding of the trade union Solidarity at Gdansk in 1980. The Polish people were encouraged to believe that the stranglehold of the U.S.S.R. was being loosened due to the election of a Polish-born Pope and the accompanying acknowledgment that the Roman Catholic church remained a power in the land. Zanussi was approached by companies representing Italian and British television to make a film about the Pope, **From a Far Country** (1981), which he accepted as a challenge. With *E Venne un Uomo* (q.v.) in mind, he makes the Pope a subsidiary character, concentrating on some imagined friends of his youth, and their reaction to events in Poland from the War to the present day. Zanussi was given carte blanche, except that he was required to use British actors so that the film would be widely seen. They do not convince as Poles and the film itself is banal, which is particularly disappointing as its director is one of the most subtle currently working in films.

Zanussi appears as himself in **Camera Buff** (1979), directed by Krzysztof Kieślowski, and *Camouflage* is held up as an influence on the film's hero (Jerzy Stuhr), a factory worker whose obsession with amateur film-making leads to the break-up of his marriage. It also results in him becoming the factory's official film-maker, which leads him into conflict with the bosses. This is a tale of integrity and the right to free speech, and those in opposition are, like those in Zanussi's films, petty officials, not so much corrupt as tired and afraid to rock the boat. The film, which is nicely made, has dialogue by the director and his leading actor, and it shared the Grand Prix at the Moscow Film Festival, suggesting that the jury sided with its young hero. Jerzy Stuhr also played the lead in **Top Dog** (1979), directed by Feliks Falk, which is somewhat fiercer in its denunciation of the authorities, and indeed it created a furore in Poland, coming as it did before the liberalisation. Its subject is the wheeling and dealing of show business. Danielak (Stuhr), a small town compère of gigs and concerts, discovers that the officials who can make or break him are as corrupt as he; accordingly, in order to placate or best them, he moves from hypocrisy to deceit to betraying his friends. He is another protagonist who looks to the West; and we may say that this film would have created no stir had it emanated from Hollywood – but it is a brave film, rich in the details of small town life.

Wajda also chose to make two films discussing the responsibilities of the media, **Rough Treatment** (1978) and **The Conductor** (1979). There may be something of himself in the two leading characters, one a prominent television journalist (Zbigniew Zapasiewicz) and the other a world famous conductor (John Gielgud, unconvincingly dubbed when he has to speak Polish) returning to his native Poland after years in America. *Rough Treatment* deals with the break-up of the journalist's marriage due to the wife's infidelity, and it was made, Wadja said, 'in a blind rage', with no further explanation. *The Conductor* examines the strains on a marriage as the couple concerned are affected by this visitor, whom they hero-worship. The first of the two films contains a number of comments on the authorities, especially in the peremptory

The Eloquence of Andrzej Wajda

Andrzej Wajda is the best-known of the Eastern bloc directors, and many of his films have had successful careers in the West, from *Ashes and Diamonds* TOP, with Ewa Krzyzanowska and Zbigniew Cybulski onwards. His work is eclectic and includes such a roaring melodrama, as *Siberian Lady Macbeth*, CENTRE, with Ljuba Tadic, Olivera Markovic and, being murdered, Miodrag Lazovic. One of his finest films is *Man of Iron*, BOTTOM, with Krystyna Janda and Jerzy Radziwilowicz.

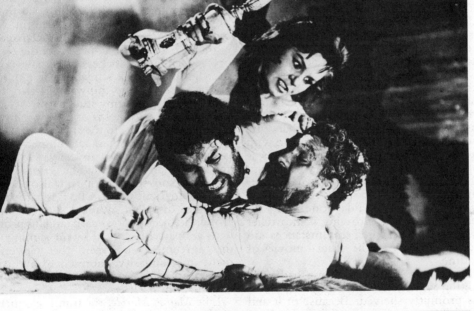

transfer of officials; the second, a minor film, seems to be a-political until the end, when the young husband (Andrzej Seweryn) opts for duty and diplomacy rather than emotion, so that his wife (Krystyna Janda) screams at him 'Those who do not love what they are doing are not free.'

Wajda's vitality and roughness of approach are fitting companions to his passion, which is in full flood in two of his greatest films, **Man of Marble** (1976) and **Man of Iron** (1981). Again the leading characters are media personalities who become caught up in greater events, but as written by Aleksandor Ścibor-Rylski both are examinations of the forces which have shaped the recent events in Poland and are still shaping them. In *Man of Marble* a film student (Krystyna Janda) chooses to make her diploma piece on Birkut (Jerzy Radziwilowicz), a folk-hero of the Fifties who has been not only forgotten but discredited. She is both brave and foolhardy, undeterred by the atmosphere of guilt and suspicion around her as she forces confessions from those who knew Birkut or watches the propaganda film which made him the people's hero in the first place. He was 'the original hayseed', a Stakhanovite bricklayer, selected by the Party, and with a party man to guide him. But if, as is implied, he is destroyed by his best friend (Michael Tarkowski), why does this gentleman also disappear, to reappear as a high Party official? Wajda wonderfully re-creates the period, throwing it into relief against today's changed circumstances and wickedly parodying the official movies of the time.

This was a film that Wajda had been wanting to make for thirteen years, and it was promptly shelved. Because of it and *Camouflage* the Minister of Culture, Josef Techma, was dismissed (though he was later reinstated). Both films were nevertheless nominated for the industry's own annual awards, and were the only contenders in the absence of any other entries. They won jointly, but Zanussi was on location and could not receive his prize, and the television cameraman who photographed Wajda receiving his award on the back steps was fired. The city of Gdansk held a festival of the now proliferating films critical of the Communist regime just after the settlement between Solidarity

and the Government, and it was while there that Wajda was asked to make a sequel to *Man of Marble* – naturally enough, for its ending had connected Birkut to the December massacres of 1970 in Gdansk.

Man of Iron is less complex than the earlier film, but typically bold in referring to the December massacres more directly. In 1980 a number of unfair dismissals have brought about more unrest among the workers; they have closed the dock gates and there is a spontaneous demonstration at the spot where some workers had died ten years earlier. A mediocre radio producer, Winkel (Marian Opania) is sent to Gdansk to prepare a report on the activities there, which must reveal the striking shipworkers as counter-revolutionaries, probably funded by the C.I.A. Winkel finds officials prepared to lie to him, he finds himself under surveillance, and in the world where 'bosses' can be replaced overnight – in dramatic contrast to the free, open world of the strikers, who have now been joined by the students (after initial doubts, because the shipworkers had not supported them during student unrest two years earlier). Winkel is craven, but he is increasingly drawn to the truth, especially when he meets Agnieska, whom we had last seen making her investigative film about the man of marble. She is now married to his son, the man of iron (also played by Mr Radziwilowicz), who is regarded as the chief dissident. Winkel slyly stamps 'Solidarity' on his press card, and his problems are partially solved by the signing of the agreement between the Government and Solidarity, represented by Lech Walesa, its leader, who has a small role in the film as himself.

Like *Man of Marble*, the film is eloquent on the responsibility of the media in representing the views of the people – who want freedom as the English wanted the Reform Bill in 1832, 'the bill, the whole bill and nothing but the bill'. Wajda hurried to finish work on the film, in order to get it to the Cannes Film Festival so that it would attract the maximum world attention. It won the Grand Prix, justifiable if only because it is, like its predecessor, a superb piece of film-making. Zanussi commented that it 'brings a nobility to the cinema it has not known before. In Poland people have always seen the film as an official medium.

Wajda's film is the first radical proof that it need not follow official policy but that it really can speak for the people.' In Britain the critic David Robinson made the salient point that 'rarely, even in the classic days of the Soviet revolutionary cinema, have film-makers felt themselves so much the instrument of history as in Poland's current political upheaval.'

In the euphoria surrounding the film's reception in the West Wajda and the Association of Polish Film Producers announced an annual film festival in Warsaw, in the hope of interesting the West in Polish cinema and so wresting control from its present chiefs. An 'honest partnership' was sought with Film Polski, 'no different from that of any other progressive film industry'. The actual shortage of film stock in Poland, plus the Western money brought in by the films of Wajda and Zanussi gave them leverage in arranging co-productions with the West. As I write both are working in the West because of the martial law which was imposed at the end of 1981 as the first step in abolishing Solidarity. I cannot help reflecting that Wajda would have been wiser to have had his conductor, Gielgud, returning from the U.S.S.R. rather than the U.S.A.

This outburst of socially critical films from Poland has not only been the outstanding event of the film industries within the Soviet bloc, but important in its own right. The reasons for it are enormous, but I find no parallel in the freer capitalist countries beyond the work of a few people like Rosi and Costa-Gavras, questioning the motives of those who rule our lives.

Further, one of the most rewarding experiences offered by the cinema in the last three decades is to have watched Wajda move to a study of his society after having raked over the coals of the Second World War, at one time the preoccupation of nine out of ten films made in the Soviet bloc. He is one of the few outstanding directors to have emerged from the state film academies, along with Zanussi and Milos Forman: he crashed through the limitations on subject matter with the voracity of his talent, while Zanussi did it with his meticulous intelligence and Forman with his sense of humour. They may not be alone in this, but they are the only ones whose work we have been allowed to see.

If we add Bulgaria, Roumania and East Germany, we may suppose that the Soviet Union and its satellites produce over five hundred films a year, and most of the few bad ones that we see are bad for the same reasons. Granted the restrictions on material and therefore the insistence on proletarian subjects, the films themselves too often are merely films made for their own sake. The camera moves from one exquisite image to another; characters wander in and out of close-up, caught at their most provocative and intense; and somehow the results are all alike – despite the separate cultural traditions of these countries, including the conglomeration of nation states within the Soviet Union itself. Occasionally, even in a film as poor as *Improperly Dressed*, there seems a voice crying to be free. What happened in Poland should have surprised none of us.

38

Italy: Traditions Maintained and Betrayed

DESPITE THE INTEREST caused by the so-called neo-realist films in the immediate postwar years, the number of Italian films widely seen overseas was not large. By the Fifties, however, the directors favoured by the art-houses were as likely to be Italian as French. The two countries reacted in different fashion. French film-makers, producers and directors alike, remained phlegmatic about the chances of foreign distribution, but their Italian counterparts became over-enthusiastic about the possibilities. The activity-zone, after thirty years, lies littered with the debris. Those directors whose flirtation with international fame destroyed their artistic credit soon retreated. The two most aggressive Italian entrepreneurs, Carlo Ponti and Dino de Laurentiis, moved their activities to the United States. Unlike, say, Pommer in the Silent era, neither of them has had the least artistic influence and, as their ratio of failures to successes shows, it is doubtful whether audiences have ever given more than a passing thought to their capability as producers. The Italian cinema has continued to reflect the preoccupations of its directors, who include at least one of genius and a few of great talent. There are as many again whose gifts have been woefully misused.

Roberto Rossellini was the first to fall and the cause was not a producer but an American star, Ingrid Bergman, who had seen *Roma, Città Aperta* and wrote to him asking whether he had a role for her in his next film. While making **Stromboli** (1950) they fell in love, and speculation that this enormously popular star might be an adulteress won the film more newspaper headlines than any yet made. R.K.O. were to release, and the company's sales chief, Ned Depinset, urged Howard Hughes to buy out Bergman and Rossellini's shares in the film, anticipating a greater success than *Gone with the Wind*. R.K.O. fell short by thirteen days of getting the film out before the birth of Miss Bergman's baby (the imminence of which had been constantly denied), and after lethal reviews there were no profits for anyone. In the film Bergman is a Czech, a displaced person, who marries an Italian soldier (Mario Vitale) and goes to live with him in his fishing village which, though remote and primitive, has many English-speaking peasants. Because she is of a different class, she makes no attempt to please him or fit in, and she forfeits sympathy further by trying to seduce the priest and the lighthouse-keeper. A documentary sequence on tuna-fishing does little to elevate this gauche and obtuse melodrama; Rossellini himself claimed that it was butchered by R.K.O.'s editors, but we may suppose the fault lay in inept handling, which their customary expertise could not disguise.

The urgency and social concern of his earlier work resurfaced in **Europa '51** (1951), with Bergman as a wealthy manufacturer's wife who feels obliged to become the conscience of the world; but so great was the *Stromboli* debacle that its good intentions were not acknowledged. With more justification, Rossellini's reputation ebbed away with the films that followed. Although he had staged Honegger's oratorio, *Jeanne au Bucher* or **Giovanna d'Arco al Rogo** (1954), in several European opera houses, he achieved little in the film version beyond a camera moving amidst purple mist, pink lights and fairyland angels. The English dialogue of **Viaggio in Italia** (1954) is composed of phrase-book sentences, which would matter less if the story, about a doomed marriage, were told with a modicum of conviction or insight. Instead, Bergman, lacking her Hollywood radiance, is a comic figure plodding around Pompeii and the Phrygian Fields, while the film itself perpetuates the tourist's view of Italy, its inhabitants feckless, cute, argumentative and mandoline-playing.

The Bergman-Rossellini collaboration concluded with the even more disastrous **Angst/La Paura** (1955), made in Germany – not inappropriately, since it is based (although modified and simplified) on a story by Stefan Zweig. Bergman is a married woman blackmailed by her lover's girlfriend, a predicament in which she behaves absurdly and which is treated by Rossellini without the least tension. The revelation that it is the husband who has initiated the blackmail momentarily rouses the piece from its torpor and only then does it make any point – though inadvertently, being affected by the off-screen domestic situation: he was Italian and she Swedish, and this German film emphasises the difference in the marital imbalance in their own countries.

The *Cahiers du Cinéma* devotees continued to trumpet Rossellini's work, in the face of public indifference elsewhere. **Il Generale della Rovere** (1959) temporarily restored him to critical favour but his films for television, shown abroad in some specialised cinemas, only confirmed the impression left by this group of films.

The career of Vittoria de Sica is slightly less disastrous, but more disturbing, since he was the greater film-maker. When the Italian film industry and critics rejected *Umberto D* as decisively as they had *Ladri di Biciclette*, he succumbed to foreign blandishments. Zavattini wrote **Stazione Termini** or **Indiscretion of an American Wife** (1953), to prove his theory that one small situation can provide a complete drama – in this case the prolonged farewell between a married woman and her lover at Rome's central station. These roles were at one point to have been played by Ingrid Bergman and Gérard Philipe, but Rossellini was unwilling to have Bergman work for anyone else; David O. Selznick still wanted to work with de Sica, and he saw the woman's role as ideal for his wife, Jennifer Jones. He constantly interfered during filming and so detested the result that he cut it to just over an hour for the American release. The critics disliked this particular alliance – they underestimated the intensity of Montgomery Clift, as the lover – and the seemingly impulsive direction, designed to build tension as to whether or not the wife will board her train; but the chief flaw is the English dialogue by Truman Capote.

A second association with Hollywood proved no happier, when Paramount cut two episodes of **L'Oro di Napoli** (1954), which it released in English-speaking territories. Originally the film consisted of six sections – anecdotes on such aspects of Neapolitan life as a bourgeois funeral, a pizza-stall, a chess game, written by Zavattini. De Sica (who had been brought up in Naples) himself appeared in the film, together with other professional players, including Sophia Loren and Silvana Mangano. Its reception further determined de Sica and Zavattini to return to the spirit of their great films: **Il Tetto** (1956) is a study of the underprivileged, played by non-professional actors. With customary affection it tells of a young couple, tired of living with in-laws, who struggle to build a modest home of their own. But the motivations of the postwar period were no longer valid, and the attitudes seem assumed for their own sake. There was also some softening of pessimism, to appease local critics, but they did not like the film any more than the others; and this time de Sica found little consolation from the reviews of their foreign colleagues. Like Frank Capra before him, his vanity stung, this celebrant of the common man turned away from directing; and decided to devote himself exclusively to acting.

He said later that the heart had gone out of him, and that was apparent when he was prevailed upon by friends – Carlo Ponti and his wife, Sophia Loren – to direct **La Ciociara** (1961). Her American career had failed to bring prestige commensurate with its attendant publicity, so Ponti felt that Alberto Moravia's novel provided an ideal vehicle, detailing as it does the sad wanderings of a plucky woman and her daughter during the confusion of the War years. Zavattini worked on the adaptation, which shows little more involvement than

The decline of Vittorio de Sica is perhaps the saddest in the history of cinema, since from making some of the greatest of all films he went on to make some of the worst. *La Ciociara* is among neither, but it was deservedly popular and has many excellent sequences, including those between Sophia Loren, as a homeless mother, and Jean-Paul Belmondo as the student who befriends her.

the direction; but, dubbed and rechristened *Two Women*, the film was particularly successful in the U.S., where it gained Miss Loren an Oscar for Best Actress. De Sica was again in demand as a director, and he elected to make **The Condemned of Altona** (1963), with an English script by Abby Mann, based on Jean-Paul Sartre's play. Its subject is German War guilt as it affects one German family; as its members are played by Loren, Fredric March, Maximilian Schell, Françoise Prévost and Robert Wagner the film may be seen to be internationalism run riot, and, therefore self-defeating.

De Sica fared little better with **Il Guidizio Universale** (1962), a whimsical confection by Zavattini, concerning the fun and pathos experienced by Neapolitans at the immediate prospect of the Last Judgment; taking part in the vignettes which comprise the film are Melina Mercouri, Ernest Borgnine, Anouk Aimée, Jimmy Durante, Lino Ventura, Akim Tamiroff, Jack Palance, Alberto Sordi, Fernandel, Vittorio Gassmann and others – but since their voices are dubbed the effect is less disturbing than in *Altona*. Zavattini also provided the impetus, and Ponti the backing, for **Boccaccio '70** (1961), with four different directors handling stories which Boccaccio might have written were he alive today. De Sica's episode, written by

Zavattini, does not recall former glories, but since it loves life, sex, Italy and Sophia Loren it is the only one that Boccaccio might have acknowledged. Its humour is sly, but it is nevertheless a *jeu d'esprit* about a shooting gallery attendant who offers herself in a raffle to pay for her sister's accouchement. Its joyful vulgarity has nothing to do with Loren shaking her breasts or adjusting her bra-straps, but she does so in such exuberant manner that it is astonishing that Visconti's flaccid episode should generally have been preferred by reviewers.

Ieri, Oggi e Domani (1964) and **Matrimonio all'Italiana** (1964) are co-starring vehicles for Loren and Mastroianni, produced by Ponti and Joseph E. Levine (whose company had distributed *La Ciociara* in the U.S.). The former is another episode film – about the working-class in Naples, a wealthy woman and her less affluent lover in Milan, a call-girl and her client in Rome – and intermittently engaging. Eduardo de Filippo wrote the first of the three stories, while his comic play – known to us as 'Filumena' – is the basis of the second film. Mastroianni's performance in that is particularly brilliant – a seedy Lothario, moustached and cigarette-holdered, who takes his mistress so much for granted over the years that he is surprised when she determines to prevent him marrying another. It is a film as Italian as *panettone* or *fritto misto*, but like *Ieri, Oggi e Domani* was destroyed in the dubbed versions shown abroad. However, while the earlier film is a little more interesting in Italian, *Matrimonio* is transformed. It is not like de Sica's masterpieces, but it is well-constructed and hugely enjoyable.

De Sica and Zavattini announced the end of their collaboration at the time of *Ieri, Oggi e Domani*, and in view of the quality of **Woman Times Seven** (1967) it is a pity that they changed their minds. This episode piece might just have worked if filmed, as intended, in Italy with Loren; but made in English in Paris, with Shirley MacLaine and assorted leading men, it fails at every level. **I Girasole** (1970) seems to have begun as an uncompromising endeavour on the part of both writer and director, albeit a vehicle for Loren and Mastroianni; the story, based on fact, concerns a peasant couple separated by the

War and her refusal to acknowledge that he is dead – and later that he prefers to remain in Russia with the woman he has married. The situations always seem less real than concocted, and it is doubtful whether the film would be improved with the removal of the Henry Mancini score imposed by Ponti. De Sica may have felt that the pessimistic nature of the material made it appropriate for him, but this is basically a romantic film, whereas his great films were cries against social injustice.

His indifference shows, and he admitted at this time that he only worked to pay his gambling debts. However, two among his last handful of films show that he wanted to retrieve his reputation before he died. He came to **Il Giardino dei Finzi-Contini** (1971) at the invitation of Arthur Cohn, its American co-producer, who was struggling with one of the six completed scripts. Its tone is that of Giorgio Bassani's novel, discreet and well-bred, with murmurs of menace, as the well-heeled youngsters of Ferrara in 1938 realise that their world is to be shattered by Mussolini's legislation against Italian Jewry. When the film won an Oscar as Best Foreign Language Film, de Sica said that it was the only one of his late films that he himself thought could be set beside the early ones. He went on to make **Una Breva Vacanza** (1973), an equally simple film which Zavattini wrote for him: a Milan factory worker (Florinda Bolkan) is sent to a sanatorium in the mountains, where she realises for the first time that people have values other than those imposed by her family, including her male chauvinist husband; the doctors treat her as a human being and some of the other inmates, more privileged than she, regard her as an equal. There are faults, but the film's triumph, as superbly photographed by Ennio Guarrino, is that every shot has been freshly thought out so that we can share the heroine's experience.

Zavattini's early work with de Sica convinced him that he no longer needed to work on pseudo-Carné subjects like *Au-delà des Grilles*, and in 1950 he worked with Luciano Emmer, a specialist in non-fiction subjects, on *Domenica d'Agosto*, a semi-documentary study of a day by the sea. His quest for realism led him to the anecdotal, which resulted in an omnibus film, **Amore in Città** (1953), which represents the worst and best of neo-realism. Falsely claiming hidden cameras, Alberto Lattuada's leering study of Rome's pretty girls is patently artificial; Dino Risi's portrait of a Roman dance-hall is dull; and Michelangelo Antonioni's examination of suicidal young girls is pretentious in form (interviews in a film studio), and ineffectual except in its revelation of the director's concept of futility. However, the tale of an unwed mother and her unwanted baby, directed by Zavattini and Francesco Maselli, and an anecdote about a matrimonial agency and its attendant dangers, directed by Federico Fellini, are riveting short stories artfully told. Returning to the form, spurred by the success of a French episode film, Zavattini made **Le Italiane e l'Amore** (1962), again with young or unknown directors and an amateur cast: but the emphasis this time was closer to fiction than documentary.

Federico Fellini (b. 1920) moved from neo-realism to its antithesis: a former comedy writer and gag-man, he was writer and assistant director on Rossellini's three most original films – *Roma, Città Aperta, Paisà* and *Il Miracolo* – and his contribution to **Luci del Varietà** (1950), co-directed with Lattuada, is patently the paramount one. If it is better than Lattuada's later films, it is also better than those of Fellini; but we recognise Fellini's preoccupations – the tatty music-hall milieu, the invincible third-rate vaudevillians and their occasional exploitation by the wealthy. Remaining among the lower echelons of show business, he offered **Lo Sceicco Bianco** (1952), in which a young bride (Brunella Bovo) deserts her husband for the blandishments of a hero (Alberto Sordi) of the *fumetti* (i.e. photo-magazine fiction). Staying with the lost and lonely, he devised **I Vitelloni** (1953), about some young layabouts in a sleepy resort, their horizons bounded by carnival, music-hall, cinema, dance-hall, and a regard for themselves which exceeds, from sheer indolence, their desire for the opposite sex. Fellini was a gently amusing critic of provincial life, and his love of it is apparent in his night-time shots of deserted piazzas, with the only light and sound coming from a small bar, almost equally empty. **La Strada** (1954) is set in just this kind of rural environment, and on the endless open road which is home for two unlikely

The portrait of rural Italy in Fellini's early films is quite remarkable. *La Strada* concerns two peripatetic street entertainers, a Strong Man and his assistant, Giulietta Masina – whose uncertain relationship does not improve when they meet up with an old rival of his, Richard Basehart.

people dependent on each other, the Strong Man (Anthony Quinn) and his subnormal companion, Gelsomina (Giulietta Masina). Despite the film's popularity, their adventures have always seemed to me too strenuously picaresque, and Signorina Masina (married to Fellini) less Chaplinesque, as intended, than a lugubrious Harpo Marx.

In her other films she had often played a rather wry whore, and it is nice to be reassured of her talent in Fellini's **Il Bidone** (1955), an engaging tale of conscience and retribution among con-men, with Broderick Crawford and Richard Basehart joining Franco Fabrizi as the schemers. Because *La Strada* had made Masina an international star he fashioned **Le Notti di Cabiria** (1956) for her, with some basic pathos and clowning. Again she is a prostitute, smiling back at all male injustice – and meant to be, at the end, after her 'respectable' sweetheart has stolen her savings, the embodiment of the indomitable human spirit.

La Strada's Oscar (for Best Foreign Language Film) encouraged Fellini to spend several years planning an elaborate and harsh panorama of Roman life, **La Dolce Vita** (1960), as witnessed by a reporter

(Marcello Mastroianni) who has been rendered emotionally bankrupt by it. He stumbles from a call-girl (Anouk Aimée) to a drunken movie star (Anita Ekberg), ending at a particularly joyless, unenthusiastic orgy, after trying to recapture true values with either his father or his intellectual mentor (Alain Cuny), who sits around playing the most commonly known Bach Toccata and Fugue. Fellini's striking visual sense and his ability to indict the foolish before they have uttered six words, now begin to desert him: there is no rule which decrees that a portrait must be realistic, but beyond a quality of incipient self-disgust the film seems fascinated by its own eccentrics. Outside Italy, in other European countries, it was regarded as trite and, at 178 minutes, self-indulgent – until, that is, it reached the U.S., where it confirmed the puritan suspicion that Europeans were irretrievably decadent. American tourists were just beginning to over-run Italy, and certainly at that time the Via Veneto at night did suggest that all manner of debaucheries were just around the corner.

As social critic, Fellini was best on the small and shabby, on the hypocritical: his episode in *Boccaccio '70* is splendid, an account of a moral campaigner (Peppino de Filippo), so upset at the prospect of a sexy lady on a poster advertising milk, removes his trousers to fling at it to prevent us seeing it. For a last time, the grotesques were held in check; henceforward, the director would publicly confess his nightmares and fantasies, so intermingled with reality and memory that no distinction could be made. Carried away by autocriticism, he no longer needed a plot, and **Otto e Mezzo** (1963) and **Giulietta delgi Spiriti** (1965) are, respectively, concerned with a film-maker (Mastroianni) who fears moral and mental bankruptcy, and a film-maker's wife (Masina) who fears she is losing her husband – both told as stream-of-consciousness conceits, with an occasional bold image. 'There would be little to say on this subject were it not for the nonsense that has been written about it,' said Namier, anticipating the theories expended on such films. Even fervent admirers fell away after two limp historical graffiti, **Fellini Satyricon** (1969) and **Casanova** (1977).

When Italian television offered *carte blanche* to a number of directors for a film of their choice, Fellini made **I Clowns** (1970), and where Antonioni chose China, Fellini showed that he had no desire to wrestle with the world's problems, or even those of the individual; he no longer wished to 'speak' to us but, as in his two memory films, **Roma** (1972) and **Amarcord** (1974), only to himself, and moreover, at inordinate length. *Roma* has motorway carnage, borrowed from *Weekend*, two minutes' intelligent comment from Gore Vidal and a number of very boring fantasies from the nether side of Roman life: it is a form of cinematic masturbation, with a music-hall sequence ten times longer than any in *Luce del Varietà* but without an iota of its charm or amused observation.

The uncertain reception of most of his earlier films, and the near-oblivion that enfolded Rossellini, surely convinced Fellini that he must be noticed at all costs; the abrupt switch from romantic reality to personal fantasy was surely dictated by the superiority of Luchino Visconti, whose *Rocco e i Suoi Fratelli* (q.v.) competed in 1960 with *La Dolce Vita* and Antonioni's *L'Avventura* (q.v.) in critical discussions of the renaissance of Italian cinema. When **Bellissima** (1951) opened in London and

New York it was the first of Visconti's films to do so, and since few reviewers had heard of *Ossessione* or *La Terra Trema* it was dismissed as merely a vehicle for Anna Magnani. As a mother fiercely determined that her child should become a movie-star she is in almost every frame. The screenplay is by Suso Cecchi d'Amico, Francesco Rosi and Visconti, from a story by Zavattini, whose preoccupations are recognisable: the exasperated artisans, the outrageously cunning con-men and women, the hangers-on; the innocence of childhood; the lonely people in the deserted streets; and the compromises forced on the poor. The conclusion is little different from that of *Ladri di Biciclette* – that love and honour transcend poverty – to remind us that de Sica's great artistic vision could render Zavattini's observations universal, whereas Visconti keeps them Roman. Zavattini, drawn to cinema, and Visconti, drawn to opera, were less able to avoid cliché, and a striving for significance tends to obscure the satiric intent.

Senso (1954) is Visconti's first historical film, and as such an excursion into the genre against which he had been rebelling when he made his debut. It owes much to such forerunners as Blasetti's *1860* and Soldati's *Piccolo Mondo Antico*, which is not to deny Visconti's own claim that the idea was born one evening at La Scala, Milan, with a desire to capture on film both opera and audience. Thus it begins at the Fenice in Venice during a performance of 'Il Trovatore' in 1848 – for Verdi had been adopted by the insurgents – and Visconti found a story about a Countess (Alida Valli) whose adulterous passion for a young Austrian officer (Farley Granger) shatters her emotional attachment to the Cause, the Risorgimento. The plan was 'to mount a whole tableau of Italian history . . . to tell a story of a war which ended in disaster and which was the work of a single class', but both the Government and the distributor objected to the script, forcing Visconti to play down the defeat at Custozza and to change the ending, which was to have shown the disillusioned Countess disappearing into the crowd and a drunken Austrian soldier crying 'Long live Austria'. The present ending – the execution of the officer, after betraying his mistress – is suitable enough for this sad tale. Visconti, aristocrat and communist, sought only a limited truth, and one that was determined further by his emotional nature. He worked all his life at extremes, from *La Terra Trema* to 'Die Rosenkavalier' in the opera house, and it is perhaps sensible to dismiss notions of artifice and to revel in the images. *Senso*, as photographed by G. R. Aldo and Robert Krasker, is one of the most beautiful of Italian films. It is obvious that the officer's cloak was planned to swing in a certain manner, that the Countess's veil would lift to reveal just this much anguish, but all artifice is valid in the spell cast by this panoply of nineteenth-century Italy, its manners, morals and expectations, its costumes and its landscapes.

Chopped to ribbons (though since restored), it was hardly a success in Italy: nor, dubbed, and retitled *The Wanton Countess*, was it much admired in London or New York – for which Visconti must share some blame, since its writers, Tennessee Williams and Paul Bowles, are credited on the original Italian print. The experience of making it strengthened Visconti's belief that 'neo-romanticism' was the logical development of neo-realism, and his version of Dostoevsky's **Le Notti Bianche** (1957) resembles nothing so much as a Griffith melodrama re-set in Carné's prewar Paris. The waif of Maria Schell makes Giulietta Masina seem both modern and full-blooded; Jean Marais is the man for whom she pines, and Mastroianni the man who entertains her while she waits. The film's failure caused Visconti to return to the mood of *La Terra Trema*, and **Rocco e i Suoi Fratelli** (1960), he claimed, was 'a kind of sequel'. The title is a reference to Thomas Mann's 'Joseph and his Brothers', and the brethren are from Lucania adjusting to life in the industrial north. Each has a 'chapter' but the film concentrates only on two – Rocco (Alain Delon) and Simone (Renato Salvatori) – which suggests great changes between original conception and what is finally on screen. If what is there suggests a leaning towards social history, the end result is soap opera. A myopic vision, an egotism and values acquired from staging Puccini and Tennessee Williams in the theatre, have been imposed upon the will that forged *La Terra Trema*, and the film is coarsened further by the passing-off of handsome nonentities as actors, a homosexual seduction scene and

a particularly misogynous rape. As an exercise in style, owing nothing to the innovations of Antonioni or the *nouvelle vague*, it is absolutely assured. This was Visconti's own favourite film.

That style, and Visconti's absorption in the nineteenth century, combined to make **Il Gattopardo** (1963), from Giuseppe Di Lampedusa's novel, as impressive as *Senso*. Though Visconti lacked de Sica's feeling for humanity, Antonioni's vision and Fellini's flair, he had great intelligence and taste, using the second to advance the first. One looks in his work for verisimilitude, for he never sacrificed authenticity to beauty but strove for both. His reputation sprang partly from the social undertones, supposedly leftist, in his films, but he was moralist rather than judge – and, like other careful, serious directors, he never had the courage really to disturb his audience. He was happiest in the past: the Milan of *Rocco* is risible, but his Sicily in *Il Gattopardo* is persuasive, from the credits onwards, as the camera moves towards the mansion on this particular morning, a light breeze disturbing the curtains as the family kneels at prayer. Carriages wind across a dusty landscape, hunters stalk through a field of yellow corn; a town nestles on a hill in the sunlight; birds fly in the morning air. The set pieces are unforgettable, including the picnic and the final dinner party, taking up the last forty minutes of the film and symbolising, as the battle-lines clear, the end of one era and the start of another. One is represented by a *nouveau riche* merchant (Paolo Stoppa), and the other by the Prince – a portrait limited by Burt Lancaster's too-often too-knowing smile, but conveying the man's wit, for instance, as he looks impatiently at his wasted daughters plying their embroidery. If in the end, the film is superficial on the Risorgimento, it is, we may feel, marvellous on the mood of the time. Physical beauty alone could not make it the enthralling experience it is: perhaps it was meant to be a dream, its characters cocooned, despite everything, against the pain of change, as was the case with Visconti's last four films.

Cut, dubbed and reprocessed in foul colour by 20th Century-Fox – its huge budget having required the participation of one of the major American companies – *Il Gattopardo* was a disaster in Britain and the U.S. Visconti, with reason, disowned

Visconti's Re-creation of the Past

Although Visconti set out to be the leading apostle of neo-realism it was clear from his first films that he was a full-blooded romantic – and he was able to combine both aspects of his talent in his period films. Perhaps the most striking of them are the two set at the time of the Risorgimento, *Senso*, LEFT, with Alida Valli and Farley Granger, and *Il Gattopardo*, BELOW, with Burt Lancaster, seated, and Rina Morelli, in the centre of the picture. The former is in fact romantic melodrama, and the latter, taken from the famous novel, a study of the effect of the Revolution on an aristocratic Sicilian family.

this version, whereas the original Italian version ran for over a year in Paris. After **Vaghe Stelle dell'Orsa** (1965), an operatic family melodrama, and **Lo Straniero** (1967), an off-centre version of Camus' 'L'Etranger', Visconti contributed to **Le Streghe** (1967), a sketch film prepared by de Laurentiis to re-launch his wife, Silvana Mangano, who had been in temporary retirement. Visconti's is the longest episode at forty-five minutes and is set in a house party in Kitzbühl where a movie star (Mangano) is a disruptive presence. The script by Giuseppe Patroni Griffi and Zavattini sets out to be satire, but is directed in such a manner as to take the rich and worldly at face value. The episode directed by Pasolini (q.v.) is equally dire, and that directed by de Sica, with Clint Eastwood as a husband no longer alive to his wife's sexual allure, only slightly better. The whole film is redolent of the worst of Italian cinema and despite bi-lingual credit-titles (in Italian and English) was hardly seen abroad.

Visconti himself took to filming in English, which is to say that English scripts were prepared for those of the international casts who could act in that language, while the rest did their best – for eventual dubbing. **The Damned** (1970) was backed by Warner Bros., since once again the budget was high; the subject was also supposedly of international appeal – an allegory of the rise and fall of Nazi Germany, as represented by a family presumably based on the Krupps. It comes to life briefly, in a re-creation of the Night of the Long Knives, a fetishistic orgy of uniforms and transvestism that surely resembles a sequence cut fifty years earlier from *The Four Horsemen of the Apocalypse* – except, that is, for the nude men and their blood-spattered bodies, all of which are most pictorial. The cast includes Dirk Bogarde, Ingrid Thulin, Florinda Bolkin, Umberto Orsini and, as the anti-hero, a young discovery of Visconti's, Helmut Berger, who moves from an impersonation of Marlene Dietrich in *The Blue Angel*, through child-molesting, to mother-rape. Berger, exuding all the chic of a second-rank male model, fascinated Visconti, to the extent that he became absorbed in Germanic culture: and his version of Thomas Mann's novella, **Death in Venice** (1971), atoned for the comic strip that is *The Damned*.

Except that the profession of Aschenbach has been changed from writer to composer (based on Gustav Mahler), and that a short tale has been extended to 130 minutes, the transcription is a literal one, even to the camera abandoned on its tripod as Aschenbach is dying. In that role, Bogarde is superb; and the use of the adagietto from Mahler's 5th Symphony as an accompaniment to the crossing of the Lagoon is one of the most emotional moments in cinema history. It was such deep-seated romanticism which caused many people to respond to this film, even those with little sympathy for an ageing man obsessed by the image of a fair youth. In the U.S., the art-house public, until then wary of Visconti, finally yielded. Americans felt happier with the obscurities of Fellini's fantasies than with the operatic and possibly decadent intrigues of the remote Visconti, but of the two the latter had been more successful in reaching the general public in Europe.

Ludwig (1973), was his first film in many a year to fail in Europe, and in New York, when it opened, it was a joke-of-the-month, along with the remake of *Lost Horizon*. M-G-M, who had taken distribution rights, cut it from three hours to two before abandoning hope, and refused to open it in Britain (they sold it later to an independent British distributor). Visconti wrote it with his customary collaborator, d'Amico, and Enrico Medioli, who joined them for Visconti's last films. Like Helmut Käutner's film on the same subject, this one starts with Ludwig's death and then proceeds to examine his life – in a manner which is dissertation rather than study. The original screenplay, lurching back and forth in time, was not only fragmentary, but so structured as to emphasise its own banality: by eventually assembling the material in chronological order the piece builds nobly enough to its final section – dealing with Ludwig's homosexuality, extravagance and insanity. The matter of homosexuality is the real trouble: whatever technical innovations Visconti might accept, he was unable to treat the subject except in the manner of a lady novelist of two decades earlier – as composed of coy voyeuristic glances or an all-guardsmen party as decorous as a church fête. As Wagner, Trevor Howard takes the film as the magnificent professional he is, but

Visconti's habitually weak casting goes beyond Berger as the King: Romy Schneider is a vulgar Sissi* and Silvana Mangano a wraith-like Cosima. As in most of Visconti's late films, the costumes, by Piero Tosi, are splendid, and the locations are spectacular – as Käutner had already proved, also using Ludwig's own castles for interiors and exteriors.

During the film's making Visconti suffered a stroke, and directed his last two films from a wheelchair. **Conversation Piece** (1975) suffered a fate similar to *Ludwig* in New York, where it was laughed off the screen at the city's annual film festival. Nevertheless it proves to be, at least technically, the handiwork of a master, which is all the more refreshing since at this time most films showed scant respect for the old rules with nothing new to replace them. Burt Lancaster returned to work with Visconti, acting less studiously than in *Il Gattopardo* as an ageing professor confronted, in his Roman apartment, with the puzzling life-style of the young – as chiefly represented by Herr Berger, an unabashed gigolo. The film provides a detailed study of the professor's mentality and is also a tale of suspense in the manner of *The Servant* (q.v.): but the professor's fixation on the young man having been established, he is allowed only one carnal look in his direction. Since the professor clearly represents Visconti, it is sad that he, so artistically courageous in his early career, fails to confront his own homosexuality on screen. He seems to have wanted to but changed his mind, which may be why this film eventually fizzles out in a number of pointless scenes. He was a contradiction in private life, for instance, insisting that his menservants wore white gloves to serve his raffish retinue while he expounded his left-wing beliefs. His later films gave no indication of these, and most of them are disappointing compared to *La Terra Trema*. I believe that his rivalry with Fellini and Antonioni intensified after they became international names, and that he made the sort of films they would not, or could not, make. He certainly showed the weakness common to many eminent directors, in that every film he made had to be an 'event'.

His last film, **L'Innocente** (1976), carries less of that aura, and it is both less and more interesting than *Conversation Piece*. It is not remotely personal and the story, by d'Annunzio, merely states the obvious, that in his time there were different rules for men and women in sexual matters. The film is an exquisite portrait of a vanished age, its pictorial style once again derived from the Academic paintings. The grand flourish is missing, but otherwise the film is representative of Visconti's work as a whole, leading us to suppose that there is nothing more here than meets the eye; so his career, resplendent at its best, ends with a sigh.

Michelangelo Antonioni (b. 1912) is the greatest of the Italians: with *L'Avventura* (q.v.) he changed the language of the cinema. Born in Ferrara, he studied economics and film – at the Centro Sperimentale – and was also journalist, scriptwriter and documentary film-maker before directing his first feature, **Cronaca di un Amore** (1950). The affair of the title is adulterous and doomed, since, as the couple (Lucia Bosè and Massimo Girotti) are only too aware, because of the unexplained and accidental death of a friend, a private detective is spying on them. They decide to murder her husband, but he dies before they can do so, which does not contribute to their happiness. With great intensity Antonioni already deals with what were to become common themes in his work: the role of fate in our lives, and our sense of guilt in being unable to control either. They recur in **La Signora senza Camelie** (1953), a morality tale of a girl (Bosè) too sensitive to be a starlet, and not talented enough to be a star; a failure playing Joan of Arc, she begs her producer husband for a second chance and when that is denied settles for dustbin epics and the clandestine liaisons of the also-ran. Better focused than *Bellissima*, it has moments of amusing, if awkward symbolism, as in the matter of the stills – Davis, Hepburn and Garbo as she makes her way to greatness, and Hedy Lamarr and Virginia Mayo as she is put in her place.

Le Amiche (1955) is, true to the title, a study of a group of friends – the high bourgeoisie of Turin, directionless, whether locked in love or out of it – as adapted from a novel by Pavese, virtually the only time Antonioni has not provided

*She had played Sissi, the Empress Elizabeth, several times in her teens, in some sugary German films.

his own source material. **Il Grido** (1957) is not a far cry from Camus' 'La Chute', about a man (Steve Cochran) who disintegrates when one love (Alida Valli) leaves him and he can find no consolation with another (Betsy Blair). Despite this progression to international star names, the four films met with little or no success. I should also mention a deserved failure, **I Vinti** (1953), filmed in three languages, the French and Italian versions concerning juvenile delinquency, and the English, ludicrously, an egomaniac killer (Peter Reynolds) and an ageing tart (Fay Compton). The catcalling and laughter that greeted *L'Avventura* at the Cannes Festival seemed to close the file on Antonioni, though there were some who, fortunately, recognised a masterpiece.

L'Avventura (1960) was, to many, mesmerising at first viewing, and I find it so after seeing it several times. It is, like *La Règle du Jeu*, which was also misunderstood by its original audiences, a novel written with a camera. Renoir's film was not revolutionary, but *L'Avventura* is, for it tells a tale of self-discovery and emotional change almost entirely in images. The dialogue is sparse, and the image itself is less important than the spatial relationships of figure to landscape, of these Roman people to the Sicilian environment. During a cruise a woman (Lea Massari) disappears on a barren island whereupon her lover (Gabriele Ferzetti), an architect, and her closest friend (Monica Vitti) undertake a search for her: as the search seems increasingly futile, they realise that they have fallen in love. The film probes the nature of loving itself, and that is the adventure of the title. Its starting point has a multitude of sources – a trip to Sicily, a love affair dying and another starting, impressions of friends. Events occur, of significance only to these people, moulded as they are by families, professions, friends and circumstances: yet they are not really aware till they are fully embarked on their emotional quest, which will lead them to a greater understanding but no greater happiness. We are sometimes ahead of them and sometimes not, depending on the image, always demanding a reconsideration of the one before, be it as they search for the lost girl on the volcanic island or meet in a hotel lobby. In *Signora senza Camelie* the audience is privy

to a telephone conversation, and only when it is over does the camera draw back to reveal another character in the room, causing a reassessment of what we had just heard. Withholding information had been a device available to novelists but not, seemingly, to film-makers, originating from stage production: it had been used in thrillers, perhaps with someone hiding, to create tension, but Antonioni was the first to use it to demand an intellectual response from his audience. True, he has one of the elements of a thriller – a disappearance – but the distinctive and growing menace devolves from the audience's awareness of Vitti's and Ferzetti's own growing awareness. That is one reason why *L'Avventura* is the cinema's most perfect matching of form and content.

The subject of **La Notte** (1961) is marital malaise, treated not as a narrative, but as another situation to be quarried in every direction. The husband (Mastroianni) is a novelist and it is only at the end, as he and his wife (Jeanne Moreau) stroll into the dawn after a smart party, that they acknowledge, albeit clumsily, that their marriage has disintegrated. She does say 'I feel like dying because I no longer love you', but her comment that he should take the job offered to him so that his life can be his own is not what one expects a writer's wife to say: it signals a defeat as hauntingly absurd as the lover's comment on his own career in *L'Avventura*. It was with *La Notte* that Antonioni exerted the most profound influence on his contemporaries, and it has tremendous force, unlike his imitators. They noted the chilly nightclub, the tower-blocks and wasteland of Milan and the platitudinous party guests, without understanding that at the heart of the film is a theme, and it concerns the self-doubts of an artist. *La Notte* is occasionally schematic, a charge to be levelled at all of **L'Eclisse** (1962) – once, that is, it has been established that its heroine (Vitti) is so bored by one affair that she is impelled to embark upon another. The title refers to the eclipse of feeling in modern life, and though elsewhere Antonioni was able to analyse contemporary *angst*, here he only sets it down, having, I think, over-intellectualised every line of dialogue, every set-up and every object seen on the screen. The air of improvisation apparent with *Le Amiche* and *L'Avventura* has been dissipated, but Antonioni's ability to communicate his excitement with the medium was to return in the next two films – though it is of the second, *Blow-Up* (q.v.), that he would claim, 'All the others I did with my stomach, this one I did with my brain.'

Il Deserto Rosso (1964) does convey a sense of having been laboured upon too long, especially in those scenes set in a street repainted in the required pastel shades. A year earlier, Bergman in *The Silence* had set his tortured ladies in a strange city, and the lady out of kilter here is Miss Vitti, then Antonioni's muse and chief protagonist. Because her life is bounded by her husband, his job and their child, she takes a lover (Richard Harris): 'There is something terrible about reality,' she tells him, 'and I don't know what it is' – which gives the film its title, though the red desert may also be the dreadful manufacturing town of Ravenna (significantly we do not see the mosaics), or the dreamed-of Patagonia, or bed, or a place of longings and frustrations, or any combination of these. It is an ambiguous title, too, because this is a very cold film, rewarding primarily to those prepared to be patient with its pessimism.

Like Bergman, Antonioni is more interesting when he is dealing with a male protagonist, and the one in **Blow-Up** (1967) is a successful London photographer (David Hemmings), who is plebeian, disgruntled and bored. Unlike the architect of *L'Avventura* and the novelist of *La Notte*, Antonioni does not seem to care for him, though he is sympathetic towards his dilemma in wanting to take 'real' pictures of vagrants instead of artful fashion stills. He claims to be confined, but his life is surely independent, able as he is to participate in an anti-war march or entertain two girls who throw themselves upon him. At one moment, in a park, he hops and skips, liberated at discovering that life holds something more, literally, than meets the eye. For his life has been galvanised by having taken, in that park, a series of photographs which may reveal a murder, and also, even less distinctly, the murderer: is he then no longer a purveyor of the real, but a conveyor of the illusion of reality (like a film director) . . . and does the final, even more symbolic sequence, mean that in future he will see? Like the

protagonists of *La Notte* and more particularly *L'Avventura*, he is an artist, disorientated in a worthless society, being pushed by new perceptions into a voyage of self-discovery.

It remains an astonishing film, too big an achievement to be dated by its portrait of 'swinging' London, though it was perhaps that which made it so popular at the time. Ponti, who had produced for M-G-M, had no difficulty in persuading that company to invest four million dollars in an American venture, **Zabriskie Point** (1970). Such plot as there is involves a student who, because he thinks he has killed a cop, steals a plane to fly to Death Valley; and such perceptions as there are are superficial – on the vulgarity of Los Angeles and the ready violence and despair of the young. American critics howled in execration and the film was only little better liked in Europe, to the gratification of some, for Antonioni could then be dismissed – like Bergman – as a bored man who made pictures about boring people.

Antonioni himself agreed that the film was a debacle, and he was only able to work with M-G-M again when, under a change of management, the company agreed to distribute **The Passenger** (1975), with Jack Nicholson in the title role as a reporter. It begins, hallucinatingly, in the North African desert, and moves to London, Munich and Barcelona, before settling in Southern Spain. Antonioni's use of his landscapes had become somewhat self-conscious, but this is, again, a film about seeing: Nicholson admits, after he has assumed the identity of another man, that he was blinkered before. When he and the girl (Maria Schneider) reach their final destination she asks what he sees, and he replies that he sees, exists and acts: therefore he is. As Kierkegaard expressed existentialism, he has re-created himself, in this specific situation and environment. Antonioni's co-authors were Mark Peploe and Peter Wollen, the latter author of a treatise on symbolism in film. The film's ultimate failure has less to do with that than with having opted for the form of a thriller, leaving too much unexplained. That might not have been a demerit, were not the characters so dehumanised – another tendency of Antonioni's which has increased over the years – so that Nicholson's natural warmth is subdued.

Antonioni the Innovator

Michelangelo Antonioni changed the language of cinema, the first director to do so since the Silent days. He may not have been the first to realise that the medium might follow literature rather than the theatre in being selective in deciding what to convey to an audience, but he was the first to do so in extended form – and often to demonstrate emotional content rather than advance the plot. He experimented with the form in some of his earlier films, and finally achieved a magnificent flowering with it in *L'Avventura*, ABOVE RIGHT, with Monica Vitti and Gabriele Ferzetti. At its most superficial the film could be described as a thriller with no solution, but it was also about the malaise of modern life, and that was a subject to which Antonioni returned in *La Notte*, ABOVE, with Jeanne Moreau and Marcello Mastroianni, and *Il Deserto Rosso*, RIGHT, with Signorina Vitti – often called upon by Antonioni to help him express his feelings upon the subject. When critics began to carp about his pessimism, he tried, in *The Passenger*, BOTTOM RIGHT, to incorporate more mysterious elements than in any of his films since *L'Avventura*: and since in the meantime others had been imitating his film language this movie is not as rewarding as that had been. But it was very entertaining, and Jack Nicholson was excellent as the man who assumes the identity of another.

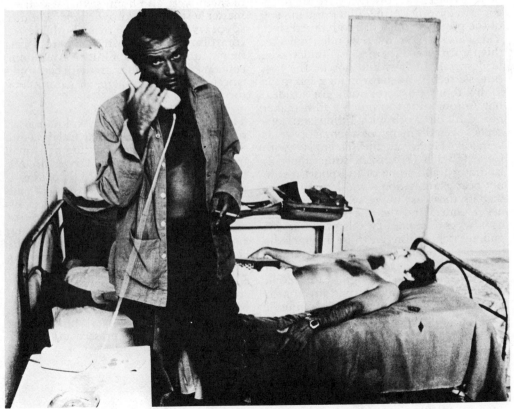

Italy: Traditions Maintained and Betrayed

Though audiences were as enthusiastic as reviewers, they were insufficient to enable Antonioni to find backing for his next venture, said to be very expensive.★

Eventually he put aside a number of projects to make **Il Mistero di Oberwald** (1980) because, he said, he wanted to experiment with the video camera. It is possible that the choice of subject – it is a remake of *L'Aigle à Deux Têtes* – was that of Monica Vitti, who plays the lead, for, predictably, it seemed one with which he was not in sympathy. He regarded it as a minor work and it carried none of his hallmarks; so it was all the more intoxicating, after his long silence, to witness again his marvellously individual style in **Identificazione di una Donna** (1982), however much this is limited to the clever use of sets and locations and deliberate obfuscation. He has said that its preoccupations are Italian but also universal, being, as the title suggests, about the nature of the loved one. A film director (Tomas Milian), while searching for the ideal woman to play in his – vaguely planned – next movie, has affairs with two women, in the process of which he realises how little he knows about either. The disappearance of the first of the women is redolent of *L'Avventura*, but in this case she leaves deliberately and he is perplexed as to why; there are references to the other earlier films, and in view of the projects which had foundered since *The Passenger* we may wonder whether this return to old themes was undertaken in desperation. It would not be the first time a director, stuck for an idea, has made a film about a director stuck for an idea, but Antonioni is too much a film-maker not to fill his work with a thousand concepts, even if many of them appear as symbols. He wrote the screenplay with Gerard Brach (Polanski's sometime collaborator), and some of its aphorisms do not bear examination – and I am not sure that its thesis is 'universal', that we can never understand the one we love. That has always been one of his themes, but, as I said, his richest films are those in which the male protagonists embark on a voyage of self-discovery: they were all aspects of Antonioni himself. It is significant that in making a movie about a movie director for the first time his hero understands himself

★He was reported at one point as seeking finance in Australia.

no better at the end than at the beginning.

As I write, Antonioni is making the first of two films with American backing; it had been shameful that a great film-maker was denied an audience while lesser ones were finding backing. In Italy there is less dichotomy between talented film-makers and less gifted ones. If we accept the declines of de Sica and Fellini as owing to exceptional and personal circumstances, an examination of any other score of Italian directors will reveal one good film – hence one international success – and several bad ones. The disturbing factor is that they have had better raw material than film-makers in most European democracies – or, rather, they have a stronger tradition of socially concerned cinema, despite the restraining mantles of Fascism and the Church. The Vatican seems not to have minded the sex dramas of the Fifties, since these invariably held a moral, and seems to have considered it prudent to ignore the increasing attacks on its authority. The fact that the majority of Italian film-makers was militantly left-wing was not a matter to which attention should be drawn, particularly as the more serious they were the more likely was their work to be appreciated only by the intellectual coteries of Rome, Milan and Turin; the fact that many of them were also homosexual was also a matter best left unacknowledged. The dual advocacy of freedom from both clerical control and sexual constraint is a recurring theme, implicit in the films of Antonioni, concerned though they are with city sophisticates – and it is there, in galumphing form, in *La Dolce Vita*.

The richest field for such explorations is rural Italy, and in particular Calabria and Sicily – and Sicily is the setting of a small triumph, Pietro Germi's **Divorzio all' Italiana** (1961). A count (Mastroianni) is married to a podgy, moustached and amorous wife (Daniela Rocca), but is anxious to bed his pretty cousin: since that would only be possible after a wedding, and since divorce is impermissible, he decides on the unlikely course of finding another man who finds his wife attractive, and then shooting her, counting on the courts to be lenient. In these crumbling palazzi the girls have pasty faces and the men, always lecherous, dark moustaches: their sexual code is expressed in Germi's follow-up, **Sedotta e Abbandonata** (1964), 'A man has the right to ask; a woman has the duty to refuse.' Agnese (Stefania Sandrelli) is the girl seduced – by Peppino her sister's fiancé; a new suitor, an impoverished *barone*, is found for the sister, but Peppino then refuses Agnese because he wants a chaste wife. Leader of the brouhaha is her father, played by an actor whose resemblance to Raimu is only physical, in which context we may be reminded that Mediterranean attitudes to sex are indeed hard to fathom. Whereas *Divorzio all'Italiana* developed its comment on Sicilian family honour logically and hilariously this one is strained – a proof that most bucolic sex comedies are strictly for local consumption.

Among Germi's writers were Age and Scarpelli, usually associated with Mario Monicelli (b. 1915), and their **I Soliti Ignoti** (1958) – *Big Deal on Madonna Street* in the U.S. – was, with *Divorzio all'Italiana*, one of the few Italian comedies to be widely popular abroad. Most of those that we see concern sex, but noticeable in the lighter moments of serious films are notions which amuse Italians about themselves: their ability to charm themselves out of situations, their predilection for idling and their cunning when the best-laid plans go awry. The vast difference between the people of the South and those of the North is another source of humour, and that is the one missing element in this film. It might be described as *Rififi* in the Ealing manner, inasmuch as it is about a heist attempted by a captivatingly incompetent band of crooks (Mastroianni, Gassmann, Toto, Salvatori). Monicelli attempted to combine comedy and social comment in both **La Grande Guerra** (1959) and his episode, cut from foreign release prints, of **Boccaccio '70**, the first an unsuccessful juxtaposition of World War I carnage and the antics of an Italian Quirt and Flagg (Gassmann, Alberto Sordi), and the second some misadventures of a young couple who marry though prohibited by her boss from doing so. Monicelli manages this with light irony, offering a milieu of neon lights and cold efficiency, of traffic and loneliness, boding well for **I Compagni** (1963), an account of strikers in Turin in the 1890s and the birth of Trade Unionism. Industrial unrest had been a favourite theme of Italian writers, painters

and film-makers until Mussolini came to power – but then for a long while it was a subject avoided by almost all national film industries. The only exception I know is Hochbaum's 1929 *Brüder*, which Monicelli could hardly have seen. *I Compagni* lacks the passion of that and of later films on the subject, but it handles the matter entertainingly, with exceptional performances by Mastroianni as the professional agitator, François Perier as the involved local schoolmaster, Salvatori as the voice of doubt and moderation, and, playing against cliché, Annie Girardot as a warm-hearted prostitute. It is all the more saddening that Monicelli's later films are, at best, undistinguished, including **Vogliamo i Colonnelli** (1973), a gross comedy which applies the situation of *I Soliti Ignoti* to a group of officers planning a Greek-style *coup d'état*.

A similar progression may be noted with Franco Rossi (b. 1919), who made his international reputation with **Amici per la Pelle** (1955), a perfect example of the film sensitive, concerning the friendship of two sub-teen boys and the misunderstandings which bring about its end. **Morte di un Amico** (1960) is, in contrast, unconcerned with the finer things in life, the relationship this time being between two layabouts (Spiros Fokas, Gianni Garko) who live off prostitution – and in this case it would not be perverse to speculate on the exact nature of the friendship. **Una Rosa**

The comedies which tumble copiously from the Italian studios are rarely exportable, though the few that have been of international standard have been very successful indeed. One of them is *I Soliti Ignoti*, directed by Mario Monicelli, about a gang of small-time hoods who experience every possible mishap in trying to pull off a burglary. Among the gang were Toto, behind the jet, Vittorio Gassmann, Memmo Carotenuto and Marcello Mastroianni.

While many of Mauro Bolognini's compatriots have startled world audiences with ambitious and/or sensational movies, he has continued to make quiet, often absorbing films, usually with a social theme, many of them set in the recent past. His sense of period is remarkable, whether filming in the streets or indoors: here are Jean-Paul Belmondo and Claudia Cardinale inside a Florentine bordello in *La Viaccia*.

per Tutti (1967) concerns a prostitute (Claudia Cardinale) who behaves in Rio very much like Melina Mercouri in Athens, and is depressing evidence that Rossi had abandoned the realism of *Amici per la Pelle* to re-enter the White Telephone era.

Among the second-rank directors Mauro Bolognini (b. 1923) holds an honourable place, since he seems incapable of making either a very bad film or a magnificent one. He studied architecture and screen design, with the result that his modern films are impeccable in appearance, and the period subjects considerably more than stylish; his social concern reflects the legacy of realism, though clearly he works in the literary mood of many years earlier – an ironic detachment leaning slightly towards the emotional and melancholic. It is a detachment taken too far: he refuses to probe beneath the surface and, lacking the melodramatic energy of Visconti, his films are often attractive but bland. **Giovani Mariti** (1958) concerns a group of young men, married but unfit for matrimony; and **La Notte Brava** (1959) returns to the theme, except that they are younger, and more inclined to stealing and whoring – with one young man prepared to sell himself to another. The wealthy buyer is representative of Rome's *jeunesse dorée* – a suitable expression, since the screenplay by Pasolini is based on French models. The hero (Mastroianni) of **Il Bell'Antonio**

(1960) also has a sexual problem, in the form of impotence. Vitaliano Brancati's novel, published ten years earlier, had hitherto been rejected by the Censor, which may be why this adaptation fatally lacks the edge of *Divorzio all'Italiana*. This particular Sicilian male has had an entirely typical upbringing, leaving him with such an odd concept of women that, confronted with the one (Cardinale) to whom he is married, he can only stand aside and worship. Sexual discontent is also the subject of **La Viaccia** (1961) and **Senilità** (1962), companion pieces: respectively, a country lout (Jean-Paul Belmondo) becomes enamoured of a girl (Cardinale) who is one of the most contented inmates of a bordello; and a bourgeois (Anthony Franciosa) moves towards self-destruction by refusing to accept the fact that the girl (Cardinale) he adores is at least a semi-whore. The source of the latter is Italo Svevo's novel, 'As a Man Grows Older', updated from the turn of the century to the Twenties – perhaps to differentiate it from *La Viaccia*. The views of Florence in the one and Trieste in the other, photographed in the rain and in harsh monochrome, are memorable.

The setting of **Agostino** (1962), from Moravia's novel, has been transferred from Viareggio to Venice – which is typical of Bolognini's approach. However, Moravia liked the film, with reservations, and reviewing in *L'Espresso* he mentioned that the small boy hero (Paolo Colombo) 'knows nothing, either, of sex or class . . . his friends make him discover, with pain, in a short season at the seaside, what Marx demonstrated: that in the depths of social and family relations there is no innocence.' On the one hand, he discovers that his mother (Ingrid Thulin) is having an affair with a wealthy playboy (John Saxon); on the other, his companions accuse him of something similar with the fisherman (Mario Bartoletti) who is their idol – and it was bold, foolhardy and romantic to make this man so handsome, masculine and sympathetic.

The mainly bleak period which followed for Bolognini included a number of the omnibus films in which most of these directors participated, including **Le Bambole** (1965), which was perhaps the most notorious. These compendia were invariably sexual in nature – advancing in such matters as the exposure of the female torso – on the assumption that it was more practical to test censorship with part of a film than the whole, since the offending sequence could simply be removed if required: in the event, censorship, more often local than national, was less virulent than the headlines and the theoretically heavy fines would indicate.

Bolognini eventually escaped from such projects with **Metello** (1970), based on a novel by Vasco Pratolini, one of his series covering Italian history from the 1890s onwards and an attempt at understanding the present by an 'enchanted remembrance of things past'. Since Bolognini has always shown interest in such matters, we may wonder whether he was in fact rather more interested in decor than in the forces which move society. This film has a wonderful evocation of turn of the century Florence – in colour – and that overwhelms the struggles of its worker hero (Massimo Ranieri), made militant by injustice on the building sites. If the film lacks the conviction of *I Compagni*, it remains to Bolognini's credit, for labour unrest was an unpopular movie subject, even at this date, in most Western democracies; and he does achieve more passion in a loose sequel, **Libera . . . Amore Mio** (1975). The source this time is a memoir by Luciano Vincenzoni, writing about his mother, an outspoken opponent of Fascism. She is Libera (Cardinale) – and that is the name given at the end of *Metello* to the unborn baby; and just as Metello was influenced by the example of his father, an anarchist, so Libera lives by the example of hers (Adolfo Celli). As the mood darkens, with battles between the partisans and the Fascisti, Bolognini proves to be no polemicist, though he may be admired for being one of the first film-makers prepared to examine that era. **Per le Antica Scala** (1975), is also set during that period, and it is an account of a mad-house where, unsurprisingly, the physicians are as mad as the patients. As the sexually-warped head of them, Mastroianni gives an exceptional performance, as does Françoise Fabian as the new doctor who clashes with him.

According to its French producers, Bolognini's **La Dame aux Camélias** (1981) is the twenty-second film version of this tale. It is almost certainly the best. It dispenses with the play by Dumas in prologue and epilogue, but he is seen as one of the admirers of Alphonsine Plessis (Isabelle Huppert), who was the model for his heroine. The film follows her from life with her drug-addicted father (Gian Maria Volonté) and poverty in Normandy to the demi-monde and death – which comes not a moment too soon in view of her debts. She is portrayed as a predatory bitch, stupid and without real feeling, while her companions are completely lacking in morals and scruples. An air of eroticism pervades the film, and there are hints of unnamed vices. As the strange man whom Alphonsine marries, Bruno Ganz is superb – and the adjective may be applied to the art direction of Mario Garbuglia and the costumes of Piero Tosi. Another collaborator of Visconti, Enrico Medioli, provided the story for the screenplay (by Jean Aurenche and Vladimir Pozner), and it may have been he who influenced Bolognini to make this the most full-blooded of his films. The world of *La Viaccia* is small and cosy in comparison.

Bolognini remains virtually unknown outside the continent; when *Per le Antiche Scala* was shown in London and New York in 1976 it went virtually unremarked by the press. It is far from being Bolognini's best film, but it is better than any made by Pier Paolo Pasolini (1922–75), who enjoyed, at least for a while, a measure of critical favour. He began in films as a writer, including collaboration on *Morte di un Amico* and several of Bolognini's, including *La Notte Brava* – and these were two films he particularly disliked. His first two films as a director, **Accattone** (1961) and **Mamma Roma** (1962) showed him to be less sensitive than Rossi (at that time) and Bolognini, but considerably more spirited than either. The first is little more than a hymn to the then amateur actor, Franco Citti, who plays the eponymous hero, and were his close-ups cut it would be at least fifteen minutes shorter. The second is also a star vehicle for Anna Magnani, playing a prostitute who has to go back on the game, and the ending in particular is as rigged as any star vehicle ever made. The accompaniment of Bach and Vivaldi to the action, like the use of suburban wasteland locations, was taken as evidence of high intent. There are isolated moments of honest observation, perhaps because Pasolini's involvement with the world of pimps and *putanas* was as personal as a Genet (Pasolini died at the hands of a homosexual drifter, on a suburban wasteland). His background (his father was an army officer), together with his outspoken Marxism and cultural references were already admired by Italian intellectuals when he contributed an anti-clerical sketch to **RoGoPaG** (1962), in the form of a movie director (Orson Welles) filming the Crucifixion. The film merely proves that Rossellini, Godard and Pasolini were among the most inept directors then working (the fourth episode was directed by Ugo Gregoretti and his sketch is no more than a minor jape). Nevertheless Pasolini was convicted of offending the Church and given a suspended sentence. His response was to make a film of the Crucifixion himself. **Il Vangelo Secondo Matteo** (1964) benefited immeasurably from its shoestring budget, for that seemed to prove that it was a labour of love; and its favourable reception was not unconnected with the hugely expensive and lifeless *Greatest Story Ever Told*. As against the myriad guest stars of that film, Pasolini's cast was composed solely of amateurs. The Christ looked like an El Greco, and the disciples might have been models for Caravaggio or Michelangelo, which was the nearest the film came to achieving any weight. That Christ may have been a poseur is hinted at, opposed to which his teachings are offered more or less complete. But the emotionalism surrounding Christ becomes a negative virtue in Pasolini's hands, not in the least compensated for by the incongruous use of 'Sometimes I Feel Like a Motherless Child'.

Pasolini's inability to put his camera at the service of his text was further demonstrated by another adaptation of an ancient text, the **Edipe Re** (1967) of Sophocles, which he regarded as his most autobiographical film. Presumably he identified with this elemental man in search of his destiny – and since it was not his way to offer Oedipus straight, there are a prologue and epilogue to remind us, impertinently, that this is a timeless story; and this timeless story turns out to be rather like a comic-strip.

The achievement of **Teorema** (1968) was to dragoon the male crotch into the realms of art, in the guise of offering a critique on the bourgeoisie: it gets many a close-up as a guest (Terence Stamp) affects a Milanese household in a manner which can only be described as disturbing. He has his way successively with maid, son, mother, daughter and father, after which each begins to behave oddly. Pasolini's approach puts the film in the 'heavy breathing' category, but when I originally saw it the audience began to titter as mother took to picking up boys and one of them peeled off his shirt before throwing himself upon her. As she progressed to picking up couples the sniggers turned to laughter, and the audience remained convulsed, cheering and clapping, as the maid began to levitate and father, after resisting the come-hither look of a young tough, disrobed on a Milan railway platform, to wander bare-arsed on the volcanic slopes of a conveniently nearby mountain. It was abundantly clear that Pasolini was 'played out', and with **Il Decamerone** (1970) he 'sold out', moving on to equally salacious versions of 'The Canterbury Tales' and 'The Thousand and One Nights'. Only a minor squeak of embarrassment greeted his posthumous version of de Sade updated to the Fascist era to serve, as he said, as a 'metaphor', **Salo, o le Centiventi Giornate di Sodoma** (1975). Great art has rarely derived from man's degradation, but this film is by turns risible, as small boys prepare for buggery; poleaxingly boring, during long discussions on masturbation, etc., and repugnant, in its graphic scatology. Banned virtually everywhere – few cinemas cared to show it, and those which did drew scant audiences – its defenders were, unsurprisingly, few and muted.

The influence of Pasolini and Fellini on their weaker compatriots has been disastrous – not to mention some downmarket films which attracted world audiences: the 'spear-and-sandal' spectaculars, and the made-in-Italy Westerns which followed them. No reputable director wished to make such films, but the showy, empty style of Serge Leone, acknowledged master director of 'spaghetti' Westerns, seems to have found its way into other films. Even veteran directors like Lattuada bowed to the prevailing vulgarity, and I pass over a great many so-called comedies, every ancient wheeze heavily over-emphasised, and photographed in appropriate bright colours and modish manner. I mention the dire **Dramma della Gelosia – Tutti i Particolari in Cronaca** (1970), a triangle mix-up with Mastroianni, Monica Vitti and Giancarlo Giannini, only to show that a director may improve – in this case Ettore Scola, whose **Una Giornata Particolare** (1977) is a neat attempt, in near-monochrome, to deal calmly with homosexuality, in the person of a radio-announcer (Mastroianni) whose private life has brought him into conflict with the Fascist authorities; at least at the moment of seduction by a – drab – housewife (Loren) he looks suitably abashed. In contrast to Scola, Elio Petri began directing with discretion but moved in the other direction. **L'Assassino** (1961) concerns an imprisoned murderer (Mastroianni), whose relationship with his victim (Micheline Presle) is laid painfully bare; in similar depth, and in the same time-jumping style, Petri offered another murderer in **Indagine su un Cittadino al di Sopra di Ogni Sospetto** (1970) – that is, a 'citizen above suspicion' (Gian Maria Volonté) because he happens to be head of homicide, now promoted to Chief of Political Intelligence. As Costa-Gavras has proved, flashiness is not necessarily a deterrent to the enjoyment of this kind of thriller, but in this case the behaviour examined is motivated entirely towards that flashiness.

A more extreme case of a once promising director is Lina Wertmuller, a former theatre and television writer who moved from assisting Fellini on *Otto e Mezzo* to directing. **I Basilischi** (1963) was made for less than $100,000 on location in a small town in Puglia, with amateur performers. One of her backers was the group called 22 Dicembre, to which Ermanno Olmi also belonged, and her study of this Southern community is not unlike his in *I Fidanzati* (q.v.), that is, in the pure style of neo-realism, without either the satire of Germi or the lyricism of Fellini's rural studies. Gianni Di Venanzo was the photographer, though one should think only of him to explain its superiority over the lady's later work, for this is very nicely made. In 1975 New York discovered Wertmuller, and her half dozen films followed each other into cinemas, to virtually unanimous rave reviews. However, she remained unknown in Britain and France since, as both *Time* and *Variety* pointed out, critics of those countries had seen her films at festivals, and were not, to put it mildly, enthusiastic. Of course, Fellini is, or was, 'big' in New York, and it is he whom Wertmuller was pathetically emulating, with her grotesques, imprisoned in their gross bodies and subject to indignities – which by some chance are usually sexual. Two stories intertwine in **Pasqualino Settebellezze** (1976) – *Seven Beauties* – and it is hard to tell which is the less interesting, the one about the concentration camp internee (Giancarlo Giannini) who decides to make love to the huge mannish commandant (Shirley Stoler), or his memories of prewar Naples, murdering and chopping up the body of the man who turned his sister into a whore. John Coleman in the *New Statesman* noted its American success, and said it 'looks like shouting, gesticulating, postured rubbish to me', offering the additional indignity of a three-line review. In *The Observer*, Russell Davies took more trouble: 'This is another lady – Liliana Cavani was the last – who seems to think that the most pointed way of illustrating a moral decline is to stage it as a kind of nightclub parody of masochistic sexual relations . . . It is my belief that this kind of thing raises interest in nothing more political than itself: boots, boobs, thighs spilling over the top of stockings, and degradation in general; and whatever else Miss Wertmuller does with her Warner Bros. contract,* it is certain to involve her in reproducing the odd bit of comparable tatty sexual charade.' It did, too: and since the film concerned was in English, American critics were able to realise how appalling her films are. As they had turned on Fellini in English (*Casanova*), so they turned on her, bringing them, in both cases, in line with the majority of European critics. As for Miss Cavani, I have not seen *The Night Porter*, to which Mr Davies was referring, since I saw the earlier **I Cannibali** (1970), a showy triviality – though deadly serious – with aspirations towards being an Italian version of Bergman's *The Shame*. I would not have brought the matter up, but it is beyond comprehension how either lady – *I Basilischi* apart – ever found backers.

*It was annulled after one film. When American critics attacked Wertmuller's subsequent films, they referred to the earlier ones that they had liked as 'dated'.

Italy: Traditions Maintained and Betrayed

Bernardo Bertolucci (b. 1940) was assistant to Pasolini on *Accattone*, but his first two films as director, **Prima Della Rivoluzione** (1964) and **Partner** (1968) are a precocious blend of Antonioni and Godard, though, alas, tending more towards the latter – not that either director is free of misogyny or hints of perversion – with a hero, in the first film, who has an affair with an aunt. Supposedly he is trying to come to terms with his Marxism, and since the film is set in Bertolucci's birthplace, Parma, it may be autobiographical; I could not tell you the subject of the other film, since it remained obscure when I left after an hour. Both films make political allusions, and are lavish with cultural references – Verdi, Shakespeare, Howard Hawks, Nicholas Ray . . . One character has seen *Viaggio in Italia* fifteen times and anyone who could sit through it even twice is likely to make films as awful as these. Amazingly, the first won the Young Critics' prize at Cannes, which led to (minimal) foreign distribution. Bertolucci did not acquire a reputation till his fourth film, **Il Conformista** (1970), and **La Strategia del Ragno** (1970), made for television. Each is still immature and employs the enigmatic, time-jumping style fashionable at the time: the enormous advance on the earlier films is due to the stronger subjects involved. *Strategia*, based on a story by Borges – transcribed from Ireland in 1824 to the lower Po Valley in the post-Fascist period – is an examination of heroism, as undertaken by the dead man's son (Giulio Brogi); *Conformista* is a study of a Fascist (Jean-Louis Trintignant), his political attitudes conditioned by suppressed homosexuality – a dénouement unsurprising after *Agostino*, since this is also based on a novel by Moravia, who publicly announced his dislike of the film.

Bertolucci's bankruptcy, moral and intellectual, was again apparent in **Last Tango in Paris** (1972), a dreary piece about a girl (Maria Schneider) who regularly turns up to be sodomised, with the help of a pat of butter, in an empty apartment, by a man (Marlon Brando) whose name she does not know. With dialogue and trimmings of similar persuasion, this footnote to Freud caused a sensation, to the delight of United Artists, which had taken the film for world-wide release on the strength of Brando's participation. The company proclaimed that it would be the most financially successful film of all time, but the sensation lasted only a few weeks, dying at the box office despite much talk of suppression and praise from two expected critics in London and New York, who claimed it an earth-shattering masterpiece. Consequently, they had to say something similar about **Novecento** (1976), this time to more general ridicule. This was Bertolucci's way of topping *Last Tango*, dirtier and longer – to the extent of almost 5½ hours, and the longest film with which a Hollywood company had been associated since *The Wedding March*. I should say several Hollywood companies, since it passed from one to the other amidst threats of litigation; and although we may again find some Hollywood names in the cast – Burt Lancaster, Robert de Niro – it bears witness to Hollywood's fascination with European production when the content is mainly sexual.

Bertolucci's model was Visconti, but he was more ambitious, covering no less than half of this century as experienced by rich boy (de Niro) and poor (Gérard Depardieu). As a political tract it is, in the words of Frank Rich in *Time*, 'maddeningly simple-minded', while as an entertainment it hovers between late Joan Crawford and Pasolini's *Salo* – and it manages the considerable feat of being even less watchable than that. There is a wedding ceremony during which the aristocratic Amelia (Laura Betti) shouts four-letter words before rushing off to the woodshed where she performs fellatio on the Fascist Attila (Donald Sutherland): discovered by a small boy, he and then *she* sodomise him before killing him by swinging him by his legs so that his head is crushed by the four walls – for which the rich boy allows his best friend to be blamed, despite his being miles away at the time. This was another Bertolucci film I failed to see to the end – in common with many others. Tried out in Europe, cut to 4½ hours in two parts, it was discovered that less than half of those who saw the first part returned for the second. Despite the respectability conferred by some festival showings, 20th Century-Fox and Paramount (taking over from United Artists) had given up hope by the time they opened it in the Anglo-Saxon market, and it was just as well. It was a surprise to no one that Bertolucci's next film featured mother-son masturbation, incest and a father-fixation, as well as the usual homosexual longings.

Following such examples the Italian cinema has developed its own school of soft pornography, where ladies have their silk underwear torn off by gentlemen, and turn to other ladies for satisfaction when the spirit moves. It is apparently essential that these tales be set during the Fascist era, or before, and be prettily photographed in the manner of Visconti and Bolognini. Typical are **Mogliamante** (1977), directed by Mario Vicario, set in the foothills of the Dolomites, involving a husband (Mastroianni) who, hidden in an attic, watches his wife receive a succession of lovers; and **Ritratto di Borghesia in Nero** (1978) – or *A Nest of Vipers* – directed by Tonino Cervi, concerning a boy who seduces his friend's mother (Senta Berger), who, on his defection, then revenges herself by seducing his fiancée (Ornella Muti). Of the same standard is **Pane e Cioccolata** (1974), directed by Franco Brusati, which starts out as a bright satire on an Italian waiter (Nino Manfredi) and conditions in present-day Switzerland, but is soon throwing conviction aside for a number of feeble jokes.

Brusati has ideas above his station. At least this film has a creditable theme – the reaction of an Italian to 'abroad' – and it is always possible that its vulgarities were imposed upon him by Manfredi, star and producer; but **Dimenticare Venezia** (1979) proves them to be his own. The twin themes of a death in the family and the return to the country home are old, and their treatment here is none the worse for being influenced by Fellini and Carlos Saura (q.v.): and what is new and different here is that they are experienced by two homosexual couples, two women of the same age and a middle-aged man (Erland Josephson) and his younger partner. Brusati deals with their sexual behaviour in a way which violates all known patterns, so that he repeats the nudes prancing in the sylvan setting from *Pane e Cioccolata*, presumably on the grounds that from such repetitions are the reputations of auteurs made. The younger gay man proving himself capable of heterosexual sex (he looks down at his organ) provides the most unintentionally funny moment in cinema since *S. A. Mann Brand*. This is an 'art'

movie, i.e. one in which life is subservient to mood, and both are subservient to effect. The amount of female flesh on display suggests that Brusati is either opportunist or voyeur; if he is homosexual himself, he joins the other gay directors in being able only to handle the subject dishonestly.

That this film is reputed to have won awards in Italy must be depressing to those film-makers who have tried to make films entertaining without recourse to salaciousness or Fellini-like excess. These directors include Nanni Loy (b. 1925), who made his reputation with **Le Quattro Giornate di Napoli** (1963), a decent reconstruction of the battle resulting in the German withdrawal from Naples, and whose best film is probably **Detenuto in Attesa di Guidizio** (1971), the story of an innocent man (Alberto Sordi) imprisoned by bureaucratic error – Kafka in a recognisable setting. Dino Risi (b. 1917) also works agreeably in a commercial context, usually with Vittorio Gassmann – whose performances can make his films worthwhile. The best of their later films is **Profumo di Donna** (1974), the adventures of a blinded, one-armed ex-officer (Gassmann) and the army student detailed to look after him: the interplay of character is so felicitous that one regrets the tendency towards the conventional elsewhere. Another actor of ease and authority, under-appreciated outside Italy, is Gian Maria Volonté, whose proud, cold Vanzetti in **Sacco e Vanzetti** (1971) is to be treasured: Sacco is Riccardo Cucciolla, the director Giuliano Montaldo, and the film is probably the best possible cinematic account of one of the century's great *causes célèbres*. The exposition is clear, the approach unemotional, and the film can only be faulted in its attitude towards the events which brought the pair to trial: Montaldo is certain that socialism and radicalism are beneficial to society, but he hedges on the matter of anarchy, clearly because he does not want to lose sympathy for his heroes.

The tradition of the Italian political film has remained not only alive but kicking, due in part to Gillo Pontecorvo (b. 1919), a former journalist and documentary director. His second feature, **Kapo** (1959), is a superficial portrait of life in the German concentration camps. **Queimada!** (1970),

The films of Gillo Pontecorvo have been few and far between, and they have been variable in quality, but *La Battaglia di Algeri* is the best film about a revolution since Eisenstein. Unlike the Soviet directors, however, Pontecorvo is fair to both sides.

an attempt to examine the roots of colonialism, is fatally flawed – possibly because of the need to change the locations from Colombia to Africa during shooting, and the publicised dissensions* with the leading actor, Marlon Brando, in a narcissistic performance as an Englishman sent by his government to exploit the natives. But between the two, **La Battaglia di Algeri** (1966), is a perfect example of the political film, presenting the facts in enthralling fashion and leaving the audience to draw its own conclusions. It treats with dignity and sympathy both the Arab population and the harassed French 'occupiers', condemning only the far-away and indifferent government in Paris. It starts in

*The experience kept Pontecorvo away from films for five years, after which several projects came to nothing. He says that he would have been more prolific had he been a novelist or a painter, 'but with films the possibility of being true to yourself is that much harder'.

1957, with the capture of the last tree member of the F.L.N., and then tracks back to show both his joining the Movement and the methods of its leader, Saari Kadar, whose terrorism, as the French colonel points out, is to revolution what guerrilla tactics are to war.

If the film was to influence Costa-Gavras, we may see that it was in turn influenced by Francesco Rosi (b. 1922), who unlike Pontecorvo has been reasonably prolific. A former law student and radio writer, he was an assistant to Visconti on *La Terra Trema*, and he collaborated with Zavattini and Antonioni, among others, as well as co-directing two films before making **La Sfida** (1958). He said, 'A director makes his first film with passion and without regard for what has gone before,' but this is in fact a reworking of *La Terra Trema*, with the Visconti arias replaced by Zavattini's naturalism. The setting is Naples, Rosi's native city, and his purpose was to expose certain business practices in what he calls 'the tomato war', with local racketeers controlling the price paid for fresh produce from the hinterland. A small-time operator tries to move into the big time, but unlike 'Ntoni in *La Terra Trema*, whose motives were philanthropic, his are selfish – and on that the film fails, since the role requires a stronger actor than it has. **I Magliari** (1959) also concerns racketeers, and they are rival con-men (Alberto Sordi, Renato Salvatori) preying on their compatriots, immigrant workers in Germany. Sordi, like the protagonist in *La Sfida*, manages to antagonise his colleagues more than his rivals – and this was to be a continuing theme in Rosi's films. For the moment it means that both films end dispiritedly, and they are further weakened by an uncertain grasp of narrative – though that is partially hidden in the vigorous handling of individual scenes and the photography of Gianni di Venanzo.

Rosi, aware of his chief fault, as he admitted, avoids narrative in **Salvatore Giuliano** (1961) and capitalises on these two virtues. There is a superb unity of the landscape and people of Sicily, and it was this dramatic but non-fictional examination of the Sicilian bandit that made Rosi's international reputation, which grew with **Le Mani sulla Citta** (1964), at once a return to Naples – though a city itself is never named – and the theme of corruption. A property speculator (Rod Steiger) is unconcerned with his methods, even when an unsafe building collapses and claims victims. He is made to show care because an election is imminent, and as a result of that the Right joins the Left in the enquiry that is ordered: but too much is at stake to allow any headway on the part of the idealists involved. Rosi explained his purpose: 'What interests me passionately is how a character behaves in relation to the collectivity of society. I'm not making a study of character but of society. To understand what a man is like in his private drama you must begin to understand him in his public life.'

The statement explains why a planned documentary of Spain became, instead, the story of a bullfighter (Miguel Mateo Miguelin), **Il Momento della Verità** (1965). Di Venanzo's superb pictures of the San Fermin fiesta in Pamplona and of the *penitentes* in Seville were incorporated into a portrait of a poor boy attracted to money and fame – at which point Rosi has little more to offer than a show business tale of a jet-setter, Linda Christian, playing 'herself', whose main interest is in seducing the bullfighter. The wide screen and colour footage of the *corrida* were incomparably superior to those seen outside Spain hitherto (the most honest accounts were in some black and white documentaries, and even they were censored in most countries; but by this time it was calculated that tourism had removed the horror from bullfighting). Also filmed in Spain was **C'era una Volta** (1967), among the brown hills, an appropriate setting for this tale of a peasant girl (Sophia Loren) who beats twelve princesses in a washing-up contest for the prince (Omar Sharif) – very much a Mediterranean fairytale and, as such, successful; but Anglo-Saxon audiences did not appreciate it. They did not get a chance to see **Uomini Contro** (1970), though the English title was already chosen – *Just Another War*: to which the response must be that it is just another war film. The cast is headed by Mark Frechette, from *Zabriskie Point*, and there is no reason why this semi-amateur American should play an Italian officer except that Rosi anticipated an international success; the cost, in any case, was such that he had had to seek Yugoslav collaboration. The Alpine battlefield has been imaginatively and bloodily re-created, and photographed in steely colours by Pasqualino de Santis, but Rosi's urge to say something important – doubtless intense after the last two films – resulted only in cliché: that military men are fanatics and war is hell.

Nevertheless, it had been clear from *Salvatore Giuliano* and *Mani sulla Città* that Rosi would one day make a great film. The occasion presented itself with **Il Caso Mattei** (1972), which again takes the form of an investigation into the nature of power and its ally, corruption. Like *Giuliano*, it is as much a quest into the man's death as his life. Enrico Mattei, played in the film by Gian Maria Volonté, was a socialist and idealist who persuaded the Government to make use of the oil deposits in the Po Valley (against its will, for it was committed to an agrarian society and that had been a Fascist policy). From his efforts grew AGIP, the vast state-owned refining company, ample proof of his belief that the state should own its country's assets. As a state industry it offered advantageous terms to the oil-producing countries of the Third World, thus incurring the wrath of the competing capitalist oil companies. Mattei's singleness of purpose was a match for their deviousness, but the implication that one or other of them was involved in his death, in a mysterious air crash, is the whole point of the film. Its enquiry consists of the necessity of half-truths, conjectures, events conveniently forgotten, and even a sequence involving Rosi himself, finding himself stone-walled as he prepared this film. His thesis is dazzlingly worked out with regard to explanations of the complicated business and political relationships – and their expression in visual terms. The film is, he said, 'a critique and a commentary', adding, 'I believe that power should be constantly renewed before it has a chance to corrupt. And by corruption I do not necessarily mean evil but also doing nothing that might interfere with the pursuit of power. Keeping quiet, hushing up, if you like. I believe profoundly that there is something wrong, not only in the West, between the ordinary people and those who exercise authority over them in their name. And what is wrong is not just political but economic, cultural, religious, and military too.' He also observed that although Mattei himself was incorruptible he 'created around him an enormous amount of corruption because he wanted to hold on to power for the sake of his vision of the future'. Mattei's beliefs become meaningless unless we believe, as Rosi intended, that it is because of them he was done away with. Only hints are offered of the involvement of the Mafia (which did not care for an impoverished society becoming self-sufficient) and the C.I.A., neither of which are mentioned, and their links with American capitalism.

The film opened in America not long after it was officially admitted that the C.I.A. had been involved in assassination plots against certain world figures in attempts to prevent the spread of Communism. It was an almost total failure, a puzzling matter explained to some extent when we know that the distributor had lopped off the film's last ten minutes in order to destroy its anti-American stance. I happened to see the idiotic potted review in *The New Yorker*,★ particularly unfavourable towards the 'new' ending, and find it incredible that so influential a journal was apparently ignorant of the excision – especially as the film had attracted widespread comment in the world press when it had won the Grand Prix at Cannes. In Britain a number of reviewers, including the normally perceptive David Robinson in *The Times*, compared it with *Citizen Kane*, which is like comparing a well-loved novel with a report on one of the multi-national corporations – except of course that Rosi's film is considerably more riveting: but the actions of real-life press barons affect few of us, while the activities of the multi-nationals do. Rosi used the investigative form again in **Lucky Luciano** (1973), which has Volonté in the title role, Steiger in a sub-plot about another dubious Italo-American, and Edmond O'Brien as a U.N. man. The American names did not help the film in the States, nor did a commendation by Norman Mailer that this movie about the Mafia was 'the most careful, the most thoughtful, the truest, and the most sensitive to the paradoxes of a society of crime'. Actually the film damaged Rosi's reputation, since, by employing arbitrary time-shifts, he made it almost impossible to follow: Rosi's old narrative difficulty had returned in curious fashion.

Whether or not he has solved this problem, **Cadaveri Eccellenti** (1976) is a film so rich, so powerful and so absorbing that it leaves the spectator breathless. His visual style is extraordinary – as Russell Davies put it in *The Observer*: 'Few directors select their shots with such flamboyant intelligence as this.' The characters scurry in the shadows of the huge monuments of Church and state, dwarfed by baroque façades and grandiose staircases – undoubtedly in Italy though the setting is not identified. Police headquarters are vast and modern; the inspector (Lino Ventura) lives in a poky modern flat while the legal eagles

★This magazine has a reputation for being wrong about movies. Not only did it originally champion *Last Tango in Paris* and the films of Lina Wertmuller, all later discredited, but it had to withdraw its original annihilating caption review of *L'Avventura* as it became accepted as a classic. (In fact, *L'Avventura* has appeared in each of *Sight and Sound*'s once-in-a-decade polls of world critics of the Ten Best Films of all time since it was made.)

Italy: Traditions Maintained and Betrayed

The vagaries of foreign distribution – and, if it comes to that, foreign appreciation – are curious, and while Americans were applauding the films of Lina Wertmuller, regarded as worthless by virtually every European critic, they were given little or no chance to see either *Il Caso Mattei*, BELOW, with Gian Maria Volonté, or *Cadaveri Eccellenti*, LEFT, with Lino Ventura, standing. Both are 'political' film-makers, but where Wertmuller makes her few and very obvious points with the subtlety of a bulldozer, Rosi, in these two brilliant films, makes every line and detail politically allusive.

whose deaths he is investigating live in overstuffed apartments reeking, like the churches and halls of justice, of centuries past. This is a film, rare in the history of cinema, in which location – as opposed to decor – is a character in its own right, commenting upon the action. There is a sequence in Lina Wertmuller's *Pasqualino Settebelleze* which takes place in the Muzeo Nazionale in Naples, and like everything else in that film the setting is obtrusive, gimmicky and pointless: Rosi stages his finale in the same building, and it becomes relevant to the action. *Cadaveri* is slow-moving for a film which could be described as a thriller, but that suits Ventura's style as he doggedly pursues a homicidal maniac before realising that more important, political, forces are at work. From interviewing small-time crooks he moves to the bigwigs – a Minister (Fernando Rey), almost certainly involved in the later murders, and a High Court judge (Max von Sydow), denouncing Voltaire and denying the possibility of judicial error. Finally Ventura finds the responsible forces, and they belong not to the revolutionary party, as in the original novel by Leonardo Sciascia, but to the Communists.

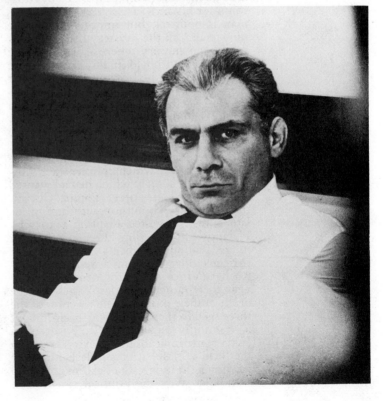

Rosi's starting point was the 'historical compromise', i.e. the alliance of the Christian Democrat and Communist Parties, and while he considered 'the C.P. the only uncorrupt party in power, the film shows that in the end it too has to take part in the maintenance of a certain political power.' When I expressed to him some disappointment that this merely meant that power corrupts, he responded that 'it has relevance to every European country with a strong Communist Party, for those Communists must, as in the film, find a democratic way to proceed.'

Invited by R.A.I., the state-owned television service, to select a subject for filming, Rosi chose the memoir by Carlo Levi, **Cristo si è Fermato a Eboli** (1979), cutting his four-part T.V. programme to a 141 minute movie of singular beauty, and since the form is experience-related rather than narrative no great harm seems to have been done. In moving from the political present to the past, Rosi has tried to explain the film as 'a journey through my own conscience', the experience of a backward rural region, Campania, by a city-bred intellectual (Volonté), exiled by Mussolini for his anti-Fascist views. Since this man is political, but impotently so, the film retains all the mystery of Rosi's best work – an enquiry where at least half the answers are withheld. In this enquiry there is a respect for the historical process, but the usual magisterial blend of art and dialectic is softened by a sympathy much deeper than that of *Il Momento della Verità*. The occasional self-conscious shot that we associate with peasantry cannot mar it.

Rosi remained in reflective mood in **Tre Fratelli** (1981), which concerns a Southern family, a subject which he had wanted to tackle for some time. Tonino Guerra, the customary co-author with him of his later films, suggested adapting a story by Platanov. In the film three brothers, a judge (Philippe Noiret), a factory-worker (Michele Placido) and a reform school teacher (Vittorio Mezzogiorno) return to visit their father (Charles Vanel) on the death of their mother. The reaction of the three men to their childhood environment is beautifully detailed, but Rosi's attempts to say something about urban terrorism, in the form of flashbacks and flash-forwards involving the judge, do not seem profound – though given the political situation in

Italy at this time his urge to make some comment is understandable. These two last films, incidentally, have received some acclaim in the U.S., but his two masterpieces, *Il Caso Mattei* and *Cadaveri Eccellenti*, remain little known there.

The sponsorship by R.A.I. of some of the country's best film-makers may seem curious to television executives elsewhere, their thoughts seldom rising above cops and robbers. The network does not expect huge ratings at home or great profits from overseas distribution, but believes that it is spending public money in the public interest. When R.A.I. entered **Padre Padrone** (1977) in the Cannes Festival, it drew attention to the work of the Taviani brothers, Vittorio (b. 1930) and Paolo (b. 1932); they wrote and directed it from an autobiographical novel by the self-educated Gavino Ledda, whose working life began as a lad herding goats in the mountains for his father – who represents all the *padre padrones* of peasant stock, initially unfeeling and later simply incapable of understanding the boy's need for learning. As a study of a young man's odyssey, or of deprivation, in Sardinia, this film is in the great tradition of Italian cinema, but is sufficiently rough and direct to suggest that the Tavianis were not looking backwards. It is touching and appropriate that one of the last actions of Rossellini, as president of the Cannes Festival, was to fight, successfully, for this film to be awarded the Grand Prix; he died a week later.

The Tavianis had begun as neo-realists, but seem to have broken away at about the time of their fourth film, in 1969. Their other best-known films, **Allonsanfa'n** (1974) and **La Notte di San Lorenzo** (1982), are made in much more florid style – and it is one, common in some of their compatriots, in which conviction and narrative are sacrificed to visual imagery and immediacy of situation. To judge by the martial theme music of both these polemical pieces they are a pair, concerning as they do political activists after the Restoration of 1816 and during the German retreat of 1944. The earlier film, which centres on a traitor (Mastroianni), grew from despair with the political situation, producing a climate – said Vittorio Taviani – leading to two opposing movements, 'one towards regression, the loss of self and of the world, and the other towards desire and the need to live with the world'. The view may be discerned in both films, if in more muddled form in the later one, and, coupled with the vitality with which they are made, they are eminently watchable; but *La Notte di San Lorenzo* is a retrogression from the films on the same subject made soon after the War.

The films of Marco Bellochio (b. 1939) have also proved uneven. He studied philosophy and cinema at the Centro Sperimentale, and for a while held a scholarship to the Slade School of Fine Arts in London. Both **I Pugni in Tasca** (1965) and **Nel Nome del Padre** (1973) are intensely Italian and Catholic, though their subjects – the family in the one and school in the other – are common to all of us. The family in *I Pugni in Tasca* consists of a blind mother, a daughter who is quarrelsome and possibly mad, and two younger sons, one of whom is an epileptic and the other mentally retarded; there is also an elder son (Marino Masè), the breadwinner and 'normal' – and it is for him that Bellochio reserves his contempt. One virtue of his approach is that he is not, like others who have treated the family as divisive, nihilistic; he works from the inside outwards, and his misfits are individually and lovingly conceived. The same is true of pupils and teachers in *Nel Nome del Padre*, but instead of the sustained invective of the earlier film he builds tension in a series of small vignettes. One leaves the cinema believing that someone's adolescence was like this – and glad to have experienced it at one remove. Bellochio's views are not entirely in accordance with our best hopes for the human race, and it is hardly surprising that he was drawn to Tchekov, in a version of 'The Seagull' made for R.A.I., *Il Gabbiano* (1977) – dark, Italianate and, in his own words, 'depressing', but as perceptive an interpretation of this comedy as we are likely to see. He would have done better to have remained with the classics, for the strife-ridden families of **Salto nel Vuoto** (1980) and **Gli Occhi, la Bocca** (1982) seem to be so for their own sake. Since the characters of both behave in absurd fashion, Bellochio's customary mysteries do not connect with life. At his best his excoriation of the second-rate takes him near to Antonioni, but with these two films he is of the level of Brusati.

That leaves Antonioni and Rosi, both pessimists, in the forefront of living Italian directors, along with the more cheerful Ermanno Olmi (b. 1931), humanist rather than polemicist. He has said (in an interview in *Sight and Sound*, 1970), 'Many of our men of culture who wish to express their ideas through the cinema, end by debasing the medium in this way: they put over their "message" in thrillers, erotic stories, romantic fables. This is not serious, indeed it is dishonest. I believe that one of the fundamental examples of absolute purity of culture is to be found in the Gospels . . .' One cannot imagine any of his confrères reaching for the Gospels, and in fact the prevailing tone of Italian cinema is anti-clerical: the clergy in Italian films tend to be either comic or like the hellfire shouting bigot of Vicario's *Mogliamante* – a far cry from the gentle parish priest of Olmi's *L'Albero degli Zoccoli* (q.v.). Olmi is not typical of Italian film-makers for he is neither 'intellectual' nor well-born, and he lives in a small town in the North of the country, believing that one of his strengths lies in his isolation from Cinecittà. In the polarisation of Italian thought since the War, he is now the only cinema representative – though Rosi's films have become increasingly humanist – of his side, drawn by instinct and upbringing rather than 'the hope of prolonging the feeling of solidarity with the working-class experienced during the Resistance', as Adrian Lyttelton put it in the *New Statesman* in 1979, speaking of the artists of the previous generation. Olmi says he makes films 'because I desire to talk about the reality of the times in which I live, in other words I desire to express ideas and propose them to the largest number of people': in the first part of the sentence we can see Zavattini's creed made a quarter of a century before, 'The important thing is to see.'

Zavattini's primary themes of earning a living, of coping, recur in all of Olmi's films. While working as a clerk for Edison Volta Olmi had persuaded the company to let him become involved with its industrial shorts and while doing so he conceived the idea for his first feature, **Il Tempo si è Fermato** (1959), about two men in a small encampment high in the Alpine snows, watching over an unfinished dam till work can recommence in the spring. One is probably in his forties and the other is a

Olmi, the True Heir of Neo-realism

Ermanno Olmi lives and works away from the mainstream of the Italian film industry, which may be why, after twenty years, his vision remains so fresh – or that may have something to do with his entry in the film industry. He was a mere clerk with the Edison company when he was rewarded with the official gift of a 16mm camera for his work with the firm's dramatic society – and he persuaded the company to put him in charge of the company's documentary films. *Il Posto*, BELOW RIGHT, his first 'commercial' film, was based on his experiences with Edison, as was the office-party sequence in *I Fidanzati*, RIGHT. Among his superb later films is *Il Recuperanti*, BELOW FAR RIGHT, about two men scavenging for metal embedded in the hills after wartime battles there. All the players are amateurs.

newcomer, perhaps a student, since he says that he plans to spend the winter studying. The film's subject is no more than their reaction to each other, in this admittedly strange environment. Neither is very communicative, but it is the younger man who makes tentative gestures of friendliness. Since there is no plot, Olmi should not have a climax, but he manages one – a particularly wild stormy night when the boy thinks he has 'flu: and all that happens is that the older man begins to feel fatherly towards him. The delicacy with which the film is handled is remarkable, its humour slight but memorable – as when each of the men takes a surreptitious peep at the other's book to see what he is reading. Also astonishing is Olmi's confidence that we might treasure the least emotion, the least detail of the daily grind, if it is presented sympathetically.

Il Posto (1961) is precisely about one man's first job, and it is confessedly autobiographical, clearly the reason it captures so accurately adolescent fears of interviews, the boss, colleagues. The piece is primarily a comedy, ironic rather than satirical, especially in the brilliantly observed office party. A coda finds the boy moving upwards in the office hierarchy, probably never to lose either aspirations or frustrations. The malevolent universe of the de Sica-Zavattini films was leavened by humour since there was no hope for their peasants in this world and precious little in the next, but Olmi uses his humour to show that his characters neither start nor finish despairingly. His world is not especially harsh and contains nothing like the venal businessmen of *Miracolo a Milano*: but increasingly in his films, as in Rosi's, there is a tension between the mere fact of existence and a world in which so much is beyond comprehension. His subject is not character, but experience, and in **I Fidanzati** (1963) his hero, Giovanni, looks about him in the same puzzled attempt at understanding as the young hero of *Il Posto*: he is a Northerner sent to work in Sicily and to him it is, at first, a very strange place.

E Venne un Uomo (1964) is firstly about a boy's experience of learning and later becomes a study in vocation – of a man very much open to the thoughts of others; but this tribute to Pope John XXIII is Olmi's one failure. Working, for the only time in his feature career, with a major collaborator – Vincenzo Labella, producer and co-scenarist – he devised a film part-documentary and part-dramatisation, with Rod Steiger, appearing humbly honoured to be present. But he remains a movie star, an unsuitable representative of John as priest or Pope: the commentary he speaks and the visuals which include him, move on different levels, and what should be a unifying force is in fact divisive, so that the spiritual struggles detailed in 'Journal of a Soul' – the source of the screenplay – remain resolutely beyond the film's grasp. Olmi blamed himself for the film's failure, believing the conception right but that it was a mistake to make a film which was 'all thought'. It was popular in Italy, but its failure elsewhere effectively closed most foreign markets to Olmi.

That failure may be the reason why in his subsequent films there is no longer any levity during the working day. Olmi refuses to satirise the advertising office which is the setting of **Un Certo Giorno** (1969): instead he concentrates on one man's quest for fulfilment – which means, firstly, an adjustment of his sense of guilt towards his wife and colleagues, and, secondly, attempts to avoid boredom. The theme, said Olmi, is 'that of a man responsible in the face of his own reality', and much of the film was improvised after he had watched the amateurs in the cast 're-creating' themselves; but it was, he said, not *'cinéma vérité*, in which you accept whatever reality is thrown at you. I was at the disposition of this particular reality and I provoked it to carry forward the theme that interested me.' The theme of **I Recuperanti** (1970) is that of *Il Tempo si è Fermato*, developed further, with greater disparity between the ages of the two men. They are scavengers, working in the mountains in search of scrap metal left from the battles of the First World War – and that was what the older actor had done in life. He had, said Olmi, 'that baggage of experience which the character we had "invented" in our script should carry with him. The real Toni then took over from our literary creation.' Since *I Recuperanti* is an affirmation, after the doubt of *Un Certo Giorno*, the old man's experience may have coloured the finished film more than intended. The time is hard and the terrain wayward, but the working alliance between the old man and his young apprentice, an army veteran (of the Second World War) is as enlivening for us as for them – no Zorba-like confrontation, nor is the old man Boudu, though Renoir comes fleetingly to mind while watching Olmi's films. Olmi has 'an unmistakable leaning towards the positive qualities of man's condition in a world prone to cynicism and destructive violence' was *Variety*'s touching comment on **Durante l'Estate** (1971), which, after the earlier films, is something of a confection. Its protagonist is an elderly drop-out who colours maps to turn an honest lira, living in what he describes as a world of colours – and that is his downfall, since he feels the same way about people, or some of them, and is ready to cater to their fantasies. His reality has nothing to do with the Milanese who scurry around him, but his view is examined and found valid before he is returned to obscurity.

Olmi's films are about the ability to see and to feel, which is why so many of them feature encounters with strangers or unexpected meetings with old friends. In **La Circostanza** (1974) several members of a family are forced into new perceptions. In dealing again with people of the middle class, Olmi discards affection and humour, thus moving closer to Antonioni's work; he has adopted a similarly elliptical style, but hardly seems comfortable with it. He may have realised this, since **L'Albero degli Zoccoli** (1978) – *The Tree of Wooden Clogs* – is the most literal of his films. It is based on stories he heard as a boy, and its key 'is the permanence of the relationship between God's land and the people who farm it'. It portrays a way of life now being eroded (by television, by the refusal of youngsters to stay on the land). It is likely that it could not have been made later, since by then recollections would have become third hand, and it could not have been made earlier because the old film-stocks do require artificial lighting which would have imposed a certain theatricality. For all the basis in fact, the film's courtship recalls that in *Due Soldi di Speranza*, though that may be because of the similarity of wooing habits; the ending – the banishment of the family – which resembles the 'hopeless' endings of the early neo-realist films, does have its roots elsewhere; the solidarity of the peasants is like

that of *Distant Thunder* (and Satyajit Ray has spoken of his debt to the neo-realists). The film, I think, lacks the flair of Sjöström's rural tales, but it is surely a beautiful counterpoint to most other retellings of the Italian past.

Frank Rich in *Time* was certain that Olmi was no fan of Bertolucci's *Novecento*, adding 'There is nothing wrong with Olmi's decision to avoid the contrivances of narrative and ideology, as long as he then goes on to reveal the truth about his characters. This he has not done.' Since that is something essential to Olmi's work up to then, he presumably had his reasons for not doing so on this occasion. He can be dangerously slow, and sometimes long-winded but, to use an analogy I think he might like, his films are like a church in which the lamps are being gradually lit: as the small lives he is examining will be illuminated. In *The New York Times*, Vincent Canby wrote a piece explaining why he could not yet be certain whether *L'Albero degli Zoccoli* was a masterpiece. I do not know either: but I have no reservations about *Il Posto, I Fidanzati, Un Certo Giorno, I Recuperanti* and *Durante l'Estate*. They are wonderful films.

Olmi had been backed, since *I Recuperanti*, by R.A.I., who were awarded a second consecutive Grand Prix at Cannes with *L'Albero degli Zoccoli* – thus ensuring distribution in the U.S. for Olmi for the first time after the failure of *E Venne un Uomo*. If America's lack of interest in Rosi's films has been because of their lack of sex – as John Francis Lane suggested in *Films and Filming* – then clearly Olmi would fare no better. It is easy enough to find sex in Fellini, Wertmuller and Bertolucci and easy enough to see that these are erratic film-makers. Their reputations, as I write, are no longer high: but if there are precedents for such judgments the reflection on the cinema culture of New York, crucial to the issue, is pretty damning.

One Italian director, Franco Zeffirelli (b. 1923) has made virtually all his films for American companies – or at least in English. A former assistant of Visconti, he was becoming established as an opera director when the Old Vic invited him to design and direct a production of 'Romeo and Juliet', which made his reputation. In 1967 he directed a film of *The Taming of the*

Franco Zeffirelli's *Romeo and Juliet*, with Michael York, left, as Tybalt and Leonard Whiting as Romeo. One reason that it was the best screen version of this particular play is that the younger generations of the Montagues and Capulets were indeed young, spirited and non-actorish.

Shrew, which he followed with **Romeo and Juliet** (1968), the first of the three English-language film versions to see it as a play about adolescents, and Italian adolescents at that; the marauding bands of Montagues and Capulets had become Renaissance versions of the youths in films like *La Notte Brava*. The leading roles are poorly spoken and performed, but the Romeo (Leonard Whiting) has an appropriately pubescent, dreamy look, and Juliet (Olivia Hussey) is at least physically adorable, small, doll-like and piquant. In compensation, the handling of the action is inventive and vigorously imaginative: Zeffirelli has made the climax Juliet's intimations of mortality, a child clasping the vial of poison in front of a vast four-poster. The rest is played out as if in a dream, the child-lovers out of their depth, and good as

it is, it is inevitably a disappointment after the buoyancy of the first half. Danilo Donati's costumes and Renzo Mongiardino's decor – a huge piazza and muralled rooms effectively disguise the fact that little of the film was made on location – contribute mightily to the only Shakespeare film to rank with Olivier's as a critical and box-office success.

Zeffirelli was accordingly encouraged to embark on a youth-orientated view of St Francis of Assisi, **Brother Sun, Sister Moon** (1972), but in that context English dialogue (e.g. 'You pathetic little creep!') and actors proved an initial handicap. The camera has so lovingly photographed their faces – and the lyrical countryside – that a mood of sensuality has been asserted even before St Francis strips coyly in the town's main square. It is quite feasible for an

Italian film-maker to see St Francis in this manner (instead of as an ascetic), but making him an exponent of Sixties 'flower-power' completes the miscalculations. The film failed so completely that Paramount were not interested in backing Zeffirelli again, so that he confined his work to the theatre till approached by two television companies, R.A.I. and the British I.T.C., to make a six-hour **Jesus of Nazareth** (1977), to be televised in two parts. With Laurence Olivier consenting to take part, a starry cast was assembled, to support the relatively unknown Robert Powell as Jesus, evidently chosen for his visible sanctity.

Apart from an emphasis on the Jewishness of its characters, this film looks like Sunday School stamps, with an occasional excursion into Renaissance painting. In *The Observer*, Clive James said, 'There is no vulgarity. There is no sensationalism. In fact it gradually dawns on you that there is not much of anything, except good taste . . . On the whole it can be said that this was a project well worth trying, especially when you consider how lousy those Hollywood Biblical epics used to be.' Yes: but two of those lousy movies were made by Stevens and Wyler, using their idea of good taste, and Pasolini's used his idea of 'imagination'. There are moments here – the gold and purple of the Court, the portrait of a fishing community, passion in an olive grove – which transcended such considerations; and there were other occasions, mainly brought about by the English dialogue of Anthony Burgess, which seemed to undermine the whole enterprise. Nevertheless it restored Zeffirelli to favour, and coinciding with M-G-M's invitation to make a film, he happened to catch on television one made by that company in 1931 which he rather foolishly decided to remake, **The Champ** (1979).

The T.V. showing re-awakened childhood traumas, he said, for as a child he had been shoved from pillar to post like the boy in the film. His version is sunny and pretty, well acted by Jon Voight in the title role and Ricky Schroder as the boy, with a manipulation of audience emotions in the final scene so shameless that children are liable to emerge in floods of tears. One might have respected it more if Zeffirelli, on a tour to promote it, had not spoken disparagingly of some infinitely more worthwhile films – *Kramer vs. Kramer* (q.v.) and *The China Syndrome* (q.v.).

If, in truth, Zeffirelli belongs only marginally to a consideration of Italian cinema, he remains more central to the mainstream of Italian culture, certainly with his opera productions and their painterly compositions. Italy in the second half of the twentieth century is a country riven by contradictions, not least in its being the most communist of Catholic Western democracies. The hill towns of Tuscany and Umbria remain unspoilt, but the marvellous centres of the old cities have to fight the encroachment of neon light and traffic, and their new suburbs of surpassing ugliness. Thus the Italian cinema: one half opts for the traditional and the other for the trashy – and it is the former which is by far the more contemporary.

39

British Cinema:
A Matter of Collusion

WHEN KORDA DIED in 1956 the British cinema virtually expired with him. The few independents left concentrated on B-movies, for which there was apparently a market, since Hollywood had all but abandoned making them. Production was otherwise mainly in the hands of the Rank Organisation, whose executives seemed capable of initiating only programme pictures to play in the company's own cinemas – which constituted almost two-thirds of those in the country. Rank's popular films were confined to some war movies and the series begun by *Doctor in the House* (q.v.) with Dirk Bogarde. When in the early Sixties the company reduced its activity to a handful of films annually its 'stars' literally disappeared from the screens. Their names had glowed from the marquees of several hundred Gaumonts and Odeons, yet with the exception of Bogarde, Peter Finch and a few others those who chose to stay in the profession could do so only by taking supporting roles.

Hollywood summoned none of them, but film directors found work there or in the American-financed movies made in Britain. American financiers, producers, stars and writers arrived regularly in Elstree and Pinewood to make 'British' pictures of local appeal and a great many more of supposed world appeal. The success of *The Bridge on the River Kwai* (q.v.) and *Tom Jones* (q.v.) was responsible for much of Hollywood's interest in British talent, but the lower costs and the quality of supporting players were considerable factors when producing costume pictures, since it was clear that audiences more readily accepted historic characters with British accents. There remained the

advantage of the British quota system, so that the Hollywood companies continued to maintain distribution offices in London; and the British, from every point of view, were glad of the patronage.

The American influx did not kill the indigenous British film, but what remained was hardly worth preserving – war films, trivial thrillers and comedies. With Ealing Studios almost defunct, comedy was in a depressed state, and I at least never found any virtue in the 'Carry On' series which began a twenty-year run with **Carry On, Sergeant** (1958), a harmless service stage farce so renamed. A talented group of eccentric comedians was embroiled in increasingly salacious situations, devoid of wit but heavy with humour – not that much of that survived the clumsy handling.

Another military comedy, **Private's Progress** (1956), is a rehash of similar japes of the war years, complete to the gormless private (Ian Carmichael) parachuted behind German lines. But the picture was memorable among all the other officer-encrusted British movies by portraying for the first time the officers as just as venal and stupid as the men they commanded; they included Terry-Thomas, whose permanently outraged major is a thing of beauty. These two actors, together with Dennis Price and Richard Attenborough, played their roles again in **I'm All Right Jack** (1959), also adapted from a novel by Alan Hackney and produced by the Boultings, with brother John directing. This examined the further progress of the Carmichael character, in the postwar world, working in a factory and being manipulated by his former officers for their own selfish ends. Carmichael has been befriended by a union leader (Peter Sellers), who approves of 'intellectuals' like him and whose greatest wish is to go to Russia. Sellers is brilliant: his Kite is defensively shifty-eyed, uncertain of his vowels – and indeed of anything he says – as he attempts an accent which is not posh but which conceals his origins.

The Boultings were said to have 'taken on' the unions, but the film, though occasionally amusing, is smug, slackly scripted and conventional. The same may be said of their other attempts at satire, also supposedly at the expense of British authoritarian institutions. **Brothers in Law** (1957), directed by John Boulting, finds Carmichael, Attenborough and Terry-Thomas in the legal profession, and **Carleton-Browne of the F.O.** (1959), directed by Jeffrey Dell and Roy Boulting, pits Terry-Thomas, a particularly dense diplomat, against Sellers, the wily native prime minister of one of Britain's forgotten colonies. **Heavens Above!** (1963) has the charming idea of a parson – Sellers in another of his fine performances – whose innate goodness is mistaken for naivety by the worldly clerics and scheming local politicos who surround him; but the film offers the standard Boulting brothers' comic solution to the dilemmas of their earnest Capraesque heroes: the breakdown of law and order. They had used that effectively in their thriller, *Seven Days to Noon*, and to little purpose in *I'm All Right Jack*, which also portrays the usual band of smarty businessmen in league to bring down the proles. These are right-wing movies posing as left-wing movies, and the most shameful of them is **Lucky Jim** (1957), because its source is of different mettle from those of the other movies. Kingsley Amis's novel, a broadside taken at the academic world, was seminal, its hero – played in the film by Carmichael – caught in the crossfire of class and culture. Such predecessors as Orwell and Priestley had chosen to understate the dislike between the classes, but Lucky Jim responded by comforting himself with beer and inner sarcasm, and building a dream world in which the enemy – the phoneys and the pseuds on the faculty – falls flat on its collective face. That aspect of the novel was all that the Boultings understood, and they used it only too literally, so that the revolutionary literary movement of which

Amis was a part was not for the moment to affect the British film industry.

Launder and Gilliat made a cheery version of Amis's second novel, 'That Uncertain Feeling', retitled **Only Two Can Play** (1961) and directed by Gilliat from a screenplay by Bryan Forbes. It is clear that they were attracted to Amis's stereotypes, such as nagging landladies and local flirts, and the many jokes about breasts; the result is a sour, but accurate, portrait of provincial life. Peter Sellers is the disaffected hero, a librarian, and the pseuds this time are local literary men who write symbolic verse plays. Unhappily, the later films of Launder and Gilliat are disappointing, but they were responsible for **The Smallest Show on Earth** (1957), a pleasing and often hilarious comedy about a young couple (Virginia McKenna, Bill Travers) running a flea-pit cinema which shakes as the trains go by. Aided by the inebriated projectionist (Sellers) and the venerable cashier (Margaret Rutherford), they counter the attraction of the local supercinema with old flicks with such titles as 'Killer Riders of Wyoming'. William Rose and John Eldridge wrote it, from Rose's story, and Basil Dearden directed. The break-up of Ealing had pushed its alumni out into the cold, and it was Dearden's customary producer, Michael Relph, who had persuaded Launder and Gilliat to sponsor it.

Sellers was also seen to advantage in **The Wrong Arm of the Law** (1963), as a seedy London gang operator working under the cover of a French couturier. The film, however, belongs to Lionel Jeffries as a Scotland Yard man of sublime obtuseness, pleased as punch with his guile and his suspicions, and desperately sycophantic towards his superiors. This is one of the last and best of the variations on *The Lavender Hill Mob*, as directed by Cliff Owen, whose later attempts to put television comics through their screen paces have little of the finesse shown on this occasion.

Among the film's seven credited writers were Alan Simpson and Ray Galton, whose radio and television scripts had done so much to establish the comic persona of Tony Hancock (1924–68). They wrote, and Robert Day directed, **The Rebel** (1961), the only film to embody that persona – though, as *Call Me Genius*, it

British Cinema: A Matter of Collusion

was a failure in the U.S. Intended as a satire on *The Moon and Sixpence*, the result is flatfooted – for instance, the regimentation of office life had been better done in many other movies – but Hancock is superb as a Sunday painter shakily convinced of his gifts. His landlady (Irene Handl) sees his daubs for what they are, but what would a landlady, detested breed, know of art? He nods sagely, if uncomprehendingly, at mention of Renoir or Cézanne, in turn not expecting his own idiotic comments on art to be any better understood; and thus with deceit practised on both sides he becomes the darling of the *rive gauche*. When praised, he offers a mock-modest shrug, certain that the world is finally coming to its senses; checked, he offers a fish-eye stare, desperately unsure as to whether the twerp before him is, after all, right. His fleeting doubts about his abilities, his subterfuges and his lies make him the most human of the self-obsessed. Offered an absurd price for a painting, he says 'Why resist fate?' – fate being as consistently fascinating as himself. Since he always expected to be exposed, he is not surprised to find his time in the sun so short, so he

retires to wait again for the world's call. In Hancock's only other starring film, **The Punch and Judy Man** (1963), directed by Jeremy Summers, he plays a resort entertainer married to a silly social climber – Sylvia Sims miscast in a role requiring the British equivalent of those ladies who played wife to W. C. Fields – which brings him into contact with a number of civic dignitaries. Whereas at other times he excelled at deflating the pompous, Hancock muffs it here; it is painful to see him struggling with this material, particularly as it cuts across the character Galton and Simpson created for him. He had rejected their script in favour of one by himself and the critic Philip Oakes; the film's failure, in conjunction with the American rejection of *The Rebel*, were factors which eventually led to his suicide.

Of the war films churned out by the plane load, the most popular were **The Dam Busters** (1955), directed by Michael Anderson, and **Reach for the Sky** (1956), directed by Lewis Gilbert. Both were adapted from factual R.A.F. exploits as put into book form by Paul Brickhill. The earlier movie details the experiments of

Barnes Wallis (Michael Redgrave) in devising a missile to bounce along the waters of the three dams which supplied the Ruhr, together with the subsequent bombing mission, led by Wing Commander Guy Gibson (Richard Todd); its superiority over other films of the genre is due to the intelligent and beautifully organised screenplay by R. C. Sherriff. It has a craftsmanship and a sense of pride lacking from *Reach for the Sky*, which does disservice to its hero, Squadron Leader Douglas Bader, a legless pilot readmitted to the R.A.F. on the outbreak of war, and a later inmate of Colditz. No one involved seems to understand what motivated him – except Kenneth More, playing Bader, and the film would be unbearable without him, with his breezy, easy way, his warm broad grin and his patent sincerity. The film may be bracketed with *Going My Way* and *The Sound of Music* as an instance of a likeable performer modifying mawkish intentions.

The biggest financial success of the decade was an Anglo-American war film, **The Bridge on the River Kwai** (1958), which was produced by Sam Spiegel, directed by David Lean and written by two Americans, Carl Foreman and Michael Wilson (though, since both were still on Hollywood's blacklist, the screenplay was credited to Pierre Boulle, author of the original novel). They were rewarded for their efforts by a total of seven Oscars, and, it would be nice to say, the contempt of the men who worked on the Kwai bridge and the Siam railway – but according to a B.B.C. documentary on the subject the survivors were unanimous in considering the film too unimportant to be repudiated. Sixteen thousand Europeans and one hundred thousand Asians died, a matter on which the film is completely silent; the malaria, beri-beri and cholera of reality are unmentioned in what appears to be an Eastern version of the *Club Méditerranée*. In fact the officers joined the men as white coolies, both because they felt it only right to do so and were threatened by machine guns if they did not: in the film the British commander (Alec Guinness) is prepared to die for the Geneva rule that P.O.W.s of commissioned rank must not do manual work and is cheered for his stand by the men – which reveals a profound ignorance of British service mentality. The cast includes William Holden and

Jack Hawkins, but the performances are uninteresting except for those by Sessue Hayakawa as the Japanese commander, digging beneath the yellow peril level of the writing, and James Donald, combining intelligence with the obligatory stiff upper lip. His famous final comment, 'Madness . . . madness', as the bridge is blown up, comes oddly after the schoolboy heroics and pretty jungle photography.

The great Japanese war films then being produced were not known in the West, but it is worth considering the extent to which the French and Italians had revitalised cinema by the time Lean and Spiegel made **Lawrence of Arabia** (1962) – especially as the notices throughout the world endorsed its makers' estimate of its importance. They had passed up Rattigan's recent play on Lawrence, 'Ross', for a screenplay by Robert Bolt,★ then best known for his play 'A Man for All Seasons'. Lawrence had fascinated film-makers since Lowell Thomas's magic lantern lectures during his lifetime, and in 1936 Korda, planning a film biography, had put the actor Walter Hudd under contract because of his physical resemblance. At another time Leslie Howard was to have played Lawrence, and twenty years later Rank projected a version with Dirk Bogarde, written by Rattigan – which became 'Ross' when the film was cancelled (that play was purchased during its West End run by Herbert Wilcox for £100,000, a fact which contributed to his bankruptcy, for Lean's film killed any prospect of his making it). During this time Richard Aldington's 1955 biography had somewhat tarnished the Lawrence legend, and Bolt's literal script pays lip-service to the revelations therein – that Lawrence was six-tenths poseur and even more partisan in the Arab cause after being sodomised in a Turkish jail. Such suggestions were heady among the empty spectacles of the time, but the film eventually concludes that Lawrence was a hero who became a nuisance to both the British and the Arabs – unless, that is, the grimaces in which Peter O'Toole indulges are meant to express paranoia. The action sequences are expertly handled and Lawrence's fascination with the desert is powerfully communicated by F. A. Young's colour photography.

★A decade later, Bolt's then-current play on Mary, Queen of Scots, was passed over as the source of a film (q.v.) on her.

1103

Young's photography may be all you care to remember of **Doctor Zhivago** (1965), a further collaboration of Bolt and Lean, this time for Carlo Ponti and M-G-M. Boris Pasternak's novel had been a news item, a piece of merchandise, a holy tabernacle, its reception not uninfluenced in the West by its being banned in Russia, the author's incarceration and his reputation as heir to Tolstoi; but on screen his story emerges as a half-cocked version of *War and Peace*, shaping the Russian Revolution into the usual pattern of unrest, war and adjustment. Facile remarks are dropped about equality being best and of the necessity of sweeping away the old order; the 'people' seem composed of *tricoteurs* borrowed from antique movies about the French Revolution; and, in the end, none of the problems facing a capitalist film on this subject are resolved. Spain, Finland and Canada deputised for Russia, but Lean often settles for mere effect – as with the ice-house, as perfect in its way as Miss Havisham's cobwebbed dining room in *Great Expectations*. With the exception of Julie Christie, warm and spirited as Zhivago's true love, and Rod Steiger, as the commissar who vainly loves her, the performances are poor. In the title role Omar Sharif's spaniel-eyes mirror less centuries of suffering than a soppy bedside manner, while Ralph Richardson, shouting 'Oh no, not another purge!' is ludicrous. The film was even more popular than its predecessors, which meant that Lean had been responsible for drawing more money into the box office than any other individual director. Since his early films are so striking, it was sad to see him engaged on these museum pieces. At any given moment **Ryan's Daughter** (1970) is exquisitely made, but it is a terrible film. Its miscalculations start with Bolt's screenplay, a vehicle for his then wife, Sarah Miles, an inadequate actress. A wisp of a plot places her as the Scarlett O'Hara of the Emerald Isle, in 1916, being unfaithful to her schoolteacher husband (Robert Mitchum) with a British officer (Christopher Jones). The film lasts 3 hours 26 minutes, heavy with effects and 'atmosphere', some of it borrowed from German Silents, as when the villagers mock the woman or the village idiot (John Mills, who is embarrassing). Lean has let the old blarney interfere with his judgment, and this born film-

maker is no longer able to recognise a cliché; a foolish screenplay encourages him to pander to his increasing proclivity towards grandiloquence. The film cost M-G-M $14 million, and brought in just over that amount at the American box office. Lean has not filmed since, due to the apparent cost of a project on the *H.M.S. Bounty* affair, which he had finally to abandon, but he is reported to be preparing *A Passage to India*.

His leading British contemporary, Carol Reed, emerged less fortunately from Hollywood backing. **The Key** (1958) continued his run of disappointing films, a trivial – and unatmospheric – wartime romance, with Sophia Loren as a girl whose doorkey is passed from one rescue boat captain to another. Carl Foreman's script makes small noises on the disillusion and degradation wrought by war but does not make its point; and it fails as a love story as neither Loren nor William Holden is interesting on this occasion. It is all the more regrettable therefore that Trevor Howard is killed at the end of the first hour. The sea sequences are magnificently handled, but with the inroads now being made by younger film-makers Reed's approach could be seen to be more impersonal than ever. Of his last half-dozen films he made only two of interest. **Our Man in Havana** (1959) lacks the élan of his earlier collaborations with Graham Greene, who adapted it from his own serio-comic novel about a vacuum-cleaner salesman inducted into the British secret service. In the role Alec Guinness substitutes Mr Polly for the drab and obsessive original, and the film is further weakened by Burl Ives, as a former Jewish refugee from Hitler, and Jo Morrow as the ingenue. But there are three superb performances: Noël Coward as the reptilian recruitment agent, Ralph Richardson as the dim, hide-bound Ministerial figure, and Ernie Kovacs as the local police chief; all of them bring a rare humour to the cat-and-mouse game. **Oliver!** (1968) is based on a British musical which succeeded on Broadway, a bastardisation of Dickens with a comic-lovable Fagin, given to ditties like 'You've Got to Pick a Pocket or Two', and orphans whose emaciated appearance and wistful rendering of 'Food, Glorious Food' is belied by their subsequent dance. The film won an Oscar for Best Picture and another for Best

Direction – the latter surprisingly justified. Reed's understanding of the medium and of Dickens are much in evidence; he had not been so artfully employed since *Kipps* almost twenty years earlier. He follows Lean's *Oliver Twist* only in his use of the decor, demonstrating a lighter touch and swinging easily back and forth from songs to dialogue. Unquestionably editing can help a director in these matters, but when a derivative score, tiresome choreography and a lacklustre cast can cheer an audience, that is as clear an evidence of a director's skill as one may find.

A few truly British films deserve mention before we look at the bulk of Anglo-American co-productions. One of the best is **A Night to Remember** (1958), at a cost of £640,000 the most expensive Rank film since *Caesar and Cleopatra*. John Davis, the head of Rank, was not enthusiastic about the project, but consented because Walter Lord's book had been a bestseller on both sides of the Atlantic. Using an understatement appropriate to the title, Lord had set down the details of that particular night when the unsinkable Titanic went down – a matter which caught the imagination of the world and has held it ever since. Eric Ambler's screenplay selects the most telling and ironic details, as well as adding some representative ones. Kenneth More was a sensible choice to play the first mate, Lightoller, who emerged from Lord's account as a natural hero and hugely likeable. 'I'll never be sure of anything again', are his last words. The film is never sufficiently nightmarish, but it is often moving, as when the ship's architect (Michael Goodliffe) realises that it is going to sink. Of the half-dozen films on this subject this remains the best, despite only workmanlike direction by Roy Baker.

Another untypical film to appear from Rank was **Victim** (1961), featuring Dirk Bogarde as a married lawyer forced to realise that an occasional fling does not make him an occasional gay: 'I wanted him, I tell you, I *wanted* him,' he screams at his wife. As in Proust, many of the characters are eventually revealed as homosexual, but what is most incredible is that it is not the affluent, eminent lawyer who is blackmailed but his young, impoverished lover. It was not unwise to present this particular subject for the first time to the British public as a thriller, following a

similar approach in *Sapphire*, a mystery with a race angle made by the same team – producer Michael Relph, director Basil Dearden and writer Janet Green, all of them earnest and glum. The subject was topical, in the light of the Wolfenden Report recommending changes in the laws against homosexuality, and Bogarde is on record as believing that the film was as much responsible as the report for the eventual change. That it was made at all was due to the new awareness in British films fostered by Woodfall (q.v.), but the subject matter was the only novelty in this well-intentioned but simplistic movie.

Alec Guinness also attempted, with the co-operation of director Ronald Neame and the backing of United Artists, to turn British films away from the War and footling comedy. Both **The Horse's Mouth** (1959) and **Tunes of Glory** (1960) are adaptations of novels, by, respectively, Joyce Cary, with a screenplay by Guinness himself, and James Kennaway, who wrote his own. Both are Ealing-influenced in their ardour for British eccentricity, and the tone of the Cary film may be judged from its frisky reworking of Prokofiev's already sprightly Lieutenant Kije Suite. Its thesis of an artist's right to indulgence in a philistine world provokes individual reaction – positively in the case of his paintings ('doubled' by John Bratby) but much less so in the case of Guinness's stubble-chinned painter, better at scrounging than expressing his love affair with the palette. *Tunes of Glory* is much more impressive. Beyond its Hugh Walpole-like conflict between two responsible men unable to understand each other, it is a nimble study of the military mind and such related matters as the mystique of the Regiment, in this case a Highland one in its peacetime mess. Guinness never immersed himself so deeply as in this role of the red-headed Scots colonel, with his bluster, his awkwardness, his goodness, his conceit and his lack of intelligence. The more interesting role is that of the university-trained disciplinarian, but John Mills so over-acts that he dissipates the conflict at the core of the film, to its consequent detriment.

Neame, not the toughest of directors, nevertheless has a certain grace when confronted with a congenial subject. **I Could Go On Singing** (1963) is the last screen work of Judy Garland, playing herself to an uncomfortable degree, a lady of accomplishment and fame, temperamental, selfish, unreliable, and treated as a spoilt child by her secretary (Aline MacMahon) and manager (Jack Klugman). That she makes us care is due to her extraordinary talent; the vulnerability of her youth has not left her, and though her one over-riding resistible quality in life at this time was self-pity, she can tear at your heart with her denunciation of her life as entertainer. 'I can't be spread so thin . . . It's just not worth all the deaths I have to die.' Neame achieves, otherwise, a welcome informality in this dated tale of an American star trying to regain the love of her young, British son. And he might have got nearer the electricity of a Garland concert, in the Palladium sequences, had she had better songs. His weaknesses are more apparent in **The Prime of Miss Jean Brodie** (1969), in which Muriel Spark's serpent-beneath-the-velvet wit has been prettied up and conventionalised, admittedly with the help of Jay Presson Allen, who had made a hit play from Spark's novel. Miss Brodie (Maggie Smith) is a Scottish teacher believing passionately in art and fascism; her favouritism, her opinionated manner, her contempt for the curriculum and the headmistress (Celia Johnson) bring about her downfall – a matter of nuance in the book, and pure melodrama in this movie. Spark's Miss Brodie was oddly moving – as was Vanessa Redgrave in the stage version – but this one, nary a hair out of place, is not. The film is stolen by Celia Johnson, playing a waiting game with humour and little ticks of malevolence. The material is sufficiently unusual for one to be grateful that Neame was in charge, rather than a lesser director, but he shows little feeling for either the period (the Thirties) or Spark's ironies. And he should never have allowed an ending opposed to hers, which makes quite clear that Miss Brodie is not to be admired.

Acknowledgment should be made of Neame's greatest success, **The Poseidon Adventure** (1972), made in Hollywood for 20th Century-Fox. At first one suspects a remake, forty years on, of Fox's *Transatlantic*, which is a masterpiece compared with this screenplay as written by Stirling Silliphant and Wendell Mayes from a novel by Paul Gallico. It follows the adventures of a particularly uninteresting bunch of people (including Gene Hackman, Shelley Winters and Carol Lynley) trapped in a liner capsized on the ocean-bed, and is at once so old fashioned and unconvincing that its popularity surprised everyone, including its makers. It is not so much directed as organised.

Like Neame, Anthony Asquith continued to choose above-average material, and **Orders to Kill** (1958) is not only the best of his later films, but the best British war movie of the period. The material is slightly doubtful, for Donald Downes's original novel claimed to be based on fact, which is not entirely true; but in Paul Dehn's screenplay it makes both a good thriller and a drama of conscience, as a young American (Paul Massie) is secreted into Paris to assassinate a mild man suspected of being a traitor to the Resistance.

Returning to Shaw, Asquith made **The Doctor's Dilemma** (1959), the seventh full-length Shaw play to reach the screen. It concentrates on the Dubedats (Leslie Caron, Dirk Bogarde) at the expense of the medical profession, which is a pity in view of the faultless interpretations of Cutler Walpole (Alastair Sim), Sir Patrick (Felix Aylmer) and Dr Blenkinsop (Michael Gwynn). Anatole de Grunwald's adaptation omits the question of whether artists are subject to the same laws as other mortals, and we might have had guidance on the issue of whether humanity would be served by saving Louis, had we been shown even one of his paintings. De Grunwald also produced Asquith's last two features, **The V.I.P.s** (1963) and **The Yellow Rolls-Royce** (1964), which, written by another old colleague, Terence Rattigan, and with all-star Anglo-American casts, were by far the most successful they made. Both have episodic narratives, and the second of the two is feeble; but *The V.I.P.s*, a 'Grand Hotel' set at Heathrow airport, has its moments, most endurably with Rod Taylor and Maggie Smith, as an Australian businessman and his timid but ever-loving secretary. Reinforced by the confidence of these players, the writing and direction are surer than elsewhere in the film, while Margaret Rutherford is in her element as a batty duchess.

There are British directors of this period whose patronage by Hollywood is more curious, and we looked at some of their films in the last Hollywood chapter. The following are chiefly British, if not British-financed, and are listed here because of the success they achieved in the international market. **Those Magnificent Men in Their Flying Machines** (1965) is an aerial, period version of *It's a Mad, Mad, Mad, Mad World*, with a bunch of heavyweight comics, some American, with jokes to match. Its subject is a promising one – international rivalry to make the first London-Paris flight – and it is often visually rewarding. Despite a healthy profit (it cost $5 million and took almost three times that in the U.S. alone), 20th Century-Fox declined a second outing with director Ken Annakin and writer Jack Davies, which was eventually made by a Franco-Italian consortium and distributed by Paramount, who called it **Monte Carlo or Bust** (1969) in Britain and *Those Daring Young Men in Their Jaunty Jalopies* in the U.S. That it is marginally the better of the two films is due to the presence of Peter Cook and Dudley Moore as two Britons with unbounded confidence in the British; the joy of both films is Terry-Thomas as a dastardly baronet who will stop at nothing to win. Paramount withdrew from **The Battle of Britain** (1969) during pre-production, and as presented by United Artists there is little evidence of the reputed £12 million budget, except in the presence of a dozen leading stars, including Laurence Olivier, Kenneth More, Susannah York, Trevor Howard and Michael Caine. There is also little sense of period as directed by Guy Hamilton; in this case the film did not perform particularly well at the American box office.

One of its two producers was Harry Saltzman, the driving economic force behind Woodfall Films and, with Albert Broccoli, responsible for the movies featuring the adventures of Ian Fleming's secret-service man, James Bond. Saltzman is a Canadian and Broccoli an American who had also worked in Britain for some years, as a partner in Warwick Films. Warwick had resolutely sought popularity by importing rather *passé* Hollywood names to star in such 'action' movies as *Zarak*, *Interpol* and *Safari* and, in view of decreasing public interest, was about to give up the ghost when Broccoli and Saltzman signed an agreement with United Artists to make a series of films about Bond,

James Bond in a typical situation, in *Diamonds are Forever* (1971), directed by Guy Hamilton and the Bond, of course, is Sean Connery. Connery was Bond in the first film drawn from the secret agent thrillers by Ian Fleming, but after disputes with the producers about his fee was replaced for one film by George Lazenby, an Australian model, and permanently by Roger Moore. Moore is almost certainly closer to the Bond of Fleming, who publicly endorsed Connery while privately deploring the casting. But Connery is the only Bond: he grew into the role while Moore, in his own words, is a 'plastic' actor.

provided that the first one was successful. Although Fleming's snobbish thrillers had been praised and their sales were improving with each publication, other producers had hesitated. **Dr No** (1962) was made on a medium budget, and there was no indication during the first weeks of its release, to indifferent response, that business would pick up to make it the first of the most successful series in cinema history.★

Fleming's formula was as old as movies: an ersatz Mabuse, now prepared to use nuclear arms in his bid for world domination; a deadly tarantula or so borrowed from a modern Fu Manchu; and a hero for whom women fall like nine-pins. Bond is the sort of man who reads *Playboy*, with his taste in cocktails and clothes meticulously detailed. He is less fussy about his women, satisfying them quickly before jetting out to the next exotic locale and on occasion (like Sam Spade) bedding down with women he knows to be his mortal foes. Apart from its Caribbean setting, *Dr No* seemed one step up from a B picture, and dowdier than it might have been because of its Bond, Sean Connery, a minor actor chosen in desperation after a number of names had turned down the role. As long as he played the role he lacked suavity, but he was to gain greatly in authority and humour.

★Though we may now suppose it to be overtaken by *Star Wars* (q.v.) and its sequels.

British Cinema: A Matter of Collusion

As popularity increased to a phenomenal degree, the Bond films became an annual event, each more expensive than the one before, and eventually having plots unconnected with the Fleming novels after which they were titled. Gimmickry was all, and probably the chief credit for the series belongs to Ken Adam, the production designer, or, in the case of **You Only Live Twice** (1967) John Stears, in charge of special effects. Bond, for instance, has a 'do it yourself' helicopter equipped with flame-throwers that can turn corners; the climax takes place in an atomic warship – claimed to be the largest set ever built for a movie – underneath a false lake in an extinct volcano. Any enthusiasm I, personally, felt was muted by the mercilessly methodical way the film was put together; as the mechanical devices abound and the killings mount, I sit glassy-eyed, wishing I were elsewhere, wondering about the dubious morality whereby named powers (Russia, China) struggle for control of the world with nuclear weapons. The success of the films perhaps reflects the paranoia of the nuclear age, with villains reduced to 'oily peril' types, and an intrepid, indestructible Britisher to put them in their place, which is of course the cold, cold ground. This particular Bond film was written by Roald Dahl, the only writer of any distinction to be employed on the series; the director was Lewis Gilbert, while Terence Young directed *Dr No*. Guy Hamilton is the other director most closely associated with the series, and it is not unkind to assume that they were employed less for their reputation as accomplished film-makers than for their ability to manipulate the weaponry involved.

Saltzman alone produced **The Ipcress File** (1965), from the novel by Len Deighton, whose Cockney secret agent, Harry Palmer (Michael Caine), was supposedly the antithesis of Bond. Sidney J. Furie directed this complot of red herrings, with more efficiency than most of the Bond directors managed. Two further Harry Palmer adventures failed to hold the public, but Bond marched on, with Roger Moore filling Connery's shoes after a conflict over his fee. Neither played Bond in **Casino Royale** (1967), based on the Fleming novel to which Broccoli and Saltzman did not hold the rights, since those were already owned by Charles K. Feldman.

When negotiations between both parties broke down it was found that most stars refused to invite comparison with Connery, so the film became a gigantic spoof with several stars, including David Niven and Woody Allen, sharing the role of Bond. The direction was shared between John Huston, Ken Hughes, Val Guest, Robert Parrish and Joe McGrath, but any competition between them was destructive, for the film belongs decisively in the category of those which tried to kill the cinema, along with *Candy* and *The Magic Christian*, its contemporaries.

Lewis Gilbert directed **The Greengage Summer** (1961), a likeable tale set, as the credits put it, in the green and gold champagne district of France. Based on Rumer Godden's novel, it tells of an abandoned adolescent (Susannah York), the debonair and mysterious Englishman (Kenneth More) on whom she gets a crush, and the lesbian-inclined hotel proprietress (Danielle Darrieux). **Alfie** (1966) concerns a Cockney tearaway (Michael Caine) who uses women as some people use Kleenex, until he gets his comeuppance, and is finally deserted. Bill McNaughton's dialogue shows the benificent influence of those scripts written by Galton and Simpson for Hancock: but if his original play was unexceptional in its morals the material makes an objectionable film, in which Gilbert's direction oscillates between *Carry On* salaciousness in the comic scenes and Aeschylian gloom to underline any point. The film's popularity was due in part to Caine, probably the first true Cockney screen hero.

Among the films which have paved the way for the lack of morals evident in *Alfie* is **I Am a Camera** (1955), adapted from John van Druten's play based on 'Sally Bowles', one of Christopher Isherwood's Berlin stories. Despite the play's success in New York, Sally's alley-cat habits had prevented any Hollywood studio from buying the rights, so they were purchased by a British company, which, in an attempt to get the M.P.A.A. approval, to ensure showings in the U.S., decreed that Sally should change her mind and not go ahead with an abortion – but it was to no avail. Nevertheless, like *The Moon Is Blue*, some American theatres booked the film, but it is hardly better than that as directed by Henry Cornelius, showing little insight into the Berlin of the period or the character of the male lead, played by Laurence Harvey. As on Broadway, Julie Harris is Sally, extravagant, reckless and somewhat tatty; this movie would be unendurable without her.

A more elevated tale, **Sons and Lovers** (1960), was produced by an American, Jerry Wald, in his bid to bring culture to the masses; but since the novel in question does not exactly have a riveting plot, its justification would have to be the re-creation of Lawrence's world – which was entrusted to Jack Cardiff, directing, and Gavin Lambert and T. E. B. Clarke, who wrote the script. The mining village on the edge of the moors is well-found; there are some family snapshots – Christmas, father in the tin bath – and a whiff of the suffragette movement and contemporary attitudes to sex. As the father, even as diminished into a half-crusty lovable, Trevor Howard excels; but as Paul, Dean Stockwell is no more than a Hollywood leading man and as mother, Wendy Hiller signals her emotions as to a West End gallery.

Peter Ustinov's **Billy Budd** (1962) is technically one of the best of sea films, excellent on the physical details and balanced on the matter of above and below decks. As director and collaborator on the screenplay, Ustinov keeps soberly and thoughtfully to Melville, but weakens after the death of Claggart (Robert Ryan) because of a quirk of casting – his own performance as the captain, established as far too reasonable to stand by the letter of the law. (He only played the role as a way of getting another 'name' into the cast without paying much for it; Allied Artists, backing it to the tune of $1,400,000, remained unenthusiastic.) Of the excellent cast Terence Stamp is fittingly impressive as Billy, and nothing else in the film is quite as good as his night-time conversation with Claggart, where the purity of the one and the evil of the other are beautifully balanced, with Claggart's strange psychology only implied.

Another distinguished sea story, **A High Wind in Jamaica** (1965) was less fortunate, apparently due to loss of nerve on the part of the director, Alexander Mackendrick, and his writers. Richard Hughes's ecstatic adventure is about some children who, taken prisoner by pirates, not only retain their self-possession but take readily to cruelty since it has been part of their fantasy world and they are unable to separate that from reality. The eldest girl uses her sexuality, both knowingly and subconsciously, when she falls ill; but all of this has become a tale of a gruff old pirate captain (Anthony Quinn) stirred by a sick child.

The most famous American star to film in Britain was Marilyn Monroe, who started **The Prince and the Showgirl** (1957) in a blaze of publicity, having persuaded Laurence Olivier to direct and co-star with her in her own production, with Warners to distribute. Terence Rattigan's screenplay was adapted from his own mock-Ruritanian comedy, 'The Sleeping Prince', which on stage had been no more than a showcase for Sir Laurence and Vivien Leigh, whose role Monroe played – an American chorus girl hired to keep company with a visiting royal. The publicists' dream turned sour as her unpunctuality and rudeness to Olivier turned the set into one of hostility (years later he gallantly tried to explain her behaviour by saying that she loved being a model and star, but dreaded acting). It says much for him that she seldom acted more resourcefully or looked more beautiful, and his own performance is a triumph. The Prince is an ageing roué, a man with a heart for something beneath the call of duty, but not much of a heart – and it is a performance which calls to mind that of Gustav Gründgens in *Liebelei*, who at one point in his career had been known as Germany's Olivier. The film itself starts sparklingly, but it is hardly surprising that the final scenes seem perfunctorily treated. One begins to wonder how Lubitsch might have handled it, but it is only superficially Lubitsch material, since it is either anti-sex or very British on the subject, with the consummation between the prince and the showgirl almost an afterthought.

During the following decade Olivier was the director of Britain's National Theatre, where his successes included his Othello, Edgar in 'The Dance of Death' and a production of 'Three Sisters'. Filmed records of these were shown in cinemas, but in each case they give only an incomplete idea of what the original had been like. His screen appearances included the Mahdi in **Khartoum** (1966), with

Charlton Heston as 'Chinese' Gordon, who managed a fair British accent and the essential vanity, but lacked any hint of the desiccated, lonely visionary. Robert Ardrey's script is a history lesson, while Basil Dearden's direction hardly makes our pulses quicken – and nothing else is as good as the introduction, a potted history of the Nile, photographed by Eliot Elisofon. The film ends with an apologia, 'We cannot be sure how long his memory will live, but a world with no room for the Gordons will return to the sands.' The American producer, Julian Blaustein, had hoped to duplicate the success of *Lawrence of Arabia*.

The best historical film of the period was **The Trials of Oscar Wilde** (1960), written and directed by Ken Hughes, then known, if at all, for some undistinguished melodramas. Its true theme is that of a major literary figure ruined by his own foolhardiness, but it could not be done without reference to its protagonist's homosexuality. That remained prohibited as a screen subject but, as we have seen, a number of London and Broadway plays had touched on the matter during the last few years; and it was the acceptance of this particular film which gave rise to the later *Victim*. Making a film about Wilde was an idea whose time had come, for Gregory Ratoff was hastily directing a rival version in Britain. Hughes's film reached cinemas first (by three days) and reached it best, being especially good on the confused friendships and rivalries of the period; in a generally veracious account he omits Bosie's insistence on carrying out the family feud before the largest possible audience. That would have made Wilde (Peter Finch) a mere pawn, and Hughes sets him up as tragic hero brought low by love: given the nature of that love that was perhaps the wisest approach at that time, though we might have preferred him as dandy, wit or social lion. The respect accorded the film did not earn Hughes more interesting projects, so that it was ten years before he obtained backing for **Cromwell** (1970), which manages to be as inaccurate as the despised historicals of the past, and even duller. It turns on the sort of spurious confrontation thought to be a simple way of explaining complex historical questions, and is made the poorer since the Cromwell of Richard Harris is hardly a

thinking man. Charles I, better acted by Alec Guinness, suffers by being saintly rather than scheming.

Becket (1964) also demonstrates the wrong approach to history. Anouilh's play, an irreverent chronicle of a friendship, has been smothered in cathedral-look gloom – except for the sex sequences, mostly involving Peter O'Toole's over-emotional Henry II. In the original each episode grew from the one before, but that is not true under Peter Glenville's direction, while Edward Anhalt's screenplay★ dampens what remains of the jokes about French misconceptions of the English and vice versa. Even in the first reel Richard Burton's Becket suffers from an overdose of piety, but oblivious to the stars and the direction John Gielgud and Pamela Brown act in the style Anouilh intended, he as a foxy King Louis and she as Queen Eleanor. The film enjoyed the same popularity as *Lawrence of Arabia*, *A Man for All Seasons* and *A Lion in Winter* (q.v.), which sent its producer, Hal Wallis, to search among old Broadway plays for another historical subject for Burton. He came up with Maxwell Anderson's 'Anne of the Thousand Days', but Charles Bluhdorn, then head of Paramount, refused to sanction any film with Burton (because Burton had agreed to speak the commentary of a Paramount film for a moderate sum, but changed his mind and asked instead for some diamond and emerald earrings to be given to his wife, Elizabeth Taylor). Wallis accordingly severed his twenty-five year association with Paramount, and moved to Universal. The film, with Burton as Henry VIII and Genevieve Bujold as Anne Boleyn, was mildly successful, but critics were unanimous in disliking the direction of Charles Jarrott, who was nevertheless retained for **Mary, Queen of Scots** (1971). He doggedly mishandles John Hale's screenplay, an adroit mixture of fact and fiction, historic dialogue and more specious speeches of his own devising. Given the approach, Vanessa Redgrave wisely interprets Mary as a storybook heroine but Glenda Jackson's Elizabeth I is a suburban harridan. Miss Jackson was more happily cast as a sluttish Emma Hamilton in **Bequest**

★Anhalt later wrote the book of a West End musical on Becket, which received about the worst notices in theatre history.

to the Nation (1973), directed by James Cellan Jones, with Peter Finch as Nelson; but both films were among the half dozen successive failures which led to Wallis's retirement in 1975.

The age of the wide screen spectacular was dying, and with it the historical drama. Both were expensive, and the adult and/or family audiences for whom they were intended were staying home with their television sets. Colour television was now available in many countries and the programmes shown had at last begun to rival the cinema in content and technique.

That the Hollywood studios had backed most of these films was proof of their continuing obsession with Britain – which would remain, for different reasons, long after it had ceased to be Hollywood's chief export market (indeed, it moved well down the list). As far as the British themselves were concerned, they were content to have their plays, novels and films dwell in the past, if only metaphorically. The British cinema was at its most hermetic, particularly when compared with some of the harshly observant Hollywood films of the late Fifties. The move towards a truly contemporary cinema began with **Room at the Top** (1959), if we are to judge from the admiring notices of the time. John Braine's original novel was the least of the three artefacts which most contributed to the upheaval in British culture, for the film of *Lucky Jim* had been contemptible, while that of *Look Back in Anger* (q.v.) was some months in the future. The tone of all three was anti-cant, but Braine's was the only one based on American models. Apart from Henry James and T. S. Eliot, American culture had impinged on the British only at the mundane level of thrillers or musicals. Braine's hero, a young man on the make, had been a constant in American fiction since Dreiser, if not before. He was also resolutely grammar-school, and, equally rare, tossed around brand names and openly indulged in sex as often as possible. The book's bestselling status interested two producers, John and James Woolf, most of whose films until then had been mediocre – none of them helped by the presence, as the critics pointed out, of an appalling actor, Laurence Harvey, who happened to be James's lover. *Room at the Top* contained a marvellous role for him, and it gave the Woolfs a chance to promote

their associate producer, Jack Clayton (b. 1921), who had just directed an acclaimed short, *The Bespoke Overcoat*. Seen today, *Room at the Top* is specious, its portrait of provincial life ungenerous without being satiric; Neil Paterson's otherwise banal screenplay is against class-consciousness, and every reference is underscored in Clayton's direction. The acting is equally unsubtle, with the glowing exception of Simone Signoret, sensual and touching as the older woman grasping at love.

Meanwhile, the moribund local industry was receiving some impetus from the government-funded British Film Institute, whose journal, *Sight and Sound*, had been publishing a number of young critics with pronounced ideas on films. They included (q.v.) Lindsay Anderson, Tony Richardson and Karel Reisz, who were scraping up money to make documentary shorts. In 1956 the Institute's National Film Theatre presented a season called 'Free Cinema', which included an American documentary, *On the Bowery*, short films by Franju, Truffaut and Godard, plus British contributions by Anderson, Richardson, Reisz, Lorenza Mazzetti (unheard of again) and (q.v.) Claude Goretta and Alain Tanner. The preoccupations of Anderson's **O Dreamland** (1953), an account of a funfair, are reflected in Richardson's and Reisz's **Momma Don't Allow** (1955), a portrait of an evening at a suburban jazz club, which the B.F.I. financed. Walter Lassally was the photographer, as on so many films of the 'Free Cinema' movement, including Anderson's **Thursday's Children** (1953), about the teaching of deaf children, co-directed with Guy Brenton, and **Every Day Except Christmas** (1957), about the workers of Covent Garden market. Both films bear witness to Anderson's admiration for Humphrey Jennings, but as creative works – one of the declared aims of the movement – few of the films produced are important. However, as a record of the Fifties many of them are far more valuable than might have been suspected. That is especially true of *Momma Don't Allow* and a further collaboration of Reisz and Lassally, **We Are the Lambeth Boys** (1959), a study of a working-class boys' club. Financed by the Ford Motor Company and at 59 minutes the longest of these films, it also marked the end of the movement. It was difficult to see how any of these people could be assimilated into a local industry so opposed to their aims and methods, and yet some were – if not at the industry's instigation.

Tony Richardson (b. 1928) arrived there first, via the theatre, repeating on film his direction of John Osborne's **Look Back in Anger** (1959). The play had been staged at the Royal Court Theatre by the English Stage Company, whose aims were little different from those of New York's Group Theatre twenty years earlier, to offer drama of substance and a left-wing tinge: that the Royal Court's work seemed pioneering is comment enough on the state of the British theatre at the time. The British critical establishment as a whole were displeased with neither theatre nor cinema, and the damp critical reception accorded the film of *Look Back in Anger* was symptomatic: the play had really been liked only by a minority, but fortunately a vociferous one. That was sufficient to interest the moguls, including Harry Saltzman, a former producer in American television, whose only film was *The Iron Petticoat*, a terrible British imitation of *Ninotchka* written by Ben Hecht, with Katharine Hepburn and Bob Hope. In forming Woodfall Films with Osborne and Richardson, Saltzman allowed them the creative control they demanded, though in negotiating the distribution deal (with Associated British) they were forced to agree to some emasculation – thus Nigel Kneale's screenplay (with additional dialogue by Osborne) has little of Jimmy Porter's rantings against a class-divided society. Thus the young man is rebelling without any causes, and he is unlikeable as he hurls invective at his wife (Mary Ure) and beds her best friend (Claire Bloom), who had loathed him till a moment or two earlier. That may be wish-fulfilment on the part of the author, and it is certainly, in plot terms, not too far removed from *A Streetcar Named Desire*. Hollow and full of hatred as it is, and because it is, it is heartbreaking to see it now, knowing that Osborne, Richardson and Richard Burton – who uses his bark to superb effect as Jimmy – would never do anything better. Richardson may have studied Bazin and the Italian neo-realists but, unlike other British contemporaries working in features, he uses locations with understanding

and not only to prevent us from recalling the film's theatrical origins. He rejected the familiar 'character' playing, with its humour and overstatement – Edith Evans is superb as an interpolated character, Ma Tanner – and he gets a balance among the players that was missing from *Room at the Top*. The film is a worthy heir to the 'Free Cinema' movement, in being virtually the only British feature of the era to say something about that time.

For his second film Richardson chose **The Entertainer** (1960) (which he had also directed on stage), Osborne's study in disenchantment, a hotchpotch of anti-right bias, music-hall jokes, second-hand dreams and family strife. The allegorical aspect of the play – that the failed comic, Archie Rice, stood for a bankrupt Britain – has gone by now. The film is primarily a study of Archie, and thus of Archie's world, from dressing-room to saloon bar. It is Olivier, repeating his stage performance, who makes it a great experience, remodelling his Archie for one of the best performances ever given on film. A lesser actor might have managed the 'public' Archie, with his hail-fellow-well-met, his sniggering one-liners, his wheedling, high-pitched familiarity, his inability to feel a snub; some might manage the plebeian accent, falling into effeminacy; but no one else could have managed the inner Archie, which is an echoing hollow, who has devoted his life to chasing a will-o'-the-wisp – a dream of his own fame, his own success – and who in doing so has closed himself to any emotion other than the pleasure of a draught Bass or a quick lay. As his loving daughter, Joan Plowright brings more to the role than was written into it; and in small roles are Miriam Karlin (as an ageing, bad-tempered soubrette), Alan Bates, Daniel Massey and Albert Finney. Another virtue of Woodfall was its bringing fresh talent to the screen. With a couple of honourable exceptions, the press notices, except for praise for Olivier's own contribution, were worse than those for its predecessor, and the industry disliked it so much that a gala premiere was cancelled and the film sneaked out in the dead summer months. Yet the fact remains that the British cinema grew up because of these two films.

As far as the critics and the public were concerned, the breakthrough came with

Woodfall, Britain's New Wave

The British cinema was dying on its feet when it was injected with new blood by a group of theatre people, including John Osborne the dramatist and Tony Richardson the director, who helped to form a company called 'Woodfall', originally designed to film Osborne's plays. The second of these was *The Entertainer*, RIGHT, with Laurence Olivier repeating his much-acclaimed stage performance, supported by Joan Plowright, who took over the role of his daughter on the stage and repeated it in the film (and in real life she married him). Karel Reisz directed *Saturday Night and Sunday Morning*, BELOW, with Albert Finney and Shirley Field, and like Richardson he was connected with both film criticism and the movement called 'Free Cinema'.

The guiding force of the Woodfall films was to put the British working class on the screen honestly, and that had seldom even been attempted before. John Schlesinger may have succeeded even better, in *Billy Liar!* RIGHT, with Tom Courtenay and Rodney Bewes and *A Kind of Loving*, FAR RIGHT, with Alan Bates and June Ritchie. The films were so much discussed, as well as imitated, that it is a tribute to the care with which they were made that they remain still fresh today.

Saturday Night and Sunday Morning (1960), which Richardson and Saltzman produced for Karel Reisz (b. 1926) to direct, and **A Taste of Honey** (1961), directed by Richardson. Both tell as much about the England of those days as one may want to know. Each, like *Room at the Top*, goes North, to the industrial cities, and where Reisz finds some of the plainest, ugliest pubs and streets, Richardson uses canals, factory chimneys and winding streets. As we may have guessed from their earlier documentaries, they are very fond of dance-halls and pubs, i.e. places where 'the people' go, and these became the clichés of the Woodfall school. But I was astonished, recently, to find these films undated. Their strength lies in the subject matter and dialogue. *Saturday Night* was adapted by Alan Sillitoe from his own novel about a factory-worker (Albert Finney) who takes up with a married woman (Rachel Roberts). *A Taste of Honey* was written by Richardson and Shelagh Delaney (from the latter's play, on which it is a considerable improvement). Its subject was – and perhaps remains – unusual in drama; a schoolgirl (Rita Tushingham) lives in mutual antagonism with her tarty mum (Dora Bryan), flitting from cheap apartment to cheap apartment as the rent becomes due. When Mum's latest fancy man (Robert Stephens) proposes, and doesn't want the girl, she lets her black sailor lover make her pregnant and with that predicament goes to live with a young homosexual misfit (Murray Melvin). Richardson's somewhat florid style is not unsuitable, since the crux of the matter is the girl's occasional moment of magic in a world all too familiarly hellish. Both films take a poor view of the working classes, but they were the first to take them seriously, finding pride, spirit and tenderness as integral as in any other milieu.

Richardson was patently anxious to give the lie to the customary British film view of Britain, and **The Loneliness of the Long Distance Runner** (1962) is light years ahead of another movie on a borstal institution, *Boys in Brown*, twelve years earlier. He is expectedly good on his young hero (Tom Courtenay), unexpectedly good on the governors and other

do-gooders. Michael Redgrave, as the warden, an old codger with no understanding of the delinquents' mentalities, or indeed anything but the therapeutic joys of sport, gives one of his best performances and the film only fails – if significantly – in its suggestion that borstal boys and public schoolboys are brothers under the skin, finding a common ground in the lousy meals they are served.

The most sympathetic exponent of this 'stunted lives' syndrome was John Schlesinger (b. 1926), a former actor and documentary film-maker. Coming from a privileged background, like Richardson, he nevertheless feels much empathy with the working classes, and if his direction is even more studied it is also more confident. **A Kind of Loving** (1962) and **Billy Liar!** (1963) are the best films of this group, although the first was dismissed by British critics as just another kitchen-sink movie (perhaps because its production team was also responsible for the *Carry On* films), till it went on to win the Golden Bear at the Berlin Festival. That Schlesinger's films have wit is due in part to his

writers, Willis Hall and Keith Waterhouse, working in the first instance from Stan Barstow's novel, and in the second from their own play, based on Waterhouse's novel. In both cases they are acute on some fond and foolish aspects of British life. Humour begins with Barstow's title, which refers to the British kind of sex, with Vic (Alan Bates) turning either to a sex-manual or a book of nudes for help. The boredom of office life is relieved by the pursuit of Ingrid (June Ritchie), who succumbs in the front parlour one Sunday afternoon when Mum (Thora Hird) is out; and it is this lady who almost ruins the subsequent, shotgun marriage – a petty little Tory, incensed that Vic cares neither for T.V. quiz shows nor coats from Marks and Spencer. That terrain of suburban terrace houses is also the world of Billy the liar (Tom Courtenay), and infinitely sadder, since he longs to escape, from his mean-spirited employer (Leonard Rossiter), his irascible dad (Wilfred Pickles), and his grandmother (Ethel Griffies), a grumbling nonentity. Help arrives in the form of a liberated, highly up-to-the-minute and very young Earth-mother (Julie Christie) – if only he can accept it. 'They're not worth it, the whole place isn't worth it,' she says.

The battle was won: British cinema had been released from its thrall to the upper and middle classes. Among those fighting the same fight on behalf of the stage was Joan Littlewood (b. 1916), whose East End Theatre Workshop had concentrated on plays about working people (including 'A Taste of Honey'). In the climate conditioned by the success of these films she was given the chance to direct a movie version of one of those plays, **Sparrows Can't Sing** (1963). She wrote the screenplay with its author, Stephen Lewis, but although she fought the studio at every step she cannot be exempted from perpetrating the myth of the East End as a haven of loveable Cockneys. As the most prominent of these, Barbara Windsor is more accurately cast than most actresses: she is found living in sin with a bus-driver (George Sewell) by her husband (James Booth) when he returns from sea, and the plot chiefly concerns his attempts to get her back. Littlewood's love for Stepney, with its barren pubs and rows of houses, is clear, and this makes the film refreshing. Penelope Gilliatt's lyrical review in *The Observer* was taken to task for inverted snobbery – but was understandable in view of her opinion that working-class films had for years been 'desolatingly bad'.

The prime recipient of overpraise was **This Sporting Life** (1963), directed by Lindsay Anderson in an attempt to turn David Storey's novel into a modern 'Wuthering Heights'. Since, as Anderson says, he has 'a very low opinion of the British film industry *and* the British public' (*The Sunday Times*, 9 June 1974), it is not surprising to find that this movie is somewhat second-hand: the rugger-playing hero (Richard Harris) is an amalgam of John Garfield and Marlon Brando; the frigid widow (Rachel Roberts) is a variation of the role played by this actress in *Saturday Night and Sunday Morning*; the oily, insinuating promoter (Alan Badel) is from *Rocco e i suoi Fratelli*; the predatory, rather cheap wife from Amis's 'That Uncertain Feeling', and the party from the film of that book; the vamp at that gathering is from *The Bachelor Party*; and the walk across the railway tracks at night from any six Hollywood dramas of the Forties.

It was nevertheless a welcome film to come from the Rank Organisation, which almost certainly had been encouraged by the fact that Karel Reisz was the producer. As across the Channel, this group of young film-makers emanating from Woodfall helped each other, and it was Richardson who produced **Girl with Green Eyes** (1964), directed by a former camera operator with Woodfall, Desmond Davis, from a screenplay and novel by Edna O'Brien. Its setting is Ireland, in itself a rarity, though its subject is not. That is the hopeless affair between a shopgirl (Rita Tushingham) and a suave, married, cosmopolitan writer (Peter Finch). But both players are superb, as is Lynn Redgrave, as the girl's sexually confident friend; the film is fresh, funny and poignant. Richardson's contribution may have been all-important, in view of **Smashing Time** (1967), with the same two actresses as Northern girls setting out to conquer 'swinging' London. The producer, Carlo Ponti, seems to have wanted a reflection of *Blow-Up*; George Melly contributed a horrendously unfunny script, and the film is less directed by Davis than assembled, with the aid of a sledge-hammer.

Another swift decline was that of Clive Donner, a former editor, who had made no mark as a director until **The Caretaker** (1964), an independent production whose slight budget – £30,000 – was collected from a group of people including Noël Coward, Richard Burton and Peter Hall. As adapted by Harold Pinter from his own play, it quickly disappeared from view, demonstrating the superior common sense of cinemagoers over theatrical devotees (in 1977 Bernard Levin, in *The Sunday Times*, was to fulminate against the play's 'emptiness, weightlessness and triviality . . . its terrible but complete absence of any subject matter or philosophical point.'). Donner really sprang into prominence with **Nothing But the Best** (1964), whose content was no more than that of *Room at the Top* restyled as black comedy, with a witty script by Frederic Raphael, adapted from Stanley Ellin's book. Alan Bates is the young man who will stop at literally nothing to achieve his goal, and Millicent Martin is the aristocratic girl who, fortunately for him, falls for him. The presence of this actress and a number of other artists from the B.B.C.'s 'That Was the Week

That Was' is evidence that this satiric, iconoclastic programme was another manifestation of the revolt against accepted British attitudes, and that programme's certainty that the wealthy and aristocratic were petty, self-satisfied and conscienceless was reflected in this film. This is virtually all it has in common with **Here We Go Round the Mulberry Bush** (1968), produced and directed by Donner, from a screenplay and novel by Hunter Davies. This is *Billy Liar!* worked over and transported south to one of the 'new' towns, Stevenage, and is an even more egregious example of the youth-orientated movie than *Smashing Time*. The additional dialogue is credited to the 'associate producer', an American, Larry Kramer, but its misinterpretation of contemporary life is too pervasive to be blamed on one man.

Suburbia is also the setting of **Live Now – Pay Later** (1962), whose subject, the association between corrupt businessmen and local politicians, was not uncommon in Hollywood but had hardly been touched upon by a British film. The hero, brilliantly played by Ian Hendry, epitomises the Sixties – a smooth-tongued heel, who works as a touting salesman required to get the goods into the home. He also tries to get into as many beds as possible, but that is typical of the approach, with anything thrown in for a laugh. Jack Trevor Story wrote the screenplay from a novel by Jack Lindsay, and the otherwise self-indulgent direction by Jay Lewis does at least move quickly. The industry by this time had managed to put aside its doubts about the two Osborne-Richardson films, unquestionably reassured by the popularity of the later Woodfall films, especially *Saturday Night and Sunday Morning*. It now proceeded to make its own working-class films but made sure that these were in the hands of talents more congenial to it.

The L-Shaped Room (1963) was directed and written by a former actor, Bryan Forbes, in which he employed the obligatory 'new' faces but could not prevent a number of them hamming it up. This account of a London rooming-house borrows only the trappings of new British cinema, being resolutely old-fashioned with its 'slice-of-life' vignettes. As adapted from the novel by Lynne Reid Banks, it strains for substance; what it achieves is the equivalent of a damned good read. **Term of Trial** (1962) does not even do that, rendering only drab the dilemma of a teacher (Laurence Olivier) accused of misconduct by a precocious adolescent (Sarah Miles); the director, Peter Glenville, wastes Simone Signoret as the teacher's contemptuous wife, but the care and detail of Olivier's work are clearly directorproof. **The Leather Boys** (1964), directed by Sidney J. Furie and written by Gillian Freeman (under a male pseudonym) is at least honest to its environment – the motor-cycle gangs, coming from the small terrace houses. It is a good study of a working-class marriage gone wrong and destroyed, when the husband (Colin Campbell) decides to leave his perky, discontented wife (Tushingham) for his easygoing homosexual friend (Dudley Sutton). The dénouement is decently handled, and if the men are the more sympathetically presented, that might be due to Mr Sutton's performance.

You would not have to like any of these films to appreciate that the British nouvelle vague did not roll in vain, but its aim was different from its brotherhood in France – it was to prise the British cinema loose from the influence of Shaftesbury Avenue. Hence its preoccupation with the working-classes; and as the movement died it gave birth to such films as *Here We Go Round the Mulberry Bush*, which saw Britain *only* in terms of working-class and upper crust. The demotic slant of these films made them more welcome in American cinemas than any British film since the heyday of the Ealing comedy. The Hollywood studios intervened more directly as their domestic audiences shrank and *The Bridge on the River Kwai* proved that a 'British' film was welcomed the world over – while the Oscar awarded to Simone Signoret for *Room at the Top* proved that prestige could be gained from an exclusively British film. The absolute confirmation, on both counts, was **Tom Jones** (1963), financed by United Artists when its cost, though low in comparison to most Hollywood-backed historical movies, proved too high for Woodfall's usual backers. It grossed over $17 million in the U.S. alone, and won Oscars for Best Picture, Best Direction for Tony Richardson and Best Screenplay for John Osborne, as adapted from Henry Fielding's classic novel. It is a tour of Merrie England with its pants down and a grimy face, the cinema equivalent of Hogarth after a lifetime of Gainsboroughs. Indeed, it rather overdoes its drunks and cripples. Its bawdry, so refreshing then, has been copied endlessly,★ and if few of Richardson's tricks were even then new – a speeded-up chase, the Silent screen parody, the wipes, the asides to the camera – they were then at least, bright and delightful. Like most critics turned directors, he was not interested in working either expensively or in academic mould, and if the film now seems tame and only mildly amusing, it has a springlike quality, a sense of happiness and of a nice cast having fun.

Richardson chose his subjects as boldly as his casts, but admiration for **The Loved One** (1965) is likely to go no further. Everything is overweighted and overloaded, and therefore quite inappropriate as a means of filming Evelyn Waugh. This is the only film made from one of his novels in his lifetime, a satire on American burial customs set mainly in a cemetery and funeral parlour. On the screen it has become a black comedy, as written by Christopher Isherwood and Terry Southern, with graftings from *Dr Strangelove* (q.v.) – to which Southern had contributed – in the form of a climax involving irresponsible military men and guided missiles. The piece is somewhat disadvantaged by Robert Morse, miscast as a Britisher and too knowing. (In an even worse film from a Waugh novel, 'Decline and Fall', Robin Phillips had the right Alice in Wonderland quality.) Richardson's earlier visit to Hollywood had been for 20th Century-Fox, to direct the film of an American novel, **Sanctuary** (1961), whose failure he blamed on studio interference. It is, nevertheless, more professional than most of his films, and its faults would seem to be due to the Production Code, not yet in its death throes, curtailing all the scenes which gave Faulkner's piece its meaning. The cast – not of Richardson's choosing – is also unfortunate, with the exception of Lee Remick, glowing at the carnal delights laid before her. Richardson's interest in unorthodox sexuality led to two disasters, **Mademoiselle** (1967) and **The Sailor from Gibraltar** (1967), both with Jeanne

★Including Richardson himself, who returned to this novelist after a run of failures. But *Joseph Andrews* (1977) has all the vices of *Tom Jones* and none of its virtues.

Moreau, the former from a story by Jean Genet, the latter from a novel by Marguerite Duras, adapted by Richardson, Isherwood and Don Magner. The first concentrates on a schoolmistress whose frustration leads her to pyromania and humiliation, i.e. baying like a dog, while fornicating with an impossibly beautiful and strong Italian woodcutter (Ettore Manni). The second is about an Englishman (Ian Bannen) who joins a wealthy widow in the search for her sailor lover who may, or may not, be imaginary. The Genet is not only unpleasantly misogynist but a desperate quest for artiness, as it borrows from *Les Amants*, *La Terra Trema*, Pagnol, *Goupi Mains Rouges*, and Buñuel. The Duras has a line, 'It's like leaving a movie before the end' which, when I saw it, brought a loudly applauded *cri de coeur* from the audience, 'What a bloody good idea.'

The Charge of the Light Brigade (1968) recalls a song by Noël Coward, 'We cheered the Charge of the Light Brigade/ No Matter why they charged', because Richardson also does not care, though he is far from cheering. A good many years too late, he seems to want to get even with those Victorian generals. When Warners filmed the Charge, they added some fiction. Charles Wood's invented additions include a young bride (Vanessa Redgrave) who falls in love with her husband's best friend (David Hemmings), plus some heavy borrowings from Cecil Woodham-Smith's 'The Reason Why', as revealed in the credits. (Well into the project, Richardson had learned that Laurence Harvey owned the film rights to that book and part of the agreement with the actor was a lump sum to him and his appearance in a cameo role – which was cut from the final print.) Where Mrs Woodham-Smith was appalled but analytic, Wood is only scurrilous, but even so the antics of the lords – Cardigan (Trevor Howard), Raglan (John Gielgud) and Lucan (Harry Andrews) – are splendidly enjoyable. However, Richardson's faults are here in abundance. His indecision when to end a scene, meaningless shots and a lack of cohesive style contrast with the physical evocation of Victorian Britain which is superlative, and wonderfully complemented by Richard Williams's linking animation, encapsulating the graphic art of the period, and concise in its exposition of the Victorians' world. The final Charge is well managed; but it should be noted that the film neither presents nor considers the reason why.

Richardson tried to keep the film from the British critics, without success. It was poorly received, but quite justly did exceptional business in what the trade calls 'better class halls'. His subsequent films received even worse notices, and certainly **Laughter in the Dark** (1969) is very bad. What seems like spontaneity in the early films has become carelessness, but equally at fault with Richardson is the film's writer, Edward Bond, who did not know how to respond to Vladimir Nabokov's text with irony or implicit sophistication. Perhaps it was too large a task to transpose the action from Berlin in the Twenties to London in the present day, but that is no excuse for a subnormal vocabulary, even on the premise that it is appropriate to the tacky French couple (Anna Karina, Jean-Claude Drouot) who prey on the unfortunate Sir Edward. In the latter role Nicol Williamson conveys obsession as well as any actor since Jannings, and he is so persuasive that the final sequences, in which he is tormented in his blindness, are powerful.

One of the films that wrecked Richardson's reputation was *Ned Kelly*, and it was a film of that title that Reisz prepared after *Saturday Night and Sunday Morning*. When Columbia turned it down, Reisz accepted an offer from M-G-M to remake **Night Must Fall** (1964), with a screenplay by Clive Exton, which tries to provide a psycho-sexual attraction between Danny and the old lady's companion (now her daughter), which does not make sense, partly because Susan Hampshire is inadequate in the role. Albert Finney, however, pulls out all the stops as Danny, and the film does chill the spine. **Morgan – a Suitable Case for Treatment** (1966) concerns an impeccable young Marxist (David Warner) so hung up on animals that he confuses them with people, and after much discussion he is in a straitjacket at the end of the film. His fantasies are borrowed from *Billy Liar!*, except that he is the victim of the Fascists rather than their leader; his wife's very-U parents are Jimmy Porter's in-laws in person; and the feeling of pastiche in David Mercer's script is reinforced by resemblances to Ken

Kesey's 'One Flew Over the Cuckoo's Nest'. Richard Lester had recently made *The Knack* (q.v.) in a larky style, but Reisz proves not the man for a similar tactic. The film's greatest asset is Vanessa Redgrave, and for Reisz she became Isadora Duncan in **Isadora** (1969). As a former critic, Reisz was more aware than most of the pitfalls of film biography, which may be why this one, like *Salvatore Giuliano* (to go no further back) is an enquiry into the very nature of Miss Duncan, contrasting her last days with her youth, as it was and as it was imagined by her. Despite this ambition, the screenplay, by Exton, Melvyn Bragg and Margaret Drabble, does no more than pass on information. Miss Redgrave cannot prevent Isadora from being tiresome, nor Reisz rid his film from the stench of mothballs.

While making the film its producers, Universal, quoted him in their publicity as saying, 'Everything must spring from the moment, so that it seems fresh and alive', but this is something Reisz seems incapable of achieving, even in two contemporary tales, made in the U.S., **The Gambler** (1974) and **Who'll Stop the Rain?** (1978), though he responds as keenly as other foreign directors to the American scene. Both compare poorly with films on the same subjects. Unlike Altman with *California Suite* (q.v.), Reisz fails to tear through the more pretentious script of *The Gambler*, while *Who'll Stop the Rain?* is no more than an exploitation piece beside *Cutter's Way* (q.v.), with its heroin-running Vietnam veteran (Nick Nolte), vicious cops and other fashionable clichés.

Nor were Reisz's care and intelligence better served with **The French Lieutenant's Woman** (1981), based on John Fowles's novel. Fowles had retained control over the material, partly because of the terrible film made from another of his novels, *The Magus*. Both stories involve a young man puzzled by the behaviour of others, in the case of the later book an enigmatic young woman. It is a slight tale, made memorable by Fowles's witty asides on Victorian life and literature. The difficulty of wrenching a workable screenplay from the material had defeated half a dozen directors, including Fred Zinnemann. The problem appeared to be solved by replacing Fowles's commentary with a modern story about two actors (Meryl

Streep, Jeremy Irons) who play the Victorian couple in a film version; but as written by Harold Pinter it is vulgar in its own right, embarrassing to watch, and it wrecks the project. The book's dual ending is mentioned and then, foolishly, not used. The film's reviews were mixed, but it achieved a certain caché among cinema patrons, tired of the scifi and blood cluttering up so many screens.

It would be unjust also to label Lindsay Anderson disappointing, since *This Sporting Life* hardly raised expectations. **If . . .** (1968) is a moderately amusing portrait of public school life, but when it was described as 'a hatchet job', Anderson countered that the term was 'misleading . . . it is a timeless and non-specific metaphor for the basic tensions between hierarchy and anarchy, independence and tradition, liberty and law.' One might have hoped that a film about rebellion, or the flouting of authority would have concerned a section of society with a right to protest, e.g. miners or dockers; but Cheltenham College (the exteriors were filmed there, and it is where Anderson himself went to school) is not a microcosm of anything of any importance. The portrait of bumbling governors and other authoritarian figures is less incisive than that in *The Loneliness of the Long Distance Runner*, and the descent into anarchy less pointed than in its inspiration, *Zéro de Conduite*. **O Lucky Man!** (1973) is equally derivative and even more self-indulgent, taking almost three hours to recount the adventures of a salesman (Malcolm McDowell) in a Kafkaesque Britain. At one point he becomes involved with the rich and is told, 'Sir James's time is worth five hundred pounds a minute. Please keep it short', a line that exemplifies the film, heavy-handed, obvious and bludgeoning. It is a Brechtian film, despising its audience, and Anderson's comments, as usual, give ammunition to those who dislike his work. To him this is 'epic satire'. The O was added to the title for 'universality', and he hoped 'to entertain with a story that would continually surprise, continually amuse. And finally enlighten.' A number of respectful reviews hinted that he had succeeded, but the public knew better. The fact that Anderson has made a reputation on three poor films is a mystery, but probably not unconnected with a chronic disposition to

lash out publicly at anyone with whom he disagrees. He apparently told Joan Plowright that she was 'not politically mature' because she did not laugh at **Britannia Hospital** (1982), in which she appeared. The British critics agreed with her on this supposed satire on contemporary Britain, and were not at all amused or respectful.

Jack Clayton, on the other hand, seemed to have improved mightily over his first feature, *Room at the Top*, even if his version of James's 'The Turn of the Screw' seems unduly influenced by the 1944 *Jane Eyre*. **The Innocents** (1961), titled after William Archibald's dramatised version, is academically sound, sufficiently ambiguous and imaginative, and selective of its horrors. One of its few minor flaws is the declamatory tone adopted by Miss Giddens, played by Deborah Kerr, usually a subtle screen actress. Subtlety is not in evidence in **The Pumpkin Eater** (1964), an account of a nervous breakdown experienced by the perpetually pregnant wife (Anne Bancroft) of a philandering scriptwriter. The original novel by Penelope Mortimer was one of those which plundered friends and acquaintances for copy, with their Habitat kitchens and shopping expeditions to Harrods. The screenplay by Harold Pinter is observant of the idiotic remarks overheard on buses and at parties, but falters at content, intent on offering 'meaningful' pauses. Since Clayton's direction is subservient to these, the piece is as long-winded as it is inferior to Bergman's similar studies. **Our Mother's House** (1967) centres on seven young children who hide the fact of their mother's death from the world, which is not among the world's most familiar plots, but it had been used some years earlier by Torre Nilsson in *La Caida* (q.v.). The children in this case resemble some of those in 'Lord of the Flies', and the sense of *déjà-vu* is completed by Dirk Bogarde repeating his role in *The Servant* (q.v.).

The Great Gatsby (1974) was a mistake. The project was started by Ali MacGraw, then married to Paramount's production chief, Robert Evans, because she wanted to play Daisy. Paramount had filmed Fitzgerald's novel twice before, but had relinquished the rights on selling the 1949 version to M.C.A. Television. The company had to repurchase them, as well as paying $350,000 to the Fitzgerald estate, and when the cost rose to $6 million, it sold shares to independent brokers. Publicity was blamed for 'overkill' when the film failed, but the fact was simply that this bright, glancing, melancholy tale had become an ornate, funereal spectacular. The script by Francis Coppola (among those rejected was one by Truman Capote, for which he was paid $100,000) was over-reverential, and Clayton's direction was over-emphatic. Endlessly the parties roll (there are only two, but they seem like two hundred) and endlessly the feet tap, the skirts bob and the camera lingers on the rolled stockings. The film lasts 146 minutes, an achievement of sorts, since the book takes less than half that time to read. Robert Redford's Gatsby lacks the raffish and slightly sinister quality that Alan Ladd brought to the role (and he was not that good); Mia Farrow and Bruce Dern come off best as the Buchanans; Karen Black, the Shelley Winters *de nos jours*, plays Myrtle in familiar style. Scott would not have liked it, but he would have loved the ballyhoo. It is ironic that because of this movie the Twenties became referred to as 'The Gatsby era', and he would have loved that too, the poor son-of-a-bitch.

Clayton's career is unhappily typical of this group, with long pauses searching for the right property – viable, unusual, and above the ordinary run of material: not for him, Richardson or Reisz the pot-boilers that kept Chabrol going. It would be hard to say which approach was the wiser, since Chabrol did return to quality movies, with impressive results, while they foundered on their derivative prestige efforts or were swamped by Hollywood projects for which they were unsuited. It is in that context that the career of John Schlesinger must be considered. When he moved on from the working-class setting, it was to satire (a rare thing in British cinema) with an original screenplay by Frederic Raphael, who was later awarded an Oscar. The film, **Darling** (1965), also won the New York Critics' award as Best of the Year, but a number of dissenters found it as empty as the life it portrayed. Schlesinger himself said ten years later; 'I think it's a madly dated film; at the time we thought it was truthfully done.' It is certainly more truthful than *La Dolce Vita*, which it resembles in being about a world of journalists and models. The heroine, Diana, is an anthology of all the nit-witted models who ever made the headlines, though played by Julie Christie with engaging warmth. As she tells her tale (supposedly dictating for magazine serialisation) the action counterpoints her words with facile irony. 'It should be so easy to be happy,' she says. 'It should be the easiest thing in the world'; and her lover (Dirk Bogarde), rejecting her, cries, 'I don't take whores in taxis'. Both lines, changing the phraseology a little, could come from a Joan Crawford vehicle. I don't find the piece dated; it is amusingly done – from a parody of those man-in-the-street interviews to an embarrassed orgy in Paris, from Diana's gay photographer pal ogling the boys on the Piccola Marina to a theatrical audition.

Raphael, adapting Thomas Hardy for Schlesinger, has allowed the countryside to speak for itself. Hardy believed that man was moulded by his environment or, to use a word more common then, Nature. In **Far from the Madding Crowd** (1967) Dorset and Wiltshire are photographed plain; the supporting faces look neither like actors nor Flaherty-like posers. Best of all, Schlesinger believed we might share the pleasures and pains of rural England under the ageing Queen – bargaining in the corn-exchange, sheep-dipping and joining a workers' supper, saving the ricks from fire and celebrating the harvest festival. The story might be by any specialist in period romance – the self-willed girl (Christie) and her three suitors: the shepherd (Alan Bates), the squire (Peter Finch) and the soldier-deceiver (Terence Stamp); but there has never been a better film about the British countryside. The British press reacted as with *The Charge of the Light Brigade*, but this film also became a popular favourite and has remained so. In the U.S. it was liked by neither press nor public.

Schlesinger, nevertheless, found his next assignment in the U.S., **Midnight Cowboy** (1969), written by Waldo Salt, a Hollywood veteran, from the novel by James Leo Herlihy. It is, ultimately, about the love of two men, though neither of them is exactly, in the film's terminology, a fag. Joe Buck (Jon Voight), a hustler, is wistful American cousin to Billy Liar, and if there is a consistent theme in Schlesinger's films it is that since life is not what one expects as a child, a thought should be spared for those who cannot cope. He

The one British
director to go
from strength to
strength was John
Schlesinger, who at
his best shows both
wit and sympathy.
After making
Darling, RIGHT, with
Dirk Bogarde and
Julie Christie – who
with it became only
the third player to
win a Best Actress
Oscar for a non-
Hollywood film –
Schlesinger was
solicited by the
Americans to direct
Midnight Cowboy,
BELOW, with Jon
Voight and Dustin
Hoffman. The
Oscars this time
went to Schlesinger
for Best Direction
and to the film itself,
as that year's Best.

made his name with a documentary short, *Terminus*, about a lost child; and here both Joe and the shabby cripple, Ratso (Dustin Hoffman), are lost in New York. The film is not only about their relationship, but about the under-belly of the city: the 42nd Street hustlers and hand-me-down conmen; lonely men in hotel rooms; cinema balconies and cheap cafeterias; a man prostrate outside Tiffany's being ignored by passers-by; of a time and a town where sex buys money and money sex, and no one cares which is which any more. Schlesinger peddles dreams with regrettable razzle-dazzle – psychedelic lighting and quick cutting – but the American dream was never more sour. This is a remarkable movie, and was recognised as such by moviegoers, critics and the Academy Award voters.

Sunday, Bloody Sunday (1971) is also about the love of two men, though the younger (Murray Head) of them is unsure whether he cares more for the other (Peter Finch) or for a lonely divorcee (Glenda Jackson). Times Square has given way to Piccadilly, and Schlesinger's locations are, as usual, percipient and evocative. His continual obsession with the uneasy roots of his urban characters enables him to home in on detail – a pile of dishes in a sink, an office-block, a long-playing record – which builds into his fabric. He needs all his expertise for what is otherwise a pot-boiler, credited to Penelope Gilliatt, but by his own admission chiefly written by himself. The screenplay is about sex *only*; it is a sexual view of the universe. Undoubtedly much that is here is based on fact, but Schlesinger's own sympathies cannot bring it to life. *Midnight Cowboy* is optimistic, because its two leading characters, both losers, recognise one positive emotion, a love for each other. Schlesinger has said that *Bloody Sunday* is positive because it is about people coping. The older man is a doctor, but unlike the doctor in *Brief Encounter*, also involved in an emotional situation he could not control, this one fails to arouse sympathy.

Schlesinger returned to the U.S., with a screenplay by Waldo Salt, but despite the Oscars awarded to *Midnight Cowboy* there were no immediate takers for **The Day of the Locust** (1975). When Warners at the last minute backed out, Paramount stepped in, seemingly embarked on a series of campus classics: but this film is even less successful than *The Great Gatsby*, and just as long, though from an equally short text. It is a travesty of Nathaniel West's novella of Hollywood misfits. Episode after episode in the film is drawn from the original, but with the point blunted or changed. West's book on characters trapped by situation and environment is a theme that excellently suits Schlesinger, but he misses the humour, the incongruities, the melancholy – finding only the grotesque, as is the way of less worthy directors.

Schlesinger made **Marathon Man** (1976) for Paramount to restore his bankability, though he commented later that it was not his favourite film; nor was it anybody's. His ability to create suspense goes for little in such situations as a pursuit in which Dustin Hoffman makes for the city freeways, instead of the bright lights and the nearest precinct. The screenwriter, questioned on its logicality, grunted, 'It's a thriller, for godsake.' He was William Goldman, writer of *Butch Cassidy and the Sundance Kid* (q.v.), and his work here is 'thin, flashy, oversold and opportunistic', to use the adjectives Russell Davies in *The* (London) *Observer* applied to the films of 1976 as a whole. What is so contemptible is that this film uses as its basis the Nazi persecution of the Jews – and we might note that it is mainly the work of Jewish talents. The only reason to see it is Laurence Olivier's performance as the head of New York's present-day coven of Nazis – and it is a sad comment on the movie industry that posterity will have a record of this tawdry monster and not of this actor's Macbeth.

Paramount turned down **Yanks** (1979), a pet project of Schlesinger's, and though Universal put up a sum for the American rights and United Artists another for the British, the bulk of the £3,000,000 budget came from Germany – ironically – since its subject is the effect of the G.I.s on the British, and *vice versa*, while stationed in England, en route for the invasion of Germany. Colin Welland – growing up in Lancashire when the Yanks were there – wrote it, with Walter Bernstein, brought from Hollywood to do the American dialogue. 'Ours is an intimate film,' Schlesinger said, but its trouble is that it is not. The score by Richard Rodney Bennett is grandiose; at 139 minutes the film is too long and though the cross section concept is unexceptionable, the necessary points on the subject are evident in the first reel, leaving no sense of urgency in what follows. However, if future generations want to know what it was like, this film will tell them. The reconstruction of the period is virtually faultless. There is one mistake (Christmas tree lights were banned during the War) and a few omissions (resentment over the G.I.s' smarter uniforms; nylons; the furtiveness of sex). There is also much that is excellent, including individual resentment of the intruding Yanks at a time of bereavement, British championing of black soldiers and a number of moments reminiscent of Schlesinger's early work, such as the busybody who takes over the queue for oranges. The film goes further back, to the days of *In Which We Serve*, with the lower orders having a 'Hokey Cokey' wedding and the lady of the manor (Vanessa Redgrave) an affair with an American officer (William Devane) that is discreet and frightfully well-conducted.

Honky Tonk Freeway (1981) is an American 'road' movie, another cross section tale, about a number of people making their way across country to a small town in Florida, whose leading inhabitants are in despair because the new freeway will bypass it. Edward Clinton's screenplay provided Schlesinger with an opportunity to make a companion picture to *Midnight Cowboy*, broader, funnier and more bitter, because middle-America does not inspire the same affection as Manhattan. The film reflects the consumer society of the good old U.S. of A., being exuberant, somewhat tacky, friendly and enterprising. American critics loathed it, possibly resenting a foreigner commenting on their country in this way. The British critics joined them in their scorn, but that is something which should be considered in the context of other Britishers working for Hollywood companies – a matter approved of only if they make cliquish, minority tales. In this case the money was provided by the British and American sections of E.M.I., and the amount of it was $30 million. I agree with those who failed to see where the money went on the screen, but this is otherwise an entertaining and often funny movie. It is by no means a great one, and is disappointing if compared to Schlesinger's early films –

but I cannot think of any more unfairly handled by the press.

Bryan Forbes followed *The L-Shaped Room* with **Seance on a Wet Afternoon** (1964), co-producing with Richard Attenborough in what seems to be a concerted attempt to draw attention to their virtuosity. The direction is as studied as Attenborough's busy performance – as the husband of a fake medium (Kim Stanley) who between them kidnap a small child. Unlike her co-star, Miss Stanley seems to have accepted that after the first clever scene there is nothing to 'act'. The performance of Edith Evans in **The Whisperers** (1967) is blessedly unlike those customarily given of pathetic old ladies in movies – gaunt, ungainly and unsmiling, her hooded eyes masking prejudice and fear. Eric Portman is also superb but, with the exception of Leonard Rossiter as a welfare man, the other performances are overdrawn. Forbes does not understand reticence and there is not a shot in the film not composed with an eye to the eyes of festival jurors. The two movies nevertheless belong to the aftermath of the Woodfall revolution, but Forbes had aspirations to Hollywood fame. He had an unhappy and unlucky two years as head of production when Associated British Pictures became E.M.I., at the start of which he failed with an American-backed film, **The Madwoman of Chaillot** (1969). He was called in by the producer Ely Landau, when John Huston quit after seventeen days' shooting. If, ideally, Jean Giraudoux's play deserved a fantasist of the order of Clair or Ophuls, Huston was at least an eclectic – but in the event Forbes is merely literal and slow. Edward Anhalt's updating of the original foolishly brings in the then topical subject of the Paris student riots, while Katharine Hepburn's performance as the recluse is one of her late film failures. She is merely an eccentric with 'concern' on her sleeve, whereas the role requires someone brought out of personal fantasy and indecision to represent the forces of right and common sense. Margaret Leighton, querulous and dotty, should have played the part, and of the all-star cast hers is the only successful performance. The largest role is that of the maid, first seen serving in the café, and then serving the Countess, though Giraudoux did not actually give her many lines. She appears constantly to the rear or side of other people's close-ups, and has a number of her own; she is in fact Nanette Newman, the wife of Mr Forbes.

When Forbes's friend Richard Attenborough became a director he showed a fondness for 'epic' films with messages. **Oh! What a Lovely War** (1969) had been a very moving stage piece in the form of an end-of-the-pier entertainment, built around the songs and statistics of the First World War. The casualty board, so eloquent on the stage, appears in the film but briefly, and it is difficult to believe that anyone concerned with this all-star effort really felt deeply about the waste, the criminality, the stupidity and pointlessness of that war – except Len Deighton, who wrote the screen adaptation but demanded that his name be removed from the credits after seeing the result. Joan Littlewood's original tight conception has been transmuted into a mish-mash of ill-digested ideas, many staged in an art director's dream decor, like the artful poppies popping into focus before the mud. American critics were much less impressed than the British, but it was an American, Joseph E. Levine, who chose Attenborough to direct **A Bridge Too Far** (1977). This is a study of one of the great debacles of the Second World War, the Battle of Arnhem, when 35,000 men were parachuted behind the German lines with the intention of taking the six strategic bridges across the Ruhr and thus shortening the war by three months. Cornelius Ryan had written a book on the subject as a follow-up to that on which *The Longest Day* was based, but the wherewithal for the operation, the tactics and the actual events seem to have been of little interest to either Attenborough or to the screenwriter, William Goldman. As the film draws to its overdue close – it lasts 175 minutes – it is clear that they, like Harlan in his wretched *Kolberg*, are trying to sell 'failure' to audiences; and they do it, incredibly, with sentimentality and artiness, borrowing an image from 'Mother Courage' and the spinning cartwheel from *Potemkin*. Of the names in the cast, Sean Connery and Anthony Hopkins impress, while the best performances are given by some lesser-known people, Frank Grimes, Edward Fox and John Stride.

It would seem from the evidence that Attenborough believes that the old-fashioned artefacts that he directs can become respectable or even 'art' if replete with liberal values – which is not to say that he is insincere. He was determined to make **Gandhi** (1982) from the moment he became a producer in the early Sixties, and the dream seemed to become a likelihood when Levine agreed to find the backing as a successor to *A Bridge Too Far*. The comparative failure of that film made him change his mind, but Attenborough had already sunk £60,000 of his own money into development. The film cost £9 million, the bulk of it coming from Goldcrest Films (q.v.), plus smaller amounts put up by an American investment company and, after an Indian maharaja had pulled out at the last minute, the Indian government. Since the film distorts what Gandhi said and believed, and since the greatest threat to Mrs Indira Gandhi's regime is from the Gandhians – with the Marxists a close second – it is not surprising that she wished to back it. At least, this is the view of the Indian critic Prabhu S. Guptara, who also objects to the presence in the film of an undue preponderance of Westerners in Gandhi's life, such as the American photographer (Candice Bergen) and reporter (Martin Sheen), a device imitative of *Lawrence of Arabia*. Guptara feels these people do not compensate for 'the major, central imbalance of the film, Gandhi's spiritual quest, which was at the centre of everything he attempted as a man and politician [and] is entirely and completely missing'; he has also pointed out that Gandhi was not against British rule but that he believed that it would not disappear until it was understood why foreigners were in power in the first place.

Gandhi is simply too important a figure for the film's distortions to pass unnoticed, particularly in the right-wing press, for the piece is violently against the Raj. Attenborough chose John Briley, an American, to write the screenplay on the basis of his work on *Pope Joan*, a film no one else seemed to like; and Briley claimed – at least before *Gandhi* won its many Oscars, including Best Picture, Best Direction and Best Actor – that what was on screen was not what he wrote. At 188 minutes it is an absurdly overlong entertainment, with none of the pretension which mars Attenborough's earlier work as a director; it has a slow, steady pace which recalls the discredited 'roadshow' epics of the Sixties. It

Ben Kingsley in Richard Attenborough's life of *Gandhi*, which won several Oscars and in other ways justified Attenborough's twenty-year struggle to complete the project. This is the young Gandhi, during his South African period, and it has to be said that Kingsley's performance was a vital factor in the film's effectiveness.

is better than most of them because it has a strong subject – even if it is not the right one – injustice and one man's fight against it. It is a biography of a major twentieth-century figure who spent most of his life in dispute with the authorities set over him. It is therefore not dissimilar in several ways to its contemporary, *Reds* (q.v.), but where that has vitality and ambiguity this marshals its facts simply, though often with subtlety. Attenborough's respect for his subject and India is always apparent – in, for instance, hiring Ravi Shankar to compose the music – while Ben Kingsley's performance in the title role is often moving. The film's exposition of goodness may be one reason for its popularity – but it would be a pity if that encouraged a return to long, expensive movies.

Attenborough's other films as director include a story of Churchill's youth, *Young Winston*, which was not a success for its

writer-producer Carl Foreman. Of the many films written and/or produced by Foreman, he himself directed only one, **The Victors** (1963), from his own script, declaring that in neither *The Bridge on the River Kwai* nor *The Guns of Navarone* had he been able 'to articulate the clear and forceful statement' that he wished to make on war. *The Victors*, like *Paisà*, offers episodes of army life from the invasion of Sicily upwards, and the gentlemen of the title are played by some young American actors, whose conquests are often restricted to a bevy of popular European female stars. Wars make nice girls whores, according to Foreman, but soldiers get dehumanised too. This particular platoon has the job of shooting a G.I. for desertion in 1943, as Frank Sinatra sings (anachronistically) 'Have Yourself a Merry Little Christmas', which is typical of Foreman's approach, as is the ending, a knife-fight between a G.I. (George Hamilton) and a Russian soldier (Albert Finney) – symbolic harbinger of the Cold War to come. The film lasts almost three hours, and never approaches the force of Wellman's *The Story of G.I. Joe*.

Another prominent black-listed American film-maker working in Britain, originally under a pseudonym, was Joseph Losey (b. 1909). A number of programmers under his own name occasioned no comment, but **Blind Date** (1959) gained several admirers in France – to the satisfaction of the Rank Organisation which, having abandoned hope of breaking into the American market, had turned to Europe, employing a number of continental stars. In this case they are Hardy Kruger and Micheline Presle, as suspect and victim in a particularly absurd murder mystery. Losey accepted an offer from France to film a pulp thriller by James Hadley Chase, but **Eva** (1962) emerged as art house fodder, helped by Gianni di Venanzo's greytoned photography of Rome and Venice and borrowings from *L'Avventura*, not to mention Jeanne Moreau in her familiar role as *femme fatale*. Stanley Baker plays a writer obsessed by her. The film impressed a few, and picked up some further admirers (as is customary in such circumstances) when it became known that the producers, the Hakim brothers, had loathed it so much that they had cut it before distribution.

Losey returned to Britain, and at last achieved a considerable reputation with **The Servant** (1963), based on Robin Maugham's novel about a curious relationship between a rich young man (James Fox) and his valet (Dirk Bogarde). Losey and Bogarde had discussed filming it some years earlier, but in the meantime Michael Anderson had bought the rights and had found backing for a screenplay by Harold Pinter. Associated British became involved, and with the aid of the Grade Organisation, agent for some of the principals, the film was financed to the modest sum of £150,000. Pinter was the ideal choice for the script, since his first and best play, 'The Birthday Party', concerned a similar exercise in who might be doing what to whom. *The Servant* was like no other English-speaking movie. Only in Antonioni would one find this mocking, acrid view of the rich, and although Osborne, and others, had more broadly characterised them as brainless nitwits, this film dropped large hints of lesbianism, drunkenness among the clergy and other decadent practices. Pinter offered, in the end, only a conundrum. The film works towards an affirmation of homosexual dependence – the whole point of Maugham's novel – and then up-ends it, in an epilogue tacked on by Losey and Pinter, who admitted that it was an attempt to deny the homosexual connotation.

For a mere £80,000 Losey made **King and Country** (1964), a drama of the trenches of World War One, with Tom Courtenay as a deserter and Bogarde as his defending officer. It is a film as heavy in irony and emotional bankruptcy as Foreman's *The Victors*. **Accident** (1967) sets a tale of interweaving loves, ambitions and jealousies against the minutiae of Oxford life, as adapted by Pinter from a novel by Nicholas Mosley, and it is a good example of the second-rate imitating its betters. In an interview in *Sight and Sound* Losey made it clear that he had seen *Muriel* and *Il Deserto Rosso*, but in his case the elliptical structure is used to confuse instead of illuminate – or to create enigma for its own sake, as in the sequence where the don (Dirk Bogarde) returns home to find another don in his dressing-gown, with a woman revealed to him, but not the audience (yet), as someone other than his wife.

M-G-M backed **The Go-Between** (1971) but disliked it so much that it sold the American rights to Columbia, just before it won the Grand Prix at Cannes, beating *Death in Venice* – to Visconti's professed annoyance. A number of theorists went to work to prove that it continued the Losey-Pinter exploration of the British class-structure, which it did, but only by violating L. P. Hartley's original novel, which concerns an affair between a young farmer (Alan Bates) and a well-born young lady (Julie Christie). She is the daughter of the manor-house, which becomes in the film the most stately of stately homes, a distance far more difficult to breach but in keeping with the film's overall vulgarity, with Michel Legrand's mock-Bach thundering on the soundtrack. Losey later observed that none of his British films – there were several others – had made money and, obviously aware that someone was trying to tell him something, decamped to France, where his reputation was less equivocally held. The first film of his sojourn, **Mr Klein** (1976), confirmed his craftsmanship, but also his relentless pursuit of an art house taste which did not exist outside his own imagination and that of the French. They awarded a César, i.e. their Oscar, to this modish piece about a Jew wanted by the Nazis for deportation, co-scripted with Franco Solinas, whose credits include *Salvatore Giuliano* and *La Battaglia di Algeri*. John Coleman's *New Statesman* review is an epitaph on Losey's work, 'God knows it is fashionable in some quarters to make puzzle-pictures, life being an enigma, etc . . . [but] after all, there was a real War, there were six million Jews killed, and super-chic, a kind of stoned mystification – however comforting to the prize-giving French – seem inapposite approaches to these facts: like running up a Dior shroud for a corpse.'

Another American working in Britain – and a former associate of Losey on British T.V. series – is Richard Lester (b. 1932), whose work on T.V. commercials developed into a fragmented, frenzied style which, added to his irreverent humour, made him an ideal director for the Sixties (and for the Beatles, the pop-group which left an indelible mark on that decade). His first film, a short, was *The Running, Jumping and Standing Still Film*, with Peter Sellers (with whom he had worked in T.V.), and he has the Beatles running, jumping and not standing still in his third feature and their first, **A Hard Day's Night** (1964). Indeed, everyone concerned seems to have St Vitus's dance, perhaps to divert us from the fact that our four heroes have no charisma as actors. A vague plot has them arriving in London for a concert, and on the assumption that audiences were curious to see *them*, it was just as well to let them play themselves. Alun Owen's inconsequential and theoretically Marxian script de-mythifies them. They are 'us', not 'them'. Their targets are the same as those of Lucky Jim, Hancock and Billy Liar – bowler-hatted gentlemen in railway-carriages, stuffed-shirt reporters, nervous shop-assistants, pompous hotel clerks and camp T.V. producers. All of these were easy targets, and the screenplay is humourless and sycophantic into the bargain.

Comment was inevitably centred on the Beatles, and it was not till **The Knack, and How To Get It** (1965) that Lester came into his own, a youthful lark about sex, and the graduation from fantasy to practice. This one has, however, dated even more horribly than *A Hard Day's Night*. We laughed then at Rita Tushingham running around London crying 'Rape'; at the journey of the new bed through the city; at the sight (or sound) of sacred cows on the soundtrack, e.g. the Queen, writers to the *Daily Telegraph*, senior citizens. They are old fogeys. Our young heroes are free spirits – literally, as they are wafted about London – and if they are preoccupied with sex, is that not because they are young and healthy? Lester does not seem really to know these emotions, but has borrowed them, with so much else, from Jean-Luc Godard. The high spirits aimed for are never comparable to such aged films as, say, *Le Million* or *Sonnenstrahl*, both of which, not coincidentally, had pleasing leading players. There were never three musketeers as lacklustre as Ray Brooks, Donal Donnelly and Michael Crawford, the latter in a particularly narcissistic performance.

A Funny Thing Happened on the Way to the Forum (1966) we owe first to Hal Prince (q.v.), creator extraordinary of Broadway musicals. Its 'anything-goes' comic-strip book, originally by Burt Shevelove and Larry Gelbart, required Lester's similar visual approach. Faced with the Beatles' lack of screen personality, he had broken their songs into fragments, and he does the same with Stephen Sondheim's songs, in keeping with the harum scarum quality of the enterprise. The final chariot race is no more inventive than that chase in *It's a Mad, Mad, Mad, Mad World*, but infinitely funnier, proving that Mack Sennett can be recycled if the spirit is right. Buster Keaton is around, if briefly. He, the flustered Michael Hordern and the ingratiating Jack Gilford take the piece from the two billed stars, Zero Mostel and Phil Silvers. Best of all is Patricia Jessel as the iron-jawed, iron-willed matron, innocently boasting to the incredulous commander that she entertained two hundred soldiers all by herself. More surprisingly, Lester proved adept at drama, or at least his frenetic handling was suitable for the special circumstances of **Petulia** (1968). The title role is played by Julie Christie, a young lady who leaves her sadistic husband (Richard Chamberlain) in search of an adulterous affair, which she achieves with a doctor (George C. Scott). Her sadness and the doctor's kindness are more important than the plot, and more important than either is the urban malaise suffocating them – specifically that of San Francisco. This was the first British film made in the U.S. since the days of the first Talkies. The camera, wielded by Nicolas Roeg (q.v.) is seldom still, and since Lawrence B. Marcus's sour screenplay is based on a novel called 'Me and the Arch Kook Petulia' it may be said that the film's visual style was appropriate for the kookiness.

On either side of *Petulia*, Lester made two comedies, *How I Won the War* and *The Bed Sitting Room*, so appallingly childish – the second concerned Britain after a nuclear attack – that his neglect over the next years was entirely understandable. He worked in Italian T.V., on commercials, until rescued by Alexander Salkind, who had envisaged **The Three Musketeers** (1973) for a new generation, with a great number of pratfalls and a kick in the groin as likely as a thrust with a sword. Lester's excesses and fussiness proved no substitute for the excitement engendered by previous versions, and Oliver Reed, Charlton Heston (Richelieu), Richard Chamberlain, Faye Dunaway, Raquel Welch, Geraldine Chaplin, Christopher Lee, Michael York and an unfunny comic, Spike Milligan, performed to less than expectations, which in most cases were not high to start with. They had, however, shot enough material for two films, and after re-negotiations involving salaries, *The Four Musketeers* turned up, to appreciably fewer spectators. Lester chose as his screenwriter George MacDonald Fraser, whose Victorian spoof novels about a character named Flashman he had been hoping to film for years. He finally did – *Royal Flash* – to no avail.

Undeterred, Lester tried once more for historical anachronism in **Robin and Marian** (1976). James Goldman provided the screenplay, with a number of thoughts on medieval kingship which he could not fit into *The Lion in Winter* (q.v.), in the process proving that more than realism, i.e. four-letter words and gallons of blood,★ was needed in attempting to redefine old

myths. The aged Robin Hood (Sean Connery) speaks as a modern radical; the peasants are merely oafish; and a number of talented people – Ian Holm, Ronnie Barker, Nicol Williamson, not to mention Audrey Hepburn as Maid Marian – are wasted. Warners offered **The Ritz** (1976) on the principle that Lester's characters are always leaping about, and this concerns a number of chases inside a gay New York bath-house, as adapted by Terence McNally from his own Broadway farce. The film features among others Jack Weston, escaping from his Mafia-minded brother-in-law, Rita Moreno as an untalented but temperamental chanteuse, and Treat Williams as a detective who only looks like Alan Ladd when he is fully clothed. There are good jokes for collectors of gay humour, and Lester's customary facetiousness gives way to that. His later work includes *Superman II* (q.v.).

His erstwhile photographer, Nicolas Roeg (who had also worked with Clive Donner and Schlesinger) became a director, but one less interested in situation and character than camera-angles and ostentatious locations. **Don't Look Now** (1973) and **The Man Who Fell to Earth** (1976) are splendid examples of mumbo-jumbo. The first, an elongation of a supernatural tale by Daphne du Maurier, takes place in a wintry Venice – much less sinister in this film, despite Roeg's tricks, than in reality – and concerns a child who might, or might not, be dead. The second is about an extraterrestrial being (David Bowie) stranded in the wilds of the U.S. and planning to take over control of the world. Paramount backed out from its involvement in the film on seeing it complete, and it was finally taken for America by a minor distributor, Cinema 5, whose president, Don Rugoff, said, 'I didn't understand the film, but the kids really do.' He cut it by 25 minutes, thereby causing Americans to wonder how many of the ambiguities were intentional.

Another director chiefly concerned with effect is John Boorman who, after a British pop film, found himself in the U.S. directing a heist tale with Lee Marvin, **Point Blank** (1967), which borrows all the tricks of Lester and Godard to such an extent that the plot is completely annihilated. One of its producers, Robert Chartoff, combined with Irwin Winkler to produce a similar

★Both elements were edited out of the television print, which I am told is quite pleasing.

movie, *The Split*, after which they backed Boorman's **Leo the Last** (1970), gallantly described by Chartoff as 'considerably ahead of its time' when it flopped with both press and public. It did, however, win the Director's Prize at Cannes, possibly because it can be seen to be directed – that is to say, derelict houses in Notting Hill Gate are painted black, the way Antonioni painted a street in *Il Deserto Rosso*, and the various orgies suggest Fellini. However, Boorman, under control, can direct, as Warners proved with **Deliverance** (1972), which offers the classic cinema suspense of chase and survival. As adapted by James Dickey from his own novel, four city men go canoeing in the Appalachian Mountains. 'The machines are gonna fail,' one (Burt Reynolds) says prophetically, 'the system's gonna fail,' and it is he who is first forced to kill – the mountain man who is raping one of his buddies. You may not care to trace the allegories, but this is the best man–against–nature thriller that films have yet done.

In the matter of showing–off, Boorman and Roeg are minor league compared with Ken Russell, who made the transition from T.V. to cinema with **Women in Love** (1969), written and produced by Larry Kramer with fidelity to its source, but also containing a subtle substitution of his own false premises for Lawrence's – most obviously in the matter of love, marital, carnal, platonic and in the nude wrestling scene between Gerald (Oliver Reed) and Rupert (Alan Bates). Apart from one lingering shot of a rearing horse (symbol of masculinity) over-emphasis is withheld till the final sequence in Zermatt, when the film goes completely off the rails, with Gudrun (Glenda Jackson) prancing round the room, while an ageing queen (Vladek Sheybal) proclaims himself Tchaikovsky. 'I'm a homosexual . . . You will be my wife and writhe on the floor of a railway carriage.' She did, too, for Miss Jackson played Tchaikovsky's wife in Russell's *The Music Lovers*, with Richard Chamberlain as the composer. Aided by some critics' quotes, United Artists was able to advertise the film as having 'raving and hysterical sex', while Russell's on-screen pyrotechnics and his penchant for publicity enabled his next film to arrive as 'Ken Russell's **The Devils'** (1971), the sort of billing it had taken other directors several

years to earn. The film itself is a catalogue of violence, viciousness and sexuality built around the seventeenth century events in Loudon concerning diabolic possession. Not only did it confirm Russell's obsession with such matters, but it proved conclusively that he lacks virtually every requirement of a film-maker. He is capable of putting spectacular and *outré* images on the screen, but he has no gift for character, situation, pacing, rhythm, tension or tone. His subsequent movies, equally bizarre, created increasingly less controversy and less business at the box-office. He blamed the critics, adding that their opinions would not prevent him from making more films. As offers died away, he returned to television. After a three-year absence from films, however, he was invited to Hollywood to film **Altered States** (1980), the adventures of a scientist (William Hurt) who becomes obsessed with taking himself on psychedelic trips. Paddy Chayevsky, who had written the original novel, chose to use a pseudonym for his screenplay credit. Russell's contribution is leaden self-plagiarism, and if the film attracted some mild attention in the States, it was dismissed elsewhere.

For a while it looked as though the young Hungarian-born Peter Medak belonged to this school of showy filmmakers. **Negatives** (1970) consists of 'kinky' games-time between a particularly tedious trio (Glenda Jackson, Peter McEnery, Diane Cilento), and **The Ruling Class** (1972) is an overlong black comedy about an English milord (Peter O'Toole), who fancies himself first as Christ and then as Jack the Ripper, behaving accordingly. Peter Barnes adapted it from his own West End play, continuing to tilt at disused windmills, and Medak was no more able to make the jokes seem fresh than he was of controlling the star, O'Toole, who was also the producer. There was, however, some consolation in the butler (Arthur Lowe), whose servility masks communist sympathies and contempt for his employers. But with a better and more difficult piece, **A Day in the Death of Joe Egg** (1972), Medak proved to be the equal of almost any of his contemporaries. Peter Nichols, adapting his autobiographical play, moves in familiar fields – suburban send-up, nostalgia, family squabbles – but he moves confidently where others toil

and stumble. Since his purpose was to stimulate laughter in detailing the troubles of a couple with a helplessly spastic child, the stage production required the utmost delicacy. Moving in with close-up, Medak achieves an admirable reticence and sympathy which is admittedly aided by the performances of Janet Suzman and Alan Bates. It is a film made with love. Columbia, releasing it, did not love it – afraid, reasonably, of euthanasia as a movie subject. It could only have succeeded at the box office with rave notices, and, opening in the wake of *The Ruling Class*, it was dismissed, with virtually no acknowledgment of its subject or the fact that Nichols's play had been one of the most admired of the past decade.

Jack Gold, who has had more success directing for television than the cinema, made a good film from **The National Health** (1975), adapted by Peter Nichols from his own play. Nichols's virtues as humorist and social historian are evident in this realistic account of life in the ward of an antiquated hospital, its amenities contrasted with the fictional one – the scene of a parody of medical soap operas which cuts into the action. The best feature of the latter is Lynn Redgrave's joyful imitation of her sister Vanessa; the best of the rest of it are the character studies, headed by Jim Dale as the cheeky orderly, and Clive Swift, Colin Blakely and Bob Hoskins as assorted patients.

Another of Nichols's plays, **Privates on Parade** (1982), came to the screen in unfortunate manner, with some palm trees stuck in a sunny English field pretending to be Singapore in 1948. The small budget was also reflected in some historical inaccuracies, but John Cleese is funny as a C.O. magnificently obtuse to the 'camping' all around him – as led by an outrageously effeminate Denis Quilley, repeating his clever and endearing stage performance. Michael Blakemore directed, as he had done for the Royal Shakespeare Company, and there are clear parallels with **The Virgin Soldiers**

(1969), directed by John Dexter, also best known for his work in the theatre. It is also set during the Malayan Emergency, in 1950; and it also has some amusement at the expense of young conscripts and their experience of sex and life in the service before becoming serious – and bloody – up country, to provide the expected antiwar message. As written by John Hopkins from the novel by Leslie Thomas, it is a much better film than *Privates on Parade*; it also reflects the changes wrought in British cinema by being almost the first accurate picture of British service life – marvellously so in its account of the monthly dance, from the hours spent before mirrors with combs and Brylcreem, to disillusion over the available ladies and the movement towards getting as drunk as possible. Hywel Bennett (the hero), Nigel Davenport (the sergeant), Michael Gwynn (the vague colonel), Jack Shepherd (the boastful corporal), Nigel Patrick (the R.S.M.), Rachel Kempson (his wife) and Lynn Redgrave (their daughter) are all splendidly right.

Nichols contributed to **Georgy Girl** (1966), writing the screenplay with Margaret Forster, author of the original novel. The Canadian-born director, Silvio Narizzano, has his predominantly young cast behave in the relentlessly facetious manner of those in the films of Richard Lester, but their antics otherwise are pleasing. The Georgy of the title is an ugly duckling, warmly and touchingly played by Lynn Redgrave, who finds herself permanent second fiddle to her glamorous and promiscuous room-mate (Charlotte Rampling). The latter spends most of her time in bed with Jos (Alan Bates) who, like Georgy's Daddy Long Legs (James Mason), gradually awakens to Georgy's considerable charms. The film was particularly popular in the U.S., where sexual activity was still more or less restricted to the comedies of Doris Day and Rock Hudson.

Narizzano directed **Loot** (1970), which arrived at the same time as **Entertaining Mr Sloane** (1970), directed by Douglas Hickox and also based on a play by Joe Orton. Of all those who cocked a snook at society in the wake of Amis and Osborne, Orton was the most individual, the most extreme and the wittiest, quietly advancing the most outrageous propositions on life behind the lace-curtains. *Mr Sloane*, briefly, concerns a middle-aged brother

(Harry Andrews) and sister (Beryl Reid) each with such lecherous intentions towards a young pick-up (Peter McEnery) that they are prepared to overlook his brutal murder of their father. *Loot* is a tale of two young thieves (Hywel Bennett, Roy Holder) prepared to do anything rather than surrender the swag they have hidden in the coffin of the mother of one of them, and a Scotland Yard man (Richard Attenborough) who has equally few scruples. On the understanding that Orton was a working-class writer, both films are burdened with pop-songs, garish suburban decor and a frenzied pace. They also dilute what was Orton's greatest strength, the Civil Servantese of his dialogue. That *Loot* is the better of the two only indicates the vulgarity of the other.

It may be typical of the British cultural climate that few critics pointed out how unworthy these two films were of their author; few complained at the inadequacy of *Privates on Parade*, and there were few to point out the virtues of *A Day in the Death of Joe Egg*; yet there was an outcry over **Charlie Bubbles** (1967), written by a much lesser figure than either Orton or Nichols, Shelagh Delaney. The film was rejected by the large London cinemas and the circuits, and the press as a whole came to the rescue – though fortunately not encouraging either the writer or the director, Albert Finney, to persevere in these occupations. The direction is, admittedly, observant, particularly on the experience of returning to once-familiar territory, now changed by circumstances and one's own experiences. Finney himself plays the lead and at the end, his problems unsolved, he grabs a balloon and floats out to sea – a final insult in a script of whoozy insignificance.

Even at this level it was clear that the sterility of the old British cinema had gone for ever. Certain talents moved ahead in their own fashion, unaffected by the American money poured into a number of projects, usually elephantine comedies, which tried and failed to unite traditional British humour with the new permissiveness. After its troubles at home at the end of the Sixties Hollywood became more selective in financing British pictures; E.M.I. had a few isolated successes, often with an American co-partner, while Rank and the television-owned I.T.C. limped along. The films of E.M.I. and I.T.C. were likely to be of supposed 'international' appeal, but Rank, too often burnt by like ambitions, backed predominately British films till deciding to quit production in 1980. The producers, directors and writers of the postwar period retired; and, as we have seen, few of those who came to prominence in the Woodfall period and afterwards had more than a precarious foothold. There were movie spin-offs from T.V. series, some very popular, and there were several one-of-a-kind films, symptomatic of an industry divided – sunk back into lethargy and desperate to know what next to put before the cameras.

20th Century-Fox financed **The Rocky Horror Picture Show** (1975), admittedly on a low budget and presumably because the original was then half way through what was to become its ten-year stage run. It is set in a Transylvanian castle where the men walk around in female underwear except for a leather-clad motor-cyclist and a robot fashioned from a physique magazine. A young American couple stumbles upon them, to the confusion of their own sexuality – but that promising idea is lost in timidity. The execution of the musical numbers is execrable and the overall lack of talent quite startling. Said the director, Jim Sharman, 'We've aimed for something tacky . . . It's trivia, but if you want to know what pop-culture in the Seventies is all about, this show will tell you.' He is apparently right: the attention paid to the stage show and the film was initially and at best dismissive, but it has become one of the most persistent items in the weekend midnight matinee repertory. A follow-up, **Shock Treatment** (1981), has not; this particular audience has available a large number of off-centre, low-budget, pornographic and scatological films more satisfying to its taste for camp.

British screen musicals have, with reason, a grim reputation, and **Bugsy Malone** (1976) is even more difficult to sit through than *The Rocky Horror Picture Show*, though made by more talented people. The idea of its writer-director, Alan Parker, was to re-create Chicago gang-warfare in terms of children, with guns firing custard-pies instead of bullets and with orange juice replacing booze; but his young cast was not accomplished enough to disguise the weakness of the musical numbers and the intended satire. Parker, like most British directors of his generation, had graduated from television commercials to television films. The latter include **The Evacuees** (1975), an enchanting, honest and funny account, written by Jack Rosenthal, of two young Jewish boys billeted on a gentile Lancashire family during the War. *Bugsy Malone* came about when Parker realised that there were no films around to which he might take his children, but given the reluctance of British banks to finance local talent Parker did not find it easy to graduate from television to cinema. In this case the government-sponsored National Film Finance Corporation advanced some money, which encouraged Rank and Paramount to supply the rest needed, for the respective British and American rights (the supposition being, as in the case of *The Slipper and the Rose*, *Chitty-Chitty Bang-Bang* and others, that children's films provide an indefinite annuity, though the only proof has been provided by Disney and by M-G-M with *The Wizard of Oz*).

Parker and the producer David Puttnam were each offered **Midnight Express** (1978) by Columbia, and they decided to do it to prove that they could make the sort of action tale which appealed to American audiences. Oliver Stone's screenplay is based on the book by Billy Hayes (played in the film by Brad Davis) about his experiences in a Turkish jail for being in possession of two kilos of drugs. It was a dishonest book, as Puttnam (by his own admission) was increasingly aware, but the film compounds the matter by being rabidly racial. It implies that Hayes was innocent; it makes much of his escape, though he was in fact released under an amnesty agreement; homosexuality was practised by everyone (the commentary informs us) but in the film it is limited to the Turkish guards, who are brutal rapists as well. The Turks as a whole are shown to be hypocrites, only pretending to take a stand on drug-trafficking. Our hero tears out the one good eye and the tongue of a Turkish prisoner, said to be an informer, and we are expected to be sympathetic. The film was popular and considered to be powerful in some quarters, but it received its just deserts in others: *Time* called it 'repulsive' and Tom Milne in *The Observer* 'repellent'.

Working in television Parker had underplayed his situations, but he goes to the other extreme in movies, to the extent of killing whatever subtleties were in Bo Goldman's original script for **Shoot the Moon** (1982). This is one of the crop of Hollywood movies on divorce which followed *Kramer vs. Kramer* (q.v.) and the break-up in question occurs in Marin County between a writer (Albert Finney) and a wife (Diane Keaton) left with several small children. Finney's performance, without any reference to his English accent, and apparently modelled on Dracula, is as showy and heavy as the direction. There is hardly a scene which rings true, and when he goes berserk at the end it seems only too fitting.

Michael Apted has proved a more attentive student of the American scene. His British films are undistinguished, including **Agatha** (1979), a rather pointless investigation into the celebrated disappearance of the thriller writer Agatha Christie in 1926, with Vanessa Redgrave in that role and Dustin Hoffman as an American reporter. The film's thesis is that Ms Christie plans an elaborate plot to murder the mistress of her husband, whom she loathes so much, while the real truth seems to be that she accused her husband of intent to murder before she disappeared and hoped by staying hidden long enough that he would be convicted and hanged. The film is carefully made, but not the polished work that is **Coal Miner's Daughter** (1980), which follows the fortunes of Loretta Lynn from courtship in a Kentucky shack to coping with the stresses of fame as a popular Country and Western singer. Tom Rickman's screenplay, based on Miss Lynn's book, has the richer material in the first half, in its portrait of a primitive community and Lynn's realisation that fame might be at hand. That fame is handled, in the second part of the film, neither mawkishly nor with particular care for the two individuals concerned. They, Miss Lynn and her husband, are admirably played by Sissy Spacek (who was awarded an Oscar) and Tommy Lee Jones.

Agatha, like *Midnight Express*, was produced by David Puttnam, who said that he backed **Chariots of Fire** (1981) because it was the antithesis of the latter – and a more accurate example of the sort of movie he wanted to make. The director, Hugh Hudson, had done some second unit work on Parker's film, and before then had worked in commercials, as is evident from his style on this occasion. Colin Welland's screenplay is founded on what may be said to be false assumptions, since it was based on fact. Harold Abrahams (Ben Cross) was not motivated by his experience of anti-Semitism, but sibling rivalry; and Eric Lidell (Ian Charleson) had long decided to do what the film presents as a huge dilemma for him. But the film's faults are as nothing to its virtues – and, indeed, it was rewarding to find the British cinema, again moribund, making a statement on anti-Semitism and making a film about Cambridge University, about Scottish Presbyterianism and the two runners from each background who went on to triumph in the 1924 Paris Olympics. The film was part-financed by an American group, The Ladd Company, and when 20th Century-Fox (who released in Britain) lost its services, they let the film go with it to Warners. It was awarded a popular Best Picture Oscar and became the most successful 'British' film ever to play in American cinemas. With local production at its lowest level – films for television apart – within living memory, Puttnam became the man on whom the hopes of the British film industry rested, as he well knew: it was to him that aspiring directors and writers brought projects, in the knowledge that the American production companies had confidence in his judgment. He has said that he intends to remain a producer or an executive producer, only working on films to which he can give individual attention. He is encouraging on every aspect of the industry: it may be that he keeps a high profile (because of the Oscar), but I cannot recall in two decades a spokesman with such sound ideas on what British films should be doing.

The local industry was also cheered at this time by **The Long Good Friday** (1981), a corkscrew thriller about an East End gang leader (Bob Hoskins), expertly directed by John MacKenzie, and **Gregory's Girl** (1980), a naive but sweet comedy directed by Bill Forsyth. Forsyth's semi-amateur **That Sinking Feeling** (1979), the adventures of some Glaswegian teenagers, is pretentious, and derivative of Richard Lester's early films. However, the jokes in *Gregory's Girl* spring not from old

movies but the whims and inconsistencies of life. Its young hero (Gordon John Sinclair) is a schoolboy in a new town near Glasgow, and his girl is a rather glamorous young lady (Dee Hepburn) who manages to get herself a place in the boys' football team. David Puttnam invited Forsyth to write and direct a film in the manner of Ealing comedy, and the result was **Local Hero** (1983), a pleasing entertainment which sets two smart American businessmen (Burt Lancaster, Peter Riegert) among some even cannier Scottish villagers, but it is not a very substantial one – at least in comparison with *The 'Maggie'*, but it is possible that Forsyth thought Ealing comedy should not be emulated at this stage.

Forsyth's obvious influences were the films of Ken Loach (b. 1936) and Tony Garnett (b. 1936), the dominant names at that point where British cinema and television meet. Loach made his name with a T.V. documentary in the B.B.C.'s 'Wednesday Play' series, 'Cathy Come Home', followed by another study of working-class life, 'Up the Junction', written by Nell Dunn. While inferior talents made a movie of the second, Joseph Janni – an old Rank hand best noted for finding the backing for Schlesinger's British films – got Loach and Dunn to collaborate on **Poor Cow** (1967), a further thesis on the deprived – in this case, the milieu of petty crooks and their women. This girl (Carol White) shacks up with a pal (Terence Stamp) of her husband's while the latter is in jail. She becomes a barmaid, poses for Sunday morning photographers and is both on the game and in the throes of divorce when the husband returns; they then settle down once more to domestic boredom. Loach was still reacting against films like *The Blue Lamp*, but the field had been long won and the flags run up.

The film is sterile, without the care that makes **Kes** (1970) exceptional. The producer here is Garnett, then a B.B.C. producer, and the director, Loach, is his most famous protégé. Together, with the backing of the short-lived American company, National General, they optioned a novel by Barry Hines and commissioned a screenplay from him, with the budget agreed at $400,000. National General then began to add overheads, etc. and changed its mind at the last minute. Tony Richard-

son, who had wanted Loach to work for Woodfall, took on the project and his clout was sufficient with United Artists for that company to back it. Set in Yorkshire, it is about a boy (David Bradley) and his pet kestrel, in the way that *The Great Adventure* was about a boy and his pet otter. It is also about the experiences of an English childhood, the morning paper-round, reading Desperate Dan, the squabbling family and above all, school – the boring soccer match, the bumptious games master, the sardonic head teacher. The lad himself is reasonably pessimistic, since the male members of the family traditionally go down the mines, and he is not sufficiently intelligent for an alternative job. His imagination has never been fired, he has never seen himself as an individual designated for special attention, and he does not know how to respond in kind to the well-meaning, platitudinous careers officer. Loach offers half-truths some of the time – the clichés of The Wednesday Play as derived jointly from Woodfall, the nouvelle vague and its off-shoot, *cinéma vérité* – but no other British film of the period is as rewarding as this.

British audiences reacted everywhere with glee, but the North Country accents were sufficiently heavy to limit appreciation in the U.S. **Family Life** (1971), however, quickly passed from sight, which is the fate it deserved. The source

Finally, the British cinema found some new talent, in the team of producer Tony Garnett and director Ken Loach, though they have worked mainly in television (and have now split, with Garnett turning director). Admittedly, their few films for the cinema have been patchy, and the only memorable one is *Kes*, about a boy (David Bradley) and his kestrel. Significantly, the boy is less like a younger version of Billy Liar than a sour, English version of the youngster in Olmi's *Il Posto*.

was a T.V. play by David Mercer, doing his own adaptation, and his dialogue is bitingly accurate: but in its dual indictment of the institution of the title and the National Health Service it falters and fails. A nineteen-year-old girl succumbs to a nervous breakdown, and, finally losing the fight, is incarcerated; her quarrelling parents are apparently to blame, and the piece is such a scream of hatred against the suburbs that it flails out in every direction. The same is true of **Bleak Moments** (1971), financed – the cost was £18,000 – mainly by Albert Finney's company, with help from the B.F.I. and written and directed by Mike Leigh, whose work for T.V. and the theatre had been grounded in improvisation. He was responsible for 'Abigail's Party', a funny play about middle-class trendies, but **Grown-Ups** (1980) is again so biased against suburban people that it is boring as entertainment and useless as the social document it pretends to be. Leigh appears not to understand that all writers and film-makers who have successfully portrayed the deprived, be it physically, mentally or financially, have brought compassion to the task.

Tony Garnett does understand that, and turning director, he made **Prostitute** (1980) – which like *Grown-Ups* played a number of festivals but was designed for television audiences rather than the cinema. As a documentary *Prostitute* is impeccable, though Garnett's sympathies lead him not only into a discursive, plotless film, but into a number of schematic devices, so that the social worker (Kate Crutchley), responsible for the welfare of the lady of the title, is not only attached to her in sublimated lesbian fashion but has an affair with a weedy, jargon-spouting sociologist, as if to prove that they are sisters under the skin.

Working for Garnett and the B.B.C., Loach produced some of the best naturalistic work done in television, including the four-part **Days of Hope** (1975), written by Jim Allen, an account of the Labour movement from the Great War to the General Strike as experienced by a nucleus of agitators. This was followed by the two-part **The Price of Coal** (1977), written by Hines, a pertinent study of a mining community in present-day Britain. Garnett's influence on his team must be something of which other producers have only

dreamed: there may further be cited Roland Joffe's **The Spongers** (1978), written by Allen, an indictment of the welfare system, and Leslie Blair's four-part **Law and Order** (1978), written by G. F. Newman, an examination of Scotland Yard corruption. Both are of the same superlative quality. We may have doubts as to whether working-class solidarity is quite such a bulwark, or whether those set in authority over us are quite as venal and inefficient, but the best purpose of polemic is to question, and television – so prodigal with its mediocrity – is a good place for it. The standard of performance in Garnett's films is as extraordinary as their sympathies, and with them should be considered the pieces written by Jack Rosenthal, culminating in **The Knowledge** (1979), a study of London cab-drivers, directed by Bob Brooks, which as pure entertainment and social record is worth all the British cinema films made on either side of it.

Loach described **Looks and Smiles** (1981) as 'very gentle', observing that he is not interested in making propaganda films, since that is limiting. The subject to him is 'about kids coming to terms with the outside world', but to most of us it is about unemployment. The film is a timely reminder of Mrs Thatcher's Britain, with its three million out of work, and it is overly discreet in not mentioning either her or her government. The film looks at two North Country youngsters on the dole, a boy and a girl. The courtship shows how such matters have changed since *A Kind of Loving*. Otherwise these kids are inarticulate and aimless. If there is a danger in the Loach-Garnett approach it is that audiences may find the lack of literacy and the implied contempt of authority somewhat wearisome. They have become clichés among some less talented practitioners of the working-class genre, if I may call it such, though the examples I am thinking of have not left television for cinemas.

With these films in mind – to leave aside the Italian example of R.A.I. – it can only be promising that both the B.B.C. and the commercial television companies (via Channel Four, which began transmissions in 1982) are investing in films for the commercial cinema. The British cinema, otherwise, is virtually dead; but then it has been a long time a-dying. Apart from a period during the war years and just after, it produced little of note till the Woodfall revolt. Between the two it reverted, ethically and intellectually, to the Edwardian period. The Sixties, as a consequence of Woodfall, were enormously vital if leaving little of actual value. Take, for instance, 1967. If we include foreign directors working in Britain, the films include *A Countess from Hong Kong, Blow-Up, Two for the Road, The Deadly Affair* (q.v.), *Half-a-Sixpence, Accident, How I Won the War, Charlie Bubbles, The Whisperers, The Sailor from Gibraltar, Billion Dollar Brain, Far from the Madding Crowd, To Sir with Love, Our Mother's House, Smashing Time, Poor Cow* and *Pretty Polly*. You would have to go back twenty years to find the British industry coping with such confidence with so many themes, most of them rooted in the real world. But vitality proved insufficient. If we accept Chaplin's film as an aberration, *Blow-Up* is the only film by a major artist; and you may otherwise only care to remember *The Deadly Affair, Two for the Road* and *Far from the Madding Crowd*, three superior entertainments. The others strive to preach to us, without success, on the perils of old age, fame, loneliness, Soviet-West relations, war, race, juvenile delinquents, malaise, contemporary London and so on. It is little wonder that the films of the following decade had even less to say.

As the American companies began to pull out of Britain, the industry was left to the old duopoly of Rank and Associated British. At the time of Korda's death British Lion had been taken over by the National Film Finance Corporation, wiping out the debts he left, and for some years it successfully released many important independent productions, including those of the Boultings, Launder and Gilliat and Woodfall, but after the Conservative government decreed an injection of private money in 1963 it underwent a number of board changes and four years later its production was reduced to a trickle. In 1969 Associated British was bought by E.M.I., the giant recording/electronics conglomerate, and under the chairmanship of Bernard Delfont the initial policy was to make films primarily for the home market; when that policy failed (under the aegis of Bryan Forbes), E.M.I. aimed its product at the international market, often with American partnership involved. However, they had a number of expensive failures, such as *Honky Tonk Freeway, Can't Stop the Music* and the 1980 remake of *The Jazz Singer*, while turning down more essentially British projects – notably *Chariots of Fire* and *Gandhi*, Britain's biggest successes world wide since *Tom Jones* twenty years earlier (always excepting the Bond films). Delfont's brother, Lew Grade, the television peer, extended his activities to films, but his I.T.C. company again looked to the international market, with results at worst disastrous and at best unmemorable. Grade was relieved of his position in 1980 after the debacle of *Raise the Titanic*, reckoned to have lost most of its $22 million cost – understandably to those of us unfortunate to have seen it. The company was bought by the millionaire Australian entrepreneur, Robert Holmes a'Court, and it has since – like E.M.I. – proceeded with the utmost caution, usually in conjunction with an American partner. The Rank Organisation reduced its programme to moderate proportions in the early Sixties, sometimes producing less than half a dozen unambitious films in a year: imbued by the renewed competition of E.M.I. and I.T.C. in the late Seventies it began again to spend lavishly, but the public refused to go to see remakes of *The 39 Steps* and *The Lady Vanishes*, as well as *The Riddle of the Sands* and Roeg's *Bad Timing*. When all four failed within the same year, 1979, the company announced that it was quitting production entirely, but might invest in films it would distribute and show in its cinemas. Thus the duopoly of the British film industry was finally broken, and few alive could recall when it had not been there, since the predecessors of Rank and E.M.I. – respectively Gaumont-British and B.I.P. – had become rivals in the Twenties.

There had been, admittedly, a brief period during the War, when Associated British was quiescent and before the rise of Rank, which had seen a large number of independent producers operating, as in France or Italy; and this is the situation today, if we regard E.M.I. as no longer a dominant power. Unlike that time during the War, the Hollywood companies are investing in British movies, which may mean a more viable cinema – for the majority of films presented by I.T.C. and

British Cinema: A Matter of Collusion

E.M.I. in the late Seventies looked like and, indeed, were projects rejected by the American studios. That would seem to be the case of the Cannon group, making some British films after purchasing from Lew Grade the Classic circuit, but Cannon is Israeli-owned and also active in America; a remake of *The Wicked Lady*, directed by Michael Winner, with Faye Dunaway, was not an auspicious start.

And that brings us back to the two Oscar-winners, *Chariots of Fire* and *Gandhi*, both the products of Goldcrest Films, the company founded by a Canadian, John D. Eberts, originally as a sideline to find financing for movies. After four years of activity he obtained backing for an animated feature, *Watership Down*, chiefly from the Pearson-Longman conglomerate, whose subsidiary, Penguin Books, published the paperback edition of the original novel. In 1979 Pearson-Longman invested heavily in Goldcrest, and with the great successes of *Chariots of Fire* and *Gandhi* it may be said that Eberts never looked back. Whether or not he is the new Korda is up to him. He stresses that his team is as important as he is; that he wants his films, preferably, to be both optimistic and British in outlook; and made with British money. But after those two successes – Columbia released *Gandhi* – he has the confidence of Hollywood. The high finan-cial risk involved can be shared with one of the major American companies and one of the American cable companies, such as Home Box Office, which will bring a much quicker return on investment than can be obtained from cinema showings.

But perhaps the most hopeful signal for the British film industry is Eberts's determination to work with as many major film talents as possible. One Puttnam and one Attenborough cannot be heirs to Korda, Balcon and del Guidice, but if a different order is required a sympathetic financier must be the next best thing. Who are to be Britain's film directors is another matter. Tony Garnett, who has an American wife, has moved to Los Angeles, and though his first American film, *Handgun*, was financed by E.M.I., it also has an American setting. Ken Loach may not adapt to the cinema as he should, and the same may be true of several others who have made reputations in television. As far as I am concerned, the jury is still out on such film-makers as Alan Parker and Ridley Scott, who made *The Duellists*, *Alien* and *Blade Runner*. Many of the directors whose work is discussed in the later part of this chapter are in theory active, even if the text implies that their credits ceased years ago. Many have not done interesting work. With the British cinema there have been too many lost chances.

40

Movies Around the World

AS AN EXPERIENCE, the film festival is one of the most ghastly ever to be endured. The two exceptions are those held in London or New York, where a selection has been made of the films shown at other festivals, programmed in reasonable comfort and without undue ballyhoo – though I have never understood the stampede for tickets, since in both cities the foreign films that are distributed usually consist of festival entries, and many festival films are deservedly never seen again. The system is rich with anomalies: the festival organisers in both cities see it as their job to offer a representative selection of world cinema, while at the same time hoping to open up commercial possibilities. Such altruism aside, many of the entries should never have been made in the first place, while others have not had the subsequent showings they deserve. The choice of foreign or foreign-language films available to us depends on the festival organisers and the art-house managers, and no one has yet devised a better system: the later career of Buñuel, the international careers of Bergman, Ray and Kurosawa are all due to showings at festivals. Their works, hitherto considered too parochial, were exposed at those circuses which are the festivals of Cannes and Venice, and it is to these, and increasingly to Berlin, that many film-makers look for the key to international fame.

It is to the festivals that we owe our knowledge of the less prolific and less spectacular native industries – but it remains a partial knowledge. Most festival organisers reserve the right to select from the competing or submitting industries – a fact highlighted when Cannes initially refused *Bugsy Malone* as insufficiently 'esoteric' to justify its inclusion, surely the most foolish criterion ever to be applied to cinema. Secondly, a festival trophy often encourages the initiating producers to over-estimate prospects in the foreign market and ask for an advance which the distributors cannot meet. Eventually, however, the foreign films we see depend less on the vagaries of festival organisers and art-house exhibitors than on the qualities of the films themselves. An art-house distributor does not buy a film from Outer Mongolia to offer his clients a novelty: he hopes to establish a director and/or producer whose work he can profitably handle over the years. It seldom happens.

In 1953, at Cannes, a Brazilian film, **O Cangaciero** – *The Bandit* – attracted some attention. It is a conventional chase story which probably owed its foreign bookings to its catchy theme-tune. Though rather flatly directed by Lima Barreto (1910–82), he might have nevertheless had an international career on the strength of it; but he was so temperamental that his next film was never completed and for the next thirty years quarrels with producers kept his endless projects from being realised. No other Brazilian director attracted world attention till Glauber Rocha (1938–81) made **Antonio-das-Mortes** (1969), another tale of banditry. A burly, bearded trouble-shooter is hired to rid the region of some marauders who prey on the villagers, but, as he discovers, local politicians are using him as a cover to preserve the status quo. Rocha had founded the *cinema novo* movement with the aim of ridding Brazilian cinema of the apparently endless stream of carnival tales which dominated it; he wanted a cinema that acknowledged such realities of Brazilian life as illiteracy, unemployment and poverty. *Antonio* begins as an examination of the place of bandits in popular mythology, but then seems less interested in Brazilian life than in imitating Sergio Leone and Godard, or borrowing from *High Noon* and *The Wild Bunch*, whose bloody conclusion it follows. The film's worst excesses are repeated, with few of its virtues, in **Der Leone Have Sept Cabecas** (1970).

Among Rocha's followers the most exceptional would seem Ruy Guerra (b. 1931), whose more conventional approach is due to his training with Jean Delannoy in France. Born in Mozambique, he examines both the terrain of Brazil and its mythology with the same fascination as Rocha, but with less wilful obscurity. **Os Fuzis** (1963) is accordingly much more successful in demanding that political and religious leaders consider the plight of the peasants. The film is overlong and sometimes arid, which is a pity, for its theme is original and interesting – the interplay of a lonely army garrison and the apathetic peasantry, either of which might ignite the spark which sets off the explosion.

Dona Flor and her Two Husbands (1978) is a very different kettle of fish as written and directed by Bruno Barreto from a novel by Jorge Amado, which uses the situation of 'Blithe Spirit' without Coward's invention or any native wit. When Vadinho (José Winkler) drops dead returning from carnival, Dona Flor (Sonia Braga) later remembers both how he ill-treated her and how rapturous were their nights – in contrast to the hesitant, rhythmic love-making of her second husband, a stuffy, bourgeois chemist (Mauro Mendonça). Barreto's contrasting of the two marriages is as subtle as his handling of the sex sequences is not, and he fails to derive any humour from the situation of the first husband turning up as a ghost. Nevertheless, the American art-house public was much amused, but in Britain the critics' scorn quickly despatched the piece – which is sad because the local colour is pleasing.

The local colour in **Pixote** (1981) is urban and reminiscent of *Los Olvidados*. It is the third film made by Hector Babenco, a Chilean now living in Brazil, who appears at the outset to explain that Brazil has three million homeless children who are prey to adult criminals who coopt them

to work for them, since those under eighteen cannot be prosecuted. Pixote himself is twelve; he spends the earlier part of the film in reform school, where violence, sudden death, brutality and homosexual rape are everyday occurrences. The tradition of films about such institutions has accustomed us to the bullying, sadistic guards and the apathy of the rest of the staff: but the details are so degrading as to suggest Babenco did first-hand research in a just mood of reforming zeal. But after Pixote has escaped he carries on a life of crime involving drugs, pornography and prostitution – all aspects which movies have glamorised, and despite some squalor this one is not entirely free of that quality. When Pixote walks away at the end, a killer twice over, we do not know whether he goes to a bleak future or more prostitutes and pornography. The film would have been more honorable, and its moral better stated, had it been the second half, rather than the first, which had been wholly pessimistic; but then it might not have enjoyed its great success.

The best-known South American director remains the Argentinian, Leopoldo Torre Nilsson (1924–78), who expressed his dissatisfaction with society in very different terms. The Government on occasion took exception to his work, critical as it was of the bourgeoisie and the decadence that he found inseparable from it. In fact he seems to have been as much attracted as repelled by his subject matter. Torre Nilsson's world is of huge cloistered mansions, their curtains drawn, their furniture baroque, their conservatories stuffed with hot-house plants. It is a world in which the old are grasping and either gossiping or reminiscing about the past – and it is there that they seem to live, with the manners and clothes of their youth. The young go about their business with the calm of an earlier time, and that business is chiefly sexual. They dream and write love letters, reluctant to form permanent relationships. The girls indulge in fantasies of being deflowered by idealised men, who are the playboys who suggest – but never seem to experience – any number of perversions which they surely have the means to buy. They are all far less creatures of action than their cousins in Buñuel – and even more isolated from reality: it is not for nothing that a Torre Nilsson heroine may be found reading Proust, since an echo of the imprisoned Albertine reappears constantly in his work. That has a consistency almost unequalled in cinema – at least from 1957, when his eighth film attracted attention at the Cannes Film Festival. The first two were made in collaboration with his father, who was also a director; the year that Cannes made him an international figure he married the novelist Beatríz Guido, who was responsible for the screenplays and/or stories of most of his subsequent films.

It is conceivable that they were both influenced by Jean Anouilh, since the theme of youth corrupted or disillusioned by hypocritical elders surfaces so often. In **La Casa del Angel** (1957) and **La Caida** (1959) a charming and somewhat withdrawn blonde actress, Elsa Daniel, plays an adolescent whose life is restricted, in the first case by a prudish mother and a politically ambitious father, and in the second by a group of infant harpies. The chief protagonist of **Fin de Fiesta** (1960) is male, but also young, and, like her, he will eventually expiate the evils and mysteries of the grown-ups' world; he is caught between meaningless feuds – and, this being a Torre Nilsson film, is seduced in a chicken-house of all places. Miss Daniel plays a gauche girl in **La Mano en la Trampa** (1961), who finds that the contempt of her elders no longer matters when she becomes infatuated with an older stranger (Francisco Rabal); and since there is a secret in the attic you may think of 'Jane Eyre'. The gothic strain plays even more beautifully in **Piel de Verano** (1962). A wealthy girl is promised a trip to Paris by her grandmother if she will nurse the son, apparently fatally ill, of that lady's lover: but he is cured when they fall in love – or seem to fall in love; and she finds that she is the reason for his death as she was for his life.

Such tales hardly indicated great seriousness, yet Torre Nilsson was not only the one Argentine film-maker able to command world attention, but the only one to do so from the South American continent – and at that time, Buñuel apart, the only one to do so from Spanish-speaking territories. Important directors are expected to tackle weighty matters, which may be why Torre Nilsson turned to a study of a young revolutionary in **El**

Ojo de la Corradura (1965). He uses the labyrinth of Latin American politics as an occasion for comedy more sardonic than usual, and in moving from his familiar territory he reveals a remarkable aptitude for the form required. Martin – played by Stathis Giallelis, the young hero of Kazan's *America, America* – temporarily has to cease his activities with a Fascist terrorist organisation, and is forced to hole up in a decaying, claustrophobic hotel, accompanied by a childhood friend, Inês (Janet Margolin): in idleness, he manages to convince himself that the theatrical troupe down the hall are assassins, their victim to be a visiting dictator whom he particularly admires. Torre Nilsson expends on this misguided idealist his customary care when confronted with the abnormal or distorted psychology of the young: but this time the increasingly nightmarish world is one of the young man's own making – but not that far away from the 'normal' world we experience every day.

It is by far the most satisfying of Torre Nilsson's films, and till we can see the dozen or so subsequent films which were not exported we must conclude that the rest of his career was an anti-climax. He was not successful with a film made in English, in Puerto Rico, **Monday's Child** (1967), with Arthur Kennedy and Geraldine Page; and, as I have implied, the films that followed did not reach the major festivals. While we did not hear from him he had, like all film-makers, moved from

The films of the Argentinian director Leopoldo Torre Nilsson made an impact on the art-house circuit in the late Fifties and early Sixties and his present neglect is inexplicable. In suggesting decadence among the bourgeoisie he is not the master Buñuel is, but he is a master nevertheless, entirely consistent in his approach to the evils unshown and unnamed. In *La Casa del Angel* Elsa Daniel grows into adolescence dreaming of seduction by a political friend of her father, Lautaro Murua. It happens at her instigation, but the aftermath is not quite what she expected.

monochrome to colour, and strangely it did not suit him.

His powerful visual style had been a matter of dark shadows, tilted angles and the soft whites of girlhood; there were whispers, remarks half-heard and old gramophone records; his elliptical narrative style had preceded that of the European directors, but both **Boquitas Pintadas** (1974) and **Piedra Libre** (1976) seem not only old-fashioned but, compared with his other films, commonplace. The first, based on a strongly satiric novel by Manuel Puig, who wrote the screenplay with Torre Nilsson, deals with a group of friends over the years, and mostly the relationship of one (Marta Gonzales) with a cheap, tubercular Lothario (Alfredo Alcón); the second concerns another virginal girl (Marlina Ross), an orphan, who becomes in time a Becky Sharp-like intruder able to take over the household because of what she has learnt. It was the last in a series of skirmishes with authority, who banned it for 'immorality' and 'attacks on family, religion and class structure'. European and American critics, after an initial fascination, dismissed Torre Nilsson as a maker of women's weepies, which is certainly less than the truth. He is a minor master, believing absolutely in his own created world, and on that matter generally persuasive.

The only other South American country to have successfully exported film is Chile, but despite the title **Valparaiso Mi Amor** (1970) Aldo Francia's film reveals that, as he said, he speaks not only for his own country: 'Our social reality in Chile and Latin America is too horrible to be reproduced as pamphletarian caricature.' The voice is that which Buñuel used in *Los Olvidados*, but is somewhat less dispassionate, as befits his indebtedness to the nouvelle vague (evidenced by stills from their films stuck on an office wall). The setting is a shanty-town, and the subject the tribulations of one of its families, somewhat too thinly drawn but with compensation in Francia's rich portrait of the city. It is an accomplished movie for a film industry a year old. The first Chilean feature had been produced with the cooperation of one of the country's six universities – **El Chacal de Nahueltoro** (1969), directed by Miguel Littin, and it would be a remarkable film under any circumstances. Based on fact, it is about a murderer, the jackal of the title: the cinema has a long history of sympathetic studies of murderers, and Littin is clever in completely avoiding sentiment, while extracting compassion for the peasantry – not, however, shown as other than illiterate and brutalised. But **La Tierra Prometida** (1974) contained all the pitfalls open to an inexperienced film-maker, and Littin fell into every one of them. His expressed undertaking was to side-step history as interpreted in 'the interests of the bourgeoisie' and 're-read the class struggle in the light of Marxism': his subject is a band of itinerant workers who, in 1932, attempted a cooperative on some acres of land which they hoped had been abandoned. The film was not started until after Allende came to power, and not finished till after the *putsch*: Littin had to flee, and in Mexico he found his favoured subject, 'the origins of the working class and the origins of Fascism and repression in Chile'. **Actas de Marusia** (1976), again based on fact, deals with an incident in 1907, when the inhumanly-treated workers in a saltpetre mine revolted against its British owners. Littin wrote the screenplay from information supplied by a fellow-Chilean, Patricio Mans, based on the 'letters' of the title, but the information he offers us is still not enough; he is too busy theorising. He has learnt to present an identifiable hero, played by Gian-Maria Volonté, but makes the mistake of assuming that we all share his view that policemen and soldiers are pigs.

The same incident serves as the source for a film by the Cuban Humberto Solás, already known for **Lucia** (1969), a prize-winner at the Moscow film festival. It conforms, alas, to stereotype, being again about revolution – though as this seems a staple of both Latin American cinema and the communist block it is perhaps inevitable in Cuba; and, as with many products of young film industries, it reflects influences – in the first section of this tripartite film, those of Buñuel, Renoir, Kurosawa, Welles and Visconti. This episode, set in 1895, is routine movie stuff, but the others, concerning later Lucias at other times of revolution, are, in contrast, concise, beautifully observed, and filmed with verve. Solás' film on the saltpetre workers,

Cantata de Chile (1976), is also based on material supplied by Patricio Mans; it too has its longueurs, as when the workers are proclaiming their solidarity or haranguing their colleagues – as always the fault of communist films, but Solás has more intelligence and imagination than most communist-bloc directors. He is violently didactic, but whereas with Littin one wants him to copy Costa-Gavras and hurl both narrative and propaganda at us simultaneously, Solás takes his own reasonable time. His exposition of the aspirations of the strikers and the moderation of their masters is exemplary. (The faces of the strikers disbelievingly comprehending that *their* government supports the *foreign* interests is one of the most eloquent images in cinema.) His purpose is to show the roots of totalitarianism in Chile from the conquistadores to the nineteenth-century presidents, and he uses any means that he thinks fit, be it tableaux, swirling mists, coloured lights or speeches addressed directly to the audience: his achievement is to have taken these theatrical devices and transformed them into pure – and very exciting – cinema. The film was designed as 'an act of solidarity with the Chilean people', but, in the director's words, 'I feel that the film's significance could transcend Latin America and operate in the same way in any context of oppression and under-development.' For once a director's claims for significance in his own work are justified.

In 1981 there were retrospectives in Berlin and London of the Portuguese director Mañoël de Oliveira (b. 1908), plus a laudatory article by John Gillett in *Sight and Sound*. De Oliveira is an interesting figure, and he can be a film-maker of force and imagination, but I do not think he is of world class. He has spent most of his life working in the family's manufacturing plant and, until recently, made only an occasional film. His first short, a documentary, was filmed in 1931, and his first feature, **Aniki-Bobó** (1942), more than a decade later. It is nicely photographed in the streets and along the river-banks of his native city, Oporto, and follows the adventures of some children,

Lucia won the Grand Prix at the 1969 Moscow Film Festival, which was not surprising since that particular festival tends to award prizes to films from other Communist countries – and in this case we may see the award as a pat on the back for a fledgling industry in a country not long converted to that way of life, Cuba. All the same, Humberto Solás's three-part epic has such verve that it is a pity that we have not seen more of his work. Playing the first of the three Lucias in the three episodes is Raquel Revuelta.

1143

among them Carlitos, who steals a doll from a shop and then returns it when the shopkeeper proves that he is not to be blamed for an accident that befell one of his friends. De Oliveira did not film again till he made **The Passion of Christ** (1963), an account of the annual passion play which takes place in the village of Chaves, some fifty miles from Oporto. The scenes of village life are engaging, but some symbolism at the end, meant to remind audiences of the Cuba crisis of the previous year, looks merely jejune.

A decade later the Gulbenkian Foundation decided to subsidise the Portuguese cinema and de Oliveira took the opportunity to make **Past and Present** (1972), based on a comedy by Vincente Sanches that he particularly admired. In investigating the antics of some wealthy friends of the upper bourgeoisie the film has moments of sour humour, particularly in respect of their marital affairs, but as a whole the piece is less taking than Buñuel's similar Mexican films. It was successful enough for de Oliveira to accept an assignment (he had been his own producer on his earlier films), but **Benilde, Virgin and Mother** (1975) is no more than a photographed play – and not a very good one. Its heroine, a strange girl, is found to be pregnant, and the resolution is found in Act III, that she was 'taken advantage of' while sleepwalking; or else the father is the village idiot heard moaning off screen. That is about the level of it. That de Oliveira might one day make a first-rate movie was not confirmed by **Ill-Fated Love** (1978), a television serial adapted for cinema showings abroad. Based on a nineteenth-century novel of passion by Camilo Castelo Branco, noted for its exuberance (and already filmed twice), the film is anything but: the cardboard characters come and go before a motionless camera – so immobile, in fact, that it lingers on long after they have left any individual scene.

Any reflection on the small Portuguese film industry could be deflected across the Peninsula and along the Mediterranean, to Greece. Conditions there were equally inauspicious for movie-making: a sparse population, with few big cities, so that films were aimed at the mainly unsophisticated audiences of rural areas – thus limiting the prospects of overseas distribution.

Film production began in the early Twenties, and consisted chiefly of theatrical melodramas and light comedies with songs. The standard and output both declined in the late Thirties and during the German Occupation, but American aid in the postwar period brought a revival of Greek cinema, in subject matter deeply indebted to what was happening in Italy at that time. Nevertheless the first Greek film-maker to receive international attention was Michael Cacoyannis (b. 1922) – which is ironic, for he was born in Cyprus under British rule. He studied and worked in London during the War and afterwards, mainly as actor and producer under the name of Michael Yannis; it is perhaps because of his British connections that his first film was shown at the Edinburgh Festival in 1954.

Windfall in Athens (1953) is a slight film, and fresh, despite its debt to French and Italian comedies of the period. The locations are pleasing and the opening is delightful, showing the leading characters rising one Sunday morning and contemplating how to spend the day. The script, by Cacoyannis himself, is not as bright, telling as it does of a girl (Elli Lambetti) who has her clothes stolen while swimming and therefore loses the lottery ticket in a pocket; there are complications for the unhappily married man who has given her a lift from the beach and for the young man (Dimitri Horn) who has purchased the ticket from the thieves. **Stella** (1955) was sent to Cannes, where it was respectfully received, though it is even more derivative – relying heavily on the low life peasant melodramas emanating from Italy. Stella is a singer, wrongly identified in the subtitles as a whore: 'When she likes a man, she goes crazy' says someone, and as played by Melina Mercouri it is a vast understatement. When she throws over her gentleman for a footballer, it is like tigers mating, but when he forces her to marry she absents herself from the ceremony to spend the night dancing with a student: and then, rather than lose her freedom, she lets him stab her to death. Helped by the photography of Walter Lassally (who would frequently work in Greece in the years to come), Cacoyannis did much more complicated work in **A Girl in Black** (1955), based on his own, more confident, screenplay. A young writer

Most Greek films are for strictly local consumption, and those that appear abroad are usually heavy-breathing bucolic dramas, dubbed for their particular market. That leaves Michael Cacoyannis, a Cypriot, as the only Greek director of international renown (if we except Costa-Gavras, who has not directed in his native land). Cacoyannis has made some poor films, including the English-language *Zorba the Greek*, but he has made one film of high quality, *A Matter of Dignity*, a study of Athenian high society. Elli Lambetti is the girl in search of a wealthy husband, and she chooses Minas Christades, right, in preference to Michel Nikolinakos, whom she really loves.

(Dimitri Horn) goes to Hydra, where he is drawn into the feud between a girl (Miss Lambetti) and a local fisherman who has been persecuting her because she has rejected him.

Moving away from peasant drama, to Athenian high society, Cacoyannis made his best film, **A Matter of Dignity** (1957). The title refers to an impoverished aristocratic family trying to keep up appearances till the daughter (Miss Lambetti) has hooked a wealthy fiancé. The story is not unlike that of *Calle Mayor* and Cacoyannis responds as easily as Bardem to time and place – an empty house after a party, a seedy café, the streets above the town at night; both films share the suggestion that 'society' is basically as unhappy as it is worthless. **Our Last Spring** (1960) also has a familiar theme, that of adolescent responsibility to the adult world, as a group of boys grope their way to manhood; but the plot is indecipherable. Warners financed, which may be why Cacoyannis chose to film in English; but

he conformed to that rule by which European directors seem bound to make bad films when they have American backing.

He restored his reputation with **Electra** (1962), based on Euripides, and considered to be the first successful film of a classic Greek tragedy. In fact, the approach is desperate to make an effect, but Lassally's photography and the locations, in and around Mycenae, somewhat disguise that; and the face and presence of Irene Papas in the title-role are assets, though she hardly gives a performance. The moderate success of the film enabled Cacoyannis to embark on **Zorba the Greek** (1964), with the backing of 20th Century-Fox and the participation of Anthony Quinn as the male equivalent of the role Mercouri played in *Stella* – 'a life force', as the studio synopsis succinctly put it. As adapted from the novel by Kazantzakis, the life force introduces a prissy young Anglo-Greek (Alan Bates) to the joys of ouzo and the sirtaki, as well as into the bed of a young widow (Miss Papas), who is consequently stoned by the villagers. The film, aspiring to the 'realism' of *La Terra Trema*, is rather like nineteenth-century academic painting – predictable, sentimental, meticulous and empty. However, Cacoyannis knew what he was doing, and the easily-assimilated message found a large response, especially in the U.S., where, following *La Dolce Vita*, it confirmed prejudices about European life. In *The New York Times*, Bosley Crowther's fulsome notice referred to 'the meanness and ignorance of the people of Crete . . . [and] the hard, barren look of the island', thereby showing his own ignorance and unwittingly explaining why the film was as much loathed in Greece as it was admired elsewhere.

20th Century-Fox rewarded Cacoyannis by letting him film a subject of his own choosing, **The Day the Fish Came Out** (1967), a crypto-homosexual comic allegory, in English, about two atom bombs lost in the Aegean. The reviews were contemptuous and business minimal, forcing Cacoyannis back to classic tragedy again to retrieve his reputation. **The Trojan Women** (1971) uses Edith Hamilton's archaic translation, with some updating ('What's up?'), and Cacoyannis' own approach is no more consistent, free of whatever restraints had been imposed earlier by the Peloponnese (this was filmed in Spain). Katharine Hepburn, misled by critics who had hailed her as a tragedienne for her performance in *Long Day's Journey into Night* (q.v.), makes a querulous Hecuba. In 1977 Cacoyannis made his last film to date, *Iphigenia*, which passed unnoticed.

The house of Atreus is to be found again in **The Travelling Players** (1975), in the guise of a theatrical troupe in Greece between 1922 and 1952, but mostly during the war years. Such plot as there is might have been compressed into ten minutes, but the film lasts almost four hours as amateurishly directed by Theodor Angelopolos, whose other films have been poorly received: why this one escaped that fate is unfathomable.

Feature film production in Canada was sporadic till recent years; traditionally aspiring directors and artists sought work in London or, preferably, Hollywood. Documentaries have a stronger tradition, following the appointment of John Grierson as Film Commissioner in 1939 and the establishment of the National Film Board of Canada, which produced cartoons as well as non-fiction pieces. The Board's most prolific exponent was Norman McLaren, whose many experiments, like scratching patterns on celluloid, were too arid for most audiences. A one-time colleague, Claude Jutra (b. 1930), directed the first Canadian film widely seen abroad, **Mon Oncle Antoine** (1971), produced by l'Office National du Film du Canada. Set in a small, snow-covered town in Quebec Province, it is a familiar story of adolescence, with the customary sexual encounters. Jutra retrogressed rapidly with **Kamouraska** (1973), an attempt to blend the plot of 'Thérèse Raquin' with the vapourings of a Barbara Cartland – and filmed with greater fidelity to romantic fiction than the Zolaesque elements.

Jutra's two films were made as a consequence of the 1967 Act of Parliament setting up the Canadian Film Development Corporation, and after the mild success abroad of the first of them the Corporation became confident of success in world markets. Canadian-born artists were encouraged to return, but there was contention over the number of American and British players acceptable, especially as some of them were paid more than their usual fees and were, in any case, of doubtful box-office standing. With Government money, therefore, being injected either wholly or partially in a score or so films annually since 1970, it is disappointing that during that time only four have been made of more than passing interest.

The Apprenticeship of Duddy Kravitz (1974) was directed by Ted Kotcheff, who had made a handful of undistinguished British films, and it is based on a novel by Mordecai Richler, also a Canadian living in Britain. Richard Dreyfuss is the Duddy of the title, with some fellow Americans in support – Randy Quaid, Jack Warden and Joseph Wiseman (who was however born in Montreal) – and the British Denholm Elliott. Elliott repeats his performance of *Nothing but the Best*, but then the piece is itself a replication, a Montreal version of Budd Schulberg's 'What Makes Sammy Run?' with some bawdiness and an attempt to portray a Jewish community with less gloss than *Goodbye Columbus* (q.v.). Like *Mon Oncle Antoine* it is set in the recent past, as is **Why Shoot**

the Teacher? (1977), directed by Silvio Narizzano, another Canadian with some British (and American) credits. Yet again the source is an autobiographical book, by Max Braithwaite, played in the film by Bud Cort. In 1935 he left home to be a teacher to a small community on the Great Plains, clearly not a congenial place for that particular profession. The yokels seem in some perverse way to have modelled themselves on Ma and Pa Kettle and, again, the piece is consistently second-hand, even to the ending, when Max returns to fight back; but there is a nice moment when he and a farmer's wife (Samantha Eggar) read scenes from 'Private Lives'.

Outrageous (1977) features Craig Russell, a female impersonator, and the source is a story by Margaret Gibson, who lived with Russell at one point: we may therefore assume autobiography again, in this tale of a schizophrenic girl (Hollis McLaren), escaped from a mental home, who is befriended by a drag queen, and later reunited with him in the U.S. They are at home: 'There are eight million of us and we're all alive and sick and living in New York.' It is a naive film, and the equation of drag and homosexuality may be offensive to some; but it is honest and funny and, to use David Robinson's surprising but accurate adjective in The Times, endearing. The director is Richard Benner, from television and Toronto-based, who made it for $165,000 (Canadian). Zale Dalen, from Vancouver and with several successful shorts to his credit, made **Skip Tracer** (1977) for $20,000 less – and it would be a considerable achievement had it cost three times that amount. The title refers to the occupation of its protagonist (David Peterson), which is to exact payment for his employer, a finance company, or repossess, which may mean stripping the house to the last ashtray. When we meet him, he is the perfect company man, almost an automaton; when he eventually cracks the film becomes a study in conscience, but it is always as tight and taut as a thriller. Both films are about people leading offbeat lives, but they are genuinely illuminating and a sure guide to the direction that subsidised cinema should take.

The most successful Canadian feature to date is **Porky's**, released in 1982 and made in Florida with an American cast and mainly with American money. The others, in order, are Quest for Fire, Meatballs, The Changeling, Murder by Decree, The Apprenticeship of Duddy Kravitz, Heavy Metal, Black Christmas, The Amateur and Why Shoot the Teacher? It is not a list to give any Canadian self-respect, even though it does not reveal the fact that most of the subsidised films made in Canada are cheap, mindless, horror films. That can make no one proud, particularly when compared with what has been happening in Australia during this time.

The Australian film industry is much older than that of Canada, and it is reputed to have had a success during the war years with **40,000 Horsemen** (1940), directed by Charles Chauvel. His uncle had been commander of the Australian Light Horse in the Sinai desert campaign, a subject which so filled Chauvel with enthusiasm that he started this film in 1938, as another world war looked imminent: but he shot the bulk of it in 1940, when the outbreak of that war had given the project new meaning. The action scenes are well managed – some sand dunes near Sydney stood in for the desert – but almost everything else is lamentably amateurish, including the performances of assorted Turks, Germans and Arabs. The 'French' heroine (Betty Bryant) dons Arab garments for the sort of adventures unseen since the early Twenties, including an oasis meeting with the Anzac hero (Grant Taylor). If this film was not laughed at on its British and American showings (I can find record of only a few) it can only be because its heart is in the right place.

Consequently, it was not until the Seventies that Australia, like Canada, decided to confront the international market. There were similar reasons – the need for star names was disappearing and most people the world over watched movies in the English language in the first place. The Australians were too modest to suppose that the world was waiting for their films, but they could be cheaply made and there was also a possibility of a television sale abroad. And a number of Australians who had learnt their craft in television wished to try it out in movies made for the cinema. Show business was burgeoning with the population and local taste was thought to be much more sophisticated than it had been. Nevertheless, some broad and blunt-witted comedies were not initially intended for overseas consumption – those featuring the fictitious Alvin Purple and his non-fictitious counterpart Barry McKenzie, whose forte is the impersonation of typical cobbers; but their popularity at home aroused some scattered foreign bookings.

Those encouraged Michael Thornhill, a former critic and documentary filmmaker, to engage a British name, Corin Redgrave, to star in **Between Wars** (1974), written with Frank Moorhouse from the latter's account of Dr Edward Trenbow, whose experience in the First World War led to his becoming a specialist in nervous disorders and a campaigner against Australia's involvement in World War II. It was an intelligent choice of subject to offer to world audiences, and it impressed those who thought the Australian cinema consisted of comedies about Alvin and Barry; but seen ten years later, the material is mishandled, the period detail often absurd and the performances, except Redgrave's, stilted.

Thornhill made other films, each less well received than the one before, while Peter Weir (b. 1944) was the one Australian director to become well known abroad. He had been making documentaries with the Commonwealth Film Unit when given the chance to put into production **The Cars That Ate Paris** (1974), part-written by him and based on his own idea. Driving in the New South Wales outback two brothers are in a strange accident which is fatal for one of them. The survivor (Terry Camilleri) finds himself overcome by inertia, a 'vegie', as the population refers to the other, numerous victims of accidents. The affable mayor (John Meillon) is clearly lying when he claims that all is well, for the older citizens are just as clearly terrified of the strangely-garbed youths and their even stranger cars. It is not a successful film artistically; it seems to proclaim that it is not what was expected of an Australian film – which is both its strength and its weakness, its originality and its showing-off. Nor was it a success locally (though it would give rise to *Mad Max*, a not dissimilar tale, which has been one of Australia's biggest hits worldwide to date).

Nevertheless, the strangeness of the idea, coupled with Weir's skill, gained the film some bookings abroad, encouraging those factions in Sydney and Melbourne who were clamouring for an indigenous industry making worthwhile films. Its members were reckoned to be Socialist, and a Socialist Government had come to power in 1972 under the leadership of Gough Whitlam, who believed it was time for Australians to be proud of being Australians instead of relying on Britain and the U.S. for their culture. Accordingly the Australian Film Commission was established in 1975, to help commercial companies finance their product: by 1980 over fifty films had received Government money, of which approximately 38% was returned from box-office receipts – most of it from only eight films. Twenty-eight of the others were a total write-off.

Prior to the establishment of the A.F.C., the state of South Australia had decided to provide funds for film-makers, and New South Wales was to follow (both under Labour administrations); by the end of the decade most of the other states had followed suit. Virtually every Australian film since to find a welcome abroad has had public money contributing to its financing, and the results, though variable, are proof overall of Whitlam's theories. Alone, the first film of the South Australian Film Corporation (in this case the sole backer) is sufficient justification for state support: for **Sunday Too Far Away** (1974) is at the same time very Australian and very accomplished, as directed by Ken Hannam, who had worked in British and Australian television. It is an account of the sheep-shearers' strike in the outback in 1955, written by John Dingwall with a fine disregard for the clichés of other tales set in remote, enclosed communities; and its star is the fine actor Jack Thompson, who more than any of his colleagues has some of the heroic stature of the great Hollywood male stars.

The film made only a mild impact in the international market, unlike an Antonioni-like mystery, **Picnic at Hanging Rock** (1975). This proved to be *the* breakthrough for the Australian cinema in most countries, except in the U.S. where the public refused to be drawn to a mystery which remained unsolved at the end. The picnic of the title was held on St Valentine's Day,

1900, when three schoolgirls disappeared: only one was found (a week later) so that Cliff Green's script, from Joan Lindsay's factual novel, does not distort historical fact, but it is more inconclusive than it need be. The director, Peter Weir, is no Antonioni, able to examine either a relationship or a society in this context. Rather, his narrative is so consistent with the pregnant looks passed between the girls as they dress in the first scene that it is hardly compelling. Weir's ambitions go more awry in **The Last Wave** (1977), an attempt to translate to Sydney his own mystical experience while visiting Roman ruins in Tunisia. At a time of strange climatic omens, a young lawyer (Richard Chamberlain) dreams about an aborigine, whom he subsequently meets when asked to defend a group of them involved in a drunken brawl; through him he meets a tribal elder who tells the lawyer that he believes him to be the descendant of a South American race which had inhabited Australia in prehistoric times, and with him he goes to see paintings by his supposed ancestors, Mayan in design and predicting a cataclysmic disaster to precede spiritual renewal for the world. Like *The Cars That Ate Paris*, the film hopes to stun with its originality, but it too is confused when it thinks it is being profound. For all that, it is likeable and proof of an energetic and confident talent.

Meanwhile, the success of *Picnic at Hanging Rock* had established, for good or ill, a temporary pattern for Australian cinema: the stories were without melodramatics, they were set in the recent past and were often factual. The second of several school stories was **The Devil's Playground** (1976), an admittedly autobiographical account written and directed by Fred Schepisi, who had worked on commercials and documentaries. He had contributed to a three-part feature, *Libido*, working with the novelist Thomas Keneally, who appears in this film as a Catholic priest. The film is set in a Roman Catholic seminary in the autumn of 1953, skittering between the adolescent discontent of one boy (Simon Burke) and the misfit masters, including one going mad from (hetero)sexual abstinence and another whose beery approaches to women disguise his fear of them. The many references to masturbation serve to

underline the fact that all the school needs is an influx of women, but despite some sharp character sketches it adds up to very little.

Storm Boy (1976) also has a young hero (Greg Rowe), and it could be termed a boy-and-pelican film. The youngster lives with his dour hermit of a father (Peter Cummins) and as well as the pelican he is friendly with an aborigine (Gulpilil); their adventures, touching if a little banal, take place along the Cooring Beach of South Australia, whose Film Corporation produced. The film was such a great success Down Under that a follow-up was planned, **Blue Fin** (1978), with most of the same team, young Master Rowe, the screenwriter Sonia Berg (again working from a novel by Colin Thiele) and the cinematographer Geoff Burton. The French-born director of *Storm Boy*, Henri Safran, was replaced by Carl Schultz, and because that film had made little impact overseas the German actor Hardy Kruger was brought in to play Rowe's father, the

Not till the Sixties was the Australian cinema fit to travel, since it was hardly of a high standard. The breakthrough came with some comedies taking advantage of the new permissiveness and, to be fair, their crudeness was offset by an amused insight into the Aussies' innocence in such matters. There followed hard upon them a tale of the Outback, which might be supposed to be for local consumption only; but *Sunday Too Far Away*, directed by Ken Hannam and acted by Jack Thompson, is an absorbing drama.

1149

captain of a small craft who despises the boy so much that he thinks him unworthy to follow in his footsteps. Uncredited, Bruce Beresford (q.v.) reshot some of Kruger's footage, using a double, to make him more sympathetic, but it was, deservedly, a failure in direct proportion to its predecessor.

Meanwhile, some more substantial films were being made. **The Mango Tree** (1977) was directed by Kevin Dobson, a newcomer from television, and adapted from a novel by Ronald McKie by the producer, Michael Pate, returning to his homeland after some years playing small roles in Hollywood. He also put his son Christopher in the lead, a rather uninteresting schoolboy who is taught the facts of life, apparently for his own good, by the French mistress – an action guessed at and approved of by his grandmother (Geraldine Fitzgerald). In other ways, too, the film contradicts our knowledge of the way people thought and behaved in 1915 (or thereabouts), so that this was another justified failure. The past was more respectfully re-created in **The Picture Show Man** (1977), directed by John Power, which follows the peregrinations of Pop (John Meillon), who, with his screen, projector, son and dog, goes from town to town hiring halls for his (Silent) movies. The film was written by Joan Long, who also wrote **Caddie** (1976) from an autobiography of a lady of that name, played in the film by Helen Morse. It details the vicissitudes endured by her from the time she runs out on her unfaithful husband, through love affairs with a bookie (Jack Thompson) and a Greek businessman (Takis Emmanuel) to working as a barmaid during the Depression. The director was Donald Crombie, whose work we shall examine again, along with a couple of other Australian directors, including Ken Hannam. But at this stage it can be said that following on *Sunday Too Far Away* Hannam's second film, **Break of Day** (1976), is a disappointment. Its subject is a Lawrentian affair between a young, married Gallipoli veteran (Andrew McFarlane) and a city-bred, 'new' woman, a painter (Sara Kestelman); possibly influenced by *Picnic at Hanging Rock* the film is far more inconclusive than it needs to be.

Despite their varying quality, these films justify a subsidised or an 'official'

cinema, affectionate towards the country's past and responsive to its landscape. They each suffer from an earnestness which has less to do with lack of humour than a pace which echoes the slowness of life, a fault which proves almost fatal to **Newsfront** (1978), which revives in otherwise heartening form the rivalry of newsreel companies as in *Too Hot to Handle*. It was directed by Philip Noyce and, set in the Forties and Fifties, it covers events fondly remembered by native audiences. Ironically the film is at its best at the end, when it gives way to Hollywood tradition in resolving the dilemma of the hero (Bill Hunter) by tempting him to give in to his natural enemy, television.

Amidst such nostalgic occasions, **End Play** (1975) was a tonic, as based on a contemporary thriller by Russell Braddon about a series of unexplained murders and two brothers (George Mallaby, John Waters), one of whom is in a wheelchair and one of whom – either one – is probably the killer. The dénouement has its weaknesses, but otherwise the film is handled with confidence by its writer-producer-director Tim Burstall, who had made the Alvin Purple films. It is a pity that this 'veteran' of Australian films has since done such disappointing work.

The director of the Barry McKenzie films, Bruce Beresford (b. 1940) has been more fortunate. He also, for the moment, eschewed nostalgia by bringing to the screen **Don's Party** (1976), based on a play by David Williamson, who is considered Melbourne's leading playwright, if not of Australia as a whole (Burstall had earlier done a less successful version of one of Williamson's plays). Williamson wrote the screenplay for a piece which might be described as a variation on 'That Championship Season' with the wives along. It quite simply charts a drunken evening, with egos, flesh and neuroses exposed as the booze takes effect: the masochistic streak of humour is richer than in the American play, as each of the men falls on his face – a hail-fellow-well-met crew, cheery, naive, complacent, and more prone to boast of lechery than actually indulging in it.

Beresford then changed course to make his 'period' film, **The Getting of Wisdom** (1977), able to raise the financing because of the success of *Picnic at Hanging*

Rock – though there were doubts as to whether the public would want two films about an Australian girls' school at the turn of the century. Henry Handel (Ethel) Richardson's novel was autobiographical, telling of Laura, the daughter of a widowed postmistress who leaves home to board at the Presbyterian Ladies' College in Melbourne. As perfectly played by an amateur, Susannah Fowle, Laura's direct manner and extrovert personality make her unpopular; she is disliked by the headmistress; she has a crush on the new chaplain (John Waters) while a dumpy newcomer, who gets a crush on her, implies that he and Laura are having an affair – a rumour which Laura does not deny; finally she becomes friends with the head girl (Hilary Ryan), who, because of her beauty and her position, is an outsider like herself. The film is quietly and skilfully made, demonstrating Beresford's increasing confidence. He turned to a thriller, again as a change of pace, **The Money Movers** (1979), writing the screenplay himself after reading a book by Devon Minchin, who had founded one of Australia's commercial security services. The members of the film's security force lead a life of some excitement, since it involves an occasional cosh-or-be-coshed operation; they also appear to be corrupt. For that reason they are not sympathetic, nor are the villains – the gangsters – an interesting bunch; but Beresford moves between the two groups with exhilarating speed.

He became very serious with **'Breaker' Morant** (1980), written by himself with others from a number of sources – since Morant (who derived his nickname from horsebreaking) was an Australian folk hero. He was English-born, and saw the Boer War as a chance of being reunited with his family in England. Instead, he was courtmartialled and executed, and that is the subject of this film. He had taken the law into his own hands and killed some Boer prisoners and a German missionary – an action of considerable consequence, for it might have brought Germany into the War; Morant's defence was that the order came from Kitchener himself, through an intermediary, now dead. The direction is somewhat self-conscious, and if Beresford makes use of the unusual setting, the South African veldt – though the film was made in South Australia and could not deceive Australians – he can do little with the British actor, Edward Woodward, who in the title role plays in vainglorious manner, denying any glimpse into Morant's character. This hollowness at the core of the film is somewhat offset by the clever performance of Jack Thompson as the defending counsel.

The Club (1980) is again based by Williamson on one of his plays, about a Melbourne rugby football club and the wrangling that ensues when a young player is acquired for a large sum, with the inference that the veteran coach (Thompson) is no longer helping the team to victory. As in *Don's Party*, the dialogue has bite, if still mainly of appeal to those interested in the Australian male: his swearing, drinking and relations with women. Beresford and Williamson make the team reasonably glamorous, but obviously do not care for the boys in the boardroom.

Overseas, **My Brilliant Career** (1979) was often bracketed with *The Getting of Wisdom*, for the good reason that both are based on autobiographical novels about growing up, written about the same time by women who published under male pseudonyms. In both cases the screenplays were written by Eleanor Witcombe, and this one is tellingly directed by Gillian Armstrong, a former art director. Miles Franklin's novel detailed her life with her impoverished family and her desire to escape into a world of what she calls culture and the arts. She does escape for a while to live with her comfortably-situated grandmother, and is proposed to by a handsome young man of a wealthy family: their relationship, beginning with teenage banter, develops into something deeper as they recognise in each other qualities of independence unlike those around them. She, Sybilla – splendidly played by Judy Davis – is tomboyish, unconventional and outspoken, but since Sam Neill's performance gives every reason why she should accept him, her rejection is clearly more faithful to the original than dramatically satisfying.

Donald Crombie, meanwhile, stayed with the past, and had been preparing **The Irishman** (1978) before the success of *Caddie*. He wrote the screenplay himself, from Elizabeth O'Connor's novel, about a teamster (Michael Craig) with twenty fine Clydesdale horses and little concern that

The new Australian cinema has made its aim clear, doubtless because there is government money in most of its projects: it is to be honest, unmelodramatic and, where possible, factual Consequently most of the films look at Australia's past, and since there isn't too much of that the films often seem alike – not surprisingly, since most of them are based on twentieth-century biographies or memoirs. Miles Franklin's story of her adolescence, *My Brilliant Career*, became unexpectedly the most rewarding of these films – due in large degree to the performances of Judy Davis and the New Zealand actor Sam Neill.

one of his rivals had brought the first motorised trucks to the area – North Queensland, with its sun, eucalyptus trees and jerry-built wooden towns. The film shows the effect of his drunkenness and fecklessness on the man's sons – but not entirely convincingly. It is hard to disagree with the Australian critic Romola Constantine, who wrote in the *Sun-Herald*, 'If this sensitive, beautiful film had come several years ago it would not have met the now predictable complaints: that Australian pictures have now worked the 1920s Australian scene to death. And here's yet another one, taking its time showing the wide open spaces, the changing age, the young man growing up, country races, pub brawls, and old folk a-dying.' Whether or not Crombie took this to heart, **Cathy's Child** (1979) is set in the recent past as written by Ken Quinnell, a Sydney film critic, and based on a book by Dick Wordley, who had been involved in the Cathy Baikas affair of 1974. The film begins by suggesting that there is a story in every newspaper item, which in this case is the abduction of a child from one parent by the other: this usually only makes headlines when the child is spirited out of the country, and this child has been taken to Greece. A mother's anguish has been with us since movies began, but *Cathy's Child* is about much more than that, including governmental responsibility and press ethics – and it is made with richness of detail. The Maltese mother is flawlessly played by Michelle Fawden and Wordley by Alan Cassell, a man seemingly conditioned by too many cigarettes and too many late nights.

If *Cathy's Child* suggests that Crombie is one of the best of contemporary directors, the same might be said of **Summerfield** (1977) and Ken Hannam. Cliff Green wrote this exercise in the genre film, that of the stranger who arrives in town to meet with instant hostility. He (Nick Tate) is the new teacher in a sleepy coastal village (the outdoor scenes were filmed at Churchill Island, south of Melbourne), and there is something menacing in the very sunlight. In his book on the Australian cinema, 'The Last New Wave', David Stratton says that the film's problem was 'all too common among Australian films: an unusual location is found, exciting incidents are conceived, but not enough thought is given to character development, relationships between characters, and – more often than not – a satisfactory ending.' This last point is certainly true, but in general scariness and making us wonder what will happen next *Summerfield* holds a high place among the thrillers of the Seventies.

In the matter of comparisons, **The Odd Angry Shot** (1979) received a glowing one when it had its belated British premiere on B.B.C. television. Its subject is the Vietnam War, and Richard West, who was there, wrote in *The Spectator*, 'Unpublicised and unpretentious, it is nevertheless incomparably more true to Vietnam than Hollywood bores like *Apocalypse Now!* and *The Deer Hunter*... Above all, it is free of the whining self-pity that seems to accompany all American films and books on Vietnam.' There is talent in Tom Jeffrey's writing and directing, from a novel by William Nagle, but if, as I suspect, he was attempting to make a large statement he misses. There are a number of minor flaws, including the casting of a T.V. star, Graham Kennedy, as the unit veteran: he is convincing as an ordinary down-to-earth joe, but is unlikely as artist and thinker. The youngsters – John Hargreaves, Bryan Brown, John Jarratt – sit around bored and foul-mouthed, except when they go to the city for R and R, when they are drunk and foul-mouthed. Every so often they stalk other groups of young men, trying to kill them: these opponents have slant eyes, they open fire first and seem like creatures from another planet – but there seems no good reason why either side should be involved in undertaking this grisly operation.

Gallipoli (1981) makes its point about war more immediately and forcefully. The film was conceived and directed by Peter Weir, who commissioned David Williamson to write the screenplay, which falls into three parts. The first is about the acquaintanceship and subsequent friendship of a smiling blond boy (Mark Lee) from the Outback and a city – Perth – boy (Mel Gibson): since they are both runners

this part of the film resembles the concurrent *Chariots of Fire*, and it is not completely compelling. The middle section, with the troops in training near Cairo, is the best account I know of naive young white men coping with the deviousness of the pedlars of the East, and the film makes the telling point that it is because they are Australians that they are tough, proud and not to be monkeyed around with. The last section, at Gallipoli itself, has a night-before-battle sequence which is a tribute to Olivier's *Henry V*, but subsequently it neither emphasises the carnage nor explains (more than perfunctorily) the reason for battle – on the reasonable assumption that it was absurd in the first place. The decency, clarity and lack of pretentiousness make this film memorable; the mainly light-hearted dialogue underlines the strong relationships often formed between soldiers. The film's subject is not the mentality of soldiers but the waste of them, which may be why it does not equal the impact of the two similar films, *All Quiet on the Western Front* and *Paths of Glory*. The producer was a new company formed by two successful Australian tycoons, Rupert Murdoch and Robert Stigwood, and the latter's connections with Paramount was the reason for that company to undertake the requisite world distribution for the film to recover its costs. As a result, it was the most successful Australian film to date, despite

Norman Kaye and Wendy Hughes in *Lonely Hearts*, which won the Best Film prize when the Australian Film Awards were handed out in 1982 – and it is nice to know that such a quiet, civilised entertainment can gain recognition. It is about a couple, approaching middle-age, who meet through a marriage bureau, a relationship handled with wit and sensitivity by the director Paul Cox, who wrote the screenplay with John Clarke.

the initial publicity tag, 'From the place you've never heard of . . . the story you'll never forget', though that was quickly changed to 'From the place you may never have heard of . . .'

Buoyed by the international interest in this film and Government and state subsidies, the Australian film industry produced forty-nine films in 1981, but that was reduced to five the following year after some cunning entrepreneurs had found a means of making tax losses out of the industry. I should imagine that it would be healthy if annual production were to settle at somewhere between the two figures. There is talent to be exploited and a beautiful and varied country – aspects to be enjoyed in the least of these films. The best of them are among the best produced anywhere in the world in the Seventies, which says much for an industry which, if not young, had hitherto been insignificant for most of its life.

Despite its advantage of language, the Australian cinema has made smaller inroads into the consciousness of Anglo-Saxon movie-buffs than has the 'New German Cinema', so-called, which came along at the same time. Both the Australian film-makers and the 'new' Germans worked conscientiously but self-consciously, aware of a void in the past. In the case of the Australians, it is a true void; in the case of the Germans, it is a twenty-five year hiatus – or so it was described by one of the exponents of the new German cinema, Werner Herzog, explaining the recovery from 'an epoch of barbarism with the Nazis'. This is disingenuous: the Nazis did not rule for a quarter of a century, but by suggesting that the films of the post-Nazi era were poor Herzog implies that the new German cinema was all the more revolutionary.

In fact the Germans did produce a number of interesting films after the War, including **Tiefland** (1954), actually made during the War, with a history going even further back. Leni Riefenstahl had planned it in 1934, as a vehicle for Heinrich George, but his schedule and her nervous breakdown forced its cancellation. She later claimed that had she made it she would not have been forced into making *Triumph des Willens*, and that by resurrecting the subject on the outbreak of war she avoided

making the propaganda films demanded by Goebbels at the time. The film's source is in an opera by Eugene d'Albert which had been popular in Berlin in the Twenties: the setting is nineteenth-century Spain and its hero an impoverished landlord (Bernhard Minetti) who marries a wealthy heiress although he is in love with a flamenco dancer (Miss Riefenstahl). The dancer marries a poor shepherd and when the landlord attempts to ravish her the two men fight with knives. It is a trumpery plot, but as with *Das Blaue Licht* the mountain scenery is superbly photographed and the direction accomplished. The film was not quite finished when the French confiscated it in 1945, and Riefenstahl did not manage to get it shown till after she had been deNazified in 1952; by that time it was considered old-fashioned and she withdrew it (and withheld it for over twenty years) though not, apparently, until it had recovered its cost. This had been considerable, bringing into question her standing with the upper echelons of the Nazi party. She said that both she and *Tiefland* were thought so unimportant that she was forced into filming the interiors in Prague, and Goebbels' diary confirms at least his own lack of interest; however, when she could no longer film the exteriors in Spain a Spanish town was constructed in Bavaria – and *Tiefland* became the most expensive film made by the Germans since the coming of Talkies. That fact, given the difficulties facing Germany in 1942, would not suggest that she was in disgrace, though there may well have been mutual disillusionment between her and the Party.

Only two German films made an international impact in the immediate post-war years. One of these is **Berliner Ballade** (1948), which is not good and could never have been good, but it was immensely cheering to the Germans themselves and interesting to the rest of the world as an entertainment rising literally from the rubble that was Berlin. It plants in those ruins a skinny soldier (Gert Fröbe), called Otto Normalverbraucher – or Otto Nobody in the English subtitles – who confronts shortages of food, jobs and housing while dreaming all the time of a café where a blonde serves him lashings of cream cakes. The film is little more than a series of revue sketches, of sophomoric humour, with a plea at the end for international harmony; but it wears a grin in the face of adversity, though one of slapstick rather than satire, after an excellent start showing the Prussian taste for militarism as more than usually absurd in the present circumstances. The director, Robert A. Stemmle, did little else of note in a twenty year career.

Die Mörder sind unter Uns (1946) was a co-production between East and West Germany taking a more serious view of the same situation, showing ordinary people coping with the horrifying living conditions and the Nazi sympathisers who believed that the overwhelming defeat was simply a setback. It is melodramatic, but handled with vigour by Wolfgang Staudte, who went on to make a good film from Heinrich Mann's 1918 satiric novel, **Der Untertan** (1951), about one Hessling (Werner Peters), a silly little man obsessed by all matters military. Hessling finds his own mediocrity assuaged by joining an absurd group of duellists, the New Teutonians, or confirmed by undertaking abject jobs as a soldier; later he only exists by kowtowing to authority or planning the further aggrandisement of the Kaiser; clearly this theme had singular relevance in the light of recent events. It was made under East German auspices, but without the smallest iota of the Soviet influence which was to seep into the East German cinema. Staudte himself went to West Germany in 1955, but succeeded in making only some increasingly flaccid films.

Helmut Käutner provided the West German film industry with a success when **Die Letzte Brücke** (1954) won the Palme d'Or and the International Critics' prize at the Cannes Festival, though it was actually an Austrian-Yugoslav co-production, and one of the few of the time to prove the feasibility of such cooperation. Käutner wrote the script with Norbert Kunze, which tells of a German doctor (Maria Schell) kidnapped by partisans to care for their wounded, and her difficulty in explaining to her fiancé (Carl Mohner) why her first loyalty is to them. Miss Schell avoids the cloying mannerisms we normally associate with her, but she remains a 'star' despite the circumstances; the partisans are too well groomed and the scenery too striking; and the approach is a mite sentimental.

Käutner's film on the mad king of Bavaria, **Ludwig II, Glanz und ende eines König** (1954), has only a few insights into its subject, a magnificent Wagner in Paul Bildt, an excellent Ludwig in O. W. Fischer and some pretty scenery photographed in colour by the British Douglas Slocombe; but **Der Hauptmann von Köpenick** (1956) is a less surefooted historical enterprise. Carl Zuckmayer wrote the screenplay from his own play, omitting practically nothing. He had been more selective in adapting it for Richard Oswald's 1931 version, to which the credits of this one acknowledge a debt. Käutner's treatment is far less invigorating; the original settings have been faithfully copied except when he seems to be imitating Clair's *Les Grandes Manoeuvres*; but period charm is not the prime requisite for Zuckmayer's biting anti-military satire. In other circumstances Heinz Rühmann might have made an excellent Wilhelm Voigt. Universal were so impressed with Käutner at this time that he was summoned to Hollywood to make two soap operas, of which I have seen **A Stranger in My Arms** (1959), a banal melodrama notable only for the performance of Mary Astor as a possessive mother.

It is not, perhaps, quite so depressing an experience as the films Fritz Lang made after returning to Germany. He later remarked that he did not consider them important, but was hoping for 'a great financial success so that I would again have the chance – as I had with *M* – to work without restrictions. It was my mistake.' It was also a gigantic miscalculation to suppose that audiences would want to see the childish fantasies of his very first film. **Der Tiger von Eschnapur** (1959) and its sequel, **Das Indische Grabmal** (1959) were based on scripts he had written with his wife in 1920. They are in colour and technically competent, but **Die Tausend Augen des Dr Mabuse** (1961) does not have even these advantages – nor indeed anything to indicate that it was made by a once formidable director. Pabst, on the other hand, made a partial return to form with **Der Letzte Akt** (1955), and it may be significant, given the preoccupations of the German industry up to this time, that, like *Die Letzte Brücke*, it is an Austrian production. It is an account of the last days of Hitler, played by Albin Skoda in a manner suggesting silliness rather than sickness.

The confined settings – most of it takes place inside the bunker – clearly did not inspire him, as if to confirm that he lost interest in realism at the time of *Kamaradschaft*. Despite the hysteria inherent in the subject, the piece comes to life only with the performance of Oskar Werner as the obligatory 'good' German. **Es Geschah am 20 Juli** (1955) retraces the plot to kill Hitler, but this second comment on the Nazi years is also made with momentary compassion but chiefly coldness.

Peter Lorre, a contemporary of Lang and Pabst, left Hollywood for Germany to make **Der Verlorene** (1951), not only as an actor, but as producer, director and part-writer. It is a psychological thriller in the manner of *M*, set during the War, but the regime under which its protagonist goes about his business might be any totalitarian one. I cannot agree with those who find in the film a condemnation of Nazi tactics, nor that its failure was due to Germany's refusal to face its recent past, since that is never an issue; I think, rather, that audiences found it old-fashioned, since its style so much resembles the films of the pre-Nazi era.

Die Brücke (1959) was one of the very few German films of the Fifties to be widely seen abroad. Its director, Bernhard Wicki, had played the partisan leader in *Die Letzte Brücke* for Käutner, whom he had assisted on a number of other films. These two films are alike in missing that element which can turn the well-made, well-intentioned into something beyond the mundane; their common subject is war, and though based on truth, both have the aura of reverentially created fictions – in this case about a group of schoolboys determined to defend the town bridge against the American advance. They are not sentimentalised, nor does the film strive too hard to condemn Nazism. As a result of its success, Wicki was invited to direct the German sequence of *The Longest Day* and then **The Visit** (1964), based on Friedrich Dürrenmatt's play. Ben Barzman's screenplay reduces the material, and the vengeful, infirm, aged lady becomes an inadequate, middle-aged Ingrid Bergman in the trappings of early Gloria Swanson, with Anthony Quinn on his usual form as the suitor who did her an injustice years before. The film is a companion to *The Condemned of Altona*, which

was also handled by 20th Century-Fox, with casts and production companies of several different nationalities.

The first German film on a contemporary subject to be extensively seen abroad was **Das Mädchen Rosemarie** (1958), and that was due to its content rather than Rolf Thiele's direction, which is rudimentary. Rosemarie Nitribitt, played in the film by Nadja Tiller, was a callgirl found murdered near Frankfurt, and subsequently revealed to have had among her clients some of Germany's most influential businessmen, several of whom she may have been blackmailing. Thiele attempts satire at the expense of the Mercedes set and strives for Brechtian significance by presenting two commentators who make sour remarks about Germany's economic miracle.

Similar motives on the part of foreign distributors brought a film by Veit Harlan to art-houses, **Anders als du und Ich** (1957). It is no less nondescript than his earlier films, but revives a subject dormant since the German Silent cinema, homosexuality. In this case, it is a false alarm, and a mother's worries have been in vain when the suspect *jugend* is caught chasing the housemaid. In the meantime we have been instructed by a number of legal and medical specialists, and amused, not intentionally, by a middle-aged gentleman whose home life consists of displays of wrestling by youths in satin swimsuits.

It was hardly to be expected that young German film buffs, fresh from watching the films of the nouvelle vague, would be empathetic to Harlan and Thiele. In 1962 a manifesto was launched to coincide with the Oberhausen Film Festival and signed by twenty-six young directors: 'The new cinema needs new forms of freedom: from the conventions and clichés of the established industry, from intervention by commercial partners, and finally freedom from . . . other vested interests.' The signatories were not part of the ramshackle German film industry, but they had been working on shorts and in television, thus creating a climate for Government discussions. In 1966 an awards system was announced, in which public money would be set aside for films and screenplays of quality. It was a system already adopted in a number of countries – primarily in Scandinavia – to encourage local production, which was always at the mercy of exhibitors preternaturally biased towards foreign, i.e. American, 'commercial' films. In Germany the situation had become critical as the state-run television channels devoured cinema patrons, and in 1974 the Government induced the two principal T.V. networks to commit the equivalent of $1.8 million to immediate film production, with control two years later over the films concerned, when their cinema career was deemed to be finished (the networks also bought seventeen existing films for $80,000 each). Two years earlier a tax had been placed on cinema attendances, to be ploughed back into the industry; a small annual fund was available to young directors; and a tax shelter scheme was devised to attract private investors – not, in fact, restricted to local film-makers and, as it turned out, of considerable benefit to a number of the more risky American productions.

Ironically, the first manifestations of the new German cinema appreciated abroad were of very limited appeal, *Abschied von Gestern*, directed by Alexander Kluge, and *Chronik der Anna Magdalena Bach*, directed by Jean-Marie Straub, both made in 1966. They impressed some on their festival showings, but, with reason, created no stir when shown in foreign art-houses, so that it was not until later that most film enthusiasts became aware that there was a new German cinema, when **Angst Essen Seele Auf** (1973) – *Fear Eats the Soul* – became a critical and popular success. It was the eighteenth film of Rainer Werner Fassbinder (1946–82), who had started making short films at the age of twenty, and who had also founded an *Anti-teater* movement. *Angst Essen Seele Auf* was not only a remarkable film to have come from Germany, hitherto untouched by any movement towards realism, but it also made a strong and subtle statement on racism: a middle-aged widow (Brigitte Mira), sheltering from the rain in a dreary prostitutes' bar, meets a young Arab *gastarbeiter*, Ali (El Hedi Ben Salem). Their eventual marriage is greeted with ridicule or scorn by her children and friends, but its destruction comes from within, when she begins to mother him. Fassbinder's unimaginative, Ozu-like style seemed right for his material, which includes aspects of the underbelly of life in Munich that few could have

imagined. The screenplay, which he wrote himself, was based on fact, and he had already used the incident in 1970 in **Der Amerikanische Soldat** as an anecdote told by a minor character. That film, according to *Sight and Sound*, is a revision of Douglas Sirk's *All That Heaven Allows*; and my own immediate desire after watching *Angst Essen Seele Auf* to see all of Fassbinder's early films was fulfilled by **Martha** (1974), a re-vamping of Sirk's *Sleep, My Love* and an excellent example of the second-rate imitating the third-rate. It was made for television and has not, with reason, been publicly seen in either Britain or the U.S.

Together *Angst Essen Seele Auf* and *Martha* showed a director capable of swinging from excellence to something worse than mediocrity. Later, I think, this polarisation became less apparent, but there were at this time two Fassbinders, the observant, lively one who had made **Händler der Vier Jahreszeiten** (1971), and the artificial, sterile director responsible for **Die Bitteren Tränen der Petra von Kant** (1972). If, as Fassbinder claimed, his movies were 'all self-contained discourses on human behaviour' the former is largely successful, losing some conviction on its insistence on cheap sexuality as it dwells on the affairs of Hans (Hans Hirschmüller), who sells fruit from a barrow, beats his wife and drinks himself

The 'new' German cinema, much discussed and written about, arouses strong passions – particularly among those who, having patronised two or three of its products, refuse to be subjected to like boredom again. The directors connected with this movement are not among the cinema's notable talents, being more concerned with effect than narrative form. Their acknowledged leader was the prolific Rainer Werner Fassbinder, who made his reputation with *Angst Essen Seele Auf*, where his compassion more than atoned for that deficiency. The leading players were Brigitte Mira and El Hedi Ben Salem, and their unlikely romance was very touching.

to death. In *Petra von Kant* a group of snake-like ladies squabble between themselves for bodily possession, and, except for that lack of inhibition, are the daughters of Sappho as movies ever presented them.

As he achieved international recognition Fassbinder announced 'About half the early films were "about" my discoveries in the American cinema . . . The others were investigations into German actualities. I thought then that if you brought people up against their own reality, they'd react against it. I now think that the primary need is to satisfy the audience, and then to deal with political comment. First, you have to make films that are seductive, beautiful, about love or whatever . . . That's the preliminary stage in a kind of political presentation.' If any of his films had any real political comment he hid it well; and if **Effi Briest** (1974) is about love, it is far from seductive. Theodor Fontane's classic novel proposes the not unfamiliar situation of a girl married to a much older man but attracted to a young one. Fassbinder attempts a visual style he supposes to be the cinema equivalent of 'literature', starting each sequence with a tableau unfreezing and finishing with a fade into white: but he succeeds in making this 148-minute film seem endless. He was too prolific, it seems, to develop any film sense. His early films are like radio with pictures, proceeding in a series of conversations either pretentious or pointless. Later he became obsessed with rather outré decor, featuring lamps, mirrors and furnishings of an Art Deco persuasion (even when inappropriate); his camera would circulate amidst it at least once in every sequence.

Bolwieser (1977) starts in this fashion, with characters glimpsed through dusty glass partitions or through lace curtains. The time and place – Bavaria in the dying days of the Weimar Republic – is well established, and the plot has possibilities, as Hanni (Elisabeth Trissenaar), married to the local stationmaster (Kurt Raab), moves from one lover (Bernhard Helfrich), the butcher, to another (Udo Kier), a hairdresser. The original novel by Oskar Maria Graf was published in 1931, and it is in the long German tradition of small town satire: but satire is not something Fassbinder understands, and the result is a betrayal of the book. Admittedly the piece was made for television and shown in two separate hundred minute parts, but as cut to two hours for showings abroad it is certainly no better than **Despair/Eine Reise ins Licht**.(1978), a travesty of Vladimir Nabokov's clever novel as written in English by Tom Stoppard and acted in self-pitying, over-emphatic manner by Dirk Bogarde. Bogarde plays a chocolate manufacturer who is schizophrenic and getting no sexual satisfaction from his wife (Andréa Ferreol), so he arranges for his own disappearance by changing clothes with a tramp (Klaus Löwitsch). There is much more plot, and the film is conceivably meant to be a thriller, but beyond the fact that it is set at the same time as *Bolwieser* and has an ending stolen from *Sunset Boulevard* all point or purpose is withheld from us.

That the tramp stands around naked for much of the time and for no good reason is evidence of Fassbinder's sexual inclination – not that he tried to hide that, and indeed in **Faustrecht der Freiheit** (1975) he played a homosexual, a rather stupid carnival worker fleeced and dunned by the wealthy middle classes. This study of exploitation would be good enough to justify its own exploitation of the gay milieu did not most of the situations seem to come from old Joan Crawford movies, in which they were handled more honestly and dramatically. If Fassbinder abandoned his early obsession with Hollywood, the European cinema remained to be plundered: **Chinesisches Roulette** (1976) is a rehash of *La Règle du Jeu*, with a dash of *The Boys in the Band*, and **In Einem Jahr mit 13 Monden** (1979) a homosexual version of *Le Feu Follet*. **Die Zartlichkeit der Wölfe** (1973) is a homosexual version of *M*, based, admittedly, on the same source – Peter Kürten, the vampire of Düsseldorf; Fassbinder produced, for one of his actors, Ulli Lommel, to direct, which he does in the same manner as his master.

Despite occasional respectful and even enthusiastic notices Fassbinder did not become a name on the American art-house circuit till **Die Ehe der Maria Braun** (1979), undoubtedly his best film since *Angst Essen Seele Auf*. It is by turns stagey and imaginative, and Hanna Schygulla's performance in the leading role was gratifying to those who had not been exposed to Fassbinder's heroines with their slit skirts, net stockings and make-up and hair-styles of the Forties. Her costume is justified to an extent, for the film follows its heroine from the aftermath of war through the economic miracle. As in *Der Blaue Engel*, she is a lady of loose morals loved to the point of self-destruction by a respectable man – played by Ivan Desny with a professionalism not evident elsewhere in the film. He is a wealthy industrialist, and Maria Braun uses his devotion to make her way in the world, while still loving the man (Klaus Löwitsch) she married. It is not original of Fassbinder – credited with the original idea of the film – to suggest that Maria loves both men in different ways, but because she believes precisely that, the film has some weight. Her progress from poverty to power is as interesting as such matters often are in movies, and as a family saga, which is what this film really is, it is often unexpected. The film's success encouraged Fassbinder to make some more on the same theme before his early death from a combination of drugs and drink.

Werner Herzog (b. 1942) appears to have something more to say than Fassbinder, but since his way of saying it is equally debilitating few would agree with his own estimate that his films are ahead of their time. He achieved a degree of success in the international market with his fifth film, **Aguirre, der Zorn Gottes** (1972): its opening sequence alone would have justified that success, and actually did, for the rest is appalling. The setting is the Andes, forested and misty: down the mountainside, across the valley, files a troop of men, to unearthly sounding choral music. After that, the photography by Thomas Mauch finds a few more stunning images, but the screenplay, by Herzog, lacks both coherence and conviction as it follows the exploits of a megalomaniac conquistador (Klaus Kinski) hoping to establish his own empire. The large number of loose ends is due to the difficult conditions of filming in the jungle, with Herzog both extemporising and omitting much of what he intended at the outset. The original soundtrack in English was jettisoned, and the German one substituted is banal.

Reviewers gave the film only a muted welcome, but most surrendered to **Jeder für Sich und Gott Gegen Alle** (1974), the story of Kaspar Hauser, who in 1828 materialised in the main square of Nuremberg and was thought to have been kept in captivity since childhood. He is treated as a side-show and eventually murdered, in the meantime establishing an odd serenity and wisdom. This material, surely among the best that any film-maker ever had to work with, finds Herzog often didactic, complex and mysterious, but always prepared to sacrifice conviction for effect. **Woyzeck** (1979) begins with little conviction, since it violates all known concepts of military dress and behaviour, and as the errors accumulate a dull movie becomes an irritating one. Herzog turned to Büchner's astonishing play after the failure a year earlier of *Nosferatu*, a literal remake of Murnau's film, with another English track which had to be replaced (because audiences laughed). Herzog's adaptation of Büchner is framed with the device used by Carson McCullers in 'Reflections in a Golden Eye', suggesting that we alone are privy to reasons for the murder it speaks of, and that we should therefore cry out on behalf of the poor murderer. We do not care, for Herzog cannot move us, as did Georg Klarens in his less painstaking 1950 version.

The goalkeeper hero of **Die Angst des Tormanns beim Elfmeter** (1972) is a modern Woyzeck: with a similar mentality, but with less reason, he strangles the woman he has slept with. This is the second feature of Wim Wenders (b. 1945), and it is an excellent example of his intention that his films 'deal with the period of time in which they were made, the cities, the landscapes . . .' He and Peter Handke wrote it, from Handke's novel, and its chief fault is its lack of dimension, which is less than in Chabrol's lesser studies in crime. As a study of despair and desperation, **Alice in den Stadten** (1974) is mainly padding, and in this instance the film to be preferred is *Paper Moon*, also about a travelling man saddled with a precocious young girl. This is one of several films Wenders made in imitation of American 'road' movies; his admiration for Hollywood cinema was again apparent with **Der Amerikanische Freund** (1977), a very free adaptation of Patricia Highsmith's 'Ripley's Game', with Bruno Ganz as a Hamburg picture-framer who has leukemia and agrees to act as a hit-man in

Paris to provide for his widow and child. As in Hitchcock's *Strangers on a Train* the murder proposal takes place on a train – Hamburg's U-Bahn. And the cast includes two third-rate American film-makers, Samuel Fuller and Nicholas Ray, known to be admired by their European counterparts. In *Alice in den Stadten* there are several references to John Ford, but better Ford than Douglas Sirk.

And better Herzog than Hans Jürgen Syberberg, whose extensive films to date have been disquisitions on Ludwig II, the pulp writer Karl May, and Hitler, told in a mish-mash of fantasy, polemic, puppetry, monologue or whatever means are at hand. **Hitler** (1976) opened in Britain to the cautiously animated notices customarily given by critics confronted with the unusual: a handful were scornful, in contrast to the American press where Francis Coppola sponsored this seven-hour conglomeration. In the meantime British television critics had seen it, cut into four parts, and were unanimous. Clive James in *The Observer* called it 'a nonsense', going on, 'this trouncingly fatuous epic went only to prove that politics have changed immeasurably for the better. Hitler was a failed artist who took his revenge by wrecking as much of Europe as he could get his hands on [according to Syberberg]. Nowadays, thanks to State subsidies there is no such thing as a failed artist.' It is doubtful that without television and Government funds these four directors would ever have been heard of outside Germany, or, indeed, within. With a couple of exceptions the public's reception has been seldom higher than indifferent. Those exceptions belong to Fassbinder, while Herzog and Wenders, between moments of self-aggrandisement, have given evidence that they can direct. Even admirers find the new German cinema ponderous.

The one outstanding German director of this period does not really belong to the movement, for he made his first film in 1966. Volker Schlöndorff (b. 1939) studied in France with Melville, among others, returning to Germany to make his feature debut with **Der Junge Törless** (1966), a rather prosaic version of Robert Musil's novel of the sexual and brutal traumas awaiting sensitive students at military school. Schlöndorff's wife, Margarethe von Trotta, acted in several of his films and was co-writer and co-director of **Die Verlorene Ehre der Katharina Blum** (1975). Heinrich Böll's novel, an attack on the yellow press, provided Schlöndorff with international recognition, and the opening sequence – a young man on a Rhine steamer – shows that he has forgotten more about cinema than Fassbinder ever learnt. The film as a whole is an over-emphatic polemic, influenced by Costa-Gavras, and if ultimately not completely satisfactory that has something to do with the colourless performance of Angela Winkler as the girl pushed around by press and police for sheltering a man they refer to as an anarchist. Fräulein von Trotta plays the lead in **Der Fangschuss** (1976), a Countess who makes an unsuccessful pass at an officer (Matthias Habich), a young man with a undefined liaison in the past and a penchant for gazing at the sleeping figure of a colleague. The dénouement will come as no surprise to readers of Julien Green, but the source is in fact a novel by Marguerite Yourcenar, 'Coup de Grâce', turned into a feminist tract by von Trotta and two other women writers. Schlöndorff directed, alone, responding keenly to the setting, a castle near Riga during the First World War.

His greatest success has been **Die Blechtrommel** (1979), the first German film ever to win Hollywood's Oscar for the Best Foreign Language film. Its source is the influential novel by Gunter Grass that we know as 'The Tin Drum'. Schlöndorff was approached by the producer, Franz Seitz, after Grass had reserved the right to withdraw his own support if he disliked the final draft of the script, written by Schlöndorff and Jean-Claude Carrière. They begin as the book does, with the antecedents and birth of Oskar (David Bennent), who decides while a child to stop growing, observing at the same time the sexuality and mortality of those around him and the rise and fall of the Nazis. Reading the book it seemed to me that on these aspects of sex and death Grass was as imaginative as he was humourless and pointless; it required no perception to portray the Nazis as morons and clowns: but Schlöndorff treats this material with wit and insight, so that the film is by turns touching and disturbing. He did not feel that the film could stretch itself to include the last part of the book, taking Oskar through the Economic Miracle, which is a pity for, in my opinion, it is then that Grass shows his real power.

Schlöndorff was working on a second film with Grass about two young teachers who travel the world in an attempt to confront reality when Grass recommended to him **Die Falschung** (1981), a novel by a friend of his, Nicholas Born, who had based it on his experiences as a reporter during the Middle East crisis. The screenplay by the director, Von Trotta, Carrière and Kai Herrmann (a colleague of Born) focuses on a journalist (Bruno Ganz), who, reporting on the Civil War in Lebanon, becomes confused and then dismayed at the prospect of communicating its stupidity, cruelty and futility; on the sidelines are a failing marriage back home and an unsatisfactory affair with the German widow (Hanna Schygulla) of an Arab. Analogies are drawn between these problems and the conflict in the streets, and the unworthiness of this concept is admitted in a foreword which claims that what follows is a work of the imagination. Alternatively, that is Schlöndorff's way of advising audiences that, like his protagonist, he feels inadequate to the events he has to portray. The introduction further states that the film is not a documentary, but in that case is defensive for no good reason: at least forty per cent of the film consists of footage of the fighting in Beirut – the ruins, the wounded, the charred bodies, the partisans posing for pictures – and the compassion inherent in the selection is reason enough to admire this deeply flawed film.

Its failure highlights the dichotomy between Schlöndorff on the one hand and Fassbinder, Herzog and Wenders on the other: he works in traditional mould, liking literary adaptations or films of significance, while they try to find an original method of conveying their own personal fantasies, or those connected with their obsession with Hollywood. Both approaches are valid. But in the end his craftmanship, put at the service of the cinema's liberal values, is preferable to limited talents on their ego-trips. The Germans themselves have few doubts as to which they like best, and for some years the one great subsidised success was **Lina Braake** (1975). It united the critics and public, but has not to date been seen in the U.S., while its showings in Britain went virtually

ignored. Its writer-director, Bernhard Sinkel, a former lawyer making his first feature, shows much skill in detailing the cares of the lady of the title, who is eighty-two and trying to adjust to life in an old people's home. She is played by Lina Carstens and is magnificently matched by a white-maned fellow-inmate played by Fritz Rasp, the great villain of the Silent era. Lina's adventures include a trip to Sardinia which is not only implausible but too strong for this particular film – which nevertheless has heart, a rare quality in German cinema.

Angst Essen Seele Auf has it, as does **In der Fremde** (1975), directed by Sohrab Shahid Saless (b. 1944), an Iranian who had studied in Vienna and Paris before making shorts and documentaries for the Iranian Ministry of Culture. His first two features, made in Iran, are virtually motionless studies of two of the country's less affluent citizens, a railway-crossing keeper and a fisherman's small son. The second was awarded a prize at the Berlin Film Festival, which encouraged him to return to Germany for *In der Fremde*, written with Helga Houzer and concerning an immigrant Turkish worker, played by the Persian writer-actor Parviz Sayyad. It is better than Saless's earlier films, but some way below Tchekov, his avowed inspiration, since the aspirations of his hero remain barred to us beyond a desire for a woman and a vague wish to adapt to his environment.

Lina Carstens in *Lina Braake*, directed by Bernhard Sinkel, one of the most popular manifestations of the new German cinema, perhaps because it is one of the few with heart and feeling. Understandably, the cinema has seldom been interested in the problems of old age, and it would have to be said that this film is much less rigorous than *Umberto D*; but Miss Carstens gives a remarkable performance.

1161

Both Sinkel's film and Saless's are effortlessly superior to those of their more famous colleagues, while **Fabian** (1980) proves its director, Wolf Gremm, as talented as Fassbinder was not – and I make the analogy since its subject is that of *Bolwieser*, Germany on the brink of the Nazi take-over. Its source is a novel by Erich Kästner, and its eponymous hero (Hans Peter Hallwach) a young man too inert to care about the encroachment of Naziism. He is a copywriter for a tobacco firm, drifting from café to brothel, embarking on an affair with a movie starlet and seemingly indifferent to the suicide of his student friend and the 'removal' by the authorities of the professor he has befriended. Finally he returns to his home town and is drowned, for, as the end title explains, 'he couldn't swim'. In his home town he had been united with a childhood friend who has joined 'the steel helmets', and the man looks fierce till they are in a brothel together, when he suddenly appears mild. Gremm constantly demands readjustments in our attitudes from scene to scene; his period sense is impeccable and has been influenced, clearly, by a study of the films of the time; he has even 're-thought' his love scenes, so that entwined naked bodies break apart for the man to reach in a pocket for a cigarette. *Fabian* is in fact a considerable achievement: that it was turned down by the committee choosing films for the Cannes Film Festival only confirms my opinion of such bodies.

Its reception abroad has been mild, so it makes a rewarding comparison with **Taxi zum Klo** (1981), which won the Max Ophuls prize for comedy at the Berlin Film Festival; and after half a dozen other festival showings it went round the world to great acclaim and popularity. Its writer-director, Frank Ripploh, a former West Berlin schoolteacher, made it on his own and friends' money. Since it is autobiographical, it can be safely said that no film-maker had hitherto revealed so much of himself, so that we can see the blotches on his skin while engaged in various sexual acts – not to mention the various parts of the body essential to such acts. That the acts are homosexual would be of little consequence were the film not surfeited with self-loathing. It is misogynist, which is one thing, but Ripploh, who plays himself, felt compelled to tell us of his searches for sex in public lavatories and his inability to be faithful to the man who loves him – a role played by an ex-lover. He must surely have been aware that the Frank of the film indulges in practices that many gays privately abhor, whatever this film in toto does for their 'image' (in Germany, many gay groups protested). He emerges from the film less a happy homosexual than a sick one, and the final scene, of his pupils rioting as he sits before them in drag, is meant to imply that the logical conclusion of flamboyant homosexuality, i.e. the loss of the heterosexual role, the insistence on transvestism, leads to chaos. The sequences of driving around a night-and-neon Berlin are fairly intoxicating, and Ripploh, if he has anything else to say, may become a professional film-maker.

In the matter of frankness, the film makes laughable earlier German films on this subject, including **Die Konsequenz** (1977), a tragic but soppy love story between a prisoner and the warden's son. Its director, Wolfgang Petersen, would not on this evidence be a candidate for handling **Das Boot** (1981), the most expensive German film yet made – and the producer was able to raise the financing because of the popularity of Lother-Günther Buchheim's original novel. The film begins in 1943 in La Rochelle with an orgy, but the men are 'too drunk to fuck' (and the line is in English); the following morning we move out to sea with a U-boat and its crew, where their daily routine consists of profanity, proximity, fear, boredom and discipline. Petersen brings slickness to his material, but little insight, and the fact that the film actually made a profit in Germany alone on its huge investment is doubtless due to its view of the nation at a critical point in its history – courageous, desperate, defeated, pro-British to a degree (the crew sings 'Tipperary' in English) and no longer under any illusions about Nazi leadership. I believe that this merely conforms to what the Germans want to believe about themselves as they were then; but of course the same might have been said about the British when they flocked to *The Cruel Sea*, which was equally meretricious.

Britain was one of the few countries not to like *Das Boot*, but then its audiences did not greatly care for an infinitely better film about the War, **Aus einem Deutschen Leben** (1977). Perhaps the distributor was

The fact and experience of the Nazi concentration camps were too overwhelming for understanding, and it was not till the Seventies that many writers began to tackle the subject. Theodor Kotulla's *Aus Einem Deutschen Leben* is an honourable film, on the life of Rudolf Höss, the first commandant of Auschwitz, and it has become required viewing for German schoolchildren.

unwise to call it *Death is My Trade*, even if it is a literal translation of the title of the original novel by Robert Merle: it made it sound like a horror movie, and it is anything but – except by implication and in the cause of historical truth. Theodor Kotulla, the writer and director, has also used as source material the autobiographical notes left by Rudolf Höss, the first commandant of Auschwitz, and where appropriate he has found his style in *Nuit et Brouillard*. He takes his early events out of chronological order so that he can stress the irony of an averagely-intelligent German (Götz George, best known as the star of some action movies) becoming a non-fanatical Nazi functionary. It is because he is of minor importance that he is appointed commander of Auschwitz; it is because he regards himself as a disciplinarian that he accepts the institution of the Final Solution. His wife's acceptance of this, during a marital tiff, is the movie's most crass moment; otherwise this film is as much an expression of Germanness as *Der Untertan*, with a hero in love with uniforms, beer, the countryside and obedience. He may seem admirable to some until the final moments when an American officer states history's verdict with a lack of emotion which is nevertheless eloquent.

Perhaps the film says less than it should and too drily, but Kotulla's manner is preferable to the offensive splashiness of Wertmuller's *Pasqualino Settebelleze*. It is an important film and has become required viewing in German schools.

If the films from the minor film industries were poor for many years, amateurish and derivative, that is no longer the case, as film festivals demonstrate. During the last months of writing this book, I have seen excellent films from many countries whose movies were until then rarely up to festival standard. There is, however, only one other national industry that requires attention, the Chinese, if only because of the enormous population not only of the country itself but of the Chinese speaking world. Because of political differences, few Chinese films have found their way to the West; and not many of us would be naive enough to compare those that have with the Japanese. Yet both countries are not only neighbours, but the product of a long civilisation, in which the arts have played a pervasive role: we might therefore at least remark on the discrepancy between the standards of their films.

It is only recently that we have been able to see more than a small sample of Chinese cinema, and those organisers who have managed to bring Chinese films to the West have been guided by Jay Leyda's book on the subject. They have therefore to some extent chosen the films selected by Leyda as the cream of Chinese film production, which raises the question as to what the others must be like. Leyda is not always reliable. **Street Angel** (1937) is not a remake of the Borzage film, as he claims, for the only common factor in each is prostitution, or, rather, the threat of it. Initially the pleasure of seeing a film shot in the streets of Shanghai almost fifty years ago is immense: but the street scenes disappear quickly and we are left with an absurd story and screenplay by Yuan Muzhi, the director. It tries to say something about the oppressed poor, but is nothing more than a turgid melodrama, interspersed with crude slapstick and songs – accompanied by subtitles and a bouncing ball to enable the audience to join in. The other music is taken from Western records, lasting as long as it took to play one 78 r.p.m. 12″ side; and the acting is elementary – happy looks, coy looks, sad looks, and so on.

Crossroads (1937) is equally simple-minded but also rather sweet, with a stronger plot, most of it set in a run-down boarding-house, where a Box and Cox situation arises between hero and heroine. The title may refer to Shanghai – the film begins with a shot of the harbour – or to that awkward period between college and work. It focuses on four unemployed graduates, and life is not smooth: one commits suicide, one leaves for the country, one is relegated to the role of hero's friend – and the hero (Zhao Don) suffers a number of reversals before he and his sweetheart (Bai Yang) can face the future with hope. The director, Shen Xiling, had to rework the script constantly, for in the original one student went to fight, and Chiang Kai-shek's Kuomintang Government was unwilling to recognise that the country was at war with Japan until the fall of Shanghai. The War of course ruined the Chinese film industry, leaving these two films, apparently, as the most important and popular of their time.

Production ceased in Shanghai, and continued sporadically in Hankow and Chungking. The first notable post-war Chinese film was **8,000 Li of Cloud and Moon** (1947), produced by the Kun Lun company, formed by some of the personnel of the old Lianhua Film Company, one of the most important studios which had been forced to close in 1937. The story is autobiographical, for the writer-director Shi Dongshan had spent some years with an itinerant theatre company, first alerting the peasants to the Japanese menace by song and dance, and later putting on patriotic shows for the troops. In the film the troupe includes two lovers (Tao Jin, Bai Yang) who marry; the second part concerns their arrival in postwar Shanghai and their efforts to understand the wholesale corruption. At first they live with wealthy relatives, who have surrendered wholeheartedly and happily to blackmarketeering and bribery. The young couple leave, he teaching and she turning to journalism – till she is hurt in an accident. The leader of the theatrical troupe, now reunited, collects money from the members to pay for the operation, in a simple but emotional scene that has more force than any in any other Communist propaganda film that I know; the Civil War between Left and Right was in progress as this film was made, and is not mentioned; the director explained his theme as an attempt to understand why, after the Japanese surrender, he and his colleagues felt only defeat.

From this film grew another, much longer and more ambitious – and also much more naive, **The Spring River Flows East** (1947), made by Kun Lun with the same two popular players, Tao Jin and Bai Yang. Its model seems to have been either *Gone with the Wind* or *The Best Years of Our Lives*, being about men returning from the War; it begins as early as 1931, and was first shown in two parts, 'Wartime Separation' and 'Darkness and Dawn'. Zhang (Tao Jin) is a respected teacher, and a patriot inveighing against Japanese aggression; the War separates him and his wife Sufen (Bai Yang), whose family suffers atrocities at the hands of the invaders. Zhang is captured, but after escaping is taken up by the wealthy Miss Wang, who provides not only work but stylish suits and eventually a place beside her in bed. Zheng Junli and Cai Chuseng, the writer-directors, seem as certain as most filmmakers that vice is more entertaining than virtue, for while Zhang's adventures are freshly-observed, those of his now-for-gotten wife are cliché-ridden. She becomes a servant in the mansion in which he now lives, the object of contention between two women: neither he nor they are pleased when she divulges herself as his wife and thereupon commits suicide. Her mother screams out that if there is a god, why does he allow such things to happen, which is an appropriately purple ending.

The film has great vitality, even if stylistically it is clumsy and frequently derivative. Zheng Junli, working alone for Kun Lun, made **Crows and Sparrows** (1949), the only one of these films of any real value, for it does appear to give a true portrait of Shanghai just before the fall of Chiang Kai-shek. As left-wing propaganda it is less obvious than the other films from this company, even if the Communists are nice and lovable while the supporters of the old regime are dastardly (as in the Soviet films of the Twenties). They are all to be found living in a boarding-house in Shanghai, and they include a school-teacher (Sun Daolin) whose vacillations on the political situation would seem to be due to weakness of character: it says much for the film that his conversion to Communism, after being wrongly imprisoned by the villains, is at once apt and convincing. Also in the cast is Zhao Don, saddled with a nagging wife and striving to evolve schemes to defeat inflation: he is also one of the six credited writers, and said that the film was partly autobiographical.

By this time the Chinese film industry was again in full swing, but its product resembles those of the Soviet Union in being no more than simple-minded propaganda. When the subject is interesting, as with **Family** (1957), the treatment is not – and the direction, by Chen Xihe and Ye Ming, is at best uninspired. This is a family saga, one of a trilogy by Ba Jin, first published in 1933 and already filmed during the war years. Here we may justly invoke the Japanese cinema, for the subject is the resistance against oppression, at the end of feudalism, within the family circle. **Two Stage Sisters** (1964) takes another subject dear to Japanese cinemagoers, the adventures of a theatrical troupe – and these are at least pretty, in colour, and seeming to take us over vast stretches of beautiful countryside. They are also so melodramatic and predictable as to be relishable: two foster

sisters suffer deprivation and disaster, until they settle in the big city, where one becomes the mistress of a corrupt entrepreneur and the other the disciple of a worthy, culture-minded young Communist reporter. Come the Revolution and it is the latter, of course, who triumphs, while the other sinks into disgrace and dissolution; the film continues on its hysterical way as the actors, now in smart uniforms, take culture out to the provinces. The film was seen briefly before the Cultural Revolution, when it vanished; on its resurfacing, its makers, including the director, Xie Jin, sent it to the West as 'an example of their finest work'.

The Cultural Revolution brought imprisonment to both the leading players of **Red Crag** (1965), the actress Yu Lan and Zhao Don (1914–80). The film is the apotheosis of this popular and much-admired actor, but it must be said that he is somewhat self-conscious as a stoic and dedicated Communist leader. The film begins in the early Forties, when the country's leaders, the army and police officers, were bowing to their American allies. The action centres on two stalwart leaders of the underground Chinese Communist party, of their betrayal, imprisonment and torture – and of the celebrations which follow the resignation of Chiang Kai-shek. The material, once again, is fascinating: its execution, by the director Shui Hua, of no interest. It is, of course, an advance on *Street Angel* and *Crossroads*, but just as they

China's turbulent twentieth-century history was not conducive to a thriving film industry, but production continued even during the War. Not until the recent détente have we been able to sample China's cinema, which turned out to be disappointingly naive. That quality becomes a virtue in *The Spring River Flows East*, which lasts over three hours and is so prodigal of incident that one would not want to miss a single second. It concerns a married couple separated by war, and while she suffers every reversal known to screen waifs he, Tao Jin, loses his idealism when taken up by Shu Xiuwen, a wealthy lady of doubtful virtue – though on this occasion he seems to be caught up by his conscience.

1165

were elementary compared to films coming from Japan – or France, or Britain, or Italy – so are *Family*, *Red Crag* and *Two Stage Sisters*. The three Kun Lun films of the Forties are at the very least interesting, and I would like to think that among the Chinese films that we have yet to see there are others of the quality of *Crows and Sparrows*.

So much is shadow. It was with confidence that I said, starting this book, that there would be nothing on the Mongolian cinema. Since then I have seen one Mongolian film and it demands inclusion, **Tsogt Taij** (1945). Of its fellows I know not, but I suspect it is the only good Mongolian film since the People's Republic of Mongolia sent it abroad in celebration of the country's Sixtieth Anniversary, when it was already aged. The Russians had made two films in the country, *Storm Over Asia* and *Son of Mongolia*, the latter in 1936. Just after this the Mongolians started turning out films themselves, at the rate of three or four a year. Clearly *Tsogt Taij* was an ambitious undertaking: the directors were M. Luysaniamts and M. Bold, and the authors of the screenplay Yury Tarich, also the artistic supervisor, and B. Rinchen, the historical adviser, both Russians. The time is the second quarter of the sixteenth century, when the Manchus were completing their conquest of Mongolia, and its hero is Prince Tsogt, an enlightened Northern chieftain and leading supporter of the claimant to the throne of Genghis Khan: he is not supported in return, which is why his heroism is so moving. The film has touches of naivety, but these are as nothing to those in the Chinese films of the period: the direction is accomplished and the film is magnificent in detailing the religious and military crosscurrents of a medieval society.

Festivals notwithstanding, we still have insufficient opportunity to see the new and re-emergent cinemas, the pleasures of which are not always due to technique or content. Before television became the window on the world, films introduced us to faraway places, and that was one of the joys of cinemagoing in the past. Of the films we have been discussing, vivid impressions remain: the dusty suburbs of Torre Nilsson's Buenos Aires, the Austrian village in *Die Angst des Tormanns beim Elfmeter*, the Athens of *A Matter of Dignity*, the Australian Outback, the dry small town of *Calle Mayor*. Tourism is an adjunct of subsidised cinema (who does not want to visit Venice after seeing *Summer Madness*?); in less commercial terms, as well, the portraits of their countries being offered by the Australian government and Italian television are to be wholeheartedly admired. In the end, the health of the minor film industries depends on the creative talents welcomed and nurtured. Buñuel rose above the limitations of the Mexican industry, Ray struck out in a direction never dreamt of by his colleagues in India – and both made films not intended for foreign audiences. The new German cinema would collapse overnight if subsidies were withdrawn, since local audiences shun it, and yet Borau, responsible for one of the best and most popular films ever made in Spain, said 'I am not interested in making films for minority groups. I believe that way is anti-social and wastes money. One cannot waste 15 million pesetas [approx. $200,000] to please oneself.' Nevertheless *Furtivos* is a personal work, infinitely more rewarding than *Diary of a Shinjuku Thief*, made by Oshima, a director who claims to make films about 'problems meaningful to anybody in the world'. It is a question of talent. As one great director said of another – both of them working in minor industries: 'He gives you so much. He has worked it out so beautifully.' That was Satyajit Ray, explaining why his favourite director is Ingmar Bergman.

41

In Hollywood the Director is King

VERY FEW AMERICAN movies of the last quarter century have dated. The television networks in the mid-Sixties often made it a policy to only programme movies in colour at prime time, with appropriate fees, and that was, effectively, the end of the black-and-white movie. At about the same time those movie-makers using the wide screen began to plan the scenes so that no action was lost in telecasting, and since there were no technical developments, it is only in matters of fashion and special effects that one can tell an American movie of the late Fifties from one of the late Seventies. Thus the Hollywood film-maker has been left to do what he had always done best: tell a story.

The content of films has also varied little. Two of the greatest changes accompanied the break up of the studios: the virtual extinction of artificial or high-flown melodrama under the onslaught of television realism (though that was not typical of T.V. drama as a whole), and the new permissiveness. Both were inevitable, since film has always followed in the wake of drama and literature. Earlier we noted how much admired Broadway plays and popular novels had contributed to the demise of the Production Code by forcing a new sexual frankness in films. That that frankness soon became explicit had much to do with the pedlars of pornography, but that it soon became widely acceptable was due to more respectable patrons than theirs, the art-house audience. At least since *Hiroshima, Mon Amour* that audience had been accustomed to gazing upon couples in ante- or post-coital poses, and with the advent in 1967 of a Swedish enquiry into sexuality, *I Am Curious – Yellow*, directed by Vilgot Sjöman, it

began to be accustomed to naked bodies humping on beds.

At the same time the 16mm films of the American pop artist Andy Warhol arrived on the scene, to be pondered over by the pseudo-intellectual. The so-called 'underground' amateur films of Kenneth Anger which preceded them had also had homosexual connotations, and since they were equally boring the idea was mooted that there must be some hidden significance. Warhol and the word 'underground' denoted a certain artistic integrity and, with the acceptance of the films associated with his name, the way was paved for the public exhibition of hard-core pornography. That remains, to date, banned in Britain (though violence, which is far more obscene, is not), but Warhol's **Flesh** (1968) achieved public exhibition in that country without much difficulty. Warhol's friend, Paul Morrissey, put together this parade of New York hustlers and transvestites, disregarding the fumblings and clumsiness of the amateur cast, not to mention the bloops on the soundtrack and the joins in the film. As improvisation it failed to catch an iota of the native wit of New Yorkers and as social commentary it did not begin to exist. In London the police seized a copy after a number of performances at an avant-garde theatre, but the Censor intervened by granting it a certificate for public showing and it opened in a Chelsea cinema at the same time as a Tate Gallery exhibition of Warhol's paintings. In *Sight and Sound* Richard Roud observed that Warhol was one of the most important film-makers to emerge in the last ten years, because he had 'pushed back the boundaries of boredom'.

The old morality was not the only

In Hollywood the Director is King

Dennis Hopper, Peter Fonda and Jack Nicholson in *Easy Rider*, three oddballs at the mercy of redneck America. Nicholson the lawyer tries to explain: 'This used to be a helluva country, I can't tell you what's wrong . . . They're scared not of you but of what you represent to them: freedom.' He apparently spoke for a lot of people, especially the young, for the film represented the feelings of its audience as few have done in the history of films. As far as Hollywood was concerned, the message was double-edged, for a mint was lost on other films hoping to find that audience again.

victim. Some prominent Americans were assassinated and there was an unpopular war in Vietnam; it was a time between two scandals, McCarthyism and Watergate, both exposing the blatant cynicism and corruption of the Establishment. Later, in July 1974, just before measures for his removal from office were instituted against President Nixon, a Gallup poll found that forty-one per cent of the population did not think Watergate important. It was a climate conducive to the so-called hippie movement and its reaction against materialistic values – even if it was a movement which attracted more than its fair share of fakes, and an easy cop-out for those who wanted to cop-out. The sexual revolution went hand in hand with disillusionment and, after Warhol's 'innocent', 'naive' sex films there appeared the Broadway musical, 'Hair', which included a sequence of hippies in the nude, and **Easy Rider** (1968). The message of *Easy Rider* was clear: 'Fuck you, America.' The film was written, with Terry Southern, by two not quite successful actors, Peter Fonda and Dennis Hopper, with Hopper directing; it has no plot and a one-sided point of

view. Wyatt (Fonda) and Billy (Hopper) sell drugs to a pusher near the Mexican border, before proceeding to New Orleans for Mardi Gras. They have no occupation, no ambition. Their journey, like the pilgrim's progress, is a series of encounters: with a hippie commune, with the hardhats who are their natural enemies, and with an alcoholic lawyer, George (Jack Nicholson), who declines 'grass' because he has enough trouble with booze, but takes it all the same. If they are in trouble, he can get them off 'least if you haven't killed anyone. Killed anyone white, that is.' He is senselessly beaten to death by the men whose motivations he had hoped to explain: Wyatt and Billy move on, to a psychedelic drug trip with two whores in a cemetery, to their own ending, the slaughter of the innocents. It is not a good ending, but it is the one necessary to the film's makers, after its feeble acts of defiance and weaker apologia for the life-style of its heroes. If it is Nicholson's brilliant performance which holds the film together, credit should also be given to Laszlo Kovacs's photography and the editing of Henry Jaglom. It is a highly and incredibly romantic film, and that distorts its message, cloying, confused but worth making.

Columbia, which had backed the film on a medium budget, found the profits huge. The studio doors were thereupon opened to newcomers – with remarkably poor results; Hopper himself directed nothing else of interest. The industry wanted to cash in on the youth movement, and that was easy enough, in theory, with the flower-people on one side and the Establishment on the other. The great disillusionment came with the massacre of a group of innocent people by Charles Manson and his hippies in Los Angeles in 1969.

There is violence and murder in **Joe** (1970), as it concerns the two generations, allying the working-class with the affluent middle-class and making no distinction between the vicious drug-pushing young and their gentle brethren. The writer, Norman Wexler, and the director, John G. Avildsen, have no sympathy for either side. Their backers were two young men in their twenties, hitherto associated with mini-budget sexploitation movies: this one, rabble-rousing and horrendously lacking in any sort of subtlety, is only a hairsbreadth away, but its comment on American society is as valid as that in the far superior *Five Easy Pieces* (q.v.). Bill (Dennis Patrick) kills the drug-pusher who has corrupted his daughter, and in a drunken moment confesses to a hard-hat (Peter Boyle); the two men find they have much in common and later start a vigilante search for the girl, which takes them to a macrobiotic food bar, a joint for hippies where they are invited to group sex and 'grass', and to the hippie commune for the finale slaughter. The film stumbles from one improbability to another, but later variations – *Death Wish, Hardcore* (q.v.) – also failed to find a non-sensational way of showing the dilemma of the times.

Joe, though its acceptance was relative, joined *Easy Rider* and *M★A★S★H* (q.v.) as one of the free-wheeling, non-establishment movies which the predominantly young audiences preferred. The studios were willing to back such films, and if they had in some cases sold their producing facilities and abdicated much of their power as such, their distribution networks were still a prime attraction for filmmakers. Without long-term contracts, one

old problem became more acute – the near impossibility of following a flop with another project, and the young turks among the directors were as prone to these as were any of their predecessors. At this time there were approximately fifty American directors of more than passing interest, and there are many more reasons for their choice of subjects – but the principal driving force was a continuation of the Hollywood tradition – to entertain. A secondary consideration, and it was a more recent tradition, was a deliberate effort to wrest the artistic laurels from Europe's brow – which resulted in imitating, and imitating late. An important factor was the presence in the industry of Stanley Kubrick, whose career is an exemplar for every director in the industry.

Killer's Kiss (1955) represents the first time a major artist entered the industry by making his own film. Stanley Kubrick (b. 1928), a staff photographer for *Look*, had made two 16mm documentaries which R.K.O. handled. Joseph Burstyn, a foreign film distributor, suggested a feature, and Kubrick made *Fear and Desire* for $50,000, about four soldiers shot down behind enemy lines. When no Hollywood distributor would take it, Burstyn released it himself, but Kubrick then proposed *Killer's Kiss* to United Artists, who financed it together with money raised from his own family. He paid more attention to the requirements of the B-film than to logic – the title has no connection with the plot – filming in a small studio in New York and, memorably, on location. Self-confidence is evident, since he was co-producer, director, writer, editor and photographer; the plot involves a boxer, the girl he protects from the advances of her dancehall boss (Frank Silvera) and the latter's attempt at revenge. The writing and direction of **The Killing** (1956) are even more manifest, but the style is no-nonsense and the plot – about a race-track heist, as based on a novel by Lionel White – a strong one. It was daring to present a B-picture with its events not set in chronological order, but that way it does expose the mechanics of the operation. The seedy and self-seeking world of crime had seldom been better portrayed and at a time when movies were getting wider and emptier it was rewarding to have a gaggle of crooks as varied as those in *The Asphalt Jungle* or *The Big Heat*.

The Films of Stanley Kubrick

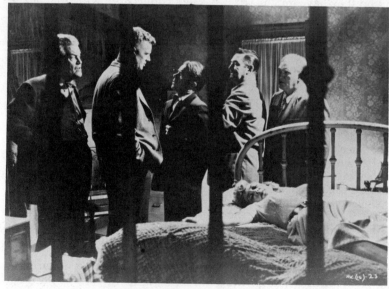

It was with *The Killing*, FAR LEFT BELOW, with Jay C. Flippen, Sterling Hayden, Elisha Cook Jr, Ted de Corsia, Joe Sawyer and, on the bed, Marie Windsor, that Stanley Kubrick established himself as one of the most exciting young directors in years. He went on to make two powerful antiwar movies, a drama, *Paths of Glory*, FAR LEFT ABOVE, and a satire, *Dr Strangelove*, LEFT, with Peter Sellers (in the wheelchair). He next directed *2001: A Space Odyssey*, BELOW, by far the best science fiction film made up to that point. Indeed, it has not been surpassed, and it is in the light of these four films that his later work is doubly disappointing.

In Hollywood the Director is King

Jim Thompson, who wrote the screenplay with Kubrick, also collaborated on **Paths of Glory** (1957), together with Calder Willingham, who had worked with Kubrick on an abortive project at M-G-M. This film, based on the novel by Humphrey Cobb, was turned down by every Hollywood company until Kirk Douglas agreed to do it, at which point United Artists put up $900,000, of which Douglas's fee was $350,000 (Douglas later claimed that Kubrick then rewrote the script to make it more commercial, but he refused to do any but the script to which he had agreed). To economise the film was made in Munich, not unsuitably since its settings are a French château and the trenches of the First World War; the subject is a court martial and the events leading up to it – a mutiny in the French army, which had been omitted from the published French records. The idealistic motives of the defending officer (Douglas) are incomprehensible to his fellow officers. The film has three endings: the final confrontation between him and the cynical C.O. (Adolphe Menjou); the execution, with the Jew between the two other victims, an analogy which would be insupportable in a lesser film; and the soldiers singing in an 'all men are brothers' gesture. At first viewing the film is so overwhelming that it takes a second one to see its faults – the ostentatious camera-work, swirling images in the style of Ophuls, and some crude devices, such as the mouthing priest and the stupid generals. The fact that these men hold outrageous beliefs does not entirely excuse Kubrick from ridiculing them: yet, paradoxically, they are exactly what the film is about. The generals converse, eat and even waltz in the château, while the men slog it out in the trenches. The generals jockey for promotion, the 'paths of glory', while the men confess that it is not death they are afraid of, but dying. The acting in every instance is worthy of the occasion, one of the finest in Hollywood history. The film was warmly praised by a few critics, but was dismissed by as many more – the same critics who had a few weeks earlier been praising *The Bridge on the River Kwai* as a serious comment on war.

Nevertheless, **Spartacus** (1960) was considered important because of Kubrick's participation. He took it over from another director to show his gratitude to Douglas, whose pet project it was (and one entirely consistent with the ambitions of the star-producers of the time), hoping that the combination of spectacle and liberal views would meet with box-office and critical success. The liberal stance is only tentative: the film purports to examine the causes of revolt and the abuses of power, but as written by Dalton Trumbo (his first credited film after his blacklisting) it states only the obvious. The director's hand is nowhere evident, but the sequences in the gladiatorial school are exciting; and despite the reputed $12 million spent, the process shots are instantly recognisable. The fundamental mistake was to make the villains more interesting than the heroes – not because heroism is necessarily boring, but because in this film it is badly acted. As the patrician Crassus, Laurence Olivier beautifully crests the huge close-ups (they all get huge close-ups), by suggesting an arrogance, ambition and intellect not written into the script; and he is matched by Peter Ustinov as the wary opportunist slave-dealer and by Charles Laughton as the cunning and experienced senator Gracchus.

The original of **Lolita** (1962), a novel by Vladimir Nabokov, was originally issued in Paris, in English, by a company associated with pornography, since the author's usual publisher thought it risked prosecution for obscenity. Its protagonist is a middle-aged professor obsessed with pubescent girls, or nymphets, a word coined in the book itself. 'How did they ever make a film of *Lolita*?' asked M-G-M's publicity, a question answered at yawn-inducing length by the critics, who do not show the same enthusiasm for their task when it is a question of a classic novel or a historical subject. By making the girl (Sue Lyon) a couple of years older, and Humbert Humbert (James Mason) younger is to answer how they made a film of it. Nabokov incorporated many of his jokes into the screenplay, but Kubrick has adopted a style which is the reverse of his vitality and, since the film was made in Britain (for economy, since anticipated bannings in the U.S. were expected to restrict its profits) he fails to retain the book's major asset, its portrait of subtopian America. The first half of the film is sustained by its situation, Humbert Humbert's marriage in order to be near the child, and the second by the juxtaposition of father-daughter/lover-mistress, a cultured man and a child whose idea of 'fun' is a lunch of French Fries and a malt. As the nemesis, Peter Sellers uses a battery of music-hall accents; and Shelley Winters is too broad as the vulgar but culture-addicted wife. Mason, all bland smiles for the world, his distaste and desperation saved for us, is now the sole reason why the piece should be seen.

Kubrick called **Dr Strangelove: or How I Learned to Stop Worrying and Love the Bomb** (1964) a 'nightmare comedy' but it is only superficially about the end of the world. It may be seen as a thriller – will-they won't-they press the right button in time? – but its purpose is less to warn of the nuclear pile-up than to expose the mentality in charge of our destinies. Like the generals in *Paths of Glory*, these scientists, politicians and high-ranking soldiers are unaware of the enormity of killing, and Kubrick, writing the screenplay with Terry Southern, from a novel by Peter George, has made the shift from drama to satire with gleaming brilliance. The visual interpretation of his thesis is perfect, and so is his cast, including Sellers in a triple role. Best of all is George C. Scott as General Buck Turgidson, a pyramid of cunning and self-satisfaction, followed by Sterling Hayden and Keenan Wynn as officers even more obtuse. The 'maybe' of the future fascinated Kubrick, but his predictions in **2001: A Space Odyssey** (1968), are trite, amusing and not very inspired – the space-station, the buttons to be pushed for phonevision, food, information, and the endless instructions. The film is visually magnificent, as 'designed and directed by' Kubrick, with a special credit; towards the end, 'the psychedelic trip', as *Variety* called it, sucks the viewer into a new dimension of sound, colour and movement, where conceptions of time and place are lost for all of its ten minutes' duration: 'Life has not many things better than this', as Dr Johnson said of travelling fast in a post-chaise. This is probably the first movie to use a simple fade to denote a time-lag of four million years, though in terms of plot, the mumbo-jumbo of the first half is preferable to that of the second. Kubrick wrote the screenplay with Arthur C. Clarke, author of the original novel; one witness, the science fiction writer, Michael Moorcock, has attested to their confusion at arriving at any ending at all. But as an abstract, *2001* is wonderful.

Unfortunately, **A Clockwork Orange** (1972) has a plot, taken from a novel by Anthony Burgess, which up-ends *Things to Come*: the people of the future are sex-obsessed, irrationally violent, and indifferent to squalor and litter. The distinction between cops and crooks has narrowed until they are interchangeable and, therefore, with all order gone, our hero (Malcolm McDowell) is of more value to society when pillaging, raping and killing than as reduced by society's more deliberate brain-washing to a vegetable. When he is sent to prison, you may think of another innocent transgressor, Paul Pennyfeather in 'Decline and Fall', a truer guide to the future than this puny, pretentious film.

Despite the fact that by this time Kubrick failed to get backing for an expensive film on Napoleon, he had achieved a position in the industry unparalleled since Capra. All his recent films had been ecstatically received, with the exception of *2001*, and that had become a great popular success – perhaps the most admired American film for a whole generation. Warners accordingly granted him complete autonomy on **Barry Lyndon** (1975), and even accepted his recommendations as to which cinema houses throughout the world it should be first offered (*Variety* reported that he employed a staff to keep track of such matters). The film opened to a panegyric in *Time* so impressive that its publicity referred to it as 'a 7-page cover story', and while *Time* undoubtedly hoped to attract those young people to whom Kubrick was a culture god, there was more than a sufficiency of hyperbole. A Warner executive was quoted as admiring Kubrick's slow methods, as that ensured a masterpiece at $11 million rather than a mediocre film at $8 million, while the article itself prophesied the 'inevitable' Oscar nominations, box-office takings to rival the record-breaking *Jaws* (q.v.) and spoke of qualities in the film 'that eluded Thackeray'. These apparently consisted of filming 'with as much beauty and grace as possible . . . all you can do is either pose questions or make truthful observations about human behaviour' – or so observed Kubrick himself, confirming his inability to understand Thackeray's malicious satire. Instead of a tale of the fashionable world of the period, peopled by the naive and gullible, fleeced and conned by the greedy and cunning, most of them snobs and hypocrites, the film is a mild series of adventures. Thackeray's Barry is at best prevaricating, hitting notes of knavery, clod-hopping cruelty, conceit and, above all, self-deceit; Kubrick's Barry is a pale shadow of Errol Flynn. He is robbed by highwaymen instead of being 'taken' by confidence tricksters; he beats the child publicly instead of privately, thus exposing the true character he tries to hide; he escapes the army with a plan involving insanity, but Thackeray's Barry does not steal a uniform from an officer bathing (who is anachronistically whispering endearments to a fellow officer). The essential visual equivalents of the book are Rowlandson and Gillray, but Kubrick has chosen Fragonard, Boucher, Gainsborough and, of all painters, Georges de la Tour.

The film united the leading critics in condemnation, and failure at this expense brings into question the wisdom of allowing any director sole control. In *The New York Times*, John Hofses tried to counter the reviews by claiming that film reviewers were literary or drama critics in disguise, unable to 'appreciate qualities of form, composition, colour, mood, music, editing rhythms' but in most of these respects the film is less advanced than M-G-M's 1938 *Marie Antoinette*. The same article quoted Kubrick as saying 'the most important parts of a film are the mysterious parts – beyond the reach of reason and language', whereas most of us, I think, would suppose these to be those which connect with an audience. This film did not, as was soon made clear to Warners' accountants.

It is sad to see a director of Kubrick's record fail, but as this disaster was followed by **The Shining** (1980) it was hard to be sympathetic. This expensive and grandiose horror film broke records in the initial weeks of its engagement, but then attendances began to plummet, taking Kubrick's reputation with them.

At the time Kubrick made his first feature, audiences were admiring **A Time Out of War** (1954), a 30-minute short about two Northern soldiers and a Southern one who, one sunny afternoon on a river bank, call an unexpected truce. Not a word or a shot is superfluous as written

and directed with elegiac grace by Denis Sanders and photographed by his brother Terry. Unlike Kubrick, the Sanders brothers could not come to terms with the industry, and their later work was again done independently. United Artists, however, released **War Hunt** (1962), another slight study of men in battle, in this case the Korean War. It owes something to *A Walk in the Sun* in trying to be honest about the nature of warfare, but fails when its young hero searches for a meaning: this may be due to the actor – Robert Redford in his film debut – who gazes around with no more than an expression of wonder.

After *Shadows*, John Cassavetes accepted an invitation to work within the industry, but was happy with neither **Too Late Blues** (1961), made for Paramount, nor **A Child is Waiting** (1963), made for Stanley Kramer. The former, a trite tale of the tensions of a jazz man, has conventional leads – Bobby Darin and Stella Stevens – and only looks fresh when compared with such contemporaries as *Tender Is the Night*; but the second film has an exceptional subject, the education of retarded children, for which the director's naturalistic approach is exactly right. Abby Mann's screenplay is hardly more than a demonstration of teaching methods, interestingly focussing on the new teacher (Judy Garland), who has at last found something useful to do with her life, and whose easy emotionalism is withheld when she realises that the head teacher (Burt Lancaster) is right on the matter of strict discipline. The film appealed neither to those interested in the subject nor to whatever audience was left for weepies, a sad postscript to Cassavetes's on-set battles with Lancaster and later with Kramer, who, he claimed, re-edited to make it more sentimental. It must be said that Kramer and Lancaster always cared more for message, image and show business than Cassavetes, who in all his films seems only interested in setting down life as it is. Unfortunately, life for him is a grim business and his subsequent independent or semi-independent films showed the need for a controlling intelligence. Whether dealing with a working-class milieu, as in **A Woman Under the Influence** (1974) or small-time hoods and strippers, as in **The Killing of a Chinese Bookie** (1976), he lacks both real understanding of his people and the old Hollywood narrative flair. He failed even with the problems of an ageing actress, played by his wife, Gena Rowlands, in **Opening Night** (1977). There is some good stuff here, but buried in the customarily excessive verbiage. Too often he attempts a shot or situation simply because other film-makers have not done so before; his aims are admirable and the results usually abysmal.

Of all American directors, none has shown such consistent interest in the working-class – or at least in the matter of earning a living – as Martin Ritt (b. 1920), a former actor, stage director and teacher at the Actors' Studio, who was recommended by Robert Alan Aurthur for **Edge of the City** (1957), the film version of his T.V. play, 'A Man is Ten Feet Tall'. Combining two concepts popular at the time, waterfront thuggery and social misfits, the film is also melodrama – which Ritt's simple approach helps to conceal; he also gets excellent performances from Cassavetes as the misfit and Sidney Poitier as his fellow teamster; this was the first American film mainly concerned with an inter-racial friendship, clearly the reason why the black must die horribly at the hands of a minor racketeer (Jack Warden). The film established Ritt as a director capable of handling the harder-edged, more honest material with which Hollywood was now preparing to deal, such as **No Down Payment** (1957), produced for 20th Century-Fox by Jerry Wald. The film takes the then unusual view that suburbanites are mundane and less interested in community relations than enslaved to materialism; as in Wald's *Peyton Place*, they also tend toward promiscuity, and in one particular case to rape.

Wald's concept of a prestige picture was an adaptation from literature, and since Ritt had become an admired director he was assigned to two adaptations of Faulkner, **The Long, Hot Summer** and **The Sound and the Fury** (1958), the second of which is especially weird. It emerges as a mixture of Tennessee Williams and Emily Brontë; if Margaret Leighton is splendid as a Blanche du Bois type, Yul Brynner is absurd as a Heathcliff figure. **Adventures of a Young Man** (1962) added the prefix *Hemingway's* to the title when it began to flop – as it was bound to do, given Richard

Beymer's interpretation of Nick Adams, reacting as he does to all the Hemingway ethos on display with one expression – that of amazement.

Ritt's reputation was helped by neither *The Black Orchid* nor *Paris Blues*, but the two Faulkner films had introduced him to the husband and wife writing team of Irving Ravetch and Harriet Frank Jr. **Hud** (1963), based on a novel by Larry McMurty, was the best picture yet for any of them, even if the influence of Williams still hangs heavy on the scenes in which Hud (Paul Newman) sweet-talks the housekeeper (Patricia Neal) and tries to rape her. The setting is a small Texas town, where the talk is mainly of cattle and where social life is restricted to movie-shows and the diner. As photographed by James Wong Howe, everything is freshly observed, even the hero-worshipping but eventually disillusioned young observer, a role already played twice in other films by this actor, Brandon de Wilde. At the end, Hud finds himself justly deserted: 'Why pick on Hud?' asks the boy. 'Everyone round here's like him,' and if that is the film's thesis it is demonstrably untrue: no one round anywhere is quite like Paul Newman.

The reviews of *Hud* seem to have restored Ritt's confidence, and **The Spy Who Came in From the Cold** (1965) clearly demonstrates the extent of his skill. John le Carré's grey-toned thriller was well-timed, coming as it did when many people were weary of James Bond and the inferior imitations: as interpreted in the screenplay (by Paul Dehn and Guy Trosper), spies are pawns, in the business solely for money and grateful for some excitement, be it even a double-cross by their own side. Ritt has the London details not only right, rare enough in itself, but amusingly right, and his vivid cast of characters is headed by Richard Burton, in the title-role, supported by Claire Bloom as the self-assured but lonely librarian who befriends him, and Oskar Werner as the East German contact. There is less action than dialogue, much of it stitched with surprises, but where most thrillers throw their surprises at the audience Ritt holds back, offering only such reaction shots as are vital. The result is a film worth all the Bonds.

Reunited with Newman, the Ravetches

In Hollywood the Director is King

Martin Ritt has never been a box-office director, as he has himself admitted, perhaps because he has always been attracted to the less sensational aspects of American society. His films are studies of environment, employment and the relationships between mundane people, in the honourable tradition of Capra; and though individually his films are not as good as we may, eventually, find his work as valuable. Ritt's films lack heart rather than conviction, but that quality is present in *Conrack*, at least in Jon Voight's customary superb performance, in this case as a teacher dedicated to educating young black children.

and Wong Howe, Ritt made **Hombre** (1967), a not unworthy successor to *Stagecoach*, whose plot it resembles. He made his most serious films to that time with **The Molly Maguires** (1970) and **The Great White Hope** (1970), but both were inadequately scripted. The 'Molly Maguires' were a secret sect operating in the hard coal region of Pennsylvania in the 1870s and dedicated to improving the heinous conditions of the workers. The conditions are glossed over and Walter Bernstein's screenplay, after refusing to either clarify or take a stand against the capitalist bosses, becomes the usual story of an undercover man (Richard Harris). 'The Great White Hope' refers to the need for another prizefighter to best the first black to win the World Heavyweight title, Jack Johnson (here called Jefferson), considered an upstart – and the title is the only subtle aspect of the screenplay. Howard Sackler, who wrote it from his own Broadway play, was intent on tragedy in the Aristotelian sense and, at the height of Johnson's career, a black Tiresias appears in the crowd to harangue him for selling out to whitey's world. Sackler's viewpoint is so consistently of the Sixties that he neglects to tell us if Johnson simply ignored racial bigotry or why his white

woman (Jane Alexander) defied society to be with him. Whether or not Johnson was a remarkable man he was in a remarkable situation, but it is left to the actor, James Earl Jones, to convey that, playing the joker or the clown.

Pete 'n' Tillie (1972) is one of Ritt's rare excursions into comedy, as written by Julius J. Epstein, from a novella by Peter de Vries, with more than a backward glance at *Penny Serenade*. Walter Matthau and Carol Burnett are much plainer, and hence more realistic, than Cary Grant and Irene Dunne. Their courtship is in a recognisable San Francisco, he punning, skittish and deliberate and she resigned: 'When you've reached my age, and your friends are beginning to worry you, blind dates are a way of life.' Ritt's detached approach is perfect, but as the material turns tragic he falters: clearly hoping for more honesty than was possible in the early Forties, the death of the child on this occasion leads not only to the break-up of the marriage but a nervous breakdown. But Hollywood had not in the meanwhile come to terms with bereavement (since audiences still did not wish to be confronted with it), and as the film strains to make any point within reach it is a pity that it left the comedy behind in reel three.

Sounder (1972) and **Conrack** (1974) are, on the other hand, splendidly brought off. *Sounder* is a story of growing-up in a black sharecropper family in the Thirties, but the script again falters, for it is no surprise that blacks have the same aspirations as the rest of us. *Conrack* concerns a young schoolteacher (Jon Voight) in an all-black community – of today, or at least a few years back – on an island just off the South Carolina coast. He is a liberal and his teachings are unorthodox, but the screenplay by the Ravetches, from Pat Conroy's autobiographical book, refuses to acknowledge that these situations have been done before, while Ritt's approach is fresher than in *Sounder*. He understates in his portrait of the community and in the teacher's battle to hold his job after meeting the disapproval of the school inspector (Hume Cronyn). And there is one sequence, as Voight's housekeeper comes to say goodbye, that is reminiscent of the first section of Satyajit Ray's *Three Daughters*.

Bernstein's screenplay for **The Front** (1976) is much better than his work on *The*

Molly Maguires, being quietly matter-of-fact on a matter which might justifiably have been handled with some hysteria – the blacklisting which operated in show business in the Fifties. Both he and Ritt had been on the list, together with other principals of the film, including Zero Mostel and Herschel Bernardi, the former playing a comic who finds that he is no longer in demand and the latter as a television executive too ineffectual to do anything about proscription. The network is shown to be avuncular, concerned but not concerned; the most telling remark in the script is spoken by the representative of the 'Freedom Information Agency', 'I don't hire, Mr Brown, I only report on Americanism.' Woody Allen plays the title-role, a cashier who passes off the work of blacklisted writers as his own.

Norma Rae (1979) is about unionisation in a backward factory in the South, and since the subject is a risky box-office prospect one may forgive Ritt and the Ravetches for indulging in a certain amount of convention and cleverness – especially in the relationship between Norma Rae (Sally Field) and the New York agitator (Ron Leibman) sent by his Union to do the organising. The relationship between the little hick girl and the city slicker – his being a Jew and cultured fascinate her – is freshly and amusingly observed, as well as being beautifully played (Miss Field won a Best Actress Oscar for her performance). The film otherwise views factory-workers without a hint of patronage and clearly expresses Ritt's own political views better than *The Molly Maguires*; its many virtues outweigh its faults.

Along with Ritt, Sidney Lumet (b. 1924) was one of the first directors to move from television into films, with **Twelve Angry Men** (1957). Henry Fonda had seen Reginald Rose's T.V. study of a dozen good men and true on jury duty, and bought it as a vehicle for himself, with Lumet redirecting. Fonda, Lee J. Cobb, E. G. Marshall, Martin Balsam, Jack Warden and George Voskovec are the leading actors in this gripping, amusing and finally too-pat drama: that their playing delights is due to the then rare practice of supposed naturalness – of overlapping dialogue, an occasional cough, of speaking off camera. Lumet's lively approach gave a lift to **Stage Struck** (1958), and as written by

Ruth and Augustus Goetz this remake of *Morning Glory* was less a tale of an aspiring actress than a witty portrait of Broadway mores and morals. Fonda is a producer and Joan Greenwood, hilariously, a temperamental star; as an ambitious young actress, Susan Strasberg offers a Juliet which in no way justifies the admiration it receives from the other characters.

That Kind of Woman (1959) was also based on old material, having reassigned the situation of *The Shopworn Angel* to World War II, with George Sanders as the wealthy businessman who almost loses his mistress, Sophia Loren, to a nice G.I., Tab Hunter. It was already clear that Lumet believed himself capable of switching from genre to genre and revitalising hoary situations, but in this case one suspected an element of mockery. He moved on to Tennessee Williams, with **That Fugitive Kind** (1960), based on the play 'Orpheus Descending'. Marlon Brando plays one of the drifters who also feature prominently in Williams's memoirs. He is one of four dreamers – together with the storekeeper's wife (Anna Magnani), the sheriff's wife (Maureen Stapleton) and the local rich girl (Joanne Woodward), dipsomaniac and nympho: and they are all threats to local red-necks (a situation to be given stronger expression, later, in *Easy Rider*). It takes a while for the piece to gather the emotional force of which Williams is capable, but Lumet is among the most successful cinema interpreters of this writer. Since he failed later, in *Blood Kin – né* 'The Seven Descents of Myrtle' – credit should perhaps be shared with Boris Kaufman, whose harsh, grainy photography had also helped to reduce the hot airs of *On the Waterfront* and *Baby Doll* to something approaching the realistic.

Lumet's reputation as an interpreter of contemporary drama increased with a television production of 'The Iceman Cometh' for Ely Landau, who subsequently produced **Long Day's Journey Into Night** (1962), also by Eugene O'Neill. The playwright's widow sold the rights only on condition that it was filmed in its entirety, which meant, among other things, no involvement by a major studio and a low budget – which was $400,000, with the four leading players getting $25,000 each, plus a percentage of the profits, if any. Consistently the best of them is Jason Robards Jr, repeating his Broadway performance, self-loathing mixed with boozy good nature; as his younger brother, Dean Stockwell understandably looks as though he expects the others to eat him alive. Father Tyrone is completely self-assured, and no one is better than Ralph Richardson at behaving as though he is no longer of this world; as the drug-addicted mother, Katharine Hepburn is also theatrical, but when the role becomes demanding she grows with it. Kaufman did the photography, and Lumet, realising that the film could hardly be a true cinematic experience, allows this tortured family to move and breathe and talk amidst their waves of emotion.

However, as with the Williams piece, he transformed Arthur Miller's **A View From the Bridge** (1962), made in fact just before *Long Day's Journey*. It was financed in France, but photographed on New York locations by Michel Kelber. In the interiors Lumet manages the claustrophobia essential to this modern tragedy, and he brings homogeneity to his cast – Raf Vallone, Miss Stapleton and Carol Lawrence as the Italo-American family, and Jean Sorel and Raymond Pellegrin as the immigrants.

Turning to a contemporary problem for the first time, Lumet directed **Fail Safe** (1964), which starts with the premise of two pilots who, due to a mechanical error, are journeying towards Moscow to drop their nuclear weapons. This potentially frightening tale, told by Lumet in plain, urgent images, is notably acted by Walter Matthau as a German-Jewish professor of strong anti-communist views; but Walter Bernstein's screenplay adds nothing to the ideas expressed in the original novel (by Eugene Burdick and Harvey Wheeler), so that the result is a long way behind *Dr Strangelove*. Following Kubrick again, Lumet attempted his own analysis of the military mentality, choosing a British military prison in North Africa during the Second World War. In its more modest way **The Hill** (1965) is as good as *Paths of Glory*, and certainly there is no film by a British director as honest about the men who choose to spend their life in uniform. The source is a play by Ray Rigby and R. S. Allen, with a screenplay by the former; the plot is not too far removed from old prison movies – as one obstinate man, a

born kicker against the pricks, decides to fight the system. That the film works so well is due in large measure to the performance of Sean Connery in this role; equally good are Michael Redgrave as the doctor, one of life's more memorable failures, and Harry Andrews, Ian Hendry and Ian Bannen as the disciplinarians, virtually drunk – when not really drunk, which is every evening – on the smell of starch in their uniforms. **The Pawnbroker** (1965) also sets out to consider the seeds of fascism, by examining a New York Jew (Rod Steiger) permanently afflicted by his memories of the concentration camp and currently trapped, though he himself is an innocent, in the criminalities of Spanish Harlem. The screenplay, by David Friedkin and Morton Fine, from a novel by Edward Lewis Wallant, is so shadowy that Lumet moves through it with unwonted speed, untypically showy. The best scenes are those between the pawnbroker and the social worker (Geraldine Fitzgerald), and the worst those with the parade of junkies, racketeers, etc. These include the Black whore who bares her breasts – the first time this had been seen in an American non-ethnic film, and permitted in view of the film's respectability, even in, for instance, Italy (after months of discussion with the Censor). This was the first American film with a Jew as a leading character in over thirty years: the fact that it was also the first American film to refer to the suffering of the Jews in the War caused it to be greatly over-rated there.

British critics much preferred **The Group** (1966), based on Mary McCarthy's novel about a clique at Vassar and their later inability to cope with sex, careers and failing marriages. Among them is a lesbian (Candice Bergen) – and that was another aspect of life that Hollywood had avoided for over thirty years, though the screenplay thoughtfully omits the book's more 'daring' passages, such as the discussions of pessaries. The film was written by Sidney Buchman, brought out of retirement by the producer, Charles K. Feldman. Lumet had liked the script while disliking the novel, and his deft, one-take approach – typical of the T.V.-trained directors – punctured the pomposity and pretension that inevitably remained. His unfailing sense of timing was eminently suited to the episodic nature of the material, but its inherent flaws meant that the finished film could never have been more than superior soap opera.

The title nevertheless could be applied to almost all of Lumet's films. Although he prides himself on his eclecticism, enjoying the challenge of moving from an adaptation of a novel or a play to a semi-documentary study, virtually all his films have been about groups of people, either friends or co-workers, people confined to a particular milieu or with common aims. The New York literary Jewish society of **Bye Bye Braverman** (1968) is viewed much more incisively and satirically than Ms McCarthy's Vassar graduates. Herbert Sargent adapted the novel by Wallace Markfield, a memoir of growing up Jewish in New York (which Lumet had also done: his father was the distinguished Yiddish actor, Baruch Lumet). This is no teen-age tale, but one about a funeral which draws a number of friends back to their shared past. The chief of these is played by George Segal, while Alan King's barbed cameo of a rabbi is a rare unflattering movie portrait of a religious leader.

The characters in **The Deadly Affair** (1967) are mainly Londoners engaged in espionage, and Lumet views both them and their setting as freshly as Ritt did in *The Spy Who Came in From the Cold*. Retained from those who worked on that film was the screenwriter, Paul Dehn, whose additions – a nymphomaniac wife and a beating-up sequence – were particularly disliked by the author of both books, John Le Carré. Le Carré did like the performance of Simone Signoret, as a suburban housewife who had survived the Nazi concentration camps, and there are also admirable portraits by James Mason as the secret agent Smiley (here called Dobbs) and Harry Andrews, Max Adrian and Maximilian Schell as civil servants who are communist sympathisers. While making the film, Lumet, Signoret and Mason decided to acquire backing for a version of Tchekov's **The Seagull** (1968), retaining also the services of Mr Andrews and David Warner, who plays Konstantin. Vanessa Redgrave unwisely portrays Nina as a Botticelli maiden, and Signoret's Arkadina is prim and selfish rather than superficial. Only James Mason, as Trigorin, valiantly attempts to bridge the gap between the various acting styles, and he is matched by Denholm Elliott and Eileen Herlie, but their roles are small. Only these three hint that the piece may be a comedy; perhaps the cold air of the Swedish locations led Lumet to his misinterpretation. Warner Bros.-Seven Arts financed, and regretted it.

It was the first of several failures for Lumet, which also include **The Appointment** (1969) and **Child's Play** (1972): both are inferior examples of currently fashionable models and miscalculations on the part of this usually intelligent director. *The Appointment*, which incited derisive laughter at the Cannes Film Festival, examines the *malaise* of some wealthy Italians, particularly Omar Sharif, who is dull as a man bewitched, bothered and bewildered by the enigmatic behaviour of Anouk Aimée, playing her customary role once too often. *Child's Play*, based on a Broadway play, is a rehash of Hugh Walpole's 'Mr Perrin and Mr Traill' with an injection of diabolism as borrowed from a best-selling novel, 'The Exorcist'; the schoolmaster protagonists are Mason and Robert Preston.

Lumet's standing within the industry was hardly affected by such films. His cast and crews adored him because he was and is the complete professional. He and his team arrive on the set knowing exactly what they are going to do, which is rare, and he invariably brings his films in under budget and under schedule. Since he enjoys working fast he is attracted to the thriller form, and he also thought Dehn's script for **Murder on the Orient Express** (1974) sufficiently good, provided that it was interpreted by stars of stature. Sean Connery, with whom he had worked before, also liked it, and he was subsequently joined by such names as Ingrid Bergman, Lauren Bacall, Richard Widmark, Miss Redgrave and John Gielgud. This old, tired Agatha Christie story deserved none of them, nor was Lumet's penchant for location shooting served, since almost all of it was set within the confines of a railway carriage: but it made a profit for its British producers, E.M.I., despite its being, at £1½ million, the most expensive film made in England for many years.

Network (1976) provided Lumet with a further success, and a more controversial one. Twenty years after they both had left television, he and Paddy Chayevsky joined forces to portray it as something

In Hollywood the Director is King

akin to the Black Death. Unfortunately, Chayevsky's gorge had so risen that he had forgotten that to explain evil it is necessary to understand it. In *The Hospital* (q.v.) he suggests that the staff and most of the patients are insane, but in *Network* his indictment extends from T.V. executives to the whole nation – that is, to all those who sit at home watching the small screen. At the end, an old T.V. hand (William Holden) rediscovers his humanity after being screwed both ways by his mistress (Faye Dunaway), who has taken his job, 'Like you, everything television touches is destroyed . . .' That is one of the more precise remarks in this combination of fantasy and hyperbole, and I should state that many within the television industry have confirmed the veracity of this film. The Academicians of Motion Picture Arts and Sciences, who should know, voted it a Best Screenplay Oscar – or were they donning their motion picture hats for a movie describing their friend/rival as a stream of mindless pap and vulgarity incarnate?

Lumet's questioning of the mentality of those set in authority over us had earlier been the subject of *The Hill* and one of his failures, **The Offence** (1972). The three films considered together confirm his strengths and weaknesses as commensurate to his material, and that of *The Offence* is poor, as based by John Hopkins on his

play about a mentally-sick policeman (Connery). Hopkins had written several episodes of a much admired British T.V. series, 'Z Cars', showing the more admirable methods of police procedure, but in trying to show the other side of the coin he managed only a superficial and humourless piece about a cop who beats up a child molester (Ian Bannen) because he himself secretly yearns to be one. The scenes in which this revelation is made are typical of Lumet's films, being crude and overemphatic. But they are only shots, instances which are apparently the price we have to pay for Lumet's skill and craftsmanship in most of his work. The opening sequences of *The Offence*, grafted on to Hopkins's original play, demonstrate Lumet's continuing ability to look with fresh vision at virtually everything in sight. In this case we see the British countryside and the British police under several new guises; and he was to do something similar on his home territory.

Indeed, Lumet's three films on New York's Finest are among the best American films of the last twenty years – an achievement which gives us reason to digress for a moment, to examine his own thoughts on his career: 'I've never been a fashionable director. The whole *auteur* nonsense is repugnant to me. I won't take the billing "a Sidney Lumet film" or "Sidney Lumet's production" . . . When I go out shooting, I'm dependent on the weather, the sun, the 120 people around me knowing their work. And I don't want to settle into a particular style, because to me the style is determined by the material itself. I think this has left me in a vacuum from the critical point of view. It's nothing that disturbs me a great deal.' He is proud of his ability to give the impression of reality, and that is essential to these three films, which would lose force if we did not believe in them completely: for **Serpico** (1973) and **Prince of the City** (1981) deal with police corruption, and **Dog Day Afternoon** (1975) is about the public's relationship with the police. All three movies are based on actual events, and as far as the two films on corruption are concerned, we may wonder to what extent the New York Police Department cooperated on location facilities. In both cases the corruption seems not much less than a hundred per cent, so that the N.Y.P.D.

must have passed both scripts with a great degree of cynicism. Lumet himself has said of *Prince of the City* that as long as he lives he will never understand the motives of anyone involved, and quotes its real life protagonist, Robert Leuci, as saying that five per cent of the police will always be dishonest, as many again will be incorruptible and the other ninety per cent will follow whichever is the stronger.

Serpico is based on a book by Peter Maas and produced by Dino de Laurentiis, who had made his American production debut with *The Valachi Papers*, adapted from Maas's book about the Mafia. Frank Serpico (Al Pacino) is an honest cop, and is said to be further a-typical, with his macho moustache, his live-in women and his bijou apartment in the Village. He likes opera, ballet, dogs and wine, and laughs when falsely accused of going down on a colleague in the john. His colleagues have a hard-hat mentality, decent enough in their sense of humour, but firmly believing that the dope-pushers and other law-breakers can afford to pay and 'it's fair shares for all.' Lumet and Jay Presson Allen wrote *Prince of the City* from a novel by Robert Daley based on the experiences of Leuci, a dedicated cop who gave evidence to a Senate commission on the corruption rampant in the N.Y.P.D. He 'ratted' while demanding reassurances that his buddies would not be arrested, but since they and he were as guilty as anyone else he finds himself sucked into a whirlpool as dangerous as it is degrading. The moral issues involved are debated for almost three hours and every minute of them is riveting. Treat Williams achieves a blend of modesty and vitality as the cop based on Leuci – who, like Serpico, found that he was no longer wanted in the police.

Dog Day Afternoon was written by Frank Pierson from accounts of a raid on a Brooklyn bank one afternoon in 1972 by three nut-cases, one of whom chickened out within minutes. The other two holed themselves up with their hostages, and it transpired that they wanted money for a sex-change operation for the boyfriend of their leader, Sonny (Pacino) – an operation that was eventually paid for by Warners, in order to get cooperation for the film to be made. Despite the brilliant editing of Dede Allen, the film does sag when it wanders from its bizarre central situation and delves back into Sonny's past. Whereas the excitement of the other two films springs from the threat to their heroes, here it is in the sly and sprightly observation of the behaviour of the hostages, the unprepossessing 'criminals', the waiting crowds and the spit-and-polish cops, only too human in their errors. The approach, as in *Network*, is satirical, but it is anecdotal instead of being hysterical.

John Frankenheimer (b. 1930) had at one time been Lumet's assistant in T.V., and had entered films at the same time. He had originally directed **The Young Stranger** (1957) on television, and we should be thankful for this transposition for it was, and remains, Hollywood's best study of adolescence. The boy (James MacArthur) is from a very comfortable home, and he is in no sense a delinquent: but when a minor incident brings him into contact with the police, he and his parents are in total conflict. He, looking for help, retreats into sarcasm; the father (James Daly), unthinking and unfeeling, does not hesitate to make matters worse; and the mother (Kim Hunter) stands weakly by, hoping the rot within her home will just go away. The happy ending robs the piece of its logic, though not of its position as one of the key films of the era; sadly, however, Frankenheimer's quiet creation of tension suggested a promise that has seldom been fulfilled. **The Young Savages** (1961) was the first deception, a meretricious

Among the best of the several interesting films of the Fifties which originated in television drama is *The Young Stranger*, with Eddie Ryder, James MacArthur, centre, and Jeff Silver, in which an incident in a movie theatre leads eventually to a crisis in a middle-class home. John Frankenheimer came from television to redirect the piece for the big screen, and he stayed; but only for a short while was the promise of this film borne out.

1181

In Hollywood the Director is King

view of juvenile criminals, adapted from a novel by Evan Hunter. The understanding D.A. was played by Burt Lancaster, whose company called in Frankenheimer on two occasions, to replace Charles Crichton on **Birdman of Alcatraz** (1962) and Arthur Penn (q.v.) on **The Train** (1964). The latter is a banal blend of *La Bataille du Rail* and Ealing comedy, about the French Resistance attempting to save a cargo of paintings, 'our national heritage', from the Germans, with Lancaster at his most self-righteous as a French superman. However, in *Birdman* this variable actor is, like the film itself, beyond good and evil. 'Twelve years I've had to look at that frozen mug of yours' says the warder (Neville Brand), and the audience is offered little other option, as Lancaster, spending the rest of his natural life in jail, becomes the world's leading authority on caged bird diseases. In life, the man was Robert Stroud: his story was written down by Thomas E. Gaddis, and Guy Trosper was the screenwriter who collaborated with Frankenheimer to make a consciously humanist, social film. It was not a huge success in cinemas, but has always been popular on television, when audiences sympathise as Stroud helps to quell riots, and perhaps become indignant as a postscript says that he was still in jail after fifty-three years and still being refused parole.

The Manchurian Candidate (1962) was almost indecently well-received, being taken for a mordant satire on American politics: it is actually a melodrama involving political conniving, the Korean War and brainwashing (though this is irrelevant to the plot). As satire, the only point the film has to make is that unscrupulous politicians have used communist-baiting as a path to power; but the screenwriter, George Axelrod, working from Richard Condon's novel, has much fun with the senator (James Gregory), a man of goonish simplicity and with a taste for booze, and his wife (Angela Lansbury), a barracuda-like all-American mom. That she turns out to be a dedicated communist makes nonsense of all that has gone before, though as a thriller the film is fair. United Artists did not care for the film, and Paramount did not like **Seven Days in May** (1964), but Frankenheimer had independent financing and the backing of President Kennedy, who lent the White House

for filming. The tale, as derived by Rod Serling from a novel by Fletcher Nebel and Charles W. Bailey II, is about a plan to oust a U.S. president (Fredric March) because he plans to sign an anti-nuclear pact with the U.S.S.R.; the leader of the coup is a fanatic general (Lancaster), whose second-in-command (Kirk Douglas) throws in his lot with the beleaguered president. Frankenheimer restricts himself to the mechanics of plotting; and the film is more penetrating than its contemporary, *Fail Safe*.

It was not long afterwards that he began to lose his reputation. John Houseman's production of **All Fall Down** (1962) had shown Frankenheimer capable of sheer carelessness, but this family drama, a poor collage as scripted by William Inge from James Leo Herlihy's decent novel, was unlikely to inspire anyone. In Europe, after a number of failures, Frankenheimer made **The Fixer** (1968), a tale of anti-Semitism in old Russia, portentously scripted by Dalton Trumbo from Bernard Malamud's novel, and apart from Dirk Bogarde and Ian Holm as lawyers, poorly acted by a mainly British cast. Frankenheimer later called it 'a lousy movie, very boring', a description surely applying also to the failures which followed it, including one made in English in France,* with French backing, which had no public showings in any English-speaking country till sold to television ten years later. Called back to Hollywood for **The French Connection II** (1975), Frankenheimer announced that he wanted to make good commercial movies in the future, but the movies he made, though commercial, were not widely liked. This one is the best. It could not be said that William Friedkin's original *French Connection* (q.v.) was worth a sequel, but this one had the excellent idea of setting down its pugnacious cop hero, 'Popeye' Doyle (Gene Hackman), in Marseille. Marseille is not the kindest city to a foreigner with no French, and both factors are extensively used; the film moves swiftly, only let down by its middle sequences, in which Doyle is forcibly turned junkie by the villain (Fernando Rey), and unconvincingly weaned 'cold turkey' by his French opposite number (Bernard Fresson).

Also coming from television was

The Impossible Object.

Arthur Penn (b. 1922), like Lumet and Frankenheimer also with theatre experience – and in that medium he was far more successful than they, continuing to direct on Broadway until 1964. His first film, **The Left-Handed Gun** (1958) was based on a T.V. play, by Gore Vidal, whose screenplay was rewritten by Leslie Stevens, at Penn's request (also dismayed by Penn's demands was the veteran photographer J. Peverell Marley, since Penn, accustomed to four cameras on a television set, insisted on two for this film). Anticipating Penn's most celebrated film, *Bonnie and Clyde* (q.v.), this one is an essay on the fusion of truth and myth, as a sycophantic journalist (Hurd Hatfield) is disappointed by the real Billy the Kid (Paul Newman), lout and psychopath. Symbolism abounds and, since there were rules governing Westerns – permitted only to be broken by the likes of *Shane* – the film was dismissed as pretentious. It was, however, liked by French critics, whose perceptions, for once, were not misplaced.

Penn was only able to return to films with **The Miracle Worker** (1962) because he had directed William Gibson's original play with success first on television and then on Broadway. There have been few American films with a theme so vital – the rescue of a human being from a state of savagery: this is the infant Helen Keller, deaf and blind, and her teacher is Annie Sullivan, from an orphanage, and with a slight affliction of her own. Gibson's writing is remarkably unsentimental, while offering some dramatic rigging in the form of opposition to Miss Sullivan's teaching methods, while Penn's loving direction errs only in allowing almost all the cast to overact – except his Annie, Anne Bancroft, and his Helen, Patty Duke, repeating their Broadway performances.

Penn has not been a prolific director, and his career might have finished with **Mickey One** (1965) had **The Chase** (1966) not already been in production. The former is a fanciful Kafkaesque fable with Warren Beatty which, unlike most of its breed, has apparently never drummed up a single supporter. As much may be said of *The Chase*, though it is at least the sort of film the industry understands. It was intended to be the definitive statement on Southern corruption, as produced by Sam Spiegel and written by Lillian Hellman – though

she expeditiously repudiated it. The attitudes towards the lynching of blacks are impeccable, but are entrenched in a story which seems of the same vintage as *They Won't Forget*: Penn manages a party sequence well, and also the atmosphere of sultry, boozy nights, but its many stars are merely stars, headed by Marlon Brando as the sheriff whose sufferings would, in another age, have brought him sainthood.

However, **Bonnie and Clyde** (1967) is one of the masterworks of the American cinema. A threnody of blood and violence, there had never been a film like it before – wholly itself, and still ahead of all other movies about America's criminals. The writers, David Newman and Robert Benton, then on the staff of *Esquire*, were movie-buffs, and patterned their screenplay on the early films of Truffaut and

The cinema's fascination with crime was never more evident than in *Bonnie and Clyde*, and only partly because it was the first of the many posthumous attempts to re-create the milieu of the gangsters of the past with anything like fidelity. Faye Dunaway played Bonnie Parker and Warren Beatty Clyde Barrow; and the film is the best of the infrequent ones directed by Arthur Penn.

In Hollywood the Director is King

Godard (both of whom, at one time, were asked to direct it), with a glance towards Hitchcock. Like Belmondo in *A Bout de Souffle*, a runt to everyone but a legend to himself, Bonnie Parker and Clyde Barrow believed in their own myth. Explaining their re-creation of these two gangsters, the writers suggest they were 'hung up' like many people today, which may explain why the film has no more depth than appears on the screen. It is a simple story brilliantly told. It does not tell the truth, but it works marvellously at that level where truth and legend meet – much better than in Penn's similar studies. Its only fault is Faye Dunaway, too film-starry in appearance and manner. And perhaps Clyde's impotence is unconvincing (used in preference, the writers said, to what they thought was the truth, that Barrow needed another man in the room). Warren Beatty – the film's producer, who invited Penn to direct – is sunny-insolent as Clyde, and is memorably supported by Gene Hackman as his brother, Estelle Parsons as the latter's giggly wife and Michael J. Pollard as the puppy-like gang member. There has never been a more awesome evocation of the U.S. during the Depression, of sleepy, dead little towns with ice-cream parlours, general stores that have not long had electric lights, and one, very surprised, bank.

Continuing his examination of the American past, Penn made **Alice's Restaurant** (1969), an inert fantasy, written by himself, built, paradoxically, around the life of a folk singer, Arlo Guthrie, son of Woody; and **Little Big Man** (1970), the story of a white man brought up as a Cheyenne, who was either 'the most neglected hero of his country or a liar of insane proportions' – a role played by Dustin Hoffman when it needs Brando or Jack Nicholson. As it happened, Penn paired these two actors in **The Missouri Breaks** (1976), and the sole virtue of Thomas McGuane's script would seem to be the provision of parts for their virtuosity. The cattle-rustler played by Nicholson is, at best, confused; the lawman played by Brando is, it would seem, a confusion of the actor's. Only the mood and tension remind us that Penn directed *Bonnie and Clyde*; the accretions are clearly the work of the man who made *Mickey One* and *Alice's Restaurant*. Penn later observed that he would never again make a film for commercial reasons.

His last two films to date were also failures, unjustly so in the case of **Night Moves** (1975). Like *Bonnie and Clyde*, it uses people, time and place beautifully, finding nuances throughout the detailed script by the English novelist Alan Sharp. Harry Moseby (Gene Hackman) is a private eye hired to find a missing girl; he does, but she is killed and he is himself the subject of an attempted murder. 'You ask all the wrong questions' says someone to him, for he is, like America, a bit of a mess; he is also like Galahad, embarking on his own voyage of discovery as he seeks to solve the mystery. The theme and the use of symbols are reminiscent of Antonioni; the start of **Four Friends** (1981) is reminiscent of *Breaking Away* (q.v.), also written by Steve Tesich. Both films begin with amiable group portraits of adolescence, but where that one was content to stay that way this one sets out to chart the American experience of the Sixties, when conformity gave way to hippiedom, when people dropped out and/or took to drugs – as represented by the hero (Craig Wasson), who had arrived from Yugoslavia as a boy. The original script dealt with the cataclysmic assassinations of the Kennedys and Martin Luther King, but at Penn's request they have been replaced (though mentioned) by the boy's father-in-law going ape with a gun on his wedding day. It had already been clear that Penn was bent on hyperbole, so it is not the scene itself which is ludicrous; but as the survivors talk afterwards they show only movie emotions, not real ones, and the film never recovers.

Another director who came from T.V. is Robert Mulligan (b. 1925), whose score of films include only a few of note. The first, **Fear Strikes Out** (1957), is one of the quietly good T.V.-orientated dramas, based on the mental illness of the baseball-player Jim Piersall of the Boston Red Sox. He is played with neurotic intensity by Anthony Perkins, without his later mannerisms, and as his father – the villain of the piece – Karl Malden acts with unusual sympathy. The illness is schizophrenia, until then treated by Hollywood as an excuse for lovely ladies to go wandering on moonlit beaches. Mulligan – whose father was a New York cop – is most at ease with a proletarian background, and

Love with the Proper Stranger (1963) is even more freshly observed. This likeable film follows the ups and downs of a romance between a jazz musician (Steve McQueen) and a Macy's store clerk (Natalie Wood) who is pregnant by him. The matter-of-fact attitude to this situation was entirely new in an American film but, having progressed that far, it could not be expected that she would subject herself to the planned abortion, especially since it is a shabby back street business. **Up the Down Staircase** (1967) was written by Tad Mosel from a best-selling book by Bel Kaufman, based on her experiences as a teacher in New York; Mulligan manages a smell of chalk-dust and the undercurrent of violence. The piece juggles with a number of issues – parental apathy, bureaucratic stranglehold, the danger of walking a slum block if you are female and pretty, the fact that no black child can feel safe in a mixed school – without pushing any one of them forward, perhaps because none has an immediate solution. Sandy Dennis is not one of the dewy-eyed teachers of Hollywood's past, but obstinate, weary and vulnerable – and likely to become as bored and cynical as her colleagues.

Mulligan's most acclaimed film has been **To Kill a Mockingbird** (1962), one of the films which re-established Universal's lost esteem after a decade of programme pictures. His treatment perfectly reproduces the virtues and vices of Harper Lee's Pulitzer-prizewinning novel – though the former are evident to me only in its portrait of the special world of children. They while away the long hot summer days in a small town in the South, as a serious drama plays around them, involving a rape, an attempted lynching and a trial. But they are precious and goody-goody, like the lawyer father (Gregory Peck) of one of them and the material itself, which is equipped with unimpeachable stances on racialism – but they are only superficial and therefore lacking in tension.

The setting of **Inside Daisy Clover** (1965) is a particularly unreal Hollywood. Gavin Lambert's novel was a collection of Hollywood myths and truths, centring on an adolescent star not wholly unlike Judy Garland. Her Prince Charming flunks out on the wedding night because, she learns later, he prefers his own sex; her family feed on her fame and fortune, but she

adjusts to fame after a nervous breakdown. The book's many and witty references to the songs, people and events of the Thirties and Forties have been omitted from the screenplay written by Lambert himself; what was a tragicomedy has become an attempt at tragedy and a particularly pretentious one. The film might just as well have been set in Timbuktu; Natalie Wood and Robert Redford are only adequate in the leads. Mulligan's other films have been equally disappointing, but **Summer of '42** (1971) was, with some justification, very popular. It begins with pictures of sunset, breaking waves, seaside villas and wild flowers – and having thus announced its intentions it proceeds to fulfil them. The Andrews Sisters are heard on the radio, *Now, Voyager* is at the local cinema and at the over-stuffed village shop the boys buy condoms (another hitherto unmentionable matter in an American film). The central situation, as adapted from the novel by Herman Raucher, is a reworking of that in *Le Blé en Herbe*: an adolescent (Gary Grimes) is taught the facts of

Robert Mulligan's *Love with the Proper Stranger* has, like many films of its time, a theme song, but in this case heard only briefly on the radio before being turned off by Natalie Wood. 'That's what love is?' she asks, 'bells and banjoes?' That is typical of the movie, which has the old malarkey going on under the new realism. The man with whom Miss Wood falls in Love is Steve McQueen.

life by an older woman (Jennifer O'Neill). Michel Legrand's theme tune sounds not at all like the music of '42, but is otherwise appropriate.

Alan J. Pakula (b. 1928) was Mulligan's producer from their days in television till they split in 1968, after the failure of *The Stalking Moon*. As the films which he has directed have maintained a higher average quality than those on which they worked together, it is tempting to suppose that Pakula's was the major contribution. His first film as a director was **The Sterile Cuckoo** (1969), another consciously lyrical and amusing look at college sexuality, written by Alvin Sargent from a novel by John Nichols. The girl, having made all the running, is not about to give up easily when the boy (Wendell Burton) tires; she is played by Liza Minnelli, with much of the vulnerability of her mother, Judy Garland. As she yields her virginity one may like to recall that at that age Mama had not long walked along the Yellow Brick Road in her red shoes. **Klute** (1971) is graphic on the details of a whore's life, which includes, on this evidence, auditioning for an off-Broadway 'Saint Joan'. Success in that field or the love of the young detective (Donald Sutherland) might lead her (Jane Fonda) back to the straight and narrow – to which extent it is very much like the prostitute films of the Silent era. The piece

Alan K. Pakula served his first decade in films as producer of those directed by Robert Mulligan. Turning director himself, he made some notable movies, including *All the President's Men*, which was in fact produced by Robert Redford, right. Redford and Dustin Hoffman play the two Washington reporters who helped to bring about the fall of Nixon, and the film's subject is, as one of them and Redford both put it, 'This is how we did it.'

is on the level of a T.V. series-episode, though Pakula's control disguises the fact. He attempted a third unusual romance, between an English spinster (Maggie Smith) and a young American (Timothy Bottoms), but **Love and Pain and the Whole Damn Thing** (1973) is tepid.

Pakula then turned to the thriller, and **The Parallax View** (1974) suffered by being released at the same time as *Chinatown* (q.v.), which also resurrected once-familiar themes and combined them with political corruption. In this case the investigative journalist (Warren Beatty) joins, as of old, an undercover organisation to get his story; he even has a sceptical editor and a frightened lady to put him on to the story in the first place. Like many modern thrillers, this one withholds facts from the audience – and not only those unknown to the hero. People speak, unheard by us, beyond glass doors, but Pakula makes great use of his structures; just as every person glimpsed is a possible killer, so every rivet is bursting with menace. The screenplay is by David Giler and Lorenzo Semple Jr, based on a novel by Loren Singer, in turn inspired by rumours about the deaths and disappearances of various figures connected with the assassination of President Kennedy. Its implication of the U.S. as a trigger-happy country is more subtle than in some well-meaning films, and stronger. The film's virtue – apart from the fact that it is far more exciting than *Chinatown* – is that its level is blood and thunder and yet its aim to touch sore spots in the American conscience is entirely well-judged. Beatty is awkward and persistent, in the tradition of reporters in movies.

The man who directed him was obviously the man to handle **All the President's Men** (1976), or so thought Robert Redford, its star and producer. The film had its origins in a report in *The Washington Post* which connected a burglary at the National Democratic headquarters with the White House, and it is about that story as researched by two reporters, Bob Woodward, played in the film by Redford, and Carl Bernstein, played by Dustin Hoffman. The book they wrote on the subject was purchased by Redford for $450,000, and Warners put up the $8½ million cost on the basis of his drawing power. The studio was uncertain whether

the public would be interested in a tale familiar from newspaper reports, while the many and salient facts needed a screenwriter of the expertise of William Goldman to knock them into dramatic shape. Even so, the meticulous Pakula did a certain amount of improvisation, using *Z* as his model – and this movie is as violently partisan: Nixon is hardly mentioned, but as the reporters burrow away they are, even with their knowledge of him, stunned by the criminal cupidity, the sheer stupidity, the arrogance and deviousness of Nixon and the men around him. The film, unlike the book, plays down the role other newspapers took in the unmasking. One of its many virtues is that it uses unfamiliar players except for the *Post* staff. The subject would have made an enthralling film if only competently dealt with, but it is superlatively well done. It commends itself to posterity, which will surely think as highly of it as the audiences and reviewers of the time.

Rollover (1981) is about the world of high finance, which apparently deterred audiences from attending; but its purpose is that of *The Parallax View* and *All the President's Men*, to show how the lives of the humble are manipulated by the rich and powerful. Again Pakula shows that he has few peers in handling such conventions of the thriller as the apparently unmotivated crime, the unexpected clue, the frightened witness; but perhaps the chief virtue of David Shaber's screenplay is the ease of the plotting, via which Jane Fonda suspects the one man in the world she can trust, Kris Kristofferson, and vice versa. Pakula has made them glamorous ikons in the manner of Hollywood stars of old, and given their capabilities it is a device that works beautifully. I have a feeling that the film will revive better than **Sophie's Choice** (1982), despite the popularity and acclaim that has greeted it. Its source is a novel by William Styron, of whom I once observed that he wrote for the sake of writing. That is the impression given by this film, which has no discernible subject. A young Southern boy (Peter MacNicol) arrives in Brooklyn in 1947 and chums up with a Jewish biologist (Kevin Kline) and his mistress (Meryl Streep), a survivor of Auschwitz. The biologist turns out to be unworthy of the boy's hero-worship, while much of the rest of the time is taken up with flashbacks to Auschwitz, when Miss Streep manages to be emotional and interesting, which she does not elsewhere. We have not yet come to grips with the concentration camp experience in drama and literature, and shall not do so by encasing it in meaningless fictions. Pakula wrote his own screenplay (for the first time), but at 157 minutes it serves only to remind us that old Hollywood made short, watchable films out of equally unpromising material.

Well before *All the President's Men* Nixon was a dirty word, if we are to believe **The Best Man** (1964), directed by Franklin J. Schaffner (b. 1920), and written by Gore Vidal from his own play. A former television director and producer, Schaffner had directed a Broadway version of 'Advise and Consent' which, in common with *The Best Man* concerns chicanery in Washington and homosexuality as the skeleton in the cupboard. The two chief contenders at a Presidential convention are Senator Russell (Henry Fonda), based on Adlai Stevenson, and Senator Cantwell (Cliff Robertson, who had recently played President Kennedy as a young man in *P. T. 109*), largely based on Nixon. It is Vidal's cruel joke that Cantwell lives to regret a youthful indiscretion, but this is not a drama *à clef*: Vidal does little to illuminate the minds and mentalities of those who seek power, clearly because he thinks little of their minds and mentalities. He loves the in-fighting, the hypocrisy, the difference between the public and private face. His text is witty and the cast of best quality: Schaffner lets both speak for themselves.

He had made his film debut with **The Stripper** (1963), in which his fresh handling concealed the tired elements in the plot – from William Inge's play, 'A Loss of Roses', concerning a showgirl (Joanne Woodward) in the suburbs, kindly seducing her old friend's adolescent son (Richard Beymer). It was not a success, nor was **The War Lord** (1965), for all its superiority to others of the genre – which may be left undefined, since there have been few enough movies set in the Dark Ages. The first and most striking quality is its understanding that man then lived by a different set of values – and the elemental tone of the piece is far closer to the sagas of the time than had been done before or

Franklin J. Schaffner's early films were modest in scale and completely realised, which led to offers to make immodest projects such as *Patton*, with George C. Scott. It was a considerable achievement, being both an excellent biographical study and a good war film, unlike many others offering some indication of how wars are planned from the battlefront.

since. In the title role, Charlton Heston plays a man of conscience, which is not an anachronism, since he alone is, and that provides the pivot of the plot. John Collier and Millard Kaufman wrote it, from a play by Leslie Stevens, and though there may be minor reservations these would not include the film's appearance – a watery, wintry world of reed and hedgerow, wattle and thatch buildings. Moving completely in the opposite direction, into the future, Heston and Schaffner made **Planet of the Apes** (1968), about some astronauts who journey not in space but time; it finishes, predictably, with the discovery of the Statue of Liberty half-buried in sand and Heston shrieking, with all the artificial anguish at his command, 'Maniacs!' – an antiwar message to remind us of the one at the end of *The Bridge on the River Kwai*, also the brainchild of Pierre Boulle. The make-up and other special effects are of outstanding quality, and there are enough good, horrific, moments to show why this spawned a number of sequels and a T.V. series.

Schaffner had a second success with

Patton (1970), controlling a large cast, a vast number of North African and European locations, and the complex character of the general himself – though written with little complexity, and requiring all George C. Scott's considerable skill to supply it. That they took a less than favourable view of its hero than is normal in such pictures undoubtedly helped the film to win a fistful of Oscars. And that brought the invitation to direct Sam Spiegel's production of **Nicholas and Alexandra** (1971), which is much more entertaining, but exactly the sort of historical epic seemingly rendered redundant by films like *Patton*. It has, moreover, a pallid, dead feel, and James Goldman's script is no more than a bland reduction of Robert K. Massie's moving biography. As the Tsar and Tsarina, Michael Jayston and Janet Suzman are dignified, humourless and somewhat unreal – which is as it should be; but if they never engage our sympathies, there are small insights, as in *Patton*, as to their inner lives. The parts of the film which do not involve the Romanovs are less satisfactory. Michael Bryant is a correct Lenin, and Brian Cox a decent Trotsky, but Tom Baker is insufficiently mesmeric as Rasputin. As Witte, Laurence Olivier alone is reason enough to see the film.

There is a superb performance by Dustin Hoffman as a myopic prisoner in **Papillon** (1973) as well as a good one by Steve McQueen in the title role, that of the Frenchman who escaped from Devil's Island and lived to tell the tale. Robert Dorfmann, another Frenchman, produced, but there was American interest because Henri Charrière's pseudo-autobiographical account had been a world bestseller. Some doubts were cast on its accuracy, which Schaffner acknowledges by using slow motion photography for one of the less credible incidents in Papillon's flight. He treats that as material for a superior adventure tale, and early strives for more authenticity – heat, sweat, proximity, deprivation, monotony – than the prison melodramas of forty years earlier.

Unjustly, the picture was not regarded as a major film by a major director, perhaps because it was designed to meet, even more than most, a popular market. Schaffner's reputation declined with **Islands in the Stream** (1977), admittedly not an entirely compelling version of Hemingway, and more reasonably with **The Boys from Brazil** (1978), based on a novel by Ira Levin. As an Austrian-Jewish Nazi hunter, Olivier has to say 'Whoever would believe such a preposterous story?' and the answer is unfathomable. The British producer, Lew Grade, had spent a fortune on a film without one believable scene, about Nazi clones growing up all over the world. The many locations show that at least one aspect of Schaffner's talent remains unimpaired.

Among the older directors, Don, or Donald, Siegel came into his own, finally fulfilling the promise of *Riot in Cell Block 11* and *Invasion of the Body Snatchers*. **Madigan** (1968) and **Coogan's Bluff** (1968) showed him to have few superiors in handling action scenes and a liking for irreverence and idiosyncrasy; the violence in both showed his antecedents to be in the thrillers of the late Fifties rather than those being made when he started his career. Both Madigan and Coogan are cops, the one, Richard Widmark, weary and resentful, the other, Clint Eastwood, wide-eyed from Arizona, but equally determined to clean New York of one particular criminal. With Eastwood, Siegel made **Two Mules for Sister Sara** (1970), about a whore (Shirley MacLaine), posing as a nun, who helps an American mercenary employed by Juarist revolutionaries; and **The Beguiled** (1971), about a wounded Union soldier sheltered in a seminary for young ladies. The latter, fastidiously made, propounds a very different view of such establishments than the one customary to nineteenth-century tales, and after wondering whether the combination of incest, lesbianism and mutilation is meant to be in emulation of lesser Jacobean tragedy, you may decide it is merely meant to be commercial – which it proved not to be. However, both **Dirty Harry** (1971) and **Charley Varrick** (1973) are so accomplished as to make one regret that Siegel has since been unable to find the same form. Charley (Walter Matthau) is a small time crook who, after a routine bank robbery, finds he has stirred up a hornet's nest, reaching right up to the Mafia; Harry (Eastwood) is a San Francisco cop hunting not the gangsters of yore but one tatty little sadist of a villain. Siegel's dual use of the city, as a place of light and space and sea,

and of scrap-dumps, seedy bars and liquor stores, was to be influential, as was the character of Harry – ruthless and cynical, a bruised, foul-tongued martyr.

If, with this handful of films, Siegel renewed the thriller genre, the transformation of the Western was the work of Sam Peckinpah (b. 1925), whose long term as director and writer of T.V. Westerns prompted him to attempt something other than the laundered version of the Old West which they offered. In **Ride the High Country** (1962) he kept to tradition by having his heroes (Joel McCrea, Randolph Scott) be true to their code; but they are ageing, paunchy and given to fond recall of the old days. And Peckinpah's mining town was not the usual constructed set, but a collection of tents, its only permanent structures the saloon and the brothel. The obligatory drunken judge is the obligatory Edgar Buchanan, but the girls all look like whores, and their boss is a gross redhead with quivering breasts. On the strength of the film's critical success, Peckinpah persuaded Columbia to put up a large budget for **Major Dundee** (1965),

Before he took to producing, and sometimes directing, his own films, Clint Eastwood appeared in a number of thrillers directed by Don Siegel, a veteran whose work took on new impetus with some cops-and-robbers films in the late Sixties. This is Eastwood in perhaps the most celebrated, *Dirty Harry*. Harry was a cop, ruthless and cynical, a bruised saint, a foul-tongued martyr – and very influential on the films and television series which followed in the wake of his success.

with Charlton Heston in the title role, chasing a bunch of Apaches into Mexico. After many rows, Columbia cut twenty minutes from the release print, and Peckinpah repudiated this rather sententious message about man's responsibility. It seemed to contradict the impression that he is a born film-maker, and **The Wild Bunch** (1969) proved conclusively that he is not. The locations are superbly chosen and photographed with all the professionalism of Lucien Ballard, and the portrait of Mexican life at the turn of the century seems authentic; but it is a boring film. So is **The Ballad of Cable Hogue** (1970), the tale of a good-natured man (Jason Robards) who survives his own stupidity and the hazards of Western life. Clichés of the new Western are in abundance: the sentimental ballad on the soundtrack and much larkiness, often consisting of the hero running around in longjohns and being bathed by the heroine, usually a somewhat bedraggled whore. The film failed at the box office; and Peckinpah resorted to the excessive and gratuitous violence which had made *The Wild Bunch* so much discussed and seen; but **Straw Dogs** (1971), made in Cornwall, England, was discussed and hardly seen. **Junior Bonner** (1972) tries for significance, in its sour portrait of contemporary America, through a story of a rodeo performer (Steve McQueen) visiting his family. Once again, Ballard did the photography, and the documentary footage of rodeos is entertaining: the rest is not, and the film's loss ($2 million) was a contributory factor in A.B.C. Pictures' abandoning film production. **The Getaway** (1972), a heist/chase movie with McQueen and Ali MacGraw, is again proof of Peckinpah's skill, making us regret that he has had few good opportunities in recent years, but it still left the impression that it might have been even better if the manifold killings and explosions had not been shown in such graphic, over-emphatic detail.

The Professionals (1966) has a similar plot to *The Wild Bunch*, concerning the expedition of a gang of mercenaries, and it is easily the better of the two films, as sharply directed and written by Richard Brooks. It opened to enthusiastic notices, but took some time to build to popular success – whereas *The Hallelujah Trail*, also with Burt Lancaster and launched at

similar expense, never got moving. The public was letting the Western die, but the faults were *sui generis*. The reasons were historical: the cattle-driving and wagon-speeding spectacles had become too difficult to mount and too costly; pro-Indian sentiment forbade the old cowboys *vs.* Indians conflict and few pro-Indian films were successful. Thus pioneering stories were out of the question, and demure gingham-clad girls now held no appeal. Lone strangers still rode into town, but like as not they were as corrupt as their opponents: we were supposed to admire their charm and strategy as they tricked their way to victory.

Brooks's best film remains **Elmer Gantry** (1960), which he adapted from Sinclair Lewis's novel, an ironic view of the mid-Western taste for revivalism. It was written not long after Aimee Semple Macpherson had been discredited, and the film's dominant virtue lies in not revealing the real ambitions of Sister Sharon (Jean Simmons) and her campaign manager (Dean Jagger). Both roles are magnificently acted, and in the compulsive first half they seem to be ardent in their mission, but realists: that she recognises Gantry (Burt Lancaster) as a charlatan and becomes his mistress does not contradict either fact. Neither the reporter (Arthur Kennedy) nor the prostitute (Shirley Jones) who conspire to bring them down is convincing: as Brooks increasingly fails to understand the motives of his characters he seems not to care what he puts on the screen as long as it is flashy.

Few of his later films were successful, including *Bite the Bullet*, one of the very few Westerns made in the Seventies. **In Cold Blood** (1967) deserved better, but unfortunately it came out at the same time as *Bonnie and Clyde*, which provided a more exciting view of old crime. People who had read Truman Capote's 'non-fiction novel' did not care to relive its grizzly matters; Conrad Hall's photography portrays Kansas only on grey days – appropriately, since its inhabitants seem to be grey; the cast is blessedly free of familiar faces. Brooks works competently in reconstructing the murder of the Clutter family, but fails to convey either its full horror or any understanding of the mentality of their killers. In the end he attempts a grim indictment of capital punishment;

withal, there have been few films on crime so honestly done.

Days of Wine and Roses (1963), directed by Blake Edwards, has an honourable place among harrowing films, as it charts the progress of a nice young couple toward alcoholism. He (Jack Lemmon) is in advertising, where boozing is used 'to entertain' and to relieve tension; she (Lee Remick) starts drinking along with him to make his drunkenness more tolerable. He can draw back, but she cannot. Lemmon, a patently honest actor, offers that Jack-in-the-box executive we had never previously seen in films, and Miss Remick refuses to allow his superb performance to overwhelm her. J. P. Miller wrote the screenplay, from his own T.V. play, and the film is as well made as Edwards's *Breakfast at Tiffany's*, which we looked at earlier.

The point about directorial quality has to be made, for Edwards's skill deteriorates when he handles his own material. He had written several of the films which Richard Quine had made for Columbia, and he began writing his own screenplays, always in collaboration, with *The Pink Panther* in 1964. This was the first of a series of so-called comedies with Peter Sellers as a bumbling French detective. I have not seen all of them, but the second one, **A Shot in the Dark** (1964), must be one of the worst-made films in cinema history. Edwards has no sense of the rhythm needed for comedy; his camera 'style', whether for one of Sellers's pratfalls or for two people in conversation is simply just to photograph them, with only an occasional close-up or long-shot. **The Great Race** (1965) is an elephantine twin to *Those Magnificent Men in their Flying Machines*, and equally unfunny, despite the presence of Jack Lemmon and Peter Falk as cod villains. The film's two set pieces, a Sennett-like custard-pie battle and a parody of *The Prisoner of Zenda*, are tedious. Given the cost and the high salaries of the stars (the others were Tony Curtis and Natalie Wood), the film, even at inflated seat prices, failed to turn a profit.

With *Darling Lili* (q.v.) Edwards began a decade of failures and near-misses, the latter including **The Tamarind Seed** (1974), a pleasing, old-fashioned cold war thriller, moving between Barbados, Paris and London. He restored his rating within the industry with another Pink Panther

film and more especially '**10**' (1979), the adventures of a bumbling lecher. The role was meant for George Segal, understandably, since both it and the situations were borrowed from *Loving* (q.v.) and *A Touch of Class*: Segal, also understandably, turned it down and the role was played by Dudley Moore, a British 'comic' whose sole claim to that description is his diminutive size. Even with Segal, these aged wheezes would have been offensive, being dragged out in a way which would have bewildered any half-decent practitioner of Hollywood comedy in the Thirties. **S.O.B.** (1981) is a satire on the movie industry, about a film director (Richard Mulligan) who turns a flop film into a hit by restaging a musical number with the girls in garter-belts and his lady-like star (Julie Andrews) baring her breasts. The film has a mildly amusing party scene, a great many unfunny scatalogical jokes and a dire second half, ending with a drawn-out funeral sequence. Since Miss Andrews is Edwards's lady-like wife – if far more talented than made to seem here – we did not need to be told that the film is partly autobiographical.

One of the flops it obliquely refers to is **Darling Lili** (1970), a costly musical

Blake Edwards started in films as a writer at Columbia, specialising in comedy, and as a director he is most renowned for some light-hearted entertainments, many of them lacking in both originality and wit. His few serious films have been much better, and especially *Days of Wine and Roses*, splendidly acted by Lee Remick and Jack Lemmon as a couple whose marriage is wrecked by too much booze.

whose failure was one reason why the industry looked askance at the genre. It has the enchanting idea of making Miss Andrews into a Mata Hari-type lady of World War I: but she and Henry Mancini's score are its sole virtues. As much may be said of **Victor/Victoria** (1982), in which Miss Andrews is an out-of-work British singer who becomes the toast of the Paris of the Thirties impersonating a female impersonator. Her mentor is a homosexual cabaret performer (Robert Preston), and there are homosexual complications when a gangster-type (James Garner) from Chicago falls in love with Andrews, believing her to be a boy. That aspect of the tale is only touched upon in Reinhold Schunzel's original, *Viktor und Viktoria*, made fifty years earlier, but much more subtly. Even when Edwards copies Schunzel, as in the night-club fight, and the final 'drag' number, he can only do so lumberingly. It is not to be expected that Edwards can reproduce the sheer vitality of Schunzel's film any more than we expect the finesse of a Lubitsch amidst the complications of the hotel bedrooms. *Darling Lili* and *Victor/ Victoria* run to two-and-a-quarter hours and I simply do not understand why Edwards, like many of today's directors, fails to understand the chief virtues of the films he is attempting to emulate – economy, pacing, brevity. *Victor/Victoria* was ecstatically received by most American critics, but was given short shrift by their British colleagues.

Miss Andrews had had a comic high spot earlier in her career, in **The Americanization of Emily** (1964), directed by Arthur Hiller (b. 1923), whose own favourite film it is. She plays a crisp English girl, a war widow, with advanced views about comforting military personnel, one of whom is Charlie (James Garner), a 'dog-robber', i.e. a rating who ensures that high-ranking officers lack for nothing in the way of comfort, be it edible, alcoholic or female. He is also a confirmed death-dodger, or coward. As written by Paddy Chayevsky from the novel by William Bradford Huie, the film makes its points far better than a number of more ambitious anti-war efforts. Hiller, from T.V., had already made a number of poor films, and there were more before **The Tiger Makes Out** (1967), Murray Schisgal's adaptation of his own play. A meek

postman (Eli Wallach) is so frustrated by his attempts at self-education and society's slights that, in revenge, he plans a kidnapping – taking, by mistake, a suburban housewife (Anne Jackson) equally discontented with her lot. This was one of the bright New York comedies of the time, more frenetic than most, but deeply alive to all sorts of human behaviour – particularly when that is conditioned by the rat race. **Popi** (1969) is about a New York Puerto Rican widower (Alan Arkin) so poor that he dreams up a scheme to get his two kids adopted as Cuban refugees. The first half is bitter, and the second bittersweet, but the whole film has Arkin extracting every ounce of penny-pinching pathos from the role.

Paddy Chayevsky turned to Hiller for his first original screenplay for more than a decade, **The Hospital** (1971) – an institution he portrays as a madhouse of weariness, fright, confusion and tension. Since the hospital itself is condemned, we may be certain of the allegory, but unlike the later *Network*, Chayevsky's observation is as keen as ever and he is marvellously served by George C. Scott as a doctor in trouble – impotent, ageing, with his wife just departed and his son 'building bombs in basements in the cause of universal brotherhood'. Hiller's tone is so much closer to *Marty* or *The Bachelor Party* than his other films, as if to prove Chayevsky's strength and his own weakness.

Hiller's box-office success with a slushy romantic drama, *Love Story*, was one reason why he was asked to direct the provocatively-titled **Making Love** (1982), regarded by the industry as a trailblazer because of its subject-matter. It was one of the many films on divorce made after the success of *Kramer vs. Kramer* (q.v.), but in this case the husband (Michael Ontkean), a doctor, leaves his wife (Kate Jackson) for another man (Harry Hamlin), a writer. Since both men are sort-of gay versions of the upright blacks Sidney Poitier used to play, the tale is little more than soap opera; but Barry Sandler's screenplay is convincing in the crucial scenes, as when the writer admits his homosexuality (a word, incidentally, never mentioned) in order to make the doctor confess that he is tempted by him. Wisely, the doctor is shown to have 'predilections' despite an apparently happy marriage –

which has no chance of surviving once they are realised.

Hiller's other films include two based on plays by Neil Simon. Filming this popular and prolific playwright is a major preoccupation for the industry – and not without reason he can be a box-office name in his own right. Admittedly, there are few adroit practitioners today of screen comedy, so that audiences gave a warm welcome to **Barefoot in the Park** (1967) and **The Odd Couple** (1968), both directed by Gene Saks from Simon's Broadway originals. They restored intimacy to Hollywood comedy, while bringing to it a new concept – that New York Jewish humour was best left to New York Jewish performers, even if gentile stars were sometimes necessary. *Barefoot* is an untidy piece about a honeymoon couple, at its best when imitative of Peter Arno, as when the bride (Jane Fonda) tries to embarrass her stuffy husband (Robert Redford) in the elevator of the Plaza Hotel, 'Mr Adams, you ever been with a fifteen-year-old girl before?' The 'odd couple' are a fastidious man (Jack Lemmon), rebounding from a broken marriage, and the slob (Walter Matthau) who gives him a home. It has some of Simon's best one-liners – 'He has 92 credit cards in his pocket. The moment he disappears America lights up' – and it teams the two most skilful light comedians in movies, even if, on this occasion, Lemmon has to work hard to make his role sympathetic. Saks's directorial method consists of little more than training his camera on the players.

As an actor, he played a supporting role in **The Prisoner of Second Avenue** (1974), the only film of Simon's work directed by one of the old guard, Melvin Frank. It is also one of Simon's failures, due perhaps to the subject, that of a man (Lemmon) who loses his job. At the end his wife (Anne Bancroft) has also lost her temporary employment, but they vow, as New Yorkers, that they will not let New York get them down. The humour is as desperate as the leading character, and its blend of the flip and the fatalistic – at the heart of all Jewish humour – goes for little in Frank's impersonal style.

Elaine May (b. 1930), the former cabaret artist, directed the best Simon film, **The Heartbreak Kid** (1972), though in this case his screenplay was based on a novel by Bruce Jay Friedman. It also poses a delicate situation, that of a honeymooner (Charles Grodin) who ditches his gauche bride (Jeannie Berlin, Miss May's daughter) for a beautiful Wasp (Cybill Shepherd). The result is iron hard, risking its laughs on our response to the heartlessness and superficiality of modern American speech. The traditional cruelty of American society goes back at least to Edith Wharton; it was treated lightheartedly in the screwball comedies of the Thirties, only to return to films in a more realistic manner with George Axelrod and Milos Forman – at least in his American film, *Taking Off* (q.v.). Miss May and Mike Nichols, in their dialogues for stage and disc, had brilliantly used the comedy of cruelty, but little of it had found its way into *The Graduate* (q.v.), with which Nichols made his reputation as a film director. On the other hand, there is a great deal of it in the first film Miss May directed, also about the country-club set, **A New Leaf** (1971), which she wrote from a story by Jack Ritchie. The Nichols-May sketches influenced the dialogue, as in the lawyer's gobbledygook about capital and income, before he gives up with: 'You have no money. I wish there was some other way of saying it.' The man who has no money is Henry Graham (Matthau), last of the New York playboys: 'All I am or was is rich,' he says, 'and that's all I ever wanted to be' – and since the only way to continue to be so is to make a wealthy match, he finds a painfully gauche spinster (May) – who happens to be the only character in the tale who is not mercenary.

Mike Nichols (b. 1931), after his cabaret work with Miss May, became one of Broadway's most successful directors, especially with Simon's plays. He made his film debut as director with **Who's Afraid of Virginia Woolf?** (1966), from Edward Albee's drama about the less endearing aspects of faculty life – drunken professors and their wives, whose screaming and shouting on this occasion permitted a number of four-letter words not heard before from the screen; and they sounded choice in the mouths of this particular husband and wife team, Richard Burton and Elizabeth Taylor. **The Graduate** (1967) also defied taboos as written by Calder Willingham and Buck Henry from a novel by Charles Webb, in showing the brazen seduction of a minor (Dustin Hoffman) by an older woman (Anne Bancroft), a family friend and mother of one of his comrades. She is a self-confessed alcoholic and he is an Alice in a wonderland of the 'silent majority', a generation who had had it and lost it in a ceaseless ritual of martinis and barbecues. The film's second half betrays the sharp observation of the first, as the boy moons around the woman's daughter and then abducts her as an act of revenge. This curious morality is in keeping with the film's bitter attitude to the older generation and its portrait of the young as honest, deceived and manipulated. If that was intended as a blatant bid for the now mainly youthful cinema audiences, it was successful, for it became the third most profitable American film yet made, a position it held until overtaken by *Love Story* three years later. Simon and Garfunkel's pleasing soundtrack songs condemned us for some years to films with cars rolling along to similar melodies.

Nichols's reputation then made him claimant to a property eyed warily by Hollywood, **Catch-22** (1970), Joseph Heller's massive debunking of the military – which remained bursting out of Buck Henry's sloppily-packed screenplay. Nichols unfortunately made matters worse by trying to instil it with meaning, which was precisely what audiences did not want – especially after the irreverence of $M\star A\star S\star H$ (q.v.) a few months earlier. However, a much better cast realised a number of Heller's superior grotesques, headed by Alan Arkin as the perplexed Yossarian, with Jon Voight as the conniving Milo Minderbinder, Anthony Perkins as the ineffectual padre, Bob Newhart as Major Major, Richard Benjamin as the smooth Major Danby and Buck Henry himself as the acolyte Korn. Another contemporary satirist, the cartoonist Jules Feiffer, wrote **Carnal Knowledge** (1971), which strove for nothing less than a summary of the American male's sex-life, from college stimulation to middle-aged doubts about potency. If there was any point or wit, it escaped Nichols, who failed more interestingly with **The Fortune** (1975), written by Carole Eastman, who as Adrien Joyce wrote the brilliant *Five Easy Pieces* (q.v.). It is a comedy of cruelty in the manner of *A New Leaf*, with an heiress (Stockard Channing) pursued

by two small-time con-men (Jack Nicholson, Warren Beatty): but it is set in the Twenties, and always hopes to evoke the comedies of Hollywood's past. At one point facsimiles of Laurel and Hardy may be discerned in their jalopy, and a couple of their gags are borrowed; but despite the screaming and slapstick the film does not succeed because Nichols has not the courage to be vulgar. Its failure is sad, since Miss Channing is virtually the only actress today with the qualities of the great comediennes of the past.

Neither Nichols nor May* has continued to work regularly in films; indeed the unexpected flowering of American comedy at the beginning of the Seventies soon died out. Other perpetrators proved to have little staying power, including Irvin Kershner (b. 1923), to whom we owe just two good films, **A Fine Madness** (1966) and **Loving** (1970), both concerning the artist as hero – and one to whom the fairer sex should not be denied. The former, written by Elliott Baker from his own novel, involves an irresponsible poet (Sean Connery), whose wife (Joanne Woodward), denied her alimony, puts him in the hands of a psychiatrist; the second, produced and written by Don Devlin from a novel by J. M. Ryan, is about a responsible commercial artist (George Segal), whose wife (Eva Marie Saint) is about to lose him to his mistress. Both films are devoted to New York; but that is not the metropolis of the films of the past, for these heroes and heroines are caught in its toils and go down fighting. The city in *A Fine Madness* is one of slum apartments and penthouses and in *Loving* it is seen from suburbia – the world of Updike and de Vries, novelists virtually ignored by the cinema. Kershner's understated reaction, catching the odd hint of absurdity, is absolutely correct.

Cy Howard (b. 1915), a former screenwriter, directed two films, of which **Lovers and Other Strangers** (1970) has merit, as written by Renée Taylor and Joseph Bologna from their play, with the aid of David Zelag Goodman. It is a pungent and funny account of a wedding, which must be one of the last times Jewish jokes were put into the mouths of Italians and/or Roman Catholics.

*In 1973 she made a film for Paramount, the subject of litigation between her and the company two years later: to date it has not been publicly shown.

A Jewish wedding is the highlight of **Goodbye, Columbus** (1969), the one good film made by Larry Peerce after *One Potato Two Potato* – and its strength is in Philip Roth's witty observation of the American Jewish milieu, as faithfully transcribed by Arnold Schulman. Undoubtedly the success of *The Graduate* caused Roth's book to be brought to the screen, since, unlike *The Pawnbroker* and *No Way to Treat a Lady* (q.v.), all the characters are Jewish, and the orientation of Howard's film indicates that the industry was not quite prepared for this. Simultaneously, each of the young Jewish heroes of *The Graduate*, *Goodbye, Columbus* and *The Heartbreak Kid* is entering an alien world, be it one of wealth, Wasps, or grown-ups, and I suspect their approach, through emotion or conviction, is the way many industry people like to refer to their past. Like Hoffman in *The Graduate*, Neil (Richard Benjamin) in *Goodbye, Columbus* observes the people with money, and is not sure that he likes them. He lives in Newark, works in a library, and is white and pasty; she (Ali MacGraw) is a Jewish princess, tanned and beautiful. His chutzpah gets him invited to stay, but the wedding – her brother's – proves her relatives no more refined than his. The implicit questioning of society's values, inherent in all the best of these films, is here; and the audiences who made this one so popular were undoubtedly refreshed by some more broken taboos – the girl hiding her diaphragm, the athlete brother washing his jockstrap, and the heroine's answer as to her summer activity, 'Growing a penis.'

Social virtues are hardly to be expected in **No Way to Treat a Lady** (1968), the best film directed by Jack Smight, otherwise well known for a slick private-eye thriller with Paul Newman, *Harper*. This one is a comedy-thriller, written by John Gay from a novel by William Goldman, and moving expertly between the antics of a camp mass-murderer (Rod Steiger) with a penchant for disguises, and the love affair of a Jewish detective (George Segal) and his gentile girl (Lee Remick). Although mother – 'I don't want to hear any more. Already I shan't sleep tonight' – is broadly acted by Eileen Heckart, she underplays compared with Ruth Gordon in **Where's Poppa?** (1970), whose whims ruin Segal's attempts at mutual seduction with his

nurse (Trish van Devere). Mother is such a menace that it is hard to understand why Segal should be catatonic at the prospect of putting her into a home, but brother Sidney (Ron Leibman) also spells trouble, running out to Central Park to be mugged and attempting rape on what turns out to be a cop in drag. Robert Kane wrote it, from his own novel, and Carl Reiner directed – poorly, clear evidence why he is best known as writer and performer. Reiner does a much smoother directorial job on **The One and Only** (1978), one of several comedies of this period, possibly autobiographical, about young Jewish guys on the make in the Fifties. This one (Henry Winkler) gives new meaning to the words 'brash' and 'extrovert', as he bounds from college to take Broadway by storm – but ends as a campy television wrestler. Neither Winkler nor Kim Darby, as his girlfriend, is quite good enough for the material, which has some marvellous satiric ideas and a few mild laughs as written by Steve Gordon, who as writer and director later had a success with *Arthur*.

Herbert Ross (b. 1927) has been an exponent of this aspect of New York, but his best and first film is very different, **Goodbye, Mr Chips** (1969). He came to it, a former choreographer, after working on the musical numbers in *Funny Lady*; like Sam Wood, director of the 1939 version, he is an American, and presumably immune from the pros and cons which surround the subject of public schools in Britain. The idea of a musical version of this particular tale was not appealing, and has been only partially solved; most of the songs are poor and they are either broken up, or used only on the soundtrack. The story itself does not especially matter: what does matter are the characters of Chips and the woman he marries, played by Peter O'Toole and Petula Clark, neither of whom ever did anything better. He is gawky, shy and stiff – and very touching, without moving into the areas of doddering lovability explored by Mr Donat. She – predictably a musical comedy star – is modest and warm and independent. The courtship between this awkward teacher and an extrovert soubrette is exquisitely rendered, against a background of Pompeii, Paestum and Naples, and beautifully written, by Terence Rattigan – who used

In Hollywood the Director is King

the occasion to add to his view of school-mastering in 'The Browning Version'. The film is one of the most unexpected of successes, but many critics, seeing only what they expected to see, trounced it: an honourable exception was John Simon, who admitted that it moved him to tears.

The coming together of two unlikely, lonely people occupied Ross again in both **The Owl and the Pussycat** (1970) and **T. R. Baskin** (1971). The couple in *Baskin* are Peter Boyle and Candice Bergen, who as the lady of the title, is possibly a high-class callgirl; in *Owl* Barbra Streisand is a low-class hooker, and George Segal is the shy writer drawn to her. The film was written by Buck Henry from Bill Man-hoff's two-handed play, its black girl changed to a Jewish one, since Ray Stark produced (both play and film), and Streisand was under contract to him. 'Hey, you straight?' she yells at Segal, examining his bedroom, and if you do not think that is funny, you should hear her say it. 'Felix? Your name Felix? – That's a sort of oogh-kie name.' Ross directed this actress again in a sequel to *Funny Girl* called **Funny Lady** (1975), and because Streisand had become, if anything, even less vulnerable with the years, it was a mistake to try and

turn the heroine, Fanny Brice, into a tragic figure. In the latter half, until that happens, the film has a splendid performance by James Caan as Fanny's second husband, the Jewish showman Billy Rose, and some funny parodies of old Follies numbers choreographed by Herbert Ross and his wife, Norah Kaye, a former ballet dancer.

Ross continued to film Broadway comedy, including **The Sunshine Boys** (1975), by Neil Simon. This aims to be the comedy of insult, and certainly the comedy of little else, as it details the attempts to reunite a vaudeville team renowned for their mutual loathing. Walter Matthau, expert in the sour, laser-beam wise-crack, is matched with George Burns, whose superb delivery reminds us of his long experience as a comic. He is the more likeable of the two, but in this context that means little. **The Goodbye Girl** (1977) has an original screenplay by Simon, and Ross's firm handling is directed towards achieving the aura of vintage romantic comedies. Unquestionably, our sympathies are being manipulated, yet not insultingly so, except in a roof dinner-party, with coloured lights: and at that point I was glad to be reminded of *Christmas in July* rather than the cliché-riddled movies which so often provide points of reference. The early part of the film, the bickering between this young mother (Marcia Mason) and her unwilling lodger (Richard Dreyfuss), resembles *The Owl and the Pussycat*: but their *détente* and *entente* make this the movies' most charming love story since *Goodbye, Mr Chips*. Dreyfuss won a Best Actor Oscar, and if the film was, in John Coleman's phrase, 'weirdly overnominated' it was in every other category beaten by *Annie Hall* (q.v.), which merely aspires to be what this film is – much funnier, more touching and more professionally made.

The reviewer in *Variety* observed that **The Seven-Per-Cent Solution** (1976) was evidence that Ross had become one of the best directors working in films; but his talent was wasted on this Sherlock Holmes pastiche written by Nicholas Meyer. It is not to be compared to Billy Wilder's similar piece, while its borrowings – from James Bond, the Marx Brothers and *The Man with the Golden Arm* – were only too typical of the movies of this time. **The Turning Point** (1977) makes deliberate reference to *Old Acquaintance*, for in his screenplay Arthur Laurents has a character also called Deedee. Both films concern the friendship of two women whose lives have diverged, one of whom becomes an influence on the other's grown-up daughter. Here, Shirley MacLaine has settled into domesticity while Anne Bancroft has become a prima ballerina. As the first film about ballet since *The Red Shoes*, it could have used more of Ross's and Miss Kaye's experience of such matters as ego, temperament, ambition and others endemic to this milieu. Mikhail Baryshnikov is found to be bedding the corps de ballet one by one, but is also dancing at gratifying length.

Much was said about the film returning women's roles to the forefront; what its success more positively did was enable Ross to make **Nijinsky** (1980). Over the years the many attempts to film this subject had foundered during the lifetime of Romola Nijinsky, who threatened legal action at any suggestion of the relationship between her husband and Diaghilev. In the event Ross and his writer, Hugh Wheeler, approach it with timidity and so cannot achieve their aim – a study of the reasons for Nijinsky's descent into madness. But if

they omit the guilt he felt, they do show that the combined emotional and professional relationship was ruinous, since their ambitions made them play dangerous games with each other. As Diaghilev, Alan Bates offers little more than an inappropriate world-weariness, George de la Pena is a lacklustre Nijinsky and Leslie Brown gets no help in explaining the enigma of Romola, depicted here as an innocent society nobody. The famous sets and costumes have been reproduced with love, but while Ross correctly attempts to avoid a ballet version of *The Great Caruso* there seems little point in photographing de la Pena from only the waist upwards or in slow motion.

Ross's delight in musicals, an endangered species, tempted him into making **Pennies from Heaven** (1981), based on a B.B.C. series which had been a success in some quarters. Other people, myself included, thought it, without hyperbole, the worst programme to be seen on television. Its writer, Dennis Potter, in an attempt to tell the truth about the Thirties, in contrast to the myth, apparently found it represented in the songs, and had the cast mime them as recorded then: he failed to see, or at least to convey, the reasons for the optimism, while his plot was an irrelevant fable about a travelling salesman who leaves his wife for a nice young teacher who becomes a whore. Ross handles the numbers in the film with the old Hollywood pizzazz, and the American cast seems at ease miming to the sweet harmony singers (the British artists on the soundtrack were working in the American idiom). Steve Martin, imitating the more spineless leading men of the period, is likeable and more relaxed than Bob Hoskins was in the original; and in his cameo as an oily wolf, Christopher Walken does a striptease – to Cole Porter's 'Let's Misbehave' – borrowed from the stage musical, 'Chicago'. Potter's screenplay, with the action transferred to the mid-West, is so witless and humourless that the film's rapid failure was not surprising.

Another former dancer and choreographer, Bob Fosse (b. 1925), made his debut as a screen director with **Sweet Charity** (1969), after a number of Broadway successes. This had been a Broadway musical, based on *Notti di Cabiria*, but despite rave notices cinema audiences were

In Hollywood the Director is King

Liza Minnelli in *Cabaret*, virtually the only hugely popular film musical since *The Sound of Music* – and the reasons must include the star, the rousing score and, undoubtedly, fascination with the film's milieu – the louche nightclubs of Berlin at the time the Nazis took over the city. Bob Fosse's vigorous handling was also a contributory factor, reminding us that he had done something similar with *Sweet Charity*, though that failed precisely because it lacked the qualities in the latter half to send the audience out cheerful.

not prepared to buy the tale a third time around. Universal, which produced, blamed the star, Shirley MacLaine, and prepared a new advertising campaign omitting her name and bearing the slogan, 'The musical with the sound of Today' – but since the sole justification of that was the worst song in the score, sung by Sammy Davis Jr, it is hardly surprising that that made no difference. Audiences may have been tired of reverently treated Broadway musicals, and Fosse's direction was brilliant in the wrong way; numbers that needed the apparent spontaneity of Gene Kelly had been chopped up with jump-cuts, stop-cuts, and Miss MacLaine posed in another part of the set; the show-stopper, 'Hey, Big Spender', like most stage numbers directed at the audience, looks fossilised on the screen. And Miss MacLaine, an agreeable talent, has shoulders too frail to carry so long a film: she is *not* Judy Garland, whose *Star is Born* had much more going for it, including a degree of optimism, whereas the last thirty minutes of this piece are downhill all the way.

On the stage, **Cabaret** (1972) was, at least in the London production, one of the great musicals; and as Sally Bowles, Judi Dench, not a great singer, came as close to breaking the collective heart of an audience as Garland ever did: replacing her in the film with Liza Minnelli, with her little mouse face, was not a bad idea, and she won an Oscar. Nor was it a bad idea to restore Herr Issyvoo (Michael York) to bisexuality; but the rest is mild, beginning with the Emcee of Joel Grey repeating his Broadway role, and nowhere near as evil or as suggestive of unspecified vices as Barry Dennen in the London production. Jay Presson Allen's infantile screenplay omits characters and complexity from the original, and a brilliant score has been abbreviated. Miss Minnelli simply has not – or had not – the temperament for the title number, and the film concludes with that, rather than the original implication of a whole city somnambulantly dancing and making love as the Nazis prepare to turn the world upside down. Fosse's direction is enlivening and energetic, and is again in **All That Jazz** (1979), a semi-musical based on his own experience as a director of Broadway shows who almost died from a heart attack. If Roy Scheider in the film is giving an accurate portrait, he is as unpleasant as he is vain: this is the greatest ego trip in the history of movies, but entertaining till towards the end, when a musical number combining the fantasies of Busby Berkeley and Fellini is staged during open-heart surgery.

Harold Prince, who had directed *Cabaret* on the stage, has had no luck with either of the films he directed. **Something for Everyone** (1970) is a black comedy set in Bavaria in pre-Nazi days, with virtually the same plot as *Teorema* but with elements of *Kind Hearts and Coronets*. **A Little Night Music** (1977) is much better and made with love, for Prince had also directed this musical version of *Smiles of a Summer Night* on Broadway and in London. His leading ladies were respectively Glynis Johns and Jean Simmons and having seen them both it is clear that the piece stands or falls by the interpretation of their role. Despite Stephen Sondheim's charming pastiche-Ravel score, the show was a dull thing in New York; in London with the enchanting Jean Simmons it sparkled. The film has Elizabeth Taylor, who is dumpy, over made-up and lacking presence. Hermione Gingold, Len Cariou (both from the Broadway show) and Diana Rigg perform stylishly, and the film is prettily set in rococo drawing rooms and on dappled lawns. But only 'A Weekend in the Country' has been staged with style; and the film's losses were a contributing factor to its Austrian production company going out of business.

George Roy Hill (b. 1922) came from Broadway, after much success in television. After three films he had a fine chance when Fred Zinnemann resigned from **Hawaii** (1966), a high budgeted film based on a small portion of James A. Michener's huge novel encompassing one thousand years of Hawaiian history. The film restricts itself to the nineteenth century, and starts with an interesting premise, the destruction of a pagan civilisation by the crusading forces of Christianity: the three hour running time crushes the audience, not to mention fire, typhoon, and numerous births and deaths. The screenplay by Dalton Trumbo and Daniel Taradash is better than their combined screen credits would suggest, if only because it has humour – a quality also to be found in the performance of Julie Andrews, as the wife of the parson (Max von Sydow), a man who, in the tradition of Victorian literature, regards himself as God's instrument on earth.

For Hill, Miss Andrews is **Thoroughly Modern Millie** (1967), to remind us that she made her American reputation in 'The Boy Friend', and where that was an affectionate spoof of the stage musicals of the Twenties, Richard Morris's screenplay does the same for the films of the era – though, of course, with songs, a number of which are charmingly staged. Few musicals of this era had so likeable a cast – apart from Miss Andrews, at her mock-innocent best, Beatrice Lillie, Carol Channing, Mary Tyler Moore, and, in emulation of Charles 'Buddy' Rogers or William Haines, James Fox and John Gavin: justly, the film was Universal's biggest moneymaker to that time. It is also, like most of the films produced by Ross Hunter, often sloppy and occasionally vulgar. Hill said that he began on the wrong foot by barring Hunter from the set, 'but he got his own back by taking me off the picture as soon as I had finished shooting. Then he cut the film himself. Twenty minutes that I had discarded were put back in – just to make it up to roadshow length. It was like putting a soufflé back into the oven for another hour. The film became tacky and cute.'

Hill said of **Butch Cassidy and the Sundance Kid** (1969) 'The critics roasted the film. If it had been a play, we'd have closed in one night. Thank God for word of mouth and my scriptwriter [William Goldman] – he said "I gave you *Shane* and you gave me *Gunga Din*." What we really got was the Laurel and Hardy of Deadwood Gulch.' What they really got was a bloodless *Wild Bunch* crossed with *Jules et Jim*, prettily photographed by Conrad Hall and played in the same manner by Paul Newman and Robert Redford. They also appeared for Hill – to equal public approval, and in this case Oscars for Best Direction and Best Picture – in **The Sting** (1973), an excessively long joke, set in the Twenties, with red herrings inside red herrings.

In his sharpest film yet, **Slap Shot** (1977), Hill examined the world of professional ice-hockey players, aided by Nancy Dowd, whose screenplay was based on observation of her brother-in-law, who was involved in that world. She is not flattering: ice-hockey players are, apparently, simple-minded hulks, given to drinking and whoring and open to manipulation. They are meant to be a reflection of a society that is all too violent – a matter grossly overstated, since in the film the games are virtually homicidal: but the lady is trying to make a number of points, including, in her treatment of the team's owner, that capitalism can play havoc with our lives. Paul Newman, loud-mouthed and easygoing, gives one of his best performances as the coach; and Hill might only be faulted, as ever, for running on too long.

Norman Jewison (b. 1926) had experience in Canadian and British T.V. before joining C.B.S., from whence he moved to Universal, to make a few forgettable comedies for Ross Hunter; he showed himself of better mettle when asked to replace Peckinpah on **The Cincinnati Kid** (1965), set in New Orleans in the Thirties, concentrating on big-time poker players, as written by Ring Lardner Jr and Terry Southern, and with a cast equally rare, including Joan Blondell, Rip Torn, Tuesday Weld, Cab Calloway, Jack Weston, and, in the leads as rival gamblers, Edward G. Robinson and Steve McQueen. 'You're good, kid' says Robinson, 'but as long as I'm around you're second best.' **The Russians Are Coming, the Russians Are Coming** (1966) features a Soviet submarine that runs aground just off the coast of Maine, to subsequent local hysteria – a subject nearly akin to Ealing comedy, but William Rose, who knew much about that, is unfortunately nearer his later form on *It's a Mad, Mad, Mad, Mad World*. The film is mainly memorable for the performance of Alan Arkin as an enterprising Russian lieutenant.

Jewison managed a more subtle portrait of a rural community in **In the Heat of the Night** (1967) – a small Mississippi town where a murder has taken place. Sterling Silliphant wrote it, from a novel by John Ball, and it added new resonances to an overworked movie subject, tensions in a small Southern town – in this case exemplified by a bigoted white cop (Rod Steiger) and his black surrogate chief (Sidney Poitier). The latter is not merely a stranger passing through, but a homicide expert from the North, to whom the white man must unwillingly defer: it is the white man who is the shell, as he confesses, while the black man has it all together. This situation, and the accompanying conflict,

evoked a warm response from audiences, as did **The Thomas Crown Affair** (1968). Jewison used an appropriately jazzy style for this tale of a complicated heist with two comely and glamorous stars, McQueen and Faye Dunaway. A soundtrack song, · 'The Windmills of Your Mind', helped Jewison to his third consecutive success.

He has been less fortunate in his subsequent films, but was responsible for introducing a more reliable talent, Hal Ashby (b. 1936), with **The Landlord** (1970). He was scheduled to direct it himself but persuaded his backers, the Mirisch brothers, to reassign the project to Ashby, his associate producer and editor. Beau Bridges plays a wealthy innocent who decides to alleviate his idleness by going into real estate, in the black ghetto of Brooklyn, where his efforts to become involved with the inhabitants lead to dislocation and misery. As a portrait of the environment, the film is far less modern than, say, *Razzia in St Pauli*. As an attack on the mendacity of the American bourgeoisie, exemplified by the hero's family, Ashby employs the style of *Petulia* and Coppola's *You're a Big Boy Now*, and in the process almost wrecks the film. Another fey comedy, **Harold and Maude** (1971), has the greatest disparity in its stars' ages since Margaret O'Brien and Wallace Beery, except that this time they are in love. The boy (Bud Cort) has a lop-sided look and the mooning expression of Harry Langdon; the woman (Ruth Gordon) is witch-like, and in fact their romance is merely a climax to the events that have gone before, mainly about young Harold's attempts at suicide, since he is in love with easeful death. His mother – marvellously played by Vivian Pickles – is dismissive, and at such moments this becomes a marvellous *comédie noire*; however, a theme song ('If you want to sing out, sing out/If you want to be free, be free . . .') reveals that the piece is pandering to the half-baked philosophies of the time – and that was also the message of *Le Roi de Coeur*, another cult film. The writer was Colin Higgins, who later became a director.

The Last Detail (1974) was written by Robert Towne from a novel by Darryl Ponicsan about two petty officers escorting a simpleton of a sailor (Randy Quaid) from Norfolk, Virginia, to the brig at

Portsmouth, New Hampshire, and what they teach him on the way. It is about their isolation and guarded friendships – of the remoteness of civilian life, of forbearance towards another's peccadilloes (it would have been different had the sailor stolen from a colleague), of shared assumptions about women and language and beer. 'Best goddam drink in the world' says 'Bad-Ass', and as spoken by Jack Nicholson the remark is sheer poetry. There is not a facet of this character, from his basic insecurity to apparent *laissez-faire* that Nicholson has not understood, in a performance that is the crown of America's most honest study of service life. In **Shampoo** (1975) Towne and Ashby kick away the props that support Californian – if not American – society: the *dolce vita* of Los Angeles turns out to be a Vanity Fair where the puppets merely jig to a new tune – with no values and no concern, which is all that may be expected since the time is Election Night, 1968, and Nixon is mouthing platitudes on television. Its message aside, the film is rather dull, and surely mystifying to anyone not versed in the mores of California. The humour, mainly sexual, includes Julie Christie under the table at the election-party, at the fly of Warren Beatty, who elsewhere takes advantage of the fact that he is considered gay because he is a hairdresser by profession. **Coming Home** (1978) is equally frank, if not quite as explicit, its *raison d'être* the affair between an army wife (Jane Fonda) and a Vietnam veteran (Jon Voight), now a paraplegic. Waldo Salt and Robert C. Jones wrote the screenplay, from a story by Nancy Dowd, and though possibly all those responsible felt deeply about Vietnam, the film is no more than an updated and highly romantic variation on *The Men*.

Ashby's **Being There** (1979) was his most warmly welcomed film since *The Last Detail*, perhaps because there had been at this time a dearth of films with ideas. The central concept in this case was borrowed from Gogol – by Jerzy Kosinski, who wrote the script from his own novel. The question arises as to whether he can pull off the situations as well as does 'The Government Inspector': a reclusive, taciturn, stupid gardener (Peter Sellers) is sent out into the great world on the death of his employer and within hours is mingling with presidents and the like, all of whom

Jack Nicholson and Randy Quaid in *The Last Detail*, directed by Hal Ashby. It belongs to that rare group of films which looks below the surface to find the emptiness of modern life – having looked where it might be found instead of where some polemic film-maker would like it to be: and if these sailors' lives are empty, it is significant that the sea is never mentioned.

consider him an expert on economics, etc. But the film does not make us believe that he does, and Kosinski merely makes statements about American gullibility and the media instead of achieving satire.

Sydney Pollack (b. 1934) is, like Ashby, chiefly concerned with the problems of contemporary America, though he has made some films about its immediate past. He moved to films from television and made a promising debut with **The Slender Thread** (1965). More than thirteen years seem to separate it from *Coming Home*, and that is partly because it appears to belong to the modestly crusading films of the Fifties. Sterling Silliphant wrote the screenplay, which for much of the time is a duologue between a would-be suicide (Anne Bancroft) and the doctor (Sidney Poitier) in the 'Crisis Clinic', at the other end of the phone. **This Property Is Condemned** (1966) was produced by John Houseman for Seven Arts, Ray Stark and Paramount, to their eventual shame. Of the fourteen writers who are reported to have worked on the screenplay three are credited, including Fred Coe and Francis Ford Coppola, who later observed that he thought his script better than the one eventually used, 'but to take a really lovely one-act play and make it into a full-length film with movie-stars is a ridiculous idea in the first place.' The play was by Tennessee Williams, and it now provides only a framing device for some drama supposedly in the style of Williams, featuring Robert

Redford and an even more negative Natalie Wood. Neither seems to have been given help by Pollack, whose direction lurches all over the place.

It had improved considerably by the time he came to make **They Shoot Horses, Don't They?** (1969) and **Jeremiah Johnson** (1972). Both, nevertheless, are weak-kneed attempts to analyse the America of some years ago. The first, based on Horace McCoy's novel about a dance marathon during the Depression era, has a remarkable performance by Jane Fonda; the second is a tribute to the pioneer spirit written by an old Hollywood hand, Edward Anhalt, and a new one, John Milius. Its star again is Mr Redford, a buddy of Pollack's from his acting days, and it is the second of their several films together. Redford was teamed with Barbra Streisand in **The Way We Were** (1973), an exercise in more recent nostalgia, moving its stars from college in the Thirties to disillusion, fame, break-up and political activity in the Fifties. Arthur Laurents wrote it, with an eye more on star appeal than honest comment. **The Electric Horseman** (1979) starts well, with its portraits of an over-the-hill rodeo star (Redford) and Las Vegas. He sells himself to some button-down-mind sponsors, and few films have managed to express so pungently the ambivalence of the world of hype, but as he lights out after his horse – his last link with integrity – and a female reporter (Jane Fonda) hopes to exploit him, one is reminded how far Hollywood can retrogress (for the situation was much better used in *Mr Deeds Goes to Town*).

Pollack's most accomplished film, **Absence of Malice** (1981), might be so because he is working from an excellent screenplay by Kurt Luedtke which, like several of the early Eighties, was based on fact. A reporter (Sally Field) on a Miami newspaper learns that an F.B.I. man (Bob Balaban) is trying to implicate Gallagher (Paul Newman) in the murder of the leader of the longshoremen's union; Gallagher has Mafia relations, but is otherwise a respectable warehouseman who is caused a great deal of grief by the tactics of the press and the F.B.I. The film confronts these less to question them than to create tension, and it is gratifying to see a thriller whose twists do not depend on murder or violence. The performances are superb,

though the film would undoubtedly have been effective with an actor of less heroic stature than Newman. Three epilogues were shot to show the development of his relationship with Miss Field – happy, unhappy and indeterminate; I cannot say that I liked the one chosen.★

Pollack's favourite interpreter, Robert Redford, turned director for **Ordinary People** (1980), which dishonourably confirmed Hollywood's misconceptions about itself by being awarded Oscars for Best Film and Best Direction. Alvin Sargent's screenplay, based on a novel by Judith Guest, probes beneath the surface of the apparent happiness of one 'average' upper-income bracket family and finds something rotten. That something is Mom (Mary Tyler Moore, known for her niceness in T.V. situation comedy), just as it was in some equally hollow plays and novels, e.g. 'All Fall Down', 'There Must Be a Pony', of the Fifties. The subject matter was presumably chosen as the least likely to have interested an actor considered one of the industry's golden boys.

Paul Newman has directed a number of films on similar themes, with more skill and an insight which proves that years of stardom had not impaired his observation – even if both **Rachel, Rachel** (1968) and **The Effect of Gamma Rays on Man-in-the-Moon Marigolds** (1972) were primarily designed as showcases for the considerable talents of his wife, Joanne Woodward. *Rachel, Rachel*, written by Stewart Stern from a novel by Margaret Laurence, is about a 35-year-old spinster schoolteacher (Miss Woodward) who feels 'This is my last ascending summer – everything from now on is just downhill . . . to the grave.' Accordingly she loses, with no particular emotion, her virginity to a city boy (James Olson); she says farewell to her lesbian friend (Estelle Parsons); and finds the courage to leave her aged, demanding mother. The title of the second film reveals its writer, Paul Zindel, as a follower of Tennessee Williams, and its monstrous mother makes the lady of 'The Glass Menagerie' seem like Snow White in comparison: but the role is well-sustained by

★The old practice of sneak-preview screenings was revived in the late Seventies, with alternative endings shown to test audience response. It was more expeditious to film several different conclusions than face the loss of the whole investment because prospective audiences left the cinema dissatisfied.

Miss Woodward until a disappointing ending. Both films are set in Connecticut and are alive to the continuity of rural life as well as such matters as earning a living and teacher-pupil relationships.

Gilbert Cates has intermittently shown himself as perceptive a director as Newman, and **Summer Wishes, Winter Dreams** (1973) has more than Miss Woodward in common with the two films in which Newman directed her. Stewart Stern wrote it, largely in the vein of his adaptation of *Rachel, Rachel*, though some jarring moments remind us that he also wrote *Rebel Without a Cause*. Rita (Woodward) suffers the death of her mother (Sylvia Sidney), and finds herself nearing a nervous breakdown on a trip to Europe with her husband (Martin Balsam). **I Never Sang for My Father** (1970) is an eloquent study of a man (Gene Hackman) attempting to come to terms with his father (Melvyn Douglas) at that delicate point when the old man has lost his wife. Robert Anderson adapted from his own play, which was indifferent on the stage. Cates brings compassion to the sad and serious themes with which he deals: the death of a parent; the discovery that an 'ordinary' person can be a failure; physical love between the middle-aged; the realisation that a son has grown up gay; the consequences of taking and giving nothing in return. Both films, unfortunately but understandably, failed to draw the public, and Cates has since worked mainly in T.V.

Robert Ellis Miller (b. 1927) has also worked chiefly in T.V., and to see most of his films is to understand why; but his version of Carson McCullers's **The Heart Is a Lonely Hunter** (1968) is very fine – as is the screenplay by Thomas C. Ryan, another gentleman with an otherwise unimposing list of credits. There are moments of stridency and self-consciousness, but the only other faults, in what must have been a difficult job of adaptation, stem from the novel itself. The small town – it was Selma, Alabama – is remarkably well rendered by James Wong Howe's camera; and Singer, the deaf-mute catalyst around whom these lonely, isolated people move, has a superlative interpreter in Alan Arkin, well supported by Sondra Locke as the plain and dreamy Mick, Stacy Keach as the drunk, Blount, and Chuck McCann as the 'dummy'. These characters have been

taken from the hothouse atmosphere of the book and out into the sunny air, and thereby becoming all the more touching.

Few claims can be made on behalf of William Friedkin (b. 1939), who caught attention with **The Night They Raided Minsky's** (1968), after some years in T.V. and two mediocre films. This one, which is enjoyable, proclaims itself a celebration of the famous burlesque house (except that the 'girls' were older and slower than in the film), and the plot about an Amish girl (Britt Ekland) taking refuge there is, to say the least, unusual. The direction appears to be frenetic, but its editor, Ralph Rosenblum, claims in his memoir that the film was dying on its feet until he rescued it in the cutting room. There are few movies more stagey than **The Boys in the Band** (1970), based on Mart Crowley's play about an all-gay New York birthday party, but **The French Connection** (1971) was awarded some justifiable Oscars – Best Picture, Best Direction and Best Actor (Gene Hackman). New York in this instance is wonderfully present, and its police department, rounding up a drugs syndicate, had seldom been so convincingly portrayed. Ernest Tidyman wrote it, from a novel based on fact, and one's chief reservations devolve upon the fact that thirty years earlier it would have made a suitable B-movie.

Paul Newman has directed his wife, Joanne Woodward, in a number of films remarkable for their quiet understanding of everyday life – all the more remarkable since it is doubtful whether either of them have been able to lead ordinary lives since they became Hollywood stars over twenty years ago. This is *Rachel, Rachel*, the only one of these films the public greatly liked, but then it says much for the Newmans that they made no attempt at box-office concessions – proving in that more adventurous than many younger talents.

Friedkin had an even bigger success with **The Exorcist** (1973), a sensational and silly account of demonic possession, and then followed it with a gigantic failure, **Sorcerer** (1977), a $21 million remake of *Le Salaire de la Peur*. He made an effort to regain favour by combining elements of two of his successful films with **Cruising** (1980), which, in fact, had been planned and then dropped ten years earlier by Philip D'Antoni, the producer of *The French Connection*. As in that film, its hero (Al Pacino) is a ruthless cop, and the boys in the band this time are the gays of the leather bars. Much shouting was heard from gay activists about its sensationalism, but I should have thought that the image presented is far healthier and better P.R. than the usual stereotyped drag queens of most films on this subject. The story, if exploitive, is no sillier than most thrillers about rough, tough New York of the present day, and it has a surrealistic ending as two men undress for either murder or sex, or both. Doubtless the effect was accidental, but since the cop gets 'corrupted' by the gay life, what are we to make of Friedkin's surely apocryphal Precinct, where a huge black cop sits around in jock-strap and Stetson just waiting to beat people up?

Mark Rydell (b. 1934) also has an uneven group of credits. None of his earlier films prepared us for the predominantly sour qualities of **The Rose** (1979), which was nevertheless partly devised to revive the musical form. More importantly it marked the first film vehicle for Bette Midler. It was not a traditional musical, since in recent years audiences had been far more sympathetic towards rock/pop concerts filmed as they were staged. Rose (Midler) is a lady in a whirlwind, or, as the latest of her casual lovers (Frederick Forrest) puts it, her 'life is like a grenade range'. Her highs are sex (including an innocent lesbian embrace), her audiences, singing in a drag club, and her lows innumerable: and to keep her going between the two, there are the pills and the booze, both responsible for many of the lows. Since she is simply unable to cope, we may recall Judy Garland, though the acknowledged source is the life of Janis Joplin; the villain of the piece is her conniving manager, who understands her well enough to play dangerously with her, but he is also

ripping her off – and it was a clever stroke to cast Alan Bates, looking cosily protective as he had done in *An Unmarried Woman* (q.v.). The film does not bother to tell us how she got this way, nor does it need to: Rydell is as completely in command of Rose's world as are Bill Kerby and Bo Goldman of her language. We are supposed to care, and we do: the sorrows of this suffering lady affected audiences as those of Mildred Pierce had done a generation earlier. This film is probably the more honest of the two, but in each case a certain mythologising is involved.

On Golden Pond (1981) proved Rydell's ability to change style as he sought different audiences, since this self-consciously lyrical film was very popular. The subject of Ernest Thompson's meretricious screenplay, from his own play, is old age, and all it really has to say is that old people are not as stuffy about sex and four-letter words as we all thought. Katharine Hepburn and Jane Fonda are mother and daughter; Henry Fonda, in his only film with his daughter – and the last that he made – won an Oscar, as did Miss Hepburn. He is superb as a crusty, querulous, outspoken old man, and so is Dabney Coleman as his daughter's lover.

Not least because of Miss Midler's performance, *The Rose* is an improvement on the last variation on the theme, **Lady Sings the Blues** (1972), in which a small, plastic Diana Ross tried to impersonate Billie Holliday. It stands halfway between *The Rose* and the artificial show business biopics of the past, and is interesting mainly because it is one of the few about a black artist (a considerable advance, for instance, on *St Louis Blues*, which in 1958 expended a superb black cast on a cheapjack biography of W. C. Handy); but, as produced by Motown the black-orientated record company, for Paramount, it is only too happy to distort in the case against whitey. Holliday did not, as far as is known, witness a lynching, as in the film, and she was not turned on to drugs by whites, but by her first, black husband. Sidney J. Furie directed, with a certain eye to period, the best of his uneven American films.

Of the British directors who have worked in Hollywood at this time, Peter Yates (b. 1929) most nearly qualifies as a native. After his third film, *Robbery*, he was offered **Bullitt** (1968), in which a San

Francisco cop (Steve McQueen) discovers the links between an underworld syndicate and a political boss (Robert Vaughn); McQueen's convincing performance and the car chases helped to make it enormously popular, and car chases, a staple of movie thrills from the very beginning, took on a new lease of life – with diminishing returns as every other film followed suit. Yates became a name director, so that much was expected of **John and Mary** (1969), since he was teamed with Dustin Hoffman, fresh from *The Graduate*, and Mia Farrow, from *Rosemary's Baby*. A respectful press was followed by public indifference, due partly to its leading players. Hoffman gives his customary impersonation of an amiable rabbit; she, playing a lovable kook, has baby-eyes, baby-voice and baby-haircut. Mervyn Jones's original novel was set in London, and it was a further mistake to have an English writer, John Mortimer, attempt the New York idiom. Yates's career went into diminuendo, but undeservedly so in the case of **The Friends of Eddie Coyle** (1973), whose bank raids and car crashes pall as they begin but which is otherwise admirable. Robert Mitchum as a petty hoodlum and fence is at his best, and Richard Jordan is equally brilliant as a plainclothes Treasury Agent. George V. Higgins, who wrote the original novel, is a Boston lawyer, and his view of crime has been honestly and unpretentiously rendered by Paul Monash, producer and writer. One thinks back to *Panic in the Streets* rather than to contemporaries like *Slither* or *The Sting*, but that is partly because of Yates's use of location – which in this case is Boston itself. The portrait of Bloomington, Indiana, in **Breaking Away** (1979) is treasurable, and one reason why the film attracted more audience affection than any in years. Bloomington seems a nice place to live, its principal drawback being that town and gown do not get on: of the four young heroes, one (Dennis Quaid) is openly resentful of the privileges accorded to the college boys. A number of clashes between the two sides suggests that Steve Tesich, the writer, may be on the verge of checking out the American class system as in no film since *Five Easy Pieces* (q.v.); he settles instead for the contrived and cute, but he is at least humorous with it – and since his humour is, if not original, likeable, and

since Yates approaches it in the manner of Capra rather than, say, Blake Edwards, all is permissible. Capra comes to mind, since audiences are rooting for the climactic cycle race to be won by the foremost (Dennis Christopher) of the young heroes.

Another British director whose films have been made chiefly in the U.S. is Anthony Harvey (b. 1931), and the first, though made in Britain, is set in the New York subway. **Dutchman** (1967) is based on LeRoi Jones's one act play about a smartly-dressed black man (Al Freeman Jr), who becomes prey to a loud-mouthed, loudly-dressed white girl (Shirley Knight). Since the piece is probably symbolical, and therefore significant, and since it is certainly well directed, Harvey was assigned to **The Lion in Winter** (1968), written by James Goldman from his play about the marriage of Henry II (Peter O'Toole) to Eleanor of Aquitaine (Katharine Hepburn). The tragic marriage has been reduced to a prolonged slanging match, and these complex people have become a wry prankster and an overemotional hell-cat, at their worst laughing over the wars they have waged against each other or bowing to the courtiers while trading insults *sotto voce* in the manner of the stars of the Thirties, e.g. Davis and Howard in *It's Love I'm After*. The public found this appealing, but if Harvey controls the wayward elements with skill, his subsequent films explain why he has since worked mostly in television.

Roman Polanski also made the transatlantic crossing, after a sojourn in Britain. Having left Poland he had paused in France, and we may assume both **Repulsion** (1965) and **Cul-de-Sac** (1966) to have been prepared in France, since Polanski's co-writer, Gerard Brach, and the leading ladies are French. *Repulsion* is a landmark in world cinema, if, intentionally, a repulsive one. It is the case-book history of a girl (Catherine Deneuve) who becomes mad and homicidal, with no one around to care, including apparently the director himself, and no probing of causes, beyond the final shot. It is Grand Guignol, the first horror film for grown-ups: we may never imagine ourselves being sucked of blood in Transylvania, but we may perhaps accept the departure from reality in a large, silent, untidy London flat. It is a film suitable only for psychopaths who do

In Hollywood the Director is King

Catherine Deneuve in *Repulsion*, directed by Roman Polanski, which confirmed his brilliance on his arrival from his native Poland. It was made in Britain, and he has since worked in the U.S., France and Italy, usually with American backing (he is no longer able to work in Hollywood after a misdemeanour caused a jail sentence passed by a California court). That did not prevent subsequent Oscar nominations for his last film to date, *Tess*, nor, probably, will it prevent Hollywood investing again in his remarkable talent.

not need it, and in the name of humanity should not see it: but its power could not be denied, nor the tension, nor the mastery with which it has been put together. *Cul-de-Sac* is a reversion to the mood of *A Knife in the Water*, slightly more humorous and perceptive, but eventually as lacking in real substance. It is also a Pinteresque fantasy, perhaps influenced by 'The Birthday Party', where two strangers turn up to menace an ordinary family. The two here are definitely crooks, and the menage consists of a bald, fussy, middle-aged man (Donald Pleasence) with transvestite tendencies and his luscious young wife (Françoise Dorléac): they, and the setting, Lindisfarne Island, are used cleverly.

Polanski was summoned to the U.S. by William Castle, producer of a number of cheap horror films, but **Rosemary's Baby** (1968), though of the same genre, is something more than that as based on Ira Levin's novel. It was a big success for all three of them, and not only with addicts of this particular form of mayhem. The pregnant heroine (Mia Farrow) is beset on all sides by people she believes to be witches, including her husband (John Cassavetes): that suspicion falls on him is perhaps the most cunning of Levin's inventions. The unthinkable impinges on the daily round to the extent that sanity is at stake: as in *Repulsion*, mundane walls have voices and therefore hidden terrors. The trump card is that everything is logically worked out:

our worst forebodings are realised. Only to be regretted is that the film's popularity caused an unending, unrewarding and relentless stream of imitations.

Polanski himself determined to film **Macbeth** (1972), with the cooperation of Kenneth Tynan, co-adapter, and *Playboy* magazine, financier. The visual conception is considerable, but as in Zeffirelli's *Romeo and Juliet* an ability to speak the verse was a talent denied the leads, Jon Finch and Francesca Annis, both chosen for their youth, but not, on this evidence, for any other qualities. The remainder of the cast, with the honourable exception of the Macduff of Terence Bayler, would seem more at home in your local bank. What attracted Polanski to the play, as might have been expected, were the dark forces, the supernatural, and the evil spirits; but there is more to the play than that. Recalled to the U.S. for **Chinatown** (1974), he ran for its producer, Robert Evans, a copy of *Che?*, that he had recently finished in Italy 'which he thought was terrific . . . [but] it was the worst picture*I ever saw in my life' said Evans, adding that Polanski could be brilliant 'if channelled properly.' Certainly Polanski responded to this material, with Jack Nicholson as the private eye who uncovers a nest of civic corruption. Robert Towne wrote it after *The Last Detail*, a film that owes nothing to old movies: this one owes everything. It was a huge success, but Polanski did not choose to be channelled further and went to France to make **The Tenant** (1976), written with Brach from a novel by the appropriately named Roland Topor. It defies description, if only because it is too painful to bear thinking about. The ad slogan, 'No one does it to you like Roman Polanski', turned out to be less inane than might have been supposed.

Polanski dedicated **Tess** (1979) to his dead wife Sharon Tate – murdered by the Manson gang in 1969 – because it was she who suggested that he make a film of Thomas Hardy's novel 'Tess of the d'Urbervilles'. In the meanwhile he had been searching for material to make a movie not unlike *Love Story*, and one may suppose that he thought that Hardy's novel might be an upmarket version: but in the event Polanski seems to have chosen it to

*I can think of only a few worse.

make his own version of *L'Albero degli Zoccoli*. It was made in France, since Britain has an extradition treaty with the U.S. and in 1977 Polanski had pleaded partial guilt to a sex-offence with a minor and had subsequently fled California while on bail: but while the terrain of Normandy and Brittany can look like Wessex, their buildings do not – and eventually the interiors look as French as the exteriors. As with his *Macbeth*, Polanski has undercast the leading roles – Nastassia Kinski as Tess, Leigh Lawson as Alexander Stoke-d'Urberville, her seducer, and Peter Firth as Angel Clare, the parson's son whom she marries. But far more crucial to the film's failure is Polanski's misunderstanding of Victorian England and the British class system. It is the latter which imbues Tess with her false pride, which causes her to accept seduction, leading therefore to her tragic conclusion. Tess has become only another film heroine, and Angel merely another priggish husband: and there is one horrendous interpolation, the slogan 'Blessed be the Merciful' painted on a gate as he bids farewell to her, as if audiences had failed to grasp the point. Nevertheless, the film is not the long slog it might have been and doubtless the popularity of the B.B.C.'s 'Classic Serial' – 'Masterpiece Theatre' in the U.S. – helped the film to a wider audience than Schlesinger's superior *Far From the Madding Crowd*.

Milos Forman, having left Czechoslovakia at the time of French investment in *The Firemen's Ball*, gravitated towards the American film industry but found himself in the midst of several years' negotiations before getting the backing for the film he wanted to do, **Taking Off** (1971), a comedy about the generation gap. He was originally interested in the subject from the point of view of the young, but made the film from the point of view of the parents – who are earnest, confused and well-meaning as they tentatively sample such habits as smoking marijuana, which they hope will give them an insight into the youngsters' world. The film was not sufficiently successful to guarantee the freedom essential to this director, and it was not until four years had passed that he directed another film, **One Flew Over the Cuckoo's Nest** (1975) – at the invitation of Michael Douglas, son of the actor Kirk Douglas. The latter had played in a

Broadway dramatisation of Ken Kesey's novel, but had been unable to find backers for a film of it; his son sought the support of Fantasy Records and the project advanced once Jack Nicholson agreed to play the lead. The screenplay is by Lawrence Hauben and Bo Goldman, though Forman's improvisatory methods are so extreme that the credited photographer, Haskell Wexler, quit before shooting ended. The film won every major Oscar – the first one to do so since *It Happened One Night*, forty-two years earlier – and became extremely popular, partly due to the cuckoo of the title, Randle P. McMurphy (Nicholson), and his battles to the death, virtually, with the ward-sister, Nurse Ratched (Louise Fletcher). Both players approach their roles by stealth: she, desiccated, unimaginative, claiming the support of discipline and her own conception of the silent majority and he a good Joe with malice towards none but with sharks' teeth when he smiles at her. He is one of the 'loonies' in this latter-day *Snake Pit*, an attempt to understand the confusions and ignominies of the mentally ill, though the film's appeal – if not the point of the original novel – seems to be its allegorical statement on the underprivileged and on authority's control over them.

Forman's sureness and energy are almost miraculous, an augury for his entanglement with the sticky subject of **Hair** (1979), a Broadway phenomenon of the

Jack Nicholson in Milos Forman's *One Flew Over the Cuckoo's Nest*, one of the most popular films of the Seventies, which proves, along with *All the President's Men* and maybe just a dozen others, that when the public is offered a film on the subject of sufficient importance, well-crafted and intelligently written, it could not care less about the feeble horror films and derivative comedies so much more often on offer. Two further examples are *The Rose* and *Melvin and Howard,* both of which, like Forman's film, have the name of Bo Goldman on the credits – and that may or may not be a coincidence.

Sixties whose time had long since gone. There were considerable doubts about its merits at the time, seemingly confirmed when revivals in London and New York, not long before the film came out, disappeared with almost indecent speed. Critics were hardly more enthusiastic about the material in the film, though Forman and his collaborators, realising that that had dated, had done a considerable job of revamping; his work at least was much admired. However, neither the generation that had flocked to the theatrical production, nor the current movie audience, was interested.

Ragtime (1981) is based upon E. L. Doctorow's popular novel of life in America from 1905 to the First World War, a panoramic and fanciful blending of fiction and such people as Houdini, Stanford White and J. P. Morgan, many of whom have been dropped from the screenplay by Michael Weller. The rights were bought by Dino de Laurentiis, who engaged Robert Altman (q.v.) to direct, but changed his mind after the failure of *Buffalo Bill and the Indians*. In separate articles in *New York* magazine David Denby and William Wolf argued that Altman would have been a more suitable choice than Forman, who is a far greater director. But they are right in view of the result, which is unconvincing in historical detail, in situation and in virtually every respect. The chief theme concerns a white family and its involvement with a black pianist (Howard E. Rollins) who refuses to accept an inferior position in society and eventually becomes an urban terrorist – a not inappropriate term since most people behave as people do today. Forman, who has been alive to the nuances of American behaviour, on this occasion is not; he and the writer fought with de Laurentiis over the actual contents, and it is worth observing that of these three principals only Weller is American. Altman had earlier said that de Laurentiis had been primarily interested in the book because of its theme of black revenge. The film cost $25 million, but few went to see it, despite the return (after twenty years of retirement) of the eighty-year-old James Cagney to play the New York police chief.

The failure of *Ragtime* has not affected Hollywood's interest in Forman, who is making *Amadeus*, based on a popular London and Broadway play. Polanski also might get American backing for most projects which interest him. Probably both of them and Peter Yates have more in common with the next generation of American film-makers, but in this matter of chronology I have preferred to place them with those of their own age group, brought up on the movies of the Thirties. Whereas most of the directors we have discussed in this chapter came from television, which hardly existed when they were young, the American directors of the next generation probably saw their first movies on television. So it seems appropriate to pause and consider their current reputations as they were, in some instances, overtaken by the new influx of talent.

On past form Stanley Kubrick is more than likely to jump back after two failures, while Arthur Penn, currently unfashionable, will always be a more interesting director than the over-productive Blake Edwards. Like him, the veterans Don Siegel and Richard Brooks have an established pattern of failures and successes; Sam Peckinpah's career as a leading proponent of extreme violence – which ultimately repulsed audiences – is a special case. So are those (in films, that is) of Nichols and May and of Bob Fosse. George Roy Hill, Arthur Hiller, Norman Jewison, Frankenheimer, William Friedkin, Franklin Schaffner and Robert Mulligan have receded into the background somewhat; Herbert Ross, Hal Ashby, Alan J. Pakula, Martin Ritt and Sidney Lumet have not – and public acceptance of their work has been as varied as that of their contemporaries. Ross seems to be regarded as one of the few reliable directors of the lighter material, while Ritt and Lumet are held in esteem for the level of, and the social content in, most of their work. I have expressed my own admiration for the efforts, or some of them, of all these people. There were a number of 'arty' disasters; a number of commercial pictures have been discussed (and others ignored). Kubrick remains an unusual case: his last three feeble films cannot hide the enduring quality present in so many of his earlier ones.

42

The Movie Brats

THE EXPRESSION 'the movie brats' was coined to describe the young Hollywood film-makers who made such a splash in the late Seventies. I hope those who coined it will permit me to extend it to include the directors who were compulsive cinema-goers in childhood and went on to study at film school. That is no more true of all those to be discussed in this chapter than my statement at the end of the last chapter that the film-makers considered there had worked in television; but it is true enough.

It may be said that a new generation of American directors begins with Francis (Ford) Coppola (b. 1939). He was certainly for a time the most successful of them. Like many of the others he studied film (at U.C.L.A.) and entered the industry by way of one of its less eminent fringes, working for Roger Corman. In 1963 Corman arranged for him to direct *Dementia 13*, a low budget horror film, after which Coppola gained a slight reputation within the industry for helping on other people's scripts. Four years later he was sufficiently well known for Seven Arts to provide backing for **You're a Big Boy Now** (1967), which, apart from some established names, was to be made with friends on minimum pay and on New York locations – in place of the London of David Benedictus's original novel. The style came from Britain too, for it was derived from Richard Lester, but the film is nonetheless very taking, as it follows a sweet nineteen-year-old (Peter Kastner) trying to lose his virginity under the tutelage of a suave colleague (Tony Bill) at the Public Library. The girl (Elizabeth Hartman) he fancies is a kook, and virtually all the characters, including the monstrous parents (Geraldine Page, Rip Torn) exemplify the manners prevalent at the time.

Coppola became, in his own expression, a 'now' director, entrusted by Warner-Seven Arts with **Finian's Rainbow** (1968), a twenty-year-old Broadway musical whose mixture of whimsy and message had either defied adaptation or unnerved the various studios which had owned it. Although it is credited to the original authors, Coppola says that he wrote the screenplay; the piece is to some extent resistible, with Tommy Steele as a leprechaun and Petula Clark as a colleen. Keenan Wynn is good as a bigoted senator, as is Al Freeman as the black man (the hero's buddy) he is bigoted about. Fred Astaire could not be bad if he tried, but a puff of wind would have wafted him off screen; the little dancing which he does was spoilt by Warners, who liked the film so much that they blew it up to 70 mm. The critics agreed with Warners, but the public did not – because, Coppola considered, it was sent out to compete with the leaden *Funny Girl* and cost, in contrast, a mere $3½ million. The dances were improvised on the back lot, in sylvan settings, and the cast takes as naturally to those as to movement. The piece is also sunny and pretty, and it put what audiences there were into a cheery mood.

Warners were so pleased that they agreed to back Coppola's own company, a dream that became an occasional reality. Its first setback came when Warners withdrew after the failure of *THX 1138*, directed by Coppola's friend George Lucas (q.v.) and **The Rain People** (1969), directed by Coppola himself. Release of both was delayed, and *The Rain People* did not appear until after *Easy Rider* had started

Al Pacino, seated, and Marlon Brando in Coppola's *The Godfather*, a film about the Mafia that became the most financially successful ever made – calling, therefore, for a sequel. It seems a long time ago that these sequels started, undisguised and boldly proclaiming, as in this case, *Part II*. The conclusions to be drawn are not kind to the industry, suggesting poverty of ideas and a desire to turn a quick buck; and very few sequels have been remotely as good as the originals.

the vogue for 'road' movies. The message of this one is too heavily loaded and too simple: a girl (Shirley Knight) runs away from home and husband, but finds that she cannot escape responsibility when, out on the open road, she becomes involved with a brain-damaged hitch-hiker (James Caan) and a cop (Robert Duvall).

Coppola's work on the script of *Patton* was one reason he was assigned to the script and direction of **The Godfather** (1972), based on Mario Puzo's bestseller.* Coppola could not turn its dross into gold, but he tightened the strands of this tenuous Mafia tale and made it watchable for three hours – with, admittedly, the excitements inherent in gang warfare, family vendettas, shoot-outs and such. The film's popularity – outstripping, at new admis-

*After the film came out the book's publisher complained to *Variety* that it had been well-received by book reviewers, but that film critics invariably referred to the novel as 'trashy'.

sion rates, any previous movie – occasioned a sequel, **The Godfather Part II** (1974), defended by Coppola on the ground that he knew from his own background that much more could be said about Italian immigration to the U.S. Thus, having covered the war years and just after, he had to go either forward or backwards for his saga, and he does both simultaneously, with Robert de Niro, in the flashbacks, preparing to become the aged Marlon Brando, who had played the Mafia chief in the first film. The film did so poorly in the U.S. that Paramount hoped that an Oscar or so would improve business, and it won a handful (this is the only time an original and a sequel have won Best Picture Oscars): but the response at the box office was only marginally improved thereby.

The screenplay for **The Conversation** (1974) had been prepared long before, and now that Coppola could get backing the topic was more timely – since the matter of wire-tapping and bugging had been brought into prominence by Watergate. Coppola himself said that he set out to make a film about privacy but found himself moving into that realm explored in *The Rain People*, i.e. responsibility. Despite their undoubted merits as director's films, each exposes an intellectual bankruptcy. *The Conversation* is as hollow as a drum. Its premise depends on a private operator (Gene Hackman) overhearing one particular, dull, conversation, and on the strength of one line – 'He'd kill us if he got the chance' – becoming obsessed with an impending murder. Conceivably a lot of conversations might lead to paranoia, but that would be moving too far from *Blow-Up*, the obvious model; instead the lone phrase leads to the wretched Hackman, being alone and unloved.

Apocalypse Now (1979) was another project which had waited for years: during its three years in production the cost rose to $31,100,000 – unsurpassed since *Cleopatra*, though some even more expensive films were in progress. A number of foreign market territories had been pre-sold, but none with an advance of more than a million dollars. United Artists put a ceiling of $20 million on their investment, which included a huge loan to Coppola, whose own involvement was $18 million – which meant placing most of his personal property at risk. The gist of his promotion was that the film is above criticism, since it is an honest endeavour to make a statement on the Vietnam War: 'I know the film is really rich and multi-levelled,' he told *Variety*, 'It's an experimental one-to-one relationship between the audience and the war. You can only dream about participating in a film like that. I feel I really showed that there could be a whole other kind of cinema . . . There are open questions in the film. The ending is like a Jungian exercise.' He lashed out at the lukewarm reception by American critics, but few would deny the salient point made by Vincent Canby in *The New York Times*: 'It's a serious attempt to deal with the manifold meanings of the American involvement in Vietnam but . . . is it to be a Philistine to suggest that though there is nothing wrong with personal movie-making, there is something slightly askew with personal movie-making on the grandiose scale of *Apocalypse Now*?' The source of the script, by Coppola and John Milius, is Conrad's 'The Heart of Darkness', but most of it is *The African Queen*, with an ending evocative of *The Black Watch* or any Tarzan movie where the hero stumbles across a mad ruler in the middle of the jungle. The character of the hero (Martin Sheen), sent on an assassination mission, is brother to some who have seen service with Graham Greene. Ichikawa's pacifist movies have also been plundered, as is, at one point, *Dersu Uzala*. What Coppola means by multi-levelled is that it is *Star Wars* (q.v.) with a message – since the cultural references within the script are to 'The Golden Bough', Eliot and Weston's 'From Ritual to Romance'; British critics, recognising them, were less flattered than amused. A photograph of Charles Manson reminds us of a time – 1968 – of American madness, of flower power and gutter-level philosophising. The ending is not, as far as I can see, a Jungian exercise, but a way of stopping a film which, having reached Kurtz's camp, has been getting gradually sillier. Up till then, it offered a number of powerful and imaginative sequences, and, it does hold our interest for most of its two and a half hours. It is an honest statement on Vietnam – on confusion, fear, a living nightmare, a world upended; and if Coppola is not, nor ever will be, Ichikawa, he is clearly to be attended to in preference

to Michael Cimino and *The Deer Hunter* (q.v.).

The film's box-office performance was not such as to relieve Coppola entirely of the financial difficulties involved in its production, thus delaying (at least) his plans to help other film-makers. He had, however, already been instrumental in United Artists handling the first feature of a documentary director, Carroll Ballard, **The Black Stallion** (1979). Based on an apparently classic novel by Walter Farley, published in 1941, it starts with a fire at sea, which strands a boy and a horse on a desert island – and there they stay for the movie's first hour, which is as magical as anything in the history of movies. The second half, after they are rescued and transported home, is of necessity more conventional, but overall this is the best children's film since *The Wizard of Oz*.

Coppola's 'empire' collapsed as he filmed **One from the Heart** (1982), a musical about 'ordinary' people set in a grandiose, stylised and studio-recreated Las Vegas, which cost over $24 million. The film was completed through various loans, from companies and individuals, some arriving only on payday. In the face of industry indifference, Coppola himself booked the film into Radio City Music Hall for previews, but when public and critical reaction was the same Paramount dropped it. It was taken up by Columbia, but only by minor distributors in foreign territories. Something similar happened with **Hammett** (1982), also produced by Coppola's Zoetrope Studios, but he could have had little hope of that saving the situation, since after seeing a roughcut he observed (reputedly) that it was the worst film he had ever seen. The trouble starts with Zoetrope, since one of his colleagues bought Joe Gore's novel and offered the direction successively to Nicolas Roeg, François Truffaut and, on the basis of *Der Amerikanische Freund*, Wim Wenders. None of them, despite that American friend, would seem to be the obvious choice for a fast-moving Thirties-type thriller, but where the book, apart from being a good pastiche of Dashiell Hammett, was flashy, and second-rate, Wenders's film is flashy, ponderous, arty and sixth-rate. The plot has been thrown out and one borrowed from Chandler's 'The Little Sister'; and a latter-day Mr

The Movie Brats

Guttmann is introduced in the person of Roy Kinnear. As he insultingly offers a lengthy explanation of the word 'gunsel' one reflects how far movie thrillers have declined since *The Maltese Falcon*.

Another young director who entered films through the good graces of Roger Corman is Peter Bogdanovich (b. 1939), who had won a degree of national fame as a critic with a fond appreciation of old movies. **Targets** (1968) mixes old movies – including one of Corman's – with the type of subject of which Corman approved, i.e. horror, but Bogdanovich cleverly used a fool-proof modern topic. A foreword notes that '7000 Americans were killed by gun-fire in 1967', with a further reference to the Texas sniper of 1966 and a call for the reformation of the gun laws. The mingling of two separate stories, we learnt later, was due to expediency, but the equation between phoney 'gothic' horror movies and a young man berserk with a gun works well enough. There are a number of fairly good jokes in the sequences between the aged star, Boris Karloff, playing himself, and the young screenwriter, Bogdanovich – also, more or less, as himself. The sniper (Tim O'Kelly), in contrast, is the all-American jock, with short hair, in sneakers and pale-coloured chinos.

The two, star and sniper, come together in a drive-in cinema: Bogdanovich not only has fun with it but he makes the most concise of all movie statements on public violence. Paramount took over the film for distribution, proof to a movie-oriented generation that it was not only in France that movie lovers were able to make their own films. Bogdanovich had demonstrated a new way into the industry, which resulted in a number of imitators, including John Carpenter and Brian da Palma, who decided that they could draw attention to themselves by splashing the screen with blood.

Bogdanovich himself turned to the subject of growing up in a small Texas town in the Fifties, **The Last Picture Show** (1971), and then to a fairly witless piece of slapstick, **What's Up Doc?** (1972), written by David Newman, Robert Benton and Buck Henry, with Barbra Streisand and Ryan O'Neal vainly striving to imitate the great comedy players of the Thirties – and if any film can be said to have begun that soon-wearisome business of referring to old Hollywood, this is it. *The Last Picture Show* had been in black-and-white, in imitation of the old movies: and so is **Paper Moon** (1973), a film as beguiling as any ever made. It is set in the Thirties,

written by Alvin Sargent from a novel by Joe David Brown, and concerns a confidence trickster (O'Neal), who finds himself constantly outsmarted by the young child (Tatum O'Neal, the actor's daughter) he is taking to an aunt in St Joseph, Missouri. The two of them are so delightful, especially the child, that it by no means matters that the film is less a narrative than a series of confrontations. This was the director's third consecutive smash hit: and he threw it all away. **Daisy Miller** (1974) was only the fourth of Henry James's stories to be filmed, but one too short and too slight to be really suitable. Frederic Raphael wrote the screenplay, the locations were prettily found at Vevey and Rome, but Bogdanovich misdirects at every turn: of the entire cast only Mildred Natwick, as Daisy's snobbish aunt, seems to have read the script, let alone the book, and James's subtleties are entirely lost. **At Long Last Love** (1975) is set in the Thirties, in that favourite derivative setting of the era, Long Island; it also has a bevy of Cole Porter songs, none of which survives this treatment – and of the stars only Burt Reynolds and Madeline Kahn show glints of the gaiety and charm which are what it is supposed to be all about. One incident is taken from Hollywood lore, as set down in Bogdanovich's own book on movies, and by standards he established himself **Nickelodeon** (1976) is pure cannibalism. After a mauling by the press, it failed almost completely at the box office, though it might surely have found an audience in those unfamiliar with its anecdotes. Bogdanovich returned to Corman for **Saint Jack** (1979), not primarily to retrieve his reputation – though that was necessary – but to prove that American movies could be made on a restricted budget, and be profitable. Paul Theroux's novel is a series of anecdotes about a pimp (Ben Gazzara) in Singapore, and the film is likeable, with some excellent local colour. It lacks a certain conviction, most obviously at the end when Jack, hitherto without a single moral scruple of any kind, finds that he cannot 'shop' a homosexual U.S. senator (George Lazenby) to the C.I.A. The complexities of human behaviour, particularly necessary in what is intended as a character study, come a close second to elementary cinema technique, like cutting away from a funeral to a postcard view. Throughout

Bogdanovich's films, even the two good ones, arbitrary incident leads only to arbitrary incident by the most artificial means: it is curious that a man who has looked so hard at old Hollywood should have failed to grasp that that was not the way they did it.

In **An Unmarried Woman** (1978), at one moment the heroine and her friends sit around reminiscing about stars of the past, and like every scene in the film it rings true; but as they agree that there is no one around today to touch Davis, Garbo, Stanwyck and Jean Arthur, you know you would rather be watching one of them. This is not a film that could have been made in their heyday, for, as in all the films of this director, Paul Mazursky (b. 1938), the people are unglamorous, they move at life's pace, they mumble: unfortunately they still throw their dilemmas at us, and this particular one concerns the reactions of a woman (Jill Clayburgh) discovering that her husband prefers another woman. I was reminded of a remark of C. A. Lejeune's, that 'it dragged its slow pace along': the film was *Cobra Woman*, and there would be no worse condemnation than to say that I would rather have been watching Maria Montez. Mazursky, a former writer, made his name with **Bob and Carol and Ted and Alice** (1969), the first comedy – indeed the first film – about wife-swapping, and so somewhat daring at that time. The film starts with a sex-therapy group session handled seriously or, at least – which is equally startling – unfunnily, and much of its humour depends on marital reactions to such everyday problems as infidelity and not feeling up to sexual intercourse. When it comes to the actual wife-swapping, the two couples of the title do not feel up to that either, which makes you wonder why they abolished the Production Code; instead they go to listen to Tony Bennett, and all concerned sing 'What the World Needs Now is Love', which is supposed to be ironic and pointed at the same time. The audience which flocked to this avoided Mazursky's second film as director, **Alex in Wonderland** (1970), which is about a director who has made a successful first film and is stumped for an idea for a second – a plot not without resemblances to Fellini's *8½*, to which this is an overt homage. There is also a discussion on masturbation, to

1213

Although critics were kind to *The Revolutionary*, the public in 1970 would have none of it – which is a pity, since it was flawlessly written by Hans Konigsberger (from his own novel) and finely directed by Paul Williams, with a performance to match by Jon Voight, centre, as a middle-class boy who takes to radicalism with fervour but with hardly a coherent thought in his well-meaning head. With him, at left, is Robert Duvall, as the factory worker who leads him towards the left, and Seymour Cassel as the nut who will take him from there to anarchy.

remind us that Mazursky in both these early films took advantage of the new permissiveness to discuss things hardly worth discussing – at least, not in this pointless manner; he was not, of course, the only one.

Michael Ritchie (b. 1939) is the social satirist which Mazursky would like to be, but it is possible that he is only as good as his script. That of **Downhill Racer** (1969) is quite literally only a study of a professional skier (Robert Redford), and we learn little about him beyond his monstrous and humourless devotion to his sport; the film was generally considered the best to date on a professional sport, a dubious compliment in view of the quality of most of the others. Ritchie's documentary approach was perfected, not without reference to *Taking Off* and *The Hospital*, by the time he directed **The Candidate** (1972) – a fragmentary, take-it-or-leave-it style particularly suitable for the purpose, which is an account of a senatorial campaign. As in *State of the Union* or *The Best Man* the details are fascinatingly set out – by Jeremy Larner, who had worked for Eugene McCarthy, and who won an Oscar for Best Original Screenplay. He is particularly adept at catching the non-committal committed remarks of both sides – which suggests satire, and that is exactly what the film is. 'There's got to be a better way' is one of the

slogans of the candidate, McKay (Redford), but he is not near to finding one: he feels deeply on a number of issues, notably pollution – but not deeply enough. He is young, ready, willing and able, but sufficiently mediocre to suggest that in thirty years' time he will be as much of a demagogue and a stereotype as his opponent. Preston Sturges would have approved of Ritchie, and **Smile** (1975) is about small-town life, an institution viewed favourably – at least by the movies – till the coming of Sturges. Ritchie himself admitted the film was influenced by *The Firemen's Ball*, but in this case we are watching a fairly dreadful group of people – though most of them are deliciously funny, as they plot and counterplot around a local beauty contest. They are also hurt and sad, given to odd revelations and moments of pomposity and pride – eventually not unlike a grown-up *American Graffiti* (q.v.), also a film of hopes and dreams. The film is so surefooted that it is disappointing to find this director working on inferior material – in **The Bad News Bears** (1976) and **Semi-Tough** (1977), presumably offered, or taken, because they also are about forms of competition. The former involves a kids' baseball team, predictably foul-mouthed – though that is the film's only joke; – and the latter concerns two football-players (Burt Reynolds, Kris Kristofferson) with distinctly playful tastes and a yen for the same girl (Jill Clayburgh). *Bears* makes a point that baseball is not the ideal game for children, especially as the ideal is not playing but winning, and the parents' obsession with winning is unlikely to turn any of the children into good citizens; the other film is merciless on weirdo groups following the latest passing fads.

Bob Rafelson (b. 1935) has also taken as his theme contemporary America – if we except **Head** (1968), starring The Monkees, a pop-group which was, by Rafelson's own admission, his creation. They had made a lot of money for the records division of Columbia Pictures, and its television subsidiary, so Rafelson felt that he was entitled 'to make a picture that would in a sense expose the process', i.e. the manufacture of a pop group. It is soon clear that The Monkees have as little acting talent as The Beatles, so, as in *A Hard Day's Night*, this group is put through a series of cut-ups interspersed with songs – and not even the semblance of a story-line. Parodies of other movies – and T.V. commercials – were not new, but they are done here charmingly; even the jokes that fail are buoyed by wit or imagination. *Head* keeps its options open; it is a more accomplished witness to the fads and fancies of the Sixties than any similar piece, and one of the few non-narrative films which offers hope for the genre. A small bonus is a brief appearance by Jack Nicholson, co-producer and co-writer. The co-sponsor was Bert Schneider, and the three of them were to be reunited on **Five Easy Pieces** (1970), with a screenplay by Adrien Joyce. (She and Nicholson had written a Western, *The Shooting*, before he became a star, and watching it I was uncertain whether they or the director, Monte Hellman, were responsible for its pretension and consequent failure.) *Five Easy Pieces* is not unlike *Easy Rider*, inasmuch as it is romantic about disillusionment and decay; it is far more honest, with points to make on the rifts in American society and a man who wants a better world and cannot find it – a theme at one time rare in American culture, perhaps more cleverly treated here than in any other version since the War. Nicholson plays the man, a construction worker, but in time we learn that he is from a wealthy and cultured family. Says his girl (Karen Black) to him, 'One thing I don't understand – how you can have this fantastic background of music and just walk away from it without a second thought', and he replies 'I did give it a second thought.'

If for no other reason, the film would be remarkable for the performance of Nicholson, who seems to *enjoy* himself as much as any good actor since Walter Huston. The theme is reprised in **The King of Marvin Gardens** (1972), in which Nicholson has a lonely night-time radio programme and would like to come in from the cold – to his family, as represented by his brother (Bruce Dern). The behaviour of the latter makes little sense, as written by Rafelson and Jacob Brackman, but one of the other players, Ellen Burstyn, explained why: 'Bob loves ambiguity. There was plenty in the script to begin with, but then after the first cut, which was about half-hour too long as they always are, he cut it for further ambiguity.' The film had little success and the much better **Stay Hungry** (1976)

attracted only a cult following. Rafelson said that he did not like Charles Gaines's novel till he realised that its conclusion was the same as that of *Five Easy Pieces* and *Marvin Gardens*; the latter had come about because 'the world was very despairing'. Yet the screenplay of *Stay Hungry*, by himself and Gaines, changes the novel's end for an optimistic one – also perhaps an arbitrary one, since he shoots in sequence and did not, with these three films, decide upon the ending until the last day of filming. Reviewing the film in the *New Statesman* John Coleman invoked 'Candide', since 'il faut cultiver notre jardin' turns up as 'Stay hungry and you'll taste life'; we may also invoke Satyajit Ray's later films, with the young hero (Jeff Bridges) searching for his identity in a changing world; but like Rafelson's earlier movies it is concerned with certain American values – those prevailing in Birmingham, Alabama. Rafelson may be the most intuitive and optimistic director of his generation, and the two qualities may be interrelated: at least, I think the acclaim that greeted *Five Easy Pieces* is reflected in this film.

Rafelson's work has been infrequent, since, as he observed, life can be happier without the stress of directing a film. In 1979 he began to direct *Brubaker*, with Robert Redford, but was removed by the

Bob Rafelson's *Five Easy Pieces* is about a hard-hat, Jack Nicholson, who likes to go bowling or to sit around swilling beer; and he has a girlfriend, Karen Black, with hardly more aspirations than he. When it turns out that he comes from a cultured middle-income family the film has a comment or so to make on class.

Jack Lemmon in John G. Avildsen's *Save the Tiger*, an executive in his forties who suddenly looks around him and doesn't like what he sees. The rumblings of Watergate had started to sound as the film was being made, but the film's pessimism is wider than that, covering a number of matters from business ethics to porno-houses.

producer; and then he and Nicholson revived **The Postman Always Rings Twice** (1981), which they had been discussing since 1973 – when Nicholson would have been the right age for the role. Hollywood is accustomed to remaking its successes rather than its failures, i.e. the good or excellent novels it mangled years ago, but in this case Rafelson should really have taken his tone from either James M. Cain's original novel or the M-G-M version of 1946. Instead, in restoring the sexual passion, he imitates the Visconti version of this story, *Ossessione*, but the reasonably explicit sex scenes have more of the flavour of cheap Italian movies like *Mogliamante* than the erotic tension Visconti achieved. Rafelson and David Mamet, his screenwriter, seem also to be in search of tragedy, and the postman now rings only once, leaving the Nicholson character crying for his lost love rather

than being accused of her murder. A further miscalculation is to have depicted the time – 1934 – as resolutely drab, confining period detail to clothes, cars, a couple of songs on the radio, and a breadline. But if the film is a disappointment from this star-director team, it has a small triumph in Jessica Lange, febrile, disturbing and far prettier and more appealing than any American film heroine in ages.

Redolent of Rafelson's best films is **Save the Tiger** (1973), with which John G. Avildsen (b. 1937) moved to the mainstream industry after the success of *Joe*. Its writer, a former assistant producer on a T.V. Tarzan series, was Steve Shagan, who adapted from his own novel: they interested Jack Lemmon but no one else, till Robert Evans at Paramount decided (in the manner of the old tycoons) that it should be made whether or not it earned a penny. It was shot in chronological order on location in Los Angeles, where Harry (Lemmon) works in the garment business. As Lemmon observed, Harry was once a nice, hustling kid who had surrendered to current values and, in the year of Watergate, is considering arson when his factory is threatened with closure: 'The Government has another word for arson and it's called fraud.' The film omits few of Harry's regrets, be they for forgotten jazz musicians or the ideals of the war years, and elsewhere it more overtly attacks the materialistic attitudes of American society. At one point there is a discussion on the ethics of Albert Speer, an indication that movies were beginning to reflect the conversations of reasonably intelligent people. Lemmon's performance won a deserved Best Actor Oscar.

Avildsen was awarded a Best Director Oscar for **Rocky** (1976), but it seems to me only marginally better than his subsequent films. The perceptions of *Save the Tiger* are largely absent in this tale of a punk (Sylvester Stallone), part-time boxer and part-time collector for a loan-shark. It was welcome to have an optimistic film in the year of *Taxi Driver* (q.v.), and since the climax is a prize-fight, with audiences rooting for Rocky, some reviewers invoked the name of Capra. Stallone wrote the screenplay as a vehicle for himself, and he has to date also directed two equally popular sequels.

Virtually all these film-makers have

been overshadowed by Robert Altman (b. 1922), who with **M★A★S★H** (1970) established himself as the most invigorating talent in the American cinema. There had not been an American film as free-wheeling and rambustious since *Shadows*, while its humour and irreverence suggested a contemporary *Duck Soup*. Ring Lardner Jr provided the dry martini cocktail script about a Mobile Army Surgical Hospital (hence the title) in Korea where, as in other recent service movies, everyone is obsessed with sex. The cast of then little-known names is headed by Donald Sutherland and Elliott Gould as medics, and the latter is very droll, given to mumbling insubordinate remarks with a knowing innocence. The lashings of blood in the operating theatre sequences give the impression that Altman was determined to be noticed at all costs, but do not detract from the circus-like effect of the film itself. It caught the mood of the anti-military young, sick of Vietnam, and there was considerable surprise when it was discovered that Altman was of another generation altogether. He had already made a number of disregarded movies, including one with a reasonably large budget, *That Cold Day in the Park*.

Altman's later work showed him youthful in his recklessness, using a seemingly rough-and-ready approach to retain his primary effect, spontaneity. Those who detected a polemic in *M★A★S★H* were not to find it again in his films, except glancingly, but they have a common theme, and it is that of Lumet (or Satyajit Ray) of people coming together and of their effect on each other. His ardour for his medium led him into a number of mindless art films, with the result that his career has been like a roller coaster. **Brewster McCloud** (1970), like Mazursky's *Alex in Wonderland*, made at the same time, is personal fantasy posing as serious or, if you like, anarchic comment, in this case on some citizens of Houston: and both films were contributory factors to the ruin of M-G-M. Its former chiefs must have been rotating in their graves since the film's major joke, repeated *ad nauseam*, is built around bird droppings, while what plot there is concerns a mild-mannered young man (Bud Cort) who yearns to be Icarus. **McCabe and Mrs Miller** (1971) is a pioneer tale set mainly in a brothel, and

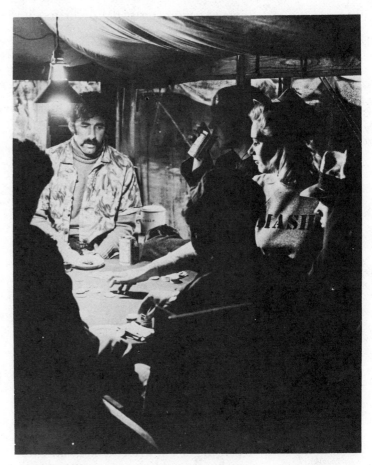

with many four-letter words exchanged between a hard-luck whore (Julie Christie) and a gambler (Warren Beatty). **Images** (1972) is about a woman (Susannah York) in the midst of a nervous breakdown, possibly from trying to sort out what is happening. Only the second of these had much success (and that was chiefly with the press). Although he was not assigned to the project, United Artists sought his advice as to the suitability of Elliott Gould playing Marlowe and Altman seized the opportunity to direct Raymond Chandler's story **The Long Goodbye** (1973) with a screenplay by Leigh Brackett. Altman suggested that by modernising it he could present a satire on modern-day California, which he has effectively done – but only at the expense of the original and a new and particularly foolish solution tagged on. And Gould is not Marlowe.

Altman hit his stride with his next three

Elliott Gould, left, Donald Sutherland, drinking from the can, and Sally Kellerman in Robert Altman's *M★A★S★H*, staff-members of a Mobile Army Surgical Hospital in Korea. Their misadventures, often hilarious, sexual and in defiance of authority, provided the basis of a television series, with different players, which ran for more than ten years and broke a number of records in that medium.

films. At moments it did occur to some that his main strength was his brilliant cinematographer, Vilmos Zsigmond, but he changed photographers, and his films remained startlingly vivid. **Thieves Like Us** (1974) is a new version of the novel once filmed as *They Live By Night*, with Keith Carradine and Shelley Duvall as the outlawed lovers; **California Split** (1974) concerns the oddball adventures of two inveterate gamblers (Gould, George Segal). Neither, despite warm notices, was successful, and he may have chosen **Nashville** (1975) because of the popularity of country and western music. The film did enable him to elaborate on the theme of *California Split* (and many other films of the time), of 'making it', of restless and funky people searching for pastures new. Those in *Nashville* aspire to political office or to a recording contract, and they are also searching for what may be described as a new lay or the ultimate in sexual satisfaction. Most of the dreams fade, or, once achieved, amount to little: the time had gone when movie heroes achieved goals or glory. We leave them more or less as we found them. One is dead, shot by a sniper at a concert, and although the atmosphere of violence had been created from the start, this cheap, cut-off ending reduces a film which for the last thirty minutes had already indicated that it did not know where to go. The first two hours are excellent, but the public failed to respond to the generally ecstatic reviews. Altman's standing had only been sustained by support from the press, but he lost that with **Buffalo Bill and the Indians** (1976) and the equally dire **Quintet** (1978), which disappeared from cinemas with uncommon rapidity, despite the presence in the cast of Paul Newman. Altman had always been prone to self-indulgence, and now it had overwhelmed him. He quarrelled with de Laurentiis, the producer of *Buffalo Bill*, and moved yet again, to 20th Century-Fox, for **The Wedding** (1978) which, like Tchekov's play and Wajda's film, is about nothing but a wedding, and **A Perfect Couple** (1979), the romance of a mismatched pair (Paul Dooley, Marta Heflin). Neither film was any more than a partial return to form, for the old energy was missing, and characters and situations of potential interest dither before disappearing altogether. As ventures in satire neither

may compare to *Stay Hungry* or *Smile*, but the cast of *A Wedding* includes Lillian Gish – Griffith's most famous actress being directed, almost seventy years later, by one who was for a while Hollywood's most stimulating film-maker.

Like Coppola, Altman has entrepreneurial ambitions and has sponsored a number of other directors, notably Robert Benton (b. 1932), who had written *Bonnie and Clyde* with David Newman. They also wrote *There Was a Crooked Man* and it was not a good idea to repeat its themes in **Bad Company** (1972) which Benton directed for producer Stanley Jaffe. In their West, there is no loyalty and no courage, and because their theme, the seduction of the young by crime, is of little dramatic interest, the film was a deserved failure. Altman enabled Benton to direct again by persuading Warners to put up the budget for **The Late Show** (1977), an improvement, as it happened, on *The Long Goodbye*, as Benton had written his own Chandleresque story, set in the present day and engagingly teaming a white-haired gammy-legged private eye (Art Carney) and a kooky dame (Lily Tomlin), a 'fruitcake' as he calls her. That again did not elicit further offers, but the producer, Jaffe, and star Dustin Hoffman decided to entrust Benton with the direction of **Kramer vs. Kramer** (1979): Benton also adapted the novel by Avery Corman, and, as David Castell observed in *Films Illustrated*, his credit, 'written for the screen' takes on 'a vivid new meaning'. The subject is a separation, a divorce, and the battle over the custody of the child (Justin Henry) – a small enough area and Benton stays rigidly within it, never straining either to move his audience or make them laugh, but succeeding simply with fresh observation. The husband (Hoffman) is in advertising, and his salary is underquoted for the purposes of the plot, since with a low-paid job he risks losing the child; but in that role Hoffman gives a magnificent, understated performance, justifying his own claim that he is 'demanding' to work with. Jane Alexander is the new lady in his life, radiant without make-up or Hepburn mannerisms; and Meryl Streep is rightly smug and unlikeable as the ex-wife. She, Hoffman, Benton and the film all won Oscars.

Hoffman has also been instrumental in furthering the career of Ulu Grosbard

(b. 1929), whom he had known when they worked together off Broadway. Grosbard's first film, **The Subject Was Roses** (1968) is an artless version of a prize-winning but derivative play, yet again unmasking the American family. Frank D. Gilroy wrote it, and the cast fortunately includes Patricia Neal, Jack Albertson and Martin Sheen. **Who Is Harry Kellerman and Why is He Saying Those Terrible Things About Me?** (1971) stars Hoffman as a Jewish, neurotic and famous pop singer. It moves uneasily from whimsy to satire (it is brilliant on his New Jersey boyhood), and Herb Gardner's screenplay reveals the same schisms as in his most famous work, *A Thousand Clowns*, that he is not as detached about New York and show business as he thinks he is. *Straight Time*, with Hoffman, was Grosbard's third failure, but he attracted favourable attention with his fourth film, **True Confessions** (1981), written by John Gregory Dunne and his wife, Joan Didion, from the former's novel. By this time Hollywood had attacked most of the institutions it had once revered, but this was the first time that it had roundly portrayed the Roman Catholic Church as having as its high ranking prelates men as greedy as they are ambitious. The film is, actually, a thriller, showing the effect on a monsignor (Robert de Niro) as his brother (Robert Duvall), a persistent L.A. cop, unmasks a wealthy supporter of the Church as the perpetrator of a particularly sadistic murder. Grosbard handles both the situations and the period detail (it is set in the Forties) with confidence, but the film is chiefly remarkable for the resource and attack of its leading players.

Grosbard may one day make a very interesting film, and so may Terrence Malick (b. 1945), a former student at the American Film Institute who entered the industry with the screenplay for an undistinguished cowboy tale, *Pocket Money*. He wrote and directed **Badlands** (1973) and **Days of Heaven** (1978), which do little more than establish that America is vast, beautiful and in places deserted (Malick was born in Texas). *Badlands* contains much spilling of blood, seemingly obligatory for directors making their first films, and though based on an actual shooting spree in Nebraska in 1958 it too often seems a combination of *Pretty Poison* and *Bonnie and Clyde*. *Days of Heaven* concentrates on immigrant farmhands in the Texas Panhandle of 1916, but in trying to come to terms with the rural past it is somewhat less successful than Richard Pearce's independently-made **Heartland** (1980), based on the autobiographical books of Elinore Randall Stewart, a widow who, in 1910, went to become housekeeper in the wilds of Wyoming to a dour Scot (Rip Torn). The hardships of her first year are told without sentimentality and in images of exceptional beauty, and she is warmly played by a stout, thirty-fiveish actress, Conchata Ferrell. Pearce, the director, had made a reputation and won the 1974 Oscar for feature documentary with his anti–Vietnam war film, *Hearts and Minds*.

John Landis may also surprise us. He had a huge success with his third film as a director, **National Lampoon's Animal House** (1978), a campus comedy which had the bright – but by now unoriginal – idea of turning the crewcut boys into prigs and villains and the slobs into heroes: but it had no other whatsoever and is at best lumberingly executed. However, **An American Werewolf in London** (1981) is a small triumph, engagingly welding together a parody of horror movies and real horror, the finale of *The Lost World* (or *King Kong*) and New York Jewish jokes with those depending on British understatement.

In the matter of humour we seem today to be dependent almost solely on the peurile and scatalogical fancies of Mel Brooks, though it is worth remarking that ever since **Blazing Saddles** (1974) broke records each of his films has been less successful at the box office. Compared to his 'anything goes' approach Woody Allen (b. 1935) seems erudite and disciplined, and he does offer four or five good lines per picture. The rest depends on recognising the references in the jokes – and his audiences of primarily young admirers are flattered at having heard of Strindberg, Zelda Fitzgerald and Marshall McLuan, not to mention his own frequent references to old movies. Most patrons, with good reasons, resisted his earlier films: **Annie Hall** (1977) was, however, enjoyed by people who normally could not stand Allen and his self-aware, self-deprecatory screen persona. We know from Ralph

The Movie Brats

You may well wonder why this particular number was staged in a saloon of the old, wild West, in *Blazing Saddles*, but then it is typical of Mel Brook's approach to comedy, which is not exactly disciplined. The lady is Madeline Kahn, who provided the film's more memorable moment.

Rosenblum's memoir that the film was a 'chaotic collection of bits and pieces' when he was asked to do the editing, 'and of all Allen's films, with the least promise for popular success.' It was he who suggested concentrating on the relationship with Annie (Diane Keaton), even though that meant shooting additional material. Allen observed 'It was originally a picture about me, exclusively . . . about my life, my thoughts, my ideas, my background,' a statement whose delusions of grandeur are perhaps only rivalled by those of his co-writer, Marshall Brickman, 'All that stuff I had written was cerebral, surreal, highly intellectual, overliterate, overeducated, self-conscious comedy.' Such revelations, of course, hardly make Allen appear disciplined and even with Rosenblum's help the film remains Hollywood's most ramshackle ego-trip since the days of Mae West.

Allen escaped from his self-absorption long enough to make **Interiors** (1978), a po-faced drama of a family, influenced by Ingmar Bergman and sporting would-be tart comments on literary society. It is as

appalling as other Hollywood attempts at an art movie, and **Manhattan** (1979) dismays as much because it is virtually a remake of *Annie Hall*. It has more plot, and finally has a point to make about certain sections of New York society – or at least Allen's own quasi-literary, show-business set with its exhaustive egos and emotional demands. The soundtrack pounds with the melodies of Gershwin, who was never so demeaned; the film further strives for 'class' by being in black and white, but that only helps to distinguish it from *Annie Hall*. The title is not inappropriate, but they could have called it *Ants in My Pants of 1979*★ to remind us how much film humour has degenerated since the days of Preston Sturges.

The director James Frawley has displayed a more positive comic talent, at any rate in **Kid Blue** (1973) and **The Big Bus** (1976). The former is the first successful spoof Western (of many) since *Cat Ballou*, and the latter a parody of disaster movies. Frawley can pick over the bones of old

★Joel McCrea was making *Ants in My Pants of 1939* in *Sullivan's Travels*.

films and still be fresh and amusing, as few other practitioners of this particular pro-liferating genre, but **The Muppet Movie** (1979) indicates that something was very wrong. It may be that he had no control over those responsible for the dismally unoriginal story-line featuring the Mup-pets, the grotesque animal puppets, or he may have been defeated by the limitations set by the producers, I.T.C., who have an internationally famous penchant for wild-ly extravagant film disasters.

In the matter of humour, the actor Alan Alda has provided some sharply satirical thrusts in the two films he wrote for him-self to appear in, **The Seduction of Joe Tynan** (1979), directed by Jerry Schatz-berg, and **The Four Seasons** (1981), directed by Alda himself. Alda returns Hollywood comedy to its old level, less by wit than observation, capturing splendidly the smugness and sentimentality of the bourgeoisie. *Joe Tynan* charts the submis-sion of a liberal senator (Alda) to the cor-ruptions attendant on success in Washing-ton, and *The Four Seasons* follows the for-tunes of three married couples as they slip into middle-age.

Jonathan Demme, a protégé of Roger Corman, has directed two films in the same vein, **Citizens Band** (1977), written by Paul Brinkman, and **Melvin and Howard** (1980), written by Bo Goldman. Both celebrate the little folk out there in middle America, the first in its cross-section portrait of some small town people brought together by C.B. radio, and the second in its curious tale, based on fact, of a young man (Paul Le Mat) who believes that Howard Hughes (Jason Robards) has left him most of his fortune. Demme's affection for his milieux is matched by the playing of Mr Le Mat, who is in both films: his round-faced optimism and in-genuity recall some heroes of the Silent era, but the inference that he is essentially mediocre is new and touching. Neither film was popular, despite particularly en-thusiastic reviews for the second of them.

Martin Scorsese (b. 1942) is, Coppola aside, the best-known of the film-makers sponsored by Corman. After his first, amateur film he was invited to make **Box-car Bertha** (1972), virtually a copy of *Bonnie and Clyde* except that Scorsese is less romantic in re-creating the bloodletting gangsters of the Depression. The film was

little seen, but Scorsese was encouraged to make **Mean Streets** (1973) by an in-dependent producer, Jonathan T. Taplin, who raised its budget of $480,000 from private sources (or, according to Scorsese himself, $350,000). The only distributor willing to handle the film was Warners, which entered it for the New York Film Festival, but it was rarely shown until revived after Scorsese's later successes. It is a New York version of *I Vitelloni*, with much blood and violence, dialogue which is less explicit except in the matter of four-letter words, and no discernible point.

Scorsese established his reputation with a film which is the reverse of that, **Alice Doesn't Live Here Anymore** (1974). He was recommended for it by Coppola when its star, Ellen Burstyn, was determined that Robert Getchell's screenplay should become a film for cinemas rather than television. Her earlier Oscar nomination was sufficient warranty for Warners to finance the $2 million budget, and she was awarded an Oscar for her portrait of Alice, an ordinary housewife who, newly widowed, sets out to fulfil her ambition of returning to Monterey. She had been a band singer, so she resorts to that, finding kindness in Phoenix and then in Tucson. As she journeys on that road she is at one with all the other travellers in American films at this time, but plucky, gently sar-castic and self-mocking in a manner unlike

Martin Scorsese was one of the most talked-about directors of the Seventies, but few people, compara-tively, actually went to see his films. The exception was *Alice Doesn't Live Here Anymore*, with Kris Kristofferson and Ellen Burstyn. Indeed, it was one of those films, like *Paper Moon* and *The Goodbye Girl*, which brought back people who had stopped going to the cinema years ago. One reason was that these films had the qualities of the films they used to like, but this was the only one of the three that did not particularly set out to be that way.

other screen heroines in many a year. Since she had been taken for granted by her husband, and is ill-treated by a lover (Harvey Keitel) in Phoenix, and as, in Miss Burstyn's words, she 'is a woman grappling with the change of consciousness we are all grappling with', the film was popular with supporters of Women's Lib, but more than the other 'road' films, its origins go back to *It Happened One Night*, with audiences wanting Alice to settle down with the gentle giant (Kris Kristofferson) who is attracted to her.

The film's success enabled Scorsese to find backing for **Taxi Driver** (1976), written by Paul Schrader (b. 1946). Schrader went on to direct two interesting films (q.v.), but we might pause to examine his antecedents since they are pertinent to this particularly unpleasant film. He had intended to become a minister in the Christian Reformed Church, and had not seen a film till he was eighteen. He subsequently studied film at U.C.L.A., and edited a movie magazine, in which he criticised some current screenwriters, 'their writing is flashy, brilliant and inherently unorganised. I am thinking primarily of certain scripts by such writers as John Milius (*Judge Roy Bean*, *Jeremiah Johnson*), Terry Malick (*Pocket Money*), Robert Dillon (*Prime Cut*), Walter Hill (*The Getaway*) and David Ward (*Steelyard Blues*). The premise of these scripts seems to be to create Great Scenes involving Great Characters, then stringing them together like beads on a rosary. The end result is not so much a well crafted script but a pastiche of touches, flashes of brilliance and momentary insights.' He might have been writing of *Taxi Driver*, which he wrote from his own experiences, according to *The Village Voice*, as 'a loner, sleeping days and wandering around Los Angeles at night. He was depressed. His nocturnal hours were spent riding aimlessly in taxicabs, drinking, and taking in an occasional porno flick': thus the protagonist (Robert de Niro) of *Taxi Driver*, except that he is a cabbie in New York, a city exclusively populated by what he calls 'garbage'. Foiled at assassinating a presidential candidate, he murders a twelve-year-old hooker and subsequently becomes a national hero, which is deeply and cheaply ironic, since audiences know that he is psychotic. The scene of the murder showed more blood

(splattered on the walls and furniture of the room in which it takes place) than I think has ever been seen in a major Hollywood movie, and many spectators found it as offensive as it was unnecessary. Scorsese explained that he had seen an episode of a T.V. series in which twenty people were killed but 'not a drop of blood was shed. That's ridiculous. It's unrealistic. I don't do things that way.' It was no surprise to learn that the young psychopath who attempted to assassinate President Reagan in 1981 had seen this film several times and was obsessed by Jodie Foster, who plays the teenage whore.

Having failed to find the truth behind the malaise of contemporary New Yorkers, Scorsese set out in **New York, New York** (1977) to find the truth behind such old Hollywood movies as *Orchestra Wives*. This truth, it would seem, is that the musicians of the Forties were bores or boors: de Niro is objectionable when first seen and never becomes likeable, as he and his wife (Liza Minnelli) row for two and a half hours – undoubtedly the reason why the film failed to find a public. It originally ran for three hours, and what remains is so superficial that the mind boggles at the content of the missing material. The truth is in Miss Minnelli's performance and nowhere else.

Interviewed during this period, little emerged from Scorsese about his craft or the medium other than that he admired Powell and Pressburger, 'because they took a lot of chances and made movie magic'. He himself could never be accused of making movie magic, but he took chances with **Raging Bull** (1980) in that, apart from the most common four-letter word, the dialogue is virtually inaudible. In humourless and pretentious fashion it strains at recounting the career of Jake La Motta, a boxing champion of the Forties. Towards the end it manages at last to make an interesting point on the aftermath of celebrity, concluding with La Motta rehearsing Brando's taxicab speech from *On the Waterfront* – and in case we have missed the point of that, it is spelled out in a biblical quotation on the end title: 'Once I was blind and now I can see.' De Niro won an Oscar for his performance, presumably for managing to put on 250 pounds to play the middle-aged La Motta, a 'first' in the annals of this award. De Niro, in other circumstances, might have been able to illuminate some facet of La Motta's interesting career and personality, but the script and direction seem resolutely opposed to any such ideas.

Since Schrader worked on the screenplay it is rewarding to find considerable content in two of the films which he wrote for himself to direct, **Blue Collar** (1978) and **Hardcore** (1979). They are too schematic, and not entirely well constructed, but they are far more successful than *Taxi Driver* in examining the reasons for the undercurrent of violence in contemporary American life. *Blue Collar* follows the exploits of three Detroit factory workers – one white (Harvey Keitel) and two black (Richard Pryor, Yaphet Kotto) – as they, apathetically at first, realise the extent of union corruption. Their surroundings – the factory canteen, the cathouse, the suburban homes – are inventively portrayed, and a reminder that the world of the artisan had hardly been seen since *On the Waterfront*. Schrader provides a more convincing ending than Brando being martyred, but whereas the earlier film was outstanding in its day, and is still powerful, this is neither. *Hardcore* is forceful only in its portrait of the seedy porno parlours of Los Angeles; perhaps its most interesting aspect is the autobiographical section at the beginning, set in the religious community of Schrader's home town, Grand Rapids, Michigan. A teenage girl fails to return there after an expedition to California, and when her father (George C. Scott) finds that she is making pornographic films he sets out to find out why; along the way he makes friends with a girl (Season Hubley) who started selling her body at fifteen, ten years ago, and can still be bruised, though she tries not to show it. Unlike *Taxi Driver* these are moral films, but they do not give the impression of a sophisticated talent, one that can teach us something about life. That quality – so prevalent in the early Thirties films of, say, Frank Borzage, Leo McCarey, et al – has gone from American movies.

It is a quality especially absent from the films by friends and colleagues George Lucas (b. 1945) and Steven Spielberg (b. 1945). Lucas began as a protégé of Coppola, and they are linked professionally with Schrader and Scorsese, if only by John Milius, writer, producer and director,

who has worked (sometimes uncredited) with all of them. Lucas and Spielberg are the products of film schools and, it would seem, endless boyhood matinees watching Flash Gordon serials when not being indoctrinated by the Sunday comics. Spielberg acquired a reputation directing for television, especially with **Duel** (1971), a simple but tense account of a car driver menaced by a truck, based on a story by Richard Matheson. It was shown to some acclaim in cinemas abroad, causing Universal to promote him to a large-budgeted cinema feature, **The Sugarland Express** (1974). It might be termed *Dog Day Afternoon* on wheels, and like that, it is based on fact and concerns petty crooks: an escaped convict (William Atherton), his wife (Goldie Hawn), their hostage and the police. During both films a massive police force is immobilised, and Spielberg, like Lumet, has much fun with the serried ranks of cops and their autos with the flashing lights and screaming sirens. It is an enjoyable movie, as is **Jaws** (1975), expertly handled by Spielberg and then the most financially successful film in cinema history. Its takings exceeded *The Godfather* in just seventy-eight days, and like that – and *Love Story* and *The Exorcist* – it had started as a manufactured bestseller of dubious merit which as a film apparently everyone wanted to see. The books have in common writers all weaned in show business: this one, by Peter Benchley, concerned a small Long Island resort whose season is threatened with ruin by the presence of a killer shark in the waters.

Yaphet Kotto, left, Harvey Keitel and Richard Pryor relaxing after a hard day in the auto-factory in *Blue Collar*, written by Paul Schrader, who with it made his debut as a director. The three of them, and especially Keitel, find that they have bitten off more than they can chew in attempting to fight union malpractices.

Mark Hamill, centre, Alec Guinness and Harrison Ford, plus, at the far left, one of the creatures of space in the hugely successful *Star Wars*. You can buy replicas of that creature and its fellows, together with the assorted robots, in toyshops the world over; undoubtedly the marketing of these artefacts, and their appeal to children, has been partly responsible for the success of this film and its two sequels, *The Empire Strikes Back* and *The Return of the Jedi*.

Meanwhile, Lucas had had a success with **American Graffiti** (1973), which Coppola had managed to set up for him after his own success with *The Godfather*. *The Last Picture Show* and *Summer of '42* had recently demonstrated that audiences were interested in the youth of yesteryear, and *American Graffiti* went back only ten years, with as much affection, but without the drama of the one or the sentimentality of the other. The three films made a fetish of getting the period details right, as if to emphasise the changes, but little has changed: life in this small Californian town is much like that anywhere else – and except that there is less booze and the youngsters are from the proletariat, they are little different from those celebrated in 'The Beautiful and the Damned'.

Simultaneously Spielberg came up with **Close Encounters of the Third Kind** (1977) and Lucas with **Star Wars** (1977), both science fiction epics. Spielberg thought up his fancy while listening to the song 'When You Wish Upon a Star' from *Pinocchio*, and the use of that song at the end (though cut from the final print) reveals that Spielberg was going where Kubrick had already trod. *Dr Strangelove* is not

the only source raided for this overblown space opera: *You Only Live Twice* is another, as well as any number of inept scifi movies of the Fifties; and the antiwar theme of *It Came from Outer Space* has been converted into a quasi-religious message. John Milius admires the film for its 'lack of pretension. Look at *Julia*. It's preachy, liberal preachy, a female macho film. *Close Encounters* is innocent, with wide-eyed, wonderful amazement.' This innocent creature was, however, considered sufficiently important to be reissued a couple of years later as *Close Encounters of the Third Kind: the Special Edition*, having become special by virtue of some minor changes made by Spielberg. This had not happened before in film history.

It is only slightly more bearable than the falsely naive *Star Wars*, where the films of the past are supposedly parodied amidst the reigning gadgetry. Like *Nickelodeon*, it is stuffed with insider's conceits and no firm narrative to hold it together. The reviews outside the U.S. were bemused or unkind, but just as *Jaws* justified the enormous pre-release publicity budget, so *Star Wars* went on to take twice the money to date of any film yet made. Significantly the expensive and much-publicised sequel – the first of a projected series – was seen by only half the number who went to the original. In America, that is: elsewhere it did even worse, if that is a word to be used about a film which was nevertheless extremely profitable. Lucas had handed the direction over to Irvin Kershner, but to little benefit, except perhaps to sub-teenage audiences. In *Newsweek* David Ansen noted what the two films 'conspicuously lack: story (as opposed to action), characters (as opposed to cartoon figures) and any real emotional resonance'.

Spielberg indulged another fantasy with **1941** (1979), with Milius working on the script, which is incoherent, and one thinks of them besottedly devouring the carrion of old Hollywood. The initial idea is based on *The Russians Are Coming, The Russians Are Coming*, that of American panic at the thought of invasion of a foreign power; the vast cast of characters chasing all over Los Angeles recalls *It's a Mad, Mad, Mad, Mad World*, and since the time is 1941 we may note that the military are portrayed as even more blockheaded than in the movies of that time – recalled by the presence of John Belushi, whose likeness to Lou Costello is not the only resemblance; while the various scenes of planes and tanks out of control seem to have been meant to appeal to those who liked the 'trips' in *2001*. Columbia, which had made a sizeable profit on its investment of $18 million in *Close Encounters*, nevertheless baulked at the budget of $32 million, so shared the risk with Universal. Both companies lost heavily, but this has been the only failure in the Lucas-Spielberg parade of hits.

However, it was in the climate of failure that every studio passed up **Raiders of the Lost Ark** (1981), except Paramount, which sunk $20 million into its imbecilities. Spielberg directed and the producer was Lucas; who explained that it was 'based on the serials I loved when I was a kid: action movies set in exotic locales with a cliff-hanger every second. I wondered why they didn't make movies like that anymore. I still wanted to see them.' So apparently did many others, for this film was hugely popular, despite more illogicalities than ever appeared in a Republic or Monogram serial. The hero (Harrison Ford) is intrepid, but he is not (like Cooper in *High Noon* or Bogart in *The African Queen*) vulnerable, or afraid. He is pushed into tight corners, but he escapes without conviction or ingenuity: guns or friendly natives materialise out of free air (he is even blown up at one point, but turns up unharmed a few minutes later). Worse, the piece is relentlessly solemn, unlike de Broca's infinitely superior *L'Homme de Rio*.

The film's popularity made Spielberg and Lucas even more the golden boys of the industry, but in the meantime Columbia dropped **E.T.: the Extra-Terrestrial** (1982) after spending $1 million in development. Universal picked it up only because it had turned down *Star Wars* (which went to 20th Century-Fox), and then saw *E.T.* become the quickest success in cinema history, overtaking all these other films at the box office. It is about the friendship of a young boy with a creature left here from another planet, and you have to believe, to start with, that small boys are not afraid of squidgey monsters. The relationship between the two is not developed, beyond a manipulative sequence where the boy at school 'feels' what E.T. is doing at home. The thinness of the plot suddenly gives way to a chase, when the scientists come for E.T., and the pursuit plagiarises that in *The Great Escape* and the end of *Miracolo in Milano*. Spielberg's now familiar style – serried rows of police cars, views of the city by night, the camera tracking back from lights mistily before it – is no consolation. In Britain, two weekly critics, John Coleman in the *New Statesman* and Peter Ackroyd in *The Spectator*, invoked Disney, and both used the word 'infantilism'. The broadcaster Kenneth Robinson called it 'the worst film I have ever seen . . . nauseating, sentimental rubbish', and I must confess that its popularity puzzles me: perhaps with so many sabre-rattlers in charge of our destinies it is nice to know that Out There there are creatures who love children, while our scientists are the forces for destruction. The best that may be said for the film was put by Joseph L. Mankiewicz, 'charming, but as intellectually demanding as the old Lassie films.'

Both Mankiewicz and Elia Kazan have observed that today's films are like comic strips, so that the dialogue should ideally be in balloons. Another who agrees is the screenwriter William Goldman, who observed that few of them prompt new

The Superman pictures – there have been three to date – are the best of the spate of movies at this time based on comic strips (or seeming like it). This is a scene from the first, which has a turgid, long beginning in that planet, Krypton, which is supposed to be the home of Superman (Christopher Reeve). The film improves mightily as it establishes him as a gauche New York journalist and is even better when he gets into his gear to fly – in this case helping fellow reporter Lois Lane (Margot Kidder) to do like- wise, not that she recognises him as the guy from the office.

perceptions, specifically mentioning *Dumbo* as a film of the past which does. I am not sure whether the compliment might be paid to **Superman** (1978) or **Superman II** (1980), but, unlike the Lucas-Spielberg fantasies, you are likely to leave the cinema feeling much more cheerful. These two films are based on an old comic strip, and were produced by Alexander Salkind, who after a quarrel with Richard Donner, who had directed *Superman*, replaced him on the second film with Richard Lester (his director on *The Three Musketeers*). The two films are interchangeable, and in any case what matters are the special effects, which vary from the fair to the miraculous. The first film has a pretentious opening, and an inadequate villain (Gene Hackman), though this actor has the knack of the villainy in the second film – and is joined by some other relishable opponents for Superman (Christopher Reeve), who is, despite his name, occasionally vulnerable and in situations done with far more relish and wit than those in *Raiders of the Lost Ark*. The film is magical whenever he starts to fly; the second of the two films was even more popular than the first, and I imagine that they and *Superman III* will enchant successive generations of children.

The chief exponent of the comic strip film has been Michael Cimino (b. 1943), though in his case they have masqueraded as serious works. After beginning as a screenwriter he wrote and directed a

derivative vehicle for Clint Eastwood, **Thunderbolt and Lightfoot** (1974). A British company, E.M.I., was virtually the only studio willing to back **The Deer Hunter** (1978), a three-hour movie on a subject Hollywood disliked, the Vietnam War, but Universal bought the American rights on the strength of Robert de Niro's participation. He plays a steelworker who is conscripted and goes to Vietnam, where his buddies play Russian roulette while he has some Errol Flynnish adventures; then he returns home disillusioned. The film particularly roused the ire of those war correspondents who had been in Vietnam: Gloria Emerson wrote in *The New York Times* that 'Cimino has cheapened and degraded the War as no one else had', and that journal reprinted John Pilger's attack in the *New Statesman*, 'The Deer Hunter and its apologists insult the memory of every American who died in Vietnam.' In Hollywood the Academy voted Oscars to the film for Best Picture and Best Direction.

Those Oscars were responsible for the budget of **Heaven's Gate** (1980) escalating from an original $11 million to $36 million, since United Artists acceded to all Cimino's demands, such as transporting cast and crew to Oxford, England, which stands in for Harvard in the prologue. One set had to be dismantled and rebuilt since it was three feet out from Cimino's calculations; a skating sequence took six months of rehearsal. We may doubt whether the entire inhabitants of Western towns took to dancing on roller skates or whether they indulged in mooning (i.e. the practice of exposing their bare buttocks, in this case on the battle field). In fact, like *The Deer Hunter*, virtually every element of this film is there to make us marvel at the skill of its maker. Its subject is The Johnson County War, and certainly the film, rich in symbolism and set-pieces, is visually handsome. The photographer is Vilmos Zsigmond, who shot *McCabe and Mrs Miller* for Robert Altman, whose brothel scenes are reproduced here; one scene is borrowed from *Days of Heaven*; while the central situation is taken from Altman's film and *Jules et Jim*, with aspects added from Eastman's films. The film opened to lethal reviews, and since most of them called it incoherent, it was withdrawn and cut from 225 minutes to 148, with some refilming and changes adding a further $7 million to the cost. It reopened to equally poor reviews and such poor business that *The New York Times* observed that at the rate of attendance it had cost United Artists $4,800 for each customer. *Variety* announced that one in four Americans was needed to see this film before it could begin to recover its cost. There were discussions of further cuts, till someone observed that it would be cheaper to show the trailer.

The film's debacle was summed up by the magazine *American Film*, 'Cimino is now less a film-maker than a·human bench-mark, as in "Post-Cimino Hollywood", the personification of the arrogant, profligate, irresponsible Young Movie Brat Director who has supposedly wrecked Hollywood's prosperity. The bitter words of veteran producer Pandro S. Berman speak for many: "When producers were supreme, Hollywood was at its peak. Now that the young director has taken over, Hollywood has gone to hell." ' This particular young director, in Cannes for a festival showing, told *Le Matin* that when Kennedy was killed many people felt better, since his brilliance reminded them that they had wasted their lives. He did not, he went on, compare himself with Kennedy, but certain journalists wanted to destroy him for not dissimilar reasons – since to them he represented success and talent.

Heaven's Gate is the most spectacular of Hollywood's follies in recent years, and it is possibly not quite the worst film. The industry which once produced entertainments for adults now caters to its teenage audiences with witless campus sex comedies and inane stories of the paranormal. There have been a few good American films in the past few years, including the enormously popular **Smokey and the Bandit** (1977), a Burt Reynolds vehicle directed by his friend Hal Needham, a former stuntman. It is clearly a committee film, and manipulative, but it is fresh and spontaneous – qualities unexpectedly found in what could have been yet another film with Reynolds as a good ol' boy involved in yet more car chases. He is a lawbreaker and a friend of whores, but withal a courtly Southerner, whereas his foe is a petty, stupid, fat sheriff (Jackie Gleason); the best of the film is in his relationship with a New York girl (Sally Field), whose cultural values centre on

'A Chorus Line' and Stephen Sondheim, neither of which he has ever heard.

Body Heat (1981) is the first film directed by Lawrence Kasdan, who also wrote it after contributing to the scripts of *The Empire Strikes Back* and *Raiders of the Lost Ark*. I am not sure that it is an admirable movie, since it is another that feeds on the films of the past, but it does so more entertainingly than most. Kasdan's sources are *Double Indemnity* and the 1946 version of *The Postman Always Rings Twice*, but when taxed with plagiarising James M. Cain he observed, soundly, that the plot had been around since Aeschylus. After the wife (Kathleen Turner) and her lover (William Hurt) have successfully bumped off her ageing husband (Richard Crenna), Kasdan provides a hundred twists, some of which strain credibility. Hurt is excellent as bungler at his job, the law, and a stud in the sack; and the bright dia-

Burt Reynolds has worked long and hard at perfecting his image, that of the good ol' boy, fallible and only too human in his weaknesses. His popularity has been steadfast now for years, most understandably when teamed with the delightful Sally Field in *Smokey and the Bandit*, an unpretentious entertainment which attracted a large proportion of the world's population into its cinemas.

Michael Douglas and Jane Fonda, co-producers and stars of *The China Syndrome*, which hoped to alert us to the dangers inherent in manufacturing nuclear energy. Those who, in the film's plot, know of a potential breakdown try to hush it up, and would have succeeded but for the two investigative television reporters that you see here – not that the film is entirely sanguine about the power of T.V.

logue is at its best when two cops, friends of his, are not sure when and how to nab him.

The China Syndrome (1979) is a thriller on the dangers of nuclear power. A generating station may be on the verge of a breakdown, which would be fatal to the local population: two investigative reporters (Michael Douglas, Jane Fonda) need the proof necessary to present their evidence, and seek the cooperation of the plant supervisor (Jack Lemmon). The director, James Bridges, uses some of the cinema's oldest tricks to heighten tension. The screenplay by Mike Gray (who originated the project) and T. S. Cook is like that of *All the President's Men* in presenting its heroes as fearless investigators into the activities of the powerful; it is concerned to the proper degree, but never as fair as its supposedly impartial approach would imply. As Lemmon prepares to spill the beans, his boss decides that they cannot

just stand by and watch this idiot wash out a billion dollar investment. As Miss Fonda, who produced the film with Douglas, observed, its subject is greed. It is also about responsibility, by inference increasingly rare in an automated society; and as the film was premiered there was an accident at a nuclear power station in Harrisburg, Pennsylvania. The three leading players, especially Lemmon, are superb.

Warren Beatty is another star who has turned producer and director as well, starting with the impertinently titled **Heaven Can Wait** (1978), sharing the second job with Buck Henry and the writing with Elaine May. It is not a remake of Lubitsch's film, but of *Here Comes Mr Jordan*, of such poor quality as to expect little of **Reds** (1981), directed by Beatty and written by him with the British dramatist Trevor Griffiths. As filming of *Reds* stretched on for two years and the budget mounted to $43 million (provided by Barclays Bank, which then bought the film and leased it back to Paramount, both companies benefiting under British tax laws) many anticipated a second *Heaven's Gate*, but *Reds* turned out to be one of the most important and stimulating films for years. It is the story of Jack Reed (Beatty) and Louise Bryant (Diane Keaton), and certain sequences are deplorable – such as the dog which whines outside their door whenever they make love. As a love story, it is mediocre, but as an extended comment on American communism it is brave and sometimes illuminating. There is no doubt that Beatty regards Reed as the Alger Hiss of his day, American enemy to the American state: after publishing his book on the Russian Revolution Reed was militant in founding the American Communist Party, so that when he disappeared inside the U.S.S.R the State Department seized the chance to dismiss him as a non-person. The first half of the film is the better, with its portrait of a pseudo-intellectual set in New York and a literary clique at Cape Cod – with Jack Nicholson, as Eugene O'Neill, taking every scene in which he appears; the second half has impressive moments, if only in giving expression to the official view that Reed's political beliefs constituted subversion. Like Bryant's spirited defence of her agnosticism and the triumphant playing of the Internationale, this is something one never expected to find in an 'American' movie. In the end it hedges its bets, though remaining ambiguous as to whether Reed became disillusioned with Soviet communism or was merely tactful. The more romantic aspects of the plot are offset by those contemporaries of Reed who interrupt the action to offer sometimes irrelevant recollections; and in the same manner reservations about Beatty's boyish Reed are offset by his obvious dedication to the project. Miss Keaton's Bryant fails to sustain the three-hour running time and is a libel on a lady who was much sharper than made to appear. Beatty was awarded an Oscar for his direction.

I doubt whether the film recovered its costs, but the only one of these films to be a clear failure was *Cutter and Bone* or **Cutter's Way** (1981) as it was renamed in an effort to attract a public which had shunned it on its first appearance. Like *Who'll Stop the Rain?*, it is about Vietnam veterans in California who have gone to the bad – the feckless philanderer Bone (Jeff Bridges), his chum Cutter (John Heard), shorn of one eye, a leg and half an arm, plus Cutter's wife (Lisa Eichhorn), who has taken to drink. The two men make it their mission to bring to justice an oil tycoon they believe to be a murderer, but this film is less a thriller than a mood piece – and the mood is mysterious and not unlike that of the *films noirs* of the Forties. Jeffrey Alan Fiskin wrote it from a novel by Newton Thornburgh, and the director is Ivan Passer, who until this sharp upturn had made increasingly feeble movies after leaving Czechoslovakia.

Another European director, Costa-Gavras, was on more predictable form with his first American film, **Missing** (1982), which created an uproar in the States, since the news media in some parts of the country have been unforthcoming about C.I.A. involvement South of the Border. The film firmly states that the U.S. government connived at the killing of a young American during the 1973 right-wing coup in Chile. Edmund Horman, his father – played in the film by Jack

Lemmon – later sued eleven high-ranking officials for $4 million, but though the case was thrown out for lack of evidence, no commentator was convinced by the three-page rebuttal by the State Department issued immediately after the film's premiere. Horman's lawyer, Thomas Hauser, wrote a book about the case, and it is that which the director and Donald Stewart drew upon for their screenplay. I did not care for the devices by which the hawkish father warms to his daughter-in-law (Sissy Spacek) and his dead son's radical views, but the facts are as persuasively presented as in *Etat de Siège*, Costa-Gavras's earlier piece about C.I.A. dirty work in Latin America. The movie is as compulsive as *Prince of the City*, which came out at the same time, and since after equally warm notices *Missing* was the more popular, we may suppose that stars, or at least names, are still a factor in audience appeal. I also make the analogy because Costa-Gavras, like Lumet, has always stressed that he is not a career director, but a 'film-maker who just gets on with the job'. In view of some of the films discussed in this chapter thank God for both of them.

Gratitude may be felt towards such films as are based on fact, like so many of the best of the early Eighties – *Reds*, *Gallipoli*, *Chariots of Fire* – even if these are only following recent European patterns. Being factual in itself is not a virtue, but since the industry cannot, or rather is unable, to return to making the sort of entertainments on which its greatness was founded, such movies are preferable to those which are no more than children's picture books. Those making films specifically aimed at the predominantly teenage audiences of today may not realise that the more intelligent films of recent years – *One Flew Over the Cuckoo's Nest*, *All the President's Men*, *Kramer vs. Kramer*, *Missing* – have all been enormously profitable. Lucas and Spielberg may be making themselves and their backers very wealthy: at the same time they are doing their medium a profound disservice.

Envoi

EVEN AS the bulk of this book was with the printer I was seeing new movies and I feel bound to include a word or so about those made by directors discussed in the text – together with a brief comment on some of the interesting new ones which have emerged.

As I do not wish to conclude this history on a graceless note I shall start with the disappointments and move on to those movies which seem to me to be successful. Ermanno Olmi, a great director, in *CamminaCammina* (1983), reconstructed the Journey of the Magi but without achieving much dramatic tension. The film is not, however, as misguided as Louis Malle's *My Dinner with André* (1981), a record of a particularly fatuous conversation between two minor New York theatre people. Nikita Mikhalkov's *Without Witnesses* (1983) is also a duologue, between a man and his ex-wife, but if it has more action it is equally devoid of humour – at least as far as this non-Soviet observer is concerned. Jerzy Skolimowski's *Moonlighting* (1982), about some Polish construction workers in London at the time of the crackdown on Solidarity, is lacking in content and in conviction, and the same is true of Martin Scorsese's *The King of Comedy* (1983), despite a typically resourceful performance by Robert de Niro as a New York schmuck with unorthodox methods of achieving fame in television. Francis Coppola followed the poor *The Outsiders* (1983) with the even worse *Rumble Fish* (1983), also based on a 'teenage' novel by S. E. Hinton – thus, as David Denby observed in *New York* magazine, signing away his reputation twice in one year.

My own expectations were less for Nagisa Oshima's *Merry Christmas, Mr Lawrence* (1983), an Anglo-Japanese production financed in New Zealand, and in the event they were met because the source, Laurens Van der Post's novel 'The Sower and the Seed', had been robbed of its point – that during the War the Japanese did not lose those qualities which were the reverse of their much-publicised barbarism. Just after I saw this thin enterprise I saw a good film with the same theme, Krzysztof Zanussi's *Wege in der Nacht* (1982), made for German television. The study of the relationship between conqueror and conquered – in this case the Germans and the Poles – is closer to *Le Silence de la Mer* than to Oshima's film, but this has intelligence as that has not.

Shyam Benegal was at less than his best with *Market Place* (1983), lingering for too long on the details of life within a *kotha* – which for the sake of brevity can be described as the Indian equivalent of a geisha house – then bringing in far too many strands of plot after the two-hour mark, which he cannot resolve in the remaining 50 minutes. Manuel Gutiérrez Aragón offered a further collaboration with his co-writer Luis Megino, *Demonios en el Jardin* (1982), which looks at a prosperous family of grocers in the Civil War and ten years later, but apart from some shafts of humour it would again seem to confirm that his best film, *Camada Negra*, owed its quality to Borau's contribution. *El Sur* (1983) is Victor Erice's first film since *El Espiritu de la Colmena*, which it too closely resembles. It is a quiet, civilised piece, but Erice's aim can only be pondered upon, since he intended a much longer film before leaving the project after a quarrel with the producer, Elias Quarejeta, who assembled what was shot into the resulting 94-

minute movie. Shohei Imamura's *The Ballad of Narayama* (1983) received the Grand Prix at the Cannes Film Festival: this remake of Kinoshita's similarly titled film included material from another novel by Fukasawa (also filmed before, by Ichikawa in 1958), but these additions turned out to be intractable, putting much of the film into the 'grunting peasants' genre. However, when Imamura remains with his central subject, the old lady who must be left on the hillside to die, he is at his magisterial best. Ichikawa himself did a new version of the novel by Junichiro Tanizaki, *The Makioka Sisters* (1983), filmed by Yutaka Abe in 1950 and Koji Shima in 1959; it is neatly told in the manner of the movies of the period when it is set, 1938, but too verbose.

Among other established directors, Wajda perhaps provided the most satisfactory work with *Danton* (1983), vividly presenting the conflicts between Danton, Robespierre and their factions; the film also has the most convincing French Revolution the cinema has given us – a time of hurry, scurry and confusion. Sidney Lumet believes that *Daniel* (1983) is his best film, which it conceivably is; but by choosing to film E. L. Doctorow's fictional account of what it was like to be the son of Jewish left-wing parents electrocuted for treachery he avoided any confrontation with the Rosenbergs and their guilt, thus bringing upon his head the wrath of American critics – not entirely without justice. However, the film deals intelligently with those who choose to be Communists in America, and passionately with the effect on children of their parents' 'aberrant' behaviour. It is its own film, going its own way, with more to say than most.

The public greatly appreciated *Tootsie* (1982), presumably because it has a cast of likeable characters played by talented people rather than because it is pointed or funny about its subject, that of an unemployed actor (Dustin Hoffman) who dons female attire to get a job in a soap opera. It is an amiable film, and with *Absence of Malice* confirms that Sidney Pollack has firm control of his directorial skills. As much may be said of George Roy Hill and *The World According to Garp* (1983), cleverly written by Steve Tesich in such a way that the confusions of John Irving's pseudo-Gunther Grass novel become

positive statements on nonconformity, fame and infidelity. Walter Hill's *48 HRS* (1983), though unforgivably foul-mouthed, is a fine audience-rousing thriller, easily exploiting the personality of a new star, Eddie Murphy. John Sayles proves himself only a competent director with *The Return of the Secaucus Seven* (1980), but his script, about some former peace protesters meeting again before the onslaught of middle age, is far better than might have been expected from the exploitation movies that he had written for other people. Woody Allen's *Zelig* (1983) is a beautifully done cod documentary on a famous figure of the Twenties and Thirties; it is not as funny as it might have been, but always likeable.

Any comments on *Daniel* may be applied to *The Ploughman's Lunch* (1983), though it is by no means as interesting. But it is such a heady experience to find a British movie even aware of politics that we may forgive some shortcomings in its story of a media figure (Jonathan Pryce) so ambitious that his integrity comes unstuck – if it was ever there. It is a first cinema movie for the director Richard Eyre and the writer Ian McEwan, even if designed to go quickly to television's Channel 4, partly responsible for its financing. Few of Channel 4's other movies have been notable but *Angel* (1982) deserved its cinema showings. Neil Jordan wrote and directed this Irish thriller in which the villains are probably IRA men, showing in his first feature a mastery of his medium. I am less sure about Geoff Murphy, the young New Zealand director of *Goodbye Pork Pie* (1981), especially as this 'road' movie is often derivative; but it is an exhilarating film, and one which uses the countryside eloquently. Australia continues to export superior works, notably Peter Weir's *The Year of Living Dangerously* (1983), a portrait of the world of the foreign correspondent as it existed in Djakarta at the time of the attempted Communist coup of 1965, and Igor Auzins's *We of the Never Never* (1982), set in the Outback at the turn of the century and based on yet another memoir by a courageous Australian lady.

I have also seen an exceptional film from Iran, *The Cycle* (1974), directed by Dariush Mehrjui, who made it clandestinely under the Shah's regime. Its subject is poverty, as

Envoi

Here is a scene from *Yol*, with Tarik Akan and Serif Sezer. One of the most moving statements about life in the Third World, the film was made despite a series of extraordinary difficulties and obstacles.

experienced by some down and outs who sell their blood to entrepreneurs who in turn sell it to the local hospital where, with the exception of one doctor, the staff are stuck in inertia and apathy. It is a film of great passion and contains images of such bleak beauty that it seems a wholly original work. These qualities it shares with the films of Yilmaz Güney (b. 1937), a former Turkish matinee idol who has directed movies the reverse of those in which he acted. Indeed, they were a new departure for the Turkish cinema, and since those that we have seen are critical of both the Turkish regime and feudal life as it is encouraged to persist it is not surprising that he has spent much of his recent life in

prison, reputedly for murder. While incarcerated he wrote and supervised *The Herd* (1978) and *Yol* (1982), both of which were directed for him by friends, respectively Zeki Ökten and Şerif Gören. Escaping into exile, he wrote and directed *Le Mur* (1983) with the aid of financing from the French government. The form of this film, a composite portrait from which emerged the dramas of certain individuals, is common to all three. It is the least of them – though still extraordinary – perhaps because of the limitations of making a film abroad, in Turkish, about conditions in a Turkish prison. *The Herd* is an exceptional piece about a fairly primitive tribesman confronted with life in modern Ankara; and *Yol*, a masterwork, follows the adventures of some prisoners allowed out on a two-week vacation. It, too, in an epic sequence, shows great compassion for the residue of feudalism.

The Pakistani director Jamil Dehlavi made *The Blood of Hossein* (1980) in his native land, but fled to Britain to complete it after the military government came to power in 1977. It is an ambitious film, criticising just such a government in a context which combines mysticism with the fates of two brothers (both played by Salmaan Peer), one caught up in the great world and the other remaining on the family estate. It could be said that the elements of soap opera were designed to appeal to an unsophisticated local population, but this is a wholly entertaining, partly magical movie by one who may be a major talent.

There are probably others now making films. There are new movies opening as I write this: perhaps it is time to quit the typewriter and look at them.

Select Bibliography

Over 5,000 films are listed in the text. Those discussed are those that I have seen (unless otherwise stated), while my viewings were supplemented by research into whatever memoirs, monographs or interviews were available. However, a list of the books consulted would run into thousands and its effectiveness accordingly diminished. What follows is a personal list, by no means exhaustive, of books for further reading.

REFERENCE AND HISTORY

Gifford, Denis: *The British Film Catalogue 1895–1970*, David & Charles, Newton Abbot, 1973
Subtitled 'A Guide to Entertainment Films' this is a listing of all of them, with casts and major credits, accompanied by a single-line plot summary – done with exemplary skill. It is not only an invaluable reference book but one to browse in, for hours and hours.

Jacobs, Lewis: *The Rise of the American Film*, Harcourt Brace, New York, 1939; Columbia University Press, New York, 1970
For many, the definitive film history, especially on early cinema, but it does stop in 1939. Jacobs's views stand the test of time much better than those of most of his contemporaries, but inevitably a few need readjustment. As I mentioned earlier, he devotes a chapter to Chaplin, but only mentions Keaton in passing.

Katz, Ephraim: *The International Film Encyclopedia*, T. Y. Crowell, New York, 1979; Macmillan, London, 1980
Without question the most informative and useful one-volume reference book on cinema, with complete credits for most directors, many producers and stars and intelligently selective credits for other movie-makers. When the author offers an opinion it tends to be conventional, but the details of individual careers are often telling; there are fewer errors than in any other book of this kind and only a couple of serious omissions.

Macgowan, Kenneth: *Behind the Screen*, Delacorte Press, New York, 1965
Subtitled 'The History and Techniques of the Motion Picture', this book is much more sound on the techniques than on the history, which is told not chronologically but as the author thinks fit – and, anyway, is chiefly concerned with Hollywood. One of the reasons the book is good is because it is told from the inside: Macgowan was a Hollywood producer.

Perry, George: *The Great British Picture Show*, Hart-Davis MacGibbon, London, 1974
A history of British cinema which manages to combine literate comments on most of the major films with splendidly researched details on financing, government intervention and many of the other minutiae involved.

René, Jeanne and Ford, Charles: *Dictionnaire du Cinéma Universel*, Robert Laffont, Paris, 1970
This, the fifth volume of the authors's *Histoire du Cinéma*, is an excellent reference work giving brief biographical and fuller filmographic details on some 4,000 directors, writers, producers, actors and technicians in the international film-making world. If not quite as accurate as it could be on the very early practitioners, it contains information on European directors not to be found elsewhere.

Robinson, David: *World Cinema, A Short History*, Eyre Methuen, London, 1973; Stein and Day, New York, 1974. Revised edition 1981
Concisely written and precisely what is claimed in its title. The first two chapters cover the cinema's pre-history with such excellence that it renders all others on the subject inadequate.

CRITICISM

Agee, James: *Agee on Film*, McDowell, Oblensky, New York, 1958; Grosset & Dunlap, 1968; Peter Owen, London, 1967
Most of the films which opened in New York between 1941 and 1948 are reviewed by a critic whose judgment is as trustworthy (still) as his writing is elegant.

Greene, Graham: *The Pleasure Dome: The Collected Film Criticism 1935–40*, Secker & Warburg, London; Oxford University Press, New York, 1980
An absorbing collection for several reasons, not least for an occasional revelation into the character of a man who would become a leading novelist. The book is a valuable insight into the mind of a serious movie-lover of the time; and it chronicles a number of films hardly written about elsewhere.

Lejeune, C. A.: *Chestnuts in Her Lap*, Phoenix House, London, 1948 (second edition)
The doyenne of London critics in her time, from 1936 (the earliest selection in this volume) till she retired in 1958. By the end she had rather lost her touch; however, she was able to analyse films brilliantly till a couple of years earlier.

Select Bibliography

These pieces from *The Observer* are a paradigm of what movie criticism should be.

Simon, John: *Movies into Film: Film Criticism 1967–70*, The Dial Press, New York, 1971. *Reverse Angle: A Decade of Films*, Clarkson S. Potter, New York, 1982

Together these two anthologies (taken from various publications) cover most of the important films shown in New York over a 15-year period, and they do so with erudition, wit, wisdom and a beautiful prose style. By the second of the two Simon has learned to curb his famous waspishness, which makes him less disturbing. He writes in the tradition of Woolcott, Agate and Tynan; there is only one critic today in Britain who might be said to be his equal and he has – as far as I know – no rivals in the U.S. These two books prove that contemporary American movie criticism does deserve to be reprinted in book form.

Winnington, Richard: *Drawn and Quartered*, The Saturn Press, London, 1948

A selection of Winnington's weekly writings on the film from 1943 to 1948 – witty, succinct and agreeably accurate by today's standards, forty years on. In 1975 Paul Rotha made a further selection of Winnington's writings on the cinema – till his death in 1953 – but it is disappointingly orthodox in choice, since Winnington could dispatch rubbish with more severity than most. What is needed is 'The Complete Winnington'.

INDIVIDUAL SURVEYS

Balio, Tino: *United Artists: The Company Built by the Stars*, University of Wisconsin, Madison, 1976

If Balio had written only a history of United Artists from published records and his viewings of the company's films this would still be a valuable book; but he had access to all the surviving papers from 1918 to 1951, when it finally lost the last of its two founders, Chaplin and Mary Pickford.

Behlmer, Rudy (editor): *Memo from David O. Selznick*, The Viking Press, New York, 1972; Macmillan, London, 1972

Selznick was a prodigious writer of memos on all aspects of the films with which he was dealing. These, selected by Mr Behlmer, take Selznick from M-G-M to Paramount to RKO to M-G-M again and finally to independent production. They provide an extraordinary portrait of the way the studio system functioned – and also, of course, the way that Selznick himself worked.

Bergan, Ronald: *Sports in the Movies*, Proteus, London and New York, 1982

One of the proliferating breed of movie books produced to meet the need for movie books, covering each of the famous sports – boxing, horse-racing – in a general essay featuring the most important films on the subject, followed by a checklist of some others. The fact that the book is livelier than most of its kind – indeed, is both enjoyable and informative – is due to a writer with an often malicious wit.

Brownlow, Kevin: *Hollywood – The Pioneers*, Collins, London, 1979; Alfred A. Knopf, New York, 1980. *The Parade's Gone By . . .* , Secker & Warburg, London, 1968; University of California Press, Berkeley and Los Angeles, 1976

The first is a beautifully illustrated book created to accompany the Thames Television series on the American Silent cinema, written by one whose knowledge of the subject is equalled by his considerable enthusiasm. The other book is described on the jacket as a 'a vivid, affectionate portrait of the golden days of Hollywood', but this is only partly true, since it covers only the Silent era and there were some golden days after that. However, Brownlow's interviews with surviving veterans are riveting; and the illustrations are marvellous.

Chierichetti, David: *Hollywood Director: Mitchell Leisen*, Curtis Books, Philadelphia, 1973

A perceptive account of Leisen's career, with comments by many of the people who worked with him. As a text, not much better than competent, despite the author's love for his subject; but as a picture of the way Hollywood functioned – or used to – as valuable as the books listed here on Selznick or by Capra.

Dunne, John Gregory: *The Studio*, Farrar, Strauss and Giroux, New York, 1969; W. H. Allen, London, 1970

Mr Dunne was given access to the conferences and committees of 20th Century-Fox during one year in the late Sixties. What emerges is not as condemnatory of the mogul mentality as 'Picture', Lillian Ross's account of the making of *The Red Badge of Courage*, but it is illuminating, and chilling.

Eyles, Allen: *The Marx Brothers, Their World of Comedy*, Zwemmer, London, 1965; A. S. Barnes, New Jersey, 1966

The films are discussed in detail by a clear-sighted enthusiast; those who have seen them may laugh out loud at this book.

Fordin, Hugh: *The World of Entertainment*, Doubleday, New York, 1975

A film-by-film account of the work of Arthur Freed, with details of production costs and changes, together with interviews with the surviving participants: so far the indispensable source book on the M-G-M musical.

Hull, David Stewart: *Film in the Third Reich*, University of California Press, Berkeley and Los Angeles, 1969

A simply written study of the films made in Germany between 1933 and 1945, taken in chronological order, without an undue stress on opinion, little theorising and much fact about the production of the films, the personalities involved and the Nazi Party interference. But to be used with caution, for research reveals that, in some cases, the author has not always seen the film under discussion.

Leprohon, Pierre: *The Italian Cinema*, Editions Seghers, Paris, 1966; Secker & Warburg, London, 1972

As I considered this booklist over the years, it was my intention to mention at least one major or source book on all the leading film industries, but it simply isn't possible (for instance, the books I have on Russian and Japanese cinema are both factually inaccurate – to judge from the films I've seen – and badly organised). Leprohon's book is not ideal, since what it covers in most detail is the already better chronicled recent period, but it is still the best book available in English on the Italian cinema from 1895 to the neo-realists.

Mankiewicz, Joseph L.: *More About 'All About Eve'*, Random House, New York, 1972

This book describes itself as 'A colloquy by Gary Carey

1234

with Joseph L. Mankiewicz', meaning that the long introduction consists of an interview by the erudite Mr Carey with Mankiewicz about his most famous film, the screenplay of which follows. Mankiewicz speaks not only of the genesis of the movie, fascinating matter in itself, but he also has witty comments to make about Hollywood and its denizens – chiefly, and appropriately, actresses.

Milne, Tom: *Mamoulian*, Thames and Hudson. London, 1969
A detailed examination of the sixteen films directed by Mamoulian by one of the best writers on the cinema.

Pratt, George C.: *Spellbound in Darkness: A History of the Silent Film*, University of Rochester Press, Rochester, 1966; The New York Graphical Society, Greenwich, Connecticut, 1977
The subtitle is justified in only a loose sense, for this is a collection of contemporary writings on movies from 1895 to 1929, with a commentary by George Pratt, master archivist or archaeologist as you will. The material gathered together here is invaluable for anyone wanting to know how the press responded to early cinema.

Sinyard, Neil and Turner, Adrian: *A Journey Down Sunset Boulevard: The Films of Billy Wilder*, B.C.W./L.S.P., 1979
This is an excellent analysis of some of the best films ever made by writers with an acute capacity for making one agree with them. Theirs is a refreshing and persuasive critical study of one of Hollywood's greatest directors. While celebrating Wilder's famed wit, the authors place particular emphasis on his European romanticism, which in turn throws fresh light on his career.

Stratton, David: *The Last New Wave – The Australian Film Revival*, Angus & Robertson, Sydney, 1980
Ten years of the Australian cinema – an exciting time for those in the film industry there, which is reflected in the text. Stratton discusses all the major films in sections under their individual directors, with a summary of the plot and all relevant details from the inception of the project to the critics' notices. One cannot imagine the subject better handled.

FILM GUIDES

Bandmann, Christa and Hembus, Joe: *Klassiker des Deutschen Tonfilm, 1930–1960*, Goldman Verlag, Munich, 1980
Brennicke, Ilona and Hembus, Joe: *Klassiker des Deutschen Stummfilm, 1910–1930*, Goldman Verlag, Munich, 1983
Both guides are fascinating reading, for the organisation of the text enables the editors to present the highlights of each year in selecting only the most outstanding films to be thoroughly discussed and portrayed in stills. This is followed by an alphabetical list of almost every important film in the years covered in each book, with production details and plot summaries that are pleasurably comprehensive. The last section is devoted to an annual production survey and film production history and innovations.

Sadoul, Georges: *Dictionary of Films*, Editions du Seuil, Paris, 1965; University of California Press, Berkeley and Los Angeles, 1972
A discussion of 1,200 films in alphabetical order, with brief production details and much common sense in the accompanying text. Sadoul's introduction mentions that he had not seen some five per cent of the films and his original has been amended in the English edition, 'translated, edited and updated' by Peter Morris. Morris has made a beautiful job of the translation – to judge it, anyway, from Sadoul's *French Film* published by the Falcon Press in London in 1953, an exceptionally lucid and informative history of French cinema, which I have not listed only because it does stop in 1950. No translator is credited, but Morris has successfully found the same style for the *Dictionary*.

INTERVIEWS

Bergman, Ingmar: *Bergman on Bergman*, P.A. Norstadt & Soners Forlag, Stockholm, 1970; London, Secker & Warburg, 1973; New York, Simon & Schuster, 1973
The great Swedish director discusses his films, his career and cinema generally with three critics, Stig Björkman, Torsten Manns and Jonas Sima.

Ciment, Michel: *Kazan on Kazan*, Secker & Warburg, London, in association with the British Film Institute, 1973
Kazan talking – with insight, modesty and eloquence – on his films and his career, with Ciment asking the questions likely to elicit the best responses.

Higham, Charles and Greenberg, Joel: *The Celluloid Muse: Hollywood Directors Speak*, Angus & Robertson, London, 1969; Henry Regnery Co, Chicago, 1971
Interviews with Robert Aldrich, Curtis Bernhardt, George Cukor, John Frankenheimer, Alfred Hitchcock, Fritz Lang, Rouben Mamoulian, Lewis Milestone, Vincente Minnelli, Jean Negulesco, Irving Rapper, Mark Robson, Jacques Tourneur, King Vidor and Billy Wilder. Most such collections are no more than gatherings from journals, often with the subject discussing his current project. The value of this particular book is that the directors were encouraged to talk about each of their films – those they considered worth analysing – in chronological order, to build a portrait of their careers and their feelings on those careers.

BIOGRAPHIES

Buñuel, Luis: *My Last Breath*, Editions Laffont, Paris, 1982; Alfred A. Knopf, New York, 1983; Jonathan Cape, London, 1983
More about the life than the films, but given the life involved we may not feel deprived. The tone is unexpectedly gentle, even if Buñuel is too honest to withhold opinions which may not please everyone.

Capra, Frank: *The Name Above the Title*, Macmillan, New York, 1971; W. H. Allen, London, 1972
The most admired and acclaimed director of Hollywood's golden years tells what it was like to be at the top of the profession and in the process offers an important insight into the way the American film industry once worked.

Dardis, Tom: *Buster Keaton, The Man Who Wouldn't Lie Down*, Andre Deutsch, London, 1979; Penguin Books, New York, 1980
Keaton's life together with his genius was so extraordinary that it would be of interest if less than well told; he has had two excellent biographers, and this one does contain more material than was available earlier to Rudi Blesh.

Houseman, John: *Front and Center*, Simon and Schuster, New York, 1979

Select Bibliography

Houseman continues his urbane account where he left off in his first book of reminiscences, 'Run Through' (published in New York by Simon and Schuster in 1972 and in London by Allen Lane in 1973); his arrival in Hollywood with Orson Welles. His lively and dispassionate style gives credibility to his opinions and anecdotes. Of all the many producers and directors who worked in Hollywood during and after World War II he was one of the most intellectual; and he furnishes the reader with an authoritative view of the industry.

Huston, John: *An Open Book*, Alfred A. Knopf, New York, 1980; Macmillan, London, 1981
Modest and frank in the manner of Buñuel's memoir, Huston writes amiably of his long career as a director. One is astonished at the range of the man's work and the standard of excellence which is evident in many of his films.

Kulik, Karol: *Alexander Korda: The Man Who Could Work Miracles*, W. H. Allen, London, 1975; Arlington House, New York, 1976
A clearly written and well researched biography with almost everything one needs to know about the films with which Korda was connected. Together with Sir Michael Balcon's memoir, 'A Lifetime of Films', it forms an almost complete history of the British cinema from the Thirties to the Fifties.

Kurosawa, Akira: *Something Like an Autobiography*, Random House, New York, 1983.
Kurosawa's account of his own life, with many revealing comments on his work and those of his colleagues.

Minnelli, Vincente, with Hector Arce: *I Remember It Well*, Doubleday, New York, 1974; Angus & Robertson, London, 1974
All that one might want to know about Minnelli's approach to the films he directed, with an incisive account of the manner in which M-G-M operated at the time.

Renoir, Jean: *My Life and My Films*, Collins, London, 1974; Atheneum, New York, 1974
I would commend the memoirs of any leading filmmaker, but Renoir's autobiography, translated by Norman Denny, is particularly interesting and it conveys the warmth and humanity that so imbue his films.

Taylor, John Russell: *Hitch: The Life and Work of Alfred Hitchcock*, Little Brown, Boston, 1978; Faber & Faber, London, 1978
A clearly written and sympathetic biography – and 'authorised', thus containing much essential information.

PICTORIAL HISTORIES

Blum, Daniel: *A Pictorial History of the Silent Screen*, Grosset and Dunlap, New York, 1953; Spring Books, London, 1961. *A Pictorial History of the Talkies*, Grosset and Dunlap, New York, 1958; Spring Books, London, 1961
A judicious selection of stills and portraits arranged year by year. It is devoted to Hollywood movies, and the occasional inclusion of foreign-language films – and British ones – comes oddly. Both books have been constantly reprinted in New York and London, but as the *Pictorial History of the Talkies* needed to be updated it was inexpertly savaged, by ripping out whole or half pages covering the years up to 1957. For anyone interested in the movies of the Thirties, Forties and Fifties it is worth searching for one of the original editions – which should not be too difficult, since the book was a vast seller.

Eames, John Douglas: *The M-G-M Story*, Octopus Books, London, 1975; Crown Publishers, New York, 1975
With very much an insider's knowledge (Eames had worked for M-G-M publicity in London) the author charts, with illustrations, every single film made by Metro-Goldwyn-Mayer after the three separate companies merged in 1924, managing in his text to mention producer, director, writer(s) and principal players. In the same format are *The Universal Story* and *The Warner Bros. Story*, both by Clive Hirschhorn, and *The RKO Story* by Richard B. Jewell and Vernon Harbin. Harbin had worked at RKO and had access to profit and loss figures on individual films as well as contract details. All the books in this series contain as much information about the history of the studios as anyone could hope for. Most of the stills in the M-G-M book are too small (in contrast to the full-page pictures, which could be said to be too big), but this fault has been rectified by the later books in the series.

Griffiths, Richard and Mayer, Arthur: *The Movies*, Simon and Schuster, New York, 1957; Spring Books, London, 1963
Along with Arthur Knight's now dated 'The Liveliest Art', published the same year, this is one of the pioneering books of film history. Since this is a picture book, it remains the more valuable of the two. The text is as packed with insights as it is debonair, but perhaps all the past fads of the movie industry should not be treated in this manner.

Hirschhorn, Clive: *The Hollywood Musical*, Octopus Books, London, 1981; Crown Publishers, New York, 1981
In the same format as the other Octopus series (see Eames: *The M-G-M Story*), covering over 1,300 musicals, with similar information about the principals involved, plus details of the musical numbers, written with enthusiasm, great good humour and erudition.

Index

1241

Index

Index

Index

Index

Index

Index

Index

Index

Index

Index

Index

Index